The School Services Sourcebook

Editorial Board

The School Services Sourcebook

A Guide for School-Based Professionals

Edited by

Cynthia Franklin

Mary Beth Harris

Paula Allen-Meares

OXFORD
UNIVERSITY PRESS
2006

OXFORD
UNIVERSITY PRESS

Oxford University Press, Inc., publishes works that further
Oxford University's objective of excellence
in research, scholarship, and education.

Oxford   New York
Auckland   Cape Town   Dar es Salaam   Hong Kong   Karachi
Kuala Lumpur   Madrid   Melbourne   Mexico City   Nairobi
New Delhi   Shanghai   Taipei   Toronto

With offices in
Argentina   Austria   Brazil   Chile   Czech Republic   France   Greece
Guatemala   Hungary   Italy   Japan   Poland   Portugal   Singapore
South Korea   Switzerland   Thailand   Turkey   Ukraine   Vietnam

Copyright © 2006 by Oxford University Press, Inc.

Published by Oxford University Press, Inc.
198 Madison Avenue, New York, New York 10016

www.oup.com

Oxford is a registered trademark of Oxford University Press

Library of Congress Cataloging-in-Publication Data
The school services sourcebook : a guide for school-based
professionals / [edited by] Cynthia Franklin, Mary Beth Harris, Paula Allen-Meares.
    p.   cm.
Summary: "A compendium of information for school-based social workers, counselors, and other
mental health professionals. Chapters include step-by-step, evidence-based interventions for a variety
of psychosocial and physical problems, as well as guidance for working with school organizations and
communities"—Provided by publisher.
Includes bibliographical references and index.
ISBN-13 978-0-19-517523-3
ISBN 0-19-517523-9
1. School social work—Handbooks, manuals, etc.   2. School children—Mental health services—
Handbooks, manuals, etc.   I. Franklin, Cynthia.   II. Harris, Mary Beth.   III. Allen-Meares, Paula, 1948–
LB3013.4.S372 2006
371.4'6—dc22   2005017096

9 8 7 6 5 4 3 2 1

Printed in the United States of America
on acid-free paper

Preface

The *School Services Sourcebook* was written to provide best practices to social workers, counselors, and mental health professionals who work in public schools or whose practices involve consultations or interventions with school systems. This book addresses effective interventions for students who are high risk because of psychosocial problems and who may have mental, neurological, or physical disorders that require special education. This book covers the mandates of the Individual With Disabilities Education Act (IDEA) and the No Child Left Behind program.

In this book, we co-mingle professional terms like school social worker, counselor, mental health practitioner, mental health worker, and special education teacher. By co-mingling these terms, it is not our intention to disparage the distinct roles of any professional group. We believe, however, that most professionals providing mental health, health, or social services in the country's approximately 15,000 school districts and 90,000 schools will find a vast number of these chapters informative and valuable to their work. Beyond the numbers of mental health and school-based services professionals who work directly in schools, mental health professionals and child and family welfare workers numbering in the thousands will welcome the resources in this volume as they transact with the crossover into schools of their practice domains with children and adolescents.

Contents of the Book

The book has three parts divided into 16 sections. Part I has six sections and covers best practice interventions with student populations with mental health diagnoses, developmental disabilities, and health and well-being issues. The first part also covers best practice resources for child abuse,

sexual abuse, out-of-home placement, dropout prevention, and interpersonal conflict and violence prevention. Part II has four sections and covers best practices for crisis intervention, group work including grief work, and staff training. Part II also covers family and parental involvement and work with multicultural groups, including the postmodern youth culture. Part III has six sections and addresses best practice interventions for school organizations and communities, including key policies and procedures that practitioners need to know. Legal and ethical guidelines are also covered along with records, assessment reports, effective organizational tools for accountability, school funding, and how to develop and sustain a school-based practice. Finally, in this section, we address the emerging mandates for the use of evidence-based practices and some of the challenges that may confront practitioners in the future.

Objectives of the Book

When planning this book, we had three main objectives in mind. First, our objective was to be a comprehensive resource for school social workers and other school-based services professionals. Of course, we were cognizant of the fact that we could not cover every issue that a school-based practitioner needs to know, but we wanted the contents of the resource book to cover the most important and timely information needed for school-based practices. For this reason, the contents of this resource book are extensive (114 chapters), and we believe that it will provide school-based practitioners with the necessary knowledge and practice tools to work successfully in the schools. We wrote this book to be like a voice-activated communication device that provides in one comprehensive volume the updated knowledge, tools, and resources that can help practitioners to improve their work in the schools.

The second objective was for this book to communicate evidence-based knowledge from research to practice and to do it so that practitioners could easily consume this knowledge. Evidence-based practices are often created and tested in universities and research centers, and it may take years for these practices to trickle down into the hands of school-based practitioners. We imagined that this book would serve as a major source for the trickle down. For this reason, we have provided the best practices through easy-to-read practice briefs, which will provide instructions for carrying out the practices in a school, and also provided additional resources for learning more. As editors, we wanted each chapter to be applied, providing practice examples and tools that can be used in the day-to-day practices of school social workers and other school-based services professionals. Each chapter follows a practice-friendly outline that includes the headings Getting Started, What We Know, What We Can Do, Tools and Practice Examples, and Key Points to Remember. It can be a challenge for researchers to communicate to practitioners in brief points and steps that can quickly be assimilated and used in practice. As editors, however, we have given this task our best effort. We hope that the practitioners who read this volume (including students) will give us feedback on how we can do this job better in future editions.

A third objective was to make this book into a relevant, research-based practice update that would be extremely useful to practitioners because its contents provide the tools and information they need. We wanted a book that school practitioners could daily use to guide their practices, prepare their presentations, review needed policies and report formats, and answer questions about issues that they could not remember or did not know. For this reason, much of the information in this book is presented in quick reference tables, outlines, and practice examples, and it includes Internet and other resources to consult.

Why Focus on Evidence-Based Practice?

Evidence-based practice is vital to all mental health settings, but nowhere is it more important than in schools because schools provide the majority of the mental health services to children and families. Evidence-based practice is a here-and-now movement, circumscribing mental health practice in all settings. At this juncture, there is no uniform definition of *evidence-based practice* that spans all fields and disciplines. We directed the contributing authors to use Rones and Hoagwood's (2000) definition from the school mental health literature as a guide when addressing chapter topics because we believe that this definition captures the spirit if not the essence of all other definitions. Rones and Hoagwood's definition follows the recommendations set by the American Psychological Association (APA), sets strict criteria for study design, and establishes a minimum number of experimental design studies required for an intervention to be considered efficacious or promising. Different fields of practice (e.g., developmental disabilities, educational researchers), however, have developed their own definitions and criteria. For this reason, we did not restrict the use of other definitions and criteria within the chapters but rather directed authors to illustrate the best practices for particular populations and concerns. This book demonstrates the best evidence-based practices; however, in some areas where evidence is lacking, experimental and best practice wisdom was also included. We hope that this approach will provide the most promising and practical ideas, as well as the best evidence, for school-based practitioners.

Who Helped Us to Develop This Sourcebook

We have received valuable direction and support for the *School Services Sourcebook* from our editorial board. The board is composed of leaders in school social work organizations as well as researchers and scholars who contribute to the practice, foundation knowledge, empirical study, and professional literature of school mental health. Throughout the process of developing the book, members of the editorial board have contributed chapters, nominated authors, and reviewed chapter manuscripts. Their colossal support and participation have been essential to the manual's development and completion.

The authors of the 114 chapters contained in this book are experts in their fields, with years of practice experience, research, and publications. They range from practicing school social workers, counselors, and psychologists, to physicians and public health specialists, and finally to researchers and scholars across disciplines whose research provides evidence and practice theory and whose writing informs and guides school mental health.

How We Selected the Chapter Topics

The topics contained in this book were identified through feedback from school social workers in six regions of the country. Social workers in California, Georgia, Michigan, New Mexico, Oregon, and Texas communicated with us through an e-mail questionnaire, individual interviews, and focus groups. We asked about the overall challenges of working in a school setting. We asked for the most urgent and frequent problems that school social workers and other school-based, practitioners encounter with students and families. We asked about the areas of practice that require continually updated training and the sources of such training. We asked about service delivery methods, such as groups, home visits, and individual contacts.

School practitioners told us that their practice requires skills in diverse areas. A primary aspect of their work is direct services to individuals (school staff as well as students), to groups, and to families. To provide these services, they need continually updated skills in conflict mediation and violence prevention, crisis management, and treating the current epidemics of substance abuse, obesity and other eating disorders, and self-mutilation. They need continual updating on psychotropic drugs and their interactions with child and adolescent development. They need cultural knowledge for engaging with increasing numbers of immigrant and refugee families and clinical tools for working with other challenging families.

Beyond direct services, they design and develop programs and program evaluation, and they do organizational and interdisciplinary team building. They report that they are more pressured than ever to produce clear evidence of their effectiveness for multiple stakeholder groups. They are being called upon to secure funding for their own programs and need to know the nuts and bolts of grant writing. The *School Services Sourcebook* covers all of these areas, as well as other topics that were suggested by our editorial board. Our goal is for this book to serve as a resource to help practitioners to be effective, marketable, and accountable.

Acknowledgments

First and foremost, we want to thank Oxford University Press for supporting this work. Our deepest gratitude goes to Joan H. Bossert and Maura Roessner for their help and guidance during this project. We owe a special gratitude to Dr. Albert R. Roberts for his encouragement and guidance in the preparation of the manuscript. The *Social Worker's Desk Reference* has also been a model and an inspiration to us. Dr. Roberts's continued support and expert reviews helped us finish this book in a timely fashion. We would also like to thank Melissa Wiersema, Tricia Cody, Katy Shepard, and Wes Baker for their editorial assistance in the management of this project and the preparation of the manuscript. We also owe gratitude to our editorial board members, who provided us very capable guidance in the planning of the book and quick assistance in reviewing the manuscripts. We give credit to all of the school social workers and school mental health professionals who participated in our survey and all those who informally gave us feedback on what this resource book should cover. Finally, we would like to thank our families, friends, and colleagues who endured the process.

Reference

Rones, M., & Hoagwood, K. (2000). School-based mental health services: A research review. *Clinical Child and Family Psychology Review, 3*(4), 223–241.

Contents

Part II

Best Practice Methods in a School-Based Environment

Section VII

Effective Crisis Intervention Methods 549

Section VIII

Effective Interventions and Resources for Group Work and Training 587

Section IX

Best School-Based Practices for Family Intervention and Parental Involvement 629

Contributors

Howard S. Adelman, PhD
Professor
Department of Psychology
Center for Mental Health in Schools
University of California, Los Angeles

Chris Ahlman, PhD
School of Social Work
Lewis-Clark State College

Eugene Aisenberg, PhD
Assistant Professor
School of Social Work
University of Washington

Craig A. Albers, PhD
Assistant Professor
School Psychology Program
University of Wisconsin, Madison

Paula Allen-Meares, PhD
Dean and Norma Radin Collegiate
  Professor of Social Work, Professor
  of Education
School of Social Work
University of Michigan

Sandra J. Altshuler, PhD
Associate Professor
School of Social Work
Eastern Washington University

Michelle Alvarez, MSW, LCSW,
  EdD
Assistant Professor
School of Social Work
University of Southern Indiana

Dawn Anderson-Butcher, PhD
Associate Professor
College of Social Work
Ohio State University

January Angeles, MPP
Research Analyst
American Institute for Research

Laura Anthony, PhD
Assistant Professor
University of Maryland

Marilyn Armour, PhD
Assistant Professor
School of Social Work
University of Texas, Austin

Ron Avi Astor, PhD
Professor
School of Social Work and School of
  Education
University of Southern California

Michelle S. Ballan, PhD
Assistant Professor
School of Social Work
Columbia University

Loren Banach
Middle School Teacher
  Houston, Texas

Oscar A. Barbarin, PhD
L. Richardson and Emily Preyer
  Bicentennial Distinguished
  Professor for Strengthening Families
School of Social Work
University of North Carolina,
  Chapel Hill

Concepcion Barrio, PhD
Associate Professor
School of Social Work
San Diego State University

Rami Benbenishty
Professor
School of Social Work
Hebrew University,
  Jerusalem

Kia J. Bentley, PhD
Professor
School of Social Work
Virginia Commonwealth
  University/University of
  Pittsburgh

Bridget K. Biggs
University of Kansas

Beverly M. Black, PhD
Associate Professor
School of Social Work
Wayne State University

Gary L. Bowen, PhD, ACSW
Kenan Distinguished Professor
School of Social Work
University of North Carolina,
  Chapel Hill

Stephen E. Brock, PhD
Professor
California State University,
  Sacramento

Ruth C. Brown
Department of Psychology
James Madison University

Noel Busch, PhD
Assistant Professor
School of Social Work
University of Texas, Austin

Lynn Bye, PhD
Assistant Professor
Rutgers University

Marilyn Camacho
Department of Child Psychiatry
Columbia University

Helen Cannella, PhD
Assistant Professor
College of Education
Ohio State University

Mo Cannistra Cuevas, PhD
Director of Social Work Program
West Texas A&M University

Cindy Carlson, PhD
Professor
Department of Educational
* Psychology*
University of Texas, Austin

Laurie M. Carpenter, MSW
Evaluation Coordinator
Princeton Center for Leadership
* Training*
Princeton, NJ

Erin A. Casey
School of Social Work
University of Washington

Kathleen A. Casey
Graduate Student
School of Social Work
University of Texas, Austin

Joanne Cashman, PhD
Project Director
National Association of
* State Directors of Special*
* Education*

Allan R. Chavkin, PhD
Professor
Department of English
Texas State University,
* San Marcos*

Nancy Feyl Chavkin, PhD
Professor
School of Social Work
Texas State University, San Marcos

Jenell S. Clarke
Doctoral Student
School of Social Work and
* Department of Psychology*
University of Michigan

Amanda Clinton-Higuita,
* PhD*
Professor
California State University,
* Northridge*

Norman H. Cobb, PhD
Associate Professor
School of Social Work
University of Texas, Arlington

Patricia A. Cody
Doctoral Candidate
School of Social Work
University of Texas, Austin

Allan Hugh Cole, Jr., PhD
Assistant Professor
Austin Presbyterian Theological
* Seminary*

Kathryn S. Collins, PhD
Assistant Professor
School of Social Work
University of Pittsburgh

Jacqueline Corcoran, PhD
Associate Professor
School of Social Work
Virginia Commonwealth University

Tamara DeHay
Graduate Student
Department of Educational
* Psychology*
University of Texas, Austin

Jorge Delva, PhD
Associate Professor
School of Social Work
University of Michigan

Laura DiGiovanni
Graduate Student
School of Social Work
University of Texas, Austin

Diana M. DiNitto, PhD
Cullen Trust Centennial Professor in
* Alcohol Studies and Education and*
* Distinguished Teaching Professor*
School of Social Work
University of Texas, Austin

David R. Dupper, PhD
College of Social Work
University of Tennessee, Knoxville

Theresa J. Early, PhD
Associate Professor
College of Social Work
Ohio State University

Chaturi Edrisinha, MED
Graduate Research Assistant
College of Education
University of Texas, Austin

Timothea M. Elizalde, MSW,
* LMSW*
Adjunct Professor
New Mexico Highlands University
School Social Worker
Highland High School
Albuquerque, New Mexico

Diane E. Elze, PhD
Assistant Professor
School of Social Work
University at Buffalo, State
* University of New York*

Anna G. Escamilla, PhD
Texas Center for Disability Studies
University of Texas, Austin

Steven W. Evans, PhD
Professor of Psychology
Director, Alvin V. Baird Attention
* and Learning Disabilities Center*
James Madison University

Kathleen Coulborn Faller, PhD,
* A.C.S.W.*
Professor, School of Social Work
Director, Family Assessment Clinic
University of Michigan

Rowena Fong, EdD
Professor
School of Social Work
University of Texas, Austin

Todd Franke, PhD
Associate Professor
Department of Social Welfare
University of California,
* Los Angeles*

Cynthia Franklin, PhD, LCSW,
* LMFT*
Stiernberg/Spencer Family Professor
* in Mental Health*
School of Social Work
University of Texas, Austin

Edith M. Freeman, PhD
Professor Emeritus
School of Social Welfare
University of Kansas

Charles D. Garvin, PhD
Professor Emeritus
School of Social Work
University of Michigan

Dorie J. Gilbert, PhD
Associate Professor
University of Texas, Austin

Linda Goldman, MS
Adjunct Professor
Counseling & Human Services
Johns Hopkins University

Vanessa Green, PhD
Assistant Professor
Department of Educational
* Psychology*
University of Texas, Austin

Roberta R. Greene, PhD
Louis and Ann Wolens Centennial
  Chair in Gerontology
School of Social Work
University of Texas, Austin

Allen B. Grove
Department of Psychology
James Madison University

Cathy L. Grover, PhD
School Social Worker
Trailblazer Alternative School
Reynoldsburg, Ohio

Jane Hanvey-Phillips
School of Social Work
University of Texas, Arlington

Mary Beth Harris, PhD
Associate Professor
School of Social Work
University of Central Florida

Bryan Harrison
Research Assistant
University of Maryland School of
  Medicine

Elayne Haymes, PhD
Associate Professor
School of Social Work
Southern Connecticut State University

Darlene M. Head-Reeves, MA
School of Education
University of North Carolina,
  Chapel Hill

Laurie Cook Heffron, MSW
Greenleaf Refugee Services
Center for Social Work Research
Austin, Texas

Brooke Hersh
Graduate Research Assistant
College of Education
University of Texas, Austin

Karen S. Hoban
Speech Language Pathologist
Cerebral Palsy of New Jersey

Merl C. Hokenstad, PhD
Professor
Mandel School of Applied Social
  Sciences
Case Western Reserve University

Lori K. Holleran, PhD
Assistant Professor
School of Social Work
University of Texas, Austin

Leslie Doty Hollingsworth, PhD
Associate Professor
School of Social Work
University of Michigan

Laura Hopson, MSSW
Graduate Research Assistant
School of Social Work
University of Texas, Austin

Esther Howe
Southern Connecticut State
  Department of Social Work

Lisa Hunter, PhD
Assistant Professor
Department of Child Psychiatry
Columbia University

Diane C. Jacobs, PhD
School of Social Work
Tulane University
New Orleans Public Schools

Srinika Jayaratne, PhD
Professor, Associate Dean of Faculty
  & Academic Affairs
School of Social Work
University of Michigan

Shane R. Jimerson, PhD
Professor
Gevirtz Graduate School of
  Education
University of California,
  Santa Barbara

Melissa Jonson-Reid, PhD
Associate Professor
George Warren Brown School of
  Social Work
Washington University

Catheleen Jordan
School of Social Work
University of Texas, Arlington

Soyon Jung
Graduate Student
School of Social Work
University of Texas, Austin

Jihye Kim, PhD
Department of Social Welfare
Daejin University, Korea

Johnny S. Kim
Graduate Student
School of Social Work
University of Texas, Austin

Karen S. Knox, PhD
Associate Professor
School of Social Work
Texas State University

Sandra Kopels, JD, MSW
Professor
School of Social Work
University of Illinois at Urbana-
  Champaign

Wynne S. Korr, PhD
Dean
School of Social Work
University of Illinois at Urbana-
  Champaign

Thomas R. Kratochwill, PhD
Professor
University of Wisconsin, Madison

Amber Kwiatkowski, MSW
Education Consultant
Ohio Department of Education

Katina M. Lambros, PhD
Child & Adolescent Services
  Research Center
Children's Hospital
San Diego, California

Giulio Lancioni, PhD
Department of Psychology
University of Bari, Italy

Julia Graham Lear, PhD
Research Professor
School of Public Health and Health
  Services
George Washington University
  Medical Center

Craig Winston LeCroy, PhD
Professor
School of Social Work
Arizona State University

Mo Yee Lee, PhD
Professor
College of Social Work
Ohio State University

Joan Letendre, PhD, LCSW
Assistant Professor
School of Social Work
University of Connecticut

Nancy Lever, PhD
Assistant Professor
Division of Child & Adolescent
  Psychiatry
University of Maryland

Brenda Coble Lindsey, EdD,
  LCSW
Assistant Clinical Professor
School of Social Work
University of Illinois at Urbana-
  Champaign

Tammy Linseisen, LCSW, ACSW
Clinical Assistant Professor
School of Social Work
University of Texas, Austin

Courtney J. Lynch, MSSW
Graduate Research Assistant
School of Social Work
University of Texas, Austin

Sean Lynch
Graduate Student
University of California, Los Angeles

Roxana Marachi, PhD
Assistant Professor
Department of Child & Adolescent Development
California State University, Northridge

Martha J. Markward, PhD
Associate Professor
School of Social Work
University of Missouri, Columbia

Carey E. Masse
Department of Psychology
James Madison University

Mark A. Mattaini, DSW
Associate Professor
Jane Addams College of Social Work
University of Illinois, Chicago

Marian Mattison, DSW
Associate Professor
Department of Social Work
Providence College

Anita McClendon
Director of Services
Center for Elders Independence
Oakland, California

Mary M. McKay, PhD
Professor
Department of Psychiatry
Mt. Sinai School of Medicine

Elizabeth Moore
University of Maryland

Reshma B. Naidoo, PhD
Graduate Student
Department of School Psychology
University of Texas, Austin

James K. Nash, PhD, MSW
Associate Professor
Graduate School of Social Work
Portland State University

Jacqueline A. Norris, EdD
Assistant Professor
Department of Education Administration
The College of New Jersey

Paula S. Nurius, PhD
Professor
School of Social Work
University of Washington

Joseph E. Nyre, PhD
University of Illinois Medical School
Hope School

Bonnie O'Reilly
Teacher
Austin Independent School District
Austin, Texas

Mark O'Reilly, PhD
Professor
College of Education
University of Texas, Austin

Dolores P. Ortega, PhD
Visiting Professor
School of Social Work
New Mexico Highlands University

David Osher, PhD
Managing Director
Children's Mental Health
American Institutes for Research

Mary Ann Overcamp-Martini, PhD
Assistant Professor
School of Social Work
University of Nevada Las Vegas

Daphna Oyserman, MSW, PhD
Professor
School of Social Work
Department of Psychology
Institute for Social Research
University of Michigan

David A. Patterson, PhD
Associate Professor
College of Social Work
University of Tennessee, Knoxville

Ronald O. Pitner, PhD
Assistant Professor
George Warren Brown School of Social Work
Washington University

Jeffrey M. Poirier, MA
Research Analyst
American Institute for Research

Elizabeth C. Pomeroy, PhD
Associate Professor
School of Social Work
University of Texas, Austin

Joelle D. Powers, PhD, MSW
School of Social Work
University of North Carolina, Chapel Hill

Carolyn B. Pryor (retired)
Wayne State University

James C. Raines, PhD
Assistant Professor
School of Social Work
Illinois State University

Gilbert A. Ramírez, MSW, LMSW
School Social Worker
Highland High School
Albuquerque, New Mexico, and Adjunct Professor
School of Social Work
New Mexico Highlands University

Camille J. Randall
University of Kansas

Albert R. Roberts, PhD
Professor of Criminal Justice
Faculty of Arts and Sciences
Rutgers University

Michelle Rosemond
Department of Psychology
University of Southern California

Mary C. Ruffolo, PhD
Associate Professor
School of Social Work
University of Michigan

Christine Anlauf Sabatino, DSW
Associate Professor
National Catholic School of Social Service
Catholic University of America

Maria Scannapieco, PhD
Associate Researcher
School of Social Work
University of Texas, Arlington

Brandon K. Schultz, EdS
Alvin V. Baird Attention and Learning Disabilities Center
James Madison University

Matthew D. Selekman, MSW, LSW
Private practice
Evanston, Illinois

Gary L. Shaffer, PhD
Associate Professor
School of Social Work
University of North Carolina,
  Chapel Hill

Katherine Shepard
Graduate Student
Department of School Psychology
University of Texas, Austin

Alphonse Shropshire, MSW,
  LCSW
Past Chair
School Social Work Practice
  Section
National Association of Social
  Workers

Jeff Sigafoos, PhD
Professor
College of Education
University of Texas, Austin

Gail H. Sims, PhD
Program Coordinator
Community Education
Austin Independent School District
Austin, Texas

John W. Sipple, PhD
Associate Professor
Department of Education
Cornell University

Renee Smith, MSW
Washington, DC

Michael S. Spencer, PhD
Associate Professor
School of Social Work
University of Michigan

David W. Springer, PhD
Associate Dean
School of Social Work
University of Texas, Austin

Sharon Stephan, PhD
Center for School Mental Health
University of Maryland

Susan Stone, JD, MD
President
Susan Stone & Associates
Austin, Texas

Calvin L. Streeter, PhD
Meadows Foundation Centennial
  Professor in The Quality of Life
  in The Rural Environment
School of Social Work
University of Texas, Austin

Danielle C. Swick, MSW
School of Social Work
University of North Carolina,
  Chapel Hill

Linda Taylor
Center for Mental Health in
  Schools
Department of Psychology
University of California, Los Angeles

Martell Teasley, PhD
College of Social Work
Florida State University

Tanya Tenor
Waterbury School District

Sanna J. Thompson, PhD
Research Associate Professor
School of Social Work
University of Texas, Austin

Mary Tierney

Elizabeth M. Timberlake
National Catholic School of Social
  Service
Catholic University of America

Meghan Tomb
Department of Child Psychiatry
Columbia University

Santos Torres, Jr., EdD
Professor
Division of Social Work
California State University,
  Sacramento

Elizabeth M. Tracy, PhD
Associate Professor
Mandel School of Applied Social
  Science
Case Western Reserve University

Dorian E. Traube, LCSW
School of Social Work
Columbia University

Stephen J. Tripodi, MSSW
Graduate Research Assistant
School of Social Work
University of Texas, Austin

John E. Tropman, PhD
Professor
School of Social Work
University of Michigan

Ernst VanBergeijk
Assistant Professor
School of Social Work
Fordham University

Hilary Ward
College of Social Work
Ohio State University

Barbara Hanna Wasik
William R. Kenan, Jr., Professor
School of Education
University of North Carolina,
  Chapel Hill

Mark Weist
The Center for School Mental
  Health Analysis and Action
University of Maryland

Arlene N. Weisz, PhD
School of Social Work
Wayne State University

Margaret White, MSW
Clinical Assistant Professor
School of Social Work
University of Illinois, Urbana

Sarah M. Woehr
University of California,
  Santa Barbara

Debra J. Woody, PhD
Associate Professor
School of Social Work
University of Texas, Arlington

Michael E. Woolley, PhD, DCSW
Assistant Professor
Schools of Social Work and
  Education
University of Michigan

Liang Zhu
Graduate Research Assistant
School of Management
Purdue University

Best Direct Practice Interventions With Student Populations

PART I

Effective Interventions and Resources for Working With Students With Mental Health Diagnoses

School social workers and other school mental health professionals report that they are at present confronted with large numbers of students who have serious mental health disorders. The chapters in this section address mental disorders that are frequently encountered in school practice settings with children and youth. The chapters provide straightforward directions in four areas: (1) The chapters provide succinct facts about suicide prevention and psychopharmacological and other prescriptive treatments for mental disorders. (2) They provide evidence-based procedures and steps for school practitioners to use when intervening with mental health issues. Prevalent issues of concern, such as disruptive behavior problems, are covered, along with a variety of other mental health challenges. (3) The chapters provide evidence-based information about mental health assessment and diagnosis and practice tools that enhance collaborative work on mental health concerns. (4) Finally, the chapters provide best practices for engaging parents and teachers as part of the supportive system for children and youth with mental health challenges.

School-Based, Adolescent Suicidality
Lethality Assessments and Crisis Intervention Protocols

Albert R. Roberts

Getting Started

Every 17 minutes, someone in this country commits suicide. This equates to 83 suicides each and every day throughout the United States. Suicides and suicide attempts take place in every age group, ethnic and racial group, gender, socioeconomic status, and geographic area (U.S. Department of Health and Human Services, 2001). Suicide is a prevalent social problem and public health problem for adults and youths. Adolescents and young adults seem to be especially vulnerable. More specifically, suicide is the third leading cause of death among young people between the ages of 15 and 24; accidents and homicides are the first and second. Suicide attempts have occurred among children as young as 7 years of age (Roberts & Yeager, 2005). Early detection and identification of acutely suicidal adolescents have the potential to dramatically decrease the prevalence of this significant social problem throughout the United States. Most children and youth who have ideas and thoughts about suicide exhibit specific warning signs, symptoms, gestures, and behaviors, which can be recognized by school social workers, mental health consultants, and crisis counselors who are trained in suicide assessment and crisis intervention.

School social workers and mental health consultants to the schools can develop competency in evidence-based suicide risk assessments and interventions. For the most part, suicidal behaviors and impulses are temporary and transient. Evidence-based studies have indicated that most individuals who have killed themselves have given some type of prior warning (Jobes, Berman, & Martin, 2005). The school social workers and mental health counselors are therefore in pivotal life-saving positions. Effective lethality assessments and evidence-based crisis intervention can certainly save lives, especially since most suicidal youth are ambivalent.

Here are three important operational definitions:

1. *Suicide*: the deliberate, intentional, and purposeful act of killing oneself
2. *Ambivalence*: having two mixed and opposing feelings at the same time, such as the desire to live and the desire to die
3. *Lethality*: the potential for a specific method and suicide plan to actually end the individual's life

What We Know

Suicide Warning Signs and Risk Factors

It is important to be aware of precipitating factors or events, risk variables, and biological or sociocultural factors that seem to put youths at imminent risk of deliberate self-harm and suicide attempts. Common triggering or precipitating events, also known as *the last straw*, include rejection or humiliation, such as a broken romance, being repeatedly bullied or teased, intense verbal abuse by parents, or the death of a parent. The key to whether or not a significant stressful life event leads to suicide or to a productive life is based on the internal meaning and perceptions that each person attaches to the event. For example, Dr. Viktor Frankel lost his wife and entire family in the concentration camps during World War II but instead of giving up, Frankel decided that no matter what torture the Nazis administered, they could not take away his will to live. His classic book, *Man's Search for Meaning*, has inspired hundreds of thousands of readers to never give up and to do their very best to lead productive lives devoted to helping others. Since the late 1970s, a number of risk variables, or suicide warning signs, have been documented (Beck, Brown, & Steer, 1997; Beck et al., 1999; Beck & Lester, 1976; Berman, 1975; Berman & Jobes, 1991; Jobes, Berman, & Martin, 2000; Kovacs, Beck, & Weissman, 1976; Maris, Berman, Maltsberger, & Yufit, 1992; Roberts, 1975, 1991). These include the following:

intense emotional pain
extreme sense of hopelessness and helplessness about oneself
socially isolated and cut off from other young people
giving away important personal possessions
prolonged feelings of emptiness, worthlessness, and/or depression
prior suicide attempts
mental confusion
prior family history of suicide
past psychiatric history
presence of weapon
alcohol or substance abuse
anger, aggression, or irritability
childhood physical or sexual abuse
sleep disturbances
loss of positive motivation
loss of interest in pleasurable things
poor personal cleanliness
excessive focus on death and dying

Specific clues to suicide include statements such as "Life sucks and I might as well end it all," "I'd be better off dead," "I wish I was dead," "I am planning on killing myself," "I bought a new dress to be buried in," or "I borrowed my uncle's gun in order to shoot myself at midnight."

The National Mental Health Association has developed the following list of warning signs of someone considering suicide:

• verbal suicide threats, such as "you'd be better off without me around"
• expressions of hopelessness and helplessness
• personality changes
• depression
• daring or risk-taking behavior
• previous suicide attempts
• giving away prized possessions
• lack of interest in future plans

All school social workers and mental health counselors should be aware of the following scales for use in assessing suicide ideation and depression:

- Beck Hopelessness Scales
- Beck Depression Inventory
- Rosenberg Self-Esteem Scale
- Linehan Reasons for Living Scale
- Brown-Goodwin Aggression Scale
- Buss-Durkee Hostility-Guilt Inventory
- Spielberger State-Trait Anxiety Scale
- Plutchik Impulsivity Scale
- Self-Rated Problem Solving Inventory
- Suicide Ideation-Worst Pt.
- European Parasuicide Study Interview Schedules I and IsI
- ICD-10 Diagnostic Schedule
- Personality Assessment Schedule

Within the current care environment, social workers are required to determine imminent, moderate, and low suicide risk. In doing so, the individual practitioner is required to assign the patient to the most appropriate level of care. The implementation of Roberts's seven-stage model provides appropriate interventions for resolution of moderate and low suicidal ideation immediately upon the individual seeking assistance. Additionally, application of the seven-stage model can provide insight in a nonthreatening manner to assist the patient in development of cognitive stabilization when completing the initial assessment and when the appropriate intervention protocol is followed.

What We Can Do

School Social Workers and Crisis Intervention Center Collaboration

Several states, including Florida, Georgia, Illinois, Massachusetts, Minnesota, New York, Ohio, Pennsylvania, Texas, Utah, Washington, and Wisconsin, maintain several 24-hour telephone crisis intervention and suicide prevention programs. These programs usually work closely with school social workers and other mental health professionals in the community. This service provides a lifeline as well as an entry point to behavioral health care for persons with major depression or suicidal thoughts and ideation. When crisis workers answer the cry for help, their primary duty is to initiate crisis intervention, beginning with rapid lethality and triage assessment and establishing rapport. In essence, crisis intervention and suicide prevention include certain primary steps in an attempt to prevent suicide:

Conduct a rapid lethality and biopsychosocial assessment.

Attempt to establish rapport and at the same time communicate a willingness to help the caller in crisis.

Help the caller in crisis to develop a plan of action which links him or her to community health care and mental health agencies. The most frequent outcome for depressed or suicidal adolescents is that they are either stabilized by the crisis social worker or transported to psychiatric screening and intake at a behavioral health care facility, hospital, or addiction treatment program.

The crisis intervention worker or mental health consultant assumes full responsibility for the case when a suicidal student arrives at school. The person cannot be rushed and handled simply by a referral to another agency. Crisis workers should follow the case until complete transfer of responsibility has been accomplished by some other agency assuming the responsibility. The crisis worker should complete the state-mandated mental health and psychiatric screening reports, which make an initial determination as to whether the person is a danger to himself or others. The ultimate goal of all crisis and suicide prevention services is to strive to relieve intense emotional pain and acute crisis episodes, while helping the person to find positive ways to cope with life (Roberts, 2000; Roberts & Yeager, 2005).

It is imperative for all crisis clinicians to establish rapport with the person in crisis by listening in a patient, hopeful, self-assured, interested, and knowledgeable manner. Skilled crisis workers try to communicate an attitude that the person has done the right thing by contacting them, and they convey willingness and an ability to help. An empathetic ear is provided to the person in crisis in order to relieve her intense stress by active listening. The crisis worker should relate to this person in a confidential, spontaneous, and noninstitutionalized manner (Yeager & Gregoire, 2000).

Suicide Assessment Measures and Tools

The author developed a seven-stage crisis intervention protocol in 1990 (Roberts, 1991). The most critical first step in applying Roberts's seven-stage crisis intervention model is conducting a lethality and biopsychosocial risk assessment. This involves a relatively quick assessment of the number and duration of risk factors, including imminent danger and availability of lethal weapons, verbalization of suicide or homicide risk, need for immediate medical attention, positive and negative coping strategies, lack of family or social supports, poor judgment, and current drug or alcohol use (Eaton, 2005; Eaton & Roberts, 2002; Roberts, 1991, 2000).

If possible, a medical assessment should include a brief summary of the presenting problem, any ongoing medical conditions, and current medications (names, dosages, and time of last dose). The highest suicide risk is among persons who express suicidal ideation, present with agitation and impulsivity, have a suicide plan, have access to a lethal weapon, exhibit poor judgment, are delusional and/or exhibiting command hallucinations, and are intoxicated or high on illegal drugs.

After listening to the story of the person in crisis and asking several key questions, the crisis worker makes a determination as to whether or not the individual has a high suicide risk. If the youth has a lethal method (e.g., a firearm) readily available and a specific plan for suicide, or has previously attempted suicide, then he is considered as having a high suicide risk. In sharp contrast, the youths evaluated as low suicide risk still need help, but they are primarily depressed and expressing ambivalent thoughts about what it's like to be in heaven versus hell. They have not yet planned the specific details of suicide. Other youths may be seeking information on how to help a friend or family member or about problems related to a broken romance, loneliness, or a sexually transmitted disease, or they may be in need of emergency medical attention due to illicit drug abuse.

With regard to inpatient versus outpatient psychiatric treatment, the most important determinant should be imminent danger—lethal means to suicide. It is also extremely important for crisis clinicians to make a multiaxial differential diagnosis using the *DSM-IV-TR*, which determines acute or chronic psychosocial stressors, dysfunctional relationships, decreased self-esteem or hopelessness, severe or unremitting anxiety, intimate partner violence, personality disorders (particularly borderline personality disorder), major depressive disorders, bipolar disorders, and comorbidity (American Psychiatric Association, 2003). See chapters 2 and 13 for discussions on how to use the *DSM-IV-TR*'s five multiaxial diagnostic criteria. Several recent studies have found that persons with suicide ideation have comorbid substance abuse and other mental disorders 60–92% of the time (Roberts, Yeager, & Streiner, 2004). Making accurate assessments and predicting short-term risk of suicide (1 to 3 days) has been found to be much more reliable than predicting long-term risk (Simon, 1992). Other serious clues to increased suicidal risk are when a person has no social support network, poor judgment, or poor impulse control and adamantly refuses to sign a contract for safety (Rudd & Joiner, 1998). Other chapters in this volume cover the assessment and evidence-based interventions for mental disorders, intimate partner violence, and substance abuse in schools.

Crisis Intervention

Crisis intervention with children and adolescents is difficult and is difficult to do well. Chapters 27 and 52 provide additional information on how to work with crisis situations. As the acuity of mental health consumers increases and the service delivery system buckles under the increasing pressure of those seeking services, it becomes clear that specific and efficacious interventions and guidelines are needed to keep the process flowing. There is growing evidence of the risk factors for suicide, including a precipitating event, such as multiple stressors, a traumatic event, major depression, increased substance abuse, deterioration in social or occupational functions, hopelessness, and verbal expressions of suicidal ideation (Weishaar, 2004). For some individuals, dealing with ambivalence—simultaneous thoughts of self-harm and thoughts of immediate gratification and satisfaction—is a day-to-day event. For some, the thought of suicide mistakenly appears to be an immediate fix to an emotionally painful or acutely embarrassing situation that seems insurmountable.

For the depressed, impulsive, and chemically dependent youth, suicide may seem like the easy way out of a downward spiral of emotional pain.

Therefore it may be helpful to include a working definition of crisis:

> *Crisis*: An acute disruption of psychological homeostasis in which one's usual coping mechanisms fail and there exists evidence of distress and functional impairment; the subjective reaction to a stressful life experience that compromises the individual's stability and ability to cope or function. The main cause of a crisis is an intensely stressful, traumatic, or hazardous event, but two other conditions are also necessary: (1) the individual's perception of the event as the cause of considerable upset and/or disruption; and (2) the individual's inability to resolve the disruption by previously used coping mechanisms. Crisis also refers to "an upset in the steady state." It often has five components: a hazardous or traumatic event, a vulnerable state, a precipitating factor, an active crisis state, and the resolution of the crisis. (Roberts, 2002)

The definition of a crisis stated above is particularly applicable to youths in acute suicidal crisis because these individuals usually seek help only after they have experienced a hazardous or traumatic event and are in a vulnerable state, have failed to cope and lessen the crisis through customary coping methods, lack family or community social supports, and want outside help. Acute psychological or situational crisis episodes may be viewed in various ways, but the definition we are using emphasizes that a crisis can be a turning point in a person's life (Roberts & Yeager, 2005).

Crisis intervention generally refers to a social worker, behavioral clinician, or crisis counselor entering into the life situation of an individual or family to alleviate the impact of a crisis episode in order to facilitate and mobilize the resources of those directly affected. Rapid assessment and timely intervention on the part of crisis counselors, social workers, psychologists, or child psychiatrists is of paramount importance.

Crisis interveners should be active and directive while displaying a nonjudgmental, accepting, hopeful, and positive attitude. Crisis interveners need to help crisis clients to identify protective factors, inner strengths, psychological hardiness, or resiliency factors which can be utilized for ego bolstering. Effective crisis interveners are able to gauge the seven stages of crisis intervention, while being flexible and realizing that several stages of intervention may overlap. Crisis intervention should culminate with a restoration of cognitive functioning, crisis resolution, and cognitive mastery (Roberts, 2000).

Tools and Practice Examples

Below is a case scenario. How would you assess the situation and how should the school social worker or mental health counselor respond?

Synopsis: Maryann

Maryann has barricaded herself in the teachers' lounge for the past 2 hours. She has called her cousin on her cell phone to offer him her favorite CDs. Her mother, Mrs. Smith, is a social studies teacher in the school. Maryann has just broken up with her boyfriend and had taken an overdose of sleeping pills 8 months ago in a similar situation.

At that previous time, Maryann had been rushed to the ER as she was distraught about the breakup with her previous boyfriend. Making matters worse, Maryann lost her father within the past year from cirrhosis of the liver. Maryann's mother usually drives her daughter home from school at 2:30 p.m. It is 4:30 and the janitor and Mrs. Smith recently found out that Maryann has barricaded herself in the teacher's lounge. Maryann has been crying. She refuses to come out, has barricaded the door with furniture, refuses to talk, and has asked her mother to put a large bottle of soda outside the lounge. Finally, Maryann said that she plans to sleep in the lounge and not come out until the morning. It is unclear whether or not Maryann has illegal drugs with her.

Application of Roberts's Seven-Stage Crisis Intervention Model

After reading the above case synopsis and reviewing the suicide risk assessment flow chart (Figure 1.1), would your preliminary rapid assessment rate Maryann as low, moderate, or high suicide risk?

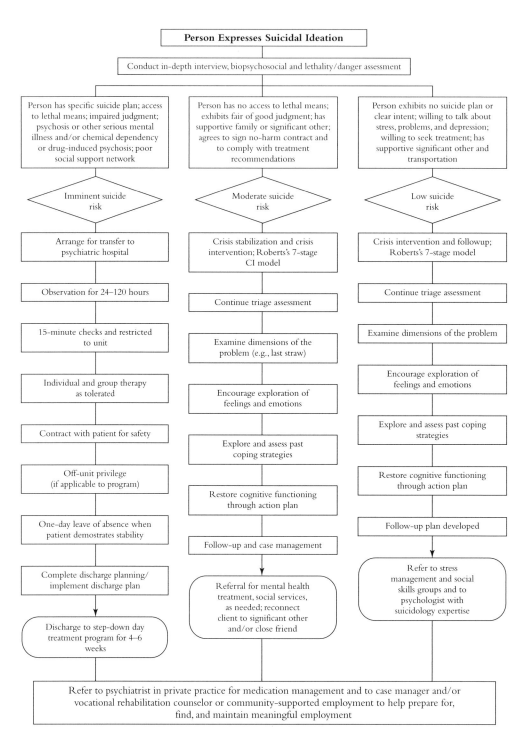

Figure 1.1. Suicide Risk Assessment and Intervention Flowchart

Source: Roberts, A. R., & Yeager, K. (2005). Lethality assessments and crisis intervention with persons presenting with suicide ideation. In A. R. Roberts (Ed.), *Crisis intervention handbook: Assessment, treatment, and research* (3rd ed.). New York: Oxford University Press. Reprinted with permission.

It is important to keep in mind that while many persons at high risk of suicide have expressed/exhibited a specific suicide plan and availability of a lethal method (e.g., firearms or a rope or belt for hanging), there are exceptions. There is a relatively small group of individuals who do not talk to anyone before making a lethal suicide attempt but do give clear clues of imminent suicide risk, for example, the honors high school student who fails a course for the first time and can't sleep may be in imminent danger. Although he has never had a problem sleeping and has been an honor student for the past 3 years, he may magnify the inconvenience of retaking a course as the worst and most shameful thing ever. Another example would be a youth or young adult who never expressed paranoid delusions and now has expressed irrational fears that a violent gang with 100 members is after him and will try to kill him tonight. These delusions are an outgrowth of a drug-induced psychosis. *Psychiatric screeners, crisis workers, counselors, social workers, family members, and close friends should be made aware of the fact that a critical clue to suicidal ideation and/or suicide attempts includes a drastic change in behavior patterns, daily routine, or actions* (e.g., youths barricading themselves in their rooms for 24 hours and refusing to come out to eat or go to the bathroom, giving away prized possessions, having paranoid delusions or command hallucinations (e.g., hearing voices that tell them to harm themselves) for the first time, or talking about how wonderful it would be to go to heaven to be with a recently deceased and loving father) (Roberts & Yeager, 2005). See chapter 11 for directions on how to recognize psychotic reactions in children and youths.

The school social worker needs to determine whether Maryann is at moderate to high risk of lethality and whether she needs to immediately call the 24-hour crisis center. The preliminary lethality assessment is based on the following six high-risk factors:

1. This is the first time that Maryann has ever barricaded herself in the teachers' lounge.
2. She seems to be depressed as shown by her not eating for 24 hours and crying for many hours.
3. She had a previous suicide attempt only 8 months ago.
4. She just gave away prized possessions—all of her favorite CDs.
5. Her father, to whom she was close, died less than 12 months ago.
6. She refuses to communicate with anyone.

You are the school social worker or crisis counselor, and you are dispatched to the school. The following application focuses on what you should say and do when you arrive. We describe this crisis situation with specific details and statements on ways in which to apply each of the seven stages in Roberts's crisis intervention model. First, it is important to be aware that stages 1 and 2 often take place simultaneously. However, in the case of life-threatening and high-risk suicide ideation, child abuse, sexual assault, or domestic violence, the emphasis is on rapid crisis, lethality, and triage assessment.

Stage 1: Assess Lethality by Talking Relatively Quickly to the Mother and Then Patiently to the Teenager

• Ask the mother if the daughter has been taking Acutane for acne. Then, ask the mother if Maryann was ever prescribed any antidepressant medication.
• If yes, does she know if the daughter has been taking her medication, what is the name of it, and who prescribed it?
• Was it prescribed by a family doctor or a psychiatrist?
• Does Maryann have access to her medications or any other drugs?
• Also, upon arrival at the school or outside the teachers' lounge, ask the mother if anything has changed in the past 20–30 minutes (since they reached you) in her daughter's situation.

The crisis worker needs to obtain background information quickly from the mother: rapid collateral assessment. Next, give the mother something to do so she is not in the way (i.e., ask her to call the ex-boyfriend or Maryann's best girlfriend to obtain background data, especially whether or not Maryann has recently taken any illegal drugs).

• Assess Maryann's danger to herself and others (suicidal or homicidal thoughts), substance abuse history, and preexisting mental disorders.
• Ask questions about symptoms, traumatic events, stressful life events, future plans, suicidal ideation, previous suicide attempts, and mental illness.
• Ask about upcoming special events or birthday celebrations that Maryann may be looking forward to, or recollections of happy events or celebrations in the past that may well be

repeated in the future (special events can instill hope for the future).

- Determine if Maryann needs immediate medical attention and if there are drugs, sleeping pills, or weapons in her possession.

Rapid Triage Assessment

1. The individual is a danger to herself or others and is exhibiting intense and acute psychiatric symptoms. These students generally require short-term emergency hospitalization and psychopharmacotherapy to protect them from self-harm or from harming other persons. (Priority I requires emergency medical treatment, ambulance or rescue transport, and admission to a psychiatric screening center.)
2. The individual is in a precrisis stage due to ineffective coping skills, a weak support system, or ambivalence about seeking the help of a therapist. These students may have mild or no psychiatric symptoms or suicide risk. They may need one to three sessions of crisis counseling and referral to a support group.
3. The third type of student may have called a suicide prevention program or indicated to a friend or a teacher that she is sad, anxious, lonely, and/or depressed (Roberts, 2002).

It is important to make a determination as to whether or not Maryann needs the mobile crisis intervention team to respond quickly to her home or school. In similar situations, the youth may have just attempted suicide or is planning to attempt suicide shortly or may be experiencing command hallucinations of a violent nature (Priority I). The student may be experiencing delusions and may be unable and fearful of leaving the teachers' lounge (Priority II), or she may be suffering from mood disturbances or depression and fleeting suicidal ideation, with no specific suicidal plan (Priority III: she is probably in need of an appointment with a caring social worker).

Stage 2: Establish Rapport

It is very important to introduce yourself as the school social worker or mental health counselor if Maryann has not met you before and speak in a calm and neutral manner.

- Social workers or mental health counselors should do their best to make a psychological connection to the 16-year-old in a precrisis or acute crisis situation.
- Part of establishing rapport and putting the person at ease involves being nonjudgmental, listening actively, and demonstrating empathy.
- Establish a bridge, bond, or connection by asking Maryann what CDs or posters she likes:

    "Do you have any posters on your wall at home right now?"

    "Do you have a favorite TV show?"

    "Do you have a favorite recording artist?"

- Another alternative approach is brief self-disclosure. For example:

    When I was 16 years old, my boyfriend broke up with me. I think I understand the emotional pain and sadness you are going through. I thought I loved my boyfriend very much. In fact, he was my first love. He broke up with me for another girl, and I was very sad just like you. But, about 2 months after the breakup, I met someone else and we had a very enjoyable long-term relationship.

- Ask Maryann what her favorite dessert or candy is.
- It is important to understand that many adolescents are impulsive and impatient, may have escape fantasies, and are very sensitive and temperamental. As a result, don't lecture, preach, or moralize. Make concise statements, be caring, display keen interest, and do not make disparaging or insulting statements of any kind.

Stages 3 and 4 sometimes take place simultaneously.

Stage 3: Identify the Major Problem, Including Crisis Precipitants or Triggering Incidents

- Ask questions to determine the final straw or precipitating event that led Maryann into her current situation.
- Focus on the problem or problems and prioritize and focus on the worst problem first.
- Listen carefully for symptoms and clues of suicidal thoughts and intent.
- Make a direct inquiry about suicidal plans and nonverbal gestures or other communication (e.g., diaries, poems, journals, school essays, paintings, or drawings).

- Since most adolescent suicides are impulsive and unplanned, it is important to determine whether or not Maryann has easy access to a lethal weapon or drugs (including sleeping pills, methamphetamines, or barbiturates).

Stage 4: Deal With Feelings and Emotions and Provide Support

- Deal with Maryann's immediate feelings or fears.
- Allow the client to tell her story and why she seems to be feeling so bad.
- Provide preliminary empathy to the impact of Maryann's breakup with her boyfriend.
- Use active listening skills (i.e., paraphrasing, reflection of feelings, summarizing, reassurance, compliments, advice giving, reframing, and probes).
- Normalize the client's experiences.
- Validate and identify her emotions.
- Examine her past coping methods.
- Encourage ventilation of mental and physical feelings.

Stage 5: Exploring Possible Alternatives

First, reestablish balance and homeostasis, also known as equilibrium:

a. Ask Maryann what has helped in the past; for example, what did she do to cope with the loss and grief of losing a loved family member after her father passed away?

b. Initiate solution-based therapy (e.g., use a full or partial miracle question): Let's just suppose that you made it home today and went to sleep and overnight a miracle happened, but you did not know it happened, and you changed your mind about dying. What would be the first thing you would notice that was different when you woke up?

c. Ask her about bright spots from her past (e.g., hobbies, birthday celebrations, sports successes, academic successes, vacations).

d. Mutually explore and suggest new coping options and alternatives.

e. It is important for the crisis worker to jog the client's memories so she can verbalize the last time everything seemed to be going well and she was in a good mood. Help the client to find untapped resources. If appropriate, it may be helpful to mention that you have specialized in helping youths and have helped hundreds of other teens in crisis.

f. Provide Maryann with a specific phone number of a therapist and a plan to follow. The therapist needs to be someone who is willing and able to work with challenging and difficult adolescents in crisis.

Stage 6: Formulating an Action Plan

In this stage, an active role must be taken by the crisis worker; however, the success of any intervention plan depends on the client's level of involvement, participation, and commitment. The crisis worker must help Maryann look at both the short-term and long-range impacts in planning intervention. The main goals are to help the client achieve an appropriate level of functioning and maintain adaptive coping skills and resources. It is important to have a manageable treatment plan, so the client can follow through and be successful. Do not overwhelm the client with too many tasks or strategies, which may set the client up for failure.

Clients must also feel a sense of ownership in the action plan, so that they can increase the level of control and autonomy in their lives and to ensure that they not become dependent on other support persons or resources. Obtaining a commitment from the client to follow through with the action plan and any referrals are important activities for the crisis worker, which can be maximized by using a mutual process in intervention planning. Ongoing assessment and evaluation are essential to determine whether the intervention plan is appropriate and effective in minimizing or resolving the client's identified problems. During this stage, Maryann should be processing and reintegrating the crisis impacts to achieve homeostasis and equilibrium in her life.

Termination should begin when the client has achieved the goals of the action plan or has been referred for additional services through other treatment providers. It is important to realize that many suicide-attempt survivors may need booster sessions from time to time or longer-term therapeutic help in working toward crisis mastery.

Stage 7: Follow-Up Phone Call, In-Person Appointment for Booster Session, or Home Visit

Let Maryann know that she can call you, and give her your beeper number. Let her know that the beeper is for an emergency. In addition, depending on the crisis worker's assessment when leaving the school, it would be useful to schedule a follow-up with the therapist to whom Maryann is being referred, so that there is a team approach. Follow-up also may include a session with the school social worker or crisis worker scheduled for 2 days or one week later (Roberts & Yeager, 2005).

Recommended Web Sites for Further Information

American Association of Suicidology (AAS): www.suicidology.org
American Foundation for Suicide Prevention (AFSP): www.afsp.org
Canadian Association for Suicide Prevention: www.suicideprevention.ca
Crisis Intervention Network: www.crisis-interventionnetwork.com
International Association for Suicide Prevention (IASP): www.med/iasp
National Alliance for the Mentally Ill (NAMI): www.nami.org
National Institute of Mental Health (NIMH): www.nimh.nih.gov
National Strategy for Suicide Prevention: www.mentalhealth.org/suicideprevention
Suicide Information and Education Center: www.siec.ca

Key Points to Remember

School-based suicide prevention programs for youths can be effective when school social workers attempt to enhance students' protective factors and resilience, support them through therapeutic groups, and educate teachers on suicide risk factors at staff workshops. It is also imperative that school social workers have strong links to learning disability specialists, crisis workers, mental health professionals, and family counselors.

Due to the increasing need for mental health professionals to work within time-limited environments, there is a critical need to find evidence-based approaches to suicide prevention with increasingly complex youthful populations. Schools face these challenges every day. The overriding goal of this chapter has been to provide a realistic framework for school-based suicide prevention and to examine different methods of suicide lethality assessment and crisis intervention. School social workers and other mental health consultants to schools should consistently consider comprehensive suicide risk assessment strategies, the utility of instruments to assess and reassess students' status, the amount of time available, prior suicide family history, and the cost and potential outcome of chosen interventions. Application of best practices and systematic approaches such as the seven-stage crisis intervention model will assist social workers by providing a stable framework for addressing crises within a continuously changing care environment. It is the challenge of all mental health practitioners to develop their skills in rapid assessment, risk and rescue strategies, problem-solving methods, and building on the strengths of the suicidal youth as outlined by the seven-stage model.

References

American Psychiatric Association Steering Committee on Practice Guidelines. (2003). *Practice guideline for the assessment and treatment of patients with suicidal behavior.* Washington, DC: Author.

Beck, A. T., Brown, G., & Steer, R. (1997). Psychometric characteristics of the scale for suicide ideation with psychiatric outpatients. *Behavior Research and Therapy, 11,* 1039–1046.

Beck, A. T., Brown, G., Steer, R., Dahlsgaard, K., & Grisham, J. (1999). Suicide ideation at its worst point: A predictor of eventual suicide in psychiatric outpatients. *Suicide and Life-Threatening Behavior, 29*(1), 1–9.

Beck, A. T., & Lester, D. (1976). Components of suicidal intent in completed and attempted suicides. *Journal of Psychology: Interdisciplinary & Applied, 92*(1), 35–38.

Berman, A. L. (1975). Self-destructive behavior and suicide: Epidemiology and taxonomy. In A. Roberts (Ed.), *Self-destructive behavior* (pp. 5–21). Springfield, IL: Thomas.

Berman, A. L., & Jobes, D. A. (1991). *Adolescent suicide assessment and intervention.* Washington, DC: American Psychological Association.

Eaton, Y. M. (2005). The comprehensive crisis intervention model of Safe Harbor Behavioral Health Crisis

Services. In A. R. Roberts (Ed.), *Crisis intervention handbook: Assessment, treatment and research* (3rd ed., pp. 619–631). New York: Oxford University Press.

Eaton, Y., & Roberts, A. R. (2002). Frontline crisis intervention: Step-by-step practice guidelines with case applications. In A. R. Roberts and G. J. Greene (Eds.), *Social workers' desk reference* (pp. 89–96). New York: Oxford University Press.

Jobes, D. A., Berman, A. L., & Martin, C. (2005). Adolescent suicidality and crisis intervention. In A. R. Roberts (Ed.), *Crisis intervention handbook* (3rd ed., pp. 395–415). New York: Oxford University Press.

Kovacs, M., Beck, A. T., & Weissman, A. (1976). The communication of suicidal intent: A reexamination. *Archives of General Psychiatry, 33*(2), 198–201.

Maris, R. W., Berman, A. L., Maltsberger, J. T., & Yufit, R. I. (Eds.). (1992). *Assessment and prediction of suicide.* New York: Guilford.

Roberts, A. R. (1975). Self-destruction by one's own hand. In A. Roberts (Ed.), *Self-destructive behavior* (pp. 21–77). Springfield, IL: Thomas.

Roberts, A. R. (1991). *Contemporary perspectives on crisis intervention and prevention.* Englewood Cliffs, NJ: Prentice-Hall.

Roberts, A. R. (2000). Glossary. In A. R. Roberts (Ed.), *Crisis intervention handbook: Assessment, treatment and research* (2nd ed., pp. 513–529). New York: Oxford University Press.

Roberts, A. R. (2002). Assessment, crisis intervention and trauma treatment: The Integrative ACT Intervention Model. *Brief Treatment and Crisis Intervention, 2*(1), 1–21.

Roberts, A. R., & Yeager, K. R. (2005). Lethality assessments and crisis intervention with persons presenting with suicidal ideation. In A. R. Roberts (Ed.), *Crisis intervention handbook: Assessment, treatment and research* (3rd ed., pp. 35–63). New York: Oxford University Press.

Roberts, A. R., Yeager, K. R., & Streiner, D. L. (2004). Evidence-based practice with comorbid substance abuse, mental illness and suicidality: Can the evidence be found? *Brief Treatment and Crisis Intervention, 4*(2), 123–136.

Rudd, M., & Joiner, T. (1998). The assessment, management, and treatment of suicidality: Toward clinically informed and balanced standards of care. *Clinical Psychology: Science and Practice, 5*, 135–150.

Simon, R. I. (1992). *Psychiatry and law for clinicians.* Washington, DC: American Psychiatric Press.

U.S. Department of Health and Human Services. (2001). *National strategy for suicide prevention: Goals and objectives for action.* Rockville, MD: Author.

Weishaar, M. E. (2004). A cognitive-behavioral approach to suicide risk reduction in crisis intervention. In A. R. Roberts and K. Yeager (Eds.), *Evidence-based practice manual: Research and outcome measures in health and human services* (pp. 749–757). New York: Oxford University Press.

Yeager, K. R., & Gregoire, T. K. (2000). Crisis intervention application of brief solution-focused therapy in addictions. In A. R. Roberts (Ed.), *Crisis intervention handbook: Assessment, treatment and research* (2nd ed., pp. 275–306). New York: Oxford University Press.

Psychopharmacological Treatment for Child and Adolescent Mental Disorders

Kia J. Bentley ▪ Kathryn S. Collins

CHAPTER 2

Getting Started

Psychopharmacological treatment as an attempt to respond to students' social, emotional, and behavioral issues began during the 1930s and since the 1980s has been rapidly increasing as the treatment of choice by many health and mental health care providers (Olfson, Marcus, Weissman, & Jensen, 2002; Popper, 2002). Of particular interest is that despite the widespread use of psychotropic medications, with a few exceptions, the specific effectiveness of most of these drugs in children and adolescents has not been thoroughly researched, *and* they are most commonly used in ways not yet approved by the Food and Drug Administration (FDA) (Center for Mental Health in Schools at UCLA, 2003). Thus, it seems that proactively treating mental disorders in children and adolescents using knowledge acquired from research and real world experiences with adults is an accepted and understandable approach that seeks to help reduce real pain, distress, and dysfunction in young human lives. The thinking of many practitioners and parents is that the positive impact of medications—or, better said, the hope and promise of it—is sufficiently beneficial to outweigh the potential harm of psychopharmacological agents; therefore the use of a wide variety of psychiatric medications is a viable but not much-needed option.

What We Know

Understanding Common Mental Disorders

Obviously, children and adolescents can and do experience the entire range of social, emotional, and behavioral problems, which are associated with significant distress to the students and their families, schools, and communities. Mental health problems are thought to affect 1 in 5 students at any given time, while 1 in 10 students experience serious emotional disturbances that severely disrupt their daily functioning (U.S. Department of Health and Human Services, 1999). When left undiagnosed and untreated, mental health problems can contribute to school failure, family conflicts, drug and alcohol abuse, violence, and suicide. School social workers can help by explaining that epidemiological studies indicate that mental and emotional disorders in children and adolescents, like those in adults, are primarily related to some complex interplay of biological and environmental factors (Rutter, 2000, 2002). Chapters in the first section of this book cover effective ways to intervene with several mental disorders that confront children and youths, which also may become a barrier to their learning. It important to note that mental disorders can remit or endure over the life span. School social workers and school-based mental health counselors can work with others (e.g., nurses, psychologists, psychiatrists, pharmacists) to develop psychoeducational programs and materials to teach students and parents about common disorders and their treatment. Such education can have an empowering effect, strengthen coping skills, provide emotional support, increase clients' hope, and promote good communication, among other things (Bentley & Walsh, 2006). Some common categories of disorders found in childhood include anxiety and mood disorders, attention deficit and disruptive disorders, autism and other pervasive developmental disorders, eating disorders, schizophrenia, and tic disorders (American Psychiatric Association, 2000).

Understanding Medications and Their Specific Use in Children

The five classes of medication are antipsychotic medications, antidepressants, anti-anxiety medications, mood stabilizers, and stimulants. Medications from all five drug classes are used with children and adolescents experiencing mental, emotional, and behavioral disorders. An important trend is that a physician's choice of type of medication may be only in part related to a student's diagnosis. That is, it is overly simplistic to say that depression will be treated with an antidepressant, anxiety with an anti-anxiety (anxiolytic) medication, ADHD with a stimulant, and so on. Instead, the choice may relate to concern over a particularly prominent symptom or the interplay of symptoms, the explicit avoidance of a side effect (in youth, for example, weight gain, acne, tremors, confusion, effects on reproductive system or sexual functioning), and especially the past effectiveness of a specific drug in clinical trials or in real-world practice with adults. Thus, in practice, physicians, for example, might choose a selective serotonin reuptake inhibitor (SSRI) for a wide variety of concerns ranging from depression, obsessive-compulsive disorder, and conduct disorder to eating disorder, anxiety disorder, and ADHD (Magno-Zito et al., 2002). Another example is that while anticonvulsant medications have been used instead of, or in combination with, lithium for the treatment of bipolar disorder, some physicians are now prescribing small doses of an antipsychotic medication for bipolar disorder in youth, often in combination with more traditional mood stabilizers (Wilens & Wozniak, 2003). Lithium, a naturally occurring salt categorized as a mood stabilizer, also has been used to treat a range of disorders from the expected bipolar disorder to posttraumatic stress, aggression, and depression. One of the highest profile drugs currently is Strattera (atomoxetine), approved in November 2002 for the treatment of ADHD in both children and adults. Because it is a nonstimulant, it is thought be safer and have less abuse potential. However, it is known to have other serious side effects, such as hallucinations and liver damage. A summary of key medications currently used with children and adolescents is provided in the "Tools and Practice Examples" section of this chapter (see also National Institute of Mental Health, 2004; Thomson Healthcare, 2003).

Controversy About the Use of Psychopharmacological Treatment With Children

Much controversy surrounds the practice of child and adolescent psychopharmacology, and the school social worker and mental health counselor sit right in the middle of it, that is, "at the nexus of the systems of home, school and community," as one social worker eloquently noted (Allen-Meares, 1991, p. 5). In embracing expanded roles in medication management, school social workers uphold their professional tradition of striving to keep students safe from harm or distress, in its many forms, and help to keep their schools on the forefront of our changing society's thinking about psychotropic medications for children and adolescents. We argue that school social workers and other mental health consultants have a crucial role of not only providing comprehensive biopsychosocial assessment information to health and mental health care providers and parents so that good decisions can be made around the prescription of psychotropic medications but also in helping to monitor the positive and negative effects of medications on students in the school system.

As new psychotropic medicines are introduced, as new methods of administration develop, and even as new philosophies about dosing and polypharmacy emerge, it will be important for school social workers and mental health counselors to expand their knowledge and skill base about the medications so that they may promote the full quality of life and well-being of the students they serve, while helping to deter any negative outcomes. Toward this end, we start with the assumption that children and adolescents are both like adults and not like adults, and these different dimensions affect pharmacological treatment and medication management. For example, the rates of absorption, distribution, and metabolism are quite different in children. Importantly, children and adolescents have different cognitive schema that may effect their descriptions of physiologic or psychological changes (Brown & Sammons, 2002). Yet, as human beings, children and adolescents have the same basic anatomy, functional systems, and all of the same basic emotional needs and psychological dimensions as everyone else. With that principle in mind, this chapter will offer ideas on four basic "how do you help" questions faced by school social workers working with children, adolescents, and their families:

- How do you help students and parents make sense of the controversy and ambiguity in child and adolescent psychopharmacotherapy?
- How do you help students and parents understand common mental disorders and the medications used to treat them?
- How do you help students and parents negotiate the referral processes and pharmacological assessment?
- How do you help students and parents in managing and monitoring medications?

Making Sense of the Controversy and Ambiguity in Child and Adolescent Psychopharmacotherapy

Worries About Physical and Psychological Developmental Impact

Clearly one of the biggest concerns about the use of medication in children and adolescents relates to uncertainties about long-term effects, both physical and psychological. These are important considerations for which some assurances can be provided, but also a place where a healthy skepticism may be appropriate. It is true that most formal clinical drug research, both with children and adults, does not help us to understand the long-term effects of medications because studies tend to focus on initial effects over just a few weeks to a few months. The further bad news is that such a lack of research opens the door to speculation and myth. For example, the early concerns that stimulants were associated with significant levels of stunted growth have been largely abandoned by most reputable providers. However, some Internet sites continue to relay what appears to be misinformation about this and closely related issues.

Another specific concern about children and adolescents who take psychiatric medications relates to the fact that brain and neurotransmitter development is occurring at the same time these drugs are being used (Floersch, 2003; Greenhill & Setterberg, 1993). What are the long-term developmental effects? Another concern: Do we fully understand how medication use should be adjusted to account for the physical development of children's renal functioning, gastrointestinal system, or hepatic enzyme system in their early years? Another compelling concern has been raised by Floersch (2003, p. 52) about the impact of taking psychiatric medication on the self-identity

and psychological development of children and adolescents. This will be especially important as school social workers and mental health counselors listen to how students make sense of their medication experience. So, as we have noted, while some argue that children are, after all, human beings and thus clinical research in humans is relevant and useful, others argue that children are still other than and different than little adults; thus, given the intrusiveness of the intervention, extreme caution is called for.

Worries About Pathologizing Human Experience

Of equal concern is that the use of psychiatric medications in children represents an inappropriate "blaming the victim." A number of vocal critics of medication use have noted that massive increases in the use of medication with kids in recent years has led to an underemphasis on other potential culprits in the seeming rise of mental, emotional, and behavioral difficulties in children, that is, the larger social context and poor school and community supports. Admittedly, it could be said that dramatic prescription increases and expanded use of medications with children and adolescents are not necessarily problematic signs, but rather represent good news about the accessibility of treatment to those in need. However, there remains a pervasive feeling among many school social workers and others in the field that too many children are being medicated without sufficient cause (see below) and that we are neglecting other environmental influences on behavior, which might have even a more powerful impact. These things might include a lack of tolerance of difference among kids, poor parenting practices, misperceptions about what is developmentally "typical" in children and adolescents, the violent media and the tendency to rely on overstimulation, the drug culture, the cultural value of immediate gratification, or more school system–focused influences like lack of school resources, high student–teacher ratios, lack of teacher training, and low teacher salaries, to name a few.

Backlash About Medication in Schools

Fears about the overmedication of children are reflected in recent legislation that has passed in Congress. In May 2003, the House of Representatives passed the Child Medication Safety Act of 2003 (H.R. 1170) authored by Representative Max Burns, a Republican from Georgia. While it did not get out of committee in the Senate that year, it (now HR 1790) has been reintroduced in 2005 by Representative John Kline with 21 cosponsors and is in committee as of this writing. The bill would require states that receive federal Department of Education funds for any program or activity to create and implement specific policies *prohibiting* school personnel from "coercing children to receive, or their parents to administer, a controlled substance in schedule II under the Controlled Substances Act, as a condition of attending school or receiving services." However, it does not prohibit classroom teachers or other school personnel from making *observations* about academic achievement and classroom behavior and relaying the information to parents or recommending evaluation regarding special education or related school and classroom services under the Individuals With Disabilities Education Act (IDEA). It should be noted that an amendment with softer wording prohibiting educational personnel from "requiring" medication for children as a condition for attending school or receiving services was attached to the reauthorization of IDEA (P.L. 108-446), which recently passed Congress. Further, the comptroller general of the Government Accounting Office (GAO) plans to research such issues as the variation of states' definitions of medication use and the extent to which school personnel actively influence parents to pursue medication, the prescription rates of psychotropic drugs used in public schools to treat children diagnosed with mental health disorders (with specific mention of ADD/ADHD), and the identification and prevalence of medications used both under the Controlled Substance Act and otherwise.

Many states are in various stages of enacting legislation specifically on this issue. Some states, such as Georgia, Washington, North Carolina, and Hawaii, have created legislation to investigate the prevalence and effects of psychotropic medications on children and develop recommendations on how to better monitor prescription rates. Other states, such as Connecticut, Maryland, Illinois, Colorado, Minnesota, and Virginia, require school policies strictly prohibiting school personnel from recommending or requiring psychotropic drug use. Further, legislation urges school personnel to use nonmedication alternatives only with students who have difficulty learning

and/or who display hyperactivity or other behavioral disruptions. Connecticut, Minnesota, Utah, and Illinois have legislation prohibiting disciplinary actions, such as reports to child protection services or charges of neglect against parents who refuse to seek a prescription for or administer psychotropic medications. It is crucial for school social workers and other personnel to be aware of legislative activities in their respective states and school districts as well as the values (and fears and concerns) they represent.

Off-Label Use by Physicians

Another issue of some concern is the widespread "off-label" use of medications with children and adolescents. *Off-label use* refers to the use of a specific medication with children in spite of the fact that it has not yet been approved by the FDA for use with children in particular. Parents and teachers should know that this practice is not only very common but obviously also quite legal, as long as the drug has been studied and received approval for use in adults. Physicians know well that the FDA is after all about the development and marketing of drugs, not the regulation of the practice of medicine. While off-label use represents up to three quarters of medication use with children, drug companies are not allowed to target their marketing or advertising of a specific nonapproved drug for use in children until sufficient safety and effectiveness has been established and FDA approval obtained. The lack of FDA approval, then, does not mean a drug is *not* safe or effective. Clinical trials with children and adolescents are relatively new (Wilens, 1999) and come with even more controversy, as we discuss below.

The Media and Clinical Drug Research With Children

Newspapers and magazines have been generously covering issues related to the testing and marketing of medications for children. Parents, social workers, and school-based mental health workers cannot help but be curious about them or, more likely, have serious questions and concerns. For example, in 2002, the issue of pediatric drug testing in general made it to the editorial pages of *USA Today* ("Why Give Kids Drugs," 2002, p. 12A). At issue was whether the FDA exceeded its authority in 1999 by requiring (one report used the word "forcing") drug companies to test their adult products on children prior to receiving approval for distribution to children. The rule, instituted mainly due to concerns around psychiatric medication use among children, was thought by most lawmakers, health care providers, and advocates to be a step *forward* in ensuring the safety of children. However, the Competitive Enterprise Institute, a think tank concerned about advancing free markets on numerous fronts, brought a successful lawsuit, which has led to alterations and an emphasis on the voluntary testing of many drugs.

The most prominent recent topic has been the FDA's concern about suicidal ideation and self-harm among some young (and not so young) users of the most popular type of antidepressant, the selective serotonin reuptake inhibitors (SSRIs). After a series of public hearings and in a surprise move in early 2004, the FDA asked the manufacturers of 10 different SSRI antidepressants to strengthen or add a suitable warning about the possible connection between drug use and suicide. The hope was that this would stimulate closer monitoring of the effects of these antidepressants. What made this bold move different from past actions is that the FDA request was not preceded by very clear evidence from clinical research about the connection between the actual medications and harm. Reactions of providers and others to the FDA action (see, for example, Elias, 2004, 2005; "FDA Seeks Warning," 2004; Sood, 2005) have ranged from relief (from those who have long thought the use of psychiatric medications among children had become too casual) to anger (from those who described it as an overreaction and completely unwarranted) to worry about the chilling effect it may have on getting treatment to children who may benefit.

Misuse by Consumers

First noticed in the mid-1990s, little is empirically known about the misuse, diversion, or illegal trading or selling of psychiatric medications among youth. Methylphenidate (Ritalin), known by such street names as "vitamin R" and "Skippy," is especially suspect. One study several years ago examined 116 students in Wisconsin with ADHD and found that 16% reported having been approached at least once to sell, trade, or give away their stimulant medication in the past 5 years (Musser, Ahmann, Mundt, Broste, & Mueller-Rizner, 1998).

Reports from those in the field, including social workers, school administrators, and law enforcement authorities, suggest the problem may be much broader and more widespread. Middle school, high school, and college students, who may be trying to balance employment and academics, use medications to become hyperalert or to give them an extra energy boost to stay up all night studying or even partying. Finally, there are reports that some youth use their medications in combination with other medications or alcohol to make "cocktails" so that they can get better effects from getting stoned or high. This abuse has led to students with ADHD selling or trading their much-needed medications to other students.

In a review, Klein-Schwartz (2002) noted disagreement about the extent of abuse and diversion. While pharmacologically similar to cocaine, some experts note lower than expected misuse of Ritalin in comparison with other drugs. However, Kollins, MacDonald, and Rush (2001) concluded that it is "not benign with respect to abuse potential" (p. 624) and called on school administrators and parents to be aware of the potential for its diversion and misuse. Importantly, they added: "This caution should, of course, be weighed against the well-documented clinical benefits of the drug for many children, adolescents, and adults" (p. 624). Likewise, Musser and colleagues (1998) sensibly called for "monitoring prescription usage, periodic reassessment of efficacy, and continuing education of family and teaching staff."

What We Can Do

Typical Rationales for Physician Referral

School social workers and other school counselors will be in the position to suggest that parents seek a psychopharmacological assessment for their child, as well as to explain to students or parents why others may have suggested following through with such a referral. In either case, there seem to be two overarching reasons for referral: first, that teachers or others are seeing the kind of difficulties in a student's behavior or mood that is thought to respond to medications, or second, that the problematic issues or symptoms in the student that have been of concern have not changed with some sort of intervention by teachers or school care providers (psychologists, social workers). Whether or not medication is conceptualized as a last resort, if a referral is being considered, there is an implication that the problems are of such severity that outside medical/psychiatric attention is warranted and likely to be helpful to all of the stakeholders in the situation.

What to Expect From a Pharmacological Evaluation (Processes and Outcomes)

A solid, comprehensive psychopharmacological assessment in children and adolescents is thought to be a bit more complicated than for adults because of the need for family input, the wide developmental differences in the age group, diagnostic ambiguities, and ethical issues around decision making and the rights of minors (Bentley & Walsh, 2006). While great variability exists in the processes and procedures used, certain common elements can be expected. The goal is to obtain the most complete, accurate, and rich information possible so that decisions about diagnosis and, if relevant, specific medication type and dosage can be made with appropriate confidence. However, it is likely that conclusions by the physician will be presented as tentative, with disclaimers about how adjustments in diagnosis and treatment may be made in the future.

It may go without saying that the process done right will involve one or more face-to-face interviews with the student and parents. A "quick and dirty" 10- or 15-minute evaluation by a single provider should be considered inadequate. The interviewer(s) may be a stranger to the student and her family, or a family may choose to use its primary care physician. Interviews should consist of one or more long sessions where a series of related questions is asked, often seeking quite detailed information on developmental history (parents) or past and current patterns of behavior, thinking, and feeling (student). Interviewers may also seek information/documentation related to the student's situation from a referral source in the school system. For example, the interviewer may want medical records from the primary care physician. Sessions where psychological tests or checklists are administered may be anticipated. Importantly, anticipating a range of emotional responses to the interview by both parents and student will be helpful. Certainly, a comprehensive psychopharmacological assessment is likely to be

anxiety producing for the student and his family, even if it is associated with great hope for positive change in the future. Disclosures by students or parents, if they become known, may shock each other. Students may welcome the opportunity for help with their difficulties, or they may respond by denying problems, attempting to diminish their severity, blaming others, or expressing fears of being different or not good enough. Questions may abound, or silence may rule the day.

Helping Students and Parents to Manage and Monitor Medications

Assessing and Maximizing Therapeutic Effects and Side Effects

School social workers and other school-based professionals are not called on to medically evaluate the impact of medications, as might be the case for physicians or nurses. We do not make final decisions about medication adjustments. Instead, our concern is to collaborate with others to help keep track of the whole picture in terms of effects and side effects, both positive and negative. *Therapeutic effects* are those that are desired and represent the positive effects of medications. This could certainly mean a reduction of behavioral problems or psychiatric symptoms or an increase in normal activity, enhanced mood, or a sense of being "more like me," with greater investment in personal interests. Negative or adverse effects, referred to as *side effects* because they are, by definition, unwanted, can be physical (such as drowsiness, weight gain, tremors), psychological (such as feeling controlled or "sick"), or social (such as being rejected by a friend). Some specific challenges in monitoring medications with children and adolescents, summarized in Bentley and Walsh (2006), include the fact that they may experience more marked side effects, like sedation or extrapyramidal symptoms (e.g., neuromuscular slowness, rigidity) with antipsychotics, but talk about them less. Hormonal changes may make measuring the effectiveness of antidepressants more problematic, as is the fact that the placebo effect is so prominent in children. Indeed, causal attributions for clinical improvement should be made with care. While children seem to tolerate long-term treatment with lithium well, there are concerns about the long-term build-up of lithium in the body. More concern is expressed over the possible precipitation of agitation or mania with Tegretol (carbamazepine) or the less common but still serious lowered seizure threshold with antihistamine use in the treatment of anxiety.

A number of authors have summarized lists of existing measurement devices that social workers and school-based mental health counselors could use to help track, for example, the positive and negative symptoms of schizophrenia, dyskinesia, or akathesia; the extent of Parkinsonism symptoms; or the levels of anxiety or depression, mania or impulsivity (e.g., Bentley & Walsh, 2006; Bond & Lader, 1996). It is, however, unclear if social workers in the field regularly use this type of assessment tool. Instead, social workers and school counselors may rely on simple graphs or checklists generated from their idiosyncratic knowledge of clients' responses or rely on charting simple, brief, descriptive statements, like a mini-mental status exam, and comparing them over time.

Direct observation and candid, open dialogue are the methods for assessing effects and side effects. Helping students to manage both kinds of effects calls for a range of techniques, including simple exercises (stretching), more education (around time lags, need for patience), concrete changes in behavior (using sunscreen, dieting), problem-solving or skills training (around what to tell people at school, how to talk to the school psychologist), or reflective discussion on meaning or stigma. Obviously, tracking the effectiveness, or lack thereof, of psychiatric medications may also call for additional consultation with the physician for possible reevaluation of dosing or medication type.

Addressing Adherence Issues

Bentley and Walsh (2006) argue that to protect against inappropriately simplistic or unidimensional explanations of medication nonadherence, social workers should be equipped with a comprehensive explanatory model of adherence. They argue that *adherence* is best understood as a complex interplay of factors that relate to the *characteristics of clients* (such as health beliefs, the desire to self-regulate, the meaning of medication, and locus of control), *aspects of treatment* (such as regimen complexity, cost, timing of effects, negative side effects, and friendliness of the aftercare environment), *aspects of the social environment* (such as family beliefs and support, and messages from the

media and popular culture), and *aspects of the illness or symptoms* (denial, paranoia, depression, hostility, cognitive impairment). A good grasp of the risk and protective factors associated with nonadherence is helpful. For example, we know that bothersome side effects, a history of substance abuse, ambivalence, anger, therapeutic delays, and a poor relationship with helpers all put people at higher risk for nonadherence. Accepting or believing that one has a mental illness, having adequate preparation for and education about medication, and feeling empathy from others are, on the other hand, protective factors. Although the research that undergirds this admittedly partial list is drawn from adult samples, applying developmental theories of adolescence might help us to hypothesize that students are going to be less concerned, for example, with the impact of medication on later life than they are on the current larger meaning and symbolism (to themselves or others) of having to take a psychiatric medication for personal difficulties. It might tell us that issues of authority and trust may have a powerful impact on nonadherence, as will the parental attitudes and beliefs (Brown & Sammons, 2002).

Categories of interventions to directly affect adherence would seem to be the same for adults as for children and adolescents, in that they are likely to rely on education, cognitive and behavioral strategies, and the assessment and management of meaning. However, opportunities to creatively tailor interventions to students can and should be exploited. For example, in getting children and adolescents to express meaning, that is, the perceived impact of taking medication on their sense of self and identity, school social workers and mental health counselors could encourage storytelling, puppet play, drawing and painting and, with older students, using existing or original contemporary music and poetry. An overarching consideration is that issues of adherence are more complicated with children and adolescents in light of their limited decision-making powers. This issue may be likely to regularly rear its head in work with students.

Maximizing the Power of Collaboration

If school social workers and other school counselors are going to fully embrace their role of being a meaningful resource to students, their families, and others in the school community, close and mutually satisfying relationships with physicians, teachers, and other school-related providers is, obviously, crucial. Some philosophical foundations that may be key include:

- Embrace a client-centered "partnership" perspective around the range of medication-related dilemmas and issues that emerge in real-world practice. This suggests working toward a nonthreatening alliance, a demystification of the helping process, and a mutual sharing of respective expertise.
- Maintain a balanced perspective about psychiatric medication in the face of admittedly complex issues related to human rights and professional roles and the very real costs and benefits of psychiatric medication use.
- Work toward the successful integration of psychosocial interventions, therapeutic services, and psychopharmacology, and recognize the intrinsic power of combined treatments.
- Work toward interdisciplinary relationships characterized by equality, flexibility, decreased professional control, mutual understanding, and shared goals, but also appreciate the ideological and practical challenges that emerge, especially in managing parallel treatments.
- Genuinely appreciate both the strengths and the limits of students and their families. Work should center on students' and families' unique strengths and aspirations and away from pathology, symptoms, or weaknesses. Yet real limits (barriers to progress), such as a lack of skills or inadequate resources, have to be appreciated. (list adapted from Bentley & Walsh, 2002)

A balanced perspective acknowledges the positive impact that medications have on the lives of many, yet is not blind to the sociopolitical dimensions of prescribing, the very real dangers involved, or the negative experiences of some. It also seems to call for a rejection of any professional arrogance that would suggest that we are the only ones who embrace a "holistic perspective," are the only ones to have the "best interest" of the client at heart, or that we alone "get it."

Instead, while social workers should recognize the potential for ideological conflict, rivalry, or awkwardness when working with those who were trained and socialized very differently, we should still strive for greater understanding of the legitimate roles and expertise of others. In-

deed, a recent survey of practicing social workers concluded that most social workers get their knowledge about psychiatric medications not from books or school, but from everyday interactions with physicians and clients (Bentley, Walsh, & Farmer, in press). Thus, school social workers and other school-based professionals working with physicians and others around medication issues should reject building a professional life around keeping insulated or second-guessing the decisions of others, and instead build one around inquiring exchanges and reciprocity of respect. This is so important because we know that off-label practices, the greater acceptability of polypharmacy (the use of multiple medications at one time), and even the use of dosages beyond what the desk references allow for are not uncommon. To automatically conclude malpractice would represent naiveté. That is not to say that seeking greater understanding of others, whether clients or other providers, means being passive or not asking the tough questions when needed: *Tell me more about how you came to choose that one first? Why are you prescribing that medication in addition? What is the purpose of different doses for different times? What are you hoping for with that unusual schedule? What would the signs of overmedication look like? Isn't that drug usually used with someone with different symptoms or diagnoses? Is that more than is typically prescribed? What is your thinking on this?* These questions are consistent with the professional mandate, not only to understand the entire service plan of any case, but to be advocates for clients and be an approachable, consumer-friendly translator of information for students and their families. Thus, social workers' efforts to maximize collaboration and increase our confidence in carrying out these roles may center on maximizing our learning about what others do as well as increasing time spent in interaction (Bentley, Walsh, & Farmer, in press). Further suggestions for discussing medications are provided in the next section.

Tools and Practice Examples

Table 2.1 provides a summary of common mental disorders that are frequently treated with medication and some case examples. Table 2.2 provides a summary of medications that are frequently provided to children.

Table 2.1 Case Vignettes of Common Mental Disorders

Category of Disorder	Common Symptomatology	Vignette
Anxiety	Excessive fear, worry, or uneasiness; social withdrawal, poor concentration, irritability; terror of certain objects or situations; anxiety and/or panic at being separated from parent or guardian; nightmares, continuous memories of traumatic events	Jana is 8 years old and has extreme separation anxiety. On the days her mother is able to get her to go to school, Jana has bouts of hyperventilating, crying spells, trembling hands, and wanting to sit by herself in the corner of the room. She states she is afraid that something bad will happen to her mother if she is not with her.
Depression	Feelings of sadness, hopelessness, worthlessness, and/or suicide; irritability, somatic complaints, poor concentration; loss of interest in friends and/or play; deterioration of school work; poor sleep and appetite, lack of motivation	Ten-year-old Colin's grades went from A's and B's to failing over the course of 6 weeks. He has lost interest in going to recess and spends most of his time alone. Colin told his school counselor that he was really sad and felt like he would never be good enough to pass fifth grade. His parents state that when he comes home from school, he is irritable and usually just wants to go to bed and doesn't even want to eat with the family.
Oppositional defiant/ conduct	Violates rights of others by lying, theft, aggression, truancy, the setting of fires, and vandalism; low self-esteem, depression; running away from home	Sonya is in tenth grade. She had to go to juvenile court twice for truancy this school year. Sonya told the judge she would never amount to anything and didn't care that her parents had to pay fines for school truancy. Recently, Sonya also confided to her friend that she has been stealing her teachers' money over the past year so that she can buy a house for herself. Her friend said that Sonya stated that if she told anyone about what she was doing, she would hurt her friend's little brother.
ADD/ ADHD	Inattentive, hyperactive, aggressive and/or defiant, impulsive, easily distracted; difficulty completing tasks, fidgets, cannot sit still; interrupts often, cannot wait turn	Jaime's teacher has noticed that she is constantly out of her chair and walking around the room, talking to the other children. Jaime's parents report that they have difficulty calming her down so that she can focus on her homework. They also say she has been teasing and hitting her younger sister.
Learning and communication	Problems with spoken and written language, coordination, attention, or self-control; struggles to explain feelings and thoughts; difficulty with math, technology, and scientific information; delayed in grade-level progress	Alex's counselor describes him as a bright and articulate 12-year-old. If he hears a story, he can tell it back to his teacher and parents verbatim. Yet, he has difficulty answering questions about the significance of characters or actions of characters in the stories. Alex's written work is poor. He

(continued)

Table 2.1 (*Continued*)

Category of Disorder	Common Symptomatology	Vignette
		cannot create simple sentences, and because he cannot comprehend short stories, he cannot complete his homework assignments without his parents reading to him. His teacher states that his written work is at a third-grade level instead of a sixth-grade level.
Autism spectrum (pervasive developmental)	Range of mild to severe problems with interpersonal interactions and communication; difficulty with cognition or thinking; struggles with understanding the feelings of others; becomes attached to one object or situation; poor eye contact, tunes people out, does not react to others (such as saying hello or waving goodbye); prefers to play alone and seems independent for stated age; general difficulty with interpreting the world	Tia just started kindergarten. She has very poor eye contact and does not smile when her teacher smiles at her or praises her. Tia's parents told her teacher that they often have to continuously repeat steps of tasks to her and that she seems "to be in her own world" and "does not hear them." During the first week of school, the teacher noticed that Tia constantly echoes what other children say in class and when she is asked to stop, she begins screaming and then has a tantrum.
Schizophrenia	Delusions, hallucinations; withdrawal from others; loss of contact with reality; catatonic or other bizarre motor behaviors, hyperactive without an apparent stimulus; flat affect, does not show emotion	Brian is 17 years old. He had a flat affect when he told the school social worker that sometimes he feels confused because he hears voices telling him to steal things and to hurt himself. He relayed that the only time he can concentrate is after praying late at night in front of the news correspondent on television. Brian believes that the correspondent is the only person who can hear him and understand what he is going through in his life. He asks the social worker if she believes him.
Tic	Involuntary twitches or movements of muscle groups, such as eye blinking, sneezing, shoulder shrugging; involuntary vocalizations, such as humming, grunting, or actual words that are expressed in a spastic or explosive manner; partial control can be obtained for short periods of time; tic behaviors fluctuate in intensity and frequency	Sam was sitting on his hands and holding his face very rigid when he visited his principal for disrupting the class. The principal told Sam that he could relax, that he just wanted to talk to him. Sam said, "I can't or I will be in trouble again." Promptly, Sam took a deep breath and started holding his breath. After a few moments, he let out his breath and his shoulders began jerking up and down a few times. The principal continued talking to Sam about his school behavior and noticed Sam's rapid eye blinking. Throughout their talk, Sam also grunted and then would hold his breath until the next grunt. The principal realized that Sam was trying to stop his motor and vocal tics due to embarrassment.

Table 2.2 Common Psychiatric Medications for Children and Adolescents

Trade Name of Drug (generic name)	Type/Class of Medication	Common Psychiatric Uses	Common Side Effects	Approved for Children?
Abilify (aripiprazole)	Antipsychotic (atypical)	Schizophrenia, bipolar, aggression	Dry mouth, weight gain, drowsiness	No
Adderall (amphetamine mixed salts)	Stimulant	ADHD	High blood pressure, rapid heart rate, gastrointestinal complaints, somnolence, weight gain, middle-ear infection	Age 3 and older
Anafranil (clomipramine)	Antidepressant	OCD		Age 10 and older for OCD
BuSpar (buspirone)	Anti-anxiety	Anxiety, phobias	Drowsiness or fatigue, dry mouth, increase in nightmares or dreams	No
Catapres (clonidine)	Alpha-adrenergic	Impulsivity, hyperactivity	Dry mouth, sedation, hypotension	
Cibalith-S (lithium citrate)	Mood stabilizer	Mania, bipolar	Diarrhea, drowsiness, lack of coordination, loss of appetite, muscle weakness, nausea or vomiting, slurred speech, trembling	Age 12 and older
Clozaril (clozapine)	Antipsychotic (atypical)	Schizophrenia	Fast or irregular heart beat, dizziness, constipation	No
Concerta (methylphenidate)	Stimulant	ADHD	Headache, stomach pain, insomnia	Age 6 and older
Cylert (pemoline)	Stimulant	ADHD	Potential for serious side effects affecting the liver	Age 6 and older
Depakote (sodium valproate)	Antiseizure, mood stablizer	Bipolar, mania	Headache, nausea, drowsiness, liver	Not for this use

(continued)

Table 2.2 (*Continued*)

Trade Name of Drug (generic name)	Type/Class of Medication	Common Psychiatric Uses	Common Side Effects	Approved for Children?
			and white cell abnormalities	Age 12 and older for seizures
Dexedrine (dextroamphetamine sulfate)	Stimulant	ADHD	Headache, restlessness, diarrhea, drowsiness, weight loss	Age 3 and older
Dextrostat (dextroamphetamine)	Stimulant	ADHD	Headache, restlessness, diarrhea, drowsiness, weight loss	Age 3 and older
Effexor (venlafaxine)	Antidepressant (SSRI)	Depression	Reduced appetite, nausea, constipation	No
Eskalith (lithium)	Mood stabilizer	Bipolar, mania, bulimia	Nausea, frequent urination, hand tremor, mild thirst	Age 12 and older
Haldol (haloperidol)	Antipsychotic	Schizophrenia, Tourette's syndrome, aggression, hyperactivity	Dry mouth, drowsiness, dizziness, confusion, tardive dyskinesia	Age 3 and older
Klonopin (clonazepam)	Anti-anxiety (benzodiazepine)	Anxiety, eating disorders, Tourette's	Drowsiness	No
Lexapro (escitalopram)	Antidepressant (SSRI)	Depression, anxiety	Nausea	No
Lithium	Mood stabilizer	Bipolar, mania	Reduced appetite, hand tremors	No
Lithobid (lithium carbonate)	Mood stabilizer	Bipolar, mania	Reduced appetite, hand tremors, blurred vision, constipation, decreased appetite, gastrointestinal problems, nausea	Age 12 and older
Luvox (fluvoxamine)	Antidepressant (SSRI)	OCD		Age 8 and older for OCD
Mellaril (thioridazine)	Antipsychotic	Schizophrenia	Nausea, gastrointestinal problems, drowsiness, tardive dyskinesia	Age 2 and older

(continued)

Table 2.2. *(Continued)*

Trade Name of Drug (generic name)	Type/Class of Medication	Common Psychiatric Uses	Common Side Effects	Approved for Children?
Orap (pimozide)	Antipsychotic	Tourette's syndrome	Dizziness, drowsiness, insomnia, nausea, diarrhea or constipation, blurred vision or sensitivity to light	Age 12 and older for Tourette's syndrome
Paxil (paroxetine)	Antidepressant (SSRI)	Depression	Drowsiness, nausea, insomnia	No
Prozac (fluoxetine)	Antidepressant (SSRI)	Depression	Anxiety, weight loss, insomnia, nervousness	Age 7 and older
Risperdal (risperidone)	Antipsychotic (atypical)	Schizophrenia	Nausea, gastrointestinal problems, drowsiness, tardive dyskinesia	No
Ritalin (methylphenidate)	Stimulant	ADHD	Headache, stomach pain, insomnia	Age 6 and older
Seroquel (quetiapine)	Antipsychotic (atypical)	Schizophrenia	Nausea, gastrointestinal problems, drowsiness, tardive dyskinesia	No
Serzone (nefazodone)	Antidepressant (SSRI)	Depression	Blurred or abnormal vision, confusion, constipation, dizziness, dry mouth, light-headedness, nausea, sleepiness, weakness	No
Sinequan (doxepin)	Tricyclic antidepressant	Depression, anxiety	Drowsiness, weight gain, dry mouth	Age 12 and older
Strattera (atomoxetine)	Nonstimulant (NRI)	ADHD	Headache, dizziness, abdominal pain, insomnia	Age 6 and older
Tegretol (carbamazepine)	Anticonvulsant, mood stabilizer	Seizure disorders, alcohol	Dizziness, drowsiness, nausea,	Not for this use; any age

(continued)

Table 2.2 (*Continued*)

Trade Name of Drug (generic name)	Type/Class of Medication	Common Psychiatric Uses	Common Side Effects	Approved for Children?
		withdrawal, cocaine addiction, depression, abnormally aggressive behavior	unsteadiness, vomiting	for seizures
Tofranil (imipramine)	Tricyclic antidepressant	Depression, bed wetting, eating disorders, ADD, OCD, panic disorder	Nervousness, sleep disorders, stomach and intestinal problems, tiredness, convulsions, emotional instability, fainting	Age 6 and older for bed wetting
Wellbutrin (bupropion)	Antidepressant	Major depression	Weight loss, constipation, dizziness, dry mouth, excessive sweating, headache, loss of appetite, sleep disturbance	No
Zoloft (sertraline)	Antidepressant (SSRI)	Depression, OCD, anxiety	Dry mouth, reduced appetite, agitation, stomach distress	Yes
Zyprexa (olanzapine)	Antipsychotic (atypical)	Schizophrenia, bipolar, mania, Tourette's	Dry mouth, weight gain, drowsiness, seizures	No

Talking with students, parents, and teachers about medication can be challenging. Following are some guidelines on how to talk to students, parents, and teachers about medication:

1. Healthy skepticism about the use of psychiatric medication is appropriate.
2. Offer chances for folks to talk about their doubts, fears, hopes, and dreams with respect to psychiatric medication.
3. Acknowledge the multiple forces influencing the use of medication with children and adolescents today.
4. Explain off-label use as both common and legal.
5. Welcome conversation on the public controversies around kids and psychiatric medication.
6. Encourage the reporting of trading or selling of medication.

7. Provide examples of the typical rationale underlying referrals to a prescriber for medication assessment.
8. Explain the usual relationship among diagnoses, symptoms, and prescriber choices of drug type and dosage.
9. Anticipate a range of emotional reactions to a referral to a prescriber and the medication assessment process itself.
10. Ask about both the positive and negative effects of medication.
11. Explain the complexity of adherence.
12. Develop easy-to-understand (noncommercial) written psychoeducational materials.
13. Offer to be a resource for information, support, and problem solving around medication-related dilemmas.
14. Give folks a chance to talk about the impact of taking medication in general but especially on their sense of self and personal identity.

Key Points to Remember

Sood (2004) noted that, after looking at all of the scientific data, a case could be made for either the overprescribing or the underprescribing of medications to children and adolescents. Certainly data show staggering increases in the number of prescriptions written and the number of children taking medications. Other data show that many children who suffer are not getting the pharmacological and other treatments that may be helpful. Sood urges us to consider the implications of our own beliefs about mental illness in children (does it exist? where does it come from?) on our attitudes toward medication and strive to deliver evidence-based practices to those in need. For school social workers and others, our goals are to help facilitate access to care, participate in multimodal approaches to service delivery, and provide much-needed supports to students, parents, teachers, and health care providers. Summarized above are the "how to's" of reaching these goals, that is, how to help students, parents, and teachers make sense of the controversy and ambiguity in child and adolescent psychopharmacotherapy, understand mental disorders and the medications used to treat them, negotiate referral processes and pharmacological assessment, and manage and monitor medication in the short and long term.

References

Allen-Meares, P. (1991). The contribution of social workers to schooling. In R. Constable, J. P. Flynn, & S. McDonald (Eds.), *School social work*. Chicago: Lyceum.

American Psychiatric Association. (2000). *Diagnostic and statistical manual of mental disorders* (4th ed., text revision). Washington, DC: Author.

Bentley, K. J., & Walsh, J. (2002). Social workers' roles in psychopharmacotherapy. In A. R. Roberts and G. J. Greene (Eds.), *Social workers' desk reference* (pp. 643–645). New York: Oxford University Press.

Bentley, K. J., & Walsh, J. (2006). *The social worker & psychotropic medication: Toward effective collaboration with mental health clients, families and providers* (3rd ed.). Pacific Grove, CA: Brooks/Cole-Wadsworth.

Bentley, K. J., Walsh, J., & Farmer, R. (in press). Roles and activities of clinical social workers in psychopharmacotherapy: Results of a national survey. *Social Work*.

Bond, A. L., & Lader, M. H. (1996). *Understanding drug treatment in mental health care*. West Sussex, England: John Wiley.

Brown, R., & Sammons, M. (2002). Pediatric psychopharmacology: A review of recent developments and recent research. *Professional Psychology, 33*(2), 135–147.

Center for Mental Health in Schools at UCLA. (2003). *A resource aid packet on students and psychotropic medication: The school's role.* Los Angeles: Author.

Elias, M. (2004, January 22). Antidepressants and suicide. *USA Today*, p. 7D.

Elias, M. (2005, February 5). Suicide alert has parents rethinking antidepressants. *USA Today*, p. 1A.

FDA seeks warning for depression drugs. (2004, March 22). *Richmond Times Dispatch*, p. A1.

Floersch, J. (2003). The subjective experience of youth psychotropic treatment. *Social Work in Mental Health, 1*(4), 51–69.

Greenhill, L. L., & Setterberg, S. (1993). Pharmacotherapy of disorders of adolescents. *Psychiatric Clinics of North America, 16*(4), 793–814.

Klein-Schwartz, W. (2002). Abuse and toxicity of methylphenidate. *Current Opinions in Pediatrics, 14*(2), 219–223.

Kollins, S. H., MacDonald, E. K., & Rush, C. R. (2001). Assessing abuse potential of methylphenidate in human and non-human subjects. *Pharmacology, Biochemistry and Behavior, 68*(3), 611–627.

Magno-Zito, J., Safer, D. J., DosReis, S., Gardner, J. F., Soeken, K., Boles, M., & Lynch, F. (2002). Rising prevalence of antidepressants among US youth. *Pediatrics, 108*(5), 721–727.

Musser, C. J., Ahmann, F. W., Mundt, P., Broste, S. K., & Mueller-Rizner, N. (1998). Stimulant use and the potential for abuse in Wisconsin. *Journal of Developmental and Behavioral Pediatrics, 19*(3), 187–192.

National Institute of Mental Health. (2004, June 3). *Treatment of children with mental disorders.* (NIH Publication No. NIH-04–4702). Available: http://www.nimh.nih.gov/publicat/childqa.cfm#link3.

Olfson, M., Marcus, S. C., Weissman, M. M., & Jensen, J. S. (2002). National trends in the use of psychotropic medications by children. *Journal of the American Academy of Child & Adolescent Psychiatry, 41*(5), 514–521.

Popper, C. W. (2002). Child and adolescent psychopharmacology at the turn of the millennium In S. Kutcher (Ed.), *Practical child and child psychopharmacology* (p. 137). Cambridge: Cambridge University Press.

Rutter, M. (2000). Psychosocial influences: critiques, findings, and research needs. *Developmental Psychopathology, 12*(3), 375–405.

Rutter, M. (2002). The interplay of nature, nurture, and developmental influences. *Archives of General Psychiatry, 59*(11), 996–1000.

Sood, A. B. (2004, May 14). *Controversy of the millennium: Drugging of America's children or catalysts for healthy minds.* Keynote address, 42nd Annual Child Psychiatry Spring Forum, Virginia Commonwealth University, Richmond, VA.

Thomson Healthcare. (2003). *PDR health.* Available: http://www.pdrhealth.com/index.html.

U.S. Department of Health and Human Services. (1999). *Mental health: A report of the surgeon general.* Rockville, MD: Author.

Why give kids drugs without pediatric testing. (2002, April 8). *USA Today,* p. 12A.

Wilens, T. E. (1999). *Straight talk about psychiatric medication for kids.* New York: Guilford.

Wilens, T. E., & Wozniak, J. (2003). Bipolar disorder in children and adolescents: Diagnostic and therapeutic issues, *Psychiatric Times, 20*(8). Accessed through http://www.psychiatrictimes.com/p030855.html

Effective Interventions for Students With Conduct Disorder

David W. Springer ■ Courtney J. Lynch

Getting Started

School-aged children and adolescents with externalizing disorders are a challenging, yet rewarding, population to help. Many school-based practitioners, teachers, and administrators may be all too familiar with the behaviors associated with a diagnosis of conduct disorder (CD), such as aggressive behavior toward others, using a weapon, fire setting, cruelty to animals or persons, vandalism, lying, truancy, running away, and theft (American Psychiatric Association, 2000). The *DSM-IV-TR* allows for coding a client with one of two subtypes of CD: childhood-onset type (at least one criterion characteristic occurs prior to age 10) and adolescent-onset type (absence of any criteria prior to age 10). A youth must be engaged in a pattern of behavior over an extended period of time (at least 6 months) that consistently violates the rights of others and societal norms.

According to findings from the Dunedin Multidisciplinary Health Study, the prevalence of adolescent-onset type of CD (24%) is higher than for childhood-onset type (7%) (Moffitt, Caspi, Dickson, Silva, & Stanton, 1996). This is good news, as the prognosis for childhood-onset type is poorer than it is for adolescent-onset type. While the focus of this chapter is on students with a diagnosis of conduct disorder, there is some indication that disruptive behavior disorders in general are on the rise (Loeber, Farrington, & Waschbusch, 1998) and that the prevalence of school-based conduct disturbance, such as bullying or fighting, is also high.

Part of what makes helping school-aged youth with conduct disorder so challenging is the multifaceted nature of their problems. Indeed, students with conduct disorder are often viewed by their teachers as experiencing a wide range of additional types of school adjustment difficulties (comorbidity) (Pullis, 1991). Fortunately, in recent years, significant advances in psychosocial treatments have been made to treat children and adolescents with disruptive behavior disorders. Unfortunately, some states operate with policies that exclude conduct-disordered students from eligibility for services in schools. Nevertheless, in keeping with a recent U.S. surgeon general's report (U.S. Department of Health and Human Services, 2001), this chapter is grounded in the assumption that conduct-disordered youth can be helped using innovative and research-based interventions. Some of these evidence-based practices are applied to the case example of Alex below. For purposes here, Rosen and Proctor's (2002) definition of evidence-based practice (EBP) has been adopted, whereby "practitioners will select interventions on the basis of their empirically demonstrated links to the desired outcomes" (p. 743).

What We Know

Classroom-based interventions of conduct problems have not received as much attention as interventions for conduct problems in the home (Fonagy & Kurtz, 2002). Little and Hudson (1998) reviewed classroom interventions, concluding that these interventions are diverse, lack empirical support, and are often not consistent with home-based interventions. Nevertheless, there are some general factors that are associated with lower levels of problem behaviors in schools, including strong positive leadership; high pupil expectations; close monitoring of pupils; good opportunities to engage in school life and take on responsibility; well-functioning incentive, reward, and punishment systems; high levels of parental involvement; an academic emphasis; and a focus on learning (Mortimore, 1995; Reynolds, Sammons, Stoll, Barber, & Hillman, 1996; cited in Fonagy & Kurtz, 2002). All of these factors have an overall positive influence on youth development, learning, and behavior management and are explored in more detail in subsequent chapters of this book.

What We Can Do

Among the effective interventions for children with conduct problems, two were found to be well-established, according to the Division 12 (Clinical Psychology) Task Force on Promotion and Dissemination of Psychological Procedures (Brestan & Eyberg, 1998). One of these is the Incredible Years Parents, Teachers and Children's Training series developed by Webster-Stratton and based on a trained leader using videotape modeling to trigger group discussion. Supporting randomized control group studies using the program as a treatment program for parents of children ages 3 to 8 years with conduct problems and as a prevention program for high-risk families include those by Reid, Webster-Stratton, and Baydar (2004); Reid, Webster-Stratton, and Hammond (2003); Spaccarelli, Cotler, and Penman (1992); Webster-Stratton (1984, 1990, 1994, 1998); Webster-Stratton, Kolpacoff, and Hollinsworth (1988); and Webster-Stratton, Reid, and Hammond (2001a). The second well-established approach is parent-training programs based on Patterson and Gullion's (1968) manual *Living With Children* (Alexander & Parsons, 1973; Bernal,

Klinnert, & Schultz, 1980; Wiltz & Patterson, 1974). See Table 3.1 for supporting studies. In short, parent management training (PMT) is the only intervention that is considered well established for the treatment of conduct disorder.

Several treatments for children with conduct problems were found to be probably efficacious, according to the same criteria (Brestan & Eyberg, 1998). Probably efficacious treatments for preschool-age children include parent–child interaction therapy, time out plus signal seat treatment, delinquency prevention program, and parent training program. Two treatments meeting the probably efficacious criteria designed for use with school-age children are problem-solving skills training and anger coping therapy. Finally, four treatments for adolescents with conduct problems were found to be probably efficacious: multisystemic therapy, assertiveness training, rational-emotive therapy, and anger control training with stress inoculation. See Table 3.2 for supporting studies.

Parent Management Training

Parent management training (PMT) is a summary term that describes a therapeutic strategy in which parents are trained to use skills for managing their child's problem behavior (Kazdin, 2004), such as effective command giving, setting up reinforcement systems, and using punishment, including taking away privileges and assigning extra chores. While PMT programs may differ in focus and therapeutic strategies used, they all share the common goal of enhancing parental control over children's behavior (Barkley, 1987; Cavell, 2000; Eyberg, 1988; Forehand & McMahon, 1981; Patterson, Reid, Jones, & Conger, 1975; Webster-Stratton, 1998).

Table 3.1 Well-Established Treatments and Supporting Studies

Best-Supported (Well-Established) Treatments	Supporting Studies
Videotape Modeling Parent Training	Reid, Webster-Stratton, & Hammond (2003); Spaccarelli, Cotler, & Penman (1992); Webster-Stratton (1984, 1990, 1994, 1998); Webster-Stratton, Kolpacoff, & Hollinsworth (1988); Webster-Stratton, Reid, & Hammond (2001b)
Parent Training Based on Living With Children	Alexander & Parsons (1973); Bernal, Klinnert, & Schultz (1980); Wiltz & Patterson (1974)

Table 3.2 Probably Efficacious Treatments and Supporting Studies

Promising (Probably Efficacious) Treatments for Preschool-Aged Children	Supporting Studies
Parent-Child Interaction Therapy	Eyberg, Boggs, & Algina (1995); McNeil, Eyberg, Eisenstadt, Newcomb, & Funderburk (1991); Zangwill (1983)
Time-Out Plus Signal Seat Treatment	Hamilton & MacQuiddy (1984)
Delinquency Prevention Program	Tremblay, Pagani-Kurtz, Masse, Vitaro, & Phil (1995); Vitaro & Tremblay (1994)
Parent Training Program for School-Aged Children	Peed, Roberts, & Forehand (1977); Wells & Egan (1988)
For School-Aged Children	
Problem-Solving Skills Training	Kazdin, Esveldt-Dawson, French, & Unis (1987a, 1987b); Kazdin, Siegel, & Bass (1992)
Anger Coping Therapy	Lochman, Burch, Curry, & Lampron (1984); Lochman, Lampron, Gemmer, & Harris (1989)
For Adolescents	
Multisystemic Therapy	Borduin, Mann, Cone, Henggeler, Fucci, Blaske, & Williams (1995); Henggeler, Melton, & Smith (1992); Henggeler, Rodick, Bourdin, Hanson, Watson, & Urey (1986)
Assertiveness Training	Huey & Rank (1984)
Rational-Emotive Therapy	Block (1978)
Anger Control Training With Stress Inoculation	Feindler, Marriott, & Iwata (1984); Schlichter & Horan (1981)

Source: This table was compiled by synthesizing information from the following: Brestan, E. V., & Eyberg, S. M. (1998). Effective psychosocial treatments of conduct-disordered children and adolescents: 29 years, 82 studies, and 5,272 kids. *Journal of Clinical Child Psychology, 27*(2), 180–189; www.effectivechildtherapy.com.

While PMT approaches are typically used for parents with younger children (Serketich & Dumas, 1996), they have been successfully adapted for parents with adolescents (cf. Bank, Marlowe, Reid, Patterson, & Weinrott, 1991; Barkley, Edwards, Laneri, Fletcher, & Metevia, 2001; Barkley, Guevremont, Anastopoulos, & Fletcher, 1992). The effectiveness of parent training is well documented and, in many respects, impressive. Still, school practitioners should be aware that studies examining the effectiveness of PMT with adolescents are equivocal, with some studies suggesting that adolescents respond less well to PMT than do their younger counterparts (Dishion & Patterson, 1992; Kazdin, 2002). In much of the outcome research, PMT has been administered to individual families in clinic settings, while group administration has been facilitated primarily through videotaped materials.

PMT has been effective in reducing conduct problems and increasing positive parenting behaviors when implemented on a large scale as part of early school intervention (Head Start) programs (Webster-Stratton, 1998; cited in Kazdin, 2004).

Problem-Solving Skills Training

Problem-solving skills training (PSST) is a cognitively based intervention that has been used to treat aggressive and antisocial youth (Kazdin, 1994). The problem-solving process involves helping clients learn how to produce a variety of potentially effective responses when faced with problem situations (D'Zurilla & Nezu, 2001). Regardless of the specific problem-solving model used, the primary focus is on addressing the

Table 3.3 Parent Management Training Sessions: Overview of the Core Sessions

1. *Introduction and overview.* This session provides the parents with an overview of the program and outlines the demands placed on them and the focus of the intervention.

2. *Defining and observing.* This session trains parents to pinpoint, define, and observe behavior. The parents and trainer define specific problems that can be observed and develop a specific plan to begin observations.

3. *Positive reinforcement (point chart and praise).* This session focuses on learning the concept of positive reinforcement, factors that contribute to the effective application, and rehearsal of applications in relation to the target child. Specific programs are outlined where praise and points are to be provided for the behaviors observed during the week. An incentive (token/point) chart is devised, and the delivery praise of the parent is developed through modeling, prompting, feedback, and praise by the therapist.

4. *Time-out form reinforcement.* Parents learn about time out and the factors related to its effective application. Delivery of time out is extensively role played and practiced. The use of time out is planned for the next week for specific behaviors.

5. *Attending and ignoring.* In this session, parents learn about attending and ignoring and choose an undesirable behavior that they will ignore and a positive behavior to which they will attend. These procedures are practiced within the session. Attention and praise for positive behaviors are key components of this session and are practiced.

6. *Shaping and school intervention.* Parents are trained to develop behaviors by reinforcement of successive approximations and to use prompts and fading of prompts to develop terminal behaviors. Also, in this session, plans are made to implement a home-based reinforcement program to develop school-related behaviors. These behaviors include individually targeted academic domains, classroom deportment, and other tasks (e.g., homework completion). Prior to the session, the therapist identifies domains of functioning, specific goals, and concrete opportunities to implement procedures at school. The specific behaviors are incorporated into the home-based reinforcement program. After this session, the school-based program continues to be developed and monitored over the course of treatment, with changes in foci as needed in discussion with the teachers and parents.

7. *Review of the program.* Observations of the previous week as well as application of the reinforcement program are reviewed. Details about the administration of praise, points, and back-up reinforcers are discussed and enacted so the therapist can identify how to improve parent performance. Changes are made in the program as needed. The parent practices designing programs for a set of hypothetical problems. The purpose is to develop skills that extend beyond implementing programs devised with the therapist.

8. *Family meeting.* At this meeting, the child and parent(s) are bought into the session. The programs are discussed along with any problems. Revisions are made as needed to correct misunderstandings or to alter facets that may not be implemented in a way that is likely to be effective. The programs are practiced (role played) to see how they are implemented and to make refinements.

9–10. *Negotiating, contracting, and compromising.* The child and parent meet together to negotiate new behavioral programs and to place these in contractual form. In the first of these sessions, negotiating and contracting are introduced, and the parent and child practice with each other on a problem/issue in the home and develop a contract that will be used as part of the program. Over the course of the sessions, the therapist shapes negotiating skills in the parent and child, reinforces compromise, and provides less and less guidance (e.g., prompts) as more difficult situations are presented.

(continued)

Table 3.3 (*Continued*)

11. *Reprimands and consequences for low-rate behaviors.* Parents are trained in effective use of reprimands and how to deal with low-rate behaviors, such as setting fires, stealing, or truancy. Specific punishment programs (usually chores) are planned and presented to the child, as needed, for low-rate behaviors.

12–13. *Review, problem solving, and practice.* Material from other sessions is reviewed in theory and practice. Special emphasis is given to role playing the application of individual principles as they are enacted with the trainer. Parents practice designing new programs, revising ailing programs, and responding to a complex array of situations in which principles and practices discussed in prior sessions are reviewed.

Source: From Kazdin, A. E. (2003). Problem-solving skills training and parent management training for conduct disorder. In A. E. Kazdin & J. R. Weisz (Eds.), *Evidence-based psychotherapies for children and adolescents* (pp. 241–262). New York: Guilford. Copyright 2003 by Guilford Press. Reprinted with permission.

thought process to help adolescents address deficiencies and distortions in their approach to interpersonal situations (Kazdin, 1994). A variety of techniques are used, including didactic teaching, practice, modeling, role playing, feedback, social reinforcement, and therapeutic games (Kronenberger & Meyer, 2001).

The problem-solving approach includes five steps for the practitioner and client to address: (1) defining the problem; (2) brainstorming; (3) evaluating the alternatives; (4) choosing and implementing an alternative; and (5) evaluating the implemented option. Several randomized clinical trials (Type 1 and 2 studies) have demonstrated the effectiveness of PSST with impulsive, aggressive, and conduct-disordered children and adolescents (cf. Baer & Nietzel, 1991; Durlak, Fuhrman, & Lampman, 1991; Kazdin, 2000; cited in Kazdin, 2002). Webster-Stratton and colleagues have developed a small-group treatment program that teaches problem solving, anger management, and social skills for children ages 4 to 8 years, and two randomized control group studies demonstrate the efficacy of this treatment program (Webster-Stratton & Hammond, 1997; Webster-Stratton & Reid, 2003a; Webster-Stratton, Reid, & Hammond, 2001b; Webster-Stratton, Reid, & Hammond, 2004). Problem-solving training produces significant reductions in conduct symptoms and improvements in prosocial behavior among antisocial youth.

Videotape Modeling Parent Program

Webster-Stratton's Videotape Modeling Parent Program, part of the Incredible Years training series, was developed to address parent, family, child,

and school risk factors related to childhood conduct disorders. The series is a result of Webster-Stratton's own research, which suggested that comprehensive videotape training methods are effective treatments for early-onset ODD/CD. The training series includes the Incredible Years Parent Interventions, the Incredible Years Teacher Training Intervention, and the Incredible Years Child Training Intervention, each of which relies on performance training methods, including videotape modeling, role play, practice activities, and live therapist feedback (Webster-Stratton & Reid, 2003b).

The parent component aims to promote competencies and strengthen families by increasing positive parenting skills, teaching positive discipline strategies, improving problem solving, and increasing family supports and collaboration, to name a few. The teacher component of the training series aims to promote teacher competencies and strengthen home-school relationships by increasing effective classroom management skills, increasing teachers' use of effective discipline and collaboration with parents, and increasing teachers' abilities in the areas of social skills, anger management, and problem solving. The child component aims to strengthen children's social and play skills, increase effective problem-solving strategies and emotional awareness, boost academic success, reduce defiance and aggression, and increase self-esteem.

Webster-Stratton and Reid (2003b) assert that the most proactive and powerful approach to the problem of escalating aggression in young children is to offer their programs using a school-based prevention/early intervention model designed to strengthen *all* children's social and

Table 3.4 Problem-Solving Skills Training: Overview of the Core Sessions

1. *Introduction and learning the steps.* The purpose of this initial session is to establish rapport with the child, to teach the problem-solving steps, and to explain the procedures of the cognitively based treatment program. The child is acquainted with the use of tokens (chips), reward menus for exchange of the chips, and response-cost contingencies. The child is trained to use the problem-solving steps in a game-like fashion in which the therapist and child take turns learning the individual steps and placing them together in a sequence.

2–3. *Applying the steps.* The second session reviews and continues to teach the steps as needed. The child is taught to employ the problem-solving steps to complete a relatively simple game. The child applies the steps to simple problem situations presented in a board-game fashion in which the therapist and child alternate turns. During the session, the therapist demonstrates how to use the problem-solving steps in decision making, how to provide self-reinforcement for successful performance, and how to cope with mistakes and failure. One of the goals of this session is to illustrate how the self-statements can be used to help "stop and think" rather than respond impulsively when confronted with a problem. The third session includes another game that leads to selection of hypothetical situations to which the child applies the steps. The therapist and child take turns, and further practice is provided using prompts, modeling, shaping, and reinforcement to help the child be facile and fluid in applying the steps. The therapist fades prompts and assistance to shape proficient use and application of the steps. A series of "supersolvers" (homework assignments) begins at this point, in which the child is asked to identify when the steps could be used, then to use the steps in increasingly more difficult and clinically relevant situations as treatment continues.

4. *Applying the steps and role playing.* The child applies the steps to real-life situations. The steps are applied to the situation to identify solutions and consequences. Then, the preferred solution, based on the likely consequences, is selected and then enacted through repeated role plays. Practice and role play are continued to develop the child's application of the steps. Multiple situations are presented and practiced in this way.

5. *Parent-child contact.* The parent(s), therapist, and child are all present in the session. The child enacts the steps to solve problems. The parents learn more about the steps and are trained to provide attention and contingent praise for the child's use of the steps and selecting and enacting prosocial solutions. The primary goal is to develop the repertoire in the parent to encourage (prompt) use of the steps and to praise applications in a way that will influence child behavior (i.e., contingent, enthusiastic, continuous, verbal, and nonverbal praise). Further contacts with the parents at the end of later sessions continue this aspect of treatment as needed.

6–11. *Continued applications to real-life situations.* In these sessions, the child uses the problem-solving steps to generate prosocial solutions to provocative interpersonal problems or situations. Each session concentrates on a different category of social interaction that the child might realistically encounter (peers, parents, siblings, teachers, etc.). Real-life situations, generated by the child or parent or from contacts with teachers and others, are enacted; hypothetical situations are also presented to elaborate themes and problem areas of the child (e.g., responding to provocation, fighting, being excluded socially, and being encouraged by peers to engage in antisocial behavior). The child's supersolvers also become a more integral part of each session; they are reenacted with the therapist beginning in session in order to better evaluate how the child is transferring skills to the daily environment.

12. *Wrap-up and role reversal.* This wrap-up session is included (1) to help the therapist generally assess what the child has learned in the session, (2) to clear up any remaining confusions the child may have concerning use of the steps, and (3) to provide a final summary for the child of what has been covered in the meetings. The final session is based on role reversal in which

(continued)

Table 3.4 (*Continued*)

the child plays the role of the therapist and the therapist plays the role of the child learning and applying the steps. The purpose of this session is to have the child teach and benefit from the learning that teaching provides, to allow for any unfinished business of the treatment ("spending" remaining chips, completing final supersolvers), and to provide closure for the therapy.

13. *Optional sessions.* During the course of therapy, additional sessions are provided to the child as needed, if the child has special difficulty in grasping any features of the problem-solving steps or their application. For example, the child may have difficulty in applying the steps, learning to state them covertly, and so on. An additional session may be applied to repeat material of a previous session, so that the child has a solid grasp of the approach. Optional sessions may be implemented at any point that the child's progress lags behind the level appropriate to the session that has been completed. For example, if a facet of treatment has not been learned (e.g., memorization of steps and fading of steps), which is associated with the particular session that has been completed, an optional session may be implemented. Also, if there is a problem or issue of the child's or parent's participation in supersolvers, a session will be scheduled with the parent and child to shape the requisite behaviors in the session and to make assignments to ensure that this aspect of treatment is carried out.

Source: From Kazdin, A. E. (2003). Problem-solving skills training and parent management training for conduct disorder. In A. E. Kazdin & J. R. Weisz (Eds.), *Evidence-based psychotherapies for children and adolescents* (pp. 241–262). New York: Guilford. Copyright 2003 by Guilford Press. Reprinted with permission.

emotional competence. Their reasons are three-fold: (1) Offering interventions in schools makes programs more accessible to families and eliminates some of the barriers (i.e., transportation) typically encountered with services offered in traditional mental health settings; (2) offering interventions in schools integrates programs before children's common behavior problems escalate to the point of needing intense clinical intervention; and (3) offering a social and emotional curriculum such as the Dinosaur School program to an entire class is less stigmatizing than a "pullout" group and is more likely to produce sustained effects across settings and time.

For more information about the Incredible Years Parent, Teacher, and Child Programs, the reader is encouraged to visit the Web site http://www.incredibleyears.com.

Tools and Practice Example

Practice Example

Alex is a 12-year-old White male who was recently arrested at school for stealing several items from his teacher, including a cell phone, $200, a watch, a lighter, and some pocket-sized school supplies. At the time of the arrest, Alex was found to be in possession of marijuana. For these offenses, Alex was placed on probation and ordered to receive mental health counseling for the length of his probation. Alex has always had minor behavior problems, but over the last year his behavior problems have escalated considerably. He lives with his parents and three siblings in a rural farming community. Though it was never confirmed, Alex's parents suspect that he was responsible for setting a small grass fire in a field behind their home last month. Alex frequently returns home from school with items that do not belong to him, and he engages in physical fights on the school bus at least once a week. Witnesses to these altercations report that Alex instigates fights with no apparent provocation. Although he tests above grade level in most subjects and his IQ falls within the normal range, Alex's teachers report that he is in danger of failing the sixth grade because he does not complete class or homework assignments. When his parents gave a blank check to his sibling for a school project, Alex stole the check, forged his parent's signature, and attempted to cash the check for $50. At home, his siblings complain that Alex steals things from them, bullies them into doing things his way, and breaks their belongings. Last month, he denied carving his

Table 3.5 Program Recommendations for Webster-Stratton Programs Depending on Degree of Risk, Treatment, or Prevention Focus

Population and Intended Use	*Minimum Core Program*	*Recommended Supplemental Programs for Special Populations*
Prevention programs for selected populations (i.e., high-risk populations without overt behavior or conduct problems) Settings: preschool, day care, Head Start, schools (grades K–3), public health centers	BASIC (12–14 2-hour weekly sessions)	• ADVANCE Parent Program for highly stressed families • SCHOOL Parent Program for children kindergarten to grade 3 • Child Dinosaur Program if child's problems are pervasive at home and school • TEACHER classroom management program if teachers have high numbers of students with behavior problems or if teachers have not received this training previously
Treatment programs for indicated populations (i.e., children exhibiting behavior problems or diagnosed with conduct disorders) Settings: mental health centers, pediatric clinics, HMOs	BASIC and ADVANCE (22–24 2-hour weekly sessions)	• Child Dinosaur Program if child's problems are pervasive at home and at school • TEACHER Program if child's problems are pervasive at home and at school • SCHOOL Program for parents if child has academic problems

Source: From Webster-Stratton, C., & Reid, M. J. (2003b). The incredible years parents, teachers, and children training series: A multifaceted treatment approach for young children with conduct problems. In A. E. Kazdin & J. R. Weisz (Eds.), *Evidence-based psychotherapies for children and adolescents* (pp. 224–240). New York: Guilford. Copyright 2003 by Guilford Press. Reprinted with permission.

initials into the bathroom wall and breaking his bedroom window with a baseball.

Among the various interventions available for use with Alex and his family, his school social worker chose to use interventions that had a solid evidence base in an effort to maximize the possibility for a successful outcome. As the first active phase of treatment, a thorough assessment is the cornerstone of a solid treatment plan (Springer, 2002). During their initial session together, the school social worker conducted a complete biopsychosocial assessment with Alex and his parents, which resulted in the following diagnoses:

Axis I   312.81: Conduct disorder, childhood-onset type, moderate
Axis II   V71.09: No diagnosis
Axis III None

Axis IV   V61.8: Sibling relational problem
          V62.3: Academic problem
          V61.20: Parent–child relational problem
          Involvement with juvenile justice system
Axis V   GAF = 45

In light of Alex's diagnosis, his age (12 years), the evidence supporting the use of PMT and PSST as probably efficacious approaches, and the availability of Alex's parents to participate in his treatment, the school social worker chose to utilize parent management training (PMT) and problem-solving skills training (PSST) with Alex and his parents. Using a combination of PMT and PSST together tends to be more effective than using either treatment alone (Kazdin, 2003). Both treatments are manualized and have core sets of themes and skills domains for treatment sessions.

PMT With Alex

One core session of PMT teaches parents to use positive reinforcement to change behavior (see step 3 in Table 3.3). Alex's social worker first spent some time training his parents to pinpoint, define, and observe problematic behavior in new ways, focusing on careful inspection of the problems. She then worked with the family to develop a token system to be implemented in their home, which would provide them a structured, consistent way to reinforce Alex's behavior. Rather than creating an exhaustive list of behaviors that would likely be difficult to track, Alex's parents began with three target behaviors/goals that they believed would be easier to manage and accomplish: respecting others' property and belongings, completing and turning in homework, and riding the school bus without fighting. In reviewing Alex's behavior, his father realized that Alex experienced very few behavior problems when he worked on outdoor projects with him. Spending time outdoors with his father, extra recreation/video game time, and an extra trip to the corner store to spend his money were the main incentives integrated into the token system. The tokens, paired with praise, were contingent on Alex's behavior specific to the targeted behaviors/goals. The social worker spent the bulk of this treatment session modeling and role playing the implementation of this token system, developing the parents' proficiency in prompting, praising behavior, and delivering consequences. The social worker reviewed the previous week's events in each subsequent session, reenacting and rehearsing problems or difficulties as needed.

The following exchange among Alex, his family, and his social worker illustrates positive reinforcement and developing effective discipline strategies:

Social worker [to parents]: You've stated that Alex's fighting is a big problem that seems to remain no matter what you do. You said that you tried time out, but that did not work. What reward do you give Alex when he does not get into fights?

Mother: I don't want to give him toys or money because it's too expensive and usually just starts more fights with his brother and sisters.

Social worker: Your husband said that Alex behaves well when he works outside with him. Is that something you would consider giving him for a reward?

Alex: I'd rather be with Dad than at home with people who pick on me and accuse me of stealing their stuff anyway!

Mother [following social worker's earlier suggestion to avoid "proving" Alex's misbehavior]: Absolutely, and if he can make it through one dinner without a fight, he can go with his father to do the evening chores outside.

The dialogue continued in this vein until the family agreed on two more problems, rewards, and consequences. The social worker met with Alex's parents to review the purpose and effective use of time out as an intervention. The last time he was in time out, Alex threw a baseball through his bedroom window. They discussed finding a safer time-out area in the house where Alex could be directly monitored and removing possibly dangerous items from his bedroom. The social worker cautioned Alex's parents that his behaviors might escalate as they begin to implement these new interventions. She encouraged them to have back-up plans in the event that their first attempt to intervene did not work. Together, they role played some possible scenarios and practiced back-up plans, alternating roles to develop proficiency. See Sells (1998) for step-by-step and detailed descriptions on developing creative and proactive interventions with parents who have challenging adolescents.

PSST With Alex

Since Alex's parents were actively participating in his treatment, the first few sessions with Alex were spent not only introducing steps in problem solving, but discussing the token system and how consequences (positive or negative) were contingent on his behavior (see steps 1–4 in Table 3.4). Alex was initially very confident in his ability but anticipated that his siblings would sabotage his efforts with their constant provocations and false accusations of stealing. Hearing this, the social worker introduced the following self-statements in problem solving in order to guide Alex's behavior and lead to developing effective solutions (Kazdin, 2003):

1. What am I supposed to do?
2. I have to look at all my possibilities.
3. I'd better concentrate and focus in.
4. I need to make a choice.
5. I did a good job (or) Oh, I made a mistake.

Alex reported that he often fought with his siblings because they provoked him, so the social worker engaged Alex in multiple role plays, repeatedly practicing how he might respond to perceived provocation. The social worker effusively praised Alex's quick recall of the self-statements and his efforts to use a "stop and think" technique that she modeled and prompted. Additionally, they practiced how to respond to mistakes and failures without exploding at others or destroying property. Alex's parents were instructed to praise and reward his efforts to avoid conflicts and employ the problem-solving steps in everyday situations at home. Subsequent treatment sessions would require Alex to use the steps in increasingly more difficult and clinically relevant, real-life situations (Kazdin, 2003).

It is important to note that medication management was not part of Alex's treatment plan. While there is survey evidence for the significant use of polypharmacy in the treatment of children with CD in the United States, "medication cannot be justified as the first line of treatment for conduct problems. A diagnosis-based approach, which defines primary or comorbid psychiatric disorders associated with aggression, should guide the pharmacological treatment of CD" (Fonagy & Kurtz, 2002, p. 192).

Had Alex been younger (ages 4 to 8 years), the social worker could have selected from the range of interventions available under the Incredible Years Training Series developed by Webster-Stratton and colleagues at the University of Washington's Parenting Clinic. One of the appealing qualities of this approach is that it has been tailored for work with youth in school settings.

Key Points to Remember

Some of the key points from this chapter are as follows:

- Conduct-disordered youth in schools can be effectively treated.
- There are two well-established and a range of probably efficacious treatment approaches from which to select when working with conduct-disordered youth.
- Using a combination of PMT and PSST together tends to be more effective than using either treatment alone (Kazdin, 2003). Both treatments are manualized and have core sets of themes and skills domains for treatment sessions.
- Medication cannot be justified as the first line of treatment for conduct problems.

- One of the well-established approaches, Webster-Stratton's videotape modeling parent program, the Incredible Years Training Series, was developed to address parent, family, child, and school risk factors related to childhood conduct disorders.
- The most proactive and powerful approach to the problem of escalating aggression in young children is to offer their programs using a school-based prevention/early intervention model designed to strengthen all children's social and emotional competence.

Despite the promising treatment effects produced by the interventions reviewed above, existing treatments need to be refined and new ones developed. We cannot yet determine the short- and long-term impact of evidence-based treatments on conduct-disordered youths, and it is sometimes unclear what part of the therapeutic process produces change. A child's eventual outcome is most likely dependent on the interrelationship among child, parent, teacher, and peer risk factors; accordingly, the most effective interventions should be those that assess these risk factors and determine which programs are needed for a particular family and child (Webster-Stratton & Reid, 2003b).

The focus in this chapter has been geared toward school social workers and other mental health practitioners working with individual students in school settings. We cannot emphasize enough that contextual issues should not be ignored. Equally important in sustaining therapeutic change with conduct-disordered youth are issues surrounding classroom management and strategies that promote positive behavior through schoolwide interventions. Accordingly, practitioners must work collaboratively with parents, teachers, peers, and school administrators to sustain change across settings. For a detailed exposition on best practice models for schoolwide interventions, the reader is referred to Bloomquist and Schnell (2002), which is an excellent source.

Additional Resources

Barkley, R. A. (1987). *Defiant children: A clinician's manual for parent training.* New York: Guilford.

Bloomquist, M. L., & Schnell, S. V. (2002). *Helping children with aggression and conduct problems: Best practices for intervention.* New York: Guilford.

Blueprints. Developed by the Center for the Study and Prevention of Violence at the University of Colorado at Boulder: http://www.colorado.edu/cspv/blueprints.

Cavell, T. A. (2000). *Working with parents of aggressive children: A practitioner's guide.* Washington, DC: American Psychological Association.

Centers for Disease Control and Prevention: http://www.cdc.gov.

Evidence-Based Treatment for Children and Adolescents: http://www.effectivechildtherapy.com.

Fonagy, P., & Kurtz, A. (2002). Disturbance of conduct. In P. Fonagy, M. Target, D. Cottrell, J. Phillips, & Z. Kurtz (Eds.), *What works for whom? A critical review of treatments for children and adolescents* (pp. 106–192). New York: Guilford.

Forehand, R. L., & McMahon, R. J. (1981). *Helping the noncompliant child: A clinician's guide to parent training.* New York: Guilford.

Henggeler, S. W., Schoenwald, S. K., Rowland, M. D., & Cunningham, P. B. (2002). *Serious emotional disturbance in children and adolescents: Multisystemic therapy.* New York: Guilford.

Incredible Years Parent, Teacher, and Child Programs: http://www.incredibleyears.com.

Lochman, J. E., Barry, T. D., & Pardini, D. A. (2003). Anger control training for aggressive youth. In A. E. Kazdin & J. R. Weisz (Eds.), *Evidence-based psychotherapies for children and adolescents* (pp. 263–281). New York: Guilford.

National Institute of Mental Health: http://nimh.gov.

Parenting Clinic, University of Washington: http://www.son.washington.edu/centers/parenting-clinic/bibligraphy.asp.

Sells, S. P. (1998). *Treating the tough adolescent: A family-based, step-by-step guide.* New York: Guilford.

Substance Abuse and Mental Health Services Administration: http://www.mentalhealth.samhsa.gov.

UCLA School Mental Health Project, Center for Mental Health in Schools: http://smhp.psych.ucla.edu.

U.S. Department of Health and Human Services, Administration for Children and Families: http://www.acf.dhhs.gov.

References

Alexander, J. F., & Parsons, B. V. (1973). Short-term behavioral intervention with delinquents: Impact on family process and recidivism. *Journal of Abnormal Psychology, 81*, 219–225.

American Psychiatric Association. (2000). *Diagnostic and statistical manual of mental disorders* (4th ed., text revision). Washington, DC: Author.

Baer, R. A., & Nietzel, M. T. (1991). Cognitive and behavioral treatment of impulsivity in children: A meta analytic review of the outcome literature. *Journal of Clinical Child Psychology.*

Bank, L., Marlowe, J. H., Reid, J. B., Patterson, G. R., & Weinrott, M. R. (1991). A comparative evaluation of parent training interventions for families of chronic delinquents. *Journal of Abnormal Child Psychology, 19*, 15–33.

Barkley, R. A. (1987). *Defiant children: A clinician's manual for parent training.* New York: Guilford.

Barkley, R., Edwards, G., Laneri, M., Fletcher, K., & Metevia, L. (2001). The efficacy of problem-solving communication training alone, behavior management training alone, and their combination for parent-adolescent conflict in teenagers with ADHD and ODD. *Journal of Consulting & Clinical Psychology, 69*, 926–941.

Barkley, R. A., Guevremont, D. C., Anastopoulos, A. D., & Fletcher, K. E. (1992). A comparison of three family therapy programs for treating family conflicts in adolescents with attention-deficit hyperactivity disorder. *Journal of Consulting and Clinical Psychology, 60*, 450–462.

Bernal, M. E., Klinnert, M. D., & Schultz, L. A. (1980). Outcome evaluation of behavioral parent training and client-centered parent counseling for children with conduct problems. *Journal of Applied Behavior Analysis, 13*, 677–691.

Block, J. (1978). Effects of a rational-emotive mental health program on poorly achieving disruptive high school students. *Journal of Counseling Psychology, 25*, 61–65.

Bloomquist, M. L., & Schnell, S. V. (2002). *Helping children with aggression and conduct problems: Best practices for intervention.* New York: Guilford.

Borduin, C. M., Mann, B. J., Cone, L. T., Henggeler, S. W., Fucci, B. R., Blaske, D. M., & Williams, R. A. (1995). Multisystemic treatment of serious juvenile offenders: Long-term prevention of criminality and violence. *Journal of Consulting and Clinical Psychology, 63*, 569–578.

Brestan, E. V., & Eyberg, S. M. (1998). Effective psychosocial treatments of conduct-disordered children and adolescents: 29 years, 82 studies, and 5,272 kids. *Journal of Clinical Child Psychology, 27*(2), 180–189.

Cavell, T. A. (2000). *Working with parents of aggressive children: A practitioner's guide.* Washington, DC: American Psychological Association.

Dishion, T. J., & Patterson, G. R. (1992). Age effects in parent training outcomes. *Behavior Therapy, 23*, 719–729.

Durlak, J., Fuhrman, T., & Lampman, C. (1991). Effectiveness of cognitive-behavior therapy for maladapting children: A meta-analysis. *Psychological Bulletin, 110*, 204–214.

D'Zurilla, T., & Nezu, A. (2001). Problem-solving therapies. In K. Dobson & S. Keith (Eds.), *Handbook of cognitive-behavioral therapies* (2nd ed., pp. 211–245). New York: Guilford.

Eyberg, S. (1988). Parent-child interaction therapy: Integration of traditional and behavioral concerns. *Child and Family Behavior Therapy, 10*, 33–45.

Eyberg, S. M., Boggs, S., & Algina, J. (1995). Parent–child interaction therapy: A psychosocial model for the treatment of young children with conduct problem behavior and their families. *Psychopharmacology Bulletin, 110,* 204–214.

Feindler, D. L., Marriott, S. A. A., & Iwata, M. (1984). Group anger control training for junior high school delinquents. *Cognitive Therapy and Research, 8,* 299–311.

Fonagy, P., & Kurtz, A. (2002). Disturbance of conduct. In P. Fonagy, M. Target, D. Cottrell, J. Phillips, & Z. Kurtz (Eds.), *What works for whom? A critical review of treatments for children and adolescents* (pp. 106–192). New York: Guilford.

Forehand, R. L., & McMahon, R. J. (1981). *Helping the noncompliant child: A clinician's guide to present training.* New York: Guilford.

Hamilton, S. B., & MacQuiddy, S. L. (1984). Self-administered behavioral parent training: Enhancement of treatment efficacy using a time-out signal seat. *Journal of Clinical Child Psychology, 13,* 61–69.

Henggeler, S. W., Melton, G. B., & Smith, L. A. (1992). Family preservation using multisystemic therapy: An effective alternative to incarcerating serious juvenile offenders. *Journal of Consulting and Clinical Psychology, 60,* 953–961.

Henggeler, S. W., Rodick, J. D., Bourdin, C. M., Hanson, C. L., Watson, S. M., & Urey, J. R. (1986). Multisystemic treatment of juvenile offenders: Effects on adolescent behavior and family interaction. *Developmental Psychology, 22,* 132–141.

Huey, W. C., & Rank, R. C. (1984). Effects of counselor and peer-led group assertiveness training on black adolescent aggression. *Journal of Counseling Psychology, 31,* 95–98.

Kazdin, A. E. (1994). Psychotherapy for children and adolescents. In A. E. Bergin, & S. L. Garfield (Eds.), *Handbook of psychotherapy and behavior change* (4th ed., pp. 543–594). New York: Wiley.

Kazdin, A. E. (2000). *Psychotherapy for children and adolescents: Directions for research and practice.* New York: Oxford University Press.

Kazdin, A. E. (2002). Psychosocial treatments for conduct disorder in children and adolescents. In P. E. Nathan & J. M. Gorman (Eds.), *A guide to treatments that work* (2nd ed., pp. 57–85). New York: Oxford University Press.

Kazdin, A. E. (2003). Problem-solving skills training and parent management training for conduct disorder. In A. E. Kazdin & J. R. Weisz (Eds.), *Evidence-based psychotherapies for children and adolescents* (pp. 241–262). New York: Guilford.

Kazdin, A. E. (2004). Psychotherapy for children and adolescents. In M. J. Lambert (Ed.), *Bergin and Garfield's handbook of psychotherapy and behavior change* (5th ed., pp. 543–589). New York: Wiley.

Kazdin, A. E., Esveldt-Dawson, K., French, N. H., & Unis, A. S. (1987a). Effect of parent management training and problem-solving skills training combined in the treatment of antisocial child behavior. *Journal of the American Academy of Child and Adolescent Psychiatry, 26,* 416–424.

Kazdin, A. E., Esveldt-Dawson, K., French, N. H., & Unis, A. S. (1987b). Problem-solving skills training and relationship therapy in the treatment of antisocial child behavior. *Journal of Consulting and Clinical Psychology, 55,* 76–85.

Kazdin, A. E., Siegel, T. C., & Bass, D. (1992). Cognitive problem-solving skills training and parent management training in the treatment of antisocial behavior in children. *Journal of Consulting and Clinical Psychology, 60,* 733–747.

Kronenberger, W. S., & Meyer, R. G. (2001). *The child clinician's handbook* (2nd ed.). Needham Heights, MA: Allyn & Bacon.

Little, E., & Hudson, A. (1998). Conduct problems and treatment across home and school: A review of the literature. *Behavior Change, 15,* 213–227.

Lochman, J. E., Burch, P. R., Curry, J. F., & Lampron, L. B. (1984). Treatment and generalization effects of cognitive-behavioral and goal-setting interventions with aggressive boys. *Journal of Consulting and Clinical Psychology, 52,* 915–916.

Lochman, J. E., Lampron, L. B., Gemmer, T. C., & Harris, S. R. (1989). Teacher consultation and cognitive-behavioral interventions with aggressive boys. *Psychology in the Schools, 26,* 179–188.

Loeber, R., Farrington, D. P., & Waschbusch, D. A. (1998). Serious and violent juvenile offenders. In R. Loeber & D. P. Farrington (Eds.), *Serious and violent juvenile offenders: Risk factors and successful interventions* (pp. 13–29). Thousand Oaks, CA: Sage.

McNeil, C. B., Eyberg, S., Eisenstadt, T. H., Newcomb, K., & Funderburk, B. W. (1991). Parent-child interaction therapy with behavior problem children: Generalization of treatment effects to the school setting. *Journal of Clinical Child Psychology, 20,* 140–151.

Moffitt, T. E., Caspi, A., Dickson, N., Silva, P., & Stanton, W. (1996). Childhood-onset versus adolescent-onset antisocial problems in males: Natural history from ages 3 to 18 years. *Developmental Psychopathology, 9,* 399–424.

Mortimore, P. (1995). The positive effects of schooling. In M. Rutter (Ed.), *Psychosocial disturbances in young people: Challenges for prevention* (pp. 333–363). Cambridge: Cambridge University Press.

Patterson, G. R., & Gullion, M. E. (1968). *Living with children: New methods for parents and teachers.* Champaign, IL: Research Press.

Patterson, G. R., Reid, J. B., Jones, R. R., & Conger, R. E. (1975). *A social learning approach to family intervention: Vol. 1. Families with aggressive children.* Eugene, OR: Castalia.

Peed, S., Roberts, M., & Forehand, R. (1977). Evaluation of the effectiveness of a standardized parent training program in altering the interaction of mothers and their noncompliant children. *Behavior Modification, 1,* 323–350.

Pullis, M. (1991). Practical considerations of excluding conduct disordered students: An empirical analysis. *Behavioral Disorders, 17*(1), 9–22.

Reid, M. J., Webster-Stratton, C., & Baydar, N. (2004). Halting the development of conduct problems in Head Start children: The effects of parent training. *Journal of Clinical Child and Adolescent Psychology, 33*(2), 279–291.

Reid, M. J., Webster-Stratton, C., & Hammond, M. (2003). Follow-up of children who received the incredible years intervention for oppositional defiant disorder: Maintenance and prediction of 2-year outcome. *Behavior Therapy, 34*(4), 471–491.

Reynolds, D., Sammons, P., Stoll, L., Barber, M., & Hillman, J. (1996). School effectiveness and school improvement in the United Kingdom. *School Effectiveness and School Improvement, 7,* 133–158.

Rosen, A., & Proctor, E. K. (2002). Standards for evidence-based social work practice: The role of replicable and appropriate interventions, outcomes, and practice guidelines. In A. R. Roberts & G. J. Greene (Eds.), *Social workers' desk reference* (pp. 743–747). New York: Oxford University Press.

Schlichter, K. J., & Horan, J. J. (1981). Effects of stress inoculation on the anger and aggression management skills of institutionalized juvenile delinquents. *Cognitive Therapy and Research, 5,* 359–365.

Sells, S. P. (1998). *Treating the tough adolescent: A family-based, step-by-step guide.* New York: Guilford.

Serketich, W. J., & Dumas, J. E. (1996). The effectiveness of behavioral parent training to modify antisocial behavior in children: A meta analysis. *Behavior Therapy, 27,* 171–186.

Spaccarelli, S., Cotler, S., & Penman, D. (1992). Problem-solving skills training as a supplement to behavioral parent training. *Cognitive Therapy and Research, 16,* 1–18.

Springer, D. W. (2002). Assessment protocols and rapid assessment instruments with troubled adolescents. In A. R. Roberts & G. J. Greene (Eds.), *Social workers' desk reference* (pp. 217–221). New York: Oxford University Press.

Tremblay, R. E., Pagani-Kurtz, L., Masse, L. C., Vitaro, F., & Phil, R. (1995). A bimodal preventive intervention for disruptive kindergarten boys: Its impact through mid-adolescence. *Journal of Consulting and Clinical Psychology, 63,* 560–568.

U.S. Department of Health and Human Services. (2001). *Youth violence: A report of the Surgeon General.* Rockville, MD: Author.

Vitaro, F., & Tremblay, R. E. (1994). Impact of a prevention program on aggressive children's friendships and social adjustment. *Journal of Abnormal Child Psychology, 22,* 457–475.

Webster-Stratton, C. (1984). Randomized trial of two parent-training programs for families with conduct-disordered children. *Journal of Consulting and Clinical Psychology, 52,* 666–678.

Webster-Stratton, C. (1990). Enhancing the effectiveness of self-administered videotape parent training for families with conduct-problem children. *Journal of Abnormal Child Psychology, 18,* 479–492.

Webster-Stratton, C. (1994). Advancing videotape parent training: A comparison study. *Journal of Consulting and Clinical Psychology, 62,* 583–593.

Webster-Stratton, C. (1998). Preventing conduct problems in Head Start children: Strengthening parenting competencies. *Journal of Consulting and Clinical Psychology, 66*(5), 715–730.

Webster-Stratton, C., & Hammond, M. (1997). Treating children with early-onset conduct problems: A comparison of child and parent training interventions. *Journal of Consulting and Clinical Psychology, 65*(1), 93–109.

Webster-Stratton, C., Kolpacoff, M., & Hollinsworth, T. (1988). Self-administered videotape therapy for families with conduct-problem children: Comparison with two cost effective treatments and a control group. *Journal of Consulting and Clinical Psychology, 56,* 558–566.

Webster-Stratton, C., & Reid, M. J. (2003a). Treating conduct problems and strengthening social emotional competence in young children (ages 4–8 years): The Dina Dinosaur treatment program. *Journal of Emotional and Behavioral Disorders, 11*(3), 130–143.

Webster-Stratton, C., & Reid, M. J. (2003b). The incredible years parents, teachers, and children training series: A multifaceted treatment approach for young children with conduct problems. In A. E. Kazdin & J. R. Weisz (Eds.), *Evidence-based psychotherapies for children and adolescents* (pp. 224–240). New York: Guilford.

Webster-Stratton, C., Reid, M. J., & Hammond, M. (2001a). Preventing conduct problems, promoting social competence: A parent and teacher training partnership in Head Start. *Journal of Clinical Child Psychology, 30*(3), 283–302.

Webster-Stratton, C., Reid, M. J., & Hammond, M. (2001b). Social skills and problem solving training for children with early-onset conduct problems: Who benefits? *Journal of Child Psychology and Psychiatry, 42*(7), 943–952.

Webster-Stratton, C., Reid, M. J., & Hammond, M. (2004). Treating children with early onset conduct problems: Intervention outcomes for parent, child, and teacher training. *Journal of Clinical Child and Adolescent Psychology, 33*(1), 105–124.

Wells, K. C., & Egan, J. (1988). Social learning and systems family therapy for childhood oppositional disorder: Comparative treatment outcome. *Comprehensive Psychiatry, 29,* 138–146.

Wiltz, N. A., & Patterson, G. R. (1974). An evaluation of parent training procedures designed to alter inappropriate aggressive behavior of boys. *Behavior Therapy, 5,* 215–221.

Zangwill, W. M. (1983). An evaluation of a parent training program. *Child and Family Behavior Therapy, 5,* 1–6.

Effective Interventions for Students With ADHD

Martell Teasley

CHAPTER 4

Getting Started

This chapter provides an overview of evidence-based practice methods for school social workers and other school counselors in the assessment and treatment of attention deficit/hyperactivity disorder (ADHD) (DuPaul & Eckert, 1997; DuPaul, Eckert, & McGoey, 1997; Erk, 1995, 2000; Hoagwood, Kelleher, Feil, & Comer, 2000; Jensen, 2000; Jensen et al., 1999; McGoey, Eckert, & Du-Paul, 2002; Olfson, Gameroff, Marcus, & Jensen, 2003; Perrin et al., 2001; Richters et al., 1995; Thomas & Corcoran, 2000). Step-by-step procedures and guidelines for assessment and treatment interventions are discussed. Resources that will assist school social workers with specific intervention procedures and methods are cited. These resources contain in-depth information supported by evidence-based research and intervention methods that are cited in the reference list for this chapter. Some examples and one case scenario that will assist school social workers with the development of a framework for understanding how to develop an intervention plan for school children diagnosed with ADHD are provided. Chapter 66 provides additional interventions and guidelines for working with parents and teachers to help adolescents with ADHD.

What We Know

Attention deficit/hyperactivity disorder is a complicated neurobiological disorder caused by malfunctioning neurotransmitters within the central nervous system (Litner, 2003). It is usually an inherited disorder "typically beginning in childhood and continuing throughout the lifespan. . . . it has been estimated that nearly 70% of children diagnosed with ADHD continue [to experience] ongoing problems as adolescents" (Litner, 2003, p. 138). Individuals with ADHD experience a host of psychological, behavioral, and cognitive problems that present them with specific challenges in their activities of daily living and interactions with their families, peers, and communities. Complications include inconsistency in sustaining attention, poor organization and planning, lack of forethought, low energy, mood swings, poor memory, overactive behavior, and impulsivity (DuPaul, Eckert, & McGoey, 1997; Erk, 2000). While coexisting learning disorders, such as conduct or oppositional disorder, are common in children diagnosed with ADHD, prevalence rates vary in research findings (Richters et al., 1995).

Attention deficit/hyperactivity disorder has multiple consequences in the school setting and presents a host of challenges for students, their families, educators, and related school services personnel. Many students diagnosed with ADHD exhibit higher than average rates of interrupting classroom activities, calling out answers or asking questions without raising their hand, getting out of an assigned seat without permission, and failing to complete assigned tasks in the classroom as well as at home. For the ADHD student, a great deal of energy and behavior in the classroom is often aimed at avoiding the completion of tasks (DuPaul et al., 1997). As a result, there is an association between individuals with ADHD and academic underachievement, school suspension, dropping out, peer rejection, the development of antisocial patterns, low self-esteem, and depression (DuPaul et al., 1997). School disciplinary problems, such as suspension and expulsion, are more characteristic of those diagnosed as hyperactive (Richters et al., 1995). Moreover, students with ADHD often do not develop the academic skills necessary for college.

What We Can Do

Assessment and Diagnosis of ADHD in Children

The *Diagnostic and Statistical Manual of Mental Disorders (DSM-IV-TR)* defines ADHD as a multidimensional disorder identified by subtypes: "Diagnosis is based on a collaborative process that involves children and adolescent psychiatrists or other physicians, the child, and the child's family, and school-based or other health care professionals as appropriate" (American Psychiatric Association, 2000, p. 1). School social workers and other mental health counselors should become familiar with the diagnostic criteria for ADHD as stated in the *DSM-IV-TR.* There are several psychometric instruments with which school social workers should become knowledgeable (Table 4.1) that are frequently used in the diagnosis of ADHD. Greater

information on clinical practice guidelines and the evaluation of ADHD in children (Perrin et al., 2001) can be found on the American Academy of Pediatrics Web site: www.help4adhd.org.

Research in Support of Treatment Interventions

Nationwide estimates of the prevalence of ADHD suggest that between 3% and 9% of children are afflicted (Richters et al., 1995). However, it is estimated that 3.4% of children ages 3 to 18 receive treatment for ADHD (Erk, 2000). There is also a high comorbidity with other mental disorders, such as conduct disorder, depression, and anxiety disorders. Although ADHD is arguably one of the most common mental health disorders challenging schools, it is also the most treatable. The most successful interventions for ADHD in school settings have been with the use of the multimodal approach consisting of pharmaceutical intervention, cognitive-behavioral training, parent training, and teacher training in classroom management techniques and special education methods. This was confirmed in separate investigations

Table 4.1 Instrumentation Used in the Assessment and Diagnosis of ADHD

1. *Child Attention Profile* (DuPaul, 1990). A 12-item scale taken from Child Behavior Checklist Teacher Report that measures rate and severity of undesirable behaviors.	Ages 6–16
2. *Child Behavior Checklist* (CBCL). Used to measure behavioral problems in children and adolescents. It relies on parent and caregiver reports and provides a total problem score in the assessment of depression, social problems, attention problems, and withdrawn, delinquent, and aggressive behavior.	Ages 3 years and older
3. *Conners's Teacher Rating Scale.* A 28-item questionnaire designed to measure various types of clinical and research applications with children. It contains four indexes including for assessment of hyperactivity and for assessment of inattention.	Ages 2–18
4. *Caregiver–Teacher Report Form.* Adapted from items in the CBCL, it replaces problems more likely observed at home with those more likely observed in daycare and preschool settings.	Ages 2–5
5. *Teacher Report Form.* Contains many of the problem items found in the CBCL but substitutes the assessment of home-specific items with school-specific behaviors and provides a standardized description of problem behaviors, academic functioning, and adaptive behaviors.	Ages 5–18
6. *Youth Self-Report for Age.* Contains specific components of the CBCL as they relate to adolescents and many items that youth may not report about themselves. Using this instrument in an interview may be the best method.	Ages 11–18
7. *ADHD Rating Scale* (DuPual, 1990). This is a scale using 14 items from the *DSM-III-R* on ADHD.	Ages 5–18

of evidence-based best practice research findings from the National Institute of Mental Health's Collaborative Multisite Multimodal Treatment Study of Children with ADHD and the American Academy of Pediatrics Committee on Quality Improvement's Subcommittee on Attention Deficit/Hyperactivity Disorder (Perrin et al., 2001). Intervention strategies suggested in this chapter are consistent with research findings from these investigations.

Approximately 70–80% of children with ADHD are treated with pharmacological intervention. In general, stimulants assist in the connection of neurotransmissions, which may help to diminish motor activity and impulsive behaviors characteristic of those diagnosed with ADHD. The clinical use of stimulant drugs has demonstrated short-term efficacy in the reduction of a range of core symptoms of ADHD, such as fidgetiness, finger tapping, fine motor movement, and classroom disturbances (Richters et al., 1995). "Stimulants have been found to enhance the sustained attention, impulse control, interpersonal behavior, and academic productivity of 70% to 80% of children with ADHD" (DuPaul & Eckert, 1997, p. 5). Additionally, stimulants have been shown to have positive effects on problem solving with peers, parent-child interactions, and a variety of controlled laboratory tasks, such as auditory and reading comprehension, spelling recall, continuous performance tasks, cue and free recall, and arithmetic computation (Richters et al., 1995). For discussion of the common medication used, see Bentley and Collins (in press).

Compliance with prescription medication protocols in the treatment of ADHD varies due to the possibility of complications from side effects (e.g., appetite reduction, insomnia, nervousness, etc.), possible addiction, or differences in environmental (home, school, or control settings) treatment reinforcement (DuPaul & Eckert, 1997). Comprehensive research studies have found that among the estimated 90% of children and adolescents with ADHD who receive prescription medication to treat ADHD, only 12–25% regularly take their medication (Smith, Waschbusch, Willoughby, & Evans, 2000). However, research on samples of children using pharmaceutical interventions in the treatment of ADHD (DuPaul & Eckert, 1997; Jensen et al., 1999; Richters et al., 1995) suggest that side effects of medication treatments may be unpleasant in the short run but are usually reversible and often dose dependent (Smith et al., 2000).

Unfortunately, previous studies are often inconsistent regarding the efficacy of pharmacological intervention in differential settings (e.g., home, school, and peer groups). The use of stimulants has demonstrated greater success in the treatment of hyperactivity than in curbing challenges with academic achievement and inattention. There is also evidence that the magnitude of stimulant benefits is not consistent across age groups. Likewise, the impact of comorbidity diagnoses in individuals with ADHD may produce differential effectiveness in the use of stimulants. Research studies have demonstrated that stabilization of treatment through pharmaceutical intervention takes approximately 14 months for school-aged children (Perrin et al., 2001). Medication regimens should be monitored closely for possible side effects (Table 4.3). Most medication side effects occur early during treatment, tend to be mild, and are short-lived. Conversely, for some children, side effects from medication have a greater effect than the reduction of problem behaviors or an increase in cognitive performance. Although rare, with high doses, some children experience mood disturbances, psychotic reactions, or hallucinations. Medication adjustments (lowering dosage or switching medication) may curb side effects. Many clinicians and physicians recommend "drug holidays"—no prescription ADHD medication on the weekends during the school year and/or during the entire summer—as a way of reducing the impact of side effects and potential long-term medical complications (Perrin et al., 2001). Overall, the use of stimulants for the treatment of ADHD may have minimal benefits in some clients, become contraindicated in others, and may be expected to yield gains beyond reduction of inattention and impulsivity in others (Richters et al., 1995).

An essential component of behavior management for school children diagnosed with ADHD is home-based treatment, with parental involvement that is coordinated with school-based interventions. Parent training in behavior modification techniques and stress management has shown improvement in school behavior and home behavior for hyperactive children and has demonstrated improvements in parent, child, and family relations (see Thomas & Corcoran, 2000, for a review of literature on family-centered approaches to ADHD). Cognitive-behavioral interventions, such as the use of token reinforcement as a reward for desired classroom behaviors, have demonstrated positive results. Successful use of behavioral

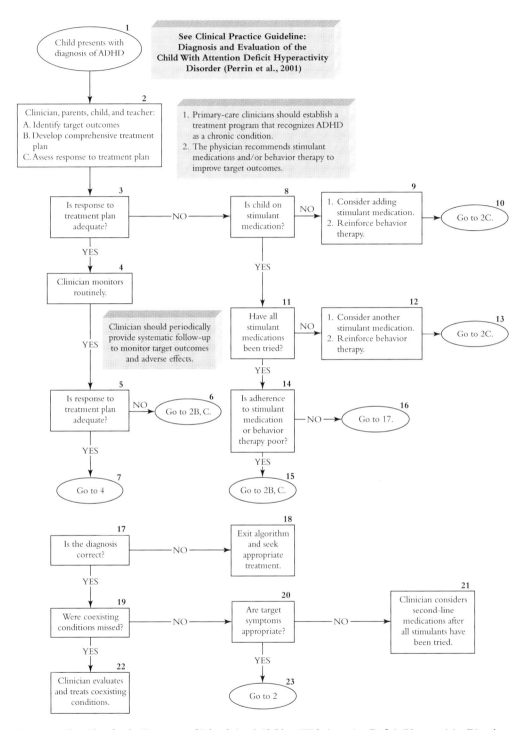

Figure 4.1. Algorithm for the Treatment of School-Aged Children With Attention Deficit/Hyperactivity Disorder
Source: Reproduced with permission from *Pediatrics, 108,* 1033–1044. Copyright 2001.

therapy in the classroom must include teacher training in classroom management techniques and individualized strategies to combat behavioral maladaptation. Techniques that encourage and accommodate students with ADHD should be at the core of a teacher's class management interventions.

Based on subgroup differences in comorbidity, age, cognitive ability, and the varied impact of pharmaceutical interventions, researchers have become increasingly interested in combined forms of treatment, or multimodal treatment strategies. *Multimodal treatment strategies* are those that tailor specific pharmaceutical and behavioral interventions to suit a client's particular needs in a given setting (e.g., home, school, and social). Treatment interventions outlined below are consistent with the multimodal approach.

Treatment Interventions

Figure 4.1 contains an evidence-based treatment algorithm developed by the American Academy of Pediatrics for children diagnosed with ADHD. Primary care clinicians should establish a management program that recognizes ADHD as a chronic condition. Prior to engaging in treatment intervention, social workers must determine the source of the ADHD diagnosis and review all accessible documentation, including those completed by psychologists, psychiatrists, and parents and teachers' evaluations of the student's classroom behavior and grades. Evidence-based treatment intervention guidelines identified from a review of the literature are outlined below.

Development of Intervention Plan

- Determine target outcomes. Desired results may include:
  - decrease in disruptive behaviors
  - improvements in relationships with parents, siblings, teachers, and peers
  - improved academic performance, particularly in completion of work, volume of work, efficiency, and accuracy
  - increased independence and self-direction
  - enhanced safety in the community, such as riding a bicycle or crossing the street without incident
  - improved self-esteem
- Treatment plan must include:
  - collaboration with other school-based professionals (e.g., school psychologists,

counselors, nurses) for special education services
  - coordination of services exterior to the school system (e.g., primary care, psychological, support groups)
  - parental and home-based intervention
  - specific cognitive-behavioral interventions
  - educational services (teachers and other faculty)
  - ongoing and outcome evaluation

Collaborative Practice

- "Collaboration between service providers and teachers is an important tool for optimizing ADHD treatment intervention" (LeFever, Villers, Morrow, & Vaughn, 2002, p. 68). An individualized approach to treatment intervention is necessary.
- Discuss findings from psychometric instrumentation used in assessment and diagnosis with the treatment team.
- Assist treatment team in the development of a functional behavioral assessment. Assist teachers with the development of a classroom individualized education program (IEP).

Medication

School social workers and mental health counselors should have a working knowledge of the most commonly used medications in the treatment of ADHD. The NIMH has developed a list of stimulants for the treatment of ADHD approved by the federal Food and Drug Administration (Table 4.2). The most common potential side effects of these medications are listed in Table 4.3; however, for more detailed information see nlm.nih.gov/medlineplus. Also, see chapter 2 in this volume for a discussion of side effects and other issues in the prescription of stimulant drugs such as Ritalin.

- Monitor medication compliance: Is the individual taking medication as prescribed by physician/psychiatrist?
- Monitor bodily movement pre- and postmedication interventions.
- Determine when medication is most beneficial (e.g., time of day, duration of effects, differences in body movement).
- Monitor side effects of medication.
- Assess parents' knowledge of medication and attitude toward use of medications.

Table 4.2 List of Medications for the Treatment of Children With ADHD

Medication	Approved Age
Adderall (amphetamine)	3 and older
Concerta (methylphenidate)	6 and older
Cylert (pemoline)	6 and older
Dexedrine (dextroamphetamine)	3 and older
Dextrostat (dextroamphetamine)	3 and older
Focalin (dexmethylphenidate)	6 and older
Metadate ER (Methylphenidate, extended release)	6 and older
Metadate CD (Methylphenidate, extended release)	6 and older
Ritalin (methylphenidate, extended release)	6 and older
Ritalin SR (Methylphenidate, extended release)	6 and older
Ritalin LA (methylphenidate, extended release)	6 and older

Table 4.3 Common Side Effects of Medications Prescribed for Children With ADHD

Generic Names	Possible Side Effects
Amphetamine	restlessness or tremors, anxiety, nervousness, headaches, dizziness, insomnia, diarrhea, constipation, dryness of the mouth, unpleasant taste in the mouth
Dexmethylphenidate	stomach pain, fever, loss of appetite, upset stomach, vomiting, difficulty falling asleep or staying asleep, dizziness, nervousness, weight loss, skin rash, headache
Dextroamphetamine	nervousness, restlessness, difficulty falling or staying asleep, false feeling of well-being, feeling of unpleasantness, dizziness, tremor, difficulty coordinating movements, headache, dry mouth, diarrhea, constipation, loss of appetite, weight loss, bad taste in mouth
Methylphenidate	nervousness, difficulty falling asleep or staying asleep, dizziness, drowsiness, upset stomach, vomiting, headache, loss of appetite
Pemoline	loss of appetite, trouble sleeping, weight loss, dizziness, drowsiness, headache, increased irritability, mental depression, stomach ache

- If necessary, provide information to parents:
  - See Medline at www.ncbi.nlm.nih.gov.
  - Provide handouts, videotapes, Internet Web sites, and support group information.

Behavioral Therapy

- Set specific goals: Develop and set clear goals; set small, reachable goals; and make certain that the child understands the goals. For example, require the child to stay focused on homework for a specified period of time or to share a toy while playing with a friend.
- Provide rewards and consequences:
  - Positive reinforcement: Provide privileges and rewards as responses to desired behavior. Instruct parents to give their child rewards when desired behavior is demonstrated or request that teachers give points

for appropriate behavior in the classroom. For example, after the completion of homework, a parent might provide free time for a desired activity, such as bike riding or playing computer games.

- Time out: Remove access to desired activities when undesirable behavior occurs. For example, a teacher might decrease recess time for inappropriate classroom behavior, or a parent might require the child to sit in the corner of a room for hitting a sibling.
- Response cost: Withdraw privileges or rewards due to unwanted behavior, for example, the loss of free time or other desired activities because homework has not been completed.
- Token economy: Combine rewards and consequences for behavior, in which the child is given a reward for desired behavior and loses privileges and rewards for unwanted behavior: (1) A teacher might give points for not daydreaming and take points away for missing assignments. (2) A teacher might give points for turning in completed assignments but deduct points if the child gets out of an assigned seat at an inappropriate time.
- The child cashes in the sum total of points daily and weekly for assessment of behavior and a possible prize if set goals are obtained.
- Maintain rewards and consequences: The benefit of constant, long-term use of rewards and consequences is the eventual shaping of the child's behavior.

Intervention With Parents

Assist parents in monitoring school assignments and require that they:

- Create a routine environment in the home:
  - Organize home: Provide specific and logical places to place the child's schoolwork and supplies.
  - Make a daily/weekly schedule.
  - Insist that the child prepare for school each evening.
  - Help the child stay on task: Make use of charts and checklists to track progress in school and with chores in the home.
  - Place items for school in highly visible areas.
  - Reduce distractions during homework and meal times, such as loud music, television,

and computer games, as such distractions can overstimulate children with ADHD.
- Engage in daily/weekly discussion of schoolwork and behavior:
  - Discuss ways to improve problem behaviors.
  - Role play and demonstrate desired behaviors and require the child to role play problem behaviors as well as desired behaviors.
  - If multiple problems persist, partialize role-playing sessions.
  - Do not use time for behavior training as a punitive measure.
- Give the child praise for completion of tasks.
- Do not overemphasize failures.
- Assist parents in the development of positive reinforcement measures.
- Obtain support and seek counseling if necessary.

Interventions With Teachers

- Assist teachers with the development of classroom management techniques:
  - Require the student to sit in the front of the classroom near the teacher.
  - Make sure that the student is away from other students who may provoke him or her.
  - Give the student classroom tasks, such as collecting books or homework.
  - Develop a plan for the student to release energy (e.g., stretching, classroom activities, educational games that require movement).
- Determine the student's ability to take notes and assist as necessary with classroom note-taking strategies.
- Assist teachers in setting up behavioral monitoring mechanisms in the classroom, including positive reinforcement measures, token economy, and time outs.
- If possible, the student should receive a copy of notes prior to class.
- Review and outline all lesson plans.
- Provide the student with written and oral instructions on homework assignments.
- Break down homework instructions into simple components.
- If available, make use of study carrel for assignment completion.
- Assist the student in the development of organizational skills.

- Provide positive reinforcement for organizational milestones (e.g., not forgetting homework for one week, completion of all homework assignments, neatness of work, preparation for class).
- Make checklist of school supplies and review with child.
- Give short but frequent assignments rather than one large assignment.
- Prepare daily or weekly report cards for home discussion.
- Assist with test taking:
  - Provide clear instructions on materials to be covered during the test.
  - Allow for additional time.
  - Consider giving verbal tests if there is no success with written tests.
  - Provide retesting on the same materials until student scores well.
  - Communicate with parents about upcoming tests.
- When possible, make use of word processors, recorded books, calculators, videotapes, and cassette recorders.
- It is important to emphasize to teachers that behavioral intervention techniques should be sustained over time.
- Schedule regular meetings with teachers.

Homework Assignments

- Make sure homework assignments are given verbally as well as in writing.
- If possible, have the student repeat and acknowledge understanding of homework assignments.
- If possible, have pre- and postclassroom group sessions in which assignments are reviewed:
  - Closely monitor students in group dynamics.
  - Anticipate problems with group dynamics, and implement changes as necessary.
- Pair the student with another student who is more patient or younger.
- Assist the student in the development of a homework log book. Parents and teachers should review the homework log with the student weekly.
- Assist parents in establishing a consistent homework protocol. Parents should personally check and verify completion of homework.

Assess Response to Treatment Plan

Develop routine monitoring to evaluate the following:

- individual and combined effects of medication and behavioral therapy
- effectiveness of behavioral interventions and any necessary revisions
- adequacy of treatment plan toward accomplishing set goals:
  - Determine cause-and-effect relationship between treatment plan and specific goals.
  - Revise treatment plan as necessary.

Base the assessment on collaborative findings using information from the IEP.

Tools and Practice Example

Case Scenario: ADHD, Predominantly Inattentive Type

Michelle is a 9-year-old girl who just started the fourth grade. Her teacher has referred her to social work services because she believes that Michelle needs special education testing. Michelle's teacher has based this request on several behavioral patterns that she has noticed during the first month of the school year. First, although homework assignments are printed on the blackboard daily, Michelle often forgets to write them down, as instructed. Second, Michelle has had poor scores on all of her tests and fails to complete her reading assignments. The teacher states that she has to call Michelle several times before getting a response. "It often appears as if she is daydreaming or mentally somewhere else," she states. During recess, the teacher also has noticed that Michelle does not play with her fourth-grade classmates but with children from the second grade instead.

In your discussion with Michelle, you record the following: She says that she does not like her sisters because they are always teasing her and that her mother treats her like a baby. When asked about her reading and her homework, Michelle states that she does not like reading because it takes too long. She states that she forgets to do her homework sometimes, and on other occasions, she gets sleepy while doing it and does not finish.

In your interview with Michelle's mother, she informs you of the following: "Michelle reminds me of my brother. He was always tripping over things, and he got into fights at school because the other kids called him goofy." Michelle's mother only lets her ride her bicycle in the backyard because Michelle was almost struck by a car twice. "Both times, Michelle stated that she thought that she could beat the car going across the street," her mother says. Michelle is also very untidy around the house: "She really makes a mess in the bathroom, so I tend to supervise her in order to avoid extra cleaning, but I don't always have time to do this." Because she makes such a mess, neither of her siblings wants to go in the bathroom after her. This sometimes starts arguments and confrontations in the mornings, when the family is preparing for the day. Her sisters, Elizabeth (age 12) and Kelly (age 8), complain that Michelle has poor cleaning habits in their room. When asked about Michelle's homework routine, her mother remarks, "It's the strangest thing. Sometimes Michelle completes her homework and forgets to take it to school or forgets that she has taken it with her and does not turn it in. I have scolded her several times for this, but nothing I do has really done much good." Sometimes, she plays too much and starts her homework late, then falls asleep; she also claims that her stomach hurts when it is time to do homework.

Assessment and Diagnosis

You suspect that Michelle is exhibiting signs of ADHD, predominantly inattentive. Follow the protocol as suggested by the American Academy of Pediatrics:

- Verify the appropriate social work protocols specific to your particular school system.
- Suggest that parents refer the ADHD child to a primary care physician for a standard history and physical.
- Coordinate school-based services in assessing a child's behavior.
- Gather evidence and make use of assessment tools.
- Document individual observations, including report cards and written comments from teachers.
- Document specific elements of behavior, including age of onset, duration of symptoms, multiple settings, and degree of functional impairment.
- Conduct a family assessment.
- Develop an individual treatment program (ITP) with the assistance of other school-based professionals (e.g., schoolteacher, counselor, psychologist, nurse).

Numerous resources exist to help school social workers and other school counselors work with youth with ADHD. Internet Web sites that are useful in the understanding and treatment of ADHD can be found in Table 4.4.

Key Points to Remember

- The diagnosis of ADHD should be made only after reliable diagnostic interviewing methods.
- Diagnosis is based on history and observable behaviors in multiple settings (e.g., home, school, play).
- Therapists should develop a comprehensive treatment plan through collaborative efforts with other school-based professionals and community service providers.
- The most successful treatment of ADHD for the context of the school setting has been with the use of the multimodal approach, consisting of pharmaceutical intervention, cognitive-behavioral training, parent training, and teacher training in classroom management techniques and special education methods.
- Provide teacher and parental support, and develop a supportive network for the client.
- Provide ongoing assessment, reassessment, and evaluation of treatment regimen.
- Follow the treatment algorithm as stated in Figure 4.1.

I would like to thank Angela Moore for her excellent work in editing this chapter.

References

American Psychiatric Association. (2000). *Diagnostic and statistical manual of mental disorders* (4th ed., text revision). Washington, DC: Author.

Bentley, K., & Collins, K. (in press). Psychopharmacological treatments for children & adolescents. In C. F. Franklin et al., *Social workers and mental health workers training and resource manual.* New York: Oxford University Press.

DuPaul, G. J., & Eckert, T. L. (1997). The effects of school-based interventions for attention deficit hyperactivity disorder: A meta-analysis. *School Psychology Review, 26*(3), 2–27.

Table 4.4 Internet Resources on ADHD

Resource	Description	Web Site
Pediatrics	Clinical guidelines for evaluation and treatment of ADHD	www.help4adhd.org
National Resource Center on ADHD, Children and Adults With ADHD (CHADD)	Major advocate for those with ADHD; contains frequently asked questions, educational resources, newsletters, conference information, membership opportunity, prescription discount card, employment information, and evidence-based research information	www.chadd.org
National Institute of Mental Health	ADHD publication: a detailed booklet that contains information on signs and symptoms of ADHD, causes, coexisting disorders, family treatment strategies, diagnostic and treatment information, behavioral , therapy, and information on help with coping	www.nimh.nih.gov/publicat/adhd 800-237-4513
MEDLINE's PubMed	Contains the latest research publication on ADHD funded by the National Institutes of Health	www.ncbi.nlm.nih.gov
Medline Plus	Contains information on pharmaceutical medications	www.nlm.nih.gov/medlineplus
ADD Kids Area, Friends and Me and ADD	Internet Web sites that contain information on explaining ADHD to children	www.helpforadd.com/talk add.org/content/kid1& add.org/content/kids/friends
PSEP Technical Assistance Center on Positive Behavioral Interventions & Supports	Contains information on behavioral interventions for unwanted behavior in the school, home, and community	www.pbis.org
American Academy of Pediatrics	Contains information on ADHD resources, symptoms and behaviors common to ADHD, diagnosis, common coexisting conditions, treatment plan, treatment with medication, unproven treatment, and evaluation methods	www.aap.org
Attention Deficit Disorder Association (ADDA)	Advocacy and support organization for individuals diagnosed with ADHD	www.ADDA.org
ADHD: A Complete and Authoritative Guide	A guidebook for families affected by ADHD. Based on evidence-based	www.aap.org

(continued)

Table 4.4 (*Continued*)

Resource	Description	Web Site
by the American Academy of Pediatrics	clinical treatment guidelines, answers the most frequently asked questions; contains the latest research on coexisting conditions and behavior therapy	
ADHA Support Company	Contains information on ADHD concerning teachers, parents, clients, medical treatment, nurses, family coping, and relationships	www.adhdsupportcompany.com

DuPaul, G. J., Eckert, T. L., & McGoey, K. E. (1997). Interventions for students with attention-deficit/hyperactivity disorder: One size dose not fit all. *School Psychology Review, 26*(3), 369–381.

Erk, R. R. (1995). A diagnosis of attention deficit disorder: What does it mean for school counselors? *School Counselor, 42*, 292–299.

Erk, R. R. (2000). Five frameworks for increasing understanding and effective treatment of attention deficit/hyperactivity disorder: Predominately inattentive type. *Journal of Counseling and Development, 78*(4), 389–399.

Hoagwood, K., Kelleher, K. J., Feil, M., & Comer, D. (2000). Treatment services for children with ADHD: A national perspective. *Journal of the American Academy of Child and Adolescent Psychiatry, 38*(7), 797–804.

Jensen, P. S. (2000). The National Institutes of Health attention-deficit/hyperactivity disorder consensus statement: Implications for practitioners and scientists. *CNS Spectrums, 5*(6), 29–33.

Jensen, P. S., Kettle, L., Roper, M. T., Sloan, M. T., Dulcan, M. K., Hoven, C., Bird, H., Bauermeister, J., & Panye, J. (1999). Are stimulants overprescribed? Treatment of ADHD in four U.S. communities. *Journal of the American Academy of Child and Adolescent Psychiatry, 38*(7), 797–804.

LeFever, G. B., Villers, M. S., Morrow, A. L., & Vaughn, E. S. (2002). Parental perceptions of adverse educational outcomes among children diagnosed and treated for ADHD: A call for improved school/provider collaboration. *Psychology in the Schools, 39*(1), 63–71.

Litner, B. (2003). Teens with ADHD: The challenge of high school. *Children and Youth Care Forum, 32*(3), 137–158.

McGoey, K., Eckert, T. L., & DuPaul, G. J. (2002). Early intervention for preschool-age children with ADHD: A literature review. *Journal of Emotional and Behavioral Disorders, 10*(1), 14–28.

Olfson, M., Gameroff, M. J., Marcus, S. C., & Jensen, P. S. (2003). National trends in the treatment of attention deficit hyperactivity disorder. *American Journal of Psychiatry, 160*(6), 1071–1077.

Perrin, J. M., Stein, M. T., Amler, R. W., Blondis, T. A., Feldman, H. M., Meyer, B. P., Shaywitz, A. B., & Wolraich, M. L. (2001). Clinical practice guideline: Treatment of the school-aged child with attention-deficit/hyperactivity disorder. *Pediatrics, 108*(4), 1033–1042.

Richters, J. E., Arnold, L. E., Jensen, P. S., Abikoff, H., Conners, C. K., Greenhill, L. L., Laurence, L., Hechtman, L., Hinshaw, S. P., Pelham, W. E., & Swanson, J. M. (1995). NIMH collaborative multisite multimodal treatment study of children with ADHD: I. Background and rationale. *Journal of the American Academy of Child and Adolescent Psychiatry, 34*(8), 987–1000.

Smith, B. H., Waschbusch, D. A., Willoughby, M. T., & Evans, S. (2000). The efficacy, safety, and practicality of treatments for adolescents with attention-deficit/hyperactivity disorder. *Clinical Child and Family Psychology Review, 3*(4), 2243–2266.

Thomas, C., & Corcoran, J. (2000). Family approaches to attention deficit hyperactivity disorder: Review of guide school social work practice. *Children & Schools, 25*(1), 19–34.

Effective Interventions for Youth With Oppositional Defiant Disorder

Tammy Linseisen

CHAPTER 5

Getting Started

"Disruptive," "mad all the time," "can't handle frustration," "touchy," "annoying," "driving me crazy," "emotionally disturbed," "passive-aggressive," "blames everyone for everything," "never takes responsibility," "doesn't listen," "noncompliant," "rude," "pushy," "oppositional," "defiant"—do any of these words or descriptions sound familiar? These are some of the terms and phrases used when parents and professionals are describing their observations of and reactions to children and adolescents who exhibit symptoms consistent with the diagnosis of oppositional defiant disorder (ODD). The prevalence of children with symptoms and/or actual diagnoses of oppositional defiant disorder has been documented in a number of publications (Eamon & Altshuler, 2004; Freeman, Franklin, Fong, Shaffer, & Timberlake, 1998; Markward & Bride, 2001; Sprague & Thyer, 2002). In fact, in the early school years, more than one half and maybe as many as two thirds of referrals made for clinical purposes are for behaviors consistent with this diagnosis (Fisher & Fagot, 1996). This diagnosis is not relegated to young children only. The following are facts about this disorder as listed in the *Diagnostic and Statistical Manual of Mental Disorders* (American Psychiatric Association, 2000):

- Evidence of the disorder is usually shown before the child is age 8.
- Evidence of the disorder will usually be shown by early adolescence.
- It is more common in families where marital difficulties exist.
- It appears more in families where at least one parent has a history of one of the following psychiatric diagnoses: mood disorder, ODD,

conduct disorder, attention deficit/hyperactivity disorder, antisocial personality disorder, or a substance-related disorder.
- Amount of oppositional symptoms seems to increase with age.
- ODD is found more often in males than in females until puberty.
- After puberty, ODD is found in both males and females at equal rates.

A critical responsibility of the school mental health professional is to accurately assess a youth's level of functioning in the school setting, although the provision of a diagnosis is not always helpful or necessary. For the orderly classification of symptoms, though, it is beneficial to work from one set of criteria. Not only are these behaviors disruptive to learning and the school setting in general, but the literature indicates that children with these kinds of behaviors are more prone to dropping out of school, substance use, peer rejection, adolescent-onset psychiatric disorders, and later antisocial behavior (Coie, Lochman, Terry, & Hyman, 1992; Kupersmidt & Coie, 1990; Kupersmidt & Patterson, 1991; Loeber, 1990). The *DSM-IV-TR* (2000) further states that significant impairment in social, academic, or occupational functioning must be caused by these behavioral disturbances. ODD should not be considered to be an accurate diagnosis if the criteria for the diagnosis of conduct disorder are met, and the same holds true if the individual is 18 years of age or older and the criteria for antisocial personality disorder are met. Even though conduct disorder and ODD are considered to be distinct, they do appear to exist on a spectrum of related disruptive behavior disorders. For this reason, the effective treatments of the two are similar, as can be seen from comparing this chapter to chapter 3 on conduct disorders.

Box 5.1

According to the *DSM-IV-TR* (2000), a youth can be diagnosed with ODD if he or she shows "a pattern of negativistic, hostile, and defiant behavior lasting at least 6 months, during which four (or more) of the following are present:

1. often loses temper;
2. often argues with adults;
3. often actively defies or refuses to comply with adults' requests or rules;
4. often deliberately annoys people;
5. often blames others for his or her mistakes or misbehavior;
6. is often touchy or easily annoyed by others;
7. is often angry and resentful;
8. is often spiteful or vindictive" (p. 102).

Reprinted with permission from the Diagnostic and Statistical Manual of Mental Disorders, Copyright 2000, American Psychiatric Association.

What We Know

A literature review of evidence-based interventions for ODD has revealed minimal results for individual practice but more promising results for group methods. Also, parent-training interventions have shown some promise, but no pharmacological treatment has been shown to be successful for the treatment of ODD in current studies. Practice wisdom as well as resiliency theory have informed the examples provided in this chapter, and information highlighting the resources not addressed in detail are located at the chapter's end.

If evidence-based programs or interventions discussed in the literature targeted youth with aggressive behaviors only, the information is not included here because two defining differences between ODD and conduct disorder, according to the *DSM-IV-TR* (2000), are that disruptive behaviors of individuals with ODD do not ordinarily involve aggression toward animals or people or the destruction of property.

The language used in research-based literature is variable when discussing behavioral problems of youth. Phrases like "disruptive school behavior," "conduct problems," "bullying and/or violent behaviors," "attachment disorders," and "emotional and/or behavioral disorders" are common when evidence-based interventions are being mentioned.

This offers a challenge to determine which of the studies is speaking to treatment of ODD specifically. Additionally, few studies have been conducted which involve youth who meet only the criteria for ODD without symptoms of other disorders or related conditions (Sprague & Thyer, 2002). This confounds the ability to define effective treatments for specified disorders, such as ODD by itself.

Certain evidence-based specifics might prove helpful to school social workers and mental health workers in their attempts to affect students via multiple systems. The following information might be useful when planning and facilitating groups with youth who meet the diagnostic criteria for ODD; when consulting with teachers who are managing students with ODD in their classrooms; or when attempting to provide effective interventions with an individual youth displaying oppositional and/or defiant behavior.

- Interventions that succeed in helping students to comply with adult directives usually lead to a decrease in disruptive behaviors (Musser, Bray, Kehle, & Jenson, 2001).
- Training parents and teachers to give commands and provide consequences effectively has been shown to improve compliance with adult requests (Musser et al., 2001).
- Delivery of requests for compliance in a firm but quiet tone of voice and also in statement form increased one program's effectiveness (O'Leary, Kaufman, Kass, & Drabman, 1970).
- Requests for compliance are more effective if specific and delivered within approximately 3 feet from the student (Van Houten, Nau, MacKenzie-Keating, Sameoto, & Colavecchia, 1982) and only once eye contact is established (Hamlet, Axelrod, & Kuerschner, 1984).
- Improving rates of students' compliance with adult requests can be achieved by obvious posting of four or five positively and behaviorally stated rules (Osenton & Chang, 1999; Rosenberg, 1986).
- Teacher movement in the classroom provides more supervision, earlier detection of potential problem situations, and increased opportunity to reward positive and prosocial behaviors (Rhode, Jenson, & Reavis, 1993).
- The use of mystery motivators can promote requests for compliance (Rhode et al., 1993). Mystery motivators are positive reinforcers that are not made known to the child, and they have been shown to help with the improvement

of inappropriate behaviors (Kehle, Madaus, Baratta, & Bray, 1998).

What We Can Do

Assessment

In order to use evidence-based interventions most effectively, an accurate assessment must be conducted in order to ensure that the youth meets the diagnostic criteria for ODD. Eamon and Altshuler (2004) highlighted the "multilayered and reciprocal nature of child, family, peer, neighborhood, and school factors in development" (p. 24). For this reason, it can be beneficial to observe children in different settings within school during a school day or week, obtain data from others in the school environment, read and review school files and referral materials, obtain data from parents regarding the youth's behavior in the home environment, as well as conduct individual interviews with the youth. The Eyberg Child Behavior Inventory (ECBI) and the Sutter-Eyberg Student Behavior Inventory (SESBI) are two of the instruments outlined in the literature that might offer some information regarding the child's behavioral functioning in the schools (Burns & Patterson, 2001). The Achenbach Child Behavior Checklist is another assessment tool utilized for home and school data, although the evidence base is not strong regarding its accuracy for diagnosis of ODD (Abolt & Thyer, 2002).

Individual Interventions

Currently, no individual interventions have been shown to be effective in producing clinically significant changes in children or adolescents who meet the criteria of ODD (Hemphill & Littlefield, 2001).

Relational and attachment theories subscribe to the notion that change can occur based on the healing power of the relationship, and although more evidence is likely in the future regarding the effectiveness of relationship to the treatment of ODD, currently there is only practice wisdom and the theory of resilience that suggest that these approaches might have a positive outcome on engaging students in a change process. In school settings, relational approaches may be integrated with evidence-based practices, such as problem-solving skills training, anger control training, and cognitive-behavioral therapies.

Resiliency

Garbarino (1999) identifies certain characteristics and conditions as directly relevant to making an impact on behaviorally disordered boys and their futures. Some of these are particularly relevant to the school environment: a stable positive emotional relationship with at least one person; actively coping with stress by finding meaning in it or making something positive out of it; an intelligence quotient (IQ) in the average range (but IQ scores can be misleading; a child's emotional intelligence is not scored on standard IQ measures); awareness of the student's own strengths and possession of a real concept of self; and positive social support from persons or institutions outside of the family (p. 168). Garbarino (1999) goes on to say that there are a number of "psychological anchors of resilience" that "are important in generating ideas for programs to save boys before they become troubled and violent" (p. 170). He defines social anchors as "the characteristics of a healthy community that holds and protects boys as they grow" (p. 170). Some of these social anchors are particularly relevant to schools and their communities:

1. Youth need some level of predictability and routine in their lives, and they thrive when this stability is present for them (the concept of stability).
2. All children need to be affirmed, which means "receiving messages of one's value and worth" (p. 171).
3. An environment that provides a sense of security allows for active exploration of the environment without fear of abandonment or danger.
4. Adults need to invest time and be physically and psychologically present with the youth.

Schools can create environments which will act as social anchors for the students, enhancing their resiliency and making a systemic impact on their overall functioning in constructive ways.

Relationship-Based Interventions

Although no efficacious individual interventions are presently documented, skilled practitioners discuss the positive effects of relational, cognitive-behavioral, and supportive individual work with children and adolescents who meet the criteria for the diagnosis of ODD. So often, these youth are disliked or disregarded by adults, and this is understandable in schools, given the challenges they can present in a classroom and with authority. Relationships with these youngsters, identified in the system as "problematic" or "defiant," can sometimes take time and require great patience from the school mental health worker or social worker. It is likely that the older the youth, the more challenging the relationship is to develop. The worker must meet the youth where he is, without pushing him to make changes in his behavior or to connect with the worker faster or more intimately than the youth can manage. By working with the youth at his own pace, the worker can gain trust and promote security and stability in the relationship. Once a relationship is established, infusion of problem-solving skill curricula or social skills training can occur, although modeling of prosocial behaviors is occurring all along within the relationship-building process. As part of the modeling process, games can be played with the youth that emphasize turn taking, promote problem solving, and de-emphasize competition.

Play Therapy

For children ages 12 and under, individual, child-centered play therapy is supported by practice wisdom to be an effective option, although adequate evaluative research does not exist to support this model. Briefly, then, the basic skills of child-centered play therapy lend themselves to creating an atmosphere that encourages the development of "necessary coping skills within safe boundaries" (Mader, 2000, p. 57). Play therapy is based on the premise that children express themselves via play, as adults express themselves via talking. Mader (2000) suggests "a framework within which one can work with the principal, teaching colleagues, and parents to develop an action plan that includes play counseling as a viable approach to changing behavior in disruptive students" (p. 56).

▌ Group Interventions

Problem-Solving and Social Skills Training in Groups

Problem-solving training and social skills training have evidence bases in the literature for affecting younger children who show symptoms of ODD

(Bierman, Miller, & Stabb, 1987; Kazdin, 1997). Dodge and Price (1994) relate that children who accurately perceive and effectively solve interpersonal problems use a five-stage, sequential, problem-solving decision-making process. See chapter 3 on conduct disorder for an additional review of problem-solving skills interventions. Group settings are ideal for teaching and practicing social problem-solving skills in the school setting. One problem-solving method using these highlighted steps is Second Step, "a violence-prevention curriculum created with the dual goals of reducing development of social, emotional, and behavioral problems and promoting the development of core competencies" (Frey, Hirschstein, & Guzzo, 2000, p. 103).

Using the group process, students practice this problem-solving model with hypothetical situations. Providing role plays and dramatic and comedic scenes for the youth to practice sometimes offers emotional distance when skills teaching and practicing begins in the group. Video clips are also useful for this purpose. Shorter role plays, scenes, and video clips might be utilized with younger children, and puppets or doll play might also benefit this age group.

Meichenbaum (1977) discusses the use of verbal mediation, or "self-talk," as a strategy, in this case, for youth to remember to manage impulses and to think about consequences of behavior or solutions. Self-talk can also be used to reward the children and adolescents for their own positive or successful behaviors. The third step of the problem-solving process is particularly important because it "establishes four basic values or norms for behavior: safety, fairness, people's feelings, and effectiveness" (Frey, Hirschstein, & Guzzo, 2000, p. 105). Values clarification is considered relevant when teaching children to problem solve, as children's problem-solving skills are improved once they are able to establish their own positive norms (Lochman, Coie, Underwood, & Terry, 1993).

Box 5.2 Problem-Solving Method

1. Identify the problem.
2. Brainstorm solutions.
3. Evaluate solutions by asking, "Is it safe? Is it fair? How might people feel? Will it work?"
4. Select, plan, and try the solution.
5. Evaluate if the solution worked and what to do next. (Frey, Hirschstein, & Guzzo, 2002, p. 105)

Anger Control and Stress Inoculation Training

Because the peer group is such an important part of adolescent development and because schools tend to have limited resources to provide mental health services to greater numbers of students in need, group treatment can be an effective modality for the youth and for the school. Anger control groups have been shown to be efficacious in treating ODD youngsters (Sprague & Thyer, 2002).

The following steps might be helpful to make the group work (see chapters 56–58 for additional ideas for how to lead successful groups in schools):

Preparation

- Review the files and referral materials of those youth indicated to be showing symptoms of ODD.
- Complete assessments of the youth by interviewing them individually and speaking with their various teachers directly about their behaviors.
- Using the written materials and the interviews, determine if the referred youth meet the criteria for ODD as indicated by the *DSM-IV-TR*.
- Consider limiting the group to no more than six to eight members if the facilitator's group experience with this type of adolescent is minimal or if the acuity of the collective behaviors is intense. The group can be limited to as few as four students, but it can be quite small then when students are absent or unable to attend.
- In this age group, it is suggested that same-sex membership might be more effective in order to minimize the heterosexual peer issues inherent in early adolescence.
- A cofacilitator is a helpful resource when working with youth who require a higher level of supervision and subsequent intervention. With cofacilitation, though, much work must be done to ensure active and open communication between facilitators in order to minimize splitting by the group members and other potential downfalls.
- Determine a plan for effective evaluation of the group treatment intervention. One might use disciplinary referrals to the office, teacher reports of in-class behavioral problems/consequences, and in-school suspensions to evaluate pre- and posttreatment outcomes. A pretest can be ad-

ministered to the group members as well, determining their own views of their behaviors or their responses to conflictual situations.
- The group meets two times per week for 5 weeks, and it would consist of 10 50-minute training sessions. This might be modified to a 9-week session of one group session per week if necessary.
- Individual meetings occur again with the group members chosen for the group, and relationship development begins between the facilitator and the student. The facilitator begins to learn more about the student and his view of the world.

Group Process

- Group 1 establishes a group contract about participation and rules for the group. The group leader will discuss behavioral rewards for participation and homework completion. Some programs use snacks and soft drinks. Others use a point system that can accumulate into rewards at the end of a session. With this age group, using rewards more quickly can provide the short-term reinforcement necessary to promote compliance and participation. Group 1 should engage group members to keep their interests and to whet their appetites for future groups. At the end of the first group session, it might be beneficial to review with the group the goals that might be accomplished in this group. If there is resistance, this question can wait until later or be asked individually of group members in separate sessions between the group meetings.
  - It is critical that the group leader use skills to prevent power struggles from occurring with these group members. Other than issues of safety, few reasons exist which warrant a struggle with the youth over power.
  - Put a structure into place in the group that offers clear and direct guidelines and expectations for behavior. Determine what will happen if a group member is not following directions or is violating any other group rule.
  - Find ways to reward group members for following the rules but also for the prosocial behavior of helping their peers to follow the rules.
  - Use group process to help in sticky situations. For example: "What do you think we need to do about Joey's behavior, guys?"

"What do you think our choices are?" "If Joey continues to break Rule #2, our group can't [pick something positive that is planned or a group reward that could be given]. I'm wondering how the group can help?" Give verbal praise to the suggestions that are beneficial, while trying to ignore or minimize the negative or threatening comments.

- It is sometimes helpful to use humor to defuse negative comments as well. "Well, Freddy, punching Joey in the face is an option. However, then, you would be in even more trouble with the group than Joey is. Great idea?"

- Group Two would teach the group about the cycle of provocation, which includes how to identify one's own cues of anger and one's own aggressive or inappropriate responses and then the consequences of these types of events. Movie clips can again be shown to demonstrate this cycle, and group members can use these to understand the way the cycle works with others. Depending on the group's willingness at this point, role plays can begin to demonstrate either predetermined situations provided on index cards to the players, or if the group is engaging more readily, they can provide their own scenarios. Inside-the-group reinforcements happen when certain students are shown how to work and commandeer the video player or they are chosen as the director of a scene (Sprague & Thyer, 2002).

- Future groups can focus on common self-control strategies as well as assertiveness versus aggression. Specific microskills must be defined for each strategy in order to teach it in a step-by-step way. Videotaping role plays of the youth engaging in a problematic situation can be extremely helpful. The group can review the tape together, with individual input from group members about what details led to the problems in the situation. They might identify details such as voice tones, facial expressions, hand gestures, defensiveness, hostile posturing, and angry eye contact. The scenes can be rehearsed then, using different types of coping and self-control strategies, and videotapes can be reviewed again during the course of the group. Voice tone, eye contact, the broken-record technique, problem solving, choosing battles, taking time outs, and other forms of relaxation for deescalation

are all suitable for the self-control strategy curricula.

- Rehearsal is a critical component of this type of program. Practice! Practice! Practice! Have different kids role play alternative responses for other kids. Practice the new skills as much as possible, and provide homework to the youth to try these new skills in other situations. Have them write about their experiences and bring

Box 5.3 Idea for Group One

Show video clips of popular movies where characters are exhibiting both negative and positive behaviors. Group discussions can occur after these video clips with specific questions offered, such as "What set the character off?" "What did you see happen?" "What were the consequences?"

Often, ODD youth do not see all of the consequences of their actions, particularly the consequences that involve their peer relationships and issues of respect or trust. This is an opportunity to point these things out without stepping on anyone's toes personally in the first meeting.

Box 5.4 Four Methods to Teach Alternative Responses to Conflict or Provocation

1. Self-Instruction: This is also called self-talk. The student might remind himself to keep cool or to ignore a situation.
2. Covert Modification of the Participant's Understanding of the Aggression-Causing Conditions: This is the "you're just jealous" reaction. The student uses self-talk to reframe the reason for the person's provocative behavior.
3. Self-Evaluation of Behavior During a Conflict and of Efficient Goal Accomplishment: This is a technique that asks the student to evaluate his own reactions as they are happening: "How am I doing here? or "How did I handle that?"
4. Cognitive Control Technique of Thinking Ahead: This method focuses on changing faulty thinking skills inherent in many troubled youth.

Sources: Feindler, Marriott, & Iwata, 1984; Sprague & Thyer, 2002.

this information back to the group. Reward them for completing assignments and bringing them back to the group.

Termination

- Begin preparing the group for termination several sessions prior to the last one. Remind them of the number of group meetings left. Anticipate that the group members might regress some or even miss a group or two while they begin the process of preparing for termination. Youth with ODD sometimes have issues with attachment and intimacy, and termination might trigger these issues. Encourage the group members to talk about termination and how endings have happened for them in the past. If the group is unable to do this as a whole, provide one more individual session to each student and discuss his progress in the group, strengths, and areas for growth. Offer the opportunity for more discussion about termination in this one-to-one meeting.
- Provide an ending to remember! Offer certificates for completion of the training, and it might even be worthwhile to frame them so that the youth are less likely to throw them away or misplace them. Provide a letter to the youth outlining the things discussed at the individual meetings, particularly the issues where growth has taken place and where strengths have been shown. If possible, this ending session might even involve a party where teachers and others are invited to celebrate the program's completion. This will depend on resources as well as the group's functioning and state of cohesion at the time of termination. Have the group members talk to each other about what they learned from each other specifically and ask what they will take with them from the group.
- Conduct a posttest to review the students' evaluation of their behaviors now that the group intervention has occurred. Review the posttreatment data to determine if changes have occurred in the students' school behavior and problem-solving abilities.

Group Assertiveness Training

Huey and Rank (1984) provided group assertiveness training to African American boys who were identified as demonstrating aggression in the classroom. The following definitions were provided to distinguish assertive, passive, or aggressive responses:

"A response that was forthright and honest without being threatening or abusive was considered an assertive response" (Sprague & Thyer, 2002, p. 68). A passive response was one that showed unwillingness for the student to stand up for his rights (Sprague & Thyer, 2002). An aggressive response was when the student "used sarcasm, insults, threats, and tried to reach his goals in an abusive way" (Sprague & Thyer, 2002, p. 68). The boys receiving assertiveness training showed significant improvement posttreatment with their aggressiveness and anger in the classroom, more so than those assigned to group discussion only or to no treatment at all (Sprague & Thyer, 2002). This provides another intervention option, then, using the group formation and implementation suggestions above.

Rational-Emotive Therapy

Finally, Block (1978) reviewed a mental health program utilized with African American and Latino youth in the 11th and 12th grades. These youth were "prone to misconduct" and were also at risk of school failure. The program was one of rational-emotive therapy (RET), which is based on cognitive theory and which was made famous by Albert Ellis, a psychologist. Barker (1999) writes that the therapy is one in which the "client is encouraged to make distinctions between what is objective fact in the environment and the inaccurate, negative, and self-limiting interpretations made of one's own behavior and life" (p. 400). The group leaders used a task-oriented approach, and they maintained a more directive stance in the group. The process used much role play, small-group directed discussion, and homework assignments. Exercises involved direct confrontations and taking risks, and the youth were asked to discuss openly their feelings and reactions to the homework and the assignments in the group (Sprague & Thyer, 2002). With more information about the RET method and more study about the processes underlying this model, group interventions could be developed in schools which utilize this evidence-based approach.

School mental health professionals starting groups should consider this important caution. Although particular cognitive-behavioral interventions have shown some promise with improving problematic behavior in adolescents, it is always a challenging practice to bring together a group of youth, especially of adolescent age, who demonstrate the same types of ego limitations or acting-out defenses. Ideally, prosocial and cognitive restructuring opportunities might happen in a group carefully selected with a balance of personality types and varied strengths. Who decided to put all the kids with behavior problems in the same class anyway, expecting them to be educated? Balancing a group with students who have various issues or varying degrees of symptoms could be beneficial for all involved.

Parent Training

Parent–child interaction therapy (PCIT) is a family therapy approach to the treatment of psychological problems of preschool children that integrates both traditional and behavioral methods (Brinkmeyer & Eyberg, 2003). Treatment is conducted in two phases, labeled child-directed interaction (CDI) and parent-directed interaction (PDI). In CDI, the parents are taught to allow their child to lead the play activity. Parents are taught to describe, imitate, and praise the child's appropriate behavior, and they are also taught not to criticize the child. In PDI, the parents are taught how to direct and redirect their child's activity. Parents are taught to use clear and positive statements and direct commands as well as consistent consequences, both positive and negative, for behavior. Quite a bit of evidence base exists for the use of parent training models with oppositional defiant children.

Pharmacological Interventions

No one type of medication is usually prescribed for ODD because no particular medication or class of medication has been shown to be beneficial. There is no evidence base for effective use of psychotropic medications to treat ODD (Hoagwood, Burns, Kiser, Ringeisen, & Schoenwald, 2001). This finding highlights the importance of accurate assessment of the child diagnosed with ODD, as there can be co-occurring disorders that might respond to pharmacological treatment (e.g., depression). It is the ethical responsibility of the school social worker or mental health worker to refer the student for psychiatric consultation should any information from the youth's assessment indicate the need for further medical intervention.

Tools and Practice Examples

Practice Example

A 13-year-old, Latino male student (Rico) was referred to a 27-year-old, Caucasian female social work intern (Polly) because of his school-based acting-out behavior, which included angry outbursts in the classroom and truancy. Rico told Polly that he did not have any problems, and when she asked specifically about why he thought he might have been referred to her, he replied, "I don't know, Miss." Polly established a consistent date and time to see Rico, and she met with him in the same office for several sessions, even though both of these issues were very difficult to achieve in her schedule and in this school setting. His attention span was reported to be short, so Polly started sessions at 30 minutes each.

Polly played cards with Rico and engaged him in discussions about things that he liked, disliked, enjoyed, and did not enjoy (his favorite movies, favorite foods, favorite sports, important people in his life, people he admired, people he did not, and so on). Polly raised questions about this in her supervision, questioning her effectiveness and purpose if this were the extent of her intervention with this young male. If Rico were absent on a day when a session was supposed to occur, Polly would call his home and leave a message and follow up on a subsequent day to see him in the school environment. She would not offer him a full session, but instead, she would notice his absence from their session and express her hope that he would be there for the next one.

Polly challenged Rico to think before he answered and to use different words to express himself, rather than "I don't know." She countered his potential resistance to engaging in the intervention by saying, "This probably won't work, or you might choose not to do it, but it might be interesting to see what happens." Rico eventually began to stop himself from answering with "I don't know" without any prompting, but Polly had to wait for him to do this in his own time frame. There were days that he did not seem interested, most often due to a problem he had in school prior to the session or to a health issue, and Polly did not pressure Rico to perform. Any outside pressure can regress the relationship to an earlier stage or push the child to cope ineffectively, as in previous times.

Polly walked around the school track and played basketball with Rico during some sessions.

She worked with Rico's teachers, assisting them to manage their own impatience regarding his change process. Work with teachers is critical for the youth's success, as the youth often experiences negativity from school professionals about the rate of his progress. This allows the teachers to express their frustrations appropriately to the worker, while also gaining wisdom about the youth's progress. Providing support to teachers can infuse energy into their work as well, and this might be demonstrated via more patience with the youth or by employing alternative techniques, such as humor or planned ignoring, to manage behavioral difficulties.

Polly implemented more one-on-one problem-solving skills training. She and Rico practiced the skills and videotaped the role plays, showing all types of responses. Polly brought professional movie clips into her sessions with Rico also and discussed what worked and what did not work for the characters in the movies. At year's end, Rico tolerated 50-minute sessions. Truancy was no longer a problem, and his classroom behavior showed significant improvement.

Resources

The following list offers resources to locate further information as needed about other relevant research.

Social Skills Training Program for Peer-Rejected Boys

Bierman, K. L., Miller, C. M., & Stabb, S. (1987). Improving the social behavior and peer acceptance of rejected boys: Effects of social skill training with instructions and prohibitions. *Journal of Consulting and Clinical Psychology, 55,* 194–200.

Webster-Stratton, C., & Reid, M. (2003). *The incredible years parents, teachers, and children training series: A multifaceted treatment approach for young children with conduct problems.* http://www.incredibleyears.com.

Community-Based Collaboration With School Professionals

Multisystemic Therapy: http://www.mstservices.com. (This evidence-based approach requires interventions outside of school with professionals trained specifically in this area. Schools will often collaborate with this type of treatment as part of a team. This treatment is appropriate for adolescent youth who engage in severe willful misconduct that places them at risk for out-of-home placement.)

Anger Management Curriculum for 8–12-Year-Olds

Larson, J., & Lochman, J. (2002). *Helping schoolchildren cope with anger: A cognitive-behavioral intervention.* New York: Guilford. (The Anger Coping Program, an empirically supported group intervention for 8–12-year-olds with anger and aggression problems, is offered in this manual. This program is supported by research to reduce teacher- and parent-directed aggression; improve on-task behavior in the classroom; and improve participants' verbal assertiveness and compromise skills, social competence, and academic achievement.)

Mystery Motivators

Rhode, G., Jenson, W., & Reavis, H. (1993). *The tough kid book: Practical classroom management strategies.* Longmont, CO: Sopris West. (This book offers further information about mystery motivators, mentioned above.)

Classroom Behavior Management

Harris, V. W., & Sherman, J. A. (1973). Use and analysis of the "good behavior game" to reduce disruptive classroom behavior. *Journal of Applied Behavior Analysis, 6,* 405–417. (The good behavior game is a school-based prevention program which has an evidence base for reducing problem behaviors in children.)

Key Points to Remember

Given the prevalence of children and adolescents with oppositional defiant disorder, it is somewhat surprising the limited number of evidence-based treatments documented to be effective with this population. Within a school setting, particular group interventions and parent training modules have been shown to be effective in treating ODD, but presently no pharmacological or individual interventions have shown clinical effectiveness.

Practice wisdom gains support from the concept of resiliency, offering that certain relational therapies can be effective in ameliorating the symptoms of ODD in youth, even though current research does not exist which demonstrates evidence-based effectiveness. Clearly, further research is necessary to expand the list of what works with these youth, and it is hoped that this research can focus specifically on the symptoms of ODD, rather than grouping it together with other disorders and, consequently, creating confounds about what really works with ODD youth.

Within the school setting, though, a number of the evidence-based interventions are appropriate for implementation. Groups targeting social skills training, problem solving, assertiveness, and anger management can be offered in the schools, and consultation regarding these issues can be provided to educators by school social workers and mental health workers. Individual relationship building seems relevant in order to model prosocial behaviors as well as build resiliency in the youth. Parent training is another possibility. From a systems perspective, a model of intervention for youth with ODD which targets multiple layers of the system is likely to offer the most chances for youth to gain the skills necessary for optimum functioning within the school environment.

References

Abolt, T., & Thyer, B. A. (2002). Social work assessment of children with oppositional defiant disorder: Reliability and validity of the Child Behavior Checklist. *Social Work in Mental Health, 1*, 73–84.

American Psychiatric Association. (2000). *Diagnostic and statistical manual of mental disorders* (4th ed., text revision). Washington, DC: Author.

Barker, P. (1999). *Talking cures: An introduction to the psychotherapies for health care professionals.* London: NT Books.

Bierman, K. L., Miller, C. M., & Stabb, S. (1987). Improving the social behavior and peer acceptance of rejected boys: Effects of social skill training with instructions and prohibitions. *Journal of Consulting and Clinical Psychology, 55*, 194–200.

Block, J. (1978). Effects of a rational emotive mental health program on poorly achieving, disrupting high school students. *Journal of Counseling Psychology, 25*, 61–65.

Brinkmeyer, M., & Eyberg, S. M. (2003). Parent–child interaction therapy for oppositional children. In A. E. Kazdin & J. R. Weisz (Eds.), *Evidence-based psychotherapies for children and adolescents* (pp. 204–223). New York: Guilford.

Burns, G., & Patterson, D. (2001). Normative data on the Eyberg Child Behavior Inventory and Sutter-Eyberg Student Behavior Inventory: Parent and teacher rating scales of disruptive behavior problems in children and adolescents. *Child and Family Behavior Therapy, 23*, 15–28.

Coie, J., Lochman, J., Terry, R., & Hyman, C. (1992). Predicting early adolescent disorder from childhood aggression and peer rejection. *Journal of Consulting and Clinical Psychology, 60*, 783–792.

Dodge, K. A., & Price, J. M. (1994). On the relation between social information processing and socially competent behavior in early school-aged children. *Child Development, 65*, 1385–1397.

Eamon, M. K., & Altshuler, S. J. (2004). Can we predict disruptive school behavior? *Children & Schools, 26*, 23–37.

Feindler, E. L., Marriott, S., & Iwata, M. (1984). Group anger-control training for junior high school delinquents. *Cognitive Therapy and Research, 8*, 299–311.

Fisher, P. A., & Fagot, B. I. (1996). Development of consensus about child oppositional behavior: Increased convergence with entry into school. *Journal of Applied Developmental Psychology, 17*, 519–534.

Freeman, E. M., Franklin, C. G., Fong, R., Shaffer, G. L., and Timberlake, E. M. (Eds.). (1998). *Multisystem skills and interventions in school social work practice.* Washington, DC: NASW Press.

Frey, K. S., Hirschstein, M. K., & Guzzo, B. A. (2000). Second step: Preventing aggression by promoting social competence. *Journal of Emotional and Behavioral Disorders, 8*(2), 102–112.

Garbarino, J. (1999). *Lost boys.* New York: Free Press.

Hamlet, C., Axelrod, S., & Kuerschner, S. (1984). Eye contact as an antecedent to compliant behavior. *Journal of Applied Behavior Analysis, 17*, 553–557.

Harris, V. W., & Sherman, J. A. (1973). Use and analysis of the "good behavior game" to reduce disruptive classroom behavior. *Journal of Applied Behavior Analysis, 6*, 405–417.

Hemphill, S., & Littlefield, L. (2001). Evaluation of a community-based group therapy program for children with behavior problems and their parents. *Behaviour Research and Therapy, 39*, 823–841.

Hoagwood, K., Burns, B., Kiser, L., Ringeisen, H., & Schoenwald, S. (2001). Evidence-based practice in child and adolescent mental health services. *Psychiatric Services, 52*(9), 1179–1189.

Huey, W. C., & Rank, R. C. (1984). Effects of counselor- and peer-led group assertive training on black adolescent aggression. *Journal of Counseling Psychology, 31*(1), 95–98.

Kazdin, A. E. (1997). Practitioner review: Psychosocial treatments for conduct disorder in children. *Journal of Child Psychology and Psychiatry, 38*, 161–178.

Kehle, T. J., Madaus, M. R., Baratta, V. S., & Bray, M. A. (1998). Employing self-modeling with children with selective mutism. *Journal of School Psychology, 36,* 247–260.

Kupersmidt, J. B., & Coie, J. D. (1990). Preadolescent peer status, aggression, and school adjustment as predictors of externalizing problems in adolescence. *Child Development, 61,* 1350–1362.

Kupersmidt, J. B., & Patterson, C. J. (1991). Childhood peer rejection, aggression, withdrawal, and perceived competence as predictors of self-reported behavior problems in preadolescence. *Journal of Abnormal Child Psychology, 19,* 427–503.

Lochman, J., Coie, J., Underwood, M., & Terry, R. (1993). Effectiveness of a social relations intervention program for aggressive and nonaggressive, rejected children. *Journal of Consulting and Clinical Psychology, 61,* 1053–1058.

Loeber, R. (1990). Development and risk factors of juvenile antisocial behavior and delinquency. *Clinical Psychology Review, 10,* 1–42.

Mader, C. (2000). Child-centered play therapy with disruptive school students. In H. G. Kaduson & C. E. Schaffer (Eds.), *Short-term play therapy for children* (pp. 53–68). New York: Guilford.

Markward, M. J., & Bride, B. E. (2001). Oppositional defiant disorder and the need for family-centered practice in schools. *Children & Schools, 23*(2), 73–83.

Meichenbaum, D. H. (1977). *Cognitive-behavior modification: An integrative approach.* New York: Plenum.

Musser, E. H., Bray, M. A., Kehle, T. J., & Jenson, W. R. (2001). Reducing disruptive behaviors in students with serious emotional disturbance. *School Psychology Review, 30,* 294–305.

O'Leary, K. D., Kaufman, K. F., Kass, R., & Drabman, R. (1970). The effects of loud and soft reprimands on the behavior of disruptive students. *Exceptional Children 37*(2), 145–155.

Osenton, T., & Chang, J. (1999). Solution-oriented classroom management: Application with young children. *Journal of Systemic Therapies, 18*(2), 65–76.

Rhode, G., Jenson, W. R., & Reavis, H. K. (1993). *The tough kid book: Practical classroom management strategies.* Longmont, CO: Sopris West.

Rosenberg, M. S. (1986). Maximizing the effectiveness of structured classroom management programs: Implementing rule-review procedures with disruptive and distractible students. *Behavioral Disorders, 11,* 239–248.

Sprague, A., & Thyer, B. A. (2002). Psychosocial treatment of oppositional defiant disorder: A review of empirical outcome studies. *Social Work in Mental Health, 1,* 63–72.

Van Houten, R., Nau, P., MacKenzie-Keating, S., Sameoto, D., & Colavecchia, B. (1982). An analysis of some variables influencing the effectiveness of reprimands. *Journal of Applied Behavior Analysis, 15,* 65–83.

Effective Interventions for Students With Separation Anxiety Disorder

Marilyn Camacho ▪ Lisa Hunter

Getting Started

Children experiencing separation anxiety display signs of distress when separated from their parents or primary caregivers. Separation anxiety is a normal phase of development typically evident between 10 and 18 months, and symptoms tend to dissipate by the time the child reaches the age of 2 or 3 years (Carruth, 2000). Separation anxiety becomes a disorder when "the expected developmental levels are exceeded, resulting in significant distress and impairment at home, school, and in social contexts" (Albano & Kendall, 2002, p. 130). The detrimental effects of separation anxiety disorder (SAD) are particularly noticeable in schools given that they are the setting where children are separated from their parents for the longest period of time. As such, school-based practitioners are in the unique position to identify and treat SAD. Their access to students, parents, and school staff facilitates the identification of the disorder and the implementation of appropriate interventions. In this chapter, we will briefly review the diagnostic criteria and epidemiology of SAD, describe the Coping Cat program (Kendall, 2000a), the intervention of choice for this disorder, and discuss how it can be implemented in a school setting.

What We Know

Diagnosis and Prevalence of Separation Anxiety Disorder (SAD)

According to the American Psychiatric Association's *Diagnostic and Statistical Manual of Mental Disorders* (*DSM-IV-TR*), separation anxiety disorder in children and young adolescents is marked by "developmentally inappropriate and excessive anxiety concerning separation from the home or from those to whom the person is attached" (American Psychiatric Association, 2000, p. 125). The *DSM-IV-TR* diagnostic criteria for SAD are listed in Table 6.1.

The prevalence rate for SAD is 4% (American Psychiatric Association, 2000). Children with SAD typically range in age from 8 to 12 years old (Compton et al., 2000) with age of onset being 9 years old in clinical samples (Tonge, 1994). SAD is more common in children from lower socioeconomic backgrounds (Saavedra & Silverman, 2002) and is more prevalent in girls than boys (Last, Hersen, Kazdin, Finkelstein, & Strauss, 1987). Overall, there is no evidence that SAD is more prevalent in any particular culture (Albano & Kendall, 2002).

Children with SAD often have other psychiatric disorders as well. Disorders that most commonly occur with SAD include generalized anxiety disorder (GAD) and social phobia (SoP) (Velting, Setzer, & Albano, 2004). There is also evidence of comorbidity between SAD and depression, obsessive-compulsive disorder, and gender identity disorder (Silverman & Dick-Niederhauser, 2004).

What Does SAD Look Like?

There are some developmental variations in the presentation of SAD among children. Younger children tend to report more symptoms than their older counterparts (Francis, Last, & Strauss, 1987). Additionally, the presentation of SAD in younger children has been described as "amorphous" while older children present more explicit concerns relating to separation (Perwien & Berstein, 2004).

Table 6.1 *DSM-IV-TR* Diagnostic Criteria for Separation Anxiety Disorder

Criterion A: Developmentally inappropriate and excessive anxiety concerning separation from home or from those to whom the individual is attached, as shown by at least three of the following:

- Recurrent excessive distress when separation from home or major attachment figures occurs or is anticipated
- Persistent and excessive worry about losing, or about possible harm befalling, major attachment figures
- Persistent and excessive worry that an untoward event will lead to separation from a major attachment figure
- Persistent reluctance or refusal to go to school or elsewhere because of fear of separation
- Persistently and excessively fearful or reluctant to be alone or without major attachment figures at home or without significant adults in other settings
- Persistent reluctance or refusal to go to sleep without being near a major attachment figure or to sleep away from home
- Repeated nightmares involving the theme of separation
- Repeated complaints of physical symptoms (such as headaches, stomachaches, nausea, or vomiting) when separation from major attachment figures occurs or is anticipated

Criterion B: Duration of disturbance is at least 4 weeks

Criterion C: Age of onset is before 18 years (specify if early onset occurs before age 6 years)

Criterion D: Disturbance causes clinically significant distress or impairment in social, academic (occupational), or other important areas of functioning

Criterion E: Disturbance does not occur exclusively during the course of a pervasive developmental disorder, or other psychotic disorder and, in adolescents, is not better accounted for by panic disorder with agoraphobia

Source: Reprinted with permission from the Diagnostic and Statistical Manual of Mental Disorders, Copyright 2000, American Psychiatric Association.

Young children may express SAD by closely shadowing their parents throughout the day and checking on their whereabouts for fear that the parents may become harmed (Fischer, Himle, & Thyer, 1999). In a school-aged child, symptoms associated with school refusal are most evident (Fischer et al., 1999). Some of these symptoms may include somatic complaints accompanied by frequent visits to the school nurse (Walkup & Ginsburg, 2002), tantrums, terror outbursts, attempts to leave the school to go home (Fischer et al., 1999), and high rates of school absence (Walkup & Ginsburg, 2002). It is important to note that although school refusal is a common symptom of SAD, it is not unique to the disorder and can be attributed to other disorders, such as specific phobia, social phobia, mood disorder, disruptive behavior disorder, or family conflict (Silverman & Dick-Niederhauser, 2004). Additional symptoms associated with SAD among school-aged children include frequent nightmares depicting threats to or separation from parents (Francis et al., 1987), refusal to participate in social activities that involve separation from parents, and a tendency to sleep with parents (Fischer et al., 1999).

Importance of Treating SAD in Schools

School personnel may not view SAD as a problem in need of immediate attention since externalizing disorders are so much more disruptive. This lack of attention may contribute to the underrecognition of SAD, leaving children suffering from the disorder significantly impaired and never referred for treatment. Left untreated, SAD may contribute to limited academic achievement, substance abuse, development of additional psychiatric disorders, and minimal social supports (Velting et al., 2004). Additionally, there may be a relationship between SAD in childhood and panic disorder in adulthood (Gittelman & Klein, 1984). Given these possibilities, it is imperative that school staff, particularly teachers, learn how to identify children with SAD. School-based practitioners can provide teachers with informational sessions on how to identify SAD behaviors and guidance on when and how to make referrals to the school-based mental health clinic.

What We Can Do

Assessing Separation Anxiety Disorder

Clinical judgment is necessary to distinguish "developmentally appropriate levels of separation anxiety from the clinically significant concerns about separation seen in SAD" (American Psychiatric Association, 2000, p. 124). Diagnostic interviews have been developed to augment clinical judgment by providing systematic means of establishing the primary diagnosis and aid in the differential diagnosis of comorbid disorders (Langley, Bergman, & Piacentini, 2002). This is especially helpful in diagnosing anxiety disorders given the high incidence of comorbidity associated with these disorders. Additionally, the use of self-report scales for anxiety disorders has proven to be useful in collecting information on patients' symptomology through multiple informants (Albano, 2003). These assessment measures may be administered in the beginning, middle, and termination phases of treatment in order to track changes in symptoms.

Clinical Interviews

There are two types of clinical interviews—structured and unstructured—that can be used to assess for anxiety disorders in children. The structured interview can be used flexibly and by clinicians with "limited clinical judgment" (Albano, 2003). Semistructured interviews "provide guidelines for adapting inquiries to the age or developmental level of the child, and also allow for some flexibility in probing for clarification and further information" (Albano, 2003, p. 134). Although there are no diagnostic interviews designed exclusively to assess SAD, there are several interviews with a SAD subscale. Some examples of clinical interviews with specific subscales for assessing SAD include the Anxiety Disorders Interview Schedule for *DSM-IV* (ADIS; Silverman & Nelles, 1988),

the Diagnostic Interview Schedule for Children (DISC-IV; Shaffer, Fisher, Lucas, Dulcan, & Schwab-Stone, 2000), the Diagnostic Interview for Children and Adolescents (DICA; Reich, 2000), the Child and Adolescent Psychiatric Assessment (CAPA; Angold & Costello, 2000), and the Children's Interview for Psychiatric Symptoms (ChIPS; Weller, Weller, Fristad, Rooney, & Schecter, 2000). Table 6.2 provides brief descriptions of these instruments.

Although clinical interviews such as those listed in Table 6.2 are useful tools for assessing SAD, they are most frequently used in research settings, can be time consuming to administer (2–3 hours), and may require clinician training. As such, they may not be practical for use in a school setting. The school-based practitioner, however, may find it useful to review these interviews to learn how to ask questions about SAD. Table 6.3 provides some sample questions that school-based clinicians can use when assessing for SAD.

Self-Report Measures

A number of self-report anxiety rating scales can be completed by children, as well as by parents. Although there is no established self-report measure for SAD, there are several assessment measures with items relevant to SAD that can be used to assess the disorder. These include the Multidimensional Anxiety Scale for Children (MASC; March, Parker, Sullivan, Stallings, & Conners, 1997), Screen for Child Anxiety Related Emotional Disorders (SCARED; Birmaher et al., 1997), and Spence Children's Anxiety Scale (SCAS; Spence, 1997). Table 6.4 describes the above-mentioned self-report measures. Additionally, the School Refusal Assessment Scale (SRAS; Kearney & Silverman, 1993) may be particularly useful for SAD in order to establish whether symptoms of school refusal are indeed a feature of SAD and not other disorders, such as school phobia. These measures are particularly useful in school settings given that they require little time to administer (10–15 minutes), do not require special equipment, and are of minimal cost (James, Reynolds, & Dunbar, 1994).

Teacher Reports

In addition to parents, teachers are also valuable informants in the assessment of SAD symptoms. Teachers are often the first to witness SAD,

Table 6.2 Clinical Interviews With Separation Anxiety Disorder Subscales

Clinical Interview	Age	Informant	Characteristic Features of Interview		Source
			Format	Administration	
Diagnostic Interview Schedule for Children (DISC-IV; Shaffer et al., 2000)	6–17	Child & Parent	Highly Structured	90–120 minutes	DISC Development Group Division of Child Psychiatry 1051 Riverside Drive, Box 78 New York, NY 10032 888-814-3472, disc@worldnet.att.net http://www.c-disc.com
Diagnostic Interview for Children and Adolescents (DICA; Reich, 2000)	6–17	Child, Parent	Structured & Semi-structured	60 minutes	Wendy Reich, PhD Division of Child Psychiatry Washington University 660 S. Euclid, Box 8134 St. Louis, MO 63110 314-286-2263 Wendyr@twins.wustl.edu
Child and Adolescent Psychiatric Assessment (CAPA; Angold & Costello, 2000)	9–17	Child & Parent	Structured	60–150 minutes	Adrian Angold, MD Department of Psychiatry & Behavioral Sciences Duke University Center, Box 3454 Durham, NC 277710 919-687-4686 Adrian.angold@duke.edu

(continued)

Table 6.2 (*Continued*)

Clinical Interview	Age	Informant	Format	Administration	Source
			Characteristic Features of Interview		
Anxiety Disorders Interview Scale for DSM-IV (ADIS; Silverman & Nelles, 1988)	6–17	Child & Parent	Semi-structured	60 minutes	Wendy Silverman, PhD Department of Psychology Florida International University University Park Miami, FL 33199 305-348-2064 Wendy.Silverman@fiu.edu
Children's Interview for Psychiatric Symptoms (ChIPS; Weller et al., 2000)	6–18	Child & Parent	Highly Structured	40 minutes	Elizabeth Weller, M.D. Department of Child Psychiatry The Children's Hospital of Philadelphia 34th Street & Civic Boulevard Philadelphia, PA 19104 212-590-7555 Weller@email.chop.edu

Table 6.3 Sample Questions for Assessing Separation Anxiety Disorder in School-Aged Children*

- Are there times when you don't want to be in places without your mother like school or at a relative's house?
- Sometimes you may know ahead of time if you are going to a place without your mother. Do you ever start feeling sick when thinking about not being with your mother?
- Do you ever feel sick (e.g., headaches or stomachaches) when you are someplace without your mother?
- Do you worry that something bad will happen to your mother? What do you worry may happen to her?
- Has your mother ever been very sick, or hurt by someone, or been in a bad situation, like a car accident or robbery?
- Does your mother complain that you follow her around too much?
- Does your mother get upset with you when you worry about being away from her?
- Do you know anyone in your family or any of your friends who is very ill?
- Do you remember a time that you were not with your mother for a long time? When was that time and why were you not with her?
- At bedtime, do you sleep by yourself or with your mother?
- Does your mother ever ask you to sleep by yourself? How often does she ask you to sleep on your own?
- Do you ever have nightmares about someone in your family getting sick, or that you get lost, or even about something happening that stops you from being with your family? How often do you have these dreams?
- Do you like sleeping over at a friend's or relative's home? How did you feel the last time you slept over at someone's home?
- Do you have trouble getting to school in the morning?
- How often are you absent from school?
- How often do you visit the school nurse's office?
- Do you often want to leave school during the day and go home to be with your mother?
- Do you think about your mother often during the day while you are in school?
- Does thinking about your mother make it difficult for you to concentrate on your schoolwork?
- When you are at home, do you get dressed or shower by yourself?
- When you are at home without your mother, who takes care of you? Do you like spending time with him or her when your mother is away?

*The term "mother" should be replaced with "father" or "caregiver" as indicated.

particularly when school refusal is one of the more prominent features. They can report on the frequency of a child's absences, presentation of symptoms, and degree to which symptoms are manifested. Although there are currently no SAD-specific teacher report measures, the Teacher Report Form (TRF; Achenbach, 1991) has been recommended when working with SAD (Perwien & Berstein, 2004).

Interventions

Once SAD has been assessed and diagnosed, the school-based practitioner has sufficient information to decide what intervention will best meet the child's needs. When selecting a treatment, practitioners should consider life stressors (e.g.,

death in family), time constraints (e.g., school setting), level of family involvement, and child's level of functioning. In the following section, we will present a cognitive-behavioral approach for treating SAD and its applicability in the school setting.

The Coping Cat Program: A Cognitive-Behavioral Approach for Treating SAD

Cognitive-behavioral therapy (CBT) for the treatment of anxiety involves both working with the child's external environment through the use of behavioral techniques, such as practice and exposure tasks, and working with the child's internal environment through the mastery of cognitive

Table 6.4 Self-Report Measures With Separation Anxiety Disorder Subscales

Interview	Age	Informant	Length	Characteristic Features of Interview	
				Assessment	*Source*
Multidimensional Anxiety Scale for Children (MASC; March et al., 1997)	8–19	Child	39 items	Four subscales: physical anxiety; harm avoidance; social anxiety; and separation anxiety	John S. March, MD Duke University Medical Center Department of Psychiatry, Box 3527 Durham, NC 27710 919-416-2404 jsmarch@acpub.duke.edu
Screen for Anxiety and Related Emotional Disorders (SCARED; Birmaher et al., 1997)	8–18	Child & Parent	41 items	Five subscales: separation anxiety; school phobia; panic/somatic symptoms, generalized anxiety; social phobia	Boris Birmaher, MD Western Psychiatric Institute & Clinic Department of Child Psychology 3811 O'Hara Street Pittsburgh, PA 15213 412-246-5788 birmaherb@upmc.edu
Spence Children's Anxiety Scale (SCAS; Spence, 1997)	8–12	Child	44 items	Six scales: separation anxiety; social phobia; obsessive–compulsive disorder; panic/agoraphobia; generalized anxiety	Susan H. Spence, PhD University of Queensland Department of Psychology Brisbane, QLD 4072 +61-7-3365-6220 sues@psy.uq.edu.au

techniques, such as positive self-talk and problem solving (Kendall, 2000b).

Although there have been no randomized clinical trials exclusively for SAD (Silverman & Dick-Niederhauser, 2004), the efficacy of using cognitive-behavioral methods for the treatment of SAD has been well documented in case studies (Hagopian & Slifer, 1993; Ollendick, Hagopian, & Huntzinger, 1991; Thyer & Sowers-Hoag, 1988). Some efficacy has been demonstrated for the use of CBT in conjunction with medication (Walkup, Labellarte, & Ginsburg, 2002). However, it is important to note that the pharmacological evidence for treating SAD is limited (Kearney & Silverman, 1998). As such, medication is not recommended as a "front-line intervention" but rather should be used with patients who experience severe SAD symptoms (Silverman & Dick-Niederhauser, 2004, p. 179).

The Coping Cat treatment program developed by Kendall and colleagues (1990) is the only treatment specifically designed to treat children with SAD in addition to related anxiety disorders (Kendall, Aschenbrand, & Hudson, 2003). Coping Cat is an individual, short-term, manualized treatment for children and young adolescents ranging in age from 7 to 13 years old with a principal diagnosis of SAD, GAD, or SoP (Kendall et al., 2003). The program uses a combination of behavioral strategies to achieve the following treatment goals (Kendall & Southam-Gerow, 1995):

- Identifying anxious feelings and the body's response to the anxiety
- Understanding the role that self-talk plays in worsening the anxiety
- Increasing the capability to deal with anxiety by utilizing problem-solving and coping techniques
- Evaluating one's use of coping strategies and provision of appropriate rewards

Empirical Support for Coping Cat

The effectiveness of the Coping Cat program has been well documented in the literature (Kendall, 1994; Kendall et al., 1997; Kendall & Southam-Gerow, 1996). It is identified as the "most widely disseminated CBT protocol for childhood anxiety" (Velting et al., 2004, p. 48) and has been used with success in the United States (Kendall, 1994), Australia (Barrett, Dadds, & Rapee, 1996), and Canada (Mendlowitz et al., 1999). Coping Cat is

highly adaptable and has proven effective when used in a group format (Barrett, 1998; Cobham et al., 1998; Flannery-Schroeder & Kendall, 2000; Silverman et al., 1999) and in conjunction with family anxiety management (Barrett et al., 1996). Additionally, the Coping Cat program is efficacious across different ethnic groups and genders (Treadwell, Flannery-Schroeder, & Kendall, 1995).

Implementing the Coping Cat Program

Detailed guidelines for implementing the Coping Cat program are found in *Cognitive-Behavioral Therapy for Anxious Children: Therapist Manual* (Kendall, 2000a). Information about purchasing this manual is available at www.WorkbookPublishing.com. In addition to the *Therapist Manual*, a *Coping Cat Workbook* (Kendall, 1992) is available for children to use throughout treatment. The workbook facilitates the implementation of the treatment manual by providing child-friendly tasks that help the child to understand and apply treatment concepts more easily. The accompanying notebook allows the child to record homework assignments (Show-That-I-Can tasks) that reinforce strategies learned during the session. In the next section we will describe the Coping Cat program for anxious youth ages 7–13. A version for older adolescents also exists: the C.A.T. program (Kendall, Choudhury, Hudson, & Webb, 2002a, 2002b).

Training and Supervision

Coping Cat requires proper training and supervision for successful program implementation. Although there is no set protocol for training clinicians in the use of Coping Cat, training in a manualized treatment generally involves introduction to the manual, reading and learning the manual through seminars and/or workshops, and group or individual supervision (Miller & Binder, 2002). Supervision addresses the extent to which session goals were met by the clinician and the degree to which the treatment meets individual patient needs while maintaining the integrity of the protocol (Kendall & Southam-Gerow, 1995). As mentioned previously, this chapter will provide an overview of the Coping Cat program and offer specific suggestions for using it in a school setting for the treatment of SAD. This chapter is not meant to replace the treatment manual or appropriate training and supervision from a clinician knowledgeable in the Coping Cat program. It is highly recommended that school-based practitioners interested in using the Coping Cat program with their clients read the manual and receive proper supervision before doing so.

Flexibility With the Manual

Research indicates that flexible application of the Coping Cat manual does not lead to poor treatment outcomes (Kendall & Chu, 2000). It is likely that school-based practitioners will have to make modifications to the manual in order to use it effectively in a school setting. For example, practitioners may need to cover less material in a given session in order to fit sessions into a school schedule. This type of flexibility is acceptable and encouraged.

Role of the Family in Implementation

Family involvement is essential when implementing the Coping Cat program. It is important that the family be involved in the assessment, planning, and execution of treatment goals. This is especially the case for children with SAD given that their fears are directly related to separation from their parents. Parents are involved during the assessment phase of treatment by providing valuable information on the manifestation of symptoms and history through verbal reports and completion of parent assessment scales. In some cases, the assessment phase may be the first interaction with the family and serves as an opportunity to establish rapport with the family (Kendall & Gosch, 1994). Parent sessions are integrated into the course of treatment in order to provide additional opportunities for open dialogue between therapist and family, to allow therapists to get feedback from parents and track the progress of treatment, and to coach parents on how to help their child cope with anxiety (Kendall & Gosch, 1994).

Role of Teachers in Implementation

Not only can teachers play an active role in the identification of SAD behaviors, they can also provide valuable information on the course of SAD symptoms and aid in the implementation of treatment. Given their everyday contact with the child, they are the most likely to notice fluctuations in behavior throughout treatment and should be encouraged to share these observations with the school-based practitioner. Additionally, teachers can facilitate treatment by participating in exposure exercises when appropriate, monitoring a child's visits to the school-based medical clinic in response to somatic symptoms associated with SAD, limiting these visits, and restricting the child's contact with parents throughout the school day (Perwien & Berstein, 2004).

The Coping Cat Program: Sequence and Content of Child Sessions

The main goal of the Coping Cat program is to teach children and young adolescents how to "recognize signs of unwanted anxious arousal and to let these signs serve as cues for the use of the strategies the child has learned" (Kendall et al., 2003, p. 84). The treatment involves 14–18 sessions completed over the course of 12–16 weeks. However, the program may need to be adapted to a shorter number of sessions in order to fit into the academic calendar. Additionally, the length of each session may need to be shortened to 40–45 minutes in order to better fit the scheduling demands of school settings.

Scheduling treatment sessions during school hours may prove to be challenging. Teachers may be reluctant to allow the child to leave the classroom to meet with the therapist during class time. As such, it is recommended that sessions be scheduled flexibly around school periods that involve elective classes (e.g., gym, music) or any free periods (e.g., study hall). It also may be difficult to schedule parent sessions during school hours. In some cases, it may be necessary for school practitioners to involve parents in treatment through telephone rather than face-to-face sessions.

Treatment includes a training phase and a practice phase. During the training phase (sessions 1–8), the child learns different techniques to cope with anxiety-provoking situations. In the practice phase, the child begins to practice learned coping techniques within the session or in vivo (sessions 9–18) (Kendall, 2000a). Show-That-I-Can (STIC) homework tasks are introduced during each session. STIC tasks give the child an opportunity to recap what is learned in the session and apply it in the form of an at-home assignment. Each session begins with a review of the assignment and positive reinforcement from the therapist for completed tasks. The following section summarizes the Coping Cat sessions while highlighting the key tasks for each. The session summaries are not meant to replace the manual but to introduce the session content to school-based practitioners.

The Coping Cat Training Phase (Sessions 1–8)

During the training phase, ideas and tasks are introduced to the child in order from simplest to more complex. The segment begins with the child's awareness of how the body reacts to anxious situations and learning to use these reactions as internal cues that anxiety is present. These concepts are presented in a child-friendly four-step plan with the acronym FEAR (*Feeling Frightened? Expecting bad things to happen? Attitudes and Actions that will help? Results and Rewards?*).

Session 1: Program Orientation

The training phase begins with the therapist establishing rapport with the child. The therapist assumes the role of a "coach" as she works together with the child throughout the Coping Cat program. In this first session, the therapist provides the child with an overview of what treatment entails while at the same time collecting information about what situations make the child anxious. Together, the therapist and child identify those situations that trigger the child's anxious reactions (e.g., when child is dropped off at school; when parent goes to bed and leaves child alone in bedroom; when parent goes away on vacation). Treatment goals are introduced as well as the utility of the *Coping Cat Workbook* and *Coping Cat Notebook* in meeting these goals.

Session 2: Identifying Anxious Feelings

The second session focuses on the link between anxious feelings and how different feelings manifest themselves in physical expressions. One of the goals of this session is to normalize the experience of fears and explain that the program is to help cope with these feelings. The therapist models having experienced anxiety-provoking situations and overcoming them. Additionally, role play ("feelings charades") is used to facilitate the child's understanding that different feelings have

different physical expressions. A "feelings dictionary" is then created to help the child identify the associated feelings.

As the child identifies the somatic feelings he experiences when feeling anxious, he begins to construct a fear hierarchy that ranks these feelings from least to most anxiety provoking. The fear hierarchy is developed over time beginning with the identification of low anxiety-provoking situations during the first sessions and then medium and high anxiety-provoking situations in subsequent sessions. For the SAD child, a low-anxiety situation may involve the mother cooking in the kitchen while the child is watching television in the living room. A medium anxiety-provoking situation may be staying home with a babysitter for a few hours while a high-anxiety situation may involve the mother leaving the home for business travel.

In the case of the school refuser, it is important to assess whether refusal is due to a phobia or to separation. Other low-stress situations that are not necessarily related to school or separation from parents are explored. Showing empathy is particularly important at this stage, given that children with SAD often experience a lot of anger from parents and teachers about missing school. Specific strategies, like making a "survival pack" (e.g., stickers, helpful positive thoughts, or coping strategies that can be brought to school), are implemented to remind the child of the learned coping strategies. Additionally, an in-school reward, such as making contact with a favorite teacher or counselor, is recommended.

Session 3: Recognizing Somatic Responses to Anxiety

Here, the child learns about the different somatic responses that are felt when in anxiety-provoking situations and how these responses serve as internal cues that anxiety is present. During this session, the first step of the coping plan—"F" (*Feeling Frightened?*)—is introduced. The therapist and child review specific somatic reactions to anxiety (e.g., stomach pains, nausea, headaches) and the differences between low and high anxiety. Imagery, modeling, and role-play strategies are used to help the child verbalize somatic feelings during an identified low-anxiety situation. Although the therapist will often take the lead in initiating these exercises, the child is encouraged to "tag along" by adding his feelings to the role play. Throughout the session, the child practices using his somatic responses as cues with higher-anxiety situations (via modeling and role-play exercises). The coping concept of "freeze frame" is introduced to allow the child to stop the anxiety-provoking situation, take a deep breath, and regroup.

Parent Session 1: Engaging the Parent

The primary purpose of the first parent session is to encourage parental cooperation in treatment. During this session, the therapist provides the parent with information about the treatment and discusses the child's progress in treatment. The parent is encouraged to ask questions regarding the treatment and to provide additional information about the child's anxiety (i.e., identify troublesome situations and somatic/cognitive reactions).

Parents often need to be reminded that the beginning sessions are only training and that reductions in symptoms will not be seen until later when the skills learned during the training are applied and practiced. During the first parent session, the therapist should also discuss with parents the active role they will be required to take in treatment (e.g., practice the relaxation techniques to be learned in session 4 at home with their child, help their child with STIC tasks).

When working with SAD children who refuse to go to school, it is important to assess stressors in the home or community that may potentially interfere with the course of treatment. The therapist should explore whether the parent is facilitating the behavior through their fears or inability to cope with disruptive behaviors (e.g., tantrums, crying). It is also important to address parental concerns and to provide strategies the parents can use to cope with their child's illness. Also, parents should be strongly encouraged to reward any attempts by the child to go to school as a means of reinforcing the behavior.

Session 4: Relaxation Training

During the fourth session, the therapist teaches the child relaxation techniques that can be used to alleviate symptoms of anxiety. Here, the child identifies the connection between anxiety and muscle tension. The therapist introduces the concept of relaxation by differentiating how the body feels when relaxed versus tense (e.g., have child lift shoulders as high as possible and then release) and by introducing relaxation procedures, such as deep breathing, visualization, and deep muscle tension and relaxation. (This exercise takes

approximately 15 minutes.) Together, the therapist and child tape-record a relaxation script and practice using relaxation, coping modeling, and role playing in anxious situations.

Session 5: Identifying Anxious Self-Talk

As the child becomes aware of his bodily responses, he is also taught to become aware of his thoughts during anxiety-provoking situations. In the fifth session, the child begins to identify his self-talk during anxiety-provoking situations with the goal of reducing anxiety-provoking self-talk and using more coping self-talk. Here, the "E" step (*Expecting bad things to happen?*) is introduced to help the child identify thoughts associated with anxiety and the differences between anxious thoughts and coping thoughts. The child can use cartoon bubbles to identify thoughts that reduce stress and thoughts that might induce stress (see workbook). Through modeling and role play, the child practices coping self-talk, detecting possible thinking traps, and coping in more anxiety-provoking situations.

Session 6: Identifying Coping Thoughts and Actions

During this session, the child is taught how to cope in an anxiety-provoking situation. The therapist introduces the "A" step (*Attitudes and Actions that will help?*). In this sixth session, problem solving is introduced and an action plan is developed to help the child cope in anxious situations. Both the therapist and the child practice problem solving with low- and moderate-stress situations and then practice with increasingly higher-anxiety situations.

Session 7: Self-Evaluation and Rewards

In the seventh session, self-rating and rewards are introduced as the final step ("R": *Results and Rewards*) of the coping plan. Here, the child learns how to evaluate his own work and reward successes. The child uses a "feelings barometer" to rate his performance and is encouraged to practice self-rating and -rewarding in stressful situations (e.g., how well did I handle the situation?).

Session 8: FEAR Plan Review

By the eighth session, the child has already learned the main anxiety coping skills covered in the Coping Cat program. To help facilitate recall of these strategies, they are conceptualized in a child-friendly four-step plan called the FEAR plan. During this session, the child creates a FEAR plan poster to illustrate the strategies learned. Additionally, a wallet-sized FEAR card is created for the child to help remember the strategies learned and to use as an anchor during anxiety-provoking situations. The FEAR plan is practiced (via modeling/role play) during the session beginning with nonstressful situations and continuing with increasingly anxious situations.

The Coping Cat Practice Phase (Sessions 9–16)

The second half of treatment is the practice phase. During this phase, the child applies the skills learned during the training phase to situations that elicit anxiety. The child is exposed to anxiety-provoking situations gradually, moving along a continuum from low-grade anxiety to higher grades of anxiety. The practice phase of treatment begins with a parent session.

Parent Session 2: Introduction to Practice Phase of Treatment

A second parent meeting is planned to introduce the parent to the practice phase of treatment. The therapist explains to the parent that the child will begin to practice the learned coping skills, and this will most probably make him appear to be more anxious. The exposure and practice goals of treatment are reviewed with the parent as well as ways in which the parent can support the child in what has been learned and continue to encourage the child's efforts.

Sessions 9–10: Exposure to Low-Anxiety Scenarios

In the 9th and 10th treatment sessions, the therapist initiates and continues to practice the FEAR plan with low-anxiety-provoking situations using exposure strategies in both imaginal and in vivo scenarios. It is important to "acknowledge that this portion of treatment will provoke greater anxiety" (Kendall et al., 2003, p. 85).

The ninth session begins with a shift from learning skills to practicing the learned skills in real situations (the fear hierarchy is reviewed). Imaginal exposure exercises are implemented using the FEAR plan with low-anxiety situations

(coping modeling) followed by in-session exposure exercises (e.g., for students with SAD, naturally occurring scenarios can be created in schools with the help of teachers and guidance counselors). In order to assess the extent to which the child experiences distress during exposure exercises, the subjective units of distress scale (SUDS) may be used. The therapist and child plan for additional exposure exercises to be implemented at home with the parents.

Imaginal and in-session exposure exercises with low-anxiety-provoking situations (implementation of FEAR plan through coping modeling) are continued through the 10th session. One anxiety-provoking scenario may have several anxiety-provoking elements, which should be tackled one at a time. It is important that the therapist collaborate with the child in planning more challenging situations to practice during the following treatment session.

Sessions 11–12: Exposure to Moderate-Anxiety Scenarios

During these sessions, the child practices the FEAR coping plan in situations that produce moderate anxiety. In addition to using imaginal and in-session exposure to practice the FEAR plan, the therapist may want to initiate the child's first out-of-office exposure.

Sessions 13–14: Exposure to High-Anxiety Scenarios

Sessions 13 and 14 focus on the application of the FEAR plan to situations that produce high anxiety. Imaginal exposure exercises with high-anxiety-provoking situations are implemented via modeling and role-play exercises. Throughout these two sessions, the child is reminded to use relaxation exercises to help control anxiety levels. As the child masters the imaginal exposure exercises, in-session exposure exercises are implemented with high-anxiety-provoking situations.

The idea of a commercial is introduced in session 14 as an informational piece, created by the child, to tell children how to manage anxiety. Producing a commercial will allow the child to act and feel like an expert on his own treatment and will provide a venue for the practitioner to observe what the child has learned over the course of therapy. The commercial can also be shared with others as evidence of the child's accomplishments.

Sessions 15–16: Making the Commercial

During sessions 15 and 16, the child continues to engage in in-vivo exposures in high-stress situations and to practice the FEAR plan. The therapist also begins to address anticipated concerns with termination while reinforcing the therapist's confidence in the child's ability to continue to progress on his own. Time is allotted in between sessions to allow the child to practice the FEAR coping skills on his own. As such, telephone check-ins are scheduled in between sessions as a means of providing more distanced support from the therapist.

The child, together with the therapist, begins to more actively plan the commercial. By session 16, the therapist reviews and summarizes the Coping Cat program. The commercial or audiotape "testimonial" is made, and the child's family is invited to view the commercial with the child and therapist.

Termination Session

The termination session, scheduled one week following the 16th session, is an opportunity for the therapist to provide feedback to the child and family on the child's overall progress in treatment and to comment on the child's strengths and weaknesses.

During this session, the child is presented with a certificate of completion ("goodbye ritual"), and the therapist establishes posttreatment plans with the parent that focus on helping the child to maintain and generalize his newly acquired skills. A check-in call is scheduled in 4 weeks, and future booster sessions are offered thereafter if needed.

Tools and Practice Example

Practice Example

Diego is an 8-year-old boy in the third grade, living in a single-parent home with his mother, Ms. Peña. His teacher, Miss Phillips, referred him to the school-based mental health clinic (SBMHC). Miss Phillips reported that Diego has been excessively absent in the last couple of months. When he does attend class, he arrives late, tearful, and in an irritable mood. When questioned about his tearfulness, he tells Miss Phillips that he feels sick and wants to go home. Attempts to go home are often unsuccessful. On these days, he seems distracted for most of the day and refuses to engage in school tasks. Miss Phillips reported that his behavior is worsening and is beginning to disrupt his learning.

The school-based therapist contacted Diego's mother following the teacher's referral. Ms. Peña recently started working in a perfume factory where she puts in long work hours and has an erratic work schedule. Although she acknowledged Miss Phillips's report of Diego's symptoms, she expressed that this is just a phase he is going through. Ms. Peña assured the therapist that she tries her best to bring Diego to school in order to force him to "get over it" but admits that she often gives in because "he acts up way too much." Additionally, Ms. Peña expressed disappointment with the school staff for being so impatient with Diego and not understanding that his refusal to go to school is just a phase. In the spirit of building rapport with Ms. Peña, the therapist acknowledged Ms. Peña's frustrations in dealing with Diego's behaviors and invited her to come to the SBMHC with Diego for a preliminary assessment.

Assessing for Separation Anxiety Disorder

The therapist met with Diego and Ms. Peña to get some information about Diego's symptoms and to assess the extent of impairment they may be causing. Ms. Peña reported that Diego has been refusing to go to school for more than 3 months. His school avoidance leaves Ms. Peña feeling distressed given that it interferes with her work and social life. On the days she is unable to get Diego to school, she calls in sick to stay home and take care of him. On the days she does get to work, his morning tantrums make her late and his somatic symptoms require her to leave work early to pick him up from school. She also finds that she has little time for herself given his refusal to go anywhere outside the home without her. Additionally, Diego has been sleeping with Ms. Peña for the past 2 months because of recurrent nightmares that something "bad" is going to happen to her. Ms. Peña reported no other psychosocial stressors.

When it was Diego's turn to meet with the therapist alone, Diego appeared quite distressed about his mother leaving the room. Throughout the session, Diego consistently sought reassurance of his mother's whereabouts by opening the door of the therapist's office to see if she was still in the waiting room. The therapist used the SAD section of the Anxiety Disorders Interview Scale (ADIS; Silverman & Nelles, 1988) as a guide while interviewing Diego regarding his SAD symptoms. During the interview, Diego shared that when he thinks of something bad happening to his mother (e.g., car accident) his "tummy hurts real bad." Although Diego identified a few friends with whom he enjoys spending time, most of his social activities are limited to home since he refuses to go to a friend's home unless his mother accompanies him.

The assessment concluded with completion of the Screen for Anxiety and Related Emotional Disorders (SCARED; Birmaher et al., 1997) measure by both Diego and his mother. The therapist explained that the SCARED would be useful for assessing the severity of Diego's symptoms and monitoring his progress throughout treatment. Scores on the SAD subscale of the SCARED reflected significant impairment. After a careful review of Diego's symptoms, the therapist concluded that Diego met *DSM-IV-TR* diagnostic criteria for SAD and decided to use the Coping Cat program as the intervention of choice.

Implementing a 12-Week Coping Cat Program

Setting Up the FEAR Plan

The primary focus of the first phase of treatment was to help Diego learn the coping strategies of the FEAR plan. In order to help Diego link his bodily reactions to an emotion, the therapist and Diego played "feelings charades." Diego enjoyed playing the game and was able to identify feelings and their associated physical expressions. Diego then worked with the therapist to construct a fear hierarchy in which a low-anxiety situation was identified as sitting in the therapist's office alone while his mother stayed in the waiting area; a medium-anxiety-provoking situation was identified as going to sleep by himself in his room; and a high-anxiety situation was spending a night at his grandma's house without contacting his mother. Beginning with the situation that caused the least stress, the therapist modeled the first step of the FEAR plan (F: Feeling Frightened?). Diego role played a low-anxiety scenario where he recognized

that the tightening of his chest was a clue that he was feeling anxious about not being able to check and see if his mother was still in the waiting room.

Mastering the second step in the FEAR plan (E: Expecting bad things to happen?) was not so easy. The therapist used the cartoons and empty thought bubbles in the Coping Cat workbook to help Diego master this concept. After much practice, Diego gradually was able to identify what thoughts made him anxious during his day-to-day experiences. The therapist coached Diego to use thoughts that reduce stress (coping self-talk) instead of those that induce it (anxious self-talk). The therapist and Diego practiced using coping self-talk when imagining Diego's fears of sleeping alone in his room. Diego repeated this exercise several times with different anxiety-provoking scenarios.

In the following sessions, the therapist and Diego explored some ideas about what he can do when he is anxious. During this problem-solving exercise (FEAR step A: Attitudes and Actions that will help?), Diego listed actions he could take, such as using deep-breathing exercises when alone in his room. The therapist referred to Diego's hierarchy of anxiety and modeled problem solving at bedtime. Diego recognized his anxious feelings and thoughts while getting ready to go to bed, joined in the role play, and acted out how he would listen to his favorite audio book while in bed.

Implementing the final coping step (R: Results and Rewards?) was challenging given the constant negative feedback Diego received from school staff and his mother in response to his SAD symptoms. Diego felt "bad" and undeserving of anything "good." His low self-esteem hindered his ability to evaluate his performance. The therapist worked with Diego on how to rate his own performance and praise his efforts even if the end result was not what he wanted. The therapist used Diego's past successes during session practices as examples of how Diego could rate himself positively. Diego enjoyed planning for potential rewards for successful efforts. When the therapist checked in with Ms. Peña, she expressed reluctance to reward Diego for behaviors such as going to school. She believed that Diego's attendance was to be expected and did not merit a reward. The therapist educated Ms. Peña on the importance of reinforcing positive behavior to sustain those behaviors that are desirable (i.e., going to school). Ms. Peña was receptive to the therapist's suggestions and rewarded Diego's efforts more consistently as she became comfortable with the concept of rewards.

By the end of the training phase, the therapist and Diego worked on creating a poster that illustrated the FEAR plan. Diego used bright-colored markers to detail each of the four steps to the FEAR plan while adding cut-outs from magazines that had phrases to help him recall different aspects of the plan. Diego then created a wallet-sized card and wrote the FEAR acronym on it. The FEAR card was in Diego's possession at all times and served as an anchor for him to refer to when confronting an anxiety-provoking situation.

Coping Cat Practice Phase

The main treatment goals of the second phase of treatment were to practice the FEAR plan in actual anxiety-provoking situations. Exposure to these situations was gradual, beginning with exposure to low-level situations and gradually progressing to higher-level situations.

During the beginning of the practice phase, the therapist met with Ms. Peña to review this phase of treatment. Ms. Peña was forewarned that Diego might appear more anxious in the next couple of weeks given his repeated exposure to anxiety-provoking situations. Ms. Peña was reminded of the importance of being a support for Diego and to continue praising his efforts and providing rewards for successes.

The first series of exposure sessions began with low-anxiety situations using both imaginal and in vivo exposure. For the imaginal exposure, the goal was for Diego to stay in his bedroom for 1 hour while his mother was cooking dinner in the kitchen. The therapist set up the situation as realistically as possible by hiding behind a bookcase in the office to represent the wall that separates Diego's room from the kitchen. Diego identified the stressor, used the feeling barometer to rate his anxiety, and problem solved how he would cope. The therapist later identified an anxiety-producing situation to be practiced in the office. Diego's goal was to stay in the therapist's office for the entire session without checking (e.g., opening the office door, calling out to his mother) to see if his mother was still in the waiting room. Additional in vivo exercises were practiced using low-level anxiety-provoking situations.

During the second series of exposures, the therapist referred to Diego's hierarchy of anxiety to select a situation of moderate anxiety for imaginal exposure. The first situation required Diego to imagine going to his cousin Jimmy's house to watch a movie without his mother. His mother would take him to Jimmy's home and pick him up when the movie was over. Through modeling and role play, Diego implemented the FEAR plan in this situation.

For the in vivo exposure, the goal was to implement the FEAR plan in the classroom upon arrival at school. The session was scheduled in the early morning and required collaboration between the therapist and Miss Phillips. On this day, Diego verbalized that he was feeling a bit queasy and recognized it was a signal that he was anxious because his mother had just dropped him off. Miss Phillips facilitated the exposure by reminding Diego to pull out his FEAR card. Diego sat through first period without requesting to go to the nurse's office. He was very proud of himself for his success and asked for his stickers as promised by Miss Phillips. Additional in vivo exposures for moderate-anxiety-provoking situations were practiced in subsequent sessions.

The third in vivo exposure involved a high-anxiety situation. For Diego, this involved a one-night stay at his grandma's house without calling his mother. The therapist helped Diego to practice this situation in session by inviting his grandma to the office. The therapist coached his grandma on how to support Diego through the exercise. Diego identified the somatic cues (e.g., feeling sick) he experiences at grandma's house. He also identified for both his grandma and therapist his anxious thoughts about sleeping over without his mother (e.g., Mom will never come back to get me!) and how he would use coping thoughts instead (e.g., Mom has shown that she loves me very much and would not leave me at grandma's). Diego planned to evaluate his efforts the next morning and reward his successes. Grandma, armed with an understanding of Diego's action plan, detailed how she would support Diego by giving him reminders of the FEAR strategy, offering to participate in relaxation techniques, and praising his efforts throughout his stay. For additional support, the therapist arranged to conduct a telephone check that night to reassure Diego that she was confident he could do it on his own.

Termination

Diego was fully aware of the progress he had made throughout the course of treatment and was looking forward to sharing what he learned with other kids. Given the limited resources at the school, the therapist and Diego opted for creating a brochure to present his message to other children rather than filming a commercial. Multiple copies of the brochure were made so that he could distribute it to family and friends.

The therapist met with Ms. Peña and devised a maintenance plan for Diego's learned coping skills. Ms. Peña reported a reduction in Diego's symptoms and seemed quite pleased with his progression throughout treatment. This was corroborated by the low SAD score on the SCARED measure completed by Ms. Peña and Diego. As a final reward for Diego's successful efforts, the therapist and Diego played basketball (Diego's favorite sport) in the school gym. The session ended with a goodbye ritual during which Diego was presented with a certificate of completion by the therapist in recognition of his participation in and successful completion of the Coping Cat program.

▎ Resources

Coping Cat Program: Cognitive-Behavioral Intervention for Anxious Youth (Ages 8–13)

Philip C. Kendall, *Cognitive-Behavioral Therapy for Anxious Children: Therapist Manual* (2nd ed.). Temple University. www.workbookpublishing.com

Philip C. Kendall, *Coping Cat Workbook*. Temple University. www.workbookpublishing.com

Ellen Flannery-Schroeder & Philip C. Kendall, *Cognitive-Behavioral Therapy for Anxious Children: Therapist Manual for Group Treatment*. Temple University. www.workbookpublishing.com

Bonnie Howard, Brian C. Chu, Amy L. Krain, Abbe L. Marrs-Garcia, & Philip C. Kendall, *Cognitive-Behavioral Family Therapy for Anxious Children: Therapist Manual* (2nd ed.). Temple University. www.workbookpublishing.com

Philip C. Kendall & W. Michael Nelson III, *Managing Anxiety in Youth: The "Coping Cat" Video*. Xavier University. www.workbookpublishing.com

The C.A.T. Project: Cognitive-Behavioral Intervention for Anxious Older Youth (Ages 14–17)

Philip C. Kendall, Muniya Choudhury, Jennifer Hudson, & Alicia Webb, *The C.A.T. Project Workbook for the Cognitive-Behavioral Treatment of Anxious Adolescents*. Temple University. www.workbook publishing.com

Philip C. Kendall, Muniya Choudhury, Jennifer Hudson, & Alicia Webb, *The C.A.T. Project Manual for the Cognitive Behavioral Treatment of Anxious Adolescents*. Temple University. www.workbookpublishing.com

Children's Books on Separation Anxiety

Elizabeth Crary & Marina Megale, *Mommy, Don't Go*. Reading level: Ages 4–8.

Irene Wineman Marcus, Paul Marcus, & Susan Jeschke, *Into the Great Forest: A Story for Children Away From Parents for the First Time*. Reading level: Ages 4–8

Judith Viorst, *The Good-Bye Book*. Reading level: Ages 4–8

Anxiety Organizations

Child & Adolescent Anxiety Disorders Clinic (CAADC). Temple University. 13th Street & Cecil B. Moore Avenue (Weiss Hall, Ground Level), Philadelphia, PA 19122. www.childanxiety.org

The Child Anxiety Network, Child and Adolescent Fear and Anxiety Treatment Program. 648 Beacon Street, 6th floor, Kenmore Square, Boston, MA 02215. 617-353-9610. www.childanxiety.net

Anxiety Disorder Association of America. 8730 Georgia Avenue, Suite 600, Silver Spring, MD 20910. 240-485-1001. www.adaa.org

▏ Key Points to Remember

SAD is one of the most frequently reported disorders in the school setting. The literature on treating SAD indicates that cognitive-behavioral therapy (CBT) is the intervention of choice for treating the disorder. The Coping Cat program is particularly useful in treating SAD in schools given its demonstrated effectiveness, transportability, and adaptability across diverse settings.

Implementing the Coping Cat program in the school setting requires some flexibility on the part of the school-based practitioner. Some of the factors that school-based therapists should keep in mind when implementing Coping Cat are summarized as follows:

- High comorbidity of SAD with other anxiety disorders requires that differential diagnoses be assessed thoroughly. This is especially true for children presenting with school refusal, given its similarity to school or social phobia.

- Teachers are instrumental in identifying SAD kids when provided with the resources to do so.
- Assessment of SAD is most comprehensive when multiple informants provide information on the manifestation of symptoms. Clinical interviews, self-reports (including parent versions), and teacher reports are strongly encouraged.
- The Coping Cat manual and accompanying workbook and notebook are essential tools for the delivery of CBT for SAD but must be used flexibly. Readers should obtain and read the manual prior to administering the treatment.
- Appropriate training and supervision are necessary for implementing Coping Cat.
- Family involvement throughout treatment will greatly enhance treatment effects. Parents are not only in the best position for reporting SAD symptoms but should participate actively in facilitating and reinforcing the strategies learned throughout treatment.

References

Achenbach, T. (1991). *Manual for the teacher's report form and 1991 profile.* Burlington: University of Vermont, Department of Psychiatry.

Albano, A. M. (2003). Treatment of social anxiety disorder. In M. A. Reinecke & F. M. Dattilio (Eds.), *Cognitive therapy with children and adolescents: A casebook for clinical practice* (2nd ed., pp. 128–161). New York: Guilford.

Albano, A. M., & Kendall, P. C. (2002). Cognitive behavioral therapy for children and adolescents with anxiety disorders: Clinical research advances. *International Review of Psychiatry, 14*(2), 129–134.

American Psychiatric Association. (2000). *Diagnostic and statistical manual of mental disorders* (4th ed., text revision). Washington, DC: Author.

Angold, A., & Costello, E. J. (2000). The Child and Adolescent Psychiatric Assessment (CAPA). *Journal of the American Academy of Child & Adolescent Psychiatry, 39*(1), 39–48.

Barrett, P. M. (1998). Evaluation of cognitive-behavioral group treatments for childhood anxiety disorders. *Journal of Clinical Child Psychology, 27*(4), 459–468.

Barrett, P. M., Dadds, M. R., & Rapee, R. M. (1996). Family treatment of childhood anxiety: A controlled trial. *Journal of Consulting & Clinical Psychology, 64*(2), 333–342.

Birmaher, B., Khetarpal, S., Brent, D., Cully, M., Balach, L., Kaufman, J., & Neer, S. M. (1997). The Screen for Child Anxiety Related Emotional Disorders (SCARED): Scale construction and psychometric characteristics. *Journal of the American Academy of Child & Adolescent Psychiatry, 36*(4), 545–553.

Carruth, S. G. (2000). Separation anxiety disorder: Planning treatment. *Pediatrics in Review, 21*(7), 248.

Cobham, V. E., Dadds, M. R., & Spence, S. H. (1998). The role of parental anxiety in the treatment of childhood anxiety. *Journal of Consulting & Clinical Psychology, 66*(6), 893–905.

Compton, S. N., Nelson, A. H., & March, J. S. (2000). Social phobia and separation anxiety symptoms in community and clinical samples of children and adolescents. *Journal of the American Academy of Child & Adolescent Psychiatry, 39*(8), 1040–1046.

Fischer, D. J., Himle, J. A., & Thyer, B. A. (1999). Separation anxiety disorder. In R. T. Ammerman, M. Hersen, & C. G. Last (Eds.), *Handbook of prescriptive treatments for children and adolescents* (2nd ed., pp. 141–154). Needham Heights, MA: Allyn & Bacon.

Flannery-Schroeder, E. C., & Kendall, P. C. (2000). Group and individual cognitive-behavioral treatments for youth with anxiety disorders: A randomized clinical trial. *Cognitive Therapy & Research, 24*(3), 251–278.

Francis, G., Last, C. G., & Strauss, C. C. (1987). Expression of separation anxiety disorder: The roles of age and gender. *Child Psychiatry & Human Development, 18*(2), 82–89.

Gittelman, R., & Klein, D. F. (1984). Relationship between separation anxiety and panic and agoraphobic disorders. *Psychopathology, 17*(Suppl. 1), 56–65.

Hagopian, L. P., & Slifer, K. J. (1993). Treatment of separation anxiety disorder with graduated exposure and reinforcement targeting school attendance: A controlled case study. *Journal of Anxiety Disorders, 7*(3), 271–280.

James, E. M., Reynolds, C. R., & Dunbar, J. (1994). Self-report instruments. In T. H. Ollendick, N. J. King, & W. Yule (Eds.), *International handbook of phobic and anxiety disorders in children and adolescents* (pp. 317–329). New York: Plenum.

Kearney, C. A., & Silverman, W. K. (1993). Measuring the function of school refusal behavior: The School Assessment Scale. *Journal of Clinical Child Psychology, 22*(1), 85–96.

Kearney, C. A., & Silverman, W. K. (1998). A critical review of pharmacotherapy for youth with anxiety disorders: Things are not as they seem. *Journal of Anxiety Disorders, 12*(2), 83–102.

Kendall, P. C. (1992). *Coping Cat workbook.* Ardmore, PA: Workbook Publishing.

Kendall, P. C. (1994). Treating anxiety disorders in children: Results of a randomized clinical trial. *Journal of Consulting & Clinical Psychology, 62*(1), 100–110.

Kendall, P. C. (2000a). *Cognitive-behavioral therapy for anxious children: Therapist manual* (2nd ed.). Ardmore, PA: Workbook Publishing.

Kendall, P. C. (2000b). Guiding theory for therapy with children and adolescents. In P. C. Kendall (Ed.), *Child and adolescent therapy: Cognitive-behavioral procedures* (2nd ed., pp. 3–27). New York: Guilford.

Kendall, P. C., Aschenbrand, S. G., & Hudson, J. L. (2003). Child-focused treatment of anxiety. In A. E. Kazdin &

J. R. Weisz (Eds.), *Evidence-based psychotherapies for children and adolescents* (pp. 81–100). New York: Guilford.

Kendall, P. C., Choudhury, M., Hudson, J., & Webb, A. (2002a). *The C.A.T. project therapist manual.* Ardmore, PA: Workbook Publishing.

Kendall, P. C., Choudhury, M., Hudson, J., & Webb, A. (2002b). *The C.A.T. project workbook for the cognitive-behavioral treatment of anxious adolescents.* Ardmore, PA: Workbook Publishing.

Kendall, P. C., & Chu, B. C. (2000). Retrospective self-reports of therapist flexibility in a manual-based treatment for youths with anxiety disorders. *Journal of Clinical Child Psychology, 29*(2), 209–220.

Kendall, P. C., Flannery-Schroeder, E., Panichelli-Mindel, S. M., Southam-Gerow, M., Henin, A., & Warman, M. (1997). Therapy for youths with anxiety disorders: A second randomized clinical trial. *Journal of Consulting & Clinical Psychology, 65*(3), 366–380.

Kendall, P. C., & Gosch, E. A. (1994). Cognitive-behavioral interventions In T. H. Ollendick, N. J. King, & W. Yule (Eds.), *International handbook of phobic and anxiety disorders in children and adolescents* (pp. 415–438). New York: Plenum.

Kendall, P. C., Kane, M., Howard, B., & Siqueland, L. (1990). *Cognitive-behavioral treatment of anxious children: Treatment manual.* (Available from P. C. Kendall, Department of Psychology, Temple University, Philadelphia, PA 19122)

Kendall, P. C., & Southam-Gerow, M. A. (1995). Issues in the transportability of treatment: The case of anxiety disorders in youths. *Journal of Consulting & Clinical Psychology, 63*(5), 702–708.

Kendall, P. C., & Southam-Gerow, M. A. (1996). Long-term follow-up of a cognitive-behavioral therapy for anxiety-disordered youth. *Journal of Consulting & Clinical Psychology, 64*(4), 724–730.

Langley, A. K., Bergman, R. L., & Piacentini, J. C. (2002). Assessment of childhood anxiety. *International Review of Psychiatry, 14*(2), 102–113.

Last, C. G., Hersen, M., Kazdin, A. E., Finkelstein, R., & Strauss, C. C. (1987). Comparison of DSM-III separation anxiety and overanxious disorders: Demographic characteristics and patterns of comorbidity. *Journal of the American Academy of Child & Adolescent Psychiatry, 26*(4), 527–531.

March, J. S., Parker, J. D. A., Sullivan, K., Stallings, P., & Conners, C. K. (1997). The Multidimensional Anxiety Scale for Children (MASC): Factor structure, reliability, and validity. *Journal of the American Academy of Child & Adolescent Psychiatry, 36*(4), 554–565.

Mendlowitz, S. L., Manassis, K., Bradley, S., Scapillato, D., Miezitis, S., & Shaw, B. F. (1999). Cognitive-behavioral group treatments in childhood anxiety disorders: The role of parental involvement. *Journal of the American Academy of Child & Adolescent Psychiatry, 38*(10), 1223–1229.

Miller, S. J., & Binder, J. L. (2002). The effects of manual-based training on treatment fidelity and outcome: A review of the literature on adult individual psychotherapy. *Psychotherapy: Theory, Research, Practice, Training, 39*(2), 184–198.

Ollendick, T. H., Hagopian, L. P., & Huntzinger, R. M. (1991). Cognitive-behavior therapy with nighttime fearful children. *Journal of Behavior Therapy & Experimental Psychiatry, 22*(2), 113–121.

Perwien, A. R., & Berstein, G. A. (2004). Separation anxiety disorder. In T. H. Ollendick & J. S. March (Eds.), *Phobic and anxiety disorders in children and adolescents* (pp. 272–305). New York: Oxford University Press.

Reich, W. (2000). Diagnostic interview for children and adolescents (DICA). *Journal of the American Academy of Child & Adolescent Psychiatry, 39*(1), 59–66.

Saavedra, L. M., & Silverman, W. K. (2002). Classification of anxiety disorders in children: What a difference two decades make. *International Review of Psychiatry, 14*(2), 87–101.

Shaffer, D., Fisher, P., Lucas, C. P., Dulcan, M. K., & Schwab-Stone, M. E. (2000). NIMH diagnostic interview schedule for children version IV (NIMH DISC-IV): Description, differences from previous versions, and reliability of some common diagnoses. *Journal of the American Academy of Child & Adolescent Psychiatry, 39*(1), 28–38.

Silverman, W. K., & Dick-Niederhauser, A. (2004). Separation anxiety disorder. In T. L. Morris & J. S. March (Eds.), *Anxiety disorders in children and adolescents* (2nd ed., pp. 164–188). New York: Guilford.

Silverman, W. K., Kurtines, W. M., Ginsburg, G. S., Weems, C. F., Lumpkin, P. W., & Carmichael, D. H. (1999). Treating anxiety disorders in children with group cognitive-behavioral therapy: A randomized clinical trial. *Journal of Consulting & Clinical Psychology, 67*(6), 995–1003.

Silverman, W. K., & Nelles, W. B. (1988). The anxiety disorders interview schedule for children. *Journal of the American Academy of Child & Adolescent Psychiatry, 27*(6), 772–778.

Spence, S. H. (1997). A measure of anxiety symptoms among children. *Behaviour Research & Therapy, 36*(5), 545–566.

Thyer, B. A., & Sowers-Hoag, K. M. (1988). Behavior therapy for separation anxiety disorder. *Behavior Modification, 12*(2), 205–233.

Tonge, B. (1994). Separation anxiety disorder. In T. H. Ollendick, N. J. King, & W. Yule (Eds.), *International handbook of phobic and anxiety disorders in children and adolescents* (pp. 145–167). New York: Plenum.

Treadwell, K. R. H., Flannery-Schroeder, E. C., & Kendall, P. C. (1995). Ethnicity and gender in relation to adaptive functioning, diagnostic status, and treatment outcome in children from an anxiety clinic. *Journal of Anxiety Disorders, 9*(5), 373–384.

Velting, O. N., Setzer, N. J., & Albano, A. M. (2004). Update on and advances in assessment and cognitive-behavioral treatment of anxiety disorders in children and adolescents. *Professional Psychology: Research & Practice, 35*(1), 42–54.

Walkup, J. T., & Ginsburg, G. S. (2002). Anxiety disorders in children and adolescents. *International Review of Psychiatry, 14*(2), 85–86.

Walkup, J. T., Labellarte, M. J., & Ginsburg, G. S. (2002). The pharmacological treatment of childhood anxiety disorders. *International Review of Psychiatry, 14*(2), 135–142.

Weller, E. B., Weller, R. A., Fristad, M. A., Rooney, M. T., & Schecter, J. (2000). Children's interview for psychiatric syndromes (ChIPS). *Journal of the American Academy of Child & Adolescent Psychiatry, 39*(1), 76–84.

Effective Interventions for Students With Obsessive-Compulsive Disorder

Meghan Tomb ■ Lisa Hunter

Getting Started

Obsessive-compulsive disorder (OCD) is characterized by recurrent obsessions (which cause marked anxiety or distress) and by compulsions (which serve to neutralize anxiety) that are severe enough to be time consuming (i.e., take more than 1 hour a day) or cause marked distress or impairment in functioning (American Psychiatric Association, 2000). Obsessions are "recurrent, persistent ideas, thoughts, images, or impulses, which are ego-dystonic, and experienced as senseless or repugnant." Compulsions are "repetitive and seemingly purposeful actions which are performed according to certain rules, or in a stereotyped fashion" (Thomsen, 1998, p. 2). Compulsions act to neutralize the threat stemming from an obsession (Clark, 2000). OCD is not an exclusionary disorder and is often associated with major depressive disorder, other anxiety disorders (e.g., specific phobia, social phobia, panic disorder), eating disorders, and obsessive-compulsive personality disorder (American Psychiatric Association, 2000; March & Mulle, 1998). Symptomatology is similar in adults and children/adolescents with OCD; however, children may not recognize the obsessions and compulsions as excessive or unreasonable (American Psychiatric Association, 2000; Foster & Eisler, 2001; Wagner, 2003a). Table 7.2 (p. 102) shows the complete diagnostic criteria for OCD (American Psychiatric Association, 2000). See chapters 6, 8, and 10 for discussions of interventions for comorbid disorders of depression, eating disorders, and other anxiety disorders.

It is important to note that some behaviors associated with OCD are common in the normal development of children. For instance, many children go through phases where they maintain superstitious beliefs, carry out certain rituals, such as bedtime rituals, or become fixed on a favorite number (Thomsen, 1998). However, these "normal" rituals typically dissipate by 8 years old, while children with OCD generally show an onset of the disorder after age 7. Only when rituals begin to interfere with daily life or cause marked distress should a diagnosis of OCD be considered. Washing, checking, and ordering rituals (see Table 7.1 for definitions) are particularly common, seen in about half the children with OCD (March & Mulle, 1998; Thomsen, 1998). However, these symptoms in children may not be ego-dystonic (disturbing to the self), and children do not frequently seek help. More commonly, parents will identify the problem and bring the child in for treatment. Like adults, children are more prone to engage in rituals at home than in front of peers, teachers, or strangers. This may make it difficult for school-based personnel (staff, practitioners) to identify children who are suffering quietly from OCD during school hours. Relatedly, gradual declines in schoolwork secondary to impaired concentration capabilities have been reported (American Psychiatric Association, 2000). Some of the common symptoms of OCD and ways these symptoms may be exhibited in the school setting are shown in Table 7.1.

What We Know

According to the APA (2000), community studies show that the estimated lifetime prevalence for OCD is 2.5% (Franklin et al., 1998) and the 1-year prevalence is 0.5–2.1% in adults and 0.7% in children. More-recent reviews have reported lifetime prevalence rates of up to 4% (Foster & Eisler, 2001), with as many as 33–50% of adults with

Table 7.1 Symptoms and Behavioral Manifestations of Obsessive-Compulsive Disorder

Symptom	Behavioral Manifestations	Examples in School Setting
Obsessions	Students may get "stuck," or fixated, on certain points and lose the need or ability to go on. Fixation on an obsessional thought may appear to be and is often mistaken for an attention problem, daydreaming, laziness, or poor motivation.	• Fixation on a thought may cause distraction from the task at hand, which delays students in completing school work or following directions and can lead to a decrease in work production and low grades • Fear of contamination, number obsessions ("safe" versus "bad" numbers), fear of harm or death
Compulsions		
Washing/ cleaning rituals	These students may feel obligated to wash extensively and according to a self-prescribed manner for minutes to hours at a time. Others may be less thorough about washing or cleaning but may engage in the act frequently each day.	• May appear as subtle behaviors not obviously related to washing or cleaning (i.e., going to the bathroom) • Students may frequently leave the classroom to go to the bathroom in order to privately carry out cleaning rituals • A physical sign of excessive washing is the presence of dry, red, chapped, cracked, or bleeding hands
Checking rituals	The student may unnecessarily check specific things over and over again.	• Getting ready for school, the student may check books over and over again to see if all the necessary books are there, sometimes causing lateness • At school, the student may want to call or return home to check something yet another time • The student may check and recheck answers on assignments to the point that they are submitted late or not at all • Repeatedly checking a locker to see if it is locked • Checking rituals may interfere with the completion of homework, can cause a student to work late into the night on assignments that should have taken 2 or 3 hours to complete
Repeating rituals	The student repeats a behavior or task over and over again (often connected with counting rituals)	• Repetitious questioning • Reading and rereading sentences or paragraphs in a book

(continued)

Table 7.1 (*Continued*)

Symptom	Behavioral Manifestations	Examples in School Setting
		• Sharpening pencils several times in a row • Repeatedly crossing out, tracing, or rewriting letters or words, erasing and re-erasing words • May interfere with student's ability to take notes, complete computer-scored tests, and open locker
Symmetry/ exactness rituals	Obsessions revolving around a need for symmetry	• Student may compulsively arrange objects in the classroom (e.g., books on a shelf, items on a page, pencils on a desk) • Student may feel the need to have both sides of the body identical (e.g., laces on shoes), take steps that are identical in length, or place equal emphasis on each syllable of a word
Other compulsive behaviors	Obsessional thoughts that lead to compulsive avoidance; individuals may go to great lengths to avoid objects, substances, or situations that are capable of triggering fear or discomfort	• Fear of contamination may cause avoidance of objects in classroom (paint, glue, paste, clay, tape, ink) • Inappropriately covering the hands with clothing or gloves or using shirttails or cuffs to open doors or turn on faucets • If an obsessive fear of harm, may avoid using scissors or other sharp tools in the classroom • Student may avoid using a particular doorway because passage through it may trigger a repeating ritual
	Compulsive reassurance seeking	• May continually ask teachers for reassurance that there are no germs on the drinking fountain or that there are no errors on a page
	Obsessions concerning fear	• Fear of cheating may cause students to compulsively seek reassurance, avoid looking at other children, and sometimes even to give wrong answers intentionally

OCD reporting onset of the disorder during childhood or adolescence (Franklin et al., 1998). There are not any differences in prevalence rates across different cultures (American Psychiatric Association, 2000). It is estimated that 1 in 200 children and adolescents has obsessive-compulsive disorder (Adams et al., 1994). Given this approximation, there may be 3–4 youths with OCD in an average-sized elementary school and possibly 20–30 in a large urban high school (Adams et al., 1994; March & Mulle, 1998). When left untreated, OCD can severely disrupt academic, home, social, and vocational functioning (Geller, Biederman, et al., 2001; March & Mulle, 1998; Piacentini et al. 2003). Without proper identification and treatment, these children and adolescents are at risk for significant difficulty in school.

Implications for School Social Workers and Other School-Based Practitioners and Staff

Classroom teachers and other school staff observe and interact with students on a daily basis for consistent periods of time and therefore have a unique opportunity to notice and identify OCD symptoms in children and adolescents (Adams et al., 1994). In some instances, school personnel may be the first adults in a child's life to identify potential OCD symptoms. It is essential, therefore, that "classroom teachers, school social workers, school psychologists, counselors, nurses, and administrators learn to identify OCD symptoms in the school setting, help make appropriate referrals, and assist, as appropriate, in the treatment of childhood OCD" (March & Mulle, 1998, p. 197).

School-based practitioners, like school social workers and counselors, play an important part in identifying children and adolescents who are suffering from OCD symptoms and in educating school personnel about OCD. When a child with OCD is properly identified and referred for services, the symptoms can be addressed, treated, and managed. If classroom teachers do not have the knowledge and tools to do this, symptoms may continue to impair the child's functioning on a greater scale and eventually cause the child to be unable to attend school (March & Mulle, 1998). One way that school-based practitioners can help this process is by educating school personnel on the specific ways that OCD symptoms can manifest themselves in the school setting. Information on OCD can be disseminated through teacher in-service trainings and seminars. These should include information on proper identification of OCD symptoms, referral options, and a description of available treatments for OCD. School-based practitioners may want to consult various resources in order to obtain the most up-to-date information on OCD and its treatment (Adams et al., 1994).

Teachers can be a valuable asset to school-based practitioners treating children with OCD. Teachers are in a position to report their own observations of the child in treatment as well as those of the child's peers in the classroom. Establishing a relationship with the teacher is imperative for this process. Teachers can also provide written records of social and academic problems the student is having (March & Mulle, 1998), as well as complete assessment measures. School-based practitioners should keep in mind that teachers may be more compliant in completing assessment measures for a referred student when the burden is kept low by short-form assessment measures (Velting et al., 2004).

What We Can Do

Cognitive-Behavioral Therapy as the First-Line Psychotherapy for OCD

After a school-based mental health practitioner diagnoses a child as having OCD, one of several different interventions may be implemented. Cognitive-behavioral therapy (CBT), alone or in combination with medication, represents the foundation of treatment for children and adolescents with OCD (American Academy of Child and Adolescent Psychiatry, 1998; March & Mulle, 1998) and is the basis for effective treatments for all anxiety disorders (Velting et al., 2004). For a complete review of the research literature supporting the efficacy of CBT for children and adolescents with anxiety disorders, see Kazdin and Weisz (1998), Ollendick and King (1998), and Albano and Kendall (2002). CBT programs for OCD utilize a combination of behavioral and cognitive information-processing approaches to alter symptoms. CBT aims to help the child with OCD to restructure unhealthy thoughts associated with the disorder in order to generate changes in the maladaptive behaviors that impair the child's daily home, school, and social functioning. The child learns specific strategies for coping with the disorder and, most important, for managing situations that may trigger certain thoughts and behavioral responses related to OCD.

The efficacy of CBT involving exposure and response prevention (E/RP) and pharmacotherapy with serotonin reuptake inhibitors (SRIs) is well established for adults (Franklin et al., 2002; Franklin et al., 2003; Kampman et al., 2002). Although fewer data exist for the use of CBT for the treatment of pediatric OCD, it is believed to be a useful and successful treatment for youth (Franklin et al., 1998; March & Mulle, 1998; Southam-Gerow & Kendall, 2000). In an open trial, March et al. (1994) used an adapted version of CBT to treat 15 children and adolescents (6–18 years old) with OCD, most of whom had been previously stabilized on medication. The authors reported significant benefit immediately following treatment and at 6-month follow-up. At posttreatment, results demonstrated a mean reduction of 50% in OCD symptomatology on the Yale-Brown Obsessive Compulsive Scale (Y-BOCS) and clinically asymptomatic ratings on the NIMH Global OC Scale (March et al., 1994). Eighty percent of patients were defined as responders to treatment. No patients relapsed after symptoms recurred, and booster sessions enabled 6 of the 9 asymptomatic patients to stop taking medication without relapse (March & Mulle, 1998). In another open trial, Franklin et al. (1998), found CBT to be effective in reducing OCD symptoms. Twelve of 14 patients (10 to 17 years old) in this trial showed at least 50% improvement over their pretreatment Y-BOCS severity scores, and 83% remained improved in severity at follow-up. The results of both of these trials are comparable to treatment studies using pharmacotherapy only (Southam-Gerow & Kendall, 2000).

Despite general acceptance of CBT as the treatment of choice for OCD in children (Franklin et al., 1998; March & Mulle, 1998), there is a lack of randomized controlled trials of CBT against control and other active comparison treatments in the empirical literature (March et al., 2001). The Pediatric Obsessive-Compulsive Disorder Treatment Study (POTS; Franklin, Foa, & March, 2003) is the first randomized trial in pediatric OCD that compares the efficacy of medication (sertraline), CBT for OCD, medication and CBT in combination, and a medication placebo. This study hopes to answer existing questions about the benefits and effectiveness of CBT and/or medication for the treatment of OCD. The current acceptance of CBT as the preferred treatment for OCD may be explained by the fact that exposure and response prevention (E/RP) is an integral part of any CBT protocol for OCD (Rowa et al., 2000). E/RP specifically has been proven to be an effective treatment for OCD (for reviews, see Abramowitz, 1998; Foa et al., 1998; Stanley & Turner, 1995). Additionally, studies measuring the effectiveness and transportability of cognitive-behavioral therapy from research-based randomized controlled trials (RCTs) to clinical and school practice are being seen in the literature (Warren & Thomas, 2001). In addition to the CBT protocol outlined in this chapter, the reader is also directed to Aureen Pinto Wagner's CBT protocol for children with OCD (see Wagner [2003a] for a review of this treatment protocol). Wagner's protocol, named RIDE Up and Down the Worry Hill (Wagner, 2002; 2003b), is a developmentally sensitive protocol designed as a flexible and feasible approach for clinicians in clinical settings treating children with OCD. Although comparative data do not exist for this protocol versus the protocol described in this chapter, both share many common features (Wagner, 2003a).

Pharmacotherapy

The literature on pharmacotherapy for pediatric OCD is more extensive than that of cognitive-behavioral treatment for OCD in children (Franklin et al., 2003). The medications most frequently used to treat OCD in children are SRIs. These include the tricyclic antidepressant (TCA) clomipramine, which is an SRI, and the selective serotonin reuptake inhibitors (SSRIs) fluoxetine, fluvoxamine, paroxetine, and sertraline. The majority of studies on psychopharmacology in pediatric OCD have focused on clomipramine (Franklin et al., 1998), which was approved by the FDA in 1989 for the treatment of OCD in children and adolescents aged 10 and older (March & Mulle, 1998). See chapter 2 for a review of psychiatric medications used with children and adolescents.

Though there have been fewer trials with the other medications listed above, all of the SSRIs are likely to be effective treatments for OCD in children and adolescents (Franklin et al., 2003; March & Mulle, 1998). Fluoxetine, fluvoxamine, and sertraline have all shown benefit in smaller trials but await further study on a larger scale. In a 12-week, double-blind, placebo-controlled trial, sertraline was found to be effective for pediatric OCD treatment, with 42% of patients rated as improved (March et al., 1998). Geller, Hoog, et al. (2001) reported the efficacy and safety of fluoxetine in the treatment of pediatric OCD after a 13-week double-blind, placebo-controlled clinical trial resulted in 55% of patients (7–18 years old) randomized to the medication being rated as improved. A more complete review of the research base for these medications is beyond the scope of this chapter. For additional information on recommended psychopharmacological treatment for OCD, see March et al., *The Expert Consensus Guideline Series: Treatment of Obsessive-Compulsive Disorder* (1997).

Although school-based practitioners are not responsible for prescribing medication to a child with OCD, they should be aware of the medications the child is taking. Practitioners should note any change in behavior, either improvement or otherwise since the start of medication treatment. Practitioners providing psychotherapy to a child should be in close contact with the child's prescribing primary physician and/or psychiatrist. Keeping these lines of communication open is essential for ensuring the best possible treatment outcome for the child.

Assessment and Initial Evaluation

Proper assessment and evaluation is critical in the treatment of OCD. This assessment process should include an initial screening, telephone contact with parents, pretreatment evaluation (including a behavioral analysis), and referral. There are a number of assessment tools that school social workers and other school-based practitioners can use. For a list and description of assessment tools, see Table 7.3 (p. 103). After these preliminary measures, a first appointment is scheduled. Following this first meeting, the practitioner should provide feedback to the child, parent(s), and teacher(s) involved. Once a treatment program has been established, the student's services team should meet with the mental health practitioners involved to decide on school-based interventions. It is also important at this stage to devise a plan for keeping the lines of communication open among the student, the parents, and the school. This component will be essential for developing and implementing the treatment intervention that provides the greatest benefit to the student with OCD (March & Mulle, 1998).

Overview of Cognitive-Behavioral Therapy for OCD

Cognitive-behavioral therapy is the most effective psychosocial treatment for OCD (March & Mulle, 1998). However, there is a lack of studies examining whether CBT protocols can be delivered by practitioners of all theoretical and clinical backgrounds with the same level of efficacy found in research trials (Velting et al., 2004). Similarly, the transportability of these treatments to nonresearch settings, such as schools, has not been examined extensively, though studies designed for this purpose are in progress (Albano & Kendall, 2002). When delivering CBT as treatment for anxious youth, school social workers and other practitioners are encouraged to be flexible, clinically sensitive, and developmentally appropriate (Albano & Kendall, 2002; Kendall & Chu, 2000). Keeping this in mind, practitioners in all settings seeking to use CBT must receive appropriate training and supervision (Velting et al., 2004). Below, the reader will find an overview of cognitive-behavioral therapy, as well as a more detailed description of a CBT protocol for OCD, developed by March and Mulle (1998). This description is not meant to replace the comprehensive protocol in *OCD in Children and Adolescents: A Cognitive-Behavioral Treatment Manual* (March & Mulle, 1998), and school social workers and other practitioners should not use it as such. At the end of this chapter, the reader will find a list of resources and information on how to obtain materials for use in the treatment of OCD, including the *CBT Manual for Children and Adolescents with OCD*.

The Treatment Process

Typically, CBT takes place over 12–20 sessions, depending on the severity and complexity of the case (March & Mulle, 1998). At the beginning of treatment, it is expected that the child has been through a pretreatment evaluation and assessment procedures. Though each session has its own specific goals, there are a few general themes consistent throughout treatment. Each time the practitioner meets with the child, he or she should:

- Check in with parents.
- Review the goals for that session.
- Review topics covered the previous session and any lingering questions or concerns the child may have.

- Introduce new material for the current session.
- Practice/role play new tasks.
- Explain and administer homework for the coming week.
- Provide any fact sheets pertinent to the topics covered at the end of the session. (March & Mulle, 1998)

Keeping these common themes in mind, the CBT treatment process for OCD can be broken into two phases: the acute treatment phase and the maintenance treatment phase. In the acute phase, treatment is geared toward ending the current episode of OCD. In the maintenance phase, treatment focuses on preventing any possible future episodes of OCD. These two phases are marked by the following components of treatment:

- Education: Education is crucial in helping patients and families learn how best to manage OCD and prevent its complications.
- Psychotherapy: Cognitive-behavioral psychotherapy is the key element of treatment for most patients with OCD. (This treatment may either be delivered in school or referred out to community-based programs depending on the available resources.)
- Medication: Medication with a serotonin reuptake inhibitor is helpful for many patients. (March & Mulle, 1998)

Within these two phases, treatment is broken up into four general steps over the course of 12–20 sessions. The following steps are fully described in the next section:

- Psychoeducation (sessions 1–2, week 1)
- Cognitive training (sessions 2–3, weeks 1–2)
- Mapping OCD (sessions 3–4, week 2)
- Exposure/response prevention (sessions 5–20, weeks 3–18) (March & Mulle, 1998)

The length of each session may vary slightly and can depend on the schedules of the parent and child as well as the location of treatment. Ideally, each session should allow 50–60 minutes to cover all of the goals and any additional concerns raised by the child and/or parent. In a school setting, it may be difficult to schedule sessions for this length of time. Some school-based practitioners have modified this type of treatment to fit within one class period to avoid taking the child out of more than one class at a time. Generally the time of each treatment session is arranged as follows:

- Check in (5 minutes)
- Homework review (5 minutes)
- Instruction of new task (20 minutes)
- Discussion of new homework (10 minutes)
- Review of session and homework with parents (10 minutes) (March & Mulle, 1998)

Step 1: Psychoeducation (Session 1)

During the first step of treatment, the practitioner is primarily focusing on establishing rapport with the child and parent as well as educating the family about OCD. This includes talking about OCD as a medical illness and giving the family a comprehensive knowledge base on treatment for the disorder.

Session 1 Goals

1. Establish rapport (initial interview). Treatment begins with the practitioner working to make the child feel safe and comfortable about being in therapy. One or both of the parents should be included in this first part of treatment, and initial conversation should be focused around the child's life apart from OCD. Once the practitioner begins to discuss OCD and how he or she will be working with the child and parent to establish the goals of treatment, the practitioner may be able to assess the level of understanding the family has of OCD and its treatment.
2. Establish a neurobehavioral framework.
   - As a first step in discussing OCD as a disorder, the practitioner provides a neurobehavioral framework around OCD for the child. This is extremely important during the onset of treatment in that it connects the disorder, OCD, and its symptoms with specific behavioral treatments and symptom reduction.
   - Within this discussion, the practitioner should use the neurobehavioral framework to compare OCD to medical illnesses, such as asthma or diabetes.
   - The practitioner should explain how OCD affects the brain and how it works to alter thoughts and behaviors. Symptoms of OCD, such as obsessions, can be described to the child as "brain hiccups."
   - The practitioner can use other illnesses to explain how treatment for OCD will work. Similar to insulin treatment for diabetes, the treatment of OCD may involve medication

(SSRIs), and in both disorders, psychosocial interventions are used (i.e., diet and exercise for diabetes, CBT for OCD). Also in both situations, not everyone completely recovers, so additional interventions are used to address any residual symptoms.

- The practitioner may take this opportunity to use information from the child's psychiatric evaluation to answer questions about and discuss OCD. When working with children who are on medication for OCD, the practitioner may want to stress how medication and CBT can work together to provide an effective treatment for the child.

3. Explain the treatment process. During the first two sessions, CBT as a treatment is explained and discussed in detail, including the following key points:
   - The practitioner should review risks and benefits of behavioral treatment for OCD.
   - Components, expectations, and goals of the treatment are reviewed. This can be a time for questions from the parents and the child about all three of these things. The practitioner should make sure the child understands each of the goals and what the different stages and components of treatment entail. Specifically, the child should have a grasp on E/RP and how they are connected. The child may be reassured that he or she will not have to do these things on his or her own but will have allies throughout treatment (practitioner, parents) and will be aided with a "tool kit" of coping strategies to use during these exercises.
   - The practitioner lays out an expected time frame for treatment, which can be revisited throughout treatment and altered, based on the child's progress. The practitioner may want to use visual handouts to show what the timeline will look like.

4. Externalize OCD.
   - Practitioners may want to encourage younger children to give OCD an unfavorable nickname, putting OCD on the "other side" of the child. This allows the child to view OCD as something that can be fought rather than something associated with a bad habit or a bad part of his or her personality.
   - Discuss the concept of "bossing back" OCD.

5. Homework. The concept of homework is introduced and discussed. The practitioner should make it clear that the child will always

have a collaborative say in what the homework will be.
- The child should pay attention to where OCD wins and where the child wins in preparation for session 2.
- If the child has not already done so, he or she should think about a nickname to be used for OCD.
- The child and parents should review any materials given them from the practitioner and generate any lingering questions they may have for the next session.
- Parents should work on redirecting their attention toward those things the child does well and away from OCD-related behaviors.
- When in a school setting, the practitioner may want to spend some time with the parents working on communicating with teachers about their child's OCD. The practitioner may also suggest ways in which teachers can use strategies in the classroom to help the child combat OCD.
- The child is asked to practice the technique of bossing back OCD for homework.

Step 2: Cognitive Training (CT): Introducing the Tool Kit (Sessions 2–3)

During the second step of treatment, the practitioner introduces cognitive training (CT), which is training in cognitive tactics for resisting OCD (March & Mulle, 1998). This can be distinguished from response prevention for mental rituals. Using CT will work to increase a sense of self-efficacy, controllability, and predictability of a positive outcome for E/RP tasks.

Session 2 Goals

1. Reinforce information around OCD and its treatment (may be introduced in session 1).
2. Make OCD the problem.
   - Introduce cognitive resistance (bossing back OCD) to reinforce the concept that OCD is external to the child.
   - The practitioner should begin by asking some general questions around how OCD has been bossing the child around since the last session and how the child has successfully bossed OCD back. Some of the settings the practitioner may want to address include home, playing with friends, school, etc. When talking about school, the practitioner

may want to ask questions around specific places and times in school and when the child is with specific people.

- It is imperative during this time to frame E/RP as the strategy used in the child's "fight" against OCD and the practitioner and parents as the child's allies in this fight.

3. Begin mapping OCD.
   - Introduce the concept of a transition zone between territory controlled by OCD and territory under the child's control.
   - March and Mulle (1998) suggest using the C-YBOCS (Goodman et al., 1989a, 1989b) Symptom Checklist and the patient's history to inventory the child's OCD symptoms. The fear thermometer, introduced in step 4 below, is used as a guide to generate subjective units of discomfort scores (SUDS) for each item on the stimulus hierarchy formulated in session.
   - The child generates the stimulus hierarchy by ranking the OCD symptoms from the easiest to the hardest to boss back. After the child has ranked his or her OCD symptoms on the stimulus hierarchy, areas where the child's life territory is free from OCD, where OCD and the child each "win" some of the time, and where the child cedes control to OCD will become apparent.
   - The transition zone will become obvious as the symptoms are ranked.

4. Introduce the fear thermometer, which encompasses the concepts of talking back to OCD and E/RP.

5. Using the tool kit. Once the child learns self-talk (bossing back OCD) and how to use positive coping strategies, introduce the cognitive tool kit for use during exposure and response prevention (E/RP) tasks, which will ease the process as well as support its effectiveness for the child.

6. Homework.
   - The child should pay attention to any OCD triggers he or she can detect and build a symptom list.
   - The C-YBOCS checklist can aid as a guide.

Step 3: Mapping OCD: Completing the Tool Kit (Sessions 3–4)

By the third step of treatment, the child has developed a knowledge base of OCD and a preliminary tool kit of strategies to fight OCD. At this point,

the child can begin to work within his or her own experience with OCD, identifying specific obsessions, compulsions, triggers, avoidance behaviors, and consequences (March & Mulle, 1998).

Session 3 Goals

1. Begin cognitive training (CT). The purpose of CT is to provide the child with a cognitive strategy for bossing back OCD. By learning these strategies, the child further solidifies his or her knowledge base of OCD and its treatment, cognitive resistance to OCD, and self-administered positive reinforcement.
   - Child reinforcement.
     - Constructive self-talk: The practitioner should identify and help correct negative self-talk.
     - Cognitive restructuring: The practitioner helps the child directly to address any negative assumptions (e.g., risk of getting sick from touching a doorknob) feeding into the child's obsessions. This will help the child's willingness to participate in exposure tasks in later sessions.
     - Separation from OCD: Continue to externalize OCD by separating OCD from the child as something that just comes and goes.
   - Short-form cognitive training: The practitioner may help the child to review and keep these concepts separate by giving repeated examples or writing the concepts down on separate cards the child may take home.

2. Continue mapping OCD and review the symptom list (trigger, obsession, compulsion, fear thermometer).
   - Complete the symptom list (stimulus hierarchy) begun in session 1.
   - Identify obsessions and compulsions using the CYBOCS Symptom Checklist as a guide.
   - Link obsessions and compulsions with the child's specific triggers.
   - Then rank each trigger, obsession, and compulsion according to fear temperature on a hierarchy (with the highest fear temperature on the top and the lowest on the bottom). The practitioner should be sure to get all of the details around each of these components from the child using specific questions aimed at alleviating any embarrassment the child may have around these behaviors.

3. Learn to use rewards as a strategy. Verbal praise, small prizes, and certificates can be used as

positive reinforcement to the child for bossing back OCD successfully and for making progress from session to session. These should be discussed with the child from the beginning of treatment.

4. Homework.
   - Have the child try to identify when OCD wins and when he/she wins as a lead-in to exposure and response prevention.
   - The child should practice cognitive interventions learned in session.

Session 4 Goals

1. Finalize the transition zone.
   - The child generates a stimulus hierarchy with the practitioner on paper which shows where the child is completely free from OCD, where the child and OCD each win the fight some of the time, and where the child feels helpless against OCD.
   - The transition zone lies in the central region and is the point where the child has some success against OCD. Essentially, the transition zone can be identified where the child and OCD overlap.
   - The practitioner should express to the child that she or he is on the child's side as an ally in the area of the hierarchy where the child is free from OCD.
   - Throughout this exercise, the practitioner will help the child work within the transition zone, recognizing and using aspects of the transition zone that will help to guide graded exposure throughout later treatment. The transition zone is recognized as being at the lower end of the stimulus hierarchy, where the high end includes those areas in which the child feels helpless against OCD.

2. Finalize the tool kit in preparation for E/RP.
   - Solidify a method for selecting E/RP targets in the transition zone.
   - Review and use the fear thermometer with specifics from the child's symptom hierarchy.
   - Review and discuss additional cognitive strategies.
   - Review the rewards discussed as a strategy to fight OCD and identify any other rewards for bossing back OCD.

3. Assign trial exposure tasks.
   - Before moving on to the final and longest phase of treatment, some initial exposure and response prevention tasks may be introduced to determine the child's levels of anxiety, understanding of concepts and tasks, and compliance and/or ability to participate in this area of treatment.
   - Some introduction to these tasks reinforces the notion that the child can successfully resist and win the fight against OCD.
   - During this trial period, the practitioner should pay particular attention to the transition zone and whether targets within this zone have been placed correctly. Identifying mistakes in this area at this point in treatment will reduce the chance for hang-ups or misdirection later in treatment.
   - Practice trial E/RP task in session.

4. Homework. The child should practice a trial exposure every day and pay attention to the level of anxiety felt during each exercise.

Step 4: Exposure and Response Prevention: Implement E/RP (Sessions 5–20, Weeks 3–18)

During the remaining sessions of treatment, graded E/RP is implemented. Some children may not need all of the additional 16 sessions. The practitioner also assists in imaginal and in vivo E/RP practice, which is actively associated with weekly homework assignments. *Exposure* occurs when the child exposes him- or herself to the feared object, action, or thought. *Response prevention* follows and is the process of blocking rituals triggered by the exposure to the feared stimulus and/or reducing avoidance behaviors (March & Mulle, 1998). The practitioner should continue to frame OCD as the enemy, with the child, parents, and practitioner all on the same side, fighting against OCD. Within this framework, the child may use the allies and the tool kit (from CT and E/RP) developed with the help of the practitioner to resist OCD. This resistance is practiced at home, in school, and throughout therapy. At the beginning of each E/RP session, the transition zone should be revisited and altered when appropriate. Throughout this process, the child should become more skillful and successful at resisting OCD. Relapse prevention should also be covered, usually in the last one or two sessions of treatment. Additionally, within the main course of treatment, at least two sessions (besides the first one) should include the parents. Finally, one or more booster sessions should be scheduled after treatment is terminated. The first booster session should occur approximately 1 month after the end of treatment (i.e., week 24).

Session 5 Goals

1. Identify OCD's influence with family members.
   - The practitioner should discuss the impact that OCD may have on the child's parents and other family members.
   - OCD symptoms involving the child's parents may be identified and placed on the hierarchy with their own fear temperature.
2. Update symptom hierarchy.
   - At the beginning of each session using exposure and response prevention, it is essential to go back to the symptom hierarchy and make any changes and/or additions necessary.
   - The fear thermometer will also change when the transition zone moves up the hierarchy as the child becomes more and more successful at bossing back OCD at different stages.
3. Continue imaginal and/or in vivo E/RP. There are a number of different components to consider when using exposure techniques.
   - *Contrived exposure* is shown when the child chooses to face a feared stimulus while *uncontrived exposure* is shown when the child comes into contact with the stimulus unavoidably. With contrived exposure the child is working to end avoidance while uncontrived exposure will force the child to pick RP targets.
   - The practitioner can also introduce the child to exposure for obsessions and/or mental rituals where the child allows him- or herself time for obsessions.
   - After the exposure here, the practitioner helps the child to break the rules that OCD usually sets. Some ways to break these rules include:
     - delay the ritual
     - shorten the ritual
     - do the ritual differently
     - do the ritual slowly
   - The practitioner should assist E/RP by modeling the exposure task with and without telling the child.
4. Homework. The child should practice the chosen exposure or response prevention tasks daily. The practitioner should make sure the child has chosen an exposure that will be relatively easy as this will be the first time the child practices on his or her own. The child should be reminded to use all of the strategies in the tool kit.

Session 6 Goals

1. Identify areas of difficulty with E/RP.
   - Since the last session involved actually doing exposure and response prevention for the first time, the practitioner should try to identify any areas of difficulty or frustration the child is having with E/RP.
   - The practitioner should pay close attention to the child's levels of anxiety and how he or she manages the anxiety during the exposure task.
2. Continue therapist-assisted E/RP.
   - After any questions or concerns have been addressed, the practitioner should continue with assisted E/RP.
   - The tasks that are practiced in session should be among those chosen for homework.
3. Homework. The child should choose one exposure task to practice.

Family Session 1 (Session 7)

At this point in treatment, the practitioner should encourage the parents and/or family to participate in a family session.

Session 7 Goals

1. Include parents in treatment.
   - The primary goal of the family session is to make sure that the parents feel they are included in the treatment. The practitioner may need to review the purpose of treatment at the outset.
   - Discuss the role of parents in treatment as a supportive force for the child and completely separate from OCD itself. The practitioner should discuss with the parents the various roles they may play in the child's treatment and how to carefully manage their own behavior around the child, OCD, and treatment.
   - The practitioner should discuss with the child and parents ways in which the parents can engage in extinction strategies. Extinction procedures should always be discussed and approved by the child.
   - Discuss the possibility of family therapy.

2. Positive reinforcement. Make a plan for special occasions to recognize the child's success (ceremonies) and to inform significant others of the child's success (notifications).
3. Continue E/RP. The practitioner should continue with an exposure task in session with the child. Based on the discussion with the parents, the exposure task may involve them.
4. Homework. The child should choose an exposure task to practice at home. If the parents are involved in corresponding rituals, the homework may include practice around the parents.

Moving Up the Stimulus Hierarchy (Sessions 8–11)

These four sessions over 4 weeks cover similar material, each session building on the last.

Sessions 8–11 Goals

1. Arrange rewards, ceremonies, and notifications.
   - The practitioner should review these three topics and decisions from the last session.
   - The practitioner should monitor how the child is responding to these reinforcements and whether they are a positive reinforcement to treatment. The practitioner may work with the child and parents to identify points where a ceremony is warranted and how to plan a party around accomplishments.
2. Address comorbidity and therapy needs. The reader is directed to the original treatment manual (March & Mulle, 1998) as well as *The Expert Consensus Guideline Series: Treatment of Obsessive-Compulsive Disorder* (March et al., 1997), for recommendations and references on treatment for comorbidity.
   - Any comorbidity that is present should be addressed, as well as any other therapy needs.
   - Comorbid symptoms should be separated from OCD and treated as such.
3. Continue practitioner-assisted E/RP.
   - Practitioner-assisted E/RP is continued with special attention to developmental considerations.
   - The practitioner should continue to encourage the child to move up the symptom hierarchy, practicing harder exposure tasks as treatment continues.

4. Homework. Homework for each session should involve practice of skills learned within the session.

Family Session 2 (Session 12)

Session 12 Goals

1. Remap OCD.
   - The practitioner should revisit how OCD involves and influences the parents and family of the child with OCD.
   - The practitioner should remap OCD with the child and family and make any changes to the symptom hierarchy that has developed over the last four sessions of E/RP.
2. Implement extinction tasks. With the child's permission, the practitioner should implement extinction tasks with the parents working as co-therapists.
3. Continue E/RP.
   - The child and parents may practice extinction tasks in session with the practitioner for those tasks in which the parents are enmeshed with OCD.
   - For parents who are not involved directly with the child's OCD, the practitioner may begin to transfer some of the management decisions around choosing exposure tasks to the parents. With the child's permission, the parents may act as co-therapists in this sense. This decision may be influenced by the relationship between the parents and child as well as the parents' understanding of OCD and willingness to be involved in treatment.
4. Homework. The child may choose a new E/RP task to practice. Additionally, an extinction procedure for the parents to practice for homework is chosen.

Completing E/RP (Sessions 13–18)

Sessions 13–18 Goals

1. Review child's overall progress. The practitioner should review the child's progress in treatment thus far.
2. Address plateaus.
   - The practitioner should address any areas where the child has exhibited a plateau point between easy and harder E/RP and the reasons for this.

- If the child is having a particularly hard time moving to the next stage in the hierarchy, the practitioner may want to schedule a ceremony to officially congratulate the child on completing one stage and moving on to the beginning of another.
3. Choose harder E/RP tasks. The practitioner can move forward by considering harder E/RP tasks for the child to practice, with an especially hard E/RP for the following weekly session.
4. Address comorbidity. The practitioner should be aware at this point in treatment of any comorbidity the child is exhibiting. This should be addressed in treatment and discussed with the parents.
5. Homework.
   - The child should practice an E/RP task based on the updated stimulus hierarchy.
   - The child may want to ask a friend or family member for help in working on a difficult exposure task at home.

Relapse Prevention (Session 19)

Relapse prevention can be covered in one session but may extend to two or more depending on the needs of the child. The practitioner may assess how the child feels about possible relapse or even "slips" after ending treatment. During these sessions, the practitioner may set up imaginal exposures for the child to practice how he or she would react if a slip were to occur.

Session 19 Goals

1. Explain concept of relapse prevention.
   - Primarily, the child should understand that slips are not a loss of efforts up to this point.
   - The practitioner may openly discuss and address any fears and/or misconceptions the child has of relapse.
2. Provide opportunity for imaginal exposure of relapse. The practitioner may ask the child to think of an example in which he or she may slip and then successfully use the tool kit to boss back OCD. The child should express his or her anxiety levels throughout the exposure, and the practitioner may help by suggesting specific tools to use (e.g., self-talk) in working through the exposure.
3. Address questions or concerns regarding the treatment. Since this session marks the last true treatment session, the child may have questions

or concerns regarding the treatment and what happens after treatment.
4. Homework. The child should practice a relapse prevention task either imaginal or in vivo.

Graduation (Session 20)

The main purpose of this "graduation" session is to have a celebration for the child upon completion of treatment.

Session 20 Goals

1. Celebrate the child's accomplishments. During this final session, the main focus is on celebration of the child's accomplishments during treatment.
2. The practitioner should present the child with a certificate of achievement.
3. Notify friends and family members. The child is encouraged to share his or her success with friends and family members.
4. Parents check in. The practitioner should check in with the parents at the end of this last session to address any lingering concerns regarding treatment and OCD.
5. Homework. Homework for the child should be simply to share his or her success with friends and family and to frame the certificate of achievement.

Booster Session (Session 21)

A booster session is scheduled at 4 weeks to reinforce the strategies learned throughout treatment.

Session 21 Goals

1. Celebrate the child's accomplishments since graduation.
2. Review the tool kit.
3. Reinforce relapse prevention.
4. Plan further notifications regarding the end of treatment.

Tools and Practice Examples

Assessment Instruments

In order to make a diagnosis of OCD in children and adolescents, a thorough review of

Table 7.2 Diagnostic Criteria for 300.3 Obsessive-Compulsive Disorder

A. Either obsessions or compulsions:

Obsessions as defined by (1), (2), (3), and (4):

(1) recurrent and persistent thoughts, impulses, or images that are experienced, at some time during the disturbance, as intrusive and inappropriate and that cause marked anxiety or distress

(2) the thoughts, impulses, or images are not simply excessive worries about real-life problems

(3) the person attempts to ignore or suppress such thoughts, impulses, or images, or to neutralize them with some other thought or action

(4) the person recognizes that the obsessional thoughts, impulses, or images are a product of his or her own mind (not imposed from without as in thought insertion)

Compulsions as defined by (1) and (2):

(1) repetitive behaviors (e.g., hand washing, ordering, checking) or mental acts (e.g., praying, counting, repeating words silently) that the person feels driven to perform in response to an obsession, or according to rules that must be applied rigidly

(2) the behaviors or mental acts are aimed at preventing or reducing distress or preventing some dreaded event or situation; however, these behaviors or mental acts either are not connected in a realistic way with what they are designed to neutralize or prevent or are clearly excessive

B. At some point during the course of the disorder, the person has recognized that the obsessions or compulsions are excessive or unreasonable. Note: This does not apply to children.

C. The obsessions or compulsions cause marked distress, are time consuming (take more than 1 hour a day), or significantly interfere with the person's normal routine, occupational (or academic) functioning, or usual social activities or relationships.

D. If another Axis I disorder is present, the content of the obsessions or compulsions is not restricted to it (e.g., preoccupation with food in the presence of an eating disorder; hair pulling in the presence of trichotillomania; concern with appearance in the presence of body dysmorphic disorder; preoccupation with drugs in the presence of a substance use disorder; preoccupation with having a serious illness in the presence of hypochondriasis; preoccupation with sexual urges or fantasies in the presence of a paraphilia; or guilty ruminations in the presence of major depressive disorder).

E. The disturbance is not due to the direct physiological effects of a substance (e.g., a drug or abuse of a medication) or a general medical condition.

Specify if:

With poor insight: if, for most of the time during the current episode, the person does not recognize that the obsessions and compulsions are excessive or unreasonable.

Source: Reprinted with permission from the Diagnostic and Statistical Manual of Mental Disorders, Copyright 2000, American Psychiatric Association.

the patient's behavior must be coupled with psychiatric interviews that are specific to an OCD diagnosis (Thomsen, 1998). Table 7.3 lists several assessment tools that may be helpful in the process of diagnosing OCD.

 Resources

OCD-Specific Organizations

Obsessive-Compulsive Foundation, Inc.
676 State Street
New Haven, CT 06511
Phone: 203-401-2070
Fax: 203-401-2076
E-mail: info@ocdfoundation.org
http://www.ocfoundation.org

Table 7.3 Recommended Assessment Tools

Assessment	Source	Description
NIMH Global Obsessive-Compulsive Scale	National Institute of Mental Health (public domain)	The scale is clinician-rated and used to generate a global rating from 1 to 15 that represents a description of the present clinical state of the patient. This rating is based on guidelines provided on the scale ranging from "minimal within range of normal or very mild symptoms" to "very severe obsessive-compulsive behavior."
Clinical Global Impairment Scale	National Institute of Mental Health (public domain)	This scale is clinician-rated and used to generate a global rating from 1 to 7 that represents how mentally ill the patient is at the current time, based on the therapist's clinical experience. The descriptions range from "normal, not at all ill" to "among the most extremely ill."
Clinical Global Improvement Scale	National Institute of Mental Health (public domain)	This scale is clinician-rated and used to generate a global rating from 1 to 7 that represents how the patient's condition has changed since the beginning of treatment. The descriptions range from "very much improved" to "very much worse."
Children's Yale-Brown Obsessive-Compulsive Scale*	Developed by Wayne K. Goodman, Lawrence H. Price, Steven A. Rasmussen, Mark A. Riddle, & Judith L. Rapoport Department of Psychiatry Child Study Center, Yale University School of Medicine; Department of Psychiatry, Brown University School of Medicine; Child Psychiatry Branch, National Institute of Mental Health	The CY-BOCS is the most useful and widely used instrument, both clinically and in research. This scale is designed to rate the severity of obsessive and compulsive symptoms in children and adolescents, ages 6 to 17 years old. A clinician or a trained interviewer can administer the scale in a semistructured fashion. Ratings are generated from the parent's and child's reports, who are interviewed together, and the final rating is determined from the clinical judgment of the interviewer. In total, 19 items are rated, and items 1–10 are scored for the total score, with 5 questions pertaining to obsessions and compulsions, respectively. Revised from an adult version, the interview contains questions regarding phenomenology of obsessions and compulsions, distress caused by the symptoms, control over OCD, avoidant behavior, pathological doubting, and obsessive slowness. The instrument is applicable for clinical use, particularly in describing symptoms and measuring any change in treatment (Thomsen, 1998).
Leyton Obsessional Inventory–Child Version	Berg, Whitaker, Davies, Flament, & Rapoport, 1988. © 1988 by Williams and Wilkins.	Transformed from a 65-item questionnaire (or card-sorting test) for adults, to a 20-item test for children and adolescents, this instrument can be used when screening for obsessive-compulsive symptoms, but does not specifically differentiate between obsessive traits and ego-dystonic symptoms (Thomsen, 1998).
Anxiety Disorders Interview Schedule for Children (ADIS-C)	Silverman & Nelles, 1988	Semistructured clinical interview for 6–17-year-olds, with child and parent as informants.

(continued)

Table 7.3 (*Continued*)

Assessment	Source	Description
Multidimensional Anxiety Scale for Children (MASC)	March, Parker, et al., 1997	Self-report measure for 8–19-year-olds; child informant, 39 items total (10-item short form available), four subscales: physical anxiety, harm avoidance, social anxiety, separation anxiety

*Investigators interested in using this rating scale should contact Wayne Goodman at the Clinical Neuroscience Research Unit, Connecticut Mental Health Center, 34 Park Street, New Haven, CT 06508 or Mark Riddle at the Yale Child Study Center, P.O. Box 3333, New Haven, CT 06510.

- Videotapes on OCD in school-age children
- Reading materials
  - Treatment
  - Symptoms
  - Comorbidity
- List of other resources and Web sites on OCD

OC Information Center
2711 Allen Boulevard
Middleton, WI 53562
608-836-8070

Anxiety-Specific Organizations

Anxiety Disorders Association of America
6000 Executive Boulevard, Suite 513
Rockville, MD 20852
301-231-9350

Child & Adolescent Anxiety Disorders Clinic (CAADC)
Temple University
13th Street & Cecil B. Moore Avenue (Weiss Hall, Ground Level)
Philadelphia, PA 19122
www.childanxiety.org

Child Anxiety Network
Child and Adolescent Fear and Anxiety Treatment Program
648 Beacon Street, 6th Floor, Kenmore Square
Boston, MA 02215
617-353-9610
www.childanxiety.net

Publications on OCD for Practitioners, Children, and Families

March, J., Frances, A., Kahn, D., & Carpenter, D. (1997). The Expert Consensus Guideline Series: Treatment of obsessive-compulsive disorder. *Journal of Clinical Psychiatry, 58*(Suppl. 4), 1–72.

March, J. S., & Mulle, K. (1998). *OCD in children and adolescents: A cognitive-behavioral treatment manual.* New York: Guilford. www.guilford.com.

Rapoport, J. (1991). *The boy who couldn't stop washing.* New York: Penguin.

VanNoppen, B., Pato, M., & Rasmussen, S. (1997). *Learning to live with obsessive compulsive disorder*, 4th ed. Milford.

Wagner, A. P. (2000). *Up and down the worry hill: A children's book about obsessive-compulsive disorder.* Rochester, NY: Lighthouse Press.

Wagner, A. P. (2002). *Worried no more: Help and hope for anxious children.* Rochester, NY: Lighthouse Press.

Handouts, Tips for Parents, and Guidelines

Expert Knowledge Systems
P.O. Box 917
Independence, VA 24348
www.psychguides.com

OCD Support Groups

http://groups.yahoo.com/group/OCDSupportGroups/ links

Practice Example: Background and Reason for Referral

Maria is a 10-year-old Hispanic female in the fifth grade, living with her mother and two older brothers. Her two brothers are significantly older and do not spend a lot of time with Maria. Maria's mother, Ms. Alba, works two jobs, and Maria is often at home by herself. Maria was initially referred to the school-based health clinic at the beginning of the school year by her teacher, who was concerned because he noticed that she was leaving to go to the bathroom a lot and had very red, chapped hands. Maria was assessed by the health clinic and referred to the partnering school-based mental health clinic for further assessment when it became apparent she had underlying symptoms in addition to those exhibited physically.

Jennifer, a social worker at the clinic, contacted Ms. Alba and obtained a verbal report over the phone of Maria's behavior at home. At home, Ms. Alba reported, Maria was very concerned with cleanliness and often spent hours rearranging her room, placing and replacing toys and books on her shelves. Ms. Alba also continually had trouble getting Maria out of the apartment on time for school because Maria would insist on checking to make sure her bed was made correctly and to make sure she had all of her school books in her bag. This could sometimes go on for 30 minutes to an hour and caused Ms. Alba to be late to work on a regular basis. Around meal times, Maria would insist on washing her plate, glass, and hands numerous times before and after her meal. Ms. Alba also noticed Maria had been staying up much later than usual since the start of the school year, completing her homework. Ms. Alba hadn't worried too much about this because she assumed that Maria had more challenging homework to do since she had moved into the fifth grade. Ms. Alba agreed to come into the school-based mental health clinic with Maria to meet with Jennifer for an initial screening and evaluation.

Jennifer also met with Maria's teacher to get a better sense of how Maria behaved in the classroom. Maria's teacher had noticed that Maria seemed extremely anxious when working in certain areas of the classroom and tended to go to the bathroom following activities in other areas of the classroom, including the reading circle and arts and crafts corner. When working at her desk independently or in a group, Maria always seemed to be falling behind, and her teacher would often catch her retracing one word or sentence over and over. When working on writing assignments or math problems, Maria would sometimes get stuck on the first sentence or problem, erasing and rewriting the same thing over and over. Maria seldom finished an assignment and would often be blamed or teased when working in a group for incomplete work.

Assessment

Given the information provided by the mother, teacher, Maria, and intake evaluation, Maria was diagnosed with OCD according to the *DSM-IV-TR* (American Psychiatric Association, 2000).

Other than OCD-related symptoms, Maria did not exhibit any impairment or symptoms for any other Axis I or II *DSM-IV-TR* diagnoses. She had had no previous psychiatric history, and her medical and developmental histories were normal. Nothing remarkable or traumatic had occurred in Maria's life at home or at school recently other than the reported symptoms. Jennifer scheduled a first session with Maria and her mother to begin cognitive-behavioral therapy for OCD. After the initial screening following standard clinic procedures, Jennifer completed an intake evaluation with Maria. Jennifer administered the symptom checklist from the Children's Yale-Brown Obsessive Compulsive Scale (CYBOCS) to determine if specific OCD symptoms were present. Jennifer assigned a baseline score on the CYBOCS showing significant impairment and gave a global rating using the NIMH Global Obsessive-Compulsive Scale. Jennifer also rated Maria's global symptom severity and functional impairment using the Clinical Global Impairment Scale. Jennifer continued to give global ratings after each session using these two scales. Beginning with session two of Maria's treatment, Jennifer assigned a global rating after each session using the NIMH Global Improvement Scale, to monitor functioning and improvement across sessions. Jennifer also checked in with Ms. Alba after each session to address any lingering questions and discuss what she and Maria covered in session.

Implementing the CBT for OCD in Children and Adolescents Treatment Program

Step 1: Psychoeducation and Building Rapport

At the beginning of treatment, Jennifer took some time to talk to Maria about what she likes to do in and out of school, with her friends and family. Maria reported that she likes to spend time with her mother when she is not working. She does not have many friends her own age and does not really like to play games with other children because they get annoyed at her for "ruining" the game by repeating certain steps and movements. Jennifer made an effort to also establish rapport with Ms. Alba by empathizing with her frustrations around struggling in the morning with Maria to get out of the house, as well as dealing with Maria's other behaviors associated with OCD.

Next, Jennifer explained OCD as a type of "hiccup" in Maria's brain that sometimes tells Maria what to think and how to act. While describing the treatment process to Maria and Ms. Alba, Jennifer explained how they will be working together to help Maria "boss back" her OCD. She asked Maria to think of a nickname to give her OCD. Maria chose to call her OCD "Weird Worry" and identified some of her "weird worries" as staying clean; not getting germs from food, other kids, or things in the classroom; keeping her room and desk neat; getting her homework right; and making sure she hasn't forgotten anything when she leaves her apartment. She explained that she makes sure these things don't happen by always washing her hands when she does something new, making sure she cleans and tidies her room before she goes to bed and to school, and checking her assignments over and over again to make sure they are the right answers, at home and at school.

At the end of the first session, Jennifer explained how "homework" would be used during treatment. Jennifer assured Maria that she wouldn't have to write anything for homework outside of treatment, but that treatment homework would involve practicing and thinking about things they talked about and did in session. Maria agreed to this, and after the first session, Jennifer asked her to think about Weird Worry until the next session and look out for where, when, and how Weird Worry bothers her.

Steps 2 and 3: Mapping OCD and Cognitive Training

Over the next three sessions, Jennifer continued to work on showing Maria that OCD is the problem and that Maria can develop skills to boss back and control Weird Worry. Maria practiced resisting

her OCD and reported that she had tried to resist copying over her work by telling Weird Worry to go away. During these reports, Jennifer asked Maria about her level of anxiety when resisting Weird Worry. Jennifer explained to Maria that they would begin "mapping" her OCD by labeling the degree of anxiety she experiences over different obsessions and compulsions. Jennifer introduced Maria to the concept of the "fear thermometer" and explained how it would be used to rate her anxiety. Jennifer explained that Maria will rank her specific OCD symptoms/triggers on a scale of 1 to 10. Jennifer helped Maria to write down her specific triggers, obsessions, compulsions, and fear ratings on a chart and labeled this symptom hierarchy as the "Weird Worry List." Jennifer explained she would be helping to coach Maria through this list from the lowest to the highest point, and they would only move on to the next level when Maria was comfortable.

After the symptom hierarchy was complete, Jennifer and Maria determined where in Maria's life she was free from OCD, where she shared control with Weird Worry, and where Weird Worry had complete control over her. Jennifer explained they would be working primarily in the middle area, the transition zone, and would slowly move the transition zone up the hierarchy until Weird Worry did not have any areas of control. Through cognitive training instruction, Jennifer reassured Maria that she could do this by using her tool kit of strategies created in treatment, including bossing back OCD, remembering that her worries/obsessions are just OCD, or Weird Worry, and are separate from her compulsions, and that she didn't have to pay attention to Weird Worry. Jennifer wrote these steps on a card for Maria to carry around with her. Maria continued to think about her symptom hierarchy for homework and began practicing the cognitive strategies she had learned.

At the end of session four, Maria had finalized her symptom hierarchy, including the transition zone, and had a complete tool kit of strategies she was comfortable using in fighting Weird Worry. Jennifer also set up a variety of appropriate rewards for levels of achievement upon which Maria had agreed, including small prizes and certificates.

Step 4: Exposure and Response Prevention (E/RP)

At the beginning of this step of treatment, Jennifer explained to Maria that they would be moving on to put E/RP into action. Maria had been practicing not erasing and rewriting her answers so many times and reported her anxiety was much lower when she only copied her answers 5 times instead of 10. Since this symptom target was low on the symptom hierarchy, Jennifer suggested they try practicing the exposure in vivo so Jennifer could help coach Maria through it. Jennifer reminded Maria of her tool kit, and by the end of the exercise Maria had done a few math problems without copying over the numbers. Maria expressed confidence that she could work on this over the next week using her classroom homework as the exposure.

Over the next couple of sessions, Maria reported to Jennifer that she was able to practice resisting Weird Worry by not copying over her answers for classroom homework. She practiced the E/RP at home and was able to reduce her anxiety so she did not copy some of the questions in her homework and, finally, her entire homework. Jennifer rewarded these accomplishments with praise and asked Maria to identify some new targets from higher up on the symptom hierarchy.

As a higher-anxiety exposure, Maria thought that she might be able to try getting through an activity in the classroom without washing her hands repeatedly afterward. Jennifer suggested trying this as an imaginal exposure first, asking Maria to imagine how she would feel if she participated in this activity and then did not wash her hands before moving on to the next activity. Maria used examples of self-talk to explain how she would lower the anxiety she would feel resisting Weird Worry. Jennifer then set up an in vivo exposure where Maria read her a story and then bossed back OCD by not washing her hands afterward. Jennifer coached Maria through the process of self-talk and pushing away Weird Worry and the urges to wash her hands. Although Maria did not make it through the response prevention the first time without washing her hands, she limited the time spent on scrubbing her hands with soap. After a few sessions of practice, Maria's anxiety around this target had diminished. Jennifer rewarded Maria for her efforts throughout her attempts and Maria agreed to practice resisting this urge in class.

Ms. Alba. Jennifer began the sessions by reviewing Maria's homework and answering any questions Ms. Alba had. Jennifer asked how Weird Worry might affect members of Maria's family. Maria talked about how Weird Worry bosses around her mom and what the fear temperature would be for her if Ms. Alba didn't listen to Weird Worry. Ms. Alba had noticed that Maria was working on practicing the exposures at home but still expressed some frustration with the time she had to take to accommodate Maria's anxiety over dirtiness in the apartment. Ms. Alba had to wash Maria's bed sheets almost every day and wash the dishes multiple times a day or else Maria would not eat off them. Jennifer reiterated the importance of Ms. Alba as a cheerleader for Maria and helped her to think of ways she could help Maria complete an exposure task at home. At first, Ms. Alba was reluctant to reward Maria for eating her dinner without washing the dishes so many times because Ms. Alba believed this was something Maria should be doing anyway. After Jennifer explained the importance of positive reinforcement from her, Ms. Alba agreed to try giving Maria small rewards for accomplishing exposure tasks such as this. Jennifer set up an in vivo exposure with Ms. Alba and Maria where Maria completed a task on her hierarchy with which she was comfortable (writing without retracing), and Ms. Alba practiced encouraging and praising her efforts. At the end of the session, Maria agreed to try sitting down to dinner without having Ms. Alba wash her dishes and glass so many times beforehand.

Throughout the E/RP step in treatment, which took place over 13 sessions in 14 weeks, Maria continued to practice in vivo E/RP as well as practicing at home and in the classroom. Jennifer continued to monitor Maria's progress through global ratings and check ins with Ms. Alba. She also held conferences with Maria's teacher to discuss any progress or possible regression in the classroom, but the teacher reported only positive results. Jennifer worked with the teacher to come up with some small rewards and examples of praise the teacher could use without singling Maria out from the rest of the class.

Family Sessions

During the E/RP step in treatment, Jennifer scheduled two family sessions with Maria and

Relapse Prevention

After the E/RP sessions were complete and Maria felt that Weird Worry had been won over, one session was devoted to discussing relapse prevention. Jennifer distinguished the concept of "relapse" from a "slip" in which Maria may feel some of her OCD symptoms coming back. Jennifer assured Maria that she should not think of possible slips as failure on her part but that they are normal occurrences that may come and go, which she can manage using the strategies learned and practiced while in treatment. Jennifer coached Maria through an imaginal exposure where she pictured herself having a slip in which she felt the urge to scrub her hands after sharing in an art project with classmates. Maria successfully used self-talk to extinguish the anxiety she felt during the exposure and felt confident she would be able to manage the same situation if it happened for real. Jennifer walked Maria through her symptom hierarchy and discussed ways in which Maria could handle various slips for each symptom. Jennifer checked in with Ms. Alba and discussed the upcoming graduation with her and Maria as well as the process for booster sessions in the future if Maria or Ms. Alba felt they were needed.

Graduation

This final session of treatment focused solely on Maria's accomplishments since first coming to the mental health clinic. Maria reflected on the treatment process and recalled specific advances she had made up the symptom hierarchy as well as all of the times she won and gained control over OCD. Jennifer supported this realization by sharing the declining scores on the CY-BOCS and the increase in global ratings over the course of Maria's treatment. Jennifer presented Maria with a certificate of achievement and encouraged Maria to share her certificate as well as her success with her friends and family members. Jennifer checked in with Ms. Alba as well to address any remaining questions she had about the treatment and what would happen now that Maria was not in treatment. Ms. Alba seemed confident that Maria had the tools to manage her OCD on her own with Ms. Alba as the primary cheerleader. Jennifer scheduled one booster session for the following month and reminded Maria that she could always come speak to her if she felt the need for additional booster sessions.

Key Points to Remember

Obsessive-compulsive disorder poses a significant risk to children and adolescents, with estimates of 1 in 200 children suffering from the disorder (Adams et al., 1994). School-based practitioners can play a valuable role in identifying, assessing, and treating children with OCD. Cognitive-behavior therapy, often in conjunction with pharmacotherapy, is the intervention most commonly used to treat OCD.

Though not thoroughly tested in school-based settings, CBT is an effective and useful treatment for school-based practitioners, given the brevity of treatment, flexibility, and transportability across settings and age groups. The school-based setting poses multiple challenges, however, and school-based practitioners should keep the following key points in mind:

- Training and supervision are crucial in learning and implementing cognitive-behavioral therapy.
- The *CBT Treatment Manual* for children and adolescents with OCD (March & Mulle, 1998) and the helpful handouts and tips within the manual are essential tools when providing this intervention.
- Teachers and parents can be a valuable asset to the school-based practitioner in identifying, assessing, and treating the child. Practitioners are encouraged to provide teachers and parents in the school and community with information about OCD as an educational and preventive measure.
- Asking parents, teachers, and other informants to complete assessments about the child in treatment can help the practitioner to obtain a comprehensive picture of the child's behavior at the outset as well as the child's improvement throughout treatment. Practitioners should be aware of the time constraints on teachers' schedules and use appropriate assessment instruments (e.g., short version self-report assessments).
- Because OCD can be exhibited differently at home and school, ongoing communication among teachers, parents, and the practitioner is instrumental in the success of the treatment. School-based practitioners should collaborate with teachers and parents on scheduling sessions and sharing information so as to best fit the needs of all parties involved.

References

Abramowitz, J. S. (1998). Does cognitive-behavioral therapy cure obsessive-compulsive disorder? A meta-analytic evaluation of clinical significance. *Behavior Therapy, 29*(2), 339–355.

Adams, G. B., Waas, G. A., March, J. S., & Smith, M. C. (1994). Obsessive-compulsive disorder in children and adolescents: The role of the school psychologist in identification, assessment, and treatment. *School Psychology Quarterly, 9*(4), 274–294.

Albano, A. M., & Kendall, P. C. (2002). Cognitive behavioural therapy for children and adolescents with anxiety disorders: Clinical research advances. *International Review of Psychiatry, 14,* 129–134.

American Academy of Child and Adolescent Psychiatry. (1998). Practice parameters for the assessment and treatment of children and adolescents with obsessive-compulsive disorder. *Journal of the American Academy of Child and Adolescent Psychiatry, 37,* 27S–45S.

American Psychiatric Association. (2000). *Diagnostic and statistical manual of mental disorders* (4th ed., text revision). Washington, DC: Author.

Berg, C. Z., Whitaker, A., Davies, M., Flament, M. F., & Rapoport, J. L. (1988). The survey form of the Leyton Obsessional Inventory–child version: Norms from an epidemiological study. *Journal of the American Academy of Child and Adolescent Psychiatry, 27*(6), 759–763.

Clark, D. A. (2000). Cognitive behavior therapy for obsessions and compulsions: New applications and emerging trends. *Journal of Contemporary Psychotherapy, 30*(2), 129–147.

Foa, E. B., Franklin, M. E., & Kozak, M. J. (1998). Psychosocial treatments for obsessive-compulsive disorder. In R. P. Swinson, M. M. Antony, et al. (Eds.), *Obsessive-compulsive disorder: Theory, research, and treatment* (pp. 258–276). New York: Guilford.

Foster, P. S., & Eisler, R. M. (2001). An integrative approach to the treatment of obsessive-compulsive disorder. *Comprehensive Psychiatry, 42*(1), 24–31.

Franklin, M. E., Abramowitz, J. S., Bux, Jr., D. A., Zoellner, L. A., & Feeny, N. C. (2002). Cognitive-behavioral therapy with and without medication in the treatment of obsessive-compulsive disorder. *Professional Psychology, 33*(2), 162–168.

Franklin, M. E., Foa, E., & March, J. S. (2003). The pediatric obsessive-compulsive disorder treatment study: Rationale, design, and methods. *Journal of Child and Adolescent Psychopharmacology, 13*(1), S39–S51.

Franklin, M. E., Kozak, M. J., Cashman, L. A., Coles, M. E., Rheingold, A. A., & Foa, E. B. (1998). Cognitive-behavioral treatment of pediatric obsessive-compulsive disorder: An open clinical trial. *Journal of the American Academy of Child and Adolescent Psychiatry, 37*(4), 412–419.

Franklin, M. E., Rynn, M., Foa, E. B., & March, J. S. (2003). Treatment of obsessive-compulsive disorder. In M. A. Reinecke, M. F. Dattilio, et al. (Eds.), *Cognitive therapy with children and adolescents: A casebook for clinical practice* (2nd ed., pp. 162–184). New York: Guilford.

Geller, D. A., Biederman, J., Faraone, S., Agranat, A., Cradock, K., Hagermoser, L., Kim, G., Frazier, J., & Coffey, B. J. (2001). Developmental aspects of obsessive-compulsive disorder: Findings in children, adolescents, and adults. *Journal of Nervous and Mental Disease, 189*(7), 471–477.

Geller, D. A., Hoog, S. L., Heiligenstein, J. H., Ricardi, R. K., Tamura, R., Kluszynski, S., Jacobson, J. G., & Fluoxetine Pediatric OCD Study Team. (2001). Fluoxetine treatment for obsessive-compulsive disorder in children and adolescents: A placebo-controlled clinical trial. *Journal of the American Academy of Child and Adolescent Psychiatry, 40*(7), 773–779.

Goodman, W., Price, L., Rasmussen, S., Mazure, C., Delgado, P., Heninger, G. R., & Charney, D. S. (1989a). The Yale-Brown Obsessive Compulsive Scale: II. Validity. *Archives of General Psychiatry, 46*(11), 1012–1016.

Goodman, W., Price, L., Rasmussen, S., Mazure, C., Fleischmann, R. L., Hill, C. L., Heninger, G. R., & Charney, D. S. (1989b). The Yale-Brown Obsessive Compulsive Scale: I. Development, use, and reliability. *Archives of General Psychiatry, 46*(11), 1006–1011.

Kampman, M., Keijsers, G.P.J., Hoogduin, C.A.L., & Verbraak, M.J.P.M. (2002). Addition of cognitive-behaviour therapy for obsessive-compulsive disorder patients non-responding to fluoxetine. *Acta Psychiatrica Scandinavica, 106,* 314–319.

Kazdin, A. E., & Weisz, J. R. (1998). Identifying and developing empirically supported child and adolescent treatments. *Journal of Consulting & Clinical Psychology, 66*(1), 19–36.

Kendall, P. C., & Chu, B. C. (2000). Retrospective self-reports of therapist flexibility in a manual-based treatment for youth with anxiety disorders. *Journal of Clinical Child Psychology, 29*(2), 209–220.

March, J. S., Biederman, J., Wolkow, R., Safferman, A., Mardekian, J., Cook, E. H., Cutler, N. R., Dominguez, R., Ferguson, J., Muller, B., Riesenberg, R., Rosenthal, M., Sallee, F. R., & Wagner, K. D. (1998). Sertraline in children and adolescents with obsessive-compulsive disorder: A multicenter randomized controlled trial. *Journal of the American Medical Association, 280*(20), 1752–1757.

March, J., Frances, A., Kahn, D., & Carpenter, D. (1997). The expert consensus guidelines series: Treatment of obsessive-compulsive disorder. *Journal of Clinical Psychiatry, 58*(Suppl. 4), 1–72.

March, J. S., Franklin, M., Nelson, A., & Foa, E. (2001). Cognitive-behavioral psychotherapy for pediatric obsessive-compulsive disorder. *Journal of Clinical Child Psychology, 30*(1), 8–18.

March, J. S., & Mulle, K. (1998). *OCD in children and adolescents: A cognitive-behavioral treatment manual.* New York: Guilford.

March, J. S., Mulle, K., & Herbel, B. (1994). Behavioral psychotherapy for children and adolescents with obsessive-compulsive disorder: An open trial of a new protocol-driven treatment package. *Journal of the American Academy of Child & Adolescent Psychiatry, 33*(3), 333–341.

March, J. S., Parker, J.D.A., Sullivan, K., Stallings, P., & Conners, C. K. (1997). The Multidimensional Anxiety Scale for Children (MASC): Factor structure, reliability, and validity. *Journal of the American Academy of Child & Adolescent Psychiatry, 36*(4), 554–565.

Ollendick, T. H., & King, N. J. (1998). Empirically supported treatments for children with phobic and anxiety disorders: Current status. *Journal of Clinical Child Psychology, 27*(2), 156–167.

Piacentini, J., Bergman, L., Keller, M., & McCracken, J. (2003). Functional impairment in children and adolescents with obsessive-compulsive disorder. *Journal of Child and Adolescent Psychopharmacology, 13*(1), S61–S69.

Rowa, K., Antony, M. M., & Swinson, R. P. (2000). Behavioral treatment of obsessive-compulsive disorder. *Behavioural and Cognitive Psychotherapy, 28*, 353–360.

Scahill, L., Riddle, M., McSwiggin-Hardin, M., Ort, S., King, R., Goodman, W., et al. (1997). Children's Yale-Brown Obsessive-Compulsive Scale: Reliability and validity. *Journal of Child and Adolescent Psychiatry, 36*, 844–852.

Silverman, W. K., & Nelles, W. B. (1988). The Anxiety Disorders Interview Schedule for Children. *Journal of the American Academy of Child & Adolescent Psychiatry, 27*(6), 772–778.

Southam-Gerow, M. A., & Kendall, P. C. (2000). Cognitive-behavioral therapy with youth: Advances, challenges, and future directions. *Clinical Psychology and Psychotherapy, 7*, 343–366.

Stanley, M. A., & Turner, S. M. (1995). Current status of pharmacological and behavioral treatment of obsessive-compulsive disorder. *Behavior Therapy, 26*(1), 163–186.

Thomsen, P. H. (1998). Obsessive-compulsive disorder in children and adolescent: Clinical guidelines. *European Child and Adolescent Psychiatry, 7*, 1–11.

Velting, O. N., Setzer, N. J., & Albano, A. M. (2004). Update on and advances in assessment and cognitive-behavioral treatment of anxiety disorders in children and adolescents. *Professional Psychology, 35*(1), 42–54.

Wagner, A. P. (2002). *What to do when your child has obsessive-compulsive disorder: Strategies and solutions.* Rochester, NY: Lighthouse Press.

Wagner, A. P. (2003a). Cognitive-behavioral therapy for children and adolescents with obsessive-compulsive disorder. *Brief Treatment and Crisis Intervention, 3*(3), 291–306.

Wagner, A. P. (2003b). *Treatment of OCD in children and adolescents: A cognitive-behavioral therapy manual.* Rochester, NY: Lighthouse Press.

Warren, R., & Thomas, J. C. (2001). Cognitive-behavior therapy of obsessive-compulsive disorder in private practice: An effectiveness study. *Anxiety Disorders, 15*, 277–285.

Effective Interventions for Adolescents With Depression

Jacqueline Corcoran ❋ Jane Hanvey-Phillips

CHAPTER 8

Getting Started

Depression occurs in about 2% of elementary-age children, but in adolescents rates increase dramatically, making depression for this age group a significant mental health issue. For this reason the focus on this chapter will be on depression in adolescence. Reviews of community studies have indicated lifetime prevalence rates for adolescent depression ranging from 15 to 20% (Birmaher et al., 1996; Lewinsohn & Essau, 2002). Point prevalence rates for major depression[1] in adolescents are estimated at between 4 and 8.3%; for dysthymia,[2] point prevalence rates range from 2 to 5% (Birmaher et al., 1996; Cottrell, Fonagy, Kurtz, Phillips, & Target, 2002). Rates of depression for females are double the rates of males (Birmaher et al., 1996; Lewinsohn & Essau, 2002). Depression in adolescents may also be comorbid with other disorders, such as anxiety disorders, ADHD, and substance abuse. Further, adolescent depression is a major risk factor for suicidal ideation, suicide attempts, and completed suicides (Cottrell et al., 2002; Waslick, Kandel, & Kakouros, 2002). See chapter 1 on how to identify and prevent suicide in adolescents. Finally, adolescent depression presents risk for the continuation of depression into adulthood (Klein, Dougherty, & Olino, 2005). For these reasons, school social workers should demonstrate the knowledge and competence to assess for depression in teenagers and offer appropriate treatment and referrals.

What We Know

Intervention research has tended to focus on cognitive-behavioral models. *Behavioral* models focus on the development of coping skills, especially in the domain of social skills and choosing pleasant daily activities, so that the youth receive more reinforcement from their environments. *Cognitive* models include assessing and changing the distorted thinking that people with depression exhibit, in which they cast everyday experiences in a negative light. Interventions based on cognitive-behavioral models include the following components:

- the identification and restructuring of depressive thinking
- social skills training (how to make and maintain friendships)
- communication and social problem solving (how to share feelings and resolve conflicts without alienating others)
- developing aptitudes pertaining to self-esteem (establishing performance goals)
- progressive relaxation training to ease the stress and tension that can undercut enjoyment of activities
- structuring mood-boosting activities into daily life

Narrative reviews (Diamond et al., 2002) and meta-analyses (Cuijpers, 1998; Reinecke, Ryan, & Dubois, 1998) of cognitive-behavioral treatment for adolescents have indicated positive outcomes in terms of reduction of depression for up to 2 years' follow-up. The meta-analysis by Reinecke et al. (1998) was conducted on 24 control/comparison studies of cognitive-behavioral therapy (CBT), 14 of which had posttest information and 10 of which included follow-up data. All but one of the studies had as their subjects dysphoric[3] adolescents who were recruited from schools. A group therapy format was used in most studies. The overall effect size posttreatment was 1.02, whereas the overall effect size at follow-up was .61. These effect sizes are defined as "large" and "moderate," respectively, by Cohen (1988), impressive findings for psychosocial treatment.

Another major review found a total of seven treatment-outcome studies involving children (grades three to eight) with depressive symptoms (Kaslow & Thompson, 1998). However, none of these studies met the criteria for well-established treatments. The work of one group of researchers, Stark and colleagues (Stark, Reynolds, & Kaslow, 1987; Stark, Rouse, & Livingston, 1991), merited the standard of a "probably efficacious treatment." The Kaslow and Thompson (1998) review also located seven treatment-outcome studies involving adolescents (ages 13–18) with either elevated depression scores or who had met *DSM* criteria for major depression or dysthymia. Since none of the studies compared an experimental condition with an already established treatment and none of the interventions had been examined by two or more research teams, criteria for a well-established treatment have not been met. However, the work of the research team of Lewinsohn and colleagues (Clark, Hawkins, Murphy, Sheeber, Lewinsohn, & Seeley, 1995; Lewinsohn, Clarke, Hops, & Andrews, 1990; Lewinsohn, Clarke, Rhode, Hops, & Seeley, 1996) merited the standard of "probably efficacious treatment."

What We Can Do

Intervention in the school system for depression could include primary prevention (for all teens in a particular school); secondary prevention (targeting teens of parents who are depressed as these teens have a high risk of becoming depressed themselves); or tertiary prevention (targeting teens who test positive when screened for depression). It is highly recommended that the social worker and mental health counselors screen for depression in the school; unlike externalizing problems (aggression, acting-out behaviors), which are better identified by a teacher or parent, internalizing problems, such as depression, are more accurately reported by the adolescent (Cottrell et al., 2002; Mufson & Moreau, 1997). As a result, we recommend that school social workers and mental health counselors use measures of proven standardization to screen for depression. A review of this literature was drawn from Myers and Winters

(2002). The interested reader may also consult Klein et al. (2005). Please see Table 8.1 for information on these measurement instruments.

Empirically tested cognitive-behavioral treatment models are available for public use. Specifically, the Lewinsohn and Clarke curriculum, Adolescent Coping With Depression Course, is available on the worldwide Web (http://www.kpchr.org/public/acwd/acwd.html). A shortened version of this curriculum will be described in this chapter and is available from the second author. (For some other empirically validated manuals, please see the list at the end of the chapter.)

The present intervention uses a group format, consisting of six 1-hour sessions offered once a week. A variety of techniques are employed, including education, group discussion, role play, and behavior rehearsal. Homework is emphasized as an important component of the intervention, with students being told that the amount of effort they invest in homework is associated with the amount of improvement they will feel. Given that teenagers may have difficulty with written assignments, participants are given credit even if they try to do tasks and report the results of their attempts to the group. Reinforcement may involve candy or small novelty items that teens find desirable. It often helps to ask the students what they find rewarding.

To make the intervention generally available to a wide variety of students, inclusion and exclusion criteria are kept to a minimum. The primary inclusion criteria for prospective participants includes clinically significant depression as shown by scores on standardized measures that suggest depression (for example, a score of 10 or greater on the Beck Depression Inventory [BDI]). Exclusion criteria include unwillingness to consent to the intervention and students who do not speak or understand English (unless the group is composed entirely of students who speak another language and a facilitator is available to speak the language effectively). Students who report suicidality or who are determined to be suicidal are referred for evaluation and additional intervention outside the school setting.

Session 1: Introduction to the Group and Social Skills

The purpose of the group is shared with the students; it is to help them learn skills for controlling their moods. The following introduces the connections among feelings, thoughts, and actions.

Table 8.1 Measures for Youth Depression

Children's Depression Inventory (Kovacs, 1992)	• 27-item, self-report inventory for children from ages 8 to 13 • measuring severity (0 to 2) of overt symptoms of depression, such as sadness, sleep and eating disturbances, anhedonia, and suicidal ideation • modified from the Beck Depression Inventory for adults • translated into several languages	Multi-Health Systems 908 Niagra Falls Blvd. North Tonawanda, NY 14120-2060 800-456-3003 www.mhs.com
Reynolds Adolescent Depression Scale (Reynolds, 1987)	• measures *DSM-III* criteria for depression over the past 2 weeks • has primarily been developed and used with school samples • recommended for screening, rather than outcome	Psychological Assessment Resources, Inc. P.O. Box 998 Odessa, FL 33549 800-383-6595 800-331-8378 http:www.parinc.com
Center for Epidemiologic Studies Depression Scale for Children (Weissman, Orvaschel, & Padian, 1980)	• comprises items empirically derived from adult depression scales • assesses symptoms over the past week • widely employed with adolescents	http://www.depression clinic.com/db/servlet/ TopicReq?Session ID=227809545. 1091164813041&Topic ID=3009&Action=view
Beck Depression Inventory II (Beck, Brown, & Steer, 1996)	• self-report measure with 21 items, each having four answer options • targeted audience includes depressed adults, adolescents, elderly individuals, inpatients, outpatients, primary care patients, patients with medical conditions • works well with a wide range of ages and cultures, both males and females	Harcourt Assessment 19500 Bulverde Road San Antonio, TX 78259

Students learn that the way they feel influences how they think and behave, which then influences their feelings and thoughts, and so on. They are told that when people "feel bad," they're less likely to engage in enjoyable activities, and they doubt their ability to be successful at those things

(for example, making new friends). When people are successful at some effort, they feel positive and gain self-confidence.

The facilitator then explains that they will work on changing *actions* by increasing pleasant activities, improving social skills, and developing effective communication and problem-solving skills. They will work on changing *thoughts* by stopping negative thoughts and increasing positive thoughts. They will work on changing *feelings* by changing their thoughts, changing their actions, and learning relaxation skills.

Rules for the group are then formulated. Although group members are encouraged to come up with their own rules, the following should be included:

- Avoid depressive talk.
- Allow each person to have equal time.
- Maintain confidentiality.
- Offer support that is constructive, caring, and nonpressuring.

The first topic for the group is social skills, which are discussed as important for positive interactions to occur and to build or improve relationships. Students are taught to make eye contact, smile, say something positive about other people, reveal information about themselves, when to start a conversation and what to say, and how to leave a conversation.

For the first session's homework, students are asked to practice their newly acquired skills at least twice in the upcoming week.

Session 2: Pleasant Activities

The session begins by asking students to report on their homework efforts from session 1. As an introduction to the topic for the day, students are told that pleasant activities are important for feelings of well-being. Teens are then given a list of possible activities to engage in during the upcoming week, including listening to music, hanging out with friends, and driving a car. It is recommended that cofacilitators brainstorm with the group about ideas for activities. Homework assigned for this session involves setting a reasonable goal for increasing the number of pleasant activities and then engaging in this number of activities during the upcoming week.

Session 3: Relaxation Training

Students are informed about the role of stress and tension in depression. They are then informed that relaxation is likely to contribute to a reduction in both anxiety and depression. The facilitators guide

the students through two different relaxation techniques: the Jacobson technique (progressive muscle relaxation) and the Benson technique (focusing on a word or phrase while doing progressive muscle relaxation). Homework for this session is to practice the Benson relaxation technique three times and to practice the Jacobson relaxation technique at least three times. The recommendation is made to do at least one of these techniques *every day* at a quiet time.

Session 4: Cognitive Restructuring

This session begins by educating students about the effects of decreasing negative thoughts and increasing positive thoughts. They are then taught how to replace negative thoughts with positive counterthoughts. Students are given instructions on how to use the A-B-C (activating event, belief, and consequences) technique to change their thoughts, and thus their moods.

To interrupt or stop negative thoughts, three techniques are taught:

1. *Thought stopping.* When alone and thinking negatively, students are instructed to yell "STOP" as loudly as possible and to then say, "I won't think about that any more." Students are told to gradually change from yelling to thinking "Stop," so the technique can be used in public.
2. *The rubber band technique.* Students are told they can wear a rubber band on their wrists and snap it every time they catch themselves thinking negatively. This technique should reduce negative thoughts.
3. *Set aside worrying time.* This involves scheduling a time each day to focus on troubling issues. The idea is to make an appointment with oneself for worrying; 15 minutes should be plenty.

Homework for this session is to use at least one thought-stopping technique at least two times during the week when negative thoughts cause problems.

Session 5: Communication Skills

This session involves a great deal of active participation from group members. Group members learn about appropriate responses that emphasize reflective, or active, listening with the facilitators modeling appropriate reflective listening techniques following a didactic presentation. Students are taught the difference between *understanding* and *judgmental* responses and are told that *understanding* responses promote healthier communication. Next, self-disclosure and the appropriateness of self-disclosure in given situations is addressed. Students are taught that appropriate self-disclosure includes talking about feelings related to events: "I feel _____ when you _____. I would prefer _____." They then practice this technique with their peers.

It is important to note that teens often have difficulty expressing negative feelings; therefore, in this session, they are educated about helpful ways to do this. Three possible situations are addressed: resisting peer pressure, telling a friend about something he or she did that bothered the person, and declining a friend's request for something. Students are assisted in identifying appropriate ways to express their feelings in these situations. For homework, group members are asked to use the self-disclosing format ("I feel . . .") two times in the coming week.

Session 6: Problem-Solving/ Negotiation and Maintaining Gains

The problem-solving process is taught in order to work out situations with others that are bothersome. The process includes defining the problem, brainstorming, examining possible options, deciding on an option, implementing an option, and evaluating the implementation. The cofacilitators model the techniques in a role play, and group members practice.

During this final session, students are asked to "change gears" and prepare for the group's termination. They are told that, not uncommonly, group members feel a void when the group disbands. They are assisted in preparing for termination by reminding them to use the cognitive-behavioral coping skills they have been learning throughout the course. Students are given a "life plan" worksheet to identify potentially stressful life situations—both positive and negative—and the plans they can make to cope with these. They are also given information on the symptoms of depression and are strongly encouraged to contact a physician, school social worker, or therapist if they notice symptoms persisting for a period of 2 weeks. They are reminded that putting off the help they need won't make the depression go away. Finally,

students are asked to complete a posttest measure of depression to determine their level of improvement (or decline) since the beginning of treatment. If appropriate and feasible, the measure could be used weekly to evaluate results via a single system design approach.

Use of Medications

For adolescent depression, selective serotonin reuptake inhibitors (SSRIs) (i.e., Prozac, Paxil, Celexa, Zoloft), as compared to tricyclic antidepressants, have shown greater therapeutic effectiveness and fewer adverse effects. Indeed, the tricyclic antidepressants are not recommended for children given the lack of evidence to support their use (Hazell, O'Connell, & Heathcote, 2003). Concerns about suicidality in children and adolescents who have taken medication have led the United Kingdom to ban the use of antidepressants for youth. However, a recent study showed that a 12-week course of medication and psychotherapy (cognitive-behavioral therapy) was more effective than either medication or psychotherapy alone, producing an improvement rate of 71% (Treatment for Adolescents With Depression Study Team, 2004). At the same time, medication alone showed more improvements than psychotherapy alone, which was not statistically significant from the placebo condition.

Often, medication must be administered in the school setting. This may be the case because the student has a dosing schedule requiring administration during the time he or she is at school, or may occur if a child forgets to take medication at home. As McCarthy, Kelly, and Reed (2000) note, budget cuts in a time of increasing demand for school-based health services require more unlicensed assistive personnel (UAP) or students themselves to administer medication at school. Controversy concerns the administration of medication by nonmedical personnel and their ability to read health care provider orders, to properly store medications, to monitor students for side effects, and to dispense medications accurately. An additional area of concern is the need to have parental permission to dispense needed medications at school (McCarthy et al., 2000). For parents who do not realize the importance of medication compliance, obtaining permission to dispense medication at school may be difficult. Additionally, it may be necessary for students to keep medication at home *and* at school, creating a financial burden for the family. Finally, there is the potential for students to abuse medication at school if proper monitoring is not in place. This might include selling or trading medication with other students or taking the wrong dose of their own medication. Clearly, medication issues create a dilemma for effective management in the school setting.

Challenges With School-Based Interventions

Although school-based interventions provide access to services that might otherwise be unavailable to depressed teens, they are not without challenges. Confidentiality remains one of the chief concerns in the implementation of interventions in the school setting, both in terms of identifying those at risk and in providing a confidential environment for provision of interventions (Atkins, Graczyk, Frazier, & Abdul-Adil, 2003; Satcher, 2004). Additional difficulties include integration of services with other providers outside the school and obtaining support from school personnel to facilitate interventions (Satcher, 2004). Parents also play a significant role in the success of school-based interventions. Without their consent, interventions may be prohibited for students; therefore it is necessary to educate parents, as well as students, about the intended outcomes of participation in school-based interventions. Despite these challenges, the benefits of providing interventions are likely to outweigh the difficulties of implementation.

Tools and Practice Examples

The following list provides an overview of interventions used with depressed students in the school setting.

Manuals

Clarke, G., Lewinsohn, P., & Hops, H. (1990). The adolescent coping with depression course. Available: http://www.kpchr.org/public/acwd/acwd.html.

Mufson, L., Dorta, K. P., Moreau, D., & Weissman, M. M. (2004). *Interpersonal psychotherapy for depressed adolescents* (2nd ed.). New York: Guilford.

Stark, K. (1990). *Childhood depression: School-based intervention.* New York: Guilford.

Stark, K., & Kendall, P. (1996a). *Taking action: A workbook for overcoming depression.* Available: www.workbookpublishing.com.

Stark, K., & Kendall, P. (1996b). *Treating depressed children: Therapist manual for "Taking action."* www.workbookpublishing.com.

Weisz, J. R., Weersing, V. R., Valeri, S. M., & McCarty, C. A. (1999a). *Therapist's manual for PASCET: Primary and secondary control enhancement training program.* Los Angeles: University of California.

Weisz, J. R., Weersing, V. R., Valeri, S. M., & McCarty, C. A. (1999b). *Act and think: Youth practice book for PASCET.* Los Angeles: University of California.

Case Example

Leah Hernandez was a 15-year-old Hispanic female who lived with her mother, stepfather, and older brother. There were economic difficulties, and the level of tension in the household was high. Leah's grades had begun to decline in the past few months; she was irritable and spent most of her free time sitting alone in her room or sleeping. At her school, social workers began screening students for depression, using the Beck Depression Inventory (BDI), to identify students who could benefit from participation in a cognitive-behavioral intervention. Leah participated in the screening and obtained a score of 23, which is considered a moderate level of depression.

The social worker met with Leah privately to explain that a training course was being offered to help students manage their moods. Leah was agreeable to participating, but since Leah was a minor, the social worker had to contact Leah's mother, Gloria Perez, and described the program to her. Mrs. Perez agreed to allow Leah to participate.

The course began 1 week after the conversation with Leah's mother. Arrangements had been made for the students to be excused from class for an hour, and they were welcomed with doughnuts and soft drinks. Two social workers introduced themselves as the group facilitators, then explained the format of the course and the rules for participation. Leah was shy about role playing in front of the other students, but said that having practiced starting a new conversation, it would probably be easier for her to do so on her own that week as homework.

During the session on pleasant activities, Leah reported that she rarely engaged in any activities she enjoyed. She told the group that her mother and stepfather would tell her she should be working rather than having fun. The social workers addressed this issue and encouraged Leah to identify activities that would not disrupt the household, such as listening to relaxing music in her room, writing poetry (which Leah said she used to enjoy), or taking bubble baths.

During the session on relaxation, the students were given the opportunity to practice progressive muscle relaxation skills. At first, Leah reported that she felt awkward trying to relax with other people in the room, but found she was able to follow instructions easily after the social worker told all of the students to close their eyes so nobody was looking. Leah reported feeling calm and comfortable at the end of the session and willingly practiced the relaxation skills at home during the week.

Leah realized during the session on cognitive restructuring that she usually exaggerated negative experiences and minimized positive experiences. During the time Leah was participating in the group, she failed a math test and told one of the social workers, "I'm just stupid. That's why I failed." The social worker pointed out that Leah usually passed tests and, in fact, her grades had been improving recently. Leah was able to acknowledge this and stated that she would ask for help before the next math test and believed she could pass it then.

The session on communication skills focused on reflective listening and the use of "I feel . . ." messages. Leah had difficulty, at first, using "I feel" statements but eventually was able to understand the concept and was encouraged to practice at home. Leah reported that during the week, she and her mother had several positive conversations and that Leah's mood had improved as a result of them.

Leah was quiet during the session on conflict resolution. She appeared to attend to the discussion but did not participate. At the end of the group time, the social workers asked if she understood the concepts of brainstorming and problem solving as ways to reduce conflict. Leah replied that they seemed like good ideas, but she didn't think they would work with her family. The social workers encouraged Leah to present the material to her parents and to ask them to try the strategies. She agreed to do so. When she returned the following week, she reported that her mother tried to use brainstorming with her but her stepfather told her he wasn't going to negotiate anything with her; she would have to do things his way. The social workers helped Leah to identify cognitive coping strategies she could use when faced with her stepfather's unwillingness to change.

As part of the final group session, students identified gains made in treatment and planned for the future. During this session, Leah reported feeling a sense of contentment: Her grades had improved; conflict with her mother was greatly reduced; and she had found pleasant activities to do that did not upset the family.

Key Points to Remember

- Depressed adolescents are at risk for serious negative outcomes and can benefit from school-based interventions.
- Cognitive-behavioral group interventions have been shown to be effective and are recommended in the school setting.
- The recommended intervention includes attention to social skills, pleasant activities, relaxation, cognitive restructuring, communication, and problem-solving and negotiation skills.
- Homework assignments are important to the intervention.
- Assessment before and after the intervention is recommended.
- For adolescents with severe depression and/or suicidal ideation, adjunctive interventions are also recommended.

Notes

1. A *major depressive episode* is a period of at least 2 weeks during which a person experiences a depressed mood or loss of interest in nearly all life activities.

2. *Dysthymic disorder* represents a general personality style featuring symptoms that are similar to, but less intense than, those of major depression. This diagnosis requires 2 years of a continuously depressed mood (1 year for children and adolescents). It generally has an early age of onset (childhood through early adulthood) and produces impairments in school, work, and social life.

3. *Dysphoria* is depression that is subclinical in nature—when teens do not meet full criteria for either dysthymia or major depression.

References

Atkins, M. S., Graczyk, P. A., Frazier, S. L., & Abdul-Adil, J. (2003). Toward a new model for promoting urban children's mental health: accessible, effective, and sustainable school-based mental health services. *School Psychology Review, 35,* 525–529.

Beck, A. T., Brown, G., & Steer, R. A. (1996). *Beck Depression Inventory II manual.* San Antonio, TX: Psychological Corporation.

Birmaher, B., Ryan, N., Williamson, D., Brent, D., Kaufman, J., & Dahl, R. (1996). Childhood and adolescent depression: A review of the past 10 years, part I. *Journal of the American Academy of Child & Adolescent Psychiatry, 35,* 1427–1439.

Clarke, G., Hawkins, W., Murphy, M., Sheeber, L., Lewinsohn, P., & Seeley, J. (1995). Targeted prevention of unipolar depressive disorder in an at-risk sample of high school adolescents: A randomized trial of a group cognitive intervention. *Journal of the American Academy of Child and Adolescent Psychiatry, 34,* 312–321.

Clarke, G., Lewinsohn, P., & Hops, H. (1990). *The adolescent coping with depression course.* Available: http://www.kpchr.org/public/acwd/acwd.html.

Cohen, J. (1988). *Statistical power analysis for the behavioral sciences* (2nd ed.). Hillsdale, NJ: Earlbaum.

Cottrell, D., Fonagy, P., Kurtz, Z., Phillips, J., & Target, M. (2002). What works for whom? A critical review of treatments for children and adolescents. In P. Fonagy, M. Target, D. Cottrell, J. Phillips, & Z. Kurtz (Eds.), *Depressive disorders* (pp. 89–105). New York: Guilford.

Cuijpers, P. (1998). A psychoeducational approach to the treatment of depression: A meta-analysis of Lewinsohn's "Coping with Depression" course. *Behavior Therapy, 29,* 521–533.

Diamond, G. S., Reis, B. F., Diamond, G. M., Siqueland, L., & Isaacs, L. (2002). Attachment-based family therapy for depressed adolescents: A treatment development study. *Journal of the American Academy of Child and Adolescent Psychiatry, 41*(10), 1190–1197.

Hazell, P., O'Connell, D., Heathcote, D., & Henryk D. (2003). Tricyclic drugs for depression in children and adolescents (Cochrane Review). In *The Cochrane Library,* Issue 1. Oxford: Update Software.

Kaslow, N., & Thompson, M. (1998). Applying the criteria for empirically supported treatment to studies of psychosocial interventions for child and adolescent depression. *Journal of Clinical Child Psychology, 27,* 146–155.

Klein, D., Dougherty, L., & Olino, T. (2005). Toward guidelines for evidence-based assessment of depression in children and adolescents. *Journal of Clinical Child and Adolescent Psychology, 34,* 412–432.

Kovacs, M. (1992). *Children's Depression Inventory manual.* (Available from Multi-Health Systems, 908 Niagara Falls Blvd., North Tonawanda, NY 14120-2060; (800) 456-3003; www.mhs.com)

Lewinsohn, P., Clarke, G., Hops, H., & Andrews, J. (1990). Cognitive-behavioral treatment for depressed adolescents. *Behavior Therapy, 21,* 385–401.

Lewinsohn, P., Clarke, G., Rhode, P., Hops, H., & Seeley,

J. (1996). A course in coping: A cognitive-behavioral approach to the treatment of adolescent depression. In E. D. Hibbs & P. S. Jensen (Eds.), *Psychosocial treatments for child and adolescent disorders: Empirically based strategies for clinical practice* (pp. 109–135). Washington, DC: American Psychological Association.

Lewinsohn, P., & Essau, C. (2002). Depression in adolescents. In I. H. Gotlib & C. Hammen (Eds.), *Handbook of depression* (pp. 541–559). New York: Guilford.

McCarthy, A. M., Kelly, M. W., & Reed, D. (2000). Medication administration practices of school nurses. *Journal of School Health, 70*(9), 371–376.

Mufson, L., & Moreau, D. (1997). Depressive disorders. In R. T. Ammerman & M. Hersen (Eds.), *Handbook of prevention and treatment with children and adolescents: Intervention in the real world context* (pp. 403–430). New York: John Wiley.

Myers, K., & Winters, N. C. (2002). Ten-year review of rating scales: II. Scales for internalizing disorders. *Journal of the American Academy of Child and Adolescent Psychiatry, 41,* 634–660.

Reinecke, M., Ryan, N., & Dubois, D. (1998). Cognitive-behavioral therapy of depression and depressive symptoms during adolescence: A review and meta-analysis. *Journal of the American Academy of Child and Adolescent Psychiatry, 37,* 26–34.

Reynolds, W. (1987). *Reynolds Adolescent Depression Scale (RADS).* Odessa, FL: Psychological Assessment Resources.

Roberts, C., Kane, R., Thomson, H., Bishop, B., & Hart, B. (2003). The prevention of depressive symptoms in rural school children: A randomized controlled trial. *Journal of Consulting and Clinical Psychology, 71,* 622–629.

Satcher, D. (2004). School-based mental health services (policy statement). *Pediatrics, 113,* 1839–1845.

Stark, K., Reynolds, W., & Kaslow, N. (1987). A comparison of the relative efficacy of self-control therapy and a behavioral problem-solving therapy for depression in children. *Journal of Abnormal Child Psychology, 15,* 91–113.

Stark, K., Rouse, L., & Livingston, R. (1991). Treatment of depression during childhood and adolescence: Cognitive-behavioral procedures for the individual and family. In P. Kendall (Ed.), *Child and adolescent therapy* (pp. 165–206). New York: Guilford.

Treatment for Adolescents With Depression Study Team. (2004). Fluoxetine, cognitive-behavioral therapy, and their combination for adolescents with depression: Treatment for adolescents with depression study (tads) randomized controlled trial. *Journal of the American Medical Association, 292,* 807–820.

Waslick, B. D., Kandel, B. A., & Kakouros, B. S. (2002). Depression in children and adolescents: An overview. In D. Shaffer & B. D. Waslick (Eds.), *The many faces of depression in children and adolescents* (pp. 1–36). Washington, DC: American Psychiatric Association Publishing.

Effective Interventions for Students With Bipolar Disorder

Kathleen A. Casey

Getting Started

Bipolar disorder, commonly referred to as manic-depressive illness, is among the least understood and most controversial psychiatric conditions in children. It is also one of the most severe, often creating significant impairment in school, family, and social functioning. Similar to other serious mental illnesses, early intervention and treatment of bipolar disorder is critical (Rivas-Vasquez, Johnson, Rey, & Blais, 2002). Despite the need for timely treatment and the steady increase in the diagnosis of bipolar disorder among school-aged children since the 1990s, there is a lack of empirical data to guide school social workers and school counselors in addressing this severe and chronic illness (Anglada, 2002). Indeed, to date, there are no evidence-based treatments specifically designed for youth under 18 years of age (Lofthouse & Fristad, 2004; National Institute of Mental Health, 2001).

In the absence of empirically supported treatments, the Clinical Child and Adolescent Division of the American Psychological Association recommends that practitioners utilize the most promising practices within the current literature (Kinscherff, 1999; Ollendick, 2003). To that end, this chapter translates the field's best practice information, including interventions currently undergoing clinical trials, to assist school personnel in recognizing, diagnosing, intervening with, and supporting students with bipolar disorder and their families. A list of additional resources is also included to aid teachers and counselors who wish to seek further assistance.

What We Know

Diagnosis

Bipolar disorder is a mental illness characterized by severe moods ranging between mania and depression. The American Psychiatric Association's *Diagnostic and Statistical Manual of Mental Disorders* (*DSM-IV*) classifies bipolar illness into four subtypes: bipolar I (BP-I), at least one manic or mixed episode; bipolar II (BP-II), at least one episode of major depression and hypomania; cyclothymia, alternating episodes of hypomania and symptoms of depression that fail to meet full diagnostic criteria; and bipolar not otherwise specified (BP-NOS), symptoms that do not meet full criteria but include mood disturbance marked by significant impairment (American Psychiatric Association, 1994). School personnel may be more familiar with bipolar disorder in adults, which typically manifests distinct episodes of mania and depression as seen in bipolar I. Research suggests that bipolar I is relatively rare in children and that, across the spectrum of other subtypes, their symptoms are expressed quite differently from adults (Lewinsohn, Klein, & Klein, 1995). For example, children tend to have much shorter mood phases or a more continuous series of changing moods rather than distinct episodes. In contrast to the classic manic behaviors of adults, such as elation, grandiosity, and spending sprees, children and adolescents are more likely to be highly irritable or quick to fly into a rage (Geller et al., 1998).

Since many of the symptoms associated with bipolar disorder, such as tantrums, high energy, and vivid imagination, are not uncommon among children in general, it can be very challenging for school personnel to distinguish appropriate developmental behaviors from the clinically ab-normal (Fristad & Goldberg Arnold, 2004). While school social workers and mental health counselors should familiarize themselves with the primary indicators of bipolar disorder, the key determinants of a proper assessment are recognizing the signs and symptoms in terms of their intensity, duration, context, and presentation across multiple settings (Pavuluri, Naylor, & Janicak, 2002). The core features of bipolar disorder in children include

• Elated mood: excessive laughter, silliness, and giddiness. The child is often highly excitable, may joke constantly, and may seem excessively happy without apparent cause.
• Irritable mood: crabby, angry, and aggressive. The child may throw tantrums that involve screaming and throwing things. Some children display rage-like behavior or remain inconsolable for extended periods of time.
• Grandiose or inflated self-esteem: Beyond age-appropriate bragging, the child may make statements such as "I don't need to go to school. I am smarter than all my teachers," or "I am the best baseball player in the world, and I plan to play for the Red Sox next year."
• Decreased need for sleep: Children may repeatedly stay up late at night, refuse to go to bed because they feel wide awake, and after just a few hours of sleep wake up early in the morning full of energy. Whereas most children require between 9 and 11 hours of sleep, children experiencing mania or hypomania may only get 4 to 6 hours without feeling fatigued.

• Pressured speech: Children may describe a sense of having their thoughts race without being able to slow them down. They may talk persistently and demand constant attention and that someone listen to them.
• Frenzied activity: Similar to hyperactivity demonstrated by children with ADHD, kids in a manic state of bipolar disorder may be constantly moving from one activity to the next.
• Impulsive behaviors: hypersexuality (not due to sexual abuse), hoarding, stealing, aggressive acts, or reckless behaviors.
• Depressive symptoms: whiny, sad, crabby, and tearful without apparent cause. Thoughts of suicide and suicide attempts are also reported in about 25% of children with bipolar disorder (Geller et al., 2002).
• Psychosis: hallucinations, delusions, or disconnected thoughts. See chapter 11 for a discussion of psychotic symptoms in children and adolescents.

Specific *DSM-IV* criteria for bipolar I and II are displayed in Tables 9.1 and 9.2.

Since its recent recognition among professionals, bipolar disorder that emerges prior to age 18 has been referred to by several names, including pediatric bipolar, childhood onset, adolescent onset, prepubescent onset, and juvenile onset. Empirical studies suggest that there are two subtypes, which are commonly termed (1) prepubertal/early adolescent onset (PEA-BD) and (2) adolescent onset (AO-BD). PEA-BD includes children under age 12 and is characterized by irritability, rapid (i.e., more than four times a year) or continuous cycling, and high rates of co-occurring

Table 9.1 Core Features of Bipolar Disorder I: *DSM-IV* Criteria

---

• Manic mood symptoms: abnormally or persistently elevated, expansive, or irritable (for at least 1 week)
• Additional symptoms: 3 out of 7 (4 out of 7 if primary mood state is irritable)
  1. inflated self-esteem/grandiosity
  2. decreased need for sleep
  3. flight of ideas/racing thoughts
  4. poor judgment or hypersexuality
  5. distractibility
  6. foolish or reckless behavior
  7. talkative (increased volume, speed, amount)
• Mood disturbance is sufficient to cause marked impairment
• Symptoms are not due to physiological effects of a substance or to a general medical condition

---

Source: Reprinted with permission from the Diagnostic and Statistical Manual of Mental Disorders, Copyright 2000, American Psychiatric Association.

Table 9.2 Core Features of Bipolar Disorder II: *DSM-IV* Criteria

- Hypomanic mood symptoms: abnormally or persistently elevated, expansive, or irritable (hypomania alternating with depression) (for 4–7 days)
- Additional symptoms: 3 out of 7 (4 out of 7 if primary mood state is irritable)
  1. inflated self-esteem/grandiosity
  2. decreased need for sleep
  3. flight of ideas/racing thoughts
  4. poor judgment or hypersexuality
  5. distractibility
  6. foolish or reckless behavior
  7. talkative (increased volume, speed, amount)
- Mood disturbance is sufficient to cause marked impairment
- Symptoms are not due to physiological effects of a substance or to a general medical condition

Source: Reprinted with permission from the Diagnostic and Statistical Manual of Mental Disorders, Copyright 2000, American Psychiatric Association.

ADHD and conduct disorder (Findling, Gracious, & McNamar, 2001; Geller et al., 2002; Wozniak et al., 1995). AO-BD affects postpubescent youth, who tend to experience more distinct mood episodes than those with PEA-BD and have higher rates of comorbidity with substance abuse and anxiety disorders (Carlson, Bromet, & Sievers, 2000; Lewinsohn, Klein, & Seeley, 2000).

Current debate over the classification of bipolar disorder among children calls into question the diagnostic criteria of discrete mood episodes, the duration of the episodes, and the manifestation of manic symptoms (Leibenluft, Charney, Towbin, Bhangoo, & Pine, 2003). Both the adult and childhood literature suggest a spectrum of disorders and, as a result, experts recently introduced the term early-onset spectrum disorder (EOSD) as a more accurate description of bipolar disorder for individuals under age 18 (Lofthouse & Fristad, 2004).

Prevalence

The exact prevalence of bipolar disorder among children is largely unknown. There are no epidemiological studies specific to children, in part because the diagnostic criteria have been in a state of change, but primarily because its existence as a childhood disorder has only recently been acknowledged. Community school surveys of 14- to 18-year olds indicate prevalence rates of .12% for BP-I and 1% for BP-II and cyclothymia (Lewinsohn, Klein, & Klein, 1995). Additional reports of symptoms associated with BP-NOS suggest a prevalence rate of 5.7%. Among adults, the prevalence of bipolar spectrum disorders is reported to be between 3 and 6%, with approximately 50%

of those adults reporting symptoms that began in childhood or adolescence.

Causal Factors

Bipolar disorder is considered a biopsychosocial disorder because evidence indicates a biological basis upon which psychosocial factors exert significant influence (Pavuluri, Naylor, & Janicak, 2002). More simply, biological factors likely cause the disorder and, perhaps, the course of mood cycling, but stressors within the child, family, school, and environment strongly affect outcomes. Genetic studies reveal that having a close relative with bipolar disorder increases the risk of developing the illness by 5–10% (Craddock & Jones, 1999). Twin studies also offer compelling evidence of a genetic link in the onset of bipolar disorder (Badner, 2003).

Neurochemical, pharmacological, and neuroimaging studies also offer strong evidence of biological influences in bipolar disorder. For example, serotonin, dopamine, various hormones, such as cortisol, and calcium levels have all been implicated as causal factors (Findling et al., 2003). Recent studies using neuroimaging techniques reveal possible involvement of the brain's frontal-striatal-limbic regions (DelBello & Kowatch, 2003).

Psychological and social factors appear to affect the severity of the illness, relapse rates, and recovery time. Research in this area has focused on three main categories of stressors: high expressed emotion within families, degree of maternal warmth, and disruptions to sleep patterns. An overly critical or hostile family environment coupled with emotional overinvolvement among household members characterize a family with high expressed emotion (EE). Several investigations have found that, among adults, high familial EE is associated with significantly higher relapse rates (Simmoneau, Miklowitz, & Saleem, 1998). Studies of children with bipolar disorder have focused more on the degree of maternal warmth and reveal that children who experienced low maternal warmth were four times more likely to relapse than those with high maternal warmth (Geller et al., 2000; Geller et al., 2003). Stress due to negative life events appears to increase recovery time by three- to fourfold in adults (Johnson & Miller, 1997). Recurrence rates, particularly for manic episodes, are also markedly increased by irregularities in sleep patterns (Malkoff-Schwartz et al., 1998).

What We Can Do

As with all mental health conditions in children, the hallmark of effective treatment is early identification and accurate assessment (Pavuluri, Naylor, & Janicak, 2002). This is especially true for childhood bipolar disorder, which can have devastating consequences if undetected or improperly diagnosed (McClure, Kubiszyn, & Kaslow, 2002).

Pharmacotherapy

Given that comorbidity is more the rule than the exception for children with bipolar disorder, it is not surprising that multiple medications are often needed to achieve stability. In a recent study of youth between the ages of 7 and 18, 80% of children who were unresponsive to one mood stabilizer effectively responded to the use of two mood stabilizers (Kowatch et al., 2003). Another well-controlled study using valproate found significant improvement in the use of valproate in combination with quetiapine than alone (DelBello et al., 2002). Among bipolar adolescents with symptoms of psychosis, better outcomes were reported for the combined use of lithium and antipsychotics than with lithium only (Kafantaris, Coletti, Dicker, Padula, & Kane, 2003).

Many school-based practitioners may be aware of the recent media attention centered on the use of antidepressant medication with children. Some of this controversy stems from reports indicating that both selective serotonin reuptake inhibitors (SSRIs) and stimulants induce mania (Biederman et al., 2000; Oldroyd, 1997). There is some evidence that stimulant medication may induce mania in some children (DelBello et al., 2002). These studies have been criticized for methodological shortcomings and refuted by subsequent reports, but the debate continues. Given the current state of the evidence, experts recommend mood stabilizers as the primary pharmacological intervention, followed by a slow and cautious introduction of SSRIs or stimulants as needed (Findling et al., 2003).

Since the majority of children with bipolar disorder are on multiple medications, side effects are very common. Table 9.3 lists some of the most common side effects and accommodations that can be made within the classroom and school environment to support the student. See chapter 2 for additional information on the potential side effects of medications. Most side effects are at their worst during the first few weeks of taking the medication, but some, such as weight gain, can remain and cause difficulty. The school social worker and school-based mental health practitioner can take several steps to maximize the child's compliance and comfort with medication maintenance. First, if medication must be taken during school hours, help ensure that the student can do this privately. Second, although privacy is important, safety is paramount. Be sure to inform the student's teachers and other school personnel who work directly with the child about the seriousness of side effects, such as stomach pain, vomiting, and dehydration. In case of these side effects, school staff should immediately contact a parent or other emergency contacts.

Psychosocial Interventions

Currently there are no evidence-based interventions for children with bipolar disorder, but a few clinical trials of the most promising interventions are under way. The interventions conform to the surgeon general's recommendations for treatment of childhood mood disorders by placing special emphasis on including families, determining functional status in addition to symptom severity, and including children with co-occurring disorders. They are also manualized and designed for practitioners to use flexibly (Pavuluri, Naylor, & Janicak, 2002).

Table 9.3 Common Side Effects of Bipolar Medications and Suggested Classroom Accommodations

Side Effect	Accommodation
Increased thirst	Allow ongoing access to water and juice
Frequent urination	Allow unlimited access to the bathroom
Drowsiness	Arrange for frequent breaks or a delayed start time in the morning
Fluctuations in energy and motivation	Provide a flexible workload for the student to work on projects consistent with energy and focus
Difficulty concentrating and remembering instructions	Record assignments in a daily notebook, provide special reminders, identify a classroom aide to help student focus on tasks
Easily overheated or dehydrated from physical activity	Allow student to waive physical education class on hot days

Source: Adapted from the Child and Adolescent Bipolar Foundation's *Educator's Guide* (Anglada, 2002). A more detailed list of symptoms and accommodations may be obtained at www.bpkids.org.

The Multi-Family Psychoeducation Group (MFPG) developed by Fristad and colleagues and its modified version, Individual Family Psychoeducation (IFP,) share the following treatment goals for parents and their children:

- Increase understanding of the disorder, symptoms, and common comorbid conditions.
- Increase knowledge of medications, psychological treatments, and school-based interventions.
- Help parents and children avoid blame for the disorder and encourage a sense of responsibility for symptom management.
- Promote better management of symptoms.
- Enhance coping skills.
- Improve family communication and problem-solving abilities.
- Improve family and peer relationships.
- Expand social support.
- Promote cooperation and cohesiveness among caregiving adults.

MFPG uses a group format for the advantages it offers in terms of peer support, feedback, and in vivo practice. It consists of a 6-week, 90-minute session design, which begins with a brief check-in for parents and children to review the previous week's assignments. Children and parents meet in separate groups for the remainder of the session. A randomized pilot test of MFPG demonstrated increases in parents' knowledge, improved parent–child relationships, and increased social support. IFP allows the practitioner to work with families on an individual basis and uses 16 50-minute sessions. It includes an additional component called "healthy habits" to improve regular sleep patterns, nutrition, and exercise to combat the side effects of medication and prevent relapse. MFPG is being tested in a multiyear NIMH clinical trial, and IFP is being tested using a randomized control study.

Both MFPG and IFP combine education, skill-building, and therapeutic techniques. The first 50% of the treatment is purely educational and guides families through developing and monitoring their own treatment goals, which they track on "fix-it lists." Parents also chart their child's moods to monitor the effects of medication. One of the most potent exercises, called "naming the enemy," helps both the child and parents distinguish the symptoms of the disorder from the child. The exercise involves dividing one sheet of paper into two columns; one column lists all of the child's symptoms, and the other column lists all of the child's positive qualities and strengths. Folding the page in half allows the family to see how symptoms can sometimes cover up the child's best characteristics and, conversely, how proper treatment can bring the child's finest attributes to the forefront. The remaining sessions combine coping-skills training with cognitive-behavioral techniques and problem-solving skills. Special emphasis is placed on anticipating times of added stress and developing the skills as a family to manage through them. The last session is dedicated to the child's strengths, areas in need of growth, and recommendations and resources. More detailed guidelines for both MFPG and IFP may be found in Fristad and Goldberg Arnold (2003).

The second manualized treatment being tested through an NIMH-sponsored clinical trial is Family Focused Treatment (FFT), which has been empirically supported for use with adults (Miklowitz & Goldstein, 1997). It is designed for adolescents aged 13 to 17 with BP-I. Similar to MFPG and IFP, it incorporates psychoeducation, problem-solving skills for the family, and communication skills. It places special emphasis on reducing expressed emotion (EE), crisis management, and relapse management.

Perhaps most inclusive of the school environment, Pavuluri and colleagues have developed a treatment program called Child and Family Focused Cognitive-Behavioral Treatment (CFF-CBT) for bipolar disorder, also referred to as RAINBOW, for youth between the ages of 8 and 12. CFF-CBT is an adaptation of Miklowitz and Goldstein's model for adults and, like FFT, it is based on the premise that life stress, in combination with genetic and biological factors, causes an increase in mood symptoms. Reducing stress, improving coping skills, and enhancing family support are key targets of the intervention.

The treatment format calls for 12 sessions for parents and children. RAINBOW stands for

- The importance of *Routine*
- *A*ffect regulation/anger control
- *I* can do it/self-esteem enhancement
- *N*o negative thoughts
- *B*e a good friend/balanced lifestyle for all family members
- *O*h, how can we solve it? (problem solving)
- *W*ays to seek and obtain support

RAINBOW emphasizes therapeutic support for parents in coping with their frustrations and questions. The treatment is designed in three phases:

- Phase I: therapeutic alliance, psychoeducation, role of medication
- Phase II (uses principles of cognitive behavior therapy): increase positive experiences, decrease negative consequences
- Phase III (uses interpersonal principles of problem solving): social skills, problem-solving skills, social support skills

The intervention is designed to be used flexibly. The treatment manual offers the following guidelines:

Sessions 1–2 (parents and child together): The emphasis of these sessions is learning about the illness as a brain disorder. The importance of maintaining regular sleep patterns, stress management, and medication adherence is specifically addressed.

Session 3 (parents only): Parents are taught skills to support their child in regulating emotions and ways to counteract dysfunctional thought patterns associated with bipolar disorder (e.g., grandiosity, paranoia, devaluing self and others).

Sessions 4–7 (child only): Emphasis is placed on the concept of regulating emotions and related skills. The therapist uses a mood chart to track progress across sessions.

Sessions 8–12 (alternate between parents only and joint therapy): Skill building for relapse prevention, problem solving, and social support skills are addressed.

The school is also a central component of treatment. The therapist provides a work folder of exercises that augment the weekly family sessions. Throughout all of the sessions, the therapist engages the child's teachers by requesting information on the child's classroom behavior and guiding them on classroom strategies to address the child's needs.

Tools and Practice Examples

Resources

- Child and Adolescent Bipolar Foundation. This national parent organization was formed in 1999 and provides education and online support. Its Web site, www.bipolarchildren.com, features a special section for educators that includes publications such as "The Student With Bipolar Disorder: An Educator's Guide."
- Juvenile Bipolar Research Foundation. This is a charitable organization founded in 2002 to support research in bipolar disorder among children. www.jbrf.org.
- Depression and Bipolar Support Alliance (DBSA), 730 N. Franklin Street, Suite 501, Chicago, IL 60610-7224. Phone: 312-642-0049. Fax: 312-642-7243. www.DBSAlliance.org
- Depression and Related Affective Disorders Association (DRADA), 2330 West Joppa Road, Suite 100, Lutherville, MD 21093.

Phone: 410-583-2919. E-mail: drada@jhmi. edu. www.drada.org.

- Fristad, M., & Goldberg Arnold, J. (2004). *Raising a moody child: How to cope with depression and bipolar disorder.* New York: Guilford.
- Packer, L. E. *Classroom tips for children with bipolar disorder.* www.schoolbehavior.com.

Case Study: David

David, a 9-year-old student in the third grade, recently began acting out in the classroom by refusing to stay in his seat, constantly interrupting the teacher, and talking out of turn. He failed to turn in his assignments because he said he was too smart to have to do homework. His homeroom teacher referred him to the school counselor after he began bragging to other students that he drank beer, watched pornography, and had sex with girls in his room on the weekends. The counselor contacted David's mother, who denied his claims but shared concerns about her son's recent behavior. Although David had been diagnosed with ADHD at age 7, his behavior was only partially improved with medication. Recently, the medication has seemed to make him worse, and he complains that his brain feels like it has race cars in it. He has been staying up late at night watching TV and waking up before the rest of the family to draw in his art book or play with his Gameboy. When his parents insist that he go to bed at night, he flies into a rage and screams at everyone to leave him alone.

As David's case illustrates, the diagnosis of bipolar disorder is often complicated by other conditions that share similar symptoms and may coexist. In fact, it is extremely rare for a child with bipolar disorder to have only one diagnosis (Geller et al., 2000). The American Association of Child and Adolescent Psychiatry (AACAP) has issued practice guidelines for assessment that recommend the use of structured or semistructured interviews, such as the NIMH DISC-IV (National Institute for Mental Health Diagnostic Interview Schedule IV), K-SADS-PE (Kiddie Schedule for Affective Disorders in Schizophrenia for School-Age Children–Present Episode), and ChIPS (Children's Interview for Psychiatric Syndromes), to aid in assessment and differential diagnosis. The most widely used scales are available to practitioners on-line at www.bpkids.org. In addition, the school-based mental health practitioner should gather information from multiple informants, including teachers, parents, and the child, to obtain a thorough history and more comprehensive understanding of the child's functioning. Given the evidence of a strong genetic link, a detailed family history is also a critical aspect of the assessment process (American Academy of Child and Adolescent Psychiatry, 1997).

Once diagnosed, best practice and treatment guidelines recommend a combination of pharmacotherapy and psychosocial intervention. Medication, especially for manic symptoms, is a critical precursor to psychosocial treatment. In the adult literature, lithium, valproate, and carbamazepine have been shown to be efficacious (Keck & McElroy, 2002). Unfortunately, few well-controlled studies of medication use with children have been published. One notable exception is the research on lithium, which has demonstrated efficacy for adolescents with BP-I, BP-II, and comorbid substance abuse (Geller et al., 1998).

Key Points to Remember

Bipolar disorder in children has only been officially recognized since the 1980s and, as a result, evidence-based treatments have yet to be established. Several promising interventions are available to school-based practitioners, but more research is needed to provide specific school-based interventions. A thorough assessment using multiple informants, including parents, teachers, and the child, is an essential precursor to effective treatment. Clinicians should be especially attentive to the high comorbidity rate with bipolar disorder and to the developmental differences in symptom presentation. Medication to treat a child's mood symptoms must also precede psychosocial interventions. Finally, best practice dictates collaboration with parents and the child, education about the chronic condition, differentiation of symptoms from the child, and strategy development for relapse prevention and management. A list of references is included to guide practitioners to more detailed information.

References

American Academy of Child and Adolescent Psychiatry. (1997). Practice parameters for the assessment and treatment of children and adolescents with bipolar disorder. *Journal of the American Academy of Child and Adolescent Psychiatry, 36*(1), 138–157.

American Psychiatric Association. (1994). *Diagnostic and statistical manual of mental disorders* (4th ed.). Washington, DC: Author.

Anglada, T. (2002). *The student with bipolar disorder: An educator's guide.* Murdock, FL: Child and Adolescent Bipolar Foundation.

Badner, J. (2003). The genetics of bipolar disorder. In B. Geller & M. DelBello (Eds.), *Bipolar disorder in childhood and early adolescence* (pp. 247–254). New York: Guilford.

Biederman, J., Mick, E., Faraone, S., Spencer, T., Wilens, T., & Wozniak, J. (2000). Pediatric mania: A developmental subtype of bipolar disorder? *Biological Psychiatry, 48,* 458–466.

Carlson, G., Bromet, E., & Sievers, S. (2000). Phenomenology and outcomes of subjects with early and adult-onset psychotic mania. *American Journal of Psychiatry, 157,* 213–219.

Craddock, N., & Jones, I. (1999). Genetics of bipolar disorder. *Journal of Medical Genetics, 36*(8), 585–594.

DelBello, M., & Kowatch, R. (2003). Neuroimaging in pediatric bipolar disorder. In B. Geller & M. DelBello (Eds.), *Bipolar disorder in childhood and early adolescence* (pp. 158–174). New York: Guilford.

DelBello, M., Schwiers, M., Rosenberg, H., & Strakowski, S. (2002). A double-blind, randomized, placebo-controlled study of quetiapine adjunctive treatment for adolescent mania. *Journal of the American Academy of Child and Adolescent Psychiatry, 41*(10), 1216–1223.

Findling, R., Gracious, B., & McNamara, N. (2001). Rapid, continuous cycling and psychiatric comorbidity in pediatric bipolar I disorder. *Bipolar Disorder, 3,* 202–210.

Findling, R., Kowatch, R., & Post, R. (2003). *Pediatric bipolar disorder: A handbook for clinicians.* London: Cromwell.

Fristad, M., & Goldberg Arnold, J. (2003). Family interventions for early onset bipolar disorder. In B. Geller & M. DelBello (Eds.), *Bipolar disorder in childhood and early adolescence* (pp. 295–313). New York: Guilford.

Fristad, M., & Goldberg Arnold, J. (2004). *Raising a moody child: How to cope with depression and bipolar disorder.* New York: Guilford.

Geller, B., Bolhofner, K., Craney, J., Williams, M., DelBello, M., & Gunderson, K. (2000). Psychosocial functioning in prepubertal and early adolescent bipolar disorder phenotype. *Journal of the American Academy of Child and Adolescent Psychiatry, 39*(12), 1486–1493.

Geller, B., Craney, J., Bolhofner, K., DelBello, M., Axelson, D., & Luby, J. (2003). Phenomenology and longitudinal course of children with a prepubertal and early adolescent phenotype. In B. Geller & M. DelBello (Eds.), *Bipolar disorder in childhood and early adolescence* (pp. 25–50). New York: Guilford.

Geller, B., Williams, M., Zimmerman, B., Frazier, J., Beringer, L., & Warner, K. (1998). Prepubertal and early adolescent bipolarity differentiate from ADHD

by manic symptoms, grandiose delusion, ultra-rapid or ultradian cycling. *Journal of Affective Disorders, 51,* 81–91.

Geller, B., Zimmerman, B., Williams, M., DelBello, M., Frazier, J., & Beringer, L. (2002). Phenomenology of prepubertal and early adolescent bipolar disorder: Examples of elated mood, grandiose behaviors, decreased need for sleep, racing thoughts and hypersexuality. *Journal of Child and Adolescent Psychopharmacology, 12*(1), 3–9.

Johnson, S., & Miller, I. (1997). Negative life events and time to recovery from episodes of bipolar disorder. *Journal of Abnormal Psychology, 106*(3), 449–457.

Kafantaris, V., Coletti, D., Dicker, R., Padula, G., & Kane, J. (2003). Lithium treatment of acute mania in adolescents: A large open trial. *Journal of the Academy of Child and Adolescent Psychiatry, 42,* 1038–1045.

Keck, P., & McElroy, S. (2002). Pharmacological treatments for bipolar disorder. In J. Nathan & J. Gorman (Eds.), *A guide to treatments that work* (2nd ed., pp. 277–299). Oxford: Oxford University Press.

Kinscherff, R. (1999). Empirically supported treatments: What to do until the data arrive (or now that they have)? *Clinical Child Psychology Newsletter, 14,* 4–6.

Kowatch, R., Sethuraman, G., Hume, J., Kromelis, M., & Weinberg, W. (2003). Combination pharmacotherapy in children and adolescents with bipolar disorder. *Biological Psychiatry, 53*(11), 978–984.

Leibenluft, E., Charney, D., Towbin, K., Bhangoo, R., & Pine, D. (2003). Defining clinical phenotypes of juvenile mania. *American Journal of Psychology, 160*(3), 430–437.

Lewinsohn, P., Klein, D., & Seeley, J. (2000). Bipolar disorder during adolescence and young childhood in a community sample. *Bipolar Disorders, 2,* 281–293.

Lewinsohn, P., Klein, J., & Klein, D. (1995). Bipolar disorder in a community sample of older adolescents: Prevalence, co-morbidity, and course. *Journal of the American Academy of Child and Adolescent Psychiatry, 34,* 454–463.

Lofthouse, N., & Fristad, M. (2004). Psychosocial interventions for children with early onset bipolar spectrum disorder. *Clinical Child and Family Psychological Review, 7*(2), 71–88.

Malkoff-Schwartz, S., Frank, E., Anderson, B., Sherill, J., Siegel, L., & Patterson, D. (1998). Stressful life events and social rhythm disruption in the onset of mania and depressive bipolar episodes. *Archives of General Psychiatry, 55*(8), 702–707.

McClure, E., Kubiszyn, T., & Kaslow, N. (2002). Advances in the diagnosis and treatment of childhood mood disorders. *Professional Psychology: Research and Practice, 23*(2), 125–134.

Miklowitz, D., & Goldstein, M. (1997). *Bipolar disorder: A family focused approach.* New York: Guilford Press.

National Institute of Mental Health. (2001). National Institute of Mental Health roundtable on prepubertal bipolar disorder. *Journal of the American Academy of Child and Adolescent Psychiatry, 40*(8), 871–878.

Oldroyd, J. (1997). Paroxetine-induced mania. *Journal of the American Academy of Child and Adolescent Psychiatry, 36*(6), 721–722.

Ollendick, T. (2003) Advances towards evidence-based practice with children and adolescents. *Clinical Child and Adolescent Psychology Newsletter, 18*(1), 1–3.

Pavuluri, M., Naylor, M., & Janicak, P. (2002). Recognition and treatment of pediatric bipolar disorder. *Contemporary Psychiatry, 1*(1), 1–10.

Rivas-Vasquez, R., Johnson, S., Rey, G., & Blais, M. (2002). Current treatments for bipolar disorder: A review and update for psychologists. *Professional Psychology: Research and Practice, 33*(2), 212–223.

Simmoneau, T., Miklowitz, D., & Saleem, R. (1998). Expressed emotion and interactional patterns in the family of bipolar patients. *Journal of Abnormal Psychology, 107*(3), 497–507.

Wozniak, J., Biederman, J., Kiely, K., Ablon, J., Faraone, S., & Mundy, E. (1995). Mania-like symptoms suggestive of childhood-onset bipolar disorder in clinically referred children. *Journal of the American Academy of Child and Adolescent Psychiatry, 34*(7), 867–876.

Effective Interventions for Students With Eating Disorders

Theresa J. Early

CHAPTER 10

Getting Started

At times it seems as if every person in the United States is "on a diet." There are reports both of rising obesity rates among children and adults (see chapter 30 for a discussion of this issue) and of unprecedented numbers of individuals attempting to stick to a diet that limits carbohydrates, fat, or both. Media images of the "ideal" body are unrealistic for most: too thin and out of proportion with real bodies, having a very small waist and overdeveloped chest. Within this context, many people, including children and youth, are dissatisfied with their bodies, and a small percentage of people develop eating disorders. Eating disorders are characterized by extreme obsessions with weight and eating, along with disordered behaviors around eating and weight control. Eating disorders are an important concern for school social workers and mental health personnel because these disorders often begin in adolescence. A number of school-based interventions aimed at prevention are described in the literature. In addition, professionals in the schools are in a position to notice eating disorders and assist with interventions, either through providing treatment or through supporting students who are participating in treatment in another setting. In this chapter, I will discuss two types of eating disorders that are diagnosed in youth, anorexia nervosa and bulimia nervosa, and strategies of effective intervention based on the small amount of existing empirical evidence.

What We Know

Anorexia nervosa is more likely to begin during early adolescence and bulimia nervosa is more likely to affect older adolescents and young adults, so both disorders may be seen in schools. Effective interventions have been identified for both bulimia nervosa and anorexia nervosa, but there is less empirical evidence regarding effective treatments for anorexia nervosa. Cognitive-behavioral therapy has been identified as an effective treatment for bulimia nervosa through several randomized clinical trials (see, for example, a review of 10 studies in Fairburn, Agras, & Wilson, 1992). Unfortunately, many of the studies of treatment effectiveness have been conducted with adults rather than among school-aged populations. However, several authors in the eating disorders field have described promising approaches that take into account adolescent development and the differences between anorexia nervosa and bulimia nervosa (Agras & Apple, 2002; Bowers, Evans, & Van Cleve, 1996; Lock, Le Grange, Agras, & Dare, 2001; Nicholls & Bryant-Waugh, 2003; Schmidt, 1998). In particular, Lock and colleagues (2001) have described a manualized family-based therapy approach for treatment of anorexia nervosa, which has evidence of effectiveness both as a primary treatment approach (Eisler, Dare, Hodes, Russell, Dodge, & Le Grange, 2000) and following failure of other treatments (Sim, Sadowski, Whiteside, & Wells, 2004).

According to the standard diagnostic criteria used in mental health practice, anorexia nervosa is the refusal to maintain a (minimal) normal body weight along with intense fear of gaining weight or becoming fat (American Psychiatric Association, 2000). In addition, anorexia nervosa includes a distorted body image, including an unrealistic appraisal of body weight/shape and an overemphasis on body weight and shape for self-evaluation. Thus, individuals with anorexia nervosa may be dangerously underweight but believe themselves to be fat. In addition, they believe that their shape and weight are the most important aspects of themselves. Some individuals with anorexia nervosa also engage in binge-eating and/or purging behavior. Weight loss is achieved through some combination of extreme restriction in the amount and type of food eaten, excessive exercise, and purging (vomiting, using laxatives or diuretics). In females who have already begun to have menstrual cycles, amenorrhea also is part of anorexia nervosa.

Bulimia nervosa, on the other hand, is indicated by recurrent binge eating—eating a larger amount of food in a specific period of time than most people would eat and feeling a lack of control over eating during the binge episode. Individuals with bulimia nervosa usually weigh in a normal range because they also engage in behaviors to compensate for their overeating, such as purging, fasting, or excessive exercise. Bulimia nervosa shares with anorexia nervosa an overemphasis on body shape in evaluation of the self and extreme dissatisfaction with body weight and shape.

Anorexia nervosa is relatively rare, with an average prevalence rate of 0.3% in young females (Hoek & van Hoeken, 2003). Bulimia nervosa, although still rare, is more common than anorexia nervosa, having a prevalence of about 1% in young women (Hoek & van Hoeken, 2003). Although females are at much higher risk for these disorders, they do also occur in young males. Further, even though only a small number of young people with eating problems would meet the strict diagnostic criteria set out in the *DSM-IV-TR* (American Psychiatric Association, 2000), a greater number of youth experience many of the same obsessions with food and body image. These youth are at risk of developing eating disorders.

Risk factors include:

- dieting, especially repeated, unsuccessful dieting (for bulimia nervosa)
- perfectionism
- family history of eating disorder
- parental problems such as obesity or alcohol abuse
- critical comments by family members about the student's body weight or eating
- competitive involvement in gymnastics, swimming, wrestling, or ballet

The consequences of eating disorders in youth are serious and include dental problems, bone loss, osteoporosis, stunted growth, suicide, or death from excessive weight loss in extreme cases of anorexia nervosa. A number of other emotional disorders may also occur along with either anorexia or bulimia nervosa, including depression, anxiety disorders, obsessive-compulsive disorder, and personality disorders.

Although the cause of eating disorders is not conclusively known, one theory of causation is that a young person's insecurity becomes focused on her or his weight and shape. The energy of the person is directed toward strictly controlling food intake and weight. In anorexia nervosa, successful efforts at restricting food and losing weight may initially result in positive feedback from parents, teachers, or others whose opinions the youth values. The youth wants to continue to experience success, and control becomes its own reward. The young person continues to believe she or he is still too fat, even though the amount of weight lost may have been dramatic and dangerous. In bulimia nervosa, efforts to restrict food backfire into binge-eating episodes. The youth may try to control eating through restricting herself from certain foods (e.g., chocolate) or for most of the day. The resulting guilt and shame at the loss of control, as well as intense fear of gaining weight, lead to attempts to compensate for the excess food, often through vomiting or taking excessive numbers of laxatives.

What We Can Do

Tasks of the school social worker/counselor in relation to eating disorders include:

- offering effective prevention programs (discussed in another chapter in this volume)
- identification of youth with eating disorders
- assessment of the seriousness of a student's physical condition and enlisting the aid of parents
- if physical condition warrants, referring the student for medical treatment
- participating in cognitive-behavioral care after medical treatment *or* carrying out cognitive-behavioral intervention if medical treatment is not indicated
- assisting in monitoring medication effectiveness and side effects, if pharmacological treatment is occurring

- providing support for students who are receiving treatment in other settings

Identifying Youth With Eating Disorders

- Physical signs include significant changes in weight, especially weight loss; failure to gain weight or height expected for age and stage of development; and delayed or disrupted puberty. In anorexia, abnormal hair growth (soft, downy) may be present on the face or back.
- Behavioral signs include limited food intake, either in terms of energy quality or nutrient range; excessive or irregular food intake.
- Social signs may include social isolation and withdrawal from friends and activities.

Other school personnel also are in a position to identify youth with eating disorders. Teachers and coaches, in particular, may have more regular, ongoing contact with students than do school social workers or counselors. Therefore, it is important for the school mental health professional to be a resource for other school personnel in regard to identifying and responding to signs of eating disorders in students.

Assessing Seriousness of Physical Condition

A diagnosis of anorexia nervosa requires that weight be 85% of normal weight for height and developmental stage (or less) and in postmenarche females, amenorrhea of at least three cycles. If a student meets these criteria, the school social worker should refer the youth for a medical checkup. Hospitalization may be necessary if the youth is 75–80% of expected body weight. Bulimia nervosa has fewer potential medical complications unless the youth is heavily abusing laxatives or diuretics, in which case electrolytes may become out of balance and cause rapid changes in blood pressure and/or pulse rate. If in doubt, the social worker should refer the student for a medical checkup.

Enlisting the Aid of Parents

The involvement and support of parents is important in treating many emotional and behavioral disorders in children and youth. In treating eating disorders, family support is critical. Although there

may be family dynamics that play into a youth's eating disorder, it is important to avoid blaming parents for their child's eating disorder. Family therapy to improve expression of emotions and general communication may be helpful in treating a youth's eating disorder. In family-based therapy for eating disorders, parents are specifically put in charge of refeeding their child; family relationships are renegotiated to increase parental monitoring for prevention of binge/purge behaviors; and youth are assisted with normal adolescent development (separation and individuation) (Lock et al., 2001).

Steps in Cognitive-Behavioral Intervention for Eating Disorders

The primary targets of CBT intervention for bulimia nervosa and anorexia nervosa are (1) modifying the beliefs and attitudes that support the importance of body shape and weight; and (2) normalizing eating. CBT for eating disorders, manualized initially by Fairburn, Marcus, and Wilson (1993) and more recently by Agras and Apple (1997), relies on a variety of behavioral and cognitive strategies. The treatment is problem-oriented, focused on the present and future, and proceeds (for bulimia nervosa) over 19 sessions in three stages.

Stage 1. The goal of the first stage is to normalize eating. During the first session, the mental health professional orients the student to the goals and processes of therapy. The youth must be willing to play an active role in therapy and must develop confidence in the mental health professional and the cognitive-behavioral approach. Illustrating the cognitive model of eating disorders, the mental health professional helps the student to draw connections between her own situation and the links among emotions, dietary restrictions, binge eating, and purging. The mental health professional emphasizes the importance of regular meals—three meals and two snacks daily, going no more than 3–4 hours (while awake) without eating—highlighting how hunger and cravings from strict dieting lead to binge eating and purging. Accurate information about food, nutrition, and weight regulation is provided. The mental health professional will ask the youth to make one change (e.g., eat something in the morning if breakfast is usually skipped).

Self-monitoring is an important strategy in cognitive-behavioral interventions. During the first session, the mental health professional teaches the youth to use the Daily Food Diary (see Figure 10.1). This form is used to track what the youth

Figure 10.1. Daily Food Diary

Name _____   Day _____   Date _____

Time	Type & Amount Food/Beverage	Place	Snack (S) Meal (M) Binge (B)	Purge (V/L)	Situation

Figure 10.2. Daily Record of Dysfunctional Thoughts

Name _____ Day _____ Date _____

Situation	Emotions	Automatic Thoughts	Rational Response

eats, when, how much, and various aspects of the context of eating, such as the location and associated thoughts and feelings about each episode of eating. The youth also classifies each episode as a meal, snack, or binge and records purging behavior. The purpose of keeping the food record is to identify eating episodes that are handled appropriately as well as patterns of problems and the factors that contribute to them. The record also can be used to track progress over time.

Stage 2. Once the student is eating more regularly and having fewer episodes of binge eating and purging, the treatment moves on to more cognitive aspects. The Daily Food Diary has probably already turned up some of the triggers of problematic situations, thoughts, and emotions. One of the basic tenets of cognitive-behavioral therapy is that individuals commit thinking errors, using faulty logic. The interpretation of events resulting from these errors causes negative emotions. To relieve negative emotions, then, the youth engages in binge eating, purging, or other control mechanisms in order to feel better (less anxious, for example). The mental health professional now teaches the student to identify and challenge the dysfunctional thoughts that are influencing both her emotions and behavior. A method for challenging dysfunctional thoughts involves using the Daily Record of Dysfunctional Thoughts (see Figure 10.2). From the first session on, the mental health professional should help the student to clarify the difference between thoughts and emotions to model the identification of emotions and the uncovering of automatic thoughts. The mental health professional then helps the student to identify more rational thoughts to substitute for the dysfunctional thoughts.

This stage also includes behavioral experiments through which the student actively challenges her dysfunctional thoughts. Usually the youth is convinced that there are certain foods that she just cannot eat because to have even a small amount would have a disastrous effect on her weight or shape. The intervention uses the Feared Foods List (see Figure 10.3) to identify these foods and rank them in terms of difficulty on a scale of 1–4, with 1 being the easiest to handle. The goal here is to experiment with adding a moderate-sized portion of one or more of these foods, starting with the easiest ones, to the eating plan once per week or every other week. The youth should record her reactions to consuming the feared food in her Daily Food Diary and process dysfunctional thoughts that arise.

Stage 3. The final stage of treatment is to create a maintenance plan. The mental health professional and student should brainstorm and problem solve about upcoming events and situations that are high risk for the student. The student should be prepared for a relapse of some of the disordered eating behaviors and have plans in place for what she will do. The student should write out plans of what she will do if/when relapse occurs. The plan should be specific, including making reframing statements to herself ("I have binged on fatty food today, but that does not mean that I am back to having an eating disorder") and returning to practicing the cognitive and behavioral strategies that were effective. The goal is for the student to be able to apply the tools she has learned before a short-term relapse gets out of hand and becomes a longer-term problem.

Monitoring Medication Effects and Side Effects

Table 10.1 lists some medications that may be used in treatment of anorexia nervosa and bulimia nervosa. Medications usually would be used in conjunction with therapy. Antidepressant medications combined with CBT seem to be an effective combination (Halmi, 2003).

If a student is receiving treatment for an eating disorder that includes medication, the school social worker or mental health professional should watch for the intended effects and side effects, as listed in Table 10.1, and communicate these observations to parents and/or medical personnel treating the student.

Practice Example

Tina was referred to the school social worker when her homeroom teacher noticed that Tina was throwing up in the bathroom after lunch. The teacher asked Tina if she were sick and needed to go home, and Tina's hesitation led the teacher to walk Tina to the social worker's office. In tears, Tina admitted to the social worker that she made herself vomit because she didn't want to gain weight. After a conference later in the week with Tina's mother, the social worker began meeting with Tina during a free period.

Figure 10.3. Feared Foods List

1. Food or beverage	*Rank Difficulty (1 = easiest to deal with)*
_____	*1 2 3 4*
_____	*1 2 3 4*
_____	*1 2 3 4*
_____	*1 2 3 4*
_____	*1 2 3 4*
_____	*1 2 3 4*
_____	*1 2 3 4*
_____	*1 2 3 4*
_____	*1 2 3 4*
_____	*1 2 3 4*
_____	*1 2 3 4*

2. Select one or more of the food items rated "1." Describe a plan for consuming moderate-sized portions each week or every other week. Describe your reaction in your Daily Food Diary.

Food/Beverage	*Amount in a Moderate Portion*	*How Often to Consume*

Table 10.1 Medications Used in Treatment of Eating Disorders

Medication/Source	Disorder	When Used	Symptoms Targeted	Side Effects
Fluoxetine (Prozac) or other SSRIs (Halmi, 2003)	Anorexia nervosa	Following some weight restoration	Prevent relapse; reduce depression, anxiety, and obsessive-compulsive symptoms	Nervousness, difficulty falling asleep or staying asleep, upset stomach, dry mouth, sore throat, drowsiness, weakness, shaking of hands
Fluoxetine (Prozac) or other SSRIs (Halmi, 2003)	Bulimia nervosa	During treatment	Reduce binge eating; improve mood; reduce preoccupation with shape and weight	See above
		Aftercare	Prevent relapse	
Topiramate (anticonvulsant) (Kotwal, McElroy, & Malhotra, 2003)	Bulimia nervosa	During treatment	Reduce binge eating and purging	Fatigue, flu-like symptoms, prickling or tingling or decreased tactile sensations of the skin, rare but serious side effects include kidney problems, eye problems (acute myopia and acute angle-closure glaucoma)

The social worker learned that Tina was the youngest child of four in the family. Growing up, she idolized her older sister, Judy. Tina had medical problems from birth and was babied a great deal by her parents and her older siblings. One day when Tina was about 13 years old, Judy remarked on Tina's shape, saying teasingly that she was "getting to be a little fatty." Tina was hurt—and enraged—and vowed to herself to "show her!" Although she was actually a normal weight, Tina began a diet immediately. For the next several weeks, she followed a pattern of eating little but thinking about food all the time. Initially she lost weight, but after a couple of months, one day she

was so hungry after school that she stopped on the way home and bought a box of chocolate-covered doughnuts. She meant to eat one, but soon realized she had eaten the whole box. Then she stopped at another store and bought a quart of milk. She drank the whole quart and then felt sick. This pattern continued for several days. Tina grew more and more concerned about her weight and began to make herself vomit after the doughnuts and milk.

Stage 1. The social worker got Tina to describe her eating pattern, which consisted of no breakfast, plain lettuce at lunch, then a binge on doughnuts, milk, roasted chicken, ice cream, and other foods on the way home. Tina would vomit after the binge, then eat dinner in her room, and vomit again before bed. The social worker explained the food record and the goal of eating something every 3–4 hours. Tina was alarmed that eating this much would make her weight go up. The social worker explained that eating a normal amount of food spread out over the day should result in a stable weight and that Tina's pattern, even though her intent is to lose weight through purging the food she eats, actually may be resulting in weight gain. Her strict restriction of food during the day leads to the cravings she experiences and gives in to on the way home. She feels guilty until she purges. The social worker explained that even though Tina is vomiting, it is likely that she is not able to get rid of all of the calories in the food she has consumed. Tina agreed to try to eat a small bowl of cereal with milk and half of a banana for breakfast.

The next week, Tina reported eating breakfast as planned and adding two crackers to her salad at lunch. However, she was still binge eating on doughnuts and/or roasted chicken on the way home and purging. She reported that she meant to eat only half of the doughnuts, but was unable to stop. She was able to then eat a normal amount for dinner and not purge. She worried about her weight, which was up 2 pounds from last week. The social worker explained that weight fluctuates as much as several pounds up or down per day, often depending on water retention (e.g., from where she is in her menstrual cycle or from eating a great deal of salty food). Pointing out to Tina that it is a long time between breakfast and the end of the school day, with only a small amount of food that amounts to anything in between, she suggested that Tina add to her lunch. Tina agreed to add cheese and crackers and tomato to her plain lettuce.

Stage 2. As Tina adopted a more regular meal and snack schedule, she was able to avoid binge eating on the way home most days. When she got a bad grade on a test, though, she binged on doughnuts once again. At this point, the intervention moved on to the thoughts and emotions that are associated with her eating disorder. All along, the social worker had tried to help Tina to recognize her emotions. Like many other people, Tina is not always able to label how she is feeling, confusing thoughts and feelings. In discussing the test grade, Tina said, "I feel like I'll never be able to get into a good college with these grades." The social worker responded, "You think your grades may

keep you from getting into a good college, and you feel scared or sad about that." Tina acknowledged that she feels scared; she is afraid she will disappoint her parents. The social worker introduced the Daily Record of Dysfunctional Thoughts (Figure 10.3) and helped Tina to fill it out with this example:

SW: The situation is getting a bad grade on a test. Your emotions—how you feel—is scared. What is it that you think automatically about this?

Tina: My parents will think I'm not smart enough to go to a good college.

SW: Okay, let's come up with a more rational thought. Do you really think that one test grade will keep you out of a good college?

Tina: No, I guess not.

SW: Is this bad grade what you usually get on tests?

Tina: No, I usually do much better.

SW: What was the grade?

Tina: I only got 85%.

SW: Aha, now I see. How about this for a more rational response: "Even though I got a B on the test, it is just one test. A few B's won't hurt my overall GPA anyway."

Tina: Okay, but my parents are still going to be upset.

SW: What will happen because they are upset about the grade?

Tina: I guess they will still love me.

Stage 3. Tina accomplished a great deal in treatment. She was eating regular meals and snacks, rarely binge eating, knew what was likely to trigger a binge-eating episode, and had begun to exercise more regularly. There were only a couple of sessions left, and school would be out soon for summer. Tina and the social worker were thinking about high-risk situations that might come up for Tina in the near future. Tina would be going away to band camp in July and had identified that as a potentially risky time. Tina decided to begin keeping the food diary again a week before she leaves for camp. In this way, she will be able to monitor her emotions and eating while she is away. If she begins to have problems sticking to a regular meal schedule or is tempted to binge, she will work on a more rational response to what she is feeling and thinking. If she does binge and/or purge while she is away, she will remind herself that she can stop again when she gets home.

Key Points to Remember

- Eating disorders (meeting full diagnostic criteria) are fairly rare but may have serious consequences. School personnel should be attuned to extreme weight loss and other signs of disordered eating behavior. A greater number of students may have disturbed eating behaviors that may later lead to a full-blown eating disorder.
- Individuals with anorexia nervosa are more likely to have medical complications. If anorexia nervosa is suspected, there should probably be a referral for a medical examination.
- Bulimia nervosa in particular is amenable to treatment with a cognitive-behavioral intervention. The treatment that is described here and in the treatment manuals referenced consists of 19 sessions in three stages.
- The first stage of treatment emphasizes restoring a normal eating pattern of three meals and two snacks per day.
- Stage 2 of treatment addresses the distorted thinking and emotions that lead to and maintain eating disorders.
- Stage 3 plans for relapse prevention.
- Medications are sometimes used along with therapy during treatment or afterward for relapse prevention.

References

Agras, W. S., & Apple, R. F. (1997). *Overcoming eating disorders: A cognitive-behavioral treatment for bulimia nervosa and binge eating disorder.* San Antonio, TX: Psychological Corporation.

Agras, W. S., & Apple, R. F. (2002). Understanding and treating eating disorders. In F. W. Kaslow & T. Patterson (Eds.), *Comprehensive handbook of psychotherapy: Vol. 2. Cognitive behavioral approaches* (pp. 189–212). New York: Wiley.

American Psychiatric Association. (2000). *Diagnostic and statistical manual of mental disorders* (4th ed., text revision). Washington, DC: Author.

Bowers, W. A., Evans, K., & Van Cleve, L. (1996). Treatment of adolescent eating disorders. In M. A. Reineke, F. M. Dattilio, & A. Freeman (Eds.), *Cognitive therapy with children and adolescents: A casebook for clinical practice* (pp. 227–250). New York: Guilford.

Eisler, I., Dare, C., Hodes, M., Russell, G., Dodge, E., & Le Grange, D. (2000). Family therapy for adolescent anorexia nervosa: The results of a controlled comparison of two family interventions. *Journal of Child Psychology and Psychiatry, 41,* 727–736.

Fairburn, C. G., Agras, W. S., & Wilson, G. T. (1992). The research on the treatment of bulimia nervosa: Practical and theoretical implications. In G. H. Anderson & S. H. Kennedy (Eds.), *The biology of feast and famine: Relevance to eating disorders* (pp. 318–340). New York: Academic.

Fairburn, C. G., Marcus, M. D., & Wilson, G. T. (1993). Cognitive-behavioral therapy for binge eating and bulimia nervosa: A comprehensive treatment manual. In C. G. Fairburn & G. T. Wilson (Eds.), *Binge eating: Nature, assessment, and treatment* (pp. 361–404). New York: Guilford.

Halmi, K. (2003). Eating disorders. In A. Martin, L. Scahill, D. Charney, & J. Leckman (Eds.), *Pediatric psychopharmacology* (pp. 592–602). New York: Oxford University Press.

Hoek, H. W., & van Hoeken, D. (2003). Review of the prevalence and incidence of eating disorders. *International Journal of Eating Disorders, 34,* 383–396.

Kotwal, R., McElroy, S., & Malhotra, S. (2003). What treatment data support Topiramate in bulimia nervosa and binge eating disorder? What is the drug's safety profile? How is it used in these conditions? *Eating Disorders, 11,* 71–75.

Lock, J., Le Grange, D., Agras, W. S., & Dare, C. (2001). *Treatment manual for anorexia nervosa: A family-based approach.* New York: Guilford.

Nicholls, D., & Bryant-Waugh, R. (2003). Children and young adolescents. In J. Treasure, U. Schmidt, & E. van Furth (Eds.), *Handbook of eating disorders* (pp. 415–433). New York: Wiley.

Schmidt, U. (1998). Eating disorders and obesity. In P. Graham (Ed.), *Cognitive-behaviour therapy for children and families* (pp. 262–281). Cambridge: Cambridge University Press.

Sim, L., Sadowski, C., Whiteside, S., & Wells, L. (2004). Family-based therapy for adolescents with anorexia nervosa. *Mayo Clinic Proceedings, 79,* 1305–1308.

CHAPTER
11

Effective Interventions for Students With Schizophrenia and Other Psychotic Disorders

Susan Stone

Getting Started

Psychosis is a rare phenomenon among school-aged children but is perhaps the most critical of mental conditions for early identification and intervention. Little reliable literature exists regarding school-based identification and interventions for children with schizophrenia or other psychotic disorders. Much of the literature that does exist is flawed because of marked changes in recent years in the way childhood psychosis is both conceptualized and diagnosed (Lewis, 2002). Psychosis is a frightening and little understood cluster of symptoms that impairs reality testing and everyday senses and perceptions. Because of the lack of public awareness about psychosis, in general, and especially in children, school-based practitioners may be the first to be aware of the changes in a child's behavior that reflect the possibility of psychosis. Identification of psychosis is difficult in adults but even more difficult in young children, as youths often do not have the communication skills to convey such complex symptoms to adults. Identification is also clouded by the rich imaginary processes of children. Distinguishing between imagination and psychosis can be difficult, even for well-trained child psychiatrists. This is particularly true in very young children, who are unable to use and communicate about adult rules of logic or notions of reality (Caplan, 1994). This chapter will focus on ways to identify childhood psychosis, the various causes of childhood psychosis, medical treatment, and school-based supportive interventions that may assist children and families in managing this potentially life-threatening situation.

What We Know

What Is Psychosis?

In overly simplistic terms, psychosis is an impairment of "reality testing," characterized by the following symptoms:

- Thought disturbance, a term used to reflect disorganization in the way thoughts are put together and expressed. Another term to describe thought disturbance is "loosening of associations," meaning that the logical relationships between thoughts and feelings become jumbled. In children, thought disturbance might be mistaken for inattentiveness, as the child's thinking might appear to be "jumping" from one thought to another.
- Hallucination, a phenomenon which involves seeing, hearing, feeling, or smelling something that is not there. The most common form of hallucination is an auditory hallucination, or hearing a voice or voices when there is no one speaking. Auditory hallucinations are truly like voices from the outside—not thoughts from the inside. Often, children will answer "yes" when asked about hearing voices, when truly they are only referring to internal thoughts and worries. Visual hallucinations, which are less common, are brief, vague flashes of visual material. More detailed pictures, such as cartoon characters or people, are more likely to be imagination than psychosis. Tactile hallucinations, or feeling things crawling across the skin, are very uncommon in children. Olfactory hallucinations, or smelling characteristic odors that are not present, are often associated with seizure disorders.
- Delusions are generally defined as "fixed false beliefs." Children with delusions develop

strongly held beliefs that cannot be swayed, despite confrontation with realities. The most common type of delusion is paranoid, or feeling that others are trying to hurt them. Especially in adolescence, paranoia can easily be mistaken for insecurity or difficulties in relating to peers. The reverse is also true. Delusions are very difficult to treat and tend to remain at least somewhat present even after treatment with psychotropic medications. Delusions often become even more "fixed" the more they are talked about, so attempting to argue a child out of a delusion is not advised.

Causes of Psychosis in Children

Schizophrenia is one of the least understood illnesses in the United States, largely because of media influence, confusing the clinical term *schizophrenia* with the lay term *split personality*. Schizophrenia is a very serious chronic mental illness, characterized by the psychotic symptoms (thought disturbance, hallucinations, and delusions) described above. While schizophrenia can appear in childhood, the more common course is for schizophrenia to emerge in early adulthood. The incidence of childhood-onset schizophrenia is approximately 1 in 40,000, contrasted with the incidence of schizophrenia in older adolescents and adults, which is approximately 1 in 100. (National Institute of Mental Health, 2003).

It is exceedingly rare to see schizophrenia emerge in children under the age of 6 (Werry, 1992). Very young children may have imaginary friends and fantasy thoughts, which are developmentally normal for this age. Concerns should arise, however, if a child of 7 years or older often hears voices, talks to himself or herself, stares at scary things that aren't there, and shows no interest in friendships.

Schizophrenia with childhood onset is conceptually the same as schizophrenia in adolescents and adults. In order to diagnose schizophrenia in childhood, the following must be present:

- at least two of the following: hallucinations, delusions, grossly disorganized speech or behavior, and severe withdrawal for at least 1 month;
- social or academic dysfunction; and
- continuous signs of the disturbance for 6 months. (Kaplan, Sadock, & Grebb, 1994)

Schizophrenia in adults is characterized by what mental health professionals refer to as a "chronic, deteriorating course." In children, however, consideration must be given to failure to achieve expected levels of social and academic functioning, instead of actual deterioration in functioning (Kaplan, Sadock, & Grebb, 1994). The symptoms of schizophrenia can often be managed with medications, but the illness itself is not curable, and often gets worse, even when adequate treatment is provided. Sadly, schizophrenia that appears at younger ages tends to be more resistant to treatment and have a worse prognosis (McClellan et al., 1999).

Schizophrenia is a biological brain disease. Images obtained from high-resolution magnetic resonance images (MRI scans) repeatedly demonstrate brain dysfunction. There is also clearly a genetic component to schizophrenia, demonstrated by family histories of schizophrenia in persons with the disease, as well as twin studies (Kaplan, Sadock, & Grebb, 1994). The prevalence of schizophrenia in the general population, for example, is approximately 1%, but children with two parents with schizophrenia have a 40% risk of developing the illness, and identical twins have a risk of almost 50%.

Other Causes of Psychosis in Children

Not all children and adolescents who exhibit psychotic symptoms actually have schizophrenia. Recent research has shown that schizophrenia tends to be overdiagnosed because of a lack of clarity about diagnostic criteria (Volkmar, 1996). The balance between overdiagnosis and early detection is important. While early diagnosis may dramatically affect the long-term prognosis, an erroneous diagnosis of schizophrenia can also have profound implications. All mental illnesses are stigmatizing in current society, but this is probably most pronounced for schizophrenia. The prognosis for children with other psychotic disorders is significantly better than for children with schizophrenia (McClellan et al., 1999). Anticipation of lifelong battles with psychosis, complicated by frightening information in the media, can send even the most stable families into turmoil. Sadly, many families dealing with psychosis in children and other family members are not stable, resulting in increased chaos and decreased ability to address the symptoms and follow through with treatment recommendations. A diagnosis of schizophrenia also has the unfortunate result of hampering future attempts to obtain health insurance. Thus, while early identification is important, the results of an erroneous diagnosis of childhood schizophrenia can have serious, lifelong implications.

Brief Psychotic Disorders

Some children exhibit psychotic symptoms that resemble symptoms of schizophrenia but that resolve over a relatively short period of time. This usually occurs in response to a significant stressful event, such as the death of a parent or sibling. Children with brief psychotic disorders may exhibit all of the characteristic features of schizophrenia, with the exception of significant deterioration in functioning or failure to meet expected social or academic functioning. Brief psychotic disorders are usually treated with medications and supportive therapy, much like schizophrenia, but it is important to attempt to discontinue the medications after a reasonable period of time to determine whether the underlying psychotic symptoms are still present.

Schizotypal Personality Disorder

A personality disorder is characterized by an inflexible pattern of behaviors that are maladaptive and interfere with normal functioning. While typically not diagnosed until adulthood, some personality disorders begin to reveal themselves in adolescence. One particularly severe personality disorder, schizotypal personality disorder, can easily be mistaken for schizophrenia. Children with schizotypal personality disorder may exhibit social isolation, eccentric thoughts, and bizarre behavior, but overt psychotic symptoms, such as hallucinations and outright delusions, are absent.

Mood Disorders With Psychotic Features

Children with mood disorders, such as major depression and bipolar disorder, can also exhibit psychotic symptoms. See chapters 8 and 9 for information on symptoms of mood disorders. These symptoms may closely resemble the psychotic symptoms of schizophrenia, but there is a distinct mood component present as well.

Treatment of psychosis accompanying mood disorders requires treatment of both the mood disturbance and the psychosis. Typically, the psychotic symptoms resolve relatively quickly, at which time treatment can be exclusively focused on the mood disorder.

Pervasive Developmental Disorder

Pervasive developmental disorders, including autism, have often been confused with schizophrenia. See chapter 12 for a discussion of autism and related disorders. In fact, much of the available literature about childhood-onset schizophrenia is now suspected of including numerous children with pervasive developmental disorders. While difficulty in social functioning, flat affect, and social withdrawal are present in both disorders, overt psychotic symptoms are usually absent in pervasive developmental disorders.

Attention Deficit Disorder and Obsessive-Compulsive Disorder

Other psychiatric disorders that may be confused with psychosis include attention deficit disorder and obsessive-compulsive disorder. In attention deficit disorder, attention problems and wandering thoughts may sometimes be misconstrued as hallucinations or evidence of a thought disorder. In obsessive-compulsive disorder, bizarre, ritualistic behaviors may also resemble the behaviors of children experiencing delusions. In neither of these disorders, however, would the overt presence of auditory hallucinations, frank delusions, or grossly disorganized thought processes be expected.

Drugs

Many illicit drugs currently available to children can cause significant psychotic symptoms. Most notable are cocaine, PCP, LSD, ecstasy, and inhalants. Psychotic states induced by drugs tend to be abrupt in onset and transient, whereas schizophrenia and psychoses associated with mood disorders tend to have a more gradual, insidious onset.

Medical Problems

There are a number of reversible medical problems that can cause psychotic symptoms, most notably brain tumors, thyroid imbalance, seizure disorders, and lupus, which is an autoimmune disorder. In addition, some medications can produce transient psychotic symptoms as a side effect.

Case Example of Differential Diagnosis

The following case example demonstrates the difficulty in distinguishing these conditions and issues.

Barry has always been a quiet kid. He never exhibited any behavior problems and did fairly well academically, but he never really seemed to fit in. When Barry entered high school, his grades started to fall somewhat. When he came home from school in the afternoons, he would go immediately to his room. He appeared to be distracted and often looked toward the ceiling. He stopped talking to his parents. He dropped out of sports. Often, when his mother would walk by his room, he would be talking to himself in a loud voice. The teachers noted that, while previously he would sit at the front of the class, he now sat at the back of the class and mumbled to himself often. Sometimes, when he was called on, his answers wouldn't make much sense, and the thoughts didn't connect very well. He would wash his hands several times per hour and seemed to be preoccupied with his health. He stopped eating in the cafeteria. The other kids began to steer clear of him.

Analysis

- "Always quiet." The fact that Barry has always been quiet only becomes significant after other psychiatric symptoms begin to emerge. A child who is quiet may be simply exhibiting shyness, or the quietness may indicate prodromal symptoms of an anxiety disorder, mood disorder, personality disorder, pervasive developmental disorder, or psychosis.
- "Did fairly well academically." While deterioration in functioning is necessary for a diagnosis of schizophrenia in adults, failure to achieve expected levels of academic and social functioning is a factor to consider in children. While some studies indicate some early language-related deficits (Kaplan, Sadock, & Grebb, 1994), most youths with schizophrenia function in the average range of academic performance prior to the onset of their illness. The drop in Barry's academic functioning, however, does not alone indicate concern related to psychosis. Often children with mood disorders, ADHD, and OCD exhibit worsening academic performance as well, especially as they reach the high school years.
- "Social withdrawal." Social withdrawal is also a nonspecific sign that is difficult to interpret. As

most parents of adolescents know, withdrawal in the home environment is a developmentally normal behavior for youths in their teenage years. On the other hand, social isolation can reflect serious mood disturbance or psychosis. Social isolation from peers is a stronger indicator of a significant problem.

- "Distracted, looking toward the ceiling, talking to himself." None of these symptoms alone cause concern that Barry is psychotic but, taken together, they raise a significant concern that Barry is experiencing auditory hallucinations. Children with auditory hallucinations have more difficulty than adults in blocking out the voices, so they can be observed being startled or distracted for no apparent reason and can sometimes be heard responding to the voices.
- "Thoughts didn't connect very well." The prime indicators of a thought disturbance attributable to schizophrenia are speech and/or thought processes that are grossly disorganized. So, while a child with attention deficit disorder or a mood disorder may exhibit some disjointed and meandering thinking patterns, the level of disturbance does not meet the criteria of gross disorganization.
- "Washing hands, health preoccupation, stopped eating." As with the other symptoms in Barry's history, these symptoms could be associated with psychosis but could also be consistent with other psychiatric problems. Excessive hand washing, for example, is a common symptom of obsessive-compulsive disorder. Children who stop eating may be exhibiting social anxiety or signs of an eating disorder. The key factor in interpreting these symptoms is to determine the reasons for the behavior.

What We Can Do

Assessment

As with all mental illnesses, assessment and diagnosis require a broad-based, biopsychosocial approach. Unlike other illnesses that are more common in children, however, most of the standardized assessment instruments helpful in the diagnosis of psychosis were designed primarily for use in adults (McClellan et al., 1999).

Box 11.1 Standardized Instruments

Structured Clinical Interview for *DSM-IV* (SCID) (First, 1997)
Schedule for Positive Symptoms (SAPS) (Andreasen, 1982)
Schedule for Negative Symptoms (SANS) (Andreasen, 1982)
Schedule for Affective Disorders and Schizophrenia for School Age Children (Kiddie-SADS) (Puig-Antich & Chambers, 1983)
Kiddie Formal Thought Disorder Rating Scale (Caplan, 1994)

As demonstrated by Barry's case, early signs of psychosis can be fairly nonspecific and can be easily confused with other social or psychological problems. Some things to look for are:

- Changes in the way the child interacts with peers
- Changes at home noticed by the family (changes in behavior in school without changes in behavior at home may reflect peer/social issues)
- Internal preoccupation or distraction
- Exhibition of fright, without cause, or suspicious nature (might reflect paranoid delusions)
- Bizarre or disorganized behavior or speech

If there *is* evidence of psychosis, look for:

- Recent major stressors in the child's life (may reflect brief psychotic disorder)
- Recent physical evaluation (to rule out thyroid or other medical causes)
- Recent neurologic evaluation and an EEG (to rule out seizure disorders)
- Recently started medications
- Sadness, irritability, or tearfulness
- Euphoria, with rapid speech and rambling thought process (may reflect bipolar disorder with psychotic features but, if acute onset, might also reflect drug use)
- Family history of any mental illness
- Suspicion of drug use

Psychotic disorders in children are not typically associated with mental retardation, but various developmental and learning problems may be present (Lewis, 2002). Psychoeducational testing should include assessment of intellectual level, assessment of adaptive behavior, and assessment of communication skills. Projective testing may also be helpful, as some children do not know how to describe their symptoms or do not exhibit flagrant thought disorder (Lewis, 2002).

Acute Intervention

Once psychosis has been identified in a child, regardless of the cause, certain steps must be taken immediately. Because people with schizophrenia are at a higher risk of suicide (Kaplan, Sadock, & Grebb, 1994), the safety of the child is the first concern. Using a stepwise process in the development of a safety plan will help to ensure that the complex factors associated with psychosis in children are addressed quickly and appropriately.

Step 1: Is Hospitalization Necessary?

The first critical component in the development of a safety plan is the assessment of whether the child can be maintained in the school or if hospitalization or another restrictive setting is necessary. Some children with suicidal thoughts talk about them readily, but others hide them, especially if the thoughts relate to command auditory hallucinations (voices that tell them to do something) or delusions. Even if suicidal thoughts are present, evaluation of the need for hospitalization can be complex. Psychiatric hospitalization, while sometimes necessary, can significantly increase the self-perceived stigma of mental illness for children. The decision about whether hospitalization is necessary must balance (1) the severity of the risk; (2) the stability and safety of the home environment; and (3) the ability to get the child into outpatient treatment immediately. Even if hospitalization is necessary, it will only be a short-term intervention, so efforts must begin immediately to establish a longer-term safety plan.

Step 2: Engaging the Family

Engaging the family is critical to treatment success for children with psychosis. While this is true when working with any sort of mental or emotional disturbance, it is markedly increased when working with psychotic children, for a number of reasons. First, the often bizarre nature of the psychotic symptoms and behaviors can be very frightening for family members who have watched them develop over time. These behaviors, in addition to elements of social withdrawal, can result in the child becoming isolated or even ostracized within the family unit. Because of the genetic nature of many illnesses that result in psychosis, many family members will have previous experience of psychosis, leading to a variety of emotions. Although, as in other areas related to childhood psychosis, the data are limited, available literature suggests that families of children with psychosis have some disturbances in the patterns of communication. It is unclear whether these abnormalities are reactions to the child's disorder or if they reflect the same underlying vulnerability exhibited more directly in the affected child (Lewis, 2002).

The first intervention with the family should be education. Education should focus on dispelling myths about schizophrenia and psychosis and preparing families for the difficulties they will likely address in dealing with the illness. Because of recent negative media attention to the use of psychotropic medications in children, many families may be resistant to using medications to control the symptoms of psychosis. These concerns must be addressed directly, with emphasis on the fact that psychosis and schizophrenia are biological disorders that must be addressed just as other medical conditions. Emphasis must be placed on the necessity of remaining consistent in taking these medications, and side effects from the medications should be addressed immediately with the prescribing physician, rather than simply stopping the medication. School-based mental health professionals can often serve as useful liaisons between families and the formal mental health system, which can often be somewhat intimidating.

Because psychosis in childhood is so rare, it may be difficult to identify peer support for family members. Linking families to support systems for other serious mental illnesses, however, may have some benefit. Communication issues within families must be addressed in an effort to enhance strengths and maintain the availability of the child for educational and other interventions (Lewis, 2002).

Step 3: Treatment

School-based treatment of children with psychotic disorders requires the services of a multidisciplinary team of professionals, including school social workers and mental health counselors, special education services, consulting psychiatrists for pharmacotherapy, and case management (Policy Leadership Cadre for Mental Health in Schools, 2001).

Pharmacotherapy

For the most part, the mainstay of treatment for schizophrenia and other psychotic disorders is antipsychotic medication. Unfortunately, as with the other issues in this area, the literature is extremely limited with regard to the benefit and safety of antipsychotic medication in children and adolescents (Schur et al., 2003). Furthermore, much of the literature that does exist addresses the use of antipsychotic medication for reasons other than psychosis, such as aggression or autism (Gage, 2003).

The first medications used in the treatment of psychosis in both children and adults were the "typical" antipsychotics, also known as traditional neuroleptics. While some children show little or no response to these medications, there is some evidence that these medications are moderately effective in dampening the symptoms of psychosis (Kaplan, Sadock, & Grebb, 1994).

The major limitation to their use, however, in both children and adults, is the side-effect profile, including hand tremors, stooped posture, drooling, shuffling gait, restlessness, irritability, muscle spasms, and a relatively rare disorder called tardive dyskinesia, which involves involuntary muscle movements of the head, limbs, and trunk. Although the data are limited, there is some evidence that some of these side effects may be increased in children and adolescents (Findling, 2000).

Newer generation antipsychotics, referred to as the "atypicals," have emerged in recent years as an alternative option to the traditional forms. The first of these atypical agents was clozapine, and it has probably been the medication most studied in childhood-onset schizophrenia (Frazier et al., 1994; Kumra et al., 1996; Remschmidt et al., 1994; Turetz et al., 1997). While it has proven to be effective in most of these trials, significant side effects can emerge from this medication, including drops in blood counts (necessitating frequent blood draws), weight gain (which appears to be more pronounced in children and adolescents) (Gage, 2003), and an increased risk of diabetes. Chapter 2 presents more information on the uses and side effects of psychotropic medications.

The keys to managing these side effects are analyzing the risks versus the benefits, making sure that the family understands these issues and agrees to using the medication, and minimizing dosages, to the extent possible. School social workers and other practitioners can be extremely helpful in assisting the family in monitoring the presence of side effects that may result in the child being resistant to taking the medications.

Kids Hate Medicines

While the symptoms of mental illness, especially psychosis, are incredibly troubling for children and adolescents, being seen as "different" by their peers may be even more troubling. Many youths would prefer to downplay their frightening symptoms when confronted with having to "go to the nurse's office" to take their medications. Parents of children with mental illness often relate significant difficulties with medication compliance. Here are a few strategies that seem to help:

- Normalize the illness. Emphasize that taking this kind of medication is much like taking an antibiotic for an ear infection or taking medicine for a cold.
- Monitor compliance regularly. Adolescents can be less than honest about whether or not they're taking the medications as prescribed. A quick count of pills can make a big difference between response versus no response.
- Be vigilant about side effects. Often, the reluctance to remain on the medications is more about side effects. Younger children usually don't have the communication skills to talk about side effects, so things like dysphoria, sexual side effects, and EPS may have to be detected by observation rather than communication.

Psychotherapy

Studies of psychotherapy in children with psychosis are limited in number and validity (because of the diagnostic issues noted above), but there is some evidence that supportive psychotherapy may be beneficial (Cantor & Kestenbaum, 1986). Supportive therapy should focus on education about the symptoms and coping strategies for dealing with them. It is important to note, for example, that, even with treatment, delusions may not totally go away. Using supportive, behavioral techniques may assist the child in diverting attention away from delusional thought processes or hallucinations. The usefulness of intensive, insight-oriented therapy is much less clear (Lewis, 2002). The benefits of psychotherapy may ultimately be dependent on the level of adaptive functioning and communication skills.

Step 4: Academic Programming

Although the emergence of schizophrenia in young adults may present as an acute psychotic episode, research has shown that schizophrenia in children may emerge more gradually, preceded by developmental disturbances, such as lags in motor and speech/language ability. Some recent research has shown that the pathophysiology of schizophrenia may involve abnormal development of language-related brain regions (National Institute of Mental Health, 2003). As with other areas of this illness, academic programming must balance the specialized learning needs of the child with minimizing self-perceived stigma. The need for special education services will be dependent upon developmental delays and intellectual issues identified during psychological testing. It must be noted, however, that children with psychosis may be higher functioning intellectually than other children in special education classes, necessitating specialized attention. Being placed in special education classes with children who have mental retardation or autism may actually increase the stigma and perception of self-shame. This decision must be made on a case-by-case basis.

Tools and Practice Examples

While there is a dearth of research findings with regard to childhood psychosis, there are a number of Internet Web sites that provide up-to-date, valid information about childhood schizophrenia and psychosis:

www.webmd.com
www.schizophrenia.com
www.nimh.com
www.psychiatry24×7.com
www.nmha.com
www.psychdirect.com
www.mentalhealth.com
www.nami.org

Key Points to Remember

Early identification and intervention are critical for children with schizophrenia and other psychotic disorders. The diagnosis of these conditions can be difficult for a number of reasons, including the rich imaginary processes of children and their relative inability to communicate the complex nature of psychotic symptomatology. Psychoses are generally biological conditions that may run in families. For this reason, a careful biopsychosocial assessment, including extensive family history, is necessary to arrive at a diagnosis. Because childhood psychosis is a very rare phenomenon, little literature exists about evidence-based practices. Development of a safety plan and engaging the family are critical first steps. Psychotropic medications may be helpful, but they often have difficult side effects, which may be more pronounced in children. Decisions about using these medications necessitate a careful analysis of risks versus benefits. Supportive psychotherapy has been generally shown to be effective, with special emphasis on education about the condition, treatments, and prognosis. Designing an educational program also requires a careful analysis of specialized needs versus minimization of stigma to the individual child. These decisions must be made on a case-by-case basis.

References

Cantor, S., & Kestenbaum, C. (1986). Psychotherapy with schizophrenic children. *Journal of the American Academy of Child and Adolescent Psychiatry, 25,* 623–630.

Caplan, R. (1994). Thought disorder in childhood. *Journal of the Academy of Child and Adolescent Psychiatry, 33,* 605–615.

Frazier J., Gordon C., McKenna, K., et al. (1994). An open trial of clozapine in 11 adolescents with childhood-onset schizophrenia. *Journal of the American Adolescent Psychiatry, 33*(5), 658–663.

Gage, A. (2003). Atypical antipsychotics in children and adolescents. *Case Management, 9*(1).

Kaplan, H., Sadock, B., & Grebb, J. (1994). *Kaplan and Sadock's synopsis of psychiatry* (7th ed.). Baltimore, MD: Williams and Wilkins.

Kumra S., Frazier, J., Jacobsen L., et al. (1996). Childhood-onset schizophrenia: A double-blind clozapine-haloperidol comparison. *Archives of General Psychiatry, 53*(12), 1090–1097.

Lewis, M. (2002). *Child and adolescent psychiatry: A comprehensive textbook* (3rd ed.). Hagerstown, MD: Lippincott/Williams and Wilkins.

McClellan, J., McCurry, C., Snell, J., & DuBose, A. (1999). Early onset psychotic disorders: Course and outcome over a 2-year period. *Journal of the American Academy of Child and Adolescent Psychiatry, 38*(11), 1380–1388.

National Institute of Mental Health. (2003). *Childhood-onset schizophrenia: An update from the National Institute of Mental Health.* Bethesda, MD: Author.

Policy Leadership Cadre for Mental Health in Schools. (2001). *Mental health in schools: Guidelines, models, resources and policy considerations.* Los Angeles: University of California, Center for Mental Health in Schools.

Remschmidt, H., Schulz, E., & Martin, P. (1994). An open trial of clozapine in thirty-six adolescents with schizophrenia. *Journal of Child and Adolescent Psychopharmacology, 4*(1), 31–41.

Schur, S., Sikich, L., Findling, R., Malone, R., Crismon, M., Derivan, A., Macintyre, I., Pappadopulos, E., Greenhill, L., Schooler, N., Van Orden, K., & Jensen, P. (2003). *Treatment recommendations for the use of antipsychotics for aggressive youth (TRAAY), part I: A review.* New York: Center for the Advancement of Children's Mental Health, Columbia University/New York State Psychiatric Institute.

Turetz, M., Mozes, T., Toren, P., et al. (1997). An open trial of clozapine in neuroleptic resistant childhood-onset schizophrenia. *British Journal of Psychiatry, 170,* 507–510.

Volkmar, F. (1996). Childhood and adolescent psychosis: A review of the past 10 years. *Journal of the American Academy of Child and Adolescent Psychiatry, 35*(7), 843–851.

Werry, J. S. (1992). Child and early adolescent schizophrenia: A review in light of the DSM III-R. *Journal of Autism Developmental Disorder, 22,* 610–614.

Effective Interventions for Students With Autism and Asperger's Syndrome

Michelle S. Ballan ▪ Karen S. Hoban

CHAPTER 12

Getting Started

Autism is a complex disorder defined by numerous developmental and behavioral features. The canopy of the autism spectrum is far reaching, with school-aged children and adolescents ranging from nonverbal with multiple developmental disabilities to mild Asperger's syndrome with advanced capabilities for mathematics and science. Autism spectrum disorders (ASDs), termed pervasive developmental disorders (PDDs) in the *Diagnostic and Statistical Manual of Mental Disorders* (*DSM-IV-TR*; American Psychiatric Association, 2000) and in the *International Classification of Diseases* (*ICD-10*; World Health Organization, 1992), is a term often used in educational and clinical settings to refer to various disorders spanning a severe form known as autistic disorder (AD), to a milder form called Asperger's syndrome or disorder (AS). If a child exhibits symptoms of AD or AS, but does not meet the specific criteria for either disorder, the child is diagnosed with an ASD identified as pervasive developmental disorder not otherwise specified (PDD-NOS) (American Psychiatric Association, 2000; Strock, 2004). Less common are two additional acute ASDs known as Rett's syndrome or disorder (RS) and childhood disintegrative disorder (CDD).

Students identified as having an ASD exhibit a tremendous range in symptoms and characteristics due to developmental maturity and varying degrees of associated cognitive limitations (Filipek et al., 1999). Many school social workers, psychologists, and special educators are familiar with the primary clinical symptomatology of the majority of ASDs, which typically falls within three major categories: (1) qualitative impairment in social interaction, such as gaze aversion or the absence of communication; (2) impairments in communication, such as mutism and lack of pretend play; and (3) restricted, repeti-

tive, stereotyped behavior, interests, and activities, such as retentive motor mannerisms (American Psychiatric Association, 2000; Bregman, 2005). Autism spectrum disorders vary with respect to age of onset and associations with other disorders. Differences among ASDs appear to be linked to intelligence, level of adaptive functioning, and number of autistic symptoms rather than to the presence of distinct symptoms (Hollander & Nowinski, 2003, p. 17).

Since the 1990s, research has revealed an upward trend in the prevalence rate for ASDs (Fombonne, 2005; Fombonne, Du Mazaubrun, Cans, & Grandjean, 1997; Fombonne, Simmons, Ford, Meltzer, & Goodman, 2001; Yeargin-Allsopp et al., 2003) due largely in part to issues regarding diagnosis. An increase in the prevalence rate may be attributable to a diverse range of factors, such as the broadening of diagnostic concepts to include milder and more atypical variants (Bregman, 2005), greater awareness among parents and professionals, the prospect of securing specialized services or benefits for children due to educational funding formulas, and the extent to which families advocate for the diagnosis during assessment (Scott, Clark, & Brady, 2000). Fombonne (2005) reported an estimate of 60 out of 10,000 for the prevalence of all ASDs. The majority of studies report that ASDs are four times more common in boys than girls (Fombonne, 1999), and approximately 75% of all individuals classified with autism have measured intelligence in the range of mental retardation (Bryson & Smith, 1998). Autism spectrum disorders are often accompanied by a range of abnormalities within cognitive, adaptive, affective, and behavioral domains of development, deficits in executive functions, limitations in adaptive skills, learning disabilities, mood instability, stereotypic and self-injurious behaviors, anxiety disorders, and aggression (Bregman, 2005). One in four children with an ASD develops seizures, often beginning in either early childhood or adolescence (Volkmar,

2000), and the rate of tuberous sclerosis appears to be 100 times higher among children with ASDs (Fombonne, 2005).

An increase or variation in prevalence rates may also be due largely in part to the utilization of different diagnostic criteria for ASDs across research studies. There are varying diagnostic groups within ASDs and varying diagnostic criteria for assessment. However, the *DSM-IV-TR* (2000) and the *ICD-10* (1992) share general agreement regarding the almost identical criteria for the diagnosis of the five subtypes of PDDs or ASDs (AD, AS, PDD-NOS, RS, and CDD).[1] For the purpose of this chapter, two of the more common ASDs (AD and AS) seen among school-aged children and adolescents will be the focus. The *DSM-IV-TR* (2000) outlines specific criteria for AD (see Table 12.1) and AS (see Table 12.2).

The most notable difference between AD and AS involves age-appropriate communication skills. Communication is presumed to be within normal limits in children with AS, although as one might expect of a school-aged youth with severe limitations in recognizing and interpreting social messages, pragmatic deficits are frequent (Scott et al., 2000). Because pragmatic deficits constitute a core area of communication functioning, this minimizes the true differences between children diagnosed with AS and AD (Scott et al., 2000).

The *DSM IV-TR* (2000) specifies a set of criteria for AS and AD which might lead one to believe that diagnosis of such disorders is made with ease. However, diagnosis can be difficult due in part to the lack of definitive diagnostic tests for AD or AS. There are currently no reliable physiological markers for diagnosis as there are in

Table 12.1 *DSM-IV* Diagnostic Criteria for Autistic Disorder

A. A total of six (or more) items from (1), (2), and (3), with at least two from (1), and one each from (2) and (3):

    (1) qualitative impairment in social interaction, as manifested by at least two of the following:
        (a) marked impairment in the use of multiple nonverbal behaviors such as eye-to-eye gaze, facial expression, body postures, and gestures to regulate social interaction
        (b) failure to develop peer relationships appropriate to developmental level
        (c) a lack of spontaneous seeking to share enjoyment, interests, or achievements with other people (e.g., by a lack of showing, bringing, or pointing out objects of interest)
        (d) lack of social or emotional reciprocity

    (2) qualitative impairments in communication as manifested by at least one of the following:
        (a) delay in, or total lack of, the development of spoken language (not accompanied by an attempt to compensate through alternative modes of communication such as gesture or mime)
        (b) in individuals with adequate speech, marked impairment in the ability to initiate or sustain a conversation with others
        (c) stereotyped and repetitive use of language or idiosyncratic language
        (d) lack of varied, spontaneous make-believe play or social imitative play appropriate to developmental level

    (3) restricted, repetitive, and stereotyped patterns of behavior, interests, and activities, as manifested by at least one of the following:
        (a) encompassing preoccupation with one or more stereotyped and restricted patterns of interest that is abnormal either in intensity or focus
        (b) apparently inflexible adherence to specific, nonfunctional routines or rituals
        (c) stereotyped and repetitive motor mannerisms (e.g., hand or finger flapping or twisting, or complex whole-body movements)
        (d) persistent preoccupation with parts of objects

B. Delays or abnormal functioning in at least one of the following areas, with onset prior to age 3 years: (1) social interaction, (2) language as used in social communication, or (3) symbolic or imaginative play

C. The disturbance is not better accounted for by Rett's disorder or childhood disintegrative disorder.

Source: Reprinted with permission from the *Diagnostic and Statistical Manual of Mental Disorders*. Copyright 2000. American Psychiatric Association.

Table 12.2 *DSM-IV-TR* Diagnostic Criteria for Asperger's Syndrome

A. Qualitative impairment in social interaction, as manifested by at least two of the following:
   (1) marked impairment in the use of multiple nonverbal behaviors such as eye-to-eye gaze, facial expression, body postures, and gestures to regulate social interaction
   (2) failure to develop peer relationships appropriate to developmental level
   (3) a lack of spontaneous seeking to share enjoyment, interests, or achievements with other people (e.g., by a lack of showing, bringing, or pointing out objects of interest to other people)
   (4) lack of social or emotional reciprocity

B. Restricted, repetitive, and stereotyped patterns of behavior, interests, and activities, as manifested by at least one of the following:
   (1) encompassing preoccupation with one or more stereotyped and restricted patterns of interest that is abnormal either in intensity or focus
   (2) apparently inflexible adherence to specific, nonfunctional routines or rituals
   (3) stereotyped and repetitive motor mannerisms (e.g., hand or finger flapping or twisting, or complex whole-body movements)
   (4) persistent preoccupation with parts of objects

C. The disturbance causes clinically significant impairment in social, occupational, or other important areas of functioning.

D. There is no clinically significant general delay in language (e.g., single words used by age 2 years, communicative phrases used by age 3 years).

E. There is no clinically significant delay in cognitive development or in the development of age-appropriate self-help skills, adaptive behavior (other than in social interaction), and curiosity about the environment in childhood.

F. Criteria are not met for another specific pervasive developmental disorder or schizophrenia.

Source: Reprinted with permission from the *Diagnostic and Statistical Manual of Mental Disorders*. Copyright 2000. American Psychiatric Association.

some other disabilities (i.e., the genetic markers associated with Fragile X syndrome). To make a diagnosis, clinicians frequently rely heavily on behavioral characteristics, which may be apparent in the first few months of a child's life or appear during the early years. The diagnosis of AD or AS necessitates a two-stage process composed of a developmental screening during "well child" checkups and a comprehensive evaluation by a multidisciplinary team (Filipek et al., 2000). Among the most promising first- and second-degree screening tools for AD are the Modified Checklist for Autism in Toddlers (M-CHAT; Robins, Fein, Barton, & Green, 2001) and the Screening Tool for Autism in Two-Year-Olds (STAT; Stone, Coonrod, & Ousley, 2000). For AS, the tools are the Autism Spectrum Screening Questionnaire (ASSQ; Ehlers, Gillberg, & Wing, 1999) and the Krug's Asperger's Disorder Index (KADI; Krug & Arick, 2003)[2] (see Table 12.3). These screening instruments do not provide a diagnosis; instead they aim to assess the need for referral for possible diagnosis of AS or AD.

The second stage of diagnosing AD or AS should include a formal multidisciplinary evaluation of social behavior, language and nonverbal communication, adaptive behavior, motor skills, atypical behaviors, and cognitive status made ideally by an experienced multidisciplinary team composed of social workers, psychologists, speech language pathologists, psychiatrists, pediatricians, educators, and family members (Howlin, 1998; National Research Council, 2001). Autistic disorder and AS often involve other neurological or genetic problems, thereby necessitating a first-line comprehensive assessment of medical conditions (Filipek et al., 2000). The diagnosis of AD or AS often entails a school-based social worker gathering information on developmental history, medical background, psychiatric or health disorders of family members, and psychosocial factors. Additionally, a social worker typically conducts a social family history by assessing the child's parents, caregivers, and environmental setting (McCarton, 2003). Psychological assessment and communicative assessment via testing, direct observation, and interviews should also inform the

Table 12.3 Screening Instruments for Autistic Disorder and Asperger's Syndrome

Instrument	Type of Screening	Age Level	Informant	Characteristics
Autistic Disorder				
M-CHAT (Robins et al., 2001)	Level 1	24 months	Parent	23-item checklist to examine child's developmental milestones
STAT (Stone et al., 2004)	Level 2	24–35 months	Clinician	12 activities for observing child's early social/communicative behaviors
Asperger's Syndrome				
ASSQ (Ehlers et al., 1999)	Level 1	>6 years	Parent/Teacher	27-item checklist for assessing symptoms characteristic of Asperger's syndrome
KADI (Krug & Arick, 2003)	Levels 1 & 2	>6 years	Individual with daily and regular contact with child for at least a few weeks	32-item norm-referenced rating scale for presence or absence of behaviors indicative of Asperger's syndrome

diagnosis. The psychological assessment helps to develop an understanding of the cognitive functioning and should address adaptive functioning, motor and visual skills, play, and social cognition (National Research Council, 2001). Communicative assessment should address communication skills in the context of a child's development (Lord & Paul, 1997) and assess expressive language and language comprehension.

Additionally, diagnostic instruments can be used to help structure and quantify clinical observations. The Childhood Autism Rating Scale (CARS; Schopler, Reichler, & Renner, 1986) is the strongest, best-documented, and most widely used clinical rating scale for behaviors associated with autism (Lord & Cosello, 2005, p. 748). Other instruments with strong psychometric data to support their use as a component of the diagnostic process include the Autism Diagnostic Interview-Revised (ADI-R; Lord, Rutter, & Le Couteur, 1994) and the Autism Diagnostic Observation Schedule (ADOS; Lord, Rutter, DiLavore, & Risi, 1999). One promising instrument for measuring symptom severity is the Social Responsiveness Scale (SRS; Constantino, 2002). No diagnosis would be complete without documentation of a child's unique

strengths and weaknesses, as this component is critical to designing an effective intervention program since unusual developmental profiles are typical (National Research Council, 2001).

Although several instruments have been proposed to formally substantiate a diagnosis of AS,[3] these instruments have little relationship to each other and have not been found to be reliable (Lord & Cosello, 2005). In addition to the aforementioned categories, when diagnosing AS, attention and mental control, auditory and visual perception, and memory should be assessed (DuCharme & McGrady, 2003). Additional observations may address components of topic management and conversational ability, ability to deal with nonliteral language, and language flexibility (National Research Council, 2001).

In regard to diagnosis, parents and professionals should serve as partners in reaching the best possible understanding of the child. The developmental, medical, and family histories that parents provide are crucial components of a diagnosis. Their description of their child's behavior across multiple settings is essential. The role of the professionals on the multidisciplinary team is to interpret the information that parents provide. Parents know their

Table 12.4 Diagnostic Instruments for Autistic Disorder

Instrument	Characteristics
CARS (Schopler et al., 1986)	15-item rating scale covering a particular characteristic, ability, or behavior on which children are rated after observation; can be administered by clinician or educator, and some studies have demonstrated use by parents
ADI-R (Lord et al., 1994)	93-item semistructured interview composed of three subscales (social reciprocity, communication, and restricted, repetitive behaviors); administered by a clinician to caregivers
ADOS (Lord et al., 1999)	Standardized protocol for the observation of social and communicative behavior of children who may have an ASD; administered by a clinician

individual child better than anyone, but professionals can offer a broad view of what is typical and where the child might differ from the norm (Wagner & McGrady, 2003).

Once a diagnosis of AD or AS is provided, parents begin to explore early intervention services to treat their child. Although early intervention has been shown to have a dramatic impact on reducing symptoms and increasing a child's ability to develop and gain new skills,[4] it is estimated that only 50% of children are diagnosed with an ASD before kindergarten (Strock, 2004). Thus, upon diagnosis, school-based interventions for youth with AD or AS often become the immediate focus of parents. Unfortunately, parents are soon faced with a prolific body of literature and disparate professional advice composed to some extent of ineffective approaches and treatment fads. Among the recommended treatments are facilitated communication, holding therapy, auditory integration training, gentle teaching, and hormone therapies, such as secretin, which are not adequately supported by scientific evidence for practice, and research has actually demonstrated some of these treatments to be harmful (Jacobson, Foxx, & Mulick, 2005; Simpson et al., 2004; Smith, 1996).

Part of the problem is that research has not demonstrated a single best treatment program for children with ASDs. Gresham, Beebe-Frankenberger, and MacMillan (1999) used conventional standards of research design and methodology and the Division 12 Task Force on Empirically Supported Treatments for Childhood Disorders of the American Psychological Association to evaluate the empirical evidence for the efficacy and effectiveness of several of the most visible and frequently

cited treatment programs for children with autism: the UCLA Young Autism Project, Project TEACCH, LEAP, applied behavior analysis programs, and the Denver Health Science Program (p. 559). Their evaluation documented no well-established or probably efficacious treatments for autism; however, almost all programs demonstrated significant developmental gains, particularly in measured IQ. Rogers (1998), however, aptly noted that it is essential to recognize that the lack of empirical demonstration of efficacy does not necessarily signify that a particular treatment is ineffective. Instead, it means that the treatment's efficacy has not been demonstrated in a carefully controlled and objective way (Gresham et al., 1999).

What We Know

School-aged children with ASDs face transitions to a new learning environment, socialization with new peers and adults, and departures from familiar routines and settings. Thus, many professionals agree that a highly structured, specialized program is optimal for this transition to an individualized learning environment. Among the many methods available for treatment and education of school-aged children with AD or AS, applied behavior analysis (ABA) has become the most widely accepted effective intervention model (Strock, 2004). A recent U.S. surgeon general's report (U.S. Department of Health and Human Services, 1999) noted that 3 decades of research has led to the demonstrated efficacy of applied behavioral methods in reducing inappropriate behavior and in increasing communication, learning, and appropriate social behavior for children with ASDs. Two evidence-based practices, discrete trial training or teaching (DTT) and pivotal response training (PRT), which use the principles of ABA, have been demonstrated as effective skill-based and behavioral treatment strategies. For the purpose of this chapter, *evidence-based practice* is defined as "the integration of best research evidence with clinical expertise and [client] values" (Sackett, Straus, Richardson, Rosenberg, & Haynes, 2000, p. 1).

Hundreds of scientific studies have demonstrated the effectiveness of ABA in building important skills and in reducing problem behaviors in children with ASDs (e.g., Jacobson et al., 1998; Lovaas, 1987; McEachin, Smith, & Lovaas, 1993; Smith, Groen, & Wynn, 2000), yet due to ethical and practical considerations (such as small sample size and the heterogeneity of participants), well-controlled studies with random assignment have been nearly impossible to conduct (National Research Council, 2001). Studies of ABA's effectiveness are primarily based on single-case design, with close to 100 published on children with autism since 1980. Applied behavior analysis as an umbrella term includes "numerous measurement procedures and many behavior-increase and behavior-decrease procedures that can be used singly or in combination to remediate various skill deficits and behavior problems" (McClannahan & Krantz, 2004, p. 93). The effectiveness of these more broadly defined ABA interventions for eliciting new skills and reducing problematic behavior has been documented by numerous studies (Anderson & Romanczyk, 1999; Harris, Handleman, Gordon, Kristoff, & Fuentes, 1991; Smith, 2001; Smith et al., 2000; Yoder & Layton, 1988, as cited in Paul & Sutherland, 2005, p. 949); however, this variation of treatment strategies causes problems with comparisons of ABA techniques. For this reason, the primary educational and treatment techniques of DTT and PRT are reviewed as important instructional systems of ABA (Arick, Krug, Fullerton, Loos, & Falco, 2005).

What We Can Do

Applied Behavior Analysis

Applied behavior analysis (ABA) is a discipline devoted to understanding the function behind human behavior and finding ways of altering or improving behaviors (Cooper, Heron, & Heward, 1987). Applied behavior analysis involves systematically applying learning theory–based interventions to improve socially significant observable behaviors to a meaningful degree and seeks to demonstrate that the improvement in behavior stems directly from the interventions that are utilized (Anderson, Taras, & Cannon, 1996; Baer, Wolf, & Risley, 1968; Sulzer-Azaroff & Mayer, 1991). The emphasis is on teaching the student how to learn from the environment and how to act on the environment in order to produce positive outcomes for himself and those around him (Harris & Handleman, 1994; Koegel & Koegel, 1995; Lovaas, 1993, 1981; Lovaas & Smith, 1989; Maurice, Green, & Luce, 1996; Schreibman, Charlop, & Milstein, 1993).

Behavior analytic treatment systematically teaches measurable units of a behavior or skill. Skills that a student with autism needs to learn are broken down into small steps. This form of teaching can be utilized for simple skills, such as making eye contact, to complex skills, like social interactions. Each step is initially taught by using a specific cue and pairing that cue with a prompt. Prompts range from physical guidance to verbal cues to very discrete gestures. Prompts should be faded out systematically by decreasing the level of prompt needed for the student to perform the target skill until, ideally, the student can perform the skill independently. In addition, skills should be taught by a variety of individuals, including teachers, aides, social workers, speech pathologists, and parents. There is strong evidence that parents can learn to employ ABA techniques and that doing so helps them to feel better in general and more satisfied and confident in their parenting role (Koegel et al., 1996; Ozonoff & Cathcart, 1998; Schreibman, 1997; Sofronoff & Farbotko, 2002, as cited in Wagner & McGrady, 2003). However, students should not become dependent on a particular individual or prompt. The student should be reinforced immediately after responding appropriately. The reinforcement should be a consequence that has been shown to increase the likelihood of the student responding appropriately again (Cooper et al., 1987). Reinforcements will vary from student to student. Inappropriate behavioral responses (such as tantrums, aggressive acts, screaming/yelling, stereotypic behaviors) are purposely not reinforced. Often, a functional analysis of antecedents and consequences is performed to determine what environmental reactions are reinforcing such behaviors (Cooper et al., 1987).

Applied behavior analysis has been proven effective across different providers (parents, teachers, therapists), different settings (schools, homes, hospitals, recreational areas), and behaviors (social, academic, and functional life skills; language; self-stimulatory, aggressive, and oppositional behaviors). Professionals who use ABA systematically and regularly measure progress on behavioral targets, leading to numerous studies of the effectiveness of ABA approaches. However, as Green (1996) pointed out, it is still unclear what variables are critical to intervention intensity (number of hours, length of the intervention, proportion of one-to-one to group instruction) and what are the expected outcomes when intervention intensity varies. It is also unclear what particular behavioral techniques (discrete trials, incidental teaching, pivotal response training) are most likely to be successful for a given child with an ASD and in what proportions particular techniques should be used (Anderson & Romanczyk, 1999). The current research is limited in that it does not allow us to draw comparisons across studies. For a review of the effectiveness of more broadly defined ABA intervention studies, see Anderson and Romanczyk (1999); Matson, Benavidez, Compton, Paclawskyj, and Baglio (1996); National Research Council (2001); New York State Department of Health (1999a); and Simpson et al. (2004).

Discrete Trial Training

It is important to understand that ABA is a framework for the practice of a science and not a specific program. Programs using ABA often utilize discrete trial training or teaching (DTT), which represents a specific type of presentation of opportunities to respond. Discrete trial training is a specialized teaching technique or process used to develop many new forms of behavior (Smith, 2001) and skills, including cognitive, communication, play, social, readiness, receptive-language, and self-help skills (Newsome, 1998). In addition, DTT can be used to reduce self-stimulatory responses and aggressive behaviors (Lovaas, 1981; Smith, 2001).

Discrete trial training involves breaking skills into the smallest steps, teaching each step of the skill until mastery, providing lots of repetition, prompting the correct response and fading the prompts as soon as possible, and using positive reinforcement procedures. Each discrete trial has five separate parts: (1) cue: the social worker presents a brief clear instruction or question; (2) prompt: at the same time as the cue or immediately thereafter, the social worker assists the child in responding correctly to the cue; (3) response: the child gives a correct or incorrect answer to the social worker's cue; (4) consequence: if the child has given a correct response, the social worker immediately reinforces the response with praise, access to toys, or other activities that the child enjoys. If the child has given an incorrect response, the social worker says "no," looks away, removes teaching materials, or otherwise signals that the response was incorrect; and (5) inter-trial interval: after giving the consequence, the social worker pauses briefly (1–5 seconds) before presenting the cue for the next trial (Smith, 2001, p. 86). The following is an example of DTT:

The social worker says, "Touch your nose." (verbal cue)
The student does not respond (response).
After a few seconds, the social worker places her hand on the student's hand. (prompt)
The child extends his index finger himself, and the social worker helps the child to touch his nose. (response)
The social worker says, "Yes, that is your nose. Good job touching your nose." (consequence)

This is an example of one trial. The correct response is considered a measurable unit of a skill. Data can be collected on the number of correct versus incorrect responses to chart a student's progress. This trial would be repeated approximately five times, as repetition of skills is a component of discrete trial teaching.

The social worker says, "What's your address?" (verbal cue)
The student says, "My address is 123 House Street, Maywood, New Jersey." (response)
The instructor gives the student behavior-descriptive praise (i.e., "Good, you said your address correctly") and 30 seconds to play with a toy of his choice. (consequence)

As one can see from the examples above, DTT can be used to teach the most basic information up to slightly more advanced knowledge. Discrete trial teaching affords children with AS and AD opportunities to respond which have been linked with improved performance on measures of academic achievement (Delquadri, Greenwood, Stretton, & Hall, 1983). This approach has also been credited with impressive gains in children with otherwise poor prognoses (Lovaas, 1987) and in accelerated skill acquisition (Miranda-Linne & Melin, 1992). An effective school-based intervention should prioritize discrimination issues by using DTT strategies that (1) carefully present stimuli in a systematic manner and with planned repetition; (2) provide a planned process for teaching the relationship of words to functional objects, people, and other important concepts; and (3) use systematic visual stimuli to teach important functional auditory discriminations (Arick et al., 2005, p. 1007). For studies documenting the effectiveness of DTT, see Cummings and Williams (2000); Dawson and Osterling (1997); Goldstein (2002); National Research Council (2001); Odom et al. (2003); Simpson et al. (2004); and Smith (2001).

Pivotal Response Training

Pivotal response training (PRT) is a model that aims to apply educational techniques in pivotal areas that affect target behaviors (Koegel, Koegel, Harrower, & Carter, 1999). Pivotal areas when effectively targeted result in substantial collateral gains in numerous developmental domains. Pivotal areas of primary focus include (a) responding to multiple cues and stimuli (i.e., decreasing overselectivity by distinguishing relevant features); (b) improving child motivation (i.e., increasing appropriate responses, decreasing response latency, and improving affect); (c) increasing self-management capacity (i.e., teaching children to be aware of their aberrant behaviors to self-monitor and to self-reinforce); and (d) increasing self-initiations (i.e., teaching children to respond to natural cues in the environment) (Simpson et al., 2004, pp. 114–115).

The goals of intervention in pivotal areas are "(1) to teach the child to be responsive to the many learning opportunities and social interactions that occur in the natural environment, (2) to decrease the need for constant supervision by an intervention provider, and (3) to decrease the number of services that remove the child from the natural environment" (Koegel et al., 1999, p. 174). Thus the primary purpose of PRT is to provide children with the social and educational proficiency to participate in inclusive settings.

Designed based on a series of studies identifying important treatment components, PRT in its fledgling stages used a discrete trial, applied behavior analysis approach. Currently, PRT uses the principles of applied behavior analysis (ABA) in a

manner that excludes negative interactions, reduces dependence on artificial prompts, and is family centered (Simpson et al., 2004, p. 114). Utilizing the strategies of PRT, target behaviors are taught in natural settings with items that are age-appropriate and meaningful as well as reinforcing to the child. Pivotal response training involves specific strategies such as (1) clear instructions and questions presented by the social worker, (2) child choice of stimuli (based on choices offered by the social worker), (3) integration of maintenance tasks (previously mastered tasks) (Dunlap, 1984), (4) direct reinforcement (the chosen stimuli is the reinforcer) (Koegel & Williams, 1980), (5) reinforcement of reasonable purposeful attempts at correct responding (Koegel, O'Dell, & Dunlap, 1988), and (6) turn taking to allow modeling and appropriate pace of interaction (Stahmer, Ingersoll, & Carter, 2003, p. 404). An example of using the specific steps of PRT to teach symbolic play might be as follows:

A child may choose to play with a doll. (choice)
The child is then given an empty cup and saucer, and asked, "What can we do with these toys?" (acquisition task)
The child is expected to use the teacup in some symbolic manner, such as having a tea party.
If the child does not respond, the social worker would model the symbolic behavior. (turn taking)
The teacup would then be returned to the child. If the child still does not respond, a new toy would be selected, or the social worker could assist the child.
When the child does respond, many of the child's dolls would be given to him to play with in any manner chosen, thus reinforcing the new behavior.

A more detailed description of using PRT to teach complex skills can be found in Stahmer (1999) and in *How to Teach Pivotal Behaviors to Children With Autism: A Training Manual* (Koegel, Schreffirnan, Good, Cerniglia, Murphy, & Koegel, n.d.).

PRT has been adapted to teach a variety of skills, including social skills (Koegel & Frea, 1993), symbolic (Stahmer, 1995) and sociodramatic play (Thorpe, Stahmer, & Schreibman, 1995), and joint attention (Whalen & Schreibman, 2003). Parents have been trained to successfully implement PRT. Schreibman, Kaneko, and Koegel (1991) found that parents appeared happier and more relaxed when they used PRT methods with their children than when they used more structured teaching techniques (Bregman, Zager, & Gerdtz, 2005). For studies documenting the effectiveness of PRT, see Koegel, Koegel, Shoshan, and McNerney (1999); National Research Council (2001); and Simpson et al. (2004).

Last, due to the widespread use of various medications for symptoms associated with autism, a review of interventions for school-aged children would not be complete without a brief discussion of psychopharmacology.

Psychopharmacology

Psychopharmacological treatment of children with ASDs appears to be common in clinical practice via the use of atypical antipsychotics, serotonin reuptake inhibitors, stimulants, and mood stabilizers (Aman, Collier-Crespin, & Lindsay, 2000; Martin, Scahill, Klin, & Volkmar, 1999). It is estimated that as many as half of all individuals with a diagnosis of an ASD are treated with one or more psychotropic medications (Martin et al., 1999). However, few studies specifically targeting a sample of children with ASDs and adhering to conventional standards of research design and methodology with efficacious results were found. The Research Units on Pediatric Psychopharmacology Autism Network (2002) and Shea et al. (2004) completed large-scale multisite, randomized, double-blind, placebo-controlled clinical trials of risperidone in children with autism. Risperidone is known as an atypical antipsychotic and is frequently used for treating severe maladaptive behavior and symptoms associated with AD (McDougle et al., 2000), such as aggression, self-injury, property destruction, or severe tantrums. The studies provided convincing evidence that risperidone is safe and effective for the short-term treatment of severe behavioral problems. The focus on severe behavior problems leaves an open question about possible additive effects of medication and applied behavioral interventions (Scahill & Martin, 2005). For example, the improvement in serious behavior problems associated with risperidone may enable a child to participate in an inclusive setting with DTT techniques employed.

Additional randomized, double-blind, placebo-controlled clinical trials have been conducted to test the effects of liquid fluoxetine, donepezil hydrochloride, and amantadine. All three had efficacious findings to some extent. The clinical trial conducted to examine the selective serotonin reuptake inhibitor liquid fluoxetine yielded results which indicate that a low dose is more effective than a placebo in the treatment of repetitive behaviors in childhood and adolescents with ASDs (Hollander et al., 2005). The study of donepezil hydrochloride found expressive and receptive speech gains, as well as decreases in severity of overall autistic behavior after 6 weeks for the treatment group (Chez et al., 2003). Last, a randomized control trial of amantadine for childhood autism reported clinician-rated improvements on behavioral ratings but showed no difference between the placebo and the active drug for parent ratings (King et al., 2001). However, a large placebo response was also found in this group. It is important to strongly caution professionals and family members that there are no medications specifically targeting the core symptoms of social and language impairments of autism in children.

Tools and Practice Example

Increasingly, school-based social workers and other mental health professionals are providing collaborative consultation (Idol, 1988; Idol, Paolucci-Whitcomb, & Nevin, 1986) to general education teachers of students with disabilities, focused on problem-solving efforts to identify students' behavioral difficulties and to devise strategies to reduce the problems (Curtis & Myers, 1988, as cited in Pryor, Kent, McGunn, & LeRoy, 1996). The following case example illustrates a school social worker employing ABA and DTT to address the classroom behavior of a child with AD in an inclusive setting.

Practice Example

John is an 11-year-old Caucasian male currently enrolled in a public middle school in a blue-ribbon school district on the East Coast. John comes from an upper-middle-class family. Though John has no siblings, he has many relatives, including cousins in his peer group, with whom he interacts frequently. Between the ages of 2 and 2½ years old, John's language development regressed significantly. His parents noticed that he was not utilizing his functional language at the same level he had in the past, and he began to consistently make syntactic and pragmatic errors, such as pronoun reversal, and experienced difficulty answering simple what, where, when, and why questions. In addition, John began to exhibit strange behaviors, such as placing his toys in perfectly straight lines and verbally repeating television shows and commercials out of context. He exhibited additional impairments in his social interactions, including difficulty making and maintaining eye contact and an inability to understand nonverbal social cues, such as the curling of one's finger to mean "come here." John also exhibited a lack of social reciprocity. At this time, John's parents consulted a myriad of specialists to search for an explanation for their son's changes in behavior and speech. John was eventually assessed by a multidisciplinary team of professionals, which resulted in an Axis I diagnosis of 299.00 Autistic Disorder.

In concert with the parents' preference, John's school district enrolled him in a school that specialized in educating young children with autism. Due to the research evidence demonstrating the effectiveness of ABA methods with young children with AD in preschool settings, the school he attended utilized this systematic approach to teach students a continuum of skills and behaviors. A school social worker was assigned to support John in the school and home, guiding him in the areas of social interaction, functional language, academic skills, and decreasing inappropriate behaviors. She worked closely with the parents to further reinforce their instruction of the structured approach in an effort to incorporate ABA techniques into their everyday routine, thereby reinforcing John's skill set across persons and settings.

During his kindergarten year, John was enrolled part time in a regular public school. He went to his specialized school for children with autism in the morning, where he received intensive skill training through discrete trial teaching. In the afternoon, John was integrated into a regular kindergarten class in a public school. The school social worker stayed in this class with John for 1 hour per day to aid in generalization of the skills taught in his specialized school and in the home setting. Generalization of skills has been defined as an important aspect to consider in designing any intervention for children with autism (Prizant & Wetherby, 1998; Smith, 2001).

Two advantages to John's social worker shadowing him in the public school class were the opportunity to train the school staff in ABA principles and instruction and to gather data on John's behaviors and skill level in the school setting. For example, the social worker took occurrence/nonoccurrence data on John's "TV talk" (verbal repetition of lines from his favorite television shows). On a data sheet, she divided the school day into 5-minute intervals and took data on whether John exhibited TV talk or did not. The social worker marked each 5-minute interval with a "+" if John demonstrated TV talk or a "−" if no TV talk occurred. This type of data was collected over a 3-day period during a 1-week interval. After the data collection was completed and the frequency of the behavior was established, the social worker performed a functional analysis of the behavior. The purpose of a functional analysis is to determine what environmental element is encouraging the student to engage in a particular behavior. To perform a functional analysis, the social worker took "ABC data." At each instance of the behavior, the social worker wrote down the (A) antecedent to the behavior: what occurred in the environment directly prior to the behavior being exhibited; the (B) behavior itself: exactly how the behavior was manifested, what the student said and did while participating in the behavior; and the (C) consequence(s) to the behavior: how the individuals in the environment responded to the behavior. Did the student receive attention? Was the student removed from a demanding task? After a functional analysis was performed on John's TV talk, the social worker established that John participated in the behavior to "escape" demanding social situations.

At this time, John was exhibiting noncontextual speech in the form of TV talk habitually throughout the day. The educator requested that the school social worker assist with the reduction of this behavior as it prevented John from interacting in a reciprocal way with his peers and caused many distractions for both John and his peers in relation to their learning. His social worker wrote a behavior modification plan to target this behavior. The plan was a differential reinforcement of appropriate behaviors (DRA). The DRA was selected as a treatment strategy as it enabled other school staff to be trained in the intervention techniques and built upon John's strengths by encouraging his appropriate behaviors. The DRA was executed throughout his day. When John would engage in appropriate activities without exhibiting TV talk, the social worker (or whoever was with him at the time) would sporadically give him a happy-face token, paired with social praise ("You're doing a nice job working on the puzzle"). When John would engage in TV talk, the social worker would give him a sad-face token paired with the verbal cue, "Tell me what you're doing now." This verbal cue taught John to comment on a present task rather than to perseverate on television shows. When John earned five happy-face tokens, he was able to choose a preferred activity (e.g., working on the computer) to engage in for a 3-minute period. If John received five sad-face tokens before earning five happy-face tokens, he was given a verbal prompt, "You need to talk about what is going on in the [classroom], not about TV." The staff of both his specialized and inclusive schools was trained to implement the plan, as were his parents. John exhibited this behavior very frequently (some instance of TV talk occurred in 80% of the 5-minute intervals during data collection) when the behavior plan was initially implemented. With the consistency of the implementation, the behavior was reduced to one or two instances a day after 6 months and was eventually eliminated by the end of the school year.

John was mainstreamed into the public school, full time, with a one-to-one aide at the start of his first-grade year. He was able to complete the full curriculum with the help of the school staff, who worked with the school social worker to learn how to break down John's assignments into manageable steps. For example, stories read in class were broken down into "chunks" and paired with visual cues to aid in comprehension. He continued to receive ABA instruction and DTT after school with the social worker. The social worker utilized role-play techniques to teach social skills, breaking down the skills into manageable steps:

SW: I'm going to pretend to be Kyle. I'm on the playground with a soccer ball. You're going to walk up to me, tap me on the shoulder, look in my eyes and say, "Can I play soccer with you?" Get ready. Go!

John: [walks up, taps the social worker on the shoulder, looks in her eyes, but says nothing]

SW: Say, "Can I play soccer with you?" (verbal cue)

John: Can I play soccer with you?

SW: That was great! Let's try it again. (social praise used as positive reinforcement)

In the example, the social worker is breaking down a social interaction into small, teachable steps. After John mastered this first step of playground interaction (initiating play) in several different play scenarios, the social worker expanded the recess role-play scenes to teach John how to maintain extended play periods. During lunch time and recess at the school, John's social worker would shadow him and deliver verbal cues such as "Ask Kyle, 'Can I play with you?'" or gestural prompts (i.e., point at a peer with whom he can play). The verbal cue was also paired with the gestural prompt: pointing at the peer while modeling "Can I play with you?" These strategies aimed to help John generalize the skills he learned during his therapy sessions. Again, the school staff was also taught these prompts to assist with John's socialization throughout the school day. For a child with AD to be included in a mainstream setting, he needs to be able to manage social experiences (National Research Council, 2001).

John's social worker continued to consult in the school setting. John was taught to respond to discrete hand gestures to help him to refocus on the teacher when environmental distractions would impede his concentration. If John would look out the window when his teacher was speaking, the social worker would touch his shoulder, and when John looked up, she would tap her ear twice and point to the teacher. John was taught that this gesture meant "listen to the teacher." The school staff was taught to utilize these hand gestures as well. These discrete gestures kept John from standing out too much from his peers, as verbal redirecting would draw attention to him. Through the use of such gestures by various staff members, John's classmates also began to respond to the gestures when they became unfocused.

John is currently enrolled in a public middle school. He continues to complete the full curriculum and plays on his town soccer and basketball teams. John does continue to experience difficulty in the area of reading comprehension and in assessing social cues at times. However, the progress John has made is quite noteworthy. He is a friendly and empathic boy who excels in math and enjoys athletic activities. John's success could not have been accomplished without the support of a multidisciplinary team effort. John's school social worker, teachers, speech therapist, and occupational therapist all collaborated through the years to utilize similar strategies and target compatible goals. John's parents employed reinforcement strategies in the home by carrying over the skills targeted in therapy and at school.

Resources

Overview of AD and AS

http://www.autism-society.org
http://www.autisminfo.com
http://www.nichcy.org
http://www.aspergers.com
http://www.udel.edu/bkirby/asperger/
   aslink.html
http://www.autism-pdd.net/autism.htm
http://www.autismwebsite.com/ari/index.htm

Educational and Therapeutic Interventions

http://www.teacch.com
http://www.autism.org
http://www.cabas.com

Treatment Centers

http://www.pcdi.org
http://gsappweb.rutgers.edu/DDDC
http://info.med.yale.edu/chldstdy/autism
http://www.behavior.org
http://www.son-rise.org

Training Materials

Arick, J. R., Loos, L., Falco, R., & Krug, D. A. (2004). *Strategies for teaching based on autism research: STAR.* Austin, TX: Pro-Ed.

Freeman, S., & Dake, L. (1997). *Teach me language.* Langley, BC: SKF Books.

Koegel, R. L., Koegel, L. K., & Parks, D. R. (1990). *How to teach self-management skills to people with severe disabilities: A training manual.* Santa Barbara: University of California.

Leaf, R., & McEachin, J. (1999). *A work in progress.* New York: DRL Books.

McClannahan, L. E., & Krantz, P. J. (1999). *Activity schedules for children with autism: Teaching independent behavior.* Bethesda, MD: Woodbine.

http://www.dttrainer.com/pi_overview.htm
http://www.nationalspeech.com
http://rsaffran.tripod.com/

http://www.users.qwest.net/~tbharris/prt.htm
http://www.education.ucsb.edu/autism/
   behaviormanuals.html

Suggested Practice Exercise Related to Intervention

Consider that a parent has received a diagnosis of AD for his 5-year-old son. How would you begin to present the options for intervention? Describe your role as a social worker in providing the information.

Key Points to Remember

- Autism spectrum disorders are defined by clinical symptomatology which typically falls within three major categories: (1) qualitative impairment in social interaction; (2) impairments in communication; and (3) restricted, repetitive, stereotyped behavior, interests, and activities.
- One of the important characteristics of children with ASDs is uneven learning ability and skill levels, and as such, individualization of intervention is necessary.
- Applied behavior analysis is the most widely accepted effective intervention model for children and adolescents with AD and AS.
- Discrete trial training is a specialized teaching technique or process used to develop new forms of behavior and skills, including cognitive, communication, play, social, readiness, receptive-language, and self-help skills, as well as reducing self-stimulatory responses and aggressive behaviors.
- The primary purpose of pivotal response training is to provide children with the social and educational proficiency to participate in inclusive settings.
- Medication cannot be justified as the first line of treatment for AD, AS, or the associated symptoms.
- Behavioral treatments are most successful when applied across settings and persons in the child's life.

Despite the promising treatment effects produced by the interventions reviewed above, existing treatments need to be refined and evaluated with rigorous testing procedures to establish efficacy. A primary goal of the research should be to determine the types of interventions that are most effective for children with different subtypes of ASDs and with specific characteristics, since the characteristics of children with ASDs and their life circumstances are exceedingly heterogeneous in nature (National Research Council, 2001). Regardless of the intervention selected, it is essential that strategies be devised to take advantage of the unique constellation of strengths and characteristics of the learner with AS or AD and to modify contexts to support the learning and behavioral style of the individual student (Klin, McPartland, & Volkmar, 2005).

The focus in this chapter has been geared toward the school social worker and mental health practitioner working with individual students in school settings. Equally important in sustaining gains in behavior and skill acquisition with school-aged children and adolescents with AD and AS are issues surrounding classroom management, group skill-based interventions, especially for students with AS, and working collaboratively with parents, teachers, peers, and school administrators to promote skill generalization across settings and persons in addition to sustaining change.

Notes

1. It should be noted that in addition to the diagnostic criteria for AS delineated in the *DSM-IV-TR* (2000) and the *ICD-10* (1992), there are at least five very different conceptualizations of AS (Ghaziuddin, Tsai, & Ghaziuddin, 1992; Klin & Volkmar, 1997; Leekam, Libby, Wing, Gould, & Gillberg, 2000; Szatmari, Bryson, Boyle, Streiner, & Duku, 2003), which represent to some extent the major differences in the conceptualization of this disorder (e.g., Asperger's syndrome as a milder form of autism, different conceptions of the timing when motor skills should be taken into account, etc.).

2. Level-one screening measures for autism are used to identify children at risk for autism from the general population, while level-two screening involves the identification of children at risk for autism from a population of children demonstrating a broad range of developmental concerns (Stone, Coonrod, Turner, & Pozdol, 2004).

3. There are two instruments specifically designed as diagnostic tools for Asperger's syndrome: the Asperger's Syndrome Diagnostic Interview and the Australian Scale for Asperger's Syndrome. Both require further testing to determine their reliability and validity prior to use as diagnostic instruments.

4. See Rogers (1998); National Research Council (2001); and New York State Department of Health (1999b) for a complete review of evidence-based early intervention programs.

References

Aman, M. G., Collier-Crespin, A., & Lindsay, R. L. (2000). Pharmacotherapy of disorders in mental retardation. *European Child and Adolescent Psychiatry, 9,* 98–107.

American Psychiatric Association. (2000). *Diagnostic and statistical manual of mental disorders* (4th ed., text revision). Washington, DC: Author.

Anderson, S. R., & Romanczyk, R. G. (1999). Early intervention for young children with autism: Continuum-based behavioral models. *Journal of the Association for Persons With Severe Handicaps, 24*(3), 162–173.

Anderson, S. R., Taras, M., & Cannon, B. O. (1996). Teaching new skills to young children with autism. In C. Maurice, G. Green, & S. C. Luce (Eds.), *Behavioral intervention for young children with autism: A manual for parents and professionals* (pp. 181–194). Austin, TX: Pro-Ed.

Arick, J. R., Krug, D. A., Fullerton, A., Loos, L., & Falco, R. (2005). School-based programs. In D. J. Cohen & F. R. Volkmar (Eds.), *Handbook of autism and pervasive developmental disorders*: Vol. 2, *Assessment, interventions, and policy* (3rd ed., 1003–1028). New York: Wiley.

Baer, D., Wolf, M., & Risley, R. (1968). Some current dimensions of applied behavior analysis. *Journal of Applied Behavior Analysis, 1,* 91–97.

Baker, L. J., & Welkowitz, L. A. (Eds.). (2005). *Asperger's syndrome: Intervening in schools, clinics and communities.* Mahwah, NJ: Earlbaum.

Bregman, J. (2005). Definitions and characteristics of the spectrum. In D. Zager (Ed.), *Autism spectrum disorders: Identification, education and treatment* (3rd ed., pp. 3–46). Mahwah, NJ: Erlbaum.

Bregman, J., Zager, D., & Gerdtz, J. (2005). Behavioral interventions. In F. R. Volkmar, R. Paul, A. Klin, & D. Cohen (Eds.), *Handbook of autism and pervasive developmental disorders: Vol. 2. Assessment, interventions and policy* (3rd ed., pp. 897–924). Hoboken, NJ: Wiley.

Bryson, S., & Smith, I. M. (1998). Epidemiology of autism: Prevalence, associated characteristics, and implications for research and service delivery. *Mental Retardation and Developmental Disabilities Research Reviews, 4*(2), 97–103.

Campbell, J. M. (2005). Diagnostic assessment of Asperger's disorder: A review of five third-party rating scales. *Journal of Autism and Developmental Disorders, 35*(1), 25–35.

Charman, T., & Baird, G. (2002). Practitioner review: Diagnosis of autism spectrum disorder in 2- and

3-year-old children. *Journal of Child Psychology and Psychiatry and Allied Disciplines, 43*(3), 289–305.

Chez, M. G., Buchanan, T., Becker, M., Kessler, J., Aimonovitch, M. C., & Mrazek, S. R. (2003). Donepezil hydrochloride: A double-blind study in autistic children. *Journal of Pediatric Neurology, 1*(2), 83–88.

Constantino, J. N. (2002). *The social-responsiveness scale.* Los Angeles: Western Psychological Services.

Cooper, J. O., Heron, T., & Heward, W. (1987). *Applied behavior analysis.* Columbus, OH: Merrill.

Courchesne, E. (2002). Abnormal early brain development in autism. *Molecular Psychiatry, 7*(Suppl. 2), S21–23.

Cummings, A. R., & Williams, W. L. (2000). Visual identity matching and vocal imitation training with children with autism: A surprising finding. *Journal on Developmental Disabilities, 7*(2), 109–122.

Dawson, G., & Osterling, J. (1997). Early intervention in autism. In M. Guralnick (Ed.), *The effectiveness of early intervention* (pp. 307–326). Baltimore: Brookes.

Delquadri, J. C., Greenwood, C. R., Stretton, K., & Hall, R. V. (1983). The peer tutoring spelling game: A classroom procedure for increasing opportunity to respond and spelling performance. *Education and Treatment of Children, 6*(3), 225–239.

DuCharme, R. W., & McGrady, K. A. (2003). What is Asperger syndrome? In R. W. DuCharme & T. P. Gullotta (Eds.), *Asperger syndrome: A guide for professionals and families* (pp. 1–20). New York: Kluwer Academic/Plenum.

Dunlap, G. (1984). The influence of task variation and maintenance tasks on the learning and affect of autistic children. *Journal of Experimental Child Psychology, 31,* 41–64.

Ehlers, S., Gillberg, C., & Wing, L. (1999). A screening questionnaire for Asperger syndrome and other high-functioning autism spectrum disorders in school-age children. *Journal of Autism and Developmental Disabilities, 29*(2), 129–141.

Filipek, P. A., Accardo, P. J., Ashwal, S., Baranek, G. T., Cook, E. H., Dawson G., et al. (2000). Practice parameter: Screening and diagnosis of autism. *Neurology, 55,* 468–479.

Filipek, P. A., Accardo, P. J., Baranek, G. T., Cook, E. H., Jr., Dawson, G., Gordon B., et al. (1999). The screening and diagnosis of autism spectrum disorders. *Journal of Autism and Developmental Disorders, 29*(6), 439–484.

Fombonne, E. (1999). The epidemiology of autism: A review. *Psychological Medicine, 29,* 769–786.

Fombonne, E. (2005). Epidemiological studies of pervasive developmental disorders. In F. R. Volkmar, R. Paul, A. Klin, & D. Cohen (Eds.), *Handbook of autism and pervasive developmental disorders: Vol. 1. Diagnosis, development, neurobiology and behavior* (3rd ed., pp. 42–69). Hoboken, NJ: Wiley.

Fombonne, E., Du Mazaubrun, C., Cans, C., & Grandjean, H. (1997). Autism and associated medical disorders in a French survey. *Journal of the American Academy of Child and Adolescent Psychiatry, 36*(11), 1561–1569.

Fombonne, E., Simmons, H., Ford, T., Meltzer, H., & Goodman, R. (2001). Prevalence of pervasive developmental disorders in the British Nationwide Survey of Child Mental Health. *Journal of the American Academy of Child and Adolescent Psychiatry, 40*(7), 820–827.

Ghaziuddin, M., Tsai, L., & Ghaziuddin, N. (1992). Brief report: A comparison of the diagnostic criteria for Asperger's syndrome. *Journal of Autism and Developmental Disorders, 22*(4), 643–649.

Goldstein, H. (2002). Communication intervention for children with autism: A review of treatment efficacy. *Journal of Autism and Developmental Disorders, 35*(2), 373–396.

Green, G. (1996). Early behavioral intervention for autism: What does research tell us? In C. Maurice, G. Green, & S. C. Luce (Eds.), *Behavioral intervention for young children with autism* (pp. 29–44). Austin, TX: Pro-Ed.

Gresham, F. M., Beebe-Frankenberger, M. E., & MacMillan, D. L. (1999). A selective review of treatments for children with autism: Description and methodological considerations. *School Psychology Review, 28*(4), 559–575.

Harris, S. L., & Handleman, J. S. (1994). *Preschool education programs for children with autism.* Austin, TX: Pro-Ed.

Harris, S. L., Handleman, J. S., Gordon, R., Kristoff, B., & Fuentes, F. (1991). Changes in cognitive and language functioning of preschool children with autism. *Journal of Autism and Developmental Disorders, 21,* 281–290.

Hollander, E., & Nowinski, C. V. (2003). Core symptoms, related disorders and course of autism. In E. Hollander (Ed.), *Autism spectrum disorders* (pp. 15–38). New York: Dekker.

Hollander, E., Phillips, A., Chaplin, W., Zagursky, K., Novotny, S., Wasserman, S., et al. (2005). A placebo controlled crossover trial of liquid fluoxetine on repetitive behaviors in childhood and adolescent autism. *Neuropsychopharmacology, 30*(3), 582–589.

Howlin, P. (1998). *Children with autism and Asperger syndrome: A guide for practitioners and carers.* Chichester, UK: Wiley.

Idol, L. (1988). A rationale and guidelines for establishing special education consultation programs. *Remedial and Special Education, 9*(6), 48–58.

Idol, L., Paolucci-Whitcomb, P., & Nevin, A. (1986). *Collaboration consultation.* Austin, TX: Pro-Ed.

Jacobson, J. W., Foxx, R. M., & Mulick, J. A. (Eds.). (2005). *Controversial therapies for developmental disabilities: Fad, fashion and science in professional practice.* Mahwah, NJ: Erlbaum.

Jacobson, J. W., Mulick, J. A., & Green, G. (1998). Cost-benefit estimates for early intensive behavioral intervention for young children with autism: General model and single state case. *Behavioral Interventions, 13,* 201–206.

King, B. H., Wright, D. M., Handen, B. L., Sikich, L., Zimmerman, A., McMahon, W., et al. (2001). Double-blind, placebo-controlled study of amantadine hydrochloride in the treatment of children with autistic disorder. *Journal of the American Academy of Child and Adolescent Psychiatry, 40*(6), 658–665.

Klin, A., McPartland, J., & Volkmar, F. R. (2005). Asperger syndrome. In F. R. Volkmar, R. Paul, A. Klin, & D. Cohen (Eds.), *Handbook of autism and pervasive developmental disorders: Vol. 1. Diagnosis, development, neurobiology and behavior* (3rd ed., pp. 88–125). Hoboken, NJ: Wiley.

Klin, A., & Volkmar, F. R. (1997). The pervasive developmental disorders: Nosology and profiles of development. In S. Luthar, J. Burack, D. Cicchetti, & J. Weisz (Eds.), *Developmental psychopathology: Perspectives on adjustment, risk, and disorder* (pp. 208–226). New York: Cambridge University Press.

Koegel, L. K., Koegel, R. L., Harrower, J. K., & Carter, C. M. (1999). Pivotal response intervention I: Overview of approach. *Journal of the Association for Persons With Severe Handicaps, 24*(3), 174–185.

Koegel, L. K., Koegel, R. L., Shoshan, Y., & McNerney, E. (1999). Pivotal response intervention II: Preliminary long-term outcome data. *Journal of the Association for Persons with Severe Handicaps, 24*(3), 186–198.

Koegel, R. L., O'Dell, M., & Dunlap, G. (1988). Producing speech use in nonverbal autistic children by reinforcing attempts. *Journal of Autism and Developmental Disorders, 18,* 525–538.

Koegel, R. L., & Frea, W. D. (1993). Treatment of social behavior in autism through the modification of pivotal social skills. *Journal of Applied Behavior Analysis, 26*(3), 369–377.

Koegel, R. L., & Koegel, L. K. (Eds.). (1995). *Teaching children with autism: Strategies for initiating positive interactions and improving learning opportunities.* Baltimore: Brookes.

Koegel, R. L., Schreffirnan, L., Good, A., Cerniglia, L., Murphy, C., & Koegel, L. K. (n.d.). *How to teach pivotal behaviors to children with autism: A training manual.* Available: http://www.users.qwest.net/~tbharris/prt.htm.

Koegel, R. L., & Williams, J. A. (1980). Direct versus indirect response-reinforcer relationships in teaching autistic children. *Journal of Abnormal Child Psychology, 8,* 537–547.

Krug, D. A., & Arick, J. R. (2003). *Krug Asperger's Disorder Index.* Austin, TX: Pro-Ed.

Leekam, S. R., Libby, S. J., Wing, L., Gould, J., & Gillberg, C. (2000). Comparison of ICD-10 and Gillberg's criteria for Asperger syndrome. *Autism, 4*(1), 11–28.

Lord, C., & Cosello, C. (2005). Diagnostic instruments in autistic spectrum disorders. In F. R. Volkmar, R. Paul, A. Klin, & D. Cohen (Eds.), *Handbook of autism and pervasive developmental disorders: Vol. 2. Assessment,* interventions and policy (3rd ed., pp. 730–771). Hoboken, NJ: Wiley.

Lord, C., & Paul, R. (1997). Language and communication in autism. In D. J. Cohen & F. R. Volkmar (Eds.), *Handbook of autism and pervasive developmental disorders* (2nd ed., pp. 460–483). New York: Wiley.

Lord, C., Rutter, M. L., DiLavore, P. C., & Risi, S. (1999). *Autism Diagnostic Observation Schedule-WPS* (WPS ed.). Los Angeles: Western Psychological Services.

Lord, C., Rutter, M. L., & Le Couteur, A. (1994). The Autism Diagnostic Interview-Revised: A revised version of the diagnostic interview for caregivers of individuals with possible pervasive developmental disorders. *Journal of Autism and Developmental Disorders, 24*(5), 659–685.

Lovaas, O. (1993). The development of a treatment-research project for developmentally disabled and autistic children. *Journal of Applied Behavior Analysis, 26*(4), 617–630.

Lovaas, O. I. (1981). *Teaching developmentally disabled children: The me book.* Austin, TX: Pro-Ed.

Lovaas, O. I. (1987). Behavioral treatment and normal educational and intellectual functioning in young autistic children. *Journal of Consulting and Clinical Psychology, 55,* 3–9.

Lovaas, O. I., & Smith, T. (1989). A comprehensive behavioral theory of autistic children: Paradigm for research and treatment. *Journal of Behavior Therapy and Experimental Psychology, 20,* 17–29.

Loveland, K. A., & Tunali-Kotoski, B. (2005). The school-age child with an autistic spectrum disorder. In F. R. Volkmar, R. Paul, A. Klin, & D. Cohen (Eds.), *Handbook of autism and pervasive developmental disorders: Vol. 1. Diagnosis, development, neurobiology and behavior* (3rd ed., pp. 247–287). Hoboken, NJ: Wiley.

Martin, A., Scahill, L., Klin, A., & Volkmar, F. R. (1999). Higher functioning pervasive developmental disorders: Rates and patterns of psychotropic drug use. *Journal of the American Academy of Child and Adolescent Psychiatry, 38*(7), 923–931.

Matson, J. L., Benavidez, D. A., Compton, L. S., Paclawskyj, T., & Baglio, C. (1996). Behavioral treatment of autistic persons: A review of research from 1980 to the present. *Research in Developmental Disabilities, 17,* 433–465.

Maurice, C., Green, G., & Luce, S. C. (Eds.). (1996). *Behavioral intervention for young children with autism: A manual for parents and professionals.* Austin, TX: Pro-Ed.

McCarton, C. (2003). Assessment and diagnosis of pervasive developmental disorder. In E. Hollander (Ed.), *Autism spectrum disorders* (pp. 101–132). New York: Dekker.

McClannahan, L. E., & Krantz, P. J. (2004). Selecting behavioral intervention programs for children with autism. In H. E. Briggs & T. L. Rzepnicki (Eds.), *Using evidence in social work practice: Behavioral perspectives.* Chicago: Lyceum.

McDougle, C. J., Scahill, L., McCracken, J. T., Aman, M. G., Tierney, E., Arnold, L. E., et al. (2000).

Research units on pediatric psychopharmacology (RUPP) autism network: Background and rationale for an initial controlled study of risperidone. *Child and Adolescent Psychiatric Clinics of North America, 9,* 201–224.

McEachin, J. J., Smith, T., & Lovaas, O. I. (1993). Long-term outcome for children with autism who received early intensive behavioral treatment. *American Journal of Mental Retardation, 4,* 359–372.

Miranda-Linne, F., & Melin, L. (1992). Acquisition, generalization and spontaneous use of color adjectives: A comparison of incidental teaching and traditional discrete-trial procedures for children with autism. *Research in Developmental Disabilities, 13,* 191–210.

National Research Council. (2001). *Educating children with autism.* Washington, DC: National Academy Press.

Newsome, C. B. (1998). Autistic disorder. In E. J. Mash & R. A. Barkley (Eds.), *Treatment of childhood disorders* (2nd ed., pp. 416–467). New York: Guilford.

New York State Department of Health, Early Intervention Program. (1999a). *Clinical practice guideline: Guideline technical report: Autism/pervasive developmental disorders, assessment and intervention for young children (ages 0–3 years)* (No. 4217). Albany, NY: Author.

New York State Department of Health, Early Intervention Program. (1999b). *Clinical practice guideline: Report of the recommendations: Autism/PDD, assessment and intervention in young children (age 0–3 years)* (No. 4215). Albany, NY: Author.

Odom, S. L., Brown, W. H., Frey, T., Karasu, N., Smith-Canter, L. L., & Strain, P. S. (2003). Evidence-based practices for young children with autism: Contributions for single-subject design research. *Focus on Autism and Other Developmental Disabilities, 18*(3), 166–175.

Paul, R., & Sutherland, D. (2005). Enhancing early language in children with autism spectrum disorders. In F. R. Volkmar, R. Paul, A. Klin, & D. Cohen (Eds.), *Handbook of autism and pervasive developmental disorders: Vol. 2. Assessment, interventions and policy* (3rd ed., pp. 946–976). Hoboken, NJ: Wiley.

Prizant, B. M., & Wetherby, A. (1998). Understanding the continuum of discrete-trial traditional behavioral to social-pragmatic developmental approaches in communication enhancement for young children with autism/PDD. *Seminars in Speech and Language, 19,* 329–353.

Pryor, C. B., Kent, C., McGunn, C., & LeRoy, B. (1996). Redesigning social work in inclusive schools. *Social Work, 41,* 668–676.

Research Units on Pediatric Psychopharmacology Autism Network. (2002). Risperidone in children with autism and serious behavioral problems. *New England Journal of Medicine, 347,* 314–321.

Robins, D. L., Fein, D., Barton, M. L., & Green, J. A. (2001). The Modified Checklist for Autism in Toddlers: An initial study investigating the early detection of autism and pervasive developmental disorders. *Journal of Autism and Developmental Disorders, 31*(2), 131–145.

Rogers, S. (1998). Empirically supported comprehensive treatments for young children with autism. *Journal of Clinical Child Psychology, 27,* 168–179.

Sackett, D. L., Straus, S. E., Richardson, W. C., Rosenberg, W., & Haynes, R. M. (2000). *Evidence-based medicine: How to practice and teach EBM* (2nd ed.). New York: Churchill Livingstone.

Safran, S. P. (2005). Diagnosis. In L. J. Baker & L. A. Welkowitz (Eds.), *Asperger's syndrome: Intervening in schools, clinics and communities* (pp. 43–61). Mahwah, NJ: Erlbaum.

Scahill, L., & Martin, A. (2005). Psychopharmacology. In F. R. Volkmar, R. Paul, A. Klin, & D. Cohen (Eds.), *Handbook of autism and pervasive developmental disorders: Vol. 2. Assessment, interventions and policy* (3rd ed., pp. 1102–1117). Hoboken, NJ: Wiley.

Schopler, E., Reichler, R. J., & Renner, B. R. (1986). *The Childhood Autism Rating Scale (CARS) for diagnostic screening and classification of autism.* New York: Irvington.

Schreibman, L., Charlop, M. H., & Milstein, J. P. (1993). Autism: Behavioral treatment. In V. P. Van-Hasselt & M. Hersen (Eds.), *Handbook of behavior therapy and pharmacotherapy of children: A comparative analysis* (pp. 149–170). Needham Heights, MA: Allyn & Bacon.

Schreibman, L., Kaneko, W. M., & Koegel, R. L. (1991). Positive affect of parents of autistic children: Comparison across two teaching techniques. *Behavior Therapy, 22,* 479–490.

Scott, J., Clark, C., & Brady, M. P. (2000). *Students with autism: Characteristics and instructional programming for special educators.* San Diego, CA: Singular.

Shea, S., Turgay, A., Carroll, A., Schulz, M., Orlik, H., Smith, I., et al. (2004). Risperidone in the treatment of disruptive behavioral symptoms in children with autistic and other pervasive developmental disorders. *Pediatrics, 114*(5), 634–641.

Simpson, R. L., de Boer-Ott, S. R., Griswold, D. E., Myles, B. S., Byrd, S. E., Ganz, J. B., et al. (2004). *Autism spectrum disorders: Interventions and treatments for children and youth.* Thousand Oaks, CA: Corwin.

Smith, T. (1996). Are other treatments effective? In C. Maurice, G. Green, & S. C. Luce (Eds.), *Behavioral intervention for young children with autism* (pp. 45–59). Austin, TX: Pro-Ed.

Smith, T. (2001). Discrete trial training in the treatment of autism. *Focus on Autism and Other Developmental Disabilities, 16*(2), 86–92.

Smith, T., Groen, A. D., & Wynn, J. W. (2000). Randomized trial of intensive early intervention for children with pervasive developmental disorder. *American Journal on Mental Retardation, 105*(4), 269–285.

Stahmer, A. C. (1995). Teaching symbolic play skills to children with autism using pivotal response training. *Journal of Autism and Developmental Disorders, 25,* 123–141.

Stahmer, A. C. (1999). Using pivotal response training to facilitate appropriate play in children with autistic spectrum disorders. *Child Language Teaching and Therapy, 15*(1), 29–40.

Stahmer, A. C., Ingersoll, B., & Carter, C. (2003). Behavioral approaches to promoting play. *Autism, 7*(4), 401–413.

Stone, W. L., Coonrod, E. E., & Ousley, O. Y. (2000). Brief report: Screening tool for autism in two-year-olds (STAT): Development and preliminary data. *Journal of Autism and Developmental Disorders, 30*(6), 607–612.

Stone, W. L., Coonrod, E. E., Turner, L. M., & Pozdol, S. L. (2004). Psychometric properties of the STAT for early autism screening. *Journal of Autism and Developmental Disorders, 34*(6), 691–701.

Strock, M. (2004). *Autism spectrum disorders (pervasive developmental disorders)* (NIH Publication No. 04–5511, pp. 1–40). Bethesda, MD: U.S. Department of Health and Human Services.

Sulzer-Azaroff, B., & Mayer, R. (1991). *Behavior analysis for lasting change.* Fort Worth, TX: Holt, Rinehart & Winston.

Szatmari, P., Bryson, S. E., Boyle, M. H., Streiner, D. L., & Duku, E. (2003). Predictors of outcome among high functioning children with autism and Asperger syndrome. *Journal of Child Psychology and Psychiatry, 44*(4), 520–528.

Thorpe, D. M., Stahmer, A. C., & Schreibman, L. (1995). Effects of sociodramatic play training on children with autism. *Journal of Autism and Developmental Disorders, 25*, 265–281.

U.S. Department of Health and Human Services. (1999). *Mental health: A report of the surgeon general.* Rockville, MD: Author.

Volkmar, F. R. (2000). Medical problems, treatments, and professionals. In M. D. Powers (Ed.), *Children with autism: A parent's guide* (2nd ed., pp. 67–90). Bethesda, MD: Woodbine House.

Volkmar, F. R., Koenig, K., & McCarthy, M. (2003). Autism: Diagnosis and epidemiology. In E. Hollander (Ed.), *Autism spectrum disorders* (pp. 1–14). New York: Dekker.

Wagner, A., & McGrady, K. A. (2003). Counseling and other therapeutic strategies for children with Asperger syndrome and their families. In R. W. DuCharme & T. P. Gullotta (Eds.), *Asperger syndrome: A guide for professionals and families* (pp. 83–134). New York: Kluwer Academic/Plenum.

Whalen, C., & Schreibman, L. (2003). Joint attention training for children with autism using behavior modification procedures. *Journal of Child Psychology and Psychiatry, 44*, 456–468.

World Health Organization. (1992). *International classification of diseases: Diagnostic criteria for research* (10th ed.). Geneva, Switzerland: Author.

Yeargin-Allsopp, M., Rice, C., Karapurkar, T., Doernberg, N., Boyle, C., & Murphy, C. (2003). Prevalence of autism in a U.S. metropolitan area [comment]. *Journal of the American Medical Association, 289*(1), 49–55.

Effective Strategies for Working With Students Who Have Co-Occurring Disorders

Stephen J. Tripodi ▪ Johnny S. Kim ▪ Diana M. DiNitto

CHAPTER 13

Getting Started

In this chapter, adolescents who have a mental disorder and a substance use disorder are referred to as having co-occurring disorders. More than 50% of adolescents with a substance use disorder have a co-occurring mental disorder, and approximately 43% of adolescents receiving mental health services have been diagnosed with a substance use disorder (Substance Abuse and Mental Health Services Administration, 2002a).

The mental disorders that most commonly co-occur with substance use disorders are conduct disorder (CD), attention-deficit/hyperactivity disorder (ADHD), depression, bipolar disorder, and posttraumatic stress disorder (Substance Abuse and Mental Health Services Administration, 2002b) (see Table 13.1). As many as 80% of adolescents in treatment for substance abuse have CD, between 20 and 40% have ADHD, up to 50% have mood disorders, and up to 40% have at least one anxiety disorder (Substance Abuse and Mental Health Services Administration, 2002b). Alcohol and drug use, combined with changes that occur during puberty, affect brain development and neuroendocrine systems that can exacerbate disorders such as CD, ADHD, and mood or anxiety disorders (Riggs, 2003). The reader should also consult other chapters in this book that address substance use disorders and mental disorders.

What We Know

Though researchers have begun to study adolescents with co-occurring disorders (Kaminer, Tarter, & Buckstein, 1999; Matson & Bamberg, 1998; Wise, Cuffe, & Fischer, 2001), controlled studies are needed on the effectiveness of various treatment approaches for adolescents with co-occurring disorders. While there are evidence-based practices for working with adolescents who have substance use disorders and adolescents with mental disorders (e.g., multisystemic therapy has been used with both types of disorders), currently there is no intervention with a strong evidence-base for working with adolescents who have co-occurring disorders. The lack of specific information is unfortunate, because, as discussed in previous chapters, rates are high for co-occurring mental health disorders (e.g., depression and anxiety) and co-occurring mental and substance use disorders.

This chapter suggests techniques for school social workers and other mental health counselors to use in working with students who have co-occurring disorders. These techniques include educating students on co-occurring disorders, screening and assessment procedures, working with the adolescent's family, creating a therapeutic alliance with the client, roles of the multisystemic school counselor, relapse prevention, and referral sources.

What We Can Do

Increasing Staff, Students, and Families' Knowledge of Co-Occurring Disorders

Efforts to assist students with co-occurring disorders are more effective when school social workers and similar professionals collaborate with teachers, administrators, and families. These groups often know little about this topic, so offer to organize

Table 13.1 Definitions for Most Common Mental Disorders That Co-Occur With Substance Use Disorders in Adolescents

Conduct Disorder	Attention-Deficit/Hyperactivity Disorder (ADHD)	Major Depressive Disorder	Bipolar Disorder	Posttraumatic Stress Disorder	Bulimia Nervosa
Repetitive and persistent pattern of behavior in which the basic rights of others or major age-appropriate societal norms or rules are broken.	Persistent pattern of inattention and/or hyperactivity-impulsivity that is more frequent and severe than is typically observed in individuals at a comparable level of development (criterion A). Some hyperactive-impulsive or inattentive symptoms that cause impairment must have been present before age 7 (criterion B). Some impairment from the symptoms must be present in at least two settings (criterion C). There must be clear evidence of interference with developmentally appropriate social, academic, or occupational functioning (criterion D).	A period of at least 2 weeks during which there is either depressed mood or the loss of interest or pleasure in nearly all activities. With children and adolescents, the mood may be irritable rather than sad. The individual must also experience at least four additional symptoms drawn from a list that includes changes in appetite or weight, sleep, and psychomotor activity; decreased energy; feelings of worthlessness or guilt; difficulty thinking, concentrating, or making decisions; or recurrent thoughts of death or suicidal ideation, plans, or attempts.	A clinical course that is characterized by the occurrence of one or more manic episodes or mixed episodes. Episodes of substance-induced mood disorder (due to the direct effects of a medication, other somatic treatments for depression, a drug of abuse, or toxin exposure) or of mood disorder due to a general medical condition do not count toward a diagnosis of bipolar disorder.	Development of characteristic symptoms following exposure to an extreme traumatic stressor involving direct personal experience of an event that involves actual or threatened death or serious injury or other threat to one's physical integrity; or witnessing an event that involves death, injury, or a threat to the physical integrity of another person; or learning about unexpected or violent death, serious harm, or threat of death or injury or injury experienced by a family member. Characteristic symptoms include persistent reexperiencing of the traumatic event, persistent avoidance of stimuli associated with the trauma and numbing of general responsiveness, and persistent symptoms of increased arousal.	Binge eating and inappropriate compensatory methods to prevent weight gain. The self-evaluation of individuals with bulimia nervosa is excessively influenced by body shape and weight. To qualify for the diagnosis, the binge eating and the inappropriate compensatory behaviors must occur, on average, at least twice a week for 3 months.

Source: American Psychiatric Association. (2000). *Diagnostic and statistical manual of mental disorders* (4th ed. text revision). Washington, DC: Author. Reprinted with permission from the *Diagnostic and Statistical Manual of Mental Disorders*, Copyright 2000. American Psychiatric Association.

in-service trainings for teachers and other staff. This may also increase administrators' support for services. Training should focus on topics such as identifying symptoms and behaviors typical of substance abuse, mental illness, and co-occurring disorders. Inviting staff from local mental health and substance abuse agencies to conduct or assist in this training and to inform school personnel about relevant community resources can also be helpful.

School social workers and other mental health counselors can also solicit teachers' invitations to give class presentations on mental health, substance abuse, and co-occurring disorders. This can arm students with knowledge and suggest ways they can help themselves or their friends. Students and teachers often know who is using drugs or exhibiting behavior common for adolescents with co-occurring disorders. For example, peers may know that a student is drinking or using nonprescribed drugs and discarding medication prescribed for a mental disorder.

Encourage school administrators or other personnel to send a letter to parents with information about substance use disorders, mental disorders, and co-occurring disorders; ways parents can help their child; and services the school's counseling department provides. Parents may not know how common it is for both types of disorders to occur together. Instruct teachers and students on how to refer students who may have co-occurring disorders. Send similar letters to teachers along with a form they can use to refer students.

Recognizing Students With Co-Occurring Disorders

Distinguishing normal adolescent developmental issues and acting-out behavior from behavioral problems resulting from chemical use alone or from co-occurring disorders can be difficult. Substance use disorders and mental disorders may occur independently of each other; a mental disorder may place the adolescent at greater risk for a substance abuse disorder; or alcohol or drug abuse may result in temporary mental disorder syndromes (Substance Abuse and Mental Health Services Administration, 2002a). An accurate mental disorder diagnosis may require that the adolescent be alcohol- and drug-free for a period of time.

Regardless of the specific disorders, adolescents with co-occurring disorders tend to act out, exhibiting anger and hostility toward their parents and other authority figures and gravitating toward peers who also use chemicals to assuage their pain (Evans & Sullivan, 2001). Figure 13.1 depicts predictors of co-occurring disorders, along with school-related problems, legal problems, and other common problems.

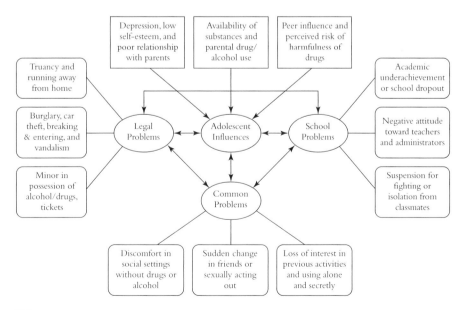

Figure 13.1

Conveying Information to Parents

Family members are often confused and hurt by the adolescent's behavior and may blame the child or themselves. Social workers and mental health counselors should explain that no one is at fault, and expressing shame to their child about his or her disorders or behaviors may ultimately lower the child's self-esteem and decrease the chances of a successful outcome. The school social worker and other mental health counselors must inform parents that professional help is likely necessary. This might mean referral to a substance abuse counselor, mental health therapist, self-help group, and/or a psychiatrist for medication. Parents should be directed to participate in their child's assessment and treatment.

Adolescent substance users are often manipulative and tend to use inconsistent parental behavior to their advantage. Parents should be encouraged to remain consistent in providing encouragement; to reward positive behavior and abstinence, including short periods of abstinence; and to follow through on consequences for negative behaviors, even though it may be difficult to do so.

Screening and Assessment

Two helpful standardized instruments for screening adolescents for co-occurring disorders are the Drug Use Screening Inventory (DUSI) (Rahdert, 1991) and the Problem-Oriented Screening Instrument for Teenagers (POSIT) (Tarter, 1990). Table 13.2 shows the completion time, required reading level, and the domains measured for both of these instruments.

Initial screening may indicate the need for a comprehensive assessment. Assessment provides an opportunity to look at the adolescent's life in a holistic manner, and it allows the social worker and other school-based practitioners to develop the necessary rapport to establish a beneficial therapeutic alliance with the adolescent and his or her family. A thorough assessment considers the adolescent's strengths; home and living situation; relationship to child welfare, mental health, juvenile justice, and school systems; educational history; family history of substance abuse and mental health problems; and medical status (U.S. Department of Health and Human Services, 1993).

Parents' or guardians' presence at the initial interview enables the social worker and school-based practitioner to obtain an early developmental history and assess family dynamics (Riggs, 2003). The social worker and mental health counselor should assess how the family enhances or reduces the potential for success by determining if there is active substance abuse or mental illness in other family members (Zweben, 1994). The social worker and counselors should also explore how the family views

Table 13.2 Screening Instruments for Adolescents With Co-Occurring Disorders

Drug Use Screening Inventory (DUSI) and Problem-Oriented Screening Instrument for Teenagers (POSIT)

Completion time	30 minutes
Required minimum reading level	Fifth grade
Domains measured	Substance abuse
	Psychiatric disorders
	Behavior problems
	School adjustment
	Health status
	Peer relations
	Social competency
	Family adjustment
	Leisure recreation
	Vocational status
	Aggressive behavior/delinquency

Sources: Rahdert, E. R. (1991). *The adolescent assessment/referral system manual* (DHHS Publication No. ADM 91–1735). Rockville, MD: National Institute on Drug Abuse; Tarter, R. (1990). Evaluation and treatment of adolescent substance abuse: A decision tree method. *American Journal of Drug and Alcohol Abuse, 16,* 1–46.

mental illness and addiction (psychological problem, illness, weak character, or the results of negative peer influences) (Zweben, 1994). Guidelines for enhancing screening and assessment include:

- Interview the parents or guardian first.
- Interview the adolescent separately to elicit information he or she may not feel comfortable disclosing in front of parents.
- Be straightforward with the adolescent.
- Be empathic, nonjudgmental, and supportive with all.
- Ask the adolescent about patterns and frequencies of use for each substance, triggers for using, perceived motivation for using, consequences for using, and treatment goals.
- To supplement information, collect data from the adolescent's family, available case studies, the school system, and health care providers. (Evans & Sullivan, 2001; Riggs, 2003; U.S. Department of Health and Human Services, 1993)

In addition to standardized instruments, Evans and Sullivan (2001) recommend the following techniques to improve the adolescent's self-report history:

- Use open-ended and specific questions.
- Recognize vague answers and be gently persistent in getting specifics.
- Periodically summarize the client's feedback.
- Avoid argumentation and confrontation.
- Express empathy through reflective listening.
- Affirm the client through compliments.
- Avoid taking the client's defenses personally.
- Avoid discussions of rationalizations.
- Start with neutral questions and ask sensitive questions later.
- Ask about past behavior before current behavior.

Major acute psychiatric symptoms, such as manic episodes, hallucinations, psychotic depression, or suicide indicators, require emergency evaluation for possible hospitalization and need for medication (Chatlos, 1994). See chapter 1 on suicide assessment.

Working With Adolescents Who Have Co-Occurring Disorders

Social workers and other professionals should not wait until substance abuse treatment is completed to treat the mental disorder (Riggs, 2003). The chances of a successful outcome increase when substance use and mental disorders are treated simultaneously. The adolescent also needs education to understand both disorders and their interactions (Chatlos, 1994). Education should include risk factors, precipitating events, and the progression of the problems. To assess the client's understanding of his or her co-occurring disorders, the social worker and school-based practitioner might ask, "What do you see as the relationship between your substance use disorder and your mental disorder?" (Manwani & Weiss, 2003). The social worker and counselors should focus on current instances of negative consequences or outcomes to enable the adolescent to recognize the effect that drug use has had on his or her life (Evans & Sullivan, 2001).

A therapeutic alliance between the school-based practitioner and the adolescent is critical. Confrontation, a technique that counselors commonly use with clients who have a substance use disorder, is not as effective as establishing trust and credibility through a positive therapeutic alliance using support, empathy, reflective listening, and validation techniques (Manwani & Weiss, 2003).

Adolescents with co-occurring disorders require a comprehensive and individualized treatment plan that may include individual therapy, group therapy, family involvement, educational services, and medication compliance, if applicable (Substance Abuse and Mental Health Services Administration, 2002a). The social worker and mental health counselors should encourage parents to commit to involvement in the treatment plan and family therapy in order to create a supportive family recovery environment (Chatlos, 1994).

During the first few counseling sessions, the school-based practitioner must work with the adolescent to establish goals in order to eliminate substance use and begin to address the co-occurring disorders and other issues (Riggs, 2003). Following goal identification, the social worker and mental health counselors should create a contract with the adolescent identifying peers with whom he or she should and should not associate (e.g., law-abiding versus non-law-abiding peers), places that should be avoided, specific hours to be home, specific hours for homework, and times for attending mutual-help groups (Chatlos, 1994). Family members should be encouraged to join community support groups like Al-Anon (for families of individuals with alcohol problems) or the National Alliance for the Mentally Ill (for families of individuals who have mental illness) and study groups for parents regarding their children's substance use disorder and mental disorder (Substance Abuse and Mental Health Services Administration, 2002a). Siblings of adolescents with co-occurring disorders or adolescents with co-occurring disorders who have substance-abusing family members might be encouraged to attend a group like Alateen. For more information, visit the Web sites of Al-Anon, Alateen, and the National Alliance for the Mentally Ill.

Each parent or guardian involved should be asked to list situations when their adolescent's drug use affected them personally in order to enable the adolescent to recognize the consequences of his or her substance use (Chatlos, 1994). Review the list in a joint session with the parents and client. If the parents cannot be involved in the client's treatment (e.g., due to incarceration), ask the client to list how his or her substance use and recent behavior affected family and friends. Adolescents often have difficulty considering future consequences. Asking the adolescent to consider a lifetime of abstinence may be overwhelming and engender hopelessness. The social worker and other school-based practitioners should focus on the here and now, encouraging the adolescent to think about one day at a time.

If the adolescent has successfully abstained from substances in the past, the school-based practitioner should compliment that accomplishment, state how difficult that must have been, and ask how the client was able to refrain from drugs. As the adolescent maintains increased periods of abstinence, the school-based practitioner should help him or her to identify areas in which his or her life is improving (Evans & Sullivan, 2001). The school-based practitioner should also compliment clients when their behavior supports maintaining stability, such as taking psychotropic medications as prescribed, participating in therapy, controlling anger, and engaging in healthy activities. Help the adolescent to identify areas where improvement in the mental disorder has resulted in changes in other areas of life, such as less acting out in the classroom. Work with the adolescents to identify reasons that they were able to behave properly in the classroom. Compliment these achievements and other positive gains to help them create those conditions more often. Inability to remain abstinent or exacerbation of mental illness may necessitate referral to residential treatment.

Multisystemic therapy (MST) is used with adolescent substance abusers and appears to fit the needs of adolescents with co-occurring disorders. MST appears to be effective in reducing acting-out behaviors, particularly illegal behaviors (Henggeler, 1999; Keys, 1999; Schoenwald, Brown, & Henggeler, 2000). MST's goals are to empower the adolescent's primary caregivers with the skills needed to address the youth's behavior problems and to empower youths to cope with the various systems in their lives (Henggeler, 1999; Schoenwald et al., 2000). MST requires knowledge of the multiple and interrelated systems (family, school, peers, and community) operating in the adolescent's life (Keys, 1999).

Implementing empirically based services is an integral aspect of MST (Henggeler, 1999; Schoenwald et al., 2000). Approaches commonly incorporated are structural family therapy, cognitive-behavioral therapy, and behavioral parental training. The counselor should choose services based on the client's individual needs. As noted in Table 13.3, the multisystemic school counselor often acts as a school-community liaison, integrated services team member, group process facilitator, systems change agent, and family advocate (Keys, 1999).

Enhancing Adolescents' Motivation

The University of Rhode Island Change Assessment Questionnaire (URICA) is a tool to measure level of motivation to change and may be useful with adolescents (Greenstein, Franklin, & McGuffin, 1999). The adolescent's level of motivation will determine the approaches the school social worker and other mental health counselors employ. Evans and Sullivan (2001) have adapted a four-level model of motivation specifically for adolescents with co-occurring disorders (originally created by Osher & Kofoed, 1989): (1) engagement, where providers work to convince clients that treatment has some value (perhaps through films, peer groups, or other techniques appealing to adolescents); (2) persuasion, which consists of attempts to convince the client of the need for help, perhaps through values clarification exercises; (3) active treatment with an emphasis on developing skills and attitudes needed to maintain sobriety and mental health; and (4) relapse prevention, in which the adolescent incorporates techniques to sustain the skills needed to maintain abstinence and mental health, such as use of an ongoing self-help group.

Relapse Prevention

Relapse prevention is a vital component of treatment for those with co-occurring disorders. Help

Table 13.3 Roles of Multisystemic School Counselor

School-Community Liaison	Integrated Services Team Member	Group Process Facilitator	Systems Change Agent	Family Advocate
• Have knowledge of community resources • Assure that treatment plans from other agencies conform to school guidelines	• Conduct meetings with applicable professionals, such as mental health professionals, health professionals, child welfare professionals, juvenile justice professionals, and substance abuse counselors	• Help create a warm climate • Establish group norms • Manage dominant group members • Empower reticent members • Negotiate conflicts between professionals	• Become a social advocate working to effect changes in policy	• Teach family how to access community services • Assure family members they are welcome at school and at meetings no matter how serious their child's behavior was

Source: Keys, S. (1999). School counselors' role in facilitating multisystemic change. *Professional School Counseling, 3*(2), 101–108.

the adolescent to identify effective methods to deal with alcohol or drug cravings and ways to recognize and avoid situations that present a high risk of relapse for both substance use and mental disorders (Manwani & Weiss, 2003). Role playing may help to decrease the chances of substance use relapse. The role playing may include situations in which friends or family members overtly or covertly encourage the client to use drugs, how to cope with emotions without using drugs, and how to socialize and have fun while clean and sober. The situations that create the highest risk for adolescent relapse for substance use and mental illness include negative emotional states like stress and interpersonal conflict (Roget, Fisher, & Johnson, 1998). Other high-risk situations include urges and temptations (parties where drugs are present), positive emotional states (the desire to celebrate achievements), negative physical states (such as sickness or physical injury), and positive interpersonal contact (interactions with potential dating partners) (Roget et al., 1998).

Before concluding treatment, a relapse prevention plan should be developed to help all of the parties involved in the adolescent's treatment. Roget et al. (1998) recommend incorporating the following in relapse prevention plans:

• Probation terms (if applicable to the client's legal situation)
• Family rules

• School attendance and grade requirements
• Participation in aftercare (e.g., outpatient therapy group or mutual-help group)
• Agreement to participate in drug testing
• Relapse consequences
• Compliance incentives (initially, a reward for each week of sobriety)

The social worker and other counselors should educate families that the overwhelming majority of individuals with substance use disorders relapse at least once. Expecting relapse does not mean accepting relapse. Parents should continue to implement immediate consequences should relapse occur.

Referrals

The ASAM Patient Placement Criteria for the Treatment of Substance-Related Disorders is a good tool to consult when considering a referral to outpatient services, intensive outpatient services with partial hospitalization, residential and intensive inpatient services, and medically managed intensive inpatient services (Mee-Lee, Shulman, Fishman, Gastfriend, & Griffith, 2001). For example, outpatient treatment is often appropriate when an adolescent suffering from co-occurring disorders admits that he or she has a problem, is not in immediate danger, and has an

Table 13.4 Summary of Techniques and Interventions for Working With Adolescents Who Have Co-Occurring Disorders

Educating Teachers and Staff	Educating Parents and Family Members	Increasing Adolescent's Motivation	Working With Adolescents
• Organize in-service training for teachers and other staff • Invite staff from local mental health and substance abuse agencies to conduct or assist in this training • Solicit teachers' invitations to give class presentations on mental health, substance abuse, and co-occurring disorders • Instruct teachers and students on how to refer students who may have co-occurring disorders • Encourage school administrators or other personnel to send a letter to parents with information about substance use disorders, mental disorders, and co-occurring disorders	• Explain to family that no one is at fault and discourage parents from expressing shame to their child • Inform parents that professional help such as a psychiatrist or substance abuse counselor may be necessary • Parents should be directed to participate in their child's assessment and treatment • Parents should be encouraged to remain consistent in providing encouragement and rewarding positive behavior like abstinence • Parents should be encouraged to follow through on consequences for negative behaviors even when difficult	• Encourage adolescent that treatment has value • Encourage adolescent of the need for help • Use active treatment with an emphasis on developing skills and attitudes necessary to maintain sobriety and mental health • Incorporate techniques to help adolescent sustain skills needed to maintain abstinence and mental health	• Screen the adolescent using the DUSI or the POSIT • Do not wait to treat the mental disorder until the completion of substance abuse treatment • Educate adolescent on both disorders and their interactions • Focus education on risk factors, precipitating events, and progression of the problems • Develop therapeutic alliance by using support, empathy, reflective listening, and validation techniques • Establish goals with the adolescent in order to eliminate substance use and begin to address the comorbid disorders and other issues • Develop comprehensive and individualized treatment plan that includes individual therapy, group therapy, family involvement, educational services, and medication compliance if needed • Encourage parents' involvement in the treatment plan and family therapy in order to create a supportive family recovery environment

intact support group (Mee-Lee et al., 2001). When circumstances indicate that residential treatment is needed, the social worker and other practitioners should look for a controlled milieu such as a therapeutic community that can address both mental and substance use disorders. Therapeutic communities have had positive outcomes with substance-abusing adolescents (DeLeon, 2000). Treatment centers that utilize immediate consequences, both positive and negative, and a reduction of privileges for upper-level residents (with longer treatment tenure and positive behavior) when lower-level residents misbehave may increase the likeliness of a successful outcome (Evans & Sullivan, 2001).

Tools

Table 13.4 summarizes the approaches presented in this chapter to help adolescents with co-occurring disorders to lead more successful and productive lives. Social workers, counselors, teachers, and other school staff need patience as well as expertise to work with youth who have co-occurring disorders. Social workers or other professionals should not blame themselves when clients misbehave or relapse. Social workers and other school mental health counselors should have a support network to discuss the challenges they face working with adolescents who have co-occurring disorders, partake in enjoyable and healthy activities, and realize the importance of perseverance for both themselves and their clients.

Key Points to Remember

Substance abuse and mental disorders frequently coexist.

The mental disorders that most commonly co-occur with substance use disorders are conduct disorders, attention deficit hyperactivity disorder, depression and other mood disorders, bipolar disorder, and posttraumatic stress disorder.

Two helpful standardized instruments for screening adolescents for co-occurring disorders are the Drug Use Screening Inventory and the Problem Oriented Screening Instrument for Teenagers.

To be effective with students who have co-occurring disorders, school professionals must make use of best practices in the treatment of the substance use and mental disorders.

The mental disorder and the substance use disorder should be addressed simultaneously.

School professionals will need a strong treatment support base rooted in the community and family to be effective with students who have co-occurring disorders. Referrals to the community are usually necessary.

Multisystemic therapy may be a promising treatment option. Utilizing the adolescents' strengths and complimenting small behavioral changes are important. Ongoing management of multiple issues and relapse prevention are also important parts of effective interventions for co-occurring disorders.

References

Chatlos, J. C. (1994). Dual diagnosis in adolescent populations. In N. S. Miller (Ed.), *Treating coexisting psychiatric and addictive disorders* (pp. 85–110). Center City, MN: Hazelden.

DeLeon, G. (2000). *The therapeutic community*. New York: Springer.

Evans, K., & Sullivan, M. (2001). *Dual diagnosis: Counseling the mentally ill substance abuser*. New York: Guilford.

Greenstein, D. D., Franklin, M. E., & McGuffin, P. (1999). Measuring motivation to change: An examination of the University of Rhode Island change assessment questionnaire (URICA) in an adolescent sample. *Psychotherapy, 36*(1), 47–55.

Henggeler, S. (1999). Multisystemic therapy: An overview of clinical procedures, outcomes, and policy implications. *Child Psychology and Psychiatric Review, 4*(1), 1–10.

Kaminer, Y., Tarter, R., & Buckstein, O. (1999). Psychotherapies for adolescent substance abusers: 15-month follow-up of a pilot study. *Journal of the American Academy of Child and Adolescent Psychiatry, 31*(6), 1046–1049.

Keys, S. (1999). School counselor's role in facilitating multisystemic change. *Professional School Counseling, 3*(2), 101–108.

Manwani, S., & Weiss, R. (2003). 5 keys to improve counseling for dual diagnosis patients: An empathic approach can be effective when treating psychiatric patients with substance use disorders. Retrieved July 14, 2004, from http://www.currentpsychiatry.com/2003_09/0903_counseling.asp.

Matson, J., & Bamberg, J. (1998). Reliability of assessment of dual diagnosis. *Research in Developmental Disabilities, 19*(1), 89–95.

Mee-Lee, D., Shulman, G., Fishman, M., Gastfriend, D., & Griffith, J. (2001). *ASAM patient placement criteria for the treatment of substance related disorders* (2nd ed.). Chevy Chase, MD: American Society of Addiction Medicine.

Osher, F. C., & Kofoed, L. L. (1989). Treatment of patients with psychiatric and psychoactive substance abuse disorders. *Hospital and Community Psychiatry, 40,* 1025–1030.

Rahdert, E. R. (1991). *The adolescent assessment/referral system manual* (DHHS Publication No. ADM 91–1735). Rockville, MD: National Institute on Drug Abuse.

Riggs, P. D. (2003). Treating adolescents for substance abuse and comorbid psychiatric disorders. *Science and Practice Perspectives, 2*(1), 18–32.

Roget, N. A., Fisher, G. L., & Johnson, M. L. (1998). A protocol for reducing juvenile recidivism through relapse prevention. *Journal of Addiction & Offender Counseling, 19*(1), 33–34.

Schoenwald, S., Brown, T., & Henggeler, S. (2000). Inside multisystemic therapy: Therapist, supervisor, and program practices. *Journal of Emotional and Behavioral Disorders, 8*(2), 83–104.

Substance Abuse and Mental Health Services Administration. (2002a). *Evidence-based practices for co-occurring disorders: Interventions for children and adolescents with co-occurring disorders.* Rockville, MD: U.S. Department of Health and Human Services.

Substance Abuse and Mental Health Services Administration. (2002b). *Prevention of co-occurring disorders: Prevention for children and adolescents.* Rockville, MD: U.S. Department of Health and Human Services.

Tarter, R. (1990). Evaluation and treatment of adolescent substance abuse: A decision tree method. *American Journal of Drug and Alcohol Abuse, 16,* 1–46.

U.S. Department of Health and Human Services. (1993). *Screening and assessment of alcohol- and other drug-abusing adolescents* (DHHS Publication No. ADM93–2009). Rockville, MD: Center for Substance Abuse Treatment.

Wise, B., Cuffe, S., & Fischer, D. O. (2001). Dual diagnosis and successful participation of adolescents in substance abuse treatment. *Journal of Substance Abuse Treatment, 21*(3), 161–165.

Zweben, J. E. (1994). Working with the family. In N. S. Miller (Ed.), *Treating coexisting psychiatric and addictive disorders* (pp. 213–230). Center City, MN: Hazelden.

Understanding the Use of Mental Health Classifications and *DSM-IV-TR* in Schools

Elizabeth C. Pomeroy ▪ Laura Hopson

Getting Started

Historically, classifying information has been a necessary human activity since the time of the ancient Greeks. Hippocrates, the ancient Greek physician, developed a medical classification system based on imbalances in the four humors: phlegm (related to apathy and sluggishness); blood (related to rapid mood changes); black bile (related to severe depression or melancholia); and yellow bile (related to irritability and anxiety). One of the purposes of a classification system is to create a common language for categorizing and understanding human difficulties. In modern times, the need to compile statistical or epidemiological information for mental disorders resulted in the most universal of modern classification systems, known as the *Diagnostic and Statistical Manual of Mental Disorders* (*DSM*) produced by the American Psychiatric Association (APA) (American Psychiatric Association, 2000). School professionals work in a collaborative environment that brings them into contact with diverse mental health professionals who rely on the diagnostic criteria of the *DSM* and use its language to describe student needs. A *DSM* diagnosis also has important implications for a student's eligibility for special education services.

While most school social workers and mental health counselors are trained in the language and the knowledge of the *DSM*, their use of the manual and its diagnostic criteria is variable. Some school-based services professionals routinely use the *DSM* (school-based therapists) while others do not routinely rely on it in their work (e.g., school social workers and guidance counselors). Teachers and other staff may not even be familiar with the mental health criteria in the manual. This chapter's goal is to help school personnel to stay abreast of the classification system used in *DSM-IV-TR* and to understand how these classifications may be used with children in schools. This chapter also provides essential knowledge for working more collaboratively with the mental health professionals and provides knowledge to help schools appropriately respond to students with mental health needs.

What We Know

The current version of the *DSM, DSM-IV-TR* (American Psychiatric Association, 2000), is the sixth publication of the manual. In the initial two versions, the manual included a listing of mental disorders with some discussion regarding the likely etiology of each disorder. Beginning with the *DSM-III* (American Psychiatric Association, 1980), several striking changes occurred. Most prominently, the emphasis in presenting disorders moved toward describing specific behavioral symptoms rather than focusing more globally on the etiology of the disorders. The motivation for this change was primarily to increase the reliability of diagnoses. Secondarily, this new focus removed from the *DSM* system the intense disagreements regarding etiology related to various theoretical approaches. The more recent versions of the *DSM* have been intentionally atheoretical (Pomeroy & Wambach, 2003).

Along with this shift toward more specific behavioral descriptions, a multiaxial classification system was introduced. The intent of this change was to communicate relevant information regarding clients' medical condition, psychosocial issues, and overall functioning, thereby more clearly describing people in their environments.

The first two axes in the five-axis classification system are used to present the clinical disorders actually listed in the manual. The majority of the mental disorders are listed on Axis I while Axis II is reserved for persistent or chronic conditions, specifically mental retardation and personality disorders. The separation of these axes is intended to assure that more-chronic conditions are not overlooked in the diagnostic process. If a client warrants multiple diagnoses on a single axis, the diagnoses are listed in order of their importance to the person's psychosocial functioning (i.e., "principal diagnosis") or in order of the focus of attention at a particular clinical interview (i.e., "reason for visit"). In instances when a client has at least one diagnosis on both Axis I and Axis II, it is assumed that the first Axis I diagnosis is the principal diagnosis unless the first Axis II diagnosis is specifically labeled as such. The *DSM* also allows for communicating the level of uncertainty regarding a particular diagnosis (see provisional diagnoses, not otherwise specified diagnoses, and deferred diagnoses for more detail) (Pomeroy & Wambach, 2003).

Axis III is designed to present general medical information. All medical conditions that may be important to understanding or treating the mental disorder(s) or that directly affect the likely prognosis of treatment should be listed on this axis. In general, this would include any medical problem related to the etiology of a mental disorder, any acute or chronic condition that affects the client's psychosocial functioning, and any condition for which the client is taking routine medication. Nonmedical practitioners should *not* diagnose general medical conditions on this axis. Instead, only conditions reported by the client, listed in a clinical record, or reported by a physician should be listed. It is strongly suggested that the source of the information about general medical conditions be included in the listing (e.g., diabetes assumed due to client's use of insulin, "bad blood" reported by client, or a concussion reported by an ER physician). Similarly, nonmedical practitioners are not encouraged to utilize International Classification of Diseases (ICD) diagnostic numbers on Axis III, an act akin to diagnosing.

Axis IV is designed to present specific information about the client's current psychosocial environment. Although only psychosocial problems that have occurred in the past year are usually listed, any psychosocial difficulty that is relevant to the client's current level of functioning may be reported. For example, childhood sexual abuse may lead to a variety of adult mental health problems and, consequently, should be included if clearly related to a disorder's etiology or if clearly pertinent in the client's perspective. A number of global categories of problem areas are suggested in the *DSM* text. Practitioners are encouraged to include specific information on Axis IV in addition to such global characterizations (such as occupational problems, problems with primary support group, or problems related to interaction with the legal system).

In some instances, specific psychosocial problems are part of the diagnostic criteria for a disorder and consequently need not be repeated on Axis IV. A child with a diagnosis of autism, for example, will clearly have problems in social relations. When such difficulties do not exceed the norm for diagnosis, for example, if the child is not forming friendships at school, they need not be listed on Axis IV. However, if that same child were being bullied on a daily basis, it would be appropriate to note that situation on Axis IV.

Finally, a Global Assessment of Functioning (GAF) score is listed on Axis V. This 100-point scale is presented in the *DSM*. At a minimum, the client's current level of functioning is included. In some instances, additional GAF scores may be given (e.g., highest level of functioning in the past year). Unfortunately, the GAF score was designed to address multiple aspects of functioning, including social relations, employment or school issues, and dangerousness to oneself or others. In some situations, an individual's functioning can be at very different levels, depending on which aspect is emphasized. It is recommended that, in those instances, the client's dangerousness to self or others should take precedence in determining the GAF score (Pomeroy & Wambach, 2003).

Although these systems have grown to be widely accepted and incorporated into the World Health Organization's *International Classification of Diseases*, controversies regarding the use of these nosologies with mental disorders have been debated since their inception. In the educational literature, some of this controversy has focused on the use of labels developed from the medical model of disease that may not be readily translatable to the classroom environment (Gresham & Gansle, 1992). Another issue has been the reliability of the diagnostic process. This issue has resulted in an increasing emphasis on descriptive (rather than etiological) diagnostic criteria for the various disorders. A third concern has focused on the stigma that placing a label on a child might have and the relevance of that label to the placement of the child within the educational system (Gresham & Gansle, 1992). More specifically stated, environmental influences on the child are ignored, thereby affixing exclusive "blame" on the individual even though the problem may well stem from or be exacerbated by people and situations in the child's environment. This set of concerns has led to the development of a multiaxial approach to diagnosis which includes consideration of medical and psychosocial situations that contribute to the disorder and/or will likely affect attempts to treat the disorder. However, it must be noted that many feel the multiaxial system in later versions of the *DSM* does not sufficiently address this concern.

In addition, fears exist about giving a child a diagnosis which inevitably results in certain stigmatized effects. For example, because mental illness is associated with a great deal of stigma, the child who has been diagnosed with an emotional or behavioral disorder may be considered "weird," "different," "crazy," "stupid," or even worse, "dangerous." These stereotypes could follow the child throughout life. Similarly, a diagnostic label may dramatically alter expectations and consequently encourage the child to measure up or down to the label. Parents, teachers, and other professionals continually wrestle with the pros and cons of diagnosing a child (even though it may be an accurate description of the child's condition), given the stereotypes in our society.

Another important issue that is currently being examined is the disproportionately high number of children from ethnic minorities who are being diagnosed with mental disorders, such as mild mental retardation (Reschly, 1996). While this problem may be due to environmental stressors and poverty, it may also be a result of culturally biased assessment instruments and categorical symptoms that are inherent in the current classification system.

Diagnostic categories have particular relevance for schools due to the requirements of special education legislation. Since 1975, with the passage of federal legislation originally known as Public Law 94–142 and later changed to the Individuals With Disabilities Education Act (IDEA), special education services in schools have grown to an estimated $32 billion program (Terman, Larner, Stevenson, & Behrman, 1996). Approximately 1 in 10 children in public schools are now being identified as in need of special education services in one form or another. The process of identification, assessment, diagnosis, and educational placement follows specific procedures according to the federal mandate. In order to be eligible for special education services, a child must meet two major criteria: first, the child must be assessed and diagnosed with at least 1 of 13 disorders outlined in IDEA (see chapter 86 for a more detailed review of the IDEA legislation). These disabilities include both physical and mental disorders. Second, special education services must be deemed necessary in order for the child to receive an appropriate education (Reschly, 1996). According to H.R. 1350:

> [A] child with a disability means a child with mental retardation, hearing impairments (including deafness), speech or language impairments, visual impairments (including blindness), serious emotional disturbance (referred to in this title as "emotional disturbance"), orthopedic impairments, autism, traumatic brain injury, other health impairments, or specific learning disabilities and who, by reason thereof, needs special education and related services. (Sec. 614, Evaluations, Eligibility Determinations, Individualized Educational Programs and Educational Placements)

In order to receive special education services, students must meet the criteria for one of the eligibility categories listed above. This has important implications because some *DSM* diagnoses fit these eligibility criteria, and others do not. A diagnosis of attention-deficit/hyperactivity disorder (ADHD), for example, was not an eligible diagnosis for receiving special education services until relatively recently. It may now be categorized as "other health impairments" and can meet eligibility requirements for special education if the student demonstrates a need for special services and has the diagnosis (U.S. Department of Education, 1999).

A diagnosis also has important implications for school accountability when it leads to placement in special education. No Child Left Behind legislation requires that schools demonstrate annual progress for all students, including those in special education classes. Schools can be held accountable for special education students who do not demonstrate progress in annual assessments, such as standardized tests (U.S. Department of Education, 2004).

What We Can Do

Despite concerns about stigma and labeling students, the *DSM-IV-TR* has become the primary language used by a variety of professionals to communicate about mental, emotional, and behavioral disorders among children and adults. Diagnostic labels serve as a shorthand for characterizing both the type and the severity of problems a client may be experiencing. In many instances, diagnoses are linked to eligibility for publicly funded treatment or special educational programs. For persons with private insurance policies, the diagnosis determines if treatment will be covered as well as limits to the amount of services a client may receive in treating the specific disorder, particularly in managed care arrangements. In short, familiarity with the *DSM-IV-TR* (American Psychiatric Association, 2000) classification system is necessary in order to function appropriately in the multidisciplinary environments of both mental health and educational systems. The purpose of this chapter is to familiarize school personnel with the usages of the *DSM-IV-TR* and how it can be used appropriately in schools. Educators who have an understanding of the *DSM* will be better able to communicate with other professionals about a child's special needs within the school system (Ronin, 2001). While teachers are not allowed by law to make diagnoses, having a working knowledge of the diagnostic system will improve their understanding of the educational needs of the child.

Because parents and children may feel stigmatized by a diagnosis, the social worker and other school mental health practitioners have the important role of helping parents to understand the diagnosis. Practitioners need to understand how the child's behaviors are connected to the diagnosis and be able to clearly explain this to parents. For some parents, it may be a relief to know that their child's behaviors are the result of a diagnosis, such as ADHD, that can be addressed with specific behavioral goals and medication. For other parents, they may worry that their children will be stigmatized or that they will not receive the same treatment as other children because of their diagnoses.

Just as the diagnosis may help a parent to view a child's behavior differently, it may also help a teacher to understand inappropriate classroom behavior. IDEA requires that special education students be placed in general education classes whenever possible (National Education Association, n.d.). Therefore, all teachers need to be aware of the diagnosis that leads to a special education placement, the behaviors associated with that diagnosis, and appropriate ways of responding to those behaviors. This means that teachers may need a great deal of assistance from school mental health practitioners to understand diagnoses of special education students.

Assessment Using the *DSM-IV-TR*

While a *DSM-IV-TR* (American Psychiatric Association, 2000) diagnosis is the abbreviated description of a client's mental health status, assessment is a much broader term/process. Certainly, initial assessment leads to diagnosis. However, assessment ideally is much more ongoing, collaborative, and detailed communication among a professional, the parents, the teachers, and the child. In this broader sense, assessment informs monitoring and evaluative processes as well as diagnostic ones.

Many factors influence the breadth and depth of the assessment process. For example, if meeting the child for the first time in a classroom situation, it is likely that only those behaviors which can be observed will be available for assessment purposes. Frequently, the amount of information a child is able to share is limited, at least initially. As the rapport between practitioner and child is established over time, the child is apt to be more comfortable in sharing sensitive information or in discussing things that don't necessarily seem relevant at first. Typically, initial assessment stretches over several interactions with the child, teachers, mental health practitioners, and parents and/or caretakers. The formation of the individual education plan under IDEA requires that specific individuals be involved in the assessment and planning for educational interventions for children.

It must also be noted that not all children enter into a helping relationship on a completely voluntary basis. Some children may be required through some legal mechanism to receive treatment or at least be evaluated for their need for special education services. In many more instances, family, friends, or school personnel pressure children to obtain help for some specified concern. Regardless of the precise mechanism, engaging the resistant child is more challenging. Generally, the practitioner must help the child find his or her own motivation or goals in order to secure any real cooperation.

Although the assessment process is obviously unique to the individual, there are some general principles that apply. Whenever possible, multiple sources of information are preferred over relying solely on the child's ability to provide information. Additional sources of assessment data include information from diverse sources and professionals, such as medical reports, psychological evaluations, educational testing and records, legal reports, and social and family data often collected by school social workers. In any particular situation, there may well be others who could provide valuable data and/or perspectives that could aid school professionals in making the correct assessment, such as peers, extended family members, probation officers, or professional child care staff in cases of residential placement.

Another guiding principle is that individual problems rarely occur in isolation. Consequently, both the child's psychosocial and medical history and his or her current life context are essential in understanding the presenting problem. So, for example, although a child may present with a specific behavioral problem, it would be far less than ideal to not review the child's prior successes and failures in coping in a variety of situations. Similarly, it would be challenging to try to address this behavioral problem without knowing basic information about the child's broader functioning within the school system, the family, and other social contexts (Jordan & Franklin, 2003).

In a related issue, it is essential to view and process assessment data within the child's context. For example, thinking that is typical of young children might be viewed as quite pathological if demonstrated by an older adolescent of normal intelligence. Beliefs that someone is trying to hurt the child or family may be viewed differently if the child is a member of an oppressed population. Practitioners must strive to become sensitive to the culture and/or circumstances that may affect the child's life and consistently interpret assessment data through a culturally competent lens (Pomeroy & Wambach, 2003).

Assessment and Diagnosis of Children in Schools

While assessment is an ongoing process in any setting (outpatient clinics, hospitals, mental health centers, or schools), the procedure for evaluating a child in a school setting involves a defined protocol.

A school professional requests that a student be evaluated for special education services. During the assessment phase, a school psychologist will use a variety of assessment instruments to evaluate the child's cognitive, emotional, social, functional, behavioral, sensory/communication, and motor skill development. The health of a child will be determined by a physician. The school psychologist will determine the primary diagnosis for the child, along with any secondary diagnoses found during the evaluation. The diagnoses for mental, emotional, behavioral, or learning disabilities often will be categorized according to the *DSM-IV-TR* criteria. This evaluation will be used to determine whether the student is eligible for special education services. The parents participate in the process of determining eligibility and may request an independent evaluation if they disagree with the results of the assessment (U.S. Department of Education, 2000).

When a student is determined to be eligible for special education services, a team of school staff, the student, and parent(s) will collaborate to create an individualized education plan (IEP). The IEP team includes the student, parent(s), counselor or social worker, teacher, special education teacher, and other relevant staff, such as speech pathologist, occupational therapist, and school psychologist. The IEP will include goals and objectives for the child's educational attainment, given the disability with which the child has been diagnosed (U.S. Department of Education, 2000). Many of the goals and outcomes that are defined in the student's IEP will be associated directly with the diagnosis and the associated behaviors. The school mental health practitioner will need to guide the parent through the process of understanding the diagnosis so that the parent will remain engaged in creating the student's IEP.

The school's progress toward helping special education students to meet stated outcomes is reevaluated annually. The IEP team looks at the plan at least once a year to review goals and outcomes. The child must be reevaluated at least once every 3 years to determine whether the child still is diagnosed with a disability that meets eligibility requirements for special education. The parent or teacher may request that the child be reevaluated at any time (U.S. Department of Education, 2000).

While this outline provides the general process that is specified in IDEA, there are significant variations to this process from state to state in terms of categorical and classification criteria (Reschly, 1996). It should be noted that, for the more severe emotional disturbances or disabilities (i.e., autism, moderate to severe mental retardation, pervasive developmental disorders), the diagnosis for special education services is relatively clear-cut. The controversies regarding assessment and diagnosis (as noted above) are related to the milder disabilities, such as mild mental retardation, mild forms of ADHD (classified as "other health impairment"), and the controversial diagnosis of bipolar disorder in children. The special education classification of these types of disabilities has been the subject of heated debate since the 1990s (Gresham & Gansle, 1992; Reynolds, 1992).

Instruments

There is a broad range of assessment instruments that can be utilized with infants, children, and adolescents in order to assess the client's psychosocial functioning and presenting problems. While some of the scales may involve evoking responses from the child or adolescent, other scales depend on interviewer observation, assessment, and report. For most of the disorders found in the *DSM-IV-TR* (American Psychiatric Association, 2000) related to infancy, childhood, and adolescence, there are assessment instruments that can be utilized to evaluate a specific problem.

For example, there are scales to measure the degree of mental retardation, motor skills deficits, perceptual problems, attention deficit disorders, depression, and behavior problems which are specifically designed to be used with children and adolescents. These scales are usually normed on a specific age range of children (i.e., 6–10 years old, 8 years old and older, 12 years old and older) and should not be used with children younger than the given age range. The following section will provide examples of some of the more common assessment instruments utilized with children and adolescents. However, there are literally hundreds of scales that can be obtained that address specific issues relevant to this age group.

Scales for Child and Adolescent Assessment

When a psychological and educational evaluation is requested for a child or adolescent, a variety of measures will be used depending on the issues

that bring the student to the attention of teachers and school counselors. In many instances, an IQ test, such as the WISC-IV, will be administered in order to obtain information about the child's level of intelligence. This is a test that must be administered by a licensed clinical psychologist, and the results of the test are provided by the psychologist. When mental retardation or other developmental delays are expected, the Differential Abilities Scale (DAS) is a particularly good measure as it provides normative data for items out of the student's age range. Thus, the tester is able to administer the most developmentally appropriate questions.

In addition, a test of adaptive behavior functioning is often used, especially for younger children or children who test below average on the measure of cognitive abilities, which is indicated by an IQ score in the range of 80–90. The Vineland Adaptive Behavior Scale measures daily living skills, such as communication, self-care, social skills, leisure skills, home safety skills, and self-direction (Sparrow, Balla, & Chicchetti, 1984). A child with an IQ score below 70–75 and significant deficits in adaptive behavior skills would be considered to have mental retardation. This diagnosis requires both a low IQ score and significant problems with adaptive behavior skills.

The Child Behavior Checklist is a global measure of functioning that assesses children's problem behaviors. The instrument is used to assess which behaviors are most problematic for the child rather than examining a specific problem area (Achenbach & Edelbrock, 1983).

The Connors Rating Scale, on the other hand, is used to assess the symptomatic behaviors associated with ADHD (Connors, 1990). A psychologist assessing a child who displays these symptoms might give a rating scale to the child's teacher and parent to evaluate these behaviors in the classroom and at home.

Cultural Considerations

The cultural background of the child and family must be taken into consideration in the assessment of the child's strengths and limitations. In some cultures, mental health issues are not discussed and are viewed as taboo. Children from these cultural backgrounds may come to the attention of teachers or other school personnel because of somatic complaints such as headaches, stomach aches, or other pain symptoms. After being examined by a physician, the child may be referred for mental health treatment if no medical reasons for the problems the child is experiencing are found.

In other cultures, mental health symptoms may be viewed as significantly related to the family's religious beliefs. For example, psychotic symptoms may be viewed as a sign from God or the Devil. Parents from certain cultures may embrace "magic realism," in which there is a belief that some action on the part of the parent brought on the symptoms in the child. For example, a parent might explain that because they dropped a knife on the floor, the child developed depressive symptoms.

In addition, it is important to keep in mind that the definition of age-appropriate behavior differs in different cultures. It is unremarkable to expect a 5-year-old child in England to be ready to go to boarding school whereas in American culture, a child of this age would be considered too young to leave home for an extended period of time. Children who are attempting to bridge two different cultures may experience problems in understanding the different normative behaviors in each. Language difficulties may be a result of learning two languages at once, rather than a psychological problem or learning disability (Pomeroy & Wambach, 2003).

Cultural differences also exist in terms of gender roles for male and female children. For example, in Indian culture, females are expected to be dependent on the males in the family, whereas in Western European and American societies, independence is a valued attribute for both genders. In some Asian cultures, female children are taught to defer to males in making major decisions. On the other hand, in American society, we teach children that there is equality between the sexes in terms of power and authority within the family.

In addition, prevalence rates for various disorders differ for male and female children. For example, boys are more likely to be assessed with a conduct disorder while girls are more frequently diagnosed with separation anxiety symptoms. Finally, children of color may experience discrimination, oppression, stigmatization, and ostracism in school situations and may display anxiety and depression related to these environmental and social factors. It is important to assess the child's entire psychosocial environment before attributing symptoms to intrapsychic factors.

Tools and Practice Examples

Tools

The referral and evaluation process follows five basic steps, which are shown in Figure 14.1.

An important function of the assessment process is to provide the practitioner with an overall understanding of the client's strengths and weaknesses in areas of psychosocial functioning (Pomeroy, Holleran, & Franklin, 2003). Table 14.1 can be completed by the practitioner during or following an assessment interview. It provides a brief and easy-to-use guideline for assessing clients in a variety of areas.

The following resources may prove useful to families in which a child is experiencing a mental disorder:

http://www.tea.state.tx.us/special.ed/explansaf/ doc/eng-ps.doc (procedural safeguards for parents of a child with a disability)

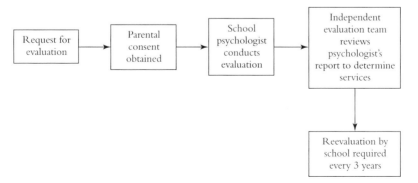

Figure 14.1. Steps in the Evaluation Process

Table 14.1 Person in Environment Assessment

Area of Functioning	Personal	Family	Friends	School/Work	Community	Intervention
Appearance						
Health						
Developmental issues/ transitions						
Coping abilities						
Stressors						
Capacity for relationships						
Social functioning						
Educational functioning						
Problem solving						
Creativity						
Cognitive functioning						
Emotional functioning						
Self-concept						
Motivation						
Ethnic identification						
Cultural barriers						
Role functioning						
Spirituality						
Other strengths						

Note: Use C to indicate a concern, S to indicate a weakness, and N/A to indicate not applicable. To rate intensity, use a 1–5 scale in which 1 = minimal intensity, 2 = mild intensity, 3 = average intensity, 4 = above-average intensity, and 5 = significant intensity.

http://www.thearc.org (Association for Retarded Citizens, a national organization of and for people with mental retardation and related developmental disabilities and their families)

http://www.autism-society.org (information on autistic disorders and treatment)

http://www.mhsource.com/disorders/tic.html (information on tic and Tourette's syndromes)

http://www.nimh.nih.gov/publicat/adhd.cfm (ADHD research and publications by the National Institute of Mental Health)

http://www.mentalhealth.com/dis/p20-ch02.html (diagnosis and treatment of conduct disorder)

http://www.mentalhealth.com/dis/p20-ch03 .html (diagnosis and treatment of separation anxiety disorder)

http://www.kennedykrieger.org/familyreso/ services/feeding.html (feeding disorders diagnosis and treatment)

http://www.mentalhealth.com/dis/p20-ch07 .html (information on Asperger's syndrome)

Case Example

Lara Hernandez is a 7-year-old Hispanic female student at Bono Elementary School. After having a fairly difficult year in first grade, Lara is now experiencing multiple problems in the beginning of second grade. Ms. Jordan, Lara's second-grade teacher, consulted with Ms. Marsh, the first-grade teacher, regarding Lara's past academic and behavior problems. Ms. Marsh stated that Lara had difficulty following directions and staying in her chair and would talk incessantly to other students. In addition, on the playground, she couldn't follow the rules of games, much to the irritation of other children. While Lara seems to want and need attention from her peers, other children tire of her excessive activity and talking and don't want to play with her any more.

In terms of academics, Ms. Marsh stated that Lara had trouble learning her alphabet and reversed letters and numbers. Ms. Marsh stated that Lara's mother had trouble getting Lara to settle down at night to do even 15 minutes of homework. Ms. Hernandez also stated that Lara had the same problem in Brownie Scouts. She bothered other children because she had difficulty sitting still and working on projects. After several weeks of class, Ms. Jordan recommended that Lara be tested by the school psychologist.

Utilizing the Child Behavior Checklist, the WISC-IV, and the Connors' Rating Scale, the psychologist determined that Lara was functioning with a normal level of intelligence. On the other hand, she did score high for hyperactivity, distractibility, and possible reading disability. The psychologist reported the results to the educational diagnostician, who called a meeting that included Lara's teacher, her parents, and the psychologist to discuss Lara's individualized education program.

Key Points to Remember

This chapter provides an overview of using the *DSM-IV-TR* to provide diagnoses in school settings. A diagnosis has the following implications for school practitioners:

- The diagnosis may facilitate dialogue and collaboration among professionals in multiple disciplines because it provides a common language for discussing a student's presenting problems.
- The diagnosis may help families and school staff to better understand and respond to a student's behavior.
- Parents and students may need help understanding the diagnosis in order to avoid feelings of stigmatization.
- The diagnosis has important implications for a student's eligibility for special education services.
- The diagnosis and associated behaviors will guide many aspects of the student's IEP.
- The diagnosis and special education placement assigns additional responsibilities to the school for demonstrating that the student is meeting the objectives stated in the IEP.

References

Achenbach, T. M., & Edelbrock, C. S. (1983). *Manual for the child behavior checklist and the revised child behavior profile.* Burlington, VT: University Associates in Psychiatry.

American Psychiatric Association. (1980). *Diagnostic and statistical manual of mental disorders* (3rd ed.). Washington, DC: Author.

American Psychiatric Association. (2000). *Diagnostic and statistical manual of mental disorders* (4th ed., text revision). Washington, DC: Author.

Connors, C. K. (1990). *Connors' rating scales manual.* North Tonawanda, NY: Mental-Health Systems.

Gresham, F. M., & Gansle, K. A. (1992). Misguided assumptions of *DSM-III-R*: Implications for school psychological practice. *School Psychology Quarterly, 7*(2), 79–95.

Individuals With Disabilities Educational Improvement Act of 2000 (Engrossed as Agreed to or Passed by Both House and Senate). H.R. 1350, Sec. 614: Evaluations, eligibility determinations, individualized education programs, and educational placements. Available: http://thomas.loc.gov/cgibin/query/F?c108:4:./temp/~c1086RnkmD:e13639.

Jordan, C., & Franklin, C. (2003). *Clinical assessment for social workers: Quantitative and qualitative methods.* Chicago: Lyceum.

National Education Association. (n.d.). Special education and the Individuals With Disabilities Education Act. Available: http://www.nea.org/specialed/index.html.

Pomeroy, E. C., Holleran, L. K., & Franklin, C. (2003). Adults. In C. Jordan & C. Franklin (Eds.), *Clinical assessment for social workers: Quantitative and qualitative methods* (pp. 215–254). Chicago: Lyceum.

Pomeroy, E. C., & Wambach, K. (2003). *The clinical assessment workbook: Balancing strengths and differential diagnosis.* Pacific Grove, CA: Brooks/Cole.

Reschly, D. J. (1996). Identification and assessment of students with disabilities. *Future of Children:*

Special Education for Students With Disabilities, 6(1), 40–53.

Reynolds, C. R. (1992). Misguided epistemological shifting, misdirected misology, and dogma in diagnosis. *School Psychology Quarterly, 7*(2), 96–99.

Ronen, T. (2001). Collaboration on critical questions in child psychotherapy: A model linking referral, assessment, intervention and evaluation. *Journal of Social Work Education, 37*(1), 91–110.

Sparrow, S., Balla, D., & Chicchetti, D. (1984). *Vineland Adaptive Behavior Scale: Interview edition, survey form.* Circle Pines, MN: American Guidance Service.

Terman, D. L., Larner, M. B., Stevenson, C. S., & Behrman, R. E. (1996). Special education for students with disabilities: Analysis and recommendations. *Future of Children: Special Education for Students With Disabilities, 6*(1), 4–24.

U.S. Department of Education. (1999). *Special education and rehabilitative services.* Available: http://www.ed.gov/policy/speced/leg/idea/brief6.html.

U.S. Department of Education. (2000). *A guide to the individualized education program.* Available: http://www.ed.gov/parents/needs/speced/iepguide/index.html#Introduction.

U.S. Department of Education. (2004). *A guide to education and No Child Left Behind.* Available: http://www.ed.gov/nclb/overview/intro/guide/guide_pg20.html#disab.

Working With Parents Regarding Their Children's Mental Disorders

Engagement

Chris Ahlman

CHAPTER 15

Getting Started

This chapter is written for those school-based practitioners who truly wish to partner with families of students with mental disorders and other educational difficulties. To engage the families, several steps must be taken; otherwise, at best, the school will have little more than a signature on its forms; at worst, the family will be hostile or disengaged. Without specific efforts to engage the family, effective change will be diminished.

Research shows us that parents' participation in their child's social, emotional, and academic growth is important for academic achievement (Walberg & Lai, 1999; Wolfendale, 1999). Our problem as school-based practitioners is that we are mandated to work with parents (Goals 2000; IDEA; No Child Left Behind, 2001), but parents are not mandated, in the same way, to work with us. We have the burden of engaging parents in the educational process. Why is this task so overwhelming in many cases? This chapter will first look at the rationale for parents' participation, then the barriers affecting participation, and finally the process by which school-based practitioners can encourage positive relationships and outcomes when working with parents of children with mental health concerns.

Most professionals who work in the public school setting have mixed attitudes about the role that parents and families should play regarding their students' education (Adelman & Taylor, 2000). However, the trend since the 1990s has been to encourage and facilitate parent involvement (Turnbull & Turnbull, 2000). The frustration of many school-based professionals is that many parents and families seem to thwart the efforts of these professionals. Until recently there have been few studies that look at why this might be. Researchers (Jivanjee,

Friesen, Kruzich, Robinson, & Pullman, 2002) have searched the literature and found that there are a limited number of studies looking for barriers to participation. However, the existing studies are a start, and this new information, offered below in a "do's and don'ts" list, is used in this chapter to help school-based practitioners not only to understand what is impeding parent participation but also what can be done to overcome these barriers. The ecological perspective dictates that we consider our clients in their environment. When we realize that children in our schools spend the majority of their time out of school, we must take this experience into consideration when defining the problem and planning the interventions. We must gain the participation of parents and families if we are to help our students with mental disorders make the changes that will help them to interact more successfully with the home and school environments (Alexander & Dore, 1999). Mental health issues are family issues. If school-based practitioners want to affect student outcomes, they must first engage and then empower families of children with mental disorders.

What We Know

The surgeon general's report on children's mental health (1999) suggests that up to 20% of all children are affected with emotional disorders. Additionally, it is imperative that we understand that "almost one-third of American women and one-fifth of American men provide evidence of psychiatric disorder.

- Sixty-five percent of these women are mothers; 52% of the men are fathers.

- Women and men with mental illness are at least as likely, if not more likely, than those without psychiatric disorder to become parents.
- The majority of adults falling into the diagnostic categories captured by the NCS (affective disorders, anxiety disorders, PTSD, and psychotic disorders) are parents.
- Parents with mental illness may be quite vulnerable to losing custody of their children, with studies reporting rates as high as 70% to 80%.
- Parents with mental illness often feel responsible or blamed for their children's difficulties, which are more prevalent than in children whose parents are well.
- Parents with mental illness are more likely to be living without partners.
- Patterns of care giving and social support vary among ethnic and racial groups; family members may be viewed as a resource or as a source of stress.
- Rates of child psychiatric diagnosis among offspring range from 30% to 50%, compared with an estimated rate of 20% among the general child population." (Nicholson, Biebel, Hinden, Henry, & Stier, 2001, pp. 1–3)

With these data on the incidence of mental illness in children and families, it is professionally and ethically responsible to work with the family of children with mental disorders, not just the child. Whether the child is the only member with symptoms or there is more than one member, school-based practitioners must be familiar with (1) *DSM-IV-TR* diagnosis, (2) mental health services, (3) family systems, and (4) the school system (Jivanjee, 2004).

What We Can Do

Other chapters in this manual address mental health disorders and the school system. This chapter will address engaging family systems and will focus on empowerment as the main service to be provided. Elizabeth Dane (1990) offers us an excellent summary of various types of family systems. Her work is focused on families of children with disabilities, and her descriptions are useful in our work with families who have children with mental disorders. Before engaging the families of our students, we need to understand family types,

for example, "healthy, fragile, disorganized, blaming, or split," the families' expectations for their children, their stage in the grieving process, and the cultural and community influences on their ability to cope (Dane, 1990).

First, as in any therapeutic relationship, practitioners must examine their own attitudes, values, and beliefs that may interfere in the engaging process. Below is a list of behaviors and attitudes that should be addressed. This list was gleaned from parent statements and research observations from various projects (Gonzalez-DeHass & Willems, 2003; Jivanjee et al., 2002; Lamb-Parker, Piotrkowski, Baker, Kessler-Sklar, Clark, & Peay, 2001; Nock & Kazdin, 2001; Pivik, McComas, & Laflamme, 2002; Reglin, King, Losike-Sedimo, & Ketterer, 2003).

Do's and Don'ts List

The parents tell us:

- Don't assume I don't care because I do not participate.
- Do be sensitive to the stigma my family feels because of mental illness.
- Don't blame me for my child's condition.
- Don't believe you know what is best for our family.
- Don't assume you can judge my parenting style without understanding me and my culture, my background, my experiences.
- Do ask me my goals for my child's education. Don't assume your goals are the same as mine.
- Do advocate for our family with other education personnel.
- Don't use educational jargon.
- Do keep information about our family confidential.
- Do understand my child's mental health condition before talking with me.
- Do be able to intervene with our family as a whole.
- Do look for our strengths as well as our weaknesses.
- Don't give me a list of what I can do for the school unless you are willing to accept my list of what the school can do for me and my family.
- Do believe that I know my child better than the school does.
- Do accommodate my work schedule. I need to support my family.

- Do have an interpreter available if you do not speak my language.
- Do accommodate my young children if I need to bring them with me.
- Do ask for my involvement from the beginning of the problem.
- Do keep open communication about concerns as well as successes.
- Do understand that I may have mental health issues also.
- Don't infer that I may lose custody of my child/children.
- Do understand that home influences my child more than school does.
- Do facilitate opportunities for me to meet other parents with children who have similar problems.
- Do help me to find resources so that we can be empowered.

After carefully considering the above list, the practitioner is ready to start work with the family. The first task in engagement is keeping an empowerment, family-strengths perspective (Dupper, 2003). A step-by-step example with explanations and definitions will be presented later in the chapter. Following you will find a checklist to be used in your work with individual families.

Parent Engagement: Rationale and Explanation

Preparation

Before you attempt to contact the family of a student, you need to gather as much information as possible. Families do not want to tell their stories, especially about the mental disorder of one or more of the members, to several different professionals. They get the sense that no one listened to them the first or second time. They may develop the attitude that you will not listen either.

1. Review the referral problem. It is important to understand what issues are of concern to the school (student's behaviors, student's academic performance, student's interactions with peers, etc.). Without a grasp on these issues, it will be impossible to engage the family in addressing them.
2. Review what is known about the student (mental health diagnosis, educational implications, specific problems). Parents report concerns when the school-based practitioners and teachers have little understanding of their child's mental disorder. There are excellent sources of information on all disorders, and practitioners must educate themselves about the disorder displayed by the student in question, as well as any idiosyncratic behaviors particular to this student.
3. Review what is known about the student's family (custodial issues, past participation, family makeup, educational levels, language spoken at home, financial issues, mental health of other members). There are many sources of information about particular families available to practitioners. First, the permanent record and registration cards should be reviewed. These documents will tell you what schools the student has attended, what grades have been received, what attendance rates have been, who are the custodial parents, scores on group tests, parents' address and phone numbers, and usually information about their work schedules. You can find out if the student is eligible for free lunch. Some registration forms indicate the language spoken at home. Next, review the student's special education folder, if applicable. Interview teachers or other school personnel who have had contact with the family. Evaluate the information given to you by others, understanding their possible biases. It is important to understand if there is an established relationship between the school and the family and whether that relationship is positive or negative.

Contact the Family

If possible, the initial contact between the practitioner and the family should give the family enough space to engage at their own rate. Phone calls are best at accomplishing this. If this is not possible, the mail should be considered next, with a home visit as the last choice. Families need to be given the opportunity to present themselves as they choose. A knock on a door without warning may put the family on the defensive for fear of being judged.

1. Introduce yourself and your role. Your title may or may not be important to the family, but your role is. It tells them the nature of the relationship you are attempting to establish. Your initial role is that of liaison between school and home. It will change and grow depending on the

needs of the family and the needs of the school. Parents tell us they want to be convinced from the beginning that the relationship is mutual. The message that they have something to offer must be given up front. Even desperate, needy families do not want to be made to feel you are there to "save" them, instruct them, or "fix" them. Practitioners must have the attitude of mutuality from the first contact.

2. Ask the family (often the mother) to set a time and place for a meeting. Be as flexible as possible, especially for the first meeting. Indicate that all family members are welcome to attend the meeting, and their input is also welcomed. Let the family decide which members need to attend. As practitioners, we would like both parents in attendance, but until we have an established relationship with the family, we must let them make these decisions.

3. At this time, indicate that you are anxious to meet with them because they are the experts on the student, and you are looking forward to their ideas and suggestions. Then, ask if there are any immediate concerns that you might address. This is also the appropriate time to briefly discuss the information you gathered from your review of the family. You are checking for accuracy. This lets the family know that you have some idea of their situation and that you want your information to be a true representation of them. There is some information, such as financial issues and mental health issues of other family members, that the parent may not want to discuss in front of the children. Asking about these over the phone with one parent allows you the opportunity to get the information without embarrassing or upsetting the parents.

4. Meet with the student before the face-to-face meeting with the family. Spend this time getting the student to describe how things are different between home and school and how they are alike. Children receive most of their socialization in the home. Practitioners need to understand the culture, traditions, and typical family functioning to help the student make the best fit between him- or herself and the school culture.

In-Person Meeting With the Family

Allow all members to introduce themselves and their place in the family structure. Again, state your role (liaison).

1. Allow family members to relate their past experiences with the school. Help them focus in on issues related to the referral problem after they have shared their more-general experiences. Van Treuren (1993) suggests a variety of ways to initiate the first session. The practitioner can use a genogram and ask the family members to assist in designing it accurately. Another activity might have all family members draw pictures of their observations on how the family has been dealing with the presenting issue. Use reflecting and reframing to help them through this process.

2. Help the family members to list their strengths individually and as a family. Initially, you might have to use your immediate observations to help them start, for example, "You were all able to come today. Family must be important to you," or "Everyone is contributing to the discussion. You must have good communication in your family." The family members may correct some of your observations, but it will help them to understand how to identify strengths.

3. Allow them to share their goals for the student for the present and for the future. These goals need not be all educationally focused. It is important to learn what the family hopes for the student in and out of the family setting.

4. Ask them to share how these goals might be accomplished. Help them to list the barriers. Help them to list the necessary resources.

5. Finish the first meeting with a summary of what was discussed. This is the time to share the school's goals and focus on common ground. List those goals shared by both the family and the school.

Ongoing Interactions With the Family

Maintaining a relationship with a family is the second half of the engagement process. Parents tell us that they are often frustrated that there is little or no communication or interaction between the school and the family after the initial contact. They can feel betrayed because they exposed their family and its vulnerabilities to public scrutiny, but now, they do not know how information about them is being used. They can believe that they were "judged unworthy or incompetent" if they are not asked to continue to participate in their child's education. Because of some cultural and class issues, many families require ongoing invitations to participate. These families do not want to "bother" the school, or assume they are no longer needed or wanted, or that they have become too burdensome and the school is trying to ignore them if invitations are not periodically made to the family by the school. This task falls often to the school-based practitioner. The rationale for maintaining the engagement is ultimately empowerment. This is accomplished with the attitude that the practitioner is a resource to the family to help them take over the task of learning to cope with the child's mental disorder and to help the child gain academic success.

There are a variety of barriers and needs with which families may present.

- Generic needs include housing, transportation, employment, recreational activities, child care, health care, and respite from the 24-hour-a-day challenges of parenting.

Table 15.1 Summary of Research on Successful Parent Education, Participation, and Intervention Programs and Projects

Program/Project and Location	*Outcomes*
First Step to Success http://www.hamfish.org	Sustained changes in adaptive behaviors; aggressive behaviors; maladaptive behaviors; and time spent engaged in assignments
Strengthening Families Program http://www.strengtheningfamilies.org	Reduction in family conflict; improvement in family communication and organization
PeaceBuilders http://www.peacebuilders.com	Reduction in teachers' estimates of aggressive behavior, referrals to principals, playground aggression, suspensions, and fights
Project ACHIEVE http://www.stopandthinksocialskills.com	Academic improvements when parents trained; improvement in teachers' perceptions of school climate; decline in disciplinary actions
Effective Black Parenting (EBPP) http://www.tyc.state.tx.us	Reduction of parental rejection; improved family quality; improved child behaviors
Parents as Teachers http://www.patnc.org	Increase in parenting knowledge and child-rearing practices; saw school district as responsive; more involved in child's schooling
Families and Schools Together (FAST) http://www.wcer.wisc.edu/fast	Improved parent–child relationships, family functioning, parental school involvement, family networking, child attention span and self-esteem, decreased behavior problems
Seattle Social Developmental Project http://ojjdp.ncjrs.org	Lower levels of aggression, antisocial behaviors, self-destructive behaviors; less delinquency initiation; increases in family management practices, communication, and attachment to family; more attachment and commitment to school
Los Ninos Bien Educados http://www.ciccparenting.org.	Improved parent–child relationships; improved child behaviors
Adolescent Transitions Program http://www.strengtheningfamilies.org.	Effective in engaging students and parents; teaching skills; improved parent–teen relationships; reduced aggressive and delinquent behaviors

Source: Center for Mental Health in Schools at UCLA, 2004.

Table 15.2 Resources for School Social Workers Regarding Parent Participation and Parent Assessments

Organization/Resource/Location	What Is Offered
National Mental Health Information Center. http://www.mentalhealth.samhsa.gov	Web site links to specific organizations related to a number of conditions; on-line manuals, guidelines, and curriculum; many sites in Spanish
Center for Health and Health Care in the Schools. http://www.healthinschools.org	Press releases; many links to a variety of health and mental health issues; some in Spanish
Research & Training Center on Family Support and Children's Mental Health. http://www.rtc.pdx.edu	Publications, research reports, articles on wide variety of mental health issues; many links; good search engine at site
UCLA Center for Mental Health in Schools. http://smhp.psych.ucla.edu	Large number of publications, articles, and brochures for mental health workers and parents; many in Spanish; good search engine
National Institute of Mental Health. http://www.nimh.nih.gov	Specific information about a variety of *DSM-IV-TR* diagnoses; publications; links; good search engine
Federation of Families for Children's Mental Health. http://www.ffcmh.org	Family-run organization; helping children with mental health needs and their families achieve a better quality of life; leadership to develop and sustain a nationwide network; goal of focusing the passion and cultural diversity of its membership to be a potent force for changing how systems respond to children with mental health needs and their families
Report of the Surgeon General's Conference on Children's Mental Health. http://www.surgeongeneral.gov	To achieve the goals of the promotion of mental health in children and the treatment of mental disorders, the Surgeon General's National Action Agenda for Children's Mental Health sets forth its guiding principles
Books Dealing With Children's Mental Health Topics for Children, Adolescents, and Their Parents http://www.baltimorepsych.com/books	A resource for practitioners and parents to read books on specific mental health issues
Connect for Kids http://www.connectforkids.org	Helps adults to make their communities better places for families and children; site provides solutions-oriented coverage of critical issues for children and families
Children's Defense Funds http://www.childrensdefense.org	"Children's Mental Health Resource Kit" is a 42-page document with facts and information for the practitioner and community

(continued)

Table 15.2 (*Continued*)

Organization/Resource/Location	What Is Offered
National Technical Assistance Center for Children's Mental Health: Communities Can! http://gucchd.georgetown.edu	Supports communities' developing systems of care that recognize the central role of the family; identifies, recognizes, and studies communities that have made substantial progress toward establishing systems to serve and support children with or at risk for disabilities and their families.

Table 15.3 Parent Engagement Checklist

1. Preparation
   - ☐ Review referral problem
   - ☐ Review what is known about the student
   - ☐ Review what is known about the student's family
2. Contact the family
   - ☐ Introduce self and role
   - ☐ Set time and place
   - ☐ Engage as experts, identify immediate concerns, check accuracy of data
   - ☐ Meet with student
3. In-person meeting with family
   - ☐ Past experiences of family with educational system
   - ☐ Family goals for student
   - ☐ Plan for goal accomplishment
     - ☐ Barriers
     - ☐ Needed resources
   - ☐ Summarize discussion
     - ☐ List goals shared by school and family
4. Ongoing interactions with family
   - ☐ Communication
   - ☐ Problem-solving activities

- Illness-related needs include the financial and emotional resources necessary to manage symptoms, obtain services, implement treatment regimes, and maintain relationships with helping professionals.
- The stigma accompanying mental illness is a pervasive factor affecting parents' access to and participation in services.
- Services tend to be problem-focused and deficit-based rather than preventive or strength-based.
- Funding streams and program eligibility requirements may limit participation to eligible adults or children, but not both.
- Services are not integrated or coordinated across or within systems. (Nicholson, Biebel, Hinden, Henry, & Stier, 2001, p. 3)

The practitioner needs to look to the school and community to suggest resources that will meet family needs. The practitioner's role has now become that of advocate, educator, and networker with the goal of family empowerment.

Tools and Practice Examples

For some established programs and projects that could be models for their interventions, the practitioner should review Table 15.1. It notes the outcomes and gives a Web site address to access more information. Use of the data gathered from these programs and projects will assist practitioners to gain an understanding of the issues that affect engagement with parents. Use of Web sites to inform practice is a fairly new concept that aids practitioners in updating and improving their services.

Table 15.2 provides practitioners and the families they serve with resources for more information about mental health disorders and interventions. It also offers resources for developing more schoolwide parent-participation programs.

Finally, Table 15.3 can be used as a checklist for the step-by-step process of engagement.

Key Points to Remember

In summary, data show that approximately 20% of the children in school have an emotional disorder. A high percentage of their families have parents or siblings who also have mental disorders. Practitioners need to work with families, as a whole. This too is research based. In order to work with these families, practitioners need to be current with research that informs practice and need to use established practices of engagement and empowerment.

References

Adelman, H., & Taylor, L. (2000). Shaping the future of mental health in schools. *Psychology in the Schools, 37,* 49–60.

Alexander, B., & Dore, M. (1999). Making the parents as partners principle a reality: The role of the alliance. *Journal of Child and Family Studies, 8*(3), 255–270.

Center for Mental Health in Schools at UCLA. (2004). *An introductory packet on parent and home involvement in schools.* Los Angeles, CA: Author.

Dane, E. (1990). *Painful passages: Working with children with learning disabilities.* Silver Springs, MD: NASW Press.

Dupper, D. (2003). *School social work: Skills & interventions for effective practice.* Hoboken, NJ: Wiley.

Goals 2000: Educate America Act of 1994, Title III, Sec. 302.

Gonzalez-DeHass, A., & Willems, P. (2003). Examining the underutilization of parent involvement in the schools. *School Community Journal, 13*(1), 85–99.

Individual With Disabilities Education Act of 1997, 20 USC §1401–1491.

Jivanjee, P. (2004). Using the parents as partners principle with SED children. In *Data trends: Summaries of research on mental health services for children and adolescents and their families.* Portland, OR: Research and Training Center for Family Support and Children's Mental Health.

Jivanjee, P., Friesen, B., Kruzich, J., Robinson, A., & Pullman, M. (2002). Family participation in systems of care: Frequently asked questions (and some answers). *CWTAC Updates: Series on Family and Professional Partnerships, 5*(1), 1–8.

Lamb-Parker, F., Piotrkowski, C., Baker, A., Kessler-Sklar, S., Clark, B., & Peay, L. (2001). Understanding barriers to parent involvement in Head Start: A research-community partnership. *Early Childhood Research Quarterly, 16*(1), 35–51.

Mental Health: A Report of the Surgeon General. (1999). Available: http://www.surgeongeneral.gov.

Nicholson, J., Biebel, K., Hinden, B., Henry, A., & Stier, L. (2001). *Critical issues for parents with mental illness and their families.* Boston: Center for Mental Health Services Research.

No Child Left Behind Act of 2001, PL. 107–110.

Nock, M., & Kazdin, A. (2001). Parent expectancies for child therapy: Assessment and relation to participation in treatment. *Journal of Child & Family Studies, 10*(2), 155–181.

Pivik, J., McComas, J., & Laflamme, M. (2002). Barriers and facilitators to inclusive education. *Exceptional Child, 69*(1), 97–108.

Reglin, G., King, S., Losike-Sedimo, N., & Ketterer, A. (2003). Barriers to school involvement and strategies to enhance involvement from parents at low-performing urban schools. *Journal of At-Risk Issues, 9*(2), 1–7.

Turnbull, H. R., & Turnbull, A. (2000). *Free appropriate public education: The law & children with disabilities.* Denver, CO: Love Publishing.

Van Treuren, R. (1993). Self perception in family systems: A diagrammical technique. In J. Rauch (Ed.), *Assessment: A sourcebook for social work practice.* Milwaukee, WI: Families International.

Walberg, H., & Lai, J. (1999). Meta-analytic effects for policy. In G. J. Cizek (Ed.), *Handbook of educational policy* (pp. 418–454). San Diego, CA: Academic.

Effective Interventions and Resources for Working With Students With Developmental Disabilities

A function of social workers and other mental health professionals in many school districts is providing or facilitating services for children and youth with developmental disabilities. In particular, school-based professionals are called upon to aid in the management of challenging behaviors with this population and need expertise in how to facilitate learning and behavior change. Many social workers and mental health counselors can benefit from more training in areas related to developmental disability. They need assistance in the knowledge of effective interventions in this burgeoning area of concern. Section II provides essential guidance for working with the three most common categories of disability: mental retardation, learning disabilities, and physical disabilities. The section provides chapters that guide practitioners on effective inclusion practices and direction on facilitating health care resources for students and schools.

Working With Students With Mental Retardation Who Exhibit Severe Challenging Behavior

Mark O'Reilly ▪ Vanessa Green ▪ Jeff Sigafoos ▪ Giulio Lancioni
Bonnie O'Reilly ▪ Helen Cannella ▪ Chaturi Edrisinha

CHAPTER 16

Getting Started

Approximately 5% of the school-age population suffers from mental retardation. Mental retardation, a form of disability, is characterized by significantly sub-average functioning both intellectually and in terms of adaptive (or everyday life skills) behavior (Drew & Hardman, 2004). The causes of mental retardation vary and include genetic and chromosomal anomalies and injuries or accidents during the developmental period. These students typically require special education support that usually occurs along a continuum of educational placement from the special education classroom to inclusion in a general education classroom with ongoing consultation from a special education teacher. In addition to difficulties in intellectual and adaptive functioning, as many as 20% of these students exhibit challenging behavior (Sigafoos, Arthur, & O'Reilly, 2003). Challenging behavior is behavior of such intensity or frequency that the safety of the student or fellow students is placed in jeopardy. Challenging behavior can take the form of aggressive outbursts (hitting, screaming, kicking), property destruction (breaking school property and instructional materials), and self-abuse (self-hitting, self-biting). Such behaviors are consistently ranked as one of the biggest problems facing the public schools in the United States (Rose & Gallop, 2003).

What We Know

A significant amount of empirical research has been conducted, and the clinical protocol for assessing and treating challenging behavior with this population of students is well established. For comprehensive reviews of the empirical literature on the assessment and treatment of aggression and self-abuse with this population, please study the following: Iwata et al. (1994), Kahng and Iwata (2002), and Matson, Dixon, & Matson (2005). In this chapter we will present the core set of clinical assessment and treatment protocol to be used when a child with such disabilities is referred within the school system. For a comprehensive yet accessible manual on how to assess and treat such behaviors, please see Carr, Levin, McConnachie, Carlson, Kemp, and Smith (1998).

What We Can Do

A Model for Understanding Challenging Behavior

The assessment and treatment protocol outlined below are premised on a particular understanding of the nature of challenging behavior exhibited by individuals with mental retardation. We believe that challenging behavior is best understood by a comprehensive examination of the context in which it occurs. We are not as much interested in "what" the child does but rather "why" the child is doing it. By understanding the context in which such behavior occurs, we may begin to understand why the child engages in challenging behavior. This model is presented in schematic form in Figure 16.1. We will briefly describe each component of the model here and further elucidate these components as we proceed through the chapter.

Setting events are bio-behavioral or social/ecological events or conditions that predispose the student to challenging behavior. For example, certain diagnoses may be associated with high levels of challenging behavior under particular contexts. Children with autism, for example, can exhibit extreme levels of aggression and self-injury when there is a change in everyday routines. Chapter 12 suggests appropriate interventions for working with children with the diagnosis of autism. Routine illnesses among children, such as inner ear infections, can also be associated with increased levels of challenging behavior. Social/ecological conditions describe the influence of environmental factors (e.g., overcrowded classroom, negative social interactions with peers or staff) that can exacerbate challenging behavior. Setting events in themselves do not cause challenging behavior, but they may predispose the student to be grumpy at a given point in time.

Antecedent conditions are those interactions that spark the challenging behavior. Examples of antecedent conditions might be the presentation of a difficult academic task by the teacher or low levels of teacher attention. Antecedent conditions are those interactions that happen immediately prior to the challenging behavior. Antecedent conditions are more likely to evoke challenging behavior for the student if setting events have occurred prior.

Challenging behaviors typically produce some predictable reaction by others such as caregivers, teachers, and fellow students. Some of the typical reactions include removal of instructional materials, removal from a current environment, attention from others in the form of reprimands, restraint, or concerned statements. These social consequences for challenging behavior can be collapsed into two major categories—behaviors that produce escape from situations or people and behaviors that produce attention from others. Researchers have demonstrated that students often use challenging behavior as a form of communication to escape from situations or to access attention from others.

Figure 16.1. A Model for Understanding Challenging Behavior

Assessment of Challenging Behavior

A thorough assessment of challenging behavior is necessary prior to putting any interventions in place. In fact the assessment results will dictate the nature of the intervention. In this section we will go through the essential protocols for assessing challenging behavior. These assessment protocols are derived from our model of understanding challenging behavior that was presented in the previous section. There are four essential steps to assessment: identify the challenging behavior, identify when the behavior occurs during the school day, identify any setting events for the challenging behavior, and identify what occurs in the school environment when the student engages in challenging behavior.

Step 1: Identify the Challenging Behavior

At face value this may seem a very easy task. However, challenging behavior is typically described in emotive terms and as personality traits (e.g., "She likes to hurt other students. He is a very stubborn child. He is aggressive"). These initial descriptions are ultimately unhelpful to the assessment process. In our example, the teacher reports that Manuel seems to get upset in class and abuses himself. Such descriptions must be translated into observable behaviors that the teacher perceives to be challenging. You can lead this discussion with the teacher by asking such questions as: "When you say he is abusive (aggressive), can you tell me what he does?" or "What does she do to hurt herself (other children)?" In other words, you must translate the initial descriptions of the student's difficulties into a description of observable behaviors.

This is an essential step in the assessment process for several reasons. First, it clarifies to all stakeholders (that is, the social worker, teacher, parent) the precise nature of the behavior to be changed. If stakeholders disagree with the focus of treatment, then new target behaviors may be selected and unnecessary interventions may be forestalled. Second, it allows for ongoing evaluation of challenging behavior during the intervention process. If desired change is not occurring, then the intervention can be altered.

There are three general guidelines for developing a clear description of challenging behavior.

1. The description should be objective, referring only to observable characteristics of the behavior and translating any inferential terms into more objective ones.
2. The description should be clear and unambiguous so that others could read the description and observe the behavior accurately.
3. The description should be complete, delineating the boundaries of what is to be included as an instance of challenging behavior and what is to be excluded.

An example of a clear description of challenging behavior arising from the statement "This student is aggressive" might be "Striking other students in a forceful manner with an open hand or closed fist, but excluding touching students with tips of fingers or with an open hand in a gentle manner." This description identifies challenging behaviors in objective terms and delineates examples of behavior to be included and excluded. Consider the following descriptions adapted from Iwata et al. (1994, p. 219), which provide clear descriptions of challenging behaviors:

- Head banging: Audible or forceful contact of the head against a stationary object.
- Biting: Closure of upper and lower teeth on any part of the body.
- Scratching: Raking the skin with fingernails or rubbing against objects.
- Pinching: Forceful grasping of skin between fingers.
- Hair pulling: Closure of fingers on hair with a pulling motion.

For our case study we defined Manuel's self-abuse as "hitting his head with a closed fist." We have moved from the global term *self-abuse* to very specific and observable behavior. Once there is agreement between all stakeholders on a description of the student's challenging behavior the next step is to begin to measure the behavior.

Step 2: Identify When the Behavior Occurs During the School Day

In this phase of the assessment process, we want to identify the times during the day when the behavior occurs. Equally important, we want to identify those times of day when the behavior does not occur, as this may provide clues for developing effective interventions. The scatterplot assessment method is probably the easiest method to use for this purpose. We find that teachers have little difficulty using this instrument with minimal instruction from a consultant. This assessment instrument provides information regarding the temporal distribution of the challenging behavior throughout the school day. Once we identify those time periods when the behavior occurs, we can then use more detailed assessment instruments to clarify the antecedents and consequences maintaining challenging behavior during those time periods (see steps 3 and 4 below).

The first step in conducting a scatterplot is to design a grid with time periods on the vertical axis and days on the horizontal axis. See Figure 16.2 for an example of a scatterplot grid. The time intervals used should suit the context. For example, you can design the intervals around a structured curriculum with each interval representing a new lesson or new activity as shown in Figure 16.2. You could also break the day into specific time segments (e.g., 15 min, 30 min, etc.) according to the exigencies of the situation. You can see from the example in Figure 16.2 that the school day (total of 3 hours) is broken into nine segments. Each of these segments represents a distinct curricular activity, and each activity lasts for 20 min. Next a decision needs to be made with regard to how to record the challenging behavior. The scatterplot technique does not require that

you record the exact frequency of occurrence of challenging behavior during each time interval. Instead, a more general recording procedure can be used. In Figure 16.2 we have decided to leave the interval empty when no behavior occurs, to place a "\" when one instance of the behavior occurs, and to shade the interval in black if more than one instance of the challenging behavior occurs during that time interval.

You can see from the results of the scatterplot in the figure that Manuel's challenging behavior seems to display a particular pattern. He tends to hit his head when he is engaged in demand or academic-type tasks. Also, his behavior seems to be a lot more severe on Monday and Wednesday during our assessment. Thus the teacher will focus further assessments of Manuel's behavior during those academic periods of the curriculum when Manuel's behavior is most problematic. We will also want to explore why his behavior is more severe on some days than on others.

Step 3: Identify Any Setting Events for the Challenging Behavior

As described earlier in our model for understanding challenging behavior, setting events are

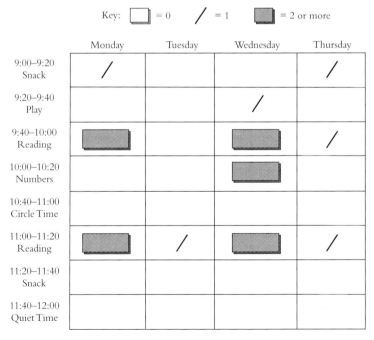

Figure 16.2. Student: Manuel. Challenging Behavior: Hitting His Head With a Closed Fist

environmental or health conditions that influence the probability or intensity of challenging behavior. Setting events can be idiosyncratic. If the results of a scatterplot assessment demonstrate large variability in challenging behavior within or across days, then it is very important to explore the influence of setting events. In our case example we saw that Manuel engaged in a lot of challenging behavior on some days but not on others. It is best to interview parents and the teacher with regard to the influence of setting events. Using the scatterplot as a springboard for such interviews can be helpful. There is no single interview format available that can tap all possible setting events. We recommend that you explore the influence of the following possibilities: prior negative social interactions, rushed through routines, changes in routines, significant others absent, major changes in living environment, changes in medication, bad mood, illness, and so on. We interviewed Manuel's mother and teacher with regard to setting events. We found that Manuel did not sleep very well on Sunday or Tuesday nights. The severe levels of challenging behavior on Monday and Wednesday might be related to the possibility that Manuel was sleep deprived on those days. Of course sleep deprivation does not explain why he engages in challenging behavior at certain periods of time during the day and not at others. To examine this issue we need to conduct our final step of the assessment process.

Step 4: Identify What Occurs in the School Environment When the Student Engages in the Challenging Behavior

During this phase of the assessment we focus on those periods of time during the day when challenging behavior is most likely. An Antecedent-Behavior-Consequence (ABC) assessment is used to identify what happened immediately before and after each occurrence of challenging behavior. We recommend that an ABC assessment be conducted for approximately 5 school days. A consultant and not the teacher should conduct this assessment, as it is not possible for a teacher to continue with normal duties and accurately implement the ABC. ABC results should provide a reasonably comprehensive picture of the immediate environmental conditions influencing challenging behavior. Essentially, the ABC assessment is designed to examine those immediate antecedent conditions that spark or evoke the challenging

behavior as well as those consequences that follow the behavior. As mentioned in our model for understanding challenging behavior, children with mental retardation typically engage in challenging behavior for two major consequences—escape a situation or gain attention from another person. So in this phase of the assessment we are trying to identify the antecedent conditions for the challenging behavior and the consequences that occur in the environment when challenging behavior occurs.

To implement an ABC assessment the consultant continuously observes the student during those time periods when challenging behavior is most problematic (these time periods have been identified by the scatterplot assessment). In our example, the consultant will observe Manuel from 9:40 a.m. to 10:20 a.m. and from 11:00 a.m. to 11:20 a.m. for five consecutive days. The consultant will use a data collection sheet similar to the one presented in Figure 16.3. The target behavior, identified in Step 1 of the assessment, is presented in the middle column. Each time the target behavior occurs, a check mark is placed in the target behavior box. The consultant then describes what happened immediately prior to the behavior. In the final column the consultant describes what people did in response to the student's behavior. Three incidents of the target behavior are included in Figure 16.3. You can see from this example that the level of detail requires significant effort on the part of those conducting the assessment. This is why we suggest that a consultant with expertise in conducting such assessments is recruited for this task. We can see from our example that Manuel engaged in head hitting immediately following an instruction from the teacher. When Manuel hits his head, the teacher withdraws the task. We can infer from the results of this assessment that Manuel's challenging behavior is motivated by escape from instructional activities. The results of our setting event assessment would indicate that when he is tired he is more likely to find instructional activities aversive and he therefore engages in more severe challenging behavior when sleep deprived. We will discuss strategies that the teacher can use to decrease such behavior in the next section.

Of course not all assessments produce such clear results as the example that we have presented here in this chapter. Sometimes it can be difficult to interpret the results of these assessments. Unclear results can occur when the student's behavior is motivated by many consequences such as

Figure 16.3.   Child: Manuel. Date and Time of Observation: April 4, 2004, 9:20–11:20

What Happened Before the Behavior	Target Behavior	What Happened After the Behavior
Teacher says: "What word is this Manuel?"	✔	Teacher moves away and asks another student
Teacher points to a letter and asks, "What letter is this Manuel?"	✔	Teachers moves on to a different topic with the class
Teacher asks Manuel to open his book	✔	Teacher does not persist but moves on to another student

escape and attention or when some unknown factor is influencing the child's behavior. In such cases a more intensive functional analysis may need to be conducted. A functional analysis would require a consultation with a professional who has expertise in behavior analysis. The process of conducting a functional analysis is beyond the scope of this chapter (see Sigafoos, Arthur, & O'Reilly, 2003, for a description of how to conduct a functional analysis).

Interventions Based on the Results of the Assessment

The specific intervention selected for a student will be derived from the results of the assessment process outlined in the previous section. Interventions can be highly idiosyncratic depending on the specific setting events that exacerbate challenging behavior, the antecedent conditions that spark such behavior, and the consequences that are produced as a result of this behavior. Other factors are also important to consider, such as student–teacher ratios, level of knowledge of the teacher, and motivation of teaching staff. In this section we will describe general guidelines for intervention selection. These guidelines are inextricably linked to the results of the prior assessment. We will discuss interventions for setting events and attention-motivated and escape-motivated challenging behavior.

Arranging positive consequences for appropriate behavior and eliminating positive consequences for challenging behavior is an important part of any intervention. In addition, other types of corrective consequences may also be necessary. Negative feedback can help the

student to learn what is right and what is wrong. In selecting consequences, it is important to consider the use of natural consequences that provide feedback without special intervention. For example, when a child rips up his coloring book, the natural consequence is that he no longer has a coloring book to use. Similarly, when a child spills her juice on the floor, the natural consequence is that she no longer has any juice to drink.

Interventions for Setting Events

As described in our model for understanding challenging behavior, setting events can be divided into two generic categories—social/ecological and bio-behavioral. Social/ecological conditions can include environmental conditions (e.g., cold classroom, cramped environment, low academic stimulation) or interactions with individuals (e.g., disliked teacher's aide, being bullied). It may be possible to remove or reduce such conditions. For example, the curriculum might be made more stimulating, a more pleasant classroom setting might be arranged, and interactions between the student with challenging behavior and a disliked aide might be minimized. In some circumstances, even when the ecological/social setting event is identified it cannot be eliminated. For example, the student may not like the teacher, but we cannot change the teacher. In such circumstances it may be necessary to focus on alternative strategies, such as teaching communication skills and enriching the current environment to manage challenging behavior.

The second broad category, bio-behavioral setting events, can be subdivided into two conditions:

a permanent or temporary influence. An example of a permanent condition would be the medical and behavioral predispositions that accompany various genetic syndromes. For example, students with Williams syndrome often display hypersensitivity to everyday sounds such as those from a vacuum cleaner or lawnmower. This sensitivity can produce aggressive behavior. Students with Prader-Willi syndrome have difficulty controlling their eating patterns and may engage in aggression when denied access to food. The impact of such genetic predispositions can be minimized by altering environmental arrangements or by direct medical monitoring and intervention.

Other bio-behavioral setting events may be temporary in nature. Conditions such as allergies, ear infections, and sleep disturbance are more common among children with mental retardation than the typical population. Such conditions may predispose students to engage in challenging behavior. These temporary bio-behavioral conditions can be treated directly (through medical/psychological intervention). Additionally, when such conditions are present, it may be advisable to eliminate or at least reduce those immediate antecedents that spark the challenging behavior during the school day. In our case example we saw that sleep disturbance might be influencing Manuel's challenging behavior. A number of strategies might be suggested in this case. A consultation may be suggested for the home to examine his bedtime routine and make suggestions to facilitate better sleep patterns. Following a night of disturbed sleep the curriculum could be modified so that Manuel is exposed to fewer academic requests on those particular days.

Interventions for Attention-Motivated Challenging Behavior

In our model for understanding challenging behavior we noted that many challenging behaviors result in or gain attention from others. That is, the consequence that maintains behavior is attention. Challenging behaviors may emerge as a means of getting attention if the person's repertoire contains few alternative responses that are effective in recruiting attention. In some situations the student's behavior may occur to gain access to items (e.g., toys, food, etc.). The intervention strategies described below would be similar for behavior that is maintained by tangible items as well as attention. We recommend that teachers use all of these techniques in combination when dealing with attention-maintained challenging behavior.

When attention is the maintaining consequence for challenging behavior one way to decrease the behavior is to *increase the overall amount of attention* that the student receives. For example, the teacher could set a kitchen timer at varying intervals of time (e.g., 30 s, 60 s) and when the timer goes off the student receives 10–20 s of positive attention. As the student starts to receive more attention than usual there is likely to be less need for that person to engage in attention-motivated challenging behavior. A variation of this strategy is to *provide attention to the student when challenging behavior is absent*. As the student learns that attention is received without having to resort to challenging behavior, then this behavior is less likely to occur. Along with attention for appropriate behavior, the teacher should *ignore challenging behavior as much as possible*. If the behavior must be attended to, then it should be done as matter-of-factly as possible. If the student has limited communication skills, then it is important to *teach more appropriate ways of gaining attention*. For example, the student might be taught to seek attention ("Will you sit with me?") so that others will come and spend time with them.

Interventions for Escape-Motivated Challenging Behavior

There are a number of interventions for escape-motivated challenging behavior. Teachers may want to use several of these strategies in combination when working with students who exhibit escape-maintained challenging behavior. If challenging behavior is reinforced by escape from nonpreferred activities, then the intervention plan should include some form of *reinforcement for increasing levels of participation*. Potential reinforcers might include praise (e.g., "Good job!"), access to preferred objects, and being allowed to take a break from task. In our example, the teacher could allow Manuel a break from instruction for 1 minute to play with a favorite toy after he correctly follows a direction. Over several weeks Manuel will be required to participate for longer periods of time before receiving a break. In this way the teacher can eventually increase participation and reduce challenging behavior. Another strategy is to *make sure that challenging behavior no longer produces escape from the task*. The teacher must be prepared to persist with instruction even if the challenging behavior escalates. In our example, when Manuel hits his head in response to a teacher direction, then the teacher must follow through with the task until Manuel completes it. In some cases challenging behavior occurs during demands because the demands are too difficult for the student to complete. In such cases *the task should be made easier by breaking it into smaller and more manageable steps or by teaching the student to request help in completing the task*. In our example, when the teacher makes an academic request of Manuel, she could immediately prompt him to ask for help. The teacher could then help Manuel to complete the task and gradually fade this assistance over time. In other cases the task presented may be less preferred than some other activities that may be available. In such a situation the teacher might *eliminate the unpreferred tasks (if possible) and introduce more preferred tasks for instruction*. Likewise, the teacher might also consider *reducing the amount of time spent on unpreferred tasks*. Manuel's teacher might consider reducing reading periods from 20 min to 10 min.

Tools and Practice Examples

For a case study, see the above discussion of how to intervene with Manuel, a 6-year-old boy with a diagnosis of Down syndrome and severe mental retardation. He attends a regular elementary school in a large urban area. In the mornings Manuel is included in the regular kindergarten class. He is the only student with a diagnosis of mental retardation in this class of 20. Overall, he seems to be adapting well to the general education setting. However, his general education teacher reports that he has begun to engage in self-abuse in class. The teacher notes that Manuel's self-abuse is beginning to upset many of the other students. The teacher has requested help in dealing with Manuel's self-abuse during class. Steps are detailed on how to help Manual in the classroom setting.

Key Points to Remember

Approximately 5% of the student population is diagnosed with mental retardation. Of this group,

some 20% exhibit severe challenging behavior, such as self-abuse and aggression. Such behaviors typically require clinical assessment and intervention. We presented an empirically validated model of assessment and treatment of challenging behavior for students with mental retardation. First, the behavior must be carefully defined in observable behavioral terms. Then the periods of time during the school day in which this behavior occurs are plotted. Next, bio-behavioral and ecological/social setting events are identified that may account for fluctuations in intensity or frequency of the behavior. The final part of thorough assessment is to identify the consequences that occur following the challenging behavior. Interventions, then, are multicomponent and are linked to the assessment results. Interventions typically involve some manipulation of setting events, modifications to the curriculum, and changes in how the teacher interacts with the student prior to and following challenging behavior.

References

Carr, E., Levin, L., McConnachie, G., Carlson, J., Kemp, D., & Smith, C. (1998). *Communication-based intervention for problem behavior: A user's guide for producing positive change*. Baltimore: Paul H. Brookes Publishing Company.

Drew, C., & Hardman, M. (2004). *Mental retardation: A lifespan approach to people with intellectual disabilities*. Columbus, OH: Pearson, Merrill, Prentice Hall.

Iwata, B., Pace, G., Dorsey, M., Zarcone, J., Vollmer, T., Smith, R., Rodgers, T., Lerman, D., Shore, B., Mazaleski, J., Goh, H., Cowdery, G., Kalsher, M., McCosh, K., & Willis, K. (1994). The functions of self-injurious behavior: An experimental-epidemiological analysis. *Journal of Applied Behavior Analysis, 27,* 215–240.

Kahng, S., & Iwata, B. (2002). Behavioral treatment of self-injury, 1964 to 2000. *American Journal on Mental Retardation, 107,* 212–221.

Matson, J., Dixon, D., & Matson, M. (2005). Assessing and treating aggression in children and adolescents with developmental disabilities: A 20-year overview. *Educational Psychology, 25,* 151–181.

Rose, L., & Gallop, A. (2003). *The 35th annual Phi Delta Kappa/Gallup poll of the public's attitudes toward the public schools*.

Sigafoos, J., Arthur, M., & O'Reilly, M. F. (2003). *Challenging behavior and developmental disability*. London: Whurr Publishers.

Improving Educational and Behavioral Performance of Students With Learning Disabilities

James C. Raines

Getting Started

Until the Education for All Handicapped Children's Act of 1975 (P.L. 94–142), students with learning disabilities were routinely unidentified (treated as "slow learners") or misidentified (treated as "mentally retarded"). Every mental health professional should be familiar with the federal definition of the term, which still relies on the conceptualization of Samuel Kirk (1962). "Specific learning disability" means:

> a disorder in one or more of the basic psychological processes involved in understanding or in using language, spoken or written, that may manifest itself in an imperfect ability to listen, think, speak, read, write, spell, or to do mathematical calculations, including conditions such as perceptual handicaps, brain injury, minimal brain dysfunction, dyslexia, and developmental aphasia. . . . The term does not include children who have learning problems that are primarily the result of visual, hearing, or motor handicaps, or mental retardation, or emotional disturbance, or of environmental, cultural, or economic disadvantage. (Assistance to the States, 1999, 34 C.F.R. §300.7(b)(10))

Thus, students with learning disabilities (LD) are a very heterogeneous group (Kavale & Forness, 1995). Since the passage of P.L. 94–142, reauthorized as the Individuals with Disabilities Education Act (IDEA) in 1990, the number of youth found to have learning disabilities has grown from 800,000 students in 1976–1977 to nearly 2.9 million students in 2000–2001. This figure accounts for 50% of all students receiving special education services and is the most common disability across all racial/ethnic groups. Students with learning disabilities have a high school graduation rate of 62.1% compared to 88% for their nondisabled peers (U.S. Dept. of Education, 2002). Furthermore, children do not simply "grow out of" learning disabilities. Their problems continue into adulthood and affect their ability to adapt and achieve in the workplace (Gerber, 2001).

The two primary mental health concerns about students with learning disabilities have been in the related areas of self-concept and social skills. Self-concept is a multidimensional construct that includes a person's perception of him/herself across several categories: academic, emotional, physical, social, and global (Harter, 1999). Social skills are a heterogeneous set of competencies that include initiating, maintaining, repairing, and ending a variety of social relationships. Regardless of the mental health problem faced by a person with learning disabilities, practitioners will want to determine how this student learns best and adapt their interventions accordingly. This chapter will first review the research support for interventions in these two areas, focusing first on general principles and secondly on specific interventions.

What We Know

Research Support for Interventions

The literature on learning disabilities/differences has also grown exponentially. PsycINFO lists over 19,000 articles, Medline lists over 8,000 entries, ERIC lists over 14,000 resources and Social Work Abstracts contains over 100 references. Thus, even a conservative estimate would put the combined total at over 30,000 articles.

Fortunately, there have been 75 meta-analyses that have systematically collected, culled, and compared the vast literature to date. Not all meta-analyses have the same methodological rigor, and readers are encouraged to see Swanson's (1996) list of criteria for evaluating syntheses of the research literature. This review will summarize the most pertinent meta-analyses and infer some general principles from them (see Table 17.1).

Table 17.1 Meta-Analyses Regarding Self-Concept or Social Skills of Students With LD

Study	Problem	Sample	Results
Bear, Minke, & Manning (2002)	Self-concepts	61 studies 1986–2000	Students with LD exhibit slightly lower global self-esteem (ES = −.18) than non-LD students and moderately lower intellectual self-esteem (ES = −.66). LD students in inclusive classrooms and resource rooms have lower intellectual self-esteem than LD students in self-contained classrooms.
Elbaum (2002)	Self-concepts across placements	38 studies 1975–1999	There were no significant differences in self-concepts across placements, except that students in self-contained classrooms had moderately lower self-concepts than those in special schools (ES = −.38).
Elbaum & Vaughn (2003)	Self-concept interventions	15 studies 1975–1997	Students w/LD have wide variations in their general self-concept. Students with the lowest self-concept at pretest improved three times as much as their average or high self-concept peers. Young adolescents were more responsive to interventions than either children or older adolescents.
Elbaum & Vaughn (2001)	Self-concept of interventions	64 studies 1975–1997	Average effects were low (ES = .19) across all age groups. Median intervention lasted 10 weeks. Elementary students benefited most from academic interventions. Middle and high school students benefited most from counseling interventions. Collateral interventions made the only impact on students' social self-concept.
Forness & Kavale (1996)	Social skills interventions	53 studies 1980–1994	Average effects were low (ES = .21) across all age groups. Average intervention was 3 hours/week over 10 weeks. Longer training was not better than brief training. Training improved self-assessment of social status, peers' assessment of communication skills, and teachers' assessment of school adjustment.
Kavale & Forness (1996)	Social skills deficits	152 studies (1980–1994)	Students w/LD demonstrate more social skills deficits (ES = .65) than their non-LD peers. Students with LD rate themselves slightly lower than peers or teachers. Teachers rated students w/LD lowest on academic competence and social interaction. Peers rated students with LD

(continued)

Table 17.1 (*Continued*)

Study	Problem	Sample	Results
			lowest on acceptance. Self-ratings showed lower academic competence, nonverbal communication ability, and social problem solving.
Ochoa & Olivarez (1995)	Peer ratings	17 studies 1978–1991	Students w/LD have much lower social status than non-LD peers (ES=−.69). Opposite-sex raters were more accepting than same-sex raters.
Nowicki (2003)	Social competence	32 studies 1990–2000	Students w/LD or low academic achievement are at greater risk for social difficulties than average or high-achieving peers. Students w/LD or low academic achievement lack accurate self-perceptions of their social acceptance.
Prout, Marcal, & Marcal (1992)	Self-reported problems	34 studies 1966–1990	Students w/LD have moderately lower self-esteem than non-LD peers (ES=.68), more anxiety (ES=.59), and more academic concerns (ES=.71).
Swanson (2001)	Academic interventions for adolescents	58 studies 1963–1997	Adolescents benefit from higher order processing interventions (ES=.82) such as extended practice with feedback, learning new skills, and advance organization of the material. High-discrepancy learners improved less than low-discrepancy learners. Ideas about self-efficacy, effort, and ability were hardest to change.
Swanson & Hoskyn (1998)	Academic interventions	180 studies 1963–1997	Students w/LD generally benefit from intervention (ES=.79). A combined model that uses direct instruction with strategic instruction worked best. Components that helped most included strategy modeling, skill demonstration, and use of small-group instruction. Effects on students' self-concept (ES=.39) and social skills (ES=.41) were low.
Swanson & Malone (1992)	Social skills deficits	117 studies 1974–1990	Students w/LD have lower social acceptance (ES=−.79) and social problem solving (ES=−.80) than their non-LD peers. White students are at higher risk for social rejection than Black students. Students with LD had more problems with nonverbal sensitivity, friendship formation, and conflict resolution.

General Principles

- Learning disabilities place children at greater risk for self-esteem and social skills deficits, but these are not universal problems, so screening is important.
- Different informants see different aspects of the problem, so it is important to triangulate both baseline and outcome measures by collecting data from teachers, parents, peers, and/or students with LD.
- There is no single cause for self-concept or social skills problems seen in students with LD. Clinicians should assess each student's dynamics individually.
- Students with LD may be more aware of social skills deficits than self-esteem problems. They may be oblivious about their "social self."

- Students who compare themselves with average or high-achieving peers may be at special risk for self-esteem issues.
- There appear to be different cultural meanings about the "LD" label, thus terms like "LD" and "special ed" should be explored with each family.
- Social skills training may improve students' self-concepts more than their social competence as rated by others in the environment.
- Elementary students' self-esteem will benefit most from academic interventions rather than counseling. Strategies and small group instruction are helpful.
- Middle school students' self-esteem will benefit most from counseling interventions. High school students may benefit from counseling.
- Collateral interventions are especially helpful in improved social self-concepts.
- Optimal duration of social skills training is about 10 weeks. Mixed gender groups may be best.

What We Can Do

Best Practices

In order to identify best practices, three methods were used. First, the four databases above were searched for specific programs that have passed methodological rigor. Roans and Hoagwood (2000) define well-established treatments as those subjected to rigorous testing involving (1) a control group (including no-treatment groups, comparative treatment groups, or multiple baseline methods); (2) standardized outcome measures; and (3) outcomes assessed at baseline and postintervention and at (3-, 6-, or 12-month) follow-up. For example, PsycInfo was searched using the following combinations of terms: (learning differences, learning disabilities, or learning disabled) AND (counseling, intervention, program, therapy, training, or treatment) AND (clinical trial, comparative, control group, experiment controls, experimental design, multiple baseline, quasi-experimental, or random sampling) AND ((self-concept, self-esteem, or self-image) OR (social adjustment, social skills, or social competence)). Second, citations were gleaned from the intervention meta-analyses for those studies that had a large effect size (ES >.80; Cohen, 1988). Finally, recent issues of core journals were hand

searched, including *Exceptional Children, Journal of Learning Disabilities, Journal of Special Education, Learning Disability Quarterly*, and *Learning Disabilities Research and Practice*. This process resulted in many promising articles, which were then read to determine which ones possessed a "goodness of fit" with the general principles drawn from the meta-analyses above as well as the seven criteria for systematic eclecticism proposed by Hepworth, Rooney, and Larsen (2002) that techniques should be empirical, efficient, specific, and ethical; use generalist skills; be culturally sensitive; and have a person-in-environment perspective. A final criterion was that the technique be *practical* in a regular education school with no special equipment. For a methodological summary of the studies chosen, see Table 17.2. Posttreatment effect size was calculated for studies that included means and standard deviations; otherwise, probability values are provided.

Screening

Because group design studies can only describe groups, not individuals, screening should be done to ensure that those who do not need socioemotional help are not pulled out of academic classes. According to Keith and Bracken (1996), there are three self-concept scales that surpass the rest in terms of being psychometrically sound. These are the Multidimensional Self-Concept Scale (MSCS), the Self-Description Questionnaire-I (SDQ-I), and the Perception of Ability Scale for Students (PASS). Likewise, Demaray and Ruffalo (1995) reviewed six social skills scales and found that the most comprehensive instrument was the Social Skills Rating System (SSRS), with others being of limited usefulness. The Tools and Practice Examples section of this chapter provides lists of the availability and grade level of each scale.

For those practitioners who cannot afford or do not have the proper training to use such scales, they may try scaled questions, such as: "On a scale from 1–10 (1 being the lowest and 10 the highest), how do your feel about yourself in each of the following areas: academic, emotional, physical, social, and overall?" (Sklare, 1997). Another option for students who have difficulty admitting any needs is to have them rank order how they are functioning, for example: "Relationships take a lot of work. Can you rank order (1 being the hardest and 4 being the easiest), which areas of relating to others you

Table 17.2 Articles Regarding Self-Concept or Social Skills

Study	Sample	Measures	Intervention	Effect size/ Probability
Fuchs, Fuchs, Mathes, & Martinez (2002)	156 children, grades 2–6 at 12 Nashville, TN elementary schools	How I Feel Toward Others (Peer rating scale; Agard et al., 1978)	Classroom-wide peer-tutoring program	ES = 1.32
Kuzell, Brassington, & Mahoney (1988)	48 children, ages 7–12 in 3 Ottawa, ON school districts	Psycho-Social Competence Incomplete Stories Test (Mondel, 1980)	Weekly parent education group	$p < .025$
Lenkowsky, Barowsky, Daybock, Puccio, & Lenkowsky (1987)	96 children, ages 12–14 in 1 New York, NY special ed. school	Piers-Harris Children's Self-concept Scale (1969)	Classroom bibliotherapy combined with group debriefing	1. ES = 1.87 2. ES = 1.80 3. ES = 0.59
Utay & Lampe (1995)	66 children, grades 3–6 in 1 Dallas, TX private special ed. school	Walker-McConnell Scale of social competence and school adjustment (1988)	Cognitive-behavioral social skills game used in a small group	1. $p < .05$ 2. $p < .05$

find hardest? (e.g., initiating, maintaining, repairing, and ending relationships)?"

Self-Esteem Interventions

The most effective interventions are ones aimed at the children and their nurturing environment. The first one addresses elementary age children and the second deals with adolescents.

Interventions With Parents

Kuzell, Brassington, and Mahoney (1988) found that a 10-week parenting course was effective in improving the self-esteem of preadolescent children with LD both at the end of the course as well as a year later. The goals of the course include: (1) teaching general parenting skills; (2) exploring how to adapt these skills for children with LD; (3) providing current information on how parents can improve their child's social and daily living skills; and (4) giving parents the chance to

share their experiences in a supportive environment. Materials include both a leader's manual and parents' manual (Kuzell & Brassington, 1985). The authors recommend using two co-leaders with the following qualifications: motivation to lead, an understanding of learning disabilities, teaching skills, and knowledge of basic parenting techniques. They also recommend that leaders present the proposal to the following constituencies before implementation: school administrators, related service personnel (i.e., school social workers, psychologists, and special educators), and the parent association to elicit suggestions before beginning the group. Participation by 8–10 families is optimal, so that the larger group can be broken into two subgroups for skills practice. The example in Box 17.1 shows how this can occur.

The group should be held in a central location with convenient parking, a comfortable room (e.g., the teachers' lounge), refreshments, a phone, and nearby washrooms. The course is designed to last 2.5 hours one night/week for 10 consecutive weeks. Ideal seasons to offer the group include September to November or January to March

Box 17.1 Identifying Strengths in the Student With LD

Preparation: Cook two pizzas with eight different toppings in separate quarters ahead of time (e.g., cheese, sausage, pepperoni, mushroom, olives, spinach, onions, and peppers).

Opening: Ask parents to define the word *pizza*. Ask if there are different kinds of pizza that all qualify under the definition. Ask if they have a favorite type of pizza. Now ask the parents to define the word *smart*. Ask if there are different kinds of smart that all qualify under the definition. Ask if they have a favorite way to learn.

Teaching: Share with the group the basics of multiple intelligences theory (Gardner, 1999), including his definition of an intelligence, the eight intelligences, their aptitudes, and their educational needs (Raines, 2003). Be sure to use visual aids and examples of each one. Armstrong (2000) has a wonderful list of prominent individuals from minority cultures that exemplify each intelligence.

Practicing: In small groups, enable parents to identify which intelligences apply to their children using Armstrong's "Checklist for Assessing Students' Multiple Intelligences" (pp. 24–27). Based on the results, empower parents to identify which tools are needed to help their children learn best. Have parents think of a recent homework assignment and how it could be adapted to fit the strengths of each child. Encourage feedback between parents about their ideas.

because of the lack of holiday interruptions. Ideal nights are Mondays or Tuesdays so that routine weekdays follow during which to practice the skills learned in the course. A flyer should contain information about sponsors, goals, leaders, time, place, cost, and registration procedures. Each week the course includes multisensory teaching about learning disabilities, some practical parenting concepts, and opportunities for parents to practice these skills in small groups. The course outline shown in Table 17.3 is supplemented by newer readings, since the authors' original book is now out-of-print. The Learning Disabilities Council (2002) also publishes a parent workbook.

Direct Interventions

Lenkowsky et al. (1987) found that bibliotherapy in classroom groups was effective for middle school children (ages 12–14) with learning disabilities. Bibliotherapy involves students in reading a story, identifying with a character, experiencing catharsis, and gaining new insight about their problem (Pardeck, 1998). This approach is especially appealing because it connects an academic means (reading) to a therapeutic end (self-esteem). The students read three age-appropriate books (e.g., Albert, 1976; Swarthout & Swarthout, 1975) about other children with learning difficulties in a "literature" class that met three times per week. They also participated in a weekly discussion group that addressed the feelings, mutual experiences, and school-related problems reflected in the books. This intervention involves collaboration between teachers, practitioners, and the school librarian to create a viable program (Lynn, McKay, & Atkins, 2003). Language arts teachers should ensure that state reading standards are met, practitioners can facilitate the group discussions, and librarians can help determine which books are currently in print and available at a group discount. For students with reading difficulties, it may be best to choose a story that is also available on audiotape. It is important to select age-appropriate books that reflect problems similar to the ones faced by the students. The Tools and Practice Examples section of this chapter provides a grade-level list of recommended bibliotherapy books for students with LD.

Sridhar and Vaughn (2002) provide a list of sample questions to be asked before, during, and after reading Polacco's (1998) story. Before reading the book, students are given a brief introduction (from the book's preface) and asked to make hypotheses about the book and the outcome of the story. During the story, students are asked to paraphrase the plot and infer the emotions of the lead characters. After reading the book, students retell the story, recount similar personal experiences, and generate possible solutions to problems shared.

Social Skills Interventions

Interventions for social skills can be done both directly and indirectly. Direct interventions aim at the student with LD while indirect interventions aim at changing others in their environment.

Table 17.3 Outline for a Parents' Group

Week	Content	New Resources
Week 1	Expectations; Philosophy of Course; Group Responsibilities; Introductions	
Week 2	Definition: Learning Disabilities Labeling: Pros and Cons Stages of Acceptance	See definition in text Sternberg & Grigorenko (1999) Higgins et al. (2002)
Week 3	Development and the Child with LD Encouragement of Strengths	Dane (1990) Raines (2003)
Week 4	Structuring the Environment Family Constellation	Cooper & Nye (1994) Dane (1990)
Week 5	Purposes of Behavior Home Activities for Specific Learning Disabilities	Raines (2002) Adelizzi & Goss (2001) Bryan et al. (2001)
Week 6	Communication Skills: Recognizing Feelings & Reflective Listening Social Skills Deficits: Nonverbal	Learning Disabilities Council (2002) Elksnin & Elksnin (2000)
Week 7	Communication Skills: "I" Messages Social Skill Deficits: Verbal	Elksnin & Elksnin (2000)
Week 8	Problem-Solving Steps Applications to Social Situations Consequences for Children with LD	Gammon & Rose (1991) Learning Disabilities Council (2002)
Week 9	Values Clarification Family Council	
Week 10	Using Resources	Adelizzi & Goss (2001)

Direct Interventions

Utay and Lampe (1995) found that the Social Skills Game, a cognitive-behavioral group play therapy by Berg, was effective in improving the peer-related social skills and academic-related skills of students with LD. They used the game with two groups of children in grades 3–4 and grades 5–6 for 50-minute sessions over 8 weeks. The game is designed to be used for children ages 8 and up. It includes three inventories to identify the students' specific skill deficits so that game cards can be preselected by the group therapist to address these problems. The cards address four social skill areas: (1) making friends; (2) responding positively to peers; (3) cooperating with peers; and (4) communicating needs. While the game can be played one-to-one, the authors felt that part of the effectiveness of the game was the group process itself. Because students with LD should spend the least amount of time possible away from core academic subjects, clinicians should consider running such groups before school, during recess or lunch, or after school. Use of a "game" may also help these students from feeling like they are missing out on the "fun" if the group is held during nonacademic times.

Interventions With Peers

Fuchs et al. (2002) found that Peer-Assisted Learning Strategies (PALS), a form of peer academic tutoring, improved the social acceptance and social standing of students with LD. This finding is especially interesting in light of Mastropieri et al.'s (2000) meta-analysis, which found that tutees generally gained more from tutoring by students with disabilities than the tutors. PALS creates 12–14 pairs of students in a classroom who work collaboratively on different learning activities, such as reading or math. It may be beneficial for the teachers to be careful not to pair students with similar learning disabilities. The class is also divided into two teams. Students earn points for their team by correct performance and good collaboration. PALS thus uses both competition and cooperation to motivate students. Teachers establish four classroom rules at the beginning: (1) talk only to your partner and only about PALS; (2) keep your voice low; (3) help your partner; and (4) try your best. The teacher gives direct instruction and clarifies understanding of each concept through a choral response (e.g., everyone, boys, or girls). Each member of the pair takes turns being either the Coach (tutor) or the Player (reader). The teacher first gives direct instructions to the Players (e.g., "M sounds like mmm . . ."). The instructor then gives strategy hints to the Coaches (e.g., "Point to the letter and say, 'What sound?'") as well as appropriate praise statements (e.g., "You could say, 'good job!'").

There are four PALS reading activities. The first activity is *Partner Reading*, during which the higher performing student reads for 5 minutes and then the lower performing student rereads the same material. As the Player works on the material, the Coach provides strategy hints, for example, "Stop, you missed that word. Can you figure it out?" After both have read, the lower performing student gets two minutes to retell what has happened. Students earn 1 point for each correctly read sentence and 10 points for the rehearsal. The second PALS activity is *Paragraph Shrinking*, during which the Player reads one paragraph at a time and tries to summarize the story in 10 words or less. If the Coach feels that they made an error, they give feedback, for example, "That's not quite right. Skim the paragraph and try again." Students earn 1 point for correctly identifying the most important idea and 1 point for stating it in 10 words or less. The third PALS activity is *Prediction Relay*, during which the Player makes a guess about what will be found in the next half page. If the Coach thinks the prediction is irrational, they can object, for example, "I don't agree. Think of something better." The Player then reads the half page aloud (with the Coach's help), confirms or contradicts the prediction, and summarizes the main point. Students earn 1 point for each reasonable prediction, 1 point for accurately confirming or contradicting the guess, and 1 point for summarization (Fuchs, Fuchs, & Burish,

2000). The final step is *Story Mapping*, where each pair combines with another pair. Each of the four students takes a turn being the leader, who identifies one part of the story (lead character, setting, problem, and result) and one major event in the story. Each leader must follow a pattern of (1) telling their answer, (2) asking group members their ideas, (3) leading discussion toward a consensus, (4) recording the group's answer on a story map, and (5) reporting the answer to the teacher. Finally, the teacher debriefs the group answers with the entire class. Each pair earns 10 points for collaborating, 2 points for each correct story part, and 1 point for each reasonable, but incorrect story part (Fuchs, Fuchs, Mathes, & Martinez, 2002). During each of these steps, the teacher roams around the class giving extra points for cooperative behavior and good tutoring.

PALS takes approximately 30 minutes three times per week. Most teachers use PALS to replace individual seatwork. Every four weeks, teachers change both pair and team assignments. Materials needed to implement PALS are minimal: teachers need an overhead projector, a folder for each pair, and a manual. Manuals help teacher partialize reading and math tasks and give strategy hints to coaches. The developers assume that beginning teachers will probably use the manual scripts verbatim while more experienced teachers will naturally paraphrase them. All teachers are encouraged to elaborate on the scripts if students do not seem to comprehend the concepts being taught. Students use their regular textbooks or library books. One-day training in PALS is arranged through PALS Outreach in Nashville, TN.

Tools and Practice Examples

As previously discussed, asking students a series of questions is a helpful reading intervention. A generic set of questions has been placed in Table 17.4.

The following measures are helpful to use to assess the emotional functioning of youth with learning disabilities.

Self-Concept Scales

Multidimensional Self-Concept Scale (Grades 5–12)

Table 17.4 General Questions Before, During, and After Reading

Key Questions	Predictions: What Might happen?	Actuality: What Really Happened?	Identification: How Are You Like That? Give an Example
1. Who are the lead characters in this story?			
2. Which one has a learning difference (LD)?			
3. What are some things that might/have happen(ed)?			
4. How does the person with LD feel about him/herself?			
5. How would this person like to be?			
6. What happens to help this person?			
7. How does this person feel about him/herself in the end?			

The Psychological Corporation
Harcourt Assessment, Inc.
19500 Bulverde Road
San Antonio, TX 78259
Phone: 800–228–0752
www.harcourtassessment.com

Perception of Ability Scale for Children (Grades 3–6)
Western Psychological Services
12031 Wilshire Blvd.
Los Angeles, CA 90025–1251
Phone: 800–648–8857
www.wpspublish.com

Self-Description Questionnaire-I (Grades 2–6)
Self-Description Questionnaire-II (Grades 7–11)
Self Research Centre
University of Western Sydney
Building 1—Bankstown Campus
Penrith South, DC 1797
Australia
Phone: 612-9772-6428
http://self.uws.edu.au

Social Skills Scales

Social Skills Rating System (Grades 3–12)
American Guidance Service
4201 Woodland Rd.
Circle Pines, MN 55014–1796
Phone: 800–328–2560
www.agsnet.com

The following resources provide help for school social workers and school-based practitioners working with youth with learning disabilities.

Peer-Assisted Learning Strategies (PALS) (Grades 2–6)
Kennedy Center
Vanderbilt University
Peabody Box 328
230 Appleton Pl.
Nashville, TN 37203–5701
(615) 343-4782
http://kc.vanderbilt.edu/kennedy/pals/index.html

Social Skills Game (Grades 3–6)
Creative Therapy Store
Western Psychological Services
12031 Wilshire Blvd.
Los Angeles, CA 90025–1251
Phone: 800-648-8857
www.creativetherapystore.com

The following list provides bibliotherapy books that may be useful for school social workers and school-based practitioners working with youth with learning disabilities.

Elementary School (Primary: Grades 1–3)

Aiello, B., & Shulman, J. (1988). *Secrets aren't always for keeps.* Frederick, MD: Twenty-first Century (48 pages).

Daly, N. (2003). *Once upon a time.* New York: Farrar, Strauss and Giroux (picture book).

Gehret, J. (1991). *The don't give up kid and learning differences.* Fairport, NY: Verbal Images (26 pages; parent guide).

Giff, P. R. (1984). *The beast in Ms. Rooney's room.* New York: Delacourte (76 pages; audio, Braille, Spanish).

Kline, S. (1985). *Herbie Jones.* New York: Puffin (95 pages; audio).

Kraus, R. (1971). *Leo, the late bloomer.* New York: Harper Collins (40 pages; audio, French, Spanish, video).

Lewis, M. (1984). *Wrongway Applebaum.* New York: Coward-McCann (63 pages).

Paterson, K. (2001). *Marvin one too many.* New York: Harper Collins (48 pages; audio).

Shreve, S. (1985). *The flunking of Joshua T. Bates.* New York: Knopf (90 pages; audio, Braille, large print).

Sinykin, S. C. (1996). *Allison walks the wire.* Portland, ME: Magic Attic (74 pages).

Elementary School (Intermediate: Grades 4–5)

Banks, J. T. (1995). *Egg drop blues.* Boston: Houghton-Mifflin (120 pages; Braille).

Carris, J. (1990). *Aunt Morbelia & the screaming skulls.* Boston: Little Brown (134 pages; audio).

Cleary, B. (1990). *Muggie Maggie.* New York: Avon (70 pages; audio, Braille, large print, Spanish).

Cutler, J. (1997). *Spaceman.* New York: Dutton (138 pages).

Greenwald, S. (1983). *Will the real Gertrude Hollings please stand up?* New York: Dell (162 pages).

Hansen, J. (1986). *Yellow Bird and me.* New York: Clarion (155 pages).

Martin, A. M. (1988). *Yours truly, Shirley.* New York: Holiday House (133 pages; audio).

McNamee, G. (2002). *Sparks.* New York: Dell/Random House (119 pages).

Polacco, P. (1998). *Thank you, Mr. Falker.* New York: Scholastic Books (unpaged, audio, Korean, Spanish, video).

Sachar, L. (1987). *There's a boy in the girls' bathroom.* New York: Knopf (195 pages; audio, Braille, large print, Spanish).

Middle School (Grades 6–8)

Betancourt, J. (1993). *My name is Brain Brian.* New York: Scholastic (128 pages; large print).

Bunting, E. (1986). *Sixth grade sleepover.* San Diego: Harcourt Brace Jovanovich (96 pages; Braille, large print).

Cassedy, S. (1987). *M. E. and Morton.* New York: Crowell (312 pages; Braille).

DeClements, B. (1985). *Sixth grade can really kill you.* New York: Puffin (146 pages; Braille, large print, teacher's guide).

Gilson, J. (1980). *Do bananas chew gum?* New York: Lothrop, Lee, & Shepard (158 pages; Braille).

Janover, C. (1995). *The worst speller in Jr. High.* Minneapolis: Free Spirit (200 pages; audio).

Lowry, L. (1984). *Us and Uncle Fraud.* New York: Dell (148 pages).

Philbrick, W. R. (1993). *Freak the mighty.* New York: Blue Sky (169 pages; audio).

Suzanne, J. (1990). *Danny means trouble.* New York: Bantam (138 pages; Spanish).

Swarthout, G., & Swarthout, K. (1975). *Whales to see the.* Garden City, NY: Doubleday (121 pages).

High School (Grades 9–12)

Adler, C. S. (1986). *Kiss the clown.* New York: Clarion (178 pages).

Albert, L. (1976). *But I'm ready to go.* Scarsdale, NY: Bradbury (230 pages; Braille).

Barrie, B. (1994). *Adam Zigzag.* New York: Delacorte (181 pages; audio).

Bezant, P. (1994). *Angie.* New York: Ballantine (170 pages).

Brown, K. (1989). *Willie's summer dream.* San Diego: Harcourt Brace Jovanovich (132 pages).

Byars, B. (1970). *The summer of the swans.* New York: Viking (142 pages; award, audio, Braille, Chinese, French, large print, Spanish, teacher's guide, and video).

Foley, J. (1986). *Falling in love is no snap.* New York: Dell (139 pages).

Hall, L. (1986). *Just one friend.* New York: Collier (118 pages).

Morton, J. (1979). *Running scared.* New York: Elsevier (118 pages).

Nelson, T. (1989). *And one for all.* New York: Orchard (182 pages).

Key Points to Remember

Students with learning disabilities represent the largest group of pupils with disabilities in American schools. They often struggle with issues of low self-esteem, low social skills, or both. Direct and indirect interventions are effective in resolving both of these issues. The best approach is to take a person-in-environment perspective by aiming interventions at both the students with LDs and their educational environment.

It is important for practitioners to remember that evidence-based practice (EBP) is a process rather than a product. Among the steps of EBP is the necessity of filtering findings through one's own education, experience, and expertise. Thus, none of the programs discussed should simply be adopted, but *adapted* to meet the unique needs of students with LD in your state, your district, and your school. EBP should never lead to a "cookbook" practice (Raines, 2004).

References

Adelizzi, J. U., & Goss, D. B. (2001). The helping hand & Appendix. In *Parenting children with learning disabilities* (pp. 79–96; 221–229). Westport, CT: Bergin & Garvey.

Agard, J. A., Veldman, D. J., Kaufman, M. J., & Semmel, M. I. (1978). *How I feel toward others: An instrument of the PRIME instrument battery*. Baltimore, MD: University Park.

Albert, L. (1976). *But I'm ready to go*. Scarsdale, NY: Bradbury.

Armstrong, T. (2000). *Multiple intelligences in the classroom* (2nd ed.). Alexandria, VA: Association for Supervision and Curriculum Development.

Bear, G. G., Minke, K. M., & Manning, M. A. (2002). Self-concept of students with learning disabilities: A meta-analysis. *School Psychology Review, 31*(3), 405–427.

Bryan, T., Burstein, K., & Bryan, J. (2001). Students with learning disabilities: Homework problems and promising practices. *Educational Psychologist, 36*(3), 167–180.

Cohen, J. (1988). *Statistical power analysis for the behavioral sciences* (2nd ed.). Hillsdale, NJ: Erlbaum.

Cooper, H., & Nye, B. (1994). Homework for students with learning disabilities: The implications of research for policy and practice. *Journal of Learning Disabilities, 27*(8), 470–479.

Dane, E. (1990). Families of children with learning disabilities. In *Painful passages: Working with children with learning disabilities* (pp. 120–156). Silver Spring, MD: NASW.

Demaray, M. K., & Ruffalo, S. L. (1995). Social skills assessment: A comparative evaluation of six published rating scales. *School Psychology Review, 24*(4), 648–672.

Elbaum, B., & Vaughn, S. (2001). School-based interventions to enhance the self-concept of students with learning disabilities: A meta-analysis. *Elementary School Journal, 101*(3), 303–329.

Elbaum, B., & Vaughn, S. (2003). For which students with learning disabilities are self-concept interventions effective? *Journal of Learning Disabilities, 36*(2), 101–108.

Elksnin, L. K., & Elksnin, N. (2000). Teaching parents to teach their children to be prosocial. *Intervention in School and Clinic, 36*(1), 27–35.

Forness, S. R., & Kavale, K. A. (1996). Treating social skill deficits in children with learning disabilities: A meta-analysis of the research. *Learning Disability Quarterly, 19*(1), 2–13.

Fuchs, D., Fuchs, L. S., & Burish, P. (2000). Peer-assisted learning strategies: An evidence-based practice to promote reading achievement. *Learning Disabilities Research & Practice, 15*(2), 85–91.

Fuchs, D., Fuchs, L. S., Mathes, P. G., & Martinez, E. A. (2002). Preliminary evidence on the social standing of students with learning disabilities in PALS and no-PALS classrooms. *Learning Disabilities Research & Practice, 17*(4), 205–215.

Gammon, E. A., & Rose, S. D. (1991). The Coping Skills Program for parents of children with developmental disabilities: An experimental evaluation. *Research on Social Work Practice, 1*(3), 244–256.

Gardner, H. (1999). *Intelligence reframed: Multiple intelligences for the 21st century*. New York: Basic Books.

Gerber, P. J. (2001). Learning disabilities: A life-span approach. In D. P. Hallahan & B. K. Keogh (Eds.), *Research and global perspectives in learning disabilities: Essays in honor of William M. Cruickshank* (pp. 167–180). Mahwah, NJ: Erlbaum.

Harter, S. (1999). *The construction of the self*. New York: Guilford.

Hepworth, D. H., Rooney, R. H., & Larsen, J. A. (2002). *Direct social work practice: Theory and skills* (6th ed.). Pacific Grove, CA: Brooks/Cole-Thomson Learning.

Higgins, E. L., Raskind, M. H., Goldberg, R. J., & Herman, K. L. (2002). Stages of acceptance of a learning disability: The impact of labeling. *Learning Disability Quarterly, 25*(1), 3–18.

Kavale, K. A., & Forness, S. (1995). *The nature of learning disabilities: Critical elements of diagnosis and classification*. Mahwah, NJ: Erlbaum.

Kavale, K. A., & Forness, S. R. (1996). Social skill deficits and learning disabilities: A meta-analysis. *Journal of Learning Disabilities, 29*(3), 226–237.

Keith, L. K., & Bracken, B. A. (1996). Self-concept instrumentation: A historical and evaluative review. In B. A. Bracken (Ed.), *Handbook of self-concept: Developmental, social, and clinical considerations* (pp. 91–170). New York: Wiley.

Kirk, S. (1962). *Educating exceptional children*. Boston: Houghton-Mifflin.

Kuzell, N., & Brassington, J. (1985). *Parenting the learning disabled child* (2 vols.). Ottawa, ON: Adlerian Centre for Counselling and Education.

Kuzell, N. D., Brassington, J., & Mahoney, W. J. (1988). Parenting the learning disabled child: Research, development and implementation of an effective course. *The Social Worker/Le Travailleur Social, 56*(3), 127–130.

Learning Disabilities Council (2002). *Understanding learning disabilities: A parent guide and workbook* (3rd ed., revised and expanded). Timonium, MD: York.

Lenkowsky, R. S., Barowsky, E. I., Dayboch, M., Puccio, L., & Lenkowsky, B. E. (1987). Effects of bibliotherapy on the self-concept of learning disabled, emotionally handicapped adolescents in a classroom setting. *Psychological Reports, 61*, 483–488.

Lynn, C. J., McKay, M. M., & Atkins, M. S. (2003). School social work: Meeting the mental health needs of students through collaboration with teachers. *Children & Schools, 25*(4), 197–209.

Mastropieri, M. A., Spencer, V., Scruggs, T. E., & Talbot, E. (2000). Students with disabilities as tutors: An updated research synthesis. In T. E. Scruggs & M. A. Mastropieri (Series & Vol. Eds.), *Advances in learning and behavioral disabilities: Vol. 14. Educational interventions* (pp. 247–279). Stamford, CT: Jai.

Mondel, S. (1980). *Psycho-social competence incomplete stories test.* Tufts-New England Medical Center.

Nowicki, E. A. (2003). A meta-analysis of the social competence of children with learning disabilities compared to classmates of low and average to high achievement. *Learning Disability Quarterly, 26*(3), 171–188.

Ochoa, S. H., & Olivarez, A. (1995). A meta-analysis of peer rating sociometric studies of pupils with learning disabilities. *Journal of Special Education, 29*(1), 1–19.

Pardeck, J. T. (1998). *Using books in clinical social work practice: A guide to bibliotherapy.* New York: Haworth.

Piers, E., & Harris, D. (1969). *The Piers-Harris Children's Self-concept Scale.* Nashville, TN: Counselor Recordings & Tests.

Polacco, P. (1998). *Thank you, Mr. Falker.* New York: Scholastic Books.

Prout, H. T., Marcal, S. D., & Marcal, D. C. (1992). A meta-analysis of self-reported personality characteristics of children and adolescents with learning disabilities. *Journal of Psychoeducational Assessment, 10*, 59–64.

Raines, J. C. (2002). Brainstorming hypotheses for functional behavioral assessment: The link to effective behavioral intervention plans. *School Social Work Journal, 26*(2), 30–45.

Raines, J. C. (2003). Multiple intelligences and social work practice for students with learning disabilities. *School Social Work Journal, 28*(1), 1–20.

Raines, J. C. (2004). Evidence-based practice in school social work: A process in perspective. *Children & Schools, 26*(2), 71–85.

Roans, M., & Hoagwood, K. (2000). School-based mental health services: A research review. *Clinical Child and Family Psychology Review, 3*(4), 223–241.

Sklare, G. B. (1997). *Brief counseling that works: A solution-focused approach for school counselors.* Thousand Oaks, CA: Corwin Press.

Sridhar, D., & Vaughn, S. (2002). Bibliotherapy: Practices for improving self-concept and reading comprehension. In B.Y.L. Wong & M. L. Donahue (Eds.), *The social dimensions of learning disabilities: Essays in honor of Tanis Bryan* (pp. 161–188). Mahwah, NJ: Erlbaum.

Sternberg, R. J., & Grigorenko, E. L. (1999). *Our labeled children: What every parent and teacher needs to know about learning disabilities.* Reading, MA: Perseus.

Swanson, H. L. (1996). Meta-analysis, replication, social skills, and learning disabilities. *Journal of Special Education, 30*(2), 213–221.

Swanson, H. L. (2001). Research on interventions for adolescents with learning disabilities: A meta-analysis of outcomes related to higher-order processing. *Elementary School Journal, 101*(3), 331–348.

Swanson, H. L., & Hoskyn, M. (1998). Experimental intervention research on students with learning disabilities: A meta-analysis of treatment outcomes. *Review of Educational Research, 68*(3), 277–321.

Swanson, H. L., & Malone, S. (1992). Social skills and learning disabilities: A meta-analysis of the literature. *School Psychology Review, 21*(3), 427–442.

Swarthout, G., & Swarthout, K. (1975). *Whales to see the.* Garden City, NY: Doubleday.

U.S. Department of Education. (2002). *Twenty-fourth annual report to Congress on the implementation of the Individuals with Disabilities Education Act.* Washington, DC: Author.

Utay, J. M., & Lampe, R. E. (1995). Use of a group counseling game to enhance social skills of children with learning disabilities. *Journal for Specialists in Group Work, 20*(2), 114–120.

Walker, H. M., & McConnell, S. R. (1988). *The Walker-McConnell Scale of Social Competence and School Adjustment.* Austin, TX: Pro-Ed.

Effective Classroom Interventions for Students With Physical Disabilities

Anna G. Escamilla

CHAPTER 18

Getting Started

Students with physical disabilities can be excellent pupils and individuals. Sometimes the lack of resources and information about how to facilitate education for these students makes daily classroom activities burdensome to all involved. In this chapter we will cover some practical ideas and exercises for the classroom. Resources will be offered to assist with the ongoing challenges. In addition the reader is encouraged to explore the topic of students with physical disabilities by using the many articles and other reading materials that are listed. This chapter is primarily an introduction to a very complex issue.

Physical disabilities can be defined as temporary or chronic conditions that affect functioning in walking, strength, coordination, fine motor and sensory abilities, and communication. These limitations may or may not affect activity in the classroom or school setting. The causes for physical disability include but are not limited to asthma, convulsive disorders, hemophilia, heart disease, cancer, AIDS, cystic fibrosis, cerebral palsy, birth defects, epilepsy, rheumatoid arthritis, brain injury, traumatic spinal cord injury, and amputations. Some students with physical disabilities use adaptive devices such as wheelchairs, crutches, white canes, special seating, or adaptive technology. Students with chronic illness may require medical attention during the school day. Students may be served both in special education classrooms as well as regular classrooms.

The philosophy of self-determination will guide you through the rest of this chapter in understanding adaptation, modifications, and other methods of inclusion for the student with physical disabilities. Self-determination is the ability to make daily decisions and life plans without the interference or influence of others unless requested. These are essential skills for lifelong success that must be developed early (Wehmeyer, Agran, & Hughes, 1998). The language you use to describe disability can be empowering and support self-determination. A simple method for communicating respect for students with disabilities is the use of person-first language. Identifying a student by their name, regardless of their disability, supports self-respect. To say the "handicapped child," or the "wheelchair student" identifies the disability and focuses on the student's lack of ability, above all personal identity. If it is necessary to refer to the disability, say "(Name) _____ who uses a wheelchair" or "(Name) _____ who has cerebral palsy." It is important to avoid pitying language to describe disability such as "suffers" and "afflicted." Pity does not help a student with a disability. Compassionate support should be the goal of any intervention. Other students model the language and attitude of the teachers, counselors, and social workers around the student with the disability. It is essential to live what you intend to teach about disability.

What We Know

Students with physical disabilities are not a homogeneous group. However, the attitudes toward these students by peers, teachers, and others in a school setting can have many commonalities. For this chapter meta-analyses and extensive literature reviews were compared in order to arrive at the best practices for working with students with disabilities in the classroom. Citations from identified studies current as of 1990 and reviews were checked for possible resources. In addition Medline, Psyclit, and Eric databases were searched for any meta-analyses or comprehensive literature reviews done on children with physical disabili-ties and children with physical disabilities in the classroom. Table 18.1 summarizes the results of these searches.

Assimilating all this information leads us to con-clude that the current research does not reliably

Table 18.1 Comparison of Meta-Analyses and Comprehensive Literature Reviews

Study	Target Problem	Sample	Results
Buysee & Bailey (1993). Behavioral and developmental outcomes in young children with disabilities in integrated and segregated settings: A review of comparative studies.	1. Strengths and limitations of existing research 2. Integrate findings relative to behavior and development 3. Identify needs for further research on integrated vs. segregated settings for young children with disabilities	22 studies reviewed of children with disabilities ages 0–6 in early intervention programs	1. Integrated environ-ments facilitate social interactions for young children with disabilities 2. These settings are not detrimental to developmental outcomes in these children
LeBovidge, Lavigne, Donenberg, & Miller (2003). Psychological adjustment of children and adolescents with chronic arthritis: A meta-analytic review.	Determine whether children and adolescents with chronic arthritis are at more risk for development of adjustment problems than controls	21 studies that report overall adjustment problems, internalizing symptoms, externalizing symptoms, or self-concept of youth with arthritis	Important to assess children & adolescents with chronic arthritis for internalizing problems. These youth were not found to be at greater risk for poor self-concept or self-esteem problems than controls. Used Child Behavior Checklist (CBCL).
McGregor & Vogelsberg (1998). Inclusive schooling practices: Pedagogical and Research Foundation: A synthesis of the literature that informs best practices about inclusive schooling	Summarizes the literature base that informs our current understanding of the best approaches to support students with disabilities in inclusive settings	54 research studies on inclusion	Practices associated with inclusive schooling practices continue to evolve as experience increases. Collective resources, strategies, and creativity of both general and special education teachers are necessary and sufficient to achieve inclusion.
Mulvihill, Cotton, & Gyaben (2004).	What are the issues and best practices	Reviewed 53 sources on inclusive practices	There is not a single set of criteria,

(continued)

Table 18.1 *(Continued)*

Study	Target Problem	Sample	Results
Best practices for inclusive child and adolescent out-of-school care: A review of the literature.	in inclusive education?	for school-age children and adolescents	recommendations, or guidelines for inclusion; however, there are guiding principles. Recommend systematic, programmatic, multidisciplinary research.
Prevatt, Heffer, & Lowe (2000). A review of school reintegration programs for children with cancer.	Review of literature that summarizes suggestions for successful reintegration	15 programs from journal articles on school reintegration programs for children with cancer specifically compared	No empirical evidence, but evidence that normalcy beneficial in facilitating adjustment of ill child's return to school. Best practices include school staff workshops, peer programs, school personnel & peer educational presentations, consultation & team building, strategies for families, school & hospital collaboration.
Ward & Barrett (2002). A review of behavior analysis research in physical education.	Overview of behavior analysis and how it contributes to physical education	5 journals focusing on behavior analysis studies in PE. 6 single-subject studies on participants with disabilities	Lack of treatment integrity in the studies. Peers as mediators main type of intervention. Lack of evidence that behaviors were maintained or generalized. The focus of most studies was interventions designed to improve teaching behaviors.

support a particular intervention. However, there is evidence that guiding principles such as integrated settings, workshops for teachers and staff, peer programs, school personnel and peer educational presentations, consultation and team building, therapeutic strategies for families, and school and hospital collaboration can be beneficial in supporting children with physical disabilities (Mulvihill, Cotton, & Gyaben, 2004). In addition, the collaboration between regular and special education teachers allows for collective creativity in designing individualized interventions in the classroom. The following section provides examples to use in the classroom based on these conclusions.

What We Can Do

School settings can be very nurturing and supportive of students. This is also true as it relates to students with physical disabilities. The following section will provide information, activities, and resources about students with disabilities, their peers, teachers, and parents.

Integrated Settings

Children with physical disabilities can participate to varying degrees in the activities of children without disabilities, including social activities. For example, the student with a wheelchair needs to have access to all or most areas of the classroom. Most deaf students included in regular classrooms will have sign language communication skills, lip readings skills, or other communication methods. Sometimes the use of adaptive equipment can help facilitate participation and inclusion. Adaptive technology is a specialized practical modification of an existing device, instrument, or apparatus used in performing a variety of daily life skills including learning. Some adaptive technology is "low tech," practical, and inexpensive. Other adaptive technology is "high tech" and includes switch devices to activate a computer, screen readers, or electronic equipment for speech (see Resources section).

There are many resources and opportunities available to students with disabilities and their teachers (see "Resources" section). For example, a student with a physical disability who uses a wheelchair may work on a desk that is elevated by wooden blocks or a student with low vision may use a lamp on his or her desk. Avoid isolating the child with a disability in the back of a classroom. Encourage them to participate with their peers in activities outside of the classroom.

- Include the child with a disability in all activities (i.e., science activities, field trips, and physical education).
- Allow space to maneuver a wheelchair.
- Change seating to make it possible for all students to see and hear better, such as circular seating in small groups (Nabors & Larson, 2002).
- Encourage the students with disabilities to interact with nondisabled peers and avoid social

isolation (Blum, Resnick, Nelson, & St. Germaine, 1991).

- Offer the same instruction to students with disabilities as is offered to the nondisabled student.
- Encourage and assist young children to include the student with the disability in activities whenever possible.
- Offer information to the student with the disability about available student activities and clubs.
- If overheads, handouts, or the blackboard is used, read them aloud.
- Present any handouts or readings in an accessible format.
- Give students with speech difficulties time to respond to a question.
- Younger children sometimes will ask direct questions about a peer's disability. This should be encouraged if at all possible.
- Encourage students to challenge attitudes and stereotyping through direct contact and reality-based interaction.
- Remember that difficulty in communicating does not mean that a person also has a cognitive deficit.

Educational Workshops for Teachers, Staff, and Peers

Teachers are including students with physical disabilities in regular classrooms. For more information on issues related to inclusion and mainstreaming of students with disabilities, see chapter 19. Most teachers welcome the opportunity to provide an enriched learning environment for all of their students. Other teachers have strong reactions to this task. Frustration may be felt or even anger at what they perceive as an extra workload. It is difficult for a teacher to provide a positive inclusive classroom if they are having strong negative emotional reactions. Some teachers feel a blow to their self-efficacy as a professional for not being able to provide a perceived quality education to all students (Forlin, 1998). Support for teachers, staff, and peers in the form of educational workshops and smaller educational groups is an excellent method of making inclusion a positive experience for all. Here are some steps toward success.

- Provide teachers and other staff with information about their students' disabilities prior to their entry into the classroom.

- Obtain information from parents, previous teachers, medical resources, and the student him- or herself.
- Provide a private, small-group environment for teachers, staff, and peers where they feel they can vent emotions constructively without hurting the student or being criticized for having a less than correct attitude.
- Attempt to utilize social work and other school-based practitioners as experts in the areas of disability to assist with these support groups.
- Arrange sensitivity training on site from professionals in the field of disabilities (see Resources section).

Peer Programs

It is likely that a student with a physical disability will be absent from classes frequently (Nabors & Lehmkuhl, 2004). The student may feel frustrated by an inability to keep up with assignments (Lightfoot, Wright, & Sloper, 1998). Here are some suggested steps to take to support the student with the physical disability.

- Assign a peer or peers who are willing to take the responsibility for getting class work to the student.
- Involve the student with the disability and their volunteer peers (buddy) in selecting who will be given this task.
- Check periodically to make sure the relationship is working for both parties.
- Make every effort to ensure a mutual, reciprocal, and empowering relationship for the child with a disability.

Consultation and Team Building

It is very helpful to assemble a team of support persons and consultants for the process of including students with physical disabilities in the classroom. The most effective team is comprised of the student, their parents, teachers (both regular and special education), school medical staff, and any current medical providers. The student with the disability should be involved in all decision making regarding what to tell other students about the disability. The student's need for confidentiality should be considered first even above the needs of their parents to openly discuss these issues. The following are some suggestions:

- Sometimes students with disabilities would like to limit their disclosure to the school nurse and/or specific teachers.
- If the student decides to share information with his or her classmates, make plans to use these as teaching opportunities.
- Include professionals that can provide accurate information (Lightfoot et al., 1998).
- Get assistance from the teachers of the visually impaired in making accommodations for students.
- Consult with the speech therapists if they are involved with the student.
- Speak to parents, as well as the student, about what methods of communication they use.

Therapeutic Strategies for Families

Have compassion and understanding of the difficulties parents face when raising a child with a disability. Adolescence poses a challenge in the case of students with disabilities as much as those students without disabilities. Students may not agree with their parents' choices regarding their activities at school. Sometimes the student with the disability feels more vulnerable to taking an opposing view against their parents because they are totally dependent on them for daily support. The use of self-determination to support the development of mature judgment and preparation for life after graduation in students with disabilities can become a very effective tool to use (Wehmeyer, 1997). Teachers and social workers need to work toward developing independence in these students just as they would with students without disabilities. These steps may assist families in dealing with the stresses of having a child with a disability in a regular classroom.

- Support students in learning skills to express their opinions, desires, and needs appropriately.
- Help parents see the importance of allowing children with disabilities to take calculated risks.
- Encourage the student to express their desires.
- Develop a transition plan for when the child leaves school.
- Assist and encourage the adolescent student and parents to investigate adult services and explore options for meaningful employment or postsecondary education.
- When appropriate encourage family and individual psychotherapy services with professionals in the community.

School and Hospital Collaboration

Some differences in teacher involvement will occur when dealing with children with physical disabilities in the classroom. Among these differences is the need for interaction with external medical professionals. This becomes important not only for education about a particular disability but also because medical professionals may need information in order to provide appropriate treatment to the student.

- Obtain written consent from the parents and student to interact with their medical team.
- Set up informative meetings with the medical team associated with the individual student if possible.
- Ask the members of the medical team to send information in the form of brochures or resources to the school staff involved with the student.
- Basic planning for emergencies and daily activity should be in place prior to the student's entering the classroom.
- Include the student and the parents in all these activities.

Collaboration Between Regular and Special Education Teachers

Collaboration between teachers is probably the most important part of successful inclusion of students with physical disabilities. Both professionals must be able to have a mutually supportive attitude that in turn carries over to the inclusive classroom. The following are some suggested ideas for making this experience successful.

- Develop a climate of mutual trust.
- Involve your principal in obtaining scheduled preparation time.
- Teachers should visit and observe the classes of teachers who have experience with successful inclusion.
- Special education teachers can work with the regular teachers to determine their need for information about the medical conditions of his or her students.
- Use problem-solving skills and good communication skills.
- Work with specific task-related issues.
- Allow time for the receiving teacher to observe the student and discuss the student's

needs with the current teacher and parents (Perner & Porter, 1998; McGregor & Vogelsberg, 1998).

Self-Determination Activity

Invite a panel of adults with disabilities to come to the classroom and talk about what they are doing in their lives. Ensure that these adults are willing to answer questions candidly. Ask them to explain what self-determination means to them.

Tools and Practice Examples

Case Example

Mary is a 10-year-old female student in the fourth grade with cerebral palsy. Cerebral palsy is a motor impairment resulting from brain damage usually during fetal development or infancy. It affects body movements and muscle coordination. She has and uses an electric wheelchair, which she operates with a joystick control. She needs assistance with eating and self-care. Mary's teacher has met with the special education consultant prior to starting the school year. They were able to assemble a team that included the student, the parents, teacher, teacher assistant, school counselor/social worker, her physical therapist, and an occupational therapist. The team worked on several parts of the needed accommodations for Mary in the classroom. Among the suggested accommodations were computer hardware and software, which allows her to use the computer by herself. Her teacher has designed class work for all students so that using the computer is routine, thereby not singling Mary out. The classroom is arranged so that all the computers face three walls and the students' backs are toward the middle of the room. In the center of the room there is a round table with chairs around it. When the students discuss parts of their lessons they come to the center of the room and sit at the table. One area of the table is cut out so that Mary's wheelchair can fit closer in with the other students. Mary agreed to let her teacher talk to the class about cerebral palsy. Her teacher, the special education consultant, and Mary prepared the lesson. Although Mary cannot speak clearly, she presented information to her classmates with support from the teacher. Mary asked for volunteers to be her buddy so that if she missed classes, she would be able to get class work to her and help her stay up with the class. Mary's teacher has informed her of the many clubs and organizations at the school and encouraged Mary to join the school Newsletter Club because Mary enjoys writing.

Resources

Here is a list of resources that are helpful to school social workers and other school counselors working with students with physical disabilities.

Hilton, A., & Ringlaben, R. (Eds.). (1998). *Best and promising practices in developmental disabilities.* Austin, TX: PRO-ED, Inc. (27 chapters dealing with developmental disabilities; includes chapters on self-determination, assistive technology, and facilitating inclusion in the classroom)

http://www.thinkquest.org/library/cat_show.html?cat_id=80 (Web site offers resources on differently abled students by students)

http://www.inclusive.co.uk (Web site with information on information technology and special needs)

http://snow.utoronto.ca (resources on best practices and self-paced [many are free] online workshops)

http://www.aucd.org (the Association of University Centers on Disabilities can provide valuable resources for training available to teachers and the public in every state)

Education for Disability and Gender Equality (EDGE): http://www.disabilityhistory.org/dshp.html (Web resource for high school students; offers facts and ideas in sciences and humanities about men, women, and disability)

Key Points to Remember

- Although research does not yet support any particular interventions, there is substantial evidence that certain ideas and guiding principles work in the successful classroom.
- Include the student with the disability in as much decision making as possible about his or her own needs and shared information.
- Inclusive settings provide good education for students with physical disabilities.

- Peer support helps the student with the physical disability to stay up with the class when medical appointments and illness take them out of the classroom.
- Teachers who use teams of the student, professionals, and family members to help plan accommodations have more success in dealing with students with physical disabilities.
- Medical professionals need to be utilized as resources for the teachers in understanding their student's physical needs.
- The special education consultant can be very valuable to teachers in preparing their class work and classroom.
- Teachers need to have compassion and understanding toward parents and help make them part of the team for their son or daughter.

It is important when dealing with children with physical disabilities to remember that the goal to be achieved is inclusion. The research is beginning to provide the guidelines; however, it is the individual teacher, counselor, social worker, and teaching assistant who will truly change everyday lives for children with physical disabilities.

References

Blum, R., Resnick, M., Nelson, R., & St. Germaine, A. (1991). Family and peer issues among adolescents with spina bifida and cerebral palsy. *Pediatrics, 88*(2), 280–285.

Buysee, V., & Bailey, Jr., D., (1993). Behavioral and developmental outcomes in young children with disabilities in integrated and segregated settings: A review of comparative studies. *Journal of Special Education, 26*(4), 434–462.

Forlin, C. (1998). Teachers' personal concerns about including children with a disability in regular classrooms. *Journal of Developmental and Physical Disabilities, 10*(1), 87–106.

LeBovidge, J., Lavigne, J., Donenberg, G., & Miller, M. (2003). Psychological adjustment of children and adolescents with chronic arthritis: A meta-analytic review. *Journal of Pediatric Psychology, 28*(1), 29–39.

Lightfoot, J., Wright, S., & Sloper, P. (1998). Supporting pupils in mainstream school with an illness or disability: Young people's views. *Child: Care, Health and Development, 25*(4), 267–283.

McGregor, G., & Vogelsberg, R. (1998). *Inclusive schooling practices: Pedagogical and research foundation: A synthesis of the literature that informs best practices about inclusive schooling.* Allegheny University of the

Health Sciences, Consortium on Inclusive Schooling Practices: Brookes Publishing Co.

Mulvihill, B., Cotton, J., & Gyaben, S. (2004). Best practices for inclusive child and adolescent out-of-school care: A review of the literature. *Family and Community Health, 27,* 52–65.

Nabors, L., & Larson, E. (2002). The effects of brief interventions on children's playmate preferences for a child sitting in a wheelchair. *Journal of Developmental and Physical Disabilities, 14*(4), 403–413.

Nabors, L., & Lehmkuhl, H. (2004). Children with chronic medical conditions: Recommendations for school mental health clinicians. *Journal of Developmental and Physical Disabilities, 16*(1), 1–15.

Perner, D., & Porter, G. (1998). Creating inclusive schools: Changing roles and strategies. In A. Hilton & R. Ringlaben (Eds.), *Best and promising practices in developmental disabilities* (pp. 317–330). Austin, TX: PRO-ED.

Prevatt, F., Heffer, R., & Lowe, P. (2000). A review of school reintegration programs for children with cancer. *Journal of School Psychology 38*(5), 447–454.

Ward, P., & Barrett, T. (2002). A review of behavior analysis research in physical education. *Journal of Teaching in Physical Education, 21*(3), 242–267.

Wehmeyer, M. (1997). Self determination as an educational outcome: A definitional framework and implications for intervention. *Journal of Developmental and Physical Disabilities, 9*(3), 175–209.

Wehmeyer, M., Agran, M., & Hughes, C. (1998). *Teaching self-determination to students with disabilities: Basic skills for successful transition.* Baltimore, MD: Brookes Publishing Co.

What Does the Research Evidence Say About Inclusion Practices?

Brandon K. Schultz ■ Steven W. Evans

CHAPTER 19

Getting Started

The education field has struggled with the notion of separate learning environments for students based on their unique characteristics for many years. Perhaps the most well-known example of this is the *Brown v. Board of Education* Supreme Court case, which, in addressing issues of racial segregation in our public schools, concluded that "separate educational facilities are inherently unequal." Although 50 years have passed since the *Brown* decision, similar questions persist in relation to students receiving special education services in segregated environments. Clearly the cultural and political implications are different than those of the *Brown* decision, but concerns such as stigma, socialization, and self-worth are analogous.

In the spirit of *Brown*, many have called for some degree of integration of special education (SE) and general education (GE) services. This viewpoint received support from the federal government with the passage of the Education for All Handicapped Children Act (Public Law 94-142) in 1975, which required that SE students learn with their nondisabled peers to the "maximum extent appropriate." With this legislation, the mandate of integrating SE students into GE environments, usually referred to in today's current vernacular as *inclusion*, and sometimes referred to in the past as *mainstreaming,* began in earnest. We will use the terms *inclusion* and *mainstreaming* generically to refer to *all* strategies devised for integrating SE students with their GE peers. Whenever inclusion strategies are considered, several questions naturally arise: (1) What are the potential benefits, if any, of educating an SE student with his or her GE peers? (2) Is there a potential for negative outcomes among the nondisabled

peers or the general education teachers who teach them? And (3) what can educators do to assure the best possible outcomes for inclusion students? Given that the vast majority of students in special education are only minimally to moderately impaired, the answers to these questions are rarely straightforward. In this chapter we address these questions based on the findings from relevant research conducted over many decades. In addition, we explore school-related conditions that appear to facilitate successful inclusion. Our focus is on students with mild to moderate disabilities, for whom inclusion decisions are particularly challenging.

What We Know

Although a thorough delineation of all inclusion or mainstreaming strategies is well beyond the scope of this chapter, most may be considered to fall into one of two categories: partial or full integration. The first category, partial integration, includes strategies such as "pull-out" programs, which involve removing students from general education classrooms during specific times when individualized attention is warranted. For example, a student might attend social studies and science classes with her GE peers, but meet with a special education teacher in a resource room for individualized reading assistance. In contrast, full integration places the special needs student in regular education classrooms on a full-time basis. Depending on the type of model used, additional supports may be provided that range from full-time assistance from a professional "co-teacher" within the GE classroom to no specialized support at all.

Inclusion is a term commonly used to refer

to either partial- or full-integration strategies that include meaningful modifications to the GE classroom learning activities. This distinction was made following criticism of early mainstreaming practices that simply placed students with mild disabilities in GE classrooms without making changes to the classrooms, providing additional supports, or making adjustments to the curriculum. Inclusive strategies call for significant changes in GE settings and require teaching flexibility and acceptance of student diversity (McLeskey & Waldron, 2002; Voltz, Brazil, & Ford, 2001). In recent years the term *inclusion* has essentially replaced the term *mainstreaming* in most discussions of the topic, as there is growing recognition of the need to modify GE environments to ensure success. Readers should be aware that these terms are often used interchangeably among educators and definitions vary from source to source.

It is important to recognize that mainstreaming or inclusion is not an intervention, but rather a broad array of placement strategies that may or may not enhance the interventions and accommodations that are outlined in an individual education plan (IEP). This means that while the research on inclusion can reflect large-scale trends, the outcomes for any individual student will depend on the quality of the interventions described in his or her IEP. Consequently, it is not surprising that the research findings in the professional literature are mixed. In fact, depending on the study cited, there appears to be support for and against most practices. In recent years, however, several literature reviews have been published in an attempt to synthesize the best data and draw practical conclusions for practitioners (see Table 19.1; e.g., Freeman & Alkin, 2000; Garrick-Duhaney & Salend, 2000; Salend & Garrick-Duhaney, 1999; Vaughn & Klingner, 1998; Manset & Semmel, 1997; Scruggs & Mastropieri, 1996).

Unfortunately, for some topics there is a paucity of research that is worth noting. For example, there is little research into inclusion practices at the secondary level (Mastropieri & Scruggs, 2001) or the preschool level (Stahmer & Ingersol, 2004). In response, research continues to expand into these and other areas. (For a sample of research that has been conducted in the United States that was not included in the literature reviews cited above, refer to Table 19.2.) Nevertheless, the research available to date sug-

gests several general answers to the questions posed above.

Question 1: What are the potential benefits, if any, of educating an SE student with his or her GE peers?

- Some SE students appear to perform better academically in GE settings. These findings have been demonstrated among children with learning disabilities (Manset & Semmel, 1997) and among children with mild mental retardation (Freeman & Alkin, 2000), and may extend to other diagnostic categories as well. Other students, however, appear to prefer more traditional/segregated SE settings (Vaughn & Klingner, 1998) and perform better academically in these settings (Salend & Garrick-Duhaney, 1999). For example, students whose behavior may disrupt the entire class and seriously compromise the learning of others may do better in restrictive placements. It is difficult to predict which students will receive greater benefit from traditional placements compared to placements including extensive inclusion. In general, the research suggests that students with mild disabilities experience the greatest academic benefits from inclusion placements, but this does not mean that students with more severe disabilities might not also benefit. Again, individual outcomes depend on additional factors, such as the quality and appropriateness of the inclusion strategy attempted.
- In terms of socialization, SE students report having more opportunities to establish friendships in integrated environments (Vaughn & Klingner, 1998). Indeed, SE students who are mainstreamed generally appear to enjoy greater social acceptance from their GE peers, but the quality of these relationships is unclear (Salend & Garrick-Duhaney, 1999). Parents of students who are included in GE commonly report that their child is better accepted by their nondisabled peers and that this has a positive impact on the child's self-image (Garrick-Duhaney & Salend, 2000).

Question 2: Is there a potential for negative outcomes among the nondisabled peers or the general education teachers in inclusion classrooms?

- As a group GE students do not appear to be negatively impacted by inclusion, even though

Table 19.1 Summary of Literature Reviews of Research Into Mainstreaming and the Reviewers' Overall Conclusions

	Number of Studies Reviewed	Publication Dates*	Type of Disabilities Included	Types of Outcome(s) Investigated	General Conclusions of the Reviewers
Freeman & Alkin (2000)	36	1957–1997	Mental retardation	Academic and social	• Overall, children with mild MR perform better academically when more fully integrated with GE peers. • Children with MR are generally less socially accepted than their nondisabled peers, regardless of school placement. • Social acceptance appears to be related to degree of similarity between SE and GE students, but can be facilitated by trained teachers.
Garrick-Duhaney & Salend (2000)	17	1987–1998	All disabilities	Parent perceptions	• Parents of GE students generally approve of inclusive classrooms, citing benefits for their children including greater awareness of disabilities and acceptance. • Parents of GE students express some concerns, including the impact of the quality of instruction, the preparedness of GE teachers, and the possibility that their children might emulate the behaviors of SE students. • The majority of parents of children receiving SE services support mainstreaming, citing positive outcomes such as greater acceptance from peers and improved self-image. • Parents of students receiving SE services also report concerns, including the loss of individualized attention, mistreatment from peers, and a lack of school-based professionals with the required training.

(continued)

Table 19.1 (*Continued*)

	Number of Studies Reviewed	Publication Dates*	Type of Disabilities Included	Types of Outcome(s) Investigated	General Conclusions of the Reviewers
Manset & Semmel (1997)	11	1984–1994	Mild disabilities (e.g., learning disabilities)	Academic	• Mainstreaming can be beneficial, but no one model appears to be ideal for all students. • A spectrum of services should be made available, including traditional SE services and mainstreaming strategies.
Salend & Garrick-Duhaney (1999)	46	1989–1998	All disabilities	Academic and social, as well as effects on nondisabled peers and teacher attitudes	• Some students perform better academically within more traditional SE delivery models. • Social outcomes appear generally positive, but the nature of interactions between SE and GE peers is unclear. SE students need training in social and behavioral skills. • Disabled students generally appear to prefer individualized SE assistance when not missing important/desirable activities in GE classes. • Nondisabled peers, as a group, do not appear to be deleteriously impacted in mainstream settings, although these students express such concerns. • Teachers' reactions to inclusion appear mixed, with fears centered on issues of training, resources, new demands/ roles, and the impact mainstreaming has on nondisabled peers.
Scruggs & Mastropieri (1996)	28	1975–1995	All disabilities	Teacher perceptions	• GE teacher support for mainstreaming appears to decrease as the degree of integration and severity of disability increases. This has been consistent since 1975.

(continued)

Table 19.1 (*Continued*)

	Number of Studies Reviewed	Publication Dates*	Type of Disabilities Included	Types of Outcome(s) Investigated	General Conclusions of the Reviewers
					• Teacher support for mainstreaming is affected by the extra demands placed on teachers rather than their emotional reaction. This has also been consistent since 1975. • Roughly half of GE teachers and two thirds of SE teachers believe that mainstreaming can provide some benefits. Only a minority of teachers feel that full integration is more effective than more traditional SE services.
Vaughn & Klingner (1998)	8	1987–1998	Learning disabilities	Student perceptions	• Students do not prefer any one mainstreaming strategy, so providing a range of models is advantageous. • Students in segregated SE settings appear to appreciate the assistance, quiet environment, and the activities they do. • Students report that mainstreaming provides more opportunities to establish friendships with their peers.

*This is the range (in years) between the oldest and most recent research article reviewed by the authors.

they commonly express such concerns (Salend & Garrick-Duhaney, 1999).

• Support for inclusion among GE teachers seems to decrease as the degree of integration or the severity of disability increases. This may be related to the additional demands these conditions create (Scruggs & Mastropieri, 1996). Parents of GE students commonly express fears that mainstreaming may negatively impact the quality of classroom instruction, that GE teachers are underprepared, and that their children may imitate the inappropriate behavior of their SE peers (Garrick-Duhaney & Salend, 2000).

Question 3: What can educators do to ensure the best possible outcomes for mainstreamed students?

• Since no one model of inclusion appears to be more effective or preferred by most students, a spectrum of services should be made available (Vaughn & Klingner, 1998; Manset & Semmel, 1997). Clearly, this requires flexibility within school systems.

• Although social acceptance appears to be related to the degree of similarity between SE and GE students, teachers can facilitate social acceptance in their classrooms, if trained to do so (Freeman & Alkin, 2000). This means that some of the social barriers that occur as a result of the dissimilarities between disabled and nondisabled students can be overcome through direct intervention. Further, research suggests that SE students can benefit from targeted social and behavioral skills training (Salend & Garrick-Duhaney, 1999).

Table 19.2 Summary of Recent Studies of Mainstreaming Conducted in the United States, Not Included in the Literature Reviews Cited in Table 19.1

	Topic	Sample	Age/ Grade Level	Type of Disability	Experimental Comparisons	Data Collection Method(s)	General Conclusion
Giangreco, Broer, & Edelman (2002)	Paraprofessional support of mainstreaming	215 Paraprofessionals	Grades K–12	All disabilities*	N/A	Questionnaires and interviews, as well as classroom observations	There has been a significant increase in the use of paraprofessionals to support mainstreamed students. The role of paraprofessionals increasingly includes instruction, even though their training may be insufficient and their impact is still unclear.
Huber, Rosenfeld, & Fiorello (2001)	Impact of mainstreaming on GE students	410 GE students	Grades 1–5	All disabilities	Academic outcomes before and after mainstreaming	Standardized test scores	Low-achieving GE students appeared to benefit from mainstream classrooms, while higher achieving GE students "lost ground" in the first year. In the second year, these trends were less pronounced.
Kasari, Freeman, Bauminger, & Aukin (1999)	Parental perceptions	262 parents of children with disabilities	Ages 2–18	Autism and Down syndrome	Parental preferences for children with autism vs. children with Down syndrome	Surveys	Parents of students with Down syndrome are more likely than parents of children with autism to prefer full integration. Parents of children with autism expressed more concerns over peer rejection and GE teacher training. Overall, parents of younger children were more likely to prefer full integration.

(continued)

Table 19.2 (*Continued*)

Krajewski & Hyde (2000)	Changes in GE student attitudes over time	459 GE students*	Grades 9–12	Mental retardation	Data from 1987/data from 1998	Questionnaires	Mainstreaming (inclusion) appears to positively influence GE students' attitudes toward peers with mental retardation.
Leyser & Tappendorf (2001)	Changes in mainstreaming practices	91 SE and GE teachers	Grades 1–8*	All disabilities*	N/A	Questionnaires	Educators do not hold unfavorable attitudes toward mainstreaming, but do not strongly support the practice either. Teachers did not generally use a wide variety of teaching strategies, as expected.
Rea, McLaughlin, & Walther-Thomas (2002)	Academic and behavior outcomes	58	Grade 8	Learning disabilities	Inclusion/pull-out	Academic outcomes, behavior outcomes, and attendance	LD students in inclusive classrooms received higher grades, higher scores on tests of achievement, comparable levels of suspensions, and higher rates of school attendance.
Robertson, Chamberlain, & Kasari (2003)	Relationship between GE teachers and children with autism	187 students (12 students with autism)	Grades 2–3	Autism	N/A	Questionnaires and interviews	Overall, GE teachers form good relationships with students with autism, but this is negatively impacted by problem behavior. The presence of a paraprofessional in the class did not appear to impact the teacher–student relationship.
Stahmer & Ingersol (2004)	Toddlers with autism in inclusive preschools	20 children	6–17 mos.	Autistic spectrum disorders	Pretest/Posttest	Standardized assessments, functional outcomes	Children with autism in mainstreamed preschool environments exhibited significant increases in social and language skills. Play skills also positively improved.

*In these instances, explicit data were not provided by the authors. We conclude the data reported in this table based on our reading of the article.

What We Can Do

In addition to evaluating student outcomes, the professional literature describes environmental conditions that appear to facilitate successful inclusion. This research has been synthesized to create the following checklist for conducting an informal needs assessment as part of the inclusion decision-making process.

- *Effective inclusion requires leadership.* Administrators must fully support the notion of inclusion and provide the leadership necessary to make inclusion work. Administrative support can have the effect of creating a climate of openness to change, which is required whenever inclusion strategies are introduced (McLeskey & Waldron, 2002). This may call for "visionary leaders" who are willing to share their vision and encourage stakeholders to take an active role in the changes (Villa & Thousand, 2003). Administrators can expect that teachers will have concerns around new demands and roles, the need for additional training, and the impact inclusion practices will have on GE classrooms (Salend & Garrick-Duhaney, 1999). These concerns generally intensify in cases where student disabilities are severe or full integration strategies are attempted (Scruggs & Mastropieri, 1996). In response, administrators must demonstrate leadership through active involvement. This is often evidenced through their approach to IEP meetings. Do they attend? Are they active contributors? Does someone usually have to go find them? These behaviors reflect the administrators' priorities and may implicitly condone teachers who do not prioritize SE students included in their classrooms. Conversely, administrators who clearly demonstrate a priority for attending meetings, who ask teachers about the progress of students in special education, and who collaborate with special education teachers to support inclusion of students will create a climate where inclusion is a priority and professionals work to make these collaborative efforts succeed.
- *GE and SE teachers must be included in the decision-making process.* Teachers must take an active role in the development and decision-making process of the IEP for inclusion to be effective (McLeskey & Waldron, 2002). This process is frequently compromised when the

GE teacher who is going to be responsible for implementing the IEP is not included in the development. As a result, GE teachers often feel as though the decisions to include children with special needs in their classroom are made without their input or consent. This is common when an IEP is being made or reviewed in the spring and no one knows who the child is going to have as a teacher in the fall. In these cases the GE portion of IEPs may be ignored until problems reappear the following year. It is also common to have educators in one school prepare the IEP in the spring without specific interventions so teachers at a new school (e.g., when going from elementary to middle) can insert the interventions when the child arrives in the fall. Since the teachers at the new school do not know much about the child at the beginning of the school year, the interventions tend to be a template and the experience from the original school years may be lost. Furthermore, in our experience attending IEP meetings, it is not uncommon for the regular education teachers to be included in the discussions simply to make the meetings "official." This usually implies a token role for the GE teacher and is inconsistent with the recommendations from the literature. Meaningful inclusion implemented by invested teachers is unlikely to occur in this type of a system.

- *Additional training and/or collaboration must be available to teachers.* Teachers commonly express concerns around their own ability to effectively teach students with special needs (Salend & Garrick-Duhaney, 1999). To ease these concerns, additional training should be made available that is thorough, offered repeatedly, and available during the school day in the form of consultation and technical assistance. In our experience, ongoing collaboration between teachers and a school psychologist has proven invaluable in supporting students with special needs in the GE classroom. GE teachers appreciate the support and the assistance when solving problems "on the fly."
- *Schools must make a continuum of integrative placements available for their SE students.* Research suggests that, given the diversity of students with special needs, a variety of inclusion strategies should be made available (Manset & Semmel, 1997). For example, one school may utilize self-contained SE classrooms, "pull-out" resource rooms, and SE co-teachers in GE classrooms, all of which are available to SE

students based on individual needs. Sometimes schools over-rely on a rigid set of services that may vary in intensity but are not flexible enough to provide a true continuum. Inclusion requires teachers to relinquish the traditional distinctions between SE and GE services. Instead, the focus should be on identifying a set of interventions that work and then sharing the responsibility for implementation (Villa & Thousand, 2003). In fact, there has been some pressure to completely eliminate the SE–GE distinction altogether, so that all students, regardless of need or ability level, will be served in one integrated environment (Fuchs & Fuchs, 1994). While most practices have yet to embrace this approach, effective inclusion does require that educators reexamine the relationship between SE and GE services.

- *Teachers in inclusion classrooms must be prepared to utilize a wide variety of teaching strategies.* Students receiving SE services are extremely diverse; therefore, interventions and accommodations conducted in inclusion classrooms need to reflect that diversity if they are to succeed. Indeed, it is true that one size does not fit all. Teachers in inclusion environments must be prepared to switch between strategies, such as direct instruction and cooperative learning, as needed (Voltz, Brazil, & Ford, 2001). Mastropieri and Scruggs (2001) state that in cases where inclusion was effective at both the elementary and secondary levels, teachers demonstrated effective teaching skills and adapted these to the special learning needs of specific students. One important element of effective and individualized teaching is the close monitoring of each student's progress. But in actual practice, some schools only measure SE students' progress annually at the IEP meetings, or when a parent complains. This system of monitoring is unlikely to be sufficient to support effective inclusion services. Frequent attention and appraisal of student progress is clearly needed, as this information informs adjustments to the teaching strategies.

- *A climate of acceptance should be cultivated within inclusion classrooms.* Although parents of GE students may express concerns, it does not appear that inclusion environments have a negative impact on the overall quality of education (Salend & Garrick-Duhaney, 1999). Rather, recent research like that conducted by Krajewski and Hyde (2000) suggests that inclusion may positively influence the attitudes of GE

students, such that they become more accepting of individuals with disabilities. In other words, GE students generally come away from their experiences in integrated classrooms with a positive outlook. This can be facilitated by teachers who are trained to discuss issues of diversity with GE students (Freeman & Alkin, 2000). What is important is that SE students are made to feel safe and accepted into the inclusion environment (Voltz, Brazil, & Ford, 2001). Common threats to feeling safe include teasing and ridicule by peers, public displays of failure, and feedback that conveys that they are not making contributions to the class. However, it appears that when these problems are prevented, inclusion has the benefit of increasing the social exposure of SE students and may possibly lead to more friendships between SE and GE peers (Freeman & Alkin, 2000; Garrick-Duhaney & Salend, 2000; Salend & Garrick-Duhaney, 1999; Vaughn & Klingner, 1998). Readers should be aware that, while a causal relationship between inclusion and social functioning is often implied in the literature (i.e., inclusion *causes* improvements in social skills), this must be interpreted with caution. Although there are reports that students who are included function socially better than students who are not, it is quite possible that students who function better socially are more likely to be included than students who are severely socially impaired. Furthermore, students with social impairment frequently perceive the social opportunities associated with GE classrooms and activities as situations to be avoided, since they experience social rejection and ridicule. It is important to remember that many children who receive SE services have achieved a very unfavorable reputation and social status prior to ever being referred for SE. The stigma of special education or individual services may pale in comparison to the reputation already established.

- *SE students, when possible, should be involved in the decision-making process.* The research has clearly shown that sentiment among SE students varies greatly in terms of which inclusion strategies they prefer (Vaughn & Klingner, 1998). It stands to reason that, especially for older and more independent SE students, extending some responsibility in the decision-making process will reinforce the sense that they, too, are a stakeholder in the outcomes. Educators should not be surprised if SE students choose the more traditional, segregated approach to SE services, as this has been shown to occur rather regularly (Salend & Garrick-Duhaney, 1999; Vaughn & Klingner, 1998). Students often report that they appreciate the more individualized attention and quiet environment that segregated environments afford. While some students may opt for these restrictive settings, it is important to consider other factors before accommodating to their choice. Children and adolescents frequently find restrictive settings less demanding, and they discover that they can achieve better grades with less effort than in a placement in a GE classroom. Restrictive settings can function as an escape from the social and academic challenges of a GE classroom. Restrictive settings may also be easier for parents and teachers, since the likelihood of problems, need for managing homework, and discipline troubles may be diminished in segregated SE settings. Sometimes restrictive settings can lead to stagnation, and the elimination of problems is due to the removal of academic, organizational, and social challenges. So while increased student involvement in the decision-making process is generally advisable, students, as well as their parents and educators, may need to be encouraged to face the obstacles and daily challenges that stand between them and real success.

Key Points to Remember

Segregation of special education services into specialized environments begs the question of whether separate is equal. In our view, true equality comes from the expectation that all students can and will achieve. If the ultimate goal is to prepare children for life after public education, then high expectations and a continuous priority placed on moving toward independent functioning is critical. After all, employers are not looking for employees for whom they have to organize their materials, prompt them to stay on task, and read or write things for them. So while educators may help students compensate for their weaknesses, the assistance should be temporary and faded to promote and support independent functioning.

Effective inclusion has the potential to raise the bar through the expectation that SE students will eventually learn to succeed in the GE setting.

But regardless of the placement decision, the ultimate goal should be for students with special needs to exhibit newly learned skills and behaviors in multiple environments. Behavior specialists often refer to this type of behavior crossover as *generalization*. Methods for achieving generalization have been described in the literature (e.g., Evans, Langberg, & Williams, 2003) and should be considered when making inclusion decisions and designing the specific interventions.

As emphasized above, inclusion in itself is a placement option, not an intervention. Simple placement alone will not result in real success for students with disabilities. In any environment, educators will need to implement meaningful academic, behavioral, and social interventions. It is this realization that resulted in the movement toward true *inclusion* of SE students in the mainstream environment and away from just passive placements. Providing the necessary interventions and support is often much more challenging in inclusion environments. At times it seems easier for parents, teachers, and students to opt for segregated self-contained classrooms and programs that do not expect students with special needs to compete or achieve.

While it is frequently popular to advocate for extensive inclusion and it is sometimes linked to societal values such as our sense of social justice (e.g., Sapon-Shevin, 2003), there are practical issues that challenge this practice. For example, schools cannot overlook the practical implications of how the modern emphasis on high-stakes testing is likely to affect these efforts (Defur, 2002). The pressures to move through high volumes of material in preparation for tests might make GE classrooms less amenable to inclusion efforts (Mastropieri & Scruggs, 2001). Furthermore, other practical limitations need to be considered such as class size, teacher/student compatibility, and number of other students in the classroom who require individualized instructions or interventions from the classroom teacher. While these are not always addressed in the professional literature, school-based practitioners will undoubtedly be faced with these issues.

In general, researchers have attempted to answer three fundamental questions that pertain to mainstreaming or inclusion: What are the benefits, if any, of inclusion? Are general education students or teachers likely to be negatively impacted by having students with special needs in their classrooms? And how can educators make inclusion effective? The findings reveal many advantages to inclusion that suggest that it should be considered for the educational planning for many SE students, particularly those with high incidence disabilities. Successful inclusion appears to depend on seven conditions that educators must consider when making decisions. These include the degree of administrative support and leadership; how involved teachers are in the decision-making process; the training and consultation available to GE teachers; how robust the continuum of SE services are in the school; how skilled GE teachers are in utilizing multiple teaching styles; the climate of acceptance in GE classrooms; and how involved students are in the decision-making process. While the research provides general guidance, the ultimate decision must be made at the school level based on strategies best able to meet the individual learning needs of the student and help him or her progress toward independent functioning in a GE environment.

References

Defur, S. H. (2002). Education reform, high-stakes assessment, and students with disabilities. *Remedial and Special Education, 23,* 203–211.

Evans, S. W., Langberg, J., & Williams, J. (2003). Treatment generalization in school based mental health. In M. Weist, S. Evans, & N. Lever (Eds.), *Handbook of school mental health.* New York: Kluwer/Plenum.

Freeman, S. F., & Alkin, M. C. (2000). Academic and social attainments of children with mental retardation in general education and special education settings. *Remedial and Special Education, 21,* 3–18.

Fuchs, D., & Fuchs, L. S. (1994). Inclusive schools movement and the radicalization of special education reform. *Exceptional Children, 60,* 294–309.

Garrick-Duhaney, L. M., & Salend, S. J. (2000). Parental perceptions of inclusive educational placements. *Remedial and Special Education, 21*(2), 121–128.

Krajewski, J. J., & Hyde, M. S. (2000). Comparison of teen attitudes toward individuals with mental retardation between 1987 and 1998: Has inclusion made a difference? *Education and Training in Mental Retardation and Developmental Disabilities, 35,* 284–293.

Manset, G., & Semmel, M. I. (1997). Are inclusive programs for students with mild disabilities effective? A comparative review of model programs. *Journal of Special Education, 31,* 155–180.

Mastropieri, M. A., & Scruggs, T. E. (2001). Promoting inclusion in secondary classrooms. *Learning Disability Quarterly, 24,* 265–274.

McLeskey, J., & Waldron, N. L. (2002). School change and inclusive schools: Lessons learned from practice. *Phi Delta Kappan, 84,* 65–73.

Salend, S. J., & Garrick-Duhaney, L. M. (1999). The impact of inclusion on students with and without disabilities and their educators. *Remedial and Special Education, 20,* 114–126.

Sapon-Shevin, M. (2003). Inclusion: A matter of social justice. *Educational Leadership, 61,* 25–28.

Scruggs, T. E., & Mastropieri, M. A. (1996). Teacher perceptions of mainstreaming/inclusion, 1958–1995: A research synthesis. *Exceptional Children, 63,* 59–75.

Stahmer, A. C., & Ingersol, B. (2004). Inclusive programming for toddlers with autistic spectrum disorders: Outcomes from the children's toddler school. *Journal of Positive Behavioral Interventions, 6,* 67–82.

Vaughn, S., & Klingner, J. K. (1998). Student's perceptions of inclusion and resource room settings. *Journal of Special Education, 32,* 79–88.

Villa, R. A., & Thousand, J. S. (2003). Making inclusive education work. *Educational Leadership, 61,* 19–24.

Voltz, D. L., Brazil, N., & Ford, A. (2001). What matters most in inclusive education: A practical guide for moving forward. *Intervention in School and Clinic, 37*(1), 23–30.

CHAPTER 20

Building Successful Alliances With Health Care Professionals

Camille J. Randall ▪ Joseph E. Nyre ▪ Bridget K. Biggs

Getting Started

Students who have been identified for special education services with emotional disturbance or other health impairments represent a significant challenge for school social workers and other school-based mental health providers. In response, a proliferation of Expanded School Mental Health models (Weist, Goldstein, Morris, & Bryant, 2003) provide increased opportunity for social workers and other school-based mental health providers to interact with greater proportions of the student body via universal and targeted prevention activities. Because of these contacts, school social workers and other school-based mental health providers are a crucial link between children and other professionals who provide related services, such as general health care, mental health services, medication management, and community supports. As school-based health centers (SBHCs) become more common practice settings for mental health professionals in the twenty-first century, the need for effective collaborative models between therapeutic staff (commonly social workers) and physicians, nurses, and psychiatrists becomes more salient (American Academy of Pediatrics, 2004; Weist et al., 2003).

Children and adolescents' visits to SBHCs are most commonly for mental health or substance abuse issues (American Academy of Pediatrics, 2004). Due to the prevalence of mental health concerns among youth seen in medical practices, health professionals such as physicians and nurses need to know how to link children with mental health staff. Similarly, mental health staff need to skillfully consult with health care providers about physical symptoms and the effects of psychotropic medication. Fortunately, many SBHCs have on-site psychiatrists for a portion of the week (Waxman, Weist, & Benson, 1999), reducing barriers for school social workers to refer children for evaluations or for them to discuss common clients on their caseloads. Regardless of whether the physicians or psychiatrists providing psychopharmacological treatment are affiliated with the school or based in the community, school social workers encounter youth who are under the care of a physician or other health professional for mental health–related issues. A significant number of children are taking medication for behavioral or emotional difficulties. For school children identified with disabilities, approximately 26% take prescription medication related to their disability; 19% take medication affecting behavior, mood, or emotion (namely, stimulants or antidepressants; Blackorby, Levine, & Wagner, 2002). Other data estimate that, among the general school-aged population, 9% of children take one or more prescription drugs for behavioral or emotional concerns, with antidepressant use increasing to about 5% of insured youth by the time they reach high school (Center for Health and Health Care in Schools, 2004).

What We Know

Much has been written about collaborative practice in schools, yet little has been empirically evaluated. Specific collaborative models addressing the interface between school social workers and health professionals can best be described as in the process of development at this time. Writings on the topic pertain to mental health professionals, broadly, or address social workers in specific settings other than schools. One model training program for behavioral health professionals incorporates didactic and practical training and emphasizes the inclusion of physicians in training activities (Bray & Rogers, 1997). Other writings address private or community-based mental health professionals' integration with primary care or family practice (Lesser, 2000; Pace, Chaney, Mullins, & Olson, 1995; Valenstein, 1999). An empirical study of a primary care pediatric team suggested positive outcomes for some family cases that were collaboratively interviewed by social work and health care staff (Pomerantz, 1984). However, because this retrospective study failed to clearly define collaboration, the application of its findings to other settings is limited. A descriptive study evaluated positive and negative collaborative experiences from both physicians' and social workers' perspectives (Abramson & Mizrahi, 1996). Although professional participants in this study practiced in hospital settings, findings suggest implications for school-based providers. Communication between professionals is upheld as critical in the collaborative process, based on the finding that both social workers and doctors emphasize this feature in recollections of positive and negative working alliances.

For a comprehensive discussion of consultation models, the reader is directed to West and Idol (1987) and Idol and West (1987).

What We Can Do

Although evidence-based best practices in building successful alliances with physicians and other health professionals are wanting at present, many writings present beneficial discussions of barriers and potential contributors to forging good working relationships with health professionals. Additionally, a current school-based treatment model for children with serious psychiatric vulnerabilities emphasizes strong collaboration between the treating therapist and all other professionals involved with a referred child (Nyre, Vernberg, & Roberts, 2003). Experience garnered while working within this model's parameters, too, provides examples of how school-based mental health professionals can communicate with health professionals, as well as offer their expertise in assisting with treatment decisions. The steps set out in

Box 20.1

1. Complete intake.
2. Obtain release/s of information.
3. Make the initial contact/s.
4. Educate school-based health care staff.
5. Educate yourself about health care perspectives and medication management.
6. Collect data on symptoms and functioning.
7. Maintain contacts with health care staff.
8. Consider joint sessions with health care staff.
9. Ensure follow-up with inpatient settings when your client is hospitalized.

Box 20.1 may not be applicable for every client and need not be addressed in order of their presentation. However, they are illustrative of the multiple avenues school-based social workers can interact with health professionals to the benefit of their clients.

1. Intake

As part of a thorough intake interview, school-based social workers should inquire about other professionals who are working with the referred student currently, as well as in the recent past. Parents or guardians should also provide information about historical and current medical conditions and should provide information about current medications that are prescribed to their child (e.g., what kinds? how much? what for?). If a child is prescribed medication to help manage behaviors or emotions, social workers will find it useful to assess the guardian's and child's perceptions of pharmacotherapy. Reluctance about taking medications or lack of belief in their utility may predict problems with medical compliance. Children who take psychotropic medications (e.g., stimulants, antidepressants, mood stabilizers) often have taken several different combinations of drugs (polypharmacy) as their treating physician has attempted to titrate medication to maximize benefits and minimize negative side effects. Complicated medication histories may signal to the social worker increased need for collaboration with the prescribing physician. When appropriate, it may be helpful to complete contact-tracking forms listing others involved in school-based or community treatment and listing medical information (see Figure 20.1). Consistent with best practice guidelines and common school policies, medication information should be shared with the school nurse to ensure appropriate and responsible health care.

2. Release of Information

Information from the intake interview will help determine whether to obtain releases to share information with a child's physician or psychiatrist. Having parents or guardians sign releases during or directly after the intake phase may be most time-efficient. Clinicians should be prepared that some parents may be wary of information exchange, especially given the perceived stigma of receiving mental health treatment. Potential reasons for and examples of information sharing should be clearly specified for the child and parent(s). Social workers should use their agency or school's specified release form and seek assent from students of adolescent age.

3. Initial Contact

Sometimes social workers may wait to contact a child's health care provider until a notable incident (e.g., unexplained mania, child's report of dizziness) or change in medication occurs. Establishing a working relationship prior to such an occurrence by making a brief, informational contact early in treatment may prevent some of the pitfalls associated with a poor alliance between treating professionals. This contact is best made by phone, as it allows providers to define their roles in treatment (Valenstein, 1999). The other professionals may need to see a copy of the release of information prior to speaking with you, so having access to the signed release is often helpful. See chapter 87 for information on safeguarding client information and meeting the requirements of HIPPA regulations. Often, physicians are not aware that their patients are concurrently receiving mental health treatment and may find the simple communication beneficial (Valenstein, 1999). Social workers can state their frequency of contact with the client and the way/s they are involved to prevent duplication of services. Role competition, role confusion, and turf issues can impair cooperation between helping professionals and health care workers (Abramson & Mizrahi, 1996; Lesser, 2000; McDaniel, 1995; Pace et al.,

1995; Waxman et al., 1999). To circumvent problematic processes, social workers can ask health care professionals how they can be helpful after they have introduced their role in working with a common child. Assistance should be volunteered, rather than asserted, as medical professionals may be especially sensitive to perceived threats to their expertise or clinical autonomy (Abramson & Mizrahi, 1996; Bray, Enright, & Rogers, 1997; Waxman et al., 1999). During the initial contact with prescribing physicians, social workers should clarify with the physician their client's current medication regimen. Of final note, communication and accessibility are especially important to physicians when working with other professionals (McDaniel, 1995); social workers can make themselves appear more accessible to physicians by requesting "good times" to call the physician, by providing the best times and means for contacting them, and by keeping written communications (e.g., reports, graphs; see step 6) as concise as possible. Before ending the initial phone call, agree on the timing and means of the next contact (e.g., "How about I call you in two weeks to discuss Jimmy's symptoms and functioning at school?")

4. Educating School-Based Health Care Staff

In cases where physical and mental health care are both located in a school, such as in SBHCs, mental health professionals can educate health staff about common symptom presentations that may necessitate mental health referrals (Weist et al., 2003). General care physicians or nursing staff often appreciate information from the mental health perspective, as some community practitioners have expressed lack of knowledge about psychiatric assessment and treatment (Valenstein, 1999). In addition to providing general information to help school-based health professionals identify appropriate referrals, referral procedures may need to be clarified and documented, so practitioners know the steps for making referrals for mental health treatment (Bray et al., 1997). In working on specific cases, as a courtesy and toward building collaboration, mental health staff should update referring physicians or nurses about the status of referred students (Bray et al., 1997). Additionally, constraints on the sharing of sensitive information should be delineated at the outset of these school-based collegial relationships (Bray & Rogers, 1997).

5. Educating Self About Health Care Perspectives and Medication Management

Many writers discuss the philosophical and training differences between mental health professionals and health care providers. Whereas social workers and other mental health professionals are trained in multiple treatment paradigms (e.g., systems, cognitive-behavioral) and, accordingly, seek multiple sources of information in attempts to understand their clients, health care professionals principally ascribe to a biomedical model (Bray & Rogers, 1997). Increasingly, however, these authors note that primary care physicians have a better grasp of a biopsychosocial model of physical illness. Nevertheless, to communicate well with health care providers, it is essential for social workers to appreciate differences associated with the medical culture.

Social workers have available to them many informational resources describing pharmacotherapy and the indications, recommended doses, and possible side effects of most medications used in treating behavioral and emotional problems. References for several common practitioners' references are provided in a section of this chapter's bibliography. Although these texts should not supplant dialogue with a client's treating physician, they can help social workers ask educated questions during contacts and meetings. Also, an understanding of what effects and side effects are possible with particular medications can help school social workers make informed observations as they meet with their clients on a regular basis. For example, knowing that specific antidepressants (namely, SSRIs) may take up to 2 weeks to show an effect and even longer to reach therapeutic levels, a school-based clinician may wait to contact their client's physician to discuss perceived mood improvement after this medication has been started. Conversely, if a client seems to be demonstrating an adverse reaction (e.g., mania, heart palpitations) to a medicine recently added or increased in dosage, her clinician may opt to contact the physician immediately.

School-based social workers need to exercise caution in conveying what they have learned about the medical management of their clients' physical and sociobehavioral ailments. They are not able to prescribe medication, lacking detailed knowledge about medications' chemical properties or mechanisms of action. During consultation, if a primary care physician indicates a lack of knowledge about how to appropriately medicate a condition, the school-based clinician should suggest a consultation with a child psychiatrist. It is outside the professional bounds of a mental health clinician to recommend the specific use of a medication or to dictate how and when a medication should be changed. Because of more regular end extensive contacts, as well as enhanced ability to confer with teachers and parents on a regular basis, it is appropriate, however, for a school-based clinician to share succinct and well-documented observations of a shared client during consultation with a medical provider. Additionally, it is appropriate for clinicians to be honest about their understanding of how medical treatment may benefit their client. Appropriate care must be taken in selecting language. ("What would be the pros and cons of using an SSRI for Jeannie's presentation?" versus "Based on the depressive symptoms I've seen, Jeannie needs to be on Zoloft.") Step 6 details monitoring mechanisms.

6. Data Collection

Each session a school-based mental health clinician has with a child is an opportunity to monitor his or her emotional and behavioral functioning. Typically, case notes record some degree of such assessment: "*Juan's mood appeared brighter, compared to the past two weeks, and he was eager to describe the fun things he and his stepfather have been doing together. He said he is less argumentative with his siblings and has been able to fall asleep quickly at bedtime.*" If a child has recently started a medication, or if changes have been made in a prior regimen, the clinician may wish to document symptom levels more systematically. Data may be gathered weekly, during sessions, or may be arranged to be collected more frequently (e.g., school social worker can consult with classroom teacher 3x/week; daily ratings possible in some programs). A sample symptom rating form is provided in Figure 20.2. This example includes common behavioral symptoms of children referred for school-based mental health services, as well as common areas to assess for side effects of psychotropic medicines (e.g., toileting, sleep, tremors). Clinicians will need to regularly consult with caregivers to obtain the most accurate information for symptom rating scales. Even though they may be somewhat idiosyncratically employed, rating forms are able to provide quasi-objective behavioral data and are able to illustrate changes across time.

Physicians may appreciate the relative simplicity and organization of numerical data, given the pragmatics of time (primary care physicians may see up to 60 patients per day; Bray & Rogers, 1997). When clinicians offer their assistance during initial contacts with physicians, they may inquire whether physicians have their own preferred rating forms. Measures may be specific to medication or diagnosis, or may be general, as the example in Figure 20.2. Further accommodating physicians' time constraints, clinicians may wish to prepare graphical summaries of ratings forms (see Figure 20.3). Hawkins and Mathews (1999) describe other methods of assessing clinical progress in school settings.

Information about a child's response to medication may help shape health professionals' diagnostic understanding of shared clients' behavioral and emotional problems. For instance, a provider, viewing a child's mood symptoms to be consistent with an anxiety disorder, prescribed an SSRI. However, soon afterward, the social worker who regularly met with the child at school was asked to work with the child one-on-one due to his erratic and seemingly "uncontrollable" behavior. During the second day of his marked behavioral change, the social worker consulted with the prescribing physician, also providing case note data indicating that irritable behavior seemed to be problematic for him at regular intervals. This information, combined with his acute response to the SSRI, led the physician to consider a bipolar working diagnosis (Lofthouse & Fristad, 2004). Medication changes, which included a mood stabilizer, eventually helped the student function well at school.

7. Maintenance

Many authors recommend that mental health professionals regularly and continually contact health professionals (e.g., pediatricians, psychiatrists, nurse practitioners) to maintain good alliance (Bray & Rogers, 1997; Valenstein, 1999). However, as suggested earlier, physicians have increasingly busy schedules and limited consultation time outside of patient visits, which often range from 15 to 20 minutes. It is therefore essential that school-based mental health professionals plan the frequency and mode of regular contact early in alliance formation with physicians. For students with special health care needs, school-based mental health professionals can adapt best practices from pediatric psychology

(e.g., pain management, medication compliance for diabetes), necessitating regular contact with treating physicians to determine how psychosocial interventions seem to be enhancing medical treatment (Weist et al., 2003). Further, Pace and colleagues (1995) suggest ways that mental health clinicians can foster health care professionals' trust in ongoing consultative enterprises. These authors suggest that clinicians "ascertain the physician's psychological hypotheses about the patient and gradually merge his or her impressions with those of the physician" and "encourage a collegial relationship by facilitating communication and seeking clarification about terminology, diagnoses, procedures, or treatments that may be unclear to either party" (p. 126).

8. Special Considerations

In certain circumstances, joint sessions between mental health professionals and physicians may be indicated (see section 4). This may be considered the most powerful method of collaboration, as many providers find it to be useful in the resolution of particularly difficult or complex problems or impasses on the part of either professional (McDaniel, 1995). Joint sessions may enable social workers to model assertiveness and begin to transfer authority back to caregivers who have been reluctant to advocate for their children during medical visits or who have difficulty formulating questions about medical procedures or prescription rationales. School-based clinicians may learn that a client has been admitted to the hospital for a medical procedure or for inpatient psychiatric observation or treatment. In such cases, it is important for clinicians to obtain needed releases to share pertinent information, as well as to obtain summary reports and to plan for aftercare and the student's transition back to school (Rappaport, Osher, Garrison, Anderson-Ketchmark, & Dwyer, 2003). The absence of such communication and collaboration may re-create or exacerbate precipitating or causative environmental triggers leading to the initial admission.

Tools and Practice Examples

The following case example demonstrates how a mental health professional may interact with a pediatrician and psychiatrist, given concerns about a child's physical and behavioral functioning that arise in the course of treatment. Additionally, it illustrates how a mental health professional may empower a parent to address his or her child's health concerns. Despite attempts to transfer skills to the parent, therapists may encounter circumstances where ethical practice dictates decision making. This vignette exhibits examples of critical decision points.

Jimmy, a 6-year-old in first grade, was referred to a therapeutic classroom in August. He had been diagnosed with ADHD and was receiving psychotropic medication from a child psychiatrist in the community. Referral concerns included aggressiveness at school and with younger siblings, developmentally inappropriate difficulty distinguishing reality from fantasy, poor parental supervision, and suspected physical and emotional abuse by his stepfather. At referral, Jimmy was prescribed Strattera and clonidine.

Setting Up

During the initial planning meeting, the classroom therapist obtained signed releases from Jimmy's mother permitting information sharing with the prescribing psychiatrist and family physician. Jimmy's classroom therapist educated herself about the indications and possible side effects of Jimmy's medications by using a prescription reference. Because the therapist had an opportunity to observe Jimmy daily and had regular contact with his parents, she had information valuable for medication management and health care that psychiatrists and pediatricians typically have difficulty accessing. Also, because of this regular contact, the therapist, along with the school nurse, were in a position to monitor whether Jimmy was receiving medications as prescribed. Given recent history of morning doses being missed, in September, the therapist arranged with Jimmy's mother and the school nurse to have him take his Strattera and his two daytime doses of clonidine at school. The therapeutic staff at school maintained daily records of Jimmy's symptom levels, noting a period of increased distractibility in September and increased irritability in October. Extreme lethargy and pallor were noted from late September forward. During early contacts with Jimmy's mother, the therapist inquired about nutrition and sleep schedules, in order to determine possible sources

of his lethargy and irritability. She encouraged the mother to discuss concerns about lethargy with Jimmy's psychiatrist during his upcoming appointment, thus supporting the mother to advocate for her child's needs and promoting the role of the psychiatrist. Additionally, she encouraged his mother to schedule a pediatric appointment to assess for anemia.

Linking

In working with Jimmy and his parents, the therapist encountered several impasses. Linking with medical personnel was vital to meeting his needs. As this case illustrates, multiple and various approaches, as well as persistence, may be needed to successfully coordinate services to meet all the needs of the child. Despite several follow-up contacts, Jimmy's mother had not scheduled a physical. Jimmy continued to present as lethargic and pale. During a home visit in October, his therapist asked if she could attend his upcoming psychiatry appointment, in order to share current concerns about Jimmy's lethargy and affect. In preparation, Jimmy's therapist used a spreadsheet program to create graphs charting key symptom ratings from the prior months (e.g., lethargy, flat affect, irritability; Figure 20.3). Jimmy and his mother did not show for the scheduled appointment. After the missed appointment, the therapist contacted the psychiatrist's nurse practitioner by phone and provided a copy of the graphs, as well as a brief note about her concerns regarding Jimmy's drowsiness. Although the medication changes could not be approved without an office checkup, the nurse practitioner acknowledged the helpfulness of the information.

During a home visit in mid-November, the therapist encouraged Jimmy's mother to schedule a physical before the end of the visit. The therapist attended this appointment with Jimmy and his mother in December, modeling appropriate ways to address health care concerns. Jimmy began taking multivitamins after this appointment. Around this time, the mother reported that Jimmy's state-assisted medical insurance had lapsed and that she had not filled out paperwork to reinstate it. Jimmy had enough clonidine to last a month. Understanding that abruptly discontinuing clonidine could cause withdrawal symptoms (e.g., headaches, agitation, rapid rise in blood pressure), the therapist emphasized that Jimmy's mother should contact his psychiatrist by the end of the week. Follow-up contact indicated this had not occurred, so the therapist initiated rescheduling a medication checkup for late December and arranged with the psychiatrist's nurse to have prescriptions available until this time. After his medication checkup, Jimmy's psychiatrist lowered his dose of clonidine and increased his Strattera.

Continuation

In January, the school's therapeutic staff noted a pattern of increased inattention and impulsivity and a few days of markedly erratic behavior. Additionally, disorganized thought symptoms reemerged. Again, the therapist's familiarity with Jimmy's medications and their indications proved important for identifying potential problems related to his medications that were influencing his behavior. The therapist consulted with the school nurse who confirmed that Jimmy had no more medicine at school. In addition, reports from home suggested that he had not been receiving clonidine consistently or at all. The therapist continued to support Jimmy's mother in resuming prescription coverage and had additional phone contacts with Jimmy's psychiatric nurse practitioner. Through this collaborative effort, his prescriptions were again available in February. During the next several months of treatment, Jimmy's therapist continued to promote regular attendance at medication checkups and maintained daily symptom records in anticipation of sharing data with his health care providers.

Forms

Figure 20.1 can be used as a guide to gather information about a student's medication usage. Figure 20.2 can be used as a guide to assess students' symptoms. Figure 20.3 provides a sample of a symptom rating graph.

The following list provides basic medical texts to assist school social workers in working with medical professionals.

Diamond, R. J. (2002). *Instant psychopharmacology: A guide for the nonmedical mental health professional* (2nd ed.). New York: W. W. Norton.

Epocrates. (2004). Epocrates Rx online premium web-based desktop reference. Retrieved from http://www2.epocrates.com/products/online_general_info.html.

Gitlin, M. J. (1996). The psychotherapist's guide to psychopharmacology (2nd ed.). New York: Free Press.

Julien, R. M. (2001). *A primer of drug action: A concise, nontechnical guide to the actions, uses, and side effects of psychoactive drugs* (9th ed.). New York: Worth.

Maxmen, J. S., & Ward, N. G. (2002). *Psychotropic drugs: Fast facts* (3rd ed.). New York: W. W. Norton.

Key Points to Remember

"A successful collaborative relationship depends on the same interpersonal skills the [clinician] uses with patients in psychotherapy: good communication, an understanding of the physician's worldview, the development of a personal relationship, a common language, shared goals, and a contract to work together" (McDaniel, 1995, p. 118). Although deference is important in all relationships with other professionals, social workers working within school settings may find it particularly important in fostering good consultative alliances with health care professionals. Traditionally, physicians are accustomed to autonomous clinical decision making and differentially espouse the biomedical model of pathology. School-based social workers, in turn, are more accustomed to the professional reciprocity inherent in interdisciplinary student improvement teams and are less likely to espouse a single explanatory model for their client's behavioral and emotional difficulties. Actions school-based social workers can take to promote successful connections with health care providers, in summary, include:

- In initial meetings with children and their families, inquire about other professionals working with the child, existing medical conditions, and medications. Get signed releases of information to contact those professionals as appropriate.
- Call health professionals early in treatment to establish contact. Explain your role and inquire how you might be helpful to the child's treatment.
- Work out a regular contact schedule with the health professional. Provide written summaries and graphs of observed symptoms when possible and appropriate.
- Clarify confidentiality constraints. Realize that mental health practitioners may have different standards than other professionals.
- Learn about the biomedical model to better understand the perspective of health care

Figure 20.1. Sample Medical Information Form

MEDICAL INFORMATION FORM

Student Name: _____

Neighborhood School: _____

Current medications, doses, and times of administration
(*include all medications the student is taking, not just medications administered at school*):

Person responsible for monitoring medications:

Psychiatric diagnosis or diagnoses:

Brief summary of medical history:

Figure 20.2. Sample Symptom Rating Scale

Symptom Rating Scale

Student _____

Rater/s _____ Date _____ Setting _____

Instructions: Please rate each symptom from 0 (absent) to 9 (serious). Circle only one number beside each item. A zero means that you have not seen the symptom in this child today (or received reliable report of the symptom), and a 9 means that you have noticed it frequently and at a high intensity level.

Symptom	n.a.	Mild or Infrequent				Moderate Frequency & Intensity				High Frequency & Intensity	
Picking or biting skin	0	1	2	3	4	5	6	7	8	9
Oppositional	0	1	2	3	4	5	6	7	8	9
Stares a lot or daydreams	0	1	2	3	4	5	6	7	8	9
Talks less with others	0	1	2	3	4	5	6	7	8	9
Uninterested in others	0	1	2	3	4	5	6	7	8	9
Appetite change (more/less)	0	1	2	3	4	5	6	7	8	9
Irritable	0	1	2	3	4	5	6	7	8	9
Stomach aches/Toileting changes	0	1	2	3	4	5	6	7	8	9
Headaches	0	1	2	3	4	5	6	7	8	9
Drowsy or lethargic	0	1	2	3	4	5	6	7	8	9
Easily frustrated	0	1	2	3	4	5	6	7	8	9

(continued)

Figure 20.2. (*Continued*)

Symptom	n.a.	Mild or Infrequent				Moderate Frequency & Intensity			High Frequency & Intensity	
Sad/Unhappy	0	1	2	3	4	5	6	7	8	9
Prone to crying	0	1	2	3	4	5	6	7	8	9
Flat affect	0	1	2	3	4	5	6	7	8	9
Anxious/Vigilant/Worried	0	1	2	3	4	5	6	7	8	9
Tremors	0	1	2	3	4	5	6	7	8	9
Euphoric/Unusually happy	0	1	2	3	4	5	6	7	8	9
Dizziness	0	1	2	3	4	5	6	7	8	9
Tics or nervous movements	0	1	2	3	4	5	6	7	8	9
Inattentive	0	1	2	3	4	5	6	7	8	9
Overactive	0	1	2	3	4	5	6	7	8	9
Impulsive	0	1	2	3	4	5	6	7	8	9
Tantrum or anger display	0	1	2	3	4	5	6	7	8	9
Other _____	0	1	2	3	4	5	6	7	8	9

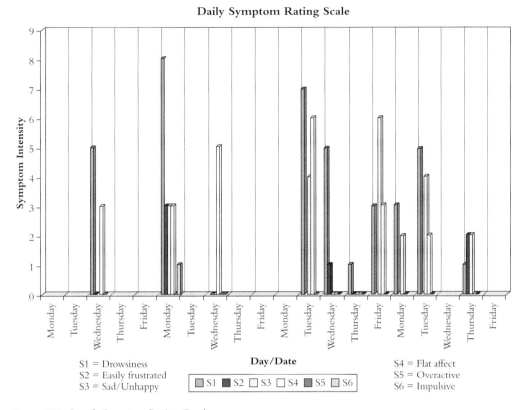

Figure 20.3. Sample Symptom Rating Graph

professionals to improve communication and ward off misunderstandings. (Helpful sources are provided below.)

• In complex cases or at times of impasse, consider conducting a joint session with the health care professional.

References

Abramson, J. S., & Mizrahi, T. (1996). When social workers and physicians collaborate: Positive and negative interdisciplinary experiences. *Social Work, 41,* 270–281.

American Academy of Pediatrics. (2004). School-based mental health services: Policy statement. *Pediatrics, 113,* 1839–1845.

Blackorby, J., Levine, P., & Wagner, M. (2002). *Behind the label: The functional implications of disability* (SRI P10656). Menlo Park, CA: SRI International.

Bray, J. H., Enright, M. F., & Rogers, J. (1997). Collaboration with primary care physicians. In J. A. Morris (Ed.), *Practicing psychology in rural settings: Hospital*

privileges and collaborative care. Washington, DC: American Psychological Association.

Bray, J. H., & Rogers, J. C. (1997). The Linkages project: Training behavioral health professionals for collaborative practice with primary care physicians. *Families, Systems, & Health, 15,* 55–63.

Center for Health and Health Care in Schools. (2004, June). *Psychotropic drugs and children: Use, trends, and implications for schools.* Washington, DC: George Washington University, School of Public Health and Health Services.

Hawkins, R. P., & Mathews, J. R. (1999). Frequent monitoring of clinical outcomes: Research and accountability for clinical practice. *Education & Treatment of Children, 22,* 117–135.

Idol, L., & West, J. F. (1987). Consultation in special education: II. Training and practice. *Journal of Learning Disabilities, 20,* 474–494.

Lesser, J. G. (2000). Clinical social work and family medicine: A partnership in community service. *Health & Social Work, 25,* 119–126.

Lofthouse, N., & Fristad, M. A. (2004). Psychosocial interventions for children with early-onset bipolar spectrum disorder. *Clinical Child and Family Review, 7,* 71–88.

McDaniel, S. H. (1995). Collaboration between psychologists and family physicians: Implementing the biopsychosocial model. *Professional Psychology: Research and Practice, 26,* 117–122.

Nyre, J. E., Vernberg, E. M., & Roberts, M. C. (2003). Serving the most severe of serious emotionally disturbed students in school settings. In M. D. Weist, S. W. Evans, & N. A. Lever (Eds.), *Handbook of school mental health: Advancing practice and research* (pp. 203–222). New York: Kluwer/Plenum.

Pace, T. M., Chaney, J. M., Mullins, L. L., & Olson, R. A. (1995). Psychological consultation with primary care physicians: Obstacles and opportunities in the medical setting. *Professional Psychology: Research and Practice, 26,* 123–131.

Pomerantz, B. R. (1984). Collaborative interviewing: A family-centered approach to pediatric care. *Health and Social Work, 9,* 66–73.

Rappaport, N., Osher, D., Garrison, E. G., Anderson-Ketchmark, C., & Dwyer, K. (2003). Enhancing collaboration within and across disciplines to advance mental health programs in schools. In M. D. Weist, S. W. Evans, & N. A. Lever (Eds.), *Handbook of school mental health: Advancing practice and research* (pp. 107–118). New York: Kluwer/Plenum.

Valenstein, M. (1999). Primary care physicians and mental health professionals: Models for collaboration. In M. B. Riba and R. Balon (Eds.), *Psychopharmacology and psychotherapy: A collaborative approach* (pp. 325–352). Washington, DC: American Psychiatric Association.

Waxman, R. P., Weist, M. D., & Benson, D. M. (1999). Toward collaboration in the growing education–mental health interface. *Clinical Psychology Review, 19,* 239–253.

Weist, M. D., Goldstein, A., Morris, L., & Bryant, T. (2003). Integrating expanded school mental health programs and school-based health centers. *Psychology in the Schools, 40,* 297–308.

West, J. F., & Idol, L. (1987). School consultation: I. An interdisciplinary perspective on theory, models, and research. *Journal of Learning Disabilities, 20,* 388–408.

Promoting Health and Well-Being: Effective Interventions and Resources

This section focuses on interventions and resources for health-related issues that school social workers and school mental health professionals identify as growing problems in their schools. Topics addressed in this section include substance abuse, HIV-AIDS, sexually transmitted diseases, self-harm and mutilation, adolescent pregnancy, and obesity. Each chapter includes concise briefs on the best practice knowledge in this area and quick reviews of the most effective interventions. Substance abuse, both drugs and alcohol, continues to present a primary challenge and is a major mitigating factor associated with other school problems such as school violence, adolescent pregnancy, academic failure, and dropout. This section includes evidence-based interventions to assist school social workers and other mental health professionals who may not have experience or specific training in the area of substance abuse assessment and treatment and yet are confronted with it in their school practice. These chapters will also serve as welcome updates for professionals with extensive training in substance abuse treatment. HIV and sexually transmitted diseases and adolescent pregnancy are also continuing health threats to adolescents, and school-based practitioners are provided resources and curricula that can help reduce these challenges among adolescents. Finally, childhood obesity serves as one of the foremost health threats of our time, and schools are being called upon to help with this problem. Best practices are offered for helping children and youth with weight management.

Substance Abuse Prevention: Effective School-Based Programs

Laura DiGiovanni

CHAPTER 21

Getting Started

According to all of the latest figures, it appears that our youth are smoking cigarettes, drinking alcohol, and using illicit drugs *less* frequently (SAMHSA, 2004). Children's attitudes have appeared to improve regarding substance use and abuse in recent years. In addition, participation in delinquent behaviors has dramatically declined in our youth. This is all good news and means that the substance abuse prevention approaches are working. However, many students in our schools continue to smoke cigarettes, drink alcohol under age, and use illicit drugs. If some children have changed, programs will need to be even more effective to reach the remaining potential users. Therefore, it is more important than ever that the programs we use are the most effective in school-based prevention programs. One program that appears to be effective is the Life Skills Training program.

The reality of substance use among our youth is still very striking. The National Institute on Alcohol Abuse and Alcoholism (NIAAA, 2004) identified alcohol as the primary psychoactive substance used by our youth. The Fiscal Year 2005 Congressional Budget Justification (NIAAA, 2004) indicates that 78% of 12th graders, 67% of 10th graders, and 47% of 8th graders have used alcohol. In addition, inhalant use among 8th graders shows a dramatic increase over the past year (SAMHSA, 2004). Although illicit drug use seems to have decreased in recent years, prescription drug use and abuse remains high (SAMHSA, 2004). Also, heroin and crack use by students have not declined and continue to present problems. According to the National Survey on Drug Use and Health (SAMHSA, 2004), 31% of children aged 12–17 had smoked cigarettes in their lifetime. These statistics highlight the need for the use of *effective* substance abuse prevention approaches.

What We Know

Although prevention programs vary regarding focus (e.g., parents, family, and communities), substance abuse prevention programs have primarily been school-based. Schools have the greatest access to the majority of the nation's children and are well known for providing education and collecting data from students about substance use/abuse (Burke, 2002).

Approaches to Substance Abuse Prevention

Traditional approaches to school-based substance abuse prevention have included information dissemination of facts, such as public service announcements. Fear arousal (e.g., trying to scare children into avoiding alcohol and drug use) is another commonly used method of traditional instruction. Another possible traditional approach has included moral appeals (e.g., doing the "right" thing). Finally, affective education, or focusing on children's feelings of self-worth and feelings about smoking, drinking, or using drugs, was included.

However, none of these approaches has seemed to be successful. The main argument for the limited or complete lack of success suggests that these methods do not address the *underlying causes* of substance use/abuse (Botvin & Botvin, 1992; Gottfredson, 1996; Kinder, Pape, & Walfish, 1980; Schinke, Botvin, & Orlandi, 1991; Sherman, 2000; Swisher & Hoffman, 1975). One of the most well-known school-based substance abuse prevention programs is Project DARE (Drug Abuse Resistance Education), which has police officers go to schools and provide factual information to students. However, studies have indicated that it is not effective (Ennett, Tobler, Ringwalt, & Flewelling, 1994; Gottfredson, 1996; Rosenbaum & Hanson, 1998; Sherman, 2000).

Beginning in the 1970s, psychosocial approaches began to emerge, including resistance skills, psychological inoculation, and personal and social skills training. These approaches address more of the *causes* of substance abuse and have produced more promising results for reducing alcohol and marijuana use, increasing knowledge, and impacts on attitudes, beliefs, and social-resistance skills (Best et al., 1984; Hops, Tildesley, & Lichtenstein, 1990; McAlister, Perry, Killen, Slinkard, & Maccoby, 1980; Schinke, Botvin, & Orlandi, 1991).

Meta-Analytic Reviews

Research suggests that these programs also have limitations. Early meta-analyses indicated that these previously employed school-based substance abuse prevention programs appeared to increase knowledge but did little to change attitudes and behaviors of students regarding drug use or abuse (Bangert-Drowns, 1988; Brunvold & Rundall, 1988; Tobler, 1986). Their findings also consistently point toward the need for an increased focus on psychosocial factors, such as school, family, media, and peer influences, and on personal competencies, cognitive expectancies, social skills, and psychological factors (Bangert-Drowns, 1988; Botvin & Botvin, 1992; Bruvold & Rundall, 1988; Tobler, 1986).

However, later analyses indicate that these meta-analytic reviews had a number of weaknesses. Bruvold (1993) indicates that these studies failed to meet a number of necessary criteria for current meta-analytic reviews: they were not comprehensive, did not use a systematic screening process to eliminate studies that were not equal or methodologically sound, did not use appropriate statistical techniques, and did not cover a specified time period.

More recent meta-analytic studies conducted in the 1990s used more sophisticated statistical analysis, more methodologically sound studies, and a more defined set of studies in the analysis (Bruvold, 1993; Tobler & Stratton, 1997; White & Pitts, 1998). These meta-analyses revealed that school-based prevention programs that addressed more psychosocial factors were more effective in changing attitudes and behaviors (Bruvold, 1993; Tobler & Stratton, 1997; White & Pitts, 1998). For example, Bruvold (1993) noted that programs that attempted to develop a student's ability to recognize social pressures to use drugs and ways to resist them, along with the ability to identify immediate social and physical consequences, were better able to change students' attitudes and behaviors. This was best accomplished through lengthier practice, role playing, a public declaration not to use, and most important, through discussion, rather than earlier lecture models. Tobler and Stratton (1997) also improved on previous meta-analyses and determined that the most effective school-based prevention programs were smaller in size (not held in auditoriums) and more interactive. They noted that failures in the programs could have been due to poor implementation. Finally, White and Pitts (1998) determined that prevention programs that increased their focus on social skills training improved students' abilities to change attitudes and behaviors, along with increasing their knowledge about drug use and misuse. Some of these social skills included a component of improving self-esteem, assertiveness and refusal skills, and life skills. In order for school-based prevention programs to be effective, an increased focus on the social aspects of student's lives and less of a traditional lecture approach seem to be common elements that the more recent meta-analytic studies have in common.

What We Can Do

Many of these school-based substance abuse prevention programs continue today and can be accessed through the Internet. The Center for Substance Abuse Prevention (1999) (CSAP) has created a National Registry of Effective Prevention Programs (NREPP) to identify, review, and disseminate effective alcohol, tobacco, and other drugs (ATOD) prevention programs (see Table 21.2 for program access information).

Life Skills Training and Previous Research

In the late 1970s, an integrative approach to school-based substance abuse prevention was developed by Gilbert Botvin, called the Life Skills Training (LST) program (Botvin, Eng, & Williams, 1980). As a research program, this effective model has received extensive study for more than 20 years, with results indicating approximately a 50–87% reduction in the prevalence of tobacco, alcohol, or illicit drug use (National Health Promotion Associates [NHPA], 2002). In a strategic plan, Botvin and colleagues have systematically studied the effectiveness of the LST program, using experimental and quasi-experimental, pre- and post-test designs. First, Botvin and colleagues focused on the program's effectiveness and produced a 75% reduction in number of new student cigarette smokers (Botvin et al., 1980). Then, Botvin and his colleagues examined the LST program with different providers (e.g., teachers, peer-led classes, and school staff) with continued success (Botvin & Eng, 1982; Botvin, Renick, & Baker, 1983).

Further studies examined and demonstrated the effectiveness of the LST program in targeting alcohol and other illicit drugs (Botvin, Baker, Renick, Filazzola, & Botvin, 1984; Botvin, Baker, Dusenbury, Tortu, & Botvin, 1990). When examining the effectiveness with different ethnicities (in particular, Hispanic and African American) and substances, findings supported not only the efficacy of the LST program but also determined that the program did not always require cultural modifications (Botvin, Baker, Botvin, et al., 1993; Botvin, Dusenbury, Baker, & James-Ortiz, 1989).

Botvin and his colleagues (1990) also examined the generalizability of the program by conducting a large-scale controlled prevention trial of 5,954 students in 56 schools with positive results up to 40 months after the training. This research indicates the effectiveness of the LST program over a six-year period with 7th, 8th, and 9th grade students (Botvin, Schinke, Epstein, Diaz, & Botvin, 1995). Given the number and variety of studies conducted on the LST program, it seems clear that it offers great opportunities for school-based substance abuse prevention.

Table 21.1 Descriptions of Meta-Analyses

Author	Type of Prevention Intervention	Substances Studies	Populations	Findings
Tobler (1986)	A variety—mostly traditional, mostly affective educational, information dissemination	143 programs—a variety, including tobacco, alcohol, and marijuana	Adolescents—a variety, causing problems with findings. A variety of programs included in criteria (some students had drug problems, some had disciplinary problems, and some no problems at all)	Programs were most effective in increasing knowledge; minor improvements in reducing behaviors; even smaller effects in improving attitudes; found that peer programs were most effective in producing positive changes. Weak methodology.
Bangert-Drowns (1988)	Mostly traditional—affective educational programs, information dissemination	Smoking prevention programs	Elementary school to college students—traditional students	Maintained support of previous findings—programs increase knowledge of substances. Changes in student attitudes were more statistically significant. Behaviors continued to show limited change. Peers in programs appear to impact changes more than didactic instruction.
Bruvold & Rundall (1988)	Mostly traditional—affective educational programs, information dissemination	19 programs—alcohol and tobacco	Adolescent school students	Increased knowledge, but failed to change attitudes or behaviors.
Bruvold (1993)	Psychosocial—personal and social skills training	94 programs—tobacco prevention, curricula mainly provided in schools	Adolescent school students	Behavioral effect sizes were found to be largest for interventions with a social reinforcement orientation, moderate for interventions with developmental or social norms orientation, and small for traditional orientation.
Tobler & Stratton (1997)	Psychosocial—personal and social skills training	120 programs—tobacco, alcohol, marijuana and illicit drugs	5th—12th graders	Most effective programs in changing adolescent drug use were interactive (groups C and D) and included comprehensive life skill training (CLST) or social influence training (SIT). Larger groups were less effective.
White & Pitts (1998)	Psychosocial—personal and social skills training	62 prevention programs	71% school-based	Most effective programs were a mix of focused interventions (assertiveness skills, refusal skills, and normative education) and generic training (life skills, decision-making, problem-solving, goal-setting, and communication skills).

Table 21.2 Overview of Major Preventive Approaches

Intervention	Focus	Methods	Source/Name of Education Program	Web Site
Traditional				
Information dissemination (fear arousal, moral appeals)	Increase knowledge of drugs, consequences of use; promote anti-drug use attitudes	Didactic instruction, discussion, audio/video presentations, displays of substances, posters, pamphlets, school assembly programs	Public-information campaigns; government agencies; community groups (e.g., American Cancer Society, National Council on Alcoholism)	American Cancer Society: http://www.cancer.org/docroot/PED/content/PED_10_14_How_to_Fight_Teen_Smoking.asp National Council on Alcoholism: http://www.ncadd-middlesex.com/
			Drug Abuse Resistance Education (DARE)	Drug Abuse Resistance Education: http://www.dare.com/home/default.asp
Affective education	Increase self-esteem, responsible decision making, interpersonal growth; generally includes little or no information about drugs	Didactic instruction, discussion, experiential activities, group problem-solving exercises	Here's Looking at You 2000	Here's Looking at You 2000: http://www.chef.org/prevention/looking.php
			Me-Me	Me-Me: http://www.ed.gov/pubs/EPTW/eptw9/eptw9m.html
Alternatives	Increase self-esteem, self-reliance; provide variable alternatives to drug use; reduce boredom and sense of alienation (arts, crafts, music, sports)	Organization of youth centers, recreational activities; participation in community services projects; vocational training	Outward Bound (wilderness program)	Outward Bound: http://www.outwardbound.org/

(continued)

Table 21.2 (*Continued*)

Intervention	Focus	Methods	Source/Name of Education Program	Web Site
Psychosocial Resistance skills training	Increase awareness of social influence to smoke, drink, or use drugs; develop skills for resisting substance-use influences; increase knowledge of immediate negative consequences; establish non–substance-use norms	Class discussion; resistance-skills training; behavioral rehearsal; extended practice via behavioral "homework"; use of same age or older peer leaders	Prevention Enhancement Protocols System (PEPS)	Prevention Enhancement Protocols System: http://www.health.org/govpubs/PHD822/aap .aspx
Personal and social skills training	Increase decision making, personal behavior change, anxiety reduction, social communication, social and assertive skills; application of generic skills to resist substance-use influences	Class discussion; cognitive–behavioral skills training (instruction, demonstration, practice, feedback, reinforcement)	General personal and social skills (Caplan et al., 1992) Project Counseling Leadership About Smoking Pressure (CLASP) Life Skills Training	General Personal and Social Skills: http://www.ncbi.nlm.nih.gov/entrez/query.fcgi? cmd=Retrieve&db=PubMed&list_uids=1556286 &dopt=Abstract Project CLASP: http://www.ssw.upenn.edu/crysp/publications/ pub14_full.html Life Skills Training: http://www.lifeskillstraining.com/old3.cfm

Source: Adapted from Schinke, Borvin, & Orlandi (1991, pp. 20–35). LifeSkills Training, Copyright © Gilbert J. Borvin, 1979–2004.

Intervention with Steps and Examples

Based on a risk and protective model, the LST program has three main goals: to teach prevention-related information, promote anti-drug norms, teach drug refusal skills, and foster the development of personal self-management skills and general social skills (National Health Promotion Associates, 2002). The main objectives of the program are:

- Provide students with the necessary skills to resist social (peer) pressures to smoke, drink and use drugs
- Help them to develop greater self-esteem, self-mastery, and self-confidence
- Enable children to effectively cope with social anxiety
- Increase their knowledge of the immediate consequences of substance abuse
- Enhance cognitive and behavioral competency to reduce and prevent a variety of health risk behaviors. (National Health Promotion Associates, 2002)

Working solely with the students, the underlying assumption of the LST program is that substance abuse prevention needs to address a number of areas in a student's life. The program accomplishes this by addressing three major domains in its curriculum: drug resistance skills and information, self-management skills, and general social skills.

The drug resistance skills portion of LST provides information on the actual number of youth in the United States who use tobacco, alcohol, or illicit drugs, as well as the short- and long-term consequences of this use (Botvin, 1996). Also included is "information about the declining social acceptability of cigarette smoking and other drug use, the physiological effects of cigarette smoking," how to avoid media pressures to smoke, drink, or use drugs, and how to resist peer pressure (Botvin, 1996, p. 223).

The personal self-management skills training encourages students to examine their self-image and how this impacts them, and how to problem solve while looking ahead at the consequences. Information on how to reduce stress, anxiety, and anger, how to identify problem situations, set goals, and how to self-monitor are also central to this domain (Botvin, 1996).

Finally, to empower students to overcome shyness, learn more effective communication skills, increase their assertiveness, and recognize their life choices, the LST program offers a general social skills component. This domain explores the topics of communication and socialization through both verbal and nonverbal skills. Through examining communication and socialization, issues about intimate relationships develop (Botvin, 1996).

The LST program spans 3 years of student development, typically either grades 6–8 or 7–9. The curriculum for the program has 15 sessions in the first year (7th grade), 10 sessions in the second year, and 5 sessions in the third year. Each session lasts approximately 45 minutes and can be taught either weekly or daily, depending on the students' needs. By reinforcing information taught the first year, the last 2 years are considered "booster" sessions in order to maintain the gains already established in the first year. The NHPA (2002) states the entire curriculum must be taught in the sequence provided in order to gain the full benefits. The curriculum has been modified for elementary students (24 session, with 8 sessions per year), and studies continue with this population. Preliminary findings suggest that this curriculum modification is successful (Botvin et al., 2003) (see Table 21.3).

The standardized curriculum offers both teacher and student manuals, enabling providers (social workers, mental health professionals, teachers, school staff, and peers) to maintain the sequence of the curriculum and provide the instruction in a variety of settings. The teacher's manual includes goals, objectives, and lesson plans that detail the content and activities for each session. The student manuals have the necessary reference material, class exercises, and homework assignments for each session (Botvin, 1996).

Intervention methods used in the sessions include "didactic teaching methods, facilitation-group discussion, classroom demonstrations, and cognitive-behavioral skills training" (Botvin, 1996, p. 224). Because the majority of the sessions include facilitated group discussions, one of the main roles of the intervention provider is skills trainer, or coach, rather than educator (Botvin, 1996).

The recommended ratio of students to provider is 25:1. In addition, studies have supported the curriculum being taught in a variety of settings, including school classrooms, after-school programs, summer camps, and community-based organizations (NHPA, 2002). However, NHPA indicates that a gymnasium is not an appropriate setting for students to learn the curriculum.

Table 21.3 Grid of Life Skills Program Structures for Elementary and Middle Schools

Program Levels	Elementary School Program Structure	Program Levels	Middle School Program Structure
Entire program comprises	24 class sessions (approximately 30–45 minutes each) to be conducted over 3 years	Entire program comprises:	30 class sessions (approximately 45 minutes each) to be conducted over 3 years
Core curriculum: level 1	• 3rd or 4th grade • Composed of 8 class sessions • Covers all skill areas	Core curriculum: level 1	• 6th or 7th grade • 15 class sessions • Cover all skill areas • Additional 3 class sessions on violence prevention (optional)
Core curriculum: level 2	• 4th or 5th grade • 8 class sessions • Reviews all skill areas	Booster session: level 2	• 7th or 8th grade • 10 class sessions • Additional 2 class sessions on violence prevention (optional)
Core curriculum: level 3	• 5th or 6th grade • 8 class sessions • Reviews all skill areas	Booster session: level 3	• 8th or 9th grade • 5 class sessions • Additional 2 class sessions on violence prevention (optional)
Middle school general information	The booster sessions provide additional skill development and opportunities to practice in key areas. The beginning of each level depends upon the transition from elementary school to middle school/junior high school.		
Elementary school general information	The elementary program can be used either alone or in combination with the middle school program. Under ideal conditions, it is intended to be implemented in a sequential manner across all three years of upper elementary school. However, the elementary program is designed to be flexible and can be implemented over one, two, or three years, depending on availability of time.		

Source: From the National Health Promotion Associates Web site: http://www.lifeskillstraining.com/program_structure1.cfm. LifeSkills Training. Copyright © Gilbert J. Botvin, 1979–2004.

One of the strengths of the LST program is its simplicity, with easy-to-follow instructions for both teachers and students. Included in each LST program is a teacher's manual, student guide, and audiocassette tape with relaxation exercises (NHPA, 2002). The curriculum also offers evaluation tools, including pre- and post-tests, fidelity checklists (to monitor implementation by providers), and quizzes for the students. Teacher training in each curriculum level is highly recommended.

Life Skills Training is comprehensive coverage of a range of topics. The first year of the curriculum includes session on self-image and self-improvement; making decisions; the myths and realities of smoking, alcohol, and marijuana (the "gateway" drugs to more intense substance abuse); biofeedback and smoking; advertising; violence and the media; coping with anxiety and anger; communication skills; social skills; assertiveness training; and resolving conflicts. The second year exposes students to new topics, such as the causes and effects of drug abuse and violence, and resisting peer pressure. Topics expanded upon in this second year include: making decisions, media influence, coping with anxiety and anger, communication skills, social skills, assertiveness training, and resolving conflicts. The final year builds on these basics, applying the knowledge to new situations that the students experience in which they have to cope.

As indicated previously, each teacher's manual specifies the goals, objectives, materials needed, special preparation that may be required prior to the session, possible vocabulary that needs to be explained to the students, homework assignments to hand out, and then the actual directions on how to complete each session. A sample of the *Teacher Manual* material for the first Social Skills training session follows:

Social Skills (A)—Teacher Manual

Session Goal: To teach students basic social skills in order to develop successful interpersonal relationships.

Major Objectives

- Recognize that many people feel shy or uncomfortable in social situations.
- Discuss how shyness can be overcome.
- Practice making social contacts.
- Practice giving and receiving compliments.
- Practice initiating, sustaining, and ending conversations.

Materials Needed

- Student Guide
- Tennis balls (2 or 3)

Special Preparation

- None

Vocabulary

- Self-confident
- Specific
- Initiating
- Sustain
- Compliment

Homework

- Student Guide: Review *Getting Over Being Shy* (page 71) and fill out *Social Activities, Worksheet 21* (page 76)

Introduction

Tell students that today you are going to cover some techniques that can help make them more socially attractive and self-confident. Many people are shy and uncomfortable in social situations, not because there is anything wrong with them, but simply because they have not learned the basic ingredients of social life.

Overcoming Shyness

1. Begin a discussion on shyness by asking students how many of them consider themselves to be shy or have been told that they were shy.
2. Ask students the following questions:
   (a) How many of you have been uncomfortable in social situations?
   (b) Why do people feel shy or uncomfortable in social situations?
   (c) Is there anything that you can do about it?
3. Tell students that many actors and well-known personalities are shy and uncomfortable being themselves but are comfortable and able to overcome their shyness by "acting" or playing a role. By learning social skills and practicing in situations that are fairly easy at first, they can develop social self-confidence. In the beginning, it helps to "act." They should develop "scripts" for various social situations and rehearse them (e.g., practice in front of a mirror).
4. Review strategies for getting over being shy (refer students to page 71 of the Student Guide).

Getting Over Being Shy

Learn to act: You can learn new social skills and become more self-confident by handling difficult social situations as if you were a performer playing a role. For many shy people, it is easier to pretend they are someone else playing a part than it is to be themselves. Thus, thinking of yourself as an actor playing a part is a good *first step* in acquiring new social skills and becoming more confident. Start small and strive for gradual improvement: Begin by practicing on easy situations, gradually working up to more difficult ones. Develop scripts: Write out a brief script of what you want to say, how you want to say it, and what you want to do in each situation you are trying to master.

Practice: Rehearse at home. Practice the skills you are learning and how to handle specific situations using the scripts you developed. Watch yourself in the mirror and listen to your voice. If you can, practice with someone playing the part of the other person. Be persistent: Keep at it. If you stick to it and continue to work on improving, you are bound to succeed.

Points to Make

- Shyness can be overcome by learning to "act" as if you are not shy (by being more outgoing) and by improving your basic social skills.
- Anxiety about social contacts can be overcome by practicing the techniques learned in the *Coping with Anxiety* session, particularly mental rehearsal and deep breathing.

Initiating Social Contacts

1. Tell students that an important step in overcoming shyness and a valuable social skill involves initiating social contacts (saying "hello" or starting conversation).
2. Calling someone they do not know very well on the phone and asking them for specific information. For example:
   (a) Call the operator to ask for phone numbers
   (b) Call the local department store to ask about some product(s)
   (c) Call your friend and talk to his or her mom on the phone
   Note: It helps to have a telephone for these exercises.
3. Have students practice greeting people by saying "hello" or by nodding, waving, smiling, etc. Have students suggest other greetings and write them on the board. Have them rehearse some of these. For example, pairs of students can rehearse:
   (a) Meeting in the hall
   (b) Sitting down in the cafeteria
4. Have students practice asking directions from someone they do not know.
5. Practice starting conversations with new people in public places (e.g., movie and grocery lines, doctor's office, sporting events). Go over the examples in the Student Guide on *Meeting*

New People page 72 and have the students suggest additional "openers" from their own experience. Sample "Openers":
   (a) "This line is so long, this must be a good movie."
   (b) "Have you heard anything about it?"
   (c) "Is that a good book? What's it about?"
   (d) "That's a nice jacket. Where did you get it?"
   (e) "Did you see the game last night? Who won?"
(Adapted from: http://www.lifeskillstraining. com/pdf/Sample_Teachers_Manual.pdf)

▓ Social Skills (A)—Student Manual

Accompanying the teacher's manual is a student manual that has information and material for each session. However, the student manuals contain more of the exercise materials, rather than the "nuts and bolts" of the items to be covered. A sample of the *Student Manual* material for the first Social Skills training session follows:

Getting Over Being Shy

Many people, even famous TV and movie personalities, can be shy and feel uncomfortable in social situations. However, you can learn to be more comfortable in social situations by learning how to deal with anxiety and nervousness (practiced in the last session) and by improving your social skills in social situations. Below are some ideas.

Learn to "act": You can learn new social skills and become more self-confident by "playing" a social situation as if you were an actor acting out a specific role.

Start small: Begin by practicing on easy situations, gradually working up to more difficult ones.

Prepare yourself: Write out a brief script and rehearse it at home, watch yourself in the mirror, and listen to your voice. This is what actors in plays and movies do.

Saying Hello

1. Another way to get over being shy is to practice saying hello to people.
2. Below are some common greetings.
   (a) "Hello" or "Hi"
   (b) "How is it going?"

(c) "Good to see you."
(d) "Have a good (nice) day."
3. Gestures (a nod, smile, or wave)
4. Get in the habit of saying hello to people. The more people you say hello to, the more people will say hello to you. Most people are shy. You can help them by saying hello first.

Meeting New People

Try to meet a lot of new people. Begin a conversation wherever you go (for example, while standing in line at the movies, grocery store, bank, a sporting event, etc.). Start the conversation with something you have in common. Again, asking questions is an effective method. Below are some examples:

- "This line is so long, this must be a good movie. Have you heard anything about it?"
- "Is that a good book? What's it about?"
- "That's a nice jacket. Where did you get it?"
- "Did you see the game last night? Who won?"

Life Skills Training. Copyright © Gilbert J. Botvin, 1979–2004.

▌ Resources

Resources for school-based substance abuse prevention programs can be found in the following list. The Web sites included in the list provide information regarding training manuals, video training tools, Web resources, books, journals, and journal articles.

Life Skills Training
National Health Promotion Associates, Inc.
711 Westchester Avenue
White Plains, NY 10604
(800) 293-4969
lstinfo@nhpanet.com

Life Skills Research
Institute for Prevention Research, Cornell University Medical College
411 East 69th Street, KB-201
New York, NY 10021
(212) 746-1270
ipr@mail.med.cornell.edu

Center for Substance Abuse Prevention
P.O. Box 2345
Rockville, MD 20847-2345
(800) 729-6686 or (240) 276-2130
http://www.prevention.samhsa.gov/

National Institute on Alcohol Abuse and Alcoholism
5635 Fishers Lane, MSC 9304
Bethesda, MD 20892-9304
http://www.niaaa.nih.gov/

National Institute on Drug Abuse
6001 Executive Boulevard, Room 5213
Bethesda, MD 20892-9561
(301) 443-1124
http://backtoschool.drugabuse.gov/

Substance Abuse and Mental Health Services Administration
P.O. Box 2345
Rockville, MD 20847-2345
(800) 729-6686 or TDD (hearing impaired): (800) 487-4889
http://www.samhsa.gov/ or www.health.org
e-mail: info@health.org

National Clearing House for Drug and Alcohol Information (NCADI)
11420 Rockville Pike
Rockville, MD 20852
(800) 729-6686
http://www.health.org

United States Department of Health and Human Services
200 Independence Avenue, S.W.
Washington, DC 20201
(877) 696-6775 or (202) 619-0257
http://www.os.dhhs.gov/

Provides Some Online Training
Drug and Alcohol Treatment and Prevention Global Network
http://www.drugnet.net/prevention.htm

▓ Key Points to Remember

Even though substance abuse has begun declining in recent years, tobacco, alcohol, and illicit drug use continues to plague our youth. Although a number of substance abuse prevention programs have been tried in the past, traditional models do not seem effective and have had poor outcomes. More recent models that include psychosocial components have had better outcomes and seem to be reducing substance use in children and adolescents.

One of the most promising substance abuse prevention programs to date is the Life Skills Training program. This program spans three grades for students, the first of which is intended to provide the foundation materials, and the last two of which are meant as "booster sessions" and are intended to maintain the progress made in the first year. Research has supported the effectiveness of this model, which continues to have positive study outcomes.

One of the reasons for its effectiveness is its simplicity of use. Each session has been broken down for the teacher and student, enabling the structure of the program to be flexible for use with a number of different providers in a variety of settings. The simple, yet clear manuals make it easy and effective to use.

References

Bangert-Drowns, R. L. (1988). The effects of school-based substance abuse education—a meta-analysis. *Journal of Drug Education, 18*, 243–264.

Best, J. A., Flay, B. R., Towson, S. M. J., Ryan, L. B., Perry, C., Brown, K. S., Kersell, M. W., & d'Avernas, J. R. (1984). Smoking prevention and the concept of risk. *Journal of Applied Social Psychology, 14*, 257–273.

Botvin, G. J. (1996). Substance abuse prevention through life skills training. In R. D. Peters & R. J. McMahon (Eds.), *Preventing childhood disorders, substance abuse, and delinquency*. Thousand Oaks, CA: Sage Publications.

Botvin, G. J., Baker, E., Botvin, E. M., Dusenbury, L., Cardwell, J., & Diaz, T. (1993). Factors promoting cigarette smoking among black youth: A causal modeling approach. *Addictive Behaviors, 18*, 397–405.

Botvin, G. J., Baker, E., Dusenbury, L., Tortu, S., & Botvin, E. M. (1990). Preventing adolescent drug abuse through a multimodal cognitive-behavioral approach: Results of a 3-year study. *Journal of Consulting and Clinical Psychology, 58*(4), 437–446.

Botvin, G. J., Baker, E., Renick, N., Filazzola, A. D., & Botvin, E. M. (1984). A cognitive-behavioral approach to substance abuse prevention. *Addictive Behaviors, 9*, 137–147.

Botvin, G. J., & Botvin, E. M. (1992). Adolescent tobacco, alcohol, and drug abuse: Prevention strategies, empirical findings, and assessment issues. *Developmental and Behavioral Pediatrics, 13*, 290–301.

Botvin, G. J., Dusenbury, L., Baker, E., & James-Ortiz, S. (1989). A skills training approach to smoking prevention among Hispanic youth. *Journal of Behavioral Medicine, 12*(3), 279–296.

Botvin, G. J., & Eng, A. (1982). The efficacy of a multicomponent approach to the prevention of cigarette smoking. *Preventive Medicine, 11*, 199–211.

Botvin, G. J., Eng, A., & Williams, C. L. (1980). Preventing the onset of cigarette smoking through life skills training. *Preventive Medicine, 9*, 135–143.

Botvin, G. J., Griffin, K. W., & Paul, E. (2003). Preventing tobacco and alcohol use among elementary school students through life skills training. *Journal of Child & Adolescent Substance Abuse, 12*(4), 1–17.

Botvin, G. J., Renick, N., & Baker, E. (1983). The effects of scheduling format and booster sessions on a broad spectrum psychosocial approach to smoking prevention. *Journal of Behavioral Medicine, 6*, 359–379.

Botvin, G. J., Schinke, S. P., Epstein, J. A., Diaz, T., & Botvin, E. M. (1995). Effectiveness of culturally focused and generic skills training approaches to alcohol and drug abuse prevention among minority adolescents: Two-year follow-up results. *Psychology of Addictive Behaviors, 9*(3), 183–194.

Bruvold, W. H. (1993). A meta-analysis of adolescent smoking prevention programs. *American Journal of Public Health, 83*(6), 872–880.

Bruvold, W. H., & Rundall, T. G. (1988). A meta-analysis and theoretical review of school based tobacco and alcohol intervention programs. *Psychology and Health, 2*, 53–78.

Burke, M. R. (2002). School-based substance abuse prevention: Political finger-pointing does not work. *Federal Probation, 66*(2), 66–72.

Caplan, M., Weissberg, R. P., & Grober, J. S. (1992). Social competence promotion with inner-city and suburban young adolescents: Effects on social adjustment and alcohol use. *Journal of Consulting & Clinical Psychology, 60*(1), 56–63.

Ennett, S. T., Tobler, N. S., Ringwalt, C. L., & Flewelling, R. L. (1994). How effective is drug abuse resistance education? A meta-analysis of Project DARE outcome evaluations. *American Journal of Public Health, 84*(9), 1394–1400.

Gottfredson, D. (1996). School-based crime prevention. In L. W. Sherman, et al., *Preventing crime: What works, what doesn't, what's promising*. Report to the United States Congress, prepared for the National Institute of Justice.

Hops, H., Tildesley, E., & Lichtenstein, E. (1990). Parent–adolescent problem-solving interactions and drug use. *American Journal of Drug & Alcohol Abuse, 16*(3/4), 239–258.

Kinder, B., Pape, N., & Walfish, S. (1980). Drug and alcohol education programs: A review of outcome studies. *The International Journal of the Addictions, 15*, 1035–1054.

McAlister, A., Perry, C. L., Killen, J., Slinkard, L. A., & Maccoby, N. (1980). Pilot study of smoking, alcohol, and drug abuse prevention. *American Journal of Public Health, 70,* 719–721.

National Health Promotion Associates, Inc. (2002). Life Skills Training program. Retrieved on July 12, 2004: http://www.lifeskillstraining.com

National Institute of Alcohol Abuse and Alcoholism. (2004). Statement by Ting-Kai Li, M.D. Fiscal Year 2005 President's Budget Request for the National Institute on Alcohol Abuse and Alcoholism. Bethesda, MD: U.S. Department of Health and Human Services. Retrieved on July 26, 2004 from: http://www.niaaa.nih.gov/about/statement04.htm

Rosenbaum, D. P., & Hanson, G. S. (1998). Assessing the effects of school-based drug education: A six-year multilevel analysis of project D.A.R.E. *The Journal of Research in Crime and Delinquency:* Beverly Hills.

SAMHSA [Substance Abuse and Mental Health Services Administration]. (2004). *Results from the 2003 National Survey on Drug Use and Health: National Findings* (Office of Applied Studies, NSDUH Series H–25, DHHS Publication No. SMA 04–3964). Rockville, MD.

Schinke, S. P., Botvin, G. J., & Orlandi, M. A. (1991). *Substance abuse in children and adolescents.* Newbury Park, CA: Sage Publications.

Sherman, L. (2000). The safe and drug-free schools program. Brookings papers on education policy (pp. 125–171). Retrieved July 28, 2004 from: http://muse.jhu.edu/journals/brookings_papers_on_education_policy/v2000/2000.1sherman.html

Swisher, J. D., & Hoffman, A. (1975). Information: The irrelevant variable in drug education. In B. W. Corder, R. A. Smith, and J. D. Swisher (Eds.), *Drug abuse prevention: Perspectives and approaches for educators* (pp. 49–62). Dubuque, IA: William C. Brown.

Tobler, N. S. (1986). Meta-analysis of 143 adolescent drug prevention programs: Quantitative outcome results of program participants compared to a control group or comparison group. *Journal of Drug Issues, 16*(4), 537–567.

Tobler, N. S., & Stratton, H. H. (1997). Effectiveness of school-based drug prevention programs: A meta-analysis of the research. *Journal of Primary Prevention, 18*(1), 71–128.

White, D., & Pitts, M. (1998). Educating young people about drugs: A systematic review. *Addiction, 93*(10), 1475–1487.

Substance Abuse at Elementary Age

Effective Interventions

Soyon Jung ▪ Lori K. Holleran

CHAPTER 22

Getting Started

Substance use/abuse is usually perceived as a problem of the adult and adolescent population and seldom seriously examined with regard to elementary school children. According to Parents' Resource Institute for Drug Education (PRIDE, 2003), however, it is not uncommon among elementary school children to experiment with various substances. The PRIDE survey analyzing data collected from 72,025 4th through 6th grade students reported that 2.7% of 4th graders, 4.4% of 5th graders, and 5.6% of 6th graders smoked cigarettes during the past year. The proportion of the elementary school students who drank beer or wine coolers in the previous year ranges from 6.3% (beer consumption among 4th graders) to 11.2% (wine coolers consumption among 6th graders). Substance use by elementary school children is not limited to tobacco or alcohol beverages. Three percent of 4th graders, 3.3% of fifth graders, and 3.9% of 6th graders reported inhalant use in the prior year. The percentages of the students using marijuana in the past year ranges from 0.7% for 4th graders to 1.8% for 6th graders.

In addition to the prevalence of substance use/abuse among elementary school children, it should be noted that the age of first substance use is getting younger (American Academy of Pediatrics, 1998). For example, the proportion of students who drank alcohol before age 13 years was about 16% for 11th and 12th grade males, but it was 33.3% for 10th grade males (Center for Disease Control and Prevention, 2004). It should be taken seriously because earlier onset of substance use is significantly related to heavier use and more addictive symptoms in later years, as

well as more difficult rehabilitation if a problem emerges (Jenson & Howard, 1991; Knowles, 2001; Sarvela, Monge, Shannon, & Newrot, 1999). The risk of early use of substances also exists physiologically. A child's brain is different from an adult's and the deleterious effects of alcohol on a developing brain are profound (Kuhn, Swartzwelder, & Wilson, 1998).

These statistics and trends of experimentation with substances might suggest that substance use/abuse prevention programs be provided to elementary school students. There is also empirical evidence that well-designed prevention programs for elementary school children significantly reduce various problem behaviors, including substance use/abuse in their later lives (e.g., Hawkins, Catalano, Kosterman, Abbott, & Hill, 1999). The elementary school is often regarded as the ideal setting for substance use/abuse prevention programs (Gibson, Mitchell, & Basile, 1993). The reasons can be summarized as follows: First, the school environment has a powerful influence on children, given time spent, learning process, and social interaction (St. Pierre, Mark, Kaltreider, & Campbell, 2001). Second, schools are the major provider of mental health services for children (Rones & Hoagwood, 2000), and a number of school-based prevention programs have been found effective (Gibson et al., 1993). Thus, many schools already have valuable resources and accumulated know-how regarding mental health services. Finally, students are more likely to obtain information about substances and talk about drugs with their schoolteachers rather than their parents (Alcoholism & Drug Abuse Weekly, 1999, April 19).

In this chapter, the authors present an overview of selective prevention interventions, a risk and protective factor paradigm, and two examples of evidence-based programs, the Strengthening Families Program (SFP) and Positive Action (PA). The two programs are particularly worth noting because they illustrate how preventive intervention can address risk, enhance protective factors, and be effectively implemented at school settings. Lastly, practical guidelines are then presented for school social workers and other school mental health professionals who envision substance use/abuse prevention targeting elementary school children.

What We Know

Understanding Selective Prevention Programs

Preventive interventions are often classified into three categories, universal, selective, and indicated prevention, based on the target populations. Universal preventions address the entire population of a community or an organization such as an elementary school. Indicated preventions are directed toward specific individuals who are showing serious precursors or are already involved in problem behavior(s) such as substance use/abuse. On the other hand, selective prevention targets "subsets of the total population that are deemed to be at risk for substance abuse by virtue of their membership in a particular population segment— for example, children of adult alcoholics, dropouts, or students who are failing academically" (National Institute on Drug Abuse [NIDA], 1997b, p.11). Selective prevention interventions are recommendable in elementary school settings, given that a majority of elementary school students do not exhibit substance use/abuse problem but a significant number of them are exposed to multiple risk factors.

Program Goal and Theoretical Background of Selective Prevention

The ultimate goal of selective prevention is to deter the onset of substance abuse among at-risk groups and to help them be equipped with proper skills and information so that they can reduce their vulnerability (NIDA, 1997a). Based on a risk and protective factor model, selective prevention approaches usually pursue such goals by minimizing the impacts of risk factors and maximizing the

effects of protective factors. Initially risk factors for substance use/abuse were limited to a narrow range of factors such as biological or psychological variables only (Jenson, 1997). Recently, however, the risk factor model is usually grounded in comprehensive ecological frameworks. Table 22.1 shows some examples of studies that present risk factors for substance use/abuse, which range from individual attributes to macro-social environmental characteristics.

While risk factors increase the likelihood of problem incidence, protective factors reduce the likelihood because they buffer the impact of risk factors by augmenting strength. Complementing the risk factor model, prevention efforts based on a protective factor model focus on the positive and also modifiable factors rather than less mutable risks such as temperament, genetic heritage, or low socioeconomic status. A major contribution of protective factor models to the prevention approach is that they shift the prevention paradigm from a psychopathological perspective to a healthy human development perspective (Holleran, Kim, & Dixon, 2004). According to 40 Developmental Assets of Search Institute (accessible at http://www.search-institute.org), one of the most widely used and effective protective factor models, protective factors can be classified into two categories, external assets and internal assets, and each category is composed of 20 factors. The external and internal assets for elementary-age children are exhibited in the Table 22.2.

Other Characteristics of Selective Prevention

Targeting at-risk groups, selective prevention usually requires more intensive care, more professional skills, more varied treatment strategies, and a longer program duration compared to universal prevention (Kumpfer, 2003). The greatest merit of selective prevention lies in program efficiency and effectiveness. Despite larger program expenditure per capita, selective prevention is often considered more efficient than universal programs because it can cut down the total program cost by targeting individuals in need (NIDA, 1997a). In addition, a selective prevention approach can increase program efficiency by choosing optimum strategies that are well matched with identified risk factors of the program participants (Sullivan & Farrell, 2002). A particularly impressive facet of selective prevention is that its effect size is in general greater than that of

Table 22.1 Risk Factors from Multidimensional Perspectives

	Study Number (see below for reference)				
	1	2	3	4[a]	5[a]
Individual					
Problematic health status (physical and mental)		O	O	O	
Constitutional factors/Sensation-seeking orientation/(genetic predisposition to chemical dependency)	O	O	O		O
Poor impulse control			O		O
Greater levels of rebelliousness					
Attention deficits			O		
Early and persistent antisocial behavior/rebellious attitudes	O	O			O
Early initiation of the problem behavior	O				O
Favorable attitudes toward the problem behavior					
Delinquency (e.g., history of trouble w/ the police)					
Decreased perception of risk					O
Lack of social bonding/alienation		O			O
Family					
Family conflict/marital discord	O	O	O		O
Family stress				O	
Family disruption and/or dysfunction due to death, divorce, and parental incarceration				O	
Poor parent–child bonding			O		
Poor parental supervision					O
Poor family management practices/discipline	O	O	O		O
Family communication			O		
Family history of mental health problem				O	
Family present use or history of substance use/abuse			O	O	O
Family history of problem behavior	O	O			
Favorable parental attitudes/parental permissiveness toward the problem behavior/substance use	O	O			O
Incidence of child abuse, neglect, and trauma		O			O
Lack of support for positive school values and attitudes				O	
Economic deprivation					O
Differential family acculturation					O
Peers					
Rejection by conforming peer group/alienation and rebelliousness	O		O		
Association with drug-using peers/friends who engage in the problem behavior	O		O		O
Alienation and rebelliousness	O	O			
Peer pressure					
Peer approval of drug use					
School					
School failure/academic failure/beginning in late elementary school	O		O		O
Low commitment to school	O	O	O		
Absenteeism and dropout		O			O
Lack of cultural grounding and resources, language difficulties, or both		O			
Dysfunction within the school environment such as high rates of substance abuse or unsafe school environment				O	O

(continued)

Table 22.1 (*Continued*)

	Study Number (see below for reference)				
	1	2	3	4[a]	5[a]
School climate that provides little encouragement and support to students				O	
Lack of clear school policies regarding drug use					O
Low teacher expectations of student achievement					O
Low teacher and student morale				O	
Community/macro-level environment					
Neighborhood disorganization	O	O	O		O
Low neighborhood attachment	O	O	O		O
Residential mobility/transitions and mobility/instability: transition and mobility	O	O	O		
High population density			O	O	
Availability of alcohol and drugs	O	O			
Low community safety/high violence/high adult crime rates/ high rates of drug abuse		O	O	O	O
Community regulation/laws favorable toward drug use, firearms, or crime	O	O	O		O
Pro-use messages specifically in advertising					O
Negative community attitudes toward youth		O			
Cultural norms about alcohol and drug use/community values and attitudes that are tolerant of substance abuse			O	O	O
Hyperactivity			O		
Lack of youth recreation opportunities/lack of cultural resources/lack of active community institutions			O	O	
Poverty and economic deprivation	O	O	O		O
Cultural disenfranchisement					O
Situational/cultural factors					
Stressful events, multiple stressors, or both		O			
High incidence of drug and alcohol use		O			
Tension around cultural identity, acculturative stress, or both		O			
Societal Factors					
National economic and employment conditions					O
Discrimination					O
Marginalization of groups					O

[a]The authors also include several other demographic risk factors such as age, gender, race/ethnicity, socioeconomic status, employment, and education. Since these factors are not specified in a useful way, however, these factors are not presented here. For example, with this information only, which gender, male or female, is risk factor is uncertain.

Study introduced
(1)—1. Hawkins, J. D., Catalano, R. F., & Miller, J. Y. (1992). Risk and protective factors for alcohol and other drug problems in adolescence and early adulthood: Implications for substance abuse prevention. *Psychological Bulletin, 112*(1), 64–105.
(1)—2. Developmental Research and Programs. (1997). *Communities that care: Risk assessment for preventing adolescent problem behaviors.* Seattle, WA: Developmental Research and Programs.
(2) Holleran, L. K., Kim, Y., & Dixon, K. (2004). Innovative approaches to risk assessment within alcohol prevention programming. In A. R. Roberts & K. R. Yeager (Eds.), *Evidence-based practice manual: Research and outcome measures in health and human services* (pp. 677–684). New York: Oxford University Press.
(3) Jenson, J. M. (1997). Risk and protective factors for alcohol and other drug use in childhood and adolescence. In M. W. Fraser (Ed.), *Risk and resilience in childhood* (pp. 117–139). Washington, DC: NASW Press.
(4) National Institute on Drug Abuse. (1997). *Drug abuse prevention for at-risk groups* (NIH No. 97-4114). Rockville, MD: U.S. Department of Health and Human Services, National Institutes of Health.
(5) Brounstein, P. J., & Zweig, J. M. (1999). *Toward the 21st century: A primer on effective programs* (DHHS Publication No. [SMA]99-3301): Substance Abuse and Mental Health Services Administration.

Table 22.2 Forty Developmental Assets for Elementary-Age Children

	External Assets		Internal Assets
Support	1. Family support 2. Positive family communication 3. Other adult relationships 4. Caring neighborhood 5. Caring out-of-home climate	Commitment to learning	21. Achievement expectation and motivation 22. Children are engaged in learning 23. Stimulating activity 24. Enjoyment of learning and bonding with school 25. Reading for pleasure
Empowerment	6. Parent involvement in out-of-home situation 7. Community values children 8. Children are given useful roles 9. Service to others 10. Safety	Positive values	26. Caring 27. Equality and social justice 28. Integrity 29. Honesty 30. Responsibility 31. Healthy lifestyle and sexual attitudes
Boundaries and expectations	11. Family boundaries 12. Out-of-home boundaries 13. Neighborhood boundaries 14. Adult role models 15. Positive peer observation 16. Appropriate expectations for growth	Social competencies	32. Planning and decision-making practice 33. Interpersonal skills 34. Cultural competence 35. Resistance skills 36. Peaceful conflict resolution
Constructive use of time	17. Creative activities 18. Out-of-home activities 19. Religious community 20. Positive, supervised time at home	Positive identity	37. Personal power 38. Self-esteem 39. Sense of purpose 40. Positive view of personal future

universal prevention (Wilson, Gottfredson, & Najaka, 2001; Gottfredson & Wilson, 2003).

Selective prevention also has some limitations and practical difficulties. The biggest challenge in selective prevention is to identify and recruit at-risk group members. Even when a valid, precise, and reliable scale or screening instrument is available, serious weakness still remains. As selective prevention is directed toward at-risk subgroups of the general population, selective prevention inherently has a high possibility of stigmatization. Another limitation or difficulty of selective prevention approaches is that parents or family involvement, the core part of selective prevention, is not a simple job in practice, although a growing body of research notes that the parent component is essential for program success. At-risk populations often include poor families and single-parent families, and many of these families do not have

enough time or resources to ensure the parents participate in and concentrate on the program.

What We Can Do

What Works? Effective Selective Prevention Programs for Elementary School Children

Although risk and protective models enhance prevention approaches, there are also some important warnings. Above all, it should be noticed that risk factors are not always causes of the problem (Fisher & Harrison, 2004). Rather, risks are correlates or covariates, which could be simple indicators or moderators of the problem (Pandina, 1996). This means that sometimes reducing the impact of risk factors does not necessarily decrease a student's substance use/abuse. This logic also applies to protective factors. Therefore, it is recommended for school social workers and other school-based practitioners to examine successful programs, refer to research on program evaluation, and develop prevention strategies based on programs whose effectiveness is empirically proven. While there is scant research that evaluates the effectiveness of selective prevention programs with rigorous scientific methods, there are some effective selective programs that can be considered model programs. Among those, selective prevention programs particularly appropriate for elementary school children are summarized in the Table 22.3.

Although all of these programs attempt to reduce the impact of risk factors and augment the effects of protective factors, they are different in terms of strength, limitations, program focus, and central strategies. Thus, it is suggested that professionals who envision substance use/abuse prevention programs scrutinize the primary resources and program strategies to select a best model program to utilize. If a model program is selected, a visit to the program Web site is recommended to glean useful information including program effectiveness, practitioner training, and economic costs of the program. Here, detailed information about the two selective prevention programs, Strengthen Families Program and Positive Action Program, are presented because these programs are considered particularly effective and applicable for elementary school settings.

The Strengthening Families Program (SFP)

The Strengthening Families Program (SFP) is a family skills training program designed to improve family life skill, parenting skills, and children's social skills (Kumpfer, Alvarado, & Whiteside, 2003). This program was developed by Karol Kumpfer and her associates in 1983, targeting elementary school age children who are at high risk for substance abuse and other problem behaviors. Over the last two decades, SFP has been revised and modified for different target populations such as junior high school students, preschool children, African Americans, and Hispanics/Latinos. SFP has shown significant effectiveness consistently in replications and various ethnic groups. For school social workers and other professionals who primarily work with elementary school children and

their families, the original version of SFP program is introduced in this chapter.

Program Goal and Objectives

The ultimate goal of SFP is to enhance the resiliency of at-risk children. For this goal, SFP put primary focus on reduction of risk factors in family environment and enhancement of protective factors. Under this goal, SFP has three specified objectives and relevant strategies as follows (NIDA, 1997a, pp. 20–21).

- To increase parenting skills by
    - Increasing positive attention and praise
    - Increasing parents' levels of empathy for their children
    - Increasing parents' use of effective discipline
    - Decreasing parents' use of physical punishment
    - Decreasing parents' use of demonstrating use of substances
- To increase children's skills by
    - Increasing their communication skills
    - Increasing their skills to resist peer pressure to use substances or engage in other inappropriate behaviors
    - Increasing recognition of feelings
    - Increasing knowledge about alcohol and drugs
    - Increasing skills for coping with anger and criticism
    - Increasing compliance with parental requests
    - Increasing their self-esteem
    - Decreasing aggressive and other problem behaviors
    - Reducing intention to use in the future and the actual use of substances
- To improve family relationships by
    - Decreasing family conflicts
    - Improving family communications
    - Increasing parent–child time together
    - Increasing planning and organization skills

Target Population

The original SFP targets at-risk children 6 to 10 years of age whose parents are substance users or abusers. Since the original version of SPF demonstrated its effectiveness in the general child

Table 22.3 Effective Selective Preventions

Program	Universal	Selective	Indicative	Target population	Duration	Program Structure	Reported Effectiveness	Personal/social competency	Academic support	In-/after-school curricula	ATOD info. dissemination	Peer resistance skill	Peer involvement	Intensive case management	Alternative activity	Family social/communi. skills	Parenting/parent discipline	Family AOD Education	Parent-child interaction	School reform	Teacher involvement	Parent-school relation	Community service	Mentoring	Community involvement	Incentives for partic. or compl.	Prob. identification/referral
Across ages http://www.temple.edu/cil/Acrossageshome.htm		O		9–13 yr. old	1–3 yr.	Intergenerational mentoring • Mentoring from qualified and trained elders • Life skills curriculum led by classroom teachers • Performing community service • Life/problem-solving curriculum • Workshop for parent & family members, which is designed to help them practice better parenting and participate in school activities	Quasi-experimental design research, the program showed desirable outcome in the following areas: • Reactions to stress & anxiety • Self-perception • Attitudes toward school, elders, & future • Problem-solving skills/self-efficacy • Knowledge about substance use • Frequency of substance use	O		O	O	O			O	O	O		O		O		●	●	●	O	
CASASTART (Striving Together to Achieve Rewarding Tomorrows) http://www.casacolumbia.org/absolutenm/templates/article.asp?articleId=287&zoneid=32		O	O	8–13 yr. old	1–3 yr.	• Case management that involves a home interview and monthly home visit • Academic support for children through tutoring and homework assistance • Social and emotional support for children through adult mentoring program • After-school curricular activities that includes recreational programs and trips • Community involvement that intends increased police presence and enhanced relationship among youth, families, and the police	Comparison of experimental subjects & control group at 1-year follow-up • Lower rate of past month use of any drugs, gateway drugs, & stronger drugs • Lower rate of past year use of any drugs & gateway drugs • Lower rate of lifetime use of any drugs or gateway drugs • Lower levels of violent crimes in the past year • Lower rate of involvement in drug sales during the past month • Lower rate of lifetime drug sales		O	O	O		O	●	O	●	●		O			O	O	O	O	O	O

(continued)

Table 22.3 (Continued)

(continued)

Program	IOM Universal	IOM Selective	IOM Indicative	Target population	Duration	Program Structure	Reported Effectiveness	Personal/social competency	Academic support	In-/after-school curricula	ATOD info. dissemination	Peer resistance skill	Peer involvement	Intensive case management	Alternative activity	Family social/commun. skills	Parenting/parent discipline	Family AOD Education	Parent–child interaction	School reform	Teacher involvement	Parent–school relation	Community service	Mentoring	Community involvement	Incentives for partic. or compl.	Prob. identification/referral
FAST (Families and Schools Together) http://www.wcer.wisc.edu/fast/	O	O	O	5–14 yr old	1–2 yr.	• Teacher identification of at-risk student • Outreach for program participants • Multifamily group sessions including parent–child play therapy (for 8 weeks) • Ongoing monthly reunions of the multifamily group (for 21 months)	• Decrease in anxiety–withdrawal of children • Increase in parent social support • Declines in attention problem and conduct disorder • Improved family cohesion • Long-term effect has been has been reported at 2–4 yr. follow-up • Program effectiveness appears consistent in more than 53 replication sites across the nation and Canada	O		O	O	O	O		O	●	●		●			O				O	O	
Positive action http://www.posaction.com/	O	O	O	5–18 yr old	0–12 yr.	• Daily classroom curriculum where teachers present 15- to 20-minute lessons (a total of 140 lessons) with various activities • School–climate program, which promotes the practice and reinforcement of schoolwide positive actions • Parent program that focuses on 42 weekly lessons for parents and encourages parent participation in school activities • Community program that is provided to community leaders so that a wide range of community service practices and cultivate positive actions within the community	• Program effectiveness has been observed in the following areas: academic achievement, absenteeism, discipline problem, violence and drug use, and criminal booking • Program effectiveness sustained in middle and high school years of the subjects • These outcome results have been replicated repeatedly	O		O	O	O	O					O		●	●	●			O		

Projective achieve

http://www.stopthinkachieve.com/

Age: 3–14 yr. old; Over 3 yr.

Strategies:
- Stop & Think Social Skills program, in-school curricula that teach students desirable social and self-management skills
- Parent training, tutoring, and support, which emphasizes ongoing parent–school collaboration
- Effective classroom teacher/staff development, which is designed to increase their skills in strategic planning, organizational analysis, effective instructional and behavioral intervention
- School reform, which intends more effective supports for social and academic development of students

Outcomes:
- Decreased discipline referrals to the principal/the office
- Improved in academic achievement
- Decreased suspension & expulsion
- Decreased grade retentions
- Decreased special education referrals & placements

Strengthen families

http://www.strengtheningfamiliesprogram.org

Age: 6–12 yr. old; 14-week courses

Strategies:
- Parent skills training that employs basic behavioral parent training techniques
- Children's skills training designed to develop and enhance children's social and problem-solving skills
- Family life skills training that utilizes family communication exercises
- Two booster sessions at 6 and 12 months after the program, which encourage positive social networking

Outcomes:
- Decreased use and intention to use ATOD among parents as well as children
- Improved parent–child bonding, family relations, & communication
- Improved children's academic achievement
- Improved parents' discipline skills and parenting self-efficacy
- Improved children's pro-social behaviors
- Reduced children's problem behaviors including substance use
- Reduced children's emotional problems including depression

● indicates primary strategy while O refers to one of the strategies utilized in the program

267

population as well as at-risk children, it can also be utilized as a universal prevention program.

Program Structure and Implementation

SFP program is composed of three primary components: parent skills training, children's skills training, and family skills training. The program participants have weekly sessions, each of which lasts 2 to 3 hours. The entire program continues for 14 consecutive weeks. For the first part of a weekly session, parents and children attend their own sessions separately. This is followed by a break, when snacks and announcements are provided. Then, the family skills training session starts, and the parents and children practice the skills together, which they learned in their own session. This format provides the participants with opportunities to learn their respective skills in their own sessions and then to practice the skills within the context of parent–child interaction. The entire program curricula for parent, children, and family skills training component are presented in the Table 22.4. As shown in the table, the topics of weekly sessions are coherent across groups so that family and children learn relevant skills at the same time and practice together.

Usually each parent skills training session starts with a review of homework and the concepts taught in the previous session. Then parents learn new concepts and skills. Finally, new homework relevant to the new concept and skills is assigned. The optimum group number for the parents' training session ranges from 8 to 12 with two skilled trainers. The basic format of the children's group session is similar to the parents'. The ideal group number is six to seven with two trainers. For smooth group work process and reinforcement of desirable behavior, children who follow group rules need to be rewarded with small prizes such as school supplies. The family training session is delivered in a format similar to that of the parents' or children's training session. Depending on the number of participants and accommodating capacity of the meeting place, family groups can be divided into several small groups or remain in one large group.

How to Implement SFP

Once a school chooses to use the Strengthening Families Program (SFP), a 2- to 3-day implementer training is conducted. A 415-page instructor manual contains a teaching outline, a script for

the videotapes, and detailed instructions for all activities. Each lesson has an "overview" section providing practical considerations for successful implementation of SFP, such as a detailed timeline, list of equipment, master copies of worksheets, and homework assignments. A separate manual contains four booster sessions. There must be a teacher/facilitator for the parent session and the youth session, held concurrently. Co-facilitators are recommended where feasible. It is suggested that meals or snacks be included as incentives, and whenever possible, childcare and transportation should be provided.

Each child and parent session contains parallel content. They spend the first hour separately in separate skill-building sessions and then come together in supervised family activities. For example, while the children are learning about the importance of following rules, parents are working on enhancing their use of consequences when rules are broken; when the two groups combine in the family session, the children and family members practice problem solving with role plays when a rule is followed or broken. The parent component has the following general goals: increase positive attention/praise, enhance empathy, teach supervision skills, decrease parents' drug use, increase positive modeling, and support the child's developmental stage. The family component provides a venue for children and families to practice and enhance listening, communication, respect, recognizing family strengths, cultural values, and effective problem-solving skills.

The groups utilize the following techniques: discussions, games, role plays, activities, videotapes, and modeling of positive relationships and behaviors. The facilitator uses the videotapes, which include time countdowns for group discussions and activities. In fact, the facilitator starts the video as the session begins and lets it run for the full session to guide the curriculum and ensure staying on task and accomplishment of session goals. Multiethnic video narrators conduct didactic presentations and are followed by family vignettes. Once the video is completed, the remaining time can be utilized for skill practice, discussions, and mutual support within the group.

Outcomes

Through extensive evaluation, the SFP has produced desirable outcomes and proved its effectiveness in various areas, including reduced use or intentions to use substances among children; reduced child problem behaviors, aggressiveness, and emotional problems; decreased substance use

Table 22.4 Strengthen Families Program Curriculum

Week	Parent Skills Curriculum	Children's Skills Curriculum	Family Skills Curriculum
1	Introduction and group building	Hello and rules	Introduction and group building
2	Developmental expectancies and stress management	Social skills I	Child's game I
3	Rewards	Social skills II	Child's game II: Rewards
4	Goals and objectives	Creating good behavior, secret rules of success	Child's game III: Goals and objectives
5	Differential attention/charts and spinners	How to say "NO" to stay out of trouble	Child's game IV: Differential attention/charts and spinners
6	Communication I	Communication I: Speaking and listening	Communication I: Speaking, listening, and coaching
7	Communication II	Communication II: Preparation for family meetings	Communication II: Family meetings
8	Alcohol, drugs, and families	Alcohol and drugs	Communication III: Learning from parents–parents' discussion
9	Problem-solving, giving directions	Problem-solving	Parents' game I: Problem-solving, giving directions
10	Limit setting I	Introduction to parents' game	Parents' game II: Consequences for noncompliance
11	Limit setting II	Coping skills I: Recognizing feelings	Parents' game III: Commands and time-out
12	Limit setting III	Coping skills II: Dealing with criticism	Parent's game IV: Parent and child interaction on commands and consequences
13	Development/implementation of behavior programs	Coping skills III: Coping with anger	Development/implementation of family meetings and behavior change programs
14	Generalization and maintenance	Graduation, resources for help, and review	Graduation party

Source: From National Institute on Drug Abuse (1997a).

among parents; improved parenting skills; and enhanced family communication skills. In a study that compared 71 SFP participating families with 47 nonparticipating families, for example, children of the SFP families were less likely to show behavioral, academic, social, and emotional problems than those of the non-SFP families (DeMarsh & Kumpfer, 1986). In addition, previously substance-using children as well as such parents showed significantly decreased use of tobacco and alcohol in pre- and post-test results (DeMarsh & Kumpfer, 1986).

Positive Action (PA)

Outlines

Positive Action (PA) is a multifaceted program integrating classroom curriculum, schoolwide program, family component, and community involvement components. Its primary goals include improvement of students' academic achievement, reduction of problem behaviors, and reinforcement of positive behaviors/attitudes. Primarily based on self-concept theories that emphasize actions rather than thoughts or feelings, PA attempts to teach students "what actions are positive, that they feel good when they do positive actions, and that they then have more positive thoughts and future actions" (Flay & Allred, 2003, p. S7). A major difference between PA and other selective prevention programs is that PA intends to affect more distal factors on student behavior in a holistic approach including school reorganization. The current PA program is the result of extensive pilot work and repeated evaluation that has been conducted since its first development by Carol Gerber Allread in 1977.

Program Goal and Objectives

PA has specified goals and objectives for the school and community as well as for the individual student and family (Flay, Allred, & Ordway, 2001, p. 76).

- Individual goals
  To give everyone the opportunity to learn and practice physical, intellectual, and emotional and social positive actions
  To understand that success and happiness means feeling good about who you are and what you are doing (being the best you can be)

To develop good character, morals, and ethics
- Family goals
  To create a positive learning environment in the home
  To contribute to adult literacy and to develop life skills in adult family members
  To prepare children to be effective learners prior to entering school
- School goals
  To bring about comprehensive school reform
  To develop lifelong skills that lead to success and happiness in school and society
  To create a positive environment conducive to teaching and learning
  To create a safe, drug-free school environment
  To promote the personal and professional development of teachers, staff members, and administrators
  To completely unite the efforts of the school, home, and community organization in promoting the social, academic, and emotional growth of children
  To teach the leadership skills that will promote high achievement and expert performance in the global marketplace
- Community goals
  To involve the whole community in learning and practicing the positive actions necessary for a good self-concept and a successful life
  To contribute to a community environment

Target Population

PA targets children and adolescents 5 through 18 years of age. It can be implemented for the general student population as universal prevention, for at-risk students as selective prevention, and also for students with problem behaviors or mental health problems as indicated prevention.

Program Structure and Implementation

The PA program consists of a detailed classroom curriculum, a schoolwide climate program, and family- and community-involvement components. The classroom curriculum is composed of over 140 lessons. Guided by the teacher's kit, which includes a program manual for teachers and necessary materials, a classroom teacher presents a lesson for about 15–20 minutes almost every school day. This teacher-led classroom curriculum is delivered in various activities including stories, games, music, questions and answers, role playing, posters, and manipulative activities. The classroom curriculum is organized in six units, which are presented in Table 22.5.

The school-climate program is designed to reinforce the practice of positive actions school-wide. For this purpose, school administrators are encouraged to utilize various activities such as assemblies, celebrations, school newspaper, community service group for students, tutoring, and diversity initiatives. There is also a guiding manual for principals, the principal's kits. This principal's manual suggests utilizing stickers, tokens, and positive notes to reinforce positive actions of

elementary school students. The parents' program has two major strategies, coordinated weekly lessons and strengthened connections between parent and school. With the purpose to help parents improve their communication skills and parenting style, the family kit introduces to parents 42 weekly lessons, which are in coordination with the PA school curriculum and school-climate activities. In addition, parents are strongly encouraged to participate in various school activities, such as the decision-making team for the PA program, the development of the mission statement, and program evaluation procedures. The PA program also intends to create a better community environment that has a positive influence on child development. For this purpose, the community kit was developed. It provides community leaders, social service workers, public servants, and

Table 22.5 The Components of Positive Action Program

Unit/Number and Topic	Content
Unit 1. Self-concept: What it is, how it's formed, and why it's important	The relationship of thoughts, feelings, and actions (behavior). Units 2–6 teach children what actions are positive in various domains of life, that they feel good when they do positive actions, and that they then have more positive thoughts and future actions
Unit 2. Positive actions for body (physical) and mind (intellectual)	*Physical*: exercise, hygiene, nutrition, avoiding harmful substances, sleeping and resting enough, safety *Intellectual*: creative thinking, learning/studying, decision making, problem solving
Unit 3. Social/emotional positive actions for managing yourself responsibly	Manage human resources of time, energy, thoughts, actions, feelings (anger, fear, loneliness, others), talents, money, and possessions. Includes self-control
Unit 4. Social/emotional positive actions for getting along with others	Treat others the way you like to be treated, code of conduct (respect, fairness, kindness, honesty, courtesy, empathy, caring, responsible, reliable), conflict resolution, communication positively (communication skills), forming relationships, working cooperatively, community service. [These are the essence of character education]
Unit 5. Social/emotional positive actions for being honest with yourself & others	Self-honesty, doing what you will say you will do (integrity), not blaming others, not making excuses, not rationalizing; self-appraisal (look at strengths and weaknesses); and being in touch with reality. [These are the essence of mental health]
Unit 6. Social/emotional positive actions for improving yourself continually	Goal setting (physical, intellectual, and social/emotional), problem solving, decision making, believe in potential, have courage to try, turn problems into opportunities, persistence
Unit 7. Review	Review of all of above

Source: From Flay & Allred (2003, p. S8). Reproduced with permission.

other stakeholders in the community with proper tools to promote positive actions, playing their roles.

Outcomes

More than 7,000 schools have used the PA program nationally or internationally. The program has consistently showed desirable outcomes in substance use, absenteeism, disciplinary problems, violence, disruptive and disrespectful behaviors, school suspension, school dropout, and academic achievement including SAT scores, reading scores, and math scores. A recent study (Flay & Allred, 2003) evaluated the long-term effects of Positive Action based on matched-school design. Below are the primary findings that show significant effects of the Positive Action program on elementary school children:

- Students in PA schools performed 45% better, on average, in the Florida Reading Test than their counterparts in matched control schools.
- PA schools have 68% less violent incidents per 100 students compared to matched schools.
- The percentage of students who received out-of-school suspensions was 33.5% lower in PA schools in comparison with matched schools.

Tools and Practice Examples

Through the several decades of experiences to prevent substance use/abuse, a substantial body of knowledge and skills has been accumulated. In the following sections, some of the critical information is summarized to guide school social workers and other professionals who are interested in at-risk children and preventive intervention programs.

What Needs to Be Done?

To be effective, school prevention programs should:

- *Be based on the needs of students, families, school, and community.* The needs assessment will shed light on program focus by specifying the strengths and weaknesses of program participants and environment. Although assessment instruments should be chosen, the list of risk

and protective factors can be utilized for a brief needs assessment.

- *Have clear objectives.* Only when the goals and objectives are properly stated, the evaluation may produce reliable results. In addition, clear goals and objectives help practitioners keep the program focus and timelines (Knowles, 2001).
- *Be based on comprehensive multidimensional perspective.* As seen earlier, risk and protective factors are situated at multisystem levels, indicating the necessity of a multidimensional approach in prevention efforts. This guideline has been supported by many empirical studies (e.g., St. Pierre et al., 2001; Tatchell, Waite, Tatchell, Durrant, & Bond, 2004).
- *Focus on parent component.* Family involvement is the key for effective prevention (Gibson et al., 1993). Programs focusing on family relationships and parenting skills are usually effective in changing negative behaviors among parents as well as children (Gonet, 1994).
- *Include competency skills.* Social competency models, such as life skills training, have shown desirable outcomes in various studies (Gonet, 1994), and the effectiveness has been validated for elementary school students (St. Pierre et al., 2001). A social competency component is considered appropriate for universal and selected prevention programs (Griffin, Botvin, Nichols, & Doyle, 2003).
- *Utilize internal resources.* For young school children, as opposed to high school students, it is recommended that internal resources be utilized (e.g., teachers as implementers) rather than external resources (i.e., programs brought to the school by outside agencies) (Marsiglia, Holleran, & Jackson, 2000). Youth implementers, such as Peer Assistance and Leader (PAL) students, may be a great resource in elementary schools. Some of the assumptions about peer-led models, such as the fear of control and discipline difficulties, are unfounded (Erhard, 1999). It is also important to note that, in the sensitive area of substance use and abuse, peer-led programs yielded twice as much participants' self-disclosure (Erhard, 1999). All in all, there are strong indications that peer-led models may possess great potential for prevention efforts.
- *Be delivered in interactive method.* Compared to a noninteractive method, an interactive method produces greater effect size (Tobler, 1992). In some cases, a program showed effectiveness only when delivered in an interaction method (Sussman, Rohrbach, Ratel, & Holiday, 2003).

- *Be implemented in an intended way.* Well-developed and empirically proven prevention models usually have specified program manuals. To achieve program effectiveness, high fidelity is a must (Hogan et al., 2003).
- *Be followed by a booster program.* It is always recommended to provide booster sessions after program completion as the booster programs are vital for long-lasting program effectiveness (Gottfredson & Wilson, 2003; Lilja, Wilhelmsen, Larsson, & Hamilton, 2003).

What Should Be Avoided?

To be effective, school prevention programs should:

- *Not target individuals with a substance abuse problem.* Only qualified specialists on drug use should provide intervention programs to identified substance users or abusers. If school social workers and counselors (given that they are not drug abuse specialists) find a student who needs intervention, they must refer the student to a proper clinical setting (Gibson et al., 1993).
- *Not provide information only.* Information or knowledge on substance use/abuse does not necessarily reduce substance use (Holleran et al., 2004; Petosa, 1992; Stoil & Hill, 1996). In the worst cases, it could increase substance use among children or adolescents (Gonet, 1994).
- *Not threaten students.* Persuading children not to use a substance in a threatening way is not effective. Rather, it could cause mistrust toward mental health professions (Gonet, 1994).
- *Not be completed in a one-shot program.* A one-shot program, such as a guest speaker or film-watching, is usually least effective (Gonet, 1994).
- *Not use a self-esteem component as a primary strategy.* Programs that put the focus on self-esteem have not been the most effective. Program results in such models are not consistent and too often disappointing (Stoil & Hill, 1996).

Key Points to Remember

In this chapter, the authors presented an overview of selective prevention interventions, explained a risk and protective factor paradigm, and provided two examples of evidence-based model programs,

the Strengthening Families Program (SFP) and Positive Action (PA). It closes with critical recommendations and practical guidelines for utilizing such interventions. As with any program, and especially with elementary school students, practitioners must be very careful to protect the confidentiality of students and families. In addition, when doing prevention interventions with children, it is vital that clinicians avoid labeling and stereotyping. It is helpful to recognize that interventions that address substance abuse prevention, as noted previously, also prevent other problematic outcomes, such as rebelliousness, aggression, and absenteeism. It is also recommended that teachers and program implementers watch students carefully for potential negative responses to the intervention (e.g., emotional overload, anxiety, depression), which might give clues that other concurrent issues or more serious problems exist. In such cases, referral to a specialist or a proper clinical setting may be necessary.

References

Alcoholism & Drug Abuse Weekly. (1999, April 19). Survey pinpoints substance use among elementary school students. *Alcoholism & Drug Abuse Weekly.*

American Academy of Pediatrics. (1998). Caring for your adolescent: Ages 12 to 21 (pamphlet).

Centers for Disease Control and Prevention. (2004). *Youth risk behavior surveillance: United States, 2003* (MMWR No. SS-2). Atlanta: U.S. Department of Health and Human Services.

DeMarsh, J. P., & Kumpfer, K. L. (1986). Family oriented interventions for the prevention of chemical dependency in children and adolescents. In S. Ezekoye, K. Kumpfer, & W. Bukoski (Eds.), *Childhood and chemical abuse: Prevention and early intervention* (pp. 117–152). New York: Haworth.

Erhard, R. (1999). Peer-led and adult-led programs—student perceptions. *Journal of Drug Education, 29*(4), 295–308.

Fisher, G. L., & Harrison, T. C. (2004). *Substance abuse: Information for school counselors, social workers, therapists, and counselors.* Boston: Pearson Education.

Flay, B. R., & Allred, C. G. (2003). Long-term effects of the Positive Action program. *American Journal of Health Behavior, 27*(Supp. 1), S6–S21.

Flay, B. R., Allred, C. G., & Ordway, N. (2001). Effects of the Positive Action program on achievement and discipline: Two matched-control comparisons. *Prevention Science, 2*(2), 71–89.

Gibson, R. L., Mitchell, M. H., & Basile, S. K. (1993). *Counseling in the elementary school: A comprehensive approach.* Boston: Allyn and Bacon.

Gonet, M. M. (1994). *Counseling the adolescent substance abuser: School-based intervention and prevention.* Thousand Oaks: CA: Sage.

Gottfredson, D. C., & Wilson, D. B. (2003). Characteristics of effective school-based substance abuse prevention. *Prevention Science, 4*(1), 27–38.

Griffin, K. W., Botvin, G. J., Nichols, T. R., & Doyle, M. M. (2003). Effectiveness of a universal drug abuse prevention approach for youth at high risk for substance use initiation. *Preventive Medicine, 36,* 1–7.

Hawkins, J. D., Catalano, R. F., Kosterman, R., Abbott, R., & Hill, K. G. (1999). Preventing adolescent health-risk behaviors by strengthening protection during childhood. *Archives of Pediatric and Adolescent Medicine, 153,* 226–234.

Hogan, J. A., Gabrielsen, K. R., Luna, N., & Grothaus, D. (2003). *Substance abuse prevention: The intersection of science and practice.* Boston: Allyn & Bacon.

Holleran, L. K., Kim, Y., & Dixon, K. (2004). Innovative approaches to risk assessment within alcohol prevention programming. In A. R. Roberts & K. R. Yeager (Eds.), *Evidence-based practice manual: Research and outcome measures in health and human services* (pp. 677–684). New York: Oxford University Press.

Jenson, J. M. (1997). Risk and protective factors for alcohol and other drug use in childhood and adolescence. In M. W. Fraser (Ed.), *Risk and resilience in childhood* (pp. 117–139). Washington, DC: NASW Press.

Jenson, J. M., & Howard, M. O. (1991). Risk-focused drug and alcohol prevention: Implications for school-based prevention programs. *Social Work in Education, 13*(4), 246–256.

Knowles, C. R. (2001). *Prevention that works: A guide for developing school-based drug and violence prevention programs.* Thousand Oaks, CA: Corwin Press.

Kuhn, C., Swartzwelder, S., & Wilson, W. (1998). *Buzzed: The straight facts about the most used and abused drugs (from alcohol to ecstasy).* New York: W. W. Norton & Company.

Kumpfer, K. L. (2003). *Identification of drug abuse prevention programs: Literature review.* Retrieved July 13, 2004, from http://www.drugabuse.gov/about/organization/despr/hsr/da-pre/KumpferLitReview.html

Kumpfer, K. L., Alvarado, R., & Whiteside, H. O. (2003). Family-based interventions for substance use and misuse prevention. *Substance Use & Misuse, 38*(11–13), 1759–1787.

Lilja, J., Wilhelmsen, B. U., Larsson, S., & Hamilton, D. (2003). Evaluation of drug use prevention programs directed at adolescents. *Substance Use & Misuse, 38*(11–13), 1831–1863.

Marsiglia, F. F., Holleran, L., & Jackson, K. M. (2000). The impact of internal and external resources on school-based substance abuse prevention. *Social Work in Education, 22*(3), 145–161.

National Institute on Drug Abuse. (1997a). *Drug abuse prevention for at-risk groups* (NIH No. 97–4114). Rockville, MD: U.S. Department of Health and Human Services, National Institutes of Health.

National Institute on Drug Abuse. (1997b). *Drug abuse prevention: What works.* Rockville, MD: U.S. Department of Health and Human Services.

Pandina, R. J. (1996, September 19–20). *Risk and protective factor models in adolescent drug use: Putting them to work for prevention.* Paper presented at the National Conference on Drug Abuse Prevention Research: Presentations, papers, and recommendations, Washington, DC.

Parents' Resource Institute for Drug Education. (2003). *2002–03 PRIDE Surveys national summary for grades 4 thru 6.* Bowling Green, KY: Author.

Petosa, R. (1992). Developing a comprehensive health promotion program to prevent adolescent drug abuse. In G. W. Lawson & A. W. Lawson (Eds.), *Adolescent substance abuse: Etiology, treatment, and prevention* (pp. 431–450). Gaithersburg, MD: Aspen.

Rones, M., & Hoagwood, K. (2000). School-based mental health services: A research review. *Clinical Child and Family Psychology Review, 3*(4), 223–241.

St. Pierre, T. S., Mark, M. M., Kaltreider, D. L., & Campbell, B. (2001). Boys & girls clubs and school collaborations: A longitudinal study of a multicomponent substance abuse prevention program for high-risk elementary school children. *Journal of Community Psychology, 29*(2), 87–106.

Sarvela, P. D., Monge, E. A., Shannon, D. V., & Newrot, R. (1999). Age of first use of cigarettes among rural and small town elementary school children in Illinois. *Journal of School Health, 69*(10), 398–402.

Stoil, M. J., & Hill, G. (1996). *Preventing substance abuse: Interventions that work.* New York: Plenum.

Sullivan, T. N., & Farrell, A. D. (2002). Risk factors. In C. A. Essau (Ed.), *Substance abuse and dependence in adolescence: Epidemiology, risk factors and treatment* (pp. 87–118). New York: Taylor & Francis.

Sussman, S., Rohrbach, L. A., Ratel, R., & Holiday, K. (2003). A look at an interactive classroom-based drug abuse prevention program: Interactive contents and suggestions for research. *Journal of Drug Education, 33*(4), 355–368.

Tatchell, T. W., Waite, P. J., Tatchell, R. H., Durrant, L. H., & Bond, D. S. (2004). Substance abuse prevention in sixth grade: The effect of a prevention program on adolescents' risk and protective factors. *American Journal of Health Studies, 19*(1), 54–61.

Tobler, N. S. (1992). Drug prevention programs can work: Research findings. *Journal of Addictive Diseases, 11*(3), 1–28.

Wilson, D. B., Gottfredson, D. C., & Najaka, S. S. (2001). School-based prevention problem behaviors: A meta-analysis. *Journal of Quantitative Criminology, 17*(3), 247–272.

Screening Substance Use/Abuse of Middle and High School Students

Lori K. Holleran ▪ Soyon Jung

CHAPTER 23

Getting Started

Adolescent substance use has been a major concern in this country. According to the Monitoring the Future (MTF) study conducted by the University of Michigan (University of Michigan Institute for Social Research, 2003) and supported by the National Institute on Drug Abuse (NIDA), high rates of American youth have tried or currently use various illicit drugs, alcohol, and tobacco. Among the 8th, 10th, and 12th graders surveyed in 2003, for example, one third currently use alcohol and one out of six smoke cigarettes. In addition, many adolescents use illegal drugs including marijuana, ecstasy, and LSD. Approximately 17% reported illicit drug use during the past month prior to the survey and 37% reported that they had tried it at least once during their lifetime.

The consequences of substance use are serious, costly, and extensive. Most substances have immediate physiological influences. They interfere with correct perception and rational judgment (McWhirter, McWhirter, McWhirter, & McWhirter, 2004). It is well established that adolescents are more likely to be involved in risk-taking behaviors under the influence of substance(s). Not surprisingly, substance use often leads to fatal accidents and crime. Alcohol consumption, for instance, is a major cause of death among youth via motor vehicle accidents, homicides, suicides, and drowning (U.S. Department of Health and Human Services [DHHS], 2000). Furthermore, heavy drinking and smoking often contribute to various diseases: cancer, heart disease, many liver-related diseases (DHHS, 2000), and sexually transmitted diseases, including HIV/AIDS (Center for Disease Control and Prevention, 2004). The economic costs of substance abuse

and drug abuse in the United States were estimated to be $167 and $110 billion, respectively, in 1995 (DHHS, 2000). Substance use has detrimental impacts on the mental health of adolescents as well. Newcomb and Bentler (1989) found that serious drug users are vulnerable to experience loneliness, depression, and suicide ideations. Moreover, substance use hinders youth from accomplishing important developmental tasks, performing expected duties, and building healthy relationships with others. Previous studies have consistently indicated that substance use is significantly associated with poor educational outcomes and academic failure (Jeynes, 2002; NCCDPHP, 2000; National Commission on Drug-Free Schools, 1990), physical fights and criminal behavior (NCCDPHP, 2000), and inadequate positive social connection (Havighurst, 1972).

Although the detrimental consequences of adolescent substance use are immense, appropriate treatment can significantly reduce the harmful effects (Winters, Latimer, & Stinchfield, 1999). Early intervention is considered especially desirable in terms of effectiveness and efficiency. The Consensus Panel for the Center for Substance Abuse Treatment (CSAT) recommends that all adolescents showing any sign of substance use be properly screened (Winters, 2001b). Thus, professionals who work with at-risk youth must have screening resources and expertise so that the adolescents can receive more comprehensive assessment and intervention services (Winters, 2001b). Since adolescents spend a large amount of time at school, the role of school mental health professionals in identifying substance users at earlier stages and providing them with intervention opportunities cannot be overemphasized.

This chapter discusses the substance use/abuse screening methods that school mental health professionals can easily utilize. A summary table of screening tools developed particularly for the adolescent population is presented. Somewhat detailed information about two screening instruments, POSIT and RAPI, which are considered most efficient at school settings, follows. This information covers how to administer the instruments and how to interpret the results. Finally, a case example is provided to demonstrate the techniques described in the chapter.

Substance users need to be aware of their problems and motivated for change with regard to substances during each screening procedure (Winters, 2001b). School mental health professionals should remember to utilize their most astute clinical techniques to make successful initial contacts with potential substance users and refer them to suitable intervention programs.

What We Know and Can Do

Screening Adolescent Substance Use/Abuse

Before examining specific screening methods and procedures, it is necessary to understand the differences between screening, assessment, and diagnosis of substance use/abuse. The primary purpose of screening is to identify potential substance users who need a through assessment (Winters, 2001b). On the other hand, comprehensive assessment aims to verify substance use/abuse of an adolescent and reveal other relevant problems and service needs (Winters, 2001b). Diagnosis is carried out based on the most comprehensive measures or highly structured criteria such as those presented in the fourth edition of the *Diagnostic and Statistical Manual of Mental Disorders* (*DSM-IV*). Diagnosis is considered a more decisive conclusion compared to assessment. While *assessment* refers to "the process of gathering information," *diagnosis* is defined as the "the conclusion that is reached on the basis of the assessment" (Fisher & Harrison, 2004, p. 84).

One important point that school mental health professionals should keep in mind is that a comprehensive substance use/abuse assessment or diagnosis is best conducted by alcohol, tobacco, and other drug (commonly referred to as ATOD) specialists in general, and those involved in the intervention plan or treatment service in particular.

Thus, it is recommended for school mental health professionals to provide screening services only, unless they have adequate qualification for substance use/abuse assessment and diagnosis (Fisher & Harrison, 2004).

Who Needs to Be Screened?

As substance use is quite prevalent among American youth and many of them are diverge from the stereotypes of ATOD users, school social workers and school counselors need to be always aware that the possibility of a substance use problem exists when they are providing any kind of service to students. Ideally, screenings for substance use/abuse would be done universally with all students. However, given limited resources and inadequate numbers of mental health professionals at school, it would be more desirable to focus on screening students at risk for substance use/abuse or showing some indication of possible substance use.

An effective way to identify potential substance users for screening is to utilize a multidisciplinary team including classroom teachers. Because classroom teachers spend much time with students and have many opportunities to observe student behaviors directly, they can make a significant contribution to problem identification (Gonet, 1994). School social workers and drug counselors can encourage participation of teachers in case identification procedures and enhance the quality of information reported by the teachers, using a form specially designed to easily detect substance use among students.

Self-Report Screening Instruments for Adolescents

Although there are various approaches available, self-report screening instruments are commonly used to identify ATOD problem among adolescents (Martin & Winters, 1998). Using standardized instruments has some advantages: it reduces potential bias (Winters, 2001a); it is less likely to threaten students than other methods (Winters, 2001a); and it makes mental health professionals look trustworthy (Orenstein, Davis, & Wolfe, 1995). If school mental health professionals plan to use self-report screening instruments, the biggest challenge is selecting the best instrument in a given situation. Fortunately, many screening

Table 23.1 Screening Instruments for Adolescent Substance or Alcohol Use/Abuse

Name of Screening Tool and Contact Info for Access	Brief Description	Number of Q (time)	Reading Level	Cost[a] and Copyright	Key Reference
Adolescent Alcohol Involvement Scale (AAIS) http://www.niaaa.nih.gov/publications/aais.htm	• *Problems measured:* alcohol use and psychosocial consequences • *Administration:* self-report • *Required qualification for use:* no specific requirement • *Reliability:* test–retest & internal consistency • *Validity:* construct & criterion (predictive, concurrent, postdictive)	14 (5 m)	No info	Cost information is not available Copyright status is unknown	Mayer & Filstead (1979)
Adolescent Drinking Index (ADI) Psychological Assessment Resources, Inc. PO Box 998, Odessa, FL 33556 (800) 331-8378 http://www.parinc.com/index.cfm	• *Problems measured:* severity of drinking problems • *Administration:* self-report or interview • *Qualification for administration:* (1) a bachelor's degree or higher in psychology or a related field; or (2) adequate training for interpreting psychological test results • *Reliability:* internal consistency • *Validity:* criterion (concurrent validity)	24 (5 m)	5th grade	Introductory kit: $82 Professional manual: $35 Test booklets (pkg/25): $53	*Mental Measurements Yearbook* (12th ed.)
Adolescent Drug Involvement Scale (ADIS) D. Paul Moberg, Ph.D. Center for Health Policy & Program Evaluation Univ. of Wisconsin at Madison 2710 Marshall Ct., Madison, WI 53705 (608) 263-1304	• *Problems measured:* levels of drug use other than alcohol • *Administration:* self-report • *Qualification for administration:* no specific requirement • *Reliability:* internal consistency • *Validity:* criterion (concurrent)	12 (4–5 m)	No info	No cost ADIS is in public domain	Moberg & Hahn (1991)
CRAFFT[b] American Medical Association Licensing and Permission 515 N. State Street Chicago, IL 60610	• *Problems measured:* substance use problem • *Administration:* self-report • *Required qualification for use:* no information available • *Reliability:* internal consistency • *Validity:* criterion	6	No info	No cost Copyrighted	Knight et al. (1999)

(continued)

Table 23.1 (*Continued*)

Name of Screening Tool and Contact Info for Access	Brief Description	Number of Q (time)	Reading Level	Cost[a] and Copyright	Key Reference
Drug and Alcohol Problem (DAP) Quick Screen Richard H. Schwartz, M.D. 410 Maple Avenue West Vienna, VA 22180 (703) 338–2244	• *Problems measured*: overall problem of alcohol and other drug use • *Administration*: self-report or interview • *Qualification for administration*: no specific requirement • *Reliability & validity*: this scale has been tested in a pediatric practice setting. However, reliability and validity of the DAP Quick Screen have not been evaluated	30 (10 m)	6th grade	No cost DAP is in public domain	Schwartz & Wirtz (1990)
Drug Use Screening Inventory Revised (DUSI-R)[c] The Gordian Group P.O. Box 1587 Hartsville, SC 29950 (843) 383–2201 www.dusi.com	• *Problems measured*: severity of disturbance in 10 domains including drug & alcohol use, substance use, behavior patterns, and health status. • *Administration*: self-report • *Qualification for administration*: drug counselors and other qualified users • *Reliability & Validity*: good levels of reliability and validity of DUSI-R have been reported	159 (20–40 m)	5th grade	A copy of paper DUSI-R: $2 DUSI-R software for computer administration: $199 Copyrighted	Kirisci, Mezzich, & Tarter (1995)
Personal Experience Screening Questionnaire (PESQ) Western Psychological Services 12031 Wilshire Blvd. Los Angeles, CA 90025 (310) 478–2061 http://www.wpspublish.com/Inetpub4/index.htm	• *Problems measured*: problem severity, psychosocial items, & drug use history • *Administration*: self-report or interview • *Qualification for administration*: no specific requirement • *Reliability*: internal consistency • *Validity*: content, construct, & criterion (postdictive & concurrent)	40 (10 m)	No info	$79.50 per kit (each kit includes 25 Autoscore Test Forms & 1 Manual) Copyrighted	Winters (1991) Winters (1992)

(continued)

Instrument	Description	Items (time)	Reading level	Cost	Reference
Problem Oriented Screening Instrument for Teenagers (POSIT)[b] Elizabeth Rahdert, Ph.D. National Institute on Drug Abuse, NIH 5600 Fishers Lane, Room 10A–10 Rockville, MD 20857 (301) 443–0107	• *Goal:* to identify substance abuse and related problems and to estimate potential service needs in 10 system areas • *Type:* paper-and-pencil questionnaire CD-ROM version is also available • *Administration:* self-report or interview • *Qualification for administration:* no specific requirement • *Reliability:* test–retest & internal consistency • *Validity:* content, criterion (concurrent & predictive), construct validity (convergent & discriminant)	139 (20–30 m)	5th grade (12–19 yrs old)	No cost POSIT is in public domain	Rahdert (1991)
Rutgers Alcohol Problem Index (RAPI) Helene Raskin White, Ph.D. Center of Alcohol Studies Rutgers University P.O. Box 969 Piscataway, NJ 08855–0969 (732) 445–3579	• *Problems assessed:* problem drinking of adolescents • *Administration:* self-report or interview • *Qualification for administration:* no training required • *Reliability:* split-half, internal consistency • *Validity:* content and criterion • RAPI is appropriate for use in clinical and nonclinical samples of adolescents and young adults	23 (10 m)	7th grade	No cost Copyrighted	White & Labouvie (1989)

[a]Cost as of July, 2004
[b]CRAFFT questions can be obtained from http://wwwslp3d2.com/rwj_1027/webcast/docs/screentest.html
[c]Indicates that Spanish version is available.

instruments for the adolescent population have been developed in recent years and now there is a wide range of appropriate instruments. Table 23.1 briefly introduces nine screening instruments for adolescents suitable for school settings. Since the characteristics of the instruments are very diverse, school mental health professions are advised to check the qualities, cost, and required conditions of the instruments thoroughly before choosing one. Among the nine instruments, Problem Oriented Screening Instruments for Teenagers (POSIT) and Rutgers Alcohol Problem Index (RAPI) are especially recommendable for school mental health professionals considering low cost, copyright, easy access, and psychometric traits of the instruments. Thus, these instruments are presented as exemplars.

Problem-Oriented Screening Instrument for Teenagers (POSIT)

Brief Description

POSIT is one of the most widely used instruments for adolescent substance use/abuse.[1] It was developed by National Institute on Drug Abuse (NIDA) to identify potential problems and service needs of adolescents aged 12 to 19 years. It is composed of 139 Yes/No questions under the following 10 subscales: Substance Use and Abuse; Physical Health Status; Mental Health Status; Family Relations; Peer Relations; Educational Status; Vocational Status; Social Skills; Leisure and Recreation; and Aggressive Behavior and Delinquency.

Format and Administration

The original POSIT is a paper-and-pencil questionnaire. Recently, a CD-ROM version became available. It can be self-administered or administered during an interview in a variety of settings including schools. No specific qualification is necessary for administration.

Scoring and Interpretation

POSIT can be scored and interpreted in two different ways, using either the original or the new scoring system. In the original scoring system, the questions are classified as general, age-related, or red-flag items. While every point-earning answer to general items adds one risk score in each subscale, the answer to age-related items does only for the teenagers in a specified age range. Either any point earning in red-flag items or expert-based cutoff score in a subscale is interpreted as indication of needs for further assessment or service in the problem area. In a new scoring system, however, red-flag items are not taken into account and the total score of each subscale is used to determine the level of risks in the area.

Psychometric Properties

The internal consistency of POSIT varies across the subscales and different studies. Some subscales, such as Substance Use/Abuse, Mental Health, and Aggressive Behavior/Delinquency exhibit high levels of internal consistency while others, such as Leisure/Recreation, Vocational Status, and Physical Health, show lower levels of internal consistency than conventionally acceptable ranges. However, it should be noticed that the Cronbach's alpha for the Substance Use/Abuse subscale has been identified as high ranging from .77 (Knight, Goodman, Pulerwitz, & DuRant, 2001) to .93 (Melchior, Rahdert, & Huba, 1994). Acceptable levels of test–retest reliability have been also reported (Dembo, Schmeidler, & Henly, 1996; McLaney & Boca, 1994). All the subscales of POSIT have successfully differentiated heavy substance users from nonusers, showing good concurrent differential validity (Melchior et al., 1994). In a study (McLaney & Boca, 1994) in which POSIT was compared with Personal Experience Inventory (PEI), Diagnostic Interview for Children and Adolescents (DICA), and the Adolescent Diagnostic Interview (ADI), POSIT also showed both convergent and divergent validity.

Brief Evaluation of the Instrument

Based on prior empirical studies, POSIT is a recommendable screening instrument especially for substance use/abuse problems among adolescents. One of the advantages of POSIT lies in its comprehensiveness. The screening results with POSIT can identify potential problems in various areas rather than assessing substance use problems only. Such comprehensiveness might help mental health professionals make better referrals for further assessment or necessary services based on various needs of the adolescents. Easy administration and cost-effectiveness are also considerable benefits of POSIT. In addition, POSIT is in the public domain and can be easily obtained at no cost by contacting NIDA or the National Clearinghouse for Alcohol and Drug Information, or by visiting the Web site of the National Institute on Alcohol Abuse and Alcoholism.

Rutgers Alcohol Problem Index (RAPI)

Brief Description

RAPI is a simple, unidimensional screening tool for problem drinking. Its target populations are adolescents and young adults aged 12 to 21 years. The researchers at the Center of Alcohol Studies, Rutgers University, developed RAPI in 1989 to create an efficient and conceptually sound instrument to assess problem drinking among adolescents. This instrument has been validated on nonclinical as well as clinical samples.

Format and Administration

RAPI is composed of 23 items describing alcohol-related problems or symptoms. The original version of RAPI asks respondents how many times they experienced each problem during the last 3 years, and provides five answer categories for each question: none; 1–2 times; 3–4 times; 6–10 times; and more than 10 times. A later version of RAPI[2] asks respondents the same questions, but the time frame was reduced to the previous year for greater specificity, as shown below. The number of answer categories was also reduced to four, ranging from "none" to "more than five times." Basically RAPI is a self-administered paper-and-pencil type instrument, but it can be easily administered also in an interview format if preferable or necessary. No special training is required for administration.

Scoring and Interpretation

Scoring of RAPI is simple. If the number assigned to each answer category is added, it forms a total scale score. It should be noted, however, that the last two answer categories of the original version

of RAPI need to be combined and three be assigned. Therefore, the total scores of both the original and later version of RAPI range from 0 to 69. The total score is considered to indicate the level of problem drinking. The necessity for a further assessment can be made based on the norms available. According to the most recent data provided by the RAPI developers, the mean scores for clinical sample range from 21 to 26, while those for nonclinical sample from 5.9 to 8.2, depending on gender and age. Specific information about RAPI mean score is exhibited in Table 23.3.

Psychometric Properties

The 23-item RAPI resulted from factor analyses conducted on a nonclinical sample of 1,308 adolescents (White & Labouvie, 1989). Its internal consistency measured was .92 and test–retest with a 3-year period marked .40 (White & Labouvie, 1989). RAPI has showed high correlation levels with Adolescent Alcohol Involvement Scale (AAIS), Alcohol Dependence Scale (ADS), DSM-III, and DSM-III-R (greater than .70), indicating good convergent validity. In addition, RAPI can differentiate seriously problematic drinkers from non- or less problematic drinkers in adolescence.

Brief Evaluation of the Instrument

As a screening instrument for adolescents, RAPI has several merits. First, it is efficient. Its administration and scoring procedures are simple and require only 15 minutes or less (10 minutes for administration and 3 to 5 minutes for scoring). It is in the public domain, and no cost is necessary. Second, RAPI has high utility. It can be used for nonclinical as well as clinical samples. Third, all the RAPI items are worded appropriately for teenage students and are easy to understand. Fourth, it can be used for various purposes. Based on RAPI scores, for example, service referral can be done properly and the effectiveness of the intervention program for adolescent drinkers can be evaluated. Furthermore, according to the scale developers, it is possible to use RAPI to assess all types of substance use problems. The only thing necessary is to use proper words for the substance instead of "alcohol" or "drinking." RAPI has also some limitations. Most notably, there is no clear cutoff

Table 23.2 Rutgers Alcohol Problem Index (RAPI)

Different things happen to people while they are drinking ALCOHOL or because of *ALCOHOL* drinking. Several of these things are listed below. Indicate how many times each of these things happened to you WITHIN THE LAST YEAR.
Use the following code:

    0 = None
    1 = 1–2 times
    2 = 3–5 times
    3 = More than 5 times

None	*1–2 Times*	*3–5 Times*	*More Than 5 Times*	*HOW MANY TIMES HAS THIS HAPPENED TO YOU WHILE YOU WERE DRINKING OR BECAUSE OF YOUR DRINKING DURING THE LAST YEAR?*
0	1	2	3	Not able to do your homework or study for a test
0	1	2	3	Got into fights with other people (friends, relatives, strangers)
0	1	2	3	Missed out on other things because you spent too much money on alcohol
0	1	2	3	Went to work or school high or drunk
0	1	2	3	Caused shame or embarrassment to someone
0	1	2	3	Neglected your responsibilities
0	1	2	3	Relatives avoided you
0	1	2	3	Felt that you needed *more* alcohol than you used to in order to get the same effect
0	1	2	3	Tried to control your drinking (tried to drink only at certain times of the day or in certain places, that is, tried to change your pattern of drinking)
0	1	2	3	Had withdrawal symptoms, that is, felt sick because you stopped or cut down on drinking
0	1	2	3	Noticed a change in your responsibility
0	1	2	3	Felt that you had a problem with alcohol
0	1	2	3	Missed a day (or part of a day) of school or work
0	1	2	3	Wanted to stop drinking but couldn't
0	1	2	3	Suddenly found yourself in a place that you could not remember getting to
0	1	2	3	Passed out or fainted suddenly
0	1	2	3	Had a fight, argument, or bad feeling with a friend
0	1	2	3	Had a fight, argument, or bad feeling with a family member
0	1	2	3	Kept drinking when you promised yourself not to
0	1	2	3	Felt you were going crazy
0	1	2	3	Had a bad time
0	1	2	3	Felt physically or psychologically dependent on alcohol
0	1	2	3	Was told by a friend, neighbor, or relative to stop or cut down drinking

point based on which adolescents with a drinking problem and adolescents without a problem can be classified. Another limitation is that RAPI measures only one problem area (e.g., alcohol use/abuse). Considering previous studies that have consistently found that substance use/abuse problems are complicated and related to many other areas, it would be more desirable to use RAPI with other instruments for more accurate screening or comprehensive assessment.

Table 23.3 Currently Available Mean Scores of RAPI

Clinical Sample	N	Mean	Nonclinical Sample	N	Mean
14–16 years old males	42	23.3	14–16 years old males	151	7.5
14–16 years old females	19	22.2	14–16 years old females	147	5.9
17–18 years old males	43	21.1	17–18 years old males	211	8.2
17–18 years old females	15	26.0	17–18 years old females	208	7.4

Tools and Practice Examples

Tools

The student behavior checklist, which is composed of the indicative signs of substance use/abuse and relevant problem behaviors as shown in Figure 23.1, is a good example of a tool used to screen for substance use. School mental health professionals can ask teachers to fill out this form and submit it to the interdisciplinary team or the professionals whenever the teachers find a potential substance user.

Case Example

Phil is 15-year-old male whose behavior has recently changed dramatically. He has a history of being a strong student with aspirations to attend college and write creatively. He had always been somewhat eccentric, dressing uniquely, with unusual hairdos, but recently appeared disheveled and unkempt. Upon noticing an undeniable drop in his grades and motivation, his English teacher utilized the student behavior checklist, particularly noting the following behaviors: excessive tardiness, frequent requests to go to the restroom, cell phone buzzing throughout class, moments of apparent disorientation, noticeable chewing of breath mints in succession, occasionally nodding off in class. When the teacher requested a meeting with Phil, she noticed that his breath smelled of alcohol. Having a strong relationship with Phil in the past, she expressed concern and requested that he meet with her to talk. She kept her comments to factual observations rather than emotional and speculative responses. She framed her interactions in empathy and supportively suggested that they invite the school social worker to talk. Phil refused initially, but with warm encouragement and strength-based, positive persuasion, he agreed to meet with the worker.

Prior to the screening, a multidisciplinary team consisting of the school social worker, classroom teachers, specialty teachers (e.g., P.E. and art), the school nurse, and principal were made aware of concerns about Phil by his English teacher. The teacher had suggested that Phil's recent change in attention span would make in-depth screening difficult, and the team and social worker decided to begin with the RAPI.

The social worker began by noting very specific strengths of the student (i.e., has aptitude for writing, his history of good grades, his bold sense of style, his sense of humor) and then gently noted the shifts that the teacher had recognized. She cleverly described that alcohol use and experimentation are common in his age group. Further, she persuaded Phil to understand that she needed to learn more about his drinking since the teacher's concerns included awareness that he drank occasionally. She also started by asking if he had any friend that drank because association is a good clue. He openly noted that a few of his friends liked to drink, but that he only did it "once in a while." Sensing his hesitancy, she clearly described that their discussion would remain confidential, except for if the information denoted danger to self or others. She stated that she would start by conducting a brief questionnaire to get a general sense of the issues. She encouraged him to be open and honest and to ask questions if he had any. She added that she would do her best to help and advocate for the student, and that she could be most effective if he was as honest as possible. This gave him the sense that she was trying to help rather than to trap or punish him. She handed him the RAPI, and he scored on the items shown in Table 23.4.

Phil's answers clearly showed a lack of concern about his own alcohol use and a belief that he could stop at any time. However, he had admitted that alcohol had played a role in his academic work, family relationships, and peer relationships (he specifically commented that his girlfriend didn't drink or smoke "pot" and was thinking of

Figure 23.1. A Sample Behavioral Checklist

Teacher Name: _____   Date: _____

_____ (student name) has been referred to the "CARE" team. Please help us by sharing information about his or her school behavior. This information will be strictly confidential. Thank you for your cooperation.

Check those behaviors you have witnessed. Use the bottom of this form if you have any further information that you think may be of help to the CARE team. Thank you.

_____ Tardy:	No. _____	_____ Nonresponsiveness
_____ Absent:	No. _____	_____ Lack of motivation
Frequent requests to go to:		_____ Change of dress (negative)
_____ Lav.	_____ Phone	_____ Defensiveness
_____ Clinic	_____ Counselor	_____ Withdrawn; loner
Other (specify) _____		_____ Erratic behavior from day to day
_____ Falling asleep		_____ Cheating
_____ Slurred speech		_____ Constantly in "wrong" area
_____ Incoherent		(specify) _____
_____ Stumbles		_____ Obscene language or gestures
Smells of:		_____ Dramatic attention-getting behavior
_____ Alcohol	_____ Mouthwash	_____ Sudden outbursts
_____ Cigarette Smoke	_____ Marijuana	_____ Verbal abuse
_____ Talk freely of drug/alcohol use		_____ Fighting
_____ Brown-stained fingertips		_____ Class interruptions for this student
_____ Bad hygiene		_____ Change of friends (negative)
_____ Unusual/frequent bruises or sores		_____ Frequent requests for schedule changes
_____ Declining grade(s)		_____ Poor work performance
From _____ to _____		
_____ Other unacceptable out-of-class behavior		_____ Other unacceptable out-of-class behavior
Example: _____		Example: _____

Use this space for any other pertinent comments: _____
_____

Please deposit this form in an envelope in the CARE Mailbox in the Main Office.

Source: From *Counseling the Adolescent Substance Abuser: School-Based Intervention and Prevention* (p. 93), by M. M. Gonet, 1994, Thousand Oaks, CA: Sage. Reprinted with permission.

Table 23.4 Phil's RAPI Test Result

None	1–2 Times	3–5 Times	More Than 5 Times	HOW MANY TIMES HAS THIS HAPPENED TO YOU WHILE YOU WERE DRINKING OR BECAUSE OF YOUR DRINKING DURING THE LAST YEAR?
0	1	X	3	Not able to do your homework or study for a test
0	X	2	3	Got into fights with other people (friends, relatives, strangers)
X	1	2	3	Missed out on other things because you spent too much money on alcohol
0	X	2	3	Went to work or school high or drunk
X	1	2	3	Caused shame or embarrassment to someone
0	X	2	3	Neglected your responsibilities
0	1	X	3	Relatives avoided you
X	1	2	3	Felt that you needed *more* alcohol than you used to in order to get the same effect
X	1	2	3	Tried to control your drinking (tried to drink only at certain times of the day or in certain places, that is, tried to change your pattern of drinking)
X	1	2	3	Had withdrawal symptoms, that is, felt sick because you stopped or cut down on drinking
0	1	X	3	Noticed a change in your responsibility
X	1	2	3	Felt that you had a problem with alcohol
0	1	2	X	Missed a day (or part of a day) of school or work
X	1	2	3	Wanted to stop drinking but couldn't
X	1	2	3	Suddenly found yourself in a place that you could not remember getting to
X	1	2	3	Passed out or fainted suddenly
0	X	2	3	Had a fight, argument or bad feeling with a friend
0	X	2	3	Had a fight, argument or bad feeling with a family member
X	1	2	3	Kept drinking when you promised yourself not to
0	1	2	X	Felt you were going crazy
0	1	2	X	Had a bad time
X	1	2	3	Felt physically or psychologically dependent on alcohol
0	1	2	X	Was told by a friend, neighbor or relative to stop or cut down drinking

breaking up with him if he did). The social worker reviewed his responses and shared his score of 23, noting that this indicates enough concern to warrant a more in-depth screening or assessment. When he protested, she showed him the means chart for his age group, noting that "clinical samples" are the individuals who needed further intervention. She assured him that she would work with him and that the school would not try to punish him. He expressed anger and fear. The social worker calmly and firmly explained the next steps and gave him some choices so that he could feel empowered. Due to the reference to marijuana, the worker noted that the follow-up should include a more extensive substance abuse history and assessment. This worker was familiar with several students in the school who were young people in 12-Step recovery. She was aware that students at this age talk more freely with peers than authorities. Thus, she offered that Phil could talk to someone who had been "in the same boat" if he would like. The social worker had already done "her homework" and had a list of referrals to be considered for Phil to participate in a substance abuse assessment. She also made another appointment with him to explore social supports and see if and who he would be willing to have involved, such as family or friends.

Key Points to Remember

This chapter aims to provide awareness of the scope and repercussions of adolescent substance abuse, directions for choosing and utilizing a screening tool in school settings, and an example of a screening scenario. Tools including the teacher's behavioral checklist, the POSIT, and the RAPI are evidence-supported, reliable, simple instruments for gathering information that can help school mental health professionals determine if an adolescent is in need of more intensive substance-related referral and triage. It is important to note, however, that screening tools, no matter how comprehensive, cannot elicit definitive diagnoses and will not be likely to fully capture the nature of an adolescent's relationship to substances. Due to the fact that adolescents almost always hide their use due to fear, shame, and a desire to maintain the option to use substances, workers must be gentle, creative, and tenacious. The critical data lie in the rapport built between worker and student. In order to do the effective "detective work" of drawing out the facts, building connection with the individual, and putting the pieces together, a worker can utilize motivational interviewing techniques described in other areas of this book (for information, trainings, and publications, see the MI Web site, http://www.motivationalinterview.org).

It is important to remember that adolescent substance use/abuse can be profoundly injurious mentally, emotionally, socially, and physically. In fact, it can be potentially fatal and should not be minimized as a "passing phase." Workers do best to err on the conservative side and, if concerns arise, to consult with and/or refer the student to a substance abuse expert.

Notes

1. The POSIT questionnaire and brief explanation are available at http://www.niaaa.nih.gov/publications/insposit.htm and http://www.niaaa.nih.gov/publications/posit.htm, respectively.

2. Recently, the RAPI authors developed a new version of the scale (18-item) and are testing its psychometric properties.

References

Center for Disease Control and Prevention. (2004). *Youth risk behavior surveillance: United States, 2003* (MMWR No. SS-2). Atlanta: U.S. Department of Health and Human Services.

Dembo, R., Schneidler, J., & Henly, G. (1996). Examination of the reliability of the Problem Oriented Screening Instrument for Teenagers (POSIT) among arrested youth entering a juvenile assessment center. *Substance Use and Misuse, 31*, 785–824.

Fisher, G. L., & Harrison, T. C. (2004). *Substance abuse: Information for school counselors, social workers, therapists, and counselors.* Boston: Pearson Education.

Gonet, M. M. (1994). *Counseling the adolescent substance abuser: School-based intervention and prevention.* Thousand Oaks, CA: Sage.

Havighurst, R. J. (1972). *Developmental tasks and education.* New York: David McKay.

Jeynes, W. (2002). The relationship between the consumption of various drugs by adolescents and their academic achievement. *American Journal of Drug Alcohol Abuse, 28,* 15–35.

Kirisci, L., Mezzich, A., & Tarter, R. (1995). Norms and sensitivity of the adolescent version of the Drug Use Screening Inventory. *Addictive Behaviors, 20*(2), 149–157.

Knight, J. R., Goodman, E., Pulerwitz, T., & DuRant, R. H. (2001). Reliability of the Problem Oriented Screening Instrument for Teenagers (POSIT) in adolescent medical practice. *Journal of Adolescent Health, 29,* 125–130.

Knight, J. R., Shrier, L. A., Bravender, T. D., Farrell, M., Bilt, J. V., & Shaffer, H. J. (1999). A new brief screen for adolescent substance abuse. *Archives Pediatrics & Adolescent Medicine, 153,* 591–596.

Martin, C. S., & Winters, K. C. (1998). Diagnosis and assessment of alcohol use disorders among adolescents. *Alcohol Health & Research World, 22*(2), 95–105.

Mayer, J., & Filstead, W. J. (1979). The Adolescent Alcohol Involvement Scale: An instrument for measuring adolescents' use and misuse of alcohol. *Journal of Studies on Alcohol, 40,* 291–300.

McLaney, M. A., & Boca, F. D. (1994). A validation of the Problem-Oriented Screening Instrument for Teenagers (POSIT). *Journal of Mental Health, 3*(3), 363–376.

McWhirter, J. J., McWhirter, B. T., McWhirter, E. H., & McWhirter, R. J. (2004). *At-risk youth: A comprehensive response.* Toronto, Canada: Brooks Cole.

Melchior, L. A., Rahdert, E., & Huba, G. J. (1994). *Reliability and validity evidence for the Problem Oriented Screening Instruments for Teenagers (POSIT).* Washington, DC: American Public Health Association.

Moberg, D. P., & Hahn, L. (1991). The Adolescent Drug Involvement Scale. *Journal of Adolescent Chemical Dependency, 2*(1), 75–88.

National Commission on Drug-Free Schools. (1990). *Toward a drug-free generation: A nation's responsibility*. Washington, DC: U.S. Government Printing Office.

Newcomb, M. D., & Bentler, P. M. (1989). Substance use and abuse among children and teenagers. *American Psychologist, 44*(2), 242–248.

Orenstein, A., Davis, R. B., & Wolfe, H. (1995). Comparing screening instruments. *Journal of Alcohol & Drug Education, 40*(3), 119–131.

Rahdert, E. R. (1991). The adolescent assessment/referral system manual. Rockville, MD: U.S. Department of Health and Human Services, Alcohol, Drug Abuse, and Mental Health Administration.

Schwartz, R. H., & Wirtz, P. W. (1990). Potential substance abuse detection among adolescent patients: Using the Drug and Alcohol Problem (DAP) Quick Screen, a 30-item questionnaire. *Clinical Pediatrics, 29*, 38–43.

University of Michigan Institute for Social Research. (2003). Results from the 2003 Monitoring the Future Study. Retrieved July 25, 2004, from http://www.nida.nih.gov/Newsroom/03/2003MTFFact-Sheet.pdf

U.S. Department of Health and Human Services. (2000). *Healthy people 2010: Understanding and improving health* (2nd ed.). Washington, DC: U.S. Government Printing Office.

White, H. R., & Labouvie, E. W. (1989). Towards the assessment of adolescent problem drinking. *Journal of Studies on Alcohol, 50*(1), 30–37.

Winters, K. (1991). *Manual for the Personal Experience Screening Questionnaire (PESQ)*. Los Angeles: Western Psychological Services.

Winters, K. C. (1992). Development of an adolescent alcohol and other drug abuse screening scale: Personal Experience Screening Questionnaire. *Addictive Behaviors, 17*, 479–490.

Winters, K. C. (2001a). Assessing adolescent substance use problems and other areas of functioning: State of the art. In P. M. Monti, S. M. Colby, & T. A. O'Leary (Eds.), *Adolescents, alcohol, and substance abuse: Reaching teens through brief interventions* (pp. 80–108). New York: Guilford.

Winters, K. C. (2001b). Screening and assessing adolescents for substance use disorders (DHHS Publication No. SMA 01–3493). Rockwall, MD: Center for Substance Abuse Treatment, U.S. Department of Health and Human Services.

Winters, K. C., Latimer, W. W., & Stinchfield, R. D. (1999). DSM-IV criteria for adolescent alcohol and cannabis use disorders. *Journal of Studies on Alcohol, 60*, 337–344.

Effective HIV Prevention in Schools

Laura Hopson

Getting Started

Although the overall incidence of AIDS in the United States is declining, there has not been any such improvement in the prevalence among American youth (Centers for Disease Control and Prevention [CDC], 2002). Between 2000 and 2003, the number of HIV/AIDS cases increased among 13- to 14-year-olds and among those between the ages of 15 and 24. There are more heterosexual adolescents infected with HIV/AIDS now than in 2000. Of those males infected with HIV/AIDS over the age of 13, the majority (62%) were men who have sex with men. The majority of females over the age of 13 living with HIV/AIDS were infected through heterosexual contact (CDC, 2003a).

American youth are more likely to have intercourse by age 15 than youth in other Western industrialized countries and are more likely to have multiple, short relationships, which puts them at greater risk (Alan Guttmacher Institute, 2002). In a national survey, over 46% of high school students reported having sexual intercourse, and over 7% had sexual intercourse before age 13. Among those who reported being sexually active, more than 14% reported having sex with four or more partners during their lifetime, only 63% of sexually active students reported using condoms the last time they had intercourse, and over 25% had used drugs or alcohol before their last sexual intercourse (CDC, 2003b).

In response to the number of HIV/AIDS cases among American youth, the Centers for Disease Control and Prevention (CDC) have made recommendations for preventing HIV/AIDS in this age group. These recommendations include the use of school-based programs because they can reach a great number of youth before they become sexually active. Most adolescents are enrolled in school prior to initiating sexual activity and when they become sexually active. Many states now require schools to offer sex education, and most require that schools teach STD/HIV education (Kirby 2002). The most helpful programs are comprehensive, emphasizing the importance of delaying sexual activity as well as providing information about protection, such as condoms, for sexually active youth (CDC, 2002).

The school setting also presents challenges for providing effective HIV prevention programs. Some schools may not allow condom distribution, for example, which is a component of many effective HIV prevention strategies (Stryker, Samuels, and Smith, 1994). Many schools will only support abstinence-based curriculums, especially for younger teens (Lohrmann et al., 2001), which eliminates the majority of research-based HIV prevention programs. Empirical evaluations of abstinence-only curriculums have not reliably demonstrated effectiveness in delaying sexual activity (Kirby, 2002). Because of such barriers, it is important that HIV prevention strategies include community intervention and planning, public information campaigns, and policy-level interventions as well as effective school-based programs (CDC, 2003c). See chapters 25 and 28 for additional information on preventing sexually transmitted diseases and adolescent pregnancies.

What We Know

Many research-based prevention programs are appropriate for school settings and have demonstrated a range of positive outcomes for adolescents. Programs have been most successful in improving condom use, knowledge about HIV, and communication skills; they have been less successful with reducing overall sexual activity (Collins et al., 2002; Johnson et al., 2003). Evidence-based prevention programs include a range of components including instruction, use of video and other media, demonstration of correct condom use, role plays, and group discussion. The programs described here are defined as evidence-based because they have been evaluated in experimental design studies that employ random assignment to treatment conditions or quasi-experimental designs that use matching or statistically corrected for any difference in experimental and comparison groups to compensate for using nonrandom assignment. The evidence-based programs also resulted in statistically significant reductions in sexual risk behaviors. See Table 24.1 for a list of evidence-based programs and their supporting studies.

The outcomes for many of the evidence-based programs included increased condom use (Coyle et al., 1999; Fisher et al., 1998; Kirby et al., 1991; Main et al., 1994; Rotheram-Borus et al., 1998; St. Lawrence et al., 1995). Other interventions have resulted in less frequent sexual intercourse and fewer sexual partners (Jemmott, Jemmott, & Fong, 1992; Main et al., 1994), as well as delayed initiation of sexual intercourse (Kirby et al., 1991). Because of the need for culturally appropriate HIV prevention, some effective programs have been tailored to meet the needs of students from particular cultural and ethnic backgrounds (Jemmott et al., 1992; Jemmott et al., 1998; Kipke, Boyer, & Hein, 1993; St. Lawrence et al., 1995). Others have been tailored for use with gay and bisexual adolescents (Remafedi, 1994; Rotheram-Borus, Reid, & Rosario, 1994). Rotheram-Borus and associates (1991, 1997) have also developed an intervention for runaway youth, although the program can be adapted for use with other adolescents. Most evidence-based HIV prevention programs share common core components. Box 24.1 displays a list of characteristics identified by Kirby (1999) that are found in effective programs.

Fisher, Fisher, Bryan, and Misovich (1998) found that students participating in a 5-day classroom curriculum increased their knowledge about HIV, were more likely to use condoms, and had more positive attitudes about HIV prevention behaviors. In the curriculum, students learn factual information about HIV, watch videos and participate in activities designed to increase motivation for reducing HIV risk behaviors, and learn skills

Box 24.1 Common Core Components of Most Evidence-Based HIV Prevention Programs

According to Kirby (1999), most evidence-based programs have the following characteristics:

1. A focus on reducing one or more sexual risk behaviors
2. A foundation in theoretical approaches that are effective in influencing the health behaviors that are the focus of the intervention
3. A clear message and consistent reinforcing of the health behaviors
4. Clear, accurate information about the risks associated with sexual behaviors and how to avoid unprotected sexual intercourse
5. A component that addresses peer pressure to engage in sexual behaviors
6. Use of modeling and opportunities for participants to practice communication, negotiation, and refusal skills
7. Diverse teaching methods that involve participants and allow them to personalize the curriculum
8. Behavioral goal setting and teaching methods that are appropriate to the age, sexual experience, and culture of participants
9. Adequate duration to allow participants time to complete activities
10. Selection of people who believe in the program to be trained and lead the curriculum

From "Reflections on two decades of research on teen sexual behavior and pregnancy," by D. Kirby, 1999. *Journal of School Health, 69*(3), 89–94.

for reducing risk behaviors. The following section provides a case example of a school that implements Fisher et al.'s (1998) program and summarizes the curriculum activities.

Tools and Practice Examples

Case Example: Newton High School

Ms. Jones, the principal at Newton High School, is concerned about the large number of pregnant and parenting teens at Newton. In order to better understand the problem, Ms. Jones meets with the school social worker, nurse, and counselors. The

Table 24.1 Evidence-Based HIV Prevention Programs

Evidence-Based Interventions	Supporting Studies	Contact Information
ARREST Program	Kipke, M. D., Boyer, C., & Hein, K. (1993). An evaluation of an AIDS risk reduction education and skills training (ARREST) program. *Journal of Adolescent Health, 14*(7), 533–539.	Michele D. Kipke, Ph.D. Children's Hospital P.O. Box 54700 Mailstop #2 Los Angeles, CA 90054-0700
Be Proud! Be Responsible!	Jemmott, J., Jemmott, L., & Fong, G. (1992). Reductions in HIV risk associated sexual behaviors among black male adolescents: Effects of an AIDS prevention program. *American Journal of Public Health, 82*(3), 372–377.	John B. Jemmott III, Ph.D. jjemmott@asc.upenn.edu Treatment manual available from www.selectmedia.org
Becoming a Responsible Teen	St. Lawrence, J., Brasfield, T., Jefferson, K., Alleyne, E., O'Brannon, R., & Shirley, A. (1995). A cognitive-behavioral intervention to reduce African-American adolescents' risk for HIV infection. *Journal of Consulting and Clinical Psychology, 63*(2), 221–237.	Janet S. St. Lawrence, Ph.D. nzs4@cdc.gov treatment manual available from www.etr.org
Cognitive and Behavioral Adaptations to HIV/AIDS among Gay and Bisexual Adolescents	Remafedi, G. (1994). Cognitive and behavioral adaptations to HIV/AIDS among gay and bisexual adolescents. *Journal of Adolescent Health, 15*, 142–148.	Gary Remafedi, MD Box 721 UMHC 420 Delaware St. SE Minneapolis, MN 55455-0392
Factors Mediating Changes in Sexual HIV Risk Behaviors among Gay and Bisexual Male Adolescents	Rotheram-Borus, M. J., Reid, H., & Rosario, M. (1994). Factors mediating changes in sexual HIV risk behaviors among gay and bisexual male adolescents. *American Journal of Public Health, 84*(12), 1938–1946.	Mary Jane Rotheram-Borus, Ph.D. rotheram@ucla.edu
Focus on Kids	Stanton, B., Li, X., Ricardo, I., Galbraith, J., Feigelman, S., & Kaljee, L. (1996). A randomized, controlled effectiveness trial of an AIDS prevention program for low-income African-American youths. *Archives of Pediatric and Adolescent Medicine, 151*(4), 398–406.	Bonita Stanton, MD bstanton@umabnet.ab.umd Educational treatment manual available from www.etr.org
Get Real About AIDS	Main, D., Iverson, D., McGloin, J., Banspach, S. W., Collins, J. L., Rugg, D. L., & Kolbe, L. J. (1994). Preventing HIV infection among adolescents: Evaluation of a school-based education program. *Preventive Medicine, 23*(4), 409–417.	Deborah S. Main, Ph.D. debbi.main@uchsc.edu Treatment manual available from AGC Educational Media at agcmedia@starnetinc.com

(continued)

Table 24.1 (*Continued*)

Evidence-Based Interventions	*Supporting Studies*	*Contact Information*
Information-Motivation-Behavioral Skills Model-based HIV Prevention Curriculum	Fisher, J. D., Fisher, W. A., Bryan, A. D., & Misovich, S. J. (1998). Information-motivation-behavioral skills model-based HIV risk behavior change intervention for inner city youth. *Health Psychology, 21*(2), 177–186.	Jeffrey Fisher, Ph.D. jeffrey.fisher@uconn.edu Videos and treatment manual available from www.films.org
Making a Difference	Jemmott, J., Jemmott, L., & Fong, G. (1998). Abstinence and safer sex HIV risk reduction interventions for African American adolescents. *Journal of the American Medical Association, 279*(19), 1529–1536.	John B. Jemmott III, Ph.D. jjemmott@asc.upenn.edu Treatment manual available from www.selectmedia.org
Making Proud Choices	Jemmott, J., Jemmott, L., & Fong, G. (1998). Abstinence and safer sex HIV risk reduction interventions for African American adolescents. *Journal of the American Medical Association, 279*(19), 1529–1536.	John B. Jemmott III, Ph.D. jjemmott@asc.upenn.edu Treatment manual available from www.selectmedia.org
Reducing the Risk	Kirby, D., Barth, R. P., Leland, N., & Fetro, J. V. (1991). Reducing the risk: Impact of a new curriculum on sexual risk-taking. *Family Planning Perspectives, 23*(6), 253–263.	Nancy Shanfeld, Ph.D. ETR Associates Treatment manual available from www.etr.org
Safer Choices	Coyle, K., Basen-Engquist, K., Kirby, D., Parcel, G., Banspach, S., Harrist, R., Baumler, E., & Weil, M. (1999). Short term impact of Safer-Choices: A multi-component, school-based HIV, other STD, and pregnancy prevention program. *Journal of School Health, 69*(5), 181–188.	Karin Coyle, Ph.D. (831) 438-4060, ext. 140 Treatment manual available from www.etr.org
Self Center	Zabin, L. S., Hirsh, M. B., Strett, R., Emerson, M. R., Smith, M., Hardy, J. B., & King, T. M. (1988). The Baltimore Pregnancy Prevention Program for urban teenagers: 1. How did it work? *Family Planning Perspectives, 20,* 182–187.	Laurie Schwab Zabin, Ph.D. Johns Hopkins University Sociometrics, Program Archive on Sexuality, Health & Adolescence http://www.socio.com
Street Smart	Rotheram-Borus, M., Van Rossem, R., Gwadz, M., Koopman, C., & Lee, M. (1997). *Street Smart.*	Mary Jane Rotheram-Borus, Ph.D. rotheram@ucla.edu Intervention manual available at: http://chipts.ucla.edu/ interventions/manuals/ intervstreetsmart.html
3 Week and 7 Week HIV Interventions	Rotheram-Borus, M. J., Gwadz, M., Fernandez, M. I., & Srinivasan, S. (1998). Timing of HIV interventions on reductions in sexual risk among adolescents. *American Journal of Community Psychology, 26,* 73–96.	Mary Jane Rotheram-Borus, Ph.D. rotheram@ucla.edu

social worker and nurse report that several students have expressed concerns related to sexually transmitted diseases and pregnancy. They feel that students need more education about reducing risk because students often ask about safe sex practices and contraception. The counselors agree that students lack adequate knowledge about sexual risks and effective protection. Ms. Jones also learns that the community surrounding Newton has higher rates of sexually transmitted diseases than other communities in the district, and HIV rates among young adults in her community are higher than average.

Ms. Jones decides that she needs an effective HIV prevention program at Newton to protect her students. Because many of her students are already sexually active, Ms. Jones chooses Fisher et al.'s (1998) classroom-based curriculum, which helps students learn skills to abstain from sexual activity as well as skills for using contraception. Because the curriculum uses videotapes to provide much of the information on HIV prevention information and skills, Ms. Jones also felt that it would be relatively easy for her teachers to implement. Ms. Quincy is one of several Newton High School teachers who volunteer to provide the curriculum to their classes. Ms. Quincy teaches an English class in which she meets with the same group of 10th graders every day. During this week, 40 minutes of class time will be devoted to the Information-Motivation-Behavioral Skills Curriculum. The following overview of sessions is based on the teacher's manual for the curriculum available from www.films.com (Misovich et al., 2000).

Information-Motivation-Behavioral Skills HIV Prevention Program

Day 1

The Information-Motivation-Behavioral Skills Curriculum consists of five 40-minute sessions that are provided to students on consecutive class days. During the first session, students learn facts about HIV transmission and prevention. The session also aims to correct common misperceptions about HIV. Students watch the video "Knowing the Facts: Preventing Infection" and participate in classroom activities. After the video, students discuss the following three ways that HIV can be transmitted from one person to another: unprotected sexual intercourse, sharing needles, and

transmission from mother to baby during pregnancy, birth, or breastfeeding. The group also discusses abstinence from sexual intercourse as an HIV prevention behavior and correct condom use as a behavior that greatly reduces risk for transmission of HIV.

In one of the activities for this session, students are given flashcards with questions about HIV risk behaviors, and they answer the questions for the group. One flashcard, for example, lists several behaviors, and students are asked to say whether the behavior is high risk, low risk, or no risk for HIV transmission. These behaviors include French kissing, oral sex, vaginal or anal intercourse using a condom correctly and without a condom, and sharing needles.

Group Discussion and Flashcard Activity With Ms. Quincy's Class

After Ms. Quincy shows her students the video "Knowing the Facts: Preventing Infection," she asks students to discuss the three ways that HIV can be transmitted from one person to another. The students were able to talk about each of the three ways: unprotected sexual intercourse, sharing needles, and from mother to baby. In response to another of Ms. Quincy's questions about ways to prevent transmission of HIV, the students say that using condoms will prevent HIV. Ms. Quincy asks the students if condoms are 100% effective at preventing transmission, and the students respond that, if a condom breaks or is not used properly, it may not be effective.

Ms. Quincy distributes flashcards to the students for the activity. Each flashcard displays a question, and the students are asked to read the question out loud and answer it. She explains that some of the flashcards ask about sexual behaviors that might be a little difficult to talk about but that the group can contribute to answering the questions. Ms. Quincy asks one of her students, Jessica, to begin. Jessica stands and reads the question on her card, "How can you tell if a person is infected with HIV?" Jessica says that she does not think that you can tell if a person has HIV by their appearance. Ms. Quincy tells Jessica that she is correct because most people with HIV do not have symptoms that are visible to others.

The next student, Jason, reads the question on his card, "What are high risk, low risk, and no risk behaviors for transmitting HIV?" Jason reads the first behavior on the flashcard, "French kissing," and says that this behavior presents no risk because

HIV cannot be passed from one person to another through saliva. Jason reads another behavior on the flashcard "Vaginal or anal intercourse always using a condom properly," and says that he thinks this behavior is no risk but he is not sure. Ms. Quincy asks the class to discuss this, and several students agree with Jason that the behavior is no risk. Other students say that the behavior presents some risk because a condom could break even if it is used properly. Ms. Quincy says that it is true that the condom can break, so the behavior would be classified as low risk instead of no risk. The group continues this activity until all of the flashcard questions have been discussed and answered.

Day 2

The second class in the curriculum aims to increase students' motivation to practice HIV prevention behaviors. The session includes showing the video "Just Like Me: Talking About AIDS," in which young people infected with HIV ask that students change their attitudes about HIV risk so they can prevent becoming infected as well. Following the video, teachers facilitate a discussion about how the attitudes and norms that led to the infection of the people in the video are common among many teens. This session also includes a group discussion about abstaining from sexual activity that includes reasons people may want to wait until they are older to have sexual intercourse, why it might be difficult to wait, and strategies for making it less difficult to wait. Following this discussion, the teacher facilitates another discussion about using condoms.

Day 2 Curriculum With Ms. Quincy's Class

After the class watches the video, Ms. Quincy asks the students, "What were some of the reasons that people in the video mentioned that made them think they could not be infected by the other person?" One of the students, Kelly, responds, "One of the assumptions was that if you are in a committed relationship with one person for a long time, you can't get HIV." Another student says, "They also thought that because they were young they couldn't get HIV." Ms. Quincy asks, "How common are these assumptions among people you know?" The students agree that many of their peers would think that they are safe if they are having sex with young people because they do

not believe that young people are going to have HIV. Ms. Quincy asks the students to also discuss how the people in the video said others can avoid getting HIV. The students respond that using condoms correctly can reduce their risk and abstaining from sex can prevent HIV altogether.

Day 3

The third session aims to further motivate participants with a third video, "Stakes are High: Asserting Yourself Part 1," which features real high school students overcoming obstacles to HIV prevention by assertively negotiating abstinence or using contraception. In the video, students also support each other for using HIV prevention strategies. Students in the group participate in classroom activities and group discussion that encourage peer support of HIV prevention behaviors. The session also includes a discussion about how to obtain and carry condoms.

Day 3 Group Discussion With Ms. Quincy's Class

The discussion following the video begins with Ms. Quincy's asking the class about two of the high school students in the video, Afiya and Tyrone. Afiya has decided that she does not want to have sex until she is married. The class discusses the strategies that Afiya uses to make it less difficult for her to abstain from sexual activity. One student says that a strategy Afiya uses is to suggest that the couple leave the apartment where they would be alone and more likely to have sex. Another student says that Afiya was also direct and firm with Tyrone in telling him that she would not have sex until she was married. Ms. Quincy asks the class to discuss another couple in the video who decided that they might want to have sex but had no condoms. The students discussed how friends in the video were able to support the couple by strongly advising them to use condoms and going with them when they went to buy condoms.

In order to encourage the students to think about the logistics of obtaining condoms, Ms. Quincy asks them to discuss a scene in the video in which students purchase condoms. She asks students about convenient places where they might go to get condoms. One of the students mentions that the drug store two blocks from the school would probably have condoms. Another student says that the school nurse might also have condoms that she would give to students. Ms. Quincy agrees that those are both places that are likely to have condoms.

Day 4

The fourth session aims to help students develop behavioral skills for abstinence and condom use. The session includes a fourth video, "Stakes Are High: Asserting Yourself Part 2," which shows adolescents demonstrating HIV prevention behaviors, such as abstaining from sex, discussing condoms, and using condoms. Students then practice these behaviors themselves. The teacher demonstrates correctly placing a condom over fingers or a model of a penis, and students then practice doing the same. The teacher gives students scripts printed on large cards from which they can practice negotiating abstinence from sex or condom use with a partner.

Practicing Negotiation Skills With Ms. Quincy's Class

Ms. Quincy distributes large cards, each of which displays an important step in practicing safer sex through condom use. The cards include statements such as "Decision to Have Intercourse," "Discuss Methods of Birth Control," "Decide to Use Condoms," "Get Condoms," "Take Condom Out of Package," and "Unroll Condom on Erect Penis." Ms. Quincy asks the students to hold their cards and form a line so that their cards are displayed in the correct order of steps for practicing safer sex. After about 15 minutes, the students have placed themselves in the correct order. Ms. Quincy then asks them to read aloud and discuss each step.

Jessica is the first in the row of students and she reads her card, "Decision to Have Intercourse." Ms. Quincy asks the students to talk about how they would make this decision. Jessica begins by saying that the couple should consider whether they both really want to have intercourse or whether one partner is putting pressure on the other. Another student, David, adds that this would be the time for the couple to think about the social and physical consequences of intercourse. Ms. Quincy asks David to give an example of a social and a physical consequence. David says that having sex might take their relationship to a more serious level and make it more painful if the

couple ended the relationship. He adds that the physical consequences could be pregnancy or getting HIV. Ms. Quincy continues to facilitate the discussion by asking each student to read their card and discuss how they would complete the step.

Day 5

The final session is a review of communication strategies. The students then form small groups and generate their own responses to common scenarios that increase risk for HIV. The group provides feedback on the students' responses according to the communication skills discussed during previous sessions. Students' responses are critiqued and modified by their peers and the teacher to become more effective for preventing HIV risk behavior. Students then have the opportunity to practice using the modified responses.

Practicing Communication in Ms. Quincy's Class

In one of the small groups, a female student, Jessica, is practicing a response to peer pressure from her boyfriend to have sexual intercourse. A male student, David, is playing the role of the boyfriend. David says to Jessica, "I don't understand why you don't want to have sex with me. You must not care about me, or maybe you're more interested in someone else." Jessica responds by saying, "That's not true. I just don't want to have sex until I'm out of high school at least." David continues to press Jessica by saying that he does not understand and feels hurt. Jessica offers the same response each time.

Ms. Quincy asks the other students in the group to help Jessica by using some of the communication skills they have learned. One of the students asks Jessica if she could tell David that she does care about David and wants to be with him but that there are other things they can do together that will strengthen their relationship. Another student suggests that Jessica be firmer in telling her boyfriend that she will not have sex. Jessica practices this response: "David, I care about you very much. Even though I won't have sex, there are a lot of things I want to do with you and I want our relationship to be strong. What else can we do together?" In order to reinforce this behavior, the group tells Jessica that she handled the situation well by communicating to David firmly that she would not have sex but that the relationship was important to her.

A description of the sessions described above is provided in Fisher et al.'s (1998) article describing the study evaluating the curriculum. A treatment manual for sessions 1 through 4 and the videos used in each session are available from www.films.org.

Additional Resources

Advocates for Youth: www.advocatesforyouth.org

The Centers for Disease Control and Prevention Division of Sexually Transmitted Diseases: http://www.cdc.gov/std/

The Centers for Disease Control and Prevention Division of HIV/AIDS Prevention: http://www.cdc.gov/hiv/dhap.htm

The Centers for Disease Control and Prevention's Compendium of HIV Prevention Interventions with Evidence of Effectiveness: http://www.cdc.gov/hiv/pubs/HIVcompendium/hivcompendium.htm

The Center for HIV Identification, Prevention, and Treatment Services (CHIPTS): http://chipts.ucla.edu/about/index.html

Sociometrics HIV/AIDS Prevention Program Archive (HAPPA): http://www.socio.com/pasha/haprogms.htm

Southwestern University's HIV Prevention Toolbox: http://www3.utsouthwestern.edu/preventiontoolbox/interven.htm

Key Points to Remember

Some of the key points discussed in this chapter were:

- The prevalence of HIV/AIDS among adolescents and young adults indicates a great need to reduce sexual risk behaviors among American youth.
- A number of evidence-based HIV prevention programs are appropriate for use in schools, and school-based curricula have the potential to reach many teens before they become sexually active as well as those who are who are already sexually active.
- Most of the effective HIV prevention curricula include educational and skill-building components.

- Fisher et al.'s (1998) Information-Motivation-Behavioral Skills curriculum is one approach that has resulted in increased condom use and more positive attitudes about HIV prevention behaviors when administered to teens in a school setting.

There is a great need for interventions that reduce risk for HIV/AIDS among youth. Fortunately, many effective and promising programs have already been developed. The challenge for the future will be to work with schools and other organizations to help them implement these evidence-based programs. Because the curricula include information about condom use as well as abstinence from sexual intercourse, school staff may face opposition when trying to implement these programs, and successful implementation may require advocating for changes in state and local school policies.

References

Alan Guttmacher Institute. (2002). Teenagers' sexual and reproductive health. *Facts in Brief, January, 2002.* New York: Alan Guttmacher Institute. Retrieved November 1, 2003 from http://www.agi-usa.org

Centers for Disease Control and Prevention. (2002). *Young people at risk: HIV/AIDS among America's youth.* Atlanta, GA: U.S. Department of Health and Human Services, Centers for Disease Control and Prevention. Retrieved December 18, 2004, from http://www.cdc.gov/hiv

Centers for Disease Control and Prevention. (2003a). *HIV/AIDS surveillance report: Cases of HIV infection and AIDS in the United States, 2003.* Atlanta, GA: U.S. Department of Health and Human Services, Centers for Disease Control and Prevention (pp. 1–9). Retrieved December 18, 2004, from http://www.cdc.gov/hiv/stats/hasrlink.htm

Centers for Disease Control and Prevention. (2003b). *Youth risk behavior surveillance 2003.* Atlanta, GA: U.S. Department of Health and Human Services, Centers for Disease Control and Prevention. Retrieved December 17, 2004, from www.cdc.gov.

Centers for Disease Control and Prevention. (2003c). *HIV strategic plan through 2005.* Atlanta, GA: U.S. Department of Health and Human Services, Centers for Disease Control and Prevention. Retrieved December 18, 2004, from http://www.cdc.gov/nchstp/od/hiv_plan/Table%20of%20Contents.htm

Collins, J., Robin, L., Wooley, S., Fenley, D., Hunt, P., Taylor, J., Haber, D., & Kolbe, L. (2002). Programs-that-work: CDC's guide to effective programs that reduce health-risk behavior of youth. *Journal of School Health, 72*(3), 93–99.

Coyle, K., Basen-Engquist, K., Kirby, D., Parcel, G., Banspach, S., Harrist, R., Baumler, E., & Weil, M. (1999). Short term impact of Safer-Choices: A multi-component, school-based HIV, other STD, and pregnancy prevention program. *Journal of School Health, 69*(5), 181–188.

Fisher, J. D., Fisher, W. A., Bryan, A. D., & Misovich, S. J. (1998). Information-Motivation-Behavioral Skills Model based HIV risk behavior change intervention for inner city youth. *Health Psychology, 21*(2), 177–186.

Jemmott, J., Jemmott, L., & Fong, G. (1992). Reductions in HIV risk associated sexual behaviors among black male adolescents: Effects of an AIDS prevention program. *American Journal of Public Health, 82*(3), 372–377.

Jemmott, J. B., Jemmott, L. S., Fong, G. T., & McCaffree, K. (1998). Abstinence and safer sex: HIV risk-reduction interventions for African American adolescents. *Journal of the American Medical Association, 279*(19), 1529–1536.

Johnson, B. T., Carey, M. P., Marsh, K. L., Levin, K. D., & Scott-Sheldon, J. (2003). Interventions to reduce sexual risk for the Human Immunodeficiency Virus in adolescents, 1985–2000. *Archives of Pediatric and Adolescent Medicine, 157,* 381–388.

Kipke, M. D., Boyer, C., & Hein, K. (1993). An evaluation of an AIDS risk reduction education and skills training (ARREST) program. *Journal of Adolescent Health, 14*(7), 533–539.

Kirby, D. (1999). Reflections on two decades of research on teen sexual behavior and pregnancy. *Journal of School Health, 69*(3), 89–94.

Kirby, D. (2002). The impact of schools and school programs upon adolescent sexual behavior. *Journal of Sex Research, 39*(1), 27–33.

Kirby, D., Barth, R. P., Leland, N., & Fetro, J. V. (1991). Reducing the risk: Impact of a new curriculum on sexual risk-taking. *Family Planning Perspectives, 23*(6), 253–263.

Lohrmann, D. K., Blake, S., Collins, T., Windsor, R., & Parrillo, A. V. (2001). Evaluation of school-based HIV prevention education programs in New Jersey. *Journal of School Health, 71*(6), 207–211.

Main, D., Iverson, D., McGloin, J., Banspach, S. W., Collins, J. L., Rugg, D. L., & Kolbe, L. J. (1994). Preventing HIV infection among adolescents: Evaluation of a school-based education program. *Preventive Medicine, 23*(4), 409–417.

Misovich, S. J., Fisher, W. A., Fisher, J. D., Figueroa-Richmond, B., Bryan, A., & Muller, L. (2000). *Information–Motivation–Behavioral Skills HIV Prevention Program: Teacher's manual and natural opinion leader training manual.* Published by Films for the Humanities and Sciences (films.com). Retrieved December 11, 2004, from http://www.films.com/Films_Home/item.cfm?s=1&bin=8801

Remafedi, G. (1994). Cognitive and behavioral adaptations to HIV/AIDS among gay and bisexual adolescents. *Journal of Adolescent Health, 15,* 142–148.

Rotheram-Borus, M. J., Gwadz, M., Fernandez, M. I., & Srinivasan, S. (1998). Timing of HIV interventions on reductions in sexual risk among adolescents. *American Journal of Community Psychology, 26,* 73–96.

Rotheram-Borus, M. J., Kooperman, C., Haignere, C., & Davies, M. (1991). Reducing HIV sexual risk behaviors among runaway adolescents. *JAMA: Journal of the American Medical Association, 266,* 1237–1241.

Rotheram-Borus, M. J., Reid, H., & Rosario, M. (1994). Factors mediating changes in sexual HIV risk behaviors among gay and bisexual male adolescents. *American Journal of Public Health, 84*(12), 1938–1946.

Rotheram-Borus, M. J., Song, J., Gwadz, M., Lee, M., Van Rossem, R., & Koopman, C. (2003). Reductions in HIV risk among runaway youth. *Prevention Science, 4*(3), 173–187.

Rotheram-Borus, M., Van Rossem, R., Gwadz, M., Koopman, C., & Lee, M. (1997). *Street smart.* Retrieved December 18, 2004 from http://chipts.ucla.edu/interventions/manuals/intervstreetsmart.html

St. Lawrence, J., Brasfield, T., Jefferson, K., Alleyne, E., O'Brannon, R., & Shirley, A. (1995). A cognitive-behavioral intervention to reduce African-American adolescents' risk for HIV infection. *Journal of Consulting and Clinical Psychology, 63*(2), 221–237.

Stanton, B., Li, X., Ricardo, I., Galbraith, J., Feigelman, S., & Kaljee, L. A. (1996). A randomized, controlled effectiveness trial of an AIDS prevention program for low-income African-American youths. *Archives of Pediatric and Adolescent Medicine, 151*(4), 398–406.

Stryker, J., Samuels, S. E., & Smith, M. D. (1994). Condom availability in schools: The need for improved program evaluations. *American Journal of Public Health, 84*(12), 1901–1906.

Effective STD Prevention

Laura Hopson

Getting Started

According to the Youth Risk Behavior Surveillance conducted by the Centers for Disease Control and Prevention (CDC), almost half of American high school students have had sex in their lifetime, and over one third reported being currently sexually active. Of these students, only 63% reported using condoms the last time they had intercourse (CDC, 2003b). The high rates of sexual activity and failure to use condoms in many cases helps to explain the large number of American adolescents infected with sexually transmitted diseases.

Although rates of gonorrhea infection have generally declined among American youth, women between the ages of 15 and 19 represent the largest proportion of women diagnosed with gonorrhea at a rate of about 635 cases per every 100,000 women in this age group. Infection rates for gonorrhea among male adolescents are about 466 per every 100,000 males between the ages of 15 and 19. chlamydia infection is widespread and especially problematic among economically disadvantaged women. The Adolescent Women Reproductive Health Monitoring Project estimates that more than 11% of adolescent women are infected with chlamydia (CDC, 2003a). Adolescent girls may be at higher risk than adult women for becoming infected with STDs because of their immature cervix. They are also more likely to have multiple partners within a short period of time and older partners who may have multiple partners themselves.

STD prevention programs for adolescents face many challenges because adolescents often do not perceive themselves to be at risk. They may hold negative beliefs about condom use and have few skills to negotiate safer sex practices with a partner. Programs may face additional barriers because those that discuss condom use are controversial in many communities. As with HIV prevention strategies, effective STD prevention may require addressing political barriers and misinformation, including the idea that sex education results in increased sexual activity among teens (CDC, 2003a).

What We Know

A summary of interventions that effectively reduce HIV risk behaviors among adolescents is provided in the previous chapter on HIV prevention programs. These programs are also effective for preventing STDs. See Table 24.1 in the HIV prevention chapter for a list of evidence-based programs that are appropriate for use in a school setting.

One of these effective programs is Street Smart, a program developed by Rotheram-Borus and associates (1997) for use with runaway youth. The treatment manual specifies that this curriculum may be easily adapted for use with other adolescents as well. In adapting the curriculum, however, it is important to maintain the critical, core components of the intervention displayed in Box 25.1 (Southwestern, n.d.). Without including all of these core components, the intervention may lose some of its effectiveness. The curriculum consists of eight 2-hour group sessions, one individual session, and a session in which the group visits a community agency. Each session of the Street Smart curriculum includes the key techniques displayed in Box 25.2.

In a study evaluating the effects of Street Smart with runaway youth, teens who received

Box 25.1 Core Elements of the Street Smart Program

Core elements are components that must be included in the program as indicated in the manual in order for the program to maintain its effectiveness. For Street Smart, these elements are:

- Opportunities to practice controlling and expressing emotions and cognitive awareness
- Teaching HIV/AIDS risks and allowing participants opportunities to apply the ideas to their own lives
- Identifying personal triggers for HIV risk behaviors
- Using peer support and skills-building in small groups
- Building skills in problem solving, assertiveness, and skills for reducing HIV/AIDS risk behaviors

Source: From *HIV prevention toolbox: Street smart*, by Southwestern, The University of Texas Southwestern Medical Center at Dallas, n.d. Retrieved December 21, 2004 from http://www3.utsouthwestern.edu/preventiontoolbox/interven/streetsmart.htm

Box 25.2 Key Components of Every Street Smart Session

1. A stack of tokens, which are $1'' \times 1''$ pieces of colored paper, are given to each participant. When participants hear or see another group member doing something that they like, they give that group member a token.
2. A feeling thermometer is a scale that ranges from 0 to 100, with 100 representing the most discomfort and 0 representing a complete absence of discomfort. Facilitators use the thermometer to help participants recognize, assess, and discuss their feelings.
3. Role playing in each session gives participants the opportunity to practice new behaviors and act out situations in a supportive environment. Role plays in Street Smart session consist of two actors playing out a scene, a coach assigned to each actor to provide suggestions, one director who determines who plays each part, and other participants assigned to observe interactions, such as eye contact and body language, during the role play.
4. The sessions are videotaped so that students can observe themselves interacting in the role play situations.
5. Participants use the SMART model to apply the following problem-solving steps:
   a. *State* the problem
   b. *Make* a goal
   c. *Actions*—list the possible actions that could be taken
   d. *Reach* a decision about which action to use
   e. *Try* doing the action and review it
6. A large flipchart on a stand is used to save written material and goals set by participants so they can be reviewed later.
7. The curriculum provides choices in the curriculum so that facilitators have different options they can use with their participants for each session.

Source: From *Street Smart*, by M. Rotheram-Borus, R, Van Rossem, M. Gwadz, C. Koopman, & M. Lee, 1997. Retrieved December 18, 2004 from http://chips.ucla.edu/interventions/manuals/intervstreetsmart.html

the intervention reduced the number of unprotected sexual acts and reduced their substance use when compared with teens who did not receive the intervention. The following description of sessions is based on information provided in the treatment manual for Street Smart, which can be downloaded from the following Web site: http://chips.ucla.edu (Rotheram-Borus et al., 1997).

Tools and Practice Examples

Case Example: Jenson High School

Ms. Davis is a social worker at Jenson High School, an alternative school for students who have experienced behavioral or academic difficulties that made it difficult for them to thrive at a traditional high school. Students often come to Ms. Davis to ask her questions about sexual health, and a number of Jenson students are pregnant or parenting teens. Because Ms. Davis suspects that many of the students engage in a

number of risk behaviors, such as unprotected sexual activity and drug use, she administers an anonymous survey to the student body. The results of the survey suggest that 60% of the students at Jenson are sexually active, and 40% use alcohol or drugs on a regular basis. Other results that concern Ms. Davis include a large number of sexually active students who indicated that they do not use condoms when they have sex or that they consume alcohol or drugs prior to having sex.

Ms. Davis takes the results to the principal and asks permission to implement a program designed to reduce sexual risk taking. The principal agrees that Ms. Davis should work to find a program that will reduce risks for Jenson students. Ms. Davis decides on the Street Smart program because it provides information about STDs and HIV, condom use, and the risks of combining alcohol or drug use with sexual activity. With the approval of the principal, Ms. Davis sends parents permission letters that describe the curriculum. Ms. Davis, gives students who have parental permission to participate the opportunity to join the group, which will take place after school.

Street Smart

Session 1: Getting the Language of HIV and STDs

The first day of Street Smart is dedicated to learning facts about HIV and STDs as well as learning about situations that present great risks for transmission of HIV and STDs. This session begins with introductions and the "Be Smart about HIV/AIDS and STDs" game in which participants form teams and answer questions about HIV/AIDS and STDs. Following the game, participants engage in role playing and discuss situations in which they would feel high, moderate, low, and no discomfort, using the feeling thermometer to illustrate. See Box 25.2 for a description of the feeling thermometer. Another activity included in this session involves giving students nametags, some of which display a small star or square indicating that the person is HIV-positive or has an STD. This activity helps students to see how easily and quickly HIV and STDs can be spread to uninfected people. The session concludes with a discussion about participants' strengths and resources that can help them achieve their goals.

Nametag Activity With Jenson High School Students

Ms. Davis provides nametags to all of the participants. Two of the nametags have a small square in the corner, and two others have a small star. The students put on the nametags, and Ms. Davis asks them to pretend they are at a party, mingling with the other group members. Ms. Davis asks the students to identify at least two situations that would be triggers for risky sexual behavior and discuss them with others. She also tells them to identify someone as a potential romantic partner.

After a few minutes of mingling, Ms. Davis asks the students to talk about the triggers for engaging in risky behavior. She then explains that two people in the group have a small star on their nametag and that these two group members represent people who are HIV positive. Two other people, she explains, have small squares on their nametags, representing people who have an STD. After a few minutes, the group members have discovered which group members are wearing the nametags in question. Ms. Davis explains that, if anyone in the group had engaged in risky sexual behavior with those people, they may have contracted and STD or HIV and passed it on to others. Ms. Davis encourages group members to discuss the exercise.

Session 2: Personalized Risk

In this session, participants begin by discussing how old they were when they had their first serious relationship. They role play a situation in which they define a risk behavior and the triggers associated with the behavior. For example, two students enact a script in which a girl tells her friend that she had sex without using protection, and the friend questions her behavior. The role play is followed by questions about what were the girl's triggers for unsafe sex and what skills might have helped her avoid unsafe sex. Students divide into two groups and create a list of possible triggers for having unsafe sex, and participants write down a personal trigger that puts them at risk for unsafe sex. In another role play, participants practice setting their own limits. The facilitator also encourages group members to express appreciation for the contributions of other members.

Session 3: How to Use Condoms

The session begins with a discussion about the best color for a box of condoms. Each participant receives several condoms to handle in order to reduce discomfort with condoms. In order to encourage the students, the facilitator may say, "Open up the condoms and do whatever you want with them—stretch them, chew on them, whatever." The group is then asked to try to figure out the correct steps in putting on a male condom. Participants practice putting male condoms on a penis model and female condoms in the female model. The facilitator can ask the participants to use the feeling thermometer to monitor any feelings of discomfort during these activities.

Session 4: Drugs and Alcohol

This session begins with a discussion about any successes students have had in practicing behavior related to previous sessions. Through a role-playing activity, participants explore the relationship between drug and alcohol use and sexual risk behavior. The students also make a list of the advantages and disadvantages of substance use. Another role play is used to help participants understand how substance use affects their ability to practice safer sex. The facilitator presents information about the effect of substance use on the brain and asks participants to identify triggers that put them at risk for using substances, along with ways to deal with those triggers. A third role play helps students deal with risky situations.

Discussing Beliefs About Alcohol and Drug Use With Jenson High School Students

Ms. Davis distributes cards to each of the group members. Each card displays a substance use belief, such as "Using is the only way to increase my creativity and productivity." She then tells the students to imagine that someone has told them that they believe the statement printed on the card and asks them to argue against the belief. In order to model this activity, Ms. Davis asks one of the students to pick a card and hand it to her. She reads the card out loud, "The only way to deal with my anger is by using." In response to the statement, Ms. Davis adds, "Actually, using does not help you deal with the anger at all. It's just a way to keep you from dealing with the thing that's really making you angry." Ms. Davis asks one of the students, Jamie, to practice the activity. Jamie reads her card, "My life won't get better, even if I stop using." Jamie then states her response, "Drug use can cause so many problems—conflicts with your

parents, problems with money, failing in school. At least if you weren't using drugs you wouldn't have those problems to deal with." Ms. Davis tells Jamie that she did a wonderful job answering the question and proceeds to ask the next student to read his card and think of a response.

Session 5: Recognizing and Coping With Feelings

Participants begin this session by describing something about themselves that makes them proud. Using the feeling thermometer, participants rate sexually risky situations according to the amount of discomfort they cause. The facilitator may ask students to think of a situation that put them at risk for acquiring an STD and caused a great deal of discomfort, a behavior that they would rate close to 100 on the feeling thermometer. The group thinks about the emotions they feel and any physical stress responses they experience when confronted with the uncomfortable situation, as well as identifying what might have triggered it.

A role-playing activity is used to help participants understand how to cope with risky situations, and a second role play helps them learn effective problem definition as a strategy for learning to focus on manageable problems. The role playing continues in this session with a situation in which participants have to get tested for HIV.

Session 6: Negotiating Effectively

Participants begin by reviewing any successes they have had relevant to the previous session. This session includes an opportunity for each group member to consider their own sexual values. In order to learn how to deal with peer pressure to engage in substance abuse and risky sexual behavior, participants practice using interpersonal problem-solving skills. They also participate in a role play in which they have to ask potential sexual partners questions to determine whether they are at risk for having HIV or STDs. The facilitator asks students to generate a list of questions that would be helpful in this situation and ensures that questions such as "Do you usually use a condom?" "Do you shoot drugs?" and "Have you had a lot of sex partners?" are included on the list.

Session 7: Self-Talk

The facilitator begins this session by asking participants to tell the group things that they say to themselves to make them feel good. The facilitator explains that we have thoughts that help us practice healthier behaviors and other thoughts that are barriers to practicing those behaviors. Through participating in a game, group members learn to distinguish between harmful and helpful thoughts related to sexual risk behavior. Group members are given the opportunity to practice moving from harmful thoughts to helpful thoughts through a role play. The facilitator helps by giving several examples of self-talk statements.

Practicing Self-Talk With Jenson High School Students

Ms. Davis explains to the group that self-talk is something we do all the time, but we do not always realize it. She goes on to say that we can make self-talk helpful for reducing our chances of engaging in risky behavior. In explaining how to use self-talk, Ms. Davis breaks it down into parts. First, she says, you make a plan to confront a situation. Then you act on the situation. If you feel that you are getting overwhelmed, use self-talk to help yourself cope. Finally, you evaluate the situation and how you handled it. Ms. Davis distributes a handout that provides examples of self-talk for each part of the process. For the planning step, examples of self-talk include "This is going to be tough, but I can handle it" and "I'll take a few deep breaths beforehand." For acting on the situation, an example of self-talk would be "Don't let him rattle me" and "I have a right to my point of view." When experiencing feeling overwhelmed, helpful self-talk includes statements such as "He wants me to get angry" and "There's no shame in leaving and coming back later." Ms. Davis asks the class if there are statements they would like to add to the list of self-talk suggestions.

Session 8: Safer Sex

In this session, the participants learn why people sometimes take sexual risks even though they know the behavior is risky. Using the feeling thermometer, participants can assess their own level of discomfort in discussing safer sex. They learn about the kinds of rationalizations that increase risk for unsafe sex and how to deal with those rationalizations. Included in this part of the curriculum is a goal-setting activity to help group members define what they want for themselves. Students make a list of their goals and rate the goals on a scale from 1 to 10, with 1 meaning that the goal is not very important and 10 meaning that the goal is very important. The facilitator personalizes the curriculum by asking group members why they and their friends might engage in risky behaviors. Students can use their creativity in an activity that involves creating a music video, commercial, or other media to create a message promoting safer sex. Since this is the final interactive group session, the participants discuss the ending of the group.

Session 9: Personal Counseling

In the personal counseling session, the facilitator assesses whether the participants are sexually active and asks them to identify priorities and goals related to safer sex. The session is also used to help the teens identify triggers that might prevent them from practicing safer sex behaviors and develop a plan for coping with these triggers. The students are then given the opportunity to ask any questions about HIV/AIDS, STDs, testing, community resources, and anything else that they would like to know.

Session 10: Looking Over a Community Resource

For this session, the facilitator takes a group of participants to visit a relevant community resource so that the group can learn more about the services available in their community and can form links with the community agency that provides those services. Before the visit, the facilitator helps the participants develop questions for the staff at the community agency. The staff and consumers at the community agency describe the resources provided by the agency and allow participants to ask questions. To allow more time for discussion, the group may also share a meal with the agency staff and consumers. The facilitator encourages the group to make specific plans to return for another visit and to thank the staff and consumers for the visit.

▦ Additional Resources

Advocates for Youth: www.advocatesforyouth.org
The Centers for Disease Control and Prevention

Division of Sexually Transmitted Diseases: http://www.cdc.gov/std/

The Centers for Disease Control and Prevention Division of HIV/AIDS Prevention: http://www.cdc.gov/hiv/dhap.htm

The Centers for Disease Control and Prevention's compendium of HIV prevention interventions with evidence of effectiveness: http:// www.cdc.gov/hiv/pubs/HIVcompendium/hivcompendium.htm

The Center for HIV Identification, Prevention, and Treatment Services (CHIPTS): http:// chipts.ucla.edu/about/index.html

Sociometrics HIV/AIDS Prevention Program Archive (HAPPA): http://www.socio.com/pasha/haprogms.htm

Southwestern University's HIV Prevention Toolbox: http://www3.utsouthwestern.edu/preventiontoolbox/

Key Points to Remember

The key points discussed in this chapter include:

- Implementation of effective STD prevention programs is greatly needed to reduce the rates of STD infection among American youth.
- One challenge to evidence-based STD prevention is opposition to curricula that discuss safer sax practices, such as condom use.
- The Street Smart program is a 10-session program that has demonstrated reductions in sexual risk taking among runaway youth and can be adapted for use with other adolescents at risk for STDs and HIV.

Many STD and HIV prevention programs have been rigorously evaluated and shown to be effective. In many cases, the authors have also provided user-friendly treatment manuals that are easily accessed. As discussed in the HIV prevention chapter, the challenge in implementing these programs will be overcoming some of the barriers to using effective programs that include instruction on safer sex strategies, such as condom use.

References

Centers for Disease Control and Prevention. (2003a). *Sexually transmitted disease surveillance, 2003: Adolescents and young adults.* Atlanta, GA: U.S. Department of Health and Human Services, September 2004. Retrieved on December 20, 2004, from http://www.cdc.gov/std/stats/adol.htm

Centers for Disease Control and Prevention. (2003b). *Youth risk behavior surveillance 2003.* Atlanta, GA: U.S. Department of Health and Human Services, Centers for Disease Control and Prevention. Retrieved December 17, 2004, from www.cdc.gov.

Rotheram-Borus, M., Van Rossem, R., Gwadz, M., Koopman, C., & Lee, M. (1997) *Street smart.* Retrieved December 18, 2004, from http://chipts.ucla.edu/interventions/manuals/intervstreetsmart.html

Rotheram-Borus, M. J., Song, J., Gwadz, M., Lee, M., Van Rossem, R., & Koopman, C. (2003). Reductions in HIV risk among runaway youth. *Prevention Science, 4*(3), 173–187.

Southwestern, University of Texas Southwestern Medical Center at Dallas (n.d.). *HIV prevention toolbox: Street smart.* Retrieved December 21, 2004, from http://www3.utsouthwestern.edu/preventiontoolbox/interven/streetsmart.htm

Effective Cognitive-Behavioral Interventions for Self-Mutilation

Katherine Shepard ▪ Tamara DeHay ▪ Brooke Hersh

CHAPTER 26

Getting Started

The expression of self-mutilation behaviors in children and adolescents is a frightening and, in some ways, puzzling phenomenon. Often referred to in the literature as *deliberate self-harm, self-mutilation behavior, parasuicidal behavior, partial suicide, antisuicide,* and *wrist-cutting syndrome,* the act of self-mutilation behavior can be defined based on its directness, social acceptability, degree of damage, frequency, and intent (Suyemoto, 1998). Specifically, it has been defined as the direct, deliberate, and repetitive destruction or alteration of body tissue, which results in minor to moderate injury, without conscious suicidal intent (Favazza & Conterio, 1989; Suyemoto, 1998). The behaviors that constitute self-mutilation are diverse and include behaviors such as cutting, burning, scratching, and skin-picking (Simeon & Favazza, 2001). It is distinguished from socially accepted forms of bodily harm such as body piercing or tattooing and from indirect forms such as drinking and driving and substance abuse.

As mentioned in the definition above, it is important to make a clear distinction between the types of self-mutilation behavior discussed here and suicidality. The three characteristics commonly cited as distinguishing between the two are lethality, intent, and repetition. Self-mutilation behavior usually results in superficial to moderate injury, with very low lethality and without suicidal intent. It is also highly repetitive, with 30% of cases repeating within 1 year. Many have come to view self-mutilation behavior as a precursor to suicide because about half of all people who commit suicide have a history of self-harm and an estimated 10% of people who engage in an act of self-harm subsequently commit suicide (Gunnell & Frankel, 1994; Harris & Hawton, 1997).

What We Know

Classifications of Self-Mutilation Behavior (SMB)

The most widely used classification system used for self-mutilation proposes four large categories (Favazza, 1998; Favazza & Rosenthal, 1990; Favazza & Simeon, 1995; Simeon & Favazza, 2001). It is important to note the four-category model is based primarily on work with adult populations. Despite this limitation, the proposed model provides a useful heuristic for school social workers and other mental health professionals who work with youth engaging in self-mutilation behaviors (Simeon & Favazza, 2001).

Stereotypic SMB

Stereotypic SMB is characterized by highly repetitive behaviors such as head-banging, self-hitting, and skin-picking. Stereotypic SMB is frequently observed in populations with mental retardation, autism, Lesch-Nyhan, Cornelia de Lange, and Prader-Willi syndrome (Simeon & Favazza, 2001).

Major SMB

Major SMB is the most severe of the four categories. This form of SMB is frequently an isolated occurrence that occurs in either a psychotic or intoxicated state. Behaviors that constitute major SMB are usually life-threatening and include limb amputation, castration, and self-removal of the eyes (Simeon & Favazza, 2001).

Compulsive SMB

The compulsive form of SMB is characterized by behaviors such as hair-pulling, skin-picking, and severe nail-biting. Individuals with this form of SMB frequently report that these behaviors have a ritualized and symbolic component. Compulsive SMB is commonly seen in individuals diagnosed with trichotillomania, obsessive-compulsive disorder, and stereotypic movement disorders (Simeon & Favazza, 2001).

Impulsive SMB

Impulsive SMB is perhaps the broadest of the four categories. The harming behaviors can occur repetitively or only occur once. The self-mutilating behavior frequently has a symbolic element, such as cleansing or punishment. Behaviors associated with this category include burning, superficial and deep cutting, and self-hitting. This form of SMB is frequently observed in individuals diagnosed with personality disorders (mainly borderline), eating disorders, depression, and post-traumatic stress disorder (Simeon & Favazza, 2001).

This review of effective practices with youth with SMB will focus primarily on youth engaging in impulsive SMB.

▌ Prevalence

The prevalence rate of self-mutilation behavior as defined above is difficult to assess, and a wide disparity exists between the rates documented in the extant literature. Many patients who have engaged in these behaviors will not report them spontaneously, and because of the lack of severity of the actual physical harm, many cases are never reported even when the individual is explicitly asked. Some research has estimated that self-mutilation behavior occurs in approximately 4% of the general population and in 4.3% to 21% of clinical populations (Suyemoto, 1998).

The age of onset of self-mutilation behaviors is usually in middle to late adolescence and the majority of documented cases have occurred in females (Favazza & Conterio, 1988; Sonneborn & Vanstraelen, 1992; Suyemoto, 1998). There is again much disagreement in the literature regarding the actual prevalence within the adolescent population. For instance, Kahan and Pattison (1984) have

reported that the incidence is relatively low at 1.2%, while Favazza, DeRosear, and Conterio (1989) found a prevalence rate of 12% in a general sample of college students.

When adolescents do engage in self-mutilation behavior, it seems that it most often includes skin-cutting and picking at existing wounds. These actions comprise about one third of adolescent self-harm (Guertin et al., 2001). They are followed in frequency by acts such as burning and self-hitting (Favazza & Conterio, 1989). A high percentage of people who engage in self-mutilation behavior will repeat the behavior within 1 year, and about 13% of cases are termed "major repeaters," with a lifetime history of five or more episodes (Kreftman & Casey, 1988).

▌ Functions of Self-Mutilation

Most research on impulsive self-mutilation suggests that this behavior is most often used as a coping strategy. Research examining self-mutilation found that self-mutilation is frequently used by youth who become stressed by the numerous demands that society places upon them as well as by the difficult social transitions that occur during this developmental stage. In a study examining why adolescents cut themselves, Allen (1995) identified three main reasons for cutting:

1. *To manage negative moods.* Most adolescents report feeling intensely angry or distressed immediately preceding the cutting. The subsequent harm serves as a form of self-medication in that the episode releases tension. In addition, adolescents who engage in self-mutilation behaviors report that it ameliorates feelings of depersonalization and alienation from the world. In particular, cutting and burning behaviors appear to make the adolescent feel alive (Allen, 1995).
2. *A response to beliefs or habitual thoughts.* Youth who engage in self-harming behavior also report that it is a way of dealing with a sense of "internal badness" and anger at other individuals. The self-harming behaviors serve as a way to inflict punishment on oneself for having inadequacies as well as to channel aggression toward others back to the self. These explanations for engaging in self-mutilation behaviors are most frequently observed in youths with a history of physical and/or sexual abuse (Allen, 1995).

3. *To manage interactions with others.* To family members and friends of adolescents who engage in SMB, the behaviors frequently are seen as a cry for help or as a method of gaining attention (Allen, 1995). Favazza (1989), however, identified an alternative role that self-mutilation might play in maintaining difficult relationships. In particular, Favazza hypothesizes that "self-mutilators who received nurturance after enduring pain of physical abuse as youngsters may harm themselves as a repetition of their childhood experience because they believe that 'after the suffering there is love and forgiveness.'" Thus, adolescents who engage in self-mutilation may do so as an attempt to obtain love and protection from significant people in their lives.

Adolescents' Experiences During Self-Mutilation

There is a surprising degree of agreement among researchers regarding the phenomenological aspects of self-mutilation behavior. Personal accounts by individuals who engage in self-mutilation behavior often include descriptions of powerful and overwhelming feelings of anger, tension, or anxiety immediately prior to the act. They frequently report experiencing little or no pain during an episode and a sense of relief and invigoration after engaging in cutting (Grossman & Siever, 2001). In this way, the self-mutilation behavior serves to relieve emotional distress and regulate the stress level of the individual. The behavior itself becomes reinforcing to the individual in that it provides a brief reprieve from the intense negative emotions that have triggered it (Favazza, 1999; Herpertz, 1995; Suyemoto, 1998).

Research examining the biological effects of self-mutilation behaviors suggests that such behaviors often trigger the release of neurotransmitters that are associated with decreased stress and increased pleasure. In particular, endogenous opiates appear to serve an important function in SMB (Sandman & Touchette, 2002). Endogenous opiates are released within the body when injury or physical trauma occurs and serve to reduce pain. Thus, one possible function of SMB is to cause the release of endogenous opiates, which results in an "opiate high" where the individual experiences a euphoric-like state. This physiological change is reinforcing because as the individual engages more in self-harming behavior to experience the release of endogenous opiates, his or her system will develop a tolerance for the chemical and require a higher dosage of endogenous opiates to produce the euphoric state. Consequently, the individual will engage in more frequent and severe SMB in order to receive the opiate high (Sandman & Touchette, 2001).

Alternatively, it has been hypothesized that SMB results from insensitivity to pain, which could be due to a chronically elevated level of endogenous opiates. The chronically increased level of these endogenous opiates would result in the individual feeling numb. The pain that they would experience when cutting would serve to counter the numb feeling and decrease sensations of depersonalization and alienation (Sandman & Touchette, 2002). Thus, youth who report cutting to feel alive may have an overabundance of opiates in their systems and cutting may serve to provide a sense of alertness. In sum, research with adult populations suggests that endogenous opiates may play a critical role in creating the positive mental state that individuals experience after cutting.

Factors Associated With Impulsive SMB

Several factors have been identified as being associated with impulsive SMB in adolescents. Among these factors is an overall increased number of risk-taking and reckless behaviors. Additionally, adolescents who engage in SMB frequently present as passive and unable to effectively solve problems. They seem to have overgeneralized memories and marked difficulty in remembering and analyzing specific situations. It may be that their limited access to specific memories renders them less able to use prior experience to find effective means of resolving current problems (Evans, 2000). As mentioned above, SMB may also be related to dissociation, which results in a feeling of numbness and disconnection from others (van der Kolk & Fisler, 1994). It is important to note that the levels of cognitive and affective disturbance in individuals who engage in SMB are generally higher compared to suicide attempters, and that this symptomatology may be expressed through multiple self-destructive channels.

Research has identified several risk factors that place youth at greater risk for engaging in SMB. Selekman's chapter in this text provides a detailed review of risk factors associated with America's current culture. This chapter focuses exclusively on empirically supported risk factors and interventions for the impulsive form of self-mutilation.

Presence of Other Forms of Psychopathology

As described previously, various forms of psychopathology place youth at greater risk for self-mutilation. Affective and behavioral symptoms such as anxiety, depression, loneliness, conduct problems, antisocial behavior, eating disorders, and anger are often associated with these behaviors. The description below provides a brief description of unique aspects of the relationship between specific diagnoses and self-mutilation. Other chapters in this volume cover in more detail several of these disorders.

Depression

Adolescents who are clinically depressed are more likely to engage in self-mutilation. Depressed females who do not receive treatment for depression are at greater risk for using SMB as a means of reducing the symptoms of distress, anxiety, and hopelessness associated with depression (Derouin & Bravender, 2004). In addition to decreasing these symptoms, female adolescents with depression also reported that cutting behaviors elicited care and concern from caregivers when they felt unheard or unnoticed by others.

Eating Disorders

Approximately 60% of adolescent females who report self-mutilation behaviors also report eating disorders (Favazza & Conterio, 1989; Zila & Kiselica, 2001). In adolescents who display both eating disorders and SMB, cutting and other forms of mutilation are utilized as a punishment for binging or failing to follow food restrictions. Yaryura-Tobias et al.'s (1995) research also demonstrated that self-mutilation behaviors frequently replace maladaptive eating behaviors in youth who are being treated for anorexia. If, however, the adolescent relapses to an anorectic state, the SMB usually subsides. Consequently, school social workers and other mental health professionals who work with youth with eating disorders must attend to signs that SMB may be occurring.

Borderline Personality Disorder

Borderline personality disorder (BPD) is characterized by intense negative emotions including depression, self-hatred, anger, and hopelessness. Furthermore, individuals with BPD usually lack the coping resources to handle these negative emotions and often resort to SMB or suicide attempts as a form of coping (Ivanoff, Linehan, & Brown, 2001). Thus, it is not surprising that approximately 80% of individuals diagnosed with BPD report having engaged in some form of self-mutilation at least once (Fryer, 1988). Moreover, BPD is the most common diagnosis found in adult populations of self-mutilators (Walsh & Rosen, 1988). Although personality disorders are not diagnosed in children and very rarely diagnosed in adolescents, school social workers and other mental health professionals working with clients who have symptoms consistent with BPD should attend carefully to any signs of suicidal ideation or self-mutilation.

Substance Abuse

An increased rate of substance abuse has been noted in adolescents who engage in SMB. Walsh and Rosen (1988) speculate that this increase is related to the self-mutilating adolescent's overall impulsive pattern of responding. It may also be the case that the substance abuse provides further relief from the adolescent's affective symptoms.

Other Disorders

Bipolar disorder, oppositional defiant disorder, and dysthymia have also been mentioned in the extant literature as disorders associated with self-mutilation behaviors. However, there is a dearth of empirical data on this association; thus, these disorders will not be covered in this chapter.

History of Severe Physical and/or Sexual Abuse

Survivors of either sexual or physical abuse are at greater risk for self-mutilation (Favazza & Conterio, 1989; Pattison & Kahan, 1983; von der Kolk et al., 1991; Zila & Kiselica, 2001). Physical and sexual abuse by primary caregivers is thought to put children at risk for SMB because the youths must muster all of their own coping resources to handle stress and anxiety without the assistance of their caregiver. Because the level of stressors frequently exceed the level of resources available, the child resorts to the use of maladaptive coping skills, such as cutting, to reduce anxiety (Himber, 1994).

Contagion Factor

Adolescents who are surrounded by peers who engage in self-mutilation practices are at a greater risk for trying these behaviors. Research has demonstrated that youth who are in residential treatment facilities or incarcerated are likely to try cutting or other forms of self-mutilation when exposed to peers who engage in these behaviors (Favazza, 1998; Taiminen, Kallio-Soukainen, Nokso-Koivistom, Kaljonen, & Helenuis, 1998). In addition, there is growing evidence for the contagion factor in "normal" adolescents in the school setting. Self-mutilation is frequently passed among social groups in schools when one child engages in the behavior and reports to peers the relief that he or she experiences as a result of the behavior (Derouin & Bravender, 2004). Thus, school social workers or mental health professionals must carefully monitor students who associate with known self-mutilators.

What We Can Do

Given the high prevalence rate and contagious nature of self-mutilation, it is important that school social workers and other mental health professionals know how to identify and successfully intervene in cases involving cutting or other forms of mutilation. This chapter focuses exclusively on empirically supported cognitive behavioral and behavioral treatments for SMB. For a review of solution-oriented and strengths-based approaches, see Selekman's chapter in this text.

Identification and Assessment of SMB

Identifying students who self-mutilate is an extremely difficult task as most youth are highly secretive about these behaviors. Some warning signs that a youth may self-mutilate include wearing long-sleeved clothing in warm weather and wearing many bracelets or wristbands to prevent cuts

and scrapes from showing. In addition, these adolescents frequently seek excuses from the school nurse to miss physical education and other outdoor activities that require their skin to be exposed. The school social worker should work closely with school nurses to identify students who demonstrate the warning signs described above (Derouin & Bravender, 2004).

Once a student has been identified as self-mutilating, it is important that the social worker complete a thorough interview to assess the extent of the mutilating behaviors and the student's current coping strategies. A sample interview will be presented later in this chapter. For additional interviewing strategies and questions, review Selekman's chapter in this text. In addition to conducting a thorough interview, self-report measures can provide greater insight into the reasons why the student self-mutilates. The Self-Injury Motivation Scale, II (SIMS-II; Osuch et al., 1999) is a useful tool for assessing the underlying reasons for SMB. This measure identifies six distinct motivations for SMB: (1) affect regulation, (2) de-isolation, (3) punitive duality, (3) influencing others, (4) magic control, and (5) self-stimulation. Although this scale was developed using adult populations, research has demonstrated that it has adequate psychometric properties for clinical use with adolescents. In addition, SIMS-II has been found to be a useful tool for identifying and quickly assessing a variety of different reasons for the adolescent's SMB. These reasons can be used to provide an initial set of dysfunctional thoughts and beliefs about cutting behavior that can be discussed and challenged in subsequent sessions (Kumar, Pepe, & Steer, 2004).

Predicting Repetition

Because a high percentage of children and adolescents who engage in SMB once will subsequently repeat the behavior (the majority within the first 2 months after the initial act), it is important for school social workers and other mental health professionals to understand the risk factors associated with repetition. Depression and a history of previous SMB significantly increase the risk of repetition. Family functioning is also an important associated factor, and poor parental mental health has been found to be the strongest predictor of repeated self-harm (Chitsabesan et al., 2003). The school social worker must take this into account when meeting with parents about their child's symptoms, and oftentimes it may be helpful to recommend that the parents seek out individual or family counseling.

The Issue of Confidentiality

At some point during the assessment process, it is likely that the school social worker or other mental health professionals will have to inform the adolescent's parents about the behavior. Because of the serious implications that informing the parents can have on rapport in subsequent sessions, it is important that the school social worker openly discusses the upcoming disclosure with the youth. During this discussion, the social worker should emphasize that parents may be helpful in the recovery process. In addition, the school social worker may want to "brainstorm" ways that the youth could be involved in the disclosure. In particular, it may be useful for the child to inform his or her parents in the presence of the school social worker during a meeting in the social worker's office (Froeschle & Moyer, 2004).

Promising Interventions

Relatively few empirical studies exist which examine the efficacy of interventions for SMB. Of the few studies that do exist, the majority only explore the efficacy of cognitive-behavioral therapy and behavioral interventions. From this limited body of research, cognitive counseling and behavior modification appear to be effective in adolescent populations. For a review of integrative and strengths-based approaches to treating self-mutilation, see Selekman's chapter in this text.

Cognitive Counseling

Cognitive therapy educates the client about the relationship between their thoughts, emotions, and their self-mutilation behaviors. During sessions, the social worker or counselor helps the client identify negative emotions and recognize the relationship between these emotions and thoughts that are associated with self-harming behavior. Then, intervention focuses on helping the client challenge the thoughts that lead to self-mutilation. According to Walsh and Rosen (1994), four beliefs are associated with self-mutilation.

1. Self-mutilation is acceptable.
2. One's body and self are disgusting and deserving of punishment.
3. Action is needed to reduce unpleasant feelings.
4. Overt action is needed to communicate feelings to other people.

Throughout the counseling process, the social worker or other professional helps the client evaluate the validity of these beliefs and others that may be affecting their negative behaviors. See Table 26.1 for example questions and strategies that could be used to challenge the aforementioned beliefs.

Another important component of cognitive therapy is to help the student develop a healthier set of coping skills. The mental health professional works with the client to develop activities such as journaling, listening to music, exercising, or engaging in relaxing activities when they experience the urge to cut. Case studies have illustrated that helping the client develop more proactive ways of dealing with concerns can reduce SMB. For example, Pipher (1994) worked with an adolescent female who engaged in self-mutilation when she became overwhelmed by societal problems such as HIV and homelessness. In addition to recommending journaling when the client is upset, the social worker or other school professional helped the adolescent to engage in activities that would address and sublimate her concerns. In this case study, the adolescent began to volunteer at a local soup kitchen, which in turn enabled the youth to feel as though she was contributing in a positive way to her concerns.

When developing coping strategies, it is often necessary to provide alternative behaviors that mimic the effects of self-mutilation without the accompanying physical harm (Alderman, 1997). This is especially important in the early phases of intervention when the adolescent may "crave" the physical effects of self-mutilation. The following are examples of replacement behaviors:

1. Have the adolescent wear a loose-fitting rubber band around his or her wrist and snap it when the urge to engage in self-mutilation occurs.
2. Have the adolescent tightly squeeze a piece of ice in the palm of his or her hand.
3. Have the adolescent submerge his or her arm in icy water.

Each of these behaviors will initiate the same physiological effects of SM but will not cause bodily harm. As counseling continues, the client

Table 26.1 Restructuring Thoughts for SMB

Core Belief	Associated Negative Thoughts	Coping Thoughts
Self-harm is acceptable.	It's okay to cut, burn, etc. Other people cut, burn, etc.	It's not okay to cut, burn, etc. Just because other people cut, burn, etc., doesn't mean that I should.
One's body and self are disgusting and deserving of punishment.	I'm ugly.	Even though sometimes I feel ugly, I have pretty hair and nice eyes.
		Most people feel ugly sometimes, but my mom and grandma tell me I'm beautiful.
	I'm fat.	Even though sometimes I feel fat most people do at times, and I am an average weight.
		The doctor isn't concerned about my weight, so I shouldn't be either.
		(for an overweight person) Even though I am a little overweight now, I may not be overweight forever. My body is in my control and I can change it if I want to.
Action is needed to reduce unpleasant feelings.	No one likes me.	Even though not everybody likes me, lots of people do: my mom, grandma, friend A, B, & C, my youth pastor, sister/brother, etc.
	I'm alone.	That's not true! I have lots of people around that care about me: my mom, counselor, teacher, etc.
	I can't handle my emotions.	I can handle my emotions by doing coping strategies, problem solving, and changing my thinking.
Self-harm is needed to communicate feelings to others.	If I hurt myself, then others will pay more attention to me.	I do not need to hurt myself to get others to pay attention to me. I can ask (mom, teacher, counselor, sister, pastor, etc.) to talk if I am feeling stressed.

should be encouraged to rely less on these strategies and engage in more active problem-solving solutions, such as journaling, engaging in social activities, and talking with others.

In summary, cognitive therapy appears to be a two-pronged approach to treating SMB. First, the intervention seeks to challenge maladaptive core beliefs that are promoting the self-mutilation behaviors. Second, the intervention provides the youth with alternative coping strategies and problem-solving skills.

Problem-Solving Therapy

Brief problem-solving therapy has shown promise in clinical trials as being efficacious in reducing the symptoms of SMB. Individuals who engage in SMB demonstrate specific deficits in their ability to effectively solve problems, and this type of therapy is helpful in teaching skills that may reduce their need to rely on maladaptive coping strategies. The primary goal of the therapy is to address the individual's current problems by identifying and defining them, deciding on goals, and using a stepwise approach to work toward their goals and improve the problems. The client is secondarily taught to practice and generalize these skills so that they can utilize them to address future problems. Problem-solving therapies have been effective not only in problem improvement but also in reducing the treated individuals' levels of depressions and hopelessness.

Emergency Card Provision

The provision of an emergency contact card in addition to other care has shown some positive effects for clients who engage in self-mutilation behaviors. The emergency card allows individuals to make an emergency contact when they have the desire to carry out the SMB. Although this strategy is not sufficient as a sole treatment, it has been helpful in reducing repetition of SMB in clinical trials.

Psychopharmacological Interventions

The U.S. Food and Drug Administration has not yet approved any psychopharmacological interventions for the treatment of SMB. Although there is a dearth of evidence-based research on this category of interventions, some medications have shown promise of efficacy in treating the symptoms of SMB in clinical trials, and many are used off-label with varying degrees of success. The selective serotonin reuptake inhibitors (SSRIs) are generally seen as the safest and most effective medications for treatment within this population. They are helpful in controlling the symptoms of impulsivity, depression, anxiety, irritability, and aggression with minimal side effects. Other classes of medications, such as mood stabilizers, opioid antagonists, beta-blockers, antipsychotics, benzodiazepines, monoamine oxidase inhibitors, and tricyclic antidepressants have shown some utility in treating the symptoms associated with SMB but should not be used as first-line treatments due to their increased negative side-effect profiles.

Tools and Practice Examples

Inquiring about self-harm behavior is a delicate undertaking. Because the behavior is contagious

and is often learned from modeling, the social worker must be cautious not to give the child or adolescent ideas. Therefore, it may be important not to question directly about self-harm behavior if there is no prior evidence of it, especially when working with a population of children who are at risk of harming themselves.

The school social worker and other professionals working with a child or adolescent engaging in SMB should be first motivated to learn the function of the harming behavior. The social worker asks him- or herself, "What purpose is the self-harm serving?" Is the self-harmer seeking attention or pity from the social worker or someone else? If this is the root of the SMB, the self-harmer will usually be vocal about their self-harming behavior. They may brag to peers, advertising the merits of cutting or burning oneself. The harmer also receives secondary gain in the way of direct attention from the social worker or other professional after the incident(s), regular check-ins by school counselors, and possibly parental activation by way of increased attention and supervision. If this is the function of the SMB, the social worker may be curious about the child or adolescent's tendencies toward borderline PD. The school-based professionals would also be concerned about the spread of SMB to other students that the self-harmer encountered.

Is the self-harmer engaging in this behavior because he or she is trying to cope with stress by using a dangerous, maladaptive strategy? If this is the function of the SMB, the harmer may not choose to engage in self-harm if properly educated about other effective strategies. Viewing the child from a strengths-based perspective may help the social worker and other counselors when working with a child who harms due to an ineffective coping repertoire. In these cases, the professionals can perceive the self-harmer as someone who is trying to cope with his or her environment but has not learned better ways of doing so. With proper therapeutic intervention, the self-harmer can learn more adaptive ways of managing distress. Oftentimes, the SMB serves both of the functions described above. In these cases, treatment must address the attention function and coping function.

It is not uncommon for a child, especially a younger child, to be confused by his or her behavior. They may be experiencing shame or guilt about the SMB on top of the angry or sad feelings which led to the self-harm.

Case Example

A 9-year-old child reported that she just woke up with all these scratches on her arm. She didn't know how it happened. Upon questioning, she insisted that she did not do it to herself, though the scratches were characteristic of self-harming behavior (vertical scratches breaking the skin about 2 to 3 inches in length).

With children like the one in the example above, it is not only necessary to conduct a thorough inquiry with the child but also inform the parents of the professional's clinical impressions. In such cases, parents should be educated about the signs of SMB and strongly encouraged to increase supervision of the child. Further recommendations to the parent might include organizing enjoyable activities for the child and parent to participate in together. The extra attention coupled with the fun activities would serve to facilitate the child's coping mechanisms.

Treatment

Cognitive-behavioral therapy focuses on first helping the child to describe the situation occurring when the child chose to self-harm. Next, the school social worker or other counselor helps the child recognize and identify negative emotions the child was feeling during that situation (before the self-harm) and the accompanying negative automatic thoughts leading to that emotion. Subsequent treatment is three-pronged, consisting of enhancing the child's repertoire of coping skills, teaching problem-solving skills, and changing negative thinking. In addition, when working with a child who engages in self-harm the helping professionals would be wise to complete a safety contract with the child. The safety contract should include people the child feels he or she can talk to when feeling the urge to harm (include phone numbers) and a coping plan with several coping strategies and positive coping thoughts listed. With some children, safer replacement behaviors, such as holding ice or snapping a rubber band on the wrist, can be added to the contract. Figure 26.1 presents the safety contract created for the child in the subsequent case study.

Treatment should also be mindful of the possibility of more permanent or severe damage. In addition to scarring from burning or cutting, serious cuts could lead to infection or hit a vein. There also may be social implications for those who engage in SMB. These children and adolescents are more isolated from peers due to their often secretive behavior. If the SMB becomes known, then they may be rejected by their peers who think the behavior is weird or fear that the self-harmer is dangerous.

Coping Skills

The child should be taught to replace the self-harm behavior with alternative coping behaviors that are engaging for the child. There are different categories of coping skills, which are differentially effective for different negative emotions. For angry or irritable feelings, coping strategies that expend energy (e.g., running, biking, playing outside) can be highly effective. For worried or anxious feelings, coping strategies that induce relaxation (e.g., deep breathing, bubble bath) can be useful. Doing something to distract one's thinking (e.g., reading a book, surfing the Web, playing a game) is often helpful with many different negative emotions. The child should also be informed that different coping skills may work at different times, so it may be necessary to try a couple of coping strategies before one works to decrease the urge to self-harm.

Problem Solving

Problem solving focuses on actions the child can take to change situations which typically lead to the urge to self-harm. A few examples of problems that have been found to lead to self-harm in children and adolescents are fighting with siblings or parents, poor grades, family violence, parental substance abuse, and teasing by peers. It is important to emphasize that problem solving is only an option when the situation is one in which the child has some control (peer teasing). For instance, the child has no control over parental substance abuse. Problem solving can be taught concisely to children in a five-step process:

1. Identify the problem. What happened that provoked thoughts of self-harm?
2. Determine the goal. What does the child want to have happen?
3. Brainstorm plans. It is important to come up with at least five plans so the child can try a different plan if one does not work. Plans can include coping skills.

Figure 26.1. Safety Contract

I, _____ , agree not to harm myself. If I am having thoughts of harming myself I will do one or more of the following coping plans until I feel better:

1. Talk to someone (mom, dad, school counselor, youth pastor, aunt, grandmother). [include all phone numbers]
2. Play Playstation.
3. Play flute.
4. Run outside.
5. Listen to music.
6. Take a bubble bath.
7. Say my coping thoughts to myself:

   - "Who cares? Like it is cool to hang out with my sister's loser friends? Lots of other people think I'm cool, like my friends and my little sister."
   - "It is not my job to take care of my sister. I am 13 years old, and we have two parents whose job it is to take care of her."
   - "It can be hard to handle such a stressful situation, but I have lots of ideas of what I can do. If I do my coping plans, then I will feel better. Plus, I have handled lots of stressful situations in the past without hurting myself, such as my parents divorcing and moving to a new school."

I understand the contract that I am signing and agree to follow it.

_____   _____

Child Signature   Parent Signature

_____

Social Worker/
Counselor

Date: _____

4. Guess the pros and cons of each plan and pick the best one(s). In this stage the child, guided by the professional, picks the best plan after estimating the pros and cons of each. Plans may be combined, too!
5. Praise yourself! The child should be encouraged for attempting to manage the situation without self-harm, even if the plan does not work out. Successful problem solvers are the ones who make an effort to remedy problems, even if the plans tried do not solve the problem.

A few suggestions for general problem-solving plans:

1. Journaling. Journaling is a cathartic process, which helps to release negative emotions. With younger kids it may be helpful to structure the activity by giving them prompts (e.g., write down five things you are grateful for, write two good and two bad things that happened today, etc.).
2. Increasing extracurricular activities. Minimizing the time the child has to engage in SMB would be helpful.
3. Drawing. Like journaling, artistic expression is a way of coping and releasing emotion.
4. Listening to music. This is a fun and distracting activity and very developmentally appropriate for teens.
5. Exercise. As previously mentioned, exercise may be especially helpful for self-harmers. Aerobic activity releases endorphins, which are natural mood enhancers. Children may enjoy playing outside with friends, jumping rope, roller-blading, riding bikes, dancing, and playing sports. Adolescents may enjoy these activities in addition to organized exercise classes (e.g., aerobics, yoga).

Changing Negative Thinking

The third domain of intervention is working with self-harmers to identify and change negative thoughts associated with the SMB. As discussed previously, there are four core negative beliefs, which each have commonly associated negative thoughts. The school social worker or other helper works with the child to restructure the negative beliefs into more positive, adaptive thoughts—thoughts that will not lead to SMB. Two techniques that are effective in restructuring negative thoughts are (1) developing a more positive explanation for the situation causing the negative thought and (2) discovering evidence that shows that the negative thought is not true.

Table 26.1 presents examples of the four core negative beliefs, commonly associated maladaptive thoughts, and potential replacement coping thoughts used in the restructuring process with adolescents who engage in SMB.

Case Example

Miranda is in sixth grade, the first year of middle school, and is 13 years old. She is Caucasian, middle socioeconomic status, and has one older sister and one younger sister. Her parents are divorced, and recently she moved in with her father (she had been living with her mother), which resulted in changing to a middle school away from her elementary school friends. Miranda was retained in the third grade, thus is a year older and more physically developed than her peers. Miranda enjoys playing the flute in the school band and following the trends in Japanese animation. She was identified by her teachers and referred to the school counselor for exhibiting what was determined to be symptoms of depression. She had been attending weekly counseling sessions with the school social worker for 1 month when her mother called the school social worker reporting that she noticed an estimated 15 cuts, about 2 inches in length, on her daughter's arm.

Upon inquiry, Miranda reported that she had no specific thoughts about killing herself. Although she reported sometimes wishing she were dead when feeling angry, she would not act upon these feelings or thoughts. When asked more about the cutting, she described two incidents. One occurred at her mother's house and one at her father's house. Both times other family members were home. Miranda reported that the incidents were triggered by feelings of anger and confusion and that the cutting was a way to redirect her emotional pain and make her feel better. She said that the first time it did make her feel better but that the second time it only helped a little bit and that she stopped doing it and tried a coping strategy (playing her flute), which worked better.

Sample Interview Addressing Self-Harming Behavior

Below is an excerpt from a sample interview[1] with Miranda where the school social worker is inquiring about the self-harming behavior. In this example, the social worker has been informed by the child's parents that the child has engaged in self-harming behavior. The social worker has had an ongoing relationship with the child. The interview picks up after rapport has been established in that session.

S: I don't know if this is the case for you, but sometimes when children/teens are feeling very stressed they may think about hurting themselves as a way to feel better. Has this happened to you?

C: Well, sort of.

S: Oh, I see. What happened?

C: My sister and I got in a huge fight on Saturday. She wanted to go hang out with her friends, who are kind of my friends too. I wanted to go with her but she didn't want me to go. She ended up leaving right in the middle of the fight and I didn't know what to do, so that's when it happened.

S: What did you do?

C: I took the scissors and made a few scratches.

S: Then what?

C: Then I played my flute.

S: Ok. So what emotion were you feeling when you picked up the scissors.

C: I don't know. I guess I was mad, and I didn't know what do to.

S: So, were you also confused?

C: Yeah, totally.

S: So, you were feeling mad and confused. What were you thinking? What thoughts were popping into your head?

C: Well, that my sister thought I wasn't cool enough to hang out with her and her friends. I was also worried about her because sometimes she does bad things when she hangs out with her friends. So, I was thinking I should make sure I go with her so I can watch out for her but I couldn't get her to let me go along with her. I was thinking this is all too much and I couldn't handle it.

At this point the social worker has captured the triggering thoughts that cause the child to feel overwhelmed with emotion, which had led to the self-harming behavior. The school social worker could choose to help the child restructure any or all of these negative thoughts using cognitive restructuring techniques, but it was more important to use the session to develop a coping plan with the child so she could avoid cutting the next time

she has these negative thoughts and emotions. It is essential that the social worker help the child to recognize that these thoughts are triggers for her wanting to cut, so that if they occur again she can recognize that she needs to use other coping strategies.

S: You did a great job remembering the thoughts that you were having right before you picked up those scissors. Do you think you really wanted to hurt yourself or did you just want to feel better and not so overwhelmed?

C: I just didn't want to be so mad and mixed up about what to do.

S: That's understandable. It sounds like you were trying to cope with a difficult situation.

C: Yeah.

S: Well, let's see if we can come up with different and healthier ways to cope so that next time you are in a difficult and overwhelming situation you don't have to cut yourself.

It is important that the social worker empathize with the child's stress and desire to cope. It is also equally necessary for the child to agree that he or she really does not want to self-harm but just wants to feel better. Now the social worker and child are working toward the same goal.

S: So, in our previous meetings we have discussed a variety of coping strategies. Let's name them.

S & C: [Together they list five categories of coping strategies: do something fun and distracting, do something that uses energy, do something soothing and relaxing, talk to someone, and look at the situation in a more positive way. The social worker guides the child in identifying her favorite thing to do in each of the categories.]

S: Great! See you are already doing one of those coping strategies now by talking to me about this.

It is important to highlight the child's successes so that she feels a sense of competence in avoiding self-harming behavior. The social worker should continually look for sources of strength that the child already has (e.g., friends, family, an important hobby, a younger sibling, etc.), because it is through a person's strengths and resources that he or she is able to overcome their challenges.

S: Now, let's look at this desire to cut as a problem that we can solve. To do that, we will work through the problem-solving steps. (The child has been taught the problem-solving procedure in past sessions.) So, what is the problem?

C: That I cut myself.

S: That's it. What is your goal?

C: Not to cut myself?

S: Right. And I think we figured out a minute ago that the goal is also to feel better. Do you agree?

C: Yeah.

S: So, what is the next step of problem solving?

C: Come up with plans?

S: Right! That's great. So, let's come up with our five plans. Remember that coping strategies can also be plans. What is one plan?

C: To talk to someone.

S: Good. Who would you talk to? [T & C list about five adults that the child could talk to. The child may want to add peers to the list, but it is important that if the child wants to talk specifically about the desire to cut, she should do so with supportive adults—not other children. If the child just wants to vent about feeling mad, sad, confused, etc., peers are good to talk to.] What is another plan?

C: I could play Playstation, or I could play my flute.

S: Yes, you could. Those are both fun and distracting activities. What else?

C: Run outside?

S: Yes! That is a great plan. Doing a coping strategy that uses energy, getting your heart rate up, is a particularly good plan when feeling mad. There are also chemicals in your brain that get released when you exercise. These chemicals are natural ways of feeling good.

It is important that if an energetic coping strategy is not on the child's list of plans, the social worker guide the child to make sure at least one is added. Replacing the cutting with another behavior that releases similar mood-enhancing chemicals can be particularly effective for reducing cutting.

S: We just need a couple more plans.

C: Listen to music? Take a bubble bath?

S: Great! Those are both soothing and relaxing activities. They may help you feel calmer if you are feeling intense negative emotions.

C: I can think something else?

S: Do you mean coming up with more positive thoughts?

C: Yeah.

S: Great idea! That is just what I was thinking, too. Let's come up with a few coping thoughts that would be really powerful for you. [S & C generate the following coping thoughts, which directly challenge the negative thoughts that led to the cutting behavior.]

Negative Thoughts	Coping Thoughts
"My sister would think I wasn't cool."	"Who cares?! Like it is cool to hang out with my sister's loser friends? Lots of other people think I'm cool, like my friends and my little sister."
"Something bad might happen to my sister."	"It is not my job to take care of my sister. I am 13 years old and we have two parents whose job it is to take care of her."
"This is too much for me to handle."	"It can be hard to handle such a stressful situation, but I have lots of ideas of what I can do. If I do my coping plans, then I will feel better. Plus, I have handled lots of stressful situations in the past without hurting myself, such as my parents divorcing and moving to a new school."

S: So, as you know, the next step of problem solving is to guess how good each plan might be for achieving the goal of feeling better/not wanting to cut. Then, rank the plans in order from most effective to least effective. Remember, you can always combine plans or do more than one plan back-to-back.

S: Ok, so now let's come up with a safety contract that will list all the great plans you came up with. [See Safety Contract.] Do you think you can agree to the contract?

C: Yeah.

S: Excellent. Then we will both sign it.

If the child is unsure whether he or she can agree to the contract, negotiate for the maximum number of days the child thinks the contract can be upheld. Upon the end of that time period, renegotiate as needed.

Key Points to Remember

- *Self-mutilation behavior* is defined as the direct, deliberate, and repetitive destruction or alteration of body tissue, which results in minor to moderate injury, without conscious suicidal intent.
- SMB is NOT the same as a suicide attempt, but an estimated 10% of people who engage in an act of self-harm subsequently commit suicide.
- SMB is most often classified into the four broad categories of stereotypic, compulsive, major, and impulsive SMB.
- The prevalence rate of SMB has been difficult to determine but has been estimated at between 1.2% and 12% in adolescent samples.
- The functions of SMB for adolescents are most often to manage negative moods, as a response to negative beliefs, and to manage their social interactions.
- SMB is believed to have a neurochemical basis and is thought to produce euphoria, relieve tension, or reduce feelings of "numbness."
- Psychopathologies commonly associated with SMB are depression, eating disorders, personality disorders, and substance abuse.
- SMB is contagious.
- Treatment strategies that have shown promise in ameliorating the symptoms of SMB are cognitive and behavioral therapies, problem-solving therapy, emergency card provision, and psychopharmacological interventions.

Note

1. This sample interview is intended to serve only as a guide for clinicians. Each client is different, and the interview process needs to be tailored according to the client's specific needs.

References

Alderman, T. A. (1997). *The scarred soul: Understanding and ending self-inflicted violence.* Oakland, CA: New Harbinger Publications.

Allen, C. (1995). Helping with deliberate self-harm: Some practical guidelines. *Journal of Mental Health, 4*(3), 243–250.

Chitsabesan, P., Harrington, R., Harrington, V., & Tomenson, B. (2003). Predicting repeat self-harm in children: How accurate can we expect to be? *European Child & Adolescent Psychiatry, 12,* 23–29.

Derouin, A., & Bravender, T. (2004). Living on the edge: The current phenomenon of self-mutilation in adolescents. *American Journal of Maternal/Child Nursing, 29*(1), 12–18.

Evans, J. (2000). Interventions to reduce repetition of deliberate self-harm. *International Review of Psychiatry, 12,* 44–47.

Favazza, A. R. (1989). Why patients mutilate themselves. *Hospital and Community Psychiatry, 40,* 137–145.

Favazza, A. R. (1998). The coming of age of self-mutilation. *Journal of Nervous and Mental Disorders, 186,* 259–268.

Favazza, A. R. (1999). Self-mutilation. In D. G. Jacobs (Ed.), *The Harvard Medical School guide to suicide assessment and intervention* (pp. 125–145). San Francisco: Jossey Bass.

Favazza, A. R., & Conterio, K. (1988). The plight of chronic self-mutilators. *Community Mental Health Journal, 24*(1), 22–30.

Favazza, A. R., & Conterio, K. (1989). Female habitual self-mutilation. *Acta Psychiatrica Scandinavica, 79,* 283–289.

Favazza, A. R., DeRosear, L., & Conterio, K. (1989). Self-mutilation and eating disorders. *Suicide and Life-Threatening Behaviors, 19,* 352–361.

Favazza, A. R., & Rosenthal, R. (1990). Varieties of pathological self mutilation. *Behavioral Neurology, 3,* 77–85.

Favazza, A. R., & Simeon, D. (1995). Self-mutilation. In E. Hollander & D. J. Stein (Eds.), *Impulsivity and aggression* (pp. 185–200). Chicester, England: John Wiley and Sons.

Froeschle, J., & Moyer, M. (2004). Just cut it out: Legal and ethical challenges in counseling students who self-mutilate. *Professional School Counseling,* 7(4), 231.

Fryer, M. R. (1988). Suicide attempts in patients with borderline personality disorder. *American Journal of Psychiatry, 145,* 737–739.

Grossman, R., & Siever, L. (2001). Impulsive self-injurious behaviors: phenomenology, neurobiology and treatment. In D. Simeon & E. Hollander (Eds.), *Self injurious behaviors* (pp. 117–148). Washington, DC: American Psychiatric Publishing.

Guertin, T., Lloyd-Richardson, E., Spirito, A., Donaldson, D., & Boergers, J. (2001). Self-mutilative behavior in adolescents who attempt suicide by overdose. *Journal of the American Academy of Child and Adolescent Psychiatry, 40*(9), 1062–1074.

Gunnell, D., & Frankel, S. (1994). Prevention of suicide: Aspirations and evidence. *British Medical Journal, 308,* 1227–1233.

Harris, L., & Hawton, K. (2005). Suicidal intent in deliberate self-harm and risk of suicide: Predictive power of the Suicide Intent Scale. *Journal of Affective Disorders, 86*(2–3), 225–233.

Herpertz, S. (1995). Self-injurious behavior: Psychopathological and nosological characteristics in subtypes of self-injurers. *Acta Psychiatrica Scandinavica, 91,* 57–68.

Himber, J. (1994). Blood rituals, self-cutting in female psychiatric patients, *Psychotherapy, 31,* 620–631.

Ivanoff, A., Linehan, M. M., & Brown, M. (2001). Dialectic behavior therapy for impulsive self-injurious behaviors. In D. Simeon & E. Hollander (Eds.), *Self injurious behaviors: Assessment and treatment* (pp. 437–459). Washington, DC: American Psychiatric Publishing.

Kahan, J., & Pattison, E. M. (1984). Proposal for a distinctive diagnosis: The deliberate self-harm syndrome. *Suicide and Life-Threatening Behavior, 14,* 17–35.

Kreftman, N., & Casey, P. (1988). The repetition of parasuicide: An epidemiological and clinical study. *British Journal of Psychiatry, 153,* 792–800.

Kumar, G., Pepe, D., & Steer, R. A. (2004). Adolescent psychiatric inpatients' self reported reasons for cutting themselves. *Journal of Mental Diseases, 192*(12), 830–836.

Osuch, E. A., Noll, J. G., & Putnam, F. W. (1999). The motivation for self-injury in psychiatric inpatients. *Psychiatry, 62,* 334–345.

Pattison, E. M., & Kahan, J. (1983). The deliberate self-harm syndrome. *American Journal of Psychiatry, 140,* 867–872.

Pipher, M. (1994). *Reviving Ophelia: Saving the selves of adolescent girls.* New York: Ballentine Books.

Sandman, C. A., & Touchette, P. (2002). Opioids and the maintenance of self-injurious behavior (pp. 191–204). In S. R. Schroeder, M. L. Oster-Granite, & T. Thompson (Eds.), *Self-injurious behavior: Gene-brain-behavior relationships* (pp. 191–204). Washington, DC: American Psychological Association.

Simeon, D., & Favazza, A. R. (2001). Self-injurious behaviors: Phenomenology & assessment. In D. Simeon & E. Hollander (Eds.), *Self-injurious behaviors: Assessment and treatment* (pp. 1–28). Washington, DC: American Psychiatric Publishing.

Sonneborn, C. K., & Vanstraelen, P. M. (1992). A retrospective study of self-inflicted burns. *General Hospital Psychiatry, 13,* 404–407.

Suyemoto, K. (1998). The functions of self-mutilation. *Clinical Psychology Review, 18*(5), 531–554.

Taiminen, T. J., Kallio-Soukainen, K., Nokso-Kovistom, H., Kaljonen, A., & Helenuis, H. (1998). Contagion of deliberate self-harm among adolescent inpatients. *Journal of the American Academy of Child & Adolescent Psychiatry, 37*(2), 211–217.

van der Kolk, B. A., & Fisler, R. E. (1994). Child abuse and neglect and loss of self regulation. *Bulletin of the Menninger Clinic, 58,* 145–168.

van der Kolk, B. A., Perry, C. J., & Herman, J. L. (1991). Childhood origins of self-destructive behavior. *American Journal of Psychiatry, 148*(12), 1665–1671.

Walsh, B. W., & Rosen, P. M. (1988). *Self-mutilation: Theory, research and treatment.* New York: Guilford.

Yayura-Tobias, J. A., Nezitoglu, F. A., & Kaplan, S. (1995). Self-mutilation, anorexia, and dysmenorrhea in obsessive-compulsive disorder. *International Journal of Eating Disorders, 17,* 33–38.

Zila, M. L., & Kiselica, M. S. (2001). Understanding and counseling self-mutilation in female adolescents and young adults. *Journal of Counseling and Development, 79,* 46–79.

Integrative, Solution-Oriented Approaches With Self-Harming Adolescents

Matthew D. Selekman

CHAPTER 27

Getting Started

Adolescents today are growing up in a highly toxic, media-driven, consumerist culture and struggling to cope with high levels of stress in all areas of their lives. Like a fast-acting pain killer, many adolescents report that self-harming behavior can offer them quick relief from emotional distress and other stressors in their lives. Several of my students have identified trying to fit in and keep up with their peers as the number one stressor they struggle with. Adolescents are plagued by "too-muchness," too many consumer choices, too many activities, too much homework, too many colleges to choose from, and so forth (Schwartz, 2004). Many of these youth are being hurried along into adulthood long before they are ready to assume these responsibilities. Their parents have overscheduled them in too many extracurricular activities and put a lot of pressure on them to pull in those high grades so that they can get into the *best* colleges possible!

Thanks to the power of media advertisements and the blatant biases of some of the major TV networks, teenagers are regularly seduced into believing that quick-fix solutions are the best way to manage stress and problems. Pharmaceutical companies are buying up more advertising time on major television network stations to market their wonder drugs for depression, anxiety, and attention deficit disorder. Several times a day young people are being bombarded by violent images and receiving messages that the way to solve problems is to respond with aggression. In other forms of the media, teenagers see images of how certain alcoholic beverages can make them more "sexy," "social," and look "cool." They may observe their parents chain smoking or misusing alcohol and other drugs to relieve stress or to manage difficulties in their lives. Today's teenagers have learned a number of shortcuts for numbing away emotional distress and escaping from the demands of life, such as self-harming behavior. When adolescents cut or burn themselves, their bodies' immediately secrete endorphins into their bloodstream to quickly numb away the pain. Two commonalities that self-harming adolescents and adults share is that close to 70% of the students tend to experience relief from emotional distress after engaging in this behavior and tend to feel guilty and ashamed, and experience a downward swing in mood a few hours later (Favazza & Selekman, 2003). This, in turn, will often lead to thoughts of wanting to self-harm again to alleviate the emotional distress. Favazza (1998) has also found that 50% of his students had concurrent difficulties with bulimia. See chapter 26 on cognitive-behavioral interventions for self-mutilation for more information on the theory and research for this idea.

Many self-harming students report feeling emotionally disconnected and invalidated by their parents and, in some cases, their peers. One major cause of the family emotional disconnection process is high technology. Today, it is more important to be in chat rooms and playing Gameboys and computer games for hours on end than physically being with family and friends. Screens do not help develop or strengthen adolescents' social skills, uphold family values, and make them more compassionate people. Many parents do not provide any guidelines around screen usage and then get upset with their kids for not wanting to spend time together as a family. In some cases, the parents are emotionally spent from their stressful jobs or are experiencing the perils of long-term unemployment and are just not available to provide emotional support to their kids. Unfortunately, this disconnection process may lead to the adolescent seeking refuge in a *second family* outside the home of unsavory peers who may be engaging in self-harming, substance-abusing, eating-distressed, and other problematic behaviors (Selekman, 2006; Taffel & Blau, 2001). As school social workers, we need to be sensitive to the role the above aggravating factors have played in the development and maintenance of a student's self-harming behavior.

What We Know

The integrative, solution-oriented brief therapy approach to stopping self-harm that is discussed in this chapter comes out of the family systems and social construction orientations to counseling. Research is just beginning to emerge on how to stop adolescent self-harm. Many of the studies that have been conducted combined adolescents and adults in their samples (Favazza & Selekman, 2003; Santisteban, Muir, Mena, & Mitrani, 2003; Selekman, 2006; Favazza, 1998; Conterio & Lader, 1998). Santisteban et al. conducted a pilot study using their borderline adolescent family therapy model with adolescents who were diagnosed with borderline personality disorder and self-harming behavior. The researchers found that 70% of their sample was retained in therapy, and the clients rated their treatment experiences highly on alliance and satisfaction measures. This is one of the first attempts to study the effectiveness of family interventions with self-harming adolescents. Chapter 26 on cognitive-behavioral interventions for self-mutilation reviews other intervention studies.

What We Can Do

Over the past 10 years, I have been using an integrative solution-oriented brief therapy approach with self-harming adolescents (Selekman, 2005, 2006; Favazza & Selekman, 2003). Case studies and my own clinical experience indicate that solution-oriented, brief therapy (O'Hanlon & Weiner-Davis, 1989; O'Hanlon, 1987; de Shazer, 1991, 1988; Berg & Steiner, 2003; Berg & Miller, 1992) can produce good outcome results with

at-risk adolescents. I have also found that it has its limitations with self-harming adolescent clients and could be improved and made more flexible by integrating compatible ideas from other therapeutic approaches, which can offer school social workers and other school-based counselors many more pathways for intervention. Two of the major limitations of the base model are (1) the strong emphasis on trying to engage self-harming adolescents as early in treatment as possible in *solution talk*, that is, eliciting from them mostly what is going *right* in their lives, which may block them from sharing their problem stories and further invalidate them, and (2) simply changing the adolescents' behavior or problem-maintaining family patterns may not alter their oppressive self-defeating thoughts and difficulties with mood management, which often contribute to the maintenance of the self-harming behavior. Many of these youth lack adequate cognitive and self-soothing skills. To address these limitations with the solution-oriented, brief therapy model, I integrated therapeutic ideas from narrative therapy (Epston, 1998; White, 1995; White & Epston, 1990), the collaborative language systems approach of Harry Goolishian and Harlene Anderson (Anderson, 1997; Anderson & Goolishian, 1988), positive psychology and cognitive therapy (Peterson & Seligman, 2004; Seligman, 2002; Seligman, Reivich, Jaycox, & Gillham, 1995; Fredrickson, 2002; Czikszentmihalyi, 1997), mindfulness meditation ideas (Hanh, 2003, 2001; Bennett-Goleman 2001), and the use of art therapy activities (Selekman, 2005, 2006, 1997).

Major Solution-Oriented Therapeutic Strategies and Experiments

In this section of the chapter, I present some of the major solution-oriented therapeutic strategies and experiments I regularly use with self-harming adolescents to empower them to achieve their treatment goals and resolve their difficulties. Since most school social workers and mental health counselors do not have access to students' parents due to their work schedules or have the luxury of doing family therapy sessions, I present only interventions that can be used with individual students.

Interviewing for Possibilities: Creating a Climate Ripe for Change in the First Session

When beginning the counseling process with new self-harming students, it is critical to take the time to elicit from them what their key strengths and resources and treatment expectations are. The students' strengths and resources can be channeled into their identified problem and goal areas to co-construct solutions. In our therapeutic conversations and with therapeutic experiment design and selection, we should use the clients' strengths, key words, beliefs, and metaphors connected to their major skill areas as much as possible to help foster a cooperative relationship with them. In addition, having the client talk about his or her strengths and resources triggers positive emotion, which can enhance his or her problem-solving capacities (Fredrickson, 2002).

In order to gain a better understanding of why the student gravitated toward self-harming behavior as a coping strategy, it is important to invite the student to share her story about how she discovered it, what specifically it does for her, when and where it is most likely to occur, and what effect this behavior has on significant others in her life. The students take the lead in determining the treatment goals they wish to work on, even if it has nothing to do with their self-harming behavior. Our job is to closely collaborate with them in negotiating small and doable behavioral goals.

Solution-Enhancement Experiment

This experiment is specifically designed for students to keep track on a daily basis of useful self-talk and coping strategies employed to avoid the urge or temptation to cut, burn, or engage in any other form of self-harming behavior (Selekman, 2005, 2006; O'Hanlon & Weiner-Davis, 1989; de Shazer, 1985). Once we identify with the student which specific self-talk tapes or coping strategies help the most, we want to have him or her increase these solution-building patterns of thinking and doing.

Prediction Task

When the student reports that his or her self-harming behavior occurs on a random basis and he or she cannot identify key precipitants, the *prediction task* is the experiment of choice (Selekman, 2005; de Shazer, 1991, 1988). The student is instructed the night before the next day whether or not a self-harming episode will occur. Later that next day, the student is to try to identify all of the reasons why a self-harming episode did not occur. Similar to the solution-enhancement experiment, we want to increase the student's awareness of what works and to do more of it.

Pretend the Miracle Happened

When the student cannot identify any pretreatment changes or presently occurring exceptions (non-problem behaviors, thoughts, or feelings), I like to offer the student the *pretend the miracle happened* experiment. For example, if the student has conflict with two of her teachers and she is failing those classes, I may have her pick 2 days over the next week to pretend to engage in the miracle-like behaviors she thinks they would like to see from her. While pretending to engage in the teachers' miracle behaviors for the student, she is to carefully notice how they respond to her. Oftentimes students are pleasantly surprised to see how people dramatically change when they alter their behavior. I have used this experiment with students who are experiencing peer difficulties as well.

Do Something Different

This experiment can be used in multiple ways in school settings. I offer it to students who are stuck engaging in unproductive ways of thinking or behaving that are further exacerbating their problem situations. For example, one of my former clients associated with a group of peers that she would be more than likely to share a razor blade with. These peers were her best friends, and she was not ready or willing to sever her ties with them. As an experiment, I had her respond differently to them whenever they would encourage her to or begin to cut themselves around her. The client came up with three useful different ways of responding to them: leave the room in which the group self-harming behavior was occurring, change the topic when the idea of cutting was brought up, and raise the volume on the stereo and start dancing. According to my client, these creative strategies helped her to successfully avoid the temptation to cut herself and at times would change her friends' behaviors as well. Similar to the pretend the miracle happened experiment, this change strategy can be used with clients who are experiencing difficulties with particular teachers.

Imaginary Feelings X-Ray Machine

When working with self-harming students who appear to have grave difficulty expressing their thoughts and feelings or have somatic complaints, I offer them the *imaginary feelings X-ray machine experiment* (Selekman, 2005, 2006, 1997). I have the student lie down on a long sheet of paper that has the durability of meat wrapping paper. The next step is to draw the outline of his or her body. I share with the adolescent to pretend that I have turned the X-ray machine on so we can see inside them what their feelings look like. The student is to draw pictures of what he or she thinks his or her feelings look like. The feelings can be depicted in scenarios from his or her life or in symbol form. On a cautionary note, before making any interpretations about the meaning of any of the student's drawings, it is important to hear what the student has to say about his or her drawing. In addition, the social worker or counselor should present his or her interpretations in a tentative way, not as definitive explanations. Once adolescents draw out their feelings on paper, it is easier for them to talk about their unresolved issues and concerns. This art experiment is a wonderful exercise to use in adolescent groups.

Famous Guest Consultant Experiment

This playful thinking-out-of-the-box experiment taps clients' imagination powers to generate solutions for their difficulties (Selekman, 2005, 2006). I have students generate the list of three famous people that they have always admired or have been inspired by. These famous people can be historic figures, TV and movie celebrities, singers and groups, star athletes, artists, authors, and characters from popular books. I ask the students to pretend to put themselves in the heads of their selected famous people and think about how they would solve their problem or achieve their goal. Adolescents have a lot of fun with this experiment and often generate some very creative solutions with the help of their famous consultants.

Visualizing Movies of Success

This highly effective visualization tool can help disrupt the student's self-harming pattern of behavior (Selekman, 2005, 2006). The student is to close her eyes and capture a sparkling moment in her past where she had achieved or accomplished something that made her very proud of herself. She is to apply all of her senses to the experience, including color and motion. I have the client project this movie of success onto a screen in her head and watch it for 10–15 minutes with her eyes remaining closed. In order to get good at accessing their movies of success, I have students practice this visualization twice a day. What is interesting to note is that this exercise generates positive emotion in the person, which has been found to create a climate ripe for high-level problem solving (Fredrickson, 2002).

Mindfulness Meditation

Many self-harming students lack the capacity to soothe themselves when experiencing emotional distress. One effective tool we can teach them is *mindfulness meditation* (Hanh, 2003, 2001; Bennett-Goleman, 2001). There are many types of mindfulness meditations. Being mindful is one's ability to focus on one specific word, bodily sensation, or object and yet embrace or label everything that enters your mind. I teach students about *mantras*, that is, a word or a line they can say to themselves for a designated period of time. If the word *mantra* is objectionable to the school or the client, another word can be used to describe the process. I also like to teach them food and sound meditation. Like the visualizing movies of success tool, it is helpful to practice meditating twice a day for 10–15 minutes at a time. Research indicates that mindfulness meditation can lower our breathing and heart rates, reduce our emotional reactivity when experiencing stress, and strengthen our self-awareness and concentration abilities (Selekman, 2006; Bennett-Goleman, 2001).

Interviewing the Problem

This very creative narrative therapy experiment (Selekman, 2006; Epston, 1998) can be used with students who have been oppressed by their self-harming behavior or other chronic difficulties for a long time. The social worker or counselor is to pretend to be a reporter for the *New York Times* newspaper covering a story on the student's identified problem (cutting, the attitude, bulimia, etc.). The student is to pretend to put herself into the shoes of the problem and gain an inside-looking-out-perspective through its eyes and mind. Like a good reporter, the social worker or counselor needs to secure as many details as possible from the problem regarding its decision to enter the student's life; whether it is a friend or foe; how it has been helpful to the student; how it has wreaked havoc in the student's life; how it brainwashes the student; and what effect it has on family members, peers, teachers, and other significant people in her life. The reporter can also ask the problem what the student and significant others do to thwart or frustrate it and what they do that works the most to undermine it when it is up to its tricks.

The power of this therapeutic experiment is that helps liberate the student from the clutches of the problem and it can help her become more aware of the problem's tricks, so she can outsmart it when it is up to no good. Most adolescents like drama and find this experiment to be fun and insightful.

Habit Control Ritual

The habit control ritual was developed by Durrant and Coles (1991) to help empower the client, his or her parents, and involved helping professionals to conquer the externalized tyrannical problem. Once the student, the parents, the social worker, and concerned school staff have externalized the problem based on the client's description of it or belief about it, as a team they can keep track on a daily basis of what they do to stand up to the problem and not allow it to get the best of them. They are also to keep track of the problem's victories over them. On a chart in the social worker's office, they can write down their effective coping and problem-solving strategies as well as the various ways the problem undermines their efforts by dividing them and promoting behavioral slips with the client. Like the interviewing the problem experiment, the client is liberated from the shackles of the problem and free to pursue a new direction with his or her life. The parents' and school staff's original way of viewing the problem situation and interactions with the client can dramatically change as well.

Bringing in Peers and Inspirational Others

Some of the self-harming students we work with are struggling to cope with very stressful home situations. There may be destructive invalidating family interactions, or the parents may be emotionally disconnected from the student. They may have a few close and concerned friends at school that can be mobilized to provide added support for them. In addition, there may be a teacher or a coach who has taken a special interest in your client and is already providing advice and support to him or her. In fact, this *inspirational other* (Selekman, 2006; Anthony, 1984) may have a lot of creative ideas for helping your client. Bringing the concerned peers and the inspirational other into sessions as resources can help put in place a strong support system to help the client get to a better place. For example, Billy had a tendency to brutalize his body with pens and sharp items when peers at school would bully or tease him. For years, his older brother treated him the same way that the peers did at school. Billy's closest friend at school was Stacy and his inspirational other was his computer teacher Mr. Simon. With the permission of the school dean and Billy's parents, I was able to set up a crisis support team composed of the school social worker, Mr. Simon, Stacy, and his friend Phil. Whenever Billy would come to school emotionally distraught or he had been verbally abused by the bullies at school, an impromptu meeting would be arranged in the school social worker's office with the other crisis support team members to provide support and brainstorm solutions. With the help of the crisis support team, we completely eliminated Billy's self-harming behavior at school.

Constructive Management of Slips and Goal Maintenance

Self-harming students will experience inevitable slips throughout the course of intervention. Therefore, it is imperative that we prepare our students for how to constructively manage slips so that they do not escalate into prolonged relapsing and demoralizing crisis situations. First off, I like to normalize slips as signs that progress has already occurred, teachers of wisdom, and a sign that more structure is needed during leisure times. It is important in second and subsequent sessions to ask consolidating questions (Selekman, 2006; O'Hanlon & Weiner-Davis, 1989) to help solidify the gains the student is making and how to quickly get back on track when slips occur. Some examples of consolidating questions are as follows:

- "What would you have to do to go backward at this point?"
- "What did you learn from that slip on Tuesday that you will put to good use the next time you are faced with a similar stressful situation?"
- "How were you able to stay on track on Monday?" "Wednesday?"
- "Let's say we got together in 3 weeks and you come in and tell me that you had a perfect vacation from counseling, what will you tell me you did to stay on track?"

Finally, we need to address any student concerns or intervene as early as possible if he or she reports that the goal maintenance situation is beginning to unravel. Otherwise, the student will feel like he or she has returned back to square one.

Tools and Practice Examples

Key Assessment Question to Ask Self-Harming Adolescents

- Where did you learn to cut or burn yourself?
- Has anyone significant in your past ever hurt you?
- What does the cutting/burning do for you?
- Are there any particular things that happen to you or thoughts experience when you are more likely to cut/burn yourself?
- Are there any particular things that happen to you or thoughts and feelings that you experience when you are more likely to cut/burn yourself?
- What effect does your cutting/burning have on your relationship with your parents and/or siblings?
- How do your friends feel about your cutting/burning yourself?
- If you could put a voice to your cutting/burning habit, what would it say about you as a person and your situation?
- When you avoid the urge to cut/burn yourself, what do you tell yourself or do that works?

Taming the Mind: The Power of Mindful Meditation

The following techniques are effective in reducing self-harming behaviors among adolescents.

The Mantra

A mantra can be a word or a line that is meaningful to the adolescent. The word or line can be taken from one of their favorite tunes, books, or from their own unique self-generated self-talk tapes. The adolescent is to become so well acquainted with their mantra that it becomes a part of them. Adolescents should practice 10–12 minutes twice a day silently saying to themselves their mantras. The mantra can help center and sooth them when faced with stressors at home and at school.

Food Meditation

I like to use a raisin when doing this simple food meditation. A single raisin is placed in the adolescent's left palm. He or she is to carefully study the raisin's coloring, indentations/crevices, and shadowing around it for a few minutes. Then he or she is to slowly pick it up and roll it around on his or her fingertips feeling its rugged texture for a few minutes. Next, he or she is to place the raisin in his or her mouth without biting down on it. This will trigger the salivation process. The adolescent should roll the raisin around his or her mouth with the use of his or her tongue. After doing this for a few minutes, he or she is to bite down on it, which will access the taste sensation. In his or her mind, the adolescent should describe its taste (sweet, tart, or sour). The adolescent is to slowly and finely chew up the raisin for a few minutes and not swallow it. Following this step, the adolescent should swallow it and pay attention to the sensations he or she experiences both while it is traveling down his or her esophagus and once it enters his or her stomach. The whole meditation process should last for approximately 10–12 minutes.

Sound Meditation

The adolescent is to find a nice quiet place to do this meditation. He or she is to sit comfortably in a chair or lie down on the floor. With eyes closed, the adolescent is to tune into all the various sounds he or she hears around him or her. While listening to each sound, the adolescent is not to get too attached to what he or she hears, just simply label it in his or her mind. This meditation should be done for 10–12 minutes.

Key Points to Remember

Self-harming students can be a challenge to work with. Their behavior can be quite intimidating for even the most seasoned of school social workers, counselors, and teachers. To further complicate matters, some of these adolescents' symptoms switch to bulimia, substance abuse, and sexual promiscuity as well. By following the guidelines below, social workers and other school professionals will be able to foster a cooperative relationship and create a context for change with self-harming students:

- Take the time to build a safe and trusting relationship.
- Provide plenty of room for the student to share his or her problem story.
- Go with whatever the student wishes to work on changing first.
- Utilize the student's key strengths and resources in presenting problem areas.
- Carefully match your intervention questions and experiments with the student's cooperative response patterns, strengths and resources, and treatment goals.
- Actively collaborate with concerned school staff.
- Involve the student's closest friends and inspirational others as resources in the counseling process.
- Normalize for the student the inevitability of future slips and teach tools for constructively managing them.

References

Anderson, H. (1997). *Conversation, language, and possibilities: A postmodern approach to therapy.* New York: Basic.

Anderson, H., & Goolishian, H. (1988). Human systems as linguistic systems: Evolving ideas about the implications for theory and practice. *Family Process, 27*, 371–393.

Anthony, E. J. (1984). The St. Louis risk research project. In N. F. Watt, E. J. Anthony, L. C. Wynne, & J. Roth (Eds.), *Children at risk for schizophrenia: A longitudinal perspective* (pp. 105–148). Cambridge, UK: Cambridge University Press.

Bennett-Goleman, T. (2001). *Emotional alchemy: How the mind can heal the heart.* New York: Harmony.

Berg, I. K., & Miller, S. D. (1992). *Working with the problem drinker: A solution-focused approach.* New York: Norton.

Berg, I. K., & Steiner, T. (2003). *Children's solution work.* New York: Norton.

Conterio, K., & Lader, W. (1998). *Bodily harm: The breakthrough treatment program for self-injurers.* New York: Hyperion.

Czikszentmihalyi, M. (1997). *Finding flow.* New York: Basic.

De Shazer, S. (1988). *Clues: Investigating solutions in brief therapy.* New York: Norton.

De Shazer, S. (1991). *Putting difference to work.* New York: Norton.

Epston, D. (1998). *Catching up with David Epston: Collection of narrative-based papers 1991–1996.* Adelaide, South Australia: Dulwich Centre Publications.

Favazza, A. R. (1998). *Bodies under siege: Self-mutilation and body modification in culture and psychiatry* (2nd ed.). Baltimore, MD: Johns Hopkins University Press.

Favazza, A. R., & Selekman, M. (2003/April). *Self-injury in adolescents.* Annual Spring Conference of the Child and Adolescent Centre, London, Ontario, Canada.

Fredrickson, B. (2002). Positive emotion. In C. R. Snyder & S. J. Lopez (Eds.), *Handbook of positive psychology* (pp. 120–135). New York: Oxford University Press.

Hanh, T. N. (2001). *Anger.* New York: Riverhead.

Hanh, T. N. (2003). *Creating true peace: Ending violence in yourself, your family, your community, and the world.* New York: Free Press.

O'Hanlon, W. H. (1987). *Taproots: Underlying principles of Milton H. Erickson's therapy and hypnosis.* New York: Norton.

O'Hanlon, W. H., & Weiner-Davis, M. (1989). *In search of solutions: A new direction in psychotherapy.* New York: Norton.

Peterson, C., & Seligman, M. E. P. (2004). *Character strengths and virtues: Handbook and classification.* New York: Oxford University Press.

Santisteban, D. A., Muir, J. A., Mena, M. P., & Mitrani, V. B. (2003). Integrated borderline family therapy: Meeting the challenge of treating adolescents with borderline personality disorder. *Psychotherapy: Theory, Research, Practice, & Training, 40*, 251–264.

Schwartz, B. (2004). *The paradox of choice: Why more is less.* New York: HarperCollins.

Selekman, M. D. (1997). *Solution-focused therapy: Harnessing family strengths for systemic change.* New York: Guilford.

Selekman, M. D. (2005). *Pathways to change: Brief therapy solutions with difficult adolescents* (2nd ed.). New York: Guilford.

Selekman, M. D. (2006). *Working with self-harming adolescents. A collaborative, strengths-based therapy approach.* New York: Norton.

Seligman, M. E. P. (2002). *Authentic happiness.* New York: Free Press.

Seligman, M. E. P., Reivich, K., Jaycox, J., & Gillham, J. (1995). *The optimistic child.* New York: Houghton-Mifflin.

Taffel, R., & Blau, M. (2001). *The second family: How adolescent power is challenging the American family.* New York: St. Martin's.

White, M. (1995). *Re-authoring lives: Interviews & essays.* Adelaide, South Australia: Dulwich Centre Publications.

White, M., & Epston, D. (1990). *Narrative means to therapeutic ends.* New York: Norton.

CHAPTER
28

Primary Prevention of Pregnancy

Effective School-Based Programs

Mary Beth Harris

Getting Started

For decades the educational, social, and economic consequences of adolescent pregnancy and childbirth have presented a compelling challenge to schools. High schools and middle schools were coping with the growing presence of teen pregnancy for more than 15 years before it caught the country's attention in the 1980s. Between 1972 and 1990 births to teenage mothers increased by 27% to an all-time high (National Campaign to Prevent Teen Pregnancy, 2004).

These numbers alone were alarming to educators and health care professionals, but it was the continuing rise in nonmarital births and welfare dependency among adolescent mothers that placed teen pregnancy at the center of legislative debate and national program initiatives. Thus began a national focus on preventing adolescent pregnancy, fueled early on with relatively small grants and more recently with $250 million for abstinence education programs provided by the 1996 Welfare Reform Law. By 2001 more than 700 public-funded pregnancy prevention programs have been established in over 47% of urban communities across the United States, in community agencies and churches, medical facilities, and schools (Jindal, 2001).

Most experts agree that the reduction in the national adolescent birthrate between 1991 and 2000 is likely the result of several factors, including not only more sex education and pregnancy prevention programs but also growing concern about HIV and STD, and a decade of widespread financial well-being that provided youth with more life opportunities. Statistics cited in a recent report from the Alan Guttmacher Institute (2004) showed that in 2000 the birthrate for adolescent women ages 15 to 17 was 29% lower than in 1991. Birth rates declined most for African American women (31%) and least (15%) for Hispanic adolescents (Alan Guttmacher Institute, 2004). This report also indicates that the birthrate for younger adolescents, who are believed to be the most at risk for negative consequences, has remained at 0.9% per 1,000. Even with these indications of progress, however, there are 820,000 teen pregnancies each year, and over 400,000 teen births (National Campaign to Prevent Teen Pregnancy, 2004). Nearly 4 out of 10 adolescent girls in this country get pregnant at least once before they reach the age of 20. This is a higher adolescent pregnancy rate, by far, than in any other industrialized nation (Singh & Darroch, 2000).

With teen pregnancy still an issue of deep concern, schools often depend on mental health staff to provide pregnancy prevention services. Programs numbering in the hundreds can be overwhelming to school-based practitioners with the responsibility to select a program that is effective and that fits with the school and the local community. Teen pregnancy and sex education remain controversial "hot topics," and programs vary in emphasis and content. When social workers and mental health services are competing for school and community resources, selecting or developing a pregnancy prevention program that demonstrates visible results is a priority.

This chapter explores school-based pregnancy prevention practices and programs currently in use in schools across the nation. It identifies programs and program components that have been evaluated and demonstrated effective in modifying adolescent sexual behavior and preventing adolescent pregnancy. It provides guidance for assessing program goodness-of-fit to the needs and values of the local school and community, and for planning and carrying out programs demonstrated effective in school settings. A bibliography of resources provides program specifics and contact information for locating programs that have been demonstrated to be effective.

What We Know

On a daily basis school-based mental health professionals witness the discouraging consequences of adolescent pregnancy for teenage parents and their children. Even though the national rate of adolescent pregnancy has diminished in the United States, the problem is still very real and present in American schools. At the forefront of concerns is the phenomenally high rate of school dropout among adolescent mothers. Across the nation, more than 60% of teen mothers who have a child before age 18 drop out of high school (National Campaign to Prevent Teen Pregnancy, 2002).

Not completing high school or a GED by the age of 20 is a heavy indicator of future poverty. Women who become mothers in adolescence, along with their children, are far more likely to live in poverty than women who postpone childbearing until their twenties. According to a National Campaign to Prevent Teen Pregnancy Fact Sheet (2002), virtually all of the increase in child poverty over the past two decades was related to the increase in nonmarital childbearing, half of which was to mothers who had their first child in their teens. Some 51% of all mothers on welfare had their first child as a teenager. About one fourth of teen mothers have a second child within 24 months of the first birth, further contributing to economic dependency and poverty (National Campaign to Prevent Teen Pregnancy, 2002).

The penalties for children born to teenage mothers are numerous and serious. They are more likely to be born prematurely and at low birth weight, leading to a number of chronic medical and developmental problems. They are 50% more likely to fall behind academically and less likely to graduate from high school (Haeman, Wolfe, & Peterson, 1997). Sons are 13% more likely to become involved with the law and to be incarcerated (Haeman, Wolfe, & Peterson, 1997). Daughters are 22% more likely to become teen mothers themselves (Terry & Manlove, 2000). They are more likely to be poor. These children are more restricted by developmental, economic, and social factors that limit their resources and life options than children born to mothers age 20 and older.

What We Can Do

Over the past two decades the number of adolescent pregnancy prevention programs has mushroomed into the hundreds, some focused on primary prevention and others on preventing subsequent pregnancies (Franklin & Corcoran, 2000). In this chapter we review programs in which the main goal is to prevent first-time pregnancies.

Program Categories and Emphasis

Pregnancy prevention programs can be categorized according to their distinctive features and special emphases. This chapter is concerned with school-based and school-linked programs where the school system takes primary responsibility. It is also helpful for school-based practitioners to be familiar with local community programs offered at social service agencies or in hospitals or clinics. The format and focus of programs that have been evaluated and demonstrated effective in changing sexual behavior and preventing pregnancy fall into three broad categories: (1) sex education with or without contraception, (2) youth development or life options programs, and (3) service learning programs (Manlove et al., 2004). Abstinence-only program goals can be found in all three of these categories, as well as program goals for reducing sexual behavior or risks related to sexual behavior. Another important distinction is whether *skill-building* is a central goal of the program (Franklin & Corcoran, 2000). Skills building has become an especially important component in the success of prevention programs, as discussed in the next sections.

Sex Education Programs

These programs focus on delaying (abstinence) or reducing sexual activity. They range from short courses of fewer than 10 hours to comprehensive courses of more than 40 hours. The focus of sex education prevention programs varies. Some programs include contraceptive information and distribution, while others exclude this content. Although a survey of school-based health clinics in the mid-1990s indicated that states and school districts are becoming more comfortable with programs that include contraception knowledge building (Schlitt et al., 1994), this can still be a controversial issue and should be researched in the local district before selecting a program. Regardless of contraception as a program feature, most sex education prevention programs contain these components:

1. Skills building, including decision making, interpersonal, and assertiveness
2. Values clarification
3. Relevant information provision
4. Peer education where teens can educate other teens
5. Youth theater projects where dramatic scenarios serve as catalysts for discussion
6. Computer-assisted instruction for parents and adolescents
7. Day-long conferences and training

Life Options/Youth Development Programs

Life options programs focus on changing sexual behaviors and reducing pregnancies through enhancing life skills and increasing options for disadvantaged youths (Philliber & Allen, 1992). The core assumption, based on research evidence (Afexentiou & Hawley, 1997; Allen, Philliber, Herrling, & Kuperminc, 1997), is that youths who have higher educational aspirations and greater opportunities are more likely to delay sexual intercourse and childbearing. Life options programs target teenagers' educational and earnings opportunities, such as postsecondary education, job training programs, and guaranteed student loans.

Youth development programs with a number of components that target both sexuality and youth development are demonstrated in a number of program evaluation studies to be the most effective interventions for pregnancy prevention (Kirby, 2001). For example, the Carrera Program, a multi-component program offered by the Children's Aid Society, was demonstrated to prevent pregnancies for as long as 3 years. This program includes interventions common to many youth development/life options programs that focus on sexuality as well as youth development, offered in combination over time. Core components of the Carrera program are (1) family life and sex education, (2) individual academic assessment and preparation for standardized tests and college prep exams, (3) tutoring, (4) self-expression activities through use of the arts, and (5) comprehensive health and mental health care (Manlove et al., 2004).

Most effective life options programs, such as the Carrera Program (Philliber, Williams Kaye, Herrling, & West, 2002) and the Quantum Opportunities Program (Taggart & Lattimore, 2001), include sexuality and sexual behavior as a focus. Skills building in all life domains, however, is the primary curricular theme. Here are some of the personal and social skills included in the developmental curriculum of the Quantum Opportunities Program (Manlove et al., 2004):

- Awareness skills focusing on building self-esteem, including strategies for coping with peer pressure, stereotyping, and prejudice
- Community skills, including how to use available resources such as public transportation, libraries, and clinics
- Decision-making skills focusing on issues such as dropping out of school, marriage, parenting, and attending college
- Health skills, including first aid and preventive care
- Relationship skills that help with communication abilities
- Safety skills, including discussions of risky behaviors related to alcohol, drugs, and sex

Target populations for youth development programs are male and female multiracial junior high and high school students, similar to target populations for other pregnancy prevention programs. A number of research studies have examined the effectiveness of life options/youth development programs in preventing pregnancy (e.g., Allen et al., 1997; Philliber, Williams Kaye, & Herrling, 2002), and the results are promising.

Service Learning Programs

Service learning is generally defined as curriculum-based community service that integrates classroom learning with community service activities (Denner, Coyle, Robin, & Banspach, 2005). As prevention programs that focus on positive decision making and enhanced self-awareness and self-worth rather than directly on sexuality, service learning programs show a great deal of promise. Programs that have been evaluated, such as the Teen Outreach Program (Philliber & Allen, 1992) and the Learn and Serve America program (Melchoir, 1998), were found effective in preventing pregnancy as well as other positive effects such as educational achievement and social attitudes and behavior. These programs require youth to volunteer in the community and to participate in journaling, group reflections, and classroom activities and discussions. Usually service learning is differentiated from community service alone in that service learning is organized in relation to a class with clearly stated objectives and classroom goals (Franklin & Corcoran, 2000). Across school districts service learning is the central intervention with a number of youth populations and prevention programs, such as dropout prevention and gang intervention and prevention (see chapter 50).

These are the primary program components of the Teen Outreach Program:

- Supervised volunteering. Students research agencies and services and select a volunteer opportunity in the community, such as peer tutoring or volunteering in a nursing home or hospital. Throughout the year they meet regularly with their volunteer supervisor and/or classroom facilitator around their experiences.
- Weekly classroom discussions and activities. Students share their volunteer experiences with one another, and lessons from the accompanying curriculum *Changing Scenes* are used to focus the discussion.

A classroom curriculum, *Changing Scenes*, is used throughout the program. These are some of the topics and lessons:

- A chapter on values includes a discussion in which students explore how they learn values and an activity that engages participants in exploring their beliefs about gender roles
- A chapter on relationships includes exercises and activities on making friends, romantic relationships, the difference between love and infatuation, and dealing with pressure in relationships
- A chapter on short-term and long-term personal goals includes activities on setting and achieving goals and looking at teen parenthood and some of the barriers it poses to achieving one's life goals

Characteristics of Effective Curriculum-Based Programs

We now recognize that effective programs exist in all three of the approaches and categories just discussed. Researcher-author Douglas Kirby (2001) identified characteristics of effective curriculum-based programs across all categories. These are in-common characteristics in programs that have been rigorously evaluated and found to increase the age of first sex, improve the use of contraception among sexually active teens, and/or actually reduce teen pregnancy. The following is a summary:

- They have a specific, narrow focus on *behavior*, such as delaying first sex or using contraception or condoms.
- They have theoretical approaches, such as cognitive behavior and planned behavior, that have been effective with other high-risk health-related behavior. These seek to impact the beliefs, attitudes, confidence, and skills that relate to sexual behavior, which may lead to voluntary change in sexual or contraceptive behavior.
- They give the clear message about sex and protection against STD that not having sex or using condoms or other contraception is the *right* thing to do, more than simply laying out the pros and cons of sexual choices.
- They provide basic, not detailed, information about contraception and unprotected sex.
- They address peer pressure related to sex and discuss misperceptions and "lines."
- They teach communication, negotiation, and refusal skills. Some provide clear scripts for role-playing situations on these issues.
- They include games, role playing, written exercises, videos, and small group discussions, all to help participants personalize the material. Some use peer facilitators and videos of people the students can identify with.
- They reflect the age, sexual experience, and culture of the youth participating. For example, curriculum for middle school adolescents focuses on postponing sexual intercourse, while for high schoolers, programs usually emphasize avoiding unprotected sex with abstinence or the use of contraception.
- The most effective programs last at least 14 hours or longer and have a greater number of different activities for participants.
- They are strident in carefully selecting leaders who believe in the program, and they provide leaders with training sessions that last from 6 hours to 3 days and include both information and practice in using the strategies and exercises in the curriculum.

Effective Programs Lists

Research determining the effectiveness of pregnancy prevention programs continues to accumulate. This section focuses on lists of programs that have been rigorously evaluated and found to be effective, compiled by four recognized groups associated with adolescent pregnancy and other youth-related issues (Solomon & Card, 2004). The programs included in these lists are believed to be credible because they are based on actual behavior changes among teens in a program compared to a group of similar youth who were not in the program. Because the groups used slightly different criteria for selecting effective programs, the lists are somewhat diverse. Some programs, however, were selected for inclusion in three or all four lists. This section includes a brief discussion of criteria considered in selecting programs for each list, as well as a list of nine programs (Table 28.1) that were included in at least three of the four lists (Solomon & Card, 2004).

- *The Kirby List* (Kirby, 2001). The programs included in this list met six key criteria: (1) The program outcome was the reduction of primary pregnancy and/or STD/HIV infection, (2) the primary target population was age 18 and younger, (3) the evaluation study used an experimental or quasi-experimental design, (4) the evaluation study had a sample of at least 100 in the combined treatment and comparison groups, (5) the evaluation study used outcome measures of behavior or health status (in addition or instead of attitude/knowledge outcome measures), and (6) appropriate statistical analysis was used in the evaluation study.
- *The Child Trends List* (Manlove, Terry-Humen, Papillo, Franzetta, Williams, & Ryan, 2001, 2002). Studies were reviewed that focused on primary pregnancy, secondary pregnancy, and/or STD/HIV prevention. Criteria included (1) a sample of youth of any age (no sample size restriction identified) and (2) evaluations with experimental design and reproductive health outcomes. Selected studies were required to measure outcomes during adolescence, regardless of whether the sample included adolescents or younger children.
- *The PASHA List 2002* (Solomon & Card, 2004; Card, Niego, Mallari, & Farrell, 1996).

The PASHA list is updated on an ongoing basis, most recently in 2002. Replication kits containing materials needed to operate and evaluate 28 programs on the list are available to practitioners through PASHA (see Bibliography of Resources in this chapter). To be considered for this list, a program must target youth ages 10–19, although STD/HIV prevention programs targeting college students are also eligible. Evaluation criteria include an experimental or quasi-experimental design and pretest and posttest assessments. A follow-up period of at least 6 months is required for pregnancy prevention programs. Program outcomes criteria include delay of initiation of intercourse, frequency of intercourse, number of sexual partners, contraceptive use, refusal or negotiation skills, values, and attitudes toward risk-taking behavior.

- *The Advocates List* (Advocates for Youth, 2003). This list of 19 programs is part of a report published by Advocates for Youth, entitled *Science and Success: Sex Education and Other Programs That Work to Prevent Teen Pregnancy*. The list includes only programs that focus on primary pregnancies and STD/HIV infection. Programs included for consideration meet these criteria: (1) target youth ranging from infancy to the teen years, (2) evaluation criteria include an experimental or quasi-experimental design with treatment and control/comparison conditions, (3) have a sample of at least 100 combined in treatment and control/comparison groups, (4) evaluation results must have been published in a peer-reviewed journal as a proxy for high-quality design and analysis, (5) programs must have had follow-up measures at least 3 months after completion of the intervention, and (6) must have had results in which two risky sexual behaviors showed significant positive change or demonstrated a significant reduction in pregnancy and/or STD/HIV rates.

Selecting a Program and Getting Started

School mental health practitioners know that simply having been demonstrated effective is not enough if a program does not fit the school, the community, and the target population of students. At the same time, altering the goals or content of an established and effective program in order to make it fit the needs of the local school is likely to diminish the program's effectiveness. These tips

Table 28.1 Programs Included in at Least Three Effective Program Lists

Name of Program	Kirby (2001)	Child Trends (2001, 2002)	PASHA (2002)	Advocates (2003)
Sex Education Approach				
Be Proud! Be Responsible!		*	*	*
Becoming a Responsible Teen	*	*	*	*
Making a Difference: An Abstinence Approach to STD, Teen Pregnancy, and HIV/AIDS Prevention	*		*	*
Making Proud Choices	*	*	*	*
Reducing the Risk	*	*		*
Safer Choices	*	*	*	*
Service Learning Approach				
Reach for Health Community Youth Sources				
Teen Outreach Program	*	*	*	*
Sex Education + Youth Development Approach	*	*		*
Children's Aid Society— Carrera Program	*	*	*	*

Source: Adapted from Solomon & Card, 2004.

can help guide the search for the best program for your particular school and community (Solomon and Card, 2004):

1. Talk with community members such as teachers, parents, local clergy and politicians, health care providers, and students, who have an investment in the program. Inquire about their preferences and values around teen pregnancy prevention, including their views on sex education and contraception. Use what you learn from these stakeholders to aim for programs that have been found effective in achieving *goals and objectives that are relevant and acceptable* to your school and community.

2. Engage with your school's administrators and interdisciplinary mental health team about initiating a prevention program, so that all of you have investment in its operation and success. Of prime consideration is the avail-

ability of resources such as space, staff, and especially funding.

3. Look for programs that were effective with youth who are as similar to your target group of students as possible. Some important characteristics are age, gender, ethnicity, acculturation, language, incarceration status, drug and alcohol use, and literacy level. All of these can influence participants' interest in the program and ability to benefit from it.

4. Once you have narrowed your program selections to two or three, determine which of these has replication kits or treatment manuals. It is far more difficult to present a program if the original program materials are not available in a user-friendly format. PASHA (http://www.socio.com/pasha.htm), for example, offers replication kits for 28 different programs and provides sources for nine additional programs that it identifies as effective.

Bibliography of Resources

Becoming a Responsible Teen
Curriculum & materials contact: Doug Kirby, Ph.D., Senior Research Scientist
4 Carbonero Way
Scotts Valley, CA 95066
Phone: 800-435-8433
FAX: 800-435-8433
E-mail: dougk@etr.org
http://www.etr.org

Be Proud! Be Responsible!
Curriculum & materials contact: Select Media Film Library, 22-D
Hollywood Avenue
Hohokus, NJ 07423
Phone: 800-343-3540
FAX: 201-652-1973
http://www.selectmedia.org

Making a Difference! An Abstinence-Based Approach to HIV/STD and Teen Pregnancy Prevention
Curriculum and materials contact: Select Media Film Library, 22-D
Hollywood Avenue
Hohokus, NJ 07423
Phone: 800-343-5540
FAX: 201-652-1973
http://www.selectmedia.org

Making Proud Choices
Curriculum and materials contact: Select Media Film Library, 22-D
Hollywood Avenue
Hohokus, NJ 07423
Phone: 800-343-5540
FAX: 201-652-1973
http://www.selectmedia.org

Children's Aid Society—Carrera Program
Curriculum and materials contact: Michael Carrera, Ed.D., Program Designer
The Children's Aid Society
105 East 22nd Street
New York, NY 10010
Phone: 212-876-9716
http://www.stopteenpregnancy.com

Teen Outreach Program
Program contact: Gayle Waden, TOP National Coordinator
One Greenway Plaza, Suite 550
Houston, TX 77046-0103

Phone: 713-627-2322
FAX: 713-627-3006
E-mail: gwaden@cornerstone.to
www.cornerstone.to

Note: Profiles of these and other programs, including goals, population, program size and duration, and curriculum, can be accessed on the Web site of the National Campaign to Prevent Teen Pregnancy (http://www.teenpregnancy.org).

Key Points to Remember

Although the United States has achieved a large reduction over the past decade, adolescent pregnancy and childbirth still looms large as a complex challenge for schools dealing with young parents. Teen pregnancy prevention programs are now available in nearly half of all American urban communities, with a large number in public schools. School-based mental health practitioners are often responsible for originating, selecting, and managing teen pregnancy prevention programs and services for students at risk in their schools. Fortunately, a substantial number of diverse programs have now been rigorously evaluated and found to be effective in postponing or diminishing adolescent sexual activity and pregnancy. Practitioners with the responsibility of selecting and establishing pregnancy prevention services in the school have many choices of effective programs that fit the needs, values, and resources of their school and community. This chapter has described three approaches to teen pregnancy prevention programs, including (1) curriculum-based sex education, (2) the youth development/life options approach, and (3) the service learning approach, with program examples of each approach.

References

Advocates for Youth. (2003). *Science and success: Sex education and other programs that work to prevent teen pregnancy, HIV, and sexually transmitted infections.* Washington, DC: Author. Accessed online November 12, 2004, at http://www.advocatesforyouth.org/publications/ScienceSuccess.pdf

Afexentiou, D., & Hawley, C. B. (1997). Explaining female teenagers' sexual behavior and outcomes: A bivariate probit analysis with selectivity correction. *Journal of Family and Economic Issues, 18*(1), 91–106.

Alan Guttmacher Institute. (2004). U.S. teenage pregnancy statistics: Overall trends, trends by race and ethnicity and state-by state information. Retrieved November 12, 2004, from www.guttmacher.org/pus/state_pregnancy_trends.pdf

Allen, J. P., Philliber, S., Herrling, S., & Kuperminc, G. P. (1997). Preventing teen pregnancy and academic failure: Experimental evaluation of a developmentally-based approach. *Child Development, 64*(4), 729–742.

Card, J. J., Niego, S., Mallari, A., & Farrell, W. S. (1996). Prevention programs in a box. *Family Planning Perspectives, 285,* 210–220. Retrieved on November 29, 2004, from www.agi-usa.org/pubs/journals/2821096.html

Child Trends. (2001). Retrieved on November 24, 2004, from http://www.childtrends.org/PDF/KnightReports/KRepro.pdf

Child Trends. (2002). Retrieved on November 27, 2004, from http://www.childtrends.org/PDF/KnightReports/KRepro.pdf

Denner, J., Coyle, K., Robin, L., & Banspach, S. (2005). Integrating service learning into a curriculum to reduce health risks at alternative high schools. *Journal of School Health, 75*(5), 151-157.

Franklin, C., & Corcoran, J. (2000). Preventing adolescent pregnancy: A review of programs and practices. *Social Work, 45*(1), 40–52.

Haeman, R. H., Wolfe, B., & Peterson, E. (1997). Children of early childbearers as young adults. In R. A. Maynard (Ed.), *Kids having kids: Economic costs and social consequences of teen pregnancy* (pp. 257–284). Washington, DC: Urban Institute Press.

Jindal, B. P. (2001). Report to House Committee on Ways and Means Subcommittee on Human Resources November 15. Washington, DC: U.S. Government.

Kirby, D. (2001). *Emerging answers: Research findings on programs to reduce teen pregnancy.* Washington, DC: National Campaign to Prevent Teen Pregnancy.

Manlove, J., Franzetta, K., McKinney, K., Papillo, A. R., & Terry-Humen, E. (2004). *A good time: After-school programs to reduce teen pregnancy.* National Campaign to Prevent Teen Pregnancy. Washington, DC: Author.

Manlove, J., Terry-Humen, E., Papillo, A. R., Franzetta, K., Williams, S., & Ryan, S. (2001). *Background for community-level work on positive reproductive health in adolescence: Reviewing the literature on contributing factors.* Washington, DC: Child Trends. Retrieved online November 23, 2004, at www.childtrends.org/PDF/KnightReports/KRepro.pdf

Manlove, J., Terry-Humen, E., Papillo, A. R., Franzetta, K., Williams, S., & Ryan, S. (2002). *Preventing teenage pregnancy, childbearing, and sexually transmitted diseases: What the research shows.* Washington, DC: Child Trends. Retrieved November 22, 2004, at www.childtrends.org/PDF/Knightreports/K1Brief.pdf

Melchoir, A. (1998). *National evaluation of learn and serve America school and community-based programs: Final report.* Abt Associates, Inc., Cambridge, MA; Brandeis University, Waltham, MA. Center for National Service.

National Campaign to Prevent Teen Pregnancy. (2002). *Teen pregnancy: Not just another single issue.* Washington, DC: Author.

National Campaign to Prevent Teen Pregnancy. (2004). *Fact sheet: How is the 34% statistic calculated?* Washington, DC: Author.

PASHA Programs Table. (2002). Accessed online at http:// www.socio.com/newpasha/pashatablebox1.htm

Philliber, S., & Allen, J. P. (1992). Life options and community service: Teen outreach program. In B. C. Miller, J. J. Card, R. L. Paikoff, & J. L. Peterson (Eds.), *Preventing adolescent pregnancy: Model programs and evaluations* (pp. 139–155). Newbury Park, CA: Sage.

Philliber, S., Williams Kaye, J., & Herrling, S. (2001). *The national evaluation of the Children's Aid Society Carrera-model program to prevent teen pregnancy.* Accord, NY: Philliber Research Associates.

Philliber, S., Williams Kaye, J., Herrling, S., & West, E. (2002). Preventing pregnancy and improving health care access among teenagers: An evaluation of the Children's Aid Society—Carrera program. *Perspectives on Sexual and Reproductive Health, 34*(5), 244–252.

Schlitt, J. J., Rickitt, K. D., Montgomery, L. L., & Lear, J. G. (1994). State initiatives to support school-based health centers: A national survey. Paper presented at NASW Annual Conference, Memphis.

Singh, S., & Darroch, J. E. (2000). Adolescent pregnancy and childbearing: Levels and trends in developed countries. *Family Planning Perspectives, 32*(1), 14–23.

Solomon, J., & Card, J. J. (2004). Making the list: Understanding, selecting, and replicating effective teen pregnancy prevention programs. Retrieved on November 23, 2004, from http://www.teenpregnancy.org

Taggart, R., & Lattimore, B. C. (2001). *Quantum opportunities program: A youth development program.* Los Altos, CA: Sociometrics.

Best School-Based Practices With Adolescent Parents

Mary Beth Harris

Getting Started

Despite the good news that teen pregnancy declined steadily during the 1990s, it remains that 34% of girls in the United States become pregnant at least once before they reach age 20 (National Campaign to Prevent Teen Pregnancy, 2004). Of these adolescents, more than 400,000 give birth every year (Henshaw, 2004). At some point, most of these young women are students in public schools, where school-based professionals face the daunting challenge of keeping them in school and helping them to navigate the heavy responsibilities of premature parenthood. These are some of the factors that make teen parents one of the most at-risk populations among American youth:

- They are significantly at risk for school dropout, with a dropout rate of 60% (National Campaign to Prevent Teen Pregnancy, 2002).
- They are more likely to become isolated and to be clinically depressed (Kalil, Spencer, Spieker, & Gilchrist, 1998).
- They are more likely than older mothers to have complications during pregnancy and less likely to receive prenatal care.
- Their children are significantly at risk for low birth weight, prematurity, developmental problems, insufficient health care, and school failure (Brooks-Gunn & Furstenberg, 1986; Maynard, 1997).
- They are likely to have family conflicts that limit support from their parents and the father or mother of their baby (Rhodes & Woods, 1995).
- As adults, they are more likely to live in poverty (Maynard, 1997; Moore et al., 1993).

Recent public policies such as TANF have restricted economic subsidies and services for mothers and children, creating further difficulties for this vulnerable population. Young mothers who formerly depended on public assistance and social services to help them transition into adulthood and secure postsecondary education or career training are now likely to have exhausted these benefits before they leave high school. Thus, preparing young parents for immediate and long-term economic self-sufficiency has become a critical task for school-based programs.

This chapter reviews methods and interventions that have been demonstrated to be effective in school settings with teen parents. We concentrate on interventions that target decision-making and behavioral skills to help young parents elude many of the associated risks identified above, graduate from high school, and ultimately become self-sufficient adults.

What We Know

Predictors of Life Outcomes for Adolescent Parents

According to Harris and Franklin (2002), adolescent parents face challenges in four domains that predict their immediate and long-term life outcomes: (1) education, (2) employment, (3) personal relationships, and (4) parenting. Studies show a high degree of interaction among these four for determining life quality and well-being. For example, evidence indicates that the more supportive a teen mother's relationships with friends and family, the more likely she is to achieve in school and to develop a career (Rhodes & Woods, 1995; Stramenga, 2003; Zupicich, 2003). In turn, the more education an adolescent parent achieves, the higher her employment income is likely to be as an adult (Sandfort & Hill, 1996). Although studies demonstrate the importance of each domain, *education* is the most immediate and well-researched predictor of long-term adjustment and economic status.

School Achievement

High school graduation or achieving a GED before age 20 may be the single strongest asset any youth can have to protect against poverty and other negative outcomes in later life (Fine, 1986; Sandfort & Hill, 1996). Thus, school dropout for teen parents may contribute to their at-risk status more than any other factor. Regular attendance and a reasonably age-appropriate grade level, which are major school-related issues for teen parents, are recognized as the most important predictors of whether a student will graduate from high school (Beck, 1991; Burdell, 1998; DeBolt, Pasley, & Kreutzer, 1990). Numerous studies (e.g., Osofsky, Osofsky, & Diamond, 1988; Olah, 1995) indicate that programs that focus on decision-making and behavioral skills that lead to improvement in attendance and grades, personal relationships, and general social competence are the most protective interventions that schools can offer for adolescents who become pregnant. Interventions related to school achievement and dropout prevention and recovery are supported by a sizable group of outcome studies (e.g., Larrivee & Bourque, 1991; Pearson and Banerji, 1993; Rodriguez, 1995; Vallarand, Fortier, & Guay, 1997), although these do not specifically address adolescent parents.

Alternative Schools of Choice

Programs and services for pregnant and parenting students (as well as other at-risk groups) in many urban school districts are located primarily in alternative schools. These programs are structured academically and provide such additional special courses as sex education, health, life planning, parenting, and job training (Franklin, 1992; Griffin, 1998; Zellman, 1981). Although alternative schools use a variety of models, one that appears to be effective for dropout prevention and retrieval with teen parents and other at-risk populations is a small *school of choice* (Franklin, 1992). The school of choice model offers flexible schedules and individualized, self-paced learning, both compatible with the needs of adolescent parents. Additionally, the school of choice model provides student support and advocacy for dealing with psychological, social, and educational barriers to learning and achievement. Although effective interventions specifically for adolescent parents may be more easily established and integrated in an alternative school setting than in a traditional middle or high school, interventions with this population are now demonstrated effective in both traditional and alternative school settings (e.g., Fischer, 1997; Griffin, 1998; Harris & Franklin, 2002).

What We Can Do

A Cognitive-Behavioral Approach

Skills-building interventions with a cognitive-behavioral foundation are gaining strong support in schools for helping adolescents with a number of problems. Curriculums that engage youth in processing logical consequences of behavior and developing mastery of general and specific life skills have been reported effective with adolescent issues such as school dropout, pregnancy prevention, adolescent parenting, drug and alcohol addiction, problem school behavior, childhood sexual abuse, and depression (e.g., Barth, 1989; Clarke, 1992; Coren, Barlow, & Stewart-Brown, 2003; Dupper, 1998; Franklin & Corcoran, 1999; Harris & Franklin, 2002; Hogue & Liddle, 1999; McWhirter & Page, 1999). Growing evidence that this approach is effective in a number of areas with pregnant and parenting adolescents (e.g., Codega, Pasley, & Kreutzer, 1990; Harris & Franklin, 2002) endorses the use of such skills-building intervention in school programs.

Conditions and Goals of Skills-Based Programs

Skills-based interventions with a cognitive-behavior foundation contain a set of four conditions found to be effective in the mastery of new skills (Hogue & Liddle, 1999):

1. The practitioner models the skill in session.
2. The adolescent role plays and practices the skill in session.
3. The adolescent is assigned homework to continue practicing the skill.
4. The practitioner debriefs the adolescents about their success in practicing the skill and adjusts skills training to accommodate learning differences.

These interventions appear to be most effective with adolescents when they promote a sense of social support, competence, and self-efficacy. Enhancing internal *locus of control*—the youth's sense that he, rather than forces outside himself, determines the conditions of his life—is often a goal, as well (e.g., McWhirter & Page, 1999; Rice & Meyer, 1994). Specific, *task-related* homework assignments that give the adolescent a chance to practice identified skills, as well as *peer support and feedback*, appear to be effective in reinforcing these personal assets.

A cognitive-behavioral approach seeks to strengthen individual skills such as *coping with stress, problem solving*, and *goal setting* (e.g., Dupper, 1998; Rice & Meyer, 1994). Some interventions target skills specifically related to school achievement, personal relationships, health, and employment (e.g., Griffin, 1998; Harris & Franklin, 2002; Jemmont, Jemmont, Fong, & McCaffree, 1999), which are recognized protectors against the risks associated with teen pregnancy.

Coping Skills

Adolescents cope with stress in a variety of ways: (1) active, problem-focused strategies, (2) emotional adjustment and acceptance, and (3) avoidance and other passive responses (Olah, 1995; Stern & Alvarez, 1992; Stern & Zevon, 1990). Zeidner and Hammer's (1990) study with teens suggests that the type of coping they use may be more important to resolving stressful situations than the severity or frequency of the stressor. Active, problem-focused coping, found to be more effective in achieving positive outcomes than emotion-focused coping and avoidance (Aspinwall & Taylor, 1992; Zeidner & Hammer, 1990), is often a skill targeted with at-risk adolescents (e.g., Harris & Franklin, 2002). For example, young parents with a tendency to use active, problem-solving coping behaviors are shown repeatedly to experience less stress and to show greater accep-

tance, warmth, and helpfulness and less disapproval with their children (Colletta & Gregg, 1981; Passino et al., 1993). Even so, studies comparing pregnant to nonpregnant teens show that pregnant teens generally use less active coping than nonpregnant teens and identify avoidance or emotion-focused coping as their most frequent strategies (Passino et al., 1993; Codega, Pasley, & Kreutzer, 1990). Thus, increasing problem-focused coping is an important goal for a skills-based intervention with teen parents.

Social Problem-Solving Skills

Social problem-solving skills are defined as a set of specific attitudes, behaviors, and skills directed toward solving a particular real-life problem in a social context (D'Zurilla, 1986). They include these tasks:

1. Defining and formulating the problem
2. Generating a list of possible solutions
3. Selecting the solution with the best chance to succeed
4. Carrying out the solution strategies
5. Evaluating the outcome

Social problem-solving skills are recognized to strengthen a person's sense of self-efficacy and mastery over one's environment (Bandura, 1999). Although these assets are vital for pregnant and parenting adolescents, research suggests that these youths are less skilled in problem-solving than their nonpregnant peers (Passino et al., 1993). We conclude that problem-solving skills are a vital target for intervention with teen parents.

Task-Centered Group Modality

With few exceptions, effective skills-based interventions with adolescents are conducted in a group (Glodich & Allen, 1998; e.g., de Anda & Becerra, 1984; Harris & Franklin, 2002; Dupper, 1998). The isolation and need for peer contact and support that often accompany adolescent pregnancy make a group context especially relevant for these youth. Participant focus groups in our outcome studies with young mothers have consistently emphasized that being in a group with other pregnant and parenting students was one of the most important aspects of the intervention (Harris & Franklin, 2004).

We recommend a *task-centered group model* for skills-based intervention with teen parents. This is a form of short-term, goal-oriented treatment in which the client carries out actions or tasks between sessions to alleviate their problems (Reid, 1996). A task-centered group is relatively structured and provides a ready format for skills-based interventions. Over 30 studies have evaluated the effectiveness of task-centered modality, including studies of children with academic problems and adolescents in academic and residential treatment settings (Reid, 1996).

Six to eight members is thought to be the ideal size for a task-centered group, although there is evidence that groups with up to 12 members can also be effective (e.g., Harris & Franklin, 2002). Characteristics such as participants' ages and literacy skills should be considered in determining group size. Two group leaders are considered ideal with this model, although a group can be led by one facilitator when necessary.

Tools and Practice Examples

Taking Charge: A Skills-Building Group for Pregnant and Parenting Adolescents

Taking Charge is a task-centered group curriculum for adolescent parents that incorporates the skills-building components and goals discussed in this chapter. Outcome studies in alternative and traditional high schools (Harris & Franklin, 2002; Harris & Franklin, 2004, in review) have demonstrated the Taking Charge curriculum to be effective in achieving these benefits with pregnant and parenting adolescent mothers:

1. School attendance and grades significantly improved.
2. Problem-solving skills significantly improved.
3. Active, problem-focused coping increased significantly.

Using the Social Problem-Solving Process in Four Life Domains

The Taking Charge program is presented in eight sessions, during which participants learn and apply

Box 29.1 Ways That Task-Centered Groups Fit the Needs of Adolescent Parents

- *Targets client's abilities.* More than some therapeutic models, task-centered intervention stresses the adolescent's abilities to identify goals and carry through with actions to obtain what she wants. The adolescent parent is assumed to have a mind and a will that are not bound by her age, past experiences, or environment.
- *Focuses on the present.* Task-centered intervention does not attempt to deal with historical origins of the client's problem but rather supports her in achieving its resolution.
- *Short-term.* Most task-centered groups are presented in 6 to 12 weeks. Short-term interventions are more likely than longer ones to meet program goals within the limited window of access to young parents.
- *Similarity of group members on target problems.* Task-centered groups are best processed when all group members are familiar with the kind of problems others are experiencing and can engage in and benefit from one another's process.

the social problem-solving process (D'Zurilla & Nezu, 1982) to four important areas of their lives: school achievement, personal relationships, parenting, and career. After learning and practicing the steps, participants use this process during the next sessions to identify and set goals for resolving or mastering problems in each of these areas of their own lives.

These are the steps of the social problem-solving process:

1. Identify a problem that is a real barrier to me in this part of my life.
2. Identify the smaller problems that support this big problem.
3. Describe my goal for resolving this problem.
4. Identify barriers that may happen to keep me from reaching my goal.
5. Name the resources I have that can help me reach my goal.
6. List as many possible strategies as I can to help me reach my goal.
7. Pick a strategy from these that I believe has the best chance to succeed.

8. Decide on two tasks I can do immediately to carry out my strategy.
9. Now . . . JUST DO IT!

Brenda: An Example of the Problem-Solving Process

Brenda, age 16, was a high school junior and the mother of a 3-month-old son. She lived with her 19-year-old boyfriend and his parents. She had lived with the family for 5 months, since before the birth of her baby. Brenda's problem-solving process is set out in Box 29.2.

Tasks Provide Practice for New Behavior

For each goal they set, group members identify two tasks that are achievable in the week between group sessions. They work with a *"this is my task"* form that guides them through identifying the task and planning how they will carry it out. Some examples of tasks that commonly appear in Taking Charge groups are these:

- Meet with my guidance counselor about my (credits, schedule, career plan, etc.).
- Talk to my (math, science, etc.) teacher about my (grade, exam, attitude, etc.).
- Talk to my boyfriend about (help with baby costs, more time together, etc.).
- Spend at least (1 hour, etc.) on homework every day this week.
- Make an appointment to (take baby for shots, apply for food stamps, etc.).

Leaders guide participants in identifying tasks by asking questions and referring to the participants' goal and strategies. They may also help participants rehearse or role-play the task in session.

Incentives Reinforce New Behavior

To ensure that members receive the greatest benefit from Taking Charge, incentives are built into the group. For example, since food is an important incentive for adolescents and Taking Charge groups often meet during the lunch period, serving lunch during group meetings is one incentive. A snack is served in groups that meet at other times. The lunch or snack is ready to eat immediately when participants arrive.

Box 29.2 My Personal Relationship Goal

1. MY PROBLEM: My mother-in-law and I don't get along. She's cold to me and criticizes the way I look and dress, how I cook, and especially the way I take care of my baby.
2. SMALLER PROBLEMS: My boyfriend won't stand up to her. I think he's afraid of her. Neither does my father-in-law, even though I get along fine with him. She takes care of my baby while I'm at school, so she's with him as much as I am. My boyfriend is in welding school and only makes minimum wage 20 hours a week at his job, so we're (financially) dependent on his parents for another year. I don't have a car, so she has to take me to appointments for the baby.
3. MY GOAL: For my mother-in-law to like me better and stop criticizing me so much.
4. POSSIBLE BARRIERS: If I try to change anything between us, it may make things worse. I'm scared of her and try to stay away from her. I don't know how to talk to her. I don't like her at all.
5. MY RESOURCES: My boyfriend loves me and wants me to stay. Another resource is my cousin, who's a probation officer. She tries to help me understand my mother-in-law better. Another is my boyfriend's sister, who is cool with me when she drops by, and tells me to ignore my mother-in-law.
6. POSSIBLE STRATEGIES: (1) Confront my mother-in-law and threaten to move out if she doesn't change. (2) Go out of my way to please her without talking about it. (3) Get to know her better. (4) Clear the air with her to find out what I can do to make things better between us. (5) Take my baby and move back to my mother's house.
7. I CHOOSE: The strategy of clearing the air with my mother-in-law and finding out how I can make things better between us.
8. MY FIRST TASK: To talk to my boyfriend's sister about my goal and get her advice on how to talk to her mother. MY SECOND TASK: To tell my mother-in-law that I want to have a good relationship with her and ask her what I can do to help that happen.

A points system is an incentive that allows group members to earn an award at the end of Taking Charge. Points are given for group and school attendance, homework, extra credit assignments, and tasks. Awards are items of particular value to participants, such as gift certificates from a favorite store. Leaders inform the group about the points system at the first session and document points each week.

At two of the eight group sessions participants receive small gifts such as personal grooming items or pizza coupons as they are about to leave the session. In order to maintain this as an incentive for group attendance, the gift is given only to those who attend the sessions at which the gifts are presented.

Implementing Taking Charge

Even though school-based clinical trials tell us that the Taking Charge curriculum is an effective intervention with adolescent mothers, the ultimate question for school professionals is how easily such a curriculum might be implemented in their school. Anyone working in a school setting knows that there are many things to consider when selecting and implementing social service and mental health programs—How will it impact budget and staff resources? Is it controversial? Is it compatible with the school's educational goals? Will the school staff support it?

Here are some important aspects of this group curriculum to consider when deciding on interventions with pregnant and parenting students.

- In the largest clinical study of the group, the group of young women who participated in the Taking Charge curriculum gained an *eight-point advantage in their GPA* during the semester over an equivalent group who did not participate in the group. The Taking Charge participant group also *increased in school attendance from 79% to 91%*, while the nonparticipants made no gains in attendance.
- A curriculum treatment manual makes it feasible for Taking Charge to be facilitated by volunteers or student interns. The curriculum is compatible with the professional training of school mental health staff, who need only minimal training to supervise volunteer leaders or to facilitate the group.
- The average cost to present the Taking Charge group is $15 to $20 per participant for incentives, in addition to minimal supplies such as paper and folders. In previous Taking Charge studies, lunch or snacks were provided by the school and occasionally donated by local restaurants and businesses.
- In some schools, awards were created using the resources of the school or community that did not involve an outlay of cash. At one school, participants who earned the highest award, and their babies, were treated to a field trip to the city zoo, with school bus transportation and picnic lunches provided by the school cafeteria. At another school, leaders arranged for award recipients to receive manicures and hair styles at a school of cosmetology. In both instances, the alternative award was received enthusiastically by group participants.
- Although the Taking Charge curriculum is not gender-specific for adolescent parents, it has only been studied with young mothers. We cannot assume that it would be as effective with young fathers as with young mothers, although similar developmental needs and societal expectations for young mothers and young fathers suggest that the curriculum may be effective for skills building with young fathers.
- To gain sufficient mastery of the Taking Charge curriculum, we recommend that leaders spend a few hours reviewing and discussing the treatment manual, perhaps with an experienced practitioner or supervisor. Leaders report that they needed to work through the problem-solving process several times with real problems of their own before they felt prepared to help group participants with that process. The extent of training should be determined by the previous training and experience of the leaders.
- The Taking Charge treatment manual is included in a book on the intervention, currently in review with Oxford University Press. Publication is anticipated in late 2005.

Key Points to Remember

Pregnant and parenting adolescents continue to be an at-risk population in schools. With a 60% dropout rate, they are far less likely than their peers to graduate from high school, and they and their children are more likely to live in poverty than parents who delay pregnancy beyond adolescence.

Skills-based interventions that include problem-solving and coping skills have been found effective in school programs with other adolescent problems, such as drugs and alcohol, school dropout, and antisocial behavior. Such interventions are gaining support as effective with teen parents. In this chapter we have examined the foundations of a cognitive-behavioral skills-based approach, as well as the compatibility of using a task-centered group for skills-building interventions. We explored the Taking Charge curriculum, a group intervention for helping adolescent mothers to achieve coping and problem-solving skills toward graduating from high school and becoming more competent parents and self-sufficient adults.

References

Aspinwall, L. G., & Taylor, S. E. (1992). Modeling cognitive adaptation: A longitudinal investigation of the impact of individual differences and coping on college adjustment and performance. *Journal of Personality and Social Psychology, 63,* 989–1003.

Bandura, A. (1999). A social cognitive theory of personality. In L. Pervin & O. John (Eds.), *Handbook of personality* (2nd ed., pp. 154–196). New York: Guilford Press.

Barth, R. P. (1989). *Reducing the risk: Building skills to prevent pregnancy.* Santa Cruz, CA: ETR Associates/Network Publications.

Beck, M. S. (1991). *Increasing school completion: Strategies that work* (Monographs in Education No. 13). Athens, GA: University of Georgia College of Education.

Brooks-Gunn, J., & Furstenberg, F. F., Jr. (1986). The children of adolescent mothers: Physical, academic, and psychological outcomes. *Developmental Review, 6,* 224–251.

Burdell, P. (1998). Young mothers as high school students: Moving toward a new century. *Education and Urban Society, 30*(2), 202–223.

Clarke, G. (1992). Cognitive-behavioral group treatment of adolescent depression: Prediction of outcome. *Behavior Therapy, 23,* 341–354.

Codega, S. A., Pasley, B. K., & Kreutzer, J. (1990). Coping behaviors of adolescent mothers: An exploratory study and comparison of Mexican-Americans and Anglos. *Journal of Adolescent Research, 5*(1), 34–53.

Colletta, N. D., & Gregg, C. H. (1981). Adolescent mothers' vulnerability to stress. *Journal of Nervous and Mental Disorders, 169,* 50–54.

Coren, E., Barlow, J., & Stewart-Brown, S. (2003). The effectiveness of individual and group-based parenting programmes in improving outcomes for teenage mothers and their children: A systematic review. *Journal of Adolescence, 26*(1), 79–103.

de Anda, D., & Becerra, R. M. (1984). Social networks for adolescent mothers. *Social Casework: The Journal of Contemporary Social Work, 65,* 172–181.

DeBolt, M. E., Pasley, B. K., & Kreutzer, J. (1990). Factors affecting the probability of school dropout: A study of pregnant and parenting adolescent females. *Journal of Adolescent Research, 5*(3), 190–205.

Dupper, D. R. (1998). An alternative to suspension for middle school youths with behavior problems: Findings from a "school survival" group. *Research on Social Work Practice, 8*(3), 354–366.

D'Zurilla, T. J. (1986). *Problem-solving therapy: A social competence approach to clinical intervention.* New York: Springer.

D'Zurilla, T. J., & Nezu, A. (1982). Social problem-solving in adults. In P. C. Kendall (Ed.), *Advances in cognitive-behavioral research and therapy* (pp. 202–269). New York: Academic Press.

Fine, M. (1986). Why urban adolescents drop into and out of public high school. *Teachers College Record, 87,* 392–409.

Fischer, R. L. (1997). Evaluating the delivery of a teen pregnancy and parenting program across two settings. *Research on Social Work Practice, 7*(3), 350–369.

Franklin, C. (1992). Alternative school programs for at-risk youth. *Social Work in Education, 14*(4), 239–251.

Franklin, C., & Corcoran, J. (1999). Preventing adolescent pregnancy: A review of programs and practices. *Social Work in Health Care, 45*(1), 40–52.

Glodich, A., & Allen, J. G. (1998). Adolescents exposed to violence and abuse: A review of the group therapy literature with an emphasis on preventing trauma reenactment. *Journal of Child and Adolescent Group Therapy, 8*(3), 135–153.

Griffin, N. C. (1998). Cultivating self-efficacy in adolescent mothers: A collaborative approach. *Professional School Counseling, 1*(4), 53–58.

Harris, M. B., & Franklin, C. (2002). Effectiveness of a cognitive-behavioral group intervention with Mexican American adolescent mothers. *Social Work Research, 17*(2), 71–83.

Harris, M. B., & Franklin, C. (2004). *Taking charge: A skills-based group intervention for adolescent mothers.* Manuscript in review. New York: Oxford University Press.

Henshaw, S. K. (2004). *U.S. teenage pregnancy statistics with comparative statistics for women aged 20–24.* New York: Alan Guttmacher Institute.

Hogue, A., & Liddle, H. A. (1999). Family-based preventive intervention: An approach to preventing substance abuse and antisocial behavior. *American Journal of Orthopsychiatry, 69,* 275–293.

Jemmont, J. B., Jemmont, L. S., Fong, G. T., & McCaffree, K. (1999). Reducing HIV risk-associated sexual behavior among African American adolescents: Testing the generality of intervention effects. *American Journal of Community Psychology, 27*(2), 161–187.

Kalil, A., Spencer, M. S., Spieker, S. J., & Gilchrist, L. D. (1998). Effects of grandmother coresidence and quality of family relationships on depressive symptoms in adolescent mothers. *Family Relations: Interdisciplinary Journal of Applied Family Studies, 47*(4), 433–441.

Larrivee, B., & Bourque, M. L. (1991). The impact of several dropout prevention intervention strategies on at-risk students. *Education, 112*, 48–63.

Maynard, R. A. (Ed.). (1997). Kids having kids: Economic costs and social consequences of teen pregnancy. Washington, DC: Urban Institute Press.

McWhirter, B. T., & Page, G. L. (1999). Effects of anger management and goal setting group interventions on state-trait anger and self-efficacy beliefs among high risk adolescents. *Current Psychology: Developmental, Learning, Personality, Social, 18*(2), 223–237.

Moore, K. A., Myers, D. E., Morrison, D. R., Nord, C. W., Brown, B. V., & Edmonston, B. (1993). The age of childbirth and later poverty. *Journal of Research on Adolescence, 3*(4), 393–422.

National Campaign to Prevent Teen Pregnancy. (2002). *Teen pregnancy: Not just another single issue.* Washington, DC: Author.

National Campaign to Prevent Teen Pregnancy. (2004). *Fact sheet: How is the 34% statistic calculated?* Washington, DC: Author.

Olah, A. (1995). Coping strategies among adolescents: A cross-cultural study. *Journal of Adolescence, 18*(4), 491–512.

Osofsky, J. D., Osofsky, H. J., & Diamond, M. O. (1988). The transition to parenthood: Special tasks and risk factors for adolescent parents. In G. Y. Michaels & W. A. Goldberg (Eds.), *The transition to parenthood: Current theory and research* (pp. 209–232). New York: Cambridge University Press.

Passino, A. W., Whitman, T. L., Borkowski, J. G., Schellenbach, C. J., Maxwell, S. E., & Keogh, D. R. (1993). Personal adjustment during pregnancy and adolescent parenting. *Adolescence, 28*(109), 97–123.

Pearson, L. C., & Banerji, M. (1993). Effects of a ninth-grade dropout prevention program on student academic achievement, school attendance, and dropout rate. *Journal of Experimental Education, 61*(Spring), 247–256.

Reid, W. J. (1996). Task-centered social work. In Francis J. Turner (Ed.), *Social work treatment: Interlocking theoretical approaches* (4th ed., pp. 617–640). New York: Free Press.

Rhodes, J. E., & Woods, M. (1995). Comfort and conflict in relationships of pregnant, minority adolescents: Social support as a moderator of social strain. *Journal of Community Psychology, 23*, 74–84.

Rice, K. G. & Meyer, A. L. (1994). Preventing depression among young adolescents: Preliminary process results of a psycho-educational intervention program. *Journal of Counseling and Development, 73*, 145–152.

Rodriguez, R. (1995). Latino educators devise sure-fire K–12 dropout prevention programs. *Black Issues of Higher Education, 12*, 35–37.

Sandfort, J. R., & Hill, M. S. (1996). Assisting young unmarried mothers to become self-sufficient: The effects of different types of early economic support. *Journal of Marriage and the Family, 58*(2), 311–326.

Stern, M., & Alvarez, A. (1992). Pregnant and parenting adolescents: A comparative analysis of coping response and psychosocial adjustment. *Journal of Adolescent Research, 7*(4), 469–493.

Stern, M., & Zevon, M. A. (1990). Stress, coping, and family environment: The adolescent's response to naturally occurring stressors. *Journal of Adolescent Research, 7*(4), 290–305.

Stramenga, M. S. (2003). The role of developmental and relational factors in the career decision-making process of adolescent mothers. *Dissertation Abstracts International: Section B: The Sciences and Engineering,* Vol. 64(6-B), 2962.

Vallarand, R. J., Fortier, M. S., & Guay, F. (1997). Psychosocial mechanisms underlying quality of parenting among Mexican-American and White adolescent mothers. *Journal of Personality and Social Psychology, 72*(5), 1161–1176.

Zeidner, M., & Hammer, A. L. (1990). Life events and coping resources as predictors of stress symptoms in adolescents. *Personality and Individual Differences, 11*, 693–703.

Zellman, G. L. (1981). *The response of the schools to teenage pregnancy and parenthood.* Santa Monica, CA: Rand.

Zupicich, S. (2003). Understanding social supportive processes among adolescent mothers. *Dissertation Abstracts International Section A: Humanities and Social Sciences,* Vol. 63(11-A), 3869.

Effective Management of Obesity for School Children

Reshma B. Naidoo

Getting Started

The incidence and prevalence of obesity in the United States has increased rapidly since the 1980s. It is estimated that approximately 64.5% of the U.S. population is overweight, with 30.5% being obese (Ogden, Flegal, Carroll, & Johnson, 2002). Current estimates indicate that 15% of school-aged children are obese (National Center for Health Statistics, 1999; Flegal, Carroll, Ogden, & Johnson, 2002). This increase in obesity has been attributed to a lack of physical activity combined with unhealthy eating patterns.

Overweight children are more likely to become overweight adolescents; who in turn are more likely to become overweight adults (Dietz, 1991; Serdula et al., 1993). Overweight and obese individuals are at increased risk for several significant health and psychosocial problems (see Table 30.1) (Epstein, Wisniewski, & Weng, 1994). Given the range of problems experienced by obese individuals, effective management of obesity in a school-aged population has to be addressed across multiple environments that include the home and school.

Body mass index (BMI) is a commonly used indicator of obesity in which weight (in kilograms) is divided by height (in meters) squared. A BMI of 25 or greater is defined as overweight and a BMI of 30 or greater is defined as obese (Bellizzi & Dietz, 1999).

What We Know

Almost all children are enrolled in schools giving us the best opportunity to introduce obesity management and prevention programs that can affect the long-term health and well-being of children. Teaching children effective ways to control their weight provides them with a foundation that they can use to maintain healthy body weights into adulthood. Furthermore, school-based programs have the potential to affect behaviors that track into adulthood (Lytle, Kelder, Perry, & Klepp, 1995).

Most school-based programs have focused on obesity prevention and weight control (Gortmaker et al., 1999; CATCH, 2003; Cheung, Gortmaker, & Dart, 2001; Carter, Wiecha, Peterson, & Gortmaker, 2001). There is a paucity of evidence-based obesity management programs or guidelines for children (Barlow & Dietz, 1998). Consequently, a consensual agreement between experts in the field resulted in the development of a list of guidelines for obesity management programs at schools (Barlow & Dietz, 1998). The major emphases of these guidelines are presented in Table 30.2.

There are several good school-based interventions that focus on decreasing the major identified risk factors for obesity and fostering a healthy lifestyle such as *CATCH* (CATCH, 2003), *Eat Well and Keep Moving* (Cheung, Gortmaker, & Dart, 2001), and *Planet Health* (Carter, Wiecha, Peterson, & Gortmaker, 2001). The goal of these programs is to teach children healthy lifestyle habits. They focus on reducing obesity, increasing physical activity, and fostering positive dietary habits. Programs range from 8 weeks to several school years in duration. However, there is a paucity of school-based individual and/or small group programs that address the treatment and interventions of obesity management. A structured school-based weight loss program would help the child to decrease his/her percentage overweight by fostering a healthy lifestyle. The advantage of a school-based program is that children are (a) able

Table 30.1 Health and Psychosocial Problems Associated With Obesity

Psychosocial Problems		*Health Problems*	
Victims of bullying	Depression	Coronary heart disease	Cancers
Lower social status	Psychosocial ailments	High blood pressure	Gallbladder disease
Poorer self-esteem	Loneliness	Angina pectoris	Stroke
Young adult eating disorders		Congestive heart failure	
Reduced quality of life		High blood cholesterol	Gout
Distorted body image		Type II diabetes Hyperinsulinemia Insulin resistance	Eye disorders Osteoarthritis Sleep apnea or sleep disorders
		Glucose intolerance Poor reproductive health Bladder control problems (stress incontinence)	

Source: Table 30.1 was compiled by synthesizing information from several sources that included Epstein, L. H., Wisniewski, L., & Weng, R. (1994). Child and parent psychological problems influence child weight control. *Obesity Research, 2,* 509–515. National Institutes of Health (1998). *Clinical guidelines on the identification, evaluation, and treatment of overweight and obesity in adults.* Bethesda, MD: Department of Health and Human Services, National Institutes of Health, National Heart, Lung, and Blood Institute. Stunkard, A. J., & Wadden, T. A. (Eds.). 1993. *Obesity: Theory and therapy* (2nd ed.). New York: Raven Press.

to lose weight and (b) maintain their weight loss into adulthood (Knip & Nuutinen, 1993). Furthermore, children who have been placed on weight loss programs are better at keeping the weight off compared to adults, even 10 years after the completion of the weight loss program (Epstein, Valoski, Wing, & McCurley, 1994; Epstein, Valoski, Kalarchian, & McCurley, 1995).

Although there has been considerable research into treatment programs since the 1970s, there is no structured school-based obesity management intervention. This intervention is based on the best practices driven by research in the field. Major research findings used to develop this program are summarized in Table 30.3.

What We Can Do

The Obesity Management Program (OMP) is a school-based weight loss and behavioral modification program for overweight and obese individuals. The OMP is an individual therapy, and the school-based segment can be modified for groups. This multipronged program focuses on developing a healthy lifestyle that facilitates weight loss. Skills are introduced gradually over a 14-week period (see Table 30.4) and are reinforced at home and school until the child/adolescent is able to practice them without assistance. The success of the program depends upon a home–school

Table 30.2 Goals for Treating Childhood Obesity

- Dietary modifications
  - Reduce intake of dietary fat
  - Increase the intake of fruits and vegetables
  - Decrease soda consumption
- Increase physical activity
- Decrease television, computer, and video game time

Source: Information extracted from Barlow, S. E., & Dietz, W. H. (1998). Obesity evaluation and treatment: Expert committee recommendations. *Pediatrics, 102,* p. E29. Retrieved November 2004 from http://www.pediatrics.org/cgi/content/full/102/3/e29

Table 30.3 Well-Established Treatments and Supporting Studies

Established Treatment Modality	Supporting Studies
Children-centered programs have long-term benefits	Epstein, Valoski, Kalarchian, et al., 1995. Epstein, Valoski, Wing, & McCurley, 1994; Epstein, Valoski, Kalarchian, & McCurley, 1995; Knip & Nuutinen, 1993; Lytle, Kelder, Perry, & Klepp, 1995
Increased lifestyle activity is more efficacious and enduring than structured exercise programs	Epstein, Wing, Koeske, Ossip, & Beck, 1982; Epstein, Valoski, Wing, & McCurley, 1994
Gradually scheduled programs provide more support for behavior modification programs	Senediak & Spence, 1985; Rees, 1990
Rewards for increasing desired or decreasing undesired behaviors are more effective reinforcers than punishment or disincentives	Coates, Jeffery, Slinkard, Killen, & Danaher, 1982; Epstein, Valoski, et al., 1995
Multimodal treatment strategies that include the family and school are more effective than unitary programs	Brownell, Kelman, & Stunkard, 1983; Epstein, Wing, Koeske, Andrasik, & Ossip, 1981; Epstein et al., 1980; Epstein, Valoski, Wing, & McCurley, 1990; CATCH, 2003; Cheung, Gortmaker, & Dart, 2001; Carter, Wiecha, Peterson, & Gortmaker, 2001; Gortmaker et al., 1999; Lytle, Kelder, Perry & Klepp, 1995
Systemic approach to behavior modification	Goetz & Caron, 1999; Raue, Castonguay, & Goldfried, 1993; Golan, Weizman, Apter, & Fainaru, 1998
Mentoring and support	Buckley & Zimmermann, 2003
24-hour recall records	Baxter & Thompson, 2002; Armstrong et al., 2000.

collaboration and requires active involvement of the family. Homework is assigned at the end of each weekly session to reinforce and practice new skills. Practicing skills and the completion of homework is essential for the success of the program.

Tools and Practice Examples

Practice Examples

Lisa had entered the sixth grade at middle school. After the first 6 weeks, Ms. Halferty, her homeroom teacher, noticed that although Lisa was making adequate academic progress, maintaining an A/B average, she had difficulty adjusting to middle school. Lisa had low self-esteem, was very self-conscious, and often sat by herself. Ms. Halferty was concerned about Lisa's isolation from her peers and attributed Lisa's social difficulties to her obesity. Lisa had always been on the heavy side, but her weight gain had accelerated in the fourth grade. She weighed 160 pounds and was 5 feet 1 inch tall at the time of this referral.

Lisa lived with her parents and her 10-year-old brother in a suburban neighborhood. Both of her parents had full-time jobs. Since Lisa and her brother were not allowed to play outside for safety reasons, they completed their homework and then watched television until their parents' return.

Table 30.4 Obesity Management Program: Weekly Goals

Week	Objective
Week 1 *Town meeting*	1. Establishing a family–child–school collaboration in weight management a. Rationale for program b. The role of the family–school collaboration c. Overview of the program, duration, and procedure d. Cost of the program e. Family commitment and contract • U.S. obesity trends 1985 to 2002 are available at: http://www.cdc.gov/nccdphp/dnpa/obesity/trend/maps/index.htm. • Parent handout: *Obesity in children: A prevention guide for parents* available at: www.nasponline.org/pdf/Obesity.pdf • Parent handout: *Obesity in children and teens:* A parent information sheet available at: http://www.aacap.org/publications/factsfam/79.htm
Week 2 *Getting started*	1. Outlining the program with the child 2. Establishing baselines 3. Completing forms 4. Homework—completion of daily record sheets for the week • BMI calculators are available at: www.cdc.gov/nccdphp/dnpa/bmi/calc-bmi.htm
Week 3 *On your marks . . .*	1. Introduction of the weekly weigh-in 2. Understanding baselines and plotting charts a. BMI b. Television viewing patterns c. Physical activity patterns d. Foods chart—what I am eating 3. Television and advertising—how it affects our eating patterns 4. Introduce the "5-a-day program" 5. Homework—completion of daily record sheets for the week. • Copies of the 5-a-day program, facts of the day, and interesting recipes can be obtained at http://www.cdc.gov/nccdphp/dnpa/5aday/index.htm
Week 4 *Get set . . .*	1. Weekly weigh-in 2. Checking in: diet, television, and physical activity logs. Plot your progress 3. What do I do when I watch TV? 4. Reading food labels 5. Homework • A Web site with information to help children learn how to read food labels: http://kidshealth.org/kid/stay_healthy/food/labels.html
Week 5 *Go!*	1. Weekly weigh in 2. Checking in: diet, television, and physical activity logs. Plot your progress 3. The food pyramid and what that means 4. How to increase my physical activity 5. Homework • A Web site with information to help children learn about the food pyramid: http://kidshealth.org/kid/stay_healthy/food/pyramid.html • *The Food Guide Pyramid* can help families make healthy eating choices and is available from the Center for Nutrition Policy and Promotion, 703-305-7600 and at www.usda.gov/cnpp/pyrabklt.pdf

(continued)

Table 30.4 (*Continued*)

Week	Objective
Week 6 *Pacing*	1. Weekly weigh-in 2. Checking in: diet, television, and physical activity logs. Plot your progress 3. Good foods versus bad foods—a review 4. Stoplight diet 5. Homework • Peer support, food logs, and weigh-ins help to keep the child on track • *The Stoplight Diet for Children: An Eight-Week Program for Parents and Children* (1988) by Leonard Epstein and Sally Squires, published by Little Brown & Company, is a comprehensive guide. The Stoplight Diet: A brief primer This is a parent–child team effort developed by Dr. Leonard Epstein. ∗ Foods are linked to the three signals on a traffic light: • High-calorie foods that contain fats, oils, and simple sugars, like soda and cookies, are "red" and should rarely be eaten. • Moderate-calorie foods, like cereal, dairy products, and meat are "yellow" and should be eaten with caution. • "Green" foods, which include most vegetables, fruits, breads, and grains get the go-ahead. ∗ This diet is aimed at changing what different foods mean, changing the meaning of snacks from red to healthy "green foods." • A useful parent resource on the health consequences of obesity is: http://diabetes.about.com/cs/kidsanddiabetes/l/blNIHkidsweight.htm
Week 7 *Steady does it*	1. Weekly weigh-in 2. Checking in: diet, television, and physical activity logs. Plot your progress 3. Increasing your physical activity—walk whenever you can 4. Homework • Resources for planning a "kids walk to school day" that include parent handouts for alternative activities: http://www.cdc.gov/nccdphp/dnpa/kidswalk/resources.htm#Train
Week 8 *Looking good!*	1. Weekly weigh-in 2. Checking in: diet, television, and physical activity logs. Plot your progress 3. Reviewing the stoplight diet 4. Progress: Calculating my BMI 5. How much television am I watching? 6. Planning a "turn your television off" week 7. Homework • A good resource for parents: Obesity and television fact sheet can be obtained at: http://www.mediafamily.org/facts/facts_tvandobchild_print. shtml • Reducing TV time: Guidelines for running the "turn your television off week" program as well as important dates and activities: http://www.tvturnoff.org/index.htm

(*continued*)

Table 30.4 (*Continued*)

Week	Objective
Week 9 *Keep on moving!*	1. Weekly weigh-in 2. Checking in: diet, television, and physical activity logs. Plot your progress 3. Brainstorm ways to increase your activity when you are sitting 4. Reviewing how the "turn your TV off week" will be run 5. Homework—"turn your TV off week" • A Web site for alternative activities to do with the "extra" time: http://www.tvturnoff.org/action.htm
Week 10 *Paying off!*	1. Weekly weigh-in 2. Checking in: diet, television, and physical activity logs. Plot your progress 3. Reevaluation of program a. How much of progress have I made? b. What is the worst part? c. What is the best part? d. How can it be improved? 4. Resetting goals
Week 11 *Yeah!*	1. Weekly weigh-in 2. Checking in: diet, television, and physical activity logs. Plot your progress 3. How do I continue when I am no longer doing this program? 4. Homework
Week 12 *Nearly there*	1. Weekly weigh-in 2. Checking in: diet, television, and physical activity logs. Plot your progress 3. Planning termination: supervise but do not assist in the weigh-in and checking in stages 4. Homework
Week 13 *On my way!*	1. Weekly weigh-in 2. Checking in: diet, television, and physical activity logs. Plot your progress 3. Working on termination: student-run session to discuss the importance of continued adherence to the program 4. Homework
Week 14 *I'm off!*	1. Weekly weigh-in 2. Checking in for the last time 3. Termination 4. Award

Establishing a Working Alliance

The focus of the initial sessions was to establish a working alliance with Lisa, her family, and the school. The problem of Lisa's obesity is viewed from a family-systemic model (Goetz & Caron, 1999), and a working alliance among the family, therapist, and child is fundamental for the success of this model (Raue, Castonguay, & Goldfried, 1993). The family, particularly parents, as the proponent of change is one of the most effective modalities of treating pediatric obesity (Golan, Weizman, Apter, & Fainaru, 1998).

Baseline psychosocial, anthropometric, and lifestyle data were collected in this phase. At the initial meeting with Lisa, the counselor discussed the referral, explored Lisa's perception of the problem and enlisted her participation in the obesity management program (OMP). Given the lack of empirically based short-term individualized obesity management programs, the counselor chose to use the multipronged OMP, in view of the fact that Lisa needed behavioral and dietary modifications with family and school support to ensure her adherence to the program.

The American Academy of Pediatricians describes childhood obesity as the most frustrating childhood condition to treat (Barlow & Dietz, 1998). There is no unitary cause for obesity. However, there is consensual data to indicate that the combination of excess caloric intake combined with low levels of physical activity result in obesity (Bray, 1987). Thus, interventions for children should be aimed at dietary and behavior modifications with increased physical activity (see Table 30.2). Higher rates of success in weight management programs were associated with supportive, interactive families demonstrating parental skills aimed at the child's development of responsibility and self-image (Epstein, 1996; Epstein, Koeske, Wing, & Valoski, 1986; Epstein, Myers, Raynor, & Saelens, 1998).

The Home–School Collaboration

A home–school collaboration was pivotal for the success of this intervention. A "town meeting" with Lisa's parents (see Week 1 in Table 30.4), Lisa, and the counselor was the next step. Lisa chose Ms. Halferty, her homeroom teacher, as her in-school support person. Ms. Halferty was also included in the planning and execution of this program. At this meeting, the psychosocial and health consequences of Lisa's body weight were explored. Educational materials on obesity management were presented to her parents. The importance of the home–school collaboration for the success of the program was expounded. The Longs agreed to participate in the OMP and signed a contract indicating their willingness to actively assist Lisa with this program. Lisa's mother agreed to be Lisa's "sponsor." The role

of the sponsor was to provide supervision, helping Lisa to complete homework assignments, stay on task, and to provide supportive nurturance at home. The structure of the 14-week OMP was outlined, and the responsibilities of the parent/sponsor were explained.

Baseline psychosocial and anthropometric data was collected at the second meeting. Psychosocial baseline data was collected on Lisa to assess her psychosocial health. There is substantive evidence to indicate that the psychosocial cost of obesity increases with the severity (Erermis et al., 2004; Wadden, Foster, Brownell, & Finley, 1984). Anxiety-depression, aggressiveness, social problems, social withdrawal, and internalizing and externalizing behavior are some of the problems that have been reported by caregivers of obese individuals (Erermis et al., 2004).

The focus of this phase of the intervention was to assess Lisa's caloric intake and expenditure and to determine her eating and activity patterns. Collecting baseline data (Figure 30.1) allows both the practitioner and the family to review the family's diet and activity patterns to identify the areas of over- and underconsumption, ascertaining problem behaviors (Barlow and Dietz, 1998).

Television (Dietz & Gortmaker, 1985; Gortmaker et al., 1996) and computer/video games have been purported to be the major cause of sedentary living among children (DuRant, Baranowski, Johnson, & Thompson, 1994; Marshall, Biddle, Gorely, Cameron, & Murdey, 2004). In addition to the sedentary lifestyle, these activities have been found to increase overall calorie consumption (Kelder, Perry, Klepp, & Lytle, 1994; Kotz & Story, 1994; Kraak & Pelletier, 1998; Jeffery & French, 1998; Coon & Tucker, 2002) through both the systematic advertising and consumption of calorie-dense snacks during these activities.

Lisa's task for the week was to complete daily (1) physical activity, (2) food, and (3) television and computer/video game logs for the next week (see Figure 30.2). The accuracy of recall records is affected by the frequency at which the record is completed. Accuracy is higher if the recording occurs close to the event (Baxter & Thompson, 2002). There is a rapid decay in memory, with poor reliability in recall after 24 hours (Armstrong et al., 2000). To facilitate Lisa's recall, both her parent sponsor and teacher provided her with

Figure 30.1. Example of Lisa Long's Baseline Data and Goal Chart

Lisa Long's Goal Chart Date: July 10, 2004

Date of Birth: 7–21–2004 Age: 11 years and 11 months

Height: 5 feet 1 inch (61 inches) Weight: 160 pounds

BMI (kg/m^2)

$=$ weight in pounds*0.455/height in inches*0.025*height in inches*0.025

$=$ (160 lbs)*0.455/(61 inches*0.025)*(61 inches*0.025)

$=$ 31.30 kg/m^2

Goals:

1. Diet:

    Improve my eating habits so that I lose weight

    Stop snacking on cookies and candy

    Stop eating doughnuts

2. Physical Activity:

    Start walking to school

    Walk around more when I am doing nothing.

3. Television:

    Watch only 2 hours of TV each day

    My ideal BMI is 24.

Figure 30.2. Individual Food, Television, and Activity Logs

Name: Date: Day:

Program	Time		
	started	ended	

	Time
Breakfast:	
Lunch:	
Dinner (e.g., 2 slices of pizza and Coke):	
Snacks (e.g., a bag of potato chips):	

Activity	Time of day	How long

Figure 30.3. Example of Note to Parents

Dear parent/guardian/sponsor, we are finally on our way.

This week Lisa will be collecting baseline data on

*   The types of food that she eats,
*   her physical activity patterns, and
*   the television programs she watches and computer and video games that she plays each day.

Lisa has been advised to complete the logs over the course of the day. Please remind her to complete the log at least once a day.

After we have collected this information, we will be better equipped to help Lisa attain her goal.

Thank you so much for helping Lisa with this program.

Sincerely,

Counselor

---

reminders to complete her record. A note was sent home to Mr. and Mrs. Long (see Figure 30.3) outlining the program for the week. As the sponsor, Mrs. Long's role was to ensure that Lisa filled in her daily logs (Figure 30.4). In addition to being reminded at home, her classroom teacher was asked to remind Lisa to complete the log at the beginning and the end of the day.

Treatment and Intervention Strategy

After baseline data had been collated, the counselor and Lisa set up both short-term and intermediate goals (see Table 30.5). The treatment and intervention phase of the OMP focused on:

1. Providing nutrition and physical activity education (weeks 3 to 10)
2. Developing mastery over diet and activity patterns
3. Establishing a working collaborative relationship between the home and school

The treatment and intervention phase was comprised of education and behavior modification components. Nutrition education was directed at making Lisa and her family more astute in their dietary choices. Reading and understanding food labels, serving sizes, and nutrient content of foods were part of the nutrition education program. The aim was to increase the consumption of high-fiber foods and fruits and vegetables and decrease simple sugar and fat consumption. This behavioral modification program was aimed at making good food choices rather than caloric restriction. This type of intervention focuses on small behavior modifications that include eating at the same place, limiting food eaten to one or two helpings, and learning to substitute low-fat and no-fat products for full-fat products. Similarly, changes in physical activity are aimed at increasing lifestyle physical activity rather than implementing a structured physical activity program. Given the low maintenance costs, lifestyle physical activity changes (e.g., walking, playing games, household chores) are more likely to have enduring results

Figure 30.4. Example of Television, Food, and Activity Logs
Baseline—Week 1: TV Viewing Log
Name: Lisa   Date: 15 July   Day: Thursday

Program	Time		
	Started	Ended	
Zoom	4:30 pm	5 pm	*(30 minutes)
Rugrats	5 pm	5:28 pm	*(28 minutes)
Simpsons	6 pm	6:30 pm	*(30 minutes)
Computer games	7 pm	9 pm	*(120 minutes)

Total amount of time spent watching television per day: 208 minutes (3 hours and 28 minutes)

Food Log
Name: Lisa   Date: 15 July   Day: Thursday

	Time	Snacks	Time
Breakfast: 1 cup of dry Frosted Flakes with a cup of 2% milk, banana, small glass of orange juice, Pop Tart, a glass of milk	8 am	Cheetos, soda	10:00 am
Lunch: 2 slices of pepperoni pizza, soda, 1 brownie	12:30 pm	Ice cream sandwich, potato chips	3 pm
Dinner: Quarter-pound burger, large fries, large soda	7 pm	Chocolate cake and chocolate milk	9 pm

Physical Activity Log
Name: Lisa   Date: 15 July   Day: Thursday

Activity	Time of day	How long
Played basketball in PE	12 pm	40 minutes
Walked home from the bus stop	4:15 pm	10 minutes

Total time spent on moderate to vigorous physical activity per day: 50 minutes
All italicized information was completed by the counselor

Table 30.5. Short-Term and Intermediate Goals

	Goal	*Objectives*
Television	Decrease fat- and sugar-dense snacks	Increase the consumption of good foods (green and yellow from the stoplight diet). Stop eating while watching TV. Measuring portions of food before eating them.
	Increase activity level during television viewing	Decrease the amount of time spent just sitting during a television program. Increase physical activity during commercial breaks. Increase the intensity of the physical activity so that metabolism is elevated.
	Limit the total time spent watching TV and playing computer and video games to 2 hours a day with the optimal goal being 1 hour a day	Plan television and computer time at the beginning of the week. Plan and have a list of alternate activities to fill in the "free" time. Plan and carry out a "turn your television off week."
Physical activity	Increase lifestyle physical activity and just keep on moving	Increase daily walking. Schedule a "walk to school" or "walk back from school day." Start walking with training buddy (mom). Find a physical activity or sport that I enjoy and increase participation in this activity. Join a club at school.
Diet	Increase good foods	Adopt and follow the 5-a-day plan. Decrease simple-carbohydrate consumption. Follow the food pyramid diet.
	Decrease soda consumption	Increase water intake; reduce or eliminate soda consumption.

(Kohl & Hobbs, 1998) compared to structured physical activity programs. Parental encouragement and support was espoused, and rewarding goal attainment was advocated. Recommended rewards included earning things that Lisa really wanted (e.g., providing her with the opportunity to gradually earn a new pair of shoes), choosing the family activity on family game night, or planning a family outing. Using food as an incentive was strongly discouraged. During this phase, both Lisa and her family learned alternative ways to eat without sacrificing palatability of foods. The decreased emphasis on television viewing had also given the family an opportunity to have more meaningful interactions with each other.

Termination

The final phase (weeks 12 to 14) of the intervention was to provide both Lisa and her family with the tools to continue with the OMP after the termination of the program. By this stage Lisa and her family had begun to employ behavioral modifications that resulted in better nutrition and physical activity choices. The increased involvement of the family in this program resulted in a renewed closeness, and the Long family was spending more time on family activities and outings. The termination process was directed toward empowering Lisa and her family to continue with positive physical activity and nutrition behaviors after the removal of active school support. By the end of the 14 weeks, Lisa had become more physically active and felt empowered to control her weight. This new confidence was also seen in her relationshiups with her peers. Lisa had not attained her goal BMI by the end of the program and decided that checking in with the counselor once a month for the rest of the academic year would provide adequate guidance for her to remain on the program.

Tools

Useful Web Sites and Additional Resources

Carter, J., Wiecha, J., Peterson, K., & Gortmaker, S. (2001). *Planet health: An interdisciplinary curriculum for teaching middle school nutrition and physical activity.* Champaign, IL: Human Kinetics.

CATCH. (2003). *Coordinated approach to child health.* Retrieved 13 July 2004.

Cheung, L., Gortmaker, S., & Dart, H. (2001). *Eat well & keep moving: An interdisciplinary curriculum for teaching upper elementary school nutrition and physical activity.* Champaign, IL: Human Kinetics.

Epstein, L. H., & Squires, S. (1988). *The stoplight diet for children: An eight-week program for parents and children.* Boston: Little Brown and Company.

National Center for Chronic Disease Prevention and Health Promotion. (2004, 23 June). *US obesity trends 1985 to 2002.* Retrieved July 5, 2004, from http://www.cdc.gov/nccdphp/dnpa/obesity/trend/maps/index.htm

National Institute on Media and the Family. (2004). *Fact sheet: Media use and obesity among children.* Retrieved July 7, 2004, from http://www.mediafamily.org/facts/facts_tvandobchild_print.html

National Institutes of Health, National Heart, Lung, and Blood Institute. (1998). Clinical guidelines on the identification, evaluation, and treatment of overweight and obesity in adults—the evidence report. *Obesity Research* 6(S2):51S-209S [Published erratum appears in *Obesity Research* 6:464]. Retrieved July 2004 from http://www.nhlbi.nih.gov/guidelines/obesity/ob_home.htm

Rimm, S. (2004). *Rescuing the emotional lives of overweight children: What our kids go though—and how we can help.* Emmaus, PA: Rodale.

TV Turnoff Network. (2004, June 3). *TV turnoff week.* Retrieved June 14, 2004, from http://www.tv-turnoff.org/index.htm

Weight Control Groups for Children

Childobesity.com
Shapedown.com/page2.htm
slimkids.com
thepathway.org

Nutrition: National Cancer Institute 5-a-Day Program

www.5aday.gov

Exercise

nutriteen.com
www.shapeup.org

Some of the key points from this chapter are:

- Changing the dietary patterns of an obese child or adolescent requires a family-based initiative.
- A healthy diet can be fostered by
  - Reducing the intake of dietary fat
  - Reducing soda consumption
  - Increasing dietary fiber
  - Increasing fruit and vegetable consumption to 5 a day
- Changes in lifestyle physical activity are more enduring than a structured physical activity program.
- Limiting television and computer viewing time increases the amount of time that is available for more meaningful engagement in lifestyle physical activities.
- Children are better able to lose weight and maintain their weight loss compared to adults.
- The key to a successful program is making enduring lifestyle changes.
- A paced program that spans a longer period of time is more effective in establishing enduring lifestyle changes.
- A collaborative family and school approach is more effective than either a family or school program.

References

Armstrong, A. M., MacDonald, A., Booth, I. W., Platts, R. G., Knibb, R. C., & Booth, D. A. (2000). Errors in memory for dietary intake and their reduction. *Applied Cognitive Psychology, 14*(2), 183–192.

Barlow, S. E., & Dietz, W. H. (1998). Obesity evaluation and treatment: Expert committee recommendations.

Pediatrics, 102(3), e29. Retrieved November 2004 from: http://www.pediatrics.org/cgi/content/full/102/3/e29

Baxter, S. D., & Thompson, W. O. (2002). Accuracy by meal component of fourth-graders' school lunch recalls is less when obtained during a 24-hour recall than as a single meal. *Nutrition Research, 22*(6), 679–684.

Bellizzi, M. C., & Dietz, W. H. (1999). Workshop on childhood obesity: Summary of the discussion. *American Journal of Clinical Nutrition, 70*(1), 173S-5.

Bray, G. A. (1987). Obesity—a disease of nutrient or energy imbalance? *Nutrition Reviews, 45,* 33–43.

Brownell, K. D., Kelman, J. H., & Stunkard, A. J. (1983). Treatment of obese children with and without their mothers: Changes in weight and blood pressure. *Pediatrics, 71*(4), 515–523.

Buckley, M. A., & Zimmermann, S. H. (2003). *Mentoring children and adolescents: A guide to the issues.* Westport, CT: Praeger Publishers.

Carter, J., Wiecha, J., Peterson, K., & Gortmaker, S. (2001). *Planet health: An interdisciplinary curriculum for teaching middle school nutrition and physical activity.* Champaign, IL: Human Kinetics.

CATCH. (2003). *Coordinated approach to child health.* Retrieved July 13, 2004.

Cheung, L., Gortmaker, S., & Dart, H. (2001). *Eat well & keep moving: An interdisciplinary curriculum for teaching upper elementary school nutrition and physical activity.* Champaign, IL: Human Kinetics.

Coates, T. J., Jeffery, R. W., Slinkard, L. A., Killen, J. D., & Danaher, B. G. (1982). Frequency of contact and monetary reward in weight loss, lipid change and blood pressure reduction with adolescents. *Behavior Therapy, 13,* 175–185.

Coon, K. A., & Tucker, K. L. (2002). Television and children's consumption patterns: A review of the literature. *Minerva Pediatrics, 54,* 423–436.

Dietz, W. (1991). Physical activity and childhood obesity. *Nutrition, 7*(4), 295–296.

Dietz, W. H., Jr., & Gortmaker, S. L. (1985). Do we fatten our children at the television set? Obesity and television viewing in children and adolescents. *Pediatrics, 75*(5), 807–812.

DuRant, R. H., Baranowski, T., Johnson, M., & Thompson, W. O. (1994). The relationship among television watching, physical activity and body composition of young children. *Pediatrics, 94,* 449–455.

Epstein, L. H. (1996). Family based behavioral intervention for obese children. *International Journal of Obesity, 20,* S14–S21.

Epstein, L. H., Koeske, R., Wing, R. R., & Valoski, A. (1986). The effects of family variables on child weight change. *Health Psychology, 5,* 1–11.

Epstein, L. H., Myers. M. D., Raynor, H. A., & Saelens, B. E. (1998). Treatment of pediatric obesity. *Pediatrics, 101,* 554–570.

Epstein, L. H., & Squires, S. (1988). *The stoplight diet for children: An eight-week program for parents and children.* Boston: Little Brown and Company.

Epstein, L. H., Valoski, A. M., Kalarchian, M. A., & McCurley, J. (1995). Do children lose and maintain weight easier than adults: A comparison of child and parent weight changes from six months to ten years. *Obesity Research, 3,* 411–417.

Epstein, L. H., Valoski, A. M., Vara, L. S., McCurley, J., Wisniewski, L., Kalarchian, M. A., Klein, K. R., & Shrager, L. R. (1995). Effects of decreasing sedentary behavior and increasing activity on weight change in obese children. *Health Psychology, 14*(2), 109–115.

Epstein, L. H., Valoski, A., Wing, R. R., & McCurley, J. (1990). Ten-year follow-up of behavioral family-based treatment for obese children. *JAMA, 264,* 2519–2523.

Epstein, L. H., Valoski, A., Wing, R. R., & McCurley, J. (1994). Ten-year outcomes of behavioral family-based treatment for childhood obesity. *Health Psychology, 13*(5), 373–383.

Epstein, L. H., Wing, R. R., Koeske, R., Andrasik, F., & Ossip, D. J. (1981). Child and parent weight loss in family-based behavior modification programs. *Journal of Consultation and Clinical Psychology, 49,* 674–685.

Epstein, L. H., Wing, R. R., Koeske, R., Ossip, D. J., & Beck, S. (1982). A comparison of lifestyle change and programmed aerobic exercise on weight and fitness changes in obese children. *Behavior Therapy, 13,* 651–665.

Epstein, L. H., Wing, R. R., Steranchak, L., Dickson, B., & Michelson, J. (1980). Comparison of family based behavior modification and nutrition education for childhood obesity. *Journal of Pediatric Psychology, 5,* 25–36.

Epstein, L. H., Wisniewski, L., & Weng, R. (1994). Child and parent psychological problems influence child weight control. *Obesity Research, 2,* 509–515.

Erermis, S., Cetin, N., Tamar, M., Bukusoglu, N., Akdeniz, F., & Goksen, D. (2004). Is obesity a risk factor for psychopathology among adolescents? *Pediatrics International, 46*(3), 296–302.

Flegal, K. M., Carroll, M. D., Ogden, C. L., & Johnson, C. L. (2002). Prevalence and trends in obesity among U.S. adults. *JAMA, 288,* 1723–1727.

Goetz, D. R., & Caron, W. (1999). A biopsychosocial model for youth obesity: Consideration of an ecosystemic collaboration. *International Journal of Obesity, 23*(S2), S58–S64.

Golan, M., Weizman, A., Apter, A., & Fainaru, M. (1998). Parents as exclusive agents of change in the treatment of childhood obesity. *American Journal of Clinical Nutrition, 67,* 1130–1135.

Gortmaker, S. L., Cheung, L. W. Y., Peterson, K. E., Chomitz, G., Cradle, J. H., Dart, H., et al. (1999). Impact of a school-based interdisciplinary intervention on diet and activity among urban primary school children: Eat well and keep moving. *Archives of Pediatrics and Adolescent Medicine, 123*(9), 975–983.

Gortmaker, S., Must, A., Sobol, A., Peterson, K., Colditz, G., & Dietz, W. (1996). Television viewing as a cause of increasing obesity among children in the United States 1986–1990. *Journal of the American Medical Association, 150*(4), 356–362.

Jeffery, R. W., & French, S. A. (1998). Epidemic obesity in the US: Are fast foods and television viewing contributing? *American Journal of Public Health, 88,* 277–280.

Kelder, R. W., Perry, C. L., Klepp, K. I., & Lytle L. L. (1994). Longitudinal tracking of adolescent smoking, physical activity, and food choice behaviors. *American Journal of Public Health, 84,* 1121–1126.

Knip, M., & Nuutinen, O. (1993). Long-term effects of weight reduction on serum lipids and plasma insulin in obese children. *American Journal of Clinical Nutrition, 54,* 490–493.

Kohl, H. W., & Hobbs, K. E. (1998). Development of physical activity behaviors among children and adolescents. *Pediatrics, 101,* 549–554.

Kotz, K., & Story, M. (1994). Food advertisements during children's Saturday morning television programming: Are they consistent with dietary recommendations? *Journal of American Dietetic Association, 94,* 1296–1300.

Kraak, V., & Pelletier, D. L. (1998). The influence of commercialism on the food purchasing behavior of children and teenage youth. *Family Economy Nutrition Review, 11,* 15–24.

Lytle, L. A., Kelder, S. H., Perry, C. L., & Klepp, K. I. (1995). Covariance of adolescent health behaviors—The class of 1989 study. *Health Education Research Theory and Practice, 10,* 133–146.

Marshall, S. J., Biddle, S. J. H., Gorely, T., Cameron, N., & Murdey, I. (2004). Relationship between media use and body fatness and physical activity in children and youth: A meta-analysis. *International Journal of Obesity, 28*(10), 1238–1246.

National Center for Health Statistics. (1999). *Prevalence of overweight among children and adolescents: United States, 1999.* Retrieved July 2004: from http://www.cdc.gov/nchs/products/pubs/pubd/hestats/overwght99.htm

National Institute on Media and the Family. (2004). *Fact sheet: Media use and obesity among children.* Retrieved July 14, 2004, from http://www.mediafamily.org/facts/facts_tvandobchild_print.shtml

Ogden, C. L., Flegal, K. M., Carroll, M. D., & Johnson, C. L. (2002). Prevalence and trends in overweight among US children and adolescents, 1999–2000. *JAMA, 288,* 1728–1732.

Raue, P. J., Castonguay, L. G., & Goldfried, M. R. (1993). The working alliance: A comparison of two therapies. *Psychotherapy Research, 3,* 197–207.

Rees, J. M. (1990). Management of obesity in adolescence. *Medical Clinics of North America, 74,* 1275–1292.

Rimm, S. (2004). *Rescuing the emotional lives of overweight children: What our kids go though—and how we can help.* Emmaus, PA: Rodale.

Senediak, C., & Spence, S. H. (1985). Rapid versus gradual scheduling of therapeutic contact in a family based behavioural weight control programme for children. *Behavioral Psychotherapy, 13,* 265–287.

Serdula, M. K., Ivery, D., Coates, R. J., Freedman, D. S., Williamson, D. F., & Byers, T. (1993). Do obese children become obese adults? A review of the literature. *Preventive Medicine, 22,* 167–177.

TV Turnoff Network. (2004). TV turnoff week. Retrieved June 14, 2004, from http://www. tvturnoff .org/index.htm

Wadden, T. A., Foster, G. D., Brownell, K. D., & Finley, E. (1984). Self-concept in obese and normal-weight children. *Journal of Consulting and Clinical Psychology, 52,* 1104–1105.

Best Practices and Resources for Intervening With Child Abuse, Sexual Abuse, and Out-of-Home Placement in a School Setting

Child abuse and the residential placement of children are considered a specialty within social work and other mental health professions. Expertise in working with children in these areas is often associated with public child-welfare practitioners and mental health clinicians who practice in community settings. But public school staff sometimes encounter students who are being abused or are living in out-of-home placement situations, so it is important that staff members be trained accordingly. Child abuse, for example, is most often discovered by public school staff. Thus, school-based mental health staff are often the professionals who report abuse and subsequently broker or provide support services for the child victim. Such a role requires the skills to recognize child abuse and neglect, knowledge of child abuse laws, and skill for working with abused children in the school setting. In addition, students who are in out-of-home placements such as foster care and the juvenile justice system are at increased risk for school failure and conduct problems. In this section, essential directives and interventions in these three areas are clearly presented, as well as guidance for developing effective alliances with child welfare, juvenile justice, and other child advocacy groups in the community.

Identifying Child Abuse or Neglect Strategies in a School Setting

Ernst VanBergeijk

CHAPTER 31

Getting Started

Why Is the Identification of Child Abuse and Neglect an Important Topic for Schools?

Schools are the single most important institution in a child's life, after his or her own family. By the nature of their relationships with a child, both in terms of proximity and duration of contact, school personnel can make a crucial difference in a child's life by detecting maltreatment. Although most school personnel likely would agree that the identification of child abuse is important, the accurate identification and reporting of child abuse (i.e., reports made based on evidence) are multifaceted and often complicated tasks. This chapter will discuss what we know about the problems associated with the identification of child maltreatment in schools and provide guidance around the identification process.

Defining Child Maltreatment

Child abuse and neglect are defined by both state and federal statutes. In 1974 Congress enacted the Child Abuse Prevention and Treatment Act, more commonly referred to as CAPTA, in which the federal government provided seed money to the states to establish 24-hour-a-day child-abuse reporting hotlines and investigatory agencies (U.S. Department of Health and Human Services, 2004). This federal statute also provided states with minimum statutory guidelines for the identification of child maltreatment. Currently, six broad categories are used typically to define child maltreatment, although only 25 of the 50 states use all six categories in their state-specific definition. These categories are physical abuse, neglect, sexual abuse, sexual exploitation, emotional maltreatment, and abandonment.

Physical abuse is defined as the nonaccidental injury of a child. This can be either through inflicting an injury or allowing a child to be injured. Neglect, in contrast, is a more abstract concept. It occurs either through the omission or commission of acts that impair or threaten to impair a child's physical, mental, or emotional condition. Sexual abuse is defined as committing or allowing the commission of a sexual offense against a child as defined by penal law. A sexual offense committed against a child is not limited to rape and sodomy. It includes fondling of the child's genitalia, oral, anal, and genital intercourse, the use of an instrument to penetrate a child's vagina or rectum, and incest (New York Society for the Prevention of Cruelty to Children, 1996). Sexual exploitation is a more specific form of sexual abuse, which includes "allowing, permitting, or encouraging a child to engage in prostitution; and allowing, permitting, encouraging, or engaging in the obscene or pornographic photographing, filming, or depicting of a child for commercial purposes" (National Center on Child Abuse and Neglect Clearinghouse, 2003). Emotional abuse may be referred to as psychological abuse or maltreatment. Like neglect, it too is an abstract concept that is difficult to operationalize. According to the National Center on Child Abuse and Neglect, emotional abuse "is a pattern of behavior that impairs a child's emotional development or sense of self-worth. This may include constant criticism, threats, or rejection, as well as withholding love, support, or guidance" (National Center on Child Abuse and Neglect Clearinghouse, 2003). Finally, abandonment has been defined as

"willful intent by words, actions, or omissions not to return for a child or failure to maintain a significant parental relationship with a child through visitation or communication, in which incidental or token visits or communication are not considered significant" (National Abandoned Infants Assistance Resource Center, 2002, p. iv).

Rarely are cases of child maltreatment clear cut, and rarely do they involve only one type of maltreatment. According to Ney, Fung, and Wickett (1994), less than 5% of instances of child maltreatment occur in isolation. Neglect is often a precursor to physical abuse in many cases, and it is the combination of physical abuse, physical neglect, and verbal abuse that has the greatest impact on children (Ney, Fung, & Wickett, 1994). Further, the younger the child when the verbal abuse and emotional neglect commence, the more severe and frequent the maltreatment tends to be (Ney et al., 1994).

In addition to knowing what constitutes the various types of maltreatment within the state, school personnel must also know what kinds of behaviors are exempt from mandatory reporting laws. All but 12 states articulate anywhere from one to four exemptions from the definition of child maltreatment. An exempted behavior is one that might otherwise fit the definition of child maltreatment but that is allowable under the state statute. The most common exemptions to mandatory reporting laws typically involve withholding medical treatment on religious grounds. Twenty-eight states and the District of Columbia have this exception. Corporal punishment is another common exemption. Fourteen states and the District of Columbia do not consider minor injuries inflicted as a result of corporal punishment to be abuse. Cultural practices (Minnesota) and poverty (six states and the District of Columbia) are other examples of exemptions. Of note, Minnesota exempts reasonable force by principal, teacher, or school employee from its definition of maltreatment. West Virginia allows an exemption to state compulsory education. The foundation of accurate identification of child maltreatment is a firm knowledge of what constitutes reportable maltreatment in one's state of practice.

What We Know

There are five primary methods of identifying child maltreatment: direct disclosure, observation, structured interview, projective tests, and screening tools. A direct disclosure is a direct verbal report by a child to an adult that he or she has been maltreated; this is the least ambiguous method of identification. The remaining methods of identification typically are used in the absence of a direct disclosure. They rest on the adult's knowledge of child maltreatment warning signs, risk and protective factors, and the use of critical thinking to evaluate the available evidence.

Observations can range from viewing an injury (e.g., a bruise), interacting with the parent or the child alone, or viewing interactions between the parent and the child or the child and his or her peers. Often in school settings, these observations are unplanned and unstructured, and they occur without the intent of assessing abuse. In clinical settings, observations may be conducted for the explicit purpose of making a child maltreatment determination. Even under clinical conditions, observational methods do not always have adequate reliability and validity (Milner & Murphy, 1995) because there are a number of biasing factors to which the observer may be responding (e.g., race, socioeconomic status, gender of the parent, dislike of the parent).

Interviews as an identification method use a question-and-answer format to gain information about characteristics of the family, parent(s), and interaction patterns. To be most useful, the interview should be planned and structured with clear objectives with regard to the types of information that the interviewer is seeking (e.g., a parent's mental health, substance abuse, and parental expectations of the child). Specific interview protocols have been designed to aid identification. For example, the Early Trauma Inventory (Bremner, Vermetten, & Mazure, 2000) is a 56-question clinician-administered interview that assesses physical, emotional, and sexual abuse as well as general trauma that results from experiences such as loss of a parent.

There are a number of specific strategies that may enhance the interview process. For example, Faller (1997) recommends that interview questions should be ordered on a continuum ranging from more general questions to focused open-ended questions (e.g., who, what, where, and when), and finally to more specific follow-up questions (e.g. "What happened after?"). In her work with sexually abused children, she has found that direct questions should be placed toward the end of the continuum and should be used when

open-ended questions are not productive (e.g., "Was it your dad who hurt you?"). Multiple choice, leading, and/or coercive questions should be avoided (e.g., "If you don't tell the truth, you're not leaving this room"). Using interview protocols requires some training, as it is important to adhere to the predetermined protocol. Interviews that become too conversational may fail to produce sufficient information to make a determination and are likely to omit pertinent areas of inquiry.

Projective tests rest on the assumption that the child is either not able or not willing to disclose maltreatment and/or discuss resulting psychological symptoms but that proxy indicators of this information may be interpreted from his or her play or art. Information garnered from these types of tests should be considered supplemental; it should not be the sole basis of an identification (Kayser & Lyon, 2000). The research in this area is equivocal as to the reliability and validity of these techniques. Administering and/or interpreting projective tests requires advanced training.

Finally, a range of standardized screening tools have been used in the identification process. These tools for the most part are issue specific (i.e., sexual abuse, psychological maltreatment) or are focused on psychological symptoms of distress associated with maltreatment (e.g., trauma symptoms). Most have been developed for either adult or adolescent populations and tested on substance abusing and/or psychiatric samples rather than on the general population of school-age children. However, there are several that are specific to child maltreatment behavior. Some are parent-focused self-report scales such as the Child Abuse Potential Inventory (CAPI) (Haz & Ramirez, 2002). For example, the CAPI has both long and short versions and aims to assess a parent's potential to maltreat his or her child. This instrument has multiple subscales, which allow the user to assess characteristics of the parent along dimensions such as social indicators, self-control, loneliness, and rigidity. Measures such as this have been empirically tested and shown to be able to distinguish at-risk parents from non-abusing parents. Other tools are child focused, such as the Gully 2000 Expectations Test (Gully, 2003). This instrument was designed for children 4–17 years of age and evaluates children in terms of sexual abuse, physical abuse, exposure to family violence, and symptoms of posttraumatic stress disorder.

What We Can Do

Though there are many empirically tested tools that can help with the identification process, it is not wise to employ them before one has a firm grasp of four core areas of relevant knowledge: (a) state laws defining child maltreatment, (b) warning signs of child maltreatment, (c) recent research on risk and protective factors, and (d) critical decision-making processes. Without this foundation and a reliance on these tools, there is a risk of failing to detect all but the most severe incidents of maltreatment. The individual will not be able to intelligently interpret screening tool results with other observable evidence. This section of the chapter is devoted to the warning signs and risk factors of child maltreatment and to procedures that may be helpful in heading off errors in critical decision making.

Warning Signs

The National Center on Child Abuse and Neglect Clearinghouse (2003) offers a complete description of the warning signs of child maltreatment in its publication *Recognizing Child Abuse: What Parents Should Know.* In this booklet, physical and behavioral indicators within the categories of maltreatment are listed for both the child victim and the potential abuser. What is particularly useful are the indicators that may be seen in the school setting. In addition to "hard" indicators such as visible injuries or poor hygiene are "soft" indicators that include abrupt changes in behavior or school performance, frequent absences from school, sudden refusals to change for physical education classes, learning problems (or difficulty concentrating) that cannot be attributed to specific physical or psychological causes, and early arrival at school or other activities and a reluctance to go home. In terms of parental behavioral indicators, the authors identify harsh or indifferent behavior; abuse of drugs or alcohol; requests for teachers to use harsh physical discipline if the child misbehaves; offers explanations for injuries that are developmentally unlikely or implausible given the nature of the injury; and/or severely limits the child's social contacts, especially with other children of the opposite sex. School-based practitioners should familiarize themselves with the complete set of warning signs at the national clearinghouse's Web site.

Risk Factors

The national clearinghouse also offers a concise list of empirically identified factors that increase the risk of child maltreatment and those that protect from abuse. Risk factors are organized into three categories: the child factors, parental and/or family factors, and social and environmental factors. It is important to note that although there are several child factors that increase the risk for maltreatment (e.g., premature birth, physical or cognitive disability, age), the majority of risk factors are parental/family or social/environmental. Families that are socially isolated, financially stressed, living in communities with high violence and high unemployment rates with substance abuse problems and/or problems with domestic violence are more likely to maltreat their children than are their more socially integrated, less stressed counterparts.

In recent decades researchers have focused their attention on protective factors associated with lower probabilities of maltreatment. Children with engaging, easygoing personalities and good social skills are less likely to experience maltreatment. Lowered rates are also associated with families with supportive relationships who are socially integrated into their neighborhoods, and with parents who are consistently gainfully employed.

Critical Decision Making

Critical thinking is a process of reasoned decision making that requires the use of rationality, self-awareness, and open-mindedness. It involves the use of evidence rather than emotion to evaluate information and guide decision making. It is an important part of the identification process because the school-based practitioner will be required to engage with complex and often emotionally charged family situations. An essential skill for practitioners is to be able to discern pertinent data from extraneous data. Training in critical thinking skills is an important tool in this process. Gambrill (1990) offers a number of rules of thumb for critical thinking that are useful in avoiding errors in causal assumptions that can be applied in the identification of child maltreatment. Among those rules of thumb are: (a) Look for alternative explanations, (b) pay attention to sources of uncertainty, (c) attend to negative information, and (d) attend to environmental causes. Using critical thinking requires one to reflect on the quality of information available, logical flaws in reasoning, awareness of one's biases, and a willingness to consider alternatives.

Approaching the Parents

Once there is sufficient cause to suspect child maltreatment, it is often advisable to discuss these concerns with the parent. Talking with the parent is not only a matter of ethical treatment; it also can provide important information to clarify the situation. It is imperative that the parent understand that school personnel are mandated reporters. This should be communicated in writing and verbally to ensure that the parent is clear about his or her rights. Meeting with the parent or parents can be uncomfortable and at times adversarial. The school-based practitioner must keep the focus of the interview, interact in an informed and professional manner, and avoid arguing and blaming language. It is best when the social worker speaks openly, professionally, and honestly about his or her concerns and legal obligations. If the school has decided to document the child's behavior and/or hygiene record in an effort to collect information more systematically, the parent should be advised of this. Approaching the parent is contraindicated if (a) it is likely to result in immediate harm to the child or others, (b) the parent appears to be under the influence of alcohol or drugs or to be psychologically unstable, (c) it interferes with an ongoing police investigation, or (d) there is a risk of flight out of the country.

Tools and Practice Examples

James is a bright, verbal 5-year-old in a kindergarten program. He has been identified as disruptive because he hits, kicks, bites, and scratches other children. At the first parent conference held at the school, the social worker meets James's parents, Mr. and Mrs. Smith. When the social worker tries to discuss James's behavior with the parents, Mr. Smith dominates the conversation and responds defensively to questions about the family. Mrs. Smith looks away from her husband and at the ground. Her arm is in a sling. The social worker notices that when Mrs. Smith does speak, she chooses her words very carefully and seems afraid she will upset Mr. Smith. At one point

during this meeting, Mr. Smith mocks James for wetting the bed at night. Toward the end of the meeting, James throws water at his toddler sister, Ann, from a water play table located in the classroom. Mr. Smith explodes in anger. He splashes James, saying, "See how you like it!" At the conclusion of this parent conference, the social worker feels intimidated by Mr. Smith and is concerned about the children. The social worker decides to conduct observations of the children's behavior and speak to their teachers.

The social worker learns that James's sister Ann is in the school's day-care program in the toddler room. She is 2½ years old and does not speak. Ann will not make eye contact with men. The social worker observes that when a man comes into the room, she hides behind the day-care worker's legs. If a man speaks in a normal tone of voice in the classroom, she often hides in a corner. The day-care worker often remarks that she is dirty "again" and that she has to clean Ann when she first comes to the day-care room. At times her buttocks and vagina are red and smell of urine. Staff members have found sticks, stones, dirt, and leaves in her diaper.

Mrs. Smith appears depressed and overwhelmed by the children and her arm injury. After several conversations with her, the staff remained unclear about how she was injured. Unemployed, Mr. Smith spends a great deal of time at home watching TV and drinking beer.

This case is an example of how complex a presenting situation can be. There are several soft warning signs of child maltreatment that James exhibits, including physically assaultive behavior toward his peers and functional enuresis. Ann also exhibits warning signs that are both soft and hard in nature. Ann's soft warning signs of maltreatment include her lack of language skills, which may indicate a developmental delay, and her fear of men. The hard warning signs have to do with her lack of adequate hygiene, an indicator of neglect.

There are a number of risk factors exhibited by this family. First are the belittling behavior and harsh treatment of James by his father. A second risk factor is the various behaviors consistent with partner violence exhibited by Mr. and Mrs. Smith. A third risk factor was Mr. Smith's potential substance abuse problem. A fourth risk factor was Mrs. Smith's depression. A final risk factor was Mr. Smith's unemployment.

In the state in which this case took place, emotional injury was not defined by state statute, so many of the behavioral indicators of potential harm were moot. The negative effects of witnessing partner violence were not considered an emotional injury. The willful or threatened harm that Ann faced through neglect was not immediately reported because of an exemption to the reporting mandates for cases in which poverty is potentially a contributing factor. Although Mr. Smith's behavior was belligerent, there were no hard indicators of physical abuse that necessitated reporting at that time.

James's and Ann's teachers, the principal, and school social worker met to discuss their concerns for these children based on the children's behavior and presentation and on their own knowledge of the risk factors for child maltreatment. They began a critical thinking process by articulating some of the biases (e.g., their dislike of Mr. Smith) that might be influencing their perceptions. They spent a few minutes brainstorming alternative explanations for James's behavior with awareness that there were many sources of uncertainty. They agreed that they needed much more substantive information. They created a form for the teacher and the child-care workers to document the children's well-being and begin a case record. The social worker agreed to contact Mrs. Smith (a) to express the school's concerns, (b) to ensure that Mrs. Smith understood that the school personnel were mandated reporters of child maltreatment, and, if required, (c) to inform Mrs. Smith of her options should it become clear that a report to child protective services would be forthcoming. They decided against asking Mr. Smith to come to the meeting, given their suspicions of domestic violence. They were concerned about provoking him. The social worker met with Mrs. Smith the next week. After reviewing the laws of mandated reporting, the social worker followed Faller's recommendations by asking Mrs. Smith some general questions about the children's care (e.g., "How often do you bathe Ann?") moving to more specific and focused questions after Mrs. Smith indicated that she felt that her husband was "hard on the kids" (e.g., "What do you mean, 'hard on the kids'?" "What does Mr. Smith do when he is hard on the kids?"). Mrs. Smith did not immediately disclose abusive behavior on her husband's part and appeared nervous. The social worker told Mrs. Smith that the school personnel were so concerned that they had decided to keep track of James's and Ann's behavior and hygiene. Although uncomfortable, the social worker continued to speak openly and professionally about her concerns. Because this was done in a nonjudgmental manner, Mrs. Smith eventually

conceded that Mr. Smith was physically abusive to both her and her children. A subsequent report was made to the proper authorities.

Rapid Assessment Instruments and Interview Protocols

Listed below are a number of instruments that may be helpful in identifying potential abuse. Please refer to the reference provided or to the Buros Center for Testing at http://www.unl.edu/buros/for psychometric properties of the scale (i.e., the reliability and validity of the instrument) and for the number of items and the length of time it takes to administer the questionnaire or interview protocol.

Rapid Assessment Instruments

Child Abuse Potential Inventory (CAPI) (Haz & Ramirez, 2002)

Conflict Tactics Scales Parent to Child version (CTSPC) (Straus, Hamby, Finkelhor, Moore, & Runyun, 1998)

Gully's 2000 Expectations Test (Gully, 2003)

Colorado Adolescent Rearing Inventory (CARI) (Crowley, Mikulich, Ehlers, Hall, & Whitmore, 2003). Available free of charge at: http://ibgwww.colorado.edu/cadd/a_drug/links/cari_home.html

Interviews

Early Trauma Inventory (ETI) (Bremner, Vermetten, & Mazure, 2000)

Resources

Books

Board of Education of the City of New York. (2000). *Identifying and reporting suspected child abuse and neglect: A practical guide for school staff.* New York: Author.

Briere, J., Berliner, L., & Bulckley, J. (2000). *The APSAC handbook on child maltreatment.* Newbury Park, CA: Sage.

Lowenthal, B. (2001). *Abuse and neglect: The educator's guide to the identification and prevention of child maltreatment.* Baltimore, MD: Paul H. Brookes.

U.S. Department of Justice, Office of Juvenile Justice and Delinquency Prevention. (1997). *Recognizing when a child's injury or illness is caused by abuse.* Washington, DC: Author.

Organizations and Government Agencies

National Center for Missing and Exploited Children
Charles B. Wang International Children's Building
699 Prince Street
Alexandria, VA 22314-3175
Web site: http://missingkids.com
Voice 703-274-3900/274-2220
Hot line: 800-THE LOST (843-5678)

National Clearinghouse on Child Abuse and Neglect Information
330 C Street, SW
Washington, DC 20447
E-mail: nccanch@calib.com
Web site: http://nccanch.acf.hhs.gov/
Voice 703-385-7565/800-394-3366
FAX 703-385-3206

Key Points to Remember

- The identification of child maltreatment is often a complex task. Rarely does child maltreatment involve a single episode and a sole form of maltreatment.
- Competent identification of child maltreatment means that school-based professionals must have a solid foundation in the four key areas of knowledge: (1) state laws defining each type of maltreatment, (2) warning signs of maltreatment, (3) recent research findings on risk and protective factors for child abuse and neglect, and (4) critical thinking and decision-making skills.
- The five methods of identification are direct disclosure from the child, observations, interviews, projective tests, and screening tools.
- As a part of ethical practice, concerns of child maltreatment should be discussed with the parent.

References

Bremner, J., Vermetten, E., & Mazure, C. (2000). Development and preliminary psychometric properties of an instrument for the measurement of childhood trauma: The Early Childhood Trauma Inventory. *Depression and Anxiety, 12*(1), 1–12.

Crowley, T., Mikulich, S., Ehlers, K., Hall, S., & Whitmore, E. (2003). Discriminative validity and clinical utility of an abuse-neglect interview for adolescents with conduct and substance use problems. *American Journal of Psychiatry, 160*(8), 1461–1469.

Faller, K. C. (1997). *Understanding and assessing child sexual maltreatment.* Thousand Oaks, CA: Sage.

Gambrill, E. (1990). *Critical thinking in clinical practice.* San Francisco: Jossey-Bass.

Gully K. (2003). Expectations test: Trauma scales for sexual abuse, physical abuse, exposure to family violence, and post-traumatic stress. *Child Maltreatment, 8*(3), 218–229.

Haz, A., & Ramirez, V. (2002). Adaptation of Child Abuse Potential Inventory in Chile: Analysis of difficulties and challenges in the application in Chilean studies. *Child Abuse and Neglect 26*(5), 481–495.

Kayser, J. A., & Lyon, M. A. (2000). Teaching social workers to use psychological assessment data. *Child Welfare, 79*(2), 197–223.

Milner, J. S., & Murphy, W. D. (1995). Assessment of child physical and sexual abuse offenders. *Family Relations, 44*(4), 478–488.

National Abandoned Infants Assistance Resource Center, School of Social Welfare, University of California at Berkeley. (2002). *Expediting permanency for abandoned infants: Guidelines for state policies and procedures.* Berkeley, CA: Author.

National Center on Child Abuse and Neglect Clearinghouse. (2003). *2003 Child abuse and neglect. State Statues Series at a glance: Definitions of child abuse and neglect.* Retrieved August 2, 2004, from http://nccanch.acf.hhs.gov

National Center on Child Abuse and Neglect Clearinghouse. (2004). *What is child abuse and neglect?* Retrieved August 2, 2004, from http://nccanch.acf.hhs.gov/pubs/factsheets/whatiscan.cfm

New York Society for the Prevention of Cruelty to Children. (1996). *NYSPCC professionals handbook: Identifying and reporting child abuse and neglect.* New York: Author.

Ney, P., Fung, T., & Wickett, A. (1994). The worst combinations of child abuse and neglect. *Child Abuse and Neglect, 18*(9), 705–714.

Straus, M., Hamby, S., Finkelhor, D., Moore, D., & Runyun, D. (1998). Identification of child maltreatment with the Parent-Child Conflict Tactics Scales: Development and psychometric data for a national sample of American parents. *Child Abuse and Neglect 22*(4), 249–270.

U.S. Department of Health and Human Services, National Center on Child Abuse and Neglect. (2004). *Child maltreatment 2002: Reports from the states to the national child abuse and neglect data system.* Washington, DC: U.S. Government Printing Office.

Laws and Procedures for Reporting Child Abuse

An Overview

Sandra Kopels

CHAPTER 32

Getting Started

The reporting of child abuse and neglect is a relatively new phenomenon that began in the late 1960s. Before that time, child abuse and neglect were covered up or denied by families and by those with whom they came in contact. The concept of reporting abuse was unknown, and there was no mechanism set up to govern what to report and to whom. Moreover, child abuse was considered to be a private family matter in which the government had no business intervening. It was not until the passage of the Child Abuse Prevention and Treatment Act (CAPTA) in 1974 that the federal government legally recognized child abuse and neglect and attempted to address it.

What We Know and Must Do

When the federal government enacted CAPTA, Congress provided incentives for states to set up programs to combat child abuse by providing a federal match to state funding for child abuse research, education, prevention, identification, and treatment. Within a few years, all 50 states had created a system to handle the reporting of child abuse cases. CAPTA has been reauthorized a number of times since its original enactment, and its scope has been expanded and refined; most recently, CAPTA was reauthorized by the Keeping Children and Families Safe Act of 2003.

In CAPTA's most recent reauthorization, Congress found that approximately 900,000 American children were victims of abuse and neglect, and that children suffer from neglect more than any other form of maltreatment. Congress found that the problem of child abuse and neglect requires a comprehensive approach that must integrate the expertise of people in social services, the law, health, mental health, education, substance abuse, and community-based organizations. Additionally, Congress noted that approaches to child abuse should be sensitive to factors of ethnic and cultural diversity that may influence child-rearing patterns.

How does child abuse reporting affect social workers and mental health professionals who work in the schools? In the course of their jobs, social workers and other counselors who attend to the mental health needs of students encounter children who are being abused or neglected at home. These professionals are required by law to report suspected abuse and neglect. At the same time, they must, as Congress has noted, be sensitive to diversity issues and cultural practices because they serve as liaisons between home, school, and the community.

In Illinois in FY 2002, of the 12,273 child abuse reports made by school personnel, 3,715 reports were made by school social workers (Illinois Department of Children and Family Services, 2002). Social workers reported more abuse and neglect than did any other category of school personnel and were responsible for making 30.27% of reports by all school personnel. Teachers, who generated the next-highest number, reported 2,682 (21.85%) cases of suspected abuse and neglect (Illinois Department of Children and Family Services, 2002). So although teachers greatly outnumber social workers in schools, and teachers have daily and ongoing contact with students, school social workers report more suspected child abuse and neglect. Because of their intensive involvement with students, teachers are most often the first school personnel to hear about or suspect abuse, but they frequently call on the social worker or other counselors to help make reports and to intervene. (See chapter 31 for strategies school-based practitioners can use to promote awareness among teachers of what constitutes child abuse, and for a discussion of evidence-based approaches to prevent abuse that can be implemented in the school in partnership with community-based agencies.)

What Is Child Maltreatment?

Child maltreatment is a term that encompasses different types of actions that harm children, including child abuse and neglect. With the passage of CAPTA, the federal government created a minimum legal definition of child abuse and neglect. According to that definition, child abuse and neglect are "any recent act or failure to act on the part of a parent or caretaker, which results in death, serious physical or emotional harm, sexual abuse or exploitation, or an act or failure to act which presents an imminent risk of serious harm" (42 U.S.C. §5106(g)). This minimum guideline must be met by each of the 50 states and U.S. territories; aside from that requirement, however, each state or territory is free to choose how to define abuse and neglect within its own laws. Generally, there is a wide variation among states as to the specific kinds of actions or conditions that constitute child abuse or neglect. Additionally, some states consider abuse and neglect together in one legal definition and do not differentiate abuse from neglect.

What Are Child Abuse and Neglect?

Chapter 33 presents a comprehensive discussion of the kinds of actions that constitute child abuse and neglect. Generally speaking, however, child abuse falls into three main categories: physical abuse, sexual abuse, and emotional abuse. Physical abuse is a physical injury that a parent or caretaker inflicts upon a child, whether or not the parent or caretaker intends to harm the child. Sexual abuse is generally defined as an act that involves the parent or caretaker who performs sexual behaviors or allows others to engage in sexual activities with the child. Emotional abuse involves acts that undermine a child's self-worth or development. Child abuse does not consist entirely of direct actions of parents or caretakers. Parents or caretakers who allow a child to be harmed also commit abuse.

Child neglect has to do with omissions: It is the failure of the parent or caretaker to provide the child with basic needs. Physical neglect occurs when the parent fails to provide the child with adequate food, clothing, shelter, or supervision. Medical neglect occurs when the parent fails to provide the child with necessary medical or mental health treatment. Educational neglect occurs when the parent fails to send the child to school or address the child's special educational needs.

Some states include particular actions in their legal definitions of abuse. Certain cultural practices that are regular practice in a parent's country of origin are considered abuse in the United States. For example, female genital mutilation, widely practiced in some African and Middle Eastern countries, is defined as child abuse in certain states. Other cultural practices, such as corporal punishment, are usually not considered to be abuse so long as the punishment is reasonable in nature. Other issues that reflect growing societal concerns may be considered to be abuse in some states. These include children who are exposed to certain negative influences, including domestic violence, substance abuse, or methamphetamine laboratories.

Some states exempt certain conduct of the parents from the legal definition of neglect if the failure to provide certain supports derives from something other than willful inaction. For example, the failure to obtain medical services such as a blood transfusion may be a result of the religious convictions of the parents rather than conscious disregard for their child. Other states include certain types of exposure within their neglect definitions; many states deem children who are born with alcohol or drugs in their system to be neglected.

Who Is Required to Report?

Each state delineates persons who are obligated to report child abuse and neglect. These individuals are known as mandated reporters because they are required by law to report maltreatment known to or suspected by them. In many states, the persons required to report are those whose occupations bring them in contact with children. Generally, mandated reporters include child care providers, mental health professionals, health care workers, law enforcement personnel, and school personnel.

In all 50 states, social workers are considered to be mandated reporters of child abuse and neglect.

Many states specifically delineate other professionals who are required to report. For example, some state statutes list funeral home directors, film processors, camp counselors, and firefighters as those specifically required to report. Some states require Christian Science practitioners or religious healers to report. Clergy, who in the past were usually exempt from reporting child abuse or neglect, are now required to report child abuse in some states. Certain states do not specify reporters by professions; instead, those states place the duty to report on every individual, regardless of his or her profession. In all states, even if there is no specific duty to report child abuse, any person may file a report. To encourage reporting, states may offer anonymity to reporters so that their identities are hidden from the alleged perpetrators. Typically, mandated reporters are not entitled to anonymity.

What Must Be Reported?

Mandated reporters are not obligated to report behaviors that do not meet a state's legal definition of abuse or neglect, nor are they required to report situations that the reporters themselves believe are wrong but are not illegal. The legal definition of abuse or neglect is more specific than the way those terms are used by laypeople or in professional practice, and the mandate to report is always dependent on these legal definitions.

It is not always clear whether certain acts meet the definitions of abuse and neglect within a particular state. Parental behavior or inaction constitutes abuse or neglect only if the acts fit the way a legislature has defined abuse or neglect. For example, a child may tell the social worker that his or her parent gets drunk every night. Though excessive drinking may not be beneficial to the parent's health or be a good model for the child, the parent's alcohol usage is not illegal, and by itself it is not injurious to the child. Unless a state defines abuse to include a child who is exposed to intoxicated behavior, the parental drunkenness is not abuse and need not be reported. However, if, while intoxicated, the parent strikes the child, operates a motor vehicle with the child as a passenger, or allows drinking buddies to mistreat the child, this could constitute abuse and be reported because the child is at risk of harm.

As I said above, some states exempt certain circumstances from the definitions of abuse or neglect; that is, the state defines what abuse or neglect means, but then it carves some conditions out of the definition. For example, a state may define neglect as the failure to provide proper food, clothing, or shelter. However, the definition may carve out an exception if the failure to provide adequately for the child is a result of poverty. A parent who has the financial means to provide proper support and chooses not to neglects the child; a parent who cannot financially provide these supports may not be neglectful (Eamon & Kopels, 2004).

States often impose other conditions on what must be reported. Typically, definitions of child abuse and neglect apply only to victims who are under 18 years of age and are acts committed by adults who are related to a child or are responsible for the child's welfare. In some states if the abuse or neglect happens to someone older than 18, or if the perpetrator is unknown to the child, then this may not constitute child abuse or neglect. For example, if a school social worker is told by a 20-year-old special education student that her father sexually abused her, the student is too old to meet the legal definition of abuse. If a child tells the school social worker that she was attacked by a stranger, this does not constitute child abuse. Therefore, because these situations do not meet the definition of child abuse and neglect, the mandated reporter would not have to report.

How Certain Must a Mandated Reporter Be That Abuse or Neglect Occurred?

Most child abuse or neglect does not occur in the presence of a mandated reporter but rather outside the school environment. See Chapter 31 for more information about who is required to report abuse. Mandated reporters need to rely on their professional judgment and skill to decide whether abuse or neglect may have happened and whether they are mandated to report an incident. As one recent article relevant to this topic noted: "The law does not require absolute certainty on the part of the mandated reporter. In fact, the law does not even require actual knowledge. Typically, state law uses language that provides for discretion on the part of the reporter. Standards for when reports are made use words such as the mandated reporter 'knows' or has 'reasonable cause to "believe" or "suspect,"' or has 'reason to believe,' or has "reason to suspect'" (U.S. Department of Health and Human Services [USDHHS], 2002b).

Sometimes, a mandated reporter will have reasonable cause to believe a child has been abused because the child actually tells the reporter about the abuse. Sometimes, a child may not disclose abuse to a mandated reporter, but the reporter notices signs, like bruising or swelling, and the reporter suspects that abuse has occurred. Other times, a child may be dirty and unkempt for months, and, when asked, the child provides an implausible explanation. Clearly, if a social worker or other counselor observes injuries or signs, or if a child's explanations are inconsistent or unbelievable given what the social worker or counselor knows, or if there have been past incidents that now seem suspicious, these are indicators that a mandated reporter has enough reason to report.

Where Does a Mandated Reporter Report?

All states have a system in place for receiving child abuse and neglect reports. However, these systems vary greatly among states. In most places, telephone reports of child abuse and neglect are made to a child abuse hotline that typically is operated 24 hours a day. Calls are sometimes made to a "central registry," a centralized database with information on previously made reports of child maltreatment in a selected geographical area that is operated by child protective services. The hotline may be part of and run by the same agency that operates the central registry. Some states have a statewide system of receiving reports that refers investigation to a smaller, regional division. Other states have divided their handling of reported abuse or neglect calls by counties, totally separate entities from one another. Still other states have reporting systems that include both child protective services and law enforcement. In these states, child abuse and neglect reports may be made to either social services or the police; these two branches work closely together and coordinate the investigation of child abuse reports depending on the type and seriousness of the allegations.

When Does a Report Have to Be Made?

Though worded differently, state statutes are consistent in requiring that mandated reporters report any suspected abuse or neglect without delay. The majority of states require that reports be made immediately. Others require that those mandated to do so report promptly, and some of these specify a time limit—for example, within 24 hours (USDHHS, 2002b). Therefore, mandated reporters must report suspected abuse or neglect as soon as they form a belief that it may have occurred. Sometimes, mandated reporters would like to consult with their supervisors prior to making a report. This would be allowable so long as the consultation occurs within a very brief period of time. For example, if the supervisor is in a 1-hour meeting or will return to the office later that day, the mandated reporter probably can wait until the supervisor is available. However, if the supervisor is on an extended vacation, the mandated reporter would violate his or her duty by waiting to report. Obviously, how "immediate" is immediately is a judgment call; however, a mandated reporter must report suspected child abuse and neglect as soon as possible for the child's protection.

What Happens When a Report Is Made?

When a reporter calls a child abuse hotline, the child protective service agency will try to gather information to determine if an investigation is warranted. Not all reports must be investigated. If a report falls outside the definitions of child abuse or neglect as established by state law, if the caller has no credible reason for suspecting child abuse, if the caller has a history of false or malicious reporting, or if there is insufficient information provided, then child protective services may decide not to investigate (Sagatun & Edwards, 1995). Mandated reporters should provide the hotline personnel as much information as possible to answer the questions that will be asked of them when they make a report. When reporters, mandated or otherwise, express vague statements of concern without underlying facts, the screener's ability to determine whether to accept the case for investigation is limited (Duncan, 2001). Though some callers may not provide enough information for child protective services to accept the report for investigation, certain calls may be referred to other community agencies or services. Child protective services may provide information and referrals to agencies better suited to meet the needs of a particular family (Duncan, 2001).

If the child protective services agency accepts the allegation as a report, an investigation will begin. CAPTA does not specify time frames for investigations. Instead, CAPTA requires that states include procedures for the immediate screening, safety assessment, and prompt investigations of the reports (42 U.S.C. § 5106a(b)(2)). States vary as to how soon an investigation must begin, what types of information needs to be collected on a family/child, who must be interviewed, and the time lines for completion of investigations (Kopels, Charleton, & Wells, 2003). Many states require an investigation to be initiated "immediately" or "promptly," and other states specify that investigations must begin within a certain amount of time, in some cases 24 hours. Other states differentiate the time allowed for the initiation of an investigation based on the seriousness of the allegations of harm to the child (Kopels et al., 2003).

In the most serious cases, child protective services may work in conjunction with law enforcement to provide immediate safety for all parties. Child protection services and the police will decide if criminal investigation is warranted and whether mandated services are required. The child may or may not be removed from the home, depending on the plan for safety and services to the children and families (Duncan, 2001). As part of the investigation, child protective services workers make home visits, interview family members, and contact other professionals who have had some involvement with the family (Sagatun & Edwards, 1995). The investigator may also talk with the reporter who initially made the report.

Mandated reporters often want to know the results of an investigation. Typically, child protective services determine whether a case is substantiated or unsubstantiated. Although these terms vary by state, a case is "substantiated" or "indicated" when an investigation determines that the allegations of abuse or neglect are warranted and that maltreatment did occur. A case is "unsubstantiated" or "unfounded" when the investigation determined that maltreatment did not occur. Some state and local child welfare agencies will inform mandated reporters of the outcome of a report. In some states, the child protection agency sends a letter to mandated reporters and may contact them about the results of an investigation. However, because families maintain a right to privacy that is built into child reporting laws, reporters may not be informed of investigations' findings and may never learn what resulted from their report (Duncan, 2001).

What Happens If a Mandated Reporter Does Not Report?

Social workers and mental health professionals who work in schools must report all child abuse and neglect known to or suspected by them. Despite this mandate, many cases of child abuse and neglect are not reported, even when suspected by professionals (USDHHS, 2003). As a consequence, 47 states impose punishment on mandated reporters who fail to report.

Certain sanctions are criminal in nature. In approximately 35 states and some U.S. territories, the failure to report is classified as a misdemeanor and is punishable by a fine and/or imprisonment (USDHHS, 2002b). Most of these states impose penalties on mandatory reporters who "knowingly" or "willfully" failed to report suspected abuse or who "should have known" that abuse was likely yet never reported their suspicions. Some states use language such as "intentionally" or "purposely" in determining standards for mandated reporters who fail to report, and other states impose penalties without providing a standard (USDHHS, 2002b).

In addition to criminal punishment, mandated reporters may also face civil lawsuits from persons who claim that the failure to report caused further injury to a child. Seven states have legislation that permits monetary recovery for the failure to comply with mandatory reporting requirements (National Association of Social Workers, 2004). In the other 43 states, unless legislation is enacted, the courts will determine whether monetary liability can be imposed on mandated reporters who fail to report. The failure to report child abuse and neglect can also subject a mandated reporter to licensure action and to disciplinary action by professional organizations.

Does Child Abuse Reporting Affect the Duty to Maintain Confidentiality?

Social workers and mental health professionals have an ethical duty, and often a legal duty, to maintain the confidentiality of information provided to them in their professional capacities. The mandatory reporting of child abuse and neglect creates a conflicting duty to report (Kagle & Kopels, 1994). In recognition of this conflict, child abuse and neglect reporting is considered to be an exception to the duty to maintain client confidentiality. Privileged communications, a concept that protects the confidentiality of certain relationships in court proceedings, does not apply to mandatory reporting in about half of the states (USDHHS, 2002b). This means that mandated reporters must report suspected child abuse and neglect, cooperate in ensuing investigations, and testify in court, if requested to do so.

CAPTA requires that states have provisions for immunity from prosecution for individuals who make a good-faith report of suspected or known child abuse and neglect (42 U.S.C. §5106a(b)(2)(A)(vii)). These immunity statutes protect mandated reporters from civil or criminal liability that could occur from the filing of a report. State statutes vary as to whether the immunity is absolute (and, therefore, is not dependent on the reasonableness of the mandated reporter's belief), or whether the immunity is limited to situations in which the reporter acts in good faith. Good faith is often presumed, giving the reporter a defense to a lawsuit. Reporters who act maliciously or negligently may not enjoy immunity from litigation or prosecution.

Do Mandated Reporters Actually Report Maltreatment?

Child abuse reporting laws are designed to ensure that children who are at risk of harm by parental action or inaction are identified and that services are provided to safeguard them from future harm. However, little empirical evidence exists to support the assumptions on which reporting laws are based (Hutchinson, 1993). The lack of clarity about what the law actually requires and the reliance on professionals' judgment leads to unevenness in the reporting of child abuse. Research has shown that various professionals respond differently to reporting requirements (Kalichman, 1999) and have different knowledge, opinions, and decision-making processes regarding the duty to report (Renninger, Veach, & Bagdade, 2002).

Research indicates that mandatory reporting laws may result in the underreporting of suspected child abuse. Kalichman (1999), who reviews literature that argues against mandatory reporting, found that some professionals feel that reporting interferes with child protection, is destructive to the helping relationships, and is harmful to children and families; they also think that reporting laws are overly vague and unenforceable. Hutchinson (1993) notes that some professionals fear a disruption in the therapeutic

alliance, hesitate to get involved in legal proceedings, fear liability if the report is not substantiated, or see no benefits to clients. Studies demonstrate that during their careers, close to 60% of professionals fail to report suspected maltreatment (Delaronde, King, Bendel, & Reece, 2000; USDHHS, 1988).

Research indicates that mandatory reporting laws lead to the overreporting of suspected child abuse as well. Lindsey (1994) noted that although reports of child abuse increased sevenfold during the period of 1975–1986, child fatalities remained relatively stable. In 2002, of the 2.6 million referrals to child protection agencies, mandated professionals initiated 56.5% of all child abuse reports (U.S. Department of Health and Human Services [USDHHS], 2002a). More than half of these reports (60.4%) were unsubstantiated, and of those, more than half came from educational, social services, legal/law enforcement personnel, and anonymous reporters (USDHHS, 2002a). Although the rate of substantiated cases has remained constant since 2000, the number of unsubstantiated cases has increased.

Ainsworth (2002) questioned whether evidence exists that children are abused and neglected less in jurisdictions that require mandatory reporting. He compared New South Wales, which requires mandatory reporting, with Western Australia, which does not. He found that mandatory reporting in New South Wales led to fewer substantiated cases of abuse and more effort and resources spent on unsubstantiated cases than Western Australia's nonmandatory reporting requirement. He suggests that mandatory reporting systems are overburdened with notifications of suspected abuse, and unsubstantiated cases overwhelm services that are supposed to target the most at-risk children. Delaronde et al. (2000) examined the level of support of social workers, pediatricians, and physician's assistants for mandated reporting versus an alternative model that allowed for more discretion. They found that mandated reporters who did not report all cases of suspected child maltreatment significantly favor a discretionary policy.

Key Points to Remember

Child abuse and neglect reporting is governed by state laws that require mandated reporters to take action to protect children. Because of the variance between states and client situations, there is no "one size fits all" way to handle child abuse reporting. The best practice approach to child abuse reporting is to learn the laws that govern practice within a particular state and follow the legal mandates. Therefore, school social workers and mental health professionals should:

- familiarize themselves with the law in the state of employment regarding child abuse and neglect
- learn where to call when abuse or neglect is suspected
- make the call as soon as possible
- know the behavioral indicators or signs of abuse and neglect in children
- gather as much information as possible before calling, such as child's name, date of birth, address, and telephone number; details of the suspected abuse; and information about the perpetrator
- report, when in doubt

References

Ainsworth, F. (2002). Mandatory reporting of child abuse and neglect: Does it really make a difference? *Child and Family Social Work, 7*, 57–63.

Child Abuse Prevention and Treatment Act. P.L. 93–247, 42 U.S.C. §5101 et seq. (1974).

Delaronde, S., King, G., Bendel, R., & Reece, R. (2000). Opinions among mandated reporters toward child maltreatment reporting policies. *Child Abuse and Neglect, 24*(7), 901–910.

Duncan, N. (2001). *When should teachers report abuse: A child abuse investigator offers tips for educators.* Retrieved May 15, 2004, from http://www.cwla.org/articles/cv0111teachers.htm

Eamon, M. K., & Kopels, S. (2004). "For reasons of poverty": Court challenges to child welfare practices and mandated programs. *Children and Youth Services Review, 26*(9), 821–836.

Hutchinson, E. D. (1993). Mandatory reporting laws: Child protective case findings gone awry? *Social Work, 38*(1), 56–63.

Illinois Department of Children and Family Services. *Child abuse and neglect statistics annual report 2002.*

Table 9. Source of Reports. Retrieved May 11, 2004, from http://www.state.il.us/dcfs/docs/cants2002table9.shtml

Kagle, J. D., & Kopels, S. (1994). Confidentiality after Tarasoff. *Health and Social Work, 19*(3), 217–222.

Kalichman, S. (1999). *Mandated reporting of suspected child abuse: Ethics, law, and policy* (2nd ed). Washington, DC: American Psychological Association.

Keeping Children and Families Safe Act of 2003. (P.L. 108-36).

Kopels, S., Charleton, T., & Wells, S. J. (2003). Investigation laws and practices in child protective services. *Child Welfare, 82*(6), 661–684.

Lindsey, D. (1994). Mandated reporting and child abuse fatalities: Requirements for a system to protect children. *Social Work Research, 18*(1), 41–54.

National Association of Social Workers. *Social workers and civil liability for failure to report child abuse.* Retrieved February 26, 2004, from http://www.socialworkers.org/ldf/legal_issue/200402.asp?back=yes

Renninger, S. M., Veach, P. M., & Bagdade, P. (2002). Psychologist's knowledge, opinions, and decision-making process regarding child abuse and neglect reporting laws. *Professional Psychology: Research and Practice, 33*(1), 19–23.

Sagatun, I. J., & Edwards, L. P. (1995). *Child abuse and the legal system.* Chicago: Nelson-Hall.

U.S. Department of Health and Human Services, Administration on Children, Youth and Families (2002a). *Child maltreatment 2002: Reports from the states to the national child abuse and neglect data systems—National statistics on child abuse and neglect.* Retrieved September 5, 2004, from http://www.acf.dhhs.gov/programs/cb/publications/cm02/cm02.pdf

U.S. Department of Health and Human Services, Administration on Children, Youth and Families. National Clearinghouse on Child Abuse and Neglect Information. (2002b). *Current trends in child maltreatment reporting laws.* Washington, DC: U.S. Government Printing Office.

U.S. Department of Health and Human Services, Administration on Children, Youth and Families. National Clearinghouse on Child Abuse and Neglect Information. (2003). *Reporting penalties.* Washington, DC: U.S. Government Printing Office.

U.S. Department of Health and Human Services, Children's Bureau, National Center on Child Abuse and Neglect. (1988). *Study findings: Study of national incidence and prevalence of child abuse and neglect: 1988.* Washington, DC: U.S. Government Printing Office.

Helping Students Who Have Been Physically or Sexually Abused

Strategies and Interventions

Kathleen Coulborn Faller

CHAPTER 33

Getting Started

Most children go to school, and they are in school for several hours 5 days a week about 10 months of the year. Thus, school is where children have the greatest exposure to professionals who can identify, report, and ameliorate sexual and physical abuse. These professionals—teachers, counselors, school social workers, and school administrators—are all mandated reporters of child abuse and neglect. It is not accidental that of all the mandated reporters, school personnel make the largest proportion of professional reports (U.S. Department of Health and Human Services [US-DHHS], 2004). Similarly, the National Incidence Studies, which examine the relationship between cases of child maltreatment that are investigated by child protective services and those identified by "sentinels," such as school staff, have found that schools accounted for reporting approximately half of the almost 3 million cases of child abuse and neglect that came to professional attention (Sedlak & Broadhurst, 1996).

Because of their centrality in the lives of school-age children, school personnel have the potential to play an instrumental role in ameliorating the effects of child physical and sexual abuse. See chapters 31 and 32 for more information on reporting and preventing child abuse in schools.

What We Know

Despite the pivotal role of school personnel in intervention with children who have been physically and sexually abused, child maltreatment literature focuses on the role of schools in identifying, reporting, and preventing child abuse and neglect (e.g., Broadhurst, 1984; Crosson-Tower, 2002; US-DHHS, 2003). This literature consists of numerous manuals and a modest number of books. In addition, the school social work literature describes abused and neglected children as a special population to be addressed by social workers and mental health professionals in the schools, but it provides very little information about specific strategies and interventions that might support maltreated children (Allen-Meares, Washington, & Welsh, 2000; Constable, McDonald, & Flynn, 2002). In fact, there is very little evidence-based literature that focuses on the role of school-based intervention to assist physically and sexually abused children. Consequently, I will draw upon school-compatible, evidence-based practice from the child welfare literature, the small body of strategies and interventions for maltreated children in the school system, and what professionals consider to be best practice for school personnel addressing the needs of physically and sexually abused children. Topics covered are (1) the consequences of physical and sexual abuse, (2) the importance of support, belief, and role modeling for victims of abuse, (3) using multidisciplinary teams with abused children, and (4) abuse-specific cognitive-behavioral treatment.

Multiple Consequences of Sexual and Physical Abuse

The research on the effects of child sexual and physical abuse indicates that abuse impairs the functioning of its victims, but not in a single, definable way (Berliner & Elliott, 2002; Kolko, 2002). The most common sequelae in sexually abused children are fears or phobias and sexualized behaviors (Chaffin, Letourneau, & Silovsky, 2002; Kendall-Tackett, Williams, & Finkelhor, 1993). The most common sequelae of physical abuse are aggression and health problems (Kolko, 2002). Both physically and sexually abused children are likely to blame themselves for their abuse and the aftermath of discovery, to have academic difficulties, and to have symptoms of posttraumatic stress disorder or other trauma symptoms (Berliner & Elliott, 2003; Kolko, 2002). The effect of sexual and physical abuse is compounded by co-morbid conditions (Allen-Meares et al., 2000; Berliner & Elliott, 2003). Children may be *both* sexually and physically abused and exposed to other traumatizing situations such as neglect, domestic violence, and substance abuse (http://www.ssw.umich.edu/icwtp/). Moreover, special needs children are at greater risk for physical and sexual abuse (Davies, 2002; Gorman-Smith & Matson, 1992).

Support, Belief, and Modeling Appropriate Adult Responses

According to a respectable body of research, a child's recovery from sexual abuse is more likely if the child has caretakers who support him or her and believe that the abuse in fact occurred (Bolen, Lamb, & Gradante, 2002; Everson, Hunter, Runyon, & Edelsohn, 1989; Heriot, 1996; Hunter, Coulter, Runyan, & Everson, 1990). By extension, support and belief provided by other important people, such as teachers, school social workers, and school counselors, can ameliorate the effects of both sexual and physical abuse. For many abused children, school is their refuge from a painful home environment.

A related finding is the importance of a mentor or role model to a child's survival of adverse home circumstances. Thus, school personnel can be central to children's recovery from abuse and can provide an alternative adult response and a different model for adult behavior for children who have been physically and sexually abused.

Multidisciplinary Response

School systems and child welfare systems have in common an appreciation of the importance of a multidisciplinary response to children's problems. In the 1970s, federal legislation in both education (P.L. 94-142, Education for All Handicapped Children Act) and child welfare (P.L. 93-247,

Child Abuse Prevention and Treatment Act [CAPTA]) provided for multidisciplinary services to aid abused children. School personnel thus can use existing skills in working as part of a multidisciplinary team to intervene with abused children. Team members include not only school staff, but also child welfare staff, therapists, and sometimes law enforcement personnel, foster parents, court workers, and judges.

What We Can Do

Efficacy of Abuse-Specific, Cognitive-Behavioral Treatment

Many communities have developed treatment programs for sexually abused children, and a smaller number have programs for physically abused children. These programs are based upon clinical experience, are likely to be experiential, and are often delivered in a group format. Most of these interventions have not been evaluated (Berliner & Elliott, 2001; Kolko, 2002). Those programs that have been demonstrated to be effective take a cognitive-behavioral approach (e.g., Berliner & Elliott, 2002; Cohen, Berliner, & Mannarino, 2003). Although group treatment may be more efficient, it has not been shown to be more effective (Berliner & Elliott, 2002).

In other communities, professionals rely on counseling to address the consequences of abuse. Research has shown that nonspecific treatment is not as effective as cognitive-behavioral abuse-specific treatment and may be ineffective with children who have a history of abuse (Berliner & Elliott, 2001).

Instructions on Intervention

The findings described in the previous section can guide school professionals as they intervene with children who have a history of physical and sexual abuse.

Addressing the Consequences of Physical and Sexual Abuse

When children not identified as physically or sexually abused display known symptoms of abuse, school personnel need to ensure that someone will inquire about the cause of the child's symptoms. School practice, local child welfare policy, and the specifics of the case determine whether school personnel talk to the child or whether it is reported to child protective services, which will then conduct an interview.

When children identified as physically or sexually abused display known symptoms, school personnel must ensure that the symptoms are understood and addressed by other staff. Many times sequelae of physical and sexual abuse are treated simply as bad behavior, which is then punished rather than understood in terms of etiology.

All relevant school staff should understand the source of the child's problems and have sensitive, consistent, and coordinated responses to these problems. Such responses may be accomplished by having a school-based team meeting or series of meetings.

School is the natural environment for dealing with academic deficits that may result from physical and sexual abuse and/or school disruption because of foster care placement. Schools can provide tutoring and other academic support services and can ensure that the child's school record follows him or her (Ayasse, 1998).

Supporting and Believing the Child

Adults often doubt children's accounts of abuse or deny its effects, especially when the allegation is sexual abuse. Research indicates that false allegations of abuse are rare (Faller, 2003). Nevertheless, adults may spend more time agonizing about the truth of the child's allegation than about the consequences of abuse to the child. School personnel must support and believe children in order to help them heal. The determination of the likelihood of child abuse is the responsibility of other professionals (child protection workers, physicians, and judges). If these professionals have determined that the child has been abused, school personnel should assume that is true, and they should provide the child with role models of concerned and fair-minded adults.

Working as Part of the Multidisciplinary Team

When children who are victims of physical and sexual abuse attend school, school personnel must appreciate that there are other professionals involved and, within the bounds of confidentiality, reach out to them. School personnel should insist that services to the child be coordinated and that they be part of the service delivery process.

Although school personnel may act in loco parentis and may spend more time with abused children than the other professionals on the team, child welfare staff and court staff have final say about how a child's abuse case will be handled. The preeminent role of child welfare and court professionals can be challenging when there is disagreement about how a particular child's situation should be handled (Bross, Krugman, Lenherr, Rosenberg, & Schmitt, 1988).

Many communities now have programs and community-based teams to assure coordination of services to abused and neglected children and their families or other caretakers. An example is Wraparound Services, which draws on school, child welfare, mental health programs, and other community services to prevent children from going into foster or residential care.

Assuring the Child Receives Appropriate Treatment

School personnel should assure that victims of physical and sexual abuse receive abuse-specific, state-of-the-art treatment with a cognitive-behavioral component. Child welfare staff often focus on a child's safety and may fail to follow through on treatment once the child is protected. Moreover, they may not be aware of the type of treatment that is effective.

In some full-service schools, treatment programs for physically and sexually abused children may actually be provided in the school setting, but in most communities, treatment is provided by community-based social services agencies.

Tools and Practice Examples

Case Example of How to Do the Intervention

Cindy is a biracial, 15-year-old girl whose Caucasian mother died of cancer when she was 8. The cancer was diagnosed when Cindy was born. Her African American father, a very accomplished electrical engineer, was overwhelmed by the loss of his wife and blamed his daughter for the mother's death. He targeted Cindy for physical, emotional, and sexual abuse. She told her school counselor about her abuse when she was 13. Cindy was very bright and sweet, but she also overate and had a problem wetting herself, problems later determined to be related to her abuse.

The school counselor never doubted Cindy's account and immediately reported the abuse to child protective services. The school stood by Cindy when her father vehemently denied the abuse. The school also advocated for Cindy when her father tried to get her declared mentally ill (because she overate, wet herself, and accused him of abuse) and committed to a day treatment center.

As a consequence of the school counselor's report, Cindy was placed in foster care with a single African American woman living in another town in the same county. The woman had three other foster children, all African American teenage girls. But they were very different from Cindy. She had played the violin in the school orchestra until her father had sold her violin because he thought her grades should be better. She was very interested in going to college.

Cindy's school was the place where she formed close relationships, both with peers and adults. She wanted to continue in her school, even though it was in a different town, and she asked her school social worker to intervene with the child welfare worker in charge of Cindy's case. Cindy's teacher, counselor, and the school social worker all attended an initial meeting with child welfare staff and were able to get her child welfare worker to agree that it was in Cindy's interest to continue at her current school.

Initially school staff assisted in arranging Cindy's transportation to and from school. Three months later, Cindy wanted to move in with the family of a close friend and schoolmate, and the school staff intervened with the child welfare worker to support Cindy's request. In addition, the school social worker persuaded the music teacher to lend Cindy a violin so she could continue to play in the orchestra.

Cindy's enuresis caused her much embarrassment, and she had a great deal of difficulty dealing with her father's utter rejection and refusal to acknowledge any wrongdoing. The school social worker and her new foster parents convinced the child welfare worker that Cindy needed therapy, and they worked together to select a female

therapist who was well-versed in behavioral (for the enuresis) and cognitive-behavioral (for abuse aftereffects) approaches. Cindy formed an excellent therapeutic alliance with her therapist. In addition, school personnel developed a program to get Cindy to ask when she needed to go to the toilet and for school staff to immediately grant her permission so she would not have an accident at school.

Cindy was fortunate, despite her misfortune, because she had strong and consistent advocates on her behalf in her school, an excellent child welfare caseworker, and a good therapist who was aware of effective treatment for physically and sexually abused children.

Forms and Exercises

The intervention checklist in Table 33.1 is designed to assist school personnel in developing and tracking interventions and strategies to help children who have been physically and sexually abused.

Resources

Books

Freeman, E., Franklin C., Fong, R., Schaffer, G., & Timberlake, E. (Eds.). (1998). *Multisystem skills and interventions in school social work practice.* Washington, DC: NASW Press.

Kluger, M., Alexander, G., & Curtis, P. (Eds.). (2001). *What works in child welfare.* Washington, DC: Child Welfare League of America.

Myers, J. E. B., Berliner, L., Briere, J., Hendrix, C. T., Jenny, C., & Reid, T. (Eds.). (2002). *APSAC handbook on child maltreatment* (2nd ed.). Thousand Oaks, CA: Sage.

Web Sites

American Professional Society on the Abuse of Children: www.apsac.org.

Child physical and sexual abuse: Guidelines for treatment. Available at www.musc.edu/cvc/guide1.htm

National Clearinghouse on Child Abuse and Neglect: www.calib.com/nccanch

Prevent Child Abuse America: www.preventchild-abuse.org

University of Michigan Interdisciplinary Child Welfare Training Program: www.ssw.umich.edu/icwtp/

Table 33.1 Intervention Checklist

Child identifying information	Name		Age	Grade in school
Types of sexual & physical abuse	1.	2.	3.	4.
Sequelae/symptoms/ problems	1.	2.	3.	4.
School-based plan for managing the problems	Behavior management		Services (e.g., tutoring, school social work services)	
School personnel involved with the child (e.g., teacher, counselor, school social worker, teacher aide)	1. 2. 3.			
Is there someone in the school the child trusts/ talks to?	Yes/No		Who?	
Community professionals involved with the child's case	Child welfare	Treatment provider	Other	
Team meetings	Frequency		Location	
	Who will attend?		Who convenes?	
Intervention	Therapy		Other intervention	
Other case management issues (e.g., custody, termination of parental rights)				

Key Points to Remember

Grade school and high school education are the only universal social programs in the United States. School personnel thereby are the most consistent professionals in the lives of physically and sexually abused children. Research suggests that there are several important interventions school staff can make on behalf of abused children. These include (1) recognizing and responding to sequelae or problems that result from having been physically or sexually abused; (2) believing, supporting, and mentoring abused children; (3) collaborating with other professionals who are involved in service delivery to abused children; and (4) ensuring that children who have been abused will receive abuse-specific therapy.

References

Allen-Meares, P., Washington, R., & Welsh, B. (2000). *Social work in the schools* (3rd ed.). Needham Heights, MA: Allyn & Bacon.

Ayasse, R. (1998). Addressing the needs of foster children: The Foster Youth Services Program. In E. Freeman, C. Franklin, R. Fong, Gary Schaffer, & E. Timberlake (Eds.), *Multisystem skills and interventions in school social work practice* (pp. 52–61). Washington, DC: NASW Press.

Berliner, L., & Elliott, D. (2002). Sexual abuse of children. In J.E.B. Myers, L. Berliner, J. Briere, C. T. Hendrix, C. Jenny, & T. Reid (Eds.), *The APSAC handbook on child maltreatment* (2nd ed., pp. 55–78). Thousand Oaks, CA: Sage.

Bolen, R., Lamb, L., & Gradante, J. (2002) The needs-based assessment of parental (guardian) support: A test of its validity and reliability. *Child Abuse and Neglect, 26,* 1081–1099.

Bross, D., Krugman, R., Lenherr, M., Rosenberg, D. A., & Schmitt, B. (Eds.). (1988). *The new child protection team handbook.* New York: Garland.

Chaffin, M., Letourneau, E., & Silovsky, J. (2002). Adults, adolescents, and children who sexually abuse children: A developmental perspective. In J.E.B. Myers, L. Berliner, J. Briere, C. T. Hendrix, C. Jenny, & T. Reid (Eds.), *The APSAC handbook on child maltreatment* (2nd ed., pp. 205–232). Thousand Oaks, CA: Sage.

Cohen, J., Berliner, L., & Mannarino, A. (2003). Psychosocial and pharmacological interventions for child crime victims. *Journal of Traumatic Stress, 16*(2), 175–186.

Constable, R., McDonald, S., & Flynn, J. (2002). *School social work: Practice, policy, and research perspectives* (5th ed.). Chicago: Lyceum.

Crosson-Tower, C. (2002). *When children are abused: An educator's guide.* Needham Heights, MA: Allyn & Bacon.

Davies, D. (2002). *Interviewing children with disabilities; Curriculum for the APSAC forensic interview clinic.* University of Oklahoma Health Sciences Center: American Professional Society on the Abuse of Children.

Everson, M., Hunter, W., Runyon, D., & Edelsohn, G. (1989). Maternal support following discovery of incest. *American Journal of Orthopsychiatry, 59*(2), 197–207.

Faller, K. C. (2003). *Understanding and assessing child sexual maltreatment* (2nd ed.). Thousand Oaks, CA: Sage.

Gorman-Smith, D., & Matson, J. (1992). Sexual abuse and persons with mental retardation. In W. O'Donohue & J. Greer (Eds.), *The sexual abuse of children: Theory and research* (Vol. 1, pp. 285–306). Hillsdale, NJ: Erlbaum.

Heriot, J. (1996). Maternal protectiveness following the disclosure of intrafamilial child sexual abuse. *Journal of Interpersonal Violence, 11*(2), 181–194.

Hunter, W., Coulter, M., Runyan, D., & Everson, M. (1990). Determinants of placement for sexually abused children. *Child Abuse & Neglect, 14,* 407–417.

Kendall-Tackett, K. A., Williams, L. M., & Finkelhor, D. (1993). Impact of sexual abuse on children: A review and synthesis of recent empirical studies. *Psychological Bulletin, 113,* 164–180.

Kolko, David (2002). Child physical abuse. In J.E.B. Myers, L. Berliner, J. Briere, C. T. Hendrix, C. Jenny, & T. Reid (Eds.), *The APSAC handbook on child maltreatment* (2nd ed., pp. 21–54). Thousand Oaks, CA: Sage.

Sas, L., & Cunningham, A. (1995). *Tipping the balance to tell the secret: The public discovery of child sexual abuse.* (Available from the London Court Clinic, 254 Pall Mall St., London, Ont. N6A 5P6 [519-679-7250])

Sedlak, A., & Broadhurst, D. (1996). *The third National Incidence Study on child abuse and neglect (NIS-3).* Washington, DC: U.S. Department of Health and Human Services.

Smith, C. (1998). The link between childhood maltreatment and teenage pregnancy. In E. Freeman, C. Franklin, R. Fong, G. Schaffer, & E. Timberlake (Eds.), *Multisystem skills and interventions in school social work practice* (pp. 190–205). Washington, DC: NASW Press.

U.S. Department of Health and Human Services. (2003). *School-based child maltreatment programs: Synthesis of lessons learned.* Washington, DC: Government Printing Office.

U.S. Department of Health and Human Services, National Center on Child Abuse and Neglect. (2004). *Child maltreatment 2002: Reports from the states to the national child abuse and neglect data system.* Washington, DC: U.S. Government Printing Office.

Building Effective Alliances With Child Protective Services and Other Child Welfare Agencies

Maria Scannapieco

CHAPTER 34

Getting Started

It is often not until the child enters the school system that child maltreatment becomes known outside the family. This may be one reason children in the middle years of childhood, 6 to 11 years old, are reported as being at high risk of maltreatment (U.S. Department of Health and Human Services [USDHHS], 2002). Although the risk of maltreatment declines after elementary school, children in middle school and high school are still at risk. Adolescents represent about one in five victims of child maltreatment (Thomlison, 1997). The highest physical abuse rates for girls occur among those between the ages of 12 and 15, and 32% of all physical abuse reports involve children between 11 and 17 (USDHHS, 2002). The greatest risk of sexual abuse occurs between the ages of 7 and 13 (Finkelhor, 1994), and the highest risk for first experience of sexual abuse peaks between 11 and 13 years of age (Bolen, 1998; Russell, 1986).

Schoolteachers, social workers, nurses, and other personnel are in an exceptional position to identify and report child maltreatment because they are in sustained contact with children and often have a trusting relationship with the child. An estimated 2 million reports of alleged child abuse or neglect were investigated by child protective service (CPS) agencies in 2002 (USDHHS, 2002). In 2002, two thirds (an estimated 1.73 million) of referrals were found to warrant investigation or assessment by CPS agencies. Of these screened referrals, 56.1% came from professionals in education, the law, law enforcement, social services, and medicine. The most common sources of reports were from education personnel (16.1%). The National Incident Study-3 (1996) points to similar report sources. Overall, school staff was the predominant source of recognition of maltreated children and adolescents.

Schools are in a unique position throughout the lifespan of a child to prevent, identify, and/or treat child abuse and neglect. It is no longer logical for schools to limit their role solely to the education of the child without consideration for the child's emotional well-being and how it affects his or her ability to learn (Cicchetti, Toth, & Hennessy, 1995). In acknowledgment of the changing responsibility of school systems, many school districts are being redesigned to address the social and emotional needs of children and families by creating school-linked/integration service schools (Allen-Meares, Washington, & Welsh, 2000). Given the limited resources in education and the often overwhelming challenges faced by school personnel in tackling the consequences and issues surrounding child maltreatment, alliances with the child welfare system will bring both needed expertise and tangible resources. Collaborating with CPS and other social service agencies to provide preventive interventions in the schools is another area of opportunity.

What We Know

An active relationship between schools and CPS agencies must be initiated to effectively accomplish the tasks and acquire the resources necessary to address school needs regarding child maltreatment. (See Chapter 20 for additional discussion on child maltreatment.) Although schools report more incidents of child maltreatment than any other institution, most identified incidents go unreported (Crenshaw, Crenshaw, & Lichtenberg, 1995; Sedlak & Broadhurst, 1996). Additionally, of all child maltreatment reports made by mandated reporters, teachers' reports have the lowest substantiation rate (Kesner & Robinson, 2002). Understanding the dynamics of child maltreatment is specialized and requires a wide range of knowledge and skill. Teachers are not necessarily provided this information in their training programs, and they often lack the specialized knowledge that might lead them to report incidents of child abuse and neglect. School social workers are often seen as the "go to" professionals in schools for reporting child abuse, as well as the provider of whatever follow-up services are needed for the child and his or her family. Additional mental health professionals may also be relied on to provide services or training opportunities designed to help education personnel identify signs of child maltreatment.

Boundaries among schools, CPS agencies, and other child welfare agencies must become more permeable, allowing information to flow more smoothly among the organizations. School social workers and other mental health professionals need to make connections with the local CPS agency and others to forge alliances that address the needs of maltreated children.

What We Can Do

Research on successful collaborations or partnerships have identified eight main characteristics of a successful alliance (Shaw, 2003): trust, flexibility, understanding, balance of power, shared mission, compatibility, communication, and commitment. Based on these characteristics, also supported elsewhere in the literature (Child & Faulkner, 1998; Franklin & Streeter, 1995; Mulroy, 2003), school social workers may want to consider the following in building partnerships with CPS and other child welfare agencies:

- Build trust among partners. This is critical. CPS agencies or others need to trust that the school is not putting its own interests before the best interests of the child.
- Identify and analyze the problem area on which you want to collaborate with CPS and/or other child welfare agencies: prevention, identification, or intervention. Establish what you want to achieve. What are your objectives?
- Choose a realistic strategy. What action is needed to meet the objectives? You may have

to start with providing training to teachers and then move to students and, finally, parents.
- Establish a shared vision. Develop a shared understanding of the projects' desired outcomes among school, CPS, and other agency staff.
- Ascertain the rewards and benefits of becoming part of the alliance for both parties (e.g., is it to your CPS agency's advantage to have prevention, identification, and treatment programs in schools?). Based on the area being addressed, decisions need to be made regarding which other child welfare agencies will benefit from the alliance. CPS staff can be helpful in this decision-making process.
- Involve the key players from the school, CPS, and other community social service agencies. Key players may also include parents and students. Commitment from the school principal is necessary. Depending on your community, CPS involvement may range from an administrator to a CPS worker or a CPS training person. Often CPS agencies designate school liaisons to a particular school district.
- Build ownership. The school, private child welfare agencies, and CPS agencies need to feel they have ownership in the process. Teachers and others will be more likely to use the services created if they have helped design the program.
- Address confidentiality issues clearly. Often there is a lack of understanding concerning the differences within systems responding to confidentiality issues and professionals' differing frame of reference, which may lead to distrust.
- Encourage free communication among the various parties in the alliance. Communication must be multidirectional to be effective (Mulroy, 2003).
- Build on success. Publicize your success, crediting all involved in the alliance.

There are, as indicated above, three broad areas regarding child maltreatment on which school social workers and mental health providers typically focus: prevention, identification, and intervention. How each of these efforts can benefit from a collaboration between schools and child welfare agencies is discussed in targeted sections below.

Prevention

Primary prevention should be the focus of collaborative programs between schools and CPS agencies.

Primary prevention services are designed to reduce the incidence or rate of occurrence of new cases (Willis, Holden, & Rosenberg, 1992) by teaching education personnel, students, and their caregivers nonviolent discipline and parenting practices.

CPS and other child welfare agencies have prevention resources that school mental health workers can access to provide primary prevention services in their schools. CPS agencies are usually willing to share their material or expertise in providing educational opportunities with the aim of child abuse prevention. Though CPS agencies are primarily focused on secondary and tertiary prevention, at some times during the year (such as April, Child Abuse Prevention Month), CPS provides resources to the community focused on primary prevention. Other child welfare agencies may focus on primary prevention and will be able to provide additional resources. The following types of programs have been found to be effective in changing behaviors and increasing knowledge (USDHHS, 2003):

- teacher education focusing on creating a nurturing classroom and building positive teacher–student relationships. These programs should also focus on the important role that teachers play in mediating the effects of child maltreatment. (Identification of maltreatment may also be dealt with as part of a prevention program; this will be addressed in the next section.)
- student education focusing on self-esteem groups and teen parenting programs. These might present specific curricula based on issues of child abuse and neglect, such as those focused on talking about touch.
- parent education focusing on nonviolent parenting techniques, child development, and age-appropriate expectations for children. Additionally, programs may be designed to present child abuse and neglect information to parents so that a parent may detect if a caregiver or other is abusing his or her child.

Identification

Recognizing the many forms of child maltreatment is challenging even for those who have extensive training in this area. Therefore it is understandable when teachers have difficulty. Kesner and Robinson (2002) found that school personnel were more likely to report physical abuse than neglect, psychological abuse, or sexual abuse, forms of maltreatment that are much more difficult to identify than bruises or black eyes. However, it was noted that if teachers were provided adequate training, reports in these areas would likely increase markedly because teachers are in an ideal position to detect these less obvious forms of abuse. School social workers have a unique opportunity to partner with CPS agencies and others in providing substantial in-service training for teachers and other school personnel in defining and identifying all forms of child maltreatment.

Steps in training teachers may include:

- identifying the key CPS and child welfare person to provide in-service training at your school. Again, CPS provides this for the community or has a partner that does.
- providing the training as a special event. School districts and CPS agencies have provided training during breakfast meetings and afternoon pizza parties. It is a good way to bring the partners together.

In order to provide the most effective training possible, it is important to go beyond the typical school district training, which focuses only on procedures for reporting. The following topics of training have been found to enhance teachers' understanding of maltreatment investigations and to increase teachers' willingness to report suspected cases of child abuse or neglect (USHHS, 2003):

- how to identify signs of child abuse or neglect, with a particular focus on ambiguous evidence (some programs provided teachers with protocols in identifying signs of child maltreatment);
- how to gather credible evidence before making a report;
- how to meet mandated reporting requirements if child maltreatment is suspected; and
- how to make referrals for services if necessary.

Intervention

School social workers and mental health professionals who work in or with the school system are afforded a unique opportunity to intervene in the lives of maltreated children. Prior to entering school, children may have experienced abuse for years. Parents may not have had any help with learning new and effective ways of child rearing or overcoming the many challenges of raising children with limited resources.

Once the child enters the educational system, the school can begin to provide him or her with positive and secure relationships with peers and adults, and can provide the family with the social support and connection that it needs. These children often have difficulty learning, and, consequently, management of their behaviors is difficult for the classroom teacher. Additionally, many children, particularly those in large urban areas, are in foster or kinship care and require special attention from school personnel, CPS staff, and other child welfare workers. Schools can provide opportunities for personal development and can help maltreated children to build self-confidence and to navigate the process of developing peer relationships.

School-based interventions can take many forms. Partnering with CPS and other child welfare agencies to establish programs will help ensure that children at risk are properly identified. Additionally, CPS is in a better position to have access to and information about community resources. Building alliances to address intervention needs of children identified as being at risk for maltreatment (experienced or at risk of experiencing) is critical in meeting the mission of the school system, educating children, and the mission of CPS and other child welfare agencies, while ensuring the safety, well-being, and permanency of the child. The school social worker and other mental health professionals must be at the forefront of coordinating alliances with CPS and other social service agencies in addressing school-age children's needs.

Children who receive intervention services have been found to improve school performance, increase attendance, and present fewer behavior problems (USDHHS, 2003). School social workers may want to consider offering direct services to at-risk children and families. (For additional information on direct services to children and families, see Chapters 6, 16, 26, and 61.) These may include such interventions as home visits, individual or group counseling, mentoring, support groups, social events, and tutoring. Some examples of specific programs that may be helpful are:

- after-school programs focusing on social, recreational, educational, or therapeutic issues;
- problem solving, assertiveness training, or conflict resolution programs;
- mentoring programs using adults for educational and social development; and
- services for special needs children that focus on

developmental and educational screening, and advocacy for services such as transportation.

Another program that may be helpful in this regard would target school personnel rather than the children: a program to develop resource guides for school personnel. CPS and other child welfare agencies often have directories of community services relevant to the needs of at-risk children in the school setting. Through the collaboration, a resource guide specific to the needs of school personnel can be developed addressing appropriate referral sources for families and children at risk of maltreatment.

Tools and Practice Examples

Prevention

In an elementary school, the school social worker took advantage of April's designation as Child Abuse Prevention Month. After getting the principal to agree, she set about forming an alliance to bring a prevention program to the school for both teachers and parents. She contacted the local CPS agency, and the CPS liaison for the schools suggested getting the Child Advocacy Program involved because it had experience in addressing the general community. To develop the program, the school social worker called a meeting that included a teacher, a parent, the CPS liaison, and a social worker from the Child Advocacy Program.

Since both teachers and parents were the focal point of the program, the group decided to present an educational program around ecological risks and protective factors related to child maltreatment. This way, emphasis would be on societal, environmental, community, family, and individual factors, which the group thought would be less threatening than other areas of concern.

The CPS agency and the Child Advocacy Program had the expertise and resources to present the material and provide handouts. The program took place in the evening and was developed to have a social component by providing a dessert buffet and coffee after the program.

Identification

A school social work supervisor of a large urban district learned that the state was switching its child maltreatment hotline from a local to a statewide system. All reports of child abuse and neglect would go to one call center rather than eleven regional offices. Additionally, teachers and other educational personnel would be able to make reports via e-mail.

The social work supervisor thought it important that teachers understand the changes in the state's system, and she also saw an opportunity to reiterate the signs of maltreatment and teacher' responsibilities for reporting suspected maltreatment. After talking with school district administrators and the CPS liaison, she organized a meeting with teachers and school social workers from the elementary, middle, and high schools, as well as CPS representatives, to plan the best way to proceed.

The group decided that a field trip was in order so that the teachers and school social workers could see firsthand how a call center functions. After a tour of the center, CPS staff provided training covering signs of abuse and neglect and detailing school employees' responsibilities concerning reporting; then the school personnel got hands–on practice reporting abuse via e-mail. During the field trip, teachers, CPS workers, and school social workers discussed and gave examples of the different policies they all had to follow concerning confidentiality.

Intervention

A school social worker employed in a middle school received numerous referrals from teachers regarding children fighting in the classroom and playground. The school social worker knew that children who have been maltreated are often aggressive and have learned to handle their problems through the use of violence. The school social worker thought that developing groups focused on conflict resolution would be beneficial to the identified children and could reduce acting-out behavior, leading to better learning outcomes.

After talking with the school principal, the school social worker realized that providing these groups was beyond the resources and expertise of the school. The school social worker made numerous contacts in the community and identified a number of child welfare agencies providing mediation and conflict resolution services. After persuading key personnel in the agencies of the immediacy of the problem, the school social worker called a meeting to create an action plan. Teachers were included as part of the alliance.

Given the size of the school and the number of referrals the school social worker received, the group decided it would be necessary to conduct at least four programs consisting of six-week group meetings. Since it was unrealistic to provide them all at one time, they decided the school social worker would begin with two groups, one for girls and one for boys. Responsibilities were divided among the alliance members. Two social workers from the child welfare agencies got administrative permission to include these groups as part of their workload. The school social worker was made responsible for getting parental consent and, along with the teachers, for tracking behavioral change in the students.

After the first two groups successfully completed the programs, the alliance was enthusiastic about the positive results. The alliance continued providing conflict resolution programs throughout the school year, and the school social worker received far fewer referrals from teachers relating to aggressive students.

Key Points to Remember

- Collaborations between school social workers and child welfare workers can effectively address the problems related to child maltreatment and its effects on education.
- Alliances between the school system and the child welfare system will move us forward in addressing the prevention, identification, and intervention needs of children and families who are at risk.

References

Allen-Meares, P., Washington, R. O., & Welsh, B. L. (2000). *Social work services in schools.* Boston: Allyn & Bacon.

Bolen, R. M. (2001). Risk factors for child sexual abuse victimization. In *Child sexual abuse: Its scope and our future* (pp. 135–161). New York: Kluwer Academic/Plenum.

Child, J., & Faulkner, D. (1998). *Strategies of cooperation: Managing alliances, networks, and joint ventures.* New York: Oxford University Press.

Cicchetti, D., Toth, S. L., & Hennessy, K. (1995). Child maltreatment and school adaptation: Problems and promises. In D. Cicchetti & S. L. Toth (Eds.),

Child abuse, child development, and social policy (pp. 301–330). Norwood, NY: Ablex.

Crenshaw, W. B., Crenshaw, L. M., & Lichtenberg, J. W. (1995). When educators confront child abuse: An analysis of the decision to report. *Child Abuse and Neglect, 19,* 1095–1113.

Finkelhor, D. (1994). Current information on the scope and nature of child sexual abuse. In *Future of children: Sexual abuse of children* (Vol. 4, pp. 31–53). Los Altos, CA: David and Lucile Packard Foundation.

Franklin, C., & Streeter, C. L. (1995). School reform: Linking public schools with human services. *Social Work, 40*(6), 773–781.

Kesner, J. E., & Robinson, M. (2002). Teachers as mandated reporters of child maltreatment: Comparison with legal, medical, and social services reporters. *Children and Schools, 24*(4), 222–231.

Mulroy, E. A. (2003). Community as a factor in implementing interorganizational partnerships: Issues, constraints, and adaptations. *Nonprofit Management and Leadership, 14*(1), 47–66.

Russell, D. E. H. (1986). *The secret trauma: Incest in the lives of girls and women.* New York: Basic Books.

Sedlak, A. J., & Broadhurst, D. D. (1996). The third National Incidence Study of child abuse and neglect. Washington, DC: U.S. Department of Health and Human Services.

Shaw, M. M. (2003). Successful collaboration between the nonprofit and public sectors. *Nonprofit Management and Leadership, 14*(1), 107–120.

Thomlison, B. (1997). Risk and protective factors in child maltreatment. In M. Fraser (Ed.), *Risk and resilience in childhood: An ecological perspective.* Washington, DC: National Association of Social Workers Press.

U.S. Department of Health and Human Services, Administration for Children and Families, Administration for Children, Youth and Families, Children's Bureau. (2002). *Child Maltreatment 2002.* Washington, DC: Government Printing Office.

U.S. Department of Health and Human Services, Administration for Children and Families, Children's Bureau. (2003). *School-based child maltreatment programs: Synthesis of lessons learned.* Washington, DC: Government Printing Office.

Willis, D. J., Holden, E. W., & Rosenberg, M. (Eds.). (1992). *Prevention of child maltreatment: Developmental and ecological perspectives.* New York: John Wiley & Sons.

Helping Children in Foster Care and Other Residential Placements Succeed in School

Dorian E. Traube ▪ Mary M. McKay

CHAPTER 35

Getting Started

Many children in out-of-home placements experience emotional or behavioral difficulties. Even children who do not exhibit overt symptoms are at risk for the development of mental health difficulties as a result of histories of child abuse and neglect, poverty, adult caregiver mental health concerns, stress related to removal from their families, or placement disruption (Cox, Orme, & Rhodes, 2003). Each year, billons of dollars are spent responding to the legal, correctional, educational, and psychological needs of children in out-of-home placements (Atkins et al., 1998). Yet despite this, children residing in out-of-home placements are also seriously affected by deteriorating supportive resources, including a shortage of mental health service providers.

Schools are one of the few existing resources consistently available within communities, and they offer a unique opportunity to provide mental health care for children in the child protective system. Among the advantages schools provide is the opportunity to intervene with a child and foster family or group home coordinator in a community setting, to enhance children's academic progress and affect children's peer relations, to increase access to underserved children via their availability in schools, and to lessen the stigma of mental health services (Atkins et al., 1998). Given the shortages of mental health resources in many communities, there is increasing awareness that schools are de facto mental health service providers for a majority of children, including those in out-of-home placements (Atkins et al., 1998).

What We Know About the Existing School-Based Mental Health Consultation Model

The predominant model for school-based mental health services is the consultation model. In this model, mental health providers, generally social workers, consult with teachers to develop services targeting the needs of the referred student. These consultations are important elements of providing child mental health care and are supported by numerous studies identifying the effectiveness of mental health–focused interventions in schools (Axelrod, 1977; Mash & Barkley, 1989).

Though there is not sufficient space to detail all empirically driven models of best practice with children in out-of-home placement, the authors refer the readers to the following school-based mental health interventions:

To Treat Emotional and Behavioral Disorders

Catron, T., & Weiss, B. (1994). The Vanderbilt school–based counseling program: An interagency, primary-care model of mental health services. *Journal of Emotional and Behavioral Disorders, 2,* 247–253.

Hawkins, J. D., Catalano, R. F., Kosterman, R., Abbott, R., & Hill, K. (1999). Preventing adolescent health-risk behaviors by strengthening protection during childhood. *Archives of Pediatric and Adolescent Medicine, 153,* 226–234.

To Treat Depression

Clarke, G., Hawkins, W., Murphy, M., Sheeber, L., Lewinsohn, P., & Seeley, J. (1995). Targeted prevention of unipolar depressive disorder in an at-risk sample of high school adolescents: A randomized trial of a group cognitive intervention. *Journal of the American Academy of Child and Adolescent Psychiatry, 34,* 312–321.

To Treat Conduct Disorders

Battistich, V., Schaps, E., Watson, M., & Solomon, D. (1996). Prevention effects of the Child Development Project: Early findings from an ongoing multisite demonstration trial. *Journal of Adolescent Research, 11,* 12–35.

See also Chapters 33 and 37. Table 35.1 describes some of the recent, innovative, empirically driven, direct intervention school mental health models that extend the reach of schools to provide for the social and emotional needs of children.

Although these school mental health models are considered advances and have substantial empirical support, many of these models and related interventions are rejected by teachers as being either too complex to manage independently or too distinct from standard educational practices for teachers and

Table 35.1 Innovative School-Based Mental Health Services

Program	Author	Description	Obtaining More Information
Success for All	Robert Slavin, Nancy Karweit, Barbara Wasik	**Elements:** Combines quality day care, academic tutoring, and parent support service. **Goal:** To prevent academic problems by providing quality early childhood education, remediate academic deficits, provide parents with education about health.	Book: *Preventing early failure: research, policy, and practice*
School of the 21st Century	Edward Zigler	**Elements:** Attracts noncompulsory parent participation, avoids deficit-based mentality of traditional mental health services. **Goal:** To increase mother–child interactions, stabilize child-care arrangements, improve academic outcomes.	Addressing the nation's child care crisis: The school of the 21st century, *American Journal of Orthopsychiatry 59* (1989), 485–491.
School Development Program	James Comer, Norris Haynes, Edward Joyner, Michael Ben-Avie	**Elements:** Modifies school climate by enhancing the relations among school staff, students, and parents in urban low-income schools. **Goal:** To increase academic gains, reduce suspensions, reduce corporal punishment, increase parent involvement.	Book: *Rallying the whole village: The Comer process for reforming education*
Constructive Discipline	Greta Mayer	**Elements:** Provides clearly stated rules for child, consistent enforcement of rules, planned rewards for appropriate behavior, staff support. **Goal:** To reduce antisocial behavior, create a positive school climate.	Preventing Antisocial Behavior in School, *Journal of Applied Behavioral Analysis, 28* (1989), 467–478

school administrators to embrace. Further, necessary financial or innovative staff resources are often not available to sustain innovative mental health service models for children. Yet, an important advantage of each of these models is that they do not specifically identify children in out-of-home placements as being in need. Since these models promote the mental health and well-being of *all* children in a school, the child in out-of-home placement is part of a supportive, stable school environment instead of being further stigmatized for needs that developed as a result of a history of abuse or neglect.

What We Can Do—Parents and Peers as Leaders in School (PALS) Approach

Another example of an innovation in the field of school-based practice has grown out of an increasing realization that childhood mental health disorders are affected by numerous factors beyond the level of the child. However, few school-based models have considered the specific, complex interactions of the multiple factors affecting children being reared in out-of-home placements. The Parents and Peers as Leaders in School (PALS) approach offers an innovative, ecological model guiding school-based mental health care, and it is a potential resource for youth in out-of-home placements. PALS, developed by Atkins, McKay, Abdul-Adil, et al. at the University of Illinois at Chicago, is intended to provide individualized, flexible, and coordinated mental health services for youth within their school settings. It targets children and adolescents who might not be successfully involved in care because of a shortage of providers, stigma associated with receipt of care, or mobility. For children in out-of-home placements, these barriers to mental health care abound. Therefore, there is an excellent opportunity for goodness-of-fit between the PALS school-based service delivery model and the needs of children in out-of-home placement.

Premises of the PALS Service Delivery Model

The PALS model proposes that empirically based strategies, including multisystemic therapy, are available to reduce child mental health difficulties across the multiple ecologies of schools: at the school level (e.g., providing appropriate and engaging classroom activities), at the peer level (e.g., providing appropriate teacher and peer models for classroom activities), at the adult caregiver level (e.g., involving adult caregivers in the child's educational and behavioral goals at school), and at the child level (e.g., social skills). For more information on these empirically based strategies, see Atkins et al. (1998, 2001, 2003a, 2003b). The PALS model is flexible and individualized by acknowledging that contexts for child mental health will differ across children and by providing services specific to those contexts. This flexibility is particularly relevant to children in out-of-home placements because their needs will vary according to their history and current placement status.

Goals of PALS

PALS seeks to improve all children's learning experiences by:

1. helping children manage their behavior at school and at home,
2. supporting children in the classroom,
3. supporting schools in planning for children's long-term needs,
4. supporting teachers in promoting positive classroom behavior and improving learning within their classroom,
5. increasing adult caregiver involvement in the child's education,
6. assisting adult caregivers in developing necessary resources for children to succeed at school,
7. offering practical ideas to adult caregivers on how to manage the child's needs,
8. supporting adult caregivers in linking to community resources, and
9. supporting adult caregiver and teacher collaboration to improve classroom behavior and learning.

Because children spend the vast majority of their time in school, coordination between schools and care providers boost the chances that the needs of children in out-of-home placements will be attended to in a systematic and synchronized way.

PALS Systematic Assessment

A key feature of the PALS model is to identify settings in which mental health issues emerge for the child throughout the school day. Once these settings have been identified, they are targeted using a social learning theory perspective. Social learning theory guides social works to focus on:

- the degree to which students are supervised or *monitored,*
- the extent to which students are *motivated* to behave appropriately, and
- the extent to which prosocial alternatives and social support are *modeled* by peers and adults.

The goal of PALS is to identify the level at which social learning principles are applicable and the degree to which factors within the school environment can be modified. For children in out-of-home placements, social learning theory provides a platform for transferable skills that they can apply within and outside the school environment.

Establishing Collaborative Working Relationships

The PALS model emphasizes the need for systematic assessment of child mental health difficulties and identifies factors that contribute to these at school and in the after-school environment. The model also specifies the need to involve teachers and adult caregivers in the systematic assessment of intervention needs. As previously noted, the goal of this assessment is to target problems and potential solutions using a social learning model approach (modeling, motivation, and monitoring). The PALS social worker brings to this collaboration a range of empirically validated interventions. Teachers and adult caregivers bring the practical realities of schools and foster families and/or residential treatment environments. It is this collaborative group that develops a menu of options specific to each child and his or her classroom's needs with the goal of intervening at multiple levels of the school ecology simultaneously (e.g., increasing student motivation, increasing teacher monitoring) and at the family/residential context (e.g., availability of homework help after school, increasing foster adult caregiver involvement in school supportive activities). However, the single most important theme in PALS is that instead of targeting individual children, PALS offers services that affect the *whole* classroom and extend to contexts after school. PALS aims to increase positive attitudes and behaviors among *all* children in a classroom and give all children the

opportunity for academic and social success. It is the premise of the PALS model that every teacher, classroom, and out-of-home placement has unique strengths and needs that could be overlooked by focusing on individual children. Potentially, focusing on the entire classroom creates a supportive environment for the foster child rather than further stigmatizing him or her via removal from class for individual sessions.

Steps in Conducting PALS Assessments

Foster Family Assessments

Once a child has been referred to PALS, it is necessary to complete two levels of assessments. The first level is a family/environmental assessment. Because the child is currently in foster care, it is necessary to speak directly to the foster care agency representing the child. The agency should be able to offer information about the child's social, emotional, and family history, including any auxiliary services the child may be receiving from the agency (e.g., supervised visits with the birth family, tutoring, medical care). The foster care agency will have to supply the worker with written consent to interview the child because it serves as the child's legal guardian.

After the worker receives consent to assess the child, he or she should proceed by contacting the foster family or residential facility staff to explain the PALS program and to request a meeting with them. Additionally, we advise that the worker make a visit to the foster or group home to assess the environment in which the child currently lives. Because children who have been removed from their biological family have had major disruptions in their lives, the PALS social worker should pay attention to elements of the environment that may contribute to further life disruptions, including poor supervision, chaotic daily schedules, and adult caregivers unable to know what is occurring while the child is out of the home. The environmental assessment allows the PALS team to identify and address situations in the foster child's life that may contribute to academic and social difficulties.

Classroom Assessment

The next step in implementing PALS involves assessing the classroom of the foster child. Because

PALS will be implemented for the entire class, it is important to determine how that class is currently operating. Below are some key assumptions to remember when visiting classrooms.

- Every classroom has strengths and needs; identification of needs without considering strengths provides a distorted view of the classroom.
- The team will always demonstrate respect for the teachers' roles and responsibilities and appreciation for the teachers' knowledge and ability to manage the classroom.
- Assessment is ongoing and continuous; it starts from the moment the team begins to meet and continues throughout the team's time together.

Initially, the assessment can be "informal," which involves the PALS social worker or counselor acting as a *participant observer* in the classroom. Formal assessment does not differ from the steps outlined above, but more specific information is gathered:

- times of day that are especially difficult and times of day when things tend to run smoothly
- activities of the day that are especially difficult and those that run smoothly
- student's activities during these times/activities
- teacher's activities and responsibilities during these times/activities
- other adults who may be present during these times/activities
- whether or not things ever run differently, and if they do, what is happening during those atypical times

A comprehensive assessment creates the basis for developing an intervention plan that best addresses the multiple needs of the child in out-of-home placement. The assessment of the classroom allows the PALS team to determine times and situations where intervention can occur on behalf of the foster child to create a supportive environment. This supportive environment is thought to serve as a corrective experience for children who may have rarely experienced such support.

PALS Intervention

Once the assessments have been completed and appropriate goals have been established for the child, intervention can begin. At this stage there will be two levels of intervention—one with the adult caregivers and one within the classroom.

Intervention With the Adult Caregiver

PALS adult caregiver goals are hierarchical. In other words, PALS focuses first on the primary goal, adult caregiver involvement in the child's education, then the second goal, increasing adult caregivers' social support. Finally, the third goal is to assist adult caregivers in building and developing their skills to care for children. These adult caregiver goals were developed with the belief that if adult caregivers are more involved in their child's education, feel supported, and have skills, they will be better able to support the child's learning and mental health. Below are two lists, one for foster parents and one for group home workers, that can be provided to help them develop their involvement skills.

Ways Foster Parents Can Support a Positive Learning Environment

- Ask the child what happened at school that day, and listen to the response.
- Always be respectful of the child's teacher in the child's presence.
- Meet with the teacher if the child is having behavior problems to discuss appropriate consequences at home and in school.
- Respond promptly to notes and phone calls from school.
- Attend adult caregiver/teacher conferences, report card pickup day, and as many other school events as possible.
- Request meetings with teachers to discuss the child's progress, especially when problems are not occurring.

Ways for Group Home Workers to Support a Child's Education at the Residential Placement

- Supervise homework. Provide a quiet place for the child to work. Turn off the TV, do not talk on the phone unless absolutely necessary, and ask visitors to return another time, if possible.
- Check child's school bag daily for necessary school supplies and homework.
- Give reasonable rewards for good work and good behavior.
- Establish a school–home report.
- Build a positive relationship with the foster child: engage in fun activities with him or her.

This support is vital to ensuring academic and mental health success because the adult caregiver will be a stabilizing force for a child who has experienced major instability throughout his or her life.

Intervention at the Classroom Level

As mentioned previously, the PALS classroom goals are interconnected. PALS goals were developed with the assumption that if the classroom is organized and the students are academically engaged and feel supported, then behavioral problems will decrease, and academic success will increase. Below are some proposed strategies to achieve the PALS classroom goals.

Strategies for Increasing Academic Engagement

- Discuss with the teacher the assumption that students who are engaged academically learn more and have fewer behavioral problems. Teachers are all different, and the goal is not to tell the teacher how to teach. On the other hand, research has demonstrated that children are more academically engaged when lessons are interesting and the teacher's presentation is animated. Encourage teachers to be creative when presenting new information.
- Encourage teachers to give clear instructions (e.g., write them on the board or repeat them several times) and examples to illustrate what should be learned.

Strategies for Improving Classroom Organization

- Review with teachers that a well-organized class can lead to a well-behaved class.
- Encourage teachers to establish rules for in-class and out-of-class behavior and to communicate clear, well-defined consequences for breaking the rules.
- Emphasize to teachers that they need to enforce the rules and stick to the consequences.
- Encourage teachers to review the rules with the class on a regular basis, especially after a violation has occurred.
- Encourage teachers to keep an organized desk and clean classroom. They can provide an example for the children to follow regarding their own desk and books.

Deciding on a classroom intervention should be based on the information gathered during the PALS practitioner's classroom observations and the teacher's needs assessment. The PALS school-based professional will generate a list of possible interventions that address the classroom needs identified during the assessment phase. Once identified, the interventions are reviewed with the classroom teacher. Thus, each PALS classroom will have its own unique treatment plan.

Tools and Practice Examples

David is a 10-year-old foster child residing in a low-income urban neighborhood. His mother lost custody of him when he was 5 years old because of her drug addiction. Last year she passed away from a drug overdose. David was placed for a year and a half with a foster family in his neighborhood. However, his mother's sister requested custody of him, and the courts decided kinship foster care was the more appropriate living arrangement. David's aunt decided 6 months later that David was too difficult to control and asked that he be removed from her custody. Over the last 3 years, David has been in five different kinship foster homes and lived in four different neighborhoods. He currently lives with his mother's cousin and her three children. He has been skipping school, picking fights in his fifth-grade class, and disobeying school rules.

Figure 35.1 shows the steps for implementing the PALS model.

Key Points to Remember

- Children living in out-of-home placements have historically been affected by high rates of community violence, poverty, and substance abuse; deteriorating support resources; and a serious shortage of mental health services.
- It is important to develop effective mental health services for urban children that attend to these environmental influences.
- To this end, schools offer a unique environment for helping children and families in low-income communities.
- Through schools, service providers are able to reach large numbers of traditionally underserved children and to interact with children and adult caregivers.
- The PALS program was developed as an alternative to existing service delivery models in clinics and in schools.

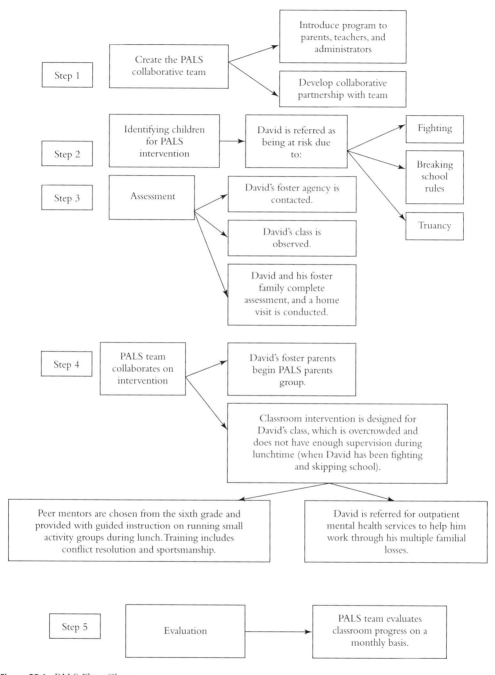

Figure 35.1. PALS Flow Chart

- PALS addresses the limitations of clinic-based consultation and school-based health clinics by (a) working directly with teachers to establish interventions that are tailored to the needs of individual teachers and classrooms and (b) involving adult caregivers in their child's education in an effort to enhance children's learning.
- It is the belief of the PALS program that classrooms have unique strengths to offer support

and continued growth for children in out-of-home placements.

Resources

Fantuzzo, J. W., & Atkins, M. S. (1992). Applied behavior analysis for educators: Teacher centered and classroom based. *Journal of Applied Analysis, 25,* 35-42.

Holtzman, W. H. (1992), *School of the future.* Washington, DC: American Psychological Association.

Lynn, C. J., McKay, M. M., & Atkins, M. S. (2003). School social work: Meeting the mental health needs of students through collaboration with teachers. *Children and School, 25*(4), 197–209.

McKay, M. M., Gonzales, J., Quintana, E., Kim, L., & Abdul-Adil, J. (1999). Multiple family groups: An alternative for reducing disruptive behavioral difficulties of urban children. *Research on Social Work Practice, 9*(5), 593–607.

McKay, M. M., Harrison, M. E., Gonzales J., Kim, L., & Quintana, E. (2002). Multiple-family groups for urban children with conduct difficulties and their families. *Psychiatric Services, 53*(11), 1467–1468.

Peters, B. R., Atkins, M. S., & McKay, M. M. (1999). Adopted children's behavior problems: A review of five explanatory models. *Clinical Psychology Review, 19*(3), 297–328.

Tolan, P. H., Hanish, L. D., McKay, M. M., & Dickey, M. H. (2002). Evaluating process in child and family interventions: Aggression prevention as an example. *Journal of Family Psychology 16*(2), 220–236.

References

Atkins, M. S., Adil, J., Jackson, M, Talbott, E., & Bell, C. (2001). School-based mental health services in urban schools: An ecological approach. *Report on Emotional and Behavioral Disorders in Youth 1*(4), 75–93.

Atkins, M. S., Graczyk, P., Frazier, S., & Adil, J. (2003a). School mental health in urban communities. In M. Weist, S. Evans, & N. Lever (Eds.), *School mental health handbook* (pp. 165–178). New York: Kluwer.

Atkins, M., Graczyk, P., Frazier, S., & Adil, J. (2003b). Toward a new model for school-based mental health: Accessible, effective, and sustainable services in urban communities. *School Psychology Review, 12,* 503–514.

Atkins, M. S., McKay, M. M., Arvantis, P., London, L., Madison, S., Costigan, C., Haney, P., Zevenbergen, A. Hess, L., Bennett, D., & Webster, D. (1998). An ecological model for school-based mental health services for urban low-income aggressive children. *Journal of Behavioral Health Services and Research 5*(1), 64–75.

Axelrod, S. (1977). *Behavior modifications for the classroom teacher.* New York: McGraw-Hill.

Battistich, V., Schaps, E., Watson, M., & Solomon, D. (1996). Prevention effects of the Child Development Project: Early findings from an ongoing multi-site demonstration trial. *Journal of Adolescent Research, 11,* 12–35.

Catron, T., & Weiss, B. (1994). The Vanderbilt school–based counseling program: An interagency, primary-care model of mental health services. *Journal of Emotional and Behavioral Disorders, 2,* 247–253.

Clarke, G., Hawkins, W., Murphy, M., Sheeber, L., Lewinsohn, P., & Seeley, J. (1995). Targeted prevention of unipolar depressive disorder in an at-risk sample of high school adolescents: A randomized trial of a group cognitive intervention. *Journal of the American Academy of Child and Adolescent Psychiatry, 34,* 312–321.

Comer, J. P., Haynes, N. M., Joyner, E. T., & Ben-Avie, M. (1996). *Rallying the whole village: The Comer process for reforming education.* New York: Teachers College Press.

Cox, M. E., Orme, J. G., & Rhodes, K. W. (2003). Willingness to foster children with emotional or behavioral problems. *Journal of Social Service Research, 29*(4), 23–51.

Hawkins, J. D., Catalano, R. F., Kosterman, R., Abbott, R., & Hill, K. (1999). Preventing adolescent health-risk behaviors by strengthening protection during childhood. *Archives of Pediatric and Adolescent Medicine, 153,* 226–234.

Mash, E. J., & Barkley, R. A. (Eds.). (1989). *Treatment of childhood disorders.* New York: Guilford.

Mayer, G. R. (1995). Preventing antisocial behavior in school. *Journal of Behavioral Analysis, 28,* 467–478.

Slavin, R., Karweit, N. L., & Wasik, B. (1994). *Preventing early school failure.* Needham Heights, MA: Allyn & Bacon.

Zigler, E. F. (1989). Addressing the nation's child care crisis: The school of the 21st century. *American Journal of Orthopsychiatry, 59,* 485–491.

Programs and Practices for Supporting School Attendance and Dropout Prevention

This section contains interventions that are empirically demonstrated as effective in several areas related to academic achievement, including increasing attendance and preventing dropout. These topics are vital to social workers and people in related mental health disciplines because doing well in school and completing school have such far-reaching effects on a youth's current and future quality of life.

Increasing School Attendance

Effective Strategies and Interventions

Johnny S. Kim ▪ Calvin L. Streeter

CHAPTER 36

Getting Started

Improving School Attendance Through Multilevel Interventions

Improving student attendance is a major preoccupation for many schools across the country. Though little educational research has focused on the relationship between attendance and student performance, some studies suggest that school attendance and student academic performance are closely associated (Borland & Howsen, 1998). (See also Chapters 37 and 38.) The assumption is that when students are not in school, they cannot learn. Though this assumption seems plausible, the implied causal ordering of the relationship is not always clear. For example, does school attendance improve academic performance or does academic performance serve as an incentive for successful students to regularly attend school? Whatever the association, it has led many school districts, school administrators, and state governments to spend tremendous resources to carefully monitor, document, and report school attendance data.

Epstein and Sheldon (2002) suggest that improving school attendance is as important as any issue that schools face today. Concern about school attendance may focus on truancy and chronic absenteeism, as when students fail to come to school on any given day. But class cutting, where students come to school to be counted but then selectively skip one or more classes each day, is seen by some a symptom of alienation and disengagement from schools and a serious issue for many urban school districts today (see Fallis & Opotow, 2003; also see chap. 38 for a discussion of dropout prevention using alternative schools and solution-focused therapy). Either way, school attendance is a serious issue and one that requires multilevel strategies to effectively address.

Truancy has been identified as a significant early warning sign that students are headed for potential delinquent activity, social isolation, and educational failure (Baker, Sigmon, & Nugent, 2001; Loeber & Farrington, 2000). Poor attendance means that students are not developing the knowledge and skills needed for later success. In addition, when not in school, many students become involved in risky behaviors such as substance abuse, sexual activity, and other activities that can lead to serious trouble within the legal system (Bell, Rosen, & Dynlacht, 1994); Dryfoos, 1990; Huizinga, Loeber, & Thornberry, 1995; Rohrman, 1993). For many youths, chronic absenteeism is a significant predictor of dropping out of school (Dynarski & Gleason, 1999). Beyond its immediate consequences for students, truancy can have significant long-term implications for youths in terms of their becoming productive members of the community. For decades, research has shown a correlation between poor school attendance and problems later in life, such as criminal activity, incarceration, marital and family problems, trouble securing and maintaining stable employment, and violent behavior (Catalano, Arthur, Hawkins, Berglund, & Olson, 1998; Dryfoos, 1990; Robins & Ratcliff, 1978; Snyder & Sickmund, 1995).

Though individual students are often blamed for truancy, school attendance may be seen as an important indicator of how well the school is functioning and the kind of educational environment created within the school. For example, large schools where students are more anonymous often have more attendance problems than small schools where a missing student is more likely to be noticed (Finn & Voelkl, 1993). In addition, students are more likely to skip school when the school environment is perceived to be boring or chaotic, when students don't feel they are being intellectually challenged, or when there are no consequences for being truant.

For schools, the consequences of truancy can be significant as well. Not only is student attendance seen as one indicator of school performance, in most states money is tied directly to student attendance. Because funding formularies often include student attendance, fewer students in the classroom mean fewer resources for academic programs. School administrators and all those involved with schools have a vested interest in getting children to school and keeping them there all day.

Truancy has important consequences for the community, too (Baker et al., 2001). These include a workforce that lacks the basic knowledge and job skills needed to fully participate in the labor market and contribute to the economy. This can result in increased costs of social services and higher rates of poverty. Local businesses are often concerned about direct losses incurred from truants' shoplifting and indirect losses from their hanging out near their businesses and fighting, using drugs and alcohol, and intimidating customers.

Thus truancy has both immediate and far-reaching consequences for individual students, families, schools, and communities. Effective interventions must understand the problem from multiple perspectives and address the problem at multiple levels.

What We Know

Most of the research literature on low school attendance has focused either on its causes or its relationship to academic performance (Corville-Smith, Ryan, Adams, & Dalicandro, 1998; Lamdin, 2001). Despite the fact that absenteeism is a concern for schools, parents, social workers, and counselors, very little research has been done to examine ways to improve school attendance (Epstein & Sheldon, 2002; Lamdin, 2001). This is especially the case when looking for evidence-based research on absenteeism and school attendance.

Some research studied schools that offer rewards or monetary incentives to improve school attendance. Sturgeon and Beer (1990) examined 14 years of data from a rural high school in the Midwest to see if an attendance reward of exemption from taking semester tests had decreased absenteeism. They examined the school's student attendance records from 1976 to 1979, when there was no attendance reward policy, and compared them with student attendance records from 1980 to 1989, when the attendance reward policy was in effect. Results showed a statistically significant decrease in the number of absences after the attendance reward was adopted. During the years 1976–1979, the average total absent days was 1750.5, which decreased to 912.5 during the years 1980–1989.

Reid and Bailey-Dempsey (1995) randomly assigned junior high and high school girls with academic or attendance problems to either a program that offered financial incentives for improving school and attendance performance, a program that offered social and educational services to the girls and their families, or to a control group. Both the financial incentive program and case management program modestly improved school attendance over the control group, but similar results were not seen the next year. Though there was no statistically significant difference between the financial and case management programs in terms of school attendance, academic improvements were better for students receiving case management services than for students receiving only financial incentives.

Recently Miller (2002) conducted a study to see if participation in a therapeutic discipline program would improve students' attitudes on attendance, increase attendance, and provide greater insight into solving attendance problems among students at a large suburban high school. Students who were truant were randomly assigned to either the therapeutic discipline program or to a control group. The therapeutic program required students to work through a bibliotherapeutic learning packet and attend a follow-up exit conference with the dean to go over the packet. Traditional methods were used on the control group: threatening students with further disciplinary measures and in-school suspension in which students were required to do schoolwork. Both programs required students to participate in a written exercise to measure insight into ways they could help solve their truancy problems. Results from this study showed students in the therapeutic program increased class attendance, had fewer absences from classes, and listed a greater number of insights into resolving their attendance problems.

What We Can Do

A Multilevel Approach to School Attendance

Across the country, hundreds of thousands of students are absent from schools each day. Many times that number cut one or more classes after being counted as present in the school's attendance records. In order to effectively address attendance problems, school administrators, teachers, and staff must understand the problem from a

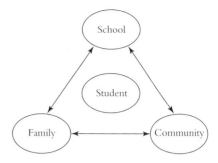

Figure 36.1. Student-Centered Multilevel Approach to School Attendance

multilevel perspective. Interventions that focus only on individual students may improve attendance in the short term for that one student. But it is unlikely that such interventions will have a widespread effect on attendance across the school. In addition, school attendance must be viewed as everyone's responsibility, not just that of the school's attendance officer. Figure 36.1 emphasizes the fact that although the individual student is at the center of our concern about truancy, an effective response must involve the school, the family, and the community.

School attendance can be influenced by a number of factors specific to the student. These might include drug and alcohol abuse, mental health problems, poor physical health, teen pregnancy and family responsibilities, student employment, and a lack of understanding of the long-term consequences of school failure.

Sometimes the school itself is largely responsible for truancy. School factors often include the school climate, such as school size and attitudes of teachers and administrators, lack of flexibility in meeting the needs of students with diverse learning styles and different cultural experiences, inconsistent policies and procedures for dealing with chronic truancy, inconsistent application of those policies, lack of meaningful consequences, a chaotic school culture and/or unsafe school environment, and a curriculum that is perceived as boring, irrelevant, or unchallenging.

Family factors that can affect student attendance include domestic violence and alcohol and drug abuse, inadequate parental supervision, poverty and low-wage jobs that require the parents to work long hours, lack of awareness of attendance laws, and parental attitudes toward education and the school.

Communities, too, can influence school attendance. They can hurt attendance when they present few opportunities for young people or lack affordable child care or accessible transportation systems. Communities with high mobility rates and large numbers of single-parent households tend to have high truancy rates. Too, differing cultural attitudes toward education can make a difference in whether a child wants to attend school.

Intervention Strategies

Individual Student Strategies

Strategies that focus on the individual student tend to focus on psychoeducational interventions and cognitive restructuring (Kearney, 2003). School social workers and other counselors assess reasons a student is absent, focusing on school- and family-related issues. Cognitive and behavioral strategies can help such a student deal with anxiety, stress, and frustrations. Behavioral strategies include relaxation, imagination, and breathing exercises the student can do in class to reduce worry and nervousness (Kearney, 2003). Cognitive strategies include the use of solution-focused and cognitive-behavioral therapy techniques. School social workers and mental health professionals should also focus on increasing student's self-esteem and social skills, since most students who frequently cut school have little self-confidence academically or socially (Corville-Smith et al., 1998). After-school tutoring programs and mentoring programs can be effective strategies for students who avoid coming to school because of academic problems.

Intervention strategies that focus on students who don't like school or don't get along with a teacher or with other students are more complex and require a multilevel approach. Perhaps the strategy should focus on the student or family; are, for example, mental health services or drug/alcohol treatment services needed? Or perhaps the focus should be on academics: would these students gain more from school if it incorporated technology into the learning process and integrated vocational and school-to-work materials into the

curriculum? Career internships might provide valuable hands-on experience that also further stresses the importance of attending classes. Or perhaps the focus should be on the social aspect of school: is the school one that makes students feel safe, respected, and welcomed? This can be accomplished by knowing students by name and recognizing their successes—no matter how small they may seem (Colorado Foundation for Families and Children, 2004).

This sort of multidisciplinary strategy—addressing truancy from three different sides: student, family, and school—is the only way to make long-term strides in improved school attendance. Though traditional approaches such as punishments and forcing attendance through parental involvement and truancy officers may be effective in the short run, the gains don't last.

Family Strategies

Family involvement is an integral part of reducing school absenteeism, and schools need to collaborate with families in order to improve student attendance (Epstein & Sheldon, 2002). Family problems spill over into the classrooms and can affect student attendance and academic performance. A study by Corville-Smith et al. (1998) found that absentee students, when compared with students who attended school regularly, perceived their families as being less accepting of them, less cohesive, less consistent and effective in discipline, and more conflicted and controlling.

School social workers and other school-based practitioners are in a unique position to help families deal with their child's attendance problem. One way practitioners can assist families is by providing resources for families and students. Family problems such as unsteady employment, lack of reliable transportation, divorce, and family conflict all affect student attendance and performance. Providing resources and connecting families with appropriate social services will help reduce family problems and improve the student's attendance.

Epstein and Sheldon (2002) provides a list of three effective family strategies available to school-based practitioners:

1. *Communicate with families when students are absent.* Collaboration between the school and

the family begins with frequent and open talks about the student's attendance problem. An increased effort needs to be made by practitioners to provide parents with information and resources from the school. This can be done by including the parents in school meetings with teachers, administrators, school social workers, and others either at the school or via conference call. Bowen (1999) recommends that practitioners solicit the parents' perceptions of and insights into their child's attendance problem. Bowen also recommends that school staff give parents ideas about activities and techniques they can use at home to improve their child's academic and behavioral problems. Having a specific school contact person for attendance problems can also help increase communication between the school and families if the families have that person's name and phone number (Epstein & Sheldon, 2002). This designated school employee should have resources and strategies available to help parents deal with the attendance problem.

2. *Hold workshops for parents.* School-based practitioners should conduct workshops that deal specifically with attendance problems. These workshops can provide parents with new strategies and tools to improve school attendance. Workshop topics might include reasons for absenteeism, strategies for improving attendance, advice on getting students up and ready for school on time, information on transportation resources, and tips for dealing with resistance. Workshops should include specific information about attendance policies, procedures, and penalties to better inform families.

3. *Visit the home.* Some school social workers, nurses, and others use home visits and phone calls to parents as part of their family-based intervention to increase parental involvement in their child's schooling (Ford & Sutphen, 1996). Making home visits is an effective strategy for reducing rates of chronic absenteeism and is usually used when students have severe attendance problems. Home visits allow school personnel to gain a more ecological perspective on the student and her or his home environment; they can see if family problems may be contributing to the attendance problem. Based on the home visit assessment, practitioners can develop a contract with the

family detailing specific goals that need to be met in order to avoid legal sanctions. See chapter 47 for guidelines on making effective home visits.

School Strategies

Changes in schools' organizational structure, curricula, and culture are needed if attendance problems are to be effectively addressed (Epstein & Sheldon, 2002). Schools should promote an environment where students feel connected to the school and invested in their learning. One way to accomplish this is to improve teacher–student relationships and engage students as active members of the school community. Reducing class sizes, if possible, will increase the interactions between student and teacher and give students the attention they need. Schools can involve students in coming up with strategies and programs aimed at reducing absenteeism. By involving students and seeking their perspectives, schools help students feel important and allow their voices to be heard (Fallis & Opotow, 2003).

Some of the more common approaches schools take to address attendance problems involve referring students to school social workers and/or truant officers. This strategy can help improve attendance rates but may not be effective with chronic absenteeism. Providing attendance awards can also be helpful, but they should be given as incentives for improved attendance and not just for perfect attendance. Another strategy is to provide after-school programs that motivate students to attend school in order to participate. These after-school programs can also be educational, covering topics on improving student self-esteem and building social skills because, as we said above, absentee students more often suffer from these deficits.

The Office of Juvenile Justice and Delinquency Prevention (OJJDP) issued a report in 1998 that highlighted some of the major research findings regarding truancy. Various programs aimed at individuals, schools, and communities were funded in 1999 through the OJJDP in an effort to develop evidence-based programs aimed at improving school attendance. Table 36.1 provides an overview of each of those federally funded projects and can also be found at http://www. ncjrs.org/html/ojjdp/jjbul2001_9_1/page3. html.

Tools and Practice Examples

Table 36.1 OJJDP-Funded Attendance Programs

Project Location	*Overview of Program*
Department of Health and Human Services: Contra Costa County, CA	An on-site probation officer assesses ninth-graders with a history of truancy and their families. The officer will refer them to appropriate resources within the school and community.
State Attorney's Office: Jacksonville, FL	School district refers students and their families to the State Attorney's Office, which has a precourt diversion program when school-based interventions fail. Following the referral, a hearing is conducted with the parent, student, school attendance social worker, and volunteer hearing officer. A contract is negotiated that includes plans for reducing truancy and accessing social services and community resources.
Clarke County School District: Athens, GA	When students at two middle schools have five or more unexcused absences, the case manager makes home visits, calls parents, organizes parent–teacher conferences to assess the causes of truancy, and provides community and social service referrals if needed. Families who do not respond to the case management approach are summoned to appear before an attendance panel.
University of Hawaii: Honolulu, HI	Attendance officers in two elementary schools provide early outreach to students and their families when absences become chronic. Community resources are used to address issues that may be affecting the student and his or her family. Saturday truancy workshops are coordinated with the police department for youth with chronic truancy problems and their families.
Suffolk County Probation Department: Yaphnak, NY	A probation officer monitors attendance, provides help with accessing school- and community-based services if needed by the student and family to improve attendance, and observes attendance and other school-based indicators to ensure that the student's attendance and engagement at school are improving.
Mayor's Anti-Gang Office: Houston, TX	A case manager identifies students with chronic truancy patterns in a high school. Through home visits and school-based supports, students and their families are provided with services, support, and resources to address truancy. The program also works with community police officers who make home visits to assess family functioning, deliver information about the law and truancy outcomes, and issue official summons to the court for a truancy petition.
King County Superior Court: Seattle, WA	Court provides an evening workshop about truancy laws and outcomes and facilitates planning between the parent and student for addressing the cause of truancy. A school-based component was added to address prevention and early intervention in 2000.
Safe Streets Campaign: Tacoma, WA	The truancy project is based in one middle school, where a coordinator monitors attendance and connects students and their families with community resources to address underlying causes of truancy.

Key Points to Remember

This chapter recognizes the challenges that school administrators, teachers, and families face in trying to improve school attendance. Overall, the highlights of this chapter include:

- Research has shown a correlation between poor school attendance and problems later in life, such as criminal activity, incarceration, marital and family problems, trouble securing and maintaining stable employment, and violent behavior.
- Though the individual student is at the center of our concern about truancy, an effective response must involve the school, the family, and the community.
- Strategies that focus on the individual student include psychoeducational interventions, cognitive restructuring, after-school tutoring programs, and mentoring programs.
- School social workers and others may also need to encourage the use of mental health and drug/alcohol treatment services for either the student or a family member of the student.
- Family interventions include providing resources and connecting families with appropriate social services to help reduce family problems, increasing communication with families when students are absent, holding workshops for parents, and visiting parents at their home.
- Changes in schools' organizational structure, curricula, and culture are needed to address serious attendance problems.

Improving school attendance is a social problem that needs to be addressed from a multilevel approach involving not only the student and the school but also the family and community. It is also not enough just to get students to show up at school by using punitive measures such as truant officers and suspensions. Schools must work to engage the student by creating a school environment that is welcoming and by addressing academic difficulties that may deter the student from attending school.

References

Baker, M. L., Sigmon, J. N., & Nugent, M. E. (2001). *Truancy reduction: Keeping students in school.* Washington,

DC: U.S. Department of Justice, Office of Justice Programs, Office of Juvenile Justice and Delinquency Prevention.

Bell, A. J., Rosen, L. A., & Dynlacht, D. (1994). Truancy intervention. *Journal of Research and Development in Education, 57*(3), 203–211.

Borland, M. V., & Howsen, R. M. (1998). Effect of student attendance on performance: Comment on Lamdin. *Journal of Educational Research, 91*(4), 195–197.

Bowen, N. K. (1999). A role for school social workers in promoting student success through school–family partnerships. *Social Work in Education, 21*(1), 34–47.

Catalano, F. R., Arthur, M. W., Hawkins, J. D., Berglund, L., & Olson, J. J. (1998). Comprehensive community- and school-based interventions to prevent antisocial behavior. In R. Loeber & D. Farrington (Eds.), *Serious and violent juvenile offenders: Risk factors and successful interventions* (pp. 248–283). Thousand Oaks, CA: Sage.

Colorado Foundation for Families and Children (2004). Ten things a school can do to improve attendance. Retrieved on October 9, 2004, from http://www.truancyprevention.org/pdf/10_ImproveAttendance.pdf

Corville-Smith, J., Ryan, B. A., Adams, G. R., & Dalicandro, T. (1998). Distinguishing absentee students from regular attenders: The combined influence of personal, family, and school factors. *Journal of Youth and Adolescence, 27*(5), 629–637.

Dryfoos, J. G. (1990). *Adolescents at risk: Prevalence and prevention.* New York: Oxford University Press.

Dynarski, M., & Gleason, P. (1999). *How can we help? Lessons from federal dropout prevention programs.* Princeton, NJ: Mathematica Policy Research.

Epstein, J. L., & Sheldon, S. B. (2002). Present and accounted for: Improving student attendance through family and community involvement. *Journal of Educational Research, 95*(5), 308–318.

Fallis, R. K., & Opotow, S. (2003). Are students failing school or are schools failing students? Class cutting in high school. *Journal of Social Issues, 59*(1), 103–119.

Finn, J. D., & Voelkl, K. E. (1993). School characteristics related to school engagement. *Journal of Negro Education, 62,* 249–268.

Ford, J., & Sutphen, R. D. (1996). Early intervention to improve attendance in elementary school at-risk children: A pilot program. *Social Work in Education, 18*(2), 95–102.

Huizinga, D., Loeber, R., & Thornberry, T. (1995). *Urban delinquency and substance abuse: Initial findings.* Washington, DC: U.S. Department of Justice, Office of Justice Programs, Office of Juvenile Justice and Delinquency Prevention.

Kearney, C. A. (2003). Bridging the gap among professionals who address youths with school absenteeism: Overview and suggestions for consensus. *Professional Psychology: Research and Practice, 34*(1), 57–65.

Lamdin, D. J. (2001). Evidence of student attendance as an independent variable in education production functions. *Journal of Educational Research, 89*(3), 155–162.

Loeber, R., & Farrington, D. (2000). Young children who commit crime: Epidemiology, developmental origins, risk factors, early interventions, and policy implications. *Development and Psychopathology, 12*(4), 737–762.

Miller, D. (2002). Effect of a program of therapeutic discipline on the attitude, attendance, and insight of truant adolescents. *Journal of Experimental Education, 55*(1), 49–53.

Reid, W. J., & Bailey-Dempsey, C. (1995). The effects of monetary incentives on school performance. *Families in Society, 76*(6), 331–340.

Robins, L. N., & Ratcliff, K. S. (1978). *Long-range outcomes associated with school truancy.* Washington, DC: Public Health Service.

Rohrman, D. (1993). Combating truancy in our schools—a community effort. *NASSP (National Association of Secondary School Principals) Bulletin, 76*(77), 40–45.

Snyder, H. N., & Sickmund, M. (1995). *Juvenile offenders and victims: A national report.* Washington, DC: U.S. Department of Justice, Office of Justice Programs, Office of Juvenile Justice and Delinquency Prevention.

Sturgeon, R., & Beer, J. (1990). Attendance reward and absenteeism in high school. *Psychological Reports, 66*(3), 759–762.

Enhancing Skills of Students Vulnerable to Underachievement and Academic Failure

Mary C. Ruffolo

CHAPTER 37

Getting Started

Many children and adolescents in educational settings today find it difficult to acquire the critical social and academic skills necessary for success in school. They are at risk of underachievement and academic failure. For these children and adolescents, the earlier they fall behind their peers, the harder it is to catch up (Durlak, 1995).

In this chapter, children and adolescents who are underachievers will be defined as students who have the critical social and academic skills but are not achieving. Underachievement can be linked to learning disabilities, behavioral difficulties, and mental health difficulties (Deschenes, Cuban, & Tyack, 2001). Academic failure is defined as the result of a student's poor social and academic performance. Underachievement and academic failure place children and adolescents at risk for dropping out of school. Each year, approximately 23% of youth aged 17 do not graduate from high school with a diploma (Kaufman, Kwon, Klein, & Chapman, 2000). Research on some of the reasons for this place responsibility on schools and teachers. Among the factors affecting a youth's academic success and failure that are within the school's purview are class size, school size, school culture, school resources, availability of after-school help and tutoring, level of conflict and violence in the school, amount of instruction time, teachers' ability to convey care and meaning, teacher–student connections, and teacher prediction of student failure (Dimmitt, 2003).

What We Know

Durlak (1995, p. 44), in a review of the literature on underachievement and academic failure, reports that the best single predictor of academic performance before a child reaches elementary school is the family's socioeconomic level, with many more children from the lowest income levels at risk of doing poorly. Research has repeatedly demonstrated that children whose work warrants failing a grade are very likely to have continued poor achievement and negative personal and social outcomes whether they are retained in that grade or promoted to the next (Owings & Magliaro, 1998). Children and youth of color and children and youth living in economically disadvantaged communities are disproportionately affected by these practices (Kao & Thompson, 2003; Scheurich, Skrla, & Johnson, 2000). Youth who identify as gay, lesbian, bisexual, and transgender also experience higher rates of academic failure (McFarland & Dupois, 2001).

It is critical that school practitioners address the challenge of underachievement and academic failure early. If the individual, family, school, and community factors that place a child at risk are not addressed, these children will become school dropouts (Richman, Bowen, & Woolley, 2004).

Using an ecologically based resiliency framework for understanding the complex factors that place children at risk for underachievement or academic failure will help school practitioners to assess what type of interventions can maximize their possibilities for academic success. In this framework, the interplay of risk and protective factors among individual child, family, school, peers, and neighborhood are assessed in order to develop interventions that promote success in school. These interventions are strength-based, developmentally appropriate, and multilevel.

Risk factors for underachievement and academic failure are conditions that contribute to barriers that may prevent a child from learning and developing. Some of the individual child and youth risk factors that can create barriers to success in school include living with chronic medical problems, having a low IQ, experiencing psychological problems, and having adjustment and temperament problems (Adelman & Taylor, 2003; Huffman, Mehlinger, & Kerivan, 2000; Richman et al., 2004). Family risk factors include poverty, violence, substance abuse, abusive caretaking, and inadequate child care provisions (Adelman & Taylor, 2003; Richman et al., 2004). School and peer factors that contribute to barriers in learning and development include poor-quality schools, negative encounters with teachers, and negative or inappropriate peer models (Adelman & Taylor, 2003; Huffman et al., 2000). Neighborhood risk factors that contribute to underachievement and academic failure include violence, presence of drug activity, minority or immigrant status, extreme economic deprivation, and community disorganization (Adelman & Taylor, 2003; Huffman, Mehlinger, & Kerivan, 2000; Richman, Bowen, & Woolley, 2004).

Protective buffers in this framework are factors that prevent or counter risk-producing conditions. Some of the individual child and youth protective buffers include having a higher cognitive ability, being able to problem solve, having a sense of purpose and hope for the future, being a girl, and having an easy temperament (Adelman & Taylor, 2003; Huffman et al., 2000). Protective buffers at the family level include having adequate financial resources, living in a nurturing, supportive family, having a safe and stable home environment, having family members who completed high school, having family members who can read, and having high-quality child care (Adelman & Taylor, 2003; Richman et al., 2004). At the school and peer level, protective buffers include experiencing academic success, having a positive relationship with one or more teachers, associating with prosocial peers, having a strong bond with others, and attending a school that has a schoolwide climate that promotes nurturing and support (Adelman & Taylor, 2003). At the neighborhood level, protective buffers include having a strong local economy; having available and accessible services; living in a stable and safe community; having opportunities to successfully participate, contribute to, and be recognized by the community;

and living in a community in which a child feels a sense of community (Adelman & Taylor, 2003; Richman et al., 2004).

Resilience emerges as a result of balancing the risk conditions and protective buffers across multiple system levels (Hawkins, Arthur, & Catalano, 1995; O'Keefe, 1994). Richman et al. (2004, p. 151) identify five primary areas of resiliency that promote school success: (1) social competence and connectedness (e.g., empathy and caring, prosocial peers); (2) autonomy (e.g., sense of power, impulse control, self-efficacy); (3) sense of purpose (e.g., healthy expectations, internal locus of control); (4) contextual factors (e.g., safe from bullying and school violence, accessible, supportive adults); and (5) problem-solving skills (e.g., alternative solutions, planning).

What We Can Do

Assessment

In order to assess underachievement and academic failure risks for individual students, school practitioners need to take into account the child's intellectual abilities and contextual factors (at school, in the family, with peers, and in the neighborhood). Intelligence testing, achievement testing, and testing for learning disabilities will help school practitioners to identify a child's intellectual strengths and weaknesses. The use of multiple informants (e.g., parents, teachers) and multiple methods (e.g., self-report, direct observation) in assessment is a strategy that can help the school practitioner to understand the child in context. In addition to these intelligence and achievement tests, school practitioners need to engage youth in assessment processes that capture how they perceive their family, peers, school, and neighborhood. Though a number of assessment tools have been developed to assess contextual issues, the tools that appear to provide the best information for youth at risk of academic failure and underachievement are the School Success Profile (SSP) and the Elementary School Success Profile (ESSP). The SSP, developed by Bowen and Richman (2001), is a survey questionnaire with 220 multiple choice items designed to help school practitioners assess middle school and high school students' perceptions of neighborhood, school, peer, and family conditions. The

SSP contains no questions about illegal behavior, substance abuse, sexual activities, or issues of child abuse that may place youth or families in self-incriminating situations (Richman et al., 2004, p. 152). Validity and reliability measures of the SSP have been empirically supported across a number of research intervention studies (Bowen & Bowen, 1999; Bowen, Woolley, Richman, & Bowen, 2001; Nash, 2002). The ESSP also includes input from parents and teachers (Richman et al., 2004). The ESSP assesses neighborhood conditions, school environment, friend networks, family relationships, parent education involvement, child well-being, social behavior at home and school, and school performance. Like the SSP, the ESSP has demonstrated good reliability and validity in national studies. The SSP and ESSP assessment tools can assist the school practitioner in developing appropriate family, peer, school, and neighborhood interventions for individual youth and will help in monitoring change over time.

Individual, Parent, and Schoolwide Interventions

Research supports the use of cognitive-behavioral interventions in assisting individual children experiencing underachievement or academic failure in building resiliency by increasing problem-solving skills, promoting prosocial peer connections, and increasing social competence (Friedberg & McClure, 2002; Stallard, 2002). Cognitive-behavioral treatment (CBT) uses a collaborative model, is time limited, focuses on the here and now, and promotes a skill-based learning approach. The empirical support for CBT for children and youth with externalizing conditions, anxiety, and depression is relatively strong (Weisz & Jensen, 1999). The results of randomized trials of CBT suggest that CBT fits into the category of "probably efficacious" interventions based on the framework developed by the American Psychological Association (Lonigan, Elbert, & Johnson, 1998). This category requires having two or more CBT studies that demonstrate superiority in outcomes when compared to wait-listed children. Cognitive-behavioral interventions help children learn to identify feelings and thoughts, to connect feelings and thoughts, and to change thoughts. Cognitive-behavioral interventions work best with children at least 7 years of age (Kazdin, 2003).

Tools and Practice Examples

Key steps for school practitioners in using CBT for children 7 years or older who are experiencing underachievement and academic failure are identified by Stallard (2002). These include:

1. developing a clear and shared understanding of the relationship between how students think, how they feel, and what they do;
2. engaging in thought monitoring, which helps students to focus on core beliefs about their situation, their negative automatic thoughts, and situations that produce overly negative or self-critical thoughts;
3. identifying common negative thoughts or assumptions;
4. testing and evaluating these assumptions and helping the student engage in balanced thinking or cognitive restructuring;
5. teaching new cognitive skills that promote positive self-talk, consequential thinking, and problem solving;
6. addressing emotional education through monitoring and managing core emotions by teaching relaxation training and other preventive strategies;
7. managing reinforcers, practicing tasks, testing predictions, doing homework assignments; and
8. role-playing, modeling, and rehearsal.

Throughout the intervention process, the school practitioner needs to establish reinforcements and rewards that address the student's commitment to the intervention process. The reinforcements and rewards may be through contingency contracts, student self-reinforcements, or plans based on performance.

The use of worksheets that address each CBT step and the use of related homework help engage students in CBT. Helping students tune into their feelings might involve using puppets, feelings charts, games, or sentence completion exercises that focus on what happens when the child feels sad, angry, upset, excited, unhappy, or disappointed. Use of metaphors like a volcano erupting or a balloon bursting may help students monitor the depth of their feelings. To help students link thoughts and feelings, students may complete a situation, thoughts, and feelings chart. Using this chart, students would record the day and time, what happened (the situation), their thoughts about what happened, and the feelings that they had when the situation occurred. To help students engage in balanced thinking or cognitive restructuring, school practitioners can use thought thermometers (ranging from 1 = don't believe at all to 10 = very strongly believe) or worksheets that have students record the day and time, what their thoughts were, what evidence there was to support these thoughts, what evidence challenges these thoughts, and what would be more balanced thoughts (Friedberg & McClure, 2002; Stallard, 2002). For children and youth experiencing underachievement or academic failure, recording their thoughts when they are studying, taking tests, or answering questions in class may be the first step in changing the way students engage in school. When asked to do schoolwork by teachers or parents, students who are experiencing academic problems may have trigger thoughts like "I know I can't do this" or "I don't know what to do" or "I'm sure I will do this wrong." Another way for students to track movement toward balanced thinking is have them respond to the following questions developed by Stallard (2002, pp. 79–80):

1. What evidence is there to support this thought?
2. What evidence is there to question this thought?
3. What would my best friend/teacher/parent say if he or she heard me thinking in this way?
4. What would I say to my best friend if he or she had this thought?
5. Am I making any thinking errors?
6. Am I having a downer on myself and forgetting my strengths?
7. Am I blowing things up (all-or-nothing thinking, magnifying the negative, or snowballing?
8. Am I predicting failure?
9. Are these feeling thoughts?
10. Am I setting myself up to fail?
11. Am I blaming myself for the things that have gone wrong?

Teaching problem-solving skills as part of CBT helps children and youth approach challenging academic situations by developing effective solutions. Kazdin (2003) developed an interpersonal cognitive problem-solving skills training program (PSST) that consists of 12 to 20 weekly individual sessions, each of which usually lasts 30 to 50 minutes. The first few sessions focus on teaching the child the steps involved in problem solving; the next sessions use role plays and games to help the child or youth practice the problem-solving steps; the remaining sessions focus on using problem-solving skills in real-life situations. Parents are involved in the middle phase of the intervention and are taught the problem-solving steps so that they can reinforce the skills in the home environment. In order to help children and youth operationalize the problem-solving steps, Kazdin (2003, p. 246) developed a series of self-statement steps to solve a problem. These self-statements steps are:

1. I must understand what I am supposed to do.
2. I have to look at all the possibilities.
3. I'd better concentrate and focus.
4. I need to make a choice.
5. I did a good job (or) Oh, I made a mistake.

Methods that help children to control their feelings include relaxing through controlled breathing (slowly drawing in the breath, holding it for 5 seconds, then slowly letting it out); engaging in physical exercise (e.g., walking briskly, jumping rope, running); and using progressive muscle relaxation methods (tensing muscles for 3 to 5 seconds).

While most children and youth benefit from CBT in schools, strong home–school collaboration appears to be particularly important for families of children and youth who are experiencing academic failure and are living in socially or economically disadvantaged communities (Raffaele & Knoff, 1999). Research indicates that effective school–home collaborations need to be proactive, sensitive to and respectful of the cultural backgrounds of students and families, and attentive to parental contributions to the educational process (Raffaele & Knoff, 1999). One model of this collaboration that has demonstrated positive outcomes for children is the Conjoint Behavioral Consultation (CBC) model. The CBC model is defined as "a structured, indirect form of service-delivery, in which parents and teachers are joined to work together to address academic, social or behavioral needs of an individual for whom both parties bear some responsibility" (Sheridan & Kratochwill, 1992, p. 122). Parents and teachers engage in a structured problem-solving process with a school practitioner to collaboratively address the needs of children at home and at school (Sheridan, Eagle, Cowan, & Mickelson, 2001).

The CBC steps involve: (1) conjoint problem identification; (2) conjoint problem analysis; (3) treatment implementation; and (4) conjoint treatment evaluation (Sheridan et al., 2001). In the first step, school practitioners help parents and teachers identify the child's needs at home and at school. The parents and teachers decide on target behaviors for intervention. The school practitioner helps parents and teachers develop procedures for collecting baseline data on the target behaviors. These procedures might include keeping a daily record of particular behaviors, noting when the child is on task, or monitoring the parents' or teacher's reactions to the child's behavior. In the second step, parents and teachers evaluate the baseline data, decide on behavioral goals for the child, and discuss conditions that might help the child reach—or deter the child from—the target behaviors (Sheridan et al., 2001). During the third step, treatment implementation, the school practitioner reinforces and supports parent and teacher intervention efforts. In the final step, parents and teachers evaluate the effectiveness of the interventions and determine if further consultation is needed.

The goals of CBC are to establish partnerships between parents and teachers that will benefit the student and to develop and enhance the skills and competencies of parents and teachers in meeting the student's needs. Studies have supported the use of CBC for children at risk for underachievement and academic failure, especially for elementary and middle school children (Sheridan et al., 2001).

While individual and parental interventions are critical to helping students who are underachieving or failing academically, a more preventive, schoolwide intervention is needed to promote school success for all students. Several federal and community initiatives have developed prevention programs, both universal and targeted, that promote positive behavioral supports in the schools and academic success. One model of a schoolwide program that has demonstrated positive outcomes is Project ACHIEVE.

Project ACHIEVE, which has been implemented in schools and school districts across the country since 1990, is a comprehensive approach to maximizing children's academic, social, emotional, and behavioral progress (Knoff, Finch, & Carlyon, 2004). Through Project ACHIEVE, all regular education teachers, special education teachers, and support staff learn how to assess and address academic and behavioral problems (Hoagwood & Johnson, 2003).

According to Knoff, Finch, and Carlyon (2004, p. 19-6), Project ACHIEVE has six primary goals: (1) to enhance the problem-solving skills of teachers and other educators; (2) to improve the classroom and behavior-management skills of school personnel and the prosocial and self-management skills of students; (3) to ensure a high-quality education to all students in the school and to intervene strategically with students who are not performing at acceptable levels; (4) to aid the social and academic progress of students by strengthening the commitment of parents and community; (5) to validate the school's comprehensive improvement process; and (6) to create a school culture in which every teacher, staff member, and parent believes that everyone is responsible for every student. Schools that have implemented Project ACHIEVE experienced declines in special education referrals, disciplining referrals, and out-of-school suspensions; they also saw improvements in student achievement in comparison to a demographically matched sample (Hoagwood & Johnson, 2003; Knoff et al., 2004).

Three of the components of Project ACHIEVE are especially useful for school practitioners: (1) behavioral consultations and interventions; (2) referral question consultation (RQC); and (3) parent training, tutoring, and support. A critical component of the behavioral consultation and intervention component involves instruction of prosocial skills using social learning theory principles that are sensitive to cultural diversity (Cartledge & Milburn, 1996). The Stop and Think Social Skills Program (Knoff, 2001) for elementary and middle school students is an example of a social learning approach that teaches students more than 60 behavioral skills that are designed to motivate them and engage them academically. The 60 skills can be organized into four areas: survival skills (e.g., listening, following directions); interpersonal skills (e.g., sharing, waiting your turn, asking for permission); problem-solving skills (e.g., asking for help, deciding what to do, accepting consequences); and conflict resolution skills (e.g., dealing with teasing, losing, peer pressure). Five problem-solving steps are taught and reinforced: (1) Stop and think! (2) Are you going to make a good choice or bad choice? (3) What are your choices or steps? (4) Do it! and (5) Good job! (Knoff, 2001). The RQC component uses a systematic, problem-solving approach that shifts school practice from refer-test-place to one that fosters consultation and classroom-based interventions when problems surface (Knoff et al.,

2004). This promotes linking assessment and intervention to student success and progress. The parent training, tutoring, and support component focuses on training parents to transfer the social skills and discipline/behavior management approaches of the school into the home and teaching them how to monitor their child's homework and academic achievement. Space in the school is dedicated to drop-in centers for parents in an effort to increase their participation in the school.

Promoting school success requires more than one level of intervention by school practitioners. Maintaining a school culture that fosters safety, caring, and positive adult involvement (parents, teachers, and staff) in the lives of students requires that schools address the challenges and risk conditions that children encounter, whether from themselves or their peers, their families, their schools, or their neighborhoods. (See Chapters 75 and 76 for additional information.) School practitioners need to promote conditions that build resiliency and school success especially for children who are doing poorly in school.

More information on the School Success Profile and the Elementary School Success Profile is available at http://www.schoolsuccessprofile.org. Information on the Stop and Think Social Skills Program is available from the National Mental Health and Education Center at http://www.naspcenter.org.

Key Points to Remember

- Children who are underachieving or failing at school can benefit from individual, parent, and schoolwide interventions that build resiliency and promote school success.
- Using an ecologically based resiliency framework for understanding the complex factors that place children and youth at risk for underachievement or academic failure will help school practitioners to assess what type of interventions can best help these children and youth.
- In assessing the causes for underachievement and academic failure, school practitioners need to take into account the child's intellectual abilities and contextual factors (at school, in the family, with peers, and in the neighborhood).
- Cognitive-behavioral treatment helps children learn how to identify their feelings and thoughts, how to connect feelings and thoughts, and how to change thoughts. Cognitive-behavioral treatment uses a collaborative model, is time limited, focuses on the here and now, and promotes skill-based learning.
- School-home collaborations join parents and teachers as partners in developing interventions that target problem behaviors. The Conjoint Behavioral Consultation model is one example of a collaboration that shows promise for children who are underachieving or failing in school.
- In order to prevent academic failure, schoolwide intervention approaches that promote school success for all students need to be implemented. Schoolwide approaches such as Project ACHIEVE offer universal and targeted interventions.

References

Adelman, H., & Taylor, L. (2003). *Addressing barriers to learning: A comprehensive approach to mental health in schools.* Los Angeles: Center for Mental Health in Schools at UCLA.

Bowen, G. L., Woolley, M., Richman, J. M., & Bowen, N. K. (2001). Brief intervention in schools: The school success profile. *Brief Treatment and Crisis Intervention, 1,* 43–54.

Bowen, N. K., & Bowen, G. L. (1999). Effects of crime and violence in neighborhoods and schools on the school behavior and performance of adolescents. *Journal of Adolescent Research, 14,* 319–342.

Bowen, N. K., & Richman, J. M. (2001). *The school success profile.* Chapel Hill: University of North Carolina Press.

Cartledge G., & Milburn, J. F. (1996). *Cultural diversity and social skills instruction.* Champaign, IL: Research Press.

Deschenes, S., Cuban, L., & Tyack, D. (2001). Mismatch: Historical perspectives on schools and students who don't fit. *Teachers College Record, 103,* 525–547.

Dimmitt, C. (2003). Transforming school counseling practice through collaboration and the use of data: A study of academic failure in high school. *Professional School Counseling, 6*(5), 340–349.

Durlak, J. A. (1995). *School-based prevention programmes for children and adolescents.* Thousand Oaks, CA: Sage.

Dwyer, K., & Osher, D. (2000). *Safeguarding our children: An action guide.* Washington, DC: U.S. Department of Education and Justice, American Institutes of Research.

Friedberg, R. D., & McClure, J. M. (2002). *Clinical practice of cognitive therapy with children and adolescents: The nuts and bolts.* New York: Guilford.

Hawkins, J. D., Arthur, M. W., & Catalano, R. F. (1995). Preventing substance abuse. In M. Tonry & D. Farrington (Eds.), *Crime and justice: A review of research. Building a safer society: Strategic approaches to crime prevention* (Vol. 19, pp. 343–427). Chicago: University of Chicago Press.

Hoagwood, K., & Johnson, J. (2003). School psychology: A public health framework; I. From evidence-based practices to evidence-based policies. *Journal of School Psychology, 41,* 3–21.

Huffman, L., Mehlinger, S., & Kerivan, A. (2000). *Research on the risk factors for early school problems and selected federal policies affecting children's social and emotional development and their readiness for school.* Child Mental Health Foundation and Agencies Network. Retrieved May 16, 2004, from www.nimh.nih.gov/childp/goodstart.cfm

Kao, G., & Thompson, J. S. (2003). Racial and ethnic stratification in educational achievement and attainment. *Annual Review of Sociology, 29,* 417–442.

Kaufman, P., Kwon, J. Y., Klein, S., & Chapman, C. (2000). *Dropout rates in the United States* (NCES 2001–2002). Washington, DC: U.S. Department of Education National Center for Education Statistics.

Kazdin, A. E. (2003). Problem-solving skills training and parent management training for conduct disorder. In A. Kazdin & J. R. Weisz (Eds.), *Evidence-based psychotherapies for children and adolescents.* New York: Guilford.

Knoff, H. M. (2001). *The stop and think social skills program (preschool–grade 1, grades 2/3, Grades 4/5, middle school 6–8).* Longmont, CO: Sopris West.

Knoff, H. M., Finch, C., & Carlyon, W. (2004). Project ACHIEVE and the development of school-wide positive behavioral self-management systems—prevention, intervention, and intensive needs approaches. In K. E. Robinson, *Advances in school-based mental health interventions: Best practices and program models* (pp. 19-1–19-28). Kingston, NJ: Civic Research Institute.

Lonigan, C. J., Elbert, J. C., & Johnson, S. B. (1998). Empirically supported psychosocial interventions for children: An overview. *Journal of Child Clinical Psychology, 27,* 138–145.

McFarland, W. P., & Dupois, M. (2001). The legal duty to protect gay and lesbian students from violence in the schools. *Professional School Counseling, 4*(3), 171–180.

Nash, J. K. (2002). Neighborhood effects on sense of school coherence and educational behavior in students at risk of school failure. *Children and Schools, 24,* 73–89.

O'Keefe, M. (1994). Adjustment of children from maritally violent homes. *Families in Society, 75,* 403–415.

Owings, W. A., & Magliaro, S. (1998). Grade retention: A history of failure. *Educational Leadership, 56*(1), 86–89.

Raffaele, L., & Knoff, H. (1999). Improving home-school collaboration with disadvantaged families: Organizational principles, perspectives, and approaches. *School Psychology Review, 28,* 448–466.

Richman, J. M., Bowen, G. L., & Woolley, M. E. (2004). School failure: An eco-interactional developmental perspective. In M. W. Fraser (Ed.), *Risk and resilience in childhood: An ecological perspective* (2nd ed., pp. 133–160). Washington, DC: NASW Press.

Scheurich, J. J., Skrla, L., & Johnson, J. F. (2000). Thinking carefully about equity and accountability. *Phi Delta Kappan, 82*(4), 293–300.

Sheridan, S. M., Eagle, J. W., Cowan, R. J., & Mickelson, W. (2001). The effects of conjoint behavioral consultation: Results of a four-year investigation. *Journal of School Psychology, 39,* 361–385.

Sheridan, S. M., & Kratochwill, T. R. (1992). Behavioral parent–teacher consultation: Conceptual and research considerations. *Journal of School Psychology, 30,* 117–139.

Stallard, P. (2002). *Think good—feel good: A cognitive behavior therapy workbook for children and young people.* Hoboken, NJ: John Wiley & Sons.

Weisz, J. R., & Jensen, P. S. (1999). Efficacy and effectiveness of child and adolescent psychotherapy and pharmacotherapy. *Mental Health Services Research, 1,* 125–157.

Guides for Designing and Establishing Alternative School Programs for Dropout Prevention

David R. Dupper

Getting Started

The purpose of this chapter is to describe best practices in designing and establishing alternative education schools and programs for students who are at risk of dropping out of school as a result of truancy, poor grades, disruptive behavior, pregnancy, repeated suspensions, or expulsions. Following a brief overview of the history of alternative education in the United States and two opposing models of alternative education, this chapter discusses those best practices, based on empirical research, that are common across successful alternative education programs. It also discusses several obstacles or challenges that may arise in implementing these best practices and provides a series of steps to build a broad base of support for alternative education programs and services as well as assist in overcome or reducing obstacles and barriers. This is followed by a case illustration that shows how a number of the best practices discussed in this chapter have been used in an alternative school in Idaho. The chapter concludes with several important points to remember and additional resources that can be used by school social workers and other student-service professionals interested in designing and establishing alternative education schools and programs.

Alternative Education in the United States

The alternative school movement began in earnest in the 1960s as a response to the failure of traditional schools to address the needs of large groups of students (Kershaw & Blank, 1993; Raywid, 1990, 1994). The mission of these early alternative schools was to reach students who were unsuccessful in traditional school settings or disaffected with schooling and provide them with an opportunity to learn in a different academic setting (Ascher, 1982; Atkins, Allen, & Meredith, n.d.; Gregg, 1998).

Over the past decade, public concerns with violence, weapons, and drugs have led to a dramatic shift from an educational purpose to a disciplinary or correctional purpose in alternative education (Gregg, 1998). For example, alternative schools today are often viewed as places where disruptive, deviant, and dysfunctional students are sent "in order to protect and benefit the students who remain in traditional schools" (McGee, 2001, p. 589). Rather than focusing on fixing the educational environment, today's public alternative schools focus on fixing the student and keeping "problem kids" out of our regular schools and off the street. See Table 38.1 for a comparison of these two opposing models of alternative education in relation to school climate (culture), staffing issues, curriculum and instruction, and entrance and exit criteria.

As seen in Table 38.1, alternative schools with an educational focus ("fix the environment") are student-centered, caring, humane learning environments where personal relationships are emphasized and the curriculum is delivered experientially. These alternative schools are more long-term in nature because they focus on the transition from school to work through vocational training (Atkins et al., n.d.). On the other hand, alternative schools with a disciplinary focus ("fix the child") are highly structured, punitive environments where student compliance is emphasized and behavior modification rather than academics is emphasized. These alternative schools and programs are more short-term in nature, and they focus on improving students' behavior and

Table 38.1 Educational Versus Disciplinary Models of Alternative Education

	Educational (fix the educational environment)	Disciplinary (fix the child)
Climate	• Challenging, caring, nurturing, supportive • Collaborative • Student-centered • Personal relationships, bonding to faculty and other students • Focus on whole child • High expectations for student achievement, behavior • Student behavior guided by norms	• Controlling • Highly structured, regulated • Student compliance • Student behavior controlled by rules • Focus on behavior • Punitive
Staffing	• Teacher chooses, not assigned • Hiring, seniority waivers may be needed • May be contracted on part-time or as-needed basis to meet graduation, IEP requirements • Teacher assumes multiple roles (teacher, mentor, counselor) • Repertoire of teaching skills, strategies • Caring, humane • Accountable for student success • Collegiality, teamwork • Professional community	• Controlling • Highly structured, regulated • Student compliance • Student behavior controlled by rules • Focus on behavior • Punitive
Curriculum and instruction	• Full instructional program • Integrated curriculum, interdisciplinary projects • Individualized (for learning styles, needs, current achievement levels) • Clear program goals • Experiential, hands-on learning • Vocational, career, community service components • Challenging, engaging, relevant • Structured for early, frequent success • Continuous progress model • Student responsibility for learning • Multidisciplinary: academic, behavioral, social contexts	• Academics not the focus • Provides only basics, no electives • Skill and drill • Lessons may be provided by home school • Behavior modification • Remediation
Entrance, exit criteria	• Students attend by choice • Long-term; students may graduate from program	• Student assigned or given limited options (e.g., alternative school or jail) • Short-term (1 day, rest of semester, rest of year); student returns to host school when time or behavior requirements met • By contract with parent, child • Transition services critical • Collaboration with home school, support system for returning students important

Source: Adapted from Appalachia Educational Laboratory. (1998). *Schools for disruptive students: A questionable alternative?* Policy Briefs Series. Charleston, WV: Author. Reprinted with permission.

returning them to their home schools (Atkins et al., n.d.). It is important to note that researchers have found that alternative schools that are correctional in nature, focusing on punitive disciplinary policies and practices, "reap no positive long-term gains and may even increase negative outcomes" (Gregg, 1998, p. 3). On the other hand, alternative schools that focus on education rather than punishment work best in improving student behavior and student achievement (Kershaw & Blank, 1993; Morley, 1991; Raywid, 1994). Research also shows that alternative schools and programs that focus primarily on therapeutic interventions may "temporarily improve student behavior and achievement[,] but results tend to fade when students return to home schools" (Gregg, 1998, p. 5).

What We Know

Empirically Supported Characteristics Common to Successful Alternative Education Programs

One of the most comprehensive definitions of today's alternative school is provided by the U.S. Department of Education. It defines an alternative school as "a public elementary/secondary school that addresses needs of students that typically cannot be met in a regular school, provides nontraditional education, serves as an adjunct to a regular school, or falls outside the categories of regular, special education, or vocational education (U.S. Department of Education, 2002, p. 55). Daniel Wiltrout, a consultant with the Wisconsin Department of Instruction, defines alternative schools as schools in a different setting that offer flexible schedules, smaller teacher–student ratios, and modified curriculum to serve students not succeeding in traditional public school environments (National Conference of State Legislatures, 2004). Rather than providing a definition, Morley (1991, p. 8) describes alternative education as "a perspective, not a procedure or program. It is based upon the belief that there are many ways to become educated, as well as many types of environments and structures within which this may occur." This viewpoint assumes that all children do not learn in the same manner and that the core of alternative education lies in varied methods of instruction and an innovative curriculum (Reimer & Cash, 2003).

Though it is possible to provide definitions and philosophical perspectives about alternative education, it is much more difficult to discuss the effectiveness of alternative schools and programs, largely because so few rigorous studies have been done in this area (Lange & Sletten, 2002). In one of the few studies to date, Cox, Davidson, and Bynum (1995) used meta-analysis to summarize empirical research on alternative schools in the years 1966–1993. Their final meta-analysis included 57 evaluations of alternative schools that met the following criteria: the program being evaluated consisted of a separate curriculum, was housed outside a conventional school, and statistically assessed at least one type of outcome (e.g., student attitudes toward school, school performance, self-esteem, delinquency). Based on their meta-analysis, these authors found that:

- alternative schools targeting a specific population (primarily low achievers or delinquents) have more impact than programs not targeting specific types of students;
- alternative schools have small positive effects on attitudes and performance outcomes;
- however, these authors also found that alternative schools do not affect delinquent behavior; that is, their effect on school performance and self-esteem is not large enough to influence delinquent behavior.

In a recent publication, Reimer and Cash (2003) have analyzed a number of empirical studies by researchers in alternative education (Kadel, 1994; Kellmayer, 1995; Public Schools of North Carolina, 2000; Raywid, 1994; Schargel & Smink, 2001; Wehlage, 1983) and contributed to the knowledge base by identifying a number of characteristics and best practices of successful alternative schools. A number of other researchers (Ascher, 1982; Barr & Parrett, 2001; Chavkin, 1993; Cox et al., 1995; Dollar, 1983; Franklin & Streeter, 1991; Ingersoll & LeBoeuf, 1997; Kraemer & Ruzzi, 2001; Morley, 1991; Northwest Regional Educational Laboratory, 2001; U.S. Department of Education, 1996; Young, 1990) have also contributed to our understanding of characteristics that distinguish successful alternative programs from unsuccessful programs.

Table 38.2 contains a comprehensive list of characteristics and best practices common to successful alternative programs based on the empirical research. Research indicates that perhaps the single most important characteristic in developing an alternative school or program is employing teachers and staff who have chosen to work with and are committed to these youth. The selection of committed and caring staff is of paramount importance because "students can overcome bad teaching but they may never recover from a bad teacher who fails to project a true sense of caring and concern" (Reimer & Cash, 2003, p. 19). Successful alternative programs provide ongoing staff development in the areas of classroom management techniques, diversity training, and alternative instructional methods because most teachers did not receive this training in their formal teacher education program (Reimer & Cash, 2003). It also appears that successful alternative programs target a specific population of at-risk students and develop a holistic, humane, flexible educational program that is individualized and responsive to the social, emotional, and academic needs of these youth. Meeting the academic needs of these youth requires a hands-on, experiential curriculum that is tailored to the unique learning style of each student. Unfortunately, there is little or no data related to what happens to alternative school graduates upon reentry into their home school. However, there is evidence to suggest that long-term outcomes may be enhanced by providing follow-up and transition services to these students (Atkins et al., n.d; Glass, 1995).

What We Can Do

Steps in Designing and Establishing Effective Alternative Education Schools and Programs

The recent emphasis on zero tolerance and punitive discipline as a response to student misbehavior poses a number of significant challenges for school social workers and other student service professionals in designing and establishing effective alternative schools and programs. With a general public clamoring for punishment and making "bad kids" pay for their school misbehavior and poor attitude, many alternative schools have evolved into dumping grounds to warehouse children. A central challenge awaiting school social workers and others is to convince the general public, as well as some teachers and administrators, that effective and humane alternative programs must offer students opportunities to learn

from their mistakes and move forward positively with their lives, rather than focusing exclusively on punishment. School social workers and counselors must be prepared to challenge comments and attitudes such as the following one made by a school superintendent in North Carolina: "I'm not going to waste my certified teachers on those kids" (North Carolina Education and Law Project, 1997, p. 3).

To overcome obstacles such as these, it is essential that school social workers and others plan and implement in a carefully thought out and systematic manner. The following series of sequential steps are based on the work of Reimer and Cash (2003), DeBlois (1994), Dugger and DesMoulin-Kherat (1996), and Harrington-Lueker (1994). They are designed to build a broad base of support in the initial phases of program development, to help overcome potential barriers and obstacles throughout the process, and to ensure that programs are built upon those characteristics and best practices outlined in Table 38.2.

1. *Establish a planning team or task force.* To ensure a broad base of support, it is recommended that this planning team or task force include representatives of local social service agencies, local businesses, law enforcement, and schools. It will work best if it has 6 to 15 members. Reimer and Cash (2003) state that teams with more than 15 members "become cumbersome to work with and may become splintered as time goes on. Conversely, a subgroup or powerful leader who wants to push through his/her own vision and agenda may sway a small group" (p. 17). It is advisable to start putting the team together at least 1 year ahead of the start-up date of a school or program. See Dupper (1993) for a detailed discussion of a community task force that was an integral part of an alternative program for potential dropouts in a middle school setting.

2. *Develop a philosophy and mission for the school or program.* A group consensus on the philosophical foundation is absolutely essential since this will guide the development of program policies and procedures (Reimer & Cash, 2003). A central question is whether the school or program is envisioned as educational (focused on providing an alternative learning experience) or disciplinary (focused on "fixing the child"). These two opposing philosophies are described and contrasted in Table 38.1. In determining which of these philosophies will be

Table 38.2 Characteristics and Best Practices Common to Successful Alternative Education Programs

- a student-to-staff ratio that is lower than in mainstream schools (i.e., maximum teacher/student ratio of 1:10) (Ingersoll & LeBoeuf, 1997; Northwest Regional Educational Laboratory, 2001; Schargel & Smink, 2001)
- small student base not exceeding 250 students (Schargel & Smink, 2001)
- a clear stated mission shared by all staff and clear rules that are enforced fairly and consistently (Ingersoll & LeBoeuf, 1997; Northwest Regional Educational Laboratory, 2001; Cox, Davidson, & Bynum, 1995; Schargel & Smink, 2001)
- A caring faculty who have chosen to teach in alternative schools and programs and who are committed to counseling, mentoring, and tutoring students in these programs (Barr & Parrett, 2001; Northwest Regional Educational Laboratory, 2001; Schargel & Smink, 2001)
- continual staff development opportunities (Schargel & Smink, 2001)
- school staff having high academic standards and high expectations for student achievement (Schargel & Smink, 2001)
- focus is on individualized learning that takes into account student's expectations and learning style within a *flexible schedule* that allows students to work at their own pace (Ascher, 1982; Chavkin, 1993; Dollar, 1983; Franklin & Streeter, 1991; Northwest Regional Educational Laboratory, 2001; Schargel & Smink, 2001)
- one-on-one interaction between teachers and students with a total commitment to have each student be successful (Morley, 1991; Young 1990; Schargel & Smink, 2001)
- a school or program that targets specific populations (i.e., primarily low school achievers or delinquents) (Chavkin, 1993; Cox, Davidson, & Bynum, 1995; Franklin & Streeter, 1991)
- strong stable, and dynamic leadership (Reimer & Cash, 2003)
- provide a supportive, informal setting where personal relationships between students and teachers and a "family-like atmosphere" of respect can flourish (Morley, 1991; Young 1990; Northwest Regional Educational Laboratory, 2001; Schargel & Smink, 2001)
- provide a curriculum that can be described as "applied," "experiential," "hands-on," or "integrated"; a curriculum that emphasizes "real life learning" and that makes connections between the school and the community or "work world" (Young, 1990; Kraemer & Ruzzi, 2001; Ingersoll & LeBoeuf, 1997; Northwest Regional Educational Laboratory, 2001; Reimer & Cash, 2003)
- holistic services are provided to meet the emotional, physical, and academic needs of students (Reimer & Cash, 2003)
- student voices in decision-making and school operations is emphasized (Morley, 1991; Young 1990; Ascher, 1982; Northwest Regional Educational Laboratory, 2001)
- broad participation of the family and community is emphasized (Ascher, 1982; Ingersoll & LeBoeuf, 1997; Chavkin, 1993; Franklin & Streeter, 1991; Reimer & Cash, 2003)
- strong working relations with all parts of the school system and with other collaborating agencies that provide critical services to youth (Northwest Regional Educational Laboratory, 2001)

chosen, it is essential that school social workers and counselors make the planning team or task force aware of current research on characteristics and best practices of alternative programs (see Table 38.2).

3. *Develop the design and operation of the school or program.* This is the point at which a building principal or program director should be hired to decide upon the nuts and bolts of the school or program with advice from school district staff. At this stage of the process it is important to consider how the school or program will receive funding (per-student costs for alternative education are higher because of the lower teacher–student ratio), where it will be located (i.e., settings for alternative schools and programs range from space in a large department store to an empty office building to a portable structure), how large it will be, whom it will serve, how transportation will be provided, and how it will be staffed. Again, it is essential that the school social worker and counselors share best practices related to each of these issues. At this point, it is also important to remember that applying for grants and holding annual fund-raising events is time consuming and

tiresome (DeBlois, 1994). If the school district is too small or lacks the financial resources to support an alternative school, look into participating in a regional program run by an education service district (Northwest Regional Educational Laboratory, 2001). However, if one of the goals of the program is for students to reenter their traditional or base school, then it may be helpful to be located in or near that school. It is essential that good two-way communication between the alternative and students' home schools be maintained, particularly as students are preparing to transition back to their home schools (Reimer & Cash, 2003).

4. *Select staff members.* Because of the deep suspicion and distrust that many students feel toward a school system that they believe has failed them, it is extremely important that a fragile bond of two-way trust between students and staff be established (Kraemer & Ruzzi, 2001). This is particularly true if students will be assigned to the alternative school or program rather than attend by choice. Since many of these youth have difficulty following traditional school rules, it is important that the principal or administrator in charge of student discipline also be flexible in dealing with discipline issues (Reimer & Cash, 2003).

5. *Design the alternative curriculum.* In this step, the planning team or task force must decide upon the teacher–student ratio, what curriculum will be offered, how the curriculum will be delivered, how technology will be integrated, how social services and counseling services will be delivered, and how to provide opportunities for teachers to collaborate and plan together. It should be emphasized that the most important role of each and every staff member is to be an *informal counselor and support person to students* (Kellmayer, 1995).

6. *Build community support.* One of the most effective ways of changing the public's negative perception of alternative education is by "inviting community members, including the local press, to visit your alternative school as well as to be able to document the ways in which students have grown while attending the alternative school" (McGee, 2001, p. 589). It is important to connect with surrounding businesses and community groups for ways that they can become involved (e.g., providing money and career-related opportunities). When possible, involve parents and family, particularly at the middle school level, by, for example, sending letters to

them and holding parenting classes and student-led parent conferences. (See Chapters 76, 77, 79, and 81 for additional information.)

7. *Establish specific enrollment and exit criteria.* Enrollment criteria must be established to prevent the alternative school or program from becoming a place where the school district dumps students who don't seem to fit anywhere else. "If the school or program becomes a dumping ground for students it was not intended to serve, it is likely that the once-enthusiastic staff will become frustrated and begin to leave the school. These teachers may be replaced with others who do not share the original vision of the school, thus causing the program's reputation to suffer and enrollment to decline" (Northwest Regional Educational Laboratory, 2001).

8. *Document and publicize program results.* To avoid closure because of school board changes, opposition from teacher's unions (Amenta, 1997), or an economic downturn (DeBlois, 1994), alternative school administrators and staff must constantly sell their program by showing that it works and that it is cost effective (e.g., it is cheaper to educate now than to build prisons later). This can be accomplished through statistics, anecdotes, and personal testimony from students and parents. To assess improvements in learning, data on changes in GPA, attendance rates, graduation rates, and dropout rates should be collected and analyzed over several years (Gregg, 1998). To assess improvements in student behavior, data on changes in the number of disciplinary referrals, suspension or expulsion rates, and in-school suspension rates should be collected and analyzed over several years (Gregg, 1998).

Tools and Practice Examples

A Case Illustration

The following is excerpted from an article titled "Where Everyone Knows Your Name! Special Programs Target at-Risk Students" from the publication *Education World* (1998). It describes Meridian Academy alternative high school in Meridian, Idaho, a suburb of Boise. It provides an example of how the best practices discussed in this article have been applied in an alternative school.

All the teachers were glad to have me. They make [me] feel important—as a person. It blew my mind. I loved it from the first day. Everybody is really welcoming.—John, a tenth-grade dropout from a large high school

There were too many kids there. I sat in the back and raised my hand, but I never got any help. . . . Here, everyone is very accepting. I know I'm going to graduate.—Anna, who failed her freshman year in a big high school

The 150-student academy is a good example of an alternative high school that incorporates a number of the characteristics and best practices contained in Table 38.2. It is described as a school where "invisible" children who got lost in the shuffle of larger schools are offered a new chance for success. Students attend small classes (15 in the average class) where teachers greet them by name every day; where teachers strive to draw every student into every lesson, engaging the students and making them feel "visible"; and where small "family group" sessions offer students an opportunity to air problems and receive support on a regular basis. The curriculum at Meridian is hands-on and student centered. Instead of reading out of a book and answering the questions in the back, students become involved by building it, or making it, or doing it. Meridian has a no-homework policy. Meridian staff recognize that many at-risk students fall behind because they can't keep up with the homework assigned in regular schools. Many come from home situations that are not conducive to doing homework, and many have after-school jobs, parenting responsibilities, or go to vocational school at night. To compensate, class time is extended, and Friday afternoons are dedicated to finishing or making up work. As an added incentive to staying on top of work, students who are caught up with their work get to leave early on Fridays. Discipline is not much of a problem at Meridian Academy. The staff and even the students recognize that structure is a key to success: lack of structure at home and in school are some of the main causes for the students' previous school problems. Each student must sign the school's student behavior policy each semester. It's a policy that the students have a hand in forming, and it spells out school rules and consequences. After three discipline referrals, students must appear before a student court where evidence is presented and students and parents have an opportunity to make their pleas. Staff members then vote to give the students another chance or to dismiss them. Academic expectations are very high. Students must achieve a 70% record in each class. Each year, 75% of students complete the school year. One teacher comments, "It only takes a few weeks and you notice they raise their heads up. Next they start looking you in the eye, and their shoulders are back. Pretty soon, they start thinking about vocational school, or technical school or college—the last thing they ever thought about in their lives."

Resources

Dupper, D. R. (1993). School–community collaboration: A description of a model program designed to prevent school dropouts. *School Social Work Journal, 18*, 32–39. (This article provides a detailed discussion of a community task force and its importance in the overall operation of an alternative program.)

Northwest Regional Educational Laboratory, Alternative schools: Caring for kids on the edge, *Northwest Education Magazine* (summer 1998). This organization can be reached at 101 S.W. Main Street, Suite 500, Portland, OR 97204, Telephone (503) 275–9500, e-mail: webmaster@nwrel.org, NWREL Web Site: http:// www.nwrel.org

The Center for Effective Collaboration and Practice. *Alternative schools: Information for families.* Available at http://cecp.air.org/family-briefs/ docs/AltSch.pdf

The National Dropout Prevention Center (NDPC) at Clemson University has become a well-established national resource for sharing solutions for student success. The center can be reached at 209 Martin Street, Clemson, SC 29631–1555, (864) 656–2599, e-mail: ndpc@clemson.edu; http://www.dropoutprevention.org/

National Coalition of Advocates for Students is a private nonprofit coalition of advocacy organizations that work on behalf of students who are traditionally underserved (e.g., students of color, immigrants, students from low-income families, and special needs students). E-mail: ncasmfe@aol.com; Web site: http://www.ncas1.org/

Quality alternative placements for suspended or expelled students: "Lessons learned" from the Center for the Prevention of School Violence's Youth Out of the Education Mainstream Initiative can be downloaded at http://www.ncdjjdp.org/cpsv/alt_learning/yoem/qareplace.htm

Kennedy, R. L. & Morton, J. H. (1999). *A school for healing: Alternative strategies for teaching at-risk students.* New York: Peter Lang.

For state-by-state information on alternative schools for disruptive students, see http://www.ecs.org/clearinghouse/15/05/1505.htm. Successful alternative education programs for troubled youth can be downloaded from http://www.ncsl.org/programs/educ/AlterEdSN.htm.

Key Points to Remember

- A major challenge that school social workers and others face in designing and establishing effective and humane alternative schools and programs is to create schools and programs that are creative outlets for students whose needs are not being met by traditional schools. It is important to create places where students will have opportunities to learn from their mistakes and move forward positively with their lives rather than be warehoused as "bad kids."
- The ultimate outcome for the majority of students in an alternative school or program is a successful reentry into their base school. Therefore, ongoing communication with the base school is essential, and adequate supports (e.g., transition specialists) must be provided to the students as they reenter. Evidence suggests that providing follow-up and transition services to students as they return to their home schools may enhance long-term outcomes.
- Target specific populations of at-risk students (e.g., low achievers or delinquents). Targeted programs have been shown to be more effective than programs that do not target specific types of students.
- Plan for the maximum level of voluntary participation by both students and teachers. Hire teachers with both the skills and the passion to teach material in an experiential, creative, and noncompetitive manner. Develop an organizational structure characterized by flexibility and autonomy, one in which students, teachers, and parents can work together to make program decisions.
- Follow the eight steps described in this chapter

focusing on the design and creation of effective alternative education schools and programs. Include as many of the characteristics contained in Table 38.2 as possible as these are, according to a number of researchers in the field of alternative education, the best practices.

References

Amenta, R. (1997). Horizon alternative school: Why promising reforms disappear. *Education Week, 16*(22), 36, 38.

Ascher, C. (1982). ERIC/CUE: Alternative schools: Some answers and questions. *Urban Review, 14*, 65–69.

Atkins, T., Allen, J., & Meredith, M. (n.d.). *Alternative schools: Information for families.* Eugene: Center for Effective Collaboration and Practice, University of Oregon. Retrieved April 6, 2004, from http://cecp.air.org/familybriefs/docs/AltSch.pdf

Barr, R. D., & Parrett, W. H. (2001). *Hope fulfilled for at-risk and violent youth.* Needham Heights, MA: Allyn & Bacon.

Chavkin, N. F. (1993). School social workers helping multiethnic families: Schools and communities join forces. In N. F. Chavkin (Ed.), *Families and schools in a pluralistic society* (pp. 217–228). Albany: State University of New York Press.

Cox, S. M., Davidson, W. S., & Bynum, T. S. (1995). A meta-analytic assessment of delinquency-related outcomes of alternative education programs. *Crime and Delinquency, 41*, 219–234.

DeBlois, R. (1994). Keeping alternatives alive. *American School Board Journal, 181*, 33–34.

Dollar, R. (1983). What is really going on in schools? *Social Policy, 13*, 7–19.

Dugger, C., & Desmoulin-Kherat, S. (1996). Helping younger dropouts get back into school. *Middle School Journal, 28*, 29–33.

Dupper, D. R. (1993). School-community collaboration: A description of a model program designed to prevent school dropouts. *School Social Work Journal, 18*, 32–39.

Education World. (1998). Where everyone knows your name! Special programs target at-risk students. Retrieved April 20, 2004, from http://www.educationworld.com/a_admin/admin098.shtml

Franklin, C., & Streeter, C. L. (1991). Evidence for the effectiveness of social work with high school dropout youths. *Social Work in Education, 13*, 307–327.

Glass, R. (1995). Alternative schools help kids succeed. *Education Digest, 60*, 21–24.

Gregg, S. (1998). *Schools for disruptive students: A questionable alternative?* Policy Briefs series. Charleston, WV: Appalachia Educational Laboratory.

Harrington-Lueker, D. (1994). Hanging on to hope. *American School Board Journal, 181*, 16–21.

Ingersoll, S., & LeBoeuf, D. (1997). *Reaching out to youth out of the education mainstream.* U.S. Department of Justice, Office of Justice Programs, Office of Juvenile Justice and Delinquency Prevention.

Kadel, S. (1994). *Reengineering high schools for student access. Hot topics: Usable research.* Palatha, FL: Southeastern Regional Vision for Education. (ERIC Document Reproduction Service No. ED366076)

Kellmayer, J. (1995). *How to establish an alternative school.* Thousand Oaks, CA: Corwin.

Kershaw, C., & Blank, M. (1993, April). *Student and educator perceptions of the impact of an alternative school structure.* Paper presented at the annual meeting of the American Educational Research Association, Atlanta, GA.

Kraemer, J., & Ruzzi, B. B. (2001). Alternative education cannot be left behind. *Education Week.* Retrieved January 23, 2004, from http://www.edweek.org/ew/newstory.cfm?slug=06kraemer.h21

Lange, C. M., & Sletten, S. J. (2002). *Alternative education: A brief history and research synthesis.* Alexandria, VA: National Association of State Directors of Special Education.

McGee, J. (2001). Reflections of an alternative school administrator. *Phi Delta Kappan, 82*, 588–591.

Morley, R. (1991). *Alternative education* (ED349652). Clemson, SC: National Dropout Prevention Center.

National Conference of State Legislatures. (2004). Successful alternative education programs for troubled youth. Retrieved May 1, 2004, from http://ncsl.org/programs/educ/AlterEdSN.htm

North Carolina Education and Law Project. (1997). *Alternative schools: Short-term solutions with long-term consequences* (2nd ed.). Raleigh, NC: Author.

Northwest Regional Educational Laboratory. (2001). *Alternative schools: Approaches for students at risk.* Retrieved May 1, 2004, from http://www.nwrel.org/request/sept97/article2.html

Public Schools of North Carolina. (2000, March). Case studies of best practices. Alternative schools and programs: 1998–99. Raleigh, NC: Author. Retrieved May 5, 2004, from http://www.ncpublicschool.org/accountability/alternative/case9899.pdf

Raywid, M. (1990). Alternative education: The definition problem. *Changing Schools, 18,* 4–5, 10.

Raywid, M. (1994). Synthesis of research: Alternative schools: The state of the art. *Educational Leadership, 52*, 26–31.

Reimer, M. S., & Cash, T. (2003). *Alternative schools: Best practices for development and evaluation.* Clemson, SC: National Dropout Prevention Center/Network.

Schargel, F. P., & Smink, J. (2001). *Strategies to help solve our school dropout problem.* Larchmont, NY: Eye on Education.

U.S. Department of Education (1996). *Safe and drug-free schools. Alternative education programs for expelled students.* Retrieved May 1, 2004, from http://www.ed.gov/offices/OESE/SDFS/actguid/altersc.html

U.S. Department of Education. (2002). *Characteristics of the 100 largest elementary and secondary school districts in the United States: 2000–01,* NCES 2002–351. Washington DC: Author.

Wehlage, G. (1983). *Effective programs for the marginal high school student. Fastback 197.* Bloomington, IN: Phi Delta Kappa.

Young, T. (1990). *Public alternative education: Options and choices for today's schools.* New York: Teachers College Press.

Interpersonal Conflict, Violence, and Classroom Management

Best Practices and Resources

This section responds to the concerns of school social workers and other school professionals about the growing incidence of violence and conflict in schools. The chapters address best practices in predicting, preventing, and coping with school violence, and they address specific situations such as conflicts between students, conflicts between students and teachers, gang behavior, rape and sexual harassment, bullying, and violent aggressiveness. Chapters provide specific guidance for working with teachers in their management of conflict and behavior in the classroom, for forming alliances between parents and school staff, and for influencing a nonviolent school environment and culture.

Evidence-Based Violence Prevention Programs and Best Implementation Practices

Ron Avi Astor ▪ Michelle Rosemond ▪ Ronald O. Pitner
Roxana Marachi ▪ Rami Benbenishty

CHAPTER 39

Getting Started

Social work as a profession has contributed to the national and international dialogue concerning violence prevention programs in schools. School social workers play an increasingly important role in shaping and implementing policy, interventions, and procedures that make U.S. schools safer. The chapters in this section provide a comprehensive guide to best practices in nearly all aspects of school conflict and violence, from organizational and procedural modifications (see especially chapters 40 and 41), to diminishing interpersonal conflict between individuals and groups on school grounds and in the classroom. The dynamics of such serious problems as bullying, physical aggressiveness, date rape, sexual harassment, and physical violence among adolescent couples are explained in tandem with full and detailed guidance to practice responses and interventions.

In order to use resources to the best advantage and to maximize program effectiveness, it is helpful for school mental health professionals to not only know the dynamics and best approaches for assessing and intervening in school violence but also be familiar with available model programs already studied and found to be effective. As an overview leading into this section of the manual, this chapter will review several examples of effective violence prevention programs as well as model school safety programs.

One great weakness in establishing evidence-based violence prevention programs is that they are often introduced to schools with a "top-down" approach, ignoring variations in local school contexts. Even model programs that have been demonstrated to be effective in large-scale research studies have a better chance for success at any given school if the program matches the needs and values of the community, the school, and the school staff. To assist readers in achieving such a match, we offer monitoring and mapping approaches as a guide to develop a bottom-up program and in tracking program interventions.

What We Know

In this section of the chapter we present examples of the most researched model school safety programs available to schools and practitioners. Table 39.1 includes the names of the programs, Web sites where the programs can be explored, program components, outcome measures, and results from studies. We also include a more extensive list of Web sites and resources for each program at the end of the chapter. The programs listed in Table 39.1 have been rated as "effective" by multiple national organizations. Our designation of effective is a composite of ratings from 11 independent scientific organizations that evaluated the most popular school violence prevention programs. Criteria considered in designating a program as effective include (1) evidence of effectiveness based on rigorous evaluations with experimental or quasi-experimental designs; (2) the clarity of the program's goals and rationale; (3) the fit between the program content and the characteristics of the intended population and setting; (4) the integration of the program into schools' educational mission; (5) the availability of necessary information and guidance for replication in other settings; and (6) the incorporation of post-treatment and follow-up data collection as part of the program. We describe in detail four of the five programs listed in Table 39.1.

What We Can Do

Bullying Prevention Program

The Bullying Prevention Program (BPP) is a comprehensive multicomponent bullying reduction and prevention program designed for students in grades 1–9. It was developed during the 1970s by Dan Olweus to reduce bully and victim problems in Norwegian schools. Since then, it has been translated into more than 12 languages and successfully established in schools in more than 15 countries. The BPP has been shown to reduce levels of bully and victim incidents by 33–64% (see Table 39.1). We also refer the reader to chapter 42 for an in-depth review of bullying as a school problem, as well as comprehensive guidance on program selection and specific examples of evidence-based interventions and tools in a bullying prevention program.

Content

As seen in Table 39.1 under Program Components, the BPP is implemented at three levels of the school environment—the total school, classroom, and the individual student. At the school-wide level, the BPP establishes antibullying policy in the school system. To raise awareness and quantify the prevalence of bullying in the school, administrators distribute an anonymous 29-item student questionnaire to all students. A school conference day about bullying is established to talk about the results of the assessment and discuss interventions. Additionally, schools create a BPP coordination team in which a representative administrator, teacher, counselor, parent, and student come together to lead the program implementation. In the BPP program, the school adopts rules against bullying and explains to students the negative consequences for bullying behavior. All staff receive training to learn about the harmful consequences of bullying, to increase supervision in areas on campus that are prone to violence, and to provide systematic reinforcement of rules applied to all students.

At the classroom level, students have regular workshops about the harmful consequences of bullying. Students have discussions about bullying and violent behaviors, watch video presentations of bullying situations, write about ways to combat the problem, and engage in role play. Students are encouraged to increase their knowledge and empathy regarding bullying.

The individual student level involves direct consequences for bullying behaviors. There are focused interventions with those identified as bullies and victims, as well as the bystanders. The parents of involved students are given help and support to reinforce nonviolence at home. School mental health workers play an essential role in

Table 39.1 Model Violence Prevention Programs and Evaluation Sources

Program (Authors)	Grade	Participants	Program Components	Outcome Measures	Results
Bullying Prevention Program (Olweus, 1993) www.clemson.edu/olweus	4th–7th grades	2,500 students in 42 primary and secondary schools in Norway. (The program is now international and is being applied in 15 countries. The materials are translated into more than 12 languages.)	Core components of the program are implemented at the school level, the class level, and the individual level. Including: • Distribution of anonymous student questionnaire assessing the nature and prevalence of bullying • Development of positive and negative consequences for students' behavior • Establishment of a supervisory system • Reinforcement of schoolwide rules against bullying • Classroom workshops with video and discussions to increase knowledge and empathy • Interventions with perpetrators and victims of bullying • Discussions with parents	Student self-report measures collected at introduction of the program, 4 months after introduction, 1-year follow-up, and 2-year follow-up. • Reports of incidents of bullying and victimization • Scale of general youth antisocial behavior • Assessment of school climate—order and discipline • Measure of social relationships and attitude toward school	The results show a 33–64% reduction in the levels of bully incidents. The author found a 30–70% reduction in aggregated peer rating variables. In addition there was no displacement of bullying to before or after school. There was also a significant reduction in antisocial behavior such as fighting, theft, and truancy. The school climate showed marked improvement, with students reporting an increased satisfaction with school in general, positive social relationships and positive attitude toward schoolwork and school. Rated effective—1, 2, 3, 4, 6, 7, 8, 9

(continued)

Table 39.1 (*Continued*)

Program (Authors)	Grade	Participants	Program Components	Outcome Measures	Results
Child Development Project (Battistich, Schaps, Watson, & Solomon, 1996) www.devstu.org/	3rd–6th grades	4,500 students in 24 elementary schools from 6 diverse districts throughout the United States.	This is a comprehensive model focused on creating a cooperative and supportive school environment. Classroom components include: • staff training in cooperative learning • implementation of a model that fosters cross-grade "buddying" activities • a developmental approach to discipline that fosters self-control • a model to engage students in classroom norm setting and decision making Schoolwide community-building activities are used to promote school bonding and parent involvement activities such as interactive homework assignments that reinforce the family–school partnership.	Data were collected after 1 year and 2 years of intervention. Teachers were assessed through four 90-minute observations and annual teacher questionnaires. Student assessments were self-report surveys of drug use and delinquent behavior.	Results showed that students experienced a stronger sense of community and more motivation to be helpful, better conflict-resolution skills, greater acceptance of people who are different, higher self-esteem, stronger feelings of social competence, less loneliness in school, and fewer delinquent acts. Statistically significant decreases were found for marijuana use, vehicle theft, and weapons. By the second year of the program, students in schools showed significantly lower rates of skipping school, carrying weapons, and stealing vehicles ($ps < .01$). Rated effective—3, 4, 5, 6, 7, 9

(*continued*)

FAST Track—Families and Schools Together *(Conduct Problems Prevention Research Group,* 2002) www.fasttrackproject.org	Three cohorts of students, grades 1–10 (still ongoing) At-risk kindergartners identified based on combined teacher and parent ratings of behavior (CBCL). Highest 10% recruited for study. *N* = 445 intervention children *N* = 446 control group children	Long-term program. Weekly enrichment program for high-risk children and their parents Students placed in "friendship groups" of 5–6 students each. Discussions, modeling stories and films, role plays Sessions focus on reviewing and practicing skills in emotional understanding and communication, friendship building, self-control, and social problem solving Parents meet in groups led by family coordinators to discuss parenting strategies, then 30-minute parent-child cooperative activity time; biweekly home visits Academic tutoring provided by trained tutors in 30-minute sessions 3X/week	Externalizing Scale of CBCL—*oppositional, aggressive, and delinquent* behaviors. • *Parent Daily Report:* degree to which child engaged in aggressive and oppositional behaviors during previous 24 hrs (given 3x) • Child behavior change • Teacher assessment of acting-out behaviors in school (Teacher Report Form, Achenbach) • Scale from the TOCA-R (Teacher Observation of Classroom Adaptation–Revised) • Authority Acceptance Scale • Peer rating of aggressive and hyperactive-disruptive behaviors.	Intervention group had higher scores on emotion recognition, emotion coping, and social problem solving compared to control group. It also had lower rates of aggressive retaliation compared to control group. Direct observation results: • Intervention group spent more time in positive peer interaction than did the control group. • Intervention group received higher peer social preference scores than control group. • Intervention group had higher language arts grades than control group. Rated effective—2, 3, 6, 8, 9, 11

(continued)

Table 39.1 (*Continued*)

Program (Authors)	Grade	Participants	Program Components	Outcome Measures	Results
PATHS curriculum (Component of FAST Track)	1st–5th grades over three cohorts (Results from grade 1 findings only are reviewed here)	198 intervention classrooms 180 control classrooms matched by school size, achievement levels, poverty, and ethnic diversity 7,560 total students 845 students were in high-risk intervention or control conditions (6,715 students non–high-risk children)	PATHS (Promoting Alternative Thinking Strategies) administered to classrooms, 57 lessons (half-hour sessions, 2–3X/week) • Skills related to understanding and communicating emotions • Skills related to increase of positive social behavior • Self-control and social problem solving Presented through direct instruction, discussion, modeling stories, or video Teachers attended 2.5 day training and received weekly consultation from FAST Track staff Quality of implementation was assessed by teacher's observer ratings	1) Teachers were interviewed about behavior of each child in class (fall/ spring of first grade) 2) Sociometric assessments (peer nominations made by students) collected to assess • Peer aggression • Peer hyperactivity/ disruptiveness • Peer social status 3) Quality of classroom atmosphere was assessed by observer ratings assessing the following: • Level of disruption • Ability to handle transitions • Ability to follow rules • Level of cooperation • Use of problem– solving skills	Hierarchical Linear Modeling (Accounting for gender, site, cohort, and intervention) Intervention classrooms had lower ratings of hyperactivity/disruptive behavior and aggression and more favorable observer ratings of classroom atmosphere. Three cohorts of intervention, so teachers administered curriculum, 1, 2, or 3 times. When teacher experience was included in analyses, teachers who taught more cohorts had higher classroom atmosphere ratings (by neutral observer). Teacher skill in program implementation was also related to positive outcomes. Rated effective—2, 3, 6, 8, 9, 11

(continued)

- Skill in teaching PATHS concepts
- Management of the classroom
- Modeling and generalizing PATHS throughout day
- Openness to consultation

- Ability to express feelings
- Ability to stay focused on task
- Criticism vs. supportiveness

Evaluating sources:

1. American Youth Policy Forum. See R. A. Mendel (2000), *Less hype, more help: Reducing juvenile crime, what works and what doesn't.* Washington, DC: American Youth Policy Forum. Programs are categorized as *Effective* (refer to www.aypf.org).
2. Blueprints for Violence Prevention. Programs are divided into *Model* and *Promising* (refer to www.colorado.edu/cspv/blueprints).
3. Center for Mental Health Services, U.S. Department of Health and Human Services, Prevention Research Center for the Promotion of Human Development. Programs are divided into *Effective* and *Promising* (refer to www.prevention.psu.edu).
4. Center for Substance Abuse Prevention, Substance Abuse and Mental Health Services Administration, Department of Health and Human Services, National Registry of Effective Programs. Programs are divided into *Model, Promising,* and *Effective* (refer to www.modelprograms.samhsa.gov).
5. Department of Education, Safe and Drug Free Schools. Programs are divided into *Exemplary* and *Promising* (refer to www.ed.gov/about/offices/list/osdfs/index.html?src=mr).
6. Communities That Care. See R. Posey, S. Wong, R. Catalano, D. Hawkins, L. Dusenbury, & P. Chappell. (2000). *Communities that care prevention strategies: A research guide to what works.* Programs are categorized as *Effective* (refer to www.preventionscience.com/ctc/CTC.html).
7. Sherman et al. (1998): *Preventing crime: What works, what doesn't, what's promising.* University of Maryland Department of Criminology and Criminal Justice. NCJ 165366. Programs are categorized as *Effective* (refer to http://www.ncjrs.org/works/).
8. *Youth violence: A report of the surgeon general.* Programs are divided into *Model* and *Promising: Level 1—Violence Prevention; Level 2—Risk Prevention* (refer to www.surgeongeneral.gov/library/youthviolence).
9. Title V (OJJDP). *Effective and promising programs guide.* Washington, DC: Office of Juvenile Justice and Delinquency Prevention, Office of Justice Programs, U.S. Dept. of Justice. Programs are divided into *Exemplary, Effective,* and *Promising* (refer to www.dsgonline.com).
10. Centers for Disease Control: National Center for Injury Prevention and Control—Division of Violence Prevention. *Best practices of youth violence prevention: A sourcebook for community action* 2002. Programs are categorized as *Effective* (refer to www.cdc.gov/ncipc/dvp/bestpractices.htm).
11. Hamilton Fish Institute on School and Community Violence. Programs are divided into *Effective and Noteworthy* (refer to www.hamfish.org/programs/).

more serious cases of bullying.

The goal of using interventions through all three levels is to ensure that students are given a consistent, coordinated, and strong message that bullying will not be tolerated. The BPP teaches students that everyone has a responsibility to prevent bullying, either by refusing to support bullying behavior or by alerting an adult to the problem.

Theoretical Rationale and Conceptual Framework

The BBP program is based on a systematic restructuring of the school environment that redirects bullying behavior and provides rewards for more prosocial behavior. The conceptual framework is based on research on the development and modification of aggressive behavior, as well as positive childrearing dimensions (Olweus, Limber, & Mihalic, 1999). The goal is to create a school environment that (1) is characterized by adults who are engaged and caring, (2) has firm limits to unacceptable behavior, (3) has consistent responses of no rewards and negative consequences for violent behavior, and (4) has adults who act as authorities and positive role models (Olweus et al., 1999).

Much of the success of the BPP can be attributed to its being a schoolwide program, so that it becomes an integral part of the school environment. Students and adults participate in most of the universal components of the program. Indeed, teachers, parents, and administrators play an important role in the success of the program. School staff and parents are expected to (1) become aware of the extent of the bullying problem in their school through assessments, (2) gain an understanding of the significance and harmful effects of bullying, and (3) take an active role in enforcing rules against bullying behavior (Olweus et al., 1999).

Evaluation

As seen in Table 39.1, the first and most comprehensive evaluation study of this program was conducted with 2,500 students in Norway (also see Olweus et al., 1999). However, since then, this program has been implemented and positively evaluated in many countries. Evaluation of this program has consistently demonstrated significant reductions in bully/victim reports across many cultures. General antisocial behaviors such as vandalism, fighting, theft, and truancy are reduced. Improvements are also found in classroom culture in that students reported improved order and discipline at school, more positive social relationships, and more positive attitudes toward school and schoolwork.

Child Development Project

The Child Development Project (CDP) is an ecological approach to intervention that collaboratively involves teachers, parents, and students working to influence all aspects of the school community (Developmental Studies Center, 1995). Its main objective is to create a cooperative and supportive school environment for children in grades K–6. Established in 1981, the CDP strives to foster shared commitment to prosocial, democratic values in two specific ways: through adult guidance and through direct participation by children (Developmental Studies Center, 1995). Throughout this process, children are able to develop a sense that the school community cares for them, and they, in turn, begin to care about the school community.

Teachers are trained to implement most components of the intervention, and ongoing consultation and support are provided by the Developmental Studies Center. Research indicates that schools should make a minimum of a 3-year commitment to the CDP if it is to be effective (Northwest Regional Educational Laboratory, 1998). The CDP has been established in 165 elementary schools, and it has been shown to be effective in both ethnically and socioeconomically diverse settings (Battistich, Solomon, Watson, & Schaps, 1997; Battistich, Schaps, Watson, & Solomon, 1996; Northwest Regional Educational Laboratory, 1998; Solomon, Watson, Battistich, Schaps, & Delucchi, 1996).

Theoretical Rationale and Conceptual Framework

The Child Development Project's theoretical framework is guided by research on socialization, learning and motivation, and prosocial development (Battistich, Schaps, Watson, Solomon, & Lewis, 2000). Its overall objective is for schools to be transformed into caring and supportive communities in which everyone works collaboratively in the learning process. Such a focus is expected to foster children's intellectual and sociomoral development, self-direction, competence, and belonging (Battistich, Schaps, Watson, Solomon, & Lewis, 2000). And where these qualities are fostered, children become attached to and invested in the school community, which in turn leads them to internalize the school norms. School norms typically promote prosocial activity (e.g., concern for others) and proscribe antisocial activity (e.g., drug use or gang activity). The program is based on the idea that children's internalization of school norms will solidify their commitment to the school's community values.

Content

There are four interrelated goals on which the components of the CDP are based: (1) building warm, stable, supportive relationships; (2) attending to social and ethical dimensions of learning; (3) honoring intrinsic motivations; and (4) teaching in ways that support students' active construction of meaning (Battistich, Schaps, Watson, Solomon, & Lewis, 2000). These goals are interwoven into the five major components of CDP, which are presented in Table 39.2. The five components are literature-based reading and language arts, collaborative classroom learning, developmental discipline, parent involvement, and schoolwide activities.

The first three components are all designed for the classroom. The literature-based readings component is most directly focused on teaching for understanding. Thus, the selection of books is designed to help teachers foster a deeper and more empathic understanding of the readings among the students. The component that involves collaborative learning emphasizes the importance of working with others in a fair and cooperative manner. The final classroom component involves building care and respect for everyone in the classroom community (Northwest Regional Educational Laboratory, 1998). The two other components' foci go beyond the classroom. Parent involvement is designed to develop meaningful conversations between adults and their children; schoolwide activities are focused on allowing participation by all and avoiding hierarchies and competition (Northwest Regional Education Laboratory, 1998).

Implementation

At least 80% of the school faculty must support their school's adoption of the CDP for it to be established there. Training is conducted by Developmental Studies Center's staff and involves initial consultation and planning to identify needs and goals; a 3-day summer institute to orient teachers on the CDP components and materials; three half-day follow-up workshops conducted during the school year; three on-site sessions, each lasting 2.5 days, which include consultation, in-class demonstrations, co-teaching, planning; and professional development support kits that can be used to train new staff (Developmental Studies Center, 2004).

Evaluation

As seen in Table 39.1, CDP strengthens students' sense of their school as a community, their ethical and social resources (e.g., conflict resolution skills, social problem-solving skills, commitment to democratic values, concern for others), their academic motivation (e.g., liking for school), and their abstention from drug use and other problem behaviors (e.g., gang-related activity) (Battistich, Schaps, Watson, & Solomon, 1996; Battistich, Schaps, Watson, Solomon, & Lewis, 2000; Battistich, Solomon, Watson, & Schaps, 1997; Northwest Regional Education Laboratory, 1998). Moreover, positive effects were reported 2 years after students left elementary school with regard to those students' conflict resolution skills, self-esteem, and involvement in extracurricular activity (Developmental Studies Center, 1995).

FAST Track

The FAST Track Project is a long-term comprehensive intervention that encompasses multiple facets of children's social contexts. The intervention is comprehensive in that it has both universal (schoolwide) components and targeted components, which attempt to provide focused assistance to both children at high risk of antisocial behaviors and to their social systems. One of the great strengths of this program is its detailed attention to the intersection of the multiple contexts that contribute to children's developmental outcomes. The FAST Track prevention program aims to im-

Table 39.2 Components of Child Development Project

Components	What Is Done
1. Literature-based reading and language arts	1. *Reading aloud* allows students to have shared experience of hearing stories told aloud. 2. *Partner reads* help students build automaticity through the support of their partner. ★In each of these scenarios, the teacher asks open-ended discussion questions about issues evoked by books and gives students an opportunity to discuss these issues with one another.
2. Collaborative classroom learning	1. *Peer collaboration* involves equal-status peers working in pairs or small groups on challenging projects that require collaboration. 2. *Adult guidance* involves the teacher monitoring peer groups. The teacher discusses the specific learning goals and behaviors required for successful cooperation at the beginning of each activity. The teacher also assists students in reflecting on group interaction at the conclusion of each task.

3. Developmental discipline	1. The teacher involves children in
	   a. shaping norms of classroom;
	   b. developing collaborative approaches to resolving conflict;
	   c. practicing skills of nonviolent problem solving;
	   d. helping them to anticipate problems so that they might be avoided;
	   e. determining source of problems, thinking about solutions, and trying its effects on others.
	 2. Playground disputes become opportunities for children to engage in many of the above activities.
	 3. The teacher avoids extrinsic incentives in order to foster personal commitment to justice.

4. Parent involvement	1. *A school "coordinating team"* of parents and teachers collectively plans schoolwide activities. 2. *Family participation* includes *"homeside activities"* that are designed to connect the home and school life. There are 18 activities per grade level, and each requires interaction between the parent and the student. For example, parents may discuss their culture and heritage with their child. The child then presents this information to the class.
5. Schoolwide activities	1. *Buddies Program* brings older and younger students together in activities, such as playing a game or going on a field trip. 2. *Grandperson's Day* draws older family members to the school to discuss their experiences. 3. *Family Read-Aloud* or *Family Film* nights bring parents and children together to engage in a learning activity.

Source: Battistich, Schaps, Watson, Solomon, & Lewis, 2000 (with permission of Springer Science and Business Media); Developmental Studies Center, 1998.

prove child competences, parent effectiveness, the school context, and school–home communications with the intention of preventing antisocial behavior across the developmental trajectory.

Theoretical Rationale and Conceptual Framework

The developmental theory guiding this intervention addresses the interaction of multiple influences on the development of antisocial behavior. These various elements include socioeconomic factors, family dynamics, peer influences, school factors, and the child's temperament.

Content

There are four FAST Track sites in the United States, with a total of 891 children (and their families) participating (with near-equal numbers of at-risk children in both intervention and control groups). The initial sample consisted of children identified as "at risk" by a combination of teacher and parent ratings of their behavior. Children in the intervention group were provided with a host of services, including weekly enrichment programs, involvement in "friendship groups," and sessions in which they were taught and had opportunities to practice social skills. The parents of the intervention children were also provided with family coordinators who conducted biweekly home visits in efforts to enhance their parenting behavior management skills, specifically in the areas of praise, time-outs, and self-restraint. Children in the intervention group were also provided with three 30-minute academic tutoring sessions each week.

When the children in the intervention group reached adolescence (grades 6–10), the group-based interventions were de-emphasized. However, the intervention retained its curriculum-based parent and youth group meetings to support children in their transition into middle school (grades 5–7). In continuation of the earlier targeted model, individual support was provided for participants and their families in order to strengthen protective factors and reduce risk factors. The targeted intervention at the adolescent phase focused on academic tutoring, mentoring, home visiting and family problem solving, and supporting positive peer-group involvement. To address the multiple contexts in the adolescents' lives, the school tried to establish relations with the community agencies that served the participants.

FAST Track also included an important universal component for children in the first through the fifth grades in the target schools. This school-based intervention consisted of teacher-led curricula called "PATHS" (Promoting Alternative Thinking Strategies), designed to provide children with strategies in understanding the development of emotional concepts, social understanding, and self-control. Since PATHS has been evaluated separately and shown to have independent positive effects, we will present PATHS separately in the next section. Some schools may choose to adopt only sections of the overall program, such as PATHS.

Evaluation

FAST Track is one of the more rigorously evaluated comprehensive violence prevention programs and has become widely known as one of the leading models of an effective approach to prevention of antisocial behaviors in youth. As shown in Table 39.1, evaluation studies of FAST Track have revealed positive outcomes for program participants. In addition to those differences highlighted in the table, the prevention revealed statistically significant improvements in the targeted children's social-cognitive and academic skills, in addition to reductions in their parents' use of harsh discipline. The intervention children also demonstrated considerable behavioral improvements at home, in the classroom, and on the playground during and following their elementary school years. In addition to these behavioral improvements, the intervention children were at a reduced risk of being placed in special education classes than children in the control conditions. The findings generalized across ethnicity, gender, and a host of child and family characteristics.

Promoting Alternative Thinking Strategies

PATHS is the classroom curriculum component of the FAST Track intervention program. We present it separately because PATHS has been adopted and studied independently of FAST Track. PATHS was designed to promote emotional and social competence and to reduce aggression and other behavior problems in children in grades K–5 (Greenberg, Kusché, Cook, & Quamma, 1995). PATHS focuses on four domains related to school success: (1) prosocial behavior and friendship skills, (2) emotional understanding and self-control, (3) communication and conflict resolution, and (4) problem-solving skills (Conduct Problems Prevention Research Group, 2002). PATHS provides teachers and counselors with training, lesson modules, and ongoing consultation and support. Additionally, parents receive information and activities to complete with their children.

PATHS can be used with all elementary school–age children, and ideally it should be ongoing, beginning in kindergarten and continuing through fifth grade. It has been field-tested and researched in regular education classroom settings and in settings that serve special needs students such as the deaf, hearing-impaired, learning disabled, emotionally disturbed, mildly mentally delayed, and gifted (see Greenberg et al., 1995; Greenberg & Kusché, 1998).

Theoretical Rationale and Conceptual Framework

PATHS is based on five conceptual models (Greenberg, Kusché, & Mihalic, 1998). First, the ABCD (Affective-Behavioral-Cognitive-Dynamic) model of development promotes skills that are developmentally appropriate. The second model is an eco-behavioral system orientation that focuses on helping the teacher use these skills to build a healthy classroom atmosphere. The third model involves neurobiology and brain organization for cognitive development. The fourth is psychodynamic education that was derived from developmental psychodynamic theory. Finally, the fifth model includes psychological issues related to emotional awareness or emotional intelligence. These conceptual models come together in this curriculum to provide a comprehensive and developmentally based program that addresses students' cognitive processes, emotions, and behaviors.

Content

The PATHS curriculum (Greenberg, Kusché, & Mihalic, 1998) is taught three times a week for a minimum of 20–30 minutes a day. The curriculum contains four units with a total of 119 lessons in each unit. They consist of the following: (1) a "Turtle Unit" focusing on classroom behavior, emotional literacy, and self-control; (2) a "Feeling and Relationship Unit" focusing on building self-esteem and social competence; (3) a "Problem-Solving Unit" with instruction on the 11-step model of social problem solving and positive peer relations; and (4) a "Supplementary Lessons Unit" containing 30 lessons that delve more in depth into PATHS concepts. The lessons are age appropriate, and as we can see in Table 39.3, the lessons for third-grade students match developmental stages and cover the conceptual domains of self-control, emotional understanding, self-esteem, peer relations, and problem solving. (Lesson 93, presented in detail in Table 39.4, covers self-control and problem solving.)

The PATHS curriculum includes comprehensive materials, and the basic PATHS kit (grades 1–5) includes an instructor's manual, five curriculum manuals, feelings photographs, feelings face cards, two wall charts, and four full-color posters. The Turtle Unit (for kindergarten classrooms) includes an instructor's manual, curriculum manual, turtle puppet with pad, turtle stamp, and poster. Teachers receive on-site training and technical assistance to ensure effective implementation of the program.

Evaluation

PATHS was evaluated between 1994 and 2003 in various research studies using randomized control groups and was found to be effective. As seen in Table 39.1, PATHS has been found to be a model or effective program by at least six groups that review violence prevention programs nationwide for effectiveness. An overview of results from all trials reveals a reduction in aggressive behavior; conduct disorder, and violent solutions to social problems. In addition, results found an increase in self-control, vocabulary for emotions, cognitive skills, ability to tolerate frustration, and to effectively use conflict-resolution strategies (SAMHSA Model Programs, 2003). The findings have been consistent across teacher reports, self-reports, and child assessments and interviews.

Tools and Practice Examples

Learning Self-Control, Volume 5— Supplementary Lesson 93, Grade 3

In the PATHS curriculum, each unit builds on the preceding units. Table 39.4 consists of an excerpt

Table 39.3 PATHS Lessons for Grade 3

Lesson Topic	Volume & Lesson #	Conceptual Domains				
		Self-Control	Emotional Understanding	Self-Esteem	Peer Relations	Problem Solving
PATHS Rules	Vol. 1, L 1	X		X	X	X
PATHS Kid/Complimenting/Self-esteem	Vol. 1, L 2	X		X	X	X
Anger Intensity	Vol. 1, L 10		X		X	
Anger Management/Control Signals	Vol. 1, L 11–12	X		X	X	X
Fear Intensity/Sad Intensity	Vol. 1, L 15–17		X		X	
Disgusted, Delighted	Vol. 1, L 21		X		X	
Frustrated, Disappointed/Hopeful, Proud/Ashamed, Guilty, Curious/Interested/Bored, Confused/Worried/Sure, Anxious/Calm, Shy/Lonely	Vol. 2, L 23–32, 37		X		X	
Embarrassed/Humiliated	Vol. 2, L 33–34		X		X	
Intentionality (Accident/Purpose), Manners	Vol. 3, L 38–44		X		X	
Jealous/Content, Greedy/Selfish/Generous, Malicious/Kind, Rejected/Included, Excluded, Forgiving/Resentful	Vol. 3, 48–56		X		X	
Informal Problem Solving	Vol. 5, 90–92	X				X
Self-Control and Problem Prevention	Vol. 5, L 93–94	X				X
Friendship	Vol. 5, L 95–97.	X	X	X	X	X
Teasing	Vol. 5, L 98–101.	X	X	X	X	X
Apply Problem-Solving Steps	Vol. 4, L 89.					X

Table 39.4 PATHS Learning Self-Control, Volume 5, Lesson 93

Introduction	"Today I'm going to tell you a story about a boy who had problems, but he learned a new way to help himself."
Story: "Thomas in Control"	This is a story about a boy who did not like to go to school. Thomas felt very upset about going to school. He wanted to run outside and play with his toys or ride his bike or watch television or play a game. Thomas did not like to sit quietly. It was hard for him to pay attention when the teacher or the other kids were talking in class. Instead, Thomas would tease whoever was sitting beside him, by grabbing their pencils and books, by making faces at them, or by whispering to them. The other kids would get angry at Thomas when he bothered them and would yell at him or would do some of the same things back. Then everyone would get caught and would get into trouble. That's why some of the kids thought that Thomas was troublemaker. Sometimes when they went out to the playground at recess, the other kids would still be mad at Thomas, and they would get into a fight. All of this hate and resentment made Thomas feel very uncomfortable inside. One day when he was feeling his worst, the playground teacher told Thomas that he had to go to the principal's office because he hadn't been following the playground rules. "You know," said the principal in a very calm voice, "you have a very big problem, but I'll share a secret with you. You already have the answer to your problem with you. You carry it with you everywhere you go. It's your ability to think. Whenever you feel upset, when you are angry or frustrated, you can use your mind and think. You can stop, take a long, deep breath, and say the problem and how you feel. When you remind yourself to stop and calm down, it's like taking a rest for a minute. You can rest until you feel calm. That is how you can control yourself. And when you can control yourself, then people will say, 'Thomas has good self-control. He thinks before he does something that will cause problems.' " The principal showed Thomas the three steps for calming down. Then the principal reminded Thomas that the next time he felt upset or angry, he could think about the control signals and could calm himself down. Thomas liked the idea and wanted to try it himself. He wanted to do well in school, he wanted his teacher to like him, and he especially wanted to make friends. . . .
On board	Begin drawing on the chalk board Feelings: comfortable and uncomfortable/ Behavior OK and not OK.
Discussion	Ask students to name the different feelings and behavior that Thomas felt and list them under the appropriate categories. Ask them to discuss the relationships between these feelings and behaviors if they are able to do so. Ask students to name the kinds of things that bug them in the classroom, playground, lunchroom, and so on, and list them in the categories. This will help students become aware of what they do that bothers others. Ask student if using the three steps to calm down would help with any of the things they listed.

Source: Story excerpt reduced for space reasons from Kusche & Greenberg (1995), available for review on www.channing-bete.com

from supplementary lesson 93 and is intended for third graders.

The objective of this lesson is to discuss the idea of self-control as an internalized process. It emphasizes the concept of using thinking to control one's behavior and to distinguish between feelings and behaviors. The teacher reads a story about a boy named Thomas who had problems with self-control, was angry, and would get into fights with other children. Throughout the story, students learn the three steps for calming down to gain control of their behavior. The lesson is followed by the teacher drawing a hierarchy of feelings and behaviors on the board and asking questions to encourage classroom discussion. Students are encouraged to talk about how they felt when they acted without thinking first, and to say whether things got out of control and how they felt about the outcome. This lesson teaches students anger management and problem-solving skills through a developmentally appropriate story that is easy to relate to and that facilitates discussion.

Monitoring and Evaluating Violence Prevention Programs

A review of the school safety literature strongly suggests that model school safety programs should be developed and implemented in a process that ensures their relevance and applicability to each specific site. These are important assumptions of the programs described in this chapter as well as program interventions described in other chapters of section VI:

- Fitting a program to a school involves grassroots participation.
- Students and teachers in the school need to be empowered to deal with the problem.
- Democracy is the core of a good school safety program.
- Schools should demonstrate a proactive vision surrounding the violence problem in their school.

Implementing interventions or components of any model program is likely to be slightly different for every school. An eye toward the overall assumptions and flexibility should enable each school to adapt the program or general principles to its unique demographic, philosophical, and organizational needs.

Data and Program Evaluation

An important element of successful school safety programs is the ongoing and interactive use of data. This perspective proposes that the continuous and ongoing analysis and interpretation of data is an essential part of the intervention process. Data are used to create awareness, mobilize different school constituencies, assess the extent of the problem, plan and implement interventions, and conduct evaluations. Information is provided on a continuous basis to different groups in each step of the intervention

process. Unfortunately, many U.S. schools purchase evidence-based programs but do not collect any data about their own district or school.

The process of building and implementing school safety programs is continual and cyclical, always changing to respond to new circumstances and emerging needs. Hence, the evaluation of the program's progress becomes a reassessment of the situation, leading to a new cycle of awareness building, planning, modifying, and evaluating. A school's failure to gather site-specific and comparative data could be a significant obstacle in (a) assessing whether that specific school has a violence problem, (b) adapting a school safety program, and (c) evaluating the implementation process and outcomes of the program.

Monitoring and school mapping can help create a "whole-school response" and help the school to identify, create, and/or adapt programs to the site. Monitoring is the ongoing process of collecting and using data to shape, fit, match, and evaluate the intervention. The value of monitoring comes from the two levels of information processing involved: description and comparison. The description of the basic frequency of certain behaviors may be quite instructive. For example, it is helpful to know how many weapon-related events or sexual assaults occur at a specific school.

Using Comparisons

In general, comparisons enhance the value of information by putting it in context. In order to adapt a program, it is imperative to ascertain (a) which acts are more problematic than others, (b) which grade levels are victimized more, and (c) how violence levels in a specific school compare over time and for different ethnic, age, and gender groups. For example, if bullying is not a major problem in the school, it does not make sense to adopt an antibullying program. Perhaps bullying is a problem only in one grade level within a large school, whereas other forms of violence are problems in other grades. Though these concerns may sound like common sense, very few schools actually collect systemic information to ascertain the extent of the school safety problem. Currently, many districts and schools across the United States are purchasing expensive violence prevention programs targeting a specific form of violence (e.g., sexual harassment, bullying, weapon use) without data about the extent of the problem in their schools. This creates a chain of difficulties through the implementation process and later in the evaluation of the program. If the problem was never established, it is difficult to know if the program ever worked. Hence, it is important to examine levels of violence over time.

Using Mapping as a Monitoring Tool

Mapping is a qualitative tool that can help monitor and generate the kind of comparisons discussed above. Chapter 95 provides further guidance on comprehensive resource mapping for the school. Mapping does not require extensive training and can provide valuable information that helps implement, monitor, and assess the ongoing health of a program. This procedure is designed to involve school constituents by revealing how forms of violence within a school building interact with locations, patterns of the school day, and social organizational variables (e.g., teacher–student relationships, teachers' professional roles, and the school's organizational response to violence; for more detail see Astor, Benbenishty, & Meyer, 2004; Astor, Meyer, & Behre, 1999; Astor & Meyer, 1999; Astor, Meyer, & Pitner, 2001). An important goal of this procedure is to allow students and teachers to convey their personal theories about why specific locations and times in their schools are more dangerous. This process greatly facilitates the implementation and evaluation of the model programs reviewed in the first sections of this chapter.

Step-by-Step Instructions

Mapping, Interviews, and Interventions

The first step in this assessment procedure is obtaining a map of the school. Ideally, the map should contain all internal school territory, including the areas surrounding the school and playground. In communities where the routes to and from school are dangerous, a simple map of the surrounding neighborhood may be added to the assessment process. The focus groups should begin with the facilitator distributing two sets of identical school maps to each individual.

Map A and B: Two photocopied maps of the school are needed for each student and teacher. One map should be used to determine where students and teachers think the most events involving violence occur. Participants should also be asked to identify the locations (on the maps) of up to three of the most violent events that have occurred within the past academic year. Next to each marked event on the map, participants should be asked to write the following information: (1) the general time frame of the event (e.g., before school, after school, morning period, afternoon period, evening sports event, between classes, etc.); (2) the grade and gender of those involved in the violence; and (3) their knowledge of any organizational response to the event (e.g., someone was sent to principal's office, suspended, sent to peer counselor, done nothing to, etc.). On the second map, members should be asked to circle areas or territories that they perceive to be unsafe or potentially dangerous. This second map provides information about areas within the school that participants avoid or fear even though they may not possess knowledge of a particular event.

Discussion of Violent Events and Areas

The first part of the group discussion should center on the specific events and the areas marked as unsafe or dangerous on their personal maps. We have asked questions such as "Are there times when those places you've marked on the maps are less safe?" "Is there a particular group of students that is more likely to get hurt there?" and "Why do you think that area has so many incidents?" The overall purpose of the group interviews is to explore why bullying or victimization occurs at those specific times and in those specific spaces. Consequently, the interviews should also focus on gathering information regarding the organizational response to the event (e.g., "What happened to the two students after the event?" or "Did the hall monitors intervene when they saw what happened?"), procedures (e.g., "What happens when the students are sent to the office after a fight?" "Did anyone call the parents of the bully or victim?"), follow-up (e.g., "Do the teachers, hall monitors, and/or administrators follow up on any consequences given to the students?" or "Did anyone check on the welfare of the victim?"), and clarity of procedures (e.g., "Does it matter who stops the bullying?" such as a volunteer, security guard, teacher, or principal).

Interviewers should also explore participants' ideas for solutions to the specific violence problems (e.g., "Can you think of ways to avoid bullying or victimization in that place?" or "If you were the principal, what would you do to make that place safer?"). In addition, the interviewer should explore any obstacles that participants foresee with implementation (e.g., "Do you think that type of plan is realistic?" "Has that been tried before? What happened?" or "Do you think that plan would work?"). Such obstacles could range from issues related to roles (e.g., "It's not my job to monitor students during lunch") to discipline policy and issues of personal safety (e.g., "I don't want to intervene because I may get hurt").

In schools that already have started model programs designed to address school violence, specific questions should be asked about the effectiveness of those interventions, why they work or do not work, and what could be done to make the current measures more effective. We recommend that the interviewer ask both subjective questions (e.g., "Do you think the antiviolence program is working? Why do you think it works, or why does it not work?") as well as specific questions related to the reduction of victimization (e.g., "Do you believe the antiviolence program has reduced the number of fights/name calling [or any other type of violence the school is interested in preventing] on the playground? Why or why not?").

Transferring all of the reported events onto one large map of the school enables students and staff to locate specific "hot spots" for violence and dangerous time periods within each individual school. The combined data are presented to all school constituencies, and they are asked to once again discuss and interpret the maps. Teachers and students use the maps and interviews to suggest ways to improve the settings and what aspects of the program are working or not working. For example, in one school, events were clustered by time, age, gender, and location. In the case of older students (11th and 12th graders), events were clustered in the parking lot outside of the auxiliary gym immediately after school, whereas for younger students (9th and 10th graders), events were reported in the lunchroom and hallways during transition periods. For this school, the map suggested that interventions be geared specifically toward older students, directly after school, by the main entrance, and in the school parking lot. Students and teachers agreed that increasing the visible presence of school staff in and around the parking lot for the 20 minutes after school had great potential for reducing the number of violent events. Younger students were experiencing violence mainly before, during, and after lunch, near the cafeteria. Many students expressed feelings of being unsafe between classes in the hallways.

This school already had an antibullying program, and it was able to incorporate this specific type of intervention into existing activities designed to stem school violence.

Compiling all the interview suggestions into themes is an important second step in adapting context-relevant interventions. Students, teachers, and administrators may have differing viewpoints regarding the organizational response of the school to a violent incident. Relaying the diversity of responses to students, teachers, and administrators can provide an opportunity for reflection and may generate ways to remedy the violence problem in certain situations. When the data are presented to students, teachers, and administrators, they can center their discussions on why those areas are dangerous and what kinds of interventions could make the location safer. Mapping methods provide data-based approaches to gathering information about bullying/victimization in schools. Moreover, they provide site-specific information, which makes it easier for schools to address these problems.

Identifying specific target groups for interventions is another way data can/should be used. A school could use this monitoring system to identify particular problem areas in their school. They could then track progress in reducing violence in these locations over time and by different groups.

Key Points to Remember

Based on our review of programs, it appears that successful schoolwide intervention programs have the following core underlying implementation characteristics:

They are comprehensive, intensive, ecological, and require "buy-in" from school and community.

They raise the awareness and responsibility of students, teachers, and parents regarding the types of violence in their schools (e.g., sexual harassment, fighting, and weapons use).

They create clear guidelines and rules for all members of the school community.

They target the various social systems in the school and clearly communicate to the entire school community what procedures should be followed before, during, and after violent events.

They focus on getting the school staff, students, and parents involved in the program.

They often fit easily into the normal flow and mission of the school setting.

They use faculty, staff, and parents in the school setting to plan, implement, and sustain the program.

They increase monitoring and supervision in nonclassroom areas.

They include ongoing monitoring and mapping, which provide information that schools can use to tailor a program to their specific needs and increase its chance of success.

Resources

Web Sites on Model Programs

Bullying Prevention Program: http://www.clemson.edu/olweus/

Child Development Project: http://www.devstu.org

FAST Track: www.fasttrackproject.org

Promoting Alternative Thinking Strategies: http://www.channing-bete.com/positive youth/pages/PATHS/PATHS.html

Web Sites That Evaluate School Violence Prevention Programs

Blueprints for Violence Prevention: www.colorado.edu/cspv/blueprints

Center for Disease Control: National Center for Injury Prevention and Control—Division of Violence Prevention: www.cdc.gov/ncipc/dvp/ bestpractices.htm

Department of Education: Safe and Drug Free Schools: www.ed.gov/about/offices/list/osdfs/index.html?src=mr

Hamilton Fish Institute on School and Community Violence: www.hamfish.org/programs/

Substance Abuse and Mental Health Services Administration: www.modelprograms.samhsa.gov

U.S. Department of Health and Human Services Prevention Research Center for the Promotion of Human Development: www.prevention.psu.edu

U.S. Office of Juvenile Justice and Delinquency Prevention & Title V: www.dsgonline.com

Youth Violence: A Report of the Surgeon General: www.surgeongeneral.gov/library/youthviolence

References

Astor, R. A., Benbenishty, R., & Meyer, H. A. (2004). Monitoring and mapping student victimization in schools. *Theory into Practice, 43*(1), 39–49.

Astor, R. A., & Meyer, H. (1999). Where girls and women won't go: Female students', teachers', and social workers' views of school safety. *Social Work in Education, 21,* 201–219.

Astor, R. A., Meyer, H., & Behre, W. J. (1999). Unowned places and times: Maps and interviews about violence in high schools. *American Educational Research Journal, 36,* 3–42.

Astor, R. A., Meyer, H. A., & Pitner, R. O. (2001). Elementary and middle school students' perceptions of safety: An examination of violence-prone school sub-contexts. *The Elementary School Journal, 101,* 511–528.

Battistich, V., Schaps, E., Watson, M., & Solomon, D. (1996). Prevention effects of the child development project: Early findings from an ongoing multi-site demonstration trial. *Journal of Adolescent Research, 11,* 12–35.

Battistich, V., Schaps, E., Watson, M., Solomon, D., & Lewis, C. (2000). Effects of the child development project on students' drug use and other problem behaviors. *Journal of Primary Prevention, 21,* 75–99.

Battistich, V., Solomon, D., Watson, M., & Schaps, E. (1997). Caring school communities. *Educational Psychologist, 32,* 137–151.

Conduct Problems Prevention Research Group. (1992). Initial impact of the Fast Track Prevention Trial for conduct problems: I. The high-risk sample. *Journal of Consulting and Clinical Psychology, 67,* 631–647.

Conduct Problems Prevention Research Group. (2002). The implementation of the Fast Track program: An example of a large-scale prevention science efficacy trial. *Journal of Abnormal Child Psychology, 30,* 1–17.

Developmental Studies Center. (1995). *Child development project.* Retrieved May 18, 2004, from http://www.ed.gov/pubs/EPTW/eptw5/eptw5a.html

Developmental Studies Center. (1998, April). *Some basics of the Child Development Project.* Paper presented at the AERA conference, San Diego. Retrieved May 23, 2004, from http://waarden.goliath.nl/studie/concepten/cdp/basics.html

Developmental Studies Center. (2004). *Comprehensive*

program: The Child Development Project. Retrieved May 27, 2004, from http://www.devstu.org/cdp/imp_prof_devt.html

Greenberg, M. T., & Kusché, C. A. (1998). Preventive interventions for school-age deaf children: The PATHS curriculum. *Journal of Deaf Studies and Deaf Education, 3*(1), 49–63.

Greenberg, M. T., Kusché, C. A., Cook, E. T., & Quamma, J. P. (1995). Promoting emotional competence in school-age children: The effects of the PATHS curriculum. *Emotions in developmental psychopathology* [Special issue], *Development and Psychopathology, 7*(1), 117–136.

Greenberg, M. T., Kusché, C., & Mihalic, S. F. (1998). *Blueprints for violence prevention, Book 10: Promoting alternative thinking strategies (PATHS).* Boulder, CO: Center for the Study and Prevention of Violence.

Northwest Regional Educational Laboratory. (1998). *The catalog of school reform models.* Retrieved May 23, 2004, from http://www.nwrel.org/scpd/catalog/ModelDetails.asp?ModelID=6

Olweus, D. (1993). *Bullying at school: What we know and what we can do.* Malden, MA: Blackwell Publishers.

Olweus, D., Limber, S., & Mihalic, S. F. (1999). *Blueprints for violence prevention, Book 9: Bullying prevention program.* Boulder, CO: Center for the Study and Prevention of Violence.

Solomon, D., Watson, M., Battistich, V., Schaps, E., & Delucchi, K. (1996). Creating classrooms that students experience as communities. *American Journal of Community Psychology, 24,* 719–748.

Creating a Violence-Free School Climate/Culture

Mark A. Mattaini

CHAPTER 40

Getting Started

In an increasingly globalized world, rates of violence among the young appear to be increasing nearly worldwide (Buvinic & Morrison, 2000). The incidence of most types of violence is much higher in the United States, however, than in most developed countries. And although schools are the safest places for children, most schools are not safe. Fourteen percent of high school students carry weapons to school; a larger number carry them outside of school (Josephson Institute on Ethics, 2001). Rates of harassment, bullying, threat, coercion, humiliation, and intentional exclusion among children and youth are much higher than adults usually recognize. Nearly a third of children are regularly involved in bullying (as bully, victim, or both), and those who are not directly involved report feeling threatened by the exposure. One third of U.S. high school students do not feel safe at school. Many others find school environments so socially toxic, so emotionally violent and threatening, that they do not wish to be there (Garbarino & deLara, 2002). Adults who are present often are not aware of the extent of these issues; Garbarino and deLara call this the "secret school life of adolescents" (p. 16). Continual exposure to physical and emotional violence produces damaging levels of stress hormones, upsets the neurochemical balance in the brain, and has a profoundly negative impact on social and academic development. The problem is serious, and it is widespread, spanning all socioeconomic groups.

What We Know

A review by the U.S. surgeon general (2001) found that many common violence prevention programs (including peer-led programs like peer counseling and peer mediation) are largely ineffective, and some (like boot camps) can actually be damaging. By contrast, the most effective programs focus on improving the social climate of the school, in conjunction with supporting other protective factors like parental effectiveness and building individual social competencies. A good deal is known about how to construct school cultures that maintain a positive school climate; combining projects targeting school climate with universal life skills training (discussed in other chapters of this volume) can be particularly powerful.

A number of existing programs for constructing cultures that discourage violence and threat and support the development of positive alternative practices are listed in Table 40.1. The Good Behavior Game, Bullying Prevention, Effective Behavior Support, and Positive Action are well-established strategies, supported by multiple controlled studies. PeaceBuilders, CommunityBuilders, and PEACE POWER, which are partial replications of one another, are based in strong science and can be viewed as probably efficacious or promising. Decisions about selecting programs draw in part on data, but also on the resources required. For example, Effective Behavior Support and CommunityBuilders as implemented so far require considerable additional staffing resources, and Positive Action and PeaceBuilders are commercial programs that can involve significant financial cost. Of the programs identified, only Bullying Prevention, the Good Behavior Game, and PEACE POWER are currently readily accessible in journal or manual form.

Table 40.1 Key Studies Related to Creating Violence-Free School Cultures.

Program and Key Reference	Findings
Community Builders (promising; incorporates well-established practices) Metzler et al. (2001)	Levels of positive reinforcement increased, aggressive behavior declined, disciplinary referrals and harassment declined among some groups, reports of verbal and physical attacks decreased (but did at comparison school as well).
Effective Behavior Support (well established) Sprague et al. (2001)	Social skills improved, and office referrals for disciplinary action declined. Students' perceptions of school safety did not improve, however.
Good Behavior Game (well established) Embry (2002)	Antisocial behaviors improved even when evaluated in long-term follow-up. Results are from approximately 20 independent replications of the Good Behavior Game used with different grade levels, different types of students, and in different settings.
PeaceBuilders (probably efficacious) Flannery et al. (2003)	Prosocial behavior increased, aggressive behavior was reduced, and social competence improved. Results are somewhat variable among age groups, but maintain over 2-year period.
PEACE POWER (promising; incorporates well-established practices) Strickland et al. (n.d.)	Levels of recognition, respect, shared power, and peacemaking increased in three of four schools.
Positive Action (well established) Flay et al. (2001)	Disciplinary referrals decreased by up to 85%, school performance improved, and number of arrests declined.

What We Can Do

Our review indicates that cultures that are effective in reducing violence are characterized by high levels of four interlocking cultural practices among multiple groups of actors (staff, students, parents, community members): (a) recognition of contributions and successes, (b) acting with respect, (c) sharing power to build community, and (d) healing (making peace) when conflicts occur (Mattaini, 2001). Each of these core practices has independent scientific support, and together they are consistent with the recommendations reported in multiple reviews. The four practices are summarized here; examples in practice are presented in a later section of this chapter.

- *Recognizing contributions and successes.* Effective programs universally aim to catalyze large increases in the frequency of reinforcement or recognition for prosocial actions, including contributions to the community and personal successes. High levels of affection and recognition increase the availability of serotonin and dopamine in critical regions of the brain and are associated with prosocial behavior and learning.
- *Acting with respect.* Within a culture of respect, individuals and groups have the opportunity to flourish and achieve their full developmental potential. Threat, harassment, violence, and coercion limit that potential. Building alternatives to adversarial and disrespectful actions and acting to interrupt those behaviors when they occur are therefore critical shifts in constructing organizational and community culture.
- *Sharing power to build community.* Simply suppressing violence is not an effective strategy; violence provides social power and protection,

and individuals will give it up only if they learn to exercise effective alternative forms of power. In an organizational community of shared power, all have opportunities to contribute from their own gifts and talents, all have a strong voice in shaping the community, and no one is excluded. (Exclusion itself is a serious risk factor for violence against self or others.)

- *Making peace.* Even in the strongest of groups and communities, conflicts will occur. In many cases, such conflicts are never really resolved, and they often are allowed to fester and spread below the surface. A real process of healing— and not just a forced handshake—is required if the overall climate of the school is to be nonviolent and empowering.

A culture of recognition, respect, nonviolent shared power, and healing emerges not from a single heroic effort but rather is a result of literally thousands of small actions occurring over an extended period of time. The most powerful efforts strive to establish a healthy culture throughout the school, although it is possible to do something meaningful even in a single classroom. Key steps for building an integrated, collective effort are outlined below.

1. *Form a working group.* Culture-building projects usually begin with one key staff person, often a social worker or a principal. Experience suggests that such a project can succeed only with strong buy-in from the top administrator, so unless the principal is the initiator, the key staff person should begin by discussing and examining printed information about the possibilities with the administrator. It can be enormously helpful to also locate one or two other strong staff supporters who can form the core of a working group. Ultimately, the strongest projects involve staff, students (especially in work with older youth), parents, and community members, so an intermediate goal should be to form a working group including representatives of each. Student energy should be harnessed to the greatest extent possible. Students are often the most hopeful of all participants and seriously interested in making a difference in school and community, even in very stressed schools. Forming the group may happen immediately or may occur after initial staff training, but it is important that everyone be made welcome to participate, so the project is not viewed as belonging to a particular subgroup. The working group should make plans to meet regularly, so the momentum of the project not be lost.

2. *Provide initial staff and student training.* Successfully shifting a school's culture requires the participation of a substantial proportion of staff members. For this reason, effective initial staff training is among the most critical steps. To the extent possible, *all staff*—teaching staff, administrators, maintenance and kitchen workers, security workers, and transportation staff— should be included, even if multiple training sessions are required. It is often useful to bring in an outside trainer to conduct training, but the initial planning group can also do the training themselves so long as the group includes staff who are well respected, knowledgeable about the model to be used, and skilled as trainers. Training should include the scientific underpinnings of the approach, an outline of the strategy including examples of how it has been applied elsewhere, and opportunities for small-group work among staff to consider adaptations of the basic strategy that are likely to be a good fit in terms of community and staff values, cultures, and resources.

Some of the best projects also hold a kick-off event for students; planning for those events should involve both staff and students, and the event should be both entertaining and challenging. Details depend on the age of students, but such events usually include videos; student role plays; serious discussion of the damage done by violence, harassment, bullying, and coercion; and specific options for making a contribution (even for being a "hero"). When possible, a presentation to parents and community leaders helps to expand the impact of the project.

3. *Provide ongoing planning and training.* Though a powerful beginning is helpful, the energy to continually innovate and maintain project activities usually comes from the working group. New members should be recruited during initial training and throughout the project, and they should be welcomed warmly into the group. Recruiting persons who have a real passion for this work is a priority, since involvement generally goes beyond the requirements of the job. As with any group, some members will need to participate for a limited period, then withdraw, so open membership is usually the best arrangement. Other staff and students should also be encouraged to make their own project contributions even if they do not wish to join the working group.

Once initial training has occurred, the group should quickly initiate one or two project activities with high visibility; momentum is critical at this stage. Activities can be selected and adapted from the ideas that emerged from staff during initial training, as well as from samples listed below, the available manuals, and the working group's own creative efforts. Local ownership of the project is critically important; responsiveness to ideas emerging from the staff, students, parents, and working group should therefore be a priority. Although there is considerable room for adaptation, preference should be for ideas consistent with the empirical base. Any that are not should be particularly carefully evaluated. The working group should also plan for periodic brief training sessions for the staff; often one additional session for each of the core practices is a useful arrangement. Those sessions should include both didactic material and opportunities for small-group work. The working group should meet regularly throughout the project, since maintaining momentum requires that new activities be initiated regularly, and existing activities continually evaluated for improvement, maintenance, or discontinuation.

Culture is actualized in continual patterns of action, so the core of culture-building projects is a series of action steps that are widely practiced within the school community. The goal is universality—every member of the culture participates in dynamically shaping and maintaining cultural practices, so everyone's efforts are needed. This means that most staff (and not just teaching staff) should be actively involved, even if in modest ways, as well as a large percentage of students. Visibility is essential, so project activities should be consistently "branded" with the name of the project ("Oh, another Project Peace activity!"). Table 40.2 lists a number of tools and activities for increasing levels of each of the core practices. This list should be seen as illustrative rather than comprehensive, since there are many possibilities and adaptations that can be useful within a project. The following sections describe a few actual examples of actions to increase each core practice in schools, to give a flavor for the level of variation possible.

4. *Implement activities and tools to build recognition.* The evidence supporting the importance of high levels of genuine recognition and reinforcement is strong; in classrooms with high (4 to 1 or better) ratios of recognition to reprimands, the level of problem behavior is much lower than in classrooms with higher relative levels of reprimands—which the research indicates are more typical. Verbal and nonverbal recognition is certainly useful with many children, but it sometimes is less so with those who struggle with behavior issues. Written Recognition Notes (sometimes called Praise Notes, Put-Ups, etc., in particular programs),

Table 40.2 Examples of Tools and Activities to Increase Rates of Core Practices.

Recognize Contributions and Successes:	*Act with Respect:*
• Recognition Notes and Boards	• Respect (Good Behavior) Game
• Recognition Circles	• Classroom Assignments
• Group Incentives	• Sportsmanship Education
• Home Recognition Notes	• Gender Fishbowl Exercises
• Peer Monitoring	• Pledge Campaigns
• Wall Charts	• Multiethnic Programs
• Celebrations of Successes	• Gay-Straight Alliances
• Community Recognition Efforts	• Poster Contests
Share Power to Build Community:	*Make Peace:*
• Murals, Sculptures, Gardens	• Use of Structured Making Peace Tool
• Video Projects Highlighting Community Strengths	• Healing Circles
• Service Learning	• Victim-Offender Mediation (not peer mediation)
• Community Service Projects	• Family Group Conferencing
• Youth/Adult Partnership in Prevention Projects	• Guided Intergroup Dialogues
• Participation in Governance	• Family Mediation
• Mentoring Projects	• Recognition of Peace Makers
• Community-Building Research	• Police–Youth Dialogues

often publicly posted, have demonstrated considerable power even with those young people and are a common program component. (In some cases, private notes are a better fit for a group.) Home recognition notes are a common variation with good empirical and experiential support. Teachers and other staff complete a home recognition note specifically noting positive action or progress by a student, and the school sends that note on to the child's parent or other caretaker. Recognition bulletin boards for staff, often in a lounge or meeting room, are helpful to stimulate active mutual recognition among staff, an important dynamic in its own right and an opportunity for modeling. In some programs, recognition slips, tickets, or notes can be "cashed in" for privileges or are centrally deposited for a random drawing, after which some are announced over the intercom.

Recognition can also be extended into the neighborhood, with students and staff preparing "wanted posters" recognizing contributions that community members and leaders have made to the neighborhood. Recognition projects shift attention away from what is wrong with the school or community, and they speak in ways that are inconsistent with much of what youth may hear about themselves and their communities from other sources. In one school, the working group distributed posters titled "Recognition: The Foundation of South" that listed examples of the kinds of things that might be recognized widely throughout the school. Tickets were made centrally available for recognizing anyone, which when completed were both publicly posted and entered in a drawing to win small "foundation stones" decorated by an art class.

Face-to-face recognition can also be very powerful. One approach for encouraging such direct communication is the use of Recognition Circles, in which one person at time is selected for the "hot seat," and the others go around the circle, completing the statement, "<Name>, what I appreciate about you is ___," and briefly explaining their comments. Some teachers do this weekly; in one middle school classroom, for example, the teacher randomly drew two popsicle sticks with one student name on each every Friday afternoon and conducted a Recognition Circle for those students, followed by an opportunity for general recognition. This can be a very emotional experience for some children who have never heard many positive messages about themselves.

5. *Implement activities and tools to build respect.* While recognition is generally delivered in discrete moments, respect is a state extending through time and can be more complicated to construct. It is important, therefore, that respect be expressed verbally quite regularly. Including explicit attention to respect in classroom assignments is one important step. This may range from essays in history class titled, say, "Someone I Respect and Why," to emphasis on one specific dimension of sportsmanship each day in physical education. Respect Months, in which multiple activities focused on respect occur in a concentrated way, are another useful approach (an example from one school is discussed below).

A simple approach with wide applicability is the use of Respect Pledges. Many schools have developed their own, in which those in the school make a daily commitment to act with respect, and to actively stop put-downs, threats, and harassment. The language of such pledges should, of course, be targeted to the developmental level of the students, as well as to the local situation. Schoolwide efforts to have everyone (staff and student) sign locally developed respect pledges in an organized campaign are another option.

The Good Behavior Game is a well-established approach to preventing problem behavior in its own right, and it can also be incorporated into larger projects. The game (which we often call the Respect Game in our projects) is a robust intervention that can be and has been effectively adapted to various age groups and levels of developmental maturity. The general principles of the game are quite straightforward. The teacher first leads a discussion about the way people like to see people act in the classroom, then indicates that they are going to play a game to try to make the classroom more like that. The class identifies a list of "fouls" that interfere with a pleasant classroom, which are posted. Students are distributed among two or three teams, which can be changed periodically. During the week, usually for one period on each of 2–5 days, the teacher announces at some point that they are now going to play the Respect Game (ideally varying subjects and days). The teacher sets a timer for a brief interval, perhaps 5 minutes in the beginning but later stretching gradually to the whole period. If a foul occurs during that interval, the teacher immediately and without discussion makes a small check mark on the scoreboard and moves on. When the timer rings, every team with no fouls for that interval gets a point, which is posted on the scoreboard. At the end of the period, the team or teams with the highest scores are proclaimed the winners (and may receive some very small privilege). Used consistently for some months, the Good Behavior Game has produced powerful lasting effects on levels of prosocial behavior in natural settings, even over periods of years.

Corrections are required when disrespect occurs in a classroom; there is good evidence that low-level aggression tends to escalate if not addressed. Very consistent but modest negative consequences, coupled with opportunities to practice acting more appropriately ("new way replays"), are usually the best place to start. See also resources listed at the end of the chapter for additional behavior management materials.

6. *Implement activities and tools to increase the sharing of power to build community.* Building an inclusive school community characterized by recognition and respect, in which everyone is encouraged and supported to contribute from her or his own gifts and power, is the ultimate goal of projects related to enhancing school culture. Such efforts entail finding ways to ensure that everyone has a strong voice, feels welcomed in making his or her own unique contributions, and experiences a sense of responsibility to the collective. This means, among other things, honoring different groups within the school, each of which brings its own gifts, while actively giving up disrespect among groups and maintaining openness to enriching intergroup contact.

Constructing culture often requires serious discussion that clarifies the importance of everyone's contribution. Organized dialogues of many kinds are particularly useful for encouraging positive and respectful action with older children. Dialogues between students and staff, for example, in which each participant feels free to honestly describe his or her own experiences while genuinely listening to the experiences of others, can support voices that are often not heard. Those dialogues may focus on envisioning a school that works better for all, identifying and supporting personal and collective strengths, and planning collective action of many kinds. Student dialogues across groups (by gender, race, culture, or sexual orientation, for example), guided by questions that are likely to elicit different perspectives on the school, the community, and the larger world, can be very powerful; small-group activities may be useful in initiating conversation for such dialogues.

One of the best ways to support the realization of multiple gifts is through service learning and community service projects. Young people who are struggling with some areas of academic and social life often blossom when the right opportunity to make a real contribution emerges. The research suggests that meaningful interpersonal contact (like tutoring) or work that makes a clear contribution produce the best results, while assignments experienced as "busy work" (like filing or cleaning) do not. Individual efforts can be life-changing, and collective projects involving collaborative partnerships (including student–staff partnerships) build community spirit. Even if significant service learning and community service is already present, expansion is always possible. (Note that community service used as a consequence of negative behavior, though useful in some cases, involves different dynamics.)

Among such projects are those in which high school youth bring their talents as resources to prevention projects in elementary schools, including those that aim to build empowered nonviolent cultures and to eliminate bullying. Planning and actively engaging in such programs in their own schools or in the neighborhood are other common options. Active work on projects like murals, community gardens and playgrounds, community sculptures, and even school redesign are other opportunities, often calling for partnerships with others outside the school. Research projects, another possibility, can provide positive new experiences; planning and conducting a respect survey in the school or a survey of personal, associational, and institutional resources in a neighborhood are examples.

7. *Implement activities and tools to increase healing of conflicts.* Conflicts will emerge among any group of people who relate to each other closely over a period of time. Learning a standard framework for addressing such conflicts through repeated practice is an important form of social skills training, especially if used as standard practice in a classroom or school. One model that draws on considerable research begins by preparing each participant to listen respectfully, and then guiding those involved through a structured process in which each participant has an opportunity, in turn, to respond to the following questions:

- What happened here?
- How did that affect you? (optionally, if participant is developmentally able, "and others?")
- What could we do now to heal the damage?
- So what is our plan?

The final step is to provide recognition for contributions that participants have made to the healing process. Staff often require structured practice to make this kind of process work, without being sidetracked into refereeing exchanges of blame.

There is also a range of restorative circle and conferencing approaches that are supported by promising outcome data. Among these are healing circles that follow processes much like the outline above, but enlarged to include other members of classroom, school, or even neighborhood communities. Healing circles draw on traditional indigenous processes; for example, most rely on a talking circle format in which each question travels around the circle, and people speak only in their turn (often by passing a talking piece of some kind). One other somewhat similar process with strong support is Family Group Conferencing, a scripted process with Maori roots, often used as an alternative to suspension or court adjudication. Space precludes further discussion here, but extensive information about Family Group Conferencing is available at www.realjustice.org. It is important in using such processes to avoid "cultural appropriation"—acting as if one owns native traditions not one's own. The meaning of sacred practices is organically grounded in an intergenerational, lived cultural and spiritual reality. Professionals can learn and adapt practices from indigenous cultures, but that learning doesn't make them urban shamans or sacred circle-keepers.

8. *Monitor progress and maintain creative enthusiasm.* Projects that do not incorporate some form of simple feedback are likely to fade in the face of competing demands and priorities. For example, although improved school culture will contribute to test scores, this is a gradual process, while legal demands to demonstrate learning (often in very narrow ways) are often immediate. One valuable approach is the "chart on the wall." One or more simple charts can track a small number of variables over time. For example, ratings by staff and students regarding the frequency of each of the core practices can be graphed on a monthly or quarterly basis, as can annual respect surveys conducted among students, and in some cases the incidence of problem categories such as suspensions, disciplinary referrals, and fights. If the latter are used, it is essential that some positive variables also be tracked, since the real power in culture-building projects lies in increasing prosocial, pro-community actions. Successes demonstrated on the chart should be celebrated periodically, giving those involved opportunities to discuss what they have done and how they made it work so well (management research indicates this is a powerful form of recognition).

Though some activities may be useful on an open-ended basis, successful projects also find ways to maintain creative energy by establishing processes for continual innovation. Changes should continue to draw from the evidence base. Still, there are an infinite number of possible program activities that can be tried, and so long as a process for evaluating each is in place, even wild creativity should sometimes be encouraged.

Tools and Practice Examples

South High School

South High School is a public school in a small midwestern city that has experienced significant demographic shifts in the past two decades. The school is now quite multiethnic, and it has experienced significant ethnic tensions in addition to problems almost universal in U.S. schools: harassment, peer group exclusion, and emotional and physical violence. A school social worker came up with a project designed to address some of these problems and began with a full staff training event. As part of its PEACE POWER project, the school established an extensive system of recognition tickets, including public posting, public address announcements, classroom efforts, and random drawings of tickets that produced awards. The school also conducts an annual Respect Month, which has included a public pledge campaign, the initiation of a Gay–Straight Alliance and a related Day of Silence, a Mix It Up Day, a powerful theatrical production, interethnic events, participation in citywide intergroup organizing, plus a dozen other events and activities that continue or repeat each year. The school is also experimenting with healing circles for certain conflicts and has developed strong youth representation in planning efforts, although the initial planning was conducted primarily by a core group of staff organized by the school social worker.

King High School

By contrast, King High School is an inner-city public school in one of the largest cities in the country. The program at King was also initiated by the school social worker, who first convinced the powerful school principal of the potential of such a project. From the beginning, the core planning group of 20 was a mix of youth and staff. They began their efforts by designing and distributing posters widely in the school to spark curiosity and interest. A recognition system used specially designed postcards that were collected twice a week from teachers and mailed out to students' homes. A system of daily public-address recognition designed by the youth began at about the same time. The group then selected activities to begin with, including a pledge, youth–staff dialogues, and an extensive poster campaign. The planners wrote small grants to initiate several student organizations under the PEACE POWER umbrella, including two specifically to support the powerful dreams and hopes of groups of African American young women. At that point the entire teaching staff participated in a brief training workshop to bring them onboard. Plans are under way for larger community activities, and there is interest in additional conflict-resolution efforts. The project works to ensure that every youth participating in the effort at King (about 60 at this writing) has a clear and meaningful role.

Hillside Elementary School

The effort at Hillside Elementary School, located in a smaller city, is typical of work with elementary schools, where full staff planning is the ideal. Training workshops for staff included an introduction and one workshop on each of the core practices. Workshops began with presentation of the scientific underpinnings of each practice and a review of evidence-based strategies for each. Staff then discussed what they were already doing in each area, and they brainstormed about ways to go even further. Many of the ideas shared were very creative. For example, one teacher discussed a technique she used for teaching young children the steps in resolving conflicts. She had a large sheet with several sets of footprints facing each other, one pair for each step. As a child completed one step correctly, he or she moved up to the next. This school conducted monthly staff surveys of the frequency of core practices in the school, and the consistent increases clearly contributed to motivation.

Each of these projects is quite different; in fact every effort to shift school culture should be unique. However, efforts that are effective attend to the identified core practices, often in multiple ways. Although there are inevitable challenges (particularly when key staff leave), positive feedback tended to help maintain each of these projects.

Resources

Olweus, D. (1993). *Bullying at school: What we know and what we can do.* Cambridge, MA: Blackwell. Complete manual for bullying prevention.

PeaceBuilders: http://www.peacebuilders.com

Real Justice: http://www.realjustice.org. Inexpensive books and videos related to Family Group Conferencing and other restorative practices available for purchase.

Saving Our Schools. (1999). Two-video set from Heartland Media available at www.at-risk.com

Sidman, M. (2001). *Coercion and its fallout* (2nd ed.). Boston: Authors Cooperative. Available at www.behavior.org

Violent Times (1996). Three-video set from Attainment Co. Available from www.boystown.org

Key Points to Remember

The following summary points provide the basic framework for a successful effort to construct a school culture of nonviolent power and respect:

- A culture of nonviolent empowerment emerges from high levels of four core cultural practices: recognition, respect, shared power, and peacemaking.
- Evidence-based tools and activities should be preferred in action planning.
- The driving force behind an effective program is a small, creative, committed working group with strong administrative support.
- Effective programs must be adapted to fit the values, cultures, resources, and environment of each program through a process of creative shared power among multiple stakeholders, including students and staff.
- Staff must lead the way as models and active participants who, with other stakeholders, are responsible for the school culture.
- Regular, simple monitoring and feedback loops are necessary to ensure that gains achieved are maintained over time.

References

Buvinic, M., & Morrison, A. R. (2000). Living in a more violent world. *Foreign Policy, 118,* 58–72.

Embry, D. D. (2002). The Good Behavior Game: A best practice candidate as a universal behavioral vaccine. *Clinical Child and Family Psychology Review, 5,* 273–297.

Erickson, C. L., Mattaini, M. A., & McGuire, M. S. (2004). Constructing nonviolent cultures in schools: The state of the science. *Children and Schools, 26,* 102–116.

Flannery, D. J., Vazsonyi, A. T., Liau, A. K., Guo, S., Powell, K. E., Atha, H., Vesterdal, W., & Embry, D. (2003). Initial behavior outcomes for the PeaceBuilders universal school-based violence prevention program. *Developmental Psychology, 39,* 292–308.

Flay, B. R., Allred, C. G., & Ordway, N. (2001). Effects of the Positive Action program on achievement and discipline: Two matched-control comparisons. *Prevention Science, 2,* 71–89.

Garbarino, J., & deLara, E. (2002). *And words can hurt forever.* New York: Free Press.

Josephson Institute on Ethics (2001). *2000 report card: Violence and substance abuse.* Available at www.josephsoninstitute.org

Kretzmann, J. P., & McKnight, J. L. (1993). *Building communities from the inside out: A path toward finding and mobilizing a community's assets.* Chicago: ACTA Publications.

Mattaini, M. A. (with the PEACE POWER Working Group). (2001). *Peace Power for adolescents: Strategies for a culture of nonviolence.* Washington, DC: NASW Press. Additional information available at www.bfsr.org/PEACEPOWER.html.

Mayer, G. R. (2001). Antisocial behavior: Its causes and prevention within our schools. *Education and Treatment of Children, 24,* 414–429.

Metzler, C. W., Biglan, A., Rusby, J. C., & Sprague, J. R. (2001). Evaluation of a comprehensive behavior management program to improve school-wide positive behavior support. *Education and Treatment of Children, 24,* 448–479.

Sprague, J., Walker, H., Golly, A., White, K., Myers, D., & Shannon, T. (2001). Translating research into effective practice: The effects of a universal staff and student intervention on indicators of discipline and school safety. *Education and Treatment of Children, 24,* 495–511.

Strickland, J., Erickson, C. L, & Mattaini, M. A. (unpublished manuscript). *Social validity of the PEACE POWER strategy for youth violence prevention.* Available from mattaini@uic.edu

U.S. Surgeon General. (2001). *Youth violence: A report of the surgeon general.* Washington, DC: Department of Health and Human Services.

Assessing and Predicting Risk of Violence

Empirically Based Methods

Gary L. Bowen

Getting Started

On May 7, 2004, in Randallstown, Maryland, a drive-by shooting following a charity basketball game at a local high school left four students critically wounded. One of the two shooters charged the following day was a 17-year-old student who attended the high school. According to the police, the shootings were retaliation for a name-calling incident involving a girl, which had occurred earlier in the day (Associated Press, 2004). The next day, May 8, 2004, in Jonesboro, Arkansas, three empty chairs at high school graduation ceremonies symbolized missing classmates who were killed in a school shooting six years earlier. The two shooters, 11 and 13 at the time of the incident, both remain in a juvenile detention center (Rousseau, 2004).

Not every incident of school violence ends in death; nonetheless, fights, gang violence, rape and sexual assault, bullying, and other forms of physical and verbal harassment are all too common in lives of students—whether they are victims or witnesses. School incident reports (administrative data) and student surveys indicate that rates of school violence vary among schools and, for any one school, across time.

Although even one serious incident of school violence is too much, school violence, like many other problems, has a "tipping point" beyond which it spreads like an epidemic and places students in serious jeopardy of physical and psychological harm. According to Cantor and Wright (2002), 60% of violence occurs in just 4% of schools, and they group schools into four categories: no crime, isolated crime, moderate crime, and violent crime. In schools with high rates of violent crime, learning and academic performance are secondary to safety.

School social workers and other school-based professionals struggle to find methods to decrease the probability of school violence. Interventions to reduce school violence are, in part, efforts to decrease the risk factors associated with its occurrence; as these risk factors decrease, the probability of school violence also decreases. Interventions also strive to increase protective factors, which decrease the probability of violence either directly or by buffering the effects of risk factors.

Intervention success depends on targeting the risk and protective factors that reside both in the ecologies of schools and in the individuals who attend those schools (Fraser, 2004). School social workers need tools to assess and monitor rates of school violence and of risk and protective factors that have probabilistic linkages to its occurrence. In addition, they need a strategy for using this information to develop intervention and prevention strategies.

This chapter addresses strategies for assessing and predicting the risk of school violence. The review is framed by a seven-step planning strategy: results-focused planning (RFP). Working with student, school, and community stakeholder groups in planning strategies to decrease school violence (the performance team), a status quo assessment is the first step in this planning strategy. Four critical status quo data collection tasks are discussed here. A survey of students, the School Success Profile, is introduced as a tool that supports the status quo assessment for school social workers and other school-based professionals.

What We Know

Results-focused planning emerged from early attempts to help federal employees with the transition to the Government Performance Results Acts (P.L. 103-62). It builds on the performance-based and accountability literature that emphasizes intended outcomes, and the associated planning process supports evidence-based school social work practice (Orthner & Bowen, 2004; Raines, 2004). A key assumption of RFP is that intervention success is promoted when planning focuses on achieving defined performance goals. A seven-step process is used to help stakeholder groups move from identifying issues and concerns that hamper the achievement of performance goals to developing strategies to overcome barriers that restrict implementation of intervention and prevention strategies.

Step 1: Conduct a status quo assessment.
Step 2: Define desired results.
Step 3: Identify key partners and allies.
Step 4: Develop an action plan with each partner and ally.
Step 5: Specify the role and responsibilities of the performance team.
Step 6: Develop a monitoring and evaluation plan.
Step 7: Develop plans to overcome potential implementation hurdles.

RFP is also referred to in the literature as Results Management (Orthner & Bowen, 2004). My colleagues and I have used RFP as a strategy for working with community and school groups addressing a variety of issues and concerns, including school violence (Bowen, Bowen, Richman, & Woolley, 2002). In our use of the RFP process in schools, we work with principals to identify a performance team that will spearhead the planning process. In most cases, such a performance team is already in place, such as the school improvement teams that operate in many schools. We request that the performance team include a variety of stakeholders—teachers, parents, community members, and students. Typically, these performance teams have 10 to 12 members.

We have found that the RFP process in schools works most effectively in the context of survey data from students. The School Success Profile (SSP) is one such survey tool for middle and high school students, which yields information important to the status quo assessment (Bowen, Richman, & Bowen, 2002; Richman, Bowen, & Woolley, 2004). The SSP provides summary information on 22 core profile dimensions of a student's social environment and individual adaptation, including both neighborhood and school safety dimensions. Results from the SSP can be used to assess and monitor levels of school violence at school and factors associated with its occurrence.

What We Can Do

Status Quo Assessment

Effective planning requires good information. The first step in the RFP process involves conducting a status quo assessment, which includes estimating the magnitude of the problem or issue and identifying predictors or correlates that explain variation in the focal issue or concern. At least four types of information are needed to assess and predict the risk of violence and to plan an intervention strategy to combat it: (a) estimates about the current rate or incidence of school violence, (b) information on the risk factors associated with its occurrence, (c) information on protective factors that decrease the likelihood of school violence—assets that may also be used as resources in planning and implementing intervention strategies, and (d) information on the groups whose members are most at risk of being perpetrators, victims, or witnesses of school violence.

Estimating Current Rates

Intervention planning begins with an assessment to determine the current rate or level of the problem, issue, or challenge. Both student-based and survey-based empirical methods may be used to arrive at estimates about the potential incidence of school violence. Both methods depend on a meaningful definition of what constitutes school violence. The definition proposed by Astor, Vargas, Pitner, and Meyer (1999, p. 140) is used for purposes of the present review: "School violence covers a wide range of intentional or reckless behaviors that include physical harm, psychological harm, and property damage."

Actual reports of school violence provide one basis for estimates about school violence. Rates of school violence may vary, depending on whether counts are determined based on perpetrators, victims, or episodes. Such counts represent the number of incidents that have come to the attention of school officials and have been formally documented as meeting the definitional parameters of school violence over a specified period. These data can be aggregated across various levels (e.g., from classroom to school). Typically, these counts represent "floor" effects—low estimates of the actual level of school violence.

Survey-based estimates rely on the administration of surveys, either to the student population or to a probability sample of the student population, which ask students about behavior that meets definitional criteria of school violence. Students may report on themselves as being perpetrators or victims of school violence, or they may provide estimates about the general level of the problem in the student body, including questions about the level of safety they feel at school.

For example, the SSP asks students to report on the extent to which a number of crime- and violence-related behaviors are a problem at school (answers include "not a problem," "a little problem," and "a big problem"). In a nationally representative sample of middle and high school students who were administered the SSP, more than one in four students mentioned the following crime- and violence-related activities as being a "big problem" at school: fights among students (28%), stealing (27%), destruction of school property (27%), and student use of alcohol (28%) or illegal drugs (30%) (Bowen, Bowen, & Richman, 1998). In the context of these findings, it is not surprising that 38% of middle school students and 24% of high school students in the same survey reported that they were "sometimes or often afraid" of being hurt or bothered at school. These counts usually represent "ceiling" effects—upper limit estimates of what may be actually going on at school.

It is interesting to compare the discrepancy between what comes to the attention of school officials (administrative reports) and what students report in surveys—the larger the gap, the greater the likelihood that school resources for addressing the presenting situation are inadequate or ineffective. In general, the number of identified cases of a problem will depend, in part, on the resources to investigate and handle these cases.

Whether estimates are based on administrative reports, survey data, or the combination of administrative reports and survey data, the level of reported violence reflects the total effect of current intervention and prevention strategies. If schools are unhappy with level of school violence (i.e., dissatisfied with the status quo), efforts to reduce violence must involve intensifying current strategies,

changing strategies, or some combination of continuity and change. Without alterations in the inputs, there is no reason to assume a decrease in negative outcomes. Such efforts are informed by knowledge about risk and protective factors associated with school violence.

Identifying Risk Factors

Risk factors are defined as influences that increase the probability of a negative outcome and decrease the probability of a positive outcome (Nash & Bowen, 2002). The social work literature is replete with studies that identify risk factors associated with high rates of school violence. For example, Bowen, Powers, Woolley, and Bowen (2004) identified risk factors associated with school violence in different ecological domains. In addition, Hawkins et al. (1998) have prepared a comprehensive and rigorous review of predictors of youth violence, and Sprague and Walker (2000) summarize major sources of threats to school safety, including school administrative and management practices. The unit of analysis in studies may be individuals, special groups, or the school as a whole.

These studies employ a variety of methodologies to predict the likelihood of violence, including both quantitative and qualitative data collection strategies. For example, examining profiles of either the victims or the perpetrators of school violence who come to the attention of school authorities can help identify risk factors. One such method is the work of the U.S. Secret Service to profile school shooters and to identify the antecedents in such exceptional cases of school violence (Vossekuil, Reddy, Fein, Borum, & Modzeleski, 2000). Risk factors may also be identified using location analysis, in which areas in the school with a high incidence of violence are mapped for intervention planning (Astor, Meyer, & Pitner, 1999) (see chapter 39, p. 438). Finally, risk factors can be identified through the analysis of student survey data in an attempt to identify factors associated with high rates of school violence at either a student or an aggregate level (Eamon & Altshuler, 2004). Table 41.1 includes five sample school violence assessment and screening resources.

Although the identification of risk factors and their relative importance as correlates of school violence will vary across studies and in relation to the research strategies employed, school social workers possess an evolving body of literature that

Table 41.1 Sample School Violence Assessment and Screening Resources

Resource	Description	Source
U.S. Secret Service national threat assessment guide	Threat assessment guide and information from the analysis of school shooters, including warning signs that may precede targeted violence.	National Threat Assessment Center U.S. Secret Service 950 H Street NW, Suite 9100 Washington, DC 20223 202-406-5470 http://www.treas.gov.usss/ntac
Early warning guide	Publication sponsored by the U.S. Department of Education, Office of Safe and Drug Free Schools, and the U.S. Department of Juvenile Justice and Delinquency Prevention, which includes early warning signs of violent behavior for youth at risk.	Dwyer, K. P., Osher, D., & Warger, W. (1998). *Early warning, timely response: A guide to safe schools.* Washington, DC: U.S. Department of Education. (ERIC Document Reproduction Service No. ED 418 372.) http://www.naea-reston.org/guide.pdf
Student-level assessment and screening procedures	An excellent journal article that includes a discussion of multiple gating approaches, including a strategy developed by the authors for use with middle school students, to identify students at high risk of committing violent and aggressive acts. The authors offer important cautions about the use of such procedures.	Sprague, J., & Walker, H. (2000). Early identification and intervention for youth with antisocial and violent behavior. *Exceptional Children, 66,* 367–379.
Mapping violence-prone public spaces	A journal article that outlines procedures for identifying and reclaiming locations at school and surrounding the school where bullying and victimization are most likely to occur.	Astor, R. A., Benbenishty, R., & Meyer, H. A. (2004). Monitoring and mapping student victimization in schools. *Theory Into Practice, 43,* 39–49.
School Success Profile (SSP)	An ecologically based survey research tool for middle and high school students that can be used for assessing and monitoring school violence and selected factors associated with its occurrence. Summary information is presented on 22 core profile dimensions, and school staff receive both individual profiles, summarizing the responses for each student, and a group profile, summarizing the responses for all students who complete the instrument. Evidence-based practice resources for each profile dimension are available for SSP users.	Bowen, G. L., Richman, J. M., & Bowen, N. K. (2002). The School Success Profile: A results management approach to assessment and intervention planning. In A. R. Roberts & G. J. Greene (Eds.), *Social workers' desk reference* (pp. 787–793). New York: Oxford University Press. www.schoolsuccessprofile.org.

informs this process. Surveys like the SSP allow school social workers to monitor risk factors associated with school violence; in situations in which risk factors exceed critical threshold points, the likelihood of school violence is increased. Thus, an important task of the performance team is to determine these critical threshold points.

Several conclusions emerge from a review of the literature. First, school violence has no single "cause"—it results from a combination of individual, relational, and situational factors that interact to increase the probability of school violence. Second, although there may be some central factors associated with every form of school violence, there are unique factors associated with each specific form of school violence. Finally, associated risk factors may vary across both population subgroups (gender) and school level (elementary, middle, and high). Consequently, although it is tempting to use risk and early-warning checklists to screen either potential perpetrators or victims of school violence, the application of such checklists to individual students may lead to many false positives and negatives and is therefore not recommended (Dwyer, Osher, & Warger, 1998; Sprague & Walker, 2000). In a recent review of school violence prevention and intervention programs, Erickson, Mattaini, and McGuire (2004) conclude that the most successful programs address the culture and social climate of the school, rather than focusing on the deficiencies and problems of students or groups of students.

Identifying Protective Factors

Few situations are either all good or all bad. Most situations include a balance between the presence of risk factors that increase the probability of a negative outcome like school violence and protective factors that decrease the probability of a negative outcome (Nash & Bowen, 2002). Protective factors may simply be the opposite end of the same continuum as risks, or they may comprise factors separate from risks. Protective factors may directly influence the probability of school violence, or they may buffer or moderate the negative effects of risk factors. It is important that the status quo assessment reflect the full picture—both negatives and positives. Interventions to decrease the incidence of school violence are likely to be more effective when they promote protection in addition to addressing risks.

The strategies involved in identifying protective factors are similar to those used to identify risks.

As is the case in assessing risk factors, the unit of analysis in studies of protective factors may be individuals, special groups, or the school as a whole. In addition, both quantitative and qualitative data collection strategies may be used. For example, examining the profiles of students who do not become victims or perpetrators of school violence can identify protective factors. In addition, protective factors can be identified through the analysis of student survey data, looking for individual, relational, and situational factors associated with low rates of school violence at either a student level or an aggregate level.

In general, the social work literature on the role of strengths and assets in decreasing school violence is less well developed than the literature on risk factors (Bowen, Powers, et al., 2004). Surveys like the SSP are invaluable in helping school social workers identify and monitor both the student- and the school-level assets and strengths that decrease the probability of school violence. The identification of protective factors requires sensitivity to the different forms of school violence and to how such strengths and assets may vary across population subgroups and across school settings.

Selecting Populations at Risk

Even in schools with high rates of school violence, students' relative risk of becoming either perpetrators or victims may vary. Selecting populations at risk involves identifying the subpopulations of students who are more likely to experience school violence directly, who are more likely to have risk factors associated with school violence, or who are less likely to have protective factors that decrease their vulnerability to violence. Although many interventions may be directed toward the whole school population (i.e., universal interventions), interventions may also be targeted to student groups on the basis on their demographic profile (i.e., selective intervention) or their risk profile (i.e., indicated intervention) (Bowen, Powers, et al., 2004). The targeting of intervention resources may be particularly important if resources are limited.

Next Steps

The six steps that follow the status quo assessment result in a plan of action. Although the performance

Box 41.1 Use of Focus Groups

Forming focus groups of students and teachers so as to better understand administrative and survey data is an important data collection strategy in the status quo assessment—satisfying the need to give a "voice" to the numbers. Recently, the School Success Profile (SSP) project team administered the SSP in a middle school in which a high proportion of students reported fights to be a "big problem." School staff agreed that fights were a problem, and this finding was documented in the administrative suspension records.

In focus groups with students, the school staff were surprised to learn that fights at school added excitement to what students perceived as boring and routine. Some students were described as fight promoters—they would select two students, who might not even have a problem with each other at the beginning of the day but who would be fighting by the end of the day. Many students reported that they attended school more as "spectators" than as participants. These findings were supported by SSP data showing low levels of student engagement and low participation in extracurricular activities. The combination of SSP data and focus group discussion shifted the focus of intervention from fights to strategies intended to increase student engagement and extracurricular participation.

team coordinates the planning process, the emphasis must be on *planning with* rather than *planning for* people. Students are seen as active participants in this process. An important focus of the RFP process is helping the performance team to value, acquire, and use information and tacit knowledge from students, employees, and other stakeholders to successfully plan, implement, and evaluate strategies to decrease the risk of violence.

Key Points to Remember

The status quo assessment, which includes the process of assessing and predicting school violence, is the cornerstone of the results-focused planning sequence. We prefer to think of the results of this assessment as providing an "image" rather than the

"reality" of the presenting situation. In addition to the tasks discussed here, the status quo assessment also involves a discussion of vision. We ask the performance team to develop a vision of a school with a low likelihood of violence. In particular, we ask participants to describe the social organizational processes in such a school, including the nature of interactions among students, between students and teachers, and among school employees. This vision is then compared to the images that result from the status quo assessment, including the use of data from the School Success Profile. The aim of RFP is to develop an action plan for closing the gap between image and vision.

References

Associated Press. (2004, May 9). Two charged in drive-by shooting at MD school. *News and Observer*, p. A8.

Astor, R. A., Benbenishty, R., & Meyer, H. A. (2004). Monitoring and mapping student victimization in schools. *Theory Into Practice*, *43*, 39–49.

Astor, R. A., Meyer, H. A., & Pitner, R. (1999). Mapping school violence with students, teachers, and administrators. In L. Davis (Ed.), *Working with African American males: A guide to practice* (pp. 129–144). Thousand Oaks, CA: Sage.

Astor, R. A., Vargas, L. A., Pitner, R. O., & Meyer, H. A. (1999). School violence: Research, theory, and practice. In J. M. Jenson & M. O. Howard (Eds.), *Youth violence: Current research and recent practice innovations* (pp. 139–172). Springfield, VA: Sheridan.

Bowen, G. L., Bowen, N. K., & Richman, J. M. (1998). *Students in peril: Crime and violence in neighborhoods and schools*. Chapel Hill: University of North Carolina, Jordan Institute for Families, School of Social Work.

Bowen, G. L., Bowen, N. K., Richman, J. M., & Woolley, M. E. (2002). Reducing school violence: A social capacity framework. In L. A. Rapp-Paglicca, A. R. Roberts, & J. S. Wodarski (Eds.), *Handbook of violence* (pp. 303–325). Hoboken, NJ: Wiley.

Bowen, G. L., Powers, J. D., Woolley, M. E., & Bowen, N. K. (2004). School violence. In L. A. Rapp-Paglicci, C. N. Dulmus, & J. S. Wodarski (Eds.), *Handbook of preventive interventions for children and adolescents* (pp. 338–358). New York: John Wiley & Sons.

Bowen, G. L., Richman, J. M., & Bowen, N. K. (2002). The School Success Profile: A results management approach to assessment and intervention planning. In A. R. Roberts & G. J. Greene (Eds.), *Social workers' desk reference* (pp. 787–793). New York: Oxford University Press.

Cantor, D., & Wright, M. M. (2002). *School crime patterns: A national profile of U.S. public schools using rates of crime reported by police.* Rockville, MD: Westat.

Dwyer, K., Osher, D., & Warger, C. (1998). *Early warning, timely response: A guide to safe schools.* Washington, DC: U.S. Department of Education.

Eamon, M. K., & Altshuler, S. J. (2004). Can we predict disruptive school behavior? *Children and Schools, 26,* 23–37.

Erickson, C. L., Mattaini, M. A., & McGuire, M. S. (2004). Constructing nonviolent cultures in schools: The state of the science. *Children and Schools, 26,* 102–116.

Fraser, M. W. (2004). The ecology of childhood: A multisystems perspective. In M. W. Fraser (Ed.), *Risk and resilience in childhood: An ecological perspective* (pp. 1–12). Washington, DC: NASW Press.

Hawkins, J. D., Herrenkohl, T., Farrington, D. P., Brewer, D., Catalano, R. F., & Harachi, T. (1998). A review of predictors of youth violence. In R. Loeber & D. P. Farrington (Eds.), *Serious and violent juvenile offenders* (pp. 106–146). Thousand Oaks, CA: Sage.

Nash, J. K., & Bowen, G. L. (2002). Defining and estimating risk and protection: An illustration from the School Success Profile. *Child and Adolescent Social Work Journal, 19,* 247–261.

Orthner, D. K., & Bowen, G. L. (2004). Strengthening practice through Results Management. In A. R. Roberts & K. R. Yeager (Eds.), *Evidence-based practice manual: Research and outcome measures in health and human services* (pp. 897–904). New York: Oxford University Press.

Raines, J. C. (2004). Evidence-based practice in school social work: A process in perspective. *Children and Schools, 26,* 71–85.

Richman, J. M., Bowen, G. L., & Woolley, M. E. (2004). School failure: An eco-interactional developmental perspective. In M. W. Fraser (Ed.), *Risk and resilience in childhood: An ecological perspective* (2nd ed., pp. 133–160). Washington, DC: National Association of Social Workers.

Rousseau, C. (2004, May 9). Graduates honor those slain in '98. *News and Observer,* p. A8.

Sprague, J., & Walker, H. (2000). Early identification and intervention for youth with antisocial and violent behavior. *Exceptional Children, 66,* 367–379.

Vossekuil, B., Reddy, M., Fein, R., Borum, R., & Modzeleski, W. (2000). *USSS safe school initiative: An interim report of the prevention of targeted violence in schools.* Washington, DC: U.S. Secret Service, National Threat Assessment Center.

Best Practices for Prevention and Intervention in Schools

Esther Howe ▪ Elayne Haymes ▪ Tanya Tenor

Getting Started

Bullying in schools has historically been a persistent problem worldwide. In the United States, heightened attention to school violence in the past 15 years has led to a focus on bullying as demanding attention. The realization that many of the perpetrators of high-profile school shootings were themselves victims of bullying has added urgency to this matter. In Europe, suicide among youngsters who could no longer face their tormentors has led to the coining of the term *bullycide*. According to a study from the National Institutes of Health, published in the *Journal of the American Medical Association*, almost one third of all children in grades 6 to 10 have experienced some form of bullying (Nansel, Overpeck, Pilla, Ruan, Simons-Morton, & Scheidt, 2001). Although bullying can and does occur in other environments, the majority of bullying takes place in and around school buildings (Smith, Ananiadou, & Cowie, 2003*)*.

Bullying is thought to be the most prevalent form of violence suffered by children (Haynie et al., 2001). For our purposes, we use English criminologist David Farrington's 1993 definition of *bullying*: "Bullying is the repeated oppression, psychological or physical, of a less powerful person by a more powerful person." In recent years, the Internet has increasingly been used for these activities, thus leaving the victims vulnerable even at home. Bullying can include saying or writing inappropriate things about a person, deliberately excluding individuals from activities, threatening or actually hurting them, making a person do things against his or her own will, and teasing. This chapter will not address two specialized forms of bullying, racial and sexual harassment; these are addressed in separate chapters.

Though other forms of violence in schools have either held constant or decreased, the reported incidence of bullying has increased (Rigby, 2002). Bullying seems to peak in middle school and decline in high school. Approximately 7% of eighth graders miss at least 1 day of school each month because they are afraid of being bullied (Banks, 1997). Every year more than 160,000 students report missing some school because they are afraid. Both the widespread nature of the problem and the potential gravity of its consequences mandate that school personnel seek and implement sound evidence-based interventions to alleviate the problem.

What We Know

Research on the effectiveness of antibullying programs instituted in schools is neither strong nor definitive. There are, however, common characteristics shared by most of the programs: a whole-school approach to the problem, involvement of the wider community, inclusion of the subject matter in the curriculum, increased monitoring of student behavior, encouragement of students to seek help and subsequent provision of counseling services, and a plan to deal with cases of bullying. According to Rigby (2002), this final component is what varies most. Some programs, such as Olweus's (1993), emphasize "the need for clear rules" and the need "to apply sanctions when rules are broken." Other programs take a problem-solving approach that is focused less on assigning blame than on generating solutions. Two meta-analyses (Rigby, 2002; Smith et al., 2003) suggest that there is not enough evidence to favor one approach over the other.

Both analyses document the importance of a whole-school approach and of full staff support for the antibullying policy. Rigby concludes that "outcomes were closely related to how thoroughly the programs were implemented," *The specifics of the program are not as significant as the thoroughness with which it is carried out.* Thus staff training is crucial to the success of any school-based antibullying program.

What We Can Do

The following interlocking program components will be discussed in descending ecological order: (1) an approach to involve the entire school staff; (2) life skills training groups in which all students participate; and (3) specific interventions targeted at individual perpetrators and victims. Though other components, such as better staff monitoring of playgrounds, hallways, and school bathrooms, parental involvement, and curriculum inclusion, are important, the focus of this chapter is to give explicit guidelines on how to implement the three components mentioned above.

Get the School Staff on Board

A significant barrier to the success of a bullying prevention program can be staff lack of understanding or compliance with the program. School social workers need to begin working with school staff as soon as a mandate has been handed down from the state or the school administration. The first step is to have the faculty and staff fill out a questionnaire (for an example, see Rigby's Bullying Pages at http://www.education.unisa.edu.au). Subsequently, the social worker should schedule several professional development meetings with the staff to discuss the findings of the questionnaire and to lay out the goals of the bullying prevention program. Any staff resistance should be dealt with openly, and staff's suggestions and concerns should be listened to. The school administration's policy on bullying should be clarified. Comprehensive guidelines on what is and is not considered bullying should be presented, as well as clear protocols on how to deal with incidents of bullying both in terms of the perpetrators and the victims. Assure the staff that all of you are in this together and that the school administration and your program will

support them as the anti-bullying efforts progress. To that end, monthly refresher meetings in which new concerns and opportunities can be voiced should be held.

Prevention Interventions With All Students

Once staff support has been secured, work should begin with programs that affect all students. The school social worker should encourage teachers to incorporate information about the effects of bullying in their curricula, and they should have access to model curricular units and other resources. (See the Resources section for a list of antibullying Web sites.) School assemblies should be called to inform all students of state law regarding bullying and the school's policies and resources for dealing with bullying.

Whatever intervention the school chooses to use, it is essential to remember the importance of simple vigilance and oversight. In some instances, closer supervision of playgrounds, hallways, and bathrooms has led to a 50% decrease in bullying behavior and physical violence (Smith et al., 2003). Coy (2001) suggests the use of student volunteers to expand the "eyes and ears" of a bullying prevention program: "Students should be encouraged to report incidents of bullying by promising the students anonymity." An essential tool for helping students access help is a suggestion box in a discreet location, which enables students to leave anonymous notes about problems they have or observe. All students should know where it is.

Parental involvement is an essential component of an effective program. Parents should be told about the school's antiviolence/antibullying program and given clear descriptions of what is and is not considered bullying behavior, what the consequence are for children who engage in such conduct, and what resources, including staff, parents can avail themselves of if they fear for their children's well-being. A brochure telling parents the behavioral indicators to look out for is a useful tool for enlisting their support. The school social work should offer to speak on this topic at a meeting of the school's parent organization.

Life Skills Groups

An essential component of a whole-school approach is a prevention-focused life skills training group conducted in collaboration with each grade's scheduled health and/or social skills/life skills curriculum. Life skills training concentrates on prosocial decision making regarding anger management, conflict resolution, peer and family relations, and so on. These groups can be run by members of the school mental health team or by specially trained teachers.

All group sessions are designed to foster self-awareness and behavioral change. Topics include, but are not limited to, developing methods of self-discipline, identifying consequences before taking action, recognizing the effect of one's behavior on others, learning alternative ways of getting what one wants, mastering angry and aggressive impulses and thoughts, and learning peaceful methods of resolving conflicts (Coloroso, 2003).

The curriculum in these life skills groups should focus in part on bullying, besides helping children develop sound decision-making skills. (A model lesson of a 4-week curriculum on bullying is included in section IV.) Life skills groups represent an opportunity to enhance all students' prosocial decision-making skills while increasing their sense of community, strengthening their social network, and thereby improving the social climate of the school as a whole. Students in such a school are less to likely to bully, more likely to report bullying if they observe it, and more likely to seek help if they are victims. Some countries have focused on improving school climate as their major effort to reduce bullying behavior (Smith et al., 2003).

Working With Perpetrators and Victims

Even interventions focusing on victims and perpetrators initially use a prevention paradigm. Prevention, as it is understood in primary intervention, is a model for service predicated on the identification of unique behavioral indicators that are associated with the potential for violent behavior toward self and others (Fraser, Richman, & Galinsky, 1999). This aspect of the intervention usually proceeds according to steps outlined below.

Step 1: Identify students who have been the victims of bullying or who have been involved in a range of experiences that are high risk for aggressive acts. This goal can be realized through an annual, whole-school population survey completed at the beginning of each year as part of an assignment in an English, health, or life skills class. (Students should be allowed to refuse to fill out the survey without repercussions.)

The survey is used to assess and prioritize students for early contact and further evaluation by the staff. The survey asks questions pertaining to a range of social and emotional experiences that have been related in the literature to violent/bullying behavior as aggressor or victim (Fraser et al., 1999). Students assessed to have a high number of risk elements or who present a significant self-description indicating potential aggression or victimization behaviors are interviewed by a staff member as quickly as possible. Risk for bullying or victimization can be assessed in greater detail, and a plan can be developed that may include one or more individual and group modalities, using the prevention components described in the previous section. Staff must gain the trust of students identified as potential victims, perpetrators, and witnesses through carefully orchestrated but informal contacts—in the lunchroom, on the playground, in brief meetings, thus weaving a safety net of social support for students (Haymes, Howe, & Peck, 2003).

Step 2: Implement individual and group interventions when bullying has occurred. The intervention component of the program consists of individual and/or group sessions with antibullying staff, perpetrators, and victims. These incidents may be identified by other students, teachers, victims, or parents. Addressing individual acts of bullying after they occur leads to continued contact with school staff and/or referrals to community social service agencies for both the perpetrators and the victims. Parents should be notified and consent obtained for the staff to meet with their child on a regular basis. Parental support and involvement are made easier by negotiating this consent.

It is at this stage that the various antibullying programs diverge, predicated on whether the program supports a "rules and sanctions" approach or a problem-solving one. Currently there is no compelling evidence that one method is more effective than the other. Some schools now favor a mixed approach, basing the intervention chosen on the severity of the bullying and the responsiveness of the perpetrators to problem-solving methods (Rigby, 2002). For a detailed description of the most well documented rules-and-sanctions approach, see the materials on the Olweus Bullying Prevention program at http://www.model-programs.samhsa.gov/print

For schools adopting a problem-solving approach, peer mediation can be used to address the actions of perpetrators and victims (Cowie & Sharp, 1996). A mental health worker or teacher trained in antibullying work, students involved in the incident, and neutral students trained in peer mediation skills are brought together for one session to hear the facts of the case from those directly involved. When possible, bystanders who saw the incident are also included. Consequences to the perpetrator for not participating in the mediation are outlined by a school administrator prior at the beginning of the meeting. Guidelines for implementing a mediation session can be found below. Research shows the effects of this intervention are strongest for the victims, who report *feeling* less bullied.

Students—victim and perpetrator—develop a behavioral contract to avoid future incidents, and the perpetrator must make symbolic or actual restitution to the victim, depending on the nature of the incident. Where indicated, students will be referred for additional interventions. Parents are informed of the mediation and its outcome, and their consent to therapeutic sessions is obtained. (See Resources to refer to other interventions using the problem-solving approach.) Treatment goals and treatment techniques are developed from evidence-based practice methods for intervening with both the bullies and the bullied.

Working With the Victims of Bullying

Students who are victims of bullying are typically anxious, insecure, and cautious. They tend to have low self-esteem and rarely defend themselves or retaliate when confronted by students who bully them (Banks, 1997). Outcomes for the child who has been bullied can include depression, isolation, poor school attendance, and diminished grades. At the extreme, bullied children can exhibit patterns of irrational retaliation or suicide.

To reduce the social isolation often exhibited by victims of bullying, teachers should implement cooperative learning techniques in their teaching methods. In addition, victims, who often suffer from poor social functioning (Haynie et al., 2001), should be involved in social skills training groups to enhance their understanding of social cues as well as to provide them with better responses to threats of bullying. Also, research by

Young and Holdorf (2003) points to the validity of implementing solution-focused brief therapy support groups for victims of bullying.

Working With the Bullies

Bullies generally exhibit poor psychosocial functioning in comparison to nonbullying classmates. In addition they tend to be unpopular—but more popular than their victims (Haynie et al., 2001). The lack of self-regulation in their behavior and their risk for future involvement in crime and delinquent behavior make focused interventions a vital part of a school's antibullying efforts. Available research suggests interventions with bullies similar to those suggested for their victims: cooperative learning techniques in the classroom and social skills support groups to reduce aggressive behaviors and strengthen positive social interactions. In addition, there must be consistent enforcement of nonpunitive, graduated consequences along with parental involvement to discuss behaviors of concern, consequences for conduct violations, and systems of support.

Underlying all the recommended interventions is the theme of social support. It is a key ingredient for any antibullying effort, helping the victims, the bullies, and the bystanders. The value of a network of social support should not be underestimated.

Family sessions are scheduled as needed to inform parents of serious aggressive behavior problems and incidents of bullying behavior or victimization. Increasing communication with parents enables them to participate more actively in the "school-family partnership" (Bowen, 1999). Parent awareness and participation are a vital component of a bullying-prevention program, essential for the support of children who are at risk of committing or who have committed acts of bullying as well as for the child who has been a victim. Telephone communication, in-school conferences, and home visits are included among valuable outreach efforts.

All aspects of the school's organizational and curricular components should be taken into consideration when adapting the basic elements of a bullying-prevention or intervention program. The various components must be tailored to the culture of the school and the specific characteristics of the community. A coordinator's clear understanding of possible barriers to implementation will enable him or her to develop the necessary relationships within the school and in the community.

Tools and Practice Examples

To reinforce the value we attach to life skills groups in the prevention of and intervention with bullying behavior, we present a comprehensive lesson plan in its entirety. This module is one part of a four-module antibullying unit within a broader life skills curriculum in a middle school. The curriculum includes most components of the evidence-based best practices delineated in this chapter. An anticipated by-product is the strengthening of social ties throughout the school.

Bullying Lesson One: What Is Bullying?

Objective: To introduce bullying and to explore its prevalence

Grades: 6/8

Time: 25–30 minutes

Materials: Board and markers, "Why Children Bully" sheet, Bully Survey

1. Tell the class that you are starting a unit to prevent bullying. Explain that the goal of this unit is to stop bullying in the classroom, hallway, and school bus. You will learn in this lesson the steps that can prevent bullying.
2. Ask the class to define a bully. You can use one of their definitions or this one: someone who hurts or intimidates other people.
3. Pass out the "Why Children Bully" sheet to the class. Go through sheet with class.
4. Under the "Ways students bully" question, give examples for each category. For physical: spitting, tripping, pushing, shoving, destroying another's things, hitting. Social: gossiping, spreading rumors, ethnic or racial slurs, excluding, humiliating. Verbal: name-calling, teasing, mocking, verbal threats of aggression. Intimidation: graffiti, making a public challenge, coercion.
5. Divide the students into groups of three to six. Ask the groups to rate 1–5 which one of the ways outlined in "Why Children Bully" happens the most at school.
6. Ask the groups to rate 1–5 which one of the ways outlined in "Who is a bully?" is the truest. Ask the groups to rate 1–4 which one of the ways outlined in "Ways students bully" happens the most at school. Ask the groups to rate 1–4

which one of the ways outlined in "Whom do bullies most often pick on?" is the truest. Ask reporters to share the group's results.
7. Pass out the Bully Survey. Make sure the students don't put their names on the top of the sheet. Questions 1 and 2 are optional. Explain that answers won't be disclosed.
8. Review what a bully is, and tell the class they will learn effective ways to deal with bullying in this unit. Ask students to hand in their surveys.

Why do students bully?

1. To gain power.
2. To get attention or become popular.
3. To get material things.
4. To act out problems at home.
5. To copy another person they admire.

Who is a bully?

1. A person who doesn't care if bad things happen to other people.
2. A person who doesn't feel bad when he or she hurts others.
3. A person who likes to be in charge and always gets his or her way.
4. A person who believes others deserve to get bullied.
5. A person who is bullied at home by his or her parents, brothers, or sisters.

Ways students bully

1. Physical aggression
2. Social alienation
3. Verbal aggression
4. Intimidation

Whom do bullies most often pick on?

1. Students who are smaller.
2. Students who don't have that many friends.
3. Students who don't stick up for themselves or get help from an adult.
4. Most anybody, if they think they can get away with it.

What can happen to people who get bullied?

1. Feel scared, alone, and sad
2. Don't like school
3. Get headaches and stomachaches
4. Don't feel good about themselves

Bully survey

1. How do you most often feel at school?_____
   Answer: (a) Very Sad (b) Sad (c) OK (d) Happy (e) Very Happy

2. The adults at my school are:_____
   (a) not helpful (b) sometimes helpful (c) always helpful
3. How do you feel in these places? (1) Unsafe
   (2) OK (3) Safe
   In the classroom_____
   On the playground_____
   In the lunchroom_____
   Going to and from school_____
4. How often do other students hit, kick, or push you?
5. How often do other students say mean things to you?
6. If you have been bullied this year, whom have you told?
7. If you have been bullied this year, who has helped?
8. How often do you hit, kick, or push?
9. How often do you say mean things?
10. How many people do you think are lonely at school?
11. Do you feel lonely at school?
12. List three students you like to do things with:
13. List three students you don't like to be with:
14. List three students who most need friends:

Additional modules deal with how students can help prevent bullying and get help.

Resources

The following sources provide access to relevant research, tools, and materials for school-based practitioners wishing to develop bullying prevention and intervention programs in their settings.

Avoid violence: Try mediation. Provided by Youth in Action, National Youth Network. http://sadonline.com/campaign/mediation.

ERIC/CASS Virtual Library on Bullying in School. ERIC Clearinghouse on Counseling & Students Services. http://ericcass.uncg.edu/virtuallib/bullying

ERIC Digest. *Bullying in schools.* (1997). http://www.ed.gov/databases/ERIC_Digests

Dr. Rigby's Bullying Pages. http://www.education.unisa.edu.au. This site also leads to comprehensive resources for both educators and school-based mental health practitioners looking for intervention strategies specific to the needs of their school's population.

Olweus Bullying Prevention. http://www.modelprograms.samhsa.gov/print.

Other Suggested Resources

The no-blame approach. This is a nonpunitive approach to dealing with bully/victim problems in schools. Generally considered to be more appropriate for use in primary schools.

Method of shared concern. This is another nonpunitive approach to bullying. Has been used successfully worldwide.

Mindmatters. A service aimed at promoting the mental health of high school students; it includes a program that addresses the issue of bullying and how it can be countered by schools.

A manual for schools and communities. This manual, provided by the California Department of Education, is comprehensive in its coverage of bullying in schools and is highly instructive.

Key Points to Remember

We conclude with the caveat that the research on the effectiveness of antibullying interventions is not strong. Rigby (2002) points out that the interventions *do* work, but not as effectively as one would hope. It is not clear, given that most interventions are multilayered, which component counts most for positive outcome. We have reviewed the most well-researched, evidence-based interventions: involvement of all the stakeholders in a school, prevention through life skills curricula, problem-solving approaches and those that focus on rules and consequences. Two factors emerge with clarity: (1) the exact components of the program do not matter as much as the quality and thoroughness with which the interventions are implemented; and (2) given the potentially severe consequences of bullying, it is a moral imperative to continue to implement such programs and to formulate and revise the programs based on solid evidence.

References

Banks, R. (1997). *Bullying in schools.* ERIC Digest. Champaign, IL: ERIC Clearinghouse on Elementary and Early Childhood Education.

Bowen, N. K. (1999). A role for school social workers in promoting success through school–family partnerships. *Social Work in Education, 21,* 34–47.

Coloroso, B. (2003). *The bully, the bullied, and the bystander.* New York: HarperResource.

Cowie, H., & Sharp, S. (1996). *Peer counselling in schools: A time to listen.* London: David Fulton.

Coy, D. R. (2001). *Bullying.* ERIC/CASS Digest. Greensboro, NC: ERIC Clearinghouse on Counseling and Student Services.

Fraser, M. W., Richman, J. M., & Galinsky, M. J. (1999). Risk, protection, and resilience: Toward a conceptual framework for social work practice. *Social Work Research, 23,* 131–143.

Haymes, E., Howe, E., & Peck, L. (2003). Whole school violence prevention program: A university–public school collaboration. *Children and Schools, 25,* 121–127.

Haynie, D. L., Nansel, T., Eitel, P., Crump, A. D., Saylor, K., Yu, K., & Simons-Morton, B. (2001). Bullies, victims, and bully/victims: Distinct groups of at-risk youth. *Journal of Early Adolescence, 21*(1), 29–49.

Nansel, T. R., Overpeck, M., Pilla, R. S., Ruan, W. J., Simons-Morton, S., & Scheidt, S. (2001). Bully behaviors among U.S. youth: Prevalence and association with psychosocial adjustment. *Journal of the American Medical Association, 285,* 2094–2100

Olweus, D. (1993). *Bullying at school: What we know and what we can do.* Cambridge, MA: Blackwell.

Rigby, K. (2000). Effects of peer victimisation in schools and perceived social support on adolescent well-being. *Journal of Adolescence 23,* 57–68.

Rigby, K. (2002). *A meta-evaluation of methods and approaches to reducing bullying in pre-schools and in early primary school in Australia.* Canberra, Australia: Commonwealth Attorney General's Department.

Smith, P. K., Ananiadou, K., & Cowie, H. (2003). Interventions to reduce school bullying. *Canadian Journal of Psychiatry, 48,* 591–599.

Young, S., & Holdorf, G. (2003). Using solution focused brief therapy in individual referrals for bullying. *Educational Psychology in Practice, 19*(4), 271–282.

An Evidence-Based Approach to Management of Students Who Wish to Harm Others

James K. Nash

Getting Started

This chapter describes an evidence-based approach to management of physical aggression in elementary and middle school students. Drawing from a public health prevention framework, the chapter presents strategies for *selective* intervention (also known as early intervention) with this population (Mrazek & Haggerty, 1994). Selective intervention targets students who display elevated levels of aggression relative to the general population of same-age students, but who do not display a level of aggression that calls for intensive treatment. In contrast, universal intervention (or primary prevention) targets all students in a school regardless of risk status, and indicated intervention (treatment) targets students who have a specific problem or diagnosis (e.g., conduct disorder). Other chapters of this volume describe universal and indicated intervention, as well as strategies for crisis intervention. It is useful to note that many programs suitable for selective intervention can also be used in primary prevention and treatment.

Evidence-based practice includes a focus on the research base of intervention. However, the term *evidence based* has a broader meaning (Gambrill, 2003). Evidence refers not only to research results regarding the effectiveness of interventions. It refers to consumer preferences and clinical wisdom. It refers to research-based knowledge of risk and protective factors and of the processes that lead to, and inhibit, a problem such as aggression. Evidence also refers to knowledge of characteristics that are unique to a particular child, family, school, or community, and to information about the influence of cultural differences. In sum, evidence-based practice is a collaborative process between practitioners and consumers in which all of these types of evidence are used to guide practice (Fraser & Galinsky, 2004).

What We Know

Understanding Student Aggression: An Overview

Aggressive behavior by students has serious consequences for individuals and schools. Victims experience physical injury and, potentially, psychological trauma. Student aggression disrupts the learning and social climate of schools and classrooms (Small & Tetrick, 2001). For perpetrators, elevated levels of aggression in elementary or middle school represent a potent risk factor for future chronic aggressive behavior, academic failure and dropout, delinquency, and substance use (Dodge & Pettit, 2003).

The rate of all aggressive acts (including simple assault) in schools fell slightly during the 1990s, from 48 per 100,000 students in 1992 to 43 per 100,000 in 1998. The reduction in rates has accelerated in this century. Rates in 2000 and 2001 were, respectively, 26 and 28 per 100,000 students. Rates of more serious types of violence (e.g., rape and aggravated assault) remained stable—at about 10 per 100,000 students—during the 1990s, although a reduction occurred by 2000 and 2001 (5 and 6 per 100,000 students, respectively). Students' perceptions of school safety also changed during this period. In 1995, 12% of students reported being afraid at school, compared with 6% in 2001 (DeVoe et al., 2003; Small & Tetrick, 2001).

Reduction in rates of student aggression is good news, to be sure. Nevertheless, ongoing attention to selective intervention is warranted. Urban schools and schools predominantly serving students of color continue to experience higher levels of student aggression compared to majority culture, suburban, and rural schools. A higher percentage of students report being afraid in the former types of schools (DeVoe et al., 2003). Moreover, rates of aggression aimed at teachers remained stable over the past several years. In 1993–1994, 10% of teachers reported being threatened with injury by a student, and 4% reported being physically attacked. Rates in 1999–2000 were 9% for threats and 4% for attacks (DeVoe et al., 2003).

Accessing and Using Evidence

School social workers are well situated to build on the gains of the past decade and to meet ongoing challenges associated with student aggression through evidence-based selective intervention. Although many programs aimed at managing student aggression have not undergone evaluation (Flannery et al., 2003), evidence of the effectiveness of a growing number of programs is available. Web-based resources that describe in detail the available evidence—and how to use evidence critically—appear in Table 43.1. Terms for categorizing programs (e.g., "proven" vs. "model") differ across Web sites, but criteria for assessing the research base of programs are consistent with those identified by Rones and Hoagwood (2000).

A Web site that may be of particular interest to school social workers is that of the Collaborative for Academic, Social, and Emotional Learning (CASEL). The site provides details (e.g., research base, target) of school-based programs that can be used as selective intervention. It also contains a book chapter that provides a rationale for school-based interventions aimed at promoting social and emotional competence in students as a means of increasing academic achievement. The Web site of the Campbell Collaboration (CC) may come to serve as a gold standard for providing evidence of program effectiveness (Gambrill, 2003). The CC includes representatives of social welfare and educational agencies and universities in the United States and abroad. Of note, the CC reviews are described as comprehensive and systematic, and they cover published and unpublished studies.

In addition to information on the research base of programs, a number of Web sites in Table 43.1 provide other content needed for evidence-based selective intervention. For example, the site of the Office of Juvenile Justice and Delinquency Prevention (OJJDP) and the report on youth violence by the U.S. surgeon general describe research into the nature, causes, and consequences of student aggression. This information can help practitioners and consumers understand how individual and environmental factors interact over time to influence students' use of aggression. Such knowledge guides selection of a suitable program or set of programs (Fraser & Galinsky, 2004; Fraser, Kirby, & Smokowski, 2004). A Web-accessible report published by the U.S. Department of Education (DOE) describes various research designs and their strengths and limitations. Practitioners can use the DOE report as a guide for assessing critically the quality of research on program effectiveness.

Research-based information about factors that contribute to student aggression and about the effectiveness of interventions is a key component of evidence-based practice. However, other types of information are needed. Fraser and Galinsky (2004) emphasized the importance of integrating research-based information about risk, protection, and intervention programs with knowledge of *local conditions*, such as the student and staff profile of a school or neighborhood characteristics. Additionally, knowledge of how risk and protective factors operate differently across cultural, racial, and gender subgroups is essential when selecting an approach. These issues highlight a need to identify characteristics of the target population and samples (e.g., European American males, Latina girls) that were included in the available research. For example, a proven program aimed at reducing aggression may be unsuitable for rural students if the program was developed and tested only in urban schools. Programs developed and tested solely with European American students may lack effectiveness with—or harm—students of color (Bernal & Scharrón-Del-Río, 2001). The Web site of the Substance Abuse and Mental Health Services Administration (SAMHSA) provides details of the target population and samples of the studies of many of the intervention programs listed on the site.

What We Can Do

Evidence-Based Selective Intervention

Goals of selective intervention with students who display elevated levels of aggression include protecting students and teachers from harm, improving school and classroom culture, preventing inappropriate special education placement, and preventing future aggression. Many selective intervention programs include a focus on increasing students' social and emotional competence, which has been linked to improved academic achievement (Zins, Bloodworth, Weissberg, & Walberg, 2004).

Ecological Focus

Attention to the broad ecology of childhood is likely to result in more successful outcomes for selective intervention with this population (Fraser et al., 2004). For example, referral of a family to community resources is a feasible strategy in many schools. Individual-focused selective intervention programs can also be delivered within a context of comprehensive primary prevention that targets the whole school (Greenberg et al., 2003).

Intervention Steps

Evidence-based selective intervention with students who display elevated levels of aggression requires completing a series of related steps:

- conducting screening and assessment
- developing an intervention plan
- implementing the plan and evaluating the effects of the intervention

There is nothing new about the steps themselves; they are central to social work practice. However, there are specific guidelines for completing the steps in a manner that is consistent with an evidence-based approach (see, e.g., Fraser & Galinsky, 2004)

Conducting Screening and Assessment

Selective intervention begins with *screening* to identify a pool of students who may be displaying problematic levels of aggression. Screening leads to an individualized *assessment* of a particular student and his or her environment to determine whether selective intervention is warranted and to identify salient risk and protective factors that are amenable to change. Assessment should also identify students who are in immediate need of more intensive treatment. Screening and assessment

often involve the use of established measures and procedures with demonstrated reliability and validity (see, e.g., Williams, Ayers, Van Dorn, & Arthur, 2004). However, existing procedures that track students' behavior (e.g., behavior referrals) can be a valuable sources of information. Assessment should always occur in collaboration with the family and teacher to develop a shared understanding of why, when, and under what circumstances a student becomes aggressive.

Tools and Practice Examples

Develop a Plan

Assessment-based knowledge of the child–environment system is linked with knowledge of risk and protective processes and available programs to develop an individualized intervention plan. An intervention plan should begin with a statement of desired short-term outcomes (e.g., reduced exposure to risk, increased availability of protective factors) and long-term outcomes (e.g., reduced use of aggression). The plan should specify the program or programs that have been selected to bring about these outcomes, and it should detail procedures for tracking progress toward targeted outcomes.

The Web sites listed in Table 43.1 are sources for assessing the quality of research-based evidence about risk, protection, and intervention in the area of student aggression. As practitioners, family members, and teachers evaluate the evidence available from these and other sources, they can use the following questions (Fraser & Galinsky, 2004; Fraser et al., 2004) to guide decision making about an intervention plan for a particular student:

- What individual and environmental risk factors are known to increase the likelihood of aggression in students who are similar to this student? Are any of these risk factors present for this student and, if so, which ones? Are the risk factors amenable to change via intervention?
- To what extent is there a shared understanding among the family and the student, the worker, the teacher, and others, that these risk factors are important?
- Is there evidence of protective factors that can modify the effects of risk for students similar to

this student? Do these protective factors exist, or can they be developed, for this student?

- Is there evidence that particular intervention strategies or programs are effective in reducing risk or building protection for students who are similar to this student? How strong is the evidence? What are the characteristics of the students (classrooms, communities, families) with whom the program or strategy was developed and tested?
- Is the strategy or program acceptable to the family and the child? Is it feasible given the unique situation of this student at this school? Are there disadvantages to its use (e.g., labeling, cost, disruption of a student's schedule or classroom climate)?
- To what extent is the program or strategy specified? Is a manual or guide available that spells out exactly what to do and how to adapt the program when this is desirable?
- Does the available evidence identify commonly used programs or strategies that do not work or that may be harmful?

Select an Evidence-Based Program

As Table 43.1 clearly shows, there is an abundance of research-based evidence on programs that can be used as selective intervention for student aggression. Recent literature (e.g., Greenberg et al., 2003) has summarized much of the evidence and provided general conclusions to guide the process of using the literature to develop an intervention plan:

- Many effective programs include a focus on skill building (e.g., problem-solving skills, peer interaction skills) as a means of promoting social and emotional competence and reducing aggression in students.
- Detailed manuals or curricula that specify exactly what to do are essential elements of many effective programs.
- Where possible, long-term programs—those continuing over 1 or more academic years—are generally considered more effective than short-term programs.
- Primary prevention programs that target an entire classroom or school, for example, by providing skills training to all students, developing schoolwide rules and contingencies for positive behavior, or strengthening the instructional practices of teachers, produce better

outcomes than do programs that focus solely on changing a particular student.
- Some effective school-based programs include a focus on family factors, for example, promoting a positive family atmosphere or building parenting skills.

Warnings: Identifying a particular student as being "at risk" carries with it a potential for labeling, and this can harm the student (Dodge & Pettit, 2003). Thus, screening should not occur in the absence of safeguards against such harm. One such example of a safeguard is to provide consultation to teachers and other school staff. A related concern involves delivering selective intervention to multiple students who display increased levels of aggression. Interventions to groups consisting solely of aggressive students has been shown to lead to negative rather than positive outcomes (see, e.g., Dishion, McCord, & Poulin, 1999).

Implement the Program

During program implementation there should be an emphasis on maintaining and tracking treatment fidelity—that is, implementing the program as it is intended—and on tracking progress toward short- and long-term outcomes. Descriptions of model programs at the SAMHSA Web site (see Table 43.1) include a section on fidelity, but this does not typically describe how to track fidelity or a student's level of exposure to the program. Manualized programs may include materials for tracking fidelity. When these are not available, simple forms can be developed to gather this information. Procedures for tracking fidelity can be burdensome, but this is a key element in being able to demonstrate the effectiveness of the program.

Tracking progress toward short- and long-term outcomes is another key process. A single-subject design is suitable for most situations (see, e.g., Abell & Hudson, 2000). Practitioners, families, students, and teachers should reach a shared decision about which outcomes to track. There should be an emphasis on using established, culturally relevant, and user-friendly measures of risk and protective factors and aggression. Ideally, an evaluation plan will also emphasize outcomes with high ecological validity for which data are already being collected. For example, students who have problems with aggression may receive referrals to the office because of their behavior.

Table 43.1 Web Resources for Selective Intervention

Site and Sponsor	URL	Content
Collaborative for Academic, Social, and Emotional Learning (CASEL). A collaborative of scholars and others from universities, institutes, and advocacy groups (including Penn State University, University of Illinois at Chicago).	www.casel.org	The site includes conceptual material that develops an argument for the importance of promoting social and emotional learning as a means of promoting academic achievement (i.e., the central mission of schools). It includes information on model and promising programs. *Safe and sound: An education leader's guide to evidence-based social and emotional learning (SEL) Programs* is available at the site. There is an emphasis on comprehensive (e.g., schoolwide) approaches and universal prevention, but many of the reviewed programs are likely to be useful as selective interventions.
The Campbell Collaboration. Domestic and international agencies and universities (e.g., University of Pennsylvania, Swedish Council for Social Research, UK Home Office).	www.campbellcollaboration.org	This site contains systematic reviews of research on educational, social, psychological, and criminological interventions. A number of these are suitable as selective interventions for managing student aggression. Currently, a limited number of reviews are available, and many more are listed as under way but not yet accessible via the Web.
Office of Juvenile Justice and Delinquency Prevention (OJJDP), U.S. Department of Justice	www.ojjdp.ncjrs.org	This Web site includes content on the prevalence of delinquency including aggressive acts, on research into the causes and consequences of delinquency, and on effective prevention strategies. Many OJJDP publications on topics of interest (e.g., school violence, creating safe schools) are available as PDF files for download. The authors of OJJDP publications are often top scholars in a particular field.
U.S. surgeon general's report on youth violence. U.S. Department of Health and Human Services (2001).	www.surgeongeneral.gov/library/youthviolence	This report is available in its entirety or in sections as a PDF file. Chapter 5 describes demonstrated and promising programs, some of which can be used as selective interventions in schools. It also identifies programs that do not work.
Identifying and implementing educational practices supported by rigorous evidence: A user friendly guide. U.S. Department of Education (December 2003).	www.ed.gov/rschstat/research/pubs/rigorousevid/rigorousevid.pdf	This report provides a definition of evidence-based practice and presents guidelines that practitioners can use to assess the quality of research on program effectiveness. It as available as a PDF file.
Substance Abuse and Mental Health Services Administration (SAMHSA)	http://www.modelprograms.samhsa.gov	The SAMHSA Web site provides details (e.g., target, elements, costs, research base) of *model*, *effective*, and *promising* programs, many of which are suitable for

(continued)

Table 43.1 (*Continued*)

Site and Sponsor	URL	Content
Model Programs, U.S. Department of Health and Human Services		selective intervention. Of note, program descriptions include information on tracking fidelity and on characteristics (e.g., race/ethnicity, urban) of the samples with whom the reviewed programs were developed and tested. Program summaries with details are available to download as PDF files.
Center for the Study and Prevention of Violence. University of Colorado	www.colorado.edu.cspv/blueprints	The "Blueprints" section of this site distinguishes model and promising violence prevention programs and describes the scope (i.e., universal, selective, or indicated), content, outcomes, and costs of programs. It summarizes the types and results of research studies on effectiveness. The site identifies other Web sites on evidence-based practice, as well as the criteria these sites use to evaluate practices.
Promising Practices Network on Children, Families, and Communities. Private foundations and institutes including Annie E. Casey and Packard Foundations, and Rand Corporation	www.promisingpractices.net	The programs described at this site target a wide variety of child and family domains, and many appear to be best suited as universal interventions. Some programs may be useful as selective interventions for managing student aggression.
What Works Clearinghouse, U.S. Department of Education	www.w-w-c.org	This site aims to serve as a central source of information on science-based education programs, some of which target social and emotional competence. The project is, apparently, in development, but it promises to be a useful resource in the future.

Many schools keep track of such referrals. Thus, indicators of progress may be the number of referrals and, relatedly, the amount of time spent outside class because of behavior.

Key Points to Remember

An evidence-based approach to selective intervention with students who display elevated levels of aggression requires using different types of information from a variety to sources to develop and implement a plan that fits the circumstances of a particular school. Research-based information about the processes that lead to aggression and about effective intervention programs is at the heart of an evidence-based approach. Equally important is information about local conditions and cultural differences, clinical wisdom, and collaboration between families and school staff. Finally, recent research clearly indicates that combining a focus on identified students with attention to the broader environment in which these students function is likely to result in more positive outcomes.

References

Abell, N., & Hudson, W. W. (2000). Pragmatic applications of single-case and groups designs in social work practice evaluation and research. In P. Allen-Meares & C. Garvin (Eds.), *The handbook of social work direct practice* (pp. 535–550). Thousand Oaks, CA: Sage.

Bernal, G., & Scharrón-Del-Río, M. R. (2001). Are empirically supported treatments valid for ethnic minorities? Toward an alternative approach for treatment research. *Cultural Diversity and Ethnic Minority, 7,* 328–342.

DeVoe, J. F., Peter, K., Kaufman, P., Ruddy, S. A., Miller, A. K., Planty, M., Snyder, T. D., & Rand, M. R. *Indicators of school crime and safety: 2003* (NCES 2004–004/NCJ 201257). Washington, DC: U.S. Departments of Education and Justice. Retrieved April 1, 2004, from http://nces.ed.gov/pubs2004/2004004.pdf

Dishion, T. J., McCord, J., & Poulin, F. (1999). When interventions harm: Peer groups and problem behavior. *American Psychologist, 54,* 755–764.

Dodge, K. A., & Pettit, G. S. (2003). A biopsychosocial model of the development of chronic conduct problems in adolescence. *Developmental Psychology, 39,* 349–371.

Flannery, D. J., Liau, A. K., Powell, K. E., Vesterdal, W., Vazsonyi, A. T., Guo, S., Atha, H., & Embry, D. (2003). Initial behavior outcomes for the Peace-Builders universal school-based violence prevention program. *Developmental Psychology, 39,* 292–308.

Fraser, M. W., & Galinsky, M. J. (2004). Risk and resilience in childhood: Toward an evidence-based model of practice. In M. W. Fraser (Ed.), *Risk and resilience in childhood: An ecological perspective* (2nd ed., pp. 385–402). Washington, DC: NASW Press.

Fraser, M. W., Kirby, L. D., & Smokowski, P. R. (2004). Risk and resilience in childhood. In M. W. Fraser (Ed.), *Risk and resilience in childhood: An ecological perspective* (2nd ed., pp. 13–66). Washington, DC: NASW Press.

Gambrill, E. (2003). Evidence-based practice: Sea change of the emperor's new clothes? *Journal of Social Work Education, 39,* 3–23.

Greenberg, M. T., Weissberg, R. P., O'Brien, M. U., Zins, J. E., Fredericks, L., Resnik, H., & Elias, M. J. (2003). Enhancing school-based prevention and youth development through coordinated social, emotional, and academic learning. *American Psychologist, 58,* 466–474.

Mrazek, P. J., & Haggerty, R. J. (1994). *Reducing risks for mental disorders: Frontiers for preventive intervention research.* Washington, DC: National Academy Press.

Rones, M., & Hoagwood, K. (2000). School-based mental health services: A research review. *Clinical Child and Family Psychology Review, 3,* 223–240.

Small, M., & Tetrick, K. (2001). School violence: An overview. *Juvenile Justice, 8*(1), 3–12. Washington, DC: U.S. Department of Justice, Office of Juvenile Justice and Delinquency Prevention. Retrieved April 1, 2004, from http://www.ncjrs.org/pdffiles1/ojjdp/188158.pdf

Williams, J. H., Ayers, C., Van Dorn, R., & Arthur, M. (2004). Risk and protective factors in the development of delinquency and conduct disorder. In M. W. Fraser (Ed.), *Risk and resilience in childhood: An ecological perspective* (2nd ed., pp. 209–249). Washington, DC: NASW Press.

Zins, J. E., Bloodworth, M. R., Weissberg, R. P., & Walberg, H. J. (2004). The scientific base linking social and emotional learning to school success. In J. Zins, R. Weissberg, M. Wang, & H. Walberg (Eds.), *Building academic success on social and emotional learning: What does the research say?* (pp. 3–22). New York: Teachers College Press.

Peer Conflict

Effective Resolution Strategies

Debra J. Woody

Getting Started

Extreme acts of violence in schools across the country have increased interest in school-based conflict resolution programs over the last 5 years. Fortunately, such horrendous violence as the acts that occurred at Columbine High School are relatively rare. However, these situations have advanced our understanding of the effects that unresolved conflicts can have on students, teachers, and the school environment and have brought to light the more common, chronic, less extreme acts of violence that occur daily at many school campuses. These chronic acts of violence occur in the form of verbal threats, cursing, name calling, insults, racial slurs, pushing, grabbing or shoving, punching or kicking, and fighting (Bastian & Taylor, 1991; Opotow, 1989). School-based conflict resolution programs have been developed to provide students with skills to better handle, manage, and resolve conflict and to teach and promote tolerance and acceptance among students and school personnel.

What We Know

Research reports on the effects of school-based conflict resolution programs have been positive throughout the literature of social work and other mental health professions. Results from these empirical investigations indicate that teaching conflict resolution skills to students increases their knowledge of nonviolent means to conflict resolution (Johnson, Johnson, Dudley, Mitchell, & Fredrickson, 1997; Woody, 2001), promotes the development of a more positive attitude about nonviolent

conflict resolution methods (Dudley, Johnson, & Johnson, 1996; Stevahn, Johnson, Johnson, & Laginski, 1996), increases students' ability to apply nonviolent methods (Johnson, Johnson, Dudley, Mitchell, et al., 1997; Stevahn, Johnson, Johnson, & Laginski, 1996; Woody, 2001), reduces the frequency of violent confrontations in the schools (DuRant, Treiber, Getts, & McCloud, 1996; Johnson, Johnson, & Dudley, 1992; Stevahn, Johnson, Johnson, Green, & Laginski, 1997), and has a positive effect on the overall school climate (Burrell, Zirbel, & Allen, 2003). Some students have transferred the skills learned in conflict resolution to nonclassroom and nonschool settings (Johnson, Johnson, Dudley, Ward, & Magnuson, 1995). These outcomes were true regardless of the age group targeted in the conflict resolution program.

School-based conflict resolution programs are also recognized as cost effective (Batton, 2003). In one report, a cost-benefit analysis compared the cost of a statewide conflict resolution program to the cost of school detentions, expulsions, in-school suspensions, Saturday schools, and other types of disciplinary actions. The cost of the conflict resolution program was less than one fourth the cost of the disciplinary programs.

What We Can Do

In selecting a conflict resolution program, it is helpful to know the characteristics of programs that have been found most effective. Several key ingredients found in successful conflict resolution programs are summarized in Box 44.1 (Dusenbury, Falco, Lake, Brannigan, & Bosworth, 1997).

Other investigators suggest several factors characteristic of ineffective violence prevention programs (Dusenbury et al., 1997). They warn that programs with these characteristics (presented in Box 44.2) may actually increase aggressive behavior.

One last consideration about effective conflict resolution programs is that they are often based on

Box 44.1 Key Components of Successful Conflict Resolution Programs

1. A comprehensive approach that includes family, peers, media, and the community (including the school community)
2. Programs that begin in kindergarten or first grade and are reinforced across the school years
3. Programs that go beyond violence prevention to include conflict resolution skills
4. Programs appropriate for the developmental level of the students targeted
5. Programs that teach students how to manage conflict instead of how to eliminate all conflict
6. Program content that promotes personal and social competencies
7. Interactive techniques that use group work, cooperative learning, discussion, and role plays or behavioral rehearsal to develop personal and social skills.
8. Program content that includes materials that are culturally sensitive to groups represented in the student body
9. Programs that include teacher training and development
10. Programs designed to promote effective classroom management strategies, including good and effective discipline and positive control in the classroom
11. Programs that include activities that foster norms against violence, aggression, and bullying
12. An approach that teaches *all* students—not just a select few—how to resolve conflicts

Adapted from Johnson & Johnson (1995), "Why violence prevention programs don't work and what does." *Educational Leadership, 52*(5), 63–68. Reprinted with permission. The Association for Supervision and Curriculum Development is a worldwide community of educators advocating sound policies and sharing best practices to achieve the success of each learner. To learn more, visit ASCD policies at www.ascd.org. Also adapted from Dusenbury, Falco, Lake, Brannigan, & Bosworth (1997), "Nine critical elements of promising violence prevention programs." *Journal of School Health, 76*(10), 409–414. With the permission of Blackwell Publishers.

Box 44.2 Six Elements of Ineffective Conflict Resolution Programs

1. Using scare tactics
2. Adding a violence prevention program to a school system that is already overwhelmed
3. Segregating aggressive students into a separate group for any purpose
4. Programs that are too brief and not supported by a positive school environment
5. Programs that focus only on self-esteem enhancement
6. Programs that only provide information

Adapted from Dusenbury, Falco, Lake, Brannigan, & Bosworth (1997, pp. 413–414). With the permission of Blackwell Publishers.

social learning theory, attribution theory, and anger replacement therapy, with specific curriculum content related to these theories included in the program. The essential content areas that should be included are listed in Box 44.3.

In addition to the elements and specific content included in conflict resolution programs, there are several different types of conflict resolution programs identified in the literature. In one approach, for example, conflict resolution material is infused into regular academic teaching materials (see, for example, Stevahn, Johnson, Johnson, Green, et al., 1997; Stevahn, Johnson, Johnson, & Laginski, 1996). In another approach, conflict resolution skills are taught to a select group of students who become peer mediators (see for example, Johnson, Johnson, Dudley, Ward, & Mag-

Box 44.3 Successful Content Areas

1. Information about the negative consequences of violence for the perpetrator as well as victims, friends, family members, and others
2. Anger management skills that teach self-control
3. Social perspective taking, which teaches students that others often have a different, equally valid, and less anger-producing perspective on the same situation
4. Decision-making and problem-solving skills
5. Active listening and effective communication skills
6. Courtesy, compassion, caring, and respect for others, with content that focuses on prejudice, sexism, and male–female relationships

nuson, 1995). And in other programs, groups of students identified as "high risk" were targeted to receive conflict resolution training (see, for example, DuRant et al., 1996; Paschall & Flewelling, 1997). However, the more comprehensive the program, the more the aspects of successful programs identified above can be included in the program.

Tools and Practice Example

A Comprehensive Conflict Resolution Model

In this section I'll present an example of a comprehensive school-based conflict resolution approach, constructed and used by two social workers in an alternative high school setting. The identified school is a relatively small high school with an average enrollment of about 350 students. The school provides a nontraditional academic environment to high school students who have performed poorly in a regular high school setting. Most students are referred to the alternative school by counselors at their home school. Although the focus for referral to the alternative school is academics, for most of these students, poor school performance is symptomatic of interpersonal and psychosocial difficulties; many have problems caused by substance abuse, truancy, lack of family support, abuse, homelessness, or poverty. In addition, some of the students are pregnant or have children. After referral, most students attend the school for the remainder of their high school years. A smaller number return to their home campus after they are able to reach their identified grade level. Thus, students enter and exit the school at various points in their academic process. Many support services, including social work services, are available to students at the school.

Before the conflict resolution program was started, conflict between students and acts of violence were typical of that described in the literature. These occurred regularly, ranging from verbal threats to physical confrontation. As is also typical, when friction arose between students prior to the presence of mental health services on the campus, they were told to ignore it or to "just get over it." When social workers were initially added to the school program, most disputes between students were referred to the social workers for resolution. For more severe acts of violence, such as fighting, students were ejected from the school.

The social workers described this type of reactive referral and intervention structure as time consuming and ineffective. They spent a great portion of their day helping students resolve conflicts. This was problematic given the many other existing psychosocial needs evident in the student body. Although many students were helped in the resolution of conflicts, relatively few students were actually learning how to resolve conflicts on their own, so many repeat referrals were received. This approach did not reduce the number of conflicts occurring in the school. Thus, the social workers developed a more extensive conflict resolution program.

Structure of the Conflict Resolution Program

Unique to the conflict resolution program developed in this high school is the comprehensive approach to program structure. With the support of the principal, the plan was to create a systematic conflict resolution process. The plan included the two aspects of comprehensive programs called for in the literature. First, it was schoolwide: all students, staff, administrators, and faculty were required to receive the conflict resolution training. Second, the training and intervention process continued throughout the school year.

Phase 1

The first phase was to provide training to all students currently enrolled. Twenty students were randomly pulled out of selected classes to attend a 4-hour group training session run by the social workers. The sessions continued until all students had received the training.

Phase 2

In the next phase, all school personnel, including administrators, staff members, and teachers, received the same conflict resolution training. They received the training as a group, in a 2-hour, in-service conference. In addition to the conflict resolution skills presented to the students, the school personnel received instruction on how to integrate the conflict resolution process into the school day. Teachers were instructed to remind students to use their skills when they observed a conflict between students. If the teacher needed to intervene in the situation, he or she was to use the conflict resolution model to help the students express their feelings, concerns, and so on and move toward resolution. If the conflict could not be resolved with the teacher's help, the teachers were instructed to refer students to social work services while the conflict was still in progress. Teachers were also instructed on how to use the conflict resolution and negotiation skills if they had a direct conflict with a student, another teacher, an administrator, and so on.

Phase 3

Phase 3 was the ongoing, follow-up training process. During homeroom, teachers reviewed a particular concept presented in the initial conflict resolution training and guided student discussion on it. For example, during one homeroom period, the definition of "I" messages was reviewed, and students were reminded to use this type of message when expressing feelings. These review sessions continued daily throughout the entire school year.

The following summer (and every summer thereafter), the social workers provided the conflict resolution program to new incoming students as part of a mandated half-day school orientation.

As additional new students enroll during the school year, the conflict resolution training is provided. Similarly, all new staff and faculty members are trained in the conflict resolution model. During the school year, all students receive "boosters" of the conflict resolution skills in homeroom classes. In addition, teachers continue to remind students to use their conflict resolution skills when they observe a conflict between students, and unresolved conflicts are referred to the social work staff for continued mediation and negotiation.

▓ Curriculum Components and Content

The social workers who created this program also developed the curriculum that they used, and there is empirical support for the effectiveness of their curriculum (see Woody, 2001). However, several other established conflict resolution curricula have empirical evidence supporting their effectiveness. Some of these are listed in the Resources section of this chapter. Consistent with other conflict resolution training, the overall focus of the conflict resolution training used by the

social workers in this program is enhancing communication and supplying students with a set of conflict resolution skills that they can use to successfully negotiate conflict situations. The specific content used by the social workers includes many of the areas identified in Box 44.3 as critical in effective conflict resolution curriculum. The social workers use a participatory, experiential format, which includes a significant number of role plays, exercises, and work sheets. The emphasis is on self-exploration and skill comprehension.

Phase 1: Styles and Definition of Conflict

Students are asked for a definition of conflict, and using Worksheet 44.1 below, students are instructed to think about a conflict they have had with another student and a conflict they have either observed or participated in with a teacher. Students are encouraged to talk about their answers and experiences. Next, students are asked to complete Worksheet 44.2, and these responses are also read aloud. Throughout the discussions during this phase, the social workers make several points:

1. Conflict is inevitable and is a part of life encounters and relationships.
2. The goal is to manage and negotiate conflict as opposed to avoiding conflict situations.
3. There are three basic responses to conflict: submission, aggression, and assertiveness.
4. How most individuals respond is directly and indirectly influenced by family and friends.

Phase 2: Personality Differences/Diversity

In phase 2 of the training discussion of various responses to conflict is continued, including a discussion of how values and personality type influence one's response in a given situation. The True Colors portrayal of personality (available at www.truecolors.org) is used for this discussion. Through various worksheets included in the True Colors package, students learn characteristics related to their personality type, how these personality characteristics are often viewed by others, and how differences in personality and perception not only contribute to conflict but often also influence how individuals often respond to conflict. For example, the students are asked about which

Worksheet 44.1

Remember a Conflict

Who was involved?

What was it about?

How did you respond?

When have you heard or had a conflict with another student? What was it about?

Teachers and students having conflict: What was it about?

---

personality color is characteristic of most teachers, and which color is characteristic of most high school students. Through this exchange, students are able to see that differences in values associated with personality (structure, rules, and organization versus fun, action, and entertainment) can result in conflict. This process often results in a revelation for many teachers as well.

Also emphasized in the training is that neither perspective is wrong or right, just different. To further illustrate this point, students participate in an exercise in which they are asked to respond to specific statements. For this exercise, signs that read either "strongly agree," "agree," "strongly disagree," or "disagree" are placed around the room. Students are instructed to place themselves in the section of the room underneath the sign that indicates their response to statements that are read aloud. Example statements include, "Females should always pay for themselves on a date," "Males should not cry or express feelings in public," "Condoms should be distributed in schools," and "Females who carry condoms are sluts." Stressed during this part of the process is

acceptance and appreciation for diverse opinions and values.

Phase 3: Communication and Negotiation Skills

In the last part of the training, specific communication and negotiation skills are taught and practiced by the students. These include themes around communication blocks, nonverbal communication, active listening, and communicating with "I" messages. Many worksheets and role plays are used to illustrate these concepts. Several examples are described below.

Example 1: Zip Your Zap

The two social workers involve themselves in a dialogue in front of the participants. The students are instructed to call out guesses identifying what the social workers are talking about. The social workers continue to talk together, but they occasionally throw out candy to a student who makes

Worksheet 44.2

Identifying Conflict Styles in Your Family			
	AVOID	CONFRONT	PROBLEM SOLVE
GRANDFATHER			
GRANDMOTHER			
MOM			
DAD			
BROTHER			
SISTER			
GIRLFRIEND			
BOYFRIEND			
AUNT			
UNCLE			
MYSELF			

a guess. This continues until someone correctly guesses that they are throwing candy to the third person who speaks, or until the set time limit is completed.

With this example, the students are able to describe their frustration and confusion as a result of not understanding what is occurring. These feelings are used by the social workers to discuss feelings about ineffective communication and times they are in an exchange with someone when the communication and intent are not clear. Also the point is made that individuals often end up in situations that they are confused about because they are unaware of or misread the communication exchange.

Example 2

Students are paired. One participant speaks while the other listens. Participants are required to stand during this exercise and are positioned in a way that those who speak have their backs to the social workers; only the listeners can clearly see the

adults. Once the dialogue begins between the student pairs, the social workers hold up a series of signs with instructions for the listening partner to follow. One sign instructs the partner to continually interrupt while the other student is talking. Another sign instructs the listener to ignore the speaker.

At the conclusion of the exercise, the social workers announce that they were holding up signs for the listeners to follow and ask the speaking partners to guess what the listeners were instructed to do. They are then asked how they felt during the exchange. The social workers iterate the irritation, dissatisfaction, disappointment, and so on that the students experienced when their partners presented poor listening skills.

The social workers use this exercise as a lead-in to describing in detail a pyramid of effective communication skills (advice giving, reassuring, asking open-ended questions, summarizing and clarifying) with advice giving at the bottom of the pyramid and empathy and reflective listening at the top. Students are then provided with the opportunity to take turns practicing these skills while the other partner articulates a concern. Students are encouraged to use empathy and reflective listening as much as possible. The participants then discuss what it was like to receive empathy and reflective listening and what it was like to offer support.

Example 3: Misfire

One volunteer from the group of students acts as the source of conflict and is placed in a chair in the middle of the room. The other students are usually already seated in a circle, so they surround the volunteer. The social workers create a scenario relevant to high school students. They might say, for example, that the student in the middle borrowed another student's car and returned it wrecked. Students are asked to consider what they would really say to this person if the car belonged to them. Each student is allowed to throw a crumpled piece of paper at the student in the middle of the circle and say what he or she would say to another in this type of conflict situation. After everyone has had a turn, the students are taught the skill of using "I"

messages in communication. Students are then given Worksheet 44.3.

Participants are asked again to respond to the scenario created under example 3, but this time to express their feelings and thoughts by completing the sentences provided in Worksheet 44.3. After students have had an opportunity to complete the sentences in writing, each participant reads his or her response to the group. Usually some participants have difficulty with this assignment and continue to use "you" statements. The social work facilitators point out the difficulty with making the transition from "you"-type blaming statements to "I" messages, and students who have difficulty with the assignment are encouraged to try again, sometimes with advice from other participants. The student volunteer is asked how each set of responses felt to him or her in an attempt to identify that the "I" messages were more tolerable than the blaming statements. Usually the student volunteer is also able to articulate that through the "I want or need" section of the sentence, they felt a resolution was possible.

A review of the concepts discussed during the training is used to wrap up the training session. Students are encouraged to use the "I"-message

---

Worksheet 44.3
_____

Using "I" Messages
Try not to use the word "You"

I feel _____

When _____

Because _____

I need or want _____

sentence to communicate effectively and to negotiate conflict situations.

Resources

Education World: www.education-world.com/a_curr/curr/71.shtm

National Service Learning Clearing House: www.servicelearning.org/wg-php/library/index.php?library-id=2655

PBS Teacher Resources: www.pbs.org/teachersource/whats_new/health/arr01.shtm

PeaceBuilders: www.peacebuilders.com/

Practitioner Assessment of Conflict Resolution Programs: www.ericdigest.org/2001–4/conflict.html

Teaching Students to Be Peacemakers: www.edubooks.com/Teaching_Students_to_be_Peacemakers_0939603225.html. D. Johnson and R. Johnson (1991), *Teaching students to be peacemakers*. Edna, MN: Interaction. www.-gigglepotz.com/peace.htm

Violence Prevention: https://secure.edc.org/publications/prodview.asp?656. D. Prothrow-Stith (1987), *Violence prevention curriculum for adolescents*. Newton, MA: Education Development Center.

Key Points to Remember

The conflict resolution program presented in this chapter continues to be effective for several reasons:

- The program is a comprehensive, schoolwide program. All students, faculty, and other school personnel receive the same conflict resolution training.
- The training continues throughout the school year.
- The conflict resolution model is used systematically throughout the school setting. When a conflict between students is observed, teachers and other school personnel prompt the students to use their conflict resolution skills.
- Teachers and administrators serve as role models to the students in that they use the conflict resolution skills in interactions with each other and with the students.

- Unresolved conflicts are referred to the social workers for continued mediation and negotiation.
- Students learn that conflict is inevitable but can be resolved.
- The conflict resolution training requires active, interactive participation by the participants.
- The content of the resolution training includes effective communication and empathy skills and appreciation for diversity.

The conflict resolution program described in this chapter was developed and implemented by two school social workers, Connie Grossman and Gary Grossman at Venture High School in Arlington, Texas. For further information about the program, write to cgrossma@aisd.net and ggrossma@aisd.net.

References

Bastian, L., & Taylor, B. (1991). *School crime: A national crime victimization survey report*. Washington, DC: Government Printing Office.

Batton, J. (2003). Cost-benefit analysis of CRE programs in Ohio. *Conflict Resolution Quarterly, 21*(1), 131–133.

Burrell, N., Zirbel, C., & Allen, M. (2003). Evaluating peer mediation outcomes in educational settings: A meta-analytic review. *Conflict Resolution Quarterly, 21*(1), 7–26.

Dudley, B., Johnson, D., & Johnson, R. (1996). Conflict-resolution training and middle school students' integrative negotiation behavior. *Journal of Applied Social Psychology, 26*(22), 2038–2052.

DuRant, R., Treiber, F., Getts, A., & McCloud, K. (1996). Comparison of two violence prevention curricula for middle school adolescents. *Journal of Adolescent Health, 19*(2), 111–117.

Dusenbury, L., Falco, M., Lake, A., Brannigan, R., & Bosworth, K. (1997). Nine critical elements of promising violence prevention programs. *Journal of School Health, 76*(10), 409–414.

Johnson, D., & Johnson, R. (1995). Why violence prevention programs don't work and what does. *Educational Leadership, 52*(5), 63–68.

Johnson, D., Johnson, R., & Dudley, B. (1992). Effects of peer mediation training on elementary school students. *Mediation Quarterly, 10*(1), 89–99.

Johnson, D., Johnson, R., Dudley, B., Mitchell, J., & Fredrickson, J. (1997). The impact of conflict resolution on middle school students. *Journal of Social Psychology, 137*(1) 11–21.

Johnson, D., Johnson, R., Dudley, B., Ward, M., & Magnuson, D. (1995). The impact of peer mediation training on the management of school and home conflicts. *American Educational Research Journal, 32*(4), 829–844.

Opotow, S. (1989). *The risk of violence: Peer conflicts in the lives of adolescents.* Paper presented at the annual meeting of the American Psychological Association, New Orleans.

Paschall, M., & Flewelling, R. (1997). Measuring intermediate outcomes of violence prevention programs targeting African-American male youth: An exploratory assessment of the psychometric properties of six psychosocial measures. *Health Education Research, 12*(1), 117–128.

Stevahn, L., Johnson, D., Johnson, R., Green, K., & Laginski, A. (1997). Effects on high school students of conflict resolution training integrated into English literature. *Journal of Social Psychology, 137*(3), 302–315.

Stevahn, L., Johnson, D., Johnson, R., & Laginski, A. (1996). Effects on high school students of integrating conflict resolution and peer mediation training into an academic unit. *Mediation Quarterly, 14*(1), 21–36.

Woody, D. (2001). A comprehensive school-based conflict resolution model. *Children and Schools, 23*(2), 115–123.

Using Social and Emotional Learning to Address Conflicts in the Classroom

Jacqueline A. Norris

Getting Started

At one time, classrooms in the United States had desks arranged in straight rows. The furniture was bolted to the floor, and the teacher's desk was on a raised platform in front of the room. Within this classroom the teacher lectured and the students spoke when they were spoken to, and when a student misbehaved, the consequences were often swift and severe (Ryan & Cooper, 2000).

It may seem as though this classroom was more fiction than reality, but it did exist. To many veteran teachers across the country, "those were the days." They long for the reverence in which teachers were once held. They believe that students today are disrespectful and lack discipline. The 35th annual PDK/Gallup Poll supports their belief. For 16 of the first 17 years that the poll was conducted, when asked, "What do you think are the biggest problems with which the public schools of your community must deal?" participants most commonly answered, "lack of discipline, more control" (Rose & Gallup, 2003). In fact, lack of discipline has never left the top 10 "biggest problems" over the 35-year history of the poll. A 2001 report on teacher turnover revealed that of teachers who left the field because of job dissatisfaction, 68% identified student discipline problems and lack of student motivation as their reason for leaving (Ingersoll, 2001). Obviously, lack of student discipline is a major concern for schools today.

With the emergence of constructivist theory and brain-based education, metaphors for the ways in which people learn have changed. No longer do we see students as empty vessels or blank slates that teachers must fill with knowledge. Now we know that students come to the classroom with a wide range of experiences and knowledge. Teachers who are able to recognize and help students make connections between their life experiences and new content are much more likely to help improve their students' academic achievement (National Research Council, 2000). This means that a different relationship must be established between teacher and student, one in which teachers know, accept, and understand their students and students trust and respect their teachers. Research shows that in classrooms where everyone feels accepted, valued, and affirmed, there are fewer conflicts, and when problems do arise they are resolved more amicably (Elias et al., 1997; Osterman, 2000; Blum, McNeely, & Rinehart, 2002; Frey & George-Nichols, 2003). What knowledge must a teacher have to establish such an environment, and what competences must students have in order to maintain it?

This chapter examines social and emotional learning (SEL) as an approach to building respectful and trusting relationships in the classroom. It will show how the school social worker or counselor and other school-based professionals can introduce SEL skills to a classroom, and how teachers can promote transference of these skills by integrating them into classroom management and instructional strategies.

What We Know

Social and Emotional Learning

SEL plays a critical role in creating the positive learning climate in many schools today. It grows out of the theory of *emotional intelligence* developed by Peter Salovey of Yale University and John

Mayer of University of New Hampshire in 1987. These two psychologists recognized that although emotions and rational thought are commonly thought to be at opposite ends of the thinking spectrum, there is a strong relationship between them. Daniel Goleman built upon their work and popularized the concept with the publication of his highly successful book *Emotional Intelligence: Why It Can Matter More Than IQ* (1995). Emotional intelligence (EQ) is a different way of being smart. Combining interpersonal and intrapersonal intelligence, two of the multiple intelligences identified by Gardner (1983), emotional intelligence refers to one's ability to know oneself and to know how one is feeling at any given time. It also means understanding and caring about others. The Collaborative for Academics Social and Emotional Learning (CASEL), a group of researchers and practitioners, looked at how schools play a critical role in disseminating and reinforcing these life skills. A book by members of the collaborative, *Promoting Social and Emotional Learning: Guidelines for Educators* (Elias et al., 1997), provides a list of skills necessary for emotional intelligence.

Key Skills in Social and Emotional Learning

Self-Awareness

- Recognizing and naming one's emotions
- Understanding the reasons for feeling as one does

Self-Regulation of Emotion

- Verbalizing and coping with anxiety, anger, and depression
- Controlling impulses, aggression, and self-destructive, antisocial behavior
- Recognizing strengths in and mobilizing positive feelings about self, school, family, and support networks

Self-Monitoring and Performance

- Focusing on tasks at hand
- Setting short- and long-term goals
- Modifying performance in light of feedback
- Mobilizing positive motivation

- Activating hope and optimism
- Working toward optimal performance states

Empathy and Perspective Taking

- Learning how to increase and develop feedback mechanisms for use in everyday life
- Becoming a good listener
- Increasing empathy and sensitivity to others' feelings
- Understanding others' perspectives, points of view, and feelings

Social Skills in Handling Relationships

- Managing emotions in relationships, harmonizing diverse feelings and viewpoints
- Expressing emotions effectively
- Exercising assertiveness, leadership, and persuasion
- Working as part of a team/cooperative learning group
- Showing sensitivity to social cues
- Exercising social decision-making and problem-solving skills
- Responding constructively and in a problem-solving manner to interpersonal obstacles

Though many educators see the importance of social skills in academic achievement, many do not know how or where to infuse instruction on social skills into their classrooms. Still others believe it is not the job of the school to teach these skills; they want children to come to school already knowing them. With the pressure of high-stakes testing and the mandates of No Child Left Behind, it is more critical than ever for classrooms to be nonthreatening, supportive, and caring. The ability to attend to academic content is directly influenced by the ability to manage emotional impulses (Salovey & Sluyter, 1997). "Researchers have found that prosocial behavior in the classroom is linked with positive intellectual outcomes (e.g., Diperna & Elliott, 1999; Feshbach & Feshbach, 1987; Haynes, Ben-Avie, & Ensign, 2003; Pasi, 2001) and is predictive of performance on standardized achievement tests (e.g., Cobb, 1972; Malecki & Elliott, 2002; Welsh, Park, Widaman, & O'Neil, 2001; Wentzel, 1993; Zins, Weissberg, Wang, & Walberg, 2004).

A recent study on managing disruptive student behavior found that effective practices for school social workers should focus not only on individual or group work but on "implementing systems change by collaborating, consulting, developing behavior plans, and training others to work with the difficult children in the context of a child's daily school experiences" (Frey & George-Nichols, 2003, p. 99). Following this train of thought, everything in the child's school environment needs to support efforts being made to change his or her behavior. Classrooms that promote the skills of social and emotional learning do not teach them just to those who appear to be lacking in them, but to all students. Everyone learns together about themselves and the people with whom they will interact. All students learn how to actively listen; how to communicate effectively, verbally and nonverbally; and how to resolve the conflicts and problems they face. Students come to see that their emotions are precursors to their actions and that controlling their emotions allows them to choose actions, especially in response to stressful situations, in a manner that preserves everyone's dignity.

As with all effective teaching, teaching these skills must proceed in an organized, well-planned, and purposeful way. Intentionality is critical because these are not just skills for occasional use; these are life skills. There is a difference between teaching a fact or concept and teaching a skill. A skill is performance based and thus requires rehearsal followed by feedback and more rehearsal (Gagne, 1965). By incorporating SEL into instructional methods, many more opportunities to rehearse can be given. As Elias et al. put this point (1997, p. 33), "It is most beneficial to provide a developmentally appropriate combination of formal, curriculum-based instruction with ongoing, informal, and infused opportunities to develop social and emotional skills from preschool through high schools."

What We Can Do

Though hundreds of packaged programs address the concept of SEL, there may be little need to purchase a program because SEL is more a philosophical approach than a program. As such, it permeates every aspect of one's life. It simply means that we treat people with respect, give them the opportunity to be responsible and caring individuals, and expect the same treatment from them. Therefore, as teachers develop their classroom management plans, discipline practices, lesson plans, and patterns of interaction between themselves and their students, SEL is an ever-present foundation. For those teachers who struggle with or may be unaware of the importance of addressing the social and emotional components of their class, the social worker or counselor can play a pivotal role in helping to create a true community of learning.

A list of programs appears at the end of this chapter for the reader to explore. What follows are tools and sample activities that represent the major components of the most effective SEL programs used in schools today (Collaborative for Academics Social and Emotional Learning [CASEL], 2003).

Tools and Practice Examples

Skills That Build Respectful and Trusting Relationships

Optimally, the time to start building respectful and trusting relationships is even before the students arrive on the first day of school. If activities are planned that allow students to begin to know each other, their likes and dislikes, their interests and the things that are important to them throughout the school year, commonalities and familiarities take root.

Class Meetings

The social worker, school counselor, or other mental health professional can be the one who introduces the concept of class meetings. Rules for conducting acceptable patterns of interaction must first be established. Common rules are: only one person will speak at a time, everyone must listen to and be respectful toward the speaker, each person will have an opportunity to speak, and put-downs will not be allowed. For young children, each of these rules will need to be explained and modeled. We should not assume that everyone knows what listening looks like or what waiting your turn to speak feels like.

Here are sample icebreaker questions for class meetings:

• If you could spend a day with someone you admire, with whom would you spend it, and why?

- If you were an animal other than human, what would you want to be and why?
- What is your favorite food, or what is your favorite restaurant?
- If you could go anywhere on a vacation, where would you most like to go, and why?
- What have you done for someone recently that you did not expect something in return for?

These questions start out as very nonthreatening but begin to offer insight into the students' values and beliefs as the year goes on. A teacher can reinforce this personal sharing process by connecting academic material to class meetings:

- What events led up to the Revolutionary War? Which do you believe was the most influential and why?
- If you could spend a day with a character from *Tuck Everlasting,* who would it be and why?
- In reviewing for the chapter test on fractions, what was the most challenging skill for you and why?

Class meetings can also incorporate role play of social situations. Here students may act out a problem or conflict that has occurred or might occur among class members or between the teacher and a student. Together the students and the teacher identify the problem, generate possible situations, and act out a plan for addressing the problem in the future. If teasing is a problem in the class, for example, have the children write skits about this problem (if they are not capable of doing this, then an adult can tell them a situation) and have them act it out for the class. In the class meeting, discuss with students the feelings they see in the role play and the things that may be done to solve the problem. Then have the actors use the solutions generated by the class to end the play.

One of the most powerful skills of communication is the ability to listen well; Daniel Goleman says it is the root of empathy (Goleman, 1995). Active listening involves being able to hear what someone has said and paraphrasing or retelling it in your own words. The retelling is a way the listener knows that he or she has understood and interpreted words the way the speaker intended. SEL also includes being able to sense what the speaker is feeling. The listener gives eye contact, pays attention to what is being said, and indicates openness to what is being said by using accepting body language (nodding, appropriate facial expressions, leaning forward slightly).

Active Listening Steps

1. Listen carefully to the speaker, and look for facial expressions and body language that might reveal how the speaker feels about what he or she is saying.
2. Rephrase the words you heard back to the speaker to check for accuracy.
3. State the feelings you perceive are being felt and tell why.

Examples of Active Listening

Case #1

Speaker: I hate going outside for recess. The kids never let me play kickball with them. I just end up being all by myself.

Listener: So you really don't like to go outside for recess because there is no one for you to play with, right?

Speaker: Yeah!

Listener: That makes you feel hurt and upset; I can tell because your face looks sad, and your voice is weak. That is a good reason for not liking recess.

Case #2

Speaker: My dad is going to go off the deep end when he sees my report card!

Listener: He's going to be mad because of your grades?

Speaker: Yeah, I sort of didn't tell him about the last two tests I took and got "D's" on.

Listener: I guess you must be scared because you think he's going to be mad with you, and you must also be sorry because you didn't tell him about the tests when you got them back, huh?

The social worker and teacher can co-teach active listening to students in a class meeting session. This way they can role play one of the above cases so students see the correct behavior being modeled.

When in an emotional state, a person may well find it easy to blame others for what has happened, but blaming does not move the situation toward a peaceful resolution. Using "I" messages eliminates placing blame on others and shows that you are responsible for the way you feel.

Steps

1. State how you are feeling: "I feel _____"
2. State what made you feel that way (without blaming or judging others): "when or because _____"
3. State what you want or need to happen (as developmentally appropriate): "I need or want _____"

Examples of "I" Messages

"I feel angry when I am teased about my braces; I need you to stop calling me names."

"I really get distracted when I'm trying to study and loud music is playing. Would you please turn it down?"

Emotional Vocabulary

Most children have a limited emotional vocabulary. They know that they are happy, sad, or mad. Yet, if we expect them to be able to name what they are feeling when they are feeling it, we must provide them with the words to do so.

Feelings vocabulary may be introduced in small-group sessions or to a whole class. Introduce several words from the emotions word list (the number will vary depending on the age and development of the children). Ask if they know what the word means and if they have ever felt that way. If they have, have them explain what happened to produce that feeling. If they do not know the word, give them a definition and create a context into which the child can place the word.

Suppose, for example that the word is *anxious*. You might say: "Do you know this word? It means to be worried about something that is going to happen or may happen. When I had to make a speech in front of a large audience, I was anxious. I was nervous because I did not want to make a mistake. Have you ever been anxious? What happened to make you feel that way?"

Again, the purpose here is to get students to accurately label what they are feeling when they are feeling it and to distinguish one intensity of an emotion from another. Also, since we know that children who are very angry or aggressive tend to interpret even the most neutral facial expression or event as being hostile (Goleman, 1995), this means they often believe that they are being attacked and must defend themselves with

aggression. Having children identify and share times when they experienced different emotions allow you to see how they interpret the world around them. It also allows you to make corrections to these perceptions when the need arises. It is extremely important to let children know that the emotion is neither negative nor positive. It is only the actions that one takes and the choices that one makes as a result of the emotions that are positive or negative.

Once children have acquired an emotions vocabulary, can recognize and identify what they are feeling, and have begun to make connections

Box 45.1 Feelings and Emotions Word List*

Affectionate	Exhausted	Pleased
Afraid	Friendly	Proud
Alarmed	Frustrated	Regretful
Alert	Frightened	Relaxed
Amazed	Glad	Resigned
Amused	Gratified	Sad
Anxious	Guilty	Scared
Attractive	Happy	Secure
Bad	Helpless	Sensitive
Baffled	Hopeful	Shocked
Bitter	Horrified	Strong
Comfortable	Impatient	Tempted
Confused	Inadequate	Tender
Courageous	Inspired	Threatened
Daring	Interested	Trouble
Depressed	Joyful	Unimportant
Despised	Lonely	Unsure
Determined	Loving	Useless
Disappointed	Moody	Vengeful
Eager	Miserable	Weak
Embarrassed	Nervous	Worn out
Enthusiastic	Optimistic	Worried

*Obviously there are many words that could be added, and students can add to this list.

Box 45.2 Calming Down Activities

Deep Breathing. People tend to breathe from the top of their lungs. Show children how to breathe using more lung capacity by expanding their diaphragms.
  1. Take a deep breath in through your nose.
  2. Hold it to the count of 5.
  3. Blow it out slowly through your mouth.
  4. Repeat as needed.
Take a walk. Physical exercise is excellent for refocusing energy.
Talk to someone.
Write. Keep a journal in which you can express your thoughts and feelings.
Draw. Use clay, color, or paint.
Listen to music.
Use visualization. Close your eyes, and imagine a quiet and calming place where you would like to be. Paint a clear picture of it in your mind. Enjoy!
Use self-talk. Change the words you are hearing by telling yourself that you are calm and in control. Whatever is happening, you are able to handle it without hurting yourself or others.

between their feelings and their actions, we can begin to teach ways for them to manage their impulses and negative social behaviors. The social worker may review the fact that when in a highly emotional or stressful state, it is very difficult to take in information or make good rational decisions.

"Here is a list of things we can do when we start to lose control. Is there something else you can add, something you do when you need to calm down? (Tell the children about something that you do as a model.) Look at the list and pick one or two things you have used or think would work for you so that you can stay calm."

Decision Making and Problem Solving

At the heart of all conflict resolution programs is the process of decision making and problem solving. The steps of problem solving vary slightly

from program to program; however, they all generally include the following steps:

1. Identify the problem.
2. Set a goal to resolve the problem.
3. Generate possible solutions.
4. Pick one solution.
5. Try it.

Each possible solution must be examined for both positive and negative consequences. "What might happen if I do this?" Planning, a step that is often omitted, requires thoughtfully designing how, where, and when one should proceed with a chosen solution. Finally, an integral step is to evaluate the action you took. Did it get you to your goal?

In effect, decision making and problem solving are the culmination of all the skills and strategies in an SEL classroom. Having a "feelings" vocabulary to accurately label what they are feeling when they are feeling it and being able to manage their emotions so that they can interact in prosocial ways and attend to content in the classroom all work together to cue into a problem that needs to be solved. Even young children can be guided through the problem-solving process with questions that will help them to think about the conflicts, problems, and decisions they face (see Table 45.1). Individuals can self-monitor behavior by using the same questions developed into a problem-solving diary. Diaries can be tools that teachers, counselors, social workers, and even administrators use when discussing progress made in behavior over time with students.

Final Thoughts

For children who are deficient in the social skills needed to function in a learning community, the classroom can be a threatening place. These are the children most likely to be involved in school conflicts (Zins et al., 2004). We now know that children are also not likely to acquire and perform these skills in any effective way unless they are generalized to the entire school environment. Administrators, teachers, and parents sometimes look for a silver bullet that will magically make schools safe and caring, protect our children, and raise the academic achievement levels so that truly no child is left behind. There is no such quick fix.

Table 45.1 Facilitative Questioning

To Help Children Think Using Problem-Solving Steps	*Consider Asking Questions Like These*
1. Look for signs of different feelings.	1. How are you feeling? You look a little upset (sad, nervous, angry, etc.). Am I right?
2. Identify the problem.	2. What do you think is the problem?
3. Decide on a goal.	3. What do you want to have happen? What is your goal?
4. Stop and think of as many solutions as possible.	4. Let's stop and think of all the different ways you might reach your goal. What could you do? What else could you do?
5. For each solution, think of all the things that might happen next.	5. If you _____, what do you think might happen? What else could happen? (Prompt for both positive and negative outcomes.)
6. Choose the best solution.	6. Which of your ideas do you think is the best for you? Which idea has the best chance of getting you to your goal?
7. Plan it and make a final check.	7. What will you have to do to make your solution work? What do you think could go wrong or block your plan?
8. Try it and rethink it.	8. What happened when you tried your plan? What did you learn that might help you next time?

Source: Adapted with permission from Elias and Tobias (1996), *Social problem solving: Interventions in the schools*. New York: Guilford.

What will improve safety and a sense of caring within classrooms are planned and purposeful efforts. The role of the school mental health professional is uniquely positioned to lead the way in building such a comprehensive approach to social competence.

The term *social and emotional learning* is fairly new on the school scene, although the understanding that SEL skills are important to success in school and in life has been around for decades. Educators, particularly with their attention so focused on the No Child Left Behind mandates, may need a broader perspective from those who see clearly that building a mentally, socially, and academically healthy individual is precluded by first building a healthy, caring, and accepting school environment (Elias et al., 2002; Zins et al., 2004). SEL is neither a silver bullet nor a quick fix. It takes time to change human behavior, but it is time well invested and recaptured when the teacher can spend less time resolving conflicts and more time in academic pursuits.

Resources

Books

Charney, R. S. (1992). *Teaching children to care: Management in the responsive classroom*. Greenfield, MA: Northeast Foundation for Children.

Educators for Social Responsibility. (1995). *Conflict resolution workshop and implementation manual*. Cambridge, MA: Educators for Social Responsibility.

Elias, M. J., Tobias, S. E., & Friedlander, B. S. (1999). *Emotionally intelligent parenting: How to raise a self-disciplined, responsible, socially skilled child*. New York: Harmony.

Elias, M. J., Tobias, S. E., & Friedlander, B. S. (2000). *Raising emotionally intelligent teenagers: Parenting with love, laughter, and limits*. New York: Harmony.

Elias, M. J., Zins, J. E., Weissberg, R. P., Frey, K. S., Greenberg, M. T., Haynes, N. M, Kessler, R., Schwab-Stone, M. E., & Shriver, T. P. (1999). *Promoting social and emotional learning: Guidelines for educators*. Alexandria, VA: Association for Supervision and Curriculum Development.

Goleman, D. (1997). *Emotional intelligence*. New York: Bantam.

Lantieri, L., & Patti, J. (1996). *Waging peace in our schools*. Boston: Beacon.

Salovey, P., & Sluyter, J. D. (Eds.). *Emotional development and emotional intelligence: Educational implications*. New York: Basic Books.

Programs

Child Development Project (CDP): www.devs0tu.org

Don't Laugh at Me (free materials): www.dontlaugh.org

PATHS (Promoting Alternative Thinking Strategies): www.colorado.edu/cspv/blueprints/model/programs/PATHS

Primary Mental Health Project: www.pmhp.org

Resolving Conflicts Creatively Program (RCCP): www.ersnation.org/about-rccp

The Responsive Classroom: www.responsiveclassroom.org

School Development Program (SDP): www.info.med.yale.edu/comer

Second Step Violence Prevention Curriculum: www.cfchildren.org

Six Seconds Emotional Intelligence Network: www.6seconds.org

Social Decision Making and Problem Solving: http://130.219.58.44/sdm/

Social Development Research Group (SDRG): www.dept.washington.edu/sdrg

Organizations

Association for Supervision and Curriculum Development: www.ascd.org

Character Education Partnership: www.character.org

The Collaborative for Academics Social and Emotional Learning: www.CASEL.org

Social and Emotional Parenting: www.EQParenting.com

Key Points to Remember

- Helping a student to develop social skills in the classroom is more effective in the long term when the classroom culture is supportive of those social skills.

- A classroom environment that promotes caring, respectful, and responsible behaviors has fewer conflicts, and when conflicts do occur they are resolved more amicably.

- Effective communication skills such as active listening and "I" messages are critical components of a caring community.

- Social and emotional learning promotes prosocial and self-management skills.

- Social and emotional learning must be integrated into regular rules, routines, and academic instruction so that ample opportunities for practice arise.

- Social and emotional learning teaches that emotions are neither good nor bad; they just are. It is the actions taken while in the midst of a strong emotion that can become problematic.

- The time it takes to teach and reinforce these skills is not wasted. In fact, time for academic content is increased as time needed to resolve conflicts is decreased.

References

Blum, R. W., McNeely, C. A., & Rinehart, P. M. (2002). *Improving the odds: The untapped power of schools to improve the health of teens*. Minneapolis: University of Minnesota, Center for Adolescent Health and Development.

Collaborative for Academics, Social and Emotional Learning. (2003). *Safe and sound: An educational leader's guide to evidence-based social and emotional learning programs*. Chicago: Author.

Elias, M. J., & Tobias, S. E. (1996). *Social problem solving: Interventions in the schools*. New York: Guilford.

Elias, M. J., Zins, J. E., Weissberg, R. P., Frey, K. S., Greenberg, M. T., Haynes, N. M, Kessler, R., Schwab-Stone, M. E., & Shriver, T. P. (1997). *Promoting social and emotional learning: Guidelines for educators*. Alexandria, VA: Association for Supervision and Curriculum Development.

Frey, A., & George-Nichols, N. (2003). Intervention practices for students with emotional and behavioral disorders: Using research to inform school social work practice. *Children and Schools, 25*(2), 97–104.

Gagne, R. M. (1965). *The conditions of learning*. New York: Holt, Reinhart, & Winston.

Goleman, D. (1995). *Emotional intelligence: Why it can matter more than IQ*. New York: Bantam.

Ingersoll, R. M. (2001). *Teacher turnover, teacher shortages, and the organization of schools*. (Document R-01-1). University of Washington, Center for the Study of Teaching and Policy.

National Research Council. (2000). *How people learn: Brain, mind, experience, and school.* Washington, DC: National Academy Press.

Osterman, K. F. (2000). Students' need for belonging in the school community. *Review of Educational Research, 70,* 323-367.

Rose, L. C., & Gallup, A. M. (2003). The 35th annual PDK/Gallup poll of the public's attitudes toward the public schools. *Phi Delta Kappan, 5*(1), 41-52.

Ryan, K., & Cooper, J. M. (2000). *Those who can, teach* (9th ed.). Boston: Houghton Mifflin.

Salovey, P., & Sluyter, D. J. (Eds.). (1997). *Emotional development and emotional intelligence: Educational implications.* New York: Basic Books.

Zins, J. E., Weissberg, R. P., Wang, M. L., & Walberg, H. J. (Eds.). (2004). *Building academic success on social and emotional learning: What does the research say?* New York: Teachers College Press.

Acquaintance Sexual Assault and Sexual Harassment Among Teens

School-Based Interventions

Erin A. Casey ▪ Paula S. Nurius

Getting Started

Nearly all youth are directly or indirectly affected by peer-to-peer sexual harassment or assault. Adolescents are more likely to be victims of sexually aggressive crimes than any other age group (American Academy of Pediatrics [AAP], 2001), and up to 15% of young women report rape (Tjaden & Thoennes, 1998). Approximately 83% of girls and 79% of boys are sexually harassed, and more than half of all adolescents of both sexes report perpetrating sexual harassment at some point during their time in school (American Association of University Women [AAUS], 2001; Fineran & Bennett, 1999). This chapter addresses adolescent peer-to-peer sexual victimization experiences, including verbal or physical sexual harassment, nonviolent verbal coercion to gain sexual contact, and physically forced sexual contact or sexual assault. Regardless of severity, sexual victimization can have immediate and long-term psychological, emotional, and physical consequences and can cause post-assault reactions that interfere with school performance and other achievement (AAUW, 2001; Fineran & Bennett, 1999; Koss & Harvey, 1991). School personnel are uniquely positioned to recognize and intervene in recent occurrences of harassment or assault and to initiate prevention programs that may reduce young people's exposure to harm. This chapter summarizes recent literature on effective sexual violence intervention approaches with adolescents and offers strategies for working with youth to address and reduce harassment and assault. A companion chapter in this volume focuses on assault and harassment prevention among teens.

What We Know

Sexually harassing behaviors between teens range from behavior such as unwanted sexual jokes, comments, gestures, name calling, anti-gay put-downs, pinching, grabbing, and spreading of sexual rumors to more invasive actions such as unwanted sexual touching (AAUW, 2001; Safe Schools Coalition, 1999). Sexual harassment can include quid pro quo harassment in which a person in a position of power or authority demands sexual contact in exchange for granting a favor or particular status, but among teens it more commonly takes the form of "hostile environment" harassment in which ongoing physical, verbal, or nonverbal conduct of a sexual nature creates a school climate that is offensive and intimidating to one or more students (Stein, 1999). Research suggests that 30% of girls and 24% of boys experience sexual harassment "often" and that up to 68% of girls who report sexual harassment encounter it weekly or daily (AAUW, 2001; Stein, 1993). Clearly, for some youth, sexual harassment is an integral part of their daily experience at school.

Though girls and boys appear to be nearly equally involved in both sexual harassment victimization and perpetration, more serious sexual victimizations primarily involve female victims and male perpetrators (Tjaden & Thoennes, 1998). Sexual coercion and assault range from unwanted touching of sexual parts of the body to attempted or completed oral, anal, or vaginal forced intercourse. Sexual contact may be obtained through coercive behaviors such as threats, false promises, attempts to intoxicate the victim, or use of physical force or weapons. Teens are most often assaulted by acquaintances, dates, or current or former partners (Vicary, Klingaman, & Harkness, 1995).

Responses to Victim Disclosures of Sexual Harassment or Assault

Little empirical research exists related to efficacious short-term interventions with adolescent victims of rape, and virtually no studies have examined school-based interventions with targets of sexual harassment (Bennice & Resick, 2002). Substantial research has documented the immediate and long-term impacts of sexual victimization, however, and has identified important factors that can ameliorate psychological distress for victims. This section briefly reviews these empirical findings and uses them to identify potentially important aspects of short-term intervention with young people who have experienced harassment or assault.

The continuum of sexually violent behaviors from harassment to rape holds serious consequences for victims. The impact of sexual harassment on young people includes increased fear, embarrassment, self-consciousness, and self-doubt (AAUW, 2001). Many young targets of harassment begin to develop avoidance behaviors, steering clear of particular people or places in school, or skipping classes or school days to evade their harassers (AAUW, 2001). Girls tend to report more severe effects than boys, and researchers have suggested that the prevalence of harassment constitutes a gender equity issue in which hostile school environments render achievement disproportionately more difficult for girls (Fineran & Bennett, 1998). Survivors of rape or attempted rape can face more serious and long-term consequences, including posttraumatic stress symptoms, depression, suicidal ideation, anxiety, disrupted relationships, and a damaged sense of safety and self-efficacy in their environments (Koss, Bailey, Yuan, Herrera, & Lichter, 2003; Petrak, 2002). Victimization has also been demonstrated to increase vulnerability to future physical and sexual abuse, creating the risk for compounded traumatic experiences over time (Arata, 2002). Finally, victimized youth are at risk for a range of medical consequences including physical trauma, increased risk of contracting sexually transmitted disease, and unplanned pregnancy.

The interventions we describe here are broadly applicable to victims of sexual aggression and appropriate to school-based response. However, this chapter cannot do justice to the full spectrum of potential physical health and mental health needs. Serious trauma-related needs may necessitate treatment by mental health professionals (Zoellner, Goodwin, & Foa, 2000).

What We Can Do

Factors that have been associated with reduced psychological distress and enhanced recovery among adult sexual assault victims include social support, a lack of self-blame, feelings of control over one's life and recovery, and a coping style that does not avoid or deny the abusive experience or its effect (Frazier, 2003; Koss, Figueredo, & Prince, 2002; Ullman, 1999). Additionally, survivors of sexual violence appear to do better when they perceive that they are believed by support systems, when they attribute the causes of their assault to factors external to themselves, and when they feel a sense of control over the process of recovering from the assault (Frazier, 2003; Ullman, 1996). In responding, the role of school personnel is to address disclosures or rumors of sexual mistreatment, to enhance emotional and physical safety at school for identified victims, and to initiate referrals that boost a student's support network and resources outside of school. Specific strategies for responding supportively to disclosures of sexual assault or harassment are summarized in Box 46.1 and are discussed below.

Enhancing Social Support

Research consistently confirms that positive responses following a disclosure of sexual victimization are associated with decreased psychological distress, whereas negative or blaming reactions can exacerbate psychological and emotional struggles (Filipas & Ullman, 2001; Ullman, 1999). Specifically, survivors who feel listened to and believed report enhanced recovery (Ullman, 1996). Conversely, increased psychological distress is associated with others' attempts to take control of a survivor's actions or recovery process or to distract the survivor from her experience (Ullman, 1996). Research also indicates that expanding the network of positive social support available to a student is a critical aspect of intervention (Koss & Harvey, 1991). School personnel can assist survivors in identifying and expanding sources of constructive support and can provide information to friends, family members, and other network members regarding the nature and importance of positive responses to the survivor (Ullman, 1999). School personnel need also to consider the larger school environment and the potential for blaming or inappropriate responses to the student. Steps to

Box 46.1 Responding to Disclosures of Sexual Harassment or Assault

- Establish a supportive relationship.
  - Express appreciation that the student came forward.
  - Explicitly express belief in the student.
  - Demonstrate a willingness to listen to the student.
  - Respond nonjudgmentally to the student's disclosure.
  - Reaffirm that the student is not to blame for the victimization.
- Restore feelings of control.
  - Allow the student to set the pace of the interview.
  - Engage the student in collaborative problem solving about safety.
  - Attend to the student's self-identified priority concerns.
  - Ask students what kind of outcome they are hoping for, and tailor interventions to honor these wishes as much as possible.
  - Be open and clear about limitations related to mandated reporting or school sexual harassment policy.
- Provide information and referral.
  - Normalize feelings or symptoms described by the student as understandable, common reactions to an upsetting event.
  - Consider providing information about common physical and emotional reactions that someone who has been victimized may experience. Reinforce that these are normal responses.
  - Offer information about sexual assault–specific resources available in the community and how to contact them.
  - Assess interest in other referrals, such as counseling services, health and reproductive health services, legal or victim advocacy services, and cultural or community support resources.
- Mobilize effective social support.
  - Talk with students about how or when to disclose their experience to family members or friends. Provide support, problem solving, or rehearsal about reaching out or disclosing to others.
  - Talk with the student about how she might respond or seek additional emotional support if she receives nonhelpful or victim-blaming responses from formal or informal support networks.
  - Provide family members with information about sexual harassment or assault, and about the kinds of responses that will be most helpful to teens (e.g., believing the student, being nonjudgmental, communicating support and validation).

enhance confidentiality, limit rumors, and help victimized students cope with inappropriate responses from peers, school personnel, or the news media may be helpful.

Restoring a Sense of Control

School personnel may help victims restore a sense of control by offering information regarding expected physical, emotional, and psychological symptoms associated with the sexual victimization (Calhoun & Atkeson, 1991; Koss & Harvey, 1991). Recent victims of sexual assault may experience sleep disturbances, intrusive thoughts about the event, irritability, difficulty concentrating, numbing or spacing out, fearfulness, and physical discomfort (Koss & Harvey, 1991; Osterman,

Barbiaz, & Johnson, 2001). Anticipating these difficulties, knowing that these are normal responses to a traumatic event, and hearing that they subside for most people may decrease young people's anxiety and help them to restore a sense of control. Practitioners should also be aware that students' cultural backgrounds and family environments will affect the meaning that they attach to assaults, the kinds of post-assault concerns they experience, and the post-assault options that they perceive as viable (Fontes, 1995). For example, some youth may feel more inclined to seek support or guidance through spiritual or community leaders than through mainstream mental health or crisis agencies. Family reactions and support needs may vary widely, underscoring the importance of staff cultural awareness in responding. Finally, the degree to which a sexually abusive experience traumatizes a victim, and the specific factors that compromise a victim's mental and physical health, vary from person to person (Gidycz & Koss, 1991; Ruch, Amedeo, Leon, & Gartrell, 1991). Thus, referral to health and mental health community services is critical.

Enhancing Safety

A primary goal with a target of sexual harassment or assault is to assess and enhance both immediate and longer term physical and emotional safety (Koss & Harvey, 1991; Resnick, Acierno, Holmes, Dammeyer, & Kilpatrick, 2000). This is especially critical for teens who have experienced sexual aggression and may have physical injuries and other medical concerns such as pregnancy and exposure to sexually transmitted diseases, or who may be at risk for further encounters with the perpetrator. In addition to medical attention, sexually assaulted students should be provided information about medical forensic services, typically available through local emergency rooms.

Once immediate physical safety is assured, targets of harassment or assault will need help in devising a plan for staying safe inside and outside school. School personnel should watch out for the student and be alert to the possibility of additional trouble, help the student find alternatives to some routines (such as using a particular walking route), identify a safe zone in the school where the student can go when feeling threatened, notify the alleged offender that he must stay away from the student, and provide ample adult supervision in places where harassment is more likely (Stein, 1999).

Responses to Perpetrators of Sexual Harassment or Assault

Appropriate school-based interventions for youth who perpetrate sexual harassment or assault are virtually absent from the literature. Bullying and aggressive behaviors tend to cluster with other antisocial conduct, placing youth at risk for a behavioral trajectory that includes delinquency (Dishion, Patterson, & Griesler, 1994; Pellegrini, 2001). Evidence suggests that boys who sexually harass or bully their peers are more likely to report being physically and verbally abusive with their dating partners (Pellegrini, 2001; Wolfe, Wurkele, Reitzel-Jaffe, & Lefebvre, 1998).

Schools should have sanctions that communicate nontolerance for violence, and they should have programs that teach alternatives to aggressive conduct. Consequences for harassing or assaultive behavior should be clearly described in school sexual harassment policy (AAUW, 2004). Additionally, researchers increasingly suggest that interventions include a teaching component that provides a young person with clear definitions of inappropriate behavior and information about the effects of his or her behavior on the target (AAUW, 2004; Stein, 1999). This may be accomplished through a letter written by the target of harassment to the harasser (only in cases where this is amenable to the complaining student), tailoring activities in antibullying or sexual harassment curricula for use by the harasser, or asking the perpetrator to write an "empathy" letter detailing his or her behavior and the effects it has had on the target and on the school environment.

Additional sanctions might include in-school suspension with time devoted to completion of a harassment curriculum, required service to the school community, an "antiharassment" behavior plan meeting with parents present, an interview with criminal justice authorities regarding legal sanctions for continued or increased harassing or assaultive behavior, or school suspension or expulsion. Charges of sexual aggression pose ramifications for the perpetrator's family as well. Inclusion of parents or caretakers is essential, with an appreciation that they may well have support and legal needs beyond what the school can provide. Sibling needs should also be considered, particularly if the perpetrator's or victim's brothers or sisters go to the same school.

Legal Considerations in Responding to Sexual Harassment and Assault

Reporting to Law Enforcement and Mandated Reporting

Adolescents who experience physically abusive sexual harassment or sexual assault should receive information about reporting to local law enforcement. The decision to formally report an assault is difficult, and young people may need information about the process and help in sorting out the pros and cons of making a report. Local sexual assault programs can provide information and often offer in-person advocacy during this process. Additionally, most jurisdictions mandate reporting if a minor has been assaulted or molested or is in ongoing danger of abuse. School personnel need to be familiar with mandated reporting requirements and sexual assault statutes in their jurisdictions.

Additional Obligations Related to Sexual Harassment

Sexual harassment in schools receiving federal funds is a prohibited form of sex discrimination under Title IX of the Federal Educational Amendments (Office of Civil Rights, 1997). Schools are required by the Office for Civil Rights to develop and disseminate procedures for registering complaints related to sex discrimination, including incidents of sexual harassment. Additionally, many states have statutes requiring schools to develop and publish policies and procedures specifically addressing sexual harassment and/or bullying. Sample school policies on sexual harassment can be found in a free document distributed by the American Association of University Women at www.aauw.org. School policies should be disseminated to students and parents, and they must be supported by prompt response to complaints of harassment. School administrators should identify a small team of trained faculty and staff who can be available to receive and respond to incident reports or rumors. Ideally, investigative procedures should include the following elements (Northwest Womens Law Center [NWWLC], 1994): an interview with the complaining student that assesses the grievance and the student's desired outcome; an interview with the alleged harasser regarding the incident; interviews with witnesses, staff, or students whom the victim or harasser told about the incident and witnesses to previous incidents; clear communication to all parties regarding time lines and expectations of confidentiality and nonretaliation; a determination of findings and remedies; a plan to monitor possible retaliation; and clear documentation of the process.

Resources

Countering Sexual Violence and Locating Local Programs

Rape, Abuse and Incest National Network: www.rainn.org. Provides comprehensive national list of local sexual assault programs.

National Sexual Violence Resource Center: www.nsvrc.org. Provides resources and links to educational and local organizing programs.

Arizona Rape Prevention and Education Program: www.azrapeprevention.org. Provides research, curriculum resources, and statistics related to sexual violence.

Countering Sexual Harassment in Schools

American Association of University Women: www.aauw.org. Provides free resources for educators addressing sexual harassment.

Office for Civil Rights—U.S. Department of Education: www.ed.gov (search site for "sexual harassment"). Provides information regarding schools' legal responsibilities related to addressing sexual harassment.

Safe Schools Coalition: www.safeschools-wa.org. Provides information, links, research, and resources related to sexual orientation–based harassment.

Key Points to Remember

Risk of sexual victimization is at its lifetime highest in adolescence through early adulthood. The high incidence of sexual victimization, together with pervasive underreporting and long-term harm to both victims and perpetrators, underscores how important it is that school personnel take an active role in the identification, intervention, and prevention of sexual harassment and assault. As much as possible, we have built recommendations on the best available evidence, at times extrapolating from research involving people beyond adolescence. There remains, however, a serious dearth of outcome research to support strong confidence in effectiveness, particularly with respect to cultural and contextual factors, necessitating careful thought in applying recommendations. Evidence consistently indicates that young people who have witnessed, experienced, or perpetrated violence earlier in their lives are at increased risk of subsequent victimization and perpetration and tend to be less responsive to universal interventions. These background factors should remain forefront in planning.

Although separated into different chapters here, there are many interlocking themes between intervention with and prevention of teen sexual assault and harassment. Early intervention, for example, can serve not only to ameliorate the effects of victimization but also to reduce risk of future perpetration and repeat victimization. Similarly, prevention activities will undoubtedly be received by students who have already perpetrated or experienced sexual victimization by a peer, potentially increasing the likelihood of identifying unmet needs. Moreover, there is considerable overlap among forms of relationship abuse. Other chapters in this volume on topics such as bullying, dating violence, and domestic violence provide guidance complementary to ours.

Finally, as we focus here on individual students and their families, we urge recognition that intervention with sexual violence inherently involves complex and often conflicting perspectives, expectations, and emotions of all involved—those of school personnel in addition to students and their support communities. The societal attitudes, norms, and structures that give rise to sexual violence are part of and shape intervention solutions. Schools need to make an unambiguous commitment to antiviolence messaging and response readiness.

References

American Academy of Pediatrics. (2001). Alcohol use and abuse: A pediatric concern. *Pediatrics, 108*, 185–189.

American Association of University Women. (2001). *Hostile hallways: Bullying, teasing, and sexual harassment in schools.* Washington, DC: Author.

American Association of University Women. (2004). *Harassment-free hallways: How to stop sexual harassment in school.* Washington, DC: Author.

Arata, C. M. (2002). Child sexual abuse and sexual revictimization. *Clinical Psychology: Science and Practice, 9*(2), 135–164.

Bennice, J., & Resick, P. (2002). A review of treatment and outcome of post-trauma sequelae in sexual assault survivors. In J. Petrak & B. Hedge (Eds.), *The trauma of sexual assault: Treatment, prevention, and practice.* West Sussex, UK: John Wiley & Sons.

Calhoun, K. S., & Atkeson, B. M. (1991). *Treatment of rape victims.* New York: Pergamon.

Dishion, T. J., Patterson, G. R., & Griesler, P. C. (1994). Peer adaptations in the development of antisocial behavior: A confluence model. In L. R. Huessmann (Ed.), *Aggressive behavior: Current perspectives.* New York: Plenum.

Filipas, H. H., & Ullman, S. E. (2001). Social reactions to sexual assault victims from various support sources. *Violence and Victims, 16*(6), 673–692.

Fineran, S., & Bennett, L. (1998). Teenage peer sexual harassment: Implications for social work practice in education. *Social Work, 43*(1), 55–63.

Fineran, S., & Bennett, L. (1999). Gender and power issues of peer sexual harassment among teenagers. *Journal of Interpersonal Violence, 14*(6), 626–641.

Fontes, L. A. (1995). *Sexual abuse in nine North American cultures.* Thousand Oaks, CA: Sage.

Frazier, P. (2003). Perceived control and distress following sexual assault: A longitudinal test of a new model. *Journal of Personality and Social Psychology, 84*(6), 1257–1269.

Gidycz, C. A., & Koss, M. P. (1991). Predictors of long-term sexual assault trauma among a national sample of victimized college women. *Violence and Victims, 6*, 175–190.

Koss, M. P., Bailey, J. A., Yuan, N. P., Herrera, V., & Lichter, E. L. (2003). Depression and PTSD in survivors of male violence: Research and training initiatives to facilitate recovery. *Psychology of Women Quarterly, 27*, 130–142.

Koss, M. P., Figueredo, A. J., & Prince, R. J. (2002). Cognitive mediation of rape's mental, physical, and social health impact: Test of four models in cross-sectional data. *Journal of Consulting and Clinical Psychology, 4*, 926–941.

Koss, M. P., & Harvey, M. R. (1991). *The rape victim: Clinical and community interventions.* Thousand Oaks, CA: Sage.

Northwest Womens Law Center. (1994). *Sexual harassment in employment and education.* Seattle: Author.

Office of Civil Rights. (1997). *Sexual harassment guidance.* Washington, DC: Author, Department of Education.

Osterman, J. E., Barbiaz, J., & Johnson, P. (2001). Emergency interventions for rape victims. *Emergency Psychiatry, 52*, 733–740.

Pellegrini, A. D. (2001). A longitudinal study of heterosexual relationships, aggression, and sexual harassment during the transition from primary school through middle school. *Journal of Applied Developmental Psychology, 21*(2), 119–133.

Petrak, J. (2002). The psychological impact of sexual assault. In J. Petrak & B. Hedge (Eds.), *The trauma of sexual assault: Treatment, prevention, and practice.* West Sussex, England: John Wiley & Sons.

Resnick, H., Acierno, R., Holmes, M., Dammeyer, M., & Kilpatrick, D. (2000). Emergency evaluation and intervention with female victims of rape and other violence. *Journal of Clinical Psychology, 56*(10), 1317–1333.

Ruch, L. O., Amedeo, S. R., Leon, J. J., & Gartrell, J. W. (1991). Repeated sexual victimization and trauma change during the acute phase of the sexual assault trauma syndrome. *Women and Health, 17*, 1–19.

Safe Schools Coalition. (1999). *They don't even know me: Understanding anti-gay harassment and violence in schools.* Seattle: Safe Schools Coalition of Washington State.

Stein, N. (1993). *Secrets in public: Sexual harassment in our schools.* Wellesley College Center for Research on Women.

Stein, N. (1999). *Classrooms and courtrooms: Facing sexual harassment in K-12 schools.* New York: Teachers College Press.

Tjaden, P., & Thoennes, N. (1998). *Prevalence, incidence, and consequences of violence against women: Findings from the National Violence Against Women Survey.* Washington, DC: National Institute of Justice.

Ullman, S. (1996). Social reactions, coping strategies, and self-blame attributions in adjustment to sexual assault. *Psychology of Women Quarterly, 20,* 505–526.

Ullman, S. (1999). Social support and recovery from sexual assault: A review. *Aggression and Violent Behavior, 4,* 343–359.

Vicary, J., Klingaman, L. R., & Harkness, W. L. (1995). Risk factors associated with date rape and sexual assault of adolescent girls. *Journal of Adolescence, 18,* 289–306.

Wolfe, D. A., Wurkele, C., Reitzel-Jaffe, D., & Lefebvre, L. (1998). Factors associated with abusive relationships among maltreated and nonmaltreated youth. *Development and Psychopathology, 10,* 61–85.

Zoellner, L. A., Goodwin, M. L., & Foa, E. B. (2000). PTSD severity and health perceptions in female victims of sexual assault. *Journal of Traumatic Stress, 13,* 635–649.

Enhancing Conflict Resolution Through Family and School Staff Alliances

Planning for Parent or Guardian Participation in Conferences

Martha J. Markward

Getting Started

School personnel are challenged to enhance alliances between parents or guardians and school staff at a time when great emphasis is placed on students' academic and behavioral outcomes. A variety of studies suggest that parent or guardian involvement in schools, especially school–home communication, accounts for a 10% to 20% improvement in achievement (Thorkildsen & Stein, 1998). When one considers that school–home communication has also been identified as an important means of preventing conflicts between parents or guardians and teachers (Hoberecht, 1999; McDermott & Rothenberg, 2000; Penney & Wilgosh, 2000), planning conferences to meet the unique needs of families takes on even more importance.

What We Know

Grimmett and McCoy (1980) found that educational outcomes were positive when teachers described to parents or guardians their child's reading program and informed them of the child's progress in the program. Fantuzzo (1993, 1995) found that students' mathematics scores were higher when school staff used notes and phone calls to communicate with parents or guardians and when both teachers and parents rewarded children for activities. Evans et al. (1994) used home visits to improve academic achievement and to reduce the number of children placed in special education.

Ames (1993, 1995) asked teachers in experimental schools to implement a variety of school–home communication strategies over time and found that these strategies advanced children's

motivation to achieve in school; these findings held even for children with learning disabilities. Ialongo, Poduska, Werthamer, and Kellam (2001) implemented a family-school partnership (FSP) intervention that included a parent–teacher and partnership building component with a subcomponent that involved training teachers to conduct problem-solving conferences with parents. The overall FSP intervention with children in first grade resulted in positive academic and behavioral outcomes for those children when they were in the sixth grade.

What We Can Do

Despite the salience of these findings, planning adequately for parent or guardian participation in school conferences takes on importance at a time when families in the United States are so diverse. Although it is commonly believed that enhancing parent–teacher communication prevents conflicts between school staff and parents and guardians, much more information is needed to understand the extent to which planning conferences to meet the needs of families enhances alliances between school staff and parents. Many school social workers, counselors, and other support personnel who practice in schools would likely agree that poorly planned school conferences result in conflicts between parents and teachers that place students in a stressful position. Teachers in most schools hold conferences twice a year; the extent to which these attract parents can be crucial to whether or not parent–teacher alliances are forged. Coleman (1991; see also Coleman, 1997a, 1997b) identifies the following steps in planning adequately for parent participation in parent–teacher conferences.

Steps in Planning for Parent Participation in Conferences

1. Identify barriers to parent participation in school conferences.
   - Which parents/guardians should participate in the conference?
   - When should the conference be held? (Before, during, or after school?)
   - How should the conference be conducted? (Face-to-face, telephone, e-mail, or with small groups of parents?)
   - Where should the conference be held? (School, home, neighborhood center, or parents' place of employment?)
2. Create a comfortable environment for offering information, asking questions, and making recommendations.
   - Schedule an adequate amount of time for the conference so that parents do not feel rushed.
   - If the conference is held at the school, point out to the parents the projects that involved their child; if held elsewhere, take examples of the child's best efforts.
   - Begin and end the conference by emphasizing something positive about the child for whom the conference was planned.
   - Communicate in a way that matches, yet shows respect for, parents' background. Be careful not to make assumptions about parents' level of knowledge or understanding, and do not talk down to parents.
   - Send nonverbal messages of respect and interest, sit facing the parent and maintain eye contact except in situations where the cultural norm is to avoid eye contact. Put aside paperwork, and postpone taking notes until after the conference.
   - Instead of offering advice, ask parents for information and suggestions about the child; offer your own impressions as a basis for negotiation.
   - Limit the number of objectives to be achieved in the conference to one or two of the most important ones that can be addressed with some ease; then break each objective into very simple steps; assign tasks to both teacher and parents that meet each objective in the home and school, respectively; plan a strategy for evaluating the objectives from the perspectives of teacher, parents, and student.
   - Follow up the conference with a thank-you note to parents This is a good opportunity to summarize the important points addressed in the conference.
3. Implement the strategy for evaluating the impact of having planned for parent participation in the conference on the educational and behavioral outcomes of students; this plan will often need to be developed before the conference to establish a baseline for change from the perspectives of parents, teachers, and students.

Tools and Practice Example

Juan Gonzalez: A Case Example

Juan Gonzalez is a fourth grader in an elementary school of a community in one southeastern state that serves a largely Mexican population. Juan's mother works as a domestic, and his father is a laborer with a tree-trimming firm. The school social worker identified, when he conducted a needs assessment at the beginning of the year, that the Mexican parents in this community prefer services provided in the neighborhood/home rather than in the school.

Because Juan's father leaves for work very early in the morning, the teacher, interpreter, and school social worker arranged with Juan's parents for the conference to be held in the home at 4:30 in the afternoon. The teacher and school social worker made face-to-face contact with Juan's parents while the interpreter translated the teacher's comments about Juan's schoolwork and behavior for the parents; the teacher's comments were positive, and she showed his parents worksheets he had completed to accompany an exercise in comprehension. Via the interpreter, Juan's teacher told his parents that the main objective of the conference was to inform them of his academic performance and behavior. She told them that another objective was to consider their concerns and suggestions about his schoolwork.

After Juan's parents were told how well the teacher thought Juan was doing in school, she asked the parents how they thought he was doing in school. Although Juan's parents said that they thought Juan was doing okay in school, they were concerned about his being shy because they think he has few friends in the neighborhood. The teacher assured them that even though Juan is shy, he has two friends with whom he interacts at school much of the time. They were very happy to hear this, and both Juan's teacher and the social worker could tell that they were relieved to receive this news.

The teacher closed the conference by telling the parents that Juan was doing quite well overall. She thanked his parents for allowing the conference to be held in their home, and they responded that this was more comfortable for them than meeting elsewhere. She told them that she would send them a thank-you note in a week and indicated that she would send a progress note home with Juan at the end of each week regarding his academic progress and peer relationships. She asked Juan's parents to send her a note if they ever have any concerns about him.

Tools and Forms

Hughes, Oakes, Lenzo, and Carpas's (2001) book, *The Elementary Teacher's Guide to Conferences and Open Houses,* provides excellent tools for planning for parent participation in conferences. These include: (a) a preconference student survey form that asks students what they want parents to know about their work, classroom, and what questions they want parents to ask the teacher; (b) a conference invitation form; (c) conference confirmation and reminder forms; (d) receipt of reminder form; and (e) a preconference parent survey form that asks parents what they want to know about their child's progress and what other questions and concerns they may have.

Most important, Hughes et al. provide forms that can be used by practitioner-researchers to evaluate the plan for parent participation in conference. Those include: (a) the teacher conference reflection form, (b) conference evaluation form, and (c) family evaluation form. For example, the conference evaluation form asks parents to use a Likert-type scale (4 = Very much; 1 = Not at all) to rate the extent to which the meeting (a) helped them understand policies and procedures of the classroom; (b) helped them understand their child's work; (c) increased their willingness to help their child at home after this meeting; (d) allowed their questions and concerns to be addressed; (e) encouraged them to meet again; and (f) lasted an appropriate length of time and was scheduled conveniently for them (p. 39).

In addition, student performance should be measured before and after the meeting so that the effect of planning for parent participation

can be assessed. For example, the revised edition of *Teacher Observation of Classroom Adaptation* (TOCA-R; Werthamer-Larsson, Kellam, & Wheeler, 1991) can be used to assess the student's performance on the core tasks in the classroom as rated by the teacher before and after the conference. Numerous reliable and valid measures can be used before and after the conference to assess the effects on various behavioral and mood outcomes, if behavioral and affective domains of functioning are of concern.

The conference evaluation form is shown in Box 47.1.

The easy-to-use *Behavior Rating Index for Children* (BRIC; Stiffman et al., 1984) is shown in Box 47.2. This scale can be accessed in the journal article cited in references at the end of this chapter.

Resources

www.aft.org/parentpage/communicating/
  parent_teacher.html
www.bridges4kids.org/articles/10–03/IDEAprac
  tices10–03.html
www.carsondellosa.com
www.kidsource.com/kidsource/content3/
  parent.teacher.3.html
www.ncrel.org/sdrs/areas/issues/envrnment/
  famncomm/pa31k9.htm
www.nea.org/parents/schoolinvolve.html
www.npin.org/library/pre1998/n00318.html
www.pta.org/parentinvolvement/helpchild/
  hc_gc_teachers_best.asp
www.topnotchteaching.com

Key Points to Remember

Planning for *meaningful* parent participation is an important means of enhancing parent and school staff alliances. The steps outlined in this chapter allow any member of a school's staff to plan conferences with parents that take into account the diversity of families in today's society, whether diversity is related to ethnicity, family structure, work schedules, or other factors. In planning conferences, staff should:

- identify and anticipate the barriers that might prevent parents from attending conferences
- create an atmosphere that will be comfortable

Box 47.1 Parent or Guardian Conference Evaluation

Please fill out the following evaluation form to help me plan for and improve future conferences and open houses. Please sign and return this form by [date]. Thank you for your help!
_____ [sender's signature]

1. This meeting helped me understand policies and procedures of the classroom.
   very much   somewhat   a little   not at all
2. This meeting helped me better understand the work my child is doing/will do in class.
   very much   somewhat   a little   not at all
3. I am more prepared to help my child at home after this meeting.
   very much   somewhat   a little   not at all
4. My child is better prepared to complete his or her work after this meeting.
   very much   somewhat   a little   not at all
5. My questions and concerns were addressed during this meeting.
   very much   somewhat   a little   not at all
6. I would like to attend another meeting like this.
   very much   somewhat   a little   not at all
7. The length and scheduling of this meeting were satisfactory.
   very much   somewhat   a little   not at all

Please list any additional comments below or on the back of this sheet.

_____ Parent Signature ____ Date

Box 47.2 Behavior Rating Index for Children

For each item, please record the number that comes closest to your observations of the child. Record your answer in the space to the left of each item, using the scale: 1 = Rarely or never; 2 = A little of the time; 3 = Some of the time; 4 = A good part of the time; 5 = Most or all of the time.
In general, how often does this child:

____ Feel happy or relaxed?
____ Hide his/her thoughts from other people?
____ Say or do really strange things?
____ Not pay attention when he/she should?
____ Quit a job or task without finishing it?
____ Get along well with other people?
____ Hit, push, or hurt someone?
____ Get along poorly with other people?
____ Get very upset?
____ Compliment or help someone?
____ Feel sick?
____ Cheat?
____ Lose his/her temper?

for parents from all types of families and backgrounds

- implement evaluation strategies to measure whether the conference positively influenced the academic and behavioral outcomes of students and whether it satisfied the needs of parents

Social workers, school counselors, and other mental health personnel who practice in schools can play a key role in enhancing alliances between parents and school staff, particularly teachers. More important, they can determine under what circumstances planning for parent participation results in positive educational and behavioral outcomes for students with particular characteristics.

References

Ames, C. (1993). How school-to-home communications influence parent beliefs and perceptions. *Equity and choice, 9*(3), 44–49.

Ames, C. (1995). Teachers' school-to-home communications and parent involvement: The role of parent perceptions and beliefs (Tech. Rep. No. 28). East Lansing: Michigan State University, Center on Families, Communities, Schools, and Children's Learning.

Coleman, M. (1991). Planning for the changing nature of family life in schools for young children. *Young Children, 46*(4), 15–20.

Coleman, M. (1997a). Challenges to family involvement. *Childhood Education, 73*(3), 144–148.

Coleman, M. (1997b). Families and schools: In search of common ground. *Young Children, 52*(5), 14–21.

Evans, I., Okifuji, A., Engler, Bromley, K., & Tishelman, A. (1993). Home–school communication in the treatment of childhood behavior problems. *Child and Family Behavior Therapy, 15*(2), 37–60.

Fantuzzo, J., Davis, G., & Ginsburg, M. (1995). Effects of parent involvement in isolation or in combination with peer tutoring on student self concept and mathematics achievement. *Journal of Educational Psychology, 87*(2), 272–281.

Grimmett, S., & McCoy, M. (1980). Effects of parental communication on reading performance of third grade children. *Reading Teacher, 34*(3), 303–308.

Heller, L., & Fantuzzo, J. (1993). Reciprocal peer tutoring and parent partnership: Does parent involvement make a difference? *School Psychology Review, 22*(3), 517–534.

Hoberecht, R. (1999). The relationship between teacher/parent perception of communication and practices for more parent involvement at a public school. *Dissertation Abstracts International, 60* (1A). (UMI No. 95013–046)

Hughes, M., Oakes, K., Lenzo, C., & Carpas, J. (2001). *The elementary teacher's guide to conferences and open houses.* Greensboro, NC: Carson-Dellosa.

Ialongo, N., Poduska, J., Werthamer, L., & Kellam, S. (2001). The distal impact of two first grade preventive interventions on conduct problems and disorder in early adolescence. *Journal of Emotional and Behavioral Disorders, 9*(3), 140–160.

Keyes, C. (2002). A way of thinking about parent/teacher partnerships for teachers. *International Journal of Early Years Education, 10*(3), 177–191.

Penney, S., & Wilgosh, L. (2000). Fostering parent–teacher relationships when children are gifted. *Gifted Education International, 14*(3), 217–229.

Rolnick, L. (1998). The study of parent–teacher communication: The social/cognitive and efficacy bases of teachers' communicative strategies. *Dissertation Abstracts International, 58* (9A). (UMI No. 95005–039)

Stiffman, A., Orme, J., Evans, D., Feldman, R., & Keeney, P. (1984). A brief measure of children's behavior problems: The Behavior Rating Index for Children. *Measurement and Evaluation in Counseling and Development, 17*(2), 83–90.

Thorkildsen, R., & Stein, M. (1998). Is parental involvement related to student achievement? Exploring the evidence. *Phi Research Bulletin, 22.* Phi Delta Kappa Center for Education, Development, and Research.

Werthamer-Larsson, L., Kellam, S., & Wheeler, L. (1991). Effect of first grade classroom environment on shy behavior, aggressive behaviors, and concentration problems. *American Journal of Community Psychology, 19*(4), 585–602.

Engaging Adolescents in Prevention of Sexual Assault and Harassment

Erin A. Casey ■ Paula S. Nurius

Getting Started

Schools place a high premium on creating safe learning environments for their students, and they possess exciting potential to foster climates of respect that render hurtful or harassing behavior rare and unacceptable. With their ability to draw staff, teachers, youth, and parents into schoolwide prevention efforts, school personnel are uniquely situated to proactively address issues of sexual mistreatment and to reduce students' exposure to this harmful conduct.

Given that more than 75% of all high school students report experiencing some form of sexual harassment at school and that approximately 5% of all youth report being sexually assaulted by other youth on school grounds at some time in their school careers (American Association of University Women [AAUW], 2001), purposeful primary prevention is critical to maintaining a safe school atmosphere. This chapter reviews approaches to the prevention of sexual harassment and assault among adolescents and is a companion to chapter 46, which focuses on interventions used with victims and perpetrators of sexual mistreatment.

What We Know

Research on prevention efforts in schools typically highlights the importance of multilevel, ecological approaches. Sexual harassment and violence prevention is best supported by strong, enforced antiharassment policies, staff who are trained to intervene in witnessed or reported incidents of harassment, parent education, and clear,

schoolwide systems for addressing inappropriate behavior (Olweus, 1994; Sanchez, Robertson, Lewis, Rosenbluth, Bohman, & Casey, 2001; Stein, 1999). Indeed, training of all staff on procedures for handling episodes of sexual harassment or violence is critical, as classroom presentations about sexual violence may increase reporting among participants. In addition to the resources listed near the end of this chapter, school district curriculum offices, local sexual assault programs, or community agencies are often able to provide staff with in-service training on preventing violence and intervening with perpetrators and victims. Further, prevention approaches may be strengthened by engaging youth in the process of planning and implementing antiviolence programs and complemented by efforts to actively support and reward respectful behavior among students.

This chapter briefly reviews literature on effective classroom interventions used to prevent sexual violence, and it provides resources that staff can use to tailor programs for their schools. Three types of prevention programs are addressed:

1. acquaintance rape prevention programs for mixed-sex or male-only audiences;
2. rape avoidance programs for female audiences; and
3. schoolwide sexual harassment prevention interventions.

Unfortunately, few widely available anti–sexual violence curricula for adolescents have been empirically tested, and those that have tend to address the related issues of dating violence or bullying (Foshee, Bauman, Greene, Koch, Linder, & MacDougall, 2000; Sanchez et al., 2001). (For guidance on those behaviors, readers should see chapter 49 on dating violence and chapter 42 on bullying.) However, empirical literature on sexual violence prevention among college students and others identifies some elements of preventive interventions that appear to increase awareness of sexual assault and decrease rape. We apply these findings to recommendations for adolescent audiences. Additional prevention resources and curricula references can be found in the Resources section below.

What We Can Do

Sexual Assault Approaches for Mixed-Sex or Male-Only Groups

Sexual violence prevention programs that target young audiences tend to consist of educational and interactive presentations in the classroom or other group settings. Although schools may invite experts from local sexual assault programs or other community agencies to provide presentations, prevention efforts are perhaps best led by teachers or other school staff who can be available for follow-up discussions and to handle disclosures or integrate prevention learning objectives into ongoing lesson planning. Prevention approaches are most effective when they involve multiple sessions, later "booster" sessions, or integration into ongoing academic curricula rather than a single encounter (Foshee et al., 2000; Lonsway, 1996). Many researchers now conclude that single-sex sessions are more effective than mixed-sex groupings, although both approaches can be successful in increasing knowledge and decreasing victim-blaming or rape-supportive attitudes among participants (Heppner, Neville, Smith, Kivlighan, & Gershuny, 1999; Lonsway, 1996).

Presentations aimed at a single sex provide the advantage of tailoring presentations for males that address risk factors for perpetration and for females that enhance self-protective capacity. Further, male-only groups allow boys to talk frankly about their attitudes, concerns, or misconceptions about sex without fear of ridicule or hostility from female participants, and single-sex interventions prevent previously victimized girls from hearing rape-supportive talk from their male peers (Berkowitz, 2002). Whether designing programs for male-only or mixed-sex audiences, it is important to defuse the defensiveness that the subject matter can raise for young men. Approaches that address males as potential allies in ending sexual violence and as part of the "solution" are more effective in changing attitudes than approaches that focus on males as perpetrators (Berkowitz, 2002; Heppner, Neville, et al., 1999). (For additional resources related to engaging boys and men as partners in antiviolence work, see the Resources section.) Finally, presenters, educational materials, content, and activities that reflect and are relevant to the cultural diversity of participants enhance the likelihood of student engagement (Heppner, Neville, et al., 1999).

Classroom presentations that incorporate interactive elements have been shown to be more effective than strictly didactic or lecture approaches (Heppner, Neville, et al., 1999; Lonsway, 1996). Interactive features of existing prevention programs have included theatrical skits performed live or on video, student role plays of assisting a victim or confronting someone on inappropriate behavior, classroom discussion based on videotaped vignettes or stories of sexual assault, or classroom exercises such as asking students to collectively generate a letter to the editor of the local paper or other periodical or an antirape brochure for younger students. Resources for locating videos on sexual assault and harassment are included in Appendix A.

Research demonstrates that providing clear definitions and concrete examples of what constitutes sexual assault can create lasting gains in students' knowledge of sexual violence (Heppner, Humphrey, Hillenbrand-Gunn, & DeBord, 1995). Addressing "rape myths" (beliefs about rape that are widely held but untrue, such as "women say no when they really mean yes" or "girls who wear revealing clothing are asking for sex") has been shown to be an effective element of reducing attitudes that are consistent with sexually aggressive behavior (Schewe, 2002). Box 48.1 offers concrete strategies for addressing rape myths in classroom settings.

Additional aspects of prevention programs that have yet to be fully empirically validated but are recommended by researchers include generating conversation about gender roles and gender socialization, defining and discussing consent in sexual relationships, building skills for bystanders to intervene on a potential victim's behalf, and building empathy for victims through information about the effects of sexual violence (Banyard, Plante, & Moynihan, 2004; Berkowitz, 2002; Schewe, 2002). A sample educational presentation outline can be found in Box 48.2.

Box 48.1 Sample Rape Myths Activities

There are many approaches to surfacing, discussing, and challenging misperceptions about sexual assault. Common "myths" about rape include:

- Most sexual assaults are committed by strangers in dark, isolated places.
- In sex, "no" can really mean "maybe" or "yes."
- People would not be raped if they didn't wear sexy clothing or drink.
- Girls who accept rides from guys, go to their homes alone, or drink on dates are signaling that they want to have sex.
- If someone has had sex with a partner before, she can't say "no" to sex later.
- During sexual activity there is a point at which it is too late to say "no."

Strategies for discussing rape myths and facts:

- Create a true/false quiz: Transform the above myths into true/false statements and supplement with other statements about rape, such as prevalence rates, definitions, and so on. After students take the quiz, discuss each answer, providing accurate information.
- Use an "attitude continuum." Designate one side of the room as the "agree" area, and the other side of the room as the "disagree" area. Pose one or more of the above statements and ask participants to physically indicate their opinion by standing in a place that reflects their beliefs (students who are unsure or who think "it depends" can stand in the middle of the room). Ask students to describe why they are standing where they are. Let students know that they can move around and change their minds after hearing their classmates speak. If rape myths are not effectively challenged by the students themselves, suggest factual information that challenges rape myths. (Adapted with permission from King County Sexual Assault Resource Center (1992), Ending Sexual Violence Workshop.)

Critical issues in facilitation:

- Keep in mind that you will have students in the room who have already been sexually assaulted. Monitor discussions for victim-blaming statements, and gently challenge them when they arise. Ensure that "hidden" victims in the room hear clear messages from you that reinforce that victims are not to blame. Consider starting activities such as the attitude continuum with a statement such as "Everyone has valuable and important opinions to share, and we want to hear what everyone thinks. Before you share your ideas about these statements, however, consider how your words would sound to a classmate who has been sexually assaulted. We also want everyone here to feel safe."
- Reinforce ground rules with students, particularly confidentiality. Remind students not to use names or tell stories about other people that would disclose private information.
- Rape-supportive attitudes are very likely to emerge during these discussions. Anticipate these responses and prepare additional questions or information that would support a student in reconsidering his or her statements.

Reducing Adolescent Girls' Vulnerability

Sexual assault prevention programs for all-female audiences typically focus on enhancing young women's ability to reduce exposure to potentially assaultive situations and to respond self-protectively when faced with the threat of rape. These programs should be designed with an understanding that some audience members will already have been assaulted and that the content of presentations should in no way suggest that victims are responsible. Factors associated with rape-avoidance for women include reducing exposure to known risks and using active, physical resistance to a potential assailant (Schewe, 2002; Ullman, 2002). Situational risk factors for sexual violence include settings involving alcohol or drug consumption,

Box 48.2   Sample Outline for Basic Sexual
Assault Presentation

   I. Make introductions, set ground rules, ac-
      knowledge difficulty of topic.
  II. Sexual assault: Give definitions and statistics.
      A. Provide clear, behaviorally specific
         definitions of assaultive behavior.
      B. Offer statistics about how many teens
         are assaulted.
 III. Rape myths: See Box 48.1.
 IV. Define consent: Understanding what one
      is consenting to and not fearing for physi-
      cal or emotional safety if one says "no."
      A. Brainstorm ways someone indicates
         consent.
      B. Brainstorm ways someone indicates
         nonconsent.
      C. List ways that someone might under-
         mine another person's ability to give
         consent, and reinforce that these tac-
         tics are sexual assault.
      D. Provide information about warning
         signals that someone might try to sex-
         ually coerce or undermine consent
         (female or mixed-sex audiences).
      E. Discuss options if someone is unsure
         whether his partner is consenting.
  V. How to get help.
      A. Provide information about resources
         for victims, including resource people
         in school.
      B. Provide information about how to
         help a friend.
 VI. End sexual violence: Brainstorm ways for all
      young people to help end sexual violence.

being in an isolated or vulnerable setting with a
male, and being in the company of a male who is
derogatory toward women, ignores boundaries, or
attempts to assert control (Marx, Calhoun, Wilson, & Meyerson, 2001; Ullman, 2002). Additionally, passive or negotiating approaches to resisting
a potential perpetrator are less effective than physical resistance or yelling in avoiding assault (Ullman, 2002). Effective preventive interventions
with girls may therefore include information
about recognizing the above risk factors and
about self-defense techniques in the face of threat.

   Research also suggests that prevention approaches should attend to the fact that the vast
majority of victimized young women are assaulted
by someone they know and perhaps trust, and that

assaults often occur during normative socializing
and dating. Young women in these settings can
face psychological and emotional barriers to resistance such as fear of embarrassment or rejection,
concerns about preserving a relationship, and
fears about physical safety if resistance is escalated
(Norris, Nurius, & Dimeff, 1996). In addition,
even though research shows that women assign
more blame to their assailants than to themselves
in assault situations, self-blame continues to hurt
women's ability to actively resist (Nurius, Norris,
Macy, & Huang, 2004). Prevention education with
young women can help women to anticipate these
psychological responses and build active resistance
skills in the face of a known assailant. Building on
the work of Nurius, Norris, and Young (2000),
Rozee and Koss (2001) propose providing young
women with the "AAA" (Assess, Acknowledge,
Act) model of recognizing and responding to sexual threats. This approach would provide girls with
tools (such as information about risk factors) to
assess a situation as potentially dangerous, empowerment in acknowledging this threat, and practice
with behavioral options for acting on their assessment. See the Resources section for additional
prevention education resources for girls.

   It is important to note the repeated finding that
prevention programs within colleges have been
significantly less effective for students with histories of sexual assault victimization or perpetration
(Hanson & Gidycz, 1993; Lonsway, 1996). Thus,
early detection and intervention using tailored approaches is likely needed to address the special
needs of previously victimized or perpetrating students. There are several inherent challenges to implementing prevention programs. One is the
"illusion of invulnerability" inherent to the developmental stage of adolescence as well as the dissonance between simultaneously pursuing safety and
social goals—for example, developing habits of
vigilance and resistance in the same circumstances
that students are seeking friend-ship, popularity,
experimentation, and intimacy (Nurius, 2000).
Prevention efforts can be enhanced by giving
young women the opportunity to explore these
complexities and to role play and practice feasible
verbal and physical responses to threats of sexual
assault (Marx et al., 2001).

Sexual Harassment Prevention

Although awareness about sexual harassment in
schools has increased dramatically over the past

decade, empirically tested sexual harassment prevention curricula are nearly nonexistent. Safe-place's Expect Respect curriculum (see Resources), which addresses both bullying and sexual harassment with elementary and middle school students, is one of the few evaluated programs discussed in the literature (Sanchez et al., 2001). Effective principles for addressing dating violence and sexual assault have emerged, however, and are likely to apply to educational programs aimed at preventing harassment:

1. Providing concrete definitions and examples of sexually harassing behavior, as well as challenging sexual harassment "myths" (such as that people invite harassment by their dress), can increase students' awareness of inappropriate behaviors.
2. Because many students who engage in harassing behavior are unaware of the effects of their conduct or see such behavior as routine

(AAUW, 2001), educating them on the emotional and psychological effects on the targets of harassment may support behavior change.
3. Many bullying curricula include "bystander" education components that aim to enhance nontargeted students' ability to speak out against harassment, intervene on behalf of a peer, or seek adult assistance. The Expect Respect program produced a positive change in young people's intention to intervene in bullying (Sanchez et al., 2001), and these findings lend support to the inclusion of bystander skill building in sexual harassment prevention education.

A sample sexual harassment presentation outline is presented in Box 48.3.

In designing sexual harassment prevention interventions, it is particularly critical to address overall school climate and responsiveness in addition to student behavior (Stein, 1999). Classroom

---

Box 48.3 Sample Outline for Basic Sexual Harassment Presentation

I. Make introductions, set ground rules.
II. Define sexual harassment.
    A. Provide a sample definition from school policy.
    B. Brainstorm list of behaviors that could be considered harassment.
    C. Discuss difference between flirting and harassment: Brainstorm characteristics of flirting vs. characteristics of harassment, and note differences (i.e., flirting is mutual, respectful, complimentary, fun; harassment is one-sided, repeated, demeaning).
    D. Address behaviors that are both antigay harassment and sexual harassment (such as using the word *gay* as a put-down, using derogatory words for sexual minorities, threatening to harm students who identify as sexual minorities).
    E. Provide information about the prevalence of harassment in schools.
III. Address myths associated with sexual harassment, such as the ones listed below, through discussion, attitude continuum exercises, or small-group discussion.
    A. People invite harassment through their dress or actions.
    B. Harassment isn't harmful if the intention is to joke around and have fun.
    C. People who complain about harassment have no sense of humor or are too sensitive.
    D. Only girls get sexually harassed.
IV. Explore the effects of sexual harassment. Goal of discussion is not only to enhance participants' knowledge of the effects of harassment but also to increase empathy and understanding that harassment can be very hurtful, regardless of the harassers' intent.
V. What to do?
    A. Brainstorm options for bystanders/witnesses of incidents. Role play potential bystander responses.
    B. Brainstorm options for targets of harassment. Provide information about reporting procedures.
    C. Brainstorm options for what people can do if they realize they have offended someone.
    D. Brainstorm options for what students in general can do to end harassment and mistreatment.
VI. Provide resources for follow-up, reporting, and community referrals.

interventions alone may be ineffective if the larger school atmosphere contains overt or subtle support for harassing behaviors or fails to respond to incident reports. Although no multilevel interventions specific to sexual harassment have been evaluated, research from related fields highlights the importance of an ecological approach to prevention (Olweus, 1994; Sanchez et al., 2001). Elements of such an approach might include the following: conducting a schoolwide survey of students' experiences of harassment and disseminating the results among staff, students, and parents as a way of highlighting the importance of prevention and of tracking progress; sponsoring a sexual harassment awareness week with antiharassment poster contests, speakers, essay contests, or student-planned educational activities; pulling together an antiharassment advisory committee of staff, students, and parents to plan schoolwide "respect" promotion campaigns; conducting a review and revision of existing sexual harassment policy with participation of students and parents; and inviting parent organizations to sponsor or attend educational opportunities for parents regarding bullying and harassment. Finally, it is critical to provide ongoing opportunities for staff to discuss approaches to addressing harassment, to collectively examine and challenge attitudes that prevent active intervention, and to receive training on responding.

Resources

Sexual Assault

Fink, M. (1995). *Adolescent sexual assault prevention curriculum and resource guide.* Learning Publications. Available through online booksellers and bookstores.

Marx, B. P., Calhoun, K. S., Wilson, A. E., & Meyerson, L. A. (2001). Sexual revictimization prevention: An outcome evaluation. *Journal of Consulting and Clinical Psychology, 69*(1), 25–32: This article describes a prevention intervention for previously victimized college women.

Men Can Stop Rape: www.mencanstoprape.org. This Washington, DC–based organization offers strategies and tangible tools for engaging boys and men in sexual violence prevention and antiviolence work.

Safe Dates. An empirically evaluated dating violence prevention curriculum by Vangie Foshee. Distributed through the Hazeldon Foundation at www.hazeldon.org.

The White Ribbon Campaign: http://www.whiteribbon.ca/. This organization's Web site details an international campaign to involve boys and men in antiviolence work. The Web site includes tangible classroom activities to address sexual and domestic violence.

Sexual Harassment

American Association of University Women: www.aauw.org

Expect Respect. For more information about this comprehensive approach to bullying, harassment, and violence prevention, see www.austin-safeplace.org

Flirting or Hurting? Curriculum for students in grades 6–12 by Nan Stein and Lisa Sjostrom. Distributed by Wellesley College Center for Research on Women: wcwonline.org

Steps to Respect. Antibullying and -harassment curriculum for Grades 3–6, currently being empirically evaluated. Distributed by Committee for Children: www.cfchildren.org.

Producers of Educational Videos Addressing Sexual Assault and Harassment

Intermedia: www.intermedia-inc.com
Coronet/MTI Film and Video: 1–800–621–2131

Key Points to Remember

School personnel can enhance their impressive efforts to foster positive, safe school climates by incorporating intervention and prevention programs that both ameliorate the effects of sexual mistreatment and reduce its occurrence. Though there remains a serious dearth of outcome research on best practices in intervention and prevention among adolescents, the preceding recommendations have been built on the best available evidence. It is worth reiterating the importance of supporting classroom prevention curriculum with efforts at every level to consistently communicate expectations of respectful treatment among members of the school community and to challenge sexually aggressive attitudes and behavior. When students are embedded in a climate characterized by equity, respect, and safety, they can more easily apply the skills and knowledge gained through prevention curricula and can assist school staff in undertaking the vital task of proactively creating violence-free schools.

References

American Association of University Women. (2001). *Hostile hallways: Bullying, teasing, and sexual harassment in school.* Washington, DC: Author.

Banyard, V., Plante, E. G., & Moynihan, M. M. (2004). Bystander education: Bringing a broader community perspective to sexual violence prevention. *Journal of Community Psychology, 32,* 61–79.

Berkowitz, A. D. (2002). Fostering men's responsibility for preventing sexual assault. In P. Schewe (Ed.), *Preventing violence in relationships: Interventions across the life span* (pp. 163–196). Washington, DC: American Psychological Association.

Foshee, V., Bauman, K. E., Greene, W. F., Koch, G. G., Linder, G. F., & MacDougall, J. E. (2000). The Safe Dates program: One-year follow-up results. *American Journal of Public Health, 90,* 1619–1622.

Hanson, K. A., & Gidycz, C. A. (1993). Evaluation of a sexual assault prevention program. *Journal of Consulting and Clinical Psychology, 61*(6), 1046–1052.

Heppner, M. J., Humphrey, C. F., Hillenbrand-Gunn, T. L., & DeBord, K. A. (1995). The differential effects of rape prevention programming on attitudes, behavior, and knowledge. *Journal of Counseling Psychology, 42*(4), 508–518.

Heppner, M. J., Neville, H. A., Smith, K., Kivlighan, D. M., & Gershuny, B. S. (1999). Examining immediate and long-term efficacy of rape prevention programming with racially diverse college men. *Journal of Counseling Psychology, 46*(1), 16–26.

Lonsway, K. A. (1996). Preventing acquaintance rape through education: What do we know? *Psychology of Women Quarterly, 20,* 229–265.

Marx, B. P., Calhoun, K. S., Wilson, A. E., & Meyerson, L. A. (2001). Sexual revictimization prevention: An outcome evaluation. *Journal of Consulting and Clinical Psychology, 69*(1), 25–32.

Norris, J., Nurius, P. S., & Dimeff, L. (1996). Through her eyes: Factors affecting women's perception of and resistance to acquaintance sexual aggression. *Psychology of Women Quarterly, 20,* 123–145.

Nurius, P. S. (2000). Women's perception of risk for acquaintance sexual assault: A social cognitive assessment. *Aggression and Violent Behavior, 5,* 63–78.

Nurius, P. S., Norris, J., Macy, R. J., & Huang, B. (2004). Women's situational coping with acquaintance sexual assault: Applying an appraisal-based model. *Violence Against Women, 10,* 450–478.

Nurius, P. S., Norris, J., Young, D. S., Graham, T. L., & Gaylord, J. (2000). Interpreting and defensively responding to threat: Examining appraisals and coping with acquaintance sexual violence. *Violence and Victims, 15,* 187–208.

Olweus, D. (1994). Bullying at school: Long-term outcomes for the victims and an effective school-based intervention program. In L. R. Huessmann (Ed.), *Aggressive behavior: Current perspectives* (pp. 97–130). New York: Plenum.

Rozee, P. D., & Koss, M. P. (2001). Rape: A century of resistance. *Psychology of Women Quarterly, 25,* 295–311.

Sanchez, E., Robertson, T. R., Lewis, C. M., Rosenbluth, B., Bohman, T., & Casey, D. M. (2001). Preventing bullying and harassment in elementary schools: The Expect Respect model. In R. A. Geffner, M. Loring, & C. Young (Eds.), *Bullying behavior: Current issues, research, and interventions* (pp. 157–180). New York: Hayworth.

Schewe, P. A. (2002). Guidelines for developing rape prevention and risk reduction interventions. In P. Schewe (Ed.), *Preventing violence in relationships: Interventions across the life span* (pp. 163–196). Washington, DC: American Psychological Association.

Stein, N. (1999). *Classrooms and courtrooms: Facing sexual harassment in K-12 schools.* New York: Teachers College Press.

Ullman, S. E. (2002). Rape avoidance: Self-protection strategies for women. In P. Schewe (Ed.), *Preventing violence in relationships: Interventions across the life span* (pp. 137–162). Washington, DC: American Psychological Association.

Effective Interventions With Dating Violence and Domestic Violence

Beverly M. Black ■ Arlene N. Weisz

CHAPTER 49

Getting Started

This chapter emphasizes the development of dating violence prevention programs in schools and briefly discusses interventions for victims and perpetrators. We have selected this emphasis because of the advantages of presenting prevention programs in schools. Schools present an ideal opportunity for offering prevention programs, because they offer universal education (prior to the legal dropout age) and have repeated contact with youth (Jaffe, Wolfe, Crooks, Hughes, & Baker, 2004). Presenting programs to all youth rather than those considered vulnerable or at risk decreases the stigma of attending the program (Durlak, 1997). Youth may be more receptive to messages that are received under less stigmatizing conditions. Some experts suggest that youth who are most at risk are the least likely to seek formal help (Avery-Leaf & Cascardi, 2002), so universal programs are advantageous for them. Since victims and perpetrators are unlikely to seek help about dating violence from adults (Bergman, 1992; Henton, Cate, Koval, Lloyd, & Christopher, 1983), it is very important to reach peers with knowledge of how to help a friend who is involved in dating violence. Having contact with adults who are clearly open to discussing dating violence may also increase youths' willingness to seek help from adults when a violent incident occurs (Weisz & Black, n.d.).

This chapter is written for school staff who wish to conduct prevention programs. However, readers should also consider contacting a local domestic violence program or free-standing youth prevention program for assistance. Many of these agencies present prevention programs at no charge to the schools. Collaborating with an external prevention program offers the advantage of having the program presented by specialists. Staff members from an outside agency will bring experience in presenting prevention and education programs, and they often bring ample experience in working with survivors and/or perpetrators that can enrich their educational programs. For schools that do decide to work with an agency to conduct a dating violence education program, the following material will help school staff think about how they would like the program to be conducted and will help staff engage in knowledgeable dialogue with an agency's staff to prepare for the program.

What We Know

The Importance of Dating Violence Prevention

Dating violence, the perpetration or threat of violence by a person in a relationship, has emerged as a significant social problem and public health concern among American youth. Studies suggest that about one third of U.S. high school students have had experiences with dating violence (Foshee, Linder, Bauman, Langwick, Arriaga, Heath, McMahon, & Bangdiwala, 1996; Jezl, Molidor, & Wright, 1996; Malik, Sorenson, & Aneshensel, 1997; Molidor & Tolman, 1998). Dating violence occurs among youth of all racial and ethnic backgrounds (O'Keefe, 1997; O'Keefe & Treister, 1998). Both girls and boys are victims and perpetrators of dating violence; perpetrating dating violence and being a victim of dating violence are often correlated with each other.

Adolescents who have experiences with dating violence are at increased risk for physical and psychological harm (Callahan, Tolman, & Saunders, 2003; Jezl et al., 1996; Molidor & Tolman, 1998) and serious health risk behaviors (Silverman, Raj, Mucci, & Hathaway, 2001). Girls are particularly at high risk; they are three to four times more likely than boys to experience emotional or physical injury from dating violence (Sugarman & Hotaling, 1989). Many times girls, in particular, fail to recognize the injuries and harm being inflicted upon them (Banister & Schreiber, 2001).

Youth increasingly appear to accept violence in their dating relationships as normal and as a version of love (James, West, Deters, & Armijo, 2000; MEE Productions, 1996; Vezina, Lavoie, & Piche, 1995). Adolescents' tendency to exaggerate gender-specific roles and accept mythical notions about romance makes them particularly vulnerable to violence in their relationships (Prothrow-Stith, 1991). Adolescent relationships may also be prone to violence because of the dependency that they place on each other for social acceptance and for social conformity (Levesque, 1997). The majority of adolescents report approval of violence toward a dating partner under some circumstances (Carlson, 1990), and the majority of those who have experienced violence in their relationship continued to date the perpetrator of the violence against them (Bergman, 1992; Bethke & DeJoy, 1993). Banister, Jakubec, and Stein (2003) found that girls' desire to have a dating partner outweighed their health and safety concerns.

Empirical Support for Dating Violence Prevention Programs

Despite the fact that numerous prevention programs have been developed, empirical evaluations of prevention programs remain rare. Among the relatively few evaluation studies of prevention programs examining change beyond the immediate effects, only a handful of studies have examined behaviors in addition to attitudes and knowledge (Foshee, Bauman, et al., 1998; Wolfe, Wekerle, Scott, Straatman, Grasley, & Reitzel-Jaffe, 2003). Even fewer evaluation studies have been conducted using samples of minority youth in the inner city. In particular, we know little about the characteristics and content of prevention programs that relate to program effectiveness. Table 49.1 summarizes current empirical research on the characteristics of dating violence prevention programs related to effectiveness.

Few research projects have examined which program components contribute to effectiveness in youth dating violence prevention (Avery-Leaf & Cascardi, 2002; Schewe, 2003). Therefore, this chapter presents the decisions that developers of prevention programs must make and, where possible, presents evidence supporting particular approaches. In some cases, knowledge gained from other types of youth prevention programs, such as substance abuse and AIDS prevention (Durlak, 1997), may be logically extrapolated to dating violence prevention without specific empirical validation. Similarly, knowledge from social learning theory (Bandura, 1977) and persuasion theory (Hovland, Janis, & Kelley, 1953; Insko, 1967) can be applied to youth dating violence prevention, but evidence to support these applications is rarely available.

What We Can Do

Steps and Issues to Consider When Beginning a Dating Violence Prevention Program

Prevention Educators

- Because dating violence issues are so sensitive, your school may require some orientation regarding the need for this program. Sudermann, Jaffe, and Hastings (1995) present some excellent suggestions of content for orienting administrators and faculty.
- School staff should have training to conduct prevention sessions (Avery-Leaf & Cascardi, 2002). Presenters need thorough knowledge of the issues, because youth will ask many questions. They also need to be trained to avoid the victim blaming that is so common in our society. School staff may seek training from a local domestic violence program to help them become more expert in dating violence issues.
- Many experts believe knowledge of youth culture or willingness to learn from youth about their culture is also necessary (Weisz & Black, n.d.). The educators must be able to help youth feel comfortable talking about sensitive issues. Because youth are reluctant to tell adults about dating violence victimization, educators must overcome this obstacle by making it clear that they are approachable and nonjudgmental.

Table 49.1 Programs That Conducted Research on Best Practices in Youth Dating Violence Prevention

Study	Format	Target	Evaluation Design	Results	Explanation of Results
Jaffe et al., 1992	School based; students received full-day or half-day program consisting of community speakers.	High school students	Pre-, post-test, 5–6 week follow-up	Significant improvement for participants in attitudes, knowledge, and behavioral intent; some males had a "backlash effect" in attitudes.	Use gender-neutral materials to prevent defensiveness among males.
Lavoie et al., 1995	School based; schools received 2 sessions or 2 sessions plus film; wrote fictional letters to victims and perpetrators.	10th grade	Pre-, post-test	Students improved to a similar degree in attitudes; students receiving shorter version improved more on knowledge; boys and girls comparably gained in shorter program. Girls improved more in the longer program.	Short programs can modify knowledge and attitudes. Short-version improvement may relate to school differences at pretest.
Foshee, Bauman, et al., 1998	School based; 10 sessions, with theater production, poster contest, community component.	8th and 9th grades	Pretest, follow-up Control group	Youth in prevention program reported less psychological abuse and sexual violence perpetration than control group.	Program effects due to changes in dating violence norms, gender stereotyping, and awareness of services.
Cascardi et al., 1999	School-based program with students receiving the 5-session program either once or twice.	Inner-city middle schools	Pre-, post-test Control group	Program increased knowledge and help-seeking intentions, decreased intent to use aggression. Double dose showed greater attitude change and behavioral intentions.	Single program dose can decrease verbal aggression and jealous and control tactics.
Wolfe et al., 2003	Community based; 18 sessions; focus on abuse dynamics, skills, and social action.	14–16 years		Physical and emotional abuse decreased; listening skills and group involvement related to a decline in physical abusiveness.	Didactic and interactive interventions are effective in changing attitudes (at least in the short run).
Schewe, 2003	School-based programs with variations in length, format, and content.	5th–12th grades	Pre-, post-test	Effective programs had more sessions of shorter duration; male/female cofacilitators, homework, role plays, discussions, healthy relationship skills, warning signs. Ineffective programs had gender role and self-defense content, videos, quizzes, anonymous question boxes, games, artwork.	Program length, content, format, and characteristics can positively and negatively relate to program effectiveness.

- There is no research demonstrating the superiority of using mixed-gender versus single-gender program presenters (Avery-Leaf & Cascardi, 2002). Black (2004) found no outcome differences in youth participating in mixed-gender versus single-gender programs. Experienced prevention practitioners often report advantages of having male presenters, but many believe females can be very successful addressing male and female youth (Weisz & Black, n.d.). Similarly, expert prevention practitioners believe an ethnic match between youth and presenters is a good idea but far from essential for a successful program (Weisz & Black, n.d.).

Recruitment of Youth

- Start before they date. Many educators believe middle school is an ideal time to start prevention programs because students have not yet established dating patterns (Avery-Leaf & Cascardi, 2002). Though middle school youth may not be officially "dating," they may be forming romantic attachments and developing patterns of behavior within these attached relationships.
- Determine whether your school requires parental consent for youth to participate in the program or in program evaluation.
- Target all youth, not just those particularly at risk (Avery-Leaf & Cascardi, 2002; Weisz & Black, n.d.). Programs generally address all youth in particular classes, operating on the principal that making programs voluntary eliminates those most in need of the program.
- Decide whether you want to separate or combine girls and boys (Weisz & Black, 2001). Some experts believe that youth are more open when they can talk in separate groups, while others believe that dialogue between genders is essential. One option is to separate genders for some sessions or some small-group exercises and combine them for others.
- Consider the optimal group size. Most educators try to avoid addressing assemblies (Hilton, Harris, Rice, Krans, & Lavigne, 1998) because they believe smaller groups enable discussions that truly capture youths' attention and enable them to participate in active learning (Weisz & Black, n.d.).

Steps to Guide Program Structure, Content, and Evaluation

Program Structure

- Plan multiple sessions. Although some programs of short duration have been found to be effective (Lavoie, Vezina, Piche, & Boivin, 1995), multiple-session programs are generally more effective (Avery-Leaf & Cascardi, 2002; Schewe, 2000; Weisz & Black, 2001). Experts recommend presenting at least three to four sessions.
- Decide how you want the sessions to be spaced. Weekly sessions allow students time to integrate the material. However, some experienced practitioners prefer presenting one session per day for several days to increase chances of students' retaining and using information from one session to the next (Weisz & Black, n.d.). Between sessions, some educators ask students to do assignments that reinforce their message.
- Make the sessions interactive. Experts recommend devoting time to discussion, role plays, and skill development (Durlak, 1997; Schewe, 2003). Practitioners agree that discussion of issues that students raise seems to attract their attention and enables the content to be locally relevant (Weisz & Black, n.d.). Empirical evaluation does not support the use of videos, games, artwork, or anonymous question boxes (Schewe, 2003). However, expert practitioners believe that judicious use of short videos attracts youths' attention and raises important issues for discussion (Weisz & Black, n.d.).
- Set guidelines for discussion at the beginning of the program. Examples of guidelines included in the curricula listed at the end of the chapter show that these guidelines are based on sound principals of group leadership, such as respect for everyone's opinions and feelings.

Content

- Find out whether the prevention material must be reviewed by anyone in your school or district. Sometimes content about dating or violence is considered controversial and must be reviewed before it is presented.
- Use a curriculum developed by experts. These people will have experience presenting their

material to many school groups. Box 49.1 includes a sample lesson from "Expect Respect" (Rosenbluth & Bradford-Garcia, 2002), and the reference list includes other recommended curricula.

- Choose a program that matches your audience. The curriculum and audiovisual materials should be sensitive to the primary cultural group of the youth who participate in your program. Youth are more likely to pay attention to images and stories about people who seem similar to them (Hovland, Janis, & Kelley, 1953). The material should address youth in sexual minorities, because dating violence is not limited to heterosexual couples. It should also address the vulnerabilities of youth with disabilities.

- Develop wide-ranging content. Content should include: forms of violence, information about the magnitude of the problem, relationship myths, power and control versus equality, warning signs and red flags, definitions of consent, healthy and unhealthy relationships, relationship rights and responsibilities, resources for seeking help, healthy relationship skills, and how peers can help friends.

- Consider whether you want your program to address larger, societal violence issues that contribute to dating violence.

- Consider combining content. Some programs combine content on sexual violence with content on dating violence prevention, but other programs separate them.

- Train students to be educators. Incorporating peer education requires training and supervision of peer educators, but it can increase the number of students that are reached. In addition, students may pay more attention and respond better to their peers (Sudermann et al., 1995). The peer educators themselves will learn a great deal. They can be influential in changing the school's atmosphere, and they will be prepared to help friends who consult them about an incident of dating violence. One approach to peer education is to train high school students to address middle school students. Other programs recruit youth to perform in interactive theatrical presentations about dating violence.

- Select gender-neutral materials. Research suggests that these are more effective than materials that consistently describe males as perpetrators and females as victims. No program will be effective if it alienates the male students (Avery-Leaf & Cascardi, 2002; Weisz & Black, n.d.).

- Include information on peer intervention. Programs using the "bystander approach" of teaching students how to intervene in peers' abusive relationships can convey a nonblaming, empowering approach to nonviolence.

Goals and Program Evaluation

- Do conduct an evaluation. This will help you to measure how effective your program is. An evaluation can also identify aspects that need improvement. It is considered optimal to test students at the outset and after the program has run its course. Conducting a 3- to 6-month follow-up on knowledge, attitudes and behaviors would be ideal. The presenters might ask classroom teachers to administer the surveys so that time is not taken away from presentation and discussion.

- Get feedback from students. Process evaluation that asks students to recommend improvements to the program can also be very helpful.

Galvanizing the School and Involving Stakeholders in Dating- and Domestic-Violence Prevention

Schoolwide Involvement

- Give the program visibility outside the classroom. Programs that create an atmosphere in the school that supports the prevention program's norms are considered most effective (Foshee, 1998). You might organize students to put up posters that are purchased or created by youth for a contest. Musical events featuring musicians who promote nonviolence can be very appealing to youth (Center for Prevention and Study of Violence, 2000).

- Offer a training session for faculty so they understand and can reinforce the information you are presenting to the students. This session can inform faculty that they might be confusing youth by expressing attitudes that are contrary to those taught in your prevention program (Sudermann et al., 1995).

Parental Involvement

- Let parents or guardians know what their children are learning. Given their influence in their children's lives (Black & Weisz, 2003), parents can be your program's most important allies and can reinforce its messages. A parent meeting can be an ideal forum in which to present information and to influence parents' own knowledge and attitudes. The information may help parents who are dealing with domestic violence and may decrease students' exposure to parental violence, which researchers think predisposes youth to violent actions (Skuja & Halford, 2004).

- Publish a newsletter. If your program is more than one or two sessions, it is helpful to send home a newsletter periodically to inform parents about the content of the program.
- We include in this chapter (Box 49.2) an exercise intended to supplement or replace a parent orientation if parents are unable to attend. This exercise asks youth to interview their parents about dating violence issues.

Preparation for Unintended Consequences of Programs

- Be prepared to help youth decide what they should and should not disclose during programs. Even though youth should be reminded about confidentiality and respect, it is important to protect survivors from revealing information that may become the source of gossip or ridicule after the program is over.
- Inform the students of your professional obligations to report child abuse or threats to harm.
- Have a plan and resources in place to respond to disclosures of child abuse or dating violence, because youth frequently approach prevention educators for help after a presentation.

Working With Survivors and Perpetrators of Dating Violence and Domestic Violence

It can be difficult to employ the best counseling and social work skills when presented with a teen survivor of dating violence, because it is upsetting to see harm inflicted on someone so young.

However, it is very important for helpers to listen with empathy instead of telling survivors what to do (Sudermann et al., 1995). Otherwise, the helper risks repeating the same type of controlling behavior used by the abuser. Within state legal guidelines, it is important not to force survivors to tell their parents or legal authorities about dating violence. It is better to help them explore the advantages and disadvantages of telling someone. Similarly, pressuring them to break up with an abuser is not empowering. The idea of breaking up with an abuser may seem very complicated and troubling to survivors and, furthermore, does not guarantee their safety. Again, it is better to explore the survivor's thoughts about safety and about remaining in the relationship versus leaving it (Davies, Lyon, & Monti-Catania, 1998). It is important for a helper to express concerns about a survivor's safety and to urge the survivor to develop a safety plan for use if violence occurs again or is imminent. Group work with survivors of dating violence can be very powerful in decreasing isolation and helping youth share safety planning ideas with each other (Levy, 1999).

Couples counseling is not recommended for abusive intimate partner relationships (Hansen & Goldenberg, 1993) because the victim cannot speak freely in a joint session—the abuser may punish her later for what she said. Most domestic violence experts recommend couples counseling only after perpetrators have received ample intervention to help them accept responsibility for their decisions to use violence and have learned not to use it.

Research supports the practice of group treatment for perpetrators. Groups decrease isolation and increase youths' openness to learning new behaviors from peers rather than from an individual adult therapist (Davis, 2004). Because many regions do not have agency-based groups available for adolescent dating violence perpetrators, you may want to consider developing a group within your school (Davis, 2004). The focus of intervention should be psychoeducational with an emphasis on learning new coping strategies and on increasing accountability for one's behavior (Peacock & Rothman, 2001).

Tools and Practice Examples

Sample Interview

Box 49.1 Sample Lesson From the Expect Respect Curriculum

Session #11 Jealousy and Control

Society is saturated with images that equate jealousy with love. As a result, many young women excuse extremely controlling behavior as a normal expression of love. Girls who are dating jealous partners may eventually withdraw from their friends and families. They may give up opportunities such as going to college or taking a good job because they don't want to upset their partner. Ultimately, they may become afraid that if they end the relationship the abuser will hurt them, friends, family members, pets, or children.

In an abusive relationship, the abuser wants to dominate or control his or her partner. The abuser may be extremely jealous of anyone or anything that interferes with his or her influence or ability to control his or her partner. Abusers will try to restrict a partner from people or activities that increase that person's self-esteem. The abuser is likely to feel most secure when his or her partner is physically and emotionally isolated.

Objectives

Identify words and actions that signal extreme jealousy.
Identify ways to handle jealousy without violence.
Understand that jealous and controlling behaviors are warning signs for further abuse.

Materials: Handout: "Is Your Relationship Based on Equality?"
Check-In: A time when I felt jealous was _____. I handled it by _____.
Activities: Jealousy

Using one or more of the situations described during the check-in, have group members create a role play about the situation and how it was handled.
Discuss and role play healthy ways of handling jealousy or responding to someone else's jealousy.
Emphasize to group members that jealousy is a normal feeling but that trying to control someone because of it is abusive. Extreme jealousy is a warning sign of dating violence.

Discussion Questions

1. What did the abusive person in the role play say or do to indicate he or she was jealous?
2. What does the abusive person want from his or her partner when he or she becomes jealous?
3. What are some things that an abusive partner might do to control his or her partner when he or she feels jealous?
4. Do people have a right to feel jealous?
5. What can the jealous person do to handle his or her feelings without violence or control?
6. How do boys control girls, girls control boys?
7. How do you know when someone is trying to control you?
8. How do you know when you're trying to control someone else?
9. Why are jealous and controlling behaviors warning signs for further abuse?

Source: From *Expect respect: A support group curriculum for safe and healthy relationships,* 3rd. ed., by Rosenbluth & Bradford-Garcia. Austin, TX: Safe Place. Copyright 2002. Reprinted with permission.

Box 49.2   Exercise for Students to Interview Parents

Parent Interview: Dating Violence Prevention Program

Interview Feedback Form*

The goal of this exercise is to enhance the communication between student and parent(s) and share in a dialogue about relationships. Students should read the question to their parent(s) and allow them time to give a response. The student then shares his or her response with the parent(s) and discusses similarities and differences that occur.

1. What components do you think contribute to a healthy relationship?
   Student shares response:
   Parents share response:
2. What do you understand dating violence to be? What are the warning signs of dating violence?
   Student shares response:
   Parents share response:
3. What steps can you take toward ending dating violence?
   Student shares response:
   Parents share response:

*This form is shortened to preserve space. Create a form with spaces for student to record their own and their parents' responses. You might want to offer an incentive for students to bring back completed forms. *Source*: This interview was developed by James Ebaugh and Beverly Black.

Resources

Curricula

Expect Respect. For more information about this curriculum, see www.austin-safeplace.org. For information about conducting the program, consult http://www.vawnet.org.

Safe Dates. For more information, contact Vangie Foshee, University of North Carolina at Chapel Hill School of Public Health, Campus Box 7400, Chapel Hill, NC 27599-7400.

Reaching and Teaching Teens to Stop Violence. For more information, contact the Nebraska Domestic Violence Sexual Assault Coalition, Lincoln, Nebraska, through http://www.ndvsac.org.

In Touch With Teens: A Relationship Violence Prevention Curriculum for Youth Ages 12–19. For more information, contact the Los Angeles Commission on Assaults Against Women through http://www.lacaaw.org/.

Videos and Other Aids

Dating in the Hood, available at http://www.intermedia-inc.com

Dangerous Games, available at http://www.intermedia-inc.com

In Love and in Danger, available at http://www.intermedia-inc.com

A list of videos is available at: http://www.nrcdv.org

Teen Power and Control Wheel, which describes different types of dating violence abuse, is available at http://www.ncdsv.org/images/Teen_PC_wheel_NCDSV.pdf. This Web site also includes power and control and equality wheels in Spanish.

Key Points to Remember

Dating violence—experienced in some form by about one third of all U.S. high school students—is the perpetration of violence or threats of violence upon a partner in a relationship. Although many prevention programs have been developed to confront this issue, few have been subjected to empirical evaluation. However, by comparing the multiple programs currently in use and the evaluation studies that are available, it is possible to establish a set of guidelines for implementing new dating violence prevention programs in a school setting:

• Staff should receive orientation regarding the need for and benefits of such a program. Though few may be needed to present the programs, all staff must be trained to handle questions from students.

• Current practice suggests that youths should be targeted for prevention programs as early as middle school, when romantic relationships may be beginning to form. Whether the program is being presented to all youths or just those in an at-risk population, parental consent may be needed for the child's participation.

- Experienced practitioners tend to advocate a program consisting of multiple sessions over a short period of time. These sessions may be presented weekly or daily, with support existing for both.
- The curriculum for the program should be chosen carefully to represent the school's primary cultural makeup, address minority sexual lifestyles, and be gender neutral.
- Parents should be kept involved with the program and their child's progress by means of parent sessions and/or newsletters (for longer programs).
- Program presenters should be trained and ready to deal with issues requiring immediate attention (e.g., children currently being abused) or exceptional care (e.g., children who have been abused or otherwise victimized).

References

Avery-Leaf, S., & Cascardi, M. (2002). Dating violence education in schools: Prevention and early intervention strategies. In P. A. Schewe (Ed.), *Preventing violence in relationships: Interventions across the life span.* Washington, DC: American Psychological Association.

Bandura, A. (1977). *Social learning theory.* Englewood Cliffs, NJ: Prentice Hall.

Banister, E. M., Jakubec, S. L., & Stein, J. A. (2003). "Like, what am I supposed to do?" Adolescent girls' health concerns in their dating relationships. *Canadian Journal of Nursing Research, 35*(2), 16–33.

Banister, E. M., & Schreiber, R. (2001). Young women's health concerns: Revealing paradox. *Health Care for Women International, 22*(7), 633–648.

Bergman, L. (1992). Dating violence among high school students. *Social Work, 37*(1), 21–27.

Bethke, T. M., & DeJoy, D. M. (1993). An experimental study of factors influencing the acceptability of dating violence. *Journal of Interpersonal Violence, 8,* 36–51.

Black, B. (2004). Evaluation of single-gender and mixed-gender dating violence and sexual assault prevention programs. Unpublished raw data.

Black, B. M., & Weisz, A. N. (2003). Dating violence: Help-seeking behaviors of African American middle schoolers. *Violence Against Women, 9*(2), 187–206.

Callahan, M. R., Tolman, R. M., & Saunders, D. G. (2003). Adolescent dating violence victimization and psychological well-being. *Journal of Adolescent Research, 18*(6), 664–681.

Carlson, B. E. (1990). Adolescent observers of marital violence. *Journal of Family Violence, 5,* 285–299.

Cascardi, M., Avery-Leaf, S., O'Leary, D., & Slep, A. M. S. (1999). Factor structure and convergent validity of the Conflict Tactics Scale in high school students. *Psychological Assessment, 11*(4), 546–555.

Center for Prevention and Study of Violence. (n.d.). *Blueprints for violence prevention: Overview of multisystemic therapy.* Retrieved May 31, 2000, from http://www.colorado.edu/cspv/blueprints/model/ten_Multisys.htm

Davies, J., Lyon, E., & Monti-Catania, D. (1998). *Safety planning with battered women: Complex lives/difficult choices.* Thousand Oaks, CA: Sage.

Davis, D. L. (2004). Group intervention with abusive male adolescents. In P. G. Jaffe, L. L. Baker, & A. J. Cunningham (Eds.), *Protecting children from domestic violence: Strategies for community intervention* (pp. 49–67). New York: Guilford.

Durlak, J. A. (1997). *Successful prevention programs for children and adolescents.* New York: Plenum.

Foshee, V. A., Bauman, K. E., Arriaga, X. B., Helms, R. W., Koch, G. G., Linder, G. F., & Fletcher, G. (1998). An evaluation of Safe Dates, an adolescent dating violence prevention program. *American Journal of Public Health, 88*(1), 45–50.

Foshee, V. A., Linder, G. F., Bauman, K. E., Langwick, S. A., Ximena, B. A., & Heath, J. L. (1996). The Safe Dates project: Theoretical basis, evaluation design, and selected baseline findings. *American Journal of Preventive Medicine, 12*(5), 39–47.

Hansen, M., & Goldenberg, I. (1993). Conjoint therapy with violent couples: Some valid considerations. In M. Hansen & N. Harway (Eds.), *Battering and family therapy* (pp. 69–92). Newbury Park, CA: Sage.

Henton, M. J., Cate, R., Koval, J., Lloyd, S., & Christopher, S. (1983). Romance and violence in dating relationships. *Journal of Family Issues 4*(3), 467–482.

Hilton, N. Z., Harris, G. T., Rice, M. E., Krans, T. S., & Lavigne, S. E. (1998). Antiviolence education in high schools: Implementation and evaluation. *Journal of Interpersonal Violence 13,* 726–742.

Hovland, C. I., Janis, I. L., & Kelley, H. H. (1953). *Communication and persuasion.* New Haven, CN: Yale University Press.

Insko, C. A. (1967). *Theories of attitude change.* New York: Appleton-Century-Crofts.

Jaffe, P. G., Sudermann, M., Reitzel, D., & Killip, S. M. (1992). An evaluation of a secondary school primary prevention program on violence in intimate relationships. *Violence and Victims, 7,* 129–146.

Jaffe, P. G., Wolfe, D., Crooks, C., Hughes, R., & Baker, L. L. (2004). The fourth R: Developing healthy relationships through school-based interventions. In P. G. Jaffe, L. L. Baker, & A. J. Cunningham (Eds.), *Protecting children from domestic violence: Strategies for community intervention* (pp. 200–218). New York: Guilford.

James, W. H., West, C., Deters, K. E., & Armijo, E. (2000). Youth dating violence. *Adolescence, 35*(139), 455–465.

Jezl, D., Molidor, C., & Wright, T. (1996). Physical, sexual, and psychological abuse in high school dating relationships: Prevalence rates and self-esteem issues. *Child and Adolescent Social Work Journal, 13,* 69–87.

Lavoie, F., Vezina, L., Piche, C., & Boivin, M. (1995). Evaluation of a prevention program for violence in teen dating relationships. *Journal of Interpersonal Violence, 10*(4), 516–524.

Levesque, R. J. R. (1997). Evolving beyond evolutionary psychology: A look at family violence. In N. L. Segal, G. E. Weisfeld, & C. C. Weisfeld (Eds.), *Uniting psychology and biology: Integrative perspectives on human development* (pp. 507–513). Washington, DC: American Psychological Association.

Levy, B. (1999). Support groups: Empowerment for young women abused in dating relationships. In B. Levy (Ed.), *Dating violence: Young women in danger* (pp. 232–239). Seattle: Seal.

Malik, S., Sorenson, S., & Aneshensel, C. (1997). Community and dating violence among adolescents: Perpetration and victimization. *Journal of Adolescent Health, 21*, 291–302.

MEE Productions. (1996). *In search of love: "Dating violence among urban youths."* Philadelphia: Center for Human Advancement.

Molidor, C., & Tolman, R. M. (1998). Gender and contextual factors in adolescent dating violence. *Violence Against Women, 4*(2), 180–194.

O'Keefe, M. (1997). Predictors of dating violence among high school students. *Journal of Interpersonal Violence, 12*(4), 546–568.

O'Keefe, M., & Treister, L. (1998). Victims of dating violence among high school students: Are predictors different for males and females? *Violence Against Women, 4*(2), 195–223.

Peacock, D., & Rothman, E. (2001). Working with young men who batter: Current strategies and new directions. National Resource Center on Domestic Violence. Retrieved May 19, 2004, from http://www.vawnet.org/DomesticViolence/Research/VAWnetDocs/AR_juvperp.php

Prothrow-Stith, D. (1991). *Deadly consequences*. New York: Harper Perennial.

Rosenbluth, B., & Bradford-Garcia, R. (2002). *Expect Respect: A support group curriculum for safe and healthy relationships* (3rd ed.). Austin, TX: Safe Place.

Schewe, P. A. (2000). *Report of results of the STAR Project to the Illinois Violence Prevention Authority.* Retrieved May 14, 2004, from http://tigger.uic.edu/~schewepa/MPApres.htm

Schewe, P. A. (2003). *The teen dating violence prevention project: Best practices for school-based TDV prevention programming.* Unpublished report.

Silverman, J. G., Raj, A., Mucci, L. A., & Hathaway, J. (2001). Dating violence against adolescent girls and associated substance use, unhealthy weight control, sexual risk behavior, pregnancy, and suicidality. *Journal of American Medical Association, 286*(5), 1–18.

Skuja, K., & Halford, W. K. (2004). Repeating the errors of our parents? Parental violence in men's family of origin and conflict management in dating couples. *Journal of Interpersonal Violence, 19*(6), 623–638.

Sudermann, M., Jaffe, P. G., & Hastings, E. (1995). Violence prevention programs in secondary (high) schools. In E. Peled, P. G. Jaffe, & J. L. Edleson (Eds.), *Ending the cycle of violence: Community responses to children of battered women* (pp. 232–254). Thousand Oaks, CA: Sage.

Sugarman, D. G., & Hotaling, G. T. (1989). Dating violence: Prevalence, context, and risk markers. In M. A. Pirog-Good & J. E. Stets (Eds.), *Violence in dating relationships* (pp. 3–32). New York: Praeger.

Vezina, L., Lavoie, F., & Piche, C. (1995). Adolescent boys and girls: Their attitudes on dating violence. Fourth International Family Violence Research Conference.

Weisz, A. N., & Black, B. M. (n.d.). *Relationships should not hurt: Programs that reach out to youth to reduce dating violence and sexual assault.* Manuscript in preparation.

Weisz, A. N., & Black, B. M. (2001). Evaluating a sexual assault and dating violence prevention program for urban youth. *Social Work Research, 25,* 89–100.

Wolfe, D. A., Wekerle, C., Scott, K., Straatman, A. L., Grasley, C., & Reitzel-Jaffe, D. (2003). Dating violence prevention with at-risk youth: A controlled outcome evaluation. *Journal of Consulting and Clinical Psychology, 71*(2), 279–291.

Effective Intervention With Gangs and Gang Members

Timothea M. Elizalde ▪ Gilbert A. Ramírez

CHAPTER 50

Getting Started

Gang presence in public schools is a growing issue across the United States. The growth of drug sales, drug use, and gun possession on school grounds is alarming. The correlation between gang presence and crime on school grounds is significant (Howell & Lynch, 2000). Research suggests that some intervention measures can be successful in working with gang members and decreasing gang-related crime and violence in schools. This chapter reviews several studies that clearly show the need for gang intervention in schools. It introduces an evidence-based program that can be used in schools with middle school and high school students who are gang members or on the verge of becoming involved with gangs. The focus of the chapter is a step-by-step guide to assessing the need for a gang intervention group, gaining support from school administration and staff, and creating a successful school-based gang intervention program.

What We Know

Research on gangs and gang prevalence in U.S. schools continues to grow. A study conducted by the U.S. Departments of Education and Justice (Chandler, Chapman, Rand, & Taylor, 1998) suggests that gang presence in schools now extends from metropolitan urban districts to suburbia, small towns, and rural areas. Although gang involvement is associated with lower income households (less than $7,500 a year), it is increasingly noted in households with income levels of $50,000 and higher (Howell & Lynch, 2000).

Student self-reports of victimization at school such as theft, theft by force or with use of weapon, and physical assault all appear to be more prevalent when gangs have been identified in a school. Although gang involvement is commonly identified in students age 13 and older, it is seen in all levels of education, including elementary through secondary levels. It is apparent that regardless of household income, residence, or school grade level, gang presence in public schools is abundant.

The Importance of Collaboration

A collaborative effort can ultimately lead to more successful reduction in gang prevalence in schools and the community. For example, increasing school security and suppression alone is not typically as successful as when they are combined with intervention and prevention measures. Research suggests that gang violence can be reduced through a comprehensive gang initiative that includes a combination of suppression, prevention, and intervention (Police Executive Research Forum, 1999). School security/suppression efforts can be effective if used in conjunction with community involvement and intervention programs that take place during school hours (Gottfredson & Gottfredson, 1999).

The Social and Psychological Paradigm of Gang Involvement

Human beings have basic social and emotional needs, for love, protection, identity, respect, friendship, loyalty, personal power, responsibility, rewards, and consequences, and rituals/rites of passage. These needs are often met for teenagers through their connections to family, schools, peers, and peer organizations. For gang members, needs such as belonging, protection, power, and family tradition are met through gang affiliation. The need to connect with others who share a common language or culture can be a strong factor, as well as the need to identify with others who share the common experience of poverty, violence, racism, and poor access to economic and educational opportunities. The primary goal of gang intervention programs is to have more of these needs met by family, school, and community, and fewer by gangs.

Through a school-based gang intervention program, youth can be helped to redefine how they use their value system and their innate social and leadership skills to get their needs met in a prosocial manner. Many gang-involved youth have such skills but are using their abilities to lead themselves and others down a dangerous path. The skills they use to participate in illegal and dangerous behaviors are the same skills they can use to complete high school, get a job, have positive relationships, and seek postsecondary education. An effective intervention program can guide them to discover better uses for these skills and shift them to activities that will provide better outcomes for their lives.

Many gang-involved youth come from disadvantaged backgrounds, and a frequent misconception is that their parents do not care about their education and are neglectful and unfit. This is not usually the case. The case is usually that one cannot know what one does not know. Thus, if parents did not attend high school or college themselves, it is difficult for them to guide their children through experiences that they themselves have not had. This is where the social worker can be crucial in engaging the family with exposing the youth to as many career and educational opportunities as possible and exploring activities that can positively channel the incredible adolescent energy.

Gang-involved populations are often completely disengaged from traditional school roles and activities such as student government, athletics, band and chorus, and drama. There are many opportunities within a comprehensive gang intervention program to assist youth in redefining their school experience and reengaging them in the school culture. As the intervention program expands and a greater sense of belonging and self-worth begins to manifest, opportunities build upon each other, and changes become more rapid and remarkable.

What We Can Do

A survey of school-based gang prevention and intervention programs by Gottfredson and Gottfredson (1999) offers a look at the gang prevention and intervention methods that have been most successful and productive across the nation. In particular, their report outlines areas that were considered to be rated as best practice when included in a prevention or intervention program. This chapter will highlight models provided by social workers, counselors, psychologists, and other therapeutic professionals. Gottfredson and Gottfredson (1999) found that programs that include these features were more effective:

- a formal assessment or diagnosis
- written treatment goals that are agreed on by the client
- a system that monitors or tracks behavior

Table 50.1 from the report of Gottfredson and Gottfredson (p. 11) describes these and other characteristics that received higher scores in the effectiveness portion of the study.

In addition to this table, Gottfredson and Gottfredson examined program adequacy and program quality for pertinence to program effectiveness. The "overall program adequacy" of programs and models was judged on a scorecard. Those with some or all of the practice measures identified in Table 50.1, in addition to counseling or therapy services offered weekly over a period of several months, were given higher program ratings.

Regarding program quality, Gottfredson and Gottfredson identify numerous factors that should be in place for a program to meet the requirements of a quality program. These factors include the following:

- extensive training of facilitator
- adequate supervision of clients during activity
- school administrative support for the proposed activity
- integration of multiple sources of information and utilization of field experts
- structured activities that have a sense of "scriptedness"
- activities that are part of the regular school day and not scheduled as an after-school program or in addition to the regular school day

Table 50.1 Measuring Best Practice (*Methods*)—Counseling, Social Work, Psychological, or Therapeutic Activity

- *Sometimes, usually*, or *always* makes formal assessments to understand or diagnose the individual or his/her situation.
- *Always* prepares a written diagnosis or problem statement for each participant.
- *Always* develops written treatment goals for each participating student.
- Student *usually* or *always* agrees to a treatment plan contract.
- A contract to implement a treatment plan is *always* agreed to by the client.
- Specific treatment goals for individuals depend on *individual needs as indicated by assessment*.
- When referrals are made, school-based personnel *contact the provider* to verify that service was provided or to monitor progress.
- The counseling or social work plans *always* include a method for monitoring or tracking student behavior over time.

Source: Gottfredson & Gottfredson (1999), p. 11.

The study goes on to address curriculum-based intervention programs and the areas each curriculum should have in place to be considered a best practice method. Overall, the study is a preliminary report, and much of the research on gang prevention or intervention effectiveness examines numerous factors depending on the type of model utilized. It is strongly recommended that this report be reviewed by practitioners to better understand the scope of factors that need to be considered when looking at best practice models.

Preparing the Ground

Conduct a Comprehensive Assessment

It is essential, in assessing the school for a gang intervention program, to identify the extent of gang presence and the amount of administrative and staff support needed to move forward. Table 50.2 presents a checklist of conditions that can be used as a general assessment tool to help determine the severity of gang activity in a particular school.

The data that schools maintain on student activity can also reveal conditions leading to an environment vulnerable to aggression, violence, or gang prevalence and can assist in securing administrative support needed to initiate a gang intervention program. The more data demonstrating the need for intervention services, the more support for moving the school toward a proactive approach to reducing or eliminating the chance of gang violence on or near the school campus.

School enrollment rates and dropout rates should be examined, and staff should be alert to pockets of students detached or isolated from general school activity. Mental health staff should become familiar with the dynamics of the surrounding community by examining crime rates and incidence of drug trafficking, violent assaults, gang arrests, and domestic violence. Also significant is the number of child protective service responses to neglect or abuse calls in the area.

Finally, it may be beneficial to notice the degree of family transition and ethnic composition in the local area. This knowledge will assist in gaining a clear portrait of the community. Since "zero tolerance" policies do not exist beyond the school, conflicts created in the community often spill onto campus grounds. A well-informed community portrait provides a framework for understanding issues that the school may encounter currently and in the future.

Establish a Foundation: Initiating the Group Process

Implementing a gang intervention program provides a good opportunity to do important work in the organizational systems of the school. In evaluating the effects of gangs on the climate of your school, it is important to meet the staff at their current tolerance level. If they are fed up with constant disputes and violence and believe that the current policies are not working, they may be ready to support a comprehensive intervention program. However, if they are resistant, you must advance more slowly, perhaps by starting a small support group or offering assistance with mediation after a conflict. In either case, it is im-

Table 50.2 Gang Assessment Tool

1. Do you have graffiti on or near your campus?	5 points
2. Do you have crossed-out graffiti on or near your campus?	5 points
3. Do your students wear colors, jewelry, clothing, flash hand signs, or display other behavior that may be gang related?	10 points
4. Are drugs available at or near your school?	5 points
5. Has a significant increase occurred in the number of physical confrontations/ stare-downs within the past 12 months in or near your school?	5 points
6. Are weapons increasingly present in your community?	10 points
7. Are beepers, pagers, or cellular phones used by your students?	10 points
8. Have you had a drive-by shooting at or around your school?	15 points
9. Have you had a "show-by" display of weapons at or around your school?	10 points
10. Is your truancy rate increasing?	5 points
11. Are an increasing number of racial incidents occurring in your community or school?	5 points
12. Does your community have a history of gangs?	10 points
13. Is there an increasing presence of "informal social groups" with unusual (aggressive, territorial) names?	15 points

Scoring and Interpretation

15 or less	No significant gang problem exists.
20–40	An emerging gang problem; monitoring and development of a gang plan is recommended.
45–60	Gang problem exists. Establish and implement a systematic gang prevention and intervention plan.
65 or more	Acute gang problem exists, meriting a total prevention, intervention, and suppression effort.

Source: Gangs in schools: Signs, symbols, and solutions by Arnold P. Goldstein and Donald W. Kodluboy, 1998, pp. 31–32. Adapted from "Gangs vs. schools: Assessing the score in your community" by Ronald D. Stephens, March 1992, School Safety Update (National School Safety Center, 141 Duesenberg Dr., Suite 11, Westlake Village, CA 91362; www.nssc1.org), p. 8.

portant to use the assessment tools (refer to Table 50.1) to gather and organize baseline community and school data to use in advocating for an intervention program.

Program Components

Gang intervention and prevention programs employ multiple levels of practice, including individuals, groups, and larger family, organizational, and community systems. Gang-involved student support groups are the initial and core activity for most school-based gang intervention programs. The following additional components and activities are added as the program expands:

1. Parent involvement
   - Parent support groups and/or family therapy
   - Fund raising
   - Award ceremonies
2. Case management
   - Referrals to health/mental health/psychiatric services
   - Referrals to income support agencies and housing

- Links to employment opportunities and job training
- Links to sports organizations, clubs, tutoring programs, mentor programs, art programs, theater programs, and so on

3. Mediation and conflict resolution training
   - Conflict resolution training for youth and opportunities to use new skills
   - Mediation in gang disputes

4. Culturally relevant activities and exposure to new experiences
   - Sales of ethnic snack foods that students and parents jointly prepare
   - Cultural events such as plays, musical productions, art exhibitions, and so on, especially those that provide strong ties to cultural traditions
   - Introduction to established clubs that help students to connect to and have pride in their cultural traditions (BSU [Black Student Union], MEChA [Movimiento Estudiantíl Chicanos de Atzlán], Asian club, and so on)
   - Sporting events, car shows, and other events of interest to the youth
   - Visits to universities, community colleges, technical/vocational schools
   - Attendance at job/career or college fairs
   - Participation in school dances, celebrations, and theme days
   - Planning of an end-of-year event; use fundraisers to help youth meet their goal
   - Exposure to fine dining, museums, and cultural centers
   - Introduction to ropes courses, rock climbing, and challenging events

5. Service learning
   - Volunteer drives for local programs for homeless, children, animals, and so on
   - Food drives for the holidays; have the youth help deliver food to families in their neighborhoods (include their families in the giving and receiving of the food)
   - Prevention presentations: As the group becomes more established and builds credibility as leaders in their community, have them make presentations to professional groups, college classes, community groups, and children advocacy groups about how to work with gang-involved youth
   - Service on a youth advisory board for a community organization
   - Preparation of a meal that the youth serve to their families at an award ceremony that celebrates their achievements both big and small

6. Community collaborations
   - Media coverage for an activity that highlights the youth's strengths and service to community
   - Solicitation of financial and in-kind donations from community merchants for scholarships or for entry into an event such as a baseball, basketball, or hockey game; zoo; water park; restaurant; or cultural/musical/artistic event
   - Links with adult mentors in the community
   - Partnerships with local businesses to provide jobs or job mentor opportunities
   - Collaboration with all outside providers that are working with the youth to provide continuity of care and to avoid duplication of services

7. Collaboration with school staff and administration
   - Maintenance of open communication with the students' teachers. If there is a problem, this is an opportunity to assist the youth in problem solving
   - Maintenance of open communication with administrators so that you are included in the loop of communication when discipline issues arise. Also, take time to communicate individual and group successes
   - Collaborations with school counselors, who can provide educational guidance and information about postsecondary options
   - Help from staff for securing caps, gowns, graduation invitations, yearbooks, and other things students may not be able to afford

With numerous other priorities in the school competing for funding and staff resources, such a comprehensive program can be challenging to start. The list above is the ideal.

▐ Additional Training for Practitioners

In establishing a support group and other services for gang-involved students, practitioners may consider professional training in areas specific to this kind of program. Mediation and conflict resolution, multiparty dispute resolution, and aggression replacement training are excellent tools for leaders. Cultural awareness/competency and bilingualism are also assets for staff involved in gang intervention services. Experiential education is a group model that we have found to be a good fit with our gang intervention groups.

Experiential education is a unique teaching and learning process that is applicable to many learning environments, including therapeutic groups. In experiential education, participants learn by doing rather than by being given answers to questions. Participants are asked to actively explore questions and solve problems through direct hands-on experience.

Experiential education is most often understood as a specific set of activities such as outdoor adventures, cooperative games, challenge courses, and ropes courses. The basic experiential learning cycle consists of goal setting, experiencing, processing, generalizing, and applying. The group begins by setting goals and then is given a challenge activity to meet those goals, therefore providing concrete experiences. After the activity, the group processes its observations and reflections. Participants are then able to form abstract concepts and generalize the learning to their own life experience. Once the experience is generalized, they can test it out in new situations.

Establishing a Student Support Group

Here are some guidelines for establishing a support group for gang-affiliated youth in the school:

1. Use a cofacilitation model to provide continuity and support for leaders.
2. Get referrals from an administrator familiar with the discipline history of students involved in gang behaviors on campus.
3. Limit group to 10 people. It should consist of students in the same gang or students associated with the same gang to ensure higher levels of trust.
4. Meet with students individually about interest in participating in a support group.
5. Check the students' class schedules. Find a time that does not take students out of a core class.
6. Speak individually with teachers about what you are doing and gain their support.
7. Contact parents in person or by phone to tell them about the support group and activities. Send a permission form home (in parents' first language) to obtain parental consent.
8. Meet again with the student for an intake interview and assessment of needs. Talk about the short-term and long-term goals he or she would like to reach. Explain the basics of confidentiality and ask for a commitment to

attend at least three group sessions before making a decision about staying or leaving the group. Give students freedom to decide about their own participation in the group.
9. Collect baseline data on behaviors you want the group to affect, such as grades, absences, suspensions, and discipline reports. This will help you and the student to better evaluate his or her progress throughout the year.
10. Find a consistent private space where there will be no interruptions during the group process. It is important that youth in the group feel they are the priority.
11. Set a schedule. Once established, groups can meet all year, and a session should last 1.5 hours.

Session Format and Content

The first session should be devoted to orientation. After making introductions, defining the limits of confidentiality, and getting the group started on initial activities, allow participants to be the key players in determining the rules, topics of interest, and activities. It is essential that the group members feel a sense of ownership.

Sticking to a predictable format lends stability and consistency to the group process, though the topics and activities will vary. This provides a sense of safety among participants, and the process of following positive rituals may transfer into participants' lives.

This is the format that we have found effective in our own school-based practice:

Snack and Settle: As group members arrive, providing them with a snack and time to settle in is a good way to get things started. (Snack food often can be obtained through local donations.) This beginning provides for informal interaction and building ritual into the group session. It meets basic needs for food and safety.

Brain Gym: Once everyone is seated, begin a brain gym activity (for more information, see Brain Gym International in the Resources section below) or have a couple of minutes of deep breathing or 2-minute melt (Goldstein, 1998). These activities help the youth to get focused as well as provide ritual for the beginning of the session.

Positive Peer Feedback: Have students design their own cards with their names. At the beginning of each session, have participants select a name card randomly. Ask the students to remember the name on the card and to notice something positive that the person does, says, or contributes during the session.

Check-in: Go around the room and have the youth check in by using a feeling word or two that best describes their feelings at that point in time and the reason they are feeling this way. This check-in gives facilitators an opportunity to see if there is a pressing issue that needs to be addressed immediately or if the scheduled topic or activity can proceed. It also often provides information about an impending dispute that requires intervention.

Business: Next, take a brief time to discuss coming activities, set group goals, or plan a community project. Keep this brief and schedule alternative times to go into more detail or actually participate in the activities.

Topic/Activity: Facilitators should have a menu of activities planned for the session, and this menu should draw from concerns of the youth present and the needs assessed for the group. However, be flexible and ready to change the plan if a gang conflict is arising. Use the session to help the youth understand their feelings about the conflict and identify strategies to confront the situation in a manner that will provide them with dignity, respect, and a way out. The leader can help the group explore the pros and cons of mediation versus a violent confrontation. Some topics and issues that are important to gang-involved youth:

- *Relationships:* family, friends, legal, gang conflicts
- *Social and economic issues:* sexuality, teen pregnancy, parenting, jobs, money, hobbies, youth activities
- *Academic issues:* goals, conflict with teachers, conflict with peers, tutoring, truancy, grades, achievement, post-secondary education plans
- *Self-esteem issues:* self-care, goal setting, acknowledgment
- *Grief and loss issues*
- *Communication and conflict resolution skills*
- *Substance abuse*
- *Aggression and anger management issues*

Once the group has defined goals and decided on topics, as co-facilitators you will plan your group sessions accordingly. For gang-involved participants, experiential education is a group method that tends to feel less intrusive to youth who have been guarded about their feelings and also provides many physical challenges. Leaders must be well trained in experiential education before working with this population. Given that experiential education provides fun, challenge, and opportunities for personal growth, students become quickly enthusiastic about attending group sessions.

Debrief: Use this time to go around the group and ask the participants about one thing that they learned or are taking away from the group session.

Positive feedback: Have the participants take turns giving positive feedback to the person whose name card they selected at the beginning of the session.

Check-out: At the closure of the session, have each member briefly disclose their feelings once again. This allows the practitioner to gauge the immediate effect of the group session, and it allows the participants to take note of any shift in their own attitudes or feelings.

Working Within the System

In order to foster change at the micro-level for gang-involved youth, working toward systemic change is vital. For example, a youth may show a positive change in attitude toward resolving personal conflict during a group or individual session, but if other gang members are threatening him or he is subject to violence at home and these larger conflicts are not addressed or mediated, the individual may feel unable to make this change.

Collaboration With Juvenile Probation and Parole System

Since many gang-involved youth have criminal records, they often have a court-mandated probation agreement and a juvenile probation and parole officer to monitor their adherence to the agreement. Collaborating with the JPPO will help your interventions coincide with probation mandates and support the youth in reaching their set goals. The group support you are offering, along with individual and family therapy and other culturally relevant activities, may also help the youth meet mandates set forth in their probation agreement, such as counseling, community service, employment, curfew, school attendance, positive interaction with peers, and abstinence from drugs and alcohol. When youth are consistently engaged in positive activities of their choosing, there is much less free time to be involved in negative behaviors. Likewise, there is a positive connection between meaningful participation and other important protective factors for the youth.

Collaboration With Other Stakeholders

Developing collaborative relationships with the school resource officer, security or police officers, school staff, parents, and administration is crucial to your ability to offer appropriate prevention and intervention strategies before, during, and after a conflict. Suppose, for example, there has been a gang altercation on campus, and students have been suspended. Because suspension deals only with immediate discipline issues and does not help resolve the original dispute, the conflict may have grown in magnitude by the time the suspended students return to campus. This is where your credibility with the youth, the police, the administration, and parents is paramount. This rapport will enable you to offer mediation to help resolve the conflict in a socially acceptable and legal manner and may help prevent a lethal altercation. Most youth who are provided with a dignified way out of the situation will want to mediate the conflict.

School social workers play an intricate role in balancing the roles of each stakeholder in the process: police, administrators, parents, and social workers. Police officers have the role of suppression and legal direction, administrators have the role of maintaining school policy, procedure, and discipline, parents have the role of advocate and caretaker of their child, and the social worker has the role of offering therapeutic intervention strategies and coordinating efforts. All these roles must be respected as separate yet equally important in ultimately serving the best interest of students and the safety of the school. Working to this end is often challenging, but the ultimate outcome is worth the collaborative effort.

When there is a peaceful agreement at the end of multiparty gang mediation, gang-involved youth, their parents, school staff and administrators, and the school community experience a sense of relief and safety. This may also demonstrate to the judge, the probation officer, and the police that the disputants are learning nonviolent ways to deal with their conflicts. These skills inevitably provide a benefit to the youth in their probation status. They learn that as they use new skills to confront their conflicts, they earn trust and freedom, something that adolescents highly value. Many of these conflict resolution skills also transfer to interactions with their families, and many experience improved relationships at home.

After the gang members have taken part in the program for a while, you'll begin to see a metamorphosis occur in them. You will be able to see the paradigm shift (Table 50.3). *Respect,* which before was gained by threats, manipulation, and fear, becomes a value that is earned, mutual, and modeled; *power,* which was acquired by guns, force, and violence, becomes an outward sign of inner strength, self-control, and personal empowerment; *friends,* once a product of the ability to provide a car, drugs, alcohol, and money, become people who are supportive, reliable, and caring.

Tools and Practice Examples

How One High School Developed a Gang Intervention Program

The gang and racial tension had built to an all-time high in this urban high school. There were daily incidents of violence and threats of violence on the campus. The environment was disruptive, and both students and staff felt unsafe. When the administration asked for faculty advice, the initial and natural responses were suppressive: "stricter policies; more police; more campus security; suspension from school." The school's social worker understood that most of the conflict was not perpetuated by personal disputes among the individuals involved but rather by gang loyalties and activities at the school. This appeared to be an opportune time for the social worker to introduce gang mediation strategies to the administration. However, when the social worker proposed multiparty gang mediation, there was great hesitation and doubt that such an intervention would have any effect. Given the resistance, the social worker offered to use mediation to help resolve individual disputes. A week later, the assistant principal called the social worker to deal with a dispute between two students who were members of rival gangs. When the mediation was held, it became evident that there were many others involved. The immediate disputants were free to speak for themselves but, according to gang culture, were not allowed to speak for others involved. Thus, a number of

Table 50.3 Paradigm Shift

Gang Definition	Individual Needs	Redefining Through Support Group and Intervention Program
Jealousy, possessiveness, manipulativeness	Love	Unconditional, supportive, caring
Guns, force, violence	Power	Empowerment, inner strength, self-control
Fearless, tough guy	Identity	Unique, individual, personality
"Us" vs. "them"	Trust	Powerful, established with time, rewarding
Threats, fear based, manipulative	Respect	Earned, mutual, modeled
"No rats"	Honesty	Without judgment, safe
Conditional: car, alcohol, drugs	Friends	Supportive, reliable, caring
Conditional	Loyalty	Requires commitment and accountability
High risk, dangerous, illegal	Fun	Natural, childlike, risk taking
Earned by criminal behavior	Honor	Earned through commitment and achievement
Expectation of illegal behavior	Duty	By choice, importance of word
Obey gang rules	Responsibility	Meaningful, important, rewarding
Veterans vs. Pee Wees Older vs. younger/newer	Authority	Veterans support Pee Wees
Instant gratification	Rewards	Earned, enjoyable, worthwhile
Severe, deadly, fear based	Consequences	Just, fair, purposeful
Sex, drug use, weapons use, probation, jail, fights, suspension	Rituals/Rites of Passage	Students become teachers, mentors; they graduate, go to college, have careers

other (student) members of the two gangs were called into the session as they were identified, and a mutual agreement for peace was reached. No student needed to be suspended, no probation officers had to be called, and, in the end, the session was a multiparty gang mediation process. This success helped the school administration to consider more favorably the idea of such an intervention.

Later in the year, a huge rival gang fight occurred on the campus, and many students were suspended. Once again the social worker suggested intervening with a multiparty gang mediation, informing administrators that although the fight was over and the participants suspended, the problem had not been resolved. In fact, the suspension time only allowed for the rivals to plan revenge, and rumors were surfacing about the use of weapons. The administration was not comfortable having such an intervention take place on campus, so the social worker offered to intervene off campus. When this was agreeable to school administration, the social worker collaborated with an organization in the community, one that worked with gang-involved youth and was familiar with the disputants, and received permission to conduct the mediation at its facility.

A date and time was set with the disputing gangs, and each member was contacted individually to ask for his participation. The disputants were anxious yet eager to resolve the problem. Many had probation agreements and a lot to lose, including school credits, their freedom, family relationships, and, worst-case scenario, their lives.

The rivals met at an office where they were first searched for weapons and then invited in for a pizza dinner. After pizza, the disputants sat at a business table where they were provided with pencil, pad, and water. The mediation was conducted by co-mediators with other gang intervention specialists present for safety. The disputants agreed to follow mediation rules and mutually decided to speak in Spanish during the mediation. After nearly 3 hours, a peace agreement was reached, and all participants signed.

When the youth returned to school, they found the social worker's office. Because of the rapport built during the mediation process, the students began dropping by and disclosing information about other conflicts in their personal lives. It quickly became evident to the social worker and to her young visitors that their common bond was that they were all dealing with complex and overwhelming life circumstances. They required an outlet other than the maladaptive ways that they were using to manage their problems. The social worker suggested a support group to help the young men with future gang, personal, family, and school problems. The young men agreed, and the onetime rivals participated in a support group that was inevitably the birth of the school's gang prevention and intervention program. The program grew and is still in place at the high school today, containing all the components for a comprehensive program that are described in this chapter.

Resources

Brain Gym International: http://www.braingym.org

National Youth Gang Center: http://www.iir.com/nygc/publications.htm

Key Points to Remember

Given the trends in school gang activity, intervention and prevention should not be ignored.

Research indicates that intervention services for gang-involved youth can be effective if they incorporate measures identified in this chapter. Initiating a comprehensive gang intervention program requires an extensive assessment of the school and community, support from administration and staff, outreach to community agencies, coordination with the juvenile justice system, and collaboration with community partners. When initiating a comprehensive program is not possible, concentrate on implementing a support group. Other components of the program can be added to this foundation. Practitioners are in a position to profoundly affect the school by redefining the way it approaches working with gang-involved youth. Youth will respond positively to the effort to support and reconnect them to the school community and culture. This outcome can perpetuate a culture in which youth are no longer viewed as gangsters but as strong individuals who can contribute to their community.

References

Chandler, K. A., Chapman, C. D., Rand, M. R., & Taylor, B. M. (1998). *Students' reports of school crime: 1989 and 1995.* Washington, DC: U.S. Department of Education, Office of Educational Research and Improvement, National Center for Education Statistics, and U.S. Department of Justice, Office of Justice Programs, Bureau of Justice Statistics.

Goldstein, A. P. (1998). *The peace curriculum: Expanded aggression replacement training.* Erie, CO: Research Press, Center for Safe Schools and Communities.

Gottfredson, G. D., & Gottfredson, D. C. (1999, July 29). *Survey of school-based gang prevention and intervention programs: Preliminary findings.* Paper presented at the National Youth Gang Symposium, Las Vegas, NV.

Howell, J. C., & Lynch, J. P. (2000). *Youth gangs in schools.* Washington, DC: U.S. Department of Justice, Office of Justice Programs, Office of Juvenile Justice and Delinquency Prevention.

Police Executive Research Forum. (1999). *Addressing community gang problems: A model for problem solving.* Washington, DC: U.S. Department of Justice, Office of Justice Programs, Bureau of Justice Assistance.

CHAPTER
51

Connecting School-Based Practices and Juvenile Justice

Karen S. Knox ▪ Albert R. Roberts

Getting Started

School social workers, counselors, and other mental health professionals are involved with many types of early intervention and prevention programs for at-risk children and adolescents, such as programs targeting school retention and truancy problems, drug and alcohol use, teen parenting, gangs, bullying, child abuse, sexual abuse/date rape, and family violence. The final report of the National Study of Delinquency Prevention in Schools reports an increase in school-based prevention programs in recent years, particularly in programs emphasizing school safety, conflict resolution skills, and adolescent decision making to reduce violence and risky behavior (Gottfredson, Gottfredson, Czeh, Cantor, Crosse, & Hantman, 2000). Continued growth and funding for these programs come from national educational funding, juvenile justice mandates, private foundations, and corporate initiatives.

Professionals in the juvenile justice system deal with the same issues these programs address and have seen an increase in the numbers of juveniles who are placed on probation. Data from the Office of Juvenile Justice and Delinquency Prevention (OJJDP) indicate that from 1985 to 2000, there was a 108% increase of adjudicated delinquency cases ordered to formal probation, as compared with a 49% increase in adjudicated delinquency cases ordered to residential placement (OJJDP, 2005). Of the 1.1 million court cases in 2000, 58% received probation, and 14% were placed in an out-of-home placement (OJJDP, 2005). The reality is that these youth on probation are living in their family homes, attending schools, and are likely receiving services from multiple community sources.

The majority of probation cases are property crimes, but from 1985 to 2000, an increase pro-portionally of crimes against persons (193%), drug/alcohol-related offenses (267%), and violations of public order (214%) were ordered to formal probati on (OJJDP, 2005). Even youth who have committed sexual offenses and other serious crimes may be placed on probation; some are monitored by electronic means or are subject to intensive supervision services, and others live in halfway houses or other supervised settings and attend public schools.

Schools are a key locus for prevention and intervention services, not only because children and adolescents spend so much of their time there, but also because it is the primary institution that influences their socialization in behavior, roles, and developmental tasks (Gottfredson et al., 2000). Although there are diverse views and values on schools' roles and activities in socializing our children beyond the educational boundaries, the reality is that schools fill a vital niche in addressing many of the problems faced by children and youth today.

What We Know

Poor academic performance is identified as a significant risk factor for delinquency. A meta-analysis of longitudinal and experimental studies by Maguin and Loeber (1996) found that poor academic performance is related to the prevalence and onset of delinquency, as well as the escalation in frequency and seriousness of offense. More specifically, the poorer the academic performance, the higher the delinquency, with the odds of delinquency involvement being twice as high for students with poor academic performance than for students with high academic performance (Howell, 2003). The studies in the meta-analysis also show some evidence that poor academic performance is related to early onset of offending (Maguin & Loeber, 1996).

School failure is a stronger predictor of delinquency than other variables such as economic class, racial or ethnic background, or peer group relationships (Siegel, Welsh, & Senna, 2003). Youth who report that they don't like school, don't do well in school, and don't do their homework are also the ones most likely to self-report delinquent acts (Thornberry, Lizotte, Krohn, Farnworth, & Jang, 1991). In contrast, at-risk youth with histories of abuse and neglect who do well in school are often able to avoid delinquent involvement (Smith, Lizotte, Thornberry, & Krohn, 1997).

Poor academic performance can stem from a variety of factors, such as learning disabilities, below-average IQ, attention-deficit hyperactivity disorder (ADHD), and other cognitive functioning problems. In a recent study comparing 10 evidence-based model juvenile programs, more than half included data documenting these types of cognitive deficits with their clients (Roberts, 2004). Data from the Texas Youth Commission reveals that 75% of juvenile offenders in the system's programs have IQs below the mean score of 100, and the median reading and math achievement level is fifth or sixth grade, which is 4–5 years behind their peers for the average 16-year-old (Roberts, 2004).

Having to repeat grades and being older than the other students in one's class also has a negative effect and puts students at risk for dropping out, being truant, and bonding weakly to school. Other factors such as a lack of family involvement, low motivation for success in school, low educational aspirations, and poor study habits are common. It is also typical for juvenile offenders to have a history of other school problems and antisocial behaviors, such as poor peer relations, authority problems with teachers and administrators, not following school rules, being suspended and expelled for school infractions, gang affiliation, and drug/alcohol use.

What We Can Do

Evidence-Based School Prevention and Intervention Programs

Research indicates that early intervention is most effective when the needs of children (early

education) and parents (parental training, family strengthening, and parental support) are addressed simultaneously and when programs target persistently disruptive and delinquent children (Loeber & Farrington, 2001). Preschool programs such as Head Start, Nurturing Programs, and Home Instruction for Parents of Preschool Youth are examples of early intervention programs that address multiple needs and problems of at-risk children and families. High-quality, intensive preschool programs show strong support for preventing delinquency by preparing children for elementary school and reducing the chances of early school failure (Siegel et al., 2003; Zieglar & Styfco, 2001).

The school's role in preventing delinquency may involve programs that target the general student body or only certain at-risk students. However, school-based prevention programs usually include the following types of interventions (Gottfredson et al., 2000):

- Social competency skills
- Behavioral management interventions
- Environmental change to increase school and behavior management
- Increased bonding and socialization
- Recreation or productive activities
- Information and psychoeducation

Some programs attempt to prevent or reduce delinquency by manipulating factors in the learning environment. The Seattle Social Development Project (SSDP), which began in 1981, is a longitudinal study of youth to evaluate strategies that reduce or prevent delinquency. The study's 800-plus participants, who are now young adults, have been interviewed annually since elementary school.

The results of the SSDP showed effectiveness at promoting school and social functioning for elementary students, and it also indicated effectiveness as an adolescent violence prevention strategy in a follow-up study (Howell, 2003). This project involved multiple components and provided social competence training for children and training for teachers and parents on how to encourage interest in school. The program started in the first grade and continued until the sixth grade with small-group skills training for the children on problem solving, communication, and conflict resolution.

The parent and teacher training focused on how to consistently reward and encourage desirable behavior and appropriately apply negative consequences for undesirable behavior. Other parent training addressed strategies to improve academic performance and information on risk factors for delinquency (Siegel et al., 2003). Six years later, a study of the long-term effects of the SSDP found improved academic achievement and commitment to school, along with reduced misbehavior and violence at school, heavy drinking, and sexual activity among the participants (Hawkins, Catalano, Kosterman, Abbott, & Hill, 1999; Howell, 2003).

Behavior management programs target youth who are impulsive, aggressive, or disorderly in conduct and are directed at tardiness, inadequate class preparation and performance, bad behavior, and poor attendance (Gottfredson et al., 2000). Environmental changes address school norms, clarify rules, improve school discipline, decrease classroom disruptions, and improve classroom management and organization. The Program Development Evaluation (PDE) method is a multicomponent middle school organizational intervention by school teams composed of teachers, parents, and administrators. PDE demonstrated effectiveness in increasing the clarity and consistency of school rules, student success, school attachment, and staff morale, and in reducing problem behavior (Gottfredson et al., 2000; Howell, 2003).

Bonding can be achieved by increasing rewarding school learning experiences through school mentors, positive role models, field trips, team projects, special interest and support groups, extracurricular activities, culture-specific activities, and values education. These types of programs, along with other recreation and youth employment programs, provide supervision of youth in after-school hours and promote attachment and a sense of school culture. Information and psychoeducational interventions usually address drug/alcohol/tobacco use, sexual abuse/date rape, family violence, teen parenting, and other criminal or risky behaviors.

Evidence-Based Juvenile Justice Treatment Programs

During the past three decades, the federal and state governments have allocated billions of dollars toward addressing juvenile delinquency. A recent change for funding sources has been toward accountability in planning and implementing outcome studies to determine program efficacy and effectiveness. A meta-analysis of 117 studies on treatment programs for noninstitutionalized juvenile offenders reports a 40% reduction on recidivism rates, with recidivism being defined as police contact or arrest. The studies evaluated programs that included counseling services (individual, family, and group), interpersonal skills training, and behavioral modification (Lipsey, Wilson, & Cothern, 2000).

A recent national survey of nine model programs that conducted systematic research with outcome measures including recidivism rates demonstrated more success than traditional institutional programs (Roberts, 2004). The similarities between these and successful school-based programs include the multisystemic focus of intervention, family/parent involvement, and an emphasis on academic achievement, vocational training, core values, behavior modification, positive socialization, family counseling, drug/alcohol counseling, group therapy, and community service. Most of the programs' populations were below grade level and/or below average IQ level and had other school problems such as truancy and disruptive behaviors.

During the 1980s, the "wraparound" philosophy developed, which refers to a service delivery system that integrates services from multiple service providers (Howell, 2003). This philosophy of care includes a definable planning process involving the child and family that results in community service and natural supports individualized for that child to obtain specific positive outcomes. These services are then said to be "wrapped" around the specific needs of that child and family (Roberts, 2004). Wraparound Milwaukee is an innovative system of care that emphasizes developing and delivering strength-based, highly individualized, community-focused services to meet the needs of youth and their families. These multiple services systems are combined into a single system of care under the auspices of the Milwaukee County Health and Human Services Department. Care coordinators conduct assessments of needs and strengths, organize team planning, identify and obtain treatment resources and supports, and monitor and evaluate the care plan (Roberts, 2004).

Caseloads are small, with up to eight families, and care coordinators receive extensive training and certification in the wraparound process. Referrals are through court order, which gives authority for a different level of care if needed. Pooled funding from various child-serving agencies and Medicaid are used to create maximum flexibility and the most sufficient funding base possible. In 2001, Wraparound Milwaukee served 869 children and their families, and for those children who were referred as a condition of their probation, recidivism rates after 1 year decreased, as shown in Table 51.1. Wraparound Milwaukee is a successful program because it provides strength-based, comprehensive, flexible, and cost-effective alternatives to institutional care and has achieved positive outcomes for the children and their families.

Another innovative, community-based program is the Bethesda Day Treatment Center, which is designed to assist youth who have been either adjudicated or are status offenders or child abuse dependency cases. The program provides both day treatment and in-home treatment services, with individualized education, substance abuse counseling, family systems counseling, and short-term foster care. An interesting aspect is that it involves the whole family and is integrated into the home, school, peer group, and community. It may require 55 hours or more per week, and the program does not suspend or expel any youth (Roberts, 2004).

The program consists of 17 treatment modules combined and customized to meet the needs of individual youth. These modules include psychological counseling, social skills, education and vocation training, life skills, family counseling, and substance abuse counseling. Two thirds of the youth are below grade level in reading, and most have committed criminal offenses. The client recidivism rate is only 10.4% within the first 12 months of discharge. Although the program evaluation did not review individual treatment modules, the program does appear to be effective as it provides the needed services and has moderately low recidivism with high-risk offenders (Roberts, 2004)

Restitution programs are another innovation in juvenile probation programs. Early studies did not show very positive effects for this approach as an independent intervention (Howell, 2003). When restitution is used only as a punitive measure, it is not as effective as when it is combined with other interventions such as academic support, self-image enhancement, rehabilitation services, and prosocial skill development. In Keene, New Hampshire, the Earn-It Program is a restitution-based youth offender program that allows the offender to repay the victim of the crime. The program does not offer psychological, family, or social skills counseling. Shoplifting, criminal mischief, and theft are the main offenses, the average age is 15.3 years old, and 79% of the youth are male, with a majority below average in school and/or coded special education (Roberts, 2004). Participants have a 14% recidivism rate after 12 months, and 72% of the participants complete the program (Roberts, 2004). Providing more services that address the youth's problems that led to the criminal behavior in conjunction with restitution could strengthen this program.

Intensive supervision services are designed to serve as an alternative to secure confinement for repeat, high-risk offenders. Intensive supervision usually requires lower case loads for probation officers and includes electronic monitoring; drug screening and treatment; individual, group, and family counseling services; restitution; and community service. The Community Intensive Supervision Project of Pittsburgh includes such services and can operate at a lower cost than traditional institutional facilities. In 1996, only 10 of the 209 juveniles were convicted on new criminal acts;

Table 51.1 Wraparound Milwaukee: Recidivism Rates

	Prior to Enrollment	*One Year Following Enrollment*
Property Offenses	40%	15%
Assaults	18%	5%
Weapons Offenses	11%	3%
Sexual Offenses	17%	2%
Drug Offenses	9%	6%
Other Offenses	32%	14%

Source: Roberts, 2004

however, the program had a 45% recidivism rate for those who completed the program (Roberts, 2004). What is not included in the study is the expected recidivism rate for this targeted repeat offender population, so it is difficult to determine whether the program is effective.

Juvenile Justice Alternative Education Programs

Youth who are expelled or placed on probation attend alternative schools until they are returned to the regular public school system. Typically, an assessment is done after 90 days to determine whether the student will remain in the alternative school. Juvenile Justice Alternative Education Programs (JJAEP) are for juvenile offenders on probation or parole who are unable to attend public school. These programs are funded by the Office of Juvenile Justice and Delinquency Prevention through block grants to states and discretionary grants to local governments and private organizations.

In Polk County, Florida, the Alternative Education Department has programs that target school dropouts, while the juvenile justice programs are only for adjudicated, court-ordered offenders. Both programs work with students who have the following problems: learning disabilities, drug addiction, teen pregnancy, mental health disorders, family crisis, juvenile delinquency, and socialization conduct disorders. Some are dropouts, 30–40% are special education students, and 40–45% are 2 years behind grade level (*Alternative Education Department Overview*, 2005). Students are evaluated using the Florida Comprehensive Aptitude Test, student exit tests, and computer gains reports that indicate student improvement of up to two or more grade levels within the length of time in their programs. More than 70% of students who take the GED pass on their first try (*Alternative Education Department Overview*, 2005).

Program evaluations reported on the OJJDP Model Programs Guide Web site, which includes a meta-analysis of 57 alternative school programs, found that alternative schools have a positive effect on school performance, attitudes toward school, and self-esteem but no effect on delinquency (Cox, Davison, & Bynum, 1995). The study also found that alternative schools that targeted at-risk youth produced better effects than other programs and that the more successful programs tend to have a curriculum and structure centered on the needs of the designated population. These effects, however, may be short term. An assessment that used an experimental design with a 1-year follow-up of a single alternative school found that these positive effects were not observed 1 year later (Cox, 1999). Therefore, after-care services or follow-up support given to students in alternative schools is important in achieving the long-term goals of the program. A 5-year evaluation of the career academy concept (the OJJDP alternative school model) covering nine schools and 1,900 students found that, compared with their counterparts who did not attend, at-risk students enrolled in career academies were one third less likely to drop out of school and were more likely to complete their courses and apply to college. The study also found that students in career academies were provided with more opportunities to set goals and reach academic and professional objectives (Kemple & Snipes, 2000).

School-Based Juvenile Probation Officers

Under this model, probation officers are housed in schools rather than the probation department. In addition to working with juveniles on probation, school-based probation officers also intervene with youths who are at risk for delinquency (Howell, 2003). One of the benefits of this model is increased contact between the probation officer and the youth with almost daily contact, rather than once a week or less in more traditional models. Contact can be either formal meetings or more informal interactions, with the goal of developing more substantial relationships and improving communication. Another benefit is access to administrators and teachers for referrals and feedback, and access to school documents such as attendance, grades, and discipline records. School-based probation officers can also

- intervene in crisis situations involving juvenile probation students;
- assist schools in handling disruptive behaviors;
- coordinate services between schools and other agencies; and
- coordinate reentry efforts for youth returning from a juvenile justice facility (Stephens & Arnette, 2000).

Related benefits may be a reduction of school crime and a more positive perspective among youth about probation officers through activities such as mentoring, classroom speaking, and role modeling (*Safe and Responsive Schools,* 2005).

Concerns about confidentiality of juvenile justice and student school records are an issue with this type of model, and it can be addressed through appropriate guidelines available through the OJJDP. Office space needs to be arranged to ensure privacy and confidentiality for the juvenile on probation (*Safe and Responsive Schools,* 2005). Privacy and confidentiality are difficult to ensure in a school, and efforts to maximize them and minimize potential stigma and negative peer interactions with nonoffending youth should be priorities.

Although this model is relatively new, preliminary studies suggest that it has a positive effect on academic performance, school attendance, school conduct, and recidivism (Griffin, 1999; Metzger, 1997). A comparison of 75 randomly selected school-based probation clients with 75 regular probation clients matched on age, race, gender, crime, and county of supervision found that school-based probation clients spent significantly more time in the community without being charged with new offenses or placed in custody and were less likely to be charged with serious crimes (Metzger, 1997). This study also found several other important benefits, including closer overall supervision, better school attendance, fewer instances of recidivism, fewer placements, and far fewer placement days—resulting in an estimated cost savings of $6,665 for every case assigned to school-based probation (*Safe and Responsive Schools,* 2005).

Recently, Torbett, Ricci, Brooks, and Zawacki (2001) surveyed probation officers, probation supervisors, and school administrators in Pennsylvania. All three groups reported high levels of satisfaction with the school-based probation program, including the services the program provides, the effect the program has on the school climate, and the communication that the program fosters between the schools and the juvenile courts. Moreover, more than 90% of the probation officers and 79% of the school administrators believed the program is effective in reducing recidivism among probationers (*Safe and Responsive Schools,* 2005). While not definitive, these results suggest that school-based probation should be considered a promising alternative in a graduated sanctions system.

Tools and Practice Examples

John, 14, is on probation for molesting two of his younger cousins. He is an outpatient at a counseling program for adolescent sex offenders. He lives at home with his mother and his 18-year-old sister. His father is in prison for family violence, but his mother continues to have contact with him, and the family visits him at the prison. He is scheduled to be released from prison in 3 months. John has been expelled from five schools and is currently attending a Juvenile Justice Alternative Education Program. He will not be allowed back in the public school system because he has a record of expulsions.

John has a fourth-grade reading level and is behind two grade levels in his other subjects. He has had problems since elementary school with acting out in class and being disruptive. He frequently got suspended or expelled for cursing and talking back to teachers and administrators, being tardy or truant, and fighting with his peers. He consistently receives failing grades, and while he does some of his homework, he also fails to turn in his completed assignments. He has low motivation for school success, and his home environment does not support academic achievement.

John and his family are receiving family counseling services through the local community mental health center, which has a contract with the county probation office to provide in-home visits and counseling services. His mother must participate and attend parent counseling with the adolescent sex offender program. His probation officer meets with John weekly and coordinates his treatment services. He does not have a history of substance abuse, but he must comply with probation rules about random urinalysis tests for drug screening. Treatment outcome evaluations are provided monthly from his sex offender treatment providers and the family counselor, and case staffings are done with the probation officer and the treatment providers on a regular basis every 3 months.

John is currently having problems at home with his sister as they bicker and fight frequently. He is upset with his mother for visiting his father, and he is worried that she will let him move back home when he gets out of prison. The family is working on these issues in counseling, and he says that things are getting better at home between him and his sister because she got a job and is out of the house more often. Her absence has created a supervision problem, though, because John is not allowed to be unsupervised at home under his sex offender probation guidelines. His probation officer is looking into community service and restitution programs to address this issue.

Since starting at the JJAEP, John's grades and attendance have improved, and he completes his homework assignments and turns them in regularly. He says that the smaller class size and individual attention he receives from his teacher helps him understand the subjects better. He has a mentor from the local college, a student volunteer, helping him with his reading and math assignments. The mentor is one of the few positive male role models with whom John has had continuing contact. This relationship has opened John up to future opportunities, as he and the mentor share many life circumstances, and John sees what successes his mentor has achieved.

John has also been making progress in his sex offender treatment. Being in the group has helped him to be more responsible and to work on his relationships with peers and his family. His communication skills are improving, and he makes better eye contact when speaking to others. He has learned how to be assertive rather than aggressive, and his peers and therapists help give him feedback on how to handle his anger management problems. Though John has made much progress, he will need intensive case services to maintain the improvements he and his family have achieved. Fortunately, he is on probation for at least 2 years, and his probation officer can request extensions every 6 months to ensure continuity of treatment. However, should John commit more offenses or not comply with his probation and treatment guidelines, he can also be reevaluated and placed in a more restrictive setting, such as residential treatment or a correctional facility.

John's case is an example of multiple community-based agencies working with juvenile probation to attempt a less restrictive, rehabilitation-focused case plan for an at-risk youthful offender. Coordination of services, along with strict supervision and probation guidelines, ensures that John is receiving the needed interventions for being successful in school, at home, and on probation. Though he and his family face many issues currently and in the future, it is hoped that he will be able to maintain his progress and ultimately graduate from both probation and high school.

Resources

The following Web sites can be useful resources for information and program referral:

The Brown Schools Alternative Education Programs: www.brownschools.com

Communities in Schools—Helping Kids Stay in School & Prepare for Life: www.cisnet.org

Center on Juvenile and Criminal Justice: www.cjcj.org

Seattle Social Development Project: http://depts.washington.edu/ssdp/

OJJDP Model Programs Guide: www.dsgonline.com

Office of Juvenile Justice and Delinquency Prevention: http://ojjdp.ncjrs.org

Alternative Education Department, Polk County, Florida: www.pcsb.k12.fl.us/AltEd

Southwest Key, Inc.—Alternative Education Programs: www.swkey.org

Texas Juvenile Probation Commission: www.tjpc.state.tx.us

Key Points to Remember

- *Behavior management programs* work with youth who have impulsive, aggressive, or conduct disordered behavior and are directed at tardiness, class preparation and performance, behavior, and attendance.
- *Day treatment programs* provide in-home treatment services, with individualized education services, substance abuse counseling, family systems counseling, and short-term foster care.
- *Intensive supervision services* are designed to serve as an alternative to secure confinement for repeat, high-risk offenders. Probation officers who work in these programs have smaller caseloads and more frequent contacts with the juvenile offenders and their families.
- *Juvenile Justice Alternative Education Programs* are for juvenile offenders who are on probation or have been paroled and are unable to attend public schools.
- *Restitution programs* provide work and community service opportunities for the offender to pay restitution to his or her victim(s) and to pay for legal and court fines.
- *School-based juvenile probation officers* are housed in schools rather than the probation department. In addition to working with juveniles

on probation, school-based probation officers intervene with youths who are at risk for delinquency.

- *Social competency programs* typically use cognitive-behavioral techniques, social skills training, rehearsal, and role playing to improve social skills, problem-solving skills, anger management skills, communication skills, and assertiveness skills training.
- *Transitional services and aftercare* are provided to the family and youth for a period of time after release, which provides continuity and helps ensure a successful transition.
- *Wraparound services* is a service delivery system that integrates services from multiple providers and individualizes them to meet the client's needs.

References

Alternative education department overview. (n.d.). Retrieved March 1, 2005, from http://www.pcsb.k12.fl.us/AltEd/overview/htm

Cox, S. (1999). An assessment of an alternative education programs for at-risk delinquent youth. *Journal of Research in Crime and Delinquency 36*(3), 323–336.

Cox, S., Davison, W., & Bynum, T. (1995). A meta-analytic assessment of delinquency-related outcomes of alternative education programs. *Crime and Delinquency 41*(2), 19–34.

Gottfredson, G. D., Gottfredson, D. C., Czeh, E. R., Cantor, D., Crosse, S., & Hantman, I. (2000). *The national study of delinquency prevention in schools: Final report.* Ellicott City, MD: Gottfredson Associates.

Griffin, T. (1999). Juvenile probation in the schools. *NCJJ In-Focus, 1–11.*

Hawkins, J. D., Catalano, R. F., Kosterman, R., Abbott, R. D., & Hill, K. G. (1999). Preventing adolescent health-risk behavior by strengthening protection during childhood. *Archives of Pediatrics and Adolescent Medicine, 153,* 226–234.

Howell, J. C. (2003). *Preventing and reducing juvenile delinquency: A comprehensive framework.* Thousand Oaks, CA: Sage.

Kemple, J., & Snipes, J. (2000). *Career academies: Impacts on students' engagement and performance in high school.* San Francisco: Manpower Demonstration Research Corporation.

Lipsey, M. W., Wilson, D. B., & Cothern, L. (2000). *Effective interventions for serious and violent juvenile offenders.* Juvenile Justice Bulletin. Washington, DC: Office of Juvenile Justice and Delinquency Prevention.

Loeber, R., & Farrington, D. P. (2001). Executive summary. In R. Loeber & D. P. Farrington (Eds.), *Child delinquents: Development, intervention, and service needs* (pp. xix–xxxi). Thousand Oaks, CA: Sage.

Maguin, E., & Loeber, R. (1996). Academic performance and delinquency. *Crime and Justice, 20,* 145–164.

Metzger, D. (1997). *School-based probation in Pennsylvania.* Philadelphia: University of Pennsylvania, Center for Studies of Addiction.

Office of Juvenile Justice and Delinquency Prevention. (n.d.). *Model programs guide.* Retrieved February 26, 2005, from http://dsgonline.com/mpg_non_flash/school_based_probtion.htm

Office of Juvenile Justice and Delinquency Prevention. (n.d.). *Statistical briefing book.* Retrieved February 26, 2005, from http://ojjdp.ncjrs.org/ojstatbb/

Roberts, A. R. (2004). Epilogue: National survey of juvenile offender treatment programs that work. In A. R. Roberts (Ed.), *Juvenile justice sourcebook: Past, present and future* (pp. 537–561). New York: Oxford University Press.

Safe and responsive schools: School-based probation officers. (n.d.). Retrieved March 2, 2005, from http://www.indiana.edu/~safeschl

Siegel, L. J., Welsh, B. C., & Senna, J. J. (2003). *Juvenile delinquency: Theory, practice, and law.* Belmont, CA: Thompson/Wadsworth.

Smith, C. A., Lizotte, A. J., Thornberry, T. P., & Krohn, M. D. (1997). Resilience to delinquency. *Preventive Researcher, 4,* 4–7.

Stephens, R., & Arnette, J. (2000). *From the courthouse to the schoolhouse: Making a successful transition.* Washington, DC: U.S. Department of Justice, Office of Justice Programs, Office of Juvenile Justice and Delinquency Prevention.

Thornberry, T. P., Lizotte, A. J., Krohn, M. D., Farnworth, M., & Jang, S. J. (1991). Testing interactional theory: An examination of reciprocal causal relationships among family, school, and delinquency. *Journal of Criminal Law and Criminology, 82,* 3–35.

Torbett, P., Ricci, R., Brooks, C., & Zawacki, S. (2001). *Evaluation of Pennsylvania's school-based probation program.* Pittsburgh, PA: National Center for Juvenile Justice.

Zieglar E., & Styfco, S. J. (2001). Extended childhood intervention prepares children for school and beyond. *Journal of the American Medical Association, 285,* 2378–2380.

Best Practice Methods in a School-Based Environment

PART II

Effective Crisis Intervention Methods

School social workers and school-based mental health professionals are aware that school crises are associated with a wide display of family, community, and societal issues. Gang violence, school shootings, natural disasters, terrorism, and increasing media attention to violence all are potential crises in the school environment, and the school-based mental health staff are central in resolving the consequences. This section provides best practice guidelines for a number of social work and mental health functions related to crisis events.

Developing School-Wide and District-Wide Crisis Prevention/Intervention Protocols for Natural Disasters

Karen S. Knox ▪ Albert R. Roberts

Getting Started

While schools have historically had emergency response plans for natural disasters, the need for crisis intervention/prevention plans and teams in school settings has become more evident with increases in school violence, terrorist threats/acts, and other traumatic situations. In the past, crisis preparedness may have seemed more important to schools at high risk for natural disasters, but it is clear that being prepared for potential crisis situations and their aftermath is today's reality for all schools. Much has been learned from research and intervention with those experiencing natural disasters and other tragic school incidents, and that knowledge and experience has contributed to more comprehensive planning and development to meet the needs of the local community and school community.

This chapter provides an overview of the research studies and literature on how to develop school crisis intervention/prevention plans and teams and a discussion of the empirical evidence that supports best practices with victims and survivors of natural disasters. A crisis intervention model is presented as a guideline for planning at the regional, district, and school levels. Specific steps for crisis intervention services and debriefing in the aftermath of a natural disaster are also provided, as are resources and Web sites that aid school personnel in crisis preparedness, training, and response. A case example then illustrates how the model can be applied as a school responds to a natural disaster. This article identifies some of the typical issues and impacts of natural disasters, but one must remember that each situation is unique and even the most comprehensive plans cannot anticipate all of the possible scenarios and effects. It is also important to present crisis plans in a supportive way and to emphasize prevention, rather than expectation, to try to minimize any anxiety and fear among those involved.

What We Know

The empirical research on children and adolescents experiencing natural disasters examines a variety of impact and treatment issues, including specific issues associated with certain types of natural disasters, that is, hurricanes, tornadoes, earthquakes, and floods (Asarnow, Glynn, Pyrnoos, Nahum, Gunthrie, Cantwell, & Franklin, 1999; Feinberg, 1999; Shaw, Applegate, & Shorr, 1996; Zenere, 2001). For example, the warning time or advance notice associated with hurricanes can give people time to gather belongings and seek refuge but also allows more time for fear and anxiety to increase. In contrast, the sudden devastation of earthquakes and tornadoes leaves people little time to prepare and may cause more confusion and panic responses.

Literature addressing other issues, such as posttraumatic stress disorder symptoms; the impacts of relocation and parental reactions; coping styles; and developmental, cultural, and ethnic considerations, contributes to the knowledge base for best practices in this field (Bolton, O'Ryan, Udwin, Boyle, & Yule, 2000; Goenjian, Molina, Steinberg, & Fairbanks, 2001; Jones, Fray, Cunningham, & Kaiser, 2001; La Greca, Silverman, Vernberg, & Prinstein, 1996; Lazarus & Gillespie, 1996; Prinstein, La Greca, Vernberg, & Silverman, 1996; Raid & Norris, 1996; Wasserstein & La Greca, 1998). This literature provides insights from previous personal experiences and research studies on how school-based mental health and social work professionals can plan and prepare for and intervene after natural disasters. Current research emphasizes collaboration among schools, communities, and state and federal organizations and programs; teaching children and adolescents effective coping strategies; fostering supportive relationships among peers and with families; and helping survivors to process their emotions and reactions (Brock, Sandoval, & Lewis, 2001; Lazarus, Jimerson, & Brock, 2002).

What We Can Do

School-Based Crisis Intervention

Those with personal experience with school crises and tragedies have authored the majority of the literature on school crisis intervention/prevention. One of the first school crisis incidents to receive national media attention was the Chowchilla school bus kidnapping in California in 1976, during which the children were buried underground for 27 hours before escaping from the kidnappers. The children received no school or local mental health services, and Terr (1983) found that 5 years later, all of the children displayed posttraumatic stress disorder symptoms. Training manuals and journal articles from the 1990s describe how school professionals responded to actual school crises in order to increase awareness about the effects on those involved and the need for crisis preparedness (Kennedy, 1999; Kline, Schonfeld, & Lichtenstein, 1995; Lichtenstein, Schonfeld, Kline, & Speese-Linehan, 1995; Pitcher & Poland, 1992; Poland & Pitcher, 1990; Young, 1997).

More current literature focuses on practical guides and steps in developing school crisis plans and teams (Allen, Burt, Bryan, Carter, Orsi, & Durkan, 2002; Brock, Lazarus, & Jimerson, 2002; Brock, Sandoval, & Lewis, 2001; Eaves, 2001; Newgrass & Schonfeld, 2000; Rock, 2000; Sandoval, 2002; Schonfeld, Lichtenstein, Pruett, & Speese-Linehan, 2002; Wanko, 2001; Watson & Watson, 2002). These manuals and handbooks are excellent resources that include strategies on how to plan and intervene in specific crisis situations, training curriculums, case vignettes, samples of forms, and ideas for supplies and crisis kits. Table 52.1 outlines the major contributors and their literature and can be used as a reference guide for the best practices in school crisis intervention.

School Crisis Response Model

A school crisis response model should address the levels and types of intervention, as well as the collaboration among the school system, the local community, state resources, and federal programs. School crisis intervention models typically have three levels:

- *Primary prevention* activities, such as emergency response planning and training, crisis drills in schools, establishing a crisis team, and preparing for medical, security, communication, and media responses
- *Secondary intervention* steps during the natural disaster or crisis to minimize its effects and to keep the situation from escalating, including evacuating students to safety, notification to family members and parents, and immediate crisis intervention strategies to address the emotional impacts and physical safety needs of those involved

Table 52.1 School-Based Crisis Intervention Literature and Manuals

Reference	Description
Brock, S. E., Lazarus, P. J., & Jimerson, S. R. (2002) *Best practices in school crisis prevention and intervention*. Bethesda, MD: NASP Publications	Chapters cover crisis theory, primary prevention plans, preparing for crises, responding to crisis events, specific types of crises, long–term treatment of trauma, and special topics such as legal and ethical issues, research needs, and advocacy in this field
Brock, S. E., Sandoval, J., & Lewis, S. (2001) *Preparing for crises in the schools: A manual for building school crisis response teams*. New York: Wiley	Training manual with curriculum that includes lectures, experiential exercises, and handouts for an intensive 2-day in-service on crisis intervention and PTSD; also included are samples of forms and evaluation instruments for safe schools
Decker, R. H. (1997) *When a crisis hits: Will your school be ready?* Thousand Oaks, CA: Corwin	10-step approach outlines district–wide planning components for crisis management; also provides various case scenarios and recommendations for specific steps and actions to take for a variety of crises
Educational Service District 105, Yakima, WA (1997) *Quick response: A step-by-step guide to crisis management for principals, counselors, and teachers*. Alexandria, VA: Association for Supervision and Curriculum Development	Training manual to develop crisis management plan and teams with specific guidelines, checklists, and resources for prevention planning and crisis intervention, including flip charts with references to local and national resources and contact information
Sandoval, J. (2002) *Handbook of crisis counseling, intervention, and prevention in the schools*. Mahwah, NJ: Erlbaum	Reference for mental health professionals on school-based crises, with discussion of the research that underlies best practice. Chapters cover crisis preparedness and counseling, types of crises during childhood and adolescence, and developmentally appropriate intervention activities
Schonfeld, D. J., Lichtenstein, R., Pruett, M. K., & Speese–Linehan, D. (2002) *How to prepare for and respond to a crisis*. Alexandria, VA: Association for Supervision and Curriculum Development	Chapters cover the crisis intervention model and how to establish crisis teams with guidelines on how to develop a school crisis plan and samples of forms, a school crisis kit, and case vignettes for training

- *Tertiary intervention* in the aftermath, including debriefing, support groups, short-term counseling, and referral to other community-based programs and long-term services as needed

These three levels of intervention require participation and support from key personnel at different levels or divisions of the school system, from the central administration to school principals and other campus faculty and staff, and may vary depending on the needs of the community and the size and number of school districts and campuses involved. Newgrass and Schonfeld (2000) recommend a hierarchical model as follows:

- *Regional resource team* composed of a multidisciplinary team with representatives from the school administration and mental health, police, academic, and social services, which meets to develop and review programs, protocols, and policies; to provide support and training to district level teams; and to act as an information clearinghouse
- *District level teams* to provide the crisis response oversight for the school system, including central office administrators and mental health staff who oversee district policies and procedures, resource allocation, staff training and supervision, and technical assistance to the schools within the district at the time of crisis
- *School-based crisis teams* consisting of the school administrator(s), the school nurse, social workers, school counselors, teachers, and support and security staff, who provide direct crisis intervention services and ongoing counseling services

This type of crisis response model allows flexibility to meet the needs of different levels of crisis situations from incidents involving only one school campus, to those involving more than one school in a district or the entire community. A comprehensive model must incorporate all of the different levels of intervention and resources to adequately plan for and respond to the variety of school crisis situations that could be anticipated. Coordinating and implementing the many needs involved in a school crisis can be confusing and cause response delays, if previous planning has not been adequate.

The following school crisis response model provides a guide for planning and developing a region-wide plan. While this model doesn't include all of the specific tasks and activities involved

at each level, it does give a framework for how to distribute and organize the various steps and procedures that need to be implemented for a timely and coordinated response. Other pertinent issues and obstacles will need to be developed for the unique needs of each school and the surrounding community. For example, larger metropolitan areas with several school districts may have more problems with coordinating services and personnel due to student body size and geographical considerations, while smaller school districts may have limitations in resources and technical assistance.

School Crisis Response Model

School-Based Crisis Teams

The purpose of the school-based crisis team is to delegate and implement the roles and duties that are needed during and after a crisis. Team size varies depending on the size of the school district and individual schools within the district, but typically ranges from four to eight members. If the team is too large, it can be unmanageable and difficult to schedule meetings and trainings. If the team is too small, then there may not be enough members to cover critical tasks. It is recommended that teams be multidisciplinary with members from the school administration, school counselors, social workers, the school nurse, teachers, security officers, and support staff. There should also be alternates or members who serve as backups or on a rotating basis to address potential problems with members being unavailable or suffering burnout. Some suggested roles and tasks for the crisis team members include:

- *team leader*: responsible for planning and presiding at team meetings; oversees the functioning of the team and its members; conducts drills and readiness checks; and reports to district level contacts
- *assistant team leader*: assists in planning and implementing tasks; coordinates training and support services for team members; and is responsible if the team leader is unavailable
- *media coordinator*: serves as the contact person for all media inquiries and as a link with the regional and district teams
- *staff notification coordinator*: establishes and initiates a telephone tree or alternate communication system to notify team members, other

Table 52.2 School Crisis Response Model

Level of Intervention	Regional	District	School
Primary Prevention	Community-level crisis response plan and team	Emergency response policies/procedures	Emergency and evacuation plans and drills
	Policies and procedures	Safety and security issues	Prevention programs
	Support and resources	Training and education	Support services
	Networking	Communication systems	Crisis intervention team
Secondary Intervention	Activate community response team and plan involving school, emergency medical personnel, police, mental health and social service providers	Activate district-level plan and procedures	Activate school crisis plan and teams
		Coordinate school-level crisis teams	Emergency and evacuation procedures
		Link to regional level	Notification/communication
		Communication and media	Debriefing/demobilization
	Technical assistance	Resource allocation for schools	Short-term crisis counseling
	Networking with community resources	Ongoing support and resources	Referrals for long-term counseling or other services
Tertiary Intervention	Policy and procedures evaluation	Program and response plan evaluation	Memorialization
	Ongoing planning and needs assessment for the region	District team meetings to improve procedures and prevention strategies	Follow up with school crisis team members
			Practice evaluation of interventions and programs

school staff, and people affected by the crisis, such as students, families, and staff, in an organized manner
- *in-house communications coordinator:* screens all incoming calls; maintains a phone log; assists the staff notification coordinator; and maintains a phone directory of regional and district-level teams, staff, and community resources
- *crowd management coordinator:* collaborates with the school security personnel, local law enforcement, and emergency departments to supervise evacuation and crowd control procedures and to assure the safe and organized movement of students and staff to minimize the risk of harm

- *evaluator:* designs questionnaires and structured interviews for evaluation; collects data on crisis team performance and outcomes; coordinates debriefing and demobilization procedures with the crisis team members as a part of the evaluation process (Brock, Sandoval, & Lewis, 2001; Schonfeld, Kline, & Members of the Crisis Intervention Committee, 1994)

Debriefing refers to stress-relieving activities and processing of the incident. Typically, this occurs between 24 and 72 hours after the critical incident and can be done individually and with the team as a group. Debriefing meetings should encourage the team members to support each other and not be critical. The purpose of debriefing is to evaluate whether any crisis team members need to be referred for counseling services and to begin the evaluation process. This type of debriefing is not intended to be therapeutic, as in critical incident stress debriefing or management, and is primarily evaluative in nature. Any clinical intervention services for crisis team members should be done by non-team, qualified professionals outside of the school setting.

Demobilization refers to evaluative information-gathering strategies for the purpose of improving responses and prevention planning. Information and feedback are gathered through written surveys or structured interviews with individuals or in a group setting after the crisis situation has been resolved. Information on the school crisis intervention process and procedures, problems with the implementation of the crisis response plan, and other unforeseen circumstances or factors affecting the efforts are examples of the type of information gathered during demobilization.

It is important to have a *building plan* to provide space for medical triage, safety, shelter, communication, and other emergency needs of the law enforcement and medical personnel who are dealing with the immediate crisis situation. There should also be designated support rooms that are adequately staffed by qualified counseling personnel and crisis team members to provide mental health triage, referral, and brief time-limited interventions. School crisis team members need to develop guidelines for referring students and monitoring their status, as well as procedures for getting parental permission for treatment, referrals for ongoing treatment or school-based support groups, and other follow-up services as needed (Schonfeld et al., 1994).

The school crisis team may also need to deal with issues of grief and loss, such as how to convey formally the condolences of the school or class; how to handle personal belongings; appropriate displays of memorials, such as flowers, candles, photos, and so on; attending funeral services; and school memorial or recognition services. The nature and timing of such memorializations need to be given careful thought and planning to ensure that they do not escalate the effects of the crisis situation or prematurely try to create closure (Schonfeld et al., 1994).

Training and resources for school crisis teams require time, money, and effort that many financially burdened school districts may be reluctant to fund. However, there are training curriculums,

manuals, and workshops available to assist in this process. School districts may want to cross-train crisis team members at various levels or provide specialized training relevant to the team members' roles and responsibilities. In-service trainers who could conduct workshops on a regular basis as needed would be cost effective and would provide continuity in the training, which should be viewed as an ongoing need. School crisis team members who are professionally qualified to provide direct counseling and crisis intervention services would need more in-depth and specialized training on specific types of crises. Collaboration with community professionals who have experience and expertise in crisis intervention could be another resource for ongoing training and clinical services.

Tools and Practice Example

Tools

Additional resources for school crisis management can be found on the Internet through these Web sites:

- www.aaets.com (American Academy of Experts in Traumatic Stress)
- www.apa.org (American Psychological Association's Disaster Response Network)
- www.compassionatefriends.org (support groups for bereaved parents)
- www.crisisinfo.org (national standards for responding to university and school-based crises)
- www.disasterhelp.gov (offers information, resources, and links for disaster responses and organizations)
- www.fema.gov (Federal Emergency Management Agency)
- www.keepschoolssafe.org (National Association of Attorneys General and National School Boards Association)
- www.ncptsd.org (National Center for PTSD: Disaster Mental Health Services offers a guidebook for clinicians and administrators and information on PTSD in children and adolescents)
- www.ojp.usdoj.gov/ovc/infores/crt/pdfwelc.htm (community crisis response team training manual from the U.S. Department of Justice's Office for Victims of Crime)

- www.schoolcrisisresponse.com (practical guide for school crisis response planning)
- www.tlcinstitute.org (National Institute for Trauma and Loss in Children)

Case Example

In July 2002, there was torrential rain and flooding in the Hill Country area of central Texas that resulted in 2–3 feet of rain in a week. According to the National Weather Service Web site, 80 counties were declared disaster areas; two lakes and eight rivers in the area flooded, with some cresting 30–40 feet above flood stage; 48,000 homes were destroyed; 25 shelters were needed for displaced families; and there were nine fatalities (National Weather Service, 2002).

One of the hardest hit areas was New Braunfels, where many families lost everything and were displaced for several weeks until the flood waters receded. That displacement continued for months for some families who had to rebuild homes that were destroyed and for others who had to relocate. When school started that fall, many children were still experiencing PTSD symptoms and other impact issues from their experiences, and even children who had not been directly affected showed signs of traumatization.

The Hill Country Mental Health/Mental Retardation Center, the Comal County School District, and the Communities in Schools Program provided counseling and support groups in the schools for the teachers, staff, and schoolchildren. Communities in Schools (CIS) is a free-standing program housed on school campuses, which targets for prevention and intervention services at-risk children, including those with problems with behaviors or peers, teen parents, and students at risk for dropping out. These multidisciplinary counseling teams provided crisis intervention, individual therapy, grief and loss groups, and ongoing peer support groups to address the psychological and emotional distress the students were experiencing. Children who had to be evacuated from the flooded areas and those whose homes were destroyed experienced sleeping problems, had nightmares, and were anxious and worried about where they would live and what would happen to them and their families. Another important treatment issue was the loss of pets and farm animals, where the students' grief and guilt feelings over not being able to rescue some of their animals were difficult to resolve. The counselors found that students were affected throughout that school year, especially whenever it rained, which triggered a lot of fear and concern, especially from the younger elementary school children. The teams also provided support services and in-service training for the schoolteachers and staff on how to address and manage any aftereffects and impact issues from the flooding and related problems during class. Many students had difficulty concentrating and focusing on their work, and others had emotional reactions and outbursts that would disrupt class and trigger other students' reactions.

School and CIS staff also worked with the families who had been displaced and lost their belongings to get them needed resources from the community and disaster relief agencies. This area has many families living in poverty who lost everything, had no resources, and were dependent on others to survive. Feelings of hopelessness and frustration increased the longer it took to receive assistance, and many families had to double up with relatives, friends, or neighbors until repairs or other living arrangements could be made. The extended time needed for relocation and rebuilding throughout the school year interfered with many students' abilities to maintain school performance and attendance.

If school had been in session at the time of the flooding, then the crisis response plans would have been implemented immediately at all three levels of intervention in order to respond to the flooding, including specific emergency, safety, evacuation, and notification procedures and coordination with the community emergency response units, such as EMS, fire, and police. With weather and building damage considerations, the schools would either have been used as emergency shelters and for medical triage, or if conditions warranted, evacuation procedures might have been necessary. With either option, resources would have needed to be mobilized, and the emergency communication and notification systems would have begun. Table 52.3 provides a summary of the three intervention levels and their respective tasks.

Key Points to Remember

Current literature and research indicate that collaboration and planning between schools and communities are necessary to develop intervention and prevention plans for natural disasters and

Table 52.3 Intervention Levels and Tasks

Intervention Level	Regional	District	School
Primary Tasks	Implement crisis response plan; establish emergency communication procedures; notification and coordination of media announcements; technical assistance	Coordinate school emergency response procedures with community first-responders; assist with evacuation and shelter needs; communication link between regional and school levels	Activate school emergency response plan and notification procedures; school crisis team assists community first-responders with evacuation, safety, medical, and shelter needs
Secondary Tasks	Assess needs and provide resources for rebuilding, staff and student safety, plans for return to school; coordinate media and notification services	Oversee the distribution of resources and plan for reconstruction of schools or reassignment of staff and students; communication link between regional and school levels	Debriefing and demobilization procedures; assist with school reopening and clean-up activities; crisis intervention services and referrals to community resources
Follow-Up Tasks	Assessment of future needs and resources; evaluation of emergency response effectiveness; ongoing policy and resource development	Coordinate ongoing resources, training, and support services for schools; team meetings to evaluate and improve prevention and response plans; media notification; memorial services	Memorial services and follow-up support services for staff, students, and family members; referral for counseling or support groups; evaluation of crisis team and response

other types of crisis situations. Important points to address in this effort include:

- *School crisis intervention models* usually have three levels: primary prevention planning and preparation, secondary intervention during the crisis situation, and tertiary intervention in the aftermath.
- *School crisis response levels* are typically at the regional, district, and school levels.
- *School crisis teams* delegate and implement the roles, duties, and responsibilities that are needed during and after a crisis situation and include a team leader; assistant team leader; coordinators for the media, staff notification, in-house communication, and crowd management; and an evaluator.

- *Debriefing* involves stress-relieving and processing activities within 24–72 hours to evaluate team members' need for referral for counseling services.
- *Demobilization* refers to strategies to gather information and feedback from the crisis team members to improve responses and procedures in the future.
- *Impact issues*, such as relocation, parental reactions, coping styles, grief and loss, and developmental, cultural, and ethnic considerations, are important to address in counseling the survivors of natural disasters.
- *Follow-up strategies* to provide support and long-term services from local community organizations and programs should also be included.

References

Allen, M., Burt, K., Bryan, E., Carter, D., Orsi, R., & Durkan, L. (2002). School counselors' preparation for and participation in crisis intervention. *Professional School Counseling, 6*(2), 96–102.

Asarnow, J., Glynn, S., Pyrnoos, R. S., Nahum, J., Gunthrie, D., Cantwell, D. P., & Franklin, B. (1999). When the earth stops shaking: Earthquake sequelae among children diagnosed for pre-earthquake psychopathology. *Journal of the American Academy of Child & Adolescent Psychiatry, 38,* 1016–1023.

Bolton, D., O'Ryan, D., Udwin, O., Boyle, S., & Yule, W. (2000). The long-term psychological effects of a disaster experienced in adolescence: II. General psychopathology. *Journal of Child Psychology and Psychiatry and Allied Disciplines, 41,* 513–523.

Brock, S. E., Lazarus, P. J., & Jimerson, S. R. (Eds.). (2002). *Best practices in school crisis prevention and intervention.* Bethesda, MD: NASP Publications.

Brock, S. E., Sandoval, J., & Lewis, S. (2001). *Preparing for crises in the schools: A manual for building school crisis response teams.* New York: Wiley.

Decker, R. H. (1997). *When a crisis hits: Will your school be ready?* Thousand Oaks, CA: Corwin.

Eaves, C. (2001). The development and implementation of a crisis response team in a school setting. *International Journal of Emergency Mental Health, 3*(1), 35–46.

Educational Service District 105, Yakima, Washington. (1997). *Quick response: A step-by-step guide to crisis management for principals, counselors, and teachers.* Alexandria, VA: Association for Supervision and Curriculum Development.

Feinberg, T. (1999). The midwest floods of 1993: Observations of a natural disaster. In A. S. Canter & S. A. Carroll (Eds.), *Crisis prevention & response: A collection of NASP resources* (pp. 223–239). Bethesda, MD: National Association of School Psychologists.

Goenjian, A. K., Molina, L., Steinberg, A. M., & Fairbanks, L. A. (2001). Post traumatic stress and depressive reactions among adolescents after Hurricane Mitch. *American Journal of Psychiatry, 158,* 788–794.

Jones, R. T., Fray, R., Cunningham, J. D., & Kaiser, L. (2001). The psychological effects of hurricane Andrew on ethnic minority and Caucasian children and adolescents: A case study. *Cultural Diversity and Ethnic Minority Psychology, 7,* 103–108.

Kennedy, M. (1999). Crisis management: Every school needs a plan. *American School & University, 71*(11), 25–27.

Kline, M., Schonfeld, D., & Lichtenstein, R. (1995). Benefits and challenges of school-based crisis response teams. *Journal of Social Health, 65,* 245–249.

La Greca, A. M., Silverman, W. K., Vernberg, E. M., & Prinstein, M. J. (1996). Symptoms of posttraumatic stress in children following hurricane Andrew: A prospective study. *Journal of Consulting & Clinical Psychology, 64,* 712–723.

Lazarus, P. J., & Gillespie, B. (1996). Critical actions in the aftermath of natural disasters. *School Administrator, 53*(2), 35–36.

Lazarus, P. J., Jimerson, S. R., & Brock, S. E. (2002). Natural disasters. In S. E. Brock, P. J. Lazarus, & S. R. Jimerson (Eds.), *Best practices in school crisis prevention and intervention* (pp. 433–447). Bethesda, MD: NASP Publications.

Lichtenstein, R., Schonfeld, D., Kline, M., & Speese-Linehan, D. (1995). *How to prepare for and respond to a crisis.* Alexandria, VA: Association for Supervision and Curriculum Development.

National Weather Service, Hydrologic Information Center. (2002). Texas flooding: July 2002. Available: www.nws.noaa.gov/oh/hic/current/TX, July_2002. sthml.

Newgrass, S., & Schonfeld, D. (2000). School crisis intervention, crisis prevention, and crisis response. In A. R. Roberts (Ed.), *Crisis intervention handbook: Assessment, treatment, and research* (pp. 209–228). New York: Oxford University Press.

Pitcher, G., & Poland, S. (1992). *Crisis intervention in the schools.* New York: Guilford.

Poland, S., & Pitcher, G. (1990). Best practices in crisis intervention. In A. Thomas & J. Grimes (Eds.), *Best practices in school psychology* (pp. 259–275). Washington, DC: National Association of School Psychologists.

Prinstein, M. J., La Greca, A. M., Vernberg, E. M., & Silverman, W. K. (1996). Children's coping assistance: How parents, teachers, and friends help children cope after a natural disaster. *Journal of Clinical Child Psychology, 25,* 463–475.

Raid, J. K., & Norris, F. H. (1996). The social influence of relocation on the environmental, social, and psychological stress experience of disaster victims. *Environment and Behavior, 28,* 163–182.

Rock, M. L. (2000). Effective crisis management planning: Creating a collaborative framework. *Education & Treatment of Children, 23*(3), 248–265.

Sandoval, J. (Ed.). (2002). *Handbook of crisis counseling, intervention, and prevention in the schools.* Mahwah, NJ: Erlbaum.

Schonfeld, D., Kline, M., & Members of the Crisis Intervention Committee. (1994). School-based crisis intervention: An organizational model. *Crisis Intervention and Time-Limited Treatment, 1*(2), 155–166.

Schonfeld, D. J., Lichtenstein, R., Pruett, M. K., & Speese-Linehan, D. (2002). *How to prepare for and respond to a crisis.* Alexandria, VA: Association for Supervision and Curriculum Development.

Shaw, J. A., Applegate, B., & Shorr, C. (1996). Twenty-one month follow up of children exposed to hurricane Andrew. *Journal of the American Academy of Child & Adolescent Psychiatry, 35,* 359–366.

Terr, L. C. (1983). Chowchilla revisited: The effects of a psychic trauma after a school bus kidnapping. *American Journal of Psychiatry, 140,* 1543–1555.

Wanko, M. A. (2001). *Safe schools: Crisis prevention and response.* Lanham, MD: Scarecrow.

Wasserstein, S. B., & La Greca, A. M. (1998). Hurricane Andrew: Parent conflict as a moderator of children's adjustment. *Hispanic Journal of Behavioral Sciences, 20,* 212–224.

Watson, R. J., & Watson, R. S. (2002). *The school as a safe haven.* Westport, CT: Bergin & Garvey.

Young, M. A. (1997). *The community crisis response team training manual.* Washington, DC: National Organization for Victim Assistance.

Zenere, F. J. (2001). Tremors of trauma: Responding to the El Salvador earthquakes. *NASP Communique, 29*(7), 10–11.

Immediate School-Based Intervention Following Violent Crises

Shane R. Jimerson ▪ Stephen E. Brock
Sarah M. Woehr ▪ Amanda Clinton-Higuita

Getting Started

Amid a decade of shootings and other violent events on school campuses, education professionals are faced with new challenges. While the vast majority of school campuses will never experience a violent death, other forms of school violence, such as assaults, are more common (Anderson et al., 2001). While there is limited research addressing schools' interventions to these crises, many lessons may be learned from those who have attended to the aftermath of school violence. The lessons learned from these events inform our crisis intervention strategies for working with students at school (Brock & Jimerson, 2004; Brock, Lazarus, & Jimerson, 2002; Brock, Sandoval, & Lewis, 2001).

This chapter provides a brief review of the practice and theory of school-based crisis intervention. To support the implementation of these activities, this chapter provides a framework for conceptualizing the elements of school crisis intervention, reviews specific school crisis interventions, and discusses relevant research. It concludes with an overview of the school crisis intervention process and provides a case illustration.

What We Know

Overview

We define *crisis interventions* as those activities, typically directed by school-based mental health professionals, that address the social and emotional consequences of a crisis event. Recognizing that

the form and content of school crisis interventions will change over time (National Institute of Mental Health, 2002), our school crisis intervention framework consists of a chronological system that divides crisis events into five phases (Valent, 2000): (a) pre-impact (the period before the crisis), (b) impact (when the crisis occurs), (c) recoil (immediately after the crisis event), (d) post-impact (days to weeks after the crisis event), and (e) recovery and reconstruction (months or years after the event). Table 53.1 illustrates this conceptualization of the time periods during which the different elements of school crisis intervention occur. This chapter will focus primarily on the impact, recoil, and post-impact phases of crisis intervention.

The impact and recoil phases of a crisis necessitate immediate crisis intervention. As can be seen in Table 53.1, the elements of this intervention include immediate prevention, support system reestablishment, psychological education, psychological first aid, and risk-screening and referral activities. Combined, these activities are designed to mitigate the social and emotional harm generated by a crisis event and to identify those individuals in need of professional mental health intervention.

Immediate School Crisis Intervention Elements and Relevant Research

No systematic, experimental research has been conducted on violent school crises due to the low incidence rate, as well as the unpredictability of their occurrence. Therefore, the crisis intervention elements discussed below have been validated via anecdotal evidence and by a review of crisis-related literature (Brock & Jimerson, 2004).

Table 53.1 Five Phases of Crisis Events

Pre-Impact *The Period Before the Crisis*	Impact *When the Crisis Occurs*	Recoil *Immediately After the Crisis*	Post-Impact *Days to Weeks After the Crisis*	Recovery/Reconstruction *Months or Years After the Crisis*
			Mental Health Intervention	
			• Cognitive-behavioral	• Cognitive-behavioral
		Psychological First Aid		
		• Individual first aid	• Individual first aid • Group first aid	• Crisis prevention/preparedness planning • Anniversary reaction support
		Psychological Education		
		• Psychoeducation groups • Caregiver training • Informational flyers	• Psychoeducation groups • Caregiver training • Informational flyers	• Anniversary preparedness • Caregiver training • Informational flyers
		Risk Screening and Referral		
		• Initial screening	• Individual screening • School wide screening • Referral procedures	• Individual screening
		Support System		
		• Reunite with/locate caregivers and loved ones	• Reunite with friends and teachers • Return to school	
	Immediate Prevention			
	• Protect from harm and danger	• Minimize crisis exposure • Ensure actual and perceived safety		

Crisis Preparedness

- Crisis education
- Crisis drills
- Crisis planning

Source: Modified from Brock & Jimerson, 2004.

Immediate Prevention

These activities focus on protecting and/or shielding students from physical and emotional harm. For example, implementing crisis response strategies, such as lockdown or evacuation procedures, would be considered part of immediate prevention. Research supports the need for immediate prevention, since a positive correlation between the degree of exposure to a crisis event and subsequent stress reactions has been established (Pynoos et al., 1987). Given these data, it is not surprising to find that exposure to crisis events via television viewing has suggested it to be a PTSD risk factor (Gurwitch, Sitterle, Yound, & Pferrerbaum, 2002).

Reestablishing Social Support Systems

Individuals with strong familial and social support systems are better able to cope with life stressors than those without such supports (Cohen & Willis, 1985). Given this assertion, it is not surprising that the reestablishment and use of naturally occurring supports (e.g., parents, peers, and teachers) is a frequently recommended and empirically supported crisis intervention (Brock & Jimerson, 2004).

Psychological Education

The primary goal of psychological education is to provide students, staff, and caregivers with knowledge that assists in understanding, preparing for, and responding to the crisis and resulting problems and reactions. There is no research assessing the effectiveness of psychological education among schoolchildren. However, there is limited research addressing the effectiveness of psychological education among adults. For example, a study by Herman, Kaplan, and LeMelle (2002) examined the effect of this intervention for governmental and nonprofit agency workers following the events of September 11, 2001. The 90- to 120-minute interventions gave information about normal and pathological emotional responses, how to help children, and practical coping strategies. Survey results revealed that the vast majority (82%) found this psychological education to be helpful.

Individual Psychological First Aid

The primary goal of individual psychological first aid is to directly facilitate coping with crisis problems and reactions in a fashion that allows for a return to pre-crisis functioning levels. Individual first aid requires school crisis interveners to make psychological contact with the person in crisis, identify crisis problems, examine possible solutions, help the person to take concrete problem-solving action, and when necessary ensure connections to appropriate helping resources (Slaikeu, 1990). Very little research exists regarding the efficacy of individual psychological first aid interventions following crisis events. However, given that these interventions facilitate active or approach coping strategies (i.e., they aim at helping students to take concrete problem-solving actions), that research has suggested that such coping is associated with lower rates of mental illness (Seiffge-Krenke, Weidemann, Fentner, Aegenheister, & Poeblau, 2001) and that avoidant coping strategies are predictive of posttraumatic stress (McFarlane, 1988), these interventions may be said to have some empirical support.

Group Psychological First Aid

These interventions actively explore and process crisis experiences and share individual crisis reactions. By doing so in a group setting, these interventions aim to help students feel less alone and more connected to their classmates by virtue of their common experiences and reactions. They also help to normalize these experiences and reactions (Brock, 2002a). There is no research regarding the use of these interventions with children, and the available research regarding group psychological first aid interventions (such as debriefing) when used with adolescents and adults has yielded mixed results. Among acute trauma victims (i.e., individuals hospitalized following car accidents and with severe burns), these interventions may at best not be helpful and at worst may increase psychological injury. This intervention appears to be most appropriate for vicarious trauma victims (i.e., those who witnessed or have learned about a crisis event happening to someone else; Brock & Jimerson, 2004).

Risk Screening and Referral

Finally, risk screening and referral (also known as psychological triage) is a dynamic process that helps school crisis intervention teams identify those individuals who *do* and *do not* need their services. All of the crisis interventions just reviewed can be considered a part of risk screening and referral. Arguably, the most important outcome that would support the effectiveness of any risk screening and referral protocol would be a low incidence of failure to identify and refer students who have significant mental health problems secondary to crisis exposure. To our knowledge, there is no research assessing the effectiveness of any school-based risk screening and referral protocol. There are, however, substantial data that can be used to validate the inclusion of specific risk factors in risk screening. These factors include physical proximity and duration of exposure to the crisis, emotional proximity to the crisis (i.e., having significant relationships with crisis victims and threat perceptions), the severity and type of crisis reactions (e.g., the diagnosis of an acute stress disorder is a powerful predictor of later PTSD), and a host of external and internal resources (Brock, 2002b).

Professional Mental Health Interventions

Although not considered an immediate crisis intervention, the longer term mental health treatment provided by mental health professionals (e.g., clinical social workers and psychologists) to individuals who develop psychopathology (e.g., posttraumatic stress disorder) subsequent to crisis exposure deserves some mention here. While there is only limited research examining immediate crisis interventions, the literature regarding these psychotherapeutic responses is much more substantial. Particularly, cognitive-behavioral treatments have been found to be effective for psychological trauma (Foa & Meadows, 1998). These treatments included exposure-based therapies, anxiety management, and cognitive therapy. From their review of the empirical literature, Foa and Meadows suggest that prolonged exposure, a form of cognitive-behavioral therapy, is the most effective and beneficial treatment approach for traumatic stress reactions.

Multicomponent Crisis Intervention

As illustrated in the discussion of various intervention strategies, no single intervention activity will provide resolution for all individuals in the aftermath of a violent school crisis event. When it comes to crisis intervention, one size does not fit all. Considering the complexity inherent in the multitude of individual and contextual factors that affect post-crisis responses, systematic and multifaceted crisis intervention approaches are encouraged. It must also be acknowledged that changes in perceptions and reactions are likely to occur over time. By making use of a chronological framework, the intervention strategies outlined above address the unique considerations of crises that affect children in the school context. Insights based on research, practical experience, and theory should be incorporated into chronologically based school crisis management plans aimed at facilitating the coping and adjustment of students in the wake of crises.

What We Can Do

The process of school crisis intervention requires a multidisciplinary school crisis team that attempts to manage the myriad challenges generated by a crisis event. Preparation for responding to the aftermath of any crisis should include a comprehensive, yet flexible, plan that takes into account a school's diverse populations. While there are many practical considerations addressed in the development of a school-based crisis intervention plan, such plans often overlook the unique needs of those who are affected. The efficacy of intervention efforts will likely be positively influenced by taking time to address a few of these special considerations, including the developmental level of the students and the ethnic and linguistic diversity of the student population.

Before reviewing the process of school crisis intervention, it is important to acknowledge that resolution of the acute crisis situation is a prerequisite to the initiation of the school mental health response (or the immediate crisis intervention). In other words, the work of emergency response personnel (e.g., police and paramedics) takes precedence over the work of school mental health responders. The meeting of emergency medical needs and ensuring physical safety is prerequisite to the work of the school crisis intervention team. It is also important to acknowledge that prerequisite to the implementation of these guidelines is the development of a crisis team with a clear leadership structure. That is, it must be understood who is in charge of the crisis intervention. Adapted from the work of Brock et al. (2001), the process of school crisis intervention is now discussed.

Preparation

The process of school crisis intervention begins with crisis planning. A comprehensive crisis intervention plan should be designed to be flexible enough to address the full range of potential crises. In order to achieve as high a level of preparedness as possible, an intervention plan that encompasses the following key elements should be developed: (a) formation and maintenance of a school/community crisis team; (b) training of teachers and support staff on crisis intervention procedures, including important developmental and cultural considerations along with annual reviews of the crisis plan; (c) formation of guidelines for school staff facilitating student coping; (d) development of an accounting system for all students immediately following a crisis; (e) coordination with the community in the event of a crisis; (f) offering of parent education programs; and (g) preparation of a longer term follow-up plan in addition to the immediate intervention plan.

Assess the Crisis Situation

Following the occurrence of a crisis event, the first task to be completed is for the crisis intervention team leadership to assess the crisis situation. This involves gathering crisis facts and estimating the event's impact on the school. This information is used to decide upon the level of crisis response required (e.g., school site level versus district level). Information sources include law enforcement, medical personnel, and the families of crisis victims.

Disseminate Crisis Information

Once the basic facts have been identified, the crisis intervention team leadership should hold a crisis management meeting, during which crisis facts are shared and initial intervention activities planned. In addition, crisis facts need to be shared with the broader school community. Sharing crisis information is critical to a school crisis intervention as crisis rumors are typically more frightening than crisis facts. Especially when being shared with students, these facts should be disseminated in as normal and natural an environment and manner as possible. An example includes an announcement read simultaneously by classroom teachers, rather than having an all-school assembly. It is important to note that when making decisions about what information to share with a school, it may be appropriate to avoid mentioning particularly frightening crisis details. If such facts are not publicly available or being speculated upon, then there will be no reason to discuss them. However, no matter how unpleasant the facts are, if students have questions about them, it will typically be appropriate to answer them as honestly as possible.

Begin to Identify Crisis Victims

As the facts are collected, the school crisis intervention team should also begin identifying both physical and psychological crisis victims. The most important factor in determining the degree of psychological trauma experience by a child is proximity to the crisis event. However, students' familiarity with crisis victims and severity of their crisis reactions are also predictors of psychological injury.

Crisis intervention guidelines must specify a procedure for identifying crisis victims. When there are large numbers of victims, a psychological triage will need to be conducted (Brock, 2002b). Part of such triage is to ensure that parents, teachers, and the school community are aware of the signs and symptoms of posttraumatic stress in students and colleagues and accept the responsibility for referring those individuals for appropriate treatment.

Provide Specific Crisis Interventions

As psychological trauma victims are identified, decisions need to be made regarding the provision of crisis intervention services (the elements of which were discussed in the first part of this chapter). These services need to ensure that the acute distress or grief experienced by students is supported in a professional, empathic manner and that the psychological equilibrium of students and faculty members is restored as soon as possible. In addition, these interventions continue the process of identifying crisis victims. While it should be expected that, with the support of their natural caregiving environments, most students will recover from their crisis event exposure, some may require more direct crisis intervention assistance, such as psychological first aid or professional mental health intervention. The presence of any degree of lethality, such as suicidal or homicidal thinking, or an inability to cope with the traumatizing circumstances are reasons for making an immediate professional mental health counseling referral.

Debrief and Evaluate the Crisis Response

Finally, it is essential that crisis response procedural guidelines include activities designed to care for the caregivers. Following a crisis response, all crisis team members will need to be offered the opportunity to debrief. In addition, they need to evaluate the effectiveness of the response. No two crises are alike. Thus, given the proper reflective thought, all crises are potential learning experiences. These debriefings also provide an opportunity to begin to develop the long-term planning that may be required (e.g., coordinating school with community mental health interventions, planning for memorials, planning for anniversaries).

Tools and Practice Examples

To illustrate the process of a school crisis intervention, we offer the following scenario and then speculate on a school's hypothetical intervention response:

> On January 28, a 6-year-old first-grader, Samantha, had a disagreement with a male classmate. The next day, while the children were lining up, the little boy approached Samantha, pulled out a gun, and fired a single shot at her. Samantha died a few hours later.

Preparation

Ideally, the school at which this crisis took place will not have waited until this crisis event to consider how it will respond to a crisis at school. The degree to which the school was prepared will facilitate all subsequent crisis intervention activities.

Assessing the Situation

Subsequent to emergency medical personnel and law enforcement officials completing their assigned tasks, such as transporting Samantha to a hospital and removing the firearm from the child who shot her, the crisis team begins to assess the crisis situation. This may occur on the same day as the crisis or a subsequent day, depending upon whether children remain in school, given the nature of the event. In the present case, facts regarding the crisis were first obtained. Specifically, Samantha's principal spoke with emergency response workers, law enforcement officials, and Samantha 's mother to determine what had happened. In the meantime, after law enforcement had completed the investigation, the mental health professionals met with Samantha's classroom teacher to gather facts about the events of the previous day.

Disseminating Information

The day following the shooting, the school's principal mental health professionals, including the school social worker and school psychologist, met in order to share the information they had gathered and gauge the degree of impact on the educational community. They decided that, first, a meeting would be held with teachers in order to help them learn how to talk to their classes. In an effort for the teachers to be supported while sharing information about Samantha's death with their students, mental health professionals from the broader educational community made themselves available.

Identifying Crisis Victims

While visiting classrooms in support of teachers, the mental health professionals paid close attention to the behavior of students in an effort to identify students demonstrating signs of acute distress, either emotional or behavioral. This was critically important due to the young age of the children in Samantha's classroom, which made it difficult for them to self-identify. Furthermore, they also offered open office hours so that students who needed additional support could be referred to them by their teachers or request to go to their offices. Parents were also asked to share with mental health professionals any significant changes in the behavior of their children.

Providing Crisis Interventions

The first crisis interventions offered were designed to minimize exposure to crisis images. Specifically, immediately after the shooting, all students were directed away from the scene of the medical emergency. Next, parents were given the crisis facts and offered psychological education regarding how they can help their children to cope with the shooting and given guidance regarding how to identify the need for mental health intervention. Especially important was the guidance offered regarding how young children look to the significant adults in their lives to gauge how threatening the event was. Given this fact, they were advised to be sure they were in control of their own emotions when they set out to comfort their children.

To facilitate the coping process, as well as to continue the process of identifying psychological trauma victims, the school social worker and school psychologist spent the first several days following the shooting in Samantha's first-grade classroom. Here they offered individual and small-group psychological first aid. Group psychological first aid also was made available to all other classrooms in the school. These sessions were facilitated by the community mental health professionals (who had been brought into the school to support this crisis intervention).

In a continuing effort to prevent the development of significant trauma and loss responses, the school social worker and the school psychologist decided to visit Samantha's first-grade classroom and offer individual counseling support daily during the next 4 weeks. They continued to provide counseling in small groups to the students in Samantha's classroom. Students who had observed the shooting were also designated for individual counseling with the mental health professionals. Voluntary counseling groups were established for other children in the school.

Throughout this time period, students continued to be monitored for signs of psychopathology that might signal the need for referral to a community mental health professional.

Debriefing and Evaluating the Crisis Response

In order to debrief, the entire crisis team met at weekly intervals during the first month following Samantha's death. Each member of the school crisis intervention team reported on her current activities and shared updated information related to the community response to Samantha's death and the status of the boy who had shot her. This was also the chance for the crisis intervention team members to offer support to each other. Clearly, such crisis intervention will take its toll on the mental health of the crisis interveners.

The school social worker and school psychologist evaluated the effectiveness of the group and individual counseling and discussed the needs of the student population. Later, to get further information, personal interviews were conducted with teachers in order to gather information about their perceptions of students' reaction to the death of their schoolmate, as well as to intervention services. From these evaluative efforts, decisions were made regarding how the school's crisis intervention plan could be improved.

Key Points to Remember

Tragic crisis events, such as shootings on school campuses, affect children, families, educational professionals, schools, and communities in innumerable ways. Thus, it is imperative that schools and communities prepare for such events (Brock et al., 2001). It is clear that while the trauma from a violent school crisis can be extensive, the damage may be addressed and recovery achieved through the use of immediate and proactive school-based crisis interventions. The ongoing preparation and training of educational and mental health professionals will assist in addressing the relevant issues by their acquiring knowledge of both the issues and methods for supportive interventions in the classroom as well as in larger group settings.

Comprehensive school crisis intervention plans and advanced preparation are essential to being ready to respond to a crisis event at school (Brock et al., 2001). Such plans must include mental health professionals, who can assist in providing appropriate support services for diverse students, families, faculty, and staff. Thus, it is strongly recommended that educational professionals engage in professional development and prepare a comprehensive crisis intervention plan. The lessons learned by numerous educational and mental health professionals responding to school crises across the country should further inspire all educational and mental health professionals to thoroughly prepare for such devastating events so that, should the need arise, they will be well equipped to respond and assist in the school community's recovery process.

References

Anderson, M., Kaufman, J., Simon, T. R., Barrios, L., Paulozzi, L., Ryan, G., Hammond, R., Modzeleski, W., Feucht, T., Potter, L., & the School-Associated Violent Deaths Study Group. (2001). School associated violent deaths in the United States, 1994–1999. *Journal of the American Medical Association, 286,* 2695–2702.

Brock, S. E. (2002a). Group crisis intervention. In S. E. Brock, P. J. Lazarus, & S. R. Jimerson (Eds.), *Best practices in school crisis prevention and intervention* (pp. 23-46). Bethesda, MD: National Association of School Psychologists.

Brock, S. E. (2002b). Identifying psychological trauma victims. In S. E. Brock, P. J. Lazarus, & S. R. Jimerson (Eds.), *Best practices in school crisis prevention and intervention* (pp. 367–383). Bethesda, MD: National Association of School Psychologists.

Brock, S. E., & Jimerson, S. R. (2004). School crisis interventions: Strategies for addressing the consequences of crisis events. In E. R. Gerler, Jr. (Ed.), *Handbook of school violence* (pp. 285–332). Binghamton, NY: Haworth.

Brock, S. E., Lazarus, P. J., & Jimerson S. R. (Eds.). (2002). *Best practices in school crisis prevention and intervention.* Bethesda, MD: National Association of School Psychologists.

Brock, S. E., Sandoval, J., & Lewis, S. (2001). *Preparing for crises in the schools: A manual for building school crisis response teams.* New York: Wiley.

Cohen, S., & Willis, T. A. (1985). Stress, social support, and the buffering hypothesis. *Psychological Bulletin, 98,* 310-355.

Foa, E. B., & Meadows, E. A. (1998). Psychosocial treatments for posttraumatic stress disorder. In R. Yehuda (Ed.), *Psychological trauma* (pp. 179–204). Washington, DC: American Psychiatric Press.

Gurwitch, R. H., Sitterle, K. A., Yound, B. H., & Pferrerbaum, B. (2002). The aftermath of terrorism. In A. M. La Greca, W. K. Silverman, E. M. Vernberg, & M. C. Roberts (Eds.), *Helping children cope with disasters and terrorism* (pp. 327–357). Washington, DC: American Psychological Association.

Herman, R., Kaplan, M., & LeMelle, S. (2002). Psychoeducational debriefings after the September 11 disaster. *Psychiatric Services, 53,* 479.

McFarlane, A. (1988). The longitudinal course of posttraumatic morbidity: The range of outcomes and their predictors. *Journal of Nervous and Mental Disease, 176,* 30–39.

National Institute of Mental Health. (2002). *Mental health and mass violence: Evidence-based early psychological intervention for victims/survivors of mass violence. A workshop to reach consensus on best practices.* [NIH Publication No. 02–5138] Washington, DC: U.S. Government Printing Office.

Pynoos, R. S., Frederick, C., Nader, K., Steinberg, A., Eth, S., Nune, F., & Fairbanks, L. (1987). Life threat and post traumatic stress in school-age children. *Archives of General Psychiatry, 44,* 1057–1063.

Seiffge-Krenke, I., Weidemann, S., Fentner, S., Aegenheister, N., & Poeblau, M. (2001). Coping with school-related stress and family stress in healthy and clinically referred adolescents. *European Psychologist, 6,* 123–132.

Slaikeu, K. (1990). *Crisis intervention: A handbook for practice and research* (2nd ed.). Newton, MA: Allyn & Bacon.

Valent, P. (2000). Disaster syndrome. In G. Fink (Ed.), *Encyclopedia of stress* (Vol. 1, pp. 706–709). San Diego, CA: Academic.

Best Practice Grief Work With Students in the Schools

Linda Goldman

Getting Started

School social workers, counselors, and other mental health professionals must create an environment for grieving children that provides a safe haven for expression and release of thoughts and feelings, a respect for their grief process, and an acknowledgment of the complex levels of loss associated with the death of a loved one. Involving children in memorializing and creating the recognition that young people are an integral part of the grief community can only enhance their self-worth and dignity as they feel acknowledged by society.

Today's children live in a world affected by death, war, terrorism, violence, sexuality, abuse, and abandonment. If young people are not affected directly, they are influenced vicariously by a media that all too often acts as a surrogate parent and extended family to many of our children. From the death of a classmate to a dad's deployment, girls and boys are becoming increasingly subject to traumatic grief by prevailing social and societal issues in their home, school, community, nation, and world.

Parents and professionals must create environments where children and teens are recognized mourners. Children become recognized mourners when they are given a voice to express their grief, an avenue to physically commemorate a loved one, and a safe haven for expression and commemoration. Training needs to be provided for social workers, educators, and parents on the topics of grief and trauma, which so affect our young people today. The University of Maryland's School of Social Work has provided such a forum in its Advanced Certification for Children and Adolescents programs, in which practical and theoretical information is presented to clinicians.

Montgomery County, Maryland, has created training for teachers and counselors on the creation and implementation of grief support in their schools, including procedures for the development of ongoing support groups. Safe Harbor, a grief support program for children and teens, provides outreach education and information for grieving children and families.

What We Know

The Nature of Grief

Fox (1988) explained that one useful way to help bereaved children to monitor their ongoing emotional needs is to "conceptualize what they must do in order to stay psychologically healthy" (p. 8). Fox emphasized that in order to assure that children's grief will be good grief, they must accomplish four tasks: understanding, grieving, commemorating, and going on. Each child's unique nature and age-appropriate level of experience can influence how he or she works through these tasks.

Bereaved children may not process grief in a linear way (Goldman, 2000). The tasks may surface and resurface in varying order, intensity, and duration. Grief work can be messy, with children being inundated with waves of feelings when they least expect it, for example, listening to music with friends, hearing a story, or even being at a birthday party. Tommy's dad was shot and killed in front of his house. A few months later, Tommy attended a birthday party. A balloon burst, and he thought it was a bullet. He ran out of the room screaming and crying. He hadn't expected to be hit with a grief bullet that day.

Children's Developmental Understanding of Death

This section has been adapted from Goldman (2005). Children's understanding of death changes as they develop, as explained by Piaget's cognitive stages of development (Ginsberg & Opper, 1969). Gaining insight into children's developmental stages allows predictability and knowledge of age-appropriate responses.

Pre-Operational Stage (Usually 2–7 Years)

The child conceptualizes death with magical thinking, egocentricity, reversibility, and causality. Young children developmentally live in an egocentric world, filled with the notion that they have caused and are responsible for everything. Children's magical thinking causes them to feel that their words and thoughts can magically cause an event. Five-year-old Sam screamed at his older brother, "I hate you and I wish you were dead!" He was haunted with the idea that his words created his brother's murder the following day. Sam's egocentric perception placed him at the center of the universe, capable of creating and destroying at will the world around him.

Alice, at age 4, displayed her egocentricity when she relayed to me that she had killed her mother. When I asked how she did that, she responded, "My mom picked me up on the night she had her heart attack. If she hadn't picked me up, she wouldn't have died, so I killed her." She felt that she was the central cause of the death. Talking about the medical facts of how Mom died, her heart condition, smoking, and lack of taking proper medicine helped to reduce the common mindset of a young child that she magically caused the death to happen.

Angela, a 6-year-old first-grader, was very sad after her dad died of cancer. She age-appropriately perceived death as reversible and told her friends and family that her dad was coming back. She even wrote him a letter and waited and waited for the mailman to bring back a response. Angela's mom explained to her the following definition of death for young children: "Death is when a person's body stops working. Usually someone dies when they are very, very old, or very, very, very sick, or their bodies are so injured that the doctors and nurses can't make their bodies work again" (Goldman, 2000).

Concrete Operations (Usually 7–12 Years)

During this stage, the child is very curious, the concept of death becomes more realistic, and he or she seeks new information. Ten-year-old Mary wanted to know everything about her mother's death. She said she had heard so many stories about her mom's fatal car crash that she wanted to look up the story in the newspaper to find out the facts. Eleven-year-old Margaret wondered about her friend who got killed in a sudden plane crash: "What was she thinking before the crash, was she scared, and did she suffer?"

Tom age-appropriately wondered if there was an afterlife and exactly where his dad was. At this stage of development, children commonly express logical thoughts and fears about death, can conceptualize that all body functions stop, and begin to internalize the universality and permanence of death. They may ponder the facts about how the terrorists got the plane to crash, wanting to know every detail. When working with this age group, it is important to ask, "What are the facts that you would like to know?" and help them to find answers through family, friends, the media, and experts.

Prepositional Operations, Implications, and Logic Stage of Development (Usually Age 13 and Older)

This stage is usually characterized by the adolescent's concept of death. Many are self-absorbed at this age, seeing mortality and death as a natural process that is remote from their day-to-day lives and something they cannot control. Young people are often absorbed with shaping their own lives and deny the possibility of their own deaths.

Sixteen-year-old Malcolm expressed the following age-appropriate thoughts when he proclaimed, "I don't want to think about death now. I want to think about living my life!" Teens benefit greatly by peer support groups as it is developmentally appropriate to value feedback and support from peers.

Common Signs of Grieving Children

Social workers, educators, parents, and other mental health professionals need to familiarize themselves with the common signs of grieving children. In this way, they can educate children and caring adults who work with children about the ways that young people feel and think. Knowing these signs helps to normalize them and reduce anxiety about them for children and adults as well. Children may

- imitate the behavior of the deceased
- want to "appear normal"
- need to tell their story over and over again
- enjoy wearing or holding something of the loved one
- speak of the loved one in the present
- tend to worry excessively about their health and the health of surviving loved ones
- become the class bully or class clown
- regress and become clingy or wet the bed
- have headaches or stomachaches
- display poor eating patterns
- appear hyperactive or impulsive or have an inability to concentrate
- begin to use drugs or alcohol or become sexually promiscuous
- show a change in grades and lack of interest in school

Grief and ADD

Often children and teens are misdiagnosed with attention-deficit disorder or learning disabilities after an experience of traumatic loss. Hyperactivity, impulsivity, distractibility, and inability to concentrate are common grief symptoms that can become the behavioral criteria to diagnose learning problems. It is essential to take a loss inventory of the grieving child to become aware of any past or present loss issues and identify if the behavior signs observed are a by-product of a grief and loss situation.

Seven-year-old Sam was a second-grader whose best friend, Adam, was killed in a car crash on the day before Christmas. He came back to school after the winter holidays with extreme restlessness and frequent swings of emotional outbursts and withdrawal. This continued for several months with decrease in attention and school performance. The grief symptoms continued well into third grade, and Sam's teacher relayed to his mom that he may be exhibiting attention deficit. She suggested that Sam receive an evaluation by his pediatrician.

Sam was placed on Ritalin and given this drug for the next 3 years. He continued to have nightmares and the bed wetting that had begun with his friend's death, and these anxieties were never

addressed inside or outside of the school system. He became a part of the learning disabled population, and his deep grief and its symptoms remained buried (Goldman, 2001).

Signs of Grieving Children in the Classroom

The bereaved child may display one or several of these behaviors:

- become the class clown
- become withdrawn and unsociable
- become restless and unable to stay seated
- call out of turn
- not complete schoolwork
- have problems listening and staying on task
- become overly talkative
- become disorganized
- engage in reckless physical actions
- show poor concentration around external stimuli
- show difficulty in following directions

Caring adults need to educate and become educated in learning the signs of normal and complicated grief. Gaining a respect for and acceptance of the feelings of anxiety and depression that occur with grief can normalize common characteristics and reduce anxiety for children and the adults around them. Social workers and other caring professionals must become a strong force in differentiating between grief and ADD signs.

What We Can Do

Normalize Grief

Professionals and parents can realize that children do not like to feel different, and often the grieving child does. When grieving children have experienced the death of someone close to them, they may choose not to talk about the death because they do not want to appear not normal. Not talking about the death allows some children to feel they still have some control over what has happened in their lives or hide any shame about feeling different.

Tom was playing on the school football team, and the final tournament was a major event. Most of the moms and dads of the team members came to support their children for the game. Tom scored the winning touchdown for his team. Charlie, Tom's coach, ran over to congratulate him, and all the other boys and their parents joined in the celebration. "Where's your dad?" Coach Charlie asked. "He's working today, and couldn't come," Tom replied. Coach Charlie was unaware that Tom's dad had died the year before. Tom needed to save face and avoid his dad's death in order to "appear normal."

As an advocate for the grieving child, school social workers, counselors, and other mental health professionals need to be sure that these girls and boys are identified and given strategies to help them work through their grief. A grief and loss inventory (e.g., Goldman, 2000, pp. 125–129) is a helpful tool for the school system, which not only provides a loss history but also accountability in keeping a record of recommendations, interventions, and follow-ups. This loss inventory becomes an avenue of communication for the school system. In this way, faculty members like Coach Charlie can review this tool in order to identify grieving students like Tom and create modifications and interventions to help them with their process.

Recognize Grief Feelings

Children gain a greater understanding of themselves when they can express previously hidden emotions. The awareness of unrecognized feelings also allows social workers, other mental health professionals, educators, and parents to be more in touch with what is going on in the grief process. Grief feelings and thoughts are continuous and ever-changing, inundating the children's lives like waves on the ocean. These thoughts and feelings may arrive without warning, and children feel unprepared for their enormity in a school setting.

Encourage Acknowledgment and Memory Sharing

The bereaved child needs to acknowledge a parent or sibling who died by using his or her name or sharing a memory. It can be useful to create a memory table where children can bring treasured objects or favorite pictures, reminding them of their person. They can leave them there for others to see, or join together in a memory circle and talk about what the picture or object means to them.

Tools and Practice Examples

Bereaved children need to tell their story over and over again. One of the common signs of grieving children under stress is this need to repeatedly share the story of their loss. We can help them do this by listening, sharing, and providing opportunities to help them retell and reframe their experience. Giving children an open-ended opportunity for relaying a hard time and expressing difficulties, remaining worries, and a new self-view gives them permission to re-create a worrisome experience. We can ask children to "tell us about a day you will never forget," and often they choose September 11, 2001.

Interventions

Working With Young Children: Projective Play

Projective play allows many young children to work through complex issues, including their grief process, by using play. Play allows them to use their imaginations to safely express thoughts and feelings. Children have a restricted verbal ability for sharing feelings and a limited emotional capacity to tolerate the pain of loss; they communicate their feelings, wishes, fears, and attempted resolutions to their problems through play (Webb, 2002).

Providing props, such as helping figures, puppets, costumes, and building blocks, allows children to re-create their experience and role play what happened and ways to work with what happened. Children feel empowered when they can imagine alternatives and possible solutions, release feelings, and create dialogue through projective play.

Many children spontaneously built towers of blocks as the Twin Towers and then knocked them down with an airplane to replay the attack. Alex explained to his nursery school teacher as the tower fell: "Airplanes make buildings go BOOM!"

Children can re-create the disaster setting with doctors, nurses, firefighters, and police officers who helped in the disaster by using props for projective play. Sally pretended to be a nurse helping those hurt at the Pentagon crash, and Jimmy put on a fire hat and gloves and said, "Don't worry, I'll save you. Run for your lives."

During a play therapy session, children who survived the death of their dad, who was a firefighter, decided to reenact the disaster. Their play illustrated their desire to become firefighters and "save as many people as possible." Kevin, age 4, watched with his family in their car as his father was murdered at a convenience store. His play presented constant replaying of the murder and "good guy/bad guy" scenarios.

Puppets and stuffed animals are a safe way for children to speak of the trauma. "I wonder what Bart the puppet would say about the trauma. Let's allow Bart to tell us about his story."

Memory Work

Memory work can be a helpful tool to safely process the events after a death. The following questions can provide a foundation for discussion:

Where were you when [the trauma] happened?
What was your first thought?
What are the facts about [the trauma]?
What sticks with you now?
Do you feel like you did anything wrong?
What is it you still want to know?
What scares you the most?
What makes you feel peaceful?
What can you do to feel better?

Memory Books

Bereaved children need to use memory work to create a physical way to remember their feelings and share them. Memory books are a collection of feelings and thoughts through drawings and writings that allow children to reexperience memories in a safe way. They serve as a useful tool to enable children to tell about their person who died and to open discussion. Children can tell about how their person died and share funny, happy, or sad memories. Melissa is a 12-year-old whose dad died of cancer. She shared her funniest memory of her dad in her memory book:

My funniest memory of my father is when . . . he came home from getting his hair shaved off after being diagnosed with lung cancer. During his cancer he always kept a good attitude. That's

just my Dad's personality—a good sense of humor. Why do the good people have to die? — By Melissa, Age 13. (Goldman, 2000, p. 90)

Memory Boxes

Memory boxes contain pictures and special objects that remind children of their person who died. They can be decorated with pictures and words that remind the children of their loved one or special containers meaningful to the person who died. Jane made a memory box with pictures and special objects that reminded her of her friend Zoe, who died suddenly in a plane crash. She included pictures, stuffed animals, a list of her top favorite memories, and other special items to remind her of her friend.

Writing, Poetry, and Journaling

Bereaved children need to use tools such as drawing, writing, role playing, and reenactment to safely project feelings and thoughts about their loss and present life outside of themselves. Letter and poetry writing are grief therapy techniques that give children concrete ways to commemorate the death of a loved one. Seven-year-old Ashley wrote the following Mother's Day letter to her mom the year after her mother died. She decided with her teacher to send off a balloon and an "I love you" note for her mother:

Dear Mom,
    I really miss you. I am doing good in school. I can't figure out what to get you yet for Mother's day.
        I love you. Ashley

Eight-year-old Julia's best friend, Anne, and her family died in the 2001 terrorist attack. She created this poem as a tribute to her friend in her memory book:

Julia
Active, funny, kind
Good Friend of Anne
Loss, anger, grief
Who misses her funny, caring and silly ways
Who worries about war and our President
Stomachaches, headaches, muscles get tense
Who heals by reading, laying down, talking
Remembers by memories and hearing her name
Who wishes for peace and unity
Strong. (Goldman, 2005)

Tools to Help Bereaved Children Feel Safe

Bereaved children often are preoccupied with their own health and the health of their loved ones. Providing a reality check, such as calling their surviving parent during the school day or allowing visits to the school nurse, is reassuring to boys and girls that they and their families are okay. Surviving parents can have a physical exam and bring a doctor's note to the child saying the exam went well. Children can also make fear boxes, safe or peaceful boxes, or a worry list.

Sandra put together a peaceful box. She found toys, stuffed animals, and pictures that made her feel safe and peaceful. Alex made a fear box. He cut out pictures from newspapers and magazines about what frightens him and pasted them around the box. He wrote down fears and put them inside. Denise created a worry list. She made a list of worries from 1 to 5. Number 1 was the biggest. Suggest that children talk about their lists with someone they trust, like a parent, sibling, teacher, or good friend.

Systems Changes and Interventions

"The goal of helping children of all ages to cope with death is to promote their competence, facilitate their ability to cope, and recognize that children are active participants in their lives" (Silverman, 2000, p. 42). Grieving children have become the norm in our educational system, with more and more children experiencing traumatic grief at earlier and earlier ages. Social workers, educators, and parents can support the concept of young people being an integral part of a family or community grief team and allow them to become recognized mourners.

Adults Can Create Interventions That Advocate for the Grieving Child

Bereaved children need interventions to accommodate their loss issues. The mental health professional, educator, or parent may serve as a liaison and advocate for the grieving child in the school. Often the suggestion and implementation of simple interventions for grieving girls and boys are useful and practical means of facilitating their process. Children should be given choices of places to which they can go within the schools, people with whom they are comfortable talking, and times that they find are best to call and be reassured about loved ones. They can choose a safe place outside the classroom when these unexpected, overwhelming feelings arise, without needing to explain why in front of fellow classmates. The following are suggestions for school interventions (adapted from Goldman, 2001):

- Allow the child to leave the room if needed.
- Allow the child to call home if necessary.
- Create a visit to the school nurse and guidance counselor periodically.
- Change some work assignments.
- Assign a class helper.
- Create some private time in the day.
- Give more academic progress reports.

Grief-Based Support Groups

Seven-year-old Tony became a member of a school-based grief therapy group, which he attended with four other children aged 6 to 9. He attended this group, led by his guidance counselor, for several months. The children made memory books, commemorated loved ones, and shared photos and stories. Tony had been diagnosed with attention-deficit disorder a year after his father's murder. After attending this group, his concentration in school became more focused, and eventually he was taken off medication. He continued going to a children's bereavement group in a neighborhood hospice program for the rest of the school year.

One of the best techniques for adolescents is peer support and discussion groups, as they are much more comfortable at this age talking with peers about death and trauma than with adults. Many teen survivors of trauma feel comforted and free to share their thoughts when they are placed in support groups only for other teens who are survivors of similar experiences. Tony's dad died in the September 11 Pentagon crash. He explained the value of his teen support group, which included other survivors of September 11 as follows: "I don't have to explain a lot of things. I already know they understand."

Adults Can Provide Activities Helpful for Bereaved Children

Several interventions that allow children safe expression of thoughts and feelings are worry lists, fear boxes, peaceful places, and reality checks. They provide safe activities for children to process their grief responses.

Thomas was the 17-year-old captain of his football team. He was killed instantly in an automobile accident the night before the first day of school. Parents and teachers provided a forum for grieving students to actively commemorate his death. The school developed a memory library shelf for Thomas where books could be donated in his name. A memory location was created on the football field where students could visit during the day and feel they were with Thomas. Friends established a memory chat room where the only prerequisite for entering was to share a memory of Thomas. The school created a memory wall with a Thomas mural that remained throughout the year. Teachers and students could write or draw a memory or note at any time during the school day.

Educators Can Benefit From a Loss and Grief Inventory

A loss and grief inventory (e.g., Goldman, 2000) is a useful tool for creating and storing history on the grieving child throughout his academic life. This history includes all losses and important dates of birthdays and deaths of loved ones that may have a great impact on the child through the years. It also provides accountability for recognizing the grieving child and accurately documenting necessary accommodations, follow-ups, and recommendations.

Educators, Parents, and Other Professionals Can Use "Teachable Moments" to Acknowledge a Loss

Teachable moments are spontaneous mini-lessons created in the moment using a life experience that is happening now. The death of Goldie, the goldfish in Mrs. Arnold's classroom, was a huge loss to her kindergarten class. Goldie's death during school provided a teachable moment when the children could express their feelings about death and commemorate the loss with a burial ritual and memorial service. The death of Rocky, Margie's dog, was very sad. Family and friends came together and participated in a ceremony for Rocky, and Margie and her sister shared a poem about how much they loved their special dog.

The shootings at Columbine High School created many teachable moments at homes and at schools across the country to dialogue about the bullying, victimization, and violence that affect so many children. One school system sent a poster signed by all of its students and teachers, sharing their concern and prayers for the Columbine students. A discussion of the terrorist attack on Russian children led a group of teens to raise money for their aid.

Adults Can Actively Involve Children and Teens in Commemorating

Here are some ways:

- Create a ceremony, such as releasing a balloon with a special note or lighting a candle.
- Create a memorial wall with stories and pictures of shared events.
- Have an assembly about the person who died.
- Plant a memorial garden.
- Initiate a scholarship fund.
- Establish an ongoing fundraiser, such as a car wash or bake sale, with proceeds going toward the bereaved family's designated charity.
- Place memorial pages and pictures in the school yearbook or school newspaper.
- Send flowers to the grieving family.

Key Points to Remember

What we can mention, we can manage. This idea is a useful paradigm for social workers, educators, parents, and other caring professionals to understand when establishing an oasis of safety for the grieving child. Allowing children to acknowledge and express thoughts and feelings involving grief and loss is an ongoing and integral piece of their grief process.

Children in the 21st century face losses in the form of sudden fatal accidents and deaths due to illness, suicide, homicide, and disease. There are also many social issues that have a similar effect on children. Loss of family stability from separation and divorce, violence and abuse, bullying and victimization issues, foster care and abandonment, unemployment, multiple moves, parental imprisonment or deployment, and family alcohol and drug addiction are a few of the many grief issues affecting today's young children. Societal and global issues of war, terrorism, and nuclear threat create an overlay of trauma on top of these preexisting issues for our students.

Educators can provide a grief vocabulary, resources, crisis and educational interventions, preventions, and follow-up procedures. Administrators, teachers, and parents can join in creating comfort zones for the grieving children within the school system. By opening communication about loss and grief issues, adults are able to create a bridge between the world of fear, isolation, and loneliness and the world of truth, compassion, and dignity for the grieving child.

Resources

CD-ROM for Teachers and Counselors

A Look at Children's Grief (with 2 CEU credits). Two 1-hour modules: Children's Loss and Grief and Grief Resolution Techniques. info@adec.org or 860-586-7503.

Books for Teachers and Parents

Kathleen Cassini and Jacqueline Rogers, *Death in the Classroom*. Cincinnati, OH: Griefwork of Cincinnati, 1990. A teacher's resource that offers guidance for working with death in the classroom.

Linda Goldman, *Breaking the Silence: A Guide to Help Children With Complicated Grief: Suicide, Homicide, AIDS, Violence and Abuse*, 2nd ed. New York: Taylor & Francis, 2002. A guide for adults to help children with complicated grief issues. Includes chapters on suicide, homicide, AIDS, violence, and abuse; guidelines for educators; national resources; and an annotated bibliography.

Linda Goldman, *Life and Loss: A Guide to Help Grieving Children*, 2nd ed. Washington, DC: Taylor & Francis, 2000. A resource for working with children and normal grief. It provides information, resources, hands-on activities, model of a goodbye visit for children, and an annotated bibliography.

Linda Goldman, *Raising Our Children to Be Resilient: A Guide to Helping Children Cope with Trauma in Today's World*. New York: Taylor & Francis, 2005. This book deals with contemporary grief and trauma issues that affect children and interventions for healing and resiliency.

Robert and Eileen Stevenson, *Teaching Students About Death*. Philadelphia, PA: Charles Press, 1996. This resource for educators and parents explains childhood bereavement in the schools.

Books for Children and Teens

J. Bode, *Death Is Hard to Live With*. New York: Bantam Doubleday Dell, 1993. Teenagers talk frankly about how they cope with loss.

Linda Goldman, *Bart Speaks Out: An Interactive Storybook for Young Children About Suicide*. Los Angeles, CA: WPS, 1996 (ages 5–10). This interactive storybook provides words to use with young children in discussing the sensitive topic of suicide.

Marge Heegaard, *When Someone Very Special Dies*. Minneapolis, MN: Woodland, 1988 (ages 4–7). A workbook for young children that uses artwork and journaling to allow them to understand and express their grief.

B. Mellonie and R. Ingpen, *Lifetimes: The Beautiful Way to Explain Death to Children*. New York: Bantam, 1983 (ages 4–10). Explains the life cycle of plants, animals, and people.

Donna O'Toole, *Aardy Aardvark Finds Hope*. Burnsville, NC: Mt. Rainbow, 1998 (ages 5–8). A story about animals that presents pain, sadness, and eventual hope after death.

Sarah Stein, *About Dying*. New York: Walker, 1974 (ages 3–6). Contains simple text and photographs to help young children understand death and provides ways to help them participate in commemorating.

Enid Traisman, *Fire in My Heart, Ice in My Veins*. Omaha, NE: Centering, 1992. A book for teenagers to explore thoughts and feelings and record grief memories.

S. Varley, *Badger's Parting Gifts*. New York: Morrow, 1984 (for all ages). Badger was a special friend to all the animals. After his death, each friend recalls a special memory.

References

Fox, S. (1988). *Good grief: Helping groups of children when a friend dies*. Boston: New England Association for the Education of Young Children.

Ginsberg, H., & Opper, S. (1969). *Piaget's theory of intellectual development*. Englewood, NJ: Prentice-Hall.

Goldman, L. (2000). *Life and loss: A guide to help grieving children*. New York: Taylor & Francis.

Goldman, L. (2001). *Breaking the silence: A guide to help children with complicated grief*. New York: Taylor & Francis.

Goldman, L. (2005). *Raising our children to be resilient: A guide to helping children cope with trauma in today's world*. New York: Taylor & Francis.

Silverman, P. (2000). *Never too young to know: Death in children's lives*. New York: Oxford University Press.

Webb, N. B. (Ed.). (2002). *Helping bereaved children: A handbook for practitioners* (2nd ed). New York: Guilford.

Grief Work With Elementary- and Middle-School Students

Walking With Hope When a Child Grieves

Eugene Aisenberg

CHAPTER 55

Getting Started

Death is a universal human experience. Yet it is deeply personal for the one who mourns the absence of a loved one. Despite the irrevocable reality of death, the loss of a loved one can shake one's core and fill a person with sadness, pain, and, in some instances, depression. For a school-aged child, a parent's death can be overwhelming. The death of a mother or father can evoke within a child powerful and at times conflicting cognitions and emotions such as guilt, anger, and love.

Previous chapters examined the role of the practitioner in addressing children who experience traumatic events and traumatic loss. The focus of this chapter is individual grief work with elementary- and middle-school children who have experienced the death of a parent due to illness or accident. Throughout the course of an academic year, school social workers and school mental health practitioners likely will encounter students who experience the death of a parent or manifest grief responses from deaths that occurred in previous years as 1 out of every 20 American children under age 15 have lost at least one parent due to death (Steen, 1998). See chapter 54 for more discussion on how to work with grief and loss.

Parental death can place elementary- and middle-school children at risk for a range of emotional and behavioral problems (Dowdney, 2000; Lutzke, Ayers, Sandler, & Barr, 1997; Worden & Silverman, 1996). Research highlights significant differences in how grieving children see themselves in terms of school performance, general behavioral conduct, and overall self-esteem within 2 years following a parent's death. Within this time period, bereaved children are at higher risk of being more socially withdrawn and are at risk of manifesting higher levels of aggressive behavior

than nonbereaved children (Worden, 1996). Without timely and effective intervention, this vulnerable population is at risk for long-term effects, such as difficulties with future intimate relationships, vocational success, and general joy of life (Wolfelt, 1996).

While the focus of the chapter is grief work, much of its content can be applied to intervening with a child living with a sibling or parent with a chronic disease or a disabling condition or whose parents are divorced. In such circumstances, a child may experience many of the feelings and thoughts of a child whose parent has died.

This chapter does not present a recipe or formula to be universally applied to grieving children. The response of children to the death of a parent varies. When children grieve, they bring the unique factors of their family and support systems, past experiences with loss or trauma, and their developmental and cognitive abilities. Just as each child's grief is unique, there is no singular way to engage a child who mourns. To promote the practitioner's effective response to a grieving child, this chapter provides guidelines and principles. They orient the practitioner to assess important areas and guide the practitioner in addressing the suffering and grief of a child, whether the death of a parent is recent or several years ago.

This chapter posits that the heart of the practitioner must be open and listening to accompany a child through the loss. To walk with hope amid the hurt, emptiness, or confusion that a child may be experiencing, the practitioner must skillfully respond to the cry of the child. This cry does not consist merely of tears. It is the ache of the heart and can be masked by such behavior as stellar academic achievement or aggression. If ignored, the cry may reveal itself through attention-getting behavior or physical symptoms. Concrete ways to walk with a child whose parent has died will be presented, but by no means are they exhaustive examples.

What We Know

A review of the research literature on children's grief and loss of a parent due to illness revealed a void. No program meets the criteria of evidence-based practice. The absence of evidence-based programs is not very surprising due to the strict criteria of best practices as strategies and programs that are deemed to be research-based by scientists and researchers from a number of organizations, including the National Institute of Mental Health, American Psychological Association, National Association of Social Workers, and Department of Education. The lack of evidence-based practices that address grief in elementary- and middle-school children does not signify, however, a scarcity of quality interventions being implemented. Some research-based interventions include the Family Bereavement Program (Sandler et al., 2003) and the Harvard/MGH Child Bereavement Study (Silverman, 2000). Also, there exists much practice wisdom in rural and urban communities and communities of color. Unfortunately, this indigenous experience of effective practice is not recognized or sanctioned as best practice. Clearly, more research is warranted in this important area.

What We Can Do

In spite of the limited evidence-based research, many resources exist for practitioners in their work with children, as well as for children, parents, and educators. Only a few can be highlighted in this chapter. See the "Tools and Case Example" section for more information about other approaches.

Goals of Intervention

Three principal goals guide grief work with elementary- and middle-school students:

1. Provide a safe place for the child.
2. Facilitate the telling of the story by the child.
3. Promote healing in order to promote life.

Provide a Safe Place

The school social worker or mental health practitioner has a wonderful privilege and responsibility—to help create a safe and welcoming environment for the student and for the school community and family. The practitioner can make a transformative difference in the life of the grieving child by helping the child to identify and understand the experience of loss and its impact. Often a teacher, coach, school administrator, or family member alerts the practitioner to a grieving child. The referring person is acting out of concern for the child and may have noticed a shift in the child's behavior, affect, or school work. In welcoming a child who has recently experienced the death of a mother or father, or whose grief has been recently triggered, the practitioner should acknowledge the referral.

The school social worker or mental health practitioner should also admit to the child that the process is painful, but the goal is growth and healing. The practitioner must gain the confidence of the bereaved child that speaking about or revisiting painful feelings is worthwhile. To many children, the process of grief work may appear to be like continually picking at a scab. It seems counterintuitive since a natural response is to avoid pain. The practitioner, in essence, is asking the child to trust that exposure to feelings and memories about the deceased is beneficial.

Throughout the engagement process, the school social worker or mental health professional should affirm that the child is the authority of her or his own feelings and experience. Also, the practitioner should recognize that the bereaved child is the true expert in the counseling relationship (Wolfelt, 1996).

Facilitate Telling the Story

Another primary goal for the practitioner is to allow the child to reveal her story as she feels comfortable in her own way and time. The telling of the story of the relationship is important as it affords a space for children to remember and honor the relationship with their deceased mother or father. The telling may be in the form of words or be expressed through sculpting, drawing, or play. The practitioner needs to help the child understand that the goal of such exposure and retelling is not to inflict more pain. Rather, the goal is healing.

To bridge understanding of this important step for the child to express feelings in manageable ways, I often use one of three images with children, depending on the circumstances. The first image is that of a pus-infected thumb: "Doing nothing only allows the condition to worsen. To heal the thumb involves pain, squeezing hard to get out the pus. It hurts! The purpose, however, is not to cause more suffering, but to heal the thumb so that it can resume its functioning." The practitioner needs to be honest; the child is likely going to hurt in the grief work. However, the goal is to help children feel and remember not only the hurt and pain but also the good things about their relationship with their deceased mother or father.

The second image is that of a scar due to a fall that required stitches: "Do you remember the pain? Yes! The scar remains a visible reminder of what took place and cannot be undone. However, in touching it today, it is not painful. The death of your mother will remain with you throughout your life. Her death can't be undone. Does this mean it must always be full of pain? No!" This example helps to contextualize the child's experience of loss and paves the way for a child to remember without hurting as much and to claim the full range of emotions pertaining to the deceased, including happiness and love in addition to sadness, anger, anxiety, or guilt.

The third image is that of a leaky cup. Hand the child a plastic cup: "What would happen if this cup had a hole in it and you put water in it? Even if you put all the water of the Pacific Ocean in this cup, it would still end up empty. Your pain can be like the hole in this cup. Unless you deal with that hole, deal with your hurt (loneliness, anger, guilt, sadness, etc.), all the joy and fun you ever have will leak out, leaving you still feeling sad and empty inside."

Receiving the child's story requires that the practitioner assess and respect the child's origins and experiences. While talking about one's experience is seen as normal in Western culture, allocentric-oriented cultures, such as Latino and Asian/Pacific Islander cultures, may have more boundaries around what is private information and what is community information in efforts to save face. As a result, it may be culturally discongruent for a child or family to share information about death and grief with a school social worker or mental health practitioner. Conversely, people from individualistic-oriented cultures will likely be less concerned with face and may find it more ego-syntonic to process feelings and experiences with a mental health professional.

There is another reason that some children may not want to disclose with the practitioner. Children do not want to appear "different" from their peers nor do they want to be treated differently: "I don't want to talk about my father's death. My friends will think I'm weird." Also, children may have a difficult time trying to sort out what their classmates and friends should be told and how to deal with the discomfort of other people in relation to the death. Many times, as a result of this discomfort, they are hesitant to play or afraid to be happy because they don't want others to think they don't care about the death of their parent (Schumacher, 1984).

It is crucial to address such reactions with the child. The practitioner may ask, "Why do you think it is important to express our feelings?" or explain, "If we don't, they really don't go anywhere, and even though we don't want them to, our feelings will continue to affect us. They may make us tired or grouchy or sick" (Lehmann, Jimerson, & Gaasch, 2001).

Two images help illustrate this last point: a teapot and a balloon. The practitioner hands the child a teapot and directs the child to the image of water being heated in the teapot: "What would happen if we blocked the hole in its lid? The water could boil over and probably hurt us. The purpose of the hole is to let the steam out. Expressing your feelings is like making the small hole in the teapot lid; it helps get out some of your hurt and pain." A balloon can also demonstrate this truth: "If we don't express our feelings in some way and just stuff them away inside us, it is like adding air to this balloon. [Blow up the balloon more.] What will happen if we continue to add air? Our feelings will burst out too, if we don't let them out little by little." Let the air out of the balloon a little at a time (Lehmann et al., 2001).

Promote Healing

A third goal of intervention is to promote healing, which necessarily involves addressing that which thwarts the growth and development of the child. In this process of grief work, a child may manifest denial, minimization, or other defense mechanisms. Denial is not necessarily a bad or negative thing; it can often serve a protective purpose for the child. Much like a youngster with a broken leg relying on the support of crutches in the healing process, a youngster may use denial as a coping mechanism. Once the leg is strengthened and healed, however, continued use of crutches serves to prevent the child from running and assuming regular activities. Similarly, continual use of denial may interfere with a child's functioning and impede healing and growth. In such circumstances, the denial must be confronted appropriately. Using evocative language is one tool. For example, instead of saying, "When you lost your mother . . . ," the practitioner can say, "When your mother died. . . ."

The blocking out of painful feelings or memories, while being a natural response, also prevents access to and enjoyment of positive emotions and responses, including spontaneity and joy. Blocking out, stuffing feelings away, or running from them consumes emotional and psychic energy. Thus, a goal of intervention is to assist the child to face and target the pain and free up the use of such energy for life-giving responses.

The practitioner must recognize that the intervention consists of two parallel rails or tracks. The rails are the rail of growth and the rail of healing. Often, we focus predominantly on one rail: the rail of healing. However, it is not enough to attend only to the healing process. To promote healing, one must also be attentive to the rail of growth. With growth comes the strength to continue to face the hurt and experience any tears. The practitioner needs to be attentive to both rails and equip the child to advance on both rails, although not necessarily at the same rate or pace. When mourning is activated at a later time or age, it does not necessarily signal pathology but rather can indicate the positive development of further strength to work through the loss. Thus, children's reaction to the reminder may not be a sign that they have failed to sufficiently heal. In actuality, it may indicate that the children have grown stronger in broken places and are now able to do more work and more healing than before.

Crucial Areas for Assessment

The school mental health practitioner should assess the following six key areas in intervening with a child whose parent has died: (1) strengths of the child and supports the child experiences; (2) how the child was informed about the parent's death; (3) previous losses the child has experienced and how the child coped with those losses

as well as the coping of the child's family; (4) the child's somatic complaints, behavior, and other signals; (5) the child's cognitive distortions; and (6) reminders of the parent's death.

Strengths

It is important to assess the strengths of the child as well as other resources that can facilitate growth and healing. They may be protective factors intrinsic to the child, such as temperament or intelligence. They may be attachment to a significant adult figure, such as the surviving parent, a friend's mother or father, a teacher, or a coach. Other resources may include engagement in activities, such as basketball, or association with an organization, such as a church.

Informing a Child

An important area to assess, especially since it is often unaddressed, is how the child learned of the parent's death. The following is a vivid example:

A family of six—mother and father, aunt and uncle, and two sisters, 8 and 12 years of age—were traveling in the family van on a Sunday morning. Traffic was light on the freeway and they were driving at the speed limit when a tractor trailer lost control and hit the van. The father was killed instantly; the other family members were gravely injured. The sisters were taken to one hospital and the adult family members were taken to another hospital. Within 2 hours, the eldest sister also died. The other family members would eventually survive the horrific crash. The 8-year-old, Marie, was the least injured but remained hospitalized for 5 days. Throughout her hospitalization, she kept inquiring about her sister and other family members. Extended family members had not informed her of the death of her father and sister. They were consumed with their own grief, visiting the other hospitalized family members, and caring for their families while carrying out their work responsibilities. It was not until the time of discharge that Marie was told of her loved ones' deaths. Upon being informed, she replied, "I know."

Marie had grown suspicious due to the lack of information being provided to her and suspected the worse. Understandably, the family was stressed and wanted to shelter Marie from the painful news. However, the lack of information had fostered mistrust. Also, it contributed to Marie's reliance upon her imagination regarding aspects of her father and sister's deaths. Later, the lack of being informed would contribute to Marie's anger and complicate her grief.

Providing clear and appropriate information about the causes and circumstances of a parent's death is an effective way to support and assist a child to process the painful and potentially overwhelming experience of death. In doing so, it is imperative to inform a child or discuss the death of a parent according to the child's developmental ability and in age-appropriate terms. For example, children ages 8–12 often seek concrete information and details regarding the death of a parent. Practitioners should encourage questions and make clear that they are available to provide answers. Do not attempt to "sugar coat" or rationalize the death, as in "Your mother is not suffering any more" or "Your father is in a better place." At times, in wanting to "protect" the child, adults withhold information or exclude the child in discussions and preparations. The lack of inclusion places children on the outside, as spectators to the family discussion and to their feelings. A child can become increasingly vulnerable as one who is acted upon by others or by thoughts and feelings without a sense of power or control. Withholding information can also leave a child to imagine and believe things in exaggeration or in ways that are detrimental to the child's coping and well-being. Children—in particular, young children—often feel they have caused and are responsible for everything. Children need to know that they did not cause their parent's death by their anger or wishing.

Research reveals that children who have been told about the impending death of a loved one and who are encouraged to ask questions and express feelings cope more successfully and report fewer depressive symptoms than children without this knowledge and opportunity (Raveis, Siegel, & Karus, 1998; Sahler, 2000). One tool is the question box. It can be a decorated shoebox. A child is invited to write a question on a piece of paper at any time and place it in the box anonymously with the assurance that the practitioner will provide a quick response. This tool is helpful when working with a classroom of children, families, and small groups of children, even with an individual child. This tool affirms open communication and trust and provides a forum to address some fears and concerns and normalize them.

Previous Losses

The school mental health professional should also assess other losses/separations a child may have experienced, such as family moves, multiple foster care placements, or the death of a grandmother or fish or other pet. In doing so, the practitioner should assess how the child coped with such losses, including assessing the child's spirituality or faith practice. In addition, the practitioner needs to assess how other family members are coping. It is likely that they are grieving as well. The more depressed or distressed the surviving parent, the less able the parent will be to act as a buffer for the child. In such circumstances, children may refrain from disclosing to family members or revealing their emotions out of a strong desire not to burden other family members or add to others' distress. Assessing the coping responses of other family members can illuminate any shifts in roles or parentification of the child, whereby the child takes on adult roles and responsibilities within the family pattern of functioning and communication. Also, this assessment can inform the practitioner of existing supports and strengths of the family and the child, which are crucial to resiliency.

A useful tool is to have children draw pictures of their families. The details of the drawings provide a wealth of information and facilitate communication. Who is included in the picture, who is absent, the proximity of family members to each other, the expressions of the family members, and the structures that may be included in the drawing reveal significant information about the child's perceptions of the family and its dynamics.

A key area to address with the child is the identification and experience of feelings, including anger. Anger is not bad, not right or wrong. It is a feeling. Children often do not receive permission, implicitly or explicitly, to feel anger and may perceive it negatively as if they should not feel angry. Instead of asking directly, "Are you angry that your mom died?" the practitioner may ask, "What do you miss about your mom?" This less direct approach can also be effective in addressing a child's guilt, anxiety, helplessness, loneliness, or sadness. A guiding principle is to get out the feeling as a live sensation. In cases where a child is experiencing anger, it is possible to help the child give expression to the anger in a safe way. One technique is to use wet sponges. Each time the child throws a sponge against a wall, the child is encouraged to vent an angry statement. The same technique can be used with other items, even sunflower seeds.

Developmentally, a child has less available coping mechanisms than an adult to face the death of a mother or father. In particular, children under 11 years of age have more limited cognitive ability to understand the nature of the person's death and the implications of the death (Baker & Sedney, 1996). Such a loss can be overwhelming for a school-aged child and precipitate a crisis. In some ways, it may be like a swimmer in the ocean who is unexpectedly knocked underwater by a wave. For a few moments that seem perilously eternal, the swimmer may begin to panic as he actively seeks to find the ocean floor, begins to reestablish balance and equilibrium, resurfaces, and breathes.

One appropriate coping response of the child is the telling of the story of the parent's death over and over. This retelling reflects children's attempt to regain equilibrium and manage their lives. The practitioner's responsibility is to help normalize the child's experience of loss and reactions to it. In doing so, the practitioner should encourage the child to acknowledge the deceased by using the parent's name and encourage as much continuity in activity as possible. The death of a parent may result in a child's heightened concern for the safety of the surviving parent (Goldman, 2000). Research has shown that up to 50% of children manifest such concern even 2 years after the death of a parent (Worden & Silverman, 1996). In the counseling relationship, the practitioner can provide the child support and reasonable assurance of safety for the child and the child's loved ones.

Somatic Signals

The following are important clues or signs of grief when assessing a child who has experienced the loss of a parent: somatic symptoms such as headaches and stomachaches, depressive-like symptoms of sleep disturbance, crying, lack of concentration, and regressive behaviors such as excessive clinging or babyish talk or behavior (Worden & Silverman, 1996). Other signals of a child's grieving may include imitating the behavior of the deceased, wearing clothing or jewelry of the deceased, expressing feeling watched by the deceased mother or father, talking to the deceased parent, and speaking of the deceased parent in the present tense. Rather than squelch or eliminate such behavior, the practitioner should recognize

that these behaviors reflect that children do not want to forget their mother or father, regardless of the strength or quality of attachment. The practitioner needs to reassure the child and normalize such behavior.

Cognitive Distortions

In grief, it is possible that a child may experience distortions, misunderstanding, or guilt: "I was always mean to my mom"; "I was never grateful to my dad and should have thanked him." Assessing cognitive distortions enables the practitioner to help children to cognitively restructure previous schemas that may be counterproductive or harmful to their self-esteem. Informed by the assessment, the practitioner is equipped to help the child challenge harmful cognitive distortions and to assist the child to get out the guilt which the child may have internalized and which may keep the child imprisoned in fear and shame.

It is not unlike the story of the young cub, Simba, in the movie *The Lion King*. Simba believed what his Uncle Scar told him, that he was responsible for his own father's death. So he fled in shame and guilt far away from his home. He chose to withdraw, abandon his inheritance, and live in relative isolation. Only later, with the help of some friends, did Simba find the strength and courage to return to his homeland to claim what he thought was the truth. Upon his return, Simba discovered that all of the shame and guilt that he had carried for so long was based on a lie. The truth was that his uncle had murdered his father. To walk with Simba is to help him come to acceptance and to discover the truth of who he is, to claim his rightful place in the circle of life, and no longer to adhere to the lies he believed about himself. To walk with the bereaved child requires that the practitioner be a patient listener and be creative in using tools and techniques to help the child identify and confront any cognitive distortions, accept the truth of the loss and pain, deal with both expressed and latent affect, readjust after the loss, and live.

Reminders

A final important area to assess is reminders of the parent's death and absence. These reminders may be anniversaries, birthdays, or holidays. Seeing friends go out with their parents to the mall or dinner can evoke painful memories of the absence and loss. The practitioner needs to pay close attention to reminders such as seeing other parents at the school's volleyball or soccer game. The occasions of Mother's Day and surrounding school activities or anticipated loss due to the parent's absence at graduation can also be poignant reminders and evoke profound pain of missing a loved one, especially if not addressed with sensitivity and inclusion. Other possible triggers may include eating at a favorite restaurant, the smell of dad's cologne, the taste of a chocolate cake similar to that baked by mom, or hearing a song that was playing in the days surrounding the parent's death. Children may receive the inappropriate message from family members, friends, or teachers that they should "move on" and "get over the loss." The practitioner should assess for the reminders that are particular to the grieving child. The response to such triggers may appear to be regressive. This is not necessarily the case. For example, a child may express, "I'm tired of hurting. I just want to play and have fun." Instead of signaling avoidance, play may represent a healthy balance in face of the heaviness or intensity of grief work.

Tools and Practice Examples

Resources for Parents, Educators, and Mental Health Professionals

Corr, C. A., & Corr, D. M. (Eds.). (1996). *Handbook of childhood death and bereavement.* New York: Springer.
Doka, K. J. (Ed.). (2000). *Living with grief: Children, adolescents, and loss.* Washington, DC: Hospice Foundation of America.
Gilko-Braden, M. (1992). *Grief comes to class.* Omaha, NE: Centering.
Goldman, L. (1996). *Breaking the silence: A guide to help children with complicated grief: Suicide, homicide, AIDS, violence and abuse.* Washington, DC: Taylor & Francis.
Goldman, L. (2000). *Life and loss: A guide to help grieving children* (2nd ed.). Philadelphia: Taylor & Francis.
Lehmann, L., Jimerson, S. R., & Gaasch, A. (2001). *Mourning child grief support group curriculum: Middle childhood edition.* Philadelphia: Brunner-Routledge.
Smith, S. C. (1999). *The forgotten mourners: Guidelines for working with bereaved children* (2nd ed.). London: Kingsley.
Wolfelt, A. (1996). *Healing the bereaved child: Grief gardening, growth through grief and other touchstones for caregivers.* Fort Collins, CO: Companion Press.
Worden, J. W. (1996). *Children and grief: When a parent dies.* New York: Guilford.

Worden, J. W. (2002). *Grief counseling and grief therapy* (3rd ed.). New York: Springer.

Resources for Children

Amos, J. (1997). *Separations: Death.* London: Zero to Ten.
Blume, J. (1981). *Tiger eyes.* New York: Bantam/Doubleday Dell.
Brown, L., & Brown, M. (1996). *When dinosaurs die.* New York: Little, Brown.
Doherty, B. (2002). *The golden bird.* London: Egmont.
Grollman, E. (1976). *Talking about death: A dialogue between parent and child.* Boston: Beacon.
Levete, S. (1998). *When people die.* Brookfield, CT: Copper Beech.
Varley, S. (1984). *Badger's parting gifts.* New York: Morrow.

Treatment Techniques

In the process of assessment of the six key areas, many of the following questions suggested by Lehmann and colleagues (2001) can be instrumental:

- Who told you about the death of your mother/father? What did the person say?
- How did you feel when you found out that your mother/father died?
- What do you remember about the last time you saw your mother/father alive?
- Were you there when your mother/father died? What was it like?
- Did you get to see the body? What was it like to see the body?
- Where is your mother/father now?

Lehmann and colleagues (2001) also provide a wealth of activities and reproducible handouts, including journal sheets, grief cards, and story cards. One tool that is especially useful is the memory cards. Have the child pull or draw one as if from a deck of cards and discuss the memory. Spend time in listening to these precious memories. Table 55.1, Memory Cards, provides some examples.

Based on the work of Worden (2002), the following are useful techniques to facilitate communication with the child, engage the child in treatment, and assist the child to remember the deceased parent as the parent was, with his or her blemishes and talents, not as someone who was perfect or someone on a pedestal. Many of the

Table 55.1 Memory Cards

Remember a gift your mom/dad gave to you	Remember something you gave your mom/dad
Remember an angry memory with your mom/dad	Remember something funny that happened with your mom/dad
Remember a happy memory with your mom/dad	Remember a way your mom/dad helped you out

following techniques provide concrete ways for children to get out and give expression to their experience of parental death. They are useful to the school mental health practitioner in providing contextual information crucial to the evolving process of intervention and walking with the child through the grief and loss.

1. Use symbols, such as photos of the deceased parent or a candle.
2. Write a letter to the deceased parent. This activity is especially helpful if the child did not have the chance to say goodbye or was not present at the time of death.
3. Drawing or other forms of art are wonderful mediums for expression of a child's feelings and experiences with the deceased.
4. Role playing various situations that children fear or feel awkward about, like telling their friends about the death of their parent, going to the funeral, or going to the soccer game without mom being there, can be useful.
5. Create a memory book and allow the child to put photos, including those of the funeral, stories, music, and other items of their memories with their deceased parent. This activity is especially appropriate when the child is ready to claim not just the sadness and hurt of the loss but also the fun times and happiness shared with the deceased parent.
6. Respect silence. Some of the deepest communication can occur during silence, when you are simply present to the child and the child's feelings.
7. Plant a flower or tree. Planting life is a wonderful way to teach a child about death and renewal as part of the fabric of life.

Here is a story a mother shared with me:

> Grandpa Tom was diagnosed with advanced prostate cancer. After some encouragement,

Grandma Maureen and Grandpa Tom came to live with us in order for Grandpa to undergo surgery and subsequent chemotherapy treatment. To prepare to welcome them, my 4-year-old daughter, Freya, and I planted a red tulip and a yellow tulip. She named the red tulip for her grandfather and the yellow tulip for her grandmother. Upon their arrival, both grandparents commented on the beautiful tulips. Each morning, the tulips greeted Grandma as she left the house to accompany Grandpa Tom during his hospitalization and treatment. Each evening, they welcomed her home. After 3 months, Grandpa died. The tulips became a wonderful teaching symbol to my daughter and family. Five years later, the tulips still bloom and remind us of Grandpa's love that remains with us.

Key Points to Remember

This chapter provides school social workers and mental health practitioners with a framework to effectively engage in grief work with elementary- and middle-school children. It provides examples and helpful techniques for practitioners to skillfully use in walking with children in and through their grief due to the death of a parent. For the practitioner's walk with hope through the tasks of strengthening a child and facilitating healing, this chapter emphasizes the importance of

- allowing children to tell their story while being respectful of difference, including cultural difference. Remember to acknowledge that the process is painful and emphasize that the goal is to heal and grow
- promoting both the rail of growth and the rail of healing

- assessing six areas:
  1. the strengths and resources of the child
  2. how the child was informed about the parent's death
  3. any previous losses the child has experienced and how the child coped with them as well as the coping of the child's family
  4. possible somatic complaints and behavioral and other signals
  5. possible cognitive distortions
  6. reminders of the parent's death
- using age-appropriate techniques to support remembering and healing

This chapter is dedicated to Sr. Mary Ann Connell and Fr. Lawrence Shelton, who have walked with me to Life.

References

Baker, J. E., & Sedney, M. A. (1996). How bereaved children cope with loss: An overview. In C. A. Corr & D. M. Corr (Eds.), *Handbook of childhood death and bereavement* (pp. 109–129). New York: Springer.

Dowdney, L. (2000). Childhood bereavement following parental death. *Journal of Child Psychology and Psychiatry and Allied Disciplines, 41*, 819–830.

Goldman, L. (2000). Helping the grieving child in school. *Phi Delta Kappa Fastbacks,* no. 460, 7–40.

Lehmann, L., Jimerson, S. R., & Gaasch, A. (2001). *Mourning child grief support group curriculum: Middle childhood edition.* Philadelphia: Brunner-Routledge.

Lutzke, J. R., Ayers, T. S., Sandler, I. N., & Barr, A. (1997). Risks and interventions for the parentally bereaved child. In S. A. Wolchik and I. N. Sandler (Eds.), *Handbook of children's coping: Linking theory and intervention* (pp. 215–243). New York: Plenum.

Raveis, V. H., Siegel, K., & Karus, D. (1998). Children's psychological distress following the death of a parent. *Journal of Youth and Adolescence, 28*, 165–180.

Sahler, O. J. (2000). The child and death. *Pediatric Review, 21*, 350–353.

Sandler, I. N., Ayers, T. S., Wolchik, S. A., Tein, J. Y., Kwok, O. M., Haine, R. A., Twohey, J. L., Suter, J., Lin, K., Padgett-Jones, S., Lutzke, J. R., Cole, E., Kriege, G., & Griffin, W. A. (2003). The family bereavement program: Efficacy evaluation of a theory-based prevention program for parentally bereaved children and adolescents. *Journal of Consulting and Clinical Psychology, 71*, 587–600.

Schumacher, J. D. (1984). Helping children cope with a sibling's death. In J. C. Hansen (Ed.), *Death and grief in the family* (pp. 82–94). Rockville, MD: Aspen Systems.

Silverman, P. R. (2000). *Never too young to know: Death in children's lives.* New York: Oxford University Press.

Steen, K. F. (1998). A comprehensive approach to bereavement. *Nurse Practitioner, 23*, 54–68.

Wolfelt, A. (1996). *Healing the bereaved child: Grief gardening, growth through grief and other touchstones for caregivers.* Fort Collins, CO: Companion Press.

Worden, J. W. (1996). *Children and grief: When a parent dies.* New York: Guilford.

Worden, J. W. (2002). *Grief counseling and grief therapy: A handbook for the mental health practitioner.* New York: Springer.

Worden, J. W., & Silverman, P. R. (1996). Parental death and the adjustment of school-age children. *Omega: Journal of Death & Dying, 33*, 91–102.

Effective Interventions and Resources for Group Work and Training

School social workers and mental health practitioners who contributed to the conceptualization of this resource book say that groups are one of the most beneficial intervention methods that they can use in schools. Using groups in schools can be both a time- and cost-efficient method for working with students. Feedback from professionals reflects a need for expanded skills in designing and facilitating a diverse range of groups in school settings. The chapters in this section respond to these needs with specific guidelines for best group practices and effective in-service and other presentations.

Designing and Facilitating Support Groups and Therapy Groups With Adolescents

Importance of the Topic for Schools

Charles D. Garvin

CHAPTER 56

Getting Started

Adolescents experience concerns and problems that have manifestations related to their stage of development. Virtually all can be observed in the school environment and affect or are affected by that environment, and all of those listed below have been treated successfully with group therapy in the school setting.[1]

- Poor relationships with peers. This is of great importance to teens as they move beyond the dominant role of the family into that of the peer culture. This problem is often associated with a deficit in social skills development.
- Emotional reactions in adolescence. Two emotions that are observed in the school environment are depression and anger. Depressed adolescents may not perform well in the classroom, may appear withdrawn, and may have a large number of absences. Angry students may vent at teachers or classmates; this anger may take the form of verbal abuse, property destruction, or frequent fighting.
- Substance abuse. Many adolescents experiment with drugs and alcohol. The use may be induced by peer pressures. Students can become seriously addicted, with devastating effects on social and educational activities.
- Posttraumatic stress. Some adolescents are exposed to traumatic events, such as family violence, school violence (such as a school shooting), or a natural disaster (explosion, flood, tornado). Afterward, the student may experience nightmares, phobias, or anxiety attacks that seriously impede the student's school performance.
- Delinquency. Some adolescents become involved in either individual or gang-related illegal acts and, as a result, perform poorly in school. They are often expelled, if the acts occur in school, or are sent to alternative schools for students labeled delinquent.

What We Know

A number of studies have been conducted that demonstrate the effectiveness of group work for the above problems. An issue is that the majority of the studies evaluated the use of a cognitive-behavioral group approach. Approaches that use other models portrayed in the literature on social work with groups are also likely to be used in schools (Garvin, 1997; Northen & Kurland, 2001; Shulman, 1999; Toseland & Rivas, 2001), but these have not been evaluated as rigorously as those derived from cognitive-behavioral theory.

Group practitioners assess individual change by using any of the instruments that have been developed for one-on-one work. Many instruments have also been developed for assessing changes in group conditions, and the major ones have been described by Toseland (2004, pp. 25–27).

Table 56.1 summarizes studies of the evidence for the effectiveness of group work with adolescents in schools. As can be seen, the effectiveness of a cognitive-behavioral group approach has been demonstrated with respect to adolescent depression, substance abuse, anger and disruptive classroom behavior, anxiety disorders, and post-traumatic disorders. A psychoeducational approach was effective with reducing risky behaviors. One study (Wagner & Macgowan, 2004) used an eclectic approach derived from cognitive theory, skills training, problem solving, and motivation enhancement. Several approaches were effective with students of color, such as narrative therapy with Hispanic adolescents and an indigenous African approach to empower inner-city African American female students. A so-called psychodynamic-cognitive group was effectively used to treat posttraumatic stress disorder and to prevent self-destructive behavior.

Groups are especially appropriate for adolescents because of their strong investments in peer relationships as they seek less dependence on their families. They use peer groups to help them to develop their identities, select appropriate sets of values, strengthen close relationships, and explore intimacy.

What We Can Do

This section will be an overview of the steps in conducting support and treatment groups for adolescents. A difficulty in providing such an overview is that, as shown above, groups are conducted to help adolescents with a variety of concerns, and different interventions are utilized for each concern. Some of these interventions are specific to the treatment approach, such as the use of role models or the examination of distortions in the members' thought processes. Other interventions are utilized in all approaches and relate to maintaining the group as the means and context of treatment, such as defining the group's purpose and increasing members' attraction and commitment to the group.

Another semantic issue is posed by the title of this chapter, which refers to "support" and "therapy." For purposes of this chapter, we define *support groups* as those in which members provide encouragement to each other, in addition to examples of their successful coping with problems. *Therapy* will include all of the above processes but, in addition, the social worker and mental health practitioner will help the members to explicitly seek changes in their behaviors and in the attitudes and emotions related to the behaviors in question.

The Pre-Group Phase

In order to have a successful group experience, the group must be well planned in advance. The following are the types of planning that must be accomplished:

- *Determine group purpose.* The group's purpose, once defined, guides all of the other activities that precede the first meeting of the actual group.
- *Recruitment.* The practitioner must plan a strategy for obtaining a sufficient number of members for the group; this relates to the size issue to be discussed next.

Composition and Size

A treatment group typically has about 7 members, although a support group may have as many as 10–12 members. It is important in any group to choose members who are likely to be compatible with each other and to be able to help one another attain both individual and group goals. Members should also find several other members of the group who are similar to themselves on

Table 56.1 Group Programs With Empirical Support

Type of Problem and Description of Intervention

Depression

Clarke, DeBar, & Lewinsohn, 2003

Cognitive-behavioral treatment for depression in 13–18-year-olds in a group or classlike setting, 16 2-hour sessions

Substance abuse

Curry et al., 2003

Cognitive-behavioral treatment (integrated group and family) for 14–18-year-olds suffering from both substance abuse and depression

Wagner & Macgowan, 2004

Explored students' beliefs and learned behaviors, enhanced coping skills to handle negative moods and engage in social interactions, managed social pressures to use, and increased students' motivation to change. Served high- and middle-school students identified on instruments as frequent users of substances

Anger/disruptive classroom behavior

Feindler et al., 1984

Behavioral treatment in which students analyzed anger cues and anger responses, then generated alternative responses, such as self-imposed time out, relaxation, assertiveness, problem solving; 10 sessions over 7 weeks. Students were junior high school students with high rates of community or classroom disruption

Lochman, Barry, & Pardini, 2003

Social cognitive treatment for aggressive boys in 4th–6th grades, 18 sessions

Reactions to trauma

Glodich, Allen, & Arnold, 2001

Psychoeducational approach for traumatized high school students, 12 sessions

Saltzman et al., 2001

Psychoeducation, trauma narrative exposure exercises, guided exploration of experiences, 16–20 sessions.

Tellerman, 2001

Program entitled Solutions Unlimited Now provided a psychodynamic/cognitive group experience for 8–10 weeks. Served high school students in order to prevent self-destructive behaviors and to manage posttraumatic disorder symptoms

Anxiety disorders

Masia et al., 2001

Program based on behavioral interventions, 14 sessions

Ethnically oriented interventions related to empowerment and strengthening identity

Malgady & Costantino, 2003

Served Hispanic adolescents to reduce such behaviors as anxiety, depression, acting out; sought to enhance ethnic identity and self-esteem through narrative therapy based on heroic models

Scott, 2001

Sought to empower African American females through employing a Kawaida philosophy using rituals, symbols, affirmations, African proverbs, rhythm, and song, 14 sessions

---

characteristics they view as important. Thus, a member of a specified ethnic group or gender will be most likely to benefit from the group if there are others who are similar in this way. Other characteristics that may be salient are age, social class, social skills, and academic skills. Davis and Proctor (1989) have described the research on group composition in relationship to race and gender.

Preparation

Research has shown that if members participate in a personal interview with the practitioner before the first meeting to prepare them for the group, they are more likely to benefit from the group than members who do not have this preparation (Meadow, n.d.; Yalom, 1995).

The preparation of members for school-based groups includes the following:

- discussion of the purpose of the group
- discussion of how the potential member's concerns relate to this group's purpose
- evidence that this type of service can benefit members
- the nature of the potential member's previous experience as a group member and how this is likely to affect her or his participation in this group
- the hopes and fears of the potential member regarding the group experience

Members during this preparation are frequently asked to sign a form indicating their understanding of the group's intent and their willingness to participate in it.

Frequency

The number of times the group will meet may be only once, for a brief period (such as six times), or for as long as a semester or an academic year. A single-session group usually has the purpose of helping members to deal with a concrete event, such as the death of a classmate. Most groups meet for a short period, such as 6–10 sessions. The advantage of this is that members are likely to be motivated to attend a group that has such short-term limits, and yet this is a sufficient length of time for members to learn a set of coping skills, solve a set of clear-cut problems, and develop the

kind of trust in the practitioner and other members that will enable them to express relatively private thoughts and feelings. Meetings are usually held on a weekly basis, although some groups with highly motivated and resilient members may meet twice a week.

Meetings are typically about 1–1.5 hours in duration, although some groups may meet for 45-minute periods. Longer periods may make it difficult for members to sustain interest or to handle intense feelings that arise in longer encounters.

Group Beginnings: The Process of Group Formation

The way that the practitioner helps the group in its initial meetings to form will have a great impact on how well the group accomplishes its purposes. This process of formation may take a full session in a group meeting only a few times; a group that is likely to continue for a full semester may spend several meetings in handling the tasks of formation. These tasks consist of the following:

Review of Group Purpose

Even though the practitioner has described the group's purpose in the initial announcements about the group and in the preparatory interviews with the members, this issue should be considered again when the group meets for the first time. This is because when members actually "see" who is present, they may decide to alter the group's purpose.

During group formation, members should be helped to create individual goals that are compatible with the purposes of the group. Members may be reminded of the goals they have selected, and it is often appropriate in adolescent groups to record the goals in a personal notebook.

Norms

It is essential that members adopt a series of norms about their behavior in the group. It is inappropriate for the facilitator to simply state the "rules" and leave it at that, as the members must have enough of a discussion to indicate that they have all agreed to the norms and understand them. One of the most universal norms is confidentiality, in which members indicate that they will not repeat to anyone outside the group who else is in the group and what anyone else has said, although they are free to talk to others about what they, themselves, have said. All group workers have reported that they seldom, if ever, hear of a breach of this rule.

Emotional Reactions

Members are likely to have mixed feelings about the group, especially when the group begins. They are likely to have positive feelings about the group because they hope it will help them. On the other hand, they may fear that it will exacerbate their difficulties or that they will fail to find acceptance from the other members.

Development of Relationships

Unless members have formed relationships with at least some other members and with the practitioner, they are unlikely to wish to remain in the group or to give and receive help from other members. At the first session, the practitioner seeks to initiate this process by having members introduce themselves in ways that help them discover commonalities. Adolescents especially respond well to the numerous "ice-breakers" that are available (Barlow, Blythe, & Edmonds, 1999).

The Middle Phases of the Group

Once the above tasks related to group beginnings have been accomplished, the group is ready to undertake activities to attain its goals. Practitioners will draw upon procedures described below, albeit with differences related to various purposes and theories. In addition, the practitioner must consider processes found in the middle phases of group development.

Characteristics of Middle Phases

It would seem that once the group has formed, all would be smooth sailing. This is often not the case. Countless practitioners have observed a conflict phase early in a group's life, undoubtedly induced by members becoming comfortable enough to question the initial leadership, norms, and purposes of the group (Toseland & Rivas,

2001, p. 90). The practitioner's role is to remain supportive during this phase and to mediate conflicts that may arise. After this period, the group is likely to return to a pursuit of its goals with renewed vigor.

Common Change Processes

Change processes in groups focus on helping members to change the way they view themselves and their world (perceptions), the way they understand themselves and their world (cognitions), the way they respond emotionally (affects), the way they behave (actions), and how they can use their reasoning to create their own approaches to change (problem solving). Let us now briefly consider how groups can help adolescents in these ways.

1. Changing perceptions. Members' difficulties may be caused by how they experience situations through what they see or hear.[2] Some of the examples of this are the student who hears from peers that there is no harm in the use of marijuana, from parents that all members of some ethnic group are bad, or from teachers that he or she is inferior. One of the powers of the group is that other members may not share these perceptions and can provide overwhelming evidence about contrary views that will lead to a valuable change in the member's perceptions.

2. Changing cognitions. We refer here to beliefs that members hold about the causes and consequences of events. Examples are member A's belief that if he is rejected by a potential girlfriend, this means that he will be rejected by all future women; member B's belief that if she gets a low grade on an examination, she will always fail examinations; or member C's idea that if he fails to start a fight with a classmate, he will be viewed as a weakling. Group members can suggest cognitions that are the opposite of these, such as that member A is likely to be acceptable to other young women; B has succeeded on examinations before and, with effort, will do so again; and C will be viewed as a stronger person if he indicates that he does not wish to solve disputes physically. Another important way of approaching cognitive change through groups is through process comments. This entails the social worker, or other members, noting interactions among members and enhancing the members' awareness of the interactions, the meaning each of the members involved attaches to the interactions, and whether

the ways that the members interact further their treatment goals and, if not, what changes they would like to make in these interactions (Garvin, 1997, p. 164).

3. Changing affects. Member affects are often the source of the members' problems in any group and especially in adolescent groups. The major examples are anxiety, anger, and depression. Each of these types of feeling can be ameliorated in groups, albeit with very different procedures. Anxiety can often be lessened by any one of several group activities. Progressive relaxation can usefully be taught in almost any group because virtually all problems are accompanied by feelings of tension. This technique involves teaching members to systematically relax each muscle group. Space does not permit us to provide details on this, but excellent resources are available (Rose, 1998, pp. 296–307). Members can also be asked to visualize peaceful scenes as a means of achieving relaxation. A third approach is based in breathing exercises (Rose, 1998, pp. 304–305). Interventions in groups to reduce anger involve teaching members to express anger in safe ways, such as discussing the anger and the internal events associated with it and expressing the anger in such a manner as to acknowledge the humanity and the needs of the other persons involved (Rose, 1998, pp. 437–459).

Reducing depression requires the practitioner to help members to grieve losses and replace inactivity with productive actions. When members remain inactive or even withdrawn, they may repeatedly think of the sadness they are experiencing, thus increasing it (Curry et al., 2001).[3]

4. Changing actions. While attention to members' affects and thoughts are likely to result in their behaving differently, several approaches are used by group practitioners to help group members acquire new behaviors. These approaches make use of the opportunities afforded by the group environment. These include members using each other as role models, members practicing new behaviors in role plays, and members reinforcing the appropriate behavior of other members. Group workers will often use activities that encourage members to act in new ways, Such activities include games, drama, dance, and crafts.

5. Problem solving. All approaches to group work make use of problem solving. This process involves members defining the problem and the goal sought, seeking alternative solutions to the problem, evaluating the alternatives, choosing an alternative, and implementing the best alternative.

The Ending Phases of the Group

The way that the practitioner facilitates the group when it is about to end will have an impact on what personal changes members retain when the group ends. The amount of time allotted to this varies, depending on how long the group has been in existence. A short-term group will usually allocate all of the final session to a termination process. A group that has been in existence for a semester or longer may spend at least two sessions on termination. The following are the tasks of the ending phase:

• Members discuss the degree to which they have attained individual goals.
• Members evaluate the degree to which the group and the practitioner have been helpful.
• Members plan activities they will undertake after the group ends to maintain positive changes.
• Members discuss both positive and negative feelings about ending. Positive ones may relate to goals they have attained and pleasures the group has afforded them. Negative ones may relate to the fact that they may not see the practitioner or other members, as a group, again.

Tools and Practice Examples

Clarke and his colleagues (2003) describe a group program for depressed adolescents. They identified potential members of the group through the use of well-tested screening instruments and included teens who used drugs as long as they were not actively using during sessions. They excluded teens who had active psychotic or bipolar disorders. They also excluded teens who were major suicidal risks.

The investigators established ground rules in the first session and explained the plan for the 16 2-hour sessions to come. They also explained a social learning theory model of depression. The program utilized in this group had two components. One, primarily used in sessions 2–5, was to help the youth increase their rates of age-appropriate and pleasant activities. Group leaders helped the members to select a list of fun activities that they would like to do more often. The youths found a relationship between their moods and these activities. The youths then set small but achievable goals for increasing their activity level. They also used problem solving to remove barriers to engaging in these activities.

The second component was based on cognitive therapy and occupied most of sessions 5–10. The practitioner explained the following model: Triggering situations lead to unexamined beliefs, which contribute to feelings. The early sessions employed cartoons to illustrate common beliefs leading to frustration, anger, or depression. Members were taught how to assess whether these beliefs are rational or not. They were then coached on ways of substituting realistic, positive thoughts, after which they rated their mood changes. The members helped each other with suggestions and ideas throughout this process. The authors noted that teens are much more likely to accept this kind of analysis from each other than from adults.

The members were also taught to relax through progressive muscle relaxation and deepbreathing techniques. Final sessions were devoted to problem solving, negotiation, and communication skills. The final session focused on maintaining gains, learning how to recognize a recurrence of depression, and developing a personal depression prevention plan. Members reviewed their progress, dealt with feelings about the group ending, and discussed ways of replacing the support that the group had provided.

Key Points to Remember

- Carefully specify the purpose of the group and state this in a way that recognizes how the problem is seen in the adolescent community.
- Select members who are likely to be compatible in terms of age, culture, and personal attributes.
- Conduct a pre-group interview with each prospective member.
- In first meetings, accomplish group formation tasks, such as clarification of purpose, initiation of relationships among members, agreement on norms, and creation of individual goals.
- After formation, plan *with the members* what the activities will be to achieve the purposes of the group. These activities will encourage changes in members' perceptions, cognitions, affects, and behaviors.
- At the end of the group, engage in such termination tasks as assessment of change, evaluation

of the group experience, expression of feelings about endings, and determination of how to maintain desirable changes.

Notes

1. Since this book is directed at school social workers and related mental health professionals, we shall use the term *group work* rather than *group therapy* in this chapter as this is the designation we believe is most employed by social workers.

2. There are, of course, other senses, but these are the ones on which we shall focus here.

3. Any of these emotional responses may require treatment from a psychiatrist, such as prescribing medications.

References

Barlow, C., Blythe, J., & Edmonds, M. (1999). *A handbook of interactive exercises for groups.* Boston: Allyn & Bacon.

Clarke, G. N., DeBar, L. L., & Lewinsohn, P. M. (2003). Cognitive-behavioral group treatment for adolescent depression. In A. E. Kazdin & J. R. Weisz (Eds.), *Evidence-based psychotherapies for children and adolescents* (pp. 120–134). New York: Guilford.

Curry, J. F., Wells, K. C., Lochman, J. E., Craighead, W. E., & Nagy, P. D. (2003). Cognitive-behavioral intervention for depressed, substance-abusing adolescents: Development and pilot testing. *Journal of the American Academy of Child and Adolescent Psychiatry, 42,* 656–665.

Davis, L., & Proctor, E. (1989). *Race, gender, and class: Guidelines for practice with individuals, families, and groups.* Englewood Cliffs, NJ: Prentice-Hall.

Feindler, E. L., Marriott, S. A., & Iwata, M. (1984). Group anger-control training for junior high school delinquents. *Cognitive Therapy and Research, 8,* 299–311.

Garvin, C. D. (1997). *Contemporary group work* (3rd ed.). Boston: Allyn & Bacon.

Glodich, A., Allen, J. G., & Arnold, L. (2001). Protocol for a trauma-based psychoeducational group intervention to decrease risk-taking, reenactment, and further violence exposure: Application to the public high school setting. *Journal of Child and Adolescent Group Therapy, 11,* 87–107.

Lochman, J. E., Barry, T. D., & Pardini, D. A. (2003). Anger control training for aggressive youth. In A. E. Kazdin & J. R. Weisz (Eds.), *Evidence-based psychotherapies for children and adolescents* (pp. 263–278). New York: Guilford.

Malgady, R. G., & Costantino, G. (2003). Narrative therapy for Hispanic children and adolescents. In A. E. Kazdin & J. R. Weisz (Eds.), *Evidence-based psychotherapies for children and adolescents* (pp. 425–438). New York: Guilford.

Masia, C. L., Klein, R. G., Storch, E. A., & Corda, B. (2001). School-based behavioral treatment for social anxiety disorder in adolescents: Results of a pilot study. *Journal of the American Academy of Child and Adolescent Psychiatry: Special Issue, 40*(7), 780–786.

Meadow, D. (n.d.). *Connecting theory and practice: The effect of pregroup preparation on individual and group behavior* (mimeographed).

Northen, H., & Kurland, R. (2001). *Social work with groups* (3rd ed.). New York: Columbia University Press.

Rose, S. D. (1998). *Group therapy with troubled youth: A cognitive-behavioral interactive approach*. Thousand Oaks, CA: Sage.

Saltzman, W. R., Steinberg, A. M., Layne, C. M., Aisenberg, E., & Pynoos, R. S. (2001). A developmental approach to school-based treatment of adolescents exposed to trauma and traumatic loss. *Journal of Child and Adolescent Group Therapy, 11*, 43–56.

Scott, C. C. (2001). The sisterhood group: A culturally focused empowerment group model for inner city African-American youth. *Journal of Child and Adolescent Group Therapy, 11*, 77–85.

Shulman, L. (1999). *The skills of helping individuals, families, and groups* (4th ed.). Itaska, IL: Peacock.

Tellerman, J. S. (2001). The Solutions Unlimited Now–SUN(sm) program: Psychodynamic/cognitive structured groups for teens, pre-teens, and families. *Journal of Child and Adolescent Group Therapy, 11*, 117–134.

Toseland, R. W., Jones, L. V., & Gellis, Z. D. (2004). Group dynamics. In C. D. Garvin, L. M. Gutierrez, & M. J. Galinsky (Eds.), *Handbook of social work with groups* (pp. 13–31). New York: Guilford.

Toseland, R. W., & Rivas, R. F. (2001). *An introduction to group work practice* (4th ed.). Boston: Allyn & Bacon.

Wagner, E. F., & Macgowan, M. J. (2004). *School-based treatment of adolescent substance abuse problems: Student assistance program group counseling.* (unpublished manuscript)

Yalom, I. (1995). *The theory and practice of group psychotherapy* (4th ed.). New York: Basic.

Designing and Facilitating Groups With Children

Craig Winston LeCroy

CHAPTER 57

Getting Started

School is the major socializing institution for children. In school, children develop social behavior in addition to learning academic skills. There is a clear link among the social, emotional, and cognitive development of children. Although schools focus on children's educational and cognitive skills and capabilities, an important but neglected area of concern is the healthy psychosocial development of children. Indeed, most educators, parents, and the public want schools to have a broader agenda and include health, character development, social competence, and civic engagement (Rose & Gallup, 2000). The National Mental Health Association Commission on the Prevention of Mental-Emotional Disabilities recommended, "[P]rograms should be developed in schools (preschool through high school) that incorporate validated mental health strategies and competence building as an integral part of the curriculum" (Long, 1986). Our schools must begin to acknowledge the importance of instructing students in a new set of basics: responsible decision making, socially competent behavior, healthy behavior, positive mental health, and positive contributions to family, peers, and their community. Without such skills, children face numerous negative consequences later in life or fail to develop to their fullest capacity.

The purpose of this chapter is to provide some guidelines for designing and facilitating therapeutic groups for children. The primary focus is on elementary- and middle-school children between the ages of 6 and 12 (see chapter 56 by Garvin for information on adolescents). Offering various small groups in schools can facilitate the socialization and academic education of children. Lela Costin (1969) argued more than 35 years ago that

social workers should apply group work methods more broadly in school settings. Groups can equip children with prosocial skills to help them replace aggressive or withdrawn behaviors with appropriate coping strategies. For example, interpersonal skills can be taught to enhance communication with peers, parents, and authority figures.

Numerous opportunities exist for the implementation of various group-based programs that can help to facilitate the successful socialization of children and adolescents in our schools. Groups have been organized to serve children and adolescents with social skills deficiencies, anger control problems, substance abuse, attention-deficit/hyperactivity disorder, trauma recovery, anxiety, coping with divorce of parents, pregnancy prevention, school dropout, stress, grief and loss, obsessive-compulsive disorder, and many combinations of these themes. School social workers and other mental health practitioners can play an important role in the design and implementation of such group programs.

There are a number of advantages of working with children in groups. The peer group is a natural part of child and adolescent development, and as such the treatment more nearly simulates their real world than the client–adult dyad. Groups also represent a more efficient way of delivering interventions than do dyads. Group membership commonly ends the sense of isolation and lack of understanding that many students experience, since they are surrounded by other children who are dealing with similar issues and problems. Groups may be divided into subgroups for certain exercises and as a way of increasing the amount and breadth of interactions in the group. Certain interventions are more accessible or more effective in small groups, for example, the use of brainstorming in teaching problem-solving skills, or the use of feedback from other members following role playing, or designing extra-group tasks and goals. Games and other recreational activities help to build cohesion and motivation. Finally, groups enhance the generalization of change since each member observes and helps to solve a diversity of problems manifested by the other clients.

What We Know

Most of the empirical evidence for interventions with children and adolescents has been conducted as part of special programs that are offered in a group setting. Durlak and Wells (1997) conducted a meta-analysis to examine the impact of more than 150 primary prevention programs; 73% of the studies were conducted in a school setting. The overall results were that programs enhanced competencies such as assertiveness, communication skills, self-image, and school achievement. Strong benefits were realized for young children aged 2–7 with interventions using a behavioral approach.

More recently, Greenberg, Domitrovich, and Bumbarger (2001) reviewed more than 130 programs for schoolchildren ranging in age from 5 to 18. The intent of the review was to examine rigorously evaluated interventions that reduced psychological symptoms, such as aggression or depression, or reduced factors associated with child mental disorders. Overall results were favorable, and the authors concluded that longer-term programs are better; multiple domain-based programs (e.g., individual, school, and family) are more effective than an exclusive child focus; and with school-age children it is better to address school ecology and school climate.

Tobler, Roona, Ochshorn, Marshall, Streke, and Stackpole (2000) examined child and adolescent outcome studies over a span of 20 years. Programs were classified as noninteractive or interactive, with interactive programs obtaining stronger effects. In particular, high-intensity interactive programs with 16 or more hours of curriculum had greater impact than low-intensity (6 hours or less) programs. Greater benefits were also found for programs that included life skills models, refusal skills, goal setting, assertiveness, communication, and coping strategies. Using this research, Zins et al. (2002) make a compelling case for the relationship between programs that promote psychosocial functioning and improved school attitudes, behavior, and performance.

Most of these empirically supported groups range in size from 5 to 15 members, although the norm is about 6–9. They range in duration from 6 to 20 sessions, depending on the complexity of the presenting problems. Most group sessions last from 45 minutes to 1.5 hours. Most groups are closed and time limited, with a fixed beginning and ending time. Note that there are some data to support smaller groups over larger groups and to support providing group structure, which permits intense interaction by everyone in the group. The more complex the problems, the longer the length of time and the more sessions that are required. Table 57.1 presents examples of key group studies with empirical support.

What We Can Do

While there are many types of therapeutic groups from which children can benefit, the remainder of this chapter will focus on social competence–based groups as one example. Social competence training is often conducted in a group format that provides support and a reinforcing context for learning new responses and appropriate behaviors in a variety of social situations. The group is a natural context for social skills training because of the peer interactions that take place as the group members work together. Additionally, the group allows for the extensive use of modeling and feedback, which are successful components of group treatment.

The following seven basic steps delineate the process that group leaders can follow when doing social skills training (based on LeCroy, 1994). These guidelines have been found to be effective in teaching social skills with middle-school students (LeCroy & Rose, 1986) and elementary-school students (King & Kirschenbaum, 1992). Table 57.2 presents these steps and outlines the process for teaching social skills. In each step, there is a request for group member involvement. This is because it is critical that group leaders involve the participants actively in the skills training. Also, this keeps the group interesting and fun for the group members.

1. Present the social skill being taught. The first step is for the group leader to present the skill. The leader solicits an explanation of the skill, for example, "Can anyone tell me what it means to resist peer pressure?" After group members have answered this question, the leader emphasizes the

Table 57.1 Group Programs With Empirical Support

Type of Problem and Description of Intervention

Aggressive behavior/violence prevention

Conduct Problems Prevention Research Group, 1992
Program that focuses on school, home, and individual treatment; goal is to increase bonds in these domains; social, cognitive, and problem-solving skills are emphasized
Olweus, 1993
Multicomponent program; attempts to restructure the school environment to reduce opportunities and rewards for bullies

Withdrawn and isolated behavior

King & Kirschenbaum, 1992
Program is based on a social skills training model for young children; emphasizes teaching new skills and reinforcement for new behaviors
Weiss & Harris, 2001
Program for autistic children that applies social skills training and behavior modification primarily to enhance social interaction skills

Peer mediation/positive youth development

Hawkins et al., 1992
School-wide, school climate program for elementary schools; promotes successful participation in family, school, peer group, and community
Begun, 1995
Curriculum for learning general social skills

Divorce

Pedro-Carroll et al., 1992
10-session program that emphasizes support and skill building for children of divorce; includes content on problem solving, anger management, and coping
Wolchik et al., 1993
Parent-based intervention that focuses on parent–child relationships

Social competence

Elias & Tobias, 1998
Curriculum-based program that promotes self-control, group participation, and social awareness; emphasis is on decision-making and problem-solving skills
LeCroy & Daley, 2001a
Broad-based universal prevention program that focuses on preteen and early adolescent girls; uses a psychoeducational and social skills training approach

---

rationale for using the skill. For example, "You would use this skill when you're in a situation where you don't want to do something that your friends want you to do, and you should be able to say 'no' in a way that helps your friends to be able to accept your refusal." The leader then requests additional reasons for learning the skill.

2. Discuss the social skill. The leader presents the specific skill steps that constitute the social skill. For example, the skill steps for resisting peer pressure are good nonverbal communication (in-

cludes eye contact, posture, voice volume), saying "no" early in the interaction, suggesting an alternative activity, and leaving the situation if there is continued pressure. Leaders then ask group members to share examples of when they used the skill or examples of when they could have used the skill but did not.

3. Present a problem situation and model the skill. The leader presents a problem situation. The following is an example of a problem situation for resisting peer pressure:

Table 57.2 A Summary of the Steps in Social Skills Training

1. Present the social skill being taught
   A. Solicit an explanation of the skill
   B. Get group members to provide rationales for the skill

2. Discuss the social skill
   A. List the skill steps
   B. Get group members to give examples of using the skill

3. Present a problem situation and model the skill
   A. Evaluate the performance
   B. Get group members to discuss the model

4. Set the stage for role playing the skill
   A. Select the group members for role playing
   B. Get group members to observe the role play

5. Group members rehearse the skill
   A. Provide coaching if necessary
   B. Get group members to provide feedback on verbal and nonverbal elements

6. Practice using complex skill situations
   A. Teach accessory skills, e.g., problem solving
   B. Get group members to discuss situations and provide feedback

7. Train for generalization and maintenance
   A. Encourage practice of skills outside the group
   B. Get group members to bring in their problem situations

You are with your friend at recess, and he suggests you both play a mean trick on another student, who is also a friend of yours.

The group leader chooses members to role play this situation and then models the skills. Group members evaluate the model's performance. Did the model follow all of the skill steps? Was his or her performance successful? The group leader may choose another group member to model if the leader believes that the student already has the requisite skills. Another alternative is to present to the group videotaped models. This has the advantage of following the recommendation by researchers that the models be similar to the trainee in age, sex, and social characteristics.

4. Set the stage for the role playing of the skill. For this step, the group leader needs to construct the social circumstances for the role play. Leaders select group members for the role play and give them their parts to play. The leader reviews how to act out their roles with them. Group members not in the role play observe the process. It is sometimes helpful if they are given specific instructions for their observations. For example, one

member may observe the use of nonverbal skills; another member may be instructed to observe when "no" is said in the interaction.

5. Group members rehearse the skill. Rehearsal or guided practice of the skill is an important part of effective social skills training. Group leaders and group members provide instructions or coaching before and during the role play and provide praise and feedback for improvement. Following a role-play rehearsal, the leader will usually give instructions for improvement, model the suggested improvements, or coach the person to incorporate the feedback in the subsequent role play. Often the group members doing the role play will practice the skills in the situation several times to refine their skills and incorporate the feedback offered by the group. The role plays continue until the trainee's behavior becomes more and more similar to that of the model. It is important that "overlearning" take place, so the group leader should encourage many examples of effective skill demonstration followed by praise. Group members should be taught how to give effective feedback before the rehearsals. Throughout the

teaching process, the group leader can model desired responses. For example, after a role play, the leader can respond first and model feedback that starts with a positive statement.

6. Practice using complex skill situations. The last phase deals with more difficult and complex skill situations. Complex situations can be developed by extending the interactions and roles in the problem situations. Most social skills groups also incorporate the teaching of problem-solving abilities. Problem solving is a general approach to helping young people to gather information about a problematic situation, generate a large number of potential solutions, evaluate the consequences of various solutions, and outline plans for the implementation of a particular solution. Group leaders can identify appropriate problem situations and lead members through the above steps. The problem-solving training is important because it prepares young people to make adjustments as needed in a given situation and is a skill with large-scale application (see Elias & Tobias, 1998, for more details).

7. Train for generalization and maintenance. The success of the social skills program depends on the extent to which the skills that young people learn transfer to their day-to-day lives. Practitioners must always be planning for ways to maximize the generalization of skills learned and promote their continued use after training. There are several principles that help to facilitate the generalization and maintenance of skills. The first is the use of overlearning. The more that overlearning takes place, the greater likelihood of later transfer of skills. Therefore, it is important that group leaders insist on mastery of the skills. Another important principle of generalization is to vary the stimuli as skills are learned. To accomplish this, practitioners can use a variety of models, problem situations, role-play actors, and trainers. The different styles and behaviors of the people used produce a broader context in which to apply the skills learned. Perhaps most important is to require that young people use the skills in their real-life settings. Group leaders should assign and monitor homework to encourage transfer of learning. This may include the use of written contracts to do certain tasks outside of the group. Group members should be asked to bring to the group examples of problem situations where the social skills can be applied. Lastly, practitioners should attempt to develop external support for the skills learned. One approach to this is to set up a buddy system where group members work together to perform the skills learned outside the group.

Practical Considerations in Conducting Social Skills Training Groups

Conducting group prevention and intervention services is an efficient use of a school social worker's and mental health counselor's time, as several students can be seen at one time. However, groups must be recruited and constructed with certain key factors in mind. First, recruitment for groups will depend on the goals of the particular program. It may be necessary to limit the number of participants involved, in which case procedures must be used to help identify the students most likely to benefit from the program. This screening process can be accomplished by administering assessment devices, identifying students who meet specified risk criteria, conducting pre-group interviews, or designing a referral system for teachers and other professionals to use to refer children directly to the group (Rose, 1998). On the other hand, limiting groups only to children who meet certain risk criteria may not be best in some groups. Some research indicates that including participants who are highly socially competent can have positive implications. Given that some groups will contain children who act out antisocially, a higher degree of poor social skills modeling could initially take place. By including high-functioning children in an antisocial group, the opportunity for prosocial modeling increases. Also, it may be less difficult to maintain order (Merrell & Gimpel, 1998). Finally, group composition includes factors such as how well the group participants know one another, how heterogeneous the group is, how large the group is, the age and developmental level of the participants, and their gender. It is important that all members of a group have the time and attention they need to practice skills and receive important feedback; therefore, the group should be 6–10 members with two leaders. Merrell and Gimpel (1998) propose that the members of the group should not vary in age by more than 2 or 3 years. It is not difficult to recognize the need for language and interventions to be age- and developmentally appropriate. Presenting group material that requires a high level of cognitive ability will not be effective for group members who are either too young or who are functioning at a lower level developmentally than the skill requires.

A Group Program for Early Adolescent Girls

A social skills training psychoeducational prevention program called Go Grrrls (LeCroy & Daley, 2001a) was developed specifically for preteens or early adolescent girls. This program was designed using empirical information about the developmental tasks critical for the successful transition to adolescence and adulthood. A randomized control group evaluation found empirical support for the short-term impact of the program (LeCroy, in press; LeCroy & Daley, 2001a). In response to common problems empirically identified, a group of core developmental tasks (e.g., development of

Table 57.3. Go Grrrls Skill-Building Goals and Treatment Approach

Program Goal	Related Social Skills Training
Core skill: Assertiveness	
Goal: To teach girls to act assertively rather than passively or aggressively	1. Discuss the skill of assertiveness
Rationale: Teaching basic assertiveness skills to girls will help them speak up in classrooms and withstand peer pressure and will serve as a foundation for learning more specific refusal skills.	2. Group leaders demonstrate assertive, passive, and aggressive responses to sample situations
	3. Group members practice identifying assertive behavior
	4. Group members practice assertiveness skills
	5. Group leaders and other members provide feedback
	Sample scenario: You are in science class, and the boy you are partners with tells you that he wants to mix the chemicals and you can be the secretary. What do you do?
Core skill: Making and keeping friends	
Goal: To equip girls with the tools they need to establish and maintain healthy peer relationships	1. Discuss the components of a successful conversation, including the beginning, middle, and end
Rationale: Disturbances in peer relationships are among the best predictors of psychiatric, social, and school problems. Teaching friendship skills can reduce these problems. Strong friendship skills can be an important protective factor.	2. Group leaders demonstrate both ineffective and effective conversational skills
	3. Group members practice identifying effective conversational skills, such as making eye contact and asking questions of the other person
	4. Group members practice conversational skills in role-play situations
	5. Group leaders and other members provide feedback
	Sample scenario: It is your first day of junior high and you don't know anyone in your homeroom. Start a conversation with the girl who sits next to you.

positive gender-role identification, body image, and self-image) were identified as program goals.

Building a Solid Foundation of Skills

We have already discussed the importance of overlearning in social skills training. The Go Grrrls program is designed to increase the odds of participants' overlearning by selecting key skills that girls need to learn and building participants' confidence and mastery of these skills over several sessions. For the focus area of "assertiveness," the Go Grrrls program provides three sessions that help girls to learn this skill. In one of the early group meetings, girls are introduced to the general concept of assertiveness and are given practice using this skill. In two later sessions, girls are given additional practice using assertiveness skills. To reinforce the skills learned, girls turn in journal assignments from a workbook (LeCroy & Daley, 2001b). Table 57.3 illustrates how social skills may be combined in a complementary fashion to help participants build strengths.

Key Points to Remember

As school social workers and other practitioners work toward the goal of enhancing the socialization process of children, methods for promoting social competence, such as social skills training, have much to offer. This direct approach to working with children has been applied in numerous problem areas and with many child behavior problems. It is straightforward in application and has been adapted so that social workers, counselors, teachers, and peer helpers have successfully applied the methodology. Social workers and mental health counselors can make an important contribution to children, families, and schools through preventive and remedial approaches like those described in this chapter. As we have seen, children's social behavior is a critical aspect of their successful adaptation to society. The school represents an ideal place for children to learn and practice social behavior. It provides the needed multipeer context and offers multiple opportunities for newly learned behaviors to be generalized to other situations and circumstances. Research supports the efficacy of prevention and intervention programs like these in the schools. These promising treatment approaches offer accountability, an opportunity to reduce some of the difficulties that children face, and the skills and abilities for them to realize their full potential.

References

Begun, R. W. (1995). *Ready-to-use social skills lessons & activities for grades 4–6.* Center for Applied Research in Education.

Conduct Problems Prevention Research Group. (1992). A developmental and clinical model for the prevention of conduct disorders: The FAST Track Program. *Development and Psychopathology, 4,* 509–527.

Costin, L. B. (1969). An analysis of the tasks of school social work. *Social Service Review, 43,* 247–285.

Durlak, J. A., & Wells, A. M. (1997). Primary prevention mental health programs for children and adolescents: A meta-analytic review. *American Journal of Community Psychology, 25,* 115–152.

Elias, M. J., & Tobias, S. E. (1998). *Social problem solving: Interventions in the schools.* New York: Guilford.

Greenberg, M. T., Domitrovich, C. E., & Bumbarger, B. (2001). The prevention of mental disorders in school-aged children: Current state of the field. *Prevention & Treatment, 4.* Available: http://journals.apa.org/prevention/volume4/pre0040001a.html

Hawkins, J. D., Catalano, R. F., Morrison, D., O'Konnell, J., Abbott, R., & Day, L. (1992). The Seattle Social Development Project: Effects of the first four years on protective factors and problem behaviors. In J. McCord & R. Tremblay (Eds.), *The prevention of antisocial behavior in children* (pp. 139–161). New York: Guilford.

King, C. A., & Kirschenbaum, D. S. (1992). *Helping young children develop social skills.* Pacific Grove, CA: Brooks/Cole.

LeCroy, C. W. (1994). Social skills training. In C. LeCroy (ed.), *Handbook of child and adolescent treatment manuals.* New York: Lexington.

LeCroy, C. W. (in press). Experimental evaluation of the "Go Grrrls" preventive intervention for early adolescent girls. *Journal of Primary Prevention.*

LeCroy, C. W., & Daley, J. (2001a). *Empowering adolescent girls: Examining the present and building skills for the future with the Go Grrrls program.* New York: Norton.

LeCroy, C. W., & Daley, J. (2001b). *Go Grrrls workbook.* New York: Norton.

LeCroy, C. W., & Rose, S. D. (1986). Evaluation of preventive interventions for enhancing social competence in adolescents. *Social Work Research and Abstracts, 22,* 8–17.

Long, B. B. (1986). The prevention of mental-emotional disabilities: A report from a National Mental Health Association commission. *American Psychologist, 41,* 825–829.

Merrell, K. W., & Gimpel, G. A. (1998). *Social skills of children and adolescents: Conceptualization, assessment, treatment.* Mahwah, NJ: Erlbaum.

Olweus, D. (1993). *Bullying at school: What we know and what we can do.* Oxford: Basil Blackwell.

Pedro-Carroll, J. L., Alpert-Gillis, L. J., & Cowen, E. L. (1992). An evaluation of the efficacy of a preventive intervention for 4th–6th grade urban children of divorce. *Journal of Primary Prevention, 13,* 115–130.

Rose, L. C., & Gallup, A. M. (2000). *The 23rd Annual Phi Delta Kappa/Gallup poll of the public's attitudes towards the public schools.* Available: http://www.pdkintl.org/kappan/kpo10009.htm

Rose, S. D. (1998). *Group therapy with troubled youth.* Thousand Oaks, CA: Sage.

Tobler, N. S., Roona, M. R., Ochshorn, P., Marshall, D. G., Streke, A. V., & Stackpole, K. M. (2000). School-based adolescent drug prevention programs: 1998 meta-analysis. *Journal of Primary Prevention, 20,* 275–337.

Weiss, M., & Harris, S. L. (2001). Teaching social skills to people with autism. *Behavior Modification, 25,* 785–802.

Wolchik, S. A., West, S. G., Westover, S., Sandler, I. N., Martin, A., Lustig, J., Tein, J., & Fisher, J. (1993). The children of divorce parenting intervention: Outcome evaluation of an empirically based program. *American Journal of Community Psychology, 21,* 293–331.

Zins, J. E., Weissberg, R. P., Wang, M. C., & Walberg, H. J. (2002). *Building school success through social and emotional learning.* New York: Teachers College Press.

Design and Utility of Life Skills Groups in Schools

David R. Dupper

Getting Started

This chapter discusses the use of social skills training (SST) groups as a preventive or remedial intervention with children and youth. It begins with a discussion of social competence as a significant developmental accomplishment of children and youth who are experiencing problems. It discusses definitional problems surrounding the concept of social skills, best practices in the assessment of social skills, and research findings on the effectiveness of school-based SST groups as a promising intervention method for developing the social competencies of children and youth. This chapter then provides a brief discussion of issues related to cultural and racial differences and issues related to gender differences that should be considered in implementing SST interventions. Following this is an illustration of actions taken by a program staff in an effort to obtain support for and commitment to a social competence group in an elementary school. This chapter concludes with a summary of major points and additional resources.

What We Know

Social Competence as an Essential Aspect of Healthy Development

The development of social competence is an essential aspect of healthy normal development (LeCroy, 2002). Social competence is demonstrated through behaviors that parents, teachers, and peers consider important, adaptive, and functional in relation to environmental demands and age-appropriate societal expectations, such as peer acceptance and friendships, teacher and parental acceptance, and school adjustment (Gresham, Sugai, & Horner, 2001). According to Gresham (2002), "[T]he ability to interact successfully with peers and significant adults is one of the most important developmental accomplishments of children and youth" (p. 1029). Without such skills and competence, children and youth are more likely to experience friendship difficulties, inappropriately expressed emotions, and an inability to resist peer pressure (LeCroy, 1992). Clearly, the development of social competence should be considered an important developmental goal for all children (Katz, McClellan, Fuller, & Walz, 1995).

Unfortunately, substantial numbers of young people today lack the social competencies that protect against high-risk behaviors (Weissberg, Kumpfer, & Seligman, 2003). According to recent data from the Youth Risk Behavior Surveillance System (YRBSS), in 2003, 30.2% of high school students had ridden with a driver who had been drinking alcohol; 17.1% had carried a weapon; 33% had been in a physical fight; 8.5% had attempted suicide; 46.7% had had sexual intercourse; and 37% of sexually active students had not used a condom during their last sexual intercourse (Centers for Disease Control and Prevention, 2004). Moreover, the negative consequences of low levels of social competence in adolescents tend to persist into their adult years (Rose, 1998). Substantial research indicates that a lack of social skills in dealing with peers can lead to later maladjustment such as delinquency, dropping out of school, low academic achievement, antisocial behavior, alcoholism, and adult psychoses (Lope & Edelbaum, 1999).

The acquisition of social skills and the development of social competency are particularly important for students who demonstrate significant delays in cognitive, academic, and emotional/behavioral functioning and who meet the criteria specified in the Individuals With Disabilities Education Act (IDEA) for specific learning disabilities, mental retardation, emotional disturbance, and attention-deficit/hyperactivity disorder (Gresham & MacMillan, 1997).

Definitional Problems

Due to its relative simplicity as a construct and the fact that a very broad group of professional disciplines (e.g., social work, education, psychology, psychiatric nursing) have interest in it as a construct, "social skills is among the most widely misunderstood and ill-defined of all psychological constructs" (Merrell & Gimpel, 1998, p. 3). Gresham (1986) has divided the various definitions of social skills into three general categories: behavioral definitions, peer-acceptance definitions, and social validity definitions. The vast majority of studies have used behavioral definitions of social skills and defined them as "situation-specific behaviors that maximize the chances of reinforcement and minimize the chances of punishment based on one's social behavior" (Merrell & Gimpel, 1998, p. 5). Gresham, Sugai, and Horner (2001) defined social skills as "specific behaviors that an individual uses to perform competently or successfully on particular social tasks (e.g., starting a conversation, giving a compliment, entering an ongoing play group)" (p. 333). Peer-acceptance definitions of social skills depend upon popularity indices in defining social skills. For example, a child is viewed as being socially skilled if she is liked and accepted by her peers (Merrell & Gimpel, 1998). According to Gresham (1986), the social validity definition of social skills is a hybrid of these two categories and has received increasing empirical support since the 1980s. Based upon their extensive review of more than two decades of research, Caldarella and Merrell (1997) have developed an empirically based taxonomy of positive child and adolescent social skills. The five most common social skills dimensions identified through their meta-analysis are peer relations skills (e.g., compliments/praises/applauds peers); self-management skills (e.g., remains calm when problems arise, receives criticism well); academic skills (e.g., accomplishes tasks/assignments independently, listens to and carries out teacher's directions); compliance skills (e.g., follows rules, shares materials); and assertion skills (e.g., initiates conversations with others, questions unfair rules).

Assessment of Social Skills: Best Practices

The assessment process is an essential link between identifying children and adolescents with social skills deficits and developing an appropriate intervention plan (Merrell & Gimpel, 1998). The most direct and objective method of assessing social skills is through *direct observation*. All observational coding systems can be broken down into four general types of procedures: event recording, interval recording, time-sample recording, and duration and latency recording (Merrell & Gimpel, 1998). Space limitations will not allow for a detailed description of each of these general types. Therefore, readers seeking a detailed explanation of these coding systems should see Merrell and Gimpel (1998, pp. 63–69).

A second method that is widely used in assessing social skills in children and adolescents is *behavior rating scales*. Some widely used standardized behavior rating scales are the Behavioral Assessment System for Children (BASC; Reynolds & Kamphaus, 1992); the Social Skills Rating System (SSRS; Gresham & Elliott, 1990); the Preschool and Kindergarten Behavior Scales (PKBS; Merrell, 1994); and the Walker-McConnell Scales of Social Competence and School Adjustment (SSCSA; Walker & McConnell, 1995).

A third method used to assess social skills in children and adolescents is *sociometric techniques*. Rather than obtaining assessment data from teachers or outside observers, the defining feature of sociometric techniques is that data are obtained that assess the child's social status based on that child's peer group, usually within a classroom setting (Merrell & Gimpel, 1998). Sociometric methods usually "involve negative ranking or nomination procedures, or the use of negative characteristics to single out peers" (Merrell & Gimpel, 1998, p. 89) and can be divided into four general categories: peer nomination, picture sociometrics, "guess who" measures, and class play. See Merrell and Gimpel (1998) for a detailed description of these four sociometric techniques.

A fourth and final method of assessing social skills in children and adolescents is through *self-reports*. Through self-reports, objective data are obtained directly from the child or adolescent rather than from observers, teachers, or peers (Merrell & Gimpel, 1998). Self-report data are obtained through interviews and self-report tests, such as the Assessment of Interpersonal Relations (AIR; Bracken, 1993).

Research on the Effectiveness of Social Skills Training: Best Practices

Once an adequate assessment is completed, interventions that target specific social deficits can be implemented. One promising intervention method in developing social competencies of children and youth is social skills training (SST). Social skills training has been shown to be "perhaps the most promising new treatment model" for children and adolescents who are aggressive, disruptive, difficult to get along with, extremely shy or quiet, or unwilling to participate or socialize (LeCroy, 2002, p. 411). Rather than focusing solely on the elimination of problem behaviors, the primary focus of SST is the teaching of prosocial responses in situations that tend to elicit antisocial responses (LeCroy, 1983, 1992).

Weissberg, Barton, and Shriver (1997) found that social competence promotion programs have had positive effects on adolescents' problem-solving skills, social relations with peers, school adjustment, and reductions in high-risk behaviors. Table 58.1 contains a listing of program components and best practices shown to be associated with positive program outcomes. Readers are encouraged to incorporate these components and best practices as possible in developing SST programs in school settings.

A number of programs have incorporated these essential components and have been found to be effective in enhancing social competencies in children and youth. See Table 58.2 for a brief description of these model or exemplary programs as well as information on how to obtain more information about each program.

Table 58.1 Essential Components of Social Skills Training Programs: Best Practices

- include an affective component (e.g., stress management)

- include a cognitive component (e.g., problem solving)

- include a behavioral component (e.g., social skills training)

- include diverse and interactive teaching methods such as *modeling,* the process of learning a behavior by observing another person in the group perform that behavior; *role playing* or *behavioral rehearsal,* in which group members are asked to "try on" new modes of verbal and nonverbal behavior; *feedback,* in which following a role play, group members receive feedback from the group leader and group members about their performance; and *prompting* or *coaching,* when the group leader, prior to or during a role-play performance, provides verbal instructions to teach new social skills (each broad skill must be broken into its component parts so that it can be learned more easily)

- focus on the selection of goals that group members will work on during the SST group

- include behavioral homework assignments where group members are encouraged to practice newly acquired skills in their natural environment

- incorporate generalization from the beginning of any SST program

- be multiyear and allow children and youth to build on previous learning programs

- emphasize a real-world application of skills to promote the generalization of skills

- be implemented as early as possible in a child's life—ideally the training should begin in primary grades and continue through high school

- focus on teaching children and youth to recognize and manage their emotions, appreciate the perspectives of others, establish positive goals, make good decisions, handle interpersonal situations and conflicts, and develop responsible and respectful attitudes and values about self, others, work, health, and community service

---

Sources: Caplan & Weissberg (1988); Gresham (2002); LeCroy (1983, 2002); Poland, Pitcher, & Lazarus (2002); Scott (n.d.); Weissberg, Kumpfer, & Seligman (2003)

Table 58.2 Model School-Based Programs Designed to Enhance Social Competence

Life Skills Training (LST) has been recognized as 1 of 10 model blueprint programs that have met the rigorous scientific standards established by the Center for the Study and Prevention of Violence at the University of Colorado at Boulder (Botvin, Mihalic, & Grotpeter, 1998). LST has also been recognized as a program that works by the Centers for Disease Control and Prevention, the American Medical Association, and the American Psychological Association. Detailed information about the *Life Skills Training program* can be found at http://www.lifeskillstraining.com.

Promoting Alternative THinking Strategies (PATHS) has been recognized as 1 of 10 model blueprint programs that have met the rigorous scientific standards established by the Center for the Study and Prevention of Violence at the University of Colorado at Boulder (Greenberg, Kusche, & Mihalic, 1998). Detailed information about the PATHS program can be found at http://www.colorado.edu/cspv/blueprints/model/programs/PATHS.html.

Second Step has been recognized as a model program by the Substance Abuse and Mental Health Services Administration, U.S. Department of Health and Human Services, and as an exemplary program by the U.S. Department of Education. Additional information about *Second Step* can be found at http://www.cfchildren.org/program_ss.shtml.

The *School Survival Group* is designed for middle/junior high school students with school behavior problems. Findings from two studies (Dupper, 1998; Dupper & Krishef, 1993) have supported the short-term effectiveness of the School Survival Group. Hoagwood and Ervin (1997), in their review of school-based mental health services for children spanning a 10-year period, found that only 16 out of 228 studies met the rigorous criteria of randomized assignment, inclusion of a control group, and use of standardized outcome measures and cited Dupper and Krishef as 1 of the 16 studies that met these three criteria. The curriculum for the School Survival Group can be found in the appendix of Dupper (2003).

The *Social Skills GRoup INtervention* (S.S. GRIN) is a generic social skills group intervention that combines social learning and cognitive-behavioral techniques. Since this group intervention was found to be equally effective across all of the subtypes of peer problems targeted, this study highlights the "potential value of utilizing generic social skills training protocols" (DeRosier, 2004, p. 196).

There is one important caveat. While social skills training shows great promise as an effective preventive intervention with many children and adolescents experiencing problematic behaviors, current research findings suggest that SST is not as beneficial for students classified into one of the high-incidence disability groups. This is particularly important, "given the documented social competence deficits of students with high-incidence disabilities" (e.g., specific learning disabilities, mental retardation, emotional disturbance, or attention-deficit/hyperactivity disorder) (Gresham, Sugai, & Horner, 2001, p. 335). Based on their meta-analysis of the relevant literature, Gresham, Sugai, and Horner (2001) suggest that social skills training "has not produced large, socially important, long-term, or generalized changes in social competence of students with high-incidence disabilities" (p. 331). These authors recommend that SST involving students with high-incidence disabilities should be more frequent and intense (because 30 hours of instruction spread over 10–12 weeks is not enough) and that social skills training must be "directly linked to the individual's social deficits. . . . treatment cannot disregard the types of social skills deficits that the individual is displaying" (p. 341). They also go on to conclude that behaviors that lead to more powerful and immediate reinforcers will be performed more frequently than alternative behaviors. It is, therefore, critically important that the group leader ensure that the newly acquired social skills are reinforced more powerfully and immediately in the classroom and in the home than the older, problematic, competing behaviors.

What We Can Do

Groups are a natural context for social skills training. Groups allow for extensive use of modeling, support, feedback, and ongoing interaction with peers—all critical components of successful SST (LeCroy, 2002). Moreover, groups are one of the most efficacious and cost-effective interventions in school settings (Krieg, Simpson, Stanley, & Snider, 2002).

Although a number of authors (Elliott & Gresham, 1991; Merrell & Gimpel, 1998) have discussed models and guidelines for the teaching of social skills to children and adolescents in a small-group setting, the series of sequential steps outlined by LeCroy and Wooten (2002) is presented here due to its clarity and directness. The guidelines developed by LeCroy and Wooten (2002) can be useful to school social work practitioners interested in designing any social skills training program for children and adolescents in small-group settings:

1. Present the social skill being taught (e.g., solicit an explanation of the skill and get group members to provide a rationale for the skill).
2. Discuss the social skill (e.g., list the skill steps and get group members to give examples of using the skill).
3. Present a problem situation and model the skill (e.g., evaluate the performance and get group members to discuss the model).
4. Set the stage for role playing the skill (e.g., select the group members for role playing and get group members to observe the role play).
5. Have group members rehearse the skill (e.g., provide coaching if necessary and get group members to provide feedback on both verbal and nonverbal elements of role play).
6. Practice using complex skill situations (e.g., teach problem-solving skills and get group members to discuss situations and provide feedback).
7. Train for generalization and maintenance (e.g., encourage practice of skills outside the group and get group members to bring in their problem situations).

A description of one session from the School Survival Group, which incorporates many of these guidelines, can be found in Box 58.1. The entire curriculum for the School Survival Group can be found in the appendix of Dupper (2003). Readers should also see *Handbook of Child and Adolescent Treatment Manuals*, edited by Craig Winston LeCroy. In chapter 5, LeCroy provides an overview of social skills training as well as a detailed description of each of the 11 group sessions of a social skills training group.

Issues Related to Cultural and Racial Differences

Cultural and racial differences must be considered in interpreting scores from standardized behavior rating scales and in developing SST programs. Cartledge (1996) discusses the teaching of social skills from a perspective of cultural diversity. In her book, she emphasizes the relationship between culture and social behavior and highlights the importance of ethnic identity relative to psychological adjustment and adaptive behavior. Cartledge argues that European- and American-based social skill assessments may not adequately reflect the social competence of culturally different students and that students' behaviors must be defined and interpreted within a cultural context. She cautions against interpreting culturally different behavior as social skills deficits or as pathological or dysfunctional. She states:

> Differences observed among racially and ethnically different groups of children may be more indicative of racial or ethnic differences than of deficits. . . . These behavioral patterns are rooted in the ways in which different groups are socialized. The issue with culturally different students, as with all students, is not to view these differences as pathological but to assess the degree to which they tend to support or interfere with success in later life. (Cartledge, 1996, p. 40)

Issues Related to Gender Differences

There are important differences between the sexes that must be taken into account in developing social skills training programs. For example, males tend to rate themselves higher than do females on measures of self-esteem in the areas of general academics, math, sports, and physical appearance (Stein, Newcomb, & Bentler, 1992). Cartledge (1996) states that, in comparison to males, "females appear to be more concerned with social relationships, more oriented toward a few close intimate relationships, more prone to avoid open conflict and express aggression in subtle exclusionary rather than physical ways, and more likely to use language to resolve conflicts" (Cartledge, 1996, p. 317). As a result of these differences, one important goal in developing SST groups is to focus on helping girls learn to behave assertively in a wider variety of situations, especially in those

Box 58.1 Description of One Session from the School Survival Group

Session Two (Five Goals to Adolescent Behavior)

The leader begins by reviewing the five group rules. The leader next asks each group member to share the best thing that happened to them *in school* since the last group session. The leader begins by sharing something positive that happened to him/her, and other group members are encouraged to share. The leader states that each group session will begin by asking this question, and, therefore, group members are asked to make sure that at least one good thing happens to them in school so that they will have something to share at the beginning of each group.

The leader next asks the question: "Why do some students have difficulty getting along with teachers and other authority figures in school? Today, we are going to discuss the reason why we all behave in certain ways. All of us behave to meet certain needs that we have. What are some of these basic needs, beyond food, shelter, and clothing?"

"The first need we all have is to get *attention*. Why do we need attention? How does it feel when someone pays attention to us? We all need attention because we know we exist if someone is paying attention to us. If no one ever notices us, no matter what we do, we begin to feel like we don't exist. We all need attention, but some of us don't know how to get it in a positive way and *negative attention is better than no attention at all*. Unfortunately, some of us have only learned how to get negative attention (e.g., being the 'class clown,' being hyperactive, bizarre dress) rather than positive attention. Later in this group we will discuss ways to get positive attention rather than negative attention."

"The second need we all have is the need for *power*. We need to feel like we have a say in what happens to us. Unfortunately, many of you do not have much of an opportunity to exert your power in school (or at home). At your age, adults are always telling you what to do and you have little or no say in things that happen to you. I believe that this need for power is behind most of the problems between teenagers and adults. The adults want power over teens and the teens fight back because they want power, also. One of the most important things to remember in this group is that *teens always lose in power struggles with adults*. For example, who loses if you tell off a teacher? Who loses if you make an obscene gesture at the assistant principal for discipline? Students always lose. You cannot give a teacher a disciplinary referral to your teacher for her misbehavior in class, but she can sure give you one. You cannot suspend the principal, but he can sure suspend you. One of the things we will discuss later in group is how to not lose when you are in a power struggle with an adult."

"The third need which motivates behavior is the desire for *revenge*. Teens who feel hurt by life will strike back at others in an attempt to get even. Some people may resort to violence and destructive behavior in their efforts to get revenge. Remember that people who act this way are hurting very deeply inside and revenge is the way they have learned to deal with their hurt feelings. During this group we will discuss more productive ways of dealing with hurt."

"The fourth need that motivates some of our behavior is the need *to be left alone*. Some of us intentionally quit easily or avoid trying to do something altogether for fear that we may fail. This fear of failing school may lead us to start skipping school and dropping out of school at the first opportunity. Our thought is that if we don't try, then teachers and parents will give up on us and leave us alone. One of the goals of this group is to help you have more confidence in yourself and what you are able to do to survive in school."

"The fifth need many of us have is the need for *excitement*. Many of us are turned off by routine and become bored easily. Many teens believe that school is sooooo boring! And the way we deal with our boredom is by daydreaming, skipping school, doing alcohol or drugs, or anything that provides excitement. I hope that this group will help you to problem-solve ways to beat the boredom and routine of school.

The leader asks if anyone has questions or comments on these needs, which motivate much of teenage misbehavior in school. The leader asks for group members to state which of these needs he/she is attempting to meet and what is the behavior that he/she engages in to meet this need at school. The leader will then ask group members to discuss the consequences of each action if a student is "caught in the act" during the school day. The leader needs to stress that having attention and power, dealing with hurt, having more self-confidence, and having more excitement are worthwhile goals. What is essential is learning how to achieve these goals in ways that do not bring about negative consequences to us in school.

The leader concludes the group with each group member being asked to complete the following statement: "Today in group, I learned. . . ."

situations involving male participation (Cartledge, 1996). On a more macro-level, Cartledge recommends that "[s]chool personnel need to examine more deliberately the way in which we socialize the sexes, taking pains to create cooperative environments and offer nonsexist curricula and literature in order to foster respect and adaptive behaviors between the sexes for the betterment of all" (1996, p. 344).

Tools and Practice Examples

Obtaining Support and Commitment: A Case Example

Prior to implementing a social skills group, it is important that the school social worker and mental health practitioner lay the necessary groundwork to ensure support and commitment to the program. The following excerpt from Rose (1998) is a good illustration of the actions taken by program staff in successfully implementing the autumn, winter, spring, and summer social competence group:

> After a series of discussions about children, classes, and teachers, the program staff and the school administrators agreed to implement a preventive social competence group work program in the third grade. The administrators indicated that several potential social competence difficulties seemed to be appearing among the third-grade children. They described incidents of quarreling in the cafeteria that were worrisome to them. The program staff and the school administrators were mature enough to grasp cognitive material presented in a preventive group. The principal discussed the ideas for a social competence development program with the three third-grade teachers who appeared amenable to a classroom approach. . . . The teacher's role included the coordination of program content with the rest of the curriculum, such as social studies and health education. The program content focused on increasing empathy, promoting a positive self-concept, and learning to analyze and apply problem-solving thinking skills in social situations involving peers. Prior to delivering the program, the leaders discussed the content and approach with the school staff who, after a

brief delay, indicated their approval. The teacher provided the leaders with a class list. . . . All parents were informed of the program through a letter the teacher sent home. The leaders came one day to observe the class and to their surprise they saw several children acting aggressively toward their peers. . . . The class was divided into four smaller groups, each of which met in a corner of the classroom. Each group selected a member who chose a name of a season out of a hat. . . . The groups met once a week for 12 weeks. . . . [The group members] played a board game the leaders had developed in which they each had to say what they felt in common school situations. . . . [T]he members role played social situations and practiced responding in kindness to one another. . . . In the middle phase, the members developed their assertiveness skills by practicing making appropriate requests of peers. . . . [T]here were many opportunities for role playing and modeling. . . . [T]he members focused on social skills involved in making and keeping friends. They practiced initiating and maintaining conversations. . . . [M]embers learned conflict identification and resolution skills and practiced using problem-solving thinking in stressful situations involving the aggressive actions of peers. . . . The final phase emphasized consolidating gains, evaluating the group, and ending. . . . Afterward, the teacher related the lessons learned to the over-all social studies curriculum, which was focused on the theme of people in the natural world. (pp. 119–122)

Resources

Skillstreaming the Elementary School Child: New Strategies and Perspectives for Teaching Prosocial Skills by Arnold P. Goldstein and Ellen McGinnis. Information about this program can be found at http://www.uscart.org/sselementary.htm.

Skillstreaming the Adolescent: New Strategies and Perspectives for Teaching Prosocial Skills by Arnold P. Goldstein and Ellen McGinnis. Information about this program can be found at http://www.uscart.org/ssadolescent.htm.

The Prepare Curriculum: Teaching Prosocial Competencies by Arnold P. Goldstein. *The Prepare Curriculum* presents a series of 10 course-length interventions grouped into three areas:

reducing aggression, reducing stress, and reducing prejudice. Information about this program can be found at http://www.uscart.org/Prepare%20Curric.htm.

An overview of the *Social Skills Training Program* by Goldstein and Pollock can be downloaded at http://www.users.globalnet.co.uk/~ebdstudy/strategy/socskils.htm.

The Overcoming Obstacles program includes a comprehensive relevant life skills curriculum taught as a stand-alone course and infused into other content areas. Information about this program can be found at http://www.overcomingobstacles.org.

Key Points to Remember

- The development of social competence is an essential aspect of healthy normal development.
- Substantial numbers of young people today lack the social competencies that protect against high-risk behaviors.
- Social skills training has been shown to be the most promising new treatment model for children and adolescents who are aggressive, disruptive, difficult to get along with, extremely shy or quiet, or unwilling to participate or socialize.
- Social competence promotion programs have had positive effects on adolescents' problem-solving skills, social relations with peers, school adjustment, and reductions in high-risk behaviors.
- Social competence is best achieved by changing students' knowledge, skills, attitudes, beliefs, or behaviors by using interactive teaching techniques (e.g., role plays with peers) rather than lectures.
- Social skills training should focus on youth during the critical middle-school/junior high years and consist of multiple years of intervention (e.g., "booster sessions") using a well-tested, standardized intervention with detailed lesson plans and student materials, delivered over extended periods of time, and continually reinforced in the school environment.
- Current research suggests that social skills training is not as beneficial for students classified into one of the high-incidence disability groups (e.g., specific learning disabilities, mental retardation, emotional disturbance, or attention-deficit/hyperactivity disorder). Consequently, it

has been recommended that social skills training involving students with high-incidence disabilities should be more frequent and intense, directly linked to the individual's social deficits, and the newly acquired social skills should be reinforced more powerfully and immediately in the classroom and in the home.

- It is important to include as many of the components and best practices, contained in Table 58.1, as possible in designing and implementing a social skills training program.
- European- and American-based social skills assessments may not adequately reflect the social competence of culturally different students.
- One important goal in developing social skills training groups is to focus on helping girls learn to behave assertively in a wider variety of situations, especially in those situations involving male participation.

References

Botvin, G. J., Mihalic, S. F., & Grotpeter, J. K. (1998). *Life skills training.* Boulder, CO: Center for the Study and Prevention of Violence, Institute of Behavioral Science, University of Colorado.

Bracken, B. A. (1993). *Assessment of interpersonal relations.* Austin, TX: Pro-Ed.

Brower, A. M., & Nurius, P. S. (1993). *Social cognition and individual change: Current theory and counseling guidelines.* Newbury Park, CA: Sage.

Caldarella, P., & Merrell, K. W. (1997). Common dimensions of social skills of children and adolescents: A taxonomy of positive behaviors. *School Psychology Review, 26,* 264–278.

Caplan, M. Z., & Weissberg, R. P. (1988). Promoting social competence in early adolescence: Developmental considerations. In G. H. Schneider, G. Attili, J. Nadel, & R. P. Weissberg (Eds.), *Social competence in developmental perspective* (pp. 371–386). Boston: Kluwer Academic.

Cartledge, G. (1996). *Cultural diversity and social skills instruction: Understanding ethnic and gender differences.* Champaign, IL: Research Press.

Centers for Disease Control and Prevention. (2004, May 21). Surveillance summaries. *MMWR, 53* (No. SS-2).

DeRosier, M. E. (2004). Building relationships and combating bullying: Effectiveness of a school-based social skills group intervention. *Journal of Clinical and Adolescent Psychology, 33,* 196–201.

Dupper, D. R. (1998). An alternative to suspension for middle school youths with behavior problems: Findings from a "school survival" group. *Research on Social Work Practice, 8,* 354–366.

Dupper, D. R. (2003). *School social work: Skills and interventions for effective practice.* Hoboken, NJ: Wiley.

Dupper, D. R., & Krishef, C. H. (1993). School-based social-cognitive skills training for middle school students with school behavior problems. *Children and Youth Services Review, 15,* 131–142.

Ellickson, P. L., & Bell, R. M. (1990). Drug prevention in junior high: A multi-site longitudinal test. *Science, 247,* 1299–1305.

Ellickson, P. L., Bell, R. M., & Harrison, E. R. (1993). Changing adolescent propensities to use drugs: Results from Project ALERT. *Health Education Quarterly, 20*(2), 227–242.

Ellickson, P. L., Bell, R. M., & McGuigan, K. (1993). Preventing adolescent drug use: Long-term results of a junior high program. *American Journal of Public Health, 83,* 856–861.

Elliott, S. N., & Gresham, F. M. (1991). *Social skills intervention guide: Practical strategies for social skills training.* Circle Pines, MN: American Guidance.

Greenberg, M. T., Kusche, C., & Mihalic, S. F. (1998). *Promoting alternative thinking strategies (PATHS).* Boulder, CO: Center for the Study and Prevention of Violence, Institute of Behavioral Science, University of Colorado.

Gresham, F. M. (1986). Conceptual issues in the assessment of social competence in children. In P. S. Strain, M. J. Guralnick, and H. M. Walker (Eds.), *Children's social behavior: Development, assessment, and modification* (pp. 143–179). New York: Academic.

Gresham, F. M. (2002). Best practices in social skills training. In A. Thomas & J. Grimes (Eds.), *Best practices in school psychology* (4th ed., Vol. 2, pp. 1029–1040). Bethesda, MD: National Association of School Psychologists.

Gresham, F. M., & Elliott, S. N. (1990). *The social skills rating system.* Circle Pines, MN: American Guidance.

Gresham, F. M., & MacMillan, D. L. (1997). Social competence and affective characteristics of students with mild disabilities. *Review of Educational Research, 67,* 377–415.

Gresham, F. M., Sugai, G., & Horner, R. H. (2001). Interpreting outcomes of social skills training for students with high-incidence disabilities. *Exceptional Children, 67,* 331–344.

Hoagwood, K., & Erwin, H. D. (1997). Effectiveness of school-based mental health services for children: A 10-year research review. *Journal of Child and Family Studies, 6,* 435–451.

Jenson, J. M., & Howard, M. O. (1999). *Youth violence: Current research and recent practice innovations.* Washington, DC: NASW Press.

Katz, L. G., McClellan, D. E., Fuller, J. O., & Walz, G. R. (1995). *Building social competence in children: A practical handbook for counselors, psychologist, and teachers.* ERIC Elementary and Early Childhood Education Clearinghouse. Washington, DC: U.S. Department of Education.

Krieg, F. J., Simpson, C., Stanley, R. E., & Snider, D. A. (2002). Best practices in making school groups work. In A. Thomas & J. Grimes (Eds.), *Best practices in school psychology* (4th ed., Vol. 2, pp. 1195–1216). Bethesda, MD: National Association of School Psychologists.

LeCroy, C. W. (Ed.). (1983). *Social skills training for children and youth.* New York: Haworth.

LeCroy, C. W. (1992). *Case studies in social work practice.* Belmont, CA: Wadsworth.

LeCroy, C. W. (1994). *Handbook of child and adolescent treatment manuals.* New York: Lexington Books.

LeCroy, C. W. (2002). Child therapy and social skills. In A. R. Roberts and G. J. Greene (Eds.), *Social workers' desk reference* (pp. 406–412). New York: Oxford University Press.

LeCroy, C. W., & Wooten, L. E. (2002). Social skills groups in schools. In R. Constable, S. McDonald, & J. P. Flynn (Eds.), *School social work: Practice, policy and research perspectives* (pp. 441–457). Chicago: Lyceum.

Lochman, J. E. (1992). Cognitive-behavioral intervention with aggressive boys: Three-year follow-up and preventive efforts. *Journal of Consulting and Clinical Psychology, 60,* 426–432.

Lochman, J. E., Lampron, L. B., Gemmer, T. C., Harris, S. R., & Wyckoff, G. M. (1989). Teacher consultation and cognitive-behavioral intervention with aggressive boys. *Psychology in the Schools, 26,* 179–188.

Lochman, J. E., & Wells, K. C. (1996). A social-cognitive intervention with aggressive children: Prevention effects and contextual implementation issues. In R. DeV. Peters & R. J. McMahon (Eds.), *Preventing childhood disorders, substance abuse and delinquency* (pp. 111–143). Thousand Oaks, CA: Sage.

Lope, M., & Edelbaum, J. (1999). *I'm popular! Do I need social skills training?* Available: http://www.personal.psu.edu/faculty/j/g/jgp4/teach/497/socialskillstraining.htm

Merrell, K. W. (1994). *Preschool and kindergarten behavior scales.* Austin, TX: Pro-Ed.

Merrell, K. W., & Gimpel, G. A. (1998). *Social skills of children and adolescents: Conceptualization, assessment, treatment.* Mahwah, NJ: Erlbaum.

Poland, S., Pitcher, G., & Lazarus, P. M. (2002). Best practices in crisis prevention and management. In A. Thomas & J. Grimes (Eds.), *Best practices in school psychology* (4th ed., Vol. 2, pp. 1057–1079). Bethesda, MD: National Association of School Psychologists.

Reynolds, C. R., & Kamphaus, R. W. (1992). *The behavioral assessment system for children.* Circle Pines, MN: American Guidance Services.

Rose, S. R. (1998). *Group work with children and adolescents: Prevention and intervention in school and community systems.* Thousand Oaks, CA: Sage.

Scott, D. (n.d.). *Program outcomes for youth: Social competence.* Available: http://ag.arizona.edu/fcs/cyfernet/nowg/social_comp.html.

Stein, J. A., Newcomb, M. D., & Bentler, P. M. (1992). The effect of agency and communality on self-esteem:

Gender differences in longitudinal data. *Sex Roles, 26,* 465–483.

Thompson, E. A., Eggert, L. L., Randell, B. P., & Pike, K. C. (2001). Evaluation of indicated suicide risk prevention approaches for potential high school dropouts. *American Journal of Public Health, 91,* 742–752.

Walker, H. M., & McConnell, S. R. (1995). *The Walker-McConnell scales of social competence and school adjustment.* San Diego, CA: Singular.

Weissberg, R. P., Barton, H. A., & Shriver, T. P. (1997). The social competence promotion program for young adolescents. In G. W. Albee & T. P. Gullotta (Eds.), *Primary prevention works* (pp. 268–290). Thousand Oaks, CA: Sage.

Weissberg, R. P., Kumpfer, K. L., & Seligman, M. E. P. (2003). Prevention that works for children and youth. *American Psychologist, 58,* 425–432.

Yung, B., & Hammond, R. (1998). Breaking the cycle: A culturally sensitive violence prevention program for African-American children. In L. Lutzker (Ed.), *Handbook of child abuse research and treatments* (pp. 319–340). New York: Plenum.

Zenere III, F. J., & Lazarus, P. J. (1997). The decline of youth suicidal behavior in an urban, multicultural public school system following the introduction of a suicide prevention and intervention program. *Suicide and Life-Threatening Behavior, 27,* 387–403.

Guidelines for Making Effective Presentations in Schools

Carolyn B. Pryor

Getting Started

Presentations are a well-accepted method of getting important information out to one's target audience, recruiting new clients, and garnering support for one's programs. In the host setting of schools, making presentations can be intimidating, but effective presentations can win the hearts and minds of students, teachers, parents, and administrators and rally them to action.

A review of the literature on presentations in schools came up with no empirical studies on this topic, but practice examples show repeatedly that presentations can be effective when skillfully prepared and delivered. There is an extensive literature on making presentations in general and on learning styles.

This chapter summarizes key steps for preparing and delivering great presentations, based on literature review, training, and experience in making presentations. It highlights some features of presentations in school settings and shows how presentations can be used effectively at many levels: classrooms, school assemblies, parent programs, teacher workshops, and school board meetings. Finally, three case examples give practical tips and inspiration.

What We Know

Four key features of schools make presentations in this venue a special challenge:

1. Your target audience can cover a wide range of ability and developmental levels.

2. Teachers and administrators are experts on training and have many demands on their time.
3. School administrators will likely view you as an outsider and be resistant to your ideas.
4. Teachers and administrators will be critiquing your knowledge and people-management skills.

The following steps will help you to overcome these obstacles:

1. Identify your goals, objectives, and presentation strategy. Document how your message is backed by research and practical application. School administrators are curriculum oriented. They want to know how your presentation will fit in with the mission of the school. Explain how your presentation will help them to meet their goals. Your success depends on their consent and support.
2. Gear your presentation content and presentation style to the developmental level and attention span of the audience.
3. Approach teachers and administrators as partners. Plan your presentations jointly and include them in the delivery as much as possible.
4. Do not expect teachers to control students for you. Meet with them ahead of time to learn what strategies and techniques you can use to keep your audience attentive and involved. (Gallagher et al., 1993)

What We Can Do

A Wedding of Art and Science

If you think of the process of making an effective presentation as similar to planning a wonderful wedding, you will be able to grasp the importance of each step in the process. These include courtship, proposal, engagement, diamond, rehearsal, ceremony, reception, and honeymoon.

Courtship and Proposal

Whether sought out as a presenter or seeking opportunities to present, you want to pick a good match, a group or organization that shares your goals, that has resources and connections that could benefit you, and that can give you the support you need. An effective presentation will take a great deal of time and effort. You will be at your best when you care deeply about your subject matter and can speak from your heart. You will want to know and respond to your audience's needs. Classroom groups will have their own personalities. It helps to visit ahead of time to see how the students behave and learn (Gallagher et al., 1993). Teachers will have had previous experiences with in-service training that will affect how your presentation will be received (Jackson, 2003). Find out what they want and need. Use your social work skills to listen carefully and assess your audience.

If you are writing the proposal for your presentation, make your topic and ideas clear and compelling. Remember that educators are curriculum driven. Be specific about your purpose, goals, and objectives. What will the audience learn? How will you deliver the presentation? Why is this important to the school or community group? How might your presentation benefit them? Make your title appealing. Be imaginative and creative. This is going to be hard work, but fun too.

If you are the one sought after, find out what's in it for you and how it will help the school. Presentation skills require practice, so if you have the time and interest, go for it. Each experience is a learning opportunity and can help you be a better presenter in the future.

Be sure you have the approval of your superiors. You will need their support and blessing if you are to get results.

The Engagement

Set the date, time, and place well in advance. You will need plenty of lead time to get everything set up and optimally planned and to get your "guests"

there for the big event. Even short and simple classroom presentations will be most effective when you have prepared carefully. Dates and places for large group presentations with ambitious goals should be set well ahead. Recruit helpers and delegate responsibilities as needed.

Select your attendants. Solo presentations are the easiest to coordinate, but co-presenters who can complement your skills and experience can add impact to your presentation and give you additional assistance and support.

Send out invitations. Publicize your event well. Save-the-date notices may need to go out to key people months ahead. Classroom groups will not need much advance notification, but classroom teachers will appreciate it. There will be times that will not work well for them, and you will have to adjust your schedule. The month before the presentation is when publicity really needs a push for events that need to attract an audience. Send out written notices as appropriate. Make your invitations personalized, classy, and intriguing. Follow up with verbal encouragement to participate wherever feasible. Good publicity will help ensure that your target audience attends. If you are trying to get parents there, a parent-calling committee can be a big help. You may also want to advertise door prizes or other incentives for attendance.

Talk about it. The best way to think about what you will say and how you will say it is to talk about your topic with anyone who is interested. You will develop an engaging conversational style and get feedback. Look for humorous and colorful examples to illustrate your points. Your best jokes and inspirational stories will come from your personal experiences, where you can poke fun at yourself. Make notes about these.

The Diamond

A diamond diagram illustrates the elements of a model presentation's content and emphasizes points (Boylan, 1988). Most presenters are well advised not to write out what they plan to say word for word, but to work from an outline. First, clarify your purpose. Outline your objectives, and prepare a sparkling agenda, including a clear statement of your objectives. Three or four objectives are about the right amount. Then plan to cover benefits, facts, and experiences. It doesn't matter which order you do it in, as long as all three parts are there. Make clear what's in this for them, report research and facts on the topic, and share personal experiences in applying this information. Prepare handouts, such as fact sheets and resource lists. (You will want to encourage folks to look at you during the presentation and pick these up at the end.) Summarize the key information you presented. Once you have worked out the body of your presentation, plan and memorize a sharp, attention-getting opening. Also, think through and memorize a passionate ending point.

Plan to interject wisdom, wit, color, and spice. Heavy intellectual content needs to be broken up with attention grabbers and offset with humor. Little stories interspersed with your message will help you connect to your audience. Questioning helps you ascertain what your audience knows and whether they comprehend your message. Impromptu humor based on audience interaction helps to build rapport. Your wisdom can come both from authorities and your own life experience. The more you can show how your key message has influenced your own life, the more your audience will see its relevance for them. Bring colorful visual images into your presentation. Make it unique.

Rehearse, Rehearse, Rehearse

Timing is critical. Working from an outline, you may be amazed at how much longer things take to deliver than you anticipated. Talk the whole thing through aloud with an eye on the clock, and then modify your presentation as needed. Once you work out your timing, practice in front of a mirror or a video camera. Be picture perfect. This can be an uncomfortable step, but it also is extremely helpful. Remember to smile. If you have co-presenters, set up a dress rehearsal with them to be sure everyone looks good and all will flow smoothly. Make sure everything is prepared and likely to go the way you desire. Then rest and relax.

The Ceremony

When the big day comes, arrive early, at least 30 minutes ahead of time, to be sure everything is set up and tested. Then prepare yourself mentally and physically. As your audience arrives, meet and greet them. Get to know their interests and motivation for being there. Then, during your presentation, you can think of them as your friends and help them to feel particularly welcomed. Start on time.

Smile. Your friendly face and demeanor will help your audience feel at ease and eager to hear what you have to say. Use 5-second eye contact with every member of the audience so that they know that your message is meant for them. You may want to refer to some of the audience members by name to keep them alert and involved. Keep your composure. If someone asks you a question to which you do not know the answer, turn it back to them or offer to look up the information. Use cues and prompts. Well-organized teaching aids will guide you.

K.I.S.S. Most authorities on public speaking agree on the importance of this acronym for "Keep it simple, sweetie." Stick to your simple outline, which you can adapt according to contingencies of the day and the audience's response. Nothing will be more moving and inspiring than your personal revelation of something about which you care strongly, expressed with deep sincerity. Let them know of your joys, sorrows, dedication, love, and concerns. Don't hold back your genuine emotions; let them come through. Let the audience experience your tears and laughter with you. Then, end with that passionate point, on time or 5 minutes early (Jackson, 2003).

The Reception

After your presentation, express love and appreciation. Answer questions and get comments which amplify your material. Provide food and beverages. Then get feedback about how your message was received and how to be more effective as a speaker in the future. Connect with your guests. Let them know how to contact you for further information and professional services. Give take-home goodies. Door prizes, goody bags, and little gifts help cap off a memorable event. Don't overdo it, but make sure everyone will have something to keep that will remind them of your message and how to contact you.

The Honeymoon

A well-prepared presentation takes lots of time and hard work. You may or may not be paid to do this. In either case, be sure to treat yourself to a celebration afterward. Follow up with thank-you notes to your sponsors, attendants, and supporters. Your thoughtfulness will help you to make a lasting positive impression. Send out announcements to the media. An article in the local newspaper, possibly with a picture or two, can help spread your key message and lay the groundwork for more presentation opportunities. Don't hesitate to toot your own horn.

Do it again and again. Although the storybook wedding is once in a lifetime, presentations are best done repeatedly. With practice, they get easier to do, and you will become more skilled and confident.

Tools and Practice Examples

Suggestions for Presenting to Diverse Groups in a School Setting

Classroom Presentations

The beginning of the school year is an excellent time to reach out to new students and parents and let them know about the services you have to offer. You become a friendly face at the school and someone to turn to when troubles arise. A short presentation in every classroom can get your message across. Here are some suggestions for what can work at various age levels.

Preschool and kindergarten. Make a presentation at an event for parents, introducing yourself. Share some vignettes about how you can help, and pass out program descriptions and business cards. Use puppets to communicate with young students. Have a puppet character that you keep in your office to which children can tell their troubles. Invite students to come to your office to talk with you or to some of your puppets. Tell them how to get permission to see you if they need help.

Elementary grades. Use a magic trick to grab attention. You can get some easy ones from a magic store or create your own, adding a meaningful message.

Magic coloring book. This can be purchased at a magic shop. Flip the pages one way, and black-and-white drawings show. Flip another way, and they are colored in. Flip a third way, and the book is blank. Tell the boys and girls that they have the whole school year ahead of them. Like the pictures in the book, they will be able to add color to their lives by the things they learn and the friends they make. If they make mistakes and get into trouble, you are there to help. If they learn from their mistakes and make amends, the mistakes can be erased, and they can get a fresh start.

Middle school. Home-room meetings are a good place for presentations at this level. A poster with a message about friendship can be given to each class, with your name, contact information, and a message, for example, "I'm here to help."

High school. A welcome event for all newcomers is an important prevention tool. You can make a talk to the new students, assisted by other school support personnel and student peer helpers. Make them feel special and connected. As the school year progresses, you will be able to organize students and staff to help with presentations (Pryor, 1991).

Teachers may ask you to come to speak to the class when they are dealing with problematic behavior. You and the teacher can work on a presentation using role play, videos, and stories to get your message across.

School Assemblies

Social workers and other school-based practitioners can make a big impact on an entire school by helping put on a school assembly. A social worker, for example, could be the featured motivational speaker, or she could recruit and introduce someone who will have important symbolic meaning and appeal to the students. Theatrical programs where such topics as child abuse are explained through skits can be a means of encouraging victims of abuse to self-disclose to the teacher, counselor, or social worker later and then receive follow-up help. School assemblies are best done by a committee which includes teachers, administrators, school support staff, and possibly parents and students. Because assemblies are large, public, and involve some risk, it is best to get input in the planning from various stakeholders.

School Board Presentations

To keep support coming for student services, it is important to keep decision makers informed of what you have accomplished. Students and parents can be useful co-presenters at this level.

In-Service Training

School districts mandate a number of days each year for in-service training. A social worker or other school-based practitioner can become a key figure in the life of a district by getting on the staff development task force or making proposals to this group. Find out what topics are wanted by the administrators, teachers, school board members, and community representatives. Think through what you believe they really need to learn.

Become familiar with the standards for staff development in schools established by the National Staff Development Council (NSDC; 2001). Their thrust is to replace one-shot workshops with ongoing learning communities, wherein groups of teachers with common goals meet periodically over the course of a school year for mutual learning and problem solving. A social worker or school mental health counselor could become the facilitator of a learning group if the topic were relevant to social work skills, such as behavior management or home–school relations. The NSDC also emphasizes that staff development should be research based and data driven. Social workers and others can help districts to review data that suggest the goals for staff development and also help to examine research about the topics to be covered. Principles of adult learning emphasize the importance of individualization and contracting for learning experiences (Worth, 1985) and follow-up hands-on application of information obtained through a presentation. Social workers and mental health counselors can help teachers to set up coaching sessions, study groups, and action research teams to make the training more than a one-shot sensitivity and awareness session.

Parent and Community Programs

The keys to successful presentations at this level are food, friends, and fun. Plan and execute something that you will enjoy and find interesting. Your audience will catch your enthusiasm and have fun with you. Get administrators, teachers, and parents to help you plan these events.

Real-World Stories

Tale of a Fourth-Grade Mini-Conference

Training peer mediators is one of Terry Bond-Manville's responsibilities as a school social worker in a small school district. She and her MSW student intern trained an entire classroom to become peer mediators, treating this as a true mini-conference. Terry loved this experience and plans to do it again. Here is what worked:

1. Stressing the importance of mediation, not just for this year but forever.
2. Stressing that conflict is natural; it is *how* you handle conflict that is important.
3. Emphasizing 100% participation. This meant pairing students up, in groups of two or three, so that less-able students could participate as well.
4. Having students dress the way that their parents dressed to go to work (jeans, suits, uniforms, shirts with a name on them, etc.).
5. Holding preregistration a week before the presentation (what they wanted to get out of the training, etc.).
6. Serving a continental breakfast, providing folders with information to use throughout the day, breaks, gym, recess, lunch at their regular time, work in groups, lots of role plays, midafternoon snack, and presentation of certificates.

The Making of an In-Service Expert

Beverly Baroni-Yeglich began her professional life as a clinical social worker and frequently made 1- to 2-hour presentations in schools to generate referrals. She also made numerous presentations at her clinic. Her skills as a gestalt therapist helped her to develop skills in involving the audience and providing experiential learning. She used her social work skills to read her audience, pick up on nonverbal cues, and quickly find out what they wanted to take with them when they left.

After getting hired as a school social worker in a large school district, she used classroom presentations as part of her intervention strategies. For example, if a student was diagnosed with cancer or someone in the classroom had died, she did a presentation with the entire class. When a teacher was accused of sexual abuse, she made a presentation to the students about this situation.

Eventually, Beverly became the crisis team coordinator for the district. Doing in-service training of teachers is an important part of her work. By helping teachers to deal with crises and problem students, the social worker becomes a significant, integral part of the district. The teachers and social workers work on how to manage difficult students in the classroom, offsetting the teachers' impulse to get troubled students out of there. To start the ball rolling with an in-service training, Beverly brainstorms ideas with her team, which includes support staff and an administrator. She finds that it is absolutely necessary to have an administrator on the team, so that things get done.

One approach that has worked well is lunch-hour sessions with teachers. She also has set up four-session after-school training where teachers earn continuing education units (CEUs) and get well fed. She brings in outside experts as appropriate. A student in recovery talked about what he wishes teachers had done for him.

Bringing the Parent Voice Into the School

Janice Fialka, cofounder of several teen health centers, began her work as a social worker in the field of adolescent health care. After her first child, Micah, was born with cognitive impairments, Janice began to write and speak nationally on the parent–professional partnership. Her writings poignantly address the range of feelings that parents experience. In her much-published "Advice to Professionals Who Must Conference Cases," she reminds professionals that when sharing information, they should

> sit patiently and attentively. . . . Sit with us and create a stillness known only in small, empty chapels at sundown. Be there with us as our witness and as our friend. Do not give us advice, suggestions, comparisons, or another appointment. (That's for later.) We want only a quiet shoulder upon which to rest our heavy heads. (Fialka, 1997, 2001)

This poetic statement in its entirety is frequently used to begin presentations and in-services. Janice's words succinctly and sensitively remind professionals of the importance and power of "concentrated listening."

In her second book, coauthored with Karen Mikus, *Do You Hear What I Hear? Parents and Professionals Working Together for Children With Special Needs* (1999), there are six scenes in the life of a mother of a young son going through the assessment process. Each scene describes the internal dialogue of the mother's worries, fears, thoughts, and wishes. In addition, the professional's inner thoughts, worries, constraints, and emotions are also honestly described. This gives the reader the ability to hear both voices. Each scene is also fol-

lowed by a practical list of "Things to Consider" from both the parent's and professional's perspective. Many in-service training sessions use these inner dialogues as a way to "hear" the voices of both partners. Often two people will take turns reading the parent's piece followed by the professional's piece. Janice models how one's life experience can provide the basis for becoming a powerful and motivating speaker.

Repeatedly giving presentations and receiving constructive feedback from the audience will be your best teacher. However, there are other excellent ways to increase your skill as a presenter. The Toastmasters organization has 80 years of experience in helping people to develop their public speaking skills. This nonprofit group can provide friendly support for increasing your ability to be an effective speaker. Another highly successful program for teaching public speaking skills is the Dale Carnegie course. This class can help you to free up your inner spirit and become a motivational and inspiring presenter. Hopefully, your presentation experience won't be once in a lifetime, but many times throughout life.

Key Points to Remember

When making professional presentations to varied school groups, remember these key points:

- The Proposal. Pick a good match. Know and respond to their needs. Speak from your heart.
- The Engagement. Set the date, time, and place well ahead. Select your attendants. Send out invitations. Talk about it.
- The Diamond. Memorize a sharp opening. Clarify your purpose. Have a sparkling agenda. Cover benefits, facts, and experience. Summarize key information. Memorize a loving point.
- Rehearse, Rehearse, Rehearse. Be picture perfect. Work out the timing. Smile. Rest and relax.
- The Ceremony. Arrive early. Meet, touch, and talk. Keep your composure. Use cues and prompts. K.I.S.S.
- The Reception. Express love and appreciation. Provide food and beverages. Get feedback. Connect with guests. Give take-home goodies.
- The Honeymoon. Treat yourself. Follow up with thank-you notes. Do it again and again.

References

Boylan, B. (1988). *What's your point? A proven method for giving crystal clear presentations.* Wayzata, MN: Point Publications.

Carrington, J. (1991). *The presentation handbook: How to prepare dynamic technical and non-technical presentations like a pro.* Saratoga, CA: R&E Publishers.

Dale Carnegie Corporation. Available: http://www.dale-carnegie.com.

Daley, K., & Daley, L. (2004). *Talk your way to the top: How to address any audience like your career depends on it.* New York: McGraw-Hill.

Fialka, J. (1997, 2001). *It matters: Lessons from my son.* Huntington Woods, MI: Author.

Fialka, J., & Mikus, K. C. (1999). *Do you hear what I hear? Parents and professionals working together for children with special needs.* Ann Arbor, MI: Proctor.

Gallagher, A., et al. (1993). *Sure-fire presentations.* ERIC document 365605.

International College. (2004). *Public speaking research resources.* Available: http://www.internationalcollege.edu/irc/humspeech.htm.

Jackson, L. (2003). Delivering *relevant* staff development. *Education World.* Available: http://www.educationworld.com/a_admin/teacher_training/teacher_training004.shtml.

Koegel, T. J. (2002). *The exceptional presenter: A proven formula to open up and own the room.* Washington, DC: Koegel Group.

Mandel, S. (1987). *Effective presentation skills: Proven techniques for more confident, enthusiastic and persuasive presentations.* Los Altos, CA: Crisp.

National Staff Development Council. (2001). *Standards for staff development.* Available: http://www.nsdc.org/standards.

Newstrom, J. W., & Scallell, E. E. (1998). *The big book of presentation games: Wake-'em-up tricks, ice breakers and other fun stuff.* New York: McGraw-Hill.

Pryor, C. B. (1991). Socio-emotional orientation of transfer students: A primary prevention project. *Iowa Journal of School Social Work, 5,* 6–17.

Slutsky, J., & Aun, M. (1997). *The Toastmasters International guide to successful speaking: Overcoming fear, winning your audience, building your business career.* Chicago: Dearborn Financial.

Wilder, L. (1999). *Seven steps to fearless speaking.* New York: Wiley.

Worth, M. A. (1985). Considering the needs of educators as learners: Implications for staff development. *Education, 106*(2), 179–182.

Conducting In-Service Training and Continuing Education for Staff and Teachers

Brenda Coble Lindsey ▪ Margaret White ▪ Wynne S. Korr

CHAPTER 60

Getting Started

Professional development activities, including in-service training and continuing education, are one way that teachers and other school professionals acquire new information in hopes of improving the overall quality of education (Kwakman, 2003). Frequently, these types of activities are presented as full-day in-service seminars by outside experts (Sandholtz, 2002). Mandatory attendance is usually required for teachers as well as school social workers and other school service professionals. It is difficult to select a single topic that is relevant to everyone. As a result, there is significant risk that participants find these one-shot workshops irrelevant and the information presented easily forgotten (Fullan, 1995; Miller, 1998). Traditional in-service seminars, organized as discrete events, reinforce the notion that professional development is separate from daily work tasks and responsibilities (Fullan, 1995). This approach falls short in its ability to ensure that the importance of acquiring new learning is integrated into everyday routines. Moreover, the deep-rooted practice of relying solely upon one-day comprehensive workshops as the conduit to promoting school cultures that promote lifelong learning is ineffective (Fullan, 1995). Professional development must be based on evidence, thoughtfully planned, and address the needs of adult learners (Hassel, 1999).

What We Know

How do the needs for learning of adults differ from children? There are several important factors that must be in place in order for adults to consider professional development activities to be worthwhile. Adults prefer interactive educational experiences that are meaningful, practical, and can be immediately integrated into daily work routines (Glathorn, 1990). Professional development activities are most effective in work environments or school cultures that demonstrate a commitment to lifelong learning. These activities must include *ongoing opportunities for people to learn from each other*, especially from those facing similar challenges; a strong value of *collaboration* and a high importance placed on working together to solve problems; and *encouragement of autonomy and creativity* in the selection of work tasks and responsibilities (Smylie, 1995). Learning is an energetic process in which new knowledge is constantly created, reflected upon, and integrated in such a way that the work environment itself becomes stimulating and celebrates innovativeness (Sandholtz, 2002).

What We Can Do

Designing Effective Professional Development Programs

Quality professional development programs place great emphasis on what is taught as well as how it is taught. Both content and delivery style are important and deserve equal consideration (Hassel, 1999). The four essential steps to establishing a comprehensive professional development program are design, implementation, evaluation, and sharing of knowledge. Specific tasks that must be accomplished during each phase are

Design. Identify stakeholders; determine the planning process; review educational goals for the state, district, and school; conduct a needs assessment; create professional development goals; identify the best available research on a chosen topic; select content and activities; pinpoint resources; develop evaluation methods; and secure sanction for the plan. (Hassel, 1999)

Implementation. Provide learning experiences that disseminate relevant content about a topic of interest; encourage a climate that values collaboration and sharing of new ideas as a way to solve problems; collect data as required for the evaluation component of the plan; remain abreast of the best available research; integrate ongoing opportunities for learning into everyday activities; offer follow-up and coaching sessions to ensure participants successfully implement new skills; provide incentives to encourage the implementation of innovative strategies; reevaluate and revise the staff development plan as needed. (Hassel, 1999)

Evaluation. Complete data collection; analyze results; disseminate findings.

Sharing. Utilize information gained from the evaluation phase to inform future professional development planning processes; circulate professional development materials to others. (Hassel, 1999)

Meaningful professional development should be an entrenched organizational practice that supports and maintains a stimulating learning environment for the school community (Hassel, 1999).

Let us consider key aspects of the implementation phase in greater depth:

1. *Encourage a climate that values collaboration and sharing to solve problems*. Collaboration promotes

the development of organizational norms that value the practice of ongoing learning (Kwakman, 2003). In turn, this practice facilitates creation of a stimulating school environment where activities are designed to support and promote the pursuit and creation of learning opportunities (Law, 1999).

2. *Integrate ongoing opportunities for further learning into everyday activities*. Schools need to be a place of learning for teachers and students alike (Kwakman, 2003). When ongoing learning is a part of everyday responsibilities, professional development can lead to improvement on the part of individuals as well as the organization (Hargreaves, 1997).

3. *Offer follow-up and coaching sessions*. It is essential to provide ongoing learning opportunities that reinforce how to apply newly acquired knowledge and skills (Sandholtz, 2002). This practice not only increases the chances of application of new learning in daily practice but also emphasizes the value of lifelong learning.

An Example of Best Practices for Professional Development: Positive Behavior Support and Intervention (PBIS)

To illustrate how to conduct staff training that incorporates principles of adult learning and focuses on an evidence-based program, we will use the positive behavior support and intervention (PBIS) model. PBIS is a promising approach that incorporates evidence-based practices on a school-wide, individual, and classroom basis. School-wide positive

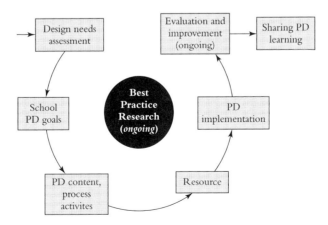

Figure 60.1. Professional Development Cycle
Source: Hassel (1999)

intervention approaches to behavior management have received increased attention in recent years and have been validated in a number of studies (Blakeslee, Sugai, & Gruba, 1999; Brooks, Todd, Tofflemoyer, & Horner, 2003; Cushing, Horner, & Barrier, 2003; Kennedy et al., 2001; Kern et al., 1994; Lewis, Sugai, & Colvin, 1998; Luiselli, Putnam, & Sunderland, 2002; Mayer et al., 1993; McCurdy, Mannella, & Eldridge, 2003; Sasso et al., 1992; Sugai, Sprague, Horner, & Walker, 2000). These proactive approaches are designed to prevent and reduce behavior problems on an individual, classroom, and school-wide basis (Sugai & Horner, 2002). Through the use of positive behavior support interventions, schools create affirmative learning environments. School-wide positive behavior support approaches include

- clear and consistent behavior expectations
- procedures for communicating expectations to staff and students, in addition to encouraging expected behaviors
- methods of preventing problem behaviors
- data collection systems used to determine decision making
- classroom behavior management practices and routines that parallel the school-wide discipline system

These approaches combine behavior analysis techniques with practices and principles of organizational behavior management (Sugai & Horner, 2002). School-wide positive behavior support approaches rely upon data-based decision making and research-validated practices in order to guide responses to behavior management issues.

Sugai and Horner (2002) reported that PBIS encompasses a number of promising practices that can also bring about improvements in school learning environments. These methods include collaborative team problem solving, ongoing professional development, ongoing evaluation and assessment, and securing support for PBIS initiatives as a means of preventing problem behaviors. Hargreaves and Fullan (1998) identified those same types of practices to be effective in creating school environments that foster success. PBIS has the potential to prevent problem behaviors while also bringing about improvements in the atmosphere in schools.

What Is Needed to Implement PBIS

Schools interested in adopting PBIS must make a commitment to utilize a team-based approach,

secure sanction from at least 80% of school staff, and possess enthusiastic administrative support (Sugai & Horner, 2002). In addition, schools must provide training to school staff so that required tasks are performed accurately, use easily managed data-collection methods, provide abundant opportunities for staff development, and offer ongoing recognition and reinforcement for staff accomplishments. School-wide PBIS approaches are more likely to be effective when all of these recommended components are in place (Sugai & Horner, 2002). Adequate staff training is essential to implementing PBIS.

Case Example: PBIS Implementation in Illinois

The Illinois State Board of Education created the Emotional and Behavioral Disabilities/Positive Behavior Interventions and Supports Network in 1990 (www.ebdnetwork-il.org). Initially developed to reduce residential placements for emotionally disturbed students, efforts were expanded in 1998 to include implementation of PBIS through a training and technical assistance model. The EBD/PBIS Network provides ongoing professional development to local schools interested in adopting school-wide positive behavior approaches. Both PBIS and the EBD network approach to professional development incorporate many best practice approaches to training and continuing education. These are highlighted below.

Outline of PBIS Professional Development Efforts: Initial Phase of PBIS Implementation

Introduction. Schools initially learn about PBIS by attending presentations made at professional educational conferences or informal gatherings for administrators (M. Dewhirst, personal communication, 2004). Those interested in implementing PBIS request technical assistance from the EBD/PBIS Network.

Overview training. This 60-minute presentation is designed to provide basic information about PBIS and secure staff support to implement the approach in their school (www.ebdnetwork-il.org). Critical components of PBIS are explained, including systemic levels of implementation, importance of data collection to guide decision making, and universal approaches to behavior management. Interactive and small-group activities are an integral part of the overview presentation. These activities are important because they allow school staff to experience firsthand the benefits of using team-based collaboration methods, which are a central element of PBIS.

Leadership team. A PBIS leadership team is created to include an administrator and representatives from various grade levels or departments within the school (Sugai & Horner, 2002).

Leadership team members attend PBIS new team initial training. This 2-day training is designed to help participants develop a preliminary plan for implementing PBIS on a school-wide basis (www.ebdnetwork-il.org). This interactive workshop utilizes a combination of large- and small-group discussion. Activities are hands-on and intended to ensure that team members can immediately integrate ideas into practice.

Implementation Phase of PBIS

Follow-up and advanced new team training. These training sessions are intensive and provided on-site by regional PBIS consultants. Teaching techniques are designed to help team members apply what they've learned to real-life situations that they encounter in their daily practice. Methods used include case analysis and consultation, dialogue with individual teachers and school service professionals regarding the application of evidence-based practices to individual client situations, and small-group discussions to problem solve implementation issues (M. Dewhirst, personal communication, 2004). During the follow-up segment of training, participants develop methods for teaching positive behavior expectations to their students and staff, create universal classroom rules and management techniques, and are introduced to behavior analysis techniques (www.ebdnetwork-il.org). The advanced training is designed to help team members apply evaluation methods to determine the effectiveness of PBIS and develop strategies to sustain the initiative over time.

Targeted team interventions training. A central tenet of PBIS is that data can be used to identify target populations of students that are at risk of ongoing problem behaviors (Sugai & Horner, 2002). This 2-day seminar teaches PBIS teams how to use data to identify, prevent, and manage problem behaviors for groups of students with intensive needs (www.ebdnetwork-il.org). The

presentation itself utilizes a combination of large- and small-group interactive, discussion-based activities. Large-group presentations focus on how to identify and intervene with specialized clusters of students who might benefit from this type of intervention. Small-group activities are designed to help teams develop initial plans for implementation of the process at their school (Scott, 2001). These activities are intended to reinforce the concept of using data to guide decisions through a collaborative team-based approach. During the training, team members develop a plan that can be implemented immediately to address issues related to specific target student populations at their school.

Functional behavior assessment training. This 2-day training provides a greater understanding of functional behavior assessment and how it can be applied for use with individual students who exhibit the most challenging and intensive behavior issues (www.ebdnetwork-il.org). Sugai, Lewis-Palmer, and Hagan-Burke (1999–2000) define functional behavior assessment as "a systematic *process* for understanding problem behavior and the factors that contribute to its occurrence and maintenance." This assessment is considered to be best practice in situations where students exhibit challenging behavior that is not easily understood or with which typical intervention strategies have proven to be unsuccessful (Crone & Horner, 2003; Horner et al., 1999–2000; Sugai, Lewis-Palmer, & Hagan-Burke, 1999–2000). A combination of large- and small-group discussion is used to facilitate a greater understanding of functional behavior assessment (www.ebdnetwork-il.org). Training activities encourage leadership teams to identify potential students at their school who might benefit from a functional behavior assessment. Participants develop a plan that can be used right away to implement the approach in their school.

Follow-up and advanced functional behavior assessment team training. A PBIS consultant from the EBD/PBIS Network provides on-site technical assistance for this phase of the training. During the follow-up phase, teams learn to apply functional behavior assessment principles to individual students with challenging behavior at their school (www.ebdnetwork-il.org). Specifically, assistance is provided in accurately identifying the antecedents and consequences of behavior as well as developing positive replacement behaviors. In the advanced segment of training, content includes sophisticated data collection and analysis methods and function-based behavior planning procedures that can be adopted as part of the PBIS efforts at school.

School-based wraparound training. This 2-day interactive training is designed to help participants understand the central concepts of the wraparound planning process and how it can be applied to students with chronic and intensive behavior problems (www.ebdnetwork-il.org). *Wraparound* is a planning process used to develop and implement intervention plans tailored to the unique individualized needs of students who exhibit chronic problem behaviors (Scott & Eber, 2003). This training includes large-group presentations about the components of the wraparound process (Eber, 2000a). The training integrates small-group activities throughout, designed so that teams develop action plans for implementation at their school.

Follow-up and advanced wraparound training. A consultant from the EBD/PBIS Network provides on-site technical assistance regarding wraparound implementation issues in local schools. Teams learn to evaluate current wraparound plans for their students and assess system-wide practices that support or impede intensive wraparound approaches (www.ebdnetwork-il.org).

Initial data management training. Participants learn how to fully integrate data-based decision making in their school (www.ebdnetwork-il.org). The training is interactive and intended to ensure that participants are able to immediately apply what they've learned. Content includes methods of identifying sources of data and how to utilize data in the development of interventions.

Follow-up and advanced data management training. This is provided as on-site technical assistance by a PBIS consultant. Teams learn how to utilize data in order to sustain PBIS efforts in their school over time (www.ebdnetwork-il.org). Evaluation is a vital component of PBIS and is built in throughout the approach. This training reflects the need for teams to conduct a comprehensive assessment of PBIS efforts and to revise plans as needed.

Coaches' training. PBIS encourages the use of school-based consultants, referred to as coaches, as a resource for school teams. Coaches are typically school social workers, school psychologists, guidance counselors, or other professionals with special knowledge and expertise about evidence-based practices related to children with emotional and behavioral disabilities. They practice in schools that have implemented PBIS and are invaluable in ensuring the sustainability of PBIS efforts in local schools. This is a 2-day training intended for persons interested in serving as a coach or leader of a school-based PBIS team. Participants learn how to support implementation efforts in order to ensure that plans are carried out as intended (www.ebdnetwork-il.org). This training includes large-group presentations that discuss ways to evaluate the effectiveness of PBIS implementation efforts coupled with small-group activities designed to encourage participants to assess the level of success of PBIS at their school (Eber, 2000b). As with other PBIS trainings, interactive discussion is a built-in component, and content is designed so that it can be immediately applied.

Follow-up and advanced coaches' training. PBIS consultants provide on-site technical assistance utilizing a "train the trainers" model (www.ebdnetwork-il.org). School-based coaches learn how to train their staff on school-wide applications of PBIS to ensure that the initiative remains in place for an extended period of time. This training module provides an opportunity to learn how to share information with others in a way that is meaningful and practical.

All of the training is designed to be interactive, meaningful, and include immediate application of training materials to routine work situations. Small-group training activities have a built-in collaboration and shared problem-solving component. The on-site technical assistance that provides follow-up training and coaching ensures the sustainability of PBIS initiatives. These components reflect essential qualities necessary for effective professional development. PBIS professional development training also reflects the application of critical steps for professional development, including design, implementation, evaluation, and sharing segments (Hassel, 1999). The integration of evidence-based practice principles throughout the PBIS approach suggests a tremendous potential to improve the learning environment for schools.

Tools and Practice Examples

Professional Development Checklist
Design
- Identify/invite stakeholders
- Identify leaders
- Determine planning process

- Review educational goals for the state, district, and school
- Conduct a needs assessment
- Create professional development goals
- Design the professional development plan
- Identify the best available research on a chosen topic
- Select content and activities
- Pinpoint resources: financial, expertise for activity and design, future needs
- Develop evaluation methods
- Secure sanction for the plan

Implementation
- Provide learning experiences that disseminate relevant content about a topic of interest
- Encourage a climate that values collaboration
- Share ideas as a way to solve problems
- Collect data for the evaluation component
- Remain abreast of the best available research
- Integrate ongoing opportunities for learning into everyday activities
- Offer follow-up and coaching sessions to ensure that participants successfully implement skills
- Provide incentives to encourage implementation of innovative strategies

Evaluation
- Complete data collection
- Analyze results
- Disseminate findings
- Reevaluate and revise the staff development plan

Sharing
- Utilize information gained from the evaluation phase in order to plan future professional development
- Circulate professional development materials

Key Points to Remember

Effective professional development requires attention to content as well as delivery (Hassel, 1999). Four essential steps to planning in-service training are:

- Design. What is to be accomplished and how?
- Implementation. The plan in action.

- Evaluation. Was it effective?
- Sharing. Let others know what works.

These practices can be adapted to any continuing education approach for teachers and other school service personnel. Professional development efforts should reinforce the importance of lifelong learning as a way to improve the quality of education.

References

Blakeslee, T., Sugai, G., & Gruba, J. (1999). A review of functional assessment use in data-based intervention studies. *Journal of Behavioral Education, 4,* 397–414.

Brooks, A., Todd, A., Tofflemoyer, S., & Horner, R. (2003). Use of functional assessment and a self-management system to increase academic engagement and work completion. *Journal of Positive Behavior Interventions, 5*(3), 144–152.

Colvin, G., Sugai, G., Good, R., & Lee, Y. (1997). Using active supervision and precorrection to improve transition behaviors in elementary school. *School Psychology Quarterly, 12,* 344–363.

Crone, D., & Horner, R. (2003). *Building positive behavior support systems in schools: Functional behavior assessment.* New York: Guilford.

Cushing, L., Horner, R., & Barrier, H. (2003). Validation and congruent validity of a direct observation tool to assess student social climate. *Journal of Positive Behavior Interventions, 5*(4), 225–237.

Eber, L. (2000a). *Applying wraparound approaches through schools: Intensive interventions and supports for students with EBD and their families and teachers.* (Available from Emotional Behavioral Disabilities/Positive Behavior Interventions and Supports Network, Illinois State Board of Education, West 40 ISC #2, 928 Barnsdale Road #254, LaGrange Park, IL 60526, www.ebdnetwork-il.org)

Eber, L. (2000b). *Illinois PBIS initiative: Implementation, progress and projections.* (Available from Emotional and Behavioral Disabilities/Positive Behavior Interventions and Supports Network, Illinois State Board of Education, West 40 ISC #2, 928 Barnsdale Road #254, LaGrange Park, IL 60526, www.ebdnetwork-il.org)

Fullan, M. (1995). The limits and the potential of professional development. In T. Guskey & M. Huberman (Eds.), *Professional development in education: New paradigms and practices* (pp. 253–268). New York: Teachers College Press.

Glathorn, A. (1990). *Supervisory leadership: An introduction to instructional supervision.* Glenview, IL: Scott Foresman.

Hargreaves, A. (1997). From reform to renewal: A new deal for a new age. In A. Hargreaves & Evans, R.

(Eds.), *Beyond educational reform: Bring teachers back in* (pp. 105–125). Buckingham: Open University Press.

Hargreaves, A., & Fullan, M. (1998). *What's worth fighting for out there?* New York: Teachers College, Columbia University.

Hassel, E. (1999). *Professional development: Learning from the best.* (Available from North Central Regional Educational Laboratory, 1900 Spring Road, Suite 300, Oak Brook, IL, www.ncrel.org)

Horner, R. (1994). Functional assessment: Contributions and future directions. *Journal of Applied Behavior Analysis, 27*(2), 401–404.

Horner, R., Sugai, G., Todd, A., & Lewis-Palmer, T. (1999–2000). Elements of behavior support plans: A technical brief. *Exceptionality, 8*(3), 205–215.

Kennedy, C., Long, T., Jolivette, K., Cox, J., Tang, J., & Thompson, T. (2001). Facilitating general education participation for students with behavior problems by linking positive behavior supports and person-centered planning. *Journal of Emotional and Behavioral Disorders, 9,* 161–171.

Kern, L., Childs, K., Dunlap, G., Clark, S., & Falke, G. (1994). Using assessment-based curricular intervention to improve the classroom behaviors of a student with emotional and behavioral challenges. *Journal of Applied Behavior Analysis, 27,* 7–19.

Kwakman, K. (2003). Factors affecting teachers' participation in professional learning activities. *Teaching and Teacher Education, 19,* 149–170.

Law, S. (1999). Leadership for learning: The changing culture of professional development in schools. *Journal of Educational Administration, 37*(1), 66–79.

Lewis, T., Sugai, G., & Colvin G., (1998). Reducing problem behavior through a school-wide system of effective behavioral support: Investigation of a school-wide social skills training program and contextual interventions. *School Psychology Review, 27,* 446–459.

Luiselli, J., Putnam, R., & Sunderland, M. (2002). Longitudinal evaluation of behavior support intervention in a public middle school. *Journal of Positive Behavior Interventions, 4*(3), 182–188.

Mayer, G., Buttersworth, T., Nafpaktitis, M., & Sulzer-Aaroff, B. (1983). Preventing school vandalism and improving discipline: A three year study. *Journal of Applied Behavior Analysis, 16,* 355–369.

McCurdy, B., Mannella, M., & Eldridge, N. (2003). Positive behavior support in urban schools: Can we prevent the escalation of antisocial behavior? *Journal of Positive Interventions, 5*(3), 158–170.

Miller, E. (1998). The old model of staff development survives in a world where everything else has changed. In R. Tovey (Ed.), *Professional development,* Harvard Education Letter Focus Series, no. 4 (1–3). Cambridge, MA: Harvard Education Letter.

O'Neill, R., Horner, R., Albin, R., Sprague, J., Storey, K., & Newton, J. (1997). *Functional assessment and program development for problem behavior: A practical handbook* (2nd ed.). Pacific Grove, CA: Brooks/Cole.

Repp, A. (1994). Comments on functional analysis procedures for school-based behavior problems. *Journal of Applied Behavior Analysis, 27*(2), 409–411.

Sandholtz, J. (2002). Inservice training or professional development: Contrasting opportunities in a school/university partnership. *Teaching and Teacher Education, 18,* 815–830.

Sasso, G., Reimers, T., Cooper, L., Wacker, D., Berg, W., Steege, M., Kelly, L., & Allaire, A. (1992). Use of discipline and experimental analyses to identify the functional properties of aberrant behavior in school settings. *Journal of Applied Behavior Analysis, 25*(4), 809–821.

Scott, T. (2001). *Targeted interventions: Facilitating systemic interventions for students with challenging behavior.* (Available from EBD/PBIS Network, Illinois Emotional and Behavioral Disabilities/Positive Behavior Interventions and Supports Network, Illinois State Board of Education, West 40 ISC #2, 928 Barnsdale Road #254, LaGrange Park, IL 60526, www.ebd-network-il.org)

Scott, T., & Eber, L. (2003). Functional assessment and wraparound as systemic school processes: Primary, secondary and tertiary systems examples. *Journal of Positive Behavior Interventions, 5*(3), 131–143.

Smylie, M. (1995). Teacher learning in the workplace: Implications for school reform. In T. Guskey & M. Huberman (Eds.), *Professional development in education: New paradigms and practices* (pp. 92–113). New York: Teachers College Press.

Sugai, G., & Horner, R. (2002). The evolution of discipline practices: School-wide positive behavior supports. *Child & Family Behavior Therapy, 24*(1–2), 23–50.

Sugai, G., Horner, R., Dunlap, G., Hieneman, M., Lewis, T., Nelson, C., Scott, T., Liaupsin, C., Sailor, W., Turnbull, A., Turnbull, H., Wickham, D., Reuff, M., & Wilcox, B. (2000). Applying positive behavioral support and functional behavioral assessment in schools. *Journal of Positive Behavioral Interventions and Support, 2,* 131–143.

Sugai, G., Lewis-Palmer, T., & Hagan-Burke, S. (1999–2000). Overview of the functional behavioral assessment process. *Exceptionality, 8*(3), 149–160.

Sugai, G., Sprague, J., Horner, R., & Walker, H. (2000). Preventing school violence: The use of office discipline referrals to assess and monitor school-wide discipline interventions. *Journal of Emotional and Behavioral Disorders, 8*(2), 94–101.

Best School-Based Practices for Family Intervention and Parental Involvement

This section addresses skills and best practice interventions for working with families and parental involvement. Active family involvement in the educational experience of children and youth has repeatedly been demonstrated to be effective in supporting success in school and life. Social workers, counselors, nurses, special education teachers, and other school-based professionals are frontline school staff in engaging and involving parents and families in their children's school experience. They need direction for helping families to cope with a range of serious problems, such as ADHD, academic failure, and dropping out of school. They need guidance for engaging effectively with a diversity of nontraditional families, such as those headed by single parents, families with immigrant status, families who hold religious fundamentalist beliefs, and families who move frequently or are homeless. To be effective, they need instruction on current family therapy, parental involvement, and home visiting. This section contains chapters that respond to these and other needs related to best practices with families and schools.

Effective Strategies for Promoting Parental Involvement
An Overview

Nancy Feyl Chavkin

Getting Started

The importance of parental involvement in education cannot be overstated; a parent is a child's first teacher and the only teacher who remains with a child throughout his education. The research is compelling about both the academic benefits (Henderson & Mapp, 2002) and the social emotional learning benefits (Zins, Bloodworth, Weissberg, & Walberg, 2004) of parental involvement. The research is clear: When parents are involved in their children's learning, children do better in school and in life. See chapter 63 for additional information on building effective family support programs.

Today, children come from families that are diverse in a variety of ways, including composition, parental working arrangements, environmental condition, economic background, language, culture, and parental education. Schools alone cannot meet the needs of these diverse students without strong parental support. Many schools are finding that parental involvement in education can play a significant role in providing necessary support for students and in helping schools to better understand their students.

In addition to the strong research and practice findings about parental involvement in education, current policy initiatives also dictate a strong role for parental involvement in education. The No Child Left Behind Act (2001) has specific requirements for parental involvement that require notification and participation of parents in their children's education.

What We Know

As Table 61.1 indicates, there are numerous research studies about the benefits of parental involvement in education. Henderson and Mapp (2002) provide evidence from more than 50 studies in three broad categories: studies on family involvement and student achievement, studies on effective strategies, and studies on parent and community organizing efforts. Their conclusion is that the evidence is beyond dispute that when parental involvement in education occurs, children benefit both academically and socially. Their findings indicate that the most accurate predictor of students' achievement is not income or social status but how much the families are able to be involved in their children's education, create home environments that support learning, and express high expectations for their children's education.

Researchers have shown that parental involvement in education is directly related to significant increases in student achievement. Herbert Walberg (1984) reviewed 29 controlled studies on school–parent programs and found that family participation in education was twice as predictive of academic learning as family socioeconomic status. Walberg also found that some parental involvement programs had effects 10 times as large as socioeconomic status and had benefits for both elementary and secondary students.

In 2001, researchers at Early Head Start from Mathematica Policy Research and the Center for Children and Families at Columbia University investigated 3,000 children and their families using control groups and found again that family involvement increased cognitive gains.

In another study of 71 Title I elementary schools, family involvement was linked to increased gains in reading and math (Westat & Policy Studies Associates, 2001). In another study, of eighth-graders, students whose families took part in a greater number of activities did better in school (Miedel & Reynolds, 1999).

In addition to the academic benefits of parental involvement in education, Rich (1993) reported that parental involvement in education helped to produce increases in student attendance, decreases in the dropout rate, positive parent–child communication, improvement of student attitudes and behavior, and more parent and community support of the school. Others

(Winters, 1993; also see Patrikakou, Weissberg, Redding, & Walberg, 2004) discuss the benefits that both parents and teachers reap from collaboration. The results are more resources, a broadening of perspectives, and sometimes personal motivation to improve themselves. There are mutually reinforcing effects that parents and children have on each other when they work together on educational outcomes.

What We Can Do

Parental Involvement Strategies

Educators and researchers have described numerous strategies for promoting parental involvement in education, but it must be emphasized that parental involvement is a broad term that encompasses many different roles and activities. The very words *parental involvement* mean different things to different people. Because the definition of parental involvement is unclear, the strategies to achieve it are complex. One approach that has been helpful for families, schools, and communities is to use a three-part process in developing their parent involvement plan.

The three parts to this process are vision, involvement, and planning (see Figure 61.1); this author prefers to call it a VIP (*Very Important Partnership*) approach. The parts are not steps that are linear and constantly moving up a ladder; they are more like a slinky that loops back and forth and thus are called phases. Because of the lack of clarity for the definition of parental involvement, one of the first issues that school social workers and mental health professionals need to consider is how to define what their vision of parental involvement is in their school and community. A second key issue is to determine how to make sure that all of the key stakeholders are involved. The third issue is how to effectively develop a systematic plan that will institute a parental involvement program that meets the needs of each particular community. All three issues take place in the contextual framework (physical and attitudinal environment) of the school and community. All schools and communities are different, and thus any discussion of how to develop a partnership must take place in the contextual framework of each particular school and community. The next sections will describe some specific strategies for each part

Table 61.1 Key Research About Parental Involvement

In schools where teachers reported high levels of outreach with parents—meeting face-to-face with parents, sending parents notes, and telephoning—test scores rose at a 40 percent higher rate for low-achieving students.

> —Westat and Policy Studies Associates. (2001). *The longitudinal evaluation of school change and performance in Title I Schools (Vol. I).* Washington, DC: U.S. Department of Education.

Programs that successfully connect with families and community invite involvement, are welcoming, and address specific parent and community needs.

> —Henderson, A. T., & Mapp, K. L. (2002). *A new wave of evidence: The impact of school, family, and community connections on student achievement.* Austin, TX: Southwest Educational Development Laboratory.

Schools' programs and teachers' practices to involve parents have important positive effects on parents' abilities to help their children across the grades; on parents' ratings of teachers' skills and teaching quality; on teachers' opinions about parents' abilities to help their children with schoolwork at home; on students' attitudes about school; and on students' reading achievement.

> —Dauber, S. L., & Epstein, J. L. (1993). Parents' attitudes and practices of involvement in inner-city elementary and middle schools. In N. F. Chavkin (Ed.), *Families and schools in a pluralistic society.* Albany: State University of New York Press.

The alterable curriculum of the home is twice as predictive of academic learning as is family socioeconomic status

> —Walberg, H. J. (1984). Improving the productivity of America's schools. *Educational Leadership, 41,* 19–27.

Dr. Comer wanted to make sure I understood that the essence of his intervention is a *process*, not a package of materials, instructional methods, or techniques. "It is the creation of a sense of community and direction for parents, school staff, and students alike."

> —Schorr, L. B. (1988). *Within our reach: Breaking the cycle of disadvantage.* Garden City, NY: Doubleday.

Children will be more successful when schools integrate efforts to promote children's academic, social, and emotional learning.

> —Patrikakou, E. N., Weissberg, R. P., Redding, S., & Walberg, H. J. (2004). *School-family partnerships: Fostering children's school success.* New York: Teachers College Press.

In schools along the Texas-Mexico border, the high performing schools were "collaborative" schools where parents and school staff "join together to serve the needs of all children."

> —Reyes, P., Scribner, J. D., & Paredes-Scribner, A. (Eds.). (1999). *Lessons from high-performing Hispanic schools: Creating learning communities.* New York: Teachers College Press.

(vision, involvement, and planning) and then present some microsteps for examining the roles of parents and teachers in the process, preparing school staff for working in the field of parental involvement, and learning from case examples.

Part 1: Vision

It is essential that school staff, parents, and the community come together and decide on their vision of what kind(s) of parental involvement they want

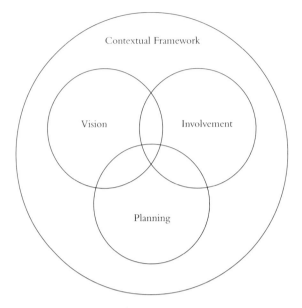

Essential Components of VIP Approach

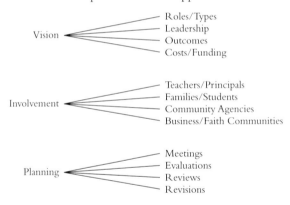

Figure 61.1. The VIP Model: Vision, Involvement, Planning

for their school. When considering vision, it is often helpful to consider types of parent involvement and the many possible roles for parents and for teachers, including how to prepare educators for working in the field of parental involvement.

The vision component of building a partnership cannot be completed unless one also simultaneously starts part 2, involvement. Visioning has to include many people from different parts of the community, and thus it needs to begin with involving as many different kinds of stakeholders as possible and focusing on their commonalities. As they explore what it is they are about and what it is they wish to change or make better, they build a relationship with each other. They start to trust each other.

Part 2: Involvement

There is no one in charge when one is trying to involve a broad spectrum of the community; the agenda is to involve key stakeholders to establish a vision. It doesn't matter whether the idea of exploring a partnership began at the top and came down or was a bottom-up phenomenon. These kinds of distinctions are blurred. The focus is on involvement and vision. The result should be an overarching goal and perhaps several possible short-term goals. These two components are essentially the beginning of a reframing of our traditional approach to working with families and communities. If we truly want change, we as professionals must change the way we approach parental involvement. We must meet the family and community on their own turf and ask them to tell us their dreams, their goals.

We need to get out of the traditional needs assessment approach where we as professionals tell families and communities what it is they need. Instead, educators should use a strength-building approach to assessment. What are the resources and capabilities of families and the community? Looking for the strengths of families and communities is an important part of the involvement component. The involvement component of building a partnership focuses on collaboration. The school and community become linked. The emphasis should be on diversity with a wide range of current skills and previous backgrounds represented.

The collaboration should include at least three main groups: the consumers, the public sector, and the private sector. The consumers are the families and communities with whom we are working— those toward whom the target goal is directed. The public sector consists of social service agencies, elected officials, media, and others in related civic or governmental positions. The private sector consists of both businesses and social service agencies. The important part of involvement is to make certain that all of the key players are involved from the beginning. The emphasis in this component is on teaming and sharing. It is a move away from a mere decision to act toward a real commitment to act.

Part 3: Planning

The planning component of building a partnership is the most misunderstood part of parental involvement partnerships. It continues the tradition of shared collaboration, of teaming, and it moves forward to be a data-driven, evaluative phase. Planning necessitates time and patience. It is an ongoing phase that never ends. Most partnerships tend to allot a short amount of time to planning and begin implementation prematurely without proper preparation. Everybody wants to see action immediately, but partnerships take time. Successful partnerships implement programs and activities, evaluate these programs and activities, reflect on these programs and activities, and then plan revisions of these programs and activities. A key concept here is *ongoing* evaluation. If the participants only evaluate at the end, they are using

an "autopsy" approach that is too late for their program. The need for formative evaluation cannot be stressed enough. The planning component is ongoing. It includes constant evaluation, reflection, feedback, and new trials. In-service training is a major part of the planning component. People need assistance when we ask them to perform new roles. We have not been taught to work in teams, to share, to relate to other professions. Financial awareness is also important. Ask: What is it we can do with the limited resources we have?— not what can't we do because we don't have the money?

Microsteps for Achieving Very Important Partnerships (VIPs): Consider Parental Roles, Prepare School Staff, and Learn From Others

Sometimes, parents work on the inside of schools as paraprofessionals or teacher aides; other times, parents simply attend Parent–Teacher Association meetings, sports events, concerts, and other student performances. Parents may also come to school to learn how to become better parents and how to help their children learn more. They may exchange information with teachers about their children's progress in person, by note, or by telephone. These contacts and assistance in the classroom are forms of active collaboration of parents and schools.

In addition to taking place inside the school, parental involvement may also take place at home. At the most basic level are family obligations to assure students' preparation for school, such as being well fed, having sufficient rest, being dressed appropriately, and being punctual. Parents also transmit their skills, knowledge, and values to children by modeling acceptable behaviors and giving direct instructions.

Some parents are involved in advocacy groups that press for educational change and reform. Sometimes, parents are able to choose the school their children attend. Some parents are actively involved in decision-making groups that influence textbook adoptions and school policies.

Chavkin and Williams (1993) list seven specific roles for parents involved in schools: (1) paid school staff: working in the school as an aide or other employee of the district; (2) school program supporter: coming to school to assist in events; (3) home tutor: helping the child learn at home; (4) audience: supporting the child by going to school performances, open houses; (5) advocate: meeting with the school board to ask for changes in policies; (6) co-learner: going to the classroom or to workshops with teachers; and (7) decision maker: being on an advisory board or school committee that makes decisions about school activities or policies.

Rutherford (1995) divides parental involvement into three broad categories: home learning: parents as the primary resource in the education of their children; school restructuring: parents as supporters and advocates for the education of their children; and district-wide programs: parents as participants in the education of all children.

Joyce Epstein (1995) presents a typology that brings together all of these important roles and conceptualizations of parental involvement in education. Table 61.2 shows her framework of the six types of involvement and sample practices with each type of involvement. Because of its

breadth, Epstein's is currently the most widely used typology. Both practitioners and researchers have used this typology as the center of their work because it covers so many aspects of parental involvement. Each of the six types can have positive results for students, parents, and teachers. For example, with Type 1 (parenting) activities, students gain respect for parents and awareness of the importance of school. Parents receive a feeling of support from both the school and other parents, and teachers gain understanding of families' cultures and views of their children. Similarly, with Type 3 (volunteering) activities, students gain skills in communicating with other adults and receive tutoring and more attention at school. Parents benefit by learning about teachers' work and feeling comfortable around educational activities, and teachers gain an appreciation for parents' talents and interest in their children and have the benefit of volunteers in their classrooms. Epstein's

Table 61.2 Epstein's Framework of Parental Involvement

Type	Definition	Examples of Practice
1. Parenting	Help families improve home environments to support the education of children	Home visits, workshops, parent education, meetings
2. Communicating	Design effective forms of communication, including both home-to-school and school-to-home communications	Conferences, translators, report cards, phone calls, newsletters, Web pages, brochures
3. Volunteering	Parent help and support	Volunteer programs, resource centers for parents, parent patrols, parents as speakers
4. Learning at Home	Provide information about how parents can help children with homework and curriculum activities	Provide information on homework policies, calendars with activities, summer learning activities, family interaction with curriculums
5. Decision Making	Parents as leaders, representatives, committee members	Active PTA/PTO, advocacy, district-level councils, elections, networks
6. Collaborating With Community	Use community resources to strengthen school and family programs	Current information to all families on community health, cultural, recreational, and social support programs; service integration with school programs

Source: Adapted from Epstein, J. L., Coates, L., Salinas, K. C., Sanders, M., & Simon, B. (1997). *Partnership 2000 schools manual: Improving school-family-community connections.* Baltimore: Johns Hopkins University Press.

typology of six types of parental involvement relies on individual schools adapting practices and programs to meet the needs and interests of their particular constituencies. Although the model has commonalities across successful programs, she is clear that good parental involvement programs can appear different in each site.

It is often helpful for new partnerships to read some of the literature about types of roles and to visit programs that use different roles. Individual schools and programs need to develop their own visions and plans. They may need to develop it in stages. For example, some schools begin with parent volunteer programs; others start with increasing communication links.

An important strategy for promoting parental involvement is to prepare school staff to work with parents. Again, there are many possible approaches to what roles should be primary and how to structure the training of school staff to work with families. It is probably less important which approach is selected and more important that preparation take place and that in-service learning continue. Most school personnel have never received any training about parental involvement or, if they have, the training has been perfunctory. School social workers and mental health workers can promote parental involvement by offering in-service training on how to work with parents.

The Harvard Family Research Project (Shartrand et al., 1997) identified seven key knowledge areas about family involvement that teachers and school staff need to know (see Table 61.3). The group also presented four approaches for how to teach the attitudes, knowledge, and skills that are needed in these seven content areas. The approaches are a functional approach that clearly describes the roles of schools and parents; a parent empowerment approach that is based on the strengths of disenfranchised families; a cultural competence approach that focuses on an inclusive, respectful school where diversity is valued; and a social capital approach that builds on community assets and parental investment in their children's education. Each of the four approaches can be used alone or in combination.

The four approaches for preparing educators about family involvement also link back to the underlying assumptions about what roles parents should have in the schools. Using the functional approach, partnerships would promote the attitude that all teachers should learn skills in working with parents. They would prepare teachers to take the lead in engaging families by providing educators with knowledge about both the benefits and the barriers to family involvement. They would advocate for teachers and administrators to involve diverse families of all backgrounds in their children's education and would emphasize developing

---

Table 61.3 Seven Key Knowledge Areas for Educators

- General Family Involvement: knowledge of the goals of, benefits, and barriers to parent involvement

- General Family Knowledge: knowledge of different families' cultures, child rearing, lifestyles, etc.

- Home–School Communication: provision of techniques and strategies for two-way communication between school and home

- Family Involvement in Learning Activities: information about how to involve parents in their children's learning at home or in the community

- Families Supporting Schools: information on ways that families can help the school, both inside and outside of the classroom

- Schools Supporting Families: information on possible ways that schools can help support the social, educational, and social services needs of families

- Families as Change Agents: information on possible roles that families can play as decision makers, researchers, and advocates in the improvement of policies, programs, and curriculums

Source: Adapted from the work of the Harvard Family Research Project: Shartrand, A. M., Weiss, H. B., Kreider, H. M., & Lopez, M. E. (1997). *New skills for new schools: Preparing teachers in family involvement.* Cambridge, MA: Harvard Family Research.

teacher knowledge and attitudes about different child-rearing practices, family structures, living environments, belief systems, and lifestyles.

The parent empowerment approach has the same basic goals as the functional approach, but it places more emphasis on the role of the family. The attitude expressed by the partnership using this approach is that all parents want the best for their children and are the most important teachers of children. This approach not only has respect for the importance of the family in a child's life but also focuses on beginning with the family and the community to find the most useful knowledge about rearing and educating children. The partnership would focus on the strengths of parents and the knowledge of power differences among groups in our society. This approach recognizes that many families belong to disenfranchised groups and works with the effects of this disadvantaged status on a family's relationship with the school.

The cultural competence approach is again similar to the other approaches, but it places the primary emphasis on the knowledge that family involvement benefits the academic achievement of minority and low-income students. Partnerships that use this approach would teach both knowledge and skills in using culturally appropriate curriculums and outreach methods. They would teach skills in understanding and combating stereotypes and prejudices.

The social capital approach is a strengths-based approach that focuses on building on and using the skills and knowledge that parents already possess. Partnerships that use this approach would teach content about differences and commonalities in norms and values across cultures. They would emphasize skills in conflict negotiation and consensus building.

Kirschenbaum (2001) presents another model that describes the components of professional preparation for parental involvement in education. Kirschenbaum uses a format (Table 61.4) that outlines the knowledge, attitudes, and skills that are important. He provides a beginning list under each category and stresses that participants need to add additional items that are relevant to their own learning needs. He stresses that it is not enough for professionals to just *know* how to develop a parental involvement program, but they must also *want* to do it and to *believe* that they can do it. He states that professional preparation must include cognitive, affective, and behavioral components.

Another important model focuses on the roles that teachers play in parental involvement. The

Table 61.4 Three Areas of Learning

Knowledge: Understandings and perspective

- Theoretical understandings
- Paradigm shift about role of professional
- Types of family involvement
- Implementation models

Attitudes

- Comfort with diverse populations
- Self-knowledge
- Receptivity about working in partnership

Skills

- Two-way communication
- Conducting parent–teacher conferences
- Conducting home visits
- Communicating across language, culture, class

self-renewing partnership model (Leuder, 1998) emphasizes changing the traditional parent involvement approach from a single-dimensional model, with parent involvement coming into the school for the sole purpose of supporting the school, to a multidimensional model, which focuses on reaching and involving the "missing families."

The goal of Leuder's model is to create learning communities, and it requires a new outreach dimension. Instead of just the traditional "energy-in" components of family involvement, where families are supporting the school by volunteering and giving their time, Leuder's model expands on traditional roles and also adds an "energy-out" component. The energy-out component is a series of strategies that the school uses to reach out to parents. In other words, the school uses its resources to create a collaborative relationship with families and communities. Leuder believes that it is the school's responsibility to work with the hard-to-reach families, and his model focuses on the active roles that educators can play in developing self-renewing partnerships with families.

Tools and Practice Examples

Case Example

Leuder's (1998) case study of Apple Hill Elementary School provides an excellent example of how to implement an effective partnership. In this particular case, the group assembled all of the stakeholders to establish a vision of what they wanted and then developed specific goals. It was an ongoing process that included a lot of planning and a lot of stages where the group met and refined its target goals. The reader can find more about the entire case in Leuder's text.

After completing the planning phase, the School Improvement Council members and the faculty of Apple Hill decided that there were two family populations that they wanted to target for interventions. These two populations were hard-to-reach families who were not involved and the parents of students who were bused in. The council decided that there was not enough good communication between the groups and the school. The members decided that their first goal was to strengthen the connections between the families and the school, and the second goal was for the families and the school to be communicating effectively. Because the second goal was largely dependent on meeting the first goal, the group focused all of its efforts on increasing the two-way communication flow between the school and parents.

The council decided on objectives for each goal and then selected and implemented best practices. For example, for the first goal, the council members changed the warning signs at the front of the building to "welcome" signs and allocated some of the parking spaces at the front of the school for parents. As the connections were made and the goals were being met, the council was able to enhance the parent partner role skills and knowledge and get the families working with the school to make sure that the partnership would continue and that the families were fully involved in the partnership to educate their children.

Reframing Our Approach

Reframing our approach to partnerships is essential to any parental involvement strategies. *Vision, Involvement,* and *Planning* are the three key ingredients of successful family-school-community partnerships, but they will not work unless we change our approach to partnerships and to family involvement in education. Many people ask if these are steps to partnerships, and the answer is "no." One cannot look at these concepts linearly. They are too interrelated, too inextricably connected to be seen as steps or even straight lines. In many ways, the vision is always being fine-tuned,

even in the planning component when the collaborators have just evaluated an activity.

Successful partnerships are like a slinky. They loop back before they move forward. There is no direct, straight path to a successful partnership. The relationships are not linear; the progress is not linear. When one is working on establishing the VIPs, one wants to be developing a process, not a project. Too often, school leaders work only on projects or pilots. These projects usually die out, and the end is always in sight. Some cynical community members have even termed them "projectitis." If participants reframe their approach, and focus on the slinky method of looping forward and then back a little and then forward again, they will see an emphasis on the partnership and on the process of creating: vision, involvement, and planning.

Creating successful partnerships is more than just a series of projects and activities; they are a process that takes time. There are no specific strategies that will work with every school and every group of families. Successful partnerships are involved in learning how to problem solve. This problem-solving approach is at the heart of all successful partnerships. Because no two communities are alike, there is no easy recipe.

In her review of three decades of research on home–school partnerships, Broussard (2003) emphasizes that school social workers and mental health professionals have both the requisite skills and an ethical obligation to collaborate with school personnel to establish not only the importance of working with families but also the value of working with families as true partners in the educational process. Building successful partnerships will take a reframing of what we as professionals see as our task, and it will take a reframing of our professional behaviors.

Examples of Successful Parental Involvement Strategies

The key commonalities of successful core programs, according to Epstein (1995), are recognition of the overlapping spheres of influence on student development; the opportunity for various types of parental involvement that promote schools, families, and communities working together; and an action team that coordinates the school's work in family and community involvement. Epstein recognizes that there are challenges to each type of involvement and offers redefinitions of key terms, such as *communication,* to mean two-way, three-way, and many-way communication.

Epstein's model suggests that the focus of community efforts should be on the strengths and talents of a community's students, families, and schools and not the traditional deficit approach of trying to fix communities with problems. The strategies described below are just a few examples of the myriad possibilities for successfully involving parents in their children's education. Additional resources for developing successful parental involvement strategies can be found in Table 61.5. There is no one way that is right for every school or every community.

Table 61.5. Resources for Increasing Parental Involvement in Education

ASPIRA Association, Inc.
  1444 I Street NW, Suite 800
  Washington, DC 20005
  http://www.aspira.org

Center on School, Family and Community Partnerships
  Johns Hopkins University
  3503 North Charles Street
  Baltimore, MD 21218
  http://www.csos.jhu.edu/p2000/center.htm

Children's Aid Society
  105 East 22nd Street
  New York, NY 10010
  http://www.childrensaidsociety.org

Commonwealth Institute for Parent Leadership
  P.O. Box 1658
  Lexington, KY 40588-1658
  http://www.cipl.org

Communities in Schools, Inc.
  277 South Washington Street, Suite 210
  Alexandria, VA 22314
  http://www.cisnet.org

Council of the Great City Schools
  1301 Pennsylvania Ave., NW, Suite 702
  Washington, DC 20004
  http://www.cgcs.org

Family Friendly Schools
  13080 Brookmead Drive
  Manassas, VA 20112
  http://www.familyfriendlyschools.org

Family Support America
  20 North Wacker Drive, Suite 1100
  Chicago, IL 60606
  http://www.familysupportamerica.org

Harvard Family Research Project
  Longfellow Hall, Appian Way
  Cambridge, MA 02138
  http://gseweb.harvard.edu/~hfrp

Institute for Responsive Education
  21 Lake Hall
  Northeastern University
  Boston, MA 02115
  http://www.responsiveeducation.org

MegaSkills Education Center
  Home and School Institute
  1500 Massachusetts Avenue, NW
  Washington, DC 20003
  http://www.megaskillshsi.org

National Association for Partners in Education
  901 N. Pitt Street, Suite 320
  Alexandria, VA 22314
  http://www.partnersineducation.org

National Center for Family and Community Connections With Schools
  Southwest Educational Development Laboratory
  211 East Seventh Street
  Austin, TX 78701
  http://www.sedl.org/connections

National Center for Family Literacy
  School Reform Initiative
  325 West Main Street, Suite 200
  Louisville, KY 40202
  http://www.famlit.org

National Coalition for Parent Involvement in Education (NCPIE)
  3929 Old Lee Highway, Suite 91-A
  Fairfax, VA 22030-2401
  http://www.ncpie.org

National Coalition of Title I/Chapter 1 Parents
  National Parent Center
  3609 Georgia Avenue, NW, 1st Floor
  Washington, DC 20036
  http://www.nctic1p.org

(continued)

Table 61.5 *(Continued)*

National Community Education Association
   3929 Old Lee Highway, Suite 91-A
   Fairfax, VA 22030
   http://www.ncea.com
	Parents as Teachers National Center, Inc.
	   2228 Ball Drive
	   St. Louis, MO 63146
	   http://www.patnc.org

National Information Center for Children
and Youth With Disabilities
   Academy for Educational Development
   1825 Connecticut Ave., NW, Suite 700
   Washington, DC 20009
   http://www.nichcy.org
	Parents for Public Schools
	   1520 North State Street
	   Jackson, MS 39202
	   http://www.parents4publicschools.
	   com

National Parent Teacher Association
   330 North Wabash Avenue, Suite 2100
   Chicago, IL 60611
   http://www.pta.org
	Project Parents, Inc.
	   46 Beach Street, Suite 502
	   Boston, MA 02111
	   http://www.projectparents.
	   org

Family Literacy

This type of project focuses on either helping parents support their children's school learning or on addressing both parent and child literacy. Many of these programs focus on reading and writing, but there is a growing emphasis on programs in science and math.

Home–School Communication

Initiatives involving home–school communication typically focus on reaching out to families. Activities often include home visits, newsletters, conferences, parent–community liaisons, and technological communications, such as e-mails, Web sites, and telephone calling systems. All of the activities are meant to empower parents by giving them more access to information about their children's learning.

Family Centers

Family centers are places where family members can meet and implement programs for their children. Sometimes these centers are located at schools, but they can also be located off-site. The important component of a family center is that it is designated as the parents' own place. It is a structural indicator of the important role that parents play in their children's education. Sometimes these centers are called parent information centers or parent resource centers.

Parent Councils or Organizing Networks

Parent involvement in decision making and advocacy has sometimes been considered controversial; however, schools that actively promote parent councils have achieved some of the best school reform results. There are a variety of decision-making and advocacy activities that can take place. Some of the groups are school-based organizations, such as PTAs and booster clubs; others are grassroots organizations with a community base.

Parent Education

There are many forms of parent education that provide specific training on parenting skills. Programs often offer support in the areas of children's developmental, academic, social, and health concerns. Sometimes, teachers and other community professionals participate together in these parent education programs.

Key Points to Remember

Both the research and the practice experience with parental involvement in education have been positive. There have been many significant improvements in the ways that educators and parents work together; many schools are successfully employing evidence-based strategies and seeing improvements in both academic and social areas. Future research is still needed in many areas, including examining points of transition within different schooling levels; testing the effectiveness of different parental involvement strategies; investigating the roles that students play in their own achievement; and exploring the role of policy in parental involvement and student achievement.

Almost a quarter of a century ago, Seeley (1981) argued for a new paradigm for parental involvement, which has not yet occurred. He argued that there must be a fundamental shift away from the delegation model in public education. He suggested that the basic structures, roles, relationships, attitudes, and assumptions must be changed if parental involvement is going to be successful. He proposed that the shift to a collaborative model would empower all of the players and produce higher levels of academic achievement.

Key questions remain. Will parental involvement include all families? Will it be based on mutual respect and true collaboration? Will it be able to deal effectively with the challenges of school violence, budget cuts, teacher strikes, low test scores, and other critical issues facing our schools?

References

Broussard, C. A. (2003). Facilitating home-school partnerships for multiethnic families: School social workers collaborating for success. *Children & Schools, 25*(4), 211–222.

Chavkin, N. F., & Williams, D. M. (1993). Minority parents and the elementary school: Attitudes and practices. In N. F. Chavkin (Ed.), *Families and schools in a pluralistic society* (pp. 73–83). Albany: State University of New York Press.

Dauber, S. L., & Epstein, J. L. (1993). Parents' attitudes and practices of involvement in inner-city elementary and middle schools. In N. F. Chavkin (Ed.), *Families and schools in a pluralistic society* (pp. 53–71). Albany, NY: SUNY.

Epstein, J. L. (1995). School/family/community partnerships: Caring for the children we share. *Phi Delta Kappan 76*(9), 701–712.

Epstein, J. L., Coates, L., Salinas, K. C., Sanders, M., & Simon, B. (1997). *Partnership 2000 schools manual: Improving school-family-community connections.* Baltimore: Johns Hopkins University Press.

Henderson, A. T., & Mapp, K. L. (2002). *A new wave of evidence: The impact of school, family, and community connections on student achievement.* Austin, TX: National Center for Family & Community Connections with Schools, Southwest Educational Development Laboratory.

Kirschenbaum, H. (2001). Educating professionals for school, family and community partnerships. In D. B. Hiatt-Michael (Ed.), *Promising practices for family involvement in schools* (pp. 185–208). Greenwich, CT: Information Age.

Lueder, D. C. (1998). *Creating partnerships with parents.* Lancaster, PA: Technomic.

Miedel, W. T., & Reynolds, A. J. (1999). Parent involvement in early intervention for disadvantaged children: Does it matter? *Journal of School Psychology, 37*(4), 379–402.

No Child Left Behind Act. (2001). Available: http://www.ed.gov/policy/elsec/leg/esea02/107–110.pdf.

Patrikakou, E. N., Weissberg, R. P., Redding, S., & Walberg, H. J. (2004). *School-family partnerships: Fostering children's school success.* New York: Teachers College Press.

Reyes, P., Scribner, J. D., & Paredes-Scribner, A. (1999). *Lessons from high-performing Hispanic schools: Creating learning communities.* New York: Teachers College Press.

Rich, D. (1993). Building the bridge to reach minority parents: Education infrastructure supporting success for all children. In N. F. Chavkin (Ed.), *Families and schools in a pluralistic society* (pp. 235–244). Albany: State University of New York Press.

Rutherford, B. (Ed.). (1995). *Creating family/school partnerships.* Columbus, OH: National Middle School Association.

Schorr, L. B. (1988). *Within our reach: Breaking the cycle of disadvantage.* New York: Doubleday.

Seeley, D. S. (1981). *Education through partnership.* Cambridge, MA: Ballinger.

Shartrand, A. M., Weiss, H. B., Kreider, H. M., & Lopez, M. E. (1997). *New skills for new schools: Preparing teachers in family involvement.* Cambridge, MA: Harvard Family Research.

Walberg, H. J. (1984). Improving the productivity of America's schools. *Educational Leadership, 41,* 19–27.

Westat & Policy Studies Associates. (2001). *The longitudinal evaluation of school change and performance in Title I Schools* (Vol. I). Washington, DC: U.S. Department of Education.

Winters, W. G. (1993). *African American mothers and urban schools: The power of participation.* New York: Lexington.

Zins, J. E., Bloodworth, M. R., Weissberg, R. P., & Walberg, H. J. (2004). The scientific base linking social and emotional learning to school success. In J. E. Zins, R. P. Weissberg, M. C. Wang, & H. J. Walberg (Eds.), *Building academic success on social and emotional learning. What does the research say?* (pp. 3–22). New York: Teachers College Press.

Effective Strategies for Involving Parents in Schools

Hilary Ward ▪ Dawn Anderson-Butcher ▪ Amber Kwiatkowski

CHAPTER 62

Getting Started

Given that parent involvement creates such beneficial outcomes (Gettinger & Guetschow, 1998; Henderson & Mapp, 2002; McKay & Stone, 2000; McNeal, 1999; Shaver & Walls, 1998), it seems strange that many schools continue to struggle with actively engaging parents as partners with schools. For instance, one elementary school serving more than 240 students in Columbus, Ohio, has only 3 members in its Parent–Teacher Organization. A different school in the community serving more than 500 middle-schoolers had only 12 parents attend parent–teacher conferences. Many schools, including these two, continue to struggle with recruiting, facilitating, and sustaining parent involvement.

What We Know

If we know that parent participation is such a powerful strategy, why is it so difficult to get parents actively engaged in schools? Although this problem can be easily discarded as the parents' lack of concern for children and schooling, nothing could be further from the truth (Christenson, 2003; Henderson & Mapp, 2002; Lawson & Briar-Lawson, 1997; Tett, 2001). Most parents want to be involved in their children's education, regardless of their race or socioeconomic status (Alameda, 2003; Cromer & Haynes, 1991; McKay & Stone, 2000; Shaver & Walls, 1998). Recruiting and retaining parents to be involved in more marginalized schools and in the education of their children, however, still proves to be an incredible challenge. Simply stated, not all parents show up at

schools and request to volunteer or engage in the ways in which schools expect them to be involved.

Creative, alternative designs are needed to recruit uninvolved parents, especially where poverty and parents representing ethnic minorities are concerned (Christenson, 2003; Lawson & Briar-Lawson, 1997; McKay & Stone, 2000). Other chapters in this volume discuss the effectiveness of parental involvement and the potential advantages of family support programs, where the school focuses on providing support to families, as well as expecting the parents to provide support to the school programs. This chapter explores several key strategies that have been shown to be essential for recruiting parents to be involved in schools (Alameda, 2003; Barton, Drake, Perez, St. Louis, & George, 2004; Christenson, 2003; Henderson & Mapp, 2002; Jacobi, Wittreich, & Hogue, 2003; Lawson & Briar-Lawson, 1997; Lynn & McKay, 2001; Raffaele & Knoff, 1999; Riggins-Newby, 2003). These strategies are grounded in new definitions of parent involvement.

Defining Parent Involvement

As discussed in other chapters, parental involvement is a broad and diverse concept that can necessitate different approaches. Strategies around parent involvement in schools are most typically defined in relation to Epstein's work (1996, 2001). The seven types of involvement she delineates are as follows: (1) Schools help families by offering parenting classes and other supports; (2) parents establish home environments to support learning; (3) effective communication is created between home and school; (4) parents volunteer in school or classrooms; (5) parents encourage learning at home by helping children with activities related to their school work; (6) parents become involved in decision making, advocacy, and committee work; and (7) parents collaborate with the community to improve education for all children.

Of these strategies, Epstein's first type of parent involvement (i.e., schools helping families) is critical to the recruitment of parents in schools within marginalized communities. As was discussed in the previous chapter, this approach is also called *family support* and is especially applicable when parents have multiple unmet needs and issues that impede their abilities to be engaged in schools and in the lives of their children. Traditional parent involvement programs initiated by schools often viewed parents as supporters of school-wide goals and student educational needs. Research identifies many limitations to this approach. Socioeconomic status, social isolation, cultural differences between parents and teachers, parents' sense of efficacy within the school, parents' educational experiences in school, parents' time commitments and family responsibilities, and race and ethnicity, if they are faced with racial discrimination, are important predictors of successful parental involvement programs (Alameda, 2003; Barton et al., 2004; Gettinger & Guetschow, 1998; Henderson & Mapp, 2002; Lynn & McKay, 2001; McNeal, 1999). Given these underlying factors that predict involvement, one of the most effective ways

to recruit parents to be involved in schools is by helping them meet their basic needs first. Figure 62.1 overviews this strategy, proposing that factors influencing parent engagement must first be addressed in order to promote traditional school- and home-based parent involvement.

Expanding the Definition of Parent Involvement

If schools are truly going to recruit all parents to be involved, they must begin addressing these underlying factors and expanding their perspectives of parent involvement.

Two-way exchanges between parents and schools that take into account the cultural, emotional, and societal issues that parents face (Barton et al., 2004) are important to engaging diverse parents in schooling. Schools must begin offering assistance, referrals, resources, and social supports to parents (Anderson-Butcher, in press; Briar-Lawson et al., 1997; Lawson & Briar-Lawson, 1997). As parent and family needs are increasingly met, parents may eventually become more engaged in schools and in their children's education. When schools are willing and able to address this aspect of the recruitment process, they send a powerful message of care and concern to parents

Figure 62.1.

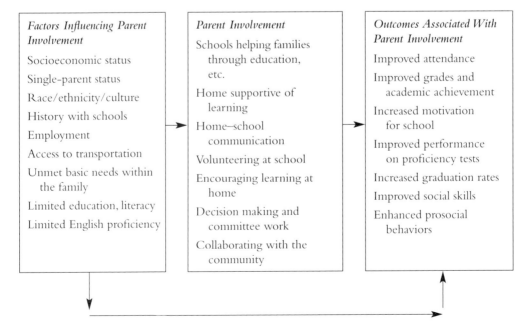

(Briar-Lawson et al., 1997; Lawson & Briar-Lawson, 1997). By addressing these needs, schools can help to increase parents' time, flexibility, skills, motivation, and energy to become involved. In essence, parents become more "recruitable" and more likely to be involved in schools in traditional ways.

What We Can Do

Steps to Recruiting Parents Through Addressing Basic Needs

Several strategies become critical to the recruitment of parents, including (1) assessing parent and family needs; (2) addressing identified needs through services and supports; (3) building relationships; (4) viewing parents as experts; (5) having parents as leaders; (6) creating spaces for parents; and (7) creating meaningful and engaging activities.

1. Assessing Parent and Family Needs

Some type of needs assessment process will be helpful to parents (Briar-Lawson et al., 1997; Chavkin & Garza-Lubeck, 1990; Jacobi et al., 2003). Several different methodologies might be used, including surveying parents, conducting focus groups, or interviewing select parent representatives from schools. Sample questions might include: What services are available to families in the community? What are parental and family needs? What are the challenges that parents and families face in accessing supports? What are the barriers to parent involvement in schools? Whatever assessment strategy is chosen, parents can be involved in the needs assessment process in creative and meaningful ways. For instance, parents might help to design the survey, determining what types of questions should be asked. They also can help to frame the questions, decide how to set up the survey items so they are easily readable and user-friendly, and determine how to get the best response rates (i.e., via phone calls, send surveys home with students, go door to door, mailings, etc.). One might also consider asking parents to help with the data collection and analysis process, thus valuing their roles as parents, experts, and leaders within the school (Kondrat & Cash, 2004; Lynn & McKay, 2001).

2. Addressing Identified Needs

Schools must address these issues by providing parents with targeted services once needs have been identified (Alameda, 2003; Anderson-Butcher, 2006; Epstein, 1996, 2001; Lawson & Briar-Lawson, 1997; McKay & Stone, 2000). Parent involvement in school now also means parents' participation in these school-linked and school-based services and supports. For instance, schools might offer General Equivalency Diploma (GED) programs, limited English proficiency classes, job training, computer classes, and literacy clubs. School-based mental health providers, health clinics, and other social service agencies might co-locate to schools, providing services onsite, where families are more likely to access them. Workshops might develop work-related competencies and life skills, allowing parents to become more employable and in turn more likely to become involved with the school (Shaver & Walls, 1998).

In addition, support service continuums within schools might be developed that link students and families to needed community resources and supports. This begins with the early identification of needs by teachers and results in referrals to school supportive service staff and other community-based services (Anderson-Butcher, in press). Student support teams and related interagency collaborations then can effectively reach out to parents and connect families to needed supports (Anderson-Butcher & Ashton, 2004).

Clearly, a variety of methods can be used to tackle the various factors that limit parent recruitment and traditional types of parent involvement. Parents will alter their perspectives toward the school, especially once the word gets out that the school, in partnership with other community-based agencies, cares about meeting student, parent, and family needs (Alameda, 1995, 2003). They will see schools and their staff as supportive, helpful, welcoming, and caring. These school attributes in turn will greatly enhance the likelihood that parents will become involved in traditional and nontraditional services offered at school.

3. Building Relationships

Parents will be more inclined to work with the schools if the schools take the time to build positive relationships with them (Chavkin &

Garza-Lubeck, 1990; Christenson, 2003; Lawson & Briar-Lawson, 1997). Schools can start developing rapport by first making positive contacts with parents. Most parents only hear from the school when their child is in trouble or is not performing well academically. Schools need to shift this paradigm so that they also communicate with parents via positive communications related to student behaviors at school (Henderson & Mapp, 2002).

This can be accomplished through a variety of methods. To name a few, teachers, administrators, and support staff can write positive newsletters related to students' achievements, provide positive phone calls to homes, encourage tours of the school, and conduct home visits to simply tell parents that they are glad their child attends the school (Henderson & Mapp, 2002; Lynn & McKay, 2001; Raffaele & Knoff, 1999). More specifically, newsletters might include stories regarding upcoming events, various classes' projects and achievements, good student reports, and how parents can support their child's learning at home (Lynn & McKay, 2001). Phone calls might describe positive student behaviors witnessed by any of the school employees (Henderson & Mapp, 2002). Teachers can also send positive progress notes home to parents, reporting good behavior and academic effort from their child.

Kumpfer and Alvarado (1998) highlight several attributes which further develop relationships and trust between school personnel and parents, including warmth, genuineness, and empathy; communication skills in presenting and listening; an openness and willingness to share; sensitivity to family and group processes; dedication to, care for, and concern about families; flexibility; humor; and credibility. These interpersonal qualities of effective service staff play a major role in building relationships between the school and parents.

4. Viewing Parents as Experts

Parents' lack of involvement in the schools can be traced back to the belief that educators and schools are the authorities on their child's education (Riggins-Newby, 2003). If schools want to recruit parents, they will have to view parents as experts in their children's education, communicating that parents' roles in the lives of their children are irreplaceable (Briar-Lawson et al., 1997; Jacobi et al., 2003; Lawson & Briar-Lawson, 1997).

One strategy that schools can employ involves holding parent–teacher conferences prior to the start of school (Jacobi et al., 2003). Here, teachers may not yet have had the opportunity to interact with the students in the classroom and hopefully have few preconceived notions regarding the students' behaviors and academic abilities. The parents will be the authority on their children and will be able to give the information they feel is pertinent regarding their children's educational needs. In this situation, parents are regarded as the experts.

An additional way to engage parents' expertise is by asking them to share their cultural traditions and skills with students at the school (Henderson & Mapp, 2002). Parents may speak to individual classes about cultural traditions and history. They might teach students how to hip-hop dance, weave baskets, or braid hair in after-school programs. Some schools take this a step further and facilitate parent-to-parent supports in the community. For instance, mothers in one community and newly immigrated refugee parents meet weekly, teaching each other about their own cultures, values, holiday traditions, and food preparation.

These and other strategies help to enhance school–family relationships and bridge the cultural gap between parents and schools (Chavkin & Garza-Lubeck, 1990). Parents have a wealth of knowledge and expertise that can be used to expand the education of students and to provide leadership and support to other families, which should be used to the fullest extent within the school.

5. Having Parents as Leaders

In addition to experts, parents also can lead efforts to recruit other parents (Briar-Lawson et al., 1997). The key is to get currently engaged parents to become actively involved in recruiting additional parents.

The first step in finding parents to be leaders involves the creation of a resource base of those parents who are already involved (Lynn & McKay, 2001; Raffaele & Knoff, 1999). The identification of some initial parents will seem obvious (i.e., the "cheerleaders"). These are the parents who are involved in the PTO, come to the parent–teacher conferences, help to run the school dances, and organize bake sales. The goal, however, is to also identify and recruit those parents who are not actively engaged in the school. Finding leaders among this group is more challenging. For this, it may be helpful to survey the school staff (teachers, coaches, aides, secretaries, etc.), asking them to list parents who have contributed to their efforts within the school. For example, school staff could name parents who have brought cookies, driven children to practices, bought gifts at holidays, made copies, or done anything else that has benefited various school efforts (e.g., Alameda, 2003). This list will give schools an idea of the parents who might be potential leaders and who can recruit other parents to be involved in the schools.

Once a list of potential parents has been created (a core of about 8–10 parents is a great start), the parents should be invited to an informational meeting related to generating parent involvement in the school (this meeting could double as a needs assessment strategy). Don't get too discouraged if only a few parents show up, as more parents will become involved as these parents recruit their friends, their children's friends' parents, and their neighbors. At this initial meeting, these parent leaders might be asked what they perceive parents want from the school, what they perceive family needs to be, what parents in the community might want to learn about, and what they might be willing to teach other parents. They also should ask parents if they would be interested in recruiting additional parents to be involved in the school.

At this point, some authors suggest that this core collection of parents receive training related to parent leadership and involvement (Alameda, 1995, 2003; Briar-Lawson et al., 1997). More specifically, parents might learn how to relate to educators, professionals, students, and other parents; might learn leadership and communication skills; and might develop problem-solving skills as they strategize about how to best reach and recruit additional parents. These skills and others will empower parents to support others in their communities, but also will empower parents to help themselves in meeting their own basic needs. Some schools have used stipends to honor parents for the work and services they provide. These stipends serve as occupational ladders into jobs as paraprofessionals, social service workers, and other helping service positions (Briar-Lawson et al., 1997).

6. Creating Spaces for Parents

While schools are creating the capacity for parent leadership and expertise, they might consider creating safe and welcoming places within the school where parents can receive communication from the school and access information about needed school and community resources. This could be set up in the form of family/parent resource centers, which send the message to parents that schools want parents involved and are willing to help families with their needs and wants (Lynn & McKay, 2001; Raffaele & Knoff, 1999; Riggins-Newby, 2003). Ideally, these centers are located within school buildings and are parent-led and parent-run. Parent liaisons (who are parents of students at the school, as opposed to professionals) staff resource centers and serve as single points of contact where other parents can go for support. These liaisons receive leadership training on how to be an advocate and support to parents. They accompany parents to meetings within the school, make home visits with school officials, and teach parents about school policies and procedures (Alameda, 2003; O'Connor, 2001). In addition, on-site services and supports from local agencies are provided at the centers; and brochures, phone numbers, and contact information for other community-based organizations are on hand for parent liaisons to distribute to interested parents (Alameda, 2003).

Resource centers also have the potential to become places where parents may give support to and receive support from other parents (Henderson & Mapp, 2002). For instance, some parents need additional supports in various personal aspects of their lives (i.e., paying bills, filling out job applications, etc.). The parent liaison and other parents at the center might assist parents with these issues, providing ongoing supports as needed within the schools.

7. Creating Meaningful and Engaging Activities

In addition to these other strategies, another key parent recruitment strategy involves offering meaningful activities in which parents can become involved (Halsey, 2004; Raffaele & Knoff, 1999). Realizing that parents will come from various skill levels and educational backgrounds, schools need to be creative in the opportunities they make available for parent involvement. They need to explore the parent and family assets and provide opportunities for parent and family involvement that match these skill sets and strengths.

One particular elementary school in Ohio valued this strategy, finding a creative way to engage even parents with limited educational backgrounds (Johnson, 2004). More specifically, this school had parents with limited literacy skills volunteer at the school by listening to students read stories aloud. These parents would challenge the students' ability to comprehend the story by asking them a variety of questions after the story was completed. At the end of the presentation, the parents would give the students standing ovations, congratulating them on their reading skills and effort.

This school found an alternative and highly meaningful way for often marginalized parents to engage "where they were at" within the school and the classroom. Additional examples of other possible ways in which parents can contribute are found in Table 62.1.

Once parents start to become involved in the schools, positive reinforcement and acknowledgment will ensure their continued support. These and other strategies, such as using certificates, stipends or honorariums and appreciation

ceremonies for parents, will increase the retention rate of parents in the school (Alameda, 2003; Briar-Lawson et al., 1997; Christenson, 2003). Furthermore, opportunities offered by and for the parents need to be fun, interactive, social, and recreational (Anderson-Butcher, Khairallah, & Race-Bigelow, 2004; Kumpfer & Alvarado, 2003). Picnics, parties, ceremonies, and fun family and community events will also help to recruit and retain parents and families (Anderson-Butcher et al., 2004; Fischer, 2003).

8. Additional Tools and Keys for Success

There are several other important factors which should be considered when recruiting parents to be involved in schools (Anderson-Butcher et al., 2004; Briar-Lawson et al., 1997; Jacobi et al., 2003; Kumpfer & Alvarado, 2003; Lawson & Briar-Lawson, 1997). These strategies target key barriers

Table 62.1 Other Meaningful Ways for Parents to Be Involved in Schools

Make phone calls to other parents for various events	Read to students
Help with crafts and other class project preplanning	Listen to students read
Recruit other parents to get involved	Support in-school suspension rooms
Invite neighbors to school events	Chaperone field trips
Pick up supplies for birthday parties	Speak at career days
Observe children in classrooms	Serve as an office assistant
Run errands for school events	Tutor children at school or in the neighborhood
Serve as a parent/teacher conference greeter	Attend parent workshops
Offer other parents support (e.g., baby-sitting)	Instruct workshops
Train children or parents on computers	Plan career days
Help run school clubs and student council meetings	Serve as a physical education instructor
Teach others about different cultures	Coordinate the school store
Coordinate newsletters	Assist in the lunchroom
Help run/facilitate boys/girls mentoring groups	Serve as a teacher aide for a day
Help set up/break down community events	Assist in the library
Decorate a classroom or bulletin board	Supervise on the playground
Serve as a fundraising drive coordinator	Coordinate food drives
Build relationships with local churches and other agencies	Organize phone trees
Organize community–school events	Facilitate family support programs
Visit neighbors and other parents	Support other parents at school conferences
Send cards to new families in the neighborhood	Help other parents with transportation
Staff the parent/family resource center	Provide birthday cards for students
Operate parent suggestion boxes	Set up car-pooling activities
Plan teacher appreciation days	Hold high expectations for the school
Network with other parents around school policies	Help other parents be better parents
Compile lists of community resources	Develop mentoring parents for parents

Sources: From Briar-Lawson et al., 1997; Chavkin & Garza-Lubeck, 1990; Christenson, 2003; Raffaele & Knoff, 1999.

related to parent recruitment and involvement and include:

- *Time*. Schedule meetings and activities right after work because once people go home, it becomes hard to leave again. Schedule breakfast meetings.
- *Location*. Place matters. Meetings and programs can be held at schools, churches, community centers, and elsewhere. Some meetings might happen at parents' place of employment.
- *Food*. Snacks and meals are great incentives for families, especially if activities are right after work so parents don't have to worry about dinner.
- *Child care*. Have teachers, students, or local agency representatives (e.g., Boys and Girls Club employees) baby-sit. Provide structured children's social and life skills programs that run simultaneously with the parents' meetings.
- *Recruitment*. Recruit participants through local recreation centers, churches, laundromats, bowling alleys, and the like. Various entities can help recruit parents in different ways.
- *Transportation*. Offer transportation to and from the school or program. Use school buses or vans from partnering community agencies.
- *Translation*. Translate materials or have people who speak the same language make contacts with parents.
- *Messenger*. Examine the strategies used to recruit parents, particularly who is relaying the message. Ask involved parents to contact and recruit other parents. Have staff from after-school programs or pastors at churches recruit parents.
- *Fun*. Make sure that parent activities also include social and recreational aspects.

Tools and Practice Examples

An example of a comprehensive parent recruitment plan exists in Columbus, Ohio, and revolves around a particular elementary school in a diverse, urban community. Approximately 50% of the students are African American, and 88.3% of the students are economically disadvantaged (Ohio Department of Education, 2004). Initially, this school had one active and two inactive members involved in its Parent–Teacher Organization. The school also had a parent liaison funded through

Title I dollars. There was limited involvement in parent-teacher conferences, classrooms, and the school in general.

The Ohio State University's P-12 Project's community and youth development partnership committee was charged with working with this school, which is adjacent to the university neighborhoods, particularly focusing on increasing parent involvement in the school and its after-school program. Members of the committee included representatives from the schools, the Boys and Girls Club, the United Way, the YWCA, local faith-based organizations, Communities in Schools, the Godman Guild, parents from the community, and faculty members from the university.

In order to better understand the needs of the families, the first thing the group did was conduct a needs assessment with the parents (Kondrat & Cash, 2004). A small group of currently involved parents was recruited and offered honorariums to support the project (honorariums were $50/month). In essence, there was a discussion about the importance of parent involvement in the school and in children's lives, as well as an overview of how many barriers and challenges exist that limit parents' ability and motivation to be truly engaged. Parents were then told that the school needed their expertise in order to truly assess parent and family needs within the school and community. Two parents and the parent liaison volunteered to help. These parents assisted in the creation of the needs assessment survey. They co-led efforts with the school and the Boys and Girls Club after-school program to organize a celebratory, end-of-the-year, community-wide event for families, where they recruited more than 75 parents to complete the surveys (parents were provided with $5 gift certificates to a grocery store to complete the survey; food was provided at the event; fun recreational activities were included). These parents then coanalyzed the data with members of the partnership committee.

After examining the results, the parents and committee members decided that one way to address the needs of parents and families was through the creation of a resource manual containing information about the various social and health services located in the neighborhoods. A 150-page resource guide was created with the direction of the parents. For example, a focus group (with food) was held with parents to discuss how the layout of the manual should look. If parents could not attend, committee members connected with these parents via phone or through home visits to get their expertise on the issue. These parents (along with friends of the original parents) are currently involved in the dissemination of this manual. They are providing input into how to best get the manual into the hands of the parents who need it most and are developing leadership strategies which involve parents in the distribution of manuals within the school and community.

Other ripple effects have occurred, where parents have learned new skills, participated in new roles, received new jobs, and engaged in new activities. To name a few, parents presented and facilitated sessions at a state-wide urban schools conference focused on addressing nonacademic barriers to learning. Parents have advocated for their own schools to be included in the P-12 Project target area. The Boys and Girls Club has successfully written a grant to fund four family liaisons charged with recruiting parents within each of their programs across the city. A master's of social work community development class was relocated to the school, focusing its mobilization strategies on engaging parents and families in new ways within the neighborhood. Relationships between parents and others in the community have been developing (one parent received support in resume and cover letter writing and now has a university faculty member to serve as a reference).

More parent involvement and leadership activities are continuing. For instance, plans are under way to develop a school-family-community coalition that focuses on strengthening the families within the neighborhood. Families and university faculty are advocating for the building of a state-of-the-art Boys and Girls Club facility in the university neighborhood. There also is discussion brewing related to the development of a time-dollar mutual support bartering system at the school (e.g., Cahn, 1998).

In summary, when parents were given the opportunity to become actively and meaningfully involved, the project took on a deeper meaning for parents, and they recruited other parents to join in the efforts. Many of the best practice strategies discussed in this chapter were used to recruit parent involvement. Parents continued their involvement and recruited others to be engaged because of the meaningful work in which they were involved and the appreciation they received for their efforts. Parent involvement at the school and in the community has been redefined, and parents are more involved in the school as a result.

Key Points to Remember

Involving parents in schools is challenging, especially given the many barriers that parents face today. A new expanded model of parent involvement, one in which schools ask how they can support parents as opposed to how parents can support schools, will help with parent recruitment and retention. This chapter provides several strategies that can be used within this new parent involvement framework. Several questions may also guide the thought process, including: Does the school have opportunities to involve parents? How does the school make parents feel welcomed at the school? Does the school examine how it can support families and parents? Does the school respond to identified parent and family needs? Does the school allow parents to have leadership roles? Are there chances for parents to become meaningfully involved? Have parent leadership classes been offered? Is there space in the school to allow parents to have their own area? Have parents been offered opportunities to expand their skills? Are parents valued as experts in their children's education? Has the school made a concerted effort to build relationships with parents? Are common barriers to parent involvement (e.g., transportation, child care, time) being addressed?

These questions and others may help schools to creatively think through the best ways in which they can involve parents. As new strategies are developed, and schools begin exploring how they can support families, parents will in turn be more likely to engage in their children's education and the school in general. The end result of these efforts will include better outcomes for youth, families, and schools.

References

Alameda, T. (1995). The healthy learners project: Bringing the community into the school. In K. Hooper-Briar & H. A. Lawson (Eds.), *Expanding partnerships for vulnerable children, youth and families* (pp. 46–56). Alexandria, VA: Council on Social Work Education.

Alameda, T. (2003). *Empowerment, social support, and self-esteem of parents involved in an elementary school program.* Unpublished doctoral dissertation, Florida International University, Miami.

Anderson-Butcher, D. (2006). Building effective family support programs and interventions. In C. Franklin, M. Harris, & P. Allen-Meares (Eds.), *The school services sourcebook.* New York: Oxford University Press.

Anderson-Butcher, D. (in press). The role of the educator in early identification, referral and linkage. In R. J. Waller (Ed.), *Child and adolescent mental health issues in the classroom.* Thousand Oaks, CA: Sage.

Anderson-Butcher, D., & Ashton, D. (2004). Innovative models of collaboration to serve children, youth, families, and communities. *Children & Schools, 26*(1), 39–53.

Anderson-Butcher, D., Khairallah, A., & Race-Bigelow, J. (2004). An in-depth examination of a mutual support group for long-term Temporary Assistance for Needy Families recipients. *Social Work, 49*(1), 131–140.

Barton, A. C., Drake, C., Perez, J. G., St. Louis, K., & George, M. (2004). Ecologies of parental engagement in urban education. *Educational Researcher, 33*(4), 3–12.

Briar-Lawson, K., Lawson, H. A., Rooney, B. J., Hansen, V., White, L. G., Radina, E., & Herzog, K. L. (1997). *From parent involvement to parent empowerment and family support: A resource guide for school community leaders.* Oxford, OH: Institute for Educational Renewal, Miami University.

Cahn, E. (1998). *Time dollars.* Chicago: Family Resource Coalition of America.

Chavkin, N. F., & Garza-Lubeck, M. (1990). Multicultural approaches to parent involvement: Research and practice. *Social Work in Education, 13*(1), 22–34.

Christenson, S. L. (2003). The family-school partnership: An opportunity to promote the learning competence of all students. *School Psychology Quarterly, 18*(4), 454–482.

Cromer, J. P., & Haynes, N. M. (1991). Parent involvement in schools: An ecological approach. *Elementary School Journal, 91*(3), 271–278.

Epstein, J. L. (1996). Perspectives and preview on research and policy for school, family, and community partnerships. In T. Alameda (2003). *Empowerment, social support, and self-esteem of parent involved in an elementary school program.* Unpublished doctoral dissertation, Florida International University, Miami.

Epstein, J. (2001). *School, family, and community partnerships: Preparing educators and improving schools.* Boulder, CO: Westview Press.

Fischer, R. L. (2003). School-based family support: Evidence from an exploratory field study. *Families in Society: The Journal of Contemporary Human Services, 84*(3), 339–347.

Gettinger, M., & Guetschow, K. W. (1998). Parental involvement in schools: Parent and teacher perceptions of roles, efficacy, and opportunities. *Journal of Research and Development in Education, 32*(1), 38–52.

Halsey, P. A. (2004). Nurturing parent involvement: Two middle level teachers share their secrets. *Clearing House, 77*(4), 135–137.

Henderson, A. T., & Mapp, K. L. (2002). *A new wave of evidence: The impact of school, family, and community connections on student achievement.* Austin, TX: National Center for Family and Community Connections with Schools, Southwest Education Developmental Laboratory.

Jacobi, E. F., Wittreich, Y., & Hogue, I. (2003). Parental involvement for a new century. *New England Readers Association Journal, 39*(3), 11–16.

Johnson, J. (2004, April). *Addressing non-academic barriers within schools.* Paper presented at the New Models for Urban School Improvement: Addressing Barriers to Academic Achievement and Successful Schools, Urban Schools Conference, Columbus, OH.

Kondrat, D., & Cash, S. (2004). *Exploring community and parent involvement in the university district neighborhood.* Columbus: Ohio State University P-12 Project.

Kumpfer, K. L., & Alvarado, R. (1998, November). *Effective family strengthening interventions.* Washington, DC: U.S. Department of Justice, Office of Justice Programs, Office of Juvenile Justice and Delinquency Prevention.

Kumpfer, K. L., & Alvarado, R. (2003). Family-strengthening approaches for the prevention of youth problem behaviors. *American Psychologist, 58*(6–7), 457–465.

Lawson, H., & Briar-Lawson, K. (1997). *Connecting the dots: Progress toward the integration of school reform, school-linked services, parent involvement, and community schools.* Oxford, OH: Institute for Educational Renewal, Miami University.

Lynn, C. J., & McKay, M. M. (2001). Promoting parent-school involvement through collaborative practice models. *School Social Work Journal, 26*(1), 1–14.

McKay, M. M., & Stone, S. (2000). Influences on urban parent involvement: Evidence from the national education longitudinal study. *School Social Work Journal, 25*(1), 16–30.

McNeal, R. B. (1999). Parental involvement as social capital: Differential effectiveness on science achievement, truancy and dropping out. *Social Forces, 78,* 117–144.

O'Connor, S. (2001). Voices of parents and teachers in a poor white urban school. *Journal of Education for Students Placed at Risk, 6*(3), 175–198.

Ohio Department of Education. (2004). *School report card.* Available: http://www.ode.state.oh.us/reportcardfiles/2002–2003/BUILD/024034.pdf.

Raffaele, L. M., & Knoff, H. M. (1999). Improving home-school collaboration with disadvantaged families: Organizational principals, perspectives, and approaches. *School Psychology Review, 28*(3), 448–466.

Riggins-Newby, C. G. (2003). Families as partners: Urban principals respond. *Educational Digest, 68*(8), 23–25.

Shaver, A. V., & Walls, R. T. (1998). Effects of Title I parent involvement on student reading and mathematics achievement. *Journal of Research and Development in Education, 31*(2), 90–97.

Tett, L. (2001). Parents as problems or parents as people? Parental involvement programs, schools and adult educators. *International Journal of Lifelong Education, 20*(3), 188–198.

Building Effective Family Support Programs and Interventions

Dawn Anderson-Butcher

CHAPTER 63

Getting Started

Family support and parent involvement strategies are typically categorized as either school- or home-based (Alameda, 2003). Parents volunteer in classrooms, serve in decision-making and leadership roles, and attend parent–teacher conferences and other school events. Parents also provide home environments that are supportive of classroom instruction, encourage their children's learning at school, and communicate regularly with teachers about what happens during the school day. As was discussed in chapters 61 and 62, parent involvement strategies are most important and have been linked to enhanced academic achievement, attendance in school, prosocial behavior, social skills, and other positive outcomes (Alameda, 2003; Epstein, 1996; Henderson & Mapp, 2002; McNeal, 1999).

Although parent involvement as typically defined is central to student learning and overall school success, many parents do not have the skills, motivation, or time to participate in their children's schools in these traditional ways (Alameda, 2003; Briar-Lawson et al., 1997). Family support programming is one emergent parent involvement strategy that expands the definition of family–school partnerships by taking these various challenges and barriers into account. Family support includes the provision of direct services to families, as well as the creation of family events and activities that encourage positive interactions among children, parents, and schools. This strategy involves providing services that strengthen the capacity of parents to support their children's healthy development (Layzer, Goodson, Bernstein, & Price, 2001). Chapter 62 discusses this approach from the perspective of parental recruitment into the programs. The current chapter focuses on many of the issues that are important to the success of the family support strategy.

What We Know

Family support interventions have incorporated the following activities into their program designs in the past (Anderson-Butcher, Khairallah, & Race-Bigelow, 2004; Briar-Lawson et al., 1997; Family Resource Coalition, 2004; Fischer, 2003; Kumpfer & Alvarado, 2003; Lawson & Briar-Lawson, 1997):

- Life skills training, including family literacy, adult education, employment or vocational training, and skill-building activities focused on problem solving, stress reduction, and communication
- Parent and family education classes aiming to teach child development, family management styles, and parent-child communication skills
- Parent and family support groups that allow parents the opportunities to share their experiences and build social support networks
- Family activities, cultural events, and recreational sports that provide opportunities for parents to spend more time with their children
- Family resource center design principles which allow for parental drop-in time and on-site informal assistance and support
- Information and referral services that link families with needed resources in schools and communities
- Occupational and educational ladders for parents, allowing for the development of work-related skills and assets
- Crisis intervention and family counseling that address specific family or child concerns

• Auxiliary support services, such as clothing exchanges, cash assistance, emergency food, and transportation

The effectiveness of these family support activities is well documented in the literature. For instance, Comer and Fraser (1998) found that family support programs contributed to gains in child development, educational attainment, and academic performance, while they also enhanced supportive home environments, parent-child interactions, health outcomes, and adult learning. Reynolds, Temple, Robertson, and Mann (2001) showed that family support in early childhood interventions reduced dropouts and juvenile arrests and increased retention and graduation rates. Fischer (2003) found that child participants in family support programs had significantly decreased behavioral problems, and families increased their sense of cohesion and adaptability. Others have described the prevention of problem behaviors and conduct disorders via family support (Anderson-Butcher et al., 2004; Kumpfer & Alvarado, 2003; Tobler & Kumpfer, 2000).

Given these benefits for children and families, family support programs and interventions have emerged as key parent involvement strategies within schools. The following best practice strategies should guide family support program designs.

What We Can Do

Below are some descriptions of the characteristics of effective family support programs, based on best practice strategies.

Addressing Family Needs

Through family support, teachers and other school personnel no longer just ask how parents can help the school. They begin thinking about what the school can do to help and support its parents (Briar-Lawson et al., 1997; Lawson & Briar-Lawson, 1997). As such, effective family support programs address the basic needs of families (Epstein, 1996, 2001). They do not solely focus on how parents can support schools and teachers through volunteerism, leadership, and monitoring children.

Links to the Community

Programs address identified family needs through their linkages to the community (Schorr, 1997; Weissbourd & Weiss, 1992). For instance, family support involves providing GED programs, limited English proficiency and literacy classes, job training, parenting education, and computer classes—all programs designed to address family needs. School-linked services connect families to cash assistance, children's health insurance programs, food banks, faith-based organizations, and other needed community resources. School-based family resource centers with on-site services and supports are created (Briar-Lawson et al., 1997; Dryfoos, 1994; Family Resource Coalition, 2004; Lawson & Briar-Lawson, 1997). Both formal and informal resources are mobilized in support of families (Family Support America, 2003; Wituk, Shepherd, Slavich, Warren, & Meissen, 2000).

Social Support/Mutual Support

The basic premise behind family support programs is that they do just that: support families. Effective programs, however, do more than support families through the provision of services. They build informal mutual support networks where parents receive social support, while simultaneously providing support to others (Anderson-Butcher et al., 2004; Riessman, 1997). Toward this end, programs strengthen social capital, build social support networks, strengthen a sense of community, and reduce social isolation and exclusion (Alameda, 2003; Family Support America, 2003; McDonald & Frey, 1999; McNeal, 1999). Families become resources to other families; friendships and interrelationships are built; and informal networks among community members are developed. These social supports in turn are preconditions to enhancing parent functioning (Powell, 1989), increasing parent involvement in low-income communities (Alameda, 2003; Kieth, 1996), and providing parents with the confidence and strength to maneuver within their environments (Alameda, 2003).

Multiple Components Aimed to Build Skill Sets

Quality family support programs are grounded in ecological perspectives, proposing that influences in the community, family, school, and peer/individual systems affect youth and family outcomes. As such, they target these multiple settings and domains, addressing the multiple risk and protective factors related to healthy youth and families (Cash & Anderson-Butcher, in press; DeMarsh & Kumpfer, 1985; Kumpfer & Alvarado, 2003). In addition, specific skill sets are developed across these systems (Kumpfer & Alvarado, 2003). For instance, programs incorporate strategies that simultaneously enhance parent and child social skills, address family conflict and management, build parent–child communication, enhance connections to schools and teachers, build social support, and strengthen a sense of community and social capital (Kumpfer & Alvarado, 2003).

Similarly, effective family support programs do not solely focus on children's needs, particularly their academic needs (Alameda, 2003). Since children are parts of family systems, programs must be family-centered, as opposed to child-centered or even parent-centered in isolation (Dunst, 1995; Family Support America, 2003; Hess, McGowan, & Botsko, 2000; Kumpfer & Alvarado, 2003). The needs of both the parent and the child are balanced (Powell, 1989). Therefore, programs focus on developing needed skills among the children and parents in developmentally appropriate ways (e.g., Alvarado, Kendall, Beesley, & Lee-Cavaness, 2000; Kumpfer & Alvarado, 2003), as well as focusing on family dynamics and interactions.

Family-Centered Programs and Parents as Equal Partners

Effective programs value parents and families as experts as they create equal relations between parents and program staff (Alameda, 2003; Alameda & Lawson, 2000; Anderson-Butcher et al., 2004; Briar-Lawson et al., 1997; Family Support America, 2003; Lawson & Briar-Lawson, 1997; Powell, 1989). For instance, collaborative processes are used where people identify their prioritized needs and develop their own solutions (Kumpfer & Alvarado, 2003; Webster-Stratton & Herbert, 1994). Families are met "where they are," and professionals strive to understand parents' and children's perspectives and wishes (Christenson, 2003). Ideal programs are family-created and -owned (Anderson-Butcher & Ashton, 2004; Briar-Lawson et al., 1997). A significant aspect of the program is prioritizing open-ended parent-dominated discussion (Powell, 1989). Parents organize the programs, determine activities and topics, serve as leaders and facilitators, and drive the program agendas. Some parents may receive stipends and honorariums in support of their

leadership and involvement (Anderson-Butcher et al., 2004; Lawson & Hooper-Briar, 1994).

Cultural Sensitivity

Quality family support programs understand and appreciate cultural sensitivity, cultural capital, and diversity. They realize that many minority groups have adopted oppositional, suspicious approaches to social institutions such as schools (Ogbu, 1978; Winters, 1993). Quality family support programs are mindful of these coping strategies; affirm families' cultural, racial, and linguistic identities (Alameda & Lawson, 2000; Family Support America, 2003); and tailor program designs and strategies to the cultural traditions of families (Kumpfer & Alvarado, 1998).

Build Relationships With Parents and Families

Families, parents, and children must feel included, welcomed, and comfortable within the programs (Anderson-Butcher et al., 2004). Relationships among key staff and family members must be developed; trust and respect must be built and earned (Anderson-Butcher et al., 2004; Henderson & Mapp, 2002). More specifically, Kumpfer and Alvarado (1998) describe nine staff characteristics and skills that are needed for program effectiveness: warmth, genuineness, and empathy; communication skills in presenting and listening; openness and willingness to share; sensitivity to family and group processes; dedication to, care for, and concern about families; flexibility; humor; credibility; and personal experience with children as a parent or childcare provider. Certain qualities are needed in a good leader or staff person, too. For instance, individuals implementing these programs need to be good facilitators. They need to encourage contributions from all participants; create a comfortable, welcoming, safe environment; have a willingness to help (i.e., a "whatever it takes" attitude); and follow up and be accountable to family needs (Anderson-Butcher et al., 2004).

Strengths-Based and Empowerment-Oriented Programs

Effective programs utilize empowerment-oriented and strengths-based approaches, as opposed to risk-focused and deficit-based ones (Dunst, 1995; Griffith, 1996; Kumpfer & Alvarado, 2003; MacLeod & Nelson, 2000; Riessman, 1997; Vakalahi & Khaja, 2000). They encourage participants to contribute from "where they are at." Some even partner with participants in the delivery of services, providing educational and occupational ladders as they teach active listening skills and empathy, support the development of self-esteem and -confidence, and promote leadership capacities among participants (Briar-Lawson, 2000; Briar-Lawson et al., 1997). Parents feel empowered to make a difference in the lives of their children, families, and communities. Some even seek out human service jobs after they experience successes with their roles in family support programs (Alameda & Lawson, 2000; Briar-Lawson et al., 1997).

Personal Readiness and Appropriate Fit

If programs are family-centered and responsive, most parents will welcome the services and support. Some families, however, will simply not respond to family support initiatives due to other unmet needs or related issues. For instance, the literature on programs serving high-risk populations suggests that program staff often become heavily involved in crisis intervention activities with families, as opposed to providing for mutual support and assistance (Halpern & Larner, 1988). Similarly, participants in parent support groups report that some individuals in need of more intensive supports will not benefit from the interactions (Anderson-Butcher et al., 2004). There also needs to be some level of motivation among program participants (i.e., a hint of some internal desire to help themselves; Anderson-Butcher et al., 2004; Riessman, 1997).

Some demographic variables, such as being shy, introverted, or easily intimidated, may also impede success (Anderson-Butcher et al., 2004). Further, the majority of participants in self-help and parent support groups are often female, potentially attracting those individuals who are more social in nature (Anderson-Butcher et al., 2004; Wituk et al., 2000). The match between the family support program and the targeted group is key.

Similarly, research documents that effective parent and family education and support programs target specific needs and characteristics of the population being served (Anderson-Butcher et al., 2004; Powell, 1989). Programs are matched to meet the particular needs of the parents and families, thus allowing for social homogeneity and the sharing of similar experiences and conditions (Riessman, 1997). For instance, some programs serve only families with children who have behavioral issues. Fischer (2003) found that targeting programs to families with moderate to high child behavioral problems produced the greatest program impacts (Fischer, 2003). Some programs will serve only teen parents or specific cultural groups or ethnic populations. Still others target families receiving Temporary Assistance for Needy Families (TANF) support or family preservation services. The targeting of certain populations allows participants to socialize with others like themselves, who experience similar challenges and needs (Anderson-Butcher et al., 2004).

Fun and Not All Work

The adoption of model programs assumes that more structured program designs and "cookie-cutter" interventions will create better outcomes. It is unclear, however, to what degree individuals will come to these structured, curriculum-based programs. As such, quality family support programs need to be fun, social, recreational, and "more than just a group" or program (Anderson-Butcher et al., 2004). Interactive, experiential, and engaging activities, such as role playing, modeling, and skills practicing, are incorporated into lessons and programs as opposed to didactic lecturing (Kumpfer & Alvarado, 2003). Programs need to incorporate picnics, barbecues, and other family meals; family games; and ceremonies (Anderson-Butcher et al., 2004; Fischer, 2003). These strategies are essential for recruiting and retaining participation among families.

The Earlier, the Better

Logically, it makes sense that family support programs focus on preventing problems before they arise (Kumpfer & Alvarado, 1998; MacLeod & Nelson, 2000). For instance, it is suggested that, in families characterized by dysfunction, interventions begin earlier in a child's life (Kumpfer & Alvarado, 2003; Webster-Stratton & Taylor, 2001). This allows families to develop skills and capacities for preventing and deterring further child behavioral problems and family conflict.

Flexibility and Responsiveness

Programs also are flexible and responsive to family needs (Anderson-Butcher et al., 2004; Dunst, 1995; Wituk et al., 2000). They address common barriers to participation, such as accessibility of meeting places and times, transportation, child care/baby-sitting, and costs (many programs are free; Riessman, 1997). Likewise, meals or snacks and rewards for attendance are critical incentives that support the retention of families within the programs (Kumpfer & Alvarado, 1998, 2003).

Implementation Fidelity and Best Practices

Effective programs must incorporate these best practices, providing evidence-based strategies that are known to create targeted outcomes for children, youth, and families (Family Support America, 2003; Kumpfer & Alvarado, 2003; Nation et al., 2003). This means that programs need to be of sufficient intensity and duration to create an effect (up to 50 hours of intervention for high-risk families; Kumpfer & Alvarado, 2003; Patterson & Narrett, 1990).

Other researchers recommend the adoption of research-based model programs, such as the Strengthening Families Program, multisystemic therapy, Homebuilders, Families and Schools Together (FAST), and Parents Anonymous (e.g., Alvarado et al., 2000). The assumption is this: If these research-based programs are implemented with fidelity in communities and schools, results are more likely to occur for families. This thesis also requires effective organizational structures, particularly related to program management and sustainability (Anderson-Butcher et al., 2004).

Tools and Practice Examples

What This Means for Program Implementation

In all, these best practice strategies must be incorporated into quality family support programs. School social workers and others organizing family support programs need to be mindful of these concepts as they plan and implement their interventions in the future. Table 63.1 organizes these concepts in a checklist format, allowing for examination of the degree to which program facilitators include these strategies within their practices. In addition, the following case example highlights this point.

A Case Example of Family Support and Leadership

School-family-community needs assessments in two communities in Salt Lake County, Utah, identified the need for additional family support and parent/community involvement programming. Data from one community pointed to high incidences of domestic violence, as well as large community and student concerns related to family conflict. Data from the other area documented social isolation among families, limited parent involvement in schools and in community events, high mobility rates, and limited English proficiency among students and families. Resource mapping identified gaps in family support services within these communities and noted large barriers related to access and affordability.

In response, several stakeholders in each community came together in monthly community coalitions to begin addressing these unmet family needs and community issues. The Boys and Girls Club, in partnership with the schools and other social service agencies, received funding to implement Parents Anonymous groups (an evidence-based model program) within each community. One group targeted individuals receiving temporary assistance for needy families and was co-led by a Department of Workforce Services eligibility worker and a parent who was a past recipient of cash assistance. The other group involved Hispanic parents whose children attended an underperforming Title I elementary school challenged by poverty transiency (150% mobility rate), language barriers, and other related needs. This second group was co-led by a vibrant, dedicated Boys and Girls Club social worker and a Hispanic parent leader in the community. Parents received honorariums for their leadership.

Groups were free of charge. They met weekly at local social service organizations but were integrally linked to school-based supportive service teams, local parent education classes, public service agencies, community events, and other

Table 63.1 Best Practice Strategies for Family Support Programs and Interventions

Addressing Family Needs and Wants

a. Are individual and collective family needs assessed?

b. What are the identified needs that families have in your school and community?

c. Are services and supports provided that target these identified needs?

d. What do parents want from the school or community?

e. Are strategies in place to help parents get what they want from the school or community?

Linking to the Community

a. Do you link families to formal and informal resources in the community that address their needs?

b. How are families referred to these services and supports?

c. How do families access these services and supports?

d. Do you have a place where families can get information and referral (e.g., family resource center, single points of contact)?

e. Are school-based and –linked services provided that target identified needs?

f. Is there a good understanding about the various resources available in the community?

g. Is it clear what are the current gaps in service delivery areas within the community?

Social Support/Mutual Support

a. Do families have opportunities to receive support?

b. Do families have opportunities to give support to others?

c. Are there opportunities for open discussions among parents and families?

d. Are friendships and social support networks fostered through the programs?

Multiple Components Aimed to Build Skill Sets

a. Is the program grounded in an ecological perspective, targeting community, family, school, and individual system needs?

b. Do program strategies address needs across these various domains?

c. Are connections built between and among these systems (e.g., families to schools, schools to communities)?

d. Do participants have the opportunity to learn new skills and knowledge?

e. Does the program explore family dynamics and patterns, not just focusing solely on parent or child individual needs?

(continued)

Family-Centered and Parents as Equal Partners

a. Are parents seen as experts on their children and families?
b. Do parents share in decision making?
c. Do parents have leadership roles within the programs?
d. Do parents help with program implementation?

Cultural Sensitivity

a. Do programs take into account the cultural traditions and backgrounds of participants?
b. Are program strategies mindful of cultural coping strategies?
c. Is diversity celebrated and invited?

Build Relationships

a. Are relationships built between program staff and families?
b. Do families feel welcome?
c. Do staff express warmth, genuineness, two-way communication, flexibility, humor, credibility, and the like?
d. Do staff provide safe contexts for families?

Strengths-Based and Empowerment-Oriented

a. Do programs build from parents' and families' strengths?
b. Do programs start from where the client is?
c. Are educational and occupational ladders provided to develop self-competencies among families and parents?
d. Do parents and families feel empowered to make a difference in their lives?

Personal Readiness and Fit

a. Does the program match personal and family needs?
b. Will the targeted parents best be served through family support or via some other more intensive type of intervention?
c. Are there personality variables that may impede parental and family involvement in family support?
d. Does the program target certain types of parents, children, and families (e.g., teen parents, parents on TANF)?
e. Are there commonalities among the participants?
f. Do families have similar shared experiences?

(continued)

Table 63.1 (*Continued*)

Fun and Not All Work

a. Is the program fun and interactive?
b. Are recreational activities incorporated into the program design?
c. Are experiential activities used, such as role playing, and skills practicing?

Earlier the Better

a. Does the program target family needs early on before major problems arise?
b. Are families and parents of younger children targeted?

Flexible and Responsive

a. Is transportation provided?
b. Are meeting times and locations appropriate for the targeted group?
c. Is child care provided?
d. Are programs offered free or at little cost to families?
e. Is food provided?
f. Are rewards or incentives given for active participation?

Implementation Fidelity Issues and Best Practices

a. Does the program incorporate a research–based model program into its strategy?
b. Is the program grounded in best practices in family support?
c. Is the program doing what it is supposed to be doing?
d. Is the program implemented effectively and efficiently?
e. Does the organizational structure support the implementation of the program?

needed resources in the communities. This ensured that parents in need of services received targeted support that most appropriately met their own family needs. School supportive services staff, child welfare workers, mental health providers, other social services personnel, and parents referred families to the groups. Groups ran in the evening hours in response to parent-identified scheduling needs. Dinners were provided (one group involved cultural potlucks). A children's social skills development program ran simultaneously with the parent support groups, and transportation was provided as needed. Groups were parent-led and -driven. Parents not only brought their issues and concerns to the groups for discussion, but they also shared information with other parents that they had learned to be helpful.

Often, the parents took on additional responsibilities outside of the group. For instance, parents served as neighborhood representatives and experts to the community-wide coalitions, ensuring that the goals and direction of the larger community services system were responsive to family and parent needs. They served on advisory boards within community projects, such as on the Parents Anonymous board. They actively worked to build a new state-of-the-art Boys and Girls Club across from the elementary school in one neighborhood (which housed a family resource center). Some were actively involved in recruiting new group members. Still others provided information at local human services agencies, discussed parent involvement and family-centered practice in front of legislative committees, mobilized phone trees and lobbying efforts around important family policies, and went to court with their peers. Informal helping and support systems also developed, as parents met for coffee or lunch, talked on the phone, and hosted picnics outside of the group.

The community also began to see the benefits of family support and involvement defined in these ways. Gradually, some of the parents who were leaders within these programs became paid parent liaisons at the schools, providing home visits and family supports under the direction of a school social worker at the school and district levels. Others were hired as staff at the Boys and Girls Club. Families felt more support and were more engaged in school and in their communities; parents and their children learned new skills and knowledge; and services in the community were more easily accessed by families (Anderson-Butcher et al., 2004).

Key Points to Remember

To conclude, family support programs and interventions can be effective strategies for supporting student achievement, increasing parent involvement, addressing family needs, strengthening community, and building child and parent skills and capacities (Anderson-Butcher et al., 2004; Briar-Lawson et al., 1997; Comer & Fraser, 1998; Fischer, 2003; Kumpfer & Alvarado, 2003; Reynolds et al., 2001; Tobler & Kumpfer, 2000). The use of these strategies and other family-centered collaborative practices, however, has not fully reached its potential in our service delivery systems and schools (Anderson-Butcher & Ashton, 2004; Anderson-Butcher et al., 2004; Kumpfer & Alvarado, 2003; Kurtz, 1990; Wituk et al., 2000). Given the aforementioned benefits, social workers and other counselors should begin incorporating family support within their practices in schools, thus building upon these best practice strategies and better supporting families in the communities where they work. This work begins with rethinking the questions related to family and parent involvement in schools. Schools should ask how they can support parents and families, as opposed to wondering how parents can help them. This perspective assumes that, once parent and family needs are met and families feel supported by the school and their communities, parents will in turn become more engaged with their children and within the school.

References

Alameda, T. (2003). *Empowerment, social support, and self-esteem of parents involved in an elementary school program*. Unpublished doctoral dissertation, Florida International University, Miami.

Alameda, T., & Lawson, M. (2000, September). *Facilitating consumer-run school community initiatives*. Paper presented at the New Century Child Welfare and Family Support National Conference, Snowbird, UT.

Alvarado, R., Kendall, K., Beesley, S., & Lee-Cavaness, C. (2000). *Strengthening America's families: Model family programs for substance abuse and delinquency prevention*. Salt Lake City: Department of Health Promotion and Education, University of Utah.

Alvarado, R., & Kumpfer, K. (2000). Strengthening America's families. *Juvenile Justice, 7*(3), 8–18.

Anderson-Butcher, D., & Ashton, D. (2004). Innovative models of collaboration to serve children, youth, families, and communities. *Children & Schools, 26*(1), 39–53.

Anderson-Butcher, D., Khairallah, A., & Race-Bigelow, J. (2004). An in-depth examination of a mutual support group for long-term, Temporary Assistance for Needy Families recipients. *Social Work, 49*(1), 131–140.

Anderson-Butcher, D., Lawson, H. A., & Barkdull, C. (2003). An evaluation of child welfare design teams in four states. *Journal of Health and Social Policy, 15*(3–4), 131–161.

Andrews, D. W. (2003, February). *Selecting evidence-based practices: What constitutes evidence?* Workshop presented at the Alternative Education Summit, Columbus, OH.

Briar-Lawson, K. (1999). Impact of welfare reform on children, parents, teachers, and schools: Interprofessional challenges and opportunities. *Teacher Education Quarterly, 26*(4), 159–172.

Briar-Lawson, K. (2000). Integrating employment, economic supports, and family capacity building. In A. Sallee, H. Lawson, & K. Briar-Lawson (Eds.), *Innovative practices with children and families* (pp. 13–31). Dubuque, IA: Bowers.

Briar-Lawson, K., Lawson, H. A., Collier, C., & Joseph, A. (1997). School-linked comprehensive services: Promising beginnings, lessons learned, and future challenges. *Social Work in Education, 19*(3), 136–148.

Cahn, E. (1998). *Time dollars.* Chicago: Family Resource Coalition of America.

Cash, S. J., & Anderson-Butcher, D. (in press). Supporting at-risk youth and their families in the community. In C. McCauly & P. Pecora (Eds.), *Enhancing the well-being of children and families through effective interventions: UK and USA evidence for practice.* London & Philadelphia: Kingsley.

Catalano, R. F., Berglund, M. L., Ryan, J. A. M., Lonczak, H. S., & Hawkins, J. D. (2002). Positive youth development in the United Sates: Research findings on evaluations of positive youth development programs. *Prevention & Treatment, 5.*

Christenson, S. L. (2003). The family-school partnership: An opportunity to promote the learning competence of all students. *School Psychology Quarterly, 18*(4), 454–482.

Collins, M. C. (1978). *Child abuser: A study of child abusers in self-help group therapy.* Littleton, MA: Publishing Sciences Group.

Comer, E. W., & Fraser, M. W. (1998). Evaluation of six family support programs: Are they effective? *Families in Society: The Journal of Contemporary Human Services, 79*(2), 134–148.

Constantino, V., & Nelson, G. (1995). Changing relationship between self-help groups and mental health professionals: Shifting ideology and power. *Canadian Journal of Community Mental Health, 14*(2), 55–70.

DeMarsh, J. P., & Kumpfer, K. L. (1985). Family-oriented interventions for the prevention of chemical dependency in children and adolescents. *Journal*

of Children in Contemporary Society: Advances in Theory and Applied Research, 18,* 117–152.

Dryfoos, J. G. (1994). *Full service schools: A revolution in health and social services for children, youth, and families.* San Francisco: Jossey-Bass.

Dunst, C. (1995). *Key characteristics and features of community-based family support programs.* Chicago: Family Support America.

Epstein, J. L. (1996). Perspectives and preview on research and policy for school, family, and community partnerships. In A. Booth & J. Dunn (Eds.), *Family-school links: How do they affect educational outcomes?* (pp. 209–246). Mahwah, NJ: Erlbaum.

Epstein, J. (2001). *School, family, and community partnerships: Preparing educators and improving schools.* Boulder, CO: Westview Press.

Family Resource Coalition. (2004). *Family support programs and the prevention of child abuse.* Available: http://www.fww.org/articles/misc/frc.htm.

Family Support America. (2003). *Guidelines for family support practice* (2nd ed.). Chicago: Author.

Fischer, R. L. (2003). School-based family support: Evidence from an exploratory field study. *Families in Society: The Journal of Contemporary Human Services, 84*(3), 339–347.

Griffith, J. (1996). Relationship of parental involvement, empowerment, and school traits to student academic performance. *Journal of Educational Research, 90,* 33–41.

Halpern, R., & Larner, M. (1988). The design of family support programs in high risk communities: Lessons learned from the child survival/Fair Start Initiative. In D. R. Powell (Ed.), *Parent education as early childhood intervention* (pp. 181–207). Norwood, NJ: Ablex.

Henderson, A. T., & Mapp, K. L. (2002). *A new wave of evidence: The impact of school, family, and community connections on student achievement.* Austin, TX: National Center for Family and Community Connections with Schools, Southwest Educational Developmental Laboratory.

Hess, P. M., McGowan, B. G., & Botsko, M. (2000). A preventive services program model for preserving and supporting families over time. *Child Welfare, 79*(3), 227–265.

Kieth, N. (1996). Can urban school reform and community development be joined: The potential of community schools. *Education and Urban Society, 28,* 237–268.

Kumpfer, K. L., & Alvarado, R. (1998, November). *Effective family strengthening interventions.* Washington, DC: U.S. Department of Justice, Office of Justice Programs, Office of Juvenile Justice and Delinquency Prevention.

Kumpfer, K. L., & Alvarado, R. (2003). Family-strengthening approaches for the prevention of youth problem behaviors. *American Psychologist, 58*(6–7), 457–465.

Kurtz, L. F. (1990). The self-help movement: Review of the past decade of research. *Social Work with Groups, 13*(3), 101–115.

Lawson, H., & Briar-Lawson, K. (1997). *Connecting the dots: Progress toward the integration of school reform, school-linked services, parent involvement, and community schools.* Oxford, OH: Institute for Educational Renewal, Miami University.

Lawson, H. A., Anderson-Butcher, D., Peterson, N., & Barkdull, C. (2003). Design teams as learning systems for complex systems change: Evaluation data and implications for higher education. *Journal of Human Behavior and the Social Environment, 7*(1–2), 159–180.

Lawson, H. A., & Hooper-Briar, K. (1994). *Serving children, youth and families through interprofessional collaboration and service integration: A framework for action.* The Danforth Foundation and The Institute for Educational Renewal at Miami University.

Layzer, J. I., Goodson, B., Bernstein, L., & Price, C. (2001). *National evaluation of family support programs: Vol. A. The meta-analysis.* Cambridge, MA: Abt Associates.

MacLeod, J., & Nelson, G. (2000). Programs for the promotion of family wellness and the prevention of child maltreatment: A meta-analytic review. *Child Abuse & Neglect, 24*(9), 1127–1149.

McDonald, L., & Frey, H. (1999). *Families and schools together: Building relationships.* Washington, DC: U.S. Department of Justice.

McNeal, R. B. (1999). Parental involvement as social capital: Differential effectiveness on science achievement, truancy and dropping out. *Social Forces, 78,* 117–144.

Nation, M., Crusto, C., Wandersman, A., Kumpfer, K. L., Seybolt, D., Morrissey-Kane, E., & Davino, K. (2003). What works in prevention: Principles of effective prevention programs. *American Psychologist, 58,* 449–456.

Ogbu, J. U. (1978). *Minority education and caste: The American system in cross-cultural perspective.* New York: Academic Press.

Patterson, G. R., & Narrett, C. M. (1990). The development of a reliable and valid treatment program for aggressive young children. *International Journal of Mental Health, 19*(3), 19–26.

Powell, D. R. (1989). *Families and early childhood programs.* Washington, DC: National Association for the Education of Young Children.

Reynolds, A. J., Temple, J. A., Robertson, D. L., & Mann, E. (2001). Long-term effects of an early childhood intervention on educational achievement and juvenile arrest: A 15-year follow up of low-income children in public schools. *Journal of the American Medical Association, 285*(18), 2339–2346.

Riessman, F. (1997). Ten self-help principles. *Social Policy,* Spring, 6–11.

Schorr, L. B. (1997). *Common purpose: Strengthening families and neighborhoods to rebuild America.* New York: Anchor.

Tobler, N., & Kumpfer, K. L. (2000). *Meta-analysis of effectiveness of family-focused substance abuse prevention programs.* Rockville, MD: Center for Substance Abuse Prevention.

Vakalahi, H. F., & Khaja, K. (2000). Parent to parent and family to family: Innovative self-help and mutual support. In A. Sallee, H. Lawson, & K. Briar-Lawson (Eds.), *Innovative practices with children and families* (pp. 271–290). Dubuque, IA: Bowers.

Webster-Stratton, C., & Herbert, M. (1994). *Troubled families, problem children: Working with parents: A collaborative process.* Chichester, England: Wiley.

Webster-Stratton, C., & Taylor, T. (2001). Nipping early risk factors in the bud: Preventing substance abuse, delinquency, and violence in adolescence through interventions targeted at young children (0–8 years). *Prevention Science, 2,* 165–192.

Weissbourd, B., & Weiss, H. (1992). Basic principles of family support programs. In M. L. Allen, P. Brown, & B. Finlay (Eds.), *Helping children by strengthening families: A look at family support programs.* Washington, DC: Children's Defense Fund Programs and Research.

Winters, W. (1993). *African American mothers and urban schools: The power of participation.* New York: Lexington Books.

Wituk, S., Shepherd, M. D., Slavich, S., Warren, M. L., & Meissen, G. (2000). A topography of self help groups: An empirical analyses. *Social Work, 45*(2), 151–156.

Best Models of Family Therapy

CHAPTER 64

Cindy Carlson

Getting Started

The link between children's school-related be-havior and the home environment is well estab-lished in research (e.g., Ryan, Adams, Gulotta, Weissberg, & Hampton, 1995). Parental compe-tence, quality of family relationships, and family stability predict a wide range of child and adoles-cent behaviors including, but not limited to, de-pression (Hammen, Rudolph, Weisz, Rao, & Burge, 1999), conduct disorders (Patterson, Dish-ion, & Bank, 1984), peer associations (Brown, Mounts, Lamborn, & Steinberg, 1993), and school performance (Christenson, Rounds, & Gorney, 1992; Dornbusch, Ritter, Leiderman, Roberts, & Fraleigh, 1987; Roesner, Eccles, & Freedman-Doan, 1999). A key factor in adolescent risk is the cumulative impact of the multiple family transi-tions associated with the dissolution of partner-ships and the repartnering of parents (Greene et al., 2003). The home lives of children today are also characterized by an unprecedented diversity of living arrangements. The 2000 Census docu-mented increases in rates of births to unmarried adolescent mothers, grandparents raising children, father-headed single-parent homes, and cohabita-tion as a precursor or substitute for marriage (U.S. Bureau of the Census, 2003). Each family struc-ture poses unique challenges to caretakers and children (Carlson & Trapani, in press; Entwisle & Alexander, 2000).

The impact of family relationships on the school-related functioning of children argues for a consideration of family-based models of interven-tion (hereafter termed family intervention) in the treatment of school problems. Family intervention "is defined broadly as a therapeutic process that helps modify individuals' psychological distress by targeting their interpersonal relationships within

the family" (Sanders, 1998, p. 427). Family inter-vention models share the assumption, rooted in systems theory, that a child's problem behaviors are related to interaction patterns within the key social systems in which the child actively partici-pates. Family intervention targets the family rela-tionship patterns that are determined through assessment to cause, maintain, or exacerbate the child's problematic functioning. Family relation-ship patterns are the priority for change because the family is viewed to be the social system with the most pervasive, emotional, and long-standing impact on the lives of children. Family interven-tion models frequently incorporate, however, an ecological perspective that recognizes the influ-ence on children's behavior of interaction patterns within other social systems, such as the school, peer group, and larger community. Models may have procedures designed to directly intervene in the multiple social systems of the child, or family intervention may be used as one component of a multicomponent treatment directed toward child or adolescent disorders.

Although few educators would argue with the notion that when children and adolescents come to school, they bring the stress or support from their family relationships with them, family inter-vention is rarely a mental health option that is available in the school setting. School-based men-tal health workers more commonly recommend to parents with troubled children that they seek family intervention from an outside source. This chapter seeks to assure, therefore, that school mental health personnel are equipped to make referrals to professionals who use empirically sup-ported family intervention models in their prac-tice, in particular those that are effective in changing the school behavior of children and ado-lescents. With the hope that family intervention will increasingly become a part of school-based mental health services, this chapter will also highlight a promising evidence-based family intervention program currently operating in the schools.

What We Know

Several recent reviews have examined the evidence base for family intervention as a method of treatment for child and adolescent disorders (Carr, 2000; Cottrell & Boston, 2002; Liddle & Rowe, 2005; Sanders, 1998; Sexton & Alexander, 2002). It is important to note that most of these reviews adopt a broad definition of family intervention that includes both family therapy, where the child is present with parents and siblings in treatment and the target for change is all of the relevant relationships in the family system, and variants of parent management training (PMT) programs where treatment is provided to the parent and the goal of change is specifically the parent–difficult child relationship dyad. With this caveat in mind, the consensus of the cited reviews is that the evidence is well established for the effectiveness of family intervention as a treatment for behavior problems in children, and, among adolescents, family intervention is effective as a treatment for conduct disorders and substance abuse problems. The evidence is promising, but not well established, for the enhanced effectiveness of child-focused treatments for anxiety, depression, eating disorders, and chronic illness, when a parent or family treatment component is included (Cottrell & Boston, 2002; Liddle & Rowe, 2005). Although parents report a change in their attitudes, there is little evidence to support that published parent education programs directly affect change in the behavior of either parents or children (Sanders, 1998).

Existing reviews of family intervention efficacy concur that PMT has received the most empirical investigation and support as a treatment for children's behavior problems (Carr, 2000; Cottrell & Boston, 2002; Liddle & Rowe, 2005; Sanders, 1998). PMT applies social learning principles to the enhancement of parents' skills with the goal of reducing coercive, ineffective parent–child interaction cycles. Patterson and colleagues have demonstrated the effectiveness of PMT with a range of ages and samples and its superiority in changing children's behavior compared with standard family therapy, peer group intervention, no

treatment, community services as usual, and attention-placebo conditions (Bank et al., 1991). Behavioral family intervention (BFI) (e.g., Sayger, Horne, Walker, & Passmore, 1988), which applies social learning principles to treatment of the family as a whole, also has demonstrated effectiveness in producing long-term changes in children's behavior (Carr, 2000; Sanders, 1998). Although PMT and BFI demonstrate strong evidence as effective treatments for child and preadolescent behavior problems, these models have not been as successful with adolescent populations (Cottrell & Boston, 2002; Sanders, 1998).

Several models of family intervention show strong evidence in clinical trials as being efficacious for the treatment of adolescent conduct problems and substance abuse (Liddle & Rowe, 2005; Sexton & Alexander, 2002). Family intervention models with an established evidence base for treatment of adolescent conduct and substance abuse problems include functional family therapy (Sexton & Alexander, 2003), multidimensional family therapy (Liddle, 2003), multisystemic therapy (Sheidow, Henggeler, & Schoenwald, 2003), and brief strategic family therapy (Szapocznik, Hervis, & Schwartz, 2003). These treatment models differ from the PMT approach in significant ways: (a) the target of change is the larger matrix of family relationships, not just the conflicted parent–child dyad; (b) there is often an emphasis on emotional, as well as behavioral, processes; (c) interventions are commonly broadened to include other relevant social systems; and (d) particular attention may be paid to strategies of engagement in treatment. These family intervention model strategies reflect the importance of acknowledging the adolescent as a partner in the therapeutic process, as well as the larger role of the peer group in the maintenance of adolescent problems.

In summary, a review of the empirical evidence for family intervention as a treatment for the problems of children and adolescents finds that behavioral approaches, both PMT and BFI, are effective in changing the behavior problems of children and preadolescents, whereas the conduct-related problems of adolescents, including substance abuse, are more effectively treated with family therapy models that also consider the broader ecological context. The clear difference between family-based models with strong evidence in effecting change in children versus adolescents highlights the importance of appropriately matching family interventions to developmental stage.

One notable limitation evident in reviews of family intervention efficacy is the lack of attention to the effectiveness of family interventions to specifically produce a change in school behavior. A recent review by the author and colleagues revealed that school outcomes are infrequently measured in clinical trials of the efficacy of family intervention, especially family therapy models (Valdez, Carlson, & Zanger, in press). Three family therapy models were identified for which school outcomes were measured: multisystemic therapy, multidimensional family therapy, and social learning (behavioral) family therapy.

The next section briefly describes several family therapy models that demonstrate the strongest empirical support for changing the behavior of children or adolescents. Family interventions that are addressed in other chapters in this volume are only briefly described, whereas the procedures for models that are not covered elsewhere are provided. Parent-focused interventions, such as parent management training, are not discussed further as these procedures are discussed elsewhere in this volume.

What We Can Do

Four family therapy models are discussed below that have strong evidence of effectiveness in multiple randomized controlled trials for the treatment of adolescent conduct and substance abuse problems. All models have demonstrated high engagement and retention rates, effectiveness with multiethnic populations, and cost effectiveness of treatment compared with usual community services. In addition, two of the four models provide evidence that treatment directed toward the family results in a change, as well, in the school-related behavior of the adolescent. A fifth school-based family-centered prevention model completes the discussion.

Multisystemic Therapy

Multisystemic therapy (MST) (Sheidow, Henggeler, & Schoenwald, 2003) is a family-based, comprehensive, multisetting intervention for adolescents with chronic behavior problems and serious emotional disturbance. It also has demonstrated efficacy with juvenile sex offenders and family

maltreatment. The model is based theoretically in family systems theory and social ecological theory. At the family level, MST seeks to reduce family conflict and ineffective communication, while improving cohesion, discipline, and parental monitoring; treatment may target parental or marital functioning if deemed related to the youth's problems. MST therapists also typically target peer-level factors, such as affiliation with deviant peers, lack of association with prosocial peers, and poor socialization skills. Finally, MST seeks to improve communication between caregivers and school personnel. All targets for change by MST have been found in research to mediate the adolescent's antisocial behavior. MST has demonstrated effectiveness in improving family relations and increasing school attendance across multiple studies (e.g., Brown, Henggeler, Schoenwald, Brondino, & Pickrel, 1999). MST has demonstrated effectiveness in reducing antisocial behavior, such as criminal activity, violence, and alcohol and drug use for up to 3 years posttreatment; MST reduced hospitalization and out-of-home placement for serious emotional disturbance and reduced recidivism for juvenile sex offenders. MST was more effective than behavioral parent training in improving parent–child interactions related to child abuse. MST is a family intervention model with demonstrated effects on school behavior.

Multidimensional Family Therapy

Multidimensional family therapy (MDFT) (Liddle, 2003) is an integrative treatment effective in reducing adolescents' drug use. The MDFT model brings together theoretically risk-factor models of drug and problem behavior, developmental psychopathology, family systems theory, peer cluster theory, social support theory, and social learning theory. The intervention targets four areas of functioning: the adolescent's intrapersonal and interpersonal functioning, parenting practices, parent–adolescent interactions, and family members' interactions with the community (e.g., school, welfare). In practice, the model uses a combination of structural family therapy, parent training, adolescent skills training, and cognitive-behavioral techniques. MDFT integrates family therapy and individual therapy. Individual therapy sessions are used to explore topics sensitive to adolescents, such as their drug use and sexual behavior. MDFT has demonstrated superior treatment effects in reducing drug use compared with individual therapy, adolescent group therapy, or multifamily psycho-educational drug counseling. It has also produced significant changes in parenting behavior and family functioning. Of importance to school mental health workers, MDFT has demonstrated positive effect on the school grades of adolescents following 6 months of treatment. MDFT has demonstrated long-term effects up to 12 months following treatment termination.

The MDFT treatment program consists of three stages (Liddle, 2003): stage 1: building the foundation (5 weeks); stage 2: prompt action and change by working the themes (6 weeks); and stage 3: sealing the changes and exit (5 weeks). The therapist works simultaneously with multiple systems and subsystems, which are termed *modules of treatment*. Four modules and procedures are delineated: (1) the adolescent module (individual therapy); (2) the parent module (therapy related to individual or conjoint work with parents, parental figures, or guardians); (3) the family interaction module (the assessment or alteration of family interaction patterns); and (4) the extrafamilial subsystem module (therapy related to work with any system in the adolescent's or parents' social world). Each area is a target of assessment, intervention, and change. The MDFT treatment manual is available from the Center for Substance Abuse Treatment (CSAT), Substance Abuse and Mental Health Services Administration (SAMHSA).

Functional Family Therapy

Functional family therapy (FFT) is a short-term family therapy intervention for adolescents and their families when the adolescent is at risk or exhibiting serious conduct problems (Sexton & Alexander, 2003). FFT is rooted in family systems, social ecological, and behavioral theories. FFT views the adolescent's clinical problems to be a manifestation of enduring family behavioral patterns that are reflected in the adolescent's and family's interactions with one another and with their larger social environment. The adolescent's problematic behavior is viewed as serving a relational function, that is, as a means by which family members maintain a learned level of connectedness or separateness from one another.

The three specific and distinct phases of FFT treatment are phase I: motivation; phase II: behavior change; and phase III: generalization. Phase I builds a therapeutic alliance and reattributes the intention and meaning of the problem, intentions, emotions, and behaviors of family members. Phase II targets specific behavioral skills of family members. Phase III shifts the focus from within-family changes to how the family responds to systems around it and planning for future crises.

With effectiveness demonstrated across multiple studies, FFT is considered a model program for the prevention and treatment of substance abuse and delinquency (Sexton & Alexander, 2003). No evidence of measurement of school outcomes, however, was identified in FFT studies; therefore, the impact of this intervention on adolescents' school attendance or performance is uncertain.

Brief Strategic Family Intervention

Brief strategic family therapy (BSFT) (Szapocznik, Hervis, & Schwartz, 2003) is a brief (8–24 sessions) family systems therapy approach to treat adolescent substance abuse and co-occurring adolescent problem behaviors. The goal of treatment is to eliminate or reduce the adolescent's substance use but also to alter the associated family interaction patterns. Techniques are rooted in structural and strategic family therapy. Particular emphasis is placed on the engagement of resistant families. Similarly to most family therapy models, intervention proceeds by forming a therapeutic alliance with the adolescent and family, diagnosing relevant family interactions, restructuring the interactions to permit more functional interaction patterns to emerge, and broadening the scope of treatment to relevant systems in the ecological context. Most recently, BSFT has demonstrated treatment superiority compared with group counseling in reducing adolescent substance use, maintaining good family functioning, or improving poor family functioning. The efficacy of BSFT has been determined primarily with Hispanic youth. The BSFT treatment manual is available at http://www.drugabuse.gov/TXManuals/bsft/BSFT7.html.

Multilevel, Family-Centered, School-Based Prevention

Systematic school-based family intervention programs, as noted earlier, are rare. Moreover, it can be argued that intensive family intervention is unnecessary for the vast majority of children and their families in schools. Schools can, however, play an important role in the prevention of serious child and adolescent problems with multilevel school-based programs that strengthen the coping and resilience of families. Preventive family interventions fall within three categories (Sanders, 1998): (a) universal interventions that are provided or available to the entire school population; (b) selective interventions targeted toward at-risk groups; and (c) indicated interventions for students exhibiting problems that are likely to worsen over time without intervention. An excellent model of an evidence-based, multilevel, school-based preventive family intervention is the Adolescent Transitions Program (ATP) (Dishion & Kavanagh, 2000), which is next described.

The ATP is an evidence-based prevention program, delivered in a middle-school setting, that is rooted in social learning and ecological theory. The three-tiered intervention strategy represents universal, selected, and indicated family intervention. At the universal level, the school contains a family resource room (FRR). The FRR disseminates information to parents about good parenting and school success through a variety of creative means, including a parent self-assessment, summer home visits, and the SHAPe (Success, Health, and Peace) curriculum. The FRR also coordinates family-school collaborative meetings. At the selected level, ATP provides the Family Check-Up (FCC), a three-session intervention, based on motivational interviewing, that is designed to support parents' accurate appraisal of their child's risk status and provide parenting resources for reducing risk. The third, indicated level of intervention provides a variety of direct professional support options to parents and families. The indicated intervention menu, which is grounded in family management practices, includes a brief family intervention, a school monitoring system, parent groups, behavioral family therapy, and case management services. A family management curriculum forms the basis for work with individual families or groups of families. The ATP model has been effective in reducing parent–child conflict on videotaped problem-solving tasks, lowering teacher ratings of adolescents' antisocial behavior, and reducing student-reported substance use. Results have been examined in a random assignment treatment study with 999 students, and positive outcomes were replicated by an independent investigator.

The ATP program provides school-based mental health workers with an excellent model of family-based prevention and intervention services that fit with the regularities of the public school context. Noteworthy aspects of the program include interventions that are based on a long-standing program of research, multiple intervention options from which parents can pick and choose, attention to the engagement of parents, and motivational strategies that encourage family participation.

Tools and Practice Examples: Case Study

This case study will illustrate the ATP model.

Howard is a single father with a son and daughter in middle school. The son has been diagnosed with ADHD but does not take medication as this is in conflict with the religious preferences of the family. The son experiences school failure often, which is related to problems with homework completion. The daughter does well in school. The school views both children to be behavior problems. The father recently assumed custody of the children from their mother because of her substance abuse problems. This resulted in the children relocating to a new city and school. The family resides in the home of the father's parents. The father is currently unemployed from a job in the high-technology industry and actively searching for employment. The school counselor referred the family to the school's family resource center following a suspension of the daughter from school.

The father was telephoned and an intake scheduled. Although strategies were employed to broaden the issue to include the grandparents in the interview, health problems prohibited their involvement. The father was sent the Family Intake Questionnaire–Adolescent version (FIQ-A) (Dishion & Kavanagh, 2003) to complete prior to the interview, in order to help the therapist focus on key areas of concern for the family.

The initial interview was scheduled for 90 minutes. Three therapists were used for the initial meeting with the family, which included a meeting with the family as a group, individual family member interviews, and the reconvening of the family to summarize the parent's decision about the appropriate next step. As noted by Dishion and Kavanagh

(2003), "The priority from a family-centered perspective is to meet with the parent" (p. 38). If multiple therapists are not available, a single therapist may meet consecutively with the family members, beginning with the parent. The goals of the initial interview were to channel individual perspectives into a family-relationship perspective and to motivate Howard to engage in the next step, a comprehensive ecological family assessment. As Howard was a concerned parent, who was also desperate for help, and both children were socially responsive to open discussion, the family readily agreed to complete the assessment step in the three-session Family Check-Up.

Assessment of this family using the ATP model consisted of videotaped assessment of the family's interaction in a structured family assessment task (in the home or resource center), collection of teacher reports on all children of concern, and daily completion of the Parent Daily Report (PDR) and Child Daily Report (CDR) (Chamberlain & Reid, 1987, cited in Dishion & Kavanagh, 2003) via telephone calls from the therapist to the home. Assessment results yielded several family relationship problems: (a) Howard was an ineffective but highly critical father; (b) the siblings had a strong bond and together engaged their father in argument until he was exhausted and gave in to them; (c) both children were resentful about having been forced to leave their mother and former home and were embarrassed that they were living with their elderly grandparents; and (d) Howard felt pressured to maintain a home environment low in conflict so that his elderly parents were not disturbed.

The family next engaged in the feedback session, which can be divided into four phases: self-assessment, support and clarification, feedback, and presentation of a choice of intervention options. In the self-assessment phase, Howard recognized that he was unable to keep from arguing with his children, and both children acknowledged that they deliberately argued with their dad to get their way. The therapist supported Howard in his efforts to seek help and provided feedback regarding the perceptions of teachers. The focus was broadened to incorporate the frame of the children feeling "out of control" of every aspect of their environment and needing strong but compassionate leadership from their father. The father was presented with several options for achieving this, and Howard elected to attend a 12-session family management group for parents of adolescents to improve his parenting.

This case illustrates the customary steps in the school-based Family Check-Up process, which may lead to a variety of forms of intervention. In the case study, Howard, the father, was not yet sufficiently empowered to elect to continue with family therapy in the face of continuous arguments from his children. The availability of a menu of therapeutic options permitted Howard to take an important step toward change in a manner that fit his personal style. Additional information about the ATP program may be found at the following Web sites:

http://www.personal.psu.edu/dept/
    prevention/ATP.htm
http://www.childtrends.org/Lifecourse/
    programs/AdolescentTransitionsProgram.htm
http://www.strengtheningfamilies.org/html/
    programs_1999/08_ATP.html

Key Points to Remember

Some of the key points of this chapter are as follows:

- The school-related behavior and learning problems of children and adolescents are frequently related to maladaptive parenting, family interaction patterns, or the stress of cumulative family transitions.
- Poor parenting and maladaptive family interaction patterns are the focus of family intervention.
- Variations of parent management training, including behavioral family intervention, are well-established treatments for child and preadolescent behavior problems.
- Conduct disorders, including substance abuse, in adolescents are more effectively treated with family therapy interventions.
- Four family therapy models are well established as models of treatment for adolescent conduct problems: multisystemic therapy, multidimensional family therapy, functional family therapy, and brief strategic family therapy.
- Although effective, family therapy models, which require a minimum of 8–24 sessions, may not be feasible within a school setting.
- More promising for schools are multilevel family-centered prevention programs, such as the Adolescent Transitions Program, which

provide an array of services for parents and families on a continuum of involvement.

The focus of this chapter has been to highlight family therapy models that have well-established efficacy in the treatment of child and adolescent problems such that school mental health workers may be informed when making referrals for treatment. A serious limitation of the family therapy literature, noted earlier, is the failure of most efficacy studies to include measures of school-based outcomes. This methodological limitation seriously constrains any conclusions that can be reached about the effectiveness of family therapy in changing the school behavior of children and adolescents, even though it is often within the school context that behavior and learning problems are first identified. The focus of the chapter has been on the referral process because all well-established family therapy models require substantial background and training on the part of the therapist, as well as considerable time to complete the full course of treatment, which is unlikely to be an option in the school setting. More promising for the school mental health worker is implementation of part or all of the multilevel, school-based, family-centered prevention program. Overall, the goal for school mental health practitioners is to consider intervention with the family context in which the child's problem may be embedded, not only treatment of the child.

References

Brown, B., Mounts, N., Lamborn, S., & Steinberg, L. (1993). Parenting practices and peer group affiliation in adolescence. *Child Development, 64,* 467–482.

Brown, T. L., Henggeler, S. W., Schoenwald, S. K., Brondino, M. J., & Pickrel, S. G. (1999). Multisystemic treatment of substance abusing and dependent juvenile delinquents: Effects on school attendance at posttreatment and 6-month follow-up. *Children's Services: Social Policy, Research, & Practice, 2*(2), 1–10.

Carlson, C., & Trapani, J. (in press). Single parenting and step-parenting. In G. Bear & K. Minki (Eds.), *Children's needs: Vol. III. Understanding and addressing the developmental needs of children.* National Association of School Psychologists.

Carr, A. (2000). Evidence based practice in family therapy and systemic consultation. Child-focused problems. *Journal of Family Therapy, 22,* 29–60.

Christenson, S. L., Rounds, T., & Gorney, D. (1992). Family factors and school achievement: An avenue to increase students success. *School Psychology Quarterly, 7,* 178–206.

Cottrell, D., & Boston, P. (2002). Practitioner review: The effectiveness of systemic family therapy for children and adolescents. *Journal of Child Psychology and Psychiatry, 43*(5), 573–586.

Dishion, T. J., & Kavanagh, K. (2000). A multi-level approach to family-centered prevention in schools: Process and outcome. *Addictive Behaviors, 25*(6), 899–911.

Dornbusch, S. M., Ritter, P. L., Leiderman, P., Roberts, D., & Fraleigh, M. (1987). The relation of parenting style to adolescent school performance. *Child Development, 58,* 1244–1257.

Entwisle, D. R., & Alexander, K. L. (2000). Diversity in family structure: Effects on schooling. In D. Demo, K. R. Allen, and M. A. Fine (Eds.), *Handbook of family diversity.* New York: Oxford University Press.

Greene, S. M., Anderson, E., Hetherington, E. M., Forgatch, M. S., & DeGarmo, D. G. (2003). Risk and resilience after divorce. In F. Walsh (Ed.), *Normal family processes* (3rd ed., pp. 96–120). New York: Guilford.

Hammen, C., Rudolph, K., Weisz, J., Rao, U., & Burge, D. (1999). The context of depression in clinic-referred youth: Neglected areas in treatment. *Journal of the American Academy of Child and Adolescent Psychiatry, 38*(1), 64–71.

Liddle, H. A. (2003). *Multidimensional family therapy for early adolescent substance abuse treatment manual.* Center for Substance Abuse Treatment. Substance Abuse and Mental Health Services Administration.

Liddle, H. A., & Rowe, C. L. (2005). Advances in family therapy research. In M. P. Nichols & R. C. Schwartz (Eds.), *The essentials of family therapy* (2nd ed., pp. 298–328). New York: Allyn & Bacon.

Patterson, G. R., Dishion, T. J., & Bank, L. (1984). Family interaction: A process model for deviancy training. *Aggressive Behavior, 10,* 253–267.

Roesner, R. W., Eccles, J. S., & Freedman-Doan, C. (1999). Academic functioning and mental health in adolescence: Patterns, progressions, and routes from childhood. *Journal of Adolescent Research, 14,* 135–174.

Ryan, B. A., Adams, G. R., Gulotta, T. P., Weissberg, R. P., & Hampton, R. L. (1995). *The family-school connection: Theory, research, and practice.* Thousand Oaks, CA: Sage.

Sanders, M. R. (1998). The empirical status of psychological interventions with families of children and adolescents. In L. L'Abate (Ed.), *Family psychopathology: The relational roots of dysfunctional behavior* (pp. 427–468). New York: Guilford.

Sexton, T. L., & Alexander, J. F. (2002). Family-based empirically supported interventions. *Counseling Psychologist, 30*(2), 238–261.

Sexton, T. L., & Alexander, J. F. (2003). Functional family therapy. In T. L. Sexton, G. R. Weeks, & M. S. Robbins

(Eds.), *Handbook of family therapy* (pp. 323–350). New York: Brunner-Routledge.

Sheidow, A. J., Henggeler, S. W., & Schoenwald, S. K. (2003). In T. L. Sexton, G. R. Weeks, & M. S. Robbins (Eds.), *Handbook of family therapy* (pp. 303–322). New York: Brunner-Routledge.

Szapocznik, J., Hervis, O., & Schwartz, S. (2003). *Brief strategic family therapy for adolescent drug abuse*. NIH Pub. No. 03–475. Washington, DC: National Institute on Drug Abuse.

U.S. Bureau of the Census. (2003). *Children's living arrangements and characteristics: March, 2002*. Available: http://www.census.gov.

Valdez, C., Carlson, C., & Zanger, D. (in press). Evidence-based parent training and family interventions for changing school behavior. *School Psychology Quarterly*.

Visher, E. B., Visher, J. S., & Pasley, K. (2003). Remarriage families and stepparenting. In F. Walsh (Ed.), *Normal family processes* (3rd ed., pp. 153–175). New York: Guilford.

Working With Oppositional Youths Using Brief Strategic Family Therapy

Patricia A. Cody

CHAPTER 65

Getting Started

Children exhibiting oppositional behavior are challenging for teachers as well as for mental health professionals working in the school system. Increasingly, school social workers and other school-based services professionals have to address these behaviors, which are not otherwise being treated. It is generally accepted that environmental contexts are important when assessing and treating oppositional behaviors and that untreated childhood delinquency often leads to adult problems in functioning (Jordan & Hickerson, 2003). Due to the strong connection between untreated delinquent behavior and problematic adult behavior, it is even more critical that school social workers and other professionals be able to assess needs and provide the most effective treatment possible for identified youth. In a study of students in Baltimore, it was found that students who were identified as needing services for problematic behavior in school were much less likely to have ever received any services than similar children who participated in a community mental health program (Weist, Myers, Hastings, Ghuman, & Han, 1999).

Although an oppositional child alone is the primary concern in a school setting, the family system as a whole should be considered for intervention. Although it may not always be possible to do family therapy in schools, the interventions can be essential in helping youths with oppositional behaviors. This chapter will focus on brief strategic family therapy (BSFT). A detailed account of BSFT will be given with a case example using BSFT in a school setting. BSFT is in line with strengths-oriented values because the approach focuses on empowering the family, emphasizing strengths, and embracing the idea of

creating healthy systems in the family and society. BSFT strengthens the family by addressing an individual problem rather than focusing solely on the problematic individual. BSFT was not developed for schools specifically but is increasingly being used in school settings, and suggestions for incorporating this model in the school setting will be given.

What We Know

There is a building body of evidence that supports the use of brief strategic family therapy models to treat oppositional youths (Szapocznik, Rio, Murray, Cohen, Scopetta, Rivas-Vasquez, Hervis, Posada, & Kurtines, 1989). In a meta-analysis done in 1987, it was found that family therapy was more effective than other treatment modalities (Hazelrigg, Cooper, & Borduin, 1987). The focus of brief strategic family interventions and other family therapy approaches is rooted in family systems theory and advocates an approach that recognizes the interrelatedness of the individuals within a family and the influence of one family member's behavior on another (Franklin, Hopson, & Barge, 2003, p. 255). The school practitioner using this approach sees maladaptive familial interaction as the problem rather than the symptom behavior that the child may be exhibiting, and the practitioner acts accordingly.

Brief strategic family therapy has been developed out of strategic family therapy and structural family therapy by Jose Szapocznik in an effort to focus on delinquent or substance-abusing adolescents. This model is particularly effective in working with families who have minority status. The family focus in dealing with a presenting problem is very appropriate for the Hispanic and African American families with whom the model was designed to be used. The Center for Family Studies at the University of Miami's School of Medicine was established in the 1970s to address the problem of adolescent drug abuse among Hispanic adolescents (Szapocznik & Williams, 2000). BSFT has significant empirical support for its effectiveness (e.g., Santisteban, Szapocznik, Perez-Vidal, Kurtines, Murray, & LaPerriere, 1996; Szapocznik, Santisteban, et al., 1989).

Clinical trials continue to support the efficacy of the BSFT model, particularly in addressing the family functioning of drug-abusing adolescents. BSFT has been shown to be particularly effective with substance-abusing adolescents although it has also been used with delinquent adolescents who are not using substances. Table 65.1 lists empirical studies supporting the efficacy of BSFT. In addition, Table 65.1 lists references for structural family therapy and strategic family therapy, out of which BSFT came.

What We Can Do

Brief strategic family therapy is based on three fundamental concepts: system, structure, and strategy. The *family system* is based on the interrelatedness of the family members. Each family member's behavior affects the other family members, creating a system that functions within the larger system of society. As BSFT has developed over time, the system that affects the child has grown to include the community, peers/friends, and school.

A family's *structure* is the set of repeated patterns and interactions that are unique to each family. A maladaptive family structure is one whose patterns and interactions continue despite the fact that the patterns and interactions do not meet the needs of the family and in many cases actually maintain problematic behavior. The third concept, *strategy*, is a deliberate set of intervention techniques. The strategies of BSFT are direct, problem-oriented, and practical. Practical strategies are used to move the family toward the particular

Table 65.1 Empirical Support for Three Family Therapy Models

Type	*Supporting Studies*
Structural Family Therapy	Harkaway, 1987
	Minuchin, Montalvo, Guerney, Rosman, & Schumer, 1967
	Minuchin, Rosman, & Baker, 1978
	Rosman, Minuchin, & Liebman, 1977
	Stanton & Todd, 1979
	Szapocznik et al., 1983
	Szapocznik, Rio, et al., 1989
	Zeigler-Driscoll, 1979
Strategic Family Therapy	Alexander & Parsons, 1973
	Cox & Ray, 1994
	Garrigan & Bambrick, 1975, 1977
	Haley & Schiff, 1993
	Ray & Keim, 1997
	Selvini-Palazzoli, 1986
	Stanton & Sadish, 1997
	Szapocznik & Williams, 2000
Brief Strategic Family Therapy	Rivas-Vasquez, Hervis, & Posada, 1989
	Santisteban et al., 2003
	Santisteban et al., 1997
	Santisteban et al., 1996
	Szapocznik et al., 1983, 1986
	Szapocznik et al., 1988
	Szapocznik, Rio et al., 1989
	Szapocznik, Santisteban et al., 1989

objectives identified by the counselor and the family.

The assessment phase of BSFT is unique in that the researchers have also developed an assessment measure that can be used. The Structural Family Systems Ratings (SFSR) measure was developed after borrowing concepts from Minuchin's Wiltwyck Family Tasks measure (Szapocznik & Williams, 2000). The administration of this measure has been standardized, increasing its reliability. The measure assesses six areas of interrelated concepts in the family system: "Structure" measures family organization; "flexibility" measures the family's ability to adapt to challenges; "resonance" measures the family's boundaries emotional distance; "developmental stage" measures the compatibility of the family member roles with what would be expected; "identified patienthood" measures whether the family members see the symptom carrier as the problem; "conflict resolution" measures the family's style in addressing problems. The measure consists of two parts: the administration of family tasks and the evaluation of family patterns based on the six areas discussed above. Good interrater reliability and internal consistency have been demonstrated, and evidence for content, factor, and construct validity exists (Szapocznik, Hervis, Rio, & Mitrani, 1991). Information about the SFSR can be accessed at the Center for Family Studies Web site (see Table 65.2). SFSR can be used initially for assessment and as an ongoing assessment for change throughout treatment.

BSFT can be implemented in a variety of settings, including schools, and includes four basic stages. Treatment generally lasts 8–12 weeks with weekly sessions of about 1–1.5 hours, although sessions may be more frequent during times of crisis. Sessions can be conducted in the home, in an office, or at school. Families may often be resistant to treatment, blaming the symptom-carrying child or adolescent. Families seeking treatment for substance-abusing adolescents rarely engage in treatment. BSFT is intended to be used with the entire family due to the assumption of the family system model. To overcome the resistance often encountered, BSFT has engagement procedures that have been developed specifically for the purpose of engaging the resistant family. One example of this strategy is for the school social worker to ally with the adolescent (if this is the primary source of resistance), thus contributing to the adolescent's sense of empowerment and feeling respected. Another example is to seek permission

from the family member seeking treatment to speak directly with the most resistant member. These strategies have been supported in a variety of studies (Coatsworth, Santisteban, McBride, & Szapocznik, 2001; Santisteban et al., 1996; Szapocznik et al., 1989). There are some cases where the family is either unavailable or unwilling to agree to engage in the treatment process. In these cases, BSFT can be used with one person. This technique will be discussed later in the chapter.

Engagement is a big part of BSFT and must be considered when working with oppositional youth and their families. Models such as BSFT regard resistance to engagement as a natural part of the therapeutic process, which should be expected (Coatsworth et al., 2001). Szapocznik and others suggest that resistance to engagement be seen as the first hurdle to overcome. Once a family has agreed to participate in therapy, it is important for a social worker or counselor utilizing BSFT to see engagement as an ongoing process. Resistance may recur throughout the treatment process as various behavior patterns are challenged and targeted for change. It is the concept that engagement must be an ongoing process throughout therapy that results in excellent retention rates among BSFT and other similar models.

Some examples of how to deal with the initial resistance are to work with a particular family member who may have influence over the others and can get them to engage or to identify a strong enough reason for the family to choose therapy over the status quo. Identifying the structure of the family may help in identifying which family member may have the most influence over other family members. For example, in many traditional Hispanic families, where BSFT has been primarily used, the father is the head of the household and often may be the entrance to the family. Although critics may suggest that utilizing the patriarchal structure is not beneficial to other members of the family, it may need to be respected and utilized to bring the family into treatment. Sometimes, the presenting behavior to be addressed can be rephrased in such a way that families have a heightened sense of urgency and are able to begin to let down initial resistance. For example, if family members are resisting treatment surrounding their teenager's drug problem, the situation may be phrased as a life-threatening problem where the teen's next overdose may be deadly. In the case of oppositional behavior in school, the school social worker or other school-based counselor may emphasize the impending expulsion. When the problem is seen from the family's perspective as urgent or grave, their initial resistance may be reduced enough to come into treatment where the engagement process becomes an ongoing part of treatment.

BSFT is a direct, problem-focused, short-term treatment, thus it must follow a specific design. This design is flexible, however, in meeting the specific needs of individual families. The design follows six phases over the course of treatment: joining, symptom identification, strengths identification, problem identification, treatment planning, and restructuring (Robbins, Szapocznik, Santisteban, Hervis, Mitrani, & Schwartz, 2003).

Joining

The first phase in BSFT is to develop a team approach. The school social worker and other mental health counselors must engage with each family member and develop a therapeutic alliance not only with each family member but also with the family as a whole. The team approach is critical for this model to succeed. One way to do this is to allow everyone a chance to speak in the initial setting. Sometimes, starting with a family member other than the one who requested treatment is a way to begin joining with the family. While listening to one family member, request respect from the others and correct interruptions by reminding the interrupter that you want to hear from him or her, but right now you are listening to the other family member. Tensions and stress in the family may be running high during the initial sessions, and there may be a tendency for family members to start pointing fingers. While observation of this behavior is helpful, try to intervene by suggesting that each member express concerns rather than placing blame.

Symptom Identification

This phase allows the school social worker to see where the symptom or presenting problem is coming from as well as the family interactions surrounding the symptom. During this phase, the school social worker should encourage family members to tell each other about the symptom. Encouraging communication between family members rather than with the school social worker provides the opportunity to observe the family patterns and interactions. Initially, the

family members have difficulty doing this and may continue to try to speak with the school social worker directly. The social worker should redirect the communication so that it occurs between family members. For example, couples who have not been communicating well with each other may start out talking directly to each other but then shift toward the social worker when it becomes difficult. The social worker should take these opportunities to underline the importance of communicating with each other about the symptom and redirect the person back to speaking directly to his or her spouse.

Strengths and Problem Identification

The third and fourth phases are to assess the strengths and problems within the relationships and subsystems in the family. It is important to identify strengths in the family at this point as they will be used to build the treatment plan later on. Strengths can be observed by the school social worker or asked about. Families sometimes have a difficult time in identifying strengths, but with encouragement often can find something that works. This will be important for the family's buy-in to the treatment plan. Problems are a little easier for the family to identify, but they may be focused on the symptom as the problem. Observation of the family patterns will help the school social worker to identify where the problems are and which problems are likely to be maintaining the symptom behavior. A frequently seen example of a relational problem is when the family members see all of their problems as a result of one person's behavior: "If he [son] would stop using drugs, we wouldn't be having all of these problems" or "If she [daughter] would do what we tell her and go to school, none of this would be going on." Other problems may be around poor conflict resolution skills, inappropriate family roles, and alliances between one parent and one child against the other parent. Most of these types of problems will be observed by the social worker if the family is encouraged to speak directly to each other when talking about the symptom. Families will often act as they normally do if they are given the opportunity.

Treatment Planning

The fifth phase is the development of the change plan. It is important for the school social worker to be direction-oriented and problem-focused. Problems that were identified in phase 4 that are linked to the symptom behavior are addressed in the treatment plan. Other problems that may have been identified, not relating to the symptom behavior, will not be addressed in the treatment plan. It may be tempting to address all of the problems, but it is important to keep to behaviors directly linked to the symptom behavior. The strengths identified in phase 3 should be used to build strategies for change. The social worker should prioritize the behaviors that are in need of change. Not only should the change strategies be built on existing strengths in the family but also the easier problems to change should be tackled first in order to create a sense of accomplishment in the family and provide motivation to continue with treatment.

Restructuring

This final phase is basically the implementation of the treatment plan. Implementation occurs during the sessions as well as between sessions through direct and specific homework assignments for the family. This includes regular reinforcement for positive behaviors as well as restructuring of relationships, shifting alliances and boundaries, and assisting parents with advice and guidance. Examples of restructuring techniques include redirecting, blocking communication, putting parents in charge, teaching new conflict resolution skills, offering more appropriate family member roles, changing family subsystems, and developing behavior management skills in the parents. Putting parents in charge is a technique that will frequently be used in families dealing with adolescent drug use. The school social worker should work to align the parents together in decision making so that the parent subsystem is not diminished by one parent's alliance with the child. One way this can be done in the session is by having the parents communicate with each other and make decisions about discipline. If the child interrupts and attempts to align with one parent, the social worker can stop the interruption and tell the child that it is very important for the parents to discuss these problems, and she will have time to talk later in the session. This acknowledges the child's need to be involved but puts the authority back in the hands of the parents as a couple.

As mentioned earlier, it is sometimes not possible to engage the family in treatment. In the case of working with schools, this may occur more frequently than in other therapeutic settings. Often, a disruptive or drug-using adolescent is brought to the attention of the school social worker first. The social worker may not have an option to refer the family for treatment, or the family may resist attempts from the school to deal with family issues. In this case, one-person BSFT is an option. When the adolescent is willing to engage in treatment, but the family is not, BSFT therapy can be used in a very similar way. The focus on family interactions and patterns remains the focus in one-person treatment. Interventions are designed around changing how the adolescent interacts within the family patterns. This may often cause a crisis as the family tries to maintain the status quo. The crisis can often be used to engage resistant family members, allowing the school social worker to move toward the traditional BSFT model. If not, the social worker can continue with the individual, with the focus remaining on the family.

The one-person model was supported by a clinical trial comparing the traditional BSFT model with the one-person model (Szapocznik, Kurtines, Foote, Perez-Vidal, & Hervis, 1983, 1986). The main reason that this model remains effective without family engagement is that it still focuses solely on family interactions and patterns rather than on the individual and the individual's behavior. This model may be useful in schools that deter school social workers and other mental health counselors from bringing families in for treatment or with families who are not willing to engage in the treatment process.

Tools and Practice Examples

Tools

Not all school professionals embrace the use of family therapy. School social workers and counselors often must deal with issues related to the children in their schools with limited resources, limited time, and sometimes limited support from the family. Despite the demands of the school setting, brief strategic family therapy, when used in schools, can be an effective approach for addressing problem behavior in students. Haley (1977) states that once a counselor engages in this model and begins to see clients from an organizational perspective, it is important to recognize that the professional is part of the organizational system. It has only been in recent years that school counseling has begun to incorporate this systems viewpoint (Davis, 2001). The following ideas are things to consider when choosing to utilize a family therapy approach in the school:

1. Discuss the plan with your administration. Getting the support of administrators is encouraged since family therapy is not a traditional school model. Be prepared to share evidence of effectiveness and be willing to compromise by working with a couple of families and then assessing results.
2. Research is emerging that suggests that a child's academic ability is related to the parent–child relationship in the home and in systems other than the school (Davis, 2001; Nicoll, 1992).
3. Davis (2001) strongly suggests that school counselors take advantage of any opportunity to take a family therapy course or attend trainings. The benefits of improved service for families in schools will be increased with training and supervision.
4. Finally, Davis (2001) cites Hinkle and Wells (1995) in stating that families are not likely to follow through on community referrals for a variety of reasons. In addition, the researchers suggest that families find schools less threatening and are more willing to engage in the change process in this environment.

Case Example

The following case is an example of how BSFT can be used in a school setting:

Michelle, a 13-year-old female, has been referred to the school social worker for disruptive behavior and suspicion of drug use. The teacher reports that Michelle has been increasingly oppositional throughout the school year. She further reports that she has suspicions about Michelle using marijuana. Michelle's school records show that her behavior in previous grades had been appropriate. She was an average student who had not been involved in any disciplinary action. During this school year, Michelle has been suspended twice for aggressive behavior toward her peers and is now being investigated by the school for suspected drug use on school property. While talking with the teacher and reviewing Michelle's

record, the school social worker learns that she has been living with her grandmother for the past few years.

When the school social worker meets with Michelle and asks about her behavior, she says that her teacher and friends were just making her mad. Initially, the social worker tries talking with Michelle about her feelings and her behavior and makes several attempts at behavioral therapy techniques. Over the course of several sessions, Michelle does not appear to be responding and her behavior continues to decline. Not only is her behavior declining, but she begins to skip her sessions with the school social worker and does not engage when she does show up. She is suspended a third time after being caught with drugs while on school property and the principal is going to expel her. At the request of the school social worker to try BSFT techniques with this family, the principal agrees to delay the expulsion for 1 month. The school social worker begins to work on overcoming Michelle's resistance by allying herself with the student. Instead of focusing on Michelle's behavior during their sessions, she focuses on family issues. This shift seems to work, and Michelle tells the social worker about her pending move back to her mother's house. The school social worker asks for Michelle's permission to speak with her grandmother, offering that perhaps her grandmother is concerned about this move as well. Michelle agrees and contact is made with the grandmother.

When the school social worker contacts the grandmother, she learns that she has been caring for Michelle because her daughter had been using drugs for years and was unable to care for Michelle. She further reveals that her daughter has recently completed an intensive drug treatment program and that Michelle is supposed to move back in with her mother in a few weeks. During this initial phone contact, the grandmother shares that she and her daughter have been recently arguing about where Michelle should live and whether or not relapse is going to occur. The grandmother confides that she doesn't know if her daughter will be able to stay clean or how things will work with Michelle living with her mother again and her taking back the role of grandmother. The social worker agrees that this could be difficult and offers help. The grandmother agrees to come in for a meeting. The social worker asks the grandmother if her daughter would be willing to come to the meeting. Upon contacting the mother on the phone, the social worker experiences resistance similar to Michelle's early resistance. The social worker spends time on the phone listening to the mother and supporting her fears about her arguments with the grandmother and the pending move of Michelle back in with her. After several phone calls, Michelle's mother agrees to come to a meeting with Michelle and the grandmother.

Joining

The first family session involved the grandmother, the mother, and Michelle. There were no other family members living in the area. During this session, the school social worker asked the family to discuss what was going on in the family, encouraging the family to speak directly to each other. The social worker repeatedly had to redirect the family members as they had a difficult time talking to each other. The social worker gave each family member time to talk, ensuring that respect was given to each family member. The school social worker made certain that each family member was respected while talking. This was critical given the resistance by Michelle and her mother prior to this meeting. The social worker supported the grandmother in her concern for Michelle and her uncertainty over how she was going to stop being the "parent" and be a grandparent instead after so many years. The mother was supported in her fear of taking the role of "mother" back. Michelle was resistant to speaking, so the social worker continued to ally herself with Michelle by suggesting that she was distressed about the current family situation and her behavior may be a result of that stress. The school social worker suspected that Michelle was not ready to move back in with her mother for fear that things would be as they were before moving in with her grandmother, where she has been happy and safe. She further suspected that Michelle's recent behavior deterioration was an attempt to prevent herself from having to move back in with her mother. In continuing to ally herself with Michelle, the social worker suggested that the move be put off until all three women were ready for this move to happen and a plan of how it was to occur was in place and agreed upon. All three women agreed to this, and the social worker noticed visible relief in all of them.

Symptom Identification

It was not difficult to identify the symptoms as the reports from the teacher were clear. The mother and grandmother were extremely upset with Michelle's aggressive behavior and possible drug use. During an early session, Michelle admitted to smoking pot and said to her mother, "It wasn't like what you did. I don't see the big deal." The primary symptoms to address were Michelle's aggression and drug use.

Strengths Identification

The family exhibited strengths in many ways. The grandmother and mother were both concerned about Michelle and were willing to engage in therapy. Michelle had been getting good grades in school and until this recent behavior change was spoken of highly by her teachers and peers. The grandmother was able to see that there was going to have to be a shift in parenting roles and was able to express fear about this not working successfully. The mother initially did not want to discuss her own drug use, but decided that she needed to share her experiences to help her daughter.

Problem Identification

The grandmother shared that she and Michelle talked about her mother in unsupportive ways. Several times in early sessions, Michelle sided with her grandmother against her mother in a way that created fighting between the grandmother and mother. The grandmother has been the parent to Michelle for many years, and while she was aware that this would change she wasn't prepared for how to deal with it. The maladaptive technique that had been in use for preparing for this change was for the grandmother and mother to fight about Michelle and the impending move in a way that Michelle was able to overhear. The main problems related to Michelle's behavior are the alliance between the grandmother and Michelle, the structure hierarchy, role responsibility, and making the mother be the parent and the grandmother be the grandparent. It became apparent that the social worker's initial suspicion that Michelle's behavior was intended to prevent a move that she was fearful of and not ready to make was accurate.

Treatment Plan

The plan that the school social worker developed would address the problems through a restructuring of the hierarchy of the family, a shifting of family boundaries so that there would not be an alliance against the mother, and improved parenting skills for the mother to take back her role as parent to Michelle. The grandmother would be supported in learning new skills about being a more traditional grandmother with regard to her interactions with Michelle. The treatment plan included a step-by-step plan of how the move would occur, what would have to be accomplished prior to the move, and how the transitional visits would be handled.

Restructuring

After the treatment plan was in place, the sessions turned to restructuring the family to address the problems. The social worker gave the grandmother and mother several directives to follow. First, they were to no longer have fights about Michelle in front of Michelle. Second, during this transition phase, decisions regarding Michelle in terms of discipline or school issues were to be made by both adults in agreement with each other. It was going to be important for Michelle to see that her grandmother supported her mother in taking over the role of parent. After the family started making these changes, the grandmother was given the directive of not talking negatively to Michelle about her mother's chances of staying clean, and the mother was given the directive to take Michelle to one of her Narcotics Anonymous meetings and share her experience with her daughter. For several sessions, the school social worker assisted the family in making these changes. Communication patterns with Michelle were worked on next. These patterns were harder to change, as they had been in place for a very long time. The grandmother became less involved with decisions to be made about Michelle, and the school social worker redirected her in sessions when she tried to interrupt in discussions concerning discipline or school issues.

Over the course of about 5 weeks, Michelle's behavior improved. Her teacher reported fewer incidents of aggression and an increase in attention to assignments. Michelle reported that she was no longer experimenting with drugs. The teacher reported that she no longer believed that

Michelle was using drugs on school property as she had believed before. The principal made the decision to not expel Michelle due to her improvements and gave the school social worker her support in continuing family therapy. Based on the success of this family in a relatively short period of time, the school was supportive of the school social worker seeking further training on the implementation of BSFT.

In this case, the school social worker began by not including the family and was not able to affect the child's behavior. Upon deciding that the family needed to be involved, the school social worker chose to utilize BSFT methods and attempted to incorporate strategies with this family. It should be noted that the BSFT discussed in this chapter has an extensive training manual, as well as training sessions that include ongoing supervision. If school social workers or counselors are interested in implementing BSFT in their schools, it is suggested that the Center for Family Studies be contacted for additional help and resources. Refer to Table 65.2 for the Web site for the Center for Family Studies. Click on "Training Programs" for information on workshops, treatment manuals, internships, externships, and supervision. There is also a phone number and e-mail address that can be used to gather additional information. The staff at the center is helpful and willing to help mental health professionals interested in learning more about implementing BSFT. Table 65.2 also includes Web sites for structural family therapy and strategic family therapy for additional reference.

Key Points to Remember

- Remember, resistance is natural and should be expected as the first obstacle to changing the symptom behavior.
- The school social worker and other school-based services professionals must consider the school as a unique and creative environment in which family therapy may be an excellent option for oppositional youth not responding to other treatment methods.
- The youth is a part of many systems: the school, the family, the community, and many others unique to each youth.
- Not all maladaptive dynamics of the family are to be addressed in BSFT. Identify the symptom behavior and work to change the dynamics

Table 65.2 Family Therapy Training Centers and Web Sites

Model	Web Site
Structural Family Therapy	Minuchin Center for the Family www.minuchincenter.org
	Philadelphia Child Guidance Clinic www.philafamily.com
Strategic Family Therapy	Brief Therapy Center at the Mental Health Research Institute (MRI) in Palo Alto, CA www.mri.org
	Haley's Family Therapy Institute in Washington, DC www.jay-haley-on-therapy.com
	Strategic Therapy Group at the Ackerman Institute www.ackerman.org
Brief Strategic Family Therapy	Center for Family Studies www.cfs.med.miami.edu
	Center for Treatment Research on Adolescent Drug Abuse (CTRADA) www.miami.edu/ctrada
	BSFT: SAMHSA Model Treatment http://modelprograms.samhsa.gov/pdfs/FactSheets/Bsft.pdf

and subsystems that have been perpetuating the symptom behavior.

- Family therapy with the family may not always be an option due to school constraints or unwillingness of the family. In these cases, consider family therapy with the child or adolescent in the school by focusing the work around the family system during the individual sessions. Take advantage of all family therapy training even if this has to be on personal time. Work with school administrators to include a family therapy model for students as a means to address oppositional behavior.

References

Alexander, J., & Parsons, B. (1973). Short-term behavioral intervention with delinquent families: Impact on family process and recidivism. *Journal of Abnormal Psychology, 81,* 219–225.

Coatsworth, J. D., Santisteban, D. A., McBride, C. K., & Szapocznik, J. (2001). Brief strategic family therapy versus community control: Engagement, retention and an exploration of the moderating role of adolescent symptom severity. *Family Process, 40,* 313–332.

Cox, R., & Ray, W. (1994). The role of theory in the treatment of substance abuse. *Contemporary Family Therapy, 16*(2), 131–144.

Davis, K. M. (2001). Structural-strategic family counseling: A case study in elementary school. *Professional School Counseling, 4*(3), 180–187.

Franklin, C., Hopson, L., & Barge, C. T. (2003). Family systems. In C. Jordan & C. Franklin (Eds.), *Clinical assessment for social workers: Quantitative and qualitative methods* (2nd ed., pp. 255–311). Chicago: Lyceum.

Garrigan, J. J., & Bambrick, A. F. (1975). Short-term family therapy for emotionally disturbed children. *Journal of Marriage and Family Counseling, 1,* 379–385.

Garrigan, J. J., & Bambrick, A. F. (1977). Family therapy for disturbed children: Some experimental results in special education. *Journal of Marriage and Family Counseling, 3,* 83–93.

Haley, J. (1977). *Problem-solving therapy.* New York: Harper & Row.

Haley, J., & Schiff, N. (1993). A model therapy for psychotic young people. *Journal of Systemic Therapies, 12,* 74–87.

Harkaway, J. E. (1987). *Eating disorders.* Rockville, MD: Aspen.

Hazelrigg, M. D., Cooper, H. M., & Borduin, C. M. (1987). Evaluating the effectiveness of family therapies: An integrative review and analysis. *Psychological Bulletin, 101,* 428–442.

Hinkle, J. S., & Wells, M. E. (1995). *Family counseling in the schools: Effective strategies and interventions for counselors, psychologists, and therapists.* Greensboro, NC: ERIC/CASS Publications.

Jordan, C., & Hickerson, J. (2003). Children and adolescents. In C. Jordan & C. Franklin (Eds.), *Clinical assessment for social workers: Quantitative and qualitative methods* (2nd ed., pp. 179–213). Chicago: Lyceum.

Minuchin, S., Montalvo, B., Guerney, B., Rosman, B., & Schumer, F. (1967). *Families of the slums.* New York: Basic.

Minuchin, S., Rosman, B., & Baker, L. (1978). *Psychosomatic families: Anorexia nervosa in context.* Cambridge, MA: Harvard University Press.

Nicoll, W. G. (1992). A family counseling and consultation model for school counselors. *School Counselor, 39,* 351–361.

Ray, W., & Keim, J. (1997). Tough teens: Mental Research Institute and Washington strategic school approaches. *Family Therapy News, 28*(5), 18, 21.

Robbins, M. S., Szapocznik, J., Santisteban, D. A., Hervis, O. E., Mitrani, V. B., & Schwartz, S. J. (2003). Brief strategic family therapy for Hispanic youth. In A. E. Kazdin & J. R. Weisz (Eds.), *Evidence-based psychotherapies for children and adolescents* (pp. 407–424). New York: Guilford.

Rosman, B. L., Minuchin, S., & Liebman, R. (1977). Treating anorexia nervosa by the family lunch session. In C. E. Schaefer & H. L. Millman (Eds.), *Therapies for children: A handbook of effective treatments for problem behavior.* San Francisco: Jossey-Bass.

Santisteban, D. A., Coatsworth, D., Perez-Vidal, A., Kurtines, W. M., Schwartz, S. J., & Szapocznik, J. (2003). The efficacy of brief strategic family therapy in modifying adolescent behavior problems and substance use. *Journal of Family Psychology, 17,* 1–17.

Santisteban, D. A., Coatsworth, J. D., Perez-Vidal, A., Mitrani, V., Jean-Gilles, M., & Szapocznik, J. (1997). Brief structural/strategic family therapy with African American and Hispanic high risk youth. *Journal of Community Psychology, 25*(5), 453–471.

Santisteban, D. A., Szapocznik, J., Perez-Vidal, A., Kurtines, W. M., Murray, E. J., & LaPerriere, A. (1996). Efficacy of intervention for engaging youth and families into treatment and some variables that may contribute to differential effectiveness. *Journal of Family Psychology, 10,* 35–44.

Selvini-Palazzoli, M. (1986). Towards a general model of psychotic family games. *Journal of Marital and Family Therapy, 12*(4), 339–349.

Stanton, D., & Shadish, W. (1997). Outcome, attrition, and family-couples treatment of drug abuse: A meta analysis and review of the controlled, comparative studies. *Psychological Bulletin, 122*(2), 170–191.

Stanton, M., & Todd, T. (1979). Structural family therapy with drug addicts. In E. Kaufman & P. Kaufman (Eds.), *The family therapy of drug and alcohol abuse.* New York: Gardner.

Szapocznik, J., Hervis, O., Rio, A. T., & Mitrani, V. B. (1991). Assessing change in family functioning as a result from treatment: The Structural Family Systems Rating scale (SFSR). *Journal of Marital and Family Therapy, 17*(3), 295–310.

Szapocznik, J., Kurtines, W. M., Foote, F., Perez-Vidal, A., & Hervis, O. (1983). Conjoint versus one person family therapy: Some evidence for the effectiveness of conducting family therapy through one person. *Journal of Consulting and Clinical Psychology, 51,* 889–899.

Szapocznik, J., Kurtines, W. M., Foote, F., Perez-Vidal, A., & Hervis, O. (1986). Conjoint versus one person family therapy: Further evidence for the effectiveness of conducting family therapy through one person. *Journal of Consulting and Clinical Psychology, 54,* 395–397.

Szapocznik, J., Perez-Vidal, A., Brickman, A., Foote, F. H., Santisteban, D. A., Hervis, O. E., & Kurtines, W. M. (1988). Engaging adolescent drug abusers and their families in treatment: A strategic structural systems approach. *Journal of Consulting and Clinical Psychology, 56,* 552–557.

Szapocznik, J., Rio, A. T., Murray, E., Cohen, R., Scopetta, M. A., Rivas-Vasquez, A., Hervis, O. E., Posada, V., & Kurtines, W. M. (1989). Structural family therapy versus psychodynamic child therapy for problematic Hispanic boys. *Journal of Consulting and Clinical Psychology, 57,* 571–578.

Szapocznik, J., Santisteban, D., Rio, A., Perez-Vidal, A., Santisteban, D. A., & Kurtines, W. M. (1989). Family effectiveness training: An intervention to prevent drug abuse and problem behavior in Hispanic adolescents. *Hispanic Journal of Behavioral Sciences, 11,* 3–27.

Szapocznik, J., & Williams, R. A. (2000). Brief strategic family therapy: Twenty-five years of interplay among theory, research and practice in adolescent behavior problems and drug abuse. *Clinical Child and Family Psychology Review, 3*(2), 117–134.

Weist, M. D., Myers, C. P., Hastings, E., Ghuman, H., & Han, Y. L. (1999). Psychosocial functioning of youth receiving mental health services in the schools versus community mental health centers. *Community Mental Health Journal, 35*(1), 69–81.

What Parents and Teachers Should Know

Effective Treatments for Youth With ADHD

Carey E. Masse ■ Steven W. Evans ■ Ruth C. Brown ■ Allen B. Grove

CHAPTER 66

Getting Started

Attention-deficit/hyperactivity disorder (ADHD) is the most common mental health disorder among children and adolescents with a prevalence rate of between 3 and 5%. ADHD is both a common disorder and one with serious consequences. The results of several longitudinal studies of children with ADHD followed into adolescence led to the consensus that 50–70% of children diagnosed with ADHD continue to meet diagnostic criteria for ADHD when they are adolescents (Barkley, 1998). Although precise figures are not available, the rate of ADHD among adolescents in special education, juvenile justice, mental health, and substance abuse treatment settings is estimated to be at least 25% (Tucker, 1999).

Presenting problems for children with ADHD typically include academic difficulties, discipline problems at school and home, and conflict with peers. Adolescents with ADHD have many of these same problems but often with more serious consequences, such as dropping out of school and legal problems. Moreover, due to physical and social maturation, adolescents encounter new sets of problems, such as automobile accidents, traffic tickets, difficulty in romantic relationships, vocational problems, and substance use or abuse (Barkley, Anastopoulos, Guevremont, & Fletcher, 1992; Barkley, Murphy, & Kwasnik, 1996).

Educators are challenged by the problems experienced by students with ADHD every day. Since 1991, schools have been required to provide psychosocial and educational interventions for adolescents with ADHD who meet eligibility criteria for special education services (Davila, Williams, & MacDonald, 1991). While there has been a great deal of research on classroom-based behavioral interventions for children with ADHD

(Pelham, Wheeler, & Chronis, 1998) and user-friendly materials to translate that research to educators and practitioners (DuPaul & Stoner, 2003), there has been very little empirical literature to guide the implementation of these interventions with adolescents (Evans, Dowling, & Brown, in press).

What We Know

The support for the effectiveness of psychosocial treatments for children with ADHD is vast and has been summarized in the literature (Pelham et al., 1998). The authors of this review concluded that behavioral parent training and behavioral interventions meet criteria for well-established treatments according to criteria reported by Lonigan, Elbert, and Johnson (1998). These conclusions have been translated into practice recommendations published by the American Academy of Pediatrics (2001) and the American Academy of Child and Adolescent Psychiatry (Dulcan & the Work Group on Quality Issues, 1997). Psychosocial treatment has been reported to produce long-term benefits, including reducing the need for stimulant medication (MTA Cooperative Group, 2004). In addition, parents report greater satisfaction when their children receive psychosocial treatment than when they receive medication alone (MTA Cooperative Group, 1999). See chapter 4 for more information on effective interventions for ADHD.

The literature on effective treatment for adolescents with ADHD is much smaller than the research literature on children (Smith, Waschbusch, Willoughby, & Evans, 2000). There are no psychosocial treatments that qualify as empirically supported for this population; however, there is growing evidence supporting some specific interventions (Evans et al., in press). Early indications are that some individual interventions, such as note taking (Evans, Pelham, & Grudberg, 1995) and family therapy (Barkley, Edwards, Laneri, Fletcher, & Metevia, 2001), appear to produce improvement, but comprehensive psychosocial programs may be what are needed to achieve meaningful overall improvement (Evans, Axelrod, & Langberg, 2004). A great deal of research and development is needed in this area before definitive conclusions can be reached.

What We Can Do

Daily report cards and contingency management are two empirically supported behavioral interventions for youth with ADHD that can be used at home and school. The procedures for each are reviewed below, but there are some specific guidelines for using these interventions that will be reviewed first.

The first guideline is *consistency*. This means that the techniques must be used in a manner that becomes expected and clearly recognized by the child. For example, if a teacher is putting a mark on the board every time a child interrupts, and the child earns classroom privileges based on the number of marks, then these conditions must be held constant for the child. Every time the teacher notices the child interrupt, a mark must go on the board. The teacher must resist the temptation to give a verbal warning that the next time he interrupts, she really will put a mark on the board. Instead, the mark needs to be placed. When an adult makes exceptions to behavioral interventions such as these, the contingencies can become personal and hurtful. For example, if a teacher frequently grants exceptions to putting a mark on the board, then the child may attribute hostility to the teacher when she really does place the mark on the board, and the consequence becomes a personal message. If the teacher is consistent, then the consequence of a mark is simply part of the system and allows the teacher to continue to be on the child's side. This is especially true if the teacher maintains a positive approach with the child even when placing the mark. For example, she may say, "I have to put this mark here since you spoke out. This is your third mark this morning. I know you

can stop before getting five. I'll remind you about raising your hand."

The second part of consistency is enforcing the *consequences* of the system. Continuing with the previous example, the child may have to eat by himself in the cafeteria if he receives five marks in the morning. Being consistent means that if the child gets five marks, he always eats by himself. As in the preceding example, the teacher should not make exceptions. If she does make exceptions, then the teacher makes the consequence a personal decision. The child comes to understand that eating alone is only partly due to interrupting. The consequence is also seen by the child as a result of whether or not the teacher likes him that day.

The second guideline is *persistence*. Behavior change frequently takes a long time. The behavioral interventions being used will take weeks and maybe months before achieving the desired change. A frequent mistake of parents and teachers is to implement a technique, and if it does not work in the next few days (or few hours), they conclude that it does not work and abandon it. When consulting with parents and teachers, it is common to hear someone say that they have tried all those behavioral techniques and nothing works. In reality, there is a chance that they did try many of them; in fact, they may have tried many in the same day and not achieved immediate satisfaction by late afternoon, so they concluded that the techniques are ineffective. This scenario is quite common since a frequent reaction from children immediately following the implementation of an intervention is to test the limits. This involves an escalation in the targeted behavior to see if the parent or adult is really going to follow through and identify any loopholes. It is during the initial stages of implementation that parents and teachers frequently need the most support to continue. Change in problematic behaviors takes time, and it is common for it to take 3 months or more to achieve notable progress.

The final guideline involves *closely monitoring* target behaviors. As can be seen from the descriptions of some of the specific interventions that follow, there are assessment systems that are part of some of the techniques. It is frequently useful to graph or chart these data to guide decisions regarding potential modifications to techniques. Sometimes, certain interventions may be ineffective or children may respond in an unexpected manner, and strategies need to be adjusted. Careful assessment and consultation with someone well trained in behavioral techniques can help teachers and parents to make these adjustments.

Behavioral interventions are effective techniques for children with ADHD; however, they are frequently oversimplified in everyday use. Adhering to these guidelines of consistency, persistence, and close monitoring along with consulting with someone trained and experienced with behavioral techniques will increase the odds of success. When possible, start with simple interventions and learn from experience. Effective, sophisticated behavioral programs have usually evolved over time and transitioned through many iterations based on data from careful assessments.

The following interventions are empirically supported treatments for children with ADHD (Pelham et al., 1998). Their application with middle and high school students will require some modifications (Evans et al., in press). Additional descriptions of these and other procedures are available through the sources listed in Table 66.1.

Overview of Daily Report Cards

Daily Report Cards (DRCs) are used to modify specific behaviors at school using home-based contingencies. A teacher should identify and operationally define three or four specific behaviors that she would like to target for a particular child. She writes these as row headings and uses the column headings for the daily rating (see Figure 66.1). Wording target behaviors positively (e.g., Michael will remember to raise his hand before speaking in class every time he speaks with no more than five times forgetting) instead of negatively (e.g., Michael will not speak without raising his hand more than five times in a day) can make the intervention user-friendly to the child and parents. Sometimes it is not practical to state them positively, and clarity may sometimes take precedence over a positive orientation. As is shown in the figure, target behaviors may be scored dichotomously, as in the example with Michael, or continuously, as in the example with Beth.

The child is responsible for taking the DRC home each day. The parents are to review it, provide feedback and support, and implement the appropriate contingencies. It is important to have the lowest level of home contingencies reserved for when the child fails to bring home the DRC so there is some incentive for bringing it home when the ratings are poor. Home contingencies should be outlined on the DRC to facilitate communication between parents and teachers and improve consistency. DRCs may be saved to serve as an assessment system to track change in the target behaviors.

Procedures

- Teachers and parents agree to implement DRCs consistently, persistently, and with close monitoring.
- Input from the child is solicited, but ultimate decisions are based on the parents' and teacher's priorities with some consideration of the child's suggestions.
- Teachers and parents establish operationally defined target behaviors for the child.
- Parents establish a set of home contingencies for the DRC.
- A parent or teacher integrates the classroom and home information into one DRC form.
- The parent and teacher review the form and make any necessary final revisions.
- The DRC is explained to the child by both the parents and the teacher, and a day is selected to initiate the intervention.
- The DRC is kept in place at least 10 days before considering any significant changes to the procedures (some minor changes may be made ahead of time).
- When the child achieves consistently high performance on a target behavior, the criteria may be adjusted toward the normal range. Continuing with the example of Michael noted above, his criteria may be changed to forgetting to raise his hand three times or less. It is important to remember that the ultimate goal is movement into the normal range for the child's age and not perfection.
- Target behaviors and home contingencies may continue to be adjusted as the child changes his behavior. Targets that are never achieved may need to be modified to include a reduced expectation with the understanding that the higher expectations will return as he progresses.
- Regular communication between parents and teachers can facilitate consistency, persistence, and close monitoring.

Limitations

The DRCs can be a very effective intervention for children with ADHD, although they do require considerable coordination between parents

Table 66.1 Sources for Behavioral/Psychosocial Interventions for Youth With ADHD

Source	Description
Abramowitz, A. J., & O'Leary, S. G. (1991). Behavioral interventions for the classroom: Implications for students with ADHD. *School Psychology Review, 20*(2), 220–234.	Review of various behavioral intervention techniques for children that can be utilized by teachers and parents
Center for Children and Families State University of New York at Buffalo http://128.205.76.10/download.html	Informative Web site that provides information for parents and teachers on assessing children with ADHD as well as treatment options
CHADD: Children and Adults With Attention–Deficit/Hyperactivity Disorder National Resource Center on AD/HD (800) 233–4050 (301) 306–7070 Fax: (301) 306–7090 http://www.chadd.org	National nonprofit organization that provides evidence–based information on ADHD to parents, educators, professionals, and the general public
Dulcan, M., & the Work Group on Quality Issues. (1997). Practice parameters for the assessment and treatment of children, adolescents, and adults with attention–deficit/hyperactivity disorder. *Journal of the American Academy of Child and Adolescent Psychiatry, 36*(Suppl. 10), 85–121.	Treatment guidelines for children with ADHD from the American Academy of Child and Adolescent Psychiatry. Includes information on medication, behavioral therapy, and family therapy for children with ADHD
Evans, S. W., Axelrod, J., & Langberg, J. M. (2004). Efficacy of a school-based treatment program for middle school youth with ADHD. *Behavior Modification, 28*(4), 528–547.	Middle–school-based psychosocial intervention program for adolescents with ADHD
Pelham, W. E., Wheeler, T., & Chronis, A. (1998). Empirically supported psychosocial treatments for attention deficit hyperactivity disorder. *Journal of Clinical Child Psychology, 27*(2), 190–205.	Review of psychosocial treatments for children and adolescents with ADHD, according to task force criteria

(continued)

Smith, B. H., Waschbusch, D. A., Willoughby, M. T., & Evans, S. W. (2000). The efficacy, safety, and practicality of treatments for adolescents with attention–deficit/hyperactivity disorder (ADHD). *Clinical Child and Family Psychology Review, 3*(4), 243–267.	Review examining the efficacy of various medication and psychosocial interventions for adolescents with ADHD
U.S. Department of Education http://www.ed.gov/about/reports/annual/osep/index.html#adhd-res2	Provides links to documents on identifying ADHD, describing ADHD, and teaching children with ADHD
Wells, K. C., Pelham, W. E. Kotkin, R. A., Hoza, B., Abikoff, H. B., Abramowitz, A., et al. (2000). Psychosocial treatment strategies in the MTA study: Rationale, methods, and critical issues in design and implementation. *Journal of Abnormal Child Psychology, 28*(6), 483–505.	Review of psychosocial techniques employed in the MTA, the largest study of treatment for children with ADHD

Note. All resources are applicable to both parents and teachers.

Michael's Daily Report Card	
Target Behavior	*October 24th, 2004*
1. Michael will raise his hand every time he wants to contribute in class with no more than 5 times forgetting.	☺
2. Michael will complete all morning classwork on time.	😐
3. Michael will not get out of his seat during class time, unless he gets permission from Mrs. Smith, with no more than 3 times forgetting.	☹
	Total Smiles: 1

Home Plan	
Forgets to bring home Daily Report Card	No privileges, 7:30 bedtime
0 smiles	No privileges, 8:00 bedtime
1 smile	8:00 bedtime, 30 minutes of TV
2 smiles	8:00 bedtime, 30 minutes of TV, does not have to clean dinner dishes
3 smiles	8:30 bedtime, 60 minutes of TV or video games, does not have to clean dinner dishes

Beth's Daily Report Card	
Target Behavior	*October 24th, 2004*
1. Beth completes her assignments on time.	① 2 3 4
2. Beth takes accurate notes during class.	1 2 ③ 4
3. Beth gets 80% or above on all quizzes and tests.	1 2 ③ 4
Total: 7	
Points Key: 1 = not at all; 2 = just a little; 3 = pretty much; 4 = very much	

Home Plan	
Forgets to bring home Daily Report Card	No privileges, 9:00 bedtime
1–4 points	No privileges, 9:30 bedtime
5–8 points	9:30 bedtime, can choose one (1) chore not to complete
9–12 points	9:30 bedtime, can choose one (1) chore not to complete and 30 minutes of TV or video games

Figure 66.1. Examples of Dichotomous and Continuous Rating Scales on Daily Report Cards

and teacher. If either the teacher or the parents are not consistent and persistent, the intervention is likely to fail. In addition, the contingencies have to be sufficiently salient to modify the behaviors and at least get the child to bring the DRC home.

If getting the DRC home is a serious obstacle, the teacher may send it home using e-mail or call and leave a voice message with the information. If parents are not consistently enforcing the contingencies, teachers may provide contingencies in the last half hour of the day for the marks on the DRC so the intervention is self-contained in the classroom. Free time; the opportunity to spend time on a computer; time in the gym with an aide, teacher, or administrator; and access to art materials are classroom reinforcers that have worked for many children in this situation.

Further Information

Additional information about the use of DRCs can be found at the Center for Children and Families at the State University of New York at Buffalo's Web site (William Pelham, director), http://128.205.76.10/download.html, and in the book *ADHD in the Schools: Assessment and Intervention Strategies* (2nd ed.) by George DuPaul and Gary Stoner (2003).

Overview of Contingency Management

According to social learning theory, people behave the way they do because they have learned to do so. They engage in a behavior because at some time that behavior was rewarded or they expected to receive a reward (e.g., verbal praise, attention, friends). Similarly, they choose not to engage in a behavior because they have been punished or expect to receive punishment (e.g., scolding, loss of friends, humiliation) if they engage in that behavior. Contingency management uses these principles to structure rewards and punishments in a way that changes the child's behavior.

The first step in changing a child's behavior is to have clearly defined expectations. These should be defined in simple terms that are age-appropriate and describe specific behaviors. These should describe behaviors in which the child should not engage, as well as behaviors in which the child should engage. For example, Billy often talks excessively, which gets him in trouble at school and is problematic at home. Billy's teachers send home notes about the problems that he causes in the classroom. Billy often interrupts his parents while they are talking to each other, talking on the phone, reading, or watching television, which makes them frustrated and upset with Billy. Rather than telling Billy to "quit talking so much" or to "quit interrupting," the behaviors that are expected of him need to be clearly labeled and defined. Billy's parents tell him that

"interrupting" means talking when someone else is talking or busy doing something, such as reading or watching television. In addition, Billy's parents tell him that when he wants to say something to someone who is busy, he should ask for permission by touching the person's arm or asking politely if he may say something.

Contingency management involves applying reinforcements and punishments to help children to modify their maladaptive behaviors. Reinforcement is used to increase how often a behavior occurs. This may be done by providing a child with something he wants after exhibiting a desirable behavior, such as the opportunity to play video games (i.e., positive reinforcement) or helping the child to avoid something he does not want, such as skipping the requirement to complete an evening chore (i.e., negative reinforcement). Punishment, on the other hand, is used to decrease how often a behavior occurs. Like reinforcement, there are two kinds of punishment. A child may be punished by providing him with something undesirable, like an extra evening task (i.e., positive punishment), or requiring him to miss something enjoyable, like skipping dessert at dinner (i.e., negative punishment). Careful and systematic manipulation of these contingencies can be effective at modifying behaviors as long as they are implemented with consistency, persistence, and close monitoring.

Procedures

The following procedures outline the steps for a token economy, which is one form of contingency management. Other forms of contingency management are described in the references in Table 66.1.

- The teacher or parent identifies a set of reinforcers that will be used in the token economy. The reinforcers should be desirable (i.e., salient), and having a variety can improve saliency. Not all reinforcers need to be tangible. For example, tokens to be a line leader, spend time in the gym with the principal, eat lunch with the teacher, and other privileges may also be included. These reinforcers are often referred to as a prize box or treasure chest, and when children have earned enough points, they may go to this area and choose items that they can afford with their points.
- The teacher or parent operationally defines a set of behaviors with specific criteria for earning

points. For example, a child may earn 5 points for going to bed within 10 minutes without negative comments after being told no more than twice. A child may earn 7 points for completing all of his assigned work in the morning work period at school.

- When starting a token economy, no more than three or four target behaviors should be included. Other target behaviors may be added later.
- Points may be recorded on a sheet on the refrigerator at home or on the student's desk at school. Young children frequently prefer tangible points, such as poker chips or tickets.
- It is frequently helpful to set designated times to visit the prize box. Otherwise, it is common for children to want to visit frequently "just to see what I might want."

Limitations

Token economies require that the teacher or parent maintain a "store" of reinforcers, including tangible items and privileges. In addition, there can be problems related to the security of earned points. Children involved in token economy systems have been known to steal tokens from other children (when they are concrete, like poker chips) or plagiarize the marking of points on recording forms. Token economies rely exclusively on reinforcement, and for many children with moderate to severe impairment, punishment may also be required. Token economies may be combined with response cost systems to add punishment to the system. Response cost involves losing points for behaviors. For example, a child may lose 5 points for hitting someone. Response cost may help to increase the saliency of the system; however, response cost systems also introduce other problems. Children with frequent problems learn that they are likely to lose points so they try to spend points as soon as they get them so they have nothing to lose. Furthermore, when a child knows that he is likely to lose points, the saliency of the reinforcement value of points is reduced, making the original system less effective.

Token economies can become quite complex, and parents and teachers may observe that students learn that they can get all of the points they need by concentrating on only one target behavior. The strength of token economies is their ability to address many problems at once; however, the complexity that results from this is also their major limitation.

Further Information

Further information about token economies and other forms of contingency management is available in a review article by Ann Abramowitz and Susan O'Leary (1991) and a parent training manual called *Defiant Children: A Clinician's Manual for Assessment and Parent Training* (2nd ed.) by Russell Barkley (1997).

Tools and Practice Example

Tools

Figure 66.1 provides examples of handouts (Daily Report Cards) frequently used to assist students with ADHD to modify their behavior.

Case Example

Brian is a 9-year-old boy with a diagnosis of ADHD in the fourth-grade class taught by Mr. O'Grady. Brian is demonstrating problems completing assignments both at home and at school and is frequently disruptive in the classroom. He speaks out during class without being called on, pesters children sitting near him, and frequently plays with items at his seat in a manner that is distracting to others. Mr. O'Grady has tried verbal reprimands and prompts and has met with Brian's parents to discuss ways to help Brian. Mr. O'Grady and Brian's parents decided to try a Daily Report Card. Mr. O'Grady developed three target behaviors to use on the card and decided to use a continuous rating scale (see Figure 66.1). Mr. O'Grady defined the three target behaviors as (1) Brian will complete and turn in all assignments on time, which requires Brian to complete all items on every assignment (seatwork and homework) and turn them in to Mr. O'Grady at or before the expected time; (2) Brian will raise his hand prior to speaking during class, which requires Brian to say things during the class time (not including transitions, PE, or lunch) only after being called on by the teacher; and (3) Brian will respect the space and quiet of others, which requires Brian to not disturb others by intruding upon their space or disrupting their quiet work area.

Mr. O'Grady met with Brian's parents to describe the procedures and to help them establish some contingencies to implement at home based on the scores from the Daily Report Card. The parents wanted to use time playing video games, bedtime, and attending soccer practice as the contingencies at home. Mr. O'Grady recommended that they choose something other than soccer practices since missing practices could result in Brian being removed from the team. In addition, Brian's participation on the soccer team is one of the only enjoyable and successful outlets for him. He suggested that participation on the soccer team should not be tied to the DRC, but should be supported and encouraged. Brian's parents agreed to initially rely on time playing video games and bedtime.

After 2 weeks of sending home the Daily Report Cards, Mr. O'Grady called Brian's parents to find out how the procedures were working at home. They reported that things were going well. Upon further questioning, Mr. O'Grady learned that Brian had not brought home the DRC on 3 days. The parents had not implemented appropriate restrictions because Brian had told them that he had a substitute teacher on those days and she did not give him his card. Mr. O'Grady informed the parents that he had not missed any days of school in the last 2 weeks. He encouraged the parents to enforce the contingencies every day regardless of the story Brian tells them. Mr. O'Grady agreed to call the parents if he is absent.

After another 2 weeks, he called them again, and Brian's parents were discouraged. They told him that they were going to discontinue using the DRC because the marks were not getting any better, and it was a battle every evening to enforce the rules. Mr. O'Grady empathized with them, but urged them to continue. He noted that if they can continue to be consistent and persistent in their implementation, he was confident that Brian would improve. He explained that many children with ADHD require 2–3 months of a well-implemented plan before exhibiting notable improvements in behavior. The parents were skeptical but agreed to continue.

Mr. O'Grady maintained contact with Brian's parents and used encouragement, coaching, and support to facilitate their collaboration. After 6 more weeks, there was a trend toward improvement with his disruptive behavior and speaking out. Problems persisted with completing homework, and the interventions targeting task completion needed to be adjusted. A homework management system for the parents and a set of immediately available reinforcement and punishment responses for use at school during seatwork time were developed. In addition to consistency and persistence, Brian was greatly aided by the communication and collaborative implementation of interventions between his parents and his teacher.

Key Points to Remember

Two examples of empirically supported treatments for children with ADHD have been described. When implemented with consistency, persistence, and close monitoring, each of these is likely to be effective in modifying the behavior of most children with ADHD. They can be applied at home and in school. Regular communication between parents and teachers can improve the success rate of these interventions. In addition, these techniques work best when coordinated by adults who take a critical-thinking and problem-solving approach to the obstacles. Finally, these techniques are most effective when delivered independent of the emotional reactions of adults. Children learn from adults' emotional reactions to their behavior, but the learning that occurs from viewing emotional reactions is different than the learning being targeted by these interventions. Punishments are not a method of retaliation, and reinforcement should not be provided because an adult likes a child. Given the frustration and tension that frequently accompany parents and teachers working with youth with ADHD (Johnston & Mash, 2001), it can be challenging to provide the consistency, persistence, and close monitoring necessary while maintaining a supportive and positive relationship.

References

Abramowitz, A. J., & O'Leary, S. G. (1991). Behavioral interventions for the classroom: Implications for students with ADHD. *School Psychology Review, 20*(2), 220–234.

American Academy of Pediatrics, Subcommittee on Attention-Deficit/Hyperactivity Disorder, Committee on Quality Improvement. (2001). Clinical practice guideline: Treatment of the school-aged child with attention-deficit/hyperactivity disorder. *Pediatrics, 108,* 1003–1044.

Barkley, R. A. (1997). *Defiant children: A clinician's manual for assessment and parent training* (2nd ed.). New York: Guilford.

Barkley, R. A. (1998). *Attention deficit hyperactivity disorder: A handbook for diagnosis and treatment.* New York: Guilford.

Barkley, R. A., Anastopoulos, A. D., Guevremont, D. C., & Fletcher, K. E. (1992). Adolescents with attention deficit hyperactivity disorder: Mother-adolescent interactions, family beliefs and conflicts, and maternal psychopathology. *Journal of Abnormal Child Psychology, 20,* 263–288.

Barkley, R. A., Edwards, G., Laneri, M., Fletcher, K., & Metevia, L. (2001). The efficacy of problem-solving communication training alone, behavior management training alone, and their combination for parent-adolescent conflict in teenagers with ADHD and ODD. *Journal of Consulting and Clinical Psychology, 69,* 926–941.

Barkley, R. A., Murphy, K. R., & Kwasnik, D. (1996). Motor vehicle driving competencies and risks in teens and young adults with attention deficit hyperactivity disorder. *Pediatrics, 98,* 1089–1095.

Cunningham, C. E., Benness, B. B., & Siegel, L. S. (1988). Family functioning, time allocation, and parental depression in the families of normal and ADHD children. *Journal of Clinical Child Psychology, 17*(2), 169–177.

Davila, R., Williams, M., & MacDonald, J. (1991). *Clarification of policy to address the needs of children with attention deficit disorders within general and/or special education.* Washington, DC: Department of Education.

Dulcan, M., & the Work Group on Quality Issues. (1997). Practice parameters for the assessment and treatment of children, adolescents, and adults with attention-deficit/hyperactivity disorder. *Journal of the American Academy of Child and Adolescent Psychiatry, 36*(Suppl. 10), 85–121.

DuPaul, G. J., & Stoner, G. (2003). *ADHD in the schools: Assessment and intervention strategies* (2nd ed.). New York: Guilford.

Evans, S. W., Axelrod, J., & Langberg, J. M. (2004). Efficacy of a school-based treatment program for middle school youth with ADHD. *Behavior Modification, 28*(4), 528–547.

Evans, S. W., Dowling, C., & Brown, R. (in press). Psychosocial treatment for adolescents with attention deficit hyperactivity disorder. In K. McBurnett, L. Pfiffner, R. Schachar, G. R. Elliot, & J. Nigg (Eds.), *Attention deficit hyperactivity disorder.*

Evans, S. W., Pelham, W., & Grudberg, M. V. (1995). The efficacy of notetaking to improve behavior and comprehension of adolescents with attention deficit hyperactivity disorder. *Exceptionality, 5*(1), 1–17.

Johnston, C., & Mash, E. J. (2001). Families of children with attention-deficit/hyperactivity disorder: Review and recommendations for future research. *Clinical Child and Family Psychology Review, 4*(3), 183–207.

Lonigan, C. J., Elbert, J. C., & Johnson, S. B. (1998). Empirically supported psychosocial interventions for children: An overview. *Journal of Clinical Child Psychology, 27,* 138–145.

MTA Cooperative Group. (1999). A 14-month randomized clinical trial of treatment strategies for attention-deficit/hyperactivity disorder. *Archives of General Psychiatry, 56,* 1073–1086.

MTA Cooperative Group. (2004). National Institute of Mental Health multimodal treatment study of ADHD follow-up: 24-month outcomes of treatment strategies for attention-deficit/hyperactivity disorder. *Pediatrics, 113,* 754–761.

Pelham, W. E., Wheeler, T., & Chronis, A. (1998). Empirically supported psychosocial treatments for attention deficit hyperactivity disorder. *Journal of Clinical Child Psychology, 27*(2), 190–205.

Smith, B. H., Waschbusch, D. A., Willoughby, M. T., & Evans, S. W. (2000). The efficacy, safety, and practicality of treatments for adolescents with attention-deficit/hyperactivity disorder (ADHD). *Clinical Child and Family Psychology Review, 3*(4), 243–267.

Tucker, P. (1999). Attention-deficit/hyperactivity disorder in the drug and alcohol clinic. *Drug and Alcohol Review, 18,* 337–344.

Solution-Focused, Brief Therapy Interventions for Students at Risk to Drop Out

Cynthia Franklin ▪ Johnny S. Kim ▪ Stephen J. Tripodi

CHAPTER 67

Getting Started

Youths from diverse cultures and backgrounds are currently dropping out of high school. The U.S. Department of Education's Institute for Education Sciences reports that high school dropout is a continuing problem for schools (What Works Clearinghouse, n.d., http://www.w-w-c.org/ comingnext/ dropout.html). The percentage of students who do not graduate from high school at the end of a 13-year program of study ranges from 11% to 28% for certain at-risk student populations. Some research suggests that high school dropouts are more likely to abuse drugs, be unemployed, and be in jail (Aloise-Young & Chavez, 2002). Every indication is that social, mental health, and family problems co-occur with high school dropout.

School social workers and other student support services professionals need effective interventions that can engage students and that can develop quick change in student behaviors and attitudes. Since the 1990s, school social workers and counselors have been experimenting with solution-focused, brief therapy (SFBT) to assist students with academic and behavioral problems. SFBT developed out of family systems theory and social construction family practice. This chapter will describe the steps in conducting SFBT and how it can be applied with students who are at risk of dropping out of high school.

What We Know

Reasons for dropping out of high school often overlap in a way that makes it difficult to develop a singular profile of at-risk school dropouts. Reviews of this topic indicate that there are both institutional and individual reasons for dropouts (Rumberger, 2004). Table 67.1 provides a summary of individual, family, and school-related reasons for dropping out based on empirical studies.

It is easy to see when examining the reasons for dropping out of high school that, in order to prevent dropout, school social workers and other professionals need to be prepared to work with students across multiple problem issues and systems (e.g., school, family, and community). Yet, for all that has been written on preventing dropout, past reviews of research studies indicate that the research in this area is limited for the scope and importance of the problem (e.g., Prevatt & Kelly, 2003; Rumberger, 2004; Slavin & Fashola, 1998). Slavin and Fashola (1998), for example, reviewed the literature on dropout prevention programs and found only two programs that met evidence-based criteria for an effective intervention. Prevatt and Kelly (2003) conducted a thorough review of research evaluating dropout prevention programs and found that few studies have evaluated program effectiveness with strong designs, and schools are not adopting research-based prevention programs. The National Dropout Prevention Center (2004) lists 15 strategies for dropout prevention that have been found to have some degree of effectiveness (http://www.dropoutprevention. org/effstrat/effstrat.htm). Alternative school programs are one of the promising practices that are mentioned across reviews. See chapter 38 in this volume for a discussion of how to design an effective alternative school program. The most comprehensive review on dropout prevention is forthcoming. Chad Nye and colleagues are conducting the study sponsored by the What Works Clearinghouse (n.d., http://www.w-w-c.org/ comingnext/dropout.html), a research arm of the Department of Education's Institute for Education

Table 67.1 Reasons for Dropping Out

Individual	*Family*	*School-Related*
• Low grades • Poor daily attendance • Misbehavior • Alcohol and drug use • Feeling alienated from other students	• Parents not engaged in child's schooling • Teen pregnancy • Student getting married • Financial and work reasons • Permissive parenting style • Negative emotional reactions and sanctions for bad grades	• Student/teacher ratio • Quality of teachers • Seeking smaller school size • School safety concerns • Not feeling welcomed at the school

Sources: Based on studies by Aloise-Young & Chavez, 2002; Jordan, Lara, & McPartland, 1996; Rumberger, 1987; Rumberger, Ghatak, Poulos, Ritter, & Dornbusch, 1990; Rumberger & Thomas, 2000.

Sciences. The What Works Clearinghouse (n.d.) uses a set of standards for evaluating studies based on rigorous, experimental criteria. This group is working in an alliance with the Campbell Collaboration to synthesize the best practices in dropout prevention. Brian Cobb (cobb@cahs.colostate.edu; personal communication, May 27, 2005) at Colorado State University and colleagues are also completing a large meta-analysis that includes approximately 50 dropout prevention programs for high-risk youths. Both of these studies will hopefully be finished in the near future and provide needed direction for practitioners.

Solution-Focused, Brief Therapy

The development of SFBT originated in the early 1980s at the Brief Family Therapy Center in Milwaukee. This approach to counseling became very popular and widely used in the 1990s mostly due to the demands for briefer counseling interventions. Practitioners also began to use the SFBT techniques in schools (Berg & Shilts, 2005; Franklin, Biever, Moore, Clemons, & Scamardo, 2001; Kral, 1995; Metcalf, 1995; Murphy, 1996; Sklare, 1997; Webb, 1999). As a result, quasi-experimental design studies began to examine the success of SFBT with students who have behavioral and academic problems. Table 67.2 presents examples of quasi-experimental studies that have been completed on SFBT in schools.

Even though the studies on the effectiveness of SFBT with at-risk students are only in the infancy stage, this approach has shown some promise with challenging and resistant students. Franklin and Streeter (2003, 2005) focused their work on using SFBT to prevent high school

dropout. These researchers and practitioners focused on training teachers and administrators in solution-focused principles and techniques. The goal was to change the school culture so that all staff used a solution-building process with students at risk to drop out. See Table 71.2 for a list of solution-focused principles for schools. These principles were developed in relationship to a study on dropout prevention.

SFBT practitioners believe that this counseling approach is effective in encouraging students to overcome personal and social barriers that are associated with dropping out of school. SFBT is helpful for adolescents at risk of dropping out because it focuses on moving students in crisis beyond their current state to a position of working through the crisis (Hopson & Kim, 2004). Students at risk of dropping out may have many different social problems or mental health or family issues. SFBT practitioners may address specific issues as barriers to student goals, but the SFBT practitioner does not try to solve all of these problems. Instead, the practitioner focuses on the functional and social outcomes of these problems (e.g., tardiness, missing classes, conflicts with teachers) and helps the students to prioritize what needs most to be changed in their future behaviors so that they can get along with others (e.g., teacher, mother, peers, boyfriend). The SFBT approach examines strengths in students and their social environment and seeks to harness those strengths to help the student to identify what is going to make a difference in their interactions. SFBT also may add resources to remove barriers that block goals and use whatever resources are available to help students succeed.

Solution-focused, questioning techniques are used to build relationships with students, engage

Table 67.2 Examples of Outcome Studies on Solution-Focused Therapy in Schools

Posttest Only

Author and Date: Littrell et al. (1995)
Population: Students (grades 9–12)
Sample Size: 61
Setting: High school
Number of Sessions: 3
Measures: Self-anchored scales
Results: No difference between brief therapy groups.

Experimental or Quasi-Experimental Designs

Author and Date: Franklin & Streeter (2005)
Population: High school dropout youths
Sample Size: 85
Setting: Alternative high school
Number of Sessions: Ongoing attendance at solution-focused high school program
Measures: School Success Profile, number of credits earned, attendance
Results: Results from the School Success Profile showed both the solution-focused group and comparison group are at high risk of dropping out with few assets or protective factors. The solution-focused group, however, rated school domain factors (school satisfaction, teacher support, school safety) as assets, while comparison group rated them as either caution or risk. The solution-focused group showed statistically significant differences on the credits earned, along with a moderate effect size. There was statistically significant difference on attendance favoring the comparison group, along with a large effect size. Authors report that the self-paced, instructional format of the solution-focused program may have confounded the attendance finding.

Author and Date: Newsome (2004)
Population: Students
Sample Size: 52
Setting: Middle school
Number of Sessions: One class period (35 minutes) for 8 weeks
Measures: Grades and attendance
Results: Grades for students in the experimental group increased from a mean pretest score of 1.58 to a mean posttest score of 1.69 while grades for the comparison group decreased from a mean pretest score of 1.66 to a posttest score of 1.48. The results of the regression testing differences between experimental and comparison groups on posttest grade point average scores was statistically significant when using pretest grade point average as the covariate; however, the proportion of variance (R^2) was not large. As for the other dependent variable, attendance, there was no statistical difference between the experimental and comparison groups.

Author and Date: Moore & Franklin (2005)
Population: Students
Sample Size: 59
Setting: Middle school
Number of Sessions:

• 4-hour teacher training on solution model
• 3–4 teacher-therapist consultations
• 1–2 formal collaborative meetings between teachers and students

• 5–7 30–45-minute individual therapy sessions with students
Measures: Teacher Report Form of the Achenbach Behavioral Checklist, Youth Self-Report of the Achenbach Behavioral Checklist

(continued)

Table 67.2 *(Continued)*

Results: Internalizing and externalizing scores for TRF showed that experimental group declined below the clinical level by posttest and remained there for follow-up. Comparison group changed little among pretest, posttest, and follow-up. Effect size for internalizing was large while effect size for externalizing was medium. Internalizing score for YSR showed no difference between experimental and comparison groups, and effect size was weak. Externalizing score for YSR showed the experimental group dropped below the clinical level and continued to drop at follow-up. A large effect size was calculated for YSR externalizing score.

Author and Date: LaFountain & Garner (1996)
Population: Students
Sample Size: 311
Setting: Elementary and high schools
Number of Sessions: 8
Measures: Index of Personality Characteristics
Results: Modest but statistically significant between-group differences were found on three subscales of the Index of Personality Characteristics: nonacademic, perception of self, and acting in. These differences suggest that students in the experimental group had higher self-esteem in nonacademic arenas; more positive attitudes and feelings about themselves; and more appropriate ways of coping with emotions.

Author and Date: Springer et al. (2000)
Population: Children
Sample Size: 10
Setting: School
Number of Sessions: 5
Measures: Hare Self-Esteem Scale
Results: Solution-focused subjects made significant pretest to posttest improvement on the Hare Self-Esteem Scale with a moderate effect size, whereas the comparison group's scores were unchanged. However, a covariance analysis of posttest scores (with pretest scores as the covariate) found no significant between-group differences. Limitations include small sample size and absence of randomization.

Single-Case and AB Designs

Author and Date: Corcoran & Stephenson (2000)
Population: Children (most referred by schools)
Sample Size: 136
Setting: University-sponsored mental health clinic
Number of Sessions: 4–6
Measures: Feelings, Attitudes and Behaviors Scale for Children, Conners's Parent Rating Scale
Results: Results showed significant improvement from pretest to posttest for some subscales in the Conners's Parent Rating Scale: conduct problems, impulsivity, and hyperactivity.

Author and Date: Franklin et al. (2001)
Population: Learning-challenged middle-school students
Sample Size: 7
Setting: Middle school
Number of Sessions: 5–10
Measures: Conners's Teacher Rating Scale
Results: 5 of 7 (71%) cases improved per teacher's report.

Author and Date: Geil (1998)
Population: Elementary-school children and teachers
Sample Size: 8 student–teacher pairs
Setting: Elementary school
Number of Sessions: 12 consultations
Measures: Instructional Environment System-II and Code for Instructional Structure and Student Academic Response
Results: Statistical difference in two of the consultation cases, only one solution-focused case.

students in a solution-building process, discover students' personal goals and strengths, and increase motivation toward desired outcomes. Selekman, in chapter 27 in this volume, illustrates several of the questioning techniques used in solution building in his chapter on self-harm. This chapter will describe the solution-building process and the structure of a typical session and illustrate questioning techniques that may be useful with students who are at risk of dropping out.

What Is Solution Building?

Solution building is a process where practitioners engage students in a purposeful conversation, resulting in changes in perceptions and social interactions. The solution-building process or conversation is often contrasted to the problem-solving process. Problem solving focuses on the resolution of presenting problems through understanding the problems, enumerating alternatives that can solve the problems, and choosing an alternative. In contrast, solution building changes the way people think about presenting problems and identifies future behaviors and tasks that have the potential to accomplish desired goals and outcomes (De Jong & Berg, 2002). Solution-building conversations result in the student discovering goals, tasks, and behaviors that change future outcomes. The SFBT practitioner acts as a catalyst or facilitator and creates an interpersonal context where the solutions emerge from the students and their ideas during the process of the conversation.

Change in SFBT comes from finding what already works and doing more of it (Miller & de Shazer, 2000). It also comes from helping students to visualize a future outcome that they desire and helping them to think through the steps to achieve it. The steps are further broken down into small tasks or solutions that are identified by the students. The reason that SFBT practitioners focus on small steps is to get students moving forward toward their goals and to help them be able to experience some success. Success builds confidence in students and has the potential to change their view of the situation (e.g., I was able to come back to school for one class with the teacher I like, so maybe I do not have to drop out). Small steps are also viewed as being capable of serving as catalysts for bigger changes.

SFBT Counseling Techniques

Exception Questions

- When does the problem not occur?
- What was different about those times when things were better between you and your teacher?
- Even though this is a very bad time, in my experience, people's lives do not always stay the same. I will bet that there have been times when the problem of being sent to the principal's office was not happening, or at least was happening less. Please describe those times. What was different? How did you get that to happen?

SFBT practitioners start solution building by exploring exceptions (Lee, 1997). Exceptions are situations when the stated complaint does not occur, occurs less often, or occurs with less intensity. Exception questions were designed to encourage students to notice evidence that not only is change possible but also that they have already had some successful attempts (Lathem, 2002). SFBT theorizes that it is more beneficial for students to increase their current successes instead of trying to eliminate the problem altogether, no matter how small the current successes appear to be (Murphy, 1996).

The school social worker and counselor must understand the students' perception of what has worked and what they think will work to achieve their goals, in addition to trusting the students in regard to seeing solutions in exceptions (Pichot & Dolan, 2003). It is important for the social worker and counselor to emphasize the exceptions and question how the student brought about these changes. Furthermore, the social worker must believe that it was not the right solution if the student walked away from it.

Relationship Questions

- What would your teacher say about your grades?
- What would your mother say?
- If you were to do something that made your teacher very happy, what would that be?
- Who would be the most surprised if you did well on that test?

Relationship questions allow students to discuss their problems from a third-person point of view, which makes the problem less threatening and allows the social worker, counselor, or teacher to assess the students' viewpoint and the students to practice thinking about the problem from the viewpoint of others. The procedure is to ask the students what their family members and teachers think about their problem and progress, as more indicators of change helping the students to develop a vision of a future appropriate to their social context. Furthermore, students develop empathy because of relationship questions as they are able to see how the severity of their problem has affected their family and significant others. Subsequently, motivation may increase as they become cognizant of the impact their problem has had on other people in their lives.

Scaling Questions

- On a scale of 1–10, with 1 being the lowest and 10 being the highest, where would you rate yourself in terms of reaching your goals that you identified last week?
- On a scale of 1–10, with 1 being that you never go to class and 10 being that you have perfect attendance, where would you put yourself on that scale? What would it take to increase two numbers on the scale?
- On a scale of 1–10, with 1 being that you are getting in trouble every day in class and 10 being that you are doing your school work and your teacher says something nice to you, where would you be on that scale?

The school social worker and other school professionals have the option to use scaling questions to quantify and measure the intensity of internal thoughts and feelings, along with helping the students to anchor reality and move forward from their problem (Franklin & Nurius, 1998; Pichot & Dolan, 2003). Many different variations of this technique can be used, such as asking for percentages of progress, holding up a ruler or string, or drawing a line on a sidewalk. Scaling questions are a technique used to determine where students are in terms of achieving their goals. Scaling is a subjective process, but it helps students to measure and assess how much progress they may or may not have made toward goals. Typically, scaling questions have students rate where they are on a scale from 1 to 10 with 1 being the worst/lowest and 10 being the best/highest. Scaling is a technique that is familiar to most students and a helpful tool for the therapist when students are having a difficult time seeing their progress.

Franklin, Corcoran, Nowicki, and Streeter (1997) describe three different uses of scaling in SFBT. First is to determine where the students are on the scale in terms of solving their own problems; second is to look for exceptions to the problem; and third is to construct a miracle or identify solution behaviors. The highest point on the scale should always represent the desired outcome. Furthermore, the scaling sequence must end with the social worker asking the students how they will move forward to another point on the scale.

The Miracle Question

Now, I want to ask you a strange question. This is probably a question no one has asked you before. Suppose that while you are sleeping tonight, a miracle happens, and the problem that brought you here is solved. However, because you are sleeping, you don't know that the miracle has happened. So, when you wake up tomorrow morning, what will be the first thing that you notice that is different that will tell you a miracle has happened and that the problem which brought you here is solved?

The miracle question strengthens students' goals by allowing them to reconstruct their story, showing a future without the students' perceived problems (Berg & De Jong, 1996; De Jong & Berg, 2001). Moreover, the social worker uses the miracle question to help students to identify ways that the solution may already be occurring in their lives. According to Pichot and Dolan (2003), the miracle question came into being by chance. One of Berg's clients suggested, "Only a miracle will help," which enabled Berg and associates to realize the power of the client imagining how the future would be without the problem.

Pichot and Dolan (2003) describe five elements that are crucial to the miracle question. The first crucial element is saying the words "suppose a miracle happens." This tells the student that a desired change is possible. Second, the student must have a basic understanding of what the miracle is, which the statement "The problem that brought you here is solved" often defines. The third crucial element to the miracle question is immediacy. The miracle must be described as happening tonight and in an environment that is realistic for students, such as in their homes. Fourth, in the hypothetical situation, the student must be unaware that the miracle has occurred. Without this, there is nothing for the student to discover, which is a vital component of the miracle question. Fifth, students must recognize the signs that indicate to them that the miracle happened.

The miracle question provides students with a vision of a problem-free future and empowers them to learn new ways of behaving. Asking this question, very gently and thoughtfully, is believed to allow a shift in the students' usual thought processes (Pichot & Dolan, 2003).

Goaling

Goaling is used as a verb in SFBT. An important distinction to make between goal setting in SFBT and other approaches to behavior change is that attaining the goal does not represent the end of counseling in SFBT; goals are considered the beginning of behavior change, not the end. The social worker and the student negotiate small, observable goals, set within a brief time frame, that lead to a new story for the student. The negotiation of goals should start immediately between the social worker and student (Franklin & Nurius, 1998). If a student is unable to think of a concrete goal, the practitioner may opt to provide multiple-choice answers. Additionally, scaling questions are beneficial to measure the student's progress toward goal attainment. Three advantages of using scales in this context are that they make goals and actions that lead to goals, they place responsibility for change on students, and students can take credit for the changes they make (Corcoran, 1998).

Walter and Peller (1996) say that goaling is the evolution of meaning about what students want to experience or what their lives may be like after the alleviation of the problem. Goaling is talking about what the student wants to do; it is not problem solving, but creative and conversational (Walter & Peller, 1996). Furthermore, goaling allows the conversation to lead to areas in students' lives that are free of the problems and where students want their lives to be.

According to Sklare (1997), the two most common types of goals that students identify are positive and negative goals. *Positive goals* are stated in terms of what the client wants and are measurable. Typical examples are "I want to get better grades" or "I want to have more friends." Most positive goals lack specific behavioral details. Asking specific details about what students will be doing when they are moving toward that goal will help students to identify specific behavioral details. So, the practitioner would say, "Let's just suppose your teacher was nicer to you. How would that help? What would you be doing differently?"

Negative goals are expressed as the absence of something. Clients will usually want themselves to stop doing something or usually want someone else to stop doing something to them. Typical examples are "I want my parents to stop bothering me" or "I want to stop getting into fights at school." When faced with negative goals, social workers must help students to reframe their goals in a way that gives students the responsibility. This can be accomplished by asking questions to help determine the students' motivation for wanting to stop doing something or wanting others to stop doing something to them. Some examples might be, "So when your parents aren't bothering you, what would that do for you?" or "When you're not getting into fights at school, what are you doing?"

The Break for Reflection

The *break* is another integral part of SFBT. It helps to transition the interview toward the final stage of the session, where the social worker or counselor develops a set of compliments for the student and a homework task. Most social workers will simply go to their desk and write down notes or just inform students that they need a minute to reflect on the discussion and make notes on their notepad. In schools, when interviews are informal and meeting places may be in classrooms or other areas, the social worker might go to the bathroom or just take some psychological space for a moment. What is important about the break is to create a strong psychological space so that when the social worker returns, the student is paying close attention to what the practitioner is going to say next (de Shazer, 1985). The social worker finishes the solution-focused session by giving the student a set of meaningful compliments, reviewing strengths and goals identified by the student, and developing a homework task to further encourage behavioral change.

Case Example Illustrating Solution-Building Conversation

Box 67.1 provides an example of a solution-building conversation between a school-based practitioner and a 16-year-old student. A teacher has sent the student for help because he is sleeping

Box 67.1 Case Example Illustrating Solution-Building Conversation

Student: I hate that teacher. She makes a big deal out of everything. I was not sleeping. I was just resting my eyes for a second. What a liar she is. Nobody likes her.

Social Worker: So, you think the teacher does not understand what you were doing in her class.

S: Yeah, that's right. She is just trying to get rid of me.

SW: Trying to get rid of you?

S: Yeah, she does not like me at all.

SW: How is it that the teacher came not to like you?

S: I do not know. You'd have to ask her.

SW: What if I did ask her, what might she say?

S: I don't know. What kind of question is that?

SW: It is an imagination question. So, let's just imagine for a moment that you did know what she might say, what might it be?

S: That's dumb.

SW: You think so?

S: Yeah!

SW: Well, sometimes I might ask dumb questions, but it is okay to answer me anyway. So, what would the teacher say about not liking you? [waits in silence, does not give up on answer, smiles, remains pleasant with student]

S: Hmm. I guess she might say that I skip the beginning or end of her class. It is *boring*! But, this sleeping thing is stupid!

SW: Of course, I know the sleeping thing you do not agree with. You were just resting your eyes. Let me see if I have this right. She would say that she does not like you because you do not come on time and stay throughout the whole class?

S: Yeah, that is it.

SW: So, I guess she might also say she wants you to keep your eyes open in her class even if you want to rest them?

S: That is hard to do because she is a terrible teacher and I just can't listen. I think she should have to take her own class to see how terrible she is.

SW: Maybe that would help?

S: I do not know.

SW: So, tell me, which is more important to your teacher right now: keeping your eyes open or coming on time and staying to the end of her class?

S: I guess keeping my eyes open because she says she is going to put me in in-school suspension.

SW: How do you feel about going to in-school suspension? I have met students who prefer that to a class.

S: No! I am going to be in worse trouble if I have to go back there again. I might have to go to the alternative learning center, and my mom is going to be mad.

SW: So, you want to stay in the teacher's class?

S: Really, I want to be moved to another class but Mr. Jones [the principal] said that was not going to happen.

SW: So, your choices are to stay in the teacher's class by finding a way to keep your eyes open or to go to the alternative learning center and face your mom?

S: It sucks!

SW: Yeah, it is a tough situation. I can see how you would feel frustrated. So, have there been times that you have somehow managed to keep your eyes open in the teacher's class?

S: Yeah.

SW: Tell me about those times.

S: Well, sometimes when it was interesting or she was reviewing for a test.

SW: You mean, sometimes the class is actually interesting? When would those times be?

S: Like when she is not lecturing and we are working on a group project.

SW: So, those times your eyes are wide open and you are participating too?

S: Yeah, I guess so.

SW: You said before that you did not close your eyes for too long. I bet sometimes in the past you managed to keep your eyes open even when she was lecturing and super-boring.

S: Yeah, I did.

SW: So, what percent of the time are you able to keep your eyes open? 5%? 10%? 25%?

S: 80% of the time!

SW: Wow! Even when she is boring.

S: Yeah, I think so.

SW: So, tell me, what percent do you think your teacher would give you?.

S: Not as high because she blows everything up.

SW: Yes, of course. Well, just suppose she improved a little and gave you more of a fair rating. What might she say?

S: Maybe about 50 or 60%.

(continued)

Box 67.1 (*continued*)

SW: That is pretty good.. How do you think you can get to 90%?

S: Get more sleep so I can stand her boring lectures.

SW: Let's just suppose you did get some more sleep. How might that help?

S: I think it would just make me more alert and patient.

SW: Are there any other things that keep you from being alert and patient? Like, for example, a lot of students I know smoke a joint or take medications before class and that makes them sleepy. Or they might have fights with their parents or girlfriend that make them distracted.

S: No, I don't smoke before class. My mom makes me take my ADHD medicine but that does not make me sleepy.

SW: For my information, how much sleep do you usually get per night?

S: About 3–4 hours.

SW: What do you do instead of sleeping?

S: Listen to the stereo and watch TV. Sometimes talk to my friends in the chat room if I can sneak into my mom's computer room.

SW: So, how much extra sleep do you think you would need to keep your eyes open in this class?

S: I do not know. Maybe 2–3 hours more.

SW: So, maybe 5–6 hours?

S: Yeah.

SW: What about the teacher's percentage? What would she say you could do to get to 60 or 70%?

S: I think she likes it when I stay in the class and ask questions.

SW: You have done that before?

S: Yeah, sometimes.

SW: If you did that, would that get you to 70% with the teacher?

S: Maybe.

[At this point, the social worker tells the student that she is going to take a few moments to think about what has been said and write down some notes]

SW: Well, you know, I am really impressed that you are able to keep your eyes open in a class that you feel is boring and that you find ways to stay in the class and ask questions in the class.. How do you manage to do that?

S: I just do it. I am not always a bad student.

SW: No, I am hearing that you know how to be a good student and that you do not want to go to the alternative learning center. I wonder if you can try an experiment for just this week? Get 5–6 hours of sleep so you can have the patience and alertness to keep your eyes open all the time during the class. Also, do what you suggested. Stay in the class from the beginning to the end. Ask questions during class. See if that will keep the teacher from kicking you out of her class.

S: Okay, I could try that.

SW: So, you could try that?

S: Yeah.

SW: So, just so I am clear about your plan for staying in the class, tell me again what you plan to do. I want to write it down here in my notes. I will talk to you at the end of the week to see how it is working.

[Student rehearses plan and social worker asks about details of the suggested approach]

during class, and she wants him to be taken out of her class because he will not participate.

The importance of this solution-building conversation is that the practitioner's dialogue with the student results in the student becoming more cooperative and selecting his own solution for the problem at hand. Notice also that the practitioner continually builds the relationship with the student, forming a desired goal to work on, and asking the student to commit to the steps to accomplish the goal. This is an example of a solution-building process. The SFBT practitioner knows that this is only a small step but will seek to build on this cooperative beginning to help the student find ways to improve his behavior in the class. At the same time, the practitioner will work with the teacher to find out in detail what the teacher wants to see different in the student's behaviors. The practitioner might give an assignment to the teacher, like noticing when the student is doing what the teacher wants in the class.

Soliciting Cooperation and Motivation in Students Who Resist

Staff in the school view most students at risk of dropping out as unmotivated, uncooperative, or resistant. SFBT practitioners believe that everyone has motivation and people are in particular motivated toward personal goals. Every student has positive aspirations, and the solution-focused practitioner will tune into what those are with individual students. The focus is always on how the goal serves to motivate socially effective behaviors or positive interactions with others. SFBT views resistance as a normal human behavior. There are two types of resistance, active and passive. Every person has the ability to be resistant and uncooperative. At the same time, every person can be cooperative. Cooperation is something that can be facilitated when people have a relationship and are working together toward a win-win outcome. Facilitating cooperative behaviors increases the student's self-esteem and enables a true partnership between the practitioner and the student to emerge (Hawkes, Marsh, & Wilgosh, 1998).

SFBT practitioners take a curious position, or "not knowing approach," when working with students who are actively resisting. They find ways to agree with the students' points of view and do not actively confront the students on points of greatest resistance. This serves to disarm students. For example, if you are playing tug-of-war with someone and stop tugging back, they often lose their balance and stop pulling against you. SFBT practitioners use the same principle in managing passive resistance. When a student gives passive responses to questions, such as "I don't know," it is important for the practitioner to pretend that she is too slow to understand and must rephrase the question. These types of conversational tactics are meant to keep the conversation and relationship moving forward in the face of resistance.

Using Emotions to Engage and Motivate Students

Sometimes SFBT practitioners will construct positive engagement by prefacing their questions about what students are doing or might do to change, coupled with acknowledging their expressions of emotions and using those emotions as a catalyst for change (Miller & de Shazer, 2000). The emotional states that SFBT practitioners are most likely to use are those associated with positive aspirations, goals, wants, and desires. They will also juxtapose positive feelings and desires against feelings and outcomes that the student wishes to avoid. This is illustrated in the solution-focused

conversation. In the example, the student wanted to remain in the class to avoid the consequences of going to the alternative learning center and facing the anger of his mom. The fears about the consequences of his behavior were used as a way to focus the student on a more positive outcome.

In another example, a student may say that she hates the school and does not like to attend but at the same time say that she really wants to graduate so she can get a better job. The SFBT practitioner would focus on the positive feeling and desire to graduate and ask questions about how that became an important goal in her life. The counselor would be curious about how the student came to feel a desire to graduate, for example. How strong is that feeling? Who else in her social network or family shares that feeling? Are there any people who do not share that feeling about the importance of graduation? How does the student keep the positive desire when others are negative? The practitioner might also assess the strength and importance of the desire to graduate through a scaling question: "On a scale of 0–10, with 0 meaning you do not care that much whether you graduate or not and 10 being that you care a great deal and are ready to do about anything to make that happen, where would you say you are?" Additionally, practitioners might make statements like "Some students do not feel like they want to graduate or just give up. What makes you feel differently?" Such statements are aimed at complimenting and encouraging the student and increasing her positive feelings and desires toward graduation.

Tools and Practice Examples

Franklin et al. (2001) suggest that, in order to conduct SFBT, the school social workers and other mental health practitioners must follow a solution-focused process and, at a minimum, implement the miracle question, ask scaling questions, and provide compliments. An SFBT session format is flexible enough to adapt to the individual needs of each student but also structured enough to provide guidance to practitioners. Following, we describe the structure of an SFBT counseling session and illustrate several of the counseling techniques.

A typical session follows the structure discussed by Franklin and Moore (1999):

Warm-up conversation to establish rapport and create relaxed environment

Identifying problem and tracking new exceptions to the problem

Using relationship questions to examine student's perception of how others view student's problem or problem resolution

Asking scaling questions and coping questions

Building goals and discovering solutions by asking the miracle question

Taking a break to formulate compliments and homework

Giving compliments and homework tasks

Structure of the Interview and Case Example

Most solution-focused interviews occur during traditional 50-minute sessions. In schools, however, these interviews may last for shorter periods of time. Interviews may last 20–30 minutes, for example. The structure of the interview is divided into three parts. The first part usually is spent making small talk with the student to find out a little bit about the student's life. During this first part, the social worker should be looking to understand the student's interests, motivations, competencies, and belief systems.

Social Worker: Hello, Charles. I understand your teacher, Mrs. Park, sent you here to see me because you're at risk of failing out of school. But I'd like to hear from you the reason you are here to see me and how this can help you. [allows student to state what the problem is]

Student: I don't know. I hate this school, and I just want to drop out so that people will leave me alone.

SW: So, if I'm understanding you correctly, you're here to see me because you hate the school and a lot of people—your teachers and maybe your parents—have been bugging you about your grades and doing homework?

S: Yeah.

SW: So what sorts of things do you like to do when you're not in school?

S: Ummm, I like to hang out with my friends.

SW: What do you and your friends talk about when you're hanging out?

S: I don't know. We talk about basketball and music and stuff. [social worker will continue to develop rapport and try to find out student's interests and belief systems]

The second part of the session, which takes up the bulk of the time—around 40 minutes in traditional sessions but maybe less time in school interviews—is spent discussing the problem, looking for exceptions, and formulating goals. One of the key components to SFBT that has been emphasized in this chapter is working with the student to identify the problem, to look for times when the problem is absent, to look for ways the solution is already occurring, and to develop attainable goals to help resolve the problem. The second part is usually initiated with questions like "How can I help you?" or "What is the reason you have come to see me?" or "How will you know when counseling is no longer necessary?" (Sklare, 1997).

SW: Okay, so how can I help you, or what can you get out of our meeting today so that you know it's been worth your time to see me?

S: I want my teachers and my parents to stop bugging me about my grades and doing homework. This school is just a waste of my time and my classes are stupid.

SW: Have you had a class that you didn't think was stupid or a waste of time? [example of looking for exceptions]

S: My English class last year was cool because we got to read some interesting books and have good discussions about them.

SW: What made the books interesting and the discussions good?

S: Well, they were books that I could understand and relate to. My teacher also made the time and effort to explain things to us and made sure we all got a turn to speak our thoughts.

SW: You said you hated this school, but yet you haven't dropped out yet. How have you managed to do that? [allows student to identify possible solutions and possible successes in what they've already been doing]

S: Well, I'm still going to some of my classes, but at this point I just don't care any more.

SW: Charles, for those classes that you do attend, what would your teachers say about your academic work? [example of relationship question]

S: I guess they might say that I don't pay attention in class, that I don't do my homework, and that I'm not trying.

SW: Do you agree with that?

S: I guess, but it's just that the classes are so stupid and boring.

SW: Charles, I'd like to ask you an unusual

question. It's probably something no one has ever asked you before. Suppose, after we're done and you leave my office, you go to bed tonight and a miracle happens. This miracle solves all of your problems that brought you here today, but because you were sleeping, you didn't know it occurred. So, the next morning you wake up and you sense something is different. What will you notice that is different that lets you know this miracle occurred and your problems are solved? [example of the miracle question]

S: I guess I wouldn't be cutting class and maybe getting better grades.

SW: What will you be doing differently to get better grades?

S: I would probably be better prepared for class.

SW: What does being better prepared for class look like? [continue to probe and elicit more details and examples]

S: I'd pay attention in class and take some notes.

SW: What else would you be doing differently when you're getting better grades?

S: Probably doing my homework and not causing trouble in class with the teacher.

SW: So, what will you be doing instead of causing trouble in class?

S: Listen and sit there and take notes, I guess.

SW: So, on a scale from 1 to 10, with 1 being I'm dropping out of school no matter what and 10 being the miracle solved my problems and I'm going to graduate, where would you say you are right now? [example of a scaling question]

S: Three.

SW: What sorts of things prevent you from giving it a 2 or a 1?

S: Well, I know I need to get my high school diploma because I always thought I might go study how to be a med tech at college. I like the TV show "CSI" and want to work in forensics.

SW: Wow! You want to study forensics. So, you need to finish school for that. So, what would need to happen for you to be a 4 or a 5?

S: I'd need to start coming to classes and doing my work. [examples of student identifying goals and solutions. Social worker would continue looking for solutions that are already occurring in Charles's life and collaborate on identifying and setting small, attainable goals]

The final part of the session lasts around 5–10 minutes. This last part involves giving the student a set of compliments, homework, and determining whether to continue discussing this topic at another time. In school settings, practitioners such as teachers and social workers have separated this last part from the rest of the conversation. The break, for example, might be extended, and the conversation might pick up in a different class period or at a different time of the day (e.g., before and after lunch).

SW: I'd like to take a minute to write down some notes based on what we've talked about. Is there anything else you feel I should know before I take this quick break?

S: No.

SW: [after taking a break] Well, Charles, I'd like to compliment you on your commitment to staying in school despite your frustrations. You seem like a bright student and understand the importance of finishing high school. I'd like to meet with you again to continue our work together. Would that be all right with you?

S: Sure.

SW: So, for next week, I'd like you to try and notice when things are going a little bit better in your classes and what you're doing differently during those times.

Internet Resources for Solution-Focused Schools

Brief Family Therapy Center: www.brief-therapy.org

Cynthia Franklin: www.utexas.edu/ssw/faculty/franklin

Garza High School: A Solution-Focused High School: http://www.austinschools.org/garza

Key Points to Remember

Youths from all backgrounds and in every place are at risk of dropping out of school. This challenge is compounded further by a lack of evidence-based interventions that school social workers and other practitioners can use to reach this challenging population.

SFBT is one intervention that can help school social workers and other school professionals engage and retrieve dropout youths. This approach builds on student strengths. SFBT offers conversational, questioning techniques that help practitioners to engage students in a solution-building process. A solution-building process helps students to discover goals, tasks, and behaviors that can change future outcomes.

The SFBT practitioner acts as a catalyst or facilitator and creates an interpersonal context where the solutions emerge from students and their ideas.

SFBT also provides specific skills for engaging, motivating, and eliciting cooperation in resistant students. Techniques include going with resistance, focusing on personal goals, taking a curious, not-knowing approach, playing dumb, and reinforcing positive emotions.

The structure of the SFBT counseling session has three parts. Case examples have given an overview of the parts and how SFBT can be used to help students at risk of dropping out.

References

Aloise-Young, P. A., & Chavez, E. L. (2002). Not all school dropouts are the same: Ethnic differences in the relation between reason for leaving school and adolescent substance use. *Psychology in the Schools, 39*(5), 539–547.

Berg, I. K., & De Jong, P. (1996). Solution-building conversation: Co-constructing a sense of competence with clients. *Families in Society: The Journal of Contemporary Human Services, 77,* 376–391.

Berg, I. K., & Shilts, L. (2005). *Classroom solutions: WOWW approach.* Milwaukee, WI: Brief Family Therapy Center.

Corcoran, J. (1998). Solution-focused practice with middle and high school at-risk youths. *Social Work in Education, 20*(4), 232–244.

Corcoran, J., & Stephenson, M. (2000). The effectiveness of solution-focused therapy with child behavior problems: A preliminary study. *Families in Society, 81*(5), 468–474.

De Jong, P., & Berg, I. K. (2001). Co-constructing cooperation with mandated clients. *Social Work, 46*(4), 361–381.

De Jong, P., & Berg, I. K. (2002). *Interviewing for solutions* (2nd ed.). Pacific Grove, CA: Brooks/Cole.

de Shazer, S. (1985). *Keys to solution in brief therapy.* New York: Norton.

Franklin, C., Biever, J., Moore, K., Clemons, D., & Scamardo, M. (2001). The effectiveness of solution-focused therapy with children in a school setting. *Research on Social Work Practice, 11*(4), 411–434.

Franklin, C., Corcoran, J., Nowicki, J., & Streeter, C. (1997). Using client self-anchored scales to measure outcomes in solution-focused therapy. *Journal of Systemic Therapies, 10*(3), 246–265.

Franklin, C., & Moore, K. C. (1999). Solution-focused brief family therapy. In C. Franklin & C. Jordan, *Family practice: Brief systems methods for social work* (pp. 143–174). Pacific Grove, CA: Brooks/Cole.

Franklin, C., & Nurius, P. (1998). Distinction between social constructionism and cognitive constructivism: Practice applications. In C. Franklin & P. Nurius (Eds.), *Constructivism in practice: Methods and challenges* (pp. 57–94). Milwaukee, WI: Families International.

Franklin, C., & Streeter, C. L. (2003). *Solution-focused accountability schools for the 21st century: A training manual for Garza High School.* Austin: University of Texas, Hogg Foundation for Mental Health.

Franklin, C., & Streeter, C. L. (2005). *Solution-focused alternatives for education: An Evaluation of Gonzalo Garza Independent High School.* Austin: University of Texas, Hogg Foundation for Mental Health.

Hawkes, D., Marsh, T., & Wilgosh, R. (1998). How to begin: The concepts of solution-focused therapy. In *Solution focused therapy: A handbook for health care professionals* (pp. 5–15). Woburn, MA: Reed.

Hopson, L. M., & Kim, J. S. (2004). A solution-focused approach to crisis intervention with adolescents. *Journal of Evidence-Based Social Work, 1*(2–3), 93–110.

Jordan, W. L., Lara, J., & McPartland, J. M. (1996). Exploring the causes of early dropout among race-ethnic and gender groups. *Youth & Society, 28*(1), 62–94.

Kral, R. (1995). *Strategies that work: Techniques for solutions in schools.* Milwaukee, WI: Brief Family Therapy Press.

LaFountain, R. M., & Garner, N. E. (1996). Solution-focused counseling groups: The results are in. *Journal for Specialists in Group Work, 21*(2), 128–143.

Lathem, J. (2002). Brief solution-focused therapy. *Child and Adolescent Mental Health, 7*(4), 189–192.

Lee, M. Y. (Ed.). (1997). A study of solution-focused brief family therapy: Outcomes and issues. *American Journal of Family Therapy, 25,* 3–17.

Littrell, J. M., Malia, J. A., & Vanderwood, M. (1995). Single-session brief counseling in a high school. *Journal of Counseling and Development, 73,* 451–458.

Metcalf, L. (1995). *Counseling toward solutions: A practical solution-focused program for working with students, teachers, and parents.* San Francisco: Jossey-Bass.

Miller, G., & de Shazer, S. (2000). Emotions in solution-focused therapy: A re-examination. *Family Process, 39*(1), 5.

Moore, K. C., & Franklin, C. (2005). *The effectiveness of solution-focused therapy with school-related behavior problems.* Manuscript under review

Murphy, J. (1996). Solution-focused brief therapy in the school. In S. Miller, M. Hubble, & B. Duncan (Eds.), *Handbook of solution-focused brief therapy* (pp. 184–204). San Francisco: Jossey-Bass.

National Dropout Prevention Center. (2004). *National Dropout Prevention Center/Network: Effective strategies.* Available: http://www.dropoutprevention.org/effstrat/effstrat.htm.

Newsome, S. (2004). Solution-focused brief therapy (SFBT) groupwork with at-risk junior high school students: Enhancing the bottom-line. *Research on Social Work Practice, 14*(5), 336–343.

Pichot, T., & Dolan, Y. (2003). *Solution-focused brief therapy: Its effective use in agency settings.* Binghamton, NY: Hawthorne.

Prevatt, F., & Kelly, F. D. (2003). Dropping out of school: A review of intervention programs. *Journal of School Psychology, 5*, 377–395.

Rumberger, R. W. (1987). High school dropouts: A review of issues and evidence. *Review of Educational Research, 57*(2), 101–121.

Rumberger, R. W. (2004). Why students drop out of school. In G. Orfied (Ed.), *Dropouts in America: Confronting the graduation rate crisis* (pp. 131–155). Cambridge, MA: Harvard Education Press.

Rumberger, R. W., Ghatak, R., Poulos, G., Ritter, P. L., & Dornbusch, S. M. (1990). Family influences on dropout behavior in one California high school. *Sociology of Education, 63*, 283–299.

Rumberger, R. W., & Thomas, S. L. (2000). The distribution of dropout and turnover rates among urban and suburban high school. *Sociology of Education, 73*(1), 39–67.

Sklare, G. (1997). *Brief counseling that works: A solution-focused approach for school counselors* (pp. 43–64). Thousand Oaks, CA: Corwin Press/Sage.

Slavin, R. E., & Fashola, O. S. (1998). *Show me the evidence: Proven and promising programs for America's schools.* New York: Corwin Press.

Springer, D., Lynch, C., & Rubin, A. (2000). Effects of a solution-focused mutual aid group for Hispanic children of incarcerated parents. *Child & Adolescent Social Work Journal, 17*(6), 431–442.

Walter, J. L., & Peller, J. E. (1996). Rethinking our assumptions: Assuming anew in a postmodern world. In S. Miller, M. Hubble, & B. Duncan (Eds.), *Handbook of solution-focused brief therapy* (pp. 9–26). San Francisco: Jossey-Bass.

Webb, W. H. (1999). *Solutioning: Solution-focused interventions for counselors.* Philadelphia: Accelerated Press.

What Works Clearinghouse. (n.d.). *Interventions for preventing high school dropout.* Available: http://www.w-w-c.org/comingnext/dropout.html.

Effective Intervening With Students From Single-Parent Families and Their Parents

Mo Yee Lee ■ Cathy L. Grover

CHAPTER 68

Getting Started

Based on March 2002 U.S. Census data, among the 72 million children (defined as the population under 18) residing in the United States, 16.5 million (23%) lived with a single mother and 3.3 million (5%) lived with a single father (U.S. Census Bureau, June 2003). Single parents are a diverse group and generally include single mothers, single fathers, and never-married and divorced parents. The challenges encountered by many single parents and their children are well documented and include the following:

1. Poverty. In 1999, the poverty rate for single-mother families with both preschool children and school-aged children was 51.3% as compared to 10.6% for married-couple families and 26.5% for single-father families (U.S. Census Bureau, May 2003). Overall, children living with a divorced parent fare better than children living with a parent who has never married (U.S. Bureau of the Census, September 1997).
2. School and behavioral problems in children. Studies on family structure reveal that children from single-parent homes tend to have higher rates of absenteeism and truancy than those from two-parent households (Kleine, 1994). Young persons who lived in one-parent households were more likely to participate in sexual intercourse, skip school, fight, and use alcohol or tobacco (Oman et al., 2002). Empirical evidence also suggests that poverty and living in a poor neighborhood are associated with school and mental health or behavioral problems (Thornberry, Smith, Rivera, Huizinga, & Stouthamer-Loeber, 1999; Wandersman & Nation, 1998).
3. Overburden and lack of social support. Based on the strain perspective (Kitson & Morgan,

1990), single parents are more apt to experience multiple losses, economic challenges, and increased childcare responsibilities when compared to married parents. Studies also indicate that single parents are more isolated than their married counterparts because of the divergent paths that they have taken (McLanahan & Booth, 1989). These factors can contribute to boundary confusion between the parent and the child in a single-parent family. The child and parent can become "peers" as exemplified by the comment: "I lost my drinking buddy when my mom started going to AA. She's no fun any more." Another possibility is role reversal in which the child takes on the role of parenting an overwhelmed parent who is struggling with financial problems and childcare responsibilities (Wallerstein, 2001).
4. Emotional stress in children. Children in a single-parent household often experience conflict over loyalty issues when dealing with parental divorce or separation (Maccoby, Buchanan, Mnookin, & Dornbusch, 1993). Children must also negotiate changes and new roles when courtship, dating, or marriage occurs in their families (Anderson et al., 1999; Bray, 1999). Emotional distress associated with family changes has been shown to be related to behavioral and emotional adjustment problems in children (Emery, 1999; Lee, 2002).

What We Know

While effective interventions with students from single-parent families and their parents should address the unique characteristics and challenges encountered by these families, it is imperative for

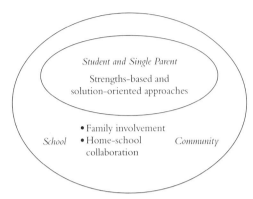

Figure 68.1. A Model of Effectiveness Intervention With Students From Single-Parent Families

school social workers and mental health counselors to recognize and respect single-parent families as a diverse and heterogeneous group. The student's idiosyncratic situation and life context is more than a simple description or label. The following trends have emerged that address prevention and remedial interventions with students from single-parent families. These trends recognize the interconnectedness of students, parents, schools, and the community (Figure 68.1). The students' school problems are systemic in nature and are not "owned" by the students or their families. Resolving students' school problems requires partnership and a focus on students' strengths and resilience.

Interventions Based on a Resilience, Strengths, and Solution-Oriented Perspective

Saleebey (1996) argued that most helping professions in the United States are saturated with practice approaches that are based upon a deficits or pathology perspective. This is likely to occur with single-parent families. For instance, studies on family structure reveal that children from single-parent homes tend to have higher rates of absenteeism and truancy and are more likely to participate in sexual intercourse, skip school, fight, and use alcohol or tobacco than those from two-parent households (Kleine, 1994; Oman et al., 2002). While these findings are helpful for us to understand the challenges encountered by students from single-parent families, such negative evaluation can be stigmatizing and not helpful in working with them. In contrast to the deficits

perspective is the *resilience* perspective, which views single-parent families as having the resources and coping skills for successfully handling their life situations (Emery & Forehand, 1999; Haggerty et al., 1994). The role of school social workers and counselors is to work with the students and their families so that they learn to tap into the resources within them. The counselor does not change people but rather serves as a catalyst for students and parents to discover and use their resources to accomplish their goals. Solution-focused therapy provides well-defined interventions that operationalize a resilience and strengths perspective in working with students and their families (Durrant, 1995; Metcalf, 1995; Murphy, 1997). The use of solution-focused interventions in a school setting showed promising evidence of effectiveness with a wide range of students' behavioral, emotional, and mental health problems on an individual basis and in groups, with students and their families, and in school-based consultations (Gingerich & Wabeke, 2001; see Table 68.1).

Interventions Focused on Family Involvement or Family–School Collaboration

As has been discussed elsewhere in this book studies consistently indicate that family involvement is a key factor in student success (Broussard, 2003). In the Goal 2000: Educate America Act, President Bill Clinton included and signed into law the goal for increasing parent participation in education (U.S. Department of Education, 1994, P.L. 103–227). Germain (1999) noted that the school social worker "stands at the interface not only of child and school, but family and school, and community and school" (p. 36). Further, the school social worker and other mental health counselors are "in a position to help child, parents, and community develop social competence and, at the same time, to help increase the school's responsiveness to the needs and aspirations of children, parents, and community" (p. 36). Research has shown that practices that invite parents to participate in their children's education are critical in determining parental involvement. These practices are more important than any family characteristic, including the parent's marital, socioeconomic, or education status; family style; and child's grade level (Bowen & Bowen, 1998). One prominent collaborative

Table 68.1 Empirical Support for Solution-Focused Therapy With Single Parents

Dielman & Franklin, 1998	Single-case study of using SFT with an adolescent boy with a diagnosis of ADHD
Durrant, 1995	Single-case study of using SFT with a Fourth-grade girl with anxiety disorder
Geil, 1998	Effectiveness of SFT school-based consultation for one student–teacher pair
LaFountain, Garner, & Eliason, 1996	Improved self-esteem and coping for elementary, middle, and high school students who participated in eight-session SFT groups
Littrell, Malia, & Vanderwood, 1995	Improved problem situation and goal attainment for one-session SFT groups with high school students with academic and personal problems
Morrison et al., 1993	One-group design to evaluate the use of SFT that guided a school discipline board in managing disciplining problems in 30 elementary students; 67% showed improvement that was maintained over a 1–2-year period
Murphy & Duncan, 1997	Single-case study of using SFT with an adolescent boy who was referred by teachers for his oppositional behaviors
Teall, 2000	Single-case study of using SFT with an 11-year-old boy and his parent regarding problems in completing homework
Zimmerman, Jacobsen, MacIntyre, & Watson, 1996	Improved role image, objectivity, communication, and limit setting for parents who participated in 6-session SFT parenting groups

Table 68.2 Empirical Support for Parental and Family Involvement in Students' Outcomes

Bempechat, 1990	Increased academic achievement in students
Bowen, 1999	Improvements in students' academic and social behavior and improved parent–teacher communications
Desimone, 1999	Raised test scores in students
Haynes, Comer, & Hamilton-Lee, 1989	Improved self-esteem, motivation, and behavior in students
Henderson, 1987	Improved attendance in students
Henderson & Berla, 1994	Reduced dropout rates in students
McDonald et al., 1997	Improved academic competence and behaviors in students, reduced family conflict, improved parent involvement in school, improved parent leadership, created friendship network in the community
Sar & Wulff, 2003	Positive changes in school's treatment of student problems, families felt empowered to engage in problem solving, improved children's psychological outcomes

family-school initiative is the Family Builders approach that was first developed by the Catholic Archdiocese of Louisville, Kentucky, in 1994 to support children's academic and social competence (Sar & Wulff, 2003; see Table 68.2). Families and School Together (FAST; McDonald, Billingham, Conrad, Morgan, & Payton, 1997) is another collaborative model that combined clinical intervention with community development to address problems in students. It is a multifamily group intervention program designed to build protective factors for children (4–12 years old) and to empower parents to be the primary prevention agents for their own children. These programs/approaches focus on general student populations, including students from single-parent homes. These approaches assume that the problems of children are usually systemic in nature and should be solved in the school setting in collaboration with other involved parties. Interventions or strategies for improvement are important; however, they are secondary to the collaborative partnership among families, schools, and other involved parties. In addition, students and families are viewed as legitimate partners in solving their own problems. The competence of families and schools is strengthened to handle the problem and to develop solutions as opposed to reliance on outside professionals (McDonald et al., 1997; Robbins & Carter, 1998; Sar & Wulff, 2003).

What We Can Do

A Strengths-Based, Solution-Focused Approach to Working With Students and Their Families

Originally developed at the Brief Family Therapy Center in Milwaukee by Steve de Shazer, Insoo Kim Berg, and their associates (Berg, 1994; De-Jong & Berg, 2002; de Shazer, 1991), the purpose of strengths-based, solution-focused interventions is to engage students and their parents in a solution-building process in which they find out what works for them. Such an approach involves the following assumptions (Berg, 1994; Lee, Sebold, & Uken, 2003): (1) There are exceptions to every problem pattern; (2) it is more helpful to focus on what students can do and their strengths

than what is lacking and the problems in the change process; (3) language is powerful in creating and sustaining reality; therefore, the preferred language is the "language of solution and change"; (4) problems and solutions are the students' construction, and they determine the goals of treatment; and (5) because everything is connected, it is not necessary for the solutions to be directly related to the problems or vice versa. Often, these interventions are used when counseling students independently or with their single parents (e.g., Dielman & Franklin, 1998; Durrant, 1995; Murphy & Duncan, 1997), in conducting student or parent groups (Littrell et al., 1995; Zimmerman et al., 1996), and in school-based consultations (Metcalf, 1995).

Initiating Change

Defining the Problem

The students and parents are immediately encouraged to give a clear and explicit statement of their presenting complaint. In a school setting, major complaints are often initiated by teachers or parents in the form of students' inabilities to do homework, cooperate in class, or other behavioral concerns independent of or in relation to other students. Sometimes, students may also self-refer for personal problems.

1. Explore the behavioral and environmental factors maintaining the complaints.
2. Assess students' and parents' help-seeking status in terms of customers, visitors, or complainants. (DeJong & Berg, 2002)

Students and Parents as Assessors

Without focusing on the history of the problems, the school-based practitioner begins strengths-based, solution-oriented assessment that assists students and parents in identifying solutions for their problems. The school-based practitioner does not assume an expert position in conducting assessment with the purpose of determining a comprehensive treatment plan for each particular student. Students or single parents are the assessors, who constantly self-evaluate what is the problem, what may be feasible solutions to the problem, what is the desirable future, what are the goals of treatment, what strengths and resources they have, what may be helpful in the process of change, how committed or motivated they are to make change a reality, and how quickly they want to proceed with the change (Lee et al., 2003).

Building Initiative for Change

A major goal of assessment is to provide a context for students to begin noticing a different reality, which focuses on their competencies and possibilities for beneficial change. The most available starting point is what they have already been doing well and what they already possess (Lee et al., 2003). Useful questions are: What are some of your recent successes? When was the last time that you successfully broke a habit that was hard to break? What kinds of things do teachers and friends compliment you on? What things are you doing now that contribute to your life in school going better?

Searching for Exception Patterns

Every problem pattern includes some sort of exception to the rule (de Shazer, 1985). Despite the multideficiencies or problems that students or single parents may perceive that they have, there are always times when they handle their school problems in a more satisfying way or in a different manner. These exceptions provide the clues for solutions (Murphy, 1997) and represent students' "unnoticed" strengths and resources to address the problems they have in schools. *Exception questions* and *coping questions* are useful to assist students in noticing, amplifying, sustaining, and reinforcing these exceptions regardless of how small or infrequent they may be (Durrant, 1995).

Envisioning a Desirable Future

For positive change to happen, students and parents need to be hopeful about the future and develop a clear vision of life in school either without the presenting complaint or with acceptable improvements in the school problem. A widely used format suggested by solution-focused therapy is the *miracle question* (Berg & Miller, 1992).

Setting Goals of Treatment

Building on visions of a desirable future is the process of helping students and parents to develop useful goals that provide a context of change. Lee,

Sebold, and Uken (2003) have described the criteria for goals:

Useful. Goal needs to be personally meaningful and useful in improving lives in school.

Interpersonal. When students work on their goals, other persons will be able to notice the changes they have made and potentially be affected by the students' changed behavior.

New. The goal needs to be something different, a behavior that the student or parent has not generally done before.

Regular. The goal has to be a behavior that the student can practice on a regular basis.

Establishing Clear Indicators of Change

Students, parents, and teachers usually easily recognize the presence of the problem. However, in terms of change, it is more important for them to know when the student is making positive progress. *Scaling questions* provide a simple tool for students and parents to quantify and evaluate their situation and progress so that they establish a clear indicator of progress for themselves (Berg, 1994).

Giving Feedback

It is important to provide *feedback* to students and families that summarizes the essence of the session so that useful discussion is highlighted and expanded. The feedback includes three components: compliments, bridging statements, and task assignments that assist students and parents in noticing and practicing solutions in their natural life context (de Shazer & Molnar, 1984).

Task Assignments

If students and parents are customers and able to identify exception behaviors to the school problem, ask them to *do more of what works*.

If students and parents are visitors or unsure of goals, use *observing tasks*: "Between now and the next time we meet, I want you to observe, so that you can tell me next time, what happens in your [school, family, relationships with friends] that you want to continue to have happen." (Molnar & de Shazer, 1987)

If students and parents perceive no control over the problem, assign them to *do something different* or use the *prediction task*. (Berg, 1994)

Consolidating Change

The primary tasks for the middle and latter phases of treatment are to expand and consolidate useful change efforts. Usually, the following responses are encountered:

Students and parents report positive experiences as a result of their change efforts.
Students and parents report not working on the goal.
Students and parents report no change or that the goal is not helpful.

When Students and Parents Report and Share Positive Changes

1. Review positive changes and stay curious about all details so that the possibilities and meanings of the change efforts can be fully examined and explored.
2. Help students to evaluate the impact their behavior has had on others who may have directly or indirectly experienced the changes.
3. Assist students and parents to make connections between what they have done and positive outcomes. This process of discovering the details and exploring the full impact of the change behavior magnifies its importance and expands the meaning that is attributed to it. Direct and indirect compliments are critical to this process not only because they offer important feedback but also because they set expectations for change. (Lee et al., 2003)

When Students and Parents Report That They Have Not Worked on the Goal

Students' and parents' response to their change effort is just a response, and there is no good or bad response.

1. Accept the statement.
2. Ask the students and parents to state their goal.
3. Look for exceptions.
4. Notice the unnoticed small events.
5. Help students and parents to evaluate their commitment to the change effort.
6. Help them to evaluate the usefulness of the goal.
7. Compliment any goal work.
8. Help students and parents detail future goal work.

When Students and Parents Report No Change or the Goal Is Not Helpful

All change efforts are helpful even when a student states that the change effort has failed to produce the desired results. Such feedback helps the student to discover what is not a solution and provides an opportunity to explore new ideas. It encourages the school-based practitioner and the student to look in other directions that will likely hold more promise.

1. Ask students and parents what their goal is.
2. Help them to be specific about their goal behavior and the responses to it.
3. Look for exceptions to "not helpful."
4. Help them to reevaluate the usefulness of their goal: Was part of the work on your goal helpful? Did you discover any clues about what would be more helpful? What do you think you will need to do differently to be more successful? Are there some adjustments that you would make?
5. Compliment any goal efforts. (Lee et al., 2003)

Strengths-based, solution-oriented interventions are often used when working with students independently or with their single parents. In addition, these interventions are useful in working with teachers and school personnel individually, in team meetings, or in parent–teacher meetings (Metcalf, 1995). For instance, the school-based practitioner can suggest an observation task to the teacher: "I am working with Johnny to help him stay focused in your class. It'll be very helpful if you can work with me in the process. Between now and Friday, I would like you to observe, so that you can share with me, what's going on in the class that helps Johnny to stay focused." Similarly, the school-based practitioner can ask everyone in a parent–teacher meeting the following questions, which naturally bring a solution-oriented spirit instead of a blaming stance to the meeting: What kinds of things about Eric would you compliment? What little things is Johnny (or his parent) doing lately that may be helpful to him being able to come to school on time? What little things can each of you do to help Susanne feel safe at school?

The school-based practitioner cautiously refrains from providing/suggesting any predetermined solutions. The practitioner is responsible for creating a dialogical context in which student, teachers, and parents experience a solution-building process that is initiated from within and grounded in student strengths.

Pragmatic Guidelines: Interventions for Family Involvement or Family–School Collaboration

While strengths-based, solution-oriented interventions focus more on a microlevel of interventions, interventions that focus on family involvement and family–school collaboration happen on a mezzo- or macrolevel that addresses the interface of school, family, and community. Effective facilitation of family–school collaboration has to be considered from diverse vantage points:

Readiness of the parents and their resources and capacities for participation
Awareness and sensitivity of the school personnel
Effective models/procedures of family–school collaboration

Readiness of Parents and Their Resources and Capacities for Participation

Single parents have been described as "one person working two full-time jobs." They are less likely to report frequent contact with schools, volunteering, or communication with their children about school (McKay & Stone, 2000). Bowen (1999) proposed that the school social worker and mental health counselor could be instrumental in facilitating parent–school communication regarding individual students.

Establish inclusion by inviting parents to school meetings where their children's academic and social progress is discussed.
Advocate for meetings at times that parents can attend.
Arrange for transportation or child care.
Promote an exchange of information at meetings such that parents' perceptions, insights, and suggestions are included in decisions.
Elicit from school staff specific activity ideas and resources for parents to use at home to address student academic and behavioral goals.
In situations in which parents cannot attend meetings, school social workers can model or coordinate efforts to ensure that parents are informed of meeting topics, have a chance to convey their concerns and insights, are given a summary of meeting outcomes, and receive specific activity ideas and resources to use at home.

Awareness and Sensitivity of the School Personnel

Home–school communication and collaboration is based on the premise that school personnel recognize diverse family contexts and cultures through respectful and effective communication. While teachers and administrators are primarily educated, middle-class Caucasians, student populations tend to be more diverse and heterogeneous. Home–school communication can be stifled when teachers and families are of differing backgrounds (Broussard, 2003). The following methods have been suggested for school personnel to increase their awareness and sensitivity in including families from diverse backgrounds, including single-parent families, as partners in education.

School personnel should work to expand their knowledge base of literature that addresses inequitable practices and its impact on students' academic and behavioral outcomes.
Systematically assess the school to determine teachers' and administrators' awareness and respect for family lifestyles outside of their experience and the extent of teacher-initiated family contact. Formal (e.g., survey) or informal (e.g., observation, discussion) assessments provide information for targeting interventions.
Engage in collaborative in-service training with teachers and administrators using family knowledge modules and strategies, such as case scenarios, role playing, classroom film analysis, and self-reflection, to increase awareness and respect for diverse family lifestyles and cultural backgrounds.
Establish parent groups and parent resource centers (see Lawson & Briar-Lawson, 1998) as well as conduct parent workshops that promote information sharing, mutual support, empathy, and a sense of community. Parents can be involved with the school through parent orientations, parent ombudspersons, or ad hoc parent-school teams.
Develop collaborative relationships with community members and institutions, school administrators, teachers, families, and youths who can contribute to and benefit from family information.

Effective Models/Procedures of Family–School Collaborative Initiatives

Home–school collaborative models provide interventions that combine remediation of problems with community development by merging micro and macro dimensions of practice. The following procedures and components have been empirically tested and found to be useful in facilitating family–school collaboration with respect to individual students' academic or behavioral problems (Bowen, 1999; McDonald et al., 1997; Sar & Wulff, 2003). Also, see chapter 72 for more information on making home visits and collaborating with parents.

- Assess the student's school functioning on the basis of interviews with teachers and parents and observation of the student's behavior in the school.
- The community of concern is identified and invited to a meeting. The *community of concern* includes individuals affected by or concerned about the problem presented by the student. They can be parents, relatives, neighbors, or family friends.
- In the meeting, the parameters of the student's problem are established by discussing the related contexts of the problem.
- School staff and families examine their strengths and offer their views on how the problem may be understood. Respect and appreciation of all viewpoints is necessary during this brainstorming process. Each participant describes a strength of the student and a concern. The student is then asked if he or she knew that people felt that way about him or her (or had these concerns). The student is given an opportunity to reflect and respond.
- The community of concern identifies strategies that have worked before and pieces together a solution or set of solutions. Consensus is reached on the solution(s) and roles are assigned. It is helpful to identify specific academic or behavioral goals for the student as well as accompanying strategies (i.e., home activity ideas) and materials for meeting the goals.
- The treatment plan should be carefully implemented with the school social worker or counselor contacting parents and teachers on a regular basis to check and monitor progress.
- When positive changes are accomplished, these changes, even subtle ones, are celebrated to affirm growth, potential, confidence, and hope. (Powell, 1996)
- Upon termination, the community of concern discusses how to maintain the positive changes. Follow-up meetings are scheduled and provisions for relapses are made. Participants also reflect on what they achieved and learned.
- After treatment completion, parents and teachers are expected to independently maintain their partnership in addressing the student's needs.

Utilizing Parents as Resources in the Community

Schools can also support and promote programs in the community that serve to address students' problems in the school setting. One useful intervention is the development of parent support groups and programs. The increasing numbers of at-risk students and dropouts correspond to changes in family structure, including the growth of single-parent families (Kottman & Wilborn, 1992). Counselors can train parents to help parents, which is a way of utilizing community resources to increase efficiency in serving students. For instance, parent study groups have been utilized to provide direct assistance to parents and indirect help to children. Weekly group discussions focusing on parents and their needs are held to establish the parents as an integral component of the school (Kottman & Wilborn, 1992). In addition, school social workers and counselors can develop and coordinate psychoeducation groups facilitated by parents who have experience with particular student problems and situations (Thomas & Corcoran, 2003). These paraprofessionals were found effective for parent–child interaction training in a low-income, ethnic minority sample (Strayhorn & Weidman, 1991). To successfully reach out to and engage the single-parent community, school professionals have to carefully consider the following strategies (Lochman, 2000; McKay & Stone, 2000):

- Adopt an active problem-solving approach with parent communities to identify, from their perspectives, factors that facilitate participation as well as barriers to participation.
- Conduct parent meetings in community settings.
- Provide child care and transportation for meetings.
- Facilitate cohesion building in parent groups through appropriate sharing of personal experiences, creating informal support networks within the group, and utilizing parents' own

ideas rather than rigidly imposing the program's techniques.

Develop parent interventions that address family communication and that contain personally relevant topics such as parental stress.

Develop programs that incorporate the relevant cultural contexts of the parent community. Programs need to be based on an understanding of family processes and family change strategies across socioeconomic, ethnic, and community backgrounds to be relevant and effective.

Tools and Practice Example

Lewis is an 18-year-old 11th-grader who failed the 9th grade due to a lack of earned credits. When Lewis was in the 7th grade, his mother, Karen, and father divorced. Since that time, Lewis has had little contact with his father. Karen works two jobs to provide financially for her son. According to Lewis's teachers, he struggles with "staying on task" and completing his schoolwork. While Lewis is of average ability, his classroom behaviors often get in the way of his working up to his potential. Lewis was referred to the school social worker because his off-task behaviors have been escalating into loud outbursts and confrontations with other students, disrupting the educational process.

The school social worker met with the teacher to obtain a description of the problem behavior in terms of frequency and intensity as well as to discover exceptions to the problem behavior. Were there days when Lewis was on task and completing his schoolwork? What was different about those times? After gathering information from the teacher, the social worker met with Lewis.

Social Worker: Lewis, your teacher, Mrs. Jones, is concerned about your behavior in class and the way it is affecting your grades. What do you think about your work and the way you are in Mrs. Jones's class?

Lewis: I'm doing okay.

SW: What would I see if I were a fly on the wall watching you in Mrs. Jones's class?

Lewis: First, I go to my folder and get my work and do the kick-off for the day. Then, Mrs. Jones gives us our assignment and how to do it. I do it. I finish before everyone else most of the time.

SW: Then what?

Lewis: I can't believe I'm in trouble. I do my work. I just want to get my stuff done. I'm not looking to cause a problem.

SW: You aren't in trouble, Lewis. Mrs. Jones shared with me that you have days that are really good where you quietly complete your work and are respectful to others. We'd like to know how you do that so there can be more of those kinds of days. How do you make those days happen?

Lewis: She said I had good days?

SW: Yes. I'm wondering how we could work together so that you have more good days.

Lewis was originally defensive when discussing the problem identified by his teacher. After sharing with him an exception to the problem and complimenting him on his good days as supported by teacher information, Lewis changed from a visitor to a customer who was interested in doing something different. Lewis was also engaged as the expert on his behavior who held the key to making changes in how he did his work and the way he acted in Mrs. Jones's class. Lewis shared that he had difficulty sitting still to complete his assignments, and while he frequently "finished" before his classmates, his work was not always complete. He indicated that on days when he had 8 hours of sleep, he was more focused and less irritable.

SW: You seem to have a good idea of what works for you. What else are you good at?

Lewis: My job. I bus tables at the Steak House. I'm fast.

SW: How is it that you are so good at your job?

Lewis: It's important to me. I want to make money to help my mom. Plus, I get to move around a lot, and I like being busy.

SW: You're a busy guy. It must be hard for you to slow down and focus on desk work in school. Suppose that after our meeting today, you go home, go to work, and go to bed. While you are sleeping, a miracle happens and your school problem is suddenly solved, like magic. Because you were sleeping, you don't know that a miracle happened, but when you wake up tomorrow morning, you will be different. How will you know a miracle has happened? What will be the first small sign that tells you that the problem is resolved?

Lewis described how he would get up after sleeping for 8 hours. His mom would have breakfast with him before school. He would go to school and do his work. Then, Lewis would go home, eat, go to work, and get to bed on time. In response to "How will others know that something is different about you?" Lewis replied that his mom would notice because he would not be up waiting for her to get home from work. Lewis explained that he liked to look after his mom by waiting up for her to get home from work. The social worker and Lewis discussed other ways that he could look after his mom and still get 8 hours of sleep. Lewis's goal was to get 8 hours of sleep on school nights. This goal fit with the teacher's goal of having Lewis complete his work and being respectful to others because these behaviors were contingent on Lewis getting 8 hours of sleep. When Lewis was asked about how confident he was about changing his sleep schedule (on a scale of 1–10), he was uncertain about giving up his responsibility of checking on his mom at night when she arrived home.

After collecting information about the problem and setting goals individually with Mrs. Jones and Lewis, a meeting was scheduled for the social worker, Mrs. Jones, Lewis, and Karen. Karen was initially disturbed by the prospect of having to meet about Lewis's class work and behavior, but she was immediately more responsive when the social worker complimented her on raising such a caring son who was so dedicated to his mother. When asked about others who might be invited as members of a community of concern, Karen reported that she could not think of anyone and that she had little contact with school personnel because of her "chaotic" life. Karen shared how it had been very difficult raising Lewis on her own and that she wondered if she was "doing it right." She enjoyed having Lewis meet her at the door at night to talk with her but had often felt guilty that he stayed up so late. She reported that he insisted on "being there" for her. The social worker asked Karen to think about other ways that Lewis could be there for her and to bring them to the meeting.

The first meeting was canceled due to Karen's work conflict, so a second meeting was scheduled in the break room of Karen's workplace. Karen greeted the group and was visibly impressed with the efforts of the school staff. Since the phone conversation, Karen and Lewis had discussed that he would go ahead and go to bed before she arrived home. He would leave the hall light on, and Karen would turn it off when she went to bed. Lewis would know that his mom was home by the "light signal." Also, Karen and Lewis would have breakfast together in the mornings before going to

work and school. Karen wondered how other single parents managed their lives and was pleased to get a list of other single parents' phone numbers to contact from time to time for support. The phone list was provided by a single-parent support group coordinated by the school social worker in collaboration with a community mental health agency. Karen also identified the best way to reach her for updates on Lewis's progress in his schoolwork and classroom behavior.

By working together as a team, a simple yet effective solution was developed for Lewis. Lewis did improve on completing his assignments. An additional intervention was developed with input from the expert, Lewis, who requested a "busy box" of activities to work on after completing assignments at the end of class. Through increasing his sleep to 8 hours and staying busy, Lewis made great strides in completing his class work and being respectful to others. A follow-up meeting was held at the school to celebrate the success. Karen and Lewis were proud of their efforts and thought they could accomplish "whatever comes next."

Key Points to Remember

Schools increasingly become the de facto mental health service system for many children and adolescents (Burns et al., 1995), and there is an increased emphasis on developing empirically supported interventions with students and their families (Adelman & Taylor, 2000). Traditional treatment of school problems in students from single-parent families is mostly influenced by an individual and deficits perspective. In essence, treatment has mostly focused on clinical practices with students and their families in resolving school problems that emphasize individual responsibilities for the problems. Recent advances, however, suggest that effective intervention with students from single-parent families requires multilevel skills that enable the school social worker or counselor to effectively work with students and their families and to facilitate home–school collaboration in the process. The described interventions recognize the systemic nature of students' problems and the interconnectedness of students, families, school, and community (Sar & Wulff, 2003). The focus is on utilizing students', and single-parent families' and community strengths in resolving the problems. Specific interventions are directed by the idiosyncratic characteristics of particular students and their family milieu, although it echoes the wisdom that "it takes a community to raise a child."

References

Adelman, H. S., & Taylor, L. (2000). Shaping the future of mental health in schools. *Psychology in the Schools, 37*, 49–60.

Anderson, E. R., Greene, S. M., Hetherington, E. M., et al. (1999). The dynamics of parental remarriage: Adolescent, parent, and sibling influences. In E. M. Hetherington (Ed.), *Coping with divorce, single parenting, and remarriage: A risk and resiliency perspective* (pp. 295–321). Mahwah, NJ: Erlbaum.

Bempechat, S. B. (1990). *The role of parent involvement in children's academic learning: A review of the literature.* New York: ERIC Clearinghouse on Urban Education.

Berg, I. K. (1994). *Family-based services: A solution-focused approach.* New York: Norton.

Berg, I. K., & Miller, S. (1992). *Working with the problem drinker: A solution-focused approach.* New York: Norton.

Bowen, N. K. (1999). A role for school social workers in promoting student success through school family partnerships. *Social Work in Education, 21*, 34–47.

Bowen, N. K., & Bowen, G. L. (1998). The effects of home microsystem risk factors and school microsystem protective factors on student academic performance and affective investment in schooling. *Social Work in Education, 20*, 219–231.

Bray, J. H. (1999). From marriage to remarriage and beyond: Findings from the developmental issues in step families research project. In E. M. Hetherington (Ed.), *Coping with divorce, single parenting, and remarriage: A risk and resiliency perspective* (pp. 253–272). Mahwah, NJ: Erlbaum.

Broussard, C. A. (2003). Facilitating home-school partnerships for multi-ethnic families: School social workers collaborating for success. *Children and Schools, 25*, 211–222.

Burns, B. J., Costello, E. J., Angold, A., Tweed, D., Stangl, D., Farmer, E. M. Z., & Erkanli, A. (1995). Children's mental health service use across service sectors. *Health Affairs, 14*, 147–159.

DeJong, P., & Berg, I. K. (2002). *Interviewing for solutions* (2nd ed.). Pacific Grove, CA: Brooks/Cole.

de Shazer, S. (1985). *Keys to solutions in brief therapy.* New York: Norton.

de Shazer, S. (1991). *Putting difference to work.* New York: Norton.

de Shazer, S., & Molnar, A. (1984). Four useful interventions in brief family therapy. *Journal of Marital and Family Therapy, 10*, 297–304.

Desimone, L. (1999). Linking parent involvement with student achievement: Do race and income matter? *Journal of Educational Research, 93*, 11–31.

Dielman, M. B., & Franklin, C. (1998). Brief solution-focused therapy with parents and adolescents with ADHD. *Social Work in Education, 20*, 261–268.

Durrant, M. (1995). *Creative strategies for school problems: Solutions for psychologists and teachers.* New York: Norton.

Emery, R. E. (1999). *Marriage, divorce, and children's adjustment.* Thousand Oaks, CA: Sage.

Emery, R. E., & Forehand, R. (1999). Parental divorce and children's well-being: A focus on resilience. In R. J. Haggerty et al. (Eds.), *Stress, risk, and resilience in children and adolescents: Processes, mechanisms, and interventions* (pp. 64–99). Cambridge: Cambridge University Press.

Geil, M. (1998). *Solution-focused consultation: An alternative consultation model to manage student behavior and improve classroom environment.* Unpublished doctoral dissertation, University of Northern Colorado, Greeley.

Germain, C. B. (1999). An ecological perspective on social work in the schools. In R. Constable, S. McDonald, & J. P. Flynn (Eds.), *School social work: Practice, policy and research perspectives* (pp. 33–44). Chicago: Lyceum.

Gingerich, W. J., & Wabeke, T. (2001). A solution-focused approach to mental health intervention in school settings. *Children and Schools, 23*, 33–47.

Haggerty, R., et al. (1994). *Stress, risk, and resilience in children and adolescents: Processes, mechanisms, and interventions.* Cambridge: Cambridge University Press.

Haynes, N., Comer, J., & Hamilton-Lee, M. (1989). School climate enhancement through parental involvement. *Journal of School Psychology, 27*, 97–100.

Henderson, A. T. (Ed.). (1987). *The evidence continues to grow: Parent involvement improves student achievement.* Columbia, MD: National Committee for Citizens in Education.

Henderson, A. T., & Berla, N. (1994). *A new generation of evidence: The family is critical to student achievement.* Columbia, MD: National Committee for Citizens in Education.

Kitson, G. C., & Morgan, L. A. (1990). The multiple consequences of divorce. *Journal of Marriage and the Family, 52*, 913–924.

Kleine, P. A. (1994). *Chronic absenteeism: A community issue.* [Report No. EA026196] East Lansing, MI: National Center for Research on Teacher Learning. [ERIC Document Reproduction Service No. ED375494]

Kottman, T., & Wilborn, B. L. (1992). Parents helping parents: Multiplying the counselor's effectiveness. *School Counselor, 40*, 10–14.

LaFountain, R. M., Garner, N. E., & Eliason, G. T. (1996). Solution-focused counseling groups: A key for school counselors. *School Counselor, 43*, 256–267.

Lawson, H., & Briar-Lawson, K. (1998). *Connecting the dots: Progress toward the integration of school reform, school-linked services, parent involvement and community schools.* Oxford, OH: Miami University, Danforth

Foundation and Institute for Education Renewal.

Lee, M.Y. (2002). A model of children's post-divorce behavioral adjustment in maternal- and dual-residence arrangements. *Journal of Family Issues, 23*(5), 672–697.

Lee, M.Y., Sebold, J., & Uken, A. (2003). *Solution-focused treatment with domestic violence offenders: Accountability for change.* New York: Oxford University Press.

Littrell, J. M., Malia, J. A., & Vanderwood, M. (1995). Single-session brief counseling in a high school. *Journal of Counseling and Development, 73,* 451–458.

Lochman, J. E. (2000). Parent and family skills training in targeted prevention programs for at risk youth. *Journal of Primary Prevention, 21*(2), 253–265.

Maccoby, E. E., Buchanan, C. M., Mnookin, R. H., & Dornbusch, S. M. (1993). Post divorce roles of mothers and fathers in the lives of their children. *Journal of Family Psychology, 7,* 24–38.

McDonald, L., Billingham, S., Conrad, T., Morgan, A. O. N., & Payton, E. (1997). Families and Schools Together (FAST): Integrating community development with clinical strategies. *Families in Society, 78,* 140–155.

McKay, M. M., & Stone, S. (2000). Influences on urban parent involvement: Evidence from the National Education Longitude Study. *School Social Work Journal, 25*(1), 16–30.

McLanahan, S. S., & Booth, K. (1989). Mother-only families: Problems, prospects, and politics. *Journal of Marriage and the Family, 51,* 557–580.

Metcalf, L. (1995). *Counseling toward solutions: A practical solution-focused program for working with students, teachers, and parents.* West Nyack, NY: Center for Applied Research in Education.

Molnar, A., & de Shazer, S. (1987). Solution focused therapy: Toward the identification of therapeutic tasks. *Journal of Marital and Family Therapy, 13*(4), 349–358.

Morrison, J.A., Olivios, K., Dominguez, G., Gomez, D., & Lena, D. (1993). The application of family systems approaches to school behavior problems on a school-level discipline board: An outcome study. *Elementary School Guidance & Counseling, 27,* 258–272.

Murphy, J. J. (1997). *Solution-focused counseling in middle and high schools.* Alexandria, VA: American Counseling Association.

Murphy, J. J., & Duncan, B. L. (1997). *Brief intervention for school problems.* New York: Guilford.

Oman, R. F., McLeroy, K. R., Versely, S., Aspy, C. B., Smith, D. W., & Penn, D. A. (2002). An adolescent age group approach to examining youth risk behaviors. *American Journal of Health Promotion, 16,* 167–176.

Powell, J. Y. (1996). A schema for family-centered practice. *Families in Society, 77,* 446–448.

Robbins, T., & Carter, M. (1998, August–September). Family builders: Counseling families in Catholic schools. *Momentum,* 31–33.

Saleebey, D. (1996). The strengths perspective in social work practice: Extensions and cautions. *Social Work, 41,* 296–304.

Sar, B. K., & Wulff, D. P. (2003). Family builders approach: Enhancing the well-being of children through family-school partnerships. *Children and Schools, 25,* 241–251.

Strayhorn, J., & Weidman, C. (1991). Follow-up one year after parent-child interaction training: Effects on behavior of preschool children. *Journal of American Academy of Child and Adolescent Psychiatry, 30,* 138–143.

Teall, B. (2000). Using solution-oriented interventions in an ecological frame: A case illustration. *Social Work in Education, 22,* 54–61.

Thomas, C., & Corcoran, J. (2003). Family approaches to attention deficit hyperactivity disorder: A review to guide school social work practice. *Children & Schools, 25*(1), 19–34.

Thornberry, T. P., Smith, C. A., Rivera, C., Huizinga, D., & Stouthamer-Loeber, M. (1999). *Family disruption and delinquency.* [Report No. UD033207] East Lansing, MI: National Center for Research on Teacher Learning. [ERIC Document Reproduction Service No. ED436604]

U.S. Bureau of the Census. (1997, September). *Census brief: Children with single parents: How they fare.* [CENBR/97–1] Washington, DC: U.S. Department of Commerce, Economics and Statistic Administration, Bureau of the Census.

U.S. Census Bureau. (2003, May). *Poverty 1999: Census 2000 brief.* [C2KBR-19] Washington, DC: U.S. Department of Commerce, Economics and Statistic Administration, U.S. Census Bureau.

U.S. Census Bureau. (2003, June). *Children' living arrangements and characteristics: March 2002.* [P20 547] Washington, DC: U.S. Department of Commerce, Economics and Statistic Administration, U.S. Census Bureau.

U.S. Department of Education. (1994). *Goals 2000: National education goals.* Washington, DC: Author.

Wallerstein, J. (2001). The challenges of divorce for parents and children. In J. Westman (Ed.), *Parenthood in America: Undervalued, underpaid, under siege* (pp. 127–139). Madison: University of Wisconsin Press.

Wandersman, A., & Nation, M. (1998). Urban neighborhoods and mental health: Psychological contributions to understanding toxicity, resilience, and interventions. *American Psychologist, 53,* 647–656.

Zimmerman, T. S., Jacobsen, R. B., MacIntyre, M., & Watson, C. (1996). Solution-focused parenting groups: An empirical study. *Journal of Systemic Therapies, 15,* 12–25.

Working With Families From Religious Fundamentalist Backgrounds

Allan Hugh Cole, Jr.

CHAPTER 69

Getting Started

Religious fundamentalism, defined below, is an influential phenomenon in the United States. It is found in various religions and faith traditions, including Christian, Jewish, Islamic, Hindu, and Buddhist movements. School social workers and other mental health consultants are particularly likely to encounter fundamentalist beliefs in schools because fundamentalism has significant numbers of adherents within Protestant Christianity (Almond, Appleby, & Sivan, 2003, p. 90). Once on the fringe of American Christianity and found mostly in the South, Christian fundamentalism has become a nationally prominent and powerful movement—religiously and politically—with such groups as the Christian Coalition, the Southern Baptist Convention (now the largest Protestant denomination), and the Believer's Bible Fellowship, among others, signifying what has been termed the "second coming" of fundamentalism (Murray, 2005).

In an increasingly pluralistic society, school social workers and mental health counselors practice with diverse religious populations which include fundamentalists. Moreover, school social workers and counselors often serve as the principal resource for educating, building and sustaining relationships, and helping to foster ongoing communication among school personnel, students, and their families. The goal is to formulate and support interventions needed for ameliorating problems in living that impact students and families in the school environment and beyond. Practitioners thus need to be familiar with a growing and increasingly diverse number of religious traditions and spiritualities that clients may embrace, including the qualities and distinctions of the religious fundamentalist worldview. Likewise, practitioners must be sensitive to particular challenges, both interpersonal and systemic, that may arise in schools with these populations. Finally, practitioners must identify and adopt resources for effective practice that respect and draw on what *clients* believe, value, and determine they need, on the one hand, and what practice standards, values, and ethics require, on the other. Attention to these matters, including the tensions that emerge, informs a need for competence and proficiency among school social workers and other school-based practitioners.

What We Know

Characteristics of Fundamentalism

Fundamentalism is a difficult term to define. This follows from the intangible nature of religious belief itself and from the divergent viewpoints found among different religions and, not infrequently, within the same religion. In other words, one person's fundamentalist is another's religious conservative is another's evangelical. Moreover, the media and broader cultures frequently identify fundamentalism inaccurately. Confusion arises because religious and nationalist or ethnic loyalties are often conflated with religiosity, so that what is called religious fundamentalism is more accurately described as religious nationalism or ethnonationalism (Almond, Appleby, & Sivan, 2003, p. 90). In the case of Christianity, orthodoxy or evangelicalism—which differ from fundamentalism but also share some of its characteristics to varying degrees—are often lumped in with fundamentalism and thus used interchangeably with it in popular thought and public discourse (Hill & Hood, 1999, p. 417). One way to think about this lack of distinction with respect to Christianity is that while many fundamentalists could be considered evangelical, not all evangelicals are fundamentalist. Both evangelicals and fundamentalists tend to hold to the tenets of classical Christian orthodoxy and embrace the God-inspired nature of the Bible. However fundamentalists tend to view the Bible's texts as inerrant and thus interpret them literally, while evangelicals vary on their views of what inspiration might mean. That includes accepting contradictions and multiple interpretations or other unresolved issues within the texts. So, the difference between fundamentalism and evangelicalism (important to theological discussions and religious communities) is often more in degree than in the kind of faith practiced, which contributes to their being conflated in popular thought. What is important to our discussion here is to understand prevalent characteristics within fundamentalist communities so that we can work successfully with adhering students and families. Before beginning that discussion, however, it is important to point out that just like issues of immigrant or ethnic-minority status (see chapters 76 and 78), there are within-group differences, and holding to a religious belief system of any sort involves matters of degree. The school social worker and mental health practitioner should always inquire about how important religion is to a client, and not assume any particular religious background or qualities thereof.

There are nine qualities, widely accepted among religion scholars, that characterize religious fundamentalism (Almond, Appleby, & Sivan, 2003, pp. 90–115). The social worker's and counselor's knowledge of these characteristics, as well as his or her awareness of the common tendency to conflate religious understandings, identity, and commitments with other facets of life, may be helpful in both assessment and ongoing practice with students and their families. These characteristics provide a heuristic structure for understanding the fundamentalist's primary frame of reference and thus may serve to guide practice accordingly, by starting where the client is.

Fundamentalism's characteristics, the first five of which are ideological in nature and the last four of which are relational, are:

- Reactivity and defensiveness, especially with respect to the marginalization of one's religion and its traditions by secularism, modernization, government, and the erosion of their religion's values and influence. Often this leads to activist efforts to assuage the marginalization and gain influence.
- Selectivity, particularly with respect to what is embraced and rejected in both the religious tradition and modernity. Selectivity often highlights valued distinctions—whether religious or secular in kind—between the fundamentalist and the mainstream.
- Dualistic worldview, where sharp distinctions are drawn between light and darkness, spiritual and material, and good and evil. This is especially evident with respect to morals and truth.
- Affirmation of inerrancy and the absolute, particularly as they concern what the fundamentalist views as divinely inspired sacred texts and religious tradition. Closely related are literal readings and understandings of texts and traditions whose instructions and truths the fundamentalist claims, applies, and advocates. This may translate into dogmatism and rigidity of beliefs, values, and behavior.
- Millennial and messianic views of history whose climax involves miraculous phenomena, including a triumph of light over darkness and good over evil. Typically inseparable from this experience is the inaugural role played by an omnipotent redeemer figure.
- Elect membership composed of divinely chosen and called persons. This often leads to a sense of superiority among the chosen and thus a devaluation of what others may have to offer.
- Sharp boundaries separating the elect and non-elect (saved and unsaved, moral and sinful, clean and unclean). This often creates an "us against them" mentality and can lead to guardedness or even distrust of those outside the religion.
- Tension between commitment to voluntary and egalitarian membership, wherein faithful insiders presumably have equal status, and yielding to the authority of a charismatic leader, who is set apart from the community.
- Strict conformity to behavioral requirements prescribed by religious commitments, so that individuality and unconventionality are devalued (if not rejected) and group norms are affirmed and maintained.

Assessment

In order to be attuned to the client's religiosity, a practitioner may make use of several diagnostic scales that measure religious fundamentalism. These include:

- Christian Fundamentalist Belief Scale (Gibson & Francis, 1996/1999)
- Fundamentalism Scale Revised (Broen, 1957/1999; Gorsuch & Smith, 1983/1999)
- Religious Fundamentalism Scale (Altemeyer & Hunsberger, 1992/1999)
- Religious Fundamentalism Scale (Martin & Westie, 1959/1999)
- Religious Fundamentalism Scale of the MMPI (Wiggins, 1966/1999)
- Religious Worldview Scale (Jennings, 1972/1999; McClean, 1952/1999)

It should be noted that only the Altemeyer and Hunsberger scale is appropriate for measuring non-Christian fundamentalism and only after making some slight modifications. That points to the fact that fundamentalism in the United States is, by and large, a Christian phenomenon. It suggests further that the school-based practitioner will need to make use of information gleaned in interviews, especially as it relates to the nine characteristics of fundamentalism cited above, perhaps along with these diagnostic scales, in assessing whether the client's principal frame of reference or worldview is in fact akin to that of the religious fundamentalist and, if so, what that may mean for practice. Greater knowledge of non-Christian religious traditions, and particularly fundamentalist movements within them, will supplement the dearth of scales that assess for fundamentalism outside Christianity. These issues, however, can become very delicate in schools, especially because of the policies to keep religion and education separate within the public schools. Asking sensitive questions as a means of getting to know the client family better might work best. For example:

Social Worker: What outside activities or groups does Josh have?

Parent: He is involved three nights a week with our church.

SW: Great! I suppose church is important to him then?

P: Yes. We raised him to believe in God, and we are very glad he is involved in our church.

SW: Sounds like your church might be important to others in your family too.

P: Yes, it is very important to everyone. My father was a minister.

SW: Really, that is interesting. So, you are a PK. [colloquial language for preacher's kid] Do you mind if I ask what church?

P: The Church of Christ. [The social worker recognizes the church as one with fundamentalist beliefs, but if one did not recognize the church, one could say something like, "I am not familiar with that church. I am curious, do you mind, and do not feel like you have to answer this, but I am always interested in the beliefs of different churches. So, what do you believe?" Most fundamentalists will be happy to share their faith with you.]

SW: So, Josh is like third generation in your faith? That must make your family proud.

P: Yes, it does.

SW: So, what other hobbies or outside interests does Josh have?

P: Well, that is about it now.

Additional scales, also useful in assessing for fundamentalism but broader in scope, include:

- Dogmatism Scale (Form E) (Rokeach, 1960)
- Religious Coping Activities Scale (Pargament, Ensing, Falgout, Olsen, Reilly, Van Haitsma, & Warren, 1990/1999)
- Religious Problem-Solving Scale (Pargament, Kennell, Hathaway, Grevengoed, Newman, & Jones, 1988/1999)
- Royal Free Interview for Religious and Spiritual Beliefs (King, Speck, & Thomas, 1995/1999)

Importantly, the social worker and mental health counselor must rely on practice wisdom and broad assessment strategies when working with this population. This prevents thin descriptions of client histories, personal traits, or perceived needs. It also guards against diagnostic reductionism. Diagnostic scales may supplement, but cannot replace, good communication between practitioners and clients, wherein the social worker seeks to gain a depth of insight pertaining not only to the client's religious orientation but also to multiple other psychosocial factors. Such communication seeks in various ways and through a variety of approaches to provide for deeper and more contextualized information, understanding, and strategies for intervention.

Challenges

School social workers and mental health counselors face several potential challenges when working with religious fundamentalists. The same is true with other religious populations, including

Christian evangelicals and conservatives of various faiths, who present with characteristics similar in kind, if not in degree, to those of fundamentalists. Some of the challenges center principally on the school-based practitioner; others center on the client; and still others play out in the relationship between them.

One challenge is that concerted efforts to engage in nonbiased practice, surely a noble and necessary objective, may lead to the social worker and counselor neglecting to identify and utilize what is of greatest value to the client, namely, the client's religion. As a result, this may prompt neglect of what orients the client's cognitions and behaviors most profoundly. That is, in an attempt to remain open and nonjudgmental practitioners, social workers may fail to privilege the client's unique and particular frame of reference, worldview, or "meaning system"—all of which are grounded in religious commitments—and also may fail to make proper use of those in practice (Denton, 1990; Stalley, 1978). This usually plays out as the practitioner's sensitivity to remaining unbiased or "objective" results in not recognizing and working with the *client's* biases and subjective experiences: in this case, religious ones. Not only does this hinder the process of gaining information and perspective, it also diminishes the resources within the client's religious faith that may be drawn on during interventions. Denton (1990) notes that along with the "polemical" side of fundamentalism, there is a "private" side, which emphasizes love and support (p. 8). Drawing on York's (1987) discussion of religion's role in hospital neonatal care, Denton points out that "fundamentalism provided families with opportunities for socialization, belongingness, increased status and role opportunities, forgiveness, ability to relinquish responsibility for one's actions and problems, and spiritual guidance in the form of rules, values, and rituals" (Denton, 1990, p. 8). Moreover, emotional distress has been found to be assuaged through participation in a fundamentalist church (Ness & Wintrob, 1980). It is an important benefit to clients as social workers recognize and affirm the potential value and resources found within the client's religious orientation as part and parcel of honoring their own commitments to nonbiased practice.

A second challenge is that fundamentalism may be foreign, suspect, or objectionable for the practitioner, which may make remaining open to the client's experience, meaning system, and values even more problematic. Here, the practitioner may be aware of the client's religious orientation and may have been attuned to its impact on the client's life, problem, and potential resources for intervention. However, the practitioner's own distaste for the client's religious worldview and commitments, and perhaps the corresponding belief that these are unhealthy or otherwise inappropriate, prevents assigning them proper significance. The result is akin to what was mentioned previously, namely, a failure to work within the client's principal fame of reference.

This particular challenge may actually be the more typical and complicating one. One reason is that psychodynamically oriented practitioners, who still make up a large portion of social workers and other counselors, tend to have an ambivalent relationship with religion in general—professionally, if not personally—and are particularly suspicious of religious fundamentalism (Northcut, 2004). Related to that, facets of the fundamentalist worldview are in tension with, if not contradictory to, many counselors' values and ethics, which may result in a prima facie bias against what the fundamentalist client reveals, values, or requires (Denton, 1990). Hodge (2002) goes as far as to claim that social work often oppresses more conservative Christians in its widespread lack of tolerance for evangelical belief systems. He notes that whereas social work is to be commended for its tolerance with respect to gender, race, ethnicity, age, sexual orientation, and class, among other variables, religion remains the glaring omission in the field's commitment to inclusion (Hodge, 2002, p. 402). If this omission is apparent in practice with evangelicals, it is likely more so in practice with fundamentalists, whose belief systems are typically more pronounced and in greater tension with social work and mental health norms, values, and ethics. Practitioners must remain sensitive to these tendencies among their profession and discern whether or any of these are inhibiting their own effective practice.

A third set of challenges relates more directly to the characteristics and inclinations of religious fundamentalism previously cited. The fundamentalist client may be suspicious, if not rejecting, of the school-based practitioner, the institution he or she represents, and what both may have to offer. Particularly difficult may be the fundamentalist client's reactionary and defensive postures toward those in the public schools, who represent the government. Tied to this may be the client's perceived marginalization by those in power, the school personnel being examples, who are often viewed as instruments of the outside, immoral world and as being complicit in its downfall. That mind-set may be joined with a corresponding suspicion of what is valued by so-called experts, who are trained by secular universities in social sciences and who represent the mainstream.

Moreover, the fundamentalist tends to hold rigidly to a dualistic, black-and-white understanding of the world. Often connected with that understanding is intolerance for ambiguity or the gray areas of life. The fundamentalist penchant for clear-cut and firm understandings, particularly with respect to morals, truth, and personal behaviors, may temper, if not prevent, the client from considering the new ideas, understandings, and behaviors that the social worker and mental health counselor offer.

Yet another difficulty may come with the primacy and authority the fundamentalist grants to sacred texts (Bible, Koran, or Torah) or to charismatic leaders. These attitudes too may minimize the value given to other kinds of authority and expertise, including what the social worker embodies and represents. Similarly, fundamentalism's strongly demarcated gender roles typically results in men having authority over women, which poses a particular challenge for the female social worker and other school-based practitioners. Difficult too may be the value placed on supernatural intercession in the form of miracles, which may limit the client's openness to interventions the social worker and mental health counselor may provide and which may result in a measure of passivity.

Two additional challenges stem from fundamentalists' suspicion of those outside their own religious group. Such suspicion may prompt a feeling of having been disloyal among those who venture beyond the group for assistance. It may also mitigate efforts that the social worker makes to help the client change behaviors away from those endorsed by group and religious norms.

Any of these tendencies may challenge the practitioner's efforts to establish rapport, acquire information, and work collaboratively with the client to formulate and implement strategies for change. Note too that fundamentalist clients' suspicions or distrust not only dissuade them from engaging the school and its personnel. They may also eventuate in the social worker or other counselor being mistrustful of the client. That is, when we perceive the client's lack of trust, we may resent this personal reaction, and thus be less open to trusting or valuing the client's perspective. In all of these scenarios, effective practice is compromised.

What We Can Do

Cultivate Awareness of Various Religions and Their Potential Resources

Social workers and other counselors must educate themselves on a variety of religions and spiritualities, particularly those represented by the client populations they serve. While one need not become an expert, a basic understanding of, and appreciation for, various religions and spiritualities fosters rapport with clients and, presumably, reduces the number of inaccurate assumptions the practitioner may otherwise make about what the client believes, values, and desires. Moreover, increased familiarity with another's frame of reference allows the practitioner to utilize that frame more generously in practice, thus facilitating more acceptable and useful interventions. When clients perceive the practitioner's sensitivity to their way of understanding and living in the world, clients tend to be more receptive to what the practitioner may say about the clients' condition and offers of strategies for change.

The following resources provide excellent information on numerous religions and spiritualities, including fundamentalist movements. These are helpful for increasing one's knowledge and sensitivities.

Books

Ammerman, N. T. (1988). *Bible believers: Fundamentalists in the modern world.* New Brunswick, NJ: Rutgers University Press.

Mead, F. S., & Hill, S. S. (2001). *Handbook of denominations in the United States* (11th ed.). Nashville, TN: Abingdon.

Web Sites

http://religiousmovements.lib.virginia.edu
http://www.adherents.com
http://www.clas.ufl.edu/users/gthursby/rel
http://pluralism.org

Social workers and other mental health counselors may benefit too from building relationships with clergy and other religious leaders in their communities. Although this alliance is not easy in public schools, ministerial resources can be helpful for persuading families to trust and cooperate. Not only does this provide educational opportunities, it may also prove helpful for collaborative work with clients whom social workers, counselors, and clergy all serve. Areas for collaboration might be in issues such as child abuse or domestic violence, for example. Building relationships with fundamentalist clergy and adherents may prove more difficult than doing so with more progressive and open religious communities, but it is important to keep in mind that most religious communities have those who are more open or who might even want to enhance the community's openness. Offering an open community forum on issues of importance to the school and inviting fundamentalist leaders may be one way to identify those who are approachable. See chapters 61 and 62 for suggestions on how to build partnerships and work with the community. Efforts to learn from and work with leaders within fundamentalist traditions may well prove to be worthwhile, particularly as this facilitates greater understanding, sensitivity, and appreciation among all parties and thus fosters more normative working partnerships.

Cultivate Self-Awareness

Just as crucial as increasing one's awareness of various religions, spiritualities, and fundamentalist movements is developing greater awareness of oneself, both as a person and as a practitioner. Keen insights pertaining to who we are and what we bring to practice by virtue of our own experiences remain essential for effective school-based practice. We must commit to a lifelong process of self-discovery and understanding, so as to mitigate our making false assumptions, acting out in inappropriate ways with clients, or otherwise obstructing practice appropriately centered on *their* experiences, needs, and goals. These insights have particular import for social work with religious fundamentalists, especially when the practitioner does not share the same religious orientation.

As Sue and Sue (1990) have noted with respect to divergent worldviews among "culturally different" practitioners and clients, "Counselors who hold a world view different from that of their clients and are unaware of the basis for this difference are most likely to impute negative traits to clients" (p. 137). Hence, school-based practitioners must put into place a framework and method for ongoing self-assessment, wherein they seek clarity about a variety of matters. The goal is to foster practice attuned to what the client values and seeks and to prevent the practitioner's biases or preconceptions from detracting from appropriate client self-determination.

Listed below are some matters (foci) that the social worker and other counselors should explore and a set of questions to promote greater self-awareness:

- *Focus*: one's own religious or spiritual orientation. To the extent we consider, comprehend, evaluate, and utilize another's religiosity in our practice, we tend to do so by appealing first to our own internal frame of reference. We are inclined to use our own religious or spiritual history, understanding, and commitments—or perhaps our lack thereof—as the baseline for interacting with the history, understanding, and commitments of another. Though this is inevitable, an unreflective appeal to our own experience hampers our commitment to begin with the client's frame of reference and to assign priority to it. When that happens, practice is compromised. Ask yourself the following questions:

  What do I believe about God, the spiritual realm, and the sacred in life?

  What value do I place on my own religious faith, and to what extent does this shape my own conceptions of life, death, hardships, relationships, meaning, values, goals, behaviors, and the like?

  On a scale of 1–10, with 1 representing "nonexistent" and 10 representing "very central," what role does my religious faith play in my daily life?

  What has been my experience with religion—my own or others'—and how has that informed my perception of religious faith, whether positively, negatively, or both?

  To what extent do my preconceptions about religion or spirituality affect my practice, particularly when religiosity plays a central role?

- *Focus*: one's preconceptions of or biases toward religious fundamentalists. For most persons, social workers and other counselors included, some experiences, practices, behaviors, or values are difficult to understand, acknowledge, or accept. Such difficulties are not limited to the religious sphere. Yet, as previously mentioned, religious fundamentalism and practice with clients who embrace it may pose particular challenges to social workers and other mental health professionals because of divergent world views and commitments. Related to this, religiosity is often closely tied to racial, ethnic, class, or cultural identities and expressions. Consequently, school-based practitioners must assess their responses to a client's religiosity while considering their feelings about those factors as well. Ask yourself the following questions:

> What do I know about the type of fundamentalism my client embraces?
>
> Do I need to know more before making an assessment of its role, meaning, and value, both for the client and for our work together? If so, how may I acquire more knowledge and understanding?
>
> What do I believe and how do I feel about my client's fundamentalism as I understand it? How may this either facilitate or hamper practice?
>
> How do I tend to react or respond to those I perceive to be substantially different from me, whether religiously or otherwise, and what informs that reactivity or response?
>
> What is particularly problematic for me, if anything, in what I understand to be my client's beliefs, values, and goals?
>
> Are there elements of my client's religious orientation that may be utilized as resources for effective practice? How open am I to working with them?

If a practitioner finds it particularly difficult to work with a client, whether due to conflicts centered on religious fundamentalism or something else, the social worker or counselor needs to seek the counsel of a supervisor. Consultation with the supervisor may elicit ways the practitioner can in fact work with the client after all. Or, if that is not possible, the supervisor may assist the practitioner with identifying another practitioner or additional resources (within the institution or agency or beyond) which will provide for the client's needs. Supervisory resources with clinical expertise are not always available in school settings. So, the practitioner must be creative in reaching out for assistance in such cases.

Appealing to the Code of Ethics

Cultivating both our understanding of a client's religious worldview and our awareness of ourselves as practitioners must always be correlated with an appeal to the profession's *Code of Ethics* (National Association of Social Workers, 2005). All counseling professionals have a code of ethics that they can use to help them with ethical and other sensitive matters related to values. Informed by the core values of service, social justice, the dignity and worth of the person, the importance of human relationships, integrity, and competence, for example, the *NASW Code of Ethics* for social workers provides ethical principles and standards meant to guide practice at all times, but particularly in instances where value disparity or ethical dilemmas threaten effective practice. As McGowan notes, "Practitioners' choice of values is always the primary determinant of what they actually do with clients" (1995, p. 28). That points to the fact that our own personal values, those of institutions like the schools we serve, and, perhaps, those tied to differing religious worldviews and commitments inevitably play a role in practice. This includes both how we assess the client context or need and how we intervene. As previously suggested, recognizing this and devising strategies for incorporating it in our work with integrity is a necessary first step for effective practice. When value conflicts arise, however, and lead to ethical dilemmas, the social work profession requires that practitioners appeal to the *Code of Ethics* as the definitive guide for practice decisions.

As McGowan (1995) emphasizes, however, complications arise when practitioners have to choose between two conflicting values, like the dignity and worth of the individual, on the one hand, and the obligation to promote social justice and the interests of the larger community, on the other. Similarly, the *Code of Ethics* is not overly prescriptive. Rather, it provides a more general guiding framework for applying ethical principles to ethical dilemmas. That means the social worker will need constantly to rely on practice wisdom and collaborative analysis with colleagues and supervisors, along with the norms proffered by the *Code of Ethics*, when dilemmas arise.

Here is an example of an ethical dilemma with respect to the social work *Code of Ethics*: "What does a commitment to the social work *Code of Ethics* allow in my practice with this client?" To explore this, ask yourself the following questions:

- To what extent, if any, does my client's faith, its norms, and its practices violate the standards, values, and ethics of social work?
- Am I identifying a concern as being ethically suspect when it is more accurately described as stemming from my own negative opinion of the client and his or her religious orientation?
- Can I work with my client in a manner consistent with the standards and values of the social

work profession and particularly the social work *Code of Ethics*?

- If I cannot work with this client, how may I make the most appropriate referral?

Becoming Culturally Capable

Augsburger (1986) puts forth a concept that social workers and mental health counselors may utilize in their practice with any client whom they perceive to be "culturally different" from themselves, including the religious fundamentalist. Specifically, practitioners must become *culturally capable*, meaning they must develop frameworks and methods for practice that promote client welfare and prevent client oppression, whatever the reasons. To that end, Augsburger lists five characteristics—which can be both measured and taught—that distinguish culturally capable professionals (1986, pp. 20–21):

- A clear understanding of one's own values and basic assumptions. This means recognizing that others' values and assumptions, though perhaps different from one's own, are nonetheless legitimate and potentially useful.
- A capacity for welcoming, entering into, and prizing other worldviews without negating their legitimacy.
- Seeking sources of influence in the person and the context, the individual and the environment.
- An ability to move beyond counseling theory, orientation, or technique and be an effective human being. This means respecting not only one's professional training and insights, as important as those are, but also one's capacities for building and sustaining human connections and relationships with the client and thus fostering deep and high-quality rapport.
- Seeing others, along with oneself, as universal citizens, marked by unity amid diversity. This means the social worker must seek connections with the client that transcend differences of religion and its constituent qualities.

Developing these capacities, in conjunction with the strategies for enhancing self-awareness described previously and in other ways that the school-based practitioner finds most helpful, will enhance practice with religious fundamentalists. This is particularly important in cases where a practitioner, the client, or both discern significant differences between them in worldviews, commitments, or practices.

Tools and Practice Examples

Case Example: The Roberts Family

As you read the following case scenario, consider how you would assess the situation and how you would respond on behalf of the school.

> Johnny Roberts, a fourth-grader, has been referred to you by his teacher, Ms. Jones. He is a conscientious student, pleasant with his peers and teachers, and slightly introverted. His performance in the classroom has declined noticeably during the last month. He seems constantly tired and unable to focus and has fallen asleep during class on at least three occasions. Exploring these concerns with Johnny, Ms. Jones learns that his family's church congregation has recently moved from one location to another and that the family is spending several late nights each week involved with the activities of building this new church. Ms. Jones shares this information with you, the school social worker, and asks you to intervene.

The following commentary focuses on what you, the social worker, should consider as you contact the family, how you may respond to particular issues that surface, and a few general strategies for intervention.

Precontact

- Given the information that Ms. Jones shared, what do you assume about Johnny's family's religion? How open are you to hearing more about this from Johnny and his parents?
- If your hunch that Johnny's family are Christian fundamentalists proves accurate, how might you establish rapport, indicating your openness to, and desire for, learning more about the family's involvement in their congregation? How specifically might you explore this with the parents? What questions might you ask?
- What challenges do you anticipate in light of

what you know about fundamentalism? If these surface, how specifically might you respond?

One need not be exhaustive. Reflections here are taking place almost exclusively in the realm of speculation. Yet, thinking about possible scenarios, far from biasing the social worker prematurely or inappropriately, actually may help to anticipate both one's own struggles and the family's before the fact. This mitigates potential breakdowns in rapport and in the forming of collaborative partnerships, which inform effective practice.

Contact

Establishing Rapport

- Telephone the parents and introduce yourself as the school social worker.
- Convey both your own and the school's affection for Johnny, and share your reason for calling as you calmly yet clearly express your concerns. Specifically, indicate that Ms. Jones and you have noticed the changes in Johnny's classroom affect and engagement, as mentioned above.
- While men in fundamentalist families typically "represent" the family in conversations with outsiders, women often have more authority and purview in matters involving children. So, either the father or mother may be the principal parental contact.
- Assuming you are speaking with the mother, explore with her some reasons that Johnny may be so tired at school. It may be best initially to refrain from sharing what you know about the family's involvement in the congregation. Leading with that knowledge may indicate that you view this negatively, and that may prompt a more defensive posture and response. If, after several attempts at encouraging disclosure of this information, the mother is not forthcoming, you may decide to ask her about it more directly.
- In whatever manner the information is put forth, convey a desire to know more about the congregation, its activities, and the family's involvement in both. A tone of genuine inquiry, not judgment, should be maintained. Conveying interest promotes deeper rapport and better partnerships and learning opportunities. You may also decide to try to build a connection

with the parents by conveying some of your own knowledge or experiences with what you perceive to be similar religious communities. The goal here, again, is to foster rapport and gain more insight concerning the family's primary frame of reference, not to convey your own knowledge or expertise. Maintain your awareness of appropriate self-disclosure throughout this process as you look for ways to make personal connections.

Through this rapport-building phase, you learn that the family does indeed present with most of the aforementioned characteristics of fundamentalism and that the only identifiable precipitator of Johnny's changed classroom affect and behavior is the family's level of involvement in the congregation. Johnny's parents demonstrate genuine care and concern for him and indicate their desire for him to do well in school. They seem to frame his behaviors, however, in terms of disrespect for his elders (for his teacher, Ms. Jones) and laziness, which you associate with their religious understandings of authority, respect, and work ethic. From the outset you have looked for any indicators of abuse or neglect and have identified none, save the fact that Johnny is not getting enough rest. While this is unacceptable, you determine that it does not yet rise to a level such that not reporting it immediately to the appropriate authorities violates either state laws or the *Code of Ethics*. Confident that you and Johnny's parents have established enough rapport to work together, you proceed to the intervention phase in hopes that you can affect positive change.

Intervention

You identify two goals for an initial intervention. The first is to reframe the way the parents perceive Johnny's decline in the classroom. That is, you want to help them understand that Johnny is not disrespectful or lazy at all, but that he is simply not getting the rest that a boy his age requires. The second goal is to encourage the parents to recognize that Johnny may need to forgo some time spent at church in order to get to bed at an earlier hour, thus feeling more rested and ready to learn.

- You may say, "I really appreciate your sensitivity to the importance of being alert and attentive in the classroom. As you said, this promotes good learning for all students. Frankly, I have never known Johnny to be anything but respectful and energetic in class. That's a credit to your parenting! It's only been about a month now that I've noticed a big change. So, I wonder if it may just be that Johnny needs to get to bed a little earlier and get more sleep."

• The parents may be unwilling, or unable, to recognize the connection between church activities and Johnny's decline in school. If so, then you may need to help them make the connection a bit more directly. You may say something like this: "It occurs to me that Johnny being sleepy and less engaged in class started at about the same time you say that your congregation moved. I realize how exciting it can be to build a new church and also how eager churches are to get people heavily involved. And it seems like this is a good place for your family, that you're happy there. But, I'm wondering whether it may help Johnny to feel better at school, and thus perform better, if you, or at least he, were to get home a bit earlier on school nights."

• The parents may refuse this and become defensive. If so, then you have to judge whether pushing the point further at this time is appropriate. You may be confident that you have established enough rapport with the parents to facilitate ongoing work and thus decide to end this conversation for now and to call again in a week or two. Or, you may invite them to a face-to-face conference. If so, thank the parents for their time, indicate your affection for Johnny once again, and express your confidence that together you'll find a solution to your shared concern, namely, Johnny and his well-being. Also, let the parents know that you plan to be in touch with them again (by phone or in person) within the time period discussed. Make sure you follow up accordingly. Your failure to do so may convey your lack of genuineness, particularly with persons who tend to think more rigidly about responsibility, one's "word," keeping commitments, and the like.

• If the parents are open to the possibility that Johnny might be leaving church too late at night or, perhaps, that he might be spending too many nights a week there, then you will want to explore ways to help them think about alternative arrangements.

• Invite the father's participation if that has not happened, but do not insist on it.

• Underscore the value you recognize that the family places on their involvement in the congregation, so as not to diminish its importance.

To do that will undermine your rapport and working relationship.

• Also remind them of the value they have already affirmed in Johnny's being alert, attentive, and participating in the classroom. You may say something like this: "I'm wondering if you could explore ways to get Johnny home and to bed earlier. Maybe he could leave early with one of you [the parents]. Or, maybe you could think about him being out fewer nights each week. Or, maybe both are good things to consider." You may also add, "I really think that if Johnny gets more sleep, he'll feel and do better not only at school, but at church too, and that's what we all want."

Follow Up

Assuming the initial conversation with Johnny's parents goes well, and that there is a basis for continued work, a follow-up conference should build on the first conversation's content and foster continued collaborative efforts to help Johnny. If challenges like those mentioned previously arise, you, the social worker, should utilize the strategies discussed as you look for ways to meet them. Remembering that a tenuous relationship is better than none at all, the school social worker must seek with zest and genuine openness to meet, understand, and work with the fundamentalist student and family to the greatest extent possible.

Key Points to Remember

• Religious fundamentalists will view, comprehend, and live in the world utilizing as their primary frame of reference and meaning the ideals, teachings, and practices of their religious tradition. Social workers and mental health counselors benefit the family with fundamentalist beliefs by enhancing their awareness and understanding of the family's religious orientation and considering ways that the strengths associated with it may be utilized in effective practice.

• Social workers and other mental health professionals typically do not share the fundamentalist's worldview and thus may be suspicious if not rejecting of both the client's right to embrace his or her religious understandings and commitments and the resources for effecting the appropriate changes that the social worker may offer in practice interventions. This means that the social worker and other professionals must commit to ongoing self-reflection and make use of frameworks like those put forth here to assess candidly their own biases and preconceptions and how those are figuring into practice.

- As is true in school-based practice with any population, ethical dilemmas may arise in practice with fundamentalists. When this happens, practitioners must appeal to their *Code of Ethics* as the principal guiding framework for decision making, consult with peers and especially with a supervisor, and seek to identify ways of working through the ethical dilemma so that both client needs and values and the social worker's ethics are maintained.

The author wishes to express his gratitude to Whitney S. Bodman, assistant professor in comparative religion, Austin Presbyterian Theological Seminary, Austin, Texas, for helpful conversation and for suggesting resources on fundamentalism; and to Britta Martin Dukes, the author's research and teaching assistant, for securing resources from libraries.

References

Almond, G. A., Appleby, R. S., & Sivan, E. (2003). *Strong religion: The rise of fundamentalisms around the world.* Chicago: University of Chicago Press.

Altemeyer, B., & Hunsberger, B. (1999). Religious fundamentalism scale. In P. C. Hill & R. W. Hood (Eds.), *Measures of religiosity* (pp. 422–425). Birmingham, AL: Religious Education Press. (Original work published 1992)

Augsburger, D. W. (1986). *Pastoral counseling across cultures.* Philadelphia: Westminster.

Denton, R. T. (1990). The religiously fundamentalist family: Training for assessment and treatment. *Journal of Social Work Education, 1,* 6–14.

Gibson, H. M., & Francis, L. J. (1999). Christian fundamentalist belief scale. In P. C. Hill & R. W. Hood (Eds.), *Measures of religiosity* (pp. 418–419). Birmingham, AL: Religious Education Press. (Original work published 1996)

Gorsuch, R. L., & Smith, C. S. (1999). Fundamentalism scale-revised. In P. C. Hill & R. W. Hood (Eds.),

Measures of religiosity (pp. 419–421). Birmingham, AL: Religious Education Press. (Original work published 1983)

Hill, P. C., & Hood, R. W., Jr. (Eds.). (1999). *Measures of religiosity.* Birmingham, AL: Religious Education Press.

Hodge, D. R. (2002). Does social work oppress evangelical Christians? A "new class" analysis of society and social work. *Social Work, 47*(4), 401–414.

King, M., Speck, P., & Thomas, A. (1999). The Royal Free Interview for religious and spiritual beliefs. In P. C. Hill & R. W. Hood (Eds.), *Measures of religiosity* (pp. 351–357). Birmingham, AL: Religious Education Press. (Original work published 1995)

Martin, J. G., & Westie, F. R. (1999). Religious fundamentalism scale. In P. C. Hill & R. W. Hood (Eds.), *Measures of religiosity* (pp. 425–427). Birmingham, AL: Religious Education Press. (Original work published 1959)

McClean, M. (1999). Religious world view scale. In P. C. Hill & R. W. Hood (Eds.), *Measures of religiosity* (pp. 59–61). Birmingham, AL: Religious Education Press. (Original work published 1952)

McGowan, B. G. (1995). Values and ethics. In C. H. Meyer & M. A. Mattaini (Eds.), *The foundations of social work practice: A graduate text* (pp. 28–41). Washington, DC: NASW Press.

Murray, B. (2005). Tracking religious membership in the United States. *Faith and Public Life* Web site. Available: http://facsnet.org/issues/faith.

National Association of Social Workers. (2005). *Code of Ethics.* National Association of Social Workers home page. Available: http://www.naswdc.org/pubs/code.

Ness, R. C., & Wintrob, R. M. (1980). The emotional impact of fundamentalist religious practice: An empirical study of intergroup variation. *American Journal of Orthopsychiatry, 50,* 302–315.

Northcut, T. B. (2004). Pedagogy in diversity: Teaching religion and spirituality in the clinical social work classroom. *Smith College Studies in Social Work, 74*(2), 349–358.

Pargament, K. I., Ensing, D. S., Falgout, K., Olsen, H., Reilly, B., Van Haitsma, K., & Warren, R. (1999). Religious coping activities scale. In P. C. Hill & R. W. Hood (Eds.), *Measures of religiosity* (pp. 344–347). Birmingham, AL: Religious Education Press. (Original work published 1990)

Pargament, K. I., Kennell, J., Hathaway, W., Grevengoed, N., Newman, J., & Jones, W. (1999). Religious problem-solving scale. In P. C. Hill & R. W. Hood (Eds.), *Measures of religiosity* (pp. 347–350). Birmingham, AL: Religious Education Press. (Original work published 1988)

Rokeach, M. (1999). The dogmatism scale: Form E. In P. C. Hill & R. W. Hood (Eds.), *Measures of religiosity* (pp. 490–493). Birmingham, AL: Religious Education Press. (Original work published 1956)

Stalley, R. F. (1978). Non-judgmental attitudes. In N. Timms & D. Watson (Eds.), *Philosophy in social work.* London: Routledge & Kegan.

Sue, D. W., & Sue, D. (1990). *Counseling the culturally different: Theory & practice.* New York: Wiley.

Wiggins, J. S. (1999). Religious fundamentalism scale of the MMPI. In P. C. Hill & R. W. Hood (Eds.), *Measures of religiosity* (pp. 427–430). Birmingham, AL: Religious Education Press. (Original work published 1966)

York, G. Y. (1987). *Religious-based denial as a coping mechanism for the rural client.* Paper presented at the Annual Conference of the National Association for Rural Mental Health, Hendersonville, NC.

Intervening With Students and Families Who Frequently Relocate or Are Homeless

Sanna J. Thompson ▪ Jihye Kim

Getting Started

Family housing instability or frequent relocation is difficult for children and adolescents and causes stress due to the loss of the central organizing structure of their lives (Rafferty, Shinn, & Weitzman, 2004). Children in these families may experience a loss of identity, disconnection from familiar surroundings, and intense sadness and loss (Walsh & Buckley, 1994). Children who frequently move are more likely to be poor, come from single-parent households, and have caregivers who are unemployed or failed to graduate from high school (Long, 1992). For families who become homeless, the loss of home is typically sudden, unexpected, and traumatic. Disruption of normal family functioning and fears concerning safety and security are heightened among the children involved. Children, feeling that parents cannot be depended on for stability and safety, may respond with anger and disruptive behavior. In situations where the family must live in a shelter situation, typical family functioning changes in response to the institutional setting's rules and hierarchy of authority.

Family housing instability often affects the continuity of the children's schooling. Research has shown that children who experience frequent relocation, including homelessness, also experience excessive school mobility, are at increased risk of failing a grade (Heinlein & Shinn, 2000; Wood et al., 1993), and have poor academic performance. Students who change schools frequently are twice as likely to have nutrition, health, and hygiene problems; are four times as likely to drop out; and are 77% more likely to have multiple behavioral problems (Simpson & Fowler, 1994; Wood et al., 1993). Teachers have limited time and resources to address most of these problems; thus, involvement

of the student, the parent(s), and the school social worker is required.

One major problem confronting highly transient students is their difficulty enrolling in school without proper documentation, such as previous school records, birth certificates, and immunization records. Delaying enrollment and missing days or weeks of school result in academic failure and increase the risk that the student will simply drop out of school. For homeless and immigrant students, the McKinney-Vento Homeless Education Assistance Improvements Act of 2001 provides a specialized liaison to help these students and families overcome barriers to enrollment. To improve the likelihood of academic success for all highly mobile students, barriers to education must be removed and helpful interventions provided that ensure accessibility to vital educational services.

What We Know

Interventions that have shown the greatest effectiveness in ameliorating youth problems encourage the inclusion of parents or caregivers. School social workers, counselors, and other school-based practitioners are indispensable in coordinating educational services to students, while providing effective interaction with parents as well. One family-oriented intervention model that has considerable empirical support and demonstrated success with high-risk and drug-using youth is multidimensional family therapy (MDFT; Hogue & Liddle, 1999; Liddle et al., 2001; Liddle & Hogue, 2000). MDFT is based on the integration of existing therapeutic theories in areas such as case management, school interventions, drug counseling methods, use of multimedia, and HIV/AIDS prevention (Liddle, 2002). Even though the research on this model has mostly demonstrated efficacy with youth who have substance abuse and other high-risk behavior problems, it appears to be an effective approach for ameliorating crisis situations.

MDFT has an integrative therapeutic philosophy and clinical approach that focuses on developing relationships with important individuals in the student's life (Diamond & Liddle, 1996; Liddle & Dakof, 1995) and is something that schools can make use of with students and families. MDFT encompasses a collaborative, individualized approach that requires a high degree of engagement by families. It relies on an empirical knowledge base of risk and protective factors associated with high-risk youth behaviors to assess and intervene in students' problems. Strategies for engagement are employed to capture the interest of the family and assess risk and protective factors within the specific ecological context of the family (Hogue & Liddle, 1999). Problems or crises provide critical assessment information that focuses intervention efforts.

In consultation with parents, teachers, shelter staff (if the family is homeless), and others, the school social worker or other school-based practitioner coordinates and facilitates interactions with the individuals most involved with the student. Sessions are held wherever the appropriate parties can be convened (home, school, shelter, juvenile court, etc.) and whenever the need arises. Change is multidimensional and multifaceted as it emerges from the interactions among systems, people, domains of functioning, and interpersonal processes. Working with multiple systems in a coordinated way, inside and outside the family, is fundamental to MDFT.

What We Can Do

Phase 1: Building the Foundation

Intervention begins with the process of building collaborative relationships with the student and the family. School social workers and counselors, recognizing the highly mobile family situation as a crisis, must establish an alliance and facilitate engagement for intervention. Working with students and their parent(s), they work to encourage treatment receptivity and motivation for change. Resistance is normal; resistant behaviors can provide

direction for intervention implementation. School social workers and other school professionals utilizing the MDFT framework create a context in which the student and parents can deal with the hopelessness, helplessness, and despair often experienced in stressful living conditions.

Once the student has been identified, the school-based practitioner must establish an alliance with the student and parent(s). The social worker or mental health counselor connects with the parent(s) and child and assists them to understand the experiences of the other. A critical component for success is helping the student and parent(s) feel that MDFT can address their concerns, assist them to convey their personal feelings about their family life, and work to overcome problem areas. Alliance building begins with demonstrating genuine interest and concern for the family's well-being.

Sample Sentences Intended to Stimulate Discussion With the Student

- "I can and will be on your side at least some of the time." Students need to be aware of the school-based practitioner's genuine interest, respect, and support for them individually. MDFT necessitates developing strong alliances with students and the subsystems that affect them.
- "When your parents and teachers understand you more fully, they can appreciate what you are going through." Recognizing the difficulties experienced by the student due to frequent housing disruption, the social worker or counselor addresses the feelings, responses, and needs of the student.
- "Some aspects of who you are will always remain private (we can talk about these things between us if you like), but it is important for your parents and teachers to know about some of the concerns you are facing. I can help with this." School-based practitioners can provide a feeling of security by discussing issues of confidentiality. In addition, students are provided support when they agree to discuss sensitive material for the purpose of enhancing others' understanding of their life and needs.

Sample Sentences Intended to Stimulate Discussion With Parent(s)

- "I've seen how difficult this is for you. My heart goes out to you, and I will do everything I can to support you." The school-based practitioner presents as an ally who will support the caregivers' attempts to provide appropriate parenting to their child and cope with their own feelings of hopelessness concerning their living situation.

- "If I hear right, what you are saying is that you feel absolutely alone in dealing with your problems. I see what a hard time you're having trying to keep your family together after losing your home." Acknowledgment of the difficult situations that impede successful parenting and family management validates the parents' challenging role. It acknowledges that the parents have individual problems, disappointments, desires, hopes, and dreams that are separate from their role as parents.

Phase 2: Identifying Themes Within Multidimensional Subsystems

An MDFT social worker's efforts focus on understanding the events, personal and family characteristics, and responses that are affected by the family's residential instability or frequent moves. Themes or problem areas are identified and assessed to determine the need for change. School-based practitioners attempt to understand the individual's functioning, as well as the mechanisms of interconnection among the multiple systems that affect the student's life.

Student Subsystem

Housing instability increases the likelihood that students may exhibit low academic achievement, disruptive classroom behaviors, or mental or physical health difficulties. Exploration of students' history and development of strategies to promote their adjustment in school are crucial.

School Attendance

Students may be frequently absent from school because of the family's relocations, students running away from home or shelter, lack of transportation to school, or low motivation or fears concerning attending a new school.

Academic Achievement

Students may exhibit poor academic performance, deficient cognitive skills, and learning disabilities. They may have had to repeat a grade. These factors often result from repeated absences or low expectations of academic success.

Classroom Behaviors

Highly mobile students may not easily conform to new classroom environments due to their chaotic home lives. They may present with a short attention span, hyperactivity, or disruptive behavior.

Basic Needs

Students may suffer from a lack of proper nutrition, appropriate clothing and shoes, and school supplies. Difficulties in transportation and lack of resources often constrain their participation in school-related activities.

Physical Health

Highly mobile students frequently are exposed to hunger and poor nutrition. They generally have more colds, diarrhea, stomach problems, skin diseases, respiratory infections, and hearing and visual impairments than students with permanent homes. They often fail to receive appropriate medical treatment due to the family's frequent moves or lack of insurance; thus, illnesses may become chronic or severe. These students also have a greater likelihood of drug or alcohol abuse, high-risk sexual behaviors, teen pregnancy, and sexually transmitted diseases.

Mental Health

Students living in highly transient situations often suffer from depression, anxiety, aggression, and suicidal ideation. They may fail to develop a sense of trust, continuity, and belongingness. Feelings of isolation, loss, and low self-esteem are increased by a sense that they are different from their peers because they do not have a stable home or fashionable clothing.

Parent Subsystem

Many parents experiencing unstable housing suffer from financial difficulties, have substance use or mental health problems, have low educational status, and have difficulties in parenting and communicating with their children. Although parents may have a positive attitude toward the education of their children, they may have limited participation in their child's academic performance due to lack of time or transportation, taking care of other children, being unfamiliar with school systems, or being reluctant to discuss their children's issues out of shame or hopelessness.

Student/Family Interaction Subsystem

Housing instability often leads to stressful situations that affect family relationships and negatively influence students' development. Students may have experienced severe conflict or violence in their family, neglect, abandonment, or physical or sexual abuse. Parents may lack the skills to provide consistent and age-appropriate limit setting. Due to their residential instability, they may be inattentive to their child's academic development and fail to monitor school attendance and performance. The communication between students and their parents should be examined. Their chaotic living conditions are likely to cause defensiveness and blame, further eroding the relationship.

Extrafamilial Subsystems

Peers

Constructing and continuing relationships with peers can be impeded by lack of stable housing, a telephone, or transportation. Students may experience stigmatization by classmates who tease them about their residential status, poor physical appearance, and lack of personal possessions. Due to feeling shame, fear, or alienation, they may respond in aggressive or hostile ways. These students also are vulnerable to association with gangs and other deviant peers who engage in antisocial behaviors.

Teachers and School Personnel

Students may not tell their teachers about their residential status due to being ashamed or afraid of differential treatment. They may feel stigmatized by school staff when enrolled with "homeless" status.

Shelters and Other Social Agencies

Students are often affiliated with shelters, the juvenile justice system, child protective services, and other social service agencies. These systems are often resources that can provide supportive connections for the student and family. Many highly mobile families living in a series of temporary homes, shelters, or hotels often experience crowded conditions and lack privacy. Finding appropriate space for the student to do homework, where noise problems are reduced, is often difficult.

Phase 3: Working With Themes

This stage of the intervention focuses on facilitating processes and fostering skills that allow the student and parent(s) to identify and work on particular problem areas that require change. MDFT involves understanding the individual's functioning, as well as the mechanisms of interconnection among the systems that affect the student's life. Social workers and other staff primarily explore risk and protective factors that affect the student's school performance directly or indirectly. They work with the many systems involved in the student's academic motivation and performance.

Identify Main Themes and Set Goals

The first step involves determining the areas of the student's life that will be most accessible for intervention. These will not be the only available areas for intervention, but are identified as those most likely to create successful change. Core themes are consistently addressed, while working minimally with other areas.

Make Plans for the Sessions

Social workers and counselors work with students inside and outside of the school setting. Sessions are provided as needed (daily or weekly), and the context of each session changes to provide maximum flexibility and opportunity to implement clinical methods. Various sessions are designed for most effective interactions, such as meeting with the family in their current residence (i.e., in the shelter and including shelter staff in the session), with the student during after-school program sessions with student peers, with the student and family while waiting to see the school principal, or with the student at a restaurant.

Work With Multiple Systems and Multiple Approaches

Utilizing multidimensional thinking, school social workers and counselors develop a variety of alliances with the student, the family (parents, siblings, other relatives), and extrafamilial systems (school, juvenile justice, shelter staff, if homeless). Facilitating the progression of interactions with these various systems must be accomplished simultaneously. Everything focuses on the students' needs, how their successful academic achievement can be facilitated, and how they can be directed to prosocial and developmentally appropriate pursuits. The school-based practitioners involved must be skilled in applying different types of interactions needed with students, parents, other family members, school staff, and juvenile justice officials. For example, addressing poor academic performance involves changing many things that currently support the behavior, such as the student's attitudes and beliefs, affiliation with and access to deviant peers, failure to bond with prosocial institutions (school), the family environment (including residential instability), and parenting practices.

Develop Successive Approximations

A step-by-step approach is utilized to encourage needed change. Small steps are identified that ultimately lead to successful outcomes. MDFT school social workers engage with the student to determine the set of circumstances, daily activities, and interpersonal and intrapersonal processes that are impeding positive change. They then identify specific steps to overcome the difficulty or improve the targeted problem area.

Provide Linking

School social workers and others may utilize *linking*, which is the process of shaping change across many areas and in a variety of environments, including school, family, and the individual. Therapeutic continuity is achieved through connecting each session to the others through a series of building blocks that generalize gains made in one problem area to another area of difficulty. Linking also involves highlighting the progress made by one family member to motivate and facilitate change in other family members.

▨ Phase 4: Sealing the Changes

The MDFT school-based practitioner establishes meaning for the changes that have occurred by

putting into words some of the successes. Specific successes and accomplishments that occurred while engaged in the intervention are discussed and used as evidence of and prompts for how new crises or problems can be managed in the future. For example, deepening the student's affiliation with school, other important social institutions, and the family can be viewed as a major accomplishment.

Tools and Case Examples

Kate is a 12-year-old, fifth-grade girl who is currently living in a homeless shelter with her mother and two younger brothers. She was admitted to a new school last week and was referred to the MDFT school social worker. This school is the third school she has been admitted to this year. The family has lived in multiple shelters since her mother divorced 2 years ago and her father abandoned them. Her mother, Megan, is currently unemployed.

▨ Phase 1: Building the Foundation

- Upon Kate's admission to the school, the social worker meets with her and listens to her story, demonstrating genuine interest in her welfare and building trust.
- The social worker meets alone with Megan, Kate's mother, and explores the family's housing situation and its impact on Kate.

▨ Phase 2: Identifying Themes

- The social worker meets with Kate and Megan together to assess various themes.
- Themes include:
  - academic failure due to extensive absences
  - feelings of loss and loneliness due to moving away from friends
  - lack of a supportive father
  - limited financial support to gain stable housing
  - Megan's poor parenting due to depression
- Kate and Megan agree that "Kate's frequent absences from school and falling behind her peers" is the first area to address with the MDFT social worker.

Phase 3: Working With Themes

- The social worker meets with Kate to set goals, including:
  - catch up on missed curriculum
  - attend school daily
  - complete all homework daily
- The social worker and Kate identify the subsystems needed to support her goals:
  - Parent subsystem
    - The social worker introduces Megan to Kate's teacher and other school staff. She talks to Megan about Kate's need to find space to complete homework and her engagement with the school.
  - Extrafamilial subsystems
    - School: The social worker holds meetings with Kate's teacher and principal to increase awareness of her situation and needs. They develop a special educational plan for Kate; A tutor is recruited to assist Kate after school.
    - Shelter: The social worker works with shelter staff to find a quiet place where Kate can study in the evening.
    - Transportation is made available for Kate's commute to school each day.
- The social worker continues to work extensively with multiple systems for approximately 3 months; discussions increasingly expand to other themes.

Phase 4: Sealing the Changes

The MDFT social worker monitors Kate's academic performance and continues to remain in contact with her and Megan, but in a more limited way. As the social worker supports Kate and Megan in their new skills, they will be provided crisis intervention when needed.

Resources

Center for Treatment Research in Adolescent Drug Abuse. (2004). Available: http://www.miami.edu/ctrada.

National Association for the Education of Homeless Children and Youth. (2004). Available: http://www.naehcy.org.

Texas Homeless Education Office. (2004). Available: http://www.utdanacenter.org/theo/resources.html.

Walsh, M. E. (1992). *Moving to nowhere: Children's stories of homelessness.* Westport, CT: Auburn House.

Key Points to Remember

- Students' unstable or highly mobile living conditions are multidimensional phenomena.
- Treatment focuses on building multiple collaborative relationships with the student, family, and other subsystems.
- Equipped with a general understanding of the situation, the MDFT school social worker explores themes needed for change to occur.
- Themes most accessible and likely to be successful are addressed initially; additional themes are addressed as appropriate.
- School social workers and other mental health counselors work extensively with multiple systems and approaches; sessions are held where and when needed.
- Changes that occur during the intervention are praised and connected to future expectations.

References

Diamond, G. M., & Liddle, H. A. (1996). Resolving a therapeutic impasse between parents and adolescents in multidimensional family therapy. *Journal of Consulting & Clinical Psychology, 64*(3), 481–488.

Heinlein, L. M., & Shinn, M. (2000). School mobility and student achievement in an urban setting. *Psychology in the Schools, 37*(4), 349–357.

Hogue, A., & Liddle, H. A. (1999). Family-based preventive intervention: An approach to preventing substance use and antisocial behavior. *American Journal of Orthopsychiatry, 69*(3), 278–293.

Liddle, H. A. (2002). *Multidimensional family therapy for adolescent cannabis users.* [DHHS pub. No. 02–3660] Rockville, MD: Center for Substance Abuse Treatment, Substance Abuse and Mental Health Services Administration.

Liddle, H. A., & Dakof, G. A. (1995). Efficacy of family therapy for drug abuse: Promising but not definitive. *Journal of Marital & Family Therapy, 21*(4), 511–539.

Liddle, H. A., Dakof, G. A., Parker, K., Diamond, G. S., Barrett, K., & Tejeda, M. (2001). Multidimensional family therapy for adolescent drug abuse: Results of a randomized clinical trial. *American Journal of Drug & Alcohol Abuse, 27*(4), 651–688.

Liddle, H. A., & Hogue, A. (2000). A family-based,

developmental-ecological preventive intervention for high-risk adolescents. *Journal of Marital & Family Therapy, 26*(3), 265–279.

Long, L. (1992). International perspectives on the residential mobility of America's children. *Journal of Marriage & the Family, 54,* 861–869.

Rafferty, Y., Shinn, M., & Weitzman, B.C. (2004). Academic achievement among formerly homeless adolescents and their continuously housed peers. *Journal of School Psychology, 42,* 179–199.

Simpson, G. A., & Fowler, M. G. (1994). Geographic mobility and children's emotional/behavioral adjustment and school functioning. *Pediatrics, 93*(2), 303–309.

Walsh, M. E., & Buckley, M. A. (1994). Children's experiences of homelessness: Implications for school counselors. *Elementary School Guidance & Counseling, 29*(1), 4–15.

Wood, D., Halton, N., Scarlata, D., Newacheck, P., & Nessim, S. (1993). Impact of family relocation on children's growth development, school function, and behavior. *Journal of the American Medical Association, 270,* 1334–1338.

Students Living in the Care of Grandparents

Roberta R. Greene

CHAPTER 71

Getting Started

Starting about 1990, policy makers, researchers, and the media first began to notice the startling increase in grandparent-headed households, prompting them to question why. More recent data suggest that this trend continues to grow (Casper & Bryson, 1998). Based on a national survey of 3,477 grandparents in 1997, Fuller-Thomson, Minkler, and Driver (1997) found that 10% of U.S. grandparents have taken on primary responsibility for raising one or more grandchildren for a period of at least 6 months at some point in their lifetimes. According to more recent Census Bureau statistics, 5.7 million grandparents care for children under 8 years of age (http://factfinder.census.gov/servlet/datasetMainPage-Servlet?_program+Dss&_lang+e).

Research on grandparenting has been conducted in four broad areas:

1. analyzing the grandparent–grandchild relationship
2. examining the mental and physical health of grandparents and grandchildren
3. profiling grandparent-maintained households and the grandparents or grandchildren living in them
4. documenting the relatively poor economic situations of these families (Casper & Bryson, 1998)

However, there appears to be little evidence-based information about how grandchildren raised by grandparents fare, especially in school (Dench, 2002), although it is documented that these grandchildren are at higher risk of adjustment problems (Rodriguez-Srednicki, 2002).

This chapter discusses the growing body of literature about caregiving grandparents in order to provide school social workers and mental health counselors with the theoretical understanding necessary to develop assessment and intervention strategies. It explores the role of school social workers and other school-based practitioners in recognizing, supporting, and including families headed by grandparents. School policy and program strategies are also discussed.

What We Know

Students from families headed by grandparents constitute an increasing proportion of students in schools (Rothenberg, 1996). Estimates of the percentage of students in urban schools living with caregivers other than their biological parents range from 30% to as high as 60% (Hampton, Rak, & Mumford, 1997). In addition to grandparent-headed families, other family forms may include multiracial families, families with gay or lesbian parents, and foster families (Schwartz, 1999). *Kin keeping* or *kinship care*, referring to relatives who step into the role of parenting, has always been a latent family resource (Chan & Elder, 2000; Kolomer, 2000). However, the 1990 census data suggest that the grandparent-headed family form is dramatically increasing, with a 44% increase over the preceding decade. In addition, the number of children in what is called a *skipped generation household*, a household in which neither biological parent is present, nearly tripled from 1990 to 1994 (Minkler, 1999).

Legislative Activity

Two major legislative actions have contributed to the increase in kinship care: The 1995 amendments to the Social Security Act require states to offer adult relatives the first foster care option; and the Kinship Care Act of 1996 places grandparents first in line as possible foster care or adoptive parents when a grandchild is removed from a parent's home for safety reasons. In some instances, the Kinship Care Act has had the effect of grandparents becoming "de facto caregivers for children of teenage mothers" (Falk & Falk, 2002, p. 59).

Demographics

According to the U.S. Census, in 1970, 2.2 million children were living in a household maintained by a grandparent. By 1997, this number had risen to 3.9 million (Casper & Bryson, 1998). Kinship care can be informal or formal, with 15.5% of grandparents having legal authority to act on the child's behalf. African American children are four to five times more likely to live with relatives in the absence of a biological parent than are White children. Among Latinos, 7.4% of children live with grandparents in the absence of their biological parents (Burnette, 2000). Half of kinship caregivers are single, while 85% are women. Ninety-five percent are under 50 years of age (Grant, 2000).

Risks

In contrast to prevalence figures, a profile of grandparents providing care to grandchildren suggests that a majority are White women in their middle 50s, with a high school degree (Fuller-Thomson & Minkler, 2001). The prevalence of such arrangements is an estimate at best. However, the profile raises important psychosocial considerations about family well-being that may affect school performance. For example, Minkler (1999) has contended that grandparent caregiving has disproportionate effects on low-income women and therefore constitutes a women's issue. There are also disproportionate representations of African Americans and Latinos as well as higher poverty rates in kinship care families, thereby raising questions about access to proper health care services and the rates of underemployment.

School social workers and mental health counselors need to evaluate the circumstances that require a grandparent to take on a parenting role as they may be stressful, such as the death of the grandchild's parent. The grandparent may blame himself or herself for what has happened. He or she can experience depression or become more vulnerable to alcohol abuse or dependence on tranquilizers. Similarly, research documents that custodial grandchildren are more likely than same-aged peers to manifest behavioral and psychological adjustment difficulties. This may be the result of such complications as in utero exposure to drugs (Rodriguez-Srednicki, 2002).

Contributing Factors

School social workers and counselors need to be familiar with the contributing factors that account for the increase in grandparents acting as parents. These may include the death of a parent, parental abandonment, or high incidences of divorce, parental imprisonment, or drug addiction. The AIDS epidemic, crack cocaine and other substance abuse, and teen pregnancy also have contributed to these numbers (Fuller-Thomson & Minkler, 2001).

These prior family difficulties may have lingering effects on both grandchild and grandparents that can present as behavior problems at school. For example, students may be depressed or exhibit other effects of past neglect, abuse, or grief over separation from their parents (Burton, 1996). School problems may result in special education referrals or legal issues around guardianship or custody; the lack of health services may become an economic stressor (Grant, 2000). Grandparents may be struggling with the shift back to child-rearing responsibilities. Therefore, according to Rothenberg (1996), "Families made up of grandparents and their grandchildren are just one of the diverse family structures with which schools are learning to work" (p. 1).

What We Can Do

Assessment of Intergenerational Family Dynamics

Intergenerational family dynamics are shaped by role transitions across the life course usually based on age and cultural norms. Research suggests that these expectations tend to govern how individual family members anticipate their lives unfolding, providing temporal markers for family events (Burton, 1996; Waldrop & Weber, 2001). That is, as the systems age, there is predictable timing to family transitions and events. School social workers and mental health practitioners need to understand that family interdependence means that changes in any one family member have a ripple effect throughout the system (Greene, 2000). The life course role transitions that occur according to expectation are called *on time*, while those that seem to violate the expected timetable are termed *off time* (Greene, 2000).

For example, Hirshorn (1998) described how a grandparent may feel when getting young children ready for school as he or she assumes the role of a parent off time:

> Grandparent caregiving stretches, reorganizes, and redefines the relationship between family members; redraws the boundaries of family and, often, of household units; and redirects the transfer of resources within the family. (p. 200)

At the same time, as people are living longer, more grandparents are available to assume child-rearing roles and to redefine what "age," "old," and "retirement" mean (Force, Botsford, Pisano, & Holbert, 2000). Practitioners should keep in mind that a rigid assessment of age-appropriate roles is useful only when examining factors that may lead to stress (Fuller-Thomson et al., 1997). Research has documented that many aspects of caregiving for a grandchild can be a mixture of burden and honor—and sometimes rewarding. For example, caregiving may be related to experiencing the joys of children, participating in grandchildren's activities, developing a new focus in life, and watching a grandchild's accomplishments. Another important protective factor is the grandparent's knowledge that he or she is holding the family together (Force et al., 2000). For example, in a study by Poindexter and Linsk (1999), respondents tended to experience difficulties with finances and housing. At the same time, they indicated that they were proud of their roles as family sustainers and nurturers.

How grandparents appraise their role can become important to how they face risks and stressors (Huyck, 1991). To what extent does the caregiver believe he or she has mastered the caregiving role (Pruchno, Hicks-Patrick, & Burant, 1997)? The practitioner must learn from the family what subjective states are associated with the various life events associated with parenting (Pruchno & McKenney, 2002). Grandparents may also develop their own coping strategies, including taking action, talking about feelings, focusing on the grandchild, reaching out to others, and having religious faith (Reitzes & Mutran, 2004; Waldrop & Weber, 2001).

Interventions

Compared to other households, grandparents raising grandchildren are more likely to be poor, to receive public assistance, and to have no health insurance (Casper & Bryson, 1998). Therefore, interventions to address these potential risks are best designed from an ecological systems perspective (Cox, 2003). That is, interventions may address the various systems and environmental pressures a family can face. That opportunity is most likely to occur in a school setting. However, Gibson (2002) has argued that schools may be unprepared for an alternative family form or misunderstand the grandparents they encounter; therefore, school personnel must become more prepared to work with child-rearing differences. Her research suggested that practitioners need to begin their work by understanding the differences between mothering and grandparent caregiving.

Child-Focused Interventions

Once engaged, schools can offer stability to children from disrupted families. This requires a welcoming and safe school environment where students are encouraged to succeed. School social workers and counselors can play a key role in providing this nurturing behavior by compiling complete information on the student and working with social service agencies to assure comprehensive holistic care (Schwartz, 1999). The more students experience a sense of mastery at school, the more likely they are to develop high self-esteem and a commitment to learning. This in turn leads to resiliency (Benard, 1991; see Table 71.1).

Assisting clients from a resiliency perspective follows in the strengths-based tradition (Greene, 2002). When working from this point of view, the school social worker and other school practitioners may be challenged to recognize that students have strengths despite their many adversities. The role of school-based practitioners is to help students and their families move toward hope and change (Saleebey, 1997; Whitley, White, Kelley, & Yorke, 1999). Rather than an emphasis on the student's past, the practitioner focuses on the student's future (De Jong & Berg, 2002; Franklin &

Table 71.1 School Strategies Intended to Help Grandchildren

Schools can help children cope with the stresses of adjusting to their living arrangements by

- Anticipating transitional or adjustment difficulties and acting to minimize them. If a grandchild has only recently come into the grandparent's home, he or she may need time to adjust to a new routine, including expectations that he or she will attend school regularly and complete schoolwork.
- Looking for children's strengths and building on them. As many as two thirds of children who have grown up in difficult circumstances have within them the resilience to grow up to lead healthy, productive lives (Benard, 1991). With support and sensitivity, these children can often meet teachers' expectations.
- Placing children living with grandparents with the most stable and experienced teachers. Whether because of long-term family instability or recent sudden trauma, children living with their grandparents may need not only extra attention during the school year but also the classroom stability that an experienced teacher can provide.
- Trying not to single out children because of their family status in front of peers or other teachers. Shame and the feeling of being different from their peers, however unjustified, can contribute to a difficult school adjustment for these children.

Source: Rothenberg, D. (1996). *Grandparents as parents: A primer for schools.* Kid Source Online. Eric Clearinghouse on Elementary and Early Childhood Education. http://www.kidsource.com/kidsource/content2/grandparents.3.html.

Streeter, 2003). The practitioner has a belief in the student's abilities and fosters competence through interventions at home, with peers, or at school.

Solution-focused therapy embodies this philosophy, and its efficacy is increasingly being supported in the research literature (De Jong & Berg, 2002). The techniques are based on a therapeutic conversation that emphasizes empowering language and the search for solutions. New positive behaviors are discovered in collaboration with the client, and the goal is to support student autonomy and problem solving. These conversational techniques are best incorporated into programs and curriculums throughout the school (see Table 71.2). Also, see chapter 27 on self-harming behavior, chapter 68 on working with single-parent families, and chapter 67 on effective interventions for those at risk of dropping out for more examples of work in schools with solution-focused therapy.

Diversity

School social workers and other counselors need to pay particular attention to the strengths and educational needs of diverse students. For example, research on resilience suggests that many individuals create meaningful lives following profound ongoing stress or adversity through the support they receive from their spiritual/religious community (Hudley, Haight, & Miller, 2003). In addition, research of Strom, Buki, and Strom (1997) revealed

differences between the needs of English- and Spanish-speaking grandparents. Spanish-speaking grandparents reported a need for more information from their schools than did English-speaking grandparents. Schwartz (2003) has urged that after-school and community technology education programs be an instrument for improving family and school communication, noting the increase in public and private grants available in this arena. In 2003, there were more than 2,000 community technology centers around the country.

Family-Centered Interventions

School social workers and other counselors can use their knowledge of family systems theory to assist the family unit as a group. Family treatment can incorporate strengths-based assessment tools designed to reveal the family's most salient assets (De Jong & Miller, 1995). The interview is used to identify the grandparent's specific problems and goals. Whitley et al. (1999) suggest that the practitioner ask the following questions to ascertain how the grandparent resolved similar problems in the past:

- What is a current problem that you also faced in the past?
- What did you do to solve the problem in the past?
- Can you now use the same resources you used in the past to solve your current problem?

Table 71.2 Practice Principles for Solution-Focused Schools

1. Develop strong interpersonal and relationship skills of school personnel. Each school staff member focuses on building warm, supportive, and affirming relationships with every student. Students are personally known by each teacher and staff member.
2. Start where students are in relationship to their academic skills, learning styles, and personal needs.
3. School culture is built around a strengths orientation, focusing on building a community of empowered learners.
4. The school culture promotes the idea that behavior, or "doing," is the key to success in school and in life. Hard work and pride in oneself are important to accomplishing life tasks like graduating from high school.
5. Positive words and compliments are seen as important for helping students to achieve their academic and life goals. School staff members identify positives in students. Compliments and positive feedback are given to students on an ongoing basis. Administrators, faculty, and staff model this type of behavior toward one another.
6. The school has a future orientation. School personnel emphasize what students can do next to achieve and improve themselves. Faculty and staff focus students on positive behaviors and what they have done in the past that works and on what they can do differently that will work for them. If you are doing something that works, do more of it, and if what you are doing does not work, do something different.
7. The school culture facilitates beliefs in choice and self-determination. The solution-focused school is a school of choice that facilitates commitment on the part of its participants.
8. The culture of the solution-focused school fosters responsibility for self and others.
9. Teaching and learning are done in a collaborative manner.
10. Faculty and staff focus on building motivation and confidence in learning and achievement. The natural capacities of students are used to help them to want to excel.
11. Goal setting and a task orientation are pivotal to the school's instructional practices. Students are taught to set clear goals and to use small steps and tasks to achieve those goals. Academic instruction is portfolio- and mastery-based and goal-driven.
12. Small increments of change are valued and praised by faculty. Students can progress as fast or slowly as needed. Instructional practices are self-paced and individualized.
13. The staff helps students to notice their positive progress and plan for additional progress through the use of scaling questions or other self-evaluative tools. For example, "On a scale of 1–10, with 10 being you have completely reached your goal of coming to school to finish your science project, where are you today?" If the student says 5, the school staff says, "That's great! How can you get to a 6?"
14. The school staff uses the miracle question or other hypothetical/pretend questions that evoke positive imagery and promote trying new behaviors. For example, "Let's just suppose that you go home from school tonight and, while you are sleeping, a miracle happens, and these difficulties that you are having in completing your school credits in math disappear. When you wake up in the morning, what will be the first thing that you notice about your life that will be different?" Staff may also ask the pretend question: "Let's just suppose that you did know how to do math for a moment. How might that change what you are doing in school?"
15. Faculty and staff help students to build confidence by solution building. Solution building differs from the traditional problem-solving approach that is used in schools. Faculty lead students through the steps of solution building and help them to master the cognitive and behavioral skills needed to solution build. These skills include but are not limited to being able to articulate what is desired instead of what is the problem, mastery of goal setting, the ability to imagine and envision a bright and successful future, a focus on doing something different, and facilitating small behavioral changes.

Source: Franklin, C., & Streeter, C. (2003). *Solution-focused accountability schools for the twenty-first century.* Austin: University of Texas, Hogg Foundation for Mental Health.

- Were there occasions in the past when the problem occurred, but did not turn into a crisis, and what did you do to keep it from turning into a crisis? (p. 4)

Grandparent–Centered Group Support Interventions

Grandparents can feel isolated in their role and alienated from their grandchild's school. Group services information can be accessed through such organizations as the Brookdale Foundation and American Association of Retired Persons' Grandparent Information Center (AARP, 1993). These programs suggest that PTAs take up the banner of providing social supports (Minkler, 1999). Practitioners may also find Web-based resources, such as the Wisconsin Alliance for Family Caregiving, which provides family caregiving education through various curriculums. Sponsored by the University of Wisconsin Extension, the Web site offers information on child development and self-care (http://www.uwex.edu/ces/flp/caregiving).

School social workers and mental health counselors may want to seek out community-based services for grandparents from their school. For example, a large, private social service and mental health agency in New England started a program known as Grandcare (Kluger & Aprea, 1999).

Finally, grandparents can also be valuable resources for schools (Reynolds, Wright, & Beale 2003). Grandparents can tell practitioners what they need from schools and communities. In a recent study from the Gerontology Institute and the Center College of Public and Community Service of Massachusetts, grandparents indicated that they wanted:

- increased outreach from schools and communities
- involvement of grandparents in community assessment and referrals

Box 71.1 Services Provided to Grandfamilies

- Support/self-help groups
- Counseling and mental health services
- Recreational opportunities
- Grandparents' groups
- Transportation
- Financial assistance/entitlements
- Respite care
- Day care

- sensitivity training for teachers on grandparent caregiver needs and concerns
- information from the schools on children's health and learning problems
- grandparent involvement in in-service training for teachers
- grandparent involvement in parent/teacher councils and other committees appointed by school board members and the administration
- respite care, such as before- and after-school child care
- fact sheets on child development
- information on grandparent support groups

Hopefully, as many school districts are working more closely with grandparents raising grandchildren, the school-based practitioner can provide the leadership necessary to accomplish these suggestions.

Tools and Case Examples

Tables 71.1, 71.2, and 71.3 can be used to guide school social workers and others who work closely with grandparents raising grandchildren.

Key Points to Remember

Since the 1990s, there has been a growing number of grandparents taking on the role of primary caregiver for their grandchildren. Although a number of studies have analyzed this trend and its impact on the health and economic situation of the grandparents and grandchildren involved, few have focused on the impact of this trend on the grandchildren's school performance. A number of factors have been found to contribute to this trend, including increased life spans and recent Social Security and foster care legislation.

School-based practitioners need to be sensitive to many issues when the grandparent is the caregiver, including:

- events that led to the grandparent assuming custody of the grandchild
- support resources available to the family
- the potential burden that the situation places on grandparent and grandchild alike

Table 71.3 School Strategies Intended to Help Grandparents

The school can support grandparents who are working to raise and educate their grandchildren by

- Examining school policies on enrollment. Existing policies may need revision to accommodate the realities of children living with grandparents.
- Having helpful information on hand for grandparents acting as parents. School social workers may write a resource list and share it with teachers and grandparents acting as parents.
- Keeping in mind that short-term respite care often tops the wish list of grandparent caregivers (Turner, 1995).
- Being sure that school policy supports appropriate referrals for educational, health, and social services, as needed.
- Keeping in mind that school may be a much different place from the schools that grandparents remember. Schools might consider scheduling extra time for grandparent–teacher conferences.
- Using family-friendly strategies to encourage surrogate parents to take an active role in their children's education. For example, when the school is sending home important notices, the teacher needs to know whether it is Grandmommy or Poppa who will read, sign, and return the forms.

Source: Based on Rothenberg, D. (1996). *Grandparents as parents: A primer for schools.* Kid Source Online. Eric Clearinghouse on Elementary and Early Childhood Education. http://www.kidsource.com/kidsource/content2/grandparents.3.html.

- how the grandparent views his or her role as caregiver

To be best prepared to handle issues arising under these circumstances, school social workers and counselors need to be aware of these issues. They should also attempt to utilize a strengths-based focus to any interventions and use solution-focused therapy when needed. Practitioners with experience can take advantage of a family systems theory approach. Additionally, many community services and Internet-based resource sites are available to help these families outside of the school.

References

American Association of Retired Persons (AARP). (1993). *Grandparents raising their grandchildren: What to consider and where to find help.* Washington, DC: Author.

Benard, B. (1991). *Fostering resiliency in kids: Protective factors in the family, school, and community.* San Francisco: Far West Laboratory for Educational Research and Development.

Burnette, D. (2000). Latino grandparents rearing grandchildren with special needs: Effects on depressive symptomatology. *Journal of Gerontological Social Work, 33*(3), 1–16.

Burton, L. M. (1996). Age norms, the timing of family role transitions, and intergenerational caregiving among aging African American women. *Gerontologist, 36*(2), 199–208.

Casper, L. M., & Bryson, K. R. (1998). *Co-resident grandparents and their grandchildren: Grandparent maintained families.* Washington, DC: U.S. Bureau of the Census, Population Division. Available: http://www.census.gov/population/www/documentation/twps0026/twps0026.html.

Chan, C. G., & Elder, G. H. (2000). Matrilineal advantage in grandchild-grandparent relations. *Gerontologist, 40*(2), 179–190.

Cox, C. B. (2002). Empowering African American custodial grandparents. *Social Work, 47*(1), 45–53.

De Jong, P., & Berg, I. K. (2002). *Interviewing for solutions* (2nd ed.). Pacific Grove, CA: Brooks/Cole.

De Jong, P., & Miller, S. (1995). How to interview for clients' strengths. *Social Work, 40*, 729–736.

Dench, G. (2002). *Grandmothers: The changing culture.* New Brunswick, NJ: Transaction.

Falk, U. A., & Falk, G. (2002). *Grandparents.* Amherst, NY: Prometheus.

Force, L. T., Botsford, A., Pisano, P. A., & Holbert, A. (2000). Grandparents raising grandchildren with and without a developmental disability: Preliminary comparisons. *Journal of Gerontological Social Work, 33*(4), 5–21.

Franklin, C., & Streeter, C. (2003). *Solution-focused accountability schools for the twenty-first century: A training manual for Gonzalo Garza Independent High School.* Austin: University of Texas, School of Social Work, Hogg Foundation for Mental Health. Available: www.utexas.edu/ssw/faculty/franklin.

Fuller-Thomson, E., & Minkler, M. (2001). American grandparents providing extensive child care to their grandchildren: Prevalence and profile. *Gerontologist, 41*(2), 201–209.

Fuller-Thomson, E., Minkler, M., & Driver, D. (1997). A profile of grandparents raiding grandchildren in the United States. *Gerontologist, 37*(3), 406–411.

Gibson, P. (2002). Barriers, lessons learned, and helpful hints: Grandmother caregivers talk about service utilization. *Journal of Gerontological Social Work, 39*(4), 55–74.

Grant, R. (2000). The special needs of children in kinship care. *Journal of Gerontological Social Work, 33*(3), 17–33.

Greene, R. R. (2000). *Social work with the aged and their families*. New York: Aldine De Gruyter.

Greene, R. R. (2002). *Resiliency theory: An integrated framework for practice, research, and policy*. Washington, DC: NASW Press.

Hampton, F. M., Rak, C., & Mumford, D. A. (1997). Children's literature reflecting diverse family structures: Social and academic benefits for early reading programs. *ERS Spectrum, 15*(4), 10–15.

Hirshorn, B. A. (1998). Grandparents as caregivers. In M. E. Szinovacz (Ed.), *Handbook on grandparenthood* (pp. 200–214). Westport, CT: Greenwood Press.

Hudley, E., Haight, W., & Miller, P. (2003). *Raise up a child*. Chicago: Lyceum.

Huyck, M. H. (1991). Predicates of personal control among middle-aged and young-old men and women in middle America. *International Journal of Aging and Human Development, 32*, 261–275.

Kluger, M., & Aprea, D. M. (1999). Grandparents raising grandchildren: A description of the families and a special pilot program. *Journal of Gerontological Social Work, 32*(10), 5–17.

Kolomer, S., McCallion, P., & Janicki, M. P. (2002). African American grandmother caregivers of children with disabilities: Predictors of depressive symptoms. *Journal of Gerontological Social Work, 37*(3–4), 45–62.

Kolomer, S. R. (2000). Kinship foster care and its impact on grandmother caregivers. *Journal of Gerontological Social Work, 33*(3), 85–102.

Minkler, M. (1999). Intergenerational households headed by grandparents: Contexts, realities, and implications for policy. *Journal of Aging Studies, 13*(2), 199–219.

Poindexter, C. C., & Linsk, N. (1998). The sources of social support for a sample of older minority caregivers. *Families in Society, 79*(5), 491–503.

Pruchno, R., Hicks-Patrick, J., & Burant, C. (1997). African-American and white mothers of adults with chronic disabilities: Caregiving burden and satisfaction. *Family Relations, 46*, 335–346.

Pruchno, R. A., & McKenney, D. (2002). Psychological well-being of black and white grandmothers raising grandchildren: Examination of a two-factor model. *Journal of Gerontology, 57B*, 444–452.

Reitzes, D. C., & Mutran, E. J. (2004). Grandparenthood: Factors influencing frequency of grandparent-grandchildren contact and grandparent role satisfaction. *Journal of Gerontology, 59B*(1), 9–16.

Reynolds, G. P., Wright, J. V., & Beale, B. (2003). The roles of grandparents in educating today's children. *Journal of Instructional Psychology, 30*(4), 316–325.

Rodriguez-Srednicki, O. (2002). The custodial grandparent phenomenon: A challenge to schools and school psychology. *NASP Communiqué, 31*(1). September. Available: http://www.nasponline.org/futures/grandparents.html.

Rothenberg, D. (1996). *Grandparents as parents: A primer for schools*. Kid Source Online. Eric Clearinghouse on Elementary and Early Childhood Education. Available: http://www.kidsource.com/kidsource/content2/grandparents.3.html.

Saleebey, D. (Ed.). (1997). *The strengths perspective in social work practice* (2nd ed.). New York: Longman.

Schwartz, W. (1999). *Family diversity in urban school*. ERIC/CUE Digest, No. 148. Eric Clearinghouse on Urban Education. Available: http://www.ericfacility.net/databases/ERIC_Digests/ed434188.html.

Schwartz, W. (2003). *After-school and community technology education programs for low income families*. ERIC Digest, Eric Clearinghouse on Urban Education. Available: http://www.ericfacility.net/databases/ERIC_Digests/ed478098.html.

Strom, R. D., Buki, L. P., & Strom, S. K. (1997). Strengths and educational needs of Mexican American grandparents. *International Journal of Aging and Human Development, 45*(1), 1–21.

Waldrop, D. P., & Weber, J. A. (2001). From grandparent to caregiver: The stress and satisfaction of raising grandchildren. *Families in Society, 82*(5), 461–471.

Whitley, D. M., White, K. R., Kelley, S. J., & Yorke, B. (1999). Strengths-based case management: The application to grandparents raising grandchildren. *Families in Society, 80*(2), 110–119.

Home Visiting

Essential Guidelines for Home Visits and Engaging With Families

Barbara Hanna Wasik ▪ Gary L. Shaffer

Visiting with people in their homes is one of the most humane and family-centered approaches to service delivery in our society. Home visiting is uniquely supportive of family life, bringing services to families, providing services in a familiar setting, and reducing obstacles to services.—Wasik & Bryant, 2001

CHAPTER 72

Getting Started

Home visiting has a long history in education, family and child welfare, and physical and mental health services (Hancock & Pelton, 1989; Levine & Levine, 1970; Oppenheimer, 1925; Richmond, 1899). Home visits are critical in serving children and youth from birth to high school and in addressing issues ranging from programs for preschool children through school-system concerns. Educational organizations rely on home visits to address a wide range of issues related to student behaviors such as attendance, discipline, physical or mental challenges, drug or alcohol abuse, depression, or antisocial activities. Other home visits focus on student characteristics relating specifically to school performance, such as risk for school failure among preschool children or low academic achievement among school-age children.

Why this enduring interest in and reliance on home visiting? Many believe that home visits help to break down barriers between professionals and families, reduce obstacles to services, and provide opportunities to respond to individual family needs. Minuchin and colleagues (Minuchin, Colapinto, & Minuchin, 1998) have written that, through home visiting, "the aura of authority that characterizes an official setting is muted and the reality of the family's life environment is acknowledged" (p. 204). By visiting in the home, we can gain an appreciation of the family's home life and can respond with more knowledge and greater sensitivity to the family's needs. Through our presence in the family's community, we can gain knowledge about the local culture, values, and languages. We also gain unique opportunities for engaging families. Regardless of the impetus for the home visit, home visitors not only need

general knowledge and skills related to home visiting (including a repertoire of appropriate clinical/interviewing skills) but also specific knowledge and skills related to the particular focus of the visit.

Today, home visiting remains a mainstay of varied services, including early childhood intervention; nursing, rehabilitation, and hospice programs; protective services; and school social work practice. Young children and their parents are served through an extensive set of national programs, such as the Parents as Teachers, Healthy Families America, Nurse–Family Partnership, Home Instruction for Parents of Preschool Youngsters, and Early Head Start programs. In addition, hundreds of local parent support programs have included home-visiting strategies (Catalano, Berglund, Ryan, Lonczak, & Hawkins, 2002; Fraser, Day, Galinsky, Hodges, & Smokowski, 2004; Gomby, Culross, & Behrman 1999; Greenberg, Domitrovich, & Bumbarger, 2001). Some of these programs have been intensely researched and tested; others have been implemented with little research or empirical evidence to guide their efforts. Some programs employ professionals as home visitors while others employ paraprofessionals. Other critical differences among these programs include the goals of the home visit, the procedures and materials used, the duration and intensity of the visits, and whether participation is voluntary.

In this chapter, we present information relevant for school social workers and others who provide services to school-age students and their families. We begin with information on the prevalence of home visiting and a brief review of program outcomes. We then include guidelines for home visiting, specific information for preparing for a home visit, and a framework and strategies to guide the actual home visit. Additional resources are included to illustrate the various types of programs, purposes, and outcomes of home visitation.

What We Know

Prevalence of Home Visiting

The acceptance of home visiting as an effective practice among school social workers is illustrated in a random sample of school social workers who were asked about school violence and personal safety. A vast majority of the 576 respondents (91%) endorsed home visits as an effective intervention for aggressive children, and 82% of those responding reported that they conduct home visits for aggressive children. This high rate of home visiting occurred despite the fact that 74% of respondents viewed home visits as potentially dangerous situations (Astor, Behre, Wallace, & Fravil, 1998).

Further evidence of the widespread use of home visiting across agencies comes from Johnson's study (2001). She found 37 states reporting the use of home-visiting programs to improve parenting skills (81%), enhance child development (76%), and prevent abuse and neglect (71%). Several states (i.e., Florida, Illinois, Michigan, New York, Ohio, Oklahoma, and Washington) have demonstrated their commitment to home visiting by budgeting $10–50 million a year for one or more such programs. Johnson (2001) concluded:

> The convergence of several policy and research trends created a policy setting conducive to the expansion of home visiting efforts. These include growing public awareness of infant and brain development research, emphasis on early education and school readiness, recognition of the importance of family support, enactment of welfare reform policies, expansion of child health coverage, and the devolution of authority and funding in many policy areas to states. (p. ix)

One outcome of this renewed interest has been the involvement of many school systems in home-visiting programs for students who are also parents of young children. Such programs often focus on helping young parents to complete their education and to acquire parenting skills.

Program Effectiveness

Since the 1990s, many authors have addressed the effectiveness of home visiting. They have both reviewed the existing research and conducted meta-analyses of these studies. The reviews have shown mixed results (Daro & Harding, 1999; Greenberg, Domitrovich, & Bumbarger, 2001; Guterman, 2000; Substance Abuse and Mental Health Services Administration, n.d.; Sweet & Appelbaum, 2004).

Reviews of studies on national programs that focused on increasing parenting skills to assure children's school readiness have yielded inconsistent findings (Gomby, Culross, & Behrman, 1999; Gomby, Larson, Lewit, & Behrman, 1993). The most consistently positive outcomes have come from the Nurse–Family Partnership and its earlier models (Olds, Henderson, Kitzman, Eckenrode, Cole, & Tatelbaum, 1999).

However, two home-visiting programs have obtained strong empirical support for their procedures. One of these is the work of Lutzker and his colleagues (Lutzker, Bigelow, Doctor, Gershater, & Greene, 1998), who developed and researched an ecobehavioral approach to address adult and child neglect, finding strong support for reducing parental behaviors associated with abuse and neglect. A second noteworthy example of an effective home-visiting program is multisystemic therapy for serious juvenile delinquents, which draws from several theories, including ecological theory, family systems theory, behavioral theory, and cognitive-behavioral theory. This home-visiting program has resulted in reduced antisocial behavior, less substance abuse, and less aggression with peers (Henggeler, Schoenwald, Borduin, Rowland, & Cunningham, 1998). See chapter 3 on effective treatments with students with conduct disorders for more information on multisystemic therapy.

Concern with the absence of positive outcome data in some experimental studies has led to detailed analyses of process and outcome data. One exemplary analysis of Hawaii's Healthy Start program questions the adequacy of the preparation and training of the home visitors (Duggan, Fuddy, Burrell, Higman, McFarlane, Windham, & Sia, 2004). In examining why child and parent outcomes were not strong, researchers found that paraprofessional home visitors were not identifying or were failing to address several key predictors of abuse and neglect: partner violence, substance abuse, and parental depression.

These findings have important implications for school social workers and others who provide home-visiting services as they provide compelling evidence of the need to assure that visitors are well trained and have the knowledge and skills essential to address the goals and objectives of the program. Home visitors need to be thoroughly acquainted with the basics of visiting, equipped with strong clinical and helping skills, and knowledgeable of the skills specific to the intervention that is being implemented. Furthermore, home visitors need access to professional development and ongoing supervision in order to reflect on and improve their practice.

What We Can Do

Home-Visiting Principles

In this section, we present principles that help to focus the work of the home visitor, information for planning the home visit, and a framework for the home visit itself. We focus on general strategies for home visits (such as the need to engage the family in a working relationship), rather than specific interventions for particular family needs. However, numerous interventions described throughout this book can be used within the context of home visits to reach specific goals. For example, home visitors can use the information described in part I of this volume for working with students with conduct disorders, learning disabilities, or substance abuse and when meeting with the families.

Guidelines

First, as illustrated in Table 72.1, we identify guidelines that help to structure the home visit. These guidelines help home visitors to recognize that they are guests in the family's home and that they need to work with the family in a collaborative and flexible manner, provide individualized services, and help families to obtain resources that can help sustain changes over time.

Preparation for the Home Visit

Preparing for a home visit may take more time than preparing to see a parent or family in an office or school setting because you must not only prepare for the content of the meeting and learn about the family but also learn about the community surrounding the home in order to gain relevant information for visiting the family. A considerable amount of preparation is essential if you have not previously visited with the family, or in the neighborhood. Specific preparation activities are listed next.

Table 72.1 Home-Visiting Guidelines

- Home visitors should view the family as a social system where changes in one individual in the family can influence other family members as well as the overall functioning of the family.
- Home-based interventions should be individualized, whether focused on a specific family member or the entire family.
- Home visitors can best conceptualize their helping relationship as a collaboration between the home visitor and the family members, which builds on the family's strengths.
- Home visitors must be flexible and responsive to the immediate needs of families as well as to their long-term goals.
- Home visitors need to continually evaluate the family's strengths, limitations, and progress and use this knowledge to modify interventions as necessary.
- Home visitors need to be able to encourage effective coping and problem-solving skills.
- Home visitors should remain attentive to the family's future needs and help the members consider ways that newly acquired skills or attitudes might be generalized to future situations.
- Home visitors need to link the family with natural helping systems in the community, resources that can support the family after services are terminated (e.g., extended family members, significant others, neighbors, clubs, and faith organizations).

Source: Adapted from Wasik, B. H., & Bryant, D. M. (2001). *Home visiting: Procedures for helping families* (2nd ed.). Thousand Oaks, CA: Sage.

Learn About the Family

What is the composition of the family? Are supportive relatives or friends nearby? When are family members most likely to be at home? Who do you expect to be present in the home? Are there special considerations involved in visiting with this family? Is this a voluntary or mandated visit? If your organization or school has provided services to this family before, what knowledge can be shared with you? Such information could include which family members are most supportive of the visit or whether any difficulties have been experienced before.

Review the Purpose of the Visit

Reflect on the goals and purposes of the visit. Think through what you hope to accomplish on the visit and what steps you think might be necessary to accomplish the goals. Ask yourself the following questions: If this is not the first visit, did you leave any adult or student informational materials during your last visit? Did you expect any tasks to be completed between the last visit and this one? Determine what materials you might need for the visit, such as school forms or records, parenting materials, or referral information.

Remember, both general and specific knowledge and skills are essential for effective home visiting. Ask yourself what specific skills and competencies are needed for this visit. For example, does a parent need to have an interpretation of a psychological report? Should the school nurse go on this home visit with you? Do you need to address the student's low school achievement? Would it be advantageous for the student's teacher to be on this visit? Did you obtain any data at the last visit that need to be considered? Is there a specific intervention protocol to be followed for this visit?

Set the Time

Make contact with the family in advance to confirm the date and time for the visit. If this time is set up more than a few days in advance, reconfirm the day and time before the visit, if possible. This task may be difficult as families may not have phones or may be unwilling to share contact information.

Learn the Characteristics of the Neighborhood

Learn how to get to the home. If necessary, make a trial trip to the home to assure that you know the location. Have a map of the community and the neighborhood available and use an online travel direction program to assist you in your preparations.

Consider Personal Safety

In today's society, safety issues can occur in any neighborhood and, as previously mentioned, the majority of school social workers view home visits as potentially dangerous situations (Astor, Behre, Wallace, & Fravil, 1998). Consequently, home visitors should attend to basic personal safety issues. Having a cell phone that can be used to make quick contact with others is prudent behavior, as is letting another responsible person know when and where you will be visiting and when you are expected back. Decide if the safety concerns call for you to visit during the day or with a coworker. In some instances, you may benefit from using the school resource officer as an escort (Wasik & Coleman, 2004).

Conducting the Home Visit

The framework we present here has relevance across home visiting for many purposes related to working with children, youth, and their families (Wasik & Sparling, 1998). Each topic presented in Table 72.2 identifies one aspect of the home visit. Reviewing each of these aspects before making a home visit will help assure that you have thoroughly thought through the overall structure of the home visit as well as made considerations for the specific visit. Reflecting on this set of items after the home visit can help you to evaluate your actions in the home and to learn from the visit. Additional detailed information appears in Wasik and Sparling (1998).

In addition to the structure provided in the table, good home visits happen when the home visitor employs strong helping skills. School social workers and other mental health counselors are introduced to these during their training, but it is helpful to list those that are especially important for home visits (see Table 72.3). In essence, you want to put the family at ease, be respectful and

Table 72.2 Aspects of Home Visits

	Visitor's Actions and Responsibilities
Greeting and engagement	Greet family members warmly and establish rapport Discuss purpose of home visit
Assessment of current family/child status	Ask about changes since last visit Discuss • current status of child or youth and parent/family • family needs and resources
Child/adolescent focus	Discuss goals/objectives for the child or adolescent Inquire about recent activities or services Jointly plan with family for any new activities or interventions Describe fully any new activities or interventions Assure that family understands
Parent–child focus	Discuss specific parent concerns regarding child/adolescent Help parent resolve difficulties in parent–child relationships Jointly plan with family for any new activities or interventions Assure that family understands
Family focus	Respond appropriately to family culture, practices, and beliefs Encourage participation of family members as appropriate Discuss family social support network as needed
Health/safety	Identify/respond to health issues Make referrals as appropriate
Parent coping and problem solving	Use effective problem-solving strategies Encourage parents to clarify concerns and problems Help parents develop strategies and follow through
Case management and coordination	Discuss other services Discuss any coordination issues Make referrals as appropriate
Closure and planning for next steps	Recap main points of visit Discuss specific goals of coming weeks Provide • time for parent/family input • encouragement for next steps Arrange for next meeting

nonjudgmental, and use procedures that engage the family and help them to make progress toward their own goals.

The clinical skills listed in Table 72.3 are important for engaging with families and helping them to accept and address concerns. Home visitors can also benefit by using a structure, such as a problem-solving strategy, to guide their interactions related to specific concerns or issues (see Table 72.4). This strategy helps home visitors in their interactions with a family by clarifying the status or progress made in the problem-solving

Table 72.3 Clinical Interviewing Skills

Visitor communicates warmth and caring.
Visitor conveys empathy.
Visitor puts parent/family at ease.
Visitor uses a collaborative manner.
Visitor individualizes services.
Visitor listens attentively.
Visitor is reflective and thoughtful.
Visitor is appropriately directive.
Visitor questions/probes as needed.
Visitor clarifies or restates client goals or needs.
Visitor provides support and encouragement.
Visitor compliments parents and students on strengths or positive activities.
Visitor is appropriately responsive to parent or student emotions.
Visitor uses appropriate clinical techniques.

process and what is needed to move forward. Using a problem-solving strategy can provide greater focus to the home visit and provide more clarity to the concerns being addressed. A strategy such as this is especially helpful when you are not using a programmed or scripted intervention. Additional information on the use of this problem-solving strategy can be found in Wasik and Bryant (2001).

raphy presents a selection of specific programs that incorporate home visiting, a brief description and focus of each, selected outcomes, and contact information. Table 72.5 lists a range of home-visiting programs serving children from infancy to late adolescence and their families. This list, although just a starting point, provides the reader with information on the breadth of issues being addressed through home-visiting services and examples of the kinds of procedures that are used.

Resource Bibliography: Programs Incorporating Home Visiting

For those providing home-visiting services, it is important to become familiar with specific programs and their empirical database. The resource bibliog-

Key Points to Remember

This chapter has provided an overview of home visiting for school social workers and others working within educational organizations. We

Table 72.4 Problem-Solving Strategy

1. *Problem definition*: describing a problem situation (a situation is defined as a problem when its resolution is not automatic)
2. *Goal selection*: describing what a person wants to happen
3. *Generation of solutions*: identifying a number of alternative responses that may address a problem or reach a goal
4. *Consideration of consequences*: identifying the positive and negative consequences of any solution in relation to time; money; personal, emotional, and social effects; immediate and long-term effects
5. *Decision making*: weighing the proposed solutions and consequences and appropriately determining which one is best for the individual at the time (decision making includes consideration of a person's priorities and values)
6. *Implementation*: carrying out those actions called for by the decision
7. *Evaluation*: reviewing the outcome to determine whether it met the person's goals

Table 72.5 Home-Visiting Programs

Resource	Description	Selected Outcomes	Contact
Parents as Teachers	Early childhood parent education and family support program. Focus: 0–5 years	Parents engage in language and literacy-promoting behaviors; children score high on kindergarten readiness tests	Parents as Teachers National Center www.patnc.org
First Steps to Success	Goal is to divert antisocial behavior in kindergarteners. Three components: universal screening, school and home intervention. Being introduced to Head Start children and families. Focus: kindergarteners	Decrease in aggression; increase in adaptive behavior and academic achievement.	Hill M. Walker, Co-Director Institute on Violence and Destructive Behavior 1265 University of Oregon, Eugene, OR 97403-1265 Phone: (541) 346-3580 E-mail: hwalker@oregon. uoregon.edu
Early Risers: Skills for Success	The program is specifically aimed at children who display early aggressive, disruptive, and/or nonconformist behaviors. Focus: 6–10 years.	Improvement in academic achievement and social skills; decreased behavior problems	Gerald J. August, Ph.D. University of Minnesota F256/2B West 2450 Riverside Avenue Minneapolis, MN 55454-1495 Phone: (612) 273-9711 Fax: (612) 273-9779 Email: augus001@tc.umn.edu
Multisystemic Therapy	Family oriented family therapy, home-based. Focus: violent, substance-abusing youth 12–17 years.	Cost-efficient reduction in substance use and antisocial behavior in serious, chronic, juvenile offenders	Scott W. Henggeler, Ph.D. Family Services Research Center, Medical University of South Carolina Henggesw@musc.edu

Source: U.S. Department of Health and Human Services, Substance Abuse and Mental Health Services Administration and the Administration for Children & Families; Program Web sites.

gave some background on the advantages of home visiting and its prevalence and general guidelines to help social workers begin to practice in this setting. We also provided helpful information for review as the social worker prepares for a home visit and a framework for conducting the home visit itself. In addition, we suggested a problem-solving strategy as a way of providing structure and guidance to the home-visiting pro-

cess. Additional resources will need to be consulted for those new to home visiting. These resources include both general sources on home visiting and sources specific to the objectives for the home visit. Seeking out other experienced home visitors for mentoring and supervision is also a way to master the skills needed to be an effective home visitor.

References

Astor, R. A., Behre, W. J., Wallace, J. M., & Fravil, K. (1998). School social workers and school violence: Personal safety, training, and violence programs. *Social Work, 43*(3), 223–232.

Catalano, R. F., Berglund, M. L., Ryan, J. A. M., Lonczak, H. S., & Hawkins, J. D. (2002). Positive youth development in the United States: Research findings on evaluations of positive youth development programs. *Prevention & Treatment, 5,* Article 15. Available: http://journals.apa.org/prevention.

Daro, D. A., & Harding, K. A. (1999). Healthy Families America: Using research to enhance practice. *Future of Children, 9*(1), 152–176.

Duggan, A., Fuddy, L., Burrell, L., Higman, S. M., McFarlane, E., Windham, A., & Sia, C. (2004). Randomized trail of a statewide home visiting program to prevent child abuse: Impact in reducing parental risk factors. *Child Abuse and Neglect, 28,* 623–643.

Fraser, M. W., Day, S. V., Galinsky, M. J., Hodges, V. G., & Smokowski, P. R. (2004). Conduct problems and peer rejection in childhood: A randomized trial of the Making Choices and Strong Families programs. *Research on Social Work Practice, 14,* 313–324.

Gomby, D. S., Culross, P. L., & Behrman, R. E. (1999). Home visiting: Recent program evaluations: Analysis and recommendations. *Future of Children: Home Visiting, 9,* 4–26.

Gomby, D. S., Larson, C. S., Lewit, E. M., & Behrman, R. E. (1993). Home visiting: Analysis and recommendations. *Future of Children: Home Visiting, 3,* 6–22.

Greenberg, M. T., Domitrovich, C., & Bumbarger, B. (2001). The prevention of mental disorders in school-aged children: Current state of the field. *Prevention & Treatment, 4,* Article 1. Available: http://journals.apa.org/prevention.

Guterman, N. B. (2000). *Stopping child maltreatment before it starts: Emerging horizons in early home visitation services.* Thousand Oaks, CA: Sage.

Hancock, B. L., & Pelton, L. H. (1989). Home visits: History and functions. *Social Casework, 70,* 21–27.

Henggeler, S. W., Schoenwald, S. K., Borduin, C. M., Rowland, M. D., & Cunningham, P. B. (1998). *Multisystemic treatment of antisocial behavior in children and adolescents.* New York: Guilford.

Johnson, K. A. (2001). *No place like home: State home visiting policies and programs.* Commonwealth Fund. Available: http://www.cmwf.org/publications/publications_show.htm?doc_id=221347.

Levine, M., & Levine, A. (1970). *A social history of the helping services: Clinic, court, school, and community.* New York: Appleton-Century-Crofts.

Lutzker, J. R., Bigelow, K. M., Doctor, R. M., Gershater, R. M., & Greene, B. F. (1998). An ecological behavioral model for the prevention and treatment of child abuse and neglect. In J. R. Lutzker (Ed.), *Handbook of child abuse research and treatment* (pp. 239–266). New York: Plenum.

Minuchin, P., Colapinto, J., & Minuchin, S. (1998). *Working with families of the poor.* New York: Guilford.

Olds, D. L., Henderson, C. R., Kitzman, H. J., Eckenrode, J. J., Cole, R. E., & Tatelbaum, R. C. (1999). Prenatal and infant home visitation by nurses: Recent findings. *Future of Children, 9,* 44–65.

Oppenheimer, J. J. (1925). *The visiting teacher movement with special reference to administrative relationships* (2nd ed.). New York: Joint Committee on Methods of Preventing Delinquency.

Richmond, M. (1899). *Friendly visiting among the poor.* New York: Macmillan.

Substance Abuse and Mental Health Services Administration, Center for Substance Abuse Prevention. (n.d.) *SAMHSA model programs: Effective substance abuse and mental health programs for every community.* Available: http://modelprograms.samhsa.gov.

Sweet, M. A., & Appelbaum, M. I. (2004). Is home visiting an effective strategy? A meta-analytic review of home visiting programs for families with young children. *Child Development, 75*(5), 1435–1456.

Wasik, B. H., & Bryant, D. M. (2001). *Home visiting: Procedures for helping families* (2nd ed.). Thousand Oaks, CA: Sage.

Wasik, B. H., & Coleman, S. (2004). *Safety issues in home visiting.* Chapel Hill: Center for Home Visiting, University of North Carolina.

Wasik, B. H., & Sparling, J. J. (1998). *Home Visit Assessment Instrument.* Chapel Hill: Center for Home Visiting, University of North Carolina.

Guidelines for Working With Multicultural Groups and Managing Diverse Relationships in a School Community Context

Dimensions of race and culture are shifting in school populations. Today's school social workers and related professionals must be competent with people from widely diverse cultural backgrounds and serve as cultural mediators and educators for school staff and the school environment. School practitioners who contributed to the planning of this volume report that practitioners often feel unprepared in this area. The knowledge to work effectively with multiple cultures, to intervene with the special needs of diverse families, and to design culturally appropriate services for growing numbers of students and families of color and low socioeconomic status are some of the immediate needs they identified. This section responds to these issues and other skills related to diversity.

Working With Culturally/Racially Diverse Students to Improve Connection to School and Academic Performance

Daphna Oyserman

CHAPTER 73

Getting Started

About half of low-income and minority youth do not graduate from high school on time. (For more information about interventions with specific low-income or minority groups, see chapters 38, 67, 70, 74, and 76–83.) For social workers in schools, an important task is to help students at risk of school failure see the connection between the mundane present with its everyday behaviors and a future self—often envisioned in terms of vague yet positive hopes and dreams. Underperformance in school and school failure are an enormous waste of human potential and increase risk of negative outcomes (delinquency, depression, substance use, early risky sexual activity) in adolescence and adulthood. Low academic attainment and especially lack of a high school diploma increase risk in adulthood—it is harder to get and keep a job, harder to earn

enough income, and, as a result, harder to provide for one's children. Thus, improving connection to school and academic performance is a central task for the prevention of problematic outcomes both during adolescence and in adulthood.

What We Know

Early research suggests that when asked about their hopes and dreams for themselves in adulthood—their hoped-for possible selves (PS)—youths have high hopes that do not differ across levels of risk (Oyserman & Markus, 1990a). Even very low income youth report high hopes and dreams. However, more variance is found when asking youth about their more proximal PS for the coming year (Oyserman & Markus, 1990a) and when asking youth if they are doing anything to try to attain these PS (Oyserman & Saltz, 1993). Content of more proximal PS (Oyserman & Markus, 1990a) and not trying to attain positive PS (or avoid negative PS) are both related to more problem behaviors (Oyserman & Saltz, 1993). Thus the question for social work interventions is how to translate already high hopes and dreams for the future into proximal PS focused on connection to school and academic attainment: that is, how to help youth link PS to current behavior.

Operationalizing PS

PS are defined as images of ourselves not as we currently are but at positive or negative end states—the self who already passed the algebra test, the self who failed to lose weight, the self who falls in with the "wrong" crowd (Oyserman & Markus, 1990a). A central life task of adolescence and early adulthood is figuring out not simply what one is like now but also who one might become; not only what is possible for the self but also how to fit together the many available images of the future (Oyserman, 2001). PS of teens are likely to include expectations and concerns about how one will do in school, how one will fit in socially, and how to get through adolescence without becoming off-track—pregnant, arrested, or hooked on drugs (Oyserman & Fryberg, in press). Indeed, existing evidence suggests that expectations and concerns about succeeding in school or being a good student are the most common PS in adolescence, even among very low income minority teens at high risk of school failure (Oyserman & Fryberg, in press).

PS and Racial-Ethnic Identity

For urban, low-income, and minority youths, PS and racial-ethnic (REI) or social identity are likely to be interwoven. Findings from studies primarily focused on Detroit, African American, middle and high school youths suggest that both PS and REI play an important role in school performance and vulnerability to depression (Oyserman, Bybee, & Terry, 2004; Oyserman, Gant, & Ager, 1995; Oyserman & Harrison, 1998; Oyserman, Terry, & Bybee, 2002). These studies document that academic outcomes improve when academic achievement is an integral part of REI (see also Oyserman, Kemmelmeier, Fryberg, Brosh, & Hart-Johnson, 2003 for research focused

on American Indian, Mexican American, and Arab youth). Simply having a positive self-image or a positive sense of connection to one's racial-ethnic group is not enough. Because PS and REI are both potential sources of academic focus, interventions that promote focus on PS as congruent with REI and on REI as congruent with school attainment are more likely to be effective.

How Might PS Influence Behavior?

But how do PS sustain effortful action to influence behavior? By articulating and detailing the look and feel of the future, PS may sustain effortful action by making the future come alive as a possible reality. Without an academic PS to consider, a student has no reason not to stay up late to see another TV show or video. Thus, PS may function to reduce the impact of moment-to-moment shifts in what is made salient by one's social context. They focus attention on successful attainment of self-goals and avoidance of anti-goals. Becoming like one's academic success PS could involve strategies such as "go to all my classes" and "set my alarm clock so I won't get up late." PS do not develop in isolation; youth need to be able to find connections between their PS and other important identities such as REI and to feel that important others (including parents and other adults who may be role models) view their PS as plausible. Low-income youth, nonheterosexual LGBT (lesbian, gay, bi- or trans-gendered) youth and youth of color may find it difficult to create positive and believable PS focused on school as a pathway to adulthood unless these PS are fostered in a social context that creates local norms highlighting the relevance of academic achievement for being part of one's social identity (including REI, social class, and LGBT identity).

What We Can Do

In their summary of research on PS for minority youth, Oyserman and Fryberg (in press) note that research is mostly correlational and necessarily leaves unanswered how to translate findings about correlations between PS, school involvement, and REI (or LGBT or social-class identity) into a framework for change. To address this gap, in our own research we have focused on experimental manipulations to capture the "active" aspects of PS and social identity (Oyserman, Bybee, & Terry, 2003; Oyserman, Bybee, Terry, & Hart-Johnson, 2004; Oyserman, Gant, & Ager, 1995; Oyserman & Markus, 1990b; Oyserman & Saltz, 1993; Oyserman, Terry, & Bybee, 2002) and used these as the basis for developing a brief intervention, outlined below. The intervention was designed, implemented, and evaluated with funding from the National Institutes of Health (Grant number MH58299, Oyserman PI) to engage low-income youth both white and of color in developing clearly articulated PS that linked current school involvement with adult futures. The underlying assumption is that if one could help youth articulate achievement-oriented PS in a positive peer-based social context that implicitly framed academic achievement as part of REI, one should be able to bolster not only youth's PS but also their sense of connection to school and involvement in school more generally (see also Oyserman, Bybee, & Terry, in press).

All too often, social work practitioners attempt to develop comprehensive interventions that require more time and resources than they are able to marshal over time. Given the need for very brief, low-budget universal interventions, we developed an intervention called School-to-Jobs with the goal of meeting the social worker's need for a brief, cheap, fun intervention that can be sustained over time in high-need schools.

The School-to-Jobs (STJ) Program aims at promoting development of PS pathways from middle to high school by (1) helping youths articulate proximal and more distal PS goals and strategies to obtain their PS; (2) increasing concern about school and academic efficacy within the context of REI; and (3) developing culturally appropriate active listening and positive communication skills.

Thumbnail Sketch of the STJ Intervention

The goal was that the intervention would highlight and elicit the relevance of school to attaining one's PS. The intervention is small-group based (groups of about 12 students) and has been tested as both an after-school (Oyserman, Terry, & Bybee, 2002) and in-school program (Oyserman, Bybee, & Terry, in press) for middle school students. The after-school test of the intervention followed youth to the end of the academic year and documented significantly reduced risk of be-

ing sent out of class, significantly improved attendance and time spent doing homework, as well as change in the youth's PS, comparing control and intervention youth and statistically controlling for previous academic attainment (Oyserman et al., 2002). A second randomized clinical trial of the intervention involved an in-school test with a 2-year follow-up (Oyserman et al., in press). Here significant change was found in grades and attendance by school records, as well as reduction in grade retention (being held back a year). Again effects were mediated by change in youth PS. In terms of efficacy, a standard criteria is that a program's success should be replicated in at least two randomized trials to provide assurance that a program is probably efficacious. The STJ program meets this standard. At the next stage, the success of the STJ program needs to be replicated with a different research team to ascertain that the program is robustly efficacious.

STJ uses a small-group, active learning paradigm with a series of small-group activities, within which youth gain a sense of their own vision for the future and learn to develop strategies to help attain this vision; parents and community members join in developing youth's skills. The name of the program, School-to-Jobs, was chosen to emphasize the connection between current action and future goals. STJ utilizes a social cognitive approach, utilizing basic social psychological theory and research on the nature of information processing and motivation (Oyserman, Terry, & Bybee, 2002). This research suggests that structured activities occurring in everyday settings can have great impact on who we think we are and what is possible for us to achieve because subtle contextual shifts can powerfully change the sense made of daily experiences. The meaning made of everyday experience in turn fuels motivation.

Specifically, the goal of STJ is to develop a sequence of activities and tasks that provide youth with experiences of creating and detailing more explicit academic PS that feel congruent with REI and other social identities and then give them practice in the skills needed to engage in and put effort into school. Helping youth define explicit PS and link them to effort is expected to improve academic outcomes, and improved outcomes are expected to help sustain PS and effort over time, producing a positive cycle of change. Activities were designed to create well-explicated PS with clear, comprehensive, plausible strategies to achieve these PS.

Parents and community members are included in two final optional sessions. Adults are brought in to anchor youth in an adult worldview, to provide opportunities to practice skills needed to obtain support from adults, and to allow youth to practice obtaining support for their emerging PS from adults. Thus, adults are brought in as tools for youth rather than as teachers or authority figures. To ensure engagement of all youth, the STJ sessions are interactive; they begin with a simple and more general future focus and gradually move toward more specific and proximal links with the present, and they build in a focus on handling failures, which we term inoculation from failure. Below is a thumbnail sketch of the sessions, followed by an example of the "cheat sheet" summary trainers use to ensure that they are following the manual and an example of the observer checklist used to assess fidelity of delivery. The intervention, summary sheets, and fidelity assessment are collected in a manual that can be obtained from the author.

Thumbnail Sketch of Sessions

1. *Creating a group.* (Goal: Create a positive sense of membership and set the stage for school involvement and adult PS). Activity: Trainers and participants discuss their expectations and concerns about program content; participants develop program rules. Activities include introducing one another in terms of skills and abilities to succeed this school year, human knot, and other activities that build the idea that group members have positive attributes related to school achievement and that others also want to do well in school. (For further information about group work with students, see chapters 56–58.)

2. *Adult images.* (Goal: Create a concrete experience of imagining adulthood). Activity: Participants choose from pictures portraying adults in the domains of adulthood (work, family, lifestyle, community service, health, and hobbies) and then describe how these represent their future images. (Pictures fit the racial/ethnic background of participants; making and hearing about choices gets participants to think about the future.)

3. *Time lines.* (Goal: Concretize the connection between present and future, and normalize failures and setbacks as part of progress to the future.) Activity: Participants draw personal time lines from the present as far into the future as they can. Trainers define *forks in the road* (choices that have consequences) and *roadblocks* (obstacles placed by others and situations—for example, lack of financial resources, racial and/or sexual discrimination), and participants draw at least one of each in their time line. Discussion connects current activities and future visions, and youth give each other feedback focused on sequences and ways to go around obstacles.

4. *PS and strategies boards.* (Goal: Concretize the connection between current behavior, next year, and adult attainments.) Activity: Using poster board and colored stickers, participants map out next year and adult PS and the strategies they are using now or could use. Then they map out all the school-related PS and strategies used so that participants using particular strategies can explain what they are doing and guide others through obstacles.

5. *Solving everyday problems I.* (Goal: Provide participants with concrete experience breaking down everyday school problems into more manageable parts.) Activity: In prior sessions, solo activities were the springboard to group discussion. The next sessions use group activity as springboard because participants are confident enough with one another to work together in small groups, and group work reinforces positive REI. Participants solve logic problems together, developing a strategy of writing down the known to solve for the unknown. Using this success as a springboard, each group develops strategies for handling a set of school-focused problems (doing poorly in math class, tackling a big history assignment) by first listing the questions they must ask themselves or get information about prior to deciding on a course of action. The session ends with full group discussion of questions raised and decisions made.

6. *Solving everyday problems II.* (Goal: Reinforce participants' ability to make school-related plans for the future and to reach out to adults to accomplish this.) Activity: Using the same small-group format as in the previous session, participants develop a list of requirements for high school graduation and prerequisites/skills needed for entry into college and other training, then work as a large group to find out about the actual requirements for local educational institutions. This is connected back to the adult visions, time lines, and strategy board

sessions—helping youth see the process by which they can attain the PS they have imagined and deal with obstacles or forks in the road.

7. *Wrapping up, moving forward.* (Goal: Organize experiences so far and set the stage for bringing parents/guardians to the group.) Activity: Participants "walk through" the program by discussing what they did in each session, what they learned in each, and what they liked and disliked about the program. Parent or other important adult involvement is discussed with a focus on how these adults from the youth's own community can help youth on their pathways to adulthood. Youth explore the similarities and differences they see between their own experiences and those they imagine their parents had.

8. *Building an alliance and developing communication skills.* (Goal: Allow youth and parents to state their concerns for the student in the coming year, see limitations of current communication skills in handling these concerns, and practice another model in a structured setting.) Activity: Parents and youth introduce one another, and youth lead a review of previous sessions. Then parents and youth separate to discuss what concerns each has about the transition to high school. These concerns form the basis for discussion of how to communicate with one another on important topics. Trainers role-play parent and youth suggestions and then operationalize communication as active listening and "taking the floor." Parents pair off with their own child to try out being an active listener and taking the floor. Both parent and child have a chance to experience the listener and the floor role, allowing both to raise and to react to a point of concern. Then participants

Box 73.1 Detailed Outline—Session 1

- Greet/welcome participants. Check names against roster. Greet latecomers.
- Introduce one another (trainers). Also identify the trait each has that helps him or her to succeed in work or school.
- Introduce observer. Emphasize role to observe trainers to help improve program (and not to grade students).
- Ask what an introduction is. (It is a way of saying who you are and what you can contribute.) Write definition on newsprint.
- Identify goals for introductions (they differ depending on context).
- Ask about skills and abilities for succeeding in school (since this is school to jobs).
- Write tasks and examples on newsprint.
- Introduce partner skills. (Pass out marbles. Ask for questions before task begins. Circulate, check for understanding.)
- Ask youth to introduce partners. Ask them to repeat names.
- Explain concepts (expectations/concerns). Use newsprint to write group responses.
- Reinforce and repeat four basic themes that will be covered (1. setting clear goals for next year and afterward; 2. developing strategies to work on these goals; 3. thinking about a path to the future; 4. working

with teachers, parents and others in the community as resources).
- Elicit group rules. Write on newsprint.
- State aim of program. Use prepared newsprint.
- State goal. Use prepared newsprint.
- Explain group naming activity. Give examples, elicit ideas.
- Explain session schedule. Provide contact information. Write on board.
- Review. Ask participant to name all names.
- Explain task, line up from youngest to oldest without talking. (Encourage. When completed, ask month of birth.)
- Congratulate. Reinforce cooperation.
- Explain task, stand in circle, cross arms in front, grab hands of two people across the circle, without letting go, uncross hands and re-form the circle. (Trainers are part of the circle.) Congratulate. Reinforce cooperation.
- Work on adult images. Ask, "What will adulthood be like for you?"
- Provide snacks. Pass out session evaluation forms. Ask for help rearranging the room.
- Pick up evaluation forms. Make sure attendance form is filled out. Say goodbyes. Rate participant participation.

Box 73.2 Detailed Outline—Session 2

- Greet participants by name. Take attendance.
- Say, "Today is session 2: adult images."
- Ask for what happened last session. (Elicit activities. Elicit rationale.)
- Ask students to choose pictures that represent visions of themselves as adults.
  - Tell them to pick at least 10 pictures.
  - Ask them to ask themselves what the pictures mean to them.
  - Ask them when these pictures will be true of them.
  - Tell them that all will discuss these pictures afterward.
- Make sure instructions are clear. Have participants begin. Pass out snacks.
- Mingle—check for understanding.
- Have everyone rejoin circle.
- Show pictures, explain to group, while group listens and pays attention to common themes.

- Explain task: Each participant writes on newsprint something similar about everyone's adult visions.
  - Ask for questions
  - Mingle, help individually as needed
- Discuss themes that are there and areas that are missing (jobs, family, friends, community involvement, lifestyle).
- Review concept of adult domains: adult images about jobs, family, friends, community involvement, lifestyle).
- Explain concept: Adult images can be goals if they are worked on, and this will be discussed in coming sessions.
- Tell them that the next session will identify role models.
- Pass out session evaluation forms. Ask for help rearranging the room.
- Pick up evaluation forms. Make sure attendance form is filled out. Say goodbyes. Rate participant participation.

talk about the experience and commit to practice this skill. This section focuses on REI by highlighting connections between parents and youth, the importance of school, and difficulties encountered along the way.

9. *Jobs, careers, and informational interviewing.* (Goal: Identify gaps in knowledge about how schooling links to careers and provide youth with skills to obtain this information.) Activity: Parents describe how they got their current jobs (or strategies they have tried to get jobs in the past if not currently employed), and youth describe how to find out about jobs and careers. Trainers highlight parent and youth frustration about connecting qualifications and experiences to desired careers and jobs, thus introducing the concept of informational interviewing. Parents and youth practice informational interviewing and then use this skill to do informational interviews with community members who join the group at this point. Then participants discuss ways that they can use informational interviewing at a number of junctures in the future. Youth talk about barriers to contacting people in the community who have jobs that seem of interest to them. Community members discuss ways to make contacts, responding to specific concerns raised by youth and giving youth a chance to role-play these strategies. This session focuses on REI by highlighting role models from youth's racial-ethnic community.

Tools and Practice Examples

Hands-On Examples

An example of an intervention session checklist for use in rating fidelity of implementation can be found in Table 73.1.

Table 73.1 School-to-Jobs Observation Form

Youth Session 1

Date ___/___/___ School Code _____

Class Code _____

Site: _____ Group _____

Trainers: _____ Observer _____

Task	Y	N	Detailed Trainer Activity	Y	N	Group Behavior	1-5
Start on time	—	—	*START TIME* _____				
Opening							
• Welcome	—	—	• Greet and welcome participants				
• Introductions	—	—	• Check names against roster	—	—	• Talk with trainers	—
			• Greet latecomers	—	—	• Talk with each other	—
			• Trainers introduce each other (name, University of Michigan)	—	—	• Listen	—
			• Introduce observer	—	—	• Acknowledge observer	—
			• Emphasize role to observe trainers to help improve program	—	—		
Introduction							
• Introduce the concept of introductions as goal oriented	—	—	• Ask what an introduction is	—	—	• Share ideas	—
			• Reinforce: is a way of saying who you are and what you can contribute	—	—		
			• Write definition on newsprint	—	—		
• Introduce school-to-jobs as success oriented	—	—	• Different goals for introductions	—	—		
			• Ask about skills and abilities for succeeding in school	—	—	• Share ideas	—
			• Write tasks and examples on newsprint	—	—		

(continued)

Table 73.1 Continued

Task	Y	N	Detailed Trainer Activity	Y	N	Group Behavior	1-5
Introduction task							
• Group creation process—is atmosphere starting to feel like a group?	—	—	• Explain activity (partners learn of partner skills, introduce)	—	—	• Take marble	—
			• Pass out marbles	—	—	• Separate into pairs	—
			• Ask for questions before task begins	—	—	• Share skills and abilities	—
• Group feeling that group as a whole has skills and abilities that can be relied on.	—	—	• Circulate, check for understanding	—	—		
			• Ask youth to introduce partners	—	—	• Introduce partner	—
			• Ask for repetition of names	—	—	• Practice saying names	—
Expectations and concerns			• Introduce new task, explain concept	—	—		
			• Ask for expectations	—	—	• Participate	—
• Give youth a voice	—	—	• Use newsprint to write group expectations	—	—		
			• Ask for concerns	—	—		
			• Use newsprint to write group concerns	—	—		
• Crystallize and focus group goals	—	—	• Reinforce and repeat four basic themes that will be covered.	—	—	• Listen	—
			• setting clear goals for next year and afterward	—	—		
			• developing strategies to work on these goals	—	—		
			• thinking about a path to the future	—	—		
			• working with teachers, parents, and others in the community as resources	—	—		

• Create group ownership (sense of being heard and a member of something)	• Elicit group rules • Write on newsprint	• Participate
Aim	• State aim (help create road map, need to think about goals, work on strategies, develop alternatives) • Use prepared newsprint	• Listen
Program aim is clarified	• State goal (a clear, more detailed sense of what you need to do and how to do it)	
Naming group	• Explain activity • Give examples, elicit ideas	• Participate • Vote
Schedule	• Explain session schedule • Provide contact information • Write on board	• Listen

Line up task
• Group creation process (is group interaction increasing? sense of collectiveness?)
	• Review: Ask participant to name all names
	• Explain task, line up from youngest to oldest without talking
	  • Encourage
	  • When completed, ask to give month of birth
	  • Congratulate
	• Reinforce cooperation
		• Participate
		• Move around, line up

(continued)

Table 73.1 (*Continued*)

Task	Y	N	Detailed Trainer Activity	Y	N	Group Behavior	1-5
Human knot task • Group creation process (is this feeling like a "group"?)		—	• Explain task, stand in circle, cross arms in front, and grab hands of two people across the circle; then, without letting go of hands, get them uncrossed so that we are again in a circle	—	—	• Participate	—
			• Trainers are part of the circle	—	—		
			• Congratulate		—		
			• Reinforce cooperation	—	—	• Move, re-form circle	—
Next session and good-byes		—	• Next session will work on adult images: What will adulthood be like for you?	—	—	• Listen	—
			• Provide snacks	—	—	• Eat	—
			• Pass out session evaluation forms	—	—	• Complete evaluation forms	—
			• Ask for help rearranging the room	—	—		
			• Say goodbyes	—	—	• Rearrange room	
			• Rate participant participation levels	—	—		—
			• END TIME _____				

References

Oyserman, D. (2001). Self and identity. In A. Tessor & N. Schwarz (Eds.), *Blackwell handbook of social psychology* (pp. 499–517). Malden, MA: Blackwell.

Oyserman, D., Bybee, D, & Terry, K. (2003). Gendered racial identity and involvement with school. *Self and Identity, 2,* 1–18.

Oyserman, D., Bybee, D., & Terry, K. (in press). Possible selves and academic outcomes: How and when possible selves impel action. *Journal of Personality and Social Psychology.*

Oyserman, D., Bybee, D., Terry, K., & Hart-Johnson, T. (2004). Possible selves as roadmaps. *Journal of Research on Personality, 38,* 130–149.

Oyserman, D., & Fryberg, S. (in press). The possible selves of diverse adolescents: Content and function across gender, race and national origin. In C. Dunkel & J. Kerpelmen (Eds.), *Possible selves: Theory, research, and application.* Huntington, NY: Nova.

Oyserman, D., Gant, L., & Ager, J. (1995). A socially contextualized model of African American identity: School persistence and possible selves. *Journal of Personality and Social Psychology, 69,* 1216–1232.

Oyserman, D., & Harrison, K. (1998). Implications of ethnic identity: African American identity and possible selves. In J. K. Swim & C. Stangor (Eds.), *Prejudice: The target's perspective* (pp. 281–300). San Diego, CA: Academic Press.

Oyserman, D., Harrison, K., & Bybee, D. (2001). Can racial identity be promotive of academic efficacy in adolescence? *International Journal of Behavioral Development, 25,* 379–385.

Oyserman, D., Kemmelmeier, M., Fryberg, S., Brosh, H., & Hart-Johnson, T. (2003). Racial-ethnic self-schemas. *Social Psychology Quarterly, 66,* 333–347.

Oyserman, D., & Markus, H. (1990a). Possible selves and delinquency. *Journal of Personality and Social Psychology, 59,* 112–125.

Oyserman, D., & Markus, H. (1990b). Possible selves in balance: Implications for delinquency. *Journal of Social Issues, 46,* 141–157.

Oyserman, D., & Saltz, E. (1993). Competence, delinquency, and attempts to attain possible selves. *Journal of Personality and Social Psychology, 65,* 360–374.

Oyserman, D., Terry, K., & Bybee, D., (2002). A possible selves intervention to enhance school involvement. *Journal of Adolescence, 24,* 313–326.

Mental Health Interventions With Latino Students in Multicultural School Environments: A Framework for Assessing Biases and Developing Cultural Competence

Katina M. Lambros ■ Concepcion Barrio

CHAPTER 74

Getting Started

Why Schools Need to Assess Biases and Level of Cultural Knowledge When Working With Latino Students and Their Families

Schools are becoming increasingly culturally and ethnically diverse environments. Research shows that ethnic minority student populations are growing in the United States, and this trend is especially true for the Latino population, which increased by more than 50% from 1990 to 2000 and constitutes the largest ethnic minority group in the country (U.S. Bureau of the Census, 2001, 2002).

The effects of culture on the academic experience and mental health functioning of Latino students are of paramount concern to families, educators, and communities alike. The *Digest of Education Statistics* (U.S. Department of Education [USDE], National Center for Education Statistics, 1993) shows that only 27% of Latino children 3 to 4 years old attended preschool in 1992, suggesting that for many families, early cognitive learning and cultural indoctrination occur at home. This at-home preschool education may result in their coming to the European American K-8 educational system with a culture-specific set of learning styles, goals, and expectations, which may make negotiating school systems difficult (Center for Mental Health in Schools at UCLA, 2001). Additionally, Latinos are at the highest risk for school failure, experience considerable academic underachievement, and are at significant risk for poor mental health outcomes (U.S. Department of Health and Human Services [DHHS], 2001). Furthermore, their participation in all levels of education continues to be low; they experience numerous grade retentions and have the highest high school dropout rate in the nation. Regarding mental health functioning, Latino youth are also more likely to report depression and anxiety and to consider suicide than non-Hispanic whites (DHHS, 2001). These statistics indeed argue for improved and more culturally relevant school-based mental health intervention for this population of children. (For additional information about working with specific populations, see Chapters 76–78 and 80.)

Unfortunately, the majority of all school-age students needing mental health services go unserved (Burns et al., 1995). Mental health intervention may be less likely for Latino youth than others in part because Latinos are underrepresented in service sectors such as schools and mental health (McCabe et al., in press). Moreover, Latinos have less overall access to mental health care, are less likely to receive needed care, and receive a poorer quality of care (Kataoka, Zhang, & Wells, 2002; Yeh, McCabe, Hough, Dupuis, & Hazen, 2003). For youth who do receive mental health services, it is important to note that *schools* are considered the primary mental health service provider and that between 70 and 80% of children who received services were seen by practitioners within a school setting (Burns et al., 1995). Special education data also reflect that the mental health needs of Latino students are not being met, as they are underrepresented in the emotionally disturbed category, which serves youth having significant emotional, behavioral, and mental health problems (McCabe et al., in press; USDE, 2002). See Section 1 for more information about working with students with mental diagnosis.

Reasons for school problems for Latino students have been attributed to inappropriate cognitive, cultural, and linguistic assessment and teaching/intervention methods (Treuba & Bartolome, 1997). Moreover, a lack of culturally appropriate and empirically supported mental health prevention and early intervention services in schools and classrooms for this population may also contribute to disparities in referral and service use. Yet, school staff working directly with youth do not readily assume that their own teaching methods or tools may contribute to students' problems. Staff may be likely to attribute difficulties to within-child problems, and thus believe that change is required in children and families, not in the practices of schools and teachers (American Association of School Administrators, 1987; Carter & Chatfield, 1986; Knapp & Shields, 1990; Means & Knapp, 1991). Teaching techniques are often assumed to be value-free and culturally neutral, and this assumption has prevented school providers from analyzing whether their teaching and intervention methods are equally effective with all student populations (Treuba & Bartolome, 1997). This practice is in contrast to several recent health policy reports (DHHS, 2000, 2001), which have called for bringing empirically supported treatments into "real world settings," such as schools, and also stressing the need to develop, test, and modify mental health interventions with ethnic minority populations.

According to Banks (1988), in order to achieve this, the ethnic identity of every Latino student must be appreciated and respected by the teacher, other school staff, and the student's peer group. This cultural awareness and recognition provides a cornerstone for the learning activities taking place in the classroom and on the school campus. In addition, Latino youth must be encouraged to recognize and appreciate their own ethnic heritage and learn to appreciate the ethnic heritages of the other children. This recognition of individual ethnic identities links the teachers and students together, constituting a learning process that requires a transactional fit among child, teacher, classroom, and the academic content to be learned (Center for Mental Health in Schools at UCLA, 2001).

The purpose of this chapter is to provide a framework that promotes the development of cultural competence for practitioners working with Latino students and their families within multicultural school settings (by "practitioners," we mean any personnel, whether in the school system or in the surrounding community, who work with a school-age child). We have examined literature from the mental health and psychotherapy

fields and the educational and school consultation fields, and have identified aspects of several models that can be adapted and applied to school social work practice settings with Latino students. First we address the definition of the concept of cultural competence, followed by an overview of several approaches and implications for practice.

What We Know

Cultural Competence Models and Approaches

There are numerous definitions of cultural competence in the health and mental health literature. The concept was first developed by the federally funded Child and Adolescent Service System Program in the 1980s. The definition of cultural competence developed by Cross and colleagues (1989) is comprehensive and has been frequently used in mental health services. "Cultural competence" refers to a set of congruent practice skills, knowledge, behaviors, attitudes, and policies that come together in a system, agency, or among consumer providers and professionals that enables the system, agency, or those professionals and consumer providers to work effectively in crosscultural situations. At the provider level, cultural competence requires an examination of one's own attitudes and values, and the acquisition of the values, knowledge, skills, and attributes that will allow an individual to work appropriately in crosscultural situations (Maternal and Child Health Bureau, 1999).

Notably, the mental health literature is replete with many approaches to cultural competence. Several models attend to the needs of specific ethnic groups, while others are applicable to diverse groups (Center for Mental Health Services [CMHS], 2000; Cross, Bazron, Dennis, & Isaacs, 1989; Sue, 1998). There are also models that address the cultural competence components related to training and staff development (Lum, 1999; Sue, Arrendondo, & McDavis, 1992). Most approaches to cultural competence emphasize the common themes of cultural awareness, knowledge, and skill that apply to the cultural competence of the organization, delivery of direct services, and training and staff development.

A model by Steven Lopez (1997) called Shifting Cultural Lenses has been received favorably by practitioners in diverse practice settings (S. R. Lopez, 2002; S. R. Lopez, Kopelowicz, & Cañive, 2002). The model was based on three decades of psychotherapy research using both qualitative and quantitative methods. It also draws heavily from anthropological perspectives, specifically the explanatory models by Kleinman (1988, 1995). Cultural competence is viewed as an ongoing process in which the provider considers cultural factors while collecting evidence to test a given cultural hypothesis that a particular diagnosis or intervention is culturally relevant or not relevant for the client or family being served (S. R. Lopez, 1997). The model depicts two simultaneous strategies to service delivery and outreach in ethnically and culturally diverse communities. The culturally specific approach considers culture from an emic (specific or insider) perspective, which incorporates an attitude of openness in the discovery, acquisition, and interpretation of knowledge. In this approach, providers occupy the role of learner/facilitator in the process of promotion of cultural relevance and development of culturally congruent services. At the same time, the provider considers clinical evidence from an etic (general) perspective where the attitude is one of distance from the cultural group and the objective is the accumulation of universal knowledge. Through this approach, providers occupy the role of teacher/expert and evaluate culture from the vantage point of mainstream values. Culturally competent approaches balance the shift in cultural lenses in eliciting and understanding the client's cultural perspective within the provider's own framework in any given treatment domain (engagement, assessment, intervention, outreach, and collaborative work).

More specifically, the Lopez (S. R. Lopez, 1997) model of cultural competence can be applied with a variety of mental health interventions in schools and requires school staff to accurately assess their own biases and cultural knowledge and the effects they have on the type and quality of services provided to Latino students. This model requires a *shifting* of cultural lenses to consider the interface between multiple cultural perspectives in successfully understanding and addressing Latino students with school problems: (a) the student and family culture-specific framework, (b) the school provider's culture-specific and culture-general framework, (c) the school culture and climate, and (d) the culture of the surrounding community.

The operating principles of the above model

can be applied in multiple settings. In order to enhance the model by Steven Lopez and align it for those who provide services in the schools, we have also included standards from a multicultural school consultation (MSC) model, which is a framework applied to various consultation models that infuse cultural considerations into the theory, research, practice, and training of consultation (Tarver Behring & Ingraham, 1998). In this model, the constructs of multicultural and cross-cultural consultation are central, and the primary school provider or "consultant" addresses the needs and cultural values of the "consultee(s)" and/or "clients." Within this consultation triad, one or more persons may differ culturally from the other members. This aspect of multicultural consultation is referred to as cross-cultural consultation (Ingraham, 2000; Tarver Behring & Ingraham, 1998) and has been developed for use within diverse school settings. This MSC model posits consultation through a multicultural lens and incorporates a broad consideration of diversity; it attends to all parties in the consultation process, considers the cultural context of consultation services, explores various issues related to school-based consultation across and within cultures, identifies competencies to develop in consultants and consultees, and increases attention to areas in need of further research (Ingraham, 2000). Many of the central features of the MSC model are well aligned with the Steven Lopez (1997) model of cultural competence, and as the provision of school-based mental health services requires the convergence of many service sectors/disciplines such as education, mental health, social work, counseling, and psychology, this model serves to link principles from these paradigms. The framework proposed bridges two conceptual models of cultural competence, which require additional empirical research; however, these authors wanted to present conceptual applications of it within diverse schools and more specifically with Latino students.

Research Support for Practice Method

Research on the efficacy of mental health interventions with racially or ethnically diverse populations is limited. Although many randomized clinical trials evaluating mental health interventions have been conducted, little or no information on race or ethnicity of the participants is available, and no study has analyzed the efficacy of the treatment by ethnicity or race (DHHS, 2001).

Despite advocacy to deliver mental health services that are responsive to the cultural concerns (i.e., languages, experiences, traditions, beliefs, values) of racial/ethnic groups, even fewer studies have examined the effects of culturally informed or culturally modified interventions with particular ethnic groups (DHHS, 2001). Although new models of service delivery that promote cultural competence have been proposed, currently those models consist primarily of a set of guiding principles that lack empirical validation and are typically applied across all ethnic groups. No data specify the key aspects of cultural competence and what influence, if any, they have on clinical outcomes for racial/ethnic minorities (e.g., Falicov, 1998; Koss-Chioino & Vargas, 1999; S. R. Lopez, 1997; Ramirez, 1991; Ridley, Mendoza, Kanitz, Angermeier, & Zenk, 1994; Sue & Sue, 1999; Sue & Zane, 1987; Szapocznik et al., 1997). However, within the mental health literature, data from consumer and family self-reports, ethnic matching, and ethnic-specific services, outcome studies suggest that tailoring services to the specific cultural needs of these groups will improve utilization and outcomes (DHHS, 2001).

Within the educational and school consultation literature, several intervention models for providing psychological and mental health services in schools have been studied (Conduct Problems Prevention Group, 1999; Conoley & Conoley, 1992; Hawkins, Catalano, Kosterman, Abbott, & Hill, 1999; Reid, Eddy, Fetrow, & Stoolmiller, 1999; Walker, Kavanagh, Stiller, Golly, Severson, & Feil, 1998). However, little has been published on the application of these interventions within diverse school settings or on the cultural modifications of these interventions for particular racial/ethnic groups. In addition, there are many school consultation models (Bergen & Kratochwill, 1990; Conoley & Conoley, 1992; Sheridan, Kratochwill, & Bergen, 1996) for implementing such interventions; however, attention to cultural issues in these models is limited (Ingraham, 2000). The MSC model can be applied to situations in which cultural issues are raised and specific tailoring of the traditional consultation process is done to fit the needs and cultural values of the consultant, consultee, and client (Tarver Behring & Ingraham, 1998). This model appears promising in terms of its cultural relevance; however, additional empirical research on its application in diverse school settings is needed.

What We Can Do

Practice Guidelines and Task Examples for Assessing Biases and Level of Cultural Knowledge

The following section begins with culturally relevant issues that must be considered and explored when working with Latino students and their families. It is important to note that these issues must not be generalized to all Latino students and families, as the great diversity among Latino groups in the United States should be acknowledged. This diversity is reflected in variations in family patterns and traditions. Differences based on country of origin, social class and economic status, immigration history, and level of acculturation are among the salient factors that should be recognized for their potential influence on parenting, communication style, and other family practices (Barrio & Hughes, 2000). The general issues listed here are highlighted for their relevance to providing school services to Latino students and families. The remainder of the section presents three case vignettes describing school-based activities in which cultural biases and knowledge were not competently assessed, and examples of how these cases could have been approached from a culturally competent perspective. Following these are more thorough discussions of each vignette within a framework of providing culturally competent (a) referral, (b) assessment, and (c) intervention for Latino students and families. Also included in this section are hands-on tips to guide school practitioners in addressing the educational and mental health needs of Latinos in a culturally relevant and competent manner.

Some cultural issues to consider in working with Latino students and families:

- Ethnic minority cultures, particularly Latino cultures, are known to be more family-centered than are Euro-American cultures (Barrio, 2000; Lin & Kleinman, 1988). The familial self or *familismo* is considered the common thread shared by Latino groups (Falicov, 1999).
- A family's cultural practices, characteristics, and coping style should be considered as cultural resources that can enhance the student's ability to meet the academic standards of the classroom. Studies have shown that acculturation to American values and behaviors can have a

negative effect on the mental health of Mexican immigrants and their families, and that the retention of Mexican traditional culture can have positive effects on mental health outcomes (Vega et al., 1998).

- For many Latino children, it may be culturally expected to respond to parents and school staff in a compliant, cooperative, nonassertive, and respectful manner. Indirect communication and an interdependent or collectivistic orientation may be reflective of the family communication pattern. Latino family practices need to be viewed within the given cultural context, without imposing labels (i.e., enmeshed, dysfunctional) that may pathologize familial relationships and interpersonal style.

- Latino families may show mistrust of Western medical models of mental health diagnoses and treatment and may access services from alternative sources (e.g., priests, spiritual healers, herbalists) (Woodward, Dwinell, & Arons, 1992).

- Latino students may be developing language skills in both English and Spanish, which may affect both academic and social performance. Therefore, the child's bilingual development and bicultural identity needs to be considered in the referral, assessment, and intervention process.

- It is critical to carefully assess the criteria underlying mental health constructs (e.g., impulsivity, anxiety, depression) with an awareness of normative behavior within the child's cultural setting (Pitts & Wallace, 2003).

Tools and Practice Examples

Case Vignette #1—Referral

A teacher has referred a fourth-grade Latino student, Frank, to the school social worker because he seems withdrawn, anxious, and depressed. According to the teacher, Frank doesn't participate in class discussions, makes poor eye contact with others, doesn't respond when called upon, and has few social interactions. Academically, Frank is at grade level in all subject areas. Socially, he seems quiet and well-behaved. He has one close friend, but he does not readily join established social groups or initiate conversations with unfamiliar peers. The social worker talked with Frank and his

parents about the teacher's concerns. His parents shared that it is important that Frank is respectful and compliant with school staff and that he behave appropriately at home, in school, and in the community, particularly at church services. Upon interviewing Frank's teacher, the school social worker discovered that this teacher encouraged her students to assert themselves and their ideas verbally in class, required them to question and challenge academic concepts and ideas, and favored highly competitive assignments, such as class debates on course topics. She also coordinated the school plays and had a dramatic and expressive teaching style. She felt Frank was anxious during public-speaking activities, could not advocate for himself, and appeared overly sad and indifferent. As such, her evaluation of Frank in the areas of effort, citizenship, and social interaction reflected low grades. Therefore, she determined that Frank was either anxious or depressed and in need of mental health treatment.

Ideas for a more culturally competent approach: Had the classroom teacher assessed her own personal values for optimal classroom behavior (advocacy, assertion, expression) and those of Frank and his family, she would have realized that they were not congruent with the values of the child's family. Knowledge about the family's cultural orientation would have allowed her to "shift" her cultural lenses and consider the child's behavior within the context of his family culture. Frank was functioning quite well, but what the teacher perceived as signs of anxiety or depression was a behavioral style that was culturally different than her own. With this insight, the teacher could have structured social and academic activities that respected his cultural orientation while also meeting her expectations for academic performance. For example, rather then expect Frank to compete for a main character in a classroom skit, explain to him the various roles that the skit involves—including writing the storyline, building the stage, or filming—and validate his selection of any one of these tasks.

Case Vignette #2—Assessment

Mexican immigrant parents been asked by the school to attend a series of student study team (SST) meetings for their second-grade daughter, Karina. The SST is a multidisciplinary team of school personnel who work with the teacher to design interventions for students preceding formal evaluation for special education. The SST is often the first pathway to receiving school services. For several months, Karina has had significant academic problems in all core areas, and exhibits high levels of off-task and inattentive behavior. Her native language is Spanish, and she is designated as an English language learner. Based on observations and screenings, her expressive and receptive language abilities are delayed in both English and Spanish. Socially, she interacts well in group activities and on the playground. Despite several academic and language interventions, Karina is not meeting grade-level standards, and her parents continue to express concerns that she "is sad and feels badly about herself." Members of the SST recommend a psychoeducational evaluation for a learning disability and explain special education services to Karina's parents. Immediately, her parents express concerns about "special education." Based on their prior experiences, they feel that these classes are for kids who are "retarded" or "crazy," and they think that attending them would bring shame on Karina and the family. They do not want her separated from her teacher, and they do not consent to the assessment process.

Ideas for a more culturally competent approach: Asking Karina's parents their thoughts about special education would have provided the SST valuable information about realistic intervention options. Connecting them with a Spanish-speaking parent facilitator who has experience with special education services may have helped the family learn about the benefits of this plan for Karina in an incremental manner. Inviting the family to visit a special education classroom during reading may have provided them a better sense about the children enrolled in these classes and the kinds of activities that take place. Introducing them to a bilingual special education teacher and establishing rapport may have helped them to gradually accept these needed services for their daughter.

Case Vignette #3—Intervention

A sixth-grade Latino student, Juan, was diagnosed with attention-deficit/hyperactivity disorder (ADHD) by a school psychologist. Juan has numerous problems in reading and math, and he has behavioral difficulties such as not paying attention, not remaining seated, and not joining peer groups in his school. In determining the course of intervention, school staff discussed with the family the efficacy of medication and recommended this for Juan's condition. The parents expressed alarm and resisted the medication intervention. Despite numerous efforts on the part of school staff to discuss a treatment plan with the family, they showed a lack of trust in school professionals, a refusal of any treatment plan involving medication, and an overall lack of engagement with the school. Further exploration by a school social worker during a home visit uncovered that the parents felt pressured by school staff to medicate the child; they regarded medication as an extreme measure and were afraid that their child could become dependent, addicted, and possibly suffer brain damage as a result of taking medication.

Ideas for a more culturally competent approach: School providers should have approached Juan's family differently by asking first about their perceptions and understanding of Juan's school and behavioral problems. This would have revealed the family's explanatory model, providing culturally specific information for shaping a culturally acceptable treatment plan that would fit with the family's values and beliefs. This would also serve to engage and build a therapeutic alliance with the family and increase their receptivity to psychoeducational information regarding ADHD. An approach founded in mutual respect and agreement between the school staff and the child's family is essential in fostering adherence to any behavioral or medication treatment plan.

Culturally Competent Referrals

There may be several referral avenues that schools use to bring students having problems to the attention of professionals, including student study teams, individual education plans, transdisciplinary teams, school nurses, and health service centers. These referrals may come from various sources including teachers, parents, other school staff, and outside professionals (e.g., pediatricians, social workers). Whatever referral mechanism is most frequent in schools, it is crucial to conduct assessment of the sociocultural framework of (a) the student and family being referred, (b) the referral source, and (c) the primary service provider and/or team that the student is referred to. For example, Vignette #1 describes a child who is not currently meeting the sociobehavioral expectations of his classroom. Upon further assessment, it is discovered that there is a cultural mismatch between the student and his teacher. The teacher-preferred behaviors (expressive, self-assertive, analytical) were in sharp contrast to those values and behaviors that the family held important for their son (respectful, mild-mannered). This generated a referral to a mental health provider, which was culturally biased. Had the classroom teacher shifted her cultural lenses to simultaneously consider (and assess) the cultural framework and values of Frank and his family and her own biases and values regarding the expected social norms within her classroom, perhaps a mental health referral would not have been necessary. Instead, she could have learned about Frank's cultural orientation and incorporated it into classroom activities that would promote rather than hinder the child's academic performance, self-esteem, and ethnic identity. It is also important to note that a child who is subjected to a culturally invalidating teaching environment can potentially develop symptoms of anxiety and depression that will indeed require mental health treatment. Such a situation may not be caused by inherent mental health problems but may instead represent an acculturative stress response in trying to cope with daily exposure to an insensitive teaching style. In summary, assessing the biases and cultural knowledge of all involved in the referral process is crucial.

Tips:

- When a student is referred for screening, evaluation, or service, carefully review the referral reason (academic and/or behavioral) and consider it within the cultural norms and expectations of the student, family, teacher, classroom environment, school, and any other relevant setting. Take into account cultural misinformation, racism, and cultural differences that may affect Latino learners.
- When examining the validity of a referral, remember that Latino families may differ in terms of their family composition, childrearing practices, response to disobedience, perceptions of disability/health, communication and interpersonal styles, and help-seeking behaviors. These cultural considerations should be examined in the context of how they influence students' functioning within classroom situations, schools, families, and communities (Lynch, 1992).
- As a school provider, refine the ability to recognize the limits of your own multicultural competence. Ask yourself what you know about the customs, values, and historical experiences of a particular child in your class or school with whom you are planning on working.
- Seek educational, consultative, and training experiences to improve multicultural knowledge. Identify individuals in your school who come from an ethnic or cultural heritage different than your own, who are bilingual, who have (bilingual) crosscultural, language, and academic development (CLAD/BCLAD) certifications and become familiar with departments specializing in dual-language services, English language learners, and other services or populations.

▌ Culturally Competent Assessment

Competent assessment practices should undoubtedly be the basis for which intervention decisions are made. For schools, assessment of problems may include a psychoeducational or mental health screening/evaluation in the areas of cognition, academic achievement, learning modalities, and sociobehavioral functioning using tools that are both norm-referenced and idiographic in nature (e.g., direct observations, achievement tests, functional assessments, curriculum-based measurements, semistructured interviews). Often, information is collected from the student, as well as other individuals familiar with the child (teacher, other school staff, parents, other relatives, etc.). Assessments also often involve several school staff who interact and assess the child (e.g., school social worker, psychologist, classroom teacher, speech pathologist, counselor). School staff *must* consider all assessment information within the sociocultural context of the student and his or her family. Remember that a student's cultural framework may not align with the school service provider's own cultural framework. Also consider that the student family's cultural orientation may not be in sync with the school's cultural context or those standards suggested by a particular discipline (social work, psychology, mental health). As an example, in Vignette #2 the school staff assumed that Karina's family held the same beliefs and views about special education as the SST did. Failure to assess their perspective resulted in hesitation, fear, and doubt as to whether the school could help Karina. Perhaps asking Karina's parents what they thought she needed to help with her schoolwork would have been a better place to start. Also, inviting them to visit a resource classroom prior to discussing special education may have given them a clearer picture about the children served and the types of learning activities offered in such classrooms. Having them meet a special education teacher with bilingual certification may have also eased their fears about having Karina change teachers. By shifting their cultural lenses, the school providers would have become aware of the family's perspective regarding the nature and description of the problem, their beliefs about the cause of the problem, and their expectations for treatment. It is important to seek and explore the immediate family's perspective on the problem, as not doing so may result in inappropriate treatments. Accurate assessment and an effective intervention depend on rapport and the school providers' understanding of students' cultural identity, social supports, self-esteem, and reticence about treatment because of societal stigma (S. R. Lopez, 1997). This information will guide school providers in determining a particular intervention to use with a student.

Tips:

- Mainstream, standardized, norm-referenced tests may not be valid measures for Latino students who are English language learners (ELLs), due to inappropriateness of norms, scores reflecting English proficiency, fairness of content, and differences in educational background, acculturation, and economic situation. Use a variety of assessment techniques to examine Latino students' functioning across a number of settings (e.g., school, home, community).
- Interpret assessment results by examining a Latino student's behavioral or mental health functioning in terms of (a) his or her familiarity with the majority culture's behavioral expectations and/or (b) the acculturation conflicts that may interfere with the student's ability to perform adequately within various social situations (CMHS, 2000).
- In most assessment situations, Latino students' performances are compared to a normative sample that is racially, ethnically, and culturally different. Throughout the assessment process, school providers can minimize bias by comparing the performance of an individual Latino student to other children of the same age, socioeconomic level, and linguistic and cultural background. Consider the application of more relevant norms for a better fit between the student's sociocultural background and the normative sample's sociocultural background (S. R. Lopez, 1997).

- Assessment of the Latino student's instructional and classroom environment is critical, and school providers must ask: Are the class materials appropriate for the language, academic, and sociocultural skills of the student? Can Latino students understand and relate to the content of the materials from their cultural perspective? Does the curriculum address the unique cultural and linguistic needs of the Latino student? Are teaching strategies sensitive to students' cultural differences in communication, attitudes, and values? Are cultural differences recognized and valued in the classroom? Are the rewards and incentives valued within the culture of the Latino student?
- As the primary service provider or school social worker involved in the assessment process, you should determine your own cultural biases and cultural knowledge regarding the environment, social issues, language development, second language acquisition, acculturation, educational history, quality of educational program, socioeconomic status, and experience of racism of Latino students.
- Strive to improve your diagnostic skills with Latino students by incorporating their cultural, social, and environmental reality into the assessment of behavioral and clinical symptoms.
- Assess the cultural framework of all others involved in the assessment/intervention process.
- If interpreters are necessary, choose personnel who have prior experience in schools, high proficiency in both languages, knowledge of regional dialects, and familiarity with the education and special education program in which the student is enrolled (E. C. Lopez, 1995).

Culturally Competent Intervention

Quite often, well-researched and validated treatments are not effective due to a mismatch between the treatment and the child's family's cultural values. In Vignette #3 a discussion with the parents regarding their explanatory model (Kleinman, Eisenberg, & Good 1977) about ADHD should have been conducted and would have guided the school staff on how to approach a discussion of interventions. The discussion should include open-ended questions about what they think their child's problem is, what they think causes it, if and how it has progressed in their child, what its consequences might be, and what their views are on how best to treat it. Each family's explanatory model of their child's behavioral problems is shaped by the *cultural background* of the family and their *experience* with the behavioral problems. Different beliefs about the causes of a particular disorder and the acceptability of treatment by clients of varied cultural backgrounds have been shown to alter diagnostic and treatment patterns for disorders (Sussman, Robins, & Earls, 1987; Westermeyer, 1987). Cultural factors may affect the acceptance of and adherence to treatment plans proposed by providers (Hu, Snowden, Jerrell, & Nguyen, 1991; S. Lopez, 1989).

In Vignette #3, knowledge about racial/ethnic disparities in medication use would have been helpful. More specifically, studies have documented that African American and Latino children receive less stimulant medication for ADHD, and their parents or caregivers report less use of medication for treating ADHD, than do European American children (Rowland et al., 2002; Safer & Malever, 2000). Perhaps a review of all the effective treatments for the condition, both medication *and* behavior modification, would have been more helpful in discussing this delicate issue with this particular family. The next step would have been to ask the family which treatments they preferred and felt would work best for their child. Intervention activities need to be framed within a school–home collaboration partnership. Empirical data are available demonstrating that Latino students achieve in programs emphasizing parent involvement in curriculum planning, school organization, classroom participation, and home activities that promote literacy in the native language (Cummins, 1989). By taking this more culturally informed approach, school providers can recognize the unique ethnocultural qualities and expectations of Latino families. The school provider can then balance culturally specific values of families with those of the intervention. This approach tests cultural and alternative hypotheses in formulating a culturally competent plan (S. R. Lopez, 1994, 1997).

For some Latino students, more direct, intensive services within the schools, such as group or individual counseling, should be considered to address mental health needs. For example, a Latino student may struggle with acculturative stress, ethnic identity confusion, and cultural reactions that can harm his or her functioning (E. C. Lopez, 1995). Latino students may also experience high levels of stress associated with learning a second language or with experiences of discrimination and racism within schools and communities. According to Lopez (1995) among the culturally sensitive techniques recommended in the literature are (a) *ethnotherapy*, whereby emphasis is placed on helping individuals develop a positive sense of ethnic identity, (b) *cuento* therapy, in which folk stories assist youth in exploring cultural identity and ego development, and (c) the use of toys and materials that reflect the students' cultural and linguistic backgrounds. Also recommended are group counseling approaches, although their utility must be evaluated for Latino children whose cultural backgrounds may not necessarily promote self-disclosure with people outside the family. Last, all implemented social skills training and counseling activities should be delivered in the students' primary or most proficient language to aid communication (CMHS, 2000; E. C. Lopez, 1995).

Tips:

- Carefully consider the cultural applicability of intervention models, but do not radically modify them on the basis of limited information about the cultural congruence between their methods and the student or family belief system. Consider lower levels of modification first (S. R. Lopez, 1997).
- Incorporate Latino experiences and cultural strengths into school interventions. Incorporating activities, interaction styles, and instructional sequences that match the students' cognitive, emotional, and behavioral styles is recommended (Tharp, 1989).
- Establish school rules that reflect both the value of diversity and respect for different cultures and the importance of a climate conducive to learning.
- When using interpreters to work with Latino families to develop, refine, and evaluate interventions, provide them with time to ask parents about intervention procedures, provide feedback on implemented interventions, and explore cultural factors that may have influenced the child's or parent's behaviors (E. C. Lopez, 1995).

Key Points to Remember

- The provision of culturally competent school-based mental health services may play a role in reducing the social, cultural, and language barriers that often impede access to services and help-seeking efforts by Latino populations.

- The framework discussed here links existing models of cultural competence from the mental health field and school psychology and consultation literature.

- This framework is well aligned with public health agendas calling for cultural competence in the treatment of mental health problems in minority groups and the linkage of research models to the provision of services in schools (DHHS, 2000, 2001).

- This framework can also be applied to key activities (i.e., referral, assessment, and intervention) in working with diverse Latino children dealing with mental health issues.

- It is crucial that school practitioners and educators capitalize on the cultural strengths of the growing population of Latino students, in large part because the economic and technological future of this country depends on their educational success (Treuba & Bartolome, 1997).

- Best practices in assessing biases and cultural knowledge will guide school practitioners in addressing the educational and mental health needs of Latinos in a culturally relevant and competent manner.

References

American Association of School Administrators. (1987). *Raising achievement among minority students.* Arlington, VA: Author. (ED 282 357)

Banks, J. A. (1988). *Multiethnic education: Theory and practice.* Boston: Allyn & Bacon.

Barrio C. (2000). The cultural relevance of community support programs. *Psychiatric Services, 51*(7), 879–884.

Barrio C., & Hughes, M. (2000). Kinship care: A cultural resource of African-American and Latino families coping with parental substance abuse. *Journal of Family Social Work, 4*(4) 15–31.

Bergen, J., & Kratochwill, T. (1990). *Behavioral consultation and therapy.* New York: Plenum.

Burns, B. J., Costello, E. J., Angold, A., Tweed, D., Stangl, D., Farmer, E. M. Z., et al. (1995). Children's mental health service use across service sectors. *Health Affairs, 14*(4), 147–159.

Carter, T. P., & Chatfield, M. L. (1986). Effective bilingual schools: Implications for policy and practice. *American Journal of Education, 95*(1), 200–232. (EJ 348–511)

Center for Mental Health in Schools at UCLA. (2001). *An introductory packet on cultural concerns in addressing barriers to learning.* Los Angeles, CA: Author.

Center for Mental Health Services. (2000). *Cultural competence standards in managed care mental health services for four underserved/underrepresented racial/ethnic groups.* Rockville, MD: Substance Abuse and Mental Health Service Administration.

Conduct Problems Prevention Research Group. (1999). Initial impact of the Fast Track prevention trial for conduct problems: II. Classroom effects. *Journal of Consulting and Clinical Psychology, 67,* 631–647.

Conoley, J., & Conoley, C. (1992). *School consultation: Practice and training* (2nd ed.). Boston: Allyn & Bacon.

Cross, T., Bazron, B., Dennis, K., & Isaacs, M. (1989). Cultural competence continuum. In *Toward a culturally competent system of care, Vol. 1: A monograph on effective services for minority children who are severely emotionally disturbed.* Washington, DC: CASSP Technical Assistance Center.

Cummings, J. (1989). *Empowering minority students.* Sacramento: California Association for Bilingual Education.

Cummins, J. (1984). *Bilingualism and special education: Issues in assessment and pedagogy.* San Diego, CA: College-Hill.

Falicov, C. J. (1998). *Latino families in therapy: A guide to multicultural practice.* New York: Guilford.

Hawkins, J., Catalano, R., Kosterman, R., Abbott, R., & Hill, K. (1999). Preventing adolescent health-risk behaviors by strengthening protection during childhood. *Archives of Pediatrics and Adolescent Medicine, 153,* 226–234.

Hu, T. W., Snowden, L. R., Jerrell, J. M., & Nguyen, T. D. (1991). Ethnic populations in public mental health services: Service choice and level of use. *American Journal of Public Health, 81,* 1429–1434.

Ingraham, C. (2000). Consultation through a multicultural lens: Multicultural and cross-cultural consultation in schools. *School Psychology Review, 29*(3), 320–343.

Kataoka, S. H., Zhang, L., & Wells, K. B. (2002). Unmet need for mental health care among U.S. children: Variation by ethnicity and insurance status. *American Journal of Psychiatry, 159,* 1548–1555.

Kleinman, A. (1988). *Rethinking psychiatry: From cultural category to personal experience.* New York: Free Press.

Kleinman, A. (1995). *Writing at the margin: Discourse between anthropology and medicine.* Berkeley: University of California Press.

Kleinman, A., Eisenberg, L., & Good, B. (1978). Culture, illness, and care: Clinical lessons from anthropologic and cross-cultural research. *Annals of Internal Medicine, 88,* 251–258.

Knapp, M. S., & Shields, P. M. (1990). *Better schooling for the children of poverty: Alternatives to conventional wisdom* (Vol. 2). Washington, DC: U.S. Department of Education. (ED 314 549).

Koss-Chioino, J. D., & Vargas, L. A. (1999). *Working with Latino youth: Culture, development, and context.* San Francisco: Jossey-Bass.

Lin, K. M., & Kleinman, A. M. (1988). Psychopathology and clinical course of schizophrenia: A cross-cultural perspective. *Schizophrenia Bulletin, 14*(4), 555–567.

Lopez, E. C. (1995). Best practices in working with bilingual children. In A. Thomas & J. Grimes (Eds.), *Best practices in school psychology III.* Washington, DC: National Association of School Psychologists.

Lopez, S. (1989). Patient variable biases in clinical judgment: Conceptual overview and methodological considerations. *Psychological Bulletin, 106,* 184–203.

Lopez, S. R. (1994). Latinos and the expression of psychopathology: A call for the direct assessment of cultural influences. In C. A. Telles & M. Karno (Eds.), *Mental disorders in Hispanic populations* (pp. 109–127). Los Angeles: Neuropsychiatric Institute, UCLA Press Mental Health.

Lopez, S. R. (1997). Cultural competence in psychotherapy: A guide for clinicians and their supervisors. In C. Z. Watkins Jr. (Ed.), *Handbook of psychotherapy supervision* (pp. 570–588). New York: John Wiley & Sons.

Lopez, S. R. (2002). Teaching culturally informed psychological assessment: Conceptual issues and demonstrations. *Journal of Personality Assessment, 79,* 226–234.

Lopez, S. R., Kopelowicz, A., & Cañive, J. M. (2002). Strategies in developing culturally congruent family interventions for schizophrenia: The case of Hispanics. In H. P. Lefley & D. L. Johnson (Eds.), *Family interventions in mental illness: International perspectives* (pp. 61–90). Westport, CT: Praeger.

Lum, D. (1999). *Culturally competent practice: A framework for growth and action.* New York: Brooks/Cole.

Lynch, E. W. (1992). Developing cross-cultural competence. In E. W. Lynch & M. J. Hanson (Eds.), *Developing cross-cultural competence: A guide for working with young children and their families.* Baltimore: Paul H. Brooks.

Maternal and Child Health Bureau. (1999). *Guidance for SPRANS grant, health resources and services administration,* U.S. Department of Health and Human Services.

McCabe, K., Yeh, M., Lambros, K. M., Hough, R., Landsverk, J., Hulbert, M., et al. (in press). Racial/ethnic representation across five public sectors of care for youth with emotional and behavioral problems: Implications for students in school settings. In P. Garner, F. Yuen, P. Clough, & T. Pardeck (Eds.), *Handbook of emotional and behavioral difficulties.* London: Sage.

Means, B., & Knapp, M. S. (1991). *Teaching advanced skills to educationally disadvantaged students.* Washington, DC: U.S. Department of Education. (ED 338 722)

Pitts, G., & Wallace, P. A. (2003). Cultural awareness in the diagnosis of attention deficit/hyperactivity disorder. *Primary Psychiatry, 10*(4), 84–88.

Ramirez, M. (1991). *Psychotherapy and counseling with minorities: A cognitive approach to individual and cultural differences.* New York: Pergamon.

Reid, J., Eddy, J., Fetrow, R., & Stoolmiller, M. (1999). Description and immediate impacts of a prevention intervention for conduct problems. *American Journal of Community Psychology, 27*(4), 483–517.

Ridley, C. R., Mendoza, D. W., Kanitz, B. E., Angermeier, L., & Zenk, R. (1994). Cultural sensitivity in multicultural counseling: A perceptual schema model. *Journal of Counseling Psychology, 41,* 125–136.

Rogers, M. R., Ingraham, C. L., Bursztyn, A., Cajigas-Segredo, N., Esquivel, G., Hess, R. S., et al. (1999). Best practices in providing psychological services to racially, ethnically, culturally, and linguistically diverse individuals in the schools. *School Psychology International, 20,* 243–264.

Rowland, A. S., Umbach, D. M., Stallone, L, Naftel, A. J., Bohlig, E. M., & Sandler, D. P. (2002). Prevalence of medication treatment for attention deficit-hyperactivity disorder among elementary school children in Johnston County, North Carolina. *American Journal of Public Health 92,* 231–234.

Safer, D. J., & Malever, M. (2000). Stimulant treatment in Maryland public schools. *Pediatrics, 106,* 533–539.

Sheridan, S., Kratochwill, T., & Bergen, J. (1996). *Conjoint behavioral consultation: A procedural manual.* New York: Plenum.

Sue, D. W. (1998). In search of cultural competence in psychotherapy and counseling. *American Psychologist, 53,* 440–448.

Sue, D. W., Arrendondo, P., & McDavis, R. J. (1992). Multicultural counseling competencies and standards: A call to the profession. *Journal of Counseling and Development, 70,* 477–486.

Sue, D. W., & Sue, D. (1999). *Counseling the culturally different: Theory and practice* (3rd ed.). New York: Wiley.

Sue, S., & Zane, N. (1987). The role of culture and cultural techniques in psychotherapy: A critique and reformulation. *American Psychologist, 42*(1), 37–45.

Sussman, L. K., Robins, L. N., & Earls, F. (1987). Treatment-seeking for depression by black and white Americans. *Social Science and Medicine, 24,* 187–196.

Szapocznik, J., Kurtines, W., Santisteban, D. A., Pantin, H., Scopetta, M., Mancilla, Y., et al. (1997). The evolution of structural ecosystemic theory for working with Latino families. In J. G. Garcia & M. C. Zea (Eds.), *Psychological interventions and research with Latino populations* (pp. 166–190). Boston: Allyn & Bacon.

Tarver Behring, S., & Ingraham, C. (1998). Culture as a central component to consultation: A call to the field. *Journal of Educational and Psychological Consultation, 9,* 57–72.

Tharp, R. G. (1989). Psychocultural variables and constants. *American Psychologist, 44,* 349–359.

Treuba, E., & Bartolome, L. (1997). *The education of Latino students: Is school reform enough?* New York: ERIC Clearinghouse on Urban Education.

U.S. Bureau of the Census. (2001). *The Hispanic population: 2000* (Census Brief C2KBR/01–3). Washington, DC: U.S. Government Printing Office.

U.S. Bureau of the Census. (2002). *Coming from the Americas: A profile of the nation's foreign born population from Latin America: 2000* (Census Brief: Current Population Survey CENBR/01–2). Washington, DC: U.S. Government Printing Office.

U.S. Department of Education. (2002). *Twenty-fourth annual report to Congress on the implementation of the Individual with Disabilities Education Act.* Washington, DC: Author

U.S. Department of Education, National Center for Education Statistics. (1993). *Digest of education statistics, 1993* (NCES 2002–130), by Thomas D. Snyder. Washington, DC: Author.

U.S. Department of Health and Human Services. (2001). *Mental health: Culture, race, and ethnicity—A supplement to mental health: A report of the surgeon general.* Rockville, MD: U.S. Department of Health and Human Services, Substance Abuse and Mental Health Services Administration, Center for Mental Health Services.

Vega, W. A., Kolody, B., Aguilar-Gaxiola, S., et al. (1998). Lifetime prevalence of DSM II-R psychiatric disorders among urban and rural Mexican Americans in California. *Archives of General Psychiatry, 55,* 771–778.

Walker, H., Kavanagh, K., Stiller, B., Golly, A., Severson, H., & Feil, E. (1998). First step to success: An early intervention approach for preventing school antisocial behavior. *Journal of Emotional and Behavior Disorders, 6,* 66–80.

Westermeyer, J. (1987). Cultural factors in clinical assessment. *Journal of Consulting and Clinical Psychology, 55,* 471–478.

Woodward, A. M., Dwinell, A. D., & Arons, B. S. (1992). Barriers to mental health care for Latino Americans: A literature review and discussion. *Journal of Mental Health Administration, 19,* 224–236.

Yeh, M., McCabe, K., Hough, R., Dupuis, D., & Hazen, A. (2003). Racial/ethnic differences in parental endorsement of barriers to mental health services for youth. *Mental Health Services Research, 5,* 65–77.

Advancing a Positive School Climate for Students, Families, and Staff

Michael E. Woolley

CHAPTER 75

Getting Started

School, along with home and neighborhood, is the primary environment that impacts child developmental outcomes. Schools with a positive climate, where children feel welcome and look forward to attending, families like to visit and volunteer, and staff like to work, are environments that promote learning and healthy growth (Haynes, Emmons, & Ben-Avie, 1997; Kuperminc, Leadbeater, Emmons, & Blatt, 1997; Noblit, Malloy, & Malloy, 2001). The adults in a child's life are the central factors in the impact of those primary developmental environments. For example, the adults in a child's school—principal, teachers, and other staff—create and sustain the climate in the school (Hoy & Tarter, 1997; Olweus, 1993). Likewise, a child's parents or guardians are the central force in the home environment. When school personnel reach out to families to get them involved in the school, a bridge is built between these two primary environments that influence academic and developmental outcomes (Johns, 2001; Noblit et al., 2001).

This chapter will first define and discuss the importance of a positive school climate. The central focus, however, is how school practitioners can grow a welcoming and positive climate for students, families, and staff. A burgeoning body of literature describes the nature and effects of school climate, as well as assessment and intervention strategies. Two goals have guided the writing of this chapter: first, to synthesize this literature into four practice principles to guide intervention planning and programming; second, to present three proven programs—a school climate assessment instrument, a comprehensive school improvement program, and a bully prevention program—each of which covers aspects of these practice principles.

What We Know

School Climate

School climate is how a school makes individuals feel. Aspects of the school environment interact in complex ways to affect how students, staff, and family members feel about a school. Anderson (1982) asserted there are three dimensions to school climate: (a) the physical building and material aspects; (b) the social interactions; and (c) the belief system, values, and shared meanings. Augmenting this structural definition, Hoy and Tarter (1997) compared the climate of a school to the personality of an individual. Haynes et al. (1997) offered a definition that captures the inputs and outputs of school climate: "the quality and consistency of interpersonal interactions within the school community that influence children's cognitive, social, and psychological development" (p. 322).

Research over the past two decades has demonstrated the importance of the social environment in schools. School environments where students feel welcomed, supported, cared for, and hopeful about their performance and potential have positive effects on student behavior, well-being, and academic performance (Brand, Felner, Shim, Seitsinger, & Dumas, 2003; Sweetland & Hoy, 2000). A meta-analysis investigating the factors that affect student learning found many important factors were aspects of school climate, such as: (a) classroom management, (b) student–teacher social interaction, (c) school culture, (d) classroom climate, and (e) parental involvement policy (Wang, Haertel, & Walberg, 1997). Poor outcomes have likewise been associated with negative school climates. For example, victimization from bullying in school has been associated with low self-esteem, depression, and suicide

(Smith & Brain, 2000). Positive school environments are especially important for the success of children from lower income and/or ethnically diverse families (Haynes et al., 1997; Johns, 2001). Similarly, it has been asserted that when African American and immigrant families feel that they and their children are welcome and the school staff care about all children, positive school–family relationships can lead to better outcomes for students (Johns, 2001; Thompson, 2003).

A group of students who are at especially high risk from a negative school climate are gay, lesbian, bisexual, and transgender students and students who are questioning their sexual identities. These students are disproportionately victimized by bullying and teasing, and research reveals that schools often fail to protect them from verbal harassment and violence (Thurlow, 2001). This widespread problem has been linked to higher rates of dropping out, substance abuse, depression, and suicide among sexual minority students (Johnson & Johnson, 2000). There are a growing number of students who have gay, lesbian, bisexual, or transgender parents who likewise face struggles when the school climate does not welcome active participation by all family constellations (Ryan & Martin, 2000). (See also Chapter 83.)

What We Can Do

The practice principles detailed here were gathered from literature either describing the nature and effects of school climate or reporting on programs to improve school climate. The complexity and diversity of school climates make creating a one-size-fits-all school climate program impossible. Cook and Payne (2002) asserted that the nature and dynamics of individual schools are so varied that for change-oriented programs to be successful, they must be modified to fit the needs of each school. Therefore, these practice principles are offered as a guide in the process to formulate an assessment strategy that fits the current context, then identify programming activities that respond to the specific needs of any one school or district.

Principle 1—Ongoing Assessment

Any system needs ongoing feedback to create positive change. Standardized test scores and student behaviors are distal student outcomes of

school climate and do not provide effective feedback to promote positive change in the social environment of a school. Therefore, the first step toward improving the climate in a school is to utilize reliable and valid assessment instruments to gather data about the current state of the school climate. This data can be gathered from the school staff in order to assess the school as a working environment (see Principle 2). Data should also be gathered from students and families in order to assess the learning climate that grows out of that working environment. Below are examples of several research-based school climate instruments with proven reliability and validity.

- *Organizational Climate Description Questionnaire* (OCDQ)—The OCDQ (Hoy & Tarter, 1997) assesses school climate from the perspective of teachers and principals and includes high school, middle school, and elementary school versions. The OCDQ is described in the Tools and Practice Examples section.
- *School Success Profile* (SSP) and *Elementary School Success Profile* (ESSP)—The SSP and ESSP are assessment instruments developed for individual and school-level practice in schools. The SSP (G. L. Bowen & Richman, 2001) measures middle and high school students' perceptions of their social environments, including school, family, neighborhood, and peer group. The ESSP (N. K. Bowen, Bowen, & Woolley, 2004) measures elementary school students' perceptions of their social environments including school, and it collects data from parents or guardians and primary teachers. For more information on the SSP and ESSP, please see http://www.schoolsuccessprofile.org/
- *Inventory of School Climate-Student* (ISC-S)—The ISC-S (Brand et al., 2003) was developed as an outcome measure for the evaluation of school improvement programs. However, it measures multiple dimensions of school climate from the student perspective—such as teacher support, clarity of rules, participation in decision making, and safety problems—and could be used as an assessment tool for intervention planning.

Principle 2—Adults Are the Key

Students display the state of the climate in a school through their behavior, socioemotional functioning, and academic performance. However, it is the adults in a school who create and maintain the climate. Focusing school climate change efforts on changing the students, without also working to make changes in the work environment and relationships among staff, is much like treating the symptoms while ignoring the problem. Therefore, assessment of the school climate and resulting change efforts should start with the adults.

- School administrators and principals who are committed to change efforts provide a foundation for success. Likewise, building commitment and motivation by teachers and parents or guardians to make changes in the school climate is key (Olweus, 1993).
- Similarly, growing a more welcoming climate for families and increasing family involvement starts with school staff who reach out to provide opportunities for families to participate in the life of the school. This can be something as simple as notes home about positive accomplishments of students whose parents typically hear from the school only when their child is in trouble (Comer & Haynes, 1991). Another effective strategy is to engage the parents or guardians who are already involved in the school community to reach out to families who are not. This can be particularly important for some immigrant families, who for cultural reasons may need to be empowered to participate in the school process (Johns, 2001).
- When teachers expect students will do well and communicate to students a belief that they can meet those learning expectations, students perform better. This factor is especially important in building a school climate that is welcoming and supportive of ethnically diverse students and families (Thompson, 2003).
- For teachers, the school is a workplace. An environment where teachers feel valued and their opinions and input are included in the decision-making process results in teachers who create a welcoming and supportive climate for students (Hoy & Tarter, 1997). (Additional information about engaging parents in their child's education may be found in Chapters 15 and 47 and in Section 9.)

Principle 3—Open and Inclusive Governance Structure

An open and inclusive governance structure and decision-making process sets the stage for all stakeholders in the school to feel empowered to participate in the life of the school. This is in contrast with the traditionally hierarchical top-down way schools are often still organized.

- Successful school improvement programs are frequently organized around an inclusive decision-making structure, which seeks ongoing input from staff, students, and families. Built on an ecological and developmental perspective, successful school climates seek to promote healthy development and successful learning by recognizing, strengthening, and promoting the interconnectedness between the social environments of school, home, and community (Noblit et al., 2001).
- Creating and sustaining an open and inclusive decision-making process requires collaborative and inclusive leadership from principals and other administrators who seek and use input from teachers, families, and students in making decisions about the management of the school. In accomplishing this goal, principals will be more likely to be successful, for example, if they encourage creativity and independence on the part of school staff and respect their professionalism, individual skills, and talents (Hoy & Sweetland, 2001).

Principle 4—Safe and Welcoming

Bullying and teasing are universal school problems, and reducing bullying should be a part of any successful school climate change effort (Smith & Brain, 2000). However, it is not enough to make the school safe. Rather, the school should feel welcoming to all students and families.

- Implement a schoolwide bully prevention program. In the Tools and Practice Examples section, the Olweus Bully Prevention Program (Olweus, 1993) is described. (Bullying and associated problems are further discussed in Chapters 39–45.)
- Establish fair and consistent rules. The rules for behavior should be clearly communicated to all students and staff, and those rules should be applied in a consistent and fair manner (Welsh, 2000).
- Promote caring and trusting relationships. Teachers who care about students and families and reflect that in their behavior and interactions contribute to a positive climate. School staff who care about each other and feel

comfortable being open and honest with each other set a stage for a welcoming climate for staff and students alike (Hoy & Sweetland, 2001).

• Personalize relations with students and families. School staff should make the effort to have personal relationships with students and families. Strive to see each student as an individual, with hopes, fears, aspirations, and struggles. This seems difficult, given the workload of school staff today, but it can be seen not as more work but a different approach to the work. This can also be a broad principle or a targeted strategy. As a targeted strategy, a school can organize a program to recruit staff to volunteer to each reach out to one at-risk student in a personal way and provide a safe and caring source of encouragement and support (Shore, 1997).

• Recognize and celebrate diversity. School assemblies and celebrations provide opportunities to share and enjoy the cultural food, customs, history, talents, and interests of the various groups within the school community. This is vital to making all students and families feel welcome as schools become increasingly diverse (Johns, 2001).

Tools and Practice Examples

Each school interested in improving school climate must find and modify proven programs to fit their needs. A comprehensive approach for any one school, covering all four practice principles, may require combining two or more proven programs. For example, a school might use a school climate assessment instrument, then implement both a comprehensive school improvement program and a bully prevention program. Examples of each of these types of programs follow. Any one of these programs would improve the climate in a school, but in combination they represent a multifaceted approach that matches the complexity of the climate of a school.

School Climate Assessment Instrument

Ongoing assessment utilizing reliable and valid instruments is the first school climate practice principle stated previously. Measuring school climate involves assessing the perceptions of the school environment by school staff, students, and parents or

guardians. However, the second practice principle asserts that it is the adults in a school who most strongly influence its climate. Therefore, when assessing school climate as part of intervention planning, it is critical to gather data from the principals and teachers, because it is within those relationships that effective change needs to start. The perceptions of students and parents or guardians are also important to assess. However, their perceptions should be seen as indicators of the state of the school climate and/or used as outcome measures.

The Organizational Climate Description Questionnaire (OCDQ) is a school climate assessment tool completed by school staff. The OCDQ has different versions for elementary, middle, and high schools, has been rigorously developed, and has demonstrated reliability and validity. (For detailed information on these instruments, see Hoy & Tarter, 1997.) Interpretation and scoring information, as well as free downloadable copies of all three versions of the instrument, can be found at http://www.coe.ohio-state.edu/whoy/instruments_6.htm.

The OCDQ takes 15 minutes for teachers and principals to complete, and includes 34 to 50 multiple-choice questions. The OCDQ measures six important features of school climate. Three of these features describe the principal: (a) supportive behavior, (b) directive behavior, and (c) restrictive behavior. Three of these features describe the teachers: (a) collegial behavior, (b) intimate behavior, and (c) disengaged behavior. Scores on these six school climate features reveal the level of openness and disengagement of the staff relationships in the school. These six scores can then be plotted on a chart providing a graphic depiction of a school's climate. Hoy and Tartar's (1997) book about these instruments include intervention strategies and examples for utilizing these measures to improve the climate in a school.

Comprehensive School Improvement Program

Aspects of all four practice principles can be addressed with a comprehensive school improvement program. Many such programs have been described, including (a) Success for All, (b) Accelerated Schools, (c) Coalition of Essential Schools, (d) Project ACHIEVE, and (f) the School Development Program (SDP). However, the SDP stands out for two reasons. First, an initial and central goal of the SDP is to improve school climate, and second, extensive research supports climate change as a consistent SDP outcome (Cook, Murphy, & Hunt, 2000; Noblit et al., 2001). The SDP does not present a scripted approach to change; rather, it is process oriented with a structure that is intentionally flexible to meet the needs of a specific school. Those processes and flexible structure include (a) a collaborative governance structure, (b) three guiding principles, and (c) three key operations.

The literature supporting the effectiveness of the SDP includes anecdotal accounts, qualitative case studies, and randomized experimental evaluations. For example, Johns (2001) anecdotally described the program's effectiveness in schools serving large populations of immigrant students, particularly in engaging immigrant families. Noblit, Malloy, and Malloy (2001) presented eight qualitative case studies that illustrated the variety of what the program can look like in response to local needs. They reported that the SDP (a) created a positive learning and working environment, (b) increased parent involvement, (c) improved teacher satisfaction, (d) increased sense of community, (e) strengthened school–community ties, (f) improved school reputation, and (g) bridged racial divisiveness and unified multiethnic communities. Two randomized experimental evaluations of the SDP have been completed. Findings in the first included positive improvements in school climate and supported the SDP theoretical model (Cook, Habib, et al., 1999). The second study found significant school climate changes in both students' and teachers' perceptions (Cook, Murphy, et al., 2000). Additionally, students' maladaptive beliefs about problem behaviors improved, acting-out behaviors were reduced, and gains were found in academic achievement.

The SDP includes three elements: (a) three guiding principles, (b) three teams, and (c) three operations. (For a detailed description, see Comer, Ben-Avie, Haynes, & Joyner, 1999.)

Three Guiding Principles

First, the No Fault Principle is intended to keep the process focused on solving identified problems and not expend time or energy assigning blame for the existence of a problem. Second, the Consensus Decision-Making Principle directs the focus on what is best for the students and guides the school community to engage in open dialogue to reach consensus on all important decisions about plans, programs, and activities at the school. Third, the Collaboration Principle reinforces the No Fault and Consensus Principles and affirms all involved to work as a team and include all interested parties.

Three Teams

First, the School Planning and Management Team includes the principal and representatives from among the teachers, parents/guardians, and school staff and is the executive decision-making body for the school. The goal of this team is to create an inclusive governance structure where all stakeholder groups are informed and included. Second, the Student and Staff Support Team includes the principal and all staff with expertise on the health and well-being of the student body, such as social workers, psychologists, counselors, special education teachers, and the nurse. The central goal of this team is to promote a positive social environment in the school, by identifying individual-, group-, and school-level needs and implementing appropriate prevention or intervention activities. The Parent Team includes parents/guardians and selects members to serve on the School Planning and Management Team. The goal of the Parent Team is to increase parent participation in the social and academic aspects of the school. Critical to the success of this team is to engage families who have not previously participated in the school by reaching out to uninvolved families across racial, ethnic, and socioeconomic lines (Johns, 2001).

Three Operations

First, the Comprehensive School Plan is the master plan for the school covering both school climate and curriculum planning. It should be based on assessment data and developed, implemented, and monitored by the School Planning and Management Team with input from the other two teams. Second, Staff Development should provide opportunities for staff to build supportive and trusting working relationships while including content on the six developmental pathways for healthy student growth: cognitive, physical, language, psychological, ethical, and social (Noblit et al., 2001). The third operation is Assessment and Modification. An SDP school should collect ongoing assessments about how staff, students, and families are doing. Such data provide critical feedback to modify the planning and activities of the school. Ongoing assessment should include all levels, from individual student needs to student and staff perception of the social climate.

Implementation of the SDP will look different from school to school. In all schools, however, creating an open and inclusive governance structure and processes, as part of growing a welcoming school climate, takes time and nurturance.

Bully Prevention Program

As stated in the fourth practice principle, for a school climate to be welcoming and supportive, it must first be safe for all students. Bullying and teasing have been shown to be universal problems in schools, occurring with similar dynamics in nearly all schools across geography and culture (Smith & Brain, 2000). Therefore, bullying should be expected to exist in most schools with varying degrees of frequency and severity. It seems clear that a school interested in creating a more positive climate for all students should assess and intervene to reduce teasing and bullying. An increasing number of bully prevention programs have been developed in many countries, with many of these programs evolving from the seminal research of Dan Olweus. His 1993 book *Bullying at School*, and Web site, http://www.clemson.edu/olweus/, provide excellent descriptions of the dynamics of bullying and teasing, and detailed information on his proven Olweus Bully Prevention Program. This program is also a Substance Abuse and Mental Health Services Administration model program, with information available at: http://modelprograms.samhsa.gov/template_cf.cfm?page=model&pkProgramID=20.

The Olweus program includes intervention components at the school, classroom, and individual levels, recognizing the complexity of school climate. Echoing the first practice principle, Olweus stresses the importance of getting the principal's support and making all adults—teachers and parents or guardians—aware of the problem and involved in the solution. Two core components of the program that Olweus identifies at the school level are: first, to present findings from the Bully/Victim Questionnaire to the staff, students, and parents or guardians to raise awareness of the problem and increase involvement in the solution and, second, to provide adequate supervision during unstructured times such as recess and lunch to immediately reduce opportunities for victimization. Two core classroom-level components are to clearly state and enforce classroom rules against

bullying and teasing and to hold regular classroom meetings to discuss the classroom climate. Core components at the individual level are serious talks between school staff and bullies and their parents or guardians and, separately, between staff and victims of bullying and their parents or guardians. Such talks, which should be focused on stopping the bullying, are critical to program success.

Key Points to Remember

- The social climate of a school grows out of the perception of the school as workplace for staff and a learning place for students and families. That climate has a direct effect on student behavior, socioemotional functioning, and academic performance.
- The climate in a school is especially important to the developmental and academic outcomes of vulnerable or at-risk students, such as culturally or ethnically diverse, economically disadvantaged, or sexual-minority students.
- Schools and their climates are complex and varied; planning effective school climate change must be tailored to the needs of each school and district.
- Four key principles in positive school climate change include (a) utilizing ongoing assessment measures, (b) recognizing that the adults create and maintain the climate, (c) building an open and inclusive governance structure, and (d) making the school safe and welcoming to all students and families.
- School climate change is complex and may require a combination of proven programs and a sustained effort by committed and motivated members of all stakeholder groups.

References

Anderson, C. S. (1982). The search for school climate: A review of the research. *Review of Educational Research, 52*(3), 368–420.

Bowen, G. L., & Richman, J. M. (2001). *The school success profile*. Chapel Hill: University of North Carolina at Chapel Hill.

Bowen, N. K., Bowen, G. L., & Woolley, M. E. (2004). Constructing and validating assessment tools for school-based practitioners: The Elementary School Success Profile. In A. R. Roberts & K. Y. Yeager (Eds.), *Evidence-based practice manual: Research and outcome measures in health and human services* (pp. 509–517). New York: Oxford University Press.

Brand, S., Felner, R. D., Shim, M., Seitsinger, A., & Dumas, T. (2003). Middle school improvement and reform: Development and validation of a school-level assessment of climate, cultural pluralism, and school safety. *Journal of Educational Psychology, 95,* 570–588.

Comer, J. P., Ben-Avie, M., Haynes, N. M., & Joyner, E. T. (Eds.). (1999). *Child by child: The Comer Process for change in education.* New York: Teachers College Press.

Comer, J. P., & Haynes, N. M. (1991). Parent involvement in schools: An ecological approach. *Elementary School Journal, 91,* 271–277.

Cook, T. D., Habib, F., Phillips, M., Settersten, R. A., Shagle, S. C., & Degirmencioglu, S. M. (1999). Comer's School Development Program in Prince George's County: A theory-based evaluation. *American Educational Research Journal, 36,* 543–597.

Cook, T. D., Murphy, R. F., & Hunt, H. D. (2000). Comer's School Development Program in Chicago: A theory-based evaluation. *American Educational Research Journal, 37,* 535–597.

Cook, T. D., & Payne, M. R. (2002). Objecting to the objections to using random assignment in educational research. In F. Mosteller & R. Boruch (Eds.), *Evidence matters: Randomized trials in education research* (pp. 150–178). Washington, DC: Brookings Institution Press.

Haynes, N. M., Emmons, C., & Ben-Avie, M. (1997). School climate as a factor in student adjustment and achievement. *Journal of Educational and Psychological Consultation, 8,* 321–329.

Hoy, W. K., & Sweetland, S. R. (2001). Designing better schools: The meaning and measure of enabling school structures. *Educational Administration Quarterly, 37,* 296–321.

Hoy, W. K., & Tarter, C. J. (1997). *The road to open and healthy schools: A handbook for change* (Elementary and middle school edition, and secondary edition). Thousand Oaks, CA: Corwin.

Johns, S. E. (2001). Using the Comer Model to educate immigrant children. *Childhood Education, 77,* 268–274.

Johnson, C. C., & Johnson, K. A. (2000). High-risk behavior among gay adolescents: Implications for treatment and support. *Adolescence, 35,* 619–637.

Kuperminc, G. P., Leadbeater, B. J., Emmons, C., & Blatt, S. J. (1997). Perceived school climate and difficulties in the social adjustment of middle school students. *Applied Developmental Science, 1,* 76–88.

Noblit, G. W., Malloy, W. W., & Malloy, C. E. (Eds.). (2001). *The kids got smarter: Case studies of successful Comer schools.* Cresskill, NJ: Hampton.

Olweus, D. (1993). *Bullying in school.* Cambridge, MA: Blackwell.

Ryan, D., & Martin, A. (2000). Lesbian, gay, bisexual, and transgender parents in the school systems. *School Psychology Review, 29,* 207–216.

Shore, R. (1997). *Creating a positive school climate.* Mt. Kisco, NY: Plan for Social Excellence.

Smith, P. K., & Brain, P. (2000). Bullying in school: Lessons from two decades of research. *Aggressive Behavior, 26,* 1–9.

Sweetland, S. R., & Hoy, W. K. (2000). School characteristics and educational outcomes: Toward an organizational model of student achievement in middle schools. *Educational Administration Quarterly, 36*(5), 703–729.

Thompson, G. L. (2003). No parent left behind: Strengthening ties between educators and African American parents/guardians. *Urban Review, 35*(1), 7–23.

Thurlow, C. (2001). Naming the "outsider within": Homophobic pejoratives and the verbal abuse of lesbian, gay, and bisexual high-school pupils. *Journal of Adolescence, 24,* 25–38.

Wang, M. C., Haertel, G. D., & Walberg, H. J. (1997). Learning influences. In H. J. Walberg & G. D. Haertel (Eds.), *Psychology and educational practice* (pp. 199–211). Berkeley, CA: McCutchan.

Welsh, W. N. (2000). The effects of school climate on school disorder. *Annals of the American Academy of Political and Social Science, 567,* 88–108.

Engaging With Culturally and Racially Diverse Families

Michael S. Spencer ▪ Jenell S. Clarke

Getting Started

The engagement process in school-based mental health services is one of the first critical junctures for successful treatment of and intervention with troubled children from culturally and racially diverse families. If professionals are unable to engage families initially in the process, children will not be served, and problems will continue to mount or multiply. Delays in treatment may result, leading children who may have benefited from preventive school-based services to later be funneled into more punitive and rigid systems, including child welfare, juvenile justice, and foster care systems. To better engage families, culturally competent school social workers must first be conscious of the needs of diverse families and the barriers to engagement in services. Once these needs and barriers are identified, school social workers should adopt philosophies of practice that reflect cultural democracy, collaboration, critical consciousness, and social advocacy and action.

This chapter focuses on innovative and empirically based practices for engaging families of diverse backgrounds, with specific attention to immigrant and refugee families. (Chapter 78 discusses effective case management with immigrant and refugee students and their families.) The purpose of this chapter is twofold. First, it will provide an overview of the existing knowledge of best practices for engaging families, including addressing some of the reasons that services are underused. Second, it will provide specific recommendations and instructions for school-based practitioners that are essential for engaging culturally and racially diverse families. (See Chapters 73 and 76 for further discussion of engaging culturally and racially diverse families.)

What We Know

Although there is a growing body of knowledge about school-based mental health interventions, empirical research on engaging culturally diverse families doesn't exist in the practice literature. Rather, the process of engaging families is often included as part of the intervention, though not specifically tested for efficacy as a separate component. The purpose of this section is to provide a brief summary of the engagement component as it is used in empirically supported interventions, particularly with immigrant populations. However, we expect that there will be a degree of generalizability beyond immigrant groups to most communities of color.

Review of the Research

A number of studies have developed school-based mental health interventions aimed at immigrant children (e.g., Armbruster & Lichtman, 1999; Garrison, Roy, & Azar, 1999; Stein et al., 2002). Much of the literature provides a review of the issues and concerns of immigrant students and school mental health services, qualities of effective programs, roles of the social worker/counselor, and recommendations for intervention (e.g., Flaherty et al., 1998; Jennings, Pearson, & Harris, 2000; Williams & Butler, 2003). Although none of the studies reviewed examine the engagement process specifically, together they provide insights and strategies for how to connect immigrant families with school-based mental health services. In the following section, we examine two dimensions of the engagement process for immigrant families: (1) identification of needs and barriers and (2) culturally competent practice philosophies.

Strategies for Engaging Diverse Families

Identification of Needs and Barriers

The first step to successfully engaging families is to understand their needs for services and the barriers they experience in accessing services. There are several key issues that are particularly relevant for immigrant and refugee families: (1) lack of language proficiency; (2) discrimination; (3) shortage of racially and culturally diverse providers; and (4) cultural attitudes and values.

Language Proficiency

The literature on service use among immigrant families states clearly that language is a critical barrier (e.g., Qin-Hilliard, 2002; Williams & Butler, 2003). In conducting a needs assessment for school-based services for immigrant families, you must examine whether or not services are accessible to families who do not speak English. The checklist shown in Box 76.1 is designed to assist you in assessing your school's efforts at addressing language barriers.

In some communities, service providers will be able to identify the one or two non-English-speaking groups within their catchment area. In other communities that serve as a portal for a number of different immigrant families, the job becomes more difficult. Translators can be costly, and presenting brochures and outreach information in a multilingual format can be complex. Optimally, having a diverse staff that is representative of the community demographics is ideal. Having native speakers of different immigrant languages is also preferable.

Discrimination

Recent research has shown that exposure to discriminatory behavior is a major life stressor that has powerful adverse effects on emotional well-being (Kessler, Mickelson, & Williams, 1994). Historical and contemporary experiences with discrimination, as well as documented abuses and perceived mistreatment by medical and mental health professionals, may precipitate mistrust of service providers. Studies that have examined discrimination in service use have found that higher proportions of African Americans and Latinos compared to whites felt that a health provider judged them unfairly or treated them with disrespect because of their race or ethnic background (Richardson, 2001). Parents who encounter the mental health system are often not adequately informed about the services or their rights as clients, and they do not receive any form of advocacy throughout the process. Furthermore, they may be apprehensive about the consequences of seeking services. They may think, "Does my child really have a problem, or are they biased against my child because of his race or ethnicity? Will my child be put in a special education classroom? Will this go on my child's permanent record and haunt her throughout her academic career?" The checklist in Box 76.2 provides an assessment of discrimination as a barrier that may affect the engagement of families.

Focus: Active Antibigotry Efforts

While this list is certainly not comprehensive, it is a means to begin the process of examining ways in which discrimination exerts its influence on decisions to utilize services. A school that is actively committed to antibigotry efforts may

Box 76.1

> Is advertisement and outreach information provided in a multilingual format? Are intake and consent forms?
>
> Are the languages of those immigrant groups most predominant in your community represented?
>
> Is there a plan or strategy for those language groups not represented?
>
> Are native speakers or translators available?

Box 76.2

> Do you know the history of race and ethnic relations of the target population in the United States? In your community? In your school? Is this history acknowledged?
>
> Does your school have antibigotry policies that are understood by the community?
>
> Are incidences of racism and bigotry documented and active steps taken?
>
> Have staff received training in antibigotry practices, and are these trainings ongoing?

increase the level of trust in the system. A school that has not examined or acknowledged past wrongdoings in a public way gives families no reason to trust it with their private information. Schools may be reluctant to acknowledge past discrimination because of guilt, fears of bad press, or perceived lack of importance. School social workers need to be on the forefront of these efforts in collaboration with school administration and personnel, as well as members of the community. The Southern Poverty Law Center's Teaching Tolerance program (see www.splcenter.org) is an excellent resource for those interested in implementing antibigotry education in schools.

Shortage of Racially and Culturally Diverse Providers

In *Mental Health: Culture, Race, and Ethnicity* (U.S. Department of Health and Human Services [DHHS], 2001), the supplement to the surgeon general's report on mental health, the authors point to the shortage of providers of color as one factor accounting for low utilization rates among some groups. For example, studies have found that lack of ethnic match is significantly associated with dropping out from service usage, and that clients of color engage in treatment longer when they are matched with ethnic-specific therapists or therapists who are fluent in their native language (e.g., Yeh, Eastman, & Cheung, 1994). For example, Manderscheid and Henderson (1998) found that of mental health professionals practicing in the late 1990s, approximately 70 Asian American providers were available for every 100,000 Asian Americans in the United States.

Bilingual and culturally diverse providers can promote an antibigotry climate in schools by providing more cultural mediators and translators for school staff, bringing diverse perspectives that can enhance problem-solving strategies, and serving families without employing translators or bilingual children or family members in the process. The checklist in Box 76.3 provides issues that may be assessed regarding diverse providers.

Focus: Lay Community Workers

Though ethnic match is not imperative to the provision of culturally competent services, providing this as an option seems reasonable. Unless the

Box 76.3

Are diverse service providers representative of the community actively recruited?

Are non-MSW staff from diverse backgrounds encouraged and supported to continue their education?

Can non-MSW community members be hired and trained to do outreach, assist, and co-facilitate sessions with MSW-level providers?

racial and ethnic profile of social workers in the United States changes radically in the near future, providers of color will continue to be in short supply. Thus, creative alternatives must be developed to utilize and empower lay community workers (i.e., paraprofessionals), who are often of diverse backgrounds and may live in the same communities as your client population. Evidence for the effectiveness of lay community workers may hold promise (DHHS, 1994). Lay workers can also provide outreach to increase the knowledge of existing school-based services. Moreover, the use of lay workers develops the capacity and skills of community members. Additionally, they provide an invaluable link to community and can serve as cultural mediators for both clients and staff.

Cultural Attitudes and Values

One of the problems with establishing culturally responsive mental health services is the incongruence between the characteristics of the mental health system and the minority group, whose special needs and concerns may not be addressed by assessment instruments, agency policies, clinicians, and practices. Uba (1982) notes several cultural barriers to service use: (1) racial and cultural biases (encountering culturally inappropriate services, differential receipt of services compared); (2) conflicts between the epistemological underpinnings and characteristics of Western psychotherapy and cultural personality syndromes, values, expectations, and interpersonal styles; and (3) cultural attitudes toward seeking help and its usefulness.

An additional barrier to engagement is the aggregation of racial and cultural groups into a singular group, such as Asians, Latinos, immigrants, or refugees. The aggregation of diverse people into monolithic groups ignores the diversity of groups and makes generalizations across these groups misleading. Differences in the myriad of national and historical backgrounds, social classes, legal statuses, migration histories, languages, religious beliefs, and other sociocultural stressors have important consequences for help seeking and service use among groups. Psychosocial factors related to immigration to the United States also pose unique risks for mental health problems. Takeuchi, Mokuau, and Chun (1992) reported that immigrant status is associated with a number of stressors related to adaptation to the host society and expectations of educational and economic attainment that can influence psychological adjustment. Groups that come to the United States as refugees and as a result of war, on the other hand, may experience more exposure to trauma and difficulties with adjustment than do groups who immigrated for work opportunities or schooling. The checklist in Box 76.4 highlights cultural attitudes and values that may affect engagement.

Box 76.4

> Do providers understand the stigma that mental health services have within the specific cultural group?
>
> Are cultural values understood, such as those that may regulate display of emotion or family harmony?
>
> Are there links between schools and informal service systems, such as churches, temples, healers, family supports?
>
> Are children and families given opportunities to promote and celebrate their own cultural backgrounds?

Focus: "Loss of Face"

Among Asian cultures, Confucian philosophies may discourage open displays of emotions to maintain familial harmony. The construct "loss of face" is identified as a key and often dominant interpersonal dynamic in Asian social relations that defines an individual's social integrity and the perception of the individual as an integral member of a group. Losing face has been found to be associated with one's ability to function effectively in society in varying degrees, including assertion and self-disclosure in help-seeking situations (Zane & Yeh, 2002). Understanding the concept of loss of face can assist service providers with outreach efforts that promote services as positive.

Practice Strategies for Engaging Diverse Families

Once needs and barriers have been adequately addressed, school social workers must then adopt philosophies of practice that reflect cultural democracy, collaboration, critical consciousness, and social advocacy and action to promote engagement and appropriate service delivery. Cultural democracy is a philosophy of practice that recognizes (1) the destructive and oppressive nature of cultural domination and marginalization; (2) the importance of ensuring cultural self-determination and integrity for oppressed communities as a precondition for multicultural unity; (3) the importance of emphasizing the relationship between power, culture, and various other oppressions, including class and gender oppression; and (4) the need to invite all of the multiple voices of oppressed communities into the disclosure of liberation (Akinyela & Aldridge, 2003). There are a number of ways in which school social workers can promote the values of cultural democracy in service of engaging immigrant families in services, including the use of community resources in collaboration with school resources, individual self-awareness and critical consciousness development, and social advocacy and action.

Collaboration

Although groups of individuals who work within schools and who have a vested interest in school may have similar goals, these groups often work in opposition to one another or in isolation from one another. These groups include school social workers, school counselors, teachers, school administrators, community-based social service and mental health agencies, ethnic-specific services, researchers and academics, as well as parents and community members. Turf wars, past politics, and different professional socialization can often keep groups from working together. Distrust and cultural conflicts may keep communities isolated from those who might provide useful services.

However, if school social workers are to have any hope of engaging immigrant communities through the principles of cultural democracy, they must better use all available resources. Social workers can act as facilitators of these collaborative efforts, bringing together divergent groups, bridging these differences, and highlighting commonalities, particularly in their mission to serve children. Collaboration is one important way in which social workers can bridge school and community institutions.

Focus: Ways to Develop Collaboration

- Plan and develop a coalition within your community. Identify the key stakeholders and partners within the ecological context of the target families, including parents and community members. Collectively, identify key issues around engagement, ascertain strengths and challenges that exist in the community, and develop an action plan for promoting engagement. The coalition should meet regularly. Coalitions can act as a powerful collaboration that is able to respond to complex problems, address important social policies, and seek funding for needed resources. Coalitions keep community members involved in the decision-making process and promote empowerment.
- Understand that engaging in collaboration helps develop intergroup communication skills. People can learn and practice contact process skills and relationship protocols or cultural ways of relating to people, including respect for authority, family roles, and communication processes (Lum & Lu, 2003). Collaboration also enhances one's knowledge about community-based resources and client support systems, both formal and informal.
- Participate in active community involvement and service. Involve teachers and other school personnel as well. This serves both learning about and from the community, as well as being identified within and becoming a part of the larger community you serve. Too often, school staff lament the lack of parental involvement in schools, but they themselves lack involvement in their communities.

Individual Self-Awareness and Critical Consciousness Development

There are several important elements of your own self-awareness that are necessary when working with diverse families, particularly immigrant families. The first is an awareness and value of children's strengths and their daily contributions. Rather than view immigrant children as a problem or challenge, you must appreciate their physical and economic contribution to family and

school. This contribution may come in the form of caring for younger siblings, providing translation skills for parents who are not literate or are not proficient in English, doing housework, mediating between the family and public institutions, and contributing to household income through wage labor (Orellana, 2001).

A second aspect of self-awareness is an understanding of your own diversity. Lum (2003) uses a framework of diversity developed by Schriver (2001) to explore understandings of diversity. He asks that social workers be able to articulate their own diversity perspective and worldview (values and beliefs, culture, family, gender, sexual orientation, socioeconomic class, spirituality, ability status, etc), the intersection between these perspectives (the implications of membership in multiple groups), and the interrelatedness and interconnectedness to other people (similarities and differences). Critical consciousness, a concept introduced by Freire (1970), takes self-awareness one step further by incorporating a greater sense of understanding of power relationships and similarities and differences among and within people. Through the examination and exploration of their own multiple identities, social workers are able to situate themselves within the world in relation to others and become better aware of their own biases and assumptions.

Social Advocacy and Action

We close this section by promoting the critical importance of social advocacy and action as an important concept and skill for school social workers to develop. Improving engagement skills requires that social workers move interpersonal practice beyond diversity and toward social justice (Reed, Newman, Suarez, & Lewis, 1997). Engagement with racially and culturally diverse families is certain to be a difficult task until the social, political, and historical macro forces influencing their lives are altered. But, how does one act to help effect this?

Freire (1970) states that such a project begins with a commitment to social justice. This requires a moral and ethical attitude toward equality and possibility, and a belief in the capacity of people as agents who can act to transform their world. He adds that people must first examine the contradiction between their espoused social principles and their lived experience. If they are unable to perceive and resolve social, political, and economic contradictions in their own lives, they will have great difficulty advocating for and taking action toward social justice for others. Through this commitment, people better position themselves for working with populations that have historically underused services that could potentially improve their lives.

Tools and Practice Examples

Exercise for Developing Critical Consciousness

There are a number of exercises that can be useful in various training situations (see Adams, Bell, & Griffin, 1997). Here we highlight one exercise that could be valuable in this process.

Intersectional Stand Up

Introduction: Ask participants to remain quiet throughout until the end. Participants will be asked to stand up if a statement is true for them and will be directed to sit again before the next statement is read. If participants choose not to participate or to stand, ask that they notice when they would have stood or remained seated. Read each statement twice.

Statements

Please stand if you were taken to museums, zoos, or other cultural activities as a child.
Please stand if you are an only child.
Please stand if your ancestors were slaves or indigenous peoples whose lands were colonized and taken over.
Please stand if you rarely, if ever, have to question whether a building or event will be accessible to someone of your abilities.
Please stand up if you can hold hands with your partner and not fear for your safety.
Please stand up if you do not fear to walk alone at night because of your gender.
Please stand if one or both of your parents or caretakers were not born in the United States.
Please stand if your grandparents or great-grandparents were not born in the United States.
Please stand if one or both of your parents or caretakers holds a college degree.

Please stand if your current spiritual or religious path is Christianity.
Please stand if you had to work for wages before you were 12 years old.
Please stand if you have experienced the loss of a loved one.
Please stand if you helped your parents or caregivers in caring for siblings so they could work.
Please stand if you have ever lived away from parents or caregivers for more than six months.
Please stand if you have ever been happy.
Please stand up if English is your first language.
Please stand if you speak another language in addition to English.
Please stand if you have ever been misunderstood.

Thank the participants for taking part in this exercise.

Possible Discussion Questions

What was it like for you to notice who stood when and who remained seated?
What did you learn about your own identities?
Did anything make you uncomfortable? Why or why not?
How might your learning from this activity apply to your work with diverse families?
How might your learning apply to engaging immigrant families?

Key Points to Consider

- Most people have intersecting target and agent identities.
- Oppression may be displayed in a multitude of ways on individual, systemic, and institutional levels.
- People have many differences in their backgrounds but also many similarities.

Social workers must always practice their listening skills—not simply listening with their ears but with their hearts. Listening with one's heart entails empathy, genuineness, and sincerity. These qualities will enhance trust and promote engagement.

Key Points to Remember

In this chapter, we highlight a number of strategies for increasing our probability of successfully engaging culturally diverse families. We move away from the reliance on stereotypes and notions of better "knowing the other" and focus instead on better knowing ourselves and our service context. The strategies we have outlined would call on social workers to:

- recognize the needs of communities and barriers to service use;
- address the schools' lack of proficiency with clients' languages rather than focus on clients' lack of proficiency in English;
- recognize, acknowledge, and take action against discrimination, both interpersonal and institutional;
- address the shortage of racially and culturally diverse providers within communities (using lay community workers may be a viable option);
- understand the diverse cultural attitudes and values of the client population to better understand how to engage them in services;
- use culturally competent practice strategies incorporating the principles of cultural democracy;
- collaborate with key stakeholders and community members to gain insight into how schools might address issues of engagement; and
- promote social advocacy and action to build the community's trust in schools and work toward addressing social, political, and historical inequalities.

References

Adams, M., Bell, L. A., & Griffin, P. (1997). *Teaching for diversity and social justice.* New York: Routledge.

Akinyela, M. M., & Aldridge, D. P. (2003). Beyond Eurocentrism, Afrocentrism and multiculturalism: Toward cultural democracy in social work education. *Journal of Race, Class, and Gender, 10*, 58–70.

Armbruster, P., & Lichtman, J. (1999). Are school based mental health services effective? Evidence from 36 inner city schools. *Community Mental Health Journal, 35*, 493–504.

Flaherty, L. T., Garrison, E. G., Waxman, R., Uris, P. F., Keys, S. G., Glass-Siegel, M., et al. (1998). Optimizing the roles of school mental health professionals. *Journal of School Health, 68*, 420–424.

Freire, P. (1970). *Pedagogy of the oppressed.* New York: Herder & Herder.

Garrison, E. G., Roy, I. S., & Azar, V. (1999). Responding to the mental health needs of Latino children and

families through school-based services. *Clinical Psychology Review, 19*, 199–219.

Jennings, J., Pearson, G., & Harris, M. (2000). Implementing and maintaining school-based mental health services in a large, urban school district. *Journal of School Health, 70*, 201–205.

Kessler, R. C., Mickelson, K. D., & Williams, D. R. (1994). The prevalence, distribution, and mental health correlates of perceived discrimination in the United States. *Journal of Health and Social Behavior, 40*, 208–230.

Lum, D. (2003). *Culturally competent practice: A framework for understanding diverse groups and justice issues* (2nd ed.). Pacific Grove, CA: Brooks/Cole/Thomson Learning.

Lum, D., & Lu, Y. E. (2003). Skill development. In D. Lum (Ed.), *Culturally competent practice: A framework for understanding diverse groups and justice issues* (2nd ed., pp. 128–164). Pacific Grove, CA: Brooks/Cole–Thomson Learning.

Manderscheid, R., & Henderson, M. (1998). *Mental health, United States.* Rockville, MD: U.S. Department of Health and Human Services, Center for Mental Health Services.

Orellana, M. F. (2001). The work kids do: Mexican and Central American immigrant children's contributions to households and schools in California. *Harvard Educational Review, 71*, 366–389.

Qin-Hilliard, D. B. (2002). Overlooked and underserved: Immigrant students in U.S. secondary schools. *Harvard Educational Review, 72*, 402–406.

Reed, B. G., Newman, P. A., Suarez, Z. E., & Lewis, E. A. (1997). Interpersonal practice beyond diversity and toward social justice: The importance of critical consciousness. In C. D. Garvin & B. A. Seabury (Eds.), *Interpersonal practice in social work: Promoting competence and social injustice* (pp. 44–77). Boston: Allyn & Bacon.

Richardson, L. A. (2001). Seeking and obtaining mental health services: What do parents expect? *Archives of Psychiatric Nursing, 15*, 223–231.

Schriver, J. M. (2001). *Human behavior and the social environment: Shifting paradigms in essential knowledge for social work practice.* Boston: Allyn & Bacon.

Stein, B. D., Kataoka, S., Jaycox, L. H., Wong, M., Fink, A., Escudero, P., et al. (2002). Theoretical basis and program design of a school-based mental health intervention for traumatized immigrant children: A collaborative research partnership. *Journal of Behavioral Health Services and Research, 29*, 318–326.

Takeuchi, D. T., Mokuau, N., & Chun, C. A. (1992). Mental health services for Asian Americans and Pacific Islanders. *Journal of Mental Health Administration, 19*, 237–245.

Uba, L. (1982). Meeting the mental health needs of Asian Americans: Mainstream or segregated services. *Professional Psychology, 13*, 215–221.

U.S. Department of Health and Human Services. (1994). *Community health advisors: Models, research, and practice, public health services.* Atlanta, GA: Centers for Disease Control and Prevention.

U.S. Department of Health and Human Services. (2001). *Mental health: Culture, race, and ethnicity—A supplement to mental health: A report of the surgeon general.* Rockville, MD: U.S. Department of Health and Human Services, Substance Abuse and Mental Health Services Administration, Center for Mental Health Services.

Williams, F. C., & Butler, S. K. (2003). Concerns of newly arrived immigrant students: Implications for school counselors. *ASCA, 7,* 9–14.

Yeh, M., Eastman, K., & Cheung, M. K. (1994). Children and adolescents in community health centers: Does the ethnicity or the language of the therapist matter? *Journal of Community Psychology, 22,* 153–163.

Zane, N., & Yeh, M. (2002). The use of culturally based variables in assessment: Studies on loss of face. In K. S. Kurasaki & S. Okazaki (Eds.), *Asian American mental health: Assessment theories and methods* (pp. 123–138). New York: Kluwer Academic/Plenum.

Building Relationships Between Diverse Families and School Personnel

Danielle C. Swick ▪ Darlene M. Head-Reeves ▪ Oscar A. Barbarin

Getting Started

Addressing the needs of students from diverse backgrounds is one of the most important challenges facing school personnel in the 21st century. The racial, ethnic, and cultural landscape of the school-age population in the United States is shifting dramatically. In 2000, nonwhite students made up nearly 40% of the public school population, an increase of 17% from 1972 (National Center for Education Statistics, 2002). The changing composition of American schools creates a critical need for school mental health workers to be sensitive to issues of ethnic diversity and to be competent in providing effective and culturally relevant mental health services to students and their families (Juntunen, Atkinson, & Tierney, 2003; Locke, 2003).

Strong and enduring relationships with students and their families are required to support learning and development of an increasingly diverse student population. At the heart of such a relationship must be genuine interest in the child, an atmosphere conducive to joint problem solving, and a commitment to school–home collaboration. Such collaborative efforts on the part of school mental health workers can lead to partnerships with families that are based on mutual respect and trust. From such relationships flow a wide range of positive benefits for students, including higher grades and test scores, increased school attendance, and greater school engagement (Henderson & Mapp, 2002). However, school mental health workers face numerous barriers in establishing and maintaining effective partnerships with diverse families, including logistical difficulties in connecting with families, a mismatch between values adopted by the school staff and those espoused by families, and the stigma associated with seeking and receiving mental health services (Boethel, 2003). This chapter will illuminate strategies that school mental health personnel can use in building relationships with diverse students and their families to promote students' optimal development and achievement. The strategies are based on empirical research as well as on theory and anecdotal reports arising from practical experience.

What We Know

A growing body of empirical and anecdotal evidence from diverse fields of study suggests that there is a set of fundamental elements that characterize relationship building and effective partnerships between families and schools. Research on issues ranging from schoolwide reform, early intervention, and special education to parental involvement and family-school-community partnerships highlights several elements of successful partnerships, including (a) trust and mutual respect between school personnel and families, (b) a family-centered focus, (c) an emphasis on empowerment and shared decision making, and (d) a commitment to collaboration (see Table 77.1 for an overview of relevant research).

Several schoolwide reforms, such as the Comer School Development Program, School of the 21st Century, Comer-Zigler Initiative, and the National Network of Partnership Schools have as the centerpiece of their intervention an effort to connect with and involve families meaningfully in the education of their children (Epstein & Hollifield, 1996; Finn-Stevenson, Desimone, & Chung, 1998; Finn-Stevenson & Stern, 1997; Haynes, 2003; Haynes, Comer, & Hamilton-Lee, 1998).

Table 77.1 Select Research on Building Relationships With Diverse Families

Study/Program	Description	Relevant Findings
Boethel, M. (2003). *Diversity: School, family, and community connections*	Synthesis of 64 studies that examine the relationship between diversity and various educational issues	Most families have high aspirations for their children's school success and are actively involved in their children's schooling. Multiple contextual and logistical barriers impede parent involvement.
Comer School Development Program (SDP)	A comprehensive, school-based program designed to support all aspects of children's development, utilizing resources from schools, families, and communities.	Students have shown significant gains in standardized test scores, school competence, behavior, and school attendance.
Comer-Zigler (CoZi) Initiative	A program that combines components of the Comer School Development Program and the School of the 21st Century model	Pilot studies have indicated this model is positively associated with higher levels of academic achievement and improved school climate.
Dunst, C. J. (2002). "Family-centered practices: Birth through high school"	Reviews research that investigates family-centered school practices	There is a large discrepancy between purported and actual family-centered school practices.
Henderson, A. T., & Mapp, K. L. (2002). *A new wave of evidence: The impact of school, family, and community connections on student achievement*	Review of 51 studies that examine the relationship between parent involvement and student achievement.	Increased involvement is related to better school outcomes. Parent involvement programs effective in connecting with families encourage involvement, are welcoming, address specific parent needs, and are aware of and respect cultural and class differences.
National Network of Partnership Schools	A program to promote ongoing collaborations among schools, families, and the community	Students have shown improvements in standardized test scores, attendance records, and classroom behavior.
School of the 21st Century (21C)	A community-based model that provides all-day, year-round child care and family support services in schools in order to promote the healthy development of children from birth to age 12	Students have shown improvements in standardized test scores, parents have experienced less stress and spend less money on child care, and schools report a decrease in school vandalism, increased parental involvement, and an improved school climate

Often they attribute the success they attain in raising student achievement in no small measure to building effective relations among diverse families, the schools, and their communities. There is ample evidence documenting the link of effective partnerships between parents, school personnel, and community members to improved school success for students (Finn-Stevenson et al., 1998; Haynes, Emmons, & Woodruff, 1998; Sanders, 1996). A common feature of the programs most successful in creating this sense of partnership is strong trust and mutual respect between school staff and the family. Building trust and mutual respect begins with creating a welcoming environment in schools, communicating the desire to be responsive to addressing specific family needs, and acknowledging cultural and class differences. This is just a starting point. Successful schools go further by expanding and institutionalizing a role for parents in school governance, encouraging parent involvement, and having shared decision making as a common value and standard operating procedure.

Another desirable quality of forming effective partnerships between families and schools that is examined in early intervention and special education literature is an emphasis on family-centered practices (Dunst, 2002). Family-centered services respond to family priorities, empower families, employ a holistic or ecological approach to services, and demonstrate insight and sensitivity to families (Harbin, McWilliam, & Gallagher, 2000; Shonkoff & Phillips, 2000). Although there is a pressing need for a larger evidence base that will advance our knowledge of the implementation and effectiveness of family-centered practices, many researchers and mental health professionals agree that a family-centered focus is critical to engaging families (Dunst, 2002; Harbin et al., 2000; Shonkoff & Phillips, 2000).

A large body of literature has focused on parental involvement and family-school-community partnerships in relation to children's school success. Parental involvement and family-school-community partnerships have been linked to a host of positive outcomes for students including increased school attendance, higher grades and test scores, higher graduation rates, and improved behavior (Henderson & Mapp, 2002). Schools that are successful in promoting parental involvement start by creating a welcoming environment, building trust, and respecting families' needs and concerns (Henderson & Mapp, 2002; Hoover-Dempsey & Sandler, 1997; McKenna, Roberts, & Woodfin, 2003). Although there is large body of research on parental involvement generally, much of this success has been demonstrated with economically advantaged families. There is a need for additional case examples and empirical studies documenting strategies to involve and build relationships with low-income and ethnic minority children and families (Boethel, 2003; Jordan, Orozco, & Averett, 2001). Additionally, parent involvement literature, in general, is fraught with methodological limitations including few experimental and quasi-experimental studies, small sample sizes, and inconsistent definitions and measurement of key constructs such as partnership, parent involvement, and collaboration (Baker & Soden, 1997; Boethel, 2003; Mattingly, Prislin, McKenzie, Rodriquez, & Kayzar, 2002). However, Epstein and colleagues (2000) take a more positive stance on the state of research, noting that parent involvement has been studied extensively over the past three decades and that the research offers valuable insights into the positive effects of family-school-community partnerships on children's school success.

As discussed above, effective strategies for building relationships between diverse families and school personnel have been examined in multiple disciplines using a variety of methodologies. Despite the limitations in the research, this broad body of literature offers promising practices for school mental health workers to use. (See Section 9 for more information about family intervention and parental involvement.)

What We Can Do

A limited but growing empirical research base as well as theory and reports arising from practical experience all suggest that trust, respect, and a spirit of true collaboration are the hallmarks of building and maintaining effective relationships between school mental health personnel and diverse families (Adams & Christenson, 2000; Comer, Haynes, Joyner, & Ben-Avie, 1996; Epstein, 2001; Goddard, Tschannen-Moran, & Hoy, 2001). The following guidelines provide practical recommendations for school mental health personnel in their efforts to build collaborative partnerships with students and their families.

Begin Building Relationships Before Problems Arise

Long before there are problems, school-based professionals must build a connection to the cultural groups represented in the school population and make them feel that they are an integral part of the school community. A family may be more receptive to working together if the beginnings of the relationship are formed in the context of positive contacts with them and favorable comments about the child (Epstein et al., 2002). The relationship is already in jeopardy if the first contact regards a problem situation.

Recommendations

- Reach out to parents and help them to feel welcomed and wanted at the school (Henderson & Mapp, 2002; Hoover-Dempsey & Sandler, 1997, McKenna et al., 2003).
  - Work with other school personnel to create or designate a space in the school for families and parents.
  - Facilitate relationships between school staff and parents.
- Recruit members of the cultural community into the formal governance and informal structures of the school and use information to energize parental response (Comer et al., 1996; Epstein, 2001).
  - Develop, promote, and sustain active parent organizations, for example, PTA, PTO, and advisory councils.
  - Use diverse media and make multiple efforts to inform parents about issues at school and elsewhere that will affect children.
  - Solicit parents' opinions and advice before making important decisions.
  - Provide information to parents about local elections concerning public schools.
- Develop programs that bring families into the school for positive events (Epstein et al., 2002).
  - Provide numerous and varied opportunities for families to visit the school and interact with teachers and other families, such as potluck dinners, school productions, and other school-based events.
- Acknowledge parents and caregivers as experts about their children and convey the willingness to learn what parents have to teach the school about how best to serve their children.
  - Encourage parents to disclose information about their child and ideas for how to address his or her difficulty.

Prepare for the Initial Meeting With the Student and His or Her Family

Before making the initial contact with a family, it is important to take several issues into consideration that may hinder building a collaborative relationship. This is an important time to reflect on your attitudes, beliefs, and expectations about the causes, sources, and solutions to the problem. Gaps in your knowledge of the culture and the family's situation may lead to inaccurate assumptions and inappropriate intervention (Lockwood & Secada, 1999; McKenna et al., 2003). It is also an important time to anticipate some issues that may arise for the family during the first meeting, including the family's past experiences with school and mental health professionals (Casas, Furlong, & Ruiz de Esparza, 2003, Whaley, 2001), effects of a class-based power differential between diverse families and schools (Delpit, 1995; Lareau & Horvat, 1999; Smrekar & Cohen-Vogel, 2001), and logistical impediments such as transportation and language barriers (Boethel, 2003; Starkey & Klein, 2000). The following steps should be taken before you meet with a family for the first time:

- Consider your own beliefs about the student, his family, his cultural background, and causes of his difficulty. Biases, both positive and negative, can be a source of misunderstanding and affect how you interact with the student and his family (Lockwood & Secada, 1999).
  - Evaluate your personal experiences with individuals from this culture and consider how those experiences may influence the relationship with the student and his family.
- Adopt a stance of open inquiry as you seek to learn about the culture and the family's specific situation in the community and the family as your guide (Casas et al., 2003; McKenna et al., 2003).
  - Develop personal networks within that ethnic community to learn about the cultural norms.
  - Read books, newspapers, or magazines for information about that cultural group.
  - Attend cultural events in that community.
- Consider how the family might view mental health issues. Individuals from different cultures may be hesitant to meet with a mental health worker for a variety of reasons (Holcomb-McCoy, 2003; Webb, 2001).
  - In your interactions with the student, his family, and other members of the commu-

nity, assess whether there is a stigma attached to seeking help from a mental health professional and disclosing private family affairs to professionals and prepare to address this concern if necessary.

- In your interactions with the family, ascertain whether family members have had limited or negative experiences with the school or are unfamiliar with what mental health professionals do and provide information and alternative perspectives about school mental health personnel.
- Consider the logistics of the first meeting (Boethel, 2003; Starkey & Klein, 2000).
  - Does transportation pose a problem for the family? If so, provide suggestions for alternative arrangements such as public transportation or meeting at a central location.
  - Is child care needed for other children in the family? If so, research resources in the school or community to address this need.
  - Should provisions be made for an interpreter? If so, determine what options are available, such as other family members, family friends, or others in the community who would be willing to serve in this role and are acceptable to the family.

Forge a Strong, Enduring Relationship With the Student's Family

At this point, you have done some background planning, and by virtue of contacts with the family or someone who knows the family, you are prepared to forge a stronger alliance with this family to work jointly on resolving the situation that may interfere with the child's adjustment to school. The following are rules of thumb to consider in this important first connection between the mental health worker and the student's family:

- Initiate contact with the family as soon as possible after referral is made.
- Concentrate on the family unit rather than the child alone (Dunst, 2002; Harbin et al., 2000).
  - Seek information about the child's family: the primary caregivers, other relatives who may be actively involved in the child's life, and siblings.
  - Probe for information about family members' goals and concerns for themselves in addition to their concerns and goals for their child.

- Determine whether extended family can be involved in treatment planning.
- Focus on strengths without minimizing problems (Patrikakou & Weissberg, 2000; Shonkoff & Phillips, 2000).
  - Where possible, consider problems in terms of strengths that have gone awry!
  - Reframe problems in terms of strengths possessed or strengths to be developed.
  - Acknowledge that family members have the best interest of the child in mind and are genuinely invested in helping the child succeed.
  - Attribute positive motives to the parents' actions and behaviors on behalf of their child.
  - Determine what interests, strengths, and talents family members possess that might be useful in helping your student overcome his difficulties.
- Identify needs and concerns of the family (Holcomb-McCoy, 2003).
  - Determine what the family's priorities are for addressing the child's needs and consider how to incorporate these goals into treatment planning.
  - Explore the role parents see for themselves and for the school in the child's education. Inquire about obstacles the family faces in carrying out its role and problem-solve with the family to overcome the obstacles.
- Be open and honest in your interactions with the family (Harbin et al., 2000; Shonkoff & Phillips, 2000).
  - Clearly articulate your goals and expectations for the student and the family.
  - Openly share your perspective about the role of families in supporting children's schooling.
  - Be frank about your limitations and areas in which you lack expertise.
  - Inform the family of your boundaries and limits.

Maintain a Lasting Relationship Built on Trust, Honesty, and Mutual Respect

Recognize that parents value clear regular communication, expressions of your interest and concern for them, a strong empathic connection with the child, and a sense that you view them as knowledgeable, competent partners in responding to the needs of their children. To increase the likelihood of success and positive outcomes for your student, it is important to continue to build and maintain a trustful and respectful relationship with your student and his or her family. Your ongoing interactions with the family should be guided by the information you have gathered from your initial efforts at collaboration as well as a desire to continue a true partnership.

Recommendations:

- Be dependable, available, and responsive (Balfour & Balfour, 2001).
    - Return phone calls, respond to requests, and provide follow-up information as needed in a timely manner.
- Reinforce what the family is doing well.
    - Provide constructive feedback on the family's efforts to support their child.
- Remind yourself that family members are experts about the child.
    - Invite ideas and assistance from the family in treatment planning.
- Maintain ongoing communication with the family (Henderson & Berla, 1994).
    - Use a variety of strategies for keeping in touch with the family, such as notes, calls, visits, invitations to come to school, and e-mail where available.
- Be an advocate for the family at the school and in the larger community (Comer et al., 1996).
    - Act as a liaison between the family and other school personnel.
    - Make referrals for services as needed.
    - Provide direct assistance in meeting families' needs with school and community resources.
- Above all, be yourself—a genuine person with foibles who gives generously of self.

Tools and Practice Examples

The following case example incorporates the evidence-based guidelines for intervention discussed above:

Claudia Gomez is a 12-year-old sixth grader and the oldest of four children in a family of Mexican farmworkers who immigrated 5 years ago. She was referred to the school social worker, Ms. Slate, for failing grades, apparently lagging interest in schoolwork, and poor attendance. Claudia's teacher told Ms. Slate that Claudia was receiving

D's in several subject areas and would often be absent from school for weeks at a time. Although Claudia seemed very bright and sociable, her lack of attendance made it impossible to keep up with her schoolwork. Since the family did not have a working telephone number, her teacher had sent notes home with Claudia asking the parents to come in to discuss concerns about Claudia's grades and attendance. There was no response from the home. Even when the notes indicated a specific time, her parents did not show up for any of the scheduled conferences. At this point, her teacher was frustrated with what she saw as lack of interest on the part of Claudia's parents and therefore approached Ms. Slate for guidance.

Although there was a large Mexican population at this elementary school, Ms. Slate had little experience working with Latino families because she was relatively new to the school. Therefore, Ms. Slate found it helpful to talk to other Mexican American mothers who attended school events and who were active in the local community. Additionally, Ms. Slate realized she had a preconceived notion that Hispanic families were respectful of teachers but uninvolved in their children's education. Ms. Slate thought critically about how this expectation might influence her attempts to work with the Gomez family.

During a home visit with Claudia's mother, Ms. Slate introduced herself as the school social worker and conveyed her enthusiasm about getting to know Claudia and her family. She began the conversation with a focus on how smart Claudia was and how much she benefited when she was at school. Ms. Slate invited Mrs. Gomez to school so that they could have a conversation with the teacher about Claudia's progress and about how best to support her learning. Mrs. Gomez was hesitant and noncommittal but said that she would ask a family member to drive her to school. Mrs. Gomez did come one day, accompanied by Claudia's two preschool-age siblings, her aunt, and a family friend who drove. Realizing that none of the adults were very comfortable in English, Ms. Slate asked a bilingual teacher aide to interpret.

During the initial meeting with Claudia's family, Ms. Slate asked who lived at home with Claudia, if the family had any previous experience with mental health services, and what they saw as Claudia's strengths. Her mother expressed that she knew Claudia was very smart and so she could not understand why Claudia was getting such poor grades. She indicated that family responsibilities were very important to her family. Claudia's father was often on the road picking crops, but Mrs. Gomez and the children remained in one place because that was better for the family. She added that because she was an only child, she had to travel to Mexico several times during the year to care for her mother, who was gravely ill. At those times, Claudia was needed at home to cook and care for the younger children. It became clear that Claudia's responsibilities at home and her anxiety about her grandmother played a major role in her school performance. Ms. Slate asked if there were other family members who could care for Claudia and her siblings when Mrs. Gomez was in Mexico and was told that an aunt could do so sometimes, but not always. Ms. Slate suggested that perhaps the school could provide Claudia with a packet of homework that would allow her to keep up with her studies during absences.

Ms. Slate talked with the teacher about the family's situation and suggested strategies to address Claudia's grades and attendance. She encouraged the teacher to work closely with Claudia's family concerning her education.

Ms. Slate nurtured the relationship with Claudia's family by sending follow-up letters and making occasional visits. She let the family know she was available if they had any concerns about Claudia. Additionally, if Ms. Slate heard about something positive that Claudia did in the classroom (e.g., if she participated in classroom discussions or helped another child with an assignment), she mentioned it to the family. Through Ms. Slate's genuine efforts to engage and collaborate with Claudia's family, Claudia's grades and school attendance improved.

Resources

Books

Delpit, L. (1995). *Other people's children: Cultural conflict in the classroom.* New York: New Press.

Epstein, J. L., Sanders, M. G., Simon, B. S., Salinas, K. C., Jansorn, N. R., & Van Voorhis, F. L. (2002). *School, family, and community partnerships: Your handbook for action* (2nd ed.). Thousand Oaks, CA: Corwin.

Neuman, R. L. (1998). *Building relationships with parents and families in school-age programs.* Nashville, TN: School-Age Notes.

Pope-Davis, D. B., Coleman, H. L. K., Liu, W. M., & Toporek, R. L. (Eds.). (2003). *Handbook of multicultural competencies in counseling and psychology.* Thousand Oaks, CA: Sage.

Sue, D. W., Carter, R. T., Casa, J. M., Fouad, J. M., Ivey, A. E., Jensen, M., et al. (1998). *Multicultural counseling competencies: Individual and organizational development.* Thousand Oaks, CA: Sage.

Webb, N. B. (2001). *Culturally diverse parent-child and family relationships.* New York: Columbia University Press.

Web Sites

Comer School Development Program (SDP): http://info.med.yale.edu/comer/

School of the 21st Century (21C): http://www.yale.edu/21c

Comer-Zigler (CoZi) Initiative: http://www.yale.edu/21C/affiliated.html

National Network of Partnership Schools: http://www.csos.jhu.edu/p2000/default.htm

Achieving the Goals: Goal 8, Parental Involvement and Participation, U.S. Department of Education: http://www.ed.gov/pubs/AchGoal8/index.html

Working With Hispanic Families: National Center for Family Literacy: http://www.famlit.org/ProgramsandInitiatives/HFLI/hfli_working.cf

The Northwest Regional Educational Laboratory: http://www.nwrel.org/cfc/frc/index.html

The Southwest Educational Development Laboratory: http//www.sedl.org/

Key Points to Remember

The following are key points for school mental health professionals to remember about building relationships with diverse families:

- Build partnerships with families on a foundation of mutual respect and trust.
- Be open to examining your biases and preconceived notions about cultures different from your own.
- Be aware of logistical barriers (e.g., lack of transportation or child care) that might prevent families from keeping scheduled appointments.
- Do not assume that your concerns about the child are the same as the family's concerns
- Recognize that every family has strengths, and use these as building blocks.
- Acknowledge that the family has the best interest of the child in mind and genuinely wants him or her to succeed.

References

Adams, K. S., & Christenson, S. L. (2000). Trust and the family-school relationship: Examination of parent-teacher differences in elementary and secondary grades. *Journal of School Psychology, 38*(5), 477–497.

Baker, A. J. L., & Soden, L. M. (1998). *The challenges of parent involvement research* (Report No. EDO-UD-98-4). New York: ERIC Clearinghouse on Urban Education. (ERIC Document Reproduction Service No. ED419030)

Barbour, C., & Barbour, N. H. (2001). *Families, schools, and communities: Building partnerships for educating children.* Upper Saddle River, NJ: Merrill Prentice Hall.

Boethel, M. (2003). *Diversity: School, family, and community connections: Annual synthesis.* Retrieved April 1, 2004, from the Southwest Educational Development Laboratory Web site: http://www.sedl.org/connections/resources/diversity-synthesis.pdf

Casas, J. M., Furlong, M. J., & Ruiz De Esparza, C. (2003). Increasing Hispanic parent participation in schools: The role of the counselor. In P. B. Pederson & J. C. Carey (Eds.), *Multicultural counseling in schools: A practical handbook* (2nd ed., pp. 105–130). Boston: Pearson Education.

Cauce, A. M., Comer, J. P., & Schwartz, D. (1987). Long-term effects of a systems oriented school prevention program. *American Journal of Orthopsychiatry, 57,* 127–131.

Comer, J. P., Haynes, N. M., Joyner E. T., & Ben-Avie, M. (Eds.). (1996). *Rallying the whole village: The Comer process of reforming education.* New York: Teachers College Press.

Delpit, L. (1995). *Other people's children: Cultural conflict in the classroom.* New York: New Press.

Dunst, C. J. (2002). Family-centered practices: Birth through high school. *Journal of Special Education, 36*(3), 139–147.

Epstein, J. L. (2001). *School, family, and community partnerships: Preparing educators and improving schools.* Boulder, CO: Westview.

Epstein, J. L., & Hollifield, J. H. (1996). Title I and school-family-community partnerships: Using research to realize the potential. *Journal of Education for Students Placed at Risk, 1*(3), 263–278.

Epstein, J. L., Sanders, M. G., Simon, B. S., Salinas, K. C., Jansorn, N. R., & Van Voorhis, F. L. (2002). *School, family, and community partnerships: Your handbook for action* (2nd ed.). Thousand Oaks, CA: Corwin.

Finn-Stevenson, M., Desimone, L., & Chung, A. (1998). Linking child care and support services with the school: Pilot evaluation of the Schools of the 21st Century. *Children and Youth Services Review, 20*(3), 177–205.

Finn-Stevenson, M., & Stern, B. M. (1997). Integrating early-childhood and family-support services with a school improvement process: The Comer-Zigler initiative. *Elementary School Journal, 98*(1), 51–66.

Goddard, R. D., Tschannen-Moran, M., & Hoy, W. (2001). A multilevel examination of the distribution and effects of teacher trust in students and parents in urban elementary schools. *Elementary School Journal, 102,* 3–17.

Harbin, G. L., McWilliam, R. A., & Gallagher, J. J. (2000). Services for young children and their families. In J. P. Shonkoff & S. J. Meisels, *Handbook of early childhood intervention* (2nd ed., pp. 387–415). New York: Cambridge University Press.

Haynes, N. M. (2003). Educating for social, emotional, and academic development: The Comer School Development Program. In M. J. Elias, H. Arnold, & C. S. Hussey (Eds.), *EQ + IQ = Best leadership practices for caring and successful schools* (pp. 109–123). Thousand Oaks, CA: Corwin.

Haynes, N. M., Comer, J. P., & Hamilton-Lee, M. (1988). The School Development Program: A model for school improvement. *Journal of Negro Education, 57,* 11–21.

Haynes, N. M., Emmons, C. L., & Woodruff, D. W. (1998). School Development Program effects: Linking implementation to outcomes. *Journal of Education for Students Placed at Risk, 3*(1), 71–85.

Henderson, A. T., & Berla, N. (1994). *A new generation of evidence: The family is critical to student achievement.* Washington, DC: Center for Law and Education.

Henderson, A. T., & Mapp, K. L. (2002). *A new wave of evidence: The impact of school, family and community connections on student achievement.* Retrieved April 1, 2004, from the Southwest Educational Development Laboratory Web site: http://www.sedl.org/connections/resources/evidence.pdf

Holcomb-McCoy, C. C. (2003). Multicultural competence in school settings. In D. B. Pope-Davis, H. L. K. Coleman, W. M. Liu, & R. L. Toporek (Eds.), *Handbook of multicultural competencies in counseling and psychology* (pp. 406–419). Thousand Oaks, CA: Sage.

Hoover-Dempsey, K. V., & Sandler, H. M. (1997). Why do parents become involved in their children's education? *Review of Educational Research, 67*(1), 3–42.

Jordan, C., Orozco, E., & Averett, A. (2001). *Emerging issues in school, family, and community connections.* Retrieved April 1, 2004, from the Southwest Educational Development Laboratory Web site: http://www.sedl.org/connections/resources/

Juntunen, C. L., Atkinson, D. R., & Tierney, G. (2003). School counselors and school psychologists as school-home-community liaison in ethnically diverse schools. In P. B. Pederson & J. C. Carey (Eds.), *Multicultural counseling in schools: A practical handbook* (2nd ed., pp. 149–168). Boston: Pearson Education.

Lareau, A., & Horvat, E. M. (1999). Moments of social inclusion and exclusion: Race, class, and cultural capital in family-school relationships. *Sociology of Education, 72,* 37–53.

Locke, D. C. (2003). Improving the multicultural competence of educators. In P. B. Pederson & J. C. Carey (Eds.), *Multicultural counseling in schools: A practical handbook* (2nd ed., pp. 171–189). Boston: Pearson Education.

Lockwood, A. T., & Secada, W. G. (1999). *Transforming education for Hispanic youth: Exemplary practices, programs, and schools.* Retrieved June 1, 2004, from George Washington University, National Clearinghouse for Bilingual Education Web site: http://www.ncela.gwu.edu/pubs/resources/hispanicyouth/hdp.pdf

Mattingly, D. J., Prislin, R., McKenzie, T. L., Rodriquez, J. L., & Kayzar, B. (2002). Evaluating evaluations: The case of parent involvement programs. *Review of Educational Research, 72*(4), 549–576.

McKenna, N., Roberts, J., & Woodfin, L. (2003). Working cross-culturally in family-school partnerships. In P. B. Pederson & J. C. Carey (Eds.), *Multicultural counseling in schools: A practical handbook* (2nd ed., pp. 131–148). Boston: Pearson Education.

National Center for Education Statistics (2002). *The condition of education 2002.* Washington, DC: U.S. Department of Education. Office of Educational Research and Improvement, National Center for Education Statistics.

Patrikakou, E. N., & Weissberg, R. P. (2000). Parents' perceptions of teacher outreach and parent involvement in children's education. *Journal of Prevention and Intervention in the Community, 20*(1–2), 103–119.

Sanders, M. G. (1996). Action teams in action: Interviews and observations in three schools in the Baltimore school-family-community partnership program. *Journal of Education for Students Placed at Risk, 1*(3), 249–262.

Shonkoff, J. P., & Phillips, D. A. (2000). *From neurons to neighborhoods: The science of early childhood development.* Washington, DC: National Academy Press.

Smrekar, C., & Cohen-Vogel, L. (2001). The voices of parents: Rethinking the intersection of family and school. *Peabody Journal of Education, 76*(2), 75–101.

Starkey, P., & Klein, A. (2000). Fostering parental support for children's mathematical development: An intervention with Head Start families. *Early Education and Development, 11*(5), 659–680.

Webb, N. B. (2001). Working with culturally diverse children and families. In N. B. Webb (Ed.), *Culturally diverse parent-child and family relationships: A guide for social workers and other practitioners* (pp. 3–28). New York: Columbia University Press.

Whaley, A. L. (2001). Cultural mistrust and mental health services for African Americans: A review and meta-analysis. *Counseling Psychologist, 29*(4), 513–531.

Case Management Intervention With Immigrant and Refugee Students and Families

Rowena Fong ■ Marilyn Armour ■ Noel Busch
Laurie Cook Heffron ■ Anita McClendon

CHAPTER 78

Getting Started

The United States has always been a multicultural society, but refugee and immigrant students are increasing in numbers and creating more complexities. Delgado, Jones, and Rohani (2005, p. 20) report: "Almost 10 percent of all newcomers are under the age of 18 years, compared to the average 28.3 years for U.S. citizens. . . . Since 1990 the number of immigrant families has increased seven times faster than the corresponding number of native-born families. . . . One out of every five youth had one foreign born parent in 1995." Many immigrant and refugee children and youth have to make adjustments that most students in the United States don't confront. Some foreign-born students overcome language and cultural barriers with apparent ease. Many more, however, endure very stressful transitions to the United States (Busch, Fong, Heffron, & McClendon, 2004; Goodman; 2004; Tazi, 2004; Zhou & Bankston, 1998). Difficulties in transition are due to problems that may even include experiences of torture, rape, and abandonment, which carry over into the classroom environments.

School social workers have the challenge of addressing these problems because they interfere with immigrant students' academic learning and performance. In working with immigrant and refugee students, social workers need to manage multiple problems, including those affecting the student personally and those tangential to the students' family because of the interconnectedness between the student and the family. For example, an immigrant or refugee child or youth from a non–English-speaking family is frequently called upon to act as interpreter for the family (Suarez-Orozco & Suarez-Orozco, 2001; Tazi, 2004; Webb 2001). This role often interferes with the student's school functioning because of missed school days. Thus, the school social worker must address the family's needs as they affect the student's academic functioning. Special skills are required to manage the multiple needs of child and family simultaneously. These skills are often found in using case management as an intervention, an evidence-based practice frequently used in mental health settings with other populations. (See Chapters 76 and 78 for more discussion on interacting with immigrant and refugee students and their families.)

What We Know

Children of immigrant families, according to Suarez-Orozco and Suarez-Orozco (2001), "follow many different pathways; they forge complex and multiply determined identities that resist easy generalizations. Some do extremely well in their new country. . . . Others struggle to survive" (pp. 1–2). Though most refugee children may initially adjust with few problems, those whose families have experienced torture either in their home countries or in their migration journeys are likely to manifest symptoms of posttraumatic stress disorder (PTSD) after resettlement. While there are stories of valedictorians and National Merit Finalists among immigrant and refugee children, these should not obscure the reality of other problems of school dropouts, substance abusers, and unwed teen mothers among the undocumented immigrant and refugee youth populations (Suarez-Orozco & Suarez-Orozco, 2001; Zuniga, 2004).

It is important for school social workers to know the difference between immigrants and refugees and to determine which status fits their foreign-born students. Understanding their status can help a social worker to understand the specific stresses that students may be dealing with. Because of the diversity within the two basic groups of immigrants and refugees, each of the different status classifications carries specific stressors that are likely to affect academic performance. Immigrant populations differ from refugees in that they have the option of returning to their home countries, whereas refugees are forced to leave their home countries. Thus an immigrant child or youth with legal documentation has adjustments to make because of struggles with acculturation and (usually) language proficiency, but the student and his or her family can go back to the country of origin and resume normal life. Undocumented immigrant youth, however, have entered the United States with their families without legal documentation. They leave their countries of origin looking for better economic opportunities and living conditions. Most of them encounter some difficulty during transition. Because of their temporary status, fears of exposure and deportation may constantly produce anxiety (Delgado, Jones, & Rohani, 2005; Zuniga, 2004).

Refugees are those children, youth, and families who are forced to leave their countries of origin because they have experienced human rights violations, fear for their lives and safety, and may have experienced torture. Asylees are non-U.S. citizens who "enter the United States either on temporary visas or as undocumented entrants and who request and receive political asylum after arrival" (Foner, 2001, p. 36). For asylees the lengthy period of waiting to find out if they have been granted asylum causes a lot of stress even when the family is living here. Students frequently pick up on the parents' stressors and bring these anxieties into the school environment.

Unaccompanied refugee minors are another category of newcomers that social workers may find in their school settings. These children have come to the United States with their refugee parents, but their parents have been separated or killed in the process of transit. Legal guardians have to be established for these children, who are temporarily parentless, homeless, and rootless. In the case of some unaccompanied refugee minors, they are legally allowed to stay in the United States, but their parents have been deported.

In both immigrant and refugee populations, school social workers may find another foreign-born group of children and youth who are called the 1.5 generation. This group is between the first and second generation. They were born and raised in their home countries or in refugee camps but arrived in the United States when they were still young enough to later forget their native tongue and traditional beliefs and customs. Delgado, Jones, and Rohani (2005) write of these children: "Although potentially able to successfully blend the best of both cultures, not all youth experience this as their reality. . . . Describing his experience of the 1.5 generation, Ryu (1992, p. 50) writes of feeling anchored in neither culture. Though bilingual, he is also 'bi-illiterate,' although bicultural, he also feels biculturally deprived" (p. 52).

These different statuses will inform the school social workers of what kind of difficulties the immigrant and refugee children and youth have endured and are continuing to experience. Dropping out, truancy, language deficiencies, poor social skills, gang involvement, and academic failure may all be indicators of family stressors and difficulties in adjusting to the United States.

What We Can Do

Working with multicultural immigrant and refugee children requires interventions that encompass both the student's school problems and the family's overall adjustment problems. Though several evidence-based interventions have been used with immigrant and refugee children and youth, most focus only on the child and his or her school-related problems. The most commonly used evidence-based interventions are individual and group work with cognitive-behavioral therapy as the primary treatment modality (Congress & Lynn, 1994; Gonzalez-Ramos & Sanchez-Nester, 2001; Kataoka, Stein, Jaycox, Wong, Escudero, Tu, et. al., 2003; Land & Levy, 1992).

Congress and Lynn (1994) used group work in public schools to help immigrant children deal with feelings of loss, depression, and alienation. Kataoka et. al. (2003) established an eight-session cognitive-behavioral therapy (CBT) group for third- through eighth-grade Latino immigrants suffering from trauma-related depression and PTSD. They found that those students who were in the intervention group had significantly greater improvement in PTSD. Though parents and teachers were eligible to receive support services and psychoeducation, there are no results reported, and there is no indication that children and their families were treated simultaneously.

What is needed in working with immigrant

and refugee children and youth in schools is an approach that focuses on the students' problems and the families' stressors simultaneously. The usual pattern in the schools is to offer services only to students, with services to families done outside of the school. In the case of immigrant and refugee students and families, an alternative model using case management services with a school social worker is important to consider because of the complexity and the interrelatedness of the child's and family's problems.

Some case management services have been established in school-based health clinics (Rose & Fatout, 2003) where the school social workers coordinate care from outside social services (Harold & Harold, 1991). School social work and school-based mental health services have focused on evidence-based interventions (Durlak, 2002) with discussions among school psychologists focusing on the need for "more emphasis on public health, prevention, and improving how schools address youngsters who manifest problems" (Adelman & Taylor, 2002, p. 83).

Used in other disciplines such as mental health, disability rehabitation, family welfare, and services with older adults, the case manager has a role in multidisciplinary teams: "a case manager coordinates the team's plan and acts as the liaison between the client, the team, and provider of social services" (Dubois & Miley, 2005, p. 348), and "case management is appropriate when the clients' situation requires multiple services" (Dubois & Miley, 2005, p. 433).

"Case management with individual clients has functions including outreach, assessment from multiple social agencies or departments, case planning, assessing resources, advocacy, monitoring, and evaluation" (Dubois & Miley, 2005, p. 435), and "case management coordinates the social services that children and families receive from multiple social agencies. . . . Multisystem children need services from multiple social agencies or departments" (Rose & Fatout, 2003, p. 158).

School social workers serving immigrant and refugee youth frequently encounter these multisystem students, whose problems belong not only to the student but also to the student's family. Often family services must be involved, and the school social worker has to coordinate with them. School social workers need to handle the immigrant or refugee youth and his or her school problems through Individualized Education Plans (IEPs) and team meetings with counselors, teachers, and other school personnel. This coordination of services is done through using case management skills. Case management is one of several interventions, including art, play, and narrative therapy, that have proved effective when used with immigrant and refugee children and families (Doktor, 1998; Scheinfeld, Wallach, & Langendorf, 1997; Tazi, 2004).

Though case management has been documented as an effective evidence-based practice intervention, its use still needs exploration because the procedure of comparing immigrants to nonimmigrants is very difficult, given the different contexts and special needs of the nonimmigrant population. Case management involving school-age children will necessarily include working with the child, family, ethnic community, and the social service providers.

Tools and Practice Examples

Case management is the "strategy for coordinating services and ensuring the accountability of service providers" (Dubois & Miley, 2005, p. 239). Case management strategies for clients with multiple needs require the social worker to "appraise their needs, identify relevant services, develop comprehensive plans, advocate client's rights to services, and monitor the actual delivery of services" (Dubois & Miley, 2005, p. 239).

These five strategies are used in case management: (1) Appraise client needs; (2) identify relevant services; (3) develop comprehensive plans; (4) advocate client's rights to services; and (5) monitor the actual delivery of services.

Appraising Needs

Appraising the needs of immigrant and refugee children and youth demands that the school social worker approach the assessment process from macro to micro levels of practice. The "Person-in-Family-in-Community" Model (Fong, 1997) helps school social workers to organize their approach and the actual questions to be used with students. The assumption is that immigrant or refugee students are not alone and are part of their community as well as their family; thus the school social worker must ask questions at the macro societal level and the mezzo family level. To find out what the student needs may also require questions about the student's home country and how those needs would manifest themselves there.

Identifying Relevant Services

To identify relevant services for immigrant and refugee students and families Chow (2001) suggests organizational assessment practice principles formulated under a "User Profile" and a "Service Profile" (p. 216). The user profile is to assess who will be using the services. The user can be a child or a family system. The suggested questions to ask are:

Who will be using the services?
What is their ethnic background?
What is their immigration history? When did they arrive in the United States?
What is their family background?
What is the family structure?
What is their citizenship status?
What is their socioeconomic background?
Are there family members who are literate in their language?
Are there family members literate in English?
Will they need an interpreter? If so, what dialect?

The service profile is to assess what kinds of services will be relevant and used by that client population, based on the information received in the user profile. Questions to ask are:

What services currently exist in the community in working with this ethnic population?
Do linguistically diverse staff members offer these services? (I.e., will the services offer the correct language dialect for the client?)
Are the staff members immigrants or refugees themselves?
Are the agencies offering the range of pre-resettlement and post-resettlement services?
Are the services easily accessible by public transportation?
Are the services offered at times when the immigrants or refugees can access them?
Is the philosophy of the agency's offering of services congruent with societal values stressed in the home countries of the immigrants and refugees?
Are there barriers (e.g., financial limitations or eligibility requirements) to accessing these services?

Developing Comprehensive Plans

Because the immigrant and refugee student is an integral part of the family system, school social workers may have to not only develop student

IEPs but also individualized family service plans (IFSP).

Advocating Clients' Rights to Services

Immigrant and refugee students are a disempowered group with many needs. Thus it is important for a school social worker to include in his or her management of the case a strong advocacy tendency toward finding the services and resources to meet these needs.

Monitoring the Actual Delivery of Services

Important in this part of the case management skills is to have skills to follow up on the actual implementation of the treatment plans (IEPs and IFSP) and the delivery of services recommended. To make sure that the treatment plans are followed and the services are actually delivered the school social worker has to carefully review the plans with an interpreter who speaks the correct language dialect.

Case Example

The A family, consisting of two parents and three sons ages 14, 16, and 19, arrived in the United States in 2003 as political refugees from Eastern Europe. There the family was persecuted because of their ethnic identity; they fled their home during a war. After experiencing traumatic incidents of kidnapping and torture, they lived in bombed-out homes before taking refuge in a camp for dislocated persons.

The family has had several difficulties in adjusting to the school system in the United States. First, it had been years since the children attended school because of the conflict in their country of origin, and all arrived without documentation of grade level. The oldest son was encouraged to find work, and the younger children were placed in Grade 9. They were placed in ESL classes, which were primarily in Spanish-English, despite the fact that neither child spoke Spanish or English upon arrival.

Class scheduling presented additional problems. For example, the middle son, whose written name resembled a Hispanic name, was placed in Spanish 3. When the school counselor was contacted to discuss this situation, she suggested placing him in a flower-arranging course. It was difficult for the counselor to understand why neither scenario would be in the best interest of the student.

Absences and school suspension proved obstacles to this family, as they do with many refugee families. Refugees are often away from school for various reasons, such as initial medical checkups. Likewise, the A family children were often needed as interpreters during food stamp interviews, medical appointments, and immigration and documentation procedures. Not fully understanding the requirement of written parental permission, both students encountered difficulties with unexcused absences. Subsequently, Mrs. A missed parent–teacher conferences because of miscommunications and the language barrier. One child was also suspended for fighting with another student who insulted Mrs. A. The student explained that in his country of origin, these sorts of verbal attacks are incredibly hostile and provoking. The student did not understand why he was punished for defending his mother.

Application

Step One: Appraise the Needs

Because the boys have not been in school for years, accurate grade levels need to be determined. And since they come from Eastern Europe, it is highly unlikely that Spanish would be a language of familiarity or choice. Language ability should be assessed, and an interpreter of the appropriate language background should be located. An assessment of the boys' strengths and interests needs to be done in order to avoid misplacement into courses neither appropriate nor of interest to the boys.

An assessment of the family's immediate needs would help explain the boys' multiple absences. The family does not seem to understand the American school system practices; case management should focus on their needs simultaneously with the needs of the boys in school.

Step Two: Identify Relevant Services

The services of an interpreter speaking the appropriate language dialect is very important because placing the boys in Spanish-speaking classes is not appropriate. The interpreter should work with the school social worker who will case manage

assessments for the boys in the areas of language ability, strengths and vocational interests, and appropriate course selections. Once the family's needs are determined, the school social worker should contact refugee resettlement agencies to see which services are available, particularly the use of appropriate interpreters.

Step Three: Develop Comprehensive Plans

The school social worker should be developing both IEPs and IFSP for these refugee students and their family. The school social worker should case manage both plans. With regard to extra curricular opportunities, both students have a keen interest in sports, especially basketball, soccer, and swimming. However, their grades have not been adequate to allow participation on school teams. Coaches have tried to recruit them for soccer and basketball and provide incentive to improve their grades, but this has been unsuccessful. An IEP plan is needed to incorporate their athletic interests as incentives to motivate their interest in learning the English language and in passing their courses.

Step Four: Advocate Client's Right to Services

School social workers should lobby their principals to develop services for the growing immigrant and refugee student populations. Minimally, every educational institution should have on hand a list of relevant interpreters to be available to the school social workers. By using case management skills, school social workers have a better way to know and advocate for the student and his family in order to get a comprehensive picture of the needs that require attention.

Step Five: Monitor the Actual Delivery of Services

The treatment intervention used with the student and his family consisted mainly of the school social worker's advocacy for the family with the school system, medical and mental health providers, and other refugee social service providers. For example, the school social worker educated school personnel about the refugee experience and other barriers faced by the family. Advocacy also involved helping each family member better understand the workings of the various American systems. The school social worker acted as a case manager in assisting the coordination of medical and mental appointments, including referrals, transportation, language interpretation, and management of medications.

Resources

Bridging Refugee Youth and Children Services (BRYCS) is a national technical assistance project, which broadens the scope of information and collaboration among service providers for refugee children, youth, and families. Access at www.brycs.org

U.S Committee for Refugees and Immigrants: The National Center for Refugee and Immigrant Children, established in 2005, provides pro bono services to unaccompanied children released from detention in the United States. Access at www.refugees.org

The Immigration Legal Resource Center (ILRC) helps abused and abandoned immigrant children in foster care become permanent U.S. residents. The ILRC consults with juvenile court judges, county workers, and children's advocates working on "special immigrant juvenile" petitions. The project promotes humane treatment for all immigrant children both at the regional and national level. Access at www.ilrc.org

Center for Applied Linguistics Cultural Orientation Resource Center: The center's Web site provides information and resources about refugee orientation and training in countries of origin and in the United States, as well as facts about new refugee groups arriving in the United States. Access at www.culturalorientation.net

Points to Remember

Immigrant and refugee children and youth have different migration journeys and statuses which impact their adjustments and acculturation experiences once they arrive into the United States. Those with no legal or with temporary permanent status (undocumented immigrants, those seeking political asylum, unaccompanied refugee minors) have additional stressors of fears of exposure and deportation. Because children and youth bring their problems and anxiety about their families

into the classroom, case management is an important intervention to address both client systems simultaneously. It is very important that school social workers become equipped and use case management skills in working with immigrants and refugee students and their families because of the complexities of their problems and the interrelatedness between the students' problems and those of their families.

References

Adelman, H., & Taylor, L. (2002). School counselors and school reform: new directions. *Professional School Counseling, 5*(4), 83–90.

Busch, N., Fong, R., Heffron, L., & McClendon, A. (2004). *Assessing the needs of refugee and asylee families: A healthy marriage initiative.* Austin: University of Texas Center for Social Work Research.

Chow, J. (2001). Assessment of Asian American/Pacific Islander organizations and communities. In R. Fong & S. Furuto (Eds). *Culturally competent practice: Skills, interventions, and evaluations* (pp. 211–224). Boston, MA: Allyn & Bacon.

Congress, P., & Lynn, M. (1994). Group work programs in public schools: Ethical dilemmas and cultural diversity. *Social Work in Education, 61*(2), 107–114.

Delgado, M., Jones, K., & Rohani, M. (2005). *Social work practice with refugee and immigrant youth.* Boston, MA: Allyn & Bacon.

Dhooper, S., & Moore, S. (2001). *Social work practice with culturally diverse people.* Thousand Oaks, CA: Sage.

Dokter, D. (Ed.). (1998). *Arts therapists, refugees and migrants reaching across borders.* London: Jessica Kingsley.

Dubois, B., & Miley, K. (2005). *Social work: The empowering profession* (5th ed.). Boston, MA: Allyn & Bacon.

Durlak, J. (2002). Evaluating evidence-based inventions in school psychology. *School Psychology Quarterly, 17*(4), 475–482.

Foner, N. (Ed.). (2001). *New immigrants in New York.* New York: Columbia University Press.

Fong, R. (1997). Child welfare practice with Chinese families: Assessment issues for immigrants from the People's Republic of China. *Journal of Family Social Work, 2*(7), 33–47.

Fong, R. (Ed.). (2004*). Culturally competent practice with immigrant and refugee children and families.* New York: Guilford.

Gonzalez-Ramos, G., & Sanchez-Nester, M. (2001). Responding to immigrant children's mental health needs in the schools: Project mi tierra/my country. *Children and Schools, 23*(1), 49–62.

Goodman, M. (2004). Balkan children and families. In R. Fong (Ed.), *Culturally competent practice with immigrant and refugee children and families* (pp. 274–288). New York: Guilford.

Harold, N., & Harold, R. (1991). School-based health clinics: A vehicle for social work intervention. *Social Work in Education, 13*(3), 185–195.

Kataoka, S., Stein, D., Jaycox, H., Wong, M., Escudero, P., Tu, W., et al. (2003). A school-based mental health program for traumatized Latino immigrant children. *Journal of American Academy of Child and Adolescent Psychiatry, 42*(3), 311–318.

Land, H. & Levy, A. (1992). A school-based prevention model for depressed Asian adolescents. *Social Work in Education, 14*(3), 165–176.

Mahoney, A. (2002). Newly arrived West Indian adolescents: A call for a cohesive social welfare response to their adjustment needs. *Journal of Immigrants and Refugee Services, 1*(1), 33–48.

Potocky-Tripody, M. (2002*). Best practices for social work with refugees and immigrants.* New York: Columbia University Press.

Rose, S., & Fatout, M. (2003). *Social work practice with children and adolescents.* Boston, MA: Allyn & Bacon.

Ryu, C. (1992). 1.5 Generation. In J. Lee (Ed.), *Asian Americans* (pp. 50–54). New York: New Press.

Scheinfeld, D., Wallack, L., & Langendorf, T. (1997). *Strengthening refugee families.* Chicago: Lyceum.

Segal, U. (2002). *A framework for immigration: Asians in the United States.* New York: Columbia University Press.

Suazez-Orozco, C., & Suarez-Orozco, M. (2001). *Children of immigration.* Cambridge: Harvard University Press.

Tazi, Z. (2004). Ecuadorian and Colombian children and families. In R. Fong (Ed.), *Culturally competent practice with immigrant and refugee children and families* (pp. 233–252). New York: Guilford.

Webb, N. (Ed.). (2001). *Culturally diverse parent-child and family relationships.* New York: Columbia University Press.

Zhou, M., & Bankston, C. (1998). *Growing up American: How Vietnamese children adapt to the life in the United States.* New York: Russell Sage Foundation.

Zuniga, M. (2004). Latino children and families. In R. Fong (Ed.), *Culturally competent practice with immigrant and refugee children and families* (pp. 183–201). New York: Guilford.

Working With First Nations Students and Families

Dorie J. Gilbert ■ Gail H. Sims

CHAPTER 79

Getting Started

The number of U.S. persons estimated to be partly or fully of American Indian or Alaska Native heritage is approximately 4.1 million, or 1.5% of the U.S. population (Ogunwole, 2002). This group is one of the fastest growing populations because of increased birth rates, decreased infant mortality rates, and a greater willingness to report Native ancestry. Although the terms "American Indian," "Indian," and "Native American" are commonly used, they represent European-imposed, colonized names that serve to oppress indigenous, First Nations, or Native peoples, the original peoples occupying lands now called the United States (Yellow Bird, 2001). In this chapter, except when quoting or describing programs, we use the terms "First Nations" or "Native people" interchangeably to refer to the group as a whole; however, when addressing individuals, the best practice is to refer to Native people by their tribal nation or indigenous affiliation.

First Nations people represent a diverse population across the United States. Most (66%) Native people reside in metropolitan areas rather than on reservations or defined tribal areas, and nationally, there are 550 federally recognized tribes with a multitude of distinct tribal languages (Yellow Bird, 2001). As a group, they have experienced collective disenfranchisement, historical trauma, and contemporary challenges to traditional ways of life (Brave Heart, 1998, 2001a, 2001b). School social workers should be knowledgeable about how risks to the psychosocial well-being of Native people are rooted in impoverished living conditions and traumatic life events associated with oppression and loss of traditional culture and identity.

Within this complex array of distressed living,

a number of mental health, social, and behavioral problems as well as protective factors have been identified among Native children. In comparison to the majority culture, Native children may be at greater risk for a variety of emotional and behavioral disorders and negative psychosocial conditions. Native children enter kindergarten or first grade with relatively low levels of oral language, prereading, and premathematics skills, and less general knowledge (Farkas, 2003). Teachers in both tribal and public schools identified the three most serious problems for Native children as parental alcohol and drug abuse, poverty, and lack of parental involvement (Pavel, 1995). Other problems often cited as affecting Native children include suicidal behavior, substance abuse, violence, and depression; however, these problems must be considered within the context of complicated economic and social-political conditions, namely, the larger issues of past and current oppression, extreme poverty, loss of cultural identity, and historical trauma (Brave Heart, 2001a; Weaver, 2001).

Strengths and protective factors among Native children and adolescents include factors retained from the original culture. These include strong family bonds; emphasis on well-being of the community; wisdom and guidance of elders; cultural practices and traditions that serve to heal, empower, and increase positive ethnic identity; and sovereignty, the formalized self-determination of reservations to make choices (Weaver, 2001).

Many school social workers are in need of guidance in working with Native people; few service providers are specifically trained to work with this population. This chapter should assist school social workers and school-oriented mental health professionals in understanding how best to address the psychosocial needs of indigenous children within the school setting.

What We Know

The literature on effective interventions with First Nations people is growing but far from an established evidence-based guide to practice with Native people, especially with regard to school-based services. Moreover, Yellow Horse and Brave Heart (2004) note that there is a "dichotomy between evidence-based models alleged to be effective with American Indian/Alaska Native populations, and culturally grounded American Indian/Alaska Natives models whose efficacy have not been demonstrated" (p. 35). Rather, nationally recognized evidence-based programs are often not used with Native populations or are used with little or no integration of cultural congruency. On the other hand, culturally-based programs designed and implemented by and for Native people often show great promise but lack the replications needed to become nationally recognized as evidence-based.

The best practices at this time are "promising practices" that draw on conventional or some combination of conventional and cultural practices but are sufficiently flexible to incorporate the cultural norms and values of Native people.

What We Can Do

Counseling and Therapeutic Interventions

Cognitive Behavioral Therapy (CBT) for Child Traumatic Stress (Schinke, Brounstein, & Garner, 2001) addresses trauma-related psychiatric symptoms in children ages 3–18. Randomized control trials showed significantly greater reductions in post-traumatic stress disorder (PTSD), depression, anxiety, problem behaviors, and parental emotional distress. Given its focus on traumatic stress and reported high incidence of trauma among Native adolescents, it may have utility for Native populations (Yellow Horse & Brave Heart, 2004).

Family systems therapy matches well with the Native worldview of family and community collectivism. It sees family as the most important social unit and, at the same time, requires family members to explore ways in which their own behavior may be maladaptive or injurious to other family members (LaFromboise & Dizon, 2003).

Social cognitive therapy incorporates new develop-ments, including the recognition of the impact of culture on personal agency (Bandura, 2002) and incorporation of family systems therapy and constructivist theory (Franklin & Jordan, 2003). In particular, constructivism—which emphasizes the personal realities, individual worldviews, and personal meanings of the client—strengthens the potential success of social cognitive therapy with Native people.

School-Based Programs

Most school-based programs are group-level prevention models and are recommended for use in conjunction with individual and/or family-based interventions. These programs primarily target areas such as drug or alcohol abuse, human immunodeficiency virus (HIV), youth violence, suicide prevention, cultural identity building, and parent–child functioning (Sanchez-Way & Johnson, 2000).

PATHS (Promoting Alternative Thinking Strategies) is an evidence-based classroom program using cognitive skill building to assist schoolchildren with identifying and regulating their emotions toward increasing social functioning and reducing acting out and aggression.

Family and Schools Together (FAST) promotes protective factors to improve family functioning for children ages 4–12 with behavioral and academic problems.

Native Liaison Programs represent a highly promising strategy for working with Native children in school districts. A Native liaison is a person who works directly with the school district and acts a liaison between Native families and the school system. This position can be funded by the Office of Indian Education through a formula grant, available to any school district with at least 10 Indian children who are members of a state-recognized or federally-recognized tribe or who have a parent or grandparent who is a member of a state-recognized or federally-recognized tribe. Though the overall purpose of these grants is to assist Native children in meeting state academic standards, most programs recognize the interrelatedness of students' mental health needs and academic performance.

Culturally Grounded Interventions

Culturally appropriate interventions are grounded in indigenous culture and may include activities such as learning traditional languages and crafts, activities that increase positive cultural identity and/or spiritual practices such as talking circles, dream work, and purification lodges (Sanchez-Way & Johnson, 2000). Yellow Horse and Brave Heart (2004) identified the following culturally congruent programs that are promising practices for Native youths:

Storytelling for Empowerment is a program designed for middle school rural or reservation Native children and Latino youth. The program aims to increase resiliency by decreasing substance abuse and other risk factors such as confused cultural identity and lack of positive parental role model.

Zuni Life Skills Curriculum, used with Zuni Pueblo adolescents, merges social cognitive, life-skills development with peer helping to increase social-emotional competence and decrease suicidal risks. Evaluation results indicate reduced suicide probability and significant reductions in hopelessness.

Historical Trauma and Unresolved Grief Intervention (HTUG) is a psychoeducational group intervention that targets parents, with the overall goal of reducing mental health risk factors and increasing protective factors for Native children (Brave Heart, 1998, 2001a, 2001b).

References, contact information, and suggested readings related to the aforementioned programs are included in the References section.

Steps in Implementing the Best Intervention(s)

This section includes a summary (in steps) of how to implement a promising intervention, social cognitive therapy, available for addressing the problems of Native children in the school system. Though no one intervention can be recommended at the time, we chose to feature social cognitive therapy because of its flexibility and ability to incorporate cultural constructs important to Native people, including:

- flexibility to include others, such as family members and community liaisons, in the helping process;
- flexibility to include culturally-based helping processes, specifically indigenous healing processes where they may apply to the child/adolescent/family;
- a focus on trauma and stress, issues relevant to Native families;
- a recognition of the racial or ethnic, cultural, and socioeconomic diversity of Native families; and

- an emphasis on social construction, that is, on the personal realities, individual worldviews, and personal meanings of the child or family.

Social cognitive therapy, as presented here, involves seven major steps:

- Step 1: *Establish contact with a Native liaison.* Utilize the natural skills of a Native liaison. If your school district does not have a Native liaison, inquire about how to establish such a position at the district level.
- Step 2: *Self and Client Assessment.*
  Self-Assess. Be clear that you understand general differences between Native belief systems and dominant culture belief systems. Engage in self-assessment to be grounded in your own personal and professional values and commitment to culturally competent practice. Note how larger societal oppression affects the lives of children, families, and larger Native communities. This includes understanding the effects of historical trauma and unresolved grief (Brave Heart, 1998, 2001a, 2001b) on Native families.
  Assess cultural orientation of client. Assess the child's or family's comfort level with mainstream interventions. The comfort level of Native people with mainstream counseling practices ranges from acceptance to total rejection in favor of traditional native healing practices, with many falling in the middle of this range. Native people come from diverse backgrounds and cultural orientations; most are bicultural, meaning they are able to operate from both mainstream and Native cultural orientations.
  Assess validity of previous or current diagnoses. Eurocentric assessments can be detrimental and inappropriate for Native populations and usually stem from a practitioner's bias and/or lack of awareness of cultural differences and/or culturally biased measurement and assessment instruments (Gilbert, 2003). Ideally, assessments of Native people should use culture-specific tests, measures of cultural/ethnic identity and acculturative stress/trauma as moderators of standardized tests, thematic apperception types of tests, and, when possible, qualitative and multiple assessment strategies (Gilbert, 2003).
- Step 3: *Research the specific cultural practices and traditions of the tribe or community.* Not all families are affiliated with a tribe or Native community.

However, most have some connection to a larger community, whether through other families or participation in tribal events associated with one or more Native communities. Find out the specific cultural practices and traditions of the tribe or community to which the child or family is most connected. Make note of the resources, coping abilities, and personal meanings the child or family and community bring to the situation. Be aware that with many Native communities, counseling is best accomplished within a family context. Native children tend to acquiesce to elders (including school counselors and personnel), and little will be accomplished without involving the family so that the child has permission from elders to express himself or herself.

- Step 4: *Establish credibility and trustworthiness.* Credibility begins with accomplishing the aforementioned steps. Building trust involves patience and flexibility. In the initial session, begin by engaging in nonthreatening material. Be unobtrusive, make silent observations, show humility, and allow for differences, especially with regard to time. In a traditional Native view, time is flowing and relative, which from a Eurocentric perspective may be viewed as being irresponsible with respect to time. Schedule longer sessions to account for family involvement and allow ample time for narrative expressions, keeping in mind the fluidity of time in traditional Native culture and a tendency for Native clients to "drop by" (Brave Heart, 2001b). You may also consider incorporating humor with Native people, or at least be aware that they may introduce their problem with a joke or a story. A generic suggestion is to incorporate Native themes and values (e.g., love of nature, legends, colors, animals) as a way to broach topics. In addition, the liaison can assist with building the rapport with families. Beginning with a brief, relevant self-disclosure is also helpful as a way to open communication and show relatedness. The idea is to establish a relationship and to provide a model for sharing information, especially when dealing with children.

- Step 5: *Solicit information and develop a definition of the problem from the child's or family's cultural point of view.* Avoid asking for written information. Techniques for soliciting information through narratives, storytelling, and indirect communication styles are relevant for Native communication styles. Mirroring is extremely

important. For one, it provides the practitioner a way of altering his or her interactions based on how the child or family interacts. For example, individual differences in Native communication styles, such as indirect or direct eye contact, should be mirrored rather than basing one's interactions on assumptions or stereotypes.

- Step 6: *Explore client's thoughts, including client's cues and reinforcements for negative behavior.* Keep in mind that the child or family may not view behavior as maladaptive. Establish an understanding of the constructs, meaning, and value associated with the behavior.

- Step 7: *Effect change in maladaptive behavior*
  Provide information, models, and opportunities for the child or family to master the necessary skills. Storytelling and imaginary play are recommended for use with the Native children and adolescents. It is useful to share experiences of others who have overcome similar situations. In keeping with an indirect communication style, models of behavior should be presented as suggestions.
  Explore successes and failures with behavior change. Praise any successes with behavior change. Address previously failed attempts and explore individual and environmental factors that have contributed to unsuccessful attempts.
  Incorporate a group experience. If possible, arrange for the child or family to meet with similar others who have experience with the behavior and endorse its effectiveness. A culturally congruent group program offers an opportunity to increase positive cultural identity and indigenous healing while promoting prosocial activities, shared responsibility, networks, and collective approaches.

Tools and Practice Examples

Eddie Snow Wolf is a 14-year-old Native ninth-grade student at Smith High School, a predominantly white and low- to middle-income public high school in the Southwest. Eddie has been at the school for 5 months, and he is struggling with the course work and having difficulty getting along with classmates. Eddie came to the attention of the school social worker, Ms. Esther Jones, after he was expelled for fighting. The vice principal referred Eddie to Ms. Jones because he felt that "some home problems" might be causing Eddie's academic and conduct problems.

Step 1: Establish Contact With a Community Liaison

Ms. Jones contacted Michael Stone, the school district's Native liaison. Ms. Jones met with Mr. Stone to brief him on what details were known about Eddie's situation, and in turn Mr. Stone briefed her on what he knew of the tribe, the Oglala Lakota, to which Eddie belonged.

Step 2: Self and Client Assessment

Self-Assessment

Ms. Jones, a 35-year-old Euro-American female, acknowledged that she had no experience working with Native populations but had read resource material with general information about Native cultural norms versus mainstream, Eurocentric norms. In addition, she understood how oppression and poverty influenced the lives of many Native families.

Assess Cultural Orientation of Client

Ms. Jones reviewed Eddie's school and transfer records and determined that just prior to entering Smith High, he had lived on a nearby reservation, and from the records, he had attended a public, nontribal school only in sixth and seventh grades. From this, she made a tentative judgment that, on a continuum, Eddie might be more aligned with traditional Native practices and somewhat uncomfortable with Eurocentric, mainstream interventions.

Assess Validity of Current and Previous Diagnoses

Ms. Jones noted that 2 years prior, when Eddie attended public school, he was identified as likely having attention deficit disorder (ADD). Knowing that Native children are often misdiagnosed, Ms. Jones decided to reevaluate the diagnosis with Mr. Stone's help.

Step 3: Research the Specific Cultural Practices and Traditions of the Tribe or Community

Mr. Stone helped Ms. Jones to research the Oglala Lakota People. Ms. Jones learned that in that tradition, communication with families is usually done along gender lines, and respect must be given to cross-gender interactions (Brave Heart, 2001b). Should both a male and female family member of Eddie's family attend the counseling session, she, as a woman, would first address the other female before addressing the male. The tribal community is very strong, with most people living in the nearby urban community but visiting the reservation frequently for cultural events. With the tribal communities, families and extended families are closely connected. A particular tribal practice is for the eldest male relative to take on the title and role of "grandfather" or "father" to younger family members. Another Lakota way of life involves a concept of *tiospaye* (a collection of related families) in which a group of blood and nonblood relatives meet as a group to discuss how to strengthen the family. Ms. Jones and Mr. Stone also recognized that Eddie's immediate family members would need to be contacted to attend the counseling, based on their understanding that many traditional Native children will not disclose personal information without the presence or permission of parents or elders.

Step 4: Establishing Credibility and Trustworthiness

At the first meeting, Ms. Jones and Mr. Stone met with Eddie and Eddie's grandfather, the only immediate family member available for the meeting. Eddie's older sister lived in a nearby city and wanted to attend but did not have transportation. The meeting was scheduled for 90 minutes rather than the usual 1 hour. Based on the Lakota practices, Ms. Jones first allowed Mr. Stone to address the grandfather. After that introduction, Ms. Jones began with a brief, informal self-disclosure. She talked about her own grandfather and how important it was for him to be involved in her life. Ms. Jones and Mr. Stone then invited Mr. Snow Wolf to discuss his role in Eddie's life. Through this they learned that Mr. Snow Wolf is Eddie's deceased father's uncle, the eldest living male. As she listened and learned about the family history, Ms. Jones discovered that Eddie's mother and father had died in a car accident 2 years earlier. She was able to connect this information to Eddie's school records and recognized that the loss of his parents coincided with teachers' identifying him as needing to be tested for ADD.

Step 5: Solicit Information

Slowly, Ms. Jones broached the topic of the fight, the reason that Eddie was expelled from school. Using indirect communication, she first talked about how school environments can be difficult at times for teens. She asked Eddie how he experienced the school as being difficult. Eddie disclosed that he felt the teachers at the school didn't care about the Native students and that they ignored other students when they called Natives names. Through this conversation, it was revealed that Eddie's fight started after he had been repeatedly harassed by a white male classmate who called Eddie a "squaw boy." Eddie felt that although the teacher heard the classmate use this term repeatedly, the teacher failed to reprimand him. Eddie felt he had to take matters into his own hands to defend himself and his honor.

Step 6: Exploring Clients' Thoughts, Including Clients' Cues and Reinforcements for Negative Behavior

Ms. Jones explored what Eddie meant by "defend himself" and learned that the term "squaw boy" is a derogatory term and that by using it, the classmate was insulting Eddie and his entire family. It insulted his manhood and was especially hurtful because he came from a strong lineage of warriors. Ms. Jones learned that in Eddie's view, anyone should know that this is a derogatory slur and that the teacher should have recognized this and reprimanded the other student.

Step 7: Effecting Change in Maladaptive Behavior

Provide Information and Opportunities for the Student and Family to Master the Necessary Skills

Ms. Jones continued to meet with Eddie over the next week to discuss strategies he could use in handling conflicts with students. She asked Eddie

to practice these skills and scheduled a second meeting with Eddie and his grandfather.

The next week, Ms. Jones received a phone call from Eddie's older sister. She wanted to know what was going on with Eddie. In the conversation, the sister said that Eddie and his grandfather were living in a trailer and often went without food. She wanted to know what resources were available for them but warned that they would not want anyone, not even the counselor, to know about their financial struggles. That same day, Eddie's grandfather dropped in to see Ms. Jones. Understanding that this type of "drop in" might occur, Ms. Jones made the time to see him and offered him coffee. The grandfather wanted to talk about Eddie's drinking problem. Ms. Jones thanked him for stopping in and listened carefully as he described how Eddie drinks in the evenings and doesn't complete his schoolwork. He wanted to know what programs were available. Ms. Jones said that she would research this. She also took the opportunity to tell him that his granddaughter, Eddie's sister, was worried that he was not eating and not staying strong enough to take care of Eddie. Mr. Snow Wolf did not respond, but when Ms. Jones handed him a piece of paper with a list of places he could go for food and other resources, he nodded and thanked her. Ms. Jones set up an appointment with the family and Mr. Stone for the following week.

Explore Successes and Failures With Behavior Change

In that session, Ms. Jones explored how Eddie was handling the dynamics of the classroom. She explored his successes and discussed more strategies. To move into the topic of substance abuse, she and Mr. Stone followed steps 5 and 6. Mr. Stone broached the topic of substance abuse by telling stories of similar students who had overcome substance abuse problems.

Incorporate a Group Experience

Ms. Jones researched and found a group-based substance abuse program for Lakota youth. Since Eddie was an enrolled member of the tribe, the program was free. Also, the program incorporated Native healing practices and included a cultural identity component that would support Eddie's sense of positive ethnic identity.

Key Points to Remember

School social workers should be knowledgeable about how risks to the psychosocial well-being of Native children, adolescents, and families are often rooted in collective disenfranchisement, historical trauma, and contemporary challenges associated with loss of traditional culture and identity.

Strong family and community bonds, wisdom and guidance of elders, and positive cultural practices, traditions, and ethnic identity are among the recognized strengths and protective factors for Native children and adolescents.

In the absence of an established evidence-based guide to practice with Native people in school settings, we recommend "promising practices" that draw on conventional or some combination of conventional and cultural practices and are sufficiently flexible to incorporate the cultural norms and values of Native people. Promising practices include a number of counseling and therapeutic techniques, school-based programs, and culturally grounded interventions.

This chapter highlights social cognitive therapy because of its flexibility and ability to incorporate cultural constructs important to Native children and families. A seven-step process of social cognitive therapy provides details on culturally relevant client assessment, information gathering, establishment of credibility and trustworthiness, exploration of problems and thoughts, and ultimately, methods of effecting the desired change in behavior. A case study further elucidates how these seven steps are accomplished.

The authors would like to thank Dawn Echo Romero, CACIII, LCDC, for her review and assistance with the chapter. Romero (who is part Oglala-Sincangu Lakota) has provided substance abuse counseling for youth and their families for 14 years in both Colorado and Texas.

References

Bandura, A. (2002). Social cognitive theory in cultural context. *Applied Psychology, 51,* 269–290.

Brave Heart, M. Y. H. (1998). The return to the sacred path: Healing historical trauma response among the Lakota. *Smith College Studies in Social Work, 68*(3), 287–305.

Brave Heart, M. Y. H. (2001a). Culturally and historically congruent clinical social work assessment with Native clients. In R. Fong and S. Furuto (Eds.), *Cultural competent social work practice: Practice skills* (pp. 163–177). Needham Heights, MA: Allyn & Bacon.

Brave Heart, M. Y. H. (2001b). Culturally and historically congruent interventions with Native clients. In R. Fong and S. Furuto (Eds.), *Cultural competent social work practice: Practice skills* (pp. 285–298). Needham Heights, MA: Allyn & Bacon.

Farkas, G. (2003). Racial disparities and discrimination in education: What do we know, how do we know it, and what do we need to know? *Teachers College Record, 105*(6), 1119–1146.

Franklin, C., & Jordan, C. (2003). An integrative skills assessment approach. In C. Jordan & C. Franklin (Eds.), *Clinical assessment for social workers: Quantitative and qualitative methods* (2nd ed.). Chicago: Lyceum.

Gilbert, D. J. (2003) Multicultural assessment: A focus on ethnic-minority clients. In C. Jordan, & C. Franklin, *Clinical assessment for social workers: Quantitative and qualitative methods* (2nd ed., pp. 351–383). Chicago: Lyceum.

Gilbert, D. J., & Franklin, C. (2001). Evaluation skills with Native American individuals and families, In R. Fong and S. Furuto (Eds.), *Cultural competent social work practice: Practice skills* (pp. 178–195). Needham Heights, MA: Allyn & Bacon.

LaFromboise, T., & Dixon, M. R. (2003). American Indian children and adolescents. In J. Taylor Gibbs, L. N. Huang, and associates (Eds.), *Children of color: Psychological interventions with culturally diverse youth.* San Francisco: Jossey-Bass.

LaFromboise, T., & Howard-Pitney, B. (1995). The Zuni Life Skills Development Curriculum: Description and evaluation of a suicide prevention program. *Journal of Counseling Psychology, 42,* 479–486.

Ogunwole, S. (2002). *The American Indian and Alaska Native population: 2000.* Washington, DC: U.S. Bureau of the Census, U.S. Department of Commerce.

Pavel, D. M. (1995). Comparing BIA and tribal schools with public schools. *Journal of American Indian Education, 35*(1).

Sanchez-Way, R., & Johnson, C. (2000). Cultural practices in American Indian prevention programs. *Juvenile Justice, 7*(92), 20–30.

Weaver, H. (2001). Organization and community assessment with First Nations people. In R. Fong and S. Furuto (Eds.), *Cultural competent social work practice: Practice skills* (pp. 178–195). Needham Heights, MA: Allyn & Bacon.

Yellow Bird, M. (2001). Critical values and First Nations peoples. In R. Fong and S. Furuto (Eds.), *Cultural competent social work practice: Practice skills* (pp. 61–74). Needham Heights, MA: Allyn & Bacon.

Yellow Horse, S., & Brave Heart, M. Y. H. (2004). A review of the literature. Healing the Wakanheja: Evidence based, promising, and culturally appropriate practices for American Indian/Alaska Native children with mental health needs. In A. D. Strode (Ed.), *Mental health best practices for vulnerable populations* (pp. 35–43). Washington State Department of Social and Health Services, Mental Health Division.

Multiple Hispanic Cultures: Considerations for Working With Students and Families

CHAPTER
80

Jorge Delva • Laurie M. Carpenter

Getting Started

The Spanish-speaking Hispanic or Latino population in the United States grew from approximately 23 million to 35.3 million in the years between 1990 to 2000 (U.S. Census Bureau, 2004). In this chapter, the term "Hispanic" will be used instead of Latino throughout. This is done to reflect the more commonly used term employed by the U.S. Census Bureau—it does not indicate a preference over the term Latino (see Acuña, 1999, and Hayes-Bautista & Chapa, 1987, for critical analyses of these terms). (See chapter 74 for additional information about effective interventions with Latino students.)

The Hispanic population currently constitutes approximately 12.5% of the total U.S. population, and Hispanics are expected to constitute nearly 25% of the total population by the year 2050. The term "Hispanic" refers to a widely diverse population that includes people from nearly two dozen countries. This population is made up of individuals and groups who are of diverse socioeconomic, religious, sociopolitical, and racial or ethnic backgrounds, and of varying geopolitical histories. Some examples of these population groups include individuals of Mexican and Puerto Rican descent, as well as those from Central America and Caribbean countries, South America, and of multiracial/ethnic backgrounds, as is the case of people of indigenous, African, and Spanish backgrounds. Many people considered Hispanic were native to what is presently the United States; others are more recent immigrants whose religious backgrounds span Catholicism, Protestantism, Judaism, Islam, and other faiths. Many adults are highly educated, and many have not completed high school. These are just a few examples of the tremendous diversity found among Hispanics. Diversity is so broad within the Hispanic population that social

workers working with this population need to pay particular attention to any stereotypes they and their school systems may hold about the particular group. This diversity suggests the need for interventions that are not only theoretically sound but also sufficiently flexible to accommodate the group's heterogeneity. Motivational Interviewing (MI) is a counseling-based intervention that has both the necessary flexibility and a strong theoretical foundation (Miller & Rollnick, 2002).

Motivational Interviewing can be applied to a range of health and mental health problems. Research has shown MI interventions to be effective at decreasing the risk of alcohol-exposed pregnancies (Ingersoll et al., 2003; Handmaker, Miller, & Manicke, 1999), promoting positive dietary change (Bowen et al., 2002; Resnicow, Jackson, Wang, & De, 2001), encouraging contraceptive use (Cowley, Farley, & Beamis, 2002), and reducing substance use (Colby et al., 1998; Stein & Lebeau-Craven, 2002; Graeber, Moyers, Griffith, Guajardo, & Tonigan, 2003; McCambridge & Strang, 2004; Baker et al., 2002). A meta-analysis of MI by Burke, Arkowitz, and Menchola (2003) established that 51% of clients in the trials who received MI interventions showed improved behaviors, while 37% of those not receiving the intervention showed improved behaviors. This effect did not appear to decrease over time. In addition, because one of the aims of MI is to build rapport in order to develop a trusting relationship between the counselor and the client, it is perfectly adaptable to the differences found among Hispanic populations.

To illustrate the use of MI with Hispanic families, this chapter includes a case study of the application of MI by a school social worker with a parent whose child is beginning to have academic problems, a risk factor for drug use initiation. The particular focus on applying MI with a

819

parent of an academically struggling child stems from the important role that parents play in a child's development, particularly in preventing children from initiating drug use (Chilcoat, Dishion, & Anthony, 1995).

What We Know

Inadequate Access to Substance Abuse Preventive and Treatment Services in Schools

Recent research shows that access to substance use prevention and treatment services (e.g., in-school counseling and referral services) has decreased over time (Terry-McElrath, O'Malley, Johnston, & Yamaguchi, 2003). Furthermore, these services, when available, do not seem to be correlated with the prevalence level of alcohol or illicit drug use in the schools: The exception is marijuana use (Terry-McElrath et al., 2003). The same authors, however, found that schools with larger numbers of racial- or ethnic-minority students are less likely to offer these services than are schools with fewer racial- or ethnic-minority students.

This trend of decreasing availability of counseling services, as well as the differential rates with which they are available to minorities, is of grave concern for the Hispanic population. Research shows that the prevalence of alcohol and illicit drug use among these youth has increased considerably through the 1990s and 2000s (Delva, Wallace, O'Malley, Johnston, Bachman, & Schulenberg, 2005). It is not clear what accounts for this large increase in drug use among Hispanic youth. It is plausible that prevention programs developed and implemented during the 1980s and 1990s may not have reached a sufficiently large number of Hispanic youth, or those that did reach the populations may have been ineffective because of cultural differences. Whatever the case might be, these findings suggest there is a need to continue to identify interventions that target factors found to place Hispanic youth at risk of initiating drug use, such as academic problems.

Prevention Programs

Research has shown that prevention programs that incorporate defining characteristics of culture—

dialect, idioms, norms, values, worldviews, mores, group history, and societal and structural responses to the group—increase the personal relevance of the interventions and are more likely to lead to enduring behavior change than are interventions that endorse behavior change without making the change relevant to the life of the client (Cacioppo & Petty, 1981; Marin, 1995). Research also has shown that culturally specific interventions are more likely to be effective in improving health and preventing or reducing risky behaviors than are interventions without a cultural base (Amaro, Nieves, Johannes, & Labault Cabeza, 1999; Kantor, 1997; Padilla, 1995; Szapocznik, 1995). In the case of Hispanics, research has shown that special attention needs to be paid to the cultural influences of family and gender roles, the value of *respeto* (respect) and family interdependence, and their influence on behaviors. Hispanic families share strong feelings of loyalty, reciprocity, and solidarity. These values, along with the value of hard work (*hay que trabajar duro*) and the need to endure (*hay que aguantar*) as a means of providing for one's family, serve as the core of the resiliency and motivation to succeed apparent among Hispanic families, whether it is among "old" residents of this country, recently arrived immigrants, or undocumented families.

Consequently, one crucial point of this chapter is that to maximize the effectiveness of any intervention to prevent school dropout and substance use, the school social worker must have more than tangential knowledge of the particular Hispanic population with which she works, as it is through this understanding that stereotypes can be avoided and a true rapport built. Furthermore, knowledge of the language will help the social worker acquire a greater appreciation of the behavioral and cultural norms of the families. (More information about interventions to prevent school dropout is in section 5; see chapters 21–23 for more information regarding interventions for students involved with or affected by drug use/abuse.)

Motivational Interviewing

Motivational Interviewing is a counseling style that arose from the field of alcohol abuse treatment (Miller, 1983, 1999). Its goal is to reduce the natural resistance that individuals tend to experience when life circumstances call for them to make a decision to change a belief and/or a behavior (e.g., a person with a diagnosis of alcohol dependence having to make a decision to discontinue drinking). MI is a directive, client-centered counseling approach intended to help clients explore and resolve ambivalence they may experience when faced with the necessity of making lifestyle changes (Rollnick & Miller, 1995; Millner & Rollnick, 2002). Persons conducting MI are trained to communicate in an empathic, direct, and supportive manner in order to minimize normal resistance. The skills required to implement MI are directly in line with the Code of Ethics of the field of social work, as established by the National Association of Social Workers (National Association of Social Workers, 2004). As the code states that social workers must place the utmost value on promoting clients' self-determination and capacity to change, while treating each individual with respect, MI compels workers to interact with empathy and to assist clients in building their personal self-efficacy. The most conducive environment to a successful intervention using MI is one that is supportive and nonjudgmental, one that conveys to people that they are perfectly capable of making changes. A nonjudgmental attitude permits people to safely explore new behaviors.

Before further discussing some of the properties of MI, it is important to briefly note that MI has often been implemented within the context of the "stage of change" (Prochaska & DiClemente, 1984) or "transtheoretical model" (TTM) (Prochaska & DiClemente, 1985). According to TTM, a person may fall within any one of five stages, often times drifting back and forth between stages. The first defined stage is the precontemplation stage, in which a person is not yet thinking in serious terms about making any changes in the next 6 months. The next stage is the contemplation stage, in which a person begins to seriously think about behavioral changes within the next 6 months. In the next stage, the preparation stage, a person is prepared to take action and intends to make a change within, for example, the next 30 days. This person may also suggest that in the past 6 months she has tried making changes. The next stage, the action stage, is that in which a person has made a change within the last 6 months. And finally, the maintenance stage is that in which a person has maintained a behavior change for longer than 6 months.[1]

Quite interestingly, when MI principles are followed, the person's readiness for change is automatically taken into consideration. This situation results from the individualized approach that MI mandates. Therefore, the MI script presented in the next section does not highlight the stage of change model, as attention to the particular stage comes naturally in the implementation of MI. As noted earlier, the MI interaction will be between a school social worker and the parent of a child who lately has begun to experience some academic problems. By using MI, the school social worker does not impose personal values and goals on the parent but helps the parent explore ways to improve the child's academic standing.

A helpful framework under which to implement MI is provided by the acronym *FRAMES,* which stands for giving *f*eedback, getting the person to take *r*esponsibility for the change that needs to take place, providing brief *a*dvice, helping the person create a *m*enu of options, using *e*mpathy throughout the interaction, and assisting the person to build his or her *s*elf-efficacy to accomplish the goals.[2] The next section provides a step-by-step illustration of MI using the FRAMES framework.

Tools and Practice Examples

MI Script: A Step-by-Step Illustration

This section consists of the first contact that the caregiver will have with the school social worker. The meeting was called by the social worker to start a discussion with Ms. Martínez, the mother of a second grader, Fernanda, who recently had begun to have academic difficulties. The meeting takes place at the school. It is important to emphasize that the dialogue presented does not capture all the different communication styles and potential topics of such a conversation between social worker and parent. Rather, it provides one particular example of how MI can be used. In a meeting of this sort, a large number of issues may surface as a result of a person's background. For example, people of some groups (mostly populations of low socioeconomic status) may expect females to take on a caregiving role with siblings and assist with chores. Or a child may have time-consuming chores if parents must work long hours. The number of possible issues is very large, and a social worker must know the population well to be well prepared when meeting with parents or other family members.

The reader is encouraged to substitute his or her own style and responses according to the corresponding circumstances (e.g., the meeting includes the student's teacher, the meeting takes place at the child's home, the meeting includes a grandparent) and issues discussed. Also, details about how the script conforms to MI are kept to a minimum to avoid cutting the flow of the interaction between the social worker and parent.

MI Script

Please note that text that is italicized and in brackets or parentheses indicates comments made to highlight a point of the particular script and is not part of the script. It is highly recommended that the client (in this case, the parent) do 70% of the talking and the social worker 30% or less; otherwise, whatever interaction takes place would not be considered Motivational Interviewing (P. Weinstein, personal communication, April 13, 2004).

Introduction

Hi, Ms. Martínez, my name is Claudia González. I am the school social worker. Thank you very much for coming to meet with me today. One of the goals at our school is to meet with parents to discuss their children's progress and experiences in school. As I mentioned in our phone conversation, I wanted to meet with you to discuss how Fernanda is doing in school. Fernanda is a very bright student. You must be really proud of her. Could you tell me some of the aspirations you have for your child's future? (*The idea here is to encourage the parent discuss the aspirations she has for her child as a way to build trust and to begin building rapport.*) These are good goals to aim for, and I am getting a good sense of what is important to you. (*Begin FRAMES.*)

Feedback

This week I spoke with Fernanda's teacher, Ms. Soledad. She tells me that in the past 3 months, Fernanda has not been very focused in class, and she seems more tired than usual. For example, . . . (*It would be helpful to provide a detailed example here.*) Why do you think Fernanda is feeling this way? (*You may encourage the parent to do most of the talking by paraphrasing or saying:*

- *"Tell me more . . ." or*
- *"What other things do you or Fernanda do that prepare her for school? and/or*

- *"Tell me about how things are at home."*
- *"How difficult is it to do all the things you do?")*

(*Praise the parent for all the work she is doing by saying:*

- *"From what you tell me, despite your busy schedule, you have given a lot of thought to helping Fernanda do well in school."*
- *"This is very good."*
- *"Caring for children's schooling while managing all the family responsibilities can also be very difficult at times. Can you tell me more about how you do it?")*

Responsibility and Advice

I admire your determination to help Fernanda succeed in school. I am sorry to hear about the circumstances affecting your family that may be having an effect on Fernanda's ability to concentrate in class. Do you know that despite these difficulties there are several things you can do to make sure Fernanda does not fall behind? That's right, by working together we can get Fernanda back on track, but a lot of the work will rest on what you can do at home. We at the school can also help in various ways. Let's talk about the things we can all do.

Menu

(*At this point, the social worker has considerable information to help the parent develop goals that will help either further assess what might be affecting Fernanda's schoolwork or to begin taking steps to ameliorate the circumstances and to help the parent enhance her self-efficacy, her belief that she can make a big difference in helping Fernanda succeed in school.*)

What are some things you are already doing to help Fernanda be focused when she comes to school?

What are some other things you could be doing, but do not currently do, that might fit in with your life and would help Fernanda?

Ms. Martínez, if you did the above things, how would they make Fernanda's school experiences even better? If you did not do these things, what would Fernanda's future look like?

Empathy

Within the FRAMES framework, empathy is listed after the menu option, but empathy is used throughout the entire process.

Self-Efficacy

(The purpose of this step is to enhance the parent's self-efficacy, the belief that she can successfully accomplish the desired goals. From the list of things the parent is already doing or wishes to be doing, identify two to three goals, potential roadblocks, and steps to overcome these

and achieve the goals. Remember, the goals should be feasible, specific, and measurable. Let her take the lead in defining the goals and how to accomplish them.)

List the goals and roadblocks facing Ms. Martínez in achieving each goal.

(List the goals from the most likely to be achieved to the least likely to be achieved.)

Table 80.1

GOAL	We want to be sure you reach your goal. Could you tell me how likely are you to (state goal)? Can you tell me why you rated it this way?	What are the most important roadblocks you might have to overcome to reach your goal?
1.	1 2 3 4 5 6 7 8 9 10 Less Very Likely Likely	
2.	1 2 3 4 5 6 7 8 9 10 Less Very Likely Likely	

Box 80.1

Goal 1: _____

_____

Steps: What steps do you think you might need to take in order to be able to reach the goal by overcoming the roadblock or not letting it get in the way? _____

❏ [Paraphrase wants/desires for child. *"Let me be sure I understand. You would like Fernanda to _____."*]

❏ COMMITMENT CHECK *"Remember, it is important that you feel this is the right goal for you and that you feel you can accomplish it. Do you think you can achieve this goal? If you are not ready yet, you do not have to make the commitment. We can reevaluate the goal if you'd like to."*

❏ GIVE COPY OF GOALS TO PARENT
I am going to give you a copy of the goals you chose, with notes about the specifics to help remind you. My name and telephone number are attached, as well.

❏ ANTICIPATE PROBLEMS
Not everything goes the way we plan. There are always challenges so please feel free to call me whenever you'd like to discuss these with me. It is important to keep working on the goals we set today even when there are problems.

❏ ENCOURAGE CONTACT
Feel free to call me if you have any problem with the goals. I would also like to call you once in a while to find out how you are doing. We can always change our goals. When is the best time to call?

Telephone number to call: _____

Day and Time: _____

"I have enjoyed working with you today making a plan for Fernanda to have a better experience at school. You have identified a good plan to achieve this."

Key Points to Remember

This case study focuses on the interaction a social worker may have with a parent of a child who is exhibiting some difficulties at school. It is highly likely that one of the goals that may arise as a result of the conversation is that the family needs assistance with referrals to social services to receive relief from material hardships (e.g., hunger, unemployment, homelessness) or other chronic stressors (e.g., divorce, death in the family). It may also be necessary to have psychological or medical testing, as the child's difficulties may be a result of psychological (e.g., trauma, depression) or health problems (e.g., nutritional deficiency).

MI has been shown to be effective in helping people address the ambivalence of exploring new and healthier behaviors. In the school context, the success of this intervention results from the social worker working in partnership with the parent rather than from a top-down educational or confrontational perspective, and building rapport and trust, as these are key components of MI. Success is also linked to following the structure of the highlighted FRAMES outline, in:

- providing *f*eedback in a nonjudgmental manner,
- encouraging the parent to take *r*esponsibility to make changes,
- providing brief *a*dvice,
- creating a *m*enu of options developed jointly with the parent,
- displaying *e*mpathy throughout the interaction, and
- helping the clients build their *s*elf-efficacy to change their and their children's behaviors.

As outlined previously, MI has been shown to be effective for clients facing a wide range of health issues. However, given the heterogeneity among and within these population groups, the effectiveness of MI needs to be constantly evaluated, as is the case with any other intervention. Should the evaluation or assessment indicate MI is not appropriate with a particular group, other interventions should be considered. This chapter gives the social worker an outline of one way to implement this efficacious intervention with at-risk Hispanic populations. As the intervention appears to touch on many of the inherent values and traditions of Hispanics, it is perfectly suited to work with this population, and has potential for encouraging significant behavioral change.

Acknowledgment: The information presented in this chapter on MI is informed by the work conducted by Philip Weinstein, a professor at the University of Washington, and that of the Detroit Center for Research on Oral Health Disparities, funded by the National Institute of Health [NIDCR Grant No. U-54 DE 14261–01]. Nonetheless, the implementation of MI as presented in this chapter reflects the author's clinical and research experiences and not the views of Dr. Weinstein and the Oral Health Center research team.

Notes

1. Readers interested in learning more about this model are encouraged to visit http://www.uri.edu/research/cprc/transtheoretical.htm. This Web site provides a series of links to important information on the stage of change model.

2. A terrific source of information on MI that can be easily obtained is available from http://www.motivationalinterview.org/training/index.html

References

Acuña, R. (1999). *Occupied America: A history of Chicanos.* Boston, MA: Addison-Wesley.

Amaro, H., Nieves, R., Johannes, S. W., & Labault Cabeza, N. M. (1999). Substance abuse treatment: Critical issues and challenges in the treatment of Latina women. *Hispanic Journal of Behavioral Sciences, 21,* 266–282.

Baker, A., Lewin, T., Reichler, H., Clancy, R., Carr, V., Garrett, R., et al. (2002). *Addiction, 97,* 1329–1337.

Bowen, D., Ehret, C., Pedersen, M., Snetselaar, L., Johnson, M., Tinker, L., et al. (2002). Results of an adjunct dietary intervention program in the women's health initiative. *Journal of the American Dietetic Association, 102,* 1631–1637.

Burke, B. L., Arkowitz, H., & Menchola, M. (2003). The efficacy of motivational interviewing: A meta-analysis of controlled clinical trials. *Journal of Consulting and Clinical Psychology, 71,* 843–861.

Cacioppo, J. T., & Petty, R. E. (1981). *Attitudes and persuasion: Classic and contemporary approaches.* Dubuque, IA: William C. Brown.

Chilcoat, H. D., Dishion, T. J., & Anthony, J. C. (1995). Parent monitoring and the incidence of drug sampling in urban elementary school children. *American Journal of Epidemiology, 141,* 25–31.

Colby, S. M., Barnett, N. P., Monti, P. M., Rohsenow, D. J., Weissman, K., Spirito, A., et al. (1998). Brief motivational interviewing in a hospital setting for adolescent smoking: A preliminary study. *Journal of Consulting and Clinical Psychology, 66,* 574–578.

Cowley, C. B., Farley, T., & Beamis, K. (2002). "Well, maybe I'll try the pill for just a few months . . ." Brief motivational and narrative-based interventions to encourage contraceptive use among adolescents at high risk for early childbearing. *Families, Systems, and Health, 20,* 183–204.

Delva, J., Wallace, J. E., O'Malley, P. M., Johnston, L. D., Bachman, J. G., & Schulenberg, J. M. (2005). The epidemiology of alcohol, marijuana, and cocaine use among Mexican American, Puerto Rican, Cuban American, and other Latin American eighth graders in the U.S.: 1991–2002. *American Journal of Public Health, 95,* 696–702.

Graeber, D. A., Moyers, T. B., Griffith, G., Guajardo, E., & Tonigan, S. (2003). A pilot study comparing motivational interviewing and an educational intervention in patients with schizophrenia and alcohol use disorders. *Community Mental Health Journal, 39,* 189–202.

Handmaker, N. S., Miller, W. R., & Manicke, M. (1999). Findings of a pilot study of motivational interviewing with pregnant drinkers. *Journal of Studies on Alcohol, 60,* 285–287.

Hayes-Bautista, D., & Chapa, J. (1987). Latino terminology: Conceptual bases for standardized terminology. *American Journal of Public Health, 77,* 61–68.

Ingersoll, K., Floyd, L., Sobell, M., Velasquez, M. M., Baio, J., Carbonari, J., et al. (2003). Reducing the risk of alcohol exposed pregnancies: A study of a motivational intervention in community settings. *Pediatrics, 111,* 1131–1135.

Kantor, G. K. (1997). Alcohol and spouse abuse ethnic differences. In M. Galanter (Ed.), *Recent developments in alcoholism, Volume 13: Alcoholism and violence* (pp. 57–79). New York: Plenum.

Marin, B. (1995). *Analysis of AIDS prevention among African-Americans and Latinos in the United States.* Washington, DC: Office of Technology Assessment, U.S. Congress.

McCambridge, J., & Strang, J. (2004). The efficacy of single-session motivational interviewing in reducing drug consumption and perceptions of drug-related risk and harm among young people: Results from a multisite cluster randomized trial. *Addiction, 99,* 39–52.

Miller, W. R. (1983). Motivational interviewing with problem drinkers. *Behavioral Psychotherapy, 11,* 147–172.

Miller, W. R. (1999). Motivational interviewing: Research, practice, and puzzles. *Addictive Behaviors, 21,* 835–842.

Miller, W. R., & Rollnick, S. (2002). *Motivational interviewing: Preparing people for change* (2nd ed.). New York: Guilford.

National Association of Social Workers. (2004). *Code of Ethics of the National Association of Social Workers.* Retrieved June 22, 2004, from http://www.social-workers.org/pubs/code/code.asp.

Padilla, A. M. (Ed.). (1995). *Hispanic psychology: Critical issues in theory and research.* Beverly Hills, CA: Sage.

Prochaska, J., & DiClemente, C. C. (1984). *The transtheoretical approach: Crossing traditional boundaries of therapy.* Homewood, IL: Dow Jones–Irwin.

Prochaska, J. O., & DiClemente, C. (1985). Common processes of self-change in smoking, weight control, and psychological distress. In S. Shiffman and T. Wills (Eds.), *Coping and substance abuse: A conceptual framework* (pp. 345–363). New York: Academic Press.

Resnicow, K., Jackson, A., Wang, T., & De, A. K. (2001). A motivational interviewing intervention to increase fruit and vegetable intake through black churches: Results of the eat for life trial. *American Journal of Public Health, 91,* 1686–1693.

Rollnick, S., & Miller, W. R. (1995). What is motivational interviewing? *Behavioral and Cognitive Psychology, 23,* 325–34.

Stein, L. A. R., & Lebeau-Craven, R. (2002). Motivational interviewing and relapse prevention for DWI: A pilot study. *Journal of Drug Issues, 32,* 1051–1069.

Szapocznik, J. (Ed.). (1995). *A Hispanic/Latino family approach to substance abuse prevention.* DHHS Publication No. (SMA) 95–3034. Washington, DC: SAMHSA.

Terry-McElrath, Y. M., O'Malley, P. M., Johnston, L. D., & Yamaguchi, R. (2003, Nov. 17). *Schools as treatment access for drug-using adolescents.* Paper presented at the 131st annual meeting of the American Public Health Association, San Francisco, CA.

U.S. Census Bureau. (2004). U.S. interim projections by age, sex, race, and Hispanic origin. Retrieved May 14, 2004, from http://www.census.gov/ipc/www/usinterimproj/

Working Collaboratively With African American Students, Their Families, Cultural Networks, and School Environments

Edith M. Freeman

Getting Started

Best practices indicate that African American youths' experiences, needs, and learning styles require culturally focused interventions in addition to the psychosocial and educational strategies often used with other youths (Cherry, 1998; Harvey & Hill, 2004; Jessor, 1993). This broader focus is important for the school to accomplish its mission of educating *all* students for life (Adelman & Taylor, 1999). Hence, this chapter reviews the problem area, synthesizes best practices literature on these types of interventions with black youths, and describes a prevention program for youths and their families. A culturally relevant family example, cognitive maps, work sheets, and exercises illustrate how to apply the interventions.

What We Know

The Educational Achievement and Psychosocial-Cultural Adjustment of African American Youth

Inadequate psychosocial-cultural adjustment is influenced by a combination of individual/familial and environmental challenges that affect black children and youth in the long term. These long-term challenges include under- and unemployment; homelessness; crime and incarceration; drug use and abuse; early parenthood; little cultural pride and self-esteem; and lack of social responsibility for oneself or one's cultural group, community, or society (Banks, Hogue, Timberlake, & Liddle, 1996; Cherry et al., 1998; Freeman, 1992; Gavazzi, Alford, & McKenry, 1996; Mauer, 1999).

Youths who are inadequately adjusted are more vulnerable to personal and environmental factors that contribute to their problems, because they may lack supportive social and cultural networks that aid in managing racial stress and poverty (Freeman, 2004). Enhanced psychosocial-cultural adjustment in black youths has been found to involve high cultural and self-esteem and bonding with cultural and community institutions/networks. These youths also make effective decisions to avoid or decrease their involvement in risky behaviors such as alcohol and other drug use and violence (Banks et al., 1996; Gavazzi et al., 1996).

Lack of educational achievement includes poor school performance and below-grade-level achievement, absenteeism, early dropout, behavioral disruptions, and a general lack of readiness to learn (Cherry et al., 1996). Moreover, Waller, Brown, and Whittle (1999) contend that inadequate psychosocial-cultural adjustment and educational failure among black youths are interrelated:

> The teens most likely to become pregnant are already oppressed by poverty, a lack of social support, persistent inequalities related to race and gender, and a dearth of opportunities for personal and professional fulfillment. . . . They are also likely to be failing in school and lacking educational or professional aspirations. (p. 468)

Other authors have documented this interrelationship through research. For example, Tolan and McKay (1996) note that violent crimes are highest among young inner-city African American and Latino males, and Harvey and Hill (2004) conclude that African American males have the highest rates of school detentions, suspensions, expulsions, and special education placements. Higher rates of teen pregnancy and early parenthood as well as heavier use of cocaine among black youths also affect their school attendance and completion rates (Alan Guttmacher Institute, 1999; Dixon, Schoonmaker, & Philliber, 2000). Most important, Cherry et al. (1998) found that individual, family, and systemic factors such as discriminatory practices and oppressive policies contribute to these crime rates and to other indicators of psychosocial-cultural maladjustment and educational failure.

Research Support for Recommended Interventions: Practice Methods

This problem review led me to do a computerized search for the evidence-based, best practices research summarized in Table 81.1. In order to be included, studies had to (1) have been published in a professional journal within the past 10 years; (2) employ experimental, quasi-experimental, or naturalistic designs; (3) explore the outcomes of a school- or community-based prevention, risk reduction, or early-intervention approach; (4) focus on African American adolescents and their families in terms of academic achievement and psychosocial-cultural adjustment; and (5) use a strengths framework in the process (see Table 81.5 for these strengths frameworks) (Rones & Hoagwood, 2000).

Table 81.1 summarizes 16 studies that were included in this best practices analysis. One mixed-methods and four qualitative studies were included for comparison (Alford, 1997; Gavazzi et al., 1996; Leslie, 1998; Linnehan, 2001; Stevens, 1997), along with 11 experimental and quasi-experimental studies. Eight or 73% of the latter studies had statistically significant results, with some reporting multiple outcomes in the three target areas for male and female youths from 10 to 19 years old.

Table 81.2 analyzes those studies' statistically significant outcomes, related interventions, and other contextual information. For example, it shows that long-term mentoring interventions ranging from 9 months to 1 year (activities with adult mentors, academic tutoring, and job training) led to improved academic outcomes in two studies (better attendance rates and higher GPAs for males and females) (Linnehan, 2001; Thompson & Kelly, 2001). Four studies reported statistically significant improvements in youths' psychosocial school behavior and cultural outcomes, such as increased rule compliance, peer assertiveness skills, and awareness of Afrocentric values. Those studies targeted group training interventions for male and female youths and their parents, such as social skills or Afrocentric rites of passage approaches (Banks et al., 1996; Belgrade, Chase-Vaughn, Gray, Addison, & Cherry, 2000; Cherry et al., 1998; Johnson et al., 1998).

Statistically significant findings from two drug abuse prevention studies documented improved knowledge outcomes for male youths and their parents, based on group training interventions ranging from 7 weeks to 3 years (Harvey & Hill, 2004; Johnson et al., 1998). Only two studies reported less alcohol consumption as a result of culturally focused life skills training groups for male and female youths (Botvin, Schinke, Epstein, & Diaz, 1994; Botvin, Schinke, Epstein, Diaz, & Botvin, 1995). Finally, one study (Dixon et al., 2000) used a 13-week culturally focused group intervention with female youths to effect statistically significant outcomes: delayed initiation of sexual intercourse, less frequent unprotected sex, and fewer pregnancies.

In summary, long-term multiple culturally focused or Afrocentric group training interventions were effective with black male and female youths and their families in academic, psychosocial, and cultural areas. A critical gap in these studies is that few used follow-up evaluations to determine if their outcomes were maintained after interventions ended; Botvin et al. (1995) and Johnson et al. (1998) are exceptions. Moreover, none of the studies explored the efficacy of cultural interventions with individual youths and families in the three areas or the outcomes of related large systems change strategies.

What We Can Do

The Recommended Interventions: Practice Approach and Steps

Table 81.3 describes five program components for the recommended 18-month prevention approach for youths and their parents, along with research literature that documents the approach's effectiveness. Figure 81.1 provides more program details such as the need for a start-up component of 3 or more months, which allows staff to complete the planning steps required for effective program implementation. The Afrocentric education module and the three culturally focused life skill modules for youths are sequenced to support the core rites-of-passage module over the program year. The follow-up component provides 6 months of booster and case management services to

Table 81.1 Summary of Intervention Research on African American Families and Youths: Psychosocial–Cultural Adjustment and Educational Achievement

Study & Date	Target Subgroup	Research Design and Procedures	Intervention Approach	Study Outcomes
Harvey & Hill, (2004) Contact person: Aminifu R. Harvey, DSW, aharvey@ssw. Umaryland.edu	African American male youths and their parents (N = 12)	Quasi-experimental comparison group design Procedures: direct observation and standardized measures	MAAT Africentric Rites of Passage Program: 3 years of weekly meetings, including an after-school component, family enhancement and empowerment activities, and individual family counseling	(a) Youths: improved self-esteem, knowledge of substance abuse & HIV, motivation for learning, racial identity, and cultural awareness (not statistically significant) (b) Parents: improved parenting skills, cultural awareness, community involvement, and racial identity (not statistically significant)
Johnson et al. (1998) Contact person: Knowlton Johnson, PhD, Kwjohn01@ulkyum. louisville.edu	Male and female youths (N = 133) and their parents (African American and white)	Randomized block comparison group design Procedures: individual interviews and written questionnaires	COPES Substance Abuse Prevention Program in youths' churches: 1-year parent training, youth training, early intervention, and follow-up case management services	(a) Youths: increased bonding with parents/siblings (statistically significant) and knowledge of and resistance to substance abuse (not statistically significant) (b) Parents: increased knowledge of substance abuse issues, use of community services, and modeling of appropriate alcohol use (statistically significant)

(continued)

Table 81.1 *(Continued)*

Study & Date	*Target Subgroup*	*Research Design and Procedures*	*Intervention Approach*	*Study Outcomes*
Cherry et al. (1998) Contact person: Valerie R. Cherry, PhD, Progressive Life Center, 1123 11th St. NW, Washington, DC 20001	African American female youths and their parents	Quasi-experimental comparison group design Procedures: a range of standardized measures	NTU Africentric Substance Abuse Prevention Program, 2 years: Rites of passage, ATOD prevention, Africentric education course, parenting and work program, in-home family therapy, annual kinship event, and training of community partners	(a) Youths: increased racial identity, happiness, and self-esteem; improved school behaviors (rule compliance and interest)(statistically significant); and enhanced antidrug attitudes, Africentric values, unity and collective responsibility, and knowledge of Africa (not statistically significant) No parental outcomes reported
Aktan et al. (1996) No contact person included	Inner-city African American families and youths	Quasi-experimental comparison group design Procedures: interviews, direct observations, standardized measures, and written questionnaires	Safe Haven Family Skills Program for Substance Abuse Prevention: family skills group intervention with parents and youths	(a) Youths: enhanced risk and protective factors and appropriate behaviors (not statistically significant) (b) Parents: improved parenting efficacy and behaviors toward their children, and reductions in parent or family use of substances (not statistically significant)
Royse (1998) Contact person: David Royse, PhD, College of Social Work, University of Kentucky, Lexington, Kentucky 40506	African American male youths 14–16 years old (N=36)	Experimental design Procedures: standardized scales, questionnaires, and data from school records on performance and behavior	The Brothers' Mentoring Project, 15 months: organized group recreational activities once monthly between assigned volunteer mentors and youths	Slight decrease in youths' minor disciplinary infractions and increase in their major infractions (not statistically significant); and no significant changes in their self-esteem, drug and alcohol attitudes, GPAs, and school absences

Banks et al. (1996) Contact person: Reginald Banks, Temple University, Philadelphia, PA	Inner-city low-income African American male youths, 10–14 years old ($N=33$)	Two-group comparison design Procedures: standardized measures	Adolescent Alternatives and Consequences Social Skills Training Program (AACT), 6 weeks: Africentric black history and cultural experiences, Africentric value system, African American images and themed role plays in a peer group format	Improvements in youths' trait anger, assertiveness, self-control, general anger, and experience of anger (statistically significant)
Botvin et al. (1994) Contact person: Gilbert J. Botvin Institute for Prevention Research, Dept. of Public Health, Cornell University Medical College, 411 E. 69th Street, New York 10021	African American male and female youths ($N=456$)	Three-group comparison control group design Procedures: written questionnaires, standardized measures, and inventories	Culturally Focused & Generic Skills Training for Alcohol and Drug Prevention: $7\frac{1}{2}$ weeks; alcohol- and drug-prevention curriculum—knowledge and attitudes; involving demonstrations, behavioral rehearsal, feedback and reinforcement, and multicultural myths/stories by peer leaders and same-race group facilitators	Youths in the two culturally relevant intervention groups had significantly higher antidrinking, antimarijuana, and anticocaine scores and lower risk-taking scores and intentions to drink beer and wine.
Botvin et al. (1995) Same contact person as above	Same participants	Same design 2-year posttreatment follow-up questionnaires, standardized measures, and inventories	Same intervention	Youths in culturally focused intervention group had statistically significant less alcohol consumption, less frequent use of alcohol, and lower risk-taking scores.

(continued)

Table 81.1 (*Continued*)

Study & Date	Target Subgroup	Research Design and Procedures	Intervention Approach	Study Outcomes
				Those in both intervention groups had statistically significant less drunkenness, and increased use of assertiveness skills and lower risk-taking scores
Alford (1997) Contact person: Keith Alford, Ph.D., School of Social Work, Syracuse University, Syracuse, New York	African American male youths in foster care (*N*=29)	Naturalistic qualitative design Procedures: individual interviews and direct observations	Africentric Rites of Passage Program (AA RITES)	Themes: the importance of learning and giving back what you've learned, family solidarity and cultural interconnectedness, condemnation of violence and unproductive behavior, spirituality
Gavazzi et al. (1996) Contact person: Stephen M. Gavazzi, Dept. of Family Relations & Human Development, Ohio State University, 171 Campbell Hall, 1787 Neil Ave., Columbia, Ohio 43210	Urban African American male youths 12–21 years (*N*=37)	Naturalistic qualitative design Procedures: individual interviews	African American Culturally Specific Rites of Passage Program (AA RITES), 1-year minimum: didactic and experiential activities for three stages (separation from childhood, transformation experiences related to African heritage curriculum, and reincorporation in five core achievement areas	Themes: enhanced individual and cultural pride (inter-related); self-direction, individual responsibility and hard work, and increased knowledge of own cultural history
Dixon et al. (2000) Contact person: William W. Philliber, Research Associate, 16 Main Street, Accord, N.Y 12404	African American female youths; program graduates (*N*=33)	Quasi-experimental comparison group design Procedures: individual interviews	A Journey Toward Womanhood Africentric Pregnancy Prevention Program, 13 weeks: group intervention, 4 hours once weekly, includes self-definition, wellness, tools for survival, field trips	Statistically significant delays in initiation of sexual intercourse for Africentric group participants, who were also less likely to have had intercourse, unprotected sex (among those sexually active), and to have been pregnant

Study	Population	Design	Intervention	Findings
Stevens (1997) Contact person: Joyce West Stevens, DSW, Boston University School of Social Work, Boston, MA	African American adolescent girls, 11–14 years	Qualitative longitudinal design Procedures: participant observation, audiotapes of sessions, and field notes	Self Image Life Skills and Role Modeling Curriculum for Pregnancy Prevention, 10 weeks: group intervention and role model mentors	Themes: personal identity and self-efficacy, self-assertion, and intergenerational value and role conflicts
Linnehan (2001) No contact person included	African American youths, 15–18 years old (N=202)	Time series design Procedures: data from school records	Work-based mentoring multischool program, 1 year: academic, mentoring, and behavioral interventions	Statistically significant improvements in GPAs and attendance rates for those participating in the program 6 months or more.
Leslie (1998) No contact person included	Low-income African American mothers (N=30)	Naturalistic qualitative design Procedures: in-depth interviews	Parents' use of indigenous storytelling experiences to teach/socialize their children to Africentric values	Themes: informed values as the basis of parents' teachings: the importance of thinking ahead (having a plan), protecting the physically defenseless against the powerful, supporting altruism
Belgrave et al. (2000) No contact person included	African American girls 10–12 years old (N=55)	Quasi-experimental comparison group design Procedures: standardized measures	Resiliency-focused Africentric group intervention, 4 months: activities and exercises for increasing self-worth	Statistically significant changes in Africentric values, ethnic identity, and self-concept in intervention group
Thompson et al (2001) No contact person included	African American at risk boys (N=12)	Experimental design Procedures: standardized measures	Big Brothers/Big Sisters Mentoring program, 9 months: matched mentors/youths intervention	Treatment group participants made statistically significant academic gains compared to control (wait list) group

Table 81.2 Analysis of Early Intervention and Prevention Research on African American Youths and Families

Types of Research	Categories of Outcomes	Effective Interventions and Practice Approaches
Quantitative Research, Statistically Significant Outcomes	Psychosocial School Behavior Outcomes: • Improved assertiveness skills with peers, self-control, expression of anger, anger frequency (males & females:10–14 years) • Increased bonding with parents and siblings (males and females: 12 to 14 years old) • Increased rule compliance and interest in school (males and females: fifth and sixth graders) Cultural Strengths Outcomes: • Enhanced cultural identity, happiness, self-esteem (male/female fifth and sixth graders) • Improved awareness of Africentric values ethnic identity, and physical appearance self-concept (girls 10–12 years of age) Associated Substance Abuse Resistance Skill Outcomes: • Improved antidrug attitudes, and decreased intentions to use beer and wine, risk taking, and alcohol consumption (fifth and sixth grade males and females) • Increased ATOD knowledge, modeling appropriate alcohol use, use of community services (parents of youths) • Enhanced knowledge about drug abuse and HIV (males: 11.5 to 14.5 years old)	• 6-week youth and parental social skills intervention: peer training groups with an Africentric curriculum (Banks et al., 1996) • Church-based ATOD prevention: parent-youth training groups, 1-year follow-up case management services (Johnson et al., 1998) • 2-year prevention program with youth Africentric rites of passage and education, substance abuse prevention, and parenting and work components (Cherry et al., 1998) • Cherry et al., 1998; intervention involving parents and youths: See above • Four-month group intervention involving exercises and activities about self-worth, ethnic and gender identity, and Africentric values (Belgrade et al., 2000) • 7½-week culturally focused life skills training groups for youths in substance abuse prevention (Botvin et al., 1994, 1995) • Johnson et al., 1998; intervention for parents and youths: See above • 3-year Africentric rites of passage groups for male youths and parents: after school, family empowerment, and individual family counseling modules (Harvey & Hill, 2004)

834

	Associated Pregnancy Prevention Outcomes: • Delayed initiation of sexual intercourse, less frequent unprotected sex, and fewer pregnancies (females: 14 to 19 years of age)	• 13-week adolescent Africentric pregnancy prevention group services on self-definition, wellness, and survival self-sufficiency tools (Dixon et al., 2000)
	Academic Achievement Outcomes: • Higher academic gains (male youths) • Higher grade point averages and improved attendance rates (male and female youths 15–18 years old)	• 9-month Big Brother/Big Sister mentoring program (Thompson et al., 2001) • Yearlong work-based mentoring program for at-risk youths (Linnehan, 2001)
Naturalistic Qualitative Research: Outcome Themes	Psychosocial and Cultural Strengths Outcomes: • Increased positive attitudes toward learning, awareness of own cultural history, and interrelated cultural and self-esteem (male adolescents from 15 to 18 years old in foster care) • Increased clarity about the cultural values lessons they teach their children from cultural stories (parents) • Sense of personal-cultural identity, self-efficacy, and self-assertion (females: 11 to 14 years of age)	• 1-year Africentric rites of passage youth program, as an adjunct to an independent living program (Gavazzi et al., 1996) • Parents' indigenous Africentric storytelling intervention involving the use of cultural stories with their children (Leslie, 1998) • 10-week self-image life skills and role modeling curriculum using college-age mentors (Stevens, 1997)
	Substance Abuse Resistance Skills: • Decreased parental and family use of illegal substances and increased parenting skills (parents and male youths)	• Family skills substance abuse prevention program with group sessions for parents and youths (Aktan et al., 1996)

Table 81.3 Overview of the Recommended Early Intervention Prevention Approach for Latency-Age African American Youths and Their Families

Program Factors	Program Description
Program Philosophy—Social Importance	Prevention and early intervention with African American youths is critical in individual, peer group, school, immediate and extended family, cultural group, and community domains (Harvey & Hill, 2004). These youths require support to become centered in an Africentric worldview, values, and beliefs, such as harmony, balance, interconnectedness, and authenticity to reduce risk factors and increase their resilience (Cherry et al., 1998)
Theory/Conceptual Framework	A combined interacting theoretical perspective is needed, including an empowerment, capacity-building, ecological, family systems, resilience, strengths-based, psychoeducation framework
Target Population and Rationale	Male and female youths from 10 to 13 years *and* their parents: Research documents this is an optimal time for preventing risk factors and influencing gains in the identified areas (Belgrade et al., 2001; Botvin et al., 1994; Stevens, 1997; Cherry et al., 1998; Johnson et al., 1998)
Expected Outcomes	For youths: academic achievement, ATOD resistance skills, life or social skills, cultural esteem-identity-knowledge, early parenting prevention. For parents: parenting skills, modeling ATOD knowledge and non-drug use, cultural knowledge-identity-esteem, use of community services
Recruitment Strategy	The ecological/family systems aspects of the theoretical framework focus on all sources for potential recruits in youths' family, peer group, school, cultural, and community environments
Program Components	This 1-year multiple-strategy intervention/prevention program for African American youths and their families includes the first four components below, and in addition a 6-month follow-up component: • Initiation, Engagement, and Orientation Component • Africentric Component • Culturally Focused Life Skills Training Component • Problem-Solving and Action Steps Component • Case Management Follow–Up Component

reinforce the participants' gains and to address current needs.

Although this comprehensive program is based on findings from the empirical research literature on black youths, a smaller, more compact approach is strongly suggested as a 2- to 3-year pilot. This incremental strategy can provide the necessary observational and self-report process data on the program's strengths and problem areas for implementing the post-pilot program effectively. Figure 81.1 shows the recommended comprehensive approach as well as the suggested scaled-down pilot approach (the pilot components and modules are identified by the * sign).

Social Importance of the Recommended Approach

Table 81.3 describes the program's importance based on the best practices research summarized in the previous section. In particular, the table's Program Philosophy–Social Importance and Theory/Conceptual Framework emphasize the importance of an Afrocentric, early intervention, prevention, strengths approach for helping African American youths and families to center themselves culturally. Being culturally centered—applying Afrocentric values and traditions in their daily lives—can help families to reduce risk factors and increase protective factors. Research has documented the high value African Americans place on family centeredness and extended family relationships and the amount of emotional and task support they receive from those cultural factors (Belgrade et al., 2000; Cherry et al., 1998). Therefore, including youths *with* their families and peers in group sessions is consistent with research findings and is a promising way of addressing academic, psychosocial, and cultural needs (see Expected Outcomes in Table 81.3) (Banks et al., 1996; Harvey & Hill, 2004).

Components of the Suggested Pilot Approach

To clarify how the pilot approach is connected to the total program, Tables 81.6A and 81.6B (in Appendices A and B) include steps for implementing content and experiential exercises for the pilot modules, and Tables 81.6C and 81.6D (in Appendices C and D) describe components and modules not included in the pilot program (e.g., the substance abuse prevention and social action coaching modules). The start-up and follow-up components

are not included in these tables because they are not curriculum based; however, those modules are part of the discussion in this section.

The pilot components' purpose, the participants, and the number and frequency of sessions are included in this discussion. For the Afrocentric and culturally focused life skills modules, the discussion includes steps for using one of the suggested instructional tools or exercises (see examples of additional instructional tools in Tables 81.6A–81.6D).

The Initiation Component

The purpose of this 3-month component is to recruit and orient the participants, build communitywide acceptance and support for the program, and complete the planning and preparation necessary for program implementation. The best practices research analysis emphasized overcoming recruitment barriers by allowing sufficient planning time and including community stakeholders (Harvey & Hill, 2004). Therefore, the participants in this component include the potential recruit families and various community partners. Potential partners include school board members and neighborhood advisory committees. There are three modules for this component: the Engagement and Training of Community Partners, Site Selection and Preparation, and Recruitment and Orientation of Participants. Staff members for this and other components consist of a combination of professionals (program director), aides (outreach workers), and volunteers (community elders).

The Afrocentric Component

This component is designed to build the participants' character; self-esteem; cultural esteem; and their family, community, and cultural unity. Another purpose is to help them develop a healthy Afrocentric value system and to make a positive transition from adolescence to adulthood. The participants are the target youths and their peers, who meet in separate gender-based groups for this and all components, along with same-gender facilitators and cofacilitators. Exceptions involve special occasions where all participants meet together, such as some field trips, naming ceremonies, and the graduation ritual. The best practices research literature documents the effectiveness of same-gender peer-group training for enhancing psychosocial-cultural and education outcomes through culturally focused and Afrocentric interventions in a long-term format

Figure 81.1 Program Timeline: Recommended Early Intervention Prevention Approach for Latency-Age African American Youths and Families

	Program Startup	Program Implementation	Program Follow-up
Months:	1 3	6 9 12	18

Initiation Component

Community Partners, Participants' Recruitment and Orientation, and Site Selection

Modules

Africentric Component
Rites of Passage/Parent Involvement Module*

Culturally Focused Life Skills Component
- Social Skills Training Module
- Substance Abuse Prevention Module
- Healthy Male/Female Relations Module

Integrated or Stand-Alone
Collaborative Problem-Solving and Action Steps Component
a) Africentric Individual Family Consultation Module (as needed)
b) Social Action Coaching Module (as needed)

Culturally Focused Life Skills Component

Africentric Component
Africentric Education Module*

Culturally Focused Life Skills Component
{+} Parenting Skills Training Module*

Academic Tutoring Module (as needed)

Follow-Up Component
- Case Management Module*
- Booster Services Module
6 Months

*Suggested for pilot program

(ranging from several months to 1 or 2 years) (Botvin et al., 1994, 1995; Cherry et al., 2000; Thompson et al., 2001).

This component consists of the Rites of Passage and Africentric Education modules. The Rites of Passage Module meets weekly in after-school sessions for a year, 3 hours per session. The module teaches participants the Seven Nguzo Saba Africentric principles and how to apply them to the rites and in their daily lives (see Table 81.4).

A goal-setting exercise can be used to address part of the component's purpose as described, because it teaches youths how to set educational and psychosocial-cultural goals for managing the transition from adolescence to adulthood. For example, the exercise worksheet (Appendix E) can be used to help participants set educational goals related to the Nguzo Saba principle of Nia (purpose). Table 81.6A describes a typical group session for this module centered on the goal-setting exercise.

First, the cofacilitators can involve the participants in brainstorming the long-term benefits of completing their education based on the youths' perspectives and aspirations. As benefits are identified, cofacilitators can list them on a flip chart and invite participants to provide more details and to discuss each benefit. Each participant can be asked to identify one or more specific goals related to the benefits, such as obtaining a college scholarship for the future benefit of having a good job. Then participants can be encouraged to identify supports (door openers), barriers (door closers), and action steps for their goals ("my" steps), with input from peers and facilitators. Future sessions can be used to review youths' goal-setting worksheets to help monitor their progress and to update and revise their supports, barriers, and action steps. Other instructional tools and exercises for this module are included in Table 81.6A. (See also Chapter 73.)

The Africentric Education Module meets weekly for Saturday sessions over a 3-month period, 2 hours per session. The content and a description of a typical session are included in Table 81.6A, along with examples of several exercises. One example is focused on values clarification. The youths participate in a structured role play in which they express and clarify their values, and then compare them to those of a historical black figure. Instructions detail the steps the facilitator takes prior to the session (preparing brief descriptions of historical black figures selected by the youths), steps taken during the role play (brainstorming examples of challenging value conflicts

with the participants before having them role-play a conflict), and post-role-play debriefings (identifying the values expressed by actors in the role plays and conflicts between their values and those of the identified historical figures). This exercise uses peers to identify and resolve common value conflicts, and cultural role models to address the conflicts and reinforce a positive cultural identity (Harvey & Hill, 2004).

The Culturally Focused Life Skills Component

This component's purpose is to improve the participants' handling and expression of feelings and to teach them the life skills of improved communication, enhanced peer/family relationships, and academic success. The Academic Tutoring and Parent Skills Training modules are the two pilot modules. The Academic Tutoring Module consists of tutoring by volunteers for those youths who need it. Tutoring sessions are scheduled on an individual basis, with a minimum of one or two sessions weekly as needed throughout the program. The modules' content, examples of exercises, and a typical session are in Table 81.6B.

One exercise is part of the orientation for all youths who receive tutoring. Tutors should discuss with each youth how he or she prepared for a recent test. The goal is to identify which of the youth's test preparation strategies worked, which were ineffective, and the connection between those strategies and the outcome (the test scores). Tutors can use the description of a typical session on Table 81.6B as a guide for helping youths to develop new study habits prior to their next exam or term paper. The study habits are culturally relevant because they address and utilize cultural values and learning styles (using the colors of African flags to highlight key areas of a book, and using rhyming words or active words to increase memory of important material) (Botvin et al., 1994, 1995).

The Parenting Skills Training Module focuses on the parents of youths in the program, and it uses a multiple-family group format. Group sessions are held weekly for a 3-month period, followed by once monthly rite-of-passage parent-involvement meetings planned by the parents. Their active involvement can lead to skills development and empowerment (Cherry et al., 1998). Individual parent training booster sessions are an important option as documented by best practices literature (Botvin et al., 1994). Content

Table 81.4 Rites of Passage: Seven Africentric Principles of the Nguzo Saba: Guidelines for Healthy Living

The Seven Principles	Related Africentric Values and Goals	Related Program Examples of African American Youths' Africentric Action Steps
Umoja: unity	To strive for and maintain unity in the family, community, nation, and race	Unity Rituals: Rites of passage sessions: Do unity circle, drum call, Nguzo Saba, libation
Kujichajulia: self-determination	To define ourselves, name ourselves, and speak for ourselves from a strengths perspective, instead of being defined incorrectly and spoken for by others	Great Leaders/Who Am I Exercise: Do report on great black leader, identify qualities leader attributed to his/her success, define self and qualities
Ujima: collective work and responsibility	To build and maintain our community together; to make our brothers' and sisters' problems our problems and to solve those problems together	Seniors/Youths Community Beautification Project: Learn horticulture, broker resources, work together on landscape/community tasks
Ujamaa: cooperative economics	To build and own our own stores, shops, and other businesses, and to profit together from them	Social Action Project: Develop family plan to patronize black businesses/avoid negative values
Nia: purpose	To make as our collective vocation the building and developing of our community in order to restore our people to their traditional greatness	Action Steps Goal-Setting Exercise: Brainstorm long-term benefits of completing education, define goals/motives re community benefits
Kuumba: creativity	To do always as much as we can, in the way we can, in order to leave our community more beautiful and beneficial than when we inherited it	Graduation Ceremony: Plan together the tangible products to be creatively produced representing knowledge and skills learned from participation
Imani: faith	To believe in our parents, our teachers, our leaders, our people, ourselves, and the righteousness of our struggle	Ancestral Transformation Role Play: Think, feel, and behave as historical figure: decreases negative self/group perceptions, increases pride and belief in self/cultural group

areas for this module and steps for a typical session are included in Table 81.6B, related to the family cultural maintenance process.

During discussions with parents on such topics as how to use family leisure time, manage cultural stress from discrimination, or enhance their children's cultural identity, group facilitators can introduce the strategy of incremental cultural maintenance. The action plan includes incremental steps a family can take to become more culturally centered, beginning with levels that require lesser commitment and time, such as reading a black history book or article. In addition to helping parents to select the level of cultural maintenance activities they will focus on, based on their individual needs and perspectives, facilitators can have them identify specific steps for implementing their action plan worksheet. Future sessions can be used to collectively monitor the families' progress and revise the plans as needed based on group feedback. Parents can involve youths in planning, action steps, and monitoring their cultural maintenance process.

The Follow-Up Component

The purpose of this component is to reinforce the gains that participants make during the program year and to address their current case management needs. Referrals might involve identifying and brokering academic and counseling services for youths in their schools; emergency food, clothing, and shelter for families; social supports from cultural and community resources; or medication and treatment compliance education through collaboration between school and mental health practitioners. The Case Management Module includes parents and youths who were involved in the pilot program. The frequency and number of sessions is based on each family's needs over the 6-month follow-up period. Content areas and specific action steps to be undertaken by program staff for this module include providing information and referrals, monitoring referrals, brokering existing resources, and developing new resources where significant gaps occur.

Challenges in Implementing the Pilot Approach

It is essential to acknowledge some of the challenges involved in implementing the pilot approach described in the previous sections. Recruiting participants and developing support for the program among community partners is a key challenge. This program emphasizes prevention, nonlabeling, and the importance of cultural support, which can help to address this challenge and to reinforce the parental empowerment that occurs from their active participation and successes. Early collaborative partnerships with community organizations can increase the support and involvement of community partners; research indicates that is an essential step for meeting this challenge (Cherry et al., 1998).

Maintaining youth participation is yet another challenge. The use of culturally relevant and age-relevant interventions from the best practices research literature is crucial, along with a focus on issues that are culturally meaningful to black youths. Meeting the latter challenge is a prerequisite for addressing the next one: finding user-friendly and participant-involved methods for documenting meaningful changes that occur as a result of the program (Banks et al., 1996). Cultural consultants can help to develop culturally relevant procedures for monitoring the identified issues, processes, and outcomes.

Tools and Case Examples

The Baker Family's Background and Recruitment to the Program

Some of these challenges are apparent in the following discussion on the experiences of an African American family in a similar early-intervention rites-of-passage program. This discussion illustrates how such programs can be effective in spite of those and other challenges. Background data and information on how the Baker family became involved in the program are described, along with outcomes from interventions that were used with different family members.

The family includes the mother, Honor Baker, and her children, Garrett, Erica, and Joleal (see the School-Community Ecomap in Appendix F for a strengths-based analysis of the family's supports and stressors). Ms. Baker agreed that the two older children could participate in the rites-of-passage program for boys and girls when the program held its orientation meeting in her church. She initially declined participation for herself because of her busy schedule (and perhaps an understandable "wait-and-see" attitude) but later decided to "sit in" on the parent-training and parent-involvement sessions.

When the program started, Mr. Baker still lived with the family, but the parents separated 3 months later because of his drug abuse. Mr. Baker took many of the family's possessions— including the children's video games, television, and bikes—and sold them for drugs. He had been a good provider and an involved parent until he started using drugs after his military service during the Gulf War.

The Family's Participation, Examples of Interventions, and Outcomes

During a discussion on giving culturally affirming messages to children, Ms. Baker mentioned that Erica was always in trouble so she seldom gave the child positive messages. When other parents agreed that acting-out children make it difficult to give positive feedback, the group facilitator gave them a group homework assignment on Catching Your Child Being Good. This assignment required them to use the Atta Girl Parents' Feedback Card in Appendix G, which Ms. Baker filled out and gave to Erica between the parent sessions. In their next session, Ms. Baker said, "This assignment was an eye opener; it gave me hope for Erica." In response to the Atta Girl Card from her mother, Erica said, "Cool." Then Erica put the card on a special area of the wall next to her bed. Ms. Baker told the project director that Erica had been suspended for fighting but that the white girl she fought with was not suspended. She thought the decision was racial. The project director suggested inviting the assistant principal and a counselor to the parent-involvement meeting later that week to talk about school discipline policies. During that session, parents discussed with the assistant principal how Erica and other students had been affected by those policies. As a result, the school suspension policy was changed to require all students involved in fights to be suspended until a hearing could be held. The assistant principal later apologized to the Baker family, a sign of respect to Ms. Baker.

Erica's Participation in the Academic Tutoring Module

Erica told her tutor during one session that she just could not learn and that her reading teacher had called her "slow" when she asked for help with a book report. The tutor told Erica that all cultural groups have their best ways of learning, and then engaged her in a discussion about African American learning styles: active learning,

involving all the senses, interactive, practical in application, uses familiar cultural language and builds on cultural strengths (rhyming and movement) (see Table 81.6B). She also had Erica to complete the Youths' Affirmation Pledge in Appendix H in spite of Erica's initial reaction that she did not have any strengths. In a later tutoring session, Erica seemed especially empowered when she read from her pledge that she is more mature now than when she was as a 10-year-old, and then she said her strength is that she tries harder and "learns better when the teacher lets us ask questions or apply our class work to real life."

Garrett's Participation in the Rites of Passage Module

In one session in which the group was discussing the Nia principle (purpose) from the Nguzo Saba, the facilitators had participants complete the Action Steps Goal Setting Worksheet (Figure 81.2E). When Garrett shared his completed worksheet later during the session, he identified not having a computer as a barrier to his education goals. He acknowledged that his father had previously sold their computer for drugs. Group members gave graphic feedback about how mad that would make them feel. Garrett openly expressed his feelings for the first time in the group by admitting he was still angry about what happened. That session was a turning point for Garrett because he gradually became less withdrawn, more expressive, and more involved in the program. His completed Field Trip Critics' Review Form in Appendix I demonstrates his increased self-confidence and enhanced cultural identity and cultural pride after participating in a field trip to an African exhibit.

Additional Tools

Table 81.5 describes African American family strengths based on different frameworks from the literature.

Key Points to Remember

The Baker family continued to participate in this yearlong program until Garrett and Erica graduated, and Garrett returned the following year as a peer leader. Their participation and other positive

Table 81.5 Culturally Relevant Strengths Frameworks for African American Youths and Families

Strengths Frameworks (From Color-Blind to Culture Specific) ⟶	Personal and Social Competence Framework (CB)	Resilience and Risk and Protective Factors Framework (CS)	African Survivals Framework (CS)	Africentric Framework (CS)
Assumptions about the sources of African Americans' strengths	Some individuals develop the universal life skills and competence required for survival through significant opportunities, role models, and other key experiences, while other individuals do not	The environment and the interface between individuals and environments contain both protective and risk factors that affect survival; some people develop unique survival capacities coping with poverty, racial stress, and oppression (resilience)	Some African cultural institutions and traditions survived the diaspora and slavery through African Americans' creative adaptations, which circumvented culturally destructive laws, and enhanced their past survival and the maintenance of their cultural traditions	Some African cultural institutions and traditions were lost during the diaspora and slavery. They should be reclaimed and recovered to help African Americans become more centered in their culture (who they are) and to enhance their present survival
Examples of African American strengths from the literature on each framework	Universal life skills: resistance skills, decision-making skills, assertiveness, self-esteem building, anxiety management, personal relationship building (Botvin et al., 1995) Sense of personal identity, self-efficacy, assertion, self-image, life skills (Stevens, 1997)	Universal resilience: family management, good communication, bonding, community help-seeking (Johnson et al., 1998) Poverty-related risk and protective factors: isolation and community drug sales vs. bonding and peer abstinence (Aktan et al., 1996)	Culture: extended family network, role flexibility, healthy enmeshment (closeness), religion and spirituality, nonverbal communication (Royse, 1996) Kinship bonds, work orientation, flexible family roles, work orientation, religious orientation (Hill, 1999)	Culture: rituals (rites of passage, naming ceremonies, mentoring circles), African values (Nguza Saba, collectivism (Harvey & Hill, 2004), eldership (griots, healers), village community (Banks, 1996) Collective responsibility, spirituality, help based on need (Schiele, 1997)

outcomes are a testimony to the effectiveness of program components from the empirical literature for best practices with African American families:

- early intervention and prevention services for youths from 10 to 15 years of age;
- Afrocentric and other culturally focused interventions that are long term and that target academic, psychosocial, and cultural areas;
- a strengths-focused framework that builds on cultural resources and emphasizes collaboration and capacity or skill building;
- a focus on systemic risk factors that impede youths in negotiating the developmental transition from adolescence to adulthood (biased policies, violence, substance abuse, early parenthood);
- systems change coaching for lobbying to end biased policies and practices that hinder these youths' academic and psychosocial-cultural successes.

References

Adelman, H. S., & Taylor, L. (1999). Mental health in schools and system restructuring. *Clinical Psychology Review, 19*, 137–163.

Alan Guttmacher Institute. (1999). *Teenage pregnancy: Overall trends and state-by-state information.* New York: Author.

Alford, K. A. (1997). *A qualitative study of an Africentric rites of passage program used with adolescent males in out of care: Looking for unexpected themes.* Unpublished doctoral dissertation, Ohio State University.

Banks, R., Hogue, A., Timberlake, T., & Liddle, H. (1996). An Afrocentric approach to group social skills training with inner-city African American adolescents. *Journal of Negro Education, 65*, 414–423.

Belgrave, F. Z., Chase-Vaughn, G., Gray, F., Addison, J. D., & Cherry, V. R. (2000). The effectiveness of a culture- and gender-specific intervention for increasing resiliency among African Americans preadolescent females. *Journal of Black Psychology, 26*, 133–147.

Botvin, G. J., Schinke, S. P., Epstein, J. A., & Diaz, T. (1994). Effectiveness of culturally focused and generic skills training approaches to alcohol and drug abuse prevention among minority youths. *Psychology of Addictive Behaviors, 8*, 116–127.

Botvin, G. J., Schinke, S. P., Epstein, J. A., Diaz, T., & Botvin, E. M. (1995). Effectiveness of culturally focused and generic skills training approaches to alcohol and drug abuse prevention among minority adolescents: Two-year follow-up results. *Psychology of Addictive Behaviors, 9*, 183–194.

Cherry, V. R., Belgrave, F. Z., Jones, W., Kennon, D. K., Gray, F. S., & Phillips, F. (1998). NTU: An Africentric approach to substance abuse prevention among African American youth. *Journal of Primary Prevention, 18*, 319–339.

Dixon, A. C., Schoonmaker, C. T., & Philliber, W. W. (2000). A journey toward womanhood: Effects of an Afrocentric approach to pregnancy prevention among African American adolescent females. *Adolescence, 35*, 425–430.

Freeman, E. M. (1992). The use of storytelling techniques with young African-American males: Implications for substance abuse prevention. *Journal of Intergroup Relations, 29*, 53–72.

Freeman, E. M. (2004, March). *Effective narrative approaches: The intersection of narratives and culture.* Paper presented at the Annual Institute of Hospital Directors, Bruce Watkins Cultural Center, Kansas City, MO.

Gavazzi, S. M., Alford, K. A., & McKenry, P. C. (1996). Culturally specific programs for foster care youth: The sample case of an African American rites of passage program. *Family Relations, 45*, 166–174.

Harvey, A. R., & Hill, R. B. (2004). Africentric youth and family rites of passage program: Promoting resilience among at-risk African American youths. *Social Work, 49*, 65–75.

Jessor, R. (1993). Successful adolescent development among youth in high-risk settings. *American Psychologist, 48*, 117–126.

Johnson, K., Bryant, D. D., Collins, D. A., Noe, T. D., Strader, T. N., & Berbaum, M. (1998). Preventing and reducing alcohol and other drug use among high-risk youths by increasing family resilience. *Social Work, 43*, 297–309.

Leslie, A. R. (1998). What African American mothers perceive they socialize their children to value when telling them Brer Rabbit stories. *Journal of Comparative Family Studies, 29*, 173–186.

Linnehan, F. (2001). The relation of a work-based mentoring program to the academic performance and behavior of African American students. *Journal of Vocational Behavior, 59*, 310–325.

Mauer, M. (1999). *Race to incarcerate.* New York: New Press.

Stevens, J. W. (1997). African American female adolescent identity development: A three-dimensional perspective. *Child Welfare, 76*, 145–173.

Thompson, L. A., & Kelly, V. L. (2001). The impact of mentoring on academic achievement of at-risk youth. *Children and Youth Services Review, 23*, 227–242.

Tolan, P. H., & McKay, M. M. (2004). Preventing serious antisocial behavior in inner-city children: An empirically based family intervention program. *Family Relations, 45*, 148–155.

Waller, A. W., Brown, B., & Whittle, B. (1999). Mentoring as a bridge to positive outcomes for teen mothers and their children. *Child and Adolescent Social Work Journal, 16*, 467–480.

Appendix A

Table 81.6A Program Components of the Recommended Early Intervention Prevention Approach for Latency-Age African American Youths and Families (suggested modules for pilot program)

Africentric Component Content	Examples of Main Intervention Steps	Examples of Experiential Activities and Exercises	Examples of Instructional Forms and Methods
Rites of Passage/P.I. Module: Kwanzaa: 7 Principles 6 Principles of Ma'at Learning motivation and practical applications Physical development Creative arts Peer relations/mutual aid Family life & quality Self- & cultural esteem Natural healers, health, nutrition, and hygiene Community service	Nia Principle (purpose): 1. Discuss the meaning of purpose related to their education (future benefits, collective responsibility) 2. Describe a historical figure or ancestor who represents the Nia principle: contributions, benefits 3. Have youths write 2–4 goals that could improve their education based on the discussion, explore: • the benefits of each goal for them, the black community, and society • cultural & other barriers/supports • action steps for reaching goals	Do action steps goal-setting exercise Other examples: 1. Participate in herb gardening project with elders 2. Develop tangible products at the end of each module on learning 3. Make African crafts (ceremonial masks, jewelry) and write a brief cultural story about them	Action Steps Goal-Setting Worksheet Other examples: 1. Pictures of garden's progress and mutual work with elders 2. Audiotape of youths speaking Kiswahili about learning from family life module 3. Cultural Story Guidelines Form
Africentric Education Module: African values/rituals African/African American history Political awareness Family and community history Spirituality Importance of culture African diversity Storytelling (griots)	Values clarification: 1. Convene youth focus group to identify racial concerns/challenges 2. Briefly write their challenging situations/the underlying values 3. Discuss a list of African values—contrast with Eurocentric values 4. Have them role play a challenging situation (#2 above) 5. Group discussion, post-role-play: • African values in situation/effects • Best strategy: theirs, an elder's?	Ancestral transformation role play (values clarification) Other examples: 1. Field trip to African exhibit or African American museum 2. Participate in storytelling event with elder or griot 3. Interview a first generation African American re transitions, cultural changes, and rituals	Ancestral Role Play Guidelines Form (values clarification) Other examples: 1. Field Trip Critics' Review Form 2. Draw picture of cultural lessons learned from the story and storytelling experience 3. Prepare 5-minute oral report on cultural transitions/rituals

Table 81.6B Program Components of the Recommended Early Intervention–Prevention Approach for Latency-Age African American Youths and Families (suggested modules for pilot program)

Culturally Focused Life Skills Component	Examples of Main Intervention Steps	Examples of Experiential Activities and Exercises	Examples of Instructional Forms and Methods
Optional Academic Tutoring Module: Good study habits Learning motivation and goal-setting skills Organization & planning African American learning styles Help-seeking skills Subject-specific tutorials	Building Effective Study Habits: 1. Engage youth in discussion on strengths and challenges in school 2. Help him/her identify 2 or more goals in challenged areas 3. Ask about steps taken in recent assignment; what worked or not 4. Integrate youth's analysis with review of 5 effective study habits 5. Use current assignment for youth to practice study habits in session	Apply study habit hints to steps planned for completing new class assignment Other examples: 1. Meet with high-achieving student to discuss his/her approach to learning and overcoming obstacles 2. Apply math tutorial problem lessons to program carpentry task	List of Five Effective Study Habits for African American Youths Other examples: 1. Do think sheet on good learning and overcoming obstacles 2. Use carpentry project as tangible product for math tutorial module
Parent Training Module: Quality of life/cultural maintenance process Africentric child development Parental supervision and discipline Parental rule setting and consistent consequences Parental communication, e.g., listening, culturally affirming messages, constructive feedback Nguzo Saba and values	Cultural Maintenance Process: 1. Define cultural maintenance and its effects (better family quality of life and coping with racial stress) 2. Have parents brainstorm examples of cultural activities they've done or would like to do 3. Group discussion: • cultural benefits of activities? • barriers to those activities (family or external obstacles), Q of L effects, how to overcome them? • priority activities for family based on children's development stages? • plan for doing priority activities?	In session practice: analyze family cultural maintenance priorities and do action plan Other examples: 1. Homework assignment: Catching Your Child Being Good 2. In session practice: role play parent coaching older youth on how to supervise younger sibling	Family Cultural Maintenance Action Plan Other examples: 1. "Atta Boy or Atta Girl" Parent Feedback Card 2. Facilitators' Feedback to Parents Role Play Form

Table 81.6C Program Components of the Recommended Early Intervention Prevention Approach for Latency-Age African American Youths and Families

Culturally Focused Life Skills Component	Examples of Main Intervention Steps	Examples of Experiential Activities and Exercises	Examples of Instructional Forms and Methods
Social Skills Module: Decision making Cultural stress: coping Anger management Self- and cultural esteem Resisting peer pressures Good communication Assertiveness Expressing feelings Developing friends	Decision Making in Action: 1. Review steps of skill with youths 2. Show videotape of a black youth's cultural story and decision dilemma 3. Group discussion: • the youth's goal in the story? • obstacles the youth encounters? • how obstacles can be overcome by applying decision-making steps? • what obstacles exist in their community; their lessons from real life?	Watch and analyze video of cultural story—skill demonstration representing peers' real-life dilemmas Other examples: 1. Journal about and discuss the effects of using social skill in real life 2. Role-play how to use a social skill as in-session practice activity	Youths' Skill Demonstration Comment Form Other examples: 1. Guidelines for Youths' Structured Journal Entries 2. Group facilitators' Feedback-Reinforcement form: In Session Practice Activities
Substance Abuse Prevention Module: Types of drugs/effects Effects on African American community Spirituality and drugs Resistance/coping skills	Consequences of Drug Use: 1. Show pictures of drugs and explain their effects on users, the community 2. Have group write 5 questions to ask person in recovery: the speaker	Listen to speaker discuss drugs, consequences, resistance, and prevention; ask written questions	Youths' Drug Abuse Interview Worksheet (5 questions)
Male-Female Relations Module: Self-definition Developing relationships Reproductive behaviors Sexual health Gender roles Tools for success	Defining/Affirming Oneself: 1. Have youths bring picture of self & negative media photo—same gender 2. Place all picture sets on board 3. Group discussion: • self-definition process & obstacles • 2 positives and effects: self picture • 2 negatives and effects: media picture	Develop written agreement to affirm self based on discussion about racial-gender media biases	Youths' Affirmation Pledge Action Steps Form

Appendix D

Table 81.6D Program Components of the Recommended Early Intervention Prevention Approach for Latency-Age African American Youths and Families

Collaborative Problem Solving and Action Component	Examples of Main Interventions	Examples of Experiential Activities and Exercises	Examples of Instructional Forms and Methods
Africentric Individual Family Consultation Module: Cultural network analysis/enhancement Solution-focused cultural questions Cultural validation Cultural value conflict analysis/resolution Broker/link resources Solution-focused action steps and monitoring	Cultural Network Analysis Mapping Process: 1. Have family identify concerns, reason for service request/referral 2. Explain how network analysis can make clear/address concerns 3. Review use of map, entries, their role as key cultural informants 4. Use solution-focused cultural questions to elicit information from member and write in entries 5. Help family identify understanding gained from process and goals	Complete cultural network analysis map over 2 or more sessions, having members listen to and respond to each other's views Other examples: 1. Do a family cultural awareness exercise to identify sources of intergenerational value conflicts 2. In-session practice: Participate in cultural self-validation role play 3. Homework assignment: Complete checklist of action steps taken	Africentric Cultural Network Analysis Map Other examples: 1. Cultural Awareness–Hidden Value Messages Exercise Form 2. Form: Steps for Cultural Self-Validation in Oppressive Situations 3. Action Step Check list Homework Card
Social Action Coaching Module: School–community analysis/intervention Cultural coaches' stories (overcoming/surviving) Coalition building Situations–options–consequences–solutions action planning and steps	Systems Analysis & Change: 1. Have family identify school–community concerns/make entries 2. Help them summarize supports and barriers in each domain 3. Gather detailed info on priority barrier and related support(s) 4. Brainstorm 3 or more culturally valued options and consequences 5. Identify optimal solution & plan	Do a family analysis of school- and community-related problems Other examples: 1. Share a cultural coaches' story about handling similar difficulties 2. Use the families' cultural analysis map to identify potential coalition members/collaborators	School–Community Ecomap for Analysis and Intervention Other examples: 1. Solution-focused cultural questions to elicit stories 2. Africentric Cultural Network Analysis Map

Figure 81.2. Action Steps Goal-Setting Worksheet

Name: Garrett Baker
Date: May 20, 2002

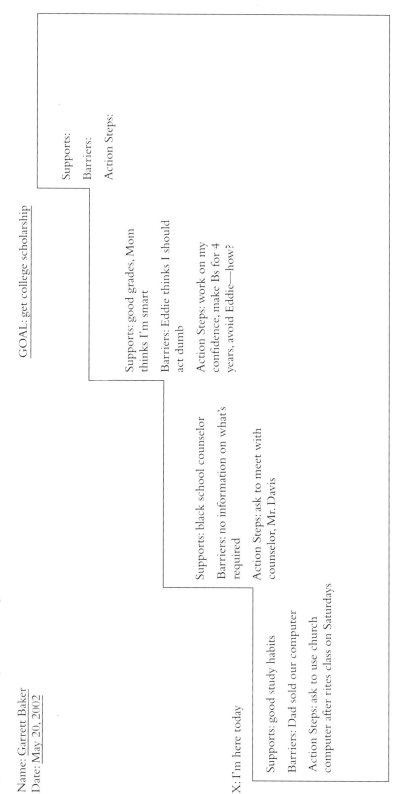

GOAL: get college scholarship

Supports:

Barriers:

Action Steps:

Supports: good grades, Mom thinks I'm smart

Barriers: Eddie thinks I should act dumb

Action Steps: work on my confidence, make Bs for 4 years, avoid Eddie—how?

Supports: black school counselor

Barriers: no information on what's required

Action Steps: ask to meet with counselor, Mr. Davis

X: I'm here today

Supports: good study habits

Barriers: Dad sold our computer

Action Steps: ask to use church computer after rites class on Saturdays

Figure 81.3. The Baker Family Example

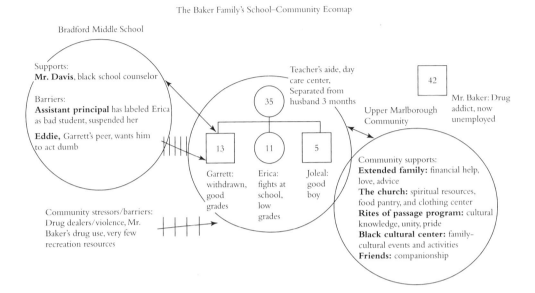

The Baker Family's School–Community Ecomap

Figure 81.4. *"Atta Girl" Parents' Feedback Card*

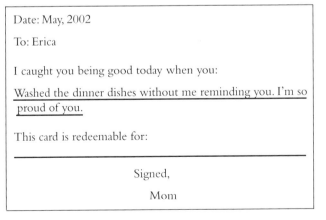

Appendix H

Figure 81.5. Youths' Affirmation Pledge–Action Steps Plan

Date: <u>May 2002</u>

Pledge:

There are many negative cultural messages and images about African Americans in newspapers, radio, video games, television, movies, magazines, music, schools, and the community. I, <u>Erica Baker</u> pledge that I will examine those messages and images for their hidden effects on me and other African Americans, and reject them starting today. I know this is hard work, but I'm committed to meeting my individual responsibility and to working with peers, family, program staff, and others to continue our efforts.

Action Steps:

Starting today, I will give positive messages to myself about me as an African American every day when I wake up. For example, I will say to myself: <u>Erica, you are a beautiful black girl and you're a good person.</u>

I will find another time during the day when I sometimes feel bad (<u>when I'm in school and think I can't learn, or the teacher says I'm slow</u>), and give myself more good messages like: <u>Erica, you're a good active learner: you're more mature and you don't give up easy.</u>

Appendix I

Figure 81.6. Field Trip Critics' Review Form

The Reviewer's Name: <u>Garrett Baker</u>
Date of Field Trip: <u>July 8, 2002</u>

Field Trip Event: <u>Museum exhibit: The Lega people of Africa (the Congo)</u>
Summary of the Review:

> The Lega people were very smart. They learned hundreds of African proverbs. Then they made art to explain their proverbs. The men were strong leaders. The families had to work together to understand the art and pass tests. They could only go to the next step if the husband and wife both passed the tests. Someone kept the Lega art so it is now in the museum. The art was amazing.

<u>Should other people see this or not see it?</u>
> It made me feel good to be a black male. All black boys and girls should see the exhibit. Parents too.

Interrace, Transrace: The Postmodern Youth Culture

Leslie Doty Hollingsworth

CHAPTER 82

Getting Started

Contemporary youth can be said to constitute a culture, defined by John Clarke, Stuart Hall, Tony Jefferson, and Brian Roberts, as a group or class of people having a "distinctive 'way of life,' [with accompanying] meanings, values, and ideas embodied in institutions and relations" (cited in Epstein, 1998, p. 9). Youth culture is characterized by, among other things, styles of dress, music, dance, and activist behaviors that some see as evidence of youth resistance to the status quo.

Contemporary youth are considered alternately as being in crisis and as having agency. From the crisis perspective, U.S. youth are seen as bombarded with problems, including "homelessness; school failure; addiction; apathy; gang involvement; police brutality and racial profiling; child-care crises; unemployment; violence in schools, neighborhoods, and families; parental neglect; excessive consumption; promiscuous sexuality and early pregnancy; the militarization of public space; the proliferation of weapons; and general alienation" (Maira & Soep, 2004, p. 252). In some cases, youth themselves are considered the problem, as when school failure is seen as their fault rather than that of the educational and larger systems (Maira & Soep). Or they may be seen as somewhat passively coping with systemic forces (Maira & Soep). In any case, it is problem behaviors such as those described that result in youth being referred to social workers in school settings for mental health counseling.

In the perspective of youth culture as characterized by agency, youth are perceived as being a source of creativity and innovation and as having the potential to positively affect their surroundings. The purpose of this chapter is to present a practice model—postmodern narrative practice, for providing mental health services to youth in school settings—that makes use of the "youth as crisis" and "youth as maintaining agency" perspectives.

The crisis and agency perspectives show up in considerations of race and ethnicity as well. Youth crisis perspectives call attention to the increased risk of problem behavior for racial and ethnic minority and immigrant youth. (See Chapters 73–81 for specific discussions of effective interventions with racial and ethnic minority/refugee and immigrant students.) The suggestion is that such youth would be better served if they were to "identify with middle-class white culture" (p. 260). An alternative view, however, is contained in the observation that many nonminority youth are "increasingly drawn to 'urban' black and latino youth culture" (Maira & Soep, 2004, p. 260). Maira and Soep write: "Sociologists of immigration who remain preoccupied with questions of (upward) class mobility fail to understand the ways in which these cross-ethnic or inter-racial affiliations may actually be adaptive for youth who find themselves marginalized within the class or racial hierarchies of the [United States] and feel distanced from the transplanted cultural rituals of their parents" (p. 260). Both problematic and positive elements associated with minority group and immigrant status should be considered in mental health intervention planning for youth.

The focus of narrative practice is on separating the problem from the identity of the person. The cliché often used is: "The person is not the problem; the problem is the problem." A practitioner using the narrative model does not disagree that a problem exists. However, the practitioner is interested in how it was possible for the problem to co-opt the youth into taking on its symptoms so that others and the youth come to perceive the youth as the problem (creating what is referred to as a *problem-saturated* identity or story). This process of shifting the paradigm in the way a problem is viewed is referred to as *externalizing the problem.*

Externalization involves actually personifying the problem so that the youth and others involved in the solution, including the practitioner, are able to recognize the power exerted by the problem and exceptions, that is, times when the youth has been able to resist giving in to the problem. The latter occasions are referred to as *historical unique outcomes.* Questions involved in externalizing the problem and identifying historical unique outcomes are referred to by some (e.g., Besa, 1994) as *relative influence questioning.* The goal is the creation of a new identity for the youth, a process referred to as *reauthoring.* Here, the youth is recognized as a key problem solver, an individual with personal agency, rather than as "the problem." A final step involves the gathering of an audience that recognizes the youth's new identity (*identifying communities of support*). The youth may be queried as to what persons are already potential celebrants of this new identity, persons who would not be surprised at such a new and different perception of the youth. Some practitioners make an effort to create communities of support for the new identity, persons who can act in association with the youth in lifting up the new identity. In school settings, school personnel should be kept in mind.

In narrative practice, the youth is considered the expert, the one with the knowledge necessary to move toward a solution of the presenting problem. Treatment is therefore collaborative, and the practitioner takes a position of curiosity and not-knowing, creating conversation and dialogue in which the youth is an active participant. The youth gives direction about who would be helpful to invite into the treatment process and what is apt to increase the potential for success in problem solving.

The social context and sociocultural conditions that surround the problem are considered important by many advocates of the narrative practice model (see White & Epston, 1990). What is there about external events, institutional structures, or societal values and ideologies that precipitate the problem? Examples in a school setting could be a tendency toward traditional and inflexible methods of educating youth, the stigmatization of contemporary youth, and overt and covert racism, sexism, ageism, or nationalism.

What We Know

The importance of an evidence base for mental health practice is increasingly stressed. Rones and Hoagwood (2000) characterize research leading to evidence-based practice as involving designs that are randomized, quasi-experimental, or multiple baseline designs. (See also chapter 114.) In the case of narrative practice, research that meets these criteria is limited. In defense of this limitation, however, it has been pointed out that holding to the requirements of a [scientific] evidence base may not be appropriate for constructionist models such as the narrative model. These models emphasize such components as personal hope and resourcefulness of the clients and the therapeutic relationship (see Larner, 2004), components that are less measurable than those associated with evidence-based practice but are more responsive to qualitative methods of inquiry (see Etchison & Kleist, 2000). As a compromise, some (e.g., Larner, 2004) recommend that continued efforts toward evidence-based practice be combined with an ethical best practice approach. Practitioners using ethical best practice approaches "choose interventions collaboratively with clients, using clinical intuition and research knowledge" (Larner, 2004, p. 31). Practitioners apply these techniques "in response to unique narratives of individuals in political, cultural, community, spiritual and family contexts" (p. 31). Case studies in the narrative practice literature often provide examples of ethical best practices.

One attempt at evidence-based research on narrative practice is David Besa's (1994) single-system design research, which uses multiple baselines in the application of the narrative model in work with six families reporting parent–child conflict. (Besa included under a description of parent–child conflict: "defiant behavior, keeping bad company, abuse of drugs, [and] school problems" [p. 309], making it relevant for this chapter.) Children in this study ranged from 8 to 17 years, with all but one being in early or middle adolescence. Parents were trained and subsequently conducted baseline measurements of the target behavior of the youth and took additional measurements during interventions and 1 month following the end of intervention. Interventions for various families were temporally staggered to ensure that the narrative therapy treatment package, and not intervening variables, was responsible for change. Improvements ranging from 88% to

98% were noted in the targeted youth behaviors for all six families, with improvements in five attributed directly to the interventions. (In the sixth family, a change in a parent's work schedule during the intervention period may have influenced the outcome.)

A caution mentioned by Besa (1994) is that in five of the six families in his study, behavioral contracts or practitioner advice were used in combination with narrative methods, in what Besa referred to as "between-session tasks" (p. 312) or later as a "treatment strategy package" (p. 323). (Though only the narrative method of externalization was used in the sixth family, it was this family in which the parental work schedule change may have affected the outcome.) In the discussion of his study, Besa acknowledges that this use of between-session tasks is in contrast to the practice used by some who wait for unique outcomes to emerge on their own. This caution is important because it suggests that an approach that combines other intervention methods, particularly behavioral ones, with the narrative method may be more effective than narrative practice alone in providing mental health services to youth. This possibility is consistent with findings from studies of clients' preferences in therapy. For example, in a study of families who unilaterally discontinued narrative therapy (Hoper, 1999), some terminations were found to be associated with an unmet desire for more guidance and solutions, more therapist alignment with parents (versus children), and incorporation of attention to cultural elements into the treatment. And in a survey of 75 persons who had received psychotherapy services, Giurelli (1999) found that the treatment events reported as most helpful were practitioner feedback, a solution focus, and practical steps that clients can carry out.

Tools and Practice Examples

The "Problem-Saturated" Story

Victoria Massey, who prefers the nickname Vicky, was referred to one of the school social workers in the public middle school she attends. The middle school is in a small suburban community in the Northeast. Vicky is a 14-year-old, African American eighth grader. Although her school attendance continued to be regular, her grades had consis-

tently dropped over the past year, to the point that she was not passing in any subjects. Teachers complained to her homeroom teacher that she had a bored, uninterested expression during classes, didn't bring in homework, and neither volunteered participation nor responded when called on. This was in contrast to her socially outgoing demeanor outside the classroom, where, teachers noted, she seemed popular with other students.

School records indicate that Vicky completed kindergarten through Grade 5 at one of the two local elementary schools in the community. She is slated to attend the one high school in the area next year. The community primarily has two-parent families, most of whom are Caucasian, in which one or both parents commute to jobs in a nearby city.

Vicky arrived promptly for the appointment that she had been excused from class to attend. She presented just slightly overweight, of average height, and dressed casually in faded jeans and a short knitted top with midlength sleeves. The social worker noted that her style of dress was similar to that of many of the girls in upper grades at the school. Her mood was pleasant, and she answered questions easily, though she did not volunteer information.

Relative Influence Questioning: Externalization of the Problem

The social worker was up front in stating her goal of making sure Vicky's experience at the school was a successful one. The observations from her teachers about her experiences in her classes suggested that wasn't totally the case right now. The social worker mentioned "boredom" as the term Vicky's teachers had used to describe the problem. She asked if Vicky would agree that boredom had taken control of her life at the school. Vicky confirmed that she was bored but had no explanation for what was different this year compared to previous ones or what would make things better. She came to school because "that's all there is to do," she said. She agreed that she got along well with other students, male and female.

Relative Influence Questioning: Historical Unique Outcomes

The social worker called attention to the fact that there seemed to be several situations in which boredom did not have a stronghold on Vicky. For example, Vicky had reported that prior to this year, boredom had not been a problem for her. She wondered how Vicky had been able to fight off boredom all those other years. Vicky thought nothing had really changed, but that was the problem. When she first came to the middle school, everything was new, and she liked being able to change classes rather than staying in the same room most of the day as she had done in elementary school. She also liked the additional subjects. She felt the school was great when students first came; but now everything seemed the same, and nothing was different enough to be of much interest. The social worker wondered what it would take to make classes interesting at this point. Vicky wasn't sure but said she'd think about it.

The social worker also noted that teachers said Vicky was popular with other students. She wondered how Vicky was able to fight off boredom enough to interact socially with other students and to be considered popular. Vicky wasn't sure she'd agree that she was popular. She had known most of the students at the school since she first started, and they knew her. She thought it may be a matter that they were familiar with each other, but she agreed that it wasn't the kind of familiarity that provided an opening for boredom like her classes did.

The social worker asked about home and whether Vicky was able to be successful at confronting boredom there. With an expression that bordered on hopelessness, Vicky said her family was the most boring of all. They didn't have anything interesting to talk about and asked the same questions or said the same thing over and over. In fact, she complained that they acted afraid most of the time. She couldn't adjust to it like her sister and brothers seemed to be able to.

Finally, the social worker asked if there were other situations or occasions when Vicky was successful at preventing boredom from taking over. Vicky thought the only other place she never felt bored was at the mall. She hung out there most afternoons and weekends with some freshmen and sophomores from the high school, along with one other girl from her school who was also in eighth grade and in some of her classes. They talk about a variety of things such as movies, concerts, and "different things that come up," but mostly they "just hang out until the mall closes." On a hunch, and knowing that only a small percentage of the students at Vicky's school were African American, the social worker asked if any of her "mall friends" were African American. Vicky acknowledged that they all were but was quick to add that it just

happened that way and that she had friends at school who were Caucasian and of other races and ethnicities as well and she was fine with them.

Vicky said she didn't mind taking part in the assessment and hearing the social worker's conclusions and recommendations. She gave the social worker permission to talk with her parents and one particular teacher she thought knew her best. She also accepted the referral to the school psychometrist for testing and evaluation.

Consideration of Social Context

Meeting Vicky's parents was immediately instructive; they were a white couple in their 40s who adopted Vicky when she was 3 months old. The parental rights of Vicky's birth mother had been terminated following Vicky's birth because the mother had been found guilty of neglect 3 years earlier, and the neglect had resulted in that child's death. The birth mother subsequently served 14 months in prison for negligent homicide. The birth mother, 20 years old at the time of Vicky's birth, had a history of heroin addiction although there was no evidence of drugs at Vicky's birth. Vicky's birth mother was unsure of the identity of the birth father, and paternity was never established. Extended family members declined responsibility for her care. None of the birth family, all of whom lived in California where Vicky was born, had ever made any effort to contact Vicky or the Massey family, and Vicky had never expressed an interest in having contact with them.

Mr. and Mrs. Massey had tried unsuccessfully for five years for a biological pregnancy before they made the decision to adopt Vicky. Ten months after they adopted Vicky, Mrs. Massey became pregnant with their younger daughter, whose birth was followed by two sons. The biological children are all two years apart. Vicky's sister, Stephanie, entered the same middle school this year, as a sixth grader and was already excelling academically and in sports. She had been selected for the varsity cheerleading squad and girls' track team captain for next year.

The Masseys described Vicky as having been "high demand from the very beginning," requiring more of their time and attention "than the other three children put together." As Vicky got older, they had "bent over backward" to make sure she didn't feel she was different or inadequate as a result of being of a race different from that of the rest of the family.

Vicky had always been very bright and quick academically, and everyone who met her commented on what a social person she was. She seemed to fit in easily wherever she went and never complained of feeling different from her sister and brothers or from other children. However, in the past year, she had become belligerent and violent at home, to the point that the other children were "afraid to cross her." Mr. and Mrs. Massey acknowledged that they had increasingly excused her from chores around the house and acquiesced to her demands to go to the mall (which was walking distance from their home), even when they knew she should be doing her homework. As a result, her grades had deteriorated badly. Things had reached the point at which the entire family basically "walked on eggshells" whenever they were around Vicky. They had wondered whether there may have been an effect of her birth mother's heroin addiction that wasn't picked up at the time of Vicky's birth or whether there may have been serious mental illness on the birth father's side since they had no records on him.

Results of the psychometric and psychological evaluations showed no indication of psychological, neurological, or learning disorder. Vicky showed cognitive ability above her grade level, in spite of her failing grades. Records from her most recent physical examination also were normal for a female adolescent of Vicky's age.

Consideration of Sociocultural Conditions

The male teacher recommended by Vicky suspected a conflict between Vicky's active, outgoing personality, one never slow to question and challenge, and the more structured, traditional style of teaching at the upper level of the middle school grades. Vicky's choice for coping with the conflict may have been to shut down. He also thought race was probably more of an issue than Vicky herself acknowledged. Although the school and community prided themselves on their socially liberal history, the environment was, for the most part, racially and ethnically homogeneous and lacking in a culturally diverse presence. The fact that racial differences often resurface during adolescence may have added to race becoming an issue for Vicky. Her sister's entry and quick success into the school setting may have threatened Vicky's identity and "place."

Creation of Between-Session Tasks

Together the teacher and social worker came up with the idea of exploring with Vicky whether she would be willing to assume a leadership role in the school with the aim of making it academically and socially more responsive to the needs of entering African American and other minority group and immigrant students. The teacher offered to serve as mentor or sponsor.

In a follow-up meeting with Vicky, the social worker disclosed the overall outcome of the testing and summarized the thoughts suggested by the male teacher. Vicky immediately brought up the idea of a Black Student Union, an organization she'd read about as existing in some other schools. At some places there was a larger organization in which members of the Black Student Union and other student groups came together to plan and collaborate. Vicky came up with the idea of a variety of new organizations that incoming students could choose from according to what was important to them. (It was a creative example of multiple perspectives on culture.) She volunteered to talk with the other African American female student she hung out with at the mall and to contact the male teacher to set up a meeting to talk about what would be involved in starting an organization. The social worker scheduled a follow-up meeting that provided Vicky with enough time to follow through on what she planned, but she told Vicky to contact her in the interim if there was a need. Vicky agreed to a follow-up meeting with her parents at which they would be told of results, progress, and plans.

Double Description: Moving From the Old Description to the New

The social worker realized, in talking with Mr. and Mrs. Massey during the follow-up meeting, that in an effort to avoid causing Vicky to feel different, the couple may have inadvertently failed to acknowledge her differentness and the positive aspects of it. In fact, through her belligerent and violent behavior, Vicky may actually have cooperated in making it easier for her to be separate from the family. Mr. and Mrs. Massey caught on right away that they needed to find ways of celebrating Vicky's racial differentness and, at the same time, of bringing her back into the family. The latter would involve having expectations of Vicky as a family member, commensurate with her age and developmental status. The social worker gave them information about a small community group of parents of multiracial families who could be good mentors and supports in working toward their new goals (*additional between-session tasks*). It would be important for Vicky to have a role as well in looking into the group. Another appointment was planned tentatively for which Vicky would be asked to coordinate scheduling. The purpose for this appointment was to make sure all were in agreement with what was to happen in the future. That meeting was held 2 weeks later.

Reauthoring: Contrasting the "Problem-Saturated Story" With an Emerging New Story

Although the social worker and Vicky waved at each other in the hallway or at school activities several times during the school year, she did not have occasion to see the family together until she attended graduation ceremonies for Vicky's class. Vicky was introduced as the organizer and outgoing president of the School's Black Student Union. She had also served as the program chair of the Union of Student Organizations. Further, Vicky was listed on the program as a member of the National Honor Society, indicating that her academic functioning and grades had much improved. The ceremony included a torch-passing activity in which graduating organizational leaders passed the torch to new officers. Vicky passed the torch to the new president of the Black Student Union. The social worker was among the many in the audience with teary eyes as Vicky was loudly applauded by all the other students.

Practice Resources

The following books and videos are useful to practitioners who want to further their skills in using the narrative practice model and to familiarize themselves with youth culture as agency. Also, regular peer consultation involving other practitioners committed to the use of this model is recommended.

- Michael White and David Epston (1990). *Narrative means to therapeutic ends.* New York: Norton. This is the seminal work on narrative practice.
- The next three chapters are found in Craig Smith and David Nylund (Eds.) (1997). *Narrative*

therapy with children and adolescents. New York: Guilford Press:

- Lisa Berndt, Victoria C. Dickerson, and Jeffrey L. Zimmerman, "Tales told out of school." Contains case studies illustrating methods specific to practice in school settings using the narrative model, along with explanations of how the structure and value system of many U.S. schools are problem-saturating for youth.
- Tom Hicks, "Sex, drugs, and postmodern therapy: A teen finds her voice." Contains a case study illustrating the use of the narrative approach with a young woman with a history of trauma and abuse and current problems of drug abuse and sexual promiscuity.
- Colin Sanders, "Re-authoring problem identities: Small victories with young persons captured by substance abuse." Contains case illustrations of applying the narrative practice method with youth in residential treatment for substance abuse.

- Stephanie Milan and Margaret Keiley. (2000). Biracial youth and families in therapy: Issues and interventions. *Journal of Marital and Family Therapy, 26,* 305–315. Recognizes the problem-saturated stories that may be directed at or internalized by interracial youth and families and provides ways that interracial families can be assisted in recognizing and re-storying their own narratives.
- *Harlem Diary: Nine voices of resilience.* The abstract for this film from the Discovery Channel describes it as following: "Terry Williams, a sociologist and author of the widely acclaimed book, *The Uptown Kids: Struggle and Hope in the Projects,* challenged nine young Harlem residents to use video cameras to record their lives over several months. The result is an award-winning program, a powerful, autobiographical collage of themselves and their unique neighborhood. Ranging in age from 12 to 26, the youth of *Harlem Diary* face incredible challenges and real-world dangers as they focus on goals that include college, careers, and parenting." A Discovery Channel Production (97 minutes, color), 1997–2004 Films for the Humanities and Sciences, PO Box 2053, Princeton, NJ, 08543-2053, Ph.: 800-257-5126, Fax: 609-671-0266. Abstract retrieved January 10, 2005, from http://www.films.com/Films_Home/Item.cfm/1/32765
- *Narrative Therapy with Dr. Stephen Madigan,* Allyn & Bacon, 75 Arlington St., Suite 300,

Boston, MA, 02116. This video demonstrates application of the narrative model in a court-ordered interview with a 13-year-old African American youth and his mother.

- *Reviving Ophelia: Saving the selves of adolescent girls.* (Video) Mary Pipher, Ph.D., writes in description: "Here, for the first time, are girls' unmuted voices from the front lines of adolescence, personal and painfully honest. By laying bare their harsh day-to-day reality, *Reviving Ophelia* issues a call to arms and offers parents compassion, strength, and strategies with which to revive these Ophelias' lost sense of self." Therapeutic Resource, Ph.: 888-331-7114. Abstract retrieved January 10, 2005, from http://www.therapeuticresources.com/0345392825text.html

- *Struggle for identity: Issues in transracial adoption.* (1998). In this 20-minute video, "transracial adoptees and their families confront difficult issues of racism, identity and sense of place in candid discussions about their lives." Photo-Synthesis Productions, Ph.: 607-272-4242. New York State Citizens Coalition for Children, 306 E. State St., #220, Ithaca, NY, 14850, Ph. 607-272-0034, office@ nysccc.org

Discussion

The case study combines the use of a structured assessment tool for assessing suicide risk with the use of ethnographic assessment methods and interventions accompanying the narrative practice approach.

Structured assessment for suicidal tendencies and other affective disturbances is important to avoid mislabeling as "boredom" symptoms that, in adolescents, may indicate the presence of serious psychiatric disorders. Winters, Myers, and Proud (2002) provide information regarding specific scales that have produced acceptable levels of reliability and validity in this regard.

Assessment processes used in the case illustration representing the narrative practice model included identification of the "problem-saturated story" and identification of historical unique outcomes, consideration of the influence of social context on the problem, and consideration of sociocultural conditions—all obtained by questioning Vicky, her parents, and the male teacher. Intervention was collaborative and included the use of between-session tasks developed in collaboration with the client, who, consistent with the

narrative model, was treated as the expert in actually formulating the tasks. Intervention also included enlisting the involvement of Vicky's parents in the reauthoring process.

These assessment and intervention methods are consistent with those identified by Etchison and Kleist (2000) in their review of narrative therapy research. The interventions used coincide with those identified by Besa (1994) as having been effective in his treatment of five out of six families presenting with parent–child conflicts. In fact, Besa reports that the results obtained when these interventions were used in his study agree with case studies showing narrative therapy to be effective. Though this would suggest validation of these interventions, Besa does not provide sufficient information about the case studies and the methodology applied in examining them to allow for conclusions about the validity of the interventions used.

The collaborative nature of the work in the case illustration, and the treatment of the client as expert both in her situation and in developing the between-session tasks, was consistent with findings of another ethnographic study (O'Connor, Meakes, Pickering, & Schuman, 1997). In that study, eight families reported valuing those elements of narrative therapy that provided them with a sense of personal agency and that allowed them to be treated as experts in their own experiences. This adds to the validity of the narrative intervention, at least within the limits of ethnographic research.

Finally, the social worker in the case illustration built on ethnic group membership and ethnic identity in presenting the context within which the intervention with Vicky (between-session tasks) could be developed. In their examination of the structure and construct validity of the Multigroup Ethnic Identity Measure (MEIM), Roberts et al. (1999) found that ethnic identity was positively correlated with measures of psychological well-being (coping, mastery, self-esteem, optimism, and happiness) and negatively correlated with loneliness and depression. These findings are consistent with those of Stalikas & Gavaki (1995), who noted better academic functioning among minority group adolescents with a strong ethnic identity. Thus, the incorporation of ethnic minority group status and ethnic identity is a valid consideration in developing the intervention.

In her meeting with Vicky's parents, the social worker used two interventions described elsewhere. First, the social worker called the parents' attention to the importance of acknowledging rather than ignoring the differentness that existed between Vicky and biological members of the family, a recommendation discussed by Kirk (1964). Finally, the social worker helped Vicky's parents to recognize that they needed to have expectations of Vicky, commensurate with her age and stage of development, as a member of the family. Kail and Cavanaugh (2004) discuss the positive relation of rules and discipline to self-esteem and self-worth in youth.

Key Points to Remember

This chapter sets forth a model of practice for use by social workers and other mental health professionals in school settings where youth present with behavior difficulties. The narrative practice model is particularly relevant where race and ethnicity and broader elements of social context are important. Though not meeting the criteria for evidence-based practice, the model is worthy of consideration as ethical best practice and includes interventions drawn from prior research or developmental theory.

Patricia Romney's paper "Reflecting on Race and Family Identity: Therapy With a Multiracial Adoptive Family" served as a guide in the development of this chapter. This paper, listed among references for this chapter, is now out of print, and I am grateful to Romney for making it available to me. For a hard copy, readers may contact Romney at romney@romneyassociates.com

References

Besa, D. (1994). Evaluating narrative family therapy using single-system research designs. *Research on Social Work Practice, 4,* 309–325.

Epstein, J. S. (1998). Introduction: Generation X, youth culture, and identity. In J. S. Epstein (Ed.). *Youth cul-* *ture: Identity in a postmodern world* (pp. 1–23). Malden, MA: Blackwell.

Etchison, M., & Kleist, D. M. (2000). Review of narrative therapy: Research and utility. *The Family Journal: Counseling and Therapy for Couples and Families, 8,* 61–66.

Giurelli, B. L. (1999). Clients as consultants: Understanding what consumers find helpful in therapy. (Doctoral dissertation, Antioch University/New England Graduate School, Keene, NH, 1990.) UMI No. 9940371.

Hoper, J. H. (1999). Families who unilaterally discontinue narrative therapy: Their story, a qualitative study. (Doctoral dissertation, Texas Woman's University, Denton.) UMI No. 9932889.

Kail, R. V., & Cavanaugh, J. C. (2004). *Human development: A life-span view.* Belmont, CA: Wadsworth/ Thomson Learning.

Kirk, H. D. (1964). *Shared fate: A theory of adoption and mental health.* London: Free Press.

Larner, G. (2004). Family therapy and the politics of evidence. *Journal of Family Therapy, 26,* 17–39.

Maira, S., & Soep, E. (2004). United States of adolescence: Reconsidering U.S. youth culture studies. *Research on Youth and Youth Cultures, 12,* 245–269.

O'Connor, T. S. J., Meakes, E., Pickering, R., & Schuman, M. (1997). On the right track: Client experience of narrative therapy. *Contemporary Family Therapy, 19,* 479–495.

Roberts, R. E., Phinney, J. S., Masse, L. C., Chen, Y. R., Roberts, C. R., & Romero, A. (1999). The structure of ethnic identity of young adolescents from diverse ethnocultural groups. *Journal of Early Adolescence, 19,* 301–322.

Romney, P. (1995). Reflecting on race and family identity: Therapy with a multiracial adoptive family. *In Session: Psychotherapy in Practice, 1,* 87–99.

Rones. M., & Hoagwood, K. (2000). School-based mental health services: A research review. *Clinical Child and Family Psychology Review, 3,* 223–241.

Stalikas, A., & Gavaki, E. (1995). The importance of ethnic identity: Self-esteem and academic achievement of second-generation Greeks in secondary school. *Canadian Journal of School Psychology, 11,* 1–9.

White, M., & Epston, D. (1990). *Narrative means to therapeutic ends.* New York: Norton.

Winters, N. C., Myers, K., & Proud, L. (2002). Ten-year review of rating scales. III: Scales assessing suicidality, cognitive style, and self-esteem. *Journal of the American Academy of Child and Adolescent Psychiatry, 41,* 1150–1181.

Working With Gay, Lesbian, Bisexual, and Transgender Students

Diane E. Elze

Getting Started

Multiple studies have shown that many gay, lesbian, bisexual, and transgender (GLBT) youths navigate family, school, and community environments marked by victimization, stigmatization, discrimination, and a lack of support from peers and adults (Bochenek & Brown, 2001; D'Augelli, Pilkington, & Hershberger, 2002; Elze, 2002, 2003; Kosciw, 2004; Mallon, 1999). Evidence exists that such experiences are associated with psychological distress, health risk behaviors (D'Augelli et al., 2002; Elze, 2002; Garofalo, Wolf, Kessel, Palfrey, & DuRant, 1998; Safren & Heimberg, 1999), and school-related problems (Russell, Seif, & Truong, 2001), although many GLBT youths do quite well (Savin-Williams, 1995).

Interventions for GLBT students must not only address their individual needs, but must transform the environmental contexts within which these young people function (D'Augelli, 1996; Elze, 2002; Mallon, 1998). School social workers are uniquely positioned to provide counseling, information, and referrals to sexual minority adolescents; to aid school-based support groups and to guide students in establishing gay-straight alliances (GSAs); and to provide training and consultation on sexual orientation and gender identity diversity to students, teachers, administrators, support staff, and parents (Elze, 2003).

What We Can Do

Preparing Yourself for Discussing Sexual Orientation and Gender Identity Issues

Become an "askable" person who signals to students that they can safely discuss issues of sexuality, sexual orientation, and gender identity with you. Researchers and practitioners have identified strategies that practitioners can use to ready themselves for talking with youths about sexual orientation and gender identity issues (Elze, 2003; Longres & Etnyre, 2004; Mallon, 1998, 1999; Ryan, 2001; Schneider, 1997; Tully, 2000). Explore your own biases, feelings, beliefs, and attitudes toward diversity in sexual orientation, gender identity, and gender expression. Educate yourself about the psychosocial strengths and needs of GLBT youths (see Table 83.2) and potential foci of interventions (see Table 83.3). Familiarize yourself with local, state, and national resources for GLBT youths and their families. Display culturally diverse, GLBT-affirmative books, posters, magazines, brochures, and symbols in your office. Regularly obtain a copy of the local GLBT newspaper. Identify mental and physical health care professionals who specialize in serving transgender adolescents.

Demonstrating That You Are Askable

The strategies that signal to GLBT youths that you are a supportive person may precipitate questions from heterosexual youths and colleagues, providing opportunities for consciousness-raising. Always correct myths, stereotypes, and other misinformation that students and colleagues articulate

Table 83.1 Glossary of Terms

Bisexual: A person whose sexual attraction, both physical and affectional, is directed toward persons of both sexes, though the degree of attraction may vary.

Coming Out: The developmental process of becoming aware of one's sexual orientation or gender identity and disclosing it to others.

Gender: Gender is an ascribed social status we are assigned at birth, based on the sex category to which we are assigned. Our society (though not all) has constructed two genders—"male" and "female."

Gender Dysphoria: Clinical symptoms of excessive discomfort, confusion, pain, and anguish from feeling an incongruity with the gender assigned to one at birth. Gender dysphoric young people often suppress and hide these feelings from others. Not all transgender youths experience gender dysphoria; some have stable identities.

Gender Expression: The communication of gender or gender identity through behaviors (e.g., mannerisms, speech patterns, dress) and appearance culturally associated with a particular gender. The ways in which people express and view gender are influenced by societal definitions of gender.

Gender Identity: A person's inner sense of being male, female, both, or something else; the gender with which one identifies, regardless of their biological sex.

Gender Role: The society's prescriptions for being male and female; the pattern of attitudes, behaviors, and beliefs dictated by society that define what it means to be male and female.

Homosexual: A person whose sexual attraction, both physical and affectional, is primarily directed toward persons of the same sex. *Gay* and *lesbian* are contemporary synonyms to refer to men and women, respectively. Some young people prefer the word *queer*, finding it more inclusive. People may be involved in same-sex sexual activities and relationships but not identify themselves as gay, lesbian, or bisexual.

Heterosexism: An ideological system that devalues and stigmatizes any nonheterosexual identity, behavior, relationship, or community. Heterosexism can exist at the personal, interpersonal, institutional, or cultural levels.

Internalized Homophobia (Biphobia, Transphobia) or Heterosexism: The acceptance and internalization of negative stereotypes and images about GLBT people by GLBT people.

Sex: In this culture, sex means biologically male or biologically female. A person is assigned to a sex category at birth on the basis of what the genitalia looks like. *Intersex* refers to a person who is born with sex chromosomes, external genitalia, or an internal reproductive system that is not considered to be society's norm for either male or female.

Sexual Orientation: The direction of one's sexual attraction, or physical and affectional attraction, which can be toward the same sex (homosexuality) or other sex (heterosexuality), both sexes (bisexuality), or neither. Gay, lesbian, and bisexual people are *gender variant* in that they are violating societal norms of sexual-object choice.

Transgender: An umbrella term that describes people whose gender identity and/or gender expression may be different from their biological sex or in violation of societal gender norms. They are, in other words, *gender variant*. This term may include preoperative transsexuals, postoperative transsexuals, nonoperative transsexuals, cross-dressers, gender benders, drag kings, and drag queens. (Not all transsexuals desire genital reassignment surgery.) Transgender people may be heterosexual, bisexual, gay, lesbian, or asexual. Gender variance in children may forecast a same-sex sexual orientation or transgenderism (with or without gender dysphoria), or may simply indicate variance in gender expression.

Table 83.2 Psychosocial Strengths and Needs to Explore With GLBT Youths

Individual

- Developmental history of same-sex attractions or gender identity issues.
- Intersection of sexual/gender identity development with racial identity development.
- Availability and accuracy of information about sexual orientation, gender identity, and GLBT people (i.e., cognitive isolation).
- Feelings and beliefs about sexual orientation or gender identity.
- Degree of social isolation (e.g., disclosure to anyone).
- Fears related to disclosure and its consequences.
- Chronic stress from managing stigmatization related to sexual, gender, and racial identity.
- Grief and loss issues (e.g., rejection by family and friends; perceived loss of status and dreams for their future).
- Coping strategies for dealing with stigmatization and other stressors.
- Spiritual or religious beliefs regarding sexual orientation and gender identity diversity.
- Awareness of HIV/AIDS, involvement in risky sexual behaviors, and use of risk reduction strategies.
- Mental health problems (e.g., depression, risk of suicide, anxiety, self-mutilation, substance use).

Family

- Cultural values, beliefs, and meanings related to sexuality, gender roles, marriage, childrearing, and parental expectations of children.
- Awareness of the youth's sexual orientation or gender identity (e.g., Do family members know? Were they told? By whom? Did they find out another way? How long have they known? How did they react?)
- Actual or anticipated risks in disclosing (e.g., violence, being thrown out of the house).
- Actual or anticipated attitudes of family members.
- Presence of other GLBT people in the lives of family members.
- Other family stressors (e.g., substance use, mental illness, family violence, financial stress).
- History of physical, sexual, or emotional abuse and/or neglect.
- Nature of family's coping responses to crises and other challenges.

Peers

- Nature of peer support (e.g., How do they describe their relationships with their peers? What kind of support have they historically received from them?)
- Disclosure history (e.g., How many friends have they confided in? What was their response? How many friends could they confide in? How open can they be with their peers?)
- Actual or anticipated attitudes of peer group.
- Conflicts in or loss of peer relationships.
- Presence of other GLBT youths in peer group.
- Availability of GLBT peers in community or on Internet.
- History of dating relationships, availability of age-appropriate dating partners.

School and Community

- The importance of attachments to ethnic community.
- Experiences with "coming out" or being perceived as GLBT.
- Expressions of heterosexism (e.g., antigay remarks, assumptions of heterosexuality).
- Experiences with harassment and discrimination from students and professionals.
- Interactions between heterosexism and racism, sexism, ableism, and classism in school and community.
- Potential sources of support (e.g., Gay-Straight Alliance, community groups, Internet, school staff, library materials).

Sources: Elze, 2002; Hershberger & D'Augelli, 2000; Mallon, 1998; Ryan, 2001; Ryan & Futterman, 1998; Savin-Williams, 1995; Schneider, 1997.

Table 83.3 Traits of an "Askable" Practitioner

Self-awareness about personal beliefs and attitudes	+	Knowledge and appreciation of GLBT youth	+	Competent social work skills	+	Privilege professional over personal values	=	Ability to work with GLBT youth

about GLBT people. Normalize sexual orientation diversity and gender variant behavior, and educate others to affirm diversity in gender expressions. When explaining to students what you do in your job, include sexual orientation, gender identity, and sexuality concerns as examples of the issues that students come and talk with you about. For example: "Jasmine, students come to see me for help with many different issues, like stress that is interfering with their studies; worries about alcohol or other drug use; fights with parents; problems with racism in school; concerns or questions about their sexual orientation or their gender identity; problems with homelessness; and a lot of other issues."

Use more inclusive language when exploring youths' dating interests, romantic relationships, sexual behaviors, and concerns about sexuality in assessments and intervention sessions. Use words like "partner," "special person," or "girlfriend or boyfriend." You may ask, for example, "Have you been dating anyone? A girl? A boy? Girls and boys?" "Have you been feeling attracted to girls or boys, or to both?" When discussing sexual behaviors, ask all youths, "Have you been or are you currently sexually active with males, females, or with both males and females?" This is particularly important when talking with young people about risk reduction strategies related to HIV or other sexually transmitted infections and pregnancy.

If a student responds angrily or with surprise at such a question, respond with a GLBT-affirmative statement, using a gentle, matter-of-fact tone of voice. Be aware that students with same-sex attractions may be testing you to see if you will agree with a homophobic statement. You also want to avoid causing young people to worry that you "saw something in them" that signaled to you that they might be GLBT. For example:

School Social Worker: "Jason, I can see that something is really bothering you that is hard for you to talk about. Is that right? (Jason nods.) So far, you've said that things are OK at home, and football is going well. You're having some problems in math, but you feel like you're handling that by getting some extra help. You've

also said that you're not involved with any drinking or drugs, especially because football is important to you. Is that right? (Jason nods.) I know that many young people have concerns about dating relationships, or about their sexual feelings. Have you been having any concerns about your sexuality, like whether you are attracted to girls or to boys? Any concerns about your sexual feelings?"

Jason: "Why are you asking me that? Do you think I'm queer or something?"

School Social Worker: "I'm glad you're checking that out with me. I ask those questions of every student who appears distressed or troubled about something. Many students do have questions about their sexuality. Some students are attracted to people of the same sex, and some students identify as gay, lesbian, or bisexual. I believe it is important that young people, if they need to, have a chance to talk about those issues in a safe and confidential setting. Does that make sense? Do you have any other concerns about why I asked you that question? It's OK to check it out with me."

With youths who are sexually active, do not assume the gender of their sexual partners, regardless of how they self-identify. We know that youths who identify as heterosexual report same-sex sexual activities, and that self-identified gay and lesbian youths report other-sex sexual activities.

Best Practices With GLBT Youths

Although specific interventions with gay, lesbian, and bisexual youths have yet to be empirically tested, a compendium of best practices frequently appears in the social work, psychology, and education literatures (Hershberger & D'Augelli, 2000; Lipkin, 2004; Longres & Etnyre, 2004; Mallon, 1998; Ryan, 2001; Schneider, 1997; Tully, 2000). Less attention has been paid to transgender adolescents. Treatment strategies with gender variant youths have often been grounded in theories that pathologize and aim to eliminate gender variant behaviors, despite the lack of empirical evidence supporting their effectiveness (Israel & Tarver, 1997; Lev, 2004). This chapter takes a gender variant affirmative approach to social work practice with transgender youths (see Mallon, 1999).

When providing services to GLBT youths, respect the students' confidentiality. Do not disclose students' sexual orientation or gender identity to parents, other caretakers, school personnel, or students. Follow your professional code of ethics. Do not assume that GLBT youths' problems are related to their sexual orientation or gender identity, and do not assume that they are not. Remember that these young people are, first and foremost, adolescents, and they may bring to you such issues as clinical depression and other mental disorders, parental substance abuse or mental illness, parental unemployment and financial stress, and domestic violence.

During a session with the school social worker, Emily, a 14-year-old lesbian, said that she felt very lonely, had no friends at school, and believed that everyone was against her because of her sexual orientation. Upon further exploration, Emily disclosed that she had always been very shy and found it difficult to initiate conversations; she had only two close friends in junior high, both of whom had moved away. After realizing her sexual orientation, she felt even more self-conscious, fearing the reactions of her peers if they found out. Emily and the social worker agreed that they would work together on developing Emily's social skills and exploring her concerns around self-disclosure. Emily did not feel ready to attend a community-based GLBT youth group, but she thought she'd talk about that again at a later date with the social worker.

Affirm, validate, and accept youths' expressions of gender variance; same-gender attractions, desires, and behaviors; and self-identification and confusion. Even under the best of circumstances, coming out can be a confusing and difficult process, with youths experiencing feelings of loneliness, anxiety, fear, isolation, shame, loss, and guilt. Remember to start where the client is starting and proceed with gentleness and patience. With transgender youths, respect their wishes by using their preferred names and pronouns, and do not demand or enforce stereotypical gender behavior.

Avoid labeling young people, but instead help them safely explore and understand their feelings, thoughts, and behaviors related to sexuality or gender identity. Follow the youth's lead in using terminology. However, be able to say the

words *gay*, *lesbian*, *bisexual*, and *transgender* comfortably and without hesitation. For example, you can reflect back the student's feelings and pose a question, as follows: "Katie, you've been having sexual feelings about your best friend, and this is worrying you. Have you been worrying that you may be gay?" When a youth discloses to you that s/he is gay, lesbian, bisexual, or transgender, respond in an affirming, supportive way; anticipate concerns about confidentiality; and give the message that you are willing to talk about any issue. For example:

"Sergio, I feel honored that you trusted me enough to share with me that you are feeling attracted to men. Please know that I will keep that confidential. I would be very interested in hearing more about your experience, if you would like to talk about it, and what it is like for you here in school and with your family. Or if there is something else that you want to talk about altogether, I'm here for that, too."

For a highly distressed youth who cries, "I don't want to be gay," encourage further expression of feelings and explore with him or her the underlying beliefs and attitudes. The distress is often grounded in myths, stereotypes, and fears of rejection and stigmatization. For example: "Joel, I can see that you are very upset at these feelings you are having. Please tell me more about what makes you say that you don't want to be gay."

Help young people build self-esteem by correcting their internalized myths and stereotypes. They may believe that they cannot enter certain occupations, will never be able to have children, or will never have a long-term relationship. Provide them with accurate and GLBT-affirming literature, including fiction and nonfiction written especially for GLBT youths. Expose students to positive and culturally diverse GLBT role models through literature, guest speakers, and films.

Suspect gender identity issues if you witness, or are informed by another person, that a youth frequently raises questions or concerns about gender, adopts an other-gender identity, and/or makes regular attempts to cross-dress (Israel & Tarver, 1997). If you suspect a youth may be experiencing gender identity issues, explore using such questions as "Who would you like to be in 5 years, when you think about your future?" "How would you like your life to look in 5 years?" Remember that sexual orientation and gender identity are different. Transgender youths may self-identify as gay, lesbian, bisexual, or heterosexual, or they may question their sexual orientation or not label themselves. Validate their sexual orientation as it unfolds. Transgender youths may need help in differentiating between their gender identity and sexual orientation (Israel & Tarver, 1997).

Explore with students how issues of sexuality, gender, and gender variance intersect with issues of race, class, and disabilities in their lives (McCready, 2001). GLBT youths are affected not only by heterosexism, but by other forms of oppression depending upon their social group memberships and racial or ethnic group memberships. Believe students when they share their experiences with discrimination and prejudice. Be willing to listen to their anger about mistreatment without becoming defensive or feeling that you need to stick up for the dominant social group (e.g., heterosexual, white). Be aware that the risks of "coming out" vary from person to person. Do not assume that coming out is the best choice for everyone. Immigrant youths, youths with disabilities, and youths of color, for example, may have more to lose by self-disclosure, especially if they are already marginalized within their schools.

Enhancing Youths' Problem-Solving, Decision-Making, and Adaptive Coping Skills

Help students problem-solve challenging situations, such as coming out to friends and family members; handling stigmatization and discrimination; dealing with name-calling; avoiding risky situations such as adult-oriented clubs; and finding age-appropriate dating partner(s), peers, and social and recreational activities. Use role play to help students practice new interactions, such as disclosing their identity to others, asking a same-sex person for a date, or calling a GLBT organization.

Assess the safety of the youths' Internet use and, if necessary, provide them with safer strategies with which to communicate with people on the Internet and guidelines for meeting people (e.g., always meet in a public place; do not disclose your home address).

Explore the youths' readiness to attend a community-based GLBT youth group. The thought of attending a group can be very frightening for a youth in the early stages of coming out. Do not push. Ask, "Would you be interested in hearing some information about a local group for young people who are gay, lesbian, bisexual,

transgender, or questioning their sexuality?" Ease the youth's exploration of the group. Anticipate and explore the questions and concerns of your client and talk with the leaders of the group about its composition, climate, and culture (e.g., age range, racial/ethnic diversity, gender diversity, location, range of activities).

Changing the School Climate: Creating a GLBT-Affirming Environment

Empirical evidence exists that gay, lesbian, and bisexual youths' comfort within their schools is associated with particular qualities of their school environments, such as teachers and administrators who act on their behalf and their own integration into heterosexual peer networks as "out" youths (Elze, 2003) (Table 83.4). Secondary school students in Massachusetts rated their schools more highly on sexual-diversity climate the more their school implemented the Safe Schools Program, which consisted of GSAs, policies prohibiting antigay harassment and violence, and training of school personnel (Szalacha, 2001). Although little research exists on the effects of GSAs and psychoeducational support groups on GLBT students' psychosocial well-being, students and adult facilitators report that such groups help break isolation, build self-esteem and supportive peer relationships, promote positive identity formation, and build self-efficacy toward advocating for GLBT-affirmative policies and programs (Blumenfeld, 1995; Sheridan, 1997). Students of color, however, may not frequent GSAs because their schools' racially defined social boundaries may influence membership in extracurricular clubs. Multilevel strategies are required that will identify, analyze, and challenge the dynamics of racial separation (McCready, 2001).

Mezzo-level interventions, as shown in Table 83.5, focus on enhancing the fit between GLBT students and their school environment by creating a safe and affirming milieu that supports their development as adolescents and their acquisition of a positive GLBT identity. School social workers, in collaboration with their colleagues, can initiate, develop, advocate for, and implement a variety of interventions that aim to change anti-GLBT attitudes and behaviors, promote the inclusion of GLBT issues in the curricula, and increase the visibility of GLBT students and school personnel within the school community.

Table 83.4 Foci of Interventions for GLBT Youths

- Clinical interventions with GLBT adolescents.
  - Support for issues related to sexual orientation or gender identity.
    - Help build a positive sexual and gender identity.
    - Help youths of color build a positive racial identity.
    - Enhance self-esteem.
    - Provide psychoeducational support and information (e.g., sexuality, sexual orientation, sexual/gender identity development).
    - Educate on the cultural and institutional nature of oppression.
    - Address internalized oppression.
    - Correct myths and stereotypes.
    - Help find social support, build social connections, and find allies.
    - Help build adaptive coping strategies to manage stigmatization.
    - Help envision and plan for a positive and productive future.
  - Support for other issues that may be related to or exacerbated by sexual orientation or gender identity issues.
    - Communication with parents.
    - Interpersonal and institutionalized marginalization of youths of color.
    - Intrafamilial victimization.
    - Problems with peers.
    - Academic problems.
  - Support for issues unrelated to sexual orientation or gender identity.
    - Parental substance abuse.
    - Parental mental illness.
    - Clinical depression.
- Clinical interventions with family members.
  - Provide psychoeducational support and information.
  - Correct myths and stereotypes.
  - Provide empathic support for feelings of grief, loss, anger, fear, shame, and guilt.
  - Refer parents to knowledgeable community professionals and GLBT-affirmative spiritual/religious leaders.
- Interventions to reduce stigmatization in school and community environments.
  - Increase the capacity of school personnel to effectively interrupt oppressive behavior.
  - Support students in developing gay-straight alliances that reflect the cultural diversity of the school.
  - Support inclusion of GLBT issues in curricula.
  - Advocate for school policies that protect GLBT students and staff.
  - Testify in support of town ordinances granting civil rights protections and domestic partnership benefits to GLBT citizens.
  - Provide consultation and training to community-based youth-serving organizations.

Source: Elze, 2002; Hershberger & D'Augelli, 2000; Ryan, 2001; Savin-Williams, 1995; Schneider, 1997

Resources

Books, Articles, and Videos

Buckel, D. (1998). *Stopping anti-gay abuse of students in public schools: A legal perspective.* New York: Lambda Legal Defense & Education Fund. Available from http://www.lambdalegal.org

Cianciotto, J., & Cahill, S. (2003). *Education policy: Issues affecting lesbian, gay, bisexual, and transgender youth.* New York: National Gay and Lesbian Task Force Policy Institute. Available from http://www.ngltf.org

Gay, Lesbian, Straight Education Network. (2000). *The GLSEN lunchbox: A comprehensive training program for ending anti-gay bias in schools.* Available from GLSEN at http://www.glsen.org.

Table 83.5 Mezzo-Level Interventions

Physical Environment

- GLBT administrators, faculty, and support staff are open and visible.
- All school personnel are aware of their legal obligation to stop anti-GLBT harassment.
- All school personnel have been trained to effectively interrupt verbal abuse and derogatory remarks.
- Transgender students can use bathrooms that correspond with their gender identity, or the faculty-staff bathroom or the bathroom in the nurse's office.
- Transgender students take physical education classes congruent with their identity and are provided with reasonable accommodations in school locker rooms.
- GLBT brochures, posters, and resource lists are displayed in school offices.
- GLBT books are in the school library.
- School dances are welcoming environments for same-sex couples and gender-variant young people. Chaperones are trained to be GLBT-affirmative.
- The school newspaper includes articles on GLBT issues.
- The school has a gay-straight alliance that is actively supported by administration, faculty, support staff, parents, and students.
- GLBT youth resources are included in student handbooks and resource lists.

Inclusive Curricula

- Bullying and violence prevention programs include harassment based on sexuality and gender nonconformity.
- Suicide, substance abuse, and dropout prevention programs integrate information about the unique stressors affecting the well-being of GLBT youths.
- Health and sexuality curricula integrate information about same-sex sexual attractions, healthy same-sex relationships, and diverse family contexts.
- Multicultural programs and community resource days should include GLBT issues.
- Teachers should be provided with consultants and peer mentors to help them appropriately integrate GLBT issues into courses.

Policies

- Enact antiharassment and nondiscrimination policies that include sexual orientation and gender expression.
- Apply school dress codes in a gender-neutral manner. Allow students to dress in a manner that reflects their gender identity.

Sources: Bochenek & Brown, 2001; D'Augelli, 1996; Elze, 2003; Lipkin, 2004; Schneider, 1997.

Governor's Commission on Gay and Lesbian Youth. (1993). *Making schools safe for gay and lesbian youth: Breaking the silence in schools and in families*. Boston: Author. Available from the commission: State House, Room 111, Boston, MA 02133, 617-725-4000, Ext. 35312, or http://www.doe.mass.edu/hssss/program/ssch.html

Human Relations Media, & GLSEN. (2003). *Dealing with difference: Opening dialogue about lesbian, gay, and straight issues*. New York: GLSEN. A 35-minute video and 82-page teacher resource book available from GLSEN at http://www.glsen.org

Lambda Legal Defense & Education Fund and the Gay, Lesbian, and Straight Education Network. (2001). *A guide to effective statewide laws/policies: Preventing discrimination against LGBT students in K-12 schools*. Author: New York. Available at http://www.lambdalegal.org

MacGillivray, I. K. (2004). *Sexual orientation & school policy: A practical guide for teachers, administrators, and community activists*. Lanham, MD: Rowman & Littlefield.

Middleton, J. (2000). *Making schools safe: An educational program from the Lesbian and Gay Rights Project of the American Civil Liberties Union*. New York: American Civil Liberties Union. Available at http://www.aclu.org

Parents, Families, and Friends of Lesbians and Gays. (2003). *From our house to the schoolhouse: A recipe for safe schools* (5th ed.). Available from PFLAG at http://www.pflag.org

Reis, B., & Saewyc, E. (1999). *Eighty-three thousand youth: Selected findings of eight population-based studies as they pertain to antigay harassment and the safety and well-being of sexual minority students*. Seattle: Safe Schools Coalition of Washington. Available at http://www.safeschoolscoalition.org

Web Sites

These Web sites provide a wealth of resources, many of them downloadable, for educators, other professionals, parents, and GLBT youths.

Advocates for Youth: www.advocatesforyouth.org
YouthResource, a project of Advocates for Youth: http://www.youthresource.com
American Psychological Association: Healthy Lesbian, Gay, and Bisexual Students Project: http://www.apa.org
Gay, Lesbian, and Straight Education Network (GLSEN): http://www.glsen.org
Lambda Legal Defense and Education Fund: http://www.lambdalegal.org
National Youth Advocacy Coalition: http://www.nyacyouth/org/ (This Web site provides a comprehensive resource database of books, journal articles, videos, and curricula. It also offers links to hundreds of youth resources, including resources specifically for GLBT youths of color, youths with disabilities, and immigrant youth.)
Parents, Families and Friends of Lesbians and Gays (PFLAG): http://www.pflag.org
PFLAG's Transgender Network: http://www.youth-guard.org/pflag-tnet/
The Safe Schools Coalition: http://www.safeschoolscoalition.org

Key Points to Remember

- School-based interventions should aim to create school environments that protect, value, and respect GLBT students and staff.
- School social workers can collaborate and intervene with multiple systems to help GLBT students establish a good fit with their school, peer, family, and community environments.
- Interventions must take into account how sexual orientation and gender identity issues intersect with issues of race, class, gender, and disability status within the social environments that youths navigate.
- GLBT youths' problems may or may not be related to their sexual orientation or gender identity, or they may be problems that are exacerbated by internal or external conflicts arising from their sexual orientation or gender identity.

- Much of the work done with GLBT youths is psychoeducational in nature, providing them with accurate and affirming information, community resources, and assistance with developing problem-solving, decision-making, and adaptive coping skills.

References

Blumenfeld, W. J. (1995). "Gay/Straight" alliances: Transforming pain to pride. In G. Unks (Ed.), *The gay teen: Educational practice and theory for lesbian, gay, and bisexual adolescents* (pp. 211–224). New York: Routledge.

Bochenek, M., & Brown, A. W. (2001). *Hatred in the hallways: Violence and discrimination against lesbian, gay, bisexual, and transgender students in U.S. schools.* New York: Human Rights Watch.

D'Augelli, A. R. (1996). Enhancing the development of lesbian, gay, and bisexual youths. In E. D. Rothblum & L. A. Bond (Eds.), *Preventing heterosexism and homophobia* (pp. 124–150). Thousand Oaks, CA: Sage.

D'Augelli, A. R., Pilkington, N. W., & Hershberger, S. L. (2002). Incidence and mental health impact of sexual orientation victimization of lesbian, gay, and bisexual youths in high school. *School Psychology Quarterly, 17*, 148–167.

Elze, D. (2002). Risk factors for internalizing and externalizing problems among gay, lesbian, and bisexual adolescents. *Social Work Research, 26*, 89–100.

Elze, D. (2003). Gay, lesbian, and bisexual adolescents' perceptions of their high school environments and factors associated with their comfort in school. *Children and Schools, 25*, 225–239.

Garofalo, R., Wolf, C., Kessel, S., Palfrey, J., & DuRant, R. (1998). The association between health risk behaviors and sexual orientation among a school-based sample of adolescents. *Pediatrics, 101*, 895–902.

Herek, G. M. (1990). The context of anti-gay violence: Notes on cultural and psychological heterosexism. *Journal of Interpersonal Violence, 5*(3), 316–333.

Hershberger, S. L., & D'Augelli, A. R. (2000). In R. M. Perez, K. A. DeBord, & K. J. Bieschke (Eds.), *Handbook of counseling and psychotherapy with lesbian, gay, and bisexual clients* (pp. 225–247). Washington, DC: American Psychological Association.

Israel, G. E., & Tarver, D. E. (1997). *Transgender care: Recommended guidelines, practical information, and personal accounts.* Philadelphia: Temple University Press.

Kosciw, J. G. (2004). *The 2003 National School Climate Survey: The school-related experiences of our nation's lesbian, gay, bisexual, and transgender youth.* New York: Gay, Lesbian, Straight Education Network.

Lev, A. I. (2004). *Transgender emergence: Therapeutic guidelines for working with gender variant people and their families.* New York: Haworth.

Lipkin, A. (2004). *Beyond diversity day: A Q&A on gay and lesbian issues in schools.* Lanham, MD: Rowman & Littlefield.

Longres, J. F., & Etnyre, W. S. (2004). Social work practice with gay and lesbian children and adolescents. In P. Allen-Meares & M. W. Fraser, *Intervention with children and adolescents: An interdisciplinary perspective* (pp. 80–105). Boston, MA: Allyn & Bacon.

Mallon, G. P. (1998). Lesbian, gay, and bisexual orientation in childhood and adolescence. In G. A. Appleby & J. W. Anastas (Eds.), *Not just a passing phase: Social work with gay, lesbian, and bisexual people* (pp. 123–144). New York: Columbia University Press.

Mallon, G. P. (Ed.). (1999). *Social services with transgendered youth.* New York: Harrington Park.

McCready, L. (2001). When fitting in isn't an option, or, why black queer males at a California high school stay away from Project 10. In K. A. Kumashiro (Ed.), *Troubling intersections of race and sexuality: Queer students of color and anti-oppressive education* (pp. 37–53). Lanham, MD: Rowman & Littlefield.

Russell, S. T., Seif, H., & Truong, N. L. (2001). School outcomes of sexual minority youth in the United States: Evidence from a national study. *Journal of Adolescence, 24,* 111–127.

Ryan, C. (2001). Counseling lesbian, gay, and bisexual youths. In A. R. D'Augelli & C. J. Patterson (Eds.), *Lesbian, gay, and bisexual identities and youth: Psychological perspectives* (pp. 224–250). New York: Oxford University Press.

Ryan, C., & Futterman, D. (1998). *Lesbian & gay youth: Care and counseling.* New York: Columbia University Press.

Safren, S. A., & Heimberg, R. G. (1999). Depression, hopelessness, suicidality, and related factors in sexual minority and heterosexual adolescents. *Journal of Consulting and Clinical Psychology, 67,* 859–866.

Savin-Williams, R. (1995). Lesbian, gay male, and bisexual adolescents. In A. R. D'Augelli & C. J. Patterson (Eds.), *Lesbian, gay, and bisexual identities over the lifespan: Psychological perspectives* (pp. 165–189). New York: Oxford University Press.

Schneider, M. S. (Ed.). (1997). *Pride and prejudice: Working with lesbian, gay, and bisexual youth.* Toronto: Central Toronto Youth Services.

Sheridan, P. (1997). Group counseling for gay male youth. In M. S. Schneider (Ed.), *Pride and prejudice: Working with lesbian, gay, and bisexual youth* (pp. 83–96). Toronto: Central Toronto Youth Services.

Szalacha, L. (2001). The sexual diversity climate of Massachusetts' secondary schools and the success of the Safe Schools Program for Gay and Lesbian Students. *Dissertation Abstracts International, 62(04A),* 1327.

Tully, C. (2000). *Lesbians, gays, and the empowerment perspective.* New York: Columbia University Press.

Best Organization, Administrative, and Community Practices in a School Context

PART
III

Interventions in the Educational Environment Through Policies and Procedures

Social workers and other mental health professionals must be well informed and up-to-date on the policies that mandate all aspects of public education. Yet, as practitioners in professional disciplines that are dissimilar to education in important ways, they often find themselves unprepared to be effective in this area. This section focuses on two groups of essential policy-related skills for school social workers and other school-based mental health professionals: (1) interpreting and understanding the wide-ranging effects of specific federal, state, and local education policies on school environment and allied programs such as mental health and social services, and (2) influencing education policies and their procedural implementation in the school and school district.

Helping Schools Meet the Mandates of Federal Policies: No Child Left Behind and Other Cutting-Edge Federal Policies

John W. Sipple ▪ Loren Banach

For too long, children suffered while jarring interests caused stalemate in the efforts to improve our schools. . . . Now, [we have] passed the most sweeping educational bill ever to come before Congress. . . . As President of the United States, I believe deeply no law I have signed or will ever sign means more to the future of America.
—President Lyndon B. Johnson's remarks at the signing of the Elementary and Secondary Education Act, April 11, 1965

Unfortunately, this bill promises more than the Federal Government can deliver, and its good intentions could be thwarted by the many unwise provisions it contains. It would unnecessarily assert Federal control over traditional state and local government functions. It establishes complex requirements under which tax dollars would be used to support administrative paperwork and not educational programs.
—President Gerald Ford's remarks at the signing of the Education for All Handicapped Children Act, November 29, 1975

You're seeing government at its best with this piece of legislation. . . . [T]his bill says . . . in return for receiving federal money, states must design accountability systems to measure—to determine whether or not children are learning to read and write and add and subtract. . . . It basically says, every child can learn. . . . It says Washington has a role of providing money, and now Washington is demanding results. But Washington should not micromanage the process. And so, this bill provides a lot more flexibility for the local folks.
—President George W. Bush's remarks on the day he signed No Child Left Behind, January 8, 2002

These three epigraphs, each a statement made by a U.S. president at the signing of a major federal education law, highlight the divisive politics, uncertain role, and multiple goals of federal education policy. Though these laws represent the most visible efforts to use federal policy to improve public schooling, research has shown that the efficacy of federal policy is a function of high-quality and comprehensive state and local policy, local educators, social workers, and health care professionals. Acting alone, federal policy at best can have a weak effect on the education of children. However, when acting in conjunction with rigorous local policy and high-quality professionals, federal education policy can be the catalyst that drives attention and resources to those students and services most in need of support and guidance.

The purpose of this chapter is to provide clarification on the intent, goals, and implications of federal education policy in general and the No Child Left Behind Act (NCLB) in particular. In doing so, this chapter

1. describes the federal role in improving public education;
2. clarifies the intent and content of the NCLB; and
3. provides research-driven guidance for local educators, social workers, and health care professionals working with children at risk of failure.

An underlying supposition of this chapter is that the NCLB is one of many factors that shape the environment in which children are growing up and being educated. However, this law has the power to drive resources toward or away from children in need and the programs serving them. For this reason, it is important that a wide range of professionals be familiar with this federal legislation so that a comprehensive set of services may be coordinated and implemented. It has long been argued that early intervention and coordinated school and community services are valuable in providing an enriched and supportive environment to meet the needs of at-risk students (Crowson & Boyd, 1993; Pennecamp, 1992; U.S. Department of Education, 1994; Warfield, 1994). This chapter intends to inform social workers and health care professionals on relevant aspects of the NCLB and to motivate coordinated services to better serve low-achieving children.

Federal Involvement in Education

When President George W. Bush signed the NCLB into law on January 8, 2002, he fundamentally altered the course of federal involvement in K-12 public education. Heretofore, the federal government limited its role to providing funds for compensatory education for poor and underachieving students, due process rights for handicapped children, free and reduced-price lunches, and other targeted programs. But under NCLB, the federal government now mandates annual quality assessments, public reporting of disaggregated results, and intervention in poorly performing schools. This act immediately generated much fanfare and political, ideological, and professional controversy, especially as initial appropriations fell short of the authorized targets for federal spending (e.g., Title 1, Sect. 1002; Elmore, 2002; Rotherham, 2002). Passed with bipartisan support, the law is designed to straddle the fence between the traditional emphasis on local and state control of U.S. public education and increasing federal involvement and oversight.

What creates this tension in federal education policy? The 10th Amendment to the U.S. Constitution states, "The powers not delegated to the United States by the Constitution, nor prohibited by it to the states, are reserved to the states respectively, or to the people." In other words, there is no constitutional provision for federal involvement in public education, and thus the plenary responsibility for education is left to states and localities. This has had the effect of dramatically limiting the involvement and power of the federal government in terms of primary and secondary education. Of course, the federal government has its fingerprints all over public education today, including what may be the most expansive of all federal education laws: the NCLB.

Two main themes of federal involvement in public schools have existed for the last half century: access and quality. Often at the prodding of the Supreme Court, access to appropriate public education has been ensured for many protected classes of students, including students with disabilities and racial and language minority students (e.g., *Brown v. Board of Education,* 1954; *Lau v. Nichols,* 1974). Although issues of access had been the province of federal education policy since the 1960s, policy regarding educational quality during this time targeted the education of poor students and math and science instruction (e.g., the National Defense Education Act). With the NCLB, however, contemporary federal policy is shifting toward measurement of quality education for *all* students in *all* schools in multiple subject areas.

It is important to highlight the strategic difference between the points of accountability for special education versus the NCLB. Whereas federal special education law targets the free and appropriate education of individual students highlighted by Individual Education Plans (IEPs), the NCLB targets school-level accountability. (See chapters 86 and 91 for further discussion on working with students who have specialized educational needs.)

ESEA/NCLB

Despite all the recent attention paid to the NCLB, some of the core provisions have been in place for the better part of 35 years, with many of the quality elements inserted in the 1994 reauthorization (the Improving America's Schools Act; see Table 84.1). In 1965 President Lyndon B. Johnson signed the Elementary and Secondary Education Act (ESEA) as a centerpiece of his War on Poverty. With this law, the federal government provided, for the first time in U.S. history, categorical aid on the basis of student poverty. This new compensatory aid was also the first significant infusion of federal dollars into the public schools. The purpose of the aid was to compensate for the lack of local resources inherent in schools serving poorer communities. The centerpiece of the ESEA was Title I, which comprised more than 80% of the law's total funding. Since its inception, the ESEA has been repeatedly reauthorized, tweaked, and revised, with the latest reauthorization resulting in the name change to the NCLB.

The NCLB is an ambitious attempt to document and measure the performance levels of every school in the nation and of subgroups of students within schools. Arguably, the law is geared to reduce the achievement gap, heighten overall performance, and hold all schools accountable by throwing a spotlight on the performance levels of schools and subgroups of students within schools. The idea is that the increased scrutiny on student and school performance will draw sufficient attention, resources, and expertise to foster improvement (Stecher, Hamilton, & Gonzalez, 2003).

Both the old (1994 reauthorization of the ESEA) and new (NCLB) laws require states to adopt state-defined standards, develop assessments, and identify schools in need of improvement. Though schools had previously been required to collect data for a range of student subgroups, under NCLB schools are required to publicly report disaggregated data by various student subgroups. This is important given the opportunity many schools had to hide the relatively low performance of certain subgroups of students. When states, districts, or newspapers simply report aggregate school means for student performance, districts with smaller proportions of poor or minority students were not required to report the measured differences between majority and minority students on standardized exams or graduation rates. With the new requirement for disaggregated reporting, potential discrepancies between groups of students will be made public. This change has the potential to alter the conversation from the traditional distinction between high- and low-performing schools to a new conversation of which schools provide more or less equitable academic programs for each or the relevant subgroups.

A second major change in the new law is the frequency with which students are required to be tested: previously once at the elementary, middle grade, and high school level, but now every year in Grades 3–8 and once during Grades 10–12. The largest change in policy has come in the area of accountability. Though the federal law established structured guidelines for accountability systems, the control over the explicit design, content, and implementation of accountability systems remains with the states. At the center of the NCLB accountability system is the demand that all students achieve proficiency in the various curricular areas by 2014—a full generation of schoolchildren or 12 years after the initial implementation of the NCLB (see http://www.ed.gov/policy/elsec/leg/esea02/index.html for a full accounting of the law's provisions).

To hold school and states accountable for student performance, all schools, districts, and states must publicly report these scores in the states' Adequate Yearly Progress (AYP) reports. AYP is a specific target for the percentage of students attaining proficient scores on the state's assessments; this applies to the overall achievement of a given school along with each subgroup's achievement. The AYP is calculated by dividing the proportion of students achieving proficiency by the number of years until 2014. The resultant number

Table 84.1 Comparison of the Title 1 Requirements in 1994 ESEA and 2002 NCLB Acts

	Old Law	New Law
Standards and assessments	States required to adopt state-defined standards, develop assessments, and identify schools in need of improvement.	Same.
Data collection	States and schools required to collect data on achievement of different groups of students by poverty, race, limited English proficiency, and disability status.	Same. But for the first time, states required to publicly report achievement data by different groups—known as disaggregated data.
Testing	Required three times: once in grades 3–5, once in grades 6–9, and once in grades 10–12.	Beginning in 2005–06, required each year from Grades 3–8 and once in Grades 10–12.
Accountability	States set up their own accountability systems. No requirement to establish timelines for full proficiency. No requirement to focus on closing achievement gaps.	Every state and school district is responsible for ensuring that students meet the state standard for proficiency within 12 years. Schools must use disaggregated data to ensure that ALL groups of students are making adequate progress.
What happens when schools don't meet their goals?	States were supposed to develop systems for requiring change in low-performing schools, but little change actually occurred.	Local leaders choose what form change should take, but real change must be implemented. States, districts, and schools are required to focus additional attention and resources on schools needing improvement. Parents have options to transfer their children to higher performing schools or to receive tutoring paid for with federal money.
Teacher quality	Not covered.	Requires states to define a qualified teacher and to ensure that low-income and minority students are not taught disproportionately by inexperienced, unqualified, or out-of-field teachers. States have until 2005–06 to get all teachers to state standards.

Source: Education Trust (2003), p. 5. Reprinted with permission.

represents the gain required to make AYP the following year.

The subgroups required for public reporting by NCLB include students of low socioeconomic status, those from major racial or ethnic groups, students with disabilities, and those who are designated as Limited English Proficient. At least 95% of students in each school and in each subgroup must be assessed in order for that school to be eligible to make AYP. If even one subgroup does not make AYP, the entire school is reported to be deficient. As argued by the Education Trust, the reporting of disaggregated data is the first-ever systematic public display of within-school performance differences of children from different racial and economic groups (Education Trust, 2003).

If a school does not meet AYP or safe harbor provisions, they will be susceptible to a series of increasingly intrusive interventions. Here is the cascade of interventions for schools not meeting the AYP provisions as outlined by the NCLB.

Every school is granted a 1-year grace period. There is no action taken if a school does not make AYP for 1 year.

If a school fails to make AYP for a second consecutive year, it will be put on the state's list of schools in need of improvement. During this time, the school must develop an improvement plan, and students must be allowed to transfer to higher performing public schools in the same district.

In the third consecutive year of not making AYP, the district must provide tutoring to low-income students in addition to regular coursework.

Corrective action must be taken during the fifth year of not making AYP. The same transfer and tutoring options are continued, but the district and state must now implement at least one of the following sanctions:

- Replace the school staff that are relevant to the failure to make AYP.
- Institute a new curriculum, with the inclusion of professional development.
- Decrease management authority.
- Appoint an outside expert to advise the school.
- Extend the school year or the school day of that school.
- Restructure the school's internal organization.

Year 6 and 7 of not making AYP require restructuring of the school include more radical interventions. Districts must develop an alternate governance plan, including the possibility of conversion to a charter school, replacing the principal and most of the staff, inviting an external group to manage the school, or allowing a state takeover.

Finally, for schools in need of improvement the NCLB mandates use of scientifically based instructional programs. To assist schools in identifying and implementing such programs, the federal government is preparing an approved list of practices. These practices and programs will meet this standard and can be found in the What Works Clearinghouse on the Internet:

The What Works Clearinghouse (WWC) was established in 2002 by the U.S. Department of Education's Institute of Education Sciences to provide educators, policymakers, researchers, and the public with a central and trusted source of scientific evidence of what works in education. . . . Through a set of accessible databases and user-friendly reports, the WWC provides education consumers with ongoing, high-quality reviews of the effectiveness of replicable educational interventions (programs, products, practices, and policies) that promise to improve student outcomes. (http://www.w-w-c.org)

In terms of research that analyzes the efficacy of this trend toward state education standards prodded by federal legislation, the evidence is varied (National Research Council, 1999). Some studies question the merit and fairness of high-stakes standards and assessments (e.g., Armein & Berliner, 2002) while others seem to suggest an overall positive effect on more equitable learning opportunities and performance (Haycock, 2002). In a national study examining the relationship between state graduation and accountability policies and student course taking and achievement, researchers found mixed effects (Schiller & Mueller, 2003). In states with more graduation requirements, greater proportions of students are enrolled in higher-level mathematics courses. However, in states with extensive testing not linked to graduation requirements, they found little effect on course taking but discernible differences in course-taking patterns by socioeconomic status. Finally, in states where testing and individual student consequences were linked, researchers found reduced differences in course taking by socioeconomic status. Similarly, other research analyzed the relationship between student performance on the National Assessment of Educational Progress and the prevalence of state minimum competency exams. The research concluded that when compared with student performance in states without these exams, students in states with them performed at higher levels (Bishop & Mane, 2001).

In addition to whether the assessments are linked to student or school performance, the timing of the student examinations may also be important. It may matter whether the student assessments are administered in the middle grades or not until the close of high school. Tests administered early may be theorized to motivate low-performing students to work harder while there is still time to improve. Conversely, early failure on state examinations may stifle motivation to continue with school and may encourage dropout. In support of this, Jacob (2001) found that at-risk students were more likely to drop out of school in states with high-stakes student assessments. Jacob also concluded that high-stakes examinations had little effect on overall achievement levels of students. In a more detailed analysis of school district programmatic responses to increased state standards in New York State, Sipple and Killeen (2004) found that districts serving higher proportions of poor children were more than twice as likely to offer the option for students to transfer to a GED program than were districts serving fewer poor students.

Parents, teachers, school social workers, and health care workers must pay close attention to course-taking patterns before and after the annual examinations called for by the NCLB.

Special Education and Limited English Proficient Students

In terms of accountability, the NCLB does not make exceptions for special education students. Like all other subgroups, 95% of special needs students need to be assessed and reported in their school's AYP report. Based on the students' IEP, disabled students can be given special accommodations in taking the exams. This can include, but is not limited to, more time in taking the exam, or special one-on-one testing conditions. Furthermore, students with significant cognitive impairments, such as mental retardation, can be given alternative assessments to satisfy the state requirements. To ensure that states do not give too many

students these alternative assessments, the NCLB has instituted an exemption cap that limits their use to 1% of all students statewide (Browder & Cooper-Duffy, 2003).

Though students with disabilities are clearly included in the new standards-based education reform, educators are not always clear on how to accomplish this in appropriate ways. As discussed by the National Research Council (1999), it is a difficult challenge for special education students to be held to the same academic standards as regular education students (see also Koenig & Bachman, 2004). Thus a conflict exists between the NCLB and the Individuals with Disabilities Education Act. The NCLB stresses systems accountability and uniformity, while the disabilities act emphasizes individual goals and learning plans for individual students. To balance this potential conflict of interest, special education teachers must work collaboratively with general education teachers to best meet the needs of the students and their schools. In the end, IEPs will need to be aligned with state standards, and educators will need to strike a balance in teaching functional and academic skills.

Strategies to Assist in Meeting the Standards

What can and should local educators, social workers, and health care workers do in response to the NCLB requirements? In terms of actual practice, the law provides little guidance beyond the technical data-reporting requirements, the definition of a highly qualified teacher, and the mandated use of scientifically based instructional programs for schools in need of improvement.

Beyond more fully understanding the broad components and implications of the NCLB, school professionals should consult some of the practical suggestions that researchers offer to meet the requirements of the NCLB (Stecher et al., 2003). These suggestions range from focusing on internal planning and capacity building (Corcoran & Goertz, 1995; Massell & Goertz, 2002; Sipple & Killeen, 2004) or tailoring staff development to the local needs of your students, school, and community in light of developing state and federal standards (Darling-Hammond & McLaughlin, 1996; Dutro, Fisk, Koch, Roop, & Wixson, 2002; Elmore & Burney, 1999; Little, 1993) to forging alliances to secure political and technical support for the school improvement efforts (Stecher et al., 2003).

Table 84.2 Summary of Research-Based Strategies on Improving Practice to Meet NCLB Requirements

Build Capacity

- Assess your own institutional capacity for improvement.
- Look for successful models in settings similar to your own.
- Engage key staff in advance planning.
- Connect with sources of knowledge outside your own school and district.
- Concentrate state and district capacity-building efforts where they are most needed.
- Remember that educational reform takes time, and the results may not be apparent immediately.

Use Standards to Improve Instruction

- Obtain a copy of your state's standards, study them, and provide opportunities for staff to discuss the standards throughout the year.
- Engage staff in the exercise of mapping your school's or district's curriculum to the standards.
- Make connections with outside institutions and experts who can provide advice on translating standards into instruction.
- Supplement state standards with materials that clarify specific learning goals.
- Communicate information about the standards to parents.

Use Assessment Results to Improve Instruction

- Require test developers to present results in a clear and useful format.
- Educate users of test information about the meaning of test scores and score reports.
- Educate users about the appropriate use of test results.
- Train teachers to translate test results into instructionally relevant information.
- Help teachers monitor student progress toward meeting standards throughout the year.
- Do not allow the standards that are tested to overshadow the standards that are not tested.
- Design the testing system so it is resistant to score inflation.
- Publish used test items annually so that everyone can see the content and format that are used.

Create Effective Incentives

- Monitor how teachers and other staff are reacting to the rewards and sanctions.
- Implement additional incentives at the school or district level.
- Create uniform incentives for students.

Help Parents Make Effective Choices

- Produce reports geared to the needs of parents.
- Engage parent groups to help design a communication strategy.
- Critically appraise the qualifications of providers of tutoring services.
- Develop programs to help parents assist their own children, whether or not transfers or tutoring services are offered.

Go Beyond the Accountability Data

- Try to diagnose the nature of the problems facing the school or district.
- Seek outside expertise for problems that accountability does not address directly.
- Be prepared to seek additional financial resources, if needed, to supplement available funds.
- Be cognizant of the political environment in which NCLB is operating.

Source: B. Stecher, L. Hamilton, & G. Gonzalez (2003). Reprinted with permission.

In addition to these recommendations and those given in Table 84.2, tremendous amounts of research over the last 30 years have focused on documenting and analyzing why some groups of children consistently outperform others. Jencks and Philips (1998) examine various explanations for the existence of the achievement gap. Among them, they find four predominant explanations, each with varying levels of research supporting the theories: test bias, heredity, family background, and cultural explanations. Within the test bias argument, they differentiate four different practices (labeling bias, content bias, methodological bias, prediction bias). As for the long-standing arguments over hereditary explanations for differential academic achievement, Jencks and Philips conclude, "We find it hard to see how anyone reading these studies with an open mind could conclude that innate ability played a large role in the black-white gap" (p. 20). Family background is a compilation of several factors that in the aggregate are strongly related to student achievement. Parsing out the different factors, however, is difficult. Finally, they identified explanations based on cultural and linguistic differences between majority and minority groups that are related to differential levels of achievement. Minority students may choose to "act white" in school and engage in linguistic *code switching* between home and school settings. These behaviors have been positively related to levels of achievement in schooling and standardized assessments. However, such behavior on the part of minority students is not without cost, some argue, resulting in additional challenges and loss of identity for racial and ethnic minorities to face (see, e.g., Fordham, 1988; O'Conner, 1997; Valenzuela, 1999).

Tools and Practice Examples

Resources for Understanding and Implementing the NCLB Act

NCLB Web site: http://www.ed.gov/nclb/
NCREL Resource Center on reducing the achievement gaps: http://www.ncrel.org/info/rc/sc.htm
Just for the Kids: www.just4kids.org. This compares every elementary and middle school's results on state assessments. It is also provides specific information on the school's location and demographics, allowing educators to see what similar schools are doing to help their students learn at higher levels
National Center for Research on Evaluation, Standards, and Student Testing. Based at the UCLA Center for the Study of Evaluation, this group studies the quality of assessments and high-stakes testing and gives recommendations for how assessments should be implemented.
Education Trust: http://www.edtrust.org/. Education Trust describes itself as an "independent nonprofit organization whose mission is to make schools and colleges work for all of the young people they serve."
Southern Regional Education Board: This organization studies the use of summer school to help low-performing students. http://www.wrightslaw.com/nclb/index.htm
Education Week: http://edweek.org/ Publication offers current news coverage of issues related to NCLB and other federal policy.
Center for Effective Collaboration and Practice http://www.air.org/cecp/. The center provides resources promoting collaborative efforts between educators and communities to improve the education of children.

Key Points to Remember

Whether the increasingly comprehensive federal education legislation known as the No Child Left Behind Act will improve school performance and reduce gaps in student achievement is not yet clear. In the meantime, one additional issue must be highlighted. With all of the attention focused on school-based activity and policy, it is paramount that attention also be paid to out-of-school issues. In other words, to improve school and student performance, the attention of policy makers and educators must look outside the walls of the school building and the traditional school day and school year. Research has identified the importance of after-school and summer school activities, given the differential experiences and resources available to children of different backgrounds (e.g., Alexander, Entwisle, & Olson, 2001). Research has also emphasized the social and economic reforms necessary to allow schools to improve (e.g., Rothstein, 2004). Whether the

NCLB stimulates school and out-of-school collaboration, including collaborations focused on social and economic development, will be up to the local educators, social and health care workers, and community leaders responsible for carrying out the goal of leaving no child behind.

References

Alexander, K. L., Entwisle, D. R., & Olson, L. S. (2001). Schools, achievement, and inequality: A seasonal perspective. *Educational Evaluation and Policy Analysis, 23*(2), 171–191.

Armein, A. L., & Berliner, D. C. (2002). High stakes testing, uncertainty, and student learning. *Education Policy Analysis Archives, 10*(18). Retrieved January 18, 2005, from http://epaa.asu.edu/epaa/v10n18/.

Bishop, J. H., & Mane, F. (2001). The impacts of minimum competency exam graduation requirements on college attendance and early labor market success of disadvantaged students. In G. Orfield & M. L. Kornhaber (Eds.), *Raising standards or raising barriers? Inequality and high-stakes testing in public education* (pp. 51–84). New York: Century Foundation Press.

Browder, D. M., & Cooper-Duffy, K. (2003). Evidence-based practices for students with severe disabilities and the requirement for accountability in "No Child Left Behind." *Journal of Special Education, 37*(3), 157.

Brown v. Board of Education, 347 U.S. 483 (1954).

Corcoran, T., & Goertz, M. (1995). Instructional capacity and high-performance standards. *Educational Researcher, 24*(9), 27–31.

Crowson, R. L., & Boyd, W. L. (1993). Coordinated services for children: Designing arks for storms and seas unknown. *American Journal of Education, 101*(2), 140–179.

Darling-Hammond, L., & McLaughlin, M. (1996). Policies and support professional development in an era of reform. In I. Oberman (Ed.), *Teacher learning: New policies, new practices* (pp. 202–219). New York: Teachers College Press.

Dutro, E., Fisk, M. C., Koch, R., Roop, L. J., & Wixson, K. (2002). When state policies meet local district contexts: Standards-based professional development as a means to individual agency and collective ownership. *Teachers College Record, 104*(4), 787–811.

Education for All Handicapped Children Act, P.L. 94–142 (1975).

Education Trust (2003). *Improving your schools: A parent and community guide to No Child Left Behind*. Washington, DC: Education Trust.

Elementary and Secondary Education Act, P.L. 89–10 (1965).

Elmore, R. F. (2002). Unwarranted intrusion. *Education Next, 2*(1), 31–35.

Elmore, R. F., & Burney, D. (1999). Investing in teacher learning: Staff development and instructional improvement. In L. Darling-Hammond & G. Sykes (Eds.), *Teaching as the learning profession: Handbook of policy and practice* (pp. 263–291). San Francisco: Jossey-Bass.

Fordham, S. (1988). Racelessness as a factor in black students' school success: Pragmatic strategy or Pyrrhic victory? *Harvard Educational Review, 58*(1), 54–85.

Improving America's Schools Act, P.L. 103–382 (1994).

Jacob, B. (2001). Getting tough: The impact of high school graduation exams. *Educational Evaluation and Policy Analysis, 23*(2), 99–121.

Jencks, C., & Phillips, M. (1998). *The black-white test score gap*. Washington, DC: Brookings Institution Press.

Koenig, J. A., & Bachman, L. F. (2004). *Keeping score for all: The effects of inclusion and accommodation policies on large-scale educational assessment*. Washington, DC: National Academy Press.

Lau v. Nichols, 414 U.S. 563 (1974).

Little, J. (1993). Teachers' professional development in a climate of educational reform. *Education Evaluation and Policy Analysis, 15*(2), 129–151.

Massell, D., & Goertz, M. E. (2002). District strategies for building instructional capacity. In A. Hightower, M. S. Knapp, J. A. Marsh, & M. W. McLaughlin (Eds.), *School districts and instructional renewal* (pp. 43–60). New York: Teachers College Press.

National Defense Education Act, P.L. 85–864 (1958).

National Research Council. (1999). *High stakes: Testing for tracking, promotion, and graduation*. Washington, DC: National Academy Press.

No Child Left Behind Act, P.L. 107–110 (2001).

O'Conner, C. (1997). Dispositions toward (collective) struggle and educational resilience in the inner city: A case analysis of six African American high school students. *American Educational Research Journal, 34*(4), 593–629.

Pennecamp, M. (1992). Toward school-linked and school based human services for children and families. *Social Work in Education, 14*(2), 125–130.

Rotherham, A. (2002). A new partnership. *Education Next, 2*(1), 37–41.

Rothstein, R. (2004). *Class and schools: Using social, economic, and educational reform to close the black-white achievement gap*. Washington, DC: Economic Policy Institute.

Schiller, K., & Mueller, C. (2003). Raising the bar and equity? Effects of state high school graduation requirements and accountability policies on students' mathematics course taking. *Educational Evaluation and Policy Analysis, 25*(3), 299–318.

Sipple, J. W., & Killeen, K. (2004). Context, capacity and concern: A district-level analysis of the implementation of standards-based reform. *Education Policy, 18*(3), 456–490.

Stecher, B., Hamilton, L., & Gonzalez, G. (2003). *Working*

smarter to leave no child behind: Practical insights for school leaders. Santa Monica, CA: Rand.

U.S. Department of Education. (1994). *Strong families, strong schools: A research base for family involvement in learning from the U.S. Department of Education.* Washington, DC: U.S. Department of Education.

Valenzuela, A. (1999). *Subtractive schooling: U.S.-Mexican youth and the politics of caring.* Albany: State University of New York Press.

Warfield, M. E. (1994). A cost-effective analysis of early intervention services in Massachusetts: Implications for policy. *Educational Evaluation and Policy Analysis, 16*(1), 87–99.

Influencing the Local Education Authority and Changing Policies in the Local School, School District, and State

Joanne Cashman

Getting Started

For decades, the American public has portrayed the behavior of policy makers in an archetypical and sometimes comic manner. The stereotype depicts a decision maker choosing among alternatives based on criteria that has little relevance to constituents' interests and, in fact, shows little understanding of their interests. This portrayal, although exaggerated, reveals the most basic problem in making public policy: choosing between competing options and multiple views on the public good.

Policy analysts and researchers understand that multiple factors affect policy decisions. Quantitative policy research is often a complex modeling of variables that approximate decision makers' behavior (Patton & Sawicki, 1993). Qualitative policy research is often a holistic presentation of the interaction between the policy decision and the real or perceived consequences (Rist, 1995). Each approach presents its own problems. Decision making is complex and difficult to generalize from one policy maker to another and one situation to the next.

The demand for good, reliable, and practical information to enable decisions on complex issues has been recently explored by researchers at the Brookings Institution and the Kennedy School of Government at Harvard University. Goldsmith and Eggers's new work, *Governing by Network* (2004), looks at the emerging strategies in which governments attempt to meet their policy goals by networking with stakeholders at all levels. The emergence of this approach underscores the importance of this chapter in developing the skill sets that will enable social workers and mental health professionals to capitalize on new opportunities.

This chapter presents practical ways for front-line workers to consider the policies that shape their work. The discussions and exercises serve as templates that service providers can use to think about and plan focused communication with decision makers that exert influence over the issues they care about. These procedures are drawn for policy analysis methodology and practices in knowledge management. Translating these methods for use by practitioners may foster action research and data collection that could become the evidence base describing what works in communicating with and influencing decision makers at all levels.

What We Know

Whether at the federal, state, or local levels, policy development is a dynamic event. The process is designed to articulate problems, information, and options that may improve outcomes. For my purpose in this chapter—helping social workers and mental health workers to find their voice in the policy process—it is useful to think of these efforts as a communication process (Dunn, 1994) that occurs in three cyclical environments: policy formulation, policy implementation, and policy evaluation (Nakamura & Smallwood, 1980).

In an ideal world, the best information informs the widest variety of options and the best choices among competing ideas; communication among researchers, practitioners, policy makers, and intended beneficiaries is open and generates high-quality strategies. In the real world, though, too many policy discussions are bounded by partial information and limited participation that excludes important perspectives. Decision makers

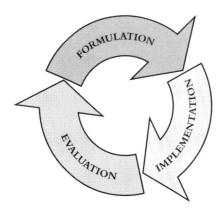

Figure 85.1. Policy as Communication

are isolated from the day-to-day realities that affect the people who must implement the policies, and, in far too many cases, policy-relevant information does not come to light until evaluation is under way.

Though timing is important in bringing practitioners' voices to policy dialogue, the ability to provide specific insights and recommendations that add value is critical. For practitioners to become respected sources of policy-relevant information, they need to acquire several new skills. First, practitioners must show that they understand policy directions that follow from mandates or other strong policy influences. Beyond identifying these influences, they must be able to target the decision points at which there exists some discretionary authority over program choices. Practitioners must also be able to identify the right decision makers. Policy direction is generally addressed at the federal or state levels, and implementation decisions are most often made at the local and site levels. As an example, local school boards cannot opt out of federal- or state-prescribed mandates, but they have considerable latitude in the ways in which they implement the mandates. Practitioners that hope to influence decisions must become familiar with mandate and its intent. Then, they must demonstrate a deep understanding of the interconnected issues and the systems designed to address them. Last, they must pose recommendations that will meet the needs of all the systems involved and publicly commit their efforts to a shared goal.

Reflections on Describing and Influencing

• Is this a problem that you can influence directly? With others? Through an association or professional group?
• Who might share your views? Who might disagree? Why?

• Who are the policy decision makers that you must reach?
• Who should deliver your message?
• Who should show support for your message?
• When should your message be delivered to achieve the desired results?

What We Can Do

Policy makers choose one option over another based on whether that policy information helps them understand the way that action will contribute to results. When practitioners try to influence policy makers, it is important that they understand the reasons that policy makers have faith in one claim over another.

When attempting to garner support for new or alternative policies, practitioners must determine what kind of information will be credible. There are at least eight ways to justify policy claims. Knowing *why* a particular policy argument influences policy makers is the first step in finding strategies that will get your opinions heard.

Tools and Practice Examples

Exercise 1

Table 85.1 will give you some important first insights about influencing the things that you care about.

Exercise 2

Use Table 85.2 to learn about the types of policy arguments. Try to recognize them in policy issues that concern you. Think about ways that you may share the information that you have in ways that will influence policy makers that seem to prefer modes for finding credible policy options.

Reflecting on Policy Arguments

Current policy decisions in education are significantly influenced by data obtained in randomized trials and experimental design research.

Table 85.1 *Exercise 1:* Accurately Describing the Problem That You See

Answer these questions to help make your own impressions explicit.	*What makes you think this?*	*How can you verify your impressions?*
Does the problem result from a federal, state or local action?		
Do you know what research or data influenced the decisions?		
Will changes require adjustments to law, regulation, agency guidance, or state and local planning processes?		
Who are the decision makers who can change the situation that you want to influence?		
Why should others support the recommendations that you are making?		

Table 85.2 What Lies Beneath a Policy Argument

Type of policy argument	*Reason policy makers have confidence in the argument*	*Examples of policies that seem to be based on this type of argument*	*Kinds of information that you might use to influence policy makers*
Authoritative	Confidence in expert testimony		
Statistical	Faith in representative samples		
Classification	Beliefs that what is true about a certain group included in the policy information is true of the larger population		
Intuitive	Reliance on insight or judgment		
Explanatory	Beliefs about theories that can account for behavior		
Pragmatic	Valuing of lessons from parallel cases and analogies		
Ethical	Beliefs about the "rightness" or "wrongness" of certain actions		

Source: Adapted from Dunn (1994).

- How might you approach decision makers who are most significantly influenced by statistical arguments?
- Are there other types of arguments that might also be persuasive? What type of argument would you choose to present? Why?

- Are there types of arguments that clearly will not be persuasive? Why?

Educational leaders are increasingly aware that their decisions must be based on implementation and outcome data.

- How can you pose new data points that may help to show connections between the academic and nonacademic barriers to achievement?
- What types of arguments might you choose to focus decision makers on the relationship between social and emotional supports and academic learning?

Stakeholder Identification

As practitioners try to influence decision makers, school-based human service workers do not have to make their case alone. Today's issues are complex and interrelated. There are many stakeholders who have the same goals and are working for the same approaches.

One of practitioners' major challenges is that they work their own "boxes." Too often, their interaction is not deep enough or frequent enough for them to recognize and identify factors that *could* bring them together with people who would support their cause. Therefore, knowing how to identify stakeholders is another important new skill that will help practitioners move their agendas at the local, state, and federal levels.

▏ Exercise 3

Exercise 3 is designed to help practitioners look across organizational boundaries and job roles to understand what might bring them together with potential collaborators. You can use this exercise as a personal exploration or use it with groups to

generate new partners and new insights about how to engage groups.

- Who are the stakeholders with shared interests? Place them around the perimeter of a large circle.
- Start with your pencil on the group with which you are affiliated.
- Draw an arrow to a group that is directly related to your work and influences your outcomes.
- How does the issue look as you consider the work of that agency? Write some key words on the arrow.
- Place yourself in the position of the other stakeholder. Think about how that stakeholder might describe the issues as they consider your involvement.
- Draw the arrow toward your group.
- Write some key words on the arrow.
- Think about all the roles along those two arrows.
- Do they hold the same picture of the issues that you do?
- Do you know how many pictures of the issues there are among these individuals with interrelated roles?
- Name and look across agencies and groups to find new colleagues that are passionate about the things you care about.
- Know the differences in the pictures that these stakeholders might hold.
- Think about how you might approach these stakeholders as new colleagues.
- Think about how you might invite these stakeholders into shared work.

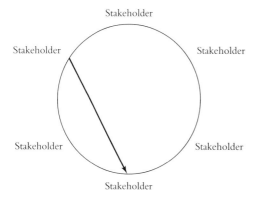

Figure 85.2. The Implementation Web

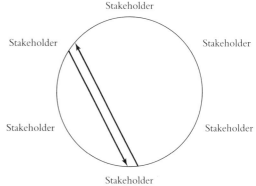

Figure 85.3. Seeing Other Points of View

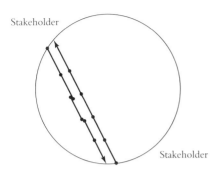

Figure 85.4. Different Roles, Different Viewpoints

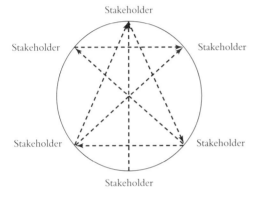

Figure 85.5. Identifying Potential Collaborators

Transformational Stories

As you have seen, the behavior of decision makers and implementers alike is affected by the way they think about issues, describe issues, and see those issues as they are perceived across groups. If you have worked through the exercises so far, you have some idea of how to make your own mental models explicit and how to detect what lies beneath the models that others hold. The exercises in this section are designed to generate some thought on how to spark new ideas and inspire action in those that hold key decision-making roles and those that do shared work.

One such new strategy is borrowed from business. Increasingly, business leaders strive to communicate the need for change and foster support for change through transformational stories. These are not the typical anecdotes that characterize debates and decisions. On the contrary, transformational stories are a strategic nar-

ration of the mental model, the policy argument and a current or prospective outcome. Transformational stories make the logic of a policy decision explicit and play out that logic in the implementation environment, where the decisions will have intended and unintended consequences.

Stories are a good avenue to convey a picture of what *could* be. But not all stories are equally powerful. An emerging strategy uncovers issues in organizational behavior, attitude toward change, and leadership qualities. This new strategy is the transformational story. In his books and electronic newsletter, noted knowledge management consultant Stephen Denning outlines storytelling as a springboard for change (Table 85.3). Many of Denning's insights are very useful in influencing the policy actors that school social workers and mental health workers want to reach.

Exercise 4: Influencing Through Transformational Stories

Imagine that a school district and county have funded "blended positions" that have filled school social work roles/dropout prevention functions for the last 2 years. Although both the county and the district are satisfied with the arrangement, budget constraints on each side are leading them to reconsider. The staff and administration have been collecting impact data but waiting until there are clear trends to make a full presentation of claims that can be made if a permanent funding stream is established for such positions. Because the argument for the program has not been made, resistance to the other options is viewed as a self-serving response on the part of the service providers.

- Think about a policy argument that you might develop to influence the county and the district. What type of policy argument would you choose? Why? (Use Table 86.1 to help you.)
- Think about the stakeholders who would share your commitment to an outcome that preserves these positions? Who are they and how do they view this problem?
- Now that you have identified the policy argument and the other stakeholders, chose an action that will drive the development of your story. What action did you chose? Why?

Table 85.3 Inspiring Action Through Stories

Objective	Story Elements	Story Narration
Sparking action	Describes how a change was implemented in the past and allows the listener to imagine how it will be useful again	Avoid excessive details that will distract the listener from the relevance to their current issues
Communicating who you are	Provides audience engaging drama and reveals some strength or vulnerability from your past	Provide meaningful details but make sure the audience has the time and inclination to hear your story
Transmitting values	Feels familiar to the audience and will prompt discussion about the issues raised by the value being promoted	Use believable, though possibly hypothetical, characters and situation and never forget that your story must be consistent with your own actions
Fostering collaboration	Movingly recounts a situation that the listeners have also experienced and that prompts them to tell their own stories on this topic	Make sure that you have an action plan to tap the energy unleashed!
Taming the grapevine	Highlights, often through humor, some aspect of a rumor that reveals it to be untrue	Avoid the temptation to be mean-spirited—and be sure the rumor is false!
Sharing knowledge	Focuses on mistakes made and shows, in some detail, how they were corrected with an explanation of why the situation worked	Solicit alternatives and, possibly, a better solution
Leading people into the future	Evokes the future you want to create without providing excess detail that will turn out to be wrong	Be sure of your storytelling skills; otherwise use a story in which the past can be a springboard to the future.

Source: This table is reproduced, with the author's permission, from Stephen Denning, 2003. *The leader's guide to storytelling: Mastering the art and discipline of business narrative.* San Francisco: Jossey-Bass.

Exercise 5: Crafting a Transformational Story of Your Own

Write a story that will increase the likelihood that the county officials and school board will favorably review the expenditure for blended funding against other necessary expenditures. Use the information in Exercises 2 and 4 to help you craft your message.

Use Table 85.4 to help you assemble the pieces.

- Write your story from the outline that you have made.
- Who should tell your story?
- Where should it be told?

Coalitions and Communities

Influencing is very often envisioned as a lobbying effort framed around a position at a decision point. In this model, several key individuals monitor strategy and inform larger groups of loosely connected people what and how they should communicate with decision makers. Although lobbying will always be an important avenue for participation in a democratic society, it is an activity that is grounded *within* efforts to formulate, implement, or evaluate policy decisions. Communication is sporadic and focused primarily at critical messages delivered within tight time frames. These efforts frequently reach large numbers of interested individuals and could be effective in drawing lessons

Table 85.4 Assembling the Pieces

Facts	Relationships	Interdependent Outcomes

across these environments, but only rarely are they continuously connected to act in this way.

New models are moving beyond coalitions built around single issues toward more thoughtful and integrated treatment of complex issues. Through the emerging field of knowledge management, new approaches conceptualize knowledge as a resource to be managed like other resources (Wenger, 2002). Some of these new efforts are organized in a social structure, a *community framework*. Communities invite coalitions, including coalitions with differing viewpoints, to pursue the issues that they care about. Within communities, members are free to express their individual and organizational positions. Over time, a community moves beyond individual positions to discover shared interests. When these individuals face challenges, they create new networks and new methods, such as those described in this chapter, to find productive channels for their work. Just as individuals can develop increased resiliency, groups can also become resilient (Smith, n.d.). A *community framework* promotes a shared vision and fosters the connections necessary to build resiliency in groups.

One interesting model is Communities of Practice, an approach derived from the business environment that has been adopted by government and education. Essentially, Communities of Practice are voluntary associations that generate excitement to attract and engage individuals that care about an issue. Communities can be particularly effective at influencing, as their membership can include many roles and many groups. When messages to decision makers are supported across groups and across roles, they are less likely to be perceived as biased accounts and are received more favorably than are single-perspective views. Consequently, they may be more effective than are the more typical lobbying efforts (Cashman, 2003).

Communities can be organized in two important ways. First, *transactional communities* join individuals who primarily want to share across locations, agencies, organizations, and roles. These groups often meet through Web-based and other technology-based mediums (phone links, video telecast, etc.). The focus of transactional communities is shaping effective policy and practice through sharing information and focused communication (Cashman, 2003).

In contrast, *transformational communities* join stakeholders at all levels of research, policy, and practice to initiate new strategies or plan cooperative efforts across locations, agencies, organizations, and roles. In a transformational community, decision makers, implementers, and consumers build information loops to keep communication flowing. Their effort is action oriented and focused on learning the lessons of shared work. Generally, an organization that has influence and direct links to individuals at all levels convenes the community and sponsors the work. Often, this is an agency or professional organization (Cashman, 2003).

Exercise 6: Connecting Through Communities

Use the information in columns 1–3 of Table 85.5 to inform your thinking. Use column 4 to generate ideas about how you can influence local and state decision makers.

Exercise 7: First Steps to Influencing

Using the exercises provided in this chapter, think about these questions, and generate your first steps!

Key Points to Remember

This chapter has presented typical and emerging methods for thinking about decision making and influencing decision makers.

- Some approaches have been adapted from accepted policy methodology; others have been translated from emerging business approaches.
- Together, they provide a framework for thinking about issues, strategy and interaction.
- Using these strategies, practitioners can initiate contact, begin dialogue and build relationships

Table 85.5 Communicating and Influencing

Community Type	Methods of Connecting	Strategies for Influencing	Potential Applications
Transactional	E-mail, Web logs, online chat, Web seminars, discussion rooms, electronic bulletin boards, list serve, document repository	Issue sensing, issue specification, stakeholder identification, focused communication, building the base of interested stakeholders, drawing on the networks of all the stakeholder groups	
Transformational	Sponsored meetings, regular telephone interchange, video conference, Webcasts, Web seminars, e-mail, Web logs, online chat, discussion rooms, electronic bulletin boards, list serve, document repository	Generate new strategies, pilot new strategies, involve decision makers in development and delivery of new strategies, identify leverage points for policy and practice, engage the full range of stakeholders, identify potential unintended consequences of policy choices, implement systems change strategies, monitor and make recommendations to adjust policy implementation strategies	

Source: Cashman (2003).

Table 85.6 Planning the First Moves

Guiding Questions	*Reflections That Inform and Support Action*
What issue do you want to influence?	
What outcome do you seek?	
How will you invite others to join your effort?	
How will you learn what others know and care about regarding this issue?	
What position(s), agency, or agencies have authority over this issue?	
What organizations, agencies, service providers, and consumers have influence over this issues?	
How do decision makers describe this issue?	
What kind of information might decision makers seek?	
Will a community strategy help build support and create a base for influencing?	
Will a transformational story help decision makers and others to focus on the benefits of your strategy?	

that can shape the policy and practice now and into the future.

- Networked governance may become the next big policy direction.

References

Cashman, J. (2003, June). *The shared responsibility for transition.* Presentation delivered at the Pennsylvania Interagency Transition Conference, Harrisburg.

Cashman, J. (2003, July). *Communities of practice: The human side of implementation.* Presentation delivered at the National Monitoring Academies for the Office of Special Education Programs. Baltimore, MD, and Salt Lake City, UT.

Denning, S. (2001). *The springboard: How storytelling ignites action in knowledge-era organizations.* Boston: Butterworth-Heineman.

Denning, S. (2003). *The leader's guide to storytelling: Mas-*

tering the art and discipline of business narrative. San Francisco: Jossey Bass.

Dunn, W. (1994). *Public policy analysis.* Englewood Cliffs, NJ: Prentice Hall.

Goldsmith, S., & Eggers, W. (2004). *Governing by network: The new shape of the public sector.* Washington, DC: Brookings Institution Press.

Nakamura, R., & Smallwood, F. (1980). *The politics of policy implementation.* New York: St. Martin's Press.

Patton, C., & Sawicki, D. (1993). *Basic methods of policy analysis and planning.* Englewood Cliffs, NJ: Prentice Hall.

Rist, R. (1995). Influencing the policy process with qualitative research. Retrieved September 15, 2004, from http://www.edpolicy/gwu.edu/resources/influencing/paper.html

Smith, C. (n.d.). Strengthening the rural community: Communities of practice. Retrieved May 6, 2004, from http://www.ncrlc.com/comm-of-practice_webdoc.html

Wenger, E., McDermott, R., & Snyder, W. (2002). *Cultivating communities of practice.* Boston: Harvard Business School Press.

Individuals With Disabilities Education Act: Translating and Implementing

Elizabeth M. Timberlake ▪ Christine Anlauf Sabatino

Getting Started

The Individuals with Disabilities Education Act of 1990, its 1997 amendments, and the accompanying federal regulations have summarized how educational systems are to accomplish the mandate to provide a free public education for children with disabilities in the least restrictive school environment appropriate for each individual child (U.S. Department of Education, 2002). For school social workers, this codification provides legal underpinnings for their services within the educational mission of the school, establishes basic procedures, and sets the stage for practice. However, it remains for school social workers to comprehend the intent of these federal mandates and the implications for service delivery, which culminates in an individualized educational program (IEP), and to translate this understanding into an IEP practice model with goals, process, and outcomes meaningful in a school setting.

What We Know

IDEA Service Eligibility and Goals

IDEA mandates a free and appropriate public education for children evaluated

> . . . as having mental retardation, a hearing impairment including deafness, speech or language impairment, a visual impairment including blindness, a serious emotional disturbance, an orthopedic impairment, autism, traumatic brain injury, other health impairment, a specific learning disability, deaf-blindness, or multiple

disabilities, and who because of these impairments needs special education and related services. (34 C.F.R. 300.7)

Statute requirements explicitly link the unique needs of each child with the services to be provided and implicitly point to education-related outcomes. A child must have one of the identified disabilities and demonstrate a need for assistance with disability-related difficulties constituting barriers to educational benefit. Since IDEA service delivery programs are associated with a child's educational progress, school personnel must show the linkage of planned interventions with educational outcomes and provide evidence of direct and indirect benefit.

For children ages 5–21 and their families, the practice process of the IDEA service delivery program culminates in the IEP, a customized planning document prepared at a formal meeting between a qualified representative of the local educational authority, the child's teacher(s), other educational personnel (where appropriate), the child's parent(s) or guardian, and the child (where appropriate) (20 U.S.C. 1401–68). These meeting participants bring together information from multiple sources to design school program modifications, services, and supports that will guide the educational experience of the child, protect the child's rights, and enable the child to:

• advance appropriately toward attaining annual goals;
• be involved and progress in the general curriculum and participate in extracurricular activities and other nonacademic activities; and
• be educated and participate with other children with disabilities and nondisabled children in extracurricular activities. (20 U.S.C. 1414 [d1, a3])

As a procedural requirement for protecting a child's rights, the IEP includes:

> present levels of educational performance, annual goals, short-term instructional objectives, specific services to be provided to the child, the extent to which the pupil will be able to be educated with nondisabled students, the projected date of initiation and anticipated duration of services, a statement of needed transition services, and various criteria for evaluating progress. (20 U.S.C. 1412 [3, 5])

As a document, the IEP represents the best thinking and planning of those persons most closely invested in the child's educational advancement and yields evidentiary benchmarks of the child's functioning at school, the child's level of service eligibility, and the parents' understanding of the strengths and needs of their child in school.

For school social workers, creating IEP documents for the IDEA service delivery program involves the practice processes of disability screening, eligibility assessment, problem formulation, goal-oriented educational problem solving, and planning. Thus, in effect, creation of IEPs is a biopsychosocial collaborative intervention process with parents on behalf of their child. In addition, a key element in IDEA service delivery by school social workers is program monitoring and practice evaluation that focus on the protection of children's rights, involvement and empowerment of parents, and enhancement of children's benefits.

IEP Program Results: Children's Rights and Parent Empowerment

IEP baseline and subsequent measurements document the climate of ongoing IDEA-related service delivery and provide an opportunity for monitoring program quality and outcomes, including the degree to which the educational rights of children with disabilities are protected in day-to-day practice and the educational benefits evidenced by children. In monitoring program quality, the following questions assist school social workers in determining the focus of their collaboration with school personnel and parents in promoting children's rights.

• Do school personnel take into account how children's needs and the right to achieve their potential, parents' expectations about their child's future, and the school environment affect IEP decisions and educational progress?
• Does the IEP team consider the fit between the school environment and the needs of children with disabilities from a child rights and parent empowerment perspective?

To measure the degree to which the ideal learning climate is found in their schools and in their own practice, school social workers and their colleagues turn to six legally mandated educational rights of children with disabilities (Turnbull & Turnbull, 1998; Whitted & Constable, 2002) as the template against which to assess results. As shown in Table 86.1, the educational rights of children with disabilities are associated with corresponding professional action principles. In turn, these rights and principles translate into protective policies and practice procedures whose fulfillment generates data for program evaluation.

For example, the educational right to *attend school and be educated* translates into the educational and social work action principles of *full access* and *zero reject*. Among others, the related protective policies involve practices such as not excluding students for lack of capacity for learning or contagious diseases, and not suspending or expelling students simply for disability-related behavioral difficulties. These practices include collaborative problem solving among school social workers, parents, and educators to identify alternative solutions that are further grounded in the protective rights to *fair evaluation* and *fair treatment*. Taken together, these four rights provide the parameters for school social work practice within the IEP's evaluative and due process procedures.

Table 86.2 illustrates how data indicators of the right to *attend school and be educated* may be counted and calculated in order to empirically substantiate that the targeted educational rights of children with disabilities have or have not been protected by school social workers and educational personnel.

Specifically, the frequencies and percentages in the table provide information about the degree to which the children are being identified as needing and receiving IDEA-related educational services and, thereby, the degree of program implementation. For example, if 47% of identified need is being met for this population, the collaborative effort of professionals and parents (as well as the school under study) is fulfilling the right to *attend school and be educated* for less than half of the children

Table 86.1 Educational Rights, Professional Action Principles, Sample of Protective Policies, and Data Generated

Educational Rights	Selected Action Principles	Selected Protective Policies	Data Indicators
1. Right to attend school and be educated	• Principle of full access • Principle of zero reject	• Identifying children with disabilities who may be at risk of experiencing barriers to benefiting from education • Not excluding children for reasons such as lack of intellectual capacity for classroom learning or having contagious diseases • Not suspending or expelling students with disability-related behavioral difficulties without further evaluation of needs and strengths and due process hearings	• # children, risks identified • # children, reasons excluded • # children, reasons suspended • # children, reasons retained
2. Right to a fair evaluation of needs	• Principle of nondiscriminatory evaluation • Principle of individualized evaluation of needs, strengths	• Evaluation not biased by race, culture, language, socioeconomic status, or religious background • Evaluation not biased by gender discrimination or type of disability • Evaluation based on facts about what students are doing in relation to education goal attainment and their capacity for achievement • Evaluation based on identifying interaction of impairments, needs, and strengths on educational goal attainment • Evaluation codified as mandated IEP	• Demographics • IEP data • # of IEPs
3. Right to benefit from school experiences	• Principle of child individuation • Principle of school adaptation	• Individualize each child's education • Follow through with the IEP to build capacities in the student with a disability and the student's educational support system of school, family, and community	• # yearly reviews • IEP data

(continued)

Table 86.1 (*Continued*)

Educational Rights	Selected Action Principles	Selected Protective Policies	Data Indicators
		• Ensure that school confers an individualized positive outcome for the target student	
4. Right to be included in the general educational curriculum and other school-related activities	• Principle of inclusivity • Principle of least restrictive environment • Principle of school adaptation	• Include student in general education curriculum with supplemental assistance and necessary services • Adapt school facilities, programs, and services as necessary and feasible to meet the educational needs of the students • Remove student from general educational curriculum only when student does not evidence benefit from supplemental assistance and necessary related services	• # of inclusions • # removed, why • #, type of adaptations
5. Right to be treated fairly	• Principle of procedural due process in decision making	• Provide parents, child with information such as notices about meetings and proposed changes in services • Provide access to records and access to fair hearing process • Follow procedures for identifying, evaluating, developing IEP, implementing IEP, assessing progress, revising IEP as indicated for goal attainment	• # timely meeting notices • # participating • Procedural checklist
6. Right to be included in the decision-making process	• Principle of child, parent inclusion • Principle of parent empowerment	• Include student and parents so that they have opportunity to affect student's education in a meaningful way	• Parent presence, IEP meeting • Parent style, level of input • Case management responsibilities assumed by parent • Leadership role taken by parent • Level of parent knowledge for decision making • Parent skill in effecting change for child

Table 86.2 Developing Indicators of Program Results

In Relation to Children Served

Data:	# of children in targeted school/region/system
	# of children screened as having disabilities
	# of children with disabilities identified as being at educational risk and eligible for IDEA services with breakdown by type of disability, risk, and service
	# of children with disabilities provided with IDEA services and breakdown by type of disability, risk, and service
Calculations:	% of children with disability in targeted system
	% of children with disability eligible for IDEA services
	% of eligible children provided IDEA services

In Relation to Services Provided

Data:	Types of special instruction	# children	# service days
	Types of specific services	# children	# service days
	Mainstreaming		
	• For instructional content	# children	# service days
	• For recreation periods	# children	# service days
	Types of transition services	# children	# service days

with disabilities. When such information is juxtaposed against the goal of 100%, the degree of success or failure becomes apparent, as does the acceptability of the stated goal.

Aggregation of such data by school social workers yields a picture of the human rights/political context of the school and school system in which children with disabilities are educated. The portrait becomes clearer as more nuanced details are filled in by additional IEP data—demographics, types and levels of disability, accommodations and resources needed and provided, and level of educational goal attainment. Over time, the static picture shifts to a longitudinal one as IEP data provide a look at the part that school social workers play and their level of success in the educational progression of cohorts of children with disabilities.

The facts and calculations shown in Tables 86.1 and 86.2 are straightforward. Competing equities, however, may cloud interpretation in day-to-day practice. Since the purpose of IDEA is protection of a vulnerable group, the law and its federal regulations provide the basis for addressing competing equities in practice among the mandated rights. For example, the right to *attend school and be educated* and the right to *be included in the general curriculum and other school-related activities* are considered universal rights for this target population. But what happens in the real world of school social work practice when high demand for services confronts scarce funds and resources?

According to 20 U.S.C. 1412 (3), children with disabilities who receive no supplemental or related educational services are to have priority over children with disabilities who receive some form of IDEA-related service. That is, the intent of this law is to provide children with disabilities the same basic educational opportunities as their nondisabled peers but not necessarily opportunities that maximize their developmental potential. In other words, this law's intent is not to fulfill the ideal that each child receives a level of service that enables the maximum benefit possible (*Board of Education v. Rowley*, 1982).

Parents, however, may not comprehend that when their child is making some progress on annual IEP goals established at IEP team meetings, the educational program is meeting the legal standard of IDEA. Although they have been included in IEP team planning meetings, research reveals that the IEP process is a passive experience for many parents (Turnbull, Turbiville, & Turnbull, 2000). Thus, the decisions and goals of the IEP may not reflect parental expectations about their child's future and parental priorities about the benefits experienced by their children. In these instances, the school social worker's practice role includes strengthening parent knowledge and involvement in a way that (1) clarifies their understanding of the type and level of benefits the educational system can provide for their child; (2) empowers their collaborative participation in

IEP decision making in their children's best interests; and (3) enhances their capacity to realistically assess their child's educational benefits in relation to their rights and goals under IDEA and its amendments. Often a key area for clarification involves the No Child Left Behind Act of 2001, which generates state report cards to assess whether children are performing at grade level in standardized reading and math tests. This law is associated with measurement of teacher and school effectiveness. It has no provision that directly addresses the educational needs of children with disabilities.

What We Can Do

IEP Practice Outcome: Child Goal Attainment

The key to determining the educational and social progress of an individual child with disabilities flows from one educational right in particular—the right to *benefit from school experiences*. In this context, the annual IEP practice outcome question is: Does the child's participation in the school experiences and resources prescribed by the IEP facilitate his or her expected level of attainment of the specified IEP goals?

To answer this question, the IEP document contains annual goal statements that specify:

- independent treatment variable—prescribed school experiences and resources;
- direction of the desired change process—decrease, maintain, or increase level of educational and psychosocial functioning; and
- outcome goal variable—level of the excess or deficit in functioning requiring attention and appraisal of the expected level of attainment in one year (Constable, 2002).

The IEP also contains benchmarks of annual progress in the form of short-term objectives through which progress toward annual goals is measured. The school social worker answers this question by addressing problems in psychosocial functioning with objectives focused on a child's psychosocial and behavioral functioning with teachers in the classroom, peers in recreation and community settings, and family members at home. In addition, the school social worker attends to family needs that are inhibiting the child's use of IEP resources and achievement of educational benefit, provides support and guidance as indicated to maintain parent involvement, and keeps the parents informed of their child's progress or lack thereof. In this way the IEP document indeed becomes "the living record of an evaluative, decision-making, and planning process . . . that has taken place among parents, school, and child" (Constable, 2002, p. 265).

The professional literature contains many descriptive studies (qualitative and quantitative) of various aspects of the IEP document. However, we were not able to locate any published studies that addressed the IEP as an intervention program yielding empirical results such as preservation of children's rights or as a practice model yielding child benefit outcomes or parent empowerment outcomes. While some literature about parent involvement was located, few outcome studies were identified (Federation for Children With Special Needs, 1999; Gorney, 1988; Zhang & Bennet, 2001). Nor was IEP outcome research identified in Sopko's (2003) synthesis of the literature since IDEA was reauthorized in 1997. Table 86.3 depicts selected reference resources and sources for research in progress.

In searching the Internet, we found multiple sites replete with protocols purporting to represent best models of IEP documents prepared through structured data collection but containing sparse supporting evidence for these claims. Therefore, these references are excluded. For the reader, a search for interventions and outcomes related to the targeted need or problem area identified in the annual IEP goal is likely to be more fruitful than a general IEP outcome search.

IEP Practice Outcome: Parent Involvement and Empowerment

Initially, IEP team members viewed parent inclusion in meetings as a symbolic gesture, allowing parents to present information but not engage in actual planning (Yoshida, Fenton, Kaufman, & Maxwell, 1978). The IDEA reauthorization law, however, includes parents in all components of educational planning for this child and views parents as equal partners in the educational processes (Sopko, 2003). Thus today, parent involvement is viewed as a value-added benefit, and school social workers are concerned with preparing parents to take an informed, collaborative role in preparing

Table 86.3 Empirical Research on IDEA and IEPs

References

Authors	Date	Focus
Fed. of Children etc.	1999	Survey of parents about IEP implementation
Gorney	1988	Parent education program about IEP process
Grigal et al.	1997	Evaluation of transition components of IEP
Orkwis et al.	2000	IDEA research supported by OSEP
Martin et al.	2004	Survey of student involvement in IEP meetings
Sopko	2003	Review of literature since 1997
Tschantz	2002	Monitoring implementation of IDEA
Zhang et al.	2001	Review of Child Find research

Current Federally Funded and Research Center Projects

National Center for Access to General Curriculum
National Center for Secondary Education and Transition
National Center for Study of Postsecondary Education Supports
OSEP Technical Assistance Center for Positive Behavioral Interventions and Supports
OSEP Special Education Elementary Longitudinal Study
OSEP National Early Intervention Longitudinal Study
OSEP Study of State and Local Implementation and Impact of IDEA Act

the IEP document, engaging in decision making and planning at IEP meetings, and monitoring IEP benefits (Goldstein & Turnbull, 1982; Martin, Marshall, & Sale, 2004). This perspective is supported by research that reports positive outcomes for both parent and child as a result of mothers' involvement in the educational process (Shonkoff, Hauser-Cram, Krauss, & Upshur, 1992). Through participation in meetings and educational services, for example, parents increase their knowledge about their child's education, parents and teachers increase communication, and children are more likely to achieve the goals set (Smith, 2001; Zhang & Bennet, 2001). Thus, besides obtaining the requisite information from parents for IEP documentation and planning, school social workers' IEP practice goals include decreasing parent and teacher resistance to parent involvement, increasing teacher–parent communication, increasing the sense of parental ownership of IEP decisions, and increasing parental ability to:

- engage in collaborative problem solving;
- mobilize the school environment for their child's educational benefit;
- help their child absorb as much educational benefit as possible; and
- monitor the level of IEP educational and social outcomes attained.

These school social work practice goals stem from the educational right of the child and parent to *be included in the decision-making process* and the corresponding action principles of *inclusion* and *empowerment*. By clarifying that the intent of parent work is the child's educational benefit, these practice goals provide direction and continuity that focus the problem formulation, problem solving, and resource allocation process on the results sought by both parents and school (Strickland & Turnbull, 1990). Furthermore, these goals suggest use of social work practice strategies that:

- build a professional relationship and support parents in their concern for their child;
- engage parents in collaborative problem-solving and decision-making processes;
- develop, clarify, and compile the biopsychosocial case history information;
- provide general information to parents about the eligibility process and requirements for IDEA services, child needs and resources, and service availability;
- provide the biopsychosocial history and social work assessment to the IEP team for collaborative decision making; and
- interpret and clarify the aggregate evidence and team recommendations for the parents.

Stemming from children's rights, these practice goals and strategies assist school social workers in monitoring progress toward goal attainment and assessing outcomes in relation to IEP formulations. In this light, one focal outcome may be stated as parent role involvement and empowerment that increases the fit between the child with disabilities and his or her school environment. This outcome has a dual legitimacy in that its sanctioning sources include both the social work profession's traditional mission and the federally mandated educational rights of children with disabilities.

For example, an involved and empowered parent is one who demonstrates:

a critical awareness and understanding of community functioning (cognitive), feelings about one's competence or ability to effect change in the community (emotional), and participatory activities focused on social change in community contexts (behavioral). (Speer & Peterson, 2000, p. 110)

Conceptually, empowering parents involves mobilizing their personal, interpersonal, and political resources and power so that their actions improve the child's overall school functioning (Gutierrez, 1995; Hardy & Leiba-O'Sullivan, 1998). Sometimes, parents are empowered to work for educational change within their child's school; other times, within the broader community. Operationally, involved and empowered parents evidence competence, political acumen, relationship skills, ability to shape educational debate, and ability to increase school responsiveness to the needs of their child.

Table 86.4 addresses contextually dependent aspects of parent role empowerment in relation to their child-in-school and takes the form of a goal attainment scale for use by school social workers. This scale provides one way in which the school social worker may rate parents' functional level of involvement and empowerment at baseline and measure change in the empowerment-related cognitions, emotions, and behaviors identified with the IEP practice goals and brief interven-

Table 86.4 Goal Attainment Indicators of Parent Role Empowerment Outcomes

Rarely	*Occasionally*	*Half the Time*	*Much of the Time*	*Consistently*

1. Understand the impact on the family and the child of the child's disability and, conversely, the impact of the family on the child.

| 1 | 2 | 3 | 4 | 5 |

2. Understand the nature of the child's disabilities in relation to functioning and learning in school.

| 1 | 2 | 3 | 4 | 5 |

3. Understand strategies for ensuring some educational benefit.

| 1 | 2 | 3 | 4 | 5 |

4. Understand school system dynamics and the external forces that shape the school environment.

| 1 | 2 | 3 | 4 | 5 |

5. Know resources and methods to produce psychosocial change.

| 1 | 2 | 3 | 4 | 5 |

6. Convey a sense of confidence, creative energy, and competence in making decisions and taking actions that affect the child.

| 1 | 2 | 3 | 4 | 5 |

7. Demonstrate assertiveness and leadership skills in obtaining appropriate accommodations to improve the child's school situation and educational benefit.

| 1 | 2 | 3 | 4 | 5 |

8. Demonstrate participatory skills in collaborative decision making and follow-through actions.

| 1 | 2 | 3 | 4 | 5 |

9. Demonstrate appropriate strategies for problem solving.

| 1 | 2 | 3 | 4 | 5 |

tion. For example, some parents need assistance in understanding the impact of the particular disability on the child and family. Others need to learn problem-solving strategies, collaborative decision-making skills, and leadership skills in obtaining appropriate educational accommodations. Since parent mastery of the IEP as a tool for their child's education is likely to be associated with child benefit, this table offers a scale for selected aspects of parent work as an example of documenting parent goals related to their children's education and assessing level of goal attainment.

Tools and Practice Examples

Child

William is a 9-year-old third-grader enrolled in his local public elementary school. He and his family have lived in this suburban community since he was born. In the third-grade classroom, he presented with extreme hyperactivity, psychomotor agitation, talkativeness with racing thoughts and ideas, and distractibility. In the first- and second-grade classrooms, by contrast, William had presented with sadness, listlessness, withdrawn behavior, uncontrollable tears, and difficulty completing school assignments. He repeated first grade. Standardized intelligence tests have consistently indicated above-average intelligence, but report card grades and standardized educational tests show below-average scholastic performance. Besides intellectual ability, William's strengths include strong investment in attending school and strong family support.

His two-parent family provides a stable family home with a good marriage, adequate housing, and above-average income. Both parents are college graduates and are employed in the business sector in moderately stressful jobs. There are no external family stressors. The large extended family in the area provides after-school care for William and his sister. Sarah, a sixth-grader, presents none of William's behavioral symptoms, performs well in school, and has good peer relationships. There is a family history of one uncle and one grandfather with mild behavioral mood swings.

Since William was 6, his parents have discussed their concerns with his pediatrician and teachers to no avail. In October of third grade, William was diagnosed at the community mental health clinic

as having a bipolar mood disorder, and he began receiving pharmacological intervention and play therapy. In November, William's community mental health team, teacher, and parents implemented a classroom and home behavioral management program to set behavioral limits and identify disciplinary practices that support effective schooling. By January, his behavior and performance in the classroom had worsened, his teacher referred him to a multidisciplinary school evaluation team, and his parents learned about IDEA for the first time.

The multidisciplinary team evaluation indicated that William met the criteria for a seriously emotionally disturbed child (SED) and was eligible for self-contained classroom education. One of William's IEP goals was managing anger and frustration with class rules and peers in a responsible manner. School social work services were identified as the responsible special education–related services. The evaluative criteria involved a behavioral contract with a student self-report, parent report, and teacher report indicating that William was or was not meeting expectations about responsible behavioral choices.

As planned, William entered the center program in April and continued through the school year. In July, however, the school board announced that all elementary school SED centers would be closed because of financial constraints and that participating children would be mainstreamed into regular educational programs with special education resources.

School Social Worker's Concurrent Parent Empowerment Goals

In addition to their child work and family work to enable a child to achieve behavioral or other goals, the authors recommend that school social workers establish concurrent goals and objectives specific to parents in order to involve them in the child's educational progress. This approach is consistent with the legal framework found in the IFSP for younger children and IDEA's reauthorization.

Parents

Therefore, work with William's parents focused on empowering them in their parent roles related to his education. Goals included (1) learning about bipolar disorder and its effects on William and his education; (2) learning about appropriate limit setting and discipline through behavior management; and (3) participating in biweekly parent–teacher conferences. The related service provider was the school social worker. Evaluation criteria included parent and school social worker reports of goal attainment.

In keeping with their person-in-environment professional tradition, additional community-related goals were added after the center's closure. That is, the school social worker engaged the parents in community and school system issues related to William's educational needs and service planning.

The second set of social work goals was established with the parents to ensure continuing educational progress for William. These goals involved (1) developing political acumen about school system dynamics and the external forces that shape the school environment and (2) shaping educational debate to bring about increased community and school responsiveness to the educational needs of their child. Their objectives included such tasks as obtaining the school report that recommended closing some special education classrooms, mobilizing other parents and the director of special education, speaking at school board meetings about the needs of children with disabilities, and obtaining publicity about the effects of this decision on children's education and lives.

Key Points to Remember

This chapter expands the traditional view of IDEA as a static law by translating its legal principles into a process view of IDEA as both a program and a practice model for intervening with children, their parents, and the school environment.

- The program model incorporates active protection of the educational rights of children with disabilities and yields empirical results couched in the terminology of best school practices.
- The practice model implements the IEP as a process for involving parents and children in educational goal attainment and actively incorporates analysis of level of goal attainment of child benefit and parent empowerment.

References

Board of Education of the Hendrick Hudson Central School District, Westchester County, et al., v. Amy Rowley et al., U.S. 176, 73 L. Ed. 2d 690, 102 S. Ct. 3034 (1982).

Constable, R. (2002). The individualized education program and the IFSP: Content, process, and the social worker's role. In R. Constable, S. McDonald, and J. Flynn (Eds.), *School social work: Practice, policy, and research perspectives* (5th ed., pp. 264–278). Chicago: Lyceum.

Federation for Children With Special Needs. (1999). *Statewide survey of individualized educational plans.* Boston: Ovid Technologies.

Goldstein, S., & Turnbull, A. (1982). Strategies to increase parent participation in IEP conferences. *Exceptional Children, 48,* 360–361.

Gorney, B. (1988). *The development and implementation of a training program through slides to facilitate parent involvement in the IEP.* Arlington, VA: ERIC Clearinghouse in Disabilities and Gifted Education.

Grigal, M., Test, D., Beattie, J., & Wood, M. (1997). An evaluation of transition components of individualized education programs. *Exceptional Children, 63,* 357–372.

Gutierrez, L. (1995). Understanding the empowerment process: Does consciousness make a difference? *Social Work Research, 19,* 229–237.

Hardy, C., & Leiba-O'Sullivan, S. (1998). The power behind empowerment: Implications for research and practice. *Human Relations, 51,* 451–483.

Martin, J., Marshall, L., & Sale, P. (2004). A 3-year study of middle, junior high, and high school IEP meetings. *Exceptional Children, 70,* 285–297.

Orkwis, R., DeCarme, J., & Glover, J. (2000). *Research, innovation, and evaluation.* Washington, DC: Office of Special Education Programs.

Shonkoff, J., Hauser-Cram, P., Krauss, M., & Upshur, C. (1992). Development of infants with disabilities and their families. *Monographs of the Society for Research in Child Development, 57*(6), serial No. 230.

Smith, S. (2001). Involving parents in the IEP process. *ERIC digest E611.* Arlington, VA: ERIC Clearinghouse in Disabilities and Gifted Education.

Sopko, K. (2003). *The IEP: A synthesis of current literature since 1997.* Prepared for Project FORUM, National Association of State Directors of Special Education, Virginia.

Speer, P., & Peterson, N. (2000). Psychometric properties of an empowerment scale: Testing cognitive, emotional, and behavioral domains. *Social Work Research, 24,* 109–118.

Strickland, B., & Turnbull, A. (1990). *Developing and implementing individualized educational programs* (3rd ed). Columbus, OH: Merrill.

Tschantz, J. (2002). Monitoring the implementation of IDEA. *Proceedings of the sixth national monitoring conference.* Salt Lake City, Utah.

Turnbull, A., Turbiville, V., & Turnbull, H. (2000). Evolution of family-professional partnerships: Collective empowerment as the model for the early 21st century. In J. Shonkoff and S. Meisels (Eds.), *Handbook of early childhood intervention* (2nd ed., pp. 630–650). Cambridge: Cambridge University Press.

Turnbull, H., & Turnbull, A. (1998). *Free and appropriate public education: The law and children with disabilities.* Denver: Love.

U.S. Department of Education. (2002). To assure the free and appropriate public education of all children with disabilities (IDEA, Section 618). *Twenty-fourth annual report to Congress on the implementation of the Individuals With Disabilities Act.* Rockville, MD: Westat.

Whitted, B., & Constable, R. (2002). Educational mandates for children with disabilities: School policies, case law, and the school social worker. In R. Constable, S. McDonald, and J. Flynn (Eds.), *School social work: Practice, policy, and research perspectives* (5th ed., pp. 122–137). Chicago: Lyceum.

Yoshida, R., Fenton, K., Kaufman, M., & Maxwell, J. (1978). Parental involvement in the special education pupil planning process: The school's perspective. *Exceptional Children, 44,* 531–533.

Zhang, C., & Bennet, T. (2001). Embracing cultural and linguistic diversity during the IFSP and IEP: Implications from DEC recommended practices. In *Serving the underserved: A review of the research and practice in Child Find, Assessment, and the IFSP/IEP process for culturally and linguistically diverse young children.* Arlington, VA: ERIC Clearinghouse on Disabilities and Gifted Education.

The Law, Ethical Guidelines, Records, Assessments, and Reports for School-Based Practice

Laws governing public education dominate in the school environment. In achieving the mandates of education policies, public school priorities can sometimes conflict with social work and mental health values. Ethical dilemmas arising from differences between education and social work or mental health priorities can be compounded when mental health practitioners are unfamiliar with laws that affect students and are without boundaries and professional procedures. Coupled with this, most schools require school-compatible formats and components for service planning, client assessments, and the maintenance of case notes and records. This section provides clear directives in these areas that will be especially valuable for social workers and related professionals new to the school setting or who require updates on laws and ethical guidelines for school-based practice.

HIPAA and the Electronic Transfer of Student Information

Mary Ann Overcamp-Martini

CHAPTER 87

Getting Started

Today's educational environment is a complex network of laws, policies, and procedures, administrative and professional relationships, and enough testing mandates and funding formulas to boggle the faint-hearted. Among these are the legal requirements to maintain the privacy of students' records. Requirements for confidentiality are not new. For social workers, counselors, and other mental health professionals, the right to privacy is generally safeguarded in the ethical responsibilities of confidentiality of client information. However, where once there were file cabinets, files, and other paper supplies, now there is the ubiquitous computer terminal. The move to electronic storage of health information has changed the processes involved in protecting client information. This chapter looks at one piece of that complicated educational maze, the law-to-policy-procedure puzzle, as it lays out issues involving the recent HIPAA (Health Insurance Portability and Accountability Act of 1996) legislation and its impact on educational records.

There are two federal privacy laws that primarily affect health records in the school environment: FERPA and HIPAA.

- FERPA is the Family Educational Rights and Privacy Act (P.L. 93–380, the Education Amendments of 1974). In general, health records in the context of educational records have been protected by FERPA since its passage in 1974.

- HIPAA refers to the Health Insurance Portability and Accountability Act of 1996, passed by Congress in August 1996. Because of the prior existence of FERPA, Congress exempted educational records from the requirements of HIPAA.

HIPAA becomes most relevant to schools in the context of electronic health transactions such as medical claims processing for third-party insurance, Medicare, and Medicaid. Outside the parameters of educational records, those electronic transactions contain what the bill refers to as "individually identifiable health information" in the educational environment (U.S. Department of Health and Human Services, 2003). HIPAA delineates individually identifiable health information as "protected health information" (PHI). The HIPAA privacy rules governing such protected health information went into effect on April 14, 2003, for most "covered entities." Although the local educational agency (LEA) is generally a covered entity under the HIPAA law, there are several exceptions to the definition of protected health information:

- Educational records under FERPA
- Records of students held by postsecondary educational institutions
- Records of students 18 years of age or older, used exclusively for health care treatment and not disclosed to other than the provider under the student's request
- Employment records maintained in the role of employer rather than health care provider

At the time of this publication, the initial rules under HIPAA will have been incorporated into the policies and procedures for the local educational agency employing school social workers. Therefore, the issues related to the impact of HIPAA on the school's procedures should already be a part of the administrative environment. Although most educational information is covered already under FERPA and not subject to HIPAA, most schools engage in some activity covered by HIPAA. In general, school-based health clinics are "covered entities" under HIPAA and therefore subject to HIPAA requirements. The services of health professionals generally bring the educational agency under HIPAA requirements in that they are among health care providers for whose services the district generally transmits protected health information electronically for billing purposes (Moore & Wall, 2003).

What kinds of activities covered under the local educational agency are of note to social workers and mental health staff? School social workers are often employees of a covered entity that transmits protected health information electronically and is generally subject to HIPAA regulations. In addition to traditional educational services, schools increasingly address the educational needs of many students covered under the Individuals with Disabilities Education Act (IDEA), including medical care for those who are chronically ill and medically fragile. In addition, schools have become a primary provider of mental health services for children (Rones & Hoagwood, 2000).

The interface between HIPAA and FERPA has been a particularly problematic consequence of the HIPAA legislation. The agency responsible for implementing HIPAA from the federal level has acknowledged that it has not adequately addressed issues important to the educational environment, although there has been a storm of questions and concerns (Bergren, 2003), particularly within the evolving interpretations of this law and corresponding policies. Eventual clarification of the interface of FERPA and HIPAA may lead to further changes in policies and procedures in many school districts.

This chapter is intended to provide introductory background information on HIPAA, as well as resource information for the use of the school social worker. This chapter is not intended to provide legal advice to school social workers. As always, questions regarding how these regulations affect school social work and mental health practice should be directed to your supervisor.

What We Know

Privacy and Confidentiality

Let us begin our look at HIPAA with a brief review regarding privacy rights. While not absolute, the individual right to privacy is considered a fundamental right in the United States. This right has been codified into state tort law in all 50 states. In the past several decades, Congress has passed a long series of privacy-related laws both deepening and broadening the legal framework of privacy protection. The U.S. Supreme Court has also upheld the constitutional right of privacy over personal health information, giving it a distinct status in relation to other privacy matters (*Whalen v. Roe*, 1977).

Several separate statutory steps have been taken to protect children in a variety of settings. One of the recent privacy laws enacted by Congress was the Children's Online Privacy Protection Act (COPPA) effective in 2000. As a response to direct marketing strategies constructing sophisticated lists of information on children for resale, the law prohibits the collection or use of information from commercial Web sites and online services directed at children under the age of 13 without verifiable parental consent (Electronic Privacy Information Center, 2004).

Since HIPAA requires compliance with more restrictive state laws and allows more restrictive professional standards, the importance of ethical standards has also been elevated in this context. The social work profession has its own historical development of the rights of confidentiality, based on the concept that the relationship necessary to provide services is one based on trust. The ethical standard of confidentiality is encoded within the NASW *Code of Ethics* (NASW, 1996), as well as those of other professional organizations. NASW recommends that social workers consider the following sections of the *Code*: Sections 1.01, Commitment to Clients; 1.02, Self-determination; 1.03, Informed Consent; and 1.07, Privacy and Confidentiality (NASW, 2002).

In addition to the NASW *Code of Ethics*, NASW has established a set of standards for school social workers. First developed in 1978, these standards were most recently updated and revised in 2002 as the NASW *Standards for School Social Work Services*. The *Standards* require compliance with local, state, and federal law, policy, and regulations as a responsibility of professional practice. Standard 7 in particular states that "school social workers shall maintain adequate safeguards for the privacy and confidentiality of information" (NASW, 2002, p. 13). In addition to compliance to the law, the *Standards* address the responsibility to inform students, parents, and other professionals of confidentiality requirements and limitations when services begin. Standard 40 further requires the development of procedures to ensure "confidentiality, documentation, and accountability" (NASW, 2002, p. 13). In legal support of such standards, the ongoing discourse regarding legal standing of the psychotherapist–patient relationship was recently decided by the U.S. Supreme Court in *Jaffee v. Redmond* (1996) that confidentiality was protected against

civil discovery under the Federal Rules of Evidence.

Within the legal and professional context briefly summarized here, the clearest precedence to the HIPAA regulations in regard to educational records is the Family Educational Right to Privacy Act of 1974 (FERPA).

FERPA

Faced with public controversy and legal challenges to educational practices concerning the confidentiality of student educational records, the U.S. Congress passed the Family Educational Rights and Privacy Act in 1974. FERPA threatens the loss of federal funds to any educational entity that allows the dissemination of information from a student's educational records to most third parties without parental consent or authorization. A process was also established for parents to challenge the information contained in a student's records. When students reach age 18, they may exercise this right on their own (Cambron-McCabe, McCarthy, & Thomas, 2004).

Because FERPA governs the privacy of educational records in schools receiving federal funds, including health information maintained by school nurses and school health providers, it is the main legislation controlling their accessibility. Even when the school district bills for services such as occupational, speech, psychological, or mental health services covered under HIPAA transactions rules, the records themselves are educational records protected by FERPA. Private educational facilities are also mandated toward privacy rights, even though they may not be subject to FERPA. Social workers who are employed by private educational facilities not receiving federal funds nor subject to FERPA need to be aware that the electronic transmission of health-related data is now covered by HIPAA regulations (Bergren, 2004a).

HIPAA

Portability of health insurance coverage is the hallmark of the HIPAA legislation, allowing individuals and their families some protection in maintaining insurance benefits in changing situations, such as a change or loss of job, divorce, pregnancy, or change of residence. Additionally, the legislation mandated reform in the health insurance industry, with specific requirements and protections regarding the electronic transmission of data. This chapter looks most closely at the privacy requirements and protections regarding the electronic transmission of data.

We are all aware of the ongoing explosion of information, with concerns expressed in many quarters regarding the time and costs involved in health care transactions. With over 450 various claims forms and procedures in use nationwide over the past couple of decades, improvement of the claims process became an emergent issue in the struggle to contain administrative health care costs and make systems function more efficiently; up to 20% of costs in health care have been reported as paperwork costs (Redhead, 2001). Efforts to standardize processes and procedures were finally mandated by the U.S. Congress in the Health Insurance Portability and Accountability Act of 1996, the first comprehensive health information policy. HIPAA requires the development and use of standardized transaction code sets among health care providers for any covered entity that does not rely entirely on paper processes.

What We Can Do

Benefits of HIPAA

Much of the HIPAA law remains in the development process, but it is expected to reduce time and costs involved in processing information regarding eligibility and claims. Benefits are expected to accrue over time as a result of the standardization of electronic data, whether involving the Internet, private networks, intranet, compact disks, magnetic tapes, digital memory cards, dial-up lines, voice response, or fax-back systems; however, dedicated fax machines (not computer fax) are considered part of a paper-to-paper transaction and therefore are not covered by HIPAA. The law defines the 10 significant electronic transactions, mandating the development of related code sets standardizing the electronic data interchange formats. These regulations are known as the Electronic Transactions and Code Sets Standards (NASW, *Understanding HIPAA*, n.d.).

Along with concerns about the burden of health care transactions, concerns regarding the protection of the privacy and security we have come to expect as U.S. citizens have grown as well. In particular, concerns about health information

and its potential uses in an interconnected technological environment have escalated in the recent past. HIPAA addresses the uses of individually identifiable health information in the school environment but outside the educational records already protected by FERPA. Just as important, it established the legal framework to protect individuals as health information systems expand and develop (Standards for Privacy of Individually Identifiable Health Information, 2000). Because even unintentional violations of HIPAA potentially can lead to monetary fines and even imprisonment, problems in implementation excesses have been common, hindering the protection of students' health needs in the educational environment. According to Bergren (2004b), some of the problematic examples of this include the physician and facility denial of parental consents or authorizations for release of information; refusal of faxed information and information regarding treatment, appointments, health accommodations, or restrictions; and even the refusal to provide immunization information necessary for school admission, without parents' hand-carrying the information from office or facility to the school. Given the daily medical care provided by local educational agencies, particularly in regard to students with medically fragile or chronically ill conditions mainstreamed in school settings under the Individuals with Disabilities Education Act (IDEA), the situation has required particular attention from educational personnel to clarify the HIPAA mandates in reference to the educational setting.

HIPAA creates two new sets of national standards for electronic transmission of protected health information, in addition to administrative simplification standards:

* HIPAA Privacy Rule
* HIPAA Security Rule

HIPAA Privacy Rule

School social workers and mental health staff are bound to compliance with local, state, and federal law regarding confidentiality, in addition to the professional obligations of their professional codes of ethics. In many ways, HIPAA builds on ethical standards and state laws regulating confidentiality, setting national standards for the protection of personally identifiable health information for the first time. More safeguards and more control over health records were established at the federal level, including several new rights briefly summarized:

- The right to access, review, and copy PHI. Clients also have the right to request a modification in the PHI.
  - This right to access, review, copy, and request modification does not extend to psychotherapy notes, if they are separated from the medical record.
  - Psychotherapy notes are defined as "notes recorded (in any medium) by a health care provider who is a mental health professional documenting or analyzing the contents of conversation during a private counseling session or a group, joint, or family counseling session and *that are separated from the rest of the individual's medical record*" (emphasis added) (U.S. Department of Health and Human Services, 2003).
  - The definition of psychotherapy notes "excludes medication prescription and monitoring, counseling session start and stop times, the modalities and frequencies of treatment furnished, results of clinical tests, and any summary of the following items: diagnosis, functional status, the treatment plan, symptoms, prognosis, and progress to date" (U.S. Department of Health and Human Services, 2003).
- The right to request restrictions on the uses and disclosures of PHI.
  - Clients may refuse the use and disclosure of information in the way that the provider may prefer. The provider does not have to agree with all requests, but must uphold those agreed upon, with the exception of emergency treatments.
  - Clients or providers may change any such agreement on restricted information, as noted previously. Clients may do so at any time, with either a written or oral notification, which must then be noted in the record. Documentation in the medical record regarding information restrictions must be maintained for 6 years.
  - Agreed-upon changes must be made on a specified timetable, beginning with a 60-day period, with the possibility of a 30-day extension. The organization is obligated to ask the client who else must be advised of any changes.
  - If the organization denies the request for an amendment, the client must be advised of

the reason for the denial and the steps to be taken to appeal the decision. They also have the right to include their request as documentation within the protected health information.
- The right to receive a list of disclosures of PHI, with exceptions. The client's rights include a written accounting statement detailing disclosures of PHI for six years prior (beginning April 2003) upon request. However, not all disclosures need to be provided to clients. Of particular importance to social workers, exclusions of disclosures include the following:
  - Health oversight agencies or law enforcement officials, who can request exclusion through an oral or written statement of an excluded time period.
  - General social services and mental health agencies.
- The right to request how and where communications of PHI occur. In other words, reasonable client requests, such as the preferred type of communication (e.g., use of a specific telephone number), must be followed in terms of time and place.
- The right to make complaints regarding handling of PHI. If clients have a complaint regarding the use and disclosure of protected health information, there are several avenues for complaints.
  - The Department of Health and Human Services
  - Organization or health plan
  - State agencies, which vary from state to state, but may include such agencies as the following: Departments of Insurance, Independent Medical Review Boards, and State Boards of Education.

Finally, HIPAA requires some administrative policies and procedures to be in place to establish compliance with the privacy rule. These include the following:

- Revision of policies and procedures to support implementation of HIPAA
- Development of a process of complaint for clients and a process of documentation of complaints and their disposition
- Safeguards to reasonably protect PHI from violations of the privacy rule
- Documentation in written or electronic form of policies and procedures and required communications and documentation

- Other—personnel, training, sanctions (NASW, *Client rights*, n.d.)

HIPAA Security Rule

Think of the extent of personal information that could be downloaded from a computer within minutes to understand the importance of the new security rules under HIPAA. Confidentiality begins with protecting access to that information (Bergren, 2001). With personally identifiable health information stored electronically rather than in paper files, different rules of security now apply under HIPAA, as of April 21, 2005. This compliance deadline refers to physical, technical, and administrative safeguards required under HIPAA. Every organization, including the local educational agency, is required to assign someone the duties of the security officer, in order to assure compliance with the law. Every organization is required to set up safeguards to protect records and monitor their use, as well as report any disuse.

For many, a disquieting part of the Security Rule is that their own access to protected health information will now likely be limited by their agency to only those parts of the record related to particular job functions. Some school employees may no longer have access, and all those who do must be informed of the legal requirements for privacy and the sanctions attached to its disregard. This is true for everyone in the agency. No one should be given unlimited access to electronic protected health information. Staff should expect their computer use to be audited electronically, as this is a requirement of the Security Rule. In many cases, these reminders may flash onto the computer screen with the entrance of a new user but certainly should be information made available to all employees as a part of ongoing security training (NASW, *HIPAA security basics*, n.d.).

No electronic records should be left unsecured, nor should the means of access to electronic records. In other words, not only should the computers themselves be protected but also any related materials, such as passwords, keys, badges, and diskettes, should be protected. Just as our home protection of personal computers has increased the use of virus detectors, firewalls, and spamware, we should encourage the heightened protection of electronic records in the workplace. Protection of login and password information is paramount. Here are some suggestions regarding password use (Bergren, 2001):

- Prefer a word not listed in a dictionary
- Prefer nonsense words, combining letters, numbers, and characters
- Prefer longer rather than short passwords
- Change passwords periodically even if the district does not require it
- Do not share passwords, even with those who have access
- Do not leave a password close to a computer, for example, sticky note on the computer!
- Expect to be subject to sanctions for password misuse under district policies

Loading personal software from home computers should be prohibited, given the propensity for virus and spyware transmission to network computer systems. Similarly, use of the Internet should be restricted to known, safe, and work-related sites. Portable computer devices constitute another avenue for leaking or destruction of electronic protected health information and should not be left unattended at any time.

An important aspect of security measures is the need to report problems in maintaining the security of the system to the security officer. Computers left unattended; screens directed toward foot traffic areas; passwords shared; software loaded for games or other personal use; doors left open or unlocked—all of these common enough workplace occurrences become security risks for electronic protected health information.

Tools and Practice Examples

Due to the changing nature of the legal environment for schools, resources providing guidance on HIPAA should be checked often. A number of sources provide general responses to questions, such as the e-journal *Health and Health Care in Schools* (http://www.healthinschools.org). There are also a number of training resources, including a series of continuing education courses offered by NASW on its Web site, www.naswdc.org. Professionals are also advised to query the federal agencies for general guidance for HIPAA and FERPA. Questions may be submitted online for general responses, with a repository of past questions and responses that may be accessed online. The federal agency that administers FERPA is the Family Policy Compliance Office, U.S. Department of Education, 400 Maryland Avenue, S.W.,

Washington, DC 20202–4605 (http://www.ed/gov/policy/gen/guid/fpco/ferpa/index.html). For HIPAA, the federal agency is the Office for Civil Rights, U.S. Department of Health and Human Services, 200 Independence Avenue, S.W., Room 509F, HHH Building, Washington, DC 20201 (http://answers.hhs.gov/cgi-bin/hhs.cfg/php/enduser/std_alp.php); e-mail: OCRPrivacy@hhs.gov; phone: (866) 627–7748.

Another governmental source for online interactive assistance comes from the Centers for Medicare and Medicaid Services, also within the U.S. Department of Health and Human Services. Called *HIPAA Online*, its web address is http://www.cms.hhs.gov/hipaa/online/default. asp. The Center for Democracy and Technology (http://www.cdt.org/) is a further Web site resource, providing updated information on legislation pertaining to electronic health information.

In addition to general guidance from sources such as these, social workers are also advised to seek guidance from state officials regarding related laws governing privacy rights in your state. The interface between federal and state law necessitates these added steps. According to the HIPAA legislation, when state law provides protection at a higher level than HIPAA, state law prevails. HIPAA is intended to act as the "federal floor" of privacy protections for individually identifiable health information when held by an entity such as a school district (U.S. Department of Health and Human Services, 2003). Therefore, state law or school district policy may most appropriately direct the activities of the social worker regarding such individually identifiable health information if they provide more protection than HIPAA. To obtain answers about the state law, questions may be addressed to your state attorney general. You may contact the attorney general for your state by checking the following directory for particular contact information: www.cslib.org/attygenl/mainlinks/tabindex9.htm.

The National Association of Social Workers (NASW) recommends that social workers participate in workshops and training sessions related to the HIPAA legislation. The NASW Web site (http://www.naswdc.org) manages a number of training sessions for social workers on different aspects of the HIPAA legislation and its impact on administrative and clinical practice. The School Social Work Association of America (SSWAA) is an additional resource for information (http://www.sswaa.org/). Questions regarding HIPAA should be handled as appropriate through district administrative guidelines, which may include the following:

- Administrative supervisor or other designated representative for educational information
- HIPAA security officer
- School attorney
- State educational agency
- State attorney general
- Department of Health and Human Services
- NASW national or state office
- State social work boards

Key Points to Remember

Much of HIPAA includes traditional measures of security and privacy for protected information held by professionals. Much of HIPAA also involves commonsense policies and procedures. However, much of HIPAA is new and more secure and private, involving more protections for clients than many of us are familiar with. Understand that the local educational agency is obligated under federal law, with the potential of monetary sanctions, to carry out the mandates of the HIPAA law.

The first step of the new regulations is to learn and follow the local educational agency's Security Plan, ask questions of supervisors and the security officer, and report any issues that would appear to breach the risks of loss of security and privacy for our clients. Changing electronic technologies will continue to necessitate ongoing training and information seeking regarding the implementation of HIPAA. Frequent review of federal guidance in regard to the interface between FERPA and HIPAA will remain necessary for the foreseeable future. Although perhaps a difficult transition, HIPAA rules create the framework for a safer, faster, and more efficient information technology system for the future.

References

Bergren, M. D. (2001). Electronic records and technology. In N. C. Schwab & M. H. B. Gelfman (Eds.), *Legal issues in school health services: A resource for school administrators, school attorneys, and school nurses* (pp. 317–334). North Branch, MN: Sunrise River Press.

Bergren, M. D. (2003). National Conference on HIPAA Privacy Rule. *NAS Newsletter, 18*(4), 20–22.

Bergren, M. D. (2004a). HIPAA-FERPA revisited. *Journal of School Nursing, 20*(2), 107–112.

Bergren, M. D. (2004b). *Testimony of Martha Dewey Bergren, DNS, RN on HIPAA and FERPA in schools, representing National Association of School Nurses.* Washington, DC: National Committee on Vital Health Statistics Subcommittee on Privacy and Confidentiality (February 19, 2004).

Cambron-McCabe, N. H., McCarthy, M. M., & Thomas, S. B. (2004). *Public school law: Teachers' and students' rights* (5th Ed.). Boston: Pearson.

Electronic Privacy Information Center. (2004). *The Children's Online Privacy Protection Act (COPPA).* Retrieved September 3, 2004, from http://www.epic.org/privacy/kids/.

Jaffee v. Redmond, 116 S. Ct. 1923 (1996).

Moore, J., & Wall, A. (2003). *Applicability of HIPAA to health information in schools.* 2003 School Attorneys' Conference. Retrieved July 13, 2004, from http://www.medicalprivacy.unc.edu/pdfs/school.pdf.

National Association of Social Workers. (1996). *Code of Ethics of the National Association of Social Workers.* Retrieved January 12, 2005 from http://www.naswdc.org/pubs/code/code.asp.

National Association of Social Workers. (2002). *NASW standards for school social work services.* Washington, DC: Author.

National Association of Social Workers. (n.d.). *Client rights.* HIPAAProf e-Learning Management System. Retrieved January 12, 2005, from http://hipaaprof.com/nasw.

National Association of Social Workers. (n.d.). *HIPAA security basics.* HIPAAProf e-Learning Management System. Retrieved January 21, 2005, from http://hipaaprof.com/nasw.

National Association of Social Workers. (n.d.). *Understanding HIPAA transactions and Code Sets Standards.* HIPAAProf e-Learning Management System. Retrieved November 13, 2004, from http://hipaaprof.com/nasw.

Redhead, C. S. (2001, April 18). *Medical records privacy: Questions and answers on the HIPAA final rule* (CRS Report for Congress, Order Code RS20500). Washington, DC: Congressional Research Service, Library of Congress.

Rones, M., & Hoagwood, K. (2000). School-based mental health services: A research review. *Clinical Child and Family Psychology Review, 3*(4), 223–241.

Standards for Privacy of Individually Identifiable Health Information, 65 Fed. Reg. 82462 (Dec. 28, 2000) (to be codified at 45 C.F.R. Parts 160 and 164). Retrieved October 27, 2004, from http://web.lexisnexis.com/congcomp/document?.

U.S. Department of Health and Human Services. (2003). Standards for privacy of individually identifiable health information; Security standards for the protection of electronic protected health information; General administrative requirements including, civil money penalties: Procedures for investigations, imposition of penalties, and hearings: Regulation text. Rockville, MD: Author. Retrieved December 27, 2004, from www.hhs.gov/ocr/combinedregtext.pdf.

Whalen v. Roe, 429 U.S. 589 (1977).

Guidelines for Confidentiality

Writing Progress Notes and Storing Confidential Information

Mo Cannistra Cuevas

CHAPTER 88

Getting Started

One of the ways social workers strive to maintain the dignity and privacy of clients is through ensuring them confidentiality when they seek services. There are times when confidentiality cannot be maintained, such as when clients disclose that they are planning to hurt themselves or someone else. Aside from these specific exceptions, values and professional codes of ethics compel social workers and other mental health professionals to do everything possible to safeguard the personal situations and life details of the clients they see (NASW, 1996). Working in the school setting, this can be difficult.

> Within the school setting, school social workers are the link between the student, the student's family, the school, and the community. . . . There is a significant connection between the efficacy of the link and the "sharing of information" between the student and the school social worker and others equally concerned about the student's education and emotional and mental well-being. (NASW, 2001, p. 1)

As discussed in other chapters, working in a system where sharing information with other professionals is an essential process can create difficulty with maintaining confidentiality. Setting up collaborative programs and working effectively with community agencies can raise still further issues related to confidentiality (Soler & Peters, 1993).

Additional concerns stem from the fact that "the concept of confidentiality is very different in a technologically advanced environment," and this adds to the issues that school social workers need to consider in their work with clients (Rock and Congress, 1999, p. 253). Taking effect in 1997, the most recent NASW *Code of Ethics* for the first time addressed directly the issues related to technology saying, "Social workers should take precautions to ensure and maintain the confidentiality of information transmitted . . . through the use of computers, electronic mail, facsimile machines, telephones and telephone answering machines, and other electronic or computer technology. Disclosure of identifying information should be avoided whenever possible" (NASW, 1996, p. 12). In the school setting, where computers are often networked and the social worker might not even be aware of the school employees who have access to the network, the issue of confidentiality becomes even more important. Butterfield (1995) discusses five levels of security that can be used to address the technology and computer access concerns, but concedes that in social service agencies, such security might not actually occur. In this chapter, the process of writing progress notes and storing the actual clients' records will be discussed in terms of the issue of confidentiality and the steps to be taken to safeguard client information.

What We Know

One of the first considerations to be discussed in this chapter is the practice setting, specifically its documentation requirements and storage policies. A school social worker, counselor, or other mental health professional might be an employee of the school district, which means that records could be considered part of the student's educational record and should be handled according to the policies and procedures for school documentation. Another possibility is that the school social worker is working in the school under the auspices of another agency that has its own policies and procedures for documentation and case files. The first step in determining how case notes need to be written, handled, stored, and eventually destroyed is to determine what rules and regulations must be known and followed.

▌ Handling Confidential Information

NASW, in the 2001 practice update, provides some practical steps to take and questions to ask in terms of handling confidential information about students and their families:

- Be proactive . . . become familiar with state laws and regulations and school district policies governing confidentiality and minors, before this information is needed.
- Become familiar with laws and regulations governing confidentiality and minors as they pertain to other school personnel (that is, school counselors, school psychologists, and school nurses). In some states, these regulations differ from those governing school social workers.
- Develop and use written guidelines for sharing confidential information with third parties.
- Develop and use written consent forms for all parties involved with students when sharing confidential information.
- Maintain written documentation indicating with whom confidential information has been shared.
- When sharing confidential information, know what information can and cannot or should or should not be shared.
- Ask the following questions when deciding to share confidential information: "Why is it important that this information be shared?" "How will the student and the student's family benefit by a decision to share or not share information?" "Does sharing the confidential information outweigh maintaining confidentiality?" "What will be the effect on the student's learning?"
- Seek direction on this issue in a wider context through professional development opportunities or in-service training for a school or school district.
- Discuss limits of confidentiality with student and student's family at the onset of services.
- When possible or appropriate, discuss breaches of confidentiality with the student and the student's family in a timely manner.

- Become familiar with limits of confidentiality and "information sharing" as they pertain to IDEA.
- When preparing social histories for students who receive special education services under IDEA, include a statement indicating that the information reported is confidential. (pp. 2–3)

Once these steps have been taken and the different aspects of confidentiality considered, the focus can now shift to handling confidentiality in terms of the notes written. Confidentiality related to progress notes is a difficult topic to address. There are many issues that can influence what is written in a progress note: what is included and what is left out. Clients often share information with social workers that is very personal because they have developed a trusting relationship with the worker. Sometimes the information shared is not relevant to the issues being addressed through their social work services and this is often information that should be protected in terms of client privacy. Once received, the social worker must decide how to record this information, how to store the recordings, and when to share this information if it is information that might be relevant to other professionals working with the student and family. "The crux of the dilemma for school social workers lies in the finding that the [confidential] information learned has educational relevance or significance—that is, an effect on learning" (NASW, 2001, p. 2).

There are many points to consider. Soler and Peters (1993) outline several reasons for protecting the privacy of children and families:

- Confidentiality restrictions protect embarrassing personal information from disclosure;
- Confidentiality provisions prevent the improper dissemination of information about children and families that might increase the likelihood of discrimination against them;
- Protecting confidential information can be necessary to protect personal security;
- Confidentiality provisions also protect family security;
- Restricting the information that human service agencies receive may also protect job security;
- Children and families also want to avoid prejudice or differential treatment by people such as teachers, school administrators, and service providers;
- Confidentiality provisions also may be necessary

to encourage individuals to make use of services designed to help them. (pp. 6–7)

It is important to consider whether personal information that is shared with the social worker needs to be specifically included in the progress note or written record of the encounter. On the other hand, information that may be helpful to other professionals working with the client and family should be included so that they can deliver the services they provide most effectively and competently. Deciding what various players need to know is a complex process that social workers face in the school setting. There are no hard-and-fast rules about what should be included, no clear guidelines that say, "Always include this information but not this." Every situation is different, and this is where the social worker depends upon his or her personal judgment to determine how detailed and/or specific to make the notes being recorded.

Reasons for Documentation

The reasons for maintaining progress notes and documentation are many. As Kagel states (1991, p. 43), progress notes "describe and assess the client-situation and the service transaction at regular intervals." Primary functions of progress notes include these (Kagel, 1991, 1996; Kirst-Ashman & Hull, 2002):

- Documenting new information related to the services to be provided
- Making changes in the service plan or activities
- Planning for termination of services
- Evaluating the effectiveness of the treatments being used
- Documenting the worker's procedures or processes with the case
- Providing information to be used in supervision or consultation
- Providing information to administrators for decision making
- Providing worker accountability

Depending upon the nature of the work with the client, the agency norms established, and the types of services provided, some of these reasons will be more important than others. Within the school, social workers are often the only link between the student, the student's family, the school

administration, and the community. The effectiveness of this link depends upon the social worker's ability to develop professional relationships with each of these individuals or groups and to communicate appropriately with each. How information is shared with these professionals and with the family members can impact the interventions being used quite significantly (NASW, 2001). Essentially, school social workers cannot fully and effectively serve students on their own, or without some level of dependence on other professionals. Because of this, school social workers often face a dilemma in "determining what information needs to be shared, with whom the information needs to be shared, when, and what information should be held in confidence. These practical considerations are often complicated by legal and ethical considerations, which vary by state" (NASW, 2001, p. 1).

At the same time, the social worker also needs to be sure that the progress notes included in the case record include the elements of good documentation so that they are beneficial to those professionals who might need the information and are an accurate reflection of the services provided. The elements of good documentation, according to Bodek (n.d.) are these:

1. Provides relevant information in appropriate detail
2. Organized with appropriate headings and logical progression
3. Thoughtful, reflecting the application of professional knowledge, skills, and judgment in the treatment/services provided
4. Appropriately concise
5. Serves the purposes of documentation (as outlined above) that are applicable to a given situation
6. Uses relevant direct quotes from the (client) and other sources
7. Distinguishes clearly between facts, observations, hard data, and opinions
8. Internally consistent
9. Written in the present tense, as appropriate (p. 4).

What We Can Do

Types of Documentation

Several different formats for progress notes are used in case management and other social work processes. Most formats are based on a problem-oriented model that assumes there is an agreed-upon problem list and an evaluation or assessment that has identified the issues to be addressed (Burrill, 1976; Cournoyer, 1991; Kagle, 1991; Martens & Holmstrup, 1974; Sheafor, Horejsi, & Horejsi, 2000). Next there is a treatment plan that identifies the worker's role, the client's role, and other resources to be utilized in addressing the identified concerns. Different agencies and settings use different forms and methods for identifying the problems to be addressed and the steps to be taken, but most complete the process with a document that lists these and incorporates both the worker's and client's perspectives of what is to be accomplished in their design. Once this has been established, writing progress notes is based on this treatment plan. Notes are written related to the problems and actions identified. Sometimes it might be that an action has been taken and the problem is resolved; sometimes the notes are saying that action was taken but did not resolve the problem, so additional steps are needed, and sometimes the notes address that action was not taken. Notes might also discuss new issues to be addressed that are being added to the treatment plan. A progress note can include a wide range of information such as "dates of meetings; names of people involved; significant facts the client provides; information given clients about agency policy; changes in the client's life circumstances; or progress attained in treatment" (Kirst-Ashman & Hull, 2002, p. 546). It is important to be particularly attentive to recording changes in the client situation that indicate new services are needed, obstacles to change or services that have come up, or unexpected results of the services delivered (Kagel, 1991). Additionally, critical incidents should be immediately documented with some detail in the case record.

Finally, progress notes should also be written to record service activities on behalf of the client. This can be useful in documenting the effort and quality of services as well as in supporting decisions and judgments rendered by the worker. Noting the date, setting, participants, and subjects discussed in such collateral contacts can demonstrate the worker's adherence to the treatment plan's objectives and goals (Kagel, 1991).

The SOAP Format

One of the most common formats for the writing of progress notes is the SOAP system. This is a structured format for writing narrative progress notes based on a problem-oriented treatment plan and documentation system. "SOAP is an acronym referring to the subjective, objective, assessment, and plan sections of a case recording for each contact with a client" (Cournoyer, 1991, p. 324). If you use the SOAP format, you'll document the following types of information, often for each problem addressed, in a session with the client or a collateral:

S—Subjective Data—information on the client's perspective of the situation or problem;
O—Objective Data—factual, measurable data collected during the session, such as observed behaviors or results of previous interventions;
A—Assessment Data—conclusions made based on the subjective and objective data such as the impact on the problem being addressed or need to reconsider treatment of the issue;
P—Plan—strategy for addressing this problem, immediate and or short-term actions as well as longer terms measures to be implemented. (Cournoyer, 1991; Kirst-Ashman & Hull 2002)

There are advantages and disadvantages to problem-oriented recording. It allows others to see the approach taken by the worker and to identify easily the problems addressed. It allows team members to communicate clearly about the issues being addressed, since they are clearly defined. It allows for ease of follow-up when the services are terminated or a worker leaves and is replaced (Kirst-Ashman & Hull, 2002; Sheafor et al., 2000). A disadvantage is that there is no clear place in this type of recording to clearly identify client strengths and focus on their utilization in treatment. Also, this format tends to focus on micro practice strategies while overlooking the mezzo and macro aspects of client problems and needs (Kirst-Ashman & Hull, 2002). Each of these concerns can be addressed by individual workers as they develop plans for recording the services they provide in the school setting.

There are some things that generally do not go into case records or progress notes. "Information regarding a client's political, religious, or other personal views does not belong in social work recording unless it has some direct bearing on the treatment process. Such bearing rarely occurs" (Wilson, 1980, p. 197). Considering possible consequences for students and their families, such as discrimination they may face or penalties in their employment, it is important not to record such information unless there is a definite need for it to be documented. Personal intimate details shared with a worker, extreme details of physical health issues, and "gossipy" information others may provide about the student or their family are generally omitted as well (Wilson, 1980). Additionally, worker frustrations with other service-providing agencies, with the educational agency or school district, with administration, or with other workers should not be noted in the process recordings, though there are likely other steps to be taken if these are impacting client services. "Highly incriminating information that could be used against the client is usually omitted from social work recordings," unless this information is relevant to the issues at hand and the services being provided (Wilson, 1980, p. 199). Finally, sensitive details that might be misinterpreted or misused by others reading the file should be omitted in situations where they do not add to the discussion of the student's situation. Once again, worker judgment in deciding what to record and what not to record becomes crucial in terms of maintaining the confidentiality of the students and their families. Gelman, Pollack, and Weiner (1999) suggest that

> social workers should be judicious in their recording of client information and should adhere to the following principles:
> * Know who the potential audience is and verify the audience's identity and the purpose for the information that is being requested.
> * Obtain informed consent and identify the limits of confidentiality.
> * Understand the potential of information technology and ensure the appropriate safeguards are in place.
> * Recorded information should be factual, accurate, objective, and necessary only for the purpose at hand.
> * Recorded information should be clear, concise, and specific.
> * Recorded information should be clearly identified.
> * The services being provided should be clearly identified.
> * The treatment being provided should be based on a professional assessment that can be supported.
> * Intuition, hypotheses, and hunches should be differentiated from facts and excluded from the record.
> * All information should be verified over

time, with corrections made in a timely fashion.
* Progress or lack of progress should be documented.
* Unmet needs should be identified.
* Obstacles to meeting needs should be indicated. (p. 249)

Storing Client Records

The second aspect of maintaining confidentiality for the students and their families in the school setting is the actual storage of the notes and case files once these have been established. Once again, familiarity with the policies and procedures of the school district, the agency, or the program employing the worker might be all that is needed, but in some cases more specific guidance is needed. Wilson (1980) provides some basic tenets for safeguarding case files that sound like common sense, but probably need to be repeated often so that workers maintain the commitment to keeping client information truly confidential. Some of the suggestions provided are especially relevant when working with children, youth, and their families.

1. Records should be kept under lock and key when not in use. When staff members go home at the end of the workday, records should be locked in a desk, file cabinet, or special storage area.
2. Records should not be left lying on top of the desk unattended for any length of time.
3. Never take records home!
4. Try not to have the client's case record visible when interviewing him.
5. A record sign-out system helps to determine readily the whereabouts of case records not filed.
6. There should be careful monitoring of all copies made of case-record materials.
7. Recorded materials are the property of the agency or school.
8. There must be specific policies stating how long records are kept before they are declared outdated and then destroyed.
9. There must be a secure method for destroying case records. (Wilson, 1980, pp. 185–188)

Computerized Recordkeeping

Additional consideration needs to be taken when case notes and other client information is computerized. Often technological advances in education and social service settings are applauded quickly, with less attention paid to the additional concerns that might be raised. As Soler and Peters (1993) warn when discussing the strengths and dangers of computerized files, "all of the information in all of the files is potentially available to anyone with a computer terminal—all without the consent of clients. Consequently, automated systems containing client information require more levels and types of security than nonautomated systems" (p. 17). See chapter 87 of this volume for a full discussion of security and recent federal requirements (HIPAA) for maintaining and sharing student information.

Butterfield (1995) suggests that there are five levels of security that can be implemented related to computer utilization and the need for controlled access and confidentiality.

- The first level is using passwords to maintain control over who can operate the computer.
- The second level is control over which individual programs on the computer can be accessed, including the operating system.
- The third level is control over access to changing or adding specific data.
- The fourth involves a means of removing a computer hard disk and locking it in a secure place.
- The fifth involves data encryption used by government agencies when a high degree of security is required. (p. 608)

The last two levels may be difficult for an individual practitioner to establish in a school setting, but the first three levels are ways school social workers can work to maintain the relative confidentiality of their client records.

Tools and Practice Examples

Documentation and Recordkeeping: A Case Example

Diane is a 13-year-old eighth-grade student. She was referred by her academic counselor after failing two courses at the last grading period. Diane lives with her mother and 10-year-old brother. Several problems have been identified, including Diane's poor socialization skills, her lack of motivation for schoolwork, her family's need for food and utility assistance, and her mother's lack of consistent employment. Strengths of the family include that her mother wants to get her GED so she is more employable, and Diane is bright and talented in art and wants to join the art club that meets after school.

The established goals:

1. Improve Diane's socialization skills
2. Enhance Diane's motivation for schoolwork, especially math
3. Secure financial assistance for the family
4. Prepare Diane's mother for consistent employment

Objectives/activities for these goals:

1. Enroll Diane in a socialization skills group
2. Encourage Diane to do schoolwork with art used as an incentive
3. Assist Diane's mother in applying for food stamps and utility stipends
4. Help Diane's mother to enroll in a GED program

The social worker calls Diane's mother to discuss the GED program she has agreed to attend. During the call the mother expresses doubts about attending, saying she is concerned with the child care arrangements for her son that were previously made. The social worker listens and asks Mom about her concerns, as well as asking if there are other things bothering her about the class. Mom tells the worker that when she was younger and tried to pass the GED exam, she was on drugs at the time and did really poorly. She discusses some of her drug history with the social worker. The social worker reiterates that Mom is in a different situation now and more able to study and think clearly in preparation and offers to send her some preparatory materials she can read before the classes to feel a bit more comfortable before going to the community college. Finally, Mom agrees to attend the classes, and the social worker ends the call. The social worker decides it will be important to call Mom next Monday to encourage her attendance and then to follow up after the first class.

The S.O.A.P. note for the call might be as follows:

Client: Diane S.
Date: 9/15/03
No. 4: Consistent employment: GED
Phone call to Mother.

S: Mom discussed concerns about child care arrangements for GED classes. Used this as a reason not to attend.

O: Mom has attempted GED in the past and not done well.

A: Mom seems to be concerned repeating failed previous attempt to take GED.

P: Send Mom prep materials; call next Monday to encourage her attendance, follow-up call after first class.

When the social worker meets Diane that afternoon to give her the GED materials, Diane mentions that she just had her math class where she was drawing pictures of the teacher she dislikes. She says she understands the assignments but does not get along with the teacher.

The social worker has recently received donated art supplies to use as incentives for students. The social worker tells Diane that if she passes her math test, she can choose some of these supplies as a reward. Diane says she will return as soon as she gets her grade and leaves the office very excited.

A second S.O.A.P. note is added for this interaction, which might be:

Client: Diane S.

Date: 9/15/03

No. 2: Lack of motivation for schoolwork

Brief meeting with Diane.

S: Diane discussed not wanting to do math homework; seemed excited about getting art supplies if she does well.

P: Have art supplies ready as reward for passing test.

In each of these situations, the social worker had additional information that she did not include. In different circumstances the same information may be important to include, but it was not relevant here, since there was no benefit to adding these details. These are judgments made by the worker based on values, skills, and experience.

Resources

Center for Mental Health in Schools at UCLA. (1996). http://smhp.psych.ucla.edu/dbsimple2.asp?primary =2306&number=9998.

Dickson, D. T. (1998). *Confidentiality and privacy in social work: A guide to the law for practitioners and students.* New York: Free Press.

National Association of Social Workers. (2001). *Confidentiality and school social work: A practice perspective.* http://www.naswdc.org/practice/update/cfs0202.htm.

Key Points to Remember

The following points are important to consider when preparing progress notes and storing information to protect confidentiality:

- Be familiar with state laws and regulations, school district policies, and agency policies and procedures governing confidentiality, documentation, and maintenance of records.
- Be familiar with confidentiality policies and procedures as they pertain to other school personnel such as school counselors, school psychologists, school nurses, teachers, and administration. Sometimes, their norms and rules are different than those used in social work.
- Have and use written guidelines for sharing confidential information with third parties, recording when information is shared in the case record.
- Protecting the confidentiality of students and their families is of utmost importance in a school setting. Take this into consideration when deciding upon what detailed information to include in progress notes.
- Take steps to ensure the physical security of written and electronic case records, including keeping records locked, using passwords to protect computer files, and limiting access to client information whether the records are electronic or paper (adapted from Rock & Congress, 1999; Kirst-Ashman & Hull, 2002; NASW, 2001; & Soler & Peters, 1993).

References

Bodek, H. (n.d.). *Basic standards for clinical documentation and record keeping.* Retrieved June 29, 2004, from http://www.clinicalsw.org/basic_standards.html.

Burrill, G. (1976). The problem-oriented log in social casework. *Social Work, 21*(1), 67–68.

Butterfield, W. (1995). Computer utilization. In R. L. Edwards (Ed.), *Encyclopedia of social work* (19th ed., Vol. 1, pp. 594–613). Washington, DC: NASW Press.

Center for Mental Health in Schools at UCLA. (1996). *An introductory packet on confidentiality and informed consent.* Los Angeles: Author. Created November 1996. Revised November 2002. Retrieved June 20, 2004, from http://smhp.psych.ucla.edu/dbsimple2 .asp?primary=2306&number=9998.

Cournoyer, B. (1991). *The social work skills workbook.* Belmont, CA: Wadsworth Publishing Company.

Dickson, D. T. (1998). *Confidentiality and privacy in social work: A guide to the law for practitioners and students.* New York: Free Press.

Gelman, S., Pollack, D., & Weiner, A. (1999). Confidentiality of social work records in the computer age. *Social Work, 44*(3), 243–253.

Kagle, J. D. (1991). *Social work records.* Belmont, CA: Wadsworth Publishing Company.

Kagle, J. D. (1996). *Social work records* (2nd ed.). Prospect Heights, IL: Waveland.

Kardon, S. (1993, October). Confidentiality: A different perspective [as readers see it]. *Social Work in Education, 15*(4), 247–250.

Kirst-Ashman, K., & Hull, G. H., Jr. (2002). *Understanding generalist practice* (3rd ed.). Pacific Grove, CA: Brooks/Cole.

Martens, W. M., & Holmstrup, E. (1974). Problem-oriented recording. *Social Casework, 55*(9), 554–561.

National Association of Social Workers [NASW]. (1996) *Code of ethics.* Washington, DC: Author.

National Association of Social Workers [NASW]. (2001) *Confidentiality and school social work: A practice perspective.* Practice Update, Vol. 2, No. 2, October 2001. Washington, DC: Author. Retrieved July 7, 2004, from http://www.naswdc.org/practice/update/cfs0202.htm.

Rock, B., & Congress, E. (1999). The new confidentiality for the 21st century in a managed care environment. *Social Work, 44*(3), 253–263.

Sheafor, B. W., Horejsi, C. R., & Horejsi, G. A. (2000). *Techniques and guidelines for social work practice* (5th ed.). Boston: Allyn & Bacon.

Soler, M., & Peters, C. (1993). *Who should know what? Confidentiality and information sharing in service integration.* Des Moines, IA: National Center for Service Integration.

Wilson, S. J. (1980). *Recording guidelines for social workers.* New York: Free Press.

Professional Ethical Codes: Applications to Common Ethical Dilemmas

Marian Mattison

Getting Started

Of all the fields of contemporary practice, school-based practitioners face some of the more challenging ethical dilemmas encountered by mental health professionals today. The sheer range of psychosocial problems presented by school-aged children and the growing severity of diagnosed and undiagnosed mental health problems require school practitioners to provide a wide range of services and manage competing obligations and loyalties to multiple parties. As members of an educational community, parents, teachers, and administrators compete for access to confidential information shared by student clients.

Upholding parental rights while simultaneously meeting one's ethical obligations to be a student advocate involves a delicate balancing act. Working almost exclusively with minors, school counselors and social workers must balance the obligation to students to protect the confidential relationship not only against the parents' legal ownership to the confidential information shared by their minor child (see chapter 88) but also against teachers' access to information about students. The practitioner's job is further complicated by the fact that state laws are uneven and offer differing opinions concerning who owns a child's confidential information. The strain inherent in meeting multiple loyalties to a variety of interested parties obligates the practitioner to meet conflicting, often competing, needs.

What We Know

Breaching Confidentiality

School practitioners routinely exercise professional discretion in judging those situations that warrant/justify a breach of confidentiality. While the legal age of majority is generally 18, it is likely that school social workers, counselors, and other mental health professionals do not rely solely on chronological age in making decisions about the disclosure of confidential information but rather they assess and account for the developmental maturity of the minor client. Students judged to be more mature or more capable are granted greater measures of confidentiality. "School counselors believe that regardless of professional ethics and rules, the age of the child is the most significant variable in dealing with dilemmas related to confidentiality," with school counselors at the secondary level protecting student confidence to a greater extent than counselors at the elementary and middle school levels (Isaacs & Stone, 2003, p. 194). Legal mandates, codes of ethics, local policies in school jurisdictions, and precedents set by individual schools must all be accounted for in balancing the obligation to protect student confidence against the duty to disclose.

Training for Ethical Decision Making

When practitioners complete graduate education, they often become quickly immersed in the demands of practice. The time available to make thoughtful decisions is overshadowed by the call for immediate action to circumstances that are often yet being revealed. Decisions involving matters of values and ethics are often made with less than sufficient consideration to the complexity of the value tensions at hand. For mental health practitioners with minimal ethics content in their own training, the lack of knowledge and skills to reason effectively about ethical issues poses an even greater challenge. Licensing standards for mental health professionals in many states have responded by requiring a prescribed number of hours in ethics training for license renewal. This development has resulted not only in many available choices of ethics seminars and continuing education classes but also in an increased focus on ethics at professional conferences and in professional journals. For school-based practitioners who feel a need for more knowledge and skill in the area of ethical decision making, this is a welcome trend.

Standards for Ethical Practice

In an effort to meet one's professional obligations competently and to circumscribe charges of ethical misconduct, school mental health staff are responsible to perform their duties in accordance with the highest standards of practice established by their discipline. For school social workers this would require acting in compliance with the duties and obligations to clients, employers, and society as described in the NASW *Code of Ethics* (1996). "The NASW Code of Ethics sets forth specific ethical standards with which the public can expect social workers to comply and to which the public can hold social workers accountable" (Reamer, 1998, p. 13). This *Code* and the codes of allied disciplines, the ASCA's *Ethical Standards of School Counselors* (American School Counselor Association, 1998) and the ACA's *Code of Ethics* (American Counseling Association, 1995), are viewed as the highest authorities and reference points to which the courts and state boards of inquiry investigating ethics complaints against practitioners will turn to determine how "an ordinary, reasonable, and prudent professional would act under the same or similar circumstances" (Reamer, 1998, p. 14).

Applying the provisions of any professional code necessarily involves degrees of interpretation, the exercise of judgment, and decisions about the applicability of given standards to individual case circumstances. "Ethical decision making in a given situation must apply the informed judgment of the individual social worker and should also consider how the issues would be judged in a peer review process where the ethical standards of the profession would be applied" (NASW *Code of Ethics*, "Purpose of the NASW Code of Ethics," 1996). Outcomes will differ because "weighing the best interests of the student may result in different courses of action depending on the student, the counselor, and the community" (Davis & Ritchie, 2003, p. 203).

What We Can Do

Ethical Dilemmas

Ethical dilemmas are those problems in which the practitioner is challenged to select a course of action when each possible alternative will result in an undesirable outcome for one or more of the interested parties. When confronted with an ethical dilemma, the school counselor must decide which competing values or obligations to meet foremost and which action to choose over the many possible courses of action under consideration. Questions such as "To whom does the counselor owe primary loyalty" and "Whose interests should be considered foremost?" involve ethical questions of "right" versus "wrong."

Systematic Ethical Decision Making

While there is no one universal analytic model for application to cases of ethical conflict, there is consensus that skillfully reasoning through ethical dilemmas can best be accomplished by following a stage approach, assuring that all facets of the dilemma are accounted for. Research suggests that "the process of ethical decision making can be taught in a rational, systematic manner" (Linzer, 1999, p. xvi). Becoming familiar with the steps associated with skillful decision making anchors ethical judgments in systematic thinking and is likely to result in decisions that account for the multitude of competing factors and a consideration of the interests of stakeholders in the case. The goal of instruction in ethical reasoning focuses on the process of making decisions (as opposed to strictly the outcome or choice of action) because "if we teach practitioners and students how to think about ethics, they will know what to do" (Linzer, 1999, p. xvi).

▌ Stages of Ethical Decision Making

When school practitioners are faced with competing values, duties, and obligations, a set of steps can be applied to *think through* the dilemma before taking action. Deliberate thinking and documenting the process of the decision making leaves the practitioner prepared to justify the decision and defend their action if called upon to do so. Referencing a decision-making model such as the one that follows will ultimately deepen the practitioner's thinking about an ethical dilemma and will assist in reaching a thoughtfully reasoned solution.

For purposes of illustrating the steps involved in the analysis and resolution of an ethical dilemma, let us use the following case example:

> Mark, a 16-year-old high school student, discloses his HIV positive status to the school counselor. Mark proudly tells the practitioner that not only is he sexually active with his girlfriend of 4 months, but with two other female students at the school. Mark is not using safe sex practices and refuses to disclose his HIV status to his sexual partners.

Step One: Gather Additional Background Information and Assess the Case Details

The analysis of the ethical dilemma begins as the school counselor gathers and assesses the details of the client's situation, asks questions, and obtains a complete picture of others who, in addition to the student client, have a vested interest in any outcome that might result. The "stakeholders" are those individuals who will possibly benefit or lose as a result of the choice of action ultimately selected. In this initial phase of information gathering, the counselor attempts to determine the answers to these and other questions:

"Can the client be 'encouraged' to disclose the potential risk to his sexual partners?"

"Can the student be 'influenced' to practice safer sex?"

"Are the identities of the third parties known to the social worker?"

"Is the diagnosis medically verifiable?"

"What are the actual/potential risks to third parties?"

Step Two: Separate Practice Considerations From the Ethical Aspects of the Case

In order to determine if the case under consideration is truly an ethical dilemma, one must be certain that the decision to select one action over others involves conflicting or competing values rather than questions answerable by the application of practice standards. If there is no ambiguity about the right or wrong action to take or principle to apply, it is likely that the decision to act can be made by applying best practice standards. If the case presents an ethical dilemma, there will be gray areas and differences of opinion about what is the "right" course of action to take. There will be questions about whose interests should be considered foremost and uncertainty about which values should take precedent over others when each cannot be met simultaneously.

Reaching professional judgments is guided by the provisions in professional codes of ethics as well as by the laws and legal imperatives established on a state-by-state basis. The practitioner must be clear about the legal obligations regulating the standards for professional behavior in one's discipline and recognize that moral responsibilities will often run contrary to legal obligations. Be aware that state laws regulating professional practice may differ for school counselors, social workers, and other mental health professionals. Here the school counselor must be aware of any legal duties to protect client confidence or a duty/obligation to warn third parties (under the interpretations and application of the *Tarasoff* decision).[1] Moreover, "all states do not treat the confidentiality of children's communication to counselors in a uniform way" (Isaacs, 2003, p. 118), and the counselor must determine state mandates regarding the student client's rights to a confidential relationship.

Clarity regarding the circumstances under which client confidentiality can be breached according to applicable laws and regulations regarding minors and HIV status is a practice consideration while the ethical considerations involve question such as:

"Does the duty to warn apply to cases of HIV/AIDS?"

"Is the school counselor's obligation solely to the infected student client or does it extend to the protection of other members of the school community?"

"Does the counselor feel a paternalistic/moral obligation to disclose, even if this necessitates overriding one's legal obligation to protect the infected student?"

Note that the answers to the ethical questions are less clear and more open to individual interpretation.

Step Three: Explicitly Identify the Value Tensions

An ethical dilemma arises when a counselor faces two or more completing values. In this case the client's right to privacy competes with protecting third parties. The practitioner is left to decide to which value he/she is more committed when both values cannot be acted upon simultaneously. "Should the rights of the infected student take priority over protecting the lives of others?" "Should the duty to protect human life take precedent over the duty to keep confidential the information shared by clients?"

An additional conflict is between the values of autonomy and paternalism. Practitioners will disagree (in this case as well as in others) over the extent to which clients have the right to engage in self-destructive behaviors. While counselors promote and encourage client autonomy, occasions do arise when the practitioner judges that clients' right to pursue their own goals must be overridden to protect clients from harming themselves or others. Counselors may justify the use of professional paternalism in order to protect those clients who fail to exercise sound judgment and present risks deemed to be imprudent. "Can the counselor justify the duty to warn/protect based on beneficence, the obligation to promote good for both the client and society?"

From a societal perspective, this case raises questions about individual rights (confidentiality) versus the public's interests (safety and protection). One could argue that not only are the client's current sexual partners at risk but also are a broader array of citizens who have the potential to become infected into the future. While it is clear that confidentiality laws were designed to reassure infected parties that they would be protected, is it ever justifiable to limit the freedoms of an infected client to protect the civil liberties of community members? Can the *Tarasoff* ruling be interpreted as obligating a school counselor to warn sexual partners of possible harm? If a known

party becomes infected, could the practitioner be charged with the failure to protect?

Step Four: Consult Relevant Codes of Ethics, Supervisors, and Colleagues

One of the challenges faced by school practitioners addressing ethical dilemmas is the variety and range of ethical codes that set standards for practitioners in school settings. A broad spectrum of mental health professionals work in schools, and each is responsible to competing and potentially contradictory professional responsibilities as delineated by professional codes of ethics. For example, "A school counselor who is a member of the American School Counselor Association (ASCA) and the American Counseling Association (ACA), who is certified by the National Board of Certified Counselors (NBCC), and who is licensed by his or her own state counseling licensure board has agreed to abide by four separate sets of ethical standards" (Remley & Huey, 2003, pp. 5–6). Generally, the standards set for allied mental health disciplines parallel one another, although there are different degrees of specificity related to the school practitioner's obligations to minors, parents, teachers, and administrators.

Discipline Specific Ethical Standards

Consulting relevant codes of ethics is important at many levels. First, it informs practitioners regarding the ethical practices expected of their discipline. Second, acting in compliance with code standards can help adjudicate allegations of misconduct, should they arise. While the conceptual guidelines put forth in codes cannot always be met in practice, practitioners must be prepared to explain their reasoning should they choose to act outside a given standard. *What is ethically acceptable may be at odds with what is legally correct and vice versa.* Even where a counselor feels a moral obligation to protect third parties through the disclosure of information received in confidence, there may be no professional or legal mandates compelling them to do so.

Understanding professional norms is further advanced through consultation and discussion with colleagues and supervisors. Most codes will require practitioners to "seek the advice and counsel of colleagues whenever such consultation is in the best interests of clients" (NASW *Code of Ethics*, Standard 2.05 a, 1996) and expect organizations to have "the necessary competencies and resources for giving the kind of consulting services needed" to its practitioners (ACA, Standard D.2.b, 1995).

In this case, the ASCA's ethical standards specifically obligate school counselors to disclose "information to an identified third party who, by his or her relationship to the counselee, is at a high risk of contracting a disease that is commonly known to be communicable and fatal. Prior to disclosure, the counselor will ascertain that the counselee has not already informed the third party about his or her disease and he/she is not intending to inform the third party in the immediate future" (ASCA, Standard A.2.c, 1998). This standard is specific in obligating members of the ASCA to notify the sexual partners of HIV-positive clients and the appropriate school officials when clients refuse to disclose on their own. School counselors from allied disciplines are not equally obligated.

Step Five: Identify Alternative Intervention Strategies and Targets for Intervention

A next step in the decision-making process is to identify the possible courses of action available and the ethical implications of each. Here, the counselor would likely be deciding between protecting the student client's confidence versus disclosing the information against client wishes. The decision maker might consider whether to act on one of these alternatives in the immediate present or possibly adopting a "wait and see" attitude with a plan to act at some predetermined point into the future. The practitioner may also be considering gradations of these choices in determining to whom they would disclose and the specificity of the information shared. Each of the alternatives should be explicitly identified and given ample consideration.

Possible choices of action:

1. To protect the client's privacy
2. To disclose confidential information to at-risk third parties
3. To notify public health authorities for the purpose of having the Partner Notification Program contact those at risk (*Note*: Program may not be available in all states.)
4. To disclose the confidential information to school administrators

Step Six: Weigh the Costs and Benefits to Various Stakeholders

For each choice of action, the impact on those who stand to benefit or to suffer harmful consequences brought about by the action selected needs to be anticipated. Practitioners should, as best they can, project anticipated consequences for each individual who has a vested interest in the outcome. While the consequences of one's action and how others will respond are not entirely predictable, consideration should be given to the interested parties that have legitimate interests at stake.

An individual practitioner may judge, for example, that a greater good would result by disclosing information to those at risk because these individuals would benefit from knowledge of the potential health threat. On the other hand, disclosure of the student client's HIV status may result in harm to the client–counselor relationship, result in social isolation and discrimination for the student client, and threaten the counselor's position because, based on state law, he/she may be legally bound to protect the rights and confidentiality of the HIV individual. The disclosure, against the client's expressed wishes, may be legally challenged by the client or school system, thereby threatening the practitioner's livelihood and reputation.

Next, the potential impacts of protecting the student's privacy (choice one) are examined. Completing a stakeholder's analysis for *each* of the choices of action identified in Step 5 encourages the decision maker to utilize a *systems perspective* in accounting for the interests of those who will be potentially impacted.

Choice One: To Protect the Client's Privacy

Potential benefits for the client:

- the therapeutic relationship is not disrupted
- trust is maintained
- client is not placed at increased risk for discrimination
- client autonomy is preserved

Potential benefits for society:

- adequate statutory protection of confidentiality and privacy for high-risk groups is maintained
- others who are HIV-positive may come forward to seek help from counselors

Potential benefits for the practitioner:

- the legal obligation (varies from state to state) to protect the confidence of HIV individuals is met
- client feels supported and may be therapeutically encouraged to disclose his health status to those at risk
- avoidance of charges of malpractice and litigation

Potential harms for the client:

- client experiences diminished sense of self over harm caused to others
- keeping the "secret" creates stress and negative health consequences
- client does not seek medical treatment; health fails

Potential harms for sexual partners:

- they are not afforded information to protect their health interests
- they may contract a fatal disease and die

Potential harms for the counselor:

- failure to protect third parties from known harm might result in death(s)
- lawsuits brought by those at risk may harm the counselor's professional reputation
- failure to protect known third parties from risk is judged a dereliction of duty, and employment is terminated

Potential harms for society:

- a rise in the numbers of AIDS-related cases and the associated social and economic costs

Step Seven: Clarify and Make Explicit Personal Values

Being aware of one's values and preferences throughout the process of decision making cannot be emphasized enough. Practitioners who openly acknowledge their value positions are less likely to unwittingly bias the decision-making process (Lowenberg, Dolgoff, & Harington, 2000). For example, practitioners should question whether personal/family experiences with persons with AIDS create bias or whether a caring relationship

with a young daughter/niece/friend influences the decision to protect those at risk.

It is wise to examine one's own decision-making style. Do I typically favor strict adherence to the policies and laws applicable to a given situation, or do I tend to act based on maximizing the good that will result? "Those whose moral development is on a rule or legalistic oriented level may well find this dilemma differently solved than those whose development is oriented more toward principled decisions and behavior" (Isaacs, 2003, p. 121).

Step Eight: Determine Which Priority or Obligation to Meet Foremost and Justify One's Choice of Action

After completing the assessment, the counselor must ultimately determine which of the competing obligations or values to honor foremost. The decision maker will draw conclusions and justify a decision based on professional standards, ethical principles, and professional judgment. The individual counselor may conclude that the decision to protect client confidence was based on the prevailing legal mandate, or that acting paternalistically to protect at-risk third parties was the moral imperative and served the greater good, or perhaps that school policy dictated the disclosure of the information to school administrators. (Note that counselors relying on a set of guidelines for decision making will not necessarily arrive at the same conclusions or select the same course of action.)

Step Nine: Document the Process of Decision Making

In much the same manner that clinical decisions are documented as part of a case record, the process followed by the counselor in addressing and resolving the ethical dilemma should be recorded. Documenting that one adhered to ethical standards or one's "professional interpretation of the standards" (Davis & Ritchie, 2003, p. 203) can serve to defend one's action and minimize the risk of litigation. To protect the counselor under charges of misconduct, the record should reflect the careful step-by-step process followed, indicate where consultation was sought, and demonstrate that thoughtful decision making occurred. The counselor must exercise discretion when deciding the extent of the detail to include in the client record.

Key Points to Remember

While a case-specific example was used to illustrate a stage approach to ethical decision making, it is hoped that the reader has an expanded appreciation for the range of considerations that warrant attention when thinking through ethical dilemmas. The process described can be generalized and applied to a variety of ethical dilemmas encountered in one's practice and will become more habitual with repeated uses. While it should be clear that the decision maker must be contemplative in musing about the various possibilities for action and the potential impacts on those affected by the decision, the reader is cautioned not to get mired in the complexities of the steps and stages but rather to appreciate that lucid and reasoned thinking will greatly improve the merits of one's decision making.

Resources

For the reader interested in additional learning on the subject of ethical challenges confronted by school counselors, *Ethical & Legal Issues in School Counseling* by Remley, Hermann, and Huey (2003) is strongly recommended. The text is a compilation of 30 articles addressing a range of issues, questions, and concerns specific to the interests of school counselors from a variety of disciplines.

Note

1. Against specified criteria, the *Tarasoff* decision releases counselors from the bonds of confidentiality and establishes a duty to warn an intended known victim in cases of impending harm.

References

American Counseling Association [ACA]. (1995). *Code of ethics.* Alexandria, VA: Author.

American School Counselor Association [ASCA]. (1998). *Ethical standards for school counselors.* Alexandria, VA: Author.

Davis, T., & Ritchie, M. (2003). Confidentiality and the school counselor: A challenge for the 1990s. In T. P. Remley, Jr., M. A. Hermann, & W. C. Huey (Eds.), *Ethical and legal issues in school counseling* (2nd ed., pp. 197–207). Alexandria, VA: American School Counselor Association.

Isaacs, M. L. (2003). The duty to warn and protect: Tarasoff and the elementary school counselor. In T. P. Remley, Jr., M. A. Hermann, & W. C. Huey (Eds.), *Ethical and legal issues in school counseling* (2nd ed., pp. 111–129). Alexandria, VA: American School Counselor Association.

Isaacs, M. L., & Stone, C. (2003). School counselors and confidentiality: Factors affecting professional choices. In T. P. Remley, Jr., M. A. Hermann, & W. C. Huey (Eds.), *Ethical and legal issues in school counseling* (2nd ed., pp. 179–196). Alexandria, VA: American School Counselor Association.

Linzer, N. (1999). *Resolving ethical dilemmas in social work practice.* Needham Heights, MA: Allyn & Bacon.

Lowenberg, F. M., Dolgoff, R., & Harington, D. (2000). *Ethical decisions for social work practice* (6th ed.). Itasca, IL: F. E. Peacock Publishers, Inc.

National Association of Social Workers [NASW]. (1996). *NASW code of ethics.* Washington, DC: Author.

Reamer, F. G. (1998). *Ethical standards in social work: A critical review of the NASW Code of Ethics.* Washington, DC: NASW Press.

Remley, T. P., Jr., Hermann, M. A., & Huey, W. C. (Eds.). (2003). *Ethical and legal issues in school counseling* (2nd ed.). Alexandria, VA: American School Counselor Association.

Remley, T. P., Jr., & Huey, W. C. (2003). An ethics quiz for school social workers. In T. P. Remley, Jr., M. A. Hermann, & W. C. Huey (Eds.), *Ethical and legal issues in school counseling* (2nd ed., pp. 5–20). Alexandria, VA: American School Counselor Association.

Schulte, J. M., & Cochrane, D. (1995). *Ethics in school counseling.* New York: Columbia University.

Tarasoff v. Regents of the University of California, 17 Cal. 3d 425, 551 P. 2d 334 (1976).

Guidelines for Writing an Effective Psychosocial Assessment Report

Dolores P. Ortega

CHAPTER 90

Getting Started

School-aged children who live in poverty are often traumatized by violent acts committed by strangers, their peers, and their parents. The struggle to comprehend the injustice of violence, as it is linked to feelings of uncertainty, hopelessness, and emotional despair, is so overwhelming that it leaves many children static. Moreover, violence serves as an oppressive force, especially in rural communities where few resources are available to combat it. The multifaceted problems faced by America's adolescents and children continue to call for our attention. The young child or adolescent who commits an act of violence may often be playing out the confusion of a developing sense of self-identity, loss of spirituality, and her or his own sense of injustice. An act of violence may give the child a short-term sense of power over the victim but in the long term only exacerbates their anguish. Many children who come from families that are experiencing these high-risk behaviors receive modeling that violence is an accepted way of problem solving. This modeling may be the result of poor social control, the negative heroics of gang violence, victimization, drugs, alcohol, unhealthy environments, and the deterioration of the family. Children who live in economically, politically, and socially depressed areas struggle with the complexities of navigating through the demands placed on them by their environments, their parents, and their teachers.

What We Know

In studying children who live in depressed areas, I found that many factors such as home life,

neighborhoods, and conditions in the classroom contribute to troubled behaviors and social relationships. Rural areas, economically depressed and crime-ridden, experience the challenge of keeping children safe. Although there are many ways to define violence and trauma, Jennifer McIntosh (2002) defined violence as a "nonthinking state of mind." This "unthinkingness" may impact children if the parents do not allow them to understand violence in a tolerable, manageable, reflective way but, rather, model violent reactions to violence. When this occurs, children are left overwhelmed by the violent experience.

There are indicators, however, that some children are resilient and are able to cope with tremendous trauma: "It is estimated that 80% of all children exposed to powerful stressors do not sustain developmental damage. Research indicates that certain factors contribute to the resilience of these children [such as] a child's characteristics and early life experiences" (Rutter, 1979; Werner, 1990). Werner (1990) first conceptualized the term *resilience* in 1984. He defined it as the ability to "effectively cope with stress by exhibiting psychological strength regardless of the developmental stage or the set of circumstances." Resilience is especially relevant when the child has adequate and healthy support systems in place or has an adult who generally sees to it that the child thrives in his or her environment and development. Again, the issue of resilience brings us to seek the answers as to why some children who share the same community, the same home environment, and the same parent experience violence differently. On one hand, many children who are living with these conditions appear to be well adjusted, are able to socialize, and are considered to be resilient high achievers. Can we assume that a network of supportive adults protects these well-adjusted children? On the other hand, the sibling of this resilient child who has been exposed to the same type of family and/or community violence exhibits symptoms of depression and anxiety and mirrors the aggressive behavior. Why is it that some children in the same family have difficulty establishing autonomy, healthy attachments, and trust?

Children who live in poverty and who live in low-income housing are at an unfair disadvantage, since they are dependent on the success or failure of their particular family and surrounding neighborhood. Children who grow up under severe conditions of poverty may find it difficult to encounter adults whom they can trust. Many low-income neighborhoods do not have the environments conducive for children to express their feelings. On the contrary, these high-risk neighborhoods are plagued with adults who inflict emotional distress on children by suppressing the children's expression of their natural emotions and fear. When children do express fear, it is often minimized or ignored by the adult, leaving little room for children to learn coping skills.

The family's failure is partly due to the daily struggle of "making ends meet," since most social programs have been drastically cut. Due to the Federal Welfare Reform Act of 1996, TANF economically disadvantaged mothers are expected to enter a competitive labor market with few resources, no job experience, and limited education. These added stressors may manifest themselves in accelerated incidents of family violence. It is difficult to predict the effect that family violence has on children and the length of time they carry the scars. The intergenerational causes of violence are complex, and prevention requires multifaceted approaches.

Studies to curb violence in the schools are helpful if the research is expanded to include the development and implementation of preventative programs, and if the programs are tracked over extended periods of time to evaluate their effectiveness. Violence has multiple meanings within multiple contexts; therefore, it is important and necessary that any research design define violence within those specific contexts.

Many young children live in these disorganized communities and carry with them the stigmas associated with living in poor, violent neighborhoods. Therefore, many strategies are in place to identify "potentially dangerous students" in our school systems. Another approach in addressing potentially violent students is by creating a climate that models emotional caring and nurturing. When these children do not have the models for violence prevention at an early age, their risk factors will increase as they grow older.

Today, the graphic image of young children physically assaulting one another is common throughout our elementary schools. These continual physical assaults on children are so brutal that many of the school personnel are overwhelmed. The stress levels of children and adults who study and work in schools confirm that it is a national crisis. Although there are no definite answers to the problems, there are specific ideas that can assist schools, communities, and parents in providing safety for our youth and children while they are at school.

School personnel have always struggled to diffuse conflict among students, but today the problem of violence has grown into an insidious complex and chaotic system within families and our schools. Due to poverty, isolation, and family violence, hopelessness and despair are prevalent in the demeanor of many young children. The violence has not appeared overnight, but is a result of intergenerational patterns within families and society. The prevention of violence requires multiple strategies to diffuse patterns within families and institutions. Early intervention is crucial in deterring the violence that could result in the student developing mental illness. The following culturally relevant psychosocial assessment will assist the social worker in working with ethnic populations who have been raised in violent environments.

What We Can Do

The culturally sensitive psychosocial assessment for multicultural students seeks to add cultural elements to better meet the needs of the populations assessed by providing a meaningful assessment within the student's cultural framework. It is important that social workers, counselors, and other mental health professionals develop an awareness of the child's cultural and social context. Many children who live in economically and socially depressed areas struggle with the complexity of mental health issues. Children who live in these depressed areas experience violent neighborhoods and families, which can contribute to troubled behaviors and social relationships at school.

According to the National Institute of Mental Health, children experience significant distress when they are exposed to violence early in their lives. Moreover, the National Association for the Education of Young Children (NAEYC) reports that children who have been exposed to frequent and continuous acts of violence in their homes and in their communities develop serious problems that impact their developmental progress in school and other learning environments.

The mental health social worker who conducts a culturally competent psychosocial assessment may facilitate the improved integration of mental health services combined with the goal of educational achievement. This assessment provides an effective method of helping the social worker understand how the students are responding to issues of violence and mental illness.

It is very important that social workers, counselors, and other mental health professionals not present themselves as intellectually superior or as saviors of humankind. The goal is to work collaboratively with the family and school system in order to integrate violence prevention strategies. However, children's violent behaviors will not be unlearned without additional community support, multifaceted approaches, and long-term interventions. It is imperative that the social worker respect the culture of *conociendo* (getting to know one another), or cooperation from the family may be difficult to achieve. If this period of building trust is not observed, the families, teachers, and children may perceive the social worker as an outsider and not part of the school community. Once the social worker is in sync with the school culture, it is common for students and their families to ask questions about the social worker's native origins, family, and employment in order to build familiarity. It is important for the social worker to meet each family member individually. Once the families know who the social worker is in relation to the community school, the social worker is able to proceed: he or she has become an insider.

In a cultural context, rapport is better established when the social worker is able to sit and talk casually with the family members about things other than the highlighted problems. This valuable meeting time allows the social worker to gain access to family time and classroom time and, ultimately, secure teacher participation in the assessment process. Another crucial factor in establishing rapport is the active involvement in developing violence prevention resources and strategies for teachers and administrators to successfully combat violence in their own educational system, neighborhood culture, and their families. It is a contextually relevant exploration of how to address issues before violence occurs, using the culture and language of the people affected. Intervention is the cornerstone of any prevention strategy.

The social worker must be sensitive to the families', teachers', and children's cultural behaviors, beliefs, and attitudes so as to work collaboratively with the system within the school in order to integrate violence prevention strategies.

Once cultural connections have been made between the social worker and the families, teachers, and children, cultural partnerships between the social worker and the parent are constructed, and agreements to work with one another are made. The establishment of mutual trust is a crucial condition of these cultural partnerships among child, parent, elder, and social worker. That trust is strengthened as the family observes the social worker engaging with the child on several occasions. This technique of establishing trust and rapport through consistent dialogue empowers parents and elders to become more active participants in the treatment process. Part of this dialogue is based on inquiry. The parents and elders inquire about the social worker's role and reason for being involved with the child. The role of the social worker is explained to the family. The family may ask about the social worker's native origins, employment, family, and extended family. The family and the social worker can then seek a common ground for knowing one another, and once this process is achieved, the relationship between the social worker and the parents and elders may be strengthened.

Consent forms in the student's native language should be given to bilingual or monolingual ethnic parents and elders. Each consent form may have to be read to them in whichever language they feel most comfortable with to make sure every family member understands what they are signing. Consent forms should be written in a language that encourages the family to participate in the child's treatment.

Confidentiality is taught as part of the consent and assessment process, an important technique for respecting the rights of children. Parents and elders contribute important input in these interdisciplinary partnerships and the assessment process. An important outcome of this more positive model for the parents is the crucial connection they are able to maintain with their children's school. Having parents and elders as allies ensures quality education and effective mental health treatment. Involving families as planners along with social workers, principals, school counselors, psychologists, and others validates them as wise and intelligent people. If parents and elders are not given community and school support, children cannot be healthy, happy, and successful in school. An inviting educational climate must be made available to parents so they can participate in the decisions made by teachers and social workers—decisions that directly affect the well-being of their children, especially parents who are at risk themselves.

Many ethnic parents are low-income homemakers who have important and useful trades: arts and crafts, weavers, chili vendors, and those who care for the elderly and for the children. This "unskilled" labor force would immensely enrich the classroom environment and children through their contributions to the school community. This invitation to participate in the assessment gives parents and elders the opportunity to legitimize their knowledge and skills, which then places them in a valuable partnership with the social worker and the teachers. As teachers become overwhelmed and at times disheartened by standardized testing and high standards, families not only are entrusted with the children's academic success but also become the driving force for viable outcomes. Families gain hands-on knowledge and experience because they are actively engaged throughout the assessment process. They feel that they have valuable contributions and are also learning from the interdisciplinary team. This may result in families themselves becoming interested in higher education and having a firm understanding of how mental health services are integrated within the school community. Parents and elders learn to become advocates for their children in school, and school administrators learn to involve and listen to them. Moreover, parents and elders with positive attitudes toward schools have been shown to have a positive effect on children's school performance. Children may also learn from their families' experience that involving themselves with social work services is valuable.

The dream of ending all intergenerational violence in the daily lives of children and their families may seem unrealistic, but the small positive steps within elementary schools for the daily prevention of violence is very realistic. The significant statements made by the literature related to children, violence, and schooling regarding (1) "nonthinking" and reactionary behavior, (2) seemingly trivial violent acts not recognized and prevented, (3) the modeling of behavior by caretakers, (4) the issue of school safety, (5) conditions schools are facing, and (6) the effective role of community partnerships have all proven significant to this approach of a culturally relevant assessment. Teaching children resiliency as a survival skill is a primary prevention tool for parents, mentors, school administrators, teachers, clergy, social workers, children, and families. This verbal and nonverbal language opens the gateway to our humanity and gives people their rightful dignity. This dignity and validation is peacemaking behavior. Advocacy for children's rights and dignity as human beings must be incorporated into any violence prevention model especially with younger children. Early intervention is the gateway to violence prevention.

The culturally relevant mental health assessment is an early intervention that may stop the cycle of violence as it deteriorates the academic and emotional development of children struggling with the culture of violence. It may heal the scars for the children, the school, and the greater community. These parents reciprocate by returning to their families of origin and modeling these new supportive behaviors. This cycle may prevent future violence in the schools, neighborhoods, and the greater community. If this modeling is sustained over many years, children will have the conditions to develop into healthy, educated, and compassionate adults.

The whole concept of wellness, education, sense of community, sense of *familia*, sense of belonging, the sense that you have the right to be a child, within the daily school climate and the school system as a whole—this ideal is sometimes difficult to achieve. It is important to confer some compassion for the monumental tasks required of schools and families today. The teachers and school personnel, due to their stressful daily environment, are expected to raise their own families, educate children, mediate conflict, refer children for social services, discipline effectively, survive in a chaotic and politically charged school peer group, and keep their sense of creativity, inspiration, and humor.

Families have a tremendous task in raising healthy, educated, and compassionate children. When systems do not cooperate and share effective resources that are readily available, the results are that the multicolored fabric of the common culture is unraveled. Violence prevention programs and culturally relevant assessments can never be carbon copies of one another. They must be created by an accurate and community-driven decision-making process that incorporates many voices to ensure cultural relevancy and diversity. This is a primary consideration for the front-end staff that implements these programs on a day-to-day and year-to-year basis. In terms of partnerships, more research must be conducted to develop models of how low-income rural communities can partner and benefit from urban communities that may already have resources and established prevention programs. Conversely, urban communities may also gain knowledge from rural communities. Our vision of a climate of partnership and a culturally relevant assessment must extend itself beyond school districts, state lines, and nations.

Tools and Practice Examples

A Culturally Competent Psychosocial Assessment for Students

Background

Name
Age
Gender
Ethnic background
Student lives with?
School student is currently attending?
Grade student is currently enrolled in?
Teacher?
Does student require bilingual Spanish services?

Cultural Strengths

1. What country are you from?
2. How many years have you been living in the United States?
3. How many years has your family been living in this country?
   A. Recent immigrant under 1 year
   B. 1–5 years or
   C. More than 5 years
4. What is your cultural identity: Hispanic, Native American, Anglo, African American?
5. What language do you prefer for treatment?
6. What is your home language?
7. What cultural value do I need to take into consideration?

8. Have you used a cultural form of healing; if so, describe?
9. Are there any cultural conflicts I need to be aware of?
10. Are there any religious or spiritual beliefs that I should know about?

Brief Psychiatric History

1. Presenting problem (for schoolchildren include home, extended family home, immigrant issues, peer functioning, and school)
2. Does student's family want services?
3. Psychiatric history
4. History of mental illness in the family?
5. Has the student been previously hospitalized? Inpatient, outpatient (include dates, providers, diagnostics, results)
6. Has the student been diagnosed by a *curandero/a* (folk healer)?
7. Current and or past medications (psychotropic, over-the-counter, and/or including the use of herbs, natural or holistic remedies)
8. Suicide ideation/attempts
9. Homicide ideation/attempts

Medical History

1. Current health problems
2. Medical referral needed
3. Cultural healer referral needed
4. Sleep
5. Appetite
6. Disabilities (physical, developmental, cognitive, or other)
7. Seizures, head injuries
8. Fetal exposure to alcohol, drugs, natural hallucinogens

School Information

1. School problems
2. Suspensions, expulsions
3. Relationship with mother
4. Relationship with father
5. Relationship with extended family member (if student is recent immigrant, please elaborate)
6. Problems within the family
7. Social problems (if student is experiencing problems with acclamation and language, please elaborate)

8. Behavior problems
9. Gang affiliation
10. Arrests
11. Current legal problems
12. Victim/perpetrator of violence

Family Employment: Source of Income of Father/Mother/Caregiver

1. Migrant field worker
2. Housekeeper
3. Rancher
4. Farmer
5. Factory worker
6. Dairy worker
7. Restaurant worker
8. Landscaping
9. Unemployed
10. Other
   Mental status:
   Disposition:

A Culturally Relevant Case Study

Gina is a 13-year-old girl who lives with her grandmother in a high-risk neighborhood. Her mother has a long history of depression; her father crosses the Mexican border to work every day. Gina's relationship with her parents is strained due to physical violence inflicted by her mother throughout her childhood. While at school, Gina has found herself continuously being referred to the school principal for bullying younger children: pulling hair, kicking, and using profanity. Gina's referral to the school principal is the typical response of the school. However, the principal is not equipped to conduct a thorough exploration of the child's background. Using a culturally competent framework, the school social worker is able to gain a more comprehensive view into the child's family, academic environment, language skills, belief system (including the use of alternative healing practices), and the use of symbolic or metaphorical interpretation.

Key Points

This chapter provides information about conducting effective psychosocial assessments in school settings. The following key points were discussed:

- A wide range of factors, such as home life, neighborhoods, and conditions in the classroom, contribute to behaviors and relationships in school settings.
- A child's resiliency helps determine whether developmental damage occurs from traumatic experiences.
- Poverty and violence greatly increase stress for children and families.
- Conducting an adequate assessment includes understanding a child's cultural and social context.
- Collaboration with the family is important in conducting psychosocial assessments.
- Families should be actively engaged in the assessment process.

References

McIntosh, J. E. (2002). Thought in the face of violence: A child's need. *Child Abuse and Neglect, 26*(3), 229–241.

Rutter, M. (1979). Protective factors in children's responses to stress and disadvantage. In M. W. Kent & J. E. Rolf (Eds.), *Primary prevention of psychopathology: Social competence in children* (Vol. 3, pp. 49–74). Hanover, NH: University Press of New England.

Werner, E. E. (1990). Protective factors and individual resilience. In S. J. Meisels & J. P. Shonkoff (Eds.), *Handbook of early childhood education* (pp. 97–116). Cambridge: Cambridge University Press.

Guidelines for Writing an Effective Service Plan for Children With Disabilities

Joan Letendre

Getting Started

The legislative victory for social equity in the education of children with disabilities has impacted the role of school social workers and other school-based services professionals as they have become increasingly included in both the evaluation and development of the service delivery plan. The role of the school social worker and other school-based services professionals in supporting the effective social and emotional functioning of children with disabilities in schools through direct (individual and group services to the child) as well as indirect services (collaboration between school, family and community) is often crucial to the success of individual educational plans. This chapter describes the multifaceted role of the school social worker or other mental health practitioner in the individual educational plan process, details the federal mandates that must be followed to be in compliance with the law, and illustrates through a case example how the school social worker collaboratively develops a strong service plan that engages parent, classroom teacher, and child in a decision-making process that will contribute to a successful educational plan.

What We Know

Federal Mandates for the Education of Children with Disabilities

Landmark legislation, the Education for Handicapped Children Act of 1975 (P.L. 94-142) and its 1997 reauthorization as the Individuals with Disabilities Act (IDEA) or (P.L. 105-17), guarantees a "free and appropriate education" for all children with disabilities who are between the ages of 3 and 21 and have not graduated from high school (Kordesh & Constable, 2002). Schools and school districts are held accountable by the federal government for the education of children with disabilities including "mental retardation, hearing impairments (including deafness), speech or language impairments, visual impairments (including blindness), serious emotional disturbance (hereinafter referred to as 'emotional disturbance'), orthopedic impairments, autism, traumatic brain injury, other health impairments, or specific learning disabilities" (IDEA, Section 1, Part A, Section 602). Federal guidelines specify that children with disabilities be evaluated by a multidisciplinary team in the child's native language to determine eligibility for special education services and that the evaluation results are used to collaboratively develop a service delivery plan (individual educational plan) for the education of the child within the least restrictive environment. Such legislation promised that children who had cognitive, developmental, communication, social, emotional, and behavioral difficulties would no longer be shuttled to classrooms or institutional programs where minimal learning took place. Strong emphasis was placed on incorporating the strengths and capabilities of the child, as well as including parental input in developing the plan.

Development of the Individual Educational Plan

What Is the Goal of the Individual Educational Plan?

The goal of the individual educational plan (IEP) is to develop an educational road map that supports the current functioning of the child with disabilities within the educational setting. The IEP is developed through the collaborative efforts of a team of professionals with the input of the parents and child (when appropriate). Four federal guidelines direct the process: (1) determining the child's current level of functioning; (2) developing clearly defined and attainable goals and objectives; (3) determining the educational modifications, educational aids, and related services that will enable the child to succeed in school; and (4) developing an evaluation plan that will determine if the expected progress is achieved.

Who Are the Members of the IEP Team?

Federal guidelines specify the following members of the IEP team:

1. The parents of the child with a disability if they choose to attend. Parental input is strongly recommended in the IEP and mandated in the individual family service plan (IFSP) that is specific to infants and toddlers with disabilities.
2. The child whenever the input would be useful or if the parent requests the child's presence. Input of children and adolescents in the specifics of service delivery can contribute to the successful implementation of the plan (Fairbanks, 1985).
3. A regular education teacher if the child is currently or will be participating in regular education classes. With the emphasis on educating children in the least restrictive environment, knowledge of the expectations of the regular education classes is important if a placement in the least restrictive environment is to apply.
4. At least one special education teacher.
5. At least one member of the local educational agency (LEA) who is knowledgeable about the curricular needs of children.
6. An individual who can interpret the instructional implications of evaluation effectively. Often the same members of the multidisciplinary team who have evaluated the child are also IEP members, particularly if they are providing services to the child.
7. Parents may also include an individual who has specific knowledge or expertise regarding the child. A therapist or staff member of a community program can provide knowledge of the child in a different context. If the child's

behavior impedes his or her learning or the learning of others, an individual who is knowledgeable about positive behavior strategies may be essential to the success of the educational plan (IDEA 97, Section 614(d)(B)). A school social worker is one of the mental health professionals who could fill this role.

What We Can Do

What Roles Does the School Social Worker or Other Mental Health Practitioner Play in the IEP Process?

Although federal regulations do not specify "school social worker" as a member of the IEP team, the teamwork and collaborative skills of the school social worker or other school-based mental health professional can greatly facilitate development of a plan that parents and school personnel accept. Knowledge of the child through pre-evaluation contacts, acquaintance with the family during the development of the social history, and expertise in development of positive behavioral strategies that recognize the child's interface with teacher and parents can be critical to the establishment and implementation of a mutually agreed upon educational plan. School social workers and other mental health practitioners may function in the roles of evaluator, advocate, mediator, and resource consultant throughout the process of developing the IEP as illustrated in the following vignettes.

Evaluator

The school social worker or other mental health practitioner first engages parents, many of whom are fearful and distressed with concerns about their child's educational difficulties, in a mutual process of developing a social developmental history that identifies the unique familial and cultural factors that contribute to the child's cognitive, language, social, and emotional functioning. The school social worker's contact with the child and family during the preintervention and evaluation process contributes to an understanding of the social-cultural-emotional factors that impact learning and behavior in school. The information is shared in the determination of eligibility meeting and included in the educational plan to support the child's learning.

Peter is a fourth-grade child who is exhibiting academic and behavioral difficulties in the classroom. Peter often does not complete classroom work and never returns completed homework. Through development of the social history, the school social worker has learned that Peter's immigrant parents have a sixth-grade level of education and do not speak English in the home. Although they believe that it is important for Peter to get an education, they do not feel competent to assist him with his schoolwork. With this knowledge, the team can develop a more realistic home–school collaboration that permits the parents to support the child's learning but relies on other resources (mentor, older sib, homework buddy) for direct help with the homework.

Educator and Advocate

School social workers and other mental health practitioners may prepare parents for their role in the development of the individual educational plan and continue to support them as they advocate for their child's needs in the meeting.

Peter's immigrant parents are fearful that a designation of "disability" will result in their son's permanent placement in a program for children who cannot learn. They do not think that they have any "say" in the decisions made by a group of American educators who know much more about these matters than they. Normalizing the concerns that the parents are experiencing as frequent fears of parents who are going through this process, the school social worker can then provide information that informs the parents of their rights and responsibilities in the determination of the type of educational placement that will benefit their child. The careful use of a translator knowledgeable about special education issues as well as the language and culture of the parents may contribute to this process. As the social worker prepares (coaches) the parents in the importance of their role, parents can learn how to ask for clarification of points that they do not understand as well as question decisions that are made related to program planning. They can be reassured that no service plan can be completed without their approval.

Mediator

Awareness of the parameters of the school as well as the concerns of the parents allows the school social worker to mediate disputes that interfere with development of consensus on a workable plan. Parents advocating for their child may find it difficult to understand that services, although uniquely mandated for their child, have to be addressed within the context of a classroom setting, whether special education or regular education (Fantuzzo & Atkins, 1992). If the educational plan is to support the child's functioning in the least restrictive environment, behavioral plans must include an understanding of the challenges that the regular education teacher experiences in managing a classroom of students as well as one with a cognitive or behavioral disability.

Sarah is a third-grade child who exhibits much creativity but numerous challenges in the classroom. Sarah is often defiant and has difficulty following classroom rules. Sarah's parents admit to spending considerable time coaxing her to finish tasks at home. They have found that when they give her choices, she is more likely to comply. Sarah is mainstreamed for three of her academic classes and Mrs. Pollard complains that she has 24 other third-graders and little time to "cater" to Sarah's "every little whim." With recognition of the importance of establishing a behavioral plan that responds to the realities of the classroom as well as the needs of the child, the school social worker can incorporate the successful strategies used by the parents (use of choices and extra time) to develop a classroom behavioral plan that will permit some choice for Sarah while appreciating the time commitments of Mrs. Pollard. Scheduling a meeting with the parents, Sarah, the school social worker, and Mrs. Pollard might facilitate this process.

Resource Consultant

Many children, especially those with severe disabilities, will need additional resources within the community if they are to experience educational success. The knowledge that the mental health practitioner has about community services and the ability to access resources not provided in the school are essential to the success of the plan (Constable, 2003).

> Anna is a 13-year-old adolescent who emigrated from Russia 2 years ago. According to her mother, she has "fallen into the wrong crowd." In addition to recognition of specific learning disabilities, Anna has displayed behaviors that her mother says were not evident in Russia, where Anna had many friends and "never got in trouble." Anna spends her time with older peers, many of whom are not in school, and several times, the police have called Mrs. P. regarding curfew violations and minor vandalism. Mrs. P works long hours at three jobs, and Anna is often left alone. One of the goals of Anna's individual educational plan is to develop positive peer relationships that will contribute to her social and emotional growth both in and out of school. Since there are no after-school programs in the school, the social worker finds a community program that is specifically designed to mentor young adolescent girls who are at risk of failure in school.

What Are the Federal Guidelines for Development of the Individual Educational Plan?

Parental Participation

Federal guidelines specify that the IEP be developed in collaboration with parents, who are expected to be major contributors to the development of their child's service delivery plan. Maximal efforts must be employed to schedule meetings to facilitate optimal parental involvement. School social workers can engage a reluctant parent in this process. It is essential that the timing of the meeting respond to the needs of the parents as well as the school district. For example, a distraught parent, who has just heard from educational experts about the severity of their child's disability and educational needs, may have difficulty fully participating in a collaborative planning process. Likewise, school personnel, overburdened by the large amounts of paperwork involved in the IEP, may bring a draft of the goals and objectives to the meeting but must understand that no final decisions about the educational plan can be made without parental approval.

What Points Must Be Addressed in an Individual Educational Plan?

Each state and local district must address the following parts of the IEP:

- A statement of the child's present levels of educational performance in academic and nonacademic areas that specifies the effect of the disability on the student's performance
- A statement of annual goals and short-term objectives or "benchmarks"
- A statement of educational and related services to be provided to the child and a statement of the program modifications or supports for school personnel that will be provided so that the child attains the annual goals and participates, whenever possible and appropriate, in the general curriculum
- The projected dates for initiation of services, frequency, and the anticipated duration of services
- Extent of participation in regular education programs
- A statement of the extent to which the child will not be able to participate in a general educational program
- A statement of how the child's progress toward the annual goal will be measured and how the parents will be informed (by means of periodic report cards) of progress toward the annual goals and short-term objectives
- An individual transition plan (ITP), which is a statement of the needed transition services (to facilitate movement to postsecondary education, employment, or additional schooling or training), including, when appropriate, a statement of the interagency responsibilities or linkages before the student leaves the school setting. An ITP is now generally developed as a child is transitioning to another school to ensure continuity of services, for example, a child transitioning to middle school from elementary school (IDEA, 300.347).

Documentation

Districts vary in the ways that school social workers and other school-based services professionals are included in the documentation of the IEP. The school social worker or other mental health practitioners are specifically concerned with documenting the current social, emotional, and behavioral functioning of the child; developing goals and objectives that support optimal age-appropriate development; and defining the services and methods of evaluation. In some states and districts, for example, school social workers complete their own individual educational plans addressing these points. In other districts, school social workers "sign off" on classroom IEPs. Likewise, state and local educational districts can develop their own IEP forms as long as each point specified by the federal mandates is addressed. Reauthorization of IDEA may include changes to state and local documentation procedures that involve greater standardization of forms to ease the amount of paperwork that has often been a complaint of school administrators (e-mail communication, Myrna Mandlawitz, 2004).

Tools and Practice Examples

A Practice Example

The following example illustrates the school social worker's process in developing a unique individual educational plan that addresses the academic and social-emotional challenges of a fourth-grade girl whose eligibility for special education services have been determined by a case study evaluation. A description of the student's social-emotional functioning in family and school contexts was obtained by the school social worker during meetings with her parents for the social developmental history and is included in the individual education plan. The summary of the student's social-emotional functioning is followed by a description of current level of performance, emphasizing strengths as well as challenges, and designation of goals and objectives for impacting school and home behaviors, services necessary to accomplish the goals, and evaluation methods to measure change.

1. Present Level of Performance

Present level of performance describes both Helen's strengths and problems in concrete and observable language. Information from the social-emotional description obtained from parents and teachers provides a baseline measurement for development of goals and objectives that encourage growth in both academic and social-emotional areas. Parental contributions focused on strengths as well as challenges are emphasized.

Social-Emotional Functioning

Box 91.1 Helen: Summary of Current Social-Emotional Functioning

Helen is a 10-year-old fourth-grade girl who exhibits impulsive and disruptive behaviors in the classroom. Helen is an excited and creative learner but is selective about what she learns and how she learns it. According to her teacher: "Helen wants what she wants when she wants it." She prefers subjects that are "hands on," such as science and math, and excels in these subjects. Helen has difficulty with independent seatwork and becomes angry and disruptive when the teacher asks her to stay on task when she is looking around the room. As a result, Helen's performance in reading, social studies, and language arts is poor. Helen consistently yells out answers before she has raised her hand. Helen also rarely follows through on homework assignments, often "forgetting" the work in her desk, which frustrates her parents and teachers. Although eager to play with classmates, Helen's demanding behaviors anger her peers, often resulting in rejection. Helen becomes angry when she does not get her way with peers and sometimes cries, causing classmates to call her "baby." Such interactions increase her frustration.

Helen is the oldest of three children and can be very nurturing with her younger brother and sister. Helen's parents report that she can occupy herself well at home with games, artwork, and outside play with her siblings and a younger neighbor girl. It is only when they ask her to comply with a task that she does not like, such as homework or setting the table, that she becomes defiant and screams and yells until she gets her way. Mrs. S. reports that since this behavior is so upsetting to the whole family, they often "give in to keep the peace."

2. Annual Goals and Short–Term Objectives or "Benchmarks"

The goals and objectives evolve from the team's determination of the gains that can be reasonably anticipated for the student during the school year. Goal setting is dependent on having established a realistic baseline functioning level for the child in both academic and nonacademic areas. Realistic goals and objectives encourage strong participation in the service plan and increase motivation

Box 91.2 Helen: Present Level of Performance

Helen actively engages in learning if she enjoys the subject. At school she is creative and enthusiastic about hands-on subjects such as math and science. At home, Helen prefers doing artwork or playing outdoors with younger siblings and neighbor. Helen is nurturing with younger children, particularly her siblings and neighbor children.

When Helen does not want to do a task (e.g., homework or chore), she yells and argues. Helen rarely completes homework assignments in reading and social studies and never brings home assignments for homework.

Helen is eager to play with peers but has trouble waiting her turn or playing by the rules.

Helen screams and cries when the group does not play by her rules.

for continued progress. In contrast, setting unrealistic goals results in discouragement and an ensuing decrease in the motivation to engage in aspects of the plan that encourage educational success. Input from the child, parent, and teacher at this stage of the development of the IEP ensure collaboration between home and school.

Goals are broad statements that describe the anticipated progress that the child can accomplish within the school year in both academic and nonacademic areas of functioning.

The related objectives or benchmarks break the goals down into concrete and specific steps that enable the goal to be achieved. Each goal should contain at least two objectives related to goal acquisition. Sanders (2003) suggests developing goals and objectives by identifying the basic needs (motivation, behavior, social skills, or self-image) that support or impede student learning in nonacademic areas. By focusing on Helen's needs for (1) motivation to comply with age-appropriate expectations related to in-school and homework assignments (2) behaviors that decrease emotional outbursts and promote age-appropriate methods of getting her needs met, and (3) social skills for interacting positively with peers, the school social worker can target specific cognitions or behaviors focused on accomplishing the goal.

3. Objectives and Evaluation Procedures and Schedule

Box 91.3 Helen: Annual Goals and Short-Term Objectives

Annual Goal 1: Helen will increase attention in classroom and compliance with academic tasks.

- Objective 1: With social work intervention and a positive behavioral plan, Helen will increase attentiveness during classroom activities. (Defines the persons involved providing the service)
  - Evaluation procedure: Teacher logs, contracting, self-monitoring checklist, observations (defines the methods for measuring the behaviors)
  - Evaluation schedule: Daily (defines how often the behavior will be monitored)
- Objective 2: With social work intervention, Helen will practice asking the teacher for help when she does not understand work.
  - Evaluation procedure: Teacher logs, contracting, observations
  - Evaluation schedule: Weekly
- Objective 3: With social work intervention and a home–school communication plan, Helen will learn responsibility for bringing homework home, completing assignments, and returning them to her teacher.
  - Evaluation procedure: Teacher–parent home–school communication reports
  - Evaluation schedule: Daily

Annual Goal 2: Helen will decrease emotional outbursts.

- Objective 1: With social work intervention individually and in a group, Helen will learn to practice relaxation techniques for use when she is angry.

(Continued)

Box 91.3. *(Continued)*

- Evaluation procedure: Observation, self-reports, disciplinary reports
- Evaluation schedule: Daily
- Objective 2: With social work intervention individually and in a group, Helen will practice calming self-statements.
  - Evaluation procedure: Home–school reports, self-reports, observations
  - Evaluation schedule: Daily
- Objective 3: With social work intervention individually and in a group, Helen will learn to verbalize her frustrations.
  - Evaluation procedures: Home–school report, self-reports, discipline reports, observations in classroom and on playground
  - Evaluation schedule: Daily

Annual Goal 3: Helen will increase positive interactions with peers.

- Objective 1: With social work intervention within a group, Helen will learn to wait her turn and contribute positively to group discussions and games.
  - Evaluation procedure: Teacher–parent home–school communication reports, self-reports, discipline reports, observation in classroom and on playground
  - Evaluation schedule: Weekly
- Objective 2: With social work intervention within a group, Helen will learn how to practice calming self-talk when she is angry.
  - Evaluation procedure: Teacher–parent home–school communication reports, self-reports, discipline reports, observation in classroom and on playground
  - Evaluation schedule: Weekly
- Objective 3: With social work intervention within a group, Helen will practice basic cooperative social skills and use these in organized games on the playground.
  - Evaluation procedure: Teacher–parent home–school communication reports, self-reports, discipline reports, observation in classroom and on playground
  - Evaluation schedule: Weekly
- Objective 4: With social work intervention within a group, Helen will learn skills for understanding how her behaviors affect peers.
  - Evaluation procedure: Teacher–parent home–school communication reports, self-reports, discipline reports, observation in classroom and on playground
  - Evaluation schedule: Weekly

4. Special Education and Related Services

The goals and objectives determine the related services needed to support them. Designating the service provider, as well as determining whether the services are direct or indirect contact with the child, ensures accountability. If the services are not available within the school, the school must contract with individuals, agencies, or other school districts to ensure their provision. Direct services designate that the school social worker meets with the child either individually or in a group to address the objectives.

Participation in a weekly social skills group can teach Helen positive ways of interacting with peers (initiating contact, taking turns, negotiating, managing conflict, giving and accepting positive as well as critical feedback, etc.). Indirect services designate collaboration with teachers and family to support the child's functioning in the classroom and collaboration between home and school. Home–school collaboration is important to provide similar structure and reinforcement for the new behaviors that Helen is learning. The social worker, teacher, and parent collaboratively develop a simple home–school report that is signed daily by parent and teacher and reports on compliance with classroom and homework behaviors. When Helen complies with the expectations, she is rewarded. Since one of Helen's strengths is nurturing younger children, the reward system might include participation in a cross-age tutoring program where fourth graders read to kindergarten students.

5. The Projected Dates for Initiation of Services, Frequency, and the Anticipated Duration of Services

Although daily, weekly, and monthly goals are monitored, depending on the unique needs of the child, yearly IEP meetings are conducted to monitor the successful attainment of goals and benchmarks and to make decisions regarding continuation of services. A statement of the time frame expected to attain objectives is included. Development of new or modified goals reflects the student's progress. Although IEP review meetings are generally held yearly, a parent or member of the IEP team can convene a meeting to make changes to a program that reflects emerging issues or needs of the student. For students with severe emotional and behavioral problems, such monitoring and changes may occur frequently. For instance, if a plan had been developed for Helen and modification was necessary, the IEP team could meet before the annual review meeting to address concerns and modify the preexisting plan. Tables 91.1 and 91.2 encapsulate Helen's service delivery plan by indicating the type of service, the provider, the dates for initiation of services, frequency and duration of services, and additional comments that reflect on service delivery.

School Social Work Checklist for IEP Process

Is the school social worker aware of district policy for documenting related services on the IEP?

Are meetings scheduled so that parents can contribute fully to the process?

If appropriate, is the child involved in the IEP process?

Are the parents knowledgeable about their rights?

Have the parents been coached in asking questions and contributing to the plan?

Does the IEP discuss strengths as well as challenges for the child?

Are the goals and objectives clearly and objectively written?

Could a stranger read the goals and objectives and know how to proceed?

Is the skill or behavior relevant to behavior in school?

Is the skill or behavior in keeping with student development?

Are the service providers identified?

Are the types of services that the school social worker provides clearly defined?

If a service is not available in the district, are alternative resources identified?

Are several methods of measuring progress delineated?

Is there a schedule for evaluating behavior change and skill acquisition?

Resources

Council for Exceptional Children: http://www.cec.sped.org/

Education Resources Information Center: http:// www.eric.ed.gov/

Table 91.1 Consultation (Indirect Services to School Personnel or Parents)

Type of Service	Focus on Goal	Person Responsible	Start Date	Frequency/ Duration per Day	Total Time/Cycle	Comments
Social work	1, 2, 3	Teacher, social worker	5/04	15 minutes 2x/week	30 minutes	Staff to consult weekly to coordinate services
Social work	1, 2	Social worker	5/05	15-minute phone contact with parents, 1x/week	15 minutes	To monitor home/school report

Table 91.2 Special Education and Related Services in Other Settings (Direct Services)

Type of Service	Focus on Goal	Person Responsible	Start Date	Frequency/ Duration per Day	Total Time/Cycle	Comments
Social work/ social skills group	3	Social worker	9/2004	Weekly/ 45 minutes 1x/week	45 minutes	Evaluation after 10 weeks for continuation schedule
Social work	1, 2	Social worker	9/2004	15 minutes/1x/ week individual session	15 minutes	To monitor and modify behavioral plan

IDEA rules and regulations: Full documentation in http://www.ideapractices.org/law/regulations/topicIndex.php

Lignugaris-Kraft, B., Marchand-Martella, N., & Martella, R. C. (2001). Strategies for writing better goals and short term objectives or benchmarks. *Teaching Exceptional Children, 34*(1), 52–58.

School Social Work Association of America. Advocacy group for school social workers. Provide current updates on changes in special education legislation. http://www.sswaa.org.

U.S. Office of Special Education and Rehabilitation and Research Services: www.ed.gov/offices/OSERS/OSEP

Web sites for Offices of Special Education in each state. The sites define the state regulations for IEP development and the forms used in each state. Individual states also have resources for completing IEPs and parent guides to the educational rights of students. These materials are not standardized but particular to the individual state.

Key Points to Remember

Schools and school districts are held accountable by the federal government for the education of children with disabilities, including "mental retardation, hearing impairments (including deafness), speech or language impairments, visual impairments (including blindness), serious emotional disturbance, orthopedic impairments, autism, traumatic brain injury, other health impairments, or specific learning disabilities" (IDEA, Section 1, Part A, Section 602).

Federal guidelines specify that children with disabilities be evaluated by a multidisciplinary team in the child's native language to determine eligibility for special education services and that the evaluation results are used to collaboratively develop a service delivery plan (individual educational plan) for the education of the child within the least restrictive environment.

The individual educational plan is developed through the collaborative efforts of a team of professionals with the input of the parents and child (when appropriate). Four federal guidelines direct the process: (1) determining the child's current level of functioning; (2) developing clearly defined and attainable goals and objectives; (3) determining the educational modifications, educational aids, and related services that will enable the child to succeed in school; and (4) developing an evaluation plan that will determine if the expected progress is achieved.

School social workers and other mental health practitioners may function in roles of evaluator, advocate, mediator, and resource consultant throughout the process of developing the IEP. IEPs require schools to follow requirements set to assure an equal and effective education for children with disabilities (summarized in this chapter), including annual benchmark assessments of student progress, transition planning, and documentation.

School districts vary in the ways that school social workers and other school-based services professionals are included in the documentation of the IEP. The school social worker or other mental health practitioner is specifically concerned with documenting the current social, emotional, and behavioral functioning of the child, developing goals and objectives that support optimal age-appropriate development, and defining the services and methods of evaluation.

References

Constable, R. (2003). The individual education program and the IFSP: Content, process, and the social worker's role. In R. Constable, S. McDonald, & J. P. Flynn (Eds.), *School social work, practice, policy, and research perspectives* (5th ed., pp. 264–278). Chicago: Lyceum.

Fairbanks, N. M. (1985). Involving children in the IEP: The car-in-the-garage technique. *Social Work in Education, 7*(3), 171–182.

Fantuzzo, J., & Atkins, M. (1992). Teacher oriented behavior management. *Journal of Applied Behavior Analysis, 25,* 37–42.

IDEA 97. Law & Regulations. Retrieved on June 30, 2004, from http://www.ideapractices.org/law/regulations/topicIndex.php

Kordesh, R. S., & Constable, R. (2002). Policies, programs, and mandates for developing social services in schools. In R. Constable, S. McDonald, & J. P. Flynn (Eds.), *School social work: Practice, policy, and research perspectives* (5th ed., pp. 83–100). Chicago: Lyceum.

Sanders, D. (2003). Annual goals and short term objectives for school social workers. In R. Constable, S. McDonald, & J. P. Flynn (Eds.), *School social work, practice, policy, and research perspectives* (5th ed., pp. 279–288). Chicago: Lyceum.

Effective Methods and Resources for Working With the Organization and Community Context of the School

Organization skills may be as important as direct service skills for school social workers and other mental health professionals. Social workers and other school-based practitioners trained as direct service practitioners report that they often feel powerless in dealing with the complex organizational structure and multiple processes of the school. To be accepted and accommodated, however, practitioners must gain understanding of a range of systems and skills that allow them to be effective within educational systems. The chapters in this section will focus on best practices for developing and maintaining effective organization and community affiliations and changing school systems.

Employed by the School? Essential Functions of a School-Based Case Manager

Debra J. Woody

Getting Started

Case management is described as one of the most common functions performed by social workers in a school setting (Dennison, 1998). But because there is a broad range of definitions for case management in general, there are various definitions and descriptions of case management in school settings. Many school social workers suggest no difference between good old-fashioned social casework and case management in a school setting (Moore, 1990). This may be because the role and responsibilities of school social workers are broad and similar to the roles and responsibilities of the school-based case manager. In addition, both share the common goal of providing services to help students take full advantage of what schooling has to offer (Allen-Meares, 1999). The objective of providing social work case management in schools is to guarantee that students receive services, treatment, and educational opportunities that the school setting can provide or facilitate (Smith & Stowitschek, 1998). Similar to social casework, case management involves linking the student to a variety of services, sometimes providing therapeutic services, and monitoring the quality of various services to which a student might be linked (Woodside & McClam, 1998).

In addition to the traditional social casework approach to case management services, a more recent trend is the development of "interprofessional" case management teams involving various school personnel, including school social workers (Smith & Stowitschek, 1998). Members of the team work together to assess the needs of individual students and/or the entire student body and identify or develop resources or programs to meet the needs of students. Usually the delivery of the services and programs provided to students are coordinated through the team, and members of the team monitor student progress. There are several variations of the case management team approach. For example, in a local alternative high school in Texas, school personnel are members of a case management team led by the school social worker. The team identifies student needs and coordinates services for their student population. Each member of the team is assigned case management responsibilities for a group of 10 or fewer students. Each case manager is required to meet weekly with assigned students to assess student needs and assist each student with identified issues and concerns. One task performed by the case managers is to monitor the daily attendance of the students assigned to them. If attendance records indicate that a student is absent, the case manager attempts to locate the student and inquire about the absences from school. The case manager then assists the student in removing obstacles to the student's return to school, including coordinating community services if needed. The case managers also monitor students' academic performance through weekly consultations with teachers and help students set weekly academic goals. The case managers use the case management team for consultation and guidance.

In other school settings, members of the case management team serve as a "core" team and representatives from additional community service agencies are added, depending on the need of the students. The C-Stars model is a good example of the case management team approach (see Stowitschek, Smith, & Armijo, 1998). The goal of the team is to develop a network of community services that are available to individual students or that are available to address the needs of the general student body.

What We Know

It is difficult to evaluate the effectiveness of case management. Providing case management necessitates flexibility in terms of goals, objectives, and intervention strategy and requires a unique intervention in response to the specific situation. The effectiveness of case management is also difficult to document because of the primary focus on linking clients to community services and resources. These aspects of case management make it difficult to create collective outcomes and measures necessary for empirical documentation. Thus, there are few empirical studies about the effectiveness of case management services in general and in school settings specifically.

Given the lack of clear distinction between case management and social casework in school settings, a review of outcomes from studies about the effectiveness of school social work services may shed some light on the effectiveness of school-based case management services. In their review and analysis of studies described in the literature, Early and Vonk (2001) found empirical support for the overall effectiveness of social work services in schools. They conclude that school-based social work services help students increase problem-solving skills, improve students' relationships with peers, and increase students' interpersonal skills. Note, however, that this review included a mixture of studies, not just the traditional social casework approach. For example, some of the interventions targeted small groups while other interventions were delivered to classroom groups.

In another study, the outcomes are reported for a social worker who performed tasks similar to social work case management (Bowen, 1999). The social worker assessed the level of school functioning among a group of elementary school students and based on the assessment-identified academic and/or behavioral goals for each student. The social worker provided strategies that a student's parents could use to help their child reach the identified goals. Each week the social worker contacted the parents for progress reports to help resolve any problems related to the strategy and to assess new problems or concerns. The social worker also served as a bridge between the teachers and parents by providing the parents with weekly feedback from the teachers concerning their student's progress. Empirically based findings indicate improvements in students' academic performance and social behavior and an increase in communication between the parents and teachers.

Case management as an intervention was studied more directly in another study (Reid & Bailey-Dempsey, 1994). Female students in grades 6 through 10 received either a $50 cash incentive or case management services to improve school attendance and academic performance. Interestingly, students who received the case management intervention showed more improvement in school attendance and academic performance than those who received the cash incentive. In addition, girls who received case management had increased self-esteem scores while the self-esteem scores of girls who received cash incentives decreased. The case management program was rated more favorably by the parents and students who received it, than was the cash incentive program rated by the parents and students who received it.

There are several reports of positive outcomes for interprofessional case management programs as well. Findings indicate a decrease in absenteeism, improvement in grades, and a reduction in behavior problems (Stowitschek, Smith, & Armijo, 1998).

What We Can Do

A Comprehensive Model of Case Management

Rothman (1991) offers a model for case management intervention that we have adapted for school-based case management in Figure 92.1. The model is presented as a flowchart to illustrate the school case management intervention process. This model was selected for this chapter because it is comprehensive and grounded in empirical findings on case management. Rothman's model is easily adapted to case management services in a school setting (Figure 92.1).

Access to Case Management Services

Even in a school setting where there is a ready and waiting population in need of case management services, the social worker may still need to do outreach. This usually involves helping school personnel, students, and parents know about the availability of social case management services, and how this service may be beneficial to students, families, and the school community. If social work services are new to the school and/or school district, the case manager will have to create a referral process including referral forms.

The case manager may also consider outreach to representatives from community programs and services. This not only helps the school-based case manager in the development of a community network for referral outside the school but also informs community groups about the availability of case management services in the school setting. Recently, a student was referred to a new school case manager by a recreational counselor at a local after-school facility. Although the student had multiple problems, school personnel were unaware

of the student's situation. It was only because the social work case manager had made recent outreach efforts to the facility that personnel in the facility were aware of case management services available at the school.

Intake and Assessment

In a school setting, multiple sources are used for intake and assessment information. This includes the student, family members, teachers, and other school personnel. Some case managers also conduct systematic observations of the student in the classroom setting (for examples, see chapter 50). Many make use of relevant clinical measures or scales.

In addition to the traditional assessment of potential psychological, social, and medical needs as presented by Rothman, case managers also assess additional psychosocial concerns such as socioeconomic, academic, and behavioral issues.

Goal Setting

In conjunction with the student, and parents and teachers if possible, both short-term and long-term goals are established, based on the outcome of the assessment. Short-term goals may include tasks such as helping the parent complete the application for the free and reduced lunch program. Long-term goals may be subdivided into short-term goals. For example, the long-term goal "improving academic performance" may have a short-term goal that the student will pass midterm exams. Rothman emphasizes the importance of considering personal and situational limitations in helping clients set goals. In other words, the case manager must guide the student in setting realistic, obtainable goals.

Intervention Planning or Resource Identification and Indexing

Rothman proposes that traditionally, case managers plan the intervention first and then seek programs, services, and so on to carry out the plan. Because resources, services, and programs are not always available to meet the needs of the client, Rothman suggests an alternative, which is to determine what is available first and then create the intervention plan based on what is available.

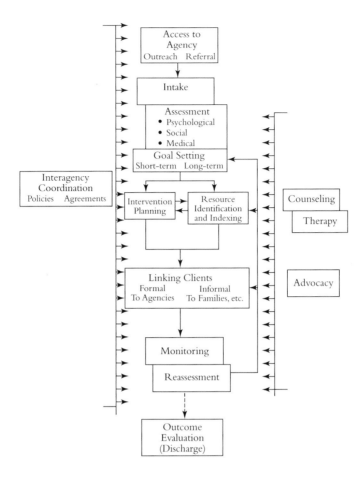

Figure 92.1.

Regardless of the process used, Rothman proposes that intervention planning in case management encompasses therapy and counseling as well as linking clients to programs and services. Case managers in a school setting should consider resources both inside and outside the school system.

The objective behind Rothman's concept of resource identification and indexing is that case managers create an accessible, up-to-date index of available resources. For case managers in the school, this index should include resources relevant to children, adolescents, and their families and may include community mental health services, parenting guidance clinics, emergency food sources, resources for clothing, medical, and dental care, applications for the reduced and free lunch and breakfast program, drug and alcohol treatment facilities, and the addresses of local public human resource centers. Resources within the school system that may be included in the index are the names

and phone numbers of all the school principals, vice principals, school counselors, and administrators over special student services, such as the special education program, teen parenting program, adult education services, homebound services, psychological services, and homeless student program. In addition, the school-based case manager should be familiar with the PTA/PTO officers.

Linking Clients

Rothman describes the act of linking clients to services as active and facilitative and requiring both concrete and emotional support. According to Rothman, concrete linkage includes carefully matching the client need with the available resource and with written permission from the student and parent, making the initial contact on behalf of the client. Emotional support includes preparing the student and family for linkage by

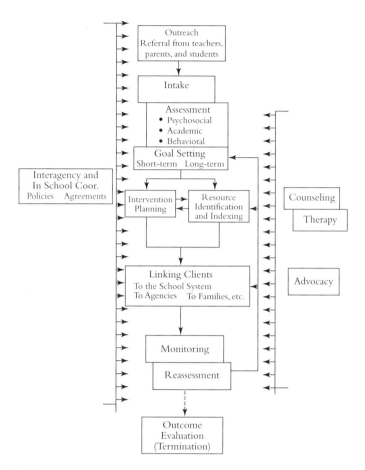

Figure 92.1 (Continued)

Source: Adapted from "A Model of Case Management: Toward Empirically Based Practice," by J. Rothman, 1991, *Social Work, 36*(6), pp. 520–528. Adapted with permission. Copyright 1991, National Association of Social Workers, Inc., Social Work.

providing detailed information about the re-source, anticipating barriers and difficulties, role playing, and, if needed, accompanying the student and/or family on the first visit.

For case managers in a school setting, linking students may also require assessing the availability of family members to participate in the interven-tion plan. As an example, an intervention plan cre-ated for a student who had missed a great amount of schoolwork required that the student participate in tutoring sessions with the teacher before school. Through discussion with the student and parent, the case manager discovered that the mother leaves home at 5:30 A.M. and takes two buses in order to arrive at work by the 7:00 A.M. starting time. Not only did the student lack transportation to the before-school tutoring sessions but also had the re-

sponsibility for helping his younger siblings dress and leave for school. The case manager was instru-mental in helping the teacher and student devise an alternative intervention plan, more realistic to the student's family situation.

Monitoring and Reassessment

Rothman suggests that an important task in case management is monitoring and reassessing the cur-rent intervention plan to determine whether the arrangements are helping the client meet the iden-tified goals. According to Rothman, this involves keeping current on the suitability of resources to which the client has been linked. In a school setting this is easily accomplished through periodically meeting with the student, if the case manager is not already working with the client on a regular basis. Rothman proposes that failed connections are directed back to goal setting or to the linking process, depending on the reason for the breakdown.

Intermittent Functions

Interagency coordination, counseling, short-term therapy, and advocacy are not rungs on the case management flowchart but are identified by Rothman as skills that facilitate the case management process. Interagency coordination refers to the formal and informal agreements between agencies that facilitate the linkage process. For example, a case manager in a school setting negotiated with a local dentist to reduce the usual rate for dental services to students referred from the school by the case manager.

Rothman describes counseling as helping clients with issues such as problem solving, reality testing, and development of socialization and life skills. According to Rothman, counseling does not need to be ongoing and can be used as needed at various points in the process.

Therapy is considered more intense than counseling and is used in the short term to help clients cope with immediate problems and/or crisis situations. Rothman proposes that the therapy can be provided to the individual, in groups, or to families. Like counseling, therapy can also be intermittent as needed throughout the case management process. For example, a case manager in a local high school had been helping a student prepare for the impending death of his mother. Through joint counseling sessions with the student and extended family members, the social work case manager helped the student and family decide on living and financial arrangements for the student and attended to the student's need for ongoing family support. On the morning of the mother's death, the student left the hospital and, unable to think of any other place to go, appeared at the school. The case manager helped the student activate the plan that he and family members had agreed on. After the funeral, when the student returned to school, the case manager provided therapy around grief and problems he was having connecting emotionally with extended family members. When the student was emotionally ready, the case manager linked the student to a support group for adolescents experiencing grief and loss.

Rothman defines *advocacy* as an assertive approach by the case manager to help clients receive services that are denied to them. Case managers in school settings must be ready to advocate for students and parents both within the school setting and in the community.

Outcome Evaluation

Rothman uses a dotted line to connect outcome evaluation to the rest of the model, because outcome evaluation is viewed as not always possible. Rothman supports the empirical evaluation of case management services whenever possible.

Tools and Practice Examples

School Case Management: A Practice Application

Vanessa Smith is a social worker employed by a school district to provide case management services to students on two middle school campuses. Ms. Smith has been employed in this position for about a year. Although the school district had social work case managers in several of the elementary schools, she is the first social worker of any type employed to work with students at the middle school campuses. Immediately after she began work, Ms. Smith made a point of introducing herself to the principals and school counselors on both campuses, as well as introducing herself to as many teachers as possible. She developed a formal system through which teachers and other school personnel could refer students for case management services and through teacher in-service training sessions was able to present the case management process and referral methods to school personnel. At first, few referrals were made, and Ms. Smith used this time to acquaint herself with school and community resources and develop an index of names and numbers. It seemed as though all at once, Ms. Smith was inundated with referrals, mainly from teachers.

Referral

When Ms. Smith checked her school mailbox on Monday morning, she found a referral form from the art teacher. She thought this was a bit unusual because up until this point, all the referral forms she had received were from classroom teachers and the school counselors. Ms. Smith decided to talk with the art teacher first before talking with the student. The art teacher showed Ms. Smith a collage she received from the eighth-grade student, Maranda. The teacher explained to Ms. Smith that in all her years of teaching she had never received a collage like this one. The assignment was for students to illustrate their life goals by creating a collage. Maranda produced a collage using pictures of graves, tombs, crosses, and red smatterings, which she told the art teacher represented blood.

The art teacher did not know much additional information about the student. She described Maranda as a quiet and withdrawn girl who kept to herself. When the art teacher talked with Maranda in private about the collage, Maranda seemed genuinely embarrassed and provided little additional information.

Intake and Assessment

Ms. Smith returned to her office and found the student's identification information in the school's database. She noted that the student has a younger brother and that she and her brother live with the mother a few miles from the school. Information about the father was not available, and an aunt was listed as an emergency contact.

Ms. Smith was able to meet with the student later in the day. During the intake session, Maranda became tearful almost immediately. She told Ms. Smith that she often thinks about death because she is fearful of her mother dying. When probed, Maranda told Ms. Smith that her mother's boyfriend had moved in with them recently and was often abusive to the mother. She described him physically assaulting the mother and threatening to kill her. Maranda denied that her mother or boyfriend had ever abused her or her brother in any way. In fact, she described the boyfriend as nice to her and her brother, often buying them expensive clothes and toys. Maranda admits, though, that she is afraid of him, and although she has more clothes and things, she liked it better when he did not live with them.

Ms. Smith asked Maranda about school. Maranda reported that she had been an A/B student, but she recently received deficiency notices in math, science, and language arts and was worried about passing these three subjects. Maranda described herself as a loner with a few good friends.

Ms. Smith talked with Maranda about making

a home visit and talking with Maranda's mother, Ms. Jenkins. Maranda hesitantly agreed that it would be okay but begged Ms. Smith not to tell her mother that she told her about the abuse.

Ms. Smith received confirmation from Maranda's teachers that she had been a good student but was currently in danger of failing the three courses. All of her teachers described her as quiet, and one teacher described Maranda falling asleep in class on several occasions.

Upon arrival at the Jenkins's home, Ms. Smith was met at the door by Ms. Jenkins, who had a black eye. Ms. Smith was surprised about how forthcoming Ms. Jenkins was about the abuse when she asked Ms. Jenkins about the black eye. Although Ms. Jenkins was not interested in leaving the home or the relationship, Ms. Smith left the name and phone number for several area abuse centers and shelters. Ms. Smith discussed the problems Maranda was having at school and suggested a connection between the abuse and Maranda's difficulties at school. Ms. Smith recommended family counseling to Ms. Jenkins, who stated that she was not interested in family counseling but agreed to seek counseling for Maranda. With agreement from Ms. Jenkins, Ms. Smith phoned the community counseling center and made the referral for Maranda in the presence of Ms. Jenkins. Ms. Smith then handed the phone to Ms. Jenkins who supplied the needed information and was given the time and day for the first appointment.

Goal Setting and Intervention Planning

A day or two later, Ms. Smith met with Maranda at school and discussed the outcome of the home visit. Together Ms. Smith and Maranda identified the following goals and intervention plans:

1. Reduce Maranda's level of anxiety
   a. participate in counseling at the community counseling center
   b. develop a exit plan when the abuse first occurs
2. Earn passing grades by the end of the semester
   a. Develop a plan with the teachers to help her catch up on work

Linking Clients

Ms. Smith had already begun this process when she connected the mother to the counseling center.

Maranda identified an aunt that she feels connected to, and with the mother's written permission, Ms. Smith contacted the aunt, who agreed to meet the children at a designated meeting place when they call for help. Maranda decided to have a bag prepacked to take with her in case she spent the night at the aunt's home. Maranda was also encouraged to phone the police during the abusive episodes.

Ms. Smith also arranged a meeting between Maranda and the three teachers from the classes she was in danger of failing. They each were already offering tutoring before school to interested students. Maranda agreed to choose one teacher each morning and attend the tutoring sessions. Maranda thought this would be a good opportunity for her to complete her homework, since she had difficulty completing it at home. Each teacher also agreed to call on Maranda more in class and to redirect her if she seemed distracted or fell asleep.

Ms. Smith phoned Ms. Jenkins to discuss the intervention plans. Ms. Jenkins agreed to the exit plan and agreed to get Maranda to the tutoring sessions.

Monitoring and Reassessment

Ms. Smith met with Maranda at the end of the following week. Maranda had not attended the counseling appointment and was not able to articulate why she had not gone. She was, however, attending the before-school tutoring and thought this was helping her with her schoolwork.

When Ms. Smith phoned the mother to see why Maranda had not attended the counseling appointment, Ms. Jenkins stated that she talked with Maranda and reassured her that the boyfriend would not kill her. Ms. Jenkins felt that this had taken care of the situation and that Maranda was no longer in need of counseling. Ms. Smith was unable to persuade Ms. Jenkins otherwise about the counseling at that time but had another opportunity a few weeks later. Ms. Smith was called to the girl's bathroom where she found Maranda sobbing uncontrollably. Through sobs, Maranda told Ms. Smith that her mother had been abused by the boyfriend the night before. Maranda and her brother did seek shelter at the aunt's home, but Maranda was upset that her mother allowed the boyfriend to stay in their home. Ms. Smith used this opportunity to call the mother and request that she come to the school immediately, since Ms. Smith was not able to cajole Maranda into returning to class. Maranda's sobbing became more intense when Ms. Jenkins

arrived at the school. Ms. Smith again emphasized the need for counseling and was able to get Maranda an emergency appointment at the counseling center. Ms. Smith drove Maranda and her mom to the center, taking the opportunity to link Maranda and the mom with the therapist.

Ms. Smith continued to monitor Maranda's progress through the teachers and by meeting with Maranda periodically to find out how the therapy sessions were going. Ms. Smith also called Ms. Jenkins occasionally to get her perception of how Maranda was progressing. She also wanted to leave the door open with Ms. Jenkins in case she needed emergency assistance in terms of the abuse.

Although Ms. Smith did not conduct a formal outcome evaluation, she did keep track of Maranda's academic performance. She also made note of the number of anxiety-producing situations like the one in the girl's bathroom.

▍ Resources

Case Management

NASW Standards for Social Work Case Management: www.naswdc.org/practice/standards/sw_case_mgmt.asp.

Reinhard, J. (2000). Limitations of mental health case management: A rationale emotive and cognitive therapy perspective. *Journal of Rational-Emotive & Cognitive-Behavior Therapy, 18*(2), 103–117.

Weaver, D., & Hasenfeld, Y. (1997). Case management practices, participant responses, and compliance in welfare-to-work programs. *Social Work Research, 21*(2), 92–100.

School-Based Case Management

Lynn, C., McKay, M., & Atkins, M. (2003). School social work: Meeting the mental health needs of students through collaboration with teachers. *Children & Schools, 25*(4), 197–209.

Shepard-Tew, D., & Creamer, D. A. (1998). Elementary school integrated services teams: Applying case-management techniques. *Professional School Counseling, 28*(2), 141–146.

▍ Key Points to Remember

Although there are many definitions of case management, there is little distinction between providing social work casework services in a school setting and in providing social work case management services. Regardless, case management is believed to be one of the main functions provided by social workers in school settings. Although there are only a few studies in which the effectiveness of case management services in a school setting has been evaluated, there is some support that it is an effective mode of intervention. Demonstrated in this chapter is the use of a case management model in a school setting.

References

Allen-Meares, P. (1999). The contribution of social workers to schooling—revisited. In R. Constable, McDonald, S., & Flynn, S. (Eds.), *School social work: Practice, policy, and research perspectives* (4th ed., pp. 24–32). Chicago: Lyceum.

Bowen, N. (1999). A role for school social workers in promoting student success through school–family partnerships. *Social Work in Education, 21*(1), 34–48.

Dennison, S. (1998). School social work roles and working conditions in a southern state. *School Social Work Journal, 23*(1), 44–54.

Early, T., & Vonk, E. (2001). Effectiveness of school social work from a risk and resilience perspective. *Children & Schools, 23*(1), 9–31.

Moore, S. (1990). A social work practice model of case management: The case management grid. *Social Work, 35*(5), 444–448.

Reid, W., & Bailey-Dempsey, C. (1994). Cash incentives versus case management: Can money replace services in preventing school failure? *Social Work Research, 18*(4), 227–236.

Rothman, J. (1991). A model of case management: Toward empirically based practice. *Social Work, 36*(6), 520–528.

Smith, A., & Stowitschek, J. (1998). School-based interprofessional case management: A literature-based rationale and a practitioner-molded model. *Preventing School Failure, 42*(2), 61–65.

Stowitschek, J., Smith, A., & Armijo, E. (1998). Organizing, implementing, and evaluating school-based management. The C-Stars experience. *Preventing School Failure, 42*(2) 73–77.

Woodside, M., & McClam, T. (1998). *Generalist case management: A method of human service delivery.* Pacific Grove, CA: Brooks/Cole.

Want to Work With Schools?

What Is Involved in Successful Linkages?

Linda Taylor ▪ Howard S. Adelman

Getting Started

Increasingly, it is evident that schools, families, and communities should work closely with each other to meet their mutual goals. Schools are located in communities but often are islands with no bridges to the mainland. Families live in neighborhoods, often with little connection to each other or to the schools their youngsters attend. Neighborhood resources, such as agencies, youth groups, and businesses, have major stakes in the community. All these entities affect each other, for good or bad. Because of this and because they share goals related to education and socialization of the young, schools, homes, and communities must collaborate with each other if they are to minimize problems and maximize results.

Recent years have seen an expansion in school–community linkages. Initiatives are sprouting in a rather dramatic and ad hoc manner. Such initiatives often are referred to as collaborations. Comprehensive collaboration is seen as a promising direction for generating essential interventions to address barriers to learning, enhance healthy development and learning, and strengthen families and neighborhoods (Adelman & Taylor, 2002b, 2003; Center for Mental Health in Schools, 2002; Franklin & Streeter, 1995; Honig, Kahne, & McLaughlin, 2001; Melaville & Blank, 1998; Southwest Regional Educational Laboratory, 2001; Taylor & Adelman, 2003, 2004; also see Table 93.1). For schools, such links are seen as a way to provide more support for schools, students, and families. For agencies, connection with schools is seen as providing better access to families and youth and thus as providing an opportunity to reach and have an impact on hard-to-reach clients. The interest in collaboration is bolstered by concern about widespread fragmentation of school and community interventions. The hope is that integrated resources will have a greater impact.

A community is not limited to agencies and organization. It encompasses people, businesses, community-based organizations, postsecondary institutions, faith-based and civic groups, programs at parks and libraries, and any facility that can be used for recreation, learning, enrichment, and support (Kretzmann, 1998; Kretzmann & McKnight, 1993). By connecting with schools, community entities can help weave together a critical mass of resources and strategies. This is especially needed in impoverished communities.

While informal linkages are relatively simple to acquire, establishing major long-term connections is complicated. This is particularly so when the aim is to evolve a comprehensive, multifaceted, and integrated intervention approach. Such an approach involves more than informally linking and integrating a few community services and activities to schools. A comprehensive approach requires weaving school and community resources together and doing so in ways that formalize and institutionalize connections and share major responsibilities. Building informal linkages into substantive partnerships requires an enlightened vision, cohesive policy, creative leadership, and new and multifaceted roles for professionals (e.g., see Adelman & Taylor, 2002b, 2003).

Toward enhancing linkages, our purpose here is to share lessons learned in recent years about connecting community and school resources and outline steps for building strong connections.

What We Know

Projects across the country demonstrate how communities and schools connect to improve results for

Table 93.1 Communities and Schools Working Together

Key Resources	Web Site Access
Strengthening schools, families, and communities: Community school models (2000) by M. Blank & L. Samberg	Coalition for Community Schools http://www.communityschools.org
School–Community Partnerships: A Guide (2002)	Center for Mental Health in Schools at UCLA http://smhp.psych.ucla.edu/pdfdocs/ Partnership/scpart1.pdf
Schools report five elements for successful partnership programs (2000)	National Network of Partnership Schools http://www.csos.jhu.edu
Fostering school, family, and community involvement (2003)	Northwest Regional Educational Laboratory http://www.safetyzone.org/pdfs/ta_guides/ packet_7.pdf
School–community partnering (2001) by P. Pardini	*The School Administrator* http://www.aasa.org/publications/sa/2001_08/ pardini1.htm
Putting the pieces together: Comprehensive school-linked strategies for children and families (1996)	U.S. Department of Education http://www.ncrel.org/sdrs/areas/issues/ envrnmnt/css/ppt/putting.htm
School-linked comprehensive services for children and families (1994)	U.S. Office of Educational Research and Improvement http://eric-web.tc.columbia.edu/families/ School-Linked

youngsters, families, and neighborhoods (see references in Table 93.1). Some embrace a wide range of stakeholders, including families and community-based organizations and agencies, such as public and private health and human service agencies, schools, businesses, youth and faith organizations, institutions for postsecondary learning, and so forth.

Various levels and forms of collaboration are being tested, including statewide initiatives in California, Florida, Kentucky, Iowa, Missouri, New Jersey, Ohio, and Oregon, among others. Most of these consist of special projects to (a) coordinate and integrate programs and services, (b) improve access to health and social services, (c) expand after-school academics, recreation, and enrichment, (d) build systems of care, (e) reduce delinquency, (f) enhance transitions to work/ career/postsecondary education, and (g) enhance life in school and community. Such "experiments" are driven by diverse and overlapping

initiatives, including efforts to reform, improve, and enhance:

• schools, including restructuring student supports
• community health and social service agencies
• community schools
• youth development
• community development

As community agencies have developed connections with schools, four not mutually exclusive formats have emerged: (1) colocation of community agency personnel and services at schools— sometimes in the context of family and parent resource centers or school-based health centers financed in part by community health organizations, (2) formal linkages with agencies to enhance access and service coordination for students and families at the agency, at a nearby satellite clinic, or in a school-based or linked center,

(3) formal partnerships between community agencies and a school district to establish or expand school-based or linked facilities that include provision of services, and (4) schools contracting with community providers to offer mandated and designated student services.

No complete catalogue of school–community initiatives exists. Analyses outlining trends are summarized in the documents cited in Table 93.1. Examples include approaches designated as school-linked and coordinated services, wrap-around, one-stop shopping, full-service schools, systems of care, community schools, programs to mobilize community and social capital, and initiatives to build community policies and structures to enhance youth support, safety, recreation, work, service, and enrichment.

A reasonable inference from available data is that school–community collaborations can be successful and cost-effective over the long run. They not only improve service access but also encourage schools to open their doors and enhance opportunities for recreation, enrichment, remediation, and family involvement. Youth development initiatives, for example, expand intervention efforts beyond services and programs. They encourage a view of schools not only as community centers where families can easily access services but also as hubs for community-wide learning and activity. Federal funding for after-school programs at school sites enhances this view by expanding opportunities for recreation, enrichment, academic supports, and child care. Adult education and training at neighborhood school sites also help change the old view that schools close when the youngsters leave. Indeed, the concept of a "second shift" at school sites is beginning to spread in response to community needs and involvements.

At the same time, it has become clear that initiatives focused mainly on integrated school-linked services are too limited in scope and are producing a new form of fragmentation, counterproductive competition, and marginalization (Adelman & Taylor, 2002a). In too many instances, school-linked services result only in co-locating agency staff on school campuses. As these activities proceed, a small number of youngsters receive services, but little connection is made with school staff and programs. The tendency is to link them to schools without integrating them with a school's education support programs and the direct efforts of classroom teachers. Failure to integrate with other services and with key programs at the school probably undermines the efficacy of a service and limits its impact on academic performance. By themselves, use of health and human services is an insufficient strategy for dealing with the biggest problems confronting schools. Services are only one facet of any effort to develop the kind of comprehensive approach that can effectively address barriers to learning and enhance healthy development.

All this underscores the importance of personnel from the school and community devoting a greater proportion of their talents and time to creating a comprehensive, integrated approach (Council of Chief State School Officers, 2000; Dryfoos & Maguire, 2002; McMahon, Ward, Pruett, Davidson, & Griffith, 2000; U.S. Department of Education, 1996). This means connecting in ways that go beyond an agenda for coordinating community services and colocation. It calls for a focus on restructuring the various learning support programs and services that schools own and operate. Such broad agendas tend to reduce tension between school-based staff and their counterparts in community-based organizations. (When "outside" professionals are brought in, school district pupil services personnel often view it as discounting their skills and threatening their jobs.) Such agendas also lead policy makers to the mistaken impression that linking community resources to schools can effectively meet the needs of schools in addressing barriers to learning. In turn, this has led some legislators to view the linking of community services to schools as a way to free up the dollars underwriting school-owned services. The reality is that even when one adds together community and school assets, the total set of resources in impoverished locales is woefully inadequate. In situation after situation, it has become evident that as soon as the first few sites demonstrating school–community collaboration are in place, community agencies find they have stretched their resources to the limit. (One response to the resource problem has been to focus on providing services that can be reimbursed through third-party payments, such as Medicaid funds. However, this often results in further limiting the range of interventions and who receives them.)

What We Can Do

For community–school connections to be most beneficial, the efforts must coalesce into a comprehensive, multifaceted, and cohesive component and use all resources in the most cost-effective manner. The development and maintenance of such a component requires (1) working within the context of a comprehensive intervention framework and (2) rethinking existing infrastructure mechanisms.

A Comprehensive Intervention Framework

A comprehensive approach encompasses a full continuum of programs and services, including efforts to promote positive development, prevent problems, respond as early after onset as is feasible, and offer treatment regimens/systems of care. Physical and mental health and psychosocial concerns are a major focus of such a continuum of interventions.

For work with schools, pioneering efforts have pursued such a continuum and also synthesized and operationalized a comprehensive component consisting of six programmatic arenas (Adelman & Taylor, 2002b, 2006a, 2006b; Center for Mental Health in Schools, 2003). The result is a framework that captures the essence of the multifaceted concerns schools must address each day. The six arenas focus intervention on

- enhancing regular classroom strategies to enable learning (e.g., improving instruction for students who have become disengaged from learning at school and for those with mild to moderate learning and behavior problems)
- supporting transitions (e.g., assisting students and families as they negotiate school and grade changes and many other transitions)
- increasing home and school connections
- responding to and, where feasible, preventing crises
- increasing community involvement and support (outreach to develop greater community involvement and support, including enhanced use of volunteers)
- facilitating student and family access to effective services and special assistance as needed

Establishing a comprehensive component requires braiding together many public and private resources. To these ends, a high-priority policy commitment is required that promotes the weaving together of school and community resources to support strategic development of comprehensive approaches (see Table 93.2). In communities, the need is for better ways of connecting agency and other resources to each other and to schools. In schools, the need is for restructuring to combine parallel efforts supported by general funds, compensatory and special education entitlement, safe and drug-free school grants, and specially funded projects. In the process, efficiency and effectiveness can be achieved by connecting families of schools, such as high schools and their feeder schools, with each other and community resources. Such a strengthened policy focus allows personnel to build the continuum of interventions needed to make a significant impact in addressing the health, learning, and well-being of all youngsters through strengthening youngsters, families, schools, and neighborhoods.

Redesigning Infrastructure as a Key to Enhancing Practice

One critical facet of efforts to promote comprehensive, multifaceted, and integrated approaches involves redesigning infrastructure to maximize resources. The focus is on designing resource-oriented mechanisms to reframe how schools provide student support and how they connect with each other and with community resources. The intent is to enhance use of existing resources and evolve a comprehensive approach. In this context, all those interested in connecting with schools are called upon to adopt a broad perspective of intervention. They also are asked to invest in the development and evaluation of interventions that go beyond one-to-one and small-group approaches and that incorporate public health and primary prevention initiatives. All this requires infrastructure mechanisms that focus on optimal deployment of resources. In linking with the school, community providers can be a catalyst in stimulating redesign of existing infrastructure to establish essential resource-oriented mechanisms.

A Learning Supports Resource Team

When we suggest establishment of a learning supports resource team (previously called a resource coordinating team), some school staff quickly respond: *We already have one!* When we explore this with them, we usually find what they have is a *case-oriented team*—that is, a team that focuses on individual students who are having problems. Such a team may be called a student study team,

Table 93.2 Policy Considerations Related to Enhancing Linkages

Policy Makers Concerned With Enhancing Community–School Collaboration Need to Focus on

1. *Broadening governance.* Existing governance needs to move toward shared decision making and appropriate degrees of local control and private sector involvement. A key facet of this is guaranteeing roles and providing incentives, supports, and training for effective involvement of line staff, families, students, and other community members.

2. *Providing change teams and change agents.* Establishing effective school–community collaboration involves major systemic restructuring. Well-trained change teams and change agents are needed to carry out the daily activities of systemic change related to building essential support and redesigning processes to initiate, establish, and maintain changes over time. Moving beyond initial demonstrations requires policies and processes that ensure what often is called diffusion, replication, roll out, or scale-up. Too often, proposed systemic changes are not accompanied with the resources necessary to accomplish essential changes. Common deficiencies include inadequate strategies for creating motivational readiness among a critical mass of stakeholders, assignment of change agents with relatively little specific training in facilitating large-scale systemic change, and scheduling unrealistically short time frames for building capacity to accomplish desired institutional changes.

3. *Delineating high-level leadership assignments and underwriting essential leadership/management training.* Appropriate leaders must be designated and prepared to accept the vision for change, understand how to effect and institutionalize the changes, and know how to generate ongoing renewal.

4. *Establishing and institutionalizing resource-oriented mechanisms to promote community–school connections.* Such mechanisms encompass such functions as analyzing, planning, coordinating, integrating, monitoring, evaluating, and strengthening resource use and linkages.

5. *Building capacity.* Policy is needed to ensure resources are available to both accomplish desired system changes and enhance intervention quality over time. A key facet of this is a major investment in staff recruitment and development using well-designed and technologically sophisticated strategies for dealing with the problems of frequent turnover and diffusing information updates; another facet is an investment in technical assistance at all levels and for all aspects and stages of the work.

6. *Ensuring a sophisticated approach to accountability.* The initial emphasis needs to be on data that can help develop effective approaches for collaboration in providing interventions and a results-oriented focus on short-term benchmarks and that evolves into evaluation of long-range indicators of impact. (Here, too, technologically sophisticated and integrated management information systems are essential.)

---

student success team, student assistance team, teacher assistance team, and so forth.

To help clarify the difference between re-source- and case-oriented teams, we contrast the functions of each in Table 93.3.

Two parables help differentiate the two types of mechanisms and the importance of both sets of functions. A *case-orientation* fits the *starfish* metaphor.

> The day after a great storm had washed up all sorts of sea life far up onto the beach, a young-ster set out to throw back as many of the still-living starfish as he could. After watching him toss one after the other into the ocean, an old man approached him and said: *It's no use your doing that, there are too many, You're not going to make any difference.*
>
> The boy looked at him in surprise, then bent over, picked up another starfish, threw it in, and replied: *It made a difference to that one!*

This parable, of course, reflects all the important efforts to assist specific students.

The *resource-oriented* focus is captured by what can be called the *bridge* parable.

> In a small town, one weekend a group of school staff went fishing together down at the

Table 93.3 Contrasting Team Functions

A Case-Oriented Team	A Resource-Oriented Team
Focuses on specific *individuals* and discrete *services* to address barriers to learning	Focuses on *all* students and the *resources, programs, and systems* to address barriers to learning and promote healthy development
Sometimes called:	Possibly called:
• Child study team	• Learning supports resource team
• Student study team	• Resource coordinating team
• Student success team	• Resource coordinating council
• Student assistance team	• School support team
• Teacher assistance team	• Learning support team
• IEP team	
Examples of functions:	*Examples of functions:*
• triage	• aggregating data across students and from teachers to analyze school needs
• referral	• mapping resources
• case monitoring/management	• analyzing resources
• case progress review	• enhancing resources
• case reassessment	• program and system planning/development
	• including emphasis on establishing a full continuum of intervention
	• redeploying resources
	• coordinating and integrating resources
	• social "marketing"

river. Not long after they got there, a child came floating down the rapids calling for help. One of the group on the shore quickly dived in and pulled the child out. Minutes later another, then another, and then many more children were coming down the river. Soon every one was diving in and dragging children to the shore and then jumping back in to save as many as they could. In the midst of all this frenzy, one of the group was seen walking away. Her colleagues were irate. How could she leave when there were so many children to save? After long hours, to everyone's relief, the flow of children stopped, and the group could finally catch their breath.

At that moment, their colleague came back. They turned on her and angrily shouted: *How could you walk off when we needed everyone here to save the children?*

She replied: *It occurred to me that someone ought to go upstream and find out why so many kids were falling into the river. What I found is that the old wooden bridge had several planks missing, and when some children tried to jump over the gap, they couldn't make it and fell through into the river. So I got someone to fix the bridge.*

Fixing and building better bridges is a good way to think about prevention, and it helps underscore the importance of taking time to improve and enhance resources, programs, and systems.

Contrasting functions differentiate the two separate teams. However, one team carefully separating the two agendas can do the work, since the talents of many of the same individuals will be called upon (e.g., a school social worker, school psychologist, counselor, nurse, behavioral specialist, special education teacher, a school administrator, and representatives from the community).

In sum, a resource-oriented team is needed to take charge of school resources used for learning support programs and systems and for weaving these together in strategic ways with community resources (Adelman, 1996; Lim & Adelman, 1997; Rosenblum, DiCecco, Taylor, & Adelman, 1995). It is a key element in managing and enhancing programs and systems in ways that integrate and strengthen interventions and connect community and school. The effectiveness of such a mechanism depends on how well it is integrated into a school's decision making.

A Resource-Oriented Mechanism for a Family of Schools

Schools in the same neighborhood or geographic area have a number of shared concerns, and schools in the feeder pattern often interact with students from the same family. Some school programs and personnel and community resources can be shared by several neighboring schools, thereby minimizing redundancy and reducing costs. A mechanism connecting schools can help ensure cohesive and equitable deployment of resources and also can enhance the pooling of resources to reduce costs. Such a mechanism can be particularly useful for integrating the efforts of high schools, their feeder middle and elementary schools, and community resources. This clearly is important in addressing barriers with those families who have youngsters attending more than one level of schooling in the same cluster or feeder pattern. It is neither cost-effective nor good intervention for several schools separately to contact the same family in instances where several children from the family need special attention. With respect to linking with community resources, a resource-oriented mechanism connecting a family of schools and its surrounding community is especially attractive to community agencies that

often do not have the time or personnel to make independent arrangements with every school. Such a mechanism can provide leadership, facilitate communication and connection, and ensure quality improvement across schools. For example, a complex learning supports resource *council* might consist of representatives from the high school and its feeder middle and elementary schools. It brings together one to two representatives from each school's resource *team*, along with community representatives (see Figure 93.1).

A mechanism such as a learning supports resource *council* helps (a) coordinate and integrate programs serving multiple schools, (b) identify and meet common needs with respect to guidelines and staff development, and (c) create linkages and collaborations among schools and with community agencies. In this last regard, it can play a special role in community outreach both to create formal working relationships and ensure that all participating schools have access to such resources. Natural starting points for councils are the sharing of need assessments, resource mapping, analyses, and recommendations for reform and restructuring. An initial focus may be on local, high-priority concerns, such as developing prevention programs and safe school plans to address community–school violence.

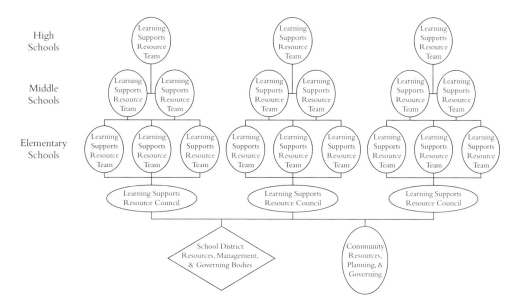

Figure 93.1. Resource-Oriented Mechanisms Across a Family of Schools

About Leadership and Infrastructure

It is clear that building a comprehensive component linking community and school requires strong leadership and new roles and functions to help steer systemic changes and construct the necessary infrastructure. Establishment and maintenance of the component requires continuous, effective teaming, organization, and accountability.

Administrative leadership at every level is key to the success of any initiative in schools that involves systemic change (Adelman & Taylor, 2006a). It is imperative that such leadership is at a high enough level to be at key decision-making tables when budget and other fundamental decisions are discussed. Besides facilitating initial development of a potent component, the administrative leaders must guide and be accountable for daily implementation, monitoring, and problem solving.

Establishing Resource-Oriented Teams and Councils

Guides to establishing resource teams and councils are listed in the Tools and Practice Examples section. To provide a sense of what is involved, Table 93.4 shows a benchmark checklist that outlines basic phases and steps. Review that checklist now. Below we underscore a few other points. And, in chapter 95, we discuss mapping the school's resources.

Building Infrastructure From Localities Outward

To ensure that interventions are implemented at the school level, it is a good idea to conceive from localities outward. The focus, first, is on mechanisms at the school–neighborhood level. Then, based on analyses of what is needed to facilitate and enhance efforts at a school, mechanisms are conceived that enable several school–neighborhood collaborations to work together to increase efficiency and effectiveness and achieve economies of scale. Then, system-wide mechanisms can be redesigned to provide support for what each locality is trying to develop.

Building Capacity

A redesigned infrastructure involves systemic changes. Systemic changes require policy support, leadership, capacity building, and nurturing. As stressed in Tables 93.2 and 93.4, policy is needed to ensure resources are available to both accomplish desired systemic changes and enhance intervention quality over time. A key facet of this is a major investment in staff recruitment and development using well-designed and technologically sophisticated strategies for dealing with the problems of frequent staff turnover and diffusing information updates (Adelman & Taylor, 2006b). Another facet is an investment in technical assistance at all levels and for all aspects and stages of the work. (Tools and resources to aid in capacity building are highlighted in the following section.)

A Caveat

In building a comprehensive, multifaceted component, teams will be confronted by the complementary challenges surrounding the needs for *evidence-based strategies* and *demonstrating results*. These matters must be addressed in ways that enhance rather than hinder development of a comprehensive component for system-wide effectiveness. The dilemma arises because of the limited nature and scope of interventions that currently have strong research support. The best (not always to be equated with good) evidence-based strategies for identifying and working with student problems are for a small number of non-comorbid disorders. Clearly, before such narrow-band strategies are seen as the answer, they must be widely implemented in community and school settings, and they must generate data that demonstrate broad impact and enhanced cost-effectiveness.

Tools and Practice Examples

Resource-oriented mechanisms are a key to establishing and sustaining effective community–school connections. Thus, community entities should focus on helping to create such mechanisms. At each site, key stakeholders and their leadership must understand and commit to restructuring, and the commitment must be reflected in policy statements and capacity building.

The checklist in Table 93.4 is designed to aid those involved in the process of organizing at a

Table 93.4 Benchmark Checklist: Steps in Establishing a Learning Supports Resource Team and Council

Site Name	Date Started	Date Completed	Current Status
I. ORIENTATION AND CREATING READINESS			
A. Building interest and consensus for developing a comprehensive component and reframing infrastructure			
B. Introducing basic ideas to relevant stakeholders			
(1) "Social marketing" strategies used to introduce basic ideas and relevant research base to key stakeholders • administrators • staff • parent representatives • business and community stakeholders			
(2) Opportunities for interchange provided and additional in-depth presentations made to build a critical mass of consensus for systemic changes			
(3) Ongoing evaluation indicates a critical mass of stakeholders are ready to pursue a policy commitment			
(4) Ratification and sponsorship by critical mass of stakeholders			
C. Establishing policy commitment and framework (follow-up meetings with decision makers to clarify the dimensions of the work and agree on how to proceed)			
(1) Negotiation of policy commitment and conditions for engagement (e.g., high-level policy established and assurance of leadership commitment for developing a comprehensive component and related resource-oriented mechanisms)			
(2) Policy translated into vision, a framework, and a strategic plan that phase in changes using a realistic time line			
(3) Policy translated into appropriate resource allocations (leadership, staff, space, budget, time for change agents and staff to work together)			

(continued)

Table 93.4 (*Continued*)

Site Name	Date Started	Date Completed	Current Status
(4) Incentives for change established (e.g., intrinsically valued outcomes, expectations for success, recognitions, rewards)			
(5) Procedural options established that reflect stakeholder strengths and from them those expected to implement change can select strategies they see as workable			
(6) Infrastructure and processes established for facilitating change efforts			
(7) Change agent(s) identified—indicate name(s) below			
(8) Initial capacity building—essential skills developed among stakeholders to begin implementation			
(9) Benchmarks used to provide feedback on progress and to make necessary improvements in creating readiness			
D. Development of specific start-up and phase-in plan			
II. START-UP AND PHASE-IN			
A. Identification of a site leader assigned to ensure development of a comprehensive component and related resource-oriented mechanisms Name: Position:			
B. Leadership and systemic change training for all who take a lead in developing the component and new infrastructure			
C. ESTABLISH RESOURCE-ORIENTED MECHANISM (e.g., learning supports resource team)			
(1) Make the case and start with schools that indicate readiness (After initial presentations have been made to potential school sites, elicit responses regarding possible interest)			
(2) At sites that are highly interested in proceeding, clarify processes and potential outcomes			
(3) Identification of potential team members			

(continued)

Table 93.4 (*Continued*)

Site Name	Date Started	Date Completed	Current Status
(4) Recruitment of team members. Name: Position:			
(5) Meet with key individuals at the site to discuss their role and functions as leaders for the intended systemic changes (e.g., meet with the site administrative leader who has been designated for this role; meet with each person who will initially be part of a resource team)			
(6) Before having the first team meeting, work with individuals to clarify specific roles and functions for making the group effective (e.g., Who will be the meeting facilitator? time keeper? record keeper?). Provide whatever training is needed to ensure that these groups are ready and able to work productively			
(7) Initial team meeting			
(8) Ongoing training and nurturing of team. It may take several meetings before a group functions well. A change agent can help them coalesce into a working group			
D. INITIAL MAPPING AND ANALYSIS OF EXISTING RESOURCES			
(1) Initial mapping—The group's first substantive task is to map learning support resources at the site (programs, services, "who's who," schedules—don't forget recreation and enrichment activities such as those brought to or linked with the school). The mapping should also clarify the systems used to ensure that staff, parents, and students learn about and gain access to these resources. The group should plan to update all of above as changes are made			
(2) Initial analyses (of needs, gaps, efficacy, coordination)—Mapping is followed by an analysis of what's worth maintaining and what should be shelved so that resources can be redeployed. Then, the focus shifts to planning to enhance and expand in ways that better address barriers to learning and promote healthy development. (What don't we have that we need? Do we have people/programs that could be more effective if used in other ways? Do we have too much in one area, not enough in others? major gaps?)			

(continued)

Table 93.4 (*Continued*)

Site Name	Date Started	Date Completed	Current Status
(3) Initial plans and steps to improve existing activity and move on in developing a comprehensive component—It helps if the focus initially is on doing some highly visible things that can pay off quickly. Such products generate a sense that system improvement is feasible and allows an early sense of accomplishment. It also can generate some excitement and increase the commitment and involvement of others			
(4) Initial maps and plans distributed—It helps if the resource maps and plans are organized into a delineated set of intervention arenas, rather than a "laundry list"			
E. REFINING INFRASTRUCTURE AND PURSUING DEEPER MAPPING AND ANALYSES			
(1) Standing work groups developed for designated intervention arenas—These work groups go into depth in mapping and analyzing resources related to each designated arena of intervention and formulate initial recommendations for enhancing interventions and related systems			
(2) Ad hoc work groups developed to enhance component visibility, communication, sharing, and problem solving			
(3) Training of area work groups Specify areas:			
F. ESTABLISH A RESOURCE-ORIENTED MECHANISM FOR THE FEEDER PATTERN OF SCHOOLS AND LOCAL COMMUNITY (e.g., a learning supports resource council) AND TRAIN THOSE WHO STAFF IT			
(1) Identification of representatives to the council (specify)			
(2) Training for council members			
(3) Initial meeting			
(4) Ongoing training and nurturance of council			

(continued)

Table 93.4 (*Continued*)

Site Name	Date Started	Date Completed	Current Status
(5) Council works on filling program/service gaps and pursuing economies of scale through outreach designed to establish formal collaborative linkages with other schools in the feeder pattern and with district-wide and community resources			
G. SYSTEM FOR QUALITY IMPROVEMENT AND EVALUATION OF IMPACT			
(1) Decisions about indicators to be used			
(2) Indicate those responsible for quality improvement and impact evaluation processes Name: Position:			
(3) Training of those responsible for processes			
(4) Initial quality improvement recommendations Made. Acted upon.			
(5) Initial impact evaluation report and recommendations			
III. MAINTENANCE AND EVOLUTION			
IV. PLANS FOR ONGOING RENEWAL			
A. Indications of planning for maintenance			
(1) Policy commitments			
(2) Regular budget allocations			
(3) Ongoing administrative leadership			
(4) A key facet of school improvement plans			
B. Strategies in use for maintaining momentum/progress (sustainability) (List most prominent examples)			
C. Strategies in use and future plans for generating renewal (List most prominent examples)			

site and establishing coordination among multiple sites in the same locale. It was developed as a formative evaluation tool to aid planning and implementation. The items should be modified to fit local strategic and action plans.

Guides to Aid Practice

Specific guides and tools have been created by the Center for Mental Health in Schools at UCLA to aid development and sustainability of school–community connections. These are packaged in a variety of resource documents. Following is a brief description of the major resources and how to access them (at no cost) on the Internet.

- *Resource-Oriented Teams: Key Infrastructure Mechanisms for Enhancing Supports.* Describes resource-oriented mechanisms designed to ensure schools systematically address how they use resources for addressing barriers to student learning and promoting health development. (http://smhp.psych.ucla.edu/pdfdocs/contedu /developing_resource_oriented-mechanisms .pdf)
- *Introduction to a Component for Addressing Barriers to Learning.* A brief overview of the needs for a component that supports learning. Useful in clarifying the "big picture" for all stakeholders. (http://smhp.psych.ucla.edu/pdfdocs/briefs/ introductionbrief.pdf)
- *Organization Facilitators: A Change Agent for Systemic School and Community Changes.* Outlines the roles and functions of a change agent to guide, support, and sustain systemic changes (http://smhp.psych.ucla.edu/pdfdocs/Report/ orgfacrep.pdf).
- *Addressing Barriers to Learning: A Set of Surveys to Map What a School Has and Needs.* Provides surveys to use as tools in the process of building a collaborative team with a shared vision for a school. Explores the systems in place at a school and focuses on six program arenas to promote what is already occurring and generate enthusiasm for expanding programs for prevention and early interventions related to (1) classrooms, (2) support for transitions, (3) home involvement in schooling, (4) community outreach for involvement and support, (5) crisis assistance and prevention, and (6) student and family assistance programs

and services. (http://smhp.psych.ucla.edu/ pdfdocs/Surveys/ Set1.pdf)
- *Sustaining School–Community Partnerships to Enhance Outcomes for Children & Youth.* Outlines phases and steps and provides a variety of tools to use in strategic efforts to plan, implement, sustain, and go to scale. (http://smhp.psych. ucla.edu/pdfdocs/sustaining.pdf)

Other useful guides and tools are provided through the *Community Tool Box* (http://ctb.lsi .ukans.edu/). This site, created in 1995 by the University of Kansas Work Group on Health Promotion and Community Development in Lawrence, Kansas, and AHEC/Community Partners in Amherst, Massachusetts, continues to grow weekly. Currently, the core is "how-to tools" (including tools for mapping). For instance, there are sections on leadership, strategic planning, community assessment, advocacy, grant writing, and evaluation.

Key Points to Remember

Fulfilling the promise of community and school collaboration requires:

- *eliciting a policy commitment*—one that supports community and school linkages for development of comprehensive approaches to addressing barriers to learning and development and promoting healthy development
- *adopting a comprehensive framework for intervention*—encompassing (a) a continuum ranging from efforts to promote positive development, prevent problems, and respond as early after onset as is feasible, through treatment regimens/systems of care and (b) a well-delineated programmatic approach to addressing the multifaceted concerns confronting schools each day
- *redesigning infrastructure*—establishing resource-oriented mechanisms from the locality outward and focused on weaving together community and school resources to support the strategic development of comprehensive approaches, sustaining linkages, and generating renewal
- *designing systemic change*—planning change strategically and using well-trained change agents

References

Adelman, H. S. (1996). Restructuring education support services and integrating community resources: Beyond the full service school model. *School Psychology Review, 25,* 431–445.

Adelman, H. S., & Taylor, L. (2002a). *Impediments to enhancing availability of mental health services in schools: Fragmentation, overspecialization, counterproductive competition, and marginalization.* Paper commissioned by the National Association of School Psychologists and the ERIC Clearinghouse on Counseling and Student Services (ERIC/CASS). Published by the *ERIC/CASS Clearinghouse.* Accessible on Internet from http://ericcass.uncg.edu/whatnew.html

Adelman, H. S., & Taylor. L. (2002b). So you want higher achievement scores? Its time to rethink learning supports. In *The State Education Standard* (pp. 52–56). Alexandria, VA: National Association of State Boards of Education.

Adelman, H. S., & Taylor, L. (2003). Creating school and community partnerships for substance abuse prevention programs. *Journal of Primary Prevention, 23,* 331–371.

Adelman, H. S., & Taylor, L. (2006a). *The school leader's guide to student learning supports: New directions for addressing barriers to learning.* Thousand Oaks, CA: Corwin.

Adelman, H.S., & Taylor, L. (2006b). *The implementation guide to student learning supports in the classroom and schoolwide: New directions for addressing barriers to learning.* Thousand Oaks, CA: Corwin.

Center for Mental Health in Schools. (2002). *School-community partnership: A guide.* Los Angeles: Author. Retrieved on August 1, 2005, from http://smhp.psych.ucla.edu/pdfdocs/Partnership/scpart1.pdf

Center for Mental Health in Schools. (2003). *Where's it happening: New directions for student support.* Los Angeles: Author. Retrieved on August 1, 2005, from http://smhp.psych.ucla.edu/pdfdocs/wheresithappening/overview.pdf

Council of Chief State School Officers. (2000). *Extended learning initiatives: Opportunities and implementation challenges.* Washington, DC: Author.

Dryfoos, J., & Maguire, S. (2002). *Inside full-service community schools.* Thousand Oaks, CA: Corwin.

Franklin, C., & Streeter, C. L. (1995). School reform: Linking public schools with human services. *Social Work, 40,* 773–782.

Honig, M. I., Kahne, J., & McLaughlin, M. W. (2001). School–community connections: Strengthening opportunity to learn and opportunity to teach. In V. Richardson (Ed.), *Handbook of research on teaching* (4th ed., pp. 998–1028). Washington, DC: American Educational Research Association.

Kretzmann, J. (1998). *Community-based development and local schools: A promising partnership.* Evanston, IL: Institute for Policy Research.

Kretzmann, J., & McKnight, J. (1993). *Building communities from the inside out: A path toward finding and mobilizing a community's assets.* Chicago: ACTA.

Lim, C., & Adelman, H. S. (1997). Establishing school-based collaborative teams to coordinate resources: A case study. *Social Work in Education, 19,* 266–277.

McMahon, T., Ward, N., Pruett, M., Davidson, L., & Griffith, E. (2000) Building full-service schools: Lessons learned in the development of interagency collaboratives. *Journal of Educational and Psychological Consultation, 11,* 65–92.

Melaville, A., & Blank, M. J. (1998). *Learning together: The developing field of school–community initiatives.* Flint, MI: Mott Foundation.

Rosenblum, L., DiCecco, M. B., Taylor, L., & Adelman, H. S. (1995). Upgrading school support programs through collaboration: Resource coordinating teams. *Social Work in Education, 17,* 117–124.

Southwest Regional Educational Laboratory. (2001). *Emerging issues in school, family, & community connections: Annual synthesis.* Austin, TX: Author.

Taylor, L., & Adelman, H. S. (2003). School–community relations: Policy and practice. In M. Fishbaugh, T. Berkeley, & G. Schroth (Eds.), *Ensuring safe school environments: Exploring issues—seeking solutions* (pp. 107–132). Mahwah, NJ: Lawrence Erlbaum.

Taylor, L., & Adelman, H. S. (2004). Advancing mental health in schools: Guiding frameworks and strategic approaches. In K. Robinson (Ed.), *Advances in school-based mental health: Best practices and program models* (pp. 2-1–2-20). Kingston, NJ: Civic Research Institute.

U.S. Department of Education. (1996). *Putting the pieces together: Comprehensive school-linked strategies for children and families.* Washington, DC: Author.

Teacher and Principal Consultations: Best Practices

Craig A. Albers ▪ Thomas R. Kratochwill

CHAPTER 94

Getting Started

At a time when a significant number of children are considered to be at risk for academic, behavioral, and social-emotional difficulties, schools are viewed as a location to address these issues through the provision of comprehensive intervention services. Illustrating the extent to which schools currently provide these services, Burns and colleagues (1995) presented data indicating that up to 80% of children's mental health services are provided within the school setting. Legislation, such as the Individuals with Disabilities Act of 2004, places emphasis on meeting the needs of students with disabilities in the regular education classroom as well as requiring interventions prior to considering eligibility for special education services. Additionally, multitiered intervention models are being advocated as a method of providing early intervention services along a continuum in which a student's needs determine the level of services that are provided. These factors indicate the necessity of having a service delivery model that allows for the provision of services in an efficient, yet cost-effective manner. The provision of services through consultation has the potential to meet these requirements.

What We Know

The effectiveness of the consultative process has been well documented within educational settings. For example, school social workers, school psychologists, special education teachers, speech-language pathologists, and school counselors have all used various consultation models within the school setting. Additionally, teachers and administrators frequently prefer collaboration and consultation with educational professionals as a method of addressing concerns (Curtis & Zins, 1988). When paired with quality interventions, consultation has effectively been used to address academic difficulties (e.g., Galloway & Sheridan, 1994), behaviors related to attention deficit hyperactivity disorder (e.g., Dunson, Hughes, & Jackson, 1994), social skills deficits and withdrawn children (e.g., Sheridan, Kratochwill, & Elliott, 1990), irrational fears (Sheridan & Colton, 1994), and disruptive behaviors (e.g., Wilkinson, 1997), among others. The use of consultation has consistently resulted in positive outcomes (Sheridan, Welch, & Orme, 1996) and has been identified as one of three interventions with empirical support (Hoagwood & Erwin, 1997).

Consultation is an indirect service delivery model in which a consultant (e.g., school psychologist, counselor, social worker) works with a consultee (e.g., teachers, administrators, paraprofessionals, parents), with the desired outcome being a change in the client's (e.g., student's) behavior. Consultation within the school setting is designed to resolve the student's immediate problem, while providing the consultee with the necessary skills to deal with similar issues in the future, which is a form of prevention (Elliott & Sheridan, 1992). Because of its indirect nature and secondary goal of increasing consultee's skills for dealing with similar difficulties in the future, consultation is considered to be a cost-effective model of service delivery.

What We Can Do

A wide variety of consultation models are available for consultants to utilize. The more common consultative models include behavioral, clinical, collaborative, conjoint behavioral, instructional, mental health, and organizational development models. Educational professionals within the school setting will likely embrace different consultative models depending on their theoretical perspectives, the type of problem being addressed, and the preferences of the consultee. Despite the wide variety of consultative models, all share certain characteristics:

- They utilize an indirect service delivery format
- They have remediation and prevention as goals
- They share similar viewpoints regarding the consultant–consultee relationship
- They utilize a problem-solving process (Gutkin & Curtis, 1999; Kratochwill & Pittman, 2002)

The consultant–consultee relationship is considered to be collaborative and voluntary and can be ended by the consultee at any time. Furthermore, since the consultee is encouraged to be an active participant, any suggestions provided by the consultant can be rejected. All the models require the consultant to have strong interpersonal skills, such as showing respect for the consultee and being trustworthy, approachable, encouraging, and pleasant (Knoff & Hines, 1995). A consultant should also be an active listener and effective facilitator.

Problem-Solving Consultation

An in-depth review of the various consultation models is beyond the scope of this chapter; readers are referred to the recommended readings for additional information. Although all of the consultation models have a literature base examining their theoretical and empirical foundations, the behavioral consultation model has been extensively examined within the school setting and is supported by empirical research. Consequently, this chapter presents an overview of the behavioral model of consultation, recently refined and renamed as *problem-solving consultation* (e.g., Kratochwill, Elliott, & Stoiber, 2002). As outlined by Kratochwill and colleagues, problem-solving consultation consists of a series of five stages: (1) entry and development of a

relationship, (2) problem identification, (3) problem analysis, (4) plan implementation, and (5) plan evaluation. Table 94.1 provides an overview of the stages within the problem-solving consultation process.

Stage 1: Development of a Consultative Relationship

The development of a consultative relationship begins well before a teacher or administrator approaches the consultant with an issue. The astute consultant will have an understanding of the school climate, such as the philosophy of the principal regarding discipline-related issues, school characteristics, teacher-related factors, and the history of prior consultative-related services that may or may not have been successful. Resistance, which is considered a natural process within consultation that impedes the problem-solving process, can result from four different sources: (a) perceptions that the plan will be ineffective, (b) a lack of knowledge regarding how to implement the plan, (c) a lack of skills to implement the plan, and (d) incompatibility between the consultee's viewpoints and the corresponding intervention plan (Mendoza, 1993). Having an understanding of the common sources of resistance and the underlying dynamics of the school system will help the school-based consultant be prepared prior to entering into a consultative relationship with an administrator or educator. Efforts to enhance the consultative relationship should continue throughout all stages of the consultative process.

Stage 2: Problem Identification

The goal of the problem identification stage is to collect information that documents if a discrepancy exists between actual and desired performance. Information is primarily collected during a meeting with the consultee. For the first-time consultee, it is beneficial to describe the process of consultation. Once the discrepancy is clarified, a plan should be formulated to collect additional information to serve as a baseline regarding levels of performance and to identify contributing factors. After finalizing a data collection plan, the consultant should provide a summary of the meeting and schedule a *problem analysis* meeting.

Stage 3: Problem Analysis

The problem analysis meeting is designed to identify factors contributing to the problem. "Admiration" of the problem should be avoided, with efforts instead focused on what needs to occur to decrease the discrepancy between actual and desired performance. Information regarding what occurs immediately prior to, during, and following the problem may provide additional information regarding what is maintaining the problem. One method of identifying the function of a behavior is to conduct a *functional behavioral assessment*, which is designed to identify functional relationships between problem behaviors and environmental variables (e.g., Crone & Horner, 2003). Once an understanding of the contributing factors relating to the problem is obtained, the focus can shift to developing an intervention plan. Interventions that have a high degree of acceptability should be considered for implementation. *Acceptability*, which refers to the degree that the consultee agrees with the intervention plan, can be enhanced by selecting interventions that (a) are positive as compared to punitive, (b) are less complex, (c) require a reasonable amount of time and resources, and (d) are perceived to be effective (Elliott, 1988).

Stage 4: Plan Implementation

After selecting an acceptable intervention, the plan is implemented. To increase the likelihood of success, three factors need to be considered. First, the steps of the plan need to be clearly defined, and the consultee needs to have the necessary skills to implement the plan. If these skills are lacking, the consultant should work with the consultee to ensure that they obtain the prerequisite skills. Second, a data collection plan should be developed. And third, if data collected while the plan is being implemented indicate that the plan is not resulting in the desired outcomes, the consultant and consultee should return to earlier stages of the process, making sure that the problem is clearly defined and that an appropriate intervention plan was selected.

Stage 5: Plan Evaluation

Plan evaluation focuses on examining data collected during the implementation phase. The consultant and consultee determine whether the intervention should be (a) continued to maintain the desired performance, (b) modified to maintain or increase the desired behavior, or (c) discontinued as the problem behavior is unlikely to reoccur. Finally, a plan should be formulated to monitor whether the problem resurfaces in the future. At the conclusion of the process, the consultant should reinforce the consultee for efforts that were made to resolve the problem, with additional encouragement provided to the consultee to engage in consultation should any additional problems arise in the future.

Tools and Practice Examples

The Problem-Solving Consultation Process: A Case Study

The case study presented is an overview of the problem-solving consultation process utilized by a school psychologist. However, the consultative process is similar whether the consultant is a school psychologist, social worker, school counselor, or any other related school service provider.

Stage 1: Development of a Consultative Relationship

The school psychologist in this case study worked in an elementary school that encouraged consultation between teachers and other school-based professionals. As part of this consultative process, the school psychologist met with the principal on a weekly basis to discuss any concerns that the principal had regarding the school. For example, the principal had recently shared her concerns regarding the lack of classroom management strategies in some of the inexperienced teachers' classrooms. Following the meeting with the principal, a third-grade classroom teacher who had 2 years of teaching experience approached the school psychologist to express her concerns regarding the behavior of a student in her classroom. A meeting designed to explore the teacher's concern was scheduled. To prepare for the meeting, the classroom teacher was asked to compile a list of behaviors that were considered problematic.

Table 94.1 Stages and Recommended Activities in the Problem-Solving Consultation Process

	Stages of Consultation	*Typical Activities*
Stage 1	Development of consultative relationship	• Establish rapport and organize materials • Plan initial meeting/collect background information
Stage 2	Problem identification	• Determine whether discrepancy exists • Provide a clear, objective definition of the problem • Collect additional information • Summarize the meeting
Stage 3	Problem analysis	• Identify what the problem is/what the problem is not • Identify what factors are contributing to the problem • Have the consultee specify what he or she would like to see • Generate possible interventions
Stage 4	Plan implementation	• Determine how to evaluate outcomes • Make sure the consultee has the skills to implement the plan • Implement the plan and monitor progress
Stage 5	Plan evaluation	• Evaluate the progress and process • If effective, plan for maintenance and follow-up • If not effective, revert back to earlier stage

Stage 2: Problem Identification

The psychologist and classroom teacher met the next day. After establishing rapport with the classroom teacher, the psychologist described the consultative process, indicating that they were going to work together to identify and define the behavior concerns and then develop an intervention plan. The teacher was informed that the consultative process was voluntary; consequently, she had the right to disagree with the plan and could terminate the consultative process at any point. The teacher indicated that the student had a difficult time getting started on assignments; instead of beginning on the assigned task, he tended to walk around the classroom and talk with his classmates. His assignment completion rate was less than 70%, which was below her expected completion rate of at least 90%. According to the teacher, when the student began working immediately, his performance on the assignments was quite acceptable, as were his quiz and test scores. She added that his lower grades were simply the result of not completing the assignments as required. At this point, the psychologist and classroom teacher agreed that the student's actual performance was less than the desired performance. The meeting concluded with the teacher agreeing to monitor the student's work completion rates for the next week, while the psychologist

agreed to conduct observations in the classroom as a way of collecting baseline data. A problem analysis meeting was scheduled for the following week.

Stage 3: Problem Analysis

Prior to the problem analysis meeting, classroom observations were conducted at various times throughout the day. These observations supported the difficulties as described by the classroom teacher; however, it was also noted that many of the students in the classroom had difficulties transitioning to new activities once entering the classroom, specifically at the beginning of the day and following lunch. The apparent need for classroom management strategies was consistent with information shared by the principal in her weekly meetings with the psychologist.

During the meeting, the psychologist and teacher examined the data and agreed that the student's difficulty was the result of a performance deficit. The teacher was asked to think about when these problems occurred and whether other students had similar difficulties. She indicated that while other students had difficulties transitioning between tasks, the student she referred for consultation was having the greatest difficulties, and thus she felt it was appropriate to address his needs first. She also noticed that these behaviors oc-curred classwide when students returned to the classroom following outside activities, such as lunch, recess, or art class. Consequently, she felt that maybe a plan could be developed to use with other students as well.

Stage 4: Plan Implementation

At this point, the psychologist offered a couple of intervention possibilities. First, he suggested that they could develop an intervention, imple-ment it with the referred student, and if it was successful, try it with other students. Alterna-tively, they could try to develop a plan that the teacher could use with the entire classroom. After the teacher expressed interest regarding a classroom-wide program, the psychologist and teacher began developing a plan that would per-mit students to have a period of time to calm down upon entering the classroom. It was also agreed that a group contingency plan would be put into place that would reinforce students, but only if the entire classroom transitioned effi-ciently between activities. Finally, the teacher agreed to provide additional reinforcement to the referred student to encourage the comple-tion of assignments.

Since the teacher indicated that the developed plan was acceptable to her, methods of data col-lection were discussed. The teacher indicated that she would simply use a timer and record the tran-sition times between activities, as well as continu-ing to record work completion rates. Assignment completion rates from the previous 3 weeks were used as baseline data. The psychologist and teacher agreed to meet in 4 weeks to review the data and determine whether the plan needed to be modi-fied. The psychologist offered to conduct addi-tional observations prior to that meeting, which the teacher readily agreed to.

Stage 5: Plan Evaluation

The psychologist and teacher met 4 weeks later to review the data. Information collected by the teacher, as well as information obtained by the psychologist during observations, indicated that the intervention was working well as the transi-tion times for the entire classroom had decreased. Additionally, the targeted student had increased his work completion rates to over 90%. As an in-dicator of her satisfaction, the teacher asked the psychologist if he would be willing to work with her regarding some other issues that were occur-ring within the classroom setting. The psycholo-gist indicated he would welcome the opportunity, and another meeting was scheduled for the fol-lowing week, with the goals of continuing to evaluate the maintenance of effects of the cur-rent intervention, as well as beginning the con-sultative process for the other issues raised by the teacher.

Resources

Bergan, J. R., & Kratochwill, T. R. (1990). *Behavioral consultation and therapy*. New York: Plenum.

Erchul, W. P., & Martens, B. K. (2002). *School consultation: Conceptual and empirical bases of practice* (2nd ed.). New York: Kluwer/Plenum.

Gutkin, T. B., & Curtis, M. J. (1999). School-based consultation theory and practice: The art and science of indirect service delivery. In C. R. Reynolds & T. B. Gutkin (Eds.), *The handbook of school psychology* (3rd ed., pp. 598–637). New York: John Wiley & Sons.

Kratochwill, T. R., & Bergan, J. R. (1990). *Behavioral consultation in applied settings: An individual guide*. New York: Plenum.

Kratochwill, T. R., Elliott, S. N., & Stoiber, K. C. (2002). Best practices in school-based problem-solving consultation. In A. Thomas & J. Grimes (Eds.), *Best practices in school psychology—IV* (pp. 583–608). Washington, DC: NASP.

Sheridan, S. M., Kratochwill, T. R., & Bergan, J. (1996). *Conjoint behavioral consultation: A procedural manual*. New York: Plenum.

Sladeczek, I. E., Kratochwill, T. R., Steinbach, C. L., Kumke, P., & Hagermoser, L. (2003). Problem-solving consultation in the new millennium. In E. Cole & J. A. Siegel (Eds.), *Effective consultation in school psychology* (2nd ed., pp. 60–86). Ashland, OH: Hogrefe & Huber.

Zins, J. E., & Erchul, W. P. (2002). Best practices in school consultation. In A. Thomas & J. Grimes (Eds.), *Best practices in school psychology—IV* (pp. 625–643). Washington, DC: NASP.

Key Points to Remember

As indicated in the case example, consultation provides a framework for addressing various is-sues that arise within the educational setting. Not only can consultation focus on specific student issues, but it can also focus on classroom, as well as schoolwide, processes. Since a secondary goal of consultation is to increase the skills of the consultee so that he or she can deal with similar issues in the future, consultation is also conceptualized as a preventive process. In summary, school-based practitioners should consider the following points when consulting with teachers and principals:

- Consultation provides an alternative to providing direct, one-on-one services (e.g., therapy, counseling).
- Numerous models of consultation exist. However, all models utilize an indirect service delivery format, are designed to resolve the referral concern and increase the skills of the consultee to deal with similar problems in the future, and view the consultant–consultee relationship as collaborative and voluntary.
- Effective consultants demonstrate appropriate interpersonal and problem-solving skills and have a knowledge base regarding the consultative process and corresponding interventions.
- Problem-solving consultation consists of a series of five stages: (1) development of a consultative relationship, (2) problem identification, (3) problem analysis, (4) plan implementation, and (5) plan evaluation. The stages can be revisited at any point if necessary.

References

Burns, B. J., Costello, J. E., Angold, A., Tweed, D., Stangl, D., Farmer, E. M. Z., & Erkanli, A. (1995). Children's mental health service use across service sectors. *Health Affairs, 14,* 148–159.

Crone, D. A., & Horner, R. H. (2003). *Building positive behavior support systems in schools: Functional behavior assessment.* New York: Guilford Press.

Curtis, M. J., & Zins, J. E. (1988). Effects of training in consultation and instructor feedback on acquisition of consultation skills. *Journal of School Psychology, 26,* 185–190.

Dunson, R. M., Hughes, J. N., & Jackson, T. W. (1994). Effect of behavioral consultation on student and teacher behavior. *Journal of School Psychology, 32,* 247–266.

Elliott, S. N. (1988). Acceptability of behavioral treatments: Review of variables that influence treatment selection. *Professional Psychology: Research and Practice, 19,* 68–80.

Elliott, S. N., & Sheridan, S. M. (1992). Consultation and teaming: Problem solving among educators, parents, and support personnel. *Elementary School Journal, 92,* 315–338.

Galloway, J., & Sheridan, S. M. (1994). Implementing scientific practices through case studies: Examples using home-school intervention and consultation. *Journal of School Psychology, 32,* 385–413.

Gutkin, T. B., & Curtis, M. J. (1999). School-based consultation theory and practice: The art and science of indirect service delivery. In C. R. Reynolds & T. B. Gutkin (Eds.), *The handbook of school psychology* (3rd ed., pp. 598–637). New York: John Wiley & Sons.

Hoagwood, K., & Erwin, H. D. (1997). Effectiveness of school-based mental health services for children: A 10-year research review. *Journal of Child and Family Studies, 6,* 435–451.

Knoff, H. M., & Hines, C. V. (1995). Finalizing the consultant effectiveness scale: An analysis and validation of the characteristics of effective consultants. *School Psychology Review, 24,* 480–496.

Kratochwill, T. R., Elliott, S. N., & Stoiber, K. C. (2002). Best practices in school-based problem-solving consultation. In A. Thomas, & J. Grimes (Eds.), *Best practices in school psychology—IV* (pp. 583–608). Washington, DC: NASP.

Kratochwill, T. R., & Pittman, P. H. (2002). Expanding problem-solving consultation training: Prospects and frameworks. *Journal of Educational and Psychological Consultation, 13,* 69–95.

Mendoza, D. W. (1993). A review of Gerald Caplan's *Theory and practice of mental health consultation. Journal of Counseling and Development, 71,* 629–625.

Sheridan, S. M., & Colton, D. L. (1994). Conjoint behavioral consultation: A review case study. *Journal of Educational and Psychological Consultation, 5,* 211–228.

Sheridan, S., Kratochwill, T., & Elliott, S. N. (1990). Behavioral consultation with parents and teachers: Delivering treatment for socially withdrawn children at home and school. *School Psychology Review, 19,* 33–52.

Sheridan, S. M., Welch, M., & Orme, S. F. (1996). Is consultation effective? *Remedial & Special Education, 17,* 341–354.

Wilkinson, L. A. (1997). School-based behavioral consultation: Delivering treatment for children's externalizing behavior in the classroom. *Journal of Educational & Psychological Consultation, 8,* 255–276.

Mapping a School's Resources to Improve Their Use in Preventing and Ameliorating Problems

Howard S. Adelman ▪ Linda Taylor

CHAPTER 95

Getting Started

To function well, every system must fully understand and manage its resources. Mapping is a first and essential step toward these ends, and done properly, it is a major intervention in efforts to enhance systemic effectiveness and change for addressing barriers to learning and teaching.

Schools have a variety of programs and services for students who manifest learning, behavior, and emotional problems. These range from entitlement programs for economically impoverished students, through extra help for low-performing students/ schools, to special education interventions. In some places, the resources devoted to such efforts may account for as much as 30% of a school's budget. However, because school improvement initiatives continue to marginalize these "learning supports," the resources are deployed in a fragmented manner. The result is that essential resources often are deployed in redundant and wasteful ways and the overall impact is undermined. And the problem usually is compounded when efforts are made to connect community resources to schools. Given that an effective system of learning supports is fundamental to improving student achievement, greater attention must be paid to using all learning support resources effectively and efficiently (Adelman & Taylor, 1997, 2002, 2006a; Marx, Wooley, & Northrop, 1998; Rosenblum, DiCecco, Taylor, & Adelman, 1995). This means that school improvement efforts must place a high priority on mapping, analyzing, and managing these resources.

What We Know

Our particular focus here is on clarifying the mapping process. However, it should be emphasized from the outset that mapping is not an end in itself. Mapping provides a basis for resource analyses in order to make informed decisions about resource deployment. Analysis of what is needed, available, and effective provides the foundation for improving cost-efficiency and setting priorities. In a similar fashion, mapping and analyses of a complex or family of schools (e.g., a high school and its feeder middle and elementary schools) provides information for decision making that can lead to strategies for cooperation and integration to enhance intervention effectiveness and garner economies of scale.

In our work, mapping provides the basis for developing a comprehensive, multifaceted, and cohesive system of learning supports. The immediate challenges in such work are to move from piecemeal approaches by coordinating and integrating existing activity and then strengthening such activity. Then, the emphasis is on filling gaps over time. To these ends, resources must be redeployed from poorly conceived activities to enhance the potency of well-conceived programs. At the same time, resources are directed at ensuring programs are in place to reduce unnecessary referrals and to follow through more effectively with necessary referrals. Over time, the challenges are to evolve existing programs so they are more effective and then to enhance resources as needed (e.g., by working with neighboring schools, community resources, volunteers, professionals-in-training, and family engagement). As resources are enhanced, these challenges encompass solving problems related to sharing space and information, building working relationships, adjusting job descriptions, allocating time, and modifying policies (Adelman & Taylor, 2006a, 2006b).

Mapping Resources for Learning Supports

In discussing resource mapping, our concern is with those assets currently at a school or that can be accessed for use by the school to provide support for students who are manifesting learning, behavior, or emotional problems. Such assets are money, personnel, programs, services, material, equipment, facilities, social and human capital, leadership, infrastructure mechanisms, and more. The focus is on detailing first what the school currently has in terms of the resources it directly "owns" and controls and then those it has access to from other schools, the district, and the surrounding community.

Why is it important to map *both* school and community resources? Schools and communities share (a) goals and problems with respect to children, youth, and families; (b) the need to develop cost-effective systems, programs, and services; (c) accountability pressures related to improving outcomes; and (d) the opportunity to improve effectiveness by coordinating and eventually integrating resources to develop a full continuum of systemic interventions.

What We Can Do

Appreciating the importance of resource mapping often creates a desire to accomplish the work quickly. Generally speaking, however, mapping usually is best done in stages and requires constant updating. Thus, most schools will find it convenient to do the easiest forms of mapping first and then build the capacity to do in-depth mapping over a period of months. Similarly, initial analyses and management of resources will focus mostly on detailing what exists with a view to coordinating resource use. Over time, the focus is on spreadsheet-type analyses, priority recommendations, and deploying, redeploying, and braiding resources to enhance cost-effectiveness and fill programmatic gaps. Ultimately, the work can provide the basis for evolving a comprehensive, multifaceted, and cohesive system of learning supports through systemic improvements and changes and enhancing collaborative arrangements.

Who Does It?

Resource mapping can be pursued by almost anyone. Indeed, one individual could accomplish a great deal. No matter how many are involved, the key to doing it effectively is to establish a formal mechanism for ongoing mapping and providing training and support so that it can be done well.

In chapter 93, we discuss use of a learning supports resource team (previously called a resource coordinating team) as a prototype mechanism for accomplishing tasks such as resource mapping. Given that establishing yet another team can be difficult, an existing team can divide its time to encompass the work. For example, a school could expand the role and functions of a school-based student study/success team or a crisis team to focus on mapping and related resource-oriented functions. Of course, in doing so, care must be taken to keep agendas separate and to include additional stakeholders, such as parent, community, and student representatives, when a resource focus is the agenda.

How to Do It

As noted previously, mapping should be done in stages, starting with a simple task and building over time.

1. A first step is to clarify people/agencies to carry out relevant roles/functions.
2. Next, clarify specific programs, activities, and services (including information on how many students/families can be accommodated).
3. Delineate the systemic mechanisms involved in processing and decision making.
4. Identify the dollars and other related resources (e.g., facilities, equipment) that are being expended from various sources.
5. Collate the various policies that are relevant to the endeavor.

At each stage, develop a set of benchmarks to guide the work. As the information is gathered, establish a computer file. In the later stages, create spreadsheet formats.

Clarify Who's Who and What They Do

One of the first mapping tasks is to develop a list that describes who provides learning supports at the school, including any representatives from community agencies who come to the school. The resulting product spells out names, titles, and general functions. Because many support staff serve several schools, it also clarifies when each individual is at the school. While it seems common sense that every school would have such a list, we find too few do.

Figure 95.1 provides a template for clarifying who's who and what they do. Once the resources are mapped, the product can be widely distributed to stakeholders as an information guide and a "social marketing" tool.

Map All Programs, Activities, and Services

After doing this, the next mapping task is to specify all existing school-based and linked learning support activities that address barriers to learning and teaching, as well as those designed to promote healthy development. This can be done initially as a "laundry list," but as soon as feasible, it needs to be organized into a logical framework. One empirically developed framework is the six areas that have been conceived as the "curriculum" of an enabling component (e.g., see Adelman & Taylor, 1997, 2002, 2006a, 2006b). These six areas are:

1. Classroom-focused enabling—helping teachers learn and develop an increasingly wide array of strategies for preventing and handling problems in the classroom.
2. Crisis response and prevention—responding to schoolwide crises, minimizing their impact, and developing prevention strategies to reduce the number of schoolwide and personal crises.
3. Support for transitions—facilitating transitions, including welcoming and providing support for new arrivals, before- and after-school activity, articulation in moving to the next level of schooling, transition to and from special education, and transition to postschool life.
4. Home involvement in schooling—facilitating comprehensive home involvement (e.g., to improve student functioning through parent education and instruction in helping with schoolwork; to meet specific parent needs through ESL classes and mutual support groups).
5. Community involvement—facilitating comprehensive volunteer and community involvement—including formal linkages with community-based health and human services, local businesses, and various sources for volunteer recruitment.
6. Student and family assistance—assisting students and families with problems that cannot be handled by the teacher alone (e.g., connecting the student and family with school and community health, human, social, psychological, and special education resources; triage; IEPs; case management).

The Center for Mental Health in Schools at UCLA has developed a set of self-study instruments that delineate many activities related to each of these areas. These provide templates to aid school personnel in mapping the status of current school site activities. Additional instruments are also available for mapping: (a) a school's systems for coordinating and monitoring student and family services and schoolwide activities and (b) school–community partnerships. All these tools are available for downloading at no cost from the center's Web site (http://smhp.psych.ucla.edu). For illustrative purposes, the school–community partnership survey is included in the Tools and Practice Examples section of this chapter.

Delineate the Systemic Mechanisms Involved in Processing and Decision Making

It is essential to clarify the "who, what, and how" of decision making related to allocating and using resources for learning support. This includes decisions about handling specific students; about establishing, maintaining, or ending programs; and about overall budget and space allocations. How many mechanisms are there? How are they connected to each other? Are the decisions made by an individual or a group? If a group, who on the group represents learning supports? Understanding mechanism deficiencies is a key to enhancing practices for specific students and their families (e.g., minimizing inappropriate referrals, providing best practice assistance) and is a critical step in taking action to end the marginalization and fragmentation of learning supports.

How Much Is Being Spent?

By this point, it should be obvious why we say mapping usually will have to be done in stages. After all these tasks has been accomplished, it is time to translate existing efforts into dollar expenditures and create spreadsheet formats. In some schools, the

Figure 95.1. Mapping Who's Who at School

Each staff member is a special resource for each other. A few individuals are highlighted here to underscore some special functions.

School Psychologist:			Resource and Special Education Teachers:		
Times at School:			Times at School:		
Provides assessment and testing of students for special services. Counseling for students and parents. Support services for teachers. Prevention, crisis, conflict resolution, program modification for special learning and/or behavioral needs			Provides information on program modifications for students in regular classrooms as well as providing services for special education		
School Nurse:			Other important resources:		
Times at School:			School-Based Crisis Team (list by name and title)		
Provides immunizations, follow-up, communicable disease control, vision and hearing screening and follow-up, health assessments and referrals, health counseling and information for students and families					
Pupil Services & Attendance Counselor:					
Times at School:			School Improvement Program Planners		
Provides a liaison between school and home to maximize school attendance, transition counseling for returnees, enhancing attendance improvement activities					
Social Worker:					
Times at School:			Community Resources		
Assists in identifying at-risk students and provides follow-up counseling for students and parents. Refers families for additional services if needed			Providing school-linked or school-based interventions and resources		
Counselor:			Who	What They Do	When
Times at School:					
General and special counseling/guidance services. Consultation with parents and school staff					
Dropout Prevention Program Coordination:					
Times at School					
Coordinates activity designed to promote dropout prevention					
Title I and Bilingual Coordinators:					
Times at School:					
Coordinates categorical programs, provides services to identified Title I students, implements bilingual master plan (supervising the curriculum, testing, and so forth)					

Figure 95.2. Mapping Resources for Student Transitions and Family–School Involvement

Support for Transitions	Current Committee Members
Enhancing school capacity to handle the variety of transition concerns confronting students and their families	(Names of those who work regularly to enhance this area of activity throughout the school)
Current Programs/Resources	
• Welcoming club • Student peer buddy social support program • Family peer buddy social support program • Before school tournaments, enrichment, and recreational activities • After-school sports, tournaments, enrichment, and recreation activities • Service learning program • Student job program • End-of-year 6-week program conducted by teacher and support staff to prepare students for the next grade • Articulation programs conducted by support staff to prepare students graduating to secondary schools • Follow-up monitoring by teachers • Design a transition program and support staff to identify and assist students who are having difficulty with transition into a new grade or school	**Priorities for Future Development in This Area** • In-service for support staff related to enhancing transition programs • Recruitment of more volunteers to aid with transition programs • Preparation of a "Welcome to Our School" video to be shown to all newcomers and visitors—for regular use in the front office or in a special welcoming space implemented by a resource teacher and support staff for students (and their families) entering and returning from special education • Enhance recess and lunch recreation and enrichment opportunities
Home Involvement in Schooling	Current Committee Members
Enhancing school capacity to provide those in the home with opportunities for learning, special assistance, and participation	(Names of those who work regularly to enhance this area of activity throughout the school)
Current Programs/Resources	

• Adult education programs at the school and neighborhood
  ○ ESL
  ○ Literacy
  ○ Job skills
  ○ Child care certification program
  ○ Citizenship exam preparation classes
  ○ Parenting and helping their youngster with school work
  ○ Aerobics/sewing
	Priorities for Future Development in this Area

(continued)

Figure 95.2. *(Continued)*

<table><tr><td>• Parent participation and parent classes • Some on-campus family assistance services and assistance in connecting with community services (see Student & Family Assistance) • Family volunteers staff school welcoming club, assist in the front office, in classrooms, on the yard • Family–staff picnic • Training for participation in school governance • Participation on school advisory and governance bodies • Regular parent–teacher communications (regular phone and e-mail discussions, in-person conferences on request, monthly newsletter) • School "beautification" program • Planning for community involvement</td><td>• Enhance outreach programs to engage and reengage family members who are seldom in contact with the school and often are hard to reach • Establish self-led mutual support groups for families • Expand opportunities for families to use school facilities during nonschool hours for enrichment and recreation • Enhance in-service for all staff to increase motivation and capability for enhancing home involvement</td></tr></table>

Note: Figure 95.2 illustrates examples of two areas, student transitions and family–school involvement, at a school that categorizes its learning support programs based on the six aspects of an enabling component. For examples of other products, see *Resource Mapping and Management to Address Barriers to Learning: An Intervention for Systemic Change* (http:// smhp. psych.ucla.edu).

large proportion of students who are not doing well has resulted in learning supports becoming a large percentage of the budget. However, because the actual dollars spent tend to be masked in various ways, decision making and accountability related to learning supports are not a major focus of school improvement planning. Mapping the dollars is a fundamental step in changing all this. It is, of course, just one step. It provides the information for the analyses that clarify how to rethink allocations to improve resource use in preventing and ameliorating problems with the aim of enhancing student achievement.

Mapping Policies

With all these tasks accomplished, it is time to clarify each of the policies that determine how resources are used. The focus is on policy that positively and/or negatively affects learning support practices at a school and in the surrounding community. Such policy is found in the regulations and guidelines that direct the work. The picture that evolves usually is a set of unconnected regulations and guidelines that were developed in an ad hoc and piecemeal manner. The lack of cohesive policy tends to work against good practice and tends to produce redundancy and waste. In

formulating recommendations for enhancing resource use, a policy map helps to identify what is feasible under existing policy, where waivers should be sought, and what should be pursued to enhance policy cohesion.

At this point, it should be evident that mapping resources is, in effect, an intervention for systemic change. By identifying and analyzing existing resources, awareness is heightened about their value in helping students engage and reengage in learning at school. Analyses also can lead to sophisticated recommendations for deploying and redeploying resources to improve programs, enhance cost-effectiveness, and fill programmatic gaps in keeping with priorities. And a focus on these matters often highlights the reality that the school's current infrastructure requires some revamping to ensure that necessary functions are carried out.

The products of mapping activity provide information for analyses and recommendations. They also can be invaluable for "social marketing" efforts designed to inform teachers, parents, and other community stakeholders about all that the school is doing to address barriers to learning and promote healthy development. One example is the document that emerges from mapping who's who and what they do (see Figure 95.1). Another source of such information is the school–community partnerships self-study survey.

Tools and Practice Examples

School–Community Partnerships Self-Study Survey

Formal efforts to create school–community partnerships to improve school and neighborhood involve building formal relationships to connect resources involved in preK–12 schooling and resources in the community (including formal and informal organizations, such as the home and agencies involved in providing health and human services, religion, policing, justice, and economic development; organizations that foster youth development, recreation, and enrichment; as well as businesses, unions, governance bodies, and institutions of higher education).

As you work toward enhancing such partnerships, it helps to clarify what you have in place as a basis for determining what needs to be done. You will want to pay special attention to:

- clarifying what resources already are available
- how the resources are organized to work together
- what procedures are in place for enhancing resource usefulness

The following survey is designed as a self-study instrument related to school–community partnerships. Stakeholders can use such surveys to map and analyze the current status of their efforts.

This type of self-study is best done by teams. For example, a group of stakeholders could use the items to discuss how well specific processes and programs are functioning and what is not being done. Members of the team initially might work separately in filling out the items, but the real payoff comes from discussing them as a group. The instrument also can be used as a form of program quality review.

In analyzing the status of their school–community partnerships, the group may decide that some existing activity is not a high priority and that the resources should be redeployed to help establish more important programs. Other activity may be seen as needing to be embellished so that it is effective. Finally, decisions may be made regarding new desired activities, and since not everything can be added at once, priorities and time lines can be established.

I. Overview: Areas for School–Community Partnership

Indicate the status of partnerships between a given school or family of schools and community with respect to each of the following areas.

II. List Current School–Community Partnerships

Make two lists: (1) those focused on improving the school and (2) those focused on improving the neighborhood (through enhancing links with the school, including use of school facilities and resources).

III. School–Community Partnerships to Improve the School

Indicate the status of partnerships between a given school or family of schools and community (Name of school(s) _____

_____

_____).

Key Points to Remember

Why Mapping Resources Is So Important

To function well, every system must fully understand and manage its resources. Mapping is a first and essential step toward these ends, and done properly, it is a major intervention in efforts to enhance systemic effectiveness and change for addressing barriers to learning and teaching.

What Are Resources?

Money, personnel, programs, services, material, equipment, real estate, facilities, social and human capital, leadership, infrastructure mechanisms, and more.

What Do We Mean by Mapping and Who Does It?

A representative group of informed stakeholders is asked to undertake the process of identifying

Table 95.1

Please Indicate All Items That Apply	Yes	*Yes, but More of This Is Needed*	No	*If No, Is This Something You Want?*
A. Improving the school (name of school(s)):				
1. the instructional component of schooling				
2. the governance and management of schooling				
3. financial support for schooling				
4. school-based programs and services to address barriers to learning				
B. Improving the neighborhood (through enhancing linkages with the school, including use of school facilities and resources)				
1. youth development programs				
2. youth and family recreation and enrichment opportunities				
3. physical health services				
4. mental health services				
5. programs to address psychosocial problems				
6. basic living needs services				
7. work/career programs				
8. social services				
9. crime and juvenile justice programs				
10. legal assistance				
11. support for development of neighborhood organizations				
12. economic development programs				

those assets currently at a school or that can be accessed for use by the school to provide support for students who are manifesting learning, behavior, or emotional problems. The focus is on detailing first what the school currently has in terms of the resources it directly "owns" and controls and then those it has access to from other schools, the district, and the surrounding community.

Why Mapping Both School and Community Resources Is So Important

Schools and communities share (a) goals and problems with respect to children, youth, and families; (b) the need to develop cost-effective systems, programs, and services; (c) accountability pressures related to improving outcomes; and (d) the opportunity to improve effectiveness by coordinating and eventually integrating resources to develop a full continuum of systemic interventions.

Doing Resource Mapping

Do it in stages (start simple and build over time). Steps include (a) clarifying who's who and what they do, (b) mapping all programs, activities, and services, (c) delineating systemic mechanisms involved in processing and decision making, (d) clarifying how much is being spent, and (e) mapping policies.

What Does This Process Lead To?

Products that can be used for analyses, recommendations, and social marketing.

Table 95.2 Overview: System Status for Enhancing School–Community Partnership

	DK	1	2	3	4	5
Items 1–7 ask what processes are in place. Use the following ratings in responding to these items. DK=don't know; 1=not yet; 2=planned; 3=just recently initiated; 4=has been functional for a while; 5=well institutionalized (well established with a commitment to maintenance						
1. Is there a stated policy for enhancing school–community partnerships (e.g., from the school, community agencies, government bodies)?	DK	1	2	3	4	5
2. Is there a designated leader or leaders for enhancing school–community partnerships?	DK	1	2	3	4	5
3. With respect to each entity involved in the school–community partnerships, have persons been designated as representatives to meet with each other?	DK	1	2	3	4	5
4. Do personnel involved in enhancing school–community partnerships meet regularly as a team to evaluate current status and plan next steps?	DK	1	2	3	4	5
5. Is there a written plan for capacity building related to enhancing the school–community partnerships?	DK	1	2	3	4	5
6. Are there written descriptions available to give all stakeholders regarding current school–community partnerships?	DK	1	2	3	4	5
7. Are there effective processes by which stakeholders learn?						
(a) what is available in the way of programs/services?	DK	1	2	3	4	5
(b) how to access programs/services they need?	DK	1	2	3	4	5
8. In general, how effective are your local efforts to enhance school–community partnerships?	DK	1	2	3	4	5
9. With respect to enhancing school–community partnerships, how effective are each of the following:						
(a) current policy?	DK	1	2	3	4	5
(b) designated leadership?	DK	1	2	3	4	5
(c) designated representatives?	DK	1	2	3	4	5
(d) team monitoring and planning of next steps?	DK	1	2	3	4	5
(e) capacity building efforts?	DK	1	2	3	4	5

Table 95.3

Please Indicate All Items That Apply	Yes	Yes, but More of This Is Needed	No	If No, Is This Something You Want?
Partnerships to improve				
1. *The instructional component of schooling*				
a. kindergarten readiness programs				
b. tutoring				
c. mentoring				
d. school reform initiatives				
e. homework hotlines				
f. media/technology				
g. career academy programs				
h. adult education, ESL, literacy, citizenship classes				
i. other _____				
2. *The governance and management of schooling*				
a. PTA/PTSA				
b. shared leadership				
c. advisory bodies				
d. other _____				
3. *Financial support for schooling*				
a. adopt-a-school				
b. grant programs and funded projects				
c. donations/fund raising				
d. other				
4. *School-based programs and services to address barriers to learning*				
a. student and family assistance programs/services				
b. transition programs				
c. crisis response and prevention programs				
d. home involvement programs				
e. pre- and in-service staff development programs				
f. other _____				
Partnerships to improve				
1. *Youth development programs*				
a. home visitation programs				
b. parent education				
c. infant and toddler programs				
d. child care/children's centers/preschool programs				
e. community service programs				
f. public health and safety programs				
g. leadership development programs				
h. other _____				
2. *Youth and family recreation and enrichment opportunities*				
a. art/music/cultural programs				
b. parks programs				
c. youth clubs				
d. scouts				
e. youth sports leagues				
f. community centers				
g. library programs				

(continued)

Table 95.3 (*Continued*)

Please Indicate All Items That Apply	Yes	Yes, but More of This Is Needed	No	If No, Is This Something You Want?
h. faith community activity				
i. camping programs				
j. other _____				
3. *Physical health services*				
a. school-based/linked clinics for primary care				
b. immunization clinics				
c. communicable disease control programs				
d. EPSDT programs				
e. pro bono/volunteer programs				
f. AIDS/HIV programs				
g. asthma programs				
h. pregnant and parenting minors programs				
i. dental services				
j. vision and hearing services				
k. referral facilitation				
l. emergency care				
m. other _____				
4. *Mental health services*				
a. school-based/linked clinics w/ mental health component				
b. EPSDT mental health focus				
c. pro bono/volunteer programs				
d. referral facilitation				
e. counseling				
f. crisis hotlines				
g. other _____				
5. *Programs to address psychosocial problems*				
a. conflict mediation/resolution				
b. substance abuse				
c. community/school safe havens				
d. safe passages				
e. youth violence prevention				
f. gang alternatives				
g. pregnancy prevention and counseling				
h. case management of programs for high-risk youth				
i. child abuse and domestic violence programs				
j. other _____				
6. *Basic living needs services*				
a. food				
b. clothing				
c. housing				
d. transportation				
e. other _____				
7. *Work/career program*				
a. job mentoring				
b. job programs and employment opportunities				
c. other: _____				

(*continued*)

Table 95.3 (*Continued*)

Please Indicate All Items That Apply	Yes	Yes, but More of This Is Needed	No	If No, Is This Something You Want?
8. *Social services*				
a. school-based/linked family resource centers				
b. integrated services initiatives				
c. budgeting/financial management counseling				
d. family preservation and support				
e. foster care school transition programs				
f. case management				
g. immigration and cultural transition assistance				
h. language translation				
i. other _____				
9. *Crime and juvenile justice programs*				
a. camp returnee programs				
b. children's court liaison				
c. truancy mediation				
d. juvenile diversion programs with school				
e. probation services at school				
f. police protection programs				
g. other				
10. *Legal assistance*				
a. legal aid programs				
b. other _____				
11. *Support for development of neighborhood organizations*				
a. neighborhood protective associations				
b. emergency response planning and implementation				
c. neighborhood coalitions and advocacy groups				
d. volunteer services				
e. welcoming clubs				
f. social support networks				
g. other _____				
12. *Economic development programs*				
a. empowerment zones.				
b. urban village programs				
c. other _____				

▍Resources

Here is a sample of Web sites describing processes and providing tools for mapping school and community resources.

1. *Resource mapping and management to address barriers to learning: An intervention for systemic change.* Center for Mental Health in Schools. http://smhp.psych.ucla.edu

Discusses the processes and provides a set of self-study surveys designed to aid school staff as they map and analyze their current programs, services, and systems for purposes of developing a comprehensive, multifaceted approach to addressing barriers to learning.

2. *Building communities from the inside out.* Asset-Based Community Development Institute. http://www.northwestern.edu/IPR/abcdci.html

Uses a "Capacity Inventory," which is an online printable questionnaire that can be presented to citizens of the community to attain their skills and use them in improving the community.

3. *Moving Through Change, Communication, Engaging People in Community, Strategic Thinking.* http://www.ael.org/rel/rural/pdf/mapping.pdf

    Determine what assets are available to help improve local education and quality of life and to help match needs and assets. Includes instructions on generating a community profile.

4. *Asset Mapping: A Powerful Tool for Communities.* Northwest Regional Educational Laboratory. http://www.nwrel.org/nwreport/dec98/article8.html

    This is part of a series of four workbooks to support community education. This workbook shows readers how to approach community development from a positive, creative perspective, one that builds on strengths and resources.

5. *Community Building Resources: Community Capacity Building & Asset Mapping©.* http://www.cbr-aimhigh.com/What_cbr_Does/philosophy.htm

    Designed as a way to animate, connect, and inform citizens and to create an environment in which relationships can build. The asset focus can be a catalyst and a spark for the people to discover, access, and mobilize their unrecognized resources, and it engages people who have not participated in the life of the community.

6. *Building Communities Through Strengths.* The Madii Institute. http://www.madii.org/amhome/amhome.html

    Identify and involve all the capabilities or capacities of a community to create community transformation or to build community self-reliance. Many communities find they have all the resources they have hoped for during the asset mapping process.

7. *A Cultural Path.* The Madii Institute. http://www.madii.org/culture/culture.html

    Examines the importance of different aspects of culture in asset mapping. Including cultural knowledge as an asset extends the current asset mapping and other community development models and broadens the possibilities for building community.

Following are some additional resources relevant to mapping school and community.

References

Adelman, H. S., & Taylor, L. (1997). Addressing barriers to learning: Beyond school-linked services and full service schools. *American Journal of Orthopsychiatry, 67,* 408–421.

Adelman, H. S., & Taylor. L. (2002). So you want higher achievement scores? Its time to rethink learning supports. *The State Education Standard* (pp. 52–56). Alexandria, VA: National Association of State Boards of Education.

Adelman, H. S., & Taylor, L. (2006a). *The school leader's guide to student learning supports: New directions for addressing barriers to learning.* Thousand Oaks, CA: Corwin Press.

Adelman, H. S., & Taylor, L. (2006b). *The implementation guide to student learning supports in the classroom and schoolwide: New directions for addressing barriers to learning.* Thousand Oaks, CA: Corwin Press.

AED. (2002). *Community youth mapping guide, tool kit, and informational video.* Washington, DC: AED Center for Youth Development and Policy Research.

Bruner, C., Bell, K., Brindis, C., Chang, H., & Scarbrough, W. (1993). *Charting a course: Assessing a community's strengths and needs.* Des Moines, IA: National Center for Service Integration.

Center for Mental Health in Schools. (1995). *Addressing barriers to learning: A set of surveys to map what a school has and what it needs.* Los Angeles: Author at UCLA. Available online at http://smhp.psych.ucla.edu.

Center for Mental Health in Schools. (1999). *School-community partnerships: A guide.* Los Angeles: Author at UCLA. Available online at http://smhp.psych.ucla.edu.

Community Building Resources. (2000) *Our book is your book—Thinking about community capacity building and asset mapping* (3rd printing). Edmonton, AB: Author.

Community Technology Center Net (1996). *Startup manual.* Chapter 2: "Mapping community resources." Available online at http://www.ctcnet.org/.

Dedrick, A., Mitchell, G., Miyagawa, M., & Roberts, S. (1997). *From model to reality—Community capacity building and asset mapping. Listen and learn . . . the answers are with communities.* Edmonton, AB: Author.

Dedrick, A., Mitchell, G., & Roberts, S. (1994). *Community capacity building and asset mapping: Model development.* Edmonton, AB: Community Development Caritas.

Dewar, T. (1997). *A guide to evaluating asset based community development: Lessons, challenges & opportunities.* Chicago, IL: ACTA.

Fisher, R., & Kling, J. (1993). *Mobilizing the community.* Newbury Park, CA: Sage Publications.

Kingsley, G. T., Coulton, C. J., Barndt, M., Sawicki, D. S., & Tatian, P. (1997). *Mapping your community: Using geographic information to strengthen community initiatives.* Washington, DC: U.S. Department of Housing and Urban Development.

Kretzmann, J. P., & McKnight, J. L. (1993). *Building communities from the inside out: A path toward finding and mobilizing a community's assets.* Evanston, IL: Center for Urban Affairs and Policy Research Neighbourhood Innovations Network.

Kretzmann, J. P., & McKnight, J. L. (1996a). *A guide to mapping and mobilizing the economic capacities of local residents.* Chicago, IL: ACTA Publications.

Kretzmann, J. P., & McKnight, J. L. (1996b). *A guide to mapping consumer expenditures and mobilizing consumer expenditure capacities.* Chicago, IL: ACTA Publications.

Kretzmann, J. P., & McKnight, J. L. (1996c). *A guide to mapping local business assets and mobilizing local business capacities.* Chicago, IL: ACTA Publications.

Kretzmann, J. P., & McKnight, J. L. (1997). *A guide to capacity inventories: Mobilizing the community skills of local residents.* Chicago, IL: ACTA Publications.

Kretzmann, J. P., McKnight, J. L., & Sheehan, G., with Green, M., & Puntenney, D. (1997). *A guide to capacity inventories: Mobilizing the community skills of local residents.* Evanston, IL: Institute for Policy Research, Northwestern University.

Marx, E., Wooley, S., & Northrop, D. (1998). *Health is academic.* New York: Teachers College Press.

McKnight, J. L. (1995). *The careless society—Community and its counterfeits.* New York: Harper Collins Publishers.

Mizrahi, T., & Morrison, J. D. (1993). *Community organization and social administration—Advances, trends and emerging principles.* Binghamton, NY: Haworth Press, Inc.

Rosenblum, L., DiCecco, M. B., Taylor, L., & Adelman, H. S. (1995). Upgrading school support programs through collaboration: Resource coordinating teams. *Social Work in Education, 17,* 117–124.

Writing a Contract With a Community Agency for a School-Based Service

Michelle Alvarez ■ Lynn Bye

CHAPTER 96

Getting Started

This chapter provides guidance for important aspects of contracting for school social work and other mental health services. Starting with the need for school social work services especially in the area of mental health, this chapter moves into the "Contract with America" and the privatization movement to provide a context for contracted services in the schools. The chapter finishes with a discussion of funding for privately contracted services, and sample contracts are provided.

The need for school social work and other mental health services stems from the role of the school social worker, which has long been to guard the right of every child to an education (Agresta, 2004). For some children this means special services must be provided to help them benefit from instruction (Adelman & Taylor, 2000b, p. 171). Although special services are important, the "quality improvement" movement in schools generally left the mental health agenda "unexplored" and full of gaps in prevention and early intervention (Weist, 1997, p. 337).

What We Know

Benefit of Contracting for Services

Contracting for services may provide school districts with an opportunity to try out school social work services and the services of other mental health professionals, and discover how these services can support the educational attainment of the students. In times of financial retrenchment, school districts' shrinking budgets often result in

staff cuts and fewer support staff such as school social workers. Due to the tremendous financial pressure school districts face, they may at times need to contract for essential social work services. Regardless of the funding, social workers providing services in the schools are under pressure to show results rather than simply perform services.

Many schools have become centers where families can access multiple school-linked services, but the outside professionals may not be aware of the school culture or potential turf issues (Adelman & Taylor, 2000b). Community partnerships between schools and social service agencies can be an attempt to help families access services without having to go to different agencies that may not understand the culture of the contracting institution (McCroskey, Picus, Yoo, Marsenich, & Robillard, 2004). With outside personnel entering the school, there is a potential for miscommunication (Adelman & Taylor, 2000b). An important role for a school-based school-employed social worker is to serve as a coordinator, keeping the lines of communication open between the different parties.

Mental Health Services in Schools

Mental health services in schools can range from preventative, where systematic assessment is done to screen for antisocial behavior (Walker, Severson, Feil, Stiller, & Golly, 1998), to crisis containment, where support staff respond to student suicide or school violence (Rones & Hoagwood, 2000). With the onslaught of school violence, more opportunities to contract for services evolved. Seven hundred cities and towns surveyed by the National League of Cities mentioned that school violence was a problem (Walker, Stiller, Severson, Golly, & Feil, 1994). The Comprehensive

Community Mental Health Program for Children and Their Families that calls for a comprehensive community mental health services program (SAMHSA, 2004) also provides further opportunity to bring mental health services into schools.

Hiring Mental Health Professionals

When hiring mental health professionals in schools that already employ school counselors, school social workers, and/or school psychologists, duplication of existing services and related territorial issues may be concerns. Franklin (2001) identified some of these issues and suggests strategies to capitalize on existing resources, such as collaborating with contracted mental health professionals to enhance student academic success. Specifically, Franklin's (2001) recommendations include the following:

- Involve school-employed mental health professionals in the contracting of supplemental mental health services
- Consult with school-employed mental health professionals on the scope of services that should be provided by supplemental mental health professionals so as not to duplicate services provided
- Facilitate the collaboration of services between school-employed and contracted mental health professionals
- Plan for office space and office equipment needs of contracted employees so as not to deplete resources for school-employed mental health professionals
- Ensure that contracted mental health professionals have the credentials necessary to provide the services for which they are contracted.

Funding Mental Health Services in Schools

The national trend is for most of the mental health funding to be "directed" toward "severe, pervasive and/or chronic psychosocial problems" rather than toward prevention (Adelman & Taylor, 2000a, p. 4). The "Contract with America" in the 1990s focused on tax cuts, dismantling social programs, and privatization of public service (Fisher, 2002). More recently there is a movement "toward tying significant portions of public financing for MH and psychosocial concerns to schools"

(Adelman & Taylor, 2000a, p. 4). Channeling mental health funding toward schools makes sense, since schools are the major providers of mental health services for children.

The privatization of educational services is defined as "the transfer of public money or assets from the public domain to the private sector" and requires school social workers and related mental health providers to have knowledge and skills related to availability of funds for services and issues related to contracting for services (Fitz & Beers, 2002, p. 137). In privatization, billing issues present a challenge. One form of privatization is contracting services by purchasing them from individuals or businesses outside of the school. For example, school bus services are often contracted with private vendors. Like school bus companies, social workers and other related mental health professionals can contract directly with schools for the provision of specific services. In times of limited education funding, contracting for school social work services can enable the school system to maximize resources through full access to a community agencies menu of services, such as access to mobile dental and health services and eligibility for hospital foundation funds for special projects when contracting with a hospital (personal communication, grant manager, D. Diehl, August 26, 2004). For example, a social worker in St. Cloud, Minnesota, who had a reputation as an excellent group worker, was contracted by the school district to conduct a certain number of social skills groups in specific schools. Faculty within a school often made requests to the school principal to contract with this social worker for a specific group of students.

School districts can obtain funds to contract for school social work services under the Individuals with Disabilities Education Act Amendments (IDEA) of 1997, through federal title funds, and through billing Medicaid and parents' private insurance. According to the U.S. Department of Education (1999), social work services covered under IDEA include the following:

- Preparing a social or developmental history on a child with a disability
- Group and individual counseling with the child and the family
- Working in partnership with parents and others on those problems in a child's living situation (home, school, and community) that affect the child's adjustment in school
- Mobilizing school and community resources

to enable the child to learn as effectively as possible in his or her educational program
- Assisting in developing positive behavioral intervention strategies. (Section 300.24(b)(13))

In addition to these IDEA categorical qualifiers, billing can be complicated. Schools can only bill an insurance company for related services with the written permission of the parent. However, under the law, with the parent's permission, the insurance company must be billed for these services. If the school does not bill for services, an outside agency providing the service can bill.

What We Can Do

Tips for Developing Contracts

Social workers and other related health professionals interested in developing private contracts with school districts can learn some valuable tips from health providers, who have been offering privately contracted services to schools for the past 30 years. Honore, Simoes, Moonesinghe, Kirbey, and Renner (2004) make the following suggestions for developing contracts:

- Develop mutually agreed upon outcomes between the independent contractor and the hiring agency
- Write expected outcomes into the contract
- Specify when and how the outcomes will be measured
- Identify in writing how the short-term contracted services will help the school accomplish its long-term objectives
- Annually update and negotiate the contract

A review of sample contracts or memoranda of understanding, which are available at http://smhp .psych.ucla.edu/qf/mou.htm, and additional resources provided by the University of California at Los Angeles Center for Mental Health in Schools (personal communication, L. Taylor, September 20, 2004) revealed the following content areas included in agreements between schools and school social workers or other related mental health providers.

- List parties involved in the agreement
- Describe the need for services

- Define the purpose of the agreement, the shared vision, and benefits of collaboration
- List strategies for addressing the needs
- Outline scope and boundaries of services to be provided, areas of collaboration/cooperation
- Specify compensation, work hours, funding options that are in place or will be pursued
- Clarify responsibilities, roles, and authority of all parties
- Describe methods for exchanging information and limits of confidentiality by all parties (e.g., recording, sharing, releases, reports of abuse)
- Identify how compliance with all applicable federal, state, and local laws, rules, regulations, and policies will be achieved
- Identify process for evaluating services provided under this agreement
- Outline a dispute-resolution plan
- Specify an agreement start date, life of the agreement (effective dates), and process for reviewing and updating agreement
- Obtain signatures of official from each party involved in the agreement and date of signature.

Under these general contract headings, it is important to include specifics regarding situations that may be faced during the agreement. Interviews conducted with a school administrator, a school principal, and an agency revealed the following issues that social workers and related mental health professionals who contract with schools would be wise to consider addressing in a written contract.

Contract Issues From a School Administrator's Viewpoint

The school administrators interviewed for this chapter suggest that it is important to include details on the following issues when contracting for services:

- Documentation of credentials of contracted employee (e.g., state-issued professional license, appropriate academic degree, criminal history check)
- Coordination of services provided between school and agency staff (e.g., when coordinated by the principal or a school-employed social worker, workable timeframes and times during the day can be provided for services)
- Evidence-based practices
- Terms for renewal of contract

- Congruence between goals of school and contracted services
- Space where confidential services can be provided with required equipment
- Conditions for termination of specific services
- Liability and indemnification
- Court subpoenas (i.e., who prepares the contracted worker for testimony)
- Use of dual release of information forms
- Familiarity with school district policies (e.g., schools could provide an orientation manual that includes procedures for reporting child abuse)
- Identification of responsibility for day-to-day supervision of contracted employee and handling of performance issues
- Creation of a schedule listing when contracted and volunteer personnel are expected to enter and exit the building for both organizational and security purposes (Diehl, personal communication, August 26, 2004; Johnson, personal communication, September 8, 2004)

Contract Issues From an Agency Staff's Viewpoint

Agency staff interviewed for this chapter identified several issues also addressed by school administrators. Additionally, agency staff identified the following items as important to include when crafting a contract:

- Scope of confidentiality (e.g., under what circumstances and with whom does the contracted school social worker or mental health provider share information?)
- Responsibility for day-to-day supervision of contracted employee and handling of performance issues
- Which party will be billing and for what specific services (Black & Wooten, personal communication, September 2, 2004)

Tools and Practice Examples

Sample Contracts

Although no contract includes all the recommended information identified in this chapter, Figures 96.1 and 96.2 show two examples of

contracts that could be used as models for drafting a contract for services.

Resources

National Assembly on School Based Health Care offers sample agreement within a training manual for a small fee: http://www.nasbhc.org/tat/toolkits.htm

Sample memorandums of agreements posted by the UCLA School Mental Health Project are listed under "Relevant Publications on the Internet": http://smhp.psych.ucla.edu/qf/mou.htm

Sample funding strategies for mental health services that could be included in a contract:

1. Funds for school-based mental health services: http://smhp.psych.ucla.edu/qf/medicaid.htm.
2. A tool kit on creative financing for school-based health services: http://www.nasbhc.org/Creative_Financing_TOC.htm.

Key Points to Remember

This chapter provided information on important aspects of contracting school social workers and other mental health professionals (e.g., school counselors, school psychologists, community mental health professional services). Suggestions for areas that should be addressed in a contract were gleaned from the literature and interviews with school administrators and agency staff. Recommendations gleaned from the information gathered for this chapter include:

- Review existing resources before negotiating a contract (e.g., services currently provided at the school, sample contract formats)
- Coordinate contracted services with school-employed school social workers, counselors, and psychologists
- Utilize school-employed school social workers, school counselors, or school psychologists to facilitate the provision of contracted mental health services in the school
- Work closely with all parties to agree upon a common goal and a common definition of services to be provided

Figure 96.1. Example Contract

MEMORANDUM OF UNDERSTANDING
Between the Department of Mental Health, Community Services Agency and District of Columbia Public School System

Parties
The Department of Mental Health, Community Services Agency (DMH-CSA), and the District of Columbia Public School System (DCPS), in order to provide prevention, assessment, and treatment services to children and adolescents enrolled in DCPS through a collaborative effort by both parties. A mental health clinician is defined as an employee of the DMH-CSA that is placed in a school to provide prevention, early intervention, and treatment services to students enrolled in the school.

SHARED VISION FOR MENTAL HEALTH IN SCHOOLS
To support a school environment in which all children are emotionally prepared, ready to learn, and able to progress toward productive adulthood.

SHARED MISSION FOR MENTAL HEALTH IN SCHOOLS
To create a child- and family-centered school-based mental health program to include prevention, early intervention and treatment in collaboration with schools, and community-based child and family serving organizations.

FUNCTIONS TO BE CARRIED OUT TO ACHIEVE THE VISION AND MISSION
A. Assessment for initial screening of problems, as well as for diagnosis and intervention planning (including a focus on needs and assets)
B. Referral, triage, and monitoring/management of care
C. Direct service and instruction (including primary prevention programs/activities, early intervention, individual, family, and group counseling, crisis intervention and planning)
D. Coordination, development, and leadership related to school-based programs, services, resources, and systems toward evolving a comprehensive, multifaceted, and integrated continuum of programs and services
E. Consultation, supervision, and in-service instruction with a multidisciplinary focus
F. Enhancing connections with and involvement of home and community resources

STRUCTURE FOR CARRYING OUT THE FUNCTIONS
Referral and Triage Teams. Participating schools will have or will establish an infrastructure for developing and implementing a school mental health program and for providing systemic approaches to prevention, early intervention, and treatment programs (including referral, triage, assessment, and other related interventions). The infrastructure will involve the Teacher Assistance Teams (TATs) or equivalent team with participation from the school principal or a designee, all other mental health clinicians working in the school (both school hired and DMH-CSA clinicians), the school nurse, and any other relevant staff members who would have input in the development of a school-based mental health intervention. Referrals to this team will be structured so that there is one point of entry at each school. The team then reviews the information provided in a timely manner and the most appropriate mental health clinician is assigned. All team members that have regular contact with the identified client will provide feedback on the development of an intervention plan. The clinician assigned to work with a student and his or her family, whether hired by the DMH-CSA or the school, will have responsibility for monitoring services offered and providing periodic progress reports to the TAT consistent with the provisions of the Mental Health Information Act.

Services Will Supplement Existing Programs. The school-based services provided through the DMH-CSA will supplement and not supplant services already in place. This includes mental health services already being provided by the DMH-CSA in various DC public schools. Although all students will have access to prevention activities and targeted students can be referred for early intervention activities, the school-based services provided through the DMH-CSA will not replace treatment services provided through the school for students involved in the special education process.

(continued)

Figure 96.1. *(Continued)*

SPECIFIC ROLE AND FUNCTIONS OF THE MENTAL HEALTH CLINICIAN OF THE DEPARTMENT OF MENTAL HEALTH, COMMUNITY SERVICES AGENCY

The clinician hired by the Department of Mental Health is placed in each participating school to assist in the development of a school mental health program and to provide prevention, early intervention, treatment, and assessment services to children and adolescents enrolled in the school. The clinician will also provide consultation, training, and support to teachers, administrators, and other school staff. Although functioning in a school setting, the clinician is still governed by the Department of Mental Health, Community Services Agency policies and procedures.

WORKING CONDITIONS RELATED TO THE MENTAL HEALTH CLINICIAN

The following are specific matters related to the mutual responsibilities and accountabilities of the clinician and the school in working together.

What DMH-CSA Provides. The Department of Mental Health, Community Services Agency provides supervision and support for mental health clinicians. The DMH-CSA will hire and supervise one or more clinicians who will be placed in participating schools. Each clinician is expected to attend a weekly supervisory and training meeting. The DMH-CSA policy dictates that mental health clinicians are expected to call their supervisors whenever troublesome cases or unusual incidents arise and will file unusual incident reports as required to both the DMH-CSA supervisor and to the Principal of the school to which they are assigned. Should a conflict arise with respect to DMH-CSA policies and procedures, it is the responsibility of the clinician's supervisor to work with the school in resolving the matter.

What the School Provides. For the DMH–CSA clinician to work effectively, the school must provide a private space, a locking filing cabinet, and a dedicated phone line for each clinician assigned to a school. In addition, schools are asked to provide necessary supplies, materials, and allow use of their office equipment so that mental health clinicians can conduct mental health services in ways that would enable them to complete their responsibilities at the school.

DMH-CSA Clinician as a Member of the School Team. Although not a school employee, the mental health clinician is expected to work closely with the school staff, to share nonconfidential and confidential information with the staff as appropriate under the conditions noted below, and to assist staff in responding to behavioral health concerns. Administrative aggregate information, such as the number of students seen, the number and theme of therapeutic groups, and general concerns raised, can be shared in accordance with the Mental Health Information Act, D.C.

Code Section 7–1201.01 *et seq.* Mental health clinicians can acknowledge receipt of a mental health referral and indicate whether that student has been seen. Compliance with a request to share any other information related to a student's treatment would require an appropriate release of information signed by the student. Monthly summary reports of aggregate mental health data will be provided to the principal. Efforts will be made to resolve dilemmas that arise from the legal confidentiality requirements that are in place for the DMH-CSA and the school so that all staff involved with a student can work together in the student's best interest while adhering to mandatory mental health laws.

DC Permits Students to Obtain Mental Health Services Without Parental Consent. The Mental Health Service Delivery Reform Act of 2001 indicates that a clinician may deliver outpatient mental health services and mental health supports to a minor who is voluntarily seeking such services without parental or guardian consent for a period of 90 days if the clinician determines that (1) the minor is knowingly and voluntarily seeking services and (2) the provision of services is clinically indicated for the minor's well-being. At the end of the 90-day period, the clinician will make a new determination that mental health services are voluntary and are clinically indicated. This important feature of DC law allows students to self-refer and to consent to confidential mental health services. Mental health clinicians routinely encourage students to inform and involve their parents in treatment, and concerted effort will be demonstrated in this regard. Schools must to clarify the law in meetings with parents.

(continued)

Figure 96.1. (*Continued*)

Meetings Outside of the School. Mental health clinicians may visit students' homes or community agencies as part of their job without obtaining permission from the school.

Referrals to the Mental Health Clinician. All referrals to mental health clinicians by school staff must be made in the referral format suggested by the Department of Mental Health, Community Services Agency and in a manner consistent with DCPS policy. All schools are requested to convene a team of relevant individuals that meet regularly to review and assign requests for services. The uniform referral process is critical to the Department's service delivery, record keeping, and accountability. All referrals, whether self-referral by the student or by the staff, contain confidential information and cannot be shared or copied without appropriate authorization.

Compensation for Services. According to the District Personnel Manual and the Department of Mental Health, Community Services Agency human resource policies, mental health clinicians cannot be financially compensated by the school for work completed as part of their normal duties.

Hours. The mental health clinicians are responsible for reporting their hours to the Department of Mental Health, Community Services Agency, but should sign in and out of the school if the school requires such a procedure. Mental health clinicians will report their schedules to the school on a monthly basis, and each carries a cell phone provided by the program to assure that they can be reached when out of the building.

Requests for Leave Time. Requests for leave time will be approved by supervisors at the Department of Mental Health, Community Services Agency with consideration given to school schedules and needs. Principals will be informed of this leave in writing.

Program Evaluation Responsibilities. In order to assure that we are having a positive and significant impact on children, youth, and families, the Department will collect information to assess the utilization of services and their quality as a basis for revising and improving the program at regular intervals. School staff (administrators and teachers), families, and students will be asked to participate on a regular basis in these evaluations. In addition, schools will be asked to share school-level data (e.g., attendance records, disciplinary actions, grades) so that we can assess impact on achievement and school behavior. Results will be shared with schools.

LEGAL CONSIDERATIONS
The following are legal requirements to which clinicians must adhere.

Mandatory Reporting Laws. Under D.C. Code 2–135 1, *et seq.* "the following personnel (in their professional or official capacity) must report any known (or) suspected case of child abuse (sexual or physical) or neglect: every physician, psychologist, medical examiner, dentist, chiropractor, registered nurse, licensed practical nurse, person involved in the care and treatment of consumers, law enforcement officer, school official, teacher, social service worker, day care worker, and mental health professional." The statute goes on to warn that "willful failure to make such a report by any of the above-mentioned persons may result in a fine . . . and/or imprisonment." Note that school staff members, as well as mental health clinicians, are mandated reporters of child abuse and neglect. Individuals who have contact with a suspected victim of abuse or neglect should make the report within the required period of time. Mental health clinicians will comply with DC statute, Department of Mental Health, Community Services Agency policy, and DCPS policy on procedures for reporting. Clinicians, in accordance with DCPS policy, are expected to inform the school principal of a report.

Mental Health Records Are Confidential and Not Part of the School Record. All mental health clinicians must abide by the Mental Health Information Act, a statute that dictates how information should be shared and with whom. When a record is developed in response to a referral for mental health services and the DMH-CSA mental health clinician assigned to a school provides these services, that record belongs to the Department of Mental Health, Community Services Agency and is not a part of the school record. As such, only those individuals authorized by the Department of Mental Health, Community Services Agency (i.e., a direct clinical supervisor), those who have a written authorization for release of information, or those with a court order can have access to information in these records.

(*continued*)

Figure 96.1. (*Continued*)

Disclosure of Mental Health Information. The DC Mental Health Information Act states that "except as specifically authorized . . . no mental health professional . . . shall disclose or permit the disclosure of mental health information to any person" (p. 249) except "on an emergency basis . . . if the mental health professional reasonably believes that such disclosure is necessary to initiate or seek emergency hospitalization of the client . . . or to otherwise protect the client or another individual from a substantial risk of imminent and serious physical injury" (p. 255). (See also D.C. Code Section 7–1203.03.) A mental health clinician may disclose information with the written authorization of a parent or legal guardian to a school staff employee; however, if disclosure of mental health information is made, that school employee may not disclose said information to any one else without the written authorization of the parent or guardian as required by the Mental Health Information Act.

Release of Mental Health Records Can Be Pursuant to a Court Order. In the District of Columbia a court order *signed by a judge* is required before a mental health record can be released to the courts or court designee. A subpoena is not sufficient for the release of a mental health record. If a court order or a subpoena is served to the "custodian of the records" and they are referring to the mental health records, the mental health clinician will be responsible for following appropriate procedures outlined by the Department of Mental Health, Community Services Agency and complying with the law in regards to this request. The Department requests that the original or a copy of the court order be given to the mental health clinician in order to submit the request for an appropriate release of the record. The mental health clinician will not be allowed to turn over the mental health record immediately, but will need to contact his or her supervisor to apprise her of the situation and then call the Corporation Counsel's office to verify the court order and to discuss procedures for complying with the request.

TERMS OF THE AGREEMENT
This agreement shall be for a period of one year beginning October 1, 2001 and ending September 30, 2002.

TERMINATION CLAUSE
Violation of client's rights as outlined in the Mental Health Information Act or violation of policies or regulations of the Department of Mental Health, Community Services Agency may result in the immediate termination of this memorandum of understanding and subsequent clinical services.

I _____
(signature of DCPS representative) have read the above and agree to follow the program procedures and expectations as defined herein as a condition of accepting the Department of Mental Health, Community Services Agency's mental health clinician in DC Public Schools.
_____(date)

I _____
(signature of DMH representative) have read the above and agree to follow the program procedures and expectations as defined herein as a condition of providing mental health services through the Department of Mental Health, Community Services Agency clinician in DC Public Schools.
_____(date)

(11/1/01)

Note: Printed with permission from the District of Columbia Public School System. An online version of this contract can be found at http://smhp.psych.ucla.edu/pdfdocs/dcmou.pdf

Figure 96.2. Example Contract

ANCILLARY SERVICES AGREEMENT

THIS ANCILLARY SERVICES AGREEMENT ("Agreement"), made and entered into as of the
_____ day of _____, 2004, by and between the EVANSVILLE-VANDERBURGH SCHOOL
CORPORATION ("EVSC") and _____, ("Service Provider"),

WITNESSETH:

WHEREAS, the Service Provider is qualified to provide certain services, which services are more
particularly described below; and

WHEREAS, the EVSC and/or students of the EVSC are in need of the Services; and

WHEREAS, the EVSC and the Service Provider wish to form a working relationship to provide
the Services, as more specifically provided herein.

NOW, THEREFORE, in consideration of the mutual promises and covenants contained herein,
the parties agree as follows:

1. *Services to be Provided.* Service Provider agrees to provide the following services:

   _____
   _____
   _____

2. *Term of Agreement; Renewal.* The term of this agreement shall be effective as of the _____ day of
   _____, 2004, shall continue until the _____ of _____, 200__, (the "Initial Term") and
   shall be automatically renewed for subsequent additional one (1) year terms unless terminated as
   provided herein.
3. *Termination of Specific Service.* EVSC may, at any time, with or without cause, terminate this
   Agreement as to any one or more of the Service(s) (as hereinabove defined) to be provided by Service Provider.
4. *Indemnification.* The Service Provider agrees to and shall indemnify and hold harmless the EVSC, its
   officers, agents, and employees, from and against any and all liability, damage, loss, cost, judgment,
   award, and expense, including attorney fees, which may accrue to or be incurred or sustained by
   the EVSC, its officers, agents, and employees, on account of any claim, suit, action, demand,
   or charge arising from, as a result of, or in any way related to, whether directly or indirectly,
   (a) the negligence or intentional conduct of the Service Provider or its employees, agents, or
   representatives, (b) in connection with the performance of services under this Agreement, (c) the
   conduct, action, or inaction of the Service Provider or its employees, agents, or representatives, or
   (d) any breach of this Agreement by the Service Provider.
5. *Relationship of Parties.* The parties agree that the relationship between them shall be that of an independent contractor and the agents, employees, or personnel of one party shall not be considered
   the agents, employees, or personnel of the other.
6. *Liability Insurance.* Service Provider shall carry in its own name, at its own cost, the following
   insurance or self-insurance (check those that apply):
   _____ Comprehensive General Liability Insurance with limits of not less than $1,000,000.00 each
   occurrence, $3,000,000.00 aggregate.
   _____ Workers' Compensation Insurance covering any liability incurred under the Indiana Workers
   Compensation Act and the Indiana Occupational Disease Act and including not less than
   $100,000.00 employer's liability insurance.
   _____ Professional Liability Insurance with limits of not less than those prescribed for health care
   providers that are _____, as required by I.C. 27–12–4–1, *et seq.*
   _____ Automobile Insurance with limits at least $1,000,000.00 Combined Single Liability per
   occurrence.

(continued)

Figure 96.2. (*Continued*)

7. *Confidentiality.* The Service Provider recognizes that EVSC student records must be kept confidential pursuant to federal and state law and agrees to maintain and preserve such confidentiality at all times.

8. *EVSC Policies.* The Service Provider shall cause all of its agents, employees, or personnel providing services hereunder to observe and comply with all rules, policies, standards and guidelines of the EVSC as may be adopted and amended from time to time by EVSC, including but not limited to procedures for reporting child abuse and neglect and building security issues, in addition to those of the Service Provider.

IN WITNESS WHEREOF, the parties hereto have hereunto set their hands and seals the day and date hereinabove first written and acknowledged the effective date of this Agreement to be the _____ day of _____, 2004.

EVANSVILLE-VANDERBURGH SCHOOL CORPORATION

By: _____

Its: *Superintendent*

NAME OF SERVICE PROVIDER

By: _____

Its: _____

1997

Note: Printed with permission from Evansville-Vanderburgh School Corporation.

- Orient contracted employees to all laws, regulations, and policies of a school setting

These steps should lead to a seamless delivery of mental health services in a school setting that positively enhance student learning and academic success.

References

Adelman, H., & Taylor, L. (2000a). *A center brief and fact sheet: Financing mental health for children & adolescents.* Los Angeles: Mental Health in Schools Training and Technical Assistance Center.

Adelman, H., & Taylor, L. (2000b). Promoting mental health in schools in the midst of school reform. *Journal of School Health, 70*(5), 171–178.

Agresta, J. (2004). Professional role perceptions of school social workers, psychologists, and counselors. *Children & Schools, 26*(3), 151–163.

Fisher, R. (2002). From Henry Street to contracted services: Financing the settlement house. *Journal of Sociology and Social Welfare, 29*(3), 25–27.

Fitz, J., & Beers, B. (2002). Education management organizations and the privatization of public education: A cross-national comparison of the USA and Britain. *Comparative Education, 38*(2), 137–154.

Franklin, C. (2001). Establishing successful relationships with expanded school mental health professionals. *Children & Schools, 23*(4), 194–197.

Honore, P., Simoes, E., Moonesinghe, R., Kirbey, H., & Renner, M. (2004). Applying principles for outcomes-based contracting in a public health program. *Journal of Public Health Management Practice, 10*(5), 451–457.

McCroskey, J., Picus, L., Yoo, J., Marsenich, L., & Robillard, E. (2004). Show me the money: Estimating public expenditures to improve outcomes for children, families, and communities. *Children & Schools, 26*(3), 165–173.

Rones, M., & Hoagwood, K. (2000). School-based mental health services: A research review. *Clinical Child and Family Psychology Review, 3*(4), 223–241.

Substance Abuse and Mental Health Services Administration (SAMSHA). (2004). *Comprehensive community mental health services program for children and their families.* Washington, DC: Author. Retrieved on October 18, 2004 from http://www.mentalhealth.samhsa.gov/publications/allpubs/CA-0013/default.asp.

U.S. Department of Education (1999). *Assistance to states for the education of children with disabilities and the early intervention program for infants and toddlers with disabilities; final regulations.* Federal Register, 64(48), 12406–12671. Washington, DC: Author.

Walker, H., Stiller, B., Severson, H., Golly, A., & Feil, E. (1994). First step to success: Intervening at the point of school entry to prevent antisocial behavior patterns. *Psychology in the Schools, 35*(3), 259–269.

Walker, H. M., Severson H. H., Feil, E. G., Stiller, B., & Golly, A. (1998). First step to success: Intervening at the point of school entry to prevent antisocial behavior patterns. *Psychology in the Schools, 35*(3), 259–269.

Weist, M. D. (1997). Expanded school mental health services: A national movement in progress. *Advances in Clinical Child Psychology, 19,* 319–352.

Best Practices for Designing and Developing School-Based Health Centers

Julia Graham Lear

Getting Started

Call them school-based health centers, school clinics, or expanded school health services, they represent a recent development in health care at school. In the past 30 years, in almost every state, a handful or more of communities have decided that their children and youth could benefit from the delivery of basic health care at or near school, and frequently the definition of basic care includes emotional and behavioral health services. Because school social workers often have a broad net of connections inside and outside the school, community, social workers may be asked to help plan or lead efforts to create new school-based health centers. This chapter describes important factors to consider during the planning and early implementation phases of such an initiative and suggests key issues to keep in mind as the project moves forward.

What We Know

Some Background

According to the most recent survey, there were about 1,500 school-based health centers across the country in 2002. The centers were found in 43 states plus the District of Columbia (Figure 97.1). Seven states did not have school-based health centers: Arkansas, Hawaii, Idaho, Nevada, North Dakota, South Dakota, and Wyoming.

The centers are located in elementary schools (37%), middle schools (18%), high schools (36%), k–12 schools (3%), alternative schools (1%), and a mix of other schools (4%). Since 1998, elementary

schools have seen the largest growth in school-based health centers (Center for Health and Health Care in Schools, 2002).

What Is a School-Based Health Center?

School-based health centers share the following characteristics:

They are located inside the school building or on the school campus. As an early architect of school-based health centers, Philip J. Porter once said, "Health services need to be where students can trip over them. Adolescents do not carry appointment books, and school is the only place where they are required to spend time" (Center for Health and Health Care in Schools, 1993).

In most instances they are sponsored by mainstream health organizations. With 32% of the approximately 1,500 centers in the United States, hospitals are the leading organizers of school-based health centers. Health departments and federal community health centers each sponsor 17%. Community-based nonprofit organizations sponsor 12%. School districts sponsor 15% of the centers (National Assembly on School-Based Health Care, 2003).

The centers are staffed by licensed health professionals. Students receive care from multidisciplinary teams of professionals, each of whom can address a broad range of problems. A medical assistant supports a nurse practitioner or physician assistant. Mental health services are typically provided by a master's-level social worker. A part-time pediatrician or family practitioner may round out the core staff. Centers also may have a part-time nutritionist, dental hygienist, substance abuse counselor, conflict resolution

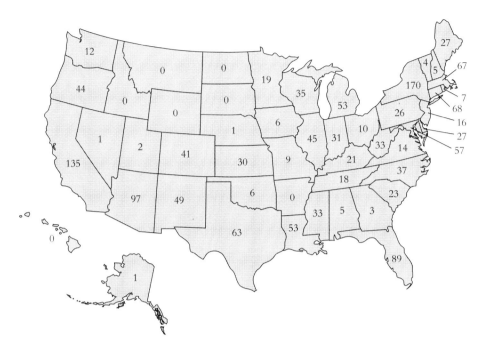

Map reports number of centers by state for school year 2001-2002.

Figure 97.1. National Survey of State SBHC Initiatives, School Year 2001–2002

Source: The Center for Health and Health Care in Schools. (2002). "State Survey of School-Based Health Centers Initiatives." George Washington University Medical Center, Washington.

counselor, and health educator, depending on the needs of students and the resources available in the community.

School-based health centers provide comprehensive services. From diagnosis and treatment of diseases to counseling for students and families, school-based health centers address a broad spectrum of health problems. A 2001–2002 survey of 1,100 centers found that leading physical health services included treatment for acute illness (94%), screenings such as vision and hearing (91%), asthma treatment (90%), comprehensive physical exams (89%), and immunizations (85%). Mental health services were provided at more than half the school-based centers. Leading services included assessments (74%), screenings (71%), grief and loss therapy (62%), and brief therapeutic interventions (62%). Most centers also provide health promotion and disease prevention programs, including tobacco use prevention (87%), alcohol and drug use topics (82%), and violence prevention and conflict resolution (82%) (National Assembly on School-Based Health Care, 2003).

School-based health centers build partnerships with parents. Typically, school-based health centers require written parental consent prior to accepting students as patients. School-based health centers also strive to get parents involved through parent newsletters, family communication seminars, and satisfaction surveys. Centers communicate with parents without compromising the confidential patient–provider relationship that teens desire and expect. Parents are immediately informed about their children's condition and treatment in life-threatening situations. While protecting teens' privacy, staff members also strongly encourage family communication.

School-based health centers build partnerships within their schools. Health centers organize open houses, attend faculty conferences, and conduct schoolwide immunization campaigns. Health center staff members meet with principals, assistant principals, teachers, coaches, guidance, and other pupil support personnel, as well as front-office staff. Health center personnel, who frequently are not school district employees, team up with the school's own health staff and with the academic and administrative staff to lead staff workshops on child and adolescent health, organize health fairs, and work in multiple ways to support the school community.

School-based health centers build partnerships with the community. To organize community support, health centers establish advisory councils of parents, students, health care providers, legislators, clergy, and community leaders. The councils advise on local needs, help develop health center policies, educate the community about child and adolescent health concerns, and educate local and state officials about the important role health centers have in working with families and communities to support healthy children and teens.

What We Can Do

First Steps

The starting point for a school-based health center may vary considerably from place to place. In some cases, it could be a response to a school crisis; in another, an opportunity may present itself in the form of a new grant program. A center may also be identified as the right response to a long-felt need, or result from the work of a community advocate who puts together the research, political, and funding pieces essential to launch a center. The remarkable thing is that those centers that do get started have a very good chance of surviving—despite ongoing financial and other challenges.

Centers that are well designed and that succeed address the following four questions.

1. *Is there an unmet need?* Documenting unmet need is essential to assure that the center will be busy, demonstrate its use to the community, and generate the funds required to sustain the center in the future. Information about student needs also provides a critical platform on which to build the service program. Limited budgets and space will require that choices be made among the types of providers to be hired, the services to be offered, and the skills or perspectives to be reflected in the staff. A solid needs analysis provides the information necessary to determine whether to move forward with a project and, if so, how to move forward.

2. *What do key stakeholders think and how will they be involved in the program?* Establishing a school-based health center is a challenging task. As with other physical and mental health programs in schools, the health center bridges two complex worlds—education and health. Key figures from both must support the initiative. Conversations with school board members, parents, the superintendent, affected principals, influential school staff, and community-based health professionals are essential for understanding their interests and involving them in the ongoing development of the program. Both during the planning phase and after the new center is launched, some of the stakeholders will serve on the health center advisory committee. The advisory committee will be the ongoing political firewall for the health center. Because members will include representatives of elected officials, parents, teachers, and recognized children's advocates, the advisory committee will reflect the community in supporting the centers.

3. *Is space available?* Finding adequate space for a school-based health center can be both a practical and political challenge. Some communities are experiencing rapid growth, and the schools are crowded. A separate facility located on the school campus may be a necessary direction. As a matter of convenience and student safety, many health center veterans argue that the center should be centrally located inside the school—across from the cafeteria or positioned off another well-traveled corridor. First floor space is generally more desirable than upper floors. If a center is to be used by community members or at times when the school is not open, ideally the center will be directly accessible from the outside. In a school with space constraints, it may be difficult to find space not already occupied by others. While principals typically determine space arrangements, health center planners will want to do what they can to assure that their new space does not generate hostility among their school colleagues. That said, securing the school principal's commitment to specific space before a final selection is announced may be a wise course of action.

4. *Are there sufficient funds to support the center, for an initial 4-year time period?* Across the country, community leaders and health professionals have launched school-based health centers with funding from a variety of sources—public

funds from city or county budgets, state grant dollars, private foundation grants, and in limited instances, funding from the federal community health center grant program. It is also possible for community organizations to pool resources, blending donated dollars, staffing, and other resources to provide the components of a school-based health center. While there is variety in the sources of funding, it is generally true that it requires several years to complete program design, start up initial operations, and get the center functioning on an even keel. The initial financial plan should ideally provide for 4 years of funding.

School-Based Health Center Nuts and Bolts

Whether a school-based health center is just starting up or fine-tuning a long-established program, the core components of a successful program include a memorandum of understanding between the school district and sponsor of the school-based health center, alignment of health services with students' unmet health needs, staffing to provide the services, a management and training structure, and a realistic budget.

A *memorandum of understanding (MOU)* helps define the mutual responsibilities of the school-based health center and the school or school district. From the perspective of the center, it is important that the school commit to providing space, heat, light, and power as an in-kind contribution. The school may also provide the Internet connection, telephone lines, janitorial services, and/or support for some staff members. For its part, the school may want to clarify the operating hours of the center, who will use the center, and the conditions under which the center may be used. Questions the MOU could answer include: Will teachers be served at the center? Will all students be permitted to use the center? What will be the hours of service, and under what conditions may a student be excused from class to visit the center? Procedures to be used in working out day-to-day problems can also be established in an MOU.

Health services and staffing are central to the success of a school-based health center. The initial determination of student problems that have not been addressed by services in the community lays the groundwork for setting service priorities. If the primary concerns of students attending a local high school are mental health and substance abuse, then it makes sense that the initial hires or service contracts would be in those two arenas. If an elementary school serves a significant number of recent immigrant families, it would be likely that service and staffing decisions would reflect this important aspect of the community. In the main, school-based health centers are staffed with nurse practitioners who can diagnose and treat diseases and clinically trained social workers to screen, assess for, and treat mental and behavioral health problems. A mix of other full- or part-time staff completes the clinic team. They include physicians, nutritionists, nurses, health educators, and health aides. Many schools host at least some health professionals and health educators—either on staff, under contract, or available through volunteer arrangements full- or part-time. Schools, particularly those in large urban school districts, may have an array of health providers. These include school nurses, mental health professionals, substance abuse counselors, and health educators. Who these people are and whether their services are full-time or part-time will have been established during the planning process. Making certain that the school-based health center complements rather than duplicates existing services is vital.

The management and training structure for a school-based health center should take into account that the center is located off-site from its institutional home. From a management perspective, a school-based health center is generally too small to justify a full-time management position. Even if a center operates within a multisite program of four or more centers, the manager will split her or his time among the sites, often maintaining an office at the sponsoring institution. Typically this means that at any one location, day-to-day center management is handled by a senior clinician, either the nurse practitioner or the mental health professional. In addition to providing clinical services, this person assures that clinic policies and protocols are observed, that records are maintained in accord with sponsor policies, and that relationships with school staff and the center advisory committee are attended to. The school-based health center program manager, who provides the interface between the sponsoring institution and the health center, is typically responsible for preparation of annual budgets, tracking revenues and expenses, and conducting long-term planning for the financial future of the organization. This person also tends to the center's important external relationships with parents, the advisory committee, the school board, and any other community leaders with a particular interest in the center.

From a clinical practice and training perspective, there are several implications for offering health services in a location other than within the sponsoring institution. First, the persons who are selected to be the school-based health professionals, whether they are nurse practitioners, nutritionists, clinical social workers, or nurses, will preferably have several years of experience in their own fields. To practice in a satellite facility means to be distant from seasoned professionals and less likely to have easy consults close at hand. Putting inexperienced providers in a school setting deprives them of the opportunity to practice their new skills with the guidance of easily accessible senior staff. A benefit of health center sponsorship by a mainstream health care organization is that these sponsoring organizations frequently maintain a rich array of clinical training opportunities that help the health center staff keep their skills sharp as well as build relationships within the sponsoring organization. Typically these organizations will require that health center staff participate in training on a regular basis.

Persistent Issues

Two issues that are critical in the development of school-based health centers are politics and financing. They must be carefully monitored and tended by health center leaders and advisors.

Politics

When the term *politics* is raised in connection with school-based health centers, the first words likely to occur to the reader are "teen pregnancy" or some other hot-button issue. While proposed school-based health centers may trigger a debate on teen sexuality and whether or how such centers should respond to this matter, in many communities the questions may center on cost, who is in charge, and the role of parents. Whatever the questions raised, however, developing and maintaining a school-based health center requires ongoing attention to political issues at many levels.

At the local level, within the school building, there are critical relationships to be established and maintained with other health professionals,

teachers, counselors, and the administrative staff. Long-time school building staff can be a resource for understanding the school's culture and the most effective way to work with students. Outside the school building, within the superintendent's office, the school board, the county commission, the mayor's office, or in the community at large, the health center must cultivate supporters who understand the work of the center and will advocate on its behalf. When seeking support, whether from voters or from local or national elected officials, the most important advocates for the health center will be the students, their parents, and representatives of the community, in that order. Professionals who draw their paycheck from the health center cannot be as persuasive as those who use and value the service.

Strategies to build relationships with state officials and federal representatives include assuring that local representatives have visited the center, have seen firsthand the support it has within the community, and understand what must be done in the state capital or in Washington to sustain the centers. In some states, school-based health centers have benefited from partnering with child advocacy organizations in the state capital. Twenty states have active school-based health center associations. The National Assembly on School-Based Health Care is a good place to start learning how to pursue these relationships. Because relationships are built over a period of time, the time to begin is when the project begins.

Financing—Making Sure There Is a Tomorrow

There is no easy road to financing school-based health centers. The very reason they fill a critical need is that they care for children and adolescents who either do not have insurance, are enrolled in poorly funded Medicaid or S-CHIP programs, or need services such as early mental health interventions that are not reimbursed or are reimbursed with difficulty. Thus, the justification for a school-based health center has within it the seeds of ongoing financial struggle. In some states, such as New York, the Medicaid program treats school-based health centers equitably, and the challenge is less. In other states, such as Oklahoma, where Medicaid reimbursement rates do not cover the cost of providing care, the challenge is profound.

A study of school-based health center funding found that the average health center budget in

Box 97.1 State SBHC Associations

Arizona	Massachusetts
California	Michigan
Colorado	New Mexico
Connecticut	New York
Florida	North Carolina
Illinois	Ohio
Kentucky	Oregon
Louisiana	Rhode Island
Maine	Texas
Maryland	West Virginia

fiscal year 1999/2000 totaled $169,000, with state governments providing 29% of the cost, city and county governments contributing 20%, in-kind contributions totaling 17%, patient care revenues 12%, private funding 14%, and federal revenues 8% (National Assembly on School-Based Health Care, 1999–2000). While individual centers might be mostly funded by a state grant or by city or county resources, this study presents the range of financial resources available to school-based health centers.

The past 20 years of rapid growth in school-based health centers suggest the following lessons about financing school-based health centers:

- It will always be hard work. Frequently the patients are uninsured or poorly insured. Moreover, the centers often provide important services such as family counseling or teacher consultations that are not covered by health insurance.
- In close-knit, smaller communities such as Wayne County (see below), it is possible to build an extraordinary school-based program using a combination of contributed resources and volunteer professionals. However, these contributions require continued outreach to build the relationships that are the foundation for community giving.
- In complex, urban environments, school-based health center resources may be more conventional: local tax dollars, state and federal grants, as well as United Ways and other private philanthropy.
- Private philanthropy and public dollars may be available to help support SBHCs even if they do not bear the specific title "school-based health center grant program." Funds targeted on children's health services, new immigrant

communities, prevention programs, health care for the uninsured, programs to prevent alcohol and substance abuse and teen pregnancy, and initiatives to build school–community partnerships are all potential resources.

Tools and Practice Examples

WISH—Wayne County Initiative for School Health

Less than 10 years ago, Wayne County, North Carolina, had one school nurse to provide professional health services to the 20,000 students enrolled in this rural school district some 60 miles east of Raleigh. David Tayloe, the head of the largest local pediatrics group in the county, noted that he and his colleagues rarely saw children after they entered the fourth or fifth grade. Concerned about this absence of care, as well as high rates of teen pregnancy and other problems among the community's adolescents, the pediatrician met with officials from a local hospital, the school system, and the health department to discuss how the community might organize an effective response. With the incentive of a grant program available from the Robert Wood Johnson Foundation, this group submitted an application, was successful, and opened centers in two county middle schools. Over the next 8 years, this group of community representatives became an independent nonprofit collaborative named the Wayne County Initiative for School Health (WISH) and began building a school-based health center network for middle and high schools in the county. By 2005, WISH was managing health centers in four middle schools and one high school that together served 2,000 students.

In 1996 when the Wayne County school health collaboration was getting started, state data identified middle school children as having the least access to health care. Parent surveys told them that parents worried about getting basic care for their children, wanted more teen pregnancy prevention, and needed greater access to children's mental health services. Barriers to care were identified as the difficulty the parents experienced in getting time off from work to take their children to the doctor and their lack of health insurance due to high cost. That parents of Wayne County truly wanted their children to have more access to health care has been demonstrated by ongoing high rates of student enrollment in the health centers. At each of the five schools, more than 85% of the children are enrolled in the centers. All students receiving services in the health centers must have a signed parental consent form on file, and parents must come to the center *in person* to enroll their child.

When the first two centers opened, they provided acute and chronic health services, mental health care, health education, nutrition education, immunizations, and physical examinations. This basic service package has been maintained. A clinic director and medical director oversee the operation of the centers. Each health center has a full-time registered nurse and aide. A group of health educators, mental health counselors, and dietitians rotate among the schools. Mental health professionals, including licensed clinical social workers, are private practice clinicians who sign MOUs with WISH and commit to a specific number of days at the health centers. These MOUs specify that the clinicians must see all students, regardless of insurance status. Clinicians are compensated by insurance payments for Medicaid and privately insured patients.

Funding for the centers remains a challenging but cooperative effort. The school system designed and built generous-sized health center offices that include a waiting room, an enclosed business and registration area, at least two exam rooms, and a room for group health education and other activities. School custodians help keep the clinic clean. The partner agencies contribute staffing and supplies. The students contribute pocket change to the "WISHing Well" and raise more than $1,000 annually to support the center. Reimbursement for patient services is received for students enrolled in public or private health insurance plans. The four health centers that meet stringent credentialing criteria established by the state are permitted to see Medicaid-enrolled children without securing prior approval from the children's medical homes.

Program performance from a community perspective is monitored through multiple satisfaction surveys. Parents, teachers, and students are all surveyed for their views on whether the school-based health centers are meeting their needs.

Denver Health School-Based Health Center Program

Denver's first two school-based health centers also started with a grant from the Robert Wood Johnson Foundation—but 10 years earlier than the Wayne County initiative. Under the leadership of the Denver Children's Hospital, the program launched clinics in Lincoln and East high schools with full-time nurse practitioners and master's-prepared mental health professionals at all sites. In contrast to Wayne County, many of these students had community-based health providers to whom they turned for annual physical exams and routine medical services. A study conducted after 10 years of operation, however, documented that when students were concerned about confidentiality, they were more likely to use the school-based health centers. As the study report noted, the school-based health centers were the students' primary source of mental health care and reproductive health services. The centers appeared to be the *only* source for substance abuse interventions and treatment. The Denver school-based health centers on average enroll 87% of the students at their schools.

As grant funds diminished, the Children's Hospital concluded that it did not have the resources to sustain the school-based health centers. Denver Health, the city's safety-net provider that included a 400-bed hospital, the public health department, and a network of community health centers, agreed to assume management of the school-based health centers. Because Denver Health receives substantial state funding for care to uninsured and low-income people in Colorado and because Denver Health, as a federally qualified health center, is entitled to receive cost-based reimbursement for care provided to Medicaid beneficiaries, the organization had a stronger financial base with which to support the school health centers.

With the transfer of program sponsorship, the network of centers began to expand. Denver Health has opened additional centers and was joined in the enterprise by St. Anthony's Hospital. In addition to Denver Public Schools, partners include Arapahoe House (a substance abuse prevention and treatment center), the Mental Health Center of Denver, and the University of Colorado School of Nursing. At present there are 11 school-based health centers operating in elementary, middle, and high schools. More than 6,000 students receive services through the clinics annually. The health centers provide basic medical care, health education, and mental health care. School health center team members include physicians, physician assistants, nurses, nurse practitioners, social workers, mental health therapists, and substance abuse counselors. In the difficult arena of substance abuse, working with Arapahoe House, the centers sponsor a 6-week course designed to decrease use of drugs and alcohol. Once school staff members identify students as substance users, the students are required to enroll in the course. During the school year 2001–2002, medical visits constituted 60% of clinic visits, mental health 27%, and substance abuse 13% (Denver Health, 2002).

In addition to routine clinical care, health center staffers organize a variety of programs for students, including immunization initiatives, insurance outreach and enrollment, asthma management, and case management of sexually active and pregnant teens.

Even with a solid financial base, Denver Health commits significant time to securing funding for its centers. In 2002, while Denver Health provided about 50% of the funding through state and federal grants as well as other resources, Denver Public Schools contributed 29% of the budget, St. Anthony's 10%, Mental Health Corporation of Denver 4%, Children's Hospital 3%, Arapahoe House 2%, and patient care revenue totaled 5%.

1. The National Assembly on School-Based Health Care (NASBHC), the national membership organization for school-based health centers, maintains a Web site, www.nasbhc.org, with how-to guides on starting a center. As well, they develop background papers and policy analyses that provide more in-depth material.

2. A number of state school-based health center organizations (see the Box 97.1) also have Web sites and resources that offer state-specific information.

3. The Center for Health and Health Care in Schools (CHHCS) located at the School of Public Health and Health Services at the George Washington University Medical Center also sponsors a Web site, www.healthin schools.org, with current information on funding resources, as well as extensive materials on school-based health services, school-based health centers, and school-based mental health services.

Key Points to Remember

The melding of primary care, mental health, and health education in one location within a school building has proven a powerful model for addressing the health needs of children but a challenging model to fund. The simplest part of starting a school-based health center will be organizing the clinical practice, arranging the staffing, and securing adequate space. The biggest job will be securing both a strong political base of support and developing a network of potential donors. The first steps in that direction will include organizing stakeholders at the school building, school district, community, and state levels and making the personal connections and collaborative relationships that result in a team of people committed to the long-term success of the center.

References

Center for Health and Health Care in Schools. (1993). *The answer is at school.* The George Washington University Medical Center.

Center for Health and Health Care in Schools. (2002). *2002 state survey of school-based health center initiatives.* School of Public Health and Health Services, The George Washington University Medical Center.

Denver Health. (2002). *Denver health school-based health centers: 2001–2002 annual report.* Denver, CO: Author.

National Assembly on School-Based Health Care. (1999–2000). *School-based health center revenues data from 1999–2000.* Accessed from the Internet on March 30, 2005 at http://www.nasbhc.org/APP/SBHC_finance_fact-sheet.pdf.

National Assembly on School-Based Health Care. (2003). *School-based health centers: Where kids learn and grow.* Washington, DC: Author.

Resources

Individuals and communities seeking to develop school-based health centers will find these organizations and Web sites of considerable help:

Best Practice in Expanded School Mental Health Services

Nancy Lever ■ Laura Anthony ■ Sharon Stephan
Elizabeth Moore ■ Bryan Harrison ■ Mark Weist

CHAPTER 98

Getting Started

In recent years a growing recognition of need has fostered an increase in comprehensive mental health services directly in schools. The expanded school mental health (ESMH) movement refers to the provision of a full continuum of mental health services (including schoolwide mental health promotion, early intervention, prevention, and treatment) to youth in special and general education through family–school–community partnerships (Weist, 1997). Expanded school mental health involves the collaborative efforts of school and community staff as guided by youth and families; it does not represent community providers coming into schools and working in relative isolation. As such, ESMH should be viewed as augmenting the more traditional mental health approach in schools, with the family–school–community partnership benefiting all three systems and moving the community toward a system of care that includes more preventive approaches (Acosta, Tashman, Prodente, & Proescher, 2002; Weist & Evans, in press).

What We Know

With the progressive development and increased prominence of school-based mental health in 7 recent years (as demonstrated in the New Freedom Initiative, see www.mentalhealthcommission.gov), the development of a quality assessment and improvement training agenda becomes increasingly more important (Power, Manz, & Leff, 2003; Weist et al., in press). The Center for School Mental Health Assistance, a national technical assistance, training, resource, and research center for advancing school mental health, currently oversees a major project funded by the National Institute of Mental Health to develop quality assessment and improvement in ESMH. Central to the project is a set of 10 principles for best practice, which was strategically developed over a 2-year period based on a qualitative research process (Weist et al., in press). The following presents practical tips for pursuing these principles for best practice, providing examples from a well-established school mental health program.

What We Can Do

Principle 1: All Youth and Families Are Able to Access Appropriate Care Regardless of Their Ability to Pay

Financing school mental health has many challenging dimensions (Evans et al., 2003; see resources of the National Assembly on School-Based Health Care, http://nasbhc.org). School-based programs usually cannot rely on grants and contracts alone, requiring fee-for-service revenue from Medicaid and other health insurance programs. While all students may not be eligible for reimbursable mental health care, program sustainability critically depends on access to reimbursement for students entitled to it. To accomplish this goal, school social workers and other clinicians can assist families to enroll in insurance programs for which they qualify.

Students who do not have health insurance may be eligible to receive it through Medicaid or the State Children's Health Insurance Program (SCHIP). SCHIP provides insurance to children and adolescents who exceed financial eligibility requirements for Medicaid but are still considered low income. To learn more about your state's insurance eligibility requirements, key Web sites to access include those developed by the U.S. Department of Health and Human Services (http://www.insurekidsnow.gov/states.htm) and the American Academy of Pediatrics (http://www.aap.org/advocacy/washing/elections/med_factsheet_pub.htm).

While clinicians cannot resolve all insurance coverage issues, they can become aware of agencies/programs that offer free care to individuals without health insurance. Clinicians can also provide reimbursable services and increase financial support for their program through advocacy, grant writing, and helping to form and foster partnerships within their school and larger community.

Principle 2: Programs Are Implemented to Address Needs and Strengthen Assets for Students, Families, Schools, and Communities

School-based mental health programs should be uniquely tailored to address school and community needs and to strengthen assets. The literature reveals a disparity between services families believe they need and those actually offered (Massey, Kershaw, Falk, & Hannah, 2000). School-based programs must engage children and families by striving to partner with families to ensure that families see services as relevant, appropriate, and effective.

To comprehend a school's needs, it helps to go directly to key stakeholders for input. Feedback from stakeholders can be obtained both formally and informally. Regular meetings, focus groups, and forums and informal meetings with students, families, teachers, administrators, and community leaders guide programs to address relevant concerns and assist in identifying key resources within the school and larger community.

Principle 3: Programs and Services Focus on Reducing Barriers to Development and Learning, Are Student and Family Friendly, and Whenever Possible, Are Based on Evidence of Positive Impact

Staff training and supervision is a critical component for accurately matching program services and appropriate treatments/interventions with the presenting needs of students. Training and supervision can assist clinicians manage their time to best serve the school and help them reduce barriers to development and learning. Clinicians should give significant thought to initial treatment planning and formulate questions such as the following: How is this student proceeding toward treatment goals? Is each goal still relevant? Do more important issues need to be addressed? Is therapy proactive or has it become reactive? Engaging students and families in developing clear treatment goals and expectations can keep treatment on track and increase satisfaction with care.

Much of the training and supervision for clinicians should focus on the delivery of effective care through empirically supported practice.

Box 98.1 Principle 1: All Youth and Families Are Able to Access Appropriate Care Regardless of Their Ability to Pay

- Compile eligibility information for Medicaid and SCHIP in your state
- Coordinate with your school health staff or school nurse on how to expedite new SCHIP enrollment
- Include insurance coverage and case management needs as standard questions in the intake process
- Post the numbers for enrolling children in insurance programs in your office (1-877-KIDS-NOW) and have necessary forms available to apply
- Help coordinate an information table or presentation about SCHIP in your state
- Write letters to local and state leaders about the value of school mental health and the necessity of funding
- Seek small grants and organize fund-raisers to support your school-based program

Box 98.2 Principle 2: Programs Are Implemented to Address Needs and Strengthen Assets for Students, Families, Schools, and Communities

- Design a questionnaire for stakeholders to assess resources within a school and local community (e.g., mental health, medical, educational, vocational)
- Regularly ask stakeholders about what works and does not work as it relates to mental health
- Have a feedback box available outside your office and specifically ask for critical feedback on how to better address school and community needs
- Keep track of community developments through diverse local media
- Make sure to partner with families and to include them as a true collaborator in treatment and as leaders in guiding and enhancing program services
- Hold semiannual forums to hear stakeholders' views on needs, strengths, and resources
- Assess resources and strengths within the school and surrounding community through open discussions, questionnaires, and forums
- Ask students and families directly about what risk factors are impacting their lives the most

Empirically supported approaches refer both to the use of formally developed evidence-based interventions (e.g., manuals that have been shown to lead to positive impacts for students in schools through randomized controlled trials) and to skills documented in a range of research studies associated with positive outcomes (e.g., cognitive behavioral skills such as self-instructional training, relaxation training, problem-solving). Through research and practical experiences in ESMH, the CSMHA developed an approach to empirically supported practice that involves four components: (1) reducing documented stress/risk factors in students' lives (e.g., exposure to violence, affiliation with acting-out peers), (2) enhancing documented internal (e.g., reading for pleasure, helping others) and external (e.g., receiving support from positive adults, being involved in faith communities) protective factors in students' lives, (3) training youth in skills shown to be associated with positive functioning

in many studies (as just reviewed), and (4) using formally developed manualized approaches with adequate training, supervision, support, and technical assistance.

Principle 4: Students, Families, Teachers, and Other Important Groups Are Actively Involved in the Program's Development, Oversight, Evaluation, and Continuous Improvement

Hodges, Nesman, and Hernandez (1999) poignantly stated: "The emergence of families as full partners in systems of care is the key to true and lasting collaboration" (p. 14). Expanded school mental health programs can benefit from involving school and community stakeholders in the original planning process. Key stakeholders (youth, families, school staff, community leaders) should then provide regular feedback on the

Box 98.3 Principle 3: Programs and Services Focus on Reducing Barriers to Development and Learning, Are Student and Family Friendly, and Are Based on Evidence of Positive Impact

- Get the client and family to agree on the problems, goals, and plans for treatment and methods to evaluate progress
- Continuously evaluate services to ensure they match presenting needs and issues
- Treat youth and families as partners and use strategies to ensure they remain engaged in therapy
- During each session ask for student/family feedback on services and ways to enhance treatment
- Focus therapy on reducing stress and risk, enhancing protective factors, and training in key cognitive behavioral skills
- Explore various evidence-based manuals to address presenting problem of students on your caseload; seek and receive training on at least one of these manuals, and begin to use it

Box 98.4 Principle 4: Students, Families, Teachers, and Other Important Groups Are Actively Involved in the Program's Development, Oversight, Evaluation, and Continuous Improvement

- Invite students, families, and teachers to participate on your advisory board
- Hold focus groups with stakeholders to elicit feedback about needs and recommendations for programs and services
- Assess needs across different stakeholders (e.g., parents, students, teachers, community leaders)
- Organize and provide training events for stakeholders based on input from them
- Follow through on stakeholder recommendations and report back on changes made
- Provide multiple forums for input: suggestion box, e-mail or Web site, voice mail, newsletters
- Invite family members or teachers to colead support or psychoeducational groups

program through informal mechanisms (e.g., meetings, phone calls) and formal feedback through advisory boards and other mechanisms (e.g., questionnaires, focus groups, surveys) (Ambrose, Weist, Schaeffer, Nabors, & Hill, 2002, p. 104). Stakeholders should assist with ongoing assessment of community needs and available resources, refining the program vision and mission, creating special programs to address needs within schools and communities, developing quality assessment and improvement guidelines and protocols, making program improvement recommendations, and securing additional funds (Acosta et al., 2002; Ambrose et al., 2002). For programs operating in multiple schools, it helps to have representation from each school on the program-wide advisory board and to consider smaller schoolwide steering committees/advisory boards that report to the larger advisory board (Hoganbruen, Clauss-Ehlers, Nelson, & Faenza, 2003).

Principle 5: Quality Assessment and Improvement Activities Continually Guide and Provide Feedback to the Program

Expanded school mental health programs should be guided by an effective quality assessment and improvement plan (Ambrose et al., 2002; Chinman, Imm, & Wandersman, 2004). Plans should specify roles and directives, as well as processes for program evaluation, dissemination of findings, and incorporating feedback into the program. A theme of continuous quality improvement (CQI) (Chinman et al., 2004; Zarin, West, & Hart, 2001) should prevail, representing a continuous feedback loop in which services are delivered, evaluated, modified, and redelivered. Quality assessment and improvement activities have many benefits, which include structuring and improving program services, increasing the likelihood of achieving positive outcomes, and providing

Box 98.5 Principle 5: Quality Assessment and Improvement Activities Continually Guide and Provide Feedback to the Program

- Provide regular training on empirically supported practices and provide support, technical assistance, strong supervision, and ongoing coaching in implementing them
- Develop a quality improvement team to oversee and guide the program
- Develop mechanisms to receive ongoing feedback from stakeholders about all aspects of your program
- Strategize as a team about how to best measure client change to document treatment effectiveness
- Conduct self-study chart reviews to ensure quality of services and adherence to ethical guidelines
- Convene a group to conduct chart reviews, quality improvement reviews, and ethics reviews
- Form a clinical peer review group (activities could include intensive case reviews, initial assessment reviews, reviews of videotapes, or role-taking activities)
- Ensure adequate procedures and training on them to address high-risk situations (e.g., suicidality, reporting abuse and neglect)

Box 98.6 Principle 6: A Continuum of Care Is Provided, Including Schoolwide Mental Health Promotion, Early Intervention, and Treatment

- Develop environment-focused interventions by assisting schools ensure safe and welcoming environments
- Implement measures such as the Psychosocial Environment Profile of the World Health Organization
- Develop a policy that states all students should have at least one meaningful positive interaction with an adult in school during the day
- Work collaboratively with educators in assisting them to implement positive classroom management strategies
- Assure that more preventive services can be offered to all youth including those without diagnoses
- Get and maintain buy-in from principal and administration for a full range of services
- Consider working with graduate student interns and externs in order to increase capacity and to help the ESMH program to better address prevention

mechanisms for documenting program outcomes and evidence of accountability (Ambrose et al., 2002).

Principle 6: A Continuum of Care Is Provided, Including Schoolwide Mental Health Promotion, Early Intervention, and Treatment

The recent report of President Bush's New Freedom Initiative on Mental Health (2003; www.mentalhealthcommission.gov) explicitly supports the improvement and expansion of school mental health programs. This report emphasizes a public health approach, indicating a full continuum of schoolwide promotion, early intervention, prevention, and treatment services in the schools. However, moving toward a complete

continuum presents considerable challenges in the United States, as the health care and payment systems focus on treatment of established problems (Evans et al., 2003). This highlights a significant advocacy and policy need; the need to expand resources and support to enable a full continuum of mental health promotion and intervention for youth in schools.

Principle 7: Staff Hold to High Ethical Standards; Are Committed to Children, Adolescents, and Families; and Display an Energetic, Flexible, Responsive, and Proactive Style in Delivering Services

School mental health programs depend on their staff to wear multiple hats (e.g., clinician, consultant, change agent, prevention specialist, and team

Box 98.7 Principle 7: Staff Hold to High Ethical Standards; Are Committed to Children, Adolescents, and Families; and Display an Energetic, Flexible, Responsive, and Proactive Style in Delivering Services

- Know the ethical guidelines of your profession
- Attend regular training that focuses on ethics and legal issues
- Attend professional conferences and workshops to keep abreast of innovative treatments and to keep you excited about your work
- Get involved in advocacy or policy work to increase public support for school mental health
- Develop a climate of open communication and reciprocal supervision about challenging situations with respected peers
- Arrange for one-to-one supervision with a more experienced clinician
- Provide cotherapy with other experienced professionals
- Pay attention to your own wellness needs

player), with each role contributing to the overall receptiveness to and impact of the program. Outstanding clinicians are energetic, flexible, responsive, and proactive in delivering services, while managing to contend with school and community stressors, paperwork, and administrative demands.

With the many demands of expanded school mental health, burnout presents a real danger. Ideally, clinicians should receive ongoing support and high-quality supervision from a licensed provider who has experience in school mental health. Supervision should be within a framework of continuous quality improvement with an emphasis on empirically supported practice. Stephan, Davis, Callan, and Weist (in press) suggest that school mental health clinicians would benefit from more intensive supervision in many realms: (1) conducting needs assessments, (2) developing referral mechanisms and building support for a full range of services, (3) maintaining positive relationships with school staff, (4) participating in school teams and committees, (5) responding to diverse school and community stakeholders, (6) understanding the resources in a community and how to refer to them, and (7) knowing education policy and regulations related to mental health.

Principle 8: Staff Are Respectful of, and Competently Address, Developmental, Cultural, and Personal Differences Among Students, Families, and School Staff

Cultural competence applies to all service systems because everyone has a culture and remains part of several subcultures (Center for Mental Health Services, 2002). Sensitivity to subcultures relates to appreciating differences both between and within groups. An effective service delivery system that addresses the mental health needs of diverse children and families must often surmount daunting barriers such as poverty, acculturation, language differences, and limited educational attainment. It is essential to adapt school mental health services and to provide ongoing training to clinicians to ensure programs are sensitive to developmental, cultural, and personal differences. Learning can occur on a formal basis with lectures and workshops, but can also stem from discussions with colleagues and clients. A major theme in cultural competence is true empathy for understanding the needs and developing responsive services for the various cultural/ethnic groups served by the school (Clauss-Ehlers & Weist, 2004).

To best facilitate a collaborative relationship with students and families served by school mental health programs, school social workers should make every effort to ensure that the program environment welcomes and respects clients. The National Association of School Psychologists advises members to remember, "It is the school's responsibility to provide a welcoming environment for all families. The school must send consistent messages to families that their contributions to forming effective partnerships are valued. Efforts should be made to work collaboratively with all families, including those whose primary language is not English and those with limited literacy skills." (1999, para. 5)

Box 98.8 Principle 8: Staff Are Respectful of, and Competently Address, Developmental, Cultural, and Personal Differences Among Students, Families, and School Staff

- Hold forums with families and youth from various cultural/ethnic groups to ask them about their needs and to seek recommendations on developing/improving services
- Provide regular training to staff on issues related to cultural competence
- Appoint advisory board members from the community so voices from all groups within the community participate in decision making
- Actively recruit multiethnic and multiracial staff
- Consider program accessibility and physical appearance of your office (e.g., pictures, literature, language) in terms of respect for different cultural groups
- Evaluate your caseload. If any minority group is underrepresented, consider how to outreach
- Learn as much as you can about each student's or family's culture, while recognizing the influence of your own background on your responses to cultural differences
- Work within and respect each student's family structure (grandparents, other relatives, friends)

Cultural awareness regarding ethnicity, disability, gender, sexual orientation, socioeconomic status, and so on, fosters a welcoming environment for students and families.

Principle 9: Staff Build and Maintain Strong Relationships With Other Mental Health and Health Providers and Educators in the School, and a Theme of Interdisciplinary Collaboration Characterizes All Efforts

Within an effective school mental health program, social workers, psychologists, nurses, psychiatrists, families, students, teachers, and school administrators work together to address the emotional and behavioral difficulties that interfere with learning and to optimize overall student well-being. One way to enhance collaboration is to develop interdisciplinary teams, such as a mental health team or student support team. When functioning well, mental health teams take on the role of agents for systematic change in the school. These teams may initiate schoolwide interventions, such as implementing crisis intervention plans, bringing relevant curricula into the school to promote the development of psychosocial competencies, conducting mental health education programs for children in classrooms, and directing peer counseling programs. In addition to participating in teams, such as student support or mental health teams, school social workers should meet regularly with school administrators and teachers to receive ongoing feedback for the program and individual students served. It is also critical to discuss issues related to limits of confidentiality and to develop a plan for how to share information to promote effective collaboration that respects student and family privacy.

Principle 10: Mental Health Programs in the School Are Coordinated With Related Programs in Other Community Settings

Researchers and practitioners express many concerns about the fragmented planning and implementation of community health and human services (Adelman & Taylor, 1997). The development of a "resource coordinating team" is one way resources can be made more accessible. According to the model described by Rosenblum, DiCecco, Taylor, and Adelman (1995), the resource coordinating team facilitates cohesion and coordination of school support programs for students and families. Roles assumed by the resource coordination team can include identifying and preparing a list of available resources at the school, in the district, and in the community; clarifying how school staff and families can gain access to resources; ensuring maintenance of needed resources; and exploring ways to improve and augment existing resources. Involving various stakeholder groups helps ensure that diverse knowledge and perspectives are taken into account.

Tools and Practice Example

Established in 1989 in four Baltimore City schools, the University of Maryland School Mental Health Program (SMHP) has expanded to 25

Box 98.9 Principle 9: Staff Build and Maintain Strong Relationships With Other Mental Health and Health Providers and Educators in the School, and a Theme of Interdisciplinary Collaboration Characterizes All Efforts

- Attend team meetings, staff meetings, and service coordination teams within your school
- Form an interdisciplinary mental health team with all school mental health and student support staff
- Develop a resource coordinating team to ascertain and use available school and community resources
- Create a service system map along a continuum of primary, secondary, and tertiary prevention for mental health service providers in the school
- Identify any areas of duplication or gaps in this map and devise collaborative ways to optimize services

Box 98.10 Principle 10: Mental Health Programs in the School Are Coordinated With Related Programs in Other Community Settings

- Develop a resource directory for your school and local community
- Contact your local mental health agency, either for your city or your state; a resource directory may already exist for your area
- Begin a resource coordinating team
- Share your resource directory with your school and local community. Ask for feedback on additional resources
- Have a "community resource fair" and invite community organizations to set up booths. Begin small-scale collaborations with organizations outside of the school (e.g., choose one student per week involved in an outside agency and try to make contact with that agency)

schools served by 30 clinicians drawn from diverse disciplines such as social work, psychology, counseling, and psychiatry. The SMHP developed in response to community stakeholder input requesting comprehensive mental health services for children and adolescents that were easily accessible and tailored to students' and families' needs (Flaherty & Weist, 1999). Quality improvement became a focus from the outset, with training and policy development reflecting many of the principles outlined here. Examples of the SMHP's efforts to achieve principles for best practice follow.

Reflecting *Principle 1*, a core tenet of the SMHP is to promote easy access to mental health for students and families, regardless of their ability to pay. Despite challenges to secure and maintain funding (Lever, Stephan, Axelrod, & Weist, 2004), the SMHP consistently serves youth and families with and without insurance. The program has done so by actively seeking "braided" funding to support the program, including local grants and contracts from the school system and health department, fee-for-service revenue, fund-raising, and city, state, and federal funding related to special initiatives in the school.

Principles 2 and *4* highlight the importance of assessing and addressing the strengths and needs of a community, as well as obtaining stakeholder input at all levels of school-based mental health program implementation. The University of Maryland SMHP ensured stakeholder participation in its development and improvement by holding focus groups with key stakeholders to elicit feedback prior to initiating services. Subsequently, the program conducted needs assessments and focus groups to determine the perceived problems faced by youth and families, as well as the relevance of school mental health in addressing these problems

(Axelrod et al., 2002). The SMHP has consistently maintained an advisory board throughout and worked to involve students, families, and community members on this board.

In addition to ensuring a strong partnership with stakeholders, the SMHP attempted to address community-wide needs in its clinical training and targeted interventions. Due to the high rate of trauma, violence exposure, and drug use in Baltimore City, clinicians have been extensively trained in these domains and been offered support to provide interventions to prevent and treat associated mental health issues in students.

In moving toward quality care in school mental health, the SMHP has taken several steps to achieve the goals described in *Principle 3*. These steps include the provision of goal-directed, student- and family-friendly services and the utilization of empirically supported interventions. All SMHP clinicians conduct a clinical evaluation and treatment plan with students and their families within the initial few sessions. When feasible, clinicians obtain feedback from students, family members, and teachers on student progress. The SMHP has actively pursued family involvement by hiring a family liaison to respond to family concerns and to accompany clinicians on home visits. Clinicians are also encouraged to partner with families in designing treatment and to outreach to families through meetings, phone calls, and letters.

The SMHP has focused efforts on using research to inform practice via the implementation of empirically supported interventions. It purchased several evidence-based treatment manuals for use by its clinicians and provided support for their implementation. Following the first implementation cycle, clinicians participated in focus groups to discuss their experience of introducing evidence-based curricula and made recommendations for adapting them to meet the needs of their student population.

Partnership with the CSMHA enhances the SMHP progress in the area of quality assessment and improvement (QAI) activities, the focus of *Principle 5*. In an effort to keep a pulse on the activities of school-based mental health services nationwide, CSMHA continuously offers suggestions to SMHP regarding quality improvement, including best practices for charting, supervision, and clinical decision making. SMHP has developed a policy and procedures manual that is continuously updated according to feedback from clinicians and program stakeholders.

Being housed within the Division of Child and Adolescent Psychiatry provides the SMHP a unique opportunity to work toward a full continuum of care, as indicated in *Principle 6*. The university provides a wide range of mental health services for children and adolescents that span the developmental spectrum and address problems across the prevention and intervention continuum. In addition to utilizing the university's comprehensive mental health services, SMHP clinicians target their own services across all levels of prevention; that is, they act as *prevention specialists* by offering classroom-based and group prevention activities, *interventionists* by providing individual and family therapy services to students with specific mental health needs, and *change agents* by addressing schoolwide issues and impacting overall school climate via participation in school teams and consultation with school staff.

Principle 7 speaks to a defining feature of the SMHP's success—its clinical staff. Comprised of energetic, flexible, and responsive individuals committed to the children and families they serve, staff impact program success enormously. Reflected in both hiring and training practices, SMHP remains acutely aware of the impact of its clinical staff on relationship building in the schools, productivity and quality of care, and program morale. The SMHP adopted several practices to ensure a highly motivated and supported staff; these practices include providing consistent, quality individual and group supervision to clinicians and supporting attendance at professional conferences and engagement in scholarly activities. Program administrators also attempt to attend to the wellness needs of clinical staff by providing in-service activities targeting staff burnout and stress reduction. In response to clinician feedback, the weekly staff meeting is supplemented on a monthly basis by a consultant with expertise in cultural competence.

This consultative experience lends itself to *Principle 8*, which recommends that staff be respectful of and competent in issues related to developmental and cultural diversity. SMHP has made efforts to achieve this standard by providing training in cultural competence, ensuring diverse representation in stakeholder meetings and advisory board membership, and by actively recruiting multiethnic and multiracial staff.

In its efforts to "fill in the gaps" in a comprehensive continuum of care for children and adolescents in Baltimore City, SMHP actively worked to achieve the goals reflected in *Principles 9* and *10*. To avoid duplication of services both within the school and surrounding community and to serve as a valuable add-on to existing services, SMHP carefully maps available mental health resources and seeks input regarding needed supplemental care. Within each school served by the SMHP, the clinician and program administrators work to establish strong relationships with other mental health and health providers in the school, to participate on school teams, and to collaborate with teachers. In order to coordinate with community programs as indicated in *Principle 10*, SMHP developed and updated a community resource directory for the past several years and has also invited several community organizations to be present at staff meetings.

Key Points to Remember

The school mental health field continues to grow. As shown by significant advantages in reaching youth and beginning evidence for positive outcomes achieved for students, families, schools, and community systems, the school mental health field has made great strides in advancing and completing the continuum of mental health and health care for youth. However, the more comprehensive approach to school mental health, such as the one reviewed in this chapter, is relatively young, leaving still many "horizons" of critical need for the field to look beyond.

Quality stands paramount among these horizons. This chapter attempted to present a set of validated principles for best practice in school mental health and how they can be used to improve practice and service impacts. As critical leaders in the work of school mental health, social workers have much to offer in the development of a systematic quality assessment and improvement agenda.

References

Acosta, O. M., Tashman, N. A., Prodente, C., & Proescher, E. (2002). Establishing successful school mental health programs: Guidelines and recommendations. In H. Ghuman, M. Weist, & R. Sarles (Eds.), *Providing mental health services to youth where they are: School and community-based approaches* (pp. 57–74). New York: Taylor Francis.

Adelman, H. S., & Taylor, L. (1997). Addressing barriers to learning: Beyond school-linked services and full-service schools. *American Journal of Orthopsychiatry, 67*(3), 408–421.

Ambrose, M. G., Weist, M. D., Schaeffer, C., Nabors, L., & Hill, S. (2002). Evaluation and quality improvement in school mental health. In H. Ghuman, M. Weist, & R. Sarles (Eds.), *Providing mental health services to youth where they are: School and community-based approaches* (pp. 95–112). New York: Taylor Francis.

Axelrod, J., Bryant, T., Lever, N., Lewis, C., Mullett, E., Rosner, L., Weist, M. D., Sorrell, J., & Hathaway, A. (2002). Reaching out to school and community stakeholders to improve mental health services for youth in an urban U.S. community. *International Journal of Mental Health Promotion, 4*, 49–54.

Center for Mental Health Services. (2002). *Cultural competence in serving children and adolescents with mental health problems.* Retrieved August 13, 2002 from www.mentalhealth.org/publications/allpubs/CA0015/default.asp

Chinman, M., Imm, P., & Wandersman, A. (2004). *Getting to outcomes 2004: Promoting accountability through methods and tools for planning, implementation, and evaluation.* Rand Corporation. Retrieved on July 14, 2004, from http://www.rand.org/publications/TR/TR101/.

Clauss-Ehlers, C., & Weist, M. D. (2004). Advancing community involvement and planning to promote resilience in youth from diverse communities. In C. Clauss-Ehlers & M. D. Weist (Eds.), *Community planning to foster resilience in children* (pp. 3–12) New York: KluwerAcademic/Plenum Publishers.

Evans, S. W., Glass-Siegel, M., Frank, A., Van Treuren, R., Lever, N. A., & Weist, M. D. (2003). Overcoming the challenges of funding school mental health programs. In M. D. Weist, S. W. Evans, & N. A. Lever (Eds.), *Handbook of school mental health: Advancing practice and research* (pp. 73–86). New York: Kluwer Academic/Plenum Publishers.

Flaherty, L. T., & Weist, M. D. (1999). School-based mental health services: The Baltimore models. *Psychology in the Schools, 36*, 379–389.

Hodges, S., Nesman, T., & Hernandez, M. (1999). Promising practices: Building collaboration in systems of care. In *Systems of care: Promising practices in children's mental health,* 1998 Series, Volume VI. Washington, DC: Center for Effective Collaboration and Practice, American Institutes for Research.

Hoganbruen, K., Clauss-Ehlers, C., Nelson, D., & Faenza, M. (2003). Effective advocacy for school-based mental health program. In M. D. Weist, S. W. Evans, & N. A. Lever (Eds.), *Handbook of school mental health programs: Advancing practice and research* (pp. 45–59). New York: Kluwer Academic/Plenum Publishers.

Lever, N., Stephan, S., Axelrod, J., & Weist, M. D. (2004). Accessing fee for service revenue in school mental health: A partnership with an outpatient mental health center. *Journal of School Health, 74,* 91–94.

Massey, O. T., Kershaw, M. A., Falk, K. K., & Hannah, S. K. (2000). *Children who drop out of treatment: A final report.* Tampa, FL: Louis de la Parte Mental Health Institute, University of South Florida.

National Association of School Psychologists. (1999). *Position statement on home–school collaboration: Establishing partnerships to enhance educational outcomes.* Adopted by NASP Delegate Assembly April 1999. Retrieved September 11, 2002, from http://www.nasponline.org/information/pospaper_hsc.html

Power, T. J., Manz, P. H., & Leff, S. (2003). Training for effective practice in the schools. In M. D. Weist, S. Evans, & N. A. Lever (Eds.), *Handbook of school mental health: Advancing practice and research* (pp. 257–273). New York: Kluwer Academic/Plenum Publishers.

Rosenblum, L., DiCecco, M. B., Taylor, L., & Adelman, H. S. (1995). Upgrading school support programs through collaboration: Resource coordinating teams. *Social Work in Education, 17*(2), 117–123.

Stephan, S., Davis, E., Callan, P., & Weist, M. D. (in press). Supervision in school mental health. In T. Neill (Ed.), *Helping others help children.*

Weist, M. D. (1997). Expanded school mental health services: A national movement in progress. In T. Ollendick & R. J. Prinz (Eds.), *Advances in clinical child psychology* (Vol. 19, pp. 319–352). New York: Plenum.

Weist, M. D., & Evans, S. W. (in press). Expanded school mental health: Challenges and opportunities in an emerging field. *Journal of Youth and Adolescence.*

Weist, M. D., Sander, M. A., Walrath, C., Link, B., Nabors, L., Adelsheim, S., Moore, E., Jennings, J., & Carrillo, K. (in press). Developing principles for best practice in expanded school mental health. *Journal of Youth and Adolescence.*

Zarin, D. A., West, J. C., & Hart, C. (2001). The American Psychiatric Association's agenda for evidence-based quality. In B. Dickey & L. I. Sederer (Eds.), *Improving mental health care: Commitment to quality* (pp. 151–160). Washington, DC: American Psychiatric Publishing, Inc.

Effective Resources for Accountability

With the enactment of the Goals 2000: Educate America Act, tax dollars are being allocated to public schools based on accomplishment of eight national goals for education. At least four goals relate directly to mental health and social services. More than ever, school social workers and mental health counselors must demonstrate that their services lead to improved educational achievement and that public and private funds supporting social and mental health services are well spent. They must not only describe what they do but also show the impact of their interventions. In planning and demonstrating effective accountability, skills are required that may be new to many school-based services professionals. This section provides distinct steps for designing and managing best practice program evaluation, as well as essential systems that facilitate accountability.

Linking School Social Work Interventions to Educational Outcomes for Schools

Todd Franke ※ Sean Lynch

CHAPTER 99

Getting Started

For many children, the challenges associated with growing up can be overwhelming. Equally overwhelming is the feeling that school social workers, teachers, and other social service providers often experience as they endeavor to help children and families overcome these challenges. While many programs are well meant and often well conducted, the outcome, even at a school site, is often an array of fragmented services that sometimes fail to help the children and families they were designed to serve. Yet all of these programs typically have a twofold goal: improve the quality of life for the children and their families and also enable the children to take advantage of the education being provided in the classroom by providing the prerequisite conditions necessary for them to succeed.

The importance of linking school social work interventions to educational outcomes is further compounded by the growing movement toward accountability at all levels of primary and secondary education, from teachers to principals to district superintendents. The importance of this connection has become more acute with the passage of No Child Left Behind in 2002. The act places an emphasis on standardized testing that has shifted educators' focus to students who are close to meeting minimum standards in order to meet targets (Rubin, 2004). This suggests that students who are further away from meeting minimum standards may be overlooked.

Educators have been critical of the No Child Left Behind Act. Their concern is that ultimately the act has not caused much change except for increased standardized testing, more penalties for substandard performance, and few financial resources to support the effort (Marshak, 2003). Critics of the act's focus on standardized testing suggest that it does not address the important issue of changing the model of schooling to a postindustrial one that combines individual success for a child with common academic standards for all students (Marshak, 2003). They suggest that instead of encouraging students to learn a curriculum that prepares them for adult life, students are taught to pass tests (Neill, 2003). Opponents of the act also argue that inadequate funding will prevent it from meeting its goals (Neill, 2003). In order to meet the new requirements, educators have shifted their focus to students who have not quite met the test standard (Rubin, 2004).

What We Know

Importance for Schools

While the No Child Left Behind Act may be a driving force behind some accountability efforts that have a questionable design, linking interventions with outcomes has several important features. When we take medication to combat illness, we expect that the medication is proven to have the desired effect of recovery. Similarly, when we intervene in order to resolve a problem that affects children's academic performance, we should use an intervention that is proven to have desirable outcomes.

Linking school social work interventions to educational outcomes is essential for schools because it allows staff members to show stakeholders how programs are achieving the outcomes the programs propose to deliver. Since schools are funded by public resources, school staff are accountable to children and their parents and the public, as well as the governments that fund them. Providing a quality education with equal access for all children is a formidable task, since many schoolchildren have limitations that affect their ability to perform successfully. Some of the more common concerns are mental, emotional, or behavioral problems that affect 12% to 22% of children under age 18 (Adelman & Taylor, 2003). This result is staggering, given that there are approximately 60.3 million children ages 3 to 17 enrolled in school in the United States (U.S. Census, 2000). Approximately 16% of all children receive mental health services, and of these about 70–80% obtain services at school

(Burns, Costello, et al., 1995). The rationale for providing these services at school is that schools should make every reasonable effort to assist children to perform to the best of their academic abilities (Adelman & Taylor, 2003). When their mental health concerns are treated, children are better able attend school ready to learn each day. To this end, many schools have implemented programs addressing a range of mental health issues as a means of improving educational outcomes.

By linking outcomes with interventions, programs can demonstrate that they are full educational team members who share the same goal of student success. Studies suggest that there is a relationship between educational outcomes such as higher test scores and nonacademic factors like overall student health, including mental health. For example, the California Healthy Kids Survey (CHKS) showed that schools have higher levels of academic achievement when students have fewer health risks and more protective factors (Hanson & Austin, 2003). The reason for supporting healthy development in order to generate the best educational outcomes is that the benefits are experienced over an individual's life span, creating well-educated, healthy people who are better able to be productive workers and will not have to rely on social services or health care as frequently during their adult years (Adelman & Taylor, 2003). When these connections are clear and mental health programs are able to provide evidence of their impact, they will be in a better position to withstand times of budget crisis. Rather than viewing these programs as superfluous, stakeholders will be more likely to consider these programs as an important part of the educational mission of schools.

Research Framework on Interventions

There is considerable research literature documenting the results of interventions for specific problems or issues. There is evidence that programs have positive outcomes, and the direct effect on academic skills is promising. Adelman has organized interventions that address barriers to learning for children into a framework of six categories (Adelman & Taylor, 2003). These categories, organized by intervention approach, are:

1. increasing the teacher's ability to handle problems and nurture development;

2. supporting the school's ability to manage transition;
3. preventing crisis situations and addressing them when they happen;
4. increasing participation of family members;
5. integrating the community; and
6. offering special assistance.

This framework helps us to select the appropriate intervention for a given issue that has some empirical evidence that supports the program's ability to achieve the outcomes it proposes. It was used to classify several national intervention programs in order to demonstrate the outcomes with which they are linked. We will discuss specific program results in the section below on outcomes.

What We Can Do

Based on our work with schools, we identified national intervention programs that school social work professionals would easily recognize and may have recently implemented. We organized these programs using the framework discussed earlier. We defined a national-level program as an intervention that fit into one of the six categories but one that was not created to be implemented exclusively within a particular school district with only local needs in mind. We believe, however, that the majority of programs implemented in schools are homegrown programs that blend local, state, and federal funding to address local needs. While national-level programs are probably less frequently used, we believe this is due to the limited availability of such programs. We include a list of the recognizable national-level programs and have categorized them according to the current research base (see Table 99.1). Most programs fall into the category "responding to, minimizing impact, preventing crisis." Programs such as Second Step, Positive Adolescent Choices Training (PACT), and Peacebuilders, which all address various forms of violence, all fit into this category. It is not surprising to find that violence prevention programs are readily available due to the recent national focus on school violence prevention following the incident at Columbine High School in Colorado. Programs that provide special assistance for students and families, such as Healthy Start and Why Try? were the second largest category.

MegaSkills, a program that teaches parenting skills, fits into the enhancing home involvement category.

Tools and Practice Example

Program Adaptation

Programs are rarely a perfect fit for a particular school's needs and must be adapted for local use. Schorr observes that successful programs cannot be imposed from the outside, but are rather shaped to meet local needs so communities have ownership (Schorr, 1997). Adaptation can take many forms and is not limited to making changes to meet particular students' needs. Common areas of concern tend to fall into these six areas: funding, dealing with school needs, relationships, time, competing interests, and demographic issues. These areas are summarized in Table 99.2; however, we would like to discuss the themes in greater detail and provide you with some suggestions for resolution.

One of the most important concerns of school social work programs is funding. Programs often receive insufficient funds to do the tasks outlined in the scope of work. The first years of implementation are frequently so busy that inadequate attention is paid to capturing service data that could affect funding decisions. Programs must constantly weather budget crises along with the end of funding streams, putting them in a constant state of flux. New programs like Why Try? are particularly susceptible to funding issues, especially during the implementation phase. Sometimes funding can switch after the first year of a program has been developed and staff have been trained. This can make staff feel that they have to start all over again. In order to meet these challenges, staff are stretched and programs creatively find ways to do more with less; however, long-term sustainability is a recurrent issue. To the degree that programs can demonstrate the connection between service delivery and educational outcomes, they will change school administrators' perception of the programs from a luxurious extra to the view that the programs are integral to the educational process.

There is an important balance to be struck between delivering program services and dealing with the school needs that are on top of the

Table 99.1 National-Level Program Classification

Program	Enhancing Teacher Capacity for Addressing Problems and Fostering Development	Responding to, Minimizing Impact, Preventing Crisis	Enhancing School Capacity to Handle Transition	Enhancing Home Involvement	Outreaching to Community to Build Linkages	Providing Special Assistance for Students/Families
Second Step	☐	☒	☐	☐	☐	☐
Positive Adolescent Choices Training (PACT)	☐	☒	☐	☒	☐	☐
Why Try?	☐	☐	☐	☐	☐	☒
California Healthy Start	☐	☐	☐	☐	☐	☒
Respect	☐	☒	☐	☐	☐	☐
Peacebuilders	☐	☒	☐	☐	☐	☐
Mega Skills	☐	☐	☐	☒	☐	☐
Beyond the Bell —Extended Learning Opportunities (No Child Left Behind)[a]	☐	☐	☒	☐	☐	☐
Homeless Children & Youth Program (No Child Left Behind)[a]	☐	☐	☐	☐	☐	☒
CASASTART	☐	☒	☐	☐	☐	☐
Caring School Community	☒	☐	☐	☐	☐	☐
Community of Caring	☒	☐	☐	☐	☐	☐
Facing History & Ourselves	☒	☐	☐	☐	☐	☐
Open Circle Curriculum	☒	☐	☐	☐	☐	☐
Positive Action	☒	☐	☐	☐	☐	☐
Project Star	☒	☐	☐	☐	☐	☐
Social Decision Making & Problem Solving	☒	☐	☐	☐	☐	☐
The Think Time Strategy	☒	☐	☐	☐	☐	☐

[a]The No Child Left Behind Act provides federal funds to states who in turn award money to school districts in order to implement a wide range of programs that improve educational outcomes. These include programs for homeless children and youth, as well as after-school programs.

Table 99.2 Common Concern Areas

Category	Issues	Suggestions for Resolution
Funding	• Inadequate funding • Funding instability • Long-term sustainability	• Show how programs affect educational outcomes • Identify ways of doing more with less
Dealing with school needs	• Program fit • Prioritizing school's daily needs • Program inflexibility	• Tailor services to schools' needs • Deal with kids where they are • Identify best practices, mutual support
Politics/relationships	• Primary relationship is to the school • Need buy-in from administrators on down to parents • Accountability exposure	• Demonstrate how academic and mental health missions are complementary • Be knowledgeable about school trends • Incorporate teacher's presence into program delivery
Time	• Lack of teacher and student time • Social worker's time management • Time-consuming program models	• Programs must be flexible and adaptable • Use more seasoned staff during program planning phase
Competing interests	• Conflict between mental health and academic missions • Social workers are caught between multiple roles	• Harness staff inventiveness/creativity • Adopt an eclectic approach
Demographic issues	• Dealing with counselor social worker burnout due to poverty effects • Clinical competence in diversity issues	• New social workers need to be better prepared to handle the effects of poverty on children • Programs need to be culturally relevant

school's agenda on a given day. Program staff recognize that when schools are paying for program services, staff must deliver what the school needs and the services should be tailored accordingly. On the program level this means that programs that are scripted and inflexible may need to be modified. When the program model must be adhered to without change, creativity is limited and teachers may not support the program. On the other hand, programs that are process driven and use the children's perspective are favored. Staff may be more willing to work with a program that is flexible enough to fit into an environment where the situation can rapidly change. A well-scripted program like Respect is preferred for this reason. A program

with components that can be easily dropped or shortened is valuable. A seasoned social worker can bring the program alive by working with whatever the children bring up, so it is important to deal with them where they are and integrate this with the program model. This is necessary because programs operate in a school context, and it may be necessary to deal with school issues at hand that day before your own service delivery agenda. Another good tool for dealing with school needs is collaboration and networking mental health professionals to identify ways to balance school needs with program delivery.

Another feature of programs' situational context is the relationship of social workers to the school and the political issues this may raise. The social worker's primary relationship is to the school, and he or she may feel tension with that relationship, especially if the social worker is part of another organizational division. In this case, the social worker may be perceived as an outsider by school administrators and teachers. This might cause the perception that the social worker is telling them what to do and may create resentment. Jealousy might arise because teachers may want the social worker to spend more time in the classroom and may not understand the purpose of some interventions. Personality conflicts that interfere with program's success can also come into play. In order to counteract these pitfalls, it is important to establish support from administrators and teachers as soon as possible. Social workers can do this by demonstrating how the academic and mental health missions are complementary. Their knowledge of school trends, such as curriculum changes, audits, teacher stress, and other major issues, can be useful in building support. Incorporating the teacher's presence into program delivery is another strategy for improving how the program works and increasing teacher buy-in and support.

Including the teacher's presence in the Second Step program has been particularly helpful. By involving the teacher in the program, the social worker is able to assist the teacher to learn better ways of handling specific children. The different scenarios contained in the program components allow the teacher to assist the child with work on anger management and social skills. Teacher involvement has been an effective tool to build teacher support of the program.

Many concerns about program adaptation revolve around time. Both teachers and social workers have insufficient time to do all the tasks they would like during their work day. For the social worker, the day's tasks can be overwhelming. There is little opportunity for preplanning during the program implementation phase. Service delivery can be time-consuming, so programs that are hard to implement quickly can be problematic. This can impact the success of a program like MegaSkills, since it often takes the social worker's involvement to get the program running. While the goal is to get parents to run the program, often getting to this point takes time and a significant amount of start-up time from the social worker. Teachers also cite lack of time as a stumbling block with intervention programs. Administrators and teachers often do not see how dealing with student issues

takes up time that could be devoted to other tasks. The concern about time also affects students. When school periods are changed, this affects the schedule for the day, which in turn influences whether a child can attend a program. Thus, lengthy program models need to be shortened to meet students' schedules. As a result of time concerns, programs must be flexible and adaptable with ease of curriculum modification. Programs may need to cut role play or questions, for example, in order to deal with time constraints.

Similar to time constraints, school social workers must also adapt programs in order to handle competing interests. School social workers may have to handle the perception on the part of school staff that there is a conflict between the mental health and academic missions. School staff may only support the academic aspects of the school's mission. Another competing interest is the multiple roles of the school social worker. The role of social workers in schools has become broad and does not just include clinical services. If the social worker has a job that has responsibilities in attendance, case management, and/or counseling, for example, interventions that take a long time can be frustrating due to the demands of the other responsibility areas. Sometimes social workers can be asked to assist school administrators with tasks that are not directly related to their mental health mission (e.g., assisting with award assemblies). Networking with other social work staff to harness collective inventiveness and creativity is a helpful way to handle these competing interests. A good way to respond to school staff requests for assistance with school duties that are indirectly related to the social worker's main job functions is to view the assignment as a way to build relationships with school staff. A strong relationship is integral to the success of a program like Peacebuilders, which requires the whole school to self-regulate as part of its violence prevention strategy.

Finally, demographic issues can also influence program adaptation to meet the needs of students. Social workers often practice in communities where poverty is an issue and therefore should be prepared to handle the effects of poverty on children during the term of their tenure in the position. Unfortunately, counselor burnout can be an issue that impacts how programs are delivered. Frequent staff turnover can affect program integrity and the quality of services. Social workers also frequently work with minority populations. As such they should be sensitive to diversity issues that may require modification of program delivery (e.g., providing the services in Spanish). This may involve the translation of program materials as well as the modification of the program model to make it more culturally sensitive.

Outcomes

The process of adapting programs for local use places programs in the best position to achieve the intended outcomes. We have summarized the empirical research on outcomes of these programs in Table 99.3. Each of the violence prevention programs shows evidence of favorable outcomes such as reduced aggression and violent behavior. Programs like Healthy Start, Why Try? and MegaSkills also demonstrate positive impact on domains such as health and social/ emotional functioning.

Evidence for the impact of intervention programs on educational outcomes is encouraging. In particular, programs in the special assistance for students/families and enhancing home involvement categories show the most promise for impacting educational outcomes. Improved GPAs, standardized test scores, and fewer absences are some of the educational outcomes of programs in these categories. While the violence prevention programs have favorable outcomes, evidence for the programs' impact on educational goals is less clear. While we may know intuitively that a program's reduction of aggressive behavior will affect a student's classroom performance, the educational outcome evidence is not always available (see Table 99.3).

Practice Example

In order to connect the implementation of a packaged program with its adaptation, we would like to discuss an example using the nationally recognized violence prevention program Second Step. There are a few main implementation points where the issues we have raised about adaptation are likely to arise. One of the initial implementation issues is identifying those individuals who have a stake in the program's success (Crowe & Sydney, 2000). We suggest that identifying stakeholders will require adaptation because of the politics/relationships issue we identified. It is imperative to have buy-in from stakeholders such as teachers and administrators. Without their support of the program, its success will be limited.

Identifying the purpose of the program, including its goals and objectives, is another important step (Crowe & Sydney, 2000). School staff may have to adapt Second Step to meet the specific goals and objectives of their school. The Second Step lessons are divided into empathy, impulse control, and anger management units. Role playing is extensively used in the curriculum, which allows students to further develop the skills they are learning. School staff must consider whether this format best suits their student population and meets their goals and objectives. If not, amendments to the topics covered or the use of techniques other than role play should be considered.

Receiving adequate funding to support the program is a step that brings up important issues such as sustainability (Crowe & Sydney, 2000). While funding for Second Step may come from more established sources such as federal and state governments, there is still a degree of instability. Funding for this program comes from federal and state violence prevention sources. Such funding sources can be unstable and insufficient to meet all the program needs. As a result, program staff must adapt by addressing the long-term sustainability of the program through searching for other resources and finding creative ways to stretch available dollars. Funding streams can easily change course for political reasons (e.g., budget crises), and this can have implications for program delivery. Second Step is designed for delivery over several years. If funding changes during this time period, this may have a negative effect on outcomes, since the full intensity of the program will not be delivered.

Hiring and training staff to implement Second Step is a time-consuming step (Crowe & Sydney, 2000). In order to implement this program, a 2-day training is required. In addition to this training time requirement, the program requires a significant instruction time investment. Second Step is comprised of 20 to 30 lessons, which range from 20 to 50 minutes. These features of the program suggest adaptation around the issue of time will probably be necessary. Programs that are long may not fit well into the children's school schedules. Additionally, a program that has large time demands may cause teachers to doubt they have the time to devote to it and may stretch social workers' time management skills. One solution may be to modify lesson plans in order to accommodate time challenges on a given day by shortening role play or questions.

Table 99.3 Program Outcomes

Program	Outcomes
Second Step	Reduced aggression, increased knowledge about violence and its prevention, and increased following directions (Orpinas, Parcel, et al., 1995).
Positive Adolescent Choices Training (PACT)	Reduced violent behavior and increased participants' ability to avoid violence (UCLA, 2004). Increased negative feedback delivery skills, problem solving, and peer pressure resistance; reduced in and out of school suspensions (Yung, 2001). Improved problem-solving communication and negotiation skills (Hammond and Yung, 1991).
Why Try?	Improved GPAs; reduced student absences and number of failed courses; more likely to graduate from high school (Why Try? 2003).
California Healthy Start	Improved health and social/emotional functioning; improved reading and math scores (UCLA, 2004). Significant increases in standardized test scores, increased parent participation, and reduced student mobility (C.D. of Education, 2004).
Respect	Corrects normative distortions and changes social perceptions of peer group, leading to increased empathy (Dranoff & Dobrich, 2003).
Peacebuilders	Reduces fighting and related injuries, as well as suspensions and community crime; also reduces other aggressive behavior, principal referrals, suspensions, and transfers (UCLA, 2004). Gains in teacher-reported social competence, child-reported peace-building behavior, and reductions in aggressive behavior (Flannery, Vazsonyi, et al., 2003).
Mega Skills	Improved scores on statewide achievement tests, higher attendance rates, fewer discipline problems (MegaSkills, 2004). More ready to learn and work cooperatively, better homework completion (MegaSkills, 2004).
Beyond the Bell—Extended Learning Opportunities (No Child Left Behind)	Improves academic achievement in reading, mathematics, and language development (LAUSD, 2004).
Homeless Children & Youth Program (No Child Left Behind)	Provides transportation to children so they can stay in the same school if their families become homeless (U.S. Dept. of Education, 2001). This ultimately has an impact on attendance.
CASASTART	Students were less likely to sell or use drugs or commit a violent crime and more likely to be promoted to the next grade (UCLA, 2004). Increased percentage of youth not using alcohol, tobacco, or drugs; increased percentage of juveniles who do not engage in violent behavior (Network, 2004).
Caring School Community	Students demonstrated more prosocial and problem-solving skills; had higher GPAs and test scores (UCLA, 2004). Significant reductions in drug use and other problem behaviors (Battistich, Schaps, et al., 2000).

(continued)

Table 99.3 *(Continued)*

Program	Outcomes
Community of Caring	Reduced nonexcused absences and disciplinary action; improved GPA (UCLA, 2004). Program participation was related to positive student character, perspective taking, and greater autonomy (Community of Caring, 2004). School climate, attendance, and homework completion also improved (Community of Caring, 2004).
Facing History & Ourselves	Students improved knowledge of historical concepts and interpersonal understanding (U.S. Dept. of Education, 1995).
Open Circle Curriculum	Students reported increases in interpersonal and problem-solving skills, as well as time on academic tasks (UCLA, 2004). Developed improved social skills and relationships (Taylor, Liang, et al., 2002).
Positive Action	Increased reading and math scores; improved attendance and decreased disciplinary referrals (UCLA, 2004).
Project STAR	Improved scores on standardized tests, fewer retentions in grade (UCLA, 2004).
Social Decision Making & Problem Solving	Improved coping and prosocial behaviors; better academic achievement (UCLA, 2004).
The Think Time Strategy	Improved social adjustment and academic performance; decreased disciplinary actions (UCLA, 2004).

Due to the environment of accountability, evaluating program results has become a major focus (Crowe & Sydney, 2000). Program evaluation brings up the competing interests adaptation issue because staff may be concerned about the possibility of unfavorable results. Teachers and social workers feel caught between their differing missions—the former is primarily concerned with the academic development of the child and the latter focuses on psychosocial development issues. What if the program shows favorable results in terms of psychosocial development (e.g., violence reduction) but unclear effects on academic performance? How does a violence prevention program serve academic needs? Evaluation results suggest that Second Step is considered to be a promising program and as mentioned in the Table 99.3, there is evidence for the program's impact on academic skills (Network, 2004). By adopting an eclectic approach by using programs that work (i.e., they have psychosocial as well as academic outcomes), the competing interests can ultimately be resolved.

Key Points to Remember

We have argued that the No Child Left Behind Act has inadvertently created a systems issue by focusing attention on accountability through standardized testing and influencing the drive for educational outcomes. If we focus solely on outcomes like standardized testing scores and GPAs, we may miss the many steps between social services provision and ultimate academic performance. Like the schools that are focusing on children who are likely to meet a minimum academic standard with a little extra help, we run the same risk if we serve children who are close to succeeding but miss the children who have greater deficits. However, this should not give the impression that accountability for outcomes is without merit. When implementing programs, we should intervene with those that have proven effects. Programs are able to demonstrate to stakeholders how they are achieving the outcomes they will deliver and show how programs are full educational team members. Packaged programs will need to be adapted for local use along the six categories we have suggested.

Children come to school with issues, which are years in the making, that hinder their academic performance. We should not expect that an intervention that lasts for a few short weeks will significantly affect academic performance in the short term. In the big picture, the child only spends a short period of time at school each day. The child spends the majority of his or her time in the environment where the elements of the intervention may not be reinforced or the work completed in the intervention may be undone. In short, we need to take the broader view that while accountability is important, it should not be the only focus.

References

Adelman, H., & Taylor, L. (2003a). *New directions in student support: Some fundamentals.* Los Angeles: UCLA Center for Mental Health in Schools: 5-1–5-21.

Adelman, H., & Taylor, L. (2003b). *Youngsters' mental health and psychosocial problems: What are the data?* Los Angeles: UCLA Center for Mental Health in Schools.

Battistich, V., Schaps, E., et al. (2000). Effects of the Child Development Project on students' drug use and other problem behaviors. *Journal of Primary Prevention, 21*(1), 75–99.

Burns, B. J., Costello, E. J., et al. (1995). Children's mental health service use across service sectors. *Health Affairs, 14*(3), 147–159.

C. D. o. Education (2004). Healthy Start Fact Sheet.

Community of Caring (2004). *Community of Caring: Results and research.* Community of Caring.

Crowe, A. H., & Sydney, L. (2000). Developing a policy for controlled substance testing of juveniles: Major steps for implementation. *Juvenile Accountability Block Grants Program Bulletin.* 2004.

Dranoff, S., & Dobrich, W. (2003). Rutgers University teaches RESPECT to students. *Education Update.* 2004.

Flannery, D. J., Vazsonyi, A. T., et al. (2003). Initial behavior outcomes for the PeaceBuilders universal school-based violence prevention program. *Developmental Psychology, 39*(2), 292–308.

Hammond, W. R., & Yung, B. (1991). Preventing violence in at-risk African American youth. *Journal of Health Care for the Poor & Underserved, 2*(3), 359–373.

Hanson, T. L., & Austin, G. A. (2003). Are student health risks and low resilience assets an impediment to the academic progress of schools? *California Healthy Kids Survey Factsheet 3.* Los Alamitos, CA: WestEd.

LAUSD (2004). Beyond the bell—extended learning opportunities.

Marshak, D. (2003). No Child Left Behind: A foolish race into the past. *Phi Delta Kappan, 85*(3), 229–231.

MegaSkills (2004). Research on MegaSkills.

Neill, M. (2003). Leaving children behind: How No Child Left Behind will fail our children. *Phi Delta Kappan, 85*(3), 225–228.

Network, P. P. (2004a). Proven and promising programs: CASASTART.

Network, P. P. (2004b). Proven and promising programs: Second Step Violence Prevention.

Orpinas, P., Parcel, G. S., et al. (1995). Violence prevention in middle schools: A pilot evaluation. *Journal of Adolescent Health, 17*, 360–371.

Rubin, J. (2004). Are schools cheating poor learners? *Los Angeles Times*, p. B1.

Schorr, L. (1997). *Common purpose: Strengthening families and neighborhoods to rebuild America.* New York: Anchor Books, Doubleday.

Taylor, C. A., Liang, B., et al. (2002). Gender differences in middle school adjustment, physical fighting, and social skills: Evaluation of a social competency program. *Journal of Primary Prevention, 23*(2), 259–271.

Why Try? (2003, December). Alpine School District Longitudinal Study.

UCLA (2004). A technical assistance sampler on a sampling of outcome findings from interventions relevant to addressing barriers to learning. Los Angeles.

U.S. Census. (2000). Table 1: Characteristics of children under 18 years by age, race, and Hispanic or Latino origin, for the United States. Washington, DC, U.S. Census.

U.S. Department of Education (1995). *Educational programs that work—1995.* U.S. Department of Education. 2004.

U.S. Department of Education (2001). *Preliminary overview of programs and changes included in the No Child Left Behind Act of 2001.*

Yung, B. (2001). Positive adolescent choices training.

Constructing Data Management Systems for Tracking Accountability

Melissa Jonson-Reid

CHAPTER 100

Getting Started

The call for public accountability is clear in the No Child Left Behind Act that mandates yearly accounting for school safety as well as academic achievement (www.ed.gov). To some it seems obvious that school social work services are a necessary support for academic achievement and reducing safety concerns, but as nonmandated parts of the educational system, school social workers must be cognizant of the need to communicate their importance—to be "visible" (Goren, 2002). Yet, school social workers often have large caseloads and provide a variety of services across different school settings rather than operating within a single program (Allen-Meares, 1994; Torres, 1999). This makes tracking accountability a daunting task. One means of increasing the capacity of school social workers to evaluate their services is to draw on the experience of social workers in child welfare who use computerized data management systems as a primary tool for accountability (Jonson-Reid, Kontak, & Mueller, 2001).

Child welfare agencies across the United States use computerized administrative data or management information systems (MIS) to track caseload characteristics, services, and limited outcomes. MIS make it possible to track the thousands of children served so that reports can be compiled to obtain state and federal funds, identify trends, and lobby for support. As these systems become more standardized, we are able to make comparisons across regions and support national advocacy efforts (Drake & Jonson-Reid, 1999; U.S. DHHS, 2004).

In the past, setting up MIS programs was too costly and required too much technical expertise to be considered a viable option for the school social worker. Now, computers with sufficient storage capacity (memory) and processing speed (RAM) have become affordable. Further, computer programs have grown from basic spreadsheet applications for accounting to user-friendly database applications. Because database applications like Microsoft Access are often part of basic software packages, many districts already possess the software needed. The creation and use of MIS is no longer beyond the reach of the school social work community.

The goal of this chapter is to provide the practicing school social worker with a step-by-step approach to the creation of an MIS. It draws from the author's experiences in creating an MIS to track school social work services in a few Missouri school districts (Jonson-Reid et al., 2001; Jonson-Reid, Citerman, Essma, Fezzi, & Kontak, 2004; Jonson-Reid et al., under review).

What We Know

Before thinking about the data elements you want to collect, it is important to consider some basic issues. Is an MIS a good idea for me? An MIS is not the answer to all evaluation needs or every practice setting. If you have a very small caseload in a well-defined program, the work involved in setting up and maintaining an MIS is probably not worth the effort. If, however, you have a large dynamic caseload, provide a wide variety of services, or work with several social work colleagues, the MIS provides some real advantages:

1. You can quickly compile reports on characteristics of the caseload or subgroups and examine their needs, services provided, and outcomes. This information can be used for billing for Medicaid funds, grants, district reports, advocacy, or even internal monitoring.
2. You can efficiently store information over time and examine trends. For example, you can calculate how many students are carried over on your caseload each year to better predict staffing needs.
3. You will have baseline information that can be used to monitor regular services when implementing and evaluating a new project.
4. You may be able to link your database to other computerized data such as attendance to allow you to monitor the progress of students on your caseload.
5. On a larger scale, the establishment of these types of systems could provide a national look at school social work practice. It would be a tremendous advantage to have the kind of descriptive data used by child welfare to advocate for services and obtain funds.

Once you decide an MIS is the right approach for you, there are still some considerations that should be addressed before you identify variables.

Software and Hardware

Check with your district's technology person to see what software your district currently owns. In the author's experience, many districts have a program like Microsoft Access that came along with the business software purchased by the district. Another common program is Filemaker. Both have several aftermarket "how to" books available. Whatever program you choose, it is important to be able to export (move) the data easily to other programs used for data analysis. Why is this important? You are likely to reach a point at which the simple reports you can produce from the database program do not adequately answer all your questions. As long as your program can export data into a ".dbf" or an ".xls" file, you will be in good shape. You will also need either a desktop or laptop computer with sufficient memory and RAM to operate the software and store the data. Most computers come standard with over 10 gigabytes of memory, which is fine. Today an adequate desktop can be purchased for under $1,000.

Confidentiality

In order to track trends in your cases or the relationship between services and outcomes, you must use individual-level data (i.e., data for each student). Of course, this means there are confidentiality concerns. The computer used should be in a secure location like your office or a secretary's office. The computer and the database you create should be password protected. If your computers are on a network, then you will want some sort of "firewall" to prevent hackers from accessing your data. Many are available, and your district information technology personnel can help you.

Data Back Up

Data loss can be a source of great anguish. Make sure you have a good virus protection package. Also, have a system in place to back up (copy) your data every so often so that if the computer hard drive should fail or your district annually wipes the network drive clean, you will not have to reenter everything. Most new computers can "burn" data onto CDs. Older computers use zip disks or tapes. These backups should be stored in a secure location.

Data Entry

Although MIS save time and increase options for accountability in the long run, the data do not enter themselves. In the author's experience, this is the largest barrier to ongoing maintenance of the MIS. Find out if your school site or district will provide clerical time for this purpose. If not, it is best to allow some time each week to enter information. This will make the task move more quickly and feel like less of a drain on your time.

Colleagues

You can create an MIS for your own individual use. If there are several school social workers in your district, however, everyone must use the same system for tracking cases in order to create a district-wide report on school social work services. It is essential that all of you be part of the planning process. Decisions must be made about what information to input, there must be clear understanding of the meaning of the data fields, and buy-in must be obtained to ensure that the information is entered in a timely and correct fashion.

Reporting

Many school social workers lack training and/or time to address analysis of data—particularly longitudinal data. The software should allow you to create basic reports on your own. You will probably begin to ask more complex questions as you collect data and think about accountability. Your district may have a data analyst who can take the exported data and perform more complicated statistical analyses. If not, consider the formation of a partnership with a local university person (e.g., Allen-Meares & Franklin, 1998; Jonson-Reid et al., 2001).

What We Can Do

Planning

Once you decide that having an MIS is a good idea, you need to spend time planning. Kettner, Moroney, and Martin (1999) suggest seven steps to build an MIS. Five of these steps are discussed in this chapter:

1. Identify the questions to be answered.
2. Identify the data elements needed.
3. Design data collection procedures.
4. Develop data entry procedures.
5. Develop a strategy for analysis and reporting

After you start implementing the system, there are bound to be changes needed. So, after these steps are completed, you should use the first semester or so as a pilot period. Do not be surprised if the data from the initial try is less useful than hoped. After the pilot period, hold a meeting with all users to review the process and data. This will allow you to make needed modifications.

Identifying the Questions to Be Answered

You have heard the saying "garbage in, garbage out." Computers only produce information based upon what you put in them. If you try to collect too many items, users will skip data fields seen as "less important" to save time or become frustrated and stop paying attention to accuracy. Collect too little information and you will be left with useless reports. To reach a balance, it is necessary to spend time thinking about the key questions you want answered.

1. What am I accountable for? In a self-contained special education classroom, a social worker may focus on behavioral goals linked to a child's individualized educational plan. Accountability for achieving those goals can be tracked by entering scores from a pre- and poststandardized measure like the Child Behavior Checklist. Some social workers serve many students across schools for many reasons. Their outcomes may be recorded as broad categories.

2. What is my district interested in? An MIS can help communicate your value to the district, providing at least some of your outcomes are of interest to the district. Typically schools are most interested in items related to their accountability reports and funding, such as attendance, high school completion, and disciplinary referrals.

3. Am I asking if my services "caused" the outcome? MIS are not typically designed to measure cause and effect. As you have learned in coursework on research, such evaluation requires random assignment to treatment and control groups or at least some form of comparison group. This does not mean you cannot use an MIS to record this information. If you are evaluating a program and using random assignment to treatment, then you can add an indicator in the database of who is in the treatment and control groups. Then you can run the data on your outcome measure by the indicator of group membership. If you are using a comparison group (not randomly assigned), your MIS can help you track other services children in your program are receiving. Identifying other services and problems that students encounter while in your program will help you identify possible alternative explanations for the outcome.

4. What other information do you want? In addition to service outcomes, you will want to describe various aspects of what you did during the year. This will probably include describing services, case characteristics, and overall numbers for later use in reports.

Tools and Practice Examples

Data Collection Procedures

Once the major questions you wish to answer have been identified, it is time to select variables and decide on a data collection method. There are two choices for data collection. Either complete hard-copy forms first and then enter the data into the computer or just enter the information directly into the computer. Even if you decide to enter data directly into the computer, you should still construct at least one hard-copy form first. It will be easier to review your variable choices and pilot the process on a few cases using a paper copy rather than constructing and then revising the data entry shell. It is also helpful to have a hard-copy option available for training or recording information when traveling. As we discuss variable selection, we will examine examples of portions of data forms. Notes in italic within the boxes provide advice about the form or categories.

Variable Selection

Identification

In order to track cases over time, you must have a consistent and unique way of identifying individuals. You can enter names into the computer or ID numbers or both. Entering only ID numbers provides additional protection against accidental disclosure, but it also means that you will have to keep a list somewhere that links the ID numbers to the names. Using the district's student ID number in your system is useful, as it is already linked to the student name and it may make it possible to link to data on the school's computer like attendance.

Demographic and Basic Case Information

Information such as gender, age or grade level, school, socioeconomic status, and some type of racial categorization are *critical*. Why? Some of the most common questions you will ask later will be related to characteristics of the students. For example, if a group of students on your caseload appears to be struggling, you will want to know what makes them different from the other cases. Or, if you wish to write a grant for elementary

school girls, then these variables allow you to summarize the data for this specific group.

Dates are also key components because caseloads are dynamic. Students may come and go from your caseload during the year. One might expect different outcomes for a student who receives 3 weeks of the program compared to another who completes the program. Thus, service start or referral date and end dates are important aspects of any MIS (see Box 100.1).

Other special program indicators can be added to the case description to correspond to funding sources or other programs that may interface with your services. For example, you might want to record participation in special education or the presence of a DSM diagnosis. These allow you to easily break down your statistics by special status (see Box 100.2).

Needs or Problems

An important aspect of accountability is tracking why a student was referred to you so that you can assess change. If you use a standardized assessment tool or checklist, the score or specific categories can be entered into the computer. The advantage of using standardized instruments is that you can compare them with available research, they provide norms based on large samples, and they often can be readministered as posttests. In Box 100.3, the MIS system includes the internalizing and externalizing scores from the CBCL, as well as some subscales of interest that relate directly to the intervention.

Other social workers receive referrals for diverse issues such as health, child abuse and neglect, and homelessness. In this case, a checklist of referral reasons can be developed. If you create such a checklist, it is important to consider the following:

- Will you track the referring party's issue, the issues identified after you assess the student, or both? Recording the referring party's understanding will help you report back on initial concerns. However, your assessment may reveal other issues.
- If there is more than one person contributing data, everyone must agree on what a created category means. Otherwise, your data will not be comparable across social workers. Try to make variable labels simple and clear to minimize confusion.

Box 100.1 Basic Demographic Information

Student ID: _____   School: _____

Referral Date: _____

Gender __ M __ F   Race __ African American   Grade __ (K–12)

   __ Asian

   __ Caucasian

   __ Hispanic

   __ Other

Note: Racial categories should describe your school's/district's population. For example, in the southwest there may be a substantial American Indian population but few Asians. There "American Indian" would be its own category, and Asian would likely be part of "Other."

Note: In this example we use grade level rather than age. You will be more likely to report information to the district that way. However, you do lack the ability to analyze whether or not the student is overage for his or her grade without capturing age or date of birth.

Eligible for Free or Reduced Lunch __ (Yes/No)

Note: You might also choose Medicaid eligibility or Title 1 designation as an indicator of socioeconomic status depending upon the link to funding in your district.

- The name of the issues should be specific enough to be useful. For example, "behavior problem" is too vague. It is better to use categories like "disruptive classroom behavior" and "aggression" that can be clearly defined.
- Balance the desire for depth with the need for

information and ease of data entry. Too many categories are hard to fill in and will be more difficult to summarize later. Imagine having a pie chart of problems with 50 slices—it is too confusing.

- When recording problems, do not forget

Box 100.2 Special Case Descriptors

DSM diagnosis __(Yes/No) Category _____

Note: It may be beneficial to note DSM diagnoses for students on your caseload, This will help you liaison with outside therapists and may help you obtain funding for services from organizations like the National Institutes for Mental Health. It can also aid you in choosing interventions. For example a child with ADHD may require a different approach than a child without ADHD.

Special Education __(Yes/No)

Note: It is likely that some of your caseload will also be served under the IDEA. This may even be a funding source for you.

Disability category   __ Emotional disturbance

   __ Vision/hearing

   __ Learning disability: visual __ auditory __

   __ Autism

   __ Mental retardation

   __ OHI

   __ Physical (paralysis, etc.)

Note: Do not forget to record the disability type. Even if all your students are ED, there may be other disabilities present. Such combinations of issues can impact intervention. For example, an ED child with an auditory disability may have difficulty benefiting from a "talk therapy" group.

Box 100.3 Example of Standardized Assessment Scores

Pre-test Child Behavior Checklist	Internalizing score: ___
	Externalizing: ___
Subscale of interest: _____	Score: ___
Subscale of interest: _____	Score: ___

Note: You can also design your form to mimic the scale or checklist summary area for ease of data entry.

funding streams or reporting requirements. Districts obtain funding through attendance, so it is a good idea to record this if you have an impact in that area. Or if funds are available for bullying prevention, specify "bullying" as a referral reason so you can track the issue for a grant. Including categories that correspond to larger scale areas of interest also allows you to compare the prevalence of a given issue on your caseload to district, state, or national figures.

Box 100.4 illustrates a portion of a referral reason checklist.

Services or Interventions

Obviously the detail you include in case file notes is not appropriate for the MIS. Select categories or brief comments that can later be summarized with ease. If you primarily provide counseling, you may wish to specify the type of counseling such as cognitive/behavioral, rational/emotive, or a specific curriculum. This will allow you to examine trends in outcomes that are associated with various practice approaches. If you provide different services according to a wide variety of needs, you will probably have to sacrifice some specificity. If some services are rarely provided, like transportation, create a broad "other services" category with a comment area for description rather than listing them all out.

In addition to type of service, there are characteristics of services to consider. The start and end dates will tell you how long a case was served but not how often or how intensely. Detail about services can be added by recording frequency of contacts rather than checking off the type of service. Of course, five individual counseling sessions is not necessarily the same as 5 hours of counseling. You may wish to record the number of hours

of each service provided to better understand intensity. These items can be recorded monthly, quarterly, or by semester. Generally it is better to keep up with entering data on smaller periods of time rather than trying to wait until the end of the year.

Boxes 100.5 and 100.6 provide examples of two service-tracking methods: one for social workers who provide only counseling and one for social workers who provide a variety of services. The social workers providing only counseling have a regular schedule and just indicate the number of sessions. In Box 100.6, the social workers track time served rather than frequency of contacts because the amount of time a service requires varies a lot from case to case. These social workers also work with outside agencies and record the name of the agency to whom they refer cases. This will allow them to identify agencies that may interact better with referred families or wish to consider joint participation in a grant.

Recording Outcomes

So far, we have recorded process and assessment information. We must also be accountable for outcomes. In a district where the school social worker provides mental health services for ED children, it makes sense to enter a standardized assessment like the CBCL as the problem and then use a posttest administration for the outcome. If you are trying to improve attendance, then you will record the attendance at the close of services. The specificity of the outcome will vary by the type of services you provide. If a social worker provides a range of services for a range of issues, a case disposition coding scheme may be better. Case dispositions may include "resolved and closed" with a date, as well as other case closure reasons like expulsion or graduation (see Box 100.7). Above all, make sure your outcomes

Box 100.4

Attendance___ Rate of attendance (Start): _____

Note: It is VERY important not to just list days missed. You have to record the days missed divided by the days possible to attend. Why? Because a child referred in the beginning of October will have few possible days to miss but might miss 75% of the days. At the end of the year, a child will have more total days missed, but will hopefully be missing a smaller percentage of the possible days. If you only look at the raw numbers, your outcome will look like failure even if the child's actual attendance improved.

Bullying ___Victim? ___ Perpetrator? ___

Note: Some problems should have a victim and perpetrator indicator. This is important when you consider that the perpetrator is also counted under disciplinary action while the victim is not. Further, interventions and outcomes are likely to vary along this dimension.

Child abuse and neglect suspected ___   Type 1: _____

Reported to child welfare? ___ (Yes/No) Date: _____

If no, why not? ___ (enter number)

(1 = other reasonable explanation for injury or condition; 2 = already reported this incident; 3 = concern does not meet the definition of reportable abuse or neglect)

                                   Type 2: _____

Reported to child welfare? _____ (Yes/No) Date: _____

If no, why not? ____ (enter number)

(1 = other reasonable explanation for injury or condition; 2 = already reported this incident; 3 = concern does not meet the definition of reportable abuse or neglect)

Note: School social workers often serve maltreated children. It is important to track the form of maltreatment to tailor services, dispel myths (sometimes districts may assume sexual abuse is highly prevalent because of media reports when it is typically neglect), and design programs and interventions. Tracking the reporting of such events keeps you in compliance with the law and helps trigger the need to collaborate with child welfare.

Family Issues _____ Type 1: ___ Type 2: ___ Type 3: ___

(1 = parenting; 2 = domestic violence; 3 = parental substance abuse; 4 = divorce; 5 = parental mental health; 6 = parental health; 7 = sibling conflict)

Note: There are many possible family issues. To save space, the form indicates a place to check this overall category and then leaves three spaces to indicate the specific number that corresponds to the reason. This saves data entry screen space.

correspond logically to the services you provide! For example, it is unlikely that you will have a dramatic impact on internalizing CBCL scores if you only provide crisis intervention.

From Data Form to Computer

Once you have identified the elements you wish to record, it is time to make the data entry shell. A database program, like Microsoft Access or File-maker, allows you to create an onscreen form that mimics the hard copy forms you created (see Box 100.8). Each case is presented to you as a separate screen, but the data is stored in a spreadsheet hidden from view. Most recent database programs have helpful "wizard" options that can guide you through all or part of the process. In addition to storing data, these programs can be set up to automatically produce reports. The following are some considerations you should think about regarding the data entry screen.

Box 100.5 Description of Counseling Services

Individual Counseling Fall __ (No. of sessions)   Type: __ Cognitive Behavioral
                                                              __ Rational Emotive
                                                              __ Object Relations
                                           __ Curriculum used: _____

Individual Counseling Spring __ (No. of sessions)   Type: __ Cognitive Behavioral
                                                              __ Rational Emotive
                                                              __ Object Relations
                                           __ Curriculum used: _____

Note: Sometimes it may be easier to identify a specific counseling curriculum followed rather than the mode of therapy.

"Forced Entry" Items

Most programs allow "forced entry" items. This means that the person entering data cannot proceed without entering information for this item. The advantage is that such items will not have missing data. However, if you use check boxes for referral reasons there will be some boxes that are supposed to be blank. Such items should not be forced entry.

Text Versus Categories

Categories are preferable to comment boxes in computer databases. Blank spaces that require a number to represent a category (e.g., the collaboration agency types in Box 100.6) or check boxes to represent categories (e.g., racial category in Box 100.1) save space, save time in data entry, and are easier to summarize in tables and graphs. You do, however, need to allow for text responses at

Box 100.6 Examples of Broad Range of Services

Individual counseling   Fall ____ (No. of hours)
                         Spring _____ (No. of hours)
Referral for services   Fall __ (Yes/No)   Agency 1: _____
                                               Agency 2: _____

                         Spring __ (Yes/No)   Agency 1: _____
                                               Agency 2: _____
Outside Agency Collaboration Fall hours __
Type 1: __ Contact: _____ phone: _____
Type 2: __ Contact: _____ phone: _____
(1 = child welfare; 2 = juvenile probation; 3 = comm. mental health; 4 = regional center)
Outside Agency Collaboration Spring hours __
Type 1: __ Contact: _____ phone: _____
Type 2: __ Contact: _____ phone: _____
(1 = child welfare; 2 = juvenile probation; 3 = comm. mental health; 4 = regional center)

Note: Referral for services and collaboration are different. While you want to limit categories to those with meaningful numbers, you also want to be sure you are capturing information of value. In this example, a space for a contact person is added. You will not report on contact people in your evaluation report, but this can be added as a help to you so that you do not have to look up the hard copy file to remember who to call.

Box 100.7 Case Dispositions

Closing Date: _____

Total Possible Attendance Days in Service Period: ____

Days Attended During Service Period (End): ____

Note: The above combination of variables will allow you to calculate a change in the rate of attendance from the time services started to case closure. You then compare this to the attendance rate at time of referral.

Other Dispositions:

Issue resolved: ___ (1 = outside services obtained; 2 = behavior improved; 3 = entered special education)

Graduated: ___ Moved: ___ Dropped Out: ___ Expelled: ___ Deceased: ____

times. For example, what happens if a student is not referred for any of the categories listed? You will want an "Other" space with a comment area to explain "other." Sometimes these are emerging issues that you will want to add to your data screen the following year.

Pull-Downs

Most programs will allow you to create a pull-down selection for multiple-choice categories like the racial category in Box 100.1. In Box 100.4 we see that the hard-copy form offers a space for numbers to identify specific types of "family issues." On the computer, you can create a pull-down list that allows the person entering data to choose from a preselected list of options (like the ones in parentheses on the hard-copy forms). These prompts help remind people of the category choices, save space on the screen, and cut down data entry time.

Archiving Old Records

To track trends over time, you must set up a system to archive (save) old records. You could enter data into the same database over time by using multiple screens linked together, but this may become diffi-

cult for your computer to handle over time. An alternative is to save the old database with a new name, then copy the student information to a new database with blank values except for the names, ID numbers, race, and gender from the prior year. Bringing forward the old demographics that do not change saves you time the next year. Be sure to use the ID numbers for students only once; otherwise, you will lose the ability to link student records over time! By archiving old records, you will have the capability of linking records to form a longitudinal database for analysis.

Key Points to Remember

In order to continue to promote the importance of school social work, practitioners must begin to use the technology available to meet accountability standards. If the process still seems too daunting after reading this chapter, a consultant or university partner can provide help with setting up the database. It is hoped that readers will increase their use of computerization of caseload data for accountability in their own practice. As such use increases, we can also look forward to having data that can provide a better picture of practice across the nation.

Box 100.8 School Social Work Services Tracking System

Student#   0   Last   First   Grade 4

Ethnicity   A = african amer   Gender ☐   F   Referral Date   1/21/2002   New reason date

School   Home School   EYWB ☐   ADC program ☐   VTS ☑

Referral Source   #Name?

Special Programs/Services

Special Educatio ☐   Sped Type   Foster Care ☐   Other DFS ☐   DFS Worke

504PLAN ☐   504 reason   Family Court ☐   DJO/other

Medication ☐   DSM Diagnosi   Therapy ☐   Tx contact

Referral Reasons/Response

Abuse ☐   Family Issues ☐   Homeless ☐   Financial Issue ☐

   HOTLINE1   Hotline1 Reas   famprob1

   Hotline2   hotline2 Reas   famprob3

   Hotline3   hotline3 Reas   famprob2

Academic ☐   Attendance ☐   ○ Part Days   ○ Tardies #Na

SSD Screen: Fall ☐   SSD Screen: Spring ☐   Days Absent ☐   Grief/loss ☐

SSD IEP: Fall ☐   SSD IEP: Sprin ☐   Depression ☐   Suicidal ☐

Aggression ☐   Disruptive Behavior ☑   Other Emotiona ☐

   OSS# ○   ISS# ○   Emotissue ☐

Sexual Assault ☐   Sexual Harrassment ☐   Health ☐   Healthissue ☐

   Victim: SA ☐   Victim: SH ☐   Substance Abuse ☐

Runaway ☐

Other Reason ☐   #Name?   Type of Substance:

Services/Time Served/Closure

Crisis Intervention: Fall ☐	Crisis Intervention: Spring ☐	Care Team: Fall ☐	Care Team: Sprin ☐
Counseling Indiv: Fall ☐	Counseling Indiv: Spring ☐	Home Liaison: Fall ☐	Home Liaison: Spring ☐
Counseling Group: Fall ☐	Group Type	Case Mng/staff consult.. Fall ☐	Case Mng/staff consult: Spring ☐
Counseling Group: Spring ☐	Group Type2	Agency Liaison: Fall ☐	Agency Liaison: Spring ☐
Referral for Service: Fall ☐	Other Agency #Name?	Referral for:	
Referral for Service: Spring ☐	Other Agency2 #Name?	Contact Hours: Fall #Name?	Contact Hours: Spring
Days Absent–End of Year #Name	Part days Absent #Nam	Tardies EOY #Nam	OSS#: Fall #Name
			OSS#: Spring
Close date for Fall #Name?	Case Status Fall #Name?	ISS#: Fall #Name?	
Close date for Spring #Name?	Case Status Spring #Name?	ISS#Spring #Name?	
Comments			

References

Allen-Meares, P. (1994). Social work services in schools: A national survey of entry-level tasks. *Social Work, 39,* 560–565.

Allen-Meares, P., & Franklin, C. (1998). Partnerships for better education: Schools, universities and communities (editorial). *Social Work in Education, 20,* 147–151.

Drake, B., & Jonson-Reid, M. (1999). Some thoughts on the increasing use of administrative data in child maltreatment research. *Child Maltreatment, 4,* 308–315.

Goren, S. (2002). The wonderland of social work in the schools or how Alice learned to cope. In R. Constable, S. McDonald, & J. Flynn (Eds.), *School social work: Practice, policy and research perspectives* (5th ed.). Chicago: Lyceum.

Jonson-Reid, M., Kim, J., Citerman, B., Columbini, C., Essma, A., Fezzi, N., Green, D., Kontak, D., Mueller, N., & Thomas, B. (under review). Maltreated children in schools: The interface of school social work and child welfare.

Jonson-Reid, M., Kontak, D., Citerman, B., Essma, A., & Fezzi, N. (2004). School social work case characteristics, services and dispositions: Year one results. *Children & Schools, 26,* 5–22.

Jonson-Reid, M., Kontak, D., & Mueller, S. (2001). Developing a management information system for school social workers: A field-university partnership. *Children & Schools, 23*(4), 198–211.

Kettner, P., Moroney, R., & Martin, L. (1999). *Designing and managing programs: An effectiveness-based approach* (2nd ed., pp. 139–166). Thousand Oaks, CA: Sage.

Torres, S. (1999). The status of school social workers in America. In E. Freeman, C. Franklin, R. Fong, G. Shaffer, & E. Timberlake (Eds.), *Multisystem skills and interventions in school social work practice* (pp. 461–472). Washington, DC: NASW Press.

U.S. Department of Health and Human Services, Children's Bureau. (2004). *Child maltreatment 2003.* Washington, DC: Government Printing Office.

Identifying and Using Effective Outcome Measures

Norman H. Cobb ▪ Catheleen Jordan

CHAPTER 101

Getting Started

Social workers and other mental health practitioners recognize that demonstrating evidence of success is necessary to continue providing services to students, faculty, and administration. An *evidence-based approach to program evaluation* depends on outcome measures that validate interventions and demonstrate changes. Prepared practitioners plan for the end of the school year when data is required to substantiate successful student outcomes. In effect, school social workers and other professionals know that their services are more likely to continue when they evaluate and document positive changes and outcomes. Most important, social workers' professional ethics require that they use the most effective services and document their value.

This chapter describes smart strategies for documenting the quality of social workers' and other professionals' efforts, demonstrating the effectiveness of their work, and confirming their ability to get the job done. These elements—program effort, effectiveness, and efficiency—are the central themes in program evaluation. They require the identification of effective outcome measures to establish successful programs for students. Although "efficiency" implies a cost-benefit analysis, this chapter focuses on outcome measures for school social workers. The contents, however, are applicable to other school-based, mental health practitioners, as well.

What We Know

Program effort in school social work includes descriptions of services rendered, the number of students served, and the degree to which social workers actively addressed the needs of students, teachers, and administrators. *Program effectiveness* becomes more complicated, because the objectives of school social work must be related to outcomes and quantified, tabulated, and summarized. In essence, teachers, administrators, legislators, and other stakeholders must be able to see the outcome data and agree that their expectations for success have been met. Finally, *program efficiency* must establish that the achieved results were worth the cost. The following steps identify a process to achieve program effort, effectiveness, and efficiency, which requires the identification and usage of effective outcome measures.

What We Can Do

Step One: Identifying the Outcomes

The smart approach is proactive. Outcome measures are selected at the beginning and are based on the goals and objectives of the services. In many school settings, the services are funded from a grant or established by a preexisting program. In these instances, the outcomes and methods of measurement are predetermined and must be utilized. Additional outcome measures may be added as unmeasured outcomes are identified.

In other settings, the outcomes for social work services are not predetermined and sometimes are not particularly identifiable. One option is to ask, "Why did the school system hire social workers? What do administrators and principals expect to accomplish? What is expected to be different after the services are delivered?" It is also important for social workers to give first priority to the mission and goals of the school. For example, outcomes that are important to schools indicate measurement and documentation of grades, attendance, graduation rates, and so forth.

Some job descriptions provide other answers: "Provide age appropriate drug education and counseling" or "provide pregnancy prevention and resources." Unfortunately, some job descriptions are less clear and suggest that social workers "support students' academic and developmental advancement." Furthermore, some administrators' expectations and objectives are vaguely written or not written down at all; however, careful, sensitive questioning from social work staff can uncover the more silent expectations.

The school social work literature may be a further source for identifying outcomes and outcome measures. For example, Dibble (1999) highlighted the variety of areas where success must typically be documented. He categorized service outcomes from 67 studies into five areas: school performance, social problem solving, family functioning, psychological coping, and home–school relations. Each area addresses a variety of goals that may be transformed into measurable objectives. Royce, Thyer, Padgett, and Logan (2001) explained the program logic model that described the relationship between objectives and outcomes. They referred to the Kellogg Foundation's Web-based Evaluation Handbook (http://www.wkkf.org/publications/evalhdbk/default.htm) as a model for planners and service providers to formalize the process from program goals and objectives to outcomes that are immediately measurable and outcomes that are measurable at some future point.

In the drug and pregnancy examples, longer range outcomes may specify a decrease in the number of students who develop drug problems or pregnancies compared to last year's rate. The difficulty of this approach is that long-range outcome data can be delayed by months or even years, and administrators and supervisors should be asked to approve the plan and, therefore, be willing to wait for future data.

Most important, when the outcome measures are integrally connected to aspects of the social work program, the validity of the program and outcomes are significantly enhanced. While short- and long-term outcomes may serve different purposes, they provide the necessary support for future services.

Step Two: Specifying Objectives and Measuring Outcomes

Objectives from school grants, job descriptions, or existing programs or services (drug education, pregnancy prevention, or support) must be translated into measurable statements. Objectives state expectations for programs and services, but outcome measures derive the data to establish success or failure. For example, one objective of a drug education program might be to reach a specific number of students. The corresponding outcome data would include the number of students in the program and number of sessions they attended. Another objective may specify that students will learn about drugs; therefore, the outcome measures may be a test to establish students' learning.

A pregnancy prevention program might specify that female and male students attend discussion groups on birth control and receive literature on healthy personal habits. The outcome measures may include the number of students who attended, the percentage of males and females, and the number and types of literature that individual students picked up and took with them. Also, if additional services are available to students, the number of students who requested them would be significant outcome data.

A well-developed plan identifies the outcome measures and data that workers will collect. It ensures that toward the end of the school year, social workers have data to document how students, parents, and school personnel benefited from specific services.

Observation

When human behavior is specifically defined and workers are trained and have the means to record the occurrence of behavior, observation is the most valid and reliable outcome measure. Observation and behavioral counts are the most logical outcome measures, but more important, they are also the most believable by administrators and other reviewers of the success or failure of programs.

In the examples of the drug and pregnancy programs, the number of participants documents the exposure of students to the services. More important, workers can count the number of students who ask questions and perhaps record or categorize the relevant questions. Additionally, the number of negative versus positive comments about attitudes of drug use (or pregnancy) could be counted during group discussions among students. Realistically, the behavioral counts may or may not indicate students' learning, interest, or future commitments, but they do give some credence to the need for certain programs.

Indirect Outcome Measures

Observation of behavior can be very difficult to obtain, and observed behavior may or may not measure intended objectives. Indirect measures may be necessary to validate observed behavior or establish that objectives have been met. One principle to keep in mind is that everything, in one form or another, is measurable.

Years ago at a conference a social worker quickly responded to that idea with, "Well, you can't measure love!" The speaker suggested that people who are in love tend to behave in rather specific ways. For example, most people would predict "love" if their partners said, "I love you," once or twice a day, came home after work and stayed home all night, greeted their beloved with a hug or kiss or some form of affection, gave tokens of love for birthdays, Valentine's Day, and so forth. While the details might differ from couple to couple or family to family, real deficits in the list might signal a relationship crisis!

Most concepts (love, feelings, depression, and so forth) can be measured by focusing on overt behaviors that relate to them. Similarly, covert behaviors (cognitions) can be quantified to assess the extent of people's feelings, beliefs, depression, and so forth. When students give self-reports about their behavior (activities in the privacy of their own homes, on a date, etc.) or their attitudes (good intentions for their behavior, feelings, or thoughts), indirect measures are your primary sources of information and may substantiate or validate students' self-reports.

For example, students might complete a test of their knowledge of the consequences of drug use or pregnancy. Their knowledge would be one piece of evidence to evaluate the educational aspect of the drug or pregnancy program. Unfortunately, students' knowledge (demonstrated on a test) may not transfer into behavioral changes; therefore, other measures may be needed. Students might be willing to complete anonymously a checklist of behaviors that they engaged in over the weekend. The checklist might include

behaviors that they might have used to avoid drug use or risky sexual behavior. Additionally, at the beginning and again at the end of the school year, a simple questionnaire might assess a program's effectiveness to change students' attitudes about drugs, their willingness to accept drug use in their friends, or their "romantic" or realistic notions of having unexpected babies.

School Records

School records may be a good source of data. Some social workers and researchers have advocated for the use of students' grades as an indirect outcome measure for social work services. Although increasing students' grades might result from social workers' interventions, the connection can be rather tenuous or even flawed. Attendance records, however, may be more connected to social work services, because some social work efforts address attendance. For example, did students' participation in an "attendance-problem-solving" workshop increase the number of classes and days attended? Similarly, how many students increased their attendance after social workers assisted their families with various problems?

Other sources of data might include pregnancy rates, the number of students who dropped out of school, tickets or arrests for driving under the influence, breath analysis of students at school proms, and intermittent urine analysis for the presence of drugs in the school's athletes. Finally, students may report on their own behavior by keeping daily journals to report their exposure to drugs or their choices concerning sexual behavior. Keep in mind that many school social workers report a surprising willingness of students to tell their stories.

Scales, Inventories, and Questionnaires

Numerous professionals have created measurement instruments for children, adolescents, and families. Although the terms *scales* and *inventories* are used interchangeably, instruments that assess the level of one concept such as depression, happiness, or anxiety are typically called *scales*. Inventories, on the other hand, usually survey a variety of topics. A single inventory may evaluate people's contentment at home, self-concept, and family relationships. In questionnaires, students may fill in the blanks of open-ended questions ("When I see someone smoking, I tend to think _____."). While questionnaires give maximum flexibility for student's responses, the results are difficult to evaluate and compare among students. Scales and inventories standardize responses.

Both scales and inventories are frequently called rapid assessment instruments, because they can be given quickly and easily to respondents. The format and content of the measures are consistent and, therefore, easily comparable across groups and settings. Frequently, they contain 5 to 30 questions, although others can be quite lengthy.

Standardized Scales

Standardized scales are typically the best assessment tools available. The authors and researchers of scales have statistically analyzed all items in their scales to determine the validity and reliability of single items and entire scales. Validity may be established by comparing participants' scores on a new scale to their scores on another well-established scale. For example, to establish the concurrent validity of the Generalized Contentment Scale (Nurius & Hudson, 1993), people's scores on the GCS were compared with their scores on the Beck Depression Inventory. To establish a scale's predictive validity, researchers and authors may compare respondents' scores on a new scale with the future occurrence of the scale's predicted behavior. While these approaches address some of the topics concerning validity (are you measuring what you think you are measuring?), reliable scales are stable and consistent. The reliability of scales is generally determined through statistical analysis. Correlations are often reported to indicate the consistency of people's scores on a scale at one time and again at a later time, when, in all likelihood, the people had not changed. Also, reliability statistics, such as Cronbach's alpha, may establish the similarity of people's answers to items within a scale to indicate a degree of consistency, which is called internal consistency. As a common rule of thumb, correlations or alpha statistics should be higher than .80. Scales should be selected that have studies to document the appropriateness of particular scales for specific populations and issues.

The following are three examples of items from standardized scales to assess children's depression, and they show different answer options for respondents.

For Birleson's Depression Self-Rating Scale (1981), children between the ages of 7 to 13 answer 18 questions, such as:

1. I look forward to things as much as I used to.
2. I sleep very well.

Children would write a 1, 2, or 3 to indicate "Most of the time," "Sometimes," or "Never."

Walter Hudson's Generalized Contentment Scale is used for children as young as 12. The 25-item scale begins with the following statements:

1. I feel powerless to do anything about my life.
2. I feel blue.

Respondents answer with a 1 to indicate "none of the time," 2 "very rarely," 3 "a little of the time," 4 "some of the time," 5 "a good part of the time," 6 "most of the time," or 7 "all of the time."

Kazdin's Hopelessness Scale for Children (1983) was developed for children 7 years and older. Each item is marked as true or false.

T   F   1. I want to grow up because I think things will be better.
T   F   2. I might as well give up because I can't make things better for myself.

The Likert formats and true–false are common components for most standardized scales and rapid assessment instruments. Other answer options might address frequency: "most of the time," "some of the time," and so on. Students' scores may be determined by adding together their numeric responses.

Sources. Literally hundreds of scales and inventories are available for use with children and adolescents (see Box 101.1). For example, Corcoran and Fischer (2000) included all three of the mentioned scales in their book of common scales for children, families, and adults. Other sources for scales focus on children's educational and psychological development (for example, Andrews, Janzen, & Saklofske, 2001; Sederer & Dickey, 1996). The Internet can be an enormous source for scales. Entering keywords into the "Search" area of Internet browsers, such as *scales, children*, and *measurement*, yields a vast array of options. While the Internet resource is impressive, one word of caution is always necessary: The Internet and many published sources of measurement instruments do not guarantee reliability and validity.

Scales and measurements that look impressive may not accurately evaluate the concept that is most relevant to study or properly evaluate the type of students in a particular school setting.

Choosing Scales

Corcoran (2001) asserted five steps to selecting outcome measures. The following is adapted from his work:

1. Determine what is to be measured.
2. Search through available measures in professional journals, books, commercial publishing houses, and the Internet.
3. Pick the measure that (a) seems to measure your students' problem(s), (b) is reliable and valid, and (c) has normative information to help you understand the problem in relation to the demographics of your students.
4. Take the measure yourself to aid your understanding of it.
5. Administer to your students.

Gambrill (1997) offered a list of 16 criteria for choosing or excluding scales (see Box 101.1). For example, the background information about scales should report the evidence of the scales' validity and reliability. Additionally, scales must be useful to understand students' problems. For example, while

Beck's Children's Depression Scale assesses the level of depression in elementary school students, it and others like it must also be acceptable to students and be easy to complete. Scales should result in numerical scores to indicate the severity or strength of students' conditions. Also, scales should be free from bias due to cultural factors of the respondents, gender-specific language, reactive language, and so forth.

A very important issue when choosing rapid assessment instruments or standardized scales is the population on which the scales were originally developed and tested. Many of the available standardized scales were standardized on white, middle- to upper-class students; therefore, their use with students from different racial, ethnic, or income groups should always raise caution. For example, low-income students from more diverse racial or ethnic backgrounds may not "fit" the responses of the "white, middle-class" standardized group and therefore, appear more deviant than is actually true.

Examples of Valid and Reliable Scales in Schools

Fortunately, many scales have considerable history. They have been highly researched and validated on a variety of people. The Conners scales (Conners, 1997) and Achenbach's Child Behavior

Box 101.1 Gambrill's Criteria for Selecting Outcome Measures

1. Validity data are available and show that the measure is valid (it measures what it is supposed to measure).
2. Data are useful in understanding problems and removing complaints.
3. Test–retest reliability is high (in the absence of real change).
4. Easy to complete and does not take much time.
5. Acceptable to clients.
6. Required reading levels match client skills.
7. Sensitive (small changes can be detected).
8. The user has the knowledge required to make effective use of the measure.
9. Norms are available for populations of concern.
10. Data concerning reactive effects are available.
11. Responses are quantifiable.
12. The false positive rate is low.
13. The false negative rate is low.
14. Biases are minimal (e.g., social desirability, response set, vested interest in an outcome).
15. Instructions for administration, scoring, and interpretation are clear.
16. Cultural differences are considered in relation to content.

Source: Gambrill, 1997, p. 362.

Checklist (CBCL) (1991) have been repeatedly used in school settings. They are recommended for program evaluation, because the Conners scales and the CBCL have undergone considerable analysis to establish their validity for students with diverse backgrounds. For example, Fantuzzo, Grim, Mordell, McDermott, Miller, and Coolaham (2001) found that the Conners was a valid instrument with young, low-income children. Similarly, the CBCL (Achenbach, 1991) has been successfully used with students from various backgrounds in the United States and foreign countries (Dumenci, Erol, Achenbach, & Simsek, 2004; Verhulst et al., 2004). Additionally, from a political perspective within the school system, their fame can lend credibility to the school-based program evaluation.

Kendall, Marrs-Garcia, Nath, and Sheldrick (1999) were responsible for documenting an enormous amount of data on "normal" children's behavior. School social workers may compare their students' CBCL scores with the normative data provided by the scale manual and determine the extent to which particular children deviate from the norm (Achenbach & Rescorla, 2001).

Conners (1997; Conners, Wells, Parker, Sitarenios, Diamond, & Powell, 1997) developed 11 scales in long and short versions (between 59 and 87 items take 15–20 minutes; 27–28 items take 5–12 minutes, respectively). They are available for various respondents: teachers, parents, and adolescents. The Conners scales have been considered the "gold standard" of ADHD measures and other concerns.

The newest group of three scales, the Conners ADHD/DSM-IV Scale for Parents (CADS-P), Teachers (CADS-T), or Adolescents (CADS-A), is used specifically to assess ADHD in children between 3 and 17 years of age. They are designed to assess the characteristics of ADHD described in the DSM-IV. The three different scales have between 26 to 30 items and take approximately 5–10 minutes to complete.

The CBCL is used with children between the ages of 6 and 18 (Achenbach, 1991). Parents and teachers can provide considerable information about their children's skills, emotions, and behavior. The scales assess social relationships, school performance, and children's activities. Each question requires the respondent to rank the item on a three-point scale: 0 = not true, 1 = somewhat or sometimes true, and 2 = very true or often true. The CBCL also comes in a version for 18-month-old to 5-year-old children.

Unstandardized Scales

In reality, not all situations can employ standardized scales. An adequate scale may not be available that addresses the expected outcomes or demographics of a group of students or their school program. When social workers are faced with the need to write their own questions or scales, they should be careful to operationalize what is to be measured. Questions should be simple, be phrased in age-appropriate language, and have easily understood responses. If possible, other professionals with expertise with the students or knowledge of possible outcomes of the program should examine the scale items or questions and determine their face validity.

Workers should pilot-test the evaluation measure with other workers and a small group of students. Together, they can identify errors in wording, misleading items, or even missing content. Finally, the results of these nonstandardized scales can be very helpful in determining success, but as a word of caution, the results should not be generalized beyond the current group of students. Boxes 101.2–101.6 are examples of nonstandardized scales that have been designed and effectively used in school social programs.

Final Notes

Many possible measures are available to assess the objectives of school social work practice. These and other scales have proven to be effective in program evaluations, but they should only be one source of evidence. Workers are encouraged to combine various types of measures to gain clearer understandings of effective programs.

Step Three: Planning

Effective programs require (and deserve) a thoughtful plan of implementation. The plan should include what outcomes and objectives will be measured and what specific measures will be used. It must also delineate the process to collect data and enlist the participation of important stakeholders, such as teachers, administrators, and parents. In addition, the plan should include a process for disseminating the results so they are helpful to program participants and influential for future planning and program development.

Social workers should also be careful to measure areas of particular interest to various stakeholders, such as parents, administrators, teachers, social workers in other school settings, local politicians who may influence school budgets, and so forth. Most important, by combining various types of outcome measures (behavioral observations, counts of behavior, reports of satisfaction, scales, inventories, and questionnaires), the true effectiveness of programs can be determined and affect future programs.

Social workers should continually remind themselves that data analysis and good record keeping are fundamentally essential to supporting their students. Furthermore, the data may ensure their own long-term job security and demonstrate ethical, professional practice.

Files for Each and Every Student

Since workers have contact with many, many students, the details of their lives and valuable outcome data can be easily lost. Also, to prepare for the inevitable moment when social workers and programs are evaluated, every student must have a standardized form on which all relevant data are recorded. The files may consist of forms stapled together in manila folders or computer files containing the forms where workers (or helpful clerical staff) can enter and store the data.

The task of data collection can be simplified by having standardized forms with spaces for students' demographic information and the data from outcome measures (behavioral counts, past and current attendance records, scores from scales, and so forth). The computerized versions may be kept in data management software such as Microsoft Access. In this format, data can be easily tabulated along a variety of dimensions.

Since the data will be continually collected, social workers may need to assess the amount of time necessary to maintain the records. In some schools, supportive administrators can assign clerical staff to assist with this task.

Involve All the Players

Everyone who has a role or a concern for the success of a program or service should be involved in planning the evaluation procedures, gathering data, preserving the information, and assessing the outcome. The most obvious "players" are the students who receive services and the staff who oversee them. Unfortunately, even though parents are obvious stakeholders, confidentiality issues frequently prohibit their involvement in data entry or analysis.

Workers must also be careful to train all participants in the evaluation aspect of programs. Data should be collected carefully and consistently to ensure the validity of all responses and outcomes. Data entry personnel should be trained to consistently enter scores and to avoid or minimize personal judgments.

Teachers, school staff, and administrators, however, should be involved in the planning and program. Workers should avoid the temptation to work silently behind the scenes or to stay "out of sight" of administrators. Instead, social workers are encouraged to invite input from school personnel and keep them informed about the goals and expected outcomes of the program. Periodically, all the "players" should be updated or reminded of the ongoing program.

Workers will be wise to keep a record of the progress of the program and its evaluation. In the event that outcomes do not match expectations or, better yet, when outcomes far exceed everyone's dreams, workers' process notes may be helpful to evaluate what went right and what went wrong. Furthermore, the notes will give invaluable information for proposing changes to future programs and data collection.

In summary, smart social workers are needed in the schools. They also must be sufficiently committed to examine the goals of their programs. Objectives must be tied to outcome measures and incorporate observations, scales, inventories, and questionnaires to document effectiveness. The Conners and CBCL scales are two examples of well-established, valid, and reliable scales. Planning is an essential step to safeguard the evaluation process, the data, and the potential outcome report.

Finally, dissemination of the outcome assessment is essential for program participants, parents, and all school personnel. A report of the program, supportive elements of workers' process notes, and the results of the outcome measures document social workers' efforts, validate their role, and contribute to future efforts. Furthermore, social workers should disseminate their reports to other school social workers at social work conferences. They should consider sharing their reports with editors of professional journals who are receptive to well-documented school social work programs and their outcomes. In the end, other social workers, students, parents, and schools may all benefit from the hard work of softhearted, smart social workers.

Tools and Practice Examples

Box 101.2 Anger Diary

- Name_____ Date_____
- How many arguments this week?_____
- Rate (1–10) how angry you were?_____
- What were your internal signals?
  _____
- Which steps did you use?
  _____
- What happened afterwards?
  _____

Box 101.3 Self-Anchored Scale Depression

- Instructions: Circle the number that applies every day before 8 am

                    1 2 3 4 5 6 7

Energetic,	Tired, no energy
feel alive	feel like lying down
and ready to go to work	and never getting up

Box 101.4 Rating Scale Communication

» Inadequate 1 2 3 4 5 6 7 8 9 10 Adequate

- Speak for self
- Sent I messages
- Use a stop action
- Ask for feedback
- Listen
- Summarize
- Validate
- Ask open questions
- Check out

Box 101.5 Conflict Avoidance Rating Scale

Inadequate 1 2 3 4 5 6 7 8 9 10 Adequate

Changes the subject,	Stays on topic,
Leaves the room,	Engages in
Refuses to talk about	conversation about
issues	conflictual issues

Box 101.6 Goal Attainment Scale

Scale Attainment Level	Education	Suicide
−2 Most unfavorable outcome	No attempt	Suicide
−1 Less than expected	Dropped out	Attempted
0 Expected success	Enrolled, skips	Impulses
+1 More than expected	Enrolled	1 Impulse
+2 Best anticipated success	Enrolled, goals	No impulses

Key Points to Remember

The following steps may be used to achieve an effective program evaluation:

Identifying outcomes
Measuring outcomes
Planning for success and reporting of the outcomes

An *evidence-based approach to program evaluation* depends on outcome measures that validate interventions and demonstrate changes. This chapter gives information on how to search for measures that are reliable and valid and may be used in school settings.

Program evaluation involves the measurement of several different areas. *Program effort* includes descriptions of services rendered, the number of students served, and the degree to which social workers actively addressed the needs of students, teachers, and administrators. *Program effectiveness* becomes more complicated because the objectives of school social work related to outcomes and the data are quantified, tabulated, and summarized. In schools, outcome measures that are important relate to the mission of the school such as grades, attendance, and graduation rates. Other important indicators of outcomes may be discovered through reviewing job descriptions or may be identified by observing and interviewing stakeholders. Finally, *program efficiency* must establish that the achieved results were worth the cost. In this regard, saving the school money is always a good outcome.

Resources

Corcoran, K. (2001). Chapter 5: Locating instruments. In B. Thyer (Ed.), *The handbook of social work research methods* (pp. 69–79). Thousand Oaks, CA: Sage.

Corcoran, K., & Fischer, J. (2000). *Measures for clinical practice: A sourcebook* (3rd ed.). New York: Free Press. A two-volume set that contains reliable and valid measures that may be used for clinical assessment and evaluation. The volumes are divided into measures for adults and measures for children and families.

Jordan, C., & Franklin, C. (2003). Clinical assessment for social workers: Quantitative and qualitative methods (2nd ed.). Chicago: Lyceum. This book discusses the assessment process, then describes ways of doing outcome measurement with children, adults, and families. Specific measures are recommended.

Jordan, C., Franklin, C., & Corcoran, K. (2004). Chapter 9: Measuring instruments. In R. Grinnell (Ed.), *Social work research and evaluation: Quantitative and qualitative approaches* (6th ed., pp. 151–180). Itasca, IL: Peacock. This chapter gives information on measuring instruments including standardized versus nonstandardized instruments and instrument construction and selection.

References

Achenback, T. M. (1991). *Manual for child behavior checklist/4–19 and 1991 Profile.* Burlington, VT: University of Vermont, Department of Psychiatry.

Achenbach, T. M., & Rescorla, L. A. (2001). *Manual for ASEBA school-age forms & profiles.* Burlington, VT: University of Vermont, Research Center for Children, Youth, & Families.

Andrews, J., Janzen, H. L., & Saklofske, D. H. (2001). *Handbook of psychoeducational assessment: Ability, achievement, and behavior in children.* San Diego: Academic Press.

Birleson, P. (1981). The validity of depression disorders in childhood and the development of a self-rating scale: A research report. *Journal of Child Psychology and Psychiatry, 22,* 73–88.

Conners, C. K. (1997). *Manual for the Conners' Rating Scales—Revised.* North Tonawanda, NY: Multi-Health Systems.

Conners, C. K., Wells, K. C., Parker, J. D. A., Sitarenios, G., Diamond, J. M., & Powell, J. W. (1997). A new self-report scale for assessment of adolescent psychopathology: Factor structure, reliability, validity, and diagnostic sensitivity. *Journal of Abnormal Child Psychology, 26,* 279–291.

Corcoran, K. (2001). Locating instruments. In B. Thyer (Ed.), *The handbook of social work research methods* (pp. 69–79). Thousand Oaks, CA: Sage.

Corcoran, K., & Fischer, J. (2000). *Measures for clinical practice: A sourcebook* (3rd ed.). New York: Free Press.

Dibble, N. (1999). *Outcome evaluation of school social work services.* Report for the Wisconsin Department of Public Instruction.

Dumenci, L., Erol, N., Achenbach, T. M., & Simsek, Z. (2004). Measurement structure of the Turkish translation of the Child Behavior Checklist using confirmatory factor analytic approaches to validation of syndromal constructs. *Journal of Abnormal Child Psychology, 32,* 337–342.

Fantuzzo, J., Grim, S., Mordell, M., McDermott, P., Miller, L., & Coolaham, K. (2001). A multivariate analysis of the Revised Conners' Teacher Rating Scale with low-income, urban preschool children. *Journal of Abnormal Child Psychology, 29,* 141–152.

Gambrill, E. (1997). *Social work practice: A critical thinker's guide.* New York: Oxford University Press.

Jordan, C., & Franklin, C. (2003). Clinical assessment for social workers: Quantitative and qualitative methods (2nd ed.). Chicago: Lyceum.

Jordan, C., Franklin, C., & Corcoran, K. (2004). Measuring instruments. In R. Grinnell (Ed.), *Social work research and evaluation: Quantitative and qualitative approaches* (6th ed, pp. 151–180). Itasca, IL: Peacock.

Kazdin, A. E. (1983). Hopelessness, depression, and suicidal intent among psychiatrically disturbed children. *Journal of Consulting and Clinical Psychology, 51,* 504–510.

Kendall, P. C., Marrs-Garcia, A., Nath, S. R., & Sheldrick, R. C. (1999). Normative comparisons for the evaluation of clinical significance. *Journal of Consulting & Clinical Psychology, 67,* 285–299.

Nurius, P. S., & Hudson, W. W. (1993). *Human services practice, evaluation, and computers.* Pacific Grove, CA: Brooks/Cole.

Royce, D., Thyer, B. A., Padgett, D. K., & Logan, T. K. (2001). *Program evaluation: An introduction.* Belmont, CA: Brooks/Cole.

Sederer, L. I., & Dickey, B. (Eds.). (1996). *Outcomes assessment in clinical practice.* Baltimore: Williams & Wilkins.

Verhulst, F. C., Achenbach, T. M., van der Ende, J., Erol, N., Lambert, M. C., Leung, P. W. L., Silva, M. A., Zilber, N., & Zubrick, S. R. (2003). Comparisons of problems reported by youths from seven countries. *American Journal of Psychiatry, 160,* 1479–1485.

CHAPTER 102

Using the School's Database System to Construct Accountability Tools

David A. Patterson

Getting Started

School databases in recent years have been established to collect data on a variety of indicators of school and student performance as well as mental health and social services delivery. The specific type of data collected by a school district or by an individual school will vary across locations and in accordance with local, community, and state data collection requirements. Despite this variability, schools and school systems typically collect in these databases information applicable for the evaluation of the efficacy and utility of school social work service delivery. There are commonalities in database structures and data extraction procedures that allow us to request data from a school database and use that data to measure and demonstrate the results of school social work interventions. Moreover, spreadsheets, generally available on almost every modern-day personal computer, can readily be used to construct accountability tools to summarize and graphically represent information from school databases. Simply stated, the purpose of this chapter is to describe how to use data from school databases to evaluate school social work interventions. Accountability tools developed with spreadsheets will be shown to both simplify and automate elements of this process so that it can become a routine procedure of school social work practice.

What We Know

Jonson-Reid, Kontak, and Mueller (2001) address the necessity of collecting information on the delivery of school social work services and the associated student outcomes. They describe collaboration between a university researcher and a school district to develop a management information system to capture school social work service delivery information and to report those services to the school district. The authors cite a number of advantages in the use of management information systems in evaluating school social work services. These advantages include the ability to evaluate targeted interventions, the production of data to support grant writing, and reduced costs when compared to more labor-intensive data collection such as paper-based records review. They point out, "Caseload characteristics, service delivery patterns, and case outcomes associated with school social work practice remain areas of research in need of substantial improvement" (Jonson-Reid, Kontak, & Mueller, 2001, p. 209).

Data collected in school database systems germane to school social work practice may include student achievement information, such as grades and results of standardized testing, attendance information, graduation data, and dropout rates. For instance, Threet (2001) describes a Web-based student information system used by the Cumberland County Schools in Crossville, Tennessee, that compiles data on more than 6,800 students. The system integrates personal and demographic information on students and family with attendance, conduct, and grading data. Raines (2002) suggested five ways to evaluate student progress, one of which is the review of student records. School database systems dramatically reduce the time and effort required to extract evaluative information from student records. Jonson-Reid, Kontak, Citerman, Essma, and Fezzi (2004), in a yearlong study of school social work service, used a management information system database to examine the relationships among student characteristics, services delivered, and case outcomes. They argue for increased use of school administrative databases for school social work services evaluation.

What We Can Do

Acquiring Necessary Data

In order to construct accountability tools, it is first necessary to obtain the essential data from the school database. In most schools and school systems, there is an individual designated as the database administrator. While the title of this person may vary from location to location, his or her role is to ensure the capture, integrity, and security of the data collected in the database. This individual typically has some level of responsibility in generation of reports compiled from the database. The database administrator generally processes requests for specific types of data or for data from the records of designated individuals. Further, while school databases can generate both routine and custom reports, the depth and specifics usually required to evaluate the utility of school social work services necessitates the extraction of data from the database and the handling of that data with the accountability tools described here.

Consequently, before requesting data from a school database via the database administrator, one must first consider what question or set of questions one wishes to answer. It may be that one would want to know, "Does this specific intervention that has been used with this designated group of students actually reduce incident reports?" Alternatively, one might ask, "Does the academic performance of students receiving school social work services improve over the course of the services delivery?" Or one might want to know whether, over the course of several months, students receiving school social work services improve their attendance when compared to a random sample of students who do not receive school social work services. Each of these questions represents a potentially valid and worthwhile accountability measure.

In order to obtain the necessary data from a school database to pursue any one of these three questions or, for that matter, any accountability question, one must first know what data are collected and available from the school database. This issue is best addressed by requesting from the database administrator a list of variables or, as they are often called in information technology circles, *data elements* or *data fields*. School databases can be very large and complex. The intention here is to request only those variables that are necessary to answer the accountability question(s) one is pursuing. Any request to a database administrator should be accompanied with an explanation for the request and a specified time by which the information is needed. Better still, in most cases it will likely be extremely helpful to have a face-to-face conversation with the database administrator to:

1. establish a working, collaborative relationship,
2. explain the question or questions one intends to address and to identify with the database administrator the variables in the data set that can be used to answer the questions posed,
3. identify personal and demographic information, such as name, age, race, gender, and grade level, that is available in the database that can be used to describe and compare groups of students,
4. to learn what procedures need to be followed to request data from the school database,
5. to specify the format of the requested data,
6. explain how the data will be secured and protected, and
7. establish how often the data will be requested.

In regard to point 5, ask that the database administrator provide requested data as an electronic file either as an email attachment or, if the file is not too large, then on some data storage medium such as a CD-ROM. Further, since this discussion of constructing accountability tools will center on the use of spreadsheets to create these tools, ask that the data be provided in a file format that can be read by spreadsheets, such as .xls (Microsoft Excel files) or .csv (comma delimited).

Spreadsheets

Spreadsheets are computer programs that display a matrix of rows and columns of cells into which information is entered and displayed. Spreadsheets can represent information in the form of numbers, text, or formulas. In addition to simply storing information, spreadsheets can be used in school social work practice settings to (a) record and graph the changes a student makes over the course of service delivery, (b) collect and analyze data on how groups of students and individuals within the groups change over time, and (c) generate graphs and tables reporting services delivery to funding sources and supervisors. These three tasks are made possible by virtue of the fact that spreadsheets have tools to (a) perform calculations/statistical analysis, (b) sort data in a variety of ways, (c) collapse and summarize information, and (d) filter data sets for subsets of data based upon selected criteria from the data set (Patterson & Basham, in press).

Spreadsheets, which are found on almost all modern-day computers, are a ready instrument for accomplishing the data analysis tasks of school social work. There are both commercial and non-commercial publishers of spreadsheets. Most of them are roughly equivalent in appearance and functionality. Far and away the most widely used spreadsheet around the globe is Microsoft Excel. For this reason, the steps for developing accountability tools described here, while applicable to most other spreadsheets, are represented with reference to and screen shots from Microsoft Excel.

Tools and Practice Examples

Spreadsheet Accountability Tools

Perhaps the most illuminating way to demonstrate how to construct accountability tools using information from a school database system is to offer a step-by-step case example. Let us suppose that we want to evaluate the effectiveness of an intervention to address truancy in a middle school. Teasley (2004) argues for greater involvement by school social workers in the identification, prevention, and intervention with children at risk of truancy and high rates of absenteeism. Absenteeism is defined as time not attending school and is distinct from truancy, which is defined as absence from school without parental consent. She asserts that truancy may be an early indicator of negative behaviors that can result in problematic personal and developmental consequences. As such, it would be important to evaluate whether an intervention program to reduce truancy succeeded in doing so.

Let us assume that we will begin our intervention in the seventh week of the fall semester. At this point, there are 6 weeks worth of attendance data in the school database. We want to target our intervention at students with high rates of truancy. We request of the database administrator a data file containing the following variables: name, student identification number, age, gender, grade level, GPA for prior school year, and days of unexcused absences per week for the first 6 weeks of the school year.

Figure 102.1 displays the data file with an additional variable created in the spreadsheet, Total Unexcused Absences. This additional variable was created with a formula in column N, row 2. That formula is displayed in the formula bar above columns F and G. The formula = SUM(H2:M2) tells the spreadsheet to calculate the sum of the values in columns H through M in row 2. In the spreadsheet, the formula in cell N2 has been copied and then pasted into rows 3 to 31. The entire data set was then selected and sorted in descending order on the variable Total Unexcused Absences. This sorting of the data set was accomplished by clicking on Data in the menu bar and then selecting Sort, Descending. It is important to note that accidentally selecting and sorting only column N would result in scrambling the relationship between the values for Total Unexcused Absences and the rest of the data associated with that student.

If we continue our examination of the data in Figure 102.1, we note that in column N, Total Unexcused Absences, there is a clear break point between students with 12 or more absences and those with 6 or less. Let us assume that we select the students with more than 12 absences for our intervention. We carry out our intervention for 6 weeks. To evaluate the effectiveness of this intervention, we again request a data file for students in our intervention group with attendance data for both the first 6 weeks of the semester and the next 6 weeks of attendance data. That data file appears in Figure 102.2. We can use these data to construct accountability tools for selected individual students and to evaluate the results of the intervention for the group.

Spreadsheet Single System Design for Individuals

Single system designs (SSDs) are likely the most widely taught method for evaluating social work practice outcomes (Bloom, Fischer, & Orme, 2003; Tripodi, 1994). Essentially, SSDs are evaluative procedures that graphically represent repeated measurement over time of an identified indicator of a problem. For our purposes, we graph the

Figure 102.1. Student Truancy Data File

	C	D	E	F	G	H	I	J	K	L	L	N	O	P
1	ID#	Age	Gender	Grade	Prior Yr GPA	Week 1	Week 2	Week 3	Week 4	Week 5	Week 6	Total Unexcused Absences		
2	684	11	Female	6	0.06	4	4	4	4	4	4	22		
3	5610	11	Male	6	0.66	4	4	4	4	4	4	22		
4	5157	14	Male	8	1.92	2	5	3	4	5	3	22		
5	752	12	Male	6	1.78	4	4	4	4	4	4	21		
6	9733	15	Male	8	3.58	4	1	4	5	1	4	19		
7	2470	13	Male	6	1.46	2	4	3	3	4	3	19		
8	4479	12	Male	6	3.29	4	0	3	5	3	3	18		
9	5503	15	Female	8	2.05	3	3	5	4	1	2	18		
10	3358	14	Male	7	0.04	3	3	3	3	3	3	17		
11	3242	15	Male	8	3.95	3	3	3	3	3	3	17		
12	6538	14	Male	7	0.02	3	3	3	3	3	3	17		
13	8465	13	Female	6	2.41	3	3	3	3	3	3	17		
14	6210	13	Male	6	0.59	4	0	3	5	1	3	16		
15	4285	14	Male	8	3.44	4	3	4	1	4	1	16		
16	9312	16	Male	8	2.84	4	3	5	1	2	1	16		
17	4051	12	Male	6	1.40	2	2	4	4	1	2	15		
18	5081	12	Male	7	1.22	2	3	3	0	4	4	15		
19	6780	14	Male	7	0.70	1	2	4	2	4	2	15		
20	2170	12	Male	6	3.23	4	1	2	4	0	4	15		
21	2133	14	Male	7	2.99	4	0	2	3	3	3	15		
22	9625	15	Male	8	0.77	1	2	2	1	3	5	14		
23	2551	13	Male	7	0.48	1	2	2	1	3	5	14		
24	9135	12	Female	6	2.25	3	0	3	2	0	2	12		
25	6179	14	Male	7	0.01	0	0	1	1	2	2	6		
26	6792	12	Female	6	2.43	1	1	1	1	1	1	6		
27	3726	12	Female	6	0.37	1	1	1	1	1	1	6		
28	8688	15	Male	8	1.51	1	1	1	1	1	1	6		
29	1326	12	Male	6	2.13	1	1	1	1	1	1	6		
39	5944	15	Male	8	2.34	3	1	0	1	0	1	6		
31	4374	13	Male	7	2.28	1	1	1	1	1	1	6		

N2 = =SUM(H2:M2)

Sheet1 / Sheet2 / Sheet3

Figure 102.2. Baseline and Intervention Data File

G26 = =AVERAGE(G2:G24)

	F	G	H	I	J	K	L	M	N	O	P	Q	R
1	Student	Week 1	Week 2	Week 3	Week 4	Week 5	Week 6	Week 7	Week 8	Week 9	Week 10	Week 11	Week 12
2	1	4	4	4	4	4	4	0	0	0	0	0	0
3	2	4	4	4	4	4	4	2	2	2	2	2	1
4	3	2	5	3	4	5	3	1	1	1	1	1	1
5	4	4	4	4	4	4	4	3	3	3	2	2	1
6	5	4	1	4	5	1	4	2	2	2	2	2	1
7	6	2	4	3	3	4	3	2	2	2	1	1	0
8	7	4	0	3	5	3	3	1	1	1	1	1	0
9	8	3	3	5	4	1	2	4	3	3	3	2	1
10	9	3	3	3	3	3	3	3	3	3	2	2	1
11	10	3	3	3	3	3	3	3	3	3	2	2	1
12	11	3	3	3	3	3	3	1	1	1	1	0	0
13	12	3	3	3	3	3	3	3	3	3	3	2	1
14	13	4	0	3	5	1	3	3	2	2	2	2	1
15	14	4	3	4	1	4	1	2	2	2	2	1	1
16	15	4	3	5	1	2	1	1	1	1	1	1	0
17	16	2	2	4	4	1	2	0	0	0	0	0	0
18	17	2	3	3	0	4	4	0	0	0	0	0	0
19	18	1	2	4	2	4	2	1	1	1	1	1	0
20	19	4	1	2	4	0	4	1	1	1	0	0	0
21	20	4	0	2	3	3	3	1	1	1	0	0	0
22	21	1	2	2	1	3	5	4	3	3	3	3	1
23	22	1	2	2	1	3	5	2	2	2	1	1	0
24	23	3	0	3	2	0	2	0	0	0	0	0	0
25													
26	Mean	3	2	3	3	3	3	2	2	2	1	1	0
27	S.D.	1.10	1.38	0.86	1.33	1.24	1.01	1.24	1.08	1.08	0.93	0.85	0.31
28	Mean+S.D.	3.97	3.70	4.03	4.35	4.00	3.97	3.03	2.66	2.66	2.28	2.09	0.76
29	Mean-S.D.	1.77	0.93	2.31	1.69	1.53	1.95	0.56	0.49	0.49	0.42	0.39	0.14
30	Week	1	2	3	4	5	6	7	8	9	10	11	12

change over time in school absences for student number 6 in Figure 102.3. This accountability tool was created by:

1. Copying the data for each 6-week period from the data file represented in Figure 102.2.
2. Once the data are copied, use the commands Edit, Special Paste, Transpose to transpose the data from its horizontal representation in rows in Figure 102.2 to its vertical representation in columns in Figure 102.3. In SSDs, it is important to mark the change of treatment phase from baseline, in this case the first 6 weeks, to the intervention phase, which occurred in Weeks 7 through 12. To accomplish this demarcation of phase, we paste the data from the different phases in separate columns.
3. As is evident in Figure 102.3, when the data in these two phases are graphed, two lines are created, each representing a distinct phase of treatment: baseline and intervention.
4. Charts and graphs are created in Microsoft Excel by selecting from the Menu Bar, Insert, Chart. This opens the Chart Wizard that leads one through the four steps of creating a chart, which include selecting the chart type, selecting the data from which to construct the chart, labeling the chart's elements, and specifying where to place the chart in the spreadsheet.

SSD charts, such as the one in Figure 102.3, are created by selecting Line Chart for chart type.

5. Note also that there is a line separating the baseline and intervention phase in Figure 102.3. This is a graphing convention for SSD charts. The line is drawn on the chart with the Line Tool available under Drawing Tools in Excel. Click on View, Toolbars, and Drawing to make the Drawing Tools available on the spreadsheet.

Spreadsheet Single System Design for Groups

One means to create an accountability tool to evaluate change in a group of individuals receiving a particular intervention is to display the group's outcome data in two ways on the same graph. In the example of truancy, we might want to know the average or mean level of truancy for each week in the baseline and intervention phases of treatment. In the intervention phase, this will show us on average how well our intervention is working. However, if we rely solely on the average, we are unable to see the variability within the group across the weeks. In this example variability is an indicator of how different or similar the students are in regards to their rates of truancy over

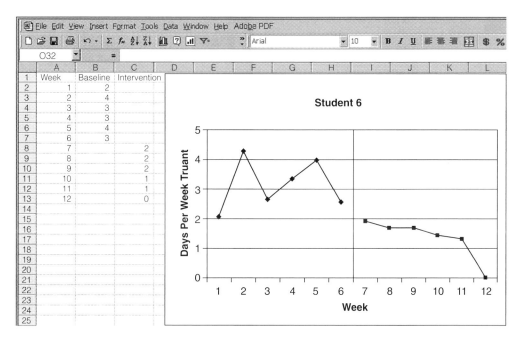

Figure 102.3. Single Case Design

the weeks. The statistical indicator of variability we will use is *standard deviation*. Lest the very mention of a statistical procedure create any anxiety, be assured that this statistic is calculated by the spreadsheet without any requisite knowledge by the user of the statistical formula. The accountability tool we are going to create is called a *standard deviation enhanced line graph* (SDELG) (Basham, 2002; Patterson & Basham, 2002).

Examining the bottom of Figure 102.2, we see there are four values that have been calculated for each week: the mean, the S.D. (standard deviation), Mean+S.D., and Mean−S.D. We create the formulas for calculating these values for Week 1 in cells G26 through G29 and then copy and paste them into the cells to the right for the remaining weeks. Note that at the top of Figure 102.2 in the formula line above columns H and I displays the formula in cell G26. This formula, =AVERAGE(G2:G24) tells the spreadsheet to calculate the mean or average value for that range of cells. In cell G26, we see that the average for those 23 values in those cells is 3.

To calculate the standard deviation:

1. From the menu bar we select Insert, Function, Statistical, STDEV.
2. This produces a dialog box with which we specify the range of cells for which we want the standard deviation calculated.
3. The standard deviation function returns a number that is the standard deviation for the specified range of cells.
4. Just as we did with the formula for the mean described previously, we then copy and paste the standard deviation function into the cells to the right for the remaining weeks.
5. Next we want to add the standard deviation for each week to the mean value for that week. In cell G28, we write a simple formula=SUM(G26+G27) and hit the Return key.
6. We then copy this formula and paste it into the cells to the right for the remaining weeks.
7. We repeat this procedure with the row labeled Mean−S.D. To subtract the standard deviation from the mean, we would use the formula=SUM(G26–G27).

In order to create a graphic depicting the change over time, we need to copy the data from the spreadsheet page seen in Figure 102.2 into a new worksheet in the same spreadsheet. Spreadsheets commonly have multiple pages or worksheets.

1. A new worksheet is created by selecting in the menu bar Insert, Worksheet.
2. Next we select the cells G26 to R29 and then use the Copy, Special Paste, Transpose command sequence described previously.
3. In the Special Paste dialogue window, be sure to select Transpose and Values. Click on the Values check box in the Special Paste dialogue box is necessary because the cells in Figure 102.2 G26 to R29 are formulas that have produced the displayed values. Pasting them into the new worksheet without selecting Values in the Special Paste dialogue box would insert errant values in the new worksheet.

Figure 102.4 displays one method of creating an accountability tool for tracking change in groups of individuals. Note that as in Figure 102.3, baseline data are not in the same columns as the data from the intervention phase. Several observations can be derived from the line graph in Figure 102.4. The mean level of truancy in the baseline phase was relatively stable. In the baseline phase, the distance between the mean and the plus and minus standard deviation lines is relatively wide and constant. In the intervention phase, there are three observable changes in the data. First, the mean level of truancy dropped on average more than 1 day per week immediately after the start of the intervention. Second, there is an obvious decline or downward trend in the mean level of truancy for the group as a whole. Third, the variation in the group, as evidenced by the decrease in the standard deviation, declined markedly during the course of the intervention. Each of these three indicators suggests the efficacy of the school social work intervention.

Key Points to Remember

We have presented here two accountability tools for evaluating school social work practice applicable for the utilization of information drawn from school databases. While attendance data was used here for the purpose of demonstration, spreadsheets are highly robust and flexible tools for the creation of single system design graphs. They can be used to track changes in a wide range of data collected in school databases that may provide evidence for the effects of school social work interventions, including graduation rates, incident reports, dropout rates, and academic performance.

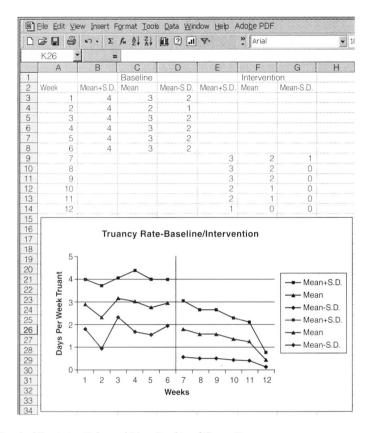

Figure 102.4. Standard Deviation Enhanced Line Graphic of Group Data

Resources

This chapter represents only an introduction to the utility of spreadsheets as accountability tools. Video examples of creating single system design graphs in spreadsheets, along with other materials on data analysis with spreadsheets, are available at http://web.utk.edu/~dap/Random/Order/Start.htm.

References

Basham, R. E. (2002). *Data visualization: Graphical representation in the evaluation of experiential group therapy education outcomes.* Proquest Digital Dissertations (UMI Dissertation Abstracts Database) ISBN: 3086821, Vol. 64–02A.

Bloom, M., Fischer, J., & Orme, J. G. (2003). *Evaluating practice: Guidelines of the accountable professional* (4th ed.). Boston: Allyn & Bacon.

Jonson-Reid, M., Kontak, D., Citerman, B., Essma, A., & Fezzi, N. (2004). School social work case characteristics, services, and dispositions: Year one results. *Children & Schools, 26*(1), 5–22.

Jonson-Reid, M., Kontak, D., & Mueller, S. (2001). Developing a management information system for school social workers: A field–university partnership. *Children and Schools, 23*(4), 198–211.

Patterson, D. A., & Basham, R. E. (2002). Data visualization procedures in the analysis of group treatment outcomes across units of analysis. *Small Group Research, 33*(2), 209–233.

Patterson, D. A., & Basham, R. E. (in press). *Data analysis with spreadsheets.* Boston: Allyn & Bacon.

Raines, J. C. (2002). Present levels of performance, goals, and objectives. *School Social Work Journal, 27*(2), 1–17.

Teasley, M. L. (2004). Absenteeism and truancy: Risk, protection, and best practice implications for school social workers. *Children & Schools, 26*(2), 117–128.

Threet, S. (2001). Administrative software: Increasing accountability. *Media & Methods, 37*(5), 32–34.

Tripodi, T. (1994). *A primer on single subject design for clinical social workers.* Washington, DC: NASW Press.

Guidelines for Writing a Report That Effectively Demonstrates Accountability

Diane C. Jacobs Alphonse Shropshire

CHAPTER 103

Getting Started

It is 9:45 A.M. The school principal walks into a meeting of the pupil services team with several student incident reports, wanting to know why no one on the mental health staff has seen *Student X* as requested. Even though the social worker has, in fact, seen the student as well as his family numerous times, there are no records to document such services.

In another school, a frustrated parent telephones the social worker's office to complain about how her child is being mishandled in the classroom by the teacher. The social worker remembers some lengthy dialogue she had with the parent previously about this situation. However, she had no record of what transpired since that talk.

A principal meets with her administrators and team leaders in preparation for the upcoming school year. The principal has learned that her student enrollment has grown and that she can hire additional staff. When asked about hiring a full-time social worker, the principal declines. She states that the part-time social worker assigned to her school never presented formal documentation on students referred for intervention. Although she appreciates the value of the social worker, she cannot justify such an addition to district administration without supporting documentation.

Each of these incidents reflects a need for the school social worker to be accountable. Yet, while most of us are aware of the need for validating our services, providing enough documentation to meet an increasing demand for accountability is a challenge for school social workers.

School social workers serve an inordinate number of students in most schools. Take, for example, a school social worker assigned to any school with a pupil enrollment of 617 students. This practitioner provides services to 223 students during the academic school year. This clientele represents just over 35% of the school's student population, which likely mirrors the number of referrals in many schools. Even with this large number, school administrators are likely to question the social worker's effectiveness unless there is documentation to demonstrate not only the volume but also the impact of services. This chapter provides a rationale, guidance, and tools for maintaining meaningful documentation and exhibiting the effects of services provided.

What We Know

Colleagues, such as teachers, can easily measure the product or service they provide. In our profession it is imperative that we report on outcome-based intervention. We must focus on the substance of interventions and avoid the tendency to report solely from the standpoint of process evaluation: the number of student or family interviews, the number of home visits made, the number of group presentations made, and the number of telephone contacts made. None of these statistics alone provides appreciation for what school social workers actually do. Process evaluations alone also make it difficult for administrators to advocate for hiring or keeping social workers in our schools. As in the previous example, a school-based mental health professional may be required to provide service to as many as 223 students during a school year. Given the need to serve such a population, social workers must determine the extent to which data collection formats must be revised. The ultimate losers when school social workers fail to substantiate their worth are the children and families who cannot be served.

In writing our reports, special care must be taken in order to ensure credibility. An example that demonstrates the importance of good qualitative and quantitative data is the Elementary and Secondary School Counseling (ESSC) program. The ESSC program was recently placed on the president's list of programs to be eliminated (School Social Work Association, 2004). The ESSC is the only federal program devoted to supporting counseling programs in schools. At this writing the School Social Work Association (SSWA) and partner associations (school counselors, school psychologists, and child and adolescent psychiatrists) are valiantly advocating to retain the ESSC. Good statistics must be readily available for such an effort. The substantiation of both quantitative and qualitative studies is used for the ESSC program to underscore the importance of school social workers incorporating evidence-based studies and accountability into their practice: "Studies show that high-quality counseling can prevent students from turning to violence, drug or alcohol abuse as well as improve grades and reduce classroom disruptions" (Secretary of Education Rod Paige announcing 2003 ESSC grantees, in National Association of Social Workers, 2004).

What We Can Do

So, where do we start? First, thanks to Microsoft Excel, the gathering and presentation of hardcore statistical data does not have to be toilsome. However, a school social worker's recording, while meeting the need for efficiency and confidentiality, must be concise and answer the questions *why and with what effect?*

A wealth of data is being produced every day in schools. Standardized test scores, school behavior incident reports, requests for exceptional student services, multidisciplinary team reports, social histories and summaries, psychiatric and psychological reports, supervisor evaluations, school principal observations, attendance reports, and school suspension/expulsion reports can be incorporated into the worker's qualitative and quantitative report. Determining the type of forms to be used in collecting these data becomes essential.

Most schools in America maintain data collection systems that utilize several standard forms. See the SSW forms in Figures 103.1–103.2 in Tools and Practice Examples for examples of those available to school social workers. Similar to forms found in most social service agencies, these forms provide detailed and succinct data for use in a variety of ways, certainly in evaluating effectiveness.

The top portion of the SSW Form 1 (see Figure 103.1) is completed at the referral stage to include information provided by the student, parent, and/or teacher. The "Reasons for Referral" section is for indicating the initial focus of intervention (i.e., Attendance, Behavior/Adjustment, Academic Problems, Home Family, Health, or Other). You may expand upon the perceived nature of the problem or make brief mention of the student's current or past grade point average, health, and/or social functioning in the "Explain Reason" section. Information obtained in this section usually assists the worker in the development of a working hypothesis. The information noted with regard to the "Student's Sibling(s) Name" usually serves as a point of reference for the school social worker in considering the student's social functioning—the emotional, relational, or interactive aspects of the student's situation at home or school.

With the example of any school in America, approximately 17% of the referral contacts relate to poor school attendance. This figure may support the claim that truancy/absenteeism may be the first sign in a series of antisocial behaviors that lead to negative personal and developmental outcomes (Teasley, 2004, p. 117). The use of an attendance sheet on the SSW Form 1 is critical in identifying patterns and may assist the school social worker in identifying underlying issues.

Written records of initial contacts made in the "Teacher/Reporter Interventions" section are also pertinent to the school social worker for purposes of assessing the strengths and weaknesses associated with home, school, and community factors impinging upon the student. Finally, signatures are required at the bottom on the front page of the Form 1; notably, the recorder's identity is essential, especially when there is a need for determining the facts of a case in the legal system.

On page 2 of the SSW Form 1 (see Figure 103.2), under the heading "To Be Completed by School Social Worker," is a space for additional intake information in order to formulate a hypothesis.

Box 103.1 Preassessment and Postassessment

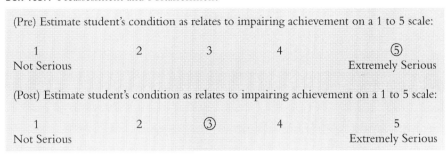

After making an assessment and identifying target systems, the report is ready to be constructed. According to Sheafor, Horejsi, and Horejsi (2000), a good report is characterized by the following: (a) shortness, (b) clarity and simplicity, (c) usefulness, and (d) organization.

The importance of documenting impact with regard to intervention cannot be overly emphasized. For example, a teacher or parent may report, "I tried what you recommended and it didn't work." The use of standardized assessment instruments or research-based methodologies (Dupper, 2003, p. 209), such as a simple rating scale, helps determine whether there has been any change relative to school social worker intervention. The SSW Form 1 includes pre- and postrating scales. A student's teacher, parent, or caregiver is interviewed and asked to submit from their standpoint a pupil rating (i.e., preassessment) on a scale from 1 to 5, with 5 being extremely serious in relationship to impairing student achievement and 1 being not serious enough to impair student achievement. For example, via use of single-system designs or classical group designs, having more than one reporter providing pre- and postratings of the student's condition helps the school social worker determine whether there has been change as a result of her or his intervention. In other words the pre- and postassessments shed light on whether there has been a change in the target behavior. Note in Box 103.1 a change from level 5 to 3.

In the section for "Student System Outcome Goals," the worker's written goal statement would be to represent observation of specific activity, and subsequently the worker would indicate if the goal was: Fully Achieved, Partially Achieved, or Not Achieved (see Figure 103.2). The importance of documenting student outcomes during the intervention process cannot be overemphasized (Rathvon, 1999, p. 44).

The "Additional Comments" section of the SSW Form 1, side 2, is where the school social worker writes the final progress note in closure. As the primary service provider, the social worker may document a review of each problem and service response. The recommendation to transfer, close, or reopen a case is made, and again the worker is obligated to sign and date this document for accountability purposes.

Throughout the intervention, the SSW Form 3 (see Figure 103.3) is used to facilitate concise record keeping in order for the worker to focus on the student's presenting and subsequent problems and the intervention to deal with his or her problem. It may be helpful to set an administrative policy for maintaining case notes for narrative recording, such as the SOAP format. Utilization of the SOAP (Sheafor et al., 2000, p. 189) format encourages concise recording, whereby specific problems are kept in focus and irrelevant information is kept out of the record.

Aggregate Reporting

As sheer numbers alone (quantity) do not always translate into effectiveness (impact), reports must reflect both volume and impact (outcome of intervention). The information collected and recorded on standardized forms, in this instance individual SSW Form 1, provides important data to show the effect that school social work intervention has on students' school adjustment. It can be readily available for scrutiny and provide documentation of interventions, intent (service goals), and results. The caseload of 223 students, given in the opening example, is not too large to review each case individually with ongoing monitoring. For illustrative purposes, imagine the utility of the SSW Form 4 and SSW 5 (see Figures 103.4 and 103.5) in representing an aggregate report from

Box 103.2 Caseload Reports at Any School in America

Caseload Results as Reported on SSW Form 4

Total Student Enrollment N=617		Total Report of Critical Cases N=47		Service Goals Fully Achieved		Service Goals Partially Achieved		Service Goals Not Achieved	
No.	%			No.	%	No.	%	No.	%
47	7.6			26	55.3	21	44.7	0	0.0

Caseload Results as Reported on SSW Form 5

Total Student Enrollment N=617		Total Report of Non-critical Cases N=176		Service Goals Fully Achieved		Service Goals Partially Achieved		Service Goals Not Achieved	
No.	%			No.	%	No.	%	No.	%
176	28.5			151	85.8	20	11.4	5	2.8

Caseload Results as Reported on SSW Forms 4 and 5

Total Student Enrollment N=617		Total Report of *Critical* and Noncritical N=223		Service Goals Fully Achieved		Service Goals Partially Achieved		Service Goals Not Achieved	
No.	%			No.	%	No.	%	No.	%
223	36.1			177	79.4	41	18.4	5	2.2

Note: Percentages gathered to show outcome of intervention provided by the school social worker.

your school giving an account of the number of students served and their outcomes.

The percentages here were based on 223 students served by the school social worker especially in consideration of the students' status being a critical case (i.e., 47 students requiring extensive treatment) or noncritical case (i.e., 176 students requiring brief therapy), and the results were attributed to the various categories of goal attainment (i.e., fully achieved, partially achieved, and not achieved).

The data from Boxes 103.2 and 103.3 above and in the pie chart below suggests an overall success rate of 79.4% of cases referred for school social work services.

This number alone would be quite significant and becomes even more compelling when you consider it with the percentage of cases where service

Box 103.3 Impact of SSW Intervention on All SSW Cases

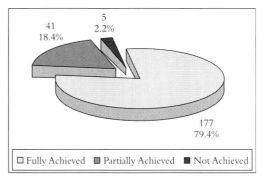

Box 103.4 Overview of Students Served by Worker

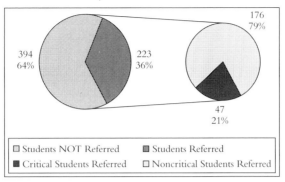

goals were partially achieved (18.4%) indicating that school social work intervention had a positive impact on 97.8% of all critical cases received.

Guidelines for Documentation: Annual Report

Evaluations of the effectiveness of interventions implemented by the school social worker and more in-depth knowledge of pupil groups and their unique situations are areas warranting attention (Huxtable & Blyth, 2002). Use of the previously described forms gives us a clear picture of the benefits of documenting reports reflecting input and output. Use of the SSW Forms 4, 5, and 6 will hopefully increase your desire to become more skillful in the arena of producing technical evaluations.

When measuring the impact of school social work services, several aspects in your service delivery plan must be considered:

- The number of critical and consult student cases served and recorded on SSW Forms 4 and 5
- The results of such service as evidenced by evaluation methods used in connection to the student's school and/or home adjustment and performances
- The intensity of the practitioner's effort in bringing about the desired change (e.g., as recorded daily on the SSW Form 6 and monthly on the SSW Form 7; see Figures 103.6 and 103.7) to represent the reason for referrals and type of interventions/direct services employed.

Box 103.5 Student Referrals and School Social Work Contacts

%	2	18	17	6	45	0	6	1	0	3	0	4
No.	18	211	200	71	535	2	70	7	3	31	0	48
Referral Contacts N=1,196	Abuse / Neglect	Academic	Attendance	Health	Behavior / Adjustment	Drug Abuse	Home / Family	Homeless	Suicidal / Homicidal	Suspension / Expulsion	Parenting Skills	Social Skills Training

The data in our example indicates that 176 noncritical (*consults*) and 47 critical-level students were referred and served by the school social worker. Please note that these numbers represent an unduplicated listing of students served.

However, when you combine these numbers you get an overview of the number of students served during the academic year. The calculations document that 223 students were served during the 2003–2004 school year, which represents 36% of the school's pupil population.

This is a very impressive number, especially when considering a social worker/student ratio at 1 to 617; in other words, the worker served one out of every three students.

Moreover, data gathered to represent the intensity of effort exerted by the school social worker come from the use of SSW Forms 6 and 7. As stated earlier, 223 students were referred by their respective school sites for school social work services. These 223 students were referred for a variety of reasons and exhibited multiple difficulties. Box 103.5 gives a descriptive example and/or overview of the difficulties precipitating student referrals and contacts made by the school social worker during the academic year 2004–2005.

It is clear from the examples in the preceding illustration that the primary reasons students are seen by the school social worker are academic, behavior adjustment, and irregular school attendance. The identification of target systems relative

Box 103.6 Populations Receiving Direct Intervention

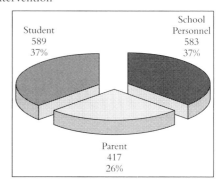

to student difficulties is made quite apparent by the data shown.

Also, the multifaceted problems presented by a referred student population directly impact the intensity of services provided by the school social worker. This intensity can be measured by intervention frequency, the inclusion of varied populations, and the duration of the intervention. Notice measurements in the pie graph in Box 103.6.

Approximately 37% (589) of all interventions rendered by the worker involved face-to-face contact with the referred student. An almost equal amount of interventions 37% (583) was provided to school personnel, primarily the instructional staff. Interventions with the household (parents) show a rate of 26% (417).

Figure 103.1. Tool 1

School Social Work Services/Child Welfare and Attendance

School Year: *04–05* Date: _____ Referral Form SS#: _____

Student Name: _____ DOB: _____ School: _____

Parent/Guardian: _____ Sp. Ed.:Yes __ No __ Grade: ___ Sex: ____
Race: _____

Father's Name: _____ Mother's Name: _____

Address:_____Zip:_____Home#:_____Work#:_____ _____

Teacher: _____ Rm.#: _____ Alt. Contact: _____ Phone#: _____

Reasons for Referral

Attendance		Behavior/ adjustment		Academic problems		Home/ family		Health		Other	
Explain reason:											
Student's sibling(s) name				DOB/age		Grade		School			

PLEASE NOTE: A for Absence   T for Tardy   D for Drop   E for Entered

@ for Excused Absence   + for Excused Tardy   S for Suspended   O for Expulsion

	M 2	T 3	W 4	T 5	F 6	M 9	T 10	W 11	T 12	F 13	M 16	T 17	W 18	T 19	F 20	M 23	T 24	W 25	T 26	F 27	M 30	T 31	W	T	F
Aug																									
Sep			1	2	3	6	7	8	9	10	13	14	15	16	17	20	21	22	23	24	27	28	29	30	
					H																				
Oct				1	4	5	6	7	8	11	12	13	14	15	18	19	20	21	22	25	26	27	28	29	
Nov	1	2	3	4	5	8	9	10	11	12	15	16	17	18	19	22	23	24	25	26	29	30			
																H	H	H	H	H					
Dec			1	2	3	6	7	8	9	10	13	14	15	16	17	20	21	22	23	24	27	28	29	30	31
																H	H	H	H	H	H	H	H	H	H
Jan	3	4	5	6	7	10	11	12	13	14	17	18	19	20	21	24	25	26	27	28	31				
											H														

(continued)

Figure 103.1. *(Continued)*

Feb		1	2	3	4	7	8	9	10	11	14	15	16	17	18	21	22	23	24	25	28				
						H	H	H																	
Mar		1	2	3	4	7	8	9	10	11	14	15	16	17	18	21	22	23	24	25	28	29	30	31	
																			H	H	H				
Apr				1	4	5	6	7	8	11	12	13	14	15	18	19	20	21	22	25	26	27	28	29
May	2	3	4	5	6	9	10	11	12	13	16	17	18	19	20	23	24	25	26	27	30	31			
Jun			1	2	3	6	7	8	9	10	13	14	15	16	17	20	21	22	23	24	27	28	29	30	

Teacher/reporter interventions:

	Type of contact				
Date	Phone	Letter	Conference	Other	Results

School Social Worker's Signature: _____ Date: _____
SSW Form 1   Side One

Figure 103.2. Tool 2

TO BE COMPLETED BY SCHOOL SOCIAL WORKER

Additional intake information:

(Preassessment) Estimate student's condition as relates to impairing achievement on a scale from 0 to 5:

Not serious   Extremely serious

0	1	2	3	4	5

Student system outcome goals	Fully achieved	Partially achieved	Not achieved
1.			
2.			
3.			
4.			
Total number of days student was absent by quarters	1st 2nd	3rd	4th

Closing/transfer summary:

(Postassessment) Estimate student's condition as relates to impairing achievement on a scale from 0 to 5:

Not serious   Extremely serious

0	1	2	3	4	5

Additional comments:

RECOMMENDATIONS: ☐ Transfer ☐ Close ☐ Reopen

Date: _____ School Social Worker: _____

Date: _____ Supervisor: _____

SSW Form 1 page 2

Figure 103.3. Tool 3

		Direct services					
Recording form				Session:			
Student:			School:				
	Direct services						
Date	STU	PAR	SCH	AG	GRP	OTH	Comments

Figure 103.4. Tool 4

REPORT OF CRITICAL CASES (*From reopened case file*)   SESSION: _____

STUDENTS	Reason for referral												Codes		
Unduplicated account:	Abuse/neglect	Academic	Attendance	Health	Behavior adjustment	Drug abuse	Home family	Homeless	Suicide/homicide	Suspensions	Parenting skills	Social skills	Fully achieved	Partially achieved	Not achieved
Totals															

Figure 103.5. Tool 5

REPORT OF NONCRITICAL (*consults*) CASES   SESSION: _____

STUDENTS	Reason for referral												Codes		
Unduplicated account:	Abuse/neglect	Academic	Attendance	Health	Behavior adjustment	Drug abuse	Home family	Homeless	Suicide/homicide	Suspensions	Parenting skills	Social skills	Fully achieved	Partially achieved	*Not/transfer critical*
Totals															

SSW Form 5

Figure 103.6. Tool 6

			Other																
Week of:	Reasons for referral	Social skills training																	
		Teen parenting																	
		Suspension/expulsion																	
		Suicide/homicide																	
		Homeless																	
		Home/family																	
		Drug abuse																	
		Behavior adjustment																	
		Health																	
		Attendance																	
		Academic																	
		Abuse/neglect																	
School:	Contacts	IEP/ISC																	
		SAT																	
		Home visits																	
		Court/FINS/ Municipal																	
		Agency professional																	
	Direct services	Small group																	
		School personnel																	
		Parent																	
		Student																	
		No. in small group																	
		No. in assembly																	
School Social Worker:		Student's name																	
			Totals:																

SSW Form 6

Figure 103.7. Tool 7

School Social Worker: _____   School: _____   Term: _____

	Monthly statistics	August	September	October	November	December	January	February	March	April	May	June (Summer School)	July (Summer School)	Totals:
Direct services	No. in assembly													
	No. in small group													
	Student													
	Parent													
	School personnel													
	Small group													
Contacts	Agency professional													
	Court/FINS/municipal													
	Home visits													
	SAT													
	IEP/ISC													
Reasons for referral	Abuse/neglect													
	Academic													
	Attendance													
	Health													
	Behavior adjustment													
	Drug abuse													
	Home/family													
	Homeless													
	Suicide/homicide													
	Suspension/expulsion													
	Teen parenting													
	Social skills training													
	Other													

Key Points to Remember

Any standard used to measure the effectiveness of social work services in schools should include a systemic approach to practice (Allen-Meares, Washington, & Welsh, 1996). Although not all-inclusive, the ideas and format for documentation presented in this chapter can guide a procedure to incorporate into one's practice as a school social worker. It includes guidelines for producing an outcome evaluation of services to individual students and the foundation for a micro/macro program and process evaluation. Although rudimentary, this design allows school social workers and administrators to critically view practices.

Dupper (2003) suggests that we go beyond focusing on the number of contacts made in providing services to youth and set our sights on the extent to which we have helped the student achieve in school. Because of the insight you have gained I trust that your reports will show: (a) that you have contributed to a student's success to some degree, (b) that you take responsibility for your work, and (c) that numbers are more than statistics.

References

Allen-Meares, P., Washington, R. O., & Welsh, B. L. (1996). *Social work services in schools* (2nd ed.). Needham Heights, MA: Allyn & Bacon.

Dupper, D. R. (2003). *School social work: Skills & interventions for effective practice.* Hoboken, NJ: Wiley.

Huxtable, M., & Blyth, E. (2002). *School social work world wide.* Washington, DC: NASW Press.

Rathvon, N. (1999). *Effective school interventions: Strategies for enhancing academic achievement and social competence.* New York: Guilford.

School Social Work Association of America. (2004, July). *Bell.* Northlake, IL: Author.

Sheafor, B. W., Horejsi, C. R., & Horejsi, G. A. (2000). *Techniques and guidelines for school social work practice* (5th ed.). Needham Heights, MA: Allyn & Bacon.

Teasley, M. L. (2004). Absenteeism and truancy: Risk, protection, and best practice II: Implications for school social workers. *Children & Schools, 26,* 117–127.

Effective Strategies for Funding School-Based Services

This section is a response to new and demanding expectations for school mental health and social service professionals in the current economy. Not only are social workers and other professionals held accountable for line-item school-allocated funds but also they often must secure funds to implement or continue essential mental health and social services. For school mental health practitioners primarily trained to provide direct client services, this may require new, unfamiliar skills. Grant writing, developing funding allies in the community, and drawing on Medicaid and other third-party sources were among the needs identified in this area by the school social workers we consulted.

Understanding the New Environment of Public School Funding

How Student Support Services Are Funded

Jeffrey M. Poirier ▪ David Osher

Getting Started

Student supports, the nature and intensity of which depend on the mental health and developmental needs of students, contribute to the development and academic success of students. School social workers and other mental health personnel play a key role in planning, coordinating, and providing this support (Rappaport et al., 2002). This is particularly true in the case of universal interventions that help create positive connections between and among students and adults, help students develop social and emotional skills, and employ positive behavioral supports, all of which contribute to safe, supportive, and successful schools (Osher, Dwyer, & Jackson, 2004; Zins, Weissberg, Wang, & Walberg, 2004). This role includes linking schools and families (Osher & Keenan, 2001). Similarly, pupil service resources are necessary not only for identifying and addressing the needs of students who are at risk of academic and behavioral problems (Dwyer & Osher, 2000) but also for ensuring active family participation in this process. Finally, pupil service personnel can play a key role in intensive interventions for those students who are at the greatest level of need, including helping students access community supports and working with the schools to align these supports. While we know a great deal about how to do this work (Greenberg et al., 2003; Osher & Hanley, 1997; Rones & Hoagwood, 2000), funding these services can be an obstacle.

In all school social worker roles, whether as provider of specific services or member of a team that plans schoolwide initiatives, it is important to support youth by ensuring that the entitlements and services they are eligible for are provided. For some youth this may consist of IDEA funds, while for others it may consist of Medicaid funding, child welfare services, juvenile justice services, or substance abuse services. Many schools and communities also receive grants such as safe and drug-free school monies, support for school health centers, and state and federal resources that support systems of care for children with emotional and behavioral disorders.

As discussed in this chapter, social workers can improve services for students by increasing current funding and improving the efficiency of how resources are used. Both strategies are particularly helpful as school districts face decreased public funding for education and increased accountability standards, which strain school budgets. When districts experience fiscal constraints and budget cuts, schools are likely to be affected; their ability to provide educational and other services to students may be diminished. This chapter outlines the basics of funding student support services, including the sources and types of funding streams used to support these services. Strategies to expand, coordinate, and redeploy funding, which may help to minimize the effect of decreased funding and even improve services, are then discussed. This chapter is intended to be a tool that you can use to understand how services are funded and how additional funding can be tapped to create a better array of services for the youth you serve. Since financial support is so important to school improvement, this chapter is written to enable you to be a change agent for your school.

What We Know

Funds for student support services largely come from public sources (i.e., federal, state, and local government) but also from insurance companies, managed care companies, charitable groups, and foundations (SMHP, 2000). Funds may be allocated to larger units, such as schools, school districts, and children who meet certain eligibility criteria, or to smaller units. It is important to understand funding streams and how the federal government allocates funds as well as your state and local funding formula (Osher et al., 2004).

A funding stream can be identified at its national or state source and traced to a local end point where districts or schools access it (Osher et al., 2004). However, funding streams often are redirected at the state and local (county, district, municipal, community) level. For example, Medicaid starts out as a federal program, but once the funding reaches the state, it takes on a state identity and is allocated through state regulations and procedures. At the local level, federal and state funds mix with local sources, creating "funding ponds" that can be accessed for student support services (Osher, McInerney, Traylor, & O'Neal, 1995; Osher et al., 2004).

Federal Funding

As of the 2000–2001 school year, approximately 7.9% of the $420 billion in public elementary and secondary school revenues came from federal sources (Cohen & Johnson, 2004). This national average varies significantly between states and across school districts within states. For example, federal sources comprised more than 13% of total revenues for public schools in six states (Alaska, Mississippi, Montana, New Mexico, North Dakota, and South Dakota); in contrast, federal revenues comprised less than 6% of total revenues in seven other states (Connecticut, Massachusetts, Minnesota, New Hampshire, New Jersey, Ohio, and Wisconsin).

Federal funds are allocated in four ways: block grants, project grants, legislative earmarks, and direct payments. Block grants use a formula to provide a fixed amount of funding. These formulas include relevant criteria, such as population, unemployment levels, and other demographic characteristics. Allocation of resources under block grants can be influenced by advocacy, since block grants are generally distributed by states based on a plan that reflects the input of state advisory groups (SAG) for the block grant. The Community Mental Health Services Block Grants and Social Services Block Grants (Title XX of the Social Security Act) are examples of formula-based federal block grants.

Project, or discretionary, grants are awarded through a competitive process and have specific purposes. Applicants may be either public or private entities, and funding is provided for particular projects or services over a fixed period of time. Project grants include evaluation grants, experimental and demonstration grants, fellowships, planning grants, research grants, scholarships, survey grants, technical assistance grants, traineeships, training grants, and unsolicited contractual agreements. For example, there are currently 6,800 schools and 1,420 communities that have received discretionary grants to fund 21st-century community learning centers in collaboration with local entities such as public agencies, businesses, postsecondary institutions, and scientific or cultural organizations. These grants can be employed to fund some types of student support. For example, a Safe School/Healthy Students grantee in Hayes, Kansas, funded the first school social workers in the county. The grant chose to employ social workers to build school–home linkages and to address the need for early interventions that provided support for families of children who were found to be at risk. Social work services included individual, family, and group interventions (Paige, Kitzis, & Wolfe, 2003). Similarly when it was a Federal Comprehensive Services for Children and Their Families grantee, Philadelphia placed school social workers in elementary schools to help the school system address the needs of children with serious emotional disturbance who were in kinship care (Woodruff et al., 1999).

Funds known as legislative earmarks are set aside for particular organizations by legislative directives in appropriations laws. These directives specify how the funding should be allocated within larger programs. Earmarks are awarded noncompetitively and occur during one fiscal year only; they do not continue over to another fiscal year. Public or private agencies are eligible for either "hard" earmarks, which are written into legislation and specify recipients and the amount of funding, or "soft" earmarks, which are awarded based on conference reports.

Federal funds may also be provided through direct payments, which are a form of federal assistance provided directly to individuals who meet eligibility requirements. Medicaid, which is described in another chapter in this handbook, is an example of such a program. Programs providing direct payments may be administered by an intermediate state agency.

The major sources of federal funding you should be familiar with are the Center for Medicare and Medicaid Services, Department of Education, Department of Health and Human Services, and Office of Juvenile Justice and Delinquency Prevention within the Department of Justice. At the end of this chapter, Table 104.1 lists major sources of federal funding, most of which are funded through one of these agencies.

State and Local Funding

On average, 49.3% of public and secondary school revenues come from state sources, which can often be used to support local school improvement efforts, while local funds comprise about 42.8% of

these revenues (Cohen & Johnson, 2004). Local funds are often limited because they are typically intended to support basic school components; however, these funds can sometimes be realigned at the school to improve efficiency and meet school objectives. Local funding for education-related initiatives, much of which may originate in federal and state budgets, may come from county or city governments as well as local agencies and school districts themselves (Flynn & Hayes, 2003).

Private Funding

In addition to public sources, various types of foundations and organizations may fund local efforts. These include community, corporate, and private foundations. You should be aware of any charitable groups or foundations that may support student support services in your local area. The Foundation Center (http://www.fdncenter.org) offers access to a directory of foundations for a monthly fee. Local foundations can often be identified by word of mouth.

The Challenge of Categorical Funding

School district revenues can be either general revenue (i.e., for any educational purpose) or categorical revenue targeted for specific purposes. Local general revenues for education are typically *lower* in school districts with *higher* levels of poverty (U.S. Department of Education, 2003). However, state general revenues and categorical funding are typically *higher* in districts with *higher* levels of poverty. Categorical revenues are therefore an important mechanism to bring programs and services to the nation's most at-risk youth. During the 1999–2000 school year, the average school district received 19% of its funds from categorical revenues (U.S. Department of Education).

Categorical revenues must be used to provide particular services to specific *categories* of entities, such as children and families. Examples of categorical funding include Head Start and IDEA. Flynn and Hayes (2003) point out that categorical funding streams are difficult to coordinate or combine because of their specific eligibility requirements, program regulations (how and when services are delivered), and funding flow and administration (who administers the program and how funds flow to programs). The nature of categorical funding can lead to fragmented services (Farrow & Joe, 1992).

Categorical funding may therefore present a challenge to providing integrated support services. For example, children in the same program may not receive the same services if program funding comes from several categorical sources that not all children are eligible to receive. In addition, program administrators must track eligibility data, tie services to their funding sources, and follow other funding regulations (Flynn & Hayes, 2003).

Still, the easiest way of funding services may be to find a categorical program that meets your needs and to draw upon these funds. Categorical funds exist to support student support efforts. Examples include services that individuals are eligible for (e.g., funding for mental health services for individuals who are identified as being eligible for services under the IDEA), as well as resources that schools are eligible for. Examples of categorical school services are comprehensive school health centers, which are funded by the Federal Health Resources Services Administration, and community schools, which are funded by some districts (e.g., Chicago and Multnomah County, Oregon).

However, there are several financing strategies that help to add flexibility so that schools and communities can coordinate categorical funding streams; these are discussed in the following section.

What We Can Do

Funding can come from your school, district, state, the federal government, or private organizations. Beyond the general school or district funds, you must draw upon resources that originate elsewhere. These are frequently referred to as funding streams. Understanding funding streams and their limits is important, since they often fund specific people, places, or services. Public funding streams are authorized by legislation that realizes specific priorities. Therefore, you should examine funding stream requirements before you try to draw upon them to fund services related to education, child welfare, juvenile justice, mental health, and substance abuse.

As you might expect, funding streams, like school budgets, are limited. Developing strategies to maximize funding are crucial, since school staff

are often confronted by fiscal constraints and funding-related challenges. In addition, you should be familiar with two other strategies that may help to improve the efficiency of current funding: coordination and redeployment. Understanding these strategies, which are discussed in the following sections, will further enable you to have a proactive approach to case advocacy, potentially increasing efficiency and making funding available for additional student support services.

Enlarging the Funding Pool

A primary financing strategy is to enlarge the funding pool (i.e., increase funding) by identifying previously untapped funding sources. It is important to take advantage of all available funding streams to maintain or enlarge services for children. Before pursuing particular funding, you should determine if:

- the district already receives funds
- the district is eligible for such funds
- the district makes allocations to schools
- the school is free to pursue additional funding independently

You should also determine the appropriate agencies (federal, state, or local) to contact and collaborate with other school staff, as well as your school district administration, to the greatest extent possible. Collaboration is discussed in greater detail later in this chapter. In addition to the references provided at the end of the chapter, you will find a list of Web-based resources that you might find useful in your efforts to enhance services for students in your school. Some of these provide information on potential grant funding, while others provide information on the financing of student support services and funding strategies. Table 104.1, listing potential funding streams, is also included at the end of the chapter.

Funding sources are not static, though. Eligibility requirements, program regulations, and the extent and purpose of funding are subject to change. For example, the Job Training Partnership Act is now the Workforce Investment Act. The Elementary and Secondary Education Act (ESEA), the largest federal elementary and secondary education program, was reauthorized in 2001 as the No Child Left Behind Act with a much greater emphasis on accountability. You should use the Web-based resources as information tools to be

Box 104.1 Enlarging the Funding Pool in Action

A member of a high school's student support staff is concerned about the school's high dropout rate relative to other schools in the state. She wants to identify potential funding sources for a school dropout prevention program, so she searches the CFDA database by applicant eligibility (elementary/secondary education as the functional area and local government as the organizational type) and finds almost 40 programs, one of which is dropout prevention. She learns that local education agencies are eligible to apply for dropout prevention program project grants. She then collaborates with the school and school district administration to apply for funding and creates a dropout prevention and reentry program in her high school.

knowledgeable of the major agencies that provide funding; these are *not* likely to change.

Sometimes schools are not eligible for categorical funds. Another approach to enlarge the funding pool is to leverage public and private resources by using available funding to qualify for additional resources, whether new or matching funds (SMHP, 2000). In this case, schools may develop relationships with other agencies (e.g., community mental health centers) or professionals (e.g., child psychiatrists), who can access these categorical funds. Medicaid is a good example of leveraging: a school that is not Medicaid eligible can develop a relationship with a Medicaid-certified provider who can bill for Medicaid services provided to Medicaid-eligible students. Medicaid, which is discussed in detail in another chapter in this handbook, can be a valuable source of funding for school-based health and mental health services. Another form of leveraging is using federal and state entitlement funding as substitutes for local expenditures, which then frees local funds for other services (SMHP, 2000).

Coordinating Funding Streams

Funding streams have specific priorities, requirements, and regulations. This may present challenges when working to coordinate funding sources (Flynn & Hayes, 2003). Yet, "the trend is toward finding ways to weave school and community resources together in a seamless manner"

(SMHP, 2000, p. 6). In fact, the U.S. Department of Education "encourages schools and districts to combine funds to more efficiently raise the achievement of the whole school community, thus increasing the capacity as a whole instead of targeting specific children" (Osher et al., 2004, p. 44). Coordination is important because fragmentation can lead to ineffective and costly interventions due to overlap across schools, social welfare, and juvenile justice; fragmentation has been blamed as the root cause of many problems associated with treating emotional and behavioral disorders (Osher & Hanley, 1996; Quinn & Poirier, 2004).

Aligning funding streams can transform traditionally separate services and programs into more integrated, comprehensive systems so that they are more responsive to children and families (Evans et al., 2003; Flynn & Hayes, 2003). Coordination also enhances collaboration for a shared goal and allows for local flexibility, a greater focus on outcomes, and greater decision making with the families of students (Bazelon, 2003; SMHP, 2000). Several coordination strategies, including braiding and blending, can be used to enhance student support services by reducing duplication, increasing the efficient use of resources, reducing the administrative burden of multiple categorical programs, and providing supports and services that are more integrated (Flynn & Hayes, 2003). Further, diversifying funding sources helps to support sustainability by ensuring that budgets are mostly covered if a particular funding stream should dry up (Bazelon, 2003; Flynn & Hayes, 2003). As a school professional you should be familiar with and utilize any community or state efforts to support funding coordination.

The first strategy of resource coordination, braiding, occurs at the school, community, and program levels. It enhances flexibility in the use of funding but has distinct features that are important to note. Specifically, funding streams are combined to support particular components of integrated service plans so that funds from different agencies can be tracked for the purpose of meeting funding requirements (Osher et al., 2004). Braiding is a useful strategy if you cannot or do not want to blend funding, which is discussed shortly. Braiding "recognizes the categorical nature of existing programs and avoids some of the conflicts that can arise in blended funding pools" (Bazelon, 2003, p. 4).

Braiding "is the most common strategy for using categorical funding streams to create more integrated and comprehensive early care and

Box 104.2 Braiding in Action

A bright, talented youth in foster care with a learning disability recently began taking drugs and engaging in gang behavior. In an effort to provide this student with the services she needs, school support staff could braid funding by using wraparound, IDEA, substance abuse, and gang abatement services. Under the provisions of IDEA, these otherwise discrete services can be integrated into one service plan.

Box 104.3 Blending in Action

Master contracting is an approach to blending that can be tailored to program or community needs. For example, in some areas agencies have replaced separate contracts from various state or county agencies with one master contract. Like other blending, this strategy depends upon state or county approval. Master contracting provides flexibility to tailor services and builds in an outcome-driven approach to accountability. Master contracting may also diminish the administrative burdens created by multiple, separate reporting requirements (Flynn & Hayes, 2003).

education initiatives [but] . . . requires a high degree of behind-the-scenes organization and record keeping" (Flynn & Hayes, 2003, p. 11). It requires a strong information management system as well as a cost-accounting system to trace expenditures to their funding sources for the purposes of resource allocation and reporting (Flynn & Hayes, 2003). States or communities must also have "a single point of responsibility for assessing services and the funding stream that can pay for them" (Bazelon, 2003, p. 4). Examples of federal programs that are commonly braided include the Child Care and Development Fund, IDEA's Grants for Infants and Families with Disabilities program, Head Start, Social Services Block Grants, Temporary Aid for Needy Families (TANF), and Title I (Flynn & Hayes, 2003).

In contrast to braiding, blended funding is a form of coordinating funding streams that is most often used by state or local policy makers, and it changes the structure and rules of funding streams to create flexibility in how funds are used (Flynn & Hayes, 2003). Blending funding may consist of combining flexible funding streams into a funding pond by overlapping roles and functions. Alternatively, it make take the form of decategorized funding, which is available when a state makes funding streams less categorical by modifying funding regulations and merging funds from different programs into one funding stream (Flynn & Hayes, 2003; SMHP, 2000).

"Blended funding—even on a small scale—has advantages over braiding of funds because it offers significant flexibility for state and local agencies and reduces the work required for reporting and accountability measures" (Bazelon, 2003, p. 4). It also allows systems to fund activities that specific categorical programs would not otherwise reimburse, helping to "plug funding gaps in the services continuum" (Bazelon, 2003, p. 4). Budgets and

functions can also be blended (SMHP, 2000). This allows funding from several state agencies and the more flexible federal programs to be combined, with authorization, to foster collaboration for a common goal, but agencies lose control due to the inability to track funds to the service-delivery point (Bazelon, 2003; Flynn & Hayes, 2003).

Blended funding can produce more money for student support services through collaboration between service providers of different agencies (Edelman, 1998). Through this collaborative process, federal funds can be accessed that might not be available otherwise. In particular, blending allows funds to be tracked for accountability to federal program administrators while still tapping into other funding streams (Bazelon, 2003; Flynn & Hayes, 2003). Blended funding can:

- Expand services without additional state or local funds
- Foster increased communication and integration among agencies
- Promote coordination of care among multiple agencies, which improves efficiency by avoiding duplicative services or approaches
- Increase cooperation among agencies (Edelman, 1998)

Schools and schoolwide teams can employ blending by coordinating the use of noncategorical resources.

Coordination has been supported by federal legislation. In fact, Subpart 14, Section 5541 of the No Child Left Behind Act of 2001 creates Grants for the Integration of Schools and Mental Health Systems that can be used to enhance, improve, or develop collaborative efforts between school-based service systems and mental health service systems to provide, enhance, or improve prevention, diagnosis, and treatment of services for students. In addition, IDEA strongly promotes interagency agreements for the coordination and delivery of services from other public agencies that are responsible for paying or providing needed services (34CFR300.142).

Redeploying Resources

If funding is invested in programs and services that are ineffective or less effective than alternatives, then resources are wasted or used inefficiently at best. Redeploying existing resources requires that schools and support staff examine how funding is used and how services are provided, and consider how funds can be used more effectively (Osher et al., 2004). In some instances funding can even be shifted from higher to comparable lower cost programs and services (SMHP, 2000). Ineffective or redundant programs should be downsized or eliminated (Osher et al., 2004).

Resources should also be targeted at programs and services, such as prevention, that help to decrease the future demand for resources. It is likely that you will not have the resources to do a formal cost-benefit analysis or evaluation of services in your school, but these are not necessary to redeploy resources. As a member of your school support staff, it is sufficiently valuable if you identify the needs of students in your school and understand what programs and services are most effective in meeting these needs. Are there programs or services that you believe would better meet the student needs? Are there services that help to decrease demand for other services, even if marginally or over a longer period of time? You should use your understanding of what is working in your school and what is not. You should also be familiar with effective, evidenced-based programs and services.

Schools and communities must increasingly shift from a short-term mind-set of "managing" social ills to a long-term vision in which they are proactively prevented. Prevention research should be linked not only with public policy (Quinn & Poirier, 2004) but also with school practice. Significantly, investing in universal and early interventions can save communities money in the long run. In the case of youth who are delinquent, effective interventions help to deconstruct the

pipeline to prison and decrease delinquency-related costs (Osher, Quinn, Poirier, & Rutherford, 2003). As prevention efforts begin to have a positive effect, it may be possible to invest funds in less costly early interventions rather than intensive interventions that have a higher per student cost.

Collaboration

Coordinating funding streams requires collaboration with agencies that provide services to students. Coordination and collaboration together help to build a comprehensive and more cost-effective support system for at-risk students and their families by reducing the fragmentation of services or "categorical drift" (agencies working in isolation), combining funds for shared purposes, and increasing service providers' awareness of the needs of students (Liontos, 1990; Osher & Keenan, 2002; Peterson, 1995). The ultimate goal of collaboration is to transform support services so that they are more responsive to children and families already receiving services from several systems (Bruner, 1991; Osher & Hanley, 1997). Children from fragile families have more complex needs that require interagency collaboration for several reasons: their families are more likely to have difficulty accessing and using all of the services they need, their families are less likely to have the skills to integrate the goals of the services they are receiving, and their families tend not to have outside resources to counteract the negative consequences when system failures occur (Bruner, 1991).

Since children are required to attend school and because schools are supposed to be concerned about the overall development of students, schools are the most accessible and appropriate place to establish collaborations with human service agencies (Ascher, 1990). As a member of your school's support staff, you can lead efforts to collaborate with other schools in your district and your school district administration to build a coalition and even to try to place a representative on one of your state's block grant state advisory group (SAG) meetings. Alternatively, you may want to work with your state school social work association to secure representation. SAGs develop priorities that determine how block grant monies will be allocated. In some cases, this can include funding for school social workers and other pupil personnel services.

Students who are at risk often receive services

from a variety of agencies, and these services tend to be fragmented because there is little cross-agency communication and coordination (Peterson, 1995). In the case of students who have disabilities, "The importance of cross-system collaborations to address the needs of children with mental or emotional disorders to receive services from various child-serving agencies—most commonly, mental health and substance abuse, child welfare, education, and juvenile justice—is increasingly recognized" (Bazelon, 2003, p. 1).

To improve the effectiveness of service delivery, it is important that both school social workers and service providers are aware of both the range of services being provided to individual students and the available information that can be used to understand individual student needs (Peterson, 1995). Effective systems of care coordinate services across schools, community mental health centers, juvenile justice programs, primary health care organizations, psychiatric treatment programs, and social service organizations to most effectively address the needs of these children.

Collaboration requires planning, commitment, thoughtful action, and openness to new approaches, as well as a willingness to evaluate and reevaluate current paradigms. Time also is an important component because trust and understanding may not be immediate. Efforts to foster collaboration may present difficult challenges: some staff or representatives of agencies may resist change; agency or government regulations may limit the extent to which staff, services, and information can be coordinated; and differences in prior training among staff from different agencies may pose a difficulty (Peterson, 1995). Successful collaborations are well documented, though. Models include system of care communities, where collaboration is institutionalized.

Systems of Care

A system of care is a coordinated network of agencies and providers that makes a full range of services available to children with mental health problems (Osher et al., 2004). Systems of care are guided by three core values:

- Child centered, family focused, and family driven
- Community-based services, management, and decision making

- Culturally competent and responsive agencies, programs, and services (Stroul & Friedman, 1986)

Among the principles embodied in a system of care are service coordination, prevention and early identification and intervention, smooth transitions among agencies, and a comprehensive array of services. Hence, a system of care is based on the notion of multiagency coordination and may require innovative funding models (Osher et al., 2004). This coordination and the aforementioned collaboration join education with child welfare, juvenile justice, and substance abuse services. These are each briefly discussed next, along with examples of relevant funding sources.

The role of child welfare services is to ensure the well-being of children and to provide services if a child is not safe or has been harmed at home (McCarthy et al., 2003). Two sources of child welfare funding include the Child Welfare Services Program (Title IV-B, Subpart 1 of the Social Security Act) and Social Services Block Grants (Title XX). Title IV-B provides grants to states for a range of child welfare services and activities, without income requirements, and Title XX provides federal funds for low-income children and families (McCarthy et al., 2003). States have a large degree of discretion in determining how Title XX monies are spent, and prevention is considered a related activity.

Additional funding and programs are available for students who may be delinquent. In order to identify students who may be involved with the justice system, schools can ask the local juvenile court to review court records in order to identify the number of students under court probation. You should also contact your department of human services to determine if prevention or intervention can by funded using TANF funds. TANF funds can sometimes be used to support community programs instead of placements for youth who are delinquent. Sources of juvenile justice funding include the Neglected and Delinquent Children Program through the Department of Education, which awards formula grants to state education agencies; Juvenile Accountability Block Grants through the Department of Justice, which awards block grants to states; the Formula Grants Program as authorized under the Juvenile Justice Delinquency and Prevention Act of 2002, also through the Department of Justice and which allocates formula grants to state agencies; and Youth Opportunity Grants through the Department of

Labor, which are competitive grants awarded to Local Workforce Investment Boards.

School mental health programs are intended to provide care for uninsured students as well as a comprehensive range of services for all students, so identifying funding sources is a major challenge facing these programs (Germaine, 1998). The federal government funds mental health services, for example, through Community Mental Health block grants through the Substance Abuse and Mental Health Services Administration, which also funds block grants for Prevention and Treatment of Substance Abuse and Indian Health Care Improvement Act grants through the Indian Health Service. Some state governments also fund school-based health and mental health services (Evans et al., 2003).

Unfortunately, "data on financing for MH are difficult to amass, especially with respect to children from zero through eighteen. Difficulty arises from many factors . . . [including] variations in where the money comes from and where it goes" (SMHP, 2000, p. 2). Some federal funds are used to support programs at the national level, while most funds are directed to states for Medicaid, block grants, and categorical programs (SMHP). Many children actually qualify for both Medicaid and IDEA services: IDEA allows for certain health-related services included in a student's individualized Education Plan to be paid for through Medicaid (Seltzer & Parker, 2003). Common sources of funding for school mental health services are Medicaid (which enrolled 19 million children in 2002); Early and Periodic Screening, Diagnosis, and Treatment (EEPSDT); Title V (Maternal and Child Health Block Grant); and private non-HMO insurance (Lewin Group, 1999). In addition, the State Children's Health Insurance Program (SCHIP) appropriated more than $4.2 billion to states in 2001 for health assistance with uninsured, low-income children.

Key Points to Remember

We have provided an overview of how student support services are funded. As discussed, you can act as a change agent in your school by helping to expand, coordinate, and redeploy funding streams. Coordination can take several forms: braiding occurs more at the program or community level, and blending typically needs involvement of state and local policy makers. Redeploying resources by identifying and eliminating waste and inefficiency is an important component of expanding school services. These strategies are not mutually exclusive; they can be combined as part of a larger approach to financing school services, which, like interagency collaboration (exemplified by systems of care communities), is essential in the new environment of school funding. A better understanding of funding, funding streams and pools, financing strategies, the role of collaboration, and the resources available to you will support your efforts to build a better array of services for the youth you serve.

Web-Based Resources

Catalog of Federal Domestic Assistance: www.cfda. gov. The Catalog of Federal Domestic Assistance (CFDA) has a comprehensive, online database of all federal programs that provide financial assistance to state and local governments, as well as other entities, such as nonprofit organizations and individuals.

CDC's Healthy Youth Funding Database: CDC provides a searchable database that provides information on federal, state, and foundation funding sources for school health programs.

The Center for Health and Health Care in Schools: www.healthinschools.org. The center provides policy analyses and program guidance on issues related to organizing and financing health programs in schools.

The Center for Medicare and Medicaid Services (CMS): http://cms.hhs.gov. The CMS Web site provides general information on service funding related to Medicaid/EPSDT and the State Children's Health Insurance Program (SCHIP).

The Finance Project: www.financeproject.org. The Finance Project is a policy research, technical assistance, and information organization. Free resources including working papers, resource guides, and toolkits are available on the Web site.

The Foundation Center: http://fdncenter.org/. The Foundation Center provides an online foundation directory with more than 2,400 annotated links to grantmaker Web sites, including community foundations, corporations, private foundations, and public charities. The "Foundation

Table 104.1 Examples of Major Funding Streams

Program	Funding Source	Local Information Source	Purpose
Alternative Strategies to Reduce Student Suspensions and Expulsions Grants	Department of Education, Office of Safe and Drug-Free Schools (www.ed.gov/offices/OSDFS)	Local educational agency	Funds projects to enhance, implement, and evaluate strategies to reduce suspensions and expulsions and to ensure continued educational progress through challenging coursework for students who are suspended or expelled.
Child Welfare Services	Title IV-B Subpart I, Social Security Act	Social services	Emergency caretaker/homemaker, financial assistance. Family preservation, mental health, alcohol and drug abuse counseling, postadoption services.
Community Development Block Grant Programs (i.e., entitlement communities, state-administered)	Department of Housing and Urban Development, Office of Community Planning and Development (http://www.hud.gov/offices/cpd/communitydevelopment/programs/index.cfm)	State, local government	Provides annual grants on a formula basis to entitled cities and counties to develop viable urban communities by providing decent housing and a suitable living environment.
Indian Child Welfare Act	Department of Interior, Bureau of Indian Affairs	Federally recognized Indian tribal government	Promotes the stability and security of American Indian tribes and families by protecting American Indian children, preventing the separation of American Indian families, and providing assistance to Indian tribes in the operation of child and family service programs.
Individuals with Disabilities Act (IDEA), part H	Department of Education, Office of Special Education Programs	Schools, districts, county offices of education	Assessment and preventive services for very young children at risk of developmental disabilities. Also transition into appropriate school setting. Requires individualized plan.
Juvenile Accountability Block Grants Program	Department of Justice, Office of Juvenile Justice and Delinquency Prevention (http://ojjdp.ncjrs.org/jaibg/)	State JABG Coordinator (http://ojjdp.ncjrs.org/jaibg/jaibg.html)	Awards grants to states to address the growing problem of juvenile crime by encouraging accountability-based reform at

Program	Administering agency	Authority/Source	Description
			the state and local levels. States and localities can use funding for activities related to any of 16 "purpose areas."
Juvenile Mentoring Program	Local educational agency	Department of Justice, Office of Juvenile Justice and Delinquency Prevention (http://ojjdp.ncjrs.org/jump/index.html)	Targets at-risk youth to provide general guidance and support; promote personal and social responsibility; increase participation in elementary and secondary education; discourage use of illegal drugs and firearms, involvement in violence, and other delinquent activity; discourage involvement in gangs; and encourage participation in service and community activities.
Medicaid	State government	Department of Health and Human Services, Title XIX, Social Security Act (http://www.cms.hhs.gov/medicaid/default.asp)	The federal government sets broad guidelines, but states have considerable flexibility in designing and administering the Medicaid program. Each state decides (1) who is eligible for coverage; (2) the type, amount, and scope of covered services; (3) which providers can obtain Medicaid reimbursement; and (4) how much providers get paid for the services they render.
Mentoring Grants	Local educational agency	Department of Education, Office of Safe and Drug-Free Schools (http://www.ed.gov/programs/dvpmentoring/applicant.html)	To promote mentoring programs for children at risk of educational failure, dropping out, or involvement in criminal or delinquent activities and without role models by assisting them in receiving support and guidance from a mentor. Supported activities will work to improve interpersonal relationships between targeted children and their peers, teachers, other adults, and family members. Additionally, funded programs will

(continued)

Table 104.1 (*Continued*)

Program	Funding Source	Local Information Source	Purpose
			work to reduce the dropout rate of at-risk children and to reduce juvenile delinquency and involvement in gangs by such children.
No Child Left Behind Act (formerly Elementary and Secondary Education Act)	Department of Education (www.nochildleftbehind.gov)	Local educational agency	To improve student achievement and change the culture of America's schools, focusing on accountability for results, an emphasis on doing what works based on scientific research, expanded parental options, and expanded local control and flexibility.
Safe Schools/Healthy Students	Department of Education, Office of Safe and Drug-Free Schools (www.ed.gov/offices/OSDFS)	Local educational agency	Provides comprehensive educational, mental health, social service, law enforcement, and juvenile justice services to students, schools, and communities.
Safe Start Initiative	Department of Justice, Office of Justice Programs (www.ojp.usdoj.gov)	State and local government	Creates comprehensive community service-delivery systems by expanding partnerships and improving access to services for young children at high risk of exposure to violence and their families.
Social Services Block Grant	Department of Health and Human Services, Administration on Children and Families, Title XX, Social Security Act (http://www.acf.hhs.gov/programs/ocs/ssbg/docs/)	State department of social/human services	Activities that promote family self-sufficiency and prevent child abuse and neglect and out-of-home placement.
Temporary Assistance For Needy Families (TANF)	Department of Health and Human Services, Administration on Children and Families, Title IV, Social Security Act (http://www.acf.hhs.gov/programs/ofa/)	Social services	Direct financial income support for families with minor children; administration of program including eligibility determination.
Twenty-First Century Community Learning Centers	Department of Education, No Child Left Behind Act, Title IV, Part B (http://www.ed.gov/programs/21stcclc)	State government	Provides expanded academic enrichment opportunities for children attending low-performing schools and provides youth development activities; drug and violence prevention programs; technology education

Program	Agency (website)	Administered by	Description
			programs; art, music, and recreation programs; counseling; and character education to enhance the academic component of the program.
Vocational and Technical Education Act (Perkins Act)	Department of Education, Office of Vocational and Adult Education (http://www.ed.gov/offices/OVAE/CTE/perkins.html)	State board for vocational education	Provides vocational–technical education programs and services to youth in secondary education. Most funds are awarded as grants to state education agencies according to a formula based on states' populations in certain age groups and their per capita income.
Workforce Investment Act—formerly the Job Training Partnership Act (e.g., Youth Opportunity Grants, State and Local Formula Youth Grants)	Department of Labor (http://www.doleta.gov/usworkforce/wia/)	State and local workforce investment boards	Provides youth opportunity grants to assist youth ages 14–21 in high-poverty areas who have one or more of the following conditions: deficient in basic literacy skills; a school dropout; homeless, runaway, or foster child; pregnant or a parent; an offender; or requiring additional assistance to complete an educational program or to secure and hold employment. Youth are prepared for postsecondary educational opportunities or employment, and programs will link academic and occupational learning.
Youth Offender Initiative Reentry Grant	Department of Justice, Office of Justice Programs (www.ojp.usdoj.gov)	State and local government	Enhances community safety by helping young offenders reintegrate into the community

Sources: Bazelon, 2003 (www.bazelon.org); SMHP, 2004.

Finder" is a free service but the "Foundation Directory Online" requires a monthly fee for access.

Georgetown University Child Development Center, "Funding Early Childhood Mental Health Services & Supports": http://gucchd.georgetown.edu/document.html#early. This provides a matrix to assist communities with developing a comprehensive financing system for early childhood mental health services.

Grants.gov: www.grants.gov. Grants.gov allows organizations to electronically find and apply for competitive grant opportunities from all federal grant-making agencies. It provides access to some 900 grant programs offered by federal grant-making agencies. The Web site allows automatic notification of grant announcements.

National Assembly on School-Based Health Care: http://www.nasbhc.org. This provides links to state SBHC Web sites and information on funding school-based health centers.

National Conference of State Legislatures, Prevention Projects Program, Funding School Health Programs: http://www.ncsl.org/programs/health/pp/schlfund.htm. NCSL has a block grant database that provides sources of school health funding by state and the requirements to access these funds. It identifies which states use six primary government grants to fund school health programs.

Schoolgrants.org: www.schoolgrants.org. Schoolgrants.org provides guidance on grant writing as well as links to federal, state, and foundation funding opportunities. State sources are listed by state, allowing for easy navigation.

UCLA School Mental Health Project (SMHP): http://smhp.psych.ucla.edu. SMHP provides technical assistance for mental health practitioners and is a significant resource for enhancing mental health in schools. It provides center briefs, guides to practice, resource aid packets, and also has a free newsletter with updates about relevant funding opportunities.

References

Ascher, C. (1990). *Linking schools with human service agencies* (ERIC/CUE Digest No. 62). ERIC Clearinghouse on Urban Education: http://www.ericdigests.org.

Bazelon Center for Mental Health Law. (2003). *Mix and match: Using federal programs to support interagency systems of care for children with mental health care needs.* Washington, DC: Author. http://www.bazelon.org.

Bruner, C. (1991). *Thinking collaboratively: Ten questions and answers to help policy makers improve children's services.* The Education and Human Services Consortium: http://www.cyfernet.org.

Cohen, C., & Johnson, F. (2004). *Revenues and expenditures for public elementary and secondary education: School year 2001–02*, NCES 2004-341. U.S. Department of Education, National Center for Education Statistics: http://nces.ed.gov/.

Dwyer, K., & Osher, D. (2000). *Safeguarding our children: An action guide.* Washington, DC: U.S. Departments of Education and Justice, American Institutes for Research.

Edelman, S. (1998). *Developing blended funding programs for children's mental health care systems.* Sacramento, CA: California Institute for Mental Health.

Evans, S. W., Glass-Siegel, M., Frank, A., Van Treuren, R., Lever, N. A., & Weist, M. D. (2003). Overcoming the challenges of funding school mental health programs. In M. D. Weist, S. W. Evans, & N. A. Lever (Eds.), *Handbook of school mental health: Advancing practice and research* (pp. 73–87). New York: Kluwer Academic/Plenum Publishers.

Farrow, F., & Joe, T. (1992, Spring). Financing school-linked integrated services. (Financing Strategy Series). The Future of Children: http://www.futureofchildren.org/.

Flynn, M., & Hayes, C. D. (2003, January). *Blending and braiding funds to support early care and education initiatives* (Financing Strategy Series). Washington, DC: www.financeproject.org.

Germaine, A. S. (1998, Spring). Funding opportunities: Promising Medicaid funding options for school mental health. *On the Move with School-Based Mental Health, 3*(1). UCLA School Mental Health Project: www.smhp.psych.ucla.edu.

Greenberg, M. T., Weissberg, R. P., Utne O'Brien, M., Zins, J. E., Fredericks, L., Resnick, H., & Elias, M. J. (2003). Enhancing school-based prevention and youth development through coordinated social, emotional, and academic learning. *American Psychologist, 58*, 466–474.

Lewin Group. (1999). Key issues for school-based health centers providing mental health environment. Retrieved June 3, 2004, from http://smhp.psych.ucla.edu.

Liontos, L. B. (1990). *Collaboration between schools and social services* (ERIC Digest Series, No. EA 48). Eugene, OR: ERIC Clearinghouse on Educational Management.

McCarthy, J., Marshall, A., Collins, J., Arganza, G., Deserly, K., & Milon, J. (2003). *A family's guide to the child welfare system.* Washington, DC: Georgetown University Center for Child and Human Development.

Mental Health in Schools Training and Technical Assistance Center, School Mental Health Project [SMHP]. (2004, February). *Financial strategies to aid in addressing barriers to learning* (Introductory Packet). Retrieved May 21, 2004, from http://smhp.psych.ucla.edu.

Mental Health in Schools Training and Technical Assistance Center, School Mental Health Project [SMHP]. (2000, November). *Financing mental health for children & adolescents* (Center Brief). Retrieved May 21, 2004, from http://smhp.psych.ucla.edu.

Osher, D., Dwyer, K., & Jackson, S. (2004). *Safe, supportive and successful schools: Step by step.* Longmont, CO: Sopris West.

Osher, D., & Hanley, T. V. (1996). Implications of the national agenda to improve results for children and youth with or at risk of serious emotional disturbance. In R. J. Illback & C. M. Nelson (Eds.), *Emerging school-based approaches for children with emotional and behavioral problems: Research and practice in service integration* (pp. 7–36). Binghamton, NY: Haworth Press.

Osher, D., & Hanley, T. V. (1997). Building upon an emergent social service delivery paradigm. In L. M. Bullock & R. A. Gable (Eds.), *Making collaboration work for children, youth, families, schools, and communities* (pp. 10–15). Reston, VA: Council for Exceptional Children.

Osher, D., & Keenan, S. (2001). From professional bureaucracy to partner with families. *Reaching Today's Youth, 5*(3), 9–15.

Osher, D., & Keenan, S. (2002). *Instituting school-based links with mental health and social service agencies* (Guides to Creating Safer Schools: Guide 6). Portland, OR: Northwest Regional Educational Laboratory.

Osher, D., McInerney, M., Traylor, K., & O'Neal, E. (1995). *Funding streams and funding ponds: An analysis of the infrastructure for financing the acquisition and use of TMM tools.* Report prepared for the Division of Innovation and Development, Office of Special Education Programs, U.S. Department of Education.

Osher, D. M., Quinn, M. M., Poirier, J. M., & Rutherford, R. B. (2003). Deconstructing the pipeline: Using efficacy and effectiveness data and cost-benefit analyses to reduce minority youth incarceration. In J. Wald & D. J. Losen (Eds.), *New direction for youth development: Deconstructing the school-to-prison pipeline* (pp. 91–120). San Francisco: Jossey-Bass.

Paige, L. Z., Kitzis, S. N., & Wolfe, J. (2003). Rural underpinnings for resiliency and linkages (rural): A safe schools/healthy students project. *Psychology in the Schools, 40*(5), 531–547.

Peterson, K. (1995). *Critical issue: Establishing collaboratives and partnerships.* North Central Regional Educational Laboratory: www.ncrel.org.

Quinn, M. M., & Poirier, J. M. (2004). Linking prevention research with policy: Examining the costs and outcomes of the failure to prevent EBD. In R. B. Rutherford, M. M. Quinn, & Sarup R. Mathur (Eds.), *Handbook of research in emotional and behavioral disorders* (pp. 78–97). New York: Guilford Press.

Rappaport, N., Osher, D., Dwyer, K., Garrison, E., Hare, I., Ladd, J., & Anderson-Ketchmark, C. (2002). Enhancing collaborations within and across disciplines to advance mental health programs in schools. In M. D. Weist, S. Evans, & N. Tashman (Eds.), *School mental health handbook* (pp. 107–118). New York: Kluwer Academic Publishing Company.

Rones, M., & Hoagwood, K. (2000). School-based mental health services: A research review. *Clinical Child and Family Psychology Review, 3*(4), 223–241.

Seltzer, T., & Parker, R. (2003). *Teaming up: Using the IDEA and Medicaid to secure comprehensive mental health services for children and youth.* Washington, DC: BazelonCenter for Mental Health Law.

SMHP. See Mental Health in Schools Training and Technical Assistance Center.

Stroul, B., & Friedman, R. (1986). *A system of care for children and youth with severe emotional disturbance* (Rev. ed.). Washington, DC: Georgetown University Child Development Center, National Technical Assistance Center for Children's Mental Health.

U.S. Department of Education, National Center for Education Statistics. (2003). *The condition of Education 2003,* NCES 2003-067. Washington, DC: U.S. Government Printing Office.

Woodruff, D. W., Osher, D., Hoffman, C. C., Gruner, A., King, M., Snow, S., & McIntire, J. C. (1999). *The role of education in a system of care: Effectively serving children with emotional or behavioral disorders.* Washington, DC: Center for Effective Collaboration and Practice, American Institutes for Research.

Zins, J., Weissberg, R., Wang, M., & Walberg, H. J. (Eds.). (2004). *Building academic success on social and emotional learning: What does the research say?* New York: Teachers College Press.

How to Obtain Medicaid Funding for School-Based Health and Mental Health Services

CHAPTER
105

January Angeles ▪ Mary Tierney ▪ David Osher

Getting Started

In the effort to meet students' educational needs, schools have become increasingly involved in delivering a broad range of services to address barriers to learning, increase school safety, and enhance learning outcomes (Learning First Alliance, 2001; Osher, Dwyer, & Jackson, 2004). For example, schools may offer individual or group counseling to youth at risk for a number of problems. Similarly, schools arrange for outside organizations to conduct school-based health, mental health, and social services. Some schools provide assessments for vision, hearing, and emotional problems.

For many students, schools are the primary point of entry to receiving needed health and social services. As such, schools have increasingly shouldered the costs and responsibilities for ensuring the health and well-being of school-aged youth. School officials and mental health staff are not always aware that Medicaid funding is available for many of the services that schools provide. Even when they do know about the availability of Medicaid, many do not take advantage of it because the process of collecting reimbursements is complicated and sometimes not perceived as worth the cost (Evans et al., 2002).

Accessing Medicaid funds can be daunting. The documentation and billing requirements may seem overwhelming. Requirements may also vary significantly from state to state. Finally, Medicaid policies and procedures change frequently, making it difficult for providers and advocates to keep up with the different requirements they have to meet. Despite the complexities involved, some schools and districts have used Medicaid as a large and reliable source of funding for school-based health and mental health services. Because Medicaid is the largest and most comprehensive source

of health care for low-income children, who are at greatest risk of developing social and emotional problems, schools cannot pass up the opportunity to use the program to strengthen and expand services for this population.

This chapter will help school staff and providers access Medicaid funding for health and mental health services provided in schools. Readers should note that this chapter contains information specific to the Medicaid program. Obtaining funding through the State Children's Health Insurance Program (SCHIP) is beyond the scope of this chapter because it is a separate program with its own requirements that are also defined on a state-by-state basis. Although many of the general principles discussed in this chapter can be applied to SCHIP, school providers who want to obtain SCHIP reimbursement should contact their state SCHIP agency for specific details.

What We Know

Medicaid is a federal-state program that provides health insurance to millions of low-income Americans. It was established in 1965 as Title XIX of the Social Security Act to help states offer medical assistance to persons with low incomes. It is jointly financed by the state and federal governments.

The federal government sets broad guidelines, but states have a great deal of flexibility in how they design and administer the Medicaid program. Within the scope of broad federal regulations, each state decides:

• who is eligible for coverage
• the type, amount, and scope of covered services

1093

- which providers can obtain Medicaid reimbursement
- how much providers get paid for their services

One of the most important things that people should know about Medicaid is that the program differs widely from state to state. Someone who is eligible for Medicaid in Arkansas may not be eligible in Florida. Along the same lines, a medical treatment that is covered by Medicaid in California may not be covered in Illinois.

Medicaid is particularly attractive as a funding source because it is an entitlement program. The program has no preset funding limit and no set number of students who can be covered. That is, schools and students do not have to compete with one another to get Medicaid funding. As long as providers follow the state rules for reimbursement, they will get paid for Medicaid services.

Maximizing Medicaid Funding

Schools can use three primary strategies for maximizing Medicaid funding for services. Because regulations vary by state, schools should check with the education, mental health, and Medicaid agencies in your state to determine how to capitalize on these sources.

- *Fee-for-Service Claiming.* Under fee-for-service claiming, Medicaid reimburses for the cost of direct services provided, such as an occupational therapy or counseling session. Schools in states that reimburse on a fee-for-service basis may be reimbursed for some or all Medicaid-eligible services, such as individual and group psychotherapy conducted by a certified Medicaid provider in the schools. Medicaid reimbursement may make it possible for schools that do not yet provide Medicaid-eligible services to do so. Claims for the cost of services are submitted to the state Medicaid agency.
- *Administrative Claiming.* Another form of Medicaid reimbursement available to schools is administrative claiming. Through administrative claiming, schools can get reimbursed for work related to the provision of direct services, such as providing referrals and case management. Its advantage is that it requires less detailed documentation of the costs for large amounts of work done by local agency staff. By using a formula to arrive at the amount of time spent

and the number of individuals involved, schools can calculate costs quickly.
- *Leveraged Funds.* Another strategy is for two or more agencies to create a formal partnership to leverage new or additional Medicaid funding. These funds are generated through an agreement between two or more agencies, at least one of which has access to Medicaid reimbursement funds and at least one of which has access to non-Medicaid funds and resources. Alone, neither the Medicaid-certified agency nor the ineligible agency can generate new revenue; together, they can. For example, schools can partner with a mental health agency that is a Medicaid-certified provider to provide services to Medicaid-eligible students in the schools.

Table 105.1 outlines these three strategies and points out some things that schools should consider when deciding which strategy to use. Keep in mind that these strategies are not mutually exclusive. Often schools that obtain Medicaid funding use a combination of fee-for-service claiming, administrative claiming, and leveraged funding.

What We Can Do

How to Get Medicaid Reimbursement for Services: Step by Step

Medicaid is a complicated program. To a certain extent, it is underused because of confusion about policies and procedures. School mental health service providers need to know three things to get Medicaid reimbursement for their services:

- *Rule 1:* Whoever provides the services must meet state Medicaid qualifications and have a provider agreement with the state Medicaid agency.
- *Rule 2:* Students receiving services must be eligible for or enrolled in Medicaid.
- *Rule 3:* Services provided must be covered under the state's Medicaid plan.

If schools adhere to these three rules, they should be able to get Medicaid reimbursement. The remainder of this chapter outlines what schools and school-based providers have to do to follow these three rules.

Table 105.1 Practical Considerations for Obtaining Medicaid Reimbursement Through Fee-for-Service, Administrative Claiming, and Leveraged Funds

	Reimbursable Services	*Advantages*	*Disadvantages*
Fee-for-service claiming	• Various clinical and rehabilitative services, as long as they are specified in the state's Medicaid plan	• Can pay for services previously funded through general funds, freeing up funds to serve more children or to offer a broader array of services	• May require start-up funding and resources in advance because it takes time to receive reimbursements • Requires intensive record keeping • Has state-determined reimbursement levels, which may not be enough to cover the costs of billing
Administrative claiming	• Outreach activities to inform parents and children about Medicaid • Activities to help enroll children into Medicaid • Certain transportation and translation services • Special education services, such as developing an individualized education plan (IEP)	• Offers funding for activities that are otherwise hard to fund, such as collaboration and case management • Requires less documentation than fee-for-service claiming	• May require significant resources for start-up because the Centers for Medicare and Medicaid Services (CMS) requires recipients to develop activity codes, conduct a time study to sample staff activity, and calculate a rate formula
Leveraged funds	• All services reimbursable through fee-for-service and administrative claiming	• Offers reimbursement for both services and administrative activities related to providing the services • Allows both partnering organizations to generate new revenue that they cannot generate individually	• Requires time to create a formal partnership because the organizations involved must have a shared vision of what the partnership entails

Step 1: Find Out What Types of Practitioners Are Eligible To Provide Medicaid Services and How They Can Become a Medicaid-Certified Provider in Their State

Whoever is providing the service has to meet provider qualifications and have a provider agreement in place with the state Medicaid program to get reimbursement. Many states give Medicaid provider status to licensed social workers, mental health practitioners, and school psychologists, but whether a particular person qualifies and can be certified as a Medicaid provider really depends on the state where he or she lives. Each state has different requirements for different types of providers, but in general, all states require providers to have the following:

• Proof of licensure or certification
• Proof of educational degree
• Proof of malpractice insurance

Check with the state Medicaid agency about other requirements for becoming a Medicaid provider. Each state Medicaid agency has a phone number (see Box 105.1) that a provider can call to discuss provider enrollment issues or to request an application.

Once the state Medicaid agency approves an application to become Medicaid certified, the provider must enter into a provider agreement. This agreement describes the responsibilities of a Medicaid provider and outlines billing and reimbursement procedures. In general, the agreement requires Medicaid-certified providers to do the following:

- *Agree to accept Medicaid payment as payment in full.* Medicaid providers cannot collect additional fees from other sources. For example, if a school bills Medicaid $100 for a service and Medicaid reimburses $80, the school cannot recover the remaining $20 that Medicaid did not pay from other funding sources.
- *Ensure that claims are processed expediently.* Providers must submit all claims to the state Medicaid agency no later than 12 months from the date of service (some states may allow less time for providers to bill).
- *Address all free care issues.* Medicaid will not pay for services that are available for free to the general public (people who are not covered by Medicaid).
- *Bill all liable third parties before billing Medicaid.* Medicaid is considered the payer of last resort. This means that if the child who receives the service has health coverage from other sources (such as a private insurance policy), providers must bill those sources before they bill Medicaid. In general, Medicaid will pay the remaining amounts not reimbursed by third parties for Medicaid-eligible services. The exception to this rule is a service provided to a child under the Individuals with Disabilities in Education Act (IDEA). Medicaid will pay prior to the Department of Education for Medicaid-covered services listed in a child's IEP or Individual family service plan (IFSP).
- *Maintain all necessary documentation.* Providers must keep organized and confidential records containing details on the service provided and the individual receiving services. Relevant documentation includes all the screening elements of an EPSDT screen; the dates, duration, and location of services; the provider of the service; any required medical documentation

related to the diagnosis or medical condition; and third-party billing information.

To Become a Medicaid-Certified Provider

1. Inquire with your state Medicaid agency if it certifies providers in your profession.
2. Find out what requirements you have to meet to become a Medicaid-certified provider.
3. Gather copies of your license or certification, academic degree, malpractice insurance, and other documents that your state Medicaid agency requires.
4. Complete and submit your state Medicaid agency's provider application.
5. Enter into a provider agreement with your Medicaid state agency.

Step 2: Find Out Whether the Student Who Needs the Services Is Eligible for or Enrolled in Medicaid

Medicaid covers three broad population groups: low-income women and their children and two-parent families in some states; individuals with disabilities; and the elderly. To qualify, individuals must have low or moderate incomes, but Medicaid eligibility is also linked to age, with specific eligibility categories for elderly persons and children. Individuals also need to meet certain criteria to be Medicaid eligible, such as residency requirements and citizenship or immigration status. Again, because Medicaid is a state-based program, the requirements that individuals need to meet depend on the state in which the person lives.

Many times students are eligible for Medicaid but are not enrolled because their parents do not know about the program or the application and enrollment process is too hard for their parents to navigate. To maximize student enrollment in the Medicaid program, it is important to address both issues. Step 2 of how to obtain Medicaid funding consists of three parts:

- Conducting outreach activities to tell students and families about the Medicaid program
- Finding out whether the student is eligible for Medicaid benefits
- Helping students and families enroll for Medicaid

Reach Out and Inform Families About Medicaid

Many families are not aware that they or their children may qualify for Medicaid coverage. Increasing awareness about Medicaid benefits and about who qualifies is essential to generating applications from potentially eligible individuals.

The following tips will help school mental health workers conduct outreach to help inform children and families about Medicaid:

- Work with the school principal or superintendent to determine which outreach activities are allowed by school policies
- Piggyback on school efforts, such as PTA meetings, parent–teacher conferences, and athletic events, to distribute information about the availability of public health insurance
- Include Medicaid information and applications in report card envelopes and back-to-school packets sent home with children in September
- Determine whether the school will add health insurance questions to mandatory health forms and free or reduced-price school lunch applications
- Present enrollment information at workshops and seminars for school staff

Keep in mind that in conducting outreach activities, it is important to target messages to children and families who fall within eligibility guidelines.

Find Out Whether a Student Is Medicaid Eligible

Often parents know about Medicaid but do not apply because they believe that they are ineligible. This represents a lost opportunity to provide needed health services to low-income families. It is important to identify individuals who might be eligible so that they can be encouraged to apply for Medicaid. As mentioned previously, eligibility for Medicaid varies from state to state, although in general an uninsured family of four with a yearly income of $33,400 is likely to qualify. Schools can also approximate whether someone qualifies by comparing his or her household income with the state income thresholds. (To check each state's threshold, visit http://www.statehealthfacts.kff.org.) Having an income that is below the state threshold will probably qualify an individual for

Medicaid. The Health Assistance Partnership has developed a screening tool with specific questions for determining eligibility status (http://www.healthassistancepartnership.org). Finally, each state Medicaid agency has staff available to help determine eligibility.

Help Students and Families Enroll in Medicaid

Even after parents find out about Medicaid and decide to apply, they may still need assistance with the process. In a nationwide survey of low-income parents, more than half indicated that they do not even attempt to enroll their children in Medicaid because the forms are too complicated and the application process is too long (Perry, Kannel, Valdez, & Chang, 2000). School social workers and staff can take several steps to help families enroll in Medicaid:

- Help parents gather the documents they need to apply, such as proof of citizenship and income
- Ensure that language assistance is available to non-English-speaking parents who want to apply
- Be available to answer questions about Medicaid or to refer parents to agencies and organizations that can help with the enrollment process

Although these tasks may seem daunting, in the end they will reap significant benefits. Schools are also uniquely positioned to undertake these tasks because access to students and parents is readily available. Fortunately, Medicaid also pays for many of these activities through the administrative claiming method.

Step 3: Find Out Whether the Services Needed Are Medicaid Eligible

For schools and mental health workers to receive reimbursement for health services, the services provided must be among those listed in the state's Medicaid statute. Although states have flexibility in shaping their state Medicaid plans, the federal government requires states to offer assistance for certain basic medical services (mandatory services). In addition to mandatory services, each state can elect to cover additional services (optional services) identified by CMS. Table 105.2 illustrates the various clinical and rehabilitative services that are defined in state Medicaid plans. Check with the state Medicaid agency for a list and definition of the services that Medicaid will pay.

IDEA Services and Medicaid

The Individuals with Disabilities in Education Act (IDEA) ensures that school-aged children with special education needs receive a free appropriate public education. It requires schools to prepare an individualized education plan (IEP) for each child needing special services. The IEP specifies all the child's special education and related health care needs.

Some health-related services specified in the IEP can be paid for through Medicaid as long as they are in the list of services outlined in the state plan. Although Medicaid and the IDEA are separate entitlements covering somewhat different populations, many children do qualify for both (Seltzer & Parker, 2003).

In this case, Medicaid is the primary payer to the Department of Education, although providers still have to bill other insurance companies (if any). In addition, Medicaid-covered services in a student's IEP are exempt from the free care rule. That is, Medicaid will still pay for services that are provided for free to non-Medicaid-eligible individuals if the services are required by the IEP.

Both Medicaid and the IDEA laws have strong entitlements to services that can benefit children with emotional and behavioral disorders. When used on behalf of children who qualify for both programs, the two statutes offer an effective way to build the comprehensive and intensive "wraparound" service package now widely understood to be necessary for many children with serious emotional or behavioral problems (Seltzer & Parker, 2003).

Preventive and Treatment Services, EPSDT, and Medicaid

Children have special status under Medicaid's Early and Periodic Screening, Diagnosis, and Treatment (EPSDT) provision. EPSDT requires states to screen eligible children under the age of 21, diagnose any conditions found through the screen, and furnish appropriate treatment to correct or ameliorate illnesses and conditions discovered through the screen. What is noteworthy about EPSDT is that when children are identified as needing services as a result of an EPSDT screen, states have to provide the services regardless of whether they are listed in the state plan.

The EPSDT program offers a comprehensive array of benefits and requires the following screening services:

- Comprehensive health and developmental history
- Comprehensive unclothed physical exam
- Appropriate immunizations and laboratory tests
- Health education, including parent education and counseling, that provides information about the benefits of healthy lifestyles and practices and about accident and disease prevention
- Vision services, including diagnosing and treating vision defects and providing eyeglasses
- Dental services, including pain relief, treatment of infections, teeth restoration, and dental health maintenance
- Hearing services, including diagnosing and treating hearing defects and providing devices such as hearing aids
- Other necessary care to diagnose and treat physical and mental health conditions discovered through an EPSDT screen

What Medicaid Will Not Pay For

Providers always need to keep in mind that in general, Medicaid will not pay for services that are offered to the general public for free, even if the services are listed in the state Medicaid plan. For example, if a school provides free vaccinations to all children in the school, Medicaid will not pay for the vaccinations given to Medicaid-eligible children even if it is a covered service. The only exception to this rule is a service that is listed in a student's IEP plan.

Gearing Up to Claim Medicaid Reimbursement

When trying to obtain Medicaid reimbursement of school-based health services, schools and providers should always ask these three questions:

- Are you a Medicaid-certified provider, and do you have a provider agreement with your state Medicaid agency?
- Are the students who need your services eligible for Medicaid, and are they enrolled in the program?
- Are the services that students need listed as a covered service under your state Medicaid plan?

If the answer to these three questions is yes, then obtaining Medicaid reimbursement should be relatively simple. Also, following these general principles will help those who wish to become established as Medicaid providers:

- *Always check with the Medicaid agency in the state about specific requirements.* Remember that Medicaid is different from state to state, so be sure to know the state's provider requirements, beneficiary eligibility requirements, and covered services.
- *Start small.* Becoming familiar with Medicaid is a complicated task. It is best not to take on other new activities while mastering the ins and outs of how to obtain and maximize Medicaid funding. Schools and providers that are already providing Medicaid-eligible services should try to get reimbursement for these services first before attempting to offer and receive reimbursement for new services.
- *Collaboration is the key.* Many organizations have the capacity and infrastructure to fulfill some, but not all, of the requirements to obtain Medicaid funding. Schools have access to Medicaid-eligible children but are not necessarily qualified as Medicaid providers. Health clinics may be Medicaid certified but do not have the ability to reach Medicaid-eligible individuals. Working together, however, schools and health clinics have the capacity to deliver a comprehensive array of services to children through Medicaid and EPSDT.
- *Documentation is the bottom line!* Medicaid agencies conduct routine audits to prevent fraud and abuse. Providers should always make sure that they keep well-maintained documentation about the services they offer and the health needs of the students receiving the services.

Practice Examples

Practice Example 1: Lafourche Parish Schools Use EPSDT Funding to Provide Screening

In Louisiana, the Lafourche Parish School District, through a partnership with the Tulane University Medical School, provides intervention, consultation, and assessment to students who are at risk for developing mental health problems. Many of the students in the schools are Medicaid eligible, and the medical school has Medicaid provider status. A partnership, therefore, allows the school district to fund many of its preventive services through Medicaid's EPSDT program.

By using Medicaid EPSDT funding to cover preventive services, the district saves money and resources in two ways:

- Medicaid funding frees up general school funds that were originally dedicated to these activities.
- Through early intervention, the school district prevents problems from starting or progressing, thereby avoiding more costly services in the future.

Practice Example 2: Los Angeles Unified School District Partnering to Leverage Funds

The Los Angeles Unified School District is an example of how a school-based mental health center successfully partnered with a provider organization to obtain Medicaid reimbursement and expand its services. With 722,000 students, LAUSD is one of the largest school districts in the United States. The district runs more than 30 school-based health clinics and four school-based child psychiatry clinics.

Originally, the district funded its mandated mental health services through general funds. In 1992, LAUSD contracted with the Los Angeles County Department of Mental Health to become a certified Medicaid provider. With the new contract in place, LAUSD began to claim Medicaid reimbursement for early and periodic screening, diagnosis, and treatment (EPSDT) services, thereby freeing up district funds. LAUSD used these funds to extend its services to other low-income children who did not qualify for Medicaid.

Practice Example 3: Innovative Practices for Enrolling Children in the State Children's Health Insurance Program (SCHIP) Through the Schools

In South Carolina, an incentive program gave $5 to each child with a completed CHIP application. Schools with the most applications were rewarded with pizza parties.

In Nevada, 70% of CHIP applicants first heard about the program through the school system. Schools used parent–teacher conferences and athletic programs to disseminate information. Also, to help facilitate enrollment, schools targeted students in the free or reduced-price lunch program as potential CHIP beneficiaries.

Resources

The Medicaid Program and CMS Guidance on Accessing Medicaid Funds

American Institutes for Research (forthcoming). *Medicaid and mental health: A consumer's guide.* Washington, DC: Center for Mental Health Services, Substance Abuse and Mental Health Services Administration.

The Medicaid resource book by Andy Schneider, Risa Elias, Rachel Garfield, David Rousseau, and Victoria Wachino, the Kaiser Commission on Medicaid and the Uninsured. Written to help the public and policy makers understand the structure and operation of the Medicaid program, this reference book contains comprehensive information about four major components of Medicaid: eligibility, benefits, financing, and administration. The book can be downloaded at http://www.kff.org/medicaid/2236-index.cfm.

Medicaid and school health: A technical assistance guide by the Centers for Medicare and Medicaid Services. This publication is a source of comprehensive technical assistance for Medicaid funding of school health programs. It explains Medicaid financing mechanisms and requirements and summarizes Medicaid regulations and policies

related to school funding. Schools seeking Medicaid funding can use the guide to ensure compliance with regulations, anticipate possible complications, and develop a broad understanding of Medicaid funding issues related to school-based health care. Download this publication at http://www.cms.hhs.gov/ medicaid/schools/scbintro.asp.

Medicaid school-based administrative claiming guide by the Centers for Medicare and Medicaid Services. This publication provides guidance to schools to ensure compliance with federal regulations on administrative claiming. It provides an overview of the regulations and requirements to obtain Medicaid funds for administrative activities, discusses the general principles of administrative claiming, and describes commonly encountered issues. The guide also features a section on how to pair administrative claiming with EPSDT and IDEA activities. The guide is available for download at http://www.cms.hhs.gov/medi-caid/schools/macguide.pdf.

Strategies for Maximizing Medicaid Funding for School-Based Health Services

Maximizing Medicaid funding to support health and mental health services for school-age children and youth by Andrew Bundy and Victoria Wegner, the Finance Project. This publication begins with a background description of Medicaid and EPSDT and then guides readers in obtaining Medicaid funding for school-based mental health services. It describes different financing options including fee-for-service and administrative claiming, leveraged funding, and statewide payment systems. For each type of funding strategy, the publication highlights case studies, practical considerations, and potential barriers and suggests ways to overcome those barriers. Download this strategy brief at www.financeproject.org/Brief5.htm.

Teaming up: Using the IDEA and Medicaid to secure comprehensive mental health services for children and youth by Tammy Seltzer and Rebekah Parker, Bazelon Center for Mental Health Law. This publication addresses the intersection of the Individuals with Disabilities Education Act (IDEA) and Medicaid as a funding possibility for mental health services. It is designed to educate attorneys who practice either

Table 105.2 Children's Clinical and Rehabilitative Services Defined in State Rules

	Clinical Services											Rehabilitative Services										
	Physician services	Individual psychotherapy	Family psychotherapy	Group psychotherapy	Medication management	Family education	Partial hospitalization	Substance abuse counseling	Independent practice psychologist: testing	Independent practice psychologist: counseling	Independent practice social workers	Intensive home based	Day treatment	After school	Summer camp/programs	Therapeutic preschool	Therapeutic nursery	Family support/wrap-around	Therapeutic foster care	Independent living skills training	Child respite care	Targeted case management for SED
AL	✓	✓	✓	✓	✓	✓	✓	✓	✓			✓	✓					✓		✓		✓
AK	✓	✓	✓	✓	✓			✓				✓	✓					✓				✓
AR	✓	✓	✓	✓	✓	✓	✓	✓	✓	✓		✓	✓	✓		✓	✓		✓	✓	✓	✓
AZ	✓	✓	✓	✓	✓	✓	✓	✓			✓	✓	✓					✓	✓	✓		✓
CA	✓	✓	✓	✓	✓							✓	✓									✓
CO	✓	✓		✓	✓	✓	✓						✓					✓		✓		✓
CT	✓	✓	✓	✓	✓	✓	✓	✓	✓	✓	✓		✓									✓
DC	✓	✓	✓	✓	✓	✓			✓	✓	✓		✓				✓					
DE		✓	✓	✓	✓	✓	✓	✓				✓	✓						✓	✓		
FL	✓	✓	✓	✓	✓		✓	✓	✓			✓	✓		✓				✓	✓		✓
GA	✓	✓	✓	✓	✓		✓	✓	✓	✓			✓	✓					✓			✓
HI	✓	✓	✓	✓	✓		✓	✓	✓													✓
IA	✓	✓	✓	✓	✓	✓		✓			✓	✓	✓								✓	
ID	✓	✓	✓	✓	✓	✓		✓	✓	✓	✓		✓							✓		
IL	✓	✓	✓	✓	✓	✓		✓				✓	✓									✓

(continued)

Table 105.2 (Continued)

	Clinical Services											Rehabilitative Services										
	Physician services	Individual psychotherapy	Family psychotherapy	Group psychotherapy	Medication management	Family education	Partial hospitalization	Substance abuse counseling	Independent practice psychologist: testing	Independent practice psychologist: counseling	Independent practice social workers	Intensive home based	Day treatment	After school	Summer camp/ programs	Therapeutic preschool	Therapeutic nursery	Family support/ wrap-around	Therapeutic foster care	Independent living skills training	Child respite care	Targeted case management for SED
IN	✓	✓	✓	✓	✓	✓	✓		✓		✓		✓							✓		✓
KS	✓	✓	✓	✓	✓	✓	✓	✓	✓	✓	✓	✓		✓	✓			✓	✓	✓	✓	✓
KY	✓	✓	✓	✓	✓	✓	✓	✓	✓	✓	✓	✓	✓	✓	✓			✓	✓			✓
LA	✓	✓	✓	✓	✓			✓	✓			✓	✓							✓		
MA		✓	✓	✓	✓		✓	✓				✓	✓				✓					
MD	✓	✓	✓	✓	✓		✓		✓			✓	✓							✓	✓	✓
ME	✓	✓	✓	✓	✓	✓		✓			✓	✓	✓					✓				
MI	✓	✓	✓	✓	✓		✓	✓	✓	✓	✓	✓	✓					✓	✓	✓		✓
MN	✓	✓	✓	✓	✓	✓	✓	✓	✓	✓	✓	✓						✓	✓			✓
MO	✓	✓	✓	✓	✓	✓			✓	✓	✓	✓										✓
MS	✓	✓	✓	✓	✓	✓		✓	✓	✓			✓									✓
MT	✓	✓	✓	✓	✓	✓	✓		✓		✓	✓	✓						✓	✓	✓	✓
NC	✓	✓		✓	✓	✓	✓		✓	✓			✓	✓					✓	✓		✓
ND	✓	✓	✓	✓	✓	✓	✓	✓	✓	✓	✓	✓	✓					✓	✓	✓	✓	✓
NE	✓	✓	✓	✓	✓	✓	✓	✓	✓	✓		✓						✓	✓			

Table 105.2 (Continued)

	Physician services	Individual psychotherapy	Family psychotherapy	Group psychotherapy	Medication management	Family education	Partial hospitalization	Substance abuse counseling	Independent practice psychologist: testing	Independent practice psychologist: counseling	Independent practice social workers	Intensive home based	Day treatment	After school	Summer camp/programs	Therapeutic preschool	Therapeutic nursery	Family support/wrap-around	Therapeutic foster care	Independent living skills training	Child respite care	Targeted case management for SED
	Clinical Services											Rehabilitative Services										
NH	✓	✓	✓	✓	✓	✓	✓	✓	✓	✓	✓	✓	✓					✓		✓		✓
NJ	✓	✓	✓	✓	✓		✓		✓	✓												✓
NM	✓	✓	✓	✓	✓		✓	✓	✓	✓	✓	✓	✓	✓					✓	✓		✓
NV	✓	✓	✓	✓	✓	✓	✓	✓	✓	✓		✓	✓					✓	✓	✓		✓
NY	✓	✓	✓	✓	✓	✓	✓	✓	✓				✓			✓			✓	✓	✓	✓
OH	✓	✓	✓	✓	✓		✓	✓	✓	✓		✓	✓					✓		✓		✓
OK	✓	✓	✓	✓	✓		✓	✓	✓			✓	✓	✓			✓	✓	✓	✓	✓	✓
OR	✓	✓	✓	✓	✓	✓	✓	✓	✓	✓	✓	✓	✓	✓	✓		✓	✓	✓	✓		✓
PA	✓	✓	✓	✓	✓	✓	✓	✓	✓	✓			✓					✓		✓		✓
RI	✓	✓	✓	✓	✓		✓	✓	✓	✓			✓									✓
SC	✓	✓	✓	✓	✓			✓		✓	✓	✓	✓			✓	✓	✓	✓	✓	✓	✓
SD	✓	✓	✓	✓	✓					✓								✓				✓
TN	✓	✓	✓	✓	✓			✓			✓						✓			✓		✓
TX	✓	✓	✓	✓	✓	✓	✓	✓	✓		✓	✓	✓							✓	✓	✓
UT	✓	✓	✓	✓	✓	✓	✓			✓		✓	✓									✓

(continued)

Table 105.2 (Continued)

	Clinical Services											Rehabilitative Services										
	Physician services	Individual psychotherapy	Family psychotherapy	Group psychotherapy	Medication management	Family education	Partial hospitalization	Substance abuse counseling	Independent practice psychologist: testing	Independent practice psychologist: counseling	Independent practice social workers	Intensive home based	Day treatment	After school	Summer camp/programs	Therapeutic preschool	Therapeutic nursery	Family support/wrap-around	Therapeutic foster care	Independent living skills training	Child respite care	Targeted case management for SED
VA	✓	✓	✓	✓	✓		✓	✓	✓	✓	✓	✓	✓		✓							✓
VT	✓	✓	✓	✓	✓	✓	✓	✓	✓	✓		✓						✓		✓	✓	✓
WA		✓	✓	✓	✓							✓	✓							✓		✓
WI	✓	✓	✓	✓	✓		✓	✓	✓	✓	✓	✓	✓							✓		✓
WV	✓	✓	✓	✓	✓		✓	✓	✓	✓	✓	✓	✓							✓		✓
WY	✓		✓	✓				✓					✓						✓	✓		✓

Source: From *Medicaid and mental health: A consumer's guide*, by American Institutes for Research (forthcoming), Washington, DC: Center for Mental Health Services, Substance Abuse and Mental Health Services Agency.

IDEA or Medicaid law on the intricacies of these mandates and how they work in conjunction with each other. The overall purpose is to provide detailed information about the program in which these attorneys do not specialize so that ultimately they can access both sources of funding to assist their clients. Although geared toward the legal advocacy community, this document is relevant to anyone interested in the funding of school-based mental health services. The publication uses case studies to illustrate how court precedents can be used to advocate for mental health service financing and how integrated financing can compensate for gaps in coverage. The publication can be downloaded at http://www.bazelon.org/issues/children/publications/teamingup/report.pdf.

Reaching Out and Enrolling Children in Medicaid

Covering kids and families back-to-school action kit by the Covering Kids Initiative of the Robert Wood Johnson Foundation. This toolkit was developed for the Covering Kids and Families Back-to-School campaign, an outreach program to inform parents about health insurance coverage for children. The toolkit contains information and materials on how to conduct outreach activities and enroll children in Medicaid and CHIP. You can download the toolkit at http://coveringkidsandfamilies.org/communications/bts/kit

Putting express lane eligibility into practice: A briefing book and guide for enrolling uninsured children who receive other public benefits into Medicaid and CHIP by the Children's Partnership and the Kaiser Commission on Medicaid and the Uninsured. This report discusses the concept of express lane eligibility, a process of linking Medicaid and CHIP applications and enrollment to other means-tested services, such as free or reduced-price lunch programs, that schools provide. The report highlights proven strategies for automatically enrolling children into public health programs and provides multiple case studies and sample program application forms that schools can adapt. It discusses factors to consider when using express lane eligibility, including confidentiality issues, adherence to current Medicaid law, and state-to-state variation in enrollment. It is available for download

at http://www.kff.org/medicaid/2211-index.cfm?RenderForPrint=1.

Medicaid and children, overcoming barriers to enrollment: Findings from a national survey by the Kaiser Commission on Medicaid and the Uninsured. This report highlights the findings from a survey of low-income parents on barriers to enrolling their children in Medicaid. It discusses how to overcome these barriers and describes various methods that schools can employ to facilitate the Medicaid enrollment process. The report is available for download at http://www.kff.org/medicaid/2174-index.cfm.

Enrolling children in health coverage programs: Schools are part of the equation by the Covering Kids Initiative of the Robert Wood Johnson Foundation. This brief demonstrates the importance of the role of schools in enrolling students in Medicaid and CHIP. It presents strategies that schools can use to reach and enroll eligible students, lists organizations dedicated to assisting schools in this effort, and highlights various ways in which schools can work with community organizations and within the state governments to enroll more students in health programs. This strategy brief is available for download at http://www.centeronbudget.org/10–1-01health2.pdf.

Children's health coverage outreach: A special role for school nurses by the Covering Kids Initiative of the Robert Wood Johnson Foundation. This strategy brief provides information on how to involve school nurses in efforts to reach out and provide information about Medicaid and SCHIP to children and their families. The brief outlines and provides case studies on various outreach strategies. The brief can be downloaded from http://www.centeronbudget.org/10–1-01health5.pdf.

Organizations That Conduct Activities Related to Medicaid, Mental Health, and Financing of School-Based Services

The Centers for Medicare and Medicaid Services: http://www.cms.gov. The Centers for Medicare and Medicaid Services (CMS) administers Medicaid and the State Children's Health Insurance Program (SCHIP). Practitioners can access general information about program rules and regulations, eligibility requirements, and billing on the Web site. Specific information about each state's Medicaid program is available through

Box 105.1 Directory of State Medicaid Agencies

Alabama
Medicaid Agency of Alabama
501 Dexter Avenue
PO Box 5624
Montgomery, AL 36103-5624
(800) 362-1504 or (334) 242-5000
http://www.medicaid.state.al.us/

Alaska
Alaska Department of Health and Human
Services
350 Main Street, Room 229
PO Box 110601
Juneau, AK 99811-0601
(907) 465-3030
http://www.hss.state.ak.us

Arizona
Health Care Cost Containment of Arizona
801 E. Jefferson Street
Phoenix, AZ 85034
(800) 962-6690 or (602) 417-7000
http://www.ahcccs.state.az.us

Arkansas
Department of Human Services of Arkansas
PO Box 1437, Slot 1100
Donaghey Plaza South
Little Rock, AR 72203-1437
(800) 484-5431 or (501) 682-8292
http://www.medicaid.state.ar.us/

California
California Department of Health Services
PO Box 942732
Sacramento, CA 94243-7320
(916) 445-4171
http://www.dhs.ca.gov/

Colorado
Department of Health Care Policy and
Financing of Colorado
1570 Grant Street
Denver, CO 80203-1818
(800) 221-3943 or (303) 866-2993
http://www.chcpf.state.co.us

Connecticut
Department of Social Services of Connecticut
25 Sigourney Street
Hartford, CT 06106-5033
(800) 842-1508 or (860) 424-4908
http://www.dss.state.ct.us

Delaware
Delaware Health and Social Services
1901 N. DuPont Highway
PO Box 906, Lewis Building
New Castle, DE 19720
(302) 255-9040
http://www.state.de.us/dhss

District of Columbia
DC Department of Health
825 North Capitol Street, NE
5th Floor
Washington, DC 20002
(202) 442-5999
http://dchealth.dc.gov/index.asp

Florida
Agency for Health Care Administration
of Florida
PO Box 13000
Tallahassee, FL 32317-3000
(888) 419-3456
http://www.fdhc.state.fl.us/index.shtml

Georgia
Georgia Department of Community Health
2 Peachtree Street, NW
Atlanta, GA 30303
(866) 322-4260 or (770) 570-3300
http://www.communityhealth.state.ga.us//

Hawaii
Department of Human Services of
Hawaii
PO Box 339
Honolulu, HI 96809
(800) 316-8005 or (808) 524-3370
http://www.med-quest.us/

Idaho
Idaho Department of Health and
Welfare
450 West State Street
Boise, ID 83720-0036
(208) 334-5500
http://www2.state.id.us/dhw

Illinois
Department of Public Aid of Illinois
201 South Grand Avenue, East
Chicago, IL 60607
(800) 226-0768 or (217) 782-2570
http://www.dpaillinois.com/

(continued)

Box 105.1 (Continued)

Indiana
Family and Social Services Administration of
Indiana
402 W. Washington Street
PO Box 7083
Indianapolis, IN 46207-7083
(800) 457-4584 or (317) 232-4966
http://www.in.gov/fssa/

Iowa
Department of Human Services of Iowa
Hoover State Office Building
5th Floor
Des Moines, IA 50319-0114
(800) 338-8366 or (515) 327-5121
http://www.dhs.state.ia.us

Kansas
Department of Social and Rehabilitation
Services of Kansas
915 S.W. Harrison Street
Topeka, KS 66612
(800) 792-4884 or (785) 274-4200
http://www.srskansas.org/hcp/

Kentucky
Cabinet Health Services of Kentucky
PO Box 2110
Frankfort, KY 40602-2110
(800) 635-2570 or (502) 564-2687
http://chs.ky.gov/dms/

Louisiana
Louisiana Department of Health and Hospital
1201 Capitol Access Road
PO Box 629
Baton Rouge, LA 70821-0629
(225) 342-9500
http://www.dhh.state.la.us

Maine
Maine Department of Human Services
442 Civic Center Drive
11 State House Station
Augusta, ME 04333-0011
(800) 321-5557 or (207) 287-3094
http://www.state.me.us/bms

Maryland
Department of Human Resources for Maryland
PO Box 17259
Baltimore, MD 21203-7259

(800) 492-5231 or (410) 767-5800
http://www.dhr.state.md.us/fia/medicaid.htm

Massachusetts
Office of Health and Human Services of
Massachusetts
600 Washington Street
Boston, MA 02111
(800) 325-5231 or (617) 628-4141
http://www.state.ma.us/dma/

Michigan
Michigan Department of Community
Health
Sixth Floor, Lewis Class Building
320 S. Walnut Street
Lansing, MI 48913
(800) 292-2550
http://www.michigan.gov/mdch

Minnesota
Department of Human Services of
Minnesota
444 Lafayette Road North
St. Paul, MN 55155
(651) 297-3933
http://www.dhs.state.mn.us/

Mississippi
Office of the Governor of Mississippi
239 North Lamar Street, Suite 801
Robert E. Lee Building
Jackson, MS 39201-1399
(800) 421-2408 or (601) 359-6048
http://www.dom.state.ms.us/

Missouri
Department of Social Services of Missouri
221 West High Street
PO Box 1527
Jefferson City, MO 65102-1527
(800) 392-2161 or (573) 751-4815
http://www.dss.state.mo.us/dms

Montana
Montana Department of Public Health and
Human Services
1400 Broadway, Cogswell Building
PO Box 8005
Helena, MT 59604-8005
(800) 362-8312 or (406) 444-5900
http://www.dphhs.state.mt.us/

(continued)

Box 105.1 (Continued)

Nebraska
Nebraska Department of Health and Human
Services System
PO Box 95044
Lincoln, NE 68509-5044
(402) 471-3121
http://www.hhs.state.ne.us

Nevada
Nevada Department of Human Resources,
Aging Division
1100 E. William Street
Suite 101
Carson City, NV 89701
(702) 486-5000
http://dhcfp.state.nv.us/

New Hampshire
New Hampshire Department of Health and
Human Services
129 Pleasant Street
Concord, NH 03301-3857
(603) 271-4238
http://www.dhhs.state.nh.us/

New Jersey
Department of Human Services of
New Jersey
Quakerbridge Plaza, Building 6
P.O. Box 716
Trenton, NJ 08625-0716
(800) 356-1561 or (609) 588-2600
http://www.state.nj.us/humanservices/

New Mexico
Department of Human Services of New
Mexico
PO Box 2348
Santa Fe, NM 87504-2348
(888) 997-2583 or (505) 827-3100
http://www.state.nm.us/hsd/mad/Index.html

New York
New York State Department of Health
Office of Medicaid Management
Governor Nelson A Rockefeller Empire State
Plaza
Corning Tower Building
Albany, NY 12237
(800) 541-2831 or (518) 747-8887
http://www.health.state.ny.us/nysdoh/
medicaid/medicaid.htm

North Carolina
North Carolina Department of Health and
Human Services
1918 Umstead Drive
Kirby Building
Raleigh, NC 27699-2501
(800) 662-7030 or (919) 857-4011
http://www.dhhs.state.nc.us/dma/

North Dakota
Department of Human Services of North
Dakota
600 E. Boulevard Avenue
Bismarck, ND 58505-0250
(800) 755-2604 or (701) 328-2332
http://lnotes.state.nd.us

Ohio
Department of Job and Family Services of
Ohio–Ohio Health Plans
30 E. Broad Street
31st Floor
Columbus, OH 43215-3414
(800) 324-8680 or (614) 728-3288
http://www.state.oh.us/odjfs/aboutus/0002
AboutUs.stm

Oklahoma
Health Care Authority of Oklahoma
4545 N. Lincoln Boulevard
Suite 124
Oklahoma City, OK 73105
(800) 522-0114 or (405) 522-7300
http://www.ohca.state.ok.us/

Oregon
Oregon Department of Human Services
500 Summer Street, NE
3rd Floor
Salem, OR 94310-1014
(800) 527-5772 or (503) 945-5772
http://www.dhs.state.or.us/

Pennsylvania
Department of Public Welfare of
Pennsylvania
Health and Welfare Building, Room 515
PO Box 2675
Harrisburg, PA 17105
(800) 692-7462 or (717) 787-1870
http://www.dpw.state.pa.us/omap/
dpwomap.asp

(continued)

Box 105.1 (Continued)

Rhode Island
Department of Human Services of Rhode
Island
Louis Pasteur Building
600 New London Avenue
Cranston, RI 02921
(401) 462-5300
http://www.dhs.state.ri.us/

South Carolina
South Carolina Department of Health and
Human Services
P.O. Box 8206
Columbia, SC 29202-8206
(803) 898-2500
http://www.dhhs.state.sc.us/Default.htm

South Dakota
Department of Social Services of South
Dakota
700 Governors Drive
Richard F Kneip Building
Pierre, SD 57501
(800) 452-7691 or (605) 773-3495
http://www.state.sd.us/social/MedElig

Tennessee
Department of Finance and Administration of
Tennessee
729 Church Street
Nashville, TN 37247
(800) 669-1851 or (615) 741-4800
http://www2.state.tn.us/health/

Texas
Health and Human Services Commission of
Texas
4900 N Lamar Boulevard
4th Floor
Austin, TX 78701
(888) 834-7406 or (512) 424-6500
http://www.hhsc.state.tx.us/

Utah
Utah Department of Health
288 North 1460 West
PO Box 143101
Salt Lake City, UT 84114-3101
(800) 662-9651 or (801) 538-6155
http://health.utah.gov/medicaid/

Vermont
Agency of Human Services of
Vermont
103 S. Main Street
Waterbury, VT 05676-1201
(800) 250-8427 or (802) 241-1282
http://www.dpath.state.vt.us/

Virginia
Department of Social Services of Virginia
600 E. Broad Street
Suite 1300
Richmond, VA 23219
(804) 726-4231
http://www.dss.state.va.us/benefit/
medicaid_coverage.html

Washington
Department of Social and Health Services of
Washington
PO Box 45505
Olympia, WA 98504-5505
(800) 562-3022 or (800) 562-6188
http://fortress.wa.gov/dshs/maa/

West Virginia
West Virginia Department of Health and
Human Resources
350 Capitol Street
Room 251
Charleston, WV 25301-3709
(304) 558-1700
http://www.wvdhhr.org/bms/

Wisconsin
Wisconsin Department of Health and Family
Services
1 W. Wilson Street
PO Box 309
Madison, WI 53701-0309
(800) 362-3002 or (608) 221-5720
http://www.dhfs.state.wi.us/medicaid/
index.htm

Wyoming
Wyoming Department of Health
147 Hathaway Building
Cheyenne, WY 82002
(888) 996-8678 or (307) 777-6964
http://wdhfs.state.wy.us/

the U.S. State and Local Government Gateway at http://www.statelocal.gov.

The Center for Health and Health Care in Schools: http://www.healthinschools.org. The Center for Health and Health Care in Schools (CHHCS) is an organization devoted to strengthening children's and youths' well-being by effectively providing health care programs and services in schools. CHHCS serves as a resource for school-based health center (SBHC) administrators, providers, and policymakers. CHHCS works to expand and include mental health services in SBHCs. The CHHCS Web site has links to mental health background information, resources about funding school-based mental health through grants or managed care, and state and local school-based initiatives.

Bazelon Center for Mental Health Law: http://www.bazelon.org. The Bazelon Center for Mental Health Law is an advocacy organization devoted to ensuring and advancing the rights of people with mental disabilities. The center acts as a legislative watchdog, communicates about court decisions affecting mental health care, and researches mental health policy implications. The center produces several fact sheets, issue briefs, and other publications on a variety of topics related to mental illness, including children's mental health.

The Finance Project: http://www.financeproject .org. The Finance Project aims to "support decision-making that produces and sustains good results for children, families and communities." The Finance Project engages in several activities, such as conducting research, organizing expert meetings and forums, and providing technical assistance specifically related to the financing of programs, projects, and initiatives. The Web site serves as the host for the Welfare Information Network, which has a section dedicated to health care and Medicaid that is a clearinghouse for health care funding information.

Key Points to Remember

This chapter has addressed issues related to obtaining Medicaid funding for health and mental health services in schools. The key points covered in the chapter are as follows:

- Issues concerning Medicaid eligibility and reimbursement

- Strategies for maximizing Medicaid reimbursement
- Helping families apply for Medicaid funding
- Obtaining Medicaid reimbursement for services specified in a student's IEP
- Tips for becoming a Medicaid services provider
- Services provided through the EPSDT program

References

Bundy, A. L., & Wegner, V. (2000). Maximizing Medicaid funding to support health and mental health services. *Finance Project Strategy Brief, 1*(5), 1–18.

Evans, S. W., Glass-Siegel, M., Frank, A., Van Treuren, R., Lever, N. A., & Weist, M. D. (2002). Overcoming the challenges of funding school mental health programs. In M. D. Weist & N. A. Lerner (Eds.), *Handbook of school mental health services* (pp. 73–86). New York: Kluwer Academic.

Fish-Parcham, C. (2003). *Screening for Medicaid and State Children's Health Insurance Program (SCHIP) eligibility.* Washington, DC: Health Assistance Partnership.

Koyanagi, C., Boudreaux, R., & Lind, E. (2003). *Mix and match: Using federal programs to support interagency systems of care for children with mental health care needs.* Washington, DC: Bazelon Center for Mental Health Law.

Learning First Alliance. (2001). *Every child learning: Safe and supportive schools.* Alexandria, VA: Association for Supervision and Curriculum Development.

Osher, D., Dwyer, K., & Jackson, S. (2004). *Safe, supportive, and successful schools: Step by step.* Longmont, CO: Sopris West Educational Services.

Perry, M., Kannel, S., Valdez, R. B., & Chang, C. (2000). *Medicaid and children overcoming barriers to enrollment: Findings from a national survey.* Washington, DC: Kaiser Commission on Medicaid and the Uninsured.

Rappaport, N., Osher, D., Dwyer, K., Garrison, E., Hare, I., Ladd, J., & Anderson-Ketchmark, C. (2002). Enhancing collaborations within and across disciplines to advance mental health programs in schools. In M. D. Weist, S. Evans, & N. Tashman (Eds.), *School mental health handbook* (pp. 107–118). New York: Kluwer Academic.

Schneider, A., Elias, R., Garfield, R., Rousseau, D., & Wachino, V. (2002). *The Medicaid resource book.* Washington, DC: Kaiser Commission on Medicaid and the Uninsured.

Seltzer, T., & Parker, R. (2003). *Teaming up: Using the IDEA and Medicaid to secure comprehensive mental health services for children and youth.* Washington, DC: Bazelon Center for Mental Health Law.

Guidelines for Writing a Successful Grant and Developing Foundation and Business Support

Allan R. Chavkin ▪ Nancy Feyl Chavkin

Getting Started

Mental health professionals across the nation are facing an unexpected crisis, a sea change in how their programs are being funded. They are being asked not only to write grants to fund their programs but also to fund their own positions. This is the new reality for funding mental health services in schools. No longer do schools see funding from external sources as a luxury; it is now a necessity. Increasingly, writing a grant is essential for maintaining the status quo; school social workers and mental health professionals are quickly learning that fund-raising is no longer just for add-on programs or extra services. Securing grants and developing foundation and business support are core requirements of the job.

This new reality has put major stresses on mental health professionals who have been trained primarily to provide direct services. Many professionals are at a loss about where to begin and how to proceed; some are so fearful of this new job requirement that they are leaving their positions in school settings for private agencies. The title of Kim Klein's book *Fundraising in Times of Crisis* (2003) is apt for our current quandary. In response to this emerging need, universities have started to add courses and assignments on grant writing; in fact, a professor at Buffalo State College recently assigned students to compile "Web Watch" columns on finding grant-writing resources online. This new column is being published by the *Phi Delta Kappan* (Anastasi & Hughes, 2003) on a regular basis and can be a current resource for new grant writers.

In the long run, there must be major changes in the existing ways we fund health, education, and social services for children; however, children in this country cannot wait for the slow wheels of bureaucracy and politics to change the funding mechanisms needed for services. In the meantime, many schools and communities will need to secure grant funds for mental health positions and for programs. It is with this realistic recognition that the authors offer some practical suggestions for what is acknowledged as short-term solutions to a long-term problem for funding mental health services in the schools.

What We Know

Best practices in grant writing lead to one clear outcome—getting funded. Those who have achieved this success offer some powerful suggestions to beginners. As the list of resources at the end of this chapter indicates, there are also numerous federal and private agencies available to assist with locating resources and providing assistance for best practices in grant writing.

Deborah Kluge (2004) suggests that there are three overarching principles: conducting research, cultivating relationships, and writing an excellent proposal. She maintains that most beginners want to start writing before they have done research on the most appropriate source of funding and before they have built relationships with their collaborators or potential funders.

David Bauer (2003) also offers mental health professionals an important suggestion when he advises grant seekers to begin proactively. Too often grant seekers have their project in mind and then try to fit it to someone else's guidelines within a short period of time. There is no time to develop a relationship with the funding agency, to understand the agenda of the grantor, or to prepare a well-conceived, winning proposal. Grant seekers sometimes begin a negative process of flooding the market with their grant requests in the hope that eventually one will be accepted, but this strategy almost never works.

Drawing on the work of Festinger (1957), Bauer uses the cognitive dissonance theory to develop his "values glasses theory" of grant seeking. Understanding the thinking and values of the grantor is critical to being successful. Too many grant writers only understand their own beliefs, and they write from a very narrow perspective. Bauer is not suggesting that grant writers should pander to the grantor's values or try to disguise a project for something it is not. What Bauer is suggesting is that grant writers first try to understand the grantor so that the grant meets the needs of the grantor, the grantee, and the grant writer. He reminds us that working proactively does not necessarily mean that grant writers will spend more time writing the grant; rather, it means that grant writers will use their time well over a longer period of time instead of trying to produce, "a last minute Herculean proposal effort." It is better to begin writing the grant well before its due date rather than at the last minute, and there are ways to begin the process of writing a grant for school mental health projects before the actual application arrives. Of course, we all know that most grants are written on short notice, but those that are funded are often those that have been in the planning stages many months before the actual application arrived. Beginning proactively means knowing the audience to whom you will be writing, and accomplishing this goal requires time.

Mim Carlson (2002) stresses that a major component of being successful in grant writing is self-assessment. Drawing on her more than 25 years of experience, she advocates for first identifying what is really happening in your agency and where you want to go. Larissa and Martin Brown (2001) also stress the importance of learning about your organization and your community before you begin to think about who will fund you. You will need to be clear about your organization's purpose and how it fits within the larger scheme of your community.

Although there many variables involved in getting funded, grant writers who have been funded many times share similar strategies for success. The next section will present some practical steps for securing grants and other external funding.

What We Can Do

Eight Steps to Successfully Securing External Funding

Step 1: Research Sources for Funding

Box 106.1 provides a number of helpful places to begin your search for an appropriate funding source. There are many different kinds of funders, and it is important to find an appropriate funder that matches your need. Primary sources of funding information include the *Federal Register*, *The Catalog of Federal Domestic Assistance*, and the *Code of Federal Regulations*; all of these are now available online through an excellent Web site (http://www. grants.gov) sponsored by the federal government. This Web site contains links to every major federal grant-awarding agency. However, many beginners find the use of primary sources overwhelming; they often prefer secondary sources that summarize the major grants, requirements, and deadlines. Examples of secondary sources often available in schools include *Education Daily* and *Federal Grants and Contracts Weekly*.

It is important to note that there are critical differences between writing a grant and seeking funds from businesses and foundations. Grants usually contain a "request for proposals" (RFP), while businesses and foundations may require only a one-page letter or brief application. Despite the differences in application procedure and length, the core requirements for conceptualizing and writing the proposal are essentially the same.

Step 2: Follow the Guidelines

When a grant writer does locate a relevant source, it is imperative to read the RFP or foundation guidelines thoroughly and follow them exactly. A number of very fine proposals are eliminated at the first stage of the review process because the authors did not comply with the requirements for submission. Grant writers should make certain that they know their audience. Key questions to consider are: Who is evaluating your proposal? What kind of projects do they want to fund? What are their interests? Often it is beneficial for writers to take the time to role play what it would be like if they were receiving this request for funding. It is helpful to see examples of other recently funded proposals. These can be requested from the agencies.

Box 106.1 Resources for Grant Writing

http://www.grants.gov: This site allows organizations to electronically find and apply for competitive grant opportunities from all federal grant-making agencies. By using colored tabs and links at the top of the screen, navigation of the site is simple.

http://www.fedgrants.gov/: The Federal Grant Opportunities site gives grantors a means to post solicitations for grants. It also gives applicants a single site for obtaining these solicitations.

http://fdncenter.org: The mission of the Foundation Center is to strengthen the nonprofit sector by advancing knowledge about U.S. philanthropy. The website collects, organizes, and communicates information about U.S. philanthropy and offers links to many funding resources.

www.schoolgrants.org: SchoolGrants was created in 1999 as a way to share grant information with PK–12 educators. SchoolGrants provides online tips for grant writing and lists a variety of opportunities available to public and private nonprofit elementary and secondary schools and districts across the United States.

http://www.cdc.gov/funding.htm: The Center for Disease Control's Procurement and Grants Office sponsors a Web site with information about funding and useful resources for grant writers. They also provide links to current statistics and data.

www.samhsa.gov/grants: SAMHSA is the federal agency charged with improving the quality and availability of prevention, treatment, and rehabilitative services in order to reduce illness, death, disability, and cost to society resulting from substance abuse and mental illnesses. They have an excellent section on current funding initiatives and guidelines for applicants.

www.grantcraft.org: The Ford Foundation provides this Web site with helpful suggestions gathered from donors and grant makers in small foundations and large, including family, corporate, and independent grant programs. These materials are meant to suggest possibilities.

www.tgci.com: The Grantsmanship Center covers all aspects of researching grants, writing grant proposals, and negotiating with funding sources. They offer a Web site, materials, and 5-day workshops on grant writing. TGCI is also active in publishing books and a magazine. TGCI's Winning Grant Proposals Online collects the best of funded federal grant proposals annually and makes them available on CD-ROM.

It is also critical that the grant writer be familiar with the criteria for review, especially the points awarded for each section of the proposal. It is only logical that if 25% of the points are awarded based on project need, then 25% of your narrative should be on project need. Box 106.2 is an example of a review criteria sheet.

Step 3: Separate the Need from the Solution

One of the biggest problems that beginning grant writers face is how to separate the need from the solution. This situation arises because we as authors have the solution in mind and we truly need the solution we are proposing. For example, school social workers might need a van to transport children to and from after-school tutoring activities. It is obvious to us how helpful that van would be. If we focus the proposal on the van, then we are focusing on the solution and not on what needs the van will meet. It would be better to document the learning needs of the students who will be transported in the van and how the van will help improve learning rather than to focus on the lack of transportation.

Perhaps the most common error with many proposals is their exclusive focus on the need for more personnel. Many times, a school principal's first response to the needs assessment question is: "I need more nurses, social workers, and aides. If I had more staff, the problems would be solved." Most likely there is an element of truth in this statement, but the statement is not a needs assessment. The statement is really the proposed solution. A better needs statement

Box 106.2 Sample Review Criteria

SELECTION CRITERIA	MAXIMUM POINTS	POINTS
1. National significance	30	_____
2. Quality of project design	30	_____
3. Quality and potential contributions of personnel	15	_____
4. Adequacy of resources	15	_____
5. Quality of management plan	10	_____
TOTAL	100	_____

Highly recommended for funding _____

Recommended for funding _____

Not recommended for funding _____

would focus on the numbers of children who are sick or without immunizations, the percentage of children who do not have adequate supervision, the low level of parental participation in school activities, or the low reading scores. Grant writers must make the connection between need and solution very early in the proposal. If you begin your proposal with the solution, you are not going to convince the reviewer why you should be funded.

The question you should always be asking is: Why should the grantor fund our project? You need to describe the problem and what will happen if you are not funded by considering all the possible negative ramifications. For example, you should inform the readers of the consequences of low reading or math scores. Charts, graphs, and facts provide the details that can help you be specific and persuasive about your needs. Painting a worst case scenario of your needs is often a useful tool. One or two case vignettes can highlight the human factor in your proposal (e.g., tell a brief story using first names).

Also, make certain you reference the current literature and state why your project is important. You should be sure to explain how your project will be a model for other sites. Explain how your program addresses the needs of similar schools and could also benefit them. The "upside-down pyramid approach" in Box 106.3 can be very useful here. Begin with the needs of your project and then build a relationship to how solving your needs will help not only your school, but the community, the state, and perhaps even the nation.

Box 106.3 The "Upside-Down Pyramid Approach" to Explaining a Project's Benefits

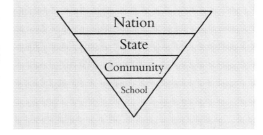

Step 4: Tell Your Story

Because school mental health projects often involve interrelated children's needs, they are sometimes difficult to describe. Because of the complexity involved in school mental health projects, telling your story well is essential for helping the funder understand exactly what your project is. Cheryl Clarke (2001) explains that storytelling is "at the core of all successful fundraising." Funders constantly report that the proposals that are easiest to understand get funded the most often.

There are many ways to tell your story, and it is often helpful to use a variety of methods to explain the needs of the project and the proposed solution. Hooking the reader with a good case example is a first step and one that is usually not difficult for school social workers and mental health professionals. Sometimes what is harder for beginners and perhaps extremely difficult for professionals who work with complex social systems

Box 106.4 Project Outline

I. Concise statement of problem/issue (whom does this problem affect? how?)

II. Documentation of severity of problem (local, state, national statistics; need hard data here)

III. Beneficiaries of your project (whom will the project help? why do it?)

IV. Strengths and resources of beneficiaries

V. Strengths and resources of community

VI. Your school's strengths and resources

VII. General goal of your project (general statement of what you will do)

VIII. Specific goal statement (try to limit your project to one major goal)

IX. Specific objectives:[a]
(no more than 3–5)

Objective 1.

Objective 2.

Objective 3.

[a] Go to Objectives Worksheet (Box 106.5) before completing this section.

is to tell the story linearly and to link your goals, objectives, needs, and resources.

Boxes 106.4, 106.5, and 106.6 are useful guides that force you to link your goal and objectives to your needs and resources. As Box 106.4 suggests, begin your thinking with a statement of the problem or issue and then ask the questions: How do your goal and objectives meet the needs? Are you building on the strengths of the beneficiaries? Are you using all the strengths and resources of the community and your group? Box 106.5 breaks the objective statement down into a series of questions that many grant writers find useful, and Box 106.6 presents a linear way of looking at goal, objectives, activities, and tasks.

Box 106.5 Objectives Worksheet

OBJECTIVE 1

Who?

Does what?

When?

Under what circumstances?

To what degree?

How will you measure it?

Be clear about the distinctions among goal, objectives, activities, and tasks. You must be very careful not to get distracted by activities and lose sight of your goal. Always refer back to your goal. As you look at these worksheets, notice that there is a connection between the goal of the project, the need for the project, existing resources, and the specific objectives.

Step 5: Demonstrating Your Organizational Capability

After establishing the need for your project and telling the story of your project by describing it in detail, the next thing you need to do is write a clear plan of operation. You should make a chart of who will do what activity, when they will do it, and where they will do it. This is especially important for school mental health projects because of the complexity of the organization. It is essential that you take the time to do this. Using Box 106.6, begin with your objectives and then list each activity that must be done to complete the objective. If possible, break the activity down into tasks. Timelines and organizational charts are very helpful at this point.

You must make it clear to the reader that you are capable of carrying out the project. You can show that you can do the project in a variety of

Box 106.6 The Linear Way of Looking at Your Proposal

Goal:

OBJECTIVE 1

Activity 1.1   how evaluated   by whom/when/what instruments/why
   Task 1.11
   Task 1.12
   Task 1.13
   Task 1.14

Activity 1.2   how evaluated   by whom/when/what instruments/why
   Task 1.21
   Task 1.22
   Task 1.23

OBJECTIVE 2

Activity 2.1   how evaluated   by whom/when/what instruments/why
   Task 2.11
   Task 2.12

Activity 2.2   how evaluated   by whom/when/what instruments/why
   Task 2.21
   Task 2.22
   Task 2.23

ways. If you have physical resources (office, equipment, library), describe them. If you have strong community support, list examples. You can include relevant letters of support in the appendix. Sometimes it is helpful to describe your previous track record with grants. Some grantors want to know if your organization can manage a budget and has been successful with other endeavors. It is critical to know your grantor, however, because some grantors are skeptical of applicants who already have too many grants. The grantor will want to know how this project is different from other previously funded projects. The grantor will want to make certain that this new request for funds is not a duplication of previous efforts. Make clear what is new about this request.

It is helpful to provide brief summaries (about a paragraph) for each person about the qualifications of key staff and how these qualifications relate to your proposal. There is no need to list extraneous positions or qualifications; be concise but laudatory about your personnel. If space permits, you can include one- or two-page vitae for key personnel in the appendix.

Visual aids can help you get organized and present a succinct but clear picture of your project. Box 106.7 is an example of a Gantt chart. Gantt charts were first developed by Henry L. Gantt in the 1900s, and they are still widely used today for establishing clear time lines and responsibilities. Funders look favorably on proposals that are well thought out and include details about time lines and the person responsible for each activity.

Sometimes grant writers use other kinds of charts to explain their activities. One might see a PERT (program evaluation and review technique) chart or a project management review chart that links goals, objectives, activities, measurement, data analysis, and outcome. A well-done graphic can be much more valuable than pages of text.

Step 6: Justifying the Project Budget

James Quick and Cheryl New (2001) are correct in their statement that just about everyone has some discomfort with budgets, and fear of budgets is a major concern for first-time grant seekers. One of their first suggestions is to clarify the term by calling it your project budget. The very act of using the more specific phrase conveys what you want to do: write a budget for your proposed project.

Your project budget should be as specific as possible, and you should justify any large or unusual expenditure. Most funding agencies like to have funds go for direct services rather than

Box 106.7 Gantt Chart

Goal: To develop a workshop for pregnant teenagers at Green County High School to improve their life skills

Objectives and Activities	Person(s) Responsible	Feb.	Time Frame March	April
Obj. 1: Locate appropriate curriculum				
Activity 1.1: Research topics	Jones & Luera	4–18		
Activity 1.2: Prepare presentations/activities	Jones & Luera	18–22		
Activity 1.3: Compile all information	Jones	22–29		
Obj. 2: Collaborate with community agencies				
Activity 2.1: Meet with agency representatives	Jones & Luera	25	11	
Activity 2.2: Organize resources	Luera	22–28		
Obj. 3: Pilot the workshop				
Activity 3.1: Recruit students	Teachers	1–15		
Activity 3.2: Conduct workshop	Jones & Luera		1–22	
Activity 3.3: Evaluate Workshop	Consultant			1–15

equipment, but you should verify that this is the assumption of your particular funding source by contacting your funder on this issue. If at all possible, secure matching funds for your proposal. Sometimes the match can be in-kind contributions, such as time or office space/equipment. Box 106.8 is an example of a project budget outline.

Sometimes funders require matching funds according to an established ratio. Cost sharing usually refers to donated services and materials. Sometimes these in-kind contributions are personnel, facilities, or services for administering the grant. In-kind services are assigned a dollar equivalency. School project proposals should be able to describe matching

Box 106.8 Example of Budget Summary

	Federal Portion	*School Match*	*Total*
Personnel	48,965	96,877	145,842
Supplies	2,000	6,000	8,000
Travel	1,000	1,000	2,000
Equipment	2,000	4,000	6,000
Communication	1,000	1,000	2,000
Printing	1,000	1,000	2,000
Contracted services	5,000	0	5,000
Miscellaneous	1,000	2,000	3,000
Direct costs	61,965	111,877	173,842
Indirect costs (8%)	4,957	8,950	13,907
Total costs	66,922	120,827	187,749

funds or cost-share with community groups, state funding, or federal grants.

Two key terms you need to know are direct costs and indirect costs. Direct costs usually include personnel (wages/salaries, fringe benefits, merit, cost-of-living raises); supplies (consumable supplies, such as pens, books, videotapes, diskettes); equipment (purchase or rental); travel (in-state and out of state; broken down by destination, purpose, mileage, per diem); communication costs (telephone equipment/installation/ charges, postage, fax); printing (publishing of brochures, handbooks, copying costs); contracted services (use of consultants, subcontracts); and miscellaneous (facility rental, repairs, anything not included in these categories).

Indirect costs are the overhead costs incurred in the administration of the grant. Your organization or the funder probably already has these calculated as a percentage of total direct costs. For example, some grants have an 8% indirect cost rate calculated on the basis of all direct costs; others have a 48% indirect cost rate calculated on the basis of only salaries/wages. Some foundations and a few state programs do not allow the inclusion of indirect costs in the budget. Check with the funding source and your administration to find out the specifics for your school or agency.

You should also include a section entitled "Budget Justification" or "Budget Rationale" in your proposal. It is an essential appendix to the budget and explains key budget line items. This narrative explanation can be used to make the rationale for each item immediately clear and is particularly helpful to grant reviewers.

you need to conduct depends on the purpose of your evaluation. Consider which of the following evaluations are appropriate for your program: effort evaluation (person hours, visits, meetings, etc.), performance evaluation (yield, results), adequacy (change in unmet need, decreased absenteeism, increased test scores), efficiency (personnel/time/ offices), process (relative success of parts of projects/aspects that could be done better), quantitative versus qualitative, formative versus summative, process versus outcome, cost-benefit versus cost-effectiveness, compliance versus quality, effectiveness versus efficiency, or inputs versus impact.

Your job is to ask the right questions. You can get assistance with the statistics, computer programs, survey design, and data collections. If you want to be successful in your project, the most important thing to remember about evaluations is to not let your project fall into the autopsy category. Many project coordinators wait until the project is over before they consider doing an evaluation. Then it is often too late to change some of the activities that could have improved the program. Cynthia Knowles (2002) reminds grant writers to build evaluation into the project from the beginning, even before the grant begins. Consider adding a process evaluation to your required evaluations of implementation and impact. You will also want to share your results and should have a plan for sharing what works in your project with others either during your program or after. Put this plan in your proposal in both the organizational plan and in the evaluation plan. Reviewers look favorably on proposals with a clear plan for dissemination of results.

Step 7: Demonstrating Accountability

If at all possible, projects should use an external evaluator because such an outside evaluator provides an objective look at your successes and failures. It is not the job of a mental health professional to do all of the evaluations, but it is clearly the responsibility of the mental health professional to make certain that the right questions are being asked. Your evaluation might consider questions in each of four areas: planning, implementation, outcome, and economic efficiency. You do not have to evaluate every activity or even every objective, but you must explain why you choose to evaluate specific parts of your project.

There are many kinds of evaluations (not all of them mutually exclusive). The kind of evaluation

Step 8: Refining Your Proposal

Writing style becomes a key factor in selecting the winning proposal when all other factors are equal. Joseph Barbato and Danielle S. Furlich (2000) make it clear that there are two parts to successful fund-raising: what you put in the proposal and how well you write it. Many grant seekers have great ideas but fall short on the second part, writing well.

Remember to always write in the active voice; avoid the unnecessarily abstract and wordy writing that often accompanies passive voice. You should avoid acronyms and jargon that are not clear to the lay reader. Use short sentences and avoid vague pronoun references. Because reviewers read many proposals in a short time, you can help them out by being as clear and precise as possible.

Include a section with appendices. This section contains supporting documents. It should not be used for essential information that needs to be in the text. It can be useful, though, for the history and background of your organization, vitae of personnel, relevant prior studies or projects, copies of support letters, evaluation instruments, or sample lesson plans.

Most important, ask outside people to read and critically review your proposal before submitting it. Do not wait until the last day to submit the proposal. It is best to have two types of readers: lay readers and experts. Lay readers are people who know nothing about your project. Have them read the proposal and see if they understand what you are saying. Expert readers know the general field and can give you feedback on missing research or a discrepancy in your organizational plans. Critique and feedback are essential to a successful proposal.

Tools and Practice Example

Forms and Samples

The forms and samples in this section were referenced in the steps previously described. As you peruse these tools, you may find it useful to refer to the steps in which they were discussed.

A Practice Example: An Abstract Containing Successful Grant Ideas

As you are putting the finishing touches on your grant proposal, do not forget the abstract. It is often helpful to wait and write the abstract of your proposal at the end of your writing endeavor because at that point you will be clear about all the parts of the proposal, and it will be easier to write a summary at the end of this process rather than at the beginning. We next present an example to show you how an abstract can pique the readers' interest with just enough detail to get the readers to want to read more. The project is clear about its goal and objectives. It gives a specific, targeted outcome (90% of students will be taking pre-algebra classes at the end of the project). The PATH Mathematics proposal also connects its demonstration project with a plan to replicate the project in the state and nation.

PATH Math (Partnership for Access to Higher Mathematics)

The goal of PATH Mathematics is to form a partnership between Southwest Texas State University (SWT), San Marcos School District (SMCISD), and San Marcos Telephone Company to significantly improve the mathematical skills of low-income students, thereby increasing these students' readiness for postsecondary education. The project uses interactive television (ITV) to achieve three key objectives:

Objective 1: Develop and implement a new pre-algebra curriculum that will allow students tracked in lower-level classes to reach algebra I by 10th grade.

Objective 2: Develop and implement a tutoring program through which tutors from SWT will work with students at the SMCISD via ITV.

Objective 3: Develop and implement a support program through which social work interns from SWT will provide mentorship, social service, and motivational activities to strengthen SMCISD students' interest in furthering their education.

Secondary students at SMCISD will receive immediate and direct benefits from this project; by the end of 3 years 90% of ninth graders will be taking pre-algebra or above mathematics courses. We will extend the project to other rural, small schools in Texas and the nation through TI-IN Network (San Antonio, TX) and United Star Network's (national) satellite broadcast systems. This model can be replicated in virtually any American community because almost every community, regardless of size, has access to a telephone company. Schools, colleges, and universities can join forces with their telephone company and use ITV to improve the mathematical skills of their high school students.

Key Points to Remember

There are many possibilities for achieving success in grant writing. Although many times proposals are not funded on the first attempt, they are often rewritten and funded on another submission. If you are rejected, write a thank-you letter to the funding agency for considering your application and request to see reviews or a summary of reviews so that you can revise and improve your grant. Few grants are funded on the first submission; a number are funded, however, after revisions and resubmissions. Writing successful proposals is not an easy task. Most of all, it takes time and commitment. School social workers and mental health professionals who want to obtain grant funding must take the time to plan and to conceptualize what they need, what resources they already have, and how they are going to organize these resources with new funding to accomplish the tasks ahead of them.

References

Anastasi, V., & Hughes, M. (2003). Grants and grant writing. *Phi Delta Kappan, 85*(2): 174.

Barbato, J., & Furlich, D. S. (2000). *Writing for a good cause: The complete guide to crafting proposals and other persuasive pieces for nonprofits.* New York: Simon & Schuster.

Bauer, D. G. (2003). *The "how to" grants manual: Successful grant seeking techniques for obtaining public and private grants* (5th ed.). Westport, CT: Praeger.

Brown, L. G., & Brown, M. J. (2001). *Demystifying grant seeking: What you really need to do to get grants.* San Francisco, CA: Jossey-Bass.

Carlson, M. (2002). *Winning grants: Step by step.* San Francisco, CA: Jossey-Bass.

Clarke, C. A. (2001). *Storytelling for grant seekers.* San Francisco, CA: Jossey-Bass.

Festinger, L. (1957). *Theory of cognitive dissonance.* Stanford, CA: Stanford University Press.

Klein, K. (2003). *Fundraising in times of crisis.* San Francisco, CA: Jossey-Bass.

Kluge, D. L (2004). Grant resources: Researching & identifying grant-making organizations. Available at: http://www.proposalwriter.com/grants.html

Knowles, C. (2002). *The first-time grant writer's guide to success.* Thousand Oaks, CA: Corwin Press, Inc.

Quick, J. A., & New, C. C. (2001). *Grant seeker's budget toolkit.* New York: John Wiley & Sons.

Grant Writing Bibliography

Coley, S. M. (2000). *Proposal writing.* Newbury Park, CA: Sage.

Edwards, R. L., Benefield, E. A. S., Edwards, J. A., & Yankey, J. A. (1997). *Building a strong foundation: Fundraising for nonprofits.* Washington, DC: National Association of Social Workers.

Geever, J. C., & McNeil, P. (2004). *The Foundation Center's guide to proposal writing.* New York: The Foundation Center.

Karsh, E., & Fox, A. S. (2003). *The only grant-writing book you'll ever need.* New York: Carroll & Graaf Publishers.

Lauffer, A. (1983). *Grantsmanship.* Thousand Oaks, CA: Sage.

New, C. C., & Quick, J. A. (1998). *Grant seeker's toolkit: A comprehensive guide to finding funding.* New York: John Wiley & Sons, Inc.

Ogden, T. E. (2002). *Research proposals: A guide to success.* New York: Raven.

Quick, J. A., & New, C. C. (2000). *Grant winner's toolkit: Project management and evaluation.* New York: John Wiley & Sons, Inc.

Ries, J. B., & Leukefeld, C. G. (1995). *Applying for research funding: Getting started and getting funded.* Thousand Oaks, CA: Sage.

Soriano, F. I. (1999). *Conducting needs assessments: A multidisciplinary approach.* Thousand Oaks, CA: Sage.

Best Practice Guides for Developing and Sustaining a Professional School-Based Practice

School-based practice is still relatively new to social work and other mental health professionals, and current practitioners are pioneers in many regards. Issues of self-care, defining one's role, supervision, professional development, and managing career advancement are often unique for school-based practitioners. This section is designed for school-based mental health professionals who are new to school-based practice, those who are the only practitioner of their kind in their school or district, and those recently moved into supervisory positions and other new responsibilities within the school. School-based practitioners will find many helpful ideas for networking, supervision, and managing their school relations. Finally, this section provides a review of the evidenced-based practice trends and predicts some of the future issues that school social workers and other mental health practitioners might face.

Licensing, Certification, and Credentialing of School Social Workers and Other School Mental Health Professionals

Santos Torres, Jr.

CHAPTER 107

Getting Started

Credentialing, certification, and licensing of school social workers and other school mental health professionals serve many purposes, but chief among these is the establishment of standards for how one is to legally function as a mental health professional in an educational environment. In general, the purpose of licensure is to assure that those involved in the delivery of professional mental health services in educational settings have received educational preparation and/or training experiences based on a set of uniform and coordinated standards and procedures, usually promulgated by state or nationally sanctioned boards, commissions, or councils in those professional disciplines, and adopted by legal

or regulatory agencies granted the authority to issue credentials, certificates, and/or licenses.

Additionally, many states have enacted title protection laws, designed to control who may use a particular label or professional identifier, such as *social worker, psychologist, nurse,* or *counselor.* Simply put, this means that one is not entitled to represent themselves as a licensed professional unless he or she has met approved legal standards for being credentialed. Title protection laws establish a set of criteria for what constitutes appropriate professional preparation and are designed to indicate that a baseline or minimum threshold of professional competence and practice has been attained by these individuals. Title protection acts carry with them legal consequences for those who inappropriately use certain professional titles and are established as a means of protecting the general public.

The public is served by these laws in that they clarify who may use certain professional titles as well as establishing, with a good measure of confidence, that those who are permitted to legally use those titles are in fact competent and ethical practitioners in their respective disciplines. Title protection laws provide direction and guidance to agencies and organizations on who is qualified to fill certain positions. Finally, when public confidence exists and the consumer believes they are the recipient of legally sanctioned service rendered by a qualified professional, then the very work itself is facilitated, since it is built upon a relationship of trust and confidence.

What We Know

There exists no one-stop shopping location for all the information one might need to learn about the licensing, certification, and credentialing of school social workers and other school mental health professionals. By and large, each educational jurisdiction promulgates its own rules and regulations on what is required to become a credentialed, certified, or licensed provider of professional mental health services in an educational setting. In the United States there are 50 educational jurisdictions, one jurisdiction per state, along with eight additional "extra-jurisdictions." Later, the reader will find a list of 50 state-level and eight extra-state-level educational jurisdictions including information such as a current telephone number, whether school social workers are certified in that jurisdiction, the degree required to be certified as a social worker in school settings, and finally, in most cases, a current Web page associated with a given jurisdiction (see Tools and Practice Examples).

As one can imagine, the numerous jurisdictions have resulted in the creation of a complex array of factors influencing the licensing, certification, and credentialing of professionals. Many states have a department of regulation and licensing that has oversight responsibility for determining who is legally eligible to serve as a professional mental health service provider in their educational system. Amazingly, information on the licensing requirements needed to do mechanical, electrical, or general construction contract work in and around schools is more clearly established, easily obtained,

or understood than that which might be required for school social workers and other mental health professionals who work directly with children, families, teachers, staff, and school administrators in public and private schools. It would appear that there is more concern about who can and should do work to the educational facility itself than with the people inside. (See also chapter 108 for more information on professional requirements for school social work and other mental health professionals.)

An important professional organization for the profession of school social work is the School Social Work Association of America (SSWAA). According to SSWAA, 34 of the 50 states in America (or 68%) certify school social workers. Additionally four of eight of the extra-state, U.S. educational jurisdictions (American Samoa, Bureau of Indian Affairs, Department of Defense, District of Columbia, Guam, North Mariana Islands, Puerto Rico, and the Virgin Islands) also certify school social workers.

The author informally surveyed the eight extra-state educational jurisdictions and learned that while Department of Defense does not currently employ school social workers, as an extra-state educational jurisdiction, they would allow the licensing, credentialing, and/or certification of a given state to be applicable to their professional social work staff. School social workers in the District of Columbia must hold both the general social work license and a public school social worker certificate issued by the D.C. Office of Academic Credentials and Standards. In the Virgin Islands, school social workers must be certified by their board of education. The Bureau of Indian Affairs, which employs a wide range of mental health professionals, including social workers, does so by utilizing the educational preparation and certification, credentialing, and licensing mechanisms of a given state.

In general, the evolution of establishing competence among professional personnel serving schools seems to have moved along the following path. The movement toward standardized assessment may have begun with successful completion and receipt of a degree to transcript review of course work on the degree (evaluating preparation in a specialized area of study) to licensing, credentialing, and certification by external organizations such as state departments of education. Additionally, there exist voluntary certification programs "which supplement legal regulation [and] . . . are based on the concept of self-regulation" (Biggerstaff, 1995, pp. 1617–1618). A primary difference between voluntary certification and legal regulation (licensing, registration, and statutory certification) is that "voluntary certification programs do not prohibit anyone from practicing a profession" (Biggerstaff, 1995, p. 1618), whereas state regulations may "restrict certain areas of practice, particularly private practice, but do not prohibit unqualified persons from practicing social work or do not regulate the practice of all people in the profession" (Biggerstaff, 1995, p. 1618). For instance, NASW launched the specialty certifications program in 2000 to help its members be competitive in the workplace. However, these certifications "provide recognition to those who have met national standards for higher levels of experience and knowledge and are not a substitute for state licenses" (NASW, 2002a). This was evidenced over 20 years ago as well, when Hawkins (1982) wrote:

> Included among the crucial elements of a good educational system are effective teachers, knowledgeable and skilled support personnel, and competent administrative forces. It is through certification at the state level that such forces are usually secured and maintained. State certification may be defined as official evidence, presented through a state's department of education, indicating successful completion of academic and practice requirements relating to the provision of competent instructional or other professional support services to the schools. (p. 41)

There are four major professional disciplines represented in educational settings that could be described as focusing on issues of mental health. These include school social workers, school psychologists, school counselors, and school nurses. Many schools have a member from each of these discipline areas represented to provide comprehensive services to its pupils. Each possesses particular knowledge and skills and are brought together to share their expertise with one another as a multidisciplinary team (Constable & Thomas, 2002). Taken together, these multidisciplinary teams provide critically needed assessment, planning, and intervention and evaluation services focused on addressing the needs of children in today's schools. It should be noted that a teamwork approach is not without problems; issues of territoriality, competition, and philosophical differences do not always lend themselves to a well-integrated and synchronized service delivery model. Similarly,

Tiefenthal argued, "There are a number of problems experienced when teams attempt to share expertise for a common purpose. The team needs to find a way to balance the power and perspectives of its members toward a genuine sharing of resources" (in Constable & Thomas, 2002, p. 156). The roles of these professionals are distinct but many times overlap with one another. According to Allen-Meares (2004), "School social workers have to be prepared to educate others about the unique aspects of their roles and to mediate the sociopolitical conflict inherent in the role confusion" (p. 296). Therefore, it is important to understand the differences in roles and expertise relative to these professional disciplines.

The School Social Worker

"As a field of practice, school social work is now nearly a century old, just a few years younger than its parent profession. Simultaneously inaugurated in three eastern U.S. cities around 1906—New York, Boston, and Hartford, Connecticut" (Torres, 1998, p. 461). It is a distinct field of social work practice with its own set of standards and expectations (see NASW, 2002b). Although all educational jurisdictions do not require the certification of school social workers, school districts hire school social workers "to enhance the district's ability to meet its academic mission, especially where home, school and community collaboration is the key to achieving that mission" (School Social Workers of America, 2004).

The School Social Workers of America (SSWA) organization provides the following as a definition of school social work: "School social work is a specialized area of practice within the broad field of the social work profession" (SSWA, 2004). Further, it states that school social workers are influential in the school system and as part of the student services team in helping to provide a setting conducive for "teaching, learning, and the attainment of competence and confidence" (SSWA, 2004). The U.S. Department of Labor similarly defines school social workers as providing "social services and assistance to improve the social and psychological functioning of children and their families and to maximize the family well-being and academic functioning of children" (U.S. Department of Labor, Bureau of Labor Statistics, 2004c). (See Tools and Practice Examples for Web-based resources pertaining to this professional group.)

The School Psychologists

The next mental health professional to be considered is the school psychologist. Focusing their efforts on the creation of a safe and healthy environment, school psychologists with specialized training in the educational and psychological needs of school-age children team with other mental health professionals to improve teaching and learning strategies (National Association of School Psychologists, 2004). Finally, "They may evaluate the effectiveness of academic programs, behavior management procedures, and other services provided in the school setting" (U.S. Department of Labor, Bureau of Labor Statistics, 2004b). School psychologists apply learning theory, promote the use of psychological theory and practice in curriculum development, and provide psychotherapeutic interventions as part of their role in the educational setting (Allen-Meares, 2004). (See Tools and Practice Examples for Web-based resources pertaining to this professional group.)

The School Counselor

School counselors at all levels help students understand and deal with social, behavioral, and personal problems. Counselors work with students individually, with small groups, or with entire classes. They consult and collaborate with parents, teachers, school administrators, school psychologists, medical professionals, and social workers in order to develop and implement strategies to help students be successful in the education system. (U.S. Department of Labor, Bureau of Labor Statistics)

According to the U.S. Department of Labor, all states require school counselors to hold a state school counseling certification. (See Tools and Practice Examples for Web-based resources pertaining to this professional group.)

The School Nurse

School nurses as a professional group are being included in this discussion on mental health professionals serving educational settings given that their role may sometimes include collecting and utilizing mental health–related information on pupils. It is a "specialized practice of professional nursing that advances the well being, academic success, and life-long achievement of students. To that end, school nurses facilitate positive student responses to normal development; promote health and safety; intervene with actual and potential health problems; provide case management services; and actively collaborate with others to build student and family capacity for adaptation, self management, self advocacy, and learning" (National Association of School Nurses, 2004, http://www.nasn.org/). (See Tools and Practice Examples for Web-based resources pertaining to this professional group.)

Tools and Practice Examples

State Departments of Education (Educational Jurisdictions)

Alabama (334) 242-9977 Certified? No http://www.alsde.edu
Alaska (907) 465-2831 Certified? Yes Degree? BSW http://www.eed.state.ak.us
Arizona (602) 542-4367 Certified? No http://www.ade.state.az.us
Arkansas (501) 682-4342 Certified? No http://arkedu.state.ar.us
California (916) 445-0184 Certified? Yes Degree? MSW http://www.ctc.ca.gov
Colorado (303) 866-6628 Certified? Yes Degree? MSW http://www.cde.state.co.us
Connecticut (860) 566-5201 Certified? Yes Degree? MSW http://www.state.ct.us/sde
Delaware (302) 739-4686 Certified? Yes Degree? BSW http://www.doe.state.de.us
Florida (850) 488-6159 Certified? Yes Degree? BSW http://www.firn.edu/doe
Georgia (404) 657-9000 Certified? Yes Degree? BSW http://www.gapsc.com
Hawaii (808) 586-3269 Certified? No http://www.doe.k12.hi.us
Idaho (208) 332-6880 Certified? Yes Degree? MSW http://www.sde.state.id.us/certification
Illinois (217) 782-2805 Certified? Yes Degree? MSW http://www.isbe.state.il.us
Indiana (317) 232-9010 Certified? Yes Degree? http://www.doe.state.in.us
Iowa (515) 281-3245 Certified? Yes Degree? MSW http://www.state.ia.us/educate

Kansas (785) 296-2288 Certified? Yes Degree? MSW http://www.ksbe.state.ks.us

Kentucky (502) 573-4606 Certified? Yes Degree? MSW http://www.kde.state.ky.us

Louisiana (504) 342-3490 Certified? Yes Degree? MSW http://www.doe.state.la.us/DOE/asps/home.asp

Maine (207) 582-8723 Certified? No http://www.state.me.us/education/homepage.htm

Maryland (410) 767-0412 Certified? No http://www.msde.state.md.us/certification/index.htm

Massachusetts (617) 388-3300 Certified? Yes Degree? MSW http://www.doe.mass.edu/educators/e_license.html

Michigan (517) 373-3310 Certified? Yes Degree? MSW http://www.michigan.gov/mde

Minnesota (651) 296-2046 Certified? Yes Degree? BSW http://www.educ.state.mn.us

Mississippi (601) 359-3483 Certified? No http://www.mde.k12.ms.us

Missouri (573) 751-0051 Certified? No http://www.dese.state.mo.us

Montana (406) 444-3150 Certified? Yes Licensing through Commerce Dept. http://www.metnet.state.mt.us/

Nebraska (402) 471-2496 Certified? No http://www.nde.state.ne.us

Nevada (702) 486-6457 or 6458 Certified? Yes Degree? Unanswered http://www.nde.state.nv.us/

New Hampshire (603) 271-2407 Certified? Yes Degree? BA in Social Work http://www.state.nh.us/doe

New Jersey (609) 292-2070 Certified? Yes Degree? BSW http://www.state.nj.us/education

New Mexico (505) 827-6581 Certified? Yes Degree? BSW http://www.sde.state.nm.us

New York (518) 474-3901 Certified? Yes Degree? BA+ http://www.nysed.gov

North Carolina (919) 733-0377 Certified? Yes Degree? BSW http://www.dpi.state.nc.us

North Dakota (701) 328-2260 Certified? No http://www.dpi.state.nd.us

Ohio (614) 466-3593 Certified? Yes Degree? MSW and social work licensure http://www.ode.state.oh.us

Oklahoma (405) 521-3337 Certified? No http://www.sde.state.ok.us

Oregon (503) 378-3586 Certified? No http://www.ode.state.or.us/

Pennsylvania (717) 787-2967 Certified? Yes Degree? MSW http://www.tcs.ed.state.pa.us/

Rhode Island (40) 277-2675 Certified? No http://www.ridoe.net/default.htm

South Carolina (803) 734-8466 Certified? Yes Degree? MSW http://www.sde.state.sc.us/

South Dakota (605) 773-3553 Certified? No http://www.state.sd.us/deca

Tennessee (615) 532-4885 Certified? Yes Degree? MSW http://www.state.tn.us/education

Texas (512) 463-8976 Certified? Yes Degree? MSW http://www.tea.state.tx.us

Utah (801) 538-7740 or 7753 Certified? Yes Degree? MSW http://www.usoe.k12.ut.us

Vermont (802) 828-2445 Certified? No http://www.state.vt.us/educ

Virginia (804) 225-2022 Certified? Yes Degree? MSW http://www.pen.k12.va.us

Washington (360) 725-6400 Certified? Yes Degree? MSW http://www.k12.wa.us/cert

West Virginia (304) 348-7712 Certified? No http://wvde.state.wv.us/

Wisconsin (608) 266-2386 Certified? Yes Degree? MSW http://www.dpi.state.wi.us

Wyoming (307) 777-7291 or 6248 Certified? Yes Degree? MSW http://www.k12.wy.us

Extra-State Educational Jurisdictions

American Samoa 001(684) 633-5237 Certified? Unknown

Bureau of Indian Affairs (505) 248-6363 Certified? Yes Degree? BSW/MSW

Department of Defense Education Activity (703) 588-3200 Certified? No http://www.odedodea.edu/

District of Columbia (202) 442-5885 Certified? Yes Degree? Must be licensed social worker

Guam (671) 475-0461 or (671) 475-0441 Certified? Unknown http://www.doe.edu.gu/

Northern Mariana Islands (670) 664-3700 Certified? Unknown

Puerto Rico (787) 763-2171 Certified? Unknown

Virgin Islands (340) 774-2810 Certified? Yes Degree? Unknown www.teachislands.vi

The preceding list was compiled from information adapted from the Web page of the School Social Work Association of American at http://www.sswaa.org/links/statedoe.html and from the personal communication by the author with representatives of the extra-state educational jurisdictions.

World Wide Web Resources on Professional Associations for School-Based Mental Health Professionals

American Association of School Administrators: AASA, founded in 1865, is the professional organization for over 14,000 educational leaders across America and in many other countries. AASA's mission is to support and develop effective school system leaders who are dedicated to the highest quality public education for all children. AASA's major focus is standing up for public education at http://www.aasa.org/.

American School Counselor Association: The American School Counselor Association (ASCA) is a worldwide nonprofit organization based in Alexandria, Virginia. Founded in 1952, ASCA supports school counselors' efforts to help students focus on academic, personal/social, and career development so they not only achieve success in school but also are prepared to lead fulfilling lives as responsible members of society. The association provides professional development, publications and other resources, research, and advocacy to more than 15,000 professional school counselors around the globe at http://www.schoolcounselor.org/.

American School Health Association: The American School Health Association unites the many professionals working in schools who are committed to safeguarding the health of school-aged children. The association, a multidisciplinary organization of administrators, counselors, dentists, health educators, physical educators, school nurses, and school physicians, advocates high-quality school health instruction, health services, and a healthful school environment at http://www. ashaweb.org/.

Association of Social Work Boards: The Association of Social Work Boards (ASWB) is the association of boards that regulate social work. ASWB develops and maintains the social work licensing examination used across the country and is a central resource for information on the legal regulation of social work. Through the association, social work boards can share information and work together. ASWB is also available to help individual social workers and social work students with questions they may have about licensing and the social work examinations at http://www.aswb.org/lic_req.shtml.

Center for School Mental Health Assistance: The Center for School Mental Health Assistance is an energetic and committed team, including youth and families, educators, social workers, psychologists, licensed professional counselors, psychiatrists, and other health and mental health staff. Our team members are advocates, clinicians, teachers, and researchers, all working on the "front lines" of effective school mental health promotion at http://csmha.umaryland.edu/.

Clinical Social Work Federation: The Clinical Social Work Federation is a confederation of 31 state societies for clinical social work. Our state societies are formed as voluntary associations for the purpose of promoting the highest standards of professional education and clinical practice. Each society is active with legislative advocacy and lobbying efforts for adequate and appropriate mental health services and coverage at their state and national levels of government at http://www.cswf.org/.

Council of Chief State School Officers: The Council of Chief State School Officers (CCSSO) is a nonpartisan, nationwide, nonprofit organization of public officials who head departments of elementary and secondary education in the states, the District of Columbia, the Department of Defense Education Activity, and five U.S. extra-state jurisdictions. CCSSO provides leadership, advocacy, and technical assistance on major educational issues. The council seeks member consensus on major educational issues and expresses their views to civic and professional organizations, federal agencies, Congress, and the public at http://www.ccsso.org/.

Council on Social Work Education: The Council on Social Work Education (CSWE) is a nonprofit national association representing over 3,000 individual members as well as graduate and undergraduate programs of professional social work education. Founded in 1952, this partnership of educational and professional institutions, social welfare agencies, and private citizens is recognized by the Council for Higher Education Accreditation as the sole accrediting agency for social work education in this country at http://www.cswe.org/.

Division of School Psychology: The Division of School Psychology is composed of scientific-practitioner psychologists whose major professional interests lie with children, families, and the schooling process. The division represents the interests of psychologists engaged in the delivery of comprehensive psychological services to children, adolescents, and families in schools and other applied settings. The division is dedicated to facilitating the professional practice of school psychology and actively advocates in domains such as education and health care reform, which have significant implications for the practice of psychology with children at http://education. indiana.edu/~div16/index.html.

Global School Psychology Network: The Global School Psychology Network is an innovative Internet community for school psychologists. It is dedicated to professional development, peer support, problem-solving assistance, and research. Its main goal is to develop and improve a true community in which participants advance their professional knowledge, provide and receive peer support, and actively involve themselves in developing the community at http:// www.dac.neu.edu/cp/consult/index.html.

International School Psychology Association: ISPA's mission is to promote the use of sound psychological principles within the context of education all over the world, to promote communication between professionals who are committed to the improvement of the mental health of children in the world's schools, to encourage the use of school psychologists in countries where they are not currently being used, to promote the psychological rights of all children all over the world, and to initiate and promote cooperation with other organizations working for purposes similar to those of ISPA in order to help children and families at http://www.ispaweb.org/en/index.html.

National Association of School Psychologists: The National Association of School Psychologists represents and supports school psychology through leadership to enhance the mental health and educational competence of all children at http://www.nasponline.org/index2. html.

National Association of School Nurses: NASN's core purpose is to advance the delivery of professional school health services to promote optimal learning in students at http://www. nasn.org/.

National Association of School Nurses for the Deaf: To enhance the quality of health education and services to deaf students through education, networking, and promoting effective communication between deaf and hearing at http:// www.nasnd.org/.

National Association of State School Nurse Consultants, Inc.: To promote the health and learning of the nation's children and youth by providing national leadership and advocacy, impacting

public policy, collaborating, and proactively influencing school health programs and school nursing practice at http://lserver.aea14.k12. ia.us/swp/tadkins/nassnc/nassnc.html.

National Association of Social Workers: NASW is the largest membership organization of professional social workers in the world, with *more than 152,000 members*. NASW works to enhance the professional growth and development of its members, to create and maintain professional standards, and to advance sound social policies at http://www.socialworkers. org/default.asp.

North American Association of Christians in Social Work: NACSW supports the integration of Christian faith and professional social work practice in the lives of its members, the profession, and the church, promoting love and justice in social service and social reform at http://www.nacsw.org/index.shtml.

School Social Work Association of America: The School Social Work Association of America is dedicated to promoting the profession of school social work and the professional development of school social workers in order to enhance the educational experience of students and their families at http://www.sswaa. org/index.html.

Social Work Examination Services: Since 1983, Social Work Examination Services has been the leader in providing on-site review courses and home study programs specifically designed to prepare social workers for license examinations throughout the United States at http://www. swes.net/.

Key Points to Remember

Secemsky and Ahlman (2003), although writing about school social work practice specifically, provide a useful set of reasons for any mental health professionals interested in working as providers of services in educational settings to attain credentialing, certification, and licensing. These authors identified the following four reasons for school social workers to pursue the license of clinical social work, but they can be extended to include the other mental health professionals considered in this chapter:

• Professional codes of ethics
• Professional standards of practice

- Credentialing, certification, and licensing may be used as a negotiation point in employment
- Licensing acts as a means of substantiating professional expertise, without which school officials may look to other school personnel who have such credentials instead of school social workers, psychologists, counselors, and nurses

References

Allen-Meares, P. (2004). *Social work services in schools* (4th ed.). Boston: Allyn & Bacon.

Biggerstaff, M. A. (1995). Licensing, regulation, and certification. In R. L. Edwards (Ed.), *Encyclopedia of Social Work* (19th ed., Vol. 2, pp. 1616–1624). Washington, DC: NASW Press.

Constable, R., & Thomas, G. (2002). Assessment, multidisciplinary teamwork, and consultation: Foundations for role development. In R. Constable, S. McDonald, & J. P. Flynn (Eds.), *School social work: Practice, policy, and research perspectives* (5th ed., pp. 153–162). Chicago, IL: Lyceum Books, Inc.

Hawkins, M. (1982). State certification standards for school social work practice. *Social Work in Education, 4,* 41–52.

National Association of School Nurses. (2004). *National association of school nurses.* Retrieved from http://www.nasn.org/.

National Association of School Psychologists. (2004). *What is a school psychologist?* Retrieved from http://www.nasponline.org/about_nasp/whatisa.html.

National Association of Social Workers [NASW]. (2002a). *Certified school social work specialist (C-SSWS): Information booklet.* Washington, DC: Author.

National Association of Social Workers [NASW]. (2002b). *Standards for school social work services: Information booklet.* Washington, DC: Author.

School Social Workers of America [SSWA]. (2004). *School social workers of America.* Retrieved from http://www.sswaa.org/index.html.

Secemsky, V. O., & Ahlman, C. (2003). Proposed guidelines for school social workers seeking clinical supervision: How to choose a supervisor. *School Social Work Journal, 27*(2), 80–88.

Torres, S. (1998). The status of school social workers in America. In E. M. Freeman, C. G. Franklin, R. Fong, G. L. Shaffer, & E. M. Timberlake (Eds.), *Multisystem skills and interventions in school social work practice* (pp. 461–472). Washington, DC: NASW Press.

U.S. Department of Labor Bureau of Labor Statistics. (2004a). *Counselors.* Retrieved from http://stats.bls.gov/oco/ocos067.htm.

U.S. Department of Labor Bureau of Labor Statistics. (2004b). *Psychologists.* Retrieved from http://stats.bls.gov/oco/ocos056.htm.

U.S. Department of Labor Bureau of Labor Statistics. (2004c). *Social workers.* Retrieved from http://stats.bls.gov/oco/ocos060.htm.

Professional Requirements for School Social Work and Other School Mental Health Professions

Sandra J. Altshuler

Getting Started

Working as a social worker within a host institution such an educational institution requires a strong awareness of professional requirements, expectations, and boundaries. Social workers need to learn about the political processes, collaborative and conflictual relationships, strengths, and challenges contained within a singular school system. A public school has been compared to a political institution (Lee, 1983), with its accompanying challenges of developing informal and formal power bases from which to effect change. Along with power, the school social worker needs to pursue successful interdisciplinary cooperation and collaboration (Allen-Meares & Pugach, 1982). To accomplish this, all mental health professionals, including social workers, need to be cognizant of each other's strengths, capacities, and limitations.

Working within a host setting requires an ability to be a "team player," in collaboration with other related professionals, not just teachers (Gibelman, 1993). As an intrinsic member of multidisciplinary teams, social workers must be familiar with the other members' strengths, knowledge base, and areas of expertise. One approach to begin this familiarity is to know about their educational and practicum experiences and the specific requirements for state certification.

This chapter begins with a general overview of the current climate for school social workers, school psychologists, and school counselors. Then, we will review the various requirements for state certification for each of the three mental health professions. Three separate tables are included in this chapter, which highlight the specific requirements, by state, for certification. Using the tables as guides, the remainder of this chapter describes in detail the similarities and differences between and

among the three professions. The chapter then concludes with each state's Department of Education Web site wherein one can find more specific information for professional requirements in that state.

What We Know

Table 108.1 highlights the certification information for school social workers across the 50 states. School social workers are employed by 43 states, 31 of which provide certification at the state level. The number of school social workers employed by states varies from almost none to more than 2,000 in both Illinois and New York. There are no apparent regional trends, and often states that do provide certification border upon states that do not. Of the states that do certify, 16 states have reciprocity with other states for certification. Indiana and Virginia have reciprocity with all 50 states, and Michigan and Wisconsin have reciprocity only on a case-by-case basis after a review.

All 50 states have certification for both school psychologists and school counselors. Table 108.2 reports on the certification information for school counselors, showing, for example, that 36 states currently have reciprocity with other states. Some states will accept certification from other states but require additional training in state law and constitution, and 38 states require some form of background check. Some states, such as Nevada, require U.S. citizenship. Many states that do not require a background check require that applicants "be of good moral character," but do not specify how this is demonstrated. As can be seen in Table 108.3, there is a significant level of agreement across the states for the certification requirements for school psychologists, which may

Table 108.1 Requirements for School Social Workers, by State

State	Employ SSWs	Certify SSWs	No. of SSWs	Education Requirements/ Specific Coursework Topics	Practicum/Internship/ Experience	Exam	Reciprocity (No. of States)	Background Check?
AL	Yes	No	<25	N/A	N/A	N/A	N/A	N/A
AK	Yes	Yes	<50	BSW; Alaska studies & multicultural/ cross-cultural communications	None	None	None	Yes
AZ	No	No	150	N/A	N/A	N/A	N/A	N/A
AR	Yes	No	<50	N/A	N/A	N/A	N/A	N/A
CA	Yes	Yes	250	MSW; school social work courses must be included in MSW program	450-hour practicum	CBEST	None	Yes
CO	Yes	Yes	403	MSW; children & the law school social work program	None	PLACE	Yes	Yes
CT	Yes	Yes	300	MSW; special education	1 school year	Praxis I	24	Yes
DE	Yes	Yes	UNK	BSW	None	Praxis I	36	No
FL	Yes	Yes	601	BSW	None	FBET & AST	Yes	Yes
GA	Yes	Yes	175	BSW	Obtain job then apply for certification	None	24	Yes
HI	Yes	No	50	BSW	Teaching experience	N/A	N/A	N/A
ID	Yes	Yes	75	MSW	300 + hour practicum	Praxis I	None	Yes
IL	Yes	Yes	2,200	MSW; disabilities & school law	600-hour practicum	Praxis II	38	Yes
IN	Yes	Yes	125	BSW	5 years experience	None	50	Yes
IA	Yes	Yes	350	MSW	2 years supervised practice	None	None	Yes
KS	Yes	Yes	200	MSW; children, youth & families, substance abuse, exceptional child, & school social work program	1 year MSW practicum or 720 hours supervised practice	None	No	Yes
KY	Yes	Yes	125	MSW; school social work program	Yes	None	Yes	Yes
LA	Yes	Yes	200	MSW	Yes or supervised employment	None	None	Yes

ME	No	No	100	N/A	N/A	N/A	N/A	N/A
MD	Yes	No	250	N/A	N/A	N/A	N/A	N/A
MA	Yes	Yes	600	MSW; school law, juvenile justice, learning disabilities	900 hours	None	Yes	No
MI	Yes	Yes	1,000	MSW; school social work program, disabilities school law & policy	500 + hours	None	Case-by-case	Yes
MN	Yes	Yes	600	BSW; human relations	None	None	None	No
MS	No	No	25	N/A	N/A	N/A	N/A	N/A
MO	Yes	No	125	N/A	N/A	N/A	N/A	N/A
MT	Yes	No	UNK	N/A	N/A	N/A	N/A	N/A
NE	Yes	No	12	N/A	N/A	N/A	N/A	N/A
NV	Yes	Yes	15	MSW; school social work program	Yes	No	No	Yes
NH	Yes	Yes	50	BSW	None	Praxis I	34	Yes
NJ	Yes	Yes	1,500	BSW; children's policies & school systems; disabilities	3 years teaching or SW experience, or MSW	None	None	Yes
NM	Yes	Yes	150	BSW	None	None	None	Yes
NY	Yes	Yes	2,500	BA + child abuse & neglect	Supervised internship	None	Yes	Yes
NC	Yes	Yes	200	BSW	Yes	None	24	Yes
ND	No	No	25	N/A	N/A	N/A	N/A	N/A
OH	Yes	Yes	350+	MSW; school social work program	Yes	None	None	Yes
OK	No	No	12	N/A	N/A	N/A	N/A	N/A
OR	No	No	40	N/A	N/A	N/A	N/A	N/A
PA	No	No	175	N/A	N/A	N/A	N/A	N/A
RI	Yes	No	100	N/A	N/A	N/A	N/A	N/A
SC	Yes	No	75	N/A	N/A	N/A	N/A	N/A

(continued)

Table 108.1 (*Continued*)

State	Employ SSW's	Certify SSW's	No. of SSW's	Education Requirements/ Specific Coursework Topics	Practicum/Internship/ Experience	Exam	Reciprocity (No. of States)	Background Check?
SD	Yes	No	12	N/A	N/A	N/A	N/A	N/A
TN	Yes	Yes	75	MSW; school social work courses	Yes	Praxis II	24	Yes
TX	Yes	Yes	225	MSW	None	License Exam	Yes	Yes
UT	Yes	Yes	50	MSW	Yes	None	30	Yes
VT	Yes	No	25	N/A	N/A	N/A	N/A	N/A
VA	Yes	Yes	350	MSW; school social work courses	400 hours or 1 year supervised FT experience	No	50	No
WA	Yes	Yes	125	MSW; school social work; courses/knowledge	Yes	Praxis II	24	Yes
WV	Yes	No	UNK	N/A	N/A	N/A	N/A	N/A
WI	Yes	Yes	500	MSW; program planning; special populations	Yes	None	Case-by-case	Yes
WY	Yes	Yes	75	MSW	Yes	None	None	Yes

Table 108.2 Requirements for School Counselors, by State

State	Employ S. Cnslrs	Certify S. Cnslrs	Education Requirements/ Specific Coursework Topics	Practicum/Internship/ Experience	Exam	Reciprocity (No. of States)	Background Check?
AL	Yes	Yes	MA counseling	2 years full-time educational experience	Varies	Yes	Yes
AK	Yes	Yes	Degree in counseling	None	Praxis I	Yes	Yes
AZ	Yes	Yes	MA school guidance & counseling	2 years full-time educational experience or 3 years teaching experience or completion of supervised practicum in school counseling	None	Yes	Yes
AR	Yes	Yes	MA school guidance & counseling	Be eligible to hold a valid AR teaching certificate or 1-year full-time teaching experience	Praxis II	Yes	Yes
CA	Yes	Yes	BA + 48 semester hours post-bacc. work in school counseling	None	CBEST	Yes	Yes
CO	Yes	Yes	MA school guidance & counseling	None	PLACE[a]	Yes	Yes
CT	Yes	Yes	MA (at least 30 semester hours in school counseling) & 36 clock hours special education	Completion of practicum and laboratory experience & be eligible for CT professional educator certificate & 30 school months teaching experience or 10-month full-time supervised internship (in addition to practicum)	Praxis I	Yes (13)	Yes
DE	Yes	Yes	MA elementary/secondary school counseling or MA (at least 27 semester hours in guidance/ counseling)	3 years professional experience in a school or 1 year full-time supervised internship	Praxis I	Yes	Yes
FL	Yes	Yes	MA school guidance & counseling or MA (at least 30 semester hours in school counseling)	None	CLAST	Yes	Yes

(continued)

Table 108.2 (*Continued*)

State	Employ S. Cnslrs	Certify S. Cnslrs	Education Requirements/ Specific Coursework Topics	Practicum/Internship/ Experience	Exam	Reciprocity (No. of States)	Background Check?
GA	Yes	Yes	MA school guidance & counseling	None	Praxis II	Yes	Yes
HI	Yes	Yes	MA from teacher education program in school counseling	None	Praxis I Praxis II	Yes	Yes
ID	Yes	Yes	MA school guidance & counseling; recency credit (6 semester credits in 5 years)	700 hours supervised field experience, 1/2 in K–12 school	None	Yes	Yes
IL	Yes	Yes	MA school guidance & counseling	3 semester hours & 100 clock hours practicum & 3 semester hours internship & be eligible for IL teaching certificate	Praxis II	No	No
IN	Yes	Yes	MA counseling or MA (at least 30 semester hours in guidance/ counseling)	Completion of supervised practicum in counseling & 2 years teaching experience or out-of-state license and 1 year experience or 1 year counseling internship	None	Yes	Yes
IA	Yes	Yes	MA	500 clock hours teaching and counseling experience	None	No	Yes
KS	Yes	Yes	MA school counseling recency credit	Eligible for a KS teaching certificate; 2 years teaching experience	Praxis II	No	Yes
KY	Yes	Yes	MA guidance & counseling	Eligible for a KY teaching certificate; 1 year full-time teaching experience	None	Yes level	Yes, required at district
LA	Yes	Yes	MA guidance & counseling	Eligible for a LA teaching certificate; 3 years experience	Praxis II	No	Yes
ME	Yes	Yes	MA guidance & counseling	1 year full-time internship as school counselor; 2 years prior work experience	None	Yes	Yes

MD	Yes	Yes	MA guidance & counseling	2 years experience as teacher or school counselor or 500 clock hours supervised school guidance/counseling practicum	None	Yes	Yes
MA	Yes	Yes	MA counseling	450 clock hour practicum	MA Test[b]	Yes	No
MI	Yes	Yes	MA school guidance & counseling	School counseling practicum	MI Test[c]	Yes	Yes
MN	Yes	Yes	MA school guidance & counseling	400-hour supervised practicum, MN human relations program: diversity & communication	Praxis I	Yes	Yes
MS	Yes	Yes	MA guidance & counseling or MA in another area & completion of guidance & counseling program or NCSC credential	Hold MS teaching certificate or 1 full year internship	Praxis II	Yes	No
MO	Yes	Yes	MA guidance & counseling	3 semester hours practicum	Praxis II	Yes	Yes
MT	Yes	Yes	MA guidance & counseling & recency credit	600 hours supervised school internship	None	Yes	No
NE	Yes	Yes	MA counseling & recency credit	Hold a NE teaching certificate & 2 years teaching experience	Praxis I	Yes	Yes, for non-NE residents
NV	Yes	Yes	MA counseling or related field or NCSC credential & coursework in US, NV constitution, NV school law	If MA in related field, must have 2 years teaching or school counseling experience	Praxis II[d]	No	Yes
NH	Yes	Yes	MA guidance & counseling or sufficient experience in education or other professions to provide competencies, skills & knowledge	None with MA; w/o MA, must have 3 months full-time teaching experience	Praxis II[e]	Yes	Yes
NJ	Yes	Yes	BA + 30 semester hours post-bacc. work in guidance & counseling	Eligible for a NJ teaching certificate & 1 year teaching experience	None	No	Yes

(continued)

Table 108.2 (Continued)

State	Employ S. Cnslrs	Certify S. Cnslrs	Education Requirements / Specific Coursework Topics	Practicum/Internship / Experience	Exam	Reciprocity (No. of States)	Background Check?
NM	Yes	Yes	MA school counseling or MA in alternate field with 36–42 graduate hours in school counseling	Non-school counseling MAs must complete practicum in a school, valid Level II NM teaching license or 3 years experience in teaching, school counseling, clinical practice, mental health, educational administration	None	No	Yes
NY	Yes	Yes	BA+30 semester hours post-B.A. work in school counseling & 2 hours training in identifying & reporting child abuse	None	None	Yes	No
NC	Yes	Yes	MA guidance & counseling	None	Praxis II	Yes	Yes, required at district level
ND	Yes	Yes	MA school counseling	450 hour internship in school	None	No	Yes
OH	Yes	Yes	MA school counseling	2 years teaching experience & 600-hour school internship or 600-hour school internship & 1 year induction under supervision of licensed school counselor or 3 years experience as a licensed school counselor in other state	Praxis II	No	Yes
OK	Yes	Yes	MA guidance & counseling; recency credit/experience	2 years related experience	OK exams[f]	Yes	Depends on district
OR	Yes	Yes	MA education & 24 quarter hours in counseling; No MA degree needed w/2 years teaching experience	6 quarter hour supervised practicum or internship or 1 year school counseling experience; must complete teaching & counseling practica	CBEST or Praxis I	Yes	Yes

State						
PA	Yes	Yes	BA school counseling	300-hour supervised school counseling internship	None	No	Yes
RI	Yes	Yes	BA & advanced degree in school counseling or MA w/24 semester hours in school counseling	3 semester hour internship; eligible for RI teaching certificate & 2 years teaching experience	None	Yes	No
SC	Yes	Yes	BA & MA school counseling	None	Praxis II	Yes	Yes
SD	Yes	Yes	BA & MA school counseling & guidance; recency credit	600 clock hours supervised school internship	None	No	No
TN	Yes	Yes	MA school counseling	1 semester school counseling internship	Praxis II	Yes	Yes, required at district level
TX	Yes	Yes	BA + 30 semester hours graduate program in counseling	Supervised practicum; hold valid TX teacher certificate & 3 years teaching	TX exam teaching	Yes	Yes
UT	Yes	Yes	MA school counseling & guidance	Practicum experience & 600-hour supervised field experience	None	Yes	Yes
VT	Yes	Yes	MA guidance	300 clock hours supervised internship in school guidance & 180 clock hours field experience	None[g]	No	Yes
VA	Yes	Yes	MA counseling	At least 200 hours clinical experience; 2 years full-time teaching/counseling experience	None	Yes	No
WA	Yes	Yes	MA counseling & 10 clock hours of coursework related to issues of abuse	None	Praxis II or NCE	Yes	Yes

(continued)

Table 108.2 (*Continued*)

State	Employ S. Cnslrs	Certify S. Cnslrs	Education Requirements/ Specific Coursework Topics	Practicum/Internship/ Experience	Exam	Reciprocity (No. of States)	Background Check?
WI	Yes	Yes	MA school counseling & guidance or MA including 30 semester hours in counseling & guidance	Eligible for a WI teaching license & 2 years teaching experience, or teaching degree & 2 years teaching experience, or 1 year full-time internship in school counseling, or 2 years experience as licensed school counselor at 3/4 time or more & 2 years teaching experience or 1 year full-time internship in school counseling	Pending review	No	Yes
WY	Yes	Yes	MA counseling & guidance	Practicum or internship in a school setting	None[h]	Yes	Yes

[a]School counseling & guidance specialty.
[b]Exams in literacy & communication only.
[c]Exams in teaching, guidance, & counseling.
[d]Exams in NV school law, NV & U.S. constitutions also required, if no courses in this area.
[e]Without MA, must also take NH exams.
[f]OK teaching exam & OK school counseling; without teaching certification, must also take OK general education exam.
[g]Says "must demonstrate competence."
[h]Exams in U.S. & WY constitutions only.

Table 108.3 Requirements for School Psychologists, by State

State	Employ S. Psychs	Certify S. Psychs	Education Requirements/ Specific Coursework Topics	Practicum/Internship/ Experience	Exam	Reciprocity (No. of States)	Background Check?
AL	Yes	Yes	NASP standards[a]	NASP standards[a]	NASP standards[a]	Yes	Yes
AK	Yes	Yes	NASP standards[a]	NASP standards[a]	NASP standards[a]	Case-by-case	Yes
AZ	Yes	Yes	MA or higher in school psychology (60 graduate semester hours)	Verified 1,000+ hour practicum	Praxis II	Yes, w/ Praxis II	Yes
AR	Yes	Yes	BA or higher in school psychology	Supervised practicum	Praxis II	Yes	Yes
CA	Yes	Yes	2 years post-B.A. study in school psychology	Practicum	CBEST	Yes	Yes
CO	Yes	Yes	NASP standards[a]	NASP standards[a]	NASP standards[a]	Yes, w/NASP standards	Yes
CT	Yes	Yes	45 semester hours in school psychology graduate program	Supervised practicum & 10-month supervised school psychology internship	Praxis I	Yes (11 states)	Yes
DE	Yes	Yes	NASP standards[a]	NASP standards[a]	NASP standards[a]	Yes	Yes
FL	Yes	Yes	MA or higher in school psychology (60 graduate semester hours) will also accept NCSP	Year-long supervised school psychology internship (6–12 semester hours)	Praxis II	Yes	Yes
GA	Yes	Yes	NASP standards[a]	NASP standards[a]	NASP standards[a]	Yes	Yes
HI	Yes	Yes	MA or higher in school psychology	Internship	Praxis II	Yes	Yes
ID	Yes	Yes	MA or higher in school psychology	Internship	Praxis II	Yes	Yes
IL	Yes	Yes	MA or higher in psychology or education psychology w/ specialization in school psychology (60 semester hours)	Practicum (at least 250 hours in school setting) & 1,200 clock hours (1 year) supervised internship	Praxis II	Yes, if IL req's met	Yes
IN	Yes	Yes	NASP standards[a]	NASP standards[a]	NASP standards[a]	No	Yes

(continued)

Table 108.3 (*Continued*)

State	Employ S. Psychs	Certify S. Psychs	Education Requirements / Specific Coursework Topics	Practicum/Internship/ Experience	Exam	Reciprocity (No. of States)	Background Check?
IA	Yes	Yes	NASP standards[a]	NASP standards[a]	NASP standards[a]	No	Yes
KS	Yes	Yes	MA or higher in school psychology (69 graduate semester hours)	1 year full-time internship	Praxis I	No	Yes
KY	Yes	Yes	MA or higher in school psychology (60 graduate semester hours)	1 year full-time internship	Praxis II	Yes	Yes
LA	Yes	Yes	NASP standards[a]	NASP standards[a]	NASP standards[a]	No	Yes
ME	Yes	Yes	NASP standards[a]	NASP standards[a]	NASP standards[a]	No	Yes
MD	Yes	Yes	NASP standards[a]	NASP standards[a]	NASP standards[a]	Case-by-case	No
MA	Yes	Yes	NASP standards[a]	NASP standards[a]	NASP standards[a]	Yes	No
MI	Yes	Yes	MA w/ a min 60 graduate semester hours in school psychology	1,200 clock hour supervised internship, at least 600 of which must be in a school setting	None	Yes	Yes
MN	Yes	Yes	MA or higher in school psychology (60 graduate semester hours)	Practicum & full-time 1-year internship	Praxis II	Yes	No
MS	Yes	Yes	MA or higher in school psychology	1 year full-time internship	Praxis I	Yes	No
MO	Yes	Yes	MA or higher in school psychology (60 graduate semester hours)	400 clock hour practicum & 2-year teaching experience	Praxis II	Yes	Yes
MT	Yes	Yes	MA or higher in school psychology	Internship	Praxis I	Yes	No
NE	Yes	Yes	MA or higher in school psychology	Internship & practicum	Praxis I	Yes	Yes[b]
NV	Yes	Yes	NASP standards[a]	NASP standards[a]	NASP standards[a]	No	Yes
NH	Yes	Yes	NASP standards[a]	NASP standards[a]	NASP standards[a]	Yes	Yes
NJ	Yes	Yes	MA or higher in school psychology	300 clock hour practicum & 1,200 clock hour supervised externship	Praxis II	No	Yes

State		Degree	Experience	Examination		
NM	Yes	MA or higher in school psychology	1,200 clock hour supervised internship	Praxis II	No	Yes
NY	Yes	MA or higher in school psychology (60 graduate semester hours)	Supervised internship/practicum	None	Yes	No
NC	Yes	MA or higher in school psychology	1,200 clock hour supervised externship	Praxis II	Yes	Yes, by district
ND	Yes	MA or higher in school psychology	1,200 clock hour supervised internship	Praxis I	No	Yes
OH	Yes	MA or higher in school psychology	4 years experience including 1–year internship	Praxis II	No	Yes
OK	Yes	NASP standards[a]	NASP standards[a]	NASP standards[a]	Yes	Yes, by district
OR	Yes	NASP standards[a]	NASP standards[a]	NASP standards[a]	Yes	Yes
PA	Yes	MA or higher in school psychology	Internship & practicum	Praxis II	No	Yes
RI	Yes	MA or higher in school psychology	Internship & practicum	None	Yes	No
SC	Yes	MA or higher in school psychology	Supervised internship	Praxis II	Yes	Yes
SD	Yes	NASP standards[a]	NASP standards[a]	NASP standards[a]	No	No
TN	Yes	MA or higher in school psychology	Internship	Praxis II	Yes	Yes, by district
TX	Yes	NASP standards[a]	NASP standards[a]	NASP standards[a]	Yes	Yes
UT	Yes	MA or higher in school psychology (60 graduate semester hours)	1,200 clock hour (1 year) supervised internship	None	Yes	Yes
VT	Yes	MA or higher in school psychology (60 graduate semester hours)	600 clock hour supervised internship	Praxis II	No	Yes
VA	Yes	NASP standards[a]	NASP standards[a]	NASP standards[a]	Yes	No

(continued)

Table 108.3 (Continued)

State	Employ S. Psychs	Certify S. Psychs	Education Requirements/ Specific Coursework Topics	Practicum/Internship/ Experience	Exam	Reciprocity (No. of States)	Background Check?
WA	Yes	Yes	NASP standards[a]	NASP standards[a]	NASP standards[a]	Yes	Yes
WV	Yes	Yes	MA or higher in school psychology	Supervised internship	Praxis II	Yes	No
WI	Yes	Yes	MA or higher in school psychology (60 graduate semester hours)	1,200 clock hour supervised internship	Praxis II	No	Yes
WY	Yes	Yes	NASP standards[a]	NASP standards[a]	NASP standards[a]	Yes	Yes

[a]National Association of School Psychologists (NASP):
• Coursework: Completion of 60 graduate semester/90 quarter hours of study through a "school psychology" program. Of these hours, a maximum of 6 semester/9 quarter hours can be in supervised practicum.
• Internship: Completion of a 1,200 hour institutionally recognized school psychology internship, at least 600 hours of which must be in a school setting.
• Examination: The National School Psychology Examination (Praxis Series of Education Testing). A minimum score of 660 must be achieved. Test scores remain valid for 5 years, after which the test must be retaken.
• Those certified by the NASP become nationally certified school psychologists (NCSPs). There is a current movement for more states to adopt these standards for their certification process.

[b]Required only for non–NE residents.

explain why all 50 states have reciprocity. The reader is encouraged to refer to Tables 108.1–3 for the remainder of the chapter's discussion.

Certification Requirements

The certification requirements for both school social workers and school counselors vary greatly by state, while the requirements for school psychologists are remarkably consistent across all the states. As you will read, school psychologists in almost all 50 states are required to have at least a master's degree in school psychology, while some school social workers and school counselors are required to have only a bachelor's degree. Similarly, the internship or practicum requirements are consistent across the 50 states for school psychologists, but vary widely for both school social workers and school counselors. The National Association of School Psychologists (NASP) has set specific standards for certification that have been adopted by 20 states. These standards include a graduate degree in school psychology, completion of a 1,200-hour internship, and a passing score on a national school psychology exam.

Educational Requirements

For school social workers, only 20 states require a master of social work (MSW) degree for certification, 10 require a bachelor of social work (BSW) degree, and 1, New York, requires a bachelor of arts (BA) in any discipline. Some of the states specify coursework as part of their requirements. For example, Illinois requires coursework in educational disabilities, school law, and school social work practice. Most other states do not cite any specific coursework beyond the foundational requirements of the degrees.

Two states, Arkansas and California, do not specifically require a master's degree for certification as a school psychologist. However, California does require 2 years of postbaccalaureate study in school psychology, which is identical to master's level work, thereby leaving Arkansas as the only state not requiring education beyond a bachelor's degree for school psychologists. All 50 states require degrees and coursework from only approved school psychology programs. All of these programs require at least five content areas of study, including psychological foundations (biological, social, and cultural bases of behavior; child

and adolescent development), educational foundations (school organization and operation, instructional design), interventions/problem solving (direct and indirect interventions, thorough assessments), statistics and research methodologies (measurement, statistics, evaluation methods), and professional school psychology (legal, ethical, professional, historical issues; role and function of school psychologist).

Similarly, all 50 states require coursework or a degree in guidance and counseling for school counselors. A master's degree in counseling, school guidance, or school counseling is required in 43 states. Alaska is the only state in the country that specifies only a "degree in counseling," while Oregon accepts either a master's degree with some courses in school counseling, or a bachelor's degree with two years of teaching experience. Five other states, California, New Jersey, New York, Rhode Island, and Texas, require a bachelor's degree with anywhere from 24 to 58 semester hours of postbaccalaureate work in school counseling, which is similar to completing master's level work. Some states also require education in specific areas such as state constitution, U.S. constitution, special education, state school law, or identification and reporting of child abuse. Most of the certified programs require the following coursework content: human growth and development, consultation skills, individual and group counseling, individual and group assessment, and professional development.

Internship/Practicum Experience

In addition to educational requirements, states often require mental health professionals working in school systems to produce proof of some type of internship or practicum experience. The nature of the requirements varies from state to state and from profession to profession. In some states a practicum or internship completed as part of their education is accepted or required as experience. Some states specify how many hours or years of experience they require, while others will accept the number of hours determined by the applicant's university.

There are 24 states that require some form of internship or practicum experience for school social work certification. Hawaii and New Jersey are the only states that accept teaching experience in lieu of social work experience, although Hawaii does not have certification for school social workers. On the minimal end, Alaska, Minnesota, New Hampshire, and New Mexico have no specific requirements for any internship or experience and accept the BSW degree for certification. Other states that accept the BSW degree, like Delaware, Indiana, New Jersey, New York, and North Carolina, all require internship hours or extensive years of experience (for example, Indiana requires 5 years of experience) for certification. On the opposite end of the spectrum, the 20 states that require an MSW also vary in their requirements for experience, with Colorado and Texas as the only states that have no internship or practicum experience specified for certification.

For school psychologist certification, all 50 states require an internship or practicum, and many require both. Missouri is the only state that requires teaching experience, but it requires significantly fewer practicum hours (400) than the other 49 states. Vermont requires 600 hours of a supervised internship, while the remaining 48 states all require at least 1,200 hours of an institutionally recognized school psychology internship. Additional specifications regarding a practicum completed within a school system range from 250 hours to the NASP standard of 600 hours.

There is a large variation in experience requirements for school counselor certification. About a dozen states do not require any experience, some states require or accept practicum hours as experience, almost half of the states require teaching licenses and teaching experience, and in some states the amount of experience needed depends upon the educational degree that the applicant possesses. For example, in Oregon, 2 years of teaching experience can negate the requirement for a master's degree. Alaska, California, New York, and South Carolina are the only four states that have no experience requirements for school counselors while accepting a bachelor's-level degree for certification. Nine other states that have no specified experience requirements accept only a master's degree in school guidance or counseling. It is likely that the vast majority of these programs require internships for students to earn their master's degrees, despite the lack of the state requirements for documenting such experiences for certification.

Examination Requirements

Many of the states utilize the Educational Testing Service (ETS), a national organization that administers a wide variety of tests, including college admission tests. The ETS has a section entitled the Praxis Series that administers the tests specific to school social work, school psychology, and school counseling for states that require it for certification. The Praxis I level of tests assesses applicants' general knowledge of basic skills (e.g., reading, writing). The Praxis II level of tests are designed to assess applicants' specific knowledge relative to their area of expertise (e.g., school social work, school psychology) and may be taken only in conjunction with the Praxis I. Therefore, on Tables 108.1–3, when the exam requirement states "Praxis II," that means that the candidate must also pass the Praxis I test. For all three mental health professionals, California has developed its own examination, reputed to be equivalent to the level of at least the Praxis I basic skills test. Colorado uses its own PLACE exam for school social workers and school counselors.

There are examination requirements in 11 states for school social work certification. Three states whose minimal educational standard is the BSW—Delaware, Florida, and New Hampshire—also require successful passage of the Praxis I or its equivalent. Of the eight states that require both an MSW and successful passage of an exam, only three—Illinois, Tennessee, and Washington—require passage of the advanced Praxis II exam or its equivalent.

To become certified as a school psychologist, applicants in 45 states must pass either the Praxis I basic skills tests or the Praxis II special subject area tests. Four states require only the Praxis I: Connecticut, Montana, Nebraska, and North Dakota. Michigan, New York, Rhode Island, and Utah have no examination requirements for certification.

The examination requirements for school counselors vary from state to state. While 20 states require applicants to pass the Praxis II, 6 states require passage of only the Praxis I exam and 17 states have no examination requirements for certification. There are a variety of state-created exams used, such as those created in California, Michigan, and Oklahoma.

What School Social Workers Can Do

In reviewing the requirements across states for the varying mental health professionals working in educational settings, there are some clear patterns that emerge. First, school psychologists appear to have the most consistent requirements across states, for education, experience, and examination expectations. Even states that do not specify the NASP requirements as their criteria appear to follow those guidelines. Second, the experience expectations for school counselors have a wide range of variance—from no hours required whatsoever to 5 years of teaching experience in a school setting. Third, school counselors are the mental health professionals most likely to be required to have a teaching certificate before they can earn their counseling certification.

As noted in the introduction to this chapter, school social workers need to pursue successful interdisciplinary cooperation and collaboration (Allen-Meares & Pugach, 1982). One tool for accomplishing this is to be cognizant of the skills and strengths of the myriad of professionals they encounter in the school system. This is difficult when the state-mandated certifications are not always clear or consistent. As a result, social workers, counselors, and psychologists working in school systems often find themselves challenging each other's turfs and boundaries because of the vagueness of the rules and mandates across states.

The information provided in this chapter is designed to provide school social workers with a clearer picture of the various states' expectations for each of the three closely aligned professions. With this picture, it is hoped that school social workers will be able to demarcate their own turf and boundaries, while simultaneously respecting their colleagues'. This will strengthen their ability to be team players, working in collaboration, rather than conflict, with psychologists and counselors, for the overall betterment of the students and school systems they serve. Rather than wasting time in protecting turf, school social workers can model the professional ethic of prioritizing the needs of clients (NASW, 1999) and supporting their colleagues' efforts in similar goals.

What is most striking, perhaps, in reviewing this information is the fact that, in comparison especially to school psychologists, school social workers have significant macro-level work to be done. School social workers lag behind other school-based mental health professionals throughout the vast majority of states in certification processes, requirements, and expectations. Illinois is one of the states with the most well-delineated set of requirements and simultaneously is a state with one of the highest numbers of employed school

social workers. The rest of the country would benefit from learning from the Illinois model, where the Illinois Association of School Social Workers has been in existence for over 30 years and has established a clear and important presence throughout the state. Without such presence, legitimacy, and qualifications recognized at the state level, school social workers will be challenged in their ability to work effectively within educational settings for the benefit of youth today.

Key Points to Remember

- Familiarity with the different state requirements can help to facilitate collaboration among school mental health professionals.
- The examination and certification requirements for both school social workers and school counselors vary greatly by state, while the requirements for school psychologists are consistent across all the states.
- Social worker certification lags behind other school mental health professions in a comprehensive standard of requirements, experience, and certification, leaving work to be done on the macro level.
- Illinois provides a model for social work certification; its requirements are clearly delineated and the state employs the highest number of school social workers.

List of Web Contacts, by State

Alabama: www.alsde.edu
Alaska: www.educ.state.ak.us
Arizona: www.ade.state.az.us
Arkansas: arkedu.state.ar.us
California: www.ctc.ca.gov
Colorado: www.cde.state.co.us
Connecticut: www.state.ct.us/sde
Delaware: www.doe.state.de.us
Washington, DC: www.k12.dc.us
Florida: www.firn.edu/doe
Georgia: gapsc.com
Hawaii: www.k12.hi.us
Idaho: www.sde.state.id.us
Illinois: www.isbe.state.il.us
Indiana: ideanet.doe.state.in.us

Iowa: www.state.ia.us
Kansas: www.ksbe.state.ks.us
Kentucky: www.kde.state.ky.us
Louisiana: www.doe.state.la.us
Maine: www.state.me.us
Maryland: www.msde.state.md.us
Massachusetts: www.doe.mass.edu
Michigan: www.state.mi.us/mde
Minnesota: www.educ.state.mn.us
Mississippi: www.mdek12.state.ms.us
Missouri: www.dese.state.ms.us
Montana: www.metnet.state.mt.us
Nebraska: www.nde.state.ne.us
Nevada: www.nde.state.nv.us
New Hampshire: www.ed.state.nh.us
New Jersey: www.state.nj.us./education
New Mexico: www.sde.state.nm.us
New York: nysed.gov
North Carolina: www.dpi.state.nc.us
North Dakota: www.state.nd.us/espb
Ohio: www.ode.state.oh.us
Oklahoma: www.sde.state.ok.us
Oregon: www.tspc.state.or.us
Pennsylvania: www.pde.psu.edu
Rhode Island: www.ridoe.net
South Carolina: www.state.sc.us/sde
South Dakota: www.state.sd.us/deca

Tennessee: www.state.tn.us/education
Texas: www.sbec.state.tx.us
Utah: www.usod.k12.ut.us
Vermont: www.state.vt.us/educ
Virginia: www.pen.k12.va.us
Washington: www.k12.wa.us
West Virginia: http://wvde.state.wv.us
Wisconsin: www.dpi.state.wi.us
Wyoming: www.k12.wy.us

References

Allen-Meares, P., & Pugach, M. (1982). Facilitating interdisciplinary collaboration on behalf of handicapped children and youth. *TASE—The Official Journal of the Teacher Education Division of the Council for Exceptional Children, 5*, 30–37.

Gibelman, M. (1993). School social workers, counselors, and psychologists in collaboration: A shared agenda. *Social Work in Education, 15*, 45–53.

Lee, L. J. (1983). The social worker in the political environment of a school system. *Social Work, 28*, 302–307.

National Association of Social Workers. (1999). *Code of Ethics of the National Association of Social Workers.* Washington, DC: Author.

When Supervisor and Supervisee Are of Different Disciplines

Guidelines and Resources

John E. Tropman ▪ Michael E. Woolley ▪ Liang Zhu ▪ Renee Smith

CHAPTER 109

Getting Started

There is a huge literature on supervision, so large that it is hard to know where, really, to get concise and core information about supervision. However, there is almost no empirical literature on the exact topic of supervision with respect to social workers. The literature that can be found is often written abroad and deals with national differences. To make matters more complicated, there are two kinds of supervision that people commonly have in mind when they speak of supervision: clinical and managerial. Clinical, or professional, supervision involves direct responsibility for the substance of the work of the clinical professional. It is essentially case review, planning, and interpretation from a professional perspective. Managerial supervision, on the other hand, looks to the organizational functioning as important. As the lead author has said elsewhere: "You are a managerial supervisor or supervisory manager when you are put in charge of overseeing one or more persons for the purpose of assisting them with the accomplishments of their jobs, and assuring that their assignments jobs are completed in a timely fashion and according to law and policy" (Tropman, in press). There is an emphasis on efficiency (doing things right), innovation (improving the job), and assisting supervisee growth and development.

Of course, it is not possible to completely separate these functions "on the ground." All supervisors do some of both. To complicate matters further, in the social work community, the term *supervisor* is usually used to refer to the professional aspect of supervision, and the term *boss* refers to the managerial aspects. That said, this chapter focuses upon the issues of managerial supervision and problems that occur when the disciplines or backgrounds of supervisor and supervisee differ. Almost all of it will apply to both functions, though the professional supervisor would need to add substantive content related to the discipline to the material reviewed here.

What We Know

Approach/Method

This chapter has been informed by previous research utilizing a focus group approach. In connection with a Children's Bureau grant to the University of Michigan School of Social Work (on which the lead author was Co-PI),[1] focus groups were conducted with supervisors in child welfare to explore the issues they seemed most concerned about, the skills they felt were most important, and the problems that seemed most central to their supervisory life. To broaden and supplement this information, the lead author met with a variety of supervisors and used them as informants and respondents. What emerged were four areas where professional and disciplinary differences matter. One was in mind-set and culture. A second was in the performance of common tasks of supervision. The last two points were cautions. Supervisors, third, stressed that disciplinary and professional differences are exacerbated in several commonly difficult areas, including feedback, giving corrective information, and dealing with difficult people. Fourth, informants cautioned us that the professional and disciplinary difference cleavages were not all that separates us. In particular, they mentioned generational differences, gender differences, and differences in temperament. These general findings are corroborated and elaborated in several books (Bittel & Newstrom, 1992; Broadwell & Dietrich, 1998; Fuller, 1990; Fuller, 1995; Gambrill & Stein, 1983; Humphrey & Stokes, 2000; Middleman & Rhodes, 1985; Perlmutter, Baily, & Netting, 2001; Whetten & Cameron, 2005) and the periodical literature as well (Buhler, 1998; Cole, 1999; Cousins, 2000; Fracaro, 2001a, 2001b; Grassell, 1989; Hull, 1999; Lindo, 1999; O'Neil, 2000; Pollock, 2000; Ramsey, 1999; Shea, 1995; Weiss, 2000; Woodruff, 1992).

Key Concerns Across Disciplines—The Mind-Set/Culture Issue

We each have our professional perspectives or ways of looking at a problem—our professional "mind-set." This mind-set often involves elements such as (a) what we think matters, (b) what we think is important, (c) what we notice as opposed to what we do not notice, and/or (d) the variables that our profession, training, or discipline prepares us to consider, manage, and discuss. Disciplines usually have a specialized vocabulary—often called jargon by others—to reflect and embody these elements. The popular phrase "if you are a hammer, everything is a nail" captures the potential problems of this conflict of mind-sets. If you are a school psychologist, political, economic, or sociological perspectives are not as likely to emerge from you, or be accepted by other psychologists if they did. If you are a principal, social work jargon or perspectives may be confusing, vague, or simply unwelcome; if you are a school social worker, educational administrative jargon or perspectives may be unclear or misinterpreted. In summation, both mind-set (the personal package of discipline) and culture (the embedded elements of discipline in groups, organizations, and polities) operate to make members of one discipline/profession strangers in a strange land when it comes to other disciplines (Heinlein, 1961). We often simply do not understand or appreciate the perspectives of "the other."

The issue of mind-set is the personal version of culture. Culture is the institutionalized set of rules and meanings that is a group property rather than an individual one. Culture assures that group norms and values are repeated. Disciplines are groups (perhaps even tribes) with norms and values—in a word, cultures. Supervising across disciplines must take both mind-set and culture into account.

A simple game, called Barnga, may help illustrate the problems that different cultures generate when they come in contact.[2] The game, named for a village in Africa, is a series of card games in which several teams play. No talking or writing is permitted, and only the word "Barnga!" in various intonations is permitted to be spoken. General instructions are given, and then written instructions are passed out to each group. One of the rules is that after playing for 5 minutes, the leading scorer of Team 1 moves to Team 2, and the lowest scorer moves to Team 5. Every high and low scorer moves. After a few rounds, debriefing is held, but by that time the room is usually in a state of chaos, with shouts of "Barnga!" going around, people standing, glaring, sighing loudly, and the like. The reason for this turmoil is that the written instructions were different for each team. As people move from team to team, they assume that the destination team is using the same rules as the team of origin. The destination teams assume that the "immigrants" come with the same rules they are already using. One can immediately picture the conflicts. Supervising across disciplines is a lot like this game, but the rules are subtler. The additional factors of communication, such as meaning, power, and the stress/default reaction, need to be taken into account when supervising.

Of course, if people could talk they might figure out that they had different sets of written rules. One might think that supervisors and supervisees could simply talk about the different rules and get everything straightened out. However, when rules are complex and buried within the deep structure of individuals and groups, mind-set, and culture, people do not necessarily begin by talking about the different rules under which they operate. Quite often they assume that others accept the same rules, and they are not even sure of which rules are relevant. Hence, communication, usually useful, does not always work as well as one might expect.

Then there is the matter of meaning. Mind-sets and cultures have both rules *and* meaning. Meaning refers to rules that are infused with values. We tend to think of our rules as, well, right, correct, the obvious thing, moral, or even sacred. It is one thing to discuss the rules for a card game and figure out that one set of written instructions had hearts as trump and another set had no trumps. However, when one person believes that one or the other of those rules is morally right, considerably more trouble may ensue. Values are not really amenable to "splitting the difference."[3] Professional values take on a sacred aspect like religious values. One would be as unlikely to say, "I am a social worker Monday, Wednesday, and Friday, and a lawyer Tuesday, Thursday, and Saturday" as one would be to say,

"I am a Jew on Monday, Wednesday, and Friday, and a Baptist on Tuesday, Thursday, and Saturday."

A third variable is power. Supervisors are more powerful than supervisees are, which gives an added weight to whatever culture or mind-set the supervisors happen to follow. The supervisor's power can privilege or sanction his or her position and make even questioning, not to mention opposition, on the part of the supervisee vastly more difficult.[4]

But let us assume that communication occurs, meaning is negotiated, and power differences are smoothed. There is still one problem remaining, the stress generated from these interactions. Behaviors driven by mind-set and culture (and temperament, as we shall see in a moment) tend to be our default choice. Under pressure and stress, we default to thinking and acting like a social worker or thinking and acting like a lawyer, even if we fully intend *not* to do so.

Table 109.1 identifies the lawyer mind-set/culture and the social worker mind-set/culture in some essential elements. We picked these professions because they have clear differences and often work together around common cases, especially in child welfare, recipients' rights, schools, and many other issues. Because the strength of professional socialization is often built upon and augments prior value dispositions, it can be exceptionally powerful. It is sometimes difficult for even well-attuned colleagues from different professions to walk in the other person's shoes. In conditions of stress, such as a court proceeding, respective practitioners may well default to their own personal/professional perspectives and dispositions. When one profession supervises the other (another stressful situation), similar defaults may occur as one tries to communicate with the other based on professional assumptions. These professional assumptions are often taken for granted by the sender but not shared by the receiver. Under stress, both the supervisor and the supervisee are likely to rely on the default "common sense" of their respective professions, thus complicating the supervisor–supervisee relationship further.

Another example would be the principals in the role of supervisor and school social workers (or other school-based practitioners) in the role of supervisee. While school-based practitioners often have professional supervisors, such as special education directors or school social work services directors, when that practitioner is in a school building, he or she will typically receive managerial supervision from the building principal. The mind-set and culture of principals (and other school administra-

Table 109.1 Default Professional Thinking Styles: Quintessential Lawyer and Social Worker Perspectives

Thinking Like a Lawyer	Thinking Like a Social Worker
Rules/law	Circumstances
Justice	Compassion
Facts	Feelings
Client forward	Person-in-situation
Fair play	Fair share
Adversarial	Mediating
Win/lose	Win/win

Note: I want to thank Kathleen C. Faller of the University of Michigan School of Social Work and Frank Vandervoort from the University of Michigan Law School for their help in constructing this table.

tors) can, and arguably should be, different from that of a school social worker. Along with disciplinary differences, their frames of reference will also vary, resulting in the previously referred to pitfall of not appreciating the perspective of "the other." For example, while a principal has the responsibility to consider all students, families, and teachers when confronting many situations, a school social worker could be focused on how to intervene and advocate for a specific student or family. Such a difference frequently leads to conflicting professional opinions on the appropriate response by the school. However, these differences represent important contributions and need to be recognized and respected by both the principals and practitioners. Essentially, school administrators employ clinicians in part to bring a different mind-set and culture to bear on school issues. Likewise, school practitioners need to be mindful of the roles and responsibilities that school administrators must assume when making decisions. Table 109.2 illustrates how a building principal and school social worker may diverge in mind-set and culture. (Chapter 94 discusses in detail best practices in teacher and principal consultations.)

These professional and disciplinary differences may well arise, as noted before, from even more basic value dispositions. Previous work on values by the lead author (Tropman, 1989, 1995, 2002a) suggests that values come in pairs that are juxtaposed to one another. Each of us has a dominant commitment and a subdominant commitment. The provisional list offered in Table 109.3 mentions some common American values with which we would all agree. The problem, as it were, is that

Table 109.2 Default Professional Thinking Styles: Quintessential Principal and School Social Worker Perspectives

Thinking Like a Principal	*Thinking Like a School Social Worker*
Situation with a student	Student-in-situation
Behavior → consequences	Assessment → intervention
What is best for the student body?	What is best for this student?
Should I suspend/expel this student?	Should I refer this student for a special education or psychological evaluation?
Can I get this family to come and pick this problematic student up?	Can I get this family to come and meet with me to try and help this problematic student?
What impact is this student having on the climate of the school?	What impact is the climate of the school having on this student?
Will I have a group of parents or teachers complaining about similar struggles?	Should I start a group for students with similar struggles?
Can/should I refer this whole situation to the social worker?	Can/should I refer this whole situation to the principal?

each of us prefers one set, in general, to the other.

The work of supervision is difficult enough when supervisor and supervisee start from the same place. Different disciplines provide us with different rules, which make the work of supervision more complex. Cultural competence, largely used in social work to refer to understanding the different cultures of ethnicity, gender, and societies, also means one needs to understand the different cultures of professions and disciplines. Encountering different professional cultures is indeed a form of culture shock. The value packages in Table 109.3 are even more difficult to address than those in Tables 109.1 or 109.2 because they exist more in our personal selves and, hence, are more in the background and deep structure of our persona. When an alpha supervisor and a beta supervisee begin working together, there can be value differences that are even deeper than profes-

sional differences that need to be understood. While reviewing Table 109.3, also consider how such values orientations may correlate with, and therefore compound, differences between supervisors and supervisees resulting from the choices individuals might make with respect to chosen discipline and career path.

Addressing these professional and personal differences is not easy. However, when differences in discipline exist, a good place to start is by focusing on value clarification. Clarification of values allows lawyers and social workers, alphas and betas, to have some awareness of their own values and those of the other. A second step is to develop an appreciation for, though not necessarily an embrace of, the different values. Cultural competence, as noted previously, involves working with different cultures in an appreciative and understanding manner. These cultures can include the

Table 109.3 Basic Value Packages that Characterize American Society

Supervisor/Supervisee Alpha	*Supervisor/Supervisee Beta*
Achievement	Equality
Fair play	Fair share
Personal fault/personal accountability	System fault/system accountability
Each tub on its own bottom	A rising tide lifts all boats
I own resources	I am a trustee of resources
Winner take all/optimizing	Winner take some/satisfying
Mountain man	Wagon train

Source: Tropman, 1995, 2002.

legal culture as well as different races and ethnicities.

Key Concerns Across Disciplines: Common Tasks in Supervision

Culture and mind-set, both professional and personal, represent the first big hurdles for supervisors of cross-disciplinary work. They represent the context of supervisory work. Professional and disciplinary differences in core skills are also important. The focus groups we worked with identified seven areas of common supervisory work, and these become places where professional and disciplinary differences can make a difference. In each case, the impact of these differences can be minimized through the establishment and use of common tools.

1. Managing the Work

Managerial supervision's job is to keep work moving along. Supervising across disciplines is hard because different disciplines have different templates and comfort levels that keep the work process moving. POSSBE is an acronym that stands for: *planning* work, *organizing* the steps that get plans accomplished, *strategizing* with supervisees about how to sequence the plans, *staffing* by getting the people you need, *budgeting* by allocating money and time, and *evaluating* by monitoring, overseeing, assessing, and appraisal. Using these POSSBE areas and following the sequence as a common template can be of great help in reducing interdisciplinary friction.

2. Setting Goals and Goal Milestones

Disciplines have different ways of goal setting, goal types, and moving toward goals. POSSBE helps, but an additional step of defining, distinguishing, and orchestrating outcomes and outputs is necessary. Supervision requires defining, with and for workers, goals (outcomes, accomplishments) and milestones toward those goals (outputs), and not mistaking outputs for outcomes.

3. Using the Supervisory Staircase

Workers arrive with different levels of competence (competence = knowledge + skill). Once on site they grow through levels of competence. Generally, these can be organized into the following levels of competence: novice worker, beginning worker, journey person or acceptably competent worker, expert worker, and master worker. Picture a staircase with the novice worker at the bottom step and the master worker on the top step. Supervision here involves working across competence levels. Supervisors need to use training, coaching, teaching, educating, and mentoring techniques up through this staircase.[5] A couple of problems can develop here. One is that the fact that just because a person is a master in one area (e.g., law) does not mean that she or he cannot also be a novice in another area (e.g., social work). This problem is one that needs to be handled with delicacy because masters tend to generalize their expertise. Hence, there can be masters in many different fields, and supervision of a master in one field by a master in another becomes difficult for obvious reasons.

Second, supervision is an administrative position, not a competence indicator. Orchestra conductors "supervise" orchestra members who play instruments, on which the conductor is (sometimes barely) a novice. So sometimes supervisors are journey persons supervising masters, as in the case of a new principal supervising a school-based mental health practitioner with 20 years' experience. In such a situation, the supervisor becomes more of a guide and attends to the fit between the master and the remaining whole, rather than reviewing work, as would be the case if the supervisor were working with a novice instead.

4. Making High-Quality Decisions

Perhaps the most important bottom line in supervision in the human services is the decisions that are made for and with clients. Different disciplines may have different criteria for determining high-quality decisions. Decisions are the products of supervisor–supervisee interaction. They should be of the highest quality (high quality = all stakeholders ahead). Many organizations cannot learn by trial and error because their first error may well be their last trial.[6] In child welfare, for example, decisions about whether a child should remain in the home or be removed are a daily occurrence. Likewise, decisions made by school professionals about whether a child needs to repeat a grade or be expelled from school can have lifelong consequences. These are critical, even life-and-death, decisions. Legal requisites come first, of course. After taking into account the legal requirements, attending to a decision framework that involves the following elements can help toward quality decision making:

1. consider the greatest good for the greatest number;
2. address the concerns of those who feel deeply;
3. address the concerns of those who have to carry out the decision(s);
4. address the issues of experts; and,
5. address the issue of what powerful people want.

A decision that meets these five criteria (1–5 + legal) has an excellent chance of being of high quality. In addition, it usually helps if some standard framework is followed in the processing of information for a decision. That way, everyone involved can be reassured that there is a process in place, which tends to assure that the relevant variables will be taken into account. Janis and Mann's (1977) steps are really excellent for this purpose, as they provide an easy-to-use process for decision making: (1) determine need, (2) develop alternatives, (3) evaluate gains/losses for self and others, (4) weigh pros and cons, (5) commit to act, and (6) implement. Decisions go better if one follows these simple steps, in order.

Supervisors need to help supervisees develop and master an orderly decision-making process to be sure that variables are not overlooked or improperly contextualized. Using such a process as a template will move supervisees along the road to high-quality decision making.

5. Using Effective Communication

Communication—what is said, how it is said, and to whom—involves at least three areas: (1) communication with self, (2) communication with others, and (3) feedback communication. While there are many kinds of communication, the focus here is on oral communication. The first area of communication, communication with self, involves what people say to themselves, is where the supervisors' mind-set is reinforced, and is one of the key points of difficulty in supervising across disciplines. Hence, supervisors need to engage in reflection, which examines their self-talk to temper their tendency toward closed-circle, self-reinforcing, self-talk.

The second area of communication is with the supervisee. Naturally that will be a better conversation if the supervisor has completed efforts in the first area of communication (the self) and

has an idea of the purposes of the meeting and what he or she hopes to get from it. That said, conversations with supervisees go more smoothly if they are focused, the communication is conjunctive, and the supervisor uses the skills of reflective listening (e.g., confirming what the supervisee has said through oral statement by noting, "I hear you saying . . . ," attentiveness, actual responses to queries and questions as opposed to evasions, and achieving conclusions for next steps at the end of the session).

The final area of communication of vital importance is feedback. Providing feedback is essential to the supervisory interaction and is perhaps its core element. Following simple rules of feedback can minimize the chance of miscommunication and misunderstanding. Constructive feedback should be (1) close to the event, (2) nonjudgmental, (3) focused on behaviors (both in terms of problems and suggestions), and (4) given in relatively small amounts. While not perfect, these tips can be very helpful in making feedback heard and used.

6. Holding Effective Meetings

Much of the supervisor's communication work, other than self-talk, is done in meetings. Running excellent meetings is a crucial skill, whether it is a staff meeting or a one-on-one meeting. While communication is an important component, structure and agenda building are vital as well. Disciplines have very different ways of approaching meetings. Developing a standard structure for meetings is extremely helpful—whether one-on-one or in a group of staff. One of the most useful practices is encompassed in the "agenda bell" (Tropman, 2002b). Supervisors have the responsibility to run good supervisory meetings. In a nutshell, these meetings should achieve decisions that are of high quality.

The agenda bell represents a graph of energy over time. As any meeting begins, the energy flow organizes itself into a "get going" phase, a "heavy work" phase, and a "decompression" phase. This appears to be true, regardless of the length of time of the meeting. For example, if there is a 2-hour staff meeting, it is the same as if it is a 20-minute supervisory session or a week-long conference. The general format is as follows: introduction, easy items, hard items, brainstorming for the future, and wrap (Tropman, 2002b). It is important that one not use reporting; rather, all participation is driven by the items upon which the group needs to act or about which they must brainstorm. This recipe is one that can be adapted and configured in terms of the local situation. Better practices for meetings can help supervisors be both effective (doing the right thing) and efficient (doing things right).

7. Managing and Developing the Supervisee/Supervisor Self

Supervisors have the responsibility to assist in the development of their supervisees. This responsibility focuses on enhancing professional growth. It means that the managerial supervisor provides increasing challenges and encourages the development of increasing skills. In this respect the supervisor can model herself or himself after a music teacher. Music teachers want their pupils to get their current music lesson right but also desire that their students migrate to more difficult music and more difficult techniques. Supervisors should take the same approach with their supervisees.

At the same time, supervisors need to develop themselves over time as well. If they are not growing, they will have a difficult time helping their supervisees grow. A key element here is that the supervisor reinforces and develops diverse interactional and cultural styles rather than growing only in their initially preferred area (preferred refers to naturally occurring realms, such as temperament). Diversity of intrapersonal and cultural styles means that one is comfortable in many modes, including, but not only, the one in which one feels the best. This is crucial in supervising across professions and disciplines because the ability to put oneself in another's shoes plays a large part in supervising across disciplines. It allows for the understanding of the other that is necessary for successful supervision anywhere, but especially when your supervisor or supervisee is from another culture or mind-set.

Key Concerns Across Disciplines: The Problem of Exacerbation

Whatever differences exist across professions and disciplines are magnified in certain situations that seem especially difficult for supervisors: providing feedback, giving corrective information, and dealing with difficult people (Pollan, 1996; Stone, Patton, & Heen, 1999). These are among the more difficult conversations the supervisor will have (think *performance appraisal*), and because each

party feels uncomfortable, the possibility for miscommunication rises sharply. Generally, good preparation is helpful (write it down) and using the "two meeting rule" helps as well (one for sharing information and perspectives, the second for action plans with reflection time in between). These especially difficult situations can also be cooled if the supervisor invites upward appraisal, where the supervisee also assesses the supervisor. One good technique for this is KSS—Keep, Stop, and Start. The supervisor asks the supervisee to share what things the supervisor is doing that are helpful and she or he should KEEP, what things are not helpful that she or he should STOP, and what things are not currently happening that she or he should START.

Key Problems Across Other Divides

Professions and disciplines are not the only differences with which supervisors might have trouble. There are gender differences in communication styles, as well as differences in temperament (as measured, for this illustration, by a Myers-Briggs Type Indicator [MBTI]) (Grey, 1992; Tannen, 1990; Keirsey & Bates, 1984). For example, Tannen argues that men tend to engage in "report" talk first—with the goal of conveying information, while women tend to engage in "rapport" talk first—with the purpose of establishing connection (Tannen, 1990). Of course each sex is able to do the other form of talking, but it may help a "Mars" man work more effectively with a "Venus" woman if they understand and are more aware of these different forms of talking (Grey, 1992).

One of the world's most popular assays in terms of behavioral repertoire is the Myers-Briggs Type Inventory (Keirsey & Bates, 1982). That assay develops 16 focal styles that have important communication properties. As long as one does not push "type" too far, it is a useful aid in improving communication. In terms of temperament, consider the extrovert (E) and the introvert (I). The extrovert tends to think through talking and surfaces a lot of ideas to which he or she may not really be attached, whereas the introvert tends to think internally first and is quiet, then shares an alternative to which she or he might well be quite committed. The E thinks the I is not responding, and the I thinks the E is babbling. Understanding type can help in understanding communication styles.

Tools and Case Examples

Table 109.4 From Novice to Master

Skill Levels	Supervisory Needs
Novice: Thumbnail • performance slow and jerky • attention to rules/facts • works with the book in hand • heavy learner *Supervisory Problem*: little reinforcement from the task	Novice: Training • understanding requirements and routines • reviewing requirements and routines • narrow policy–practice gap
Beginner: Thumbnail • performance faster and smoother • begins rule fade (acting automatically) • patterns not mentioned in rules • uses book less frequently *Supervisory Problem*: embarrassments	Beginner: Coaching • understands the requirements need to be accomplished by the employee • provides tips and suggestions
Journeyperson: Thumbnail • performance usual in terms of speed and smoothness • rule fade mostly complete • selecting most important cues • calculated, educated risk taking • uses book only for exceptions *Supervisory Problem*: may think it's the end	Journeyperson: Teaching • mastering requirements and routines • improving requirements and routines • some policy–practice gap • pass along information • set standards • the employee studies on her or his own, checks in with the teacher for review
Expert: Thumbnail • performance becomes fluid • rule fade complete • calculation and rationality diminish • no plan is permanent • attention shifts with cues • holistic, intuitive grasp • can write the book *Supervisory Problem*: possible "culture lock"	Expert: Educating • questions/improves routines and requirements, as possible • brings best practices from elsewhere
Master: Thumbnail • performance is seamless • exactly the right speed; appears effortless • understands the deep structure of the effort • holistic recognition of cues • performance is solid, confident, and sure • deeply understand; sees beyond the obvious *Supervisory Problem*: finding/arranging/managing access to the master's knowledge and self	Master: Mentoring • employee growth is the focus • looking to the future • personal connection with employee • mentoring begins when one goes beyond her/his job responsibilities in a voluntary, caring, sharing, and helping relationship

Key Points To Remember

Social work has long believed in the adage "start where the client is." In another voice, Stephen Covey has Habit 5, "seek first to understand, then be understood"[7] (Covey, 1990). The application of these dicta is vital to the managerial (and the professional) supervisor. The translation is simple: begin with the supervisee. Start where they are, rather than slipping into the default self, which is so usual and comfortable to you that it is easy to do.

Notes

1. Training Program for Child Welfare Supervisors, Children's Bureau No. 90CT0080 (University of Michigan #F003707).

2. http://www.interculturalpress.com/shop/barnga text.html. There is a good bit of material on Barnga on the Web.

3. However, where we have competing values, as in achievement versus equality, we do have ways of balancing them, including averaging, alternating, sectoring, and having a rule that specifies the occasion where we use one or the other value.

4. The lead author can serve as an example here. When I went to social work school, students were still being "counseled out" as opposed to flunking out. Basically one was "counseled out" if the faculty perceived that the student did not have the proper values. In my case I came close to being clipped by that perception. I had come from an undergraduate school where we were taught to challenge the professors. As I began to activate that behavior in social work school, the assistant dean called me in and asked if I was "resisting" social work education. Luckily for me, I learned one did not "question" professors at that time, but rather "shared feelings."

5. The Tools and Practice Examples section gives an outline of the supervisory staircase and the supervisory issues associated with each step from novice to master.

6. Other organizations where this is an issue are air traffic controllers, operators of nuclear power plants, delivering babies, and so on. These are discussed in Karl Weick's *Sensemaking in Organizations* (Weick, 1995).

7. See http://www.leaderu.com/cl-institute/habits/habit5.html

References

Bittel, L., & Newstrom, J. (1992). *What every supervisor should know* (6th ed.). New York: McGraw Hill.

Broadwell, M., & Dietrich, C.B. (1998). *The new supervisor* (5th ed.). Cambridge: Perseus Books.

Buhler, P. M. (1998). A new role for managers: The move from directing to coaching. *Supervision, 59*(10), 16–18.

Cole, M. (1999). The leader followers want to follow. *Supervision, 60*(12), 9–11.

Cousins, R. B. (2000). Active listening is more than just hearing. *Supervision, 61*(9), 14–15.

Covey, S. R. (1990). *The seven habits of highly effective people.* New York: Fireside.

Fracaro, K. (2001a). Empathy: A potent management tool. *Supervision, 62*(3), 10–13.

Fracaro, K. (2001b). Two ears and one mouth. *Supervision, 62*(2), 3–5.

Fuller, G. (1990). *Supervisor's portable answer book.* Englewood Cliffs, NJ: Prentice Hall.

Fuller, G. (1995). *The first time supervisor's survival guide.* Englewood Cliffs, NJ: Prentice Hall.

Gambrill, E., & Stein, T. (1983). *Supervision: A decision making approach.* Thousand Oaks, CA: Sage.

Grassell, M. (1989). How to supervise difficult employees. *Supervision, 50*(7), 3.

Grey, J. (1992). *Men are from Mars, women are from Venus.* New York: Harper Collins.

Henlein, R. (1961). *Strangers in a strange land.* New York: Avon.

Hull, W. W. (1999). Passing the buck vs. making an assignment. *Supervision, 60*(3), 6–7.

Humphrey, B., & Stokes, J. (2000). *The 21st century supervisor.* San Francisco: Jossey Bass.

Janis, I., & Mann, L. (1977). *Decision making.* New York: Free Press.

Kiersey, D., & Bates, M. (1984). *Please understand me: Character and temperament types.* Del Mar, CA: Prometheus Nemesis Books.

Lindo, D. (1999). Will you ever get it right? *Supervision, 60*(12), 6–8.

Middleman, R., & Rhodes, G. (1985). *Competent supervision.* Englewood Cliffs, NJ: Prentice Hall.

O'Neil, M. A. (2000). How to implement relationship management strategies. *Supervision, 6*(7), 3–4.

Perlmutter, F., Baily, D., & Netting, F. E. (2001). *Managing human resources in the human services: Supervisory challenges.* New York: Oxford University Press.

Pollan, S. (1996). *Lifescripts: What to say to get what you want in 101 of life's toughest situations.* New York: Macmillan.

Pollock, T. (2000). Sharpening your dialogue skills. *Supervision, 61*(8), 13–15.

Ramsey, R. D. (1999). Do you have what it takes to be a mentor? *Supervision, 60*(3), 3–5.

Shea, G. (1995). Can a supervisor mentor? *Supervision, 56*(11), 3.

Stone, D., Patton. B., & Heen, S. (1999). *Difficult conversations: How to discuss what matters most.* New York: Viking.

Tannen, D. (1990). *You just don't understand: Men and women in conversation.* New York: Harper Business.

Tropman, J. (1989). *American values and social welfare.* Englewood Cliffs, NJ: Prentice Hall.

Tropman, J. (1995). *The catholic ethic in American society.* San Francisco: Jossey-Bass.

Tropman, J. (2002a). *The catholic ethic and the spirit of community.* Washington, DC: Georgetown University Press.

Tropman, J. (2002b). *Making meetings work* (2nd ed.). Thousand Oaks, CA: Sage Publications.

Tropman, J. (in press). *Supervision and management in nonprofits and the human services: How not to become the manager you always hated.*

Weick, K. (1995). *Sensemaking in organizations.* Thousand Oaks, CA: Sage Publications.

Weiss, W. H. (2000). The art and skill of delegating. *Supervision, 61*(9), 3–5.

Whetten, D., & Cameron, K. (2005). *Developing management skills* (6th ed.). Upper Saddle River, NJ: Prentice Hall.

Woodruff, M. J. (1992). Understanding & supervising the twenty somethings. *Supervision, 53*(4), 10.

www.amacombooks.org/books/catalog/MGS.htm

www.amanet.org/selfstudy/super.htm

www.calib.com/nccanch/pubs/usermanuals/supercps/supercps.pdf

www.mapnp.org/library/mgmnt/prsnlmnt.htm

www.orgchanges.com

CHAPTER 110

Coping With Isolation

Guidelines for Developing a Professional Network

Joelle D. Powers ▪ Gary L. Bowen

Getting Started

School social workers and mental health professionals are key members of multidisciplinary teams in schools, working to remove barriers to students' educational success through student, family, peer, classroom, and community interventions. Interprofessional collaborations and relationships with teachers, school psychologists, nurses, and administrators are central to the successful performance of school social workers (Bronstein, 2003; Dupper, 2003; Franklin, 2004). Similarly, strong intraprofessional links and active connections with peers who share similar training and a common set of practice values and ethics are also imperative for these professionals, in order to successfully meet their responsibilities and duties.

What We Know

Approximately 5% of the estimated half a million social workers are employed in schools (NASW, 2004). Social workers provide services in 44% of the public schools in the United States (Brener, Martindale, & Weist, 2001). In many cases, there is only one social worker in a school; in other cases, school social workers work in a semiautonomous manner.

Professional isolation is common in schools, as "individualized work patterns are a prominent feature" (Avila De Lima, 2003, p. 197). Professional isolation, defined by Dussault, Deaudelin, Royer, and Loiselle (1999) as the "unpleasant experience that occurs when a person's network of social relations at work is deficient in some important ways" (p. 943), can be problematic for school-based social

workers. Feelings of professional isolation among individuals employed in helping professions have been linked to high stress levels (Dussault et al., 1999), to frustration (Lewandowski, 2003), and to professional burnout (Henning-Stout & Bonner, 1996). (See also chapter 112.)

In order to prevent a sense of isolation and seclusion in the workplace, practitioners must work to build a professional network to assist them in forging strong alliances of support and collaboration with peers. Coping with isolation through professional networks can be viewed through the lens of social exchange theory. This theoretical framework posits that the process of social exchange is based on individuals' expectations for potential rewards (Bakkenes, de Brabander, & Imants, 1999). School practitioners may desire to pursue professional networks if they perceive that there will be beneficial outcomes. Potential rewards from professional networks include increased accountability, encouraging the utilization of evidence-based practices, and increasing the probability that all students will benefit from their educational experience.

Summary of Evidence

The positive effects of social support for clients are well established in the literature (Lincoln, 2000), yet there is very little known about social support for social workers. There is preliminary evidence identifying instrumental and informational support in the workplace to have buffering effects on burnout among social workers (Himle & Jayaratne, 1991), while emotional support has proven to have little or no impact on perceived stress and strain (Jayaratne & Chess, 1984). Also, supervision and team support may be protective factors against stress and burnout (Lloyd, King,

& Chenoweth, 2002). Surprisingly few empirical studies on professional isolation and how to effectively cope with it exist (Wright, 2003). There is likewise a dearth of research about the effects of social support and collaboration for social workers (Gable, Mostert, & Tonelson, 2004).

With the exception of Franklin (2001, 2002), little discussion exists about the nature of professional networks (PNs) and the role of social support in the lives of school social workers. Consequently, we turn to the related disciplines of school psychology, education, and nursing for information regarding the risks of professional isolation and the potential benefits of developing PNs for practitioners in our field. Although none of the studies meets Rones and Hoagwood's (2000) criteria for evidence-based programs, they represent the *best knowledge currently available* and provide helpful suggestions about how and why to develop PNs.

PNs can play a key role in preventing and alleviating professional isolation among school social workers and mental health providers. PNs consist of occupational peers who provide one another with opportunities for professional development and social support. These peer networks can involve dyads, small groups, or larger scale group associations.

Professional and psychological benefits represent two distinct advantages of professional networks. Professionally, PNs can increase the informed practice of school social workers and therefore positively impact the quality of services provided to students (Henning-Stout & Bonner, 1996). This may be accomplished through case consultation, resource sharing, and practice-related skills training. Psychologically, PNs are a source of social and emotional support, which can decrease feelings of isolation, reduce occupational stress, and increase job satisfaction (Acker, 2004). PNs foster increased psychological well-being through improved access to peers, opportunities for collaboration, and social support.

What We Can Do

Intervention

Informal PNs

PNs can be divided into two categories: informal and formal. Informal PNs provide social support

and opportunities for casual learning, which might take place over lunch or in passing, whereby two or more school practitioners sound out practice ideas and problems with one another (Freeman & Pennekamp, 2002). Informal PNs function as "communities of practice" and provide the opportunity to engage in collaborative reflection on current practices that may improve the services provided to students and their families (Wesley & Buysse, 2001). Informal PNs include activities such as mentoring, problem solving, case consultation, brainstorming, and encouragement among colleagues.

The literature provides several helpful suggestions for increasing professional development opportunities and combating isolation through informal PNs. One option is to develop small peer support or supervision groups that meet regularly for case consultation (Henning-Stout & Bonner, 1996; Logan, 1997; Pryzwansky, 1996). The groups can be interprofessional and consist of on-site colleagues from multiple disciplines that may promote collaboration at your school (Bronstein & Abramson, 2003), or they can be intraprofessional to increase networking among discipline-specific school practitioners. Either method of establishing a cohort of peers that meets regularly to collaborate, to discuss ethical dilemmas, and to share best practices ideas can provide helpful insights and can raise the standard of services provided to students and their families (Freud & Krug, 2002).

Telephones and the Internet are also promising media that can be utilized to efficiently connect and collaborate with peers and to build a stronger sense of professional community (Kruger et al., 2001; Kruger & Struzziero, 1997). Telephone calls and e-mail are easy and accessible informal networking methods that do not depend on physical proximity (Garrett & Barretta-Herman, 1995). Technology-based collaboration can enhance work-related skills by expediting planning and decision making (Schopler, Abell, & Galinsky, 1998). An online chat room or a specifically established Web site or e-mail Listserv may provide faster and more convenient access to peers than face-to-face, structured opportunities (Kruger et al., 2001).

Formal PNs

Formal PNs also offer positive skill development opportunities. Formal PNs may assist school practitioners in better practicing within the framework described in the NASW's *Standards for School Social Work Services* (2002). More specifically, Standard 27 outlines the responsibility of the school practitioner to continue professional development through professional organizations, coalitions, conferences, and training events.

For the school social worker, becoming a member of national associations or organizations is among the most basic ideas for establishing formal PNs (Bredeson, 2003; Cooper & Kurkland, 2002; Franklin, 2002). The National Association of Social Workers (NASW) and the School Social Work Association of America (SSWAA) are viable options; both organizations offer an array of opportunities for professional development and networking. The NASW holds national meetings and offers a school social work section that provides additional resources for school-based practitioners. The SSWAA also holds national conferences and provides opportunities to connect with and learn from leading experts about critical school issues.

Local training opportunities also assist in further developing a practice skill set and in staying abreast of current literature and information that informs school social work practice (Bredeson, 2003). Ultimately, attending conferences and local training events will increase connections to the field and familiarize school practitioners with important trends and information.

Acquiring new knowledge and honing practice-related skills through journals (Franklin, 2002; Freeman & Pennekamp, 2002) and supervision (Lloyd, King, & Chenoweth, 2002) are also helpful components of formal PNs. Subscribing to peer-reviewed journals that focus on delivering mental health services in schools, such as *Children & Schools* and *School Social Work Journal*, will increase access to information about evidence-based practice. Professional or paid supervision by a more advanced colleague is another formal method for expanding professional networks and encouraging the development and refinement of practice skills and knowledge (Garrett & Barretta-Herman, 1995). Preliminary research found fewer that 25% of school social workers receive supervision from another social worker (Garrett & Barretta-Herman, 1995). This is unfortunate as supervision may increase job satisfaction (Staudt, 1997) and may help prevent professional stress and burnout (Lloyd et al., 2002; Soderfeldt, Soderfeldt, & Warg, 1995) and so is worth pursuing. (See also chapter 113 for more information about professional development and continuing education.)

Promising Steps for Reducing Professional Isolation Among School Social Work Practitioners

1. Become involved with both local and national organizations.
2. Subscribe to appropriate and applicable journals.
3. Locate local conferences for training with other school social workers.
4. Become involved with statewide communication for school social work through a committee or newsletter.
5. Collaborate with universities for research in the areas of school success for students.
6. Build alliances with educators to develop strategies for influencing education agencies in your area.
7. Get involved with local school-related initiatives that may be instrumental for model programs and interventions for students.
8. Pursue additional credentials and certifications for school social work.
9. Increase your knowledge of best practices and evidence-based strategies.
10. Ensure that there are practice guidelines for school social work in your district.
11. Report outcome data from interventions and promote your work.
12. Keep the mission of school social work in the forefront of your mind to assist with establishing and reaching goals to help students succeed. (Adapted from Franklin, 2001, 2002)

Tools and Practice Examples

Case Example

Danielle was a school social worker in an elementary school located in a poor community in Southern California. Danielle started working at the school soon after graduating from her MSW program, 2 years earlier. The job was quite challenging because many students were at risk; more than 70% of the student population was eligible for free and reduced-price lunches and more than half were second-language learners. Additionally, there were two special classrooms housed on the campus: one for students with severe emotional and behavioral problems and another for students with severe physical disabilities.

Although Danielle enjoyed her job immensely, she felt stress from her responsibilities at the school. She worried about cultural and behavioral issues, and about identifying the best practices for working with students. She felt isolated much of the time because she was the only social worker at the school. Danielle often felt overwhelmed by professional responsibilities, as she had few people to turn to for consultation about difficult cases and crises. The school psychologist was a good resource, but he was not very accessible because he worked only 2 days a week. The school nurse provided wonderful medical care for students on campus but had limited knowledge about the kinds of social and emotional problems that Danielle faced in practice.

Danielle was part of a student study team, which comprised Danielle, the school psychologist, the school nurse, a resource specialist, and two teachers. The team met to discuss possible strategies for students who were finding it difficult to be successful at school. This interdisciplinary collaboration was helpful for developing strategies for working with at-risk students, but the sporadic meeting times did not provide consistent feedback and practice reflection opportunities with peers.

Danielle decided to pursue professional networks for herself in an attempt to increase her professional development and improve the quality of services that she provided to students. The first step for Danielle was to create a stronger support system in her immediate school environment by setting up regular meetings with the resource specialist at her school. This increased her frequency of interdisciplinary collaboration and allowed time for practice reflection with a colleague who was familiar with the specific culture of the school, the students, and teachers. Danielle and the resource specialist agreed to meet over lunch once a week to discuss cases and brainstorm practice interventions with one another.

Danielle was also concerned that she was not connected with discipline-specific peers who shared her professional values and practice models and might assist her in providing better social work services at her school. In an effort to expand her professional networks outside of her school campus, Danielle contacted the district office to ask for the names and contact information for other school social workers in the district. Because there were only two other school social workers, she also contacted three additional local school districts and asked for the same information. With the contact information for 11 school social workers in four school districts, Danielle phoned and e-mailed each to invite them to join a peer consultation group.

Six of the 11 invited practitioners attended the first meeting of the peer consultation group. Danielle learned that other school social workers in the area also shared her concern about the lack of contact with peers and experienced comparable job stresses. The group set goals for what they would like to accomplish during regular meetings. They determined that sharing best practice resources, problem solving, and case consultation were their highest priorities, and that monthly meetings would enable them to begin collaborating on these issues.

Over the next few months, the peer consultation group met regularly. The discussions in meetings helped to increase members' knowledge and practice skills and provided a sounding board for difficult cases. They discussed ethical dilemmas, evidence-based practices, and evaluation strategies. Danielle felt empowered by the collaboration and less isolated in her work. When a difficult case presented itself and required more immediate action, Danielle now had several people she could contact by phone or e-mail for feedback and advice.

Danielle also decided to expand her professional networks on a larger scale by joining several social work associations. The SSWAA and the school section of the NASW both provided professional development opportunities and resources to strengthen her practice. When she became a member of these associations, Danielle learned about local chapters in California and about annual state and national conferences. Training opportunities highlighted important national trends, legislation affecting school social work practice, and evidence-based practices. Danielle also convinced her principal to subscribe to the NASW journal *Children & Schools* for updates on the best available interventions and strategies for students.

Danielle had effectively expanded her professional networks and increased practice strategies through informal and formal methods. She was meeting regularly with the resource specialist at her school and the school social work peer group for case consultation and resource sharing. She was registered to attend a local and national conference during the school year, and she was receiving a journal that provided her with best practice information. Danielle's expanding practice knowledge base and access to professional social work resources promoted her work with students and fostered her ability to participate in discussions with interdisciplinary student study team members. These professional networks expanded Danielle's formal and informal infrastructure for school social work practice.

Tools

Social workers have demanding and crucial jobs in school settings. PNs can effectively reduce professional isolation and increase positive student outcomes by increasing inter- and intradisciplinary collaboration and resource sharing among

Table 110.1 Resources for Building Professional Networks Bibliography

Resource	Description	Contact Information
Center for School Mental Health Assistance	An organization through the University of Maryland that promotes the advancement of school-based mental health programs. Annual conferences are available that highlight critical issues and strategies for the field.	University of Maryland Baltimore, Dept. of Psychiatry 680 W. Lexington St, 10th Floor Baltimore, Maryland 21201-1570 410-706-0980 csmha.umaryland.edu
Children & Schools	A journal that provides practitioners with helpful information on social work practice.	750 First Street, NE Suite 700 Washington, DC 20002-4241 www.naswpress.org
National Association of Social Workers (NASW)	A national organization of social workers that offers publications, opportunities for professional development, advocacy, and resource information to members. There is also a specialty practice section for school social work, which provides additional resources.	750 First Street, NE Washington, DC 20002-4241 www.naswdc.org
Peer Consultation Group: Doing What Works for Counselors	A journal article that describes the establishment, maintenance, and results of a peer consultation group for school practitioners.	Logan, W. L. (1997). Peer consultation group: Doing what works for counselors. *Professional School Counseling, 1*(2), 4–7.
Research on Social Work Practice	A journal that contains information on evidence-based practices and current research information for multiple social work settings, including schools.	2455 Teller Road Thousand Oaks, CA 91320 800-818-7243 www.sagepub.com/Journalhome.aspx
School Social Work Association of America (SSWAA)	An organization dedicated to promoting the profession of school social work. The Web site offers helpful resources, conference information, and links to state and regional organizations.	P.O. Box 2072 Northlake, IL 60164 847-289-4527 www.sswaa.org
School Social Work Journal	A journal directed primarily at the interests of social work practitioners in the public schools and of school social work educators. Articles are related to the improvement of social work practice in the schools.	*School Social Work Journal* 341 N. Charlotte Street Lombard, Illinois 60148 www.lyceumbooks.com/ sswjournal.htm

(continued)

Table 110.1 *(Continued)*

Resource	Description	Contact Information
Social Work Access Network (SWAN)	A Web site that includes a listing of conferences, chat rooms, and resources. A list of all schools of social work is also available, which can inform practitioners about local schools that may be key partners for future research collaboration.	http://cosw.sc.edu/swan/index.html
Social Work and Social Services Web sites	A Web site through Washington University in St. Louis that provides convenient links to a variety of Web sites for social work related organizations, resources, and research information.	gwbweb.wustl.edu/websites.html
Social Work Cafe	A Web site that offers an Internet community for the global exchange of information for social workers. Helpful links, chat rooms, and message boards are available to enhance the connections between social workers.	www.geocities.com/Heartland/4862/
Society for Social Work and Research (SSWR)	A national organization dedicated to supporting and improving research for social work practice. Annual conferences highlight recent research findings in the field.	www.sswr.org

practitioners. By utilizing PNs to resolve student- or school-related dilemmas, to increase awareness of best practices, to strengthen social support, and to further professional development opportunities, school-based social workers can increase their professional effectiveness and accountability as practitioners.

We highlight several key methods to build informal and formal professional networks and to thus reduce professional isolation among school social workers. While *the steps are not empirically driven*, we consider them to be *promising strategies*.

Building Informal PNs

- Establish relationships and share resources with interdisciplinary peers in your immediate environment and intradisciplinary colleagues through peer supervision or practice consultation groups.
- Utilize technology such as the telephone, e-mail, and social work chat rooms for quick

feedback from and case consultation with peers.

Building Formal PNs

- Become involved with both local and national organizations, such as the NASW and the SSWAA.
- Increase knowledge of best practices and evidence-based strategies by attending social work conferences and training events, as well as by subscribing to journals such as *Children & Schools*.

In the context of the isolation that many school social workers may confront in their professional practice, the lack of information about this issue and about evidence-based strategies for reducing professional isolation is rather surprising, given the considerable attention that social workers themselves give to the social networks and support systems of clients. Further attention to this deficit is warranted.

References

Acker, G. M. (2004). The effect of organizational conditions (role conflict, role ambiguity, opportunities for professional development, and social support) on job satisfaction and intention to leave among social workers in mental health care. *Community Mental Health Journal, 40*, 65–73.

Avila De Lima, J. (2003). Trained for isolation: The impact of departmental cultures on student teachers' views and practices of collaboration. *Journal of Education for Teaching, 29*, 197–218.

Bakkenes, I., de Brabander, C., & Imants, J. (1999). Teacher isolation and communication network analysis in primary schools. *Education Administration Quarterly, 35*, 166–202.

Bredeson, P. V. (2003). *Designs for learning: A new architecture for professional development in schools.* Thousand Oaks, CA: Corwin Press, Inc.

Brener, N. D., Martindale, J., & Weist, M. D. (2001). Mental health and social services: Results from the school health policies and programs study 2000. *Journal of School Health, 71*, 305–312.

Bronstein, L. R. (2003). A model for interdisciplinary collaboration. *Social Work, 48*(3), 297–306.

Bronstein, L. R., & Abramson, J. S. (2003). Understanding socialization of teachers and social workers: Groundwork for collaboration in schools. *Families in Society: Journal of Contemporary Services, 84*, 323–330.

Cooper, C. D., & Kurkland, N. B. (2002). Telecommuting, professional isolation, and employee development in public and private organizations. *Journal of Organizational Behavior, 23*, 511–532.

Dupper, D. R. (2003). *School social work: Skills and interventions for effective practice.* Hoboken: John Wiley & Sons, Inc.

Dussault, M., Deaudelin, C., Royer, N., & Loiselle, J. (1999). Professional isolation and occupational stress in teachers. *Psychological Reports, 84*, 943–946.

Franklin, C. G. (2001). Now is the time for building the infrastructure of school social work practice. *Children & Schools, 23*, 67–71.

Franklin, C. G. (2002). Exemplary practices. *Children & Schools, 24*, 203–204.

Franklin, C. G. (2004). The delivery of school social work services. In P. Allen-Meares (Ed.), *Social work services in schools* (4th ed., pp. 295–325). Boston: Pearson A & B.

Freeman, E. M., & Pennekamp, M. (2002). *Social work practice: Toward a child, family, school, and community perspective* (2nd ed.). Springfield, IL: Charles C. Thomas Publisher, Ltd.

Freud, S., & Krug, S. (2002). Beyond the code of ethics, Part 1: Complexities of ethical decision making in social work practice. *Families in Society: Journal of Contemporary Human Services, 83*, 474–482.

Gable, R. A., Mostert, M. P., & Tonelson, S. W. (2004). Assessing professional collaboration in schools: Knowing what works. *Preventing School Failure, 48*(3), 4–8.

Garrett, K. J., & Barretta-Herman, A. (1995). Missing links: Professional development in school social work. *Social Work in Education, 17*, 235–244.

Henning-Stout, M., & Bonner, M. (1996). Affiliation and isolation in the professional lives of school psychologists. *Journal of Education and Psychological Consultation, 7*, 41–60.

Himle, D. P., & Jayaratne, S. (1991). Buffering effects of four social support types on burnout among social workers. *Social Work Research & Abstracts, 27*, 22–28.

Jayaratne, S., & Chess, W. A. (1984). The effects of emotional support on perceived job stress and strain. *Journal of Applied Behavioral Science, 20*, 141–154.

Kruger, L. J., Maital, S. L., Macklem, G., Shriberg, D., Burgess, D. M., Kalinsky, R., et al. (2001). Sense of community among school psychologists on an Internet site. *Professional Psychology: Research and Practice, 32*, 642–649.

Kruger, L. J., & Struzziero, J. (1997). Computer-mediated peer support of consultation: Case description and evaluation. *Journal of Educational and Psychological Consultation, 8*, 75–90.

Lewandowski, C. A. (2003). Organizational factors contributing to worker frustration: The precursor to burnout. *Journal of Sociology and Social Welfare, 30*, 175–185.

Lincoln, K. D. (2000, June). Social support, negative social interactions, and psychological well-being. *Social Service Review*, pp. 231–252.

Lloyd, C., King, R., & Chenoweth, L. (2002). Social work, stress and burnout: A review. *Journal of Mental Health, 11*, 255–265.

Logan, W. L. (1997). Peer consultation group: Doing what works for counselors. *Professional School Counseling, 1*(2), 4–7.

NASW. (2002). *NASW standards for school social work services.* Retrieved May 4, 2004, from www.naswdc.org/practice/standards/NASW_SSWS.pdf

NASW. (2004). *Issue fact sheet: School social work.* Retrieved May 5, 2004, from www.socialworkers.org/pressroom/features/issue/school.asp

Pryzwansky, W. B. (1996). Professionals' peer-mediated learning experiences: Another idea whose time has come. *Journal of Educational and Psychological Consultation, 7*, 71–78.

Rones, M., & Hoagwood, K. (2000). School-based mental health services: A research review. *Clinical Child and Family Psychology Review, 3*, 223–241.

Schopler, J. H., Abell, M. D., & Galinsky, M. J. (1998). Technology-based groups: A review and conceptual framework for practice. *Social Work, 43*, 254–266.

Soderfeldt, M., Soderfeldt, B., & Warg, L. (1995). Burnout in social work. *Social Work, 40,* 638–646.

Staudt, M. (1997). Correlates of job satisfaction in school social work. *Social Work in Education, 19,* 43–52.

Wesley, P. W., & Buysse, V. (2001). Communities of practice: Expanding professional roles to promote reflec-tion and shared inquiry. *Topics in Early Childhood Special Education, 21,* 14–123.

Wright, S. (2003). The development of a worker loneli-ness scale. *Australian Journal of Psychology, 55,* 150.

Effective Strategies for Marketing a School-Based Practice in the School and Community

Christine Anlauf Sabatino

Getting Started

The fundamental purpose of school is "to provide a setting for teaching and learning in which all children can prepare themselves for the world they now live in and the world they will face in the future" (Costin, 1987, p. 538). The purpose of school-based social work services is to help each student reap the full benefit of their education and to assist vulnerable children and their families in making the educational process a success (Constable, 2002; Costin, 1969a).

The context and direction of school social work has shifted dramatically over the last century, given various social, political, and economic circumstances and different local, state, and federal initiatives (Hare & Rome, 2002). At the beginning of the 20th century, local public schools recognized there were forces in the environment that impeded the teaching–learning process (Oppenheimer, 1925). Visiting teachers were hired in recognition of the interplay among the home, school, and community that supported or thwarted endeavors to educate schoolchildren. They supplemented the teacher's understanding of the student, interpreted to the school the child's out-of-school life in the community, and interpreted to parents the demands of the school system (Culbert, 1916).

At the end of the 20th century, the U.S. government recognized the need to address the learning needs of economically disadvantaged preschool children in the community (Project Head Start, 1965; Head Start Program Reauthorization, 1994), provide compensatory education to low-income and educationally disadvantaged school-age children (ESEA, 1966), educate children with disabilities in the local community (IDEA, 1997), and generate a report card for families on statewide school performance levels (No Child Left Behind Act, 2001). Today's school social workers blend together the original framework of visiting teacher services, as well as the implementation of federal laws by addressing population trends, mental health concerns, socioeconomic issues, and educational matters that influence school achievement.

Given the historical breadth of our role, the sheer magnitude of social problems, and the rate of unexpected changes that potentially impinge on school performance, what are effective strategies for establishing successful school-based professional social work and mental health services?

What We Know

Marketing School Social Work and Mental Health Services

The school system structure has been deeply affected over the last decades by its engagement with public health care and managed mental health care. Some schools systems are engaging with public health systems to provide school-based health services that now include mental health services (Dryfoos & Maguire, 2002). Other systems are expanding school-based services for at-risk students financed through Medicaid, managed care organizations (MCO), and health maintenance organizations (HMO) (Greene & Lee, 2001; Koppleman & Lear, 1998; Streeter & Franklin, 2002). This market-oriented, business-driven service delivery system mentality requires school social workers and mental health workers to develop new knowledge and skill sets that fall outside their formal professional education (Franklin, 1999).

At this point in time, social work does not have a well-documented professional literature based on business practices. Barker (2003) defines "marketing strategies" in relationship to social welfare policy. The term "social marketing," however, is more in keeping with business practices. It is defined as "activities designed to generate interest and demand by consumers, resource suppliers, licensing and credentialing organizations, and the general public for the services of social agencies" (p. 403).

Most information in this area is found in the popular literature. Materials aim to assist private practitioners to design, develop, and market themselves (Lawless, 1997; Lawless & Wright, 2000; Grand, 2002). Materials fall into three categories: how to relate to the local community, how to work with managed care organizations, and how to network with the World Wide Web. Practice building is discussed using classical marketing tools, such as the yellow pages, newspaper ads, business cards, brochures and flyers, as well as establishing a niche market in one's area of expertise (APA, 1996; Baum & Henkel, 2004). Managed care strategies for the behavioral health care provider are a large part of these materials, since only six firms provide services for almost the entire United States (Psychotherapy Finances Online). Legal and financial issues are also considered. World Wide Web sites, such as www.psyfin.com and ww.therapyshop.com, guide the reader to books, software, practice newsletters, continuing education materials, online newsletters, therapist directories, and classified ads.

The Work Group on Health Promotion and Community Development at the University of Kansas, Lawrence, has developed a Web-based community tool box (http://ctb.ku.edu/tools) that provides practical skill-building information to promote community health and development partnerships. One project is devoted to "Social Marketing of Successful Components of the Initiative." It distinguishes between commercial and social marketing and provides further links to the Social Marketing Place (www.social-marketing.com), the Social Marketing Network of Canada (www.hc-sc.gc.ca), and the Social Marketing Manual (www. ilgard.ohiou.edu) for definitions, resources, and ethics.

To date most materials related to marketing have been written by others in the helping professions (Jones, 2001; Van Doren, Durney, & Darby, 1993). Professional social work literature contains very little that addresses marketing a school-based practice (McCroskey, Picus, Yoo, Marsenich, & Robillard, 2004). School mental health and health services, however, have started adopting the methods of social marketing in school-based practices (Franklin, in press). School social workers must take leadership roles in building and sustaining partnerships between schools and community agencies to provide seamless services in school settings (Poole, 2002). Without giving up our professional identity, values, and traditions, we must take the opportunity to learn about marketing, branding, and selling. Behind these business concepts are fundamental social work functions that improve learning, youth development, family well-being, and community life in an era of shrinking resources.

What We Can Do

Unique Challenges

With that in mind, it is important to examine several unique aspects of school social work that may come into play as the school social worker builds professional relationships with other stockholders, including students, families, school administration, and support workers. The challenges are many in this host setting; however, the fundamental fact is that "supportive services," whether school-based or community-based, are essential to schools and help make possible academic success (Nelson & Barbaro, 1985).

Administrative Issues: The Role of Organizational Structures and Political Environments

The school system is a hierarchical bureaucratic structure consisting of various subsystems that operate within specific policies and procedures and limit the power delegated to positions at every level in the school system. School social workers are traditionally part of the subsystem known as pupil personnel services, a "support service" that includes a variety of professional staff including psychologists, special education teachers, nurses, guidance counselors, attendance officers, and speech therapists. Other professionals, such as physicians, psychiatrists, and dentists, may become part of this subsystem on a contractual basis. Each professional discipline provides a distinct service. However, there may be overlap at times as the school meets identified needs.

A thorough understanding of the school subsystems includes the crucial role played by nonprofessional staff. Clerical staff, cafeteria workers, and custodians are central to the day-to-day operations of the school system. Further, teacher aides, parent volunteers, and community workers are an integral part of the school system (Winters & Easton, 1983). The working arrangements among these various subsystems create a culture and climate that varies for each school and school district, requiring social workers to recalibrate their roles and functions for each separate school assignment.

Within this organizational structure, the pupil personnel director, principal, and multidisciplinary team members are the key personnel with whom one must establish an effective working relationship and delineate duties and responsibilities. Through formal and informal channels of communication, school social workers and mental health providers instruct others about their professional knowledge, always using this information to enrich the schools' efforts to bring about student success. They bring attention to the fact that there are numerous skills needed to further academic achievement and no one person or profession has the training to address the biopsychosocial-educational needs of all students or overcome the ecological barriers that impede educational progress.

It is critical to note that social workers employed within a school system have a unique role because they must address the needs of two clients: (1) the school system and (2) the child and family. School-based practitioners must always represent the school system under whose auspices they serve. At the same time, the professional code of conduct requires them to support the child and family. They must examine the transactions between the student and school system, taking this information back to the system and activating both the student and the school to respond in ways that support the fit between them. In other words, school-based social workers and mental health workers may not tilt their efforts toward one side or the other of the person-in-environment equation because they are employed by the school system.

Legal Issues: Ethics and Confidentiality

Social workers are bound by the NASW Code of Ethics (NASW, 1999), which assists practitioners in applying ethical principles and standards when dealing with practice and policy issues that have implicit and explicit ethical concerns. For school-based social workers, dilemmas may arise within multiple arenas because of the many stakeholders in American education. When assessing and intervening in problems of school functioning, professionals must use a sophisticated ethical decision-making process and apply the proper standards to the problem because personal, professional, organizational, societal, and general ethical matters may all be reflected in school failure (Joseph, 1983; Lowenberg, Dolgoff, & Harrington, 2000).

For school social workers, standards of confidentiality are particularly complex, and confidentiality is never absolute in the school system. For example, a holistic assessment includes private information collected from a number of sources that often becomes part of a larger record of the student's educational needs. Facts are collected from the family, the student, the school staff and other professionals, and agencies within the community. The student and family have the right to be informed about what information will be included in the pupil personnel record, what will be disclosed to members of the pupil personnel team, and what will be used for multidisciplinary educational evaluations.

The school social worker must be cognizant that some members of the multidisciplinary team are not bound by a professional code of ethics or rules of confidentiality. While school social workers respect the privacy of their clients and hold in confidence all information obtained in the course of professional services, informal channels of communication are usually well developed within the social system of the school. Therefore, one needs to exercise careful judgment in deciding what information will be shared orally or in writing. Further, these decisions are to be informed by federal, state, and local laws and policies (Raines, 2004).

Legal Issues: The Role of Education Policy

The Education for All Handicapped Children Act (P.L. 94–142) is the single most important piece of federal legislation in terms of sponsoring school social work services. For the first time, federal law specifically mandated school social work services for school-age children found eligible for special education services. As amended and reauthorized, the collective special education laws are known today as the Amendments to the Individuals with Disabilities Education Act of 1997 (IDEA) (P.L. 105–17). Part C of IDEA addresses programs and services to preschool children with special needs and their families.

Under IDEA and Part C, school social workers have a crucial role in the development of the individualized education program (IEP) and the individualized family services plan (IFSP), which document overall and specific instructional goals for the child receiving special education services. The IEP endorses the social work assessment of the child's development, including the impact of culture, family history, and community context; the IFSP expresses the family statement on their priorities, resources, and concerns for their preschool child's developmental delay.

It is essential that school social workers know the federal laws, court decisions, state regulations, and local mandates that serve as a path for social work and mental health services in the schools. A greater imperative, however, is to withstand yielding to narrow legal procedures and administrative processes as the primary role. One must move beyond federally mandated services and promote programs that meet the needs of regular education as well as special education students.

Professional Issues: The Function of Interdisciplinary Collaboration

Providing first-rate support services requires interdisciplinary team collaboration in the school system. This obliges professional and nonprofessional team members to exchange information, share expertise, and offer diverse perspectives for the purpose of achieving a common goal—academic achievement and stable home–school–community relations. It entails recognition of each other's competencies and reliance on each other's work to achieve student well-being. It requires awareness of professional differences and acceptance of these differences. Mutual respect, trust, open communication, and an understanding of the various professional orientations are prerequisites to successful collaboration. This process makes services more comprehensive and effective and enables many different team members to gain a measure of success and satisfaction.

It takes time, but it is critical to collect information about each team member, their professional background, areas of expertise, and interests. See chapter 95 on resource mapping. Explore each teammate's perspective on various school problems and how these differ from the traditional paradigm used in one's own profession. Do this within the context of clarifying the goals of interdisciplinary collaboration and establishing clear roles and assignments. Further, commit to systematically reviewing interdisciplinary collaborative processes. Examine successes and failures in order to refine the team's performance standards and to make changes the team believes will help it function more effectively.

Interdisciplinary collaboration in a school system also includes discussion of tasks that are unique to certain group members and those that may be shared. Make arrangements for including information that does not arise from within the team and for supplying pertinent information to others outside the team. Build toward joint planning and shared decision making and guard against excessive specialization and fragmentation of services (Hancock, 1982). Applying different professional viewpoints through interdisciplinary team collaboration enriches the school's understanding of the child's difficulty and its impact on the school and family (Sabatino, 2002).

What We Can Do

Valuable Practice Models for School-Based Services

Educators may have differing views on whether school social workers and other providers of mental health services should be an integral part of the school. In fact, some would say school-based and school-linked mental health services are not consistent with the mission of education. They see this activity as taking away resources from instruction. Others do not see how school-based mental health services may be of help to the school or community. In fact, they view them as an attempt to infringe upon family rights and values. This is the point where knowledge and marketing meet.

Current research indicates that more than 20% of children and adolescents have mental health problems (American Academy of Pediatrics, 2004). Schools have become the "de facto" mental health service system for them (Early & Vonk, 2001). Research confirms that the school system is the most common point of entry and provider of mental health services across all age groups (Farmer, Burns, Phillips, Angold, & Costello, 2003). In addition, there are numerous federal programs, literature bases, and process and outcome research that show school-based and school-linked mental health services are central to school success (see Center for School Mental Health Assistance; Center for Mental Health in the Schools).

School social work and mental health services must be characterized and marketed as an approach that addresses barriers to child development, learning, and societal success. It is critical to describe these services as embedded within the continuum of school interventions that comprise a comprehensive and integrated service model for instructional programs (Adelman & Taylor, 2000). Mental health education services help school systems achieve a deeper understanding of students' behaviors in school, benefit students' school performance, and strengthen social networks in the neighborhood (Hoagwood & Erwin, 1997). Two models of consultation are presented that may be used to promote mental health in schoolchildren.

Tools and Practice Examples

Education and Training

The breadth of issues that may confound educational progress is endless, requiring schools, families, and communities to study new and creative ways to bring about student success. Education and training is an important way to impart information that supports the teaching–learning process. It is a cost-effective, information-centered method of disseminating specialized concepts and information to expand the school staff's view of a topic.

Teachers understand education and training approaches to learning new information. It is a method consistent with their professional education. Through lectures, materials, structured learning experiences, small group discussions, role modeling, seminars, or workshops, school social workers and mental health providers establish positive collaborative relationships and expand teachers' knowledge about problems that interfere with academic success.

Gallessich (1982) identifies the following characteristics of effective education and training programs:

- they are carefully designed in collaboration with the school;
- the training objectives are derived from a needs assessment;
- the program is unique to the needs of this particular school or community;
- the program is flexible to meet unexpected needs;
- programs have a clear connection to educational goals and objectives;
- the program is paced so it does not overload, bore, or exhaust the attendees;
- participation is voluntary;
- the presentation environment is comfortable;
- norms are developed to support group learning;
- learning includes activities to develop skills;
- feedback is solicited; and
- the trainer has school support if problems arise.

When the client base for the school system literally grows and develops during their school years, there is limitless subject matter for training and education programs. Dupper (2002) categorizes topics that easily lend themselves to presentations. For teachers, one might focus on issues of externalizing child behaviors, such as classroom behavior problems, bullying, peer harassment, suspension, and expulsion. Conversely, teachers may puzzle over internalizing child behaviors, such as anxiety, loneliness, grief, and depression.

Social problems that affect the home, school, and community include gangs, truancy, dropouts, homelessness, foster care, abuse and neglect, divorce and separation, substance abuse, teen sexual behavior, and teen pregnancy and parenting. There are groups of vulnerable schoolchildren, such as students returning from residential or juvenile justice settings and those with issues of sexual orientation, for whom it is beneficial to provide information about how to facilitate their transitions into the school and community.

General education teachers may profit from a descriptive profile of specific disability categories because they may be involved in the early detection of a student's handicapping condition. Schools may benefit from discussions about the ways the majority and minority staff and student groups overtly or covertly impede school success.

School systems need to explore the ways in which the parents and communities are involved in the organizational structure of the school. Community agencies and their staffs may profit from learning about neurological, cognitive, and motor disabilities found in schoolchildren and how these impact childhood ecology and school functioning.

Education and training programs for teachers serve a twofold function. First, they let school personnel see the vast amount of information available to assist them in their roles and tasks. Second, each program will remind teachers of other issues they are experiencing, which often leads them to invoke further assistance from the practitioner. Education and training programs may also be offered to school families and school communities to further an understanding of how the school system assesses and intervenes to promote school success. They advance collaborative partnership between school personnel, the family, and the community agency, who are all involved in efforts to bring about successful academic and social development.

Mental Health Consultation

Analyses of school social work tasks consistently identify consultation as a central function of school-based practice (Constable, Massat, McDonald, & Flynn, 2005; Costin, 1969b; Allen-Meares, 1977; Timberlake, Sabatino, & Hooper, 1982). Mental health consultation in the schools is one of the most clearly articulated, frequently researched, and significant forms of preventive mental health services (Caplan & Caplan, 1993; Mannino, MacLennan, & Shore, 1975; Mannino & Shore, 1980; Sabatino, 2002). Caplan and Caplan (1993) discuss one type of mental health consultation, consultee-centered case consultation, which is most applicable for school social workers and mental health workers serving school personnel. School staffs ask for help with problems every day. Consultee-centered case consultation is meant to help improve their capacity to work more effectively with an identified problem and to benefit similar students in the future. The goal is to understand the consultee's or teacher's problem in handling the situation rather than investigating all aspects of the student's condition. The format involves listening to the description of the problem to identify the areas where improvements in work performance are needed.

These two practice models are easily marketed to schools by either school-based or community-based mental health workers. They offer early detection and prevention services for conditions that bring about school failure. They are meant to increase academic performance, decrease school failure, and improve the quality of the educational system. They are extremely cost-effective. Finally, they help establish "comprehensive, multifaceted approaches that help ensure schools are caring and supportive places that maximize learning and well-being and strengthen students, families, schools and neighborhoods" (UCLA, 2004, p. 1).

Key Points to Remember

This chapter has offered a brief overview of the current landscape of school social work and mental health services, along with pathways to consider for a successful practice journey.

Some of the most effective strategies for institutionalizing school-based professional social work and mental health services are:

- understanding the commerce of school systems through their organizational structure, political milieu, legal mandates, and interdisciplinary workforce;
- marketing one's professional knowledge in the service of educational goals; and
- promoting proven practice models to meet educational concerns.

Resource Centers

Center for School Mental Health Analysis and Action, University of Maryland School of Medicine: http://csmha.umaryland.edu
Center for Mental Health in the School, UCLA Mental Health Project, University of California at Los Angeles: http://smhp.psych.ucla.edu
Coalition for Community Schools, Washington, DC: www.communityschools.org
International Alliance for Child and Adolescent Mental Health and Schools, University of Maryland: www.intercamhs.org
National Assembly on School-Based Health Care, Washington, DC: www.nasbhc.org

National Association of Social Workers, Washington, DC, The Section Connection: Linking schools, students, community, and family, School Social Work Association of America: www.socialworkers.org
School Social Work Association of America, Northlake, IL: www.sswaa.org/links.html

References

Adelman, H. S., & Taylor, L. (2000). Looking at school health and school reform policy through the lens of addressing barriers to learning. *Children's Services: Social Policy, Research, and Practice, 3*(2), 117–132.

Allen-Meares, P. (1977). Analysis of task in school social work. *Social Work, 22,* 196–201.

Amendments to the Individuals with Disabilities Act of 1997. P.L. 105–17.

American Academy of Pediatrics. (2004). School-based mental health services. *Pediatrics, 113*(6), 1839–1846.

American Psychological Association. (1996). *Marketing your practice: Creating opportunities for success* (Practitioner's Toolbox Series). Washington, DC: APA Press.

Barker, R. L. (2003). *The social work dictionary* (5th ed.). Washington, DC: NASW Press.

Baum, N., & Henkel, G. (2004). *Marketing your clinical practice* (3rd ed.). Boston: Jones and Bartlett Publishers, Inc.

Caplan, G., & Caplan, R. (1993). *Mental health consultation and collaboration.* New York: Jossey-Bass.

Constable, R. (2002). Developing and defining the school social worker's role. In R. Constable, S. McDonald, & J. Flynn (eds.), *School social work: Practice, policy, and research perspectives* (5th ed., pp. 353–363). Chicago: Lyceums Books, Inc.

Constable, R., Massat, C., McDonald, S., & Flynn, J. (2005). *School social work: Practice, policy, and research perspectives* (6th ed.). Chicago: Lyceum Books.

Costin, L. B. (1969a). A historical review of school social work. *Social Casework, 50*(8), 439–453.

Costin, L. B. (1969b). An analysis of the tasks in school social work. *Social Service Review, 43*(3), 274–285.

Costin, L. B. (1987). School social work. In A. Minahan (Ed.), *Encyclopedia of social work* (18th ed., pp. 538–545). Silver Spring, MD: National Association of Social Workers.

Culbert, J. (1916). In *Proceedings of the national conference of charities and corrections.* Chicago: Heldman Printing.

Dryfoos, J., & Maguire, S. (2002). *Inside full-services community schools.* Thousand Oaks, CA: Corwin Press.

Dupper, D. (2002). *School social work: Skills and interventions for effective practice.* Hoboken, NJ: John Wiley & Sons, Inc.

Early, T., & Vonk, M. E. (2001). Effectiveness of school social work from a risk and resilience perspective. *Children & Schools, 23*(1), 9–31.

Education for All Handicapped Children Act of 1975. P.L. 94–142.

Elementary and Secondary Education Amendments of 1966. P.L. 89–750.

Farmer, E. M., Burns, B., Phillips, S., Angold, A., & Costello, E. J. (2003). Pathways into and through mental health services for children and adolescents. *Psychiatric Services, 54*(1), 60–66.

Franklin, C. (1999). Coming to terms with the business of direct practice social work. *Research on Social Work Practice, 11*(2), 235–244.

Franklin, C. (in press). The future of school social work practice. Special issue: The future of social work practice.

Gallessich, J. (1982). *The profession and practice of consultation* (5th ed.). San Francisco, CA: Jossey-Bass.

Grand, L. C. (2002). *The therapist's advertising and marketing kit.* New York: John Wiley & Sons, Inc.

Greene, G., & Lee, M. Y. (2001). School social workers and students' mental health: Current trends and innovative programs. *Children & Schools, 23*(1), 3–5.

Hancock, B. (1982). *School social work.* Englewood Cliffs, NJ: Prentice-Hall.

Hare, I., & Rome, S. (2002). The developing social, political, and economic context for school social work. In R. Constable, S. McDonald, & J. Flynn (Eds.), *School social work: Practice, policy, and research perspectives* (5th ed., pp. 101–121). Chicago: Lyceums Books, Inc.

Head Start Program Reauthorization of 1994. P.L. 103–252.

Hoagwood, K., & Erwin, H. D. (1997). Effectiveness of school-based mental health services for children: A 10-year research review. *Journal of Child and Family Studies, 6,* 435–451.

Individuals With Disabilities Education Act of 1997. P.L. 105–17. U.S.C. 11401 et seq.

Jones, D. (2001). Marketing psychological services: Using client problem and solution perceptions to design help offering promotional appeals. *Psychology & Marketing, 18*(3), 261.

Joseph, M. V. (1983). Ethical decision-making in clinical practice: A model for ethical problems solving. In C. B. Germain (Ed.), *Advances in clinical practice.* Silver Spring, MD: NASW.

Koppleman, J., & Lear, J. G. (1998). The new child health insurance expansions: How will school-based health centers fit in? *Journal of School Health, 68,* 441–451.

Lawless, L. L. (1997). *How to build and market your mental health practice.* New York: John Wiley & Sons, Inc.

Lawless, L. L., & Wright, G. J. (2000). *How to get referrals: The mental health professional's guide to strategic marketing.* New York: John Wiley & Sons, Inc.

Lowenberg, F., Dolgoff, R., & Harrington, D. (2000). *Ethical decisions for social work practice* (6th ed.). Itasca, IL: F. E. Peacock.

Mannino, F. V., MacLennan, B. W., & Shore, M. F. (1975). *The practice of mental health consultation.* DHEW (ADM) 74–112.

Mannino, F. V., & Shore, M. F. (1980). *History and development of mental health consultation.* Washington, DC: NIMH.

McCroskey, J., Picus, L., Yoo, J., Marsenich, L., & Robillard, E. (2004). Show me the money: Estimating public expenditures to improve outcomes for children, families and communities. *Children & Schools, 26*(3), 165–173.

NASW (1999). *Code of ethics of the National Association of Social Workers* (revised). Washington, DC: NASW.

Nelson, G., & Barbaro, M. B. (1985). Fighting the stigma: A unique approach to marketing mental health. *Health Marketing Quarterly, 2*(4), 89–102.

No Child Left Behind Act of 2001. P.L. 107–110.

Oppenheimer, J. J. (1925). *The visiting teacher movement with special reference to administrative relationships* (2nd ed.). New York: Joint Committee on Methods of Preventing Delinquency.

Poole, D. L. (2002). Community partnerships for school based services. In A. R. Roberts & G. J. Greene (Eds.), *Social worker's desk reference* (pp. 539–544). New York: Oxford University Press.

Project Head Start. (1965). 45 CFR.

Raines, C. (2004). To tell or not to tell: Ethical issues regarding confidentiality. *School Social Work Journal, 28*(2), 61–78.

Sabatino, C. A. (2002). School social work consultation and collaboration: Integration of services across professional boundaries. In R. Constable, S. McDonald, & J. Flynn (Eds.), *School social work: Practice, policy, and research perspectives* (5th ed., pp. 208–230). Chicago: Lyceums Books, Inc.

Streeter, C. L., & Franklin, C. (2002). Standards for school social work in the 21st century. In A. R. Roberts & G. J. Greene (Eds.), *Social worker's desk reference* (pp. 612–618). New York: Oxford University Press.

Timberlake, E., Sabatino, C., & Hooper, S. (1982). School social work practice and P.L. 94–142. In R. Constable & J. Flynn (Eds.), *School social work: Practice and research perspectives* (pp. 49–72). Homewood, IL: Dorsey.

UCLA (2004). *About mental health: An overview.* Los Angeles: UCLA Center for Mental Health in Schools.

Van Doren, D., Durney, J., & Darby, C. (1993). Key decisions in marketing plan formulation for geriatric services. *Health Care Management Review, 8*(3), 7–20.

Winters, W. G., & Easton, F. (1983). *The practice of social work in schools.* New York: Free Press.

Best Practices for Avoiding Burnout

Srinika Jayaratne

Getting Started

Burnout is characterized by emotional exhaustion, cynicism or depersonalization, detachment from the job, and feelings of inadequacy and lack of personal accomplishment (Dentsen, 2002; Freudenberger, 1980; Maslach, 1982, 2003). Additionally, burnout is associated with many other psychological and health symptoms, such as depression, anxiety, and somatic complaints. While there is debate about whether there is a "process of burnout" with preliminary symptoms, there is little disagreement that the ramifications of burnout are serious. In addition to personal distress, burnout is associated with absenteeism, poor performance, and high turnover rates. In sum, the human costs of burnout have a negative impact on not only the service provider but also the service recipients and the institution. When one considers the fact that schools and children represent two of society's most important attributes, it is essential that we do whatever we can to sustain and maintain good workers.

What We Know

Organizational Factors

There is considerable evidence to support the view that organizational factors contribute significantly to burnout, with practitioners in large, impersonal bureaucracies appearing to be the most susceptible (Maslach, 2003; Maslach, Schaufeli, & Leiter, 2001). This research points to the important role played by the culture, climate, and structure of the organization. However, there are some

things individuals can do to protect themselves and handle the strains associated with burnout (Meltsner, 1989; Pines, 1982). Indeed, some research suggests that the process begins at the point of hire (Koeske & Kirk, 1995).

The complex environments school social workers practice in could be characterized as "high risk" for burnout. Ambiguities and conflicts in roles, often coupled with value dilemmas, lack of autonomy, high workload, job insecurity, and violence, all precursors of burnout, characterize the context of practice in school social work (Astor, Benbenishty, & Marachi, 2004; Pincus, 1997). In addition, the so-called paradigm shift involving "collaboration between schools and community agencies" creates an even more complicated system (Allen-Meares, 2004). While the number of social workers who are experiencing symptoms of burnout may be low, failure to deal with relevant stressors may result in an emotionally exhausted, cynical, and inadequate worker.

Research Support for Interventions and Practice Methods

The Maslach Burnout Inventory, characterized by its emphasis on *transactions* between the person and environment, is considered the gold standard in the measurement of burnout (Maslach & Jackson, 1986). Burnout is conceptualized and measured by the three dimensions: emotional exhaustion, depersonalization, and personal accomplishment. While there is a strong body of research on the phenomenon of burnout, evidence-based interventions to deal with burnout are limited (Maslach, 2003). Most interventions focus on the individual worker, not on organizational characteristics, which, according to the literature, play a significant role in the development of burnout. Furthermore, while notions of person–environment or job–person fit introduce a general framework for analysis, burnout is considered more an "end state," something that may be the result of "chronic misfit" (Maslach et al., 2001). Interventions, therefore, focus on the negative attributes of chronicity and attempt to develop preventive strategies aimed at increasing worker resilience to burnout (Skovholt, Grier, & Hanson, 2001).

There is considerable evidence that a supportive workplace environment will mitigate or "buffer" against the negative consequences of stress. However, it is essential to distinguish between different types of support—emotional, instrumental, informational, and appraisal (Acker, 1999; Barak, Nissly, & Levin, 2001; Baruch-Feldman, Schwartz, Brondolo, & Ben-Dayan, 2002; Greenglass, Fiksenbau, & Burke, 1996; Himle, Jayaratne, & Thyness, 1989a; Jayaratne & Chess, 1984)—as well as different sources of support, such as coworkers and supervisors (Hagihara, Tarumi, & Miller, 1998; Himle, Jayaratne, & Thyness, 1989b), which appear to have differential impacts on stress and burnout. In contrast, social undermining behaviors and actions heighten the process of burnout (Duffy, 2002; Gant, Nagda, Brabson, & Jayaratne, 1993; Tepper, Duffy, & Shaw, 2001).

Figure 112.1 identifies the widely accepted dimensions central to burnout assessment. The model indicates that there are direct effects on burnout from the person, organization, and client. This model also denotes that social support and undermining falls between the preceding domains and burnout, suggesting the notions of buffering or heightening. Table 112.1 presents the definitions of the various elements in the model. This robust model is supported by research conducted around the world with numerous professional populations (e.g., Cropanzano, Rupp, & Byrne, 2003; Guterman & Jayaratne, 1994; Lee & Ashforth, 1996; Maslach et al., 2001; Zapf, Seifert, Schmutte, Mertini, & Holz, 2001). According to this model, burnout interventions *must* consider personal, organizational, and client factors. Each dimension plays a role in the susceptibility to or likelihood of developing or producing symptoms of burnout.

It is important to note that state-of-the-art burnout intervention is rudimentary at best. There are no empirically validated or controlled studies, and there are few studies on burnout among school social workers. As such, the ensuing discussion provides a model with a generic but proven base and is useful for school social workers.

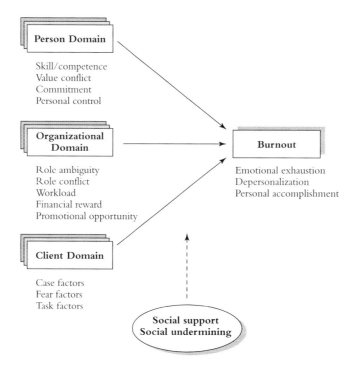

Figure 112.1. Conceptual Model on the Situational Correlates of Burnout

Table 112.1 Definitions of Situational Correlates

PERSONAL DOMAIN

Skill/Competence	The extent to which individuals believe they possess the necessary training and skills to perform their job
Value Conflict	The extent to which individuals feel their personal values are in conflict with what is required in the job
Commitment	The extent to which individuals believe in the "goodness" of the work and have an attachment to the organization
Personal Control	The extent to which individuals believe that there are sufficient resources and authority to conduct their work in the most efficacious and autonomous manner

ORGANIZATIONAL DOMAIN

Role Ambiguity	The extent to which there is absence of clarity about the nature of the job
Role Conflict	The extent to which there are conflicting demands from different parts of the organization and frustrations encountered by fulfilling one goal while contradicting another
Workload	The extent to which there is an excessive quantity of work that is expected on the job
Financial Reward	The degree of satisfaction with the compensation and benefits received by individuals for what they do
Promotional Opportunity	The extent to which an individual believes there is a career ladder and fair opportunities for promotion

CLIENT DOMAIN

Case Factors	The extent of difficulties inherent to a client and his/her context that an individual perceives to be present in the provision of services
Fear Factors	The extent to which an individual believes there is personal danger in the conduct of work activities
Task Factors	The extent to which an individual feels confident in carrying out the activities necessary in a given situation
SOCIAL SUPPORT	The extent to which the individual perceives a supportive environment at work and outside work
SOCIAL UNDERMINING	The extent to which individuals in the workplace are viewed as actively demonstrating negative and demoralizing behaviors

What We Can Do

Stress is usually caused by two broad conditions:"the occurrence of discrete events *and* the presence of relatively continuous problems" (Pearlin, Lieberman, Menaghan, & Mullan, 1981). Since some aspects of a stressful work environment are unchangeable, many activities associated with burnout intervention are "individual-oriented" stress management techniques (Azar, 2000; Leyden-Rubenstein, 1998; Meltsner, 1989). While personal strategies help in the short run and may help develop resiliency, long-term interventions must consider workplace modifications. Burnout prevention is the responsibility of not only the worker but also the organization.

The proposed interventions employ a two-pronged approach, one aimed at helping the

Table 112.2 Daily Symptom Checklist

	Day 1	Day 2	Day 3	Day 4	Day 5	Day 6	Day 7
Physical Symptoms							
Fatigued and exhausted	☐	☐	☐	☐	☐	☐	☐
Headaches or other bodily pains	☐	☐	☐	☐	☐	☐	☐
Having trouble sleeping	☐	☐	☐	☐	☐	☐	☐
Feeling lethargic	☐	☐	☐	☐	☐	☐	☐
Emotional Symptoms							
Feeling depressed	☐	☐	☐	☐	☐	☐	☐
A general sense of anxiety	☐	☐	☐	☐	☐	☐	☐
Feeling irritable and quick to anger	☐	☐	☐	☐	☐	☐	☐
Feeling like you are not achieving anything	☐	☐	☐	☐	☐	☐	☐
Thinking about quitting	☐	☐	☐	☐	☐	☐	☐
Behavioral Symptoms							
Unwilling to ask for help	☐	☐	☐	☐	☐	☐	☐
Unwilling to accept help	☐	☐	☐	☐	☐	☐	☐
Taking longer than usual to get something done	☐	☐	☐	☐	☐	☐	☐
Wanting to be by yourself	☐	☐	☐	☐	☐	☐	☐
Resisting change	☐	☐	☐	☐	☐	☐	☐
Increased use of alcohol or medications	☐	☐	☐	☐	☐	☐	☐
Other Symptoms							
Feel like you are not doing well in your job	☐	☐	☐	☐	☐	☐	☐
Feel like your co-workers are doing better than you	☐	☐	☐	☐	☐	☐	☐
Criticizing yourself	☐	☐	☐	☐	☐	☐	☐
Second-guessing your decisions and actions	☐	☐	☐	☐	☐	☐	☐
Feel like you are not getting any positive feedback	☐	☐	☐	☐	☐	☐	☐

worker manage stress and the other focusing on organizational change, a decidedly more difficult task. These interventions rely on the works of several authors and constitute widely identified key dimensions and strategies (Bell, Kulkarni, & Dalton, 2003; Leiter & Maslach, 2000; Maslach, 1982; Pearlin & Schooler, 1978; Skovholt et al., 2001).

Personal Strategies

The popular press is full of books on stress management with prescriptions ranging from good eating and exercise, to Yoga, meditation, or kick boxing. There is nothing wrong with any program that helps you deal with stress; what matters is finding strategies that work for you.

Identifying the Symptoms

An array of psychological, behavioral, and physical symptoms are associated with burnout. As with most psychosocial symptomology, it is the subjective experience that matters (Azar, 2000). The more prevalent and consistent the symptoms, the greater the need to take action. Check yourself on the symptom checklist and keep track for 2 to 3 weeks (Table 112.2). If the pages become filled with check marks, it is time to do something about it.

Coping With Stress

Now that you know you are "stressed out," how do you cope? Pay careful attention to your social resources. *Social resources* are individuals or offices you can talk with or rely on when you need help and support. Think about family, friends, and coworkers, as well as institutional resources in the school or your church, temple, or mosque. Be specific. If you are not sure how to handle a bullying student, talk it over with a colleague. If you had a really bad day, go out in the evening with a friend. Simple solutions—but the research tells us they do work. This is the time to use your network of resources.

Problem-Focused Coping

When thinking about your psychological resources, what can you do to increase your mastery and control over the situation? If you feel overworked and overburdened, run-of-the-mill problems may take on lives of their own. You may begin to wonder about your competence and your ability to handle difficult situations. You are reluctant to talk with the family of a child who is failing most of his classes because you are not sure whether anything will help. Ask yourself why. Is this family belligerent? You worked with this family before and it did not do any good? To regain mastery over the situation, it is necessary to regain confidence. Work with a colleague or observe someone else at work; do some additional reading on the topic; try something different. Remember that it is probably not lack of skill that is making you reluctant, but the demands and context that are making you feel helpless.

Emotion-Focused Coping

If, on the other hand, you are dealing with a situation where the stress producers are structural and unchangeable, consider what you can do to minimize its impact. You have to work many hours after school, and you worry about spending more time with your family. You feel that if you see one more child coming to school without breakfast, you are going to get sick. These may be realities of the job over which you have little or no control, and this is where personal well-being programs come into play. Consciously engage in and plan these activities; do not leave them up to chance. Developing control over your life will enhance your personal well-being and make you a more effective professional.

Maximize the Possibility of Success

All of us want to be successful at our work, but what do we mean? There are, of course, the obvious markers such as a pay raise, bonus, or a promotion, but these are infrequent. We should validate our successes more frequently to nourish our emotional well-being, as well our self-efficacy in our work. The tendency in this regard is to rely on uncontrollable external sources: a good word from the principal, a thank you note from a student, a teacher asking you for advice. While these are affirming, relying on external validation as the only legitimate avenue of efficacy can, in the long run, prove harmful (Acker, 1999; Raquepaw & Miller, 1986).

In contrast, there are two aspects of work that you control: professional expertise and personal relationships. According to Harris and Franklin (2004), "The breadth of knowledge and skills needed to work effectively in schools is more than any one individual may possess" (p. 281). However, keeping abreast of what is new in the field will result in greater self-confidence and mastery of theory, skills, and strategy. Go to workshops, attend relevant lectures, and read the latest journals; this knowledge will hold you in good stead going forward. It is possible that your school district does not provide financial support for these types of activities. That should not dissuade you. It is your health and performance, and the price you pay now will be well worth the benefits you derive.

Of equal importance is building relationships with helpful people and resources, within both the school and the local community. These relationships will undoubtedly pay off, if not with this student, then with another student in the future. In other words, do everything you can do to make yourself believe you have the confidence, knowledge, skills, and connections to help resolve your clients' problems (see Franklin, 2004). Bandura (1977) called this "efficacy expectation" the "conviction that one can successfully execute the behavior required to produce outcomes" (p. 79).

Set Realistic Goals

Just as you may need to pay greater attention to the definitions of success, it is also necessary to recognize smaller accomplishments. It is easy to get frustrated by the sheer number of students you are dealing with, the lack of time you have, or the inability of the system or resources to address them adequately. The fact that a student dropped out in order to work is not necessarily a failure if it prevented this student from failing in school; there is always the possibility that the student can return to school. You do not have the resources or the authority to handle the economic circumstances in this situation, but you may have helped the student deal with current reality so that he or she can move on with life without remorse and with hope—that is, the alternative reality, and also your responsibility.

Often, workload may not allow you to accomplish activities that you think are important. In a study of school social work practice, Staudt (1991) noted that practitioners wanted to do more group work, but they also wanted to work with individual students. How you perceive these types of situations and choices will help define your goals. The more realistic you are, the more successful you will be.

Diversify

In the world of stocks and bonds, the mantra has always been "diversify!" Similarly, there is a substantial body of research suggesting that a more diverse caseload, more variety in problems and challenges, and more participation in nondirect service activities mediate against the negative effects of stress (Acker, 1999; Bell et al., 2003; Proctor & Steadman, 2003; Rafferty, Friend, & Landsbergis, 2001; Skovholt et al., 2001). Doing multiple tasks and activities, engaging in non-school-related professional activities, taking a continuing education course, and so on will not only increase your intellectual excitement but also help control the development of stress. In this

sense, diversifying one's work activities serves as a preventive exercise.

Do Something Different

Feelings of helplessness are a sure route to burnout. Helplessness can lead to anger, frustration, and emotional exhaustion. Believing that if you simply try harder or do more of something it will result in change is probably a lost cause, particularly if you are beginning to feel frustrated and angry about lack of change. Change your tactics; it may not work, but it will keep you motivated to see whether this "experiment" will work. There is evidence to suggest that if nothing else, doing something different provides a psychological boost and enhances one's feelings of autonomy. And remember, you do not have to invent all of your "new" activities. Talk with your colleagues, observe others, read articles—they may all have suggestions on something you simply have not thought of before.

"Take Five"

The "water cooler" and the "coffee break" have become social phenomena and folklore. Strategically, however, this may be one of the most immediately effective tactics for handling stress. It is time out. In the context of service delivery, the social worker who tells the client, "That's a good question. Let me think about it" is buying important time. Getting up and leaving your office for a few minutes "to pick up some papers" when dealing with a particularly belligerent and disrespectful student allows you to regain your composure. Not providing an immediate response is far better than providing an answer you may regret later. These "moments for thought" are necessary ingredients of good practice.

There is nothing wrong with working the occasional evening or weekend to catch up, but if it is your normal routine, check your symptom checklist again. Time away from work is there for a reason. Make the time; take the time.

The *first* defense against burnout is you. What you do for yourself personally and professionally will help you be a better practitioner. These strategies and tips have a proven track record across men and women of all ages in allaying the symptoms of burnout. The focus, as you probably noted, is on your work. Undoubtedly life stresses may also impact your work, and work stresses may spill over to your personal life. Some of the noted techniques should be helpful regardless of the source of stress. Perhaps the most important point is not to leave things up to chance, but to take control over the situation.

Organizational Strategies

The bad news is that research tells us burnout has less to do with personal characteristics, and much to do with the organization. But that is also the good news. Many attributes of a workplace are changeable. Just as much as individuals need to be cognizant of their mental health and health status, organizations need to be sensitive to their organizational climate. Far too often, organizations wait until there is absenteeism, turnover, and poor performance—the organizational equivalent of burnout—before taking action. It is up to administrators, supervisors, *and* workers to ensure that the "system" is sensitive enough to notice problems, open enough to discuss them, and flexible enough to address them. The best practices that follow reflect activities that are feasible within budget-constrained environments. In addition, they also affirm an active status for the social worker in the process of organizational change. They offer opportunities for practitioners to engage in change activities as enablers, collaborators, mediators, and advocates. They also reflect the responsibility of school social workers.

Orientation to the Workplace

The old saying "forewarned is forearmed" is apropos to organizations interested in helping prevent burnout. *Orientation* means providing information about the formal manuals and handbooks as well as unwritten rules, formal and informal protocols within the organization, the key players and decision makers in the organization, and access to and availability of resources. Such an orientation would help you identify the realities of the work context, and therefore, you would not have to learn through trial and error. In abstract, this is a form of critical support called *information support* (House, 1981). School social workers often work in multiple schools, which, in addition to having different key personnel, may have different procedures and expectations. Research on school psychologists suggests that individuals employed in a single setting fare better than those who serve multiple settings (Proctor & Steadman, 2003). This research underscores the importance of an orientation provided by the principals and key

teachers, as well as a supervisor if present. A comprehensive and realistic orientation will go a long way toward helping the school social worker get a better handle on the job by reducing role ambiguity and conflict and by maximizing autonomy. If such an orientation does not exist, you should request it and, if necessary, establish procedures to ensure that such an orientation will occur for future hires.

Quality of Supervision

There is considerable evidence that the quality of supervision can make a significant difference in the quality of work and work life (Azar, 2000; Baruch-Feldman et al., 2002; Gant et al., 1993; Rafferty et al., 2001). Supervisors provide leadership, direction, and feedback on activities and performance, as well as offering support and mentoring. Good supervision not only helps reduce the negative effects of stress but also helps produce better quality service. However, there is nothing intrinsic to good supervisory practices; they require knowledge, skill, and expertise. As such, organizations should foster training and encourage supervisors to attend workshops that facilitate their growth and skills as supervisors. (See also chapter 109.)

Continued Training and Education

There is considerable evidence supporting the contention that young workers are more at risk of developing stress symptoms and, consequently, feelings of burnout (Barak et al., 2001; Maslach et al., 2001). This is not surprising, in that younger individuals are likely to have less expertise and mastery over professional tasks. In essence, these younger workers are likely to lack confidence and self-efficacy in their abilities. To the extent that this notion of self-efficacy holds true, it is of institutional value to maximize the probability of high worker self-efficacy by providing opportunities for training, workshops, mentoring, and supervision. When workers are confident, it is likely to mitigate against the negative effects of stress (Schaubroeck & Merritt, 1997). Thus, school districts should require social workers to pursue continuing education classes. School social workers should pressure their school districts and unions to engender and enforce these activities. (See also chapter 113 for further information about continuing education and professional development.)

Develop Support Systems

The evidence is in, and social support does make a positive difference. This could be as simple as having time set aside during the day for workers to talk things over or to go over some situations with teachers, counselors, and others. Sharing concerns, expressing thanks, helping out, and clarifying procedures can reduce stress and strain. Support is not merely emotional, it is also practical and often affirming. To assume that the workplace provides these types of support may be erroneous. Supervisors and administrators should make a conscious effort to build the community of support within the workplace. It should be part of the work routine. (See also chapter 110 for additional ideas on how to cope with isolation and build personal and professional networks.)

Safety and Comfort

Recent research and public events suggest that violence prevention is an increasingly important component of school social work practice (Astor et al., 2004). Thus, quiet work space and safety are not merely bywords, but critical to good practice. Administrators and school districts must have plans in place and be prepared to provide a safe and comfortable work environment. School social workers should make it their responsibility to affirm these rights and not let it slide by under the guise of crowded schools.

Key Points to Remember

Preventing burnout in the schools requires both individual and organizational action. While individual social workers can do much to increase their resilience to stress, organizations can do even more to help their workers become even better workers.

- Learn about the sources of stress both personal and situational. Pay attention to your symptoms.
- Take care of yourself—mind, body, and spirit. Take control of your personal health and well-being.

- Never stop learning. Take classes, talk with colleagues, and observe interactions.
- Set realistic goals.
- Be active in changing the workplace for the better. You will not only help yourself but also make it better for the students and the next worker.

References

Acker, G. M. (1999). The impact of clients' mental illness on social workers' job satisfaction and burnout. *Health & Social Work, 24*, 112–119.

Allen-Meares, P. (2004). School social work: Historical developments, influences, and practices. In P. Allen-Meares (Ed.), *Social work services in schools* (4th ed., pp. 23–51). Boston: Allyn & Bacon.

Astor, R. A., Benbenishty, R., & Marachi, R. (2004). Violence in schools. In P. Allen-Meares (Ed.), *Social work services in schools* (4th ed., pp. 149–182). Boston: Allyn & Bacon.

Azar, S. T. (2000). Preventing burnout in professionals and paraprofessionals who work with child abuse and neglect cases: A cognitive behavioral approach to supervision. *Psychotherapy in Practice, 56*, 643–663.

Bandura, A. (1977). *Social learning theory*. Englewood Cliffs, NJ: Prentice Hall.

Barak, M. E., Nissly, J. A., & Levin, A. (2001). Antecedents to retention and turnover among child welfare, social work, and other human service employees: What can we learn from past research? A review and meta-analysis. *Social Service Review, 75*, 625–661.

Baruch-Feldman, C., Schwartz, J., Brondolo, E., & Ben-Dayan, D. (2002). Sources of social support and burnout, job satisfaction and productivity. *Journal of Occupational Health Psychology, 7*, 84–93.

Bell, H., Kulkarni, S., & Dalton, L. (2003). Organizational prevention of vicarious trauma. *Families in Society, 84*, 463–471.

Cropanzano, R., Rupp, D. E., & Byrne, Z. S. (2003). The relationship of emotional exhaustion to work attitudes, job performance, and organizational citizenship behaviors. *Journal of Applied Psychology, 88*, 160–169.

Dentsen, I. L. (2002). Re-thinking burnout. *Journal of Organizational Behavior, 22*, 833–847.

Duffy, M. K. (2002). Social undermining in the workplace. *Academy of Management Journal, 45*, 331–351.

Franklin, C. (2004). The delivery of school social work services. In P. Allen-Meares (Ed.), *Social work services in schools* (4th ed., pp. 295–325). Boston: Allyn & Bacon.

Freudenberger, H. J. (1980). *Burnout: The high cost of achievement*. Garden City, NJ: Anchor Press.

Gant, L. M., Nagda, B. A., Brabson, H. W., & Jayaratne, S. (1993). Effects of social support and undermining on African American workers' perceptions of coworker and supervisor relationships and psychological well-being. *Social Work, 38*, 158–164.

Greenglass, E., Fiksenbau, L., & Burke, R. J. (1996). Components of social support, buffering effects and burnout: Implications for psychological functioning. *Anxiety, Stress & Coping: An International Journal, 9*, 185–197.

Guterman, N. B., & Jayaratne, S. (1994). "Responsibility at risk": Perceptions of stress, control and professional effectiveness in child welfare direct practitioners. *Journal of Social Service Research, 20*, 99–120.

Hagihara, A., Tarumi, K., & Miller, A. S. (1998). Social support at work as a buffer of work stress-strain relationship: A signal detection approach. *Stress Medicine, 14*, 75–81.

Harris, M. B., & Franklin, C. (2004). The design of social work services. In P. Allen-Meares (Ed.), *Social work services in schools* (4th ed., pp. 277–294). Boston: Allyn & Bacon.

Himle, D. P., Jayaratne, S., & Thyness, P. A. (1989a). The buffering effects of four types of supervisory support on work stress. *Administration in Social Work, 13*, 19–34.

Himle, D. P., Jayaratne, S., & Thyness, P. A. (1989b). The effects of emotional support on burnout, work stress and mental health among Norwegian and American social workers. *Journal of Social Service Research, 13*, 27–45.

House, J. S. (1981). *Work stress and social support*. Reading, MA: Addison-Wesley.

Jayaratne, S., & Chess, W. A. (1984). The effects of emotional support on perceived job stress and strain. *Journal of Applied Behavioral Science, 20*, 141–153.

Koeske, G. F., & Kirk, S. A. (1995). The effect of characteristics of human service workers on subsequent morale and turnover. *Administration in Social Work, 19*, 15–31.

Lee, R. T., & Ashforth, B. E. (1996). A meta-analytic examination of the correlates of the three dimensions of job burnout. *Journal of Applied Psychology, 81*, 123–133.

Leiter, M. P., & Maslach, C. (2000). *Preventing burnout and building engagement: A complete program for organizational renewal*. San Francisco: Jossey-Bass.

Leyden-Rubenstein, L. A. (1998). *The stress management handbook: Strategies for health and inner peace*. New Canaan, CT: NTC Contemporary.

Maslach, C. A. (1982). *Burnout: The cost caring*. Englewood Cliffs, NJ: Prentice Hall.

Maslach, C. A. (2003). Job burnout: New directions in research and intervention. *Current Directions in Psychological Science, 12*, 189–192.

Maslach, C. A., & Jackson, S. E. (1986). *Maslach burnout inventory manual* (2nd ed.). Palo Alto, CA: Consulting Psychologist Press.

Maslach, C. A., Schaufeli, W. B., & Leiter, M. P. (2001). Job burnout. *Annual Review of Psychology, 52*, 397–422.

Meltsner, S. (1989). *Burnout protection: Survival handbook*. King George, VA: American Foster Care Resources.

Pearlin, L. I., Lieberman, M. A., Menaghan, E. G., & Mullan, J. T. (1981). The stress process. *Journal of Health and Social Behavior, 22*, 337–356.

Pearlin, L. I., & Schooler, C. (1978). The structure of coping. *Journal of Health and Social Behavior, 19*, 2–21.

Pincus, L. L. (1997). *An exploratory analysis of the phenomenon of burnout in the school social work professional*. Dissertation Abstracts International Section A: Humanities & Social Sciences, 58 (1-A), p. 0293.

Pines, A. M. (1982). Changing organizations: Is a work environment without burnout impossible? In W. S. Paine (Ed.), *Job stress and burnout: Research, theory and intervention perspectives* (pp. 189–212). Beverly Hills, CA: Sage Publications.

Proctor, B. E., & Steadman, T. (2003). Job satisfaction, burnout, and perceived effectiveness of "in-house" versus traditional school psychologists. *Psychology in the Schools, 40*, 237–243.

Rafferty, Y., Friend, R., & Landsbergis, P. A. (2001). The association between job skill discretion, decision authority and burnout. *Work & Stress, 15*, 73–85.

Raquepaw, J. M., & Miller, R. S. (1986). Psychological burnout: A componential analysis. *Professional Psychology: Research and Practice, 20*, 32–36.

Schaubroeck, J., & Merritt, D. E. (1997). Divergent effects of job control on coping with work stressors: The key role of self-efficacy. *Academy of Management Journal, 40*, 738–754.

Skovholt, T. M., Grier, T. L., & Hanson, M. R. (2001). Career counseling for longevity: Self-care and burnout prevention strategies for counselor resilience. *Journal of Career Development, 27*, 167–176.

Staudt, M. (1991). A role perception study of school social work practice. *Social Work, 36*(6), 496–498.

Tepper, B. J., Duffy, M. K., & Shaw, J. D. (2001). Personality moderators of the relationship between abusive supervision and subordinates' resistance. *Journal of Applied Psychology, 86*, 974–983.

Zapf, D., Seifert, C., Schmutte, B., Mertini, H., & Holz, M. (2001). Emotion work and job stressors and their effects on burnout. *Psychology & Health, 16*, 527–545.

Resources for Professional Development and Continuing Education

Elizabeth M. Tracy ▪ Merl C. Hokenstad

CHAPTER 113

Getting Started

This chapter will assist school social workers and school-based mental health workers in implementing their own professional development plan, as well as present ways to become supportive of the development and expansion of social work and mental health services in schools.

Professional development for social workers and other helping professions necessitates a commitment to and a plan for continuing professional education following the completion of a degree program. The expanding knowledge base resulting from new research and the increasingly specialized skills needed for effective practice are two important reasons why continuing education is needed throughout a social work or mental health career. Professional competence requires updated knowledge and skills. For example, the National Association of Social Workers Code of Ethics mandates that social workers should keep current with emerging knowledge relevant to social workers and should participate in continuing education relevant to social work practice and ethics (NASW, 1999).

What We Know

Professional Development

Formal continuing education requirements for social workers and other helping professions have resulted in broader recognition of the need for postdegree professional development. Societal insistence on high-quality professional practice and the resulting certification of social workers have led to an increasing emphasis on continuing education. Legal regulation of social work includes mandatory continuing education for licensure in most states (Strom & Green, 1995). Thus, the mandate for professional development comes from both the profession and the larger society.

There are additional mandates for school-based workers to develop a professional education plan. The National Association of Social Workers' *Standards for School Social Work Services* (2002) states that school social workers shall assume responsibility for their own professional development. The standards indicate the importance of continuing education to keep those professionals working within schools current in educational reforms and best practice models. It also helps practitioners to maintain competence in an area of practice, to contribute to the knowledge base of the profession, and to deliver in-service training and consultation within the local education agency. The specialized knowledge and skills needed for social service work in the school system also are further developed through postdegree education. The NASW, for example, can provide certification as a school social work specialist to school social workers and school-based mental health practitioners with sufficient experience and continuing education credits.

Licensure or certification through a state department of education or other state entity is often a basic requirement for school social work practice. In many states, licensure as a social worker is a prerequisite to licensure or certification as a member of the pupil personnel team, and the periodic requirement for a specified number of continuing social work professional education credits or hours applies to school-based social workers as well. But beyond the basic duties to uphold a professional license, school-based workers also have the force of current education legislation policies driving high levels of professional development. The No Child Left Behind Act calls for school districts to hire the "most highly qualified" education professionals as a way to improve the quality of education children receive. Many school districts interpret "highly qualified" to be those workers who have been certified or licensed by their respective states. Therefore, in order to maintain employment, school social workers and school-based mental health workers often must seek and maintain licensure or certification as a school social worker.

There are also special features of practice within schools that hold implications for the types of professional development to pursue and the content for continuing education. Some of these are as follows:

- *Working in a Host Setting*—The school is a secondary setting hosting social work and mental health providers, among other supportive services, and therefore is an interdisciplinary setting in nature. Whenever mental health or social workers work in a host setting (e.g., hospital, correctional facility, or school), it is important to establish relationships within and be knowledgeable about that setting. Practitioners must possess an understanding of the school as a social organization, the roles of other educational staff, and policies and legislation affecting education at the local, state, and national levels. Such an understanding is essential to engaging with school staff and maintaining positive school relationships. (See chapter 13 for more in-depth discussion of these issues.)
- *Assessment of Child Within Context of School*—School-age children may be referred for social work or mental health services for a variety of reasons: learning difficulties, behavior problems, needs at home, or family factors. Assessment within the context of the schools requires an understanding of the child's learning style, results of educational testing and assessments, peer relationships, and the effects of the school and classroom environment. School-based workers must be familiar with a variety of assessment methods to gather information from multiple sources. They must also be familiar with assessment methods used by other school staff, such as psychologists, speech pathologists, and other learning specialists.
- *Interdisciplinary Teams*—Most school social workers and school-based mental health providers work within the context of interdisciplinary teams, including teams to assess student needs (as in a functional behavioral assessment), to document learning goals and services (as in an individual education plan), or to resolve problem behaviors in the classroom (as in intervention assistance teams). Knowledge of the roles and responsibilities of other professions is crucial to effective communication and teamwork. In addition, school-based workers often assume a mediating role between the team and the child's family, home, and community; the worker typically communicates school policy to the family and, vice versa, the family's needs and wishes to the team.
- *Combined Micro/Macro Roles*—Social work and mental health interventions in schools may focus on changing the student, changing the environment, or both. As system change agents, school-based workers, practicing from an ecological perspective, address multiple levels of the child's environment, and school-based interventions may serve wide-reaching purposes— from directly meeting the child's needs to fostering schoolwide, community, and neighborhood level changes that promote a more supportive environment for children and families. It is not unusual, then, that school social workers and school-based mental health providers find themselves writing a grant proposal, facilitating a community task force or work group, or developing school policy statements around truancy, parent involvement, or discipline. Knowledge of macro-level social work skills, such as community and team building, needs and asset assessments, or resource development and policy analysis, becomes central to the delivery of social work and mental health services in schools.

Suggested Content Areas for Continuing Education

Given the need and rationale for professional development just presented, we now turn to suggested content areas that may be most relevant for school social workers and school-based mental health practitioners. Because school-based workers, by definition, provide a wide variety of services to link school, home, and community, the number of possible content areas could be quite large. Decisions as to what training to pursue are best made in the context of a specific school district. In deciding areas for continued education, workers should consider their individual previous training and experience, the needs of their school population (staff, students, and family), length of service within the school district, and their overall plan for delivery of services in any given school year. For example, a school principal may decide that social skills groups are needed; therefore, the school-based worker may want to pursue continuing education around group work and skills training.

Entry-level school-based social worker positions often require basic knowledge of professional tasks (such as intake assessments, record keeping, confidentiality), ability to serve as a liaison between the home and school, and ability to facilitate the child's best use of school resources and the family's use of community resources (Allen-Meares, 1977). Within the context of special education legislation (Individual with Disabilities Education Act of 1990, P.L. 101–476), school social work tasks include preparing social or developmental histories, providing group or individual counseling, working with problems in the child's living situation that affect adjustment to school, and mobilizing school and community resources.

More recently, the combination of education reforms and fundamental changes in the delivery and funding of social and mental health services has led to an increase in school-linked health and mental health services and collaborative approaches to the delivery of comprehensive services (Streeter & Franklin, 2002). The practical effect is that many more community agencies are now providing services in schools and the school-based worker, rather than working in a host setting, is moving toward a transdisciplinary team setting (Waxman, Weist, & Benson, 1999). School social workers already working in schools must take the initiative in coordinating services provided to students by outside agencies. At the same time, school-based mental health workers need to learn about education laws and the school climate. Therefore, collaboration, coordination, and teamwork may be key skills called for in the current context of service delivery in schools.

Recent trends and new areas of knowledge development also suggest areas for continued education. These include the movement toward evidence-based practice (Roberts & Yeager, 2004), family-focused interventions (Robinson, 2004), multisystemic treatment models (Henggeler, Schoenwald, Borduin, Rowland, & Cunningham, 1998), new knowledge on the impact of trauma (Perry, 1997; Singer, Miller, Guo, Flannery, Frierson & Slovak, 1999; Teicher, 2002; Webb, 2004),

and brain development and brain-based learning (Gardner, 1999; Silver & Hanson, 1998). We include but a small sample of possible resources to explore these and other topics of interest in Tools and Practice Examples.

What We Can Do

Best practice principles suggest that professional development be approached in a thoughtful manner. The steps to developing a professional development plan are similar to developing and negotiating a school-based service plan: assessing self, developing trust and sanction for social services, assessing data and dynamics of school and community, negotiating a plan and priorities for work, and evaluating and developing an annual report (Allen-Meares, Washington, & Welsh, 2004).

1. The first consideration is you and your current job description. What are you expected to do? Who expects this of you (e.g., school principal, parent organization, union)? Then assess your knowledge and skills levels as well as your interests. Do you have the skills to carry out these activities? What resources, skills, or knowledge do you need to carry out your job expectations?

2. Do you have or can you create an atmosphere supportive of continued professional development? This may require adequate supervision and consultation, time for professional training relevant to social work, and a structure that rewards continued growth and improvement. It may also be necessary to organize with others in the same or similar positions as your own in order to establish appropriate professional development supports. At a minimum, the school principal or your direct supervisor should know about the goals you set for yourself in terms of professional development so that they can help create opportunities for you to accomplish those goals.

3. Examine the school environment in which you work and determine key service needs, as these would likely influence your professional development plan. Make sure you take into consideration your length of service in the school, as what you plan to accomplish in your first year may look quite different from what can be accomplished if you remain connected

with a school over time. Be sure to establish priorities and to negotiate this plan with the appropriate administrator.

4. At the same time, examine and explore the use of strengths and resources in your environment (e.g., a well-functioning team, an accessible resource center, a supportive principal). Some resources will be formal supports while others will be informal, such as the relationships you have with social workers or mental health providers in other school districts or agencies. Use this information to establish areas of professional growth and experience. Be as specific as you can, and set realistic time lines (as you do with student case planning).

5. Routinely evaluate and report on your progress. Which professional development goals were met, in whole or in part? What obstacles or barriers prevented you from completing the goal? Evaluating the reasons why goals were not met may reveal a lack of important resources, or systems issues that need to be addressed. Consider the use of a professional portfolio to document professional activities, accomplishments, and lifelong learning (Cournoyer & Stanley, 2002). Portfolios are used to organize and demonstrate talents, skills, and significant components of practice.

Tools and Practice Examples

Resources for Continuing Education and Professional Development: Web Sites of Interest to School-Based Workers

School Social Work Association of America: http://www.sswaa.org/. A national organization of School Social Workers dedicated to promoting the profession of school social work and the professional development of school social workers in order to enhance the educational experience of students and their families.

International Network for School Social Work: http://internationalnetwork-schoolsocial work.htmlplanet.com/index.htm. Provides information about school social work around the world.

NASW: School Social Work section: http://www.socialworkers.org/sections/

default.asp. A specialty practice section of the National Association of Social Workers. Provides links to state and regional school social work associations and publishes *The Section Connection*, a school social work newsletter.

Council on Social Work Education: www.cwse.org. Provides information on schools of social work education.

Wrightslaw: www.wrightslaw.com. Information about special education law and advocacy for children with disabilities.

Center for Mental Health in Schools: http://www.smhp.psych.ucla.edu/. Web site of the UCLA School Mental Health Project. Contains information on theory, research, policy, and practice related to mental health services in schools.

Collaborative for Academic, Social, and Emotional Learning (CASEL): www.casel.org. Works to establish social and emotional learning as an essential part of education.

NASW Certified School Social Work Specialist (C-SSWS): http://www.naswdc.org/ credentials/specialty/c-ssws.asp. Specialty certification in school social work.

A Resource and Planning Guide for School Social Work: http://www.dpi.state.wi.us/dpi/ dltcl/eis/pubsales/pplsvc8a.html. Sponsored by Wisconsin Department of Public Instruction.

National Clearinghouse on Child Abuse and Neglect Information: http://nccanch.acf .hhs.gov/profess/workforce/index.cfm. Provides information on training organizations and training materials on child welfare practice.

Council for Exceptional Children: www.ced.sped.org/. Includes links to Web sites focusing on children with special needs, as well as a resource catalog and training resources for special education.

Harvard Family Research Project: www. gseweb.harvard.edu/~hfrp. Offers publications on early childhood care and education, family involvement in education tools and resources.

Educational Resource Information Center (ERIC): www.access.eric.org. Extensive database of resources for educational research and information.

U.S. Department of Education: www.ed.gov. Information and access to online ordering system for educational resources.

Resources for Continuing Education and Professional Development: Conferences and Training Institutes

Annual International School Social Work Conference sponsored by the International Network for School Social Work

Annual national school social work conference held each spring by the School Social Work Association of America (SSWAA)

Legislative summit held each summer in Washington, DC, sponsored by SWAA

Training tutorials, continuing education modules, and quick training and presentation aids available from the UCLA School Mental Health Project Web site

Regional and state school social work conferences and training workshops

Continuing education workshops offered by local schools of social work, such as the summer course, Social Work in School Settings, offered by the University of Michigan

Resources for Continuing Education and Professional Development: Key Journals and Texts

Allen-Meares, P., Washington, R. O., & Welsh, B. L. (2004). *Social work services in schools* (4th ed.). Boston, MA: Pearson/Allyn & Bacon.

Children & Schools (published by NASW, formerly Social Work in Education).

Christophersen, E. R., & Mortweet, S. L. (2001). *Treatments that work with children: Empirically supported strategies for managing childhood problems.* Washington, DC: American Psychological Association.

Constable, R., McDonald, S., & Flynn, J. P. (2002). *School social work: Practice, policy and research perspectives* (5th ed.). Chicago: Lyceum Books.

Dupper, D. R. (2003). *School social work: Skills & interventions for effective practice.* Hoboken, NJ: Wiley & Sons.

Freeman, E. M., Franklin, C. G., Fong, R., Shaffer, G. L., & Timberlake, E. M. (1998). *Multisystem skills and interventions in school social work practice.* Washington, DC: NASW Press.

Huxtable, M., & Blyth, E. (2002). *School social work worldwide.* Washington, DC: NASW Press.

Journal of School Social Work (published by Iowa School Social Work Association).

Natasi, B. K., Moore, B. M., & Varjas, K. M. (2004). *School-based mental health services: Creating comprehensive and culturally specific programs.* Washington, DC: American Psychological Association.

Robinson, K. E. (Ed.). (2004). *Advances in school-based mental health interventions: Best practices and program models.* Kingston, NJ: Civic Research Institute.

School Social Work Journal (published by the Illinois Association of School Social Workers).

The Section Connection (newsletter published by NASW School Social Work Section).

Key Points to Remember

By taking advantage of the following professional development and networking opportunities, every school social worker or school-based mental health provider can also support the growth and development of school-based services.

1. One of most significant and well-established ways to support the profession is to become credentialed as appropriate to your locality. School social work credentials may involve certification or licensure, depending on the state. See chapters 107 and 108 in this volume for a review of licensing and certification credentials. Some schools of social work offer specialized training leading to state certification or licensure. Social work schools that provide specialized training in school social work often provide a mechanism for those social workers already employed in school districts to complete the educational requirements for state licensure or certification on a postgraduate basis.

2. Join one national association and one local or state association devoted to school social work or school-based mental health services (some suggestions are included in Tools and Practice Examples).

3. Plan to attend a national, regional, or state school social work or school-based services conference (such as those listed in Tools and Practice Examples) and explore continuing education workshops relevant to school-based practice. Training workshops are more likely to be available through national, regional, state, and local school social work or mental health associations and/or schools of social work that offer continuing education.

4. Become involved in meetings or training sessions offered by your local school social work organization. This provides a way to form informal relationships with other school social workers and school-based mental health providers. Better yet, become an active board or committee member.

5. Keep yourself informed by reading newsletters and professional journals, both social work and education related. E-mail newsletters are a convenient way to keep up to date, such as the weekly "e-bell" disseminated by the School Social Work Association of America. E-mail list serves also provide a way to network and contact others for advice and support.

6. It is critical for practitioners to contribute to knowledge development and policy planning. Plan to prepare a newsletter submission, for example, to NASW's *School Social Work Section Newsletter* or a paper to present at conferences: local, state, and/or national.

7. Connect with your local college or university and identify faculty members interested in schools. These contacts may lead to collaborative research studies or program evaluations. Since funded programs typically require an evaluation component, your school district may already have established relationships with a university researcher or a research consultant. These contacts may help you stay on top of evidence-based practices as well as being key resources for training, collaboration for knowledge development, and publication.

8. Plan to provide field instruction and supervision for school-based interns. This contributes to the development of the profession and helps to maintain connections with current research and literature.

9. Consider doctoral level training in school social work, both to provide leadership to the field and to contribute to research on effectiveness of school-based services.

10. Finally, and most important, identify yourself as a *school social worker or other school-based services professional* whenever you present yourself professionally. In addition, if you are a professional social worker, make sure that your job title is school social worker, whenever possible, as this title most accurately identifies the educational background, profession, and function of a social worker employed by a local education agency (NASW, 2002).

References

Allen-Meares, P. (1977). Analysis of tasks in school social work. *Social Work, 22*(3), 196–201.

Allen-Meares, P., Washington, R. O., & Welsh, B. L. (2004). *Social work services in schools* (4th ed.). Boston, MA: Pearson/Allyn & Bacon.

Cournoyer, B. R., & Stanley, M. J. (2002). *The social work portfolio: Planning, assessing and documenting lifelong learning in a dynamic profession.* Pacific Grove, CA: Brooks Cole.

Gardner, H. (1999). *Intelligence reframed: Multiple intelligences for the 21st century.* New York: Simon & Schuster.

Henggeler, S. W., Schoenwald, S. K., Borduin, C. M., Rowland, M. D., & Cunningham, P. B. (1998). *Multisystemic treatment of antisocial behavior in children and adolescents.* New York: Guilford.

National Association of Social Workers. (1999). *Code of ethics.* Washington, DC: NASW.

National Association of Social Workers. (2002). *NASW standards for school social services.* Washington, DC: NASW.

Perry, B. D. (1997). Incubated in terror: Neurodevelopmental factors in the "cycle of violence." In J. D. Osofsky (Ed.), *Children in a violent society* (pp. 124–149). New York: Guilford Press.

Roberts, A. R., & Yeager, K. R. (2004). *Evidence-based practice manual: Research and outcome measures in health and human services.* New York: Oxford University Press.

Robinson, K. E. (Ed.) (2004). *Advances in school-based mental health interventions: Best practices and program models.* Kingston, NJ: Civic Research Institute.

Silver, H. F., & Hanson, J. R. (1998). *Learning styles and strategies* (3rd ed.). Woodbridge, NJ: Thoughtful Education Press.

Singer, M. I., Miller, D. B., Guo, S., Flannery, D. J., Frierson, T., & Slovak, K. (1999). Contributors to violent behavior among elementary and middle school children. *Pediatrics, 104*(4), 878–884.

Streeter, C. L. & Franklin, C. (2002). Standards for school social work in the 21st century In A. R. Roberts & G. J. Greene (Eds.), *Social workers' desk reference* (pp. 612–618). New York: Oxford University Press.

Strom, K., & Green, R. (1995). Continuing education. In R. Edwards et al. (Eds.), *Encyclopedia of social work* (19th ed., pp. 622–632). Washington, DC: National Association of Social Workers.

Teicher, M. H. (2002). Scars that won't heal: The neurobiology of child abuse. *Scientific American, 286*(3), 68–75.

Waxman, R. P., Weist, M., & Benson, D. M. (1999). Toward collaboration in the growing education–mental health interface. *Clinical Psychology Review, 19*, 239–253.

Webb, N. B. (2004). *Mass trauma and violence: Helping families and children cope.* New York: Guilford Press.

Where Do We Go From Here?

Mental Health Workers and the Implementation of an Evidence-Based Practice

Paula Allen-Meares

CHAPTER 114

Getting Started

The primary purpose of this *School Services Sourcebook* is to provide social workers and related school-based professionals with current and diverse empirical data on interventions and approaches that address the mental health needs of various pupil groups. Between 4 million and 6 million students are thought to have serious mental health issues, which, if left untreated, can affect their futures, their lives, and society in general (Rogers, 2003). Most of these children attend school, either public or private. Therefore, the school setting becomes one of the more likely places for effective mental health services. But what is necessary to deliver these services? Where will the future of school-based intervention take us?

In this discussion, we will highlight the future of school social work, a practice that will be firmly rooted in a growing evidence base. In addition, we add a brief summary of issues specific to the selection of evidence-based interventions, methods of getting school social workers to accept and utilize evidence-based practices, and why school and communities should create partnerships for mental health services for children and adolescents.

What We Know

Evidence-Based: Definitions

The future of school social work may very well rest on the emerging concept of evidence-based practices, theories, interventions, and treatments. Although there is not currently a consensus about the definition of this concept (Hoagwood, 2003), many disciplines utilize the concept, and various definitions may be found within them. In this chapter, we attempt to define *evidence-based* in a manner that can be commonly understood.

There are two different understandings of what constitutes evidence-based in use. The first comes from the medical field, where evidence-based practice has been evolving as a standard for quite some time. In medicine, evidence-based practice is described as utilizing the best available evidence to guide decisions about patient health care and choices. Furthermore, these best practices are typically combined with what the physician has experienced in the clinical setting, as well as the patient's, beliefs and experiences (Mullen, 2002).

The second understanding comes from a social work and a social science perspective, particularly, in mental health, where the evidence-based movement is starting to truly take hold (Mullen, 2002). In the mental health field, evidence-based is considered to be "any practice that has been established as effective through scientific research according to some set of explicit criteria" (Mullen, n.p.). Criteria may include treatment standardization, treatment evaluation, controlled trials, or other scientifically tested or measured outcomes. Once those criteria are selected, theories or practices that meet them are considered part of the evidence base or best practices.

"'Evidence-based practice' refers to a body of scientific knowledge about service practices . . . or about the impact of clinical treatments or services on the mental health problems of children and adolescents" (Hoagwood, Burns, Kiser, Ringeisen, & Schoenwald, 2001, p. 1179). In other words, evidence-based practice stresses that the need for a scientific base in theories and methods applied to social work practice. The theoretical must be tested and proven in order to generate best practices, which ultimately support a sound knowledge base, and to ensure the very same effectiveness and efficiency in service delivery mentioned previously. According to Huang, Hepburn, and Espiritu (2003):

> Evidence-based practice is an emerging concept and reflects a nationwide effort to build quality and accountability in health and behavioral health care service delivery. Underlying this concept is (1) the fundamental belief that children with emotional and behavioral disorders should be able to count on receiving care that meets their needs and is based on the best scientific knowledge available, and (2) the fundamental concern that for many of these children, the care that is delivered is not effective care. (p. 1)

It is important to remember that utilizing any evidence-based treatment with children, regardless of its efficacy, will bring with it special challenges due to the fact that children and adolescents are not the same as adults. These differences in physical changes ("children undergo more rapid psychological, neuronal, and psychological changes over a briefer period than adults" [Hoagwood et al., 2001, p. 1181]) must be considered. In addition, practitioners must take into consideration their interactions with family, as well as their environment, whether on the playground, at school, or at home (Hoagwood et al., 2001).

The School

Given the very fact that children spend a large portion of their time in school (7 hours a day, 5 days a week, 10 months a year), it makes sense that the educational community plays a strategic role in the lives of children and their families. Indeed, the school has historically been a location in which social workers felt they could assist in children's health and welfare. "Seventy to 80% of children who receive mental health services receive them in schools; for many children the school system provides their only form of mental health treatment" (Hoagwood et al., 2001, p. 1183).

The *Report of the Surgeon General's Conference on Children's Mental Health* (U.S. Department of Health and Human Services, 2000) calls atten-

tion to the growing numbers of youth suffering needlessly because their emotional, behavioral, and developmental needs are not being met. It strongly suggests that it is time for the nation to treat and prevent mental illness in our youth.

Furthermore, the surgeon general's report recognizes that the responsibility for mental health care for our youth is dispersed across numerous settings and organizations: schools, primary care, the juvenile justice system, and child/family welfare systems, to name only a few. Even when evidence-based treatments are available for use by providers, utilization of those treatments, in many instances, remains low.

Unfortunately, families often cannot turn to the community anticipating relief and assistance. Rogers (2003) documents the lack of community-based services for youth with serious emotional disturbances. While appropriate and timely intervention can prevent a host of problems, such as substance abuse, juvenile delinquency, and other behavioral problems, community-based services often come up lacking.

Jessie Taft, an early leader in the functionalist movement, wrote: "The only practical and effective way to increase the mental health of a nation is through its school system. Homes are too inaccessible. The school has the time of the child and the power to do the job" (Taft, 1923, p. 398). More recently, S. Hyman, then the director of the National Institute of Mental Health, spoke to the importance of the school system as the context for the identification and treatment of school-children needing mental health treatment (Rees, 1997).

While ripe for identifying and treating children who exhibit social and mental health needs, the educational system itself is often at the mercy of institutional, local, or federal pressures or demands. As Sipple (2004) states, "The American public educational system is a beleaguered public institution fraught with relentless criticism," adding that "schools are facing ever-challenging and complex educational situations while at the same time an unprecedented inspection and expectation of practice and performance" (p. 1). Services such as special education are underfunded, and state support is either erratic or dwindling, depending on the means of each state. Schools have to involve the multiple stakeholders in its governance and decision making, reform and restructure itself to obtain excellence and relevancy, and do all of this while being cost-efficient and effective. In addition, today's educational system has numerous responsibilities on its doorstep: federal, state, and local standards, desegregation, student diversity, underachieving students, and what to do with overachievers. Add to this the expectation that physical, emotional, and behavioral problems will be addressed, and you have an environment that is overwhelmed with multiple agendas and roles (Allen-Meares, 2004). Clearly, the school and its personnel cannot achieve these multiple and important imperatives in isolation of other relevant and interested parties (e.g., community, parents).

Pertinent professional providers located in the community in collaboration with parents and school personnel will need to become a part of the solution and respond to the mental health and health issues that are going undiagnosed among pupils. We envision unusual and innovative collaborations and partnerships between the school and its community network of service providers in the decades ahead. What are currently atypical contractual arrangements between schools and their communities must become more common. Furthermore, knowledge from a cross-section of practices and empirical literatures is needed to arm these professionals with new ways to identify, treat, and prevent mental illness among children and adolescents. "No one discipline has a privileged view of either pathogenesis or treatment of mental disorders" (Rees, 1997, p. 8).

What We Can Do

Criteria for the Selection of Evidence-Based Intervention

As reflected in this book, various interventions have different levels of scientific sophistication or rigor undergirding them. When considering what interventions to utilize in a school setting or a school–community provider collaboration, the following criteria should be taken into consideration (please note that this list is not exhaustive):

1. Where does the study fall on the continuum of scientific rigor? A treatment is considered to be well established if two or more studies find it superior to wait-listed control conditions, one experiment must meet criteria for a well-established treatment, or three single case studies must be conducted (Rogers, 2003). Outcome measures must be relevant

and evaluation measurements must be of high quality and meet appropriate psychometric standards.

2. Was the design of the study effective? Evidence-based treatment should be supported by group design or single-subject experiments (Rogers, 2003).

3. Is the study transportable? One of the challenges of utilizing evidence-based interventions is transportability—that is to say, will the outcomes of the scientific study that validated this intervention in a laboratory or a clinical setting be consistent when applied in a school setting (Hoagwood et al., 2001)?

4. Are there contextual variables required for optimal outcomes? Services to children/youth are delivered in a variety of unique contexts—schools, child and family agencies, family, correctional systems, and community mental health centers. It is therefore urgent for the practitioner to know the context in which the research on the intervention was conducted (Hoagwood et al., 2001).

5. What were the characteristics of the experimental/treatment group in terms of important demographics and problems in functioning? Attention to the fit with the population that is the target of the intervention is important (Hoagwood et al., 2001). In other words, there should be congruency between the experimental sample and those that are the target of application in practice.

6. Does the intervention consider co-occurring disorders? Often the intervention focuses on one specific disorder and does not adequately take into account the possibility of other disorders that are present and/or the heterogeneity of the mental health problems broadly defined within childhood and adolescence (Hoagwood, 2003).

7. Is the intervention age appropriate or developmentally sensitive? For example, an intervention found to be effective with preadolescent youth to reduce depression may well be ineffective for adolescent youths (Hoagwood et al., 2001), and similarly, effective treatments used with adults may not affect children in the same manner.

8. When should a practitioner consider a specific drug to be effective? A drug is considered efficacious if studied through random assignment and control group comparison, and with replicated results in one or more similarly well-controlled studies. Drugs can be considered

efficacious following one randomized trial (Ringeisen, 2003).

9. Is the intervention culturally sensitive? Was the target group in the experiment or clinical group or single-case design comparable in terms of race, ethnicity, and so on? As the population of the United States continues to become larger and more diverse, this factor will become increasingly important (Rogers, 2003).

Implementation in Practice Setting

The use of evidence-based knowledge is, as mentioned, gaining a foothold in social work and social science theory. How then do practitioners make the move from what they know to what science proves to be effective? Huang et al. (2003) state that "changing practice is a formidable task that occurs at a painstakingly slow pace, often requiring not only changes in practice behaviors, but restructuring programs and allocating an infusion of upfront resources" (p. 1). So how do we make this move to a more effective service delivery?

According to a meta-analysis, several strategies have been used to influence behavioral health care professionals to incorporate evidence-based practices into their professional behaviors (Gira, Kessler, & Poertner, 2004). These include:

1. *Dissemination.* One of the most important aspects of getting practitioners to explore and utilize new approaches and scientific data is simply ensuring they are exposed to it. A simple way to do this is through dissemination. This approach can range from the publication of guidelines, mass mailings, Web sites, compiled notebooks, and so on.

2. *Continuing education.* Continuing education coursework and seminars are a part of many professions, encouraging practitioners to stay current on methods and literature after obtaining their degrees. This approach has been found to be effective in exposing practitioners to evidence-based materials and theory in randomized controlled trials, when small group activities and practice sessions are available to participants.

3. *Educational outreach.* Thomson O'Brien, et al. (2001) define an educational outreach visit as a visit paid by a trained educator with the intent of providing information to the practitioner. The educator brings the practitioner up-to-date on current practices through education, materials, and feedback.

4. *Local opinion leaders.* These individuals are defined by their colleagues as "educationally influential" (p. 73). Although it is sometimes unclear what their exact role in the professional community is, local opinion leaders typically serve as role models who assist in the dissemination, acceptance, and implementation of evidence-based practice.

5. *Audit and feedback.* Audit and feedback is a snapshot of a practice over a period of time. Experts review a practitioner's interaction with clients and provide documentation regarding the practitioner's use of evidence-based theories and methods. Documentation may also include feedback about the "congruency between practice and best evidence" (p. 73).

6. *Continuous quality improvement (CQI).* Much like quality programs in the business world, this approach looks not at an individual's performance, but instead at the organizational level. One difference between this and other quality programs is that CQI seeks to improve both the management of administrative procedures and clinical practices.

7. *Technology.* Technology may be utilized in a variety of ways, whether tracking practice statistics, educating patients, or accessing patient data during consultation. Social workers typically use technology to keep records and collect data, not to choose or document effective treatments, although the potential to plan or choose interventions is a distinct possibility.

8. *Mass media campaigns.* Campaigns target the consumer of intervention services, working on the patient's right and ability to ask the right questions, press for different treatments, and basically manage their own care. These campaigns might include TV ads, pamphlets, and so on.

Where Do We Go From Here?

Social work practitioners, both in and out of school settings, are seeing a definite shift from traditionally accepted practices to the cutting-edge best practices. It is important to remember that whether a practitioner is quick to embrace new and better practices or moves slowly and deliberately toward the future, the ultimate goal of treatment and intervention should be concerned with the health and mental health of the children they are charged with helping.

The 2000 Surgeon General's Report (U.S. DHSS, 2000) identified several key goals that are crucial to the treatment of children with mental health issues as social work and other social sciences move from the tried and true to the tested and approved. They are as follows:

1. The development, dissemination, and implementation of best practices derived from a scientific evidence base must continue.
2. Knowledge on a variety of factors, including social and psychological development, must be researched in order "to design better screening, assessment, and treatment tools, and to develop prevention programs" (p. 5).
3. Research on contexts (e.g., school, family, culture) must be supported. This research will assist us in identifying opportunities "for promoting mental health services and for providing effective prevention, treatment, and services" (p. 5).
4. Research to develop and test innovative behavioral, pharmacological, and other "mixed" interventions must also be encouraged.
5. Research on proven treatments, practices, and services developed in a lab must be increased, particularly the assessment of their effectiveness in "real-world settings" (p. 5).
6. Similarly, the effectiveness of clinical and community practices must also be studied in context.
7. Development of model programs should be encouraged, particularly those that can be sustained on a community level.
8. Private and public partnerships are key elements in facilitating the dissemination and cross-fertilization of knowledge.
9. The understanding of children's mental health care needs must increase. Additionally, training to assist practitioners to address the various mental issues among children with special health care needs and their families is necessary and urgent.
10. Research on factors that facilitate or impede the implementation of scientifically proven interventions must take place as part of the evaluation process.

Key Points to Remember

In order for practitioners, particularly those involved in mental health services for children and adolescents, to successfully take a step toward a future practice undergirded by scientific evidence, the following must be kept in the forefront of their minds:

- Evidence-based practice is built upon a scientific foundation, meaning that it has been tested using specific criteria and proven effective. Implementation of evidenced-based theories and practices into real-world application will ensure that social workers and other mental health professionals are utilizing the best practices for the children they serve.
- The use of these evidence-based best practices may be useful in a school setting if additional criteria, such as scientific rigor, are considered.
- School is one area where a large portion of children may be diagnosed and assisted with mental health or other social issues.
- When appropriate to do so, the creation of partnerships with family, community agencies, and other resources will help to sustain change.
- Sustainability is critical. Involving family members, other professionals, and relevant institutional providers in intervention planning, where and when appropriate, increases the likelihood that the change will be sustained.
- Training, further research, and technical support opportunities are needed to increase the likelihood that practitioners will adopt an evidenced-based practice.

May this book be a catalyst for change.

References

Allen-Meares, P. (2004). School social work: Historical development, influences, and practices. In P. Allen-Meares (Ed.), *Social work services in schools* (pp. 23–51). Boston: Pearson Education, Inc.

Gira, E. C., Kessler, M. L., & Poertner, J. (2004). Influencing social workers to use research evidence in practice: Lessons from medicine and the allied health professions. *Research on Social Work Practice, 14*(2), 68–79.

Hoagwood, K. (2003). Evidence-based practice in children's mental health services: What do we know? Why aren't we putting it to use? *Data Matters, 6,* 4–5.

Hoagwood, K., Burns, B. J., Kiser, L., Ringeisen, H., & Schoenwald, S. K. (2001). Evidence-based practice in child and adolescent mental health services. *Psychiatric Services, 52*(9), 1179–1189.

Huang, L. N., Hepburn, M. S., & Espiritu, R. C. (2003). To be or not to be . . . evidence-based? *Data Matters, 6*, 1–3.

Mullen, E. J. (2002, July). *Evidence-based social work-theory & practice: Historical and reflective perspective.* Minutes from the Campbell collaboration and evidence-based social work practice session at the International Conference on Evaluation for Practice, Tampere, Finland.

Rees, C. (1997). Ask the doctor: On children and mental illness. *NAMI Advocate, 8,* 10.

Ringeisen, H. (2003). Identifying efficacious interventions for children's mental health: What are the criteria and how can they be used? *Data Matters, 6,* 10–11.

Rogers, K. (2003). Evidence-based community-based interventions. In A. J. Pumariega & N. C. Winters (Eds.), *The handbook of child and adolescent systems of care* (pp. 149–170). San Francisco, CA: Jossey-Bass.

Sipple, J. (2004). Major issues in American schools. In P. Allen-Meares (Ed.), *Social work services in schools* (pp. 1–21). Boston: Pearson Education, Inc.

Taft, J. (1923). The relation of the school of mental health of the average child. *Proceedings of the National Conference of Social Work* (p. 398). Chicago: University of Chicago Press.

Thomson O'Brien, M. A., Oxman, A. D., Davis, D. A., Haynes, R. B., Freemantle, N., & Harvey, E. L. (2001). Educational outreach visits: Effects on professional practice and health care outcomes. Cochrane Effective Practice and Organisation of Care Group Cochrane Database of Systematic Reviews, 1. Retrieved August 22, 2005, from http://www.cochrane.org/cochrane/revabstr/AB000409.htm.

U.S. Department of Health and Human Services (2000). *Report of the surgeon general's conference on children's mental health: A national action agenda.* Washington, DC: Department of Health and Human Services.

Index